**TUNE-UP**
Section 1

**FUEL SYSTEMS**
Section 2

**ELECTRICAL**
Section 3

**STEERIN**
Section

**WHEEL ALIGNMENT**
Section 8

**ENGINES**
Section 5

**CLUTCHES**
Section 6

SUSPENSION
Section 9

BRAKES
Section 7

DIAGRAMS
ction 4

# PREFACE

This is the 1978 edition of Mitchell Manuals' Imported Car Tune-Up/Mechanical Service and Repair Manual. This book, like the many Mitchell publications which have preceded it, represents our commitment to professionalism in the automotive service market.

The automotive industry advances every year, and Mitchell Manuals pledges to advance and improve its products as we maintain the quality and usefulness of all Mitchell Manuals' publications.

We cordially acknowledge the good will and mutual goals that exist in the automotive business, and it is in this spirit that we thank the automotive manufacturers, distributors, dealers and the entire automotive industry for their fine cooperation and assistance which has made this publication possible.

Over 50 Years of Service
**National Service Data**

# 1978
# Imported
# Cars & Trucks

## Tune-Up·Mechanical
## Service & Repair

**Published By:**
MITCHELL MANUALS, INC.
A Cordura Company

P.O. BOX 80427
SAN DIEGO, CALIFORNIA 92138

ISBN 0-8470-5778-X

## ACKNOWLEDGEMENT

Mitchell Manuals thanks the automotive and equipment manufacturers, distributors, dealers and the entire automotive industry for their fine cooperation and assistance which makes the publication of this manual possible.

# MITCHELL MANUALS, INC.

A Cordura Company

Vice President and Publisher
W. Gardner Barker, Jr.

Director of Publications
Paul W. Kelm

Managing Editor
Jerry H. Cole

Composition Manager
Doris J. Williams

Art Director
Eloise S. Stiverson

Technical Editors
Kenneth R. Major
Kenneth A. Young
Dennis L. Bailey
Gary L. Haley
Daniel M. Kelley, Jr.
Don C. McComas
Daryl F. Visser
Robert B. Johnson
Steven L. Hansen
Michael Roeder
Mark L. Hawes
Terry L. Blomquist

PUBLISHED BY

MITCHELL MANUALS, INC.
4926 Savannah Street
P.O. Box 80427
San Diego, California 92138

a subsidiary of
CORDURA PUBLICATIONS, INC.
C.L. Kobrin, President
John Opelt, Vice President of Finance & Administration
Malcolm Ferrier, Vice President of Operations
1200 Prospect Street, Suite 460
La Jolla, California 92037

ISBN 0-8470-5778-X

©1979 MITCHELL MANUALS, INC. LITHO IN U.S.A.

# Introduction

You now have the most complete and up to date Service and Repair Manual currently available to the professional mechanic. Our staff of experts have spent many hundreds of hours gathering and processing service and repair information from sources throughout the automotive world. More than 300 separate articles provide specific step by step testing, adjusting and repair procedures for 1978 Imported Cars.

To use this manual in the most efficient and profitable way possible, please take the time to read the following section, "How to Find the Information". This will enable you to quickly locate the model car, and the mechanical procedure you desire, without wasting precious time thumbing through unnecessary pages.

# HOW TO FIND THE INFORMATION
## 3 Quick Steps

(1) On the inside cover you'll find the contents of this manual. Locate the section you want, and notice that it has a black square next to it.

**THUMB INDEX SPOT**

TUNE-UP
Section 1

(2) Looking along the right edge of the book you'll notice additional black squares.

Match the black square of the section listed inside the cover, with the black square in line with it on the book's edge, then turn directly to that section.

(3) Review the section contents page.

After locating the specific article and starting page needed, turn to the beginning of the article.

**ATTENTION** Be sure to read note at bottom of contents page

# OR...

Go directly to the GENERAL INDEX located at the back of the book.
Use this alphabetical index as you would any type of reference index.

# Section Highlights

## TUNE-UP SPECIFICATIONS
### Section T

**KEY FEATURES**

In this section you will find all 1978 model tune-up specifications listed in chart form. This is for fast reference when you need ignition or emission specifications.

- Models with Electronic Ignition are called out.
- Although complete information on Renault Gordini and Peugeot 504 & 604 models is not available, tune-up specifications for these models can be found in this section.
- Emission settings are listed in chart form.

## TUNE-UP
### Section 1

The TUNE-UP section in this manual is divided alphabetically by manufacturer and then by engine size. Included in this section are Engine Indentification, to determine precisely what engine you are working on: Complete Servicing Information, which covers maintenance items such as Belt Adjustments, Filters and Cleaners, Capacities and Electrical Applications: Illustrations and Diagrams showing Timing Marks, Firing Orders and other items which become clearer when shown in an illustration.

**KEY FEATURES**

- You'll find critical metric conversion specifications printed in RED type.
- All Chrysler Corp. Imports in one article.
- Transmission and Axle Lubricant types are listed in the Capacities table.

## FUEL SYSTEMS
### Section 2

The FUEL SYSTEMS section covers such vital points as, Carburetor and Fuel Injection Trouble Shooting, Carburetor and Fuel Injection (both gasoline and diesel), Adjustment, Inspection and Overhaul procedures. Complete specification tables and exploded views of carburetors are included in this section. The last part of this section is devoted to Electric Fuel Pumps, and includes thorough testing and adjustment procedures.

**KEY FEATURES**

- Bosch Lambda Fuel Injection System
- Bosch Diesel Injection System
- Full coverage of electrical fuel pumps.

# ELECTRICAL
## Section 3

**KEY FEATURES**

Within the ELECTRICAL section you will find comprehensive Distributor Applications and Specifications. Testing, Adjustment and Overhaul procedures for Ignition Systems, as well as Regulators and Alternators are included here. The last part of the section is comprised of complete data for Switches, Gauges, Speedometers and Instrument Panels.

- General Servicing and Trouble Shooting for Alternators.
- Hazard and Turn Signal flasher locations.
- All Electronic Ignition System testing and overhaul.

# WIRING DIAGRAMS
## Section 4

**KEY FEATURES**

The WIRING DIAGRAM section covers Chassis Wiring for nearly all imported cars, with full schematics spread across several pages for easy reading and comprehension. In addition, there is a Sub-System section which includes schematics for cars with Fuel Injection systems, Seat Belt Warning systems, and Windshield Wiper Systems. The last part is devoted to Fuses and Circuit Breakers and their applications.

- On selected models with complex electrical systems, a 4 page Chassis Wiring diagram is included.
- Detailed views of electrical componet internal parts.
- Illustrations of Fuses and Circuits on models which may be confusing otherwise.

# ENGINES
## Section 5

**KEY FEATURES**

Within the ENGINE section you will find detailed articles covering Oil Pan Removal, Engine Removal, Valve Removal and Overhaul, Crankshaft and Connecting Rod Bearing Fitting and Camshaft Inspection and Replacement. At the end of each individual article you will find tables listing complete Engine Component Specifications as well as Tightening Specifications. This makes it easier to find specifications when procedural information isn't required.

- Porsche 928 Engine information with specifications.
- Coverage of Fiesta 1.6 Liter transverse engine.
- Engine Identification is in most articles.

# CLUTCHES

## Section 6

In the CLUTCH section you will find thorough Removal, Adjustment, Overhaul and Installation procedures for all aspects of clutches. This includes Master Cylinders, Release Bearings and Slave Cylinders.

**KEY FEATURES**
- Complete coverage of Porsche 928 Clutch.
- Detailed procedures for Toyota Corolla cable operated clutch system.
- Descriptions of clutch systems used in all cars.


# BRAKES

## Section 7

At the beginning of the brake section you will find a Trouble Shooting guide to help you locate and solve most problems associated with brake systems. Individual articles include Master Cylinder and Power Brake Unit coverage, with detailed explanations for Removal, Adjustment, Overhaul and Installation of both drum and disc brake systems. At the end of each article you'll find specifications listed for Disc Brake Rotors and Brake Drums, as well as Tightening Specifications.

**KEY FEATURES**
- Datsun 510 Brake System coverage.
- Hydraulic Brake System Bleeding procedures.
- Coverage (as available) of porportioning and combination values.


# WHEEL ALIGNMENT

## Section 8

The WHEEL ALIGNMENT ssction contains a Trouble Shooting Guide and comprehensive Wheel Alignment Specifications at the beginning of the section. Procedures covered include Wheel Alignment, Wheel Bearing Adjustment and Ball Joint Checking. Jacking and Hoisting diagrams are also included.

**KEY FEATURES**
- Camber and Caster adjustment procedures.
- Riding Height adjustment for certain models.
- Wheel Alignment specifications listed in tables.

# SUSPENSION

## Section 9

This section covers all front and rear suspension components with complete Removal, Adjustment and Overhaul procedures. Such items as Coil Springs, Strut Assemblies, Stabilizer Bars and Control Arms are given detailed procedural coverage. Large and easy to understand illustrations which show proper positioning of suspension components eliminate guesswork.

### KEY FEATURES

- A complete Trouble Shooting Guide at the front of the section saves time.
- Detailed procedures for MacPherson Strut Suspension Overhaul and Adjustment.
- Complete Torque specifications are given.

# STEERING

## Section 10

The STEERING section covers all aspects of steering components. Steering Column and Switches, Steering Gears and Linkage as well as a comprehensive Power Steering section are included. At the start of the section is a Manual and Power Steering Trouble Shooting Guide to locate possible problems. Detailed diagrams and illustrations clearly show proper positioning of steering assemblies, and complete Tightening Specifications are given at the end of each article.

### KEY FEATURES

- Thorough coverage of Porsche 928 Power Steering.
- Steering Wheel Removal procedures are given.
- Steering Column Removal procedures with diagrams are included.

# LATEST CHANGES and CORRECTIONS

This section is printed on blue paper and contains information on changes and corrections from the car manufacturers which arrived too late to be included among the regular stories. This information also may refer to previous model automobiles which were covered in other editions of Mitchell's Imported Car books.

# GENERAL INDEX

The final section of the Imported Manual is the GENERAL INDEX. This section is a quick, easy reference to help you locate the information you need. It is arranged alphabetically and is broken down into all of the vehicle's major components and then divided into models under component headings.

# Section T

# QUICK-CHECK
# TUNE-UP SPECS.

*NOTE — ALSO SEE GENERAL INDEX.*

# 1978 Tune-Up Specifications

| CAR MODEL | SPARK PLUGS | | CARBURETOR | | VALVE CLEARANCE | | DISTRIBUTOR | | No. |
|---|---|---|---|---|---|---|---|---|---|
| | Type | Gap | Make & Model | | Int. | Exh. | Point Gap | Cam Angle | |
| **ARROW** 1600 & 2000 2600 | NGK BPR-6ES-11 BPR-5ES-11 | .041" .041" | Solex Solex | 28-32 DIDTA① 30-32 DIDTA | .006" H .006" H | .010" H .010" H | .020" .020" | 49-55° 49-55° | 1 2 |
| **AUDI** Fox 5000 | Bosch W175T30 W175T30 | .028" .035" | Bosch Bosch | Fuel Inj. Fuel Inj. | .010" C .010" C | .018" C .018" C | .016" Ele. Ign. | 44-50° Ele. Ign. | 3 4 |
| **BMW** 320i 530i 633SCi & 733i | Bosch W145T30 W125T30 W145T30 | .024" .024" .025" | Bosch Bosch Bosch | Fuel Inj. Fuel Inj. Fuel Inj. | .007" C .011" C .011" C | .007" C .011" C .011" C | .016" .014" Ele. Ign. | 59-65° 35-41° Ele. Ign. | 5 6 7 |
| **CAPRI II** 2300 2800 | Mtrcraft AWRF-42 AWSF-42 | .034" .034" | Mtrcraft Mtrcraft | 2150 2150③ | Hyd. Lifter .014" H | Hyd. Lifter .016" H | Ele. Ign. Ele. Ign. | Ele. Ign. Ele. Ign. | 8 9 |
| **CHALLENGER** 1600 & 2000 2600 | NGK BPR-6ES-11 BPR-6ES-11 | .041" .041" | Solex Solex | 28-32 DIDTA① 30-32 DIDTA | .006" H .006" H | .010" H .010" H | .020" .020" | 49-55° 49-55° | 10 11 |
| **COLT** 1600 & 2000 2600 | NGK BPR-6ES-11 BPR-5ES-11 | .041" .041" | Solex Solex | 28-32 DIDTA① 30-32 DIDTA | .006" H .006" H | .010" H .010" H | .020" .020" | 49-55° 49-55° | 12 13 |
| **COURIER** 1800 2300 | Mtrcraft AGR-32 AGRF-52 | .031" .031" | Hitachi Hitachi | 2-Bbl. 2-Bbl. | .012" H Hyd. Lifter | .012" H Hyd. Lifter | .020" Ele. Ign. | 49-55° Ele. Ign. | 14 15 |
| **DATSUN** B210 & F10 200SX, 510 & Pickup 280Z 810 | NGK BP5ES-11① BP6ES-11 B6ES-11 B6ES-11 | .041"② .041" .041" .041" | Hitachi Hitachi Bosch Bosch | DCH-306 DCH-340 Fuel Inj. Fuel Inj. | .014" H .010" H .010" H .010" H | .014" H .012" H .012" H .012" H | Ele. Ign. Ele. Ign. Ele. Ign. Ele. Ign. | Ele. Ign. Ele. Ign. Ele. Ign. Ele. Ign. | 16 17 18 19 |
| **FIAT** 124 Brava & Super Brava 128 & X1/9 | Champion N9Y N9Y N9Y | .025" .025" .025" | Weber Weber Weber | 32 ADFA 32 ADFA 32 DATRA | .018" C .018" C .012" C | .020" C .020" C .016" C | .016" .016" .016" | 52-58° 52-58° 52-58° | 20 21 22 |
| **FIESTA** 1600 | Mtrcraft AWRF-32 | .050" | Weber | 740 | .010" C | .021" C | Ele. Ign. | Ele. Ign. | 23 |
| **HONDA** Civic Civic CVCC & Accord | NGK BP-6ES B6-EB | .030" .030" | Keihin Keihin | 2-Bbl. 2-Bbl. | .005" C .006" C | .005" C .008" C | .020" .020" | 49-55° 49-55° | 24 25 |

# 1978 Tune-Up Specifications

| No. | IGNITION TIMING | HOT IDLE RPM | | FAST IDLE RPM | EXHAUST CO READING At Idle Speed | Remarks |
|-----|-----------------|-------------|-------------|----|----|------|
| | | Man. Trans. | Auto. Trans. | | | |
| 1 | 5°BTDC ② | 600-700 | 650-750 | 2000 | 0.1% Max. | ① — 2000cc — 30-32 DIDTA |
| 2 | 7°BTDC | 800-900 ③ | 800-900 ④ | 2000 | 0.1% Max. | ② — 1600 Hi Alt. — 10°BTDC |
| | | | | | | ③ — Calif. — 650-750 RPM |
| | | | | | | ④ — Calif. — 700-800 RPM |
| 3 | 3°ATDC | 850-1000 | 850-1000 | ..... | ① | ① — Fed. M/T — 1.5%;Fed. A/T — 1.0%;Calif. — 0.3% |
| 4 | 3°ATDC | 850-1000 | 850-1000 | ..... | 0.9% ② | ② — Calif. — 0.3% |
| 5 | 25°BTDC | 850-1050 | 850-1050 | ..... | 2.0% Max.① | ① — Calif. — 2.5-3.0% |
| 6 | 22°BTDC | 850-1050 | 850-1050 | ..... | 1.5-3.0% | |
| 7 | 22°BTDC | 850-1050 | 850-1050 | ..... | 1.5-3.0% | |
| 8 | 6°BTDC ① | 850 | 750 | 1800 ② | ..... | ① — A/T — 20°BTDC |
| 9 | 12°BTDC | 850 ④ | 750 | 1700 | ..... | ② — Fed. MT — 1600 RPM |
| | | | | | | ③ — Calif. — Mtrcraft 2700vv |
| | | | | | | ④ — Calif. — 800 RPM |
| 10 | 5°BTDC ② | 600-700 | 650-750 | 2000 | 0.1% Max. | ① — 2000 cc — 30-32 DIDTA |
| 11 | 7°BTDC ③ | 650-750 | 700-800 | 2000 | 0.1% Max. | ② — Hi Alt. — 10°BTDC |
| | | | | | | ③ — Hi Alt. — 12°BTDC |
| 12 | 5°BTDC ② | 600-700 | 650-750 | 2000 | 0.1% Max. | ① — 2000cc — 30-32 DIDTA |
| 13 | 7°BTDC | 800-900 ③ | 800-900 ④ | 2000 | 0.1% Max. | ② — 1600cc Hi Alt. — 10°BTDC |
| | | | | | | ③ — Calif. — 650-750 RPM |
| | | | | | | ④ — Calif. — 700-800 RPM |
| 14 | 8°BTDC | 700-750 | ..... | ..... | 2.0% | |
| 15 | 6°BTDC | 800-850 | 700-750 | ..... | 4.0% | |
| 16 | 10°BTDC ③ | 700 | 650 | 2300 ④ | 1.0-3.0% ⑤ | ① — 5-Sp. Hatchback — BP5EQ-13 |
| 17 | 12°BTDC | 600 | 600 | 2300 ④ | 0.3-2.0% | ② — 5-Sp. Hatchback — .047" |
| 18 | 10°BTDC | 800 | 700 | ..... | 1.0% Max. | ③ — 5-Sp. Hatchback — 5°BTDC; All Fed. A/T — 8°BTDC |
| 19 | 10°BTDC | 700 | 650 | ..... | 1.0% Max. ⑥ | ④ — A/T — 2800 RPM |
| | | | | | | ⑤ — 5-Sp. Hatchback — 0.3-2.0% |
| | | | | | | ⑥ — Calif. — 0.5% Max. |
| 20 | TDC | 800-850 | ..... | 1600 | 1.5-2.5% | ① — 5°BTDC for A/T and All With Cat. Converter |
| 21 | TDC ① | 800-850 | 700-750 | 1600 ② | 1.5-2.5% | ② — A/T — 1300 RPM |
| 22 | TDC | 800-850 | ..... | ..... | 1.5-2.5% | |
| 23 | 12°BTDC | 800-900 | ..... | 1800 | ..... | |
| 24 | 2°BTDC | 650-750 | 650-750 | 1800 | 0.35% Max. | ① — Calif. & Hi Alt. — 2°BTDC |
| 25 | 6°BTDC ① | 650-750 | 600-700 | 2600 ② | 0.4% Max. | ② — Accord — 3000 RPM |

# 1978 Tune-Up Specifications

| CAR MODEL | SPARK PLUGS | | CARBURETOR | | VALVE CLEARANCE | | DISTRIBUTOR | | No. |
|---|---|---|---|---|---|---|---|---|---|
| | Type | Gap | Make & Model | | Int. | Exh. | Point Gap | Cam Angle | |
| **JAGUAR** | Champion | | | | | | | | |
| XJ6 | N12Y | .035" | Bosch/Lucas | Fuel Inj. | .013" C | .013" C | Ele. Ign. | Ele. Ign. | 26 |
| XJ12 & XJS | N10Y | .035" | Bosch/Lucas | Fuel Inj. | .013" C | .013" C | Ele. Ign. | Ele. Ign. | 27 |
| **LANCIA** | Champion | | | | | | | | |
| All Models | N9Y | .025" | Weber | 32 DATRA | .018" C | .020" C | .016" | 52-58° | 28 |
| **LUV** | NGK | | | | | | | | |
| Pickup | BPR-6ES | .030" | Hitachi | DCP-340 | .006" C | .010" C | .018" | 47-57° | 29 |
| **MAZDA** | NGK | | | | | | | | |
| GLC | BP-6ES | .031" | Hitachi | DCG-306 | .010" H | .012" H | .020" ① | 49-55° | 30 |
| B1800 | BP-6ES | .031" | Hitachi | DCJ-328 | .012" H | .012" H | .020" | 49-55° | 31 |
| RX-4 & Cosmo | B6-ET | .041" | Hitachi | 4-Bbl. | ..... | ..... | .018" | 55-61° | 32 |
| **MERCEDES-BENZ** | Bosch | | | | | | | | |
| 230 | W145T30 | .032" | Stromberg | 175CDTU | .004" C | .008" C | Ele. Ign. | Ele. Ign. | 33 |
| 240D | ..... | ..... | Bosch | Diesel Inj. | .004" C | .012" C | ..... | ..... | 34 |
| 280 Series | W145T30 | .032" | Bosch | Fuel Inj. | .004" C | .010" C | Ele. Ign. | Ele. Ign. | 35 |
| 300D, CD & SD | ..... | ..... | Bosch | Diesel Inj. | .004" C | .012" C ① | ..... | ..... | 36 |
| 450 Series | W145T30 | .032" | Bosch | Fuel Inj. | Hyd. Lifter | Hyd. Lifter | Ele. Ign. | Ele. Ign. | 37 |
| 6.9 | W145T30 | .032" | Bosch | Fuel Inj. | Hyd. Lifter | Hyd. Lifter | Ele. Ign. | Ele. Ign. | 38 |
| **MG** | Champion | | | | | | | | |
| Midget | N12Y | .025" | Zen-Strom | 150CD4T | .010" C | .010" C | Ele. Ign. | Ele. Ign. | 39 |
| MGB | N9Y | .035" | Zen-Strom | 175CD5T | .013" H | .013" H | Ele. Ign. | Ele. Ign. | 40 |
| **OPEL** | NGK | | | | | | | | |
| 1.8 | BPR-6ES | .030" | Nikki | 2-Bbl. | .006" C | .010" C | .018" | 47-57° | 41 |
| **PORSCHE** | Bosch | | | | | | | | |
| 911SC | W145T30 | .031" | Bosch | Fuel Inj. | .004" C | .004" C | Ele. Ign. | Ele. Ign. | 42 |
| 930 Turbo | W280P21 | .024" | Bosch | Fuel Inj. | .004" C | .004" C | Ele. Ign. | Ele. Ign. | 43 |
| 924 | W200T30 | .028" | Bosch | Fuel Inj. | .004" C | .016" C | Ele. Ign. | Ele. Ign. | 44 |
| 928 | W145T30 | .030" | Bosch | Fuel Inj. | Hyd. Lifter | Hyd. Lifter | Ele. Ign. | Ele. Ign. | 45 |
| **RENAULT** | Champion | | | | | | | | |
| R-5 | L87Y ① | .025" | Weber | 32 DIR | .006" C | .008" C | .018" | 55-59° | 46 |
| R-17 Gordini | N3 ③ | .025" | Bosch | Fuel Inj. | .010" C | .010" C | .018" | 55-59° | 47 |
| **SAAB** | NGK | | | | | | | | |
| 99 | BP-6ES | .026" | Bosch | Fuel Inj. | .009" C | .017" C | Ele. Ign. | Ele. Ign. | 48 |
| Turbo | BP-6ES | .028" | Bosch | Fuel Inj. | .014" | .022" | Ele. Ign. | Ele. Ign. | 49 |
| **SAPPORO** | NGK | | | | | | | | |
| 1600 & 2000 | BPR-6ES-11 | .041" | Solex | 28-32 DIDTA ① | .006" H | .010" H | .020" | 49-55° | 50 |
| 2600 | BPR-6ES-11 | .041" | Solex | 30-32 DIDTA | .006" H | .010" H | .020" | 49-55° | 51 |
| **SUBARU** | NGK | | | | | | | | |
| 1600 & BRAT | BP-6ES | .032" | Hitachi | DCJ-306 | .010" C | .014" C | .018" ① | 52° | 52 |

| No. | IGNITION TIMING | HOT IDLE RPM | | FAST IDLE RPM | EXHAUST CO READING At Idle Speed | Remarks |
|---|---|---|---|---|---|---|
| | | Man. Trans. | Auto. Trans. | | | |
| 26 | 4°BTDC | ..... | 800 | ..... | 0.5-1.5% | ① – Calif. – 4°ATDC |
| 27 | 10°BTDC① | ..... | 750 | ..... | 1.0-2.0% | |
| 28 | TDC① | 800-850 | ..... | 1600 | 1.5-2.5% | ① – 10°BTDC With Cat. Converter |
| 29 | 6°BTDC | 900 | 900 | 3400① | ..... | ① – A/T – 3200 RPM |
| 30 | 11°BTDC② | 700-750 | 600-650 | 3500 | 1.5-2.5% | ① – Fed. Models – Electronic Ignition |
| 31 | 8°BTDC | 700-750 | ..... | 3500 | 1.5-2.5% | ② – Fed. M/T – 7°BTDC |
| 32 | 5°ATDC③ | 725-775 | 725-775 | 3250 | 0.1% Max. | ③ – Leading; Trailing – 25°ATDC |
| 33 | 10°BTDC | ..... | 850 | 1800 | 0.4-2.0% | |
| 34 | ..... | 650-750 | 650-750 | ..... | ..... | ① – 300SD – .014" Cold |
| 35 | TDC | ..... | 800 | ..... | 0.4-2.0% | ② – 300SD – 650-850 RPM |
| 36 | ..... | ..... | 650-750② | ..... | ..... | |
| 37 | TDC | ..... | 750 | ..... | 0.5-2.0% | |
| 38 | TDC | ..... | 600 | ..... | 0.5-2.0% | |
| 39 | 10°BTDC① | 700-900 | ..... | | 3.0-7.0%② | ① – Calif. – 2°ATDC |
| 40 | 10°BTDC | 750-950 | ..... | | 4.5-6.5% | ② – Calif. – 0.5-6.5% |
| 41 | 6°BTDC | 875-925 | 875-925 | 3400① | ..... | ① – M/T. Fed. A/T, 3200; Calif. A/T, 3000 |
| 42 | 5°BTDC | 900-1000 | ..... | | 1.5-3.5% | ① – Calif. – 5°ATDC |
| 43 | 10°ATDC① | 950-1050 | ..... | | 2.0-3.0% | ② – Calif. – 0.8-1.2% |
| 44 | 3°ATDC | 900-1000 | 900-1000 | | 0.5-1.0%② | ③ – At 3000 RPM |
| 45 | 31°BTDC③ | 750-850 | ..... | | 2.0-4.0% | |
| 46 | TDC | 750-850 | ..... | 1900② | 0.5-3.0% | ① – Calif. & Hi Alt. – L92Y |
| 47 | 12°BTDC | 750-950 | 750-950 | ..... | 2.0% | ② – Calif. & Hi Alt. – 1500 RPM |
| | | | | | | ③ – Calif. – N7 |
| 48 | 20°BTDC① | 825-925 | 825-925 | ..... | 0.5-2.0%② | ① – At 2000 RPM |
| 49 | 19°BTDC① | ..... | ..... | | ..... | ② – Calif. – 0.5-1.0% |
| 50 | 5°BTDC② | 600-700 | 650-750 | 2000 | 0.1% Max. | ① – 2000cc – 30-32 DIDTA |
| 51 | 7°BTDC③ | 650-750 | 700-800 | 2000 | 0.1% Max. | ② – Hi Alt. – 10°BTDC |
| | | | | | | ③ – Hi Alt: – 12°BTDC |
| 52 | 8°BTDC | 850② | 850② | ..... | 1.0-2.0%③ | ① – Calif. – Electronic Ignition |
| | | | | | | ② – Calif. – 900 RPM |
| | | | | | | ③ – Calif. – 0.5-1.0% |

# 1978 Tune-Up Specifications

| CAR MODEL | SPARK PLUGS | | CARBURETOR | | VALVE CLEARANCE | | DISTRIBUTOR | | No. |
|---|---|---|---|---|---|---|---|---|---|
| | Type | Gap | Make & Model | | Int. | Exh. | Point Gap | Cam Angle | |
| **TOYOTA** | NGK | | | | | | | | 53 |
| 3KC Engine | BP5ES-L | .031″ | Aisan | 2-Bbl. | .008″ H | .012″ H | Ele. Ign. | Ele. Ign. | 54 |
| 2TC Engine | BP5ES-L | .031″ | Aisan | 2-Bbl. | .008″ H | .013″ H | Ele. Ign. | Ele. Ign. | 55 |
| 20R Engine | BP5ES-L | .031″ | Aisan | 2-Bbl. | .008″ H | .012″ H | Ele. Ign. | Ele. Ign. | 56 |
| 4M Engine | BPR5ES | .031″ | Aisan | 2-Bbl. | .011″ H | .014″ H | Ele. Ign. | Ele. Ign. | 57 |
| 2F Engine | BP5EZ | .040″ | Aisan | 2-Bbl. | .008″ H | .014″ H | Ele. Ign. | Ele. Ign. | |
| **TRIUMPH** | Champion | | | | | | | | 58 |
| Spitfire | N12Y | .025″ | Zen-Strom | 150CD4T | .010″ C | .010″ C | Ele. Ign. | Ele. Ign. | 59 |
| TR7 | N12Y | .025″ | Zen-Strom | 175CDFEVX | .008″ C | .018″ C | Ele. Ign. | Ele. Ign. | |
| **VOLKSWAGEN** | Bosch | | | | | | | | 60 |
| Type 1 | W145M1 | .028″ | Bosch | Fuel Inj. | .006″ C | .006″ C | .016″ | 44-50° | 61 |
| Type 2 | W145M2 | .028″ | Bosch | Fuel Inj. | Hyd. Lifter | Hyd. Lifter | .016″ | 44-50° | 62 |
| Dasher | W175T30 | .028″ | Bosch | Fuel Inj. | .010″ C | .018″ C | .016″ | 44-50° | 63 |
| Rabbit & Scirocco | W175T30 | .026″ | Bosch | Fuel Inj. | .010″ C | .018″ C | .016″ | 44-50° | 64 |
| Rabbit Diesel | ..... | ..... | Bosch | Diesel Inj. | .008″ C | .016″ C | ..... | | |
| **VOLVO** | Bosch | | | | | | | | 65 |
| 240 Series | W175T30 | .030″ | Bosch | Fuel Inj. | .015″ C | .015″ C | Ele. Ign. | Ele. Ign. | 66 |
| 260 Series | WA200T30 | .030″ | Bosch | Fuel Inj. | .005″ C | .011″ C | Ele. Ign. | Ele. Ign. | |

# 1978 Tune-Up Specifications

QUICK CHECK TUNE UP SPECS

| No. | IGNITION TIMING | HOT IDLE RPM | | FAST IDLE RPM | EXHAUST CO READING At Idle Speed | Remarks |
|---|---|---|---|---|---|---|
| | | Man. Trans. | Auto. Trans. | | | |
| 53 | 8°BTDC | 700-800 | 700-800 | ..... | 4.5% Max. | ① — Calif. & Hi Alt. — 3000 RPM |
| 54 | 10°BTDC | 800-900 | 800-900 | 3200② | 4.5% Max. | |
| 55 | 8°BTDC | 750-850 | 800-900 | 2400 | 4.5% Max. | |
| 56 | 10°BTDC | ..... | 700-800 | 2500 | 4.5% Max. | |
| 57 | 7°BTDC | 600-700 | ..... | 1800 | ..... | |
| 58 | 10°BTDC① | 700-900 | ..... | ..... | 3.0-7.0%② | ① — Calif. — 2°ATDC |
| 59 | 10°BTDC① | 700-900 | ..... | ..... | 3.0-7.0% | ② — Calif. — 0.5-6.5% |
| 60 | 5°ATDC | 800-950 | ..... | ..... | 1.5% Max① | ① — Calif. — 1.0% Max. |
| 61 | 7.5°BTDC | 800-950 | 900-1000 | ..... | 1.0-1.5% | ② — Fed. A/T — 1.0% Max.; Fed. M/T — 1.5% Max.; |
| 62 | 3°ATDC | 850-1000 | 850-1000 | ..... | ② | |
| 63 | 3°ATDC | 850-1000 | 850-1000 | ..... | ② | Calif. — 0.3% Max. |
| 64 | ..... | 770-870 | ..... | ..... | ..... | |
| 65 | 12°BTDC | 850-950 | 850-950 | ..... | 0.7-1.3%① | ① — Calif. — 1.0-2.5% |
| 66 | 10°BTDC | 850-950 | 850-950 | ..... | 0.7-1.3% | |

# Section 1
# TUNE-UP

## Contents

*NOTE — ALSO SEE GENERAL INDEX*

## TUNE-UP

**Fox**

## ENGINE IDENTIFICATION

Engine number is stamped on left side of engine block near distributor.

### Engine Code Numbers

| Application | Code |
|---|---|
| Man. Trans | YG |
| Auto. Trans. | YH |

## MODEL IDENTIFICATION

### VEHICLE IDENTIFICATION

Vehicle may be identified by the chassis number which is embossed on rear wall of engine compartment, on left windshield pillar (visible through windshield), and on safety sticker on left door jamb.

## COMPRESSION PRESSURE

With engine at normal operating temperature, throttle wide open and engine at cranking speed, compression pressure should be as follows:

| Application | ①Stand. Pressure psi (kg/cm²) | ①Min. Pressure psi (kg/cm²) |
|---|---|---|
| All Models | 142-184 (10-13) | 107 (7.5) |

① — Maximum difference per cylinder is 42 psi (2.95 kg/cm²).

## VALVE TAPPET CLEARANCE

**1)** Adjust valves with engine at normal operating temperature. Clearance adjustments are to be checked and made according to firing order sequence (1-3-4-2). Rotate crankshaft until cam lobes for No. 1 cylinder valves point upward, then measure valve clearances of No. 1 cylinder.

**2)** If adjustment is necessary, use special tools 10-208 (disc removal tool) and VW546 (tappet depressing tool) to remove and install adjusting discs. Rotate camshaft until cam lobes no longer rest on adjusting discs of cylinder to be adjusted. Turn tappet until notches are at 90° to camshaft. Insert tool VW546 and depress tappet. Using tool 10-208, grasp tappet disc and rotate it out from under camshaft.

**3)** Thickness is stamped on bottom side of disc. Using clearance measurement, determine thickness of adjusting disc necessary to bring valve clearances within specifications. Discs are available in .0019" (.05 mm) increments from .1181" (3.0 mm) to .1673" (4.25 mm). Reverse removal procedure to install proper disc. Repeat procedure as required for remaining valves.

### Valve Tappet Clearance

| Application | Specification |
|---|---|
| Intake | ①.008-.012" (.2-.3 mm) |
| Exhaust | ①.016-.020" (.4-.5 mm) |

① — Adjust with engine warm.

### VALVE ARRANGEMENT

E-I-E-I-I-E-I-E (front to rear).

## SPARK PLUGS

| | |
|---|---|
| Gap | .028" (.7 mm) |
| Torque | 22 ft. lbs. (3 mkg) |

### Spark Plug Type

| Application | Bosch | Beru | Champion |
|---|---|---|---|
| All Models | W175T30 | 175/14/3A | N8Y |

## HIGH TENSION WIRE RESISTANCE

Carefully remove ends of wire from spark plug and distributor. Using an ohmmeter, check resistance of wire while gently twisting wire. If resistance is not to specification, or fluctuates from infinity to any value, replace wire.

### Resistance (Ohms) Per Wire

| Application | Resistance |
|---|---|
| All Models | 25,000-30,000 |

## DISTRIBUTOR

| | |
|---|---|
| Point Gap (All Models) | .016" (.4 mm) |
| Cam Angle (All Models) | 47°±3° |
| Condenser Capacity (All Models) | .22 mfd. |

*Fig. 1   Firing Order and Distributor Rotation*

## IGNITION TIMING

With timing light connected, engine speed set to specified RPM and vacuum hoses connected, rotate distributor until specified timing is obtained.

## TUNE-UP (Cont.)

### Ignition Timing Specifications

| Application | RPM | Timing |
|---|---|---|
| All Models | 850-1000 | ①3°ATDC |

① — With vacuum hoses connected.

**Fig. 2  Ignition Timing Mark Location**

### IDLE SPEED & MIXTURE

1) With engine at normal operating temperature, check and make sure that ignition timing, valve clearance, spark plug gap and compression pressures are within specifications. Turn headlights on high beam and, if equipped, turn air conditioning off. Leave vacuum hoses connected.

2) Adjust idle speed to specifications by means of the idle control screw at the throttle plate housing.

3) To adjust CO level, remove plug from mixture control unit between fuel distributor and venturi. Insert suitable adjusting tool (P 377) and turn clockwise to raise CO% or counterclockwise to decrease CO% until the specified CO level is obtained.

**NOTE** — *Engine will stall if pressure is exerted on adjusting tool. Use very small adjustments or CO level will be changed greatly.*

4) Remove adjusting wrench and accelerate engine briefly. Wait until CO meter has stabilized for idle speed reading. Check idle speed and CO level and adjust if necessary.

### Idle Speed (RPM) & CO Level (%)

| Application | Idle RPM | ①CO% |
|---|---|---|
| Federal | | |
| Man. Trans. | 850-1000 | 1.5 Max. |
| Auto. Trans | 850-1000 | 1.0 Max. |
| Calif. | 850-1000 | 0.3 Max. |

① — With vacuum hoses connected and air conditioning off.

### FUEL PUMP PRESSURE

| | | |
|---|---|---|
| Pressure | | |
| All Models | | 64-74 psi (4.5-5.2 kg/cm²) |
| Delivery Rate | | Approx. 1 quart in 40 seconds |

**Other Data & Specifications** — *See Tune-Up and Bosch CIS Fuel Injection in FUEL SYSTEMS Section.*

### EMISSION CONTROL SYSTEMS

*See Mitchell Manuals' Emission Control Manual.*

# GENERAL SERVICING

## IGNITION

### DISTRIBUTOR

All models are equipped with Bosch single point distributors.

**Other Data & Specifications** — *See Tune-Up & Bosch Distributors in ELECTRICAL Section.*

### IGNITION COIL

#### Resistance Specifications

| Application | Primary (Ohms) | Secondary (Ohms) |
|---|---|---|
| All Models | 1.7-2.1 | 7,000-12,000 |

## FUEL SYSTEMS

### FUEL INJECTION

All models are equipped with Bosch CIS Fuel Injection System.

**Other Data & Specifications** — *See Tune-Up and Bosch Fuel Injection in FUEL SYSTEMS Section.*

## ELECTRICAL

### BATTERY

**12 Volt** — Negative Ground

| Application | Amp. Hr. Capacity |
|---|---|
| W/O Air Conditioning | 45 |
| W/Air Conditioning | 54 |

## GENERAL SERVICING (Cont.)

**Battery Location** — Right side of engine compartment.

### STARTER

All models are equipped with Bosch Starters.

**Other Data & Specifications** — *See Bosch Starters in ELECTRICAL Section.*

### ALTERNATOR

| Application | Rated Amp. Output |
|---|---|
| W/O Air Conditioning | 55 |
| W/Air Conditioning | 65 |

**Other Data & Specifications** — *See Bosch and Motorola Alternators & Regulators in ELECTRICAL Section.*

### ALTERNATOR REGULATOR

Motorola and Bosch — Non-adjustable, integral with alternator.

Operating Voltage ......................... 12.5-14.5 Volts

**Other Data & Specifications** — *See Bosch & Motorola Alternators & Regulators in ELECTRICAL Section.*

---

### FILTERS & CLEANERS

| Filter or Cleaner | Service Interval (Miles) |
|---|---|
| Oil Filter | Replace every 7,500 |
| Air Cleaner | Replace every 15,000 |
| Fuel Filter | Replace every 15,000 |

### BELT ADJUSTMENT

**All Models** — With a 20 lbs. (9.1 kg) pressure, belt should be able to be depressed .40" (9.8 mm).

### CAPACITIES

| Application | Quantity |
|---|---|
| Crankcase (Includes Filter) | ①3.2 qts. |
| Cooling System | ②6.9 qts. |
| Man. Trans. (SAE 80W or 80W/90) | 1.6 qts. |
| Auto. Trans. (Dexron) | ③3.2 qts. |
| Auto. Trans. Final Drive (SAE 90) | 1.5 pts. |
| Fuel Tank | ④11.9 gals. |
| Windshield Washer Container | 2.0 qts. |

① — 2.6 qts. without filter.
② — Includes 0.6 qts. in expansion tank.
③ — Refill. Dry fill is 6.2 qts.
④ — Includes 1.3 gals. in reserve.

## TUNE-UP

**5000**

## ENGINE IDENTIFICATION

Engine number is stamped on left side of block near distributor.

### Engine Code Numbers

| Application | Code |
|---|---|
| Federal | WD |
| Calif. | WE |

## MODEL IDENTIFICATION

### VEHICLE IDENTIFICATION

Vehicle may be identified by the chassis number which is embossed on rear wall of engine compartment, on left windshield pillar (visible through windshield), and on safety sticker on left door jamb.

## COMPRESSION PRESSURE

With engine at normal operating temperature, throttle wide open and engine at cranking speed, compression pressure should be as follows:

| Application | ①Stand. Pressure psi (kg/cm²) | ①Min. Pressure psi (kg/cm²) |
|---|---|---|
| All Models | 120-170 (8.4-12) | 100 (6.9) |

① Maximum difference per cylinder is 42 psi (2.95 kg/cm²).

## VALVE TAPPET CLEARANCE

**1)** Adjust valves with engine at normal operating temperature. Remove accelerator linkage and cylinder head cover. Clearance adjustments are to be checked and made according to firing order sequence (1-2-4-5-3). Rotate crankshaft until cam lobes for No. 1 cylinder valves point upward; then, measure valve clearances of No. 1 cylinder.

**2)** If adjustment is necessary, use special tools 10-208 (disc removal tool) and 2078 (tappet depressing tool) to remove and install adjusting discs. Turn tappet until notches are at 90° to camshaft. Insert tool 2078 and depress tappet. Using tool 10-208, grasp tappet disc and rotate it out from under camshaft.

**3)** Thickness is stamped on bottom side of disc. Using clearance measurement, determine thickness of adjusting disc necessary to bring valve clearance within specifications. Discs are available in .0019" (.05 mm) increments from .1181" (3.0 mm) to .1673" (4.25 mm). Reverse removal procedure to install proper disc. Repeat procedure as required for remaining valves.

### Valve Tappet Clearance

| Application | Specification |
|---|---|
| Intake | ①.008-.012 (.2-.3 mm) |
| Exhaust | ①.016-.020 (.4-.5 mm) |

① — Adjust with engine warm.

## VALVE ARRANGEMENT

E-I-E-I-I-E-I-I-E-I-E (front to rear)

## SPARK PLUGS

| | |
|---|---|
| Gap | .035" (.9 mm) |
| Torque | 22 ft. lbs (3 mkg) |

### Spark Plug Type

| Application | Bosch | Beru | Champion |
|---|---|---|---|
| All Models | W175T30 | 175/14/3A | N8Y |

## HIGH TENSION WIRE RESISTANCE

Carefully remove ends of wire from spark plug and distributor. Using an ohmmeter, check resistance of wire while gently twisting wire. If resistance is not to specification, or fluctuates from infinity to any value, replace wire.

### Resistance (Ohms) Per Wire

| Application | Resistance |
|---|---|
| All Models | 25,000-30,000 |

**Fig. 1  Firing Order and Distributor Rotation**

## DISTRIBUTOR

All models are equipped with a breakerless, transistorized ignition system.

| | |
|---|---|
| Air Gap | .010" (.25 mm) |
| Dwell Angle (Non-Adjustable) | 43-65° |

## TUNE-UP (Cont.)

### IGNITION TIMING

With timing light connected, engine speed set to specified RPM and vacuum hoses connected, rotate distributor until specified timing is obtained.

#### Ignition Timing Specifications

| Application | RPM | Timing |
|---|---|---|
| All Models | 850-1000 | ①3°ATDC |

① — With vacuum hoses connected.

**Fig. 2   Ignition Timing Mark Location**

### IDLE SPEED & MIXTURE

1) With engine at normal operating temperature, check and make sure that ignition timing, valve clearance, spark plug gap and compression pressures are within specifications. Turn headlights on high beam and, if equipped, turn air conditioning off. Leave vacuum hoses connected.

2) Adjust idle speed to specifications by means of the idle control screw at the throttle plate housing.

### 3) To adjust CO level, remove plug from mixture control unit between fuel distributor and venturi. Insert suitable adjusting tool (P 377) and turn clockwise to raise CO% or counterclockwise to decrease CO% until the specified CO level is obtained.

**NOTE** — *Engine will stall if pressure is exerted on adjusting tool. Use very small adjustments or CO level will be changed greatly.*

4) Remove adjusting wrench and accelerate engine briefly. Wait until CO meter has stabilized for idle speed reading. Check idle speed and CO level and adjust if necessary.

#### Idle Speed (RPM) & CO Level (%)

| Application | Idle RPM | CO % |
|---|---|---|
| Federal | 850-1000 | ①0.9 Max. |
| Calif. | 850-1000 | ①0.3 Max. |

① — With vacuum hoses connected and air conditioning off.

### FUEL PUMP PRESSURE

Pressure
All Models .................................. 64-74 psi (4.5-5.2 kg/cm²)
Delivery Rate ......................... Approx. 1 quart in 40 seconds

**Other Data & Specifications** — *See Tune-Up and Bosch CIS Fuel Injection in FUEL SYSTEMS Section.*

### EMISSION CONTROL SYSTEMS

*See Mitchell Manuals' Emission Control Manual.*

## GENERAL SERVICING

### IGNITION

#### DISTRIBUTOR

All models are equipped with Bosch breakerless ignition system.

**Other Data & Specifications** — *See Tune-Up & Bosch Distributors in ELECTRICAL Section.*

#### IGNITION COIL

##### Resistance Specifications

| Application | Primary (Ohms) | Secondary (Ohms) |
|---|---|---|
| All Models | .95-1.4 | 5,500-8,000 |

### FUEL SYSTEMS

#### FUEL INJECTION

All models are equipped with Bosch CIS Fuel Injection System.

**Other Data & Specifications** — *See Tune-Up and Bosch Fuel Injection in FUEL SYSTEMS Section.*

### ELECTRICAL

#### BATTERY

**12 Volt** — Negative Ground

| Application | Amp. Hr. Capacity |
|---|---|
| All Models | 63 |

## GENERAL SERVICING (Cont.)

**Battery Location** – Right side of engine compartment.

### STARTER

All models are equipped with Bosch Starters.

**Other Data & Specifications** – *See Bosch Starters in ELECTRICAL Section.*

### ALTERNATOR

| Application | Rated Amp. Output |
|---|---|
| All Models | 75 |

**Other Data & Specifications** – *See Bosch Alternators & Regulators in ELECTRICAL Section.*

### ALTERNATOR REGULATOR

Bosch – Non-adjustable, integral with alternator.

| | |
|---|---|
| Operating Voltage | 12.5-14.5 Volts |

**Other Data & Specifications** – *See Bosch Alternators & Regulators in ELECTRICAL Section.*

---

### BELT ADJUSTMENT

**All Models** – With a 20 lbs. (9.1 kg) pressure, belt should be able to be depressed 3/8 -9/16" (10-15 mm).

---

### FILTERS & CLEANERS

| Filter or Cleaner | Service Interval (Miles) |
|---|---|
| Oil Filter | Replace every 7,500 |
| Air Cleaner | Replace every 15,000 |
| Fuel Filter | Replace every 15,000 |

---

### CAPACITIES

| Application | Quantity |
|---|---|
| Crankcase (Includes Filter) | ① 5.3 qts. |
| Cooling System | 8.6 qts. |
| Man. Trans. (SAE 80) | 2.6 qts. |
| Auto. Trans. (Dexron) | ② 3.2 qts. |
| Auto. Trans. Final Drive (SAE 90) | 1.1 qts. |
| Fuel Tank | ③ 15.9 gals. |
| Windshield Washer Container | 1.8 qts. |

① – 4.8 qts. without filter.
② – For refill.
③ – Includes 2.1 gals. in reserve.

# 1978 BMW 4 Tune-Up

## TUNE-UP

### 320i

## ENGINE IDENTIFICATION

The engine number of the 1990 cc 4-cylinder, single overhead camshaft engine is located on the rear of the cylinder block above the starter near the left-hand side.

## MODEL IDENTIFICATION

### VEHICLE IDENTIFICATION NUMBER

The chassis number is located on a label attached to the upper steering column and on the support plate of the right-hand wheel arch in the engine compartment.

## COMPRESSION PRESSURE

With battery fully charged, engine at normal operating temperature, throttle fully open and engine at cranking speed, compression pressure should be as follows:

Good............................ Above 149 psi (10.5 kg/cm²)
Normal............................ 135-149 psi (9.5-10.5 kg/cm²)
Poor .............................. Below 128 psi (9.0 kg/cm²)

## VALVE TAPPET CLEARANCE

With engine either cold or at normal operating temperature, loosen nut on rocker arm and adjust position of eccentric cam to obtain proper clearance. Adjust valves in firing order sequence at TDC of compression stroke.

| Adjust Cylinder at Top Dead Center | When Valves Of Cylinder Overlap |
|---|---|
| No. 1 ................................................ | No. 4 |
| No. 3 ................................................ | No. 2 |
| No. 4 ................................................ | No. 1 |
| No. 2 ................................................ | No. 3 |

### Valve Clearance Specifications

| Application | Clearance In. (mm) |
|---|---|
| Cold, Intake & Exhaust ........................... | .006-.008 (.15-.20) |
| Warm, Intake & Exhaust ......................... | .008-.010 (.20-.25) |

### VALVE ARRANGEMENT
Left Side  — All Intake.
Right Side  — All Exhaust.

Fig. 1   Firing Order and Distributor Rotation

## SPARK PLUGS

Gap ....................................... .024-.028" (.6-.7mm)
Torque .............................. 18-22 ft. lbs. (2.5-3 mkg)

### Spark Plug Type

| Application | Champion | Bosch |
|---|---|---|
| All Models ..................... | N-10Y ..................... | W 145 T30 |

## HIGH TENSION WIRE RESISTANCE

Carefully remove ends of wire from spark plug and distributor. Using an ohmmeter, check resistance of wire while gently twisting wire. If resistance is not to specification, or fluctuates from infinity to any value, replace wire.

### Resistance (Ohms) Per Wire

| Application | Resistance |
|---|---|
| All Models ................................................... | 25,000-30,000 |

## DISTRIBUTOR

Point Gap ..................................... .016" (.41 mm)
Cam Angle ............................................. 59-65°
Breaker Arm Spring Tension .............. 17-22 oz. (475-620 g)
Condenser Capacity ......................... .2±.02 mfd.

Fig. 2   Ignition Timing Mark Location

## IGNITION TIMING

With engine at normal operating temperature, connect a timing light and tachometer to vehicle. Disconnect and plug distributor vacuum line. Start engine and adjust speed to specifications shown in following table. To adjust ignition timing, rotate distributor until center of ball embedded in flywheel is visible at edge of inspection hole. On models with automatic transmission, a long pin is used instead of the ball.

### Ignition Timing Specifications

| Application | RPM | Dynamic Timing |
|---|---|---|
| California ....................... | 2400 ....................... | 25° BTDC |
| Federal ......................... | 2200 ....................... | 25° BTDC |

# 1978 BMW 4 Tune-Up

## TUNE-UP (Cont.)

### IDLE SPEED & MIXTURE

1) With air cleaner element in good condition, engine at normal operating temperature, ignition timing and valve clearance to specifications, disconnect air injection pump hose and plug check valve. Connect tachometer and exhaust gas analyzer to vehicle.

2) Adjust idle speed to specifications by adjusting idle air screw on throttle valve housing. Remove access plug, located next to fuel distributor. Insert a suitable Allen wrench (or special wrench 130 010) into plug hole and adjust to specified CO level.

CAUTION – Do not accelerate engine while adjusting CO level.

3) Reinstall plug and reconnect air hose.

### Idle Speed (RPM) & CO Level (%)

| Application | Idle RPM | CO% |
|---|---|---|
| Federal | 850-1050 | 2.0 Max. |
| Calif | 850-1050 | 2.5-3.0 |

### FUEL PUMP PRESSURE

| Application | psi (kg/cm²) |
|---|---|
| All Models | 64-74 (4.5-5.2) |

### EMISSION CONTROL SYSTEMS

See Mitchell Manuals' Emission Control Manual.

## GENERAL SERVICING

### IGNITION

**DISTRIBUTOR**

All models are equipped with Bosch single point distributors.

**Other Data & Specifications** – See Tune-Up & Bosch Distributors in ELECTRICAL Section.

**IGNITION COIL**

| Resistance | Ohms at 68°F (20°C) |
|---|---|
| Primary | 1.7-2.1 |

### FUEL SYSTEMS

**FUEL INJECTION**

All models are equipped with Bosch Continuous Injection System (CIS) fuel injection.

**Other Data & Specifications** – See Bosch CIS Fuel Injection in FUEL SYSTEMS Section.

### ELECTRICAL

**BATTERY**

**12 Volt** – Negative Ground.

| Application | Amp. Hr. Rating |
|---|---|
| All Models | 55 |

**Battery Location** – In engine compartment.

### STARTER

All models are equipped with Bosch Starters.

**Other Data & Specifications** – See Bosch Starters in ELECTRICAL Section.

### ALTERNATOR

| Application | Rated Amp. Output |
|---|---|
| All Models | 55 |

**Other Data & Specifications** – See Bosch Alternators & Regulators in ELECTRICAL Section.

### ALTERNATOR REGULATOR

All models are equipped with Bosch Alternator Regulators with an operating voltage of 13.9-14.2 volts at 68°F (20°C).

**Other Data & Specifications** – See Bosch Alternators & Regulators in ELECTRICAL Section.

# 1978 BMW 4 Tune-Up

## GENERAL SERVICING (Cont.)

### BELT ADJUSTMENT

**Fan Belt** — Adjust tension until it is possible to depress belt 3/16-3/8" (5-10 mm) midway between fan and alternator pulleys.

**Air Pump** — Adjust tension until it is possible to depress belt 3/16 - 3/8" (5-10 mm) midway between pulleys.

### FILTERS & CLEANERS

| Filter or Cleaner | Service Interval (Miles) |
| --- | --- |
| Oil Filter | Replace every 6,000 |
| Air Cleaner | Clean every 6,000 |
| | Replace every 12,500 |
| Fuel Filter | Replace every 12,500 |
| Main Fuel Filter (Electric Pump) | Replace every 37,500 |

### CAPACITIES

| Application | Quantity |
| --- | --- |
| Crankcase (Includes Filter) | 4.5 qts. |
| Cooling System (Includes Heater) | 7.4 qts. |
| Man. Trans. (SAE 80) | 2.0 pts. |
| Auto. Trans. (Dexron) | ①2.1 qts. |
| Rear Axle (SAE 90) | 2.0 pts. |
| Fuel Tank | ②16.0 gals. |

① — Refill. Total capacity: 6.4 qts.
② — Includes 2 gals. in reserve.

## TUNE-UP

530i
633CSi
733i

### ENGINE IDENTIFICATION

The 530i model is equipped with a 2985 cc engine; 633CSi and 733i models are equipped with a 3210 cc engine. Engine numbers for all models are located at rear of cylinder block above starter (left side).

### MODEL IDENTIFICATION

#### VEHICLE IDENTIFICATION NUMBER

Number is stamped on vehicle identification plate, which is located on the support plate of the right-hand wheel arch at the rear of the engine compartment.

### COMPRESSION PRESSURE

With battery fully charged, engine at normal operating temperature, throttle fully open and engine at cranking speed, compression pressure should be as follows:

530i

| | |
|---|---|
| Good | Above 156 psi (11 kg/cm²) |
| Normal | 142-156 psi (10-11 kg/cm²) |
| Poor | Below 142 psi (10 kg/cm²) |

633 CSi & 733i
| | |
|---|---|
| Good | Above 142 psi (10 kg/cm²) |
| Normal | 121-142 psi (8.5-10 kg/cm²) |
| Poor | 114 psi (8 kg/cm²) |

### VALVE TAPPET CLEARANCE

With engine cold, loosen nut on rocker arm and adjust position of eccentric cam to obtain proper clearance. Adjust valves in firing order sequence at TDC of compression stroke. Use feeler gauge to measure clearance between rocker arm eccentric and valve stem.

| Adjust Cylinder at Top Dead Center | When Valves Of Cylinder Overlap |
|---|---|
| No. 1 | No. 6 |
| No. 5 | No. 2 |
| No. 3 | No. 4 |
| No. 6 | No. 1 |
| No. 2 | No. 5 |
| No. 4 | No. 3 |

#### Valve Clearance Specifications

| Application | Clearance In. (mm) |
|---|---|
| Intake & Exhaust | ①.010-.012 (.25-.30) |

① — Adjust with engine cold.

### VALVE ARRANGEMENT

Left Side — All Intake.
Right Side — All Exhaust.

### SPARK PLUGS

| | |
|---|---|
| Gap | .024" (.6 mm) |
| Torque | 18-22 ft. lbs. (2.5-3.0 mkg) |

#### Spark Plug Type

| Application | Bosch | Champion |
|---|---|---|
| 530i | W 125 T30 | N-10Y |
| 633CSi & 733i | W 145 T30 | N-10Y |

### HIGH TENSION WIRE RESISTANCE

Carefully remove ends of wire from spark plug and distributor. Using an ohmmeter, check resistance of wire while gently twisting wire. If resistance is not to specification, or fluctuates from infinity to any value, replace wire.

#### Resistance (Ohms) Per Wire

| Application | Resistance |
|---|---|
| All Models | 25,000-30,000 |

FIRING ORDER 1-5-3-6-2-4

*Fig. 1 Firing Order and Distributor Rotation (BMW 530i)*

FIRING ORDER 1-5-3-6-2-4

*Fig. 2 Firing Order and Distributor Rotation (BMW 633CSi and 733i)*

## TUNE-UP (Cont.)

### DISTRIBUTOR

The 530i model uses a breaker point type distributor; 633CSi and 733i models use a breakerless, transistorized ignition system.

**530i**
Point Gap ...................... .014-.016" (.35-.40 mm)
Cam Angle ............................................. 35-41°
Breaker Arm Spring Tension ............ 18-22 oz. (500-630 g)
Condenser Capacity ........................................ .18-.22 mfd.
**633CSi & 733i**
Air Gap ........................ .014-.027" (.35-.70 mm)
Dwell Angle (Non-Adjustable) ................................ 32-52°

### IGNITION TIMING

**1)** Check and adjust timing with engine at normal operating temperature and distributor vacuum hoses disconnected. Connect timing light, start engine and increase engine speed to specified timing RPM. Steel ball embedded in flywheel (long pin on Auto. Trans. models) should line up with pointer attached to hole in flywheel housing.

**2)** Loosen distributor clamp, turn distributor until proper timing is achieved and tighten clamp. Connect distributor vacuum hoses and set idle speed to specified RPM.

#### Ignition Timing Specifications

| Application | RPM | Dynamic Timing |
|---|---|---|
| **530i** | | |
| Federal | 1700 | 22°BTDC |
| Calif. | 2700 | 22°BTDC |
| **633CSi & 733i** | | |
| Federal | 2400 | 22°BTDC |
| Calif. | 2750 | 22°BTDC |

### IDLE SPEED & MIXTURE

**1)** With engine at normal operating temperature, check for clean air cleaner and make sure ignition timing and valve clearance are to specifications. Disconnect hose from collector to charcoal canister, but do not plug openings. Disconnect and plug hose from air injection pump.

**2)** Adjust engine idle speed to specified RPM by means of the adjusting screw located below throttle butterfly switch.

**3)** Remove plug from air flow sensor. Use suitable tool (13 1 060) to turn by-pass air screw in air flow sensor until specified CO level is obtained. Reinstall air flow sensor plug. Reconnect hoses.

#### Idle Speed (RPM) & CO Level (%)

| Application | Idle RPM | CO % |
|---|---|---|
| All Models | 850-1050 | 1.5-3.0 |

### FUEL PUMP PRESSURE & VOLUME

Pressure ................................................. 43 psi (3.0 kg/cm²)
Volume ........................ 106 qts. in 1 hr. (1.75 pts. in 30 sec.)

### EMISSION CONTROL SYSTEMS

*See Mitchell Manuals' Emission Control Manual.*

**Fig. 3  Showing Ignition Timing Mark**

## GENERAL SERVICING

### IGNITION

#### DISTRIBUTOR

The 530i model uses a Bosch breaker point type distributor; 633CSi and 733i models use a Bosch breakerless, transistorized ignition system.

**Other Data & Specifications** — *See Tune-Up & Bosch Distributors in ELECTRICAL Section.*

### IGNITION COIL

| Resistance | Ohms at 68°F (20°C) |
|---|---|
| **Primary** | |
| 530i | 1.7-2.1 |
| 633CSi & 733i | 0.4 |

## GENERAL SERVICING ( Cont.)

### FUEL SYSTEMS

**FUEL INJECTION**

All models are equipped with Bosch Electronic Fuel Injection System.

**Other Data & Specifications** — *See Tune-Up and Bosch Electronic Fuel Injection in FUEL SYSTEMS Section.*

### ELECTRICAL

**BATTERY**

**12 Volt** — Negative Ground.

| Application | Amp. Hr. Rating |
| --- | --- |
| All Models | 66 |

**STARTER**

All models are equipped with Bosch Starters.

**Other Data & Specifications** — *See Bosch Starters in ELECTRICAL Section.*

**ALTERNATOR**

| Application | Rated Amp. Output |
| --- | --- |
| All Models | 65 |

**Other Data & Specifications** — *See Bosch Alternators & Regulators in ELECTRICAL Section.*

**ALTERNATOR REGULATOR**

All models are equipped with Bosch Alternator Regulators with an operating voltage of 13.5-14.2 volts at 68°F (20°C)

**Other Data & Specifications** — *See Bosch Alternators & Regulators in ELECTRICAL Section.*

---

### BELT ADJUSTMENT

Adjust tension until belt depresses .2-.4″ (5-10 mm) midway between pulleys.

---

### FILTERS & CLEANERS

| Filter or Cleaner | Service Interval ( Miles) |
| --- | --- |
| Oil Filter | Replace every 6,000 |
| Air Cleaner | Clean every 6,000 |
| | Replace every 12,500 |
| Fuel Pump Filter | Clean every 12,500 |
| EGR Filter | Replace every 25,000 |
| Mesh Fuel Filter (In Tank) | Replace every 37,500 |

---

### CAPACITIES

| Application | Quantity |
| --- | --- |
| Crankcase (Includes Filter) | 6.0 qts. |
| Cooling System (Includes Heater) | |
| 530i | 12.5 qts. |
| 633CSi & 733i | 13.0 qts. |
| Man. Trans. (SAE 80) | 2.3 pts. |
| Auto. Trans.(Dexron) | ①2.1 qts. |
| Rear Axle (SAE 90) | 3.1 pts. |
| Fuel Tank | |
| 530i | 16.4 gals. |
| 733i | 22.0 gals. |
| 633CSi | ②17.0 gals. |

① — Refill capacity.
② = Includes 2 gals. in reserve.

# 1978 Capri II 4 Tune-Up

## TUNE-UP

**Capri II 2300 cc**

### ENGINE IDENTIFICATION

Engine code designation is located on bottom line of vehicle identification plate which is riveted to top of right fender apron. Engine code for 2300 cc engine is "YA".

### MODEL IDENTIFICATION

**VEHICLE IDENTIFICATION NUMBER**

Vehicle Identification Number is located on vehicle identification plate which is riveted to top of right fender apron. Number is also stamped on driver's side windshield pillar and can be observed through windshield. Third and fourth digits of number identify model type. Code for Capri is "EC".

### COMPRESSION PRESSURE

Check compression pressure with battery fully charged and engine at normal operating temperature. Remove all spark plugs and set carburetor throttle plates in wide open position. Crank engine at least five compression strokes and note highest reading cylinder. Lowest reading cylinder must be at least 75% of highest reading cylinder.

### HYDRAULIC LASH ADJUSTERS

**NOTE** — *Lash adjustment is not a part of regular maintenance, but should be performed after cylinder head overhaul.*

**Fig. 1   Checking Hydraulic Lash Adjustment**

To check valve clearance, rotate camshaft until cam lobe of valve to be checked is up. Position suitable valve spring compressor tool (T74P-6565-B) under camshaft and over rocker arm end of hydraulic lash adjuster. Compress lash adjuster to fully collapsed position and insert feeler gauge (from valve side) between cam lobe and rocker arm. If clearance is not within specifications, inspect rocker arm, valve spring, camshaft and lash adjuster for wear and replace worn part(s).

| Application | Clearance |
| --- | --- |
| Base of Lobe-to-Rocker Arm | .035-.055" (0.9-1.4 mm) |
| Leak-down Rate | 2-8 Seconds |

### VALVE ARRANGEMENT

E-I-E-I-E-I-E-I (front to rear).

### SPARK PLUGS

| | |
| --- | --- |
| Gap | .034" (.86 mm) |
| Torque | 10-15 ft. lbs. (1.4-2.1 mkg) |

#### Spark Plug Type

| Application | Autolite No. |
| --- | --- |
| All Models | AWRF-42 |

### HIGH TENSION WIRE RESISTANCE

Carefully remove high tension wires from spark plugs and distributor cap. Using an ohmmeter, check high tension wire resistance while gently twisting wires. If resistance is not to specifications, or fluctuates from infinity to any value, replace high tension wire(s).

#### Resistance (Ohms) Per Wire

| Application | Ohms |
| --- | --- |
| All Models | 25,000-30,000 |

### DISTRIBUTOR

All models are equipped with Breakerless Ignition System and no adjustments are required.

**Fig. 2   Firing Order and Distributor Rotation**

### IGNITION TIMING

Check or adjust ignition timing using a timing light or suitable monolithic timing equipment. Set timing with engine at normal operating temperature, idle speed reduced to 600 RPM and distributor vacuum line disconnected and plugged.

#### Ignition Timing Specifications

| Application | Timing |
| --- | --- |
| Man. Trans. | 6°BTDC |
| Auto. Trans. | 20°BTDC |

## TUNE-UP (Cont.)

**Fig. 3  Ignition Timing Mark Location**

### HOT (SLOW) IDLE RPM

**Preparation —** 1) With air cleaner removed and vacuum hoses plugged, check timing and adjust if required, then reconnect distributor vacuum advance hose.

2) Disconnect and plug EGR valve vacuum hose. Remove spark delay valve (if equipped) and route primary vacuum hose directly to distributor vacuum advance. Leave distributor retard connected (if equipped).

3) With A/C "OFF", place Man. Trans. in neutral or Auto. Trans. in "D". Adjust curb idle screw in or out to obtain specified idle RPM.

#### Idle Speed (RPM)

| Application | RPM |
| --- | --- |
| Man. Trans. | 850 |
| Auto. Trans. | 750 |

### IDLE MIXTURE

#### ARTIFICIAL ENRICHMENT METHOD

**Preparations —** 1) With engine at normal operating temperature and idle speed correct, disconnect air cleaner-to-vapor canister hose. If applicable, disconnect PCV-to-air cleaner hose and cap air cleaner connection. Disconnect thermactor by-pass valve air hose at check valve.

**NOTE** — *When taking readings, air cleaner must be in place. Each time idle speed is adjusted, thermactor must be connected.*

2) Plug a suitable adjusting tool with bottled gas (Rotunda T75L-9600-A) into air cleaner at vapor canister hose nipple. Place manual transmission in neutral or automatic transmission in "D".

3) With engine at idle speed, richen mixture (using bottled gas) to obtain maximum RPM. Continue to richen mixture until RPM drops.

**NOTE** — *If speed does not drop with valve fully open, check bottle gas supply.*

**Correct RPM Gain —** If RPM gain is within specification given on engine compartment tune-up decal, remove tool and reconnect all hoses. Recheck idle speed and mixture settings.

**Excessive RPM Gain —** If RPM gain was higher than specified, richen mixture screw (without injecting gas) until RPM increase is equal to the excess increase. *EXAMPLE — If increase was 80 RPM and desired increase was 50 RPM, adjust mixture screw rich for 30 RPM increase. Remove limiter cap if necessary to obtain excess RPM. Readjust idle speed after each mixture screw adjustment.*

**Insufficient RPM Gain —** If speed increase was lower than specified, lean mixture screw (without injecting gas) until RPM decrease is equal to the RPM lag. *EXAMPLE — If increase was zero RPM and desired increase was 20 RPM, adjust mixture screw lean for a 20 RPM loss. Readjust idle speed after each mixture screw adjustment.*

### COLD (FAST) IDLE RPM

Set fast idle with engine at normal operating temperature, ignition timing set to specifications and EGR vacuum hose disconnected and plugged. Remove spark delay valve (if equipped) and route primary vacuum hose directly to distributor vacuum advance. Place air conditioning in "OFF" position and transmission neutral. Set throttle so fast idle adjusting screw contacts kickdown step of choke cam, and adjust screw to obtain specified RPM.

#### Fast Idle Specification

| Application | RPM |
| --- | --- |
| Federal | |
|   Man. Trans. | 1600 |
|   Auto. Trans. | 1800 |
| Calif. | 1800 |

### AUTOMATIC CHOKE SETTING

| Application | Setting |
| --- | --- |
| All | Refer To Tune-Up Decal |

### FUEL PUMP PRESSURE & VOLUME

Make all tests of the mechanical diaphragm type fuel pump at normal operating temperature and at idle speed with transmission in neutral. When making pressure test, pinch off pump-to-tank fuel return line.

| | |
| --- | --- |
| Pressure | 3.5-5.5 psi (.25-.39 kg/cm²) |
| Volume (Minimum) | 1 pt. in 25 sec. |

### EMISSION CONTROL SYSTEMS

*See Mitchell Manuals' Emission Control Manual.*

# 1978 Capri II 4 Tune-Up

## GENERAL SERVICING

### IGNITION

#### DISTRIBUTOR

All models use Bosch Breakerless Ignition System.

**Other Data & Specifications —** *See Tune-Up and Bosch Distributors in ELECTRICAL Section.*

#### IGNITION COIL

**Resistance**

| | |
|---|---|
| Primary at 68° F (20° C) | 1.3-1.6 ohms |
| Secondary at 68° F (20° C) | 7000-9300 ohms |
| Resistor Wire at 68° F (20° C) | 1.3-1.6 ohms |

### FUEL SYSTEM

#### CARBURETOR

| Application | Model |
|---|---|
| 2300 cc 2-Bbl | Motorcraft 2150 |

**Other Data & Specifications —** *See Tune-Up and Motorcraft Carburetors in FUEL SYSTEMS Section.*

### ELECTRICAL

#### BATTERY

**12 Volt —** Negative Ground.

| Application | Amp. Hr. Rating |
|---|---|
| Man. Trans. | 55 |
| Auto Trans. | 66 |

**Battery Location —** Engine compartment.

#### STARTER

Bosch Pre-Engaged Type.

| | |
|---|---|
| Engine Cranking Speed | 180 RPM |
| Starter Current Draw | 100-130 Amps. |

**Other Data & Specifications —** *See Bosch Starters in ELECTRICAL Section.*

#### ALTERNATOR

| Application | Rated Amp. Output |
|---|---|
| With A/C | 35 |
| Without A/C | 55 |

**Other Data & Specifications —** *See Bosch Alternators & Regulators in ELECTRICAL Section.*

### ALTERNATOR REGULATOR

Bosch — Non Adjustable; externally mounted.

| | |
|---|---|
| Operating Voltage | 13.7-14.4 |

**Other Data & Specifications —** *See Bosch Alternators & Regulators in ELECTRICAL Section.*

### ENGINE

#### INTAKE MANIFOLD TIGHTENING

**2300 cc —** Check intake manifold bolts in two steps for 14-21 ft. lbs. (1.9-2.9 mkg) torque.

---

### BELT ADJUSTMENT

**Tension (Lbs.) Using Strand Tension Gauge**

| Application | New Belt | ① Used Belt |
|---|---|---|
| ¼ " Belt | 80 | 60 |
| 3/8 , 15/32 & ½ " Belt | 140 | 110 |

① — Any belt operated for more than 10 minutes is considered used.

---

### FILTERS & CLEANERS

| Filter or Cleaner | "A" | "B" |
|---|---|---|
| Oil Filter | 10,000 | 10,000 |
| Air Cleaner | 20,000 | 30,000 |
| Crankcase Filter | 30,000 | 30,000 |
| PCV Valve | 20,000 | 30,000 |
| Fuel Filter | ①20,000 | ①15,000 |

① — Replace only one time.

---

### CAPACITIES

| Application | Quantity |
|---|---|
| Crankcase (Includes Filter) | 4.5 qts. |
| Cooling System | 8.5 qts. |
| Man. Trans. (SAE 80 E.P.) | 2.8 pts. |
| Auto. Trans. (ESW-M2C33-F) | |
| Refill | 8 qts. |
| Rear Axle (ESW-M2C105-A) | 2.3 pts. |
| Fuel Tank | 11.8 gals. |

## TUNE-UP

**Capri II 2800 cc**

### ENGINE IDENTIFICATION

Engine code designation is located on bottom line of vehicle identification plate which is riveted to top of right fender apron. Engine code for 2800cc engine is "PX".

### MODEL IDENTIFICATION

#### VEHICLE IDENTIFICATION NUMBER

Identification number is located on vehicle identification plate which is riveted to top of right fender apron. Number is also stamped on drivers side windshield pillar. Third and fourth digits of number identify model type. Code for Capri is "EC".

### COMPRESSION PRESSURE

Check compression pressure with battery fully charged and engine at normal operating temperature. Remove all spark plugs and set carburetor throttle plates in wide open position. Crank engine at least five compression strokes and note highest reading cylinder. Lowest reading cylinder must be at least 75% of highest reading cylinder.

### VALVE CLEARANCE

Adjust valve clearance with engine at normal operating temperature and idling. Set clearance using a step-type feeler gauge only (go and no go).

**Fig. 1   Adjusting Valve Clearance**

To adjust, turn adjusting screw until correct clearance is obtained. Adjusting screws are self-locking. Adjust valves in the following sequence, turning camshaft after adjusting each cylinder.

| Valves Open | ①Adjust Valves |
|---|---|
| No. 5 Cylinder | No. 1 Cylinder |
| No. 3 Cylinder | No. 4 Cylinder |
| No. 6 Cylinder | No. 2 Cylinder |
| No. 1 Cylinder | No. 5 Cylinder |
| No. 4 Cylinder | No. 3 Cylinder |
| No. 2 Cylinder | No. 6 Cylinder |

① — If turned by hand from crankshaft.

| Application | Clearance |
|---|---|
| Intake | .014" (.36mm) |
| Exhaust | .016" (.41mm) |

### VALVE ARRANGEMENT

I-E-E-I-E-I (Left bank, front to rear).
I-E-I-E-E-I (Right bank, front to rear).

**Fig. 2   Firing Order and Distributor Rotation**

### SPARK PLUGS

| | |
|---|---|
| Gap | .034" (.86 mm) |
| Torque | 15-20 ft. lbs. (2.1-2.8 mkg) |

**Spark Plug Type**

| Application | Autolite No. |
|---|---|
| All Models | AWSF-42 |

### HIGH TENSION WIRE RESISTANCE

Carefully remove ends of wire from spark plug and distributor. Using an ohmmeter, check resistance of wire while gently twisting wire. If resistance is not to specification, or fluctuates from infinity to any value, replace wire.

**Resistance (Ohms) Per Wire**

| Application | Resistance |
|---|---|
| All Models | 25,000-30,000 |

### DISTRIBUTOR

All models are equipped with Breakerless Ignition System and no adjustments are required.

## TUNE-UP (Cont.)

**Fig. 3  Showing Ignition Timing Marks**

### IGNITION TIMING

Check or adjust ignition timing using a timing light or suitable monolithic timing equipment. Set timing with engine at normal operating temperature, idle speed reduced to 600 RPM and distributor vacuum lines disconnected and plugged.

#### Ignition Timing Specifications

| Application | Timing |
|---|---|
| All Models | 12°BTDC |

### HOT (SLOW) IDLE RPM

**1)** Remove air cleaner, then disconnect and plug vacuum hoses. Check timing and adjust if necessary, then reconnect distributor vacuum advance hose.

**2)** Disconnect and plug EGR valve vacuum hose. Remove spark delay valve (if equipped) and route primary vacuum hose directly to distributor vacuum advance. Leave distributor retard hose connected.

**3)** Place A/C in "OFF" position. Check and adjust fast idle RPM and place Man. Trans. in neutral or Auto. Trans. in "D". Adjust curb idle speed screw in or out to obtain specified idle RPM.

#### Idle Speed (RPM)

| Application | RPM |
|---|---|
| Man. Trans. | |
| Federal | 850 |
| Calif. | 800 |
| Auto. Trans. | 750 |

### IDLE MIXTURE

#### ARTIFICIAL ENRICHMENT METHOD

**1)** With engine at normal operating temperature and idle speed correct, disconnect air cleaner-to-vapor canister hose. If applicable, disconnect PCV-to-air cleaner hose, and cap air cleaner connection. Disconnect thermactor by-pass valve air hose at check valve.

**2)** Plug suitable idle adjusting tool with bottled gas (Rotunda T75L-9600-A) into air cleaner at vapor canister hose nipple. Place manual transmission in neutral or automatic transmission in "D".

**NOTE** — *When taking readings, air cleaner must be in place. Each time idle speed is adjusted, thermactor must be connected.*

**3)** With engine at idle speed, richen mixture (using bottled gas) to obtain maximum RPM. Continue to richen mixture until RPM drops.

**NOTE** — *If RPM does not drop, check bottle gas supply.*

**Correct RPM Gain** — If RPM gain is within specifications shown on engine compartment tune-up decal, remove tool and reconnect all hoses. Recheck idle speed and mixture settings.

**Excessive RPM Gain** — If RPM gain was higher than specified, richen mixture screw (without injecting gas) until RPM increase is equal to excess increase. *EXAMPLE — If increase was 80 RPM and desired increase was 50 RPM, adjust mixture screw rich for 30 RPM increase. Remove limiter cap if necessary to obtain excess RPM. Readjust idle speed after each mixture screw adjustment.*

**Insufficient RPM Gain** — If speed increase was lower than specified, lean mixture screw (without injecting gas) until RPM decrease is equal to RPM lag. *EXAMPLE — If increase was zero RPM and desired increase was 20 RPM, adjust mixture screw lean for a 20 RPM loss. Readjust idle speed after each mixture screw adjustment.*

### COLD (FAST) IDLE RPM

Set fast idle with engine at normal operating temperature, ignition timing set to specifications and EGR vacuum hose disconnected and plugged. Remove spark delay valve (if equipped) and route primary vacuum hose directly to vacuum advance unit on distributor. Place air conditioning in "OFF" position and transmission in neutral. Set throttle so fast idle adjusting screw contacts kickdown step of choke cam, and adjust screw to obtain specified fast idle RPM.

#### Fast Idle RPM

| Application | RPM |
|---|---|
| All Models | 1700 RPM |

### AUTOMATIC CHOKE SETTING

| Application | Setting |
|---|---|
| All | Refer To Tune-Up Decal |

### FUEL PUMP PRESSURE & VOLUME

Check the mechanical diaphragm type fuel pump at idle RPM with engine at normal operating temperature and transmission in neutral.

| | |
|---|---|
| Pressure | 3.5-5.5 psi (.25-.39 kg/cm²) |
| Volume | 1 pint in 25 seconds. |

### EMISSION CONTROL SYSTEMS

*See Mitchell Manuals' Emission Control Manual.*

## GENERAL SERVICING

## IGNITION
### DISTRIBUTOR

All models use Bosch Breakerless Ignition System.

**Other Data & Specifications** —*See Tune-Up and Bosch Distributors in ELECTRICAL Section.*

### IGNITION COIL

**Resistance**

Primary at 68° F (20° C) ............................ 1.3-1.6 ohms
Secondary at 68° F (20° C) ..................... 7000-9300 ohms
Resistor Wire at 68° F (20° C) ..................... 1.3-1.6 ohms

## FUEL SYSTEMS
### CARBURETOR

| Application | Model |
|---|---|
| Federal | Motorcraft 2150 |
| Calif. | ①Motorcraft 2700 VV |

① — Variable venturi carburetor.

**Other Data & Specifications** —*See Tune-Up and Motorcraft Carburetors in FUEL SYSTEMS Section.*

## ELECTRICAL
### BATTERY

**12 Volt** — Negative Ground.

| Application | Amp. Hr. Rating |
|---|---|
| All | 66 |

**Battery Location** — In engine compartment.

### STARTER

Bosch Pre-Engaged Type.

Engine Cranking Speed .......................... 180 RPM
Starter Current Draw........................... 100-130 Amps.

**Other Data & Specifications** — *See Bosch Starters in ELECTRICAL Section.*

### ALTERNATOR

| Application | Rated Amp. Output |
|---|---|
| With A/C | 35 |
| Without A/C | 55 |

**Other Data & Specifications** — *See Bosch Alternators & Regulators in ELECTRICAL Section.*

### ALTERNATOR REGULATOR

Bosch — Non-Adjustable; externally mounted.

Operating Voltage ........................... 13.7-14.4

**Other Data & Specifications** —*See Bosch Alternators & Regulators in ELECTRICAL Section.*

## ENGINE
### INTAKE MANIFOLD TIGHTENING

Tighten intake manifold-to-cylinder head bolts in four steps to a final torque of 15-18 ft. lbs. (2.1-2.5 mkg). Tighten intake manifold-to-cylinder head stud nuts to 10-12 ft. lbs. (1.4-1.7 mkg).

### CAPACITIES

| Application | Quantity |
|---|---|
| Crankcase (Includes Filter) | 5.0 qts. |
| Cooling System | 8.5 qts. |
| Man. Trans. (SAE 80 E.P.) | 2.8 pts. |
| Auto. Trans. (Refill - ESW-M2C33-F) | 8.0 qts. |
| Rear Axle (ESW-M2C105-A) | 2.3 pts. |
| Fuel Tank | 11.8 gals. |

### BELT ADJUSTMENT

Tension (Lbs.) Using Strand Tension Gauge

| Application | New Belt | ① Used Belt |
|---|---|---|
| ¼" Belt | 80 | 60 |
| ⅜, ⁵⁄₃₂, & ½" Belt | 140 | 110 |

① — Any belt operated for more than 10 minutes is considered used.

### FILTERS & CLEANERS

**NOTE** — *Refer to Vehicle Emission Control Information decal in engine compartment for maintenance schedule code.*

Replacement Interval (Miles) Per Maintenance Schedule

| Filter or Cleaner | "A" | "B" |
|---|---|---|
| Oil Filter | 10,000 | 10,000 |
| Air Cleaner | 20,000 | 30,000 |
| Crankcase Filter | 30,000 | 30,000 |
| PCV Valve | 20,000 | 30,000 |
| Fuel Filter | ①20,000 | ①15,000 |

① — Replace only one time.

## TUNE-UP

**Arrow**
**Colt**
**Challenger**
**Sapporo**

### ENGINE IDENTIFICATION

Engine model and serial numbers are stamped on top edge of right front side of cylinder block. Engine model and serial numbers are as follows:

| Displacement | Engine Model | Serial Number |
|---|---|---|
| 1600 cc | G32B | 2A00101 & Up |
| 2000 cc | G52B | 52A00101 & Up |
| 2600 cc | G54B | 54A00101 & Up |

### MODEL IDENTIFICATION

#### VEHICLE IDENTIFICATION NUMBER

The 13-digit Vehicle Identification Number is stamped on a plate riveted to left front corner of instrument panel and visible through windshield.

### COMPRESSION PRESSURE

Check compression pressure with engine at normal operating temperature, choke and throttle valves wide open and engine at cranking speed (250 RPM). Maximum variation between cylinders should not exceed 15 psi (1.1 kg/cm²).

| Application | Pressure psi (kg/cm²) |
|---|---|
| All Models | 149 (10.5) |

**Fig. 1 Firing Order and Distributor Rotation**

FRONT OF VEHICLE

FIRING ORDER 1-3-4-2

### VALVE TAPPET CLEARANCE

Check or adjust valve clearance with engine off and at normal operating temperature. To adjust valves, loosen lock nut and turn adjusting screw until specified clearance is obtained.

**CAUTION** — Jet valve clearance must be adjusted before adjusting intake valve clearance. Loosen intake valve adjusting screw at least 2 full turns before adjusting jet valve.

#### Valve Clearances

| Application | Clearance |
|---|---|
| Jet | .006" (.15 mm) |
| Intake | .006" (.15 mm) |
| Exhaust | .010" (.25 mm) |

### VALVE ARRANGEMENT

Right Side — All Exhaust. Left Side — All Intake.

### SPARK PLUGS

| | |
|---|---|
| Gap | .039-.043 (1.0-1.1 mm) |
| Torque | 14-21 ft. lbs. (1.9-2.9 mkg) |

#### Spark Plug Type

| Application | NGK | Champion |
|---|---|---|
| 1600 & 2000 cc | BPR-6ES-11 | RN-9Y |
| 2600 cc | BPR-5ES-11 | RN-12Y |

### HIGH TENSION WIRE RESISTANCE

Carefully remove high tension wires from spark plugs and distributor cap. Using an ohmmeter, check resistance of wire while gently twisting wire. If resistance is not to specification, or fluctuates from infinity to any value, replace wire.

#### Resistance (Ohms) Per Wire

| Application | Resistance |
|---|---|
| All Models | Less Than 22,000 |

### DISTRIBUTOR

| | |
|---|---|
| Point Gap | .018-.021" (.45-.55 mm) |
| Cam Angle | 49-55° |
| Breaker Arm Spring Tension | 17-21 oz. (482-595 g) |
| Condenser Capacity | .22 mfd |

2000 cc & 2600 cc          1600 cc

**Fig. 2 Ignition Timing Mark Location**

## TUNE-UP (Cont.)

### IGNITION TIMING

**1)** With engine at normal operating temperature and point gap and idle speed set to specifications, connect timing light. Remove rubber plug from retard side of distributor vacuum unit (dual diaphragm distributors only). Start engine.

**2)** Loosen distributor nut and rotate distributor as necessary to adjust timing. Tighten mounting nut when timing is set to basic timing specification.

**3)** On models with dual diaphragm distributor, reinstall rubber plug and check actual ignition timing.

#### Ignition Timing Specifications

| Application | ①Basic Timing | ②Actual Timing |
|---|---|---|
| 1600 & 2000 cc | | |
| Fed. & Calif. ............ | 5°BTDC±1° | ..... |
| High Alt. ................ | 10°BTDC±1° | ..... |
| 2600 cc | | |
| Federal .................... | 7°BTDC±1° | ..... |
| Calif. ...................... | 7°BTDC±1° | 3°ATDC±3° |
| High Alt. ................ | 12°BTDC±1° | 2°BTDC±3° |

① — On dual diaphragm distributors, rubber plug removed from retard side of vacuum diaphragm.

② — On dual diaphragm distributors, rubber plug installed on retard side of vacuum diaphragm.

### IDLE SPEED & MIXTURE

**1)** Run engine at idle until normal operating temperature is reached. Check ignition timing and adjust to specification if necessary. Place transmission in neutral and ensure that air conditioner is OFF.

**NOTE** — *On High Altitude models, ensure altitude compensator knob on carburetor is in correct position. Slot in knob should be verticle at altitudes above 4000 ft., horizontal at altitudes below 4000 ft.*

**2)** Using idle speed adjusting screw, adjust idle to 80 RPM **above** specified idle speed.

**3)** Using idle mixture adjusting screw, adjust mixture to obtain a CO level of 1.0%. Use mixture adjusting screw again to lower idle speed to specified RPM.

**4)** Recheck idle CO%. Reading should now be at specified level. If engine misfires or CO% is incorrect, repeat steps **2)** and **3)**.

#### Idle Speed (RPM) and CO Level (%)

| Application | RPM | CO% |
|---|---|---|
| 1600 & 2000 cc | | |
| Man. Trans. ............... | 600-700 | Below 0.1 |
| Auto Trans. ............... | 650-750 | Below 0.1 |
| 2600 cc | | |
| Federal | | |
| Arrow & Colt ........... | 800-900 | Below 0.1 |
| Challenger & Sapporo | | |
| Man. Trans. ........... | 650-750 | Below 0.1 |
| Auto. Trans. ........... | 700-800 | Below 0.1 |
| Calif. | | |
| Man. Trans. ............. | 650-750 | Below 0.1 |
| Auto. Trans. ............. | 700-800 | Below 0.1 |

### COLD (FAST) IDLE RPM

With choke valve fully closed, adjust fast idle adjusting screw to obtain specified fast idle RPM.

#### Fast Idle Specification

| Application | RPM |
|---|---|
| All Models ............................................................. | 2000 |

### AUTOMATIC CHOKE SETTING

Automatic choke is properly set when yellow punch mark on bimetal case is aligned with center projection on choke housing.

### FUEL PUMP PRESSURE

All models are equipped with a mechanical diaphragm type pump. Pump is located on cylinder head and is operated by an eccentric cam on the camshaft.

#### Fuel Pump Pressure

| Application | psi (kg/cm²) |
|---|---|
| 1600 cc .................................................... | 3.7.5.1 (.26-.36) |
| 2000 & 2600 cc ......................................... | 4.6-6.0 (.32-.42) |

### EMISSION CONTROL SYSTEMS

*See Mitchell Manuals' Emission Control Manual.*

## GENERAL SERVICING

### IGNITION

**DISTRIBUTOR**

California and High Altitude models with 2600 cc engine use Mitsubishi dual diaphragm distributors. All other models use Mitsubishi single diaphragm distributors.

**Other Data & Specifications** — *See Tune-Up and Mitsubishi Distributors in ELECTRICAL Section.*

**IGNITION COIL**

| Application | Resistance (Ohms) |
|---|---|
| Primary | 1.05 |
| Secondary | 17,000 |

### FUEL SYSTEMS

**CARBURETORS**

| Application | Model |
|---|---|
| All Models | Solex DIDTA 2-Bbl. |

**Other Data & Specifications** — *See Tune-Up and Solex Carburetors in FUEL SYSTEMS Section.*

### ELECTRICAL

**BATTERY**

12 Volt — Negative Ground.

| Application | Amp. Hr. Rating |
|---|---|
| 1600 cc | 45, 60 |
| 2000 cc | 45, 60, 65 |
| 2600 cc | 65 |

**Battery Location** — Front left side of engine compartment.

**STARTER**

All models use Mitsubishi overrunning clutch type starter.

**Other Data & Specifications** — *See Mitsubishi Starters in ELECTRICAL Section.*

**ALTERNATOR**

Models equipped with 1600 cc engine use Nippondenso or Mitsubishi alternators. All other models use Mitsubishi alternators.

| Application | Rated Amp. Output |
|---|---|
| Arrow & Colt | |
| 1600 cc | 45 |
| 2000 & 2600 cc | 50 |
| Challenger & Sapporo | 50 |

**Other Data & Specifications** — *See Mitsubishi and Nippondenso Alternators and Regulators in ELECTRICAL Section.*

**ALTERNATOR REGULATOR**

Models equipped with 1600 cc engine use a Nippondenso alternator regulator. All other models use a Mitsubishi alternator regulator.

Operating Voltage ........................ 14.5-15.3 @ 68°F (20°C)

**Other Data & Specifications** — *See Mitsubishi and Nippondenso Alternators and Regulators in ELECTRICAL Section.*

### BELT ADJUSTMENT

| Application | Deflection |
|---|---|
| Fan Belt | .28-.38" (7.1-9.7 mm) |
| A/C Belt | ① |

① — Check A/C belt using strand tension gauge. Tension should be 100-110 lbs. (45-50 kg).

### FILTERS & CLEANERS

| Filter or Cleaner | Service Interval (Miles) |
|---|---|
| Oil Filter | Replace every 10,000 |
| Air Cleaner | Replace every 30,000 |
| Fuel Filter | Replace every 15,000 |
| Canister Filter | Replace every 30,000 |

### CAPACITIES

| Application | Quantity |
|---|---|
| Crankcase (Includes Filter) | |
| 1600 cc | 4.2 qts. |
| 2000 cc | 4.5 qts. |
| Cooling System | |
| 1600 cc | 7.7 qts. |
| 2000 cc | 9.5 qts. |
| 2600 cc | 5.2 qts. |
| 2600 cc | 9.7 qts. |
| Man. Trans. (SAE 80 Gear Oil) | |
| 4-Speed | 1.8 qts. |
| 5-Speed | |
| 1600 cc | 2.1 qts. |
| 2000 & 2600 cc | 2.4 qts. |
| Auto. Trans. (Dexron) | 6.8 qts. |
| Rear Axle (SAE 90 Gear Oil) | 1.2 qts. |
| Fuel Tank | |
| Arrow & Colt | |
| Station Wagon | 11.0 gals. |
| Sedan & Coupe | 13.2 gals. |
| All Others | 13.5 gals. |
| Challenger & Sapporo | 15.3 gals. |

## TUNE-UP

Courier

### ENGINE IDENTIFICATION

The engine identification number is stamped on right side of engine block below distributor and on model identification plate attached to body at right rear corner of engine compartment.

### MODEL IDENTIFICATION

#### VEHICLE IDENTIFICATION NUMBER

Vehicle identification number is stamped on model identification plate which is attached to body at right rear corner of engine compartment.

### COMPRESSION PRESSURE

Check compression pressure with engine at normal operating temperature, all spark plugs removed, throttle valve wide open and engine at cranking speed. Compression pressure is within specifications if lowest reading cylinder is more than 75% of highest.

### VALVE TAPPET CLEARANCE

**1800 cc**      **Clearance**

Intake and Exhaust (Hot) ............................. .012" (.30 mm)

### HYDRAULIC LASH ADJUSTERS

**2300 cc**      **Clearance**

Desired Clearance ...................... ①.040-.050" (1.0-1.3 mm)
Allowable Clearance ................... ①.035-.055" (0.9-1.4 mm)

① — Measured between base circle of cam lobe and cam follower, with adjuster collapsed. Leakdown rate is 2-8 seconds.

### VALVE ARRANGEMENT

1800 cc
  Right Side — All Exhaust
  Left Side — All Intake
2300 cc — E-I-E-I-E-I-E-I

### SPARK PLUGS

Gap .......................................................... .029-.033" (.7-.8mm)
Torque............................................10-16 ft. lbs. (1.4-2.2 mkg)

#### Spark Plug Type

| Application | Autolite No. |
| --- | --- |
| 1800 cc | AGR-32 |
| 2300 cc | AGRF-52 |

*Fig. 1  Distributor Rotation and Firing Order*

### DISTRIBUTOR ①

1800 cc
  Point Gap ........................................ .018-.022" (.45-.55 mm)
  Cam Angle .......................................................... 49-55°
  Breaker Arm Spring Tension .......... 17-23 ozs. (525-652 g)
  Condenser Capacity ................................... .20-.24 mfd
2300 cc
  Armature Tooth-to-Magnetic
    Pickup Gap ................................ .008-.024" (0.2-0.6 mm)

① — 1800 cc engine has breaker point type distributor; 2300 cc engine has magnetic pulse type.

### HIGH TENSION WIRE RESISTANCE

Carefully remove ends of wire from spark plug and distributor. Using an ohmmeter, check resistance of wire while gently twisting wire. If resistance is not to specification, or fluctuates from infinity to any value, replace wire.

#### Resistance (Ohms) Per Wire

| Application | Resistance |
| --- | --- |
| All Models | ①25,000-30,000 |

① — Resistance should not exceed 1000 ohms per inch of wire.

### IGNITION TIMING

Check or adjust ignition timing with engine at normal operating temperature, at correct idle speed, and with distributor vacuum advance line disconnected and plugged.

#### Ignition Timing Specifications

| Application | Timing |
| --- | --- |
| 1800 cc | ①8°BTDC |
| 2300 cc | ①6°BTDC |

① — ±1°

## TUNE-UP (Cont.)

*Fig. 2  Ignition Timing Mark Locations*

### IDLE SPEED & MIXTURE

1) With engine at normal operating temperature, Man. Trans. in neutral or Auto. Trans. in "D", connect a tachometer to engine. Adjust curb idle RPM to specifications using curb idle adjusting screw.

2) Stop engine. Disconnect hose between air pump and check valve at check valve, and plug check valve port. Start engine and turn idle mixture adjusting screw in or out to obtain specified CO level.

3) Reconnect air pump hose. Recheck idle speed and readjust if necessary.

#### Idle Speed (RPM) & CO Level (%)

| Application | RPM | ①CO% |
|---|---|---|
| 1800 cc | 700-750 | 2.0 |
| 2300 cc | | |
|   Man. Trans. | 800-850 | 4.0 |
|   Auto. Trans. | ②700-750 | 4.0 |

① — With air injection disconnected.
② — Transmission in "D".

### COLD (FAST) IDLE RPM

With choke plate fully closed, measure clearance between primary throttle plate and wall of throttle bore. If clearance is not within specifications, bend fast idle lever where it contacts throttle lever tang until proper clearance is obtained.

#### Fast Idle Specifications

| Application | Clearance |
|---|---|
| 1800 cc | .071"(1.8 mm) |
| 2300 cc | |
|   Federal | .071"(1.8 mm) |
|   Calif. | .062"(1.6 mm) |

### DASH POT ADJUSTMENT

Check engine idle speed and carburetor air-fuel mixture. With engine at operating temperature and air cleaner removed, attach tachometer to engine.

Loosen dash pot lock nut. *See Fig. 3.* Move throttle lever and hold in place to maintain specified engine speed. Turn dash pot until dash pot rod contacts throttle lever. Release throttle lever and tighten lock nut. Move throttle lever until it contacts dash pot rod and check engine speed again. Repeat adjustment if necessary.

*Fig. 3  Adjusting Dash Pot*

#### Engine Speed for Dash Pot Adjustment

| Application | RPM |
|---|---|
| Federal | 2500±100 |
| Calif. | 2200±100 |

### FUEL PUMP PRESSURE & VOLUME

| | |
|---|---|
| Pressure | 2.8-3.6 psi (.20-.25 kg/cm²) |
| Volume | 1 pt. in 30 seconds |

### EMISSION CONTROL SYSTEMS

*See Mitchell Manuals' Emission Control Manual.*

## GENERAL SERVICING

### IGNITION

#### DISTRIBUTOR

All models have Mitsubishi distributors. The 1800 cc uses a single point distributor; the 2300 cc a magnetic pulse distributor.

**Other Data & Specifications** — *See Mitsubishi Distributors in ELECTRICAL Section.*

# 1978 Courier 4 Tune-Up

1-25

T
U
N
E

U
P

## GENERAL SERVICING (Cont.)

### IGNITION COIL

**Resistance**

Primary
1800 cc ............................................. 1.42 ohms
2300 cc ........................................... .81-.99 ohms
Secondary
1800 cc ............................................. 8610 ohms
2300 cc ...................................... 6800-9200 ohms
Magnetic Pickup Coil
2300 cc ...................................... 760-840 ohms
Ballast Resistor
1800 cc .............................................. 1.6 ohms

## FUEL SYSTEMS

### CARBURETORS

| Application | Model |
|---|---|
| All Models | Hitachi DCJ 328 2-Bbl. |

**Other Data & Specifications** — *See Tune-Up and Hitachi carburetors in FUEL SYSTEMS Section.*

## ELECTRICAL

### BATTERY

**12 Volt** — Negative Ground. Located at right front of engine compartment.

| Application | Amp. Hr. Rating |
|---|---|
| All Models | |
| Standard | 60 |
| Optional | 70 |

### STARTER

Nippondenso solenoid-actuated with overrunning clutch.

Free Speed Voltage ..................... 11 at 5000 RPM
Free Speed Amperage ................... 50 at 5000 RPM

**Other Data & Specifications** — *See Nippondenso Starters in ELECTRICAL Section.*

### ALTERNATOR

| Application | Rated Amp. Output |
|---|---|
| Courier | 35 |

**Other Data & Specifications** — *See Mitsubishi Alternators and Regulators in ELECTRICAL Section.*

### ALTERNATOR REGULATOR

Mitsubishi — Non-adjustable, externally mounted.

**Other Data & Specifications** — *See Mitsubishi Alternators and Regulators in ELECTRICAL Section.*

## ENGINE

### INTAKE MANIFOLD TIGHTENING

Tighten intake and exhaust manifold-to-cylinder head bolts, starting at center and working out.

**Manifold Torque Specifications**

| Application | Ft. Lbs. (mkg) |
|---|---|
| 1800 cc | |
| Intake | 13.5-19 (1.9-2.6) |
| Exhaust | 16-21 (2.2-2.9) |
| 2300 cc | |
| Intake | 14-21 (1.9-2.9) |
| Exhaust | 16-23 (2.2-3.2) |

---

### BELT ADJUSTMENT

| Application | ①Deflection New Belt | ①Deflection Used Belt |
|---|---|---|
| 1800 cc | 0.4-0.5" | 0.5-0.6" |
| | (10.2-12.7 mm) | (12.7-15.2 mm) |
| 2300 cc | 0.6-0.7" | 0.8-0.9" |
| | (15.2-17.8 mm) | (20.3-22.9 mm) |

① — Deflection is with 22 lbs. (10 kg) pressure applied midway on longest belt run.

---

### FILTERS & CLEANERS

| Filter or Cleaner | Service Interval (Miles) |
|---|---|
| Oil Filter | Replace every 6,250 |
| Air Cleaner | ①Replace every 25,000 |
| Fuel Filter | Replace every 12,500 |
| PCV Valve | ②Replace every 25,000 |
| Canister Filter | Inspect every 25,000 |

① — Inspect and clean air filter every 12,500 miles.
② — Inspect every 12,500 miles.

---

### CAPACITIES

| Application | Quantity |
|---|---|
| Crankcase (Includes Filter) | 5.0 qts. |
| Cooling System | |
| 1800 cc | 7.6 qts. |
| 2300 cc | 8.8 qts. |
| Man. Trans.(SAE 90 with EP) | |
| 4-Speed | 1.5 qts. |
| 5-Speed | 1.8 qts. |
| Auto. Trans. (Type F Trans. Fluid) | 6.6 qts. |
| Rear Axle (Hypoid Gear Lubricant) | 2.8 pts. |
| Fuel Tank | |
| Standard | 15 gals. |
| Optional | 17.5 gals. |

**TUNE-UP**

F10
B210
200SX
510
Pickup

## ENGINE IDENTIFICATION

Engine model number followed by engine serial number is stamped on right side of cylinder block, just below the No. 4 spark plug. Model numbers are as follows:

| Application | Engine Model Number |
|---|---|
| F10 | A14 |
| B210 | A14 |
| 200SX | L20B |
| 510 | L20B |
| Pickup | L20B |

## MODEL IDENTIFICATION

### VEHICLE IDENTIFICATION NUMBER

Vehicle identification number is stamped on a plate attached to instrument panel and is visible through windshield from outside of vehicle. Number on Pickup is on upper face of right side member. An identification plate also is found inside the engine compartment.

## COMPRESSION PRESSURE

Check compression pressure with engine at normal operating temperature, all spark plugs disconnected, electrical lead to anti-dieseling solenoid disconnected, choke and throttle valves wide open and engine at cranking speed.

Lowest cylinder pressure should be at least 80% that of the highest cylinder pressure. Compression pressure should be as follows:

**Compression Pressure
@350 RPM**

| Application | psi (kg/cm²) |
|---|---|
| F10 & B210 | 178-192 (12.5-13.5) |
| All Others | 128-171 (9-12) |

## VALVE TAPPET CLEARANCE

### A14 ENGINE

Adjust valve clearance to specifications with engine off and at normal operating temperature. Rotate crankshaft to bring No. 1 cylinder to TDC on compression stroke. Adjust the following valves while engine is still hot.

| Location in Fig. 1 | Valves to Adjust |
|---|---|
| Location ① | Exhaust Valve No. 1 |
| Location ② | Intake Valve No. 1 |
| Location ③ | Intake Valve No. 2 |
| Location ⑤ | Exhaust Valve No. 3 |

Rotate crankshaft until No. 4 cylinder is at TDC on compression stroke. Adjust the following valves:

**Fig. 1   Adjusting Valve Clearance
(F10 and B210)**

| Location in Fig. 1 | Valves to Adjust |
|---|---|
| Location ④ | Exhaust Valve No. 2 |
| Location ⑥ | Intake Valve No. 3 |
| Location ⑦ | Intake Valve No. 4 |
| Location ⑧ | Exhaust Valve No. 4 |

After adjustment, tighten lock nuts firmly.

**Fig. 2   Adjusting Valve Clearance
(200SX, 510 and Pickup)**

### L20B ENGINE

Adjust valves with engine off and at normal operating temperature. Insert feeler gauge between end of cam and pivot arm from valve side of head. Use suitable wrench (ST1064001) to loosen pivot locking nut and a second wrench to turn pivot adjuster until specified clearance is obtained. Tighten locking nut and recheck clearance.

## TUNE-UP (Cont.)

A14 Engine
Cold ........................ .010" (.25 mm) ........ .010" (.25 mm)
Hot ......................... .014" (.35 mm) ........ .014" (.35 mm)
L20B Engine
Cold ........................ .008" (.20 mm) ........ .010" (.25 mm)
Hot ......................... .010" (.25 mm) ........ .012" (.30 mm)

### VALVE ARRANGEMENT

All Models — E-I-I-E-E-I-I-E (front to rear).

### SPARK PLUGS

Gap
B210 5-Spd. Hatchback ................ .043-.051" (1.1-1.3 mm)
All Others .................................... .039-.043" (1.0-1.1 mm)
Torque ........................ 11-14 ft. lbs. (1.5-2.0 mkg)

#### Standard Spark Plug Type

| Application | Hitachi No. | NGK No. |
|---|---|---|
| F10 | L46PW-11 | BP5ES-11 |
| B210 | | |
| 5-Spd. Hatchback | L46PM-13 | BP5EQ-13 |
| All Others | L46PW-11 | BP5ES-11 |
| All Others | L45PW-11 | BP6ES-11 |

### HIGH TENSION WIRE RESISTANCE

Remove distributor cap from distributor but do not disconnect high tension wires from cap. Disconnect high tension wires from spark plugs. Using an ohmmeter, check resistance from contact at spark plug end of wires to contact inside of distributor cap. Resistance should be less than 30,000 ohms. If resistance is more, disconnect wire from cap and recheck resistance. Replace wire if resistance still exceeds specification.

### DISTRIBUTOR

All models are equipped with breakerless, transistorized ignition systems.

Air Gap ............................................. .008-.016" (.2-.4 mm)

### IGNITION TIMING

Check or adjust ignition timing with engine at normal operating temperature, cam angle or air gap set within specifications and engine idle speed correct for vehicle.

To adjust, loosen distributor set screw and rotate distributor until correct timing is achieved. Lock set screw and recheck timing setting.

#### Ignition Timing Specifications

| Application | Man. Trans. | ①Auto. Trans. |
|---|---|---|
| F10 | 10°BTDC | ..... |
| B210 | | |
| Federal | ②10°BTDC | 8°BTDC |
| Calif. | ②10°BTDC | 10°BTDC |
| All Others | 12°BTDC | 12°BTDC |

① — Transmission in "D".
② — Hatchback with 5-Spd. Trans.: 5°BTDC.

**Fig. 3   Firing Order and Distributor Rotation (F10 and B210 Models)**

**Fig. 4   Firing Order and Distributor Rotation (200SX, 510 and Pickup Models)**

**Fig. 5   Ignition Timing Mark Location (F10 and B210 Models)**

**Fig. 6   Ignition Timing Mark Location (200SX, 510 & Pickup Models)**

# 1978 Datsun 4 Tune-Up

## TUNE-UP (Cont.)

### IDLE SPEED & MIXTURE

#### EXHAUST GAS ANALYZER METHOD

**1)** Warm engine to normal operating temperature and ensure ignition timing is set to specification. On all models except B210 5-Speed Hatchback, disconnect and plug hose from air check valve. *See Figs. 7 and 8.* On B210 5-Speed Hatchback model, remove short hose from between air induction pipe and air cleaner housing and plug induction pipe.

*Fig. 7 Disconnecting Air Hose at Check Valve (F10 and B210 Shown)*

*Fig. 8 Disconnecting Air Hose at Check Valve (200SX, 510 and Pickup Shown)*

**2)** With Man. Trans. in neutral or Auto. Trans. in "D", adjust idle speed screw to obtain specified idle RPM. Then, adjust mixture screw to obtain specified CO level. If mixture screw limiter cap must be removed, reinstall it with stop tab on cap positioned so screw can be turned ⅛ of a turn in rich (counterclockwise) direction. Reconnect air hose and recheck idle speed.

### Idle Speed (RPM) & CO Level (%)

| Application | RPM | CO% |
|---|---|---|
| F10 | 700 | 1.0-3.0 |
| B210 | | |
| Man. Trans. | 700 | ①1.0-3.0 |
| Auto. Trans. | ②650 | 1.0-3.0 |
| All Others | ②600 | 0.3-2.0 |

① — Hatchback with 5-Spd. Trans.: 0.3-2.0%.
② — Auto. Trans. in "D".

### TACHOMETER (LEAN DROP) METHOD

**NOTE** — *Manufacturer advises use of this method only if exhaust gas analyzer is not available.*

**1)** Warm engine to normal operating temperature and ensure ignition timing is set to specification. On all models except B210 5-Speed Hatchback, disconnect and plug hose from air check valve. *See Figs. 7 and 8.* On B210 5-Speed Hatchback model, remove short hose from between air induction pipe and air cleaner housing and plug induction pipe.

**2)** With Man. Trans. in neutral or Auto. Trans. in "D", adjust idle speed and mixture screws until best idle is obtained at specified enriched idle RPM.

### Enriched Idle RPM Specifications

| Application | RPM |
|---|---|
| F10 | 740 |
| B210 | |
| Man. Trans | ①740 |
| Auto. Trans. | ②665 |
| All Others | ②650 |

① — Hatchback with 5-Spd. Trans.: 765 RPM.
② — Auto. Trans in "D".

**3)** Now turn mixture screw clockwise (lean) until idle speed **drops** by specified RPM.

### Idle RPM Drop Specifications

| Application | RPM |
|---|---|
| F10 | 35-45 |
| B210 | |
| Man. Trans. | ①35-45 |
| Auto. Trans. | ②10-20 |
| All Others | 45-55 |

① — Hatchback with 5-Spd. Trans.: 60-70 RPM.
② — Auto. Trans. in "D".

**4)** If mixture screw limiter cap was removed, reinstall it with stop tab on cap positioned so screw can be turned ⅛ of a turn in rich (counterclockwise) direction. Reconnect air hose and recheck idle speed.

# 1978 Datsun 4 Tune-Up

## TUNE-UP (Cont.)

### COLD (FAST) IDLE RPM

With engine at normal operating temperature, transmission in neutral and fast idle arm on second highest step of fast idle cam, turn fast idle screw as required to obtain specified fast idle RPM.

#### Fast Idle RPM

| Application | Man. Trans. | Auto. Trans. |
|---|---|---|
| F10 | 1900-2700 | |
| B210 | 1900-2700 | 2400-3200 |
| All Others | 1900-2800 | 2200-3200 |

### DASHPOT ADJUSTMENT

With engine at normal operating temperature and idle speed and mixture correctly set, turn throttle valve by hand and read engine speed when dashpot just contacts stop lever. Adjust position of dashpot by turning nut until engine speed is in specified range. Tighten locknut and make sure that engine decelerates smoothly from 2000 RPM to 1000 RPM in about three seconds.

#### Dashpot Adjusting Specifications

| Application | Man. Trans. | Auto. Trans. |
|---|---|---|
| F10 | | |
| Federal | 2300-2500 | |
| Calif. | 1900-2100 | |
| B210 | | |
| Federal | ①2300-2500 | 1900-2100 |
| Calif. | 1900-2100 | 1900-2100 |
| All Others | 1900-2100 | 1650-1850 |

① — Hatchback with 5-Spd. Trans.: 1900-2100 RPM.

### FUEL PUMP PRESSURE & VOLUME

Pressure
Pickup With A/C ............... 4.6psi (.32 kg/cm²)
All Others ............... 3.0-3.8 psi(.21-.27 kg/cm²)
Volume (at 1000 RPM)
F10 & B210 ............... 1 pt./min.
200SX & 510 ............... 3.5 pt./min.
Pickup
With A/C ............... 3 pts./min.
Without A/C ............... 2 pts./min.

### EMISSION CONTROL SYSTEMS

See Mitchell Manuals' Emission Control Manual.

## GENERAL SERVICING

### IGNITION

#### DISTRIBUTOR

All models are equipped with Hitachi breakerless, transistorized ignition systems.

**Other Data & Specifications** — See Tune-Up & Hitachi Distributors in ELECTRICAL Section.

#### IGNITION COIL

| Resistance | Ohms at 68°F (20°C) |
|---|---|
| Primary | .84-1.02 |
| Secondary | 8,200-12,400 |

### FUEL SYSTEMS

#### CARBURETORS

| Application | Model |
|---|---|
| F10 & B210 2-Bbl. | DCH 306 |
| All Others | DCH 340 |

**Other Data & Specifications** — See Tune-Up & Hitachi Carburetors in FUEL SYSTEMS Section.

### ELECTRICAL

#### BATTERY

**12 Volt** — Negative Ground.

| Application | Amp. Hr. Rating |
|---|---|
| All Models | 60 |

**Battery Location** — Engine Compartment.

#### STARTER

Hitachi solenoid actuated with overrunning clutch.

Free Speed Voltage
F10 & B210 ............... 12@7000 RPM
All Others
Man. Trans. ............... 12@7000 RPM
Auto. Trans. ............... 12@6000 RPM
Free Speed Amperage
F10 & B210 ............... 60 Max.@7000 RPM
All Others
Man. Trans. ............... 60 Max.@7000 RPM
Auto. Trans. ............... 60 Max.@6000 RPM

**Other Data & Specifications** — See Hitachi Starters in ELECTRICAL Section.

## GENERAL SERVICING (Cont.)

### ALTERNATOR

| Application | Rated Amp. Output |
|---|---|
| F10 & 510 | |
| Standard | 50 |
| With A/C | 60 |
| B210 & 200SX | 50 |
| Pickup | |
| Standard | 35 |
| With A/C | 38 |

**Other Data & Specifications** — *See Hitachi Alternators & Regulators in ELECTRICAL Section.*

### ALTERNATOR REGULATOR

All models use a Hitachi alternator regulator with an operating voltage of 14.3-15.3 volts at 68°F (20°C).

**Other Data & Specifications** — *See Hitachi Alternators & Regulators in ELECTRICAL Section.*

## ENGINE

### INTAKE MANIFOLD TIGHTENING

Check manifold attaching nuts for 11-14.5 ft. lbs. (1.5-2.0 mkg) torque on F10 and B210 models or 9-12 ft. lbs. (1.2-1.6 mkg) on all other models.

### FILTERS & CLEANERS

| Filter or Cleaner | Service Interval (Miles) |
|---|---|
| Oil Filter | Replace every 7,500 |
| Air Cleaner | Replace every 30,000 |
| Fuel Filter | Replace every 30,000 |
| PCV Valve & Filter | Replace every 30,000 |
| Canister Filter | Replace every 30,000 |

### BELT ADJUSTMENT

| Application | ①Deflection |
|---|---|
| F10 | |
| Air Pump | 3/16-5/16" (5-8 mm) |
| All Other Belts | 5/16-1/2" (8-12 mm) |
| All Others | 5/16-1/2" (8-12 mm) |

① — Deflection is with 22 lbs. (10 kg) pressure applied midway on longest belt run.

### CAPACITIES

| Application | Quantity |
|---|---|
| Crankcase (Includes Filter) | |
| F10 | 3.5 qts. |
| B210 | 3.9 qts. |
| All Others | 4.5 qts. |
| Cooling System (Includes Heater) | |
| F10 & B210 | 6.3 qts. |
| 200SX | 7.9 qts. |
| 510 | 9.4 qts. |
| Pickup | ①9.25 qts. |
| Manual Transmission (API GL-4) | |
| F10 | 4.9 pts. |
| B210 | |
| 4-speed | 2.75 pts. |
| 5-speed | 3.6 pts. |
| 200SX & 510 | 3.6 pts. |
| Pickup | |
| 4-speed | 3.6 pts. |
| 5-speed | 4.25 pts. |
| Automatic Transmission (Dexron) | |
| B210 | 5.6 qts. |
| All Others (Except F10) | 5.9 qts. |
| Rear Axle (API GL-5) | |
| B210 | 1.9 pts. |
| 200SX | 2.75 pts. |
| 510 | 2.4 pts. |
| Pickup | 2.1 pts. |
| Fuel Tank | |
| F10 | 10.6 gals. |
| B210 | |
| Sedan | 11.6 gals. |
| Coupe | 11.4 gals. |
| 200SX | 15.9 gals. |
| 510 | 13.25 gals. |
| Pickup | 11.9 gals. |

① — Add .25 qts. for models with Man. Trans.

## TUNE-UP

**280Z**
**810**

### ENGINE IDENTIFICATION

Engine serial number is stamped on right rear side of cylinder block at cylinder head contact surface. Serial number is preceded by engine model number.

#### Engine Model Number

| Application | Model No. |
|---|---|
| 280Z .......................................... | L28 |
| 810 ........................................... | L24 |

### MODEL IDENTIFICATION

#### VEHICLE IDENTIFICATION NUMBER

Vehicle identification number is stamped on a plate attached to instrument panel and is visible through windshield from outside of vehicle.

### COMPRESSION PRESSURE

Test compression with engine at normal operating temperature, spark plugs removed, throttle and choke open, and engine at cranking speed. Lowest reading cylinder must be at least 80% of highest reading cylinder. Compression pressure should be as follows at 300-400 RPM:

| Application | Min. Pressure psi (kg/cm²) | Max. Pressure psi (kg/cm²) |
|---|---|---|
| 280Z ...................... | 164 (11.5) | 178 (12.5) |
| 810 ........................ | 164 (11.5) | 185 (13) |

### VALVE TAPPET CLEARANCE

Adjust valves with engine off and at normal operating temperature. Insert feeler gauge between heel of cam and pivot arm from valve side of head. Use suitable wrench (ST1064001) to loosen pivot locking nut and a second wrench to turn pivot adjuster until specified clearance is obtained. Tighten locking nut and recheck clearance.

| Application | Intake | Exhaust |
|---|---|---|
| Cold Engine.............. | .008" (.20 mm) | .010" (.25 mm) |
| Hot Engine................ | .010" (.25 mm) | .012" (.30 mm) |

#### VALVE ARRANGEMENT

E-I-I-E-I-E-E-I-E-I-I-E (front to rear).

### SPARK PLUGS

| | |
|---|---|
| Gap .............................................. | .039-.043" (1.0-1.1 mm) |
| Torque ....................................... | 11-14 ft. lbs. (1.5-2.0 mkg) |

#### Spark Plug Type

| Application | Hitachi No. | NGK No. |
|---|---|---|
| 280Z & 810 ................. | L45W-11 | B6ES-11 |

**Fig. 1    Firing Order and Distributor Rotation**

FRONT OF VEHICLE

FIRING ORDER 1-5-3-6-2-4

### HIGH TENSION WIRE RESISTANCE

Remove distributor cap from distributor but do not disconnect high tension wires from cap. Disconnect high tension wires from spark plugs. Using an ohmmeter, check resistance from contact at spark plug end of wires to contact inside of distributor cap. Resistance should be less than 30,000 ohms. If resistance is more, disconnect wire from cap and recheck resistance. Replace wire if resistance still exceeds specifications.

### DISTRIBUTOR

All models use a single pickup transistor ignition system, which uses no breaker points. The only adjustment provided is for air gap between the reluctor and pickup coil.

Measure air gap using a non-magnetic feeler gauge. If gap is not to specifications, loosen pickup coil screws and adjust gap.

Air Gap ............................................. .008-.016" (.2-.4 mm)

Crankshaft Pulley

Rotation

**Fig. 2    Ignition Timing Mark Location**

### IGNITION TIMING

With engine at normal operating temperature, connect a timing light and tachometer to engine. Check air gap and idle speed and adjust to specifications if necessary. With Man. Trans. in neutral or Auto. Trans. in "D", adjust timing by loosening set screw and rotating distributor until timing is set to specifications. Tighten set screw and recheck timing.

## TUNE-UP (Cont.)

### Ignition Timing Specifications

| Application | ①Timing |
|---|---|
| 280Z | 10°BTDC |
| 810 | |
| Federal | 8°BTDC |
| Calif. | 10°BTDC |

① — Auto. Trans. in "D".

## IDLE SPEED & MIXTURE

1) With engine at normal operating temperature and ignition timing set to specification, connect tachometer and exhaust gas analyzer. With Man. Trans. in neutral or Auto. Trans. in "D", turn idle adjusting screw on throttle chamber to obtain specified idle RPM.

2) After engine has idled for about 10 minutes after idle adjustment, check CO%. If CO% is not within specifications, proceed to step 4).

**Fig. 3    Adjusting Idle Speed**

### Idle Speed (RPM) & CO Level (%)

| Application | Idle RPM | CO% |
|---|---|---|
| 280Z | | |
| Federal | | |
| Man. Trans. | 800 | 1.0 Max. |
| Auto. Trans. | ①700 | 1.0 Max. |
| Calif. | | |
| Man. Trans. | 800 | 0.5 Max. |
| Auto. Trans. | ①700 | 0.5 Max. |
| 810 | | |
| Federal | | |
| Man. Trans. | 700 | 1.0 Max. |
| Auto. Trans. | ①650 | 1.0 Max. |
| Calif. | | |
| Man. Trans. | 700 | 0.5 Max. |
| Auto. Trans. | ①650 | 0.5 Max. |

① — Transmission in "D".

4) Remove throttle valve switch harness connector. See *Fig. 4*.

**NOTE** — *If adjusting idle CO% at altitude of 2,500 ft. (750 m) or higher, or if vehicle is a California model, unhook altitude switch connector.*

5) With a piece of electrical wire, connect No. 3 and No. 18 terminals of throttle valve switch connector.

**NOTE** — *This procedure short circuits the enrichment system and allows the idle mixture to run at full load enrichment. This step is necessary to enrichen the CO% at idle enough to be read by an exhaust gas analyzer.*

6) Remove rubber plug to gain access, and turn air by-pass screw in air flow meter clockwise for richer mixture, counter-clockwise for leaner mixture. Enriched idle CO% must correspond to altitude at which adjustment is being made.

### Enriched Idle CO Level (%)

| Altitude | Idle CO% |
|---|---|
| 0-2000 ft. (0-600 m) | 3.3% |
| 2000-4000 ft. (600-1200 m) | 4.7% |
| 4000-6000 ft. (1200-1800 m) | 5.7% |
| Above 6000 ft. | 6.7% |

**Fig. 4    Idle Mixture Ratio Adjustment**
**(280Z Shown — 810 Similar)**

7) Once correct CO values are obtained, remove wire from throttle valve switch connector. Reinstall connector to proper location. Plug altitude switch connector back into original position (if removed on Calif. models only).

8) Install new rubber plug in air by-pass screw opening. Recheck idle speed and readjust if necessary. Recheck CO%.

## TUNE-UP (Cont.)

**Fig. 5 Dashpot Adjustment**

### DASHPOT ADJUSTMENT

**Man. Trans. Only** — With engine speed at 2000 RPM, clearance between idle set screw and throttle lever should be .075" (1.9 mm). Check that dashpot rod end touches throttle lever when rod is fully extended (or when no back pressure is present at diaphragm). If necessary, loosen lock nut and turn dashpot until rod just touches throttle lever, then tighten lock nut. See *Fig. 5.*

### FUEL PUMP PRESSURE

Pressure ................................................ 36.3 psi  (2.6 kg/cm²)

### EMISSION CONTROL SYSTEMS

*See Mitchell Manuals' Emission Control Manual.*

## GENERAL SERVICING

### IGNITION

#### DISTRIBUTOR

All models are equipped with Hitachi Transistor Ignition System.

**Other Data & Specifications** — *See Tune-Up & Hitachi Distributors in ELECTRICAL Section.*

#### IGNITION COIL

| Resistance | Ohms at 68°F (20°C) |
|---|---|
| Primary | .84-1.02 |
| Secondary | 8,200-12,400 |

### FUEL SYSTEMS

#### FUEL INJECTION

All models are equipped with Bosch Electronic Fuel Injection System.

**Other Data & Specifications** — *See Tune-Up and Bosch Electronic Fuel Injection in FUEL SYSTEMS Section.*

### ELECTRICAL

#### BATTERY

**12 Volt** — Negative Ground.

All Models ................................................................. 60

**Battery Location** — Right side of engine compartment.

### STARTER

| Hitachi | Overrunning Clutch |
|---|---|
| Free Speed Voltage | 12 at 4300 RPM |
| Free Speed Amperage | 100 (Max.) at 4300 RPM |

**Other Data & Specifications** — *See Hitachi Starters in ELECTRICAL Section.*

### ALTERNATOR

| Application | Rated Amp. Output |
|---|---|
| All Models | 60 |

**Other Data & Specifications** — *See Hitachi Alternators & Regulators in ELECTRICAL Section.*

### ALTERNATOR REGULATOR

All models use a Hitachi alternator regulator with an operating voltage of 14.3-15.3 volts at 68°F (20°C).

**Other Data & Specifications** — *See Hitachi Alternators & Regulators in ELECTRICAL Section.*

### ENGINE

#### INTAKE MANIFOLD TIGHTENING

Check manifold attaching bolts for the following torque:

## GENERAL SERVICING (Cont.)

### Intake Manifold Tightening

| Application | Ft. Lbs. (mkg) |
|---|---|
| 8 mm Bolts | 10-13 (1.4-1.8) |
| 10 mm Bolts | 25-36 (3.5-5.0) |

### BELT ADJUSTMENT

| Application | ① Deflection |
|---|---|
| All Belts | 5/16-1/2" (8-12 mm) |

① — Deflection is with 22 lbs. (10 kg) pressure applied midway on belt run.

### FILTERS & CLEANERS

| Filter or Cleaner | Service Interval (Miles) |
|---|---|
| Oil Filter | Replace 7,500 |
| Air Cleaner | Replace 30,000 |
| Fuel Filter | Replace 30,000 |
| PCV Valve | Replace 30,000 |
| Canister Filter | Replace 30,000 |

### CAPACITIES

| Application | Quantity |
|---|---|
| Crankcase (Includes Filter) | |
| 280Z | 4.75 qts. |
| 810 | 5.9 qts. |
| Cooling System (Includes Heater) | |
| 280Z (Man. Trans.) | 10.9 qts. |
| 280Z (Auto. Trans.) | 10.6 qts. |
| 810 | 11 qts. |
| Man. Trans. (API GL-4) | |
| 280Z 4-Speed | 3.6 pts. |
| 280Z 5-Speed | 4.25 pts. |
| 810 | 3.6 pts. |
| Auto. Trans. (Dexron) | 5.9 qts. |
| Rear Axle (API GL-5) | |
| 280Z (Man. Trans.) | 2.75 pts. |
| 280Z (Auto. Trans.) | 2.13 pts. |
| 810 Sedan | 2.75 pts. |
| 810 Station Wagon | 2.13 pts. |
| Fuel Tank | |
| 280Z | 17.13 gals. |
| 810 Sedan | 15.9 gals. |
| 810 Station Wagon | 14.5 gals. |

## TUNE-UP

124
128
131
  Brava
  Super Brava
X1/9

### ENGINE IDENTIFICATION

**124 & 131 Models** — Engine code and identification numbers are stamped on crankcase near oil filter mount.

**128 & X1/9 Models** — Engine code and identification numbers are stamped on crankcase (flywheel end).

| Application | Engine Code | |
|---|---|---|
| | Federal | California |
| 124 | 132 A1.040.6 | 132 A1.031.6 |
| 131 | 132 A1.040.6 | 132 A1.031.6 |
| 128 | 128 A1.040.6 | 128 A1.031.6 |
| 128 3P | 128 A1.040.6 | 128 A1.031.6 |
| X1/9 | 128 AS.031.5 | 128 AS.031.6 |

### MODEL IDENTIFICATION

#### VEHICLE IDENTIFICATION NUMBER

Model can be identified by prefix of vehicle identification number, which is stamped on a plate attached to top of instrument panel between instrument cluster and windshield. Number also is found on engine compartment bulkhead of 124 and 131 models, on right-hand front wheel suspension mounting on 128 and 128 3P models, and in front trunk compartment, right-hand rear wall of X1/9 models. Model codes are as follows:

| Application | Code |
|---|---|
| 124 Models | |
|   Sport Spider | 124 CS1 |
| 128 Models | |
|   Sedan | 128 A1 |
|   Station Wagon | 128 AF1 |
| 128 3P Models | 128 AC |
| 131 Models | |
|   Sedan | 131 A3 |
|   Station Wagon | 131 AF2 |
| X 1/9 | 128 AS |

### VALVE TAPPET CLEARANCE

| Application | ①Intake | ①Exhaust |
|---|---|---|
| 124 & 131 Models | .018" (.45 mm) | .020" (.50 mm) |
| 128 & X 1/9 Models | .012" (.30 mm) | .016" (.40 mm) |

① — Set valves with engine cold.

### VALVE ARRANGEMENT

124 & 131 Models
  Right Side — All Exhaust.
  Left Side — All Intake.
128 & X1/9 Models — E-I-I-E-E-I-I-E

### SPARK PLUGS

| | |
|---|---|
| Gap | .023-.027" (.6-.7 mm) |
| Torque | |
|   131 Models | 29 ft. lbs. (4.0 mkg) |
|   All Others | 25 ft. lbs. (3.5 mkg) |

#### Spark Plug Type

| Application | Champion No. | AC No. |
|---|---|---|
| All Models | N-9Y | 42 XLS |

### HIGH TENSION WIRE RESISTANCE

Carefully remove ends of high tension wire from spark plug and distributor cap. Using an ohmmeter, check resistance of wire while gently twisting wire. If resistance is not to specification, or if resistance fluctuates from infinity to any value, replace high tension wire(s).

#### Resistance (Ohms) Per Wire

| Application | Resistance |
|---|---|
| All Models | 25,000-30,000 |

**Fig. 1    Firing Order and Distributor Rotation (124 & 131 Models)**

**Fig. 2    Firing Order and Distributor Rotation (128, 128 3P, & X1/9 Models)**

## TUNE-UP (Cont.)

### DISTRIBUTOR

Point Gap ............................... ①.015-.017" (.37-.43 mm)
Cam Angle ............................................ 55±3°
Breaker Arm Spring Tension
  124 & 131 Models ................ ②19.4±1.8 ozs. (550±50 g)
  128 & X 1/9 Models .................. 15.9±1.8 ozs. (450±50 g)
Condenser Capacity
  124 & 131 Models .................................... .20-.25 mfd.
  128 & X 1/9 Models ................................. .22-.23 mfd.

① — On models with dual point distributors, set secondary
point gap to .012-.019" (.31-.49 mm)

② — Tension on secondary points should be 14.1±1.8 ozs.
(400±50 g)

**128 Models**    **124, 131 & X1/9 Models**

### Fig. 3 Ignition Timing Mark Location

### IGNITION TIMING

Check or adjust ignition timing with engine at normal
operating temperature, Man. Trans. in neutral or Auto. Trans.
in "D" and point gap and idle speed set to specifications. To
adjust timing, align mark on drive pulley or flywheel with
specified pointer by turning distributor.

#### Ignition Timing Specifications

| Application | Timing |
|---|---|
| 131 | |
|   Man. Trans | |
|     Federal | TDC |
|     Calif. | 5°BTDC |
|   Auto. Trans. | 5°BTDC |
| All Others | TDC |

### IDLE SPEED & MIXTURE

**1)** With engine at normal operating temperature and ignition
timing set to specification, connect a tachometer and exhaust
gas analyzer. Disconnect or pinch off air injection hose.

**2)** With Man. Trans. in neutral or Auto. Trans. in "D", turn idle
speed adjusting screw to obtain specified idle RPM. Then, turn
mixture adjusting screw to obtain specified CO%. Recheck idle
speed.

**3)** Reconnect or unpinch air injection hose. Idle speed should
increase by 50 RPM.

#### Idle Speed (RPM) & CO Level (%)

| Application | Idle RPM | CO% |
|---|---|---|
| Man. Trans. ................... | 800-850 ......................... | 1.5-2.5 |
| Auto. Trans. ................. | ①700-750 ......................... | 1.5-2.5 |

① — Transmission in "D".

### COLD (FAST) IDLE RPM

#### 124 & 131 MODELS ONLY

To adjust fast idle RPM, depress button on firewall in engine
compartment, which energizes control electrovalve, and turn
fast idle adjusting screw until engine RPM is within
specifications.

#### Fast Idle RPM

| Application | RPM |
|---|---|
| 124 .................................................. | 1550-1650 |
| 131 | |
|   Man. Trans. ................................................. | 1550-1650 |
|   Auto. Trans. ................................................. | ①1250-1350 |

① — Transmission in "N".

### EMISSION CONTROL SYSTEMS

*See Mitchell Manuals' Emission Control Manual.*

## GENERAL SERVICING

### IGNITION

#### DISTRIBUTOR

All 124 and 131 models are equipped with Marelli dual point
distributors. All 128 and X 1/9 models are equipped with
Ducellier single point distributors.

**Other Data & Specifications** — *See Tune-Up, Marelli &
Ducellier Distributors in ELECTRICAL Section.*

### IGNITION COIL

| Resistance | Ohms at 68°F (20°C) |
|---|---|
| Primary | |
|   Bosch Coil ............................................. | 2.6-3.1 |
|   Marelli Coil ............................................. | 3.2-3.4 |
|   Martinetti Coil ......................................... | 3.0-3.3 |
| Secondary | |
|   Bosch Coil ............................................. | 8,500-12,000 |
|   Marelli Coil ............................................. | 9,000-11,000 |
|   Martinetti Coil ......................................... | 6,500-8,000 |

# 1978 Fiat 4 Tune-Up

T U N E U P

## GENERAL SERVICING (Cont.)

### FUEL SYSTEMS

#### CARBURETORS

| Application | Model |
|---|---|
| 124 & 131 | Weber 32 ADFA |
| 128 & X1/9 | Weber 32 DATRA |

**Other Data & Specifications** — *See Tune-Up & Weber Carburetors in FUEL SYSTEMS Section.*

### ELECTRICAL

#### BATTERY

**12 Volt** — Negative Ground.

| Application | Amp Hr. Rating |
|---|---|
| All Models | 60 |

**Battery Location** — Battery is located in engine compartment on all except 124 sports models. On these models, battery is located in trunk.

#### STARTER

All models are equipped with Fiat starters.

Free Speed Voltage
124 & 131 .................. 12 at 5200±500 RPM
128 & X1/9 ............... 11.7 at 7000±500 RPM
Free Speed Amperage
124 & 131 .................. 28 at 5200±500 RPM
128 & X1/9 ............... 35 at 7000±500 RPM

**Other Data & Specifications** — *See Fiat Starters in ELECTRICAL Section.*

#### ALTERNATOR

The 124 and 131 models are equipped with Bosch alternators; 128 and X1/9 models are equipped with Marelli alternators.

| Application | Rated Amp. Output |
|---|---|
| 124 | 55 |
| 128 | |
| Sedan & Wagon | 53 |
| 3P | 60 |
| 131 & X1/9 | 60 |

**Other Data & Specifications** — *See Bosch & Marelli Alternators & Regulators in ELECTRICAL Section.*

### ALTERNATOR REGULATOR

The 124 and 131 models are equipped with Bosch regulators; 128 and X1/9 models are equipped with Marelli regulators. With headlights on and heater fan on high speed, operating voltage should be 12.5-14.5 volts at 2500 RPM.

**Other Data & Specifications** — *See Bosch & Marelli Alternators & Regulators in ELECTRICAL Section.*

### BELT ADJUSTMENT

Belt tension is correct when under a pressure of about 22 lbs. (10 kg) belt can be depressed .4-.6" (10-15 mm)

### FILTERS & CLEANERS

| Filter or Cleaner | Service Interval (Miles) |
|---|---|
| Oil Filter | Replace every 6000 |
| Air Cleaner | Replace every 12,500 |
| Fuel Filter | Replace every 12,500 |
| Charcoal Canister | Replace every 25,000 |

### CAPACITIES

| Application | Quantity |
|---|---|
| Crankcase (Includes Filter) | |
| 124 & 131 Models | 4.0 qts. |
| 128, 128 3P, & X1/9 Models | 4.5 qts. |
| Cooling System | |
| 124 Models | 8.5 qts. |
| 128 Models | 6.8 qts. |
| 128 3P Models | 7.4 qts. |
| 131 Models | 8.5 qts. |
| X1/9 | 11.4 qts. |
| Man. Trans. (SAE 90) | |
| 124 Models | 3.5 pts. |
| 131 Models | 3.5 pts. |
| Auto. Trans. (Dexron) | |
| 131 Models Only (Refill) | 6.0 pts. |
| Rear Axle (SAE 90) | |
| 124 Models | 2.8 pts. |
| 131 Models | 2.8 pts. |
| Transaxle (SAE 90) | |
| 128 & X1/9 Models | 6.6 pts. |
| Fuel Tank | |
| 124 Models | 11.4 gals. |
| 128 Sedan & Wagon | 9.5 gals. |
| 128 3P Models | 12.5 gals. |
| 131 Models | 12.2 gals. |
| X1/9 Models | 12.2 gals. |

## TUNE-UP

**Fiesta**

### ENGINE IDENTIFICATION

Engine identification code is located on bottom line of vehicle identification plate, which is riveted on the panel above right front headlight just under hood.

| Application | Code |
|---|---|
| 1600 cc | L4 |

### MODEL IDENTIFICATION

#### VEHICLE IDENTIFICATION NUMBER

Vehicle identification number is stamped on vehicle identification plate, which is riveted on the panel above right front headlight just under hood. Number is also stamped on a plate attached to left front windshield pillar and visible through windshield.

### COMPRESSION PRESSURE

Check compression pressure with engine at normal operating temperature, all spark plugs removed, throttle valve wide open and engine at cranking speed. Compression pressure is within specifications if lowest reading cylinder is at least 75% of highest reading cylinder.

### VALVE TAPPET CLEARANCE

Adjust valves with engine cold. To adjust, turn adjusting screw until correct clearance is obtained.

**NOTE** – *Do not use Go/No-Go type feeler gauge. Check clearance fore and aft parallel to crankshaft centerline. Any other method will result in an incorrect reading.*

Adjust valves in the following sequence.

| Valves Open | Adjust Valves |
|---|---|
| No. 1 & 6 | No. 3 & 8 |
| No. 2 & 4 | No. 5 & 7 |
| No. 3 & 8 | No. 1 & 6 |
| No. 5 & 7 | No. 2 & 4 |

#### Valve Tappet Clearance

| Application | Clearance |
|---|---|
| Intake | ①.010" (.25 mm) |
| Exhaust | ①.021" (.53 mm) |

① – Adjust with engine cold.

### VALVE ARRANGEMENT

E-I-I-E-E-I-I-E

### SPARK PLUGS

| | |
|---|---|
| Gap | .050" (1.27 mm) |
| Torque | 10-15 ft. lbs. (1.4-2.1 mkg) |

**Spark Plug Type**

| Application | Autolite No. |
|---|---|
| All Models | AWRF-32 |

### HIGH TENSION WIRE RESISTANCE

Remove distributor cap from distributor, but do not disconnect high tension wires from cap. Disconnect high tension wires from spark plugs. Using an ohmmeter, check resistance from contact at spark plug end of wires to contact inside of distributor cap. Resistance should be less than 5,000 ohms per inch. If resistance is more, disconnect wire from cap and recheck resistance. Replace wire if resistance still exceeds specifications.

**Fig. 1 Firing Order and Distributor Rotation**

### DISTRIBUTOR

All models are equipped with Dura Spark II ignition system. No adjustments are required.

### IGNITION TIMING

Check and adjust ignition timing with engine at normal operating temperature, idle speed set to specification and distributor vacuum hose disconnected and plugged.

#### Ignition Timing Specifications

| Application | Timing |
|---|---|
| All Models | 12°BTDC |

**Fig. 2 Ignition Timing Mark Location**

## TUNE-UP (Cont.)

### HOT (SLOW) IDLE RPM

1) With engine off and at normal operating temperature, connect suitable tachometer. Disconnect radiator fan switch and attach a jumper wire so fan operates continuously. Remove air cleaner assembly.

2) If equipped with any of the following, perform appropriate action:

- Spark Delay Valve (in Dist. Vacuum Line) — Remove valve and connect line back together.
- Fuel Decel Valve — Disconnect from carburetor and plug hose.
- EGR PVS — Disconnect hose coming from EGR valve at PVS and plug hose.

3) Start engine, ensure normal operating temperature, raise engine speed to 2500 RPM for 15 seconds, then allow it to return to normal idle.

4) Turn idle speed screw as required to obtain specified idle RPM. If unable to obtain specified idle RPM, check dashpot (if equipped) to be sure clearance to throttle lever exists.

5) Reinstall air cleaner assembly after restoring other components to original positions. Recheck idle speed.

#### Idle Speed (RPM)

| Application | RPM |
| --- | --- |
| All Models | 800-900 |

### IDLE MIXTURE

#### PROPANE ENRICHMENT PROCEDURE

1) Apply parking brake and block drive wheels. Air cleaner may be removed as necessary to make adjustments; however, be sure to remove No. 3 and 4 spark plug wires from snorkel first.

2) Connect suitable tachometer and bring engine to normal operating temperature. Disconnect radiator fan switch and attach a jumper wire so fan operates continuously.

3) Detach fuel evaporation hose from air cleaner. Disconnect crankcase ventilation hose from air cleaner and plug hole in air cleaner.

4) Adjust curb idle as specified for idle mixture check (on Emission Control/Tune-Up decal). If "Idle Mixture Speed" is not specified on decal, use idle speed as previously outlined.

5) Run engine at 2500 RPM for 15 seconds before each speed check. Idle speed must be set with air cleaner installed.

NOTE — If idle mixture screw limiter cap is missing, turn mixture screw clockwise until lightly seated; then, turn screw counterclockwise 2 complete turns.

6) Plug propane enrichment tool (T75L-9600-A or equivalent) into air cleaner fuel evaporation purge nipple. With engine idling, slowly open propane supply valve until engine speed reaches maximum RPM and then begins to drop. Note maximum speed increase.

7) If speed increase is within specifications, replace air cleaner and all hoses. Recheck idle speed.

8) If speed increase is greater than specifications, turn mixture screw counterclockwise to richen mixture, and retest until gain is correct.

9) If speed increase is less than specifications, turn mixture screw clockwise to lean mixture, and retest until gain is correct.

10) If vehicle Tune-up Decal specifies a "0" RPM gain, use the following speed drop test procedure to adjust mixture. Decal will specify the number of turns to adjust mixture screws.

- If limiter is installed, turn to maximum rich position. Then, lean mixture by turning limiter clockwise by specified amount. Note RPM drop.
- If limiter has been removed, lean mixture by turning screw clockwise by specified amount. Note RPM drop.
- If RPM drop is equal to or greater than specification, return limiter to maximum rich position or mixture screws to pretest position.
- If RPM drop is less than specification, lean mixture screw until RPM drop meets specification. Repeat procedure to be sure settings are correct.

11) If limiters were removed, install service replacements at maximum rich stop position. Install air cleaner assembly and reconnect all systems as required. Recheck idle speed.

#### Propane Enriched RPM Gain & Reset Specifications

| Application | RPM Gain | Reset RPM |
| --- | --- | --- |
| All Models | 10-30 | 10 |

### COLD (FAST) IDLE RPM

1) Prepare the vehicle for fast idle adjustment by performing steps 1), 2) and 3) of "HOT (SLOW) IDLE RPM" procedure.

2) Remove electric choke cap unit, noting setting and relationship between choke lever and bimetal spring. Place fast idle screw on kickdown step of fast idle cam, against shoulder of high step.

3) Turn fast idle speed screw as necessary to obtain specified fast idle RPM. Reinstall choke cap and reset to specification. Reinstall air cleaner assembly after restoring other components to original positions. Recheck fast idle speed.

#### Fast Idle RPM

| Application | RPM |
| --- | --- |
| All Models | 1800 |

### AUTOMATIC CHOKE SETTING

| Application | Setting |
| --- | --- |
| All Models | INDEX |

# 1978 Fiesta 4 Tune-Up

## TUNE-UP (Cont.)

### FUEL PUMP PRESSURE

Pressure (At Idle) ........................ 3.5 psi (.25 kg/cm²)

### EMISSION CONTROL SYSTEMS

See Mitchell Manuals' Emission Control Manual.

## GENERAL SERVICING

### IGNITION

#### DISTRIBUTOR

All models are equipped with Motorcraft Dura-Spark II breakerless, electronic ignition system.

**Other Data & Specifications** — See Motorcraft Solid State Ignition in ELECTRICAL Section.

#### IGNITION COIL

**Resistance**

Primary ........................................ 1.13-1.23 ohms
Secondary .................................... 7,700-9,300

### FUEL SYSTEMS

#### CARBURETORS

| Application | Model |
|---|---|
| All Models | Weber Model 740 2-Bbl. |

**Other Data & Specifications** — See Tune-Up and Weber Carburetors in FUEL SYSTEMS Section.

### ELECTRICAL

#### BATTERY

**12 Volt** — Negative Ground. Located at right front of engine compartment.

| Application | Amp. Hr. Rating |
|---|---|
| All Models | 54 |

#### STARTER

Bosch Pre-Engaged Type.

Maximum Current Draw ...................... 350 Amps.

**Other Data & Specifications** — See Bosch Starters in ELECTRICAL Section.

#### ALTERNATOR

Air conditioned models are equipped with Bosch alternators. All other models are equipped with Motorcraft alternators.

| Application | Rated Amp. Output |
|---|---|
| Bosch | 55 |
| Motorcraft | |
| Color Code Orange | 40 |
| Color Code Green | 60 |

**Other Data & Specifications** — See Bosch & Motorcraft Alternators & Regulators in ELECTRICAL Section.

#### ALTERNATOR REGULATOR

Air conditioned models are equipped with Bosch alternator regulators. All other models are equipped with Motorcraft alternator regulators.

Operating Voltage ................................ 13.6-14.5

**Other Data & Specifications** — See Bosch & Motorcraft Alternators & Regulators in ELECTRICAL Section.

### ENGINE

#### INTAKE MANIFOLD TIGHTENING

Tighten intake manifold-to-cylinder head bolts and nuts to 12-15 ft. lbs. torque.

### BELT ADJUSTMENT

**Tension (Lbs.) With Strand Tension Gauge**

| Application | New Belt | ①Used Belt |
|---|---|---|
| All Belts (Exc. ¼") | 120-160 | 75-120 |
| ¼" Belts | 50-80 | 40-60 |

① — Any belt operated for 10 minutes or longer.

### FILTERS & CLEANERS

| Filter or Cleaner | Service Interval (Miles) |
|---|---|
| Oil Filter | Replace every 7,500 |
| Air Cleaner | Replace every 30,000 |
| Fuel Filter | ①Replace 20,000 |
| PCV Valve | Replace every 30,000 |

① — Replace only one time

### CAPACITIES

| Application | Quantity |
|---|---|
| Crankcase (Includes Filter) | 3.5 qts. |
| Cooling System | 7.0 qts. |
| Transaxle (ATF) | 5.0 pts. |
| Fuel Tank | 10 gals. |

## TUNE-UP

Accord
Civic
Civic CVCC

### ENGINE IDENTIFICATION

Engine serial number is stamped on a machined surface at rear of engine, near starter. Engine serial number is preceded by engine model number. Model numbers are as follows:

| Application | Model Code |
|---|---|
| Accord ..................................................... | EFI |
| Civic ....................................................... | EB3 |
| Civic CVCC | |
|   Sedan ................................................. | ED3 |
|   Station Wagon ...................................... | ED4 |

### MODEL IDENTIFICATION

Model identification number is stamped on a metal tag and riveted to dash. Tag is visible through windshield. Number also appears on left door post, and on body under hood behind air cleaner.

### COMPRESSION PRESSURE

Check compression with engine at normal operating temperature, air cleaner and spark plugs removed, throttle and choke valve wide open.

**Compression Pressure
@ 400 RPM**

| Application | Pressure |
|---|---|
| Accord ..................................... | 170 psi (12 kg/cm²) |
| Civic ....................................... | 155 psi (11 kg/cm²) |
| Civic CVCC .............................. | 136-192 psi (10-14 kg/cm²) |

### VALVE TAPPET CLEARANCE

**1)** Adjust valve clearance to specifications with engine cold.

**2)** With piston of No. 1 cylinder at TDC (camshaft keyway pointing up), adjust intake valves 1 and 2; exhaust valves 1 and 3; and, on Accord and Civic CVCC models, auxiliary valves 1 and 2.

**3)** Rotate crankshaft one full turn until piston of No. 4 cylinder is at TDC (camshaft keyway pointing down). Adjust intake valves 3 and 4; exhaust valves 2 and 4; and, on Accord and Civic CVCC models, auxiliary valves 3 and 4.

**4)** To adjust, loosen lock nut and turn adjusting screw until feeler gauge slides back and forth with slight drag. Tighten intake and exhaust valve lock nuts to 12-16 ft. lbs. (1.8-2.2 mkg) and auxiliary valve lock nuts to 9-12 ft. lbs. (1.2-1.6 mkg). Recheck clearance.

**Valve Clearance Specifications**

| Application | Clearance |
|---|---|
| Accord & Civic CVCC | |
|   Intake & Auxiliary ...................... | .005-.007" (.12-.18 mm) |
|   Exhaust ..................................... | .007-.009" (.12-.18 mm) |
| Civic | |
|   Intake & Exhaust ......................... | .004-.006" (.10-.16 mm) |

### VALVE ARRANGEMENT

Accord & Civic CVCC
  Left Side — I-E-E-I-I-E-E-I
  Right Side — All Auxiliary.
Civic
  Left Side — All Intake.
  Right Side — All Exhaust.

FRONT OF VEHICLE

FIRING ORDER 1-3-4-2

**Fig. 1 Firing Order and Distributor Rotation (Accord and Civic CVCC)**

FRONT OF VEHICLE

FIRING ORDER 1-3-4-2

**Fig. 2 Firing Order and Distributor Rotation (Civic)**

### SPARK PLUGS

| | |
|---|---|
| Gap ........................................... | .028-.032" (.7-.8 mm) |
| Torque | |
|   Accord & Civic CVCC .............. | 11-18 ft. lbs. (1.5-2.5 mkg) |
|   Civic ....................................... | 9-12 ft. lbs. (1.3-1.7 mkg) |

## TUNE-UP (Cont.)

### Spark Plug Type

| Application | Nippondenso | NGK |
|---|---|---|
| Accord | ①W-20ES-L | ②B-6EB |
| Civic | W-20EP | BP-6ES |
| Civic CVCC | ①W-20ES-L | ②B-6EB |

① — Cold Climates — W-1635-L
② — Cold Climates — B-5EB

## HIGH TENSION WIRE RESISTANCE

Carefully remove ends of wire from spark plug and distributor. Using an ohmmeter, check resistance of wire while gently twisting wire. If resistance is not to specification, or fluctuates from infinity to any value, replace wire.

### Resistance (Ohms) Per Wire

| Application | Resistance |
|---|---|
| All Models (2 ft. length) | 25,000 Max. |

## DISTRIBUTOR

| | |
|---|---|
| Point Gap | .018-.022″ (.45-.55 mm) |
| Cam Angle | 49-55° |
| Breaker Arm Spring Tension | 18-23 ozs. (500-650 g) |
| Condenser Capacity | .20-.24 mfd. |

## IGNITION TIMING

**Accord & Civic CVCC — 1)** With engine at normal operating temperature, idle speed set to specification and Man. Trans. in neutral or Auto. Trans in "2", connect a timing light and tachometer to engine. Then, remove rubber inspection cap from inspection window on cylinder block (at flywheel housing).

**2)** To adjust timing, loosen distributor retaining bolt and rotate distributor until specified mark on flywheel aligns with index pointer. Tighten retaining bolt and recheck timing.

**Civic — 1)** With engine at normal operating temperature, idle speed set to specification and Man. Trans. in neutral or Auto. Trans. in "2", connect a timing light and tachometer to engine.

**2)** To adjust timing, loosen distributor retaining bolt and rotate distributor until red timing mark on pulley aligns with index mark. Tighten retaining bolt and recheck timing.

### Ignition Timing Specifications

| Application | Federal | Calif. & High Alt. |
|---|---|---|
| **Accord & Civic CVCC** | | |
| Man. Trans. | 6°BTDC | 2°BTDC |
| Auto. Trans. | ①6°BTDC | ①2°BTDC |
| Civic | ①2°BTDC | ①2°BTDC |

① — Auto. Trans. in "2".

**Fig. 3 Ignition Timing Mark Location (Civic)**

**Fig. 4 Ignition Timing Mark Location (Accord & Civic CVCC)**

## IDLE SPEED & MIXTURE

### EXHAUST GAS ANALYZER METHOD

**1)** With engine at normal operating temperature, connect an exhaust gas analyzer and tachometer to vehicle. Turn headlights and cooling fan on.

**2)** Place Man. Trans. in neutral or Auto. Trans. in "2".

**3)** Adjust idle speed screw until idle speed is set to specifications. Remove mixture screw limiter cap and adjust mixture screw until CO level is within specifications.

**4)** Recheck idle speed and CO level and adjust as necessary to obtain best balance between idle speed and CO level. Install new limiter cap on mixture screw.

### Idle Speed (RPM) and CO Level (%)

| Application | Idle RPM | CO% |
|---|---|---|
| **Accord & Civic CVCC** | | |
| Man. Trans. | 650-750 | 0.4% Max. |
| Auto. Trans. | ①600-700 | 0.4% Max. |
| Civic | ①650-750 | 0.35% Max. |

① — Auto. Trans. in "2".

## TUNE-UP (Cont.)

### TACHOMETER (LEAN DROP) METHOD

**1)** With engine at normal operating temperature and Man. Trans. in neutral or Auto. Trans. in "2", turn on headlights and cooling fan.

**2)** Remove mixture screw limiter cap and turn screw counter-clockwise (rich) until highest RPM is obtained.

**3)** Adjust idle speed screw to obtain specified enriched RPM. Then, turn mixture screw clockwise (lean) until idle speed drops to specified idle RPM. Replace limiter cap with point 180° away from boss on carburetor body.

#### Lean Drop RPM Specifications

| Application | Enriched RPM | Idle RPM |
|---|---|---|
| Accord | | |
| Federal | | |
| Man. Trans | 790 | 700 |
| Auto. Trans.① | 710 | 650 |
| Calif. & High Alt. | | |
| Man. Trans. | 810 | 700 |
| Auto. Trans.① | 730 | 650 |
| Civic | | |
| Man. Trans. | 800 | 700 |
| Auto. Trans.① | 750 | 700 |
| Civic CVCC | | |
| Man. Trans. | 810 | 700 |
| Auto. Trans.① | 730 | 650 |

① — Transmission in "2".

### COLD (FAST) IDLE RPM

**Accord** — With engine off and hot, remove air cleaner cover and filter element. Hold choke valve closed and open and close throttle to engage fast idle cam. Start engine, run for one minute, and check fast idle RPM. Turn fast idle adjusting screw to obtain specified fast idle RPM.

**Civic** — With engine at normal operating temperature, align choke lever arm with boss at top of carburetor. Start engine and note fast idle RPM. To adjust, alter size of slot in throttle link lever. Narrow slot to lower RPM; widen slot to increase RPM.

**Civic CVCC** — With engine at normal operating temperature and choke knob pulled out to second detent, note fast idle RPM. To adjust, alter size of slot in fast idle adjusting link. Narrow slot to lower RPM; widen slot to increase RPM.

#### Fast Idle RPM

| Application | RPM |
|---|---|
| Accord | 2500-3500 |
| Civic | 1400-2200 |
| Civic CVCC | 2100-3100 |

### FUEL PUMP PRESSURE & VOLUME

| | |
|---|---|
| Pressure | 2-3 psi (.13-.18 kg/cm²) |
| Volume | .4 pts. in 30 sec. |

### EMISSION CONTROL SYSTEMS

See Mitchell Manuals' Emission Control Manual.

## GENERAL SERVICING

### IGNITION

#### DISTRIBUTOR

All models are equipped with Hitachi single point distributors.

**Other Data & Specifications** — *See Tune-Up and Hitachi Distributors in ELECTRICAL Section.*

#### IGNITION COIL

| Resistance | Ohms at 68°F (20°C) |
|---|---|
| Primary | 1.35-1.65 |
| Secondary | |
| Accord & Civic CVCC | 8,000-12,000 |
| Civic | 6,800-10,200 |

### FUEL SYSTEMS

#### CARBURETORS

| Application | Model |
|---|---|
| All Models | Keihin 2-Bbl. |

**Other Data & Specifications** — *See Tune-Up and Keihin Carburetors in FUEL SYSTEMS Section.*

### ELECTRICAL

#### BATTERY

**12 Volt** — Negative Ground.

| Application | Amp. Hr. Rating |
|---|---|
| All | 47 |

**Battery Location** — In engine compartment.

#### STARTER

| Application | Type |
|---|---|
| Accord | Nippondenso Overrunning Clutch |
| Civic | Hitachi Overrunning Clutch |
| Civic CVCC | Nippondenso Overrunning Clutch |
| Free Speed Voltage | |
| Accord | 11.5 at 5000 RPM (Min.) |
| Civic | 11 at 6000 RPM |
| Civic CVCC | 11.5 at 7000 RPM |
| Free Speed Amperage | |
| Accord | 90 Amps. (Max.) at 5000 RPM (Min.) |
| Civic | 70 Amps. (Max.) at 6000 RPM |
| Civic CVCC | 80 Amps. (Max.) at 7000 RPM |

**Other Data & Specifications** — *See Hitachi or Nippondenso Starters in ELECTRICAL Section.*

# 1978 Honda 4 Tune-Up

## GENERAL SERVICING (Cont.)

### ALTERNATOR

All models are equipped with Nippondenso alternators.

| Application | Rated Amp. Output |
|---|---|
| Accord | 50 |
| Civic | 45 |
| Civic | 40 |
| Civic CVCC | |
| Without A/C | 35 |
| With A/C | 45 |

**Other Data & Specifications —** *See Nippondenso Alternators and Regulators in ELECTRICAL Section.*

### ALTERNATOR REGULATOR

All models are equipped with Nippondenso alternator regulators with an operating voltage of 13.5-14.5 volts.

**Other Data & Specifications —** *See Nippondenso Alternators and Regulators in ELECTRICAL Section.*

## ENGINE

### INTAKE MANIFOLD TIGHTENING

Tighten intake manifold attaching bolts to the following specifications.

#### Intake Manifold Tightening Specifications

| Application | Ft. Lbs. (mkg) |
|---|---|
| Accord | 14-17 (2.0-2.4) |
| Civic | 13-17 (1.8-2.4) |
| Civic CVCC | 16 (2.2) |

### FILTERS & CLEANERS

| Filter or Cleaner | Service Interval (Miles) |
|---|---|
| Oil Filter | Replace every 5000 |
| Air Cleaner | Replace every 15,000 |
| Fuel Filter | ① |
| Charcoal Canister | Replace every 30,000 |

① — Replace at first 15,000 miles and then every 30,000 miles thereafter.

### BELT ADJUSTMENT

**All Models —** Deflection of belt should be .47-.67" (12-17 mm) when 19.8-24.3 lbs. (9-11 kg) pressure is applied midway between alternator and fan pulleys.

### CAPACITIES

| Application | Quantity |
|---|---|
| Crankcase (Includes Filter) | |
| All Models | 3.2 qts. |
| Cooling System (Includes Heater) | |
| Accord | 5.3 qts. |
| All Other Models | 4.2 qts. |
| Man. Trans. (SAE 10W-40) | |
| 4-Speed | 2.6 qts. |
| 5-Speed | 2.8 qts. |
| Auto. Trans. (Dexron) | 2.6 qts. |
| Fuel Tank | |
| Accord | 13.2 gals. |
| Civic CVCC Station Wagon | 11.1 gals |
| All Other Models | 10.6 gals |

## TUNE-UP

**XJ6L**

### ENGINE IDENTIFICATION

Engine number is stamped on top of cylinder block at rear of engine. Number is also stamped on Commission Plate, which is located in the engine compartment. Suffix following engine number indicates compression ratio, "L" — Low.

### MODEL IDENTIFICATION

#### VEHICLE IDENTIFICATION NUMBER

Number is stamped on a metal tag and attached to the left side rear pillar. Information on tag identifies production date and chassis number.

### COMPRESSION PRESSURE

Check compression pressure with engine at normal operating temperature, throttle valve wide open, all spark plugs removed and coil wire disconnected. Compression pressure is normal if all cylinders are within 5 psi (.35 kg/cm$^2$) of each other.

### VALVE TAPPET CLEARANCE

| Application | Clearance (Cold) |
|---|---|
| Intake | .012-.014" (.30-.35 mm) |
| Exhaust | .012-.014" (.30-.35 mm) |

#### VALVE TAPPET ADJUSTMENT

1) With camshaft covers removed, rotate camshafts and record clearance between heel of each cam lobe and its respective tappet. If adjustment is necessary, rotate camshaft and install valve timing gauge (C.3993) before removing final camshaft retaining nut. If required, disconnect sprockets from camshafts.

**NOTE** – *DO NOT rotate engine while camshaft sprockets are disconnected.*

**Fig. 1   Position of Valve Timing Gauge**

2) Remove camshaft bearing caps and lift off camshaft. Remove each tappet that requires adjustment and note its location for reassembly in its original position. Remove adjusting pad. Subtract specified valve clearance from initial clearance measured. Select appropriate adjusting shim which will equal this measurement. Adjusting pads are available in increments of .001" (.03 mm) from .085" (2.16 mm) to .110" (2.79 mm) and are marked with letters from "A" to "Z" respectively.

3) Insert correct adjusting pads and install tappets. Attach camshafts (using timing gauge). Torque camshaft bearing cap nuts to 9 ft. lbs. (1.2 mkg), connect camshaft sprockets, and install camshaft covers.

### VALVE ARRANGEMENT

Left Side  — All Exhaust
Right Side — All Intake

### SPARK PLUGS

| | |
|---|---|
| Gap | .035" (.9 mm) |
| Torque | 27 ft. lbs. (3.7 mkg) |

#### Spark Plug Type

| Application | Champion No. |
|---|---|
| All Models | N12Y |

### HIGH TENSION WIRE RESISTANCE

Carefully remove high tension wires from spark plugs and distributor cap. Using an ohmmeter, check resistance of each wire while gently twisting wire. If resistance is not to specifications, or fluctuates from infinity to any value, replace wire.

#### Resistance (Ohms) Per Wire

| Application | Resistance |
|---|---|
| All Models | 25,000-30,000 |

### DISTRIBUTOR

**NOTE** – *All models are equipped with Opus Electronic System.*

Pick-Up Module Air Gap ............. ①.014-.016" (.36-.41 mm)

① — Measured between rotor and pick-up module.

### IGNITION TIMING

Check or adjust ignition timing with engine at normal operating temperature, idle speed set to specification and distributor vacuum line connected. If timing is not correct, loosen distributor clamp bolt and rotate distributor to achieve specified timing. Then tighten clamp bolt.

#### Ignition Timing Specifications

| Application | Timing |
|---|---|
| All Models | 4°BTDC at 800 RPM |

## TUNE-UP (Cont.)

Left Side
Lower Timing
Chain Cover

**Fig. 2  Ignition Timing Mark Location**

← FRONT OF VEHICLE

FIRING ORDER 1-5-3-6-2-4

**Fig. 3  Firing Order and Distributor Rotation**

### HOT (SLOW) IDLE RPM

1) Connect a tachometer and CO% meter to engine (at exhaust manifold test points). Run engine until normal operating temperature is reached.

2) Adjust idle with air volume screw at overrun valve housing. Use $7/32$" Allen wrench and turn clockwise to lower idle; counterclockwise to raise engine idle.

3) Remove plastic plug on airflow meter to locate mixture adjustment screw. Disconnect oxygen sensor and allow engine to idle for 1 minute to stabilize mixture.

4) Turn mixture screw clockwise to richen mixture and counterclockwise to lean mixture. If correct setting cannot be attained, check all electrical connections and all hoses for proper location.

5) Replace oxygen sensor lead and disconnect test instruments.

### Idle Speed (RPM) & CO Level (%)

| Application | Idle RPM | CO % |
|---|---|---|
| All Models | 750-850 | .5-1.5 |

### FUEL PUMP PRESSURE

Pressure .................................................. 36 psi (2.5 kg/cm²)

### EMISSION CONTROL SYSTEMS

*See Mitchell Manuals' Emission Control Manual.*

# GENERAL SERVICING

## IGNITION

### DISTRIBUTOR

All models are equipped with Lucas Opus Electronic Ignition System.

**Other Data & Specifications —** *See Tune-up & Lucas Distributors in ELECTRICAL Section.*

## FUEL SYSTEMS

### FUEL INJECTION

All models are equipped with Lucas-Bosch fuel injection.

**Other Data & Specifications —** *See Tune-up and Lucas-Bosch Fuel Injection in FUEL SYSTEMS Section.*

## ELECTRICAL

### BATTERY

**12 Volt** — Negative Ground.

| Application | Amp. Hr. Capacity |
|---|---|
| All Models | 66 |

### STARTER

All models are equipped with Lucas pre-engaged Starters.

| Free Speed Amperage All Models | 100 at 5000-6000 RPM |
|---|---|

**Other Data & Specifications —** *See Lucas Starters in ELECTRICAL Section.*

## GENERAL SERVICING (Cont.)

**ALTERNATOR REGULATOR**

Lucas — Non-Adjustable; Integral with Alternator.

**Other Data & Specifications** — *See Lucas Alternators & Regulators in ELECTRICAL Section.*

**ALTERNATOR**

| Application | Rated Amp. Output |
|---|---|
| All Models | 65 |

**Other Data & Specifications** — *See Lucas Alternators & Regulators in ELECTRICAL Section.*

### BELT ADJUSTMENT

| Belt | ① Deflection |
|---|---|
| Fan/Steering Pump | Self Adjusting |
| Alternator | .15" (3.8 mm) |
| Air Conditioning | .17" (4.3 mm) |

① — Deflection is with pressure applied midway on longest belt run.

### CAPACITIES

| Application | Quantity |
|---|---|
| Crankcase (Includes Filter) | 8.7 qts. |
| Cooling System | 19.5 qts. |
| Auto. Trans. (ATF Type F) | 9.9 qts. |
| Rear Axle (SAE 90 E.P.) | 3.25 pts. |
| Fuel Tank | |
| Right Side | 12.6 gals. |
| Left Side | 12.6 gals. |

### FILTERS & CLEANERS

| Filter or Cleaner | Service Intervals (Miles) |
|---|---|
| Oil Filter | Replace every 6000 |
| Air Cleaner | Replace every 12,000 |
| Engine Breather Filter | Replace every 12,000 |
| Fuel Filter | ① |
| Charcoal Canister | Replace every 50,000 |

① — Replace at 1000 miles and then every 6,000 miles.

## TUNE-UP

XJ12
XJS

### ENGINE IDENTIFICATION

Engine identification number is stamped on rear of crankcase between cylinder heads.

### MODEL IDENTIFICATION

#### VEHICLE IDENTIFICATION NUMBER

Vehicle identification number is stamped on a plate which is located on right side of firewall adjacent to the heater.

### COMPRESSION PRESSURE

Check compression pressure with engine at normal operating temperature, spark plugs removed, throttle wide open and engine at cranking speed. Pressure should be 120-140 psi (8.4-9.8 kg/cm²) with a maximum variation between cylinders of 5 psi (.35 kg/cm²).

### VALVE TAPPET CLEARANCE

| Application | Clearance (Cold) |
|---|---|
| All Models | |
| Intake | .012-.014″ (.30-.35mm) |
| Exhaust | .012-.014″ (.30-.35mm) |

1) With intake manifolds and camshaft covers removed, check clearance between each tappet and heel of each cam. Record clearance for each valve and then subtract appropriate valve clearance from clearance obtained. Select suitable adjusting pads which equal this new measurement.

2) To install new adjusting pads, proceed as follows to remove camshaft and tappets: Bend back locking tabs and remove two camshaft sprocket retaining bolts. Rotate engine until access to remaining bolts is obtained. Bend back locking tabs, mark position of camshaft to sprocket, and remove bolts.

3) Using suitable tool (Jaguar Sprocket Retaining Tool JD.40) hold sprocket in place. Lift camshaft out of tappet block. Remove tappets and install adjusting pads.

NOTE — *Do not rotate engine with camshaft disconnected.*

4) Reinstall tappets, camshaft, bearing caps, washers and nuts. Tighten bearing cap nuts evenly to 9 ft. lbs. (1.2 mkg). Recheck valve clearance, reassemble, replace camshaft cover and manifolds.

NOTE — *Adjusting pads are available in .001″ (.03 mm) increment sizes from .085-.110″ (2.16-2.79 mm). Pads have a letter stamped on surface which indicates size ("A" through "Z" respectively).*

### VALVE ARRANGEMENT

E-I-E-I-E-I-I-E-I-E-I-E (both banks, front-to-rear)

### SPARK PLUGS

| | | |
|---|---|---|
| Gap | | .035″ (.9 mm) |
| Torque | | 25 ft. lbs. (3.5 mkg) |

#### Spark Plug Type

| Application | Champion No. |
|---|---|
| All Models | N-10Y |

### HIGH TENSION WIRE RESISTANCE

Carefully remove high tension wires from spark plugs and distributor cap. Using an ohmmeter, check high tension wire resistance while gently twisting wires. If resistance is not to specifications, or fluctuates from infinity to any value, replace high tension wire(s).

#### Resistance (Ohms) Per Wire

| Application | Ohms |
|---|---|
| All Models | 25,000-30,000 |

← FRONT OF VEHICLE

FIRING ORDER
1A-6B-5A-2B-3A-4B-6A-1B-2A-5B-4A-3B

**Fig. 1   Firing Order and Distributor Rotation**

### DISTRIBUTOR

NOTE — *All models equipped with Lucas Opus Electronic Ignition System.*

| | | |
|---|---|---|
| Pick-Up Module Air Gap | ①.020-.022″ | (.50-.55mm) |

Resistance
| | | |
|---|---|---|
| Center Terminal to Outer Terminal with Red Cable | | 2.25-2.75 ohms |
| Center Terminal to Outer Terminal with Black Cable | | .81-.99 ohms |

① — Measured between rotor and pick-up module.

**Fig. 2   Ignition Timing Mark Location**

## TUNE-UP (Cont.)

### IGNITION TIMING

Set ignition timing with engine at specified idle RPM and distributor vacuum hose connected. If timing is not 10° BTDC, adjust distributor to achieve specified timing. *See Fig. 2.*

#### Ignition Timing Specifications

| Application | RPM | Timing |
|---|---|---|
| Federal | 750 | 10° BTDC |
| California | 750 | 4° ATDC |

### HOT (SLOW) IDLE RPM

**1)** Idle speed is controlled by Auxiliary Air Valve which is located on left cylinder bank rear water pipe. With engine at normal operating temperature, throttle linkage correctly set, and transmission in neutral, adjust idle screw to obtain specified idle speed RPM.

**NOTE** — *Idle CO should be checked with air injection system inoperative. Remove blanking plug from diverter valve diaphragm housing.*

**2)** Use an exhaust gas analyzer to check CO level. Electronic Control Unit (ECU), located in trunk of vehicle, is used to control CO level. Adjust ECU control knob one "click" at a time until specified level is reached.

**3)** With engine running at idle, check CO levels at sample points located in air injection distribution rails.

**4)** Check both banks for correct CO level. A high reading on one bank could indicate a leaking injector or cold start injector.

**NOTE** — *If adjusting procedures take over two minutes, engine must be run at 2500 RPM for 30 seconds. A hot engine may operate thermostatic vacuum switch and advance ignition timing.*

#### Idle Speed (RPM) & CO Level (%)

| Application | Idle RPM | Idle CO % |
|---|---|---|
| All Models | 750 | 1-2 |

### FUEL PUMP PRESSURE

| | |
|---|---|
| Pressure | 28.5-31.3 Psi (2.0-2.2 kg/cm²) |

### EMISSION CONTROL SYSTEMS

*See Mitchell Manuals' Emission Control Manual.*

## GENERAL SERVICING

### IGNITION

#### DISTRIBUTOR

All models are equipped with Lucas Opus Electronic Ignition System.

**Other Data & Specifications** — *See Tune-Up and Lucas Distributors in ELECTRICAL Section.*

#### IGNITION COIL

| Resistance | Ohms at 68° F (20° C) |
|---|---|
| Primary | |
| XJ12 | 0.8-1.0 |
| XJS | 0.9-1.1 |

### FUEL SYSTEMS

#### FUEL INJECTION

All models are equipped with Lucas-Jaguar Electronic Fuel Injection System.

**Other Data & Specifications** — *See Tune-Up and Lucas-Jaguar Electronic Fuel Injection in FUEL SYSTEMS Section.*

#### THROTTLE LINKAGE ADJUSTMENT

**1)** Release throttle cross-rods from throttle pulley. Loosen clamps securing levers to rear of throttle shafts. With butterfly valves closed against their stops, relay arm against its stop and play in coupling taken up in opening direction, tighten clamp-to-lever on rear of throttle shaft. Repeat procedure for the other side of engine.

**2)** Now try to refit cross-rods to ball connectors on pulley; rods must fit without moving pulley or linkage. If rods will not fit without moving pulley or linkage, loosen lock nut on cross-rods and adjust length until attachment can be accomplished without moving any part of linkage. Tighten lock nuts and ensure ball joints remain free.

*Fig. 3   Throttle Linkage Adjustment Points*

# 1978 Jaguar V12 Tune-Up

## GENERAL SERVICING (Cont.)

3) Loosen lock nut on throttle pulley and back out stop screw to full extent of travel. Hold throttle relay arm pulley fully open and check that butterfly stop arms are against throttle housing. Adjust stop to just touch throttle pulley and tighten lock nut.

## ELECTRICAL

### BATTERY

12 Volt — Negative ground.

| Application | Amp. Hr. Rating |
|---|---|
| All Models ............................................. | 68 |

**Battery Location** — Under hood on right side.

### STARTER

All models are equipped with a Lucas pre-engaged Starter.

Free Speed Amperage
XJS ......................................... 100 at 5000-7500 RPM
XJ12 ....................................... 100 at 5000-6000 RPM

**Other Data & Specifications** — *See Lucas Starters in ELECTRICAL Section.*

### ALTERNATOR

| Application | Rated Amp. Output |
|---|---|
| All Models .............................................. | 65 |

**Other Data & Specifications** — *See Lucas Alternators & Regulators in ELECTRICAL Section.*

### ALTERNATOR REGULATOR

Lucas — Non-Adjustable; integral with alternator.

**Other Data & Specifications** — *See Lucas Alternators & Regulators in ELECTRICAL Section.*

### BELT ADJUSTMENT

**Alternator Belt** — With a pressure of 3.2 lbs. (1.5 kg) applied midway on longest belt run, belt deflection should be .16" (4.3 mm).

**All Other Belts** — With a pressure of 6.4 lbs. (2.9 kg) applied midway on longest belt run, belt deflection should be .13-.22" (3.3-5.6 mm).

### FILTERS & CLEANERS

| Filter or Cleaner | Service Interval (Miles) |
|---|---|
| Oil Filter................................. | Replace every 6,000 |
| Air Filter ................................ | Replace every 12,500 |
| Fuel Line Filter ....................... | Replace every 12,500 |
| Crankcase Breather ................. | Clean every 12,500 |
| Charcoal Canister .................... | Replace every 25,000 |

### CAPACITIES

| Application | XJS Quantity | XJ12 Quantity |
|---|---|---|
| Crankcase (Inc. Filter) .. | 11 qts. | 11 qts. |
| Cooling System .......... | 22.2 qts. | 22.2 qts. |
| Auto. Trans. (Type F) ... | 9.9 qts. | 9.9 qts. |
| Rear Axle (SAE 90 EP) . | 3.3 pts. | 3.25 pts. |
| Fuel Tank | | |
| XJS .......................... | 24 gals. | |
| XJ12 R.H. ................. | | 12.6 gals. |
| XJ12 L.H. ................. | | 12.6 gals. |

## TUNE-UP

Lancia Beta, All Models

### ENGINE IDENTIFICATION

Engine identification number is found on top edge of firewall in engine compartment.

| Application | Code |
|---|---|
| 1800 cc | |
| Federal | 828 A1.040.6 |
| California | 828 A1.031.6 |

### MODEL IDENTIFICATION

Vehicle identification number appears on left side of instrument panel, visible through windshield. Chassis number also appears on trailing edge of left door.

| Application | Code |
|---|---|
| Coupe | 828 AC.1 |
| Sedan | 828 CB.6 |
| HPE | 828 AF.1 |

### COMPRESSION PRESSURE

With engine at normal operating temperature and NOT running, remove spark plugs and disconnect lead from ignition coil. Starting with cylinder No. 1 (front of engine), check compression by cranking with accelerator fully depressed.

#### Compression Pressure

| Application | psi | (kg/cm²) |
|---|---|---|
| All Models | ① 114 | (8) |

① — Maximum allowable variation between cylinders not to exceed 10%.

### VALVE TAPPET CLEARANCE

1) Remove air cleaner, choke control valve, spark plug wires, intermediate tubing and EGR valve. Remove both valve tappet covers.

NOTE — *Perform check with engine cold.*

2) Turn crankshaft to bring cylinder No. 1 to TDC of ignition stroke (noted by camshaft lobes of appropriate tappets pointing upward).

3) Use feeler gauge to check and note clearance at intake and exhaust valves. Adjustment may be made by use of shims. Recheck clearance after adjustment. Repeat procedure for each cylinder.

#### Valve Clearance Specifications

| Application | Intake In. (mm) | Exhaust In. (mm) |
|---|---|---|
| All Models | .016-.019 (.41-.48) | .018-.021 (.45-.51) |

### VALVE ARRANGEMENT

**Left Side** — All Intake. (Viewed from flywheel end).

**Right Side** — All Exhaust. (Viewed from flywheel end).

### SPARK PLUGS

Gap (All Models) ............................ .023-.027" (.58-.68 mm)

#### Spark Plug Type

| Application | Champion No. |
|---|---|
| All Models | N9Y |

FIRING ORDER 1-3-4-2

FRONT OF VEHICLE ↓

**Fig. 1   Firing Order and Distributor Rotation**

### DISTRIBUTOR

Point Gap
Exc. Calif. .................................... .012-.019" (.30-.48 mm)
Calif. .......................................... .015-.017" (.38-.43 mm)
Cam Angle ..................................................... 55°±3°

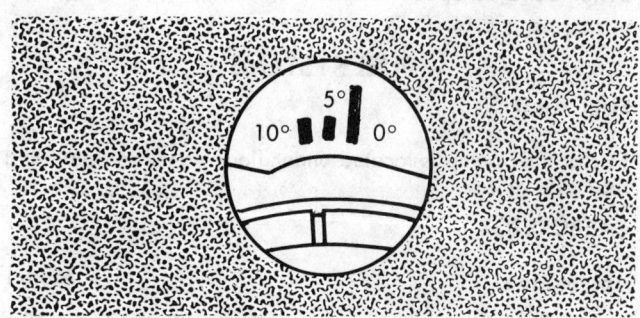

**Fig. 2   Ignition Timing Mark Location
(Viewed From Right Front Wheel Well)**

### IGNITION TIMING

1) Turn front wheels fully to right to gain access to right wheel well. Remove rubber plug from inner fender panel.

2) Connect timing light and run engine until normal operating temperatures are reached. Set engine at normal curb idle. Check "fixed advance" setting.

3) Increase engine RPM to 3600 and check "automatic advance" setting. Adjust distributor position as necessary to attain settings. Recheck timing after adjustment.

#### Ignition Timing Specifications

| Application | Fixed Advance @850±50 RPM | Auto. Advance @3600 RPM |
|---|---|---|
| All Models | | |
| Exc. Calif. | 0° | 36° |
| Calif. | 10° | 28° |

## TUNE-UP (Cont.)

### IDLE SPEED & MIXTURE

**1)** Run engine until normal operating temperatures are reached (cooling fan cuts in). With air cleaner and cover installed, set air cleaner to "SUMMER" position (reset to appropriate season after adjustment).

**2)** Using vise grip pliers, pinch off air injection hose to exhaust manifold (between diverter valve and non-return valves). After cooling fan cuts out, turn idle speed adjusting screw to obtain smoothest engine operation at specified RPM setting.

**3)** If further adjustment is necessary to obtain RPM setting, turn throttle adjusting screw.

**4)** Insert exhaust gas analyzer probe into tail pipe. Be sure air cleaner is still in "SUMMER" position. If CO level is not to specification, use idle adjusting screw to bring it within range. Recheck idle speed. It should remain within specifications.

**5)** Remove vise grips from air injection hose. Engine speed should increase 50 RPM. Do not alter this setting.

### Idle Speed (RPM) & CO Level (%)

| Application | RPM | CO% |
|---|---|---|
| All Models | 800-850 | 2±.5 |

### COLD (FAST) IDLE

After setting curb idle, depress fast idle checking button (located near right front suspension mounting in engine compartment). Hold button down while opening and closing throttle. Fast idle should register within specification. Adjust with fast idle screw, if necessary.

#### Cold (Fast) Idle Specification

| Application | RPM |
|---|---|
| All Models | 1550-1650 |

### EMISSION CONTROL SYSTEMS

*See Mitchell Manuals' Emission Control Manual.*

## GENERAL SERVICING

### IGNITION

**DISTRIBUTOR**

Federal models use a Marelli 401 P1 distributor; California models a Marelli 401 P3 distributor.

**Other Data & Specifications** — *See Tune-Up and Marelli distributors in ELECTRICAL section.*

### FUEL SYSTEMS

**FUEL PUMP**

Electric fuel pump is located under floor panel on right-hand rear side of car.

**CARBURETOR**

| Application | Model |
|---|---|
| Federal Models | Weber 32 DATRA 13/100 |
| California Models | Weber 32 DATRA 12/101 |

**Other Data & Specifications** — *See Tune-Up and Weber carburetors in FUEL SYSTEMS section.*

### ELECTRICAL

**BATTERY**

**12-Volt** — Negative Ground.

| Application | Amp. Hr. Rating |
|---|---|
| Sedan | 60 |
| All Other Models | 45 |

**Battery Location** — In engine compartment on left side.

**STARTER**

| | |
|---|---|
| Bosch | Overrunning Clutch |
| Free Speed Voltage | 11-11.5 at 4800 RPM |
| Free Speed Amperage | 27-40 at 4800 RPM |

**Other Data & Specifications** — *See Bosch starters in ELECTRICAL section.*

### ALTERNATOR

All models use a Bosch K1 14-volt alternator with built-in electronic regulator.

| Application | Rated Amp. Output |
|---|---|
| All Models | 55 |

**Other Data & Specifications** — *See Bosch alternators in ELECTRICAL section.*

### BELT ADJUSTMENT

| Application | ①Deflection |
|---|---|
| All Models | .39-.49" (9.9-12.5 mm) |

① — Deflection is with 11 pounds (4.99 kg) pressure applied midway between water pump and alternator.

### FILTERS & CLEANERS

| Filter or Cleaner | Service Interval (Miles) |
|---|---|
| Oil Filter | Replace Every 6,000 |
| Air Cleaner | Replace Every 12,500 |
| Fuel Filter | Replace Every 12,500 |
| EGR Valve & Cat. Converter | ①Inspect Every 25,000 |
| Evap. Canister Filter | Replace Every 25,000 |

① — Clean, inspect and reset warning light.

### CAPACITIES

| Application | Quantity |
|---|---|
| Crankcase (Includes Filter) | ①5.2 qts. |
| Cooling System (Includes Heater) | 8.8 qts. |
| Transaxle (SAE 40/50) | 2.56 qts. |
| Fuel Tank | ②12.5 gals. |

① — 4.25 qts. without filter change.
② — Includes 2.1 gals. in reserve.

## TUNE-UP

LUV

### ENGINE IDENTIFICATION

Engine serial number is stamped on pad between distributor and cylinder head.

### MODEL IDENTIFICATION

#### VEHICLE IDENTIFICATION NUMBER

Vehicle Identification Number is stamped on a plate attached to driver's door lock pillar.

### COMPRESSION PRESSURE

Test compression with engine at normal operating temperature, spark plugs removed, throttle valve wide open and engine at cranking speed. Maximum variation between cylinders should not exceed 8.5 psi (.6 kg/cm²).

**Compression Pressure**
**@ 300 RPM**

| Application | Min. Pressure psi(kg/cm²) | Std. Pressure psi(kg/cm²) |
|---|---|---|
| All Models | 119(8.4) | 171(12) |

### VALVE TAPPET CLEARANCE

**NOTE** — *Before adjusting valve tappet clearance, check torque of cylinder head and camshaft bolts. Valves should be adjusted every 15,000 miles.*

**1)** Measure valve clearance between rocker arm and valve stem. Position piston number one on compression stroke at TDC. Adjust intake valves 1 and 2 and exhaust valves 1 and 3.

**2)** Turn crankshaft one full turn until number four cylinder is at TDC. Adjust intake valves 3 and 4 and exhaust valves 2 and 4.

**Valve Tappet Clearance**

| Application | Clearance (Cold) |
|---|---|
| Intake | .006" (.015 mm) |
| Exhaust | .010" (.025 mm) |

#### VALVE ARRANGEMENT

All Models
  Right Side — All Intake
  Left Side — All Exhaust

Fig. 1    *Firing Order and Distributor Rotation*

### SPARK PLUGS

Gap ........................................................ .030"(.8 mm)
Torque ..................................... 18-25 ft. lbs.(2.5-3.5 mkg)

**Spark Plug Type**

| Application | AC | NGK |
|---|---|---|
| All Models | R44XLS | BPR6ES |

### HIGH TENSION WIRE RESISTANCE

Carefully remove high tension wires from spark plugs and from distributor cap. Using an ohmmeter, check resistance of wire while gently twisting wire. If resistance is not to specification, or fluctuates from infinity to any value, replace wire.

**Resistance (Ohms)**

| Application | Resistance |
|---|---|
| All Models | 25,000-30,000 |

### DISTRIBUTOR

Point Gap ................................... .016-.020"(.41-.51 mm)
Cam Angle ................................................. 47-57°
Breaker Arm Spring Tension ............ 14-19 ozs.(400-540 g)
Condenser Capacity ........................................ .20-.24 mfd.

### IGNITION TIMING

With engine at normal operating temperature and idle speed set to specification, connect a timing light to No. 1 or No. 4 cylinder. Disconnect distributor vacuum line and plug end. Check timing with marks on crankshaft pulley and rotate distributor to adjust timing.

## TUNE-UP (Cont.)

**Fig. 2    Ignition Timing Mark Location**

Timing Mark

Crankshaft Pulley

BEFORE
6 4 2 8 4 O

### Ignition Timing Specifications

| Application | Timing |
|---|---|
| All Models | ①6° BTDC |

① — With engine running at 900 RPM.

### IDLE SPEED & MIXTURE

Set idle with engine at normal operating temperature, valve clearance correctly set and ignition timing to specifications. Choke should be open, air conditioning off and air cleaner installed. Disconnect distributor vacuum line and hot idle compensator vacuum line and plug both. Then proceed as follows:

1) Turn mixture adjusting screw all the way in, then back out three complete turns. Adjust idle speed screw until 900 RPM is reached. Adjust idle mixture screw for maximum RPM.

2) Readjust idle speed screw for 900 RPM. Turn mixture adjusting screw clockwise (lean) until 850 RPM is reached. Then turn idle mixture screw ½ turn counterclockwise (rich).

## GENERAL SERVICING

### IGNITION

#### DISTRIBUTOR

All Models are equipped with a Nippondenso single point distributor.

**Other Data & Specifications** — *See Tune-Up & Nippondenso Distributors in ELECTRICAL Section.*

#### IGNITION COIL

| Resistance | Ohms |
|---|---|
| Primary | 1.3-1.4 |
| Secondary | 7,650-9,350 |

3) Adjust idle speed screw for a final idle speed of 900 RPM.

4) On vehicles with air conditioning, turn air conditioning on max cold and high blower. Open throttle enough to allow speed-up solenoid to reach full travel. Then adjust speed-up controller adjusting screw for an idle speed of 900 RPM.

#### Idle Speed (RPM)

| Application | RPM |
|---|---|
| All Models | 900 |

### COLD (FAST) IDLE RPM

Automatic choke fast idle is adjusted by opening angle of throttle valve on carburetor, rather than by engine speed. Adjust valve opening at 1st step of fast idle cam to 16-18°.

Disconnect and plug distributor, hot idle compensator and EGR valve vacuum lines after engine warm up. Adjust idle speed as follows:

#### Fast Idle Specifications

| Application | Engine Speed |
|---|---|
| Man. Trans. | 3400 RPM |
| Auto. Trans. | 3200 RPM |

### AUTOMATIC CHOKE

Automatic choke is correctly set when thickest line on the thermostat housing is aligned with index mark on thermostat cover.

### FUEL PUMP PRESSURE

| Pressure | 3.6 psi (.25 kg/cm²) |
|---|---|

### EMISSION CONTROL SYSTEMS

*See Mitchell Manuals' Emission Control Manual.*

### FUEL SYSTEMS

#### CARBURETORS

| Application | Model |
|---|---|
| All Models | Hitachi 2-Bbl. |

**Other Data & Specifications** — *See Tune-Up & Hitachi Carburetors in FUEL SYSTEMS Section.*

### ELECTRICAL

#### BATTERY

**12 Volt** — Negative Ground.

## GENERAL SERVICING (Cont.)

| Application | Amp. Hr. Rating |
|---|---|
| LUV ...............................................................50 | |

**Battery Location** — Engine compartment, left side of engine.

### STARTER

| Hitachi | Overrunning Clutch |
|---|---|
| Free Speed Voltage | 12 at 6000 RPM |
| Free Speed Amperage | 60 at 6000 RPM |

**Other Data & Specifications** — *See Hitachi Starters in ELECTRICAL Section.*

### ALTERNATOR

| Application | Rated Amp. Output |
|---|---|
| LUV | 35 |

**Other Data & Specifications** — *See Hitachi Alternators & Regulators in ELECTRICAL Section.*

### ALTERNATOR REGULATOR

All models utilize a Hitachi adjustable alternator regulator with an operating voltage of 13.8-14.8 volts.

**Other Data & Specifications** — *See Hitachi Alternators & Regulators in ELECTRICAL Section.*

### BELT ADJUSTMENT

Belt deflection for both drive belts should be .4" (10mm) with pressure applied midway on belt run.

### FILTERS & CLEANERS

| Filter or Cleaner | Service Interval (Miles) |
|---|---|
| Oil Filter | ①Replace every 15,000 |
| Air Cleaner | Replace every 30,000 |
| Fuel Filters | Replace every 15,000 |
| PCV Valve | Replace every 15,000 |

① — Replace at 7500 miles and then every 15,000 miles.

### CAPACITIES

| Application | Quantity |
|---|---|
| Crankcase (Includes Filter) | 4.2 qts. |
| Cooling System | 6.4 qts. |
| Auto. Trans. (Dexron II) | 6.5 qts. |
| Man. Trans. (SAE 30) | 2.7 pts. |
| Rear Axle (SAE 90) | 2.7 pts. |
| Steering Gear (SAE 90) | .63 pts. |
| Fuel Tank | 13.2 gals. |

TUNE UP

## TUNE-UP

GLC
B1800

### ENGINE IDENTIFICATION

Engine serial number and model code are stamped on right front upper wall of cylinder block.

| Application | Code |
|---|---|
| GLC | TC |
| B1800 | VB |

### MODEL IDENTIFICATION

#### VEHICLE IDENTIFICATION NUMBER

Number is stamped on plate riveted to right rear corner of engine compartment. On GLC models, number is also stamped on plate located at left inner corner of windshield and visible from outside of vehicle.

### COMPRESSION PRESSURE

Check compression pressure with engine at normal operating temperature, spark plugs removed, throttle valve wide open and engine at cranking speed. Crank engine until maximum pressure is reached at each cylinder. Compression is normal if lowest cylinder reading is at least 75% of highest reading.

#### Compression Pressure @300 RPM

| Application | Pressure psi(kg/cm²) |
|---|---|
| GLC | 164(11.5) |
| B1800 | 169(11.9) |

### VALVE TAPPET CLEARANCE

| Application | ①Intake | ①Exhaust |
|---|---|---|
| GLC | .010″(.25 mm) | .012″(.30 mm) |
| B1800 | .012″(.30 mm) | .012″(.30 mm) |

① — Adjust valves with engine hot.

### VALVE ARRANGEMENT

All Models
Right Side — All Exhaust.
Left Side — All Intake.

### SPARK PLUGS

| | |
|---|---|
| Gap | .029-.033″ (.75-.85 mm) |
| Torque | 11-15 ft. lbs.(1.5-2.1 mkg) |

#### Spark Plug Type

| Application | Nippondenso | NGK |
|---|---|---|
| All Models | W-20EP | ①BP6ES |

① — Use BPR6ES where required for radio interference suppression.

### HIGH TENSION WIRE RESISTANCE

Carefully remove high tension wires from spark plugs and distributor cap. Using an ohmeter, check resistance of wires while gently twisting wire. If resistance is not to specification, or fluctuates from infinity to any value, replace wire.

#### Resistance (Ohms) of Wire

| Application | Resistance |
|---|---|
| All Models | 4875 Ohms per Foot |

**Fig. 1   Firing Order and Distributor Rotation**

### DISTRIBUTOR

B1800 models and California GLC models are equipped with breaker point type distributors. Federal GLC models are equipped with a breakerless, electronic ignition system.

| | |
|---|---|
| Point Gap | .018-.022″(.45-.55 mm) |
| Air Gap① | .010-.014″(.25-.35 mm) |
| Cam Angle | 49-55° |
| Breaker Arm Spring Tension | 16-21 ozs.(450-600 g) |
| Condenser Capacity | .20-.24 mfd. |

① — Federal GLC models only.

### IGNITION TIMING

With engine at normal operating temperature, idle speed set to specification and Man. Trans. in neutral or Auto. Trans. in "D", connect timing light, start engine and rotate distributor until specified mark on crankshaft pulley aligns with indicator pin.

**NOTE** — After checking and setting timing on Federal GLC models with Man. Trans., disconnect wires from accelerator switch and check advanced timing.

## TUNE-UP (Cont.)

### Ignition Timing Specifications

| Application | Man. Trans. | ①Auto. Trans. |
|---|---|---|
| GLC | | |
| Federal | ②7°BTDC | 11°BTDC |
| Calif. | 11°BTDC | 11°BTDC |
| B1800 | 8°BTDC | |

① — Transmission in "D".
② — Advanced timing: 11°BTDC.

**Fig. 2   Ignition Timing Marks for GLC**

**Fig. 3   Ignition Timing Marks for B1800**

### IDLE SPEED AND MIXTURE

1) Set parking brake and block wheels. Turn accessories off. Connect tachometer and exhaust gas analyzer. Disconnect canister purge hose from air cleaner.

2) With Man. Trans. in neutral or Auto. Trans. in "D", turn idle speed adjusting screw as necessary to obtain specified idle RPM.

3) On Federal GLC models, disconnect hose between air silencer and reed valve. On California GLC models and all B1800 models, disconnect hose between air pump and check valve, and plug check valve port.

4) Turn mixture adjusting screw as necessary to obtain specified CO%. Reconnect hose, recheck idle speed, and readjust if necessary. Install mixture screw limiter cap (if removed).

### Idle Speed (RPM) and CO Level (%)

| Application | ①Idle RPM | ②CO% |
|---|---|---|
| Man. Trans. | 700-750 | 1.5-2.5% |
| Auto. Trans.③ | 600-650 | 1.5-2.5% |

① — Air injection connected.
② — Air injection disconnected.
③ — Transmission in "D".

## COLD (FAST) IDLE RPM

1) Connect tachometer to engine. Warm up engine to operating temperature. Ensure slow idle speed and mixture are correct.

2) Stop engine and remove air cleaner. Restart engine and run at idle. Loosen screw holding choke outer cable to carburetor. Hold choke valve wide open and pull choke cable fully out. Engine speed should be 3000-4000 RPM.

3) If adjustment is needed, remove carburetor from engine and bend choke connecting rod to obtain specified clearance between lower edge of primary throttle valve and wall of bore with choke valve closed.

### Fast Idle Specifications

| Application | Clearance |
|---|---|
| GLC | .048-.060"(1.22-1.52 mm) |
| B1800 | .063-.079"(1.61-2.11 mm) |

## FUEL PUMP PRESSURE & VOLUME

Pressure (At Idle)
 GLC (Mechanical) ............... 2.84-3.84 psi (.20-.27 kg/cm²)
 B1800 (Electric) .................... 2.8-3.6 psi (.20-.25 kg/cm²)
Volume (At Idle)
 GLC (Mechanical) ........................................ 1.1 qts. in 1 min.
 B1800 (Electric) .......................................... .8 qts. in 1 min.

## EMISSION CONTROL SYSTEMS

*See Mitchell Manuals' Emission Control Manual.*

# 1978 Mazda 4 Tune-Up

## GENERAL SERVICING

### IGNITION

#### DISTRIBUTOR

B1800 models and California GLC models are equipped with Mitsubishi breaker point type distributors. Federal GLC models are equipped with a Mitsubishi breakerless, electronic ignition system.

**Other Data & Specifications** — *See Tune-Up & Mitsubishi Distributors in ELECTRICAL Section.*

#### IGNITION COIL

Primary Resistance
  B1800 & Calif. GLC ............................................. 1.5 ohms
  Federal GLC ........................................................ 1.28 ohms
Secondary Resistance
  B1800 & Calif. GLC ............................................. 9,000 ohms
  Federal GLC ........................................................ 13,500 ohms

### FUEL SYSTEMS

#### CARBURETORS

| Application | Model |
|---|---|
| GLC .......................................... | Hitachi DCG 306 2-Bbl. |
| B1800 ..................................... | Hitachi DCJ 328 2-Bbl. |

**Other Data & Specifications** — *See Tune-Up and Hitachi Carburetors in FUEL SYSTEMS Section.*

### ELECTRICAL

#### BATTERY

**12 Volt** — Negative Ground.

| Application | Amp. Hr. Rating |
|---|---|
| GLC | |
|   Federal ............................................. | 45 |
|   Calif. ................................................ | 35 |
| B1800 ................................................... | 45 |

#### STARTER

Mitsubishi ................................................. Overrunning Clutch

Free Speed Voltage ..................... 11.5 at 6800 RPM
Free Speed Amperage ................. 53 Max. at 6800 RPM

**Other Data & Specifications** — *See Mitsubishi Starters in ELECTRICAL Section.*

#### ALTERNATOR

| Application | Rated Amp. Output |
|---|---|
| All Models ............................................... | 35 |

### ALTERNATOR REGULATOR

All models are equipped with a Mitsubishi adjustable alternator regulator with an operating voltage of 14-15 volts.

**Other Data & Specifications** — *See Mitsubishi Alternators & Regulators in ELECTRICAL Section.*

### ENGINE

#### INTAKE MANIFOLD TIGHTENING

Tighten intake manifold attaching bolts to 14-19 ft. lbs. (1.9-2.6 mkg).

---

**BELT ADJUSTMENT**

| Application | New ①Deflection | Used ①Deflection |
|---|---|---|
| Alternator Belt | .3-.4" | .4-.5" |
| | (8-11 mm) | (11-12 mm) |
| Air Pump Belt | .3-.4" | .4-.5" |
| | (8-11 mm) | (11-12 mm) |

① — Deflection is with 22 lbs. (10 kg) pressure applied midway on longest belt run.

---

**FILTERS & CLEANERS**

| Filter or Cleaner | Service Interval (Miles) |
|---|---|
| Oil Filter ............................................. | Replace every 6000 |
| Air Cleaner ........................................ | Clean every 12,500 |
| | Replace every 25,000 |
| Fuel Filter .......................................... | Replace every 12,500 |
| Charcoal Canister ............................ | Replace every 25,000 |

---

**CAPACITIES**

| Application | Quantity |
|---|---|
| Crankcase | |
|   GLC ................................................ | 3.2 qts. |
|   B1800 ............................................. | 3.8 qts. |
| Cooling System (Includes Heater) | |
|   GLC ................................................ | 5.8 qts. |
|   B1800 ............................................. | 7.6 qts. |
| Man. Trans. (SAE 80W-90) | |
|   4-Speed .......................................... | 1.5 qts. |
|   5-Speed .......................................... | 1.8 qts. |
| Auto. Trans. (Type F) ..................... | 6.0 qts. |
| Rear Axle (SAE 80W-90) | |
|   GLC ................................................ | 1.6 pts. |
|   B1800 ............................................. | 2.8 pts. |
| Fuel Tank | |
|   GLC ................................................ | 10.6 gals. |
| B1800 | |
|   Standard ......................................... | 14.8 gals. |
|   Long Bed ........................................ | 17.4 gals. |

## TUNE-UP

**RX-4**
**Cosmo**

### ENGINE IDENTIFICATION

Engine type code is stamped on rear rotor housing, to the rear of oil filter. Engine serial number is stamped on front rotor housing behind distributor. Engine type codes are as follows:

#### Engine Type Codes

| Application | Code |
|---|---|
| All Models ................................................. | 13B |

### MODEL IDENTIFICATION

#### VEHICLE IDENTIFICATION NUMBER

Number is stamped on identification plate, located at left, lower inner corner of windshield, and is visible from outside of vehicle.

### COMPRESSION PRESSURE

| Application | Pressure |
|---|---|
| All Models .............................................. | ① 85 psi (6 kg/cm²) |

① — At 250 RPM.

### SPARK PLUGS

| | |
|---|---|
| Gap ................................................. | .039-.043" (1-1.1 mm) |
| Torque .......................................... | 9-13 ft. lbs. (1.3-1.8 mkg) |

#### Spark Plug Type①

| Make | Standard | Cold Type |
|---|---|---|
| NGK ........................ | B-7ET, BR-7ET | B-8ET, BR-8ET |
| Nippondenso ......... | W22EB, W22EBR | W25EB, W25EBR |
| Champion ............. | N280B, RN280B | N278B, RN278B |

① — Second plug listed in each application is for use in areas requiring suppression of radio interference.

### HIGH TENSION WIRE RESISTANCE

Carefully remove high tension wires from spark plugs and distributor cap. Using an ohmmeter, measure resistance of wires while gently twisting wires. If resistance is not to specifications, or fluctuates from infinity to any value, replace high tension wire(s).

#### Resistance (Ohms) Per Wire

| Application | Resistance |
|---|---|
| All Models ........................................... | 4785 Ohms per Foot |

### DISTRIBUTOR

| | |
|---|---|
| Point Gap ............................................. | .016-.020" (.4-.5 mm) |
| Cam Angle .......................................... | 55-61° |
| Breaker Arm Spring Tension ....... | 17.6-22.4 ozs. (500-650 g) |
| Condenser Capacity .......................... | .24-.30 mfd. |

**Fig. 1   Firing Order and Distributor Rotation**

### IGNITION TIMING

**NOTE** — *On vehicles equipped with automatic transmission, place selector lever in "D" position and block the wheels.*

#### ALL MODELS

1) Ensure all point gaps are properly set. Warm up engine to operating temperature and connect tachometer to engine.

2) Connect timing light to leading spark plug on front rotor housing. *See Fig. 2.* Start engine and run at idle speed.

**Fig. 2   Connecting Timing Light**

3) Check leading timing. If not to specifications, adjust timing by rotating distributor housing until correct. Tighten lock nut.

## TUNE-UP (Cont.)

**4)** Recheck leading timing. Then, connect timing light to trailing spark plug cable on front housing. Start engine and check trailing timing. If not to specifications, loosen vacuum unit attaching screws and move unit in or out to adjust trailing timing.

25° ATDC (Trailing) (Red)    5° ATDC (Leading) (Yellow)

Front Drive Belt Pulley

**Fig. 3  Ignition Timing Mark Location**

### Ignition Timing Specifications

| Application | Timing |
|---|---|
| Leading | 4-6° ATDC |
| Trailing | 23-27° ATDC |

## IDLE SPEED & MIXTURE

**1)** Ensure engine is warmed up to normal operating temperature. Run engine at 2000 RPM for about 3 minutes.

**2)** Turn OFF all accessories. Unhook and plug idle compensator hose. Remove fuel filler cap. Connect exhaust gas analyzer to exhaust pipe and tachometer to engine.

**3)** With Man. Trans. in neutral or Auto. Trans. in "D", turn air adjustment screw (located on carburetor body above mixture screw) to obtain specified idle speed. Check CO level. If within specifications and idle speed is stable, mixture adjustment is not required.

**4)** If CO level is not within specifications, remove idle limiter cap from mixture adjusting screw. Turn screw clockwise until idle speed begins to fluctuate.

**5)** Slowly turn mixture adjusting screw counterclockwise until maximum specified CO level is obtained. Then, turn mixture screw an additional ¼ turn in counterclockwise direction. Recheck idle speed and readjust if necessary. Replace idle limiter cap and restore all components to original positions.

### Idle Speed (RPM) & CO (%)

| Application | RPM | CO% |
|---|---|---|
| All Models | 750 | 0.1% Max. |

## COLD (FAST) IDLE RPM

**All Models — 1)** Connect tachometer to engine and run engine until normal operating temperature is reached. Stop engine.

**2)** Pull choke knob out fully. Restart engine. Engine speed should reach RPM shown in chart within 10 seconds of starting.

**3)** If fast idle speed is not within specifications, remove carburetor from engine. With carburetor removed, be sure choke valve is held fully closed.

**4)** Measure clearance between PRIMARY throttle valve and wall of throttle bore. Clearance should be as shown in chart. If not, bend fast idle rod until correct clearance is reached.

### Fast Idle Specifications

| Application | RPM | Bore Clearance |
|---|---|---|
| Federal | 3000-3500 | .039-.047" (1.0-1.2 mm) |
| Calif. | 3000-3500 | .052-.060" (1.3-1.5 mm) |

## FUEL PUMP PRESSURE

| | |
|---|---|
| Pressure | 4.3-5.3 psi (.30-.38 kg/cm²) |
| Volume | 1.3 qts. per min. |

## EMISSION CONTROL SYSTEMS

*See Mitchell Manuals' Emission Control Manual.*

# GENERAL SERVICING

## IGNITION

### IGNITION COIL

**Resistance**                                    **Ohms @ 68°F (20°C)**

Primary ...................................................................... 1.4

## DISTRIBUTOR

All models are equipped with Mitsubishi distributors with two sets of ignition points.

**Other Data & Specifications —** *See Tune-Up & Mitsubishi Distributors in ELECTRICAL Section.*

## GENERAL SERVICING (Cont.)

### FUEL SYSTEMS

#### CARBURETOR

| Application | Model |
|---|---|
| All Models | Hitachi 4-Bbl. |

**Other Data & Specifications** — *See Tune-Up and Hitachi & Nikki Carburetors in FUEL SYSTEMS Section.*

### ELECTRICAL

#### BATTERY

**12 Volt** — Negative Ground.

| Application | Amp. Hr. Capacity |
|---|---|
| Federal | |
| Man. Trans. | 45 |
| Auto. Trans. | 55 |
| Calif. | 45 |

**Battery Location** — In engine compartment.

#### STARTER

| | |
|---|---|
| Mitsubishi | Overrunning Clutch |

Free Speed Voltage
| | |
|---|---|
| All Models | 11.5 @ 5600 RPM |

Free Speed Amperage
| | |
|---|---|
| Man. Trans. | Less than 50 @ 5600 RPM |
| Auto. Trans. | Less than 100 @ 6600 RPM |

**Other Data & Specifications** — *See Mitsubishi Starters in ELECTRICAL Section*

#### ALTERNATOR

| Application | Rated Amp. Output |
|---|---|
| All Models | 63 |

**Other Data & Specifications** — *See Mitsubishi Alternators in ELECTRICAL Section.*

#### ALTERNATOR REGULATOR

All models are equipped with Mitsubishi adjustable alternator regulators with an operating voltage of 14-15 volts.

**Other Data & Specifications** — *See Mitsubishi Alternator Regulators in ELECTRICAL Section.*

### ENGINE

#### INTAKE MANIFOLD TIGHTENING

Tighten all intake manifold attaching bolts to 12-17 ft. lbs. (1.6-2.3 mkg) of torque.

---

### FILTERS & CLEANERS

| Filter or Cleaner | Service Interval (Miles) |
|---|---|
| Oil Filter | Replace every 6000 |
| Air Cleaner | Replace every 25,000 |
| Fuel Filter | Replace every 12,500 |

---

### BELT ADJUSTMENT

| Application | ①Deflection |
|---|---|
| Alternator Belt | .51-.67" (13-17 mm) |
| Air Pump Belt | .43-.51" (11-13 mm) |
| A/C Belt | .31-.39" (8-10 mm) |
| Pow. Steering Belt | .31-.39" (8-10 mm) |

① — Deflection is with 22 lbs. (10 kg) pressure applied midway on longest belt run.

---

### CAPACITIES

| | |
|---|---|
| Crankcase | 5.3 qts. |
| Cooling System (Includes Heater) | 10.6 qts. |
| Man. Trans. (SAE 90) | 3.6 pts. |
| Auto. Trans. (Type F) | 6.6 pts. |
| Rear Axle. (SAE 90) | 2.6 pts. |
| Fuel Tank | 16.4 gals. |

## TUNE-UP

### 230

#### ENGINE IDENTIFICATION

**Engine Code Designation** — First six digits of engine identification number, located on tag at rear left side of engine crankcase, identify engine as follows:

| Application | Code |
|---|---|
| 230 | 115.954 |

#### MODEL IDENTIFICATION

##### VEHICLE IDENTIFICATION NUMBER

First six digits of identification number, located above instrument panel and visible through windshield, identify model as follows:

| Application | Code |
|---|---|
| 230 | 123.023 |

#### COMPRESSION PRESSURE

Check pressure with engine at normal operating temperature and throttle valve wide open, crank engine a minimum of eight revolutions to obtain following specifications:

| Application | Pressure |
|---|---|
| Normal | 128-142 psi (9-10 kg/cm²) |
| Min. Pressure | 107 psi (7.5 kg/cm²) |

#### VALVE TAPPET CLEARANCE

| Engine Temp. | Intake | Exhaust |
|---|---|---|
| Cold | .004″ (.10 mm) | .008 (.20 mm) |
| Hot | .006″ (.15 mm) | .010″ (.25 mm) |

#### VALVE ARRANGEMENT

All Models — E-I-I-E-E-I-I-E (front to rear).

**Fig. 1   Firing Order and Distributor Rotation**

#### SPARK PLUGS

| | |
|---|---|
| Gap | .032″ (.8 mm) |
| Torque | 18-22 ft. lbs. (2.5-3.0 mkg) |

#### Spark Plug Type①

| Application | Bosch No. | Champion No. |
|---|---|---|
| 230 | W145 T 30 | N-10Y |

① — Beru No. is 145/14/3A.

#### HIGH TENSION WIRE RESISTANCE

Carefully remove high tension wires from spark plugs and distributor cap. Using an ohmmeter, check resistance of wires while gently twisting wires. If resistance is not to specification, or fluctuates from infinity to any value, replace wire.

##### Resistance (Ohms) Per Wire

| Application | Resistance |
|---|---|
| All Models | 25,000-30,000 |

#### DISTRIBUTOR

All models are equipped with a breakerless, transistorized ignition system.

**Fig. 2   Illustration of Timing Marks**

#### IGNITION TIMING

Check or adjust ignition timing with engine at normal operating temperature, idle speed set to specifications and vacuum lines connected.

##### Ignition Timing Specifications

| Application | RPM | Timing |
|---|---|---|
| 230 | 850 | 10°BTDC |

#### IDLE SPEED & MIXTURE

1) Check spark plug gap, ignition timing, and check for leaks in intake system.

## TUNE-UP (Cont.)

2) Run engine until normal operating temperature is reached, preferably 140-176° F (60-80° C) oil temperature. Do not disconnect air injection hose.

3) Cruise control cable should rest tension-free against throttle lever. Adjust if necessary. Adjust idle speed using idle mixture adjusting screw. Connect a CO tester to the exhaust pick-up tube (must be in front of catalyst), using a hose with adapter No. 700 589 07 07 00.

4) Adjust idle speed CO level with idle air adjusting screw. Accelerate engine briefly and recheck CO value and idle speed. Readjust as necessary.

5) Adjust linkage at idle speed so that it is free of play at its completely extended position. With engine running at idle speed, remove hose from vacuum governor and adjust screw at throttle valve lever to achieve 1200-1400 RPM. See Fig. 3. Replace vacuum hose. Check clearance between lever and screw for .020" (.5 mm). If necessary, adjust at large adjusting nut.

Spring
Adjusting Nut
Adjusting Screw
Throttle Valve Lever

**Fig. 3   Adjusting Vacuum Governor**

6) Place gear selector lever in "D" position. Turn steering to full lock position and turn on air conditioning. Engine should run smoothly. If not, readjust idle speed with adjusting nut on vacuum governor.

### Idle Speed (RPM) & CO Level (%)

| Application | Idle RPM | CO% |
|---|---|---|
| All Models | 850 | 0.4-2.0 |

## BASIC IDLE SPEED ADJUSTMENT

**NOTE** — Do not perform this adjustment unless specified idle speed and mixture adjustment values cannot be obtained using preceding idle speed and mixture adjustment procedure.

1) Run engine until oil temperature reaches 176° F (80° C). Turn idle mixture adjusting screw counterclockwise until highest speed is obtained.

2) Remove plastic cap from throttle valve adjusting screw and adjust to 1000 RPM level. Replace plastic cap and adjust idle speed with idle mixture adjusting screw to 800-900 RPM. Then turn idle AIR adjusting screw clockwise to stop.

3) On Federal models, adjust fuel adjusting screw until an idle CO level of 3.5% is obtained. Then, turn idle air adjusting screw to obtain a CO level of 0.4-2.0%.

4) On California models, remove safety cap by breaking it. Adjust fuel adjusting screw until 3.5% CO level is achieved. Press on new safety cap, 000 988 51 35, using special tool 115 589 00 15 00. Adjust idle CO value with idle air adjusting screw to 0.4-2.0%.

## COLD (FAST) IDLE & MIXTURE

1) With engine at operating temperature and engaging lever on second step of fast idle cam, check fast idle speed is to specifications. If not, adjust idle mixture adjusting screw.

2) Attach exhaust gas analyzer and check CO level. If necessary to adjust, use auxiliary air adjusting screw on automatic choke housing.

### Fast Idle Speed (RPM) & CO Level (%)

| Application | Fast Idle RPM | CO% |
|---|---|---|
| All Models | 1800 | 5.0-6.0% |

## AUTOMATIC CHOKE

Choke is pretensioned at factory and should be reset at mark at second service period (6000 miles). Do not attempt to adjust set screw in diaphragm cover. Only use the auxiliary air adjusting screw in choke housing, when adjusting CO levels.

## FUEL PUMP PRESSURE

Pressure
At Cranking Speed ................... 3.6-5.4 psi (.25-.38 kg/cm²)

## EMISSION CONTROL SYSTEMS

See Mitchell Manuals' Emission Control Manual.

## GENERAL SERVICING

### IGNITION

#### DISTRIBUTOR

All models are equipped with a Bosch breakerless, electronic ignition system.

**Other Data & Specifications** — *See Tune-Up & Bosch Distributors in ELECTRICAL Section.*

#### IGNITION COIL

| Resistance | Ohms At 68°F (20°C) |
|---|---|
| Primary | .38-.45 |
| Secondary | 8,000-11,000 |

### FUEL SYSTEMS

#### CARBURETORS

| Application | Model |
|---|---|
| All Models | Zenith-Stromberg 175 CDTU |

**Other Data & Specifications** — *See Tune-Up & Zenith-Stromberg Carburetors in FUEL SYSTEMS Section.*

### ELECTRICAL

#### BATTERY

**12 Volt** — Negative Ground.

| Application | Amp. Hr. Rating |
|---|---|
| 230 | 66 |

**Battery Location** — In engine compartment.

#### STARTER

All models are equipped with Bosch starters.

| Free Speed Voltage | |
|---|---|
| All Models | 11.5 at 8000-10,000 RPM |
| Free Speed Amperage | |
| All Models | 50-80 at 8000-10,000 RPM |

**Other Data & Specifications** — *See Bosch Starters in ELECTRICAL Section.*

### ALTERNATOR REGULATOR

Bosch — Non-Adjustable; integral with Alternator.

**Other Data & Specifications** — *See Bosch Alternators & Regulators in ELECTRICAL Section.*

### ALTERNATOR

| Application | Rated Amp. Output |
|---|---|
| All Models | 55 |

**Other Data & Specifications** — *See Bosch Alternators & Regulators in ELECTRICAL Section.*

### BELT ADJUSTMENT

| Application | ①Deflection |
|---|---|
| Power Steering Belt | .20" (5 mm) |
| All Other Belts | .40" (10 mm) |

① — Deflection is with 13 lbs. (6 kg) pressure applied midway on longest belt run.

### FILTERS & CLEANERS

| Filter or Cleaner | Service Interval (Miles) |
|---|---|
| Oil Filter | Replace every 6,000 |
| Air Cleaner | Clean every 12,500 |
| | Replace every 37,500 |
| Fuel Filter | Replace every 37,500 |
| Auto. Trans. Filter | Replace every 37,500 |

### CAPACITIES

| Application | Quantity |
|---|---|
| Crankcase (Includes Filter) | ①5.8 qts. |
| Cooling System (Includes Heater) | 10.6 qts. |
| Auto. Trans. (Dexron) | ②5.1 qts. |
| Rear Axle (SAE 90) | 2.1 pts. |
| Fuel Tank | ③21.1 gals. |

① — 5.3 qts. without filter change.
② — 6.45 qts. at initial fill.
③ — Includes 3 gals. in reserve.

## TUNE-UP

### 240 D

## ENGINE IDENTIFICATION

First six digits of engine identification number, located on a tag at the rear, left side of engine crankcase, identify engines as follows:

| Model | Code |
|---|---|
| 240D | 616.912 |

## MODEL IDENTIFICATION

### VEHICLE IDENTIFICATION NUMBER

First six digits of vehicle identification number, located on a tag on left, front window post (visible through windshield) and on rear firewall in engine compartment, identify model as follows:

| Model | Code |
|---|---|
| 240D | 123.123 |

## COMPRESSION PRESSURE

Check compression pressure with engine at normal operating temperature and throttle valve fully open. Crank engine through at least 8 revolutions.

| Application | Pressure |
|---|---|
| Normal | 319-348 psi (22.5-24.5 kg/cm²) |
| Minimum | 218 psi (15 kg/cm²) |
| Maximum Variation | 44 psi (3 kg/cm²) |

## VALVE TAPPET CLEARANCE

Valves must be adjusted at ignition TDC and in firing order of individual cylinders. With engine cold, measure clearance between rocker arm and base circle of cam. Adjust valves to following specifications:

### Valve Clearance Specifications

| Application | Intake | Exhaust |
|---|---|---|
| Cold | .004" (.10 mm) | .012" (.30 mm) |
| Warm | .006" (.15 mm) | .014" (.35 mm) |

## VALVE ARRANGEMENT

**All Models** — E-I-I-E-E-I-I-E (front to rear).

## FIRING ORDER

**All Models** — 1-3-4-2

## GLOW PLUGS

Torque................................................ 36 Ft. Lbs. (5mkg.)

### Glow Plug Type

| Application | Bosch Part No. | Beru Part No. |
|---|---|---|
| 240D | 0 250 001 016 | 382 GK |

## DIESEL FUEL INJECTION SYSTEM

**NOTE** — *For complete information on the Diesel fuel injection system, see Bosch Diesel Fuel Injection (Mercedes-Benz) in the FUEL SYSTEMS Section. Information includes description, system components, service procedures, removal and installation, as well as idle speed adjustment and start of delivery timing.*

## IDLE SPEED ADJUSTMENT

**NOTE** — *For adjustment procedure, see Bosch Diesel Fuel Injection (Mercedes-Benz) in FUEL SYSTEMS Section.*

| Application | Idle RPM |
|---|---|
| 240D | 650-750 |

# GENERAL SERVICING

## FUEL SYSTEMS

### FUEL INJECTION

All Models use Bosch Diesel Fuel Injection.

**Other Data & Specifications** — *See Tune-Up and Bosch Diesel Fuel Injection in FUEL SYSTEMS Section.*

## ELECTRICAL

### BATTERY

**12 Volt** — Negative Ground.

| Application | Amp. Hr. Rating |
|---|---|
| All Models | 88 |

## STARTER

All models are equipped with Bosch Starters.

| | |
|---|---|
| Free Speed Voltage | 11.5 at 6500-8500 RPM |
| Free Speed Amperage | 65-95 at 6500-8500 RPM |

**Other Data & Specifications** — *See Bosch Starters in ELECTRICAL Section.*

## ALTERNATOR

| Application | Rated Amp. Output |
|---|---|
| All Models | 55 |

**Other Data & Specifications** — *See Bosch Alternators & Regulators in ELECTRICAL Section.*

## GENERAL SERVICING (Cont.)

### ALTERNATOR REGULATOR

Bosch — Non-Adjustable; integral with alternator.

**Other Data & Specifications** — *See Bosch Alternators & Regulators in ELECTRICAL Section.*

### CAPACITIES

| Application | Quantity |
| --- | --- |
| Crankcase (Includes Filter) | ①6.8 qts. |
| Cooling System | 10.5 qts. |
| Man. Trans. (SAE 10W/20) | 3.4 pts. |
| Auto. Trans. (Dexron) | ②5.1 qts. |
| Rear Axle (SAE 90) | 2.1 pts. |
| Fuel Tank | ③21.5 gals. |

① — Without filter, 5.3 qts.
② — Refill shown. Initial fill, 6.5 qts.
③ — Includes 3.0 gals. in reserve.

### FILTERS & CLEANERS

| Filter or Cleaner | Service Interval (Miles) |
| --- | --- |
| Oil Filter | Replace every 3,000 |
| Air Cleaner | ①Clean every 12,500 |
| Fuel Filter | Replace every 37,500 |

① — Replace every 37,500 miles.

### BELT ADJUSTMENT

| Application | ①Deflection |
| --- | --- |
| Power Steering Belt | .20" (5 mm) |
| All Other Belts | .40" (10 mm) |

① — Deflection is with a pressure of 13 lbs. (6 kg) applied midway on longest belt run.

## TUNE-UP

**300 D**
**300 CD**
**300 SD**

### ENGINE IDENTIFICATION

First six digits of engine identification number, located on a tag on the rear, left side of engine crankcase, identify engine as follows:

| Model | Engine Code |
|---|---|
| 300 D, CD | 617.912 |
| 300 SD | 617.950 |

### MODEL IDENTIFICATION

#### VEHICLE IDENTIFICATION NUMBER

First six digits of vehicle identification number, located on a tag on left, front window post and on rear firewall in engine compartment, identify model as follows:

| Model | Model Code |
|---|---|
| 300D | 123.130 |
| 300 CD | 123.150 |
| 300 SD | 116.120 |

### COMPRESSION PRESSURE

Check compression pressure with engine at normal operating temperature and throttle valve wide open, crank engine a minimum of eight compression strokes to obtain following specifications:

| Application | Pressure |
|---|---|
| Normal | 319-348 psi (22.5-24.5 kg/cm²) |
| Minimum | 218 psi (15 kg/cm²) |
| Maximum Variation | 44 psi (3 kg/cm²) |

### VALVE TAPPET CLEARANCE

Valves must be adjusted at ignition TDC and in firing order of individual cylinders. With engine cold, measure clearance between rocker arm and base circle of cam.

### Valve Clearance Specifications

| Application | Intake | Exhaust |
|---|---|---|
| Engine Cold | | |
| 300 D, CD | .004" (.10 mm) | .012" (.30 mm) |
| 300 SD | .004" (.10 mm) | .014" (.35 mm) |
| Engine Warm | | |
| 300 D, CD | .006" (.15 mm) | .014" (.35 mm) |
| 300 SD | .006" (.15 mm) | .016" (.40 mm) |

### VALVE ARRANGEMENT

E-I-I-E-E-I-I-E-E-I (front-to-rear)

### FIRING ORDER

1-2-4-5-3

### GLOW PLUGS

Torque .................. 36 ft. lbs.(5 mkg)

#### Glow Plug Type

| Application | Bosch Part No. | Beru Part No. |
|---|---|---|
| 300 D, CD | 0 250 001 016 | 382 GK |
| 300 SD | 0 250 200 054 | GV 843/5 |

### DIESEL FUEL INJECTION SYSTEM

For complete information on the Diesel fuel injection system, see Bosch Diesel Fuel Injection (Mercedes-Benz) in the FUEL SYSTEMS Section. Information includes description, system components, service procedures, removal and installation, as well as idle speed adjustment and start of delivery timing.

### IDLE SPEED ADJUSTMENT

NOTE — For adjustment procedure, see Bosch Diesel Fuel Injection (Mercedes-Benz) in FUEL SYSTEMS Section.

| Application | Idle RPM |
|---|---|
| 300 D, CD | 650-750 |
| 300 SD | 650-850 |

## GENERAL SERVICING

### ELECTRICAL

#### BATTERY

**12 Volt** — Negative Ground.

| Application | Amp. Hr. Rating |
|---|---|
| All Models | 88 |

### STARTER

All models are equipped with Bosch starters.

Free Speed Voltage .......... 11.5 at 6500-8500 RPM
Free Speed Amperage .......... 65-95 at 6500-8500 RPM

**Other Data & Specifications** — See Bosch Starters in ELECTRICAL Section.

## GENERAL SERVICING (Cont.)

**ALTERNATOR**

| Application | Rated Amp. Output |
|---|---|
| All Models | 55 |

**Other Data & Specifications** — *See Bosch Alternators & Regulators in ELECTRICAL Section.*

**ALTERNATOR REGULATOR**

Bosch — Non-Adjustable; integral with alternator.

**Other Data & Specifications** — *See Bosch Alternators & Regulators in ELECTRICAL Section.*

---

### BELT ADJUSTMENT

| Application | ①Deflection |
|---|---|
| A/C Compressor | .20" (5 mm) |
| All Other Belts | .40" (10 mm) |

① — Deflection is with a pressure of 13 lbs. applied midway on longest belt run.

---

### FILTERS & CLEANERS

| Filter or Cleaner | Service Interval (Miles) |
|---|---|
| Oil Filter | Replace every 3,000 |
| Air Cleaner | Replace every 12,500 |
| Fuel Filter | Replace every 37,500 |

---

### CAPACITIES

| Application | Quantity |
|---|---|
| Crankcase (Includes Filter) | |
| 300 D, CD | 6.8 qts. |
| 300 SD | 7.9 qts. |
| Cooling System | |
| 300 D, CD | 11.6 qts. |
| 300 SD | 13.1 qts. |
| Auto. Trans. (Dexron) | |
| 300 D, CD | ①5.1 qts. |
| 300 SD | ②5.6 qts. |
| Rear Axle (SAE 90) | 2.1 pts. |
| Fuel Tank | |
| 300 D, CD | 21.1 gals. |
| 300 SD | 21.7 gals. |

① — Refill shown. Initial fill is 6.5 qts.
② — Refill shown. Initial fill is 7 qts.

## TUNE-UP

**280 E**
**280 CE**
**280 SE**

### ENGINE IDENTIFICATION

First six digits of engine identification number, located on tag on front left side of engine crankcase, identify engine as follows:

| Application | Code |
|---|---|
| 280 E, CE ............................................. | 110.984 |
| 280 SE ................................................. | 110.985 |

### MODEL IDENTIFICATION

#### VEHICLE IDENTIFICATION NUMBER

First six digits of identification number, located above instrument panel and visible through windshield and on a tag on rear firewall of engine compartment, identify models as follows:

| Application | Code |
|---|---|
| 280 E ................................................... | 123.033 |
| 280 CE ................................................. | 123.053 |
| 280 SE ................................................. | 116.024 |

### COMPRESSION PRESSURE

Check compression pressure with engine at normal operating temperature and throttle valve fully open. Crank engine a minimum of eight revolutions to obtain following specifications:

| Application | Pressure |
|---|---|
| Normal Pressure .......................... | 130-144 psi (9-10 kg/cm²) |
| Minimum Pressure ............................... | 108 psi (7.5 kg/cm²) |
| Maximum Variation ............................. | 21 psi (1.5 kg/cm²) |

### VALVE TAPPET CLEARANCE

| Engine Temp. | Intake | Exhaust |
|---|---|---|
| Cold ....................... | .004" (.10 mm) | ......... .010" (.25 mm) |
| Hot ......................... | .006" (.15 mm) | ......... .012" (.30 mm) |

### VALVE ARRANGEMENT

All Models
Right Side — All Exhaust.
Left Side — All Intake.

### SPARK PLUGS

| | |
|---|---|
| Gap ......................................................... | .032" (.8 mm) |
| Torque ...................................... | 18-22 ft. lbs. (2.5-3.0 mkg) |

#### Spark Plug Type①

| Application | Bosch No. | Champion No. |
|---|---|---|
| All Models .............. | W 145 T 30 | ....................... N-10Y |

① — Beru Spark Plug No. 145/14/3A.

### HIGH TENSION WIRE RESISTANCE

Carefully remove high tension wires from spark plugs and distributor cap. Using an ohmmeter, measure resistance while gently twisting wire. If resistance is not to specifications or fluctuates from infinity to any value, replace wire(s).

#### Resistance (Ohms) Per Wire

| Application | Ohms |
|---|---|
| All Models ................................................. | 25,000-30,000 |

**Fig. 1   Firing Order and Distributor Rotation**

### DISTRIBUTOR

Mercedes-Benz 6-cylinder vehicles are now equipped with breakerless, transistorized ignition systems.

**Fig. 2   Timing Marks for 6-Cylinder Engines**

### IGNITION TIMING

Check or adjust ignition timing with engine at normal operating temperature, idle speed set to specifications and distributor vacuum lines connected.

#### Ignition Timing Specifications

| Application | RPM | Timing |
|---|---|---|
| All Models ....................... | 800 | ................................ TDC |

### IDLE SPEED & MIXTURE

**NOTE** — *Be sure spark plug gap and ignition timing are to specifications, and check air intake system for leaks. Turn off air conditioning system when making adjustment.*

## TUNE-UP (Cont.)

**1)** Run engine until it reaches normal operating temperature, about 140-176° F (60-80° C) oil temperature. Remove air cleaner and be sure cruise control cable rests tension-free against throttle lever.

**2)** Disconnect the control rod at the bell crank and be sure throttle valve is at the idle speed stop. Then, reconnect control rod tension-free. Cam roller should be resting free of play in the gate lever.

**3)** Adjust idle to correct RPM, using idle air adjusting screw. Connect a CO gas analyzer at the exhaust pick-up tube (exhaust back pressure line), using adapter 700 589 07 07 00.

**4)** Check CO value without air injection. To do so, remove blue vacuum line on blue thermo-vacuum valve and plug the line. To adjust for proper CO value, remove plug from mixture control regulator, insert Allen wrench and turn idle mixture adjusting screw clockwise to richen, or counterclockwise to lean the mixture.

**5)** Close bore for idle mixture adjusting screw, accelerate engine briefly, and check CO value at idle speed. Readjust if necessary. Install air cleaner and recheck both idle speed and CO value. Connect vacuum line to thermo-vacuum valve. Place Auto. Trans. in "D", switch on air conditioning and turn steering to full lock position. Engine should continue to run smoothly. If not, readjust idle speed.

## GENERAL SERVICING

### IGNITION

#### DISTRIBUTOR

All models are equipped with Bosch breakerless, transistorized distributors.

**Other Data & Specifications** — *See Tune-Up & Bosch Distributors in ELECTRICAL Section.*

#### IGNITION COIL

| Resistance | Ohms at 68°F |
|---|---|
| Primary | .33-.46 |
| Secondary | 7,000-12,000 |

### FUEL SYSTEM

#### FUEL INJECTION

| Application | Model |
|---|---|
| All Models | Bosch CIS Fuel Injection |

**Other Data & Specifications** — *See Tune-Up & Bosch CIS Fuel Injection in FUEL SYSTEMS Section.*

### Idle Speed (RPM) and CO Level (%)①

| Application | Idle RPM | CO% |
|---|---|---|
| All Models | 850 | 0.4-2.0 |

① — Without air injection.

### COLD (FAST) IDLE RPM

There is no fast idle speed adjustment, as fast idle is controlled by the cold start valve.

### FUEL PUMP DELIVERY RATE

**1)** Remove fuel return hose from fuel distributor. Connect short length of hose at point of removal. Hold end of hose in 1 liter measuring vessel.

**2)** Turn on ignition. Disconnect plug on safety switch for 30 seconds and reinstall plug. If delivery rate is below specifications, check for 11.5 volts at fuel pump, kinks in lines, faulty fuel filter or accumulator. If all check out, then replace fuel pump and reconnect return line.

#### Fuel Pump Delivery Rate

| | |
|---|---|
| Delivery Rate | 1.06 qts. (1 liter) in 30 seconds |

### EMISSION CONTROL SYSTEMS

*See Mitchell Manuals' Emission Control Manual.*

### THROTTLE CONTROL LINKAGE

**1)** Check control linkage for easy operation and straightness. Disconnect throttle control rod and check whether throttle valve rests against idle stop. Reconnect control rod. Adjust control rod so that the roller rests tension-free in slot of gate lever. See Fig. 3.

**Fig. 3  Adjusting Accelerator Linkage**

**2)** With engine stopped, press down accelerator pedal inside vehicle until it rests on kickdown switch. Throttle valve lever should rest against full throttle stop. If necessary, adjust con-

## GENERAL SERVICING (Cont.)

trol linkage at hex. nut (arrow in *Fig. 3*) until throttle valve lever rests against full throttle stop.

**3)** If full throttle stop or the idle stop is not reached with this adjustment, adjust control rod connecting the horizontal shaft to the accelerator pedal.

**4)** Adjust automatic transmission control pressure rod at idle position. Disconnect rod and push toward rear against the stop. Reconnect rod tension-free, adjusting ball socket if necessary. *See Fig. 4.*

### Control Rod Length Adjustments

| Application | Length In. (mm) |
|---|---|
| Throttle Control Rod | 13.50 (343) |
| Control Rod (Over Top of Engine) | 12.05 (306) |
| Accelerator Pedal Control Rod | 7.32 (186) |

Control Rod

A/T Control Pressure Rod

**Fig. 4 Adjusting Automatic Transmission Linkage**

## ELECTRICAL

### BATTERY

**12 Volt** — Negative Ground.

| Application | Amp. Hour Rating |
|---|---|
| All Models | 55 |

**Battery Location** — In engine compartment.

### STARTER

All models are equipped with Bosch starters.

| | |
|---|---|
| Free Speed Voltage | |
| All Models | 11.5 at 8000-10,000 RPM |
| Free Speed Amperage | |
| All Models | 50-80 at 8000-10,000 RPM |

**Other Data & Specifications** — *See Bosch Starters in ELECTRICAL Section.*

### ALTERNATOR

| Application | Rated Amp. Output |
|---|---|
| All Models | 55 |

**Other Data & Specifications** — *See Bosch Alternators & Regulators in ELECTRICAL Section.*

### ALTERNATOR REGULATOR

Bosch — Regulating voltage of 13.7-14.5 volts; integral with alternator; transistorized.

**Other Data & Specifications** — *See Bosch Alternators & Regulators in ELECTRICAL Section.*

---

### FILTERS & CLEANERS

| Filter or Cleaner | Service Interval (Miles) |
|---|---|
| Oil Filter | Replace every 6,000 |
| Air Cleaner | Clean every 12,000 |
| | Replace every 37,500 |
| Fuel Filter | Replace every 37,500 |
| Auto. Trans. Filter | Replace every 37,500 |

---

### BELT ADJUSTMENT

| Application | ① Deflection |
|---|---|
| Power Steering Belt | .20" (5 mm) |
| All Other Belts | .40" (10 mm) |

① — Deflection with 12 lbs. pressure applied midway on belt run.

---

### CAPACITIES

| Application | Quantity |
|---|---|
| Crankcase (Includes Filter) | 6.9 qts. |
| Cooling System | |
| 280 E, CE | 10.6 qts. |
| 280 SE | 11.6 qts. |
| Auto. Trans. (Dexron) | ① 5.6 qts. |
| Rear Axle (SAE 90) | 2.1 pts. |
| Fuel Tank | |
| 280 E, CE | 21.1 gals. |
| 280 SE | 25.3 gals. |

① — Refill shown. Initial fill is 7 qts.

# 1978 Mercedes-Benz V8 Tune-Up

## TUNE-UP

450 SEL
450 SL
450 SLC
6.9

### ENGINE IDENTIFICATION

First six digits of engine identification number, located on tag attached to engine crankcase (6.9, at front; 450 Series, at rear left side of block), identify engines as follows:

| Application | Code |
|---|---|
| 450 SEL | 117.986 |
| 450 SL | 117.985 |
| 450 SLC | 117.985 |
| 6.9 | 100.985 |

### MODEL IDENTIFICATION

#### VEHICLE IDENTIFICATION NUMBER

First six digits of identification number, located on a tag at left side of instrument panel (visible through windshield) and in engine compartment (6.9 on rear firewall; 450 Series to left of hood latch), identify models as follows:

| Model | Number |
|---|---|
| 450 SEL | 116.033 |
| 450 SL | 107.044 |
| 450 SLC | 107.024 |
| 6.9 | 116.036 |

### COMPRESSION PRESSURE

Check compression pressure with engine at normal operating temperature and throttle valve fully open. Crank engine a minimum of eight revolutions to obtain following specifications:

| Application | Pressure |
|---|---|
| Normal Pressure | 130-144 psi (9-10 kg/cm²) |
| Minimum Pressure | 108 psi (7.5 kg/cm²) |
| Maximum Variation | 21 psi (1.5 kg/cm²) |

### VALVE TAPPET CLEARANCE

**Hydraulic Valve Lifters —** *For adjustment see Mercedes-Benz V8 Engines in ENGINE Section.*

#### VALVE ARRANGEMENT

450 Series
  Right Bank — E-I-E-I-E-I-I-E (front to rear).
  Left Bank — E-I-I-E-I-E-I-E (front to rear).
6.9 Models
  Right Bank — I-E-I-E-I-E-I-E (front to rear).
  Left Bank — E-I-E-I-E-I-E-I (front to rear).

### SPARK PLUGS

Gap ...................................... .032" (.8 mm)
Torque ...................... 18-22 ft. lbs. (2.5-3.0 mkg)

### Spark Plug Type①

| Application | Bosch No. | Champion No. |
|---|---|---|
| All Models | W 145 T 30 | N-10Y |

① — Beru Spark Plug No. is 145/14/3A.

### HIGH TENSION WIRE RESISTANCE

Carefully remove high tension wires from spark plugs and distributor cap. Using an Ohmmeter, check resistance of wires while gently twisting wire. If resistance is not to specifications, or fluctuates from infinity to any value, replace wire(s).

#### Resistance (Ohms) Per Wire

| Application | Ohms |
|---|---|
| All Models | 25,000-30,000 |

FIRING ORDER 1-5-4-8-6-3-7-2

***Fig. 1  Firing Order and Distributor Rotation***

## DISTRIBUTOR

All models feature a breakerless, transistorized ignition system.

***Fig. 2  Timing Marks Illustrated (All Models)***

## TUNE-UP (Cont.)

### IGNITION TIMING

Check or adjust ignition timing with engine at normal operating temperature, idle speed set to specifications and distributor vacuum lines connected. *See Fig. 2.*

**Ignition Timing Specifications**

| Application | Timing |
|---|---|
| All Models ................................. | TDC at 800 RPM |

### IDLE SPEED & MIXTURE

**NOTE** — *Be sure spark plug gap and ignition timing are to specifications, and check air intake system for leaks. Turn off air conditioning system when making adjustments.*

1) Run engine until oil reaches 140-176° F (60-80° C). Remove air cleaner. Be sure cruise control cable rests tension-free against throttle lever. If necessary, adjust screw.

2) Disconnect control rod at bell crank. Check that throttle valve is at idle speed stop. Reconnect control rod so that it is tension-free. Use idle speed air adjusting screw to set correct idle speed.

3) Connect a CO gas analyzer at the exhaust pick-up tube (exhaust back pressure line). Connection must be in front of catalyst. Use a 700 589 07 07 00 Adapter. Check CO value WITH air injection on Federal 450 models. Check WITHOUT air injection on 6.9 models and California 450 models.

**NOTE** — *To disconnect air injection, remove the blue/purple vacuum line on the straight connection of the blue thermo-vacuum valve. Plug the valve connection.*

4) To adjust the CO level, remove plug from center of mixture control unit, and insert Allen wrench into idle mixture adjusting screw. Turn counterclockwise to make mixture more lean; clockwise to enrichen. Then, plug adjusting screw bore, accelerate engine briefly, and check CO value at idle speed. Readjust as necessary.

5) Install air cleaner. Recheck idle RPM and CO value. Again, readjust if necessary. Remove the air cleaner and reconnect vacuum line to thermo-vacuum valve. Place Auto. Trans. in "D", turn on air conditioning and turn steering to full lock position. The engine should continue to run smoothly. Readjust idle RPM if necessary. Install air cleaner.

**Idle Speed (RPM) and CO Level (%)**

| Application | Idle RPM | CO% |
|---|---|---|
| 450 Series | | |
| Federal ........................ | 750 | ①0.5-2.0 |
| Calif. ........................... | 750 | ②0.5-2.0 |
| 6.9 Models ................... | 600 | ②0.5-2.0 |

① — With air injection.
② — Without air injection.

### COLD (FAST) IDLE RPM

There is no fast idle speed adjustment, as fast idle is controlled by the cold start valve.

### FUEL PUMP PRESSURE & VOLUME

| | |
|---|---|
| Volume ................................. | 1 qt. in 30 seconds |

**NOTE** — *For rest, system, and warm and cold control pressures, see Bosch CIS Fuel Injection in FUEL SYSTEMS Section.*

### EMISSION CONTROL SYSTEMS

*See Mitchell Manuals' Emission Control Manual.*

## GENERAL SERVICING

### IGNITION

#### DISTRIBUTOR

All models are equipped with Bosch breakerless ignition system.

**Other Data & Specifications** — *See Tune-Up & Bosch Distributors in ELECTRICAL Section.*

#### IGNITION COIL

| Application | Ohms At 68° F (20° C) |
|---|---|
| Primary ............................................. | .33-.46 |
| Secondary ......................................... | 7,000-12,000 |

### FUEL SYSTEMS

#### FUEL INJECTION

All models use Bosch Continuous Injection System fuel injection.

**Other Data & Specifications** — *See Tune-Up & Bosch CIS Fuel Injection in FUEL SYSTEMS Section.*

### ELECTRICAL

#### BATTERY

**12 Volt** — Negative Ground.

| Application | Amp. Hr. Rating |
|---|---|
| 450 SL, SLC ................................................. | 88 |
| 450 SEL & 6.9 ............................................ | 66 |

## GENERAL SERVICING (Cont.)

**Battery Location** — Battery is located in engine compartment on 6.9 and 450 SEL models and in right side of trunk on 450 SL and 450 SLC models.

### STARTER

All models are equipped with Bosch starters.

Free Speed Voltage
450 Series ................................. 11.5 at 8,000-10,000 RPM
6.9 Models ............................... 11 at 8,500-10,000 RPM
Free Speed Amperage
450 Series ................................. 50-80 at 8,000-10,000 RPM
6.9 Models ............................... 55-85 at 8,500-10,000 RPM

**Other Data & Specifications** — *See Bosch Starters in ELECTRICAL Section.*

### ALTERNATOR

| Application | Rated Amp. Output |
|---|---|
| 450 Series | 55 |
| 6.9 Models | 75 |

**Other Data & Specifications** — *See Bosch Alternators & Regulators in ELECTRICAL Section.*

### ALTERNATOR REGULATOR

Bosch — Integral with alternator; regulating voltage of 13.7-14.5 volts.

**Other Data & Specifications** — *See Bosch Alternators & Regulators in ELECTRICAL Section.*

---

### BELT ADJUSTMENT

| Application | ① Deflection |
|---|---|
| A/C Compressor Belt | .20" (5 mm) |
| All Other Belts | .40" (10 mm) |

① —Deflection with 12 lbs. pressure applied midway on belt run.

---

### FILTERS & CLEANERS

| Filter or Cleaner | Service Intervals (Miles) |
|---|---|
| Oil Filter | |
| 450 Series | Replace every 6,000 |
| 6.9 Models | Replace every 12,500 |
| Air Cleaner | Clean every 12,500 |
| | Replace every 37,500 |
| Fuel Line Filter | Replace every 37,500 |
| Fuel Tank Filter | Replace every 37,500 |
| Auto. Trans. Filter | Replace every 37,500 |

---

### CAPACITIES

| Application | Quantity |
|---|---|
| Crankcase (Including Filter) | |
| 450 Series | ①8.5 qts. |
| 6.9 | ①11.7 qts. |
| Cooling System | |
| 450 Series | 15.8 qts. |
| 6.9 Models | 16.9 qts. |
| Auto. Trans. Refill (Dexron) | ②8.3 qts. |
| Rear Axle (SAE 90) | 2.7 qts. |
| Fuel Tank | |
| 450 SEL & 6.9 | ③25.4 gals. |
| 450 SL, SLC | ③23.8 gals. |

① — Without filter change, subtract 1.6 qts. for 6.9 models or .5 qt. for 450 series vehicles.

② — Initial fill is 9.4 qts.

③ — Includes 3.4 gals. in reserve.

## TUNE-UP

Midget
MGB

### ENGINE IDENTIFICATION

Engine number on the Midget is stamped either on a plate or directly onto cylinder block on the left side of engine. On the MGB number is stamped on a plate attached to right side of cylinder block. Engine may be identified by prefix of engine number as follows:

| Application | Engine Code |
|---|---|
| Midget | FP |
| MGB | |
| With Overdrive | |
| Federal | 18V 884 |
| Calif. | 18V 891 |
| Without Overdrive | |
| Federal | 18V 883 |
| Calif. | 18V 890 |

### MODEL IDENTIFICATION

#### VEHICLE IDENTIFICATION NUMBER

Vehicle identification number is stamped on a plate attached to left hand door post and to rear underside of hood.

### COMPRESSION PRESSURE

| Application | Pressure |
|---|---|
| Midget | 145 psi (10.2 kg/cm²) Min. |
| MGB | 130 psi (9.1 kg/cm²) Min. |

### VALVE TAPPET CLEARANCE

Remove valve cover and observe opening and closing of valves. Measure clearance between rocker arms and valve stems for a "sliding" fit. To check clearance, turn crankshaft until valves in first column are fully open, then check or adjust valves in second column. Adjust in following order:

**NOTE** — *Count valves from front to rear.*

| Valve Open | Valve to Adjust |
|---|---|
| 8 | 1 |
| 6 | 3 |
| 4 | 5 |
| 7 | 2 |
| 1 | 8 |
| 3 | 6 |
| 5 | 4 |
| 2 | 7 |

| Application | ①Clearance |
|---|---|
| Midget (Cold) | .010" (.25 mm) |
| MGB (Hot) | .013" (.33 mm) |

① — Intake and exhaust valves set to same clearance.

#### VALVE ARRANGEMENT

E-I-I-E-E-I-I-E (front to rear).

### SPARK PLUGS

| Gap | |
|---|---|
| Midget | .025" (.64 mm) |
| MGB | .035" (.90 mm) |
| Torque | |
| Midget | 20 ft. lbs. (2.8 mkg) |
| MGB | 18 ft. lbs. (2.5 mkg) |

#### Spark Plug Type

| Application | Champion No. |
|---|---|
| Midget | N-12Y |
| MGB | N-9Y |

### HIGH TENSION WIRE RESISTANCE

Remove high tension wires from spark plugs and distributor cap. Using an ohmmeter, check high tension wire resistance while gently twisting wire. If resistance is not to specifications, or fluctuates from infinity to any value, replace wire(s).

#### Resistance (Ohms) Per Wire

| Application | Ohms |
|---|---|
| All Models | 25,000-30,000 |

### DISTRIBUTOR

All models are equipped with breakerless, electronic ignition systems.

Air Gap ............... .014-.016" (.35-.40 mm)

*Fig. 1   Firing Order and Distributor Rotation (Midget)*

*Fig. 2   Firing Order and Distributor Rotation (MGB)*

# 1978 MG 4 Tune-Up

## TUNE-UP (Cont.)

### IGNITION TIMING

Check or adjust ignition timing with engine at normal operating temperature and point or air gap set to specifications. Disconnect and plug distributor vacuum hose on Federal Midget models. Rotate distributor housing to achieve correct timing. Tighten distributor lock nut and reconnect vacuum hose.

#### Ignition Timing Specifications

| Application | RPM | Timing |
|---|---|---|
| Midget | | |
|   Federal | 800 | ①10°BTDC |
|   Calif. | 800 | 2°ATDC |
| MGB | 1500 | 10°BTDC |

① — With distributor vacuum hose disconnected and plugged.

**Fig. 3   Ignition Timing Mark Location (MGB)**

**Fig. 4   Ignition Timing Mark Location (Midget)**

### IDLE SPEED & MIXTURE

**NOTE** — *Before checking idle speed and CO% level, be sure valve clearance, spark plug gap and ignition timing are to specifications. Install tachometer on engine.*

**1)** Run engine until it reaches normal operating temperature. Remove air cleaner. Ensure choke is off and fast idle screw is not in contact with fast idle cam. Make sure oil in carburetor damper is ¼" below top of piston guide rod.

**Fig. 5   Adjusting Idle Speed and CO% Level**

**2)** Disconnect air injection pump outlet hose and plug the hose. Do not plug air pump outlet, or damage to pump may occur. Disconnect float chamber vent pipe from carburetor. See Fig. 5.

**3)** Run engine at 2500 RPM for 30 seconds and check idle speed. Adjust idle speed to specifications, using idle adjusting screw.

**4)** Connect an exhaust gas analyzer to vehicle. If CO% level is not within specifications, turn FINE idle CO screw clockwise to enrich and counterclockwise to weaken mixture. If correct CO% level cannot be achieved, proceed to specific instructions for vehicle.

### MGB VEHICLES ONLY

**1)** Turn FINE idle CO screw clockwise as far as possible, and then counterclockwise 2½ turns. This places screw in mid-point of adjustment range.

**2)** Remove suction chamber cover, spring and air valve from carburetor. Check that initial needle adjustment is correct (shoulder of needle should be flush with air valve underside).

## TUNE-UP (Cont.)

**Fig. 6  Setting Initial Needle Adjustment**

**3)** If needle requires adjustment, remove air valve damper from suction chamber. Carefully insert inner part of adjusting tool (S353) into hexagon hole in needle adjuster plug. See Fig. 6. Turn tool to properly adjust needle position.

**4)** Install air valve with diaphragm tab in housing recess. Align and install suction chamber cover and damper. Recheck idle speed and CO% level as previously instructed.

**5)** If it is still impossible to obtain correct CO% level, adjust FINE idle CO screw to mid-point of adjustment range (step **1**). Then, adjust COARSE idle CO NUT clockwise to enrich and counterclockwise to lean mixture.

**6)** If CO% level is still not within specifications, turn NUT clockwise as far as possible without forcing, and then counterclockwise 2 turns to mid-point of its adjustment range. Proceed to step **1**) of following procedure.

## ALL MODELS

**1)** If CO% level is still not achieved, remove air valve damper and insert adjusting tool (S353) into dashpot until outer tool engages the air valve and inner tool engages hexagon hole in needle adjuster plug.

**NOTE** — *Lug of outer tool must engage slot in air valve or diaphragm may be torn. See Fig. 6.*

**2)** Hold outer tool firmly and turn inner tool clockwise to enrich or counterclockwise to weaken mixture. Remove tool. Top up hollow piston rod with oil (¼" below top of piston guide rod) and install damper.

**3)** Recheck CO% level and if necessary repeat this final adjusting procedure (steps **1**) and **2**) above) until correct level is achieved.

**4)** Remove plug from air manifold hose and install hose to air pump and float chamber vent pipe to carburetor. Increase engine speed to 2500 RPM for 30 seconds and readjust idle screw to achieve required idle speed. Restore all components to original positions.

### Idle Speed (RPM) and CO Level (%)

| Application | Idle RPM | ①CO% |
|---|---|---|
| Midget | | |
| Federal | 700-900 | 3.0-7.0 |
| Calif. | 700-900 | 0.5-6.5 |
| MGB | 750-950 | 4.5-6.5 |

① — With air injection disconnected.

## COLD (FAST) IDLE RPM

**1)** All models are equipped with automatic chokes for fuel enrichment. To check and adjust, remove carburetor. Open throttle butterfly and wedge open. Remove bolt and washer holding water jacket and three screws retaining heat mass.

**Fig. 7  Setting Fast Idle Clearances**

# 1978 MG 4 Tune-Up

## TUNE-UP (Cont.)

2) Rotate the operating arm and check vacuum kick piston and rod for full, free movement; fast idle cam and thermostat lever freeness to pivot; and spring operation on cam and lever.

3) Remove wedge from throttle opening.

4) Set gap between choke and throttle levers to proper clearance. Adjust by turning idle speed screw.

5) Adjust throttle stop screw to obtain proper clearance between end of fast idle pin and cam. Lock adjusting screw with lock nut.

6) Install parts previously removed, being sure to align index marks on heat mass and automatic choke body. Reinstall carburetor and check or adjust idle speed and CO% level.

**Fast Idle Gap Settings**

| Application | Clearance |
|---|---|
| Choke Lever-to-Throttle Lever | .094" (2.4 mm) |
| Fast Idle Pin-to-Cam | |
| Midget | .035" (.9 mm) |
| MGB | .025" (.6 mm) |

## FUEL PUMP PRESSURE & VOLUME

| | |
|---|---|
| Pressure (At Idle) | 2.8-3.8 psi (.20-.27 kg/cm²) |
| Volume | |
| MGB | 1 pt. in 30 sec. |

## EMISSION CONTROL SYSTEMS

*See Mitchell Manuals' Emission Control Manual.*

# GENERAL SERVICING

## IGNITION

### DISTRIBUTOR

All models are equipped with Lucas Opus breakerless, electronic ignition systems.

**Other Data & Specifications** — *See Tune-Up & Lucas Distributors in ELECTRICAL Section.*

### IGNITION COIL

| Resistance | Ohms at 68°F (20°C) |
|---|---|
| Primary | |
| Midget | 1.3-1.45 |
| MGB | 1.43-1.58 |
| Ballast Resistor | |
| Midget | 1.3-1.5 |
| MGB | 1.3-1.4 |

## FUEL SYSTEMS

### CARBURETORS

| Application | Model |
|---|---|
| Midget 1-Bbl. | 150CD4T |
| MGB 1-Bbl. | 175CD5T |

**Other Data & Specifications** — *See Tune-Up & Zenith-Stromberg Carburetors in FUEL SYSTEMS Section.*

## ELECTRICAL

### BATTERY

**12 Volt** — Negative Ground.

**Battery Location** — Battery is located in engine compartment on Midgets and under floor in rear of passenger compartment on MGB models.

| Application | Amp. Hr. Rating |
|---|---|
| Midget | |
| Standard | 40 |
| Optional | 50 |
| MGB | 66 |

### STARTER

All models are equipped with Lucas Starters.

| Free Speed Amperage | |
|---|---|
| Midget | 65 at 8000-10,000 RPM |
| MGB | 40 at 6000 RPM |

**Other Data & Specifications** — *See Lucas Starters in ELECTRICAL Section.*

### ALTERNATOR

| Application | Rated Amp. Output |
|---|---|
| Midget | 34 |
| MGB | 43 |

**Other Data & Specifications** — *See Lucas Alternators & Regulators in ELECTRICAL SECTION.*

### ALTERNATOR REGULATOR

Lucas — Non-Adjustable; Integral with Alternator.

**Other Data & Specifications** — *See Lucas Alternators & Regulators in ELECTRICAL Section.*

## GENERAL SERVICING ( Cont.)

### BELT ADJUSTMENT

| Application | ①Deflection |
|---|---|
| Alternator Belt | |
| Midget | ¾" |
| MGB | ½" |
| Air Pump Belt | ½" |

① — Deflection is with moderate hand pressure applied midway on longest belt run.

### FILTERS & CLEANERS

| Filter or Cleaner | Service Interval (Miles) |
|---|---|
| Oil Filter | Replace every 6,500 |
| Air Cleaner | Replace every 12,500 |
| Fuel Filter | Replace every 12,500 |
| Charcoal Canister① | Replace every 25,000 |

① — Replace every 50,000 miles in Midget.

### CAPACITIES

| Application | Quantity |
|---|---|
| Crankcase (Includes Filter) | |
| Midget | 4.8 qts. |
| MGB | 3.6 qts. |
| Cooling System (Includes Heater) | |
| Midget | 5.7 qts. |
| MGB | 7.2 qts. |
| Man. Trans. | |
| Midget (H.D. 90) | 1.75 pts. |
| MGB (SAE 20W-50) | ①6.0 pts. |
| Rear Axle | |
| Midget (H.D. 90) | 2.1 pts. |
| MGB (H.D. 90) | 2.0 pts. |
| Fuel Tank | |
| Midget | 7.7 gals. |
| MGB | 13.0 gals. |

① — With overdrive add 1.25 pts.

# 1978 Opel 4 Tune-Up

## TUNE-UP

Opel

### ENGINE IDENTIFICATION

Engine serial number is stamped on a machined pad at the top right front corner of engine block.

### MODEL IDENTIFICATION

#### VEHICLE IDENTIFICATION NUMBER

Number is stamped on a plate which is attached to left side of dash (driver's side) and visible through windshield.

### COMPRESSION PRESSURE

Check compression pressure with engine at normal operating temperature, all spark plugs and air cleaner element removed, and throttle valve fully open. Compression should be within specifications with a maximum variation between cylinders of 9 psi (.63 kg/cm²).

#### Compression Pressure @ 300 RPM

| Application | Standard psi (kg/cm²) | Limit for Use psi (kg/cm²) |
|---|---|---|
| All Models | 170 (11.95) | 120 (8.44) |

### VALVE TAPPET CLEARANCE

Check valve clearance with engine cold. Make sure rocker arm shaft nuts are torqued to 16 ft. lbs. (2.2 mkg). Bring piston number one to top dead center on compression stroke by aligning notch on crankshaft pulley with "O" on front cover. Adjust valves as listed in table. Then rotate crankshaft 360° until number four cylinder is at TDC and adjust remaining valves.

#### Piston No. 1 at TDC

Adjust Valves
Intake ......................................................... 1, 2
Exhaust ..................................................... 1, 3

#### Piston No. 4 at TDC

Adjust Valves
Intake ......................................................... 3, 4
Exhaust ..................................................... 2, 4

#### Valve Tappet Clearance

| Application | Clearance (Cold) |
|---|---|
| Intake | .006" (.15 mm) |
| Exhaust | .010" (.25 mm) |

### VALVE ARRANGEMENT

#### All Models

Right Side — All Intake
Left Side — All Exhaust

### SPARK PLUGS

Gap ............................................................ .030" (.8 mm)
Torque ................................. 15-22 ft. lbs. (2-3 mkg)

#### Spark Plug Type

| Application | AC | NGK |
|---|---|---|
| All Models | R44XLS | BPR6ES |

### HIGH TENSION WIRE RESISTANCE

Carefully remove high tension wires from spark plugs and distributor cap. Using an ohmmeter, check resistance of wires while gently twisting wires. If resistance is not to specifications or fluctuates from infinity to any valve, replace wire(s).

#### Resistance (Ohms) Per Wire

| Application | Ohms |
|---|---|
| All Models | 25,000-30,000 |

### DISTRIBUTOR

Point Gap ................................ .016-.020" (.4-.5 mm)
Cam Angle ..................................................... 47-57°
Breaker Arm Spring Tension ............ 14-19 ozs. (397-540 g)
Condenser Capacity ...................................... .25 mfd.

**Fig. 1 Firing Order and Distributor Rotation**

### IGNITION TIMING

Make sure distributor point gap is set correctly and engine is idling smoothly and at correct RPM. Adjust timing as follows:

1) Start engine and run until engine is at normal operating temperature. Stop engine and connect tachometer and a timing light to No. 1 cylinder.

2) Adjust timing by rotating distributor clockwise or counterclockwise until notch on pulley aligns with 6° BTDC mark on machined pad on front cover ("0" mark is TDC). Turning distributor clockwise advances timing, while counterclockwise retards timing.

#### Ignition Timing Specifications

| Application | RPM | Timing |
|---|---|---|
| All Models | 900 | 6°BTDC |

## TUNE-UP (Cont.)

**Fig. 2  Ignition Timing Mark Location**

### IDLE SPEED & MIXTURE

Make sure spark plug gap, distributor point gap, and accelerator control are adjusted properly. Ignition timing and valve clearance should be properly adjusted. Carburetor float level should be set to specifications. With transmission in neutral, air conditioning off (if equipped), air cleaner installed, vacuum lines to distributor and idle compensator disconnected and plugged, adjust idle speed as follows:

**NOTE** — *Information (RPM and number of turns) enclosed in parentheses applies to California and High Altitude vehicles only.*

1) Turn mixture adjusting screw all the way in, then back out 4½ (3) turns. Adjust idle speed screw until 950 (900) RPM is reached. Adjust idle mixture screw for maximum RPM.

2) Readjust idle speed screw for 950 (900) RPM. Turn mixture adjusting screw clockwise (lean) until 900 (850) RPM is reached. Then turn idle mixture screw ½ turn counterclockwise (rich).

3) Adjust idle speed screw for a final speed of 900 RPM.

4) On vehicles with air conditioning, after making these adjustments, turn air conditioning on maximum cold and high blower. Open throttle enough to allow speed up solenoid to reach full travel. Then adjust speed up controller adjusting screw for an idle speed of 900 RPM.

#### Idle Speed (RPM)

| Application | RPM |
| --- | --- |
| All Models | 900 |

### DASHPOT ADJUSTMENT

1) Check that the engine speed at which the dashpot shaft contacts the throttle lever is within 2600-3000 RPM for Federal vehicles and 2400-2800 RPM for California vehicles.

2) If not within specifications, hold engine speed to specification by using throttle lever. Loosen lock nut and turn dashpot until end of shaft contacts throttle lever. Tighten lock nut.

3) Repeat step 1), and check that idle speed is to specification.

### COLD (FAST) IDLE RPM

1) Adjust with engine at normal operating temperature and distributor, EGR and hot idle compensator vacuum hoses disconnected and plugged. Remove air cleaner cover.

2) With engine off, open throttle slightly, close choke valve and release throttle. Start engine without moving throttle. Using fast idle speed screw, set fast idle speed to specifications.

#### Cold (Fast) Idle Specifications

| Application | Man. Trans. RPM | Auto. Trans. RPM |
| --- | --- | --- |
| Federal | 3400 | 3200 |
| Calif. | 3400 | 3000 |

### FUEL PUMP PRESSURE & VOLUME

| | |
| --- | --- |
| Pressure | 2.4-3.3 psi (.17-.23 kg/cm²) |
| Volume | .85 qts. in 1 minute |

## GENERAL SERVICING

### IGNITION

#### DISTRIBUTOR

All models are equipped with Nippondenso single point distributors.

**Other Data & Specifications** — *See Tune-Up & Nippondenso Distributors in ELECTRICAL Section.*

#### IGNITION COIL

| | |
| --- | --- |
| Primary Resistance | 1.33-1.47 Ohms |
| Secondary Resistance | 7,650-9350 Ohms |

### FUEL SYSTEMS

#### CARBURETOR

| Application | Type |
| --- | --- |
| All Models | Nikki 2-Bbl. |

**Other Data & Specifications** — *See Tune-Up and Nikki Carburetors in FUEL SYSTEMS Section.*

# 1978 Opel 4 Tune-Up

## GENERAL SERVICING (Cont.)

### ELECTRICAL

#### BATTERY

**12 Volt** — Negative Ground.

| Application | Amp. Hr. Rating |
|---|---|
| All Models | 50 |

**Battery Location** — Under hood in right front corner of engine compartment.

#### STARTER

Hitachi .................................. Overrunning Clutch

**Other Data & Specifications** — *See Hitachi Starters in ELECTRICAL Section.*

#### ALTERNATOR

| Application | Rated Amp. Output |
|---|---|
| All Models | 40 |

**Other Data & Specifications** — *See Nippondenso Alternators & Regulators in ELECTRICAL Section.*

#### ALTERNATOR REGULATOR

All models are equipped with Nippondenso alternator regulators with an operating voltage of 13.8-14.8 volts at an engine speed of 1400-1850 RPM.

**Other Data & Specifications** — *See Nippondenso Alternators & Regulators in ELECTRICAL Section.*

### ENGINE

#### INTAKE MANIFOLD TIGHTENING

Tighten all intake manifold attaching bolts to 29 ft. lbs. (4.0 mkg) of torque.

### BELT ADJUSTMENT

Belt deflection for drive belts should be .4" (10 mm) with pressure applied midway on belt run.

### FILTERS & CLEANERS

| Filter or Cleaner | Service Interval (Miles) |
|---|---|
| Oil Filter | ①Replace every 7,500 |
| Air Cleaner | Replace every 30,000 |
| Fuel Filter | Replace every 15,000 |
| Vapor Canister Filter | Replace every 15,000 |
| Auto. Trans. Strainer | ②Replace every 30,000 |

① — At first oil change and then every second change.
② — Under severe conditions, replace every 15,000 miles.

### CAPACITIES

| Application | Capacity |
|---|---|
| Crankcase (Includes Filter) | 4.4 qts. |
| Cooling System | 6.8 qts. |
| Man. Trans. (SAE 30) | |
|   4-Speed | 2.65 qts. |
|   5-Speed | 3.25 qts. |
| Auto. Trans. (Dexron II) | 6.5 qts. |
| Rear Axle (SAE 90) | 2.5 pts. |
| Fuel Tank | 13.7 gals. |

## TUNE-UP

924

### ENGINE IDENTIFICATION

Engine identification number is located on the left side of the engine crankcase next to the clutch housing.

| Application | Displacement | Code |
|---|---|---|
| Federal | 1984 cc | XG |
| California | 1984 cc | XE |

### MODEL IDENTIFICATION

#### VEHICLE IDENTIFICATION NUMBER

The vehicle identification number is visible through the windshield and is stamped on a plate attached to left windshield pillar.

### COMPRESSION PRESSURE

Test compression pressure with fully open throttle, oil temperature above 140° F (60° C), all spark plugs removed and engine at cranking speed. Each cylinder should be allowed about 12 compression strokes. Differences between cylinders should not exceed 43 psi (3 kg/cm²).

| Application | Standard Pressure psi (kg/cm²) | Minimum Pressure psi (kg/cm²) |
|---|---|---|
| All Models | 114-156 (8-11) | 85 (6) |

*Fig. 1  Adjusting Valve Clearance*

### VALVE TAPPET CLEARANCE

It is recommended that valve clearances be checked and adjusted with engine oil temperature at 176° F (80° C). To adjust, remove cylinder head cover and turn crankshaft until cam lobes of cylinder to be adjusted point upward.

Check valve clearance. Correct by making complete turns of adjusting screw, using US 8005 adjusting tool. *See Fig. 1.* One turn changes clearance by .002" (.05 mm). Various adjusting screws are available. Camshaft must be removed to replace screws.

#### Valve Clearance Specifications

| Application | Clearance |
|---|---|
| Cold | |
| Intake | .004" (.10 mm) |
| Exhaust | .016" (.40 mm) |
| Warm | |
| Intake | .008" (.20 mm) |
| Exhaust | .018" (.45 mm) |

### VALVE ARRANGEMENT

Both Banks — I-E-I-E-I-E

### SPARK PLUGS

| | |
|---|---|
| Gap | .028" (.7 mm) |
| Torque | 21 ft. lbs. (3 mkg) |

#### Spark Plug Type

| Application | Bosch | Champion |
|---|---|---|
| All Models | W200T30 | N-8Y |

### HIGH TENSION WIRE RESISTANCE

Carefully remove high tension wires from spark plugs and distributor cap. Using an ohmmeter, check resistance of high tension wires while gently twisting wire. If resistance is not to specification, or fluctuates from infinity to any value, replace high tension wire(s).

#### Resistance (Ohms) Per Wire

| Application | Ohms |
|---|---|
| All Models | 6,000 |

## TUNE-UP (Cont.)

**Fig. 2   Firing Order and Distributor Rotation**

### DISTRIBUTOR

Air Gap (Rotor-to-Stator) ............................................. .010"
Dwell Angle
  At 1500 RPM ............................................... 52-70°
  At 5000 RPM ............................................... 42-68°

### IGNITION TIMING

Check or adjust ignition timing with engine at specified RPM and both distributor vacuum advance hoses connected. Adjust timing by turning distributor until mark on flywheel aligns with reference edge on clutch housing.

#### Ignition Timing Specifications

| Application | RPM | Timing |
|---|---|---|
| All Models ................. | 900-1000 ..................... | 3° ATDC |

**Fig. 3   Flywheel Ignition Timing Marks**

### HOT (SLOW) IDLE RPM

**NOTE** — *Ignition timing and valve clearance should be to specifications prior to setting idle RPM.*

1) With engine at normal operating temperature, connect tachometer and exhaust gas analyzer following manufacturer's instructions.

**NOTE** — *On models equipped with catalytic converter, connect suitable exhaust probe (VW 1311) in front of converter.*

2) Disconnect and plug air injection hose at air pump. Clamp hose from air cleaner to charcoal canister. On California vehicles, detach air hose at diverter valve and plug.

3) Adjust idle speed to specifications by turning idle air by-pass screw on throttle valve housing. Remove plug in mixture control unit between fuel distributor and venturi or puncture plastic cap with small screwdriver.

4) Insert adjusting wrench (P377) and adjust CO% level.

**NOTE** — *Always adjust CO% from lean to rich. (Example: If setting is too rich, turn idle adjusting screw all the way counterclockwise, and adjust back toward richer setting.) Never apply pressure to wrench during adjustment.*

5) Remove wrench and accelerate engine. Check CO% level and repeat procedure, if necessary. Recheck idle speed, adjusting as necessary.

6) Insert plug or secure adjusting screw with new blue plastic cap.

#### Idle Speed (RPM) & CO Level (%)

| Application | Idle RPM | CO%① |
|---|---|---|
| Federal ................. | 900-1000 ................. | 0.5-1.0 |
| California ................. | 900-1000 ................. | 0.7 |

① — With charcoal canister disconnected, measure in front of catalytic converter.

### FUEL PUMP PRESSURE

Pressure at 104°F (40°C)
  All Models ............................................. 36 psi (2.5 kg/cm²)
  Delivery Rate .......................................... 1 qt. in 40 seconds

### EMISSION CONTROL SYSTEMS

See Mitchell Manuals' Emission Control Manual.

## GENERAL SERVICING

### IGNITION

#### DISTRIBUTOR

All models are equipped with Bosch transistorized ignition system.

**Other Data & Specifications** — *See Tune-Up & Bosch Distributors in ELECTRICAL Section.*

#### IGNITION COIL

Primary Resistance .......................................... 1.0-1.35 Ohms
Secondary Resistance ............................. 5,500-8,000 Ohms

### FUEL SYSTEMS

#### FUEL INJECTION

All models are equipped with Bosch CIS Fuel Injection.

**Other Data & Specifications** — *See Tune-Up & Bosch CIS Fuel Injection in FUEL SYSTEMS Section.*

### ELECTRICAL

#### BATTERY

CAUTION — *Battery should be disconnected before charging. Precaution will prevent damage to fuel injection control unit.*

**12 Volt** — Negative Ground.

| Application | Amp. Hr. Rating |
|---|---|
| All Models | 63 |

**Battery Location** — Battery is located at right rear corner of engine compartment.

#### STARTER

Bosch ................................................. Overrunning Clutch

Free Speed Voltage ...................... 11.5 at 5500-7500 RPM
Free Speed Amperage ................, 30-50 at 5500-7500 RPM

**Other Data & Specifications** — *See Bosch Starters in ELECTRICAL Section.*

### ALTERNATOR

| Application | Rated Amp. Output |
|---|---|
| All Models | 75 |

**Other Data & Specifications** — *See Bosch Alternators in ELECTRICAL Section.*

#### ALTERNATOR REGULATOR

All models are equipped with Bosch alternator regulators. With rear window defogger and headlights turned on, operating voltage should be 13.5-14.5 volts at 2000 RPM.

**Other Data & Specifications** — *See Bosch Alternator Regulators in ELECTRICAL SECTION.*

---

### BELT ADJUSTMENT

Tension is correct when center portion of belt can be depressed approximately $3/16$ to $3/8$" (5-10 mm) by firm thumb pressure. Adjustment is made by shifting position of alternator. Remove small plate from alternator cover for access to adjustment lock screw.

---

### FILTERS & CLEANERS

| Filter or Cleaner | Service Interval (Miles) |
|---|---|
| Oil Filter | Replace every 15,000 |
| Air Cleaner | Replace every 15,000 |
| Fuel Filter | Replace every 15,000 |
| Air Pump Filter | Replace every 15,000 |

---

### CAPACITIES

| Application | Quantity |
|---|---|
| Crankcase (Includes Filter) | 5.28 qts. |
| Cooling System(With Heater) | 8.4 qts. |
| Manual Transaxle (SAE 80) | 2.75 qts. |
| Auto. Transaxle (ATF Dexron) | 6.4 qts. |
| Differential (SAE 90) | 1.1 qts. |
| Fuel Tank | ①16.4 gals. |

① — Includes approximately 1.3 gals. reserve.

# TUNE-UP

**911SC**
**Turbo**

## ENGINE IDENTIFICATION

Engine identification number is stamped on engine crankcase near oil temperature sensor. The first three digits in engine number identify engine type and year.

| Application | Engine Type | Code |
|---|---|---|
| 911SC | | |
| Federal | 930/04 | 628 |
| California | 930/06 | 658 |
| Turbo | | |
| Federal | 930/61 | 688 |
| California | 930/63 | 688 |

## MODEL IDENTIFICATION

### VEHICLE IDENTIFICATION NUMBER

Number is located on left windshield post and can be seen from outside of vehicle. Number is also located on rear door post on the drivers side on the Safety Compliance Sticker and on the identification plate. The identification plate is located on right side of luggage compartment.

## COMPRESSION PRESSURE

Perform compression test with wide open throttle and oil temperature not less than 140°F (60°C). Remove all spark plugs and allow about 12 piston strokes per cylinder test. Pressure difference between cylinders should not exceed 22 psi (1.5 kg/cm²).

## VALVE TAPPET CLEARANCE

Adjust valve clearance to specificatins with engine cold.

| Application | Clearance |
|---|---|
| All Models (Intake & Exhaust) | .004(.1 mm) |

### VALVE ARRANGEMENT

Engine cylinders have individual heads and contain one intake and one exhaust valve per head. Upper valves are intake and lower valves are exhaust.

## SPARK PLUGS

| Gap | |
|---|---|
| 911SC | .031" (.8 mm) |
| Turbo | .024" (.6 mm) |
| Torque | 18-22 ft. lbs.(2.5-3.0 mkg) |

### Spark Plug Type

| Application | Bosch |
|---|---|
| 911SC | W 145T30 |
| Turbo | W 280P21 |

## HIGH TENSION WIRE RESISTANCE

Carefully remove high tension wires from spark plugs and distributor cap. Using an ohmmeter, check high tension wire resistance while gently twisting wires. If resistance is not to specifications, or fluctuates from infinity to any value, replace high tension wire(s).

### Resistance (Ohms) Per Wire

| Application | Ohms |
|---|---|
| All Models | 25,000-30,000 |

*Fig. 1  Firing Order and Distributor Rotation*

## DISTRIBUTOR

All models use Bosch breakerless electronic distributors. No adjustments are necessary.

## IGNITION TIMING

With engine idling at normal operating temperature, adjust ignition timing to specifications. Vacuum hose should be connected to distributor. Appropriate mark on pulley should be aligned with mark on blower housing. Connect tachometer to black/purple wire at ignition control box.

**CAUTION** — *When engine is running, about 450 volts are present at this connection. DO NOT allow wires to touch vehicle ground.*

*Fig. 2  911 Ignition Timing Marks*

## TUNE-UP (Cont.)

**Fig. 3　Turbo Ignition Timing Marks**

Crankshaft
Pulley

### Ignition Timing Specifications

| Application | RPM | Timing |
|---|---|---|
| 911SC | 900-100 | 5° BTDC |
| Turbo |  |  |
| Federal | 950-1050 | 10° ATDC |
| California | 950-1050 | 5° ATDC |

## HOT (SLOW) IDLE RPM

**1)** Ignition timing should be to specifications and engine should be in perfect mechanical condition. With engine at normal operating temperature, remove air cleaner and detach and plug air hose at air pump.

**2)** Connect exhaust gas analyzer at fitting in front of catalytic converter. Be sure oil tank cap is tight; leaks can affect mixture and engine speed. Connect appropriate tachometer or tester to record RPM. See *instructions under Ignition Timing.*

**3)** Adjust air correction screw on throttle valve housing until specified idle speed is reached. Use special tool (P 229c).

**4)** Adjust CO% level. On Turbo models, insert long allen wrench (P 9156) into mixture control unit and engage screw. Press down ¾" to turn mixture control screw. On 911SC models, use adjusting wrench (P 377) and do not press down while adjusting. Turn clockwise to richen mixture, counterclockwise to lean mixture.

NOTE — *Always make adjustment from lean to rich. EXAMPLE: If idle screw setting is too rich, turn counterclockwise until too lean and then adjust clockwise toward richer setting. Never apply pressure to wrench while adjusting.*

**5)** Turn control screw very slightly, as even smallest turn changes CO% considerably. When checking or adjusting CO% level, plug adjusting hole before taking CO reading.

**6)** Remove wrench. Accelerate engine briefly. When CO is to specification, install air cleaner and recheck idle and CO% level.

### Idle Speed (RPM) and CO Level (%)

| Application | Idle RPM | ①CO% |
|---|---|---|
| 911SC | 900-1000 | 1.5-3.5 |
| Turbo | 950-1050 | 2.0-3.0 |

① — Measured before catalytic converter; air hose plugged.

## FUEL PUMP PRESSURE & VOLUME

| | | |
|---|---|---|
| 911SC (One Pump①) | 64-74 psi | (4.5-5.2 kg/cm²) |
| Turbo (Two Pumps①) | 87-97 psi | (6-6.7 kg/cm²) |

Volume

| | |
|---|---|
| 911SC | Min. 1.6 pts. in 30 sec. |
| Turbo | 2.5 pts. in 30 sec. |

① — Electric roller cell pumps.

## EMISSION CONTROL SYSTEMS

See *Mitchell Manuals' Emission Control Manual.*

# GENERAL SERVICING

## IGNITION

### DISTRIBUTOR

All models are equipped with Capacitive Discharge Ignition systems with Bosch breakerless distributors.

**Other Data & Specifications** — *See Tune-Up and Bosch Distributors in ELECTRICAL Section.*

## FUEL SYSTEMS

### FUEL INJECTION

All models are equipped with Bosch Continuous Injection System (CIS). Turbo has an exhaust gas turbocharger.

**Other Data & Specifications** — *See Tune-Up and Bosch Continuous Injection System (CIS) in FUEL SYSTEMS Section.*

## GENERAL SERVICING (Cont.)

### ELECTRICAL

#### BATTERY

**12 Volt** — Negative Ground.

| Application | Amp. Hr. Rating |
| --- | --- |
| All Models | 66 |

**Battery Location** — Battery is located on left in front luggage compartment, under the floor mat.

#### STARTER

| | |
| --- | --- |
| Bosch | Overrunning Clutch |
| Free Speed Voltage | 11.5 at 7300-9300 RPM |
| Free Speed Amperage | 50-80 at 7300-9300 RPM |

**Other Data & Specifications** — *See Bosch Starters in ELECTRICAL Section.*

#### ALTERNATOR

| Application | Rated Amp. Output |
| --- | --- |
| All Models | 70 |

**Other Data & Specifications** — *See Bosch or Motorola Alternators & Regulators in ELECTRICAL Section.*

### BELT ADJUSTMENT

| Application | Deflection |
| --- | --- |
| Fan Belt① | .5-.75" (13-19 mm) |
| Air Pump Belt | .3-.6" (8-15 mm) |

① — Deflection is with thumb pressure applied midway on longest belt run. To adjust add or delete spacers between pulley halves.

### FILTERS & CLEANERS

| Filter or Cleaner | Service Interval (Miles) |
| --- | --- |
| Oil Filter | Replace every 15,000 |
| Air Cleaner | Replace every 15,000 |
| Fuel Filter | Replace every 15,000 |
| Air Pump Filter | Replace every 15,000 |
| EGR Filter | Replace every 15,000 |

### ALTERNATOR REGULATOR

All models are equipped with Bosch or Motorola alternator regulators with an operating voltage of 14.2 volts at 2500 RPM.

**Other Data & Specifications** — *See Bosch or Motorola Alternators & Regulators in ELECTRICAL Section.*

### CAPACITIES

| Application | Quantity |
| --- | --- |
| Crankcase | |
| 911SC | |
|   Total Capacity | 11.6 qts. |
|   Oil Change | 10.6 qts. |
| Turbo Carrera | |
|   Total Capacity | 13.8 qts. |
|   Oil Change | 10.6 qts. |
| Transaxle (SAE 90) | |
| 911SC | 3.2 qts. |
| Turbo | 3.9 qts. |
| Fuel Tank | ①21 gals. |

① — Includes 2.1 gals. reserve.

## TUNE-UP

### 928

### ENGINE IDENTIFICATION

The engine identification number is stamped on the front rein-forcing rib in the top half of the crankcase, directly behind the fan. The first three digits (828) indicate engine type for the 928 model.

### MODEL IDENTIFICATION

#### VEHICLE IDENTIFICATION NUMBER

The vehicle identification number is located on the left front windshield pillar, visible from the outside. It is also found on the left doorsill.

### COMPRESSION PRESSURE

With engine at normal operating temperature, remove all plugs and allow 12 compression strokes per cylinder. Pressure should not vary more than 21 psi (1.5 kg/cm²) between cylinders.

### VALVE TAPPET CLEARANCE

Porsche 928 models are equipped with hydraulic valve lifters and no adjustments are necessary.

#### VALVE ARRANGEMENT

Both Banks — I-E-I-E-I-E-I-E

### SPARK PLUGS

Gap ................................................... .028-.032″ (.6-.8 mm)
Torque ................................................. 18 ft. lbs. (2.5 mkg)

#### Spark Plug Type

| Application | Bosch | Champion |
|---|---|---|
| All Models ................ | W 145T30 .......................... | N-8Y |

### HIGH TENSION WIRE RESISTANCE

Carefully remove high tension wires from spark plugs and dis-tributor cap. Using an ohmmeter, check resistance of high ten-sion wires while gently twisting wires. If resistance is not to specification, or fluctuates from infinity to any value, replace wires.

#### Resistance (Ohms) Per Wire

| Application | Ohms |
|---|---|
| All wires ....................................................... | 2,500 |

### DISTRIBUTOR

All models use Bosch breakerless electronic ignition and no ad-justment in distributor is necessary.

Fig. 1   Firing Order and Distributor Rotation

### IGNITION TIMING

1) With engine at normal operating temperature, disconnect hose to distributor. Stop engine and connect timing light to No. 1 cylinder wire and tachometer to ignition coil.

**CAUTION** — *Ignition must be off when attaching test equip-ment, as extremely high voltage can cause fatal electrical shock when ignition is on.*

2) Start engine and increase speed to 3000 RPM. Timing should be 31° BTDC. Adjust as necessary by turning dis-tributor. Increase engine speed to 5500 RPM and check that timing is now 33-37° BTDC.

3) Return engine to idle and reconnect vacuum hose to dis-tributor. Timing should now read TDC (±2°). If not, distributor should be removed and tested on machine.

#### Ignition Timing Specifications

| Application | RPM | Timing |
|---|---|---|
| All Models ...................... | 3000 ...................... | 31°BTDC |

Fig. 2   Timing Marks on Crankshaft Pulley

### HOT (SLOW) IDLE

1) With engine at normal operating temperature, disconnect air pump hose at the diverter valve and plug. Stop engine and connect tachometer. Insert gas analyzer probe in tailpipe.

2) Restart engine. Adjust control screw on throttle housing to set RPM to specification. Screw is located behind oil filler con-tainer.

## TUNE-UP (Cont.)

**3)** Adjust mixture by inserting mixture wrench (9134) into funnel opening in air cleaner. Press down to engage mixture screw.

**NOTE** — *Always adjust CO% from lean to rich. (Example: if mixture is too rich, turn idle adjusting screw counterclockwise further than necessary. Then adjust from lean to rich, turning clockwise).*

**4)** Remove wrench and accelerate engine. Check CO% and repeat mixture adjustment if necessary. Recheck idle speed and adjust if necessary. Unplug air hose and reconnect to diverter valve.

### Idle Speed (RPM) & CO Level (%)

| Application | Idle RPM | CO% |
|---|---|---|
| All Models | 750-850 | ①2.0-4.0 |

① — With air pump hose disconnected; measured at tailpipe.

### FUEL PUMP PRESSURE

Pressure (Two electric pumps) ....................................... 65 psi

### EMISSION CONTROL SYSTEMS

See Mitchell Manuals' Emission Control Manual.

## GENERAL SERVICING

### IGNITION

#### DISTRIBUTOR

All models are equipped with Bosch transistorized ignition systems.

**Other Data & Specifications** — See Tune-Up and Bosch Distributors in ELECTRICAL Section.

#### IGNITION COIL

Primary Resistance ......................................... .33-.46 Ohms
Secondary Resistance ........................... 7000-12,000 Ohms

### FUEL SYSTEMS

#### FUEL INJECTION

All models are equipped with Bosch CIS Fuel Injection.

**Other Data & Specifications** — See Tune-Up and Bosch CIS Fuel Injection in FUEL SYSTEMS Section.

### ELECTRICAL

#### BATTERY

**12 Volt** — Negative Ground.

| Application | Amp. Hr. Rating |
|---|---|
| All Models | 88 |

**Battery Location** — Battery is located under spare tire in rear of passenger compartment.

#### STARTER

Bosch ............................................. Overrunning Clutch

Free Speed Voltage ..................... 11.5 at 8500-10,500 RPM
Free Speed Amperage ............. 55-85 at 8500-10,500 RPM

**Other Data & Specifications** — See Bosch Starters in ELECTRICAL Section.

### ALTERNATOR

| Application | Rated Amp. Output |
|---|---|
| All Models | 90 |

**Other Data & Specifications** — See Bosch or Motorola Alternators in ELECTRICAL Section

### ALTERNATOR REGULATOR

All Models use Bosch or Motorola solid state alternator regulators.

**Other Data & Specifications** — See Bosch or Motorola Regulators in ELECTRICAL Section.

### BELT ADJUSTMENT

Tension is correct when belts can be depressed .4" (10 mm) by thumb pressure on center portion of belt.

### FILTERS & CLEANERS

| Filter or Cleaner | Service Interval (Miles) |
|---|---|
| Oil Filter | Replace every 15,000 |
| Air Cleaner | Replace every 15,000 |
| Fuel Filter | Replace every 15,000 |
| Air Pump Filter | Replace every 15,000 |

### CAPACITIES

| Application | Quantity |
|---|---|
| Crankcase (Includes filter) | 8.5 qts. |
| Cooling System | 17 qts. |
| Man. Transaxle (ATF Dexron) | 8 pts. |
| Automatic Transmission (ATF Dexron) | 6.4 qts. |
| Differential (SAE 90) | 4.2 pts. |
| Fuel Tank | ①23 gal. |

① — Including 2.9 gals. reserve.

## TUNE-UP

**R-5**

### ENGINE IDENTIFICATION

Type of vehicle and engine number is marked on a number plate riveted to the left rear side of the engine block. Plate is located just below cylinder head mating surface. First five digits indicate engine type.

#### Engine Codes

| Application | Code |
| --- | --- |
| R-5 | 810-28 |

### MODEL IDENTIFICATION

#### VEHICLE IDENTIFICATION NUMBER

The vehicle identification number is located on a diamond shaped plate in the engine compartment. An oval plate is also used to indicate different models and options. The VIN number is composed of sections "A" and "B" on the diamond plate. Federal or California designations are shown by number "3" on the oval plate. Federal vehicles are numbered 141, California vehicles are numbered 143.

**Fig. 1   Typical Identification Plates**

#### Vehicle Identification Codes

| Application | Codes |
| --- | --- |
| R-5 | R-1228 |

### VALVE TAPPET CLEARANCE

| Application | Intake | Exhaust |
| --- | --- | --- |
| R-5① | .006" (.15 mm) | .008" (.2 mm) |

① — Set valves with engine cold. After 50 minutes cooling, setting would be .007" (.18 mm) for intake and .010" (.25 mm) for exhaust.

### VALVE ARRANGEMENT

R-5 — E-I-I-E-E-I-I-E (Front to Rear)

### SPARK PLUGS

| | |
| --- | --- |
| Gap | .025-.028" (.6-.7 mm) |
| Torque | Maximum 20 ft. lbs. (2.77 mkg) |

#### Spark Plug Type

| Application | AC | Champion |
| --- | --- | --- |
| R-5 | | |
| Federal | 42FS | L87Y |
| Calif. & High Alt. | 43FS | L92Y |

### HIGH TENSION WIRE RESISTANCE

Carefully remove high tension wires from spark plugs and distributor cap. Using an ohmmeter, check resistance of high tension wires while gently twisting wires. If resistance is not to specification, or fluctuates from infinity to any value, replace high tension wire(s).

#### Resistance (Ohms) Per Wire

| Application | Ohms |
| --- | --- |
| All Models | 25,000-30,000 |

### DISTRIBUTOR

| | |
| --- | --- |
| Point Gap | .016-.020" (.4-.5 mm) |
| Cam Angle | |
| R-5 | 55-59° |
| Breaker Arm Spring Tension | 16 ozs. (454 g) |

**Fig. 2   R-5 Firing Order and Distributor Rotation**

### IGNITION TIMING

Check or adjust ignition timing with vacuum line disconnected and plugged and engine running at idle speed. To adjust, turn distributor until specified mark on flywheel is aligned with specified graduation mark on clutch housing. Reconnect distributor vacuum hose.

#### Ignition Timing Specifications

| Application | RPM | Timing (±1°) |
| --- | --- | --- |
| R-5 | | |
| Federal & Calif. | 850 | TDC |
| High Alt. | 800 | TDC |

**Fig. 3   R-5 Timing Mark Location**

## TUNE-UP (Cont.)

### HOT (SLOW) IDLE RPM

1) Cut off air injection system by clamping hose from diverter valve. Warm engine to operating temperature. Connect tachometer and CO meter.

**Fig 4   R-5 Idle and Mixture Adjusting Screws**

2) Turn throttle plate screw until idle speed is 775 RPM. Turn mixture screw to obtain CO reading of .5-3%. Repeat adjustments until mixture is correct and speed is 775 RPM.

3) Remove clamp and check idling speed. It should be between 750 and 850 RPM. Correct by adjusting throttle plate screw, then recheck mixture and CO%.

4) If no CO meter is available, set engine speed at 775 RPM, and using lean drop method, adjust engine for drop of 25 RPM without losing smoothness. Remove air hose clamp and check idle speed.

### Idle Speed (RPM) & CO Level (%)

| Application | Idle RPM | CO% |
|---|---|---|
| R-5 | 750-850 | .5-3.0 |

### FUEL PUMP PRESSURE

R-5 (Mechanical) .......................... 2.5-4 psi (.18-.28 kg/cm²)

### EMISSION CONTROL SYSTEMS

*See Mitchell Manuals' Emission Control Manual.*

## GENERAL SERVICING

### IGNITION

#### DISTRIBUTOR

All models are equipped with Ducellier single point distributors.

**Other Data & Specifications** – *See Tune-Up and Ducellier Distributors in ELECTRICAL Section.*

#### IGNITION COIL

R-5 models use a Mallory 12 volt coil.

**Other Data & Specifications** – *See Tune-Up & Weber Carburetors in FUEL SYSTEMS Section.*

### ELECTRICAL

#### BATTERY

**12 Volt** – Negative Ground.

| Application | Amp. Hr. Rating |
|---|---|
| R-5 | 50 |

#### ALTERNATOR

| Application | Rated Amp. Output |
|---|---|
| R-5 (SEV Marchal) | 50 |

**Other Data & Specifications** – *See SEV Marchal Alternators and Regulators in ELECTRICAL Section.*

#### STARTER

All models are equipped with a Paris Rhone starter.

**Other Data & Specification** – *See Paris Rhone Starters in ELECTRICAL Section.*

#### ALTERNATOR REGULATOR

All models are equipped with a Ducellier regulator with an operating voltage of 13.8-14.8.

**Other Data & Specifications** – *See Ducellier Alternators & Regulators in ELECTRICAL Section.*

### BELT ADJUSTMENT

| Application | ①Deflection |
|---|---|
| Alternator Belt | .22-.26" (5.5-6.5 mm) |
| Water Pump Belt | .10-.14" (2.5-3.5 mm) |
| Air Pump Belt | .31-.39" (8-10 mm) |

① – Deflection is with pressure applied midway on longest belt run.

### FILTERS & CLEANERS

| Filter or Cleaner | Service Interval (Miles) |
|---|---|
| Oil Filter | ①Replace every 13,000 |
| Air Cleaner | Replace every 12,500 |
| Air Pump Filter | Replace every 12,500 |

① – Replace filter after first 6,000 miles, then every 13,000 miles after that.

### CAPACITIES

| Application | Quantity |
|---|---|
| Crankcase (Includes Filter) | |
| R-5 | 3.5 qts. |
| Cooling System (Includes Heater) | |
| R-5 | 6.5 qts. |
| Manual Transmission (SAE 90) | 2 qts. |
| Fuel Tank | |
| R-5 | 10 gals. |

## TUNE-UP

99
Turbo

### ENGINE IDENTIFICATION

Engine number is stamped on a machined pad on engine block below CIS throttle housing.

| Application | Code |
|---|---|
| 99 | |
| Federal Models | |
| Man. Trans. | BI PO6 |
| Auto. Trans. | BI PO3 |
| Calif. Models | |
| Man. Trans. | BI PO4 |
| Auto. Trans. | BI PO5 |
| Turbo | |
| All Models | BSI 20CA |

### MODEL IDENTIFICATION

#### VEHICLE IDENTIFICATION NUMBER

Chassis number is stamped on body under left side of rear seat. Number is also stamped on a plate attached to upper left hand corner of instrument panel and is visible through windshield.

### VALVE TAPPET CLEARANCE

Bring camshaft into correct position for checking valves. Using a suitable go and no-go feeler gauge, check that clearance between valve tappet and heel of cam is to specifications given under "Preliminary Check." If within specifications, no further adjustment is necessary. If not, proceed as follows:

**NOTE** — *Turbo valve clearances are critical. Use only specifications listed for Turbo.*

1) Using special tool (8391450) and a dial indicator, measure clearance of each valve. With measuring point of dial indicator resting on tip of cam, zero dial indicator.

2) Lift valve depressor with special tool and note movement of dial indicator, indicating present valve clearance. Any valve not within "Adjustment Limit" specifications should be adjusted as follows:

3) Remove camshaft, valve depressors and adjusting pads of valves needing adjustment. Measure thickness of adjusting pad with special tool (8391633) and calculate thickness of new pad required to bring valve clearance within "Adjustment Limit" specifications.

4) Measured valve clearance plus adjusting pad thickness equals total distance between valve and cam. This total distance less the specified valve clearance, determines thickness of new adjusting pad to be installed.

5) Install new adjusting pad, valve depressors, and camshaft and recheck that clearances are correct.

### Valve Clearances①

| Application | Clearance |
|---|---|
| 99 | |
| Preliminary Check | |
| Intake | .006-.012" (.15-.30 mm) |
| Exhaust | .014-.020" (.35-.50 mm) |
| Adjustment Limit | |
| Intake | .008-.010" (.20-.25 mm) |
| Exhaust | .016-.018" (.40-.45 mm) |
| Turbo | |
| Preliminary Check | |
| Intake | .008-.010" (.20-.25 mm) |
| Exhaust | .018-.020" (.45-.50 mm) |
| Adjustment Limit | |
| Intake | .010" (.25 mm) |
| Exhaust | .020" (.50 mm) |

① — When checked 30 minutes after driving vehicle at normal operating temperature.

### VALVE ARRANGEMENT

E-I-I-E-E-I-I-E (front to rear).

### SPARK PLUGS

| | |
|---|---|
| Gap | .024-.028" (.6-.7 mm) |
| Torque | 18- 22 ft. lbs. (2.5-3.0 mkg) |

### Spark Plug Type

| Application | Bosch No. | NGK No. |
|---|---|---|
| All | W 175 T 30 | BP-6ES |

### HIGH TENSION WIRE RESISTANCE

Carefully remove high tension wires from spark plugs and distributor cap. Using an ohmmeter, check high tension wire resistance while gently twisting wires. If resistance is not to specifications, or fluctuates from infinity to any value, replace high tension wire(s).

### Resistance (Ohms) Per Wire

| Application | Ohms |
|---|---|
| All Models | |
| Wires to Cylinder 1 & 2 | 2600-3900 |
| Wires to Cylinder 3 & 4 | 2400-3600 |
| Wire from Coil to Distributor | 800-1200 |

*Fig. 1  Firing Order and Distributor Rotation*

## TUNE-UP (Cont.)

### DISTRIBUTOR

All models are equipped with Bosch breakerless electronic ignition systems. No adjustments are required for distributor.

### IGNITION TIMING

**1)** Connect tachometer and timing light. Disconnect vacuum hose and place transmission in neutral position. Check timing at 2000 RPM.

**2)** If not within specifications, loosen distributor retaining screw and rotate distributor housing. Turn clockwise for earlier ignition; counterclockwise for later.

**3)** Reconnect vacuum hose and adjust engine idle speed.

#### Ignition Timing Specifications

| Application | RPM | Timing |
|---|---|---|
| All Models | 2000 | 20° BTDC |

**Fig. 2   Location of Saab 99 & Turbo Timing Marks**

### HOT (SLOW) IDLE RPM

**1)** Remove thick hose at charcoal canister. On vehicles with air injection, remove and plug hose from air pump. On all models with Lambda system, disconnect oxygen sensor.

**CAUTION** — *Do not allow disconnected wire from Lambda oxygen sensor to touch an engine or chassis ground.*

**2)** With engine at normal operating temperature, adjust idle speed to specifications by turning adjusting screw on throttle valve by-pass duct. See *Fig. 3*.

**3)** Check CO level and, if necessary, adjust using Allen "T" wrench (8392482) to turn adjustment screw in air flow sensor. Turn clockwise to richen mixture.

**4)** Repeat idle speed and mixture adjustments until specified idle speed and CO% is obtained.

**CAUTION** — *Remove Allen "T" wrench from adjustment screw after each adjustment. If key is left in screw and engine is accelerated, lever could be damaged.*

**5)** Replace hoses and oxygen sensor wire. Then, recheck idle speed and adjust if necessary.

**Fig. 3   Adjusting Idle Speed**

#### Idle Speed (RPM) & CO Level (%)

| Application | RPM | CO% |
|---|---|---|
| 99 | | |
| Federal | 825-925 | .5-2.0 |
| Calif. & High Alt. | 825-925 | ①.75 |
| Turbo | | |
| All Models | 825-925 | ①.75 |

① — With sensor disconnected. With sensor connected, a maximum of .4% is permissible. Permissible deviation while checking is .25-1%.

### DECEL VALVE ADJUSTMENT

**1)** To adjust the decel valve, located in the inlet manifold and connected by means of a hose to the throttle housing, connect a tachometer and run engine until warm.

**2)** Unscrew the adjusting screw until valve closes completely. Set specified idle speed by adjusting idling adjusting screw. Turn down adjusting screw until engine speed is 1600 RPM.

**3)** Then back off adjusting screw two turns. Set specified idling speed with the idling adjusting screw. Check deceleration time and make any necessary fine adjustments.

**CAUTION** — *To prevent faulty deceleration readings, disconnect cooling fan cable from thermal switch during check.*

**4)** To check deceleration valve, increase engine speed to 3000 RPM. Release throttle and note how long it takes for engine to return to idle speed. Be sure engine is warm.

#### Deceleration Time Requirements

| Application | Time Required |
|---|---|
| Federal & Calif. | 4-6 seconds |
| High Alt. | 3-4 seconds |

## TUNE-UP (Cont.)

### FUEL PUMP PRESSURE

Pressure ....................................... 64-72 psi (4.5-5.1 kg/cm²)
Volume ............................ ①45.7 cu. in. (750 cc)/30 seconds

① — Measured in return fuel line.

### EMISSION CONTROL SYSTEMS

*See Mitchell Manuals' Emission Control Manual.*

## GENERAL SERVICING

### IGNITION

#### DISTRIBUTOR

All models are equipped with Bosch electronic breakerless distributors.

**Other Data & Specifications** — *See Tune-Up and Bosch Distributors in ELECTRICAL Section.*

#### IGNITION COIL

| Resistance | At 75°F (23°C) |
|---|---|
| Primary | 1.05-1.35 Ohms |
| Secondary | 5500-8500 Ohms |

### FUEL SYSTEMS

#### FUEL INJECTION

All models are equipped with Bosch Continuous Injection System (CIS). On California and Turbo models, the Lambda system is also used, with an oxygen sensor, feedback system and catalytic converter.

**Other Data & Specifications** — *For Federal Models, see Tune-Up and Bosch Continuous Injection System (CIS) in FUEL SYSTEMS Section. For California Models, see Tune-Up and Bosch Lambda Continuous Injection System in FUEL SYSTEMS Section.*

### ELECTRICAL

#### BATTERY

**12 Volt** — Negative Ground.

| Application | Amp. Hr. Rating |
|---|---|
| All Models | 60 |

**Battery Location** — In engine compartment on right side.

#### STARTER

| Bosch | Overrunning Clutch |
|---|---|
| Free Speed Voltage | 11.5 at 6500-8500 RPM |
| Free Speed Amperage | 35-55 at 6500-8500 RPM |

**Other Data & Specifications** — *See Bosch Starters in ELECTRICAL Section.*

### ALTERNATOR

| Application | Rated Amp. Output |
|---|---|
| 99 Models | 55 |
| Turbo Models | 65 |

**Other Data & Specifications** — *See S.E.V. Marchal and Bosch Alternators and Regulators in ELECTRICAL Section.*

### ALTERNATOR REGULATOR

All models are equipped with S.E.V. Marchal or Bosch alternator regulators.

**Other Data & Specifications** — *See S.E.V. Marchal and Bosch Alternators and Regulators in ELECTRICAL Section.*

### FILTERS & CLEANERS

| Filter or Cleaner | Service Interval (Miles) |
|---|---|
| Oil Filter | Replace every 5000 |
| Air Cleaner | Replace every 15,000 |
| Fuel Filter | Replace every 15,000 |
| Charcoal Canister | ①Replace every 30,000 |

① — First change at 15,000 miles.

### BELT ADJUSTMENT

| Application | ①Deflection |
|---|---|
| Alternator Belt | .4"(10 mm) |

① — Deflection is with 3.3 lbs (1.5 kg) pressure applied midway on longest belt run.

### CAPACITIES

| Application | Quantity |
|---|---|
| Crankcase (Includes Filter) | 3.7 qts. |
| Cooling System | 8.5 qts. |
| Man. Trans. including Final Drive (SAE 10-30W) | 2.6 qts. |
| Auto. Trans. (Dexron) | 8.5 qts. |
| Auto. Trans. Final Drive (SAE 80) | 1.3 qts. |
| Fuel Tank | 14.5 gals. |

# 1978 Subaru 4 Tune-Up

## TUNE-UP

**1600
BRAT**

## ENGINE IDENTIFICATION

Engine can be identified by a letter-number combination stamped on machined pad on side of engine, near distributor (below carburetor). Engine codes are as follows:

4-Speed Transmission
Federal ......................................... EA71AA
California ...................................... EA71AC
High Altitude ................................ EA71AH
4-Speed 4-WD (Including BRAT)
Federal ......................................... EA71WA
California ...................................... EA71WC
High Altitude ................................ EA71WH
5-Speed Transmission
Federal ......................................... EA71GA
California ...................................... EA71GC
High Altitude ................................ EA71GH
Automatic Transmission
Federal ......................................... EA71TA
California ...................................... EA71TC
High Altitude ................................ EA71TH

## MODEL IDENTIFICATION

The vehicle identification number is located on the left side of the instrument panel and is visible through the windshield. The chassis number may be found on firewall in engine compartment.

## COMPRESSION PRESSURE

Check pressure with engine warm, plugs removed, throttle valve wide open and engine at cranking speed. Pressure should be as specified with a variation of 7 psi (.5 kg/cm²) maximum between cylinders.

| Application | Pressure | |
| --- | --- | --- |
| | psi | (kg/cm²) |
| 1600 @ 250 RPM | 149 | (10.5) |
| 1600 @ 350 RPM | 156 | (10.97) |

## VALVE TAPPET CLEARANCE

With engine cold, bring piston to be checked to top dead center of compression stroke. Loosen lock nuts and turn adjusting screws to proper clearance. Adjust valves in firing order sequence (1-3-2-4) using valve clearance adjusting tool 398760100 (or equivalent).

### Valve Clearance Specifications

| Application | Clearance | |
| --- | --- | --- |
| Intake | .009-.011" | (.23-.27 mm) |
| Exhaust | .013-.015" | (.33-.37 mm) |

## VALVE ARRANGEMENT

I-E-E-I (both banks, front to rear).

## SPARK PLUGS

Gap .......................................................... .032" (.8 mm)
Torque.......................... 13-17 ft. lbs. (1.8-2.4 mkg)

### Spark Plug Type

| Manufacturer | Spark Plug No. |
| --- | --- |
| NGK | BP6ES |
| Nippondenso | W20EP |
| Hitachi | L45PW |

## HIGH TENSION WIRE RESISTANCE

Carefully remove high tension wires from spark plugs and ignition coil. Remove distributor cap with wires still in place. Using an ohmmeter, check high tension wire resistance between free end of wire and distributor cap electrode. If resistance is not to specifications, or fluctuates from infinity to any value, replace high tension wire(s).

### Resistance (Ohms) Per Wire

| Application | Ohms |
| --- | --- |
| All Models | 15,000 (Max.) |

**Fig. 1   Firing Order and Distributor Rotation**

## DISTRIBUTOR

Point Gap (Federal) ...................... .016-.020" (.40-.50 mm)
Air Gap (California)
 Nippondenso ................................ .008-.016" (.20-.40 mm)
 Hitachi ........................................ .012-.016" (.30-.40 mm)
Cam Angle ................................................... 49-55°
Breaker Arm Spring Tension ............ 14-19 oz. (.40-.55 kg)
Condenser Capacity ..................................... .22 mfd

## IGNITION TIMING

**1)** Adjust timing with shift lever in "N" or "P" position. Disconnect and plug vacuum hoses from distributor retard and advance mechanism. Connect timing light to No. 1 cylinder ignition wire.

## TUNE-UP (Cont.)

**2)** Adjust engine idle speed to 850 RPM for Federal and 900 RPM for California models. To set timing, loosen distributor lock down bolt and turn distributor to specified setting. Tighten lock down bolt.

### Timing Specifications

| Application | RPM | Timing |
|---|---|---|
| Federal | 850 | 8°BTDC |
| California | 900 | 8°BTDC |

**Fig. 2  Subaru Timing Marks on Flywheel**

## IDLE SPEED & MIXTURE

Be sure ignition timing and valve clearance are to specifications. Adjust with air cleaner in place.

### USING CO METER

**With AIR Disconnected — 1)** Warm engine to normal operating temperature. Disconnect air suction hose from silencer. Cap open end of silencer with tape.

**2)** Adjust both throttle adjusting screw and idle mixture adjusting screw to obtain the specified idle speed and CO percentage.

### Idle Speed (RPM) & CO Level (%) Without AIR①

| Application | Idle RPM | CO% |
|---|---|---|
| Federal | 850 | 1.0-2.0 |
| California | 900 | 0.5-1.0 |

① — Shift lever in "N" or "P".

**With AIR Connected — 1)** Remove tape from end of silencer. Connect the air suction hose from the air cleaner to the silencer.

**2)** Check that idle and CO level are to following specifications without further adjustment:

### Idle Speed (RPM) & CO Level (%) With AIR①

| Application | Idle RPM | CO% |
|---|---|---|
| Federal | 850 | 0.5-1.5 |
| California | 900 | 0.1-0.5 |

① — Shift lever in "N" or "P".

## COLD (FAST) IDLE RPM

With cam adjusting lever on fourth step of fast idle cam, primary throttle valve opening angle and clearance should be as follows. If not, adjust fast idle screw.

### Fast Idle Specifications

| Application | Throttle Valve Opening Angle | Clearance Valve-to-Body |
|---|---|---|
| Federal | 16° | .043" (1.09 mm) |
| Calif. & High Alt. | 19° | .060" (1.53 mm) |

**NOTE** — *Repair carburetors (DCJ306-8) are adjusted to Federal Low Altitude specifications. For use on California models, readjust primary throttle valve opening angle from 16° to 19° by turning fast idle adjusting screw 3 turns clockwise.*

## EMISSION CONTROL SYSTEMS

*See Mitchell Manuals' Emission Control Manual.*

# GENERAL SERVICING

## IGNITION

### DISTRIBUTORS

Nippondenso single point distributors are used on all Federal and High Altitude vehicles. Nippondenso breakerless distributors are used on California vehicles with manual transmissions, and Hitachi breakerless distributors on California vehicles with automatic transmissions.

**Other Data & Specifications** — *See Tune-Up and Hitachi and Nippondenso Distributors in ELECTRICAL section.*

# 1978 Subaru 4 Tune-Up

## GENERAL SERVICING (Cont.)

### IGNITION COIL

| Resistance | Ohms |
|---|---|
| **Primary** | |
| Hitachi | |
| Federal & High Altitude | 1.35-1.65 |
| California (Auto. Trans.) | .81-.99 |
| Nippondenso | |
| California (Man. Trans.) | 1.33-1.63 |
| **Secondary** | |
| Hitachi | |
| Federal & High Altitude | 6,800-10,200 |
| California (Auto. Trans.) | 8,500-12,900 |
| Nippondenso | |
| California (Man. Trans.) | 11,100-13,700 |

## FUEL SYSTEMS

### FUEL PUMP

12 Volt Electromagnetic Fuel Pump.

### CARBURETORS

| Application | Model |
|---|---|
| High Altitude | Hitachi DCJ306-9 |
| All Other Models | Hitachi DCJ306-8 |

**Other Data & Specifications** — *See Tune-Up and Hitachi Carburetors in FUEL SYSTEMS section.*

## ELECTRICAL

### BATTERY

12 Volt — Negative Ground.

| Application | Amp. Hr. Capacity |
|---|---|
| All | 60 |

**Battery Location** — Engine compartment; front.

### STARTER

Nippondenso — Magnetic Switch Type

| | |
|---|---|
| Free Speed Voltage | |
| All Models | 11 at 5000 RPM |
| Free Speed Amperage | |
| All Models | 50 (Max.) at 5000 RPM |

**Other Data & Specifications** — *See Nippondenso Starters in ELECTRICAL Section.*

### ALTERNATOR

| Application | Rated Amp. Output |
|---|---|
| All Models | 50 |

**Other Data & Specifications** — *See Hitachi Alternators and Regulators in ELECTRICAL Section.*

### ALTERNATOR REGULATOR

All models are equipped with Hitachi alternator regulators with an operating voltage of 14.0-14.5 volts.

**Other Data & Specifications** — *See Hitachi Alternators and Regulators in ELECTRICAL Section.*

## ENGINE

### INTAKE MANIFOLD TIGHTENING

Tighten intake manifold attaching bolts to 13-16 ft. lbs. (1.8-2.2 mkg).

### BELT ADJUSTMENT

| Application | ①Deflection |
|---|---|
| 4-Wheel Drive Models | .35-.43" (9-11 mm) |
| All Other Models | .51-.55" (13-14 mm) |

① — Deflection is with 22 lbs. (10 kg) pressure applied midway on longest belt run.

### FILTERS & CLEANERS

| Filter or Cleaner | Service Interval (Miles) |
|---|---|
| Oil Filter (BRAT) | Replace every 5000 |
| Oil Filter (All Others) | Replace every 6250 |
| Air Cleaner | Replace every 12,500 |
| Fuel Filter | Replace every 12,500 |
| Charcoal Canister Filter | Replace every 25,000 |

### CAPACITIES

| Application | Quantity |
|---|---|
| Crankcase (Includes Filter) | ①3.8 qts. |
| Cooling System | 6.3 qts. |
| **Transmission** | |
| Manual | |
| 4-Speed (SAE 85-90W) | 2.64 qts. |
| 5-Speed (SAE 85-90W) | 2.85 qts. |
| 4-Speed w/4WD (SAE 80-85W) | 3.17 qts. |
| Automatic (Dexron) | 5.9-6.3 qts. |
| **Differential** | |
| 4-Wheel Drive | 0.85 qts. |
| Automatic Transmission | 0.9-1.3 qts. |
| **Fuel Tank** | |
| Sedan, Coupe & Hardtop | 13.2 gals. |
| Station Wagon, 4-WD, BRAT | 11.9 gals. |

① — 3.5 qts. without filter.

## TUNE-UP

Celica
Corolla
Corona
Pickup

## ENGINE IDENTIFICATION

Each engine serial number contains an identifying engine code number. Engine codes are the first group of numbers and letters on Corolla models and the last group on other models.

On Corolla 1166 cc engines (3K-C), the serial number appears on the right side of the cylinder block below the spark plugs. On Corolla 1588 cc engines (2T-C), the serial number appears on the left side behind dipstick.

Engine serial numbers of Celica, Corona and Pickup models, featuring the 2189 cc engine (20R), are on right side of cylinder block. Engine codes are as follows:

### Engine Codes

| Application | Displacement | Code |
|---|---|---|
| Corolla | 1166 cc | 3K-C |
| Corolla | 1588 cc | 2T-C |
| Corona, Celica & Pickup | 2189 cc | 20R |

## MODEL IDENTIFICATION

### VEHICLE IDENTIFICATION NUMBER

Vehicle identification number is located on top of instrument panel on all models, and on firewall of engine compartment on all but Pickup models. On Pickups, number appears on front left fender apron, near windshield fluid tank. First two digits of number identify engine and model series.

| Application | Engine | Model Code |
|---|---|---|
| Corolla | | |
| 1166 cc | 3K-C | KE |
| 1588 cc | 2T-C | TE |
| Corona | 20R | RT |
| Celica | 20R | RA |
| Pickup | 20R | RN |

## COMPRESSION PRESSURE

With engine at normal operating temperature, spark plugs removed, throttle valve wide open and engine at cranking speed, compression pressures should be as follows with a maximum variation between cylinders of 14 psi (1 kg/cm²):

| Application | Stand. Pressure psi(kg/cm²) | Min. Pressure psi(kg/cm²) |
|---|---|---|
| Corolla | | |
| Calif. & Alt. | 164(11.5) | 121(8.5) |
| Federal | 171(12) | 128(9) |

## VALVE TAPPET CLEARANCE

Check or adjust valve clearance with engine at normal operating temperature.

## Valve Clearance Specifications

| Application | Intake | Exhaust |
|---|---|---|
| Corolla (2T-C) | .008" (.20 mm) | .013"(.33 mm) |
| All Other Models | .008" (.20 mm) | .012"(.30 mm) |

## VALVE ARRANGEMENTS

Corolla (3K-C) — E-I-I-E-E-I-I-E (front to rear)
All Other Models
Right Side — All Intake
Left Side — All Exhaust

Fig. 1   *Firing Order and Distributor Rotation (Corolla — 3K-C & 2T-C Engines)*

Fig. 2   *Firing Order and Distributor Rotation (Corona, Celica & Pickup — 20R Engine)*

## SPARK PLUGS

| | |
|---|---|
| Gap | .031"(.8 mm) |
| Torque | 11-15 ft. lbs.(1.5-2.1 mkg) |

### Spark Plug Type

| Application | NGK No. | Nippondenso No. |
|---|---|---|
| All Models | BP5ES-L | W16EP |

## HIGH TENSION WIRE RESISTANCE

Carefully remove high tension wires from spark plugs and distributor cap. Using an ohmmeter, check high tension wire resistance while gently twisting wires. If resistance is not to specifications, or fluctuates from infinity to any value, replace high tension wire(s).

### Resistance (Ohms) Per Wire

| Application | Ohms |
|---|---|
| All Models | 25,000 Maximum |

# 1978 Toyota 4 Tune-Up

## TUNE-UP (Cont.)

### DISTRIBUTOR

All models use transistorized ignition which eliminates breaker points. Reluctor-to-pickup air gap is the only adjustment. Measure air gap with a non-magnetic feeler gauge and move pickup if necessary to correct air gap.

All models ............................................. .008-.016" (.2-.4 mm)

### IGNITION TIMING

With engine at normal operating temperature, connect a tachometer. Check air gap in distributor, then start engine and adjust to correct idle speed. Adjust timing as follows with transmission in "N" position:

### COROLLA (3K-C ENGINE)

Pinch off vacuum line to hot idle compensation (HIC) valve on air cleaner and vacuum line to 4-way connector from carburetor heat insulator. Check timing with timing light and turn distributor to correct.

**Fig. 3   Ignition Timing Mark Locations**

### COROLLA (2T-C ENGINE)

**Engines Without High Altitude Compensation (HAC) –**
1) Check timing with timing light. If not to specifications, turn distributor to correct. If only slightly out of adjustment turn octane selector on distributor.

2) If engine has cold weather distributor, pinch hose between Bimetal Vacuum Switching Valve (BVSV) and carburetor. Timing should read 20° BTDC. Tighten clamp securely.

**Engines With High Altitude Compensation (HAC) – 1)**
Disconnect hose between HAC valve and distributor. Plug end of hose removed from distributor sub-diaphragm. Timing should be 10° BTDC at 700-900 RPM.

2) If not within specifications, turn distributor or for minor adjustment, adjust octane selector on distributor. Reconnect hose

to sub-diaphragm and recheck timing for about 20° BTDC. If still not to specification, pinch hose between HAC valve and three-way connector. Timing should be 20° BTDC.

### ALL OTHER MODELS (20R ENGINE)

**Engines Without High Altitude Compensation (HAC) –**
Timing should be 8° BTDC at 800 RPM (man. trans.) or 850 RPM (auto. trans.). Correct timing by adjusting octane selector or by turning distributor.

**Engines With High Altitude Compensation (HAC) – 1)**
Disconnect hose between HAC valve and plug end removed from distributor sub-diaphragm. Timing should be 8° BTDC at 700-900 RPM.

**2)** If out of specification, adjust octane selector or turn distributor. Reconnect hose to sub-diaphragm. Timing should now be about 13° BTDC.

**3)** If still about 8° BTDC, pinch vacuum hose between HAC valve and three-way connector. Timing should then be 13° BTDC.

#### Ignition Timing Specifications

| Application | RPM | Timing |
|---|---|---|
| Corolla (3K-C) | 750 | 8° BTDC |
| Corolla (2T-C)① | 850 | 10° BTDC |
| All Other Models② | | |
| Man. Trans. | 800 | 8° BTDC |
| Auto. Trans. | 850 | 8° BTDC |

① – With HAC, hose disconnected, 10° BTDC@700-900 RPM. After reconnecting hose, 20° BTDC.

② – With HAC, hose disconnected, 8° BTDC@700-900 RPM. After reconnecting hose, 13° BTDC.

### HOT (SLOW) IDLE RPM

1) With engine at normal operating temperature and ignition timing to specification, be sure choke valve is fully open and all accessories are in "OFF" position. Place transmission in neutral and see that air cleaner is installed, vacuum lines connected, and carburetor fuel level is correct. On 3K-C engine, pinch off vacuum lines to HIC valve and 4-way connector (EVAP hose).

2) Adjust idle speed to maximum by means of idle mixture screw. Adjust idle speed to specified mixture adjustment speed by means of idle speed adjusting screw. Continue adjusting screws until maximum speed obtainable by idle mixture screw is same as mixture adjustment speed. Then screw in idle mixture screw to obtain specified initial idle speed.

#### Idle Speed and Mixture

| Application | Mixture Adjust. RPM | Initial Idle RPM |
|---|---|---|
| Corolla (3K-C) | 830 | 700-800 |
| Corolla (2T-C) | | |
| Federal | 920 | 800-900 |
| Calif. & High Alt. | 910 | 800-900 |
| All Other Models (20R) | | |
| Man. Trans. | 870 | 750-850 |
| Auto. Trans. | 920 | 800-900 |

## TUNE-UP (Cont.)

**Fig. 4 Carburetor Adjusting Screws**

### COLD (FAST) IDLE RPM

1) With engine at normal operating temperature, close choke and throttle valves. On models equipped with 20R engine, disconnect EGR vacuum hose from valve and pinch the vacuum hose between the advancer port and the TVSV or VTV valves.

**NOTE** — *This is the Thermostatic Vacuum Switching Valve on Corona and Celica models; the Vacuum Transmitting Valve on Pickups.*

2) Start engine without stepping on accelerator pedal. Check engine speed against fast idle specifications. Adjust by turning fast idle adjusting screw. Replace all hoses.

3) On vehicles with 20R engine, release hose and reconnect EGR valve.

**Fast Idle Specifications**

| Application | RPM |
|---|---|
| Corolla (3K-C) ................................................ | ① |
| Corolla (2T-C) | |
|   Federal ..................................................... | 3000-3400 |
|   Calif. & High Altitude ............................. | 2800-3200 |
| All Other Models (20R) ................................. | 2200-2600 |

① — No fast idle on this model.
② — With EGR hose disconnected and main vacuum hose pinched off.

### AUTOMATIC CHOKE

On 2T-C engines, an electric assist choke is used. The system consists of a choke breaker diaphragm, an electrically-heated bimetal choke cap, and a choke control relay. On 20R engines, the system consists of a choke breaker diaphragm and a coolant water-heated bimetal choke cap.

### FUEL PUMP PRESSURE & VOLUME

| Pressure | |
|---|---|
| Corolla ....................................... | 2.8-4.3 psi(.2-.3 kg/cm²) |
| All Other Models ...................... | 2.1-4.3 psi(.15-.3 kg/cm²) |
| Volume | |
| Corolla ................................... | ①.9 pts. in 30 sec. |
| All Other Models ................................... | 1.3 pts. in 30 sec. |

① — Models with electric fuel pumps — 1.3 pts. in 30 sec.

### EMISSION CONTROL SYSTEMS

See Mitchell Manuals' Emission Control Manual.

## GENERAL SERVICING

### IGNITION

#### DISTRIBUTOR

All models are equipped with transistorized ignition systems.

**Other Data & Specifications** — *See Tune-Up and Nippondenso Distributors in ELECTRICAL Section.*

#### IGNITION COIL

| Resistance | Ohms |
|---|---|
| Primary | |
|   All Models ........................................................ | 1.3-1.7 |
| Secondary | |
|   All Models ................................................. | 12,000-16,000 |

### FUEL SYSTEMS

#### CARBURETORS

| Application | Make |
|---|---|
| All Models ........................................................ | Aisan 2-Bbl. |

**Other Data & Specifications** — *See Tune-Up and Aisan Carburetors in FUEL SYSTEMS Section.*

### ELECTRICAL

#### BATTERY

**12 Volt** — Negative Ground.

## GENERAL SERVICING (Cont.)

| Application | Amp. Hr. Rating |
|---|---|
| Corolla (3K-C) | 48 |
| All Other Models | |
| Standard | 50 |
| Optional | 60 |

**Battery Location** — In engine compartment.

### STARTER

All models are equipped with Nippondenso starters.

Free Speed Voltage
| | |
|---|---|
| Corolla (3K-C) | |
| Reduction Gear | 11@3500 RPM |
| Conventional | 11@5000 RPM |
| Corolla (2T-C) | |
| Reduction Gear | 11.5@3500 RPM |
| Conventional | 11.5@4000 RPM |
| All Other Models (20R) | |
| Reduction Gear | 11.5@3500 RPM |
| Conventional | 11@5000 RPM |

Free Speed Amperage
| | |
|---|---|
| Corolla (3K-C) | |
| Reduction Gear | 55@3500 RPM |
| Conventional | 50@5000 RPM |
| Corolla (2T-C) | |
| Reduction Gear | 90@3500 RPM |
| Conventional | 90@4000 RPM |
| All Other Models (20R) | |
| Reduction Gear | 80@3500 RPM |
| Conventional | 50@5000 RPM |

**Other Data & Specifications** — See Nippondenso Starters in ELECTRICAL Section.

### ALTERNATOR

| Application | Rated Amp. Output |
|---|---|
| Corolla (3K-C) | 50 |
| Corolla (2T-C) | 40, 50 |
| All Other Models | |
| Standard | 40 |
| Optional | 45, 55 |

**Other Data & Specifications** — See Nippondenso Alternators and Regulators in ELECTRICAL Section.

### ALTERNATOR REGULATOR

All models are equipped with Nippondenso alternator regulators with an operating voltage of 13.8-14.8 volts.

**Other Data & Specifications** — See Nippondenso Alternators and Regulators in ELECTRICAL Section.

## ENGINE

### INTAKE MANIFOLD TIGHTENING

| Application | Ft. Lbs. (mkg) |
|---|---|
| Corolla (3K-C) | 13-18 (1.8-2.5) |
| Corolla (2T-C) | 15-22 (2.0-3.0) |
| All Other Models (20R) | 11-15 (1.5-2.1) |

### FILTERS & CLEANERS

| Filter or Cleaner | Service Interval (Miles) |
|---|---|
| Oil Filter | Replace every 7,500 |
| Air Filter | Replace every 30,000 |
| Fuel Filter | Replace every 30,000 |
| PCV Valve | Replace every 30,000 |
| Charcoal Canister | Replace every 60,000 |

### BELT ADJUSTMENT

| Application | ①Deflection |
|---|---|
| Fan Belt | |
| Corolla (2T-C) | .31-.47" (8-12 mm) |
| All Other Models | .31-.51" (8-13 mm) |
| Air Pump Belt | |
| Corolla | .51-.71" (13-18 mm) |
| All Other Models | .31-.51" (8-13 mm) |
| A/C Belt | .43-.55" (11-14 mm) |

① — Deflection is with 22 lbs. (10 kg) pressure applied midway on longest belt run.

### CAPACITIES

| Application | Quantity |
|---|---|
| Crankcase (Includes Filter) | |
| Corolla (3K-C) | 3.7 qts. |
| Corolla (2T-C) | 4.6 qts. |
| Corona & Celica | 5.3 qts. |
| Pickup | 4.8 qts. |
| Cooling System | |
| Corolla (3K-C) | 5.8 qts. |
| Corolla (2T-C) | 8.1 qts. |
| All Other Models | 7.4 qts. |
| Man. Trans. | |
| Corolla (3K-C) | |
| 4-Speed | 3.6 pts. |
| 5-Speed | 5.2 pts. |
| Corolla (2T-C) | 3.2 pts. |
| Corona & Celica | |
| 4-Speed | 5.8 pts. |
| 5-Speed | 5.4 pts. |
| Pickup | |
| 4-Speed | 4 pts. |
| 5-Speed | 5.6 pts. |
| Auto. Trans. | |
| All Models | 6.7 qts. |
| Rear Axle | |
| Corolla (3K-C) | 2.2 pts. |
| Corolla (2T-C) | |
| 6.38" Differential | 2.2 pts. |
| 6.7" Differential | 2.6 pts. |
| Pickup | 3.4 pts. |
| All Other Models | 2.6 pts. |
| Fuel Tank | |
| Corolla | |
| Sedan and Hardtop | 13.2 gals. |
| Station Wagon | 12.4 gals. |
| Corona & Celica | 16.1 gals. |
| Pickup | |
| Short Bed | 12.2 gals. |
| Long Bed | 16.1 gals. |

## TUNE-UP

**Cressida**
**Land Cruiser**

### ENGINE IDENTIFICATION

Engines can be identified by prefix of engine serial number. Serial number is stamped on left side of block on Cressida; on right side of block on Land Cruiser.

#### Engine Model Number

| Application | Engine Number |
|---|---|
| Cressida ............................................................ | 4M |
| Land Cruiser ...................................................... | 2F |

### MODEL IDENTIFICATION

#### VEHICLE IDENTIFICATION NUMBER

The vehicle identification number is located on the firewall, top of dash, and driver's door post on Cressida models. Land Cruiser number is on right front fender apron on Land Cruiser and left front fender apron on station wagon models.

### COMPRESSION PRESSURE

Check compression pressure with engine at normal operating temperature, all spark plugs removed, throttle valve wide open and engine at cranking speed. Maximum variation between cylinders should not exceed 14 psi (1.0 kg/cm²). Standard and minimum pressures are as follows:

| Application | Standard psi (kg/cm²) | Minimum psi (kg/cm²) |
|---|---|---|
| Cressida ..................... | 156 (11) | 128 (9) |
| Land Cruiser .............. | 149 (10.5) | 114 (8) |

### VALVE TAPPET CLEARANCE

**NOTE** — *Check or adjust valve clearance with engine at normal operating temperature.*

| Application | Intake | Exhaust |
|---|---|---|
| Cressida ................. | .011" (.28 mm) | .014" (.36 mm) |
| Land Cruiser ........... | .008" (.21 mm) | .014" (.36 mm) |

#### VALVE ARRANGEMENT

**Cressida** — All valves on left side are intake, all on right side are exhaust (viewed from driver's seat).

**Land Cruiser** — E-I-I-E-E-I-I-E-E-I-I-E (front-to-rear).

### SPARK PLUGS

Gap
Cressida .................................................... .036" (0.9 mm)
Land Cruiser ............................................. .039" (1.0 mm)
Torque ..................................... 10-15 ft. lbs. (1.4-2.1 mkg)

**Fig. 1   Cressida Firing Order and Distributor Rotation**

**Fig. 2   Land Cruiser Firing Order and Distributor Rotation**

#### Spark Plug Type

| Application | NGK | Nippondenso |
|---|---|---|
| Cressida ..................... | BPR5ES | W16EPR |
| Land Cruiser ................. | BP5EZ | W14EX |

### HIGH TENSION WIRE RESISTANCE

Carefully remove high tension wires from spark plugs and distributor cap. Using an ohmmeter, check high tension wire resistance while gently twisting wires. If resistance is not to specifications, or fluctuates from infinity to any value, replace high tension wire(s).

#### Resistance (Ohms) Per Wire

| Application | Ohms |
|---|---|
| All Models .................................................... | 16,000-25,000 |

### DISTRIBUTOR

Both the Cressida (with 4M engine) and Land Cruiser (with 2F engine) are fitted with Nippondenso Transistorized Electronic Ignition Systems. The only in-service adjustment possible to distributor is the air gap. Measurement for air gap is in the table.

Air Gap ............................................. .008-.016" (.2-.4 mm)

## TUNE-UP (Cont.)

### IGNITION TIMING

**1)** Check or adjust ignition timing with engine at normal operating temperature and choke valve fully open. Connect tachometer and dwell meter to engine. See that idle speed and cam angle are set to specifications and distributor vacuum line is connected.

**2)** To adjust timing, loosen distributor clamp and rotate distributor until timing is to specification.

#### Ignition Timing Specifications

| Application | RPM | Timing |
|---|---|---|
| Cressida | 750 | 10° BTDC |
| Land Cruiser | 650 | 7° BTDC |

*Fig. 3  Cressida Timing Marks
(Crankshaft Pulley)*

7° BTDC Mark
On Flywheel

*Fig. 4  Land Cruiser Timing Marks
(Flywheel Window)*

### HOT (SLOW) IDLE RPM

**1)** With engine at normal operating temperature, choke valve fully open, all accessories off, all vacuum lines connected, ignition timing set to specifications and transmission in neutral, check that fuel level is aligned with dot on sight glass of carburetor float bowl. Adjust float level if necessary.

**2)** With air cleaner installed, adjust idle mixture screw until fastest idle RPM is obtained. Then, adjust idle speed screw until specified mixture adjustment RPM is achieved.

**3)** Repeat procedure until RPM cannot be increased by adjusting mixture screw. Set idle to specified initial idle RPM by adjusting idle speed screw in a clockwise direction.

#### Idle Speed Specifications

| Application | Mixture Adjust. RPM | Initial Idle RPM |
|---|---|---|
| Cressida | 820 | 750 |
| Land Cruiser | 690 | 650 |

*Fig. 5  Carburetor Adjusting Screw Locations*

### COLD (FAST) IDLE RPM

**Cressida** — With engine stopped, disconnect and plug hose from choke opener diaphragm. Close choke valve. Start engine without touching accelerator. Adjust fast idle speed screw until engine reaches specified speed. Reconnect hose and check operation.

**Land Cruiser** — Pull choke knob out fully. On California and High Altitude models, clamp the hose coming from the EGR port. Open choke valve with a screwdriver and start engine. Adjust to correct speed, then push knob in, unclamp hose, and check for proper operation.

#### Fast Idle Specifications

| Application | RPM |
|---|---|
| Cressida | 2300-2700 |
| Land Cruiser | ①1600-2000 |

① — Calif. & High Alt. — EGR off and vacuum advance and retard disconnected.

### FUEL PUMP PRESSURE & VOLUME

Pressure
Cressida .................................. 4.2-5.4 psi (.30-.38 kg/cm²)
Land Cruiser .......................... 3.4-4.8 psi (.24-.34 kg/cm²)
Volume (at 2000 RPM)
Cressida ................................................. 2 pts. in 60 sec.
Land Cruiser ........................................ 2.5 pts. in 30 sec.

### EMISSION CONTROL SYSTEMS

*See Mitchell Manuals' Emission Control Manual.*

# GENERAL SERVICING

## IGNITION

### DISTRIBUTOR

All models are equipped with Nippondenso Transistorized Electronic Ignition Systems.

**Other Data & Specifications** − *See Tune-Up and Nippondenso Distributors in ELECTRICAL Section.*

### IGNITION COIL

| Resistance | Ohms |
|---|---|
| Primary | |
| Cressida .................................................. | 1.3-1.7 |
| Land Cruiser ............................................ | 1.3-1.6 |
| Secondary | |
| Cressida .................................. | 12,000-16,000 |
| Land Cruiser ............................. | 9500-14,500 |
| Ballast Resistor .......................................... | 1.2 |

## FUEL SYSTEMS

### CARBURETORS

| Application | Model |
|---|---|
| All Models ...................................... | Aisan 2-Bbl. |

**Other Data & Specifications** − *See Tune-Up and Aisan Carburetors in FUEL SYSTEMS Section.*

## ELECTRICAL

### BATTERY

12 Volt − Negative Ground.

| Application | Amp. Hr. Rating |
|---|---|
| All ................................................................ | 70 |

**Battery Location** − In engine compartment.

### STARTER

All models are equipped with Nippondenso Starters.

| | |
|---|---|
| Free Speed Voltage .......................... | 11 at 5000 RPM |
| Free Speed Amperage .............. | 50 (Max.) at 5000 RPM |

**Other Data & Specifications** − *See Nippondenso Starters in ELECTRICAL Section.*

### ALTERNATOR

| Application | Rated Amp. Output |
|---|---|
| Cressida ................................................. | 60 |
| Land Cruiser | |
| Standard ......................................... | 40 or 50 |
| Optional .......................................... | 50 or 55 |

**Other Data & Specification** − *See Nippondenso Alternators and Regulators in ELECTRICAL Section.*

## ALTERNATOR REGULATOR

All models are equipped with Nippondenso alternator regulator with an operating voltage of 13.8-14.8 volts.

**Other Data & Specifications** − *See Nippondenso Alternators and Regulators in ELECTRICAL Section.*

## ENGINE

### INTAKE MANIFOLD TIGHTENING

Tighten bolts on Cressida to 11-15 ft. lbs. (1.5-2.1 mkg), bolts on Land Cruiser to 28-37 ft. lbs. (4-5 mkg) on Federal models and 37-51 ft. lbs. (5-7 mkg) on California models.

### BELT ADJUSTMENT

| Application | ①Deflection |
|---|---|
| Alternator Belt | |
| Cressida ................................ | .4-.55"(10-14 mm) |
| Land Cruiser ........................... | .5-.6"(13-15 mm) |
| Air Pump Belt | |
| Cressida ................................. | .3-.4"(8-10 mm) |
| Land Cruiser ........................... | .3-.4"(8-10 mm) |
| Air Conditioning Belt | |
| Cressida ................................. | .4-.5"(10-13 mm) |
| Land Cruiser ........................... | .6-.7"(15-18 mm) |

① − Deflection is with 22 lbs. (10 kg) pressure applied midway on longest belt run.

### FILTERS & CLEANERS

| Filter or Cleaner | Service Interval (Miles) |
|---|---|
| Oil Filter ..................... | Replace every 7,500 |
| Air Filter ..................... | Replace every 30,000 |
| Fuel Filter .................... | Replace every 30,000 |
| PCV Valve .................... | Replace every 30,000 |
| Charcoal Canister .......... | Replace every 60,000 |

### CAPACITIES

| Application | Quantity |
|---|---|
| Crankcase (Includes Filter) | |
| Cressida .................................. | 5.7 qts. |
| Land Cruiser .............................. | 8.5 qts. |
| Cooling System | |
| Cressida .................................. | 11.6 qts. |
| Land Cruiser | |
| Station Wagon ...................... | 17.6 qts. |
| All Other Models .................... | 16.8 qts. |
| Man. Trans. (SAE 90) ................... | 6.6 pts. |
| Auto. Trans. (ATF F) ................... | 2.3 qts. |
| Differentials (SAE 90) ................ | 5.2 pts. |
| Transfer Case (SAE 90) .............. | 3.6 pts. |
| Fuel Tank | |
| Cressida | |
| Sedan ................................ | 17.2 gals. |
| Station Wagon ...................... | 16.2 gals. |
| Land Cruiser | |
| Station Wagon ...................... | 21.7 gals. |
| All Others .............................. | 16.4 gals. |

# TUNE-UP

**Spitfire 1500**
**TR7**

## ENGINE IDENTIFICATION

Engine number is stamped on engine boss on left side of block below number four spark plug on Spitfire models and is stamped on the cylinder head between carburetors on TR7 models. The following engine codes (prefix letters) denote engines designed specifically for the USA market.

| Application | Displacement | Code |
|---|---|---|
| Spitfire | | |
| Federal | 1493 | FM XXXX U |
| Calif. | 1493 | FM XXXX C |
| TR7 | | |
| Federal | 1998 | CL XXXX U |
| Calif. | 1998 | CL XXXX C |

## MODEL IDENTIFICATION

### VEHICLE IDENTIFICATION NUMBER

Number is stamped on a metal plate attached to the driver's door on TR7 models and to door post on Spitfire models. Number is also stamped on a small plate and mounted on left corner of instrument panel, visible through the windshield.

## COMPRESSION PRESSURE

Check compression with engine at normal operating temperature, spark plugs removed and throttle wide open. Crank engine through four compression strokes before taking reading. On Spitfire models, minimum pressure is 145 psi (10.2 kg/cm²). On both Spitfire and TR7 models, lowest pressure should be at least 85% that of highest cylinder.

## VALVE TAPPET CLEARANCE

**Spitfire — 1)** Disconnect battery, then remove valve cover and spark plugs. Check valve clearance with engine cold. Adjust valves in outlined sequence (numbered front to rear):

| Valves Open | Adjust Valves |
|---|---|
| No. 8 & No. 6 | No. 1 & No. 3 |
| No. 4 & No. 7 | No. 5 & No. 2 |
| No. 1 & No. 3 | No. 8 & No. 6 |
| No. 5 & No. 2 | No. 4 & No. 7 |

**2)** Turn crankshaft until appropriate valves in first column open. Then check and adjust valves listed in second column.

**3)** To adjust, loosen lock nut and turn slotted adjusting pin clockwise to decrease clearance and counterclockwise to increase clearance. Tighten lock nut when correct.

**TR7 — 1)** Disconnect battery and remove camshaft cover. Loosen camshaft bearing cap nuts and retighten to 10-14 ft. lbs. (1.4-1.9 mkg). Rotate engine. Check and record clearance between cam heel and tappet. Maximum clearance is present when cam is in vertical position.

**2)** If clearance is not within specifications, remove camshaft and individually lift out each tappet and adjusting shim.

**3)** Using a micrometer, measure thickness of adjusting shim removed. Add to this the measured valve clearance and subtract the specified clearance from the total. This will offer you the thickness of adjusting shim necessary to bring the clearance within specifications.

**4)** Install tappets and add shims as needed. Install camshaft and tighten bearing caps. Recheck valve clearance, and, when correct, replace camshaft cover.

### Valve Clearance Specifications

| Application | Clearance (Cold) |
|---|---|
| Spitfire | |
| Intake & Exhaust | .010" (.25 mm) |
| TR7 | |
| Intake | .008" (.20 mm) |
| Exhaust | .018" (.50 mm) |

## VALVE ARRANGEMENT

E-I-I-E-E-I-I-E (front to rear).

**Fig. 1   Firing Order and Distributor Rotation (Spitfire)**

**Fig. 2   Firing Order and Distributor Rotation (TR7)**

## SPARK PLUGS

| | |
|---|---|
| Gap | .024-.026" (.61-.66 mm) |
| Torque | 20 ft. lbs. (2.8 mkg) |

### Spark Plug Type

| Application | Champion No. |
|---|---|
| Spitfire & TR7 | N-12Y |

## TUNE-UP (Cont.)

### HIGH TENSION WIRE RESISTANCE

Carefully remove high tension wires from spark plugs and distributor cap. Using an ohmmeter, check high tension wire resistance while gently twisting wires. If resistance is not to specifications, or fluctuates from infinity to any value, replace high tension wire(s).

#### Resistance (Ohms) Per Wire

| Application | Ohms |
|---|---|
| All Models | 25,000-30,000 |

### DISTRIBUTOR

All models are equipped with Opus Electronic Ignition System and the only adjustment required is adjusting the Pick-Up Module air gap.

CAUTION — *DO NOT insert feeler gauge into pick-up air gap when the ignition circuit is energized.*

Pick-Up Module Air Gap............... ①.014-.016″ (.35-.40 mm)

① — Measured between timing rotor and pick-up module.

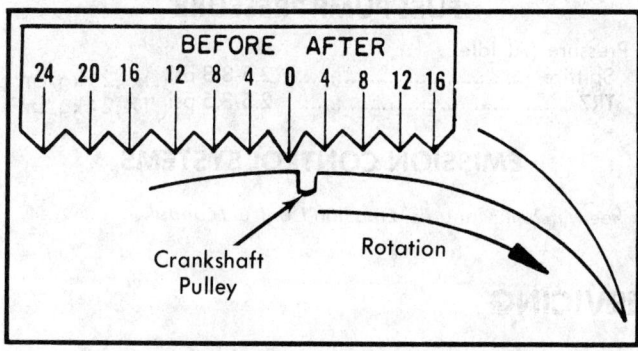

**Fig. 3  Ignition Timing Mark Location**

### IGNITION TIMING

Check or adjust ignition timing with engine at normal operating temperature, idle speed at specification and distributor vacuum retard hose connected. If correction is necessary, rotate distributor.

#### Ignition Timing Specifications

| Application | RPM | Timing |
|---|---|---|
| Spitfire & TR7① | | |
| Federal | 700-900 | 10° BTDC |
| Calif. | 700-900 | 2° ATDC |

① — Static timing on all models is 10° BTDC.

### IDLE SPEED & MIXTURE

NOTE — *See Fig. 4.*

1) Remove air cleaner and fresh air duct (dual carburetor models only), then ensure oil in carburetor damper is ¼″ below top of damper tube. With engine at normal operating temperature, connect a tachometer and exhaust gas analyzer to vehicle. Back off on fast idle adjusting screw until it no longer contacts fast idle cam.

2) On models with a single carburetor, adjust idle speed to specifications by adjusting throttle adjusting screw. On models with dual carburetors, use an air flow balance meter and synchronize carburetors, then adjust idle speed to specifications by adjusting throttle adjusting screw on each carburetor an equal amount.

3) On all models, stop engine and disconnect and plug air pump outlet hose. Start engine and check CO level. If CO level is not within specifications, adjust idle trim screw(s) clockwise to richen mixture or counterclockwise to lean mixture until CO level is within specified limit. If CO level cannot be adjusted within correct limits by adjusting the idle trim screw(s), proceed to step 4).

**Fig. 4  Screws for Adjusting Idle Speed, Mixture, & Decel Valve**

## TUNE-UP (Cont.)

4) Remove piston damper from carburetor(s). Then carefully insert needle adjusting tool (S 353) into dashpot until outer tool engages air valve and inner tool engages hexagon in needle adjuster. Hold outer tool stationary and turn inner tool clockwise to richen mixture or counterclockwise to lean mixture until CO level is within specified limit. Remove tool and reinstall piston, then recheck CO level and idle RPM and adjust as necessary.

### Idle Speed (RPM) & CO Level (%)

| Application | Idle RPM | ①CO% |
|---|---|---|
| Spitfire | | |
|   Federal | 700-900 | 3.0-7.0 |
|   California | 700-900 | 0.5-6.5 |
| TR7 | 700-900 | 3.0-7.0 |

① — Air pump disconnected.

## COLD (FAST) IDLE RPM

### MANUAL CHOKE

1) With engine at normal operating temperature, ensure that choke cam lever on carburetor(s) returns fully to its stop. Adjust choke cable, if necessary. Then pull choke knob out approximately ¼″ until fast idle cam(s) engage spring-loaded detent ball(s).

2) Loosen lock nut on carburetor(s) and turn fast idle screw against cam until engine reaches fast idle speed. Be sure carburetors are in balance. Tighten lock nut and push in choke knob fully.

### AUTOMATIC CHOKE

On models with automatic chokes, remove cover and turn fast idle screw until the gap between base circle of cam and fast idle pin is within .035″ (.89 mm) on TR7 and .020″ (.5 mm) on Spitfire.

### Fast Idle Specifications

| Application | RPM |
|---|---|
| Spitfire | ①1700-1900 |
| TR7 | ②1600 |

① — Corresponds to 1100-1300 RPM cold setting.
② — Corresponds to 1300 RPM cold setting.

### DECEL VALVE ADJUSTMENT

With engine at normal operating temperature, disconnect and plug distributor vacuum retard line. Engine speed should increase to approximately 1300 RPM. If engine speed increases to 2000-2500 RPM, decel valve will need to be adjusted. To adjust, turn by-pass valve adjusting screw until speed drops to 1300 RPM, then turn screw an additional ½ turn to fully seat valve.

NOTE — See Fig. 4.

### FUEL PUMP PRESSURE

Pressure (At Idle)
| | |
|---|---|
| Spitfire | 2.5-3.8 psi (.17-.26 kg/cm²) |
| TR7 | 2.5-3.5 psi (.17-.24 kg/cm²) |

### EMISSION CONTROL SYSTEMS

See Mitchell Manuals' Emission Control Manual.

# GENERAL SERVICING

## IGNITION

### DISTRIBUTOR

All models are equipped with Lucas Opus Electronic Ignition System.

**Other Data & Specifications** — See Tune-Up & Lucas Distributors in ELECTRICAL Section.

### IGNITION COIL

| Resistance | Ohms at 68°F (20°C) |
|---|---|
| Primary | |
|   All Models | 1.30-1.45 |
| Ballast Resistor | |
|   All Models | 1.30-1.50 |

## FUEL SYSTEMS

### CARBURETORS

| Application | Model |
|---|---|
| Spitfire | 1 Zenith-Stromberg 150 CD4T |
| TR7 | 2 Zenith-Stromberg 175 CDFEVX |

**Other Data & Specifications** — See Tune-Up and Zenith-Stromberg Carburetors in FUEL SYSTEMS Section.

## ELECTRICAL

### BATTERY

**12 Volt** — Negative Ground.

| Application | Amp. Hr. Capacity |
|---|---|
| Spitfire | 40 |
| TR7 | 50 |

**Battery Location** — In engine compartment, on firewall.

## GENERAL SERVICING (Cont.)

### STARTER

Lucas ...................................... Overrunning Clutch

Free Speed Amperage
Spitfire ........................... 65 at 8000-10,000 RPM
TR7 ....................................... 40 at 6000 RPM

**Other Data & Specifications** — *See Lucas Starters in ELECTRICAL Section.*

### ALTERNATOR

| Application | Rated Amp. Output |
|---|---|
| Spitfire | 36 |
| TR7 | 65 |

**Other Data & Specifications** — *See Lucas Alternators & Regulators in ELECTRICAL Section.*

### ALTERNATOR REGULATOR

Lucas — Non-Adjustable, integral with alternator, with an operating voltage of 13.6-14.4 volts.

**Other Data & Specifications** — *See Lucas Alternators & Regulators in ELECTRICAL Section.*

## ENGINE

### INTAKE MANIFOLD TIGHTENING

Tighten intake manifold attaching bolts to 25 ft. lbs. (3.5 mkg) on Spitfire models and to 15-20 ft. lbs. (2.1-2.7 mkg) on TR7 models.

### BELT ADJUSTMENT

| Application | ①Deflection |
|---|---|
| All Models | |
| Fan Belt | .75-1" (19-25 mm) |
| Air Pump Belt | .25-.50" (6-13 mm) |

① — Deflection is with pressure applied midway on longest belt run.

### FILTERS & CLEANERS

| Application | Service Interval (Miles) |
|---|---|
| Oil Filter | ①Replace every 12,000 |
| Air Cleaner | Replace every 12,500 |
| Fuel Filter | Replace every 12,500 |
| Carbon Canister Assy. | Replace every 50,000 |

① — Replace after first 6,000 miles and then at 12,000 mile intervals.

### CAPACITIES

| Application | Quantity |
|---|---|
| Crankcase (Includes Filter) | 4.8 qts. |
| Cooling System (Includes Heater & Reservoir) | |
| Spitfire | 4.75 qts. |
| TR7 | 7.8 qts. |
| Man. Trans. (SAE 75 EP) | |
| Spitfire | |
| Without Overdrive | 1.8 pts. |
| With Overdrive | 3.25 pts. |
| TR7 | |
| 4-Speed | 2.4 pts. |
| 5-Speed | 3.3 pts. |
| Auto. Trans. (ATF Type F) | 5.7 qts. |
| Rear Axle (SAE 90 EP) | |
| Spitfire | 1.2 pts. |
| TR7 | |
| 4-Speed | 2.7 pts. |
| 5-Speed | 2.4 pts. |
| Fuel Tank | |
| Spitfire | 8.7 gals. |
| TR7 | 14.4 gals. |

# 1978 Volkswagen 4 Tune-Up

## TUNE-UP

Type 1
Type 2
Dasher
Rabbit
Scirocco

## ENGINE IDENTIFICATION

Engine code prefixes are placed in the following locations:

**Type 1** — Engine serial number is stamped on alternator support flange.

**Type 2** — Engine serial number is stamped on crankcase below breather and also near ignition coil.

**All Other Models** — Engine serial number is stamped on left side of engine near ignition distributor.

### Engine Codes

| Application | Code |
| --- | --- |
| Type 1 | |
| Fuel Injected ................................................ | AJ |
| Type 2 ........................................................... | GD |
| Dasher | |
| Federal | |
| Man. Trans. ............................................. | YG |
| Auto Trans. ............................................. | YH |
| California ................................................... | YK |
| Rabbit & Scirocco | |
| Man. Trans. ............................................. | EE |
| Auto. Trans. ............................................. | EF |

## MODEL IDENTIFICATION

### VEHICLE IDENTIFICATION NUMBER

The Vehicle Identification Number is stamped on a plate attached to left windshield pillar on Dasher and Scirocco models. Number also appears on Dasher models at rear of engine compartment above windshield washer reservoir and on Rabbit and Scirocco models atop the suspension strut mounting of the right-hand front wheel housing. Type 1 & 2 and Rabbit vehicles have number stamped on instrument panel. All models feature numbers visible through the windshield.

## COMPRESSION PRESSURE

| Application | Stan. Pressure psi (kg/cm²) | ①Min. Pressure psi (kg/cm²) |
| --- | --- | --- |
| Type 1 ................ | 107-135 (7.5-9.5) | 85 (6.0) |
| Type 2 ................ | 85-135 (6.0-9.5) | 71 (5.0) |
| All Other Models ... | 142-185 (10.0-13.0) | 107 (7.5) |

① — Maximum variation between cylinders should not exceed 28 psi (2 kg/cm²) on Type 1 and 2 vehicles or 42 psi (3 kg/cm²) on all other vehicles.

## VALVE TAPPET CLEARANCE

**Type 1** — Perform adjustment with engine cold. Turn the crankshaft until No. 1 cylinder is at TDC position and distributor rotor points to No. 1 cylinder position. Loosen lock nut

and adjust rocker arm adjusting screw until valve clearance is to specification. Check clearance between adjusting screw and valve stem of both valves. Tighten lock nut. Turn crankshaft 90 degrees, while observing distributor rotor travel. Adjust valves of No. 2, 3, and 4 cylinders in turn.

**Type 2** — Hydraulic lifters used; no adjustment necessary.

**All Other Models** — Remove distributor cap and set engine at TDC. Align distributor rotor with No. 1 cylinder mark on distributor body. Adjust by replacing tappet discs. Discs are available in 26 thicknesses from .119-.166" (3.0-4.25 mm). Adjust valves in firing order, 1-3-4-2, according to following procedure:

### Valve Adjusting Sequence①

| Check or Adjust | When Valves Overlap |
| --- | --- |
| No. 1 ................................................... | No. 4 |
| No. 3 ................................................... | No. 2 |
| No. 4 ................................................... | No. 1 |
| No. 2 ................................................... | No. 3 |

① — Turn crankshaft 180° in normal direction of rotation after adjusting valves of each cylinder.

**NOTE** — *Use special tool VW546 to press down cam follower, so that adjusting disc can be readily removed with tool 10-208. When depressing cam followers, turn so that openings are at 90° angle to camshaft.*

### Valve Clearance Specifications

| Application | Clearance Cold | Clearance Hot |
| --- | --- | --- |
| Type 1 | | |
| Intake & Exhaust ...... | .006" (.15 mm) | ..... |
| All Other Models | | |
| Intake ........................ | .006-.010" (.15-.25 mm) | .008-.012" (.20-.30 mm) |
| Exhaust ..................... | .014-.018" (.36-.46 mm) | .016-.020" (.40-.50 mm) |

## VALVE ARRANGEMENT

**Type 1 & 2** — E-I-I-E (both banks, front-to-rear).
**All Others** — E-I-E-I-I-E-I-E (front-to-rear).

FRONT OF VEHICLE →

FIRING ORDER 1-4-3-2

*Fig. 1   Firing Order and Distributor Rotation (Type 1 & 2)*

## TUNE-UP (Cont.)

**Fig. 2  Firing Order and Distributor Rotation (Dasher)**

**Fig. 3  Firing Order and Distributor Rotation (Rabbit & Scirocco)**

## DISTRIBUTOR

| | |
|---|---|
| Point Gap | .016″ (.4 mm) |
| Dwell Angle | 44-50° |
| Breaker Arm Spring Tension | 14-21 ozs. (450-600 g) |
| Condenser Capacity | .20 mfd. |

## SPARK PLUGS

Gap
| | |
|---|---|
| Rabbit & Scirocco | .024-.028″ (.6-.7 mm) |
| All Other Models | .028″ (.7 mm) |
| Torque | 22 ft. lbs. (3 mkg) |

### Spark Plug Type

| Application | Bosch | Champion |
|---|---|---|
| Type 1 | W145M1 | L-288 |
| Type 2 | W145M2 | N-288 |
| Dasher | W175T30 | N-8Y |
| Rabbit, Scirocco | W175T30 | N-8Y |

## HIGH TENSION WIRE RESISTANCE

Carefully remove high tension wires from spark plugs and distributor cap. Using an ohmmeter, check high tension wire resistance while gently twisting wires. If resistance is not to specifications, or fluctuates from infinity to any value, replace high tension wire(s).

### Resistance (Ohms) Per Wire

| Application | Ohms |
|---|---|
| All Models | 25,000-30,000 |

## IGNITION TIMING

Connect timing light and tachometer to vehicle. On all models check or adjust ignition timing with engine at normal operating temperature and distributor vacuum lines connected. Adjust timing with engine at specified RPM. To correct timing, loosen distributor holddown bolt, turn distributor, and retighten bolt to 14 ft. lbs. (1.94 mkg).

### Ignition Timing Specifications

| Application | RPM | Timing |
|---|---|---|
| Type 1 | 800-950 | 5° ATDC |
| Type 2 | | |
|   Man. Trans | 850-950 | 7.5° BTDC |
|   Auto. Trans. | 900-1000 | 7.5° BTDC |
| Dasher | 850-1000 | 3° ATDC |
| Rabbit & Scirocco | 850-1000 | 3° ATDC |

**Fig. 4  Ignition Timing Mark Location (Type 1)**

**Fig. 5  Ignition Timing Mark Location (Type 2)**

## TUNE-UP (Cont.)

**Fig. 6    Ignition Timing Mark Location
(Dasher)**

**Fig. 7    Ignition Timing Mark Location
(Rabbit & Scirocco)**

### IDLE SPEED & MIXTURE

**Type 1 & 2 — 1)** With engine at normal operating temperature, remove hose between charcoal filter and air cleaner. Turn idle speed adjusting screw (by-pass screw) on throttle valve housing until speed is to specification. Turn clockwise to decrease speed, counterclockwise to increase speed.

**2)** With idle properly adjusted, adjust mixture (CO%). Connect an exhaust gas analyzer as instructed by manufacturer, but ahead of catalytic converter, if so equipped.

**3)** If adjustment is required, remove rubber plug from air flow sensor housing and turn mixture adjusting screw until CO% is to specification. Turn screw clockwise to increase CO% level, counterclockwise to decrease CO%. Recheck idle speed and adjust if necessary.

**Dasher, Rabbit & Scirocco — 1)** With warm engine, set brake, turn on high beams and A/C, connect tachometer. Check auxiliary air regulator to ensure it is fully closed. Turn bypass screw on throttle valve housing in to decrease idle speed; out to increase idle speed.

**2)** Disconnect evaporative emission control purge hose from charcoal filter to air cleaner. Connect exhaust gas analyzer according to manufacturer's instructions. Insert probe into tailpipe (even if equipped with catalytic converter).

**3)** If CO% is not correct at specified idle speed, remove rubber plug from top of mixture control unit. Use P377 adjusting tool (or equivalent) to turn idle mixture screw to correct CO% setting. Turn screw clockwise to increase CO% or counterclockwise to reduce CO% level. Recheck idle and adjust if necessary. Disconnect all test equipment and reconnect hose.

### Idle Speed (RPM) and CO Level (%)

| Application | Idle RPM | Maximum CO% |
|---|---|---|
| Type 1① | | |
| California | 800-950 | 1.0 |
| Federal | 800-950 | 1.5 |
| Type 2① | | |
| Man. Trans. | 800-950 | 1.0 |
| Auto. Trans. | 900-1000 | 1.0 |
| Dasher② | | |
| California | 850-1000 | 0.3 |
| Federal | | |
| Man. Trans. | 850-1000 | 1.5 |
| Auto. Trans. | 850-1000 | 1.0 |
| Rabbit & Scirocco② | | |
| California | 850-1000 | 0.3 |
| Federal | | |
| Man. Trans. | 850-1000 | 1.5 |
| Auto. Trans. | 850-1000 | 1.0 |

① — Probe inserted in front of catalytic converter.
② — Probe inserted in tailpipe.

## EMISSION CONTROL SYSTEMS

*See Mitchell Manuals' Emission Control Manual.*

# GENERAL SERVICING

## IGNITION

### DISTRIBUTOR

All models are equipped with Bosch single point distributors.

**Other Data & Specifications —** *See Tune-Up and Bosch Distributors in ELECTRICAL Section.*

## FUEL SYSTEMS

### FUEL INJECTION

**Type 1 & 2 —** All models use Bosch AFC Electronic Fuel Injection.

**Dasher, Rabbit & Scirocco —** All models use Bosch Continuous Injection System (CIS).

**Other Data & Specifications —** *See Tune-Up and Bosch AFC Electronic or Bosch CIS Fuel Injection Systems in FUEL SYSTEMS Section.*

# 1978 Volkswagen 4 Tune-Up

## GENERAL SERVICING (Cont.)

### ELECTRICAL

#### BATTERY

**12 Volt** — Negative Ground.

| Application | Amp Hr. Capacity |
|---|---|
| Type 1 | 45 |
| Type 2 | 54 |
| Dasher, Rabbit & Scirocco | |
| Standard | 45 |
| With Air Conditioning | 54 |

**Battery Location** — Battery is located under the rear seat, on right side (Type 1 models) or in engine compartment (all other models).

#### STARTER

All models are equipped with Bosch starters.

**Other Data & Specifications** — *See Bosch Starters in ELECTRICAL Section.*

### ALTERNATOR

| Application | Rated Amp. Output |
|---|---|
| Type 1 | 50 |
| Type 2 | 55 |
| Dasher, Rabbit & Scirocco | |
| Standard | 55 |
| With Air Conditioning | 65 |

**Other Data & Specifications** — *See Bosch & Motorola Alternators & Regulator in ELECTRICAL Section.*

#### ALTERNATOR REGULATOR

Bosch & Motorola — Non-Adjustable; integral with alternator.

**Other Data & Specifications** — *See Bosch & Motorola Alternators & Regulators in ELECTRICAL Section.*

### BELT ADJUSTMENT

| Application | ① Deflections |
|---|---|
| All Models | .4-.6"(10-15 mm) |

① Deflection is with thumb pressure, about 16.5 lbs. (7.5 kg), applied midway on longest belt run.

### FILTERS & CLEANERS

| Filter or Cleaner | Service Interval (Miles) |
|---|---|
| Oil Strainer (Type 1) | Clean every 5,000 |
| Oil Filter (All Other Models | Replace every 15,000 |
| Air Cleaner | |
| Dasher Only | Clean every 15,000 |
| All Models | Replace every 30,000 |
| Fuel Filter | |
| Rabbit & Scirocco | Replace every 30,000 |
| All Other Models | Replace every 15,000 |
| EGR Filter | Replace every 15,000 |

### CAPACITIES

| Application | Quantity |
|---|---|
| Crankcase | |
| Type 1 | 2.6 qts. |
| Dasher | ①3.2 qts. |
| All Other Models | ②3.7 qts. |
| Cooling System | |
| Dasher | ③6.3 qts. |
| Rabbit & Scirocco | 4.9 qts. |
| Man. Trans. & Final Drive (SAE 80 — API GL 4) | |
| Type 1 | 2.6 pts. |
| Type 2 | 7.4 pts. |
| Dasher | 3.2 pts. |
| Rabbit & Scirocco | 2.6 pts. |
| Auto. Trans. Refill (Dexron) | ④3.2 qts. |
| Auto. Trans. Final Drive (SAE 90 — API GL 5) | |
| Type 2 | 2.6 pts. |
| Dasher, Rabbit & Scirocco | 1.6 pts. |
| Fuel Tank | |
| Type 1 | |
| Beetle | 10.6 gals. |
| Convertible | 11.5 gals. |
| Type 2 | 14.6 gals. |
| Dasher | 11.9 gals. |
| Rabbit & Scirocco | 10.5 gals. |

① — Includes oil filter (w/o filter, 2.6 qts.).
② — Includes oil filter (w/o filter, 3.2 qts.).
③ — 6.9 qts. with expansion tank.
④ — Dry fill is 6.4 qts.

## TUNE-UP

**Rabbit Diesel**

### ENGINE IDENTIFICATION

The first two letters of the engine identification number, stamped on the cylinder block just below the glow plug of cylinder number 3, identifies the engine as:

| Model | Code |
|---|---|
| Rabbit ............................................................ | CK |

### MODEL IDENTIFICATION

#### VEHICLE IDENTIFICATION NUMBER

The vehicle identification number is located on the left side of the instrument panel and is visible through the windshield.

### COMPRESSION PRESSURE

Remove electrical wire from stop control on injection pump. Insulate wire end and remove injector pipes and injector. Use special adapter (VW 1323/2) or its equivalent and compression tester (VW 1323).Be sure old heat shield is between adapter and head. Operate starter and read compression.

| Application | ①Pressure |
|---|---|
| New ........................................ | 483 psi (34 kg/cm²) |
| Wear Limit ............................... | 398 psi (28 kg/cm²) |

① — 71 psi (5 kg/cm²) maximum difference between cylinders.

### VALVE CLEARANCE

**CAUTION** — *When adjusting valves, pistons MUST NOT be at TDC. Turn crankshaft ¼ turn past TDC so valves do not hit pistons when tappets are depressed.*

**CAUTION** — *When adjusting valves, do not turn engine by turning camshaft pulley. This will stretch the drive belt. Place vehicle in 4th gear and push to turn engine.*

1) Valves may be checked when engine is either warm or cold. If warm, coolant should be 95°F (35°C). Check valve clearance in firing order, 1-3-4-2.

2) Measure between cam lobes and adjusting disc, when both lobes to be checked point upward. Adjust clearance to specifications by changing disc thickness. Twenty six discs are available in thicknesses from .118-.167" (3.00-4.25 mm).

3) To remove adjusting discs, use a 10-208 removal tool, while holding cam follower down with special tool VW 546 (10-209).

### Valve Clearance Specifications

| Application | Intake | Exhaust |
|---|---|---|
| Engine Warm ............. | .008-.012" (.2-.3 mm) | .016-.020" (.4-.5 mm) |
| Engine Cold ................ | .006-.010" (.15-.25 mm) | .014-.018" (.35-.45 mm) |

### VALVE ARRANGEMENT

**All Models** — E-I-E-I-I-E-I-E (right of vehicle to left)

### FIRING ORDER

**All Models** — 1-3-4-2

*Fig. 1   Idle and Maximum Speed Adjustment*

### DIESEL FUEL INJECTION SYSTEMS

**Rabbit** — For complete information on the Diesel fuel injection system, see Bosch Diesel Fuel Injection (Volkswagen) in the FUEL SYSTEMS Section. Information includes description, system components, removal, installation, and service procedures.

### IDLE SPEED ADJUSTMENT

Run engine until warm. Mount tachometer sensor (US 1324) on valve cover and connect to battery. Attach tachometer to sensor and check idle speed. If adjustment is needed, loosen locknut on idle screw. Turn in to increase idle, out to decrease. Apply thread sealer and tighten locknut.

| Application | Idle RPM |
|---|---|
| Rabbit ........................................................ | 770-870 |

## TUNE-UP (Cont.)

### MAXIMUM SPEED ADJUSTMENT

Run engine until warm and install tachometer sensor (US 1324). Connect tachometer and set idle speed. Accelerate engine briefly to full throttle. If maximum speed does not match specifications, loosen speed locknut and adjust. Turning screw out raises speed, turning screw in lowers speed. Apply thread sealer and tighten locknut.

| Application | Maximum RPM |
|---|---|
| Rabbit | 5400-5450 |

## GENERAL SERVICING

### FUEL SYSTEMS

**FUEL INJECTION**

The Rabbit uses Bosch Diesel Fuel Injection.

**Other Data & Specifications** — *See Tune-Up and Bosch Diesel Fuel Injection in FUEL SYSTEMS Section.*

### ELECTRICAL

**BATTERY**

**12 Volt** — Negative Ground.

| Application | Amp. Hr. Rating |
|---|---|
| Rabbit | 63 |

**STARTER**

The Rabbit is equipped with Bosch Starter.

**Other Data & Specifications** — *See Bosch Starters in ELECTRICAL Section.*

**ALTERNATOR**

| Application | Rated Amp. Output |
|---|---|
| Rabbit | 55 |

**Other Data & Specifications** — *See Bosch & Motorola Alternators in ELECTRICAL Section.*

**ALTERNATOR REGULATOR**

Bosch & Motorola — Non-Adjustable; integral with alternator.

**Other Data & Specifications** — *See Bosch Alternators & Regulators in ELECTRICAL Section.*

### FILTERS & CLEANERS

| Filter or Cleaner | Service Interval (Miles) |
|---|---|
| Oil Filter | 7,500 |
| Air Cleaner | 15,000 |
| Fuel Filter | 30,000 |

### CAPACITIES

| Application | Quantity |
|---|---|
| Crankcase (includes filter) | ①3.7 qts. |
| Cooling System | 6.8 qts. |
| Man. Trans. (SAE 80W/90) | 2.6 pts. |
| Fuel Tank | 10.5 gals. |

① — 3.2 without filter change.

### BELT ADJUSTMENT

| Application | ①Deflection |
|---|---|
| Thumb Pressure | 3/8 - 5/8" (10-15 mm) |

① — Measured half way between camshaft sprocket and fuel injection pump sprocket. If special tool (VW 210) is used, scale should read 12-13.

# 1978 Volvo 4 Tune-Up

## TUNE-UP

**240 Series**

### ENGINE IDENTIFICATION

Engine identification code is stamped on left side of engine block. Code numbers for the B21F engine are also found on the model plate on the front right-hand suspension strut mounting in the engine compartment (digits 4, 5 and 6 of code number).

| Application | Code |
|---|---|
| Federal | 453 & 459 |
| California | 459 |

### MODEL IDENTIFICATION

**VEHICLE IDENTIFICATION NUMBER**

The vehicle identification number is located on a plate attached to the left windshield pillar. It also appears on model plate located on right front suspension strut mounting.

### COMPRESSION PRESSURE

With engine at normal operating temperature, spark plugs removed, throttle valve wide open and cranking speed at 250-300 RPM, compression should be as follows:

| Application | psi (kg/cm²) |
|---|---|
| All Models | 128-156 (9-11) |

### VALVE TAPPET CLEARANCE

1) Valve clearance is adjusted with engine shut off and either warm or cold. Remove valve cover. Turn crankshaft center bolt until camshaft is in position for firing No. 1 cylinder. Both cam lobes should point up at equally large angles. Pulley timing mark should be at 0°.

2) Check valve clearance of No. 1 cylinder, using a feeler gauge between camshaft lobe and adjusting discs. Intake and exhaust valves have same clearances.

3) If clearances are incorrect adjust by changing thickness of discs, which are available in .05 mm increments from 3.30 to 4.50 mm.

4) After valves for No. 1 cylinder are properly adjusted, rotate crankshaft to firing position for No. 3, No. 4, and No. 2 cylinders in sequence and complete adjustment.

**Valve Clearances**

| Application | Cold In. (mm) | Hot In. (mm) |
|---|---|---|
| Checking | .010-.018 (.25-.45) | .012-.020 (.30-.50) |
| Setting | .014-.016 (.35-.40) | .016-.018 (.40-.45) |

### VALVE ARRANGEMENT

E-I-E-I-E-I-E-I (front to rear).

### SPARK PLUGS

| | |
|---|---|
| Gap | .028-.032" (.7-.8 mm) |
| Torque | 25-29 ft. lbs. (3.5-4.0 mkg) |

**Spark Plug Type**

| Application | Bosch No. |
|---|---|
| All Models | W175T30 |

### DISTRIBUTOR

All models are equipped with Breakerless Electronic Ignition System and no adjustments are required.

**Fig. 1   Firing Order and Distributor Rotation**

### IGNITION TIMING

**NOTE** — *Preliminary to setting ignition timing, it is necessary to adjust throttle linkage and micro switch (on California vehicles) first. Procedures are given below.*

1) Install CO meter and timing light. Disconnect air hose at air pump and plug hose. Disconnect and plug EGR vacuum hose at EGR valve.

2) Disconnect throttle link and cable at throttle control pulley. Loosen lock nut and screw out throttle shaft adjusting screw. Turn screw in until it just touches boss, then in one additional turn. Lock with lock nut. Check that throttle valve does not bind.

3) Ensure that throttle control link (from pulley to lever ball), can be attached to lever ball without changing the pulley position.

4) Attach throttle cable to pulley. Adjust cable sheath so that cable is snug but does not change pulley position. Depress throttle completely; pulley should touch the full throttle boss.

5) Adjust throttle cable to automatic transmission so that cable clip will travel 2" (51 mm) from idle position to full throttle position. At idle there should be .040" (1 mm) clearance between clip and adjusting sheath.

## TUNE-UP (Cont.)

**6)** On California vehicles, micro switch must be adjusted: Connect test lamp to micro switch and turn ignition to "ON". Place a .060" (1.5 mm) feeler gauge between throttle screw and boss. Light should stay on. Insert a .080" (2 mm) feeler gauge; light should go out.

**7)** To adjust micro switch, place original feeler gauge between throttle screw and boss. Loosen lock nut and screw out micro switch adjusting screw (test lamp should go off). Turn in screw until a click is heard from the micro switch and test lamp comes on. Tighten lock nut, remove feeler gauge and lamp.

**8)** On all models, disconnect and plug vacuum hose at distributor. Use air adjusting screw to set idle speed to 700-800 RPM, then set ignition timing to specification. Reconnect distributor hose.

**Fig. 2   240 Series Timing Mark Location**

### Ignition Timing Specifications

| Application | RPM | Timing |
|---|---|---|
| All Models | 700-800 | 12°@BTDC |

## IDLE SPEED & MIXTURE

After making all preliminary adjustments and ignition timing adjustment as described above, turn out idle air adjusting screw until idle speed is to specifications. On California and High Altitude models disconnect oxygen sensor. Make final CO adjustment with engine still at idle. Turn clockwise to increase and counterclockwise to decrease CO% level. After adjustment, reconnect EGR valve, air pump and oxygen sensor, if so equipped.

### Idle Speed (RPM) & CO Level (%)

| Application | RPM | CO% |
|---|---|---|
| Federal | | |
| Man. Trans. | 850-950 | 0.7-1.3 |
| Auto. Trans. | ①750-850 | 0.7-1.3 |
| California | 850-950 | ②1.0-2.5 |

① — 800 RPM is for setting CO level only. Normal idle speed should be 850-950.

② — When oxygen sensor is reconnected, CO should drop below 1%.

### FUEL PUMP PRESSURE

Pressure .......................................... 64-74 psi(4.5-5.2 kg/cm²)

### EMISSION CONTROL SYSTEMS

See Mitchell Manuals' Emission Control Manual.

## GENERAL SERVICING

### DISTRIBUTOR

All models are equipped with Bosch Electronic Ignition System.

**Other Data & Specifications** — See Tune-Up & Bosch Distributors in ELECTRICAL Section.

### IGNITION COIL

Starting Voltage ............................................... 20,000 Volts
Maximum Voltage ............................................. 25,000 Volts

## FUEL SYSTEM

### FUEL INJECTION

California, High Altitude, and some other models use oxygen sensor feedback system (Lambda). Most Federal models are equipped with Bosch Continuous Injection System (CIS).

**Other Data & Specifications** — See Tune-Up and Bosch Continuous Injection System (CIS) and Lambda System in FUEL SYSTEMS Section.

### ELECTRICAL

#### BATTERY

**12 Volt** — Negative Ground.

| Application | Amp. Hour Rating |
|---|---|
| All | 60 |

**NOTE** — On models equipped with electronic fuel injection it is important to disconnect battery cables before charging battery. Damage may result to the electronic components if battery is not disconnected.

#### STARTER

Bosch .................................................. Overrunning Clutch

Free Speed Voltage
  All Models ................................... 11.5 at 5500-7500 RPM
Free Speed Amperage
  All Models ......................... 30-50 at 5500-7500 RPM

**Other Data & Specifications** — See Bosch Starters in ELECTRICAL Section.

## GENERAL SERVICING (Cont.)

### ALTERNATOR

| Application | Rated Amp. Output |
|---|---|
| All Models | 55 |

**Other Data & Specifications** — *See Bosch Alternators & Regulators in ELECTRICAL Section.*

### ALTERNATOR REGULATOR

All models are equipped with Bosch Alternator Regulators with an operating voltage of 13.9-14.8 volts at 4000 RPM.

**Other Data & Specifications** — *See Bosch Alternators & Regulators in ELECTRICAL Section.*

### CAPACITIES

| Application | Quantity |
|---|---|
| Crankcase (Includes Filter)① | |
| Early Production | 4.0 qts. |
| Late Production | 4.2 qts. |
| Cooling System | ②10.0 qts. |
| Transmissions | |
| Auto. Trans. (ATF Type F) | 7.0 qts. |
| Man. Trans. (ATF Type F) | 0.8 qts. |
| Man. Trans. with Overdrive (ATF Type F) | 2.4 qts. |
| Rear Axle (SAE 90) | 1.7 qts. |
| Fuel Tank | 15.8 gals. |

① — .5 qt. less without filter replacement.
② — Includes 1 qt. in expansion tank.

### BELT ADJUSTMENT

| Application | ①Deflection |
|---|---|
| All Belts | 5⁄16" (8 mm) |

① — Deflection is with thumb pressure applied midway on longest belt run.

### FILTERS & CLEANERS

| Filter or Cleaner | Service Interval (Miles) |
|---|---|
| Oil Filter | Replace every 7,500 |
| Air Cleaner | Replace every 30,000 |
| Fuel Filter | Replace every 30,000 |
| Fuel Tank Filter | Clean every 15,000 |
| EGR Valve | Replace every 30,000 |
| Evap. Canister Filter | Replace every 45,000 |

## TUNE-UP

### 260 Series

### ENGINE IDENTIFICATION

The B27F Engine may be identified by the number stamped on left side of engine block just forward of distributor. Number also is found on model plate, located on front, right-hand suspension strut mounting in engine compartment (digits 4, 5 and 6).

| Application | Code |
| --- | --- |
| Federal ........................................ | 653 & 659 |
| California ..................................... | 659 |

### MODEL IDENTIFICATION

#### VEHICLE IDENTIFICATION

The vehicle identification number is located on a plate attached to the left windshield pillar. It also appears on model plate located on right front suspension strut mounting.

### COMPRESSION PRESSURE

With engine at normal operating temperature, spark plugs removed, throttle valve wide open and cranking speed at 250-300 RPM, compression should be as follows:

#### Compression Pressure

| Application | psi (kg/cm²) |
| --- | --- |
| All Models .................................. | 114-156 (8-11) |

**NOTE** — *When checking compression pressure disconnect triggering contact cable on distributor to shut off fuel flow to injector while engine is being cranked.*

### VALVE TAPPET CLEARANCE

**1)** Adjust valves with engine shut off. Valve clearance may be checked with engine hot or cold. Rotate crankshaft so that No. 1 cylinder is at TDC of ignition stroke (both rocker arms for No. 1 cylinder have clearance).

**NOTE** — *Crank pulley has two notches. When No. 1 cylinder is at TDC, upper notch will align with "0" notch on timing marker and lower crank pulley notch will be 150° counterclockwise from upper notch. (Second notch is TDC for No. 6 cylinder when aligned with "0" on timing marker.*

**2)** Adjust valves in sequence as follows:

| Intake | Exhaust |
| --- | --- |
| Cyl. 1..................................... | Cyl. 1 |
| Cyl. 2..................................... | Cyl. 3 |
| Cyl. 4..................................... | Cyl. 6 |

**3)** Now, rotate crankshaft one complete turn, so that crank pulley notches line up as indicated in previous step. This will set No. 1 cylinder at TDC of exhaust stroke (rocker arms for No. 1 cylinder rock, indicating no clearance). Adjust valves in following sequence:

| Intake | Exhaust |
| --- | --- |
| Cyl. 3..................................... | Cyl. 2 |
| Cyl. 5..................................... | Cyl. 4 |
| Cyl. 6..................................... | Cyl. 5 |

#### Valve Clearance Specifications

| Application | Cold In. (mm) | Hot In. (mm) |
| --- | --- | --- |
| Intake ................... | .004-.006 (.10-.15) | .006-.008 (.15-.20) |
| Exhaust ................. | .010-.012 (.25-.30) | .012-.014 (.30-.35) |

### VALVE ARRANGEMENT①

**Right Bank:** E-I-E-I-E-I (front to rear).
**Left Bank:** I-E-I-E-I-E (front to rear).

① — Intake valves are inside the engine's "V"; exhaust valves are on outer sides of heads.

### SPARK PLUGS

| | |
| --- | --- |
| Gap ................................................ | .028-.032" (.7-.8 mm) |
| Torque ..................................... | 13-14.5 ft. lbs. (1.8-2.0 mkg) |

#### Spark Plug Type

| Application | Champion No. | Bosch No. |
| --- | --- | --- |
| All Models ...................... | BN9Y ...................... | WA200T30 |

**Fig. 1 Firing Order and Distributor Rotation**

## TUNE-UP (Cont.)

### DISTRIBUTOR

All models are equipped with Breakerless Solid State Ignition System and no adjustments are required.

### IGNITION TIMING

**NOTE** — *Preliminary to setting ignition timing, it is necessary to adjust throttle linkage, set balance screws, and micro switch (on California vehicles) first. Procedures are included below.*

1) Using "T" valve and hoses, install CO meter at plugs on each exhaust manifold. Connect timing light. Disconnect A.I.R. hose at air pump and plug hose. Disconnect and plug EGR vacuum hose at EGR valve. Turn air conditioning off.

2) Disconnect throttle link and cable at throttle control pulley. Loosen lock nut and screw out throttle shaft adjusting screw. Now, turn screw in until it just touches boss, then in one additional turn. Lock with lock nut. Check that throttle valve does not bind.

3) Ensure that throttle control link (from pulley to lever ball) can be attached to lever ball without changing the pulley position.

4) Attach throttle cable to pulley. Adjust cable sheath so that cable is snug but does not change pulley position. Depress throttle completely; pulley should touch the full throttle boss.

5) Adjust throttle cable to automatic transmission so that cable clip will travel 2" (51 mm) from idle position to full throttle position. At idle there should be .040" (1 mm) clearance between clip and adjusting sheath.

6) Locate the set balance screws; there are three in a row just ahead of the carburetor. Turn in the front two screws until they bottom, then back each one out 4 turns.

7) On California vehicles, micro switch must be adjusted: Connect test lamp to micro switch and turn ignition to "ON". Place a .060" (1.5 mm) feeler gauge between throttle screw and boss. Light should stay on. Insert a .080" (2 mm) feeler gauge; light should go out.

8) To adjust micro switch, place original feeler gauge between throttle screw and boss. Loosen lock nut and screw out micro switch adjusting screw (test lamp should go off). Turn in screw until a click is heard from the micro switch and test lamp comes on. Tighten lock nut; remove feeler gauge and lamp.

**Fig. 2  Ignition Timing Mark Location**

9) On all models, disconnect and plug vacuum hose at distributor. Use air adjusting screw (set balance screw No. 3) to set idle speed to 700-800 RPM. Now set timing to specification by adjusting position of distributor. Reconnect vacuum hose.

### Ignition Timing Specifications

| Application | RPM | Timing |
|---|---|---|
| All Models | 700-800 | 10±2° BTDC |

### IDLE SPEED & MIXTURE

1) After making preliminary adjustments and ignition timing adjustment, make sure engine is at normal operating temperature. Stop engine, disconnect oxygen sensor, then restart engine.

2) Using air adjustment screw (third screw back), turn screw in until it bottoms. Engine speed should drop to 500-600 RPM. Turn screw back out until 900 RPM is reached. Replace air cleaner and any other hoses before proceeding.

**Fig. 3  Setting Idle Speed With Air Adjusting Screw**

3) Using CO meter, adjusting screws on boss behind air sensor and two front balance screws, adjust idle CO to specifications. An Allen wrench is required to turn adjusting screws, and access hole must be covered or plugged while checking CO. Adjust each bank of engine separately, then check together to ensure correct CO.

### Idle Speed (RPM) & CO Level (%)

| Application | RPM | CO% |
|---|---|---|
| All Models | 850-950 | ①0.7-1.3 |

① — With sensor reconnected, CO level should drop below 1% level.

### FUEL PUMP PRESSURE

Pressure ..................................... 64-74 psi (4.5-5.2 kg/cm²)

### EMISSION CONTROL SYSTEMS

*See Mitchell Manuals' Emission Control Manual.*

# 1978 Volvo V6 Tune-Up

All models are equipped with Bosch Breakerless Solid State Ignition System.

**Other Data & Specifications** — *See Tune-Up & Bosch Distributors in ELECTRICAL Section.*

### FUEL SYSTEM

**FUEL INJECTION**

California, High Altitude, and some other models use oxygen sensor feedback system (Lambda). Most Federal models are equipped with Bosch Continuous Injection System (CIS).

**Other Data & Specifications** — *See Tune-Up and Bosch Continuous Injection System and Lambda System in FUEL SYSTEMS Section.*

### ELECTRICAL

**BATTERY**

12 Volt — Negative Ground.

| Application | Amp. Hr. Rating |
|---|---|
| All Models | 70 |

**NOTE** — *Battery must be disconnected before charging.*

**Battery Location** — In engine compartment on right side.

**STARTER**

Bosch .................................... Overrunning Clutch

Free Speed Voltage
All Models ................................. 11.5 at 5500-7500 RPM
Free Speed Amperage
All Models ............................... 30-50 at 5500-7500 RPM

**Other Data & Specifications** — *See Bosch Starters in ELECTRICAL Section.*

**ALTERNATOR**

All models are equipped with SEV Marchal alternators.

| Application | Rated Amp. Output |
|---|---|
| All Models | 55 |

**Other Data & Specifications** — *See SEV Marchal Alternators in ELECTRICAL section.*

**ALTERNATOR REGULATOR**

Some early models had SEV Marchal alternator regulators. Later models were equipped with Bosch, non-integral, non-adjustable regulators.

Operating Voltage ......................... 13.5-14.1 Volts

**Other Data & Specifications** —, *See Bosch Alternator Regulators in ELECTRICAL section.*

## FILTERS & CLEANERS

| Filter or Cleaner | Service Interval (Miles) |
|---|---|
| Oil Filter | Replace every 7500 |
| Air Cleaner | Replace every 30,000 |
| Fuel Filter | Replace every 30,000 |
| Fuel Tank Filter | Clean every 15,000 |
| EGR Valve | Clean every 15,000 |
| Evap. Canister Filter | Replace every 45,000 |

## BELT ADJUSTMENT

| Application | ①Deflection |
|---|---|
| All Belts | 5/16" (7.9 mm) |

① — Deflection is measured with thumb pressure applied at midpoint of longest belt run.

## CAPACITIES

| Application | Quantity |
|---|---|
| Crankcase (Including Filter) | ①6.8 qts. |
| Cooling System | 11.5 qts. |
| Transmissions | |
| Man. Trans. w/Overdrive (Type F) | 2.4 qts. |
| Auto. Trans. (Type F) | 7.0 qts. |
| Rear Axle (SAE 90) | 1.7 qts. |
| Fuel Tank | 15.8 gals. |

① — 6.3 qts. without filter.

# Section 2
# FUEL SYSTEMS

# Contents

*NOTE – ALSO SEE GENERAL INDEX.*

## CARBURETION TROUBLE SHOOTING

**NOTE** — *This is a general troubleshooting guide. Not all steps will apply to all carburetors. When using this guide, locate the symptom in column one that corresponds to your problem and determine the possible causes in column two. Match the number of the possible cause with the same number in column three, and you will have the correction required.*

| CONDITION | POSSIBLE CAUSE | CORRECTION |
|---|---|---|
| **COLD STARTING SYMPTOM** | | |
| ▶ Engine cranks but will not start | 1) Choke not closing (frozen) | 1) Inspect choke plate and coil; free up and adjust |
| | 2) Choke cable or linkage binding or out of adjustment | 2) Free up and adjust |
| | 3) Faulty cold start or thermo-start valve | 3) Test, replace if needed |
| | 4) No fuel to carburetor | 4) Add fuel if needed, check for pinched or blocked fuel line or filter |
| | 5) Faulty fuel pump | 5) Test and/or replace |
| ▶ Flooding | 1) Faulty fuel inlet needle and/or seat | 1) Replace |
| | 2) Dirt holding needle off seat | 2) Clean and reinstall |
| | 3) Excessive fuel pump pressure | 3) Test, replace if needed |
| | 4) Improper fuel/float level (too high) | 4) Adjust float level and drop |
| | 5) Restricted (dirty) air cleaner | 5) Clean and/or replace |
| | 6) Ruptured, split internal carburetor seals or gaskets | 6) Replace as needed |
| | 7) Choke plate setting (vacuum kick) too narrow | 7) Adjust, check linkage |
| | 8) Wrong fast idle cam index | 8) Check linkage, adjust fast idle cam setting |
| | 9) Fast idle RPM too low | 9) Adjust RPM |
| ▶ Engine stalls after starting | 1) Choke plate setting (vacuum kick) too wide | 1) Adjust, check linkage |
| | 2) Fast idle RPM too low | 2) Adjust RPM |
| | 3) Wrong fast idle cam index | 3) Check choke control lever; set cam index correctly |
| | 4) Vacuum leak | 4) Locate and repair |
| | 5) Low fuel pump output | 5) Test and/or replace |
| | 6) Fuel/float level too low | 6) Adjust float level and float drop |
| | 7) Faulty intake manifold gasket | 7) Replace gasket |
| | 8) Incorrect fuel/air mixture setting | 8) Adjust fuel/air mixture |
| | 9) Faulty idle fuel shut off valve | 9) Replace shut off valve |
| | 10) Idler jet blocked | 10) Clean |
| | 11) Damaged idle adjust screw | 11) Replace screw |
| ▶ Engine starts; idles rough and erratic | 1) Flooding in carburetor | 1) *See Flooding in this table* |
| | 2) Vacuum leak | 2) Locate and correct |
| | 3) Incorrect idle RPM | 3) Adjust fast idle RPM |
| | 4) Damaged idle adjust screw | 4) Replace screw |
| | 5) Clogged slow jet | 5) Clean |
| | 6) Incorrect fast idle cam index setting | 6) Adjust fast idle cam setting |
| | 7) Carburetor seals leaking | 7) Locate and replace |
| | 8) Carburetors not synchronized; dual carburetor models only | 8) Synchronize carburetors |
| | 9) Incorrect fuel/float level | 9) Adjust float drop and float setting |
| | 10) Idling air and/or bypass holes blocked | 10) Clean |
| | 11) Faulty anti-dieseling solenoid valve | 11) Replace solenoid |
| | 12) Worn throttle shafts | 12) Replace |
| | 13) Stuck anti-stall dashpot | 13) Replace dashpot |

## CARBURETION TROUBLE SHOOTING (Cont.)

| CONDITION | POSSIBLE CAUSE | CORRECTION |
|---|---|---|
| **HOT STARTING SYMPTOM** | | |
| ▶ Engine cranks but will not start | 1) Engine flooded, fuel level too high | 1) Adjust float drop and setting; inspect needle and seat for proper seating; check for dirt |
| | 2) Fuel vapors in carburetor bowl | 2) Inspect bowl vent operation and correct |
| | 3) Fuel line hot, touching engine block or exhaust | 3) Inspect and reroute fuel line |
| **COLD ENGINE DRIVEABILITY SYMPTOM** | | |
| ▶ Engine stalls when put in gear | 1) Incorrect choke vacuum kick setting | 1) Inspect and correct |
| | 2) Fast idle RPM too low | 2) Adjust fast idle RPM |
| | 3) Incorrect fast idle cam setting | 3) Correct cam positioning |
| | 4) Improper choke adjustment | 4) Adjust choke |
| ▶ Hesitation, stalling during acceleration<br><br>Backfire<br><br>Stumble | 1) Defective choke control switch | 1) Test, replace if needed |
| | 2) Incorrect choke vacuum kick setting | 2) Adjust vacuum kick |
| | 3) Low fuel/float level | 3) Adjust float drop and setting; check fuel level |
| | 4) Faulty accelerator pump or blocked pump discharge | 4) Inspect, adjust pump stroke, plunger; test fuel discharge quantity; check pump spray direction |
| | 5) Secondary throttle not closed, wrong lockout adjustment | 5) Adjust secondary throttles |
| | 6) Bypass holes and ducts blocked | 6) Clean preheater assembly |
| | 7) Incorrect intake air preheater setting | 7) Set to proper season |
| | 8) Incorrect carburetor synchronization; on dual carburetor models | 8) Synchronize carburetors |
| | 9) Main and/or air corrector jets blocked | 9) Inspect and clean |
| | 10) Faulty power valve | 10) Replace |
| | 11) Plugged heat crossover system | 11) Clean and test heat crossover valve; clean passages |
| **WARM ENGINE DRIVEABILITY SYMPTOM** | | |
| ▶ Low power, Surging high speed operation | 1) Main jets clogged | 1) Clean |
| | 2) Fuel filter dirty (restricted) | 2) Replace filter |
| | 3) Pinched, blocked fuel line | 3) Inspect and repair |
| | 4) Air cleaner dirty (restricted) | 4) Replace air cleaner |
| | 5) Faulty power valve | 5) Adjust or replace |
| | 6) Throttle linkage out of adjustment; not opening fully | 6) Inspect and adjust linkage |
| | 7) Low fuel pump output | 7) Replace after testing |
| | 8) Improper fuel level | 8) Adjust float/fuel level |
| | 9) Carburetor seals leaking | 9) Replace seals, gaskets |
| ▶ Carburetors cannot be synchronized<br><br>(Dual Carburetor models) | 1) Weak return springs | 1) Replace springs |
| | 2) Linkage binding, needs adjusting | 2) Inspect, clean and adjust |
| | 3) Blocked idler jets | 3) Clean jets |
| | 4) Faulty mixture control screw(s) | 4) Replace screw(s) |
| | 5) Faulty carburetor seals | 5) Replace seals as needed |
| | 6) Vacuum leak(s); Check for leak at brake unit | 6) Locate and correct leak |
| | 7) Carburetors not tightened to intake manifold properly | 7) Evenly tighten carburetor screws; check torque |

## CARBURETION TROUBLE SHOOTING (Cont.)

| CONDITION | POSSIBLE CAUSE | CORRECTION |
|---|---|---|
| ▶ High fuel consumption | 1) Fuel system leak<br>2) Wrong size jets<br>3) Faulty fuel inlet needle and/or seat<br>4) Fuel mixture setting incorrect<br>5) Dirty air cleaner<br>6) Excessive accelerator pump discharge<br>7) Intake air preheater not ON or OFF according to season<br>8) Enrichment system does not switch off<br>9) Choke valve not opening all the way<br>10) Secondary throttle opens too early | 1) Locate and repair leak<br>2) Install correct jets<br>3) Replace needle and seat<br>4) Adjust idle RPM and mixture<br>5) Clean or replace<br>6) Test and adjust fuel discharge quantity<br>7) Temperature above 50°F (10°C), preheater should be OFF<br>8) Free up vacuum plunger<br>9) Adjust choke valve<br>10) Inspect secondary throttle linkage, adjust or repair as needed |

## GASOLINE FUEL INJECTION TROUBLE SHOOTING

| CONDITION | POSSIBLE CAUSE | CORRECTION |
|---|---|---|
| **COLD START SYMPTOM** | | |
| ▶ Engine cranks, will not start | 1) Fuel pump not working<br>2) "Cold" control pressure incorrect (CIS)<br>3) Auxiliary air valve does not open<br>4) Cold start valve does not operate<br>5) Cold start valve leaking<br>6) Sensor plate stop set incorrectly (CIS)<br>7) Sensor plate and/or plunger sticking<br>8) Vacuum leak<br>9) Fuel system leak<br>10) Faulty Thermo Time switch<br>11) Distributor triggering contacts (AFC & EFI)<br>12) Temperature sensors 1 & 2 (AFC & EFI) | 1) Check fuel pump and double fuse relay, replace as necessary<br>2) Replace warm-up regulator if pressure not to specification<br>3) Replace valve<br>4) Check electrical power to valve, replace valve if necessary<br>5) Replace valve<br>6) Adjust to specifications<br>7) Free up or replace as needed<br>8) Repair vacuum leaks<br>9) Repair fuel leaks<br>10) Replace switch<br>11) Repair or replace as needed<br>12) Replace as necessary |
| ▶ Engine hard starting | 1) "Cold" control pressure incorrect (CIS)<br>2) Auxiliary air valve does not open<br>3) Cold start valve does not open<br>4) Cold start valve leaking<br>5) Sensor plate stop set incorrectly (CIS)<br>6) Sensor plate and/or plunger stuck (CIS)<br>7) Vacuum leak(s)<br>8) Fuel leak(s)<br>9) Thermo Time switch does not close | 1) Replace warm-up regulator<br>2) Replace valve<br>3) Check for electrical power to valve, replace valve if necessary<br>4) Replace cold start valve<br>5) Adjust sensor plate stop to specifications<br>6) Free up or replace as necessary<br>7) Repair vacuum leak(s)<br>8) Repair fuel leak(s)<br>9) Replace Thermo Time switch |

## GASOLINE FUEL INJECTION TROUBLE SHOOTING (Cont.)

| CONDITION | POSSIBLE CAUSE | CORRECTION |
|---|---|---|
| **HOT STARTING SYMPTOM**<br><br>▶ Engine cranks, will not start | 1) Electric fuel pump not operating<br><br>2) "Warm" control pressure incorrect (CIS)<br>3) Sensor plate stop adjustment incorrect (CIS)<br>4) Sensor plate and/or plunger stuck (CIS)<br>5) Vacuum leak(s)<br>6) Fuel system leak(s)<br>7) Injectors leaking<br>8) Idle mixture out of adjustment | 1) Check fuel pump and relay fuse, replace as needed<br>2) Replace warm-up regulator<br>3) Adjust sensor plate stop<br>4) Free up or replace<br><br>5) Repair vacuum leak(s)<br>6) Repair fuel leak(s)<br>7) Clean or replace as necessary<br>8) Adjust mixture to specifications |
| ▶ Engine Hard Starting<br>(Long Cranking Time) | 1) "Warm" control pressure incorrect (CIS)<br>2) Auxiliary air valve does not close<br>3) Sensor plate stop adjustment incorrect (CIS)<br>4) Sensor plate and/or plunger stuck (CIS)<br>5) Vacuum leak(s)<br>6) Fuel system leaks<br>7) Injectors leaking<br>8) Idle mixture out of adjustment | 1) Replace warm-up regulator<br>2) Replace valve<br>3) Adjust to specification<br>4) Free up or replace as necessary<br>5) Repair vacuum leak(s)<br>6) Repair fuel leak(s)<br>7) Clean or replace as necessary<br>8) Adjust mixture to specifications |
| **COLD ENGINE DRIVEABILITY SYMPTOM**<br><br>▶ Rough Idle During Warm-Up | 1) "Cold" control pressure incorrect (CIS)<br>2) Auxiliary air valve does not close<br>3) Auxiliary air valve does not open<br>4) Cold start valve leaking<br>5) Vacuum leak<br>6) Fuel system leak(s)<br>7) Injectors leaking | 1) Replace warm-up regulator<br><br>2) Replace valve<br><br>3) Replace valve<br><br>4) Clean or replace valve<br>5) Repair vacuum leaks<br>6) Repair fuel leaks<br>7) Clean or replace as necessary |

## GASOLINE FUEL INJECTION TROUBLE SHOOTING (Cont.)

| CONDITION | POSSIBLE CAUSE | CORRECTION |
|---|---|---|
| **HOT ENGINE DRIVEABILITY SYMPTOM** | | |
| ▶ Rough idle with warm engine | 1) "Warm" control pressure incorrect (CIS)<br>2) Auxiliary air valve does not close<br>3) Faulty cold start valve<br>4) Sensor plate and/or plunger stuck (CIS)<br>5) Vacuum leak(s)<br>6) Fuel system leak(s)<br>7) Injectors leaking<br>8) Idle mixture out of adjustment | 1) Replace warm-up regulator<br>2) Replace air valve<br>3) Clean or replace as necessary<br>4) Free up or replace as necessary<br>5) Repair vacuum leak(s)<br>6) Repair fuel leak(s)<br>7) Clean or replace injectors<br>8) Adjust mixture to specifications |
| ▶ CO level too high at idle | 1) "Warm" control pressure incorrect (CIS)<br>2) Cold start valve leaking<br>3) Sensor plate and/or plunger stuck (CIS)<br>4) Fuel system leaking<br>5) Idle mixture out of adjustment | 1) Replace warm-up regulator<br>2) Replace valve<br>3) Free up or replace as necessary<br>4) Repair fuel leak(s)<br>5) Adjust mixture to specifications |
| ▶ CO level too low at idle | 1) "Warm" control pressure incorrect (CIS)<br>2) Vacuum leak<br>3) Idle mixture out of adjustment | 1) Replace warm-up regulator<br>2) Repair vacuum leak(s)<br>3) Adjust mixture to specifications |
| ▶ Poor engine performance | 1) "Warm" control pressure incorrect (CIS)<br>2) Cold start valve leaking<br>3) Sensor plate and/or plunger stuck (CIS)<br>4) Idle mixture out of adjustment<br>5) Throttle valve does not open completely | 1) Replace warm-up regulator<br>2) Clean or replace valve<br>3) Free up or replace as necessary<br>4) Adjust mixture to specifications<br>5) Check and adjust as necessary |
| ▶ Excessive fuel consumption | 1) "Warm" control pressure incorrect (CIS)<br>2) Cold start valve leaks<br>3) Fuel system leaking<br>4) Idle mixture out of adjustment | 1) Replace warm-up regulator<br>2) Clean or replace as necessary<br>3) Repair fuel leak(s)<br>4) Adjust mixture to specifications |
| ▶ Engine misfire at high speed | 1) Loose electrical contact at fuel pump<br>2) Primary pressure too low or too high<br>3) Fuel system leaking | 1) Check and repair as necessary<br>2) Check pressure and adjust if not within specifications<br>3) Repair fuel leak(s) |
| ▶ Engine "Diesels" | 1) Sensor plate and/or plunger stuck (CIS)<br>2) Injectors leaking<br>3) Faulty cold start valve | 1) Free up or replace as necessary<br>2) Clean or replace as necessary<br>3) Clean or replace as necessary |

## GASOLINE FUEL INJECTION TROUBLE SHOOTING (Cont.)

| CONDITION | POSSIBLE CAUSE | CORRECTION |
|---|---|---|
| ▶ Idle Speed Too High and Cannot Be Adjusted Lower | 1) Auxiliary air valve does not close | 1) Replace valve |
| ▶ Engine Backfires into Intake Manifold | 1) "Warm" control pressure incorrect (CIS)<br>2) Vacuum leak(s)<br>3) Idle mixture out of adjustment | 1) Replace warm-up regulator<br>2) Repair vacuum leaks<br>3) Adjust mixture to specifications |
| ▶ Engine Backfires into Exhaust Manifold | 1) "Warm" control pressure incorrect (CIS)<br>2) Cold start valve leaks<br>3) Fuel system leaking<br>4) Idle mixture out of adjustment | 1) Replace warm-up regulator<br>2) Clean or replace as necessary<br>3) Repair fuel leaks<br>4) Adjust mixture to specifications |

## DIESEL FUEL INJECTION TROUBLE SHOOTING

| CONDITION | POSSIBLE CAUSE | CORRECTION |
|---|---|---|
| **HARD STARTING SYMPTOMS**<br>▶ Engine cranks but will not start: | 1) Incorrect fuel or no fuel<br>2) Glow plug not working properly<br>3) Air in fuel system<br>4) Faulty injector(s)<br>5) Injection pump faulty | 1) Fill or replace fuel as necessary<br>2) Repair or replace as necessary<br>3) Bleed fuel system<br>4) Repair or replace<br>5) Repair as necessary |
| ▶ Engine starts but will not run: | 1) Air in fuel system<br>2) Modulator valve out of adjustment<br>3) Fuel lines, filter or tank plugged<br>4) Idle speed adjustment incorrect | 1) Bleed fuel system<br>2) Adjust modulator valve<br>3) Clear fuel system<br>4) Adjust as necessary |
| **LOW SPEED DRIVEABILITY SYMPTOM**<br>▶ Engine runs rough: | 1) Air or dirt in fuel system<br>2) Fuel system leak<br>3) Fuel flow uneven<br>4) Incorrect fuel<br>5) Governor or timing incorrect | 1) Clean or Bleed fuel system<br>2) Repair fuel leaks<br>3) Repair as necessary<br>4) Change to correct fuel<br>5) Adjust to specifications |
| ▶ Engine idle speed too high: | 1) Idle speed set incorrectly<br>2) Modulator valve jammed<br>3) Governor improperly adjusted<br>4) Vacuum leaks in manifold | 1) Adjust to specifications<br>2) Repair as necessary<br>3) Adjust to specifications<br>4) Repair vacuum leaks |
| ▶ Poor acceleration: | 1) Incorrect fuel<br>2) Timing device stuck in idle position<br>3) Fuel pump not operating correctly | 1) Change to correct fuel<br>2) Repair as necessary<br>3) Repair or replace |
| ▶ Engine knocks: | 1) Incorrect fuel<br>2) Air in fuel system<br>3) Incorrect injection timing<br>4) Dirt in pump or injectors | 1) Change to correct fuel<br>2) Bleed fuel system<br>3) Adjust timing<br>4) Clean and replace filter |

## DIESEL FUEL INJECTION TROUBLE SHOOTING (Cont.)

| CONDITION | POSSIBLE CAUSE | CORRECTION |
|---|---|---|
| **HIGH SPEED DRIVEABILITY SYMPTOM**<br>▶ Engine smokes: | 1) Incorrect fuel<br>2) Air leak in fuel system<br>3) Injection pump misadjusted | 1) Change to correct fuel<br>2) Repair air leak<br>3) Adjust to specifications |
| ▶ Engine has power loss: | 1) Throttle valve not fully open<br>2) Clogged air filter<br>3) Badly worn pump plungers<br>4) Low fuel pressure<br><br>5) Timing device stuck in idling position<br>6) Control rod stuck<br>7) Incorrect fuel | 1) Adjust as necessary<br>2) Replace filter<br>3) Replace injection pump<br>4) Repair or replace fuel pump or injector pump<br>5) Repair<br><br>6) Repair<br>7) Change to correct fuel |
| ▶ Engine exceeds maximum permissible speed: | 1) Maximum speed stop misadjusted<br>2) Faulty governor<br>3) Control rod sticks open<br>4) Vacuum leaks | 1) Adjust to specifications<br>2) Repair or replace<br>3) Repair or replace<br>4) Repair vacuum leaks |
| ▶ Engine will not stop: | 1) Stop cable broken or misadjusted<br>2) Idle speed misadjusted<br>3) Governor malfunction | 1) Replace or Repair<br>2) Adjust to specifications<br>3) Repair or replace |

## ELECTRIC FUEL PUMP TROUBLE SHOOTING

**NOTE** — *This is a general trouble shooting guide. Not all steps will apply to all fuel pumps. Most electrical fuel pumps are sealed units and must be replaced if found defective.*

**CAUTION** — *Be sure to relieve fuel pressure on systems which maintain fuel pressure at all times. Do not allow smoking, open flames or sparks in area while performing work on any fuel system components. Fuel vapors may be present and danger of fire or explosion exists. Disconnect battery while working on fuel system.*

| CONDITION | POSSIBLE CAUSE | CORRECTION |
|---|---|---|
| ▶ Pump motor not operating; no fuel output: | 1) Check wiring to pump, check for blown pump fuse<br>2) Check for damaged pump body | 1) Repair wiring, ensure proper electrical current to pump<br>2) Replace if damaged |
| ▶ Pump operating; low fuel output: | 1) Check for restricted fuel line, filter or accumulator<br>2) Check fuel tank venting (may cause vacuum in tank if blocked)<br>3) Check for air leak on inlet side of pump | 1) Repair or replace<br>2) Repair tank venting system. Test pump output with gas cap removed to check venting.<br>3) Repair air leak |

## ELECTRIC FUEL PUMP TROUBLE SHOOTING (Cont.)

| CONDITION | POSSIBLE CAUSE | CORRECTION |
|---|---|---|
| ▶ Pump operating; no fuel output | 1) Check fuel supply | 1) Add fuel |
| | 2) Check for pinched or blocked fuel line from pump to carburetor | 2) Locate and repair |
| | 3) Check for blocked fuel filter | 3) Replace |
| | 4) Check fuel cut-off valve | 4) If blocked, disconnect outlet hose at valve and apply low air pressure to valve to reseat check ball. Recheck pump output. |
| | 5) Check contact points in pump | 5) Clean or replace points |
| ▶ Pump noisy | 1) Check for air leak on inlet (suction) side of pump | 1) Locate and repair leak |
| | 2) Pump loose, vibrating against other parts | 2) Tighten pump evenly |
| | 3) Pump lines (metal) touching body parts | 3) Reroute lines for clearance |
| | 4) Check foam rubber insulation at pump mounting | 4) Position insulation correctly or replace |
| ▶ Excessive pump pressure | 1) Defective pressure relief valve | 1) Replace pump assembly |

# 1978 Aisan Carburetors

## AISAN 2-BARREL — TOYOTA 2F ENGINE

Land Cruiser

### DESCRIPTION

Carburetor is a 2-barrel, downdraft type. It is equipped with a vacuum operated choke breaker. Choke design improves cold engine operation. A secondary slow port helps fuel mixing at start of secondary valve opening. Improvement of operation is noticed during low speed load. A carburetor throttle positioner prevents throttle from completely closing during deceleration. A throttle stop solenoid is also used to prevent dieseling during engine shut down.

### CARBURETOR IDENTIFICATION

| Application | Carburetor No. |
| --- | --- |
| Federal | 21100-61024 |
| California | |
| Station Wagon | 21100-61064 |
| Hardtop | 21100-61074 |
| High Altitude | 21100-61091 |

### ADJUSTMENTS

#### HOT (SLOW) IDLE RPM

See appropriate article in TUNE-UP Service Procedures.

#### IDLE MIXTURE

See appropriate article in TUNE-UP Service Procedures.

#### COLD (FAST) IDLE RPM

See appropriate article in TUNE-UP Service Procedures.

**NOTE** — For performing the outlined adjustment and disassembly procedures, use Toyota carburetor adjusting kits, No. 09240-00011 and No. 09860-11010.

#### FAST IDLE (OFF VEHICLE)

1) With choke valve fully closed, check clearance between throttle bore and primary throttle valve.

2) Adjust fast idle by turning fast idle adjusting screw until a clearance of .051" (1.3 mm) is obtained between bore and throttle blade. See Fig. 1.

Fig. 1   Making Fast Idle Measurement and Adjustment

#### THROTTLE POSITIONER ADJUSTMENT

1) Remove carburetor. Turn carburetor upside-down.

2) Place throttle positioner adjustment screw against tab on throttle lever.

3) Check clearance between throttle bore and primary valve. Turn throttle positioner adjustment screw until correct clearance is obtained. See Fig. 2.

Fig. 2   Aisan 2-Barrel Throttle Positioner Adjustment

#### FLOAT LEVEL ADJUSTMENT

Turn air horn assembly upside-down. Measure clearance between upper surface of float and gasket surface of air horn. Bend center float tab until float level is correct. See Fig 3.

Fig. 3   Measuring Carburetor Float Level

#### FLOAT DROP ADJUSTMENT

1) Turn air horn assembly upside-down. Measure clearance between needle push pin and float tab. Clearance should be as shown in Fig. 4.

## AISAN 2-BARREL — TOYOTA 2F ENGINE (Cont.)

2) Bend both outside float tabs until correct clearance is obtained.

**Fig. 4 Measuring Carburetor Float Drop with Gauge**

### PRIMARY & SECONDARY THROTTLE VALVE ADJUSTMENT

1) Open primary throttle valve. Then, open secondary throttle valve. Make sure valves are perpendicular to flange surface when fully opened.

2) Bend throttle lever stopper(s) until proper opening is obtained.

### ACCELERATOR PUMP ADJUSTMENT

1) Accelerator pump stroke should be .374" (9.5 mm).

2) Bend accelerator pump link to obtain right setting.

**NOTE** — Measurement should be taken at boot end of accelerator pump lever.

### CHOKE BREAK ADJUSTMENT

1) Push choke vacuum break diaphragm rod to open choke valve. Measure choke valve angle. See Fig. 5.

**Fig. 5 Choke Break Adjustment**

2) Bend choke-to-vacuum break diaphragm rod at existing bend. Release diaphragm rod and check operation. Movement of choke valve should be easy.

### SECONDARY THROTTLE OPENING ANGLE (KICK-UP)

1) Remove carburetor. Turn carburetor upside-down. Open primary throttle valve all the way.

2) Check angle between secondary throttle bore wall and secondary throttle valve with angle gauge. See Fig. 6.

3) Bend secondary throttle lever to obtain right clearance.

4) Clearance is correct when opening angle is 25° (from bore) for Federal models or 28° (from bore) for California models.

**Fig. 6 Adjusting Secondary Throttle Opening Angle (Kick-Up)**

## OVERHAUL

### DISASSEMBLY

1) Remove pump arm, pump connecting link, choke connecting link, fast idle connecting link, and throttle positioner assembly. Remove screws securing air horn to main body and carefully lift off air horn assembly. Disassemble air horn by removing float and needle assembly, fuel shut-off solenoid, power piston assembly, accelerator pump piston assembly and fuel inlet fittings.

2) From main body assembly, remove the following parts: both venturis, pump outlet check ball and spring, pump dampening spring, inlet check ball, slow metering jet, AAP assembly and check ball, power valve, main jet and secondary operating diaphragm.

3) Remove the throttle body from main body. Remove only those parts from throttle body which are necessary to proper cleaning and inspection.

### CLEANING & INSPECTION

Clean all parts in suitable carburetor solvent and blow dry with compressed air. Inspect all parts for wear or damage and replace necessary components.

## AISAN 2-BARREL — TOYOTA 2F ENGINE (Cont.)

Accel. Pump Lever

Choke Vacuum Break Diaphragm

Secondary Throttle Operating Diaphragm

Power Piston

Fuel Shut-Off Solenoid

Accel. Pump Piston Assy.

Needle Valve

Accel. Pump Outlet Check Ball

Check Balls for AAP Device

Slow Jet

Fuel Bowl Sight Glass

Venturi

Main Jets

Throttle Positioner Adjustment Screw

AAP Device

Fast Idle Speed Screw

Idle Mixture Screw

Idle Speed Screw

*Fig. 7   Carburetor Assembly for Toyota Models with 2F Engines*

## AISAN 2-BARREL — TOYOTA 2F ENGINE (Cont.)

**REASSEMBLY**

Put carburetor together in reverse of disassembly procedure. Make note of the following cautions:

1) Peen over choke valve retaining screws.

2) Make sure power piston operates smoothly after installing retaining screw.

3) Make sure that needle valve, spring and plunger are properly installed in correct order. Float must be correctly adjusted.

4) Make sure that longer (larger) jet is installed on secondary side. Make sure brass colored main jet is installed in primary side.

5) When installing AAP check balls, smaller ball should be placed in pump inlet (outside of fuel bowl) and larger should be placed inside fuel bowl in pump outlet. AAP spring should be placed with its small end away from diaphram or toward the cover.

6) When installing air horn to main body, take care not to damage pump plunger leather.

| | CARBURETOR ADJUSTMENT SPECIFICATIONS | | | | | | | |
|---|---|---|---|---|---|---|---|---|
| Application | Idle Speed (Engine RPM) | | Float Level Setting In. (mm) | Float Drop In. (mm) | Fast Idle Opening Clearance In. (mm) | Choke Breaker Angle | Accel. Pump Stroke In. (mm) | Throttle Positioner In. (mm) |
| | Hot | Fast | | | | | | |
| Land Cruiser | 600-700 | 1600-2000 | .295 (7.5) | .043" (1.1) | .051" (1.3) | 38° | .374" (9.5) | .031" (.8) |

## AISAN 2-BARREL — TOYOTA 2T-C ENGINE

**Corolla 1600**

### DESCRIPTION

Carburetor is of 2-barrel, downdraft design and is equipped with automatic choke which is heated by an electrically operated bimetal heating coil. A piston type accelerator pump is incorporated into the primary barrel and an auxiliary accelerator pump system aids in cold engine acceleration. Other equipment includes diaphragms which open secondaries at high speed and full throttle operation. California and high altitude vehicles are all equipped with throttle positioners, as well as mixture control systems on manual transmission vehicles. Other features include choke breaker, choke opener, deceleration fuel cut (Federal), and high altitude compensation devices.

### Carburetor Part Numbers

| Application | Part No. |
| --- | --- |
| Federal | 21100-26800 |
| California | 21100-26395 |
| High Altitude | 21100-26602 |

**Fig. 1  Assembled View of Aisan 2-Barrel Carburetor**

### ADJUSTMENTS

#### HOT (SLOW) IDLE RPM

*See appropriate article in TUNE-UP Service Procedures.*

#### IDLE MIXTURE

*See appropriate article in TUNE-UP Service Procedures.*

#### COLD (FAST) IDLE RPM

*See appropriate article in TUNE-UP Service Procedures.*

### FLOAT LEVEL

**NOTE** — *When top and bottom lever positions are properly adjusted, float will maintain specified fuel level (glass level mark) when engine is running.*

**Fig. 2  Carburetor Float with Float Lever Points Called Out**

Hold air horn upside-down. Allow float to hang by its own weight. Measure gap between float lip and air horn gasket surface. Bend float lip (top lever) until gap is correct. See *Fig. 2 and 3.*

.256" (6.5 mm)

**Fig. 3  Float Level Measurement Points and Gauge**

### FLOAT DROP

Lift up float. Measure gap between needle valve and float lip. Gap should be .047" (1.2 mm). Bend float tang (bottom lever) until gap is correct. See *Fig. 2 and 4.*

.047" (1.2 mm)

**Fig. 4  Measuring Carburetor Float Drop for Adjustment**

## AISAN 2-BARREL — TOYOTA 2T-C ENGINE (Cont.)

### THROTTLE VALVE ADJUSTMENT

1) Open primary throttle valve. Then, open secondary throttle valve. Make sure valves are perpendicular to flange surface when fully opened.

2) Bend throttle lever stopper(s) until proper opening is obtained.

**NOTE** — *After adjusting, check links to see that they move lightly and do not bind.*

### CHOKE UNLOADER ADJUSTMENT

Insert angle gauge. Adjust angle of choke valve so it will be 47° from fully closed position when primary throttle valve is fully open. Bend fast idle cam follower or choke shaft lip to obtain correct angle. See *Fig. 5*.

*Fig. 5   Choke Unloader Adjustment with Gauge Inserted*

### SECONDARY THROTTLE OPENING ANGLE (KICK-UP)

Bend secondary throttle lever to obtain .008″ (.2 mm) clearance between secondary throttle valve and body when primary throttle valve opening is between 64° (from bore) and full open.  See *Fig. 6*.

*Fig. 6   Carburetor Kick-Up Adjustment*

### THROTTLE POSITIONER (CALIF. & HIGH ALTITUDE ONLY)

To operate properly, the throttle positioner diaphragm, spring, and vacuum hose must be in in good condition. Check links and levers for freedom of movement. Primary throttle valve angle should be 16° on manual transmission vehicles or (15° on automatic) when throttle positioner rod contacts throttle lever tab. This should provide setting speeds of 1300-1500 RPM for manual transmission vehicles; 1100-1300 RPM for automatic. If adjustment is required, turn adjusting screw. See *Fig. 7*.

*Fig. 7   Throttle Positioner Adjusting Screw Position When Measuring Throttle Valve Angle*

### AUTOMATIC CHOKE ADJUSTMENT

1) With choke valve fully opened, turn coil housing counterclockwise. Check if choke valve closes. Set coil housing scale to center line of thermostat case.

**NOTE** — *Choke valve closes fully at atmospheric temperature of 77°F (25°C).*

2) Turn coil housing and adjust engine starting mixture to conform with vehicle operating conditions. When mixture for starting is too rich, turn clockwise, when too lean, turn counterclockwise. One graduation of scale on thermostat case is equal to 9°F (5°C) change.

### FAST IDLE ADJUSTMENT (OFF CAR)

Close choke valve. Check clearance between throttle valve and throttle bore with a wire gauge. This clearance should be as shown in *Fig. 8*. Turn fast idle screw until correct clearance is obtained.

## AISAN 2-BARREL — TOYOTA 2T-C ENGINE (Cont.)

**Fig. 8    Fast Idle Adjustment**

### ACCELERATOR PUMP STROKE ADJUSTMENT

1) Place a straightedge on top of air horn and measure full travel of pump plunger. Make measurement at boot end. Travel distance should be .197" (5.0 mm). See *Fig. 9* .

2) Bend accelerator pump actuating rod at existing bend to obtain correct travel.

**Fig. 9    Carburetor Accelerator Pump Stroke Adjustment**

## OVERHAUL

### DISASSEMBLY

**Air Horn** — 1) Loosen air horn arm set screw, and remove pump lever together with connecting rod. Remove throttle positioner connecting link and loosen six bolts. Remove air horn from body of carburetor.

2) Remove float lever pin and float. Remove needle valve, spring, push pin, and seat. Remove power piston, spring, and pump plunger. Remove plug, gasket and strainer.

**Automatic Choke** — 1) Remove coil housing, gasket, and housing plate. Remove cam float and sliding rod.

**NOTE** — *Perform step 2 only if required.*

2) File off peened part of valve set screw and remove choke valve. Remove connector set screw and take out choke shaft and vacuum piston.

3) Remove thermostat case.

**Body Parts** — 1) Remove gasket, stopper, discharge weight, and ball. Remove back spring and diaphragm from diaphragm lever.

2) Remove four flange set screws and separate flange from body. Remove solenoid valve. Remove check ball retainer and steel ball.

3) Remove slow jet, loosen 4 screws and remove second small venturi and then first small venturi. Remove power valve with wrench. Remove plugs and take out secondary main jet and primary main jet.

**NOTE** — *Perform step 4 only if required.*

4) Remove cover, gasket, and thermostatic valve. Remove level gauge clamp, level gauge glass, and gasket.

5) Remove diaphragm housing and take out housing, diaphragm, spring, and gasket.

**NOTE** — *It is important to mark the relative positions of housing, and spring bracket and diaphragm.*

**Flange Parts** — 1) Remove idle adjustment screw.

**NOTE** — *Perform steps 2 and 3 only when required.*

2) File off peened part of valve set screws and take off the throttle valves. Remove secondary throttle shaft and remove throttle lever.

**Fig. 10    Primary Throttle Valve Adjustment Points**

## AISAN 2-BARREL — TOYOTA 2T-C ENGINE (Cont.)

Vacuum Break Diaphragm

Automatic Choke Assembly

Accel. Pump Operating Lever

Needle Valve

Venturi

Power Piston

Thermostatic Valve Assy.

Accel. Pump Piston

Check Ball

Power Valve

Fuel Bowl Sight Glass

Accel. Pump Discharge Nozzle

Main Jets

AAP Device

Fuel Shut-Off Solenoid

Throttle Positioner (Calif. & H. Altitude Only)

Secondary Throttle Operating Diaphragm

Idle Speed Screw

Idle Mixture Screw

*Fig. 11  Carburetor Assembly for Toyota 2T-C Engine*

# 1978 Aisan Carburetors

## AISAN 2-BARREL — TOYOTA 2T-C ENGINE (Cont.)

**3)** Remove idle adjusting lever with throttle shaft arm attached. Remove retainer ring and take out primary throttle shaft.

### CLEANING & INSPECTION

Clean all parts in suitable solvent (carburetor cleaner) and blow dry. Do not attempt to clean jets or other passages with wire or other metal objects. Inspect all parts for wear or damage and replace necessary parts.

### REASSEMBLY

Use all new gaskets, reverse disassembly procedure and note the following:

**1)** When assembling accelerator pump components, install smaller of two steel balls at bottom of pump plunger orifice.

**2)** When installing primary throttle valve, center throttle shaft in bore using shims on shaft. See *Fig. 10*. Centering is correct when shaft notch is adjusted to bore center. Peen new set screw.

| CARBURETOR ADJUSTMENT SPECIFICATIONS | | | | | | | | |
|---|---|---|---|---|---|---|---|---|
| Application | Idle Speed (Engine RPM) | | Float Level Setting | Float Drop | Fast Idle Opening Clearance | Choke Unloader Angle | Accel. Pump Stroke | Throttle Positioner |
| | Hot | Fast | In. (mm) | In. (mm) | In. (mm) | | In. (mm) | In. (mm) |
| Corolla | 920① | 3000-3400② | .256 (6.5) | .047 (1.2) | .043 (1.1) | 47° | .197 (5) | 16° M/T 15° A/T |

① — Federal idle mixture speed. California, 910 RPM. Idle speed is 800-900 RPM.
② — Federal. California & High Altitude is 2800-3200 RPM.

## AISAN 2-BARREL — TOYOTA 3K-C ENGINES

**Corolla 1200**

### DESCRIPTION

Two barrel downdraft type carburetor, similarly constructed as two single barrel carburetors, but built into one unit. Both primary and secondary systems are provided with double venturi. Each system consists of an air horn, main nozzle, and throttle valve, with one set forming the primary side and the other the secondary side. Primary system is comprised of low speed, high speed, power, acceleration, and choke systems, and is able to supply air-fuel mixture for normal operation. With primary throttle valve fully open, secondary system also operates to supply air-fuel mixture, along with the primary system. The throttle valves of both primary and secondary sides are operated by linkage and are inter-locked, thus making it possible for both throttle valves to be fully opened at the same time.

On deceleration, manifold vacuum pressure passes through a sensing line and displaces a diaphragm, opening a mixture control valve, allowing maximum air-fuel mixture into intake manifold. Other features include a choke breaker, choke return, deceleration fuel cut, anti-dieseling solenoid and hot idle compensation.

### ADJUSTMENTS

#### HOT (SLOW) IDLE RPM

See appropriate article in TUNE-UP Service Procedures.

#### IDLE MIXTURE

See appropriate article in TUNE-UP Service Procedures.

#### COLD (FAST) IDLE RPM

See appropriate article in TUNE-UP Service Procedures.

**NOTE** — To conform with International Organization of Standardization (ISO) standards, the pitch (distance between threads) of many bolts, nuts and screws has been changed. DO NOT install other than ISO standard parts to avoid stripping or breaking carburetor parts.

#### FLOAT LEVEL ADJUSTMENT

With air horn inverted and using suitable measuring gauge, check clearance between end of float and air horn surface. If gap is not as shown in Fig. 1, adjust by bending center float tab. See Fig. 3.

.295" (7.5 mm)

**Fig. 1   Measuring Float Level**

#### FLOAT DROP ADJUSTMENT

Lift up float. Using a wire gauge, measure the gap between needle valve push pin and float lip. Dimension should be as shown in Fig. 2. If not, bend outer float tabs as necessary. See Fig. 3.

.024" (.6 mm)

**Fig. 2   Measuring Float Drop**

Center Tab

Outer Tabs

**Fig. 3   Float Tab Location**

#### PRIMARY & SECONDARY THROTTLE VALVES

When primary throttle valve is fully opened (90°), secondary throttle valve should also be completely open (90°). If adjustment is necessary, bend throttle shaft link.

**NOTE** — The secondary throttle valve should begin to open when primary throttle valve is open 61° from bore surface, or when gauge (installed as in Fig. 4) shows 29°.

Throttle Shaft Link

Primary Throttle Arm

Float Angle Gauge

61°

29°

**Fig. 4   Throttle Valve Opening**

## AISAN 2-BARREL — TOYOTA 3K-C ENGINES (Cont.)

### ACCELERATOR PUMP

Upper (left) hole in accelerator pump connecting rod link is the setting for normal weather operation. Other hole is used for extremely cold weather operation.

Total pump stroke should be .191" (4.85 mm).

### SECONDARY THROTTLE STOP LEVER

Measure distance between high speed shaft arm and stop lever just as secondary throttle valve begins to open. Clearance should be to specification shown in *Fig. 5*.

**Fig. 5   Stop Lever Measurement**

### HIGH SPEED VALVE CLEARANCE

When high speed valve is fully open, clearance between valve and bore should be .008-.016" (.2-.4 mm). If not, adjust by loosening the valve set screws and shifting high speed valve.

### FAST IDLE ADJUSTMENT (OFF CAR)

Using suitable wire gauge, measure, and if necessary, adjust clearance between throttle valve end and body with choke fully closed. Adjust fast idle screw to obtain clearance shown in *Fig. 6*.

**Fig. 6   Fast Idle Adjustment**

### OVERHAUL

#### DISASSEMBLY

1) Disconnect fast idle connector and pump lever connecting link. Remove pump lever retaining screw, pump lever, and disconnect pump connecting link.

2) Remove four air horn retaining screws and carefully lift off air horn assembly straight up.

3) Remove pump plunger and dampening spring. Invert carburetor and remove pump discharge weight and check ball, using extreme caution not to lose check ball. Remove solenoid valve. Remove four flange set screws, and lift air horn from flange.

**NOTE** — *Remove two screws from lower side. Screw with hole also serves as vacuum passage.*

4) Remove float lever pin, float, needle valve with push pin and spring, then remove seat with gasket. Remove power piston stopper retaining screw, and remove power piston and spring. Remove pump plunger boot. Loosen and remove main passage plug, take out strainer.

5) Remove small primary venturi retaining screws, then remove venturi with gasket. Also remove small secondary venturi. Remove thermostatic valve. Using tweezers, take out check ball retainer from bottom of pump cylinder. Invert carburetor and remove check ball. Unscrew and remove slow jet, being careful not to damage threads. Remove primary and secondary main jets along with gaskets.

6) Remove drain plug with gasket, then remove power valve, using a suitable tool. Remove power jet from power valve. Remove idle adjusting screw along with spring.

#### CLEANING & INSPECTION

1) Wash all parts in clean gasoline and blow all fuel passages dry with compressed air. Clean exterior parts with gasoline and a soft wire brush, remove carbon deposits from around throttle valve. Never use wire for cleaning jets. Check thermostatic valve and solenoid valve contacting surfaces, "O" ring, and valve action.

2) Inspect air horn for cracks, nicks, or burrs at gasket surfaces. Check power piston operation by breathing in and out from the hole at center of air horn, check for air leak and smooth piston movement. Inspect float for damage, then inspect "O" ring. Check float needle valve for proper seating by inverting air horn and assembling needle valve and float. Suck in on main fuel passage; if any linkage, valve seating is not satisfactory. Inspect plunger boot for damage or cracks.

3) Inspect strainer for damage or rust. Check choke valve for operation, smooth movement and see that excessive shaft play does not exist, replace as necessary. Inspect main body for cracks, nicks, or burrs at gasket surfaces. Check power valve for smooth operation and proper seating by blowing against valve. Inspect jets for damaged threads or passages. Check for pump plunger wear, then check spring for rust or weakness.

4) Check high speed valve for smooth movement; be sure shaft play is minimal. If necessary, replace high speed shaft. Inspect flange for cracks, nicks, or burrs at gasket surfaces.

## AISAN 2-BARREL — TOYOTA 3K-C ENGINES (Cont.)

Accelerator Pump Lever

Throttle Positioner

Choke Shaft

Stop Lever

Accel. Pump Piston

Needle Valve Assy.

Fuel Shut-Off Solenoid

Float

Venturi

Power Valve Assy.

Slow Jet

Secondary Main Jet

Accel. Pump Discharge Weight & Ball

Idle Speed Screw

"E" Clip

Fast Idle Speed Screw

High Speed Valve Shaft

Idle Mixture Screw

Thermostatic Valve

Primary Throttle Shaft

Primary Throttle Shaft Arm

Secondary Throttle Shaft

*Fig. 7   Aisan 2-Barrel — 3K-C Engine (Typical)*

# 1978 Aisan Carburetors

## AISAN 2-BARREL — TOYOTA 3K-C ENGINES (Cont.)

Check idle adjusting screw for damaged threads and good seating surface, also check idle spring for weakness. Check operation of primary and secondary throttle valves, also check for excessive shaft play. Primary throttle shaft play (in direction of shaft) can be adjusted using shims.

### REASSEMBLY

Reverse removal procedure noting the following:

**Choke Valve Replacement** — Remove choke valve retaining screws by removing staking, then remove choke valve from shaft; remove shaft along with return spring and relief spring. Reassemble in reverse order using multipurpose grease.

**High Speed Shaft Replacement** — Remove staked screws, then remove high speed valve from shaft. Remove retaining ring and pull out high speed shaft. Reassemble in reverse order, noting that it may be necessary to use shims to remove excessive shaft play. Shims may be installed on either or both sides of shaft.

**Throttle Valve Replacement** — If necessary to replace, disconnect throttle shaft link, remove throttle lever retaining nut, and remove primary throttle shaft arm and fast idle lever. Remove staking, then remove retaining screws and primary throttle valve.

Remove retaining ring and pull out primary throttle shaft. Remove secondary throttle shaft and valve in the same manner as primary valve and shaft. To reassemble, follow the disassembly procedures and note that the thin valve plate must be installed to the primary side, while the thick valve plate goes to the secondary side. Also, it may be necessary to install shims on one or both sides of primary throttle shaft, to eliminate excessive shaft play.

**Idle Mixture Screw** — Lightly seat mixture screw and back out three turns as a preliminary adjustment.

| | CARBURETOR ADJUSTMENT SPECIFICATIONS | | | | | | | |
|---|---|---|---|---|---|---|---|---|
| Application | Idle Speed (Engine RPM) | | Float Level Setting In. (mm) | Float Drop In. (mm) | Fast Idle Clearance In. (mm) | Choke Breaker Opening Angle | Accel. Pump Stroke In. (mm) | Throttle Positioner In. (mm) |
| | Hot | Fast | | | | | | |
| Corolla | 700-800① | ..... | .295 (7.5) | .024 (.6) | .037 (.95) | 42° | .191 (4.85) | ..... |

① — Idle mixture speed is 830 RPM.

## AISAN 2-BARREL — TOYOTA 20R ENGINE

Celica
Corona
Pickup

### DESCRIPTION

Carburetor is a two barrel downdraft design with primary and secondary venturi. An automatic choke containing a bimetal spring heated by coolant provides proper air/fuel mixture control during engine warm-up. Secondary throttle valve is actuated by a vacuum diaphragm unit with a kick-up (open) lever. Secondary valve begins to open when primary throttle valve opening angle exceeds 55°. During deceleration, a throttle positioner opens primary throttle valve slightly to maintain proper combustion of air/fuel mixture. A thermostatic valve provides air flow under secondary throttle valve when ambient air temperature is high. System helps maintain proper combustion. Other features include choke breaker, auxiliary accelerator pump and deceleration fuel cut.

### ADJUSTMENTS

#### HOT (SLOW) IDLE RPM

*See appropriate article in TUNE-UP Service Procedures.*

#### IDLE MIXTURE

*See appropriate article in TUNE-UP Service Procedures.*

#### COLD (FAST) IDLE RPM

*See appropriate article in TUNE-UP Service Procedures.*

**NOTE** — *It is recommended that Toyota carburetor adjustment kit 09240-00011 be used to make the following adjustments.*

#### ACCELERATOR PUMP STROKE ADJUSTMENT

Measure distance from top of accelerator pump operating lever to top of air horn. Make measurement with throttle valves in idle position. Make measurement again, but with throttle valves in wide open position. Difference between the two measurements is total stroke travel. Travel should be .177" (4.5 mm). *See Fig. 1.*

177" (4.5 mm)

*Fig. 1   Accelerator Pump Adjustment and Measurement*

#### FLOAT LEVEL ADJUSTMENT

1) Allow float to hang down by its own weight. Check clearance between float tip and air horn for .276" (7 mm). See Fig. 2.

**NOTE** — *Measurement must be made without gasket on air horn.*

2) Adjust by bending float lip (A).

"A"

Gauge Tool

*Fig. 2   Adjustment Points for Float Level*

#### FLOAT DROP ADJUSTMENT

1) Lift up float. Check clearance between needle valve plunger and float lip.

2) Clearance should be .04" (1 mm). Adjust by bending float tab (B). *See Fig. 3.*

B

Gauge Tool

*Fig. 3   Float Drop Adjustment Using Angle Gauge*

#### UNLOADER ADJUSTMENT

1) Open primary throttle valve. Check choke valve angle with 50° gauge. *See Fig. 4.*

2) If angle is not correct, bend fast idle cam follower lip.

Cam Follower Lip    Choke Valve    Angle Gauge 50°

Choke Shaft Tab

Throttle Shaft

*Fig. 4   Choke Unloader Adjustment Points and Measurements*

# 1978 Aisan Carburetor

## AISAN 2-BARREL — TOYOTA 20R ENGINE (Cont.)

### PRIMARY-TO-SECONDARY ANGLE AT FULL THROTTLE

When primary throttle valve is fully opened (90° from bore), check that secondary is also at full open position (90° from bore). If adjustment is necessary, bend throttle lever stoppers at primary and secondary throttle linkage. *See Fig. 5.*

*Fig. 5   Adjusting Secondary Valve Angle*

### SECONDARY THROTTLE KICK-UP

Fully open primary throttle valve. Check secondary throttle valve opening. Clearance between secondary throttle valve and bore should be .008" (.2 mm). *See Fig. 6.* Bend secondary throttle lever.

*Fig. 6   Secondary Kick-Up Measurement and Adjustment*

### AUTOMATIC CHOKE

Choke plate should close at 77°F (25°C). Index cover with center mark on housing. One increment of movement of choke cover equals 9°F variation.

### FAST IDLE (BENCH ADJUSTMENT)

With choke valve fully closed, check clearance between primary throttle valve and throttle bore. If clearance is not to specifications found in *Fig. 7*, adjust by turning fast idle screw.

*Fig. 7   Bench Adjustment of Carburetor Fast Idle*

### CHOKE BREAKER ADJUSTMENT

Push (depress) choke breaker rod to open choke valve. Check choke valve angle (38° from bore). Bend relief lever until correct measurement is obtained.

### CHOKE OPENER ADJUSTMENT

Push in choke opener rod. Check choke valve angle (50° from bore). Bend choke opener link until correct measurement is obtained. *See Fig. 8.*

*Fig. 8   Choke Opener Adjustment*

### THROTTLE POSITIONER

With throttle positioner adjusting screw on center of lever tab, measure clearance between primary throttle valve and bore. Measurement should be .009" (.22 mm). If not, set adjusting screw to provide proper clearance. When in operation, setting speed should be 1050 RPM.

## OVERHAUL

### DISASSEMBLY

1) Remove the following parts from the air horn assembly: Pump arm with connecting rod; connecting links and seven air

## AISAN 2-BARREL — TOYOTA 20R ENGINE (Cont.)

Choke Opener

Air Horn

Choke Breaker

Automatic Choke Assembly

Accel. Pump Operating Lever

Needle Valve and Seat

Float

Power Valve

Accel. Pump Piston

Venturi

Accel. Pump Discharge Nozzle

Check Ball

Fuel Bowl Sight Glass

Thermostatic Valve

Metering Jet

Main Jets

Float Chamber

Secondary Throttle Operating Diaphragm

Fast Idle Cam

AAP Device

Idle Mixture Screw

Fuel Shut-Off Solenoid

Throttle Positioner

Flange

Throttle Lever

Throttle Positioner Adjusting Screw

Fast Idle Adjusting Screw

Idle Speed Screw

*Fig. 9  Exploded View of Toyota 20R Engine Carburetor*

## AISAN 2-BARREL — TOYOTA 20R ENGINE (Cont.)

horn screws; choke opener; air horn (lift off); float pivot pin and float; needle valve assembly; and pump plunger and power piston.

2) Disassemble the following components from the automatic choke: Water and coil housing, plate and gasket; choke lever and coil housing body; and breaker, relief lever and link.

3) From the main body remove or disassemble: Venturi; pump jet, "O" ring, spring and ball; damping spring, retainer and ball; slow jet and power valve; thermostatic valve and "O" ring; and sight glass and throttle positioner.

4) Continue to disassemble body by removing: Auxiliary accelerator pump inlet plug and ball; outlet plug, spring, and ball; auxiliary pump housing; diaphragm, spring, and gasket; spring, link and diaphragm assembly; solenoid valve and fast idle cam; and carburetor body and insulator.

5) From the flange, remove: Mixture screws; throttle lever, spring and collars; and throttle positioner lever.

### CLEANING

**CAUTION** — Do not immerse synthetic components (gaskets, plastics, rubber) or thermostat and diaphragm valves in carburetor cleaner.

Immerse metal parts in carburetor cleaner and agitate until clean. Remove parts from cleaner, wash in solvent and blow dry with compressed air.

### REASSEMBLY

Reassembly of carburetor components is performed by following reverse order of disassembly. To complete carburetor assembly correctly, refer to the notes listed below:

1) Install new gaskets throughout carburetor where required. Discard all old gaskets. Check for smooth operation of all valves and linkage.

2) DO NOT overtighten power piston stop screw. If screw is too tight, the bore may be distorted resulting in sticking piston operation.

3) DO NOT install fuel level gauge glass backwards. Dot on glass should be to inside of float bowl and bubble facing outward.

4) When carburetor body is viewed from sight glass end, secondary main jet (aluminum) is located in right side opening and primary main jet (brass) in left side opening. Install both jets with flat washers.

5) Ensure flange gasket is installed correctly. Gasket will fit backwards easily, so ensure all holes are aligned properly for correct positioning.

6) Torque carburetor flange nuts (with lock washers) to **5** ft. lbs.

| | CARBURETOR ADJUSTMENT SPECIFICATIONS | | | | | | | |
|---|---|---|---|---|---|---|---|---|
| Application | Idle Speed (Engine RPM) | | Float Level Setting In. (mm) | Float Drop In. (mm) | Fast Idle Clearance In. (mm) | Choke Breaker Angle | Accel. Pump Stroke In. (mm) | Throttle Positioner In. (mm) |
| | Hot | Fast | | | | | | |
| 20R Engine | M/T 870① A/T 920① | 2200-2600② | .276 (7) | .040 (1) | .047 (1.2) | 38° | .177 (4.5) | .009 (.22) |

① — Idle mixture speed shown. Idle speed is 800±50 RPM for Man. Trans.; 850±50 RPM for Auto. Trans.

② — With EGR disconnected and vacuum advance hose unhooked and plugged.

## AISAN 2-BARREL — TOYOTA 4M ENGINE

Cressida

### DESCRIPTION

Carburetor is a 2-barrel downdraft design which incorporates a primary and secondary system. Primary system consists of; low speed circuit, high speed circuit, power circuit, acceleration circuit and automatic choke. Secondary system consists of low and high speed circuits. Secondary throttle valve is operated by vacuum diaphragm. Diaphragm operation is governed by venturi vacuum in both primary and secondary main venturis.

Throttle positioner, choke breaker and choke opener systems are used to reduce emissions and provide more efficient combustion.

### ADJUSTMENTS

### HOT (SLOW) IDLE RPM

See appropriate article in TUNE-UP Service Procedures.

### IDLE MIXTURE

See appropriate article in TUNE-UP Service Procedures.

### COLD (FAST) IDLE RPM

See appropriate article in TUNE-UP Service Procedures.

**NOTE** — It is recommended that Toyota carburetor adjustment kits No. SST 09860-11011 and 09240-00011 be used to aid in the following adjustments and disassembly.

**Fig. 1   Carburetor Choke Unloader Adjustment**

### UNLOADER ADJUSTMENT

Hold primary throttle valve wide open. Choke valve should be opened approximately 39-41° from horizontal. Bend fast idle lever to make correct adjustment. See Fig. 1 for correct use of gauge.

### THROTTLE POSITIONER

The throttle positioner diaphragm, spring and vacuum hose must be in good condition for proper operation. Check links and levers for freedom of movement. Primary Throttle Valve angle should be 15° when throttle positioner rod contacts throttle lever tab.

### FLOAT LEVEL ADJUSTMENT

1) Remove air horn and turn upside-down. Allow float tang to rest on needle valve. See Fig. 2.

2) Measure distance from end of float to air horn gasket surface. Distance should be .512" (13 mm). Bend float tang to adjust.

**Fig. 2   Making Float Level Adjustment**

### FLOAT DROP ADJUSTMENT

Lift up float. Check clearance between needle valve plunger and float lip. See Fig. 3. Clearance should be .039" (1.0 mm). Bend lower float lip to make adjustment.

**Fig. 3   Measuring Carburetor Float Drop**

**NOTE** — Fuel level is correct when fuel is between lines on sight glass.

### THROTTLE VALVE OPENING ADJUSTMENT

1) Open primary throttle valve. Then open secondary throttle valve. Throttle valves must be perpendicular to flange surface when fully opened. See Fig. 4.

2) Bend throttle lever stopper(s) to make adjustment.

# 1978 Aisan Carburetors

## AISAN 2-BARREL — TOYOTA 4M ENGINE (Cont.)

**Fig. 4   Throttle Valve Opening Adjustment Points**

### SECONDARY THROTTLE VALVE (KICK-UP) ADJUSTMENT

1) Open primary throttle valve to wide open position. Clearance between secondary throttle valve and bore should be .016" (.4 mm). See Fig. 5.

2) Adjust by bending secondary kick-up arm.

3) Check primary throttle valve opening at the time secondary throttle valve just begins to open. Primary throttle should be 64° from base plane when secondary throttle valve begins to open.

4) Adjust primary kick lever to obtain correct angle.

**Fig. 5   Measuring Secondary Kick-Up**

### CHOKE OPENER ADJUSTMENT

1) Close choke valve. Check clearance between fast idle cam pin and choke opener lever. Clearance should be .020-.059" (.5-1.5 mm).

2) Bend choke opener diaphragm-to-fast idle link.

**NOTE** — When choke opener is fully pushed in, the throttle link should not catch on fast idle cam.

### ACCELERATOR PUMP STROKE ADJUSTMENT

Measure pump stroke from closed to wide open throttle. Plunger stroke should be .217" (5.5 mm). Bend pump connecting link. See Fig. 6.

**Fig. 6   Accelerator Pump Adjustment**

### CHOKE BREAK ADJUSTMENT

Depress choke break rod. Check clearance between choke valve and bore. Measurement should be .098-.106" (2.5-2.7 mm). Adjust by bending relief lever tang. See Fig. 7.

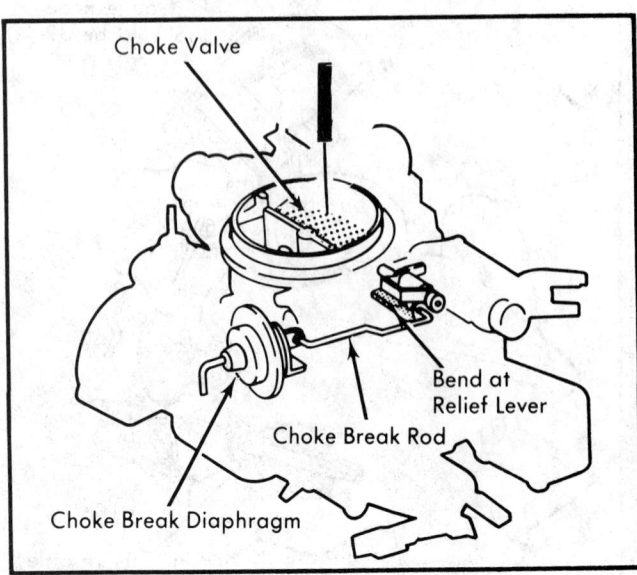

**Fig. 7   Choke Break Adjustment**

## AISAN 2-BARREL — TOYOTA 4M ENGINE (Cont.)

Accelerator Pump Lever

Air Horn

Automatic Choke Assembly

Fuel Union

Choke Breaker

Choke Operating Lever

Throttle Positioner or Dashpot

Choke Shaft

Accel. Pump Piston

Power Valve Assembly

Float Needle & Seat

Accel. Pump Rod

Accelerator Pump Discharge Nozzle

Fuel Shut-Off Solenoid

Accel. Pump Discharge Check Ball

Float

Air Bleed

Float Chamber

Fuel Bowl Sight Glass

Venturi

Venturi

Fast Idle Speed Screw

Main Jets

Fast Idle Cam

Secondary Throttle Initial Opening Link

Idle Speed Screw

Primary Throttle Shaft

Secondary Throttle Shaft

Idle Mixture Screw

Flange

Secondary Throttle Operating Diaphragm

**Fig. 8  Exploded View of Aisan 2-Barrel Carburetor Used on 4M Engines**

## AISAN 2-BARREL — TOYOTA 4M ENGINE (Cont.)

### OVERHAUL

#### DISASSEMBLY

**1)** From air horn, remove: fuel inlet fitting, accelerator pump lever and link, fast idle cam connecting rod, choke opener, and fitting clamp. Remove choke breaker and throttle positioner or dashpot. Remove air horn from main body. Remove float and needle valve, power piston and spring, automatic choke coil housing and choke valve, shaft and levers.

**2)** To disassemble body, remove first and second small venturi, power valve and power jet, plug and steel ball, accelerator pump plunger, pump jet, spring and steel ball. Remove second slow jet, main passage plug and gasket, first main jet and gasket, and second main jet and gasket. Remove fuel level gauge and clamp, solenoid valve, fast idle cam and lever.

**3)** Remove body from carburetor flange. Remove idle mixture adjusting screw and spring and diaphragm housing cap and diaphragm. Remove primary and secondary throttle shafts, valves and linkage.

### CLEANING & INSPECTION

**Cleaning** — Soak all parts (except non-metallic parts) in a suitable carburetor cleaner. Wash parts with water and use compressed air to blow out jets and passage ways.

**Inspection — 1)** Inspect air horn and body for cracks or wear. Check fuel strainer for rust and inspect needle valve and seat assembly for wear.

**2)** Check power piston and valve for wear. Make sure power piston moves freely in bore and inspect pump plunger for wear.

**3)** Check choke coil for deformation, springs for rust or distortion and steel balls for rust and pitting. Inspect diaphragms for leaks or deterioration.

### REASSEMBLY

Using all new gaskets, reverse disassembly procedure and note the following:

**1)** When installing main jets, make sure yellow colored jet is installed in primary side and white colored jet is installed in secondary side.

**2)** When installing power piston make sure piston stop is installed in correct direction and that piston operates smoothly.

**3)** When installing air horn to main body, make sure that float does not strike against body. When installing fuel inlet fitting to air horn assembly, make sure that fuel return side of fitting is facing upward.

| CARBURETOR ADJUSTMENT SPECIFICATIONS | | | | | | | | |
|---|---|---|---|---|---|---|---|---|
| Application | Idle Speed (Engine RPM) | | Float Level Setting In. (mm) | Float Drop In. (mm) | Choke Opener Clearance In. (mm) | Choke Breaker Clearance In. (mm) | Accel. Pump Stroke In. (mm) | Throttle Positioner Angle |
| | Hot | Fast | | | | | | |
| Cressida | 700-800 | 2300-2700 | .512 (13) | .039 (1.0) | .020-.059 (.5-1.5) | .098-.106 (2.5-2.7) | .217 (5.5) | 15° |

## MOTORCRAFT 2150 2-BARREL

**Capri**
**2800 cc (Federal & High Alt.)**

Fig. 1  Accelerator Pump Stroke Adjustment Holes with Rod

### DESCRIPTION

Motorcraft 2150 carburetors have two main assemblies, air horn and main body. Air horn serves as main body cover and contains choke plate and choke diaphragm. Throttle plate, accelerating pump, power valve and fuel bowl are in main body. Each bore contains main and boost venturis, main fuel discharge, accelerator pump discharge and throttle plate. The boost venturis contain high speed bleed orifices and mechanical high speed bleed control system. This system consists of mechanical lift rod that actuates reverse tapered metering rods in high speed bleed jets. This system allows control of air/fuel mixture (to boost venturis) for more precise high speed operation and improved low speed response.

### CARBURETOR IDENTIFICATION

Carburetor number prefix and suffix (example D3ZF-EA) is stamped on tag attached to carburetor. First letter of second line on tag ("A" etc.) indicates design changes. Changes may effect parts replacement. Other letters indicate assembly code, designating time of manufacture.

| Application | Ford Carburetor No. | |
| --- | --- | --- |
| | Man. Trans. | Auto. Trans. |
| 2800 cc | | |
| Federal ...................... | 77TF-KA | 77TF-LA |
| High Altitude ............. | 77TF-KA | 77TF-LA |

### ADJUSTMENTS

#### HOT (SLOW) IDLE RPM

*See appropriate article in TUNE-UP Service Procedures.*

#### IDLE MIXTURE

*See appropriate article in TUNE-UP Service Procedures.*

#### COLD (FAST) IDLE RPM

*See appropriate article in TUNE-UP Service Procedures.*

### ACCELERATOR PUMP STROKE

**NOTE** — *Accelerator pump stroke has been preset at factory for each particular engine application. Additional holes are only provided for different engine applications.*

Check to be sure pump connecting rod is in inner hole (hole nearest carburetor body) of pump lever. Connecting rod should be in specified hole on lever. *See Fig. 1.*

### FLOAT LEVEL (WET SETTING)

With air horn and gasket installed temporarily on carburetor, idle engine for at least three minutes to stabilize fuel level in bowl, then remove air horn and gasket. With engine idling, use "T" scale to measure from top machined surface of bowl to surface of fuel at a point at least 1/4" away from any vertical surface. If fuel level not correct, stop engine and adjust by bending float tab toward or away from inlet needle as required. Repeat entire procedure to recheck fuel level. After adjustment is completed, install air horn and gasket and make necessary carburetor adjustments.

**CAUTION** — *Do not allow float tab to contact needle while making adjustment.*

## MOTORCRAFT 2150 2-BARREL (Cont.)

**Fig. 2   Fuel Level Measurement with Appropriate Gauge**

### FLOAT LEVEL (DRY SETTING)

**NOTE** — *Dry float setting is preliminary adjustment only. Final adjustment (wet setting) must be made after carburetor is mounted on vehicle.*

With air horn removed, depress float tab to seat fuel inlet needle. Measure distance from top of main body (gasket removed) to float, at point 1/8" from free end of toe. If adjustment is necessary, bend float tab. See *Fig. 3.*

**NOTE** — *Do not allow float tab to contact needle while making adjustment, as Viton needle tip may be damaged.*

**Fig. 3   Making Dry Float Level Measurement and Adjustment**

### INITIAL CHOKE VALVE CLEARANCE (CHOKE VALVE PULL-DOWN)

With fast idle screw set on high step of fast idle cam, note index position of choke cover and loosen retaining screws. With retaining screws loose, rotate cover 90° in rich direction and tighten screws. Use outside vacuum source (or seat by hand) to seat diaphragm. Insert specified gauge between lower edge of choke valve and air horn wall. If necessary to adjust, turn diaphragm adjusting screw, located in end of diaphragm. Reset choke to proper index position and tighten retaining screws. See *Fig. 4.*

**Fig. 4   Choke Pull-Down Diaphragm Adjustment Screw Location**

### AUTOMATIC CHOKE

Loosen choke cover retaining screws and rotate cover and thermostatic coil assembly in "Rich" or "Lean" direction to align reference mark on cover with correct scale graduation on housing. See *Fig. 5.*

**NOTE** — *"Index" setting is with reference mark on cover aligned with longer center mark on housing.*

**Fig. 5   Automatic Choke Adjustment**

## OVERHAUL

### DISASSEMBLY

**Air Horn** — 1) Remove air cleaner anchor screw and automatic choke control rod retainer. Remove air horn attaching screws, lockwashers, carburetor I.D. tag, then remove air horn and gasket. Remove choke control rod by loosening screw attaching choke shaft lever to choke shaft. Remove rod from air horn and slide plastic dust seal out of air horn.

## MOTORCRAFT 2150 2-BARREL (Cont.)

High Speed Bleed Metering Rod Yoke & Lift Rod

Booster Venturi Screw

Weight

Accel. Pump Discharge Check Ball

Booster Venturi

Retainer

Elastomer Valve

Idle Mixture Screw

Idle Limiter Cap

Kickdown Screw

Throttle Shaft Lever Assembly

Kickdown Lever

Spring

Vent Valve Actuating Lever

Return Spring

Throttle Plates

Retainer Clip

Accel. Pump Rod

Accel. Pump Over-Travel Lever

Decel Valve Connection

Fuel Bowl Vent Valve

Choke Plate

Choke Plate Shaft

Throttle Positioner Solenoid

Choke Plate Lever

Curb Idle RPM Adjusting Screw

Choke Plate Rod

Dust Shield

Retainer

Choke Clean Air Tube

Float

Main Jets

Float Shaft

Solenoid Off Idle Speed Adjusting Screw

Fuel Inlet Needle & Seat

Diaphragm Link

Choke Linkage

Fast Idle Cam

Retainer

Choke Pull-Down Diaphragm Assy.

Link

Shield

Choke Housing

Choke Lever

Enrichment Valve

Thermostatic Housing

Fast Idle Adjusting Screw

Fast Idle Lever

**Fig. 6  Exploded View of Motorcraft 2150 Carburetor Assembly**

# 1978 Ford Carburetors

## MOTORCRAFT 2150 2-BARREL (Cont.)

2) Remove choke diaphragm assembly, then if necessary to remove choke plate, remove staking marks on attaching screws and remove screws. Remove choke plate by sliding it out of shaft from top of air horn, then remove shaft from air horn.

**Automatic Choke — 1)** Remove fast idle cam retainer, thermostatic choke spring housing screws and then remove clamp, housing and gasket.

2) Remove choke housing assembly, gasket, fast idle cam rod and cam lever. Remove choke lever screw, washer and lever assembly.

**Main Body — 1)** Pry float shaft retainer from fuel inlet seat with screwdriver, then remove float, float shaft retainer and fuel inlet needle assembly. Remove retainer and float shaft from float lever.

2) Remove fuel inlet needle, seat, filter screen and main jets. Remove booster venturi screw (accelerator pump discharge), air distribution plate, booster venturi and gasket. Invert main body and catch accelerator pump discharge weight and ball as they fall out. Remove accelerator pump operating rod from over-travel lever and retainer by pressing the ends of the retainer together, while at the same time, pressing the rod away from the retainer until free. Remove rod and retainer.

3) Remove accelerator pump cover, diaphragm assembly and spring. If necessary to remove Elastomer valve, grasp firmly and pull it out. Elastomer valve must always be replaced whenever it has been removed from carburetor.

**NOTE** — *If valve tip breaks off during removal, don't forget to remove tip from fuel bowl.*

4) Invert main body and remove power valve cover and gasket. Using a suitable wrench, remove power valve and remove gasket. Take out idle fuel mixture adjusting needles and springs. If necessary, remove nut and washer securing fast idle adjusting lever assembly to throttle shaft and lift off lever assembly. Remove anti-stall dashpot or solenoid. If throttle plates are to be removed, scribe plates along shaft and mark each plate to match its original location (which bore) for reassembly. Slide throttle shaft from main body.

## CLEANING & INSPECTION

Clean all parts, except accelerator pump diaphragm, power valve, secondary operating diaphragm. Check all parts for wear, damage, nicks and burrs. Blow out all passages with compressed air. Replace all parts as necessary.

## REASSEMBLY

Use all new gaskets and reverse disassembly procedure while noting the following:

**Throttle Valve Installation** — Refer to scribe lines and marks made at disassembly. Install throttle valves with attaching screws snug. Close valves and check fit by holding assembly up to a light. Little or no light should show between valve edges and bore. Tap valves lightly to centralize, then tighten and stake screws securely while supporting shaft on metal bar.

**Choke Valve Installation** — Install choke valve with attaching screws snug. Check valve fit and free movement by moving valve from closed to open position. Binding can be corrected by grinding edge of valve. Tighten screws securely while holding valve closed. Stake screws while supporting with a metal bar.

**Choke Valve Rod and Seal Installation** — Assemble choke rod seal between two brass washers. Slide into position on seal retainer. Insert choke rod through seal and air horn to engage choke shaft lever clevis nut.

**Accelerating Pump Elastomer Valve Installation** — Lubricate tip of new valve and insert valve tip in center hole in pump cavity. Use needle nosed pliers inserted in fuel bowl to pull valve in until it is fully seated. Cut off valve tip at retaining shoulder and remove tip from fuel bowl.

**Accelerating Pump Diaphragm Installation** — Position return spring on boss in pump chamber. Assemble diaphragm and cover and install two cover screws that do not retain vent valve bracket. Insert a new plug in vent rod and install vent rod and bracket assembly on pump.

**Idle Mixture Screw** — Install idle mixture needles and springs. Turn screws in until lightly seated, then back out 1½ turns for initial adjustment.

**Power Valve Cover Installation** — Use new gasket and position cover so that limiter stops are in position to provide positive stops for tabs on idle mixture screw limiter caps.

## MOTORCRAFT MODEL 2700 VV 2-BARREL

**Capri
2800 cc (Calif. only)**

**NOTE** — *There was no 1978 model Capri. 1977 models were marketed throughout 1978, pending availability of 1979 models.*

### DESCRIPTION

Motorcraft 2700 VV (Variable Venturi) carburetor is different than all other Motorcraft units in that it has the ability to change the area of its venturi for varying demands of the engine. This assembly uses a dual-element venturi valve that moves in and out of air stream flowing into two carburetor throats. Valve is controlled by throttle position and engine vacuum. 2700 VV unit has fuel inlet, main metering, control vacuum, cranking and cold enrichment, idle trim and accelerator pump systems and is externally vented to a carbon canister. Auxiliary systems such as idle, pullover and power systems are not needed or used. *See Fig. 1.*

### CARBURETOR IDENTIFICATION

Model identification is stamped on top of carburetor on flat surface of venturi valve cover plate.

| Application | Carburetor No. | |
| | Man. Trans. | Auto. Trans. |
| Capri California | 77TF-NA | 77TF-MA |

### ADJUSTMENTS

#### HOT (SLOW) IDLE RPM

See appropriate article in *TUNE-UP Service Procedures.*

#### IDLE MIXTURE

See appropriate article in *TUNE-UP Service Procedures.*

#### COLD (FAST) IDLE RPM

See appropriate article in *TUNE-UP Service Procedures.*

#### ACCELERATOR PUMP (INTERNAL VENT)

With curb idle speed properly adjusted, insert .010" feeler gauge between pump operating link and pump stem. Slight drag should be felt when gauge is removed. If adjustment is necessary, turn nylon adjusting nut until correct clearance is obtained. *See Fig. 2.*

**NOTE** — *Check this adjustment whenever curb idle speed is adjusted.*

**Fig. 2  Accelerator Pump (Internal Vent) Adjustment**

**Fig. 1  Motorcraft Model 2700 VV Carburetor**

## MOTORCRAFT MODEL 2700 VV 2-BARREL (Cont.)

### FUEL LEVEL (DRY SETTING)

**1)** Remove upper carburetor body assembly and old gasket. Install new gasket prior to making adjustment. Invert upper body assembly and, using suitable gauging tool, place gauge on CAST surface of upper body. *See Fig. 3.*

**NOTE** — *Do not rest gauge on gasket.*

**2)** Measure distance from cast surface to float bottom. Bend float lever away from fuel inlet needle to decrease setting and toward to increase. Float pontoon should be parallel with gasket. Check float drop adjustment.

Float Lever

Float

**Fig. 3    Fuel Level Adjustment**

### FLOAT DROP

With upper body assembly removed, hold in upright position and place gauge against cast surface of upper body (not on gasket). Measure distance between cast surface and float bottom. To adjust, bend stop tab on float lever toward hinge pin to decrease setting and away to increase. *See Fig. 4.*

Float Lever Stop Tab

Float

Gauge

**Fig. 4    Float Drop Adjustment**

### HIGH CAM SPEED POSITIONER

With high cam speed positioner in corner of correct cam step, place fast idle lever in corner of high cam speed positioner. Firmly hold throttle in closed position. With diaphragm cover removed, turn diaphragm assembly clockwise until bottomed on casting. Now rotate counterclockwise ½ turn to 1½ turns until vacuum port is aligned with diaphragm hole. Install diaphragm cover.   *See Fig. 5.*

Fast Idle Lever

Step 1

H.C.S.P.

Vacuum Port & Diaphragm Hole Must Line Up

**Fig. 5    High Cam Speed Positioner Adjustment**

### COLD ENRICHMENT ROD

Remove choke cap. With stator cap tool (T77L-9848-A or equivalent) installed, ensure cold enrichment rod is seated. Mount dial indicator with tip on top surface of enrichment rod and zero indicator. Remove stator cap and reinstall to index position. Dial indicator should read .125" ± .005". To adjust, turn nut clockwise to increase height or counterclockwise to decrease. Put on choke cap and set to proper position. *Fig. 6.*

Adjusting Nut

Enrichment Rod

Stator Cap

**Fig. 6    Adjusting Cold Enrichment Rod**

## MOTORCRAFT MODEL 2700 VV 2-BARREL (Cont.)

### CONTROL VACUUM

With tachometer installed, start engine and ensure idle is set to specification. Use an allen wrench to turn venturi valve adjusting screw clockwise to close valve. Connect vacuum gauge to vacuum tap on venturi valve cover. With engine at operating temperature, at curb idle, turn venturi bypass adjusting screw (allen screw) to reach specified vacuum setting. See Fig. 7.

**NOTE** — *Throttle must be cycled while adjusting to obtain proper vacuum drop. Check and/or reset curb idle.*

*Fig. 7   Control Vacuum Adjustment*

*Fig. 8   CVR Adjustment*

### VENTURI VALVE LIMITER

Remove carburetor, remove venturi valve cover and roller bearings. Take out expansion plug at rear of the main body on throttle side of carburetor. Center punch until loose. With allen wrench, remove venturi valve W.O.T. stop screw. Block throttle plates wide open. While applying light closing pressure on venturi valve, measure gap between valve and air horn wall. Move valve to wide open position and insert allen wrench in hole from which stop screw was removed. Turn limiter adjusting screw clockwise to increase gap and counterclockwise to decrease. With allen wrench removed, apply closing pressure to valve and recheck gap. Install venturi valve W.O.T. stop screw and turn clockwise until it touches valve. Press valve to wide open position and check gap between air horn wall and valve. Turn stop screw until gap is correct. Install new expansion plug in access hole. Install venturi valve cover and roller bearings. Replace carburetor on vehicle. See Fig. 9.

### CONTROL VACUUM REGULATOR (CVR)

**NOTE** — *Cold enrichment rod adjustment must be properly set prior to making this adjustment.*

Turn choke cap ½ turn in rich direction (clockwise) from index and cycle throttle to set fast idle speed cam. Press lightly on CVR rod and note any down travel. If present, rod is not correctly seated and requires adjustment. Turn screw counterclockwise until some down travel is felt and proceed with adjustment. Rotate CVR rod clockwise until adjusting nut just begins to rise. Recheck down travel on rod. If any spring-back is evident, rod is not fully seated. Turn adjusting screw clockwise in ¼ turn increments until spring-back is cancelled. Reset choke cap. See Fig. 8.

*Fig. 9   Venturi Valve Limiter Adjustment*

# 1978 Ford Carburetors

## MOTORCRAFT MODEL 2700 VV 2-BARREL (Cont.)

*Fig. 10  Exploded View of Upper Carburetor Body*

## MOTORCRAFT MODEL 2700 VV 2-BARREL (Cont.)

### OVERHAUL

#### DISASSEMBLY

**Upper Body** — 1) With carburetor mounted on a suitable stand, remove fuel inlet fitting, filter, gasket and spring. Remove "E" rings on accelerator pump and choke control rods and unhook rods. Take off air cleaner stud. Remove seven attaching screws and lift off upper body, noting position of two longer screws. Remove float hinge pin and float assembly.

2) Lift off float bowl gasket and take out fuel inlet valve, seat and gasket. Remove accelerator pump rod, dust seal, pump link retaining pin and link. Remove pump swivel and adjusting nut. Unhook choke control rod. Carefully lift retainer and slide out dust seal. Remove choke hinge pin. Remove cold enrichment rod nut, lever, swivel, control vacuum regulator and adjusting nut as an assembly. Only disassemble if required for parts replacement.

3) Slide cold enrichment rod from casting, and remove venturi valve cover plate and roller bearings. Take off venturi air bypass screw. Using tool (T77P-9928-A or equivalent), press tapered plugs from venturi valve pivot pins. Push out pivot pins and slide venturi valve rearward until free of casting. Remove pivot pin bushings and metering rod pivot pins (on outboard sides of venturi valves). Lift out metering rods and springs.

**NOTE** — *Note position of rods (throttle or choke side) for assembly.*

**CAUTION** — *Block venturi valve wide open while working on jets.*

4) Remove cup plugs recessed in upper body casting, with jet plug removal tool (T77L-9533-B).

**NOTE** — *Due to importance of main metering jet setting, following steps must be carefully adhered to.*

5) With jet wrench (T77L-9553-A or equivalent), turn each main jet clockwise, noting number of turns, until bottomed in casting. Record to nearest $\frac{1}{4}$ turn. Rotate jet assembly counterclockwise to remove. Take off "O" rings and identify throttle or choke side jets for assembly. Remove accelerator pump assembly and idle trim (mixture) screws. Remove venturi valve limiter adjusting screw from venturi valve (throttle side). If required for cleaning, remove $\frac{1}{8}$" plug from fuel inlet boss.

**Main Body** — 1) Remove starting enrichment solenoid and "O" ring seal. Remove valve diaphragm cover assembly, spring guide and spring. Loosen diaphragm and slide from main body. Remove diaphragm adjusting screw and valve wide open stop screw. *See Fig. 11.*

**NOTE** — *Center punch access hole plug until loose.*

2) Remove starting fuel control assembly only if there is evidence of damage. If necessary to remove, bend bimetal to expose discharge port. Using jet plug removal tool (T77L-9533-B), extract control assembly.

3) Invert carburetor on clean surface (catch check ball and weight), and remove five throttle body retaining screws. Remove throttle body and gasket. Remove choke heat shield.

*Fig. 11  Exploded View of Main Body*

**Throttle Body** — 1) Take off throttle return control (sol-a-dash), solenoid, dashpot and bracket. Remove choke housing. Remove choke thermostatic lever; slide choke shaft and lever assembly from casting and remove fast idle cam. Remove high cam speed positioner assembly, cover screws, cover, spring, diaphragm and rod. *See Fig. 12.*

*Fig. 12  Exploded View of Throttle Body*

## MOTORCRAFT MODEL 2700 VV 2-BARREL (Cont.)

2) Choke housing bushing is pressed in casting and staked. If replacement is needed, carefully press out bushing while supporting casting. File off staking prior to removal. Remove choke heat tube fitting, curb idle screw, throttle shaft nut, fast idle lever and adjusting screw. If removing throttle plates, scribe line along shaft and mark plates for proper assembly.

**NOTE** — *Throttle plate screws are staked in position; file ends before removal. If removing throttle shaft assembly, drive limiter lever stop pin down until flush with shaft. Slide shaft assembly from casting (remove kickdown screw if necessary). Remove venturi valve limiter lever, bushing and spring (if equipped).*

## ASSEMBLY

**NOTE** — *Prior to installation, support throttle assembly and drive limiter stop pin out. Install new pin after throttle plates are installed and staked, leaving about ⅛" exposed.*

To assemble, reverse removal procedures noting the following steps.

Adjust high cam speed positioner diaphragm before installing cover. Lubricate all "O" rings with mild solution of soapy water before installing. Ensure venturi valve diaphragm stem engages venturi valve when assembling upper body to main body.

## MOTORCRAFT 5200 2-BARREL

### Capri
### 2300 cc

**NOTE** — *There was no 1978 model Capri. 1977 models were marketed throughout 1978, pending availability of 1979 models.*

### DESCRIPTION

Carburetor is two stage, two venturi type with primary venturi smaller than secondary. Secondary stage is operated by mechanical linkage. Primary stage includes curb idle, accelerator pump, idle transfer, main metering jet, and power enrichment systems. Secondary stage includes transfer, main metering jet, and power enrichment systems. A single fuel bowl supplies fuel for both stages.

### CARBURETOR IDENTIFICATION

Carburetor identification number may be found stamped on side of float bowl or on a metal tag attached to carburetor.

|  | Ford Carburetor No. | |
| Application | Man. Trans. | Auto. Trans. |
| --- | --- | --- |
| Capri 2300 cc | | |
| Federal | 777F-AA① | 777F-BA① |
| | 777F-EA② | 777F-GA② |
| California | 777F-Cb① | 777F-DA① |
| | 777F-HA② | 777F-JA② |
| High Altitude | D7RE-EA① | 777F-BA① |
| | D7RE-LA② | 777F-GA② |

① — Without Air Conditioning
② — With Air Conditioning

### ADJUSTMENTS

#### HOT (SLOW) IDLE RPM

*See appropriate article in TUNE-UP Service Procedures.*

#### IDLE MIXTURE

*See appropriate article in TUNE-UP Service Procedures.*

#### COLD (FAST) IDLE RPM

*See appropriate article in TUNE-UP Service Procedures.*

#### FLOAT LEVEL

Hold carburetor bowl cover in an inverted position with float tang resting on needle valve. Measure clearance between edge of float and bowl cover. Adjust to specifications by bending float tang. See Fig. 1.

#### SECONDARY THROTTLE STOP SCREW

Back off secondary throttle stop screw until secondary throttle plate seats in its bore. Now turn screw inward until it touches tab on secondary throttle lever; turn screw in an additional ¼ turn.

**Fig. 1** *Float Level Measurement with Drill for Gauge*

#### CHOKE PLATE PULL-DOWN

1) Remove choke thermostatic spring cover.

2) Set fast idle cam on top step. Push diaphragm stem back against stop. Insert gauge *(Fig. 2)* between lower edge of choke plate and air horn wall.

3) Take up slack in linkage by pressing down on top edge of choke plate. Remove plug from diaphragm. Turn adjusting screw until clearance is right.

**Fig. 2** *Adjustment of Choke Pull Down with Related Tools*

#### CHOKE UNLOADER

Put throttle lever in wide open position. Insert a drill or gauge between lower edge of choke valve and air horn wall. If a slight drag is not felt on gauge, bend tang on fast idle lever. See Fig. 4.

# 1978 Ford Carburetors

## MOTORCRAFT 5200 2-BARREL (Cont.)

Typical Decel. Port

Fuel Inlet

Fuel Inlet Filter

High Speed Bleed

Main Well Tubes

Power Enrichment Valve

Accel. Pump Discharge Nozzle

Check Balls

Idle Jet

TSP

Fuel Inlet Needle & Seat

Main Metering Jets

Accel. Pump Operating Lever

Throttle Return Spring

Secondary Operating Return Spring

Accel. Pump

Fuel Mixture Screw

Bushing

Idle Jet

Fast Idle Adjust Screw

Choke Lever

Secondary Throttle Adjust Screw

Fast Idle Lever

Idle Adjust Screw

Fast Idle Cam

Throttle Lever Assy.

Fast Idle Rod

TSP "OFF" Adjusting Screw

Overcenter Spring

Choke Pull-Down Diaphragm

*Fig. 3  Exploded View of Motorcraft 5200 Carburetor Assembly*

## MOTORCRAFT 5200 2-BARREL (Cont.)

Drill or Gauge Rod

Fast Idle Lever

Fast Idle Cam

Throttle Lever

*Fig. 4   Choke Unloader Adjustment*

### FAST IDLE CAM CLEARANCE

Position fast idle speed screw on bottom step of fast idle cam. Insert specified gauge between lower edge of choke valve and air horn wall. Measure distance between tang on choke arm and fast idle cam. If clearance is not correct, bend tang on choke lever. *See Fig. 5.*

Drill or Gauge Rod

Choke Tang

Check Clearance Here

Fast Idle Cam

*Fig. 5   Using Drill to Measure Fast Idle Cam Clearance*

### FAST IDLE SPEED (ON CAR)

Run engine to reach normal operating temperature. Position fast idle screw on second step of fast idle cam, against shoulder of first stop. Fast idle speed can now be properly adjusted. Refer to *Fig. 5* for screw location.

### AUTOMATIC CHOKE

Choke cover can be rotated slightly after loosening three screws. It is not necessary to loosen or remove water cover. Adjust choke cover to make setting correct.

## OVERHAUL

### DISASSEMBLY

1) Remove fuel inlet filter and screen assembly. Remove bowl cover screws, retaining clips from choke rod, and bowl cover. Remove choke shaft, float, inlet needle, then remove vacuum diaphragm screws, washers, and diaphragm.

2) Remove choke housing and gasket. Slip housing away from main body and disengage fast idle rod (noting location of long screws). Remove "O" ring from vacuum passage, then remove choke shaft nut and lock washer. Note position of fast idle cam and spring.

3) Remove pump cover, diaphragm, and return spring. Remove pump discharge valve assembly and discharge nozzle. Then remove two pump discharge check balls.

4) Remove primary and secondary high speed bleed and main wells, noting sizes for reinstallation. Remove primary and secondary main metering jets, noting sizes for reinstallation. Remove power valve and primary and secondary idle jets.

5) Turn idle limiter caps to stop, remove caps, and lightly seat screws. After noting number of turns to seat, remove screws. Remove secondary operating lever return spring, then remove primary throttle lever. Remove idle adjusting lever spring, noting how primary throttle return spring is hooked. Remove secondary throttle lever and adjusting screw.

### CLEANING & INSPECTION

Clean all parts in suitable solvent and blow dry. Inspect all parts for excessive wear and replace if necessary.

NOTE — *Do not place any diaphragm or plastic parts in solvent, these should be cleaned with a soft brush or cloth.*

### REASSEMBLY

To reassemble, reverse disassembly procedure. Refer to *Fig. 3* and note the following points:

1) Use all new gaskets. Install idle mixture screw and spring until screw lightly bottoms. Back out same number of turns recorded on disassembly.

2) Make sure primary and secondary main jets are installed in correct positions. Make sure primary and secondary main well tubes and high speed bleeds are installed in correct positions. Adjust float position before installing bowl cover.

## HITACHI DCG 306, DCH 306 & DCJ 306 2-BARREL

Datsun F10 & B210
Mazda GLC
Subaru

### DESCRIPTION

Carburetor is a two barrel downdraft design with primary and secondary throttle systems. A choke valve and idle circuit are used in primary system only. Both primary and secondary venturis have main fuel nozzles. When the primary throttle valve is nearly wide open, secondary throttle valve begins to open. An auxiliary throttle valve, located above secondary throttle valve, provides smooth operation as secondary begins to open. A mechanical accelerator pump and vacuum operated power valve are used for increased fuel requirements. An anti-dieseling solenoid valve is used to stop fuel flow in idle circuit (on some models) when the ignition switch is turned off. To control exhaust emissions, Subaru uses a coasting by-pass system, Mazda an anti-afterburn valve and throttle opener system, and Datsun (except B210 5-Speed) uses a throttle positioner. Subaru and Datsun feature electric automatic chokes, while Mazda uses a manual choke equipped with an automatic return feature. California Datsuns are equipped with a hand-operated altitude compensator.

### CARBURETOR IDENTIFICATION

| Application | Hitachi Carb. No. | |
|---|---|---|
| | Man. Trans. | Auto. Trans. |
| Datsun | | |
| B210 | | |
|   Federal | ①DCH 306-60 | DCH 306-14 |
|   California | DCH 306-11 | DCH 306-15 |
| F10 | | |
|   Federal | DCH 306-64 | |
|   California | DCH 306-65 | |
| Mazda GLC | DCG 306 | DCG 306 |
| Subaru | | |
|   Federal | DCJ 306-8 | DCJ 306-8 |
|   California② | DCJ 306-8 | DCJ 306-8 |
|   High Altitude | DCJ 306-9 | DCJ 306-9 |

① — DCH 306-37 on B210 5-Speed.

② — When installing a DCJ 306-8 repair carburetor on a California vehicle, change fast idle opening angle from 16° to 19° by turning fast idle adjusting screw clockwise until throttle valve clearance becomes .060" (1.53 mm).

### ADJUSTMENTS

#### HOT (SLOW) IDLE RPM

*See appropriate article in TUNE-UP Service Procedures.*

#### IDLE MIXTURE

*See appropriate article in TUNE-UP Service Procedures.*

#### COLD (FAST) IDLE RPM

*See appropriate article in TUNE-UP Service Procedures.*

Bend tang to adjust to specifications. See *Carburetor Adjustment Specifications* table for correct specifications.

**Fig. 1** *Float Level Measurement and Adjustment Points*

#### FLOAT DROP

After checking float level, raise float until float stop contacts air horn projection. With float held up in this position, measure clearance between float tang and needle valve seat. If clearance is not to specifications, adjust by bending float stop. See *Carburetor Adjustment Specifications* table for correct specifications.

**Fig. 2** *Float Drop Measurement and Adjustment Points*

#### FAST IDLE (OFF CAR)

**Datsun** — With choke cover removed, place fast idle adjusting screw on second step of fast idle cam and measure clearance between primary throttle plate and throttle bore. To adjust, turn fast idle adjusting screw until a clearance of .039-.045" (1-1.14 mm) for automatic transmission vehicles or .029-.034" (.73-.87 mm) for manual transmission vehicles is obtained. See *Fig. 3.*

## HITACHI DCG 306, DCH 306 & DCJ 306 2-BARREL (Cont.)

**Mazda GLC** – With choke plate fully closed, measure clearance between primary throttle plate and bore wall. Clearance should be .048-.060" (1.22-1.52 mm). If not, bend fast idle connecting rod until correct clearance is obtained.

**Subaru** – Place fast idle lever on 4th step of fast idle cam. Adjust throttle plate-to-throttle bore clearance to .060" (1.53 mm) on California and High Altitude vehicles and .047" (1.20 mm) on Federal vehicles. If not to specifications, adjust fast idle adjusting screw.

**Fig. 3   Fast Idle Bench Adjustment**

### SECONDARY THROTTLE INITIAL OPENING

**All Models** – With primary-to-secondary throttle connecting rod contacting end of slot in primary throttle lever, measure clearance between primary throttle plate and bore. If adjustment is necessary, bend connecting rod to obtain specified clearance. See *Carburetor Adjustment Specifications* table for correct specifications. See *Fig. 4.*

**Fig. 4   Secondary Throttle Initial Opening Adjustment**

### VACUUM BREAK

**All Models** – Open throttle and close choke. Release throttle lever first, to trap choke closed. Remove choke cover, and using rubber band, hold choke valve closed. Manually pull vacuum break diaphragm stem out fully (keep straight) in order to compress diaphragm. Measure clearance between choke valve and air horn wall. If adjustment is necessary, bend vacuum break connecting rod. See *Fig. 5.*

**Fig. 5   Vacuum Break Adjustment**

### CHOKE UNLOADER

**Datsun & Subaru** – Open throttle valve to wide open position. Hold choke valve closed with rubber band (See *Fig. 6*). With throttle wide open and choke closed by rubber band, measure clearance between choke valve and air horn wall. If adjustment is necessary, bend choke unloader tang. See *Carburetor Adjustment Specifications* table for correct specifications. See *Fig. 6.*

**Fig. 6   Choke Unloader Adjustment**

# 1978 Hitachi Carburetors

## HITACHI DCG 306, DCH 306 & DCJ 306 2-BARREL (Cont.)

Throttle Valve
Switch Assembly
(Fed. 5-Spd. B210 Only)

Stroke Limiter

Dash Pot

Vacuum Break
Diaphragm

Secondary
Throttle
Diaphragm

Primary
Slow
Air Bleed

Accel. Pump Lever

Primary Main Air Bleed

Secondary Main Air Bleed

Accel. Pump Discharge Weight

Power Valve

Accel. Pump
Piston Assy.

Needle Valve

Float

Secondary Slow Jet

Primary
Slow Jet

Accel. Pump Rod

Fast Idle
Adjust
Screw

Aux. Valve

Anti-Dieseling
Solenoid

Secondary Main Jet

Throttle Return
Spring

Primary
Main Jet

Idle Adjust Screw

Throttle Adjust Screw

**Fig. 7  Exploded View of 1978 Datsun F10 and B210 Carburetor**

## HITACHI DCG 306, DCH 306 & DCJ 306 2-BARREL (Cont.)

**Fig. 8  Exploded View of 1978 Subaru Carburetor**

# 1978 Hitachi Carburetors

## HITACHI DCG 306, DCH 306 & DCJ 306 2-BARREL (Cont.)

Air Horn

Fuel Inlet Assembly

Accelerator Pump Lever

Vacuum Diaphragm and Bracket

Secondary Slow Air Bleed

Primary Slow Air Bleed

Needle Valve Assembly

Float

Accelerator Pump Piston & Boot

Power Valve

Secondary Main Air Bleed

Secondary Slow Jet

Accelerator Pump Spring & Check Ball

Main Body

Primary Main Air Bleed

Discharge Weight

Primary Slow Jet

Secondary Main Jet

Primary Main Jet

Gasket

Throttle Body

Fast Idle Lever

Throttle Lever

**Fig. 9** *Exploded View of 1978 Mazda GLC Carburetor*

## HITACHI DCG 306, DCH 306 & DCJ 306 2-BARREL (Cont.)

### OVERHAUL

#### REMOVAL & INSTALLATION

1) Remove air filter unit, disconnect fuel line, vacuum line, automatic choke wires and anti-dieseling solenoid wires (if equipped).

2) Remove throttle lever or cable. Remove carburetor flange nuts and carburetor. To install, reverse removal procedure.

#### DISASSEMBLY

1) Main jets and needle valves on both primary and secondary sides are accessible from outside carburetor. Remove for service as necessary.

2) Remove throttle return spring, accelerator pump lever and connecting rod. Remove spring hanger and choke linkage if equipped and choke housing. Remove carburetor main body cover being careful not to damage float.

3) Remove accelerator piston, return spring and check ball. Remove float, needle valve and filter. Remove air bleeds and emulsion tubes. Remove slow jets and power valve. Remove drain plugs and main jets. Remove servo diaphragm by-pass jet and air bleed.

4) Remove throttle body from main body with (3) set screws. Do not remove anti-dieseling solenoid except to replace. Throttle body should not be disassembled unless a throttle valve or rod is being replaced.

#### CLEANING & INSPECTION

Replace all parts contained in service overhaul kits. Soak metal parts (except anti-dieseling solenoid) in a suitable cleaner. Blow air through passages to clean and dry. Inspect all parts for wear and replace as necessary.

#### REASSEMBLY

Reverse disassembly procedure and note the following: Check each link system for smooth operation. Adjust float and linkage as required.

## CARBURETOR ADJUSTMENT SPECIFICATIONS

| Application | Idle Speed (Engine RPM) | | Float Level Setting | Float Drop Setting | Choke Linkage | Secondary Throttle | Unloader Setting | Vacuum Break |
|---|---|---|---|---|---|---|---|---|
| | Hot① | Fast | In. (mm) | In. (mm) | In. (mm) | In. (mm) | In. (mm) | In. (mm) |
| Datsun B210 | | | | | | | | |
|   Man. Trans. | 700 | 1900-2700 | .59 (15) | .051-.067 (1.3-1.7) | ..... | .23 (5.83) | .093② (2.36)② | .071-.078③ (1.80-1.98)③ |
|   Auto. Trans. | 650 | 2400-3200 | .59 (15) | .051-.067 (1.3-1.7) | ..... | .23 (5.83) | .093 (2.36) | .071-.078 (1.80-1.98) |
| F10 | 700 | 1900-2700 | .59 (15) | .051-.067 (1.3-1.7) | ..... | .23 (5.83) | .093 (2.36) | .071-.078 (1.80-1.98) |
| Mazda GLC | 700-750④ | 3000-4000 | .44 (11) | .051-.067 (1.3-1.7) | ..... | .22-.26 (5.4-6.6) | ..... | .044-.056⑤ (1.12-1.42)⑤ |
| Subaru | 800-900⑥ | ..... | .41 (10.5) | .051-.067 (1.3-1.7) | ..... | .24 (6) | .110⑦ (2.80)⑦ | .047⑧ (1.18)⑧ |

① — Auto. Trans. in DRIVE.
② — 5-Speed Federal Hatchback is .085" (2.17 mm).
③ — 5-Speed Federal Hatchback is .079-.085" (1.98-2.17 mm).
④ — Auto. Trans. is 600-650 RPM.
⑤ — Federal. California is .063-.077" (1.65-1.95 mm).
⑥ — Federal & High Altitude. California is 850-950 RPM in NEUTRAL.
⑦ — Federal. California is .098" (2.48 mm); High Altitude is .102" (2.59 mm).
⑧ — Federal. California is .060" (1.42 mm).

## HITACHI DCH 340 & DCP 340 2-BARREL

**Datsun**
**200SX**
**510**
**620 Pickup**
**LUV Pickup**

*Fig. 1   Float Level Measurement Point*

### DESCRIPTION

Carburetor is a 2-barrel downdraft type equipped with piston type accelerator pump. Carburetor consists of low speed (primary) barrel and high speed (secondary) barrel integrated into a single unit with common fuel bowl. Secondary throttle is actuated by vacuum diaphragm when primary throttle is opened a predetermined amount. Additional equipment includes an anti-dieseling solenoid, electric choke, altitude compensator and dash pot.

### CARBURETOR IDENTIFICATION

| | Carburetor No. | |
|---|---|---|
| **Application** | **Man. Trans.** | **Auto. Trans.** |
| Datsun 200SX | | |
|   Federal ................... | DCH340-93A ............ | DCH340-94A |
|   Calif. ...................... | DCH340-91A ............ | DCH340-92A |
| Datsun 510 | | |
|   Federal ................... | DCH340-93A ............ | DCH340-94A |
|   Calif. ...................... | DCH340-99 ............ | DCH340-92A |
| Datsun 620 Pickup | | |
|   Federal ................... | DCH340-97 ............... | DCH340-98 |
|   Calif. ...................... | DCH340-95 ............... | DCH340-96 |
| LUV Pickup | | |
|   All Models ............. | DCP340 ....................... | DCP340 |

### ADJUSTMENTS

#### HOT (SLOW) IDLE RPM

*See appropriate article in TUNE-UP Service Procedures.*

#### IDLE MIXTURE

*See appropriate article in TUNE-UP Service Procedures.*

#### COLD (FAST) IDLE RPM

*See appropriate article in TUNE-UP Service Procedures.*

#### FLOAT LEVEL

**NOTE** — *Fuel bowl is equipped with a sight glass. Line on sight glass indicates proper fuel level. If adjustment must be made to correct improper level, use following procedure.*

**Datsun** — With sight glass removed and carburetor main body inverted, measure distance from top of float to top of float bowl. If distance is not to specifications, bend float tang. *See Fig. 1.*

**LUV** — With sight glass removed and carburetor main body inverted, bend float tang until float is parallel with top of float bowl.

### FLOAT DROP

With float bowl removed and held upright, measure clearance between needle valve and float tang. If clearance is not .059" (1.5 mm), adjustment will be necessary. Adjust by bending float tang which contacts needle valve. *See Fig. 2.*

*Fig. 2   Float Drop Measurement Point*

### VACUUM BREAK

**Datsun** — Close choke and hold closed with rubber band stretched between choke piston and stationary part of carburetor. Grip stem of vacuum break diaphragm and pull straight outward (stem extended). Adjust gap between choke plate and air horn wall, by bending vacuum break rod. *See Fig. 3.*

**LUV** — Fully depress vacuum break diaphragm stem and measure distance between bi-metal lever side stopper and stop on choke thermostatic cover. If distance is not as specified, turn adjusting screw. *See Fig. 4.*

## HITACHI DCH 340 & DCP 340 2-BARREL (Cont.)

Pull Stem Straight Out
Measure Here
Vacuum Break Diaphragm
Choke Control Lever
Choke Valve
Vacuum Break Connecting Rod Bend Here to Adjust

**Fig. 3  Vacuum Break Adjustment for Datsun Models**

Adjusting Screw
Bi-Metal Lever Side Stop
Measure Distance Here
L

**Fig. 4  Vacuum Break Adjustment for LUV Models**

### CHOKE UNLOADER

**Datsun — 1)** Close choke plate. Hold in position with a rubber band. Place throttle in wide open position.

**2)** Measure clearance between choke plate and air horn wall. Clearance should be as specified in table. Bend unloader tang to adjust. See Fig. 5.

**NOTE** — It is important to check that throttle valve opens fully when carburetor is mounted on vehicle. If throttle does fail to open, unloader becomes inoperative.

Measure Here
.096" (2.45 mm)
Air Horn
Choke Plate

**Fig. 5  Datsun Choke Unloader Adjustment**

### SECONDARY THROTTLE INITIAL OPENING

When primary throttle valve opens 50° (47° on LUV), primary throttle lever tang contacts secondary throttle lock-out. Any further opening of throttle valve will force secondary throttle lock-out lever to actuate secondary throttle lever and secondary throttle valve will begin to open. Check and adjust as follows:

Open primary throttle valve until it is observed that secondary is just begining to open. Hold throttle in this position and measure clearance between primary throttle valve and throttle bore. If clearance is not to specifications, adjust by bending primary throttle tang. See Fig. 6.

Secondary Throttle Lockout Lever
50° on Datsun 47° on LUV
Bend Tang To Adjust
Secondary Throttle
Primary Throttle

**Fig. 6  Secondary Throttle Initial Opening Adjustment**

### CHOKE LINKAGE (FAST IDLE BENCH)

With fast idle speed screw on first step of fast idle cam, invert carburetor and close choke valve. Measure clearance between throttle plate and throttle bore. If adjustment is necessary, turn fast idle speed screw. See Fig. 7.

Fast Idle Cam
Throttle Plate
Fast Idle Screw On First Step of Cam
Measure Here

**Fig. 7  Choke Linkage Adjustment**

## OVERHAUL

### DISASSEMBLY

**1)** With carburetor removed, perform the following steps:

- Disconnect accelerator pump lever.
- Remove throttle return spring.
- Remove choke thermostat housing and wire.

# 1978 Hitachi Carburetors

## HITACHI DCH 340 & DCP 340 2-BARREL (Cont.)

Choke Chamber

Accel. Pump Lever

Accel. Pump Actuating Rod

Accel. Pump Assy.

Fuel Inlet Needle & Seat

Float Bowl Cover with Sight Glass

Coasting Air Bleed

Enricher Jet

Choke Thermostat Cover

Secondary Main Air Bleed

Power Valve

Accel. Pump Check Weight & Ball

Primary Slow Jet

Primary Slow Air Bleed

Float

Float Collar

Coasting Jet

Secondary Slow Jet

Float Chamber

Primary & Secondary Small Venturi (Remove on Federal Models Only)

Secondary Slow Air Bleed

Choke Connecting Rod

Anti-Dieseling Solenoid

Main Jets

B.C.D.D. (Federal Exc. Pickup)

Fast Idle Cam

Secondary Throttle Operating Diaph.

Fuel Shut-Off Solenoid

Idle Mixture Screw

Idle Speed Screw

B.C.D.D. (Calif. Exc. Pickup)

Throttle Valves

Throttle Body

**Fig. 8 Exploded View of Hitachi DCH Carburetor Assembly**

## HITACHI DCH 340 & DCP 340 2-BARREL (Cont.)

- Remove fuel pipe nipple and strainer.
- Remove screw attaching choke lever to choke shaft.
- Move choke lever toward choke chamber.
- Remove choke connecting rod from counter lever.
- Disconnect vacuum hose from float chamber.

2) Remove bolts attaching choke chamber from float chamber. Remove choke chamber from float chamber, then perform the following steps:

- Remove cotter pin between diaphragm rod and secondary throttle lever.
- Separate lever and diaphragm.
- Remove the two solenoid valve harness clips.
- Remove diaphragm attaching screws.
- Remove diaphragm assembly.

**Fig. 10    Inspection of Automatic Choke**

- Invert float chamber.
- Remove accelerator air bleed, main air bleeds and emulsion tubes. *See Fig. 9.*
- Remove injector weight plug.
- Invert float chamber and remove injector weight.
- Remove power jet, main jet plugs and main jets.
- Remove primary vacuum jet.

**NOTE** — *Do not remove throttle valves or choke valve unless components are damaged.*

**Fig. 9    Location of Jets and Small Venturi in Float Chamber**

### INSPECTION

**Choke Chamber** — Inspect choke shaft holes for wear, vacuum piston and choke valve for smoothness of operation. *See Fig. 10.*

**Float Chamber** — Inspect body for cracks, jointing surfaces and threaded holes for damage. Check power valve for leaks and smoothness of operation. Inspect float needle valve and float pin hole for wear. Check accelerator pump plunger for damage, wear and smoothness of operation.

**Throttle Chamber** — Check throttle valves and shafts for wear, slow and idle ports for clogging. Inspect mixture screw seating and mixture screw for step wear.

3) Separate float chamber from throttle valve body. These parts are attached by one screw on the upper part and three screws on the lower part. One of the three lower screws is used to remove the negative pressure developed in the venturi. Remove this screw carefully.

4) Remove accelerator pump plunger attaching screws. Invert float chamber and remove plunger assembly. Then perform the following:

- Remove float needle valve assembly.
- Remove float level gauge cover. Do not lose the float collar.

5) To disassemble rest of carburetor, proceed as follows:

- Remove screws attaching diaphragm cover.
- Remove diaphragm cover, spring and diaphragm. Do not lose ball and small spring.
- Remove all jets from upper part of float chamber.
- Remove small venturi from both primary and secondary venturi (on Federal models only).

### REASSEMBLY

Reverse disassembly procedures and note following: Make sure jets are installed in correct positions. If choke and throttle valves have been removed, install valves making necessary adjustments and seal screws with a suitable sealer. Check accelerator pump operation by filling cylinder with gasoline and operating plunger by hand.

# 1978 Hitachi Carburetors

## HITACHI DCH 340 & DCP 340 2-BARREL (Cont.)

| Model No. | Idle Speed (Engine RPM) | | Float Level Setting | Float Drop Setting | Choke Linkage | Secondary Throttle | Unloader Setting | Vacuum Break |
|---|---|---|---|---|---|---|---|---|
| | Hot | Fast | In. (mm) | In. (mm) | In. (mm) | In. (mm) | In. (mm) | In. (mm) |
| **CARBURETOR ADJUSTMENT SPECIFICATIONS** | | | | | | | | |
| Datsun (All Models) Man. Trans. | 600 | 1900-2800 | .283 (7.2) | .059 (1.5) | .055 (1.4) | .291 (7.4) | .096 (2.5) | .059④ (1.5) |
| Auto. Trans. | 600① | 2200-3200 | .283 (7.2) | .059 (1.5) | .065 (1.7) | .291 (7.4) | .096 (2.5) | .059④ (1.5) |
| LUV All Models | 900 | 3400② | ③ | .059 (1.5) | .051 (1.3) | .270 (6.9) | ..... | .285 (7.3) |

① — Transmission in DRIVE.
② — Manual transmission. Automatic transmission is 3200.
③ — See adjustment procedure.
④ — Calif. models. Federal models should be .069" (1.75 mm)

## HITACHI DCJ 328 2-BARREL

Courier
Mazda B1800

### DESCRIPTION

Carburetor is a 2-barrel downdraft type. The primary stage includes an idle system, a piston-type accelerator pump system, idle transfer system, main metering system and power enrichment system. The secondary stage includes an idle transfer system and main metering system. Carburetor is equipped with a cable-operated manual choke with an automatic choke release system. The 1800 cc engines are equipped with diaphragm assemblies, the 2300 cc engine with a coasting richer (deceleration) valve.

### CARBURETOR IDENTIFICATION

| Application | Carburetor No. |
|---|---|
| Courier | |
| 1800 cc | |
| Federal Man. Trans. | DCJ 328-8-3879 |
| Calif. Man. Trans. | DCJ 328-9-3882 |
| 2300 cc | |
| Federal | DCJ 328-30-3877 |
| Calif. Man. Trans. | DCJ 328-31-3874 |
| Calif. Auto. Trans. | DCJ 328-32-3876 |
| Mazda | ① |

① — Not available at time of publication.

### ADJUSTMENTS

**NOTE** — *All carburetor adjustments are similar, however there are some physical differences between the various carburetors.*

#### HOT (SLOW) IDLE RPM

*See appropriate article in TUNE-UP Service Procedures.*

#### IDLE MIXTURE

*See appropriate article in TUNE-UP Service Procedures.*

#### COLD (FAST) IDLE RPM

*See appropriate article in TUNE-UP Service Procedures.*

**Fig. 1   Measurement for Float Level Adjustment
(Carburetor Upside-Down)**

### FLOAT LEVEL

With engine running, check fuel level in bowl sight glass. If fuel level is not within specified range, remove carburetor from engine. Remove fuel bowl cover and invert carburetor. Allow float to lower by its own weight. Measure clearance between float and edge of bowl. If clearance is not to specifications, bend float tang to achieve proper clearance. *See Fig. 1.*

### FLOAT DROP

**Mazda B1800 Only** — With carburetor upright, measure clearance between lowest tip of float and fuel bowl bottom. *See Fig. 2.* If clearance is not within specifications, bend float stopper until correct clearance is obtained.

**NOTE** — *Float drop adjustment procedures similar for other models equipped with this carburetor.*

**Fig. 2   Float Drop Measurement Location
Mazda B1800 Shown**

### VACUUM BREAK DIAPHRAGM

**1)** Disconnect electrical connectors from water thermo switch and connect jumper wire to both connectors. With ignition switch in "ON" position, pull choke knob to fully close choke plate.

**2)** Disconnect vacuum supply hose from vacuum diaphragm. Using a variable outside vacuum source, apply 6.7-8.3 in. Hg to vacuum diaphragm. Choke valve should just begin to open.

**3)** Then apply 11.0-13.4 in. Hg vacuum to diaphragm. Using wire gauge, measure clearance between top of choke valve and air horn.

#### Choke Valve-to-Air Horn Clearance

| Application | In. (mm) |
|---|---|
| 1800 cc | |
| Federal | .048-.066 (1.22-1.68) |
| California | .057-.075 (1.45-1.91) |
| 2300 cc | |
| Federal | .057-.075 (1.45-1.91) |
| California | .066-.084 (1.68-2.14) |

**4)** If clearance is not to specifications, adjust by bending choke-to-vacuum break diaphragm connecting rod.

# 1978 Hitachi Carburetor

## HITACHI DCJ 328 2-BARREL (Cont.)

### CHOKE ADJUSTMENT

**Cable Adjustment** — 1) Push choke knob all the way in. Loosen choke cable screws at choke cable bracket and at choke lever.

**NOTE** — *Be sure choke plate is fully open.*

2) With choke cable inserted into choke lever, tighten attaching screw. See *Fig. 3*. Remove all slack between choke lever and choke cable bracket by pulling outward. Tighten attaching screws at bracket. Operate choke to be sure of smooth movement without binding of cable or choke plate.

**Automatic Choke Release System** — 1) Turn ignition switch to "OFF" position. Choke can be manually operated by knob and cable from instrument panel. Cable is attached to electromagnetic and thermo switches. These allow choke to be closed or set to intermediate positions automatically, preventing high exhaust manifold temperatures which occur when choke is pulled out for extended periods of time.

2) When engine warms to 118-126°F (50-52°C), the water thermo switch shuts Off, causing the electromagnet to lose force. The choke return spring pulls choke to "OFF" position.

Cable Attaching Screws

**Fig. 3   Choke Cable Attachment Points (Courier Shown)**

## OVERHAUL

### DISASSEMBLY

**NOTE** — *Slight variances may occur in procedures when disassembling carburetors, depending upon vehicle equipment and engine size.*

1) Disconnect accelerating pump connecting rod from pump lever. Remove pump lever from main body. Remove choke cable support bracket from main body and disconnect throttle return spring.

2) Disconnect fast idle rod from lever. Remove coasting richer (deceleration) valve from main body, if so equipped. Disconnect secondary throttle rod from throttle shaft. Remove secondary throttle actuator from main body.

3) Unscrew slow fuel cut valve (solenoid) from main body. Remove left rear screw attaching air horn to body. Remove bolt lock from fuel inlet assembly. Remove two remaining air horn attaching screws and remove air horn.

4) Remove bolt, fuel strainer, fuel inlet fitting, fuel inlet bolt and needle valve assembly. Remove fuel bowl sight glass cover, gasket and glass assembly.

5) Remove float lever pin and float. Remove accelerating pump cover from main body and remove pump assembly. Invert carburetor and remove inlet check ball.

6) Remove screw retaining pump discharge weight and ball. Invert carburetor and remove weight and ball. Remove idle jets, main jets and all air bleeds from main body. Remove power valve from main body.

7) Remove curb idle adjusting screw and spring and idle mixture screw and spring from lower body. Remove primary and secondary discharge nozzles, retaining screws amd washers. Remove air bleed srews from discharge nozzles and remove air emulsion tubes.

8) Remove lower body from main body. Remove retaining nut and washer from end of primary throttle shaft, and remove throttle operating lever washer and servo diaphragm operating lever, if so equipped.

9) Remove accelerating pump actuating lever, choke actuating lever, throttle return lever and idle adjusting lever.

10) Mark the primary throttle plate location in reference to its bore and to its relative position on throttle shaft. Remove throttle plate and shaft from lower body.

### INSPECTION & CLEANING

Clean all parts thoroughly in solvent and check all passages and parts for wear or damage. Make sure that all jets are clear and clean. Do not attempt to clean jets by using wire or other objects which might damage calibrated orifices. Discard old gaskets and use new gaskets for assembly.

### REASSEMBLY

Reassemble carburetor in reverse order of disassembly. Make sure that primary and secondary components are installed in their correct locations. When installing throttle valve or choke valve, make sure to eliminate gap between valve and wall of carburetor.

## HITACHI DCJ 328 2-BARREL (Cont.)

*Exploded View of Hitachi DCJ 328 Carburetor*
*(Courier Shown)*

## CARBURETOR ADJUSTMENT SPECIFICATIONS

| Application | Idle Speed (Engine RPM) | | Float Level Setting | Float Drop Setting | Choke Linkage | Secondary Throttle | Unloader Setting | Vacuum Break |
|---|---|---|---|---|---|---|---|---|
| | Hot | Fast | In. (mm) | In. (mm) | In. (mm) | In. (mm) | In. (mm) | In. (mm) |
| Courier | 700-750① | ② | .236 (6) | ..... | ..... | ..... | ..... | ③ ③ |
| Mazda B1800 | 700-750 | 3000-4000 | .236 (6) | .047 (1.2) | ..... | .186-.209 (4.73-5.30) | ..... | ③ ③ |

① — 800-850 RPM for 2300 cc engine with manual transmission.

② — See Emission Control Tune-Up Decal

③ — 1800 cc Federal, .048-.066" (1.22-1.68 mm)
1800 cc California, .057-.075" (1.45-1.91 mm)
2300 cc Federal, .057-.075" (1.45-1.91 mm)
2300 cc California, .066-.084" (1.68-2.14 mm)

# 1978 Hitachi Carburetors

## HITACHI 4-BARREL

**Mazda Rotary**
**RX-4**
**Cosmo**

### DESCRIPTION

Carburetor is of four barrel, two stage design. Primary stage includes idle system, slow speed circuit, accelerator pump system, and main metering system. In addition, fluid from sub-zero starting device, if equipped, and oil from metering oil pump is admitted into primary stage. Secondary stage contains secondary vacuum diaphragm operating system, stepping circuit, and main metering system. Choking is accomplished by semi-automatic choke. Carburetor also contains fuel return circuit and electric idle switch.

Mazda RX-4 and Cosmo models feature an altitude compensator in the intake manifold. All California models are equipped with a choke return delay valve, and automatic transmission models for California have a choke delay valve.

### ADJUSTMENTS

#### HOT (SLOW) IDLE RPM

See appropriate article in TUNE-UP Service Procedures.

#### IDLE MIXTURE

See appropriate article in TUNE-UP Service Procedures.

#### COLD (FAST) IDLE RPM

See appropriate article in TUNE-UP Service Procedures.

#### FLOAT LEVEL

1) With engine operating, check fuel level in float bowl sight glass. If fuel level is not within specified limits, remove air horn and adjust as follows:

2) Invert air horn and allow float to lower by its own weight. Measure distance from air horn gasket surface to top of float. If clearance is not to specifications, adjust by bending float seat lip. See Fig. 1.

**Fig. 1  Making Float Level Measurement for Adjustment**

3) Recheck fuel level in float bowl sight glass as a final test as to correct float level.

#### FLOAT DROP

With air horn removed and held upright, measure clearance between air horn gasket surface and bottom of float. If clearance is not to specifications, adjust by bending float drop stopper. See Fig. 2.

**Fig. 2  Making Float Drop Measurement for Adjustment**

#### ACCELERATOR PUMP

**NOTE** – Accelerator pump is adjusted by manufacturer and should only be adjusted when it is apparent that factory setting has been disturbed.

1) Remove carburetor and position over drip pan. Fill a burette or other cubic centimeter measuring device with 10-22 cc of fuel. Attach and hold burette in position shown in Fig. 3.

2) Operate carburetor linkage to wide open throttle (WOT) 10 times and check that correct amount of fuel has been drawn from burette.

3) Check position actuating rod in pump arm and/or pump piston condition.

**Fig. 3  Tool Hook Up for Accelerator Pump Discharge Test**

## HITACHI 4-BARREL (Cont.)

### CHOKE VALVE OPENING

1) Disconnect the vacuum sensing tube from the vacuum diaphragm. Fully pull out on choke lever link and hold in this position.

**RX-4 & Cosmo**

Make Clearance Measurement Here

*Fig. 4   Choke Valve Clearance Measurement Point*

2) Apply 15.7 in. Hg to vacuum diaphragm. Measure temperature surrounding bimetal sensor, then compare to specifications shown in *Fig. 5*.

3) If choke valve clearance is not correct, proceed as follows: Check clearance between stopper and bimetal spring lever. See *Fig. 6*. Clearance should be .248-.264" (6.3-6.5 mm). If not within specifications, turn adjusting screw until correct. See *Fig. 6*. Check clearance of choke valve (*Fig. 4*), measuring temperature around bimetal and comparing findings with specifications in *Fig. 5*.

*Fig. 5   Choke Valve Clearance Based on Ambient Temperature*

### CHOKE BREAK DIAPHRAGM

1) Remove air cleaner. Start engine and run at idle speed.

2) Disconnect vacuum sensing tube from choke diaphragm. The diaphragm shaft should come outward from diaphragm.

Adjusting Screw

Measure Here

Diaphragm Stroke

*Fig. 6   Choke Break Diaphragm Adjustment*

**Diaphragm Stem Travel**

| Application | In. (mm) |
| --- | --- |
| RX-4 & Cosmo | |
| Calif. Auto. Trans. | .421-.437 (10.7-11.1) |
| Other Models | .299-.315 (7.6-8.0) |

### CHOKE DELAY VALVE (CALIF. AUTO. TRANS. ONLY)

1) Warm engine to normal operating temperature. Stop engine and remove air cleaner assembly. Place shift lever in "D" position and block wheels.

2) Disconnect vacuum sensing tube from choke break diaphragm. Start engine and run it at idle. Reconnect vacuum sensing tube to diaphragm. Shaft should pull in completely within 10 to 20 seconds.

Choke Delay Valve

*Fig. 7   Choke Delay Valve (California Models with Automatic Transmission)*

## HITACHI 4-BARREL (Cont.)

### CHOKE RETURN DELAY VALVE (CALIF. ONLY)

1) Warm up engine to normal operating temperature. Stop engine and remove air cleaner assembly. Disconnect vacuum sensing tube from choke return diaphragm. Place shift lever in "N" position.

2) Start engine and run at idle speed. Reconnect vacuum sensing tube to choke RETURN diaphragm. Diaphragm shaft should pull fully into diaphragm within 20 to 70 seconds.

### CHOKE LINKAGE (FAST IDLE OPENING ANGLE)

1) With choke valve fully closed, measure the clearance between the primary throttle valve and the throttle bore.

2) Clearance should be as shown in specifications table. If clearance is not within specifications, bend fast idle rod until proper clearance is achieved. See Fig. 8.

*Fig. 8   Choke Linkage Adjustment*

## OVERHAUL

### DISASSEMBLY

**NOTE** — *Disassembly and assembly procedures will vary slightly between vehicles, due to differing equipment. Therefore, some carburetors may not have all parts referred to below. See Figs. 9 and 10.*

1) Remove choke delay and choke return delay valves (Calif. only). Remove choke heater lead and dash pot delay valve (Man. Trans. only). Disconnect throttle opener and bracket and dash pot diaphragm (Man. Trans. only).

2) Disconnect vacuum sensing tube and remove screws attaching choke thermostatic housing to carburetor. Remove throttle return spring.

3) From air horn, disconnect choke connecting rod by removing cotter pin, plain washer and spring. Remove throttle sub-return spring. Remove "E" clip and choke lever, choke return diaphragm and bracket (Calif. only), the hot start assist lever spring, fast idle rod and bracket.

4) Remove accelerator pump connecting rod by removing cotter pin. Remove bolt attaching fuel inlet fitting and remove fitting and filter. Remove screws which attach air horn to main body. Remove air horn carefully, so gasket does not tear.

5) From air horn, remove float retaining pin, float and needle assembly. Remove accelerator pump lever and piston. If equipped, remove starting assist fluid inlet fitting. Remove primary slow air bleeds.

6) From main body remove accelerator pump rod and secondary throttle valve rod. Remove accelerator pump spring, check ball and retainer plate. On manual transmission vehicles, remove idle switch by removing attaching bolt and spring. Disconnect connecting rod from secondary operating diaphragm and remove diaphragm. Remove screws attaching main body to throttle body.

7) Remove accelerator pump injection nozzle, weight and check ball from main body.

**NOTE** — *Before removing jets and air bleeds, write down their position and number of each for use in later assembly procedures.*

8) Remove all jets and air bleeds from main body. See Fig. 9. On vehicles with automatic transmission, remove power valve solenoid.

9) From throttle body, remove mixture adjusting screw and throttle adjusting screw. On manual transmission equipped vehicles, remove richer solenoid. Remove throttle lever attaching hardware.

*Fig. 9   Jet Location in Hitachi 4-Barrel Carburetor*

## HITACHI 4-BARREL (Cont.)

Accel. Pump Boot

Accel. Pump Lever

Air Vent Solenoid

Accel. Pump Actuating Rod

Elec. Asist Auto. Choke

Fuel Inlet Fitting

Choke Delay Valve

Dashpot Delay Valve

Accel. Pump Piston Assy. & Check Ball

Vacuum Break Diaphragm

Choke Return Delay Valve

Dashpot

Float Assembly

Slow Air Jet

Throttle Opener

Main Air Bleed

Idle Switch

Accel. Pump Nozzle

Main Air Bleed

Slow Air Bleed

Transition Jet

Choke Connecting Rod

Idle Air Adjust Screw

Secondary Throttle Operating Diaphragm

Main Jets

Power Solenoid

Idle Speed Screw

Throttle Return Spring Plate

Throttle Return Spring

Throttle Adjust Bracket

Richer Solenoid

**Fig. 10  Exploded View of Hitachi 4-Barrel Carburetor Assembly**

# 1978 Hitachi Carburetors

## HITACHI 4-BARREL (Cont.)

### CLEANING & INSPECTION

1) Wash all parts in suitable carburetor solvent and blow dry with compressed air.

**NOTE** — *Never use wire for cleaning jets or passageways.*

2) Inspect air horn, main body and throttle body for signs of wear or damage. Inspect choke and throttle shafts for wear. Check all linkage and connecting rods for bends. Inspect return springs and needle valve and seat.

3) Inspect float for deformation, damage or holes. Inspect filter for rust or damage. Check choke valve for excessive shaft play. Check all jets for damage or wear. See that primary and secondary throttles seat properly in their bores.

4) Test air vent, richer , and power solenoids for proper operation. When battery current is applied to richer and air vent solenoids, valve stem should be pulled into valve body. Current applied to power solenoid should cause valve stem to extend from valve.

### REASSEMBLY

Reverse disassembly procedure, use all new gaskets and note the following:

Both primary and secondary circuits have their own respective parts; do not get them mixed up during reassembly. When installing choke housing to carburetor body, carefully and accurately fit choke shaft lever to bimetal spring. Close choke valve and pull on diaphragm shaft to see that it operates and closes properly.

| CARBURETOR ADJUSTMENT SPECIFICATIONS | | | | | | | |
|---|---|---|---|---|---|---|---|
| Application | Idle Speed (Engine RPM) | | Float Level Setting In. (mm) | Float Drop Setting In. (mm) | Choke Linkage (Off Car) In. (mm) | Accelerator Pump Volume① | Choke Valve Opening② In. (mm) |
| | Hot | Fast | | | | | |
| RX-4 & Cosmo | 750±25 | 3000-3500 | .45-.49 (11.5-12.5) | 2.11-2.15 (53.5-54.5) | .067-.079 (1.7-2.0) | 6.8-9.2 | .169-.185 (4.3-4.7) |

① — Measured in cubic centimeters (cc). Amount of fuel that should have been drawn from container (burette) in 10 strokes.

② — Measured between stopper and bimetal spring lever.

## KEIHIN 2-BARREL – EXC. HONDA CVCC ENGINE

**Honda Civic**

### DESCRIPTION

Honda Civic models, except for those with CVCC engines, are equipped with a Keihin 2-bbl. carburetor for 1978. Carburetor is a downdraft design with a primary and secondary throttle system. Unit is equipped with an internal choke valve which is manually operated by a knob and cable assembly. Both primary and secondary bores have main jets which draw fuel from a common float bowl. Accelerator is a lever and diaphragm type. Manual transmission equipped vehicles utilize a vacuum operated throttle opener system which acts similar to a dashpot.

### ADJUSTMENTS

#### HOT (SLOW) IDLE RPM

*See appropriate article in TUNE-UP Service Procedures.*

#### IDLE MIXTURE

*See appropriate article in TUNE-UP Service Procedures.*

#### COLD (FAST) IDLE RPM

*See appropriate article in TUNE-UP Service Procedures.*

#### FLOAT LEVEL

**1)** Remove carburetor air horn and hold it upside down. Float needle valve should touch arm gently or have less than .004" (1 mm) clearance.

**2)** Measure distance from air horn gasket to center of float. *See Fig. 1.* Measurement should be 1.39-1.47" (35.4-37.4 mm).

**3)** Adjust by turning needle valve seat.

**NOTE** – *Do not allow valve seat to stick out above its threaded housing. Prevent needle valve from falling out.*

**4)** After adjustment, be sure needle valve seat is clean and that float moves freely.

**Fig. 1    Float Level Adjustment**

#### ACCELERATOR PUMP

**1)** Measure total travel of accelerator pump arm.

**2)** Adjust to .445" (11.3 mm) by bending the arm as shown in *Fig. 2.*

**Fig. 2    Accelerator Pump Arm Travel**

#### IDLE ADJUSTING SCREW

**1)** If idle adjusting screw has been removed or is out of adjustment, install screw and turn it until it bottoms gently.

**2)** Back out screw $2\frac{1}{2} \pm \frac{1}{2}$ turns. Install limiter cap so tab on cap is facing 180° away from stop on carburetor.

#### THROTTLE & CHOKE CABLE TENSION

**Throttle Cable Tension** – **1)** Turn adjusting nut on carburetor bracket until inner cable play is zero with throttle valve fully closed.

**2)** Back out adjusting nut .079" (2 mm). Inner cable play should be about .157-.394" (4-10 mm) between throttle link and bracket (*Fig. 3*).

**3)** Be sure carburetor throttle valve opens fully when accelerator pedal is pushed all the way down. Check to see linkage returns freely and smoothly to idle position.

**Fig. 3    Adjusting Throttle Cable Tension**

**Choke Cable Tension** – **1)** Turn adjusting nut until there is no clearance between choke lever and bracket. *See Fig. 3.*

**2)** Pull choke knob OUT all the way. Choke valve should close completely.

**3)** Push choke knob all the way IN. Choke valve should be fully open.

# 1978 Keihin Carburetors

## KEIHIN 2-BARREL — EXC. HONDA CVCC ENGINE (Cont.)

### THROTTLE OPENER (MAN. TRANS.)

1) Engine should be warmed up to operating temperature. Ignition timing (2° BTDC), idle speed (700±50 RPM), and distributor point gap (.018-.022" or .45-.55 mm) should be correct.

2) Connect hand operated vacuum pump to throttle opener as shown in *Fig. 4*. Apply a vacuum of at least 16 in. Hg.

**NOTE** — *If pump is not available, connect throttle opener directly to intake manifold vacuum source while bypassing control valve.*

**Fig. 4   Vacuum Pump Connection to Throttle Opener**

3) Engine speed should increase to 1400± 300 RPM. Cycle accelerator a few times to stabilize engine speed.

4) If RPM is not correct, check for loose vacuum tube connection or faulty vacuum tube. Check for broken diaphragm in throttle opener and replace as necessary.

5) Bend throttle link lever forks apart to increase RPM; bend together to decrease RPM. *See Fig. 5* .

**Fig. 5   Throttle Link RPM Adjustment**

6) Increase engine speed to 3500 RPM. Release throttle suddenly. Throttle should close in 2-6 seconds.

7) If adjustment is required, loosen control valve lock nut. Turn adjusting nut clockwise to decrease time; counterclockwise to increase time. *See Fig. 6* .

8) Tighten lock nut. Repeat step **6)**. If correct time cannot be obtained within full range of adjustment, replace control valve and repeat testing procedure.

**Fig. 6   Adjusting Control Valve**

## OVERHAUL

### DISASSEMBLY

1) Remove accelerator pump rod clip. Remove (5) air horn-to-throttle body screws. Lift off air horn carefully.

2) Pull out cotter pin retaining rocker arm and remove rocker arm. Remove accelerator pump rod and rubber cap.

**NOTE** — *Do not take choke valve out of air horn unless it is to be replaced.*

3) Gently remove float arm pin with pin punch.

**NOTE** — *Tap pin out from long leg side; install from short leg side ( Fig. 7). Do not tap on float support leg.*

**Fig. 7   Removing Float Pivot Pin**

4) Remove needle valve seat assembly. Use care not to damage "O" ring.

## KEIHIN 2-BARREL — EXC. HONDA CVCC ENGINE (Cont.)

Air Jets

Emulsion Tubes

Needle Valve Seat

Slow Cut Solenoid Valve

Rocker Arm

Slow Air Jets

Idle Limiter Cap

Power Jets

Main Jets

Adjusting Screw

Air Horn

Float

Throttle Opener (M/T)

Link Plate

Accelerator Pump Diaphragm

Throttle Lever

Pump Cover

Link Lever (M/T)

Bracket

**Fig. 8  Exploded View of Keihin 2-Barrel Carburetor (Honda Civic Application Shown)**

5) Remove primary and secondary air jets. Disconnect emulsion tubes. Remove primary and secondary slow air jets. *See Fig. 9.*

6) Take off clip plate. Remove main jets and valve seat.

7) Remove throttle opener by pulling out link plate cotter pin. Remove bracket retaining screw and remove assembly.

8) Remove fast idle ring. Remove throttle cable bracket, throttle lever and spring.

**NOTE** — *Do not disassemble auxiliary and throttle valves.*

9) To disassemble accelerator pump, refer to *Fig. 10.*

10) To disassemble throttle opener, refer to *Fig. 11.*

Power Jet

Primary Air Jet

Secondary Air Jet

Primary Slow Air Jet

Primary Main Jet

Secondary Main Jet

Secondary Slow Air Jet

**Fig. 9  Location of Various Jets**

Diaphragm

Spring

"U" Rings

Cover

**Fig. 10  Exploded View of Accelerator Pump**

# 1978 Keihin Carburetors

## KEIHIN 2-BARREL — EXC. HONDA CVCC ENGINE (Cont.)

**Fig. 11  Exploded View of Throttle Opener
(Man. Trans. Only)**

### INSPECTION

1) Wash parts in suitable cleaning solution.

**NOTE** — *Do not place plastic or rubber parts, or assemblies containing diaphragms into solution.*

2) Clean jets and orifices with compressed air. Do not use wire to clean jets and openings to avoid damage to parts.

3) Inspect gasket surfaces for cracks or defects.

4) Ensure parts are clean and dry before reassembly.

### REASSEMBLY

To assemble carburetor, reverse disassembly procedure and note the following:

1) Do not get primary and secondary emulsion tubes and jets mixed up, as they have a similar appearance.

2) Replace all gaskets, seals, "O" rings, and cotter pins with new ones.

3) When installing piston dust cover, place it on choke chamber first. Securely engage cover lip in chamber.

4) Tighten air horn-to-throttle body screws evenly. Do not over-tighten attaching screws, as this could cause warping or breakage of carburetor parts.

5) Be sure all moving parts operate smoothly with no binding.

## KEIHIN 2-BARREL — HONDA CVCC ENGINE

Civic (CVCC)
Accord (CVCC)

### DESCRIPTION

Carburetor is a two barrel, three venturi downdraft design. Carburetor contains two systems, primary and auxiliary. Primary system utilizes primary and secondary venturis, float system, accelerator pump system, and on idle system. Auxiliary system utilizes an auxiliary venturi with a float and idle system. Auxiliary system provides fuel to the pre-combustion chamber.

Carburetor components include: automatic choke on Accord, manual choke on Civic, choke opener diaphragm, secondary throttle operating diaphragm, primary throttle opener diaphragm, fuel shut-off solenoid, primary/secondary main and auxiliary main fuel shut-off solenoids.

### ADJUSTMENTS

#### HOT (SLOW) IDLE RPM

See appropriate article in TUNE-UP Service Procedures.

#### IDLE MIXTURE

See appropriate article in TUNE-UP Service Procedures.

#### COLD (FAST) IDLE RPM

See appropriate article in TUNE-UP Service Procedures.

#### AUTOMATIC CHOKE

Both the choke valve setting and fast idle position are controlled during engine warmup by the automatic choke. It consists of a 5 ohm resistor on the firewall, an air intake sensor in the air cleaner assembly, the voltage regulator and the choke controller.

**Choke Bimetal Tension and Linkage** — Remove air cleaner and open and close throttle fully to engage fast idle cam. If choke valve does not close to less than 1/8" (3 mm) clearance between valve and body, remove choke cover and inspect linkage. Reinstall cover, aligning index marks.

**Choke Opener and Linkage** — Start engine. Choke valve should partially open. If it does not, check linkage, leaks in diaphragm, blocked vacuum port at carburetor or leaks in "O" ring. If still inoperative, replace choke opener and adjust opener levers.

**Choke Bimetal Tension and Heater** — As engine warms up, choke valve should open to full position. If choke does not open at all, check voltage across connectors of choke cover. If no voltage, check external resistor, fuses and voltage regulator wiring. If voltage, check for 18 to 26 ohms resistance across choke cover. If choke does not open fully, disconnect air sensor wires, start engine and measure for 9.5 to 12 volts across choke cover. If more than 12 volts, replace external resistor. If still ineffective, replace choke cover assembly.

**Air Temperature Sensor** — Disconnect and remove sensor from air cleaner. Check continuity across sensor lead wires.

Continuity should be present above 57°F, (14°C), but absent below that temperature.

#### CHOKE OPENER

**Testing** — 1) Pull choke knob to second detent position. While cranking engine observe that choke butterfly valve moves between partially open and fully closed.

2) Now start engine and check to see if butterfly is partially open. If butterfly valve is not operating properly, remove screws securing choke opener diaphragm and proceed with testing.

3) Swing choke opener assembly upward until it is straight up and down above carburetor See Fig. 1. Holding opener assembly in this position, press downward.

Cover Vacuum Port With Finger

Press Choke Opener Down from Upright Position

*Fig. 1  Testing Choke Opener Diaphragm*

4) Choke opener diaphragm is now actuated. Place finger over vacuum port and hold for about five seconds. Check that diaphragm does not leak off during this time. If it does leak down, replace diaphragm unit.

5) If diaphragm assembly does not leak down, check carburetor vacuum port for vacuum and repair as necessary.

**Adjustment** — 1) Pull choke cable out to 1st detent. Depress choke opener diaphragm by hand. See Fig. 2.

2) Insert plug gauge or shank end of No. 20 drill between upper edge of choke valve and air horn wall. Clearance should be .151-.171" (3.85-4.35 mm).

3) If adjustment is needed, open or close slot in relief lever. To increase clearance widen slot; to decrease, close up slot.

4) Set choke knob at 2nd detent position. Depress choke opener diaphragm by hand. Insert shank end of No. 40 drill between choke valve and air horn wall. Clearance should be .094-.102" (2.4-2.6 mm).

5) If adjustment is needed, bend stop tab and recheck clearance.

## KEIHIN 2-BARREL – HONDA CVCC ENGINE (Cont.)

*Fig. 2   Choke Opener Adjustment*

*Fig. 4   Choke Cable Adjustment*

### CHOKE CABLE

1) Check that choke control operates smoothly with no binding or sticking. Push choke knob all the way in and remove carburetor air cleaner. Be sure that choke plate is fully open against stop tab in air horn *(Fig. 3)*.

*Fig. 3   Checking the Position of Choke Butterfly*

2) Loosen lock nut of choke cable and tighten adjusting nut to move choke plate away from stop tab. Now turn adjusting nut until plate returns to stop tab. Tighten lock nut. See *Fig. 3*.

3) Have assistant pull out choke knob to second detent position, while observing action in carburetor air horn. As choke knob is pulled to second detent position, choke plate should just close. If it does not close, inspect choke plate and return spring for signs of binding.

4) Have assistant pull choke knob all the way out and observe that choke plate remains in the closed position. Replace air cleaner. Check operation of choke indicator light with ignition switch in ON position.

### THROTTLE CABLE

1) Check that throttle cable operates smoothly with no binding or sticking. Check free play at linkage. Cable should deflect .16-.40" (4-10 mm).

2) If not within specifications, turn adjusting nut until cable has no deflection. Loosen adjusting nut until cable deflects .16-.40" (4-10 mm). Tighten lock nut.

3) Depress accelerator pedal and check full throttle condition at carburetor. Readjust cable adjusting nut to obtain full throttle condition. Test throttle return to full position when cable is released.

### FLOAT LEVEL

**NOTE** – *Float level gauge set, part number 07501-7570001, must be used to check and adjust float level. Gauge set contains a see thru adapter, with a red line as a fuel level indicator. Gauge set is installed where primary/secondary and auxiliary solenoids mount to body.*

1) With air cleaner removed and carburetor installed on vehicle, remove primary/secondary and auxiliary main jet solenoids. Attach special float level gauge, catch tray, and drain bottle to carburetor.

2) Start engine and allow it to stabilize. Float level should remain at red line on gauge. If not, adjustment is made by turning external float level adjusting screws *(Fig. 5)*.

3) Allow time for fuel level to stabilize and check again. When correct float level is achieved, paint adjusting screws to keep adjustment from changing.

## KEIHIN 2-BARREL — HONDA CVCC ENGINE ( Cont.)

To Adjust Auxiliary Float Level, Turn This External Adjusting Screw

To Adjust Primary/Secondary Float Level, Turn This External Adjusting Screw

Catch Tray (07501-6570201)

Float Level Gauge (07501-6590101) Bolted on Carb. in Place of Primary/Secondary and Auxiliary Main Jet Covers

Drain Bottle

*Fig. 5   Keihin Float Level Adjustment — External*

### ACCELERATOR PUMP

Accelerator pump stroke is adjusted by bending accelerator pump lever tang. Bend tang to get a clearance of .46-.48" (11.7-12.3 mm) between tang and throttle body stop tab (See Fig. 6).

Accelerator Pump Lever

Throttle Body Stop Tab

Bend ONLY THIS Tang To Adjust

Accelerator Pump Travel Should Be .57-.60" (14.5-15.1 mm)

*Fig. 6   Keihin Accelerator Pump Adjustment*

### THROTTLE CONTROLLER (ALL MODELS)

1) Connect tachometer to engine. Start engine and run until at normal operating temperature.

2) Unhook hose from throttle controller diaphragm. Connect a hand vacuum pump. See *Fig. 8.*

3) With engine running, apply at least 15.75 in. Hg of vacuum for more than one minute.

4) Speed should increase to RPM shown below:

Man. Trans.
With Throttle Opener Control .................. 2700±500 RPM
Without Throttle Opener Control Valve ..... 2200±500 RPM
Hondamatic ............................... 2000±500 RPM

5) If engine RPM is low, widen adjustment slot in dashpot speed adjustment lever using a screwdriver. If RPM is too high, narrow slot with pliers. If speed cannot be adjusted, or diaphragm will not maintain a vacuum, replace diaphragm.

6) Reconnect vacuum hose. Increase engine speed to 3500 RPM and hold for 2 or 3 seconds. Release throttle suddenly. Engine should return to idle within 1 to 4 seconds and arm on throttle linkage should extend fully.

**If Throttle Closes in Less Than 1 Second — 1)** Disconnect vacuum hose from throttle opener diaphragm and connect vacuum gauge to hose. At 4000 RPM there should be at least 1.2 in. Hg.

2) If there is vacuum (Federal and all Hondamatic vehicles), replace dashpot check valve and repeat the 3500 RPM test in step **6)** above.

3) If there is vacuum (California and High Altitude vehicles), bypass throttle control valve. If throttle return time is within specification, replace control valve. If throttle still returns in less than 1 second, check for vacuum at dashpot. If present, replace dashpot check valve. If no vacuum, check hoses for leaks. Remove throttle control valve bypass, reinstall hoses, and repeat 3500 RPM test in step **6)** above.

**NOTE** — *To bypass control valve, disconnect two hoses from atop the valve and connect them together.*

4) If there is no vacuum at throttle opener diaphragm, check for vacuum at carburetor vacuum port. If vacuum is present, check hoses for leaks or blockage. If there is no vacuum, clean port. In either case, repeat 3500 RPM test in step **6)** above.

**If Throttle Takes Longer Than 4 Seconds to Return — 1)** On Federal and all Hondamatic vehicles, replace dashpot check valve and repeat 3500 RPM test in step **6)** above.

2) On California and High Altitude vehicles with manual transmission, bypass throttle control valve. Repeat 3500 RPM test in step **6)** above.

**NOTE** — *To bypass control valve, disconnect two hoses from atop the valve and connect them together.*

3) If throttle still takes longer than 4 seconds after bypassing valve, replace dashpot check valve. If within specifications, check voltage at throttle opener solenoid valve. If present, replace speed sensor in speedometer; if not, replace throttle opener solenoid valve. Repeat 3500 RPM test in step **6)** above.

# 1978 Keihin Carburetors

## KEIHIN 2-BARREL — HONDA CVCC ENGINE (Cont.)

Auxiliary Needle
Valve Assy.

Main Needle
Valve Assy.

Choke Opener
Diaphragm

Accel. Pump Rod

Auxiliary
Needle Valve

Air Horn

Accel. Pump Lever

Main Needle Valve

Auxiliary Float

Main Float

Throttle Cable Brace

Auxiliary Jet Assy.

Primary Jet Assy.

Secondary Dashpot
Diaphragm

Main
Body

Auxiliary Idle
Mixture Screw

Idle Cutoff
Solenoid

Auxiliary Main
Jet Assy.

Throttle Controller
Diaphragm

Primary/Secondary
Main Fuel Shut-Off
Solenoids

Main Jet
Assy.

Accel. Pump

Throttle Body

Primary Idle
Adjusting Screw

Accel. Pump Linkage

*Fig. 7 Exploded View of Keihin Carburetor*

## THROTTLE CONTROLLER (CALIF. & HIGH ALT.)

**1)** Complete preliminary testing as described under "Throttle Controller (All Models)". Proceed to next step.

**2)** Bypass speed sensor with a jumper wire from battery positive post to yellow/black connector at emissions control box.

**3)** Raise engine speed to 3500 RPM and release throttle. Engine should return to idle within 6 seconds. Elapsed time normally is greater than dashpot test.

**4)** If not within specifications, remove throttle control valve cover. Loosen lock nut on control valve and turn adjusting nut clockwise to decrease return time, counterclockwise to increase return time. Repeat step **3)**.

**5)** Disconnect battery jumper from control box connector and stop engine.

Throttle Controller Diaphragm

Vacuum Pump

*Fig. 8 Keihin Throttle Controller Adjustment*

## KEIHIN 2-BARREL – HONDA CVCC ENGINE (Cont.)

### AUXILIARY IDLE MIXTURE

Auxiliary idle mixture screw position should be marked before removal. If screw is removed and not marked, lightly seat screw then back out 1¾ turns.

### AUXILIARY (LAMBDA) LINKAGE

**Adjustment With Dial Indicator** – 1) Back out throttle stop screw. Install dial indicator holder (07974-6570500) with dial indicator. Loosen auxiliary linkage adjustment screw lock nut. See Fig. 9.

2) Tighten adjustment screw until primary throttle plate just opens. At this point, set dial indicator to zero. Loosen adjustment screw until dial indicator has a reading of .004± .0004" (.10± .01 mm). See Fig. 10.

3) Tighten lock nut without changing position of adjustment screw. Readjust throttle stop screw when carburetor is installed on vehicle.

**Fig. 9   Dial Indicator Positioning On Throttle Plate**

**Fig. 10   Auxiliary (Lambda) Linkage Adjustment With Dial Indicator**

## NIKKI 2-BARREL

### Opel

## DESCRIPTION

Carburetor is a Nikki 2-barrel, downdraft type. It is equipped with an electric automatic choke, an anti-dieseling solenoid, a coasting richer system (fuel enrichment) solenoid, and on manual transmission models, a throttle closing dashpot. A double venturi provides for high air flow velocity at the venturi under all operating conditions, resulting in more efficient atomization of fuel for smooth combustion.

## ADJUSTMENTS

### HOT (SLOW) IDLE RPM

See appropriate article in TUNE-UP Service Procedures.

### IDLE MIXTURE

See appropriate article in TUNE-UP Service Procedures.

### COLD (FAST) IDLE RPM

See appropriate article in TUNE-UP Service Procedures.

### AUTOMATIC CHOKE SETTING

Align the setting mark on the thermostat case with the setting mark on the thermostat housing and then install and tighten the set screws securely.

### CHOKE PISTON STROKE

Hold the bimetal lever against the stopper then move choke piston link and check that stroke, as measured at clip end, is ³⁄₁₆-⁷⁄₃₂". If stroke is not within specifications, bend piston link at point shown in *Fig. 1*.

Fig. 1 Checking Choke Piston Stroke

## PRIMARY & SECONDARY THROTTLE VALVE ANGLES

**NOTE** — *Relative angles between primary and secondary throttle valves should be adjusted or checked only during overhaul or replacement.*

1) Slowly open primary throttle valve until secondary throttle arm starts to move. Using set gauge (J-26618 or equivalent), check angle of primary valve. *See Fig. 2* .

2) If adjustment is needed, bend throttle link. (See *Fig. 9* for location).

Fig. 2 Checking Relative Angles Between Primary & Secondary Throttle Valves

### FLOAT LEVEL ADJUSTMENT

Adjust float level by adding or removing copper gaskets to or from the float valve seat. The float level increases with additional gaskets. The fuel level is normal when it is even with the mark on the float bowl glass window when engine is running or stopped.

### CHOKE UNLOADER ADJUSTMENT

1) Apply light pressure on choke valve in closing direction.

2) Open throttle valve to wide open position. This will force choke valve open part way.

3) Measure distance from lower edge of choke valve to air horn wall. Measurement should be .215" (5.5 mm).

4) To adjust, remove choke heater coil cover. Bend choke unloader tang to obtain correct clearance.

### ACCELERATOR PEDAL HEIGHT

Adjust accelerator pedal height by changing the setting of the accelerator switch. The distance between the accelerator pedal and brake pedal should be held to 2.4" (61 mm), as shown in *Fig. 3*. Depress accelerator and set pedal stopper so carburetor throttle valve opens fully.

## NIKKI 2-BARREL (Cont.)

**Fig. 3   Setting Accelerator Pedal Height**

### ACCELERATOR CONTROL CABLE

1) After completing adjustment of accelerator pedal height, as described above, adjust the control cable setting. Turn the adjusting nut until throttle valve begins to open. See Fig. 4.

2) Move control cable about .35" (8.9 mm), or the equivalent of 7-7½ turns of adjusting nut, inward toward the carburetor. Lock control cable in this position with the lock nut.

3) Depress the accelerator pedal slowly and check that carburetor throttle valve does not open while accelerator switch plunger is in contact with the accelerator pedal. Readjust control cable setting if required.

**Fig. 4   Setting Accelerator Control Cable**

## OVERHAUL

### DISASSEMBLY

**NOTE** – *During disassembly, be sure to keep components in groups as removed; particularly be sure not to interchange primary and secondary components.*

**Air Horn** – 1) Remove pump arm return spring, then take out snap ring and remove pump arm and pump link. *See Fig. 5.*

2) Remove fuel pipe union cap nut, then remove union and strainer. Disconnect automatic choke lead wire from its connector.

3) Remove snap ring from select lever rod, disconnect select rod from select lever, then detach rod at choke piston assembly.

**Fig. 5   Parts Removal for Air Horn Disassembly**

4) Remove six air horn mounting screws and detach air horn assembly.

5) Disconnect automatic choke vacuum hose from choke diaphragm cover. Raise the automatic choke lead wire clip and remove lead wire from clip.

6) Remove three thermostat case cover attaching screws and remove the case cover. Remove four choke diaphragm cover attaching screws and remove the diaphragm cover.

**Fig. 6   Link Holder & Select Arm Removal**

# 1978 Nikki Carburetors

## NIKKI 2-BARREL (Cont.)

7) Remove the link holder on the choke diaphragm rod and remove the choke diaphragm. *See Fig. 6.*

8) Remove nut retaining select lever and disconnect the select lever and select arm.

**Float Bowl & Throttle Body** — 1) Remove nut retaining primary throttle lever; then, remove the throttle lever, rods, and link levers (keeping these in proper order for reassembly).

2) Remove two screws attaching the second throttle link and remove the link. Raise the solenoid valve lead wire clip and remove the lead wire from the clip. Remove the clip from the secondary throttle arm and remove the secondary diaphragm rod from the secondary throttle arm. Remove the secondary throttle arm.

3) Remove three diaphragm chamber attaching screws and remove the secondary diaphragm chamber. Remove three bolts connecting float bowl to throttle body and separate the two.

**NOTE** — *One of the three bolts is installed from the lower side of throttle body. Remove this bolt carefully, as it also serves as the vacuum outlet for the power circuit.*

4) Remove three float chamber cover attaching screws and then remove the glass, float pin collar, float, and float valve. Remove the float valve body, accelerator pump plunger, and solenoid valves.

5) Carefully remove the following jets (match number given to number shown in *Fig. 7*):

1. Primary Second Slow Air Bleed
2. Primary Slow Jet
3. Accelerating Pump Discharge Valve
4. Primary Main Air Bleed
5. Power Valve Jet
6. Secondary Main Air Bleed
7. Secondary Step Jet
8. Secondary Step Air Bleed
9. Coasting Jet

*Fig. 7  Carburetor Jet Identification*

6) Remove plugs and then primary and secondary main jets (the jet with the smallest hole is the primary side).

7) Remove screws attaching the small venturi and remove the primary and secondary small venturis. Remove the secondary diaphragm cover attaching screws, then remove the cover, spring and diaphragm.

## INSPECTION

1) Thoroughly clean all parts and use compressed air to clean jet and fuel ports (DO NOT use a wire brush).

2) Check the following for wear, distortion, or damage: fitting face of air horn; choke valve; choke shaft; fast idle cam; select lever; select arm; tape bushing; and bimetal choke coil.

*Fig. 8  Alignment of Choke Bimetal*

3) Heat bimetal to 88°F (31°C) for 5 minutes, then move bimetal lever until it contacts the stop. Check that end of bimetal coil is about 180° from the stop. *See Fig. 8.*

4) Check heater coil for an opening or oxidation. Check insulator for cracking or damage. Measure heater coil resistance. The standard resistance should be 10.5-11.5 ohms. Check choke diaphragm for breakage or deterioration.

5) Check the following portions of the float bowl assembly for any wear or damage: float bowl and threaded portions and jet fitting face; jet orifices, threaded portions, fitting face and slit; accelerator pump; springs; and boots.

## NIKKI 2-BARREL (Cont.)

Thermostat Case

Pump Arm

Pump Connecting Rod

Auto. Choke Diaphragm

Choke Dia. Rod

Coasting Richer Solenoid

Select Arm Lever

Select Arm

Cap Nut

Strainer

Accel. Pump Plunger

Primary Main Air Bleed

Float Valve

Power Valve Jet

Slow Jet

Step Jet

Anti-Diesel Solenoid

Coasting Jet (Exc. Fed. A/T)

Throttle Wire Lever

Fast Idle Lever

Speed-up Controller Adjusting Screw

Secondary Main Air Bleed

Step Air Bleed

Select Lever Rod

Primary Small Venturi

Auto. Trans. Only

Primary Throttle Arm

Secondary Small Venturi

Select Lever

Choke Piston Assy.

Float

Choke Piston Arm

Throttle Link

Secondary Throttle Shaft Arm

Secondary Throttle Return Arm

Idle Adjust Screw

Idle Nozzle

Diaphragm Chamber Assy.

Auto. Choke Vac. Hose

**Fig. 9   Exploded View of Nikki 2-Barrel Carburetor**

# 1978 Nikki Carburetors

## NIKKI 2-BARREL (Cont.)

6) Check movement of parts within pump housing. Check for seepage of fuel into the float. Again, check the following for wear or damage: float lever pin and bore, float needle and seat; float needle spring; anti-dieseling solenoid valve (also check its operation); coasting richer valve; springs; and "O" rings.

7) Check the following portions of the throttle body for wear or damage: throttle body; throttle valves and shafts; idle adjusting screw fitting face, threaded portion, and end of screw; and secondary throttle valve diaphragm and spring.

### REASSEMBLY

To reassemble, reverse disassembly procedures, noting the following: Make sure jets are installed in correct positions (all jets in the secondary side are plated with the exception of the coasting richer jet). Securely tighten the jets.

| | CARBURETOR ADJUSTMENT SPECIFICATIONS | | | | | | | |
|---|---|---|---|---|---|---|---|---|
| Application | Idle Speed (Engine RPM) | | Float Level Setting | Unloader Setting | Throttle Valve Closing Angle | | Choke Valve Closing Angle | Sec. Throttle Valve Opening Angle |
| | Hot | Fast | | | Primary | Secondary | | |
| Opel | 900 | 3400 ① | ② | .215" | 7° | 20° | 20° | 51° |

① — With vacuum lines plugged. Specification given is for all Man. Trans. models. Set Federal Auto. Trans. to 3200 RPM and Calif. Auto. Trans. to 3000 RPM.

② — Fuel level must be even with sight bowl line.

## SOLEX 32 BICSA & 34 BICSA 1-BARREL

**Peugeot 504**

### DESCRIPTION

Two 1-barrel carburetors are used together to form a compound carburetion system. Only the primary carburetor (32 BICSA) is equipped with a butterfly type choke valve. Both carburetors are equipped with a diaphragm type accelerator pump. Both carburetors also have a fuel cut-off solenoid switch which prevents engine dieseling by shutting off fuel supply when ignition is turned off. Linkage between the carburetors allows throttle valve of secondary unit (34 BICSA) to begin opening at ⅓ throttle of primary carburetor. System is equipped with a fast idling control for exhaust emission reduction purposes.

### CARBURETOR IDENTIFICATION

**Carburetor No.**

| Application | Primary | Secondary |
|---|---|---|
| Federal & Calif. .... | 32 BICSA PEU 190 ... | 34 BICSA PEU 191 |
| High Altitude ........ | 32 BICSA PEU 187 ... | 34 BICSA PEU 194 |

**NOTE** — *To change for high altitude use, convert No. 1 carburetor (32 BICSA) by substituting a 115 Main Jet for the original 120 Main Jet and a 180 Air Correction Jet for the original 170 Air Correction Jet. To convert No. 2 carburetor (34 BICSA), replace original 110 Main Jet with a 105 Main Jet and the original 50 Idle Jet with a 47 Idle Jet.*

### ADJUSTMENTS

#### HOT (SLOW) IDLE RPM

*See appropriate article in TUNE-UP Service Procedures.*

#### DECELERATION VACUUM SYSTEM (FAST IDLE RPM)

**1)** With engine at operating temperature and idle adjusted to 900 (+50) RPM, place gear selector lever in "N" and turn all electrical accessories to "OFF" position.

**2)** Disconnect hose (with red ring) from deceleration vacuum unit. Disconnect hose (with green ring) from "T" connector at deceleration valve and attach it where previous hose was removed from vacuum unit.

**Fig. 1   Adjusting Deleration Valve and Vacuum Unit**

VACUUM UNIT                     VALVE

**3)** Remove domed nut "1" in *Fig. 1*. Loosen lock nut "2" and start engine. Engine speed should be 1500 (+50) RPM.

**4)** If engine speed is not correct, adjust screw "3" to specification, using a 3 mm Allen wrench. Tighten lock nut "2" and install domed nut "1", making sure gasket is in place.

**5)** Replace vacuum hoses, previously removed, to their original locations. Loosen lock nut "4" on deceleration valve (not on vacuum unit).

**NOTE** — *Do not use mixture control screw in threaded rod "5" of deceleration valve to obtain proper fast idle speed.*

**6)** Increase engine speed to 3000 RPM without load, and allow engine speed to decrease. Unscrew threaded rod "5" one-half a turn at a time until normal idle (900 RPM) is obtained.

**7)** Then unscrew threaded rod one additional half turn and tighten lock nut.

**NOTE** — *Always hold part "6" with wrench when loosening or tightening lock nut on deceleration valve, so as not to exert force on diaphragm.*

#### ACCELERATOR PUMP

**1)** Remove carburetor from intake manifold.

**2)** Invert carburetor and insert a drill bit or pin gauge between lower edge of throttle plate and bore wall while holding throttle plate open.

**3)** Release throttle until plate touches drill bit. Use ⁹⁄₆₄" (3.5 mm) drill bit on 32 BICSA and ⁵⁄₆₄" (2.0 mm) for 34 BICSA carburetor.

**4)** Adjust accelerator pump by loosening nut on pump lever spring rod and slowly retightening until contact is made with tab on pump lever.

**5)** Install carburetors on manifold.

### CARBURETOR SPECIFICATIONS①

| Application | 32 BICSA | 34 BICSA |
|---|---|---|
| Venturi ................ | 24± .05 .................. | 26± .05 |
| Main Jet ................ | 120± 5② .................. | 110± 5② |
| Air Correction Jet ..... | 170± 20② .............. | 185± 20② |
| Idle Jet ................ | 62± 10② .................. | 50± 10② |
| Pump Injector ............ | 40± 10 .................. | 40± 10 |
| Economizer ................ | ..... .................. | 120± 20 |
| Float (weight) ......... | 5.7± gram .............. | 5.7± gram |
| Needle Valve ............ | 1.2± .20 ................. | 1.5± .20 |

① — Measurements in micromillimeters unless noted otherwise

② — Replacement jets must be same size

# 1978 Solex Carburetors

## SOLEX 32 BICSA & 34 BICSA 1-BARREL (Cont.)

Needle Valve & Seat

Needle Valve & Seat

Air Correction Jet

Air Correction Jet

Choke Connecting Rod

Accel. Pump Injection Nozzle

Accel. Pump Injection Nozzle

Main Jet Assy.

Main Jet Assy.

Accel. Pump Actuating Rod

Actuating Rod

Interconnecting Throttle Rod

Fuel Shut-Off Solenoid

Fuel Shut-Off Solenoid

Accel. Pump Ball & Screen

Accel. Pump Ball & Screen

Fast Idle Diaphragm

**Fig. 2  Exploded View of 32 BICSA & 34 BICSA Carburetors**

## SOLEX 34 TBIA 1-BARREL & SOLEX 35 CEEI 2-BARREL

**Peugeot 604**

### DESCRIPTION

The carburetion for the 1978 Peugeot 604 is made up of a primary one barrel carburetor and a secondary two barrel unit. These carburetors are mounted inline and are both downdraft designs. The secondary two barrel is vacuum controlled, while the primary carburetor operates directly from the throttle linkage. Opening of the secondary carburetor is progressive. With only slight accelerator pedal depression, a mechanical stop prevents secondary unit from opening. As pedal depression increases, stop moves and allows the rear carburetor to begin operation. Vacuum pickup for secondary carburetor operation is located at the main venturis of both the carburetors.

Idle system on both carburetors operate continually to ensure smooth transfer of operation when secondary unit begins to open. Primary uses an anti-dieseling solenoid cut-off valve. High Altitude models are different in that internal jetting sizes are reduced to compensate for difference in air density.

### CARBURETOR IDENTIFICATION

Carburetor is identified by a metal tag attached to front part of unit on driver's side and is held on by one of the air horn screws.

|  | Carburetor No. | |
| --- | --- | --- |
| **Application** | **Solex 34 TBIA** | **Solex 35 CEEI** |
| Federal | PEU 182 | PEU 186 |
| California | | |
|   Man. Trans. | PEU 182 | PEU 186 |
|   Auto. Trans. | PEU 183 | PEU 186 |
| High Altitude① | | |
|   All Man. Trans. & | | |
|   Federal Auto. Trans. | PEU 195 | PEU 196 |
|   Calif. Auto. Trans. | PEU 214 | PEU 196 |

① — Converted from Federal and California models by changing jets. If carburetor is modified, be sure to change vehicle emission control information label.

**NOTE** — *To convert low-altitude carburetors for high altitude use requires replacement of main and idle jets. To change 34 TBIA carburetors for high altitude, replace 140 Main Jet with 137.5 Main Jet and 50 Idle Jet with 48 Idle Jet. To convert 35 CEEI carburetors for high altitude, replace 145 Main Jet with 142.5 Main Jet and 47 Idle Jet with 45 Idle Jet.*

### ADJUSTMENTS

#### HOT (SLOW) IDLE RPM

*See appropriate article in TUNE-UP Service Procedures.*

#### DECELERATION VACUUM SYSTEM (COLD FAST IDLE RPM)

**1)** With engine at operating temperature and idle adjusted to 900 (+50) RPM, place gear selector lever in "N" and turn all electical accessories to "OFF" position.

**2)** Disconnect hose (with red ring) from deceleration vacuum unit. Disconnect hose (with green ring) from "T" connector at deceleration valve and attach it where previous hose was removed from vacuum unit.

**Fig. 1  Adjusting Deceleration Vacuum Unit and Valve.**

**3)** Remove domed nut "1" in *Fig. 1.* Loosen lock nut "2" and start engine. Engine speed should be 1450 (+50) RPM.

**4)** If engine speed is not correct, adjust screw "3" to specification, using a 3 mm Allen wrench. Tighten lock nut "2" and installed domed nut "1", making sure gasket is in place.

**5)** Replace vacuum hoses, previously removed, to their original locations. Loosen lock nut "4" on deceleration valve (not on vacuum unit).

**NOTE** — *Do not use mixture control screw in threaded rod "5" of deceleration valve to obtain proper fast idle speed.*

**6)** Increase engine speed to 3000 RPM without load, and allow engine speed to decrease. Unscrew threaded rod "5" one-half turn at a time until normal idle (900 RPM) is obtained.

**7)** Then unscrew threaded rod one additional half turn and tighten lock nut.

**NOTE** — *Always hold part "6" with wrench when loosening or tightening lock nut on deceleration valve, so as not to exert force on diaphragm.*

### THROTTLE CONTROL

**1)** Rotate throttle drum to full open position. Stop should be against washer to opposite side of flat area.

**2)** Loosen lock nuts and turn throttle link to adjust. Clearance of .067" (1.7 mm) should exist between fixed stop and movable stop.

**3)** With engine warmed up, bring release lever against its stop in clockwise direction. Do not allow 1-barrel carburetor throttle plate to open.

**4)** Clearance of .157" (4 mm) should exist between control quadrant stop and return link.

## SOLEX (MIKUNI) DIDTA 2-BARREL

Arrow
Colt
Challenger
Sapporo

### DESCRIPTION

The Solex (Mikuni) 28-32 DIDTA Carburetor is used on all 1600 cc models and the 30-32 DIDTA on all 2000 cc and 2600 cc models. These two barrel, two stage carburetors utilize primary and secondary circuits. Components include a solenoid fuel shut-off, water heated automatic choke, diaphragm type accelerator pump, a vacuum actuated secondary (power enrichment) circuit and a mixture control valve (deceleration device). 1600 cc models destined for high altitude operation are also equipped with an altitude compensator.

### CARBURETOR IDENTIFICATION

#### Arrow & Colt Carburetor No.

| Application | Man. Trans. | Auto. Trans. |
| --- | --- | --- |
| 1600 cc | | |
| Federal | 28-32DIDTA-74 | 28-32DIDTA-75 |
| California | | |
| Station Wagons | 28-32DIDTA-170 | 28-32DIDTA-172 |
| Other Models | 28-32DIDTA-70 | 28-32DIDTA-72 |
| High Altitude | | |
| Station Wagons | 28-32DIDTA-176 | |
| Other Models | 28-32DIDTA-76 | |
| 2000 cc | | |
| Federal | 30-32DIDTA-74 | 30-32DIDTA-75 |
| California | 30-32DIDTA-70 | 30-32DIDTA-72 |
| 2600 cc | | |
| Federal | 30-32DIDTA-174 | 30-32DIDTA-175 |
| California | 30-32DIDTA-170 | 30-32DIDTA-172 |

#### Challenger & Sapporo Carburetor No.

| Application | Man. Trans. | Auto. Trans. |
| --- | --- | --- |
| 1600 cc | | |
| Federal | 28-32DIDTA-70 | 28-32DIDTA-76 |
| California | 28-32DIDTA-170 | 28-32DIDTA-172 |
| High Altitude | 28-32DIDTA-176 | |
| 2600 cc | | |
| Federal | 30-32DIDTA-174 | 30-32DIDTA-175 |
| California | 30-32DIDTA-170 | 30-32DIDTA-172 |
| High Altitude | 30-32DIDTA-176 | |

### ADJUSTMENTS

#### HOT (SLOW) IDLE RPM

See appropriate article in TUNE-UP Service Procedures.

#### IDLE MIXTURE

See appropriate article in TUNE-UP Service Procedures.

#### COLD (FAST) IDLE RPM

See appropriate article in TUNE-UP Service Procedures.

#### FUEL LEVEL

Check fuel level through sight glass on float chamber. Fuel level should be even with center of glass. If fuel level is not as specified, increase or decrease packing under needle valve seat until correct fuel level is obtained. A sheet of packing .039" thick will change float level .118". If fuel level is within .16" (4 mm) above or below level mark on sight glass, it is acceptable.

#### MIXTURE CONTROL VALVE

Some models have a mixture control valve (MCV) built into the carburetor to decrease HC emissions during deceleration. Air is supplied into the intake manifold, decreasing intake manifold vacuum. During constant speed operation, an orifice in the MCV maintains a balanced vacuum in the spring chamber and reservoir. The valve is closed by spring force. See Fig. 1.

**Fig. 1  Mixture Control Valve Operation**

When throttle valve is closed suddenly, high vacuum from intake manifold in spring chamber forces diaphragm to open the valve, causing air flow to the intake manifold. The valve then slowly closes again, as pressure equalizes between spring chamber and reservoir through the orifice.

If engine racing (from idle to 2500 RPM) causes the valve to operate, MCV is good. If it does not operate, replace MCV valve.

#### AUTOMATIC CHOKE

1) Loosen screws holding metal ring around choke housing. This allows housing to be turned but not removed.

2) Align yellow punch mark on bimetal case with center projection on carburetor choke case. See Fig. 2.

## SOLEX (MIKUNI) DIDTA 2-BARREL (Cont.)

3) Tighten screws around holding ring.

4) Automatic choke temperatures should be set as follows:

### Automatic Choke Set Temperatures

| Application | Temperature |
| --- | --- |
| 1600 cc | |
|   All Station Wagons | 71.2°F (21.5°C) |
|   All Other Models | 73.8°F (23.5°C) |
| 2000 cc and 2600 cc | |
|   Federal | 73.8°F (23.5°C) |
|   California | 71.2°F (21.5°C) |

Fig. 2  Aligning Choke Valve Cover and Housing

## ACCELERATOR PEDAL ADJUSTMENT

To provide proper pedal-to-floor clearance, adjust bolt so that .71-.75" (18-19 mm) extends through support arm and rests against stopper. See Fig. 3.

Fig. 3  Adjusting Accelerator Pedal Linkage

## OVERHAUL

### DISASSEMBLY

NOTE — Do not remove inner venturi, by-pass screw (sealed with white paint), throttle shaft or valve. Do not disassemble parts of the automatic choke body.

1) Disconnect carburetor linkage, water hose to choke body and choke rod. Remove float chamber cover, float, and related parts. Disassemble and remove depression chamber.

2) Remove accelerator pump, cover, spring, and membrane from main body. Take out accelerator pump weight and ball. Remove enrichment cover, spring, and valve body, but do not disassemble valve body. Remove both main jet and pilot jet.

3) Disassemble throttle body by removing throttle lever nut, throttle lever, collar, abatement plate, collar, and intermediate lever.

### INSPECTION

1) Clean all parts in suitable solvent and dry with compressed air. Check all parts for wear or damage and replace if necessary. Inspect all diaphragms for cracks or holes and check rubber parts for leakage. Do not use wires when cleaning jets, as damage to orifices could occur.

NOTE — It is best to replace "O" rings, gaskets, diaphragms, and plastic parts with new ones when carburetor is disassembled.

2) Check carburetor body and water case for cracks, scaling, or clogging. Check needle valve and seat for contact. Inspect strainer screen for damage or clogging. Be sure pilot screw seat contact surface is not damaged.

3) Throttle valve and choke valve shafts should operate smoothly without binding or sticking. Be sure accelerator pump operates properly. Move the throttle lever with force to open throttle valve from idle position to an opening of 70° or more. Check delivery from pump nozzle. If none, check for clogged fuel passage or broken pump diaphragm.

4) Push the rod of the depression chamber in, seal off nipple and release rod. Rod should not return. If it does, check for defective diaphragm. If necessary, replace chamber.

5) Connect wire from positive battery post to coupler side of fuel cut-off solenoid. Connect second wire from negative post to other lead wire. Check to see that needle moves in toward solenoid. If it moves out as soon as battery is disconnected, solenoid is good.

6) Check throttle valve initial opening (clearance between throttle bore and valve) at initial step of fast idle cam. If not to specifications, turn fast idle adjusting screw in clockwise direction to increase opening, counterclockwise to decrease opening. See Fig. 5.

## SOLEX (MIKUNI) DIDTA 2-BARREL (Cont.)

Depression Chamber

Automatic Choke

Mixture Control Valve

Water Hose

Cover Assembly

Fuel Inlet

Gasket

Float

Choke Rod

Filter

Secondary Pilot Jet

Needle Valve

Throttle Lever

Sec. Main Jet

Venturi

Altitude Comp.

Mixing Body Assembly

Spring

Idle Screw

Fast Idle Screw

Enrichment Body Assembly

Abatement Plate

Intermediate Lever

Primary Main Jet

Gaskets

By-pass Screw

Primary Pilot Jet

Throttle Stop Screw

Mixture Screw

Fuel Cut-off Solenoid

Throttle Body Assembly

EGR Valve

Gasket

Accelerator Pump Assembly

*Fig. 4 Exploded View of Solex (Mikuni) DIDTA 2-Barrel Carburetor*

## SOLEX (MIKUNI) DIDTA 2-BARREL (Cont.)

### Throttle Valve Initial Opening

| Application | Clearance |
|---|---|
| 1600 cc .................................................. | .047" (1.2 mm) |
| 2000 cc .................................................. | .051" (1.3 mm) |
| 2600 cc .................................................. | .051" (1.3 mm) |

### REASSEMBLY

1) Oil choke shaft and throttle shaft interlocking section. Reassemble throttle body and all related parts, making sure that all parts move smoothly. Set throttle stop screw with throttle in full closed position and give adjustment screw additional 1/4 turn. Be sure to secure it. with lock nut.

2) Reassemble main body and related parts, making sure that pilot jet "O" ring fits well into groove. Install enrichment valve, accelerator pump, and pump cover.

3) Reassemble main body to throttle body. Install depression chamber to float cover and automatic choke assembly to body.

**Fig. 5   Checking Throttle Valve Initial Opening**

## WEBER 32 ADFA 2-BARREL

Fiat 124
Fiat 131
  Brava
  Super Brava

### DESCRIPTION

Carburetor is a two stage, two barrel downdraft type unit. Primary stage is mechanically operated by accelerator linkage. Secondary stage is operated by mechanical linkage and a vacuum diaphragm. Primary stage includes idle and transition, main metering system and acceleration system. Secondary stage includes power enrichment, secondary main metering and transfer circuits. A single fuel bowl supplies fuel for both stages. A coolant heated choke bi-metal spring operates the choke plate through linkage and is completely automatic. An idle stop solenoid shuts off fuel supply when ignition switch is in "OFF" position.

### CARBURETOR IDENTIFICATION

Carburetor number is located on lower edge of main body base on the side facing the engine. It can be quickly found by looking just above the gasket between main body and throttle plate housing.

| Application | Carburetor |
|---|---|
| Fiat 124 | |
|   Without Catalytic Converter | |
|     Before Car No. 1898385 | 32 ADFA 12/100 |
|     After Car No. 1898384 | 32 ADFA 11/100 |
|   With Catalytic Converter | |
|     Before Car No. 1898385 | 32 ADFA 15/101 |
|     After Car No. 1898384 | 32 ADFA 14/101 |
| Fiat 131 Brava & Super Brava | |
|   Without Catalytic Converter | |
|     Man. Trans. | 32 ADFA 11/102 |
|     Auto. Trans. | 32 ADFA 13/102 |
|   With Catalytic Converter | |
|     Man. Trans. | 32 ADFA 14/102 |
|     Auto. Trans. | 32 ADFA 16/102 |

### ADJUSTMENTS

#### HOT (SLOW) IDLE RPM

See appropriate article in TUNE-UP Service Procedures.

#### IDLE MIXTURE

See appropriate article in TUNE-UP Service Procedures.

#### COLD (FAST) IDLE RPM

See appropriate article in TUNE-UP Service Procedures.

#### FLOAT LEVEL & FLOAT DROP

1) Remove air horn from carburetor. Hold vertical and ensure gasket is in place. Weight of float should gently depress needle valve. Measure distance between top of float and gasket surface. Distance should be .217-.295" (5.5 - 7.5 mm). If adjustment to float level is needed, bend float arm where it joins float. See Fig. 1 .

2) To measure float drop, hold air horn in upright position and allow float to hang down fully. Measure distance from gasket surface to float top at leading edge. Distance should be .551" (14.0 mm). If necessary to adjust, bend float drop tang.

**Fig. 1 Float Level & Float Drop Adjustment (Fiat 124 & 131)**

## WEBER 32 DATRA 2-BARREL

**Fiat 128**
**Fiat X 1/9**
**Lancia Beta**

### DESCRIPTION

Carburetor is two barrel downdraft design. This unit uses a diaphragm type accelerator pump, a crankcase ventilation device, carbon monoxide idling control device, excess fuel recycling device (from carburetor to fuel tank), anti-dieseling solenoid and a dashpot. A choke unloader is used to prevent excessively rich mixtures when cold starting. This system operates both by vacuum and mechanical lever and spring action. Also featured is a coolant-heated automatic choke system.

### CARBURETOR IDENTIFICATION

Carburetor numbers are located on the lower edge of main body. Refer to chart in right hand column for carburetor numbers and application.

**Carburetor Identification Numbers**

| Application | Carburetor No. |
|---|---|
| **Fiat 128** | |
| Without Catalytic Converter | 32 DATRA 11/100 |
| With Catalytic Converter | 32 DATRA 14/100 |
| | |
| **Fiat X1/9** | |
| Without Catalytic Converter | |
| Without Air Conditioning | 32 DATRA/201 |
| With Air Conditioning | 32 DATRA/101 |
| Without Catalytic Converter | |
| Without Air Conditioning | 32 DATRA 10/200 |
| With Air Conditioning | 32 DATRA 10/100 |
| | |
| **Lancia** | |
| Scorpion | 32 DATRA 9/101 |
| All Other Models | 32 DATRA 13/100 |

**Fig. 1  Exploded View of Weber 32 DATRA 2-Barrel Carburetor (Fiat Shown, Lancia Similar)**

## WEBER 32 DATRA 2-BARREL (Cont.)

### ADJUSTMENTS

**NOTE** — *Lancia Beta carburetors are similar to Fiat applications, except for some minor differences in outer attachments. Procedures shown are applicable to all Weber 32 DATRA carburetors.*

### HOT (SLOW) IDLE RPM

*See appropriate article in TUNE-UP Service Procedures.*

### IDLE MIXTURE

*See appropriate article in TUNE-UP Service Procedures.*

### COLD (FAST) IDLE RPM

*See appropriate article in TUNE-UP Service Procedures.*

### FLOAT LEVEL

Remove air horn. With gasket in place on underside of air horn, hold vertically so weight of float closes needle valve gently. Measure distance from surface of gasket to float. This measurement should be .236-.315" (6 - 8 mm). If adjustment is needed, bend tang beneath float arm and recheck measurement.

### FLOAT DROP

Remove air horn and hold in upright position so that weight of float allows it to fully drop. Measure from top leading edge of float to gasket surface. Ensure gasket is firmly in place on air horn. Measurement should be .590" (15 mm). If adjustment is needed, bend lug on rear of float arm and recheck float drop. Total float travel should be .275-.354" (7-8 mm).

## WEBER 32 DIR 2-BARREL

Renault
R-5

### DESCRIPTION

The Weber 32 carburetor is a two barrel downdraft type. It is equipped with a manual choke and carburetor base is heated by engine coolant flowing through it. Fuel filter is a metal screen type located in carburetor fuel inlet.

### CARBURETOR IDENTIFICATION

| Application | Carb. No. |
| --- | --- |
| Renault R-5 | |
|   Federal ..................................................... | 32 DIR 56 |
|   California ................................................. | 32 DIR 55 |
|   High Altitude ........................................... | 32 DIR 53 |

### ADJUSTMENTS

#### HOT (SLOW) IDLE RPM

See appropriate article in TUNE-UP Service Procedures.

#### IDLE MIXTURE

See appropriate article in TUNE-UP Service Procedures.

#### COLD (FAST) IDLE RPM

See appropriate article in TUNE-UP Service Procedures.

#### FLOAT LEVEL & FLOAT DROP (TRAVEL)

Float level and drop are checked and adjusted with float bowl removed. Place float bowl in a vertical position. See Fig. 1. Allow weight of float to close needle valve without allowing ball to enter valve. Measure dimension "A" (Fig. 1) to check float level. Measurement should be .281" (7 mm). If necessary, adjust by bending float arm. Measure dimension "B" (Fig. 1) to check float drop. Measurement should be .315" (8 mm). If necessary, adjust by bending float arm tab.

Fig. 1    Float Level & Drop Adjustment

#### INITIAL THROTTLE VALVE OPENING ADJUSTMENT

With choke valve completely closed, measure throttle valve opening. Measurement should be .047" (1.2 mm) for Federal and .049" (1.25 mm) for California models. If necessary, adjust opening by loosening lock nut and turning adjustment screw at choke cam. See Fig. 2.

Fig. 2    Initial Throttle Valve Opening Adjustment

#### INITIAL CHOKE VALVE OPENING ADJUSTMENT

NOTE – Two adjustments are required. Both mechanical and vacuum adjustments are necessary.

Mechanical – With choke valve fully closed, push on sleeve until it contacts cam lever. Measure opening at bottom of choke valve. Measurement should be as noted in Specifications Table at end of article. If adjustment is needed, bend link as shown in Fig. 3.

Fig. 3    Choke Valve Adjustment (Mechanical)

## WEBER 32 DIR 2-BARREL (Cont.)

**Vacuum** — Push diaphragm link in as far as possible. Now close choke plates with choke arm until spring on link is slightly compressed. Measure opening at bottom of choke valve.

Measurement should be to specifications. If adjustment is needed, remove screw from end of diaphragm and turn set screw until opening is correct. See *Fig. 5.*

Fig. 4   Choke Valve Adjustment (Vacuum)

Fig. 5   Choke Valve Adjustment (Vacuum)
Set Screw Adjustment

| CARBURETOR ADJUSTMENT SPECIFICATIONS | | | | | | | | |
|---|---|---|---|---|---|---|---|---|
| Carb. No. | Idle Speed (Engine RPM) | | Float Level Setting | Float Drop Setting | Choke Plate (Vacuum) | Choke Plate (Mech.) | Unloader Setting | Vacuum Break |
| | Hot | Fast | In. (mm) | In. (mm) | In. (mm) | In. (mm) | In. (mm) | In. (mm) |
| DIR 53 | 750-800① | 1500② | .281 (7) | .313 (8) | .234 (6) | .203 (5) | ..... | ..... |
| DIR 55 | 800-900 | 1500② | .281 (7) | .313 (8) | .276 (7) | .197 (5) | ..... | ..... |
| DIR 56 | 800-900 | 1900② | .281 (7) | .313 (8) | .281 (7) | .157 (4) | ..... | ..... |

① — With air pump — 750-850 RPM
② — ±100 RPM

## WEBER 740 2-BARREL

**Ford Fiesta**

### DESCRIPTION

The Weber Model 740 2-Bbl. carburetor is a two stage, two venturi downdraft unit. Primary and secondary bores are the same size, 1.338" (34 mm). The primary throttle plate is operated directly by the throttle linkage. Secondary throttle plate is connected by linkage to the primary plate.

The Model 740 has five basic metering systems; choke system, idle and main metering systems, acceleration and power enrichment systems. Vacuum ports for distributor vacuum advance and EGR system are located in the primary venturi area of the carburetor.

### CARBURETOR IDENTIFICATION

| Application | Carburetor No. |
|---|---|
| Fiesta | |
| Federal ..................................... | 771F9510GC |
| | 771F9510GD |
| California ................................. | 771F9510HA |
| | 771F9510HB |

### TESTING

#### AUTOMATIC ELECTRIC CHOKE

**1)** Bring engine to normal operating temperature and turn off engine. Remove air cleaner and check all vacuum hoses, solenoids, and choke wires. Be sure all linkage operates freely.

**2)** Be sure choke cap is properly aligned with index mark. Choke plates should be fully open. If not, disconnect electric choke lead from cap terminal and connect to test light. Ground second test light lead. With engine running, if light does not light, suspect faulty alternator or open circuit in choke lead. If light glows, replace choke cap.

**3)** Hold throttle 1/4 open and move choke plates to closed position. Release plates. They should return to fully open position. If not, clean or repair choke system.

**4)** Using an LRE-34618 Rotunda Choke Tester or its equivalent, cool choke bi-metal. Hold throttle open and insert tester into choke housing's fast idle speed screw opening. Apply cool air for 8 minutes or until choke plates seat themselves lightly in air horn. If seating does not occur in this time, clean and repair choke system.

**5)** Hold choke plates 1/4 open and remove tester. Allow throttle to close. Choke plates should remain partially open and throttle will be in kickdown position. Without touching throttle, start and run engine. Open throttle momentarily and then release it. Choke plates should be vertical and engine speed should drop to normal idle. If not, replace electric choke cap unit.

**6)** Turn off engine, remove test equipment and reinstall all components.

#### FUEL BOWL VENT

**1)** Apply parking brakes and block wheels. Remove air cleaner. Remove bowl vent hose from canister. Check fuel bowl vent solenoid for external damage and electrical connections.

Attach a Rotunda T75L-9487-A tool or equivalent to end of canister hose.

**2)** Turn ignition switch off and hold choke plates open. Force air into fuel bowl vent system by squeezing tool's rubber bulb. If no fuel is displaced through metering system, start engine and run for 2 minutes. Turn off engine, and repeat test.

**3)** If still no fuel is displaced, remove carburetor air horn. Switch ignition on and off. Solenoid plunger should retract when switch is on and extend when off. If not, replace solenoid, plunger, seal and plunger spring. Reassemble carburetor.

**4)** With ignition switch on and tool still connected, again force air into fuel bowl vent system. If rubber bulb resists rapid squeezing (pressure build up), bowl vent is working properly. If not, disconnect electrical lead to bowl vent solenoid and connect it to test light. Ground second test light lead.

**5)** Turn ignition switch on. If test light does not glow and battery is okay, solenoid lead has an open circuit. Repair or replace. If light glows, remove test light and reconnect lead to solenoid. Remove all test equipment and reassemble all components. Install air cleaner and check all hose connections. Start and run engine at 2500 RPM for 15 seconds and turn off engine.

### ADJUSTMENTS

#### HOT (SLOW) IDLE RPM

*See appropriate article in TUNE-UP Service Procedures.*

#### IDLE MIXTURE

*See appropriate article in TUNE-UP Service Procedures.*

#### COLD (FAST) IDLE RPM

*See appropriate article in TUNE-UP Service Procedures.*

#### CHOKE PLATE VACUUM PULL-DOWN

**NOTE** — *DO NOT perform this adjustment unless replacement choke pull-down adjusting screw SEAL is available.*

**1)** Remove carburetor from vehicle.

**2)** Remove (3) choke retaining screws, ring, housing and heat shield.

**3)** Open throttle to wide open position.

**4)** Close choke valve.

**5)** Place fast idle adjusting screw on FIRST step of fast idle cam and close throttle.

**6)** Using an outside vacuum source of 17 in. Hg, apply vacuum to vacuum channel on pump bore under base of carburetor.

**7)** Measure clearance between LOWER edge of choke plate and bore wall.

**NOTE** — *Make measurement using applied vacuum of 17 in. Hg and light thumb pressure closing choke plates.*

**NOTE** — *Modulator spring should NOT be compressed.*

# 1978 Weber Carburetors

## WEBER 740 2-BARREL (Cont.)

Secondary Choke Shaft
Choke Valve
Dirt Seal
Bushing
Bimetal Shaft
Primary Choke Shaft
Sec. Choke Link
Bushings
AIR HORN
Primary Choke Link
Bimetal Lever
Retaining Ring
Electric Choke Unit
Choke Assist Spring
Fuel Return Line Check Valve & Fitting
Choke Lever
Choke Pull-down Adj. Screw
Fuel Filter
Choke Housing Vacuum Seal "O" Ring
Float
Adjusting Screw Seal
Fuel Inlet Needle & Seat
Fast Idle Speed Adjusting Screw
Float Hinge Pin
Fuel Discharge Nozzles
Locking Tab
Air Bleeds
Throttle Lever
Viton Bowl Vent Seal
Well Tubes
Idle Jet Holder
Return Spring
Pump Shooter
Idle Jet
Spacer
Bushing
Bowl Vent Arm
Spacer
Seal
Fuel Bowl Vent Solenoid
Main Jet
Stop Screw
Idle Stop Lever
"O" Ring Seal For Pump Nozzle
Return Spring "A"
MAIN BODY
Bushings
Dash Pot
Locater Washers
Power Valve Diaphragm
Idle Speed Screw
Power Valve Cover
Dash Pot Adjusting Lock Nut
"O" Ring
Idle Fuel Shut-Off Solenoid
Pump Spring
Limiter Cap
Accelerator Pump Cam
Pump Diaphragm
Idle Mixture Screw
Primary Throttle Return Spring "B"
Pump Cover

***Fig. 1  Exploded View of Weber Model 740 2-Bbl. Carburetor***

## WEBER 740 2-BARREL (Cont.)

8) If adjustment is needed, turn vacuum diaphragm adjusting screw in or out as required.

9) When correct clearance has been obtained, install carburetor on engine.

10) Reinstall shield, choke cap, ring and (3) screws.

### FLOAT LEVEL

1) Remove air cleaner.

2) Remove carburetor air horn from carburetor main body.

3) Remove gasket from air horn.

4) Hold carburetor in vertical position. *See Fig. 2.*

Float

Air Horn Assy.

Drill Bit or Gauge .276" (7 mm)

**Fig. 2    Float Level Adjustment (Hold Air Horn As Shown)**

5) Insert drill bit or pin guage of correct size (.276" or 7 mm) between float and air horn casting gasket surface. To adjust, bend float arm as necessary, at float.

**NOTE** — *Needle and seat assembly are spring loaded. Air horn must be held vertically to obtain accurate float setting.*

## OVERHAUL

### DISASSEMBLY

**NOTE** — *To prevent damage to throttle plates, install carburetor legs or four 2¼" bolts into base, using eight nuts. Use separate containers for parts removed from various assemblies.*

**Bowl Cover — 1)** Remove fuel filter. Remove six bowl cover screws and washers. Open throttle sufficiently to clear fast idle screw. Remove cover.

2) Remove float hinge pin, float and inlet needle. Remove inlet needle seat and gasket, bowl cover gasket and fuel return line check valve and fitting.

**Automatic Electric Choke — 1)** Remove bowl cover. Remove three choke cap retaining screws, retaining ring, cap unit and heat shield.

2) Remove three screws securing choke housing to bowl cover and disengage choke link. Remove "O" ring from vacuum passage.

3) Remove three choke pull down cover screws. Remove cover, spring and diaphragm assembly.

**Accelerator Pump — 1)** Remove four pump cover screws and cover, pump diaphragm and pump return spring.

2) To remove internal pump shooter, the bowl cover must be removed. Remove "O" ring with shooter.

**Main Body — 1)** Remove idle fuel shut-off solenoid and washer. Remove fuel bowl vent solenoid and washer. Remove three power valve cover screws, power valve cover, spring, and diaphragm.

**NOTE** — *To remove fuel shut-off solenoid, remove the outboard vacuum connector tube, pressed into carburetor housing. The brass tube can be removed with a slide hammer tool with a 3/32" sheet metal screw inserted into the bore of the tube. Do not use pliers. Before removal, scribe line on tube so it may be reinstalled to exact depth. To install tube, use plastic hammer and tap lightly.*

2) Remove dash pot (if so equipped). Remove throttle kicker (air conditioned cars only). Remove idle limiter cap, mixture screw and spring.

3) Remove fuel discharge nozzles, primary idle jet holder, secondary idle jet holder and high speed air bleeds.

**NOTE** — *Idle jets are located in bottom of holders. The air bleeds, main well tubes and main jets are a press fit assembly, but may be removed and assembled by hand.*

### INSPECTION

Thoroughly clean all parts and use compressed air to clean jets and fuel ports. Do not use wire brush. Check parts for wear or damage and replace plastic or rubber parts if questionable. Check all diaphragms for cracks or other defects.

### REASSEMBLY

To assemble carburetor, reverse disassembly procedure, noting the following. Do not intermix parts. Replace gaskets, seals and "O" rings with new ones, and check that all linkage moves freely without binding or sticking. Do not overtighten attaching screws.

## CARBURETOR ADJUSTMENT SPECIFICATIONS

| Ford Carb. Number | Idle Speed (Engine RPM) | | Fast Idle Cam Setting | Accel. Pump Setting | Float Level Setting | Choke Pull-Down Setting | Unloader Setting | Auto. Choke Setting |
|---|---|---|---|---|---|---|---|---|
| | Hot | Fast | | | | | | |
| 771F9510XX | ① | ① | .079"② (2 mm) | ..... | .276"③ (7 mm) | .197"② (5 mm) | .157"④ (4 mm) | INDEX |

① — See Emission Control Tune-Up Decal.
② — ±.020" (.5 mm).
③ — ±.031" (.8 mm).
④ — Minimum.

## ZENITH-STROMBERG CD TYPE 1-BARREL

**Mercedes-Benz 230**
**MG (All)**
**Triumph (All)**

### DESCRIPTION

Stromberg CD type carburetor is a constant depression carburetor, which operates on the principle of varying effective areas of choke and jet openings. This variation depends upon the degree of throttle opening, engine speed and engine load requirements.

The Mercedes, MG and Spitfire models all have single carburetors; the Triumph has twin carburetors. All carburetors feature automatic chokes.

The Mercedes 230 has an idle shut off valve built into the intake manifold and a solenoid valve to vent the float chamber. The choke housing also has an air adjustment screw for more accurate air/fuel mixture adjustment during choke operation. A mixture enrichment valve in the choke housing aids in cold starting. A pull down relay prevents an excessively lean mixture immediately after starting, allowing the egine to run smoothly after a cold start. It consists of a thermo-time switch, solenoid switch-over valve, vacuum lines & wiring harness. California vehicles have a safety cap over the fuel mixture screw to prevent unauthorized resetting or adjusting. The throttle valve adjusting screw on the Mercedes 230 is factory-set and should only be adjusted in extreme cases.

### CARBURETOR IDENTIFICATION

| Application | Type No. |
| --- | --- |
| Mercedes-Benz | |
| 230 | 175CDTU |
| M.G. | |
| Midget | 150 CD4T |
| MGB | 175 CD5T |
| Triumph | |
| Spitfire | 150 CD4T |
| TR-7 | 175 CDFEVX |
| TR-8 | 175 CDSET |

### ADJUSTMENTS

**HOT (SLOW) IDLE RPM**

*See appropriate article in TUNE-UP Service Procedures.*

**IDLE MIXTURE**

*See appropriate article in TUNE-UP Service Procedures.*

**COLD (FAST) IDLE RPM**

*See appropriate article in TUNE-UP Service Procedures.*

### FLOAT

With float cover removed and carburetor body inverted, measure distance from gasket surface of body to highest point of float. This distance should be .624-.672" (16-17 mm).

**NOTE** — *Use care to prevent misaligning floats when making adjustment. If necessary to adjust, bend float tab that contacts fuel inlet needle. Be sure tab rests on needle valve at a 90° (right) angle. See Fig. 1.*

**Fig. 1   Float Level Adjustment Points**

### ALTITUDE COMPENSATION
### FEDERAL MERCEDES 230 ONLY

1) Two markings are found on small handwheel attached to carburetor. These markings are "NORMAL" and "4000 ft." When handwheel is moved clockwise, fuel nozzle is moved upwards. This effectively leans out fuel mixture.

2) Set handwheel to "NORMAL" for vehicle operations at levels lower than 4000 ft. Set wheel to "4000 ft." for vehicle operation above that level.

3) Recheck vehicle idle speed and CO% level after resetting altitude compensator.

### OVERHAUL

**NOTE** — *The following overhaul procedure is based upon MG Midget suggested procedures, but may be generally applicable to all Stromberg CD type carburetors. Certain variations exist in external components and some models will have automatic chokes, but all carburetors (of this type) are generally similiar in their internal workings.*

1) With carburetor removed, unscrew the damper cap. Reach in through air filter side of carburetor bore and with finger, raise piston while carefully lifting oil retainer cap (on damper rod). Pull plug out of bottom of float chamber and drain fuel and oil from carburetor. Remove "O" ring on float bowl plug. Remove screws securing float chamber to bottom of carburetor. Remove float assembly by gently prying float shaft out of clip on carburetor body. Remove needle valve and washer. Remove screws securing top cover to body. Remove top cover, spring and air valve assembly.

## ZENITH-STROMBERG CD TYPE 1-BARREL (Cont.)

Front Throttle Spindle

Main Body

Throttle By-Pass Valve

Air Leak Screw & Plug

Diaphragm

Valve Body

Damper

Idle Trim Screw

Temperature Valve

Throttle Idle Speed Screw

Bi-Metal Strip

Temperature Compensating Body

Top Cover

Stop Lever

Float Needle Valve

Choke Cable Connection

Air Valve Spring

Fast Idle Cam

Fast Idle Screw

Fuel Enrichment Device (Choke)

Float Chamber

Diaphragm

CDSET Auto. Choke

Air Valve

Needle

**Fig 2  Exploded View of Stromberg CDSE/CDSET Carburetor
(CDSET Carburetor has an Automatic Choke)**

## ZENITH-STROMBERG CD TYPE 1-BARREL (Cont.)

*Fig. 3  Exploded View of CD4T Carburetor Assembly*

## ZENITH-STROMBERG CD TYPE 1-BARREL (Cont.)

**2)** From air valve assembly, remove screws securing diaphragm and retaining ring. Loosen set screw holding needle in air valve and insert needle removing tool (S353) into stem of air valve. Turn tool counterclockwise two turns, withdrawing needle assembly by pulling straight upward.

**Fig. 4   Removing Needle Valve with Appropriate Tool**

**3)** Remove choke retaining screws and remove choke assembly from side carburetor body. From removed choke assembly, remove EGR air bleed valve, nut and lock washer from choke spindle, choke cable lever, fast idle cam, and choke (starter) disc.

**4)** Remove screws securing idle air regulator. Remove screws securing deceleration by-pass valve. From deceleration by-pass valve body, remove screws in base plate, spring, valve and gaskets. Remove star washer to release adjustment screw from valve housing. Remove "O" ring seal from adjustment screw and unscrew lock nut. Remove split pin and withdraw clevis pin and washers to disconnect throttle linkage from throttle spindle lever. Remove throttle lever.

## CLEANING & INSPECTION

Wash all components in clean fuel or suitable carburetor solvent and blow dry with compressed air. Examine all parts for wear, paying particular attention to needle and seat, air valve and diaphragm.

**NOTE** — *The parts previously mentioned should be replaced, unless all are in excellent condition.*

## REASSEMBLY

Reverse disassembly procedures and note the following:

**1)** When fitting deceleration valve, ensure that register for the spring is toward the valve body.

**2)** Refit disc assembly to choke body, ensuring that lug with detent ball is between slot of disc and largest series of holes. Refit cam lever and choke cable lever (to choke body) ensuring that cam lever is located on detent ball.

**3)** When installing air valve needle assembly with tool S353, make sure tool is turned clockwise to engage threads of needle valve assembly with adjusting screw. Continue to turn until slot in needle housing is aligned with set screw. Tighten set screw carefully.

**4)** When fitting diaphragm to air valve, locate inner tag of diaphragm into recess of air valve. Now fit diaphragm retaining ring and secure with screws. Fit air valve assembly to carburetor body, by locating outer tag and rim of diaphragm with complimentary recesses of body. Fit carburetor top cover with bulge on housing neck toward air intake.

**5)** Fill carburetor damper dashpot with lightweight engine oil or Dexron automatic transmission fluid. Fill until resistance is felt to insertion of damper piston when screw cap of damper piston is about .25" (6 mm) above top cover.

**Fig. 5   Expanded View of Vacuum Piston and Diaphragm**

# 1978 Bosch Fuel Injection

## BOSCH AFC FUEL INJECTION SYSTEM

**BMW 530i, 633CSi & 733i**
**Datsun 280Z & 810**
**Volkswagen Type 1 & 2**

### DESCRIPTION

The Bosch Air Flow Controlled (AFC) fuel injection system is electronic and uses sensors to detect engine conditions. These sensors send signals to the Electronic Control Unit (ECU) and the ECU then determines amount of fuel and length of time that fuel is to be injected into the engine. See *Fig. 1.*

An air flow meter, mounted between the throttle chamber and air cleaner, measures amount of intake air. Fuel injector open-valve time is based on amount of intake air required for one rotation of engine. System maintains a constant fuel pressure and accurately balances air/fuel mixture under all operating conditions. System consists of air flow meter, various sensors and switches, air cleaner assembly, Electronic Control Unit, throttle chamber, air and pressure regulators, injectors and connecting wires, lines and hoses.

BMW models have a high altitude compensation feature, which should be hooked up if vehicle is to be operated above 4,000 feet. The altitude feature is automatic on other models. The intake air sensor transmits air flow information to the ECU while the distributor supplies engine RPM data.

### OPERATION

Fuel under pressure from electric fuel pump, flows through a pulsation damper (some models) and fuel filter and is injected into intake manifold branch to mix with incoming air. Surplus fuel returns through a fuel pressure regulator to the fuel tank. A pressure regulator controls fuel pressure so that a constant difference of 35 psi (2.55 kg/cm$^2$) exists between fuel pressure and intake manifold vacuum. To aid in cold engine starting, a cold start valve is activated by a thermo-time switch to increase quantity of fuel to be injected.

Each engine cylinder is supplied fuel by an injector. Ignition signal from ignition coil determines frequency of injections while the ECU determines length of each injection.

Air is drawn in through air cleaner and is measured by the air flow meter. Air then travels through throttle chamber and into intake manifold. A throttle valve in the chamber controls air flow while driving. At idle, throttle valve is almost closed and air is drawn through a by-pass port in throttle chamber. Idle speed adjusting screw controls quantity of air intake at idle. During warm-up operation, extra air is by-passed through air regulator to increase engine RPM.

### AIR FLOW METER & POTENTIOMETER

The throttle valve housing provides method for air to enter engine under controlled conditions. Throttle valve sliding

*Fig. 1   Diagram of Typical Bosch AFC Fuel Injection System*

## BOSCH AFC FUEL INJECTION SYSTEM (Cont.)

switch is a potentiometer which functions as sensor for informing control unit (ECU) of throttle valve position. Datsun & Volkswagen models also have a fuel pump relay contact in potentiometer section of air flow meter. During starting, fuel pump receives power from starter solenoid through fuel pump relay. Once engine starts, fuel pump relay receives power contact in potentiometer section of air flow meter. Fuel pump contacts turn ON only after flap in air flow meter turns 11° or more. Contact turns OFF when flap returns to less than 11° rotation. See Fig. 2.

### INTAKE AIR SENSOR (TEMPERATURE SENSOR I)

The intake air sensor provides the control unit with voltage signals. The intensity of these signals, depends upon intake air volume and air temperature. The incoming air moves the stator flap against the force of the return spring. As more air is drawn in, stator flap opens even more. This rotary motion of the stator flap actuates a special potentiometer (both are physically connected together) and thus varies the strength of the signal sent to the electronic control unit (ECU). Connected to the stator flap is a dampening flap which prevents rapid oscillations of the stator flap. One of the contacts on the potentiometer operates the fuel pump as the stator flap is opened by air flow. Temperature Sensor I is an intergal part of the potentiometer and its operation modifies the signal sent to the ECU. See Fig. 2.

**Fig. 2   Air Flow Meter and Air Flow Sensor Pickup**

### ENGINE COOLANT SENSOR (TEMPERATURE SENSOR II)

This sensor provides the ECU with engine temperature information relating to cold starting and warm-up enrichment operation. The temperature sensing unit uses a thermister which is sensitive in the lower temperature ranges. Electrical resistance of the thermister decreases as coolant temperature rises.

### THROTTLE VALVE SWITCH

**NOTE** — *Volkswagen models for 1978 do not have throttle valve switch or microswitch, previously used.*

Throttle valve switch is attached to throttle chamber. Accelerator pedal movement activates the switch which has two sets of contact points. One monitors idle position and the other monitors full throttle position. Idle contacts close when throttle valve is positioned at idle and open when it is at any other position. Full throttle contacts close only when throttle valve is positioned at full throttle (at more than 34° opening of valve). See Fig. 2. Throttle valve switch compensates for enrichment at idle and after idle, and at full throttle positions. Idle circuit of switch also is responsible for sending out the fuel cut-off signal. See Fig. 3.

**Fig. 3   Throttle Valve Switch (Datsun 280Z Shown)**

### ELECTRONIC CONTROL UNIT (ECU)

The electronic control unit is a pre-programmed computer. Its function is to process the incoming signal from each sensor to determine air volume (by flow sensor), engine speed, engine temperature, air temperature and throttle position. From this information, ECU determines correct injection time and quantity. See Fig. 4.

### PRESSURE REGULATOR

The non-adjustable pressure regulator controls fuel pressure, maintaining a constant 35 psi (2.55 kg/cm²) difference between fuel pressure and intake manifold vacuum. Fuel exerts pressure against spring-loaded diaphragm, which deflects uncovering return line to fuel tank. Engine vacuum also works with fuel pressure against diaphragm when high vacuum is present. Diaphragm then deflects at about 28 psi (2.0 kg/cm²) instead of 35 psi (2.55 kg/cm²). See Fig. 5.

## BOSCH AFC FUEL INJECTION SYSTEM (Cont.)

*Fig. 4   Electronic Control Unit (ECU)*

Mounting Brackets

*Fig. 5   Typical View of Pressure Regulator*

To Fuel Tank

Fuel Inlet

To Intake Manifold

*Fig. 6   Auxiliary Air Regulator*

Electrical Plug

Bi-Metal Spring

Heating Element

Air OUT

Gate Valve

Air IN

### AUXILIARY AIR REGULATOR

To provide for cold starting and engine warm-up, more air and fuel are required. The auxiliary air regulator is fully open when engine is cold and therefore provides additional air required. As engine warms up, the gate valve is closed by operation of the electrically heated bi-metal spring. *See Fig. 6.*

### THERMO-TIME SWITCH

The thermo-time switch controls the time the cold start valve is switched on. This time limit is usually between 5 and 20 seconds depending upon engine. The time switch has a bimetal contact, surrounded by a heating coil. The heating coil receives current during cranking. The bimetal contact breaks the ground circuit of the cold start valve whenever the heating coil is about 95°F or when the delay time is up. Delay time is shortened as temperature raises.

### PRE-RESISTORS

The purpose of the pre-resistor (if they are used) is mainly to reduce the response time of the injectors. The pre-resistors are connected in series between the injectors and the dual relay.

### DUAL RELAY

The dual relay is composed of two relays which control current supply for entire electronic fuel injection system and which disengages system (electrically) from battery when ignition is turned to off position. When ignition switch is on, the main relay points close, providing voltage to the ECU and pre-resistors (if used) of the electronic fuel injection system. The other relay (within the dual relay), controls current to the electric fuel pump. These points close during cranking and when points of air flow valve are closed. This design is to cut off current to fuel pump in the event that engine stops (air flow meter closed).

## TESTING

**NOTE** — *This fuel injection system maintains constant fuel pressure in fuel lines and component parts at all times. Be sure to relieve pressure before attempting to open system at any point for testing. Do not allow fuel to flow onto engine or electrical parts. Do not allow open flame in area while testing fuel system components.*

### ELECTRONIC CONTROL UNIT (ECU)

Do not attempt to test electronic control unit, as permanent damage could result. It is possible to check plug wires for continuity. The electronic control unit should only be judged faulty after compression is checked, the ignition system (particularly breaker points) has been tested and found problem-free, and all other fuel injection components have been thoroughly tested (including wiring).

### FUEL PRESSURE

**Volkswagen — 1)** Warm engine and turn it OFF. Disconnect ring main fuel hose from cold start valve and install a fuel pressure gauge to the hose. Disconnect (and plug) vacuum hose from pressure regulator.

## BOSCH AFC FUEL INJECTION SYSTEM (Cont.)

**2)** Start engine. Gauge should read approximately 35 psi (2.5 kg/cm²) or at least within a 33-37 psi (2.35-2.65 kg/cm²) range. If within specifications, repeat test with vacuum hose connected. Gauge should read approximately 28 psi (2.0 kg/cm²) or within 26-30 psi (1.85-2.15 kg/cm²) range. If pressure is too high or too low in either test, replace pressure regulator.

**3)** Correct pressure is most important at idle. However, if engine lacks power, check for large pressure drop at full throttle. If so, look for a restricted fuel line, clogged filter, dirt in tank, or defective fuel pump.

**BMW & Datsun — 1)** Disconnect ground cable from battery and release pressure in fuel system. Connect fuel pressure gauge between fuel tube and hose to fuel filter. Disconnect lead wire from "S" terminal of starter.

**2)** Connect ground cable to battery. Turn ignition switch to START position to operate fuel pump. Gauge readings should be:

**Fuel Pressure Specifications**

| Application | Pressure |
| --- | --- |
| BMW | 33.4-39 psi (2.2-2.7 kg/cm²) |
| Datsun | 36.3 psi (2.55 kg/cm²) |

**3)** If pressure is not as specified, replace fuel pressure regulator. Then, repeat test. If below pressures listed, fuel pump is defective. If within specifications, fuel pump is functional.

**NOTE** — *On BMW 733i, detach plugs at air sensor. Connect terminals 36 and 39 with jumper wire. Turn ignition ON. A click indicates pump relay is good; a humming sound means fuel pump is running. If no fuel is delivered, the pressure relief valve or check valve in fuel pump is defective. Fuel pump pressure should be 32-38 psi (2.4-2.7 mk/cm²).*

### TEMPERATURE SENSOR I (INTAKE AIR SENSOR)

**Datsun** — Disconnect battery ground cable, air flow meter, and record outside air (ambient air) temperature. Measure resistance between terminals 27 and 6, on air flow meter electrical connector. As point of reference, at 50°F. the resistance should be between 3250 and 4150 ohms or at 120°F. the resistance should be between 740 and 940 ohms. If resistance is completely outside of this range, replace temperature sensor and air flow meter as an assembly.

**Volkswagen — 1)** Disconnect plug from intake air sensor. Connect an ohmmeter between air sensor terminals 36 and 39. See *Fig. 7*. Operate air sensor flap by hand. With flap closed there should be no continuity. When flap is opened slightly, there should be continuity. If not, replace intake air sensor.

**2)** To check potentiometer, connect an ohmmeter to terminals 6 and 9 of intake air sensor. Resistance should be between 200 and 400 ohms (Type 1) or 100 and 300 ohms (Type 2). Now, connect ohmmeter between terminals 7 and 8. Reading should be between 100 and 500 ohms (Type 1) or 80 and 200 ohms (Type 2).

**Fig. 7  Air Flow Sensor & Potentiometer**

**3)** If reading is not to specification, replace air sensor.

**NOTE** — *Temperature sensor I can be tested separately if sensor is at 68° F (20° C) or above by connecting ohmmeter to terminals 6 and 27. If resistance exceeds 2500 ohms sensor I is faulty. However, entire sensor unit must be replaced.*

**BMW** — Manufacturer recommends replacement of both temperature sensor and control valve if sensor is defective.

**NOTE** — *Check resistance across air sensor. At 14° F (-10° C), check for 8,250-10,560 ohms; at 68° F (20° C), 2,280-2,720 ohms; and at 122° F (50° C), 760 to 910 ohms.*

### AUXILIARY AIR REGULATOR

**All Models Exc. Datsun — 1)** Remove auxiliary air regulator and connect ohmmeter to both terminals of regulator. Reading should be about 30 ohms.

**2)** Apply compressed air to regulator; passage must be open while engine is cold.

**3)** Connect battery voltage to both terminals. As temperature increases, opening in regulator should become smaller.

**4)** If ohmmeter reading is incorrect or if regulator fails to close with voltage applied, replace unit.

**NOTE** — *If regulator resistance is correct, use test light to check voltage at regulator plug while engine is running. If no voltage, check double relay. Also check that starter solenoid wires on terminals 30 and 50 are not reversed.*

**Datsun — 1)** Pinch hose between throttle chamber and air regulator with fingers. Engine speed should drop. If not, proceed to Step 2).

**2)** Unhook hoses at each end of regulator. Visually check opening in valve. Valve should be open when cold, and close as temperature increases.

# 1978 Bosch Fuel Injection

## BOSCH AFC FUEL INJECTION SYSTEM (Cont.)

**Fig. 8   Electronic Fuel Injection Electrical Diagram**
*Showing Electrical Terminal Numbers for Testing with Ohmmeter*
*(Datsun 280Z Shown — Others Similar)*

3) Check continuity of air regulator at electrical connector. If continuity does not exist, air regulator is defective and should be replaced.

4) Check smoothness of operation by carefully prying air regulator valve open with a flat bladed screwdriver and then close valve again. Replace valve if operation is not smooth.

### THERMO-TIME SWITCH

**All Models — 1)** Unhook battery ground cable. Disconnect electrical plug from cold start valve. Connect ohmmeter between terminal 46 and switch body.

2) If engine termperature is below 57° F (14° C), resistance should be zero. If temperature is above 72° F (22° C), resistance should read infinity. When temperature is 57-72° F (14-22° C), resistance will be zero or infinity.

3) Measure resistance between terminals 45 and switch body. Reading should be 51-62 ohms.

**Volkswagen —1)** Cool thermo-time switch with ice until below operating temperature marked on its housing, usually 95° F (35° C).

2) Disconnect electrical plug from cold start valve. Disconnect ignition primary wire from terminal 1 of ignition coil to prevent engine from starting. Tape disconnected wire to prevent shorting.

3) Attach test lamp leads to terminals of plug. Operate starter for 12 seconds or more. Test lamp should glow brightly at first, and then dim or go out within time period marked on switch (usually 8-11 seconds). If lamp lights but does not dim, replace switch.

4) If lamp does not light, attach leads from one terminal to ground. Repeat test using other terminal and ground. If lamp does not light, wire to double relay or double relay may be the problem. Also check for bad connections and check wire from terminal 50 of starter solenoid to double relay terminal 86a.

5) If current is reaching plug, but test lamp does not light (and test lamp is good), replace thermo-time switch.

## BOSCH AFC FUEL INJECTION SYSTEM (Cont.)

**BMW 733i** — 1) Pull off plugs from cold start relay. Connect ohmmeter between line 45 (relay terminal 86, connection G on thermo-time switch) and ground. Check for 40-70 ohms.

2) Connect ohmmeter between terminal 85 ("W" on thermotime switch) and ground. Connect terminal 86 with 30 (+) which is "G" on thermo-time switch. For temperatures above 59° F (15° C), you should have infinite reading. Below 59° F (15° C), you should have zero reading for 0 to 8 seconds.

### COLD START VALVE

**All Models Exc. Datsun** — Connect pressure gauge to injector supply line. Operate starter to build up fuel pressure. Unhook plug from cold start valve. Connect wires from negative (−) terminal of coil to cold start valve. Observe fuel pressure reading. It should slowly decrease. If the pressure does not drop, replace cold start valve.

**NOTE** — On BMW 733i, remove cold start valve from collector. Pull plugs from air flow sensor. Connect jumper wire from terminal 36 to 39. Pull plugs from cold start relay. Connect relay terminal 87 with terminal 30 (+). Turn ignition ON. Cold start valve must eject. If not, remove cold start relay. Pull off plugs. Connect terminal 85 with ground. Connect terminal 30 and 86c to battery positive terminal. Test lamp connected to terminals 86 or 87 and ground should light. If not, replace relay.

**Datsun** — 1) Disconnect lead wire from the "S" terminal of starter motor. Disconnect electrical connector of cold start valve. Turn ignition switch to START position, making sure fuel pump is operating properly.

2) Disconnect battery ground cable.

3) Remove (2) screws holding cold start valve to intake manifold. Remove clip and disengage fuel hose from valve. Take care to contain fuel spillage from valve.

4) Place cold start valve into glass container of over 20 cc capacity. Block remaining opening at top of container with a rag.

5) Connect battery ground cable. Turn ignition switch to START position. Cold start valve should NOT inject fuel.

**NOTE** — Prior to applying test voltaage to relay, install inline fuse in series with lead wire to avoid circuit damage. If possible, use a 7 Volt tester in place of a 12 volt tester.

6) Turn ignition switch OFF. Connect jumper wire between cold start valve and battery terminals. Ensure cold start valve is in container and container is covered with rag.

7) Cold start valve should now inject fuel. If not, replace.

### TEMPERATURE SENSOR II (ENGINE COOLANT SENSOR)

**All Models** — 1) Disconnect plug and connect an ohmmeter between temperature sensor II (engine coolant sensor) and ground. Sensor is temperature sensitive. As temperature increases, resistance will decrease.

2) Resistance readings should be approximately as follows:

### Temperature-Resistance Relationship

| Temperature Of Coolant | Resistance (Ohms) |
|---|---|
| -22° F (-30° C) | 20,300-33,000 |
| 14° F (-10° C) | 7,600-10,800 |
| 50° F (10° C) | 3,250-4,150 |
| 68° F (20° C) | 2,250-2,750 |
| 122° F (50° C) | 740-940 |
| 176° F (80° C) | 290-360 |

**NOTE** — On BMW 733i, readings are slightly different. At 14° F (-10° C) check for 7,000-11,600; at 68° F (20° C), check for 2,100-2,900; and at 176° F (80° C), 270-390 ohms.

### DECELERATION VALVE

**All Models (Exc. Datsun)** — 1) Check vacuum controlled valves by detaching hose from deceleration valve to intake air sensor at sensor. Start engine and run at about 3000 RPM.

2) Close throttle suddenly. If no suction is present at end of disconnected hose at instant of throttle closing, replace deceleration valve.

3) Check electrically controlled decel valves by, first turning ignition switch ON. Remove wire from decel valve to ATF pressure switch at switch.

4) Ground disconnected wire and listen for "click". If no click is heard, replace decel valve or pressure switch and recheck using above procedure.

5) If deceleration valve is defective, idle speed will be too fast. To check, if valve is at fault, pinch closed the valve's large fabric-covered hose. If speed drops, replace deceleration valve.

## REMOVAL & INSTALLATION

**NOTE** — This fuel injection system maintains constant fuel pressure in fuel lines and component parts at all times. Be sure to relieve pressure before attempting to open system at any point for testing. Do not allow fuel to flow onto engine or electrical parts. Do not allow open flame or sparks in area while servicing or testing fuel system components.

### AIR FLOW METER & AIR CLEANER (AFC SYSTEM)

**Removal (BMW)** — Disconnect electrical plug and loosen clamps on both sides of air flow meter. Remove air cleaner and lift air flow meter out of its holder.

**NOTE** — Use only air flow meter with yellow dot as replacement part.

**Installation (BMW)** — Reverse removal procedure.

**Removal (Datsun)** — Disconnect battery ground cable. Disconnect rubber hose from both sides of air flow meter. Disconnect air flow meter ground cable and remove three bolts securing air flow meter bracket. Move air flow meter upward. Disconnect electrical connector and remove air flow meter.

## BOSCH AFC FUEL INJECTION SYSTEM (Cont.)

**Installation (Datsun)** — To install, reverse removal procedure.

**Removal (Volkswagen)** — 1) Remove air cleaner top and filter, then carefully remove electrical connector from sensor. Loosen hose clamp then disconnect elbow duct from sensor.

**2)** Remove nuts securing air cleaner body to vehicle chassis. Remove sensor and air cleaner body as a unit. Now remove sensor from air cleaner body.

**Installation (Volkswagen)** — To install sensor, reverse removal procedure. Make sure sensor is properly adjusted after installation.

### THROTTLE VALVE HOUSING

**Removal (BMW)** — Remove throttle valve housing cover. Disconnect electrical plug of throttle valve sliding switch. Disconnect vacuum control hose and red electrical cut-off valve hose, at collector. Disconnect warm air hose. Disconnect accelerator linkage and engine vent hose. Disconnect ignition control vacuum hose. Remove cylinder head cover and un-screw lower left stud.

**Installation (BMW)** — To ease installation problems, saw slot in end of stud which was removed on installation. Replace gasket and reverse removal procedure.

**Removal (Datsun)** — Disconnect battery ground cable. Remove distributor cap and remove rubber hoses from throttle chamber. Remove throttle valve switch and disconnect B.C.D.D. device. Disconnect rod from auxiliary throttle shaft. Remove four screws securing throttle chamber to intake manifold. Throttle chamber can now be removed together with B.C.D.D. device and dashpot.

**Installation (Datsun)** — To install, reverse removal procedure.

**Removal (Volkswagen)** — 1) Remove intake air sensor and air cleaner as a unit. Loosen clamp and remove elbow ducting from top of throttle valve housing.

**2)** Disconnect throttle return spring from bracket on EGR valve body. Detach operating rod from EGR valve. Disconnect throttle linkage from arm on throttle valve shaft. Detach upper end of ball link from arm.

**3)** Disconnect vacuum hoses from throttle valve housing, mark hoses for correct position when installing. Remove screws securing throttle valve housing to manifold and remove throttle valve housing.

**Installation (Volkswagen)** — To install throttle valve housing, reverse removal procedure. Always use a new gasket when installing housing.

### CONTROL UNIT (ECU)

**Removal (BMW)** — Press back on clip (located on wire end of electrical connector) and swing cable assembly to right side. Remove screws retaining control unit.

**Installation (BMW)** — Reverse removal procedure.

**Removal (Datsun)** — Turn ignition switch OFF or disconnect battery negative (−) cable. Remove bolt securing control unit cover to left dash side panel. Remove cover and three bolts securing control unit to side panel bracket. Carefully disconnect 35-pin connector and remove control unit.

**Installation (Datsun)** — Reverse removal procedure.

**Removal (Volkswagen)** — Disconnect battery ground strap. ECU is located in right-hand side of luggage compartment, behind rear seat backrest (Type 1) and above battery (Type 2). Remove composition board cover. Use a screwdriver to carefully remove control unit plug. Position it where it cannot be damaged physically or electrically. Remove control unit from body.

**Installation (Volkswagen)** — To install ECU, reverse removal procedure. Make sure cable plug is carefully and completely engaged in ECU. Be sure new ECU has same part number as one removed. Reattach battery ground cable.

### COLD START VALVE

**Removal (BMW)** — Remove electrical connector and retaining screws. Remove cold start valve.

**Installation (BMW)** — Reverse removal procedure.

**Removal (Datsun)** — Disconnect ground cable from battery. Disconnect cold start valve connector. Release fuel pressure. Remove two screws securing cold start valve to intake manifold and remove cold start valve.

**NOTE** — *To relieve fuel pressure, connect terminals of cold start valve to battery terminals, using jumper wires. Connect for 2 to 3 seconds, using care to keep terminals separate to avoid short circuit. See Fig. 9.*

**Fig. 9   Releasing Fuel Pressure at Cold Start Valve**

**Installation (Datsun)** — To install, reverse removal procedure.

## BOSCH AFC FUEL INJECTION SYSTEM (Cont.)

**Removal (Volkswagen)** — Relieve fuel pressure and disconnect battery. Disconnect electrical connector and fuel hoses at cold start valve. Remove screws securing cold start valve to air distributor and remove valve with gasket.

**Installation (Volkswagen)** — To install cold start valve, reverse removal procedure.

### AUXILIARY AIR REGULATOR

**Removal (BMW)** — 1) Disconnect air hoses attached to auxiliary air regulator.

**NOTE** — *Auxiliary air regulator is installed in the cooling system.*

2) When removing auxiliary air regulator from cooling system, either have another regulator ready for immediate installation or drain cooling system below level of regulator. Remove screws securing regulator to block and remove regulator.

**Installation (BMW)** — To install auxiliary air regulator, reverse removal procedure.

**Removal (Datsun)** — Disconnect battery ground cable. Disconnect electrical connector from regulator and remove hose clamp. Remove two set screws.

**Installation (Datsun)** — Reverse removal procedure.

**Removal (Volkswagen)** — Disconnect air hoses and the electrical connector at auxiliary air regulator. Remove screws securing regulator to its mounting bracket. Remove auxiliary air regulator.

**Installation (Volkswagen)** — To install auxiliary air regulator, reverse removal procedure. Always use a new gasket upon installation.

### TEMPERATURE SENSOR II

**Removal (Datsun)** — Disconnect battery ground cable. Remove radiator cap. Remove drain plug from radiator and drain approximately 1-5/8 quarts of coolant. Disconnect radiator upper hose and sensor harness connector. Remove sensor.

**Installation (Datsun)** — Reverse removal procedure. Be sure to install copper washers under sensor and also to add coolant.

### THERMO-TIME SWITCH

**Removal (BMW)** — From beneath pressure regulator, remove electrical connector to thermo-time switch. Drain sufficient coolant to allow removal of switch (below level of switch). Use socket and remove switch.

**Installation (BMW)** — Reverse removal procedure.

**Removal (Datsun)** — Remove radiator cap, drain coolant to level below thermostat housing. Disconnect water hose from

thermostat housing. Disconnect battery ground cable. Disconnect lead wires from thermal transmitter and remove transmitter. Disconnect electrical connector and unscrew thermo-time switch.

**Installation (Datsun)** — Reverse removal procedure.

**Removal (Volkswagen)** — Disconnect electrical connection then remove screws securing switch. Then remove thermo-time switch from bracket.

**Installation (Volkswagen)** — To install thermo-time switch, reverse removal procedure.

### PRESSURE REGULATOR

**Removal (BMW)** — Relieve pressure in fuel system and disconnect battery. Disconnect intake pipe of number four cylinder. Disconnect pressure regulator fuel lines. Disconnect vacuum hose at collector and remove pressure regulator.

**Installation (BMW)** — To install pressure regulator, reverse removal procedure. When installing intake pipe onto cylinder head, use a new gasket.

**Removal (Datsun)** — Disconnect negative battery cable. Disconnect cold start valve connector and release fuel pressure. Remove vacuum hose connecting pressure regulator to intake manifold. Remove pressure regulator.

**Installation (Datsun)** — To install, reverse removal procedure.

**Removal (Volkswagen)** — 1) Disconnect battery and relieve pressure in fuel system. Disconnect vacuum hose from regulator. Clamp or plug fuel hoses to prevent leakage. Disconnect fuel hoses from regulator.

2) From underneath vehicle, remove ring nut securing pressure regulator to engine front cover. Remove pressure regulator.

**Installation (Volkswagen)** — To install pressure regulator, reverse removal procedure.

### INJECTORS

**Removal (BMW)** — Disconnect battery and relieve pressure in fuel system. Disconnect and plug fuel lines to injector(s) being removed. Disconnect electrical connections. Remove retaining screws and remove injector(s).

**Installation (BMW)** — To install injectors, reverse removal procedure.

**Removal (Datsun)** — 1) Disconnect negative battery cable. Remove cold start valve connector and relieve fuel pressure.

**NOTE** — *To relieve fuel pressure, connect terminals of cold start valve to battery terminals, using jumper wires. Connect*

## BOSCH AFC FUEL INJECTION SYSTEM (Cont.)

for 2 to 3 seconds, using care to keep terminals separate to avoid short circuit. See Fig. 9.

2) Disconnect electrical connectors from injectors. Disengage harness from fuel pipe wire clamp. Remove blow-by hose at rocker cover side. Remove air regulator pipe. Place rag around pipe and unfasten hose clamps on feed and return hoses. Remove fuel pipe bolts and cold start valve mounting bolts and all screws securing fuel injectors.

**Installation (Datsun)** — To install injectors, reverse removal procedure.

**Removal (Volkswagen)** — 1) Remove the large air duct between fan housing and heat exchangers on exhaust system. Disconnect battery and relieve pressure in fuel system.

2) Disconnect electrical connector and fuel lines from injectors to be removed. Remove screw securing injector to intake manifold. Remove injector with seals and retainer plate.

**Installation (Volkswagen)** — To install injectors, reverse removal procedure.

# ADJUSTMENTS

## HOT (SLOW) IDLE RPM

See appropriate article in TUNE-UP Service Procedures.

## IDLE MIXTURE

See appropriate article in TUNE-UP Service Procedures.

## THROTTLE VALVE SWITCH

**BMW** — 1) Throttle valve switch should start to operate when throttle valve is opened 2° from its normally closed position.

**NOTE** — On 733i, the idle angle (between idle cut-in position and idle stop on switch) should be 4.5° ; full throttle angle (between idle stop and full throttle cut-in should be 62° ; and maximum throttle gap angle should be 90°.

2) To check and adjust throttle valve switch, use Bosch tester No. 0684100202.

3) Use tester manufactures instructions for switch positions on tester. Readings on tester should show zero resistance for off, infinity resistance for part throttle and zero resistance for full throttle.

4) If throttle switch does not perform as described, loosen throttle switch screws. Rotate throttle valve switch clockwise until needle on tester moves from an infinity reading to a zero reading. Then rotate throttle switch counterclockwise one graduation (one graduation equals 2°). Tighten throttle valve switch screws. Recheck operation of switch.

**Datsun** — 1) Disconnect battery ground cable. Remove throttle valve switch connector.

2) Connect ohmmeter between terminals 2 and 18. Continuity should exist when throttle valve is in IDLE position and should NOT exist when valves opens about 4°. See Fig. 7.

3) Now connect ohmmeter between terminals 3 and 18. Gradually open throttle valve from fully closed position.

4) Ohmmeter reading should be at its lowest point at about 34° of throttle valve rotation. If ohmmeter reading is greater at all other valve positions, throttle valve switch is functioning properly.

## BOSCH CIS INJECTION SYSTEM – AUDI & VOLKSWAGEN

**Audi 5000
Volkswagen
    Dasher
    Rabbit
    Scirocco**

### DESCRIPTION & OPERATION

The Bosch Continuous Injection System (CIS) is a mechanically operated system. It injects fuel to each cylinder in amounts determined by the volume of air flow through the air intake system. Intake air required by the engine is metered by an air flow sensor located in the air inlet. Sensor is activated by a circular plate attached to an arm and pivot assembly which is extremely sensitive to air flow. This sensor plate is raised or lowered by the incoming flow of air, and in turn, raises or lowers a plunger in the fuel distributor. This plunger acts to increase or decrease amount of fuel to be injected at each cylinder. See Fig. 6.

Main components of the CI System are: Control Pressure Regulator, Air Sensor, Fuel Distributor, Thermo-Time Switch, Auxiliary Air Regulator, Cold Start Valve and Injectors, Electric Fuel Pump, Fuel Accumulator, Auxiliary Air Valve and a fuel filtering system. The Audi also has a deceleration valve on Federal models with manual transmission.

### TESTING

**CAUTION** – *Before making any electrical tests on an engine that is not running, but has ignition ON, disconnect plug from air sensor (if so equipped) and positive wire from alternator. Also disconnect high tension cable from terminal 4 of ignition coil so engine will not start when you run starter.*

**NOTE** – *Cold start valve receives power from terminal 50. All other electrical components of fuel system receive positive current from the pump relay. Terminal 30 is permanently connected to positive current, terminal 50 only while starter is operated (connected to control circuit of starter); and terminal 15 only when ignition is ON.*

#### FUEL PUMP OPERATION

Remove fuel pump relay. Install bridging adaptor (US4480/3) and turn adaptor switch ON. Fuel pressure should climb to 49-54 psi (3.4-3.8 kg/cm²). Turn switch OFF and check for 28-37 psi (2.0-2.6 kg/cm²).

#### MIXTURE CONTROL UNIT (AIR FLOW SENSOR)

1) Activate fuel pump with bridging adaptor switch (US4480/3). Leave ignition OFF. Remove air duct assembly.

2) Lift sensor plate with magnet or by hand until it is slightly unseated. Gradually raise plate to limit of upward travel.

3) Steady resistance should be felt over entire travel of sensor plate. No tight or binding spots should be evident. If so, check for dirty pivot or need for lubrication.

4) Ensure sensor plate is centered in inlet cone. If adjustment is needed, use suitable tool (1109 or equivalent) or insert a .004" (.10 mm) feeler gauge around outside of sensor plate while in seated position. Centering bolt should be slightly loosened. Apply Loctite to threads and tighten bolt after adjustment.

5) When sensor plate is pushed down quickly there should be no resistance felt. If binding or sticking is evident, replace sensor unit.

**NOTE** – *Now, lift sensor plate and push down quickly, but stop plate before bottoming out. Control pressure resistance should be felt. If not, clean control plunger or replace fuel distributor as necessary.*

6) If sensor plate lever is hard to move in upward direction but moves freely when pushed down, control plunger is sticking or binding. Remove fuel distributor and clean the control plunger in appropriate solvent.

7) Reinstall plunger and recheck. Replace fuel distributor if plunger still sticks or binds.

8) To adjust sensor plate position for height in cone, loosen fuel line to control pressure regulator where line is connected to fuel distributor.

**NOTE** – *Fuel is under pressure and some fuel will escape when fitting is loosened at fuel distributor. Wrap cloth around fitting to avoid spillage of fuel in engine area.*

9) Upper edge of sensor plate must not be above edge of air cone. See Fig. 1. Plate may be positioned slightly lower, but not more than .020" (.5 mm). If too high or too low, adjust by bending wire bracket beneath sensor plate. See Fig. 2.

**Fig. 1    Sensor Plate Position**

10) Check idle speed and CO% and readjust after making sensor plate adjustment.

**Fig. 2    Adjusting Location for Sensor Plate Height**

## BOSCH CIS INJECTION SYSTEM — AUDI & VOLKSWAGEN (Cont.)

### INSTALLING AND BLEEDING PRESSURE GAUGE AND VALVE

**NOTE** — *Before any pressure tests can be completed, it is necessary to install and bleed air from a gauge and valve, such as VW1318 or P378.*

1) Although pressure testing valves and gauges may appear identical to those pictured in this article, DISREGARD handle position shown when making pressure tests on fuel system.

**NOTE** — *Valves from the same manufacturer may appear the same, but may vary in interior design. When checking rest pressure or control pressure (either cold or warm), be sure valve on tester is OPEN. When checking system (line) pressure, be sure valve is CLOSED.*

2) Install gauge and valve between control pressure regulator and fuel distributor, with valve toward control pressure regulator.

3) To bleed air from valve, hang gauge downward below valve and connecting lines. Open and close valve 4 or 5 times at 10 second intervals. Raise gauge so that it is now above valve and lines and proceed with testing.

### COLD ENGINE CONTROL PRESSURE TEST

**NOTE** — *Engine must be cold for this test, preferably having set overnight at test site without operation.*

1) Install pressure gauge and valve in fuel line between fuel distributor and control pressure regulator.

2) Valve assembly should be on control pressure regulator side of gauge. See Fig. 3 .

**Fig. 3    Connecting Fuel Pressure Gauge and Valve To Test Control Pressure**

3) Turn ignition ON. With fuel pump running, bleed and then OPEN valve.

4) Unplug electrical connector from control pressure regulator. Start engine and idle for maximum of 1 minute.

5) Note control pressure and refer to graph in *Fig. 4*. At normal room temperature, about 68° F (20° C), pressure should read between 18-24 psi (1.3-1.7 kg/cm²).

6) If pressure does not read within specifications, replace control pressure regulator.

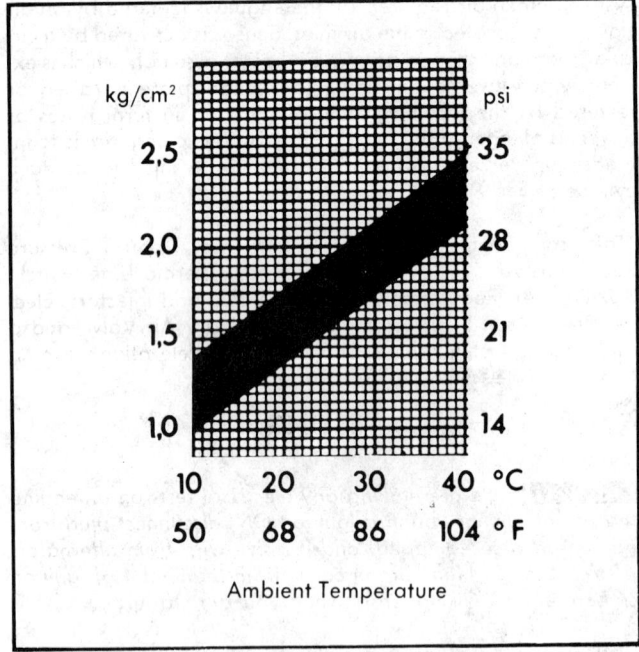

**Fig. 4    Graph Showing Cold Control Pressure at Various Temperatures**

### WARM ENGINE CONTROL PRESSURE TEST

**NOTE** — *Connect pressure testing gauge and valve in same manner as for Cold Engine Control Pressure Test. Keep pump relay bridged.*

1) Be sure to connect control pressure regulator electrical plug, previously removed. OPEN valve. See Fig. 3.

2) Start engine and idle until fuel pressure stabilizes. Reading should be 48-54 psi (3.4-3.8 kg/cm²). If not, replace control pressure regulator.

**NOTE** — *On Audi 5000, pressure should be 49-53 psi (3.5-3.8 kg/cm²) with control pressure regulator vacuum hose connected; 39-43 psi (2.8-3.1 kg/cm²) with hose disconnected.*

### REST PRESSURE

**NOTE** — *Connect pressure testing gauge and valve and check Warm Engine Control Pressure first.*

Then remove bridge from fuel pump relay. Pressure should drop to 28-37 psi (2.0-2.6 kg/cm²). If pressure drops below 28 psi (2.0 kg/cm²) the fuel pump check valve is probably defective.

## BOSCH CIS INJECTION SYSTEM — AUDI & VOLKSWAGEN (Cont.)

### SYSTEM (LINE) PRESSURE TEST

**NOTE** — *Connect and bleed pressure gauge and valve in same manner as for Control Pressure Test. Keep fuel pump relay bridged. Be sure electrical plugs are connected to control pressure regulator and auxiliary air regulator.*

1) Ensure electric fuel pump activates when ignition switch is turned ON and that fuel filter is clean.

2) CLOSE valve (*Fig. 3*). Start engine and run at idle.

3) System (line) pressure should be 64-74 psi (4.5-5.2 kg/cm²). If not within specifications, clean, check and adjust fuel distributor pressure regulator (relief) valve.

**Fig. 5  Components of Pressure Regulator Valve**

4) System pressure may be adjusted by adding to or removing shims from valve. *See Fig. 5.* Pressure will be changed 1 psi (.06 kg/cm²) by a .004" (.1 mm) shim or 4 psi (.3 kg/cm²) by a .020" (.5 mm) shim.

5) If system pressure is low, check for leaks between fuel pump and control pressure regulator. Also check for defective fuel pump.

### LEAK TEST

1) Check for correct system (line) pressure of 64-74 psi (4.5-5.2 kg/cm²). Then remove bridge from fuel pump relay.

2) Wait 10 minutes. Pressure should hold at 25 psi (1.8 kg/cm²). After 20 minutes, pressure should still hold at 23 psi (1.6 kg/cm²). If not, replace fuel pump check valve.

3) If pressure holds, but engine operates with an excessively lean mixture, replace fuel filter and test delivery rate. With filter in good condition and pump running for exactly 30 seconds, delivery volume should be 24 oz. (750 cc).

**NOTE** — *With system pressure correct on Audi 5000, pinch intake hose between fuel tank and fuel pump and turn ignition OFF. If pressure does not drop, replace fuel pump check valve. If it continues to drop, replace "O" ring in fuel distributor pressure regulator valve.*

### COLD START INJECTION VALVE & THERMO-TIME SWITCH

1) Unplug electrical connector from cold start valve but do not disconnect fuel line. Tape electrical connections to prevent accidental sparking. Disconnect electrical plug from air sensor unit and positive wire from alternator. Also disconnect high tension cable from terminal 4 of ignition coil so engine will not start.

2) Remove cold start valve from engine and place into fuel resistant container with nozzle pointing down into container.

3) Connect jumper wire from one terminal of cold start valve to ignition coil terminal #15 (hot terminal). Connect another jumper wire from remaining terminal on cold start valve to a good ground.

4) Activate electric fuel pump by removing fuel pump relay and bridging pump relay terminals L13 and L14.

5) Turn ignition switch ON. Fuel should spray from cold start valve into container in a steady cone-shaped pattern.

6) Turn ignition switch OFF (pumps will still run). Wipe nozzle of cold start valve dry with clean cloth. No drops of fuel should form on tip of valve within one minute.

7) If cold start valve leaks or does not perform to specifications, replace it.

8) To check thermo-time switch, engine must be cold. Coolant temperature should be below 95° F (35° C) on Volkswagen models and 104° F (40° C) on Audi models.

9) Remove electrical plug from cold start valve on end of intake manifold. Disconnect terminal 4 on ignition coil. Connect test light across harness plug terminals.

10) Operate starter for 15-20 seconds. Test light should come ON for 1-8 seconds and then become noticeably dimmer or go OUT.

**NOTE** — *Instead of test light, a voltmeter can be used. Voltage should register at first and then drop off to zero.*

11) If test lamp does not light, attach leads to ground and to one terminal of harness plug. Operate starter. If test lamp does not light, repeat test with leads reversed (connected to other terminal and ground). If lamp does not light, wiring to starter solenoid is defective (if test bulb is good).

12) If test lamp lights without starter operating, wires may be reversed at starter solenoid (wire for terminal 50 may be on terminal 30).

13) If voltage is reaching the test lamp, but the test lamp did not light for the 1-8 seconds when starter was operated for 15-20 seconds in step 10), replace thermo-time switch.

### AUXILIARY AIR REGULATOR

**NOTE** — *Test must be performed on cold engine only.*

**Audi** — 1) Remove electrical connector from auxiliary air regulator. Start engine and check idle speed. Pinch hose from

## BOSCH CIS INJECTION SYSTEM — AUDI & VOLKSWAGEN (Cont.)

auxiliary air regulator to rubber air duct. Idle speed should drop.

**2)** Reconnect electrical connector to auxiliary air regulator. Repeat test with a warm engine. Idle speed should remain constant with hose pinched. If not, replace auxiliary air regulator.

**Volkswagen — 1)** Disconnect both hoses from auxiliary air regulator. Disconnect electrical plugs from control pressure regulator and mixture control unit and positive wire from alternator. Turn ignition ON.

**2)** With aid of a mirror and light, observe gate valve opening in regulator. Valve should be OPEN.

**3)** Run engine at idle to warm up. Observe gate valve as engine warms up. Valve should close within 5 minutes (longer if testing is done outside in cold weather).

**4)** If valve does not close in alloted time, shut engine OFF and remove electrical plug from auxiliary air regulator. Measure resistance across terminals for 30 ohms. If ohmmeter reads infinity or considerably below 30 ohms, replace regulator. If within specification check for voltage at plug. If none, check power relay or pump relay.

### CONTROL PRESSURE REGULATOR

**1)** Check control pressure regulator (cold and warm). If not to specifications, replace regulator.

**2)** Disconnect electrical plug from air flow sensor and the positive wire from alternator. Turn ignition ON without starting engine.

**3)** Disconnect electrical plug from control pressure regulator and measure voltage at plug. If none, check power relay and pump relay. If voltage is available at pump relay, problem lies with wire connecting control pressure regulator and pump relay.

**4)** If voltage is reaching regulator plug, check resistance across regulator terminals for 20 ohms. If resistance varies greatly, replace control pressure regulator.

### INJECTOR NOZZLES

**NOTE** — *Do not allow open flame or sparks in area while testing and servicing fuel system components, to avoid possibility of fire or explosion.*

**1)** Remove one injector from manifold tube, leaving fuel hose attached to injector. Pull injector straight out. Disconnect high tension cable from terminal 4 of ignition coil to prevent engine from starting.

**2)** Point injector into a glass jar. Have someone operate starter for 15 seconds while you observe spray pattern, which should be steady and cone-shaped.

**3)** Turn ignition switch OFF. Hold injector horizontally. No fuel should drip from injector nozzle. If injector does not perform to specifications, replace it. Repeat test for each injector.

**NOTE** — *When installing injectors, soak rubber seals in gasoline briefly. Be sure injectors are fully pressed into seat.*

### DECELERATION VALVE
### (AUDI FEDERAL MAN. TRANS. ONLY)

**1)** Remove hose from side of deceleration valve and plug hose. Start engine and run for a few seconds at 3000 RPM. Let throttle snap closed. At the same time, check for suction at connection where hose was removed.

**2)** Remove vacuum hose at "T" fitting and plug hose. Start engine and run a few seconds at 3000 RPM. Let throttle snap closed. No suction should be felt at connection in side of valve (where first hose was removed). If so, replace valve.

## REMOVAL & INSTALLATION

### MIXTURE CONTROL UNIT

**CAUTION** — *On all models, disconnect battery ground cable and relieve fuel pressure before removing mixture control unit.*

**1)** Clean all fuel connections completely and disconnect them, tagging each one to insure correct installation later.

**2)** Disconnect air duct from air sensor and throttle valve housing.

**3)** Use tip of screwdriver to snap loose the retainers holding bottom part of air cleaner. Prevent unit from falling. Carefully remove mixture control unit, taking care that fuel does not spill on engine or electrical connections.

**4)** To install, reverse removal procedure. Use new gasket beneath upper section of mixture control unit.

### FUEL DISTRIBUTOR

**NOTE** — *California 1978 models have aluminum castings and a revised diaphragm for fuel distributor.*

**CAUTION** — *On all models, disconnect battery ground cable and relieve fuel pressure before removing fuel distributor.*

**1)** Clean and remove fuel lines at fuel distributor. Remove fuel distributor retaining bolts.

**2)** Carefully lift fuel distributor up and away. Use care to avoid control plunger falling out from underside of fuel distributor.

**3)** If control plunger has been removed, dampen with fuel before installing.

**NOTE** — *Small shoulder of plunger must be inserted first.*

**4)** Install fuel distributor using new O-rings.

### CONTROL PRESSURE REGULATOR FOR WARM RUNNING COMPENSATION

**CAUTION** — *On all models, disconnect battery ground cable and relieve fuel pressure before removing control pressure regulator.*

## BOSCH CIS INJECTION SYSTEM – AUDI & VOLKSWAGEN (Cont.)

**1)** Clean fuel lines and disconnect. Remove electrical connections to regulator.

**2)** Remove two screws holding regulator to engine block. Remove regulator and gasket.

**3)** To install, reverse removal procedure, using new gasket.

### AUXILIARY AIR REGULATOR

**1)** Remove vacuum hose connections to valve. Remove electrical connection(s).

**2)** Remove two screws holding regulator to No. 4 cylinder manifold tube of the intake air distributor.

**3)** To install, reverse removal procedure.

### THERMO-TIME SWITCH

**1)** Relieve any cooling system pressure and drain enough coolant from system to bring level below that of time switch.

**2)** Switch is located on coolant adaptor on engine block. Unplug electrical harness plug from thermo-time switch.

**3)** Using a deep socket (to avoid damaging electrical terminals on top of switch), remove thermo-time switch.

**4)** To install switch, reverse removal procedure. Suitable sealing compound may be needed to ensure proper seal of new switch.

### COLD START VALVE

**CAUTION** – *On all models, disconnect battery ground cable and relieve fuel pressure before removing cold start valve.*

**1)** Cold start valve is bolted to intake manifold behind throttle valve housing. Clean around fuel line and remove line from valve.

**2)** Remove electrical connector from cold start valve.

**3)** Remove bolt(s) holding cold start valve and lift out valve.

**4)** To install, reverse removal procedure.

### INJECTORS

**NOTE** – *New injectors are used for 1978 with an opening pressure of 46-54 psi (3.2-3.8 kg/cm$^2$).*

**CAUTION** – *On all models, disconnect battery ground cable and relieve fuel pressure before removing injectors.*

**1)** Clean fuel line connection at injector thoroughly. Remove fuel line from injector with special tool (P384) or equivalent.

**2)** Pull steadily upward on injector to remove.

**3)** To install, reverse removal procedure. Be sure "O" rings are soaked in gasoline for a few minutes prior to installation.

***Fig. 6*** *Functional Diagram of Volkswagen & Audi Bosch CIS Fuel Injection System*

# 1978 Bosch Fuel Injection

## BOSCH CIS INJECTION SYSTEM — BMW MODEL

**BMW 320i**

### DESCRIPTION & OPERATION

The Bosch Continuous Injection System (CIS) is a mechanical system. It injects fuel to each cylinder in amounts determined by the volume of air flow through the air intake system. Intake air required by the engine is metered by an air flow sensor located in the air inlet. Sensor is activated by a circular plate attached to an arm and pivot assembly which is extremely sensitive to air flow. This sensor plate is raised or lowered by the incoming flow of air, and in turn, raises or lowers a plunger in the fuel distributor. This plunger acts to increase or decrease amount of fuel to be injected at each cylinder. *See Fig. 1.*

Main components of the CI System are: Control Pressure Regulator, Air Sensor, Fuel Distributor, Thermo-Time Switch, Auxiliary Air Regulator, Cold Start Valve and Injectors, Electric Fuel Pump, Fuel Accumulator, Auxiliary Air Valve, a fuel filtering system and Vacuum Regulator.

### TESTING

#### AIR/FUEL MIXTURE CONTROL (AIR FLOW SENSOR)

**BMW — 1)** Detach and remove intake cowl at mixture control unit and throttle housing.

**2)** Turn ignition switch ON for about 5 seconds, then turn it OFF again. During this time, raise sensor plate by using magnet or pliers. As plate is slowly raised, resistance felt should be even throughout range of travel.

**3)** When sensor plate is quickly pushed down, no resistance should be felt. Do not allow plate to scrape on air horn wall. If necessary to center sensor plate, loosen centering bolt in middle of plate and adjust.

**4)** Check sensor plate height. Plate should be even with beginning of taper in air cone. If plate is no more than .019" (.5 mm) deeper than edge of tapered area, adjustment is not needed.

**5)** To adjust height of sensor plate, remove mixture control unit and bend spring beneath plate assembly.

**6)** If sensor plate is too high in air cone, engine will diesel or run on. If plate is too low, poor cold or warm engine starting will result.

**7)** Check for sticking or binding fuel control piston (plunger) in fuel distributor. Remove fuel distributor, remove plunger and clean thoroughly with gasoline.

**8)** Plunger binding or sticking is evident when resistance to sensor plate movement is uneven.

*Fig. 1 System Diagram of Bosch CIS System Used on BMW*

## BOSCH CIS INJECTION SYSTEM — BMW MODEL (Cont.)

### COLD ENGINE CONTROL PRESSURE TEST

**NOTE** — *Before pressure test can be done, it will be necessary to install a fuel pressure gauge, 2-way valve and 3-way "T" fitting in fuel line between fuel distributor and control pressure regulator.*

1) Install valve so that it is between gauge and control pressure regulator. See *Fig. 2*. Hang gauge from convenient point above level of units to be tested.

2) Unplug electrical connector at auxiliary air regulator to avoid overheating unit. Disconnect electrical connector at mixture control unit. Turn ignition ON.

3) Set 2-way valve for flow-through operation (open).

**Fig. 2   Connecting Gauge & Valve for Control Pressure Test on BMW Models**

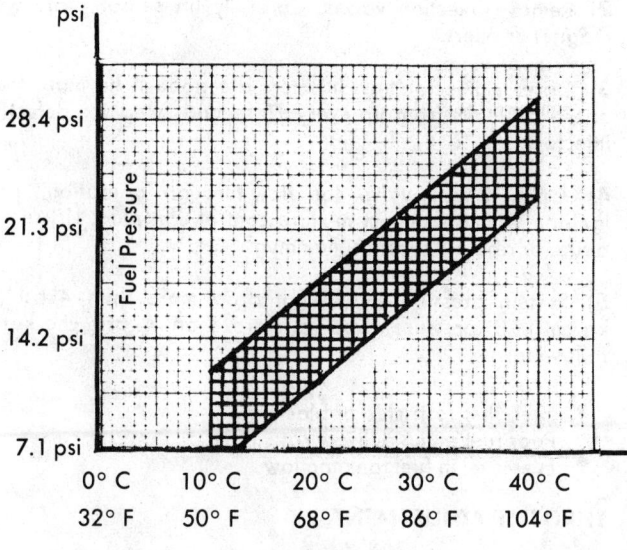

**Fig. 3   Graph Showing Fuel Pressure & Temperature Relationship**

4) Control pressure is dependant upon coolant temperature. Refer to *Fig. 3* graph for temperature and pressure relationship.

5) If fuel pressure reads too low, warm-up regulator is defective and should be replaced. If fuel pressure reads too high, regulator is defective or fuel return flow is insufficient or restricted. Turn OFF ignition.

### WARM ENGINE CONTROL PRESSURE TEST

**NOTE** — *Connect special pressure tester as outlined in cold engine testing.*

1) Open 2-way valve for flow-through operation. Disconnect electrical connector to mixture control unit.

2) Turn ignition ON. Do not start engine. Control pressure should rise steadily for about 3 minutes to 48-54 psi (3.4-3.8 kg/cm²).

3) If not, check for voltage at electrical connector. If voltage is satisfactory, heating coil is defective. Replace warm-up regulator.

4) Install air inlet assembly. Reconnect electrical connectors to auxiliary air regulator and mixture control unit. Start engine.

5) Allow engine to idle. Control pressure should stabilize at 48-54 psi (3.4-3.8 kg/cm²).

### SYSTEM PRESSURE TESTING

**NOTE** — *Refer to Cold Engine Control Pressure Test for special pressure tester connecting procedure.*

1) With engine stopped, close 2-way valve to stop flow-through of fuel. Disconnect mixture control unit electrical connector.

2) Turn ignition ON. System pressure should be 64-74 psi (4.5-5.2 kg/cm²). If system fuel pressure is too low, check the following:

- Leak at fuel lines or connections
- Clogged/restricted fuel filter
- Engine dieseling (run on condition)
- Fuel pump not delivering enough fuel
- Incorrect system pressure adjustment

3) If system fuel pressure is too high, check the following:

- Fuel return flow insufficient
- Incorrect system pressure adjustment
- Pressure regulator control piston binding

4) Adjust system pressure by adding or removing shims to system pressure regulator. See *Fig. 4*.

| Shim Thickness | Amount of Pressure Change |
|---|---|
| .020" (.5 mm) | 4.3 psi (.30 kg/cm²) |

5) Transfer valve (See *Fig. 4*) should open at 50-57 psi (3.5-4.0 kg/cm²). If not, engine will be difficult to start. Check by replacing valve and restarting engine.

## BOSCH CIS INJECTION SYSTEM — BMW MODEL (Cont.)

*Fig. 4    System Pressure Regulator Adjustment (Located in Fuel Distributor Housing)*

*Fig. 5    Cold Start Valve Terminal Locations for Testing*

### REST PRESSURE & LEAK TEST

**NOTE** — *Refer to Cold Engine Control Pressure Test for pressure tester connecting procedure.*

1) Open 2-way valve for flow-through operation. Turn ignition ON.

2) Unplug electrical connector at mixture control unit, and then plug it in again.

3) Turn ignition OFF. Observe cut-off pressure on gauge. Pressure should not drop below 24 psi (1.7 kg/cm²) for several minutes.

4) If pressure drops too soon, check the following:

- One or both "O" rings in pressure regulator leaking.
- Warm-up regulator or supply line leaking.
- Fuel pump check valve leaking.
- Pressure reservoir leaks.

5) Repair or replace parts as necessary and recheck system.

### COLD START INJECTION VALVE & THERMO-TIME SWITCH

1) Disconnect electrical plug at thermo-time switch. Connect brown/black wire (W) to ground. *See Fig. 5* .

2) Disconnect wire from lowest terminal of starter solenoid to prevent engine from starting during test.

3) Remove cold start valve. Remove fuel pump relay from relay plate. Apply battery voltage to terminal marked 87 on relay plate. This will activate fuel pump.

4) Cold start valve should spray fuel. If not, replace cold start valve and recheck.

5) Replace fuel pump relay. Reattach all electrical connectors.

6) Check thermo-time switch by disconnecting electrical plug at thermo-time switch. Connect test light to battery positive terminal (+) and terminal "W" of time switch (See Fig. 5).

7) Test light should come ON at coolant temperatures below 95° F (35° C) and should NOT come on when coolant temperature is above that level. Light should not remain on for more than 8 seconds. If switch is defective, replace it.

### AUXILIARY AIR VALVE

1) Engine must be cold to perform this test. Start engine.

2) Engine speed should be higher than specified engine speed for fast idle for a brief period. Normal idle speed should be 850-950 RPM.

3) If no increase in idle speed is evident, or idle speed fails to return to normal level after a few minutes, replace auxiliary air valve.

### INJECTOR NOZZLES

1) Install pressure tester (13 3 060 or equivalent) to measure fuel pressure applied to injector. *See Cold Engine Control Pressure Test.*

2) Remove injection valves. Carefully lift sensor plate with magnet or pliers.

3) Observe injector tips. Injectors are good if no more than one drop leaks from tip every 15 seconds. Replace defective injectors.

4) Open 2-way valve for flow-through operation. Turn ignition ON. Disconnect mixture control unit plug. Lift sensor plate for about 4 seconds maximum.

5) System pressure should not drop more than 4 psi (.3 kg/cm²). If pressure drop is more than 4 psi, check the following:

- Fuel filter restricted or blocked
- Poor fuel pump delivery rate
- Fuel level in fuel tank too low

### THROTTLE ADJUSTMENT

1) Disconnect accelerator cable.

2) Loosen lock nut and screw on adjuster stand. Adjust distance between stop and lever to .039-.058" (1-1.5 mm).

## BOSCH CIS INJECTION SYSTEM – BMW MODEL (Cont.)

3) When correct clearance has been achieved, tighten lock nut and adjusting screw.

4) Now loosen throttle lever shaft set screw. Position throttle valve in housing so that there is no play or slack. Retighten set screw.

5) Now loosen lock nut on adjuster stand. Do not allow adjusting screw to turn while loosening lock nut.

6) With lock nut loose, turn adjusting screw one full turn clockwise and tighten lock nut.

### REMOVAL & INSTALLATION

**CAUTION** – *On all models, when any fuel system component is being serviced or removed, disconnect battery ground cable and relieve fuel system pressure. Do not allow open flame or sparks in area due to danger of fire and explosion.*

#### MIXTURE CONTROL UNIT

1) Remove intake cowl. Loosen (3) screws on top of fuel distributor. Bend wire fuel line clips open and remove wire holder.

2) Carefully lift off top of fuel distributor. Do not allow control piston to fall out bottom. Disconnect mixture control unit electrical plug and remove all vacuum hoses.

3) Loosen (2) bracket nuts on side of control unit and lift out mixture control unit assembly.

**NOTE** – *Whenever venturi is to be replaced, take notice that there are two different shapes numbered as to application. Federal vehicles use Bosch No. 0 438 120 030; California vehicles use Bosch No. 0 438 120 039.*

4) Reverse removal procedure to install mixture control unit. Be sure to replace gasket between upper and lower halves of unit and replace "O" ring seal beneath fuel distributor at control piston opening.

#### FUEL DISTRIBUTOR

1) Relieve fuel pressure and disconnect all fuel lines at fuel distributor. Remove (3) screws on top of distributor unit.

2) Carefully lift fuel distributor off of mixture control unit, using care not to drop control piston from beneath distributor housing.

3) When installing fuel distributor, be sure to replace "O" ring beneath distributor head around control piston opening. Check control piston for dirt or any damage. Clean piston in new gasoline thoroughly before installing.

#### WARM-UP REGULATOR (CONTROL PRESSURE REGULATOR)

1) Disconnect fuel control line and fuel return line fittings at regulator.

2) Unplug electrical connector. Remove altitude control line (if equipped). Remove retaining bolt and remove warm-up regulator. See Fig. 6 .

**Fig. 6** *Warm-Up (Control Pressure) Regulators on BMW*

#### AUXILIARY AIR REGULATOR

1) Disconnect electrical plug from end of regulator.

2) Detach (2) hoses and remove. Remove auxiliary air regulator from cylinder head cover.

#### THERMO-TIME SWITCH

1) Remove electrical plug from time switch. Lower coolant level.

2) Remove time switch from engine using deep socket or suitable tool to avoid damaging electrical connections on top of switch. When installing, use appropriate sealer on threads.

#### COLD START VALVE

1) Clean thoroughly around fuel connection. Remove fuel line at fitting.

2) Detach electrical connector. Remove attaching bolt(s) or Allen screws and remove cold start valve.

3) To install, reverse removal procedure, ensuring that valve is firmly seated and connections are tight.

#### INJECTORS

1) Remove intake cowl and intake pipes at No. 2 and No. 3 cylinders.

2) Using suitable tool (screwdriver), gently lift injectors out of intake. Remove injectors from fuel lines and mark location of each injector.

3) To install, ensure insulator is properly seated in opening in intake. Press rubber "O" ring type seal in place in intake opening. Insert injector.

4) Install new gaskets when reinstalling intake pipes.

## BOSCH CIS INJECTION SYSTEM – MERCEDES BENZ

**Mercedes Benz**
280
450
6.9

### DESCRIPTION & OPERATION

The Bosch Continuous Injection System (CIS) is a mechanically operated system. Amount of fuel that is continuously injected to each cylinder is determined from air flow by the air sensor plate. This sensor plate is raised or lowered by the air flowing through the intake system to the engine. This, in turn, raises or lowers a plunger in the fuel distributor which increases or decreases amount of fuel to be injected at each cylinder.

Main components of the system are: Control Pressure Regulator (Warm-Up/Full Load Enrichment Compensator), Air-flow Sensor Assembly, Fuel Distributor, Thermo-Time Switch, Auxiliary Air Valve, Cold Start Valve, Injectors, Electric Fuel Pump, Fuel Accumulator, and a fuel filtering system. See *Fig. 9* for system diagram.

### TESTING & ADJUSTMENT

#### AIR/FUEL MIXTURE CONTROL (AIR FLOW SENSOR)

1) Check sensor plate lever for freedom of movement. Remove safety switch plug *(Fig. 1)*, and turn ON ignition to build up fuel control pressure.

2) Turn ignition OFF and push sensor plate down by hand. Even resistance should be felt over entire range of travel. Release sensor plate suddenly. No binding should be evident. Sensor plate should quickly return and lever should follow more slowly.

**Fig. 1    Air Flow Sensor & Control Plunger Assembly (Mixture Control Unit)**

#### COLD ENGINE CONTROL PRESSURE TEST

**NOTE** — *Before pressure testing can be done, it will be necessary to install special testing gauge and 3-way valve*

assembly. Mercedes Benz recommends unit No. 100 589 13 21 00 for this procedure. Gauge installation will remain the same for all pressure testing operations.

**Fig. 2    Pressure Testing Gauge & Valve Assembly**

1) Install tester assembly in fuel line between fuel distributor and control pressure regulator as directed in *Fig. 2*. Ensure engine is cold for this test. Remove plug from control pressure regulator.

2) Open valves for lines "A" and "B" on tester. Start engine and idle. QUICKLY read control pressure. Pressure should agree with that shown in graphs in *Fig. 3* and *Fig. 4* for ambient (surrounding) temperature.

**Fig. 3    Temperature/Control Pressure Graph**

## BOSCH CIS INJECTION SYSTEM — MERCEDES BENZ (Cont.)

**Fig. 4   Temperature/Control Pressure Graph**

**3)** If correct value is not obtained, replace the control pressure regulator (warm-up/full load enrichment compensator). Reinstall plug in regulator.

### WARM ENGINE CONTROL PRESSURE TEST

**NOTE** − *See Cold Engine Test for correct pressure tester installation.*

**1)** Tester valves "A" and "B" must be open. With fuel pumps activated, control pressure should read as follows:

| Application | Control Pressure |
|---|---|
| Federal | 49-55 psi (3.4-3.8 kg/cm²) |
| California | 42-48 psi (2.9-3.3 kg/cm²) |
| High Altitude | 52-58 psi (3.6-4.0 kg/cm²) |

**2)** If correct values are not obtained, check manifold vacuum. Disconnect vacuum hose from control pressure regulator and install "T" fitting and vacuum gauge into line.

**3)** Note vacuum reading and refer to *Fig. 5* for correct intake vacuum and control pressure relationship.

**4)** Check voltage at control pressure regulator with engine running. Remove electrical plug to check. Voltage should be minimum of 13.5 volts.

**5)** Check regulator heating coil with ohmmeter. Reading should be about 35 ohms. If not, replace control pressure regulator.

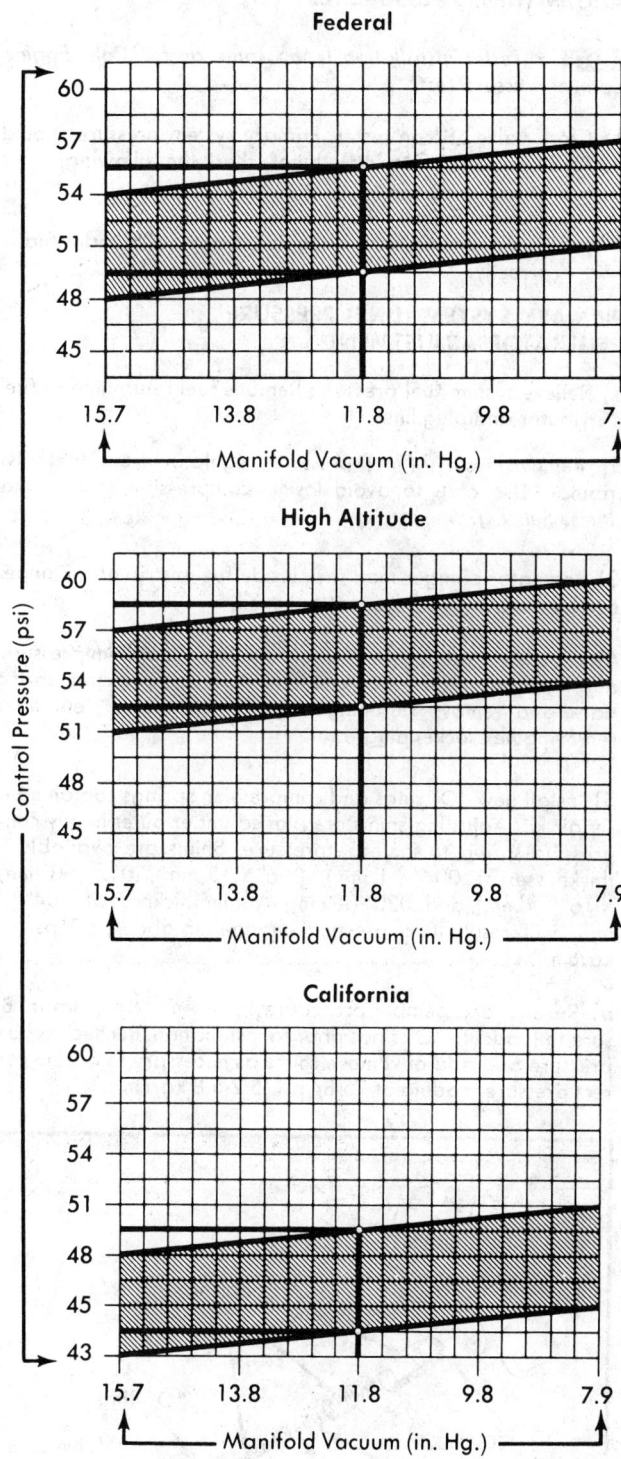

**Fig. 5   Intake Vacuum/Control Pressure Diagrams**

**6)** To check full load enrichment, remove vacuum line from control pressure regulator. Pressure should drop to 41-46 psi (2.8-3.2 kg/cm²). If not, replace regulator.

**7)** Turn OFF engine. Remove pressure tester assembly. Avoid fuel spillage on engine. Reconnect fuel lines and electrical connectors. Run engine and check for leaks.

## BOSCH CIS INJECTION SYSTEM – MERCEDES BENZ (Cont.)

### SYSTEM (LINE) PRESSURE TEST

**NOTE** – *Tester installation is the same as for Cold Engine Control Pressure Test.*

1) Close valve "B" on tester. Primary system pressure should be 75-84 psi (5.2-5.8 kg/cm²). If not, check the following:

- Fuel pump delivery may not be enough.
- Primary system pressure regulator may not be adjusted correctly.

### PRIMARY SYSTEM (LINE) PRESSURE REGULATOR ADJUSTMENT

1) Relieve system fuel pressure. Remove fuel return line at fuel distributor and plug line.

2) Remove system (line) pressure regulator from fuel distributor. Use care to avoid losing compression spring and shims. See *Fig. 6.*

3) Regulator plunger may stick inside fuel distributor. Plunger can be removed with magnet or pencil.

4) In order to add or remove shims to change system pressure, regulator must be disassembled. Push compression spring back and remove retaining ring. Remove valve stem after removing hex socket plug.

5) Install new "O" rings and compression springs contained in repair kit. Adjusting shims are placed under outer heavy compression spring to increase pressure. Shims are available in thicknesses of .004" (.1 mm), .006" (.15 mm), .012" (.3 mm), .016" (.4 mm), and .020" (.5 mm). A shim thickness of .004" (.1 mm) will result in a pressure change of about 2.9 psi (.2 kg/cm²).

6) Reverse disassembly procedure to assemble regulator. Be sure to lubricate "O" rings prior to installation. Recheck system pressure and add or remove shims as necessary to obtain correct pressure reading of 75-84 psi (5.2-5.8 kg/cm²).

### COLD START VALVE & THERMO-TIME SWITCH

1) Disconnect fuel line at cold start valve. Remove valve. Loosen fuel line on fuel distributor and turn so that cold start valve can later be reconnected. Point cold start valve down into fuel resistant container. Disconnect safety switch plug.

2) Turn ignition ON. Connect a jumper wire from cold start valve to positive (+) terminal of battery. Valve should spray a cone-shaped pattern of fuel.

**CAUTION** – *Connect jumper wire to cold start valve first to prevent electric arcing.*

**NOTE** – *When coolant temperature is below 59° F (15° C), jumper wire is not needed. Instead, reconnect harness plug.*

3) Now disconnect jumper wire from valve. Using clean cloth, wipe excess fuel from tip of valve. No fuel should leak out of nozzle.

4) Turn ignition OFF. Install cold start valve using new gasket. Reconnect safety switch plug and cold start valve plug.

5) Thermo-time switch is responsible for activating cold start valve at temperatures below 59° F (15° C). Actuating period increases with decreasing temperatures to a maximum of 12 seconds at −4° F (−20° C).

6) At coolant temperatures below 59° F, connect voltmeter to cold start valve terminal. Operate starter. Voltmeter should indicate 10 volts for amount of time that thermo-time switch is closed.

7) At coolant temperatures above 59° F, switch can be checked with an ohmmeter. Disconnect thermo-time switch plug. Connect test lead to terminal marked "W" in plug (brown/black wire), and other lead to ground. See *Fig. 7.* Reading should be about 270 ohms.

8) Connect test lead to other terminal in plug. Ohmmeter should read about 62 ohms. If not, replace switch.

**Fig. 6  Exploded View of System Pressure Regulator**

**Fig. 7  Testing Thermo-Time Switch**

## BOSCH CIS INJECTION SYSTEM — MERCEDES BENZ (Cont.)

### AUXILIARY AIR VALVE

1) When engine is initially cold started, engine speed should be about 800-1000 RPM. Engine speed should then increase to about 1200-1300 RPM.

2) As coolant temperature warms up to 158° F (70° C), engine RPM should again drop to normal range. Air valve is operating correctly if engine performs to these specifications.

### INJECTOR NOZZLES

**NOTE** — *Manufacturer recommends using testing tool (EFEP 60 H or Bosch No. 0 681 200 502) for this test. If not available, use pressure gauge assembly No. 100 589 13 21 00. See Fig. 8.*

1) Remove air filter assembly. Unscrew fuel lines at injector nozzles. Ensure nozzles do not rotate when unscrewing fittings. Catch escaping fuel with cloth.

2) Remove hold down brackets. Hold nozzles in place to avoid pulling out nozzles and insulators. Pull out injectors while keeping insulators in place in opening of intake. If insulators accidently come out, new "O" rings must be installed before placing them back into intake.

3) Connect injector nozzles to tester. Bleed pressure line with shut-off valve open and pressure line nut loose. Several strokes of hand lever should be sufficient for bleeding.

4) Tighten pressure line nut. With shut-off valve still open, depress hand lever slowly to build up pressure to maximum of 22 psi (1.5 kg/cm²). If injector leaks (solid stream from nozzle), replace it with a new one.

5) Close shut-off valve on tester and flush out valve with several rapid hand lever strokes. Open shut-off valve and slowly build up pressure with hand lever. Leak test again.

6) No fuel droplets should form within 15 seconds. Replace injectors that do not meet specifications. After installation, start engine and check for fuel leaks.

*Fig. 8  EFEP60 H Injection Nozzle Tester*

## REMOVAL & INSTALLATION

**NOTE** — *On all models, disconnect battery ground cable and relieve fuel pressure before opening fuel system at any point. Do not allow open flame or sparks in area while servicing fuel system components due to danger of fire and explosion.*

### MIXTURE CONTROL UNIT

**Air Flow Sensor Housing** — 1) Remove air filter. Remove all fuel and injection lines at injection nozzles and fuel distributor.

2) Plug all disconnected fuel supply and return lines. Remove safety switch connector. Remove retaining bolts and nuts on air flow sensor housing. Remove housing with gasket.

3) When installing housing, use new gasket. Torque hex head bolts and nuts to 6.5-7.2 ft. lbs. Reconnect all fuel lines and wiring. Start engine and check for leakage.

**Fuel Distributor** — 1) Remove air filter. Remove all fuel supply lines at fuel distributor and injectors. Plug disconnected lines.

2) Unscrew fitting for control pressure line on fuel distributor. Remove (3) retaining screws and remove distributor.

**NOTE** — *Use care not to drop control plunger from beneath fuel distributor.*

3) Install fuel distributor using reversed removal procedure. Use new "O" ring (lubricated) and carefully install distributor. Reinstall all lines. Check sensor plate and lever for freedom of movement. Check control plunger for sticking or binding. Start engine and check for leaks. Adjust idle speed if necessary.

### THERMO-TIME SWITCH

When removing thermo-time switch, use care not to damage electrical contacts on top of switch. Coolant level should be drained to a point lower than level of switch. When reinstalling switch it may be necessary to apply suitable sealing compound to threads to avoid leakage.

### INJECTORS

1) Remove air filter. Remove all fuel lines at injectors and fuel distributor. Do not allow injectors to rotate while loosening fittings.

2) Remove hold down brackets. Hold nozzles in place so insulators will not pull out with injectors. If they are accidentally pulled out, new "O" rings must be installed on insulators prior to replacement.

3) Carefully pull out injectors.

4) When installing injectors, be sure that noses on hold down brackets face to the LEFT. Do not allow injectors to rotate while tightening fittings. Run engine and check for leaks.

# 1978 Bosch Fuel Injection

## BOSCH CIS INJECTION SYSTEM — MERCEDES BENZ (Cont.)

*Fig. 9  Diagram of Mercedes-Benz CIS Injection System*

## BOSCH CIS INJECTION SYSTEM – PORSCHE

**Porsche
All Models**

### DESCRIPTION & OPERATION

The Bosch Continuous Injection System (CIS) is a mechanical system. Its entire operation is based upon the metering or sensing of the amount of intake air required to run the engine under different conditions. All intake air must pass through the mixture control unit which contains an air sensor plate within a cone shaped venturi. This plate is movable and is very sensitive to the incoming flow of air. Plate is mounted on a pivoting lever which is connected to a fuel control piston (plunger) in the fuel distributor. As the sensor plate is raised or lowered by differences in amount of air flow, the plunger is raised or lowered in the fuel distributor and determines amount of fuel to be injected into each cylinder.

System is made up of Mixture Control Unit (Air Flow Sensor & Fuel Distributor), Control Pressure Regulator, Auxiliary Air Valve, Auxiliary Air Regulator, Thermo-Time Switch (924, 928, and California 930 Turbo), Thermo-Valve (911SC & 930 Turbo), Cold Start Valve and Injectors, Electric Fuel Pump(s), Fuel Accumulator, a fuel filtering system and connecting lines and hoses.

On 911SC, 928, and 930 Turbo models, the control pressure regulator vacuum connections have been reversed. The tapping below the throttle is now connected to the side of the regulator rather than the top. *See Fig. 1.*

Control pressure regulators on 911SC and 930 Turbo work differently. On 911SC, when engine is stationary or vacuum is low, control pressure is low. Only the external spring is effective on control valve. At idling, internal spring is activated as diaphragm is lifted by vacuum. Control pressure is increased. Near full throttle, vacuum decreases, the internal spring pressure decreases and control pressure is lowered. Fuel mixture becomes richer.

On 930 Turbo models, when engine is stationary, during normal operation or at low boost pressures up to about 1.5 psi (.1 kg/cm²), both springs are effective and control pressure is high. A drop in pressure (full throttle enrichment) takes place when a pressure in excess of 1.5 psi (.1 kg/cm²) exists above the diaphragm. Then the internal spring is no longer effective.

On 930 Turbo, full throttle enrichment cannot be checked until boost pressure reaches about 4.35 psi (.3 kg/cm²).

*Fig. 1  CIS System on Porsche 930 Turbo*

## BOSCH CIS INJECTION SYSTEM – PORSCHE (Cont.)

### TESTING & ADJUSTMENT

#### AIR/FUEL MIXTURE CONTROL (AIR FLOW SENSOR)

**1)** Remove air cleaner assembly on 924 or 911SC. Working through air inlet opening, raise sensor plate lever from below. On other models, push down on sensor plate from above.

**NOTE** – *On 924 and 911SC models air flow is upward around sensor plate; on 928 and 930 Turbo models, air flow is downward. See Fig. 2.*

**2)** Resistance to sensor plate movement should be even and constant throughout entire range of travel.

**3)** Loosen line to control pressure regulator at fuel distributor to relieve fuel pressure. Upper edge of sensor plate should be flush with lip of venturi.

**4)** On 924 models, adjust height of sensor plate by bending wire clip beneath sensor plate. On 911SC models, a screw and lock nut assembly is used to adjust sensor plate height. A rubber stopping block limits downward movement of lever. On 928 and 930 Turbo models, the spring-loaded sensor plate stop is set at factory and cannot be adjusted.

**5)** Now check sensor plate position with control pressure applied. Turn ignition ON and remove electrical plug on air flow sensor. If sensor plate drops slighty on 924 or 911SC models (or raises slightly on other models) by a maximum of .04" (1 mm), operation is satisfactory. Plate may not move at all under control pressure and this condition is also satisfactory. See Fig. 2. If necessary, replace leaf spring on sensor plate stop.

**6)** To center sensor plate within air cone, loosen and remove retaining bolt. Coat bolt threads with Loctite or suitable compound and install bolt finger tight.

**7)** Using a feeler gauge, center sensor plate so that a .004" (.10 mm) gap exists between plate and air cone wall at all points around the circle. Tighten retaining bolt to 43-48 INCH lbs. (50-55 cmkg). Recheck gap after tightening.

#### INSTALLING PRESSURE TEST GAUGE

Before conducting pressure tests to determine control pressure (warm or cold) and system pressure, install a pressure testing gauge and valve assembly in the line between the control pressure regulator and the fuel distributor. A typical installation is shown in *Fig. 3*. Bleed valve before use.

**NOTE** – *Although pressure testing valves and gauges may appear identical to those pictured in this article, DISREGARD handle position when making pressure tests on fuel system. Valves from the same manufacturer may APPEAR the same, but may vary in internal design. When checking rest or control pressure (either warm or cold), be sure valve on tester is OPEN. When checking system or line pressure, be sure valve is CLOSED.*

#### COLD ENGINE CONTROL PRESSURE TEST

**NOTE** – *Engine must be cold for this test. Vehicle should sit overnight where test is to be conducted.*

**1)** Turn ignition ON. Remove air sensor and control pressure regulator plugs. On 928 remove plug from auxiliary air regulator. Pull out fuel pump relay (in passenger's footwell) and bridge terminals 30 and 87 to turn on fuel pump.

**2)** Open valve and read pressure on gauge. On 928, cold engine control pressure should be as indicated in the following table. Pressures for other models are shown in *Fig. 4*.

**Fig. 2   Correct Sensor Plate Positioning**

**Fig. 3   Pressure Tester Assembly for Checking Control Pressure**

## BOSCH CIS INJECTION SYSTEM – PORSCHE (Cont.)

**NOTE** – *Cold engine control pressure cannot be measured on 930 Turbo due to the difference in design of its control pressure regulator.*

### 928 Cold Engine Control Pressure
(At 68° F or 20° C)

| Application | psi (kg/cm²) |
|---|---|
| Engine Not Running | 16.7-21.0 (1.17-1.48) |
| Engine at Idle Speed | 23.9-28.3 (1.68-1.99) |

**3)** If cold engine control pressures are not within specifications, replace control pressure regulator.

Fig. 4   Cold Engine Control Pressure Charts

### WARM ENGINE CONTROL PRESSURE TEST

**NOTE** – *Pressure tester installation is the same as for Cold Engine Test.*

**1)** Be sure that plug to control pressure regulator is installed. Disconnect electrical plug at air flow sensor. On 928 models, be sure plug to auxiliary air regulator is installed.

**2)** Open valve on pressure gauge. Turn ignition ON. Wait 2 or 3 minutes. Take pressure reading with engine stopped.

**3)** Start engine and run at idle speed until engine reaches normal operating temperature. Take pressure reading again. Compare with the following table:

### Warm Engine Control Pressures

| Application | Stopped psi (kg/cm²) | Idling psi (kg/cm²) |
|---|---|---|
| 924 | 49.3-55.1 (3.47-3.88) | 49.3-55.1 (3.47-3.88) |
| 911SC | 39.2-45.0 (2.75-3.16) | 46.4-52.2 (3.26-3.67) |
| 928 | 41.3-45.7 (2.91-3.21) | 50.0-54.4 (3.52-3.82) |
| 930 Turbo① | 49.3-55.1 (3.47-3.88) | 49.3-55.1 (3.47-3.88) |

① – With boost pressure above 4.36 psi (.32 kg/cm²), warm control pressure should be 39.2-45.0 psi (2.75-3.16 kg/cm²). Boost pressure at 4000 RPM should be 11.6-12.6 psi (.82-.89 kg/cm²).

**4)** If pressure does not reach this level, control pressure regulator is defective and should be replaced.

### SYSTEM (LINE) CONTROL PRESSURE

**NOTE** – *Tester hook-up is the same for Cold and Warm Control Pressure Testing.*

**1)** Be sure fuel supply, fuel pump(s) and filter are in good working order. Close valve on test equipment. Disconnect electrical plug at air flow sensor terminal and turn ignition ON. Pressure should be as shown in following table:

### System (Line) Pressure

| Application | psi (kg/cm²) |
|---|---|
| 924 | 65.27-75.42 (4.59-5.30) |
| 911SC | 65.3-72.53 (4.59-5.10) |
| 928 | 72.52-84.12 (5.10-5.91) |
| 930 Turbo | 87.02-97.18 (6.12-6.83) |

**2)** If pressure is not within specifications, adjust pressure by adding or removing shims beneath outer spring in system pressure regulator, located in fuel distributor housing.

## BOSCH CIS INJECTION SYSTEM — PORSCHE (Cont.)

### LEAKAGE TEST

1) With pressure gauge connected as for measuring system (line) pressure, run engine until it reaches normal operating temperature. Shut engine OFF.

2) After 10 and 20 minute periods, record gauge readings. They should be as shown in following table:

#### Leakage Test Gauge Readings

| Application | After 10 Min. psi (kg/cm²) | After 20 Min. psi (kg/cm²) |
|---|---|---|
| 924 | 24.66 (1.73) | 21.76 (1.53) |
| 928 | 24.66 (1.73) | 21.76 (1.53) |
| 911SC & 930 Turbo | ① | ① |

① — Not available at time of publication.

3) If pressure is not maintained after 20 minutes test, check for defective "O" ring in pressure regulating valve of fuel distributor or check valve on fuel pump, leaking cold start valve, leaking control pressure regulator, or defective accumulator.

**NOTE** — *Be sure to remove bridge from fuel pump relay upon completion of pressure tests.*

### INJECTOR OPENING TEST

Injectors must be tested (after removal from engine), using an injector tester. Opening pressure for 924 is 36.26-52.21 psi (2.55-3.67 kg/cm²) and for 928 is 43.51-59.47 psi (3.06-4.18 kg/cm²).

**NOTE** — *Specifications for 911SC and 930 Turbo not available at time of publication.*

### COLD START VALVE & THERMO-TIME SWITCH

1) Ensure engine is cold. Remove cold start valve. Do not disconnect wire or fuel line. Disconnect hot lead at ignition coil. Point cold start valve down into fuel resistant container (See Fig. 5).

2) Turn ON ignition and have assistant operate starter. Valve must spray even cone shaped pattern for about 1-8 seconds. If not, replace cold start valve.

3) Check valve for leaks by turning ignition ON again. Remove electrical plug at air flow sensor. Fuel pump(s) should still be operating.

4) With clean cloth, wipe cold start valve tip dry. No fuel should leak from valve within one minute. Replace valve if defective.

5) To check thermo-time switch, remove electrical plug at cold start valve. Connect voltmeter to the plug.

6) Disconnect hot lead at ignition coil and operate starter. Voltmeter should deflect for about 1-8 seconds. Replace thermo-time switch if defective.

**NOTE** — *Ensure that coolant temperature is below 95° F (35° C) when performing test. Above that temperature, thermo-time switch does not operate and cannot be tested with voltmeter.*

With Ignition "ON" Check For Even, Conical Spray Pattern

*Fig. 5   Testing Cold Start Valve*

### THERMO-VALVE

**NOTE** — *The 930 Turbo has a thermo-valve which acts on the distributor vacuum unit. Thermo-valve is electrically-heated and is controlled by the fuel pump relay. 911SC models have an electrically-heated thermo-valve installed (by "T" fitting) in vacuum retard line. Vacuum passes through thermo-valve to side inlet of control pressure regulator.*

**930 Turbo** — 1) The thermo-valve is closed when cold. This prevents any vacuum from reaching the distributor vacuum unit (no vacuum retard). The engine now runs for a period of 15 to 20 seconds at increased idle (approximately 2000 RPM).

2) When engine starts and valve is actuated, it opens. This permits vacuum to reach the distributor and the vacuum retard will now operate. Idle speed drops to its specified 950-1050 RPM. If these conditions occur, the thermo-valve is operating properly. If not, replace thermo-valve.

**911SC Models** — 1) Remove vacuum hose from side fitting of control pressure regulator (hose from thermo-valve). Turn ignition ON.

2) Remove air sensor plug. Blow through disconnected hose. Valve should not leak air when closed. Valve should open after 20-33 seconds at 68° F (20° C). Replace valve if faulty.

### AUXILIARY AIR REGULATOR

1) Detach hose at regulator. Using mirror and flashlight, check to see that air passage in regulator is open.

2) Disconnect electrical plug at air flow sensor. Turn Ignition ON. Air passage in regulator should close after 5 minutes. If not, replace regulator. See Fig. 7.

## BOSCH CIS INJECTION SYSTEM — PORSCHE (Cont.)

Control Pressure
Line Fitting

Fuel Distributor

"O" Ring

.5 mm Shim

.1 mm Shim

Seal

Control
Piston

Air Flow Sensor Housing

Fuel Dist. Seal

Gasket

Ball

C-Clip

Sensor Plate

Pivot Lever

Operating Lever

Leaf Spring

Counterweight

Stop Bracket

*Fig. 6  Exploded View of Mixture Control Unit for Porsche 924 Model
(911SC Similar — 928 and 930 Turbo Have Downdraft Design)*

# 1978 Bosch Fuel Injection

## BOSCH CIS INJECTION SYSTEM — PORSCHE (Cont.)

Fig. 7  *Checking Operation of Auxiliary Air Regulator*

### CONTROL PRESSURE REGULATOR (WARM-UP COMPENSATOR)

**NOTE** — *911SC models have a thermo-valve installed in vacuum retard line (by "T" fitting), and vacuum passes through the electrically-heated thermo-valve to the control pressure regulator.*

**1)** Ensure engine oil temperature is above 120° F (50° C) and that engine is fully warmed up. Disconnect wires at warm-up regulator.

**2)** Remove plug at air flow sensor and turn ignition ON. Using voltmeter, check voltage at disconnected regulator plug. Voltage should be a minimum of 11.5 volts.

**3)** Using ohmmeter, check resistance of heating coil. Reading should be about 20 ohms. Replace warm-up regulator if defective.

## REMOVAL & INSTALLATION

**NOTE** — *CIS system maintains fuel pressure at all times. Before opening fuel system at any point, disconnect battery ground cable and relieve fuel pressure in system. Do not allow open flame or sparks in area while servicing fuel system components due to danger of fire and explosion.*

### MIXTURE CONTROL UNIT

**1)** Remove rubber boot or air cleaner attachment from air sensor. Clean around all fuel line fittings. Remove fuel line fittings from fuel distributor.

**2)** Detach wire plugs, loosen (6) Allen bolts and remove mixture control unit.

**3)** Reverse removal procedure to install, using new gaskets for housing and a new "O" ring beneath fuel distributor, if removed.

### FUEL DISTRIBUTOR

**1)** Clean area around fuel fittings and remove. Remove (3) retaining screws from top of fuel distributor.

**2)** Carefully lift fuel distributor off. Use care not to drop control piston out from bottom of fuel distributor.

**3)** When installing, reverse removal procedure. Ensure control piston is clean. Use new "O" ring seal between fuel distributor housing and mixture control housing.

### CONTROL PRESSURE REGULATOR (WARM-UP COMPENSATOR)

**1)** Remove electrical connectors at warm-up regulator. Loosen hollow fuel line bolts.

**2)** Loosen (2) Allen bolts and remove warm-up regulator.

**3)** When replacing the regulator, torque lower hollow bolt to 7 ft. lbs. (.97 mkg) and upper bolt to 11 ft. lbs. (1.52 mkg).

### AUXILIARY AIR VALVE

Pull wire plug off regulator and loosen hose clamps. Remove Allen screws and regulator. To install, reverse removal procedure.

### INJECTORS

**1)** Unscrew coupling nut from injector line. Install special tool (P384 or equivalent) on end of injector and pull straight upward.

**2)** Remove rubber bushing if it sticks in support sleeve.

**3)** When installing, use drop of oil on bushing and install in head. Press injector firmly into support sleeve. Press until bottomed. Replace fuel line and check for leaks.

## BOSCH CIS & LAMBDA CIS INJECTION SYSTEM — SAAB & VOLVO

**BOSCH CIS**
 Federal Only
  Saab 99
  Volvo 240 Series
  Volvo 260 Series
**BOSCH/LAMBDA CIS**
 Calif. & High Altitude
  Saab 99
  Volvo 240 Series
  Volvo 260 Series

### DESCRIPTION

**BOSCH CIS**

**NOTE** — *See Schematic Drawing of Bosch CIS Fuel Injection System in Figs. 1 and 3.*

This is a mechanical system which determines the amount of fuel to be injected into each cylinder by measuring the amount of intake air required to run the engine. Once the volume of air being drawn into the engine is known, the system can inject the correct amount of fuel to achieve a balanced air/fuel mixture. An air flow sensor, made up of a round plate and lever assembly, moves up and down in relation to the air being brought into the engine. This assembly, in turn, raises or lowers a fuel control plunger or piston in the fuel distributor, resulting in exact measurement of fuel allowed to the injectors.

**NOTE** — *On Saab 99 and Volvo 240 Series, air flows from air cleaner UP through air sensor to intake manifold. On Volvo 260 Series, air is drawn DOWN from the air cleaner, through throttle valves and to intake manifold.*

System is composed of an Air Flow Sensor, Fuel Distributor, Air Cleaner and Fuel Filter Assemblies, Warm-Up Regulator, Throttle Valve Housing, Cold Start Valve, Thermo-Time Switch, Injectors, Auxiliary Air Valve and Deceleration Valve.

**BOSCH/LAMBDA CIS**

**NOTE** — *See Schematic Drawing of Bosch/Lambda CIS Fuel Injection System in Figs. 2 and 3.*

The Bosch/Lambda CIS System consists of a conventional CIS fuel injection system, described at left, with the addition of an oxygen sensor (located in exhaust manifold), a frequency or modulating valve, a throttle valve switch (Saab 99 only), a relay switch, and an electronic control unit (ECU). The final component of the Lambda system is a three-way catalytic converter, consisting of a honey-combed ceramic material coated with rhodium and platinum.

The Lambda system operates in much the same manner as a conventional Bosch CIS system, but offers more precise fuel metering. This closer tolerance of injected fuel is controlled by the oxygen sensor which sends impulses to the electronic control unit (ECU) which in turn sends control impulses to the frequency or modulating valve. This valve controls the time the injectors are injecting fuel. The special three-way catalytic converter further reduces the three most prevalent pollutants, CO, HC, and NOx.

*Fig. 1  Diagram of Bosch CIS Injection System*

# 1978 Bosch Fuel Injection

## BOSCH CIS & LAMBDA CIS INJECTION SYSTEM – SAAB & VOLVO (Cont.)

**NOTE** – *On Saab 99 and Volvo 240 Series, air flows from air cleaner UP through air sensor to intake manifold. On Volvo 260 Series, air is drawn DOWN from the air cleaner, through throttle valves and to intake manifold.*

### TESTING

#### AIR/FUEL MIXTURE CONTROL ( AIR FLOW SENSOR )

**NOTE** – *On Saab 99 and Volvo 240 Series, air flows from air cleaner UP through air sensor to intake manifold. On Volvo 260 Series, air is drawn DOWN from the air cleaner, through throttle valves and to intake manifold.*

1) Remove the duct from top of air flow sensor. Turn on ignition for about 5 seconds and then switch it off. Remaining fuel pressure in system will press control plunger against sensor plate lever. Lift sensor plate by hand, magnet or pliers (push sensor plate down on 260 Series). A steady resistance should be felt as a result of control plunger action.  *See Fig. 4.*

2) No resistance should be noticed when the sensor plate is suddenly pushed down and is not acting against plunger (released or pulled upward on 260 Series). If sensor plate is hard to move, replace entire sensor unit. If control plunger is hard to move, replace fuel distributor.

**NOTE** – *Do not confuse control pressure resistance with binding or seizing.*

3) Be sure sensor plate is centered in the air venturi. Use centering tool 8392474 (Saab) to check for uniform clearance around edge of plate. If no tool is available, loosen retaining bolt in center of plate, adjust plate for .010" (.25 mm) clearance at all points around plate, and tighten centering bolt.

**NOTE** – *Use suitable compound such as Loctite on threads to prevent centering bolt from vibrating loose during engine operation.*

*Fig. 2  Diagram of Bosch-Lambda CIS Injection System*

## BOSCH CIS & LAMBDA CIS INJECTION SYSTEM — SAAB & VOLVO (Cont.)

NOTE — On 260 Series vehicles, air flows from air cleaner DOWN through air sensor to intake manifold.

Fuel Filter

Control Pressure Regulator

Auxiliary Air Valve

Cold Start Injector

Fuel Distributor

AIR FLOW

Air Sensor

To Fuel Tank

Injector

Fuel Distributor

Frequency (Modulating) Valve

(With Oxygen Sensor Feedback System)

**Fig. 3   Diagram of Volvo 260 Series CIS Injection System
(240 Series Similar)**

## BOSCH CIS & LAMBDA CIS INJECTION SYSTEM — SAAB & VOLVO (Cont.)

**4)** Turn ignition switch OFF, so that fuel pump is inoperative. Check rest position of air flow sensor plate. On Saab 99 and Volvo 240 Series, top of plate should be no higher than the bottom edge of air venturi. A position below lower edge of venturi is permissable if within specifications shown in table. Also see *Fig. 4*. For 260 Series plate clearance, see *Fig. 4*.

**Air Flow Sensor Plate Rest Position**

| Application | Lowest Maximum Position |
|---|---|
| Saab | .020″ (.5 mm) |
| Volvo | |
| 240 Series | .040″ (1 mm) |
| 260 Series | .020″ (.5 mm) |

**5)** If adjustment is necessary on Saab 99 or Volvo 240 Series vehicles, bend wire clip beneath sensor plate and lever. See *Fig. 4*. On 260 Series, check that plate stop does not touch plate. Contact pin is adjustable inward using a drift and mallet (tap lightly). To drive pin outward, air sensor must be removed.

### PRESSURE TESTS

**NOTE** — *Although pressure testing valves and gauges may appear identical to those pictured in this article, DISREGARD handle position when making pressure tests on the fuel system. Valves from the same manufacturer may appear the same, but may vary in interior design. When checking rest pressure or control pressure (either cold or warm), be sure valve on tester is OPEN. When checking system or line pressure, be sure valve is CLOSED.*

**Tester Installation — 1)** Before conducting pressure tests to determine system pressure, and control pressure for warm or cold engine, install special pressure testing gauge (8392516 for Saab; 999 5011 for Volvo).

**Fig. 5  *Correct Installation of Pressure Gauge (Saab Shown, Volvo Similar)***

**2)** Disconnect the control pressure line (top center) from fuel distributor and connect pressure gauge between fuel distributor and the line to control pressure regulator (warmup regulator). See *Fig. 5*.

**3)** Before testing fuel pressure, bleed pressure gauge.

**Bleeding Pressure Gauge — 1)** On Saab vehicles, remove fuel pump relay and install jumper wire from terminals 30 to 87 in relay holder. On Volvo models, install 5170 Test Relay as shown in *Fig. 6*.

**2)** This permits fuel pump to operate with ignition ON and engine not running. Check that all equipment is properly installed.

**Fig. 4  *Checking Operation of Air Flow Sensor Plate***

## BOSCH CIS & LAMBDA CIS INJECTION SYSTEM — SAAB & VOLVO (Cont.)

**Fig. 6    Installation of Volvo 5170 Test Relay (Saab Uses Jumper Wire)**

**3)** Turn ignition switch ON and let pressure gauge hang lower than hose connections to engine. To bleed gauge, repeatedly open and close valve 3 or 4 times. Now place pressure gauge higher than hose connections.

**Control Pressure Test (Cold Engine) — 1)** Open valve. Disconnect electrical connector on control pressure regulator and turn ignition ON.

**NOTE** — *This test can only be carried out when the engine is cold. To ensure engine is at ambient temperature, let vehicle set overnight without running engine.*

**2)** Volvo vehicles with V6 engine have a vacuum connection from control pressure regulator to intake manifold (Federal) or to open air (California or other vehicles with Lambda CIS system). Pressure reading will vary depending on whether this hose is connected or disconnected. *See Fig. 8.*

**3)** Compare pressure gauge reading with pressure recommended in temperature/pressure graph. *See Fig. 8.*

**4)** If pressure reading is not to specifications, replace control pressure regulator.

**Fig. 7    Schematic View of New Line Pressure Regulator**

**Control Pressure Test (Warm Engine) — 1)** Turn pressure gauge knob or lever to OPEN position. Connect electrical plug to control pressure regulator. Turn ignition ON and allow pressure to stabilize.

**2)** Volvo vehicles with V6 engine, have a vacuum connection from control pressure regulator to intake manifold (Federal) or to open air (California and other Lambda CIS equipped vehicles). Pressure reading will vary depending on whether this hose is connected or disconnected.

**3)** If pressure is not to specifications listed below, replace control pressure regulator:

### Control Pressures (Warm Engine)

| Application | psi (kg/cm²) |
|---|---|
| Saab | 48.5-54.0 (3.4-3.8) |
| Volvo | |
| 240 Series | 50-55 (3.5-3.9) |
| 260 Series | |
|    Federal | 50-55 (3.5-3.9) |
|    California (Lambda) | 45-49 (3.15-3.45) |

**System Rest Pressure Test** — Open valve on pressure gauge. Connect electrical plug to control pressure regulator. Turn ignition switch ON until rest pressure is present. Rest pressure should be 24-34 psi (1.7-2.4 kg/cm²). If pressure is greatly different, replace control pressure regulator. *Also see step* **4)** *of System Line Pressure Test.*

**System Line Pressure Test — 1)** With pressure gauge installed and bled and valve closed, turn ignition switch ON. Pressure should be 64-72.5 psi (4.5-5.1 kg/cm²).

**2)** If pressure is too low, check for low fuel pump pressure, clogged fuel tank strainer, leakage in fuel line or defective line pressure regulator in fuel distributor.

**3)** If pressure is too high, check for blocked fuel return line or defective line pressure regulator in fuel distributor.

**4)** Line and rest pressure can be adjusted by adding or removing shims from line pressure regulator in fuel distributor. Pressure can be increased by adding shims, decreased by removing them. Shims are available in .004" (.1 mm) thickness to provide pressure change of .85 psi (.06 kg/cm²) or .020" (.5 mm) to provide pressure change of 4.3 psi (.3 kg/cm²). Thicker shims should be used first when adjusting. Thinner shims should be used when line pressure is more than 70 psi (4.9 kg/cm²) and rest pressure is below 24 psi (1.7 kg/cm²). *See Fig. 7.*

### COLD START INJECTION VALVE & THERMO-TIME SWITCH

**1)** Remove plug from cold start valve and unscrew valve from throttle valve housing. Leave fuel line connected. Connect a wired plug to cold start valve and attach to battery or head light connections for power source.

**2)** Install Volvo 5170 Test Relay or jumper wire on Saab so that fuel pump will operate with ignition switch ON but with engine not running. Place cold start valve over a container. With ignition switch ON and voltage available to valve, fuel should spray for a short period (30 second maximum). Check for conical spray pattern. *See Fig. 9.*

# 1978 Bosch Fuel Injection

## BOSCH CIS & LAMBDA CIS INJECTION SYSTEM — SAAB & VOLVO (Cont.)

**CAUTION** — *Use caution when fuel is atomized, so that risk of fire is held to minimum.*

**3)** Dry off nozzle and let fuel pump run another minute. No fuel should pass through the valve. When operating properly spray will be present when engine temperature is below 113° F (45° C) and will not occur at temperatures above that figure.

**NOTE** — *Cold start valve is controlled by a thermo-time switch. As a point of reference, at an engine temperature of -4° F (-20° C), valve should spray for approximately 8 seconds.*

**4)** If engine temperature is within range that cold start spray should operate, but none occurs, check voltage at cold start valve. With starter energized, connect test lamp in series across valve contacts. Voltage indicates defective cold start valve.

**Fig. 9   Checking Cold Start Valve Efficiency**

---

**SAAB**
**Federal**

psi (kg/cm²)

42.6 (3.0)
35.6 (2.5)
28.4 (2.0)
21.3 (1.5)
14.2 (1.0)
7.1 (0.5)

| 0 | 10 | 20 | 30 | 40 | ° C |
| 32 | 50 | 68 | 86 | 104 | ° F |

**California**

psi (kg/cm²)

42.6 (3.0)
35.6 (2.5)
28.4 (2.0)
21.3 (1.5)
14.2 (1.0)
7.1 (0.5)

| 0 | 10 | 20 | 30 | 40 | ° C |
| 32 | 50 | 68 | 86 | 104 | ° F |

**VOLVO**
**260 Series**

psi (kg/cm²)

56.9 (4.0)
52.6 (3.7)
42.6 (3.0)
35.6 (2.5)
28.4 (2.0)
21.3 (1.5)
14.2 (1.0)

Vacuum Hose Connected

Vacuum Hose Disconnected

| 0 | 10 | 20 | 30 | 40 | 50 | 60 | 70 | 80 | ° C |
| 32 | 50 | 68 | 86 | 104 | 122 | 140 | 158 | 176 | ° F |

**240 Series**

psi (kg/cm²)

56.9 (4.0)
52.6 (3.7)
42.6 (3.0)
35.6 (2.5)
28.4 (2.0)
21.3 (1.5)
14.2 (1.0)

| 0 | 10 | 20 | 30 | 40 | 50 | 60 | 70 | 80 | ° C |
| 32 | 50 | 68 | 86 | 104 | 122 | 140 | 158 | 176 | ° F |

**Fig. 8   Graphs Showing Temperature/Pressure Relationship for Cold Control Pressure for Saab & Volvo Models**

## BOSCH CIS & LAMBDA CIS INJECTION SYSTEM – SAAB & VOLVO (Cont.)

5) Connect test lamp (with starter energized) to blue/yellow cable of cold start valve and ground. Voltage indicates defective thermo time-switch or defective wire between switch and cold start injector.

6) If voltage is not present, check for defective wire between starter motor and cold start injector.

7) If engine is warm (above 113° F or 45° C), and fuel injection occurs when starter is energized, either the switch or injector is defective. Remove connector from cold start injector. If there is injection when starter is energized, cold start injector is defective. If not, switch is defective.

### AUXILIARY AIR VALVE

**NOTE** — *This test can only be performed on a cold engine.*

1) The auxiliary air valve maintains proper idling speed by compensating for losses due to friction and condensation in the intake manifold and combustion chamber during cold starting.

2) The valve by-passes the throttle valve housing, but air passes through air flow sensor prior to auxiliary valve. A bimetal strip opens valve completely when engine is cold, about -22° F (-30° C), and fully closes valve at about 158° F (70° C) or after 5 minutes engine operation.

3) Install Volvo 5170 Test Relay or jumper wire (Saab) in fuel pump circuit. Disconnect plug at control pressure regulator. With engine cold, check with light and, if necessary, a mirror to see that there is an elliptical opening in the auxiliary air valve. *See Fig. 10.*

4) Turn ignition switch ON. The opening should close within 5 minutes. If valve does not close and power supply is proper, replace auxiliary air valve.

### CONTROL PRESSURE REGULATOR

1) Disconnect plug at control pressure regulator. With voltmeter, check for 11.5 volts at plug.

2) Install Volvo 5170 Test Relay or jumper wire (Saab) in fuel pump circuit and remove positive wire at alternator. Connect

ohmmeter between positive terminal on control pressure regulator and ground. If ohmmeter reads infinity, replace regulator.

### INJECTOR NOZZLES

**Saab — 1)** Remove rubber bellows from air flow sensor. Unscrew injection valves from intake manifold. Place valves in a suitable container without disconnecting fuel lines.

2) Install jumper wire in fuel pump circuit and turn ignition ON to activate fuel pump. Lift lever in air flow sensor. Injectors should spray an even cone-shaped pattern of fuel. If not, clean or replace defective injectors.

3) Turn ignition switch OFF to obtain line pressure. With clean cloth, wipe injector nozzles dry. Lift sensor lever again and check for leakage at injector nozzle tips. No fuel should leak within 15 seconds. If so, replace defective nozzles.

**Volvo — 1)** Use Bosch injector nozzle tester EFEP 60 H or Volvo tester 9999934-4 to test nozzles See Fig. 11. Connect injector to tester and pump up pressure until injector opens. Pressure should be 37-51 psi (2.6-3.6 kg/cm²).

*Fig. 11  Bosch Injector Tester (EFEP 60 H)*

**CAUTION** — *Do not exceed 85 psi (6 kg/cm²). If injector still does not open, replace.*

2) Lower pressure to 34 psi (2.4 kg/cm²). Observe nozzle tip. No fuel droplets should form within 15 seconds. If nozzles leak, replace as necessary.

**Volvo Quick Check** — With ignition ON, 5170 Test Relay installed so that fuel pump is activated, open air flow sensor plate. Injectors should whine. When sensor plate is allowed to close, injector whine should stop. Continued whining would indicate jammed control plunger in fuel distributor.

**NOTE** — *Perform this test quickly to prevent excessive fuel from being injected into engine.*

*Fig. 10  Checking Auxiliary Air Valve Operation*

## BOSCH CIS & LAMBDA CIS INJECTION SYSTEM — SAAB & VOLVO (Cont.)

### OXYGEN SENSOR FEEDBACK SYSTEM

**NOTE** — A malfunction of this system may appear as difficult starting at normal operating temperature, erratic idle, poor engine performance especially in lower speed ranges, and poor gas mileage. For components, see Fig. 12.

**Volvo — 1)** Use Bosch injector nozzle tester EFEP 60 H or Volvo tester 9999934-4 to test nozzles. See Fig. 11. Connect injector to tester and pump up pressure until injector opens. Pressure should be 37-51 psi (2.6-3.6 kg/cm²).

**2)** If no buzzing sound occurs (or defective system is strongly suspected), connect dwell meter to check duty cycle (open/close ratio) of frequency valve. Connect between instrument pickup connector and ground. Meter should be of high quality, capable of reading at least 70°.

**3)** Disconnect Lambda oxygen sensor from exhaust manifold. Check dwell reading (duty cycle), setting meter as you would for a 4-cylinder engine. Readings should be:

### Frequency Valve Duty Cycle Readings

| Application | Degrees |
| --- | --- |
| Volvo | |
| 240 Series | 49-59 |
| 260 Series | |
| Engine at 60° F (15° C) or above | 40-50 |
| Engine Below 60° F (15° C) | 71-81 |

**4)** If there is a buzzing sound, but dwell reading is incorrect, check dwell meter or short circuiting of electronic control unit.

**5)** If no buzzing sound and dwell meter is 0°, check ground wires for electronic control unit at intake manifold. Then check that terminal 8 of control unit is "live." Check voltage between terminals 8 and 16 and between 5 and 8. If voltage is found between both of these sets of connections, electronic control unit is defective.

**6)** If no buzzing sound and dwell meter reading is either 49-59° or 90°, check voltage at frequency valve. If voltage is present, check resistance at valve for 2-3 ohms. Replace valve if not within specifications. If resistance is okay, reconnect frequency valve, switch off ignition, disconnect electronic control unit and switch on ignition. Check for voltage at terminal 15 in connector. If no voltage, repair wire; if voltage, try new electronic control unit.

**7)** If buzzing sound exists at frequency valve, but there is no reading on dwell meter, check that instrument is suited for its purpose and is correctly connected. Check wire (instrument is plugged into) which is transferring the signal from the electronic control unit to dwell meter. To check, disconnect connector at electronic control unit. Use ohmmeter to check for closed circuit from terminal 17 of connector to pick-up point for dwell meter.

**Saab — 1)** Manufacturer recommends using a Bosch KDJE 7453 tester to measure the pulse relationship (open to close relationship of frequency or modulating valve) of the oxygen

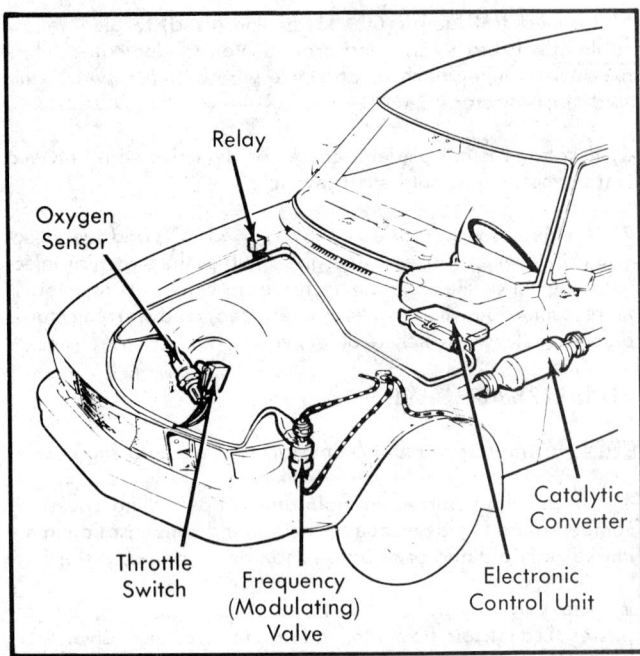

**Fig. 12 Components of Oxygen Sensor Feedback System**

sensor system. The tester is connected to a special 2-pole socket located near relay holder. With ignition switch OFF and jumper wire connected from terminal 30 to 87 in relay holder, hook up tester. The modulating or frequency valve should operate and be easily heard.

**2)** With oxygen sensor connected, meter reading should be 60±10%. This is fixed pulse relation existing before sensor has reached operating temperature or in event of defective sensor.

**3)** Disconnect cable from sensor and ground it. Reading in excess of 75% is possible. Regulating system would enrich fuel/air mixture. Disconnect sensor from ground and mixture will first become leaner and reading will drop below 50%. It then will again increase and level off at 60±10%. Reconnect sensor cable.

**4)** Fully open throttle valve and reading will level off at 45±10%.

**5)** With engine running, observe variations due to pulse relation regulation. When oxygen sensor is still cold (about 1 minute after starting), a fixed pulse relation of 60±10% will occur.

**6)** When engine is warm and CO value is correctly set at idling speed, the reading should vary back and forth between 40 and 60% readings.

**7)** If system is operating close to either end of scale, satisfactory regulation is usually not possible. If this occurs an automatic monitoring system will cut in regulating the system at a fixed pulse relation of 60% to open.

## BOSCH CIS & LAMBDA CIS INJECTION SYSTEM – SAAB & VOLVO (Cont.)

### REMOVAL & INSTALLATION

**CAUTION** – *On all models, when removing component parts, disconnect battery ground cable first and relieve fuel pressure.*

#### FUEL PUMP

**Saab – 1)** Roll back carpet in trunk compartment. Remove circular cover plate on top of pump mounting. Remove rubber cover from pump and disconnect electrical terminals at pump.

**2)** Disconnect fuel line. Hold pump with open-ended spanner wrench when loosening connection. Use special tool 88392433 to turn pump mounting counterclockwise to unlock bayonet socket from groove. Lift out pump and save "O" ring.

**NOTE** – *Pump can only be removed in one position, because one bayonet is wider than the others.*

**3)** Reverse removal procedure to install. Cover tank opening while pump is removed.

**Volvo Main Fuel Pump** – Main fuel pump is located on cross member under floor beneath rear seat. After gaining access, remove battery ground cable, electrical connections and fuel lines. Remove pump from mounting bracket.

**Volvo Fuel Feed Pump (In Tank) – 1)** Disconnect battery ground cable and remove gas cap to relieve tank pressure. Remove trunk floor mat or rear floor panel. Remove cover over pump armature after disconnecting electrical wires and ground wire screw.

**2)** Remove vent hose, fuel feed hose and fuel return hose. Clean area around armature to prevent dirt from entering tank. Lift out armature assembly using special tool 5016 or 5169.

**NOTE** – *Use care not to damage electrical wiring, float lever or filter stocking.*

**3)** To install, clean area around tank opening. Use a new "O" ring and a glycerin-type lubricant. Carefully install armature assembly and tighten with special tool 5016 or 5169. Be especially careful to connect electrical wires properly, check overall length of pump for 10.5-10.62" (267-271 mm) measurement, and check filter position that it does not interfere with float arm.

#### MIXTURE CONTROL UNIT (AIR FLOW SENSOR)

**Saab – 1)** Thoroughly clean the area around fuel connections on fuel distributor. Disconnect fuel lines from fuel distributor. Disconnect lines to injection nozzles before disconnecting control pressure line from distributor.

**2)** Remove rubber bellows from air flow sensor and throttle valve housing. Remove retaining bolts and remove mixture control unit from air cleaner.

**3)** To install, reverse removal procedure making sure air cleaner element is properly positioned first.

**Volvo** – Clean around fuel connections before removing fuel lines. Remove rubber bellows and strap for injection lines.

Remove injection lines and control pressure line from fuel distributor. Remove mixture control unit. Reverse procedure to install.

#### FUEL DISTRIBUTOR

**1)** Remove mixture control unit from vehicle. Remove attaching screws from top of fuel distributor.

**NOTE** – *Use care that control plunger does not fall out bottom of distributor when lifted off. Avoid touching plunger, if possible. Do not attempt to disassemble fuel distributor (other than line pressure regulator), but replace as a unit, if necessary.*

**2)** To install fuel distributor, reverse removal procedure, using new "O" ring and making sure control plunger does not fall from distributor. Check movement of parts of mixture control unit when assembled. There should be no binding or sticking.

#### CONTROL PRESSURE REGULATOR

**1)** Clean area around fuel fittings on regulator. Remove fuel lines. Disconnect electrical plug and remove attaching bolts.

**2)** To install, reverse removal procedure. Check that fittings are tight and leak-free.

#### AUXILIARY AIR VALVE

Remove and plug hoses. Remove electrical connections. Unscrew auxiliary air valve. To install, reverse procedure.

#### THERMO-TIME SWITCH

**1)** Drain coolant below level of thermo-time switch or have second switch ready to install as soon as old one is removed.

**2)** Disconnect electrical connector. Use a socket with sufficient depth to prevent damage to electrical contacts on top of switch. To install, reverse removal procedure.

#### COLD START VALVE

Disconnect electrical plug at cold start valve. Clean around fuel fitting and remove fuel lines. Remove retaining screws and valve. To install, reverse removal procedure. Make sure fittings are tight and leak-free.

#### INJECTORS (INJECTION NOZZLES)

**1)** Clean area around fuel line fittings at injectors. Remove fuel lines. Hold injectors to prevent them from turning, while fuel lines are being removed.

**2)** Remove screws and retaining plate. Carefully pull injectors straight up and out of opening. If insulators are used, do not pull them out with injectors.

**3)** To install, reverse removal procedures. Be sure insulators are firmly in place and new "O" ring has been installed on insulator if it has been removed. Press injectors firmly into place and tighten fuel lines. Do not allow injectors to turn when installing fuel lines. Check for leaks.

# 1978 Lucas Fuel Injection

## LUCAS-JAGUAR ELECTRONIC INJECTION SYSTEM

### Jaguar (All Models)

### DESCRIPTION

Lucas manifold pressure controlled (MPC) injection system is a pulsed, port injection system with one injector per cylinder. The amount of fuel injected depends upon engine load, speed and atmospheric pressure. Manifold pressure control regulator (MPC) measures the amount of pressure differential in the intake manifold and transmits an electric signal to electronic control unit (ECU). This signal modifies all other signals sent to ECU by the other sensors. The ECU electronically analyzes all sensor information and transmits a signal to the injectors, which determines the amount of time each injector will be open. This Bosch electronic injection system consists of three sub-assemblies; fuel delivery, air induction system, and electronic sensing and control. Major components of fuel delivery system include: twin fuel tanks, fuel vibration damper, fuel pump, change-over valves, fuel rails, injectors, fuel pressure regulator, fuel cooler and fuel filter. Major components of the electronic sensing and control are: ECU, power amplifier, thermo-time switch, incoming air and engine coolant temperature sensors, cold start injector valve, MPC (manifold pressure control sensor), throttle switch, distributor trigger unit, main relay, and pump relay.

### TESTING

**NOTE** — *Failure of any component in the system, effects balance of entire system. Installation of any new component will not automatically restore system to normal state of balance since the new component will have slightly different characteristics than original part being replaced. Although balancing the system is accomplished by the ECU, a certain amount of time is required for ECU to make this adjustment (normal road test will be sufficient time). This period of time required for the system to reach equalibrium is also required when replacing ECU.*

### FUEL PUMP

1) Switch on ignition, pump should run one or two seconds and then stop. Switch off ingnition and operate change-over switch to select other tank. Switch on ignition and pump should operate for one or two seconds, then stop. Switch off ignition. If pump operates as described, test procedure is complete, however if pump either does not run or does not stop, proceed as follows: *See Fig. 1.*

***Fig. 1   Diagram of Fuel Pump Circuit for Testing***

2) Check inertia switch (located on right front kick pad) by removing screws attaching switch to kick pad and checking that both cables are secure. Pull cables off switch and check continuity across switch terminals. Pull button out and check that an open circuit exists. Push button inward and check that resistance is either zero or less than 5 ohms. If inertia switch checks out good, ground pump relay terminal 85, switch on ignition and check circuitry as follows:

3) Use voltmeter to check voltage at test point V1. If battery voltage is present, faulty pump or bad ground connection is indicated. If no voltage is present at test point V1, make sure changeover switch is selecting correct tank and continue testing. Check voltage at test point V2. If voltage is present, faulty changeover valve or bad ground connection is indicated. If no voltage at V2, faulty switch or wiring connection is indicated. Now check voltage at test point V3 and V4. If voltage is present, an open circuit in wire to changeover valve(s) is indicated. If no voltage is present, make sure test is being carried out at correct changeover position and continue testing.

4) Check voltage at test point V5. If voltage is present, faulty switch is indicated. If necessary, replace switch and continue testing. Check voltage at V6. If voltage is present, an open circuit between terminal 87 and changeover switch is indicated. If no voltage at test point V6 check voltage at V7. If voltage is present at V7, pump relay is not energized or pump contacts are bad. If no voltage is present, check voltage at test point V8. If voltage is present, faulty pump relay is indicated. If no voltage was present at test point V8, continue testing.

5) Check voltage at test point V9. If voltage is present, an open circuit exists between test point V8 and V9. If no voltage is present at test point V9, check for voltage at test point V10. If voltage is present at this test point, main relay is not energized or contacts are faulty. If no voltage is present, check power supply from battery and continue testing. Check for voltage at test point V11. If no voltage is present, check battery voltage supplied through ignition switch via inertia switch. If voltage was present, proceed with testing. At test point V12 disconnect ground lead and connector and check for battery voltage at terminal 85. If no voltage, replace main relay. If voltage is present, check cable and ground connection from terminal 85. If relay energizes, check for battery voltage at terminal 87. If still no voltage, or relay does not energize, replace relay.

### ELECTRONIC CONTROL UNIT (ECU)

Due to the complexity of the ECU unit, Jaguar recommends the use of their "EPITEST" test unit. When using this tester, follow manufactures operating instructions. The only other method of checking out an ECU is to replace a suspected bad ECU with a known good unit and test drive the vehicle. There is no field repairs for ECU's. If ECU is bad, it should be replaced.

### FUEL PRESSURE REGULATOR

1) Depressurize fuel system. Loosen pipe clamp securing left-hand cold start injector to fuel rail and pull pipe from rail. Connect pressure gauge to fuel rail and tighten pipe clamp. Pull negative "VE" lead from ignition coil and switch on ignition. Connect pump relay terminal 85 to ground. Check pressure gauge reading, it should be 28.5-30 psi. **NOTE** — *Pressure reading may drop slowly though either regulator valve or pump non-return valve. A slow steady drop is permissable, but a fast drop should be investigated.*

## LUCAS-JAGUAR ELECTRONIC INJECTION SYSTEM (Cont.)

**2)** Operate fuel tank change-over valve and repeat step **1)**. Remove ground connection to terminal 85 of pump relay. **NOTE** — *If satisfactory pressure readings are not obtained, it will be necessary to either adjust the pressure regulator or repair the leak-down condition, before proceeding with test procedure. If satisfactory results were obtained, loosen pipe clamp and remove pressure gauge from fuel rail. Reconnect cold start injector supply pipe and tighten pipe clamp. Switch off ignition.*

### MANIFOLD PRESSURE CONTROL VALVE (MPC)

Pull connector off of pressure control valve and use ohmmeter to check the following resistances: Between terminals 7 and 15, resistance should be 85-95 ohms. Between terminals 8 and 10, resistance should be 346-354 ohms. Between all terminals and ground, resistance should be infinity. If readings are outside these values, replace MPC. *See Fig. 2.*

### INJECTORS

**Injector Windings** — Use ohmmeter to measure resistance of each injector winding. This can be accomplished by disconnecting electrical connection to each injector and measuring across both terminals. Resistance should be 2.4 at 68°F (20°C). Now check for short circuit between ground and windings by connecting ohmmeter from injector terminals to ground (injector body). Resistance should be infinity. If injector fails either of these tests, replace that injector.

**Electrical Pulses and Cable** — **1)** Injectors are connected in two groups to power amplifier and each group is divided into parallel sets of three (see table). *See Fig. 3.*

| Group 1 | | | Group 2 |
|---------|----|----|---------|
| 1A | 6B | 6A | 1B |
| 5A | 2B | 2A | 5B |
| 3A | 4B | 4A | 3B |

**Fig. 3  Firing Order Illustration**

RIGHT

1A  2A  3A  4A  5A  6A

4A  5B
3B  1B
1A  6A
6B  4B
5A  2B  3A

FIRING ORDER
1A-6B-5A-2B-3A-4B-
6A-1B-2A-5B-4A-3B

FRONT

1B  2B  3B  4B  5B  6B

LEFT

**2)** Disconnect coolant temperature sensor and terminal 85 of pump relay. Disconnect injectors electrical connection. Connect voltmeter or test light across terminals of each injector electrical plug. **NOTE** — *Start with injector at cylinder 1A. Crank engine, test light should flash or meter should deflect as amplifier pulses. Repeat test for all injectors in first set of group 1, before continuing with second set of group 1, then test group 2 etc.* **NOTE** — *If only one result (injector) per set is incorrect, check for faulty connection of that injector. If all*

Check Resistance Between the Two End Pins

15
7

For a Final Check, Test Resistance Between Each Pin and Ground

90 Ohms

Check Resistance Between the Center Two Pins

10
8

350 Ohms

**Fig. 2   Test Connections for Manifold Pressure Sensor Test**

## LUCAS-JAGUAR ELECTRONIC INJECTION SYSTEM (Cont.)

three results (injectors) in same set are incorrect, either amplifier is faulty or faulty connection is indicated. If all six results (injectors) are incorrect, defect could be faulty connection of cable, bad amplifier or bad ECU.

**NOTE** — Before performing the delivery test, take all precautions against fire and explosion; because fuel vapor will be present in engine compartment during test procedure.

**Delivery Test — 1)** Remove two set screws securing each fuel rail to intake manifold. Remove two nuts and spring washers securing each injector clamp to ram pipes. Raise fuel rail as far as possible and support with blocks of wood. **NOTE** — Take care not to strain pipe joints and locate a container beneath each injector to catch discharged fuel. Pull negative "VE" connection off of ignition coil and connector on thermo-time switch.

**2)** Crank engine and observe that each injector sprays fuel. If one injector is not operating, check that injector electrical connection and if necessary replace that injector. If three injectors are not operating, suspect power amplifier. If six injectors are not functioning, either power amplifier or ECU should be replaced. After testing is complete, reverse disassembly procedure.

### COLD START INJECTION VALVE

**NOTE** — When testing cold start system, fuel vapors will be present in engine compartment, therefore you should take all precautions necessary to prevent fire or explosion.

**Preparations For Testing** — Remove cold start injector valves from intake manifold. Place suitable container beneath each cold start valve, to catch discharged fuel. Disconnect negative "VE" connection at ignition coil.

**Engine Below 58°F (15°C) — 1)** Switch on ignition and check that injectors do not leak. Crank engine one or two revolutions and make sure that injectors spray fuel. If each injector does operate, reverse preparations for testing. If any injector fails to operate properly, continue tests.

**Fig. 4   Diagram of Cold Start Circuit for Testing**

**2)** At test point V1 (on diagram), check for battery voltage. If battery voltage is present when cranking engine and injectors still do not spray, check electrical connections to each injector. If both positive and negative connections are good, the injector is bad and should be replaced. If no voltage was present at test point V1, check for voltage at test point V2. See Fig. 4.

**3)** If voltage is present at V2, check cables between cold start injector relay and cold start injectors. If no voltage was pre-

sent at V2, check for voltage at V3. If no voltage is present at V3, check supply voltage from pump relay. If voltage was present at V3, cold start relay is not functioning properly. Check for voltage at V4.

**4)** If no voltage was present at V4, check supply voltage from starter relay. If voltage was present at V4, disconnect terminal 85 of cold start relay and check for voltage at terminal 86. If no voltage is present, replace relay. If voltage is present, bridge terminal 85 to ground and relay should energize. Now check voltage at terminal 87, if no volatge, replace relay. If voltage present at 87, check cable and connections to thermo-time switch. If cables are in good condition and making proper connections, continue test procedure.

**5)** Replace cold start injectors and all cables and connections. Crank engine and check for voltage at terminal 87. Voltage at terminal 87 should be zero. If voltage present at terminal 87, disconnect terminal 85. Crank engine and recheck for voltage at terminal 87. If terminal 87 has no voltage, thermo-time switch should be replaced. If voltage is present at 87, replace relay. **NOTE** — If injectors spray fuel while voltage at 87 is zero, injector should be replaced.

### COOLANT TEMPERATURE SENSOR

Disconnect battery and pull connector from sensor. Connect ohmmeter between the terminals and note the resistance reading. Compare reading obtained with following table, which is based upon temperature. Check each terminal to ground and make sure resistance is infinity. See Fig. 5.

Make Resistance Check Between the Two Terminals, Then Between Each Terminal and Ground. Check These Results Against Figures in Fig. 6

Ohmmeter

Two Sensor Terminals

Ground

**Fig. 5   Test Connections and Equipment for Evaluating Engine Coolant Temperature Sensor**

## LUCAS-JAGUAR ELECTRONIC INJECTION SYSTEM (Cont.)

**Fig. 6  Engine Coolant Temperature Sensor Resistance Chart**

### AIR TEMPERATURE SENSOR

Disconnect battery and pull electrical connector off sensor. Connect ohmmeter between the terminals and note reading. Compare reading with table to determine whether or not sensor is functioning properly. If reading is outside of range, replace sensor. See *Fig. 6 and 7.*

**Fig. 7  Air Temperature Sensor Resistance Chart**

### THROTTLE SWITCH

**NOTE** — *Before testing, ensure that throttle plates and throttle linkage are correctly adjusted.*

**Preparations** — Disconnect battery and pull connector off of throttle switch. See *Fig. 8.*

**Idle Position** — Connect ohmmeter between terminals 12/47 (ground) and terminal 17 of throttle switch. See *Fig. 9.* Meter

reading should be very low resistance or zero. If reading is not very low, adjust throttle switch.

**Fig. 8  Diagram of Throttle Position Switch**

**Temporary Enrichment (Acceleration)** — Connect ohmmeter between terminals 9 and 12/47 (ground). Watch ohmmeter and turn throttle by hand. Meter needle should swing smoothly between very low resistance and very high resistance (to point on open circuit). If meter does not swing smoothly, replace throttle switch.

**Fig. 9  Test Connections For Throttle Switch Testing**

## LUCAS-JAGUAR ELECTRONIC INJECTION SYSTEM (Cont.)

### AUXILIARY AIR VALVE

Remove auxiliary air valve and fully close adjustment screw. Immerse valve bulb in container of boiling water. With bulb immerased, watch valve action, through side port. Valve should move smoothly to closed position. Quickly blow through a hose attached to side port, no air should pass. Allow blub to cool. Valve should move smoothly to open position. If valve performance is not satisfactory, replace with new unit. If valve action is acceptable, reset adjustment screw and install valve. See Fig. 10.

*Fig. 10   Cutaway View of Auxiliary Air Valve*

### THERMO-TIME SWITCH

**NOTE** — *Engine should either be below 32°F (0°C) or in cold condition. If coolant is above 50°F (10°C), connect ohmmeter between terminal "W" of switch and ground. Reading should be either very high or infinity.*

Pull connector from thermo-time switch and use ohmmeter across terminals. Reading should be very low or zero ohms. Use stop watch and apply voltage to terminal "G" of switch. Note delay time according to coolant temperature (see table). If time delay is clearly outside of specifications given in table, replace unit. See Fig. 11.

*Fig. 11   Thermo-Time Switch with Details of Electrical Connections*

| Coolant Temperature °F | Delay (Seconds) |
| --- | --- |
| -4 | 8 |
| 14 | 5.7 |
| 32 | 3.5 |
| 50 | 1.2 |
| 59 | 0 |

### DISTRIBUTOR TRIGGER UNIT

Disconnect cable from pump relay terminal 85. Disconnect negative "VE" terminal from ignition coil. Seperate in-line connector to distributor trigger unit. Connect ohmmeter between terminals 21 and 12 on distributor side of in-line connector. Crank engine, ohmmeter should show even swing between low resistance (a current limiting resistor is fitted inside trigger unit) and very high resistance. Transfer ohmmeter to terminals 22 and 12, an identical result should be obtained. If meter display reading remains steady during cranking or if the swing is uneven or intermittent, the trigger unit should be replaced.

## REMOVAL & INSTALLATION

**NOTE** — *On all procedures where the fuel lines are to be disconnected, the fuel system should be relieved of its pressure. To do this, disconnect the cable (connection 85) from ECU to pump relay (see Fig. 1 for location of cable). Switch on ignition and crank engine. Engine may run for a few seconds until fuel pressure is reduced. Switch off ignition and reconnect cable to terminal 85 of pump relay.*

### FUEL PUMP

Fuel pump is located beneath the trunk compartment floor, to remove fuel pump proceed as follows:

1) Disconnect battery and remove spare tire. Clamp fuel lines on both sides of pump, then disconnect hoses from pump.

2) Disconnect electrical plug from pump. Remove screws attaching pump to mounting bracket then remove clamp from pump body. To install fuel pump, reverse removal procedure.

### ELECTRONIC CONTROL UNIT (ECU)

The ECU is located in the trunk compartment up against the rear seat panel. The ECU has an idle CO adjustment knob on it, this knob should NOT be moved. If it is, the CO level will have to be readjusted.

1) Disconnect battery. At the front end of trunk compartment (toward front of vehicle), remove the ECU cover. Disconnect ECU retainer band or clamp.

2) Remove the cable clamp screws and clip. Remove the end cover. Locate handle on cable harness plug and withdraw plug. To install, reverse removal procedure. Also, check the idle CO level.

## LUCAS-JAGUAR ELECTRONIC INJECTION SYSTEM (Cont.)

### FUEL PRESSURE REGULATOR

There are two fuel pressure regulators, one located between the third and forth intake manifold runners on each side of engine.

1) Depressurize system and disconnect battery. Remove screws securing regulator bracket. Carefully lift regulator and bracket up. Take note of how regulator is installed in bracket (which line goes to pump and which goes to fuel rails).

2) Clamp fuel lines, then disconnect fuel lines from regulator. Then disconnect regulator from bracket. To install, reverse removal procedure. Be sure to install regulator in bracket the same way it was removed, inlet to fuel pump and outlet to fuel rails.

### MANIFOLD PRESSURE CONTROL VALVE (MPC)

Manifold pressure control valve is located on the top left side of the radiator. To remove valve, proceed as follows: Disconnect battery and unplug electrical connector from valve. Disconnect hose from valve and then remove screws securing valve to bracket. To install, reverse removal procedure.

### INJECTORS

1) Depressurize system and disconnect battery. Clamp fuel line between filter and fuel rails. Disconnect electrical plug from injector(s) to be removed.

2) Remove screws securing fuel rail to intake manifold, then release clips attaching supply fuel rail to return fuel rail. Remove the 12 screws attaching injectors to intake manifold.

3) Carefully lift fuel rail, with injectors, clear of intake manifold. Plug injector holes and wipe up any spilled fuel. Now disconnect injector(s) from fuel rail as needed. As injector(s) are removed, note the location of the electrical socket. This will aid in installation.

4) To install, reverse removal procedure and note the following. Install new "O" rings on all injectors. Make sure the electrical plug is located in the right direction (as removed).

### COLD START VALVE

Depressurize system and disconnect battery. Clamp fuel line and remove electrical connector. Remove screws securing cold start valve and remove valve. **NOTE** — *There are two cold start valves on the Jaguar V12 engine.* To install, reverse removal procedure.

### COOLANT TEMPERATURE SENSOR

1) Disconnect battery and remove pressure from coolant system by loosening radiator cap. Disconnect electrical connector from sensor. **NOTE** — *Since the sensor is mounted in the block below the coolant level, it will be necessary to either drain part of the coolant or have another sensor (or other suitable plug) ready to install the moment the old sensor is removed.* Remove coolant temperature sensor.

2) When installing new sensor be sure to coat threads with a suitable sealing compound.

### AIR TEMPERATURE SENSOR

Air temperature sensor is located in the left side air cleaner. Disconnect electrical connector and remove sensor. To install, reverse removal procedure.

### THROTTLE SWITCH

1) Throttle switch is located beneath throttle pulley. Disconnect battery and remove throttle cross rods from throttle pulley. Disconnect electrical connector from switch.

2) Remove the four nuts securing throttle pulley plate to throttle pedestal and lift plate clear. Now remove the two screws and washers securing throttle switch and remove switch from spindle.

3) To install, place switch on spindle so that connector socket faces to rear. To complete installation, reverse removal procedure. Be sure to adjust switch after installation.

### AUXILIARY AIR VALVE

Auxiliary air valve is located on the left cylinder head rear coolant pipe. To remove valve, proceed as follows:

1) Disconnect battery and relieve coolant pressure. Disconnect air hoses connected to air valve. Disconnect air valve from coolant pipe.

2) Clean gasket material from coolant pipe. Scribe a mark on adjusting screw and on air valve. Now count the number of turns it takes to fully seat adjusting screw.

3) On the new auxiliary air valve, seat adjusting screw then turn out the number of turns counted in step 2). To complete installation, reverse removal procedure.

### THERMO-TIME SWITCH

**NOTE** — *Replacement of the thermo-time switch must be done on a cold engine only.*

1) Switch is located in the thermostat housing. Disconnect the battery and remove the electrical connector. Relieve pressure in coolant system.

2) Coat threads of new thermo-time switch with suitable sealer and make sure a new sealing washer is installed on new switch. Now remove old thermo-time switch and immediatly replace it with the new one.

### TRIGGERING CONTACTS

1) Disconnect battery and separate manifold pressure sensor hose at "tee". Move hoses out of way. Mark spark plug wires and disconnect them either from distributor cap or spark plugs. Remove distributor cap and rotor cap.

2) Remove four screws securing triggering contact plate to distributor housing. Now remove triggering plate, disengaging the rubber grommet from distributor housing at same time. Disconnect triggering contact cable from pump relay.

3) To install triggering contacts, reverse removal procedure.

## LUCAS-JAGUAR ELECTRONIC INJECTION SYSTEM (Cont.)

### ADJUSTMENTS

#### HOT (SLOW) IDLE RPM

*See appropriate article in TUNE-UP Service Procedures.*

#### IDLE MIXTURE

*See appropriate article in TUNE-UP Service Procedures.*

#### FUEL PRESSURE REGULATOR

**NOTE** — *Fuel pressure regulator should only be adjusted after complete system has been throughly checked.*

1) Remove bolts securing both pressure regulators to intake manifold. Crimp off fuel line between "B" bank pressure regulator inlet and fuel rail. Loosen hose clamp securing left-hand cold start injector supply line to fuel rail and remove line from rail. Connect pressure gauge to fuel rail and tighten hose clamp.

2) Start engine and loosen lock nuts on both pressure regulators. Set adjusting bolt on bank "A" regulator, until pressure gauge reads 29.6 psi (2.1 kg/cm²). Release crimp on "B" bank regulator and transfer to "A" bank regulator. Set adjusting bolt on "B" bank regulator to read 29.6 psi (2.1 kg/cm²) on pressure gauge.

3) Release crimp on "A" bank inlet line to pressure regulator, tighten lock nuts on both regulators and install bolts securing both pressure regulators to intake manifold. Switch off ignition, depressurize fuel system and remove pressure gauge. Switch on ignition and check for leaks.

#### THROTTLE SWITCH

1) Disconnect battery, remove cross rods from throttle pulley and pull connector off of throttle switch. Remove four nuts and washer securing throttle pulley plate to throttle pedestal and lift plate clear. Loosen two screws securing throttle switch. Insert .030" feeler gauge between pulley and closed throttle stop.

2) Connect ohmmeter between terminals 12 and 17 of throttle switch. Turn throttle switch slowly until meter just flips over to very low resistance (short circuit) and tighten two screws securing throttle switch. Remove feeler gauge and meter should read very high resistance when pulley is against closed stop. Reassemble and adjust throttle linkage, if necessary.

#### THROTTLE LINKAGE

**Testing** — 1) In order to determine whether or not throttle linkage needs adjusting, perform the following tests: Make sure throttle return springs are correctly attached and that throttle pulley moves freely, coming to rest against the closed stop position. Check that throttle butterfly valve (closed) stop position screw has not been moved.

**Fig. 12   Top View of Jaguar Fuel Injection System**

## LUCAS-JAGUAR ELECTRONIC INJECTION SYSTEM (Cont.)

**Fig. 13   Throttle Linkage with Detail of Linkage Connections**

Cross-Rods
Throttle Pulley
Relay Arm
Clamp Bolt
Throttle Shaft

**NOTE** — If throttle butterfly stop screw has been tampered with, do not continue this test and adjustment procedure until the throttle butterfly valves have been properly adjusted.

**2)** Check that throttle pulley can be rotated to full open position and that throttle butterfly valve arm is touching the throttle housing. If these conditions are not as specified, then it will be necessary to adjust the throttle linkage. See Fig. 13.

**Adjusting** — **1)** Release throttle cross-rods from throttle pulley. Loosen clamps securing levers to rear of throttle shafts. With butterfly valves closed against their stops, relay arm against its stop and play in coupling taken up in opening direction, tighten clamp-to-lever on rear of throttle shaft. Repeat this operation for the other side of engine.

**2)** Now try to refit cross-rods to ball connectors on pulley; rods must locate without moving pulley or linkage. If rods will not locate without moving pulley or linkage, loosen locknut on cross-rods and adjust length of rod until attachment can be accomplished without moving any part of linkage. Tighten locknuts and make sure ball joints remain free.

**3)** Loosen locknut on throttle pulley and back out stop screw to full extent of travel. Hold throttle relay arm pulley fully open and check that butterfly stop arms are against throttle housing. Adjust stop to just touch throttle pulley and tighten locknut. Check operation of throttle switch and kickdown switch.

### THROTTLE BUTTERFLY VALVE ADJUSTMENT

**CAUTION** — Any adjustment must be carried out on both butterfly valves. It is not recommended to adjust one valve only. See Fig. 14.

Remove both air cleaners, loosen locknut on throttle butterfly stop screw and turn in screw until butterfly valve is completely closed. Insert .004″ feeler gauge between top of valve and housing, to hold valve open. Set stop screw to just touch stop arm and tighten locknut with feeler gauge still in position. Press stop arm against stop screw and withdraw feeler gauge. Repeat same operation on other side of engine. Seal threads of adjusting screws with blob of paint and refit air cleaners.
**NOTE** — After adjusting throttle butterfly linkage, check throttle linkage, operation of throttle switch and kickdown switch operation.

Adjusting Screw
Locknut
Feeler Gauge (.004″)

**Fig. 14   Measuring Throttle Butterfly Valve (Using a Feeler Gauge)**

## BOSCH DIESEL INJECTION — MERCEDES-BENZ

**Mercedes-Benz**
**240D**
**300D**

### DESCRIPTION

Fuel injection system consists of the following components. See *Fig. 1:*

- Pre-filter
- Main Fuel Filter
- Fuel Injection Pump with Fuel Pump
- Mechanical Centrifugal Governor
- Automatic Altitude Compensating Device
- Vacuum Control Unit
- Injection Nozzles
- Glow Plugs
- Key-starting System

**Fig. 1 Components of Bosch Diesel Fuel Injection System for Mercedes-Benz**

Fuel is pumped from fuel tank, through a pre-filter and main fuel filter into suction chamber of injection pump. Pump's camshaft operates injection pump plungers, which force fuel through delivery valves, reverse-flow dampening valves, and pressure lines to fuel injection nozzles.

When pressure stroke is completed, spring-loaded valves close pressure lines. Plungers return to original position.

### TESTING

Manufacturer recommends that ALL tests be conducted on an injection pump test stand, using tests sheets furnished by manufacturer.

### SYSTEM COMPONENTS

#### FUEL INJECTION PUMP

Injection pumps used on 240D and 300D Diesel engines are similar. See *Fig. 2.* Major difference is the number of pumping elements, five on 300D and four on 240D — one for each cylinder.

**Fig. 2 Fuel Injection Pump Components**

Built-in mechanical centrifugal governor has eliminated need for previously-used throttle valve in intake manifold. Engine shut-off is achieved by vacuum control unit. Pumps are lubricated by engine lubrication system. Note oil inlet and outlets. See *Fig. 2.*

An automatic altitude compensating device has been added to governor housing to meet exhaust emission standards at varying altitudes.

**Fig. 3 Control Lever and Adjusting Screws for Mercedes-Benz 240D**

## BOSCH DIESEL INJECTION – MERCEDES-BENZ (Cont.)

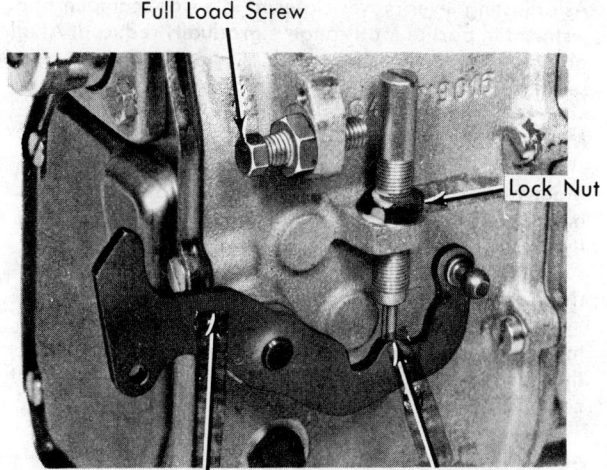

Full Load Screw

Lock Nut

Control Lever

Idle Adjusting Screw

**Fig. 4   Control Lever and Adjusting Screws for Mercedes-Benz 300D**

Fuel pump, attached to fuel injection pump, is driven by injection pump camshaft and features a hand primer pump.

Injection pumps both feature new control levers, full load stop screws and idle adjusting screws. See Figs. 3 and 4. On 240D engine, control pressure rod for automatic transmission is connected to control lever. See arrow in Fig. 3.

### GOVERNOR

Governor is an idle-maximum RPM governor. See Fig. 5 Springs are designed and adjusted so no regulating takes place in intermediate range except for compensation. Between idle and maximum RPM cutout, main rack is operated only by accelerator pedal. Pedal is connected through linkage with fulcrum lever of governor.

When engine RPM increases, flyweights move outward as soon as centrifugal force exceeds spring pressure. Movement of flyweights is transmitted through the angle lever, adjusting screws and control lever to main rack.

When reaching maximum RPM, main rack is moved toward the cutout position, reducing the amount of fuel and limiting engine RPM. As engine RPM decreases, the function is reversed.

Through governor action, engine RPM is held constant at idle speed, regardless of engine operating conditions — cold engine, air conditioner operation, power steering, or automatic transmission. At 5000-5100 RPM, governor limits RPM by pulling main rack back, until balance exists between engine RPM and fuel delivery.

### AUTOMATIC ALTITUDE COMPENSATING DEVICE

Governor is equipped with an automatic altitude compensating device to control exhaust emissions at varying altitudes. See Figs. 6 and 7.

Starting Position
Full Load Position
Idle Position
Maximum RPM Cutout Spring
Full Load Stop Lever
Main Rack Direction of Travel
Main Rack
Fulcrum Lever
Full Load
Angle Lever
Control Lever
Idle Speed Spring
Idle
Swing Lever
Full Load Stop Cam
Compensating Spring
Flyweights
Linkage
Sliding Block

**Fig. 5   Typical Governor Linkage for Mercedes-Benz (Start Position Illustrated)**

## BOSCH DIESEL INJECTION — MERCEDES-BENZ (Cont.)

**Fig. 6** *Automatic Altitude Compensating Device and Vacuum Control Unit*

With increasing altitude, atmospheric pressure is decreased. This causes two aneroid (non-fluid) compensators to expand. At specified atmospheric pressure, internal force of compensators becomes greater than pretension of aneroid compression spring. Push rod moves downward, moving linkage. This causes main rack to move in direction "D", causing less fuel to be injected. See *Fig. 7.*

As adjusting lever moves closer to idle stop, compensating adjustment in partial load range is gradually reduced. At idle it is almost completely eliminated. At low altitudes, governor settings are not affected by compensators.

### MAIN FUEL FILTER

Main fuel filter is composed of a throwaway-type filter element, which is part of lower filter housing. See *REMOVAL AND INSTALLATION.*

### INJECTION NOZZLES

Injection nozzles are used to spray fuel into the cylinder under the proper pressure and spray pattern for optimum combustion. See *Fig. 8.*

**Fig. 8** *Fuel Injection Nozzle, Holder and Glow Plug*

**Fig. 7** *Diagram of Automatic Altitude Compensating Device and Linkage*

### KEY-STARTING SYSTEM

#### Starting the Engine

To start engine, turn key to position "2" of starter switch. When indicator light in bottom of speedometer goes out, preglow time is optimum for ignition. See *Fig. 9.*

**NOTE** — *If engine does not start immediately, preglow system remains energized for approximately 2 minutes and then shuts down to prevent battery drain. Use care when working in engine compartment during this time, as resistor wires are very hot.*

## BOSCH DIESEL INJECTION — MERCEDES-BENZ (Cont.)

*Fig. 9  Wiring Diagram of Preglow System*

With key in position "2", current flows over terminal 15 of starter switch to control relay and coil of preglow relay. Preglow relay closes, permitting current to flow to glow plugs over terminal 30.

System is equipped with a temperature sensor, which turns off dash-mounted indicator light when most favorable preglow temperature is sensed. System is protected by a 50 ampere fuse box in engine compartment.

If temperature is below 59°F (15°C) and engine is cold, depress accelerator. This releases main rack in injection pump into its starting position. Turn starter switch key clockwise to "start" position. After engine starts, release accelerator pedal, allowing main rack to return to idle position. At higher temperatures and with engine warm, accelerator pressure is not required.

With starter switch in "start" position, current is supplied to solenoid switch of starter and to preglow time relay over terminal 50. Two circuits are then energized. The coil of control

relay is energized and relay is held closed by current supplied over terminal 15. During cranking, glow plugs remain energized through direct connection from terminal 50 to coil of preglow relay. Preglow relay contact remains closed.

### Driving the Vehicle

When engine begins running, release key which will return to position "2". Current is then interrupted to terminal 50 and to coil of preglow relay. Coil of control relay remains energized, however, over terminal 15. Current to glow plugs is turned off.

### Shutting Off Engine

To shut off engine, turn key to position "1" or "0". A cam-operated valve, attached to starter switch opens, connecting the vacuum line from the vacuum pump to the injection pump. *See Fig. 10.*

## BOSCH DIESEL INJECTION — MERCEDES-BENZ (Cont.)

*Fig. 10   Vacuum Diagram Showing Vacuum Pump,
Valve, and Vacuum Control Unit on Injection Pump*

Diaphragm of pump-mounted vacuum control unit reacts, pulling main rack to "stop" position.. If engine fails to stop, push "stop" lever on cylinder head. This manually moves main rack to "stop" position. *See REMOVAL AND INSTALLATION, VACUUM CONTROL UNIT and Fig. 11.*

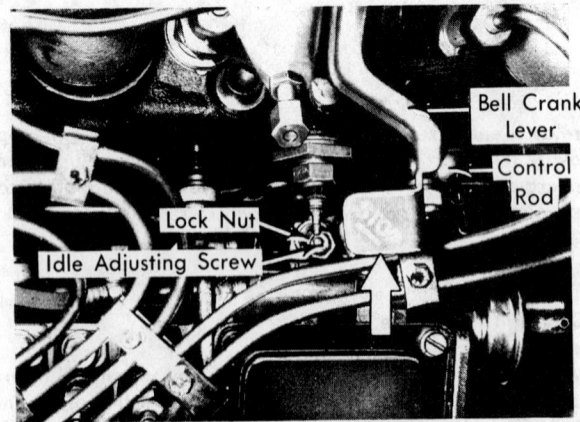

*Fig. 11   Manual "Stop" Lever Controlling
Injection Pump Main Rack*

### Starting Lock Position

To lock engine, so vehicle cannot be started by towing or coasting downhill, remove key or turn key to position "1" or "0". Vacuum control unit will then pull main rack to "stop" position.

### REVERSE FLOW DAMPENING VALVE

The disc-type reverse flow dampening valve is crimped into place above each delivery valve compression spring. Valves permit free fuel flow toward injection nozzles, opening in direction of nozzles.

Closing needle valve in nozzle causes a pressure wave to return toward injection pump. Since delivery valve is already closed, pressure wave would normally return to injection nozzle and open it briefly again. This would cause higher HC content of exhaust gases.

Pressure wave is eliminated, however, by orifice in dampening valve disc, preventing secondary injection.

## SERVICING COMPONENTS

### INJECTION NOZZLES

If exhaust gives off intermittent clouds of black smoke, this usually means one or more nozzles are operating unevenly. If exhaust offers a rumbling noise, it usually indicates one cylinder is partly or completely out of action. *See Fig. 8.* To check injection nozzles:

1) At idle, loosen each injection pipe cap nut (in turn) one-half turn. If sound of engine does not change, part of problem is a defective nozzle or inadequate sealing between pipe union and nozzle holder.

## BOSCH DIESEL INJECTION – MERCEDES-BENZ (Cont.)

**2)** Raise engine RPM above idle speed and repeat test procedure. If engine still does not run erratically with nut loosened, repair or replace that particular nozzle. If engine runs erratically when nut is loosened, nozzle is operating properly. Tighten one-half turn and check next nozzle.

### Nozzle Opening Pressures

Nozzle opening pressure should be 1635-1750 psi (115-123 kg/cm²) for new nozzles, and a minimum of 1422 psi (100 kg/cm²) for used nozzles. Difference in opening pressures in one engine should never exceed 71 psi (5 kg/cm²).

### Replacement Nozzles

Beginning with year model 1978, center hole pintle nozzle DNOSD 240 is installed on 240D and 300D engines. This nozzle is also used in earlier engines to correct excessive diesel knocking. Replace in complete sets only. Identification number DNOSD 240 is stamped on nozzle body.

When testing injection nozzles, the most important factors in order of importance are:

- Correct nozzle opening pressure setting.
- Tightness of valve seat to minimum 280 psi (19.7 kg/cm²) below opening pressure of nozzle.
- Correct spray pattern.

Always install new seal between nozzle and prechamber. Tighten nozzles to specified torque. Use accurate torque wrench so seals and nozzles are not damaged. Coked-up seals speed clogging of nozzle throttling gaps, causing distorted spray pattern and diesel knock.

### FUEL PUMP

Fuel pump must deliver fuel under constant pressure and without bubbles. Insufficient pressure could cause engine problems. Pressure is kept constant by a by-pass valve which does not open until specified pressure is reached.

### Checking Delivery Pressures

**1)** Install a suitable tester (000 589 49 21 00) between main fuel filter and fuel injection pump. See *Fig. 12.* Check for proper delivery pressure, delivery end (final) pressure, and opening pressure of by-pass valve.

**2)** Using tester's glass tube, check for air bubbles in fuel at same time pressure is read.

**3)** Bleed tester and fuel system. See *REMOVAL AND INSTALLATION, Main Fuel Filter.* Check pressure at tester with engine running at idle speed. Pressure should be 8.5-11.4 psi (0.6-0.8 kg/cm²).

**4)** Raise engine speed up to 3000 RPM. Pressure should read 11.4 psi (0.8 kg/cm²). If pressure is much higher or lower, check that by-pass valve is opening properly. If excessively high, check for crushed or restricted fuel lines.

**NOTE** – *When making pressure tests, observe glass tube for air bubbles. If bubbles appear, check system thoroughly for leaks. Check hose porosity, hairline cracks in fuel lines or hoses, deteriorated or scuffed hoses, or slack hose clips.*

**5)** Next, check delivery end (final) pressure. Using fingers, squeeze hose between tester and injection pump. If pump is working properly, pressure should be at least 15.6 psi (1.1 kg/cm²) at idle and at least 18.5 psi (1.3 kg/cm²) at 3000 RPM.

**6)** If pressure is lower than specified, either the valve requires replacing, or pump requires repair or replacement.

**7)** If pressure is higher than specified, and opening pressure of by-pass valve is greater than 11.4 psi (0.8 kg/cm²), remove, clean and check by-pass valve for leaks. Replace valve if necessary.

### LEAKING FUEL LINE FITTINGS

If external fuel leakage occurs between pipe connection fitting (union) and adjusting plate of injection pump, install new "grooved" fittings. See *Fig. 13.*

**Fig. 12   Pressure Tester (000 589 49 21 00) Hook-Up (Earlier Model Injection Pump Shown)**

**Fig. 13   Old Style and New "Grooved" Style Connection Fittings (Unions)**

## BOSCH DIESEL INJECTION — MERCEDES-BENZ (Cont.)

1) If pump is equipped with non-grooved fittings, replace ALL fittings with new "grooved" fittings. If equipped with "grooved" fittings, replace only leaking fittings.

**NOTE** — *Do not loosen adjusting plate, as this would require recalibration of injection pump on a test stand.*

2) Whenever new fittings are installed or fittings are removed for any purpose, install new copper gaskets under delivery valve carriers. Grooved end of valve carrier should be installed downward. Reinstall other valve components previously removed.

3) Oil fitting threads and tighten to 29-36 ft. lbs. (4-5 mkg), using one continuous motion.

4) Install injection lines and operate hand primer until by-pass valve opens (audible sound). Run engine and check for further leaks.

### DIESEL KNOCK

Diesel knock can be traced to mechanical causes, diesel fuel properties, or a combination of both. Knock is a pinging noise caused by excessive combustion pressure.

To eliminate or reduce knock, use fuel best suited for your area and check and correct the following:

- Beginning of fuel delivery to assure optimum compression temperature and air charge.
- Valve lash.
- Correct nozzle spray pattern and opening pressure.
- Reverse flow dampening valve for proper operation.
- Insufficient compression pressure (compression check and cylinder leak test).

### CHECKING GLOW PLUGS

Glow plugs provide ignition during starting. Use dash-mounted indicator light to locate faulty glow plugs.

1) Hold starting switch key in preglow position "2". Using screwdriver, have assistant short plugs to ground, one at a time. Each plug should spark if working properly. When grounded in this manner indicator light should be "lit."

2) If light stays on, when ground is disconnected, a short to ground exists in system. Check for leads touching cylinder head and then for carbon-fouled plug electrodes.

3) If leads appear correct, turn key to preglow position "2". Disconnect one glow plug power lead at a time, starting from ground end. Indicator light will go out when faulty plug is disconnected.

4) Check grounding of glow plug bus bar. Be sure control rods do not rest against bus bar or glow plugs.

5) Remove glow plugs with special tool (617 589 00 03 00). Ream bores with suitable reamer (636 589 03 53 00). Prevent dust from entering prechamber by greasing reamer prior to use.

6) Visually check glow plugs for damage from burning, cracks, or foreign metallic particles. If glow plug is burned out, check next plug in circuit also, since a short between threaded glow plug body and outer electrode or between outer electrode and cylinder head may result from metallic particles.

7) Remove all dirt or deposits from threaded bore.

### DEFECTIVE VACUUM CONTROL UNIT

On 5-cylinder 300D engine, engine oil can enter vacuum system through a defective diaphragm in the vacuum control unit. Sometimes vacuum pump has been mistakenly blamed. If complaints are received that engine does not shut off or shuts off with difficulty, check vacuum control unit first:

1) Remove brown and blue line from vacuum control unit. Check for traces of oil. If present, replace unit and oil-filled vacuum lines. Also repair vacuum pump and replace brake booster if oil is found at connecting fitting for vacuum line.

2) If no traces of oil are found at control unit or in vacuum lines, start engine and run at idle. Pull off brown vacuum line from "T" fitting between vacuum pump and brake booster. See *Fig. 10.* Check for vacuum. If none present, remove and check "T" fitting and clean with compressed air.

3) If vacuum is present, connect vacuum control unit directly to "T" fitting (by-pass the valve). Pump is now free to act directly upon diaphragm of control unit. If engine does not shut off immediately, replace control unit.

**NOTE** — *When installing new unit, be sure control linkage in pump governor is properly engaged and is not holding main rack in full-load position.*

4) If engine shuts off immediately, vacuum control unit is not to blame. Problem could then be jammed vacuum valve in steering lock.

5) Be sure all vacuum lines are connected as shown in *Fig. 10.* Start engine, check vacuum control unit, valve in steering lock and injection pump for leaks.

### INJECTION TIMER DRIVE

240D and 300D engines have an injection timer drive installed in the end of intermediate gear shaft. Drive is now pressure-lubricated (previously splash-lubricated).

Use care in servicing engines, as bores in bearing bushing have been eliminated in new design. Never use a new injection timer and bearing bushing with earlier version intermediate gear shafts, since no oil would reach bearing bushing.

However, the new intermediate gear shaft may be used along with previous injection timer and bearing bushing. **Never install only a bearing bushing separately.**

## REMOVAL AND INSTALLATION

### FUEL INJECTION PUMP

**Removal — 1)** Remove battery and battery frame. Clean pump and fuel lines to prevent entrance of dirt into system. Disconnect all injection, vacuum, fuel and oil lines at injection pump. Plug injection lines and fuel hose unions at pump.

**2)** Detach connecting rods and all cables from pump.

**3)** Remove mounting nuts at rear support and front flange, using a 13 mm (45° rebent) box wrench. Lift injection pump rearward from crankcase.

**NOTE** — *If drive collar is to be replaced, observe markings on flange, collar, and pump shaft for reassembly reference.*

**Installation — 1)** Remove plug and fill injection pump with ½ pint of engine oil. Turn crankshaft in direction of rotation until 45° BTDC mark aligns with pointer. Piston of No. 1 cylinder must be in compression stroke.

**2)** Slide coupling sleeve onto drive collar of injection pump. Now, slide coupling forward onto drive shaft in crankcase.

**3)** Set injection pump to "start delivery" position by turning pump shaft until drive collar tooth gap aligns with pump shaft and pump flange marks. See *Fig. 14.*

**Fig. 14   Aligning Marks on Injection Pump Shaft Drive Collar and Flange**

**4)** When applying light counterclockwise pressure (opposite direction of rotation) to drive collar, cam pressure action causes drive collar to jump back two teeth to cam base circle. Second tooth must then coincide with marking on injection pump housing.

**NOTE** — *Before installing pump, be sure piston of No. 1 cylinder is in compression stroke and crankshaft is 45° BTDC.*

**5)** Apply grease to either side of new paper gaskets and place gaskets on crankcase. Install injection pump in coupling sleeve. Be sure stud bolts are centrally positioned within slotted holes. This permits later alignment in either direction.

**NOTE** — *After aligning injection pump, there must be a clearance of 3.15" (80 mm) between crankcase and center of injection line fitting. This is to permit glow plug removal.*

**6)** Place washers in position and slightly tighten injection pump nuts.

**NOTE** — *Use special spacer washer (116 990 14 40) and M8 x 16 hex head screw to fasten rear support bracket.*

### Checking for Start of Delivery

**1)** Turn crankshaft further in direction of rotation, until 24° BTDC mark aligns with pointer. Piston of No. 1 cylinder must again be in compression stroke position.

**2)** Screw out pipe connection fitting (union) of first pumping element and remove valve parts. Reinstall fitting and attach overflow pipe.

**NOTE** — *During test adjust control lever on injection pump to full throttle (full-load) position.*

**Fig. 15   Installing Auxiliary Fuel Container on Injection Pump (Typical)**

## BOSCH DIESEL INJECTION — MERCEDES-BENZ (Cont.)

Solid Fuel     Begins to Drip     Slow Drip

*Fig. 16   Checking Fuel Dripping From Overflow Pipe*

**3)** Connect auxiliary fuel container (000 589 05 23 00) to injection pump. *See Fig. 15.* Turn engine over slowly in normal direction of rotation until fuel stream from overflow pipe stops dripping. *See Fig. 16.*

**NOTE** — *Another drop may follow 10-15 seconds later, but this is normal.*

**4)** Start of delivery should occur when pipe stops dripping Crankshaft pointer should then be on 24° BTDC mark. Turn crankshaft two more full turns. Fuel should stop dripping again at end of second full turn. If so, tighten injection pump in this position.

**5)** If crankshaft position does not prove true, loosen injection pump mounting nuts and turn pump TOWARD engine to advance start of delivery and AWAY FROM engine to retard start of delivery. When adjustment is correct, tighten mounting nuts of pump and recheck position.

**6)** Remove overflow pipe and connection fitting (union). Reinstall valve parts using new gasket. Tighten fitting to 29-36 ft. lbs. (4-5 mkg) in one continuous motion. Remove auxiliary fuel container.

**7)** Connect all fuel, vacuum and lubricating oil lines. Install all control rods, cables, and other parts previously removed. Adjust as necessary.

**8)** Bleed fuel system and install battery and battery frame. Bring engine to operating temperature. Check all connections for leaks. Check idle speed and adjust as necessary. *See ADJUSTMENTS.*

Hollow (Bleed) Bolt
Mounting Bolt

*Fig. 17   Removing, Installing and Bleeding Fuel Filter*

### FUEL FILTER

Every 37,500 miles, the main fuel filter and lower housing should be replaced. Loosen mounting bolt. *See Fig. 17.* Pull downward on one-piece element and lower housing.

Install new lower housing and element. Tighten mounting bolt. After installation, bleed fuel filter and fuel injection pump.

### Bleeding Fuel Filter

Loosen hollow bolt. *See Fig. 17.* Pump hand primer pump until fuel emerges free of bubbles. Retighten hollow bolt.

### Bleeding Injection Pump

Pump hand primer until by-pass valve on injection pump opens. You will hear a buzzing sound when this occurs. Run engine and check for leaks.

### VACUUM CONTROL UNIT

**Removal — 1)** Unscrew lower right-hand mounting screw from vacuum control unit. *See Fig. 18.*

*Fig. 18   Removing and Installing Vacuum Control Unit*

**2)** Depress "stop" lever on cylinder head cover. Measure position of main rack by inserting punch into screw bore until it touches main rack. Mark this position on punch.

**3)** Unscrew remaining three mounting screws and remove control unit.

**Installation — 1)** Install new gasket and steel ring. Make sure tang on vacuum control unit engages in main rack. Install last three mounting screws removed.

**2)** Insert punch in lower right-hand screw bore. Check main rack position with mark on punch. When punch touches main rack, press lightly on punch and move control lever on injection pump from "stop" position to "full load" stop. Punch must follow the main rack smoothly. If correct, install remaining screw.

## BOSCH DIESEL INJECTION – MERCEDES-BENZ (Cont.)

### AUTOMATIC ALTITUDE COMPENSATING DEVICE

**NOTE** – *Do not attempt to remove upper cover of governor housing. Governor linkage is assembled to altitude compensating device.*

**Removal** – Hold altitude compensating device by small nut, while loosening larger nut. *See Fig. 19.* Unscrew altitude compensating device and remove shims.

**Installation** – Using previously removed shims, screw compensating device into place. Be sure vent tube is positioned at lowest point to drain off any possible condensation. Hold small nut and tighten large nut.

*Fig. 20   Measuring Distance Between Collar and Spring*

.040" (1.0 mm) Clearance

Vent — Small Nut — Large Nut

*Fig. 19   Removing and Installing Automatic Altitude Compensating Device*

## ADJUSTMENTS

### IDLE SPEED AND IDLE SPEED REGULATOR

**1)** Check throttle linkage for free movement and wear. Run engine until oil temperature reaches 140-176° F (60-80° C). Turn idle speed regulator knob on dashboard as far as it will go. Distance between collar and spring should be .040" (1.0 mm). *See Fig. 20.* Adjust as necessary, making sure spring is properly adjusted.

**2)** Depress "stop" lever. *See Fig. 11.* Bowden cable of cruise control should rest tension-free against bell crank. If necessary, adjust cable with adjusting nut. Release "stop" lever. Cable should have play.

**3)** Disconnect control rod at bell crank lever. Check idle speed with tachometer. Loosen lock nut. *See Figs. 3 and 4.* Using adjusting screw, adjust idle speed to 650-750 RPM. Reconnect control rod free of tension. Adjust throttle linkage, if necessary.

**4)** Place automatic transmission selector lever in a driving position. Turn on air conditioner and turn power steering to full lock position. Engine must run smoothly. If necessary, readjust idle speed.

**5)** Depress accelerator pedal slightly. Simultaneously, turn idle speed regulator knob counterclockwise to "stop." Release accelerator pedal. Engine speed should be 1000-1100 RPM. If necessary, readjust idle speed by turning adjusting screw.

**6)** Let engine run for a short period. If engine speed increases by itself, reduce engine speed with adjusting screw.

**CAUTION** – *If engine speed is adjusted higher, it will be above controlled idle speed range of governor. Engine speed could automatically increase up to maximum RPM (without load).*

### TIGHTENING SPECIFICATION

| Application | Ft. Lbs. (mkg) |
|---|---|
| Rocker Arm Cover | 3.6 (0.5) |
| Glow Plugs | 36.0 (5.0) |
| Precombustion Chamber | 118.5 (16.5) |
| Nozzle-to-Holder | 54.0 (7.5) |
| Nozzle Holder-to-Head | 54.0 (7.5) |
| Nozzle Holder Connector | 54.0 (7.5) |
| Injection Pump Shaft Nut | 50.6 (7.0) |
| Connecting Fitting (Union) | 29.0-36.0 (4.0-5.0) |
| Injection Pipe Cap Nuts | 18.0 (2.5) |

### SYSTEM SPECIFICATIONS

| | |
|---|---|
| Idle Speed | 650-750 RPM |
| Fuel Pump Delivery Pressure | |
|   Idle Speed | 8.5-11.4 psi (0.6-0.8 kg/cm²) |
|   3000 RPM | 11.4 psi (0.8 kg/cm²) |
| Fuel Pump Final Delivery Pressure | |
|   Idle Speed | 15.6 psi (1.1 kg/cm²) |
|   3000 RPM | 18.5 psi (1.3 kg/cm²) |
| Start of Delivery | 24° BTDC (In Compression Stroke) |
| Nozzle Opening Pressure | 1635-1750 psi (115-123 kg/cm²) |

# 1978 Bosch Diesel Fuel Injection

## BOSCH DIESEL INJECTION — VOLKSWAGEN

**Volkswagen Rabbit**

### DESCRIPTION

Fuel injection system (*Figs. 1 and 2*) consists of the following components:

- Fuel tank.
- Fuel filter.
- Distributor-type injection pump.
- Glow plugs.
- Throttle pintle injection nozzles.
- Car application speed governor.

A vane-type fuel pump, built into the injection pump, supplies fuel from tank to fuel filter to injection pump. Injection pump supplies fuel to nozzles under high pressure, according to 1-3-4-2 firing sequence. Excess fuel is returned to fuel tank by return lines.

**Fig. 2  Fuel System Components for Volkswagen Diesel**

*Fig. 1  Fuel Supply System for Volkswagen Diesel*

## BOSCH DIESEL INJECTION — VOLKSWAGEN (Cont.)

### SYSTEM COMPONENTS

#### FUEL INJECTION PUMP

Bosch distributor-type injection pump (*Fig. 1*) consists of a low-pressure, vane-type fuel pump, a high-pressure, plunger-type injection pump, a car application speed governor and an injection timer. Pump features an electric on-off switch.

High pressure is generated by a rotating plunger, which also distributes fuel to the four cylinders.

Vane-type fuel pump, roller ring, distributor plunger and mechanical, centrifugal governor are all powered by injection pump shaft.

An injection timer on bottom of pump varies injection timing, as required by engine speed, increasing fuel pressure inside pump casing as engine speed increases.

This activates spring-loaded plunger in injection timer. Plunger rotates roller ring by means of driving pin. This has the effect of displacing its point of contact with eccentric disc, opposite pump's direction of rotation, and of advancing injection timing by 2.5°.

#### INJECTION NOZZLES

Bosch DNOSD 193 injection nozzles, mounted in KDA SD 27/4 sockets, inject fuel at 1700-1850 psi (123-130 kg/cm²). See *Fig. 3*.

A pressurized mist of fuel is injected into a round swirl chamber. Fuel swirls around chamber, mixing with hot air, compressed at a 23:1 ratio.

Combustion begins in rich swirl chamber, continues on through small passageway, and into leaner, main chamber. As peak cylinder pressures build in swirl chamber, rather than main chamber, loads on connecting rods and crankshaft are reduced.

#### GLOW PLUGS

Fast, easy starting is assured by resistor-type glow plugs, installed in swirl chambers. *See Figs. 3 and 4.* Glow plugs have stubby-finger design rather than wire-type design used on many Diesel engines. Heat is applied to swirling fuel upon injection.

Fig. 3   *Cutaway View Showing Relationship of Injection Nozzle, Glow Plug and Swirl Chamber to Piston*

Fig. 4   *Cutaway View of Resistor-Type Glow Plug*

Fig. 5   *Start Switch Key Positions (On and Pre-glow Positions Combined on Some Switches)*

## BOSCH DIESEL INJECTION — VOLKSWAGEN (Cont.)

To start a cold engine, pull out cold start knob, located left of steering column. Turn start switch key to pre-glow position. See Fig. 5.

**NOTE** — *Some switches combine the on and pre-glow positions.*

Glow plug light on dash will come on. When light goes out (approximately 15 seconds in warm climates; 60 seconds in cold), turn key to start position.

**NOTE** — *When temperature is below freezing, accelerator must be fully depressed during starting. Pre-glowing is not necessary if engine is already warm.*

After engine starts and runs for two minutes, push cold start knob fully inward. To stop engine, turn key to off position.

### CAR APPLICATION SPEED GOVERNOR

A mechanical, car application speed governor provides acceleration similar to a well-groomed spark ignition engine. See Figs. 1 and 6. Low speed range of modified part-load governor was expanded to also govern maximum engine speed.

**Fig. 6   Position and Function of Springs in Mechanical Car Application Speed Governor**

When operating at low speeds, governor assures smooth load absorption on starting.

Governor operates at starting, idling, and full-load ranges. At part-load speed range, governor has no effect, the injection pump being controlled directly by the accelerator.

Operating range is determined by type of springs used and geometry of governor levers. See Fig. 6.

### FUEL FILTER

Early model fuel filters were equipped with hand primer pump and vent screw for bleeding fuel system. See Fig. 7.

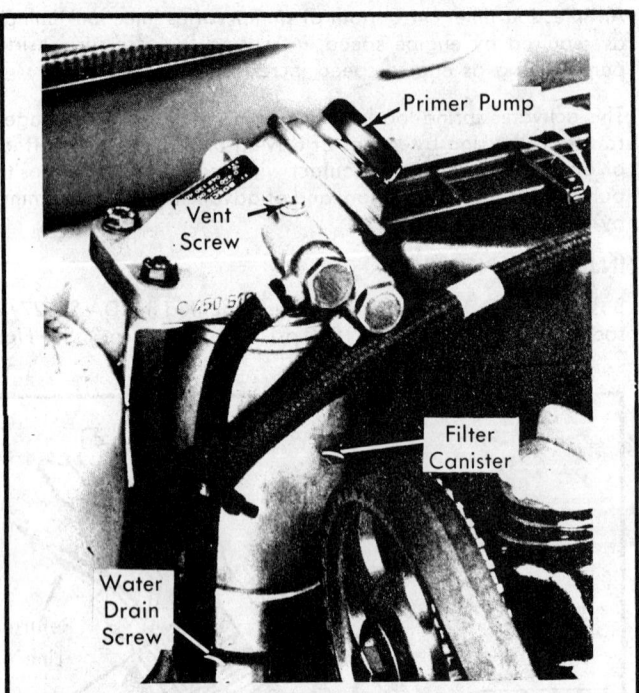

**Fig. 7   Early Model Fuel Filter With Primer Pump**

Later model filter has no primer pump. Regardless, which filter is used, bleeding is unnecessary. Vane-type fuel pump supplies fuel at starting speeds and is capable of automatically bleeding fuel supply system.

## SERVICING COMPONENTS

### FUEL INJECTION PUMP

**NOTE** — *When working on injection system, keep all components clean. Clean all injection line unions before loosening.*

If injection pump is faulty, it must be replaced. Special test equipment is necessary for making repairs.

**Removal** — 1) Remove belt cover and cylinder head cover.

**2)** Turn engine until No. 1 cylinder is at TDC. See Fig. 8. Lock camshaft in position with locking tool (2065).

**3)** Remove drive belt.

## BOSCH DIESEL INJECTION — VOLKSWAGEN (Cont.)

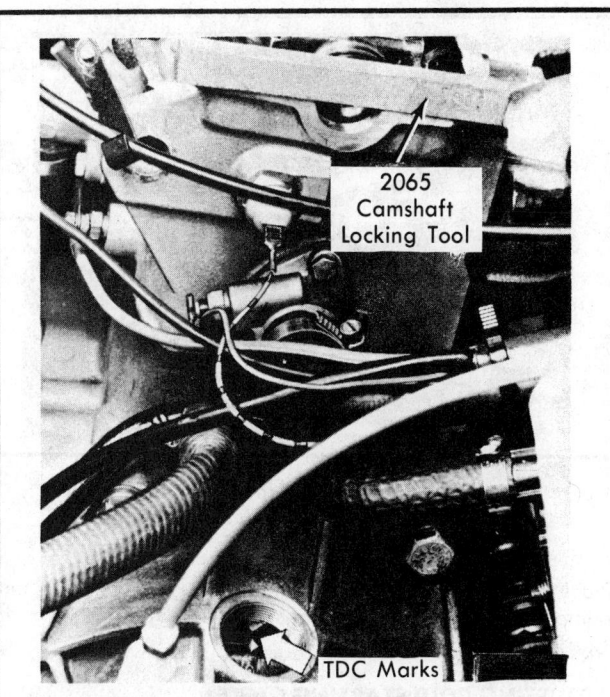

**Fig. 8    Adjusting No. 1 Cylinder to TDC and Locking Camshaft**

**Fig. 10    Aligning Reference Marks When Installing Injection Pump Gear**

**Installation — 1)** Install pump, aligning marks on pump and mounting plate. See Fig. 10. Torque mounting bolts to 18 ft. lbs. (2.5 mkg).

**2)** Install pump gear, turning it until mark on gear aligns with mounting plate mark. Torque nut to 33 ft. lbs. (4.5 mkg). Lock pump gear with setting pin (2064). See Fig. 10.

**3)** Loosen camshaft gear bolt one-half turn. Using rubber hammer, knock gear off taper.

**4)** Be sure TDC mark on flywheel aligns with reference mark. Install drive belt.

**5)** Remove setting pin (2064) from pump gear. Tension belt by turning tensioner to right. Check belt tension between camshaft and pump gears. Scale should read "11-12" on special tool (VW 210).

**6)** Tighten camshaft gear bolt to 33 ft. lbs. (4.5 mkg). Remove locking tool (2065) from camshaft. Turn crankshaft two turns in direction of engine rotation.

**7)** Using a rubber hammer, strike belt at point of measurement. Recheck belt tension, and check injection pump timing. When connecting injection nozzle lines, attach as follows:

- Line A to Cylinder No. 1.
- Line B to Cylinder No. 3.
- Line C to Cylinder No. 4.
- Line D to Cylinder No. 2.

### INJECTION NOZZLES

Injection nozzle problems usually appear as follows:

- Knocking in one or more cylinders.
- Engine overheating.
- Loss of power.
- Smoky black exhaust.
- Increased fuel consumption.

**Fig. 9    Pulling Fuel Injection Pump Gear**

**4)** Loosen (but do not remove) injection pump gear nut. Attach puller (VW 203b). See Fig. 9. Be sure jaws are at right angles to cross bar and point in direction of spindle rotation. Carefully apply tension to puller. Using a light hammer, strike puller bolt lightly, until gear loosens from injection pump shaft taper.

**5)** Remove puller and nut. Take gear off by hand.

**6)** Remove all fuel lines from pump. Cover unions with clean cloth. Disconnect wire from stop control on pump and remove accelerator cable.

**7)** Remove bolts from injection pump mounting plate. Support and remove pump.

To locate faulty injection nozzles, loosen line union on each injection nozzle (one at a time) with engine running at fast idle. If engine speed remains constant with line removed, that nozzle is defective.

## BOSCH DIESEL INJECTION – VOLKSWAGEN (Cont.)

**Removal** – 1) Detach injector line or lines.

2) Use special tool (US 2775) to remove injection nozzles.

**Installation** – 1) Install a new heat shield with recess pointing upward.

2) Torque injection nozzles to 51 ft. lbs. (7.0 mkg) and lines to 18 ft. lbs. (2.5 mkg).

**NOTE** – *Bleeding is not required.*

### FUEL FILTER

To replace filter, remove old canister and install new one. Bleeding is not required.

On early models, bleeding can be accomplished, if desired, by loosening vent screw on top of filter. See *Fig. 7*. Operate primer pump until fuel appears free of air bubbles. Then tighten vent screw and start engine.

**NOTE** – *If engine will not start, loosen line unions on two injection nozzles. Crank engine without using glow plugs. When fuel appears at unions, tighten unions and start engine.*

If water is present in system, loosen vent screw and open water drain screw on bottom of filter. Operate primer pump until clean fuel appears. Tighten water drain screw. Operate primer pump again until fuel appears free of air bubbles at vent screw. Tighten vent screw.

**NOTE** – *Later model has no primer pump. Such bleeding should not prove necessary with either filter.*

## ADJUSTMENTS

### ADJUSTING ACCELERATOR CABLE

Be sure ball pin on pump lever is pointing upward and is in line with mark on edge of elongated hole. See *white arrow in Fig. 11*. Accelerator cable should be attached at upper hole (black arrow) in bracket.

**Fig. 11   Checking Accelerator Cable Attaching Points**

**Fig. 12   Adjusting Points for Accelerator Cable, Idle Speed, and Maximum Speed**

Place pedal in full throttle position. Adjust cable with nuts until pump lever contacts stop free of strain. See *white arrow in Fig. 12*.

### ADJUSTING COLD STARTING CABLE

Insert washer onto cable. See *Fig. 13*. Install cable in bracket with rubber bushing.

**Fig. 13   Adjusting Cold Starting Cable To Provide 2.5° Timing Advance**

Insert cable in pin and install lock washer. Move lever as far as possible in direction of arrow. Pull cable tight and secure pin with clamping screw.

**NOTE** – *When cold start knob (left of steering column) is pulled out, timing of fuel injection pump is advanced 2.5°, improving starting.*

### ADJUSTING INJECTION PUMP TIMING

1) Turn engine until TDC mark on flywheel is in line with boss on bell housing and the marks on pump and mounting plate are aligned. See *Figs. 8 and 10*.

## BOSCH DIESEL INJECTION — VOLKSWAGEN (Cont.)

**Fig. 14  Setting No. 1 Cylinder at TDC With Engine Removed**

*2068 Tool*

*TDC Mark*

**NOTE** – *If engine is removed from vehicle, turn engine until TDC mark on flywheel aligns with end of setting bar (2068). See Fig. 14.*

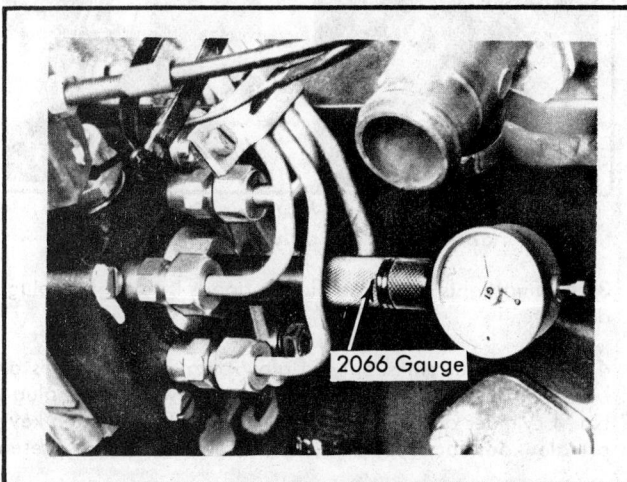

*2066 Gauge*

**Fig. 15  Preloading Injection Pump With Dial Gauge (2066)**

**2)** Remove plug from injection pump cover. Install adapter and dial gauge (2066) in plug hole. See Fig. 15. Preload gauge to .097" (2.5 mm).

**3)** Turn engine counterclockwise (opposite normal rotation) until gauge needle stops moving. Zero gauge with .039" (1 mm) preload.

**4)** Turn engine clockwise (normal rotation) until TDC on flywheel is aligned with reference mark. Gauge should read .032" (0.83 mm).

**NOTE** – *If necessary, loosen mounting plate and support bolts. Set lift to .032" (0.83 mm) by turning pump.*

### CHECKING VALVE TIMING

See *CHECKING VALVE TIMING* in ENGINE Section.

### MEASURING ENGINE SPEED

Use the following tools when measuring engine speed:

- Adapter (VW 1324).
- Bosch Dwell-Tach (EFAW 166C).
- Sun Dwell-Tach (TDT-12) as alternate.

### ADJUSTING IDLE SPEED

**1)** Operate engine until oil temperature reaches 122-158° F (50-70° C).

**2)** Set engine speed to 770-870 RPM, by turning idle adjusting screw. See Fig. 12.

**3)** Lock screw in place and seal it.

### ADJUSTING MAXIMUM SPEED

**1)** Operate engine until oil temperature reaches 122-158° F (50-70° C).

**2)** Open throttle fully and set speed at 5400-5450 RPM. See Fig. 12.

**3)** Lock screw in place and seal it.

### CHECKING INJECTION NOZZLES

**1)** To disassemble, place upper part of nozzle in vise and loosen lower part.

Upper Part
Shim
Spring
Thrust Pin
Nozzle Holder
Needle
Nozzle
Lower Part
Heat Shield

**Fig. 16  Inspecting Injection Nozzle Components**

**2)** To prevent parts from falling out, reverse position with lower part of nozzle in vise. Remove parts carefully. See Fig. 16.

## BOSCH DIESEL INJECTION — VOLKSWAGEN (Cont.)

**NOTE** — When disassembling, keep all individual parts together. Do not interchange parts from one nozzle to another.

**3)** To reassemble, reverse procedure. Tighten upper and lower parts to 51 ft. lbs. (7.0 mkg) torque.

### TESTING

#### TESTING INJECTION NOZZLES

**CAUTION** — Do not expose hands to injector spray during testing, as working pressure will cause fuel oil to penetrate skin.

Nozzles should be tested for:

- Spray formation.
- Noise.
- Breaking pressure.
- Leakage.

**Fig. 17   Testing Injection Nozzles for Spray Formation, Noise, Breaking Pressure, and Leakage**

#### Spray Formation Test

Isolate gauge (VW 1322). See Fig. 17. Use short, rapid strokes of testing pump lever (4-6 strokes per second). Spray should be even and stop cleanly. Nozzles should not drip.

#### Noise Test

Isolate gauge (VW 1322). See Fig. 17. Use long, slow strokes of testing pump lever (1-2 strokes per second). If nozzle is working properly it will "ping" as fuel emerges.

#### Breaking Pressure Test

**1)** With gauge (VW 1322) working, move pump lever down slowly. See Fig. 17. Watch pressure at which injector works.

**2)** Adjust, if necessary, by changing shims until working pressure reaches 1700-1850 psi (123-130 kg/cm²).

**3)** Using a thicker shim increases pressure. Using thinner shim decreases pressure.

**NOTE** — A shim thickness of .0019" (0.05 mm) increases pressure by 71 psi (5.0 kg/cm²). Shims are available in thicknesses of .039-.070" (1.00-1.95 mm) in .0019" (0.05 mm) steps.

#### Leakage Test

With gauge working, press pump lever down slowly and hold pressure at about 1564 psi (110 kg/cm²) for 15 seconds. See Fig. 17. No fuel should leak from nozzle tip.

#### CHECKING GLOW PLUGS

**1)** To check glow plug condition, remove glow plug wire and bus bar connector.

**2)** Connect test lamp to positive battery connector and in turn to each glow plug. See Fig. 18.

**Fig. 18   Checking Glow Plug Condition (Left) and Current Supply to Plug (Right)**

**3)** If lamp lights up, glow plug is good. If not, glow plug is defective.

**4)** To check current supply to glow plug, reinstall wires and bus bar connector. Connect test lamp between glow plug of No. 4 cylinder and ground. (See Fig. 18). Turn ignition key to pre-glow position. Test lamp should light if current is present.

### SYSTEM SPECIFICATIONS

| | |
|---|---|
| Injection Nozzle Pressure | 1700-1850 psi (123-130 kg/cm²) |
| Leakage Pressure | ①1564 psi (110 kg/cm²) |
| Injection Pump Timing | ②.032" (0.83 mm) |

① — Pressure must hold for 10 seconds.
② — Plunger stroke at engine TDC.

### TIGHTENING SPECIFICATIONS

| Application | Ft. Lbs. (mkg) |
|---|---|
| Injection Pump Mounting Bolts | 18 (2.5) |
| Fuel Injection Line Unions | 18 (2.5) |
| Fuel Injection Pump Gear Nut | 33 (4.5) |
| Camshaft Gear Bolt | 33 (4.5) |
| Injection Nozzle-to-Socket | 51 (7.0) |
| Nozzle (Upper-to-Lower Part) | 51 (7.0) |

## BOSCH ELECTRIC FUEL PUMPS

BMW
Datsun
 280Z & 810
Jaguar
 XJS & XJ12
Mercedes-Benz
Peugeot
Porsche
Volkswagen
 Fuel Injection Models (Gas)
Volvo

### DESCRIPTION

Bosch electric fuel pumps are positive displacment roller cell type, operated on 12 volts D.C. Operating pressure is determined by one or more external fuel regulators on most models. Pumps with a return line have an internal pressure relief valve which is designed to open between 43 and 65 psi depending on model application. Some applications use two pumps in series, with a combined output of about 1700 cc of fuel in 30 seconds. Single pump applications should pump about 715 cc of fuel in 30 seconds.

Pumps are activated by relays when ignition switch is in "START" or "RUN" position, and protected from electrical overload by fuses and/or fusible links. A check valve in the discharge side prevents abrupt pressure drop when stopping the engine. Some installations incorporate an impact safety switch which shuts off the pump in event of an accident.

**NOTE** — *Sequence of operations may vary between individual applications. Bosch fuel pumps are sealed and no repair or disassembly is possible.*

### OPERATION

Two methods of fuel control are used by Bosch pumps:

**1)** On pumps which have no fuel return line, fuel is taken from inlet, through pump to delivery connection. In this type both rotor and brushes are immersed in fuel. To maintain uniform fuel pressure, a ball valve is located in delivery connection. In addition, pump has a pressure relief by-pass which disconnects suction and delivery lines at approximately 73.5 psi. Delivery rate is approximately 2.11 quarts per minute at 2500 RPM.

**2)** On pumps which have a fuel return line, fuel is circulated through pump rotor and brushes. On this type, all fuel line connections are on one end of fuel pump. When pump starts operating and there is air in pump, air is vented by a spiral groove around the side of a spring loaded valve. When air has been vented and fuel pressure increases, the spring loaded valve actuates, shutting off fuel return line and opening fuel delivery line. If fuel pump pressure goes beyond proper operating pressure, 64 psi (4.5 kp/sq. cm.), spring loaded valve opens further and allows excess pressure and fuel to be returned to fuel tank.

**Fig. 2 Non-Return Type Fuel Pump (Datsun Shown)**

**Fig. 1 Return Line Type Fuel Pump**

**Fig. 3 Wiring Diagram of Datsun Fuel Pump Control System**

## BOSCH ELECTRIC FUEL PUMPS (Cont.)

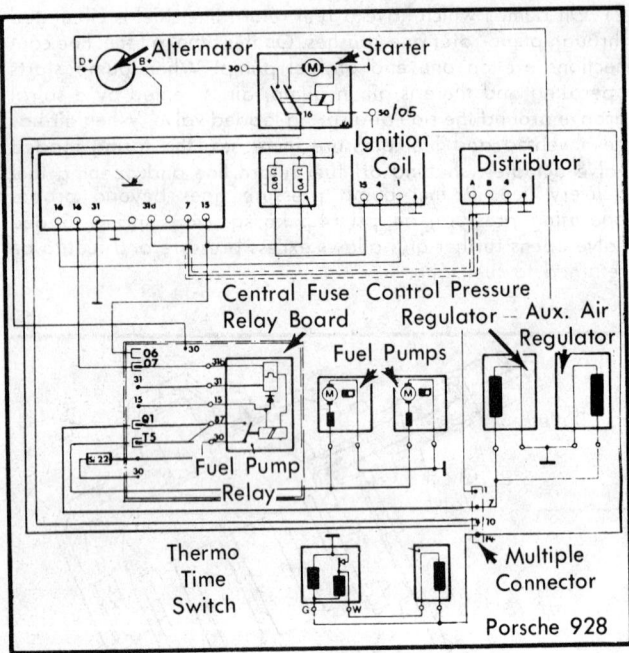

**Fig. 4  Wiring Diagram of Porsche 928 Fuel Pump Control System**

## REMOVAL & INSTALLATION

### FUEL PUMP

**CAUTION** — Do not allow smoking, open flame or sparks in area while servicing fuel system components. Disconnect battery ground terminal prior to removing pump. Danger of fire or explosion exists.

**Removal** — **1)** Fuel pressure must be relieved prior to any component removal. Carefully remove and plug fuel lines to prevent spillage. Disconnect electrical connections.

**NOTE** — Depending on make and model, it may be necessary to jack car up or remove carpeting and panels in order to gain access to fuel pump.

**2)** Remove mounting bolts and retain rubber insulating grommets for reinstallation. Tip pump as required to clear chassis and remove from car.

**Installation** — Reverse removal procedure while noting the following:

**1)** Be sure rubber grommets and insulation are installed correctly or noise and vibration will result.

**2)** Hook all fuel lines and return lines to proper fittings and be sure they are tight to avoid air and/or fuel leaks.

**3)** Route fuel lines so they will not vibrate or rub against other body parts.

**4)** Test system for leaks with engine running.

**Fig. 5  Wiring Diagram of Volvo Fuel Pump Control System**

## DATSUN & LUV ELECTRIC FUEL PUMPS

**Datsun**
 Pickup with Air Conditioning
**LUV**

### DESCRIPTION

Electro-magnetic type fuel pump is attached to the frame adjacent to gas tank (right side on Datsun, left side on LUV). Pump is cylindrical in shape with electrical lead, carburetor feed line and tank suction line protruding from the same side.

### OPERATION

Twelve volt electrical circuit is protected by fuses (number 4 and 5 for LUV) and/or fusible link. Electrical relay further feeds pump. Plunger operated by pulsating action of electro-magnetic core draws fuel from suction line and delivers discharge pressure to carburetor fuel line.

**NOTE** — *Entire pump should be replaced in event of faulty operation. Pump is totally enclosed and should not be disassembled.*

### REMOVAL & INSTALLATION

#### FUEL PUMP

Remove electrical lead and fuel lines from tank and carburetor. Remove mounting bolts and nuts and take pump off frame. To install, reverse removal procedure.

*Fig. 1   Fuel Pump Installation (LUV Shown)*

*Fig. 2   Fuel Pump Electrical Circuit
(LUV Shown, Datsun Similar)*

# 1978 Electric Fuel Pumps

## HONDA ELECTRIC FUEL PUMPS

**Accord**
**CVCC**

### DESCRIPTION

Electric fuel pump is located near gas tank at left side of vehicle. CVCC pump is mounted on fuel tank bracket with insulator bolts. Accord pump mounts to fuel pump cover with insulator bolts. Cover is bolted to frame. Fuel pump cut-off relay allows pump to run ONLY when engine is running or ignition switch is in start position.

### OPERATION & TESTING

A solid-state relay senses negative pulsations at the ignition coil and switches the pump on when the engne is running or the starter is engaged. Relay is located under dash panel at left side of driver's cmpartment. Circuit is protected by fuse in fuse box as well as main in-line fuse.

**Electrical Testing — 1)** With ignition switch OFF, connect positive probe of voltmeter to black/yellow wire terminal of fuel pump relay connector, and negative probe to ground (black) terminal. Turn ignition switch on and check for voltage. If no voltage, check fuse and continuity of black/yellow wire.

**2)** If voltage available, crank engine until points are open. Connect positive probe of voltmeter to blue wire at pump cut-off relay and ground positive probe. Turn ignition on. Voltmeter should indicate battery voltage. If not, check blue wire circuit between connector and negative terminal of ignition coil.

**3)** With voltage present from previous step, jumper the 2 black/yellow wires of relay connector and turn ignition switch ON. If fuel pressure is now available, replace fuel cut-off relay and re-test. If relay checks satisfactory, connect positive probe of voltmeter to black/yellow wire at fuel pump. Ground negative probe and turn ignition switch ON. If no voltage, check black/yellow wire continuity.

**Fuel Pump Operational Testing — 1)** Attach jumper between black/yellow wires in fuel pump cut-off relay connector.

Disconnect fuel hose to carburetor and install pressure gauge to fuel hose. Turn ignition switch ON and check for normal pressure of 2-3 psi (.13-.18 kg/cm$^2$)

**2)** Remove pressure gauge and hold measuring beaker under fuel hose. Turn ignition on and measure amount of fuel flow in 60 seconds. With 10 volts minimum battery voltage, flow should be at least 15.2 ozs. (450 ml).

### REMOVAL & INSTALLATION

#### FUEL PUMP

From underneath car, disconnect electrical leads and fuel lines. On CVCC, remove mounting bolts and take off pump. On Accord, remove fuel pump cover bolts and remove pump with cover attached. To install, reverse removal procedure.

*Fig. 1  Fuel Pump Electrical Circuit and Components*

## MAZDA ELECTRIC FUEL PUMPS

Courier
Mazda
RX-4
Cosmo
B1800

### DESCRIPTION

Pulsating electric powered fuel pump is mounted near fuel tank on frame member.

### OPERATION & TESTING

NOTE — *In line fuel filter must be changed within recommended mileage interval before performing tests. If in doubt, install new filter.*

Electrical power is supplied when ignition switch is in "RUN" position. Circuit is protected by 15 amp fuse (20 amp fuse on Cosmo) at fuse panel.

**Pressure Test** — 1) Remove air cleaner assembly and disconnect fuel line at carburetor. Connect suitable pressure gauge with restrictor and a flexible hose as illustrated in *Fig. 2.*

2) Turn ignition on and briefly vent the system into container by opening hose restrictor. Pressure should stabilize within specifications. If not within specifications and lines and filter are in satisfactory condition, pump must be replaced.

**Volume Test** — With fuel pressure within limits, open restrictor for one minute and measure fuel expelled. If not within specifications, check for restrictions in tank, line or filter. Replace pump if required.

### REMOVAL & INSTALLATION

NOTE — *Negative cable should be disconnected at battery when working on fuel pump.*

1) On Cosmo and RX-4, open trunk lid and remove floor mat. Raise rear of vehicle and support on stands. Remove fuel pump cover attaching bolts, then remove cover.

2) On all models, disconnect inlet and outlet hoses and wiring connector. Remove attaching bolts and nuts and take pump off vehicle. To install, reverse removal procedure.

### SPECIFICATIONS

| Application | Pressure (PSI) | Volume |
| --- | --- | --- |
| Courier | 2.8-3.6 | 2 pints/minute |
| Cosmo | 4.3-5. | 1.2 quarts/minute |
| RX-4 | 4.3-5.4 | 1.3 quarts/minute |
| B1800 | 2.8-3.6 | .8 quarts/minute |

**Fig. 1   Fuel Pump Circuit Schematic**

**Fig. 2   Fuel Pump Pressure and Volume Test**

## S.U. AUF TYPE ELECTRIC FUEL PUMPS

**MGB**

### DESCRIPTION

Diaphragm type pump is operated by electro-magnetic plunger controlled by adjustable contact points. Fuel flow direction is controlled by internal disc valves. Pump is located at forward end of fuel tank on right side. Pump should deliver about 1 pint of fuel in 30 seconds with a pressure of 2.3-3.8 psi.

**NOTE** — *A fuel pump inertia (safety) switch is located under the left side of the instrument panel. This switch interrupts electrical supply to fuel pump in event of impact. To reset, remove bottom panel, reach under dash and depress plunger.*

### ADJUSTMENTS

#### CONTACT PLATE POSITIONING

1) Points are correctly positioned when they contact each other on the center of the curved point and wipe across evenly.

2) Lower rocker points. Check that contact plate on top of pedestal rests on narrow pedestal bridge. Contact plate should be square with rocker points. Contact plate points should be slightly forward of rocker points.

3) If adjustment is required, use contact plate attaching screw to adjust to proper position.

*Fig. 1   Correct Contact Point Alignment*

#### SETTING CONTACT GAPS

1) Ensure rocker points are touching contact plate points. Measure distance contact points are pushed (lifted) above pedestal when cycled. Lift should be .035" (.9 mm).

2) Adjust by bending upper rocker finger beneath pedestal.

3) Now check gap between lower rocker finger and housing. Gap should be .070" (1.8 mm). To adjust, upper rocker finger may again need to be bent. **NOTE** — *Both adjustments require bending same upper rocker finger. Be careful because this finger is used to set both adjustments and they must be proportioned correctly.*

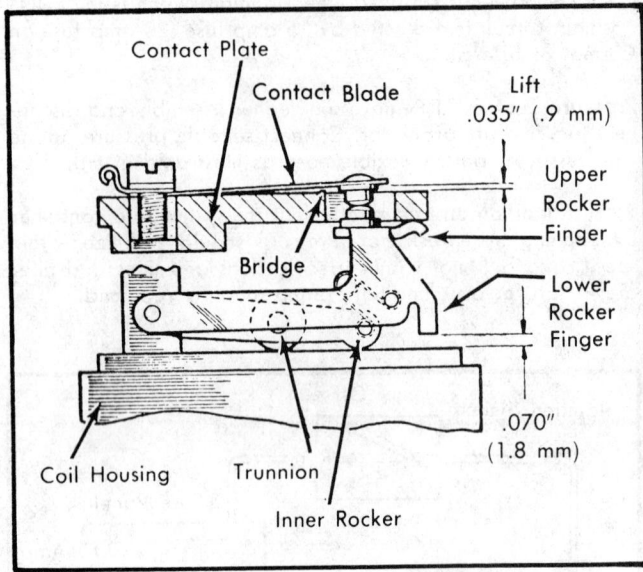

*Fig. 2   Adjusting Contact Gaps*

### REMOVAL & INSTALLATION

#### FUEL PUMP

**Removal** —1) Disconnect battery. From inside trunk, remove retaining screws and take off fuel pump guard.

2) Loosen clamp retaining pump in supporting rubber insulator. Disconnect electrical terminal from pump.

3) Working under car, disconnect inlet and outlet lines, breather pipe and electrical connection. Remove pump from support.

**Installation** — Reverse removal procedure, ensuring that pump tubing connections are fitted at the proper angle.

## S.U. AUF TYPE ELECTRIC FUEL PUMPS (Cont.)

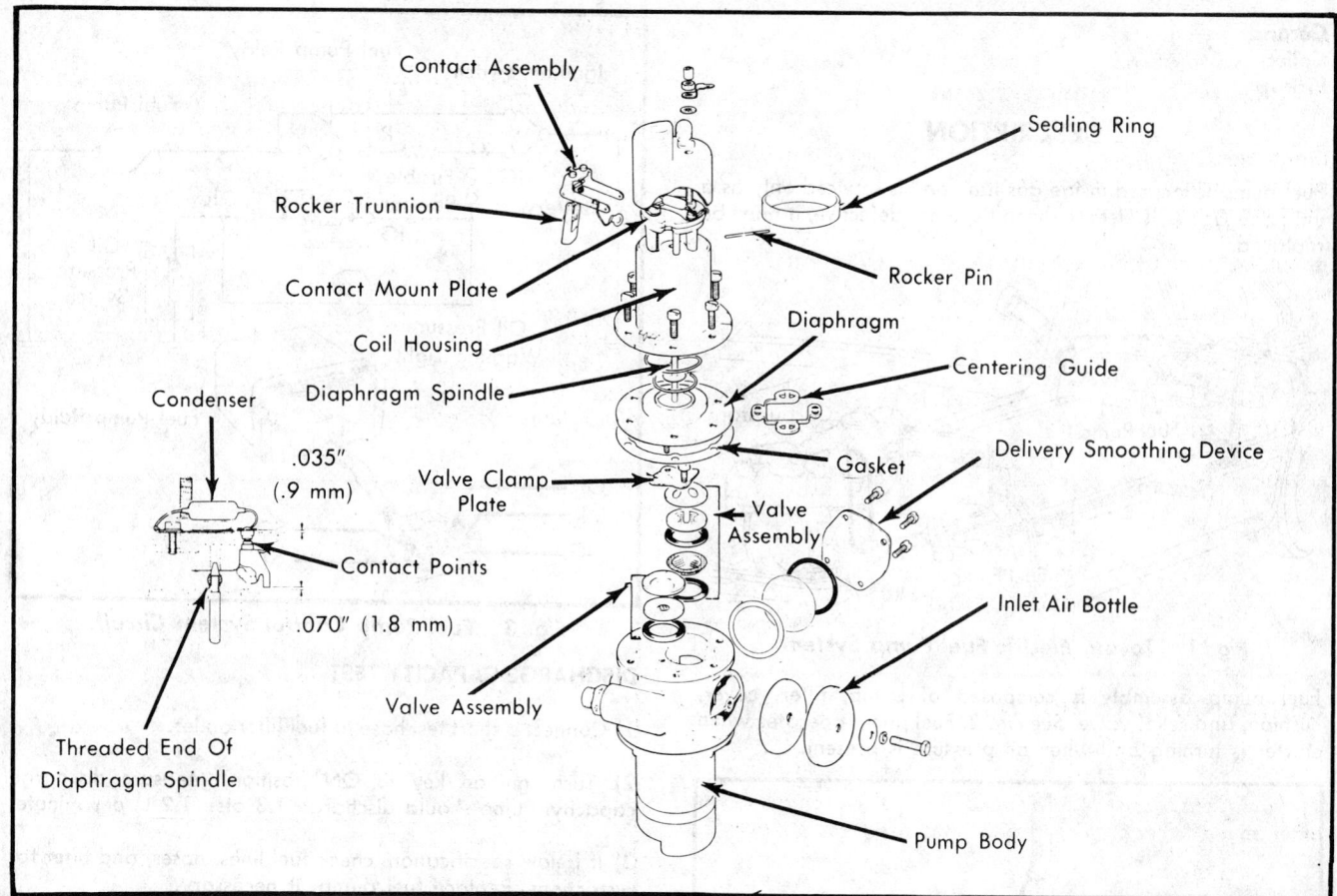

**Fig. 3   S.U. AUF 300 Electric Fuel Pump**

# 1978 Electric Fuel Pumps

## TOYOTA ELECTRIC FUEL PUMPS

**Corona
Celica
Pickup**

### DESCRIPTION

Fuel pump is located inside gas tank and is serviced only as a unit. See *Fig. 1*. If electric pump becomes defective, it must be replaced.

*Fig. 1   Toyota Electric Fuel Pump System*

Fuel pump assembly is composed of pump, filter, cover, cushion, and relief valve. See *Fig. 2*. Fuel pump operates when starter is turning and when oil pressure is present.

*Fig. 2   Exploded View of Electric Fuel Pump*

### TESTING

**CAUTION** — *Do not operate electric fuel pump unless it is immersed in gasoline. Do not attempt to test pump without resistor.*

#### PUMP OPERATION CHECK

1) Check oil pressure switch operation.

2) Disconnect connector from oil pressure switch, to operate fuel pump relay. See *Fig. 3*.

3) Turn ignition key to ON position.

4) Check pump for steady, smooth operation. Replace pump if abnormal noise is present. If pump does not run, check pump resistor, relay and pump.

*Fig. 3   Fuel Pump Control System Circuit*

### DISCHARGE CAPACITY TEST

1) Connect a short test hose to fuel filter outlet.

2) Turn ignition key to ON position. Measure discharge capacity. Pump should discharge 1.3 qts. (1.2 L) per minute.

3) If below specification, check fuel lines, hoses, and filter for restrictions. Replace fuel pump, if necessary.

### DISCHARGE PRESSURE TEST

1) Connect pressure gauge to fuel filter outlet.

2) Turn ignition key to ON position. Measure discharge pressure at gauge. Reading should be 2.1-4.3 psi (0.15-0.30 kg/cm²). If not within specified limits, check fuel level. Replace pump if necessary.

### COMPLETING TESTS

After tests, necessary repairs or replacement of parts, turn off ignition. Reconnect fuel hoses and lead to oil pressure switch.

### REMOVAL AND INSTALLATION

**Removal** — Remove fuel pump from tank. On pickup, remove fuel tank. Remove negative battery cable.

**Installation** — Install fuel pump into tank, using a new gasket. Reconnect electrical leads and fuel lines. Connect negative battery cable and check fuel system for leaks.

### FUEL PUMP RESISTOR TEST

Check for continuity between two terminals of resistor connector. If no continuity, replace resistor and check fuel pump. Resistance of 1.4 ohms required.

# Section 3
# ELECTRICAL

## Contents

*NOTE — ALSO SEE GENERAL INDEX.*

# 1978 Distributor Specifications

## DISTRIBUTOR APPLICATION TABLES

### ARROW/COLT & CHALLENGER/SAPPORO

| Application | Fed. | Calif. & High Alt. |
|---|---|---|
| Mitsubishi | | |
| 1600 cc | T3T05771 | ①T3T05772 |
| 2000 cc | | |
|   Man. Trans. | T3T04581 | T3T04581 |
|   Auto. Trans. | T3T04587 | T3T04581 |
| 2600 cc | | |
|   Man. Trans. | T3T04589 | ②T3T04887 |
|   Auto. Trans. | T3T04581 | ②T3T04887 |

① — Challenger & Sapporo — T3T05775.
② — Challenger & Sapporo — T3T04874.

### AUDI

| Application | Fed. | Calif. |
|---|---|---|
| Bosch | | |
| Fox | 049 905 205A | 049 905 205A |
| 5000 | 035 905 205C | 035 905 205C |

### BMW

| Application | Fed. | Calif. |
|---|---|---|
| Bosch | | |
| 733i① | 0 237 304 002 | 0 237 304 002 |

① — Information on remaining BMW models was not available at time of publication.

### CAPRI

| Application | Fed. | Calif. |
|---|---|---|
| Ford① | | |
| 2300 cc | | |
|   Auto. Trans. | | D7FZ-C |
|   Man. Trans. | D7FZ-D | D7FZ-E |
| Bosch② | | |
| 2800 cc③ | 305 052 | 308 010 |

① — Ford basic part number 12127.
② — Bosch basic part number 0231.
③ — Auto. Trans. models use 0231 308 012.

### COURIER

| Application | Fed. | Calif. |
|---|---|---|
| Mitsubishi | | |
| 1800 cc | T3T07182-3879 | T3T07182-3879 |
| 2300 cc | T3T60772-3877 | T3T60774-8786 |

### DATSUN

| Application | Fed. | Calif. |
|---|---|---|
| Hitachi | | |
| F10 | D4F5-04 | D4F5-04 |

### DATSUN (Cont.)

| Application | Fed. | Calif. |
|---|---|---|
| B210 | | |
|   Auto. Trans. | D4F6-03 | D4F5-05 |
|   Man. Trans. | D4F5-03 | D4F5-03 |
|   Hatchback | D4F7-01 | D4F7-01 |
| Pickup | | |
|   Auto. Trans. | D4F6-06 | D4F6-07 |
|   Man. Trans. | D4F6-05 | D4F7-02 |
| 200SX | | |
|   Auto. Trans. | D4F6-04 | D4F5-07 |
|   Man. Trans. | D4F5-06 | D4F5-06 |
| 510 | | |
|   Auto. Trans. | D4F6-04 | D4F5-07 |
|   Man. Trans. | D4F5-06 | D4F5-06 |
| 810 | | |
|   Auto. Trans. | D6F4-03 | D6F4-03 |
|   Man. Trans. | D6F6-01 | D6F5-02 |
| 280Z | | |
|   Auto. Trans. | D6F5-03 | D6F4-03 |
|   Man. Trans. | D6F5-02 | D6F4-03 |

### FIAT

| Application | Fed. | Calif. |
|---|---|---|
| Ducellier | | |
| 128 | 4480 B | 525044 B |
| X1/9 | 525047 A | 525047 A |
| Marelli | | |
| 124 | S 144 CBY | S 144 CBY |
| Brava | ① | ① |

① — Information not available at time of publication.

### FIESTA

| Application | Fed. | Calif. |
|---|---|---|
| Ford① | | |
| Fiesta | D8RZ-A | D8RZ-A |

① — Ford basic part number is 12127.

### HONDA

| Application | Fed. | Calif. & High Alt. |
|---|---|---|
| Honda Distributors | | |
| Civic | | |
|   Auto. Trans. | D412-99 | D412-99 |
|   Man. Trans. | D417-67 | D417-67 |
| Civic CVCC | | |
| Sedan | | |
|   Auto. Trans. | D409-66 | D411-B1 |
|   Man. Trans. | D409-66 | D411-B2 |
| Wagon | | |
|   Auto. Trans. | D409-66 | D4J6-06 |
|   Man. Trans. | D409-66 | D411-B1 |
| Accord① | | |
|   Auto. Trans. | | 663-791 |
|   Man. Trans. | 657-674 | 657-812 |

① — Honda basic part number is 30100.

## DISTRIBUTOR APPLICATION TABLES (Cont.)

### JAGUAR

| Application | Fed. | Calif. |
|---|---|---|
| Lucas | | |
| XJS | 36 DE 12 | 36 DE 12 |
| XJ6 | 45 DE 6 | 43 DE 6 |
| XJ12 | 36 DE 12 | 36 DE 12 |

### LANCIA

| Application | Fed. | Calif. |
|---|---|---|
| Marelli | | |
| Beta | S144CBY | S144M |

### LUV

| Application | Fed. | Calif. |
|---|---|---|
| Nippondenso | | |
| LUV | 029 100 3281 | 029 100 3281 |

### MAZDA

| Application | Fed. | Calif. |
|---|---|---|
| Mazda Distributor | | |
| GLC | 395818200 | 802818200A |
| B1800 | 387918200 | 387918200 |
| RX-4 & Cosmo | 876118200 | 876118200 |

### MERCEDES-BENZ

| Application | Fed. | Calif. |
|---|---|---|
| Bosch① | | |
| 230 | 002 024 | 002 024 |
| 280 | 304 003 | 304 003 |
| 450 & 6.9 | 405 002 | 405 002 |

① — Bosch basic part number is 0237.

### MG

| Application | Fed. | Calif. |
|---|---|---|
| Lucas | | |
| Midget | 45DE4 | 45DE4 |
| MGB | 45DE4 | 45DE4 |

### OPEL

| Application | Fed. | Calif. |
|---|---|---|
| Nippondenso | | |
| Opel | 029 100 3281 | 029 100 3281 |

### PORSCHE

| Application | Fed. | Calif. |
|---|---|---|
| Bosch | | |
| 911SC | 930 602 02 1.02 | 930 602 02 1.02 |
| Turbo | 930 602 10 1.07 | 930 602 10 1.08 |
| 924 | 047 905 205C | 047 905 205C |
| 928① | 0237 401 006 | 0237 401 006 |

① — Bosch part number.

### RENAULT

| Application | Fed. | Calif. |
|---|---|---|
| Ducellier | | |
| R-5 | 4441 | 525 003 |

### SAAB

| Application | Fed. | Calif. |
|---|---|---|
| Bosch | | |
| 99 | 0237 002 023 | 0237 002 023 |

### SUBARU

| Application | Fed. | Calif. |
|---|---|---|
| Nippondenso | | |
| All Models | 0291100 4220 | 0291100 4270 |
| Hitachi | | |
| All Models | | D4H6-01 |

### TOYOTA

| Application | Fed. | Calif. |
|---|---|---|
| Nippondenso① | | |
| 3K-C Engine | 24180 | 24180 |
| 2T-C Engine | 26280② | 26231 |
| 20R Engine | | |
| Celica | 38081③ | 38091 |
| Corona | 38050④ | 38060 |
| Pickup | 38150⑤ | ⑤38150 |
| 4M Engine | 45150 | 45160 |
| 2F Engine | 61100⑥ | 61061 |

① — Toyota basic part number is 19100.
② — 26290 optional.
③ — Auto. Trans. uses 38091.
④ — High Altitude uses 38070.
⑤ — Auto. Trans. uses 38180.
⑥ — High Altitude uses 61110.

### TRIUMPH

| Application | Fed. | Calif. |
|---|---|---|
| Lucas | | |
| Spitfire | 45DE4 | 45DE4 |
| TR7 | 47DE4 | 47DE4 |

### VOLKSWAGEN

| Application | Fed. | Calif. |
|---|---|---|
| Bosch | | |
| Type 1 | 043 905 205H | 043 905 205H |
| Type 2 | 021 905 205P | 022 905 205S |
| Dasher | 049 905 205A | 049 905 205A |
| Rabbit | 049 905 205A | 049 905 205A |
| Scirocco | 049 905 205A | 049 905 205A |

### VOLVO

| Application | Fed. | Calif. |
|---|---|---|
| Bosch | | |
| 240 Series | 0237 002 007 | 0237 003 009 |
| 260 Series | 0237 402 004 | 0237 402 004 |

# 1978 Distributor Specifications

## BOSCH DISTRIBUTOR ADVANCE & RETARD SPECIFICATIONS

NOTE — FOR DISTRIBUTOR RPM & DEGREES, DIVIDE SPECIFICATIONS BELOW BY 2

| Distributor Part No. | Rot. ⊖ | Centrifugal Advance (Engine Degrees @ RPM) | Vacuum Advance (Engine Degrees @ In. of Hg) | Vacuum Retard (Engine Degrees @ In. of Hg) |
|---|---|---|---|---|
| 021 905 205P | C | 0 @ 1000-1200; 8-13 @ 1600; 20-25 @ 3400 | 0 @ 5.1; 8.5-11 @ 7.9 | — |
| 022 905 205S | C | 0 @ 1000-1200; 8-13 @ 1600; 20-25 @ 3400 | 0 @ 5.1; 8.5-11 @ 7.9 | — |
| 035 905 205C | C | 0 @ 1000; 6-12 @ 1600; 17-23 @ 2500; 22-26 @ 3000; 21-25 @ 4500 | 6.3-79; 8; 8.7-9.4 | 1.6-4.3; 10; 5.5-8.3 |
| 043 905 205H | C | 0 @ 1000-1200; 6-12 @ 1500; 20-23 @ 3500 | 6.1; 5 @ 5.8; 4.9 @ 7.9 | 0 @ 5.9; 11-13 @ 9.1 |
| 047 905 205C | C | 1150; 10 @ 1500; 20 @ 26 @ 4000; 29 @ 4500 | 0 @ 3; 3 @ 5; 5 @ 6.3; 6.5 @ 6.5 | — |
| 049 905 205A | C | 1120-1400; 11-21 @ 2000-2400; 25-29 @ 4800; 26-30 @ 5200 | 3.2; 10; 2 @ 4; 4-8; 4.9; 11.5 | 0; 8 @ 8-10; 11 |
| 0231 305 052 | C | 0 @ 600; 2 @ 800; 3 @ 1200; 12; 21 | 0; 3 @ 2; 3.5 @ 2.5; 6 @ 6; 6.5 | — |
| 0231 308 010 | C | 0 @ 600; 3 @ 1200; 6 @ 1600; 12 @ 2400; 18 @ 3200 | 0; 3; 2 @ 3; 4 @ 5.5; 6; 6 | 6; 11 @ 12; 14 |
| 0237 002 007 | C | 1200; 10; 18; 22 @ 4800; @ 4100; @ 2200 | 4.3 | 4; 5.1 @ 10; 5.9 |
| 0237 002 023 | CC | 0 @ 700; 3 @ 2000; 7 @ 3000; 12 @ 4000; 17 @ 5000 | 0; 4.7; 8; 7.7 @ 12; 9; 17; 11.4 | — |
| 0237 002 024 | C | 15-20 @ 1500; 27-32 @ 3000; 42-48 @ 4500 | — | — |
| 0237 003 009 | C | 0 @ 1200; 10 @ 2060; 20 @ 3500; 29 @ 5000 | 0; 6.1; 4 @ 4; 7.1 @ 10; 8.7; 15; 9.1 | 4; 7.5 @ 7; 7.9 |
| 0237 304 002 | C | 11-15 @ 1000; 15-21 @ 1700; 25-31 @ 3000; 32-38 @ 4500 | — | — |
| 0237 304 003 | C | 16-26 @ 1500; 27-34 @ 3000; 28 | 0-2; 4.5 @ 2.5; 6.3 | 3-6; 7.1 @ 4-6; 7.9 |
| 0237 401 006 | C | 0 @ 800; 5 @ 1200; 24 @ 2600; 28 @ 4900 | — | — |
| 0237 402 004 | C | 0 @ 1200; 10 @ 1800; 20 @ 3100; 28 @ 4500 | 0; 3.9 @ 5; 6.3 @ 10; 8.3 | 0; 4.9 @ 10; 5.9 |
| 0237 405 002 | C | 9-17 @ 1500; 26-34 @ 3500 | 4.7 | — |
| 930 602 02 1.02 | CC | 0 @ 1200; 10 @ 1900; 18 @ 2400; 17 @ 3500; 24 @ 5200 | 0; 2.8 @ 1.5; 5.5 @ 2.5; 5.9; 3.5 | — |
| 930 602 10 1.07 | CC | 1300; 5 @ 1600; 18 @ 2700; 16 @ 6000 | 0; 4.7 @ 5; 8.3 @ 10; 9.4 | — |
| 930 602 10 1.08 | CC | 0 @ 1300; 5 @ 1600; 18 @ 2700; 16 @ 600 | 0; 4.7 @ 5; 6.3 @ 10; 8.3; 9.4 | — |

⊖ — C (Clockwise), CC (Counterclockwise), viewed from rotor end.

ELECTRICAL

## DUCELLIER DISTRIBUTOR ADVANCE & RETARD SPECIFICATIONS

*NOTE – FOR DISTRIBUTOR RPM & DEGREES, DIVIDE SPECIFICATIONS BELOW BY 2.*

| Distributor Part No. | Rot. ⊖ | Centrifugal Advance (Engine Degrees @ RPM) | Vacuum Advance (Engine Degrees @ In. of Hg) | Vacuum Retard (Engine Degrees @ In. of Hg) |
|---|---|---|---|---|
| 4441 | C | 0 @ 1100, 14 @ 1600, 36 @ 4500 | 0 @ 7, 22 | …… |
| 4480 B | C | 0 @ 1000, 10 @ 1700, 16 @ 2800, 22 @ 3800, 28 @ 4800 | 3 @ 8, 7 @ 16, 13 @ 22 | …… |
| 525 003 | C | 0 @ 1100, 26 @ 2750, 46 @ 5200 | 0 @ 3.5, 8, 10 | …… |
| 525 044 B | C | 0 @ 1000, 10 @ 1700, 16 @ 2800, 22 @ 3800, 28 @ 4800 | 4 @ 6, 10 | 0 @ 7, 3 @ 9, 6.5 @ 11, 10 @ 13 |
| 525 047 A | C | …… | 0 @ 7, 11 | …… |
| 525 089 | C | 0 @ 1200, 8 @ 1500, 10.6 @ 2000, 16 @ 3000, 26 @ 4900 | 0 @ 3, 8 @ 4.5, 17 @ 7, 22 @ 9.5 | 0 @ 3, 4 @ 4, 9 @ 5, 12 @ 6 |

⊖ – C (Clockwise), CC (Counterclockwise), viewed from rotor end.

## FORD DISTRIBUTOR ADVANCE & RETARD SPECIFICATIONS

*NOTE – FOR DISTRIBUTOR RPM & DEGREES, DIVIDE SPECIFICATIONS BELOW BY 2.*

| Distributor Part No. | Rot. ⊖ | Centrifugal Advance (Engine Degrees @ RPM) | Vacuum Advance (Engine Degrees @ In. of Hg) | Vacuum Retard (Engine Degrees @ In. of Hg) |
|---|---|---|---|---|
| D7FZ-C | C | …… | …… | …… |
| D7FZ-D | C | …… | …… | …… |
| D7FZ-E | C | …… | …… | …… |
| D8RZ-A | CC | …… | …… | …… |

⊖ – C (Clockwise), CC (Counterclockwise), viewed from rotor end.

# 1978 Distributor Specifications

## HITACHI DISTRIBUTOR ADVANCE & RETARD SPECIFICATIONS

*NOTE – FOR DISTRIBUTOR RPM & DEGREES, DIVIDE SPECIFICATIONS BELOW BY 2.*

| Distributor Part No. | Rot. ⊙ | Centrifugal Advance (Engine Degrees @ RPM) | Vacuum Advance (Engine Degrees @ In. of Hg) | Vacuum Retard (Engine Degrees @ In. of Hg) |
|---|---|---|---|---|
| D4F5-03 | CC | 0 @ 1100 / 28 @ 4600 | 0 @ 15 / 4.13 @ 15.4 | |
| D4F5-04 | CC | 0 @ 1100 / 28 @ 4600 | 0 @ 15 / 4.13 @ 15.4 | |
| D4F5-05 | CC | 0 @ 1100 / 28 @ 4600 | 0 @ 9 / 4.13 @ 11.8 | |
| D4F5-06 | CC | 0 @ 1200 / 22 @ 3900 | 0 @ 10 / 2.8 @ 7.7 | |
| D4F5-07 | CC | 0 @ 1200 / 22 @ 3900 | 0 @ 3 / 3.54 @ 5.5 | |
| D4F6-03 | CC | 0 @ 1100 / 28 @ 4600 | 0 @ 6.5 / 6.7 @ 11.8 | |
| D4F6-04 | CC | 0 @ 1200 / 22 @ 3900 | 0 @ 4 / 3.54 @ 6.3 | |
| D4F6-05 | CC | 0 @ 1200 / 22 @ 3900 | 0 @ 12.5 / 2.76 @ 9.8 | |
| D4F6-06 | CC | 0 @ 1200 / 22 @ 3900 | 0 @ 10 / 3.94 @ 9.8 | |
| D4F6-07 | CC | 0 @ 1200 / 22 @ 3900 | 0 @ 6.5 / 3.94 @ 9.8 | |
| D4F7-01 | CC | 0 @ 1100 / 28 @ 4800 | 0 @ 14.5 / 3.15 @ 13 | |
| D4F7-02 | CC | 0 @ 1200 / 14 @ 2400 / 22 @ 3900 | 0 @ 12.5 / 3.94 @ 11.8 | 7.5 / 10.8 |
| D4H6-01 | CC | 0 @ 1000 / 28 @ 4800 | 0 @ 10 / 2 @ 11.8 | 0 / 3 |
| D6F4-03 | CC | 0 @ 1200 / 17 @ 2500 | 0 @ 1.5 / 7.8 @ 13.8 | |
| D6F5-02 | CC | 0 @ 1200 / 17 @ 2500 | 0 @ 18 / 5.9 @ 11.6 | |
| D6F5-03 | CC | 0 @ 1200 / 17 @ 2500 | 0 @ 10 / 5.9 @ 9.8 | |
| D6F6-01 | C | 0 @ 1200 / 17 @ 2500 | 0 @ 2.5 / 2.8 @ 9.5 | |

⊙ – C (Clockwise), CC (Counterclockwise), viewed from rotor end.

## HONDA DISTRIBUTOR ADVANCE & RETARD SPECIFICATIONS

*NOTE — FOR DISTRIBUTOR RPM & DEGREES, DIVIDE SPECIFICATIONS BELOW BY 2*

| Distributor Part No. | Rot. ① | Centrifugal Advance (Engine Degrees @ RPM) | Vacuum Advance (Engine Degrees @ In. of Hg) | Vacuum Retard (Engine Degrees @ In. of Hg) |
|---|---|---|---|---|
| D409-66 | CC | 0@950-1200; 5-7@2000; 7-10@2700 | 0@6.5-8.5; 4.3-5.1@7.8-8.9 | ···· |
| D411-B1 | CC | 0@950-1200; 7-8.5@2500; 10-12.5@3400 | 0@6.5-8.5; 5.5-6.3@11.5-12.5 | ···· |
| D411-B2 | CC | 0@1100-1500; 6.5-7.5@3000; 10-12.5@4400 | 0@6.5-7.5; 5.5-6.3@11.5-12.5 | ···· |
| D412-99 | CC | 0@1200; 4@2000; 6@3000; 12@4000; 14@4200 | ···· | 0@2.6; 8@3.9; 11@4.5 |
| D417-67 | CC | 0@1000; 8.7@1900; 11@2500; 14@3500; 15.5@4000 | 0@2.95; 2.6@5; 3.9@9 | ···· |
| D4J6-06 | CC | 0@1200; 6@2000; 10@2500; 14@3000; 16@3400 | 0@11; 5.5@13; 11@14 | 0@2.5; 4@3.5; 7@4; 9@4.5 |
| 30100657-674 | CC | 0@950; 12@1700; 20@2800 | 0@8; 5.8@17; 4.3@7.7 | ···· |
| 30100657-812 | CC | 0@950; 12@1700; 24@3350 | 0@11.6; 4@17; 5.5@7.9 | ···· |
| 30100663-701 | CC | 0@1250; 10@2500; 16@3350 | 0@10; 5.5@9.8; 9.8@12.9 | 0@2.5; 9@4.3 |

① — C (Clockwise), CC (Counterclockwise), viewed from rotor end.

## LUCAS DISTRIBUTOR ADVANCE & RETARD SPECIFICATIONS

*NOTE — FOR DISTRIBUTOR RPM & DEGREES, DIVIDE SPECIFICATIONS BELOW BY 2*

| Distributor Part No. | Rot. ① | Automatic Advance (Distr. Degrees @ RPM) | Vacuum Advance (Distr. Degrees) Operate Distr. @ 1000 RPM | Vacuum Retard (Distr. Degrees) Operate Distr. @ 1000 RPM |
|---|---|---|---|---|
| 45DE4 (Midget) | CC | 1-7@1200; 7-13@1500; 13-17@2600; 15-19@3300 | ···· | 0@3; 10-14@11; 10-14@15 |
| MGB | CC | 13-17@2000; 28-32@3500; 33-37@4500 | 0@3; 22-26@11 | ···· |
| Spitfire | CC | 8-12@1600; 11-15@2600; 12-16@3200; 12-16@5000 | 0@1 | ···· |
| 47DEA, 47DE4 (TR7) | CC | 2-8@1300; 8-12@1900; 13-17@2800; 14-18@5000 | ···· | 0@1; 10-14@15; 10-14@20 |
| 36DE12 (XJS, XJ12) | CC | 22-26@2000; 29-33@4000; 34-38@6200 | 0@6; 4@10 | 0@3; 10-14@11; 10-14@15 |
| 43DE6, 45DE6 (XJ6) ② | CC | ···· | ···· | ···· |

① — C (Clockwise), CC (Counterclockwise), viewed from rotor end.  ② — Specifications not furnished by manufacturer.

# 1978 Distributor Specifications

## MARELLI DISTRIBUTOR ADVANCE & RETARD SPECIFICATIONS

NOTE – FOR DISTRIBUTOR RPM & DEGREES, DIVIDE SPECIFICATIONS BELOW BY 2

| Distributor Part No. | Rot. ☉ | Automatic Advance (Distr. Degrees @ RPM) | | | | | Vacuum Advance (Distr. Degrees) Operate Distr. @ 1000 RPM | Vacuum Retard (Distr. Degrees) Operate Distr. @ 1000 RPM |
|---|---|---|---|---|---|---|---|---|
| S 144 CBY | C | 0 / 1000 | 9 / 1400 | 21 / 2000 | 32 / 3200 | 36 / 3600 | ..... | ..... |
| S 144 M | C | 0 / 1000 | 10 / 1600 | 16 / 2000 | 21 / 3400 | 28 / 5800 | ..... | ..... |

☉ – C (Clockwise), CC (Counterclockwise), viewed from rotor end.

## MAZDA DISTRIBUTOR ADVANCE & RETARD SPECIFICATIONS

NOTE – FOR DISTRIBUTOR RPM & DEGRESS, DIVIDE SPECIFICATIONS BELOW BY 2

| Distributor Part No. | Rot. ☉ | Centrifugal Advance (Engine Degrees @ RPM) | | | | Vacuum Advance (Engine Degrees @ In. of Hg) | | | | Vacuum Retard (Engine Degrees @ In. of Hg) | | | |
|---|---|---|---|---|---|---|---|---|---|---|---|---|---|
| 3879 18200 | C | 0 / 1200 | 12 / 2500 | ..... | 20 / 3900 | 0 / 9 | 2.4 / 11.8 | ..... | ..... | ..... | ..... | ..... | ..... |
| 3958 1820P | C | 0 / 1200 | 10 / 3200 | ..... | 25 / 5500 | 0 / 6 | 8.7 / 15.4 | ..... | ..... | ..... | ..... | ..... | ..... |
| 8028 18200A | C | 0 / 1200 | 10 / 2500 | ..... | 25 / 5500 | 0 / 13 | 4.7 / 13.8 | ..... | ..... | ..... | ..... | ..... | ..... |
| 8761 8200 Leading | C | 0 / 1000 | 11 / 2000 | ..... | 25 / 4000 | 0 / 5 | 4 / 15.7 | ..... | ..... | ..... | ..... | ..... | ..... |
| Trailing | | 0 / 1000 | 11 / 2000 | ..... | 25 / 4000 | 0 / 17.5 | 4 / 15.7 | ..... | ..... | ..... | ..... | ..... | ..... |
| 8826 18200 Leading | C | 0 / 1000 | 10 / 2000 | ..... | 20 / 3000 | 0 / 7.5 | 3.9 / 15.7 | ..... | ..... | ..... | ..... | ..... | ..... |
| Trailing | | 0 / 1000 | 10 / 2000 | ..... | 20 / 3000 | 0 / 15 | 7.9 / 15.7 | ..... | ..... | ..... | ..... | ..... | ..... |
| 8827 18200 Leading | C | 0 / 1000 | 10 / 2000 | ..... | 20 / 3000 | 0 / 7.5 | 3.9 / 15.7 | ..... | ..... | ..... | ..... | ..... | ..... |
| Trailing | | 0 / 1000 | 10 / 2000 | ..... | 20 / 3000 | 0 / 15 | 7.9 / 15.7 | ..... | ..... | ..... | ..... | ..... | ..... |

☉ – C (Clockwise), CC (Counterclockwise), viewed from rotor end.

## MITSUBISHI DISTRIBUTOR ADVANCE & RETARD SPECIFICATIONS

NOTE — FOR DISTRIBUTOR RPM & DEGREES, DIVIDE SPECIFICATIONS BELOW BY 2

| Distributor Part No. | Rot. ⊖ | Centrifugal Advance (Engine Degrees @ RPM) | | Vacuum Advance (Engine Degrees @ In. of Hg) | | Vacuum Retard (Engine Degrees @ In. of Hg) | |
|---|---|---|---|---|---|---|---|
| T3T04581 | C | 0 @ 1200 | 20 @ 6000 | 0 @ 20 | 3.15 @ 14.2 | | |
| T3T04587 | C | 0 @ 1200 | 20 @ 6000 | 23 | 3.15 @ 11 | | |
| T3T04589 | C | 0 @ 1200 | 20 @ 6000 | 0 @ 15 | 5.1 @ 11.8 | | |
| T3T05771 | C | 0 @ 1000 | 20 @ 4400 | 0 @ 23 | 3.15 @ 11 | | |
| T3T05772 | C | 0 @ 1000 | 20 @ 4400 | 0 @ 20 | 2.4 @ 14.2 | | |
| T3T05776 | C | 0 @ 1000 | 20 @ 4400 | 0 @ 28 | 2.4 @ 9.5 | | |
| T3T05775 | C | 0 @ 1000 | 20 @ 4400 | 0 @ 20 | 3.2 @ 14.2 | | |
| T3T04874 | C | 0 @ 1200 | 20 @ 6000 | 0 @ 20 | 3.2 @ 14.2 | 0 @ 10 | 9.1 @ 12.2 |
| T3T04887 | C | 0 @ 1200 | 20 @ 6000 | 0 @ 15 | 5.1 @ 11.8 | 0 @ 10 | 8.1 @ 12.2 |
| T3T07182-3879 | C | | | | | | |
| T3T60772-3877 | C | | | | | | |
| T3T60774-8786 | C | | | | | | |

⊖ — C (Clockwise), CC (Counterclockwise), viewed from rotor end.

## NIPPONDENSO DISTRIBUTOR ADVANCE & RETARD SPECIFICATIONS

NOTE — FOR DISTRIBUTOR RPM & DEGREES, DIVIDE SPECIFICATIONS BELOW BY 2

| Distributor Part No. | Rot. ⊖ | Centrifugal Advance (Engine Degrees @ RPM) | | | Vacuum Advance (Engine Degrees @ In. of Hg) | | | Vacuum Retard (Engine Degrees @ In. of Hg) | |
|---|---|---|---|---|---|---|---|---|---|
| 19100-24180 | C | 0 @ 1000 | 23 @ 3400 | 28 @ 5400 | 0 @ 12 | 4.3 @ 7.9 | 18 / 10.2 | | |
| 19100-26231 | C | 0 @ 1100 | 5.2 @ 1550 | 16 @ 2400 / 24 @ 4200 / 22.6 @ 6000 | 0 @ 13.6 | 6 @ 8.7 | 3.5 @ 18 / 4.7 @ 11.8 | | |

⊖ — C (Clockwise), CC (Counterclockwise), viewed from rotor end.

## NIPPONDENSO DISTRIBUTOR ADVANCE & RETARD SPECIFICATIONS (Cont.)

NOTE – FOR DISTRIBUTOR RPM & DEGREES, DIVIDE SPECIFICATIONS BELOW BY 2

| Distributor Part No. | Rot. ⊖ | Centrifugal Advance (Engine Degrees @ RPM) | | | | | Vacuum Advance (Engine Degrees @ In. of Hg) | | | Vacuum Retard (Engine Degrees @ In. of Hg) | | | |
|---|---|---|---|---|---|---|---|---|---|---|---|---|---|
| 19100-26280 | C | 0/1000 | 4.2/1750 | 12.4/2800 | 20/5400 | 19.6/6000 | 0/8.2 | 20/26 | .... | .... | .... | .... | .... |
| 19100-26290 | C | 0/1000 | 4.2/1750 | 12.4/2800 | 16/4100 | 14.6/6000 | 4.3/6.3 | 10.2/13 | .... | .... | .... | .... | .... |
| 19100-38050 | C | 0/1100 | 9.4/2000 | 14/2800 | 19.2/4400 | 20.2/6000 | 0/7.4 | 18.4/24 | .... | .... | .... | .... | .... |
| 19100-38060 | C | 0/1100 | 9.4/2000 | 14/2800 | 19.2/4400 | 20.2/6000 | 4.3/8.3 | 10.2/13 | .... | .... | .... | .... | .... |
| 19100-38070 | C | 0/1100 | 8.4/2000 | 14/2800 | 19.2/4400 | 20.2/6000 | 0/4 | 17.8/22 | .... | .... | .... | .... | .... |
| 19100-38081 | C | 0/1100 | 9.4/2000 | 14/2800 | 19.2/4400 | 20.2/6000 | 0/3.6 | 23.6/28 | .... | .... | .... | .... | .... |
| 19100-38091 | C | 0/1100 | 9.4/2000 | 14/2800 | 19.2/4400 | 20.2/6000 | 3.9/4.7 | 10.6/15.8 | .... | .... | .... | .... | .... |
| 19100-38150 | C | 0/1100 | 9.4/2000 | 14/2800 | 19.2/4400 | 20.2/6000 | 0/3.6 | 23.6/28 | .... | .... | .... | .... | .... |
| 19100-38180 | C | 0/1100 | 9.4/2000 | 14/2800 | 19.2/4400 | 20.2/6000 | 3.9/4.7 | 10.6/15.8 | .... | .... | .... | .... | .... |
| 19100-45150 | C | 0/1500 | 4.4-8.4/1800 | 8.2-11.2/2400 | 12.4-15.4/4400 | 13.4-17.4/6000 | 0/3.5 | 10-13.8/14-18 | .... | .... | .... | .... | .... |
| 19100-45160 | C | 0/1500 | 4.4-8.4/1800 | 8.2-11.2/2400 | 12.4-15.4/4400 | 13.4-17.4/6000 | 0/8.3 | 9.8-14.6/15 | .... | 0/3.2 | .... | .... | 10/5.5 |
| 19100-61061 | C | 0/1000 | .... | 20/3200 | 20/.... | 17.8/6000 | 0/8.3 | 10.6/15 | .... | .... | .... | .... | .... |
| 19100-61100 | C | 0/1200 | 10/1800 | .... | 20/3800 | 18.4/6000 | 0/3.9 | 10/6.3 | .... | 0/3.2 | .... | .... | 6/5.5 |
| 19100-61110 | C | 0/1200 | 10/1800 | .... | 20/3800 | 18.4/6000 | 0/3.9 | 10/6.3 | .... | .... | .... | .... | .... |
| 029 100 3281 | CC | 0/1250 | 5/1800 | 10/2300 | 20/3500 | 26/4400 | 0/5 | 8/7.1 | 10/8.5 | .... | .... | .... | .... |
| 0291 100 4220 | CC | 0/800 | .... | 10/2000 | 26/4500 | .... | 0/2 | 10/12 | .... | 0/3 | 5/8 | 7/12 | 8/16 |
| 0291 100 4270 | CC | .... | .... | .... | .... | .... | .... | .... | .... | .... | .... | .... | .... |

⊖ – C (Clockwise), CC (Counterclockwise), viewed from rotor end.

## BOSCH SINGLE BREAKER DISTRIBUTOR

Audi
BMW
Volkswagen

### DESCRIPTION

Conventional single breaker distributor with centrifugal advance and vacuum advance and/or retard unit. Vacuum units may be single or dual diaphragm and are linked to the moveable portion of the breaker plate assembly to advance or retard spark.

**NOTE** — *Some distributors may use a dual diaphragm unit to provide retard only (vacuum advance side not used.)*

### SPECIFICATIONS

**Point Gap & Cam Angle** — *See Tune-Up Data on Car Model Tune-Up Pages.*

**Centrifugal & Vacuum Advance (Or Retard)** — *See Specification Tables in this section.*

### ADJUSTMENT

**Point Gap, Alignment, & Cam Angle** — With rubbing block on high point of cam lobe, insert a feeler gauge blade between contacts and check reading against specification. To correct, loosen retaining screw and move stationary contact point until correct gap is obtained, then tighten screw. Align points if necessary by bending stationary contact support only. Check cam angle with a dwell meter; compare indicated reading with specification and correct if necessary.

**Fig. 1    Adjusting Contact Points**

Lock Screw    Slot    Bosses

**Breaker Arm Spring Tension** — To check spring tension, place hook end of spring scale as close as possible to the movable breaker point. Pull scale at a right angle (90 degrees) to the movable arm and note reading just as points begin to open.

**Centrifugal Advance** — 1) Check distributor in test stand according to test equipment manufacturers instructions. Operate distributor both up and down the RPM range and check advance at all RPM settings specified. Adjust or replace springs, weights or cam as necessary.

2) If distributor has adjustable driving collar for centrifugal advance(see *Fig. 2*), disassemble distributor and lift shaft out. (It is not necessary to remove breaker cam assembly from shaft.) To adjust, loosen screws retaining driving collar. If driving collar is turned in direction of rotation, the advance curve rises; turning drive collar in opposite direction of rotation will lower the curve.

**CAUTION** — *Centrifugal advance curve must not be adjusted by bending spring clamps of driving collar.*

Driving Collar

Move in direction of rotation to increase advance curve or against direction of rotation to retard advance curve.

Springs

Centrifugal Advance Adjustment Slot and Screws

**Fig. 2    Centrifugal Advance Adjustment (Driving Collar)**

3) If distributor does not have adjustable driving collar, adjustment may be made by bending spring anchor tabs to modify spring tension (see illustration). To adjust for low speed operation, bend primary spring anchor tab outward to decrease advance, and inward to increase advance. For high speed operation, bend secondary spring anchor tab in or out to obtain specified settings.

Weight Return Springs

Screwdriver

Anchor Tabs

Bend Inward To Increase Advance
Bend Outward To Decrease Advance

**Fig. 3    Centrifugal Advance Adjustment (Spring Anchor Tabs)**

**Vacuum Advance** — 1) With distributor in test stand, check advance at vacuum settings shown in specifications. If tests indicate vacuum diaphragm unit is inoperative, out of calibration, or leaking, replace vacuum unit.

## BOSCH SINGLE BREAKER DISTRIBUTOR (Cont.)

**2)** Most types of vacuum diaphragm units are factory pre-set and cannot be adjusted. However, on some dual diaphragm vacuum units, the vacuum advance may be increased or decreased by turning an Allen screw located in end of diaphragm unit.

**Fig.4    Disassembled View of Bosch Distributor**

**Vacuum Retard — 1)** With distributor in test stand, check retard at vacuum setttings shown in specifications. If tests indicate vacuum diaphragm unit is inoperative, out of calibration, or leaking, replace vacuum unit.

**2)** Most types of vacuum diaphragm units are factory pre-set and cannot be adjusted. However, on some dual diaphragm units, the maximum vacuum retard setting may be raised or lowered if necessary by turning an eccentric, located at side of vacuum unit (see illustration).

**Fig. 5    Adjusting Maximum Vacuum Retard (Eccentric Location)**

## OVERHAUL

**NOTE** — *All parts should be marked or set aside separately or in groups so that same combination can be reinstalled. Keep screws with the component they attach, as screws are different lengths and damage could occur if installed in wrong position.*

**Disassembly — 1)** Disconnect and remove vacuum unit. Remove breaker points and condenser, then remove breaker assembly. Note positioning of centrifugal advance parts and mark for assembly reference. Disconnect and remove centrifugal advance springs (do not distort). Using 2 screwdrivers, carefully pry upward on the lower edge of breaker cam to disengage cam retaining ring. Lift cam, washer, retaining ring and lubricating felt pad from shaft, then remove advance weights.

**2)** Drive out retaining pin, then remove coupling (or gear) from end of distributor shaft. Remove shaft from distributor housing.

**NOTE** — *Before removing coupling (if equipped), note relationship of coupling end, then mark position of coupling on end of shaft for reassembly reference.*

**Reassembly** — Install centrifugal weights and breaker cam on distributor shaft, then install advance springs. Secure breaker cam with washer and retaining ring, then install lubricating felt pad. Install shaft in distributor housing. Complete reassembly by reversing disassembly procedure.

## BOSCH TRANSISTORIZED BREAKERLESS IGNITION SYSTEM

Audi
BMW
Mercedes Benz
Porsche
Saab
Volvo

### DESCRIPTION & OPERATION

Bosch Transistorized Ignition System includes an electronic control module, a breakerless distributor, and a high output coil. Inside the distributor a trigger wheel rotates past a magnetic pick-up coil and stator winding. This builds up and then collapses a magnetic field producing a low voltage electrical signal. This signal passes to the module which controls the dwell angle and at the same time interrupts the ignition primary current to the coil. The interruption of primary current induces the high secondary coil output voltage to the spark plugs. Standard centrifugal and vacuum advance units are used.

### SPECIFICATIONS

**Dwell Angle** — *Controlled by Electronic Control Module. Not adjustable; see Tune-Up Data on Car Model Tune-Up Pages.*

**Centrifugal & Vacuum Advance (and/or Retard)** — *See Specification Tables in this section.*

### TESTING

NOTE — *Use full page diagnosis chart for testing ignition system. Repair or replace components as indicated by chart.*

### ADJUSTMENT

NOTE — *No adjustment is required or possible with this breakerless ignition system other than maintenance of .010" (Min.) air gap between armature rotor and stator. Rotor teeth may be bent to establish proper gap.*

### OVERHAUL

#### DISASSEMBLY

1) Remove distributor cap, rotor and dust cover. Remove vacuum unit screws and lock clasp screws. Remove screws securing electrical leads and remove leads by carefully pulling straight out.

CAUTION — *Keep screws with component they attach, as screws are different lengths and damage could occur if installed in wrong position.*

**Fig. 2  *Removing or Installing Pick-Up, Stator, and Carrier Plate***

**Fig. 1  *Wiring Diagram of Typical Bosch Transistorized Ignition System***

## TESTING BOSCH BREAKERLESS IGNITION

Run starter holding coil high tension lead 3/4" from engine ground

Spark available?
- No → Check for voltage between coil terminal 15 and ground.
  - Voltage at coil terminal 15?
    - No → Check ballast resistor, ignition switch and spark plug wires.
    - Yes → Check for voltage drop across the transistor by connecting voltmeter to coil terminal 1 and ground.
      - Voltmeter reading 0.5-2.0 volts?
        - No → Voltage drop across transistor (Ignition coil terminal 1 and ground) more than 0.5-2.0 volts?
          - No → less than 0.5 volts. Check for open primary circuit in ignition coil by connecting ohmmeter across terminals 1 and 15. Correct value is 1-2 Ohms.
            - Open circuit in ign. coil?
              - No → Replace electronic module.
              - Yes → Replace ignition coil.
          - Yes → Turn ignition on, connect voltmeter across terminals 15 and ground of module.
            - Voltage at terminal 15?
              - No → Repair wire from ballast resistor(s).
              - Yes → Turn ignition on, connect voltmeter across terminals 16 and ground of module.
                - Voltage at terminal 16?
                  - No → Repair wire from ignition coil terminal 1.
                  - Yes → Check for proper grounding of electronic module. Disconnect plug at module and connect voltmeter across plug terminal 31 and ground. Reading should be zero volts.
                    - Is module grounded correctly?
                      - No → Repair ground wire.
                      - Yes → Replace electronic module.
        - Yes → Check magnetic pick-up coil resistance. Connect ohmmeter across terminals 7 and 31d of disconnected module plug. Correct value at 75° F is: 4 Cyl. approx. 1000 Ohms All others approx. 600 Ohms
          - Pick-up coil resistance correct?
            - No → Replace pick-up coil or distributor.
            - Yes → Check for grounded circuit in coil of pick-up by connecting ohmmeter to one of the pick-up terminals and ground. Reading should be infinite.
              - Coil grounded? (Ohmmeter reading not infinite)
                - No → Replace electronic module.
                - Yes → Replace pick-up coil or distributor.
- Yes → Ignition timing correct?
  - No → Adjust ignition timing.
  - Yes → Voltage measured across coil term. 1 and ground should be 0.5-2.0 volts.
    - Voltage Correct?
      - No → Replace electronic module.
      - Yes → Does engine start?
        - No → Check and repair if necessary: spark plugs, rotor, cap, wires and fuel system.
        - Yes → Check dwell angle.
          - Dwell angle correct?
            - No → Replace electronic module.
            - Yes → Correct secondary voltage is 20kV min. measured by tester or holding coil lead 3/4" from ground.
              - Secondary voltage correct?
                - No → Check and repair if necessary: rotor, cap, spark plug wires.
                  - Secondary voltage still below 20kV?
                    - No → System correct.
                    - Yes → Replace ign. coil.
                      - Secondary voltage still below 20 kV?
                        - No → System correct.
                        - Yes → Reinstall original coil. Replace electronic module.
                - Yes → Ignition system is good.

## BOSCH TRANSISTORIZED BREAKERLESS IGNITION SYSTEM (Cont.)

**2)** Remove trigger wheel snap ring and then shims. Remove carrier plate attaching screws. Remove trigger wheel and small lock pin. Remove snap ring and lift carrier plate straight up off shaft. Remove three screws to separate stator winding from carrier plate.

**3)** Disconnect springs to centrifugal governor. Mark drive shaft relation to distributor shaft then secure drive shaft in a soft-jawed vise. Carefully tap on distributor housing using a plastic mallet until circlip releases. If equipped, remove triggering contacts and attaching screws.

**4)** Remove resilient ring then mark location of flange to distributor shaft. Support distributor shaft and using a pin punch, remove pin. Remove flange and distributor shaft. Remove lock springs for centrifugal weights then remove weights.

### REASSEMBLY

**1)** To reassemble distributor, reverse disassembly procedure while noting the following: Place a light coat of grease on weights and breaker cam. Oil distributor shaft before installing shaft in housing. Soak felt lubricator in oil.

**2)** When attaching stator to plate, the connector pins should be positioned opposite and above the attachment ear for carrier plate. Install lock pin with lift facing ridge on distributor shaft. Slot on trigger wheel should be opposite ridge on distributor shaft.

**Fig. 3 Installing Trigger Wheel (Armature) and Lock Pin**

### INSPECTION

Springs for weights must not be deformed or damaged. Holes in centrifugal governor weights must not be oval or deformed. Distributor shaft to cam clearance should not exceed .004" (.1 mm). Distributor shaft to housing clearance should not exceed .008" (.2 mm).

**Fig. 4 Exploded View of Bosch Breakerless Distributor**

## DUCELLIER DISTRIBUTORS

Fiat
128 & X1/9
Renault

**Fig. 1  Adjusting Vacuum Advance
(Renault Shown)**

### DESCRIPTION

Single breaker, fully automatic type distributor. Centrifugal advance is conventional type with weights and springs. Unit may or may not be equipped with vacuum advance device.

### SPECIFICATIONS

**Point Gap, Cam Angle & Breaker Arm Spring Tension** — See Tune-Up Data on Car Model Tune-Up Pages.

**Centrifugal & Vacuum Advance** — See Specification Tables in this section.

### ADJUSTMENT

**Point Gap, Alignment, & Cam Angle** — With rubbing block on high point of cam lobe, insert a feeler gauge blade between contacts and check reading against specification. To correct, loosen retaining screw and move stationary contact point until correct gap is obtained, then tighten screw. Align points if necessary by bending stationary contact support only. Check cam angle using a dwell meter; compare indicated reading with specification and correct if necessary.

**Breaker Arm Spring Tension** — To check spring tension, place hook end of spring scale as close as possible to the movable breaker point. Pull scale at a right angle (90 degrees) to the movable arm and note reading just as points begin to open.

**Centrifugal Advance** — Check distributor in test stand according to test equipment manufacturers instructions. Operate distributor both up and down the RPM range and check advance at all RPM settings specified. If not within specifications, adjust by bending spring anchor tabs to modify tension, or replace springs.

**Vacuum Advance** — With distributor in test stand, check advance at vacuum settings shown in specifications. Adjust if necessary by altering the adjusting cam setting (see illustration). If tests indicate vacuum diaphragm unit is inoperative, out of calibration, or leaking, replace vacuum unit.

### OVERHAUL

**Disassembly** — **NOTE** — *All parts should be marked or set aside separately in groups so that same combination can be reinstalled. Remove rotor, dust cover (if equipped), and condenser. Remove vacuum diaphragm unit (if equipped), then remove breaker plate assembly. Remove pin retaining spring, then remove pin, coupling, and related parts from end of distributor shaft. Remove shaft from distributor housing. Note positioning of cam, springs and weights on distributor shaft, then remove cam attaching screw and remove cam, governor springs and weights.*

**Reassembly** — Reassemble distributor in reverse order of disassembly.

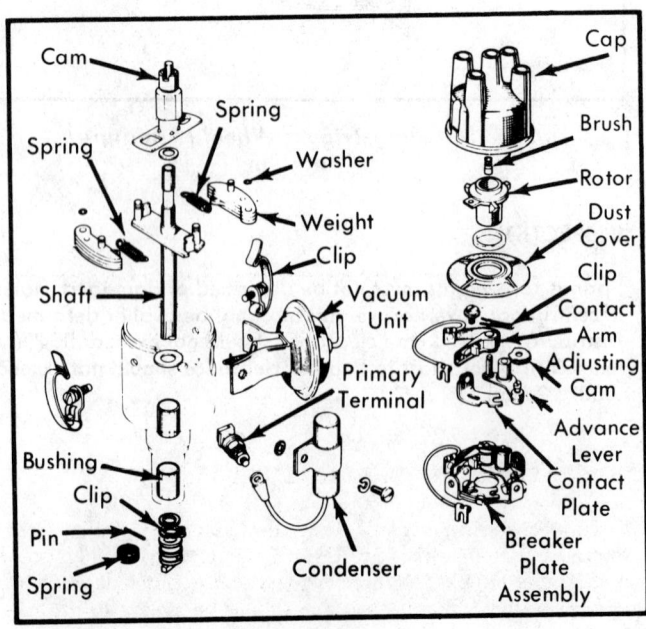

**Fig. 2  Disassembled View of Ducellier Distributor
(Vacuum Advance Version Shown)**

## HITACHI ELECTRONIC IGNITION SYSTEM

**Datsun**
 **All Models**
**Subaru**
 **Calif. with Auto. Trans.**

### DESCRIPTION

Hitachi electronic distributor consists of a housing, rotor, and distributor cap. A reluctor and pickup coil replace the breaker points and cam of a conventional distributor. A transistor ignition unit makes and breaks the electric current in the primary circuit of the ignition coil, with the duty control circuit of this unit setting the rate at which current is broken. This creates what is equal to dwell angle in a conventional distributor.

### SPECIFICATIONS

**Air Gap & Cam Angle** — *See Tune-Up Data on Car Model Tune-Up Pages.*

**Centrifugal & Vacuum Advance** — *See Specification Tables in this section.*

### ADJUSTMENTS

**Air Gap** — Align high point on reluctor with pole piece on pickup coil, then loosen pickup coil screws. Using feeler gauge, move pickup coil to specified air gap and tighten screws.

**Fig. 1   Adjusting the Air Gap**

### TESTING

#### POWER SUPPLY WIRING & BATTERY TEST

Disconnect wiring harness from the transistor ignition unit, then turn ignition switch to "ON". Connect the positive lead of a voltmeter to "BW" wire of harness and negative lead to "B" wire of harness. Battery voltage should be present. If battery voltage is not present, check and correct as necessary the following conditions: Battery cables for proper connection. Charge condition of battery. "BW" and "B" wires for continuity.

**Fig. 2   Checking Power Supply Wiring and Battery**

#### PRIMARY CIRCUIT CONTINUITY TEST

Disconnect wire "L" from ignition unit. Turn ignition switch on. Connect positive lead of voltmeter to wire "L" and negative lead to wire "B". Battery voltage should be indicated, if not proceed as follows:

1) Check wire "L" continuity.
2) Check ignition coil.
3) Check ignition coil for no continuity.

**Fig. 3   Checking Primary Circuit**

#### IGNITION COIL & RESISTOR TEST

Disconnect engine harness from ignition coil external resistor terminals. Connect an ohmmeter to terminals of resistor and note reading. If reading is more than 1.8 ohms, coil requires replacement.

#### PICKUP COIL CONTINUITY CHECK

Disconnect "R" and "G" wires from ignition unit. Connect negative side of ohmmeter to wire "G" and positive lead to wire "R". Reading should be approximately 720 ohms. Reading far below or above 720 ohms indicates need for new pickup assembly.

## HITACHI ELECTRONIC IGNITION SYSTEM (Cont.)

### PICKUP COIL POWER SIGNAL PULSE CHECK

Disconnect electronic fuel injection harness connector (280Z Calif. models) or anti-dieseling solenoid valve connector (all other models). Connect an ohmmeter to wires "R" and "G", then rotate starter motor and note reading. If needle on ohmmeter moves slightly, pickup coil is good. If needle on ohmmeter does not move, replace pickup coil.

### OVERHAUL

**Disassembly** — Remove distributor cap and rotor. Remove screws securing vacuum unit and remove vacuum unit. Remove pickup coil and adjuster plate screws. Remove pin and collar from bottom of distributor shaft. Remove shaft and adjuster plate assembly from housing. Remove rotor shaft set screw then remove rotor shaft with adjuster plate from distributor shaft.

**Reassembly** — Reassemble in reverse order of disassembly procedure. Lubricate all moving parts. Adjust air gap, phase angle, and set timing to specifications.

**Fig. 4  Disassembled View of Distributor**

## HONDA SINGLE BREAKER DISTRIBUTOR

**Honda
All Models**

### DESCRIPTION

Single breaker, fully automatic type of conventional design. Breaker plate assembly consists of a fixed lower plate, with breaker points mounted on movable upper plate. Centrifugal advance is conventional type with weights and springs. Vacuum advance (or retard) is controlled by a vacuum diaphragm unit mounted on distributor housing and linked to the movable portion of the breaker plate assembly.

**NOTE** — *Distributor operation with either vacuum advance or vacuum retard is the same except that on distributors with vacuum retard, the breaker plate rotates in the reverse direction.*

### SPECIFICATIONS

**Point Gap, Cam Angle & Breaker Arm Spring Tension** — *See Tune-Up Data on Car Model Tune-Up Pages.*

**Centrifugal & Vacuum Advance (Or Retard)** — *See Specification Tables in this section.*

### ADJUSTMENT

**Point Gap, Alignment, & Cam Angle** — With rubbing block on high point of cam lobe, insert a feeler gauge blade between contacts and check reading against specification. To correct, loosen retaining screw and move stationary contact point until correct gap is obtained, then tighten screw. Align points if necessary by bending stationary contact support only. Check cam angle using a dwell meter; compare indicated reading with specification and correct if necessary.

**Breaker Arm Spring Tension** — To check spring tension, place hook end of spring scale as close as possible to the movable breaker point. Pull scale at a right angle (90 degrees) to the movable arm and note reading just as points begin to open.

**Fig. 1 Typical Vacuum Advance System**

**Centrifugal Advance** — Check distributor in a test stand according to test equipment manufacturers instructions.

Operate distributor both up and down the RPM range and check advance at all RPM settings specified.

**Vacuum Advance (Or Retard)** — With distributor in test stand, check advance (or retard) at vacuum settings shown in specifications. If tests indicate vacuum diaphragm unit is inoperative, out of calibration, or leaking, replace vacuum unit.

### OVERHAUL

#### DISTRIBUTOR

**Disassembly** — Remove vacuum diaphragm unit. Disconnect lead and remove breaker points. Disconnect primary side terminal and remove breaker plate. Mark position of driven gear (or coupling) on shaft for reassembly reference, then drive out roll pin and remove gear (or coupling) from end of shaft. Remove shaft from distributor housing. Note positioning of cam, springs and weights on distributor shaft, then remove cam attaching screw and remove cam, governor springs and weights.

**Reassembly** — Reverse disassembly procedure and note the following: When reassembling cam, governor weights and springs to shaft, be sure to attach spring with loop end to governor weight, the pin of which is fitted into the longer slot in cam plate. Attach the spring with rectangular hook end to governor weight, the pin of which is fitted into the shorter slot.

**Fig. 2 Disassembled View of Distributor**

## LUCAS "OPUS" ELECTRONIC IGNITION SYSTEM

Jaguar
  All Models
MG
  Midget
  MGB
Triumph
  Spitfire
  TR7

### DESCRIPTION

Lucas "OPUS" (Oscillating Pick-Up System) electronic ignition includes an amplifier unit mounted on distributor on MG, Triumph, and Jaguar XJ6, or externally mounted on XJ12 and XJS; a ballast resistor wire, except on XJ12 and XJS which use a ballast resistor unit; an ignition coil; a drive resistor on MG, Triumph, and XJ6; and a breakerless distributor.

**Distributor —** 1) Consists of a centrifugal advance mechanism, a retard-type vacuum unit, a high-tension rotor, electronic timing rotor, and a pick-up module assembly.

2) The timing rotor and pick-up module, working in conjunction with a separate amplifier unit, replace the contact breaker and cam of a conventional distributor. Timing rotor is a glass-filled nylon disc with small ferrite rods embedded into its outer edge, the number and spacing of rods corresponding with the number of cylinders and firing angles of the engine. An air gap (adjustable to specified limits) exists between rotor and ferrite core of the stationary pick-up module. The pick-up module assembly comprises a magnetically balanced small transformer, with primary (input) and secondary (output) windings. **CAUTION** — *Pick-up module is magnetically balanced during manufacture and setting must not be altered. The sealed ferrite adjusting screw must not be disturbed.*

3) Automatic control of retard-ignition timing is provided by a vacuum unit which varies the static timing position of pick-up module in relation to the ferrite rods in timing rotor. The distributor timing rotor and pick-up module generate an electronic timing signal, which is fed to the amplifier unit via external cables. **CAUTION** — *The length of this triple-core extruded type cable must not be altered, and the cables must not be separated or replaced by loose individual cables.*

**Fig. 2** *Wiring Diagram of Triumph TR7 Lucas "OPUS" Ignition System Spitfire, MG and XJ6 Similar*

**Amplifier Unit —** Interprets timing signals from distributor. A power transistor incorporated in the printed circuit then functions as an electronic switch in primary circuit of ignition coil. Unit is connected to ignition coil via a ballast resistance unit and external cables.

**Drive Resistor —** An externally mounted unit which functions as part of the amplifier. External mounting is required because of size and heat dissipation requirements.

**Ballast Resistor Unit (XJ12, XJS) —** Includes three resistors enclosed in an aluminum heat sink. Two of the resistors are wired in series to coil primary winding and the third resistor functions with a transistor in the amplifier.

**Ballast Resistor Wire (XJ6, MG, Triumph) —** Connected in series between ignition switch and coil primary winding.

**Ignition Coil —** A specially designed fluid-cooled, high-performance, ballast-ignition coil. Coil terminals are marked "+" and "−" and have different types of connectors to prevent incorrect cable connection. **CAUTION** — *The "OPUS" coil is NOT interchangeable with any other type.*

**Fig. 1** *Wiring Diagram of Jaguar XJ12 and XJS Lucas "OPUS" Ignition System*

## LUCAS "OPUS" ELECTRONIC IGNITION SYSTEM (Cont.)

### SPECIFICATIONS

**Pick-Up Module Gap & Cam Angle** — *See Tune-Up Data on Car Model Tune-Up Pages.*

**Centrifugal Advance** — *See Specification Tables in this section.*

**Vacuum Retard** — *See Specification Tables in this section.*

### OPERATION

1) With ignition off and engine stopped, distributor timing rotor will normally be in a position where none of the ferrite rods will be in close proximity with ferrite core of pick-up module. When ignition is switched on, a power transistor in amplifier unit is in a conductive state, and ignition coil primary winding circuit is complete via the emitter/collector electrodes of the power transistor. Simultaneously, a pulsating alternating current voltage is applied by amplifier unit to distributor pick-up module primary windings, and a small residual alternating current voltage is produced at pick-up secondary windings, which at this stage is magnetically balanced. The voltage at pick-up module secondary terminals is applied to amplifier unit, but residual voltage at this stage is insufficient to have any effect on transistor circuits, which control the switching off of the power transistor in the output stage of amplifier unit.

2) When engine is cranked, one of the ferrite rods in the rotor, now brought into close proximity with ferrite core of module causes "magnetic unbalancing" of module core, resulting in an increase in voltage at module output terminals. This "unbalancing" and voltage increases to maximum as rotor rod passes center and upper legs of the module "E" shaped core. Maximum voltage is then applied to amplifier unit, where it is rectified. The resulting direct current is then used to operate the transistor circuits which control switching off of the power transistor in the output stage. With power transistor switched off, its emitter/collector electrodes cease to conduct, and coil primary winding is disconnected which causes a rapid collapse of the primary winding magnetic field through the secondary windings of ignition coil, resulting in a high-tension voltage being produced at ignition coil.

### TESTING

**NOTE** — *It is important that the following tests be made in order outlined below.*

**Battery (Circuit Test)** — Battery should be fully charged. Disconnect lead from coil terminal marked "−", then connect voltmeter between battery ground terminal and frame. Operate starter, voltmeter reading should not exceed 0.5 volts. If higher voltage is registered, correct faulty connection between frame and battery.

**Ignition Coil (Applied Voltage Test)** — 1) Connect voltmeter between coil "+" terminal and ground. With ignition switch ON, voltmeter should read 4-6 volts.

2) If voltmeter reads below 4 volts, check value of ballast resistor. Resistor wire resistance value should be 1.3-1.5 Ohms. Ballast resistor block values should be 7.6-9.2 Ohms (resistor 1), 0.72-0.80 Ohms (resistor 2), and 0.9-1.0 Ohms (resistor 3). Replace resistor wire or resistor if not within specifications.

3) Check battery supply voltage to resistor. If voltmeter reads above 6 volts, remove distributor cap, crank engine until two of the timing rotor sensors are equally spaced on each side of pick-up module core. Recheck voltage.

*Fig. 4   Timing Rotor Rod Location for Applied Voltage Test*

4) Check ignition coil for continuity and resistance of primary winding between "+" and "−" terminals. Replace coil if outside limits of 0.8-1.0 ohms, or if open circuited.

*Fig. 3   Exploded View of Lucas Breakerless Distributor Used on Jaguar XJ12 and XJS*

Cap

High-Tension Rotor

Electronic Timing Rotor

Pick-Up Module

Spring

Pick-Up Arm

Vacuum Retard Unit

Rotor Carrier

Weight

Support

Weight

# Distributors & Ignition Systems

## LUCAS "OPUS" ELECTRONIC IGNITION SYSTEM (Cont.)

**Ignition Coil (Voltage Drop Test)** — Connect voltmeter between "—" terminal of coil and ground. DO NOT disconnect coil wires. Switch on ignition and note meter reading. Replace amplifier unit if above 2 volts.

**Amplifier Unit (Switching Action Test)** — Remove distributor cap, then crank engine until one of the ferrite rods is in line with timing mark on module. Connect voltmeter between "—" terminal of coil and ground. DO NOT disconnect coil wires. Switch on ignition and note meter reading. If below battery voltage (12 volts), test amplifier unit, then test pick-up module.

*Fig. 5 Connections for Testing Amplifier Switching Action*

**Amplifier Unit Test** — Crank engine until two of the ferrite rods in the timing rotor are equally spaced on each side of pick-up module core. Disconnect lead from "SW" terminal of ballast unit. Connect an ammeter (0-20A range) in series with lead and terminal. Switch on ignition, ammeter should read 5-6.5 amperes. Separate connector between distributor and amplifier unit. Connect outside terminals of amplifier plug alternately to center terminal. Ammeter reading should remain unchanged. If reading increases by more than 0.5 ampere, replace amplifier unit.

*Fig. 6 Connections for Amplifier Unit Test*

**Pick-Up Module Test** — 1) Connect one lead of ohmeter to center terminal of pick-up module connector, and other lead alternately to each of the outside terminals.

2) Primary (input) winding resistance, measured between center terminal and outer terminal (red wire) should be 2.5 ohms nominal at 68°F (20°C).

3) Secondary (output) winding resistance, measured between center terminal and outer terminal (black wire), should be 0.9 ohms nominal at 68°F (20°C).

4) If readings shown above are obtained, remove pick-up module and check sealed adjusting screw near bottom leg of "E" shaped core. Replace module assembly if seal is broken.

5) If readings are not as shown above, replace module assembly.

6) On models with drive resistor, check for 9-10 Ohms resistance by testing across drive resistor terminals. Replace drive resistor if not within specifications.

## ADJUSTMENT

**Pick-Up Module Gap & Cam Angle** — Slightly loosen two screws retaining pick-up module to pick-up arm. Using feeler gauges, adjust gap between pick-up module "E" core faces and timing rotor outer edge to .020-.022" (.50-.55 mm) XJ12 and XJS, or .014-.016" (.25-.40 mm) all other models. Tighten pick-up retaining screws and recheck clearance. Check cam angle with a dwell meter.

**Centrifugal Advance** — Check distributor in test stand according to test equipment manufacturers instructions. Operate distributor both up and down the RPM range and check advance at all RPM settings specified.

**Vacuum Retard** — With distributor in test stand, check retard at vacuum settings shown in specifications. If tests indicate vacuum diaphragm unit is inoperative, out of calibration, or leaking, replace vacuum unit.

## OVERHAUL

**Disassembly (Jaguar XJ12 and XJS)** — 1) Remove distributor cap. Crank engine to align No. 1 cylinder mark on timing rotor with mark on pick-up module. Disconnect vacuum hose to retard unit and electrical lead plug. Release three Allen screws (accessible through slots in micro housing) and remove distributor. **CAUTION** - *Do not crank engine with distributor removed.*

2) Remove high-tension rotor, then remove snap ring, wave washer, and electronic timing rotor. Lift vacuum unit operating rod from peg on pick-up arm. Pry cable grommet from distributor housing. Remove pick-up arm bearing spring. Slide pick-up arm sideways to disengage it from bearing, then lift from micro housing while pulling cable through hole. Detach pick-up module.

3) Drive out roll pin and remove vacuum unit from micro housing. Remove three spring loaded screws and lift micro housing from distributor body. Remove felt pad and screw from top of rotor carrier shaft. Remove control springs from retaining posts, lift rotor carrier shaft from distributor shaft, then remove centrifugal weights.

## LUCAS "OPUS" ELECTRONIC IGNITION SYSTEM (Cont.)

Cap

Rotor

Anti-Flash Cover

Magnetic Pick-Up Coil

Snap Ring

Washer

"O" Ring

Timing Rotor

Base Plate

Spring

Shaft

Centrifugal Weights

Retard Unit Pin

Amplifier

Housing

Thrust Washer

"O" Ring

Vacuum Retard Diaphragm

Drive Gear

Pin

*Fig. 7 Exploded View of Lucas Breakerless Distributor Used on MG, MGB, Triumph and Jaguar XJ6*

**Inspection** — Check control springs for correct length. Check pivot holes in centrifugal weights for wear or deformation. Check distributor shaft for excessive play. **NOTE** — *If any part of distributor body assembly is found to be defective, the complete assembly must be replaced.*

**Reassembly** — 1) Lubricate centrifugal advance mechanism with Mobilgrease No. 2 or equivalent, then install weights on pivot posts. Lubricate bore of rotor carrier shaft with clean engine oil, install on distributor shaft, then install retaining screw and felt oil pad. Install control springs.

2) **NOTE** — *Be sure the three Allen screws and plain washers are in place through slots in distributor body base. Install micro housing on distributor body, being sure micro adjustment eccentric peg engages in slot. Tighten micro housing to body using screws, plain washers and springs (tighten screws to just short of coil binding).*

3) Loosely secure pick-up module to pick-up arm. Pass pick-up module connector and cable out through hole in micro housing and install pick-up arm on rotor carrier shaft. Install bearing spring. Engage wide part of cable grommet in hole and pry into position. Place vacuum unit in position and install new roll pin. Connect vacuum operating rod to peg on pick-up arm. Install electronic timing rotor and secure with wave washer and snap ring.

4) Using feeler gauges, adjust gap between pick-up module "E" core faces and timing rotor outer edge to specified clearance. Tighten both pick-up module retaining screws and recheck clearance. Install high-tension rotor.

**Disassembly (Jaguar XJ6, MG, Triumph)** — 1) With distributor removed from engine, remove cap, rotor, anti-flash cover and felt pad. Remove screws and washers from magnetic pick-up coil. Do not remove magnetic pick-up coil at this time. Remove screws securing amplifier module to distributor. Carefully disengage retard link from moving plate pin, then remove the two cover clips.

2) Pull out wire grommet, then remove amplifier module and magnetic pick-up coil (amplifier and coil are connected by wires). Tap out retard unit pin and then remove retard unit. Remove snap ring, washer and "O" ring. Carefully remove timing rotor.

3) Remove screws securing base plate then remove base plate. Remove drive gear pin, drive gear and thrust washer. Make sure shaft is free of burrs, then remove shaft. Remove distance collar and centrifugal weight springs.

**Inspection** — Check control springs for correct length. Check pivot holes in centrifugal weights for wear or deformation. Check distributor shaft for excessive play. **NOTE** — *If any part of distributor body assembly is found to be defective, the complete assembly must be replaced.*

**Reassembly** — To reassemble distributor, reverse disassembly procedure noting the following: Lubricate weight assembly, shaft and moving plate with Rocol "Moly Pad" or equivalent. Make sure retard link is properly attached to moving plate pin. Timing rotor tang must fit into slot on shaft. With distributor assembled and replaced in vehicle, set air gap and ignition timing to specifications.

## MARELLI DISTRIBUTORS

**Fiat 124 & 131**
**Lancia**

### DESCRIPTION

Distributors may be single or dual breaker type. Centrifugal advance is accomplished with conventional weights and springs which may be located either beneath breaker plate, or at top of distributor shaft above cam. On distributor with top mounted centrifugal advance, the rotor also serves as a cover for the advance mechanism. Distributors may or may not be equipped with a vacuum advance device.

**Dual-Breaker** — Each point set operates independently; one set for normal operation, and the other set for cold starting only. The second set provides additional spark advance. A control circuit activates the advance breaker set for cold start operation and then switches ignition circuit to the other breaker set for normal operation.

### SPECIFICATIONS

**Point Gap, Cam Angle & Breaker Arm Spring Tension** — *See Tune-Up Data on Car Model Tune-Up Pages.*

**Centrifugal & Vacuum Advance** — *See Specification Tables in this section.*

**Fig. 1  Distributor Assembly with Centrifugal Advance Under Rotor**

### ADJUSTMENT

**Point Gap, Alignment, & Cam Angle** — With rubbing block on high point of cam lobe, insert a feeler gauge blade between contacts and check reading against specification. To correct, loosen retaining screw and move stationary contact point until correct gap is obtained, then tighten screw. Align points if necessary by bending stationary contact support only. Check cam angle using a dwell meter; compare indicated reading with specification and correct if necessary. If distributor is equipped with dual breaker points, adjust each set separately to obtain the specified dwell.

**Breaker Arm Spring Tension** — To check spring tension, place hook end of spring scale as close as possible to the movable breaker point. Pull scale at a right angle (90 degrees) to the movable arm and note reading just as points begin to open.

**Centrifugal Advance** — Check distributor in test stand according to test equipment manufacturers instructions. Operate distributor both up and down the RPM range and check advance at all RPM settings specified.

**Vacuum Advance** — With distributor in test stand, check advance at vacuum settings shown in specifications. If tests indicate vacuum diaphragm unit is inoperative, out of calibration, or leaking, replace vacuum unit.

**Fig. 2  Distributor Assembly with Centrifugal Advance Below Breaker Plate**

## MITSUBISHI PISTON ENGINE BREAKER TYPE DISTRIBUTOR

Arrow, Colt, Challenger & Sapporo
  All Models
Mazda
  B1800
  GLC (California Only)

### DESCRIPTION

Mitsubishi distributors are fully automatic and of conventional design. Breaker plate assembly consists of a fixed lower plate, with breaker points mounted on movable upper plate. Centrifugal advance is conventional type with weights and springs. Vacuum advance/retard is controlled by a vacuum diaphragm unit mounted on distributor housing and linked to moveable portion of breakerplate assembly.

### SPECIFICATIONS

**Point Gap, Cam Angle & Breaker Arm Spring Tension —**
*See Tune-Up Data on Car Model Tune-Up Pages.*

**Centrifugal & Vacuum Advance —** See *Specification Tables* in this section.

**Vacuum Advance —** With distributor in test stand, check advance at vacuum settings shown in specifications. If tests indicate vacuum diaphragm unit is inoperative, out of calibration, or leaking, replace vacuum unit.

*Fig. 1   Adjusting Point Gap in Mitsubishi Distributor (Colt, Arrow, Challenger, Sapporo; Mazda Similar)*

### ADJUSTMENT

**Point Gap, Alignment, & Cam Angle —** With rubbing block on high point of cam lobe, insert a suitable feeler gauge blade between contacts and check reading against specification. To correct, loosen retaining screws and move stationary contact point until correct gap is obtained, then tighten screws. Align points if necessary by bending stationary contact support only. Check cam angle using a dwell meter; compare indicated reading with specification and correct if necessary.

**Breaker Arm Spring Tension —** To check spring tension, place hook end of spring scale as close as possible to the movable breaker point. Pull scale at a right angle (90 degrees) to the movable arm and note reading just as points begin to open.

**Centrifugal Advance —** Check distributor in test stand according to test equipment manufacturers instructions. Operate distributor both up and down the RPM range and check advance at all RPM settings specified.

**Ignition Timing Adjustment (Exc. Mazda) — 1)** Set point gap (dwell angle). Rotate crankshaft so that No. 1 piston is at top dead center on firing stroke (notch on crankshaft pulley aligned with basic timing mark).

**2)** Loosen distributor mounting nut and rotate distributor to point where breaker contacts just begin to open. Tighten mounting nut.

**3)** Remove rubber plug from distributor vacuum control retard side (dual diaphragm type only). Start engine and set at proper RPM.

**4)** Using a timing light, set timing by rotating distributor. Tighten mounting nut and replace rubber plug on dual diaphragm distributor. (Note that timing retards when plug is replaced.)

**Ignition Timing Adjustment (Mazda) —** Connect timing light to number one cylinder spark plug. Start engine and set idle to specifications. Loosen distributor bolt and rotate distributor until mark on crankshaft aligns with indicator on timing cover. Tighten distributor bolt.

## MITSUBISHI PISTON ENGINE BREAKER TYPE DISTRIBUTOR (Cont.)

### OVERHAUL

**Disassembly** – **1)** With distributor removed from engine, remove rotor, condenser, cam lubricating felt, vacuum diaphragm and breaker plate.

**2)** Mark position of driven gear on distributor shaft for reassembly reference. Drive out retaining pins and remove gear, thrust collar, washers and "O" ring from shaft.

**3)** Remove distributor shaft from housing. Note positioning of cam, springs and weights on shaft for reassembly reference. Remove cam attaching screw, cam, governor springs and weights.

**Reassembly** – Assemble distributor in reverse order of disassembly. Apply small amount of suitable lubricant to distributor cam, breaker arm spindle and vacuum link.

*Fig. 2  Exploded View of Typical Mitsubishi Distributor*

## MITSUBISHI ROTARY ENGINE BREAKER TYPE DISTRIBUTOR

**Mazda**
**All Rotary Engine Models**

### DESCRIPTION

Rotary engines use a 2-contact breaker type distributor. One set of points is used for the leading side and the other for the trailing side. Leading and trailing breaker points are attached to individual moveable breaker plates which are connected to their own vacuum advance units. A 2-level distributor cap and a 2-level rotor are used, one level for the leading side and the other for trailing side. Conventional centrifugal advance with weights and springs is used.

### SPECIFICATIONS

**Point Gap & Cam Angle** — See *Tune-Up Data on Car Model Tune-Up Pages.*

**Centrifugal & Vacuum Advance** — See *Specification Pages in this section.*

*Fig. 2 Two Breaker Distributor Adjustments*

*Fig. 1 Rotor/Distributor Cap Relationship*

### ADJUSTMENT

**Point Gap, Alignment, & Cam Angle** — With rubbing block on high point of cam lobe, insert a feeler gauge blade between contacts and check reading against specifications. To correct, loosen retaining screw and move stationary contact point until correct gap is obtained, then tighten screw. Align points if necessary by bending stationary contact support only. Check cam angle using a dwell meter; compare indicated reading with specification and correct if necessary.

**Breaker Arm Spring Tension** — To check spring tension, place hook end of spring scale as close as possible to the movable breaker point. Pull scale at a right angle to the movable arm and note reading just as points begin to open, reading should be 1.1-1.4 lbs. (.5-.65 kg).

**Centrifugal Advance** — Check distributor in test stand according to test equipment manufacturers' instructions. Operate distributor both up and down the RPM range and check advance at all RPM settings specified.

**Ignition Timing** — 1) Connect timing light to front leading spark plug lead. With engine at specified idle speed (transmission selector in "D" if equipped with auto trans.), check timing with light aimed at timing indicator pin.

2) If leading timing does not line up with pin and mark, loosen distributor lock nut and rotate distributor housing until correct timing is obtained. Tighten distributor lock nut and recheck timing.

3) Connect timing light to trailing front spark plug and check trailing timing. If adjustment is required, loosen mounting screws of trailing vacuum unit. Move unit out to advance, in to retard timing. Tighten mounting screws and recheck trailing timing.

**NOTE** — *Leading timing must be set BEFORE trailing timing. Trailing vacuum unit has a circled "T" marked on chamber housing. Leading mark on pulley is 5°ATDC and trailing mark is 25°ATDC.*

## MITSUBISHI ROTARY ENGINE BREAKER TYPE DISTRIBUTOR (Cont.)

**Fig. 3   Timing Marks**

## OVERHAUL

**Disassembly — 1)** Remove distributor cap and rotor. Disconnect primary wires from leading and trailing contact points, and couplers from condenser leads.

**2)** Remove rubber block with primary wires from housing. Remove clips holding vacuum links to breaker plates. Remove screws attaching vacuum units to housing and take off vacuum units.

**3)** Remove bearing stopper set screws and lift out breaker base plate and bearing assembly. Remove cam attaching screw and lift cam off of shaft.

**4)** Drive lock pin out of driven gear and remove gear and washers. Remove shaft through top of housing. Remove governor weight springs and take off the weights.

**Reassembly —** Reassemble in reverse order of disassembly. When installing in engine, tally marks on distributor housing must line up with pin of driven gear and timing pin must align with leading mark on pulley. Adjust points and timing to specifications.

**Fig. 4   Exploded View of Distributor**

# Distributors & Ignition Systems

## MITSUBISHI TRANSISTORIZED BREAKERLESS IGNITION SYSTEM

**Mazda**
**GLC Federal**

NOTE — *California models use the standard Mitsubishi breaker type distributor.*

### DESCRIPTION

Mitsubishi Transistorized Ignition System includes a breakerless distributor, ignition coil, ignitor (electronic module), ballast resistor, and ignition switch. The distributor utilizes a reluctor (trigger wheel), magnetic pick-up coil, and standard type centrifugal advance weights and vacuum advance units.

### OPERATION

The reluctor, turning with the distributor shaft, passes by the pick-up coil. This makes and breaks a magnetic field which produces a low voltage electrical signal. The ignitor receives this signal and turns on and then turns off the ignition primary current to the coil. This action induces the ignition secondary voltage back to the distributor and on to the spark plugs.

### SPECIFICATIONS

**Air Gap & Cam Angle** — *See Tune-Up Data on Car Model Tune-Up Pages.*

**Centrifugal & Vacuum Advance** — *See Specification Pages in this section.*

*Fig. 1  Ignition Coil & Ignitor Wiring Connections (GLC Federal Breakerless Ignition)*

### ADJUSTMENT

**Cam Angle** — Cam angle (dwell) is automatically set and manual adjustment is not required.

**Reluctor-to-Pick-Up Air Gap** — Check air gap between reluctor teeth and magnetic pick-up coil using a .010-.014" (0.25-0.36mm) flat feeler gauge. If not to specification, loosen retaining screws and move breaker plate to adjust air gap. Recheck to insure that air gap is equal at each reluctor tooth.

### TESTING

CAUTION — *Do not attempt to operate engine with one or more spark plug wires disconnected.*

#### PICK-UP COIL RESISTANCE TEST

Test pick-up coil by connecting ohmmeter across distributor wire harness connector pins. Resistance should be between 670-790 ohms. If not, replace pick-up coil.

#### IGNITION COIL TESTS

**Primary Resistance Test** — Connect ohmmeter between coil positive and negative posts. Resistance should be 1.28 ohms. Replace if not to specification.

**Secondary Resistance Test** — Resistance should be approximately 13,500 ohms. Replace if not to specifications.

NOTE — *Coil must be heated to normal operating temperature before testing.*

#### CENTRIFUGAL & VACUUM ADVANCE TESTS

Check distributor in test stand according to test equipment manufacturers' instructions. Refer to distributor test specifications in this section and check advance at all RPM and vacuum settings specified.

### OVERHAUL

**Disassembly** — 1) With distributor removed from vehicle, remove distributor cap and rotor. Remove screws retaining pick-up coil to breaker plate. Remove pick-up coil and wire harness from distributor.

2) Remove screws retaining vacuum advance unit to distributor housing and remove vacuum unit.

3) Using a pin punch remove lock pin from distributor drive gear. Remove gear and washers from shaft.

4) Remove screws retaining breaker plate to housing. Push shaft with breaker plate out through top of distributor housing.

5) Remove reluctor from distributor shaft after removing reluctor retaining screw. Remove governor weights by removing governor springs.

**Reassembly** — Reassemble distributor in reverse order of disassembly. Adjust reluctor-to-pick-up coil air gap.

# Distributors & Ignition Systems

## MITSUBISHI TRANSISTORIZED BREAKERLESS IGNITION SYSTEM (Cont.)

*Fig. 2   Exploded View of Mitsubishi Distributor.*

## MOTORCRAFT SINGLE BREAKER DISTRIBUTOR

**Courier
1800cc**

### DESCRIPTION

Distributor is of single breaker, fully automatic design. Breaker plate assembly consists of a fixed lower plate, with breaker points mounted on movable upper plate. Centrifugal advance is conventional type with weights and springs. Vacuum advance is controlled by a vacuum diaphragm unit mounted on distributor housing and linked to movable portion of breaker plate assembly.

### SPECIFICATIONS

**Point Gap, Cam Angle & Breaker Arm Spring Tension —** *See Tune-Up Data on Car Model Tune-Up Pages.*

**Centrifugal & Vacuum Advance —** *Information was not available at time of this publication.*

### ADJUSTMENT

**Point Gap, Alignment & Cam Angle —** With rubbing block on high point of cam lobe, insert a feeler gauge blade between contacts and check reading against specification. To correct, loosen retaining screw and move stationary contact point until correct gap is obtained, then tighten screw. Align points if necessary by bending stationary contact support only. Check cam angle using a dwell meter; compare indicated reading with specification and correct if necessary.

**Breaker Arm Spring Tension —** To check spring tension, place hook end of spring scale as close as possible to the movable breaker point. Pull scale at a right angle (90°) to the movable arm and note reading just as points begin to open.

### OVERHAUL

**Disassembly —** 1) Remove terminal cover retainer and cover, rotor and condenser. Remove breaker points and primary terminal block. Remove "C" clip securing vacuum advance diaphragm link to breaker plate. Remove cam attaching screw, vacuum diaphragm attaching screws and reinforcing plate.

**2)** Remove distributor cap clamps. Disconnect link from breaker plate and remove diaphragm. Lift breaker plate and subplate from housing. Remove cam, unhook springs from weights and remove weights and springs.

**Reassembly —** Reverse disassembly procedure and lubricate all pivot pins, shafts, cam, and lubricating wick with suitable lubricant.

*Fig. 1   Exploded View of Motorcraft Single Breaker Point Distributor*

## MOTORCRAFT SOLID STATE IGNITION

Capri
Fiesta

### DESCRIPTION & OPERATION

Motorcraft Solid State Ignition used on Capri and Fiesta utilizes a Bosch built breakerless distributor and Motorcraft electronic control module and coil. When ignition switch is on, primary circuit is on and coil is energized. As distributor shaft rotates, the distributor generates signals causing module to break the primary current and induce secondary voltage in coil. A timing circuit in module turns primary circuit on again to energize coil for next spark cycle. Dwell varies with engine speed and cannot be altered, so measurement and adjustment is not required.

**Electronic Module** — Module contains seven color coded wires as shown in *Fig. 2*. Module receives power from ignition switch through Red wire while engine is running and through White wire while engine is cranking. Orange and Purple wires transmit signals from distributor while Green wire receives primary ignition current from coil which is then transmitted to ground at distributor through Black wire. System protection is provided through Blue wire, which is a fusible link. The electronic module cannot be repaired.

**Distributor** — The Solid State distributor is similar in appearance to conventional distributors with the following differences: The cam and advance plate assembly has been replaced by a sleeve and advance plate assembly. The spring loaded upper and lower breaker plate assembly is replaced by a base plate mounted to base casting and fitted with a magnetic pickup assembly secured by a retaining ring. The breaker cam is replaced by an armature with poles and secured to sleeve and plate assembly. Movement of these poles passing by core of magnetic pickup assembly signals module to turn primary current off. Diaphragm assembly has a different rod. The shaft gear, weights, springs, cap and rotor have not been changed.

**Coil** — Coil is oil filled and can easily be identified by tower terminals which are labelled "BAT" (battery) and "DEC" (distributor electronic control). Solid state system coil and standard coils cannot be interchanged.

**System Protection** — System is protected against electrical currents produced or used by any vehicle component during normal operation. **NOTE** — *Damage to ignition system can occur if proper testing procedures are not followed.*

**Fig. 1   Electronic Control Module**

### TESTING

**CAUTION** — *Do not use volt-amp test procedure or any test equipment that utilizes a knife switch on battery terminal. Only test procedures as outlined in this section are to be used.*

If the ignition system is suspected of a malfunction, inspect for loose connections and tighten as necessary, then check secondary ignition circuit as follows:

**1)** Remove coil high tension lead from distributor cap and turn ignition switch on. Hold high tension lead 3/16" from a good ground and crank engine. If spark is good then trouble is in secondary circuit.

**2)** If no spark is observed, ensure that high tension lead is good. If high tension lead is good, disconnect the 3-way and 4-way connectors at electronic module and test (see test procedure tables) system at harness connectors. **NOTE** — *Do not make tests at module terminals. If all of the following tests comply with specifications, replace electronic module with a*

**Fig. 2   Schematic of Breakerless Ignition System**

## MOTORCRAFT SOLID STATE IGNITION (Cont.)

new module and test to see if there is spark. If there is spark with new module and not with old module, replace old module.

**NOTE** — *When testing module operation, it is not necessary to remove old module. Just unplug old module and plug in new module. New module does not require mounting to function.*

### MODULE BIAS TEST

With key on, measure voltage at pin #4 (Red wire) to engine ground. If observed voltage is less than battery voltage, repair voltage feed wire (Red wire) to the module.

### BATTERY SOURCE TEST

Without disconnecting coil, connect voltmeter between coil BAT terminal and engine ground. Connect a jumper wire from coil DEC terminal to a good ground. Turn all lights and accessories off and ignition on. A voltmeter reading between 4.9 and 7.9 volts indicates primary circuit from battery to coil is satisfactory. If reading is less than 4.9 volts, inspect primary wiring and resistance wire for worn insulation, broken strands and loose or corroded terminals. If reading is greater than 7.9 volts, check and replace resistance wire as necessary.

Pin # 6 (Blue Wire)
Pin # 3 (Orange Wire)
Pin # 1 (Green Wire)
Pin # 5 (White Wire)
Pin # 4 (Red Wire)
Pin # 8 (Black Wire)
Pin # 7 (Purple Wire)

**Fig. 3   Harness Connector Pins**

### CRANKING TEST

With engine cranking, measure voltage from pin #5 to engine ground. If voltage is not between 8 and 12 volts, repair voltage feed wire (White wire) to the module.

### STARTING CIRCUIT TEST

If reading is not over 6 volts, the ignition by-pass circuit is open or grounded from either the starter solenoid or the ignition switch to pin #5. Check primary connections at coil.

### DISTRIBUTOR HARDWARE TEST

Disconnect distributor 3-way pigtail. With voltmeter on 2.5 volts scale and connected between pin #3 and pin #7 and engine cranking, meter needle should oscillate. If meter does not oscillate, remove distributor cap and check for visual damage or incorrect assembly. Armature must be tight on sleeve and roll pin, aligning armature, in position. Iron stator must not be broken and armature must rotate when engine is cranking. If internal components are all good and voltmeter still will not oscillate, replace magnetic pickup (stator assembly).

### MAGNETIC PICKUP (STATOR ASSEMBLY) TEST

With key off, there should be no continuity between pin #3 and pin #7. Check resistance between pin #8 and engine ground to read zero ohms. Check resistance between pin #3 and engine ground; then, between pin #7 and engine ground. Both readings should be more than 70,000 ohms. If it fails any of the tests , the distributor magnetic pickup is inoperative and must be replaced.

### IGNITION COIL TEST

With key off, check secondary resistance between pin #4 and coil tower to be 7,000 to 13,000 ohms. Check primary resistance between pin #1 and pin #6 to be 1.0-2.0 ohms. If coil is within limits but the coil is still suspected, test coil on a standard coil tester. If reading differs from the original test, check for a defective harness.

### SHORT TEST

If resistance between pin #1 and engine ground is less than 4.0 ohms, check for a short to ground at coil "DEC" terminal or in primary wiring (Green wire) to coil.

### PRIMARY RESISTANCE WIRE TEST

Resistance between pin #4 and pin #6 should be 1-2 ohms. If not within limits, replace ignition resistance wire.

## OVERHAUL

**NOTE** — *Overhaul of the Bosch distributor is not recommended by the manufacturer. With the exception of the rotor and cap, if components of the distributor are found defective or damaged, the distributor must be replaced.*

## MOTORCRAFT SOLID STATE IGNITION

**Courier
2300cc**

### DESCRIPTION

Courier Solid State Ignition consists of an electronic control module, coil, and distributor. When ignition switch is on, primary circuit is on and coil is energized. As distributor shaft rotates the distributor generates signals causing module to break the primary current and induce secondary voltage in coil. A timing circuit in module turns primary circuit on again to energize coil for next spark cycle. The dwell varies with engine speed and can not be altered, so measurement and adjustment is not required.

*Fig. 1  Wiring Diagram of Module Test for
2300 cc Courier*

### TESTING

**NOTE** — *Insure that battery is fully charged and in good condition before making any tests.*

#### HIGH VOLTAGE SPARK TEST

**1)** Connect a remote starter switch in starting circuit and remove high tension wire from center of distributor cap.

**2)** Turn on ignition switch and hold the high tension lead 0.2-0.4 inch from a good ground. Crank engine, if no spark or a weak spark, perform following tests:

#### CONNECTORS AND WIRES

Inspect all connectors, wires and related equipment.

#### COIL RESISTANCE

Turn ignition switch to "OFF" position, check the resistance of primary and secondary coil circuits. Primary circuit should be $0.9\pm0.09$ ohms and secondary $8.0\pm1.2$K ohms. If not within specifications, replace coil.

#### ARMATURE GAP

Insure that a tooth of the armature is lined up with the magnetic pickup. Use a feeler gauge to check gap which should be $0.016\pm0.008$ inch. If gap is not within specifications, replace the distributor.

**NOTE** — *No adjustments are to be made to ignition system except initial ignition timing and spark plug gap.*

### REMOVAL & INSTALLATION

#### DISTRIBUTOR

**Removal** — **1)** Remove distributor cap, rubber cap from timing chain cover and vacuum hose from distributor vacuum.

**2)** Scribe marks between distributor body and cylinder block, and on distributor body indicating position of rotor. Scribe mark showing position of cam gear to cam gear indicator. (Primarily used for installation.)

**3)** Disconnect wiring, remove lock plate bolt, then pull distributor from cylinder block.

**NOTE** — *Do not crank engine after distributor has been removed.*

**Installation** — **1)** If engine has been cranked, turn crankshaft where number one piston is coming up on compression stroke. The mark on the cam gear should be in line with the cam gear indicator. The TDC mark on crankshaft pulley in line with pointer on timing chain cover.

**2)** If engine has not been cranked, install distributor reversing removal procedure.

## NIPPONDENSO BREAKER TYPE DISTRIBUTORS

LUV
Opel
Subaru
  Federal

### DESCRIPTION

Single breaker, fully automatic type of conventional design. Breaker points are mounted on movable portion of breaker plate assembly. Centrifugal advance is conventional type with weights and springs. Vacuum advance (or retard) is controlled by a vacuum diaphragm unit mounted on distributor housing and linked to movable portion of breaker plate assembly.

### SPECIFICATIONS

**Point Gap, Cam Angle & Breaker Arm Spring Tension** — *See Tune-Up Data on Car Model Tune-Up Pages.*

**Centrifugal & Vacuum Advance (Or Retard)** — *See Specification Tables in this section.*

### ADJUSTMENT

**Point Gap, Alignment, & Cam Angle** — With rubbing block on high point of cam lobe, insert a feeler gauge blade between contacts and check reading against specification. To correct, loosen retaining screws and move stationary contact point until correct gap is obtained, then tighten screws. Align points if necessary by bending stationary contact support only. Check cam angle using a dwell meter; compare indicated reading with specification and correct if necessary.

**Breaker Arm Spring Tension** — To check spring tension, place hook end of spring scale as close as possible to the movable breaker point. Pull scale at a right angle (90 degrees) to the movable arm and note reading just as points begin to open.

**Centrifugal Advance** — Check distributor in test stand according to test equipment manufacturers instructions. Operate distributor both up and down the RPM range and check advance at all RPM settings specified.

**Vacuum Advance (Or Retard)** — With distributor in test stand, check advance (or retard) at vacuum settings shown in specifications. If tests indicate vacuum diaphragm unit is inoperative, out of calibration, or leaking, replace vacuum unit.

### OVERHAUL

**Disassembly** — 1) Remove rotor, dust cover, and breaker point assembly. Remove vacuum advance unit retaining screw and adjuster cap, then disconnect unit from breaker plate and remove. If necessary, remove terminal insulator and attaching hardware, noting sequence for reassembly reference. Remove

cap hold-down springs if necessary, noting difference in springs and location of each.

**NOTE** — *Record the quantity, type, sequence, and thickness of washers in use at each location during disassembly.*

2) Remove breaker plate assembly. Note positioning of cam, springs and weights on distributor shaft, then remove attaching screw, cam, governor springs and weights. Mark position of driven gear on shaft for reassembly reference. Remove retaining pin(s), then remove gear, and spacing collar if so equipped, from end of shaft. Remove shaft from distributor housing.

**Reassembly** — Reassemble distributor in reverse order of disassembly.

*Fig. 1 Disassembled View of Breaker Type Distributor*

## NIPPONDENSO TRANSISTORIZED IGNITION SYSTEM

**Subaru**
  Calif. with Manual Transmission
**Toyota**
  All Models

### DESCRIPTION

Nippondenso Transistorized Ignition System includes a breakerless distributor, special ignition coil, ignition signal generating mechanism and ignition switch. Distributor consists of timing rotor, a magnet and pick up coil.

**Fig. 1   Wiring Diagram of Nippondenso Transistorized Ignition System**

**Fig. 2   Low Voltage (Firing Position) of Signal Rotor**

### OPERATION

1) The distributor pick up unit consists of a signal rotor and signal generator. As the air gap changes, the amount of flux varies which determines the amount of voltage produced across the signal generator pick up coil terminals.

2) When signal rotor lobe is not lined up with pick up coil, pick up coil generated voltage will be high resulting in restricted current flow from battery.

3) When rotor turns and a tooth passes pick up coil, *Fig. 2*, generated voltage drops to zero and allows battery current flow to pick up coil. High voltage is induced in secondary coil and spark is released to spark plug.

4) The ignitor is the ignition sensing unit. It senses the distributor ignition signal, determines ignition timing and ignition coil current passage time.

### ADJUSTMENT

**Timing Rotor-to-Pick Up Coil Projection** — Using a flat feeler gauge check air gap. Air gap should be .008-.016" (0.2-0.4 mm). If not, loosen screws and adjust to specification.

### TESTING

**CAUTION** — *Insure all wire connections are correct as reverse battery polarity within the system will damage ignitor. Do not disconnect battery while engine is running or transistors may be damaged. Do not allow water to enter ignitor. If a tachometer is connected to system, connect tachometer positive lead to coil negative terminal.*

#### IGNITION COIL TESTS

**NOTE** — *All tests are made with an ohmmeter and if the resistance for any test is not within specification, replace coil.*

**Primary Coil Resistance** — Between terminal c and e, 1.35 to 1.65 ohms.

**Secondary Coil Resistance** — Between terminal c and d, 12,-800 to 15,200 ohms.

**Resistor Resistance** — Between terminal a and b, 1.3 to 1.7 ohms.

**Insulation Resistance** — Between terminal c and f, infinity.

**Fig. 3   Ignition Coil Test Points**

## NIPPONDENSO TRANSISTORIZED IGNITION SYSTEM

### SIGNAL GENERATOR TEST

Check resistance across signal generator terminals with an ohmmeter. Resistance should be 130 to 190 ohms.

### IGNITOR TEST

**No Load Voltage Test — 1)** Turn ignition switch to "ON" position.

**2)** Check voltage between ignition coil negative (—) terminal and resistor terminal using a voltmeter. Voltage should be 12 volts.

**Voltage Test with Load — 1)** Disconnect wiring connector from distributor.

**2)** Use a 1 to 10 ohm range ohmmeter to provide resistance to the two terminals of the ignitor as illustrated.

**CAUTION** — *Do not intermix positive (+) and negative (—) terminals of the ohmmeter.*

**3)** Turn ignition switch to "ON" position.

**4)** Check voltage between ignition coil negative (—) terminal and resistor terminal using a voltmeter. Voltage should be nearly zero.

### OVERHAUL

**Disassembly — 1)** With distributor removed from vehicle, remove distributor cap, rotor and dust cover. Remove signal generator, breaker plate, wire connector and vacuum advancer from distributor.

**2)** Grind shank of gear removing flare from head of pin. Using a pin punch, drive out pin and remove gear from shaft.

**3)** Loosen two screws on bottom side of distributor housing and carefully remove shaft using a plastic hammer for tapping to prevent damage.

**4)** Remove governor spring, loosen screw at end of governor shaft and remove signal rotor from distributor. Remove governor snap ring and weight.

**Reassembly —** Reassemble distributor in reverse order of disassembly. Adjust timing-to-pick up coil projection air gap.

***Fig. 4 Exploded View of Nippondenso Fully Transistorized Distributor***

# Alternators & Regulators

## GENERAL SERVICING

### TESTING

In order to properly diagnose charging system performance, the following conditions and precautions should be observed:

**Battery Voltage** — Battery must be fully charged before conducting alternator test. Charge or replace battery as necessary.

**Battery Charging** — Both battery cables should be disconnected if using a Quick Charger in order to prevent damage to alternator and regulator components.

**Battery Boost (For Engine Start)** — Do NOT use a Quick Charger to provide starting voltage. Booster battery must be connected with negative lead to negative terminal of vehicle battery and positive lead to positive terminal of battery.

**On Car Testing** — Perform tests at normal operating temperatures. Engine should be accelerated gradually to desired testing RPM and returned to lower RPM as soon as possible. Do NOT race engine.

**CAUTION** — *Never disconnect battery or alternator leads while alternator is running. Reverse polarity or excessive voltage will severely damage the charging system.*

**Electrical Connections** — All electrical connections must be clean and snug for proper system operation. It is recommended that battery cables be disconnected, cleaned and tightened whenever performing charging system maintenance. Regulator must be properly grounded also.

**Component Replacement** — In order to prevent stray voltage or shorts, always disconnect battery prior to alternator or regulator removal.

**Drive Belt** — Drive belts must not be cracked, glazed or oily, and must be set at proper tension. A glazed belt may slip even though belt is not loose.

**NOTE** — *Excessive drive belt tension can cause bearing or case failure. Do NOT overtighten to correct for slippage.*

**Disassembly** — Case halves and stator should be scribed prior to separation for proper orientation when reassembling.

**Diode Test and Replacement** — Never use a high voltage source to test diodes. Use a low voltage source to check for one-way current flow. If replacement is required, soldering operations must be performed quickly to prevent diode damage. Diode lead should be pinched with pliers to prevent heat transfer to diode.

**Rotor and Stator Testing** — Continuity with minimum resistance should be noted between slip rings. No continuity should exist between either slip ring and rotor core or shaft. Stator conduction is normal when there is continuity between leads of stator coil but NOT between stator coil leads and stator core.

*Fig. 1    Rotor Coil Continuity Test*

*Fig. 3    Rotor Coil Ground Test*

*Fig. 2    Stator Coil Continuity Test*

*Fig. 4    Stator Coil Ground Test*

## GENERAL SERVICING (Cont.)

### CHARGING SYSTEM TROUBLE SHOOTING

| CONDITION | POSSIBLE CAUSE | CORRECTION |
|---|---|---|
| ▶ No output | 1) Sticking brushes.<br>2) Dirty brushes and slip rings.<br>3) Loose or dirty connections.<br>4) Broken leads.<br>5) Open stator winding.<br>6) Open rotor winding.<br>7) Open diodes.<br>8) Shorted rotor.<br>9) Shorted stator.<br>10) Grounded terminal.<br>11) Broken fan belt.<br>12) Blown fuse or defective contact. | 1) Replace brushes and springs.<br>2) Clean.<br>3) Clean and tighten.<br>4) Replace.<br>5) Repair or replace stator.<br>6) Replace rotor.<br>7) Replace diodes.<br>8) Replace rotor.<br>9) Replace or repair stator.<br>10) Replace insulator.<br>11) Replace belt.<br>12) Replace or repair. |
| ▶ Excessive output | 1) Broken neutral wire.<br>2) Defective voltage regulator.<br>3) Poor ground of alternator and regulator terminals.<br>4) Broken ground wire. | 1) Replace wire.<br>2) Check and repair or replace.<br>3) Clean and tighten mountings and terminals.<br>4) Replace wire. |
| ▶ Low output. | 1) Loose or worn fan belt.<br>2) Sticking brushes.<br><br>3) Low brush spring tension.<br>4) Defctive regulator.<br>5) Dirty slip rings.<br>6) Partial short, ground, or open in stator winding.<br>7) Partial short, ground or open in rotor winding.<br>8) Open diode. | 1) Adjust or replace belt.<br>2) Correct or replace brushes and/or springs.<br>3) Replace springs.<br>4) Adjust or replace.<br>5) Clean.<br>6) Replace stator.<br><br>7) Replace rotor.<br><br>8) Replace diode. |
| ▶ Noisy alternator | 1) Loose mounting.<br>2) Loose drive pulley.<br>3) Defective alternator bearing.<br>4) Brushes improperly seated. | 1) Tighten mounting bolts.<br>3) Tighten pulley.<br>3) Replace bearing.<br>4) Seat brushes correctly. |

# Alternators & Regulators

## BOSCH ALTERNATORS

Audi
BMW
Capri
Fiat
Fiesta
Lancia
Mercedes-Benz
Porsche
Saab
Volkswagen
Volvo

## DESCRIPTION

Bosch alternators are conventional 3 phase, self rectifying type alternators. Nine rectifier diodes are connected to stator windings (3 to each phase lead). Diodes change alternator A.C. voltages to D.C. voltages coming out of the "B+" and the "D+" terminals of the alternator.

## APPLICATION

| Model | Volts/Amps | Bosch Part No.① |
|---|---|---|
| Audi | | |
| Fox | 14/55 | 489 520 |
| 5000 | 14/55 | 489 659, 489 660 |
| All With A/C | 14/65 | 469 613, 469 614 |
| BMW | | |
| 320i | 14/55 | 489 648 |
| 530i | | |
| Early | 14/55 | 489 650 |
| Late | 14/65 | 489 619 |
| 633CSi, 733CSi | 14/65 | 489 619 |
| Capri | | |
| 4 Cyl. | 14/35 | 489 665 |
| | 14/45 | 489 669 |
| | 14/55 | 489 671 |
| V6 | 14/45 | 489 590 |
| | 14/55 | 489 595 |
| | 14/65 | 489 615 |
| Fiat (All) | 14/55 | 489 642 |
| | | 489 743 |
| Fiesta | 14/55 | 489 667 |
| Lancia | 14/55 | 489 541 |
| Mercedes-Benz | | |
| 230 | 14/55 | 489 556 |
| 280CE | 14/55 | 489 527 |
| | 14/35 | 489 751 |
| 280E, 280SE | 14/55 | 489 526 |
| | | 489 751 |
| 450 | 14/55 | 489 556 |
| | 14/75 | 469 501 |
| 6.9 | 14/75 | 469 500 |
| 240D | 14/55 | 489 556 |
| 300D, 300CD | 14/55 | 489 527 |
| 300SD | 14/35 | 489 683 |
| Porsche 924 | 14/75 | 469 503 |
| Saab | | |
| 99 | 14/55 | 400 922 |
| Turbo | 14/65 | 489 709 |
| Volkswagen | | |
| Type 2 | 14/70 | 450 001 |

## APPLICATION (Cont.)

| Model | Volts/Amps | Bosch Part No.① |
|---|---|---|
| Dasher | 14/55 | 489 622 |
| Rabbit/Scirocco | 14/55 | 489 622 |
| With A/C | 14/65 | 489 714 |
| Rabbit Diesel | 14/35 | 489 745 |
| | 14/55 | 489 747 |
| | 14/65 | 489 712 |
| Volvo 4 Cyl. | 14/55 | 400 913, 400 933 |

① — Bosch part numbers are preceded by 0 120 for alternators. Integral regulator models are numbered 469 and 489, while separate regulator models are numbered 400 and 450.

## SPECIFICATIONS

**Field Coil Resistance** — Measured at slip rings, resistance should be 3.4-3.74 ohms for Capri, 4.0-4.4 ohms for other models.

**Stator Windings Resistance** — Measure resistance between phase output terminals. Capri with air conditioning and Fiesta should indicate .14-.16 ohms, Capri without air conditioning should indicate .25-.28 ohms, and remaining models should indicate .2 to .22 ohms.

NOTE — See APPLICATION for rated outputs.

## ON VEHICLE TESTING

NOTE — Off vehicle testing is explained as part of Overhaul procedure in this article.

### WIRING CONTINUITY TEST
Disconnect terminal plug from rear of alternator and connect a voltmeter negative terminal to ground. With ignition "ON", connect positive lead to each of the connector wires, in turn. Voltmeter should read battery voltage as each positive connection is made. If proper voltage is not read, trace each wire to find fault.

### VOLTAGE DROP TEST — GROUND SIDE
Connect voltmeter between negative terminal of battery and alternator housing. Start engine and run at approximately 3000 RPM. If voltmeter reading exceeds .25 Volts, a high resistance in negative side of charging circuit is indicated. If so, check for loose, dirty, or corroded connections.

### OUTPUT TEST
Disconnect terminal plug from rear of alternator and connect ammeter, in series, between alternator center terminal and corresponding socket in terminal plug. Also connect a jumper lead between the "D+" terminal and its corresponding socket in terminal plug. Start engine and run at approximately 3000 RPM. Turn on headlights and leave on for five minutes. Ammeter should read maximum alternator amperage at normal operating temperature.

### REGULATOR CONTROL VOLTAGE TEST

Connect voltmeter between battery terminals. Connect ammeter in series between "B+" terminal of alternator and corresponding terminal of connector plug. Connect a jumper

## BOSCH ALTERNATORS (Cont.)

*Fig. 1   Disassembled View of Bosch Alternator*

lead between alternator "D+" terminal and corresponding terminal of connector plug. Start engine and increase speed to approximately 3000 RPM. Run engine until charging rate falls below 3-5 amps. Voltmeter should then read 13.7-14.4 volts. If these readings are not obtained, replace regulator.

NOTE — *Test cables should not be removed or load excessively reduced during testing procedure. Considerable load variations may damage the diodes. Control lamp should not go on at any time during the test.*

## OVERHAUL

### DISASSEMBLY

NOTE — *On 0 120 400 600 series alternators, lift carbon brushes with a hook and secure them, prior to disassembly (see illustration).*

1) Remove nut, pulley, hub and key. Mark location of alternator in blower housing. Unscrew brush plate assembly and remove from alternator. Remove bolts from end frame, then remove frame and field rotor. Press rotor out of end frame. Press ball bearing off rotor. Remove insulating conduit from wires and cut wires as close to soldered joints as possible.

2) The diodes may be tested at this point, prior to further disassembly. Care should be exercised with insulating bushings under positive diode carrier. To remove negative carrier, extract threaded studs. When one rectifying diode has been damaged due to short circuiting, the three complementing diodes must be replaced also. Unscrew nuts on both "B+" terminal bolts and lift positive diode carrier (heat sink) up and back.

*Fig. 2   Lifting Carbon Brushes on 0120 400 600 Series*

### TESTING & REPAIRING

**Diode Assemblies** — Test diodes with a suitable alternator tester (EFAW 192) before dismantling slip ring end frame further. CAUTION — *Do not lay positive diode carrier on housing or false reading will be obtained.* Disconnect conductor from "D+" to the exciter diodes at the exciter diodes heat sink. Unscrew spring and brush holder and remove from alternator. Unsolder stator lead and negative diode connections. Unscrew exciter diodes heat sink and remove together with positive diodes heat sink.

NOTE — *Before further testing, lightly clean all components in gasoline or trichlorethylene, but do not soak.*

**Stator** — Test stator for short circuits to ground, using suitable tester (EFAW 84). Test voltage should be 40V AC. Measure resistance of stator windings between phase connections. *See Specifications for proper value.*

**Rotor** — 1) Test claw pole rotor for short circuits to ground. Test voltage should be 40V AC. Measure resistance of exciter

## BOSCH ALTERNATORS (Cont.)

(field coil) in rotor with ohmmeter. *See Specifications for proper value.* Turn down slip rings on a lathe, using suitable tailstock chuck (EFAW 75 or GDF 85 R 3).

**2)** After turning, check concentricity of slip rings with dial gauge. Runout should not exceed .001″ (.03 mm). Minimum diameter of slip rings may be 1.25″ (31.5 mm). Maximum runout of pole wheel must not exceed .002″ (.05 mm).

**Diode Replacement** — In case diodes are found to be defective, replacement of entire diode plate assembly is recommended. Care must be exercised in soldering near diodes due to possible damage from excess heat. Use flat-jawed pliers as heat sink applied to leads when soldering diode connections.

**Drive End Frame** — Check ball bearings for wear and replace as necessary. Lubricate bearings on one side. Press ball bearing into drive end frame with shielded side downward. Screw on retainer plate. Press ball bearing onto rotor (slip ring end), then press drive end frame onto rotor.

**Carbon Brushes** — Minimum brush length is .2″ (5 mm). If replacement is required, grip brush lead with flat-jawed pliers and unsolder brushes. Do not allow solder to run into strands of brush leads. Brush must be free to slide in holder with normal spring tension of 10-14 ozs.

**REASSEMBLY**

**1)** Solder stator and diode connections using caution not to overheat diodes. Place stator and diode assembly in rear housing and secure with screws.

**2)** Lubricate new rear bearing and press onto rotor shaft, assuring that shielded side of bearing faces slip rings. Place front bearing in housing with shielded side rearward. Install retainer plate.

**3)** Place spacer ring on rotor shaft and install rotor assembly into front housing. Press front bearing retaining ring over shaft and into front housing with a socket.

**4)** Coat bearing bore of rear housing with grease and install spring washer. Assemble front housing with rotor to rear housing, using a turning or twisting motion to seat rear bearing. Line up scribed alignment marks and install screws through housing.

**5)** Install shaft key, washer, fan, spacer, pulley, lock washer and nut. Install brush and connector plug assembly and retain with screws.

## BOSCH REGULATORS

Audi
BMW
Capri
Fiat
Fiesta
Lancia
Mercedes-Benz
Porsche
Saab
Volkswagen
Volvo

**NOTE** — *For models using integral alternator regulators, see Bosch Alternators in this section.*

## DESCRIPTION

Bosch regulators are provided in either transistorized solid state or the vibrating contact type. Vibrating type is mounted separate from alternator. Solid state type may be integral with alternator or separately mounted. Vibrator model is designated "ADN" and externally mounted solid state type is designated "ED". Integral mounted solid state regulator is designated "EE".

## TESTING

### ON CAR TEST

**Vibrator Type** — Install a battery post adapter at the positive post of the battery. Connect voltmeter across battery. Connect a tachometer to ignition system. Make sure all electrical acessories are turned off. Start engine with battery post adapter switch closed; open switch as soon as engine is started. With engine speed at 4000 RPM, after voltage reading stabilizes, any reading between 13.7 and 14.8 volts is satisfactory.

**Transistorized (Solid State) Regulators** — All applicable regulators are designed to maintain from 13.7 to 14.5 volts at a load current of 5 to 7 amps. Alternator should be driven at 4000 RPM and load current set at load current rating. Resistance and speed of alternator may be readjusted if necessary. Read voltage within 1 minute. If not within specifications, regulator requires replacement.

## ADJUSTMENT

**NOTE** — *If regulator fails to keep voltage within specified limits, it must be replaced. No adjusting procedures are recommended.*

**Fig. 1   Bosch Vibrator Type Alternator Regulator**

**Fig. 2   Typical Bosch Transistorized Voltage Regulator Wiring Diagram**

## HITACHI ALTERNATORS

**Datsun (With IC Regulator)**
**LUV**
**Subaru**

### DESCRIPTION

Hitachi alternators are conventional 3 phase, self rectifying type alternators. Six diodes (3 positive and 3 negative) are used to rectify current.

### APPLICATION

| Model | Hitachi Type No. |
|---|---|
| Datsun | |
| B210 & F10 | |
| W/O Air Conditioning | LR150-36 |
| W/Air Conditioning | LR160-46 |
| 200SX & 510 | |
| W/O Air Conditioning | LR150-35 |
| 510 | |
| W/Air Conditioning | LR160-47 |
| 620 Pickup | |
| W/O Air Conditioning | LR135-44 |
| W/Air Conditioning | LR138-01 |
| 280Z & 810 | LR160-42 |
| LUV | LT135-30 |
| Subaru | LT150-21 |

### SPECIFICATIONS
#### Output@2500 Alternator RPM

| Alternator | Amps | Volts |
|---|---|---|
| LT135-30 | 28 | 14 |
| LR135-44 | 27.5 | 14 |
| LR138-01 | 30 | 14 |
| LT150-21 | 40 | 14 |
| LR150-35 | 40 | 14 |
| LR150-36 | 40 | 14 |
| LR160-42 | ①60 | 14 |
| LR160-46 | 45 | 14 |
| LR160-47 | 45 | 14 |

① — Output @ 500 RPM.

#### Nominal Output

| Alternator | Amps | Volts |
|---|---|---|
| LT135-30 | 35 | 12 |
| LR135-44 | 35 | 12 |
| LR138-01 | 38 | 12 |
| LT150-21 | 50 | 12 |
| LR150-35 | 50 | 12 |
| LR150-36 | 50 | 12 |
| LR160-42 | 60 | 12 |
| LR160-46 | 60 | 12 |
| LR160-47 | 60 | 12 |

### TESTING

**NOTE** — *Some testing is described as part of Overhaul procedure in this article. The following testing is performed with alternator on the vehicle.*

#### ALTERNATOR SPEED TEST

**Datsun Models** — Ensure battery has a full charge, then connect a 30-volt voltmeter as shown in illustration, and test as follows:

1) Detach connectors at alternator. Connect a test probe from voltmeter positive terminal to "N" or "BAT" terminal. Connect

*Fig. 2  Alternator Testing Connections for Datsun*

*Fig. 1  Disassembled View of Typical Hitachi Alternator*

# Alternators & Regulators

## HITACHI ALTERNATORS (Cont.)

other test probe to ground. Check that voltmeter registers battery voltage.

2) Turn on headlights to high beam. Start engine and increase speed to approximately 1000 RPM and observe voltmeter. If voltmeter registers below 12.5 volts, alternator is defective. If above 12.5 volts, alternator is good.

**Subaru Models** — 1) Connect a voltmeter and leads to battery as shown in *Fig. 3*. Operate the alternator and turn off the switch "SW" when alternator speed reaches approximately 800 RPM. Increase speed in small increments while watching voltmeter deflection and read alternator speed when at 14 volts. Speed should be approximately 1000 RPM.

2) Make test connections using a 30-50 ampere variable resistor, battery, ammeter, and voltmeter as shown in *Fig. 4*. Operate alternator with switch "SW-1" closed. When alternator speed reaches approximately 800 RPM, set the variable resistor to maximum and turn on switch "SW-2". Increase alternator speed while maintaining a constant 14 volts by adjusting resistance. Read current at 2500 RPM and 5000 RPM. Readings should be 37-43 amperes at 2500 RPM and 48-54 at 5000 RPM.

**Fig. 3   Alternator Testing Connections for Subaru**

### RESISTANCE & CONTINUITY TESTING

**All Models** — 1) Measure resistance, using an ohmmeter, across "F" and "E" terminals for rotor coil resistance. Rotor coil circuit is normal if resistance is 4-5 ohms. If resistance is high, there is poor contact between brushes and commutator. If no continuity exists between "F" and "E" terminals, there is either an open rotor coil circuit, brush sticking or a broken lead wire. If resistance is low, it indicates a rotor coil layer short or grounded circuit.

2) **NOTE** — *The following test will not indicate a open state of the diodes. Tester will indicate a continuity regardless of diode conditions if tester leads are connected to the terminals with polarities reversed.* Connect positive lead of tester to alternator "N" terminal and tester negative lead to alternator "A" terminal. If continuity is observed on the tester, there exists one or more shorted positive diodes.

3) Next, connect tester positive lead to alternator "E" terminal and tester negative lead to alternator "N" terminal. If continuity is present, it indicates that one or more of the negative diodes are shorted.

**Fig. 4   Alternator Test Connections for Subaru**

### INTEGRATED CIRCUIT (IC) REGULATOR

Except for LUV and Subaru installations, an integrated circuit (IC) voltage regulator is used. This unit is soldered to the brush assembly mounted inside the alternator.

**Testing** — 1) Remove brush assembly and with suitable tester, connect wiring as shown in *Fig. 6*. If V-1 voltage is not within 10-13 volts, charge or replace battery as necessary. Disconnect lead at terminal "S" and check voltage between terminals "F" and "E". If less than 2.0 volts, regulator is functioning properly.

**Fig. 5   Front and Rear Views of IC Regulator (Datsun)**

2) Measure total voltage (V-3) of batteries 1 and 2. If not within 20-26 volts, recharge or replace. Gradually decrease variable resistance (Rv) from 300 ohms and check voltage (V-2) between terminals "E" and "F". At some point, V-2 should increase to equal V-1 measured in step 1). If no V-2 variation occurs as described, regulator is defective.

3) Measure voltage (V-4) between center tap of variable resistor (Rv) and terminal "E". With resistance set as in previous step, voltage should be 14.7±.5 volts at 68°F (20°C). At ex-

# Alternators & Regulators

## HITACHI ALTERNATORS (Cont.)

tremely high case temperatures, voltage may be 1 volt lower, while at extremely cold temperatures, voltage may be 1 volt higher.

**4)** Remove test lead from terminal "S" and connect to terminal "B". Repeat steps **2)** and **3)** and check for voltage (V-4) .5-2.0 volts higher than in step **3)**. If testing specifications are not met, it will be necessary to replace the IC regulator/brush assembly.

*Fig. 6   Regulator Test Arrangement*

## OVERHAUL

### DISASSEMBLY

**1)** Remove nut and take out pulley, fan, and washers. Pull out spacer. Remove screws securing brush holder and brush holder cover. Withdraw brush and brush holder. **NOTE** — *Leave "N" lead wire connected to stator coil lead.*

**2)** Unscrew through bolts and separate front and rear housings. Remove three set screws from bearing retainer and separate rotor from front cover. Pull rear bearing from rotor assembly, if replacement is necessary.

**3)** Remove diode cover and disconnect stator coil lead wire from diode terminal, using a soldering iron. Remove the diode assembly by unscrewing the terminal nut and diode-setting nuts. Remove stator from rear cover.

### INSPECTION & REPAIR

**Rotor** — Apply tester probes to slip rings of rotor. If ohm reading is within specifications, rotor conduction is satisfactory. If not, a disconnection of field coil may exist. Next, apply probes to slip ring and rotor core, to check ground. If conduction exists, replace rotor assembly.

**Stator** — The stator is normal when there is conduction between individual stator coil terminals. When there is no conduction between terminals, cable is broken; replace stator assembly. If each lead wire of stator coil (including neutral wire) is not conductive with stator core, condition is satisfactory. If conduction exists, stator is grounded and must be replaced.

**Diodes** — **1)** Perform a conduction test on all diodes, in both directions, using an ohmmeter. Test the conduction between each terminal and plate. Diode installed on "+" plate is a positive diode which allows current to flow from terminal to "+" plate only; current does not flow from "+" plate to the

*Fig. 7   Rotor Field Coil Conduction Test*

terminal. A diode installed on the "−" plate is a negative diode and allows current to flow from the "−" plate to the terminal only; current does not flow from the terminal to the "−" plate.

**2)** If current flows in both directions, the diode is short-circuited. If current does not flow in either direction, the diode is open. If any diode is defective, replace the entire diode assembly (individual diodes are not serviceable).

**Brushes & Brush Springs** — Inspect brushes for freedom of movement in holder. Clean brush holder if necessary. Check brushes for cracks and wear; replace if beyond limits (.28" or 7.0 mm for LT135-30, LT150-21 and LR160-42; .30" or 7.5 mm for all others). Check brush springs for corrosion, damage and proper tension (9-12.2 oz. with .08" or 2 mm protrusion from holder). Test brush holder to assure that no continuity exists between holders; replace if required.

*Fig. 8   Brush Assembly with Wear Indicators*

### REASSEMBLY

Reinstall diode assembly and stator to rear cover. Connect lead wires of stator coil to terminals of diode assembly. **NOTE** — *Solder quickly to avoid damage to diodes.* Reinstall diode cover. Reinstall rotor to front cover. Place assembly in vise and replace pulley and components. Insert and tighten housing through bolts. Assemble brushes to brush holder and insert holder into alternator. Perform, as previously described.

## HITACHI REGULATORS

LUV
Subaru

### DESCRIPTION

The regulator system consists basically of a voltage regulator and a charge relay. The voltage regulator has two sets of contact points, a lower set and upper set, to control alternator voltage. An armature plate placed between the two sets of contacts moves upward, downward, or vibrates. The lower contacts, when closed, complete the field circuit direct to ground. The upper contacts, when closed, complete field circuit to ground through a resistance (field coil), and thereby produces alternator output. The charge relay is similar in construction to voltage regulator. When upper contacts are closed, ignition warning lamp goes on.

### APPLICATION

| Model | Hitachi No. |
|---|---|
| LUV | TLIZ-87 |
| Subaru | TLIZ-94 |

### TESTING

**VOLTAGE REGULATOR**

1) Connect voltmeter and ammeter as illustrated. Start and maintain engine speed at 2500 RPM for a few minutes, then check to make sure that reading of ammeter is 5 amps or less. If ammeter remains higher than 5 amps, disconnect battery in use and connect a battery known to be fully charged. Recheck to be sure reading of ammeter is lower than 5 amps.

**Fig. 1   Test Connections for Voltage Regulator**

2) Lower engine speed to idle and again increase it gradually to 2500 RPM, then note voltmeter reading. Function of regulator is normal if measured value is within specified regulating voltage. If reading of voltmeter deviates from specified range, it indicates regulator is in need of adjustment.

### ADJUSTMENT

NOTE – *Charge relay is adjusted in same manner as voltage regulator.*

1) Disconnect and remove voltage regulator from vehicle. If contact points are roughened, smooth with fine sand paper. Check and adjust gaps: core gap first, then point gap. NOTE – *Adjustment of yoke gap is unnecessary on some models.*

2) Adjust core gap by loosening screws attaching contact set to yoke. Move contact set upward or downward as required. Adjust point gap by loosening screw attaching upper contact. Move upper contact up or down as required to set gap to specification.

3) Adjust regulated voltage by means of adjusting screw. Turn screw in to increase regulated voltage or out to decrease voltage. When correct voltage adjustment is obtained, secure with lock nut. When adjustment procedure is complete, reinstall regulator and perform on car check.

**Fig. 2   Adjustment Points for Charge Relay**

**Fig. 3   Adjustment Points for Voltage Regulator**

# Alternators & Regulators

## HITACHI REGULATORS (Cont.)

| VOLTAGE REGULATOR SPECIFICATIONS | | | | | | |
|---|---|---|---|---|---|---|
| Regulator | Battery Voltage | Regulated Voltage | Voltage Coil Resistance (Ohms) | Yoke Gap In. (mm) | Core Gap In. (mm) | Point Gap In. (mm) |
| TLIZ-87 | 12 | 13.8-14.8 | 10.3 | ① | .024-.039(.6-1.0) | .012-.016(.3-.4) |
| TLIZ-94 | 12 | 14.0-15.0 | 10.3 | .035(.9) | .024-.039(.6-1.0) | .012-.016(.3-.4) |

① — No yoke gap adjustment required.

| VOLTAGE RELAY SPECIFICATIONS | | | | | |
|---|---|---|---|---|---|
| Regulator | Released Voltage | Voltage Coil Resistance (Ohms) | Yoke Gap In. (mm) | Core Gap In. (mm) | Point Gap In. (mm) |
| TLIZ-87 | 5② | 31.9 | ① | .032-.039(.8-1.0) | .016-.024(.41-.61) |
| TLIZ-94 | 8-10 | 31.9 | .035(.9) | .032-.039(.8-1.0) | .016-.024(.41-.61) |

① — No yoke gap adjustment required.

② — Measured at "A" terminal.

## LUCAS ALTERNATOR WITH INTEGRAL REGULATOR

**Jaguar**
**MG**
**Triumph**

**NOTE** — *Some Jaguar models may be fitted with Motorola alternators.*

### DESCRIPTION

Lucas "ACR" model alternators have an integral voltage regulator mounted in the slip ring end bracket. The stator consists of star-connected, three phase windings on a ring end cover and drive end bracket. The rotor is either an eight or twelve pole type with the field windings connected to two face-type slip rings, and is supported in drive-end bracket by a ball bearing and in the end cover by needle roller bearings. One positive and one negative carbon brush ride against concentric brass slip rings. The heatsink-rectifier, terminal block assembly incorporate six silicon diodes, forming a full wave rectifier bridge circuit, and three diodes which supply current to the rotor windings. **NOTE** — *Up to a ten milliamp battery drain is normal, even with the ignition in the "OFF" position.*

### APPLICATION

| Model | Type No. |
|---|---|
| Jaguar | |
| XJ-6 Without Air Cond. ................. | 18 ACR |
| XJ-6 With Air Cond. .............. | 20 ACR or 25 ACR |
| XJ-12, XJS ...................... | 20 ACR |
| MG | |
| Midget ........................ | 16 ACR |
| MGB ........................ | 18 ACR |
| Triumph | |
| Spitfire 1500 .................... | 16 ACR |
| TR-7 | |
| Without Air Cond. ................ | 17 ACR |
| With Air Cond. .................. | 20 ACR |

### SPECIFICATIONS

#### Nominal Output

| Alternator | Amps @ RPM | Voltage |
|---|---|---|
| 16 ACR .................. | 34 @ 6000 | 12 |
| 17 ACR .................. | 36 @ 6000 | 12 |
| 18 ACR .................. | 45 @ 6000 | 12 |
| 20 ACR .................. | 66 @ 6000 | 12 |
| 25 ACR .................. | 66 @ 6000 | 12 |

### TESTING

#### ON CAR TESTING

**NOTE** — *Alternator drive belt must be properly adjusted, battery and connections in good condition and charge warning bulb and circuit continuous in order to test charging system. Polarity of alternator and battery terminals MUST be observed to prevent system damage. Warm engine 3-4 minutes before testing. (Output may be slightly higher when alternator is cold.) Battery ground cable should be disconnected when attaching jumper wires to alternator and regulator.*

**Alternator Output Test — 1)** Disconnect multi-socket connector and remove molded cover from rear of alternator. (Cover may be pierced with a probe on some models in order to ground the field winding brush and by-pass the regulator.) Provide a test circuit as illustrated.

**2)** Start engine and run to give 1,500 alternator RPM (approximately 650-800 engine RPM). Test circuit bulb should be out.

**3)** Increase engine speed to 2500-3,000 RPM to give 6,000 alternator RPM. Adjust variable resistor so voltmeter reads 14 volts and note ammeter reading equal to the nominal output rating for the appropriate alternator. If readings are not correct, alternator requires overhaul or replacement.

**NOTE** — *Do not connect variable resistor across battery for longer than is necessary to complete the test.*

**Regulator Test — 1)** Provide Regulator Test Circuit as shown and gradually increase engine speed to approximately 640 RPM (1,550 alternator RPM). Test lamp should go out.

**2)** Increase engine speed to approximately 2,500 RPM (6,000 alternator RPM). Voltmeter should be steady at 13.6-14.4 volts. If reading is not steady and satisfactory Output Test has been performed, regulator should be replaced.

*Fig. 1  Alternator Output Test Circuit*
*(Spitfire 1500 Shown)*

## LUCAS ALTERNATOR WITH INTEGRAL REGULATOR (Cont.)

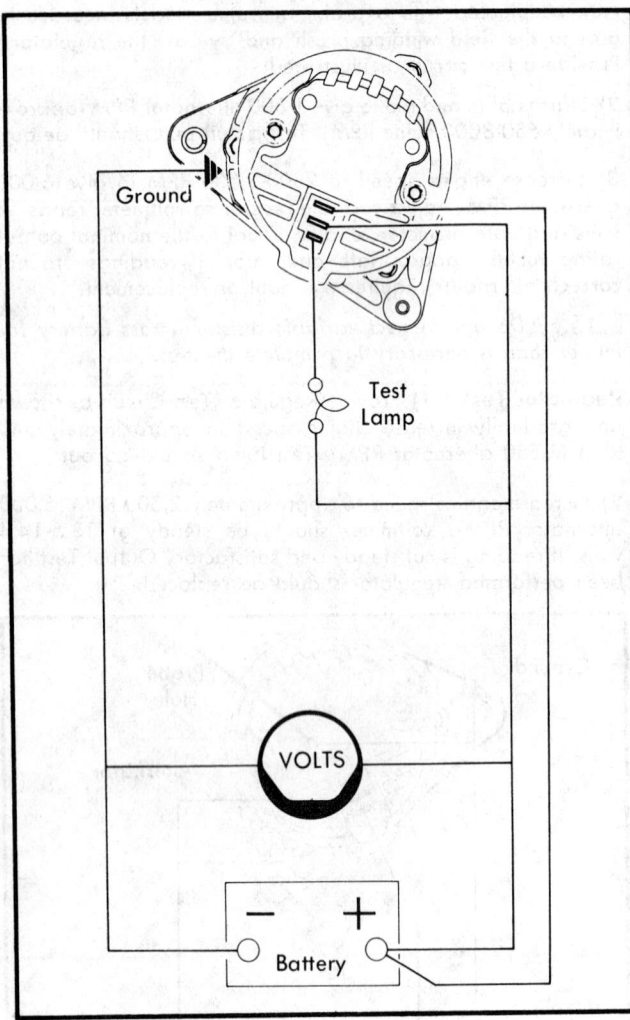

*Fig. 2  Regulator Test Circuit*
*(Spitfire 1500 Shown)*

## OVERHAUL

### DISASSEMBLY

1) Remove end cover and note wire positions and color. Remove screws attaching surge protection diode and brush assembly. Lift out brush assembly and surge protection diode. Regulator may be removed if desired.

2) Unsolder stator wire connections and remove rectifier pack grounding strip. Withdraw rectifier pack. Remove through bolts.

**CAUTION** — *When necessary to solder or unsolder leads from diodes, use pliers as a heat sink by pinching diode pin with jaws of pliers. Solder connections quickly to prevent heat damage to diodes.*

3) Remove through bolts from alternator frame and carefully slip end bracket and stator off of rotor. (It may be necessary to

tap lightly on an extractor or tube placed against outer bearing journal to separate rotor from end bracket.)

4) Complete disassembly, if required, by removing pulley and drive key. Press rotor from drive end bracket and remove screws retaining end bearing in position. Replace as necessary.

**NOTE** — *Position of all washers, spacers and insulators must be noted for proper assembly.*

### TESTING

**Rotor** — Connect an ohmmeter and read resistance of field coil (across slip rings). Using a 110-volt A.C. supply and 15-watt test lamp, check for insulation between one of the slip rings and any rotor pole. If lamp lights, rotor is shorted.

**Stator** — Connect 12-volt battery and 36-watt test lamp to two of the stator connections. Then repeat test using any other combination of two of the three connections. If lamp fails to light in either test, stator has an open coil. Using a 110-volt A.C. supply and a 15-watt test lamp, check for insulation between any one of the three stator connections and stator laminations. If lamp lights, stator should be replaced.

**Diodes** — Connect a 12-volt battery and a 1.5-watt test lamp in turn to each of the nine diode pins and its corresponding heat sink on the rectifier pack, then reverse the connections. Lamp should light (with current flow) in one direction only. If lamp lights in both directions or fails in either, rectifier pack must be renewed.

### PARTS REPLACEMENT

**Regulator** — Aluminum casing of control unit must not make contact with alternator body when installed. (Shorted field circuit could result in maximum alternator output at all times regardless of battery condition.)

**Diodes** — In event of defective diodes, heatsink and rectifier assembly should be replaced. Protect diodes from excess heat when soldering by using pliers on diode pin as a thermal shunt.

**Brushes** — Installed brushes must extend at least .2" (5 mm) from housing and springs should indicate 9-13 oz. tension when brush is pushed back flush with housing. If beyond limits, replace brush assembly.

### REASSEMBLY

Reverse disassembly procedure, noting the following: When installing slip ring end bearing, ensure it is fitted with open side facing rotor and that it is seated fully. When replacing rotor to drive end bracket, support inner track of bearing with suitable piece of tubing. DO NOT use drive end bracket as the only support for bearing when fitting rotor.

## MARELLI ALTERNATORS

### Fiat
### All Models

**NOTE** — *Some models may be equipped with Bosch alternators.*

## DESCRIPTION

Marelli alternators are conventional three-phase, self-rectifying type alternators. Six silicone rectifier diodes are connected to form a full-wave, three phase rectifying bridge. The three negative rectifier diodes are pressed directly in the end frame. Three positive diodes are located in a heat sink which is insulated from the end frame.

## APPLICATION

| Model | Fiat No. |
| --- | --- |
| 124 ...................................... | A 12M 124/12/42M |
| 128, 131 & X1/9 ............................ | A 124/14V/53A |

## TROUBLE SHOOTING

### INDICATOR LIGHT ON WITH
### IGNITION SWITCH IN OFF POSITION

Output current and voltage will be slightly lower than specifications. One or more positive diodes are shorted.

### INDICATOR LIGHT ON AT LOW RPM

Stator winding has a phase open.

### NO OUTPUT VOLTAGE

Rotor winding is open.

### INDICATOR LIGHT ON
### WITH ENGINE RUNNING

One or more negative and energizing diodes shorted.

### HIGH OUTPUT VOLTAGE

One energizing diode open. Improper operation of voltage regulator.

### INDICATOR LIGHT GLOWS DIMLY
### WITH KEY ON OR ENGINE RUNNING

Faulty connection in ignition system. Brushes stuck in housing or worn excessively.

## TESTING

### ASSEMBLED ALTERNATOR

**Rotor Windings** — Connect ohmmeter leads to positive blade brush holder (terminal 67) and a good ground. Resistance of 2.5-2.7 ohms should be noted at 68°F. Extremely high resistance indicates possible open circuit in rotor windings.

**Stator Phase Windings** — Check resistance at stator winding connectors. Resistance should be near zero. Extremely high resistance indicates open circuit in one or more windings.

**Diode Checks** — 1) Connect leads of an ohmmeter to terminal 30 and stator winding connector. Check resistance, then reverse leads and recheck. Both readings should show high resistance with one reading being slightly higher than the other. If both readings are low, a positive diode is bad.

2) Check resistance between ground and stator winding connector. Reverse leads and check reading. If both readings are low, a negative diode is bad.

3) Check resistance between energizing diode plug and stator winding connector. Reverse leads and check reading. If both readings are low, an energizing diode is bad.

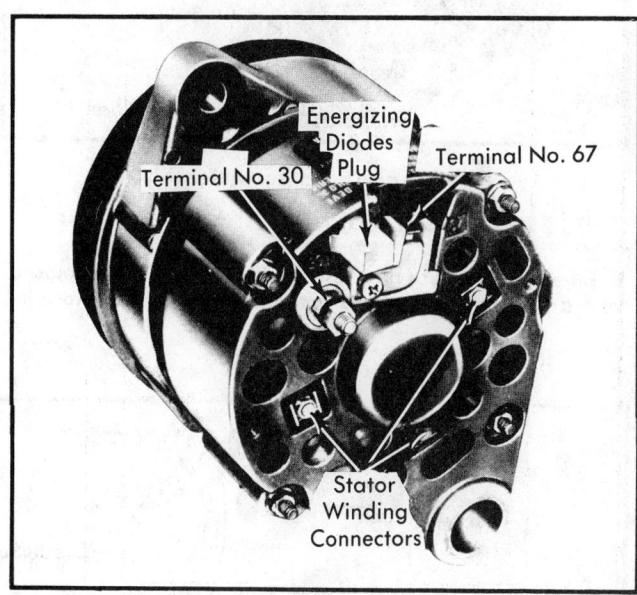

**Fig. 1   Marelli Alternator Test Points**

## OVERHAUL

### DISASSEMBLY

1) Remove drive and ventilation components from rotor shaft. Remove brush holder (with brushes) by backing out its mounting screw on diode end head. Remove Woodruff key on shaft.

2) Unscrew nuts of the four through bolts, remove drive end frame and rotor. Before removing stator, unscrew from inside (of housing), three nuts securing stator winding phase ends to diode ends. Remove stator.

3) To disassemble diode end frame, unscrew the nut of terminal "30". The frame with negative diodes and the support with positive diodes will thus be separated.

### TESTING

**Stator Winding Resistance** — With stator disassembled from alternator and leads disconnected, connect ohmmeter probes between each pair of stator leads. Ohmmeter must show equal readings for each pair of stator leads. Replace stator if readings are not equal.

**Rotor Winding Resistance** — Check rotor resistance with ohmmeter leads on slip rings. Resistance should be 2.5-2.7 ohms at 68°F.

# Alternators & Regulators

## MARELLI ALTERNATORS (Cont.)

**Brushes** — The spring pressure on slip ring brushes should be about one pound (0.43 kg), with new brushes in operation position.

**Fig. 2   Brush Holder Assembly**

### PARTS REPLACEMENT

**Brushes** — To ensure best results, brushes should be replaced with a new brush holder as a complete assembly. Before in-stalling holder assembly, clean all parts of grease and carbon dust, lubricate bearings with suitable grease (Fiat MR 3).

### REASSEMBLY

The alternator is reassembled by reversing the order of dis-assembly procedure.

### SPECIFICATIONS

| Application | Test Data |
|---|---|
| Cut-In-Speed (Max.) @ 12V (68°F) ................. | 1200 RPM |
| Current Output @ 14V | |
|   A 12M 124/12/42M ............................. | 44 amps. min. |
|   A 124/14V/53A ................................ | 57 amps. min. |
| Maximum Output Current | |
|   A 12M 124/12/42M ...................................... | 53 amps. |
|   A 124/14V/53A ................................................. | 70 amps. |
| Max. Cont. Alternator RPM ........................... | 13,000 |

**Fig. 3   Disassembled View of Typical Marelli Alternator**

## MARELLI REGULATORS

**Fiat 124**

### DESCRIPTION

Fiat voltage regulators are of the dual stage vibrating contact type. An induction auxiliary coil, considerably smaller than the magnetizing coil, is mounted near contact side of the yoke. In addition to two regulating resistors, an additional resistor works in series with the main voltage coil. The regulator is grounded through the mounting flanges. Resistors are protected from impacts by a metal shield secured to mounting flange.

### APPLICATION

| Model | Part No. |
|---|---|
| 124 | RC2/12B |

### SPECIFICATIONS

| Application | Specification |
|---|---|
| Alternator Test RPM | 5000 RPM |
| 1st Stage Testing (Amps) | 25-35 |
| 2nd Stage Testing (Amps) | 2-12 |
| 2nd Stage Testing (Volts) | 14.2±3 |
| Resistance Values (Ohms) | |
| Plug 15 & Ground | 27.7±2 |
| Plug 15 & 67 W/Contacts Open | 5.6±.3 |
| Armature Air Gap | |
| Point "A" | .055-.063" |
| Point "B" | .014-.022" |

**Fig. 1   Marelli Voltage Regulator**

### TESTING

#### BENCH TESTING

1) Install alternator and regulator on test bench equipped with gradual speed control. Connect ammeter, voltmeter, and rheostat as shown in illustration. Regulator must be placed vertically, with terminals "15" and "67" at base. Regulator must be checked without removing cover.

2) **CAUTION** – *DO NOT operate regulator with switch "I" open (battery disconnected) since this will damage regulator contacts. Operate voltage regulator in an ambient temperature of 122±5.4°F for 30 minutes (thermal stabilization). Start with rheostat fully inserted, then adjust current output to one sixth of maximum alternator output. Alternator should be operated slowly at first and then be SLOWLY brought up to 5000 RPM.*

3) **NOTE** – *Suitable thermostatic equipment must be available in order to maintain regulator at specified temperature throughout test. Operate alternator at 5000 RPM. Adjust rheostat for specified current output. See specifications.*

4) Check first stage immediately after second stage, and ensure that the conditions specified in step **2)** are still met. At 5000 RPM, adjust rheostat until specifications are met for 1st Stage Testing. Regulated voltage should be .2-.7 volts (model 124) or 0-.5 volts (all other models) less than the voltage recorded for the second stage. **NOTE** – *When testing the first and second stages, check that regulated voltage is stable, without any sudden surges or drops.*

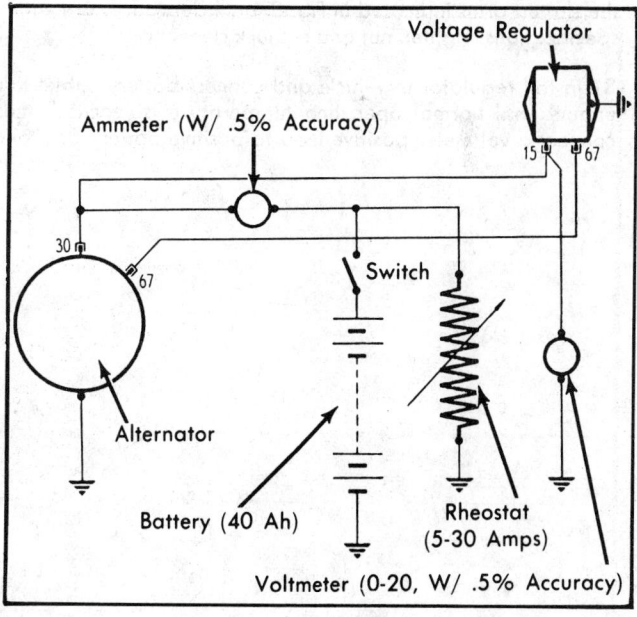

**Fig. 2   Circuit for Conducting Bench Test**

### ADJUSTMENT

#### VOLTAGE REGULATOR

1) Disconnect positive battery cable then remove dust cover on voltage regulator. Inspect contact points for pitting and burn marks, then clean minor pitting and burn marks. **NOTE** – *Extreme damage to points requires regulator replacement.* Use a feeler gauge to check measurements at point "A" and "B" as shown in *Fig. 3*.

# Alternators & Regulators

## MARELLI REGULATORS (Cont.)

*Fig. 3  Adjusting Voltage Regulator*

2) If clearances are not within specifications, remove the regulator from vehicle. Loosen nut and adjust gaps by moving the slotted arms indicated in *Fig. 3*. until clearances are within specifications. Tighten nut and recheck clearances.

3) Install regulator in vehicle and connect battery cable. Run engine until normal operating temperature is reached, then connect a voltmeter positive lead to positive battery post and negative lead to a good ground. Voltmeter should read 13.9-14.5 volts at 2500 RPM with all electrical components off. If reading is not within specifications carefully apply slight pressure to lower spring bracket to adjust. Bending bracket down increases reading while bending bracket up decreases reading. **NOTE** — *Bend bracket a very small amount as a slight change will adjust voltage. Disconnect voltmeter and install dust cover.*

## MITSUBISHI ALTERNATORS

Arrow/Colt
Challenger/Sapporo
Courier
Mazda

### DESCRIPTION

Mitsubishi alternators are conventional three-phase, self-rectifying type units containing six diodes (three positive and three negative) which are used to rectify current.

### APPLICATION

| Model | Part No. |
|---|---|
| Arrow/Colt | |
| 2000cc & 2600cc ............................ | AH2050M1 |
| Challenger/Sapporo | |
| 1600cc ........................................... | AH2250L1 |
| 2000cc & 2600cc ........................... | AH2050M1 |
| Courier .............................................. | ①D47Z-10346-A |
| Mazda | |
| RX-4, Cosmo ................................. | 8527 18 300 |
| B1800 Pickup ................................. | 0571 18 300A |
| GLC ................................................. | 0483 18 300 |

① — Ford part number. (Check number stamped on housing for individual application.)

### SPECIFICATIONS

#### Nominal Output at 2500 RPM

| Application | Amps. | Voltage |
|---|---|---|
| AH2050M1 ........................ | 42 | 14 |
| AH2250L1 ........................ | 42 | 14 |
| D47Z-10346-A ................ | 35 | 14.5 |
| 8527 18 300 .................... | 56 | 14 |
| 0571 18 300A .................. | 30 | 14 |
| 0483 18 300 .................... | 30 | 14 |

#### Coil Resistance (Ohms)

| Application | Rotor | Stator |
|---|---|---|
| Arrow/Colt, | | |
| Challenger/Sapporo ......... | ① | ① |
| Courier ............................ | 5-6 | ① |
| Mazda ............................. | 5-6 | ① |

① — Test must show continuity, no given value.

**Brush Wear Limit** — To limit line, one third of original length, or .22″ (5.5 mm), whichever is greater.

**Brush Spring Pressure** — Standard tension should be 12-16 oz. Replace if less than 8 oz. or if springs are corroded.

### TESTING

**NOTE** — *Some testing is done as part of Overhaul procedure.*

#### ON CAR TEST

Whenever battery is discharged and charging rate is low, following test should be made to determine whether fault lies

in alternator or regulator. First, place ammeter between "A" terminal of regulator and battery. Disconnect wire at "F" terminal of regulator and touch lead "A" terminal of regulator. If charging rate remains constant, alternator is defective. If current increases greatly, then regulator is faulty.

### OVERHAUL

#### DISASSEMBLY

1) Remove brush cover and through bolts. Separate diode end housing from drive housing by tapping front bracket lightly with a soft mallet.

2) Place rotor shaft in padded vise, using caution. Remove pulley nut, pulley, fan, and spacer. Remove rotor drive end housing by lightly tapping end housing with a soft mallet.

3) To separate stator from diode end housing, unsolder three negative diode leads and connections between diodes.

#### TESTING

**Diode Assemblies** — Disconnect heat sink and check each diode with tester on continuity in forward or reverse direction. If the diode shows large resistance in one direction and small resistance in other direction, diode is normal. If it shows small resistance in both directions it is shorted. If large resistance is shown in both directions, diode is open.

**CAUTION** — *If excessive temperature is allowed, diode will become inoperative.*

**Rotor Field Continuity** — Check continuity across field coil slip rings. No continuity indicates broken wire. Rotor must be replaced.

**Rotor Field Coil Ground** — Check continuity between individual slip rings and rotor core/shaft. If there is continuity, coil or slip ring is grounded. Rotor must be replaced.

**Stator Coil Ground** — Check to ensure no continuity between stator coil leads and stator core.

**Fig. 1  *Using Special Tool to Install Diode***

# Alternators & Regulators

## MITSUBISHI ALTERNATORS (Cont.)

**Stator Coil Continuity** — Check continuity between leads of stator coil. If there is no continuity, coil has broken wire and must be replaced.

## PARTS REPLACEMENT

**Diodes** — To remove diode, use a suitable tool to support heat sink and remove diode by use of a suitable press. Press out carefully to avoid damaging mounting bore of heat sink.

`CAUTION` — *Do not strike diode as shock may damage other diodes.* To install diode, support heat sink as in removal, select correct type diode (positive diodes have red markings;

negative diodes have black markings), and press diode into heat sink.

**Drive End Bearing** — Remove bearing retainer by unscrewing set screws and press out bearing, using a suitable press.

**Rear Bearing** — Remove rear bearing from housing assembly, using a suitable press or bearing puller.

## REASSEMBLY

Reassemble by reversing disassembly procedures, making sure polarity of diodes is correct.

**Fig. 2   Exploded View of Mitsubishi Alternator**

# Alternators & Regulators

## MITSUBISHI REGULATORS

Arrow/Colt, Challenger/Sapporo
(2000 cc & 2600 cc Models)
Courier
Mazda

### DESCRIPTION

Regulator consists of two elements: constant-voltage relay and pilot lamp relay. Both relays consist of an electromagnet, contacts, frame, moving element and coil side plate. This regulator has a temperature compensation gradient as an improvement over the constant voltage charging system. It has functions for automatically compensating the adjusted value of the constant-voltage relay so that the adjusted value will be lower in summer and higher in winter.

### APPLICATION

| Model | Part No. |
|---|---|
| Arrow/Colt, Challenger/Sapporo | RQB-2D |
| Courier | D27Z-10316-A |
| Mazda | 0453 18 391 |

### TESTING

CAUTION — Ensure that voltage regulator protecting fuse is functional before conducting any charging system diagnosis. Verify condition by substituting known good fuse.

To check adjusted value of constant voltage relay, connect a voltmeter between terminal "A" and E" of the regulator. Place generator at no load by disconnecting one of the battery terminals during operation at idling speed, then increase alternator speed to approximately 4000 RPM (Approximately 2000 engine RPM). In this condition, satisfactory voltage is 14.5-15.8 volts.

### ADJUSTMENT

NOTE — Adjustment procedures furnished for Mazda only. Manufacturers recommend installation of new regulator when tolerance not within limits for other models.

Adjust voltage of the constant voltage relay by bending end of coil side plate up or down as shown in illustration. If plate is bent up, the adjusted value becomes higher. If it is bent down, value becomes lower. Adjust pilot lamp relay by same method.

**Fig. 1   Regulator Harness Connector**

**Fig. 2   Voltage Adjustment Point**

| | MITSUBISHI ALTERNATOR REGULATOR SPECIFICATIONS | | | | | | |
|---|---|---|---|---|---|---|---|
| | | VOLTAGE REGULATOR | | | PILOT LAMP RELAY | | |
| Reg. No. | Output Volts | Air Gap in. (mm) | Back Gap in. (mm) | Point Gap in. (mm) | Air Gap in. (mm) | Back Gap in. (mm) | Point Gap in. (mm) |
| 045318391 | 14-15 | .028-.051 (.71-1.3) | .028-.059 (.71-1.5) | .012-.018 (.31-.45) | .039-.059 (1.0-1.5) | .028-.059 (.71-1.5) | .020-.035 (.71-1.1) |

## MOTORCRAFT ALTERNATORS

**Fiesta**

### DESCRIPTION

Alternator is belt driven from engine. An external regulator controls charging rate by switching rotor field current in and out as required through brushes contacting slip rings. Alternating current is produced and converted to direct current by the diode rectifier assembly.

### IDENTIFICATION & SPECIFICATIONS

Alternator is stamped with "Motorcraft" trademark in either orange or green.

### APPLICATION

| Color | Rating | RPM (Hot) |
|-------|--------|-----------|
| Orange | 40 Amps@15 V | 2900 |
| Green | 60 Amps@15 V | 2900 |

### TESTING

#### FUSE LINK

Fuse links are provided in the charging system to prevent damage to the harness and alternator in case the harness becomes grounded or a booster battery is connected with reverse polarity. Insulation which is rippled or bubbled indicates that the link is blown and must be replaced. In case of vehicles with two fuse links, check the accessories link by turning headlamps or an accessory on. If fuses are not blown and they still fail to function, the link is probably blown and must be replaced.

#### INDICATOR LIGHT

Warning light should come on when starting engine and go off after engine is idling. If no light, check bulb and replace if burned out. If bulb is not burned out check for open circuit between switch and regulator. If light does not go out until engine reaches high RPM, check 15 ohm resistor connected in parallel with light.

#### VOLTAGE OUTPUT TEST

**1)** Attach voltmeter to battery and record voltage. Start engine and increase engine speed to 1500 RPM when normal operating temperature is reached. With NO electrical load on system, voltage should increase to at least 1 volt but not more than 2 volts above original reading.

**2)** Turn on heater blower motor to high speed and headlights to high beam. Increase engine speed to 2000 RPM and note battery voltage at least 0.5 volt above original reading with engine off.

**3)** If no-load voltage in step **1)** exceeds 2 volts, assure that ground connections between regulator, alternator and engine are tight. Disconnect wiring plug from regulator and recheck no-load voltage. If voltmeter now indicates battery voltage throughout the test, replace voltage regulator and recheck.

**4)** If voltage increase is excessive with regulator disconnected, repair shorted wiring harness between alternator and regulator.

**NOTE** – *If harness is shorted, regulator will have been damaged and must be replaced.*

**5)** If load voltage in step **2)** did not increase or increase was less than 0.5 volt, check battery voltage at alternator "BAT" terminal. Disconnect regulator plug and check battery voltage at "A" terminal. If no voltage present at these terminals, repair wiring and repeat output test.

**6)** If battery voltage is present at both "BAT" and "A" terminals, connect jumper across "A" and "F" terminals of regulator plug. If field circuit is grounded, jumper will spark and heat. Check field circuit for ground and regulator for open before continuing.

**7)** To check field circuit, measure resistance between "F" terminal on regulator plug and negative battery cable clamp. Ohmmeter should read between 4 ohms and 250 ohms. No resistance indicates that the field circuit is grounded and requires alternator removal and repair.

**8)** Check resistance between "I" and "F" terminals with plug removed. Ohmmeter should indicate zero resistance. A reading of 10 or more ohms indicates an open connection in the regulator. Replace regulator and repair alternator field circuit

**9)** If load voltage is still less than specified, remove jumper from regulator wiring plug and install a jumper between alternator "BAT" and "FLD" terminals. Repeat output test. If results are satisfactory, wiring harness is at fault and must be repaired or replaced. If load voltage increase is still less than 0.5 volt, alternator must be removed from vehicle for bench testing.

Jumper Wire Connected to
Alternator "BAT" and "FLD"
Terminals

Regulator with
Connector Plug Removed

*Fig. 1  Alternator with Jumper for Testing*

## MOTORCRAFT ALTERNATORS (Cont.)

### OVERHAUL

#### DISASSEMBLY

**1)** Scribe mark across front and rear housings and stator for alignment during reassembly. Remove through bolts and separate front housing and rotor from rear housing and stator.

**2)** Remove terminal nuts and insulators from rear housing and separate stator/rectifier assembly from housing. Remove brushes and brush holder.

**3)** To remove stacked type rectifier, remove stator terminal screw and grounded screw by turning them ¼ turn to unlock from rectifier. Unsolder leads from rectifier using caution not to overheat rectifier assembly. To remove flat type rectifier, remove stator terminal screw by pressing straight out of rectifier. Do NOT turn screw or remove grounded screws. Unsolder leads from rectifier.

**4)** Remove front pulley and fan, then separate rotor from housing and bearing. Bearing may be replaced by removing retainer screws and retainer.

#### TESTING

**1)** Using 12 volt test lamp, check rotor continuity at slip rings and absence of ground between slip ring and rotor shaft. With ohmmeter, check for resistance of 4.0 to 4.4 ohms between slip rings.

**2)** Check resistance of .14 to .16 ohms between stator wires with ohmmeter. Check that windings are not grounded and have winding continuity with 12 volt test lamp.

**3)** Check diodes for continuity (approximately 60 ohms) in one direction only. If no continuity is observed in either direction, diode is open. If continuity is observed in both directions, diode is shorted. Rectifier assembly must be replaced if open or shorted diodes are found.

#### REASSEMBLY

**1)** Install bearing and retainer in front housing. Install rotor in housing to stop-ring, then install spacer, fan, pulley and nut with lock washer.

**2)** Assemble brush holder with brushes and springs, holding brushes in retracted position by inserting length of wire (paper clip) in holder. Solder leads from stator to rectifier pack and reverse disassembly procedure noting that scribe marks are aligned.

**3)** Remove brush retracting wire (paper clip) and seal hole with waterproof cement. Install and test alernator.

*Fig. 2  Exploded View of Motorcraft Alternator*

## NIPPONDENSO ALTERNATORS

Arrow/Colt
(1600 cc Engine)
Honda
Opel
Toyota

### DESCRIPTION

Nippondenso alternators are conventional 3 phase, self rectifying type alternators. Six diodes (3 positive and 3 negative are used to rectify current.

### APPLICATION

| Model | Amps | Part No. |
|---|---|---|
| Arrow/Colt | 35 | 021000-6420 |
| Honda | | |
| Accord | 50 | 62720-671-014① |
| Civic | 40 | 65042-634-671① |
| Civic CVCC | | |
| W/O Air Cond. | 35 | 59473-657-024① |
| W/Air Cond. | 50 | 62720-671-014① |
| Toyota② | | |
| Corolla | | |
| 3KC | 50 | 24071 |
| 3KC | 55 | 24090 |
| 2TC | 40 | 26091 |
| Corona | | |
| 20R | 55 | 38061 |
| Celica | | |
| 20R | 45 | 38051 |
| 20R | 55 | ③38061 |
| 20R | 55 | 38090 |
| Cressida | | |
| 4M | 55 | 45100 |
| 4M | 60 | ③45110 |
| Land Cruiser | | |
| 2F | 55 | 24020 |
| Pickup | | |
| 20R | 40 | 38012 |
| 20R | 40 | 38013 |

① — 31100 identifies Honda alternator.
② — All Toyota numbers are preceded by 27020.
③ — Without regulator.

### SPECIFICATIONS

#### Coil Resistance (Ohms)

| Application | Rotor |
|---|---|
| All Models | 4.1-4.3 |

#### Minimum Brush Length

| Application | In.(mm) |
|---|---|
| All Models | .22 (5.5) |

### TESTING

#### ON CAR TEST

**Preliminary Inspection** — Check alternator mounting and belt tension. Inspect turn signal fuse and gauge fuse. Check alternator and regulator wire connections for tightness.

**No Load Test** — 1) Connect a suitable test meter (09081-00010 alternator tester for models with special connector from regulator, or a common regulator tester) as shown in illustrations. Start engine and increase speed gradually to 2000-2300 RPM. Read "B" terminal voltage. Voltage should be 13.5-14.8 with a current draw of not more than 10 amps. If current is over specifications, battery is discharged or internally shorted.

2) If voltage is not steady, dirty regulator points or defective connection at "F" terminal may be the cause.

3) If voltage reading is too high, one of the following problems may be indicated: Regulator low speed gap too wide. High speed point gap too wide. High speed point gap resistance too high. Open circuit regulator coil or voltage relay coil. Open circuit regulator "N" terminal or "B" terminal. Low speed point contact tension too heavy. Loose regulator ground connection.

**"F" Terminal Voltage Test** — 1) With regulator tester, stop engine, disconnect alternator wiring connector, turn ignition switch to "ON" and measure voltage between "F" and "E" terminals of connector. Voltage should be 12 volts. If voltage is zero or very low, note the following possible causes; blown fuse, regulator "IG" terminal open, or regulator high speed points are burned.

*Fig. 1 Connections for Tester 0981-00010*

2) With alternator tester (09081-00010) connected and engine idling, press switch "F" on tester. Gradually increase engine speed to 2300 RPM. Needle on tester should deflect in small steps from 12-7 volts, 6-4 volts and 3-1 volts. If voltage does not drop as specified, regulator is defective or out of adjustment.

**Regulator Circuit Resistance** — Disconnect regulator connector plug and check resistance between regulator "IG" and "F"

## NIPPONDENSO ALTERNATORS (Cont.)

terminals with an ohmmeter. If there is any resistance, the low speed contact in regulator is defective.

**Fig. 2    Connections for Regulator Tester**

**Load Test** — With regulator tester connected as shown in illustration, start engine and turn on all lights and accessories. Run engine at 1100 RPM. Read amperage and voltage. It should be as specified. If battery is fully charged and reading is low, discharge battery by cranking engine (without spark) for about 15 seconds. Now if amperage is low, the rectifiers are open, shorted, or stator coil is open or shorted.

**Performance Test Using Conventional Tester** — 1) Attach tester as illustrated and increase engine speed until reverse current (approximately 2.5 amp.) ceases to flow to rotor field coil.

**2)** Turn off No. 1 switch and increase speed until voltmeter indicates 14V. If speed is under 1000 RPM, alternator performance is satisfactory.

**3)** Increase load resistance to near maximum so that nearly no current will flow. Close switches 1 and 2 while gradually increasing speed. Rated output should be reached by approximately 5000 RPM with satisfactory alternator.

**Fig. 3    Conventional Tester Connections**

## OVERHAUL

### DISASSEMBLY

1) Remove three retaining screws and insert screwdrivers into notches in drive end frame, pry with screwdrivers to separate

drive end frame from stator. If necessary, tap lightly on drive end frame with a mallet.

**2)** Secure rotor core in padded vise, remove pulley attaching nut, and withdraw pulley, fan, and spacer. Remove rotor from drive end frame, utilizing a press. Remove bearing retainer from drive end frame, then remove bearing, felt cover and felt ring.

**3)** Remove four rectifier holder securing nuts and two brush holder securing screws; separate stator with rectifier holders and brush holders from rectifier end frame. Remove brush lead terminal and stator coil "N" terminal from brush holder, utilizing a small screwdriver. **CAUTION** — *When removing brush holder assembly, do not remove it by cutting "N" terminal lead or melting the solder.*

### TESTING

**Rotor** — Check rotor for open field windings by connecting an ohmmeter across the slip rings. Coil resistance should be approximately as specified. Next check bearing and replace if necessary. Check slip rings for rough condition.

**Stator** — Use ohmmeter to check stator coil for ground. To check stator for open circuit, stator leads must be disconnected from diode leads. To disconnect leads from diodes, unsolder as quickly as possible with a low watt iron. Check 4 leads of stator coil for continuity between each lead. If ohmmeter shows no continuity, stator coil is open and must be replaced. Resistance should be zero.

**Fig. 4    Testing the Diodes**

**Diode Test** — With diode assembly on bench, make test connections as illustrated, using an ohmmeter. Contact diode plate with one probe and contact each of the three diode leads with the other probe. Note ohmmeter reading, then reverse probes and repeat test. Check both positive and negative diodes in this manner. All diodes should show a low reading in one

## NIPPONDENSO ALTERNATORS (Cont.)

*Fig. 5   Disassembled View of Nippondenso Alternator*

direction and no reading in opposite direction. If any one rectifier is defective, always replace positive or negative holder assembly.

### PARTS REPLACEMENT

**Brushes** — Check for cracks and wear. If brushes are worn beyond specifications, replace. Brushes should slide smoothly. Install new brush spring when replacing brush. Solder brush lead wire keeping protruded length to .51" (13 mm).

**NOTE** — *Brush length for Heavy Duty alternators is .73" (18.5 mm).*

### REASSEMBLY

Reassemble alternator by reversing disassembly procedure, noting the following points:

**1)** Press brushes, against spring tension, into brush holder. Insert a wire through access hole in rectifier and frame, and into hole in brush holder. This will prevent brushes from falling. Remove wire after assembly to end frame is completed.

**2)** Pack multipurpose grease into rear bearing and press bearing onto rotor shaft.

**3)** Install felt ring and felt cover so that convex surface of cover will face toward pulley side onto drive end frame. Next pack multipurpose grease into bearing and install bearing.

## NIPPONDENSO REGULATORS

Arrow/Colt, Challenger/Sapporo
1600 cc Engine Equipped
Honda
Opel
Toyota

### DESCRIPTION

Nippondenso regulators are of two designs: a single element type and a two element type. Two element types consists of a voltage regulator and voltage relay. The single element type has a voltage regulator only.

### APPLICATION

| Model | Part No. |
|---|---|
| Arrow/Colt, Challenger/Sapporo | 026000-1764 |
| Honda (All Models) | 56979-31400-657-673 |
| Opel | 94208462 |
| Toyota | |
| Celica | 27700-45020 |
| Corolla | 27700-38100 |
| Corona | 27700-45020 |
| Cressida | 27700-38060 |
| Land Cruiser | 27700-24020 |
| Pick-Up | 27700-38060 |

### TESTING

#### VOLTAGE REGULATOR

**Opel and Toyota** — Connect test meters as shown in illustrations. Vary alternator RPM and check voltmeter reading. Increase alternator RPM and note voltage when ammeter registers ½ of maximum rated output. Voltage should be 13.8-14.8 volts. Increase alternator speed to 3,000 RPM and note voltage again from 13.8-14.8 volts. If voltage is not within specified range, adjust regulator by bending arm to obtain correct setting.

**Honda, Arrow/Colt and Challenger/Sapporo** — Connect voltmeter between terminals A and E (except Toyota) or pin 6 (battery) and positive battery post (Toyota only). With engine idling, disconnect battery ground cable from negative post. Accelerate engine momentarily to 2000-4000 RPM and note voltage of 13.5-14.5 (Toyota) or 14.5-15.8 (except Toyota). If not within specifications, adjust or replace regulator as required.

**Fig. 1   Test Circuit for Single Element Type**

**Fig. 2   Test Circuit for Two Element Type**

#### VOLTAGE RELAY

**Charge Warning Lamp Type** — Connect test meters as shown in *Fig. 3 thru 6*. Increase alternator RPM gradually and note voltage when charge lamp goes out. Cut-in voltage should be 4.0-5.8 volts. If voltage is not as specified, bend voltage relay adjusting arm to obtain correct setting.

**Fig. 3   Test Circuit for Relay-Warning Lamp Type**

**Ammeter Type** — Connect test meters as shown in *Fig. 4 thru 6*. Increase alternator RPM gradually and note voltage. Voltage should be 4.5-5.8 volts. If necessary, adjust voltage by bending adjusting arm.

**Fig. 4   Test Circuit for Relay-Ammeter Type**

## NIPPONDENSO REGULATORS (Cont.)

**Fig. 5   Terminal Position for Honda Connector P55**

**Fig. 6   Terminal Position for 6 Pin Connector (Toyota Indicated in Italics)**

## ADJUSTMENT

**NOTE** — *Adjustments are not applicable to sealed units. If points are slightly oxidized or pitted, dress contacts with suitable emery cloth (about 400 grit). If points are oxidized or pitted excessively, replace regulator assembly.*

**Voltage Relay** — Connect voltmeter between "N" terminal (white wire) and ground then increase engine speed gradually. Voltmeter reading should be 4.0-5.8 volts when indicator light goes out. Adjust cut-in voltage by adjusting armature core gap and point gap using following procedures.

**1)** If cut-in voltage is too high, adjust by bending core adjusting arm down. Bend arm up if cut-in voltage is too low.

**2)** If adjustment of core arm does not correct cut-in voltage, proceed with point gap adjustment. Disconnect negative cable from battery. Check armature core gap with armature depressed until moving point is in contact with "B" side point. Armature core gap should be .012" or more. Adjust by bending point arm "B".

**3)** Release the armature and adjust the gap between the "B" side point and the moving point by bending point arm "A". Point gap should be .016" to .047".

**4)** After point gap adjustment, recheck cut-in voltage. If not within 4.0-5.8 volts, repeat cut-in voltage adjustment.

**Voltage Regulator** — If the no load regulated voltage is not within the 13.8-14.8 volt range, adjust regulator as follows.

**1)** If regulated voltage is too high, adjust by bending armature adjusting arm down. If voltage is too low, bend arm up.

**2)** If core arm adjustment will not correct regulated voltage, proceed to point gap adjustment.

**3)** Disconnect battery ground cable. Depress armature arm until the moving point contacts "B" side point. Bend point arm "B" to obtain armature gap of .012" or more.

**4)** Release armature and adjust gap between "B" side point and moving point by bending point arm "A". Gap should be .012" to .018".

**5)** After gap adjustment is made, recheck no load regulated voltage under operating test. Repeat core arm adjustment if necessary.

**Fig. 7   Adjustments for Voltage Relay**

**Fig. 8   Adjustments for Voltage Regulator**

# Alternators & Regulators

## SEV MARCHAL ALTERNATORS

Renault
Saab
Volvo

### DESCRIPTION

Alternator is a conventional three-phase, self-rectifying type. Six silicon rectifier diodes are connected to form a full-wave, three-phase rectifying bridge. Three exciter diodes are connected to stator windings and have a common junction point.

### APPLICATION

| Model | Part No. |
|---|---|
| Renault 5 | ① |
| Saab 99 | S.E.V. 71212002 |
| Volvo 260 Series | |
| Original Equipment | S.E.V. 7160410 |
| Replacement Alternator | ②71655302 |

① — See number stamped on housing or tag attached to housing.

② — Uses molded wiring harness and black plastic diode guard.

### SPECIFICATIONS

| Application | Data |
|---|---|
| Output @ 3000 Alternator RPM | 48 amps. |
| Output @ 5000 Alternator RPM | 55 amps. |
| Rotor Resistance between Slip Rings | 3.7-4.3 ohms |
| Stator Windings Resistance | .18 ohms±10% |
| Minimum Brush Protrusion from Holder | .16"(4 mm) |

### OVERHAUL

#### DISASSEMBLY

1) Remove brush holder attaching screws and carefully remove brush holder. Scribe a mark on end frames for reassembly reference, then remove four through bolts. Separate end frames by inserting two screwdrivers into notches on sides of alternator. **CAUTION** — *Do not insert screwdrivers deeper than .08" (2 mm) or damage may occur to stator windings.*

2) Remove nuts and washers for positive and negative diode holders from end frame. Carefully remove stator from end frame. Hold rotor in a vise using special wood blocks so no damage will occur to rotor. Remove nut, washer, pulley, fan, key and spacer. **NOTE** — *Check which way spacer faces for reassembly reference.*

3) Remove three attaching screws for bearing cap, then push rotor shaft from end frame. Press bearing from end frame. Use a puller to remove bearing from slip ring end of rotor.

#### BENCH TESTING

**Rotor** — Check rotor winding resistance across slip rings with ohmmeter and insulation between slip rings and rotor with test lamp. Replace rotor if resistance not within specifications or windings grounded.

**Stator** — Check stator for resistance with leads disconnected using ohmmeter. Check for shorts between core and leads with test lamp. Replace stator if grounded or resistance not within specifications.

**Diodes** — Use ohmmeter to perform conduction test on diodes. Observe current flow in one direction only from terminal to plate for positive diodes and from plate to terminal for negative diodes. If open or shorted, replace entire diode assembly.

**NOTE** — *Diodes may be either cylindrical or spherical in construction. Terminals must be disconnected during testing.*

#### REASSEMBLY

1) Press on inner race of bearing to position bearing on slip ring end of rotor shaft. Press on outer race to press bearing into end frame. Install bearing cap and three attaching screws. Press end frame with bearing assembly firmly onto rotor shaft. Install spacer, key, fan, pulley, washer and nut onto rotor shaft. Tighten nut to 29 ft. lbs.

2) Install insulating washers and sleeves onto positive diode holder, then install stator to end frame while inserting brush holder through opening in end frame. Install nuts and washers to secure diode holders. Check that "O" ring in end frame bearing seat does not block vent hole.

3) Assemble two end frames along with stator and rotor assemblies together, then secure with four through bolts. Install brush holder attaching screws and tighten.

*Fig. 1  Exploded View of Alternator*

# Alternators & Regulators

## SEV MOTOROLA ALTERNATORS

Audi
  Fox
Porsche
Volkswagen

### DESCRIPTION

SEV Motorola alternators are conventional three-phase, self-rectifying type alternators. Six silicon diodes (three positive and three negative) are used to rectify AC current.

**NOTE** — *Both SEV Motorola and Bosch alternators are used by Audi, Porsche and Volkswagen. Due to the wide variance in application and output for the various models, not all individual part numbers and ratings may be shown.*

### APPLICATION

| Model | Rating | ①Part No. |
|---|---|---|
| **Audi Fox** | | |
| W/Out Air Cond. | 55 Amps | 049 903 015 |
| W/Air Cond. | 65 Amps | 056 903 015E |
| **Porsche** | | |
| 911 & Turbo | 70 Amps | 911 603 120.02 |
| 924 | 75 Amps | 063 903 017 |
| 928 | | 928 603 113.03 |
| **Volkswagen** | | |
| Type 1 | 55 Amps | 043 903 023C |
| Type 2 | 55 Amps | 021 903 023F |
| **Dasher, Rabbit & Scirocco** | | |
| W/O Air Cond. | 55 Amps | 049 903 015J |
| W/Air Cond. | 65 Amps | 056 903 015E |

① — Audi, Porsche or VW part numbers.

### SPECIFICATIONS

#### Nominal Test Output

| Application | Amps/RPM | Voltage |
|---|---|---|
| Audi Fox | 25@3000 | 12.5-14.5 |
| Porsche | ① | 12.5-14.5 |
| **Volkswagen** | | |
| Type 1 | 45@3000 | 12.5-14.5 |
| Type 2 | 36@1000 | 14 |
| **Dasher, Rabbit & Scirocco** | | |
| W/O Air Cond. | 25@3000 | 12.5-14.5 |
| W/Air Cond. | 44@3000 | 12.5-14.5 |

① — Data not furnished by manufacturer.

### TESTING

#### ON CAR TEST

**1)** Disconnect battery cables and install cutout switch, variable resistance, ammeter and voltmeter as shown. Connect ground cable and check that cutout switch is in closed position.

**2)** Start engine and run at test RPM. Adjust variable resistance to give amperage readings as follows: Type 1 and models with air conditioning — 45 Amps, Type 2 — 30 Amps, other VW's without air conditioning and Audi Fox — 25 Amps. Open battery cutout switch, separating battery from test circuit. Load current is now determined by variable resistance.

**3)** Readjust variable resistance to provide Test Output Amperage. Voltage should be as specified.

**CAUTION** — *Never run alternator without battery connected unless variable resistor is installed to provide load. Alternator or regulator or both could be severely damaged without providing current load.*

**Fig. 1   Alternator Testing Set-Up**

### OVERHAUL

**NOTE** — *Since battery current reaches the alternator when the ignition is not on, battery ground strap should be disconnected when removing or installing alternator.*

**1)** Remove drive pulley and cooling fan. Remove regulator and brush assembly. Mark front and rear housing along with stator for proper orientation during reassembly.

**2)** Remove through bolts and carefully separate front housing with rotor from rear housing with stator. Rotor may be removed from housing after bearing retaining plate screws have been removed.

**NOTE** — *Bearings must be removed and installed using press with suitable adaptors. Never reinstall used bearings.*

**3)** Remove nuts holding diode assembly to rear housing and separate housing and stator. If diodes are faulty, complete assembly must be replaced rather than individual diodes. Use heat sink when making solder connections.

### TESTING

**Stator** — Check stator for short-circuiting. If one or more of the coils are burned, there must be a short-circuit in stator. Connect test lamp (12 volt, 2-5 watt) between stator plates and a terminal on stator (see illustration). If lamp lights, isolation between stator winding and stator plates must be burned, in which case stator should be replaced. **NOTE** — *Use only test lamp as specified. DO NOT use a 110-volt or 220-volt test lamp on this or any alternator test procedure.*

## SEV MOTOROLA ALTERNATORS (Cont.)

**Diodes** — Check diodes with a diode tester. If any of the rectified diodes are shorted or open, the diode holder must be replaced. If any isolation diode is faulty, replace holder, complete with isolation diodes. If diode tester is not available, diodes should be unsoldered and tested with an ohmmeter. Diodes should show high resistance in reverse direction and low resistance in flow direction.

**Rotor** — Check to make sure slip rings are not dirty or burned. Check winding for breakage or damaged isolation. Measure resistance between slip rings. It should be as specified. If winding is faulty, rotor must be replaced. **NOTE** — *It is recommended that bearings be replaced whenever alternator is disassembled.*

Fig. 3  Checking the Stator

*Fig. 2  Checking the Brush Holder*

**Brush Holder** — Connect a test lamp between the brushes. Lamp should not light. Next connect test lamp between "DF" terminal and the "+" brush. Lamp should give steady light even if brush or terminal cable is moved (see illustration). Connect test lamp between brush holder frame and "−" brush. Lamp should give steady light. If test results are not satisfactory or brush length is less than ³⁄₁₆" (5 mm), replace brush holder. **NOTE** — *Brush length is measured between brush contact surface and holder, with brush resting against spring.*

### PARTS REPLACEMENT

**Diodes** — Mark leads connecting stator to diodes, then unsolder leads. Place new diode holder in exact position of holder being replaced. Solder new leads, holding with pliers (this is to conduct heat from soldering point, to avoid damaging new diode). Use a minimum 100-watt, well-heated soldering iron. Never change places of diode holders. Positive holder is isolated from frame by means of isolation washers and sleeves and its diodes are marked in red. Negative diode holder is not isolated and its diodes are marked in black.

### REASSEMBLY

Alternator is reassembled by reversing disassembly procedures while noting the following: Rotor must be pressed into drive end shield. Connect a test lamp between "B+" terminal and alternator frame, then reverse connections. Lamp should light only in one direction. After completion of reassembly, test run alternator on bench, using same procedure as described for On Car Testing.

*Fig. 4  Disassembled View of SEV Motorola Alternator (Volkswagen Shown)*

# Starters

## BOSCH

Audi
BMW
Capri
Fiesta
Lancia
Mercedes-Benz
Porsche
Saab
Volkswagen
Volvo

## DESCRIPTION

Starter is a brush type, series wound, electric motor, equipped with an overrunning clutch (inner-wedge or outer-wedge type). Unit may or may not be equipped with a solenoid. Field frame is enclosed by commutator end frame and drive bushing and carries the pole shoes and field coils. A spline, located on drive end of armature, carries overrunning clutch and pinion assembly. Armature shaft is supported in sintered bronze bushings in the commutator end frame and drive end housings (these bushings are packed with lubricant at assembly and require no further lubrication).

## APPLICATION

| Model | ①Bosch Part No. |
|---|---|
| **Audi** | |
| 5000 | 311 122 |
| Fox | 211 218 |
| **BMW** | |
| 320i | 311 045 |
| 530i, 633CSi, 733i | 311 042 |
| **Capri** | |
| 4 Cyl. | 311 121 |
| V6 | 311 120 |
| **Fiesta** | 211 227 |
| **Lancia** | 311 116 |
| **Mercedes-Benz** | |
| 230, 280, 450 | 314 018 |
| 6.9 | 312 101 |
| 240D, 300D, 300CD, 300SD Turbo | 362 047 |
| **Porsche** | |
| 924 | 311 122 |
| 911SC & Turbo | 312 100 |
| 928 | 312 102 |
| **Saab 99** | 311 108 |
| **Volkswagen** | |
| Type 1 | |
| M/T | 211 993 |
| A/T | 212 005 |
| Type 2 | |
| M/T | 211 221 |
| A/T | 211 206 |
| Dasher | |
| M/T | 211 218 |
| A/T | 211 206 |
| Rabbit & Scirocco | |
| M/T | 211 223 |
| A/T | 212 206 |
| Diesel | 314 012 |
| **Volvo** | |
| 4 Cyl. | 311 103 |
| V6 | 311 105 |

① — Bosch starter basic part number is 0 001.

## TESTING

**Lock Test—** Mount starter in a test stand to allow starter torque measurement (follow manufacturers instructions). With voltage adjusted to specifications, ammeter reading and starter torque should be within specifications.

**Free Running Test—** With starter in test bench, take readings of starter current, voltage and RPM. Readings should be within specifications.

**NOTE** — Starter must be mounted to prevent meshing of pinion and ring gear even in engaged position. If starter has warmed up during previous tests, RPM will be higher.

## SPECIFICATIONS

### Brush Length & Spring Tension

| Application | In.(mm) | Lbs. (g) |
|---|---|---|
| 211 xxx | .52(13) | 2.5-3.0(1150-1300) |
| 211 xxx | .52(13) | 2.4-2.7(1080-1220) |
| 212 xxx | .52(13) | 2.4-2.7(1080-1220) |
| 311 xxx | .39(10) | 2.5-2.9(1150-1300) |
| 312 xxx | .39(10) | 1.8-2.0(800-900) |
| 314 xxx | .52(13) | 2.5-2.9(1150-1300) |
| 362 xxx | .61(15.5) | 2.5-2.9(1150-1300) |

## OVERHAUL

### DISASSEMBLY

1) Clamp starter in vise and remove nut and washer from solenoid main terminal connection. Remove solenoid mounting screws and guide solenoid body away from drive end housing and plunger. Disconnect plunger from actuating lever.

2) Remove screws and cap with rubber seal from commutator end housing. Wipe grease from armature shaft and remove "C" clip with shims. Remove through bolts or nuts from studs and lift off commutator end housing.

3) Lift springs clear of brushes and slide brushes from holders. Remove brush plate from housing. Separate drive end housing and armature assembly from yoke by tapping apart.

4) Remove armature assembly from drive end housing while at the same time uncoupling actuating arm. If necessary to remove actuating arm, first remove rubber insert from drive end housing. Remove pivot arm screw and nut and extract actuating arm.

5) To remove drive pinion assembly from armature shaft, separate thrust collar from over "C" clip. Remove "C" clip from its groove and drive pinion assembly off armature shaft.

### CLEANING & INSPECTING

Clean all parts with suitable cleaning agent. Inspect for wear or damage, then apply thin coat of oil to running surfaces.

## BOSCH (Cont.)

### PARTS REPLACEMENT & TESTING

**Brushes & Springs** —Check brush spring pressure with suitable spring scale. Check brushes for minimum length and freedom of movement in holders. If replacement is necessary, replace all brushes by cutting old brush leads midway between connection and old brush. Solder new brushes to original leads.

**Armature** — Check coil and commutator to shaft (or core) for short circuit, with 110 volt ac control lamp. Control lamp should not illuminate (slight illumination is possible due to dampness). Check coil to commutator for short circuit with a 6 volt DC control lamp, touching every coil on armature and its corresponding bar, brightness of lamp should not change. Check coils on armature for short circuit between windings using a growler.

Check out of round of commutator to core, it should not exceed .00197" (0.5 mm). Commutator should have a smooth greyish-blue surface with no grooves or burned spots otherwise, it must be turned. Minimum commutator diameter is 1.32" (33.5 mm). After turning commutator, undercut insulation to a depth of .0197-.0236" (0.5-0.8 mm), decrease

diameter by .0039" (0.1 mm). Do not use emery cloth, turn on a lathe only.

**Drive Assembly** — Replace drive when damaged or teeth are worn. See *Disassembly*.

**Bushings** — Self-lubricating bushings should be replaced only when worn or damaged. Force out bushings, using a suitable mandrel, remove burrs and clean hole. Before pressing in new bushing, soak bushing in a suitable oil for not less than 30 minutes. After replacing, cross check inner diameter of bushing by pulling a smoothing mandrel through.

### REASSEMBLY

**1)** Slide drive pinion assembly and thrust washer onto armature shaft. Install "C" clip into groove in armature shaft and pull thrust washer up over clip. Align fork in drive end housing and insert pivot pin. Slide armature assembly into drive end housing, coupling the shift fork onto the drive pinion flange.

*Fig. 1  Disassembled View of Typical Bosch Starter*

## BOSCH (Cont.)

**2)** Install rubber insert in drive end housing. Guide yoke assembly over armature while aligning notch with rubber insert. Tap yoke into full contact with drive end housing.

**3)** Install brush assembly noting that cutouts in brush plate slide over through bolts on models so equipped. On models with screws, brush plate cutouts align with loops in field windings. Plates are properly positioned when screws are installed in commutator end housing. Install brushes and springs assuring that field winding brush leads do not contact yoke.

**4)** Slide commutator end housing into position and secure with nuts and washers or screws, as appropriate. Install drive end housing. Install shims onto armature shaft at commutator end to eliminate end play and install "C" clip in groove.

**5)** Install bearing cap seal on commutator end housing. Lubricate end of armature shaft with lithium based grease and install bearing cap. Lubricate plunger hook and place in position over shift fork in drive end housing. Install solenoid body with return spring properly positioned, then tighten mounting screws and field connections.

| Model① | No Load Test | | Lock Test | | |
|---|---|---|---|---|---|
| | Amps. | RPM | Amps. | Volts | Torque |
| 211 xxx | 30-50 | 6000-9000 | 300-390 | 9.0 | 8.7 ft.lbs. |
| 211 9xx | 30-50 | 6500-9500 | 320-410 | 8.5 | 8.3 ft.lbs. |
| 212 xxx | 35-55 | 6000-8000 | 320-410 | 8.5 | 9.4 ft.lbs. |
| 311 xxx | 30-50 | 5500-7500 | 350-450 | 8.5 | 13.0 ft.lbs. |
| 312 1xx | 55-85 | 8500-10500 | 650-730 | 6.0 | 13.7 ft.lbs. |
| 314 xxx | 50-80 | 7300-9300 | 690-780 | 6.0 | 16.6 ft.lbs. |
| 362 xxx | 65-95 | 6500-8500 | 1100-1300 | 7.0 | 32.5 ft.lbs. |

**STARTER PERFORMANCE SPECIFICATIONS**

① — Bosch Basic Part Number is 0 001.

# Starters

## FIAT

**Fiat
All Models**

## DESCRIPTION

Fiat starter is a 12 volt system with four poles and field windings are in series. Overrunning clutch pinion drive mounted directly on armature shaft. Pinion drive and battery connection to starter motor are controlled by a solenoid mounted on starter frame.

## APPLICATION

| Model Application | Fiat No. |
|---|---|
| 128 & X1/9 Models | E 84-0.8/12 |
| 124 & 131 Models | E 100-1.3/12 |

## TESTING

### PERFORMANCE TESTS

**Cranking Amperage Draw** — Mount starter on starter test stand. Make wiring connections as shown in illustration. Starter test stand should have a ring gear and a brake dynomometer. Ring gear should have minimum pinion/ring ratio of 1.0-10. If test stand is not equipped with correct pinion/ring ratio, follow manufacturers instructions in use of test stand. Test should be made with ambient temperature of 77°F. Observe amperage draw, voltage reading, and delivered torque while operating starter and check against specifications.

**No Load Test** — With starter mounted on test stand so pinion cannot contact ring gear, operate starter. Amperage draw, voltage reading and armature RPM should be within specifications.

**Stall (Lock) Test** — With starter mounted in test stand and ring gear locked, adjust test stand rheostat to values specified (see specifications) and observe torque on dial indicator.

**Fig. 1   Performance Test Wiring Diagram**

## CRANKING SPECIFICATIONS

| Starter No. | Amps @RPM | Torque (Ft. Lbs.) |
|---|---|---|
| E 84-0.8/12 | 170@1950±100① | 2.89±.14 |
| E 100-1.3/12 | 280@1600±100② | 5.78±.14 |

① — At 10.3 volts.
② — At 9.5 volts.

**Brush Spring Tension** — E 84-0.8/12 — 2.5-2.9 lbs. (1.15-1.3 kg); E 100-1.3/12 — 2.2±.2 lbs. (1±0.1 kg).

**Rotation (Pinion End)** — Clockwise.

**Armature End Play** — E 84-0.8/12 — .0039-.0197" (0.1-0.5 mm); E 100-1.3/12 — .003-.027" (0.07-0.70 mm).

## STARTER PERFORMANCE SPECIFICATIONS

| Model | No Load Test ① | | Lock Test | | |
|---|---|---|---|---|---|
| | Amps. | RPM | Amps. | Volts | Torque (Ft. Lbs.) |
| E 84-0.8/12 | Below 35 | 7000±500 | 370 | 8.3±0.3 | 7.9±.36 |
| E 100-1.3/12 | Below 28 | 5200±500 | 530 | 7±0.3 | 12.58±.7 |

① — At 12 volts.

## OVERHAUL

### DISASSEMBLY

The starter motor can be disassembled into the following components: Solenoid, commutator end plate, frame (containing field coils and pole pieces), armature, overrunning clutch and pinion drive gear, and pinion end housing.

1) With the metal band (brush cover) removed from starter frame, disconnect lead from solenoid terminal and remove nuts from rod attaching solenoid to pinion end head of the motor and remove solenoid.

2) Disconnect positive brush holder (insulated). Lift brushes and arrange ends of brush springs against sides of brushes to hold them off commutator.

# Starters

## FIAT (Cont.)

3) Remove nuts on tie-rods of the two supports, and remove brush holder bracket. Be careful not to lose thrust washers (one fibre, and one steel) on the pin.

4) Slide frame off pinion end. Take out split pin from engaging lever pivot and remove pivot.

5) The armature and thrust washers can be taken out with drive and fork lever. Remove the snap ring from armature shaft and remove drive parts in their proper order.

### CLEANING

Do not immerse starter components in solvent. Use compressed air to blow dirt and worn brush dust from field coils and armature. Use cleaning brush dipped in solvent to clean drive unit, then blow dry with air.

### PARTS REPLACEMENT

**Field Coils** — Mount starter frame in press-type screwdriver stand and remove pole piece attaching screws. Remove pole pieces and field coils. Prior to installing new coils, heat windings to 122°F in order to obtain added flexibility and facilitate seating the coils under pole shoes. Use press-type screwdriver stand to completely tighten attaching screws. After installation is completed, measure pole shoes inner diameter. To assure proper air gap between pole shoes and armature,

inner diameter must be between 2.175-2.182" (55.25-55.42 mm) on starter No. E 84-0.8/12 and between 2.675-2.677" (67.95-68.00 mm) on starter No. E 100-1.3/12. Do not bore out inner diameter to obtain specified diameter. If diameter is not within tolerance, coils and shoes have been improperly installed.

### REASSEMBLY

Lubricate inner splined face of drive assembly with SAE 10 motor oil before installing drive on armature shaft. Reverse disassembly procedure to complete overhaul.

### TROUBLE SHOOTING & DIAGNOSIS

**Starter Inoperative** — Battery terminals corroded. Starter switch or battery terminals loose. Battery discharged or defective. Worn brushes (not contacting commutator). Starter switch (solenoid) contacts burned or worn. Commutator segment dislodged by centrifugal force.

**Starter Operation Sluggish** — Worn brushes. Part of field or armature windings shorted. Poor battery cable connections. Battery charge low, or defective cell.

**Starter Motor Noisy** — Worn armature shaft bushing. Pinion gear disengagement exceptionally late (worn or defective overrunning clutch).

**Fig. 2   Disassembled View of Fiat Starter Motor**

# Starters

## HITACHI & MITSUBISHI

Arrow/Colt, Challenger/Sapporo
Datsun
Honda (Except Calif. Civic)
LUV
Mazda
Opel

### DESCRIPTION

Starter is a 12-volt, four-pole unit of conventional design. Magnetic switch assembly is mounted on gear case. Starters have a overrunning clutch connected by a shift lever to magnetic switch plunger. Brushes and springs are retained inside yoke assembly by holders.

### APPLICATION

#### Hitachi

| Model | Part No. |
|---|---|
| Datsun | |
| B210 | |
| Man. Trans. | S114-160B |
| Auto. Trans. | S114-163E |
| F10 | S114-161E |
| 510 | |
| Man. Trans. | S114-170E |
| Auto. Trans. | S114-180F |
| 200SX | |
| Man. Trans. | S114-170E |
| Auto. Trans. | S114-180F |
| 810 | S114-254 |
| 620 Pickup | |
| Man. Trans. | S114-170E |
| Auto. Trans. | S114-180F |
| 280Z | S114-254 |

#### Hitachi (Cont.)

| Model | Part No. |
|---|---|
| LUV | S114-202 |
| Honda | 65274 31200 657 025 or 59480 31200 657 671 |
| Opel | 9420 4438 |

#### Mitsubishi

| Model | Part No. |
|---|---|
| Arrow/Colt, Challenger/Sapporo | |
| 1600cc | |
| Man. Trans. | M3T12572 |
| Auto. Trans. | M3T15772 |
| 2000cc | |
| Man. Trans. | M3T15772 |
| Auto. Trans. | M4T14771 |
| 2600cc | |
| All | M4T14771 |
| Mazda | |
| 1300cc | |
| Man. Trans. | 0324 18 400A |
| Auto. Trans. | 0324 18 400B |
| 1800cc | |
| All | 0426 18 400A |
| All Others | |
| Man. Trans. | 1757 18 400C |
| Auto. Trans. | 1758 18 400C |

## STARTER PERFORMANCE SPECIFICATIONS

| Model | No Load Test | | Lock Test | | |
|---|---|---|---|---|---|
| | Amps. | RPM | Amps. | Volts | Torque |
| **HITACHI** | | | | | |
| S114-160B | below 60 | 7000 | ..... | ..... | ..... |
| S114-161E | below 60 | 700 | ..... | ..... | ..... |
| S114-163E | below 60 | 7000 | ..... | ..... | ..... |
| S114-170E | below 60 | 7000 | ..... | ..... | ..... |
| S114-180F | below 60 | 6000 | ..... | ..... | ..... |
| S114-202 | below 60 | 6000 | below 330 | 5.0 | over 5.8 ft.lbs. |
| S114-254 | below 100 | 4300 | ..... | ..... | ..... |
| 31200-657-671① | below 70 | 6000 | below 380 | 5.5 | over 6.15 ft.lbs. |
| 94204438② | ..... | ..... | ..... | ..... | ..... |
| **MITSUBISHI** | | | | | |
| M3T12572 | below 53 | 5000 | below 400 | 6.0 | 6.7 ft.lbs. |
| M3T15772 | below 55 | 6500 | below 560 | 6.0 | 10.8 ft.lbs. |
| M4T14771 | below 62 | 4500 | below 730 | 6.0 | 18.0 ft.lbs. |
| 0324 18 400A & B | below 53 | 6800 | below 310 | 5.0 | 5.4 ft.lbs. |
| 0426 18 400A | below 53 | 6800 | below 310 | 5.0 | 5.4 ft.lbs. |
| 1757 18 400C | below 50 | 5600 | below 600 | 5.0 | 6.9 ft.lbs. |
| 1758 18 400C | below 100 | 6600 | below 1050 | 5.0 | 15.9 ft.lbs. |

① — Honda part number.
② — Buick part number.

## HITACHI & MITSUBISHI (Cont.)

### TESTING

#### PERFORMANCE TESTS

**No Load Tests** — Connect starter in series with a 12 volt battery, being certain ammeter used is capable of 1000 ampere reading. Connect voltmeter to starter (see illustration). Compare readings with specifications.

**Lock (Torque) Test** — Mount starter in a test stand to allow starter torque measurement (follow manufacturers instructions). With voltage adjusted (see specifications), ammeter reading and starter torque should be within specifications.

**Fig. 1   Connections for No Load Test**

### OVERHAUL

#### DISASSEMBLY

1) Loosen nut securing connecting plate to magnetic switch "M" terminal, remove screws securing magnetic switch and remove switch assembly. Remove two through bolts and brush cover assembly, then tap yoke assembly with a wooden hammer and remove it. Remove armature assembly shift lever.

2) Remove pinion stop ring from end of armature shaft by pushing stop ring to the clutch side. Remove snap ring and then remove stop ring with overrunning clutch. Remove overrunning clutch assembly from armature shaft.

#### PARTS REPLACEMENT & TESTING

**Brushes & Springs** — Check brush spring tension using a suitable spring scale (see specifications). Check brush contact surface condition. If brush contact is loose, replace brush. If brush length is less than specified, replace brushes. Check lead clip and wire connection, check condition of brush holders and spring clip, repair or replace parts as necessary.

### Brush Spring Tension

| Application | Lbs. (Kg) |
| --- | --- |
| Arrow, Colt | 3.3 (1.5) |
| Datsun | 3.1-4.0 (1.4-1.8) |
| Honda, LUV, Mazda, Opel | 3.5 (1.6) |

### Brush Length (Minimum)

| Application | In. (mm) |
| --- | --- |
| Arrow, Colt, Mazda | .45 (11.5) |
| Datsun | .47 (12.0) |
| Honda | .16 (4.0) |
| LUV, Opel | .47 (12.0) |

**Armature** — Check external condition of armature. Measure shaft for distortion or bending, using a dial indicator gauge. Replace armature shaft if bending exceeds .0031" on Datsun, .006" on Luv and .004" on all other models.

**Commutator** — Inspect commutator for roughness, if surface is pitted or grooved, it should be sanded lightly with no. 500 emery paper. Also check commutator for being out-of-round. If out-of-round is more than .0079", or insulating mica depth is less than .0079" from the cummutator surface, turn commutator in a lathe until out-of-round is less than .002". Insulating mica should be undercut to depth of .0197-.0315". Wear limit of commutator diameter is .0787", if excessively worn, it must be replaced.

**Field Coil** — Check field coil continuity by connecting test probe of a circuit tester or a resistance counter to the field coil positive terminal and positive brush holder, if tester shows no continuity, field circuit or coil is open. Check for grounded field coils by placing one probe of a circuit tester on yoke and other probe to field coil positive terminal, if resistance is read, field coils are grounded.

**Overrunning Clutch Assembly** — Inspect pinion assembly and sleeve. Sleeve should slide freely along armature shaft spline and if damage or resistance is noted, replace assembly. Inspect pinion teeth for excessive rubbing, replace as necessary. Check flywheel ring gear for damage or wear.

**Magnetic Switch Assembly** — After checking starter motor, magnetic switch assembly should also be checked. Connect jumper cables between negative battery terminal and starting motor "M" terminal, and positive battery terminal and starting motor "S" terminal, connecting ignition switch in series (see illustration). With ignition switch on, measure distance between the pinion front edge and pinion stopper (see illustration). Clearance should be .012-.059" on Hitachi starters and .02-.08" on Mitsubishi starters. If not within specifications, adjust by changing washer between magnetic switch and gear case.

**Fig. 2   Circuit for Testing Magnetic Switch Assembly**

## HITACHI & MITSUBISHI (Cont.)

Switch Assy.

Pinion Case Bearing

Front Bracket

Shift Lever Assy.

Lever Spring Cap

Lever Springs

Shim

Washer

Ring

Stop Ring

Seat

Overrunning Clutch

Field Coil

Armature

Yoke Assy.

Pole

Washer

Insulating Washer

Rear Cover

Rear Bushing

Brush

Through Bolt

Brush Spring

**Fig. 3  *Disassembled View of a Typical Mitsubishi Starter***

# Starters

## HITACHI & MITSUBISHI (Cont.)

**Pinion Case Bearing** — Inspect bearing for wear and check side play. Clearance between bearing and armature shaft should not exceed .0079". If limit is exceeded, replace bearing. Clearance with new bearing installed should be .001-.004" on Hitachi starters and .002-.004" on Mitsubishi starters.

**NOTE** — *Be sure bearing is installed so that end of bearing is flush with gear case end plane.*

## CLEANING & INSPECTION

Clean all disassembled parts, being careful not to use a grease dissolving solvent on overrunning clutch, armature assembly, magnetic switch assembly or field coils, as damage could result. Check all parts for damage or excessive wear, replace as required.

### REASSEMBLY

To reassemble, reverse disassembly procedure and be certain to fill rear case with grease and to lightly oil rear cover metal bearing and pinion.

**Fig. 4   Measuring Pinion Edge-to-Pinion Stopper Clearance**

**Fig. 5   Disassembled View of a Typical Hitachi Starter**

# Starters

## LUCAS

**Jaguar
MG
Triumph**

### DESCRIPTION

The Lucas starter is a series wound, four-pole, four-brush motor. Two brushes are grounded and two are insulated and connected to the ends of field coils. Some models have an extended shaft which carries a conventional inertia drive. Other models incorporate a roller clutch drive on the shaft.

### APPLICATION

| Car Model | Model No. |
| --- | --- |
| Jaguar | |
| 6 Cylinder | 3M100 |
| 12 Cylinder | M45 |
| MG | |
| Midget | M35J |
| MGB | 2M100 |
| Triumph | |
| TR7 | 2M100 |
| Spitfire | M35J |

### TESTING

#### PERFORMANCE TESTS

**No Load Test** — With starter on bench and using a good 12-volt battery, connect an ammeter in series to starter. Starter should rotate smoothly. See specifications for RPM, and current draw.

**Lock Test** — To perform lock test, follow instructions and procedures outlined in instruction manual furnished with tester. With starter locked in test stand, and voltage adjusted to specified figure, ammeter reading and starter torque should be as specified (see specifications).

### OVERHAUL

#### DISASSEMBLY

**NOTE** — *Disregard Step 1) when working on inertia drive models.*

1) Disconnect link between lower solenoid terminal and starting motor yoke. Remove nuts securing solenoid unit. Remove solenoid from drive end bracket, being careful to disengage solenoid plunger from starter drive engagement lever.

*Fig. 1   Exploded View of Lucas Inertia Starter*

# Starters

## LUCAS (Cont.)

2) Remove metal band cover, hold back brush springs and remove brushes from their holders. Remove the two through bolts and remove commutator end bracket from yoke.

3) On inertia type starters, remove drive end bracket with armature and drive from yoke. If it is necessary to remove drive end bracket from armature, it can be removed after the drive is dismantled.

4) On all other models, extract rubber seal from drive end bracket. Remove nut securing eccentric pin on which drive engagement lever pivots and remove pin. Separate drive end bracket from armature and intermediate bracket assembly. Remove washer from end of armature shaft extension and slide assembly and engagement lever off shaft. Remove intermediate bracket retaining ring from armature shaft extension and slide bracket and brake assembly off shaft.

### PARTS REPLACEMENT & TESTING

**Armature** — Check armature for open, shorted, or grounded circuits. Check for lifted commutator segments and loose turns in armature winding. A damaged armature must always be replaced and no attempt should be made to machine armature core or to true a distorted shaft. A scored armature may indicate a bent shaft or a loose pole shoe.

**Commutator** — Clean commutator with a cloth moistened in gasoline and if this is not effective, carefully polish with a strip of fine glass paper while rotating armature. To correct a badly worn commutator, disassemble starter as previously described and remove armature from end bracket. Mount armature in a lathe and rotate at high speed, taking a light cut on commutator with a very sharp tool. Do not remove more metal than is absolutely necessary. **NOTE** — *Insulators, between commutator segments, must not be undercut.*

**Brushes & Springs** — Check that brushes move freely in holders by holding back brush springs and pulling gently on the flex connectors. If movement is sluggish, remove brush from holder and clean sides with a gasoline moistened cloth. Replace brushes and springs when they have reached minimum specifications in specification table.

| Starter Model | Min. Brush Length | Min. Spring Tension |
|---|---|---|
| M35J | 3/8" | 28 ozs. |
| M45PE | 5/16" | 30 ozs. |
| 2M100/PE | 3/8" | 36 ozs. |
| 3M100 | 5/16" | 30 ozs. |

**Field Coils** — Check for open or grounded coils using test lamp or voltmeter and battery, connected in series. If coil is found to be defective, replace all coils as they should not be serviced individually. Mark yoke and pole shoes so shoes may be installed in original position. Remove fiber insulating washers and sleeve from field coil terminal post and remove insulating band from commutator end of yoke. Install a suitable tool (Pole Piece Expander) in starter and expand tool against pole pieces. Remove pole piece screws. Remove field coils and pole pieces from yoke. Carefully unsolder the field coil tappings from terminal post. To install, reverse removal procedure.

**Bushings** — 1) Armature shaft is supported by three bushings. Commutator and driving end brackets each carry porous bronze bushings, while intermediate bracket carries a graphite-impregnated brass bushing. Bushings which are worn to the extent that they allow excessive side play of the armature must be replaced.

2) The drive end bushing and intermediate bracket bushings can be pressed out. The commutator end bracket bushing is removed by inserting a suitable tap and withdrawing the tap with the bushing attached. New bushings are installed using a shouldered highly polished mandrel of same diameter as shaft to be fitted in the bushing. **CAUTION** — *Do not ream bronze bushings, as the porosity of the bushing may be altered.*

3) Before installing a new porous bronze bushing, it should be immersed in clean engine oil for 24 hours. This process can be speeded up in case of an emergency, by heating oil to 212°F (100°C) and allowing bushing to soak for two hours. Allow oil to cool before removing bushings from oil.

### REASSEMBLY

Clean all parts with a clean cloth and reassemble in the reverse order of disassembly while noting the following:

1) To facilitate installing the solenoid unit to drive end plate, ease drive assembly forward along armature shaft.

2) Set pinion movement before tightening the eccentric pivot pin securing nut. After completing reassembly, connect the small center terminal on the solenoid unit by way of a switch to a 12-volt battery. Connect other side of battery to one of the solenoid studs. Close switch (throwing drive assembly forward into the engaged position) and measure the distance between

| | STARTER PERFORMANCE SPECIFICATIONS | | | | | |
|---|---|---|---|---|---|---|
| **Model** | **No Load Test** ① | | | **Lock Test** | | |
| | Amps. | RPM | Amps. | Volts | | Torque |
| M35J | 0 65 | 8,000-10,000 | 350-375 | ① | | over 7 ft.lbs. |
| M45PE | 100 | 5,000-7,000 | 940 | ① | | over 29 ft.lbs. |
| 2M100PE | 40 | 6,000 | 463 | ① | | over 14.4 ft.lbs. |
| 3M100 | 100 | 5,000-6,000 | 940 | ① | | over 29 ft.lbs. |

① — Use 12 volt fully charged battery.

## LUCAS (Cont.)

the pinion and the washer on the armature shaft extension. Make this measurement with the pinion pressed lightly towards armature to take up slack in engagement linkage. Measurement should be .005-.015".

3) To adjust, turn pivot pin until the correct measurement is obtained. The arc of the adjustment is 180° and the arrow on pivot pin should be set between the arrows on the drive end bracket. Tighten pivot pin locking nut.

*Fig. 2  Exploded View of Lucas Pre-Engaged Starter*

# Starters

## NIPPONDENSO DIRECT DRIVE

Courier
Honda
  Civic (Cal.)
Subaru
Toyota

### DESCRIPTION

The Nippondenso starter has four pole pieces and four sets of field coils. Four commutator brushes are installed; two are grounded, and two are insulated and are connected to the ends of field coils. Field coil is connected with armature coil through brushes and commutator segments in series. Starter clutch is engaged to armature shaft with helical splines. The turning of the pinion is due to these helical splines which result in a smooth engagement of pinion and flywheel.

### APPLICATION

| Model | Part No. |
|---|---|
| Courier ........................................ | D77Z |
| Honda Civic (Cal.) ........................... | 62522-31200-657-016 |
| Subaru | |
|   Man. Trans. .............................. | 2970 |
|   Auto. Trans. (Calif.) ..................... | 4210 |
|   Auto. Trans. (Fed.) ...................... | 4721 |
| Toyota | |
|   2F Engine ............................. | 28100-60041, 60061 |
|   3K Engine ............................. | 28100-24080 |
|   4M Engine ............................. | 28100-42020, 45033 |
|   20R Engine | |
|     Federal .............................. | 28100-34052 |
|     Calif. ................................ | 28100-33020 |

### TESTING

#### PERFORMANCE TESTS

**No Load Test** — With starter on bench, and using a fully charged 12-volt battery, make connections as shown. The starter should rotate smoothly. See specification chart for RPM, voltage, and current draw.

**Fig. 1  Circuit for No Load Test**

**Lock Test** — To perform lock test follow instructions and procedures outlined in instruction manual furnished with tester. With starter locked in test stand, and voltage adjusted to specified figure, ammeter reading and starter torque should be within limits (see specifications).

### OVERHAUL

#### DISASSEMBLY

**1)** Disconnect field coil wire from starter solenoid main terminal and remove solenoid attaching bolts. Remove solenoid by moving it up and down to unhook unit from drive lever.

**2)** Remove bearing cover and pull out armature shaft lock plate, washer, seal and spring. Remove through bolts, commutator end frame, brush holder and yoke.

**3)** Remove drive lever set bolt, rubber piece, plate, armature and drive lever from housing. Remove pinion stop collar from armature shaft end and remove starter clutch.

| STARTER PERFORMANCE SPECIFICATIONS | | | | | |
|---|---|---|---|---|---|
| | No Load Test ① | | Lock Test | | |
| Model | Amps. | RPM | Amps. | Volts | Torque |
| D77Z | below 50 | over 5000 | ..... | ..... | ..... |
| 2970 | below 50 | over 5000 | below 600 | 7.7 | over 9.4 ft.lbs. |
| 4210 | below 50 | over 5000 | below 600 | 7.7 | over 9.4 ft.lbs. |
| 4721 | below 60 | over 5000 | below 600 | 7.0 | over 13.0 ft.lbs. |
| 657-016 | below 70 | over 6000 | below 380 | 5.5 | over 6.15 ft.lbs. |
| 60041 | below 50 | over 5000 | ..... | ..... | ..... |
| 60061 | below 50 | over 5000 | ..... | ..... | ..... |
| 24080 | below 55 | over 3500 | below 450 | 8.5 | 9.4 ft.lbs. |
| 42020 | below 50 | over 5000 | ..... | ..... | ..... |
| 45033 | below 50 | over 5000 | ..... | ..... | ..... |
| 34052 | below 50 | over 5000 | ..... | ..... | ..... |
| 33020 | below 50 | over 5000 | ..... | ..... | ..... |

① — At 11.5 volts on Toyota; 11 volts all others.

# Starters

## NIPPONDENSO DIRECT DRIVE (Cont.)

### PARTS REPLACEMENT & TESTING

**Armature** — Check armature for open, shorted or grounded circuits. Inspect armature shaft for bend; if bend is excessive replace armature. **NOTE** — *Do not attempt to straighten a bent shaft.* Inspect armature shaft to bushing clearance. If clearance exceeds .008", replace bushing.

**Commutator** — If condition warrants, carefully polish commutator with a strip of fine glass paper. If surface is scored, rough or burnt, dress with lathe just enough to remove defective area. If out-of-round exceeds .012", commutator must be turned. After turning, out-of-round must not exceed .004". Check mica depth and file off mica if depth is less than .008". Correct depth is .020-.032".

**Brushes & Springs** — 1) Check brush holder insulation. Connect one lead of ammeter to brush holder positive side and other lead to negative side of brush holder. If tester needle moves, the brush holder is shorted due to defective insulator. Replace brush holder.

**2)** Check brush length and if less than .16" (Honda), .39" (Toyota 3K), .51" (Toyota 2F), or .47" (all others), replace brushes. Check minimum spring tension of 21 ozs. New brush springs should have 37-48 ozs. tension. Brushes must move freely in holders.

**Starter Solenoid** — Test pull-in motion of solenoid by connecting test leads to the "50" terminal and the main "F" terminal. Apply 8 volts. Plunger should be pulled in. If switch does not pull in, it is defective. Disconnect the "F" terminal lead only. If plunger remains pulled in, then switch is satisfactory. Test plunger returning movement by connecting the battery positive lead to the "F" terminal and the negative lead to the switch

body. Depress plunger by hand and release it. If plunger returns to its original position with 12 volts, switch is satisfactory.

**Field Coils** — Check field coils for open circuit using a circuit tester. Connect one test prod to field coil lead and the other prod to soldered portion of brush lead. If meter does not register, field coil is open. Repair or replace as necessary. Check field for ground by connecting one test prod to field coil and other lead to starter housing. If meter registers, coil is grounded. Remove field coil and repair or replace as necessary.

### REASSEMBLY

Clean all parts and coat the sliding surface of armature shaft splines, starter clutch bushing, drive lever and moving stud with multipurpose grease. Reassemble in the reverse order of disassembly while noting the following: After completing reassembly, operate starter under a no load condition and check clearance between pinion gear and pinion stop collar. If clearance is not within specifications, adjust length of solenoid plunger shaft. Standard length of shaft is 1.34". To increase clearance, lengthen plunger. To decrease clearance, shorten plunger length.

| Pinion Gear Clearance | |
|---|---|
| **Application** | **Clearance** |
| Ford Courier ................................................. | .080-.160" |
| Honda .......................................................... | .012-.059" |
| Subaru ......................................................... | .004-.160" |
| Toyota .......................................................... | .040-.160" |

**Fig. 2 Disassembled View of Starter Motor**

# Starters

## NIPPONDENSO REDUCTION GEAR

**Honda**
 Accord and Civic
**Toyota**
 Models with 2T-C Engine

### DESCRIPTION

Starter is a 12 volt, 4 brush, solenoid actuated, gear reduction type and is equipped with an overrunning clutch. Brush holder assembly retains brushes and springs in starter housing. Starter may be .8, .9 or 1.4 kilowatt rated, however testing and procedures are similar for all models.

**NOTE** — *Brushes and commutator may be on gear end or end away from reduction gear.*

### APPLICATION

| Model | Part No. |
|---|---|
| Honda | |
| Accord | |
|   Standard | 62174-31200-657-671 |
|   Optional | 65578-31200-676-641 |
| Civic (Federal) | 59480-31200-657-671 |
| Toyota | |
|   .9 KW | 28100-26070, 26120 |
|   1.4 KW | 28100-26110 |

### TESTING

#### PERFORMANCE TESTS

**No Load Tests** — With starter motor connected to a 12 volt battery, connect an ammeter in series (*Fig. 1*) with starter. Connect voltmeter in parallel with battery. Compare readings with specifications.

**Fig. 1  Ammeter Hook-Up for No Load Test
(Toyota Shown)**

#### No Load Specifications

| Application | RPM | Amps@Voltage |
|---|---|---|
| Honda | | |
| Accord | | |
|   Standard | 3000 | 90 @ 11.5 |
|   Optional | 3500 | 90 @ 11.5 |
| Civic | | |
|   Federal | | 80 @ 11.5 |
| Toyota | | |
|   .9KW | 4000 | 90 @ 11.5 |
|   1.4KW | 3500 | 90 @ 11.5 |

### OVERHAUL

#### DISASSEMBLY

1) With starter removed from vehicle, disconnect wire(s) to magnetic switch. Remove bolts and remove field frame with armature from magnetic switch. Remove "O" ring and felt seal.

2) Remove screws and then remove starter gear housing from magnetic switch. Pull out clutch assembly and gears. Remove ball from clutch shaft hole or from magnetic switch. Remove brushes from brush holder then pull armature out of field frame.

#### PARTS REPLACEMENT & TESTING

**Brushes & Springs** — Measure brush length and replace if less than specified. Check brush spring tension with suitable spring scale and replace if tension is less than 2.6 lbs. (1.2 kg) or more than 4.3 lbs. (1.96 kg). Check insulation between the plus and minus brush holders, repair or replace if continuity is shown. Check condition of brush holders and spring clip, repair or replace parts as necessary.

#### Brush Length

| Application | In. (mm) |
|---|---|
| Honda | .394-.571 (10-14.5) |
| Toyota | .394-.571 (10-14.5) |

**Commutator** — Inspect commutator for roughness, if surface is pitted or grooved, it should be sanded lightly with a no. 500 emery paper. Also check commutator for being out-of-round. If out-of-round is more than .002" (.05 mm), turn commutator in a lathe until out-of-round is less than .002" (.05 mm). Insulating mica should be undercut to a depth of .024-.035" (.6-.9 mm) if it is less than .008" (.2 mm). Wear or cutting limit of commutator is 1.14" (29 mm).

**Armature Coil** — Check commutator and armature coil core for continuity, if continuity exists, replace armature. Check armature with an armature tester (growler) for shorts, if shorts exist, replace armature. Check for continuity between segments on commutator, if no continuity exists replace armature.

**Field Coil** — Check field coil for open circuits. There should be continuity between lead wire and field coil brush lead, if not, replace field coil. Check for no continuity between field coil end and end frame, if continuity exists, replace field coil.

**Overrunning Clutch Assembly** — Inspect gear teeth for wear and damage. Replace gears if damaged. Also, if gears are damaged, check flywheel ring gear. Rotate pinion. Pinion should rotate freely in a clockwise direction and lock up in a counterclockwise direction.

**Bearings** — Turn each bearing by hand, replace bearings if they stick or have a high resistance to turning.

## NIPPONDENSO REDUCTION GEAR (Cont.)

**Fig. 2   Magnetic Switch Pull-In Coil Hook-Up**

**Fig. 3   Magnetic Switch Hold-In Test Hook-Up**

**Magnetic Switch Assembly** — Connect a 12 volt battery to magnetic switch "ST" terminal, main terminal and ground (Fig. 2). Plunger should extend firmly, if not, replace magnetic switch. Next disconnect battery from main terminal. (Fig. 3) Plunger should remain extended, if not, replace magnetic switch.

**REASSEMBLY**

To reassemble, reverse disassembly procedures and note the following: Coat all sliding or moving surfaces of shaft splines, bushings and solenoid with multi-purpose grease. Apply grease to clutch assembly cavity to retain steel ball when assembling.

**Fig. 4   Exploded View of Nippondenso Reduction Gear
Starter**

## PARIS RHONE

Renault

### DESCRIPTION

Starter is a 12-volt, four-pole unit of conventional design. Solenoid assembly is mounted on starter case. Starters have a overrunning clutch (pinion-free wheel assembly) connected by a shift lever to the solenoid plunger.

### APPLICATION

| Application | Paris Rhone No. |
|---|---|
| Renault |  |
| R-5 | D8 E121 |

### TESTING

#### PERFORMANCE TEST

**Lock Test** — To perform lock test, follow instructions and procedures outlined in instruction manual furnished with tester. Use a fully charged battery and carry out the test at a temperature of 77°F. Ammeter reading and starter torque should be within limits (see specifications).

### LOCK TEST SPECIFICATIONS

| Starter No.① | Amps. | Torque (Ft. Lbs.) |
|---|---|---|
| D8 E121 | 400 | 9 |

① — Number stamped on starter housing or plate attached to starter must be verified. Only specifications available at this time are shown.

### OVERHAUL

#### DISASSEMBLY

1) Remove two nuts on through bolts. Remove the rear shield.
2) Lift out brushes and retaining shaft for connecting fork between the solenoid and pinion. Remove bolts securing solenoid and remove solenoid.
3) Remove the body and armature.

#### PARTS REPLACEMENT & TESTING

**Brushes** — Inspect brush length. If less than 5/16", replace brushes.

**Commutator** — If commutator surface is scored, rough or burnt, dress with a lathe just enough to remove defective area and polish with a strip of fine emery paper. Check insulation undercut depth and it must be .02" deep.

**Armature** — Check armature for open, shorted or grounded circuits. Inspect armature shaft for bend; if bend is excessive replace armature. **NOTE** — *Do not attempt to straighten a bent shaft.*

**Bearings** — Inspect bearings for excessive wear and clearance between armature shaft and bearing. Replace as necessary.

**Pinion-Free Wheel Assembly** — If it is necessary to change the pinion assembly, remove the stop collar, slide assembly off and replace with a new pinion assembly. Reinstall stop collar and snap ring.

#### REASSEMBLY

Clean all parts and coat the sliding surface of armature shaft, splines, and bushings with multipurpose grease. Reassemble in the reverse order of disassembly while noting the following:

1) After completing reassembly, disconnect the field terminal from solenoid. Connect solenoid to battery and measure clearance of pinion gear to stop collar. Clearance should be .02-.099".

2) If clearance is not within limits, adjust by screwing the plunger fork or adjusting screw in or out to change clearance. Solenoid must be removed to adjust plunger fork (if equipped).

*Fig. 1   Disassembled View of Paris Rhone Starter*

## BOSCH

### DESCRIPTION

Bosch Starter (Solenoid) switch is used on pre-engaged screw-push starter motors. Mounted on starter, solenoid activates a soft iron plunger (armature) which is connected to the overrunning clutch shift lever, in starter motor. Two coils are used in the solenoid. A "pull-in" coil to engage starter and a "hold-in" coil to hold cranking starter into flywheel. After cutting in starter motor current, the pull-in coil is short circuited, and only hold-in coil remains energized. When starter motor is switched off, current to solenoid stops and armature returns to outer position.

### TESTING

#### SOLENOID REMOVED FROM STARTER

With armature disconnected from overrunning clutch shift lever, armature must move freely in and out of solenoid. If corroded, clean thoroughly before proceeding with tests.

A — AMMETER
B — BATTERY
C — PULL-IN COIL
D — HOLD-IN COIL
M — SOLENOID

**Fig. 1    Typical Jumper Connections for Pull-In Test**

**Pull-In Coil** — Connect jumper wires between a 12 volt battery and the solenoid as shown in *Fig. 1*. The armature should pull-in suddenly and return when electrical connection is broken

A — AMMETER
B — BATTERY
C — PULL-IN COIL
D — HOLD-IN COIL
M — SOLENOID

**Fig. 2    Typical Jumper Connections for Hold-In Test**

**Hold-In Coil** — Connect jumper wires between a 12 volt battery and solenoid as shown in *Fig. 2*, at the same time, press the armature into the solenoid by hand. The armature should remain held-in. Disconnect jumper to terminal 50 and armature should immediately return to its outer position.

Do not attempt to repair solenoid. If it fails either test, replace it with a new one.

## HITACHI & MITSUBISHI

### DESCRIPTION

The starter solenoid is mounted directly to the starter yoke (gear case). Current flows through "Series" (Pull-in) and "Shunt" (Hold-in) coils to excite the solenoid. A plunger, inside the solenoid is pulled into the solenoid, in turn pulling the shift lever that engages the starter pinion gear with the engine flywheel ring gear. When the contacts of the solenoid close, the starter cranks the engine and the pull-in coil is cut out. The magnetic force of the hold-in coil holds the plunger in until the engine starts. When the ignition is switched from START to ON, the starting current is broken and the pull-in coil demagnitizes the hold-in coil and the plunger returns to its original position.

**Fig. 1   Starting Circuit Diagram and Solenoid Terminals**

### TESTING

Clean solenoid plunger and sleeve with fine sand paper and alcohol and blow off with air before performing tests.

**NOTE** — *Make tests with solenoid removed from starter, or remove starter to solenoid lead before testing.*

**Pull-in Coil Test** — Using a 12 volt battery, connect a jumper wire between the negative battery post and the "S" terminal. Connect a second jumper to the positive battery post, and just touch the "M" (MT) terminal. Plunger should pull-in immediately.

**Hold-in Coil Test** — Connect a ground lead between the "M" (MT) terminal and the solenoid case. Apply 8 volts to the "S" terminal, this will pull-in the plunger. Disconnect lead to "M" (MT) terminal and the plunger should remain held in.

**Fig. 2   Test connections for Pull-In Coil and Hold-In Coil**

**Return Test** — Push plunger into solenoid by hand. Apply 12 volts between the "M" (MT) terminal and the solenoid case. If solenoid case is short circuited the plunger will be attracted. If nothing happens, the solenoid is satisfactory.

**Pinion Gear Clearance** — The clearance between the pinion gear and stop collar should be .012-.059" (.305-1.52 mm) on Hitachi and .02-.08" (.51-2.03 mm) on Mitsubishi. This is adjusted by placing shims between solenoid and starter yoke.

## LUCAS

### DESCRIPTION

Starter solenoids are electro-magnetic actuators mounted externally on the yokes of pre-engaged starting motors. These solenoids contain a soft iron plunger (linked to engaging lever), starter switch contacts and a coil with two windings (a heavy gauge pull-in winding and lighter gauge hold-in winding). Initially, both windings are energized in parallel when starter device is operated, but the pull-in winding is shorted out by the starter switch contacts at the instant of closure. Solenoids described here are sealed in a rolled steel outer case or body and cannot be disassembled. Most ground return starter solenoids have three terminals (two large and one small) with the exception having an additional small terminal marked "IGN" which is used in conjunction with the ignition coil ballast resistor. These units have an auxiliary phosphor bronze contact which serves to cut out the ballast resistor during starting, thereby ensuring that terminal voltage of the coil remains unaffected by the drop in battery voltage.

### TESTING

#### SOLENOID CONTACTS

1) Disconnect all cables and connectors from solenoid terminals and connect a 10 volt power supply in series with a switch between "STA" terminal and small, unmarked terminal of solenoid. Connect a test lamp across the solenoid main terminals and insert a stop (⅛" thick) between drive end bracket and pinion gear.

2) Close switch to energize series windings and test lamp should light, indicating contacts are closed. Open switch and remove pinion stop. Close switch and hold pinion gear in engaged position. Open switch and light should go out indicating that contacts have opened.

#### WINDING CONTINUITY

Connect ohmmeter between "STA" terminal and a good ground on solenoid body. A reading of 1.01-1.07 ohms should be obtained. If reading is not to specifications, replace solenoid.

#### PULL-IN WINDING

Connect ohmmeter between small unmarked terminal of solenoid and "STA" terminal. If resistance is not within specifications, closing (series) windings are defective and solenoid must be replaced.

| Vehicle Application | Resistance (Ohms) |
|---|---|
| MGB | .25-.27 |
| TR7, Spitfire | .25-.27 |
| Jaguar V12 | .36-.42 |

#### HOLD-ON WINDING

Connect ohmmeter between small unmarked terminal of solenoid and a good ground on solenoid body. If resistance is not within specifications, hold-on (shunt) windings are bad, replace solenoid.

| Vehicle Application | Resistance (Ohms) |
|---|---|
| MGB | .76-.80 |
| TR7, Spitfire | .76-.80 |
| Jaguar V12 | 1.49-1.71 |

*Fig. 1 Lucas Starter Solenoid*

# Starter Controls

## NIPPONDENSO

### DESCRIPTION

The starter solenoid is an electromagnetic switch, activating a plunger by means of a "pull-in" coil and a "hold-in" coil. The plunger is pulled in, which engages the starter, and then is held in, while the engine starts. When the hold-in coil is activated the pull-in coil is short circuited and only the hold-in coil remains effective. When the current flow to the starter is stopped, the hold-in force is lost and the plunger returns to its rest position.

### TESTING

All tests should be performed with the starter assembled and the "M" (field) lead from the starter disconnected at the solenoid.

**NOTE** — *If plunger and or sleeve are corroded, clean with fine sand paper and alcohol, and blow out with air before performing tests.*

**Pull-In Test** — Apply 8 volts momentarily between the "S" terminal and the "M" terminal of the solenoid. If the plunger is pulled in strongly the pull-in coil is satisfactory.

**Fig. 1    Test Connections for Pull-In Coil**

**Hold-In Test** — Connect leads from an 8 volt source onto the solenoid case and to the "M" terminal. Connect a jumper wire between "M" terminal and the "S" terminal. This will pull-in the

plunger. Disconnect the jumper wire from the "M" terminal and if the plunger remains held in, the hold-in coil is satisfactory.

**Fig. 2    Test Connections for Hold-In Coil**

**Plunger Return Test** — Apply 12 volts between "M" terminal and solenoid case. Pull out starter pinion gear with fingers until it stops. If plunger returns to original position when pinion is released, solenoid is satisfactory.

**Fig. 3    Test Connections for Plunger Return**

**Solenoid Resistance Values**

Pull-In Coil — About 0.4 ohms
Hold-In Coil — About 1.1 ohms

## ARROW

### INSTRUMENT CLUSTER

To remove instrument cluster, pull out air intake control knob, ash tray, and heater control knobs. Remove radio tuning knob and 2 ring nuts. Remove 8 attaching screws from around panel and pull panel out far enough to disconnect speedometer, radio, and electrical connections. Remove instrument cluster. To install, reverse removal procedure using caution not to over-tighten mounting screws.

**Fig. 1  Arrow Instrument Cluster**

### SPEEDOMETER & GAUGE

After removing instrument panel, remove bezel and lens. Loosen attaching screws and remove speedometer and combination gauge.

### HAZARD WARNING & TURN SIGNAL FLASHER

Located at lower center of instrument panel. A separate flasher unit is used for hazard warning and turn signals.

### STOP LIGHT SWITCH

Mechanical type, mounted on bracket above brake pedal. Switch also serves as pedal stop and free travel adjustment screw.

### NEUTRAL SAFETY SWITCH

Switch is located under console box on cars with automatic transmission. Provides for starting with selector lever in "Park" or "N" position only, and completes backup light circuit in "R" position. If removal required, console box must be removed first with selector lever in "L" position. Disconnect control rod and remove selector lever assembly from car. Disconnect handle from lever, loosen indicator panel screw, then draw out panel, slider, and light holder. Remove switch and check for starter circuit continuity in park and neutral positions, backup light circuit continuity in reverse position only. Assure that switch and selector positions line up when in "N" position during reinstallation.

## AUDI

### INSTRUMENT CLUSTER

**Audi Fox —** Disconnect battery ground cable and remove lower instrument panel trim. Disconnect speedometer shaft at speedometer and multiple plug at back of cluster. Disconnect left and right mounting springs using suitable long nose pliers. Remove cluster by pulling it forward.

**Audi 5000 —** Disconnect battery ground cable. Loosen screws at bottom and side of instrument panel trim, remove trim at top first, then at bottom. Loosen cluster mounting screws, detach speedometer cable and multi-point connector. Carefully pull cluster assembly straight out.

### SPEEDOMETER, CLOCK & GAUGES

Speedometer, clock and all gauges may be removed after first removing instrument cluster from panel.

### HAZARD WARNING & TURN SIGNAL FLASHER

**Audi Fox —** Single plug-in type unit mounted on fuse block. Connectors can be installed in one position only. Be sure that flasher connector blades are properly positioned and indexed with receptacle sockets when installing.

**Audi 5000 —** Flasher unit fits in bracket behind instrument panel near multi-point connector. Plug in connector attaches to unit.

### STOP LIGHT SWITCH

Stop light switch is hydraulically operated by fluid pressure and is attached to brake master cylinder. Models with cruise control have 3 terminals, others use 2 terminals.

## BMW

### INSTRUMENT CLUSTER

CAUTION — *Disconnect battery ground cable prior to removing instrument cluster on all models.*

**320i —** Remove steering wheel. Detach lower center instrument panel trim and disconnect speedometer cable. Unscrew knurled nut at base of instrument cluster and pull out instrument cluster. Disconnect wiring at connector.

**530i —** Remove steering wheel. Detach instrument panel trim at lower left corner. Unscrew speedometer shaft and retain felt washer between upper and lower sections. Loosen knurled nut under instrument panel and pull cluster out far enough to disconnect multiple plugs at either side. Disconnect remaining wires and remove instrument cluster.

## BMW (Cont.)

**633CSi** — Disconnect negative (−) battery cable and remove steering wheel. Detach lower center instrument panel trim and remove mask from inquiry unit. Detach printed circuit board leaving wiring attached. Remove light and fog light switch, and disconnect wiring at back of switch. Remove left air control knob and cover. Loosen screws on instrument cluster, steering wheel control base and disconnect speedometer cable. Press down on instrument cluster upper section and steering column far enough to allow removal of instrument cluster at an angle.

**733i** — Loosen screws at bottom left and under steering column attaching trim panel to instrument panel. Detach trim at tray and disconnect window control cutout wires. Remove 3

### INSTRUMENT CLUSTER

**1)** Disconnect battery ground cable and remove lower steering column shroud. Release clip securing upper steering column shroud. Remove ashtray.

**2)** Remove hazard flasher switch and disconnect wiring. Remove turn signal switch and allow it to hang on wiring. Remove screws securing lower dash trim panel and pull trim panel forward and down. Disconnect wiring to clock and cigarette lighter and remove trim panel.

**3)** Pull off instrument panel light control knob. Remove lower screws securing instrument cluster, pull cluster downward and disconnect seat belt warning light wiring and oil pressure line union. Remove screws securing cluster to panel and disconnect speedometer cable and wiring. Remove cluster.

screws beneath upper instrument panel trim. Loosen steering column control and pull wheel all the way out. Tip cluster back, disconnect all plugs and wires, then remove cluster by turning out to right rear.

### SPEEDOMETER & GAUGES

Speedometer and all guages may be removed after first removing instrument cluster.

### STOP LIGHT SWITCH

Mechanical type switch mounted on brake pedal bracket. Adjust switch so that .20-.24" (5-6mm) of contact button is extended when brake pedal is fully back.

## CAPRI

### SPEEDOMETER & GAUGES

Speedometer and all gauges may be removed after first removing instrument cluster.

### HAZARD WARNING & TURN SIGNAL FLASHER

Combination flasher is located to the left of the steering column beneath instrument panel. Unit is secured by clamp with a single screw and connected by a plug type mechanical connector.

### STOP LIGHT SWITCH

Mechanical type mounted on bracket at brake pedal lever.

*Fig. 2 Capri Instrument Cluster*

## CHALLENGER & SAPPORO

### INSTRUMENT CLUSTER

To remove instrument cluster, remove ash tray bracket and panel just under column cover. Remove lenses as illustrated, then disconnect speedometer cable. Remove mounting screws, disconnect all connections and remove instrument cluster.

To further disassemble, remove all indicator lights, bezel and lens. Remove attaching nuts of speedometer, fuel gauge, temperature gauge, tachometer and ammeter. Remove as required.

**CAUTION** — *Handle cluster with care to avoid damaging printed circuit board. Do not overtighten nuts when reassembling.*

**Fig. 3   Challenger/Sapporo Instrument Cluster**

### HAZARD WARNING & TURN SIGNAL FLASHERS

Separate hazard warning and turn signal flasher units are mounted below instrument panel on driver's side with a single screw.

### STOP LIGHT SWITCH

Mechanical type stop light switch is mounted under instrument panel to left of steering column. Spring loaded push rod contacts brake lever linkage and closes circuit when brake pedal is depressed.

### NEUTRAL SAFETY (INHIBITOR) SWITCH

**NOTE** — *If inhibitor switch does not operate properly after installation of console and selector lever, it will be necessary to readjust location of the switch.*

Switch is located under console box on cars with automatic transmission. Provides for starting with selector lever in "Park" or "N" position only, and completes backup light circuit in "R" position. If removal required, console box must be removed first with selector lever in "L" position. Disconnect control rod and remove selector lever assembly from car. Disconnect handle from lever, loosen indicator panel screw, then draw out panel, slider, and light holder. Remove switch and check for starter circuit continuity in park and neutral positions, backup light circuit continuity in reverse position only. Assure that switch and selector positions line up when in "N" position during reinstallation.

## COLT

### INSTRUMENT CLUSTER

#### Coupe and Sedan

To remove instrument cluster, pull out air intake control knob, ash tray, and heater control knobs. Remove radio tuning knob and 2 ring nuts. Remove 8 attaching screws from around panel and pull panel out far enough to disconnect speedometer, radio, and electrical connections. Remove instrument cluster. To install, reverse removal procedure using caution not to overtighten mounting screws.

#### Station Wagon

Remove instrument panel od by lifting at an angle, using caution to prevent catching and bending clock and odometer knobs. Disconnect speedometer cable and all gauge connections. Remove peripheral mounting screws and lift cluster away from instrument panel. Further disassembly requires removal of clock knob and instrument cluster glass.

**Fig. 4   Colt Instrument Cluster
(Station Wagon Shown)**

## COLT (Cont.)

### SPEEDOMETER & GAUGES

Speedometer and all gauges may be removed after first removing instrument cluster.

### HAZARD WARNING & TURN SIGNAL FLASHER

Located at lower center of instrument panel. A separate flasher is used for hazard warning and turn signals.

### STOP LIGHT SWITCH

Mechanical type, mounted on brace above brake pedal. Switch also serves as a brake pedal free travel adjustment screw.

### INSTRUMENT CLUSTER

Disconnect battery ground cable. Remove four screws securing cluster to instrument panel. Pull cluster out sufficiently to gain access and disconnect speedometer cable and wiring. Remove cluster from vehicle.

### SPEEDOMETER & GAUGES

Speedometer and all gauges may be removed after first removing instrument cluster.

### INSTRUMENT CLUSTER

**200SX —** 1) Disconnect battery ground cable. Remove steering wheel and shell cover. Remove all knobs and nuts.

2) Remove upper and lower screws from instrument cluster. Pull cluster forward and disconnect wiring connectors, speedometer cable and remove rear window defogger switch. Remove instrument cluster.

**B210 —** 1) Disconnect battery ground cable and remove shell covers. **NOTE** — *To facilitate removal of cluster, remove steering wheel and turn signal switch.* Pull out ashtray and remove ashtray cover. Remove switch knobs and retaining rings.

2) Remove radio knobs and retaining knobs, if equipped. Remove nine screws securing cluster cover to dash (four on upper side, three under cover, one at ash tray outer case and one in glove box). Pull cluster cover out slightly and disconnect wiring. Remove cluster cover.

3) Remove four instrument cluster retaining screws and pull cluster out slightly. Disconnect wiring and speedometer cable. Remove instrument cluster assembly.

**F-10 —** Disconnect battery ground cable, then remove knobs and nuts from switches and radio controls. Remove ash tray, cover and meter retaining screws. Disconnect speedometer cable and electrical connections. Cluster may be removed by pulling out toward steering wheel.

### NEUTRAL SAFETY SWITCH

Switch is located under console box on cars with automatic transmission. Provides for starting with selector lever in "Park" or "N" position only, and completes backup light circuit in "R" position. If removal required, console box must be removed first with selector lever in "L" position. Disconnect control rod and remove selector lever assembly from car. Disconnect handle from lever, loosen indicator panel screw, then draw out panel, slider, and light holder. Remove switch and check for starter circuit continuity in park and neutral positions, backup light circuit continuity in reverse position only. Assure that switch and selector positions line up when in "N" position during reinstallation.

## COURIER

### HAZARD WARNING & TURN SIGNAL FLASHER

Combination flasher is located to the left of the steering column beneath instrument panel. Unit is secured by clamp with a single screw and connected by a multiple connector type plug.

### STOP LIGHT SWITCH

Mechanical type mounted on bracket at top of brake pedal.

## DATSUN

**510 —** 1) Disconnect battery ground cable, remove steering column covers and disconnect hazard warning switch connector. Pull out ash tray and heater control knobs. Remove wiper control switch. Remove heater trim panel by inserting screwdriver in fan lever slot, then pulling panel out. Remove radio knobs, nuts and washers.

2) Remove choke and defroster control knobs. Remove small rectangular trim finisher at right center of cluster lid. Remove 9 screws securing left half of cluster lid, then disconnect the following wire harness connectors: Center lighting, cigarette lighter, rear defogger switch, clock, and turn signal switch.

3) Remove cluster lid, then remove retaining screws holding instrument cluster in place. Disconnect speedometer cable and remaining electrical connectors. Remove instrument cluster.

**620 Pickup —** Disconnect battery ground cable. Remove screws securing cluster to instrument panel and from under panel remove screw securing cluster to dash. Withdraw cluster slightly, then from behind cluster disconnect speedometer cable and wiring. Remove screws securing cluster cover to cluster and remove cluster assembly.

**810 —** 1) Disconnect battery ground cable. Remove knobs and nuts on radio switch and choke control wire. Remove ash tray.

2) Remove screws and shell covers from steering column. Disconnect main harness connectors, screws retaining cluster and remove instrument cluster.

## DATSUN (Cont.)

**Fig. 5   Typical Datsun Instrument Cluster (Model 710 Shown)**

**280Z** —Gauges are individually removable after removal of center trim panel and duct hoses from 3 way duct. Remove spring bracket retaining screw, pull gauge out backwards and disconnect each connector.

## SPEEDOMETER & GAUGES

**All Exc. 280Z Models** — Speedometer and all gauges may be removed after removing instrument cluster.

**280Z Models** — Tachometer must be removed before speedometer can be removed. Take out 2 screws retaining tachometer at top and side. Pull tach out slightly, disconnect harness and remove tachometer. To remove speedometer, disconnect cable, wires and lights from back of speedometer. Working through tachometer mounting hole, loosen trip meter reset cable screw and remove cable. Take out 2 screws retaining speedometer to panel, pull speedometer out and remove instrument harness connector.

## HAZARD WARNING & TURN SIGNAL FLASHER

**All Models** — Separate flasher units located under the instrument panel are used. Turn signal flashers are larger than hazard warning flashers and may be either clip or screw mounted. Units are further located as follows:

**280Z** — Under left side trim panel.
**Pickup** — Hazard flasher left of steering column, turn signal flasher to right of steering column under dash.
**All Other Models** — Beneath and behind instrument panel, near center.

## STOP LIGHT SWITCH

Mechanical type stop light switch mounted on bracket at top of brake pedal lever. Must be adjusted so that plunger extends and closes circuit when brake pedal is depressed.

# FIAT

## INSTRUMENT CLUSTER

Disconnect battery. Remove five screws holding cluster to panel, slide cluster forward and disconnect electrical connectors and speedometer cable. Remove instrument cluster.

## SPEEDOMETER & GAUGES

Speedometer and all gauges may be removed after removing instrument cluster.

## STOP LIGHT SWITCH

Mechanical type mounted on brake pedal bracket.

## FIESTA

### INSTRUMENT CLUSTER

**1)** Disconnect battery. Snap off upper steering column shroud, then remove screws below dashboard storage space and drop lower panel (where applicable). Reach behind cluster and snap off speedometer cable locking catch with thumb, then pull cable off speedometer.

**2)** Pull instrument bezel off with fingers. Remove 4 screws from front of cluster and pull assembly out. Disconnect multiplug connectors and remove cluster.

### SPEEDOMETER & GAUGES

Speedometer, tachometer (if equipped), and gauges may be removed after first removing instrument cluster.

### INSTRUMENT CLUSTER

**Accord** — Remove steering column lower cover. Detach speedometer cable from speedometer by reaching under panel. Remove 2 screws from under cluster beside steering column. Disconnect wiring harness couplers from rear of cluster and remove cluster assembly.

**Civic** — Unscrew 3 wing nuts from behind instrument panel, disconnect speedometer and electrical connections, and remove assembly.

**CVCC** — Remove nuts and lockwashers holding cluster housing to instrument panel and tip assembly toward steering wheel.

### INSTRUMENT CLUSTER

**NOTE** — *Always disconnect battery prior to removing instrument cluster.*

**XJS** — Remove drivers side dash casing and trim from around front of instrument cluster. Remove covers from screw holes in panel and take out screws holding cluster to panel. Disconnect speedometer cable and electrical connections at back of unit. If necessary, move adjustable steering wheel and extract instrument cluster.

**NOTE** — *Instruments are removed individually from remaining Jaguar models.*

### INSTRUMENT CLUSTER

Disconnect battery positive cable and speedometer drive cable from the gear box differential unit. Remove all knurled knobs and screws securing instrument cluster to the dashboard. Lower steering wheel and remove instrument cluster. To install, reverse removal procedure.

### HAZARD WARNING & TURN SIGNAL FLASHER

Single flasher unit is mounted on relay bracket under dash panel to left of steering column.

### STOP LIGHT SWITCH

Mechanical switch is attached to bracket at top of brake pedal. Adjust switch so that it does not operate for first .2" (5.0 mm) of brake travel but operates within .8" (20.0 mm) of brake travel.

## HONDA

Disconnect speedometer cable and electrical couplers, then remove instrument cluster.

**NOTE** — *Always disconnect battery ground cable prior to removing instrument cluster.*

### SPEEDOMETER, TACHOMETER & GAUGES

Speedometer, tachometer (if equipped) and all other gauges may be removed after first removing instrument cluster.

### STOP LIGHT SWITCH

Mechanical type mounted on brake pedal bracket. Switch also serves as brake pedal stop. Adjust switch to give .039-.196" (1-5 mm) freeplay at center of brake pedal.

## JAGUAR

### SPEEDOMETER & TACHOMETER

**XJS** — Remove speedometer and tachometer from instrument cluster after removing cluster from panel.

**Except XJS** —Speedometer and tachometer may be removed by pressing on rim and turning counter-clockwise until free of locking tabs in panel. Disconnect speedometer cable and electrical connections, then remove from panel.

### HAZARD WARNING & TURN SIGNAL FLASHERS

Two separate flashers are used and are located under center of instrument panel.

### STOP LIGHT SWITCH

Mechanical type mounted on brake pedal bracket.

## LANCIA

### SPEEDOMETER & GAUGES

Remove ring nuts and extract trip distance recorder knob with cable and instrument light switch. Release the plastic retainers and remove the rim from the instrument cluster. Remove desired instrument. To install, reverse removal procedure.

### 'STOP LIGHT SWITCH

Mechanical type mounted on brake pedal bracket.

## LUV

### INSTRUMENT CLUSTER

To remove the instrument cluster, it is necessary to first detach and remove the speedometer cable and position it out of way. Now, remove the wing nuts from the rear of the instrument cluster, to free the cluster assembly, and pull cluster only part way out. Then, disconnect all necessary wiring. Remove instrument cluster assembly from panel.

### SPEEDOMETER & GAUGES

Speedometer and all gauges may be removed after first removing instrument cluster.

### STOP LIGHT SWITCH

Stop light switch is mechanical type mounted on brake pedal bracket and requires .079 to .110" free travel.

## MAZDA

### INSTRUMENT CLUSTER

**NOTE** — *Disconnect battery cable prior to removing instrument cluster.*

**Cosmo & RX-4** — Remove steering wheel, steering column cover and instrument cluster cover. Remove choke and ventilator controls (if equipped). Remove radio and light control switches, knobs and mounting nuts. Remove cluster attaching nuts or screws, then tip cluster back to disconnect speedometer cable and multiple connectors. Remove instrument cluster.

**GLC & Pickup** — Remove screws holding meter hood to panel and remove hood. Remove center panel and crash pad. Disconnect speedometer cable, remove mounting screws and tip out instrument cluster. Remove multiple connector plugs from rear of unit and remove cluster.

### SPEEDOMETER & GAUGES

Speedometer and all gauges can be removed when cluster is removed.

### STOP LIGHT SWITCH

Mechanical type mounted on brake pedal bracket and is used for pedal adjustment. Adjust for free pedal travel of .280 to .350" (7.0 to 9.0 mm)

## MERCEDES-BENZ

### INSTRUMENT CLUSTER

Instrument cluster is held in a recess by a rubber section. Remove instrument plate glass, prying out and lifting up, using a non-metalic device to prevent damage to the glass.

Remove the speedometer shaft from the cable strap under the left floormat. Pull instrument cluster out, loosen speedometer shaft, electrical connections and oil pressure line. Remove the instrument cluster sideways and to the right. To install, reverse removal procedure.

**Fig. 6  Instrument Cluster Removal**

### SPEEDOMETER & GAUGES

Speedometer and all gauges can easily be removed after removing instrument cluster.

### STOPLIGHT SWITCH

Mechanical type mounted on brake pedal bracket and is used for pedal adjustment. Switch contact button should extend for .236 to .315" (6 to 8 mm) from housing and free pedal travel should be .590 to .798" (15 to 20 mm).

## MG

### SPEEDOMETER

**MG Midget — 1)** Disconnect battery and speedometer cable from the speedometer. Remove center console retaining screws and move console back and aside toward the steering column.

**2)** Remove two knurled retaining nuts from behind speedometer and the knurled nut retaining the trip remote control in its bracket. Pull speedometer forward from dash.

## MG (Cont.)

*MG Midget Instrument Cluster*

**MGB — 1)** Disconnect the battery. Remove lower left hand instrument panel cover. Unscrew the knurled nut and disconnect speedometer cable.

**2)** Push in and turn speedometer clockwise for 30 degrees until the three studs located on the body of the speedometer are aligned with the cut-aways in the dash. Pull speedometer forward from the dash and disconnect wiring.

### INSTRUMENT CLUSTER

Disconnect battery ground cable and remove steering wheel. Disconnect speedometer cable, remove wing nut and instrument cluster retaining screws. Rotate cluster outward, disconnect two electrical connectors and remove instrument cluster. To install, reverse removal procedure.

## PORSCHE

### INSTRUMENT CLUSTER

**928 Models —** Disconnect battery ground lead. Remove steering wheel, steering column switch and instrument cover mounting screws. Disconnect both 12 pin connector plugs at instrument cluster. Lift instrument cover carefully and tilt to rear. Unscrew mounting bolt and remove instrument cluster.

### SPEEDOMETER, TACHOMETER & GAUGES

**928 Models —** Instruments may be removed from assembly individually with cluster out of car. Use caution so that printed circuit board is not damaged when disassembling cluster.

**924 Models —** Disconnect battery. Put hand underneath instrument panel to back of instrument to be removed. Press instrument forward out of instrument panel. Disconnect wiring or speedometer cable.

**NOTE** — *Remove tachometer and combination gauge before removing speedometer.*

### TACHOMETER

**All Models —** Disconnect the battery and remove the lower left hand instrument panel cover. Push in and turn 30 degrees until the three studs on the body of the tachometer are aligned with the cut-aways in the dash. Pull tachometer forward from dash and disconnect the wiring.

### GAUGES

To remove fuel, oil pressure and temperature gauges, remove components listed below to gain access to unit, then unscrew knurled nuts. Pull instrument from dash and disconnect wiring.

| To Remove | First Remove |
|---|---|
| Fuel Gauge | |
|   MG Midget | Speedometer |
|   MGB | None |
| Oil Pressure Gauge (MGB) | Tachometer |
| Temperature Gauge (MGB) | Heater Control |
| Combination Gauge (MG Midget) | Tachometer |

### STOP LIGHT SWITCH

**All Models —** Mechanical type mounted on brake pedal bracket. Free movement adjustment is .125" (3 mm).

## OPEL

### SPEEDOMETER & GAUGES

Speedometer and all gauges can be removed after first removing instrument cluster.

### STOP LIGHT SWITCH

Mechanical, mounted on brake pedal bracket.

## PORSCHE

**911 Models —** Connecting terminals and wires of all instruments are accessible from luggage compartment side of instrument panel after luggage compartment carpet is removed.

**1)** Disconnect and detach all cables and wire from instrument that is to be removed. In case of speedometer, also remove drive shaft knurled nut and withdraw shaft from speedometer.

**2)** Remove small knurled nuts securing instrument, remove retaining clamp and take instrument out from passenger compartment side.

### TURN SIGNAL FLASHER (911 MODELS)

Flasher is located adjacent to fuse block in luggage compartment, and is a plug in type.

### STOP LIGHT SWITCH

To adjust switch, loosen jam nut and adjusting screw. Clamp a piece of sheet metal .16" (4 mm) thick between brake pedal lever and pedal stop at brake pedal center. Turn adjusting screw until brake lights operate. Remove switch and lock adjusting screw. Reinstall switch and check switch operation.

# Switches, Gauges & Instrument Panels 3-97

## RENAULT

### INSTRUMENT CLUSTER

**R-5 Models** — Disconnect battery cable and speedometer cable in engine compartment. Unclip instrument panel cowel and remove. Press left and right side clips until support plate is cleared and remove instrument panel. Disconnect two electrical junction blocks and speedometer cable.

### SPEEDOMETER & GAUGES

Speedometer and all gauges may be removed after instrument cluster is removed.

### STOP LIGHT SWITCH

Mechanically operated switch attached to the steering column.

## SAAB

### INSTRUMENT CLUSTER

**99 Models** — Remove safety padding. Remove four self tapping screws. Disconnect speedometer cable and wiring. Remove bulb holders. Lift out instrument cluster.

### SPEEDOMETER & GAUGES

**99 Models** — Speedometer and all gauges may be removed after first removing instrument cluster.

### TURN SIGNAL FLASHER

Located under instrument panel on left hand side of steering column.

### STOP LIGHT SWITCH

Mechanical type mounted on brake pedal bracket.

## SUBARU

### INSTRUMENT CLUSTER

Remove instrument cluster cover screws and remove cover with rear window defogger switch. Remove cluster retaining screws and tip cluster out. Disconnect speedometer cable and wiring harness, then remove cluster.

### SPEEDOMETER & GAUGES

Speedometer and all gauges may be removed after first removing instrument cluster.

### HAZARD WARNING & TURN SIGNAL FLASHER

Located under instrument panel.

### STOP LIGHT SWITCH

Mechanical type mounted on brake pedal bracket. Adjust switch so there is .24-.55" (6-14 mm) free pedal movement before switch turns on brake lights.

## TOYOTA

### INSTRUMENT CLUSTER

**NOTE** — *Always disconnect battery prior to removing instrument cluster.*

**All Models** — Loosen instrument cluster trim panel screws and remove panel. Loosen steering column clamp bolts. Remove screws, bolts or nuts mounting the cluster to instrument panel. Disconnect speedometer cable and all instrument wire harness connectors, then remove instrument cluster.

**NOTE** — *Removal procedures are similar for all models, however all steps may not apply to each model.*

### SPEEDOMETER & GAUGES

**All Models** — Speedometer and all gauges may be removed after first removing instrument cluster.

### HAZARD WARNING & TURN SIGNAL FLASHER

**All Models** — Mounted near steering column behind instrument center panel.

### STOP LIGHT SWITCH

Mechanical type mounted on brake pedal bracket. Free travel should be .120 to .240" (3 to 6 mm).

# TRIUMPH

## INSTRUMENT CLUSTER

**Spitfire** — Disconnect battery and remove heater control knobs. Remove four screws and cup washers and lower cluster. Remove bulb holders, disconnect wiring and remove cluster.

**TR7** — Remove radio speaker grill and top instrument panel trim pad. Remove steering column shrouds, loosen odometer reset knob and remove knob with cable. Loosen clock reset knob and remove with cable. Disconnect speedometer cable, remove retaining screws and pull out instrument cluster slightly. Disconnect all wiring and remove cluster.

## TACHOMETER

**Spitfire & TR7** — Tachometer may be removed after removing instrument cluster.

## SPEEDOMETER

**Spitfire** — Disconnect battery. Lower center dash, remove tachometer and depress lever releasing catch from annular groove in the boss. Detach speedometer cable, unscrew trip reset and remove two knurled nuts. Disconnect two connectors, bulb holders and remove speedometer.

**TR7** — Speedometer may be removed after removing instrument cluster.

## GAUGES

**Spitfire & TR7** — All gauges may be removed after removing instrument cluster.

## HAZARD WARNING & TURN SIGNAL FLASHER

**Spitfire** — Separate units are mounted under dash and held in position by spring clips.

**TR7** — Separate turn signal and flasher units are mounted behind lower panel at rear of glove compartment. To gain access, open glove box and remove cover panel.

## STOP LIGHT SWITCH

Mechanical type mounted on brake pedal bracket.

# VOLKSWAGEN

## INSTRUMENT CLUSTER

**Type 1 (Beetle)** — Disconnect battery ground cable. Remove five screws securing cluster. **NOTE** — *Cluster screws are covered by small strips on left and right and by a cap in the center.* Disconnect speedometer cable and wiring, remove cluster.

**Type 2 (Bus)** — Disconnect battery ground cable. Remove cluster securing screws and tilt cluster outward. Disconnect speedometer cable and wiring and remove cluster.

**Rabbit & Scirocco** — Remove trim plate for fresh air control and remove radio or glove box. Disconnect speedometer cable and wiring. Remove retaining screw on right side of cluster (visible after radio or glove box is removed) and remove cluster.

**Dasher** — Disconnect battery ground cable and speedometer cable. Using long nosed pliers, detach springs securing left and right sides of cluster then swing cluster outward.

## SPEEDOMETER

**All Models** — Speedometer can be removed after removing instrument cluster and speedometer retaining screws.

## HAZARD WARNING & TURN SIGNAL FLASHER

**Type 1** — Flashers are mounted seperately on a bracket above the fuse box. Relays can be reached by removing the access panel from rear of the front luggage compartment.

**All Other Models** — Flasher is a plug-in unit on fuse block.

## STOP LIGHT SWITCH

Hydraulic type mounted on brake master cylinder.

# VOLVO

## INSTRUMENT CLUSTER

**All Models** — Disconnect battery ground cable and proceed as follows:

1) Remove steering column shrouds. Loosen bracket screw and allow bracket to drop down steering column. Remove instrument cluster mounting screws. Disconnect speedometer cable.

2) Press upwards on back of speedometer until snap lock on upper edge releases. Lift cluster forward and disconnect wiring. Disconnect tachometer drive cable (if equipped). Cluster may now be removed.

## SPEEDOMETER & GAUGES

**All Models** — Speedometer and all gauges can be removed after removing instrument cluster.

## HAZARD WARNING & TURN SIGNAL FLASHER

**240 Series** — Flasher is mounted behind left side kick panel.

**260 Series** — Flasher is mounted behind instrument cluster.

## STOP LIGHT SWITCH

Mechanical type mounted on brake pedal bracket. Adjust switch to provide .16" (4 mm) clearance between brake pedal and end of switch plunger.

# Section 4
# WIRING DIAGRAMS

## Contents

### CHASSIS WIRING

NOTE — ALSO SEE GENERAL INDEX.

# Contents (Cont.)

*NOTE — ALSO SEE GENERAL INDEX*

# Contents (Cont.)

## ARRANGEMENT OF DATA

The Wiring Diagram Section contains chassis wiring diagrams spread across two pages for efficient reading. The diagrams are arranged alphabetically by car model or make.

Appearing on each wiring diagram is a legend of Accessory Power Feeds. The letters preceding the titles of the accessory circuits are codes which are also shown somewhere on the diagram. These codes indicate where the sub-system wiring connects to car chassis wiring system.

Also contained in this section are Fuel Injection wiring diagrams and diagrams for various sub-systems.

*NOTE – ALSO SEE GENERAL INDEX*

# 1978 Arrow

LEGEND
ACCESSORY POWER FEED

A AIR CONDITIONING (MANUAL SYSTEM)
B SEAT BELT WARNING SYSTEM
D WIPER WASHER SYSTEM (WINDSHIELD)

- - - - A/T ONLY

# 1978 Audi

# 1978 BMW

# 1978 Capri

# 1978 Colt

# 1978 Colt

LEGEND
ACCESSORY POWER FEED

A  AIR CONDITIONING (MANUAL SYSTEM)
B  SEAT BELT WARNING SYSTEM
C  REAR WINDOW DEFROSTER
D  WIPER WASHER SYSTEM (WINDSHIELD)

# 1978 Courier

# 1978 Datsun

# 1978 Datsun

# 1978 Datsun

# 1978 Datsun

# 1978 Datsun

# 1978 Datsun

# 1978 Fiat

LEGEND
ACCESSORY POWER FEED
B. SEAT BELT WARNING SYSTEM
D. WIPER/WASHER SYSTEM (WINDSHIELD)

# 1978 Fiat

128 Sedan & Station Wagon

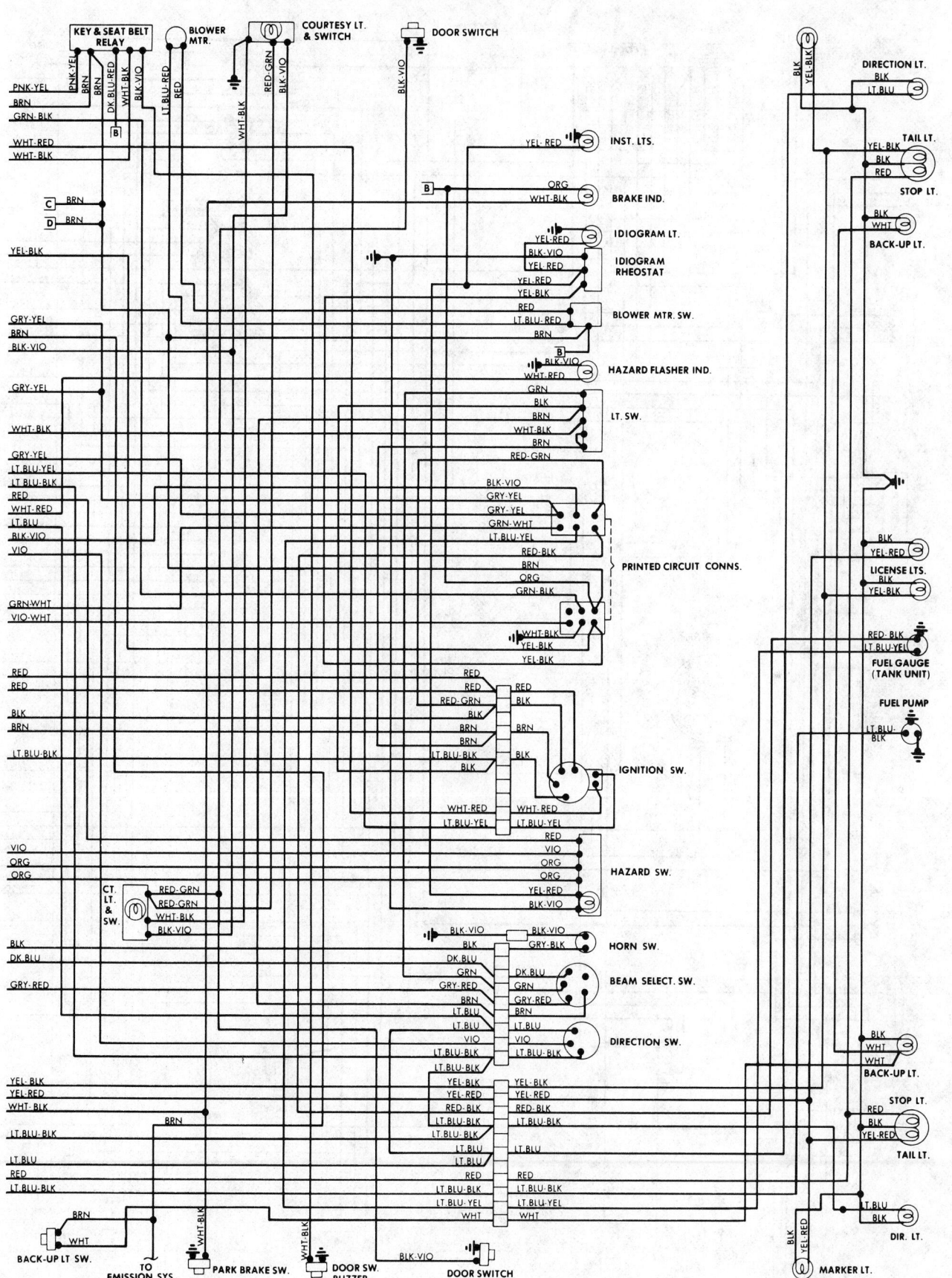

**WIRING DIAGRAMS**

# 1978 Fiat

LEGEND
ACCESSORY POWER FEED
B  SEAT BELT WARNING SYSTEM
C  REAR WINDOW DEFROSTER
D  WIPER WASHER SYSTEM (WINDSHIELD)

# 1978 Fiat

# 1978 Fiat

# 1978 Honda

# 1978 Jaguar

# 1978 Jaguar

# 1978 LUV

# 1978 Mazda

# 1978 Mazda

# 1978 Mazda

# 1978 Mercedes-Benz

# 1978 Mercedes-Benz

# 1978 MG

# 1978 MG

MARKER LT.

RED
RED
BLACK

DIRECTIONAL LT.

GREEN
RED

PARK LT.

HIGH BEAM
LOW BEAM

BLACK

HORNS

HIGH BEAM
LOW BEAM

DIRECTIONAL LT.

GREEN
RED

PARK LT.

MARKER LT.

BLACK
RED

GREEN
RED
BLUE-WHITE
BLUE-RED
PURPLE-BLACK
GREEN-RED

GREEN-WHITE

PURPLE

FUSE BOX

RED
RED
GREEN
GRN
PURPLE
B

WHITE    WHITE

GREEN-WHITE
BLUE WHITE
BLUE-RED
PURPLE-BLACK
GREEN-RED
WHITE
WHITE
GREEN-BROWN
RED
RED
GREEN-PURPLE
PURPLE
PURPLE

FUSIBLE LINK

BROWN-YEL
RED-GREEN

BROWN
BROWN

ALL BROWN

BROWN-YELLOW
RED-GREEN
GREEN
BROWN
BROWN

BATT+  IND
ALTERNATOR & REGULATOR

STARTER

ALL BROWN

WHT-RED

BLACK
BLACK

OIL PRESS. SWITCH

DISTRIBUTOR

WHITE
WHT-BLU
WHT-BLK

COIL
+  −

BATTERY

GREEN
GREEN

ALL BLACK

GREEN-BROWN

GREEN

GREEN
WHT-BRN
WHT-RED
BROWN

WHITE-LT.GREEN

WHT-BLK

WHT-BLK

WHT

GREEN

WHITE-LT.GRN
RESIST. WIRE
RESISTOR

WHT

ALL GREEN

1  2  3  4

LT.GREEN BLACK
BROWN-LT.GREEN
BLUE-LT.GRN
RED-LT.GRN
LT.GREEN-GRN.
GREEN

INST. VOLTAGE REG.

GREEN
LT.GREEN-GREEN

BLOWER MOTOR

BLACK    BLACK
GRN-YELLOW    GRN-YELL

LOW BRAKE SW.

GREEN-ORANGE
GREEN

BACK-UP LT. SW.

GREEN
GREEN-BROWN
GREEN

STOPLIGHT SW.

GREEN    GREEN
GRN-PURPLE    GRN-PURPLE

GREEN

GREEN-ORANGE

TEMPERATURE SENDER

GRN-BLU

WINDSHIELD WASHER PUMP

LT.GREEN-BLACK
GREEN
BLACK

PURPLE

WHT-BLACK
GREEN

WINDSHIELD WIPER MTR.

BLACK
BLUE-LT.GREEN
RED-LT.GREEN
GREEN
BROWN-LT.GREEN

GREEN YELLOW

LEGEND
ACCESSORY POWER FEED
B SEAT BELT WARNING SYSTEM

# 1978 Porsche

# 1978 Porsche

INSTRUMENT LIGHTS (2 USED)

DOOP SWITCH

MARKER LIGHT

CIGAR LIGHTER

WINDSHIELD WIPER & WASHER SW

BLUE-WHT
BLUE-GREEN
BLUE-RED
BLUE-YELLOW

HEATER SW & BLOWER MOTOR

RED-YELLOW

STOPLIGHT
GREEN
BLACK
RED

TAIL LIGHT
BLACK
GREEN-RED

DIR. LT.

RED
RED-YEL
RED

LIGHT SWITCH

BLACK
BLACK
BACK-UP-LIGHT

GREEN
BLUE
BLACK-YELLOW
BLACK-RED
BLACK
BLACK-WHITE
YELLOW

IGNITION SWITCH

STOP & DIR. LT.
GRN-BLK
BLACK
RED
TAIL LIGHT

BLACK
RED-YEL
BACK-UP LT.

BLUE-RED
BLUE-WHITE

HEATED REAR WINDOW

RED-YELLOW
RED-BLUE

INST LIGHTS (5 USED)

YELLOW-RED
BLACK+WHITE

LOW BRAKE INDICATOR

YELLOW-BLACK
BLACK-WHITE

OIL PRESS IND

WHITE-RED
BLACK-WHITE

ALTERNATOR IND

RED-WHT

HIGH BEAM INDICATOR

GRN-RED

R. & L. DIRECT INDICATORS

GRN-BLU
YEL-GRN
BLACK-WHT

TEMP GAUGE

FUEL GAUGE

YELLOW

TACHOMETER

PRINTED CIRC'T

BLUE-RED

HEATED REAR WINDOW IND

GREEN-WHITE

HORN BUTTON

RED-GREEN
GREEN-RED
GREEN-BLU
GREEN
GREEN-BLK
GREEN-YEL
GREEN

DIRECTIONAL & HAZARD SWITCH

BLACK-WHITE

DOME LIGHT SWITCH

STA. WGN & 4 WD ONLY

GREEN
STOP LT SW
GRN

BACK-UP LIGHT SW M/T

BLACK-WHITE
GREEN-WHITE

4WD IND

PARKING BRAKE SWITCH

YELLOW
BLACK-RED

KEY WARNING BUZZER

DOOR SWITCH

BLK-YELLOW
BLACK

HEATED REAR WINDOW

BLACK

LICENSE LIGHT
RED
RED

BLACK

FUEL GAUGE (TANK UNIT)

RED-GREEN

GEAR SELECT SWITCH

BLACK

BACK-UP-LIGHT
RED-YEL
BLK

TAIL LIGHT
RED
BLK

STOP & DIR LT.
GRN-RED

BACK-UP-LIGHT
GRN-YEL
BLK

DIR. LT.
BLK
GRN-BLU

TAIL LIGHT
RED
GRN

STOPLIGHT

MARKER LIGHT
RED
BLACK

Left side labels:
BLUE
GREEN-RED
BLUE-GREEN
BLUE-RED
BLUE-YELLOW
BLUE-WHITE
BLACK-YELLOW
RED
BLUE
YELLOW
BLUE-WHITE
BLACK-RED
GREEN
RED
YELLOW-BLK
RED-WHITE
WHT-RED
YELLOW-GRN
YEL-BLUE
BLK-WHT
BLUE-WHITE
BLACK-WHT
GREEN-YEL
BLACK
GREEN
RED
BLACK
GREEN
RED-YEL
GREEN-BLUE
GREEN-WHITE
BLUE-WHITE
GREEN-WHITE
GREEN-YEL

# 1978 Toyota

# 1978 Toyota

MARKER LT.

DIRECTION LT.
GRN-YEL

WH-BLK
GRN

PARK LT

BATTERY

HEAD LTS.
RED-GRN
RED-YEL
RED

RED-GRN
RED

W/ INTEG.
REGULATOR
ONLY

ALTERNATOR
RELAY
N  B  E

WHT-LT.BLU
WHT-LT.GRN
BLK-YEL

ALTERNATOR
REGULATOR
(ONLY)
N    F    B

WHT-LT.BLU
WHT-LT.GRN
WHT

R WIND
DEFOG. RLY.

WHT-BLK
WHT
RED-YEL
GRN-YEL

FUSIBLE LINK  BLK  (A/C ONLY)

FUS. LINK

BLK-RED
BLK-WHT

FUSIBLE LINK

STARTER

BLK

BLK

ALTERNATOR

WHT-BLK  E

F

B  N    WHT

WHT-GRN
YEL
WHT-LT.BLU

BLK-YEL

WH-BLK   IG  F  L   B   WHT

REGULATOR

BLK
GRN-YEL

WHT-BLK
BLK

FAST IDLE SOL.
(A/C ONLY)

BLK-WH

MAGN.
CLUTCH
(A/C ONLY)

YEL-WHT

RES. WIRE  BLK-YEL

RED

BLK-YEL

BLK

HORNS
GRN-RED
GRN-WHT

GRN-WHT
GRN-RED

COIL   RED
BLK

FILTER  BLK

BLK-RED

DISTRIBUTOR

RED
WHT

BLK

BLK-YEL

IGNITER

WHT-BLK

LT.BLU-YEL

LT.BLU

WINDSHIELD
WASHER MTR.

GRN RED

LT.BLU-YEL

LT.BLU

YEL-BLK   WH-BLK

OIL PRESSURE SW.

YEL BLK

1  2  3  4

TEMP SWITCH
YEL-GRN

RED
YEL GRN
RED-YEL
GRN YEL

RED-GRN
YEL-LT.BLU

RED-WHT
GRN
BLK-WHT
GRN-BLK
RED-LT.BLU

NEUTRAL
SAFETY SW.
(A/T ONLY)

WHT
BLK-YEL
GN-ORG

LT.GRN-
RED

HEAD LTS.
RED-GRN
RED

RED-GRN
RED-YEL
RED

VAC. SOL.

WHT-LT.BLU

LT.BLU-WHT

SPEED
SENSOR

BRN

FUEL
PUMP

GRN-L.BLU   BLK-YEL

VAC. SOL.

RES

BLK YEL

BLK-YEL

FUSE BOX

GRN
ORG   DIR      HORN   GRN-WH

BLK-YEL

LT.BLU  WIPER   TAIL   WHT

BLK-YEL  ENG   LIGHTER   RED

RED-YEL  DEFOG  RADIO   RED
LT.BLU

TO
RADIO

LT.BLU-RD

TO
R. WINDOW
DEFOG. GRID

PARK LT
GRN

WHT-BLK

GRN-BLK

DIRECTION LT.

WHT-LT.BLU
BLK-RED
LT.BLU-WHT
BRN
BLK-RED
WHT-GRN
GRN-LT.BLU
BLK-YEL

WHT-BLU
WHT-GRN

ELECTRONIC CONTROL
COMPUTER

FUEL CUT
OFF SOL

BLK-WHT
WHT-RED
BLK
BLK-YEL

FUEL PUMP
RELAY

WHT-BLK
RED-LT.BLU

WHT-BLU
YEL-LT.BLU

LOW BRAKE SWS.

RED

RED-WHT

BLK

HEAD LT
RELAY

GRN-WHT
GRN

GRN
WHT-GRN-RD
RED-WHT

TAIL LT.
RELAY

MARKER LT.

# 1978 Toyota

MARKER LT.

BATTERY

DIRECTION LT.
GRN-YEL

PARK LT.
GRN

HEADLIGHTS
RED-YEL
RED-GRN
RED
RED-YEL
RED

BLK-RED

FUSIBLE LINK RED    RED-BLU
FUSIBLE LINK RED    WHT
BLK-RED

LT.BLU    LT.BLU
BLK-YEL

RED    GN-WHT    R.D-BLK    LT.BLU    LT.BLU    B    GN-    GRN-    BLK-YEL
                                      RED              RED

TO RADIO

WHT
LT.BLU-RED
LT.BLU
GRN-WHT
GRN-RED
RED-BLK

WHT-RED    NEUTRAL SAFETY SW.
BLK-YEL
BLK    RED-WHT

TO EMISSION CONTROL COMP.

TO EMISSION CONTROL
WHT    RED    BLK    BLK-WHT

STARTER

ALTERNATOR
E    F    N    B

RED

HORN
GRN-WHT
GRN-RED

WHT-RED    WHT-BLK    WHT.RED    GRN    BLU    WHT

REGULATOR
E    G    F    N    B    L

WHT
YEL-WHT

TEMP. SWITCH
YEL-GRN

WHT
YEL-WHT
YEL-GRN

WHT    BALLAST RES.    BLK-YEL

COIL
BLK

DISTRIBUTOR
①    ③    WHT    RED
②    ④

YEL    BLK-YEL    RED    WHT-BLK
IGNITER

YEL-BLK

BLK-WHT

① ② ③ ④

1    2    3    4

HEADLIGHTS
RED-YEL
RED

BLK-YEL
GRN-WHT

RED-WHT

OIL PRESSURE SW.
YEL-BLK

RED-YEL
RED-GN
RED

GRN
GRN-RED

RED-YEL
RED-GRN
RED

PARK LT.
GRN

GRN-BLK
GRN-YEL

DIRECTION LT.
GRN-BLK

RED-YEL    WHT-BLU    YEL-BLK    BLK-RED    BLK-WHT

RESISTOR
BLK-RED

GRN

MARKER LT.

LEGEND
ACCESSORY POWER FEED
B. SEAT BELT WARNING SYSTEM

RED    RED-WHT    RED-BLU
HEADLIGHT RELAY

WHT-BLU    YEL-BLK    BLK-RED    BLK-WHT
FUEL PUMP RELAY

# 1978 Triumph

MARKER LT.

DIRECTION LT.
GRN

PARK LT.
RED
BLK

HEADLIGHT
BLU-WHT
BLU-RED
BLK

HORNS
PPL-BLK
PPL-BLK

HEADLIGHT
BLU-WHT
BLU-RED
BLK

PARK LT.
RED
BLK

BLK
GRN
DIRECTION LT.

MARKER LT.
BLK
RED

BATTERY

WHT-RED
WHT YEL
WHT-ORG
WHT-RED
BRN
BRN

B

STARTER

COIL
WHT-BLK
WHT-BLK
WHT-YEL

1  2  3  4

DISTRIBUTOR
1  2
3  4

WHT-BLU

RESISTOR
WHT        WHT

TEMP. SENDER
GRN-BLU

OIL PRESSURE SWITCH
WHT-BRN
WHT-PPL

ALTERNATOR-REGULATOR
BRN-YEL
BRN
BRN

BRN  BRN

RESISTANCE WIRE
WHT WHT

ANTI DIESEL VALVE

BLOWER MOTOR
GRN  GRN
GRN  GRN
GRN  GRN

FUSE BOX
RED-GRN    BRN   WHT  WHT
RED  RED   PPL PPL  GRN GRN
PPL  PPL   GRN GRN GRN

WHT    WHT
BLK
BLK-PPL
LOW BRAKE SW.

WHT-RED
GRN
V/HT
BRN-YEL
GRN
GRN
BRN
BRN-RED
GRN-BLU
BLK-PPL
WHT-BRN
WHT
WHT-BLK
BRN
RED
PPL-BLK
PPL
BLU WHT
BLU RED
GRN-WHT
WHT
RED-GRN
WHT
WHT
GRN
GRN
PPL
PPL
RED
RED
PPL
GRN RED

GRN-WHT
PPL-BLK
BLK-PPL

# 1978 Triumph

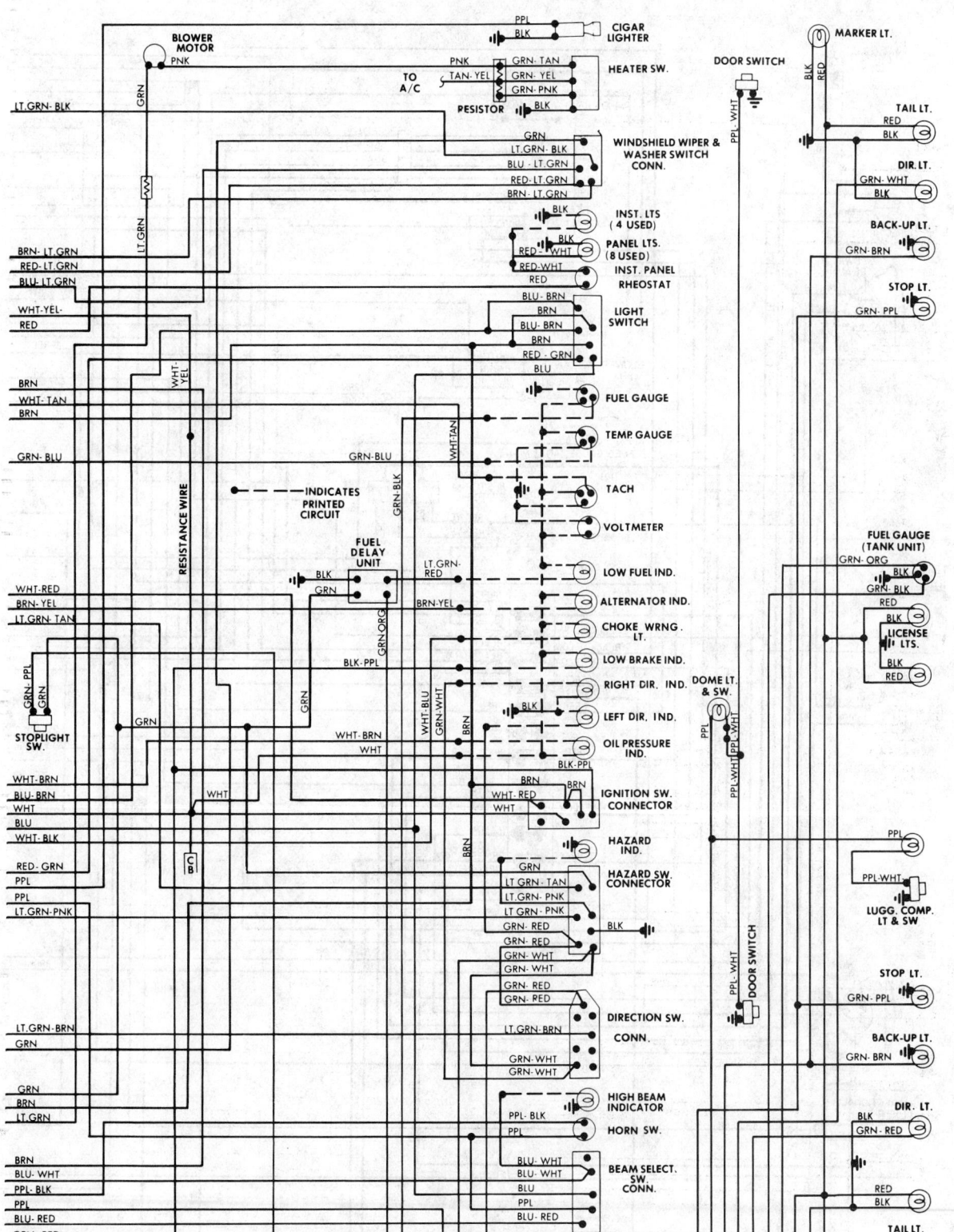

WIRING DIAGRAMS

# 1978 Volkswagen

# 1978 Volkswagen

# 1978 Volvo

## FUSE AND RELAY CONTROL BOX

**Fuse and Relay Control Box**
**Fiat 131**

## FUSE AND RELAY CONTROL BOX (Cont.)

FUSES

| | |
|---|---|
| 6 | RED |
| 3 | YEL-BLK |
| 1 | LT BLU |
| 2 | L.BLU-BLK |
| 4 | YEL-RED |
| 9 | GRY-RED |
| 8 | L.BLU-YEL |
| 10 | BRN |
| 7 | VIO-WHT |
| 5 | L.BLU-WH |
| 11 | BLK |
| 12 | BLANK |
| 13 | WHT-BLK |

CONNECTOR NO. 6

| | |
|---|---|
| 12 | L.BLU-BLK |
| 26 | OG-WHT |
| 24 | RED-BLK |
| 23 | L.BLU-RD |
| 10 | GRY-YEL |
| 8 | GN-WHT |
| 9 | RD-GRN |
| 2 | BN-WHT |

CONNECTOR NO. 7

| | |
|---|---|
| 16 | WHT-BLK |
| 14 | PNK-BLK |
| 17 | BLK |
| 21 | YEL-BLK |
| 13 | VIO-WHT |
| 31 | RED |
| 8 | WHT |
| 5 | ORG |
| 19 | GRY-RED |
| 28 | RED |

CONNECTOR NO. 8

| | |
|---|---|
| 27 | DK.BLU |
| 15 | YEL-RED |
| 11 | LT.BLU |
| 25 | LBLU-WH |
| 22 | VIO |
| 20 | GRN-BLK |
| 7 | PNK-YEL |
| 3 | WH-RED |
| 29 | PNK |
| 1 | LBLU-WH |
| 6 | DBLU-RD |
| 4 | GRY-BLK |

CONNECTOR NO. 9

| | |
|---|---|
| 30 | RED |

CONN. NO. 10

HIGH BEAM RLY.

HORN RLY.

| | |
|---|---|
| 36 | GRY |
| 35 | GRN-BLK |
| 34 | PNK |
| 33 | GRN |
| 32 | BRN |
| 37 | YEL |

CONNECTOR NO. 11

**Fuse and Relay Control Box**
**Fiat 131**

## FUSE AND RELAY CONTROL BOX (Cont.)

*Fuse and Relay Control Box*
*Porsche 924*

## FUSE AND RELAY CONTROL BOX (Cont.)

**Fuse and Relay Control Box**
**Porsche 924**

## AUTOMATIC TRANSMISSION SYSTEM

*Automatic Transmission System*
*(Datsun 200SX)*

## FUEL INJECTION SYSTEMS

*Fuel Injection System Wiring Diagram*
*(BMW 633CSi and 733i)*

## FUEL INJECTION SYSTEMS (Cont.)

*Fuel Injection System Wiring Diagram*
*(Jaguar XJ6)*

## FUEL INJECTION SYSTEMS (Cont.)

*Fuel Injection System Wiring Diagram*
*(Jaguar XJ12 and XJS)*

*Fuel Injection System Wiring Diagram*
*(Volkswagen Type 1 & 2)*

## HEATER AND AIR CONDITIONING SYSTEM

*Heater and Air Conditioning System
(Datsun 810)*

## SEAT BELT WARNING SYSTEMS

*Seat Belt Warning System Wiring Diagram
(Colt and Arrow)*

*Seat Belt Warning System Wiring Diagram
(Colt Station Wagon)*

*Seat Belt Warning System Wiring Diagram
(BMW 320i)*

## SEAT BELT WARNING SYSTEMS (Cont.)

Seat Belt Warning System Wiring Diagram
(BMW 530i)

Seat Belt Warning System Wiring Diagram
(BMW 633CSi and 733i)

Seat Belt Warning System Wiring Diagram
(Capri)

Seat Belt Warning System Wiring Diagram
(Courier)

Seat Belt Warning System Wiring Diagram
(Datsun F10)

Seat Belt Warning System Wiring Diagram
(Datsun B210)

Seat Belt Warning System Wiring Diagram
(Datsun 200SX)

## SEAT BELT WARNING SYSTEMS (Cont.)

Seat Belt Warning System Wiring Diagram
(Datsun 810)

Seat Belt Warning System Wiring Diagram
(Fiat 124)

Seat Belt Warning System Wiring Diagram
(Fiat X1/9)

Seat Belt Warning System Wiring Diagram
(Fiat 128)

Seat Belt Warning System Wiring Diagram
(Fiat 3P)

Seat Belt Warning System Wiring Diagram
(Fiat 131)

## SEAT BELT WARNING SYSTEMS (Cont.)

*Seat Belt Warning System Wiring Diagram*
*(Honda)*

*Seat Belt Warning System Wiring Diagram*
*(Mazda Cosmo and RX4)*

*Seat Belt Warning System Wiring Diagram*
*(Jaguar)*

*Seat Belt Warning System Wiring Diagram*
*(Mercedes Benz)*

*Seat Belt Warning System Wiring Diagram*
*(LUV)*

*Seat Belt Warning System Wiring Diagram*
*( MG Midget)*

*Seat Belt Warning System Wiring Diagram*
*(Mazda GLC)*

*Seat Belt Warning System Wiring Diagram*
*(Porsche 924)*

# SEAT BELT WARNING SYSTEMS (Cont.)

*Seat Belt Warning System Wiring Diagram (Porsche 911SC and Turbo)*

*Seat Belt Warning System Wiring Diagram (Toyota Land Cruiser )*

*Seat Belt Warning System Wiring Diagram (Renault R-5)*

*Seat Belt Warning System Wiring Diagram (Triumph TR7 & Spitfire)*

*Seat Belt Warning System Wiring Diagram (Saab 99)*

*Seat Belt Warning System Wiring Diagram (Volkswagen Type 1)*

*Seat Belt Warning System Wiring Diagram (Subaru)*

*Seat Belt Warning System Wiring Diagram (Volvo 240 & 260)*

## WINDSHIELD WIPER SYSTEMS

*Windshield Wiper System Wiring Diagram*
*(Arrow and Colt)*

*Windshield Wiper System Wiring Diagram*
*(BMW 633CSi and 733i)*

*Windshield Wiper System Wiring Diagram*
*(BMW 320i)*

## WINDSHIELD WIPER SYSTEMS (Cont.)

Windshield Wiper System Wiring Diagram
(Capri)

Windshield Wiper System Wiring Diagram
(Courier)

Windshield Wiper System Wiring Diagram
(Datsun 510)

## WINDSHIELD WIPER SYSTEMS (Cont.)

*Windshield Wiper System Wiring Diagram (Datsun 200SX)*

*Windshield Wiper System Wiring Diagram (Datsun 810)*

*Windshield Wiper System Wiring Diagram (Datsun B210)*

*Windshield Wiper System Wiring Diagram (Datsun F10)*

## WINDSHIELD WIPER SYSTEMS (Cont.)

Windshield Wiper System Wiring Diagram
(Fiat X1/9)

Windshield Wiper System Wiring Diagram
(Fiat 128 Sedan)

Windshield Wiper System Wiring Diagram
(Fiat 124)

Windshield Wiper System Wiring Diagram
(Fiat 128 3P)

Windshield Wiper System Wiring Diagram
(Fiat 131)

Windshield Wiper System Wiring Diagram
(Honda Accord)

## WINDSHIELD WIPER SYSTEMS (Cont.)

*Windshield Wiper System Wiring Diagram
(Jaguar)*

*Windshield Wiper System Wiring Diagram
(Mazda Cosmo and RX4)*

*Windshield Wiper System Wiring Diagram
(Mercedes Benz 230, 240D, 280, 280CE, 300D and
300CD)*

*Windshield Wiper System Wiring Diagram
(Porsche 924)*

## WINDSHIELD WIPER SYSTEMS (Cont.)

*Windshield Wiper System Wiring Diagram*
*(Porsche 911SC and Turbo)*

*Windshield Wiper System Wiring Diagram*
*(Renault R-5)*

*Windshield Wiper System Wiring Diagram*
*(Volkswagen Type 1 and 2)*

## ARROW

### FUSE BLOCK

Fuse block Is located on the wall cover to the left of the drivers seat and contains 14 fuses and three spare fuses. Circuits protected are as follows:

① — 10 Amp. Right High Beam.
② — 10 Amp. Left High Beam.
③ — 10 Amp. Taillights.
④ — 5 Amp. Parking Lights.
⑤ — 15 Amp. Rear Window Defogger.
⑥ — 10 Amp. Back-Up Lights.
⑦ — 10 Amp. Turn Signals, Volt. Regulator.
⑧ — 10 Amp. Right Low Beam.
⑨ — 10 Amp. Left Low Beam.
⑩ — 15 Amp. Cig. Lighter, Radio, Horn.
⑪ — 10 Amp. Windshield Wiper/Washer.
⑫ — 15 Amp. Heater.
⑬ — 15 Amp. Hazard Warning Flashers.
⑭ — 5 Amp. Dome Light.

### FUSIBLE LINK

**All Models** — Fusible link is located in wire between battery and alternator near battery terminal. Purpose of fusible link is to protect the power and charging circuits from excessive current.

Spare Fuses

*Fig. 1   Arrow Hatchback Fuse Block (Colt the Same)*

## AUDI

### FUSE BLOCK

**Fox** — Fuse block is located on left behind dashboard bin attached to the steering column. It contains 15 fuses arranged horizontally. Circuits protected by the fuses are, from left to right:

① — 8 Amp. Low Beam Left.
② — 8 Amp. Low Beam Right.
③ — 8 Amp. High Beam Left, High Beam Warning Light.
④ — 8 Amp. High Beam Right.
⑤ — 16 Amp. Rear Window Defogger.
⑥ — 8 Amp. Stop Lights, Hazard Flasher.
⑦ — 8 Amp. Cig. Lighter, Radio, Clock, Interior Light.
⑧ — 8 Amp. Fuel & Temperature Gauge, Warning Lights, Turn Signals, Wiper/Washer (Automatic).
⑨ — 8 Amp. Back-Up Lights, Shift Console Light.
⑩ — 16 Amp. Fresh Air Fan, Rear Window Defogger, Voltmeter.
⑪ — 8 Amp. Horn, Windshield Wiper/Washer.
⑫ — 8 Amp. License Plate Light.
⑬ — 8 Amp. Tail, Parking & Side Marker Lights (Right).

⑭ — 8 Amp. Tail, Parking & Side Marker Lights (Left)
⑮ — 16 Amp. Radiator Fan.

**5000 Models** — Fuse block is located in passenger compartment under dashboard. Fuse block contains 17 fuses. Circuits protected are, from right to left:

① — 8 Amp. Turn Signals
② — 25 Amp. Rear Window Defogger
③ — 16 Amp. Back Up Lights, Windshield Wiper Motor
④ — 8 Amp. Low Beam Headlight, Left
⑤ — 8 Amp. Low Beam Headlight, Right
⑥ — 16 Amp. Cigar Lighter, Clock, Radio
⑦ — 16 Amp. Brake Lights
⑧ — 25 Amp. Radiator Fan
⑨ — 16 Amp. Horn, Instrument Cluster Lights
⑩ — 8 Amp. Glove Box Light, License Plate Light
⑪ — 8 Amp. Left Parking and Side Marker Lights
⑫ — 8 Amp. Right Parking and Side Marker Lights
⑬ — 16 Amp. Fuel Pump
⑭ — 8 Amp. High Beam Headlight, Right
⑮ — 8 Amp. High Beam Headlight, Left
⑯ — 8 Amp. Fog Lights
⑰ — 25 Amp. Heater, Air Conditioning

## BMW

### FUSE BLOCK

**All Models** — Fuse block is located in engine compartment above wheel arch on left side. Circuits protected are listed on fuse block cover.

**320i** — Fuse block contains 18 fuses, arranged in 5 rows of 3 fuses each. Starting at top left and going down, fuses are as follows:

① — 8 Amp. Right Fog Light
② — 8 Amp. Left Fog Light
③ — 16 Amp. Fuel Pump
④ — 8 Amp. Low Beam Headlight, Right
⑤ — 8 Amp. Low Beam Headlight, Left
⑥ — 8 Amp. Right Parking, Tail, Side Marker Lights, License Light
⑦ — 16 Amp. High Beam Headlight
⑧ — 16 Amp. High Beam Headlight

## BMW (Cont.)

⑨ — 8 Amp. Left Parking, Tail, Side Marker Lights
⑩ — 25 Amp. Heated Rear Window
⑪ — 25 Amp. Heater Blower, Auxiliary Fan Control, Air Conditioning Blower
⑫ — 8 Amp. Brakes, Horn, Radio
⑬ — 25 Amp. Auxiliary Fan Motor
⑭ — 16 Amp. Back Up, Brake Warning Lights, Fuel Gauge, Tachometer, Vacuum Advance
⑮ — 16 Amp. Windshield Wiper and Washer
⑯ — 16 Amp. Cigar Lighter
⑰ — 8 Amp. Turn Signal, Hazard Light, Dome Light, Glove Box Light, Clock, Warning Buzzer
⑱ — Spare

**633CSi, 733i** — Fuse block contains 17 fuses, arranged in 3 rows.

① — 16 Amp. Fuel Delivery
② — 8 Amp. Low Beam Headlight, Right
③ — 8 Amp. Low Beam Headlight, Left
④ — 16 Amp. Cigar Lighter
⑤ — 8 Amp. Clock, Instrument Lights, Turn Signals, Hazard Lights, Seat Belt Warning, Central Locking System
⑥ — 8 Amp. Back Up, Engine Instruments, Warning Light, Buzzer
⑦ — 8 Amp. High Beam Headlight, Right
⑧ — 8 Amp. High Beam Headlight, Left
⑨ — 8 Amp. Parking, Side Marker, License Lights, Right Side
⑩ — 8 Amp. Left Parking Light
⑪ — 16 Amp. Power Mirror, Horn, Windshield Washer/Wipers
⑫ — 8 Amp. Brake Light, Glove Box Light, Radio, Safety Check
⑬ — 16 Amp. Rear Window Heater, Sunroof
⑭ — 25 Amp. Auxiliary Fan Relay, Heating, Air Conditioning
⑮ — 8 Amp. Right Fog Light
⑯ — 8 Amp. Left Fog Light
⑰ — 25 Amp. (2) Auxiliary Fan Motor

## CAPRI

Fuse block is located on left hand side of engine compartment and contains 7 fuses. Circuits protected by the fuses are, from left to right:

1 — 8 Amp. Cigarette Lighter, Clock, Interior Light, Hazard Flasher.
2 — 8 Amp. License Plate Light, Instrument Lights, Map Light.
3 — 8 Amp. Right Tail, Parking and Side Marker Lights.
4 — 8 Amp. Left Tail, Parking and Side Marker Lights.
5 — 8 Amp. Horn, Heater Blower.
6 — 16 Amp. Front and Rear Wiper Motors, Back-Up Light, Instrument Lights.
7 — 8 Amp. Turn Signals, Stop Lights.

**NOTE** — *Four additional 16 Amp. fuses are located on the bottom of the headlight relay to protect headlight circuits. Relay is located near fuse block. One additional 16 Amp. fuse is located inside the plastic cover of the heated backlight relay. Relay is located under dash below ash tray.*

## CHALLENGER & SAPPORO

### FUSE BLOCK

Fuse block is located beneath the instrument panel on the drivers side, and contains 10 fuses. Circuits protected are, from front to back:

① — 10 Amp. Voltage Regulator
② — 10 Amp. Back up Lights
③ — 10 Amp. Turn Signals, Gauges, Belt Warning Lights
④ — 15 Amp. Radio, Cigar Lighter
⑤ — 15 Amp. Windshield Wipers and Washer
⑥ — 15 Amp. Heater, Horn
⑦ — 15 Amp. Tail Lights, Dash Lights
⑧ — 20 Amp. Rear Window Defogger
⑨ — 15 Amp. Door & Hazard Warning Lights
⑩ — 15 Amp. Dome & Stop Lights

## COLT

### FUSE BLOCK

Hardtop fuse block is located on the wall cover to the left of the drivers seat and contains 10 fuses and three spare fuses. Circuits protected are as follows:

① — 15 Amp. Cigar Lighter, Radio, Horn.
② — 15 Amp. Windshield Wiper/Washer.
③ — 10 Amp. Headlights (Upper).
④ — 10 Amp. Headlights (Lower).
⑤ — 5 Amp. Dome & Instrument Lights.
⑥ — 15 Amp. Stop & Hazard Lights.
⑦ — 15 Amp. Rear Window Defogger.
⑧ — 15 Amp. Heater.
⑨ — 15 Amp. Turn Signals, Back-Up Lights, Voltage Regulator.
⑩ — 15 Amp. Tail & Parking Lights.

*Fig. 2   Colt Hardtop Fuse Block*

## COLT (Cont.)

Station wagon fuse block is located on the wall cover to the left of the drivers seat and contains 10 fuses. Hardtop models have the fuse block mounted vertically, station wagons mounted horizontally. Circuits protected are as follows:

① — 15 Amp. Stop Lights, Dome Light
② — 15 Amp. Hazard Light
③ — 15 Amp. Heater, Horn, Air Conditioning
④ — 15 Amp. Windshield Wipers, Washers
⑤ — 15 Amp. Radio, Cigar Lighter
⑥ — 15 Amp. Tail Lights
⑦ — 15 Amp. Rear Window Defogger

⑧ — 10 Amp. Turn Signals, Gauges
⑨ — 10 Amp. Back Up Lights
⑩ — 10 Amp. Voltage Regulator, Fuel Cut

**Fig. 3   Colt Station Wagon Fuse Box**

## COURIER

### FUSE BLOCK

Fuse block is located on left side of engine compartment near windshield. Block contains 9 fuses and 2 spares. Circuits protected are, from front to rear:

① — 15 Amp. Horn, Stop Lights, Hazard Warning Flasher, Interior Light, Cigar Lighter.
② — 15 Amp. Hood & Glove Box Light, Electric Rear Window Defroster.

③ — 15 Amp. Headlights (High Beam).
④ — 15 Amp. Headlights (Low Beam).
⑤ — 10 Amp. Tail, License, Front Parking, Front Side Marker, Instrument Lights.
⑥ — 10 Amp. Windshield Wipers/Washers.
⑦ — 15 Amp. Heater/Defroster Blower Motor, Radio.
⑧ — 10 Amp. Front & Rear Turn Signal Lights, Fasten Seat Belt, Oil Pressure & Brake Warning Lights, Fuel Gauge, Temperature Gauge, Back-Up Lights.
⑨ — 15 Amp. Engine.

## DATSUN

### FUSE BLOCK

**200 SX** — Fuse block is located under instrument panel, left of steering column and contains 8 fuses. Circuits protected are as follows:

① — 10 Amp. Gauges, Flasher, Back-Up Lights.
② — 15 Amp. Windshield Wiper/Washer, Heater.
③ — 15 Amp. Stop Light, Hazard Warning Lights, Horn.
④ — 15 Amp. Cigar Lighter, Clock, Dome Light.
⑤ — 15 Amp. Seat Belt Warning.
⑥ — 10 Amp. Headlights.
⑦ — 10 Amp. Tail, Parking & Interior Lights.
⑧ — 20 Amp. Radio, Rear Window Defogger.

**B210** — Fuse block is located under instrument panel to left of steering column and contains 8 fuses. Circuits protected are as follows:

1 — 10 Amp. Kickdown Switch, Neutral Safety Switch, Turn Signals, Back-Up Lights, Gauges, Warning Lights, Tachometer.
2 — 15 Amp. Windshield Wiper/Washer, Heater.
3 — 15 Amp. Hazard Warning System, Stop Lights, Horn.
4 — 15 Amp. Interior Light, Theft Protection System, Cigarette Lighter.
5 — 10 Amp. EGR and Catalyst Warning System.
6 — 15 Amp. Headlights.
7 — 10 Amp. Parking, Tail, Side Marker and Instrument Lights.
8 — 20 Amp. Rear Window Defogger, Radio.

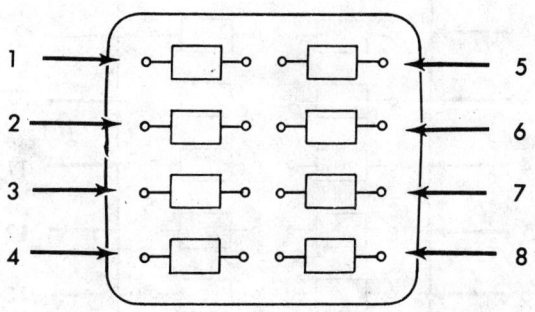

**Fig. 4   Datsun B210 Fuse Block**

**510** — Fuse block is located under the instrument panel and contains 8 fuses. Circuits protected are as follows:

① — 15 Amp. Horn, Cigar Lighter
② — 15 Amp. Interior & Stop Lights
③ — 15 Amp. Tail Lights
④ — 15 Amp. Heater, Radio
⑤ — 10 Amp. Windshield Wipers & Washer
⑥ — 10 Amp. Engine Control
⑦ — 10 Amp. Emergency Flasher, Meters
⑧ — 20 Amp. Rear Window Defogger

**810** — Fuse block is located under the instrument panel on the right kick panel and contains 11 fuses. Circuits protected are as follows:

① — 20 Amp. Rear Window Defogger.
② — 10 Amp. Flasher.

## DATSUN (Cont.)

③ — 5 Amp. Solenoid
④ — 20 Amp. Air Conditioning
⑤ — 10 Amp. Windshield Wiper/Washer
⑥ — 10 Amp. Headlights (Left).
⑦ — 10 Amp. Side Marker & Tail Lights
⑧ — 10 Amp. Dome Light.
⑨ — 10 Amp. Common
⑩ — 20 Amp. Stop Lights, Horn.
⑪ — 10 Amp. Headlights (Right).

**280Z** — Fuse block is located on right side kick panel and contains 14 fuses. Circuits protected are as follows:

① — 10 Amp. Right Headlight.
② — 10 Amp. Left Headlight.
③ — 10 Amp. Flashers.
④ — 10 Amp. Gauges.
⑤ — 20 Amp. Air Conditioner.
⑥ — 15 Amp. Windshield Wiper/Washer.
⑦ — 10 Amp. Radio.
⑧ — 15 Amp. Parking & Tail Lights.
⑨ — 10 Amp. Interior Lights.
⑩ — 10 Amp. Cigar Lighter, Clock, Map Light.
⑪ — 15 Amp. Horn, Stop Lights.
⑫ — 10 Amp. Hazard Warning Lights.
⑬ — 20 Amp. Rear Window Defogger.
⑭ — 1 Amp. Catalyst Warning Light.

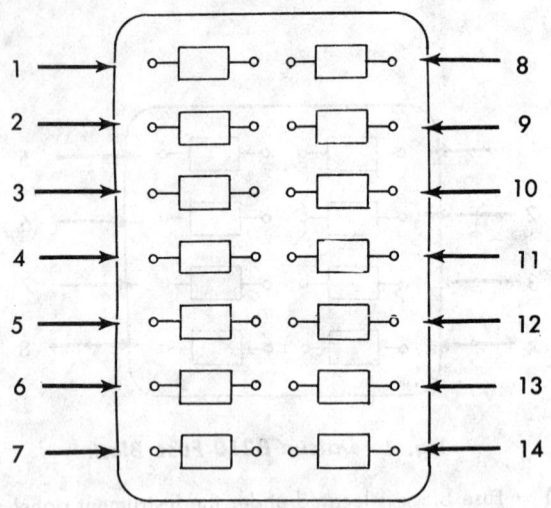

*Fig. 5  Datsun 280Z Fuse Block*

**F10** — Fuse block is located under instrument panel to left of steering column and contains eight fuses. Circuits protected are as follows:

① — 15 Amp. Headlights.
② — 10 Amp. Tail Lights.
③ — 15 Amp. Horn, Stop Lights, Hazard Warning Lights.
④ — 15 Amp. Fan Motor.
⑤ — 20 Amp. Rear Window Defogger, Cig. Lighter, Clock.
⑥ — 15 Amp. Windshield Wiper/Washer, Heater, Radio.
⑦ — 10 Amp. Cooling Fan, Gauges, Turn Signals.
⑧ — 10 Amp. Auto. Choke, EGR Solenoid, Throttle Opener.

**Pickup** — Fuse block is located under instrument panel to the left of steering column and contains six fuses. Circuits protected are as follows:

1 — 10 Amp. Heater, Emission Control.
2 — 15 Amp. Windshield Wiper/Washer, Heater Blower.
3 — 10 Amp. Back-Up, Warning and Turn Signal Lights, Gauges, Kickdown Switch, Voltage Regulator.
4 — 10 Amp. Side Marker, Tail, License, Engine Compartment, Instrument and Control Illumination Lights.
5 — 15 Amp. Headlights.
6 — 15 Amp. Hazard Warning System, Horn, Stop Lights.

**Pickup** — In addition, pickup models have fusible links protecting the interior lights, cigarette lighter and clock.

*Fig. 6  Datsun Pickup Fuse Block*

### FUSIBLE LINK

**All Models** — Fusible link is located in wire between battery and alternator near the battery. Its purpose is to protect the alternator and related circuits.

## FIAT

### FUSE BLOCK

**124 Sport Spider** — Fuse block is located under instrument panel to left of steering column. Block contains 10 fuses. Circuits protected by the fuses are as follows:

① — 8 Amp. Turn Signals, Stop Lights, Gauges, Back Up Lights Tachometer
② — 8 Amp. Windshield Wipers & Washer, Heater Fan
③ — 8 Amp. Left High Beam Headlights, High Beam Indicator

④ — 8 Amp. Right High Beam Headlight
⑤ — 8 Amp. Right Low Beam Headlight
⑥ — 8 Amp. Left Low Beam Headlight
⑦ — 8 Amp. Front Left Parking Light, Tail, License & Instrument Lights
⑧ — 8 Amp. Front Right Parking Light
⑨ — 16 Amp. Horn, Engine Fan
⑩ — 25 Amp. Buzzers, Cigar Lighter, Clock, Hazard, Aerial

**128 (Except 3P Coupe)** — Fuse block is located under instrument panel to left of steering column and contains eight fuses.

## FIAT (Cont.)

Two additional fuses, in separate holders, protect Fuel Pump and Relay (8 Amp.) and Rear Window Defogger (16 Amp.). Fuses in block protect the following circuits:

1 — 8 Amp. Gauges, Warning Lights, Turn Signals, Stop Lights, Back-Up Lights, Heater, Windshield Wiper, Seat Belt Buzzer Relay, Emission Control System
2 — 16 Amp. Interior Lights, Horns, Engine Fan Motor, Hazard Warning Flasher, Remove Key & Seat Belt Buzzer.
3 — 8 Amp. Left Headlight High Beam and High Beam Indicator.
4 — 8 Amp. Right Headlight High Beam.
5 — 8 Amp. Left Headlight Low Beam.
6 — 8 Amp. Right Headlight Low Beam.
7 — 8 Amp. Left Front Parking and Side Marker Lights, Parking and Tail Lights, Right Tail and Side Marker Lights, and Left License Plate Light.
8 — 8 Amp. Right Parking and Side Marker Lights, Left Rear Tail and Side Marker Lights, Right Side License Plate Light, Instrument Cluster Lights, Hazard Warning Flashers, Instrument Control Knob Illumination.

**128 3P Coupe** — Fuse block is located under instrument panel to left of steering column and contains 10 fuses. One additional fuse in separate holder, protects Fuel Pump and Relay (8 Amp). Fuses in block protect the following circuits:

1 — 8 Amp. Stop and Back-Up Lights, Windshield Wiper/Washer, Diverter Valve Relay.
2 — 8 Amp. Gauges, Indicator Lights, Turn Signals, Heater Blower, Key and Seat Belt Buzzer Relay, Diverter Solenoid Valve.
3 — 8 Amp. Left Headlight High Beam and High Beam Indicator.
4 — 8 Amp. Right Headlight High Beam.
5 — 8 Amp. Left Headlight Low Beam.
6 — 8 Amp. Right Headlight Low Beam.
7 — 8 Amp. Left Front Parking and Side Marker Lights, Parking and Tail Lights Indicator, Right Rear Tail and Side Marker Lights, Left License Plate Light.
8 — 8 Amp. Right Front Parking and Side Marker Lights, Left Rear Tail and Side Marker Lights, Right License Plate Light, Instrument Lights, Heater Control Illumination Light, Hazard Warning Flashers.
9 — 16 Amp. Horn Relay, Engine Fan Motor, Courtesy Light.
10 — 16 Amp. Cigar Lighter, Remove Key/Fasten Seat Belts Buzzer.

**X1/9** — Fuse block is located under instrument panel to left of steering column. Fuse block contains 12 fuses. Fuses in block protect the following circuits:

1 — 8 Amp. Gauges, Indicator Lights, Turn Signals, Stop Lights, Back-Up Lights, Heater Blower, Windshield Wiper/Washer, Seat Belt & Key Buzzer System.
2 — 8 Amp. Headlight Motors, Carburetor Fan Relay, Courtesy Light, Key/Seat Belt Buzzer.
3 — 8 Amp. Left Headlight High Beam and High Beam Indicator.
4 — 8 Amp. Right Headlight High Beam.
5 — 8 Amp. Left Headlight Low Beam.
6 — 8 Amp. Right Headlight Low Beam.
7 — 8 Amp. Left Front Parking and Side Marker Lights, Parking and Tail Lights Indicator, Right Rear Tail and Side Marker Lights, Left License Light, Control and Instrument Illumination Lights.
8 — 8 Amp. Right Front Parking and Side Marker Lights, Left Rear Tail and Side Marker Lights, Right License Plate Light.
9 — 16 Amp. Hazard Warning Flashers and Indicator, Cigarette Lighter, Rear Window Defogger.
10 — 16 Amp. Engine Fan, Horn and Relay.
11 — 3 Amp. Headlight Concealing Relay.
12 — 3 Amp. Headlight Raising Relay.

**131** — Fuse block is located under glove compartment and contains one row of 12 fuses, and another row of 2 fuses. Four spares are included. Fuses number 7 & 8 are the 2 fuses in a separate row. Circuits protected are as follows:

① — 8 Amp. Stop & Back-Up Lights, Warning Indicators, Gauges, Heater Fan Motor, Electronic Tachometer; Rear Window, Air Conditioner, Starter Inhibitor Switch & Fasten Seat Belt Relays.
② — 10 Amp. Windshield Wiper/Washer
③ — 10 Amp. Left Tail & Right Front Parking Lights, Right Front & Left Side Marker Lights.
④ — 8 Amp. Left Front Parking & Right Tail Lights, Left Front & Right Side Marker Lights, License Plate Lights, Instrument Lights.
⑤ — 8 Amp. Left Outboard Headlight (Low Beam).
⑥ — 8 Amp. Right Outboard Headlight (Low Beam).
⑦ — 16 Amp. Inboard Headlights (High Beam)
⑧ — 16 Amp. Outboard Headlights (High Beam), High Beam Indicator.
⑨ — Horn, Horn Relay Winding, Engine Fan Motor.
⑩ — 16 Amp. Clock, Courtesy Lights, Cigar Lighter, Radio Antenna Motor (When Installed).
⑪ — 16 Amp. Rear Window Defogger, Hazard Warning System.
⑫ — 16 Amp. Air Conditioner Compressor & Evaporator Fan & Condenser Motor.
⑬ — 16 Amp. Remove Key Buzzer
⑭ — Spare Fuse.

## HONDA

### FUSE BLOCK

**Civic & Civic CVCC** — Fuse block is located in front of the right door hinge pillar. Block contains 8 fuses. Circuits protected are, from bottom to top:

① — 10 Amp. Voltage Regulator.

② — 10 Amp. Windshield Wiper/Washer.
③ — 10 Amp. Turn Signals, Back-Up Lights, Fuel Gauge.
④ — 15 Amp. Heater, Radio, Rear Window Defogger.
⑤ — 15 Amp. Hazard Warning Light, Horn, Stop Lights.
⑥ — 10 Amp. Cig. Lighter, Clock, Interior Lights.
⑦ — 15 Amp. Taillights, License Light, Instrument Lights.
⑧ — 15 Amp. Headlights.

# Fuses & Circuit Breakers

## HONDA (Cont.)

**Accord** — Fuse block is located under the dashboard on drivers side. Block contains 10 fuses. One row of 8 and a row of 2. Numbers 9 & 10 are the 2 fuses in a separate row, along with 2 spares and 1 spare main fuse. Circuits protected are as follows, from top to bottom:

① — 10 Amp. Windshield Wiper/Washer.
② — 10 Amp. Voltage Regulator, Fuel Pump.
③ — 10 Amp. Turn Signals, Back-Up Lights, Fuel Gauge.
④ — 15 Amp. Headlight High Beam.
⑤ — 15 Amp. Headlight Low Beam.
⑥ — 15 Amp. Taillights, Instrument Lights

⑦ — 10 Amp. Cig. Lighter, Clock Interior Lights.
⑧ — 15 Amp. Hazard Warning Lights, Horn, Stop Lights.
⑨ — 15 Amp. Heater.
⑩ — 15 Amp. Radio, Rear Window Defroster.

### IN-LINE FUSES

One large 55 Amp. in-line fuse is installed in main battery cable to prevent damage to main wiring harness. Fuse is located in engine compartment near battery.

## JAGUAR

### FUSE BLOCK

**XJ6 Models** — Fuse block is located behind instrument panel. Access to fuses is obtained by turning access panel retaining pin counterclockwise until it unlocks. Panel will then drop slightly and bottom edge may be lifted clear of opening. Circuits protected are as follows:

① — 20 Amp. Fog Lights
② — 15 Amp. Hazard Warning System
③ — 35 Amp. Map & Interior Lights, Cigar Lighter, Clock, Trunk Light
④ — 15 Amp. Back Up Lights, Gauges
⑤ — 15 Amp. Turn Signals
⑥ — 35 Amp. Stop Lights, Battery Cooling, Horn Relay, Windshield Washer
⑦ — 15 Amp. Instrument Lights
⑧ — 15 Amp. Left Side Marker and Tail Lights
⑨ — 15 Amp. Right Side Marker and Tail Lights
⑩ — 50 Amp. A/C and Heater Relay
⑪ — 20 Amp. Windshield Wipers
⑫ — 15 Amp. Air Conditioning

**XJS Models** — Fuse block is located under dashboard on right side. Circuits protected are as follows:

① — 25 Amp. Fog Lights

② — 15 Amp. Hazard Warning
③ — 35 Amp. Map & Interior Lights, Cigar Lighter, Electric Aerial, Clock, Seat Belt Warning Light.
④ — 10 Amp. Instrument Lights
⑤ — 15 Amp. Turn Signals
⑥ — 10 Amp. Back Up Lights
⑦ — 10 Amp. Panel Switches, License Light, Trunk Light, Gear Selector Light, Cigar Lighter Light, Fibre Optic Unit
⑧ — 10 Amp. Left Side Marker & Tail Lights
⑨ — 10 Amp. Right Side Marker & Tail Lights
⑩ — 50 Amp. Air Conditioning Motor
⑪ — 35 Amp. Windshield Wipers & Washer, Horn Relay, Cooling Fan relay, A/C Relay & Clutch
⑫ — 35 Amp. Heated Back Light

**XJ12** — Fuse Information not available at time of publication.

### IN-LINE FUSES

**Head Lights** — High beam is protected by a 25 Amp. in-line fuse and low beam is governed by a 10 amp in-line fuse.

**Horn Relay** — Circuit is protected by a 35 Amp. in-line fuse.

## LANCIA

### FUSE BLOCK

Fuse block is fitted to the engine compartment and is provided with a pressure tight cover. Block contains 11 fuses. Circuits protected are, from right to left:

① — 8 Amp. Right Front Side Light, Right License Light, Rear Left Side Light
② — 8 Amp. Engine Compartment Light, Trunk Light, Cigar Lighter, Front Left & Rear Right Side Lights, Instrument Light, Left License Light
③ — 8 Amp. Right Low Beam Headlight
④ — 8 Amp. Left Low Beam Headlight
⑤ — 8 Amp. Right High Beam Headlight
⑥ — 8 Amp. Left High Beam Headlight, High Beam Indicator
⑦ — 8 Amp. Stop Lights, Windshield Washer Motor, Radio

⑧ — 16 Amp. No. 14 Solenoid Switch, Heating & Ventilation Booster, Windshield Wipers
⑨ — 16 Amp. No. 12 Solenoid Switch, Turn Signals, Coil, Handbrake Warning Light, Instrument & Warning Lights, Cooling Fan Switch
⑩ — 8 Amp. Courtesy Light, Door Lights, Clock, Glove Box Light
⑪ — 25 Amp. Horn, Cigar Lighter, Clock, Heated Rear Window

### IN-LINE FUSES

In-line fuses protect engine cooling fan (16 Amp), air conditioning booster fan (16 Amp), and an air conditioning compressor solenoid switch (25 Amp). Auxiliary fuse box is located near the left inner wheel well.

# Fuses & Circuit Breakers

## LUV

### FUSE BLOCK

Fuse block is located in engine compartment on left inner valance panel. Fuse block contains 6 fuses and 4 spares. Circuits protected by fuses are as follows:

① — 15 Amp. Tail Lights, Instrument Lights

② — 15 Amp. Turn Signals, Stop Lights, Horn
③ — 15 Amp. Dome Light, Air Conditioning
④ — 15 Amp. Heater, Back Up Lights
⑤ — 15 Amp. Fuel Pump, Voltage Regulator
⑥ — 15 Amp. Radio, Windshield Wiper & Washer, Cigar Lighter

## MAZDA

### FUSE BLOCK

**Cosmo** — Fuse block is located just below glove box and contains 14 fuses. Circuits protected are as follows:

① — 10 Amp. Ignition Reminder Switch
② — 15 Amp. Panel Lights, Left Side Marker, Tail Lights, Parking Lights, License Light
③ — 15 Amp. Right Side Marker, Tail Lights
④ — 10 Amp. Left Side High Beam Headlight, High Beam Indicator
⑤ — 10 Amp. Right Side High Beam Headlight
⑥ — 10 Amp. Left Low Beam Headlight
⑦ — 10 Amp. Right Low Beam Headlight
⑧ — 15 Amp. Courtesy Light, Clock, Cigar Lighter, Glove Box Light, Trunk Light.
⑨ — 20 Amp. Horn, Hazard Warning Flasher Switch
⑩ — 15 Amp. Defogger, Air Conditioner
⑪ — 15 Amp. Stop Lights
⑫ — 20 Amp. Heat Hazard Warning Light, Ignition Coil, Fuel Pump, Emission Control, Choke Switch
⑬ — 10 Amp. Kickdown Switch, EGR Warning, Voltage Regulator

**RX-4** — Fuse block is located just below glove box and contains 13 fuses. Circuits protected are as follows:

① — 20 Amp. Horn, Stop Lights, Hazard Warning Flasher Switch
② — 15 Amp. Interior Light, Clock, Cigar Lighter, Trunk Light, Key Buzzer, Glove Box Light, Step & Spot Lights
③ — 20 Amp. Tail Lights, Front Parking Light, Side Markers, License Light, Instrument Panel Lights
④ — 10 Amp. Left High Beam Headlight
⑤ — 10 Amp. Right High Beam Headlight, High Beam Indicator
⑥ — 10 Amp. Back Up Lights, Warning Lights, Fuel & Temperature Gauge, Turn Signals
⑦ — 15 Amp. Voltage Regulator, Kick Down Solenoid, EGR Warning
⑧ — 20 Amp. Fuel Pump, Heat Hazard Warning Light, Ignition Coil, Choke Switch, Emission Control
⑨ — 10 Amp. Left Low Beam Headlight
⑩ — 10 Amp. Right Low Beam Headlight
⑪ — 20 Amp. Rear Window Defogger, Air Conditioning
⑫ — 20 Amp. Heater, Radio
⑬ — 10 Amp. Windshield Wipers & Washers

**GLC** — The fuse block is located under the instrument panel and contains 10 fuses. Circuits protected are as follows:

① — 15 Amp. Horn, Stop & Turn Signal Lights.
② — 15 Amp. Interior Light, Cigar Lighter, Clock, Key Reminder Buzzer.
③ — 15 Amp. Tail & License Lights, Parking & Side Marker Lights, Instrument Lights.
④ — Not Used.
⑤ — Not Used.
⑥ — 10 Amp. Rear Window Defogger.
⑦ — 10 Amp. Windshield Wiper/Washer, Rear Window Wiper/Washer
⑧ — 15 Amp. Heater, Remote Control Hatchback Release.
⑨ — 10 Amp. Back-Up Lights, Kickdown Switch, Warning Lights, Gauges, Seat Belt Warning Light, Turn Signal Indicator.
⑩ — 10 Amp. Hazard Warning Lights, Choke Switch, Regulator

**Pickup** — Fuse block is located in left rear corner of engine compartment and contains six fuses. Circuits protected by fuses in block are as follows:

① — 15 Amp. Horn, Stop Lights, Interior Light, Cigar Lighter, Hazard Flashers
② — 10 Amp. Front Parking Lights, Side Lights, License Light, Tail Lights, Instrument Panel Lights
③ — 10 Amp. Back Up Lights, Warning Lights, Fuel Gauge, Water Temperature Gauge, Turn Signals
④ — 15 Amp. Choke Switch, Voltage Regulator, Fuel Pump, Fuel Cut
⑤ — 15 Amp. Heater, Radio
⑥ — 10 Amp. Windshield Wipers & Washer

### IN-LINE FUSES

A fuse block containing large in-line fuses is installed in engine compartment near battery. Fuse amperage and circuits protected is printed on fuse block cover.

## MERCEDES-BENZ

### FUSE BLOCK

**All (Exc. 450 SL & SLC)** — Main fuse block is located under hood on left inner fender panel. Fuse capacities and circuits protected are marked on fuse block cover.

**450 SL & SLC** — Main fuse block is located on right side kick panel. Fuse capacities and circuits protected are marked on fuse block cover.

### IN-LINE FUSES

Additional fuses for optional equipment and/or standard extras such as sliding sun roof, heated rear window, radio, automatic antenna, electric windows and air conditioning are located in engine compartment.

# Fuses & Circuit Breakers

## MG

### FUSE BLOCK

Fuse block is located on right hand side of engine compartment. Fuse block contains four 35 Amp. fuses and two spares. Circuits protected are, from top to bottom:

① — 35 Amp. One Parking Light, One Tail Light, One License Plate Light, One Front & Rear Side Marker Light.

② — 35 Amp. One Parking Light, One Tail Light, One Licence Plate Light, One Front & Rear Side Marker Light.

③ — 35 Amp. Turn Signal Indicator, Stop Lights, Back-Up Lights, Seat Belt & Brake Warning Lights.

④ — 35 Amp. Horn, Interior & Luggage Compartment Lights, Headlight Flasher, Cigar Lighter.

### IN-LINE FUSES

**Auxiliary Equipment** — A 35 Amp. in-line fuse located above fuse block (MG Midget) or below fuse block (MGB) protects Windshield Wipers/Washer, Heater Blower Motor, and Radio.

**Fan Thermostat** — A 35 Amp. in-line fuse protects the fan thermostat circuit.

**Hazard Warning** — A 35 Amp. in-line fuse located behind Hazard Warning Switch protects Warning Lights.

**Radio** — A separate additional in-line fuse protects Radio.

## OPEL

### FUSE BLOCK

Fuse block is located on the right side kick panel. Block contains 13 fuse positions and four spare fuses. Circuits protected are as follows:

① — 10 Amp. High Beam Headlights
② — 15 Amp. Windshield Wiper/Washer, Radio.
③ — 15 Amp. Horn, Turn Signals.
④ — 15 Amp. Rear Window Defogger.
⑤ — 15 Amp. Cig. Lighter, Interior Light.
⑥ — 15 Amp. Air Conditioning.
⑦ — 15 Spare Circuit.
⑧ — 10 Amp. Headlights Low Beam.
⑨ — 10 Amp. Instrument Lights, Emission Control System
⑩ — 15 Amp. Ignition Coil, Voltage Regulator, Fuel Pump
⑪ — 15 Amp. Heater, Back-Up Lights.
⑫ — 15 Amp. Lighting Switch.
⑬ — 15 Amp. Taillights.

### FUSIBLE LINKS

Fusible links and in-line fuses are utilized throughout the wiring system to prevent short circuits. Main fusible link is located near the battery.

## PORSCHE

### FUSE BLOCK

**924 Models** — Fuse block is located under instrument panel to left of steering column and contains 15 fuses. Circuits protected are, from left to right:

① — 8 Amp. Left Headlight (Low Beam)
② — 8 Amp. Right Headlight (Low Beam).
③ — 8 Amp. Left Headlight (High Beam).
④ — 8 Amp. Right Headlight (High Beam).
⑤ — 16 Amp. Additional Headlights.
⑥ — 8 Amp. Interior Lights, Retractable Headlights.
⑦ — 8 Amp. Emergency Flashers.
⑧ — 8 Amp. Turn Signal Indicator, Brake Warning Light.
⑨ — 8 Amp. Horn, Back-Up Lights, Rear Window Wiper.
⑩ — 8 Amp. Fresh Air Blower.
⑪ — 8 Amp. Windshield Wipers.
⑫ — 8 Amp. License Plate & Luggage Compartment Lights.
⑬ — 8 Amp. Side Marker Light (Right)
⑭ — 8 Amp. Side Marker Light (Left).
⑮ — 16 Amp. Fan, Fog Lights.

**911SC & Turbo Models** — Main fuse block is located inside luggage compartment on left side and contains 21 fuses. An additional fuse block is located in the engine compartment on left side under regulator cover. Secondary fuse block protects Sportomatic and Fan Relay (5 Amp.), Heater Fan (25 Amp.) and Rear Window Defogger (25 Amp.). Main fuse block protects the following circuits, front to rear:

1 — 16 Amp. Fog Lights.

2 — 5 Amp. License Plate & Control Lights, Fog Light Relay.

3 — 5 Amp. Right Front and Rear Parking Lights.

4 — 5 Amp. Left Front and Rear Parking Lights.

5 — 8 Amp. Right Headlight Low Beam.

6 — 8 Amp. Left Headlight Low Beam.

7 — 8 Amp. Right Headlight High Beam.

8 — 8 Amp. Left Headlight High Beam, High Beam Indicator.

9 — 5 Amp. Right Front Flasher Light.

10 — 5 Amp. Left Front Flasher Light.

11 — 16 Amp. Flasher Relay, Brake and Back-Up Lights.

12 — 25 Amp. Rear Window Defroster Relay, Fresh Air Blower, Rear Window Defroster Control Light.

13 — 25 Amp. Windshield Wiper/Washer, Air Conditioner.

14 — 25 Amp. Electric Sunroof, Rear Window Wiper.

15 — 16 Amp. Cigar Lighter, Blower Switch Control Light.

16 — 25 Amp. Fuel Pump

17 — 16 Amp. Emergency Flasher.

18 — 5 Amp. Interior, Glove Compartment, and Luggage Compartment Lighting, Clock.

19 — 16 Amp. Headlight Washer.

20 — 25 Amp. Blower for Air Conditioner.

21 — 25 Amp. Power Windows

# Fuses & Circuit Breakers

## PORSCHE (Cont.)

**928** — Fuse block is located in the passenger foot well and contains 34 fuses and 22 relays. Circuits protected by fuses are as follows, from left to right:

1 — 16 Amp. Fog Lights
2 — Not Connected
3 — 8 Amp. License Light, Engine Compartment Light
4 — 8 Amp. Switch Illumination Light
5 — 8 Amp. Cigar Lighter, Instrument Lights
6 — 16 Amp. Windshield Wipers
7 — 8 Amp. Rear Window Wipers
8 — 8 Amp. Sliding Roof
9 — 8 Amp. Back Up Lights, Outside Mirror
10 — 8 Amp. Brake Lights, Automatic Speed Control
11 — 8 Amp. Left Side Instrument Warning Lights
12 — 8 Amp. Right Side Instrument Warning Lights
13 — Not Connected
14 — 25 Amp. Power Seats
15 — 16 Amp. Power Antenna
16 — 25 Amp. Electric Radiator Fan
17 — 25 Amp. Heater, Air Conditioning Blower
18 — 25 Amp. Rear Window Defogger
19 — 25 Amp. Headlight Motor
20 — 16 Amp. Headlight Washer
21 — 25 Amp. Power Windows
22 — 16 Amp. Fuel Pump
23 — 8 Amp. Interior Lights, Clock
24 — 8 Amp. High Beam Headlights Left
25 — 8 Amp. High Beam Headlights Right
26 — 8 Amp. Low Beam Headlights Left
27 — 8 Amp. Low Beam Headlights Right
28 — 8 Amp. Left Side Markers
29 — 8 Amp. Right Side Markers
30 — 8 Amp. Front Left Turn Signal
31 — 8 Amp. Rear Left Turn Signal
32 — 8 Amp. Front Right Turn Signal
33 — 8 Amp. Rear Right Turn Signal
34 — Not Connected

**Fig. 4   Porsche 928 Fuse and Relay Block**

Relay circuits are located below the fuses on the block.

1-2 — Rear Defogger
3 — Headlight Motor Control Relay
4 — Main Headlight Power Supply Relay
5 — Turn Signal Flasher Unit
6 — Window Controls
7 — Headlight Washer Pump
8 — Not Occupied
9 — Seat Belt Time Relay
10 — Two-Tone Horn
11 — Current Limiting Diode Pack
12 — Fog Lights
13 — Headlight Beam Power Supply Relay
14 — High/Low Beam Relay
15 — Bridge
16 — Safety Relay Headlights
17 — Fuel Pump
18 — Extra Cooling Fan for Air Conditioning
19 — Wiper Intermittent
20 — Intensive Cleaner Pump
21 — Heating and Air Conditioning Blower
22 — Defroster

## RENAULT

**FUSE BLOCK**

**R-5** — Fuse block is located under the dashboard and to the right of the steering column. Circuits protected are, from left to right:

① — 8 Amp. Windshield Wiper.
② — 8 Amp. Cig. Lighter, Interior Lights.
③ — 5 Amp. Turn Signals.
④ — 8 Amp. Heater Motor.
⑤ — 15 Amp. Rear Window Defogger, Back-Up Lights.
⑥ — 5 Amp. Solenoids.

## SAAB

**FUSE BLOCK**

**99 Models** — Electrical system is protected by 12 fuses. Fuse block is mounted on the right wheel housing in the engine com-

partment. All parts of the system are fused except the headlights and the ignition system. A label by the fuse box shows which fuses protect which circuits.

## SUBARU

**FUSE BLOCK**

**All Models** — Fuse block is located on left side under instrument panel and contains 8 fuses. Circuits protected are as follows, from right to left:

① — 25 Amp. Lighting Switch
② — 20 Amp. Windshield Wiper & Washer, Fan Motor, Heater, Radio, Cigar Lighter
③ — 15 Amp. Hazard Light, Horn, Clock, Dome Light, Stop Lights

## SUBARU (Cont.)

④ — 15 Amp. Ignition Coil, Fuel Pump, Gauges
⑤ — 15 Amp. Back Up Lights, Turn Signals, Rear Window Defogger

⑥ — 15 Amp. Parking Lights, Tail Lights, License Light
⑦ — 15 Amp. Headlight Low Beam
⑧ — 11 Amp. Headlight High Beam

## TOYOTA

### FUSE BLOCK

**Cressida** — Fuse block is located on left side of drivers compartment under instrument panel. Circuits protected are as follows:

① — 15 Amp. Front Parking Lights, Side Markers, Tail Lights, License Light, Glove Box Light, Trunk & Panel Lights
② — 15 Amp. Stop Lights, Emergency Lights
③ — 15 Amp. Cigar Lighter, Clock, Dome, Courtesy, Luggage Light
④ — 15 Amp. Radio, Stereo
⑤ — 15 Amp. Emission Control Computer, Electric Choke
⑥ — 15 Amp. Turn Signals, Windshield Wipers & Washers, ESP
⑦ — 15 Amp. Back Up Lights, Warning Lights, Heater Relay, Rear Window Defogger Relay

**Corona** — Fuse block is located on left side of drivers compartment under instrument panel. Circuits protected are:

1 — 5 Amp. Radio, Tape Player.
2 — 10 Amp. Cigar Lighter, Door Warning Light.
3 — 15 Amp. Light Control Relay, Parking, Side Marker, Instrument Panel, Tail, and License Plate Lights.
4 — 15 Amp. Horn, Hazard Warning Lights, Stop Lights, Seat Belt Warning Light and Buzzer.
5 — 10 Amp. Interior Lights.
6 — 15 Amp. Spare Terminal.
7 — 15 Amp. Windshield Wiper/Washer.
8 — 10 Amp. Ignition Coil.
9 — 15 Amp. Turn Signal Lights, Regulator, Main Relay.
10 — 15 Amp. Heater Blower, Gauges, Back-up Lights, Brake Warning Lights.
11 — 15 Amp. Rear Window Defogger.

**Celica** — Fuse block is located on left side of drivers compartment under instrument panel. Circuits protected are:

① — 15 Amp. Front Parking Lights, Front & Rear Side Marker Lights, Tail, License, Glove Box & Instrument Lights.
② — 15 Amp. Stop Lights, Hazard Warning Lights
③ — 15 Amp. Cigar Lighter, Clock; Interior, Door Courtesy & Luggage Compartment Lights
④ — 20 Amp. Rear Window Defogger
⑤ — 15 Amp. Instrument Warning Lights, Gauges, Heater Relay, Defogger Switch
⑥ — 15 Amp. Turn Signal Lights, Windshield Wiper/Washer
⑦ — 15 Amp. Main Relay, Regulator IG Terminal.
⑧ — 15 Amp. Radio & Tape Player.

**Corolla** — Fuse block is located on left side of drivers compartment under instrument panel. Circuits protected are:

① — 15 Amp. Stop Lights, Emergency Flasher
② — 15 Amp. Parking, Side Marker, Instrument Panel, Ashtray, Tail Lights, License Light
③ — 15 Amp. Cigar Lighter, Interior Lights, Clock, Spot Light
④ — 15 Amp. Radio, Stereo Tape Player
⑤ — 15 Amp. Heater
⑥ — 15 Amp. Turn Signals, Windshield Wiper & Washer
⑦ — 15 Amp. Voltage Regulator, Fuel Cut Solenoid, Emission Control, Choke Coil, Electric Fan
⑧ — 15 Amp. Defogger, Back Up Lights, Warning Lights, Gauges

**Pickup** — Fuse block is located on left side of drivers compartment under instrument panel. Circuits protected are:

① — 15 Amp. Instrument Panel, Parking, Side Marker, Tail Lights, License Light
② — 20 Amp. Horns, Stop Lights
③ — 15 Amp. Cigar Lighter, Dome Light, Emergency Flasher, Fan
④ — 20 Amp. Radio, Windshield Wipers & Washer
⑤ — 20 Amp. Heater Blower, Gauges, Back Up Lights
⑥ — 15 Amp. Turn Signals
⑦ — 15 Amp. Emission Control, Alternator Regulator
⑧ — 20 Amp. Spare

**Land Cruiser** — Fuse block is mounted under dash to left of steering column (Station Wagon Models) or on left hand kick panel (All exc. Station Wagon Models). Fuse block contains 8 fuses. Circuits protected are, from end of block labeled "TOP":

1 — 15 Amp. Instrument, Parking, Side Marker, Tail and License Plate Lights.
2 — 20 Amp. Stop Lights, Horn and Hazard Warning System.
3 — 20 Amp. Cigarette Lighter, Interior Lights and Inspection Light Socket.
4 — 20 Amp. Radio, Windshield Wiper and Washer Motors.
5 — 20 Amp. Back-Up Lights, Heater and Gauges.
6 — 15 Amp. Turn Signal Lights.
7 — 15 Amp. Ignition Coil, Emission Control System, Voltage Regulator, Fuel Cut Solenoid.
8 — 20 Amp. Headlights.

### FUSIBLE LINKS

**All Models** — A fusible link is located in main battery feed wire near the battery. Protects all circuits except for starter motor.

## TRIUMPH

### FUSE BLOCK

**Spitfire** — Fuse block is mounted on left hand side of firewall in engine compartment, adjacent to clutch master cylinder.

Block contains 3 fuses and 2 spares. Circuits protected are as follows:

# Fuses & Circuit Breakers

WIRING DIAGRAMS

## TRIUMPH (Cont.)

① — 35 Amp. Windshield Wipers, Gauges, Stop & Reverse Lights, Turn Signals, Seat Belt Warning Light

② — 10 Amp. Side Marker Lights, Front Parking Lights, Tail Lights, License Light, Instrument Panel Lights

③ — 35 Amp. Headlight Flasher, Courtesy Light, Horn, Key & Hazard Warning Lights

**TR7** — Fuse block is located on a relay plate and is accessible after removal of cover panel at front of glovebox. Block contains four 35 Amp. fuses. Circuits protected are as follows:

① — 35 Amp. Air Conditioner.

② — 35 Amp. Cigar Lighter, Horn, Clock, Hazard Warning System, Courtesy Light.

③ — 35 Amp. Back-Up Lights, Heater, Windshield Wiper/Washer, Stop Lights, Turn Signals, Air Conditioner Control System.

④ — 35 Amp. Interior Lights, Parking & Side Marker Lights, Tail Lights.

---

## VOLKSWAGEN

### FUSE BLOCK

**Type 1 (Beetle)** — Fuse block is located under instrument panel near the center of vehicle and contains 12 fuses. Additional in-line fuses are located and protect circuits as follows: An 8 Amp. fuse located in engine compartment above coil, protects the Back-Up Lights. An 8 Amp. fuse located under the rear seat, left side, protects the Rear Window Defogger. A 16 Amp. fuse located in front luggage compartment near heater protects the auxiliary heater. Fuse block circuits protected are, from left to right:

① — 8 Amp. Left Tail Light.

② — 8 Amp. Right Tail Light, Parking & Side Marker Lights, License Plate Light.

③ — 8 Amp. Left Low Beam.

④ — 8 Amp. Right Low Beam.

⑤ — 8 Amp. Left High Beam, High Beam Warning Light.

⑥ — 8 Amp. Right High Beam.

⑦ — 8 Amp. Not Used.

⑧ — 8 Amp. Emergency Flasher.

⑨ — 16 Amp. Interior Light.

⑩ — 16 Amp. Windshield Wiper, Fresh Air Fan, Rear Window Defogger.

⑪ — 8 Amp. Safety Belt Warning System, Stop Lights, Brake Warning Light, Horn.

⑫ — 8 Amp. Turn Signals, Gauges, Warning Lights, Emission System (EGR).

**Type 2 (Transporter)** — Fuse block is located under instrument panel on right side of steering column. Fuse block contains 12 fuses. Two additional in-line fuses are used as follows: An 8 Amp. fuse, located in engine compartment near ignition coil on manual transmission models, protects the Back-Up Lights. A 16 Amp. fuse, located in engine compartment near blower motor protects the Warm Air Blower. Fuses in block protect the following circuits, left to right:

① — 8 Amp. Left Tail Light, Left Rear Marker Light.

② — 8 Amp. Right Tail Light, Parking Lights, License Plate Light, Right Rear Side Marker Light, Front Side Marker Lights.

③ — 8 Amp. Left Low Beam.

④ — 8 Amp. Right Low Beam.

⑤ — 8 Amp. Left High Beam, High Beam Indicator.

⑥ — 8 Amp. Right High Beam.

⑦ — 8 Amp. Accessories.

⑧ — 8 Amp. Emergency Flasher, Interior Lights.

⑨ — 16 Amp. Accessories.

⑩ — 16 Amp. Windshield Wipers, Rear Window Defogger

⑪ — 8 Amp. Horn, Stop Lights, Brake Warning Light.

⑫ — 8 Amp. Turn Signals Warning Lights, Back-Up Lights.

**Rabbit & Scirocco** — Fuse block is located under instrument panel on left side of vehicle and contains 15 fuses in one centralized unit. Two additional in-line fuses are used as follows: An 8 Amp. fuse located above fuse block, protects Rear Window Wiper. A 16 Amp. fuse located above fuse block, protects Electric Fuel Pump. Circuits protected by fuses in block are:

① — 8 Amp. Left Headlight Low Beam.

② — 8 Amp. Right Headlight Low Beam.

③ — 8 Amp. Left Headlight High Beam and Indicator.

④ — 8 Amp. Right Headlight High Beam.

⑤ — 16 Amp. Rear Window Defogger.

⑥ — 8 Amp. Stop Lights, Hazard Warning Flasher.

⑦ — 8 Amp. Interior Lights, Cigar Lighter.

⑧ — 8 Amp. Turn Signal System.

⑨ — 8 Amp. Back Up Lights, Shift Console Light, Horn.

⑩ — 16 Amp. Fresh Air Fan.

⑪ — 8 Amp. Windshield Wiper & Washer.

⑫ — 8 Amp. Luggage Compartment & License Plate Lights.

⑬ — 8 Amp. Right Parking, Tail & Side Marker Lights.

⑭ — 8 Amp. Left Parking, Tail & Side Marker Lights

⑮ — 16 Amp. Radiator Fan.

**Dasher** — Fuse block is located on the left side behind the dashboard bin and contains 15 fuses. One additional fuse is located above fuse No. 7. A 16 Amp. fuse protects the Fuel Pump Relay. Circuits protected by fuses in the block are, from left to right:

① — 8 Amp. Left Low Beam.

② — 8 Amp. Right Low Beam.

③ — 8 Amp. Left High Beam & Warning Light.

④ — 8 Amp. Right High Beam.

⑤ — 16 Amp. Rear Window Defogger.

⑥ — 8 Amp. Stop Lights, Hazard Warning Flasher.

⑦ — 8 Amp. Cigar Lighter, Clock, Radio, Interior Light.

⑧ — 8 Amp. Gauges, Warning Lights, Turn Signal Indicator.

⑨ — 8 Amp. Back-Up Lights, Shift Console Light.

⑩ — 16 Amp. Fresh Air Fan, Rear Window Defogger (Switch Current)

⑪ — 8 Amp. Horn, Windshield Wiper/Washer.

⑫ — 8 Amp. License Plate Light.

⑬ — 8 Amp. Right Tail, Parking & Side Marker Lights.

⑭ — 8 Amp. Left Tail, Parking & Side Marker Lights.

⑮ — 16 Amp. Radiator Fan.

# Fuses & Circuit Breakers

## VOLVO

**FUSE BLOCK**

**240 Series** — Fuse block is located in front of front left door pillar. Circuits protected are, from top to bottom:

① — 16 Amp. Cigar Lighter, Wipers Front & Rear
② — 16 Amp. Heater Fan, Horn, Radio
③ — 16 Amp. Rear Defogger, Overdrive
④ — 8 Amp. Back Up Lights, Air Conditioning
⑤ — 8 Amp. Instrument Lights, Turn Signals, Warning Lights, Fuel Injection Relay
⑥ — 8 Amp. Stop Lights, Trunk Light, Rear Interior Light
⑦ — 16 Amp. Fuel Pump
⑧ — 8 Amp. Clock, Glove Box Light, Dome & Hazard Light
⑨ — 8 Amp. Seat Belt Warning
⑩ — 16 Amp. Spare
⑪ — 8 Amp. Side Marker Left, Parking Light, License Light
⑫ — 8 Amp. Side Marker Right, Parking & License Light

**260 Series** — Fuse block is located in front of front left door pillar and contains 12 fuses. Circuits protected are, from top to bottom:

① — 16 Amp. Cigar Lighter, Wipers Front & Rear
② — 16 Amp. Heater Fan, Horn, Radio
③ — 16 Amp. Rear Defogger, Overdrive
④ — 8 Amp. Back Up Light, A/C, Heated Driver Seat
⑤ — 8 Amp. Instrument Lights, Turn Signals, Warning Lights, Fuel Injection Relay, Electric Side Mirrors
⑥ — 8 Amp. Stop Lights, Trunk Light, Rear Interior Light
⑦ — 16 Amp. Fuel Pump
⑧ — 8 Amp. Clock, Glove Box Light, Dome & Hazard Light
⑨ — 8 Amp. Seat Belt Warning
⑩ — 16 Amp. Window Lifts
⑪ — 8 Amp. Side Marker Left, Parking Light, License Light
⑫ — 8 Amp. Side Marker Right, Parking Light, License Light

# Section 5
# ENGINES

# Contents

*NOTE — ALSO SEE GENERAL INDEX.*

## FOX 4 CYLINDER

### ENGINE CODING

#### ENGINE IDENTIFICATION

Engine number is stamped on distributor side of engine block, just above the fuel pump. Number prefix indicates engine/transmission application as follows:

| Application | Engine Code |
|---|---|
| 1.6 Liter Calif. ....................................... | YG |
| 1.6 Liter Fed. ....................................... | YK, YH |
| Man. Trans. ....................................... | XK |
| Auto. Trans. ....................................... | ET |

### ENGINE & CYLINDER HEAD

#### ENGINE

**NOTE** — *Leave all fuel injection lines connected to components.*

**1)** Disconnect battery ground cable. Loosen clutch adjusting nut and remove clutch cable. Disconnect electrical plug connector and pressure regulator lines. Remove vacuum hoses, ignition and emission control systems from intake manifold. Remove cold start valve, pull out injectors and remove accelerator cable.

**2)** Disconnect electrical wires at: ignition coil, fan motor, radiator thermo switch, alternator and oil pressure switch. Drain and remove radiator and radiator grille. Remove starter and exhaust pipe nuts.

**3)** On vehicles with air conditioning, remove intake air duct, radiator, radiator grille and cooling fan. Remove condenser (do not loosen or remove air conditioner hoses) and hang up with wire. Remove air filter, intake air distributor, EGR valve, horn and A/C Compressor.

**4)** Remove front engine mount and lower mounting bolts at engine block. Remove flywheel guard. On automatic transmission vehicles, remove torque converter cover and torque to drive plate bolts. Support transmission with floor jack or stand.

**5)** Using suitable engine sling (tool No. US1105) lift engine and transmission, until transmission housing contacts steering drive. Adjust jack or stand to make contact with transmission. Remove upper mounting bolts at engine block. Pry engine and transmission apart and remove intermediate plate.

**6)** On manual transmission vehicles, engine must be turned and lifted, to prevent damage to transmission main shaft, clutch and body. On automatic transmissions models lift engine straight out. Secure torque converter with suitable tool (tool No. 32-200).

**Installation** — To install engine, reverse removal procedure. Check that torque converter is fully seated on one-way clutch, and can be easily turned by hand. Check that all engine mounts are free of strain, realign if necessary.

#### CYLINDER HEAD

**Removal & Installation** — **1)** Disconnect battery ground cable. Drain coolant system and disconnect hoses which are connected to cylinder head. Disconnect exhaust pipe and electrical wires. Disengage accelerator linkage and disconnect at holder. Loosen alternator tensioner and remove camshaft drive belt and "V" belt.

**2)** Loosen head bolts in reverse of tightening sequence (See Fig. 1). To install, place head gasket with word "top" facing cylinder head. Position cylinder head on gasket and install bolts. Tighten bolts, in steps, in sequence shown in *Fig. 1*. Reinstall remaining components and retime camshaft. Retighten head bolts after 1000 miles.

**NOTE** — *On some models 11 mm cylinder head bolts with 12 mm polygon socket heads have been installed in place of 10 mm hexagon socket head bolts. Torque new head bolts to 55 ft lb (7.5 mkg), then tighten ¼ turn more. New head bolts do not have to be retorqued after 1000 miles.*

**Fig. 1** *Cylinder Head Tightening Sequence*

## VALVES

### VALVE ARRANGEMENT

E-I-E-I-I-E-I-E (front to rear).

### VALVE GUIDE SERVICING

**1)** Before taking measurements, clean valve guides with a cleaning broach. To measure, attach a suitable device with a dial indicator (VW 689/1) to mounting surface of cylinder head. Insert a new valve into valve guide until stem is flush with end of guide. Rock valve against dial indicator and check amount of guide-to-stem clearance. Maximum valve rock should not exceed .039" (1.0 mm) for intake valves, and .051" (1.3 mm) for exhaust valves.

**2)** Use suitable press and adaptor (10-206) to remove and install valve guides. Press worn guides out from combustion chamber side. Coat new guide with oil and press into cold cylinder head from camshaft side. Do not use more than 1 Ton of pressure or guide shoulder may break. Ream guide by hand to proper size.

### VALVE STEM OIL SEALS

**NOTE** — *Valve stem seal, may be removed with cylinder head installed on vehicle.*

## FOX 4 CYLINDER (Cont.)

**1)** With camshaft removed, remove spark plug, turn crankshaft until piston is at BTC. Install pressure hose (tool No. VW 653) in spark plug hole and apply constant pressure.

**2)** Remove valve keepers and spring with compressor (VW 541). Lift seal off valve stem with seal remover (10-218). Slide plastic sleeve on valve stem, lubricate seal and push in place with installing tool (10-204).

### VALVE SPRINGS

With tappets removed, install suitable valve spring compressor (Tool No. 10-210). Compress springs and remove valve keepers and collar. Lift out valve springs. To install, reverse removal procedure.

### MECHANICAL VALVE LIFTER ASSEMBLY

With camshaft and tappet discs removed, lift out tappets. Inspect for wear or damage, replace as necessary. Oil tappet lightly and replace in original position.

### VALVE CLEARANCE ADJUSTMENT

**1)** Adjust valve clearances in firing number order (1-3-4-2). Rotate camshaft until number four cylinder valves overlap and measure number one cylinder valve clearances. Clearance is measured with engine warm. With a feeler gauge, measure clearance of each cylinder in turn and note clearance. If clearance is within .002" (.05 mm) of specifications, no adjustment is necessary.

**2)** Determine thickness of tappet disc installed. Using tappet clearance previously noted, calculate required thickness of disc needed to achieve proper tappet clearance. Tappet discs are available in .0019" (.05 mm) increments, from .1181" (3.0 mm) to .1673" (4.25 mm). Thickness is stamped on bottom side of tappet disc.

**3)** Special tools (tool No. VW 546 and US 4476) are required to remove tappet clearance discs. Rotate camshaft so cams of one cylinder overlap and cams of cylinder to be changed no longer rest on tappets. Rotate tappet until openings are at 90° angles to camshaft. Install tool No. VW 546 to depress tappets. Using tool No. US 4476, grasp tappet disc through opening in side of tappet and rotate out from under camshaft. Install proper disc and remove tool No. VW 546. Repeat procedure until all tappets are adjusted.

### Valve Clearances

| Application | In. (mm) |
| --- | --- |
| Intake | |
|   Hot | .008-.012 (.20-.30) |
|   Cold | .006-.010 (.15-.25) |
| Exhaust | |
|   Hot | .016-.020 (.41-.51) |
|   Cold | .014-.018 (.36-.46) |

**NOTE** – Cold settings are given for reference as initial settings after engine rework. Final adjustments are to be made with engine at operating temperature.

## PISTONS, PINS & RINGS

### OIL PAN

Drain engine oil. Attach a suitable lifting device to engine, and apply supporting tension to engine. Remove auxiliary bolts (alternately), then remove left and right engine mounts. Unscrew oil pan bolts and remove pan. When installing, gasket is installed dry, and oil pan bolts are to be tightened in a criss-cross pattern.

### PISTON & ROD ASSEMBLY

**1)** Before removing connecting rods, mark rod and cap for proper reinstallation. Remove rod bolts and caps and carefully push piston and rod assembly out top of cylinder.

**2)** On reassembly of piston and rod assemblies, cast bosses on rod and cap, as well as locating projections of bearing inserts face toward intermediate shaft. All connecting rods must be of same weight class. Weight class numbers are stamped on bottom of connecting rod caps. Using a suitable ring compresser, install piston and rod assemblies with arrow on crown of piston facing forward.

Forged Marks on Bosses Point to Intermediate Shaft

Bosses

***Fig. 2   Location of Connecting Rod Bosses***

### FITTING PISTONS

**1)** Measure cylinder at three points: .39" (10 mm) from top and bottom, and at center of cylinder bore. Take measurements in line with thrust face and at 90° to thrust face.

**2)** Measure pistons at .63" (16 mm) from bottom of piston skirt (measuring at 90° to pin bore). Combining this measurement with measurement of corresponding cylinder bore, if piston-to-cylinder clearance exceeds .003" (.08 mm), oversize pistons must be installed.

**3)** Place piston rings squarely in top of cylinder bore (above ring ridge) and measure end gap; replace as necessary. Measure ring side clearance; replace rings and/or pistons if clearance exceeds .006" (.15 mm). Install rings on piston with end gaps 120° offset to each other and stamped word "TOP" on rings facing upward.

## FOX 4 CYLINDER (Cont.)

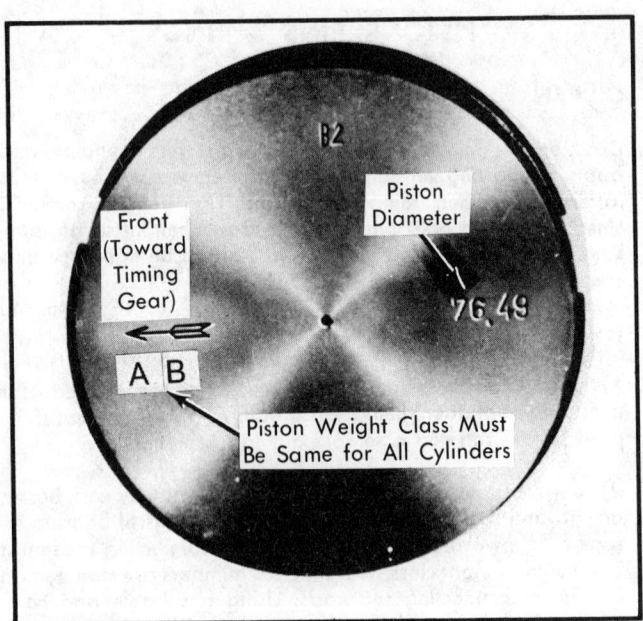

**Fig. 3   Piston Markings**

### PISTON PINS

Use pin-drift to lift circlip from piston groove. Use tool (VW 207c) to remove and install piston pins. If pins are too tight it may be necessary to warm pistons to about 140°F (60°C) for removal and replacement.

## CRANKSHAFT MAIN & CONNECTING ROD BEARINGS

### MAIN & CONNECTING ROD BEARINGS

**1)** Push crankshaft toward one end and measure crankshaft end play at No. 3 (thrust) bearing. Main bearing caps are stamp-numbered "1" to "5" (front to rear) and must return to original positions upon reassembly. Measure end play of connecting rods. Remove rod and main bearing caps and check bearing clearance, using Plastigage method.

**2)** Measure crankshaft journals with a micrometer to determine if crankshaft is out-of-round. Maximum ovality permissible is .0012" (.03 mm). Install main inserts with bearing half having oil groove into block. Lubricate bearings and install caps.

#### Crankshaft Journal Diameters

| Size | Main Bearing Inches (mm) | Connecting Rod Inches (mm) |
|---|---|---|
| Std. | 2.124(53.95) | 1.809(45.95) |
| 1st US | 2.114(53.70) | 1.799(45.70) |
| 2nd US | 2.104(53.45) | 1.789(45.45) |
| 3rd US | 2.094(53.20) | 1.779(45.20) |

### REAR MAIN BEARING OIL SEAL

Rear main bearing oil seal may be replaced with engine in vehicle, if transmission and flywheel are removed. Carefully

pry oil seal from crankcase. Install guide tool (2003/2A) on crankshaft and press seal into position as far as possible by hand. Press seal in until properly seated with installing tool (2003/1).

### INTERMEDIATE SHAFT OIL SEAL

Press seal out of flange. Using suitable tool (Tool No. 10-203), press new seal into flange until it is flush.

### FRONT MAIN BEARING OIL SEAL

**1)** Front main bearing oil seal may be replaced with engine in vehicle. Remove license plate, radiator grille and camshaft belt guard. Rotate crankshaft to TDC. Use a screwdriver to lock crankshaft from turning (through opening in transmission case). Remove pulley bolt. Loosen camshaft belt tensioner and alternator adjuster. Remove both belts.

**2)** Pry seal out of front cover with extractor tool (10-219). Using installation tool (10-203), press new seal into position, first level with cover, and finally to installed depth of 3/32" (2 mm) below cover lip. To install remaining components, reverse removal procedure and check valve timing.

## CAMSHAFT

### TIMING BELT

**1)** Remove radiator grille. Loosen alternator mounting bolts and remove "V" belt. Remove camshaft belt guard. Loosen mounting nut of camshaft belt tensioner arm and remove tension from belt. Slide belt forward off camshaft sprocket.

**2)** Install new belt and adjust tensioner arm until belt can be turned 90° with thumb and index finger at a point midway between camshaft sprocket and intermediate sprocket. Check valve timing.

**Fig. 4   Camshaft Drive Sprocket Timing Mark Alignment**

### CAMSHAFT

Remove bearing caps 5, 1 and 3. Diagonally loosen bearing caps 2 and 4 in steps, remove caps and lift out camshaft. To in-

# Audi Engines

## FOX 4 CYLINDER (Cont.)

stall, lubricate bearing surfaces and reverse removal procedures. Tighten bearing caps 2 and 4 diagonally, then tighten remaining cap nuts.

**CAUTION** — *Bearings must be installed in proper order and off center position. Bearing cap numbers may not always be on same side.*

### VALVE TIMING

Turn camshaft sprocket until punch mark on rear of camshaft sprocket is in alignment with rocker cover gasket on left side of engine. Turn crankshaft pulley and intermediate shaft sprocket until notch on pulley is aligned with punch mark on intermediate shaft sprocket. Slide camshaft belt in place and adjust tension as previously described.

**Fig. 5  Intermediate Shaft Sprocket Aligned with TDC Mark on Crankshaft Pulley**

### ENGINE OILING

**Crankcase Capacity** — 3.2 qts. with filter.

**Oil Filter** — Replaceable spin-on type.

**Normal Oil Pressure** — 28 psi at 2000 RPM with oil temperature 176°F (80°C).

### ENGINE OILING SYSTEM

Oiling system is a pressure feed system. A gear type oil pump lifts oil from oil pan and pressure feeds it to crankshaft journals, camshaft bearings and intermediate shaft. Other parts of system receive oil mist or splash for lubrication.

### OIL PUMP

Remove oil pan and two oil pump mounting bolts. Pull pump straight down and out of engine. Remove two pump cover bolts and separate cover from pump body. Ensure that oil pump gear backlash is .002-.008" (.05-.20 mm). Check that rotor end clearance is not more than .006" (.15 mm). Remove pump drive shaft and gears. Bend up metal edges and remove filter screen. To assemble, reverse disassembly procedure.

### ENGINE COOLING

**Cooling System Capacity**
  Without expansion chamber — 6½ qts.
  With expansion chamber — 7qts.

**Thermostat**

Opens at — 176° F (80° C)

**Radiator Cap** — 14 psi.

**Cooling Fan** — Cut-in 194-203°F (90-95°C). Cut-out 185-194°F (85-90°C).

### WATER PUMP

**1)** Drain coolant and remove alternator. Remove camshaft belt guard, hose clamps and pump hoses. Remove water pump mounting bolts and lift out pump by turning slightly.

**2)** Remove pulley and pump body mounting screws. Separate pump assembly from housing. To reassemble, reverse diassembly procedure using new gasket and pump-to-block seal.

## ENGINE SPECIFICATIONS

### GENERAL SPECIFICATIONS

| Year | Displ. | | Carburetor | HP at RPM | Torque (Ft. Lbs. at RPM) | Compr. Ratio | Bore | | Stroke | |
|------|--------|------|-----------|-----------|--------------------------|--------------|------|------|--------|------|
| | cu. ins. | cc | | | | | in. | mm | in. | mm |
| 1978 | 97 | 1588 | Fuel Inj. | ①78@5500 | ..... | 8.0:1 | 3.13 | 79.5 | 3.15 | 80.0 |

①Calif. — 76 HP.

### VALVES

| Engine & Valve | Head Diam. In. (mm) | Face Angle | Seat Angle | Seat Width In. (mm) | Stem Diameter In. (mm) | Stem Clearance In. (mm) | Valve Lift In. (mm) |
|----------------|---------------------|------------|------------|---------------------|------------------------|-------------------------|---------------------|
| 1588 cc Intake | 1.338 (34) | 45° | 45° | .079 (2.0) | .314 (7.97) | ..... | ..... |
| Exhaust | 1.220 (31) | 45° | 45° | .094 (2.4) | .313 (7.95) | ..... | ..... |

# Audi Engines

## FOX 4 CYLINDER (Cont.)
### ENGINE SPECIFICATIONS (Cont.)

### VALVE SPRINGS

| Engine | Free Length In. (mm) | PRESSURE Lbs. @ In. (kg @ mm) | |
|---|---|---|---|
| | | Valve Closed | Valve Open |
| 1588 cc Inner | ..... | ..... | 46-51@.72 (21-23@18.3) |
| Outer | ..... | ..... | 96-106@.92 (44-48@22.3) |

### PISTONS, PINS, RINGS

| Engine | PISTONS | PINS | | RINGS | | |
|---|---|---|---|---|---|---|
| | Clearance In. (mm)① | Piston Fit In. (mm) | Rod Fit In. (mm)③ | Rings | End Gap In. (mm)④ | Side Clearance In. (mm)⑤ |
| 1588 cc | .0012 (.031) | ② | .0011-.0034 (.028-.088) | Comp. | .012-.017 (.30-.43) | .0008-.002 (.02-.05) |
| | | | | Oil | .010-.016 (.25-.40) | .0008-.002 (.02-.05) |

① — Wear limit .003" (.07 mm). ② — Push fit at 140°F (60°C). ③ — Wear limit .004" (.12 mm).
④ — Wear limit .039" (1.0 mm). ⑤ — Wear limit .006" (.15 mm).

### CRANKSHAFT MAIN & CONNECTING ROD BEARINGS

| Engine | MAIN BEARINGS | | | | CONNECTING ROD BEARINGS | | |
|---|---|---|---|---|---|---|---|
| | Journal Diam. In. (mm) | Clearance In. (mm)① | Thrust Bearing | Crankshaft End Play In. (mm)② | Journal Diam. In. (mm) | Clearance In. (mm)③ | Side Play In. (mm) |
| 1588 cc | 2.124 (53.95) | .001-.003 (.028-.088) | No. 3 | .003-.007 (.07-.17) | 1.809 (45.95) | .001-.003 (.028-.088) | .015 (.40) |

① — Limit .007" (1.7 mm). ② — Limit .015" (.37 mm). ③ — Limit .004" (.12 mm).

### TIGHTENING SPECIFICATIONS

| Application | Ft. Lbs. (mkg) |
|---|---|
| Head Bolts (In Steps) | |
| Cold | 54 (7.5) |
| Warm | 62 (8.5) |
| Main Bearing Caps | 47 (6.5) |
| Connecting Rod Caps | 33 (4.5) |
| Flywheel (Use Loctite) | 54 (7.5) |
| Intermediate Shaft Sprocket | 58 (8.0) |
| Crankshaft Pulley | 58 (8.0) |
| Oil Pan Bolts | 6 (0.8) |
| Exhaust Manifold | 17 (2.3) |
| Intake Manifold | 18 (2.5) |
| Camshaft Bearing Caps | 15 (2.0) |
| Camshaft Sprocket | 58 (8.0) |
| Oil Pressure Switch | 9 (1.3) |

## 5000 5 CYLINDER

### ENGINE CODING

#### ENGINE IDENTIFICATION

Engine number is stamped on left side of block just ahead of distributor. 2.2 liter, 5 cylinder engine is coded WD and includes North American imports except for California. California models are coded with a WE prefix.

### ENGINE & CYLINDER HEAD

#### ENGINE

NOTE — *Leave all fuel injection lines connected unless otherwise specified.*

**Removal — 1)** Disconnect battery ground cable. Remove coolant expansion tank cap, place A/C control in "COLD" position and drain coolant. Disconnect coolant hoses, remove radiator cowl, shroud, electric fan and radiator.

**2)** Remove control pressure regulator, cold start valve, fuel supply line, fuel injectors, and air cleaner cover with filter. Detach air duct and vacuum hoses from throttle valve assembly. Pull hood latch cable guide off of bracket at right front alignment hole.

**3)** Remove and suspend power steering pump, leaving hose connected. On air conditioned models, remove grill and tip condenser outwards. Dismount A/C compressor and tie back with wire, but do not disconnect refrigerant hoses. On all models, remove windshield washer and power steering reservoirs from holders. Remove distributor cap, wires and rotor.

**4)** Take off circlip and remove throttle cable (manual transmission) or throttle push rod (automatic transmission). Disconnect electrical leads from distributor, oil pressure and water temperature senders. Detach exhaust pipe from manifold and from transmission bracket. Remove front engine mount, starter and alternator.

**5)** On automatic transmission models, work through starter hole and remove torque converter mounting bolts. On all models, remove lower engine/transmission bolts and install transmission supporting tool. Remove upper engine/transmission bolts.

**6)** Attach suitable sling to engine and lift engine/transmission enough to remove left and right engine bracket. Lift engine so that front pulley is behind grill opening and support transmission. Detach engine from transmission and lift from car while turning slightly to right.

**Installation —** To install engine, reverse removal procedure noting that metal lip on gasket between exhaust manifold and pipe faces exhaust pipe. Straight adaptor on EGR temperature control valve goes to EGR valve while angled adaptor goes to vacuum amplifier. It is recommended that engine mounting bolts be tightened with the engine running at idle speed.

#### CYLINDER HEAD

**Removal — 1)** Disconnect battery ground strap and drain cooling system. Disconnect coolant hoses from head and exhaust pipe from manifold. Remove electrical and vacuum leads

from distributor. Disconnect accelerator linkage, fuel and vacuum lines and air filter from manifold.

**2)** Remove valve cover and timing belt cover. Rotate crankshaft so that number 1 cylinder is at TDC on firing stroke. Remove drive belt sprocket from camshaft, but do NOT separate from timing belt. Loosen head bolts in reverse order of tightening sequence and lift off head.

**Installation —** Install head gasket with part number facing UP. (Guide pins may be used at opposite corners of head to ease alignment.) Install head using bolts 9 and 11(See *illustration*) to center head, then tighten bolts in sequence illustrated. Complete assembly in reverse order of removal and assure that timing marks are properly positioned.

NOTE — *Early models may be equipped with hexagonal socket bolts which require re-torquing when warm. Polygon socket head bolts are tightened to 55 ft. lbs. (7.5 mkg) with engine cold, and then tightened ¼ more. No further tightening is required.*

**Fig. 1    Tighten Cylinder Head in Sequence Shown (Loosen in Reverse Order)**

### VALVES

#### VALVE ARRANGEMENT

E-I-E-I-I-E-I-E-I-E (front to rear).

#### VALVE GUIDE SERVICING

**1)** With head disassembled, insert new valve and check for wear with dial indicator. See *Fig. 2.* If wear exceeds .039" (1.0 mm) for intake, or .051" (1.3 mm) for exhaust valve, guides should be replaced.

**2)** Press worn guides out of head from combustion chamber side with suitable tool (10-206). Coat new guides with oil and press into cold head from camshaft side. Press guides in as far as they will go, but DO NOT use more than 1 ton pressure once shoulder is seated. Ream guide by hand to proper size.

#### VALVE STEM OIL SEALS

NOTE — *Valve stem seals may be replaced with cylinder head installed on vehicle.*

With camshaft and followers removed, remove spark plug and turn crankshaft until piston of cylinder concerned is at BDC position. Install pressure hose (VW 653/3) in spark plug hole and apply low pressure air to keep valve seated. Remove valve

## 5000 5 CYLINDER (Cont.)

springs with compressor (VW 541/1 or 2036) and lift off seal with pliers (1-218). Place seal protector over valve stem, lubricate seal and push in place with installing tool (10-204).

Fig. 2 Checking Valve Guide for Wear

### VALVE SPRINGS

With camshaft and followers removed, compress spring with suitable tool (US 1020 and 1020/1 or 2037) and remove valve locks (keepers). Lift off valve springs. If required, valve spring seats may be removed using pliers (10-218). To install, reverse removal procedure.

### CAM FOLLOWERS (TAPPETS)

With camshaft removed, lift off followers and adjusting discs. Inspect for wear or damage and replace as necessary.

NOTE — Cam followers and valve system components must be kept in order and installed in original positions. Coat with oil when installing.

### VALVE CLEARANCE ADJUSTMENT

1) Disconnect accelerator linkage and remove valve cover. Turn crankshaft so that both cam lobes of cylinder to be adjusted point upward. Check valve clearances between cam and follower in firing order (1-2-4-5-3). If clearance is greater than .002" (.05 mm) from specifications, select thicker or thinner disc.

2) To replace valve adjusting discs, use follower depressor tool (2078) to press follower down, then remove adjusting disc with tool (10-208 or US4476). Insert appropriate disc and recheck clearance. Discs are available in .0019" (.05 mm) increments from .1181" (3.0 mm) to .1673" (4.25 mm). Thickness is etched on bottom of disc and should be assembled with etched mark toward follower.

#### Valve Clearances

| Application | Hot In. (mm) | Cold In. (mm) |
|---|---|---|
| Intake | .008-.012 (.20-.30) | .006-.010 (.15-.25) |
| Exhaust | .016-.020 (.40-.50) | .014-.018 (.35-.45) |

NOTE — Cold settings are given for reference as initial setting after engine rework. Final adjustments are to be made after engine is warm (at least 95 °F or 35 °C), and checked again after 1000 miles.

## PISTONS, PINS & RINGS

### OIL PAN

Drain engine oil and remove both bolts on front sub frame. Remove pan bolts and take pan from engine. Install new pan gasket and tighten pan bolts in a criss-cross pattern.

### PISTON & ROD ASSEMBLY

Note that rod cap and rod are marked for proper installation and remove cap nuts. Push piston and rod assembly out of cylinder from bottom. When assembling, note that arrow on piston top points toward timing gear. Raised forge marks on connecting rod bosses also must point to front of engine.

### FITTING PISTONS

1) Measure cylinder at 3 points: .39" (10 mm) from top and bottom, and at center of cylinder bore. Take measurements in line with thrust face and at 90° to thrust face.

2) Measure pistons at .63" (16 mm) from bottom of piston skirt (measuring 90° to pin bore). Compare this measurement with corresponding cylinder bore. If clearance exceeds .003" (.08 mm), oversize pistons must be installed.

3) To check ring gap, push ring into bottom of cylinder about .65" (16 mm) and check gap with feeler gauge. Measure ring side clearance in piston with feeler gauge. If clearance is greater than .004" (.1 mm) with new rings, piston replacement is required. Install rings with gaps 120° apart and "TOP" mark toward piston crown.

### PISTON PINS

Use pin-drift to remove circlip from pin boss in piston and press out pin. If pin is too tight, heat piston to approximately 140°F (60°C) and use tool (VW 207c) for both removal and installation. Assemble piston on connecting rod so that arrow on piston top faces forward when assembly is correctly installed.

## CRANKSHAFT MAIN & CONNECTING ROD BEARINGS

### MAIN & CONNECTING ROD BEARINGS

Check crankshaft end play at number 4 main bearing with feeler gauge. Check main bearing clearance using Plastigage method. Bearings are numbered 1 through 6 with 1 at front and 6 at flywheel end, and must be installed in original positions. Install bearing shells with lubrication grooves in block and shells with grooves in bearing caps. Check connecting rod bearing clearance with Plastigage and replace as required.

## 5000 5 CYLINDER (Cont.)

### Crankshaft Journal Diameters

| Size | Main Bearing In. (mm) | Connecting Rod In. (mm) |
|------|-----------------------|-------------------------|
| Std. | 2.260 (57.96) | 1.790 (45.96) |
| 1st US | 2.250 (57.71) | 1.780 (45.71) |
| 2nd US | 2.240 (57.46) | 1.770 (45.46) |
| 3rd US | 2.230 (57.21) | 1.760 (45.21) |

### REAR MAIN BEARING OIL SEAL

With flywheel removed, pry old seal out with tool (2086). Coat lips of new seal with oil and press into position by hand, then use installing tool (2003/1) to press in until properly seated.

### FRONT CRANKSHAFT OIL SEAL

1) Hold crankshaft front pulley with tool (2084) and remove crankshaft bolt. Loosen water pump and take tension off drive belt. Remove "V" belt pulley and drive belt sprocket from crankshaft. Pry out oil seal with tool (2086).

2) Coat lips of new seal with oil and place in position on crankshaft. Use pulley bolt and tool (2080) to press seal in housing until flush. If crankshaft shows signs of scoring, drive seal all the way in until it bottoms. Align pulley and sprocket with Woodruff key and replace componentsin reverse order of removal.

## CAMSHAFT

### TIMING BELT

Remove "V" drive belts and take off drive belt cover. Engine should be in number 1 firing position (TDC). Loosen water pump bolts and turn pump counterclockwise to loosen belt. Install new belt and adjust by turning water pump clockwise to tighten. Belt is properly adjusted when it can just be twisted 90° with thumb and index finger between camshaft and water pump sprockets. Ensure that valve timing is correct.

### CAMSHAFT

Remove bearing caps 2 and 4, then diagonally loosen bearing caps 1 and 3. Remove camshaft from head. When installing, caps must go in original position. Lubricate bearings and journals and install caps with off-center position properly aligned.

**CAUTION** — *Front oil seal must not be installed beyond flush position or oil return will be blocked.*

### VALVE TIMING

Rotate crankshaft until notch on "V" belt pulley aligns with mark on oil pump housing (engine out of vehicle) or TDC "0" mark on flywheel aligns with lug cast on clutch housing (engine installed). Fully loosen belt tension by loosening and turning water pump counterclockwise. Turn camshaft sprocket so that punch mark on rear aligns with rocker cover gasket on left side of engine. Install and adjust belt.

Cover Mounting Stud

Sprocket Marking Aligns with Upper Edge of Gasket

Camshaft Bearing Caps

Camshaft Sprocket

Distributor

Cylinder Head Gasket (Install with Numbers Facing UP)

Timing Belt Cover (Rear)

Timing Belt Cover (Front)

Timing Belt

Water Pump (Adjusts Timing Belt Tension)

*Fig. 3   Cylinder Head and Camshaft Assembly with Timing Belt and Cover*

## 5000 5 CYLINDER (Cont.)

### ENGINE OILING

**Crankcase Capacity** — 5.3 quarts (includes filter change).

**Oil Filter** — Replaceable spin-on type.

**Normal Oil Pressure** — 14 psi at idle, 85 psi at 5500 RPM with oil temperature 176°F (80°C).

### OIL PUMP

Gear type pump is mounted at front of engine, driven by crankshaft with oil suction pipe extending to oil pan. To remove, take off timing belt cover and front "V" belt pulley/drive belt sprocket. Drain engine oil and remove oil pan and oil suction pipe. Unbolt pump and remove from front of engine. Inspect endcover, housing and gears for wear or scoring. Replace pump gears in pairs only, with triangle marking toward endcover (rear). To install, reverse removal procedure.

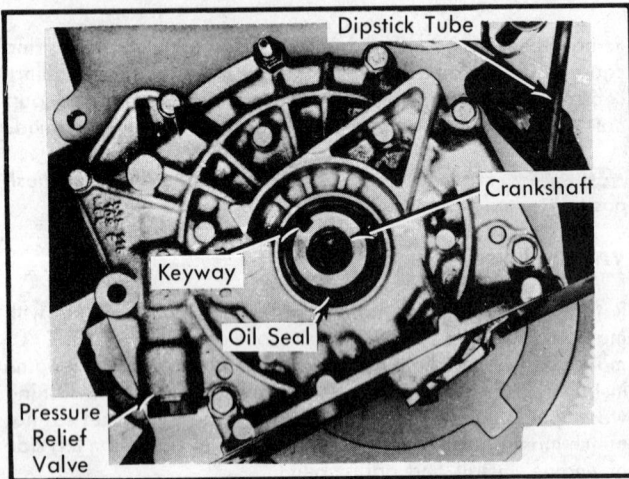

**Fig. 4   Engine Oil Pump with Crankshaft Oil Seal**

### ENGINE COOLING

**Cooling System Capacity** — 8.6 quarts.

**Thermostat** — Opens at 194°F (90°C).

**Expansion Tank Cap** — Relief valve opens at 17-19 psi.

**Radiator** — Cross flow type with electric cooling fan and coolant expansion tank. Fan cuts in at 194-203°F (90-95°C) and cuts off at 185-194°F (85-90°C).

### WATER PUMP

Water pump is driven by timing belt and is mounted at lower left front of engine block. To remove, drain cooling system and remove timing belt cover. Loosen and remove water pump mounting bolts. Remove pump and check for wear. To install, use new "O" ring and reverse removal procedure. Add coolant mixture until tank is full and replace cap. Run engine until cooling fan turns on. Check coolant level and top off if necessary.

### ENGINE SPECIFICATIONS

| | Displ. | | | | | | Bore | | Stroke | |
|---|---|---|---|---|---|---|---|---|---|---|
| Year | cu. ins. | cc | Carburetor | HP at RPM | Torque (Ft. Lbs. at RPM) | Compr. Ratio | in. | mm | in. | mm |
| 1978 | 130.8 | 2144 | Fuel Inj. | 103@5300 | 112.4@4000 | 8.0:1 | 3.13 | 79.5 | 3.40 | 86.4 |

**GENERAL SPECIFICATIONS** (table title)

**VALVES**

| Engine & Valve | Head Diam. In. (mm) | Face Angle | Seat Angle | Seat Width In. (mm) | Stem Diameter In. (mm) | Stem Clearance In. (mm)① | Valve Lift In. (mm) |
|---|---|---|---|---|---|---|---|
| 2144 cc Intake | 1.496 (38.0) | 45° | 45° | .079 (2.0) | .314 (7.97) | .039 (1.0) | ..... |
| Exhaust | 1.220 (31.0) | 45° | 45° | .094 (2.4) | .313 (7.95) | .051 (1.3) | ..... |

① — Maximum allowable clearance.

## 5000 5 CYLINDER (Cont.)

### ENGINE SPECIFICATIONS (Cont.)

#### PISTONS, PINS, RINGS

| Engine | PISTONS Clearance In. (mm) | PINS | | RINGS | | |
|---|---|---|---|---|---|---|
| | | Piston Fit In. (mm) | Rod Fit In. (mm) | Rings | End Gap In. (mm)② | Side Clearance In. (mm)③ |
| 2144 cc | .001-.003 (.025-.080) | ① | ..... | All | .010-.020 (.25-.50) | .0008-.003 (.02-.08) |

① — Push fit at 140°F (160°C).　　② — Wear limit .040" (1.0 mm).　　③ — Wear limit .004" (.1 mm).

#### CRANKSHAFT MAIN & CONNECTING ROD BEARINGS

| Engine | MAIN BEARINGS | | | | CONNECTING ROD BEARINGS | | |
|---|---|---|---|---|---|---|---|
| | Journal Diam. In. (mm) | Clearance In. (mm) | Thrust Bearing | Crankshaft End Play In. (mm) | Journal Diam. In. (mm) | Clearance In. (mm) | Side Play In. (mm) |
| 2144 cc | 2.26 (57.96) | .0006-.006 (.016-.160) | No. 4 | .003-.010 (.07-.25) | 1.790 (45.96) | .0006-.005 (.016-.120) | .016 (.40) |

#### TIGHTENING SPECIFICATIONS

| Application | Ft. Lbs. (mkg) |
|---|---|
| Head Bolts | |
| 　Cold① | 55 (7.5) |
| 　Warm (Hex Socket Head Only) | 61 (8.5) |
| Main Bearing Caps | 47 (6.5) |
| Connecting Rod Caps | 36 (5.0) |
| Flywheel/Drive Plate (Use Loctite) | 54 (7.5) |
| Crankshaft Pulley/Sprocket | 235 (35) |
| Oil Pan Bolts | 7 (1.0) |
| Exhaust Manifold | 18 (2.5) |
| Intake Manifold | 18 (2.5) |
| Camshaft Bearing Caps | 14 (2.0) |
| Camshaft Sprocket | 58 (8.0) |
| Oil Pump Mounting Bolts | 7 (1.0) |
| Timing Belt Cover | 7 (1.0) |
| Cylinder Head Cover | 7 (1.0) |
| Water Pump Mounting Bolts | 14 (2.0) |
| Engine Mount Bolts | 33 (4.5) |

① — Tighten polygon socket head bolts ¼ turn past specified torque and DO NOT retighten.

## 320i 4 CYLINDER

### ENGINE CODING

**ENGINE IDENTIFICATION**

Engine identification number is on engine block at left hand side above starter motor.

### ENGINE & CYLINDER HEAD

**ENGINE**

**NOTE** — *The "A" behind model number is for automatic transmission models.*

**Removal** — **1)** On 320i models, remove all mounting bolts accessible from above. Remove exhaust support and exhaust pipe at manifold. Remove drive shaft at transmission, remove center bearing. Remove drive shaft at center journal. Remove speedometer cable, disconnect back-up light switch.

**2)** Remove center console from transmission, remove circlip and washer, pull out selector rod. Remove clutch slave cylinder, support transmission with jack or stand. Remove crossmember and remaining transmission mounting bolts. Remove transmission towards rear of vehicle.

**3)** On 320i A, remove accelerator cable. Remove all mounting bolts accessible from above. Remove oil filler neck and drain oil. Remove exhaust support and exhaust pipe at manifold. Remove speedometer drive cable. Remove drive shaft at transmission, remove center bearing and remove drive shaft at center journal. Remove selector rod at selector lever.

**4)** Remove drive plate bolts from torque converter. Remove transmission oil cooler lines, support transmission with jack or stand. Remove crossmember at body, remove remaining transmission mounting bolts. Remove transmission and torque converter from vehicle.

**5)** On all models, drain cooling system and disconnect hoses. Remove fan shroud and radiator. Disconnect and remove battery. Remove intake cowl and disconnect wires and fuel lines to injection system. Detach and suspend A/C compressor (if equipped). Do NOT disconnect hoses.

**6)** Disconnect wires, fuel and coolant lines, and control cables between engine and chassis. Install engine sling (tool No. 11 0 000) to eyes at front and rear of engine. Detach left engine mount and upper engine damper. Detach right engine mount and lift engine from vehicle.

**Installation** — To install, reverse removal procedure ensuring that torque converter (if equipped) is properly positioned on drive plate. When filling with coolant, set heater control to "warm" and fill radiator slowly. Bleed system after engine is warm by turning cap to catch 1, then remove cap and fill radiator.

**CYLINDER HEAD**

**Removal** — **1)** Pull off breather tube, then pull hose with connector out of tube. Dismantle air cleaner assembly. Disconnect ground lead from battery. Drain cooling system. Disconnect accelerator cable. Remove cylinder head cover (rocker arm cover).

**2)** Remove wires to injection valves (mark for reassembly). Remove pressure converter hoses, water hoses at cylinder head and crankcase hoses at throttle housing and thermo valve (marking for reassembly). Remove upper timing case cover, disconnect plug connectors and ignition coil wires. Remove distributor cap and pull plugs off cold start valve, auxiliary air valve and timing valve. Disconnect oil pressure switch wire.

**3)** Set piston of No. 1 cylinder at TDC, (rotor points to notch in distributor housing, indicator points to notch in pulley). Remove timing chain tensioner and timing chain sprocket. Remove exhaust pipe at manifold and holder to transmission. Remove cylinder head bolts in reverse sequence of tightening, remove cylinder head.

*Fig. 1    Correct Procedure to Set No. 1 Piston at TDC*

**Installation** — Ensure installation guides extend .197" (5 mm) beyond cylinder head mounting surface. Also be sure there is no oil in blind holes, or head bolts will not be able to exert required holding force on head. Replace cylinder head and components in reverse of removal procedure. Tighten head bolts in 3 steps according to sequence illustrated in *Fig. 2*. See *TIGHTENING SPECIFICATIONS*. Start and run engine until normal temperatures are reached, then allow to cool to about 95°F (35°C) and tighten to final torque.

**NOTE** — *Head bolts should be re-checked for final torque after 600 miles. Always check torque with engine cool.*

*Fig. 2    Tighten Cylinder Head in Sequence Shown
(Remove in Reverse Sequence)*

## 320i 4 CYLINDER (Cont.)

**Fig. 3  Measure Dowel Projection as Shown**

## VALVES

### VALVE ARRANGEMENT

**Right Side** — All exhaust.

**Left Side** — All intake.

### ROCKER ARM ASSEMBLY

**Removal** — 1) With camshaft removed, push back thrust ring and rocker arm so rocker shaft circlip may be removed (See Fig. 4). Remove distributor mounting flange.

2) Drive rocker arms out with drift (11 3 040) from rear (distributor) end. Retain all springs, washers, rocker arms and thrust rings in proper order for assembly.

**NOTE** — *Rocker arm shaft on intake side is open. Exhaust rocker shaft is plugged.*

**Fig. 4  Rocker Shaft Circlip Removal & Installation**

**Installation** — Install all parts in original location. Replace worn rocker arms and shafts, and any rocker arms with loose contact pads. When installing rocker arm shafts, notches must be aligned to allow cylinder head bolts to fit in openings. Install circlip and ensure that plug in exhaust side rocker shaft is tight.

**Fig. 5  View Showing Rear Exhaust Rocker Shaft Plugs**

### VALVE SPRING SERVICE

Compress spring and remove keepers. Remove spring and retainer. Check spring free length and pressure and replace as required. Install springs with tight winding (painted mark) facing cylinder head. Install retainers and keepers.

### VALVE GUIDE SERVICE

1) Check valve guide for wear. If replacement is necessary, press out guide toward combustion chamber. Measure guide bore in cylinder head. If bore exceeds .5512" (14 mm), ream head and install oversize guide.

2) Heat cylinder head to 428-482°F (220-250°C) and press in new guide from top side until tapered groove end protrudes .591" (15 mm) for standard guide, or .531" (13.5 mm) for modified guide. Ream guide to obtain specified clearance. Valve guides are available in the following sizes:

### Valve Guide Sizes

| Application | Guide O.D. In. (mm) |
| --- | --- |
| Standard | .5532 (14.05) |
| 1st Oversize | .5551 (14.10) |
| 2nd Oversize | .5590 (14.20) |
| 3rd Oversize | .5630 (14.30) |
| Standard Length | 2.047 (52.0) |
| Modified Length | 1.988 (50.5) |

### VALVE SEAT SERVICE

Refer to illustration and note minimum valve seat and valve head thicknesses. If either specification is not met, replace necessary component. When replacing valve seat, remove old seat by turning out with suitable cutting tool. Drill out bore to appropriate oversize: note valve seat oversize to be used and rebore head allowing for shrink-fit of replacement seat. When installing new seat, heat head to approximately 392°F (200°C) and chill valve seat to approximately —94°F (—70°C). Replacement seats are available in the following oversizes:

## 320i 4 CYLINDER (Cont.)

### Replacement Valve Seat Rings

| Application | Measurement In. (mm) |
|---|---|
| Intake | |
| 1st Oversize | 1.864 (47.35) |
| 2nd Oversize | 1.872 (47.55) |
| Exhaust | |
| 1st Oversize | 1.589 (40.35) |
| 2nd Oversize | 1.596 (40.55) |

Minimum Thickness After Machining
Intake — .034" (.85 mm)
Exhaust — .076" (1.4 mm)

B =
Intake - .063" (1.6 mm)
Exhaust - .079" (2.0 mm)

A =
Intake - .059" (1.5 mm)
Exhaust - .079" (2.0 mm)

*Fig. 6  Checking Valve Head & Seat Thickness*

### VALVE CLEARANCE ADJUSTMENT

Adjust valves in firing order sequence (1-3-4-2) with No. 1 cylinder at TDC of compression stroke. Using a feeler gauge between rocker eccentric and valve stem, set clearance to .008-.010" (.20-.25 mm) with engine hot or to .006-.008" (.15-.20 mm) with engine cold. Loosen nut of rocker eccentric, insert a rod in eccentric hole and rotate until proper clearance is obtained (*See Fig. 7*).

**NOTE** − *Never measure or adjust valve clearance between camshaft and rocker arm pad.*

Feeler Gauge

Lock Nut

Eccentric

*Fig. 7  Correct Procedure to Perform Tappet Adjustment*

## PISTONS, PINS & RINGS

### OIL PAN

With engine installed, remove bolts securing steering to front axle carrier, move steering out of way. Drain oil, remove bolts securing oil pan, swing pan down. Turn crankshaft and remove oil pan. Coat crankcase ends where timing cover and rear main bearing cover join crankcase with sealing compound before reassembly.

### PISTON & ROD ASSEMBLY

**Removal** − After removing oil pan and cylinder head, rotate crankshaft to TDC of piston and rod assembly to be removed. Unscrew connecting rod cap nuts and push assembly out top of engine. Replace worn or damaged parts as necessary, according to appropriate service procedure indicated in this article.

**Installation** − Place rings on piston with marking "TOP" facing upward and ring end gaps 180° apart. Install piston with arrow facing forward and oil hole in wrist pin end of connecting rod facing timing chain. Ensure connecting rod and bearing cap numbers match, with No. 1 rod nearest the timing chain.

### CONNECTING ROD BUSHING

Wrist pins and pistons are matched to each other and must be replaced together. To remove piston pin from assembly, remove circlip and push out wrist pin. In event of excess clearance, new wrist pin bushing may be pressed in rod. Bushing seam should be at 90° to oil bore. Drill and deburr oil holes, then ream bushing so that pin is a light push fit through connecting rod.

### FITTING PISTONS

Piston crowns are marked with arrow for direction of installation and a "+", "−" or no sign to show weight classification. All pistons should have same weight mark. Measure piston and cylinder diameter to determine clearance (see specifications). Measure piston diameter at 90° to wrist pin bore near bottom of piston skirt, see following table for distance from bottom of piston.

### Piston Measuring Location

| Piston | In. (mm) |
|---|---|
| Mahle | .622 (15.8 mm) |
| KS | .923 (23.45 mm) |

### Piston Sizes

| Application (Grade) | Diameter In. (mm) |
|---|---|
| Standard | 3.5027 (88.97) |
| Intermediate | 3.5059 (89.05) |
| No. 1 Oversize | 3.5126 (89.22) |
| No. 2 Oversize | 3.5224 (89.47) |

## 320i 4 CYLINDER (Cont.)

### CRANKSHAFT MAIN & CONNECTING ROD BEARINGS

#### MAIN BEARING SERVICE

Plastigage method is used to determine connecting rod and main bearing journal clearances. Standard or undersize crankshafts are marked red or blue. Color coded inserts must agree with crankshaft color code (See Figures 8 & 9 ). The following table shows color code and undersizes available:

*Fig. 8   View Showing Original Crankshaft Marks*

#### Main Bearing Journal

| Application | In. (mm) |
|---|---|
| Original | 2.165 (55.0) |
| 1st Stage | 2.156 (54.75) |
| 2nd Stage | 2.146 (54.50) |
| 3rd Stage | 2.136 (54.25) |

*Fig. 9   View Showing Undersize Crankshaft Marks*

#### Connecting Rod Journal

| Application | In. (mm) |
|---|---|
| Original | 1.889 (48.0) |
| 1st Stage | 1.879 (47.75) |
| 2nd Stage | 1.870 (47.50) |
| 3rd Stage | 1.860 (47.25) |

**CAUTION** — *Crankshaft should only be factory ground due to tenifer hardening.*

### THRUST BEARING ALIGNMENT

Attach a dial indicator to crankcase with shaft touching flywheel. Move flywheel in and out to determine endplay of crankshaft. If endplay is excessive, replace center main bearing inserts.

### REAR MAIN BEARING OIL SEAL SERVICE

With flywheel removed, unscrew six attaching bolts from rear crankshaft seal holder. Carefully run a knife blade between seal holder and oil pan gasket to break seal. Remove seal holder and press out old seal, press in new seal. Coat oil pan gasket at either side with sealing compound and replace seal holder.

### FRONT COVER OIL SEAL

Seal may be replaced with engine in car. Remove radiator and fan belt. Lock flywheel with suitable tool (11 2 100), remove front pulley nut and take off pulley. Remove seal and inspect pulley for wear. Pack lips of new radial seal with grease and install with suitable tool (11 1 270). Position Woodruff key correctly and install pulley.

### ENGINE FRONT COVER

**Upper Cover** — Remove cylinder head cover and detach EGR check valve pipe from exhaust manifold. Take out bolts (8) attaching cover to head and block. Remove, clean and inspect cover. To install, use new gasket and apply suitable sealant to mating surfaces. Place cover in position and insert all bolts, tightening lower bolts at block slightly. Tighten bolts evenly to specifications starting at lower head and finishing with bolts fastening cover to block.

**Lower Timing Case Cover** — **1)** Disconnect battery ground cable and remove water pump. Remove upper timing case cover and chain tensioner piston. Remove alternator with bracket and tensioning bar. Remove air pump and bracket with tensioning bar.

**2)** Take off front pulley and remove bolts on timing case cover and front of oil pan. Carefully separate oil pan gasket from timing case cover with knife blade and remove lower cover.

**3)** To install, apply sealant and new gaskets. Ensure that chain tensioner take-up land is in oil pocket and reverse removal procedures.

### CAMSHAFT

#### CAMSHAFT

**Removal** — **1)** With cylinder head removed, loosen clamping screw and pull out distributor. Attach head assembly to a suitable holding tool (No. 11 1 040). Remove oil line and cold start valve.

**2)** Adjust valve clearance to maximum possible. Attach a suitable compression frame to preload the rocker assembly . Check end play between guide plate and camshaft. Remove guide plate and carefully withdraw camshaft.

**Installation** — **1)** When replacing camshaft, note the following: After guide plate has been installed, it must be possible to

## 320i 4 CYLINDER (Cont.)

easily rotate the camshaft. Make sure that notch in flange aligns with cast tab on cylinder head. Adjust valve clearances, note position of oil pipe sealing rings.

2) When replacing distributor, turn rotor counterclockwise by about 1.4" (3.5 mm) from notch in distributor housing, bring distributor drive into mesh with camshaft drive. Ensure vacuum advance has been located in original position. Adjust ignition timing.

Fig. 10 **Lower Timing Case and Cover**

### TIMING CHAIN REPLACEMENT

**Removal & Installation** — 1) Remove distributor cap, set piston of No. 1 cylinder at TDC. Remove upper and lower timing case covers. Remove sprocket. Remove circlip and unscrew pivot pin until guide rail rests on cylinder head gasket. Remove timing chain from sprocket and crankshaft. Remove guide rail by pulling down and swinging to the right.

2) If timing chain sprockets need replacing. Remove oil pan, remove sprocket from oil pump. Remove timing chain. Remove sprocket with suitable puller (No. 11 2 000). To install: Heat sprocket, reverse removal procedure.

### VALVE TIMING

Rotate engine to TDC of No. 1 piston. Position camshaft so that timing mark on camshaft flange is straight up and locating pin hole is straight down. Without moving crankshaft or camshaft, install camshaft sprocket so that it engages locating pin hole in camshaft flange.

### TIMING CHAIN TENSIONER SERVICE

NOTE — *Chain tensioner is correct if chain gives under slight thumb pressure.*

1) Unscrew tensioner plug and remove piston and spring.

CAUTION — *Tensioner plug is under high spring pressure, use care when removing plug.*

2) Press piston out of sleeve. Remove ball bearing and perforated disc. Clean all parts thoroughly.

3) Reassemble sleeve, perforated disc, ball bearing and piston, making sure perforated disc does not block bleed slots (See Fig. 11)

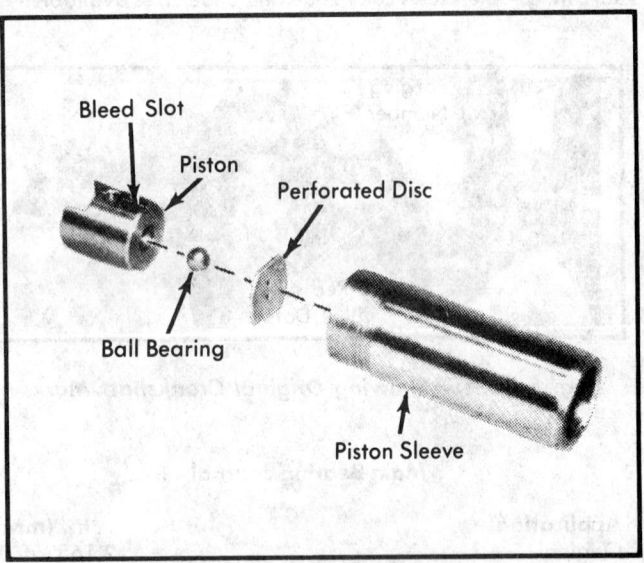

Fig. 11 **Exploded View of Chain Tensioner Piston Assembly**

4) Install piston in tensioner body. Place spring with tapered end facing tensioner plug. Screw tensioner plug slightly into tensioner body. Fill oil pocket with engine oil and move tensioner rail back and forth until oil comes out around plug threads. Tighten tensioner plug.

## ENGINE OILING

### ENGINE OILING SYSTEM

A chain driven rotor type oil pump pressure feeds oil to a full-flow oil filter. From oil filter, oil is circulated through passages to all moving parts of the engine.

**Crankcase Capacity** — 4.25 qts. (4.0 liters) with filter.
**Oil Filter** — Full-Flow
**Oil Pressure** — 57psi@4000RPM
**Pressure Regulator Valve** — Non-adjustable

### OIL PUMP

1) Remove oil pan and oil pump sprocket. Remove bolts attaching pump pick-up. Remove two bolts mounting pump to crankcase and lift out pump.

2) Unscrew union and remove spring and plunger from pump body. Remove pick-up tube and cover from pump body.

3) Measure clearance between outer rotor-to-pump body, rotor-to-rotor and rotor face-to-pump body flange (see specifications).

## 320i 4 CYLINDER (Cont.)

**4)** Using suitable puller, remove drive flange from rotor shaft. Press drive flange on new rotor shaft to a distance of 1.68" (42.7 mm) between flange and rotor face (See Fig. 12).

**5)** To install, reverse removal procedure noting that normal length (colored red) and extra long (colored green) chains are available. Further adjustment is possible by using shims between pump body and block. Oil hole in shims must line up with oil hole in pump. Chain tension is correct if chain gives under slight thumb pressure.

**Fig. 12  Measuring Distance Between Flange and Rotor Face**

### Oil Pump Specifications

| Application | Measurement In. (mm) |
|---|---|
| Rotor-to-Pump Body | .006-.011 (.150-.275) |
| Inner-to-Outer Rotor | .0047-.0079 (.12-.20) |
| Cover-to-Rotor | .0014-.0037 (.035-.095) |
| Pressure Relief Spring | |
| Free Length | 2.677 (68.0) |
| Installed Length | 2.618 (66.5) |

### ENGINE COOLING

**Thermostat** — Opens at 176°F (80°C).
**Cooling System Capacity** — 7.4 qts. (7 liters)

### WATER PUMP

**1)** Loosen alternator bracket. Remove fan and drive belt. Loosen hose clamps and remove water pump.

**2)** Using a suitable puller, remove fan hub from impeller shaft. Extract circlip and spacer ring from front of pump.

**3)** Press impeller off shaft and pump bearing out of housing. Drive friction seal out of housing and lift out cover ring.

**4)** Replace any worn or damaged parts. Using suitable tool, press impeller onto shaft until there is clearance of .031-.047" (.79-1.2 mm) between impeller and pump face.

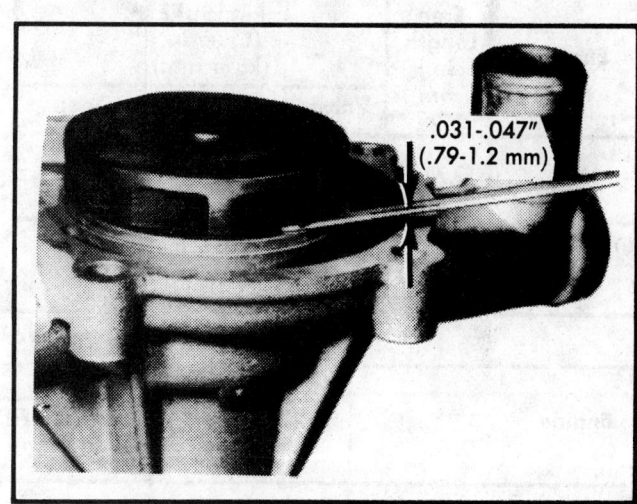

**Fig. 13  Measuring Clearance Between Water Pump Impeller and Pump Face**

**5)** Press fan hub onto shaft until shaft extends .118-.138" (3.0-3.5 mm) beyond hub face. Install pump and fan, assuring that lockplates are crimped fan bolts.

## ENGINE SPECIFICATIONS

### GENERAL SPECIFICATIONS

| Year | Displ. | | Carburetor | HP at RPM | Torque (Ft. Lbs. at RPM) | Compr. Ratio | Bore | | Stroke | |
|---|---|---|---|---|---|---|---|---|---|---|
| | cu. ins. | cc | | | | | in. | mm | in. | mm |
| 1978 | 121.4 | 1990 | Fuel Inj. | ①110@5800 | ②112@3750 | 8.1:1 | 3.504 | 89 | 3.150 | 80 |

① — Calif. 105@5800
② — Calif. 108.5@3750

# BMW Engines

## 320i 4 CYLINDER (Cont.)
### ENGINE SPECIFICATIONS (Cont.)

### VALVES

| Engine & Valve | Head Diam. In. (mm) | Face Angle | Seat Angle | Seat Width In. (mm) | Stem Diameter In. (mm) | Stem Clearance In. (mm) | Valve Lift In. (mm) |
|---|---|---|---|---|---|---|---|
| 320i Intake | 1.805 (45.84) | 45° 30' | 45° | .059-.083 (1.50-2.10) | .3134-.3139 (7.960-7.975) | .0010-.0020 (.025-.055) | ..... |
| Exhaust | 1.490 (37.84) | 45° 30' | 45° | .061-.081 (1.55-2.05) | .3129-.3134 (7.945-7.960) | .0015-.0030 (.040-.070) | ..... |

### VALVE SPRINGS

| Engine | Free Length In. (mm) ① | PRESSURE Lbs. @ In. (kg @ mm) Valve Closed | Valve Open |
|---|---|---|---|
| 320i | 1.712 (43.5) | 64@1.48 (29@37.6) | 154@1.12 (70@28.5) |

### VALVE TIMING

| Engine | INTAKE Open (BTDC) | Close (ALDC) | EXHAUST Open (BLDC) | Close (ATDC) |
|---|---|---|---|---|
| 320i | 18° | 66° | 66° | 18° |

① — May be 1.811" (46.0 mm) for some makes.

### PISTONS, PINS, RINGS

| Engine | PISTONS Clearance In. (mm) | PINS Piston Fit In. (mm) | Rod Fit In. (mm) | Rings | RINGS End Gap In. (mm) | Side Clearance In. (mm) |
|---|---|---|---|---|---|---|
| 320i | .0018 (.045) | ①.0008-.0024 (.002-.006) | .0001-.0004 | No.1 | ①.012-.020 (.30-.50) | .0024-.0036 (.06-.092) |
| | | | | No.2 | .008-.016 (.20-.40) | ②.0016-.0028 (.040-.072) |
| | | | | No.3 | .010-.020 (.25-.50) | ②.0012-.0024 (.030-.062) |

① — Mahle Pistons — .0004-.0020" (.001-.005 mm)
② — Mahle Pistons No. 2 — .0012-.0024" (.030-.062 mm)
   No. 3 .0008-.0020" (.020-.052 mm)

### CRANKSHAFT MAIN & CONNECTING ROD BEARINGS

| Engine | MAIN BEARINGS Journal Diam. In. (mm) | Clearance In. (mm) | Thrust Bearing | Crankshaft End Play In. (mm) | CONNECTING ROD BEARINGS Journal Diam. In. (mm) | Clearance In. (mm) | Side Play In. (mm) |
|---|---|---|---|---|---|---|---|
| 320i Red | 2.165 (55.0) | .0012-.0027 (.030-.070) | Center | .0033-.0068 (.085-.174) | 1.8898 (48.0) | .0012-.0027 (.030-.070) | ..... |
| Blue | 2.165 (55.0) | .0012-.0026 (.030-.068) | Center | | 1.8898 (48.0) | .0012-.0026 (.030-.068) | ..... |

## 320i 4 CYLINDER (Cont.)

### ENGINE SPECIFICATIONS (Cont.)

| CAMSHAFT | | | |
|---|---|---|---|
| Engine | Journal Diam. In. (mm) | Clearance In. (mm) | Lobe Lift In. (mm) |
| 320i No. 1 | 1.3769-1.3795 (34.975-35.041) | .0013-.0029 (.033-.074) | ..... |
| No. 2 | 1.6525-1.6551 (41.975-42.041) | .0013-.0029 (.033-.074) | |
| No. 3 | 1.6919-1.6945 (42.975-43.041) | .0013-.0029 (.033-.074) | |

① — End play is .0008-.005" (.020-.127 mm).

| TIGHTENING SPECIFICATIONS | |
|---|---|
| Application | Ft. Lbs. (mkg) |
| Cylinder Head Studs ① | |
| Step 1 | 25-32 (3.5-4.5) |
| Step 2 | 49-52 (6.8-7.2) |
| Step 3 | 56-59 (7.8-8.2) |
| Main Bearing Caps | 42-46 (5.8-6.3) |
| Connecting Rod Bolts | 38-41 (5.2-5.7) |
| Flywheel-to-Crankshaft ② | 76-83 (10.5-11.5) |
| Rocker Arm Lock Bolts | 7-8 (0.9-1.1) |
| Oil Pan Bolts | 7-8 (0.9-1.1) |
| Camshaft Oiler (Hollow Bolt) | 8-9 (1.1-1.3) |
| Crankshaft Pulley | 101-108 (14-15) |
| Fuel Pump | 7-10 (1.0-1.4) |
| Timing Cover | 7-18 (0.9-2.5) |

① — With engine cool, 95°F (35°C).
② — Coat bolts with Loctite.

## 530i, 633CSi & 733i 6 CYLINDER

### ENGINE CODING

#### ENGINE IDENTIFICATION

Engine serial number is same as chassis serial number. Engine serial number is stamped in crankcase above starter.

### ENGINE, CYLINDER HEAD & MANIFOLDS

#### ENGINE

1) Remove hood and disconnect battery ground cable. Remove radiator and air cleaner with fuel injection air volume control unit. Disconnect distributor vacuum line and wires from ignition coil. Disconnect fuel feed hose at fuel filter, hose at charcoal filter and vacuum hoses from brake booster. Disconnect all remaining fuel and coolant hoses.

2) Remove engine ground cable. Remove distributor cap and secondary wiring. Disconnect plug from fuel injection control unit and pull harness into engine compartment. Remove all remaining electrical connections. Detach A/C compressor (if equipped) and suspend from wire. Do NOT disconnect hoses.

3) Disconnect wires from starter and alternator. Disconnect accelerator linkage. Remove nuts from engine mounts. Remove protective cover from under engine. Remove power steering pump (if equipped). Attach a hoist to lifting holes at front and rear of engine.

4) Remove transmission. See *Manual Transmission Removal and Automatic Transmission Removal.* On Manual Transmission models, push back rubber boot on slave cylinder, remove circlip and pull slave cylinder out toward front. Disconnect exhaust pipes at front and rear manifolds.

5) Remove throw-out bearing lever and bearing from clutch housing. Raise engine and swing out to right to remove. To install, reverse removal procedure. Install drive pulley in correct position and lubricate contact surfaces of throw-out bearing lever with Molykote Longterm 2 paste.

#### MANUAL TRANSMISSION

1) Pull up boot from shift lever, remove circlip and pull shift lever up and out. Remove exhaust pipe support bracket. Disconnect drive shaft at transmission, loosen threaded coupling of drive shaft at rear of center support bearing.

2) Remove center support bearing and pull drive shaft from transmission. Remove speedometer cable and disconnect back-up light switch connection. Disconnect transmission from clutch housing. Support front of engine, remove transmission crossmember and transmission.

3) To install, reverse removal procedure. When installing drive shaft, push center support bearing forward .08" (2 mm) to preload bracket, and tighten nuts.

#### AUTOMATIC TRANSMISSION

1) Disconnect accelerator cable at transmission and take off of counterholder. Drain oil from transmission and remove filler tube. Plug filler tube opening and disconnect oil cooler lines at transmission. Remove web from bottom of driveshaft tunnel. Detach exhaust suspension mounting and disconnect wire harness to transmission.

2) Rotate torque converter and remove four bolts securing converter to drive plate. Disconnect shift rod from lever. Disconnect drive shaft coupling at rear of transmission and loosen threaded coupling at rear of center support bearing.

3) Remove center support bearing and pull drive shaft down and out to remove. Disconnect speedometer cable and back-up light connection. Remove transmission crossmember, allowing engine oil pan to rest on front axle crossmember.

4) Place a jack under transmission and remove ground strap. Separate transmission from engine, making sure torque converter stays in housing in transmission. Remove transmission.

5) To install, reverse removal procedure. When installing, make sure center support of torque converter is below edge of transmission. Push center support forward .08" (2 mm) to preload center bearing and tighten nuts. Adjust accelerator cable lever.

#### INTAKE MANIFOLD

Remove all hoses and lines from manifold. Remove EGR valve and bellows to air volume meter. Remove electrical connector from throttle switch. Detach manifold from supports and bend back supports slightly. Remove intake manifold. To install, reverse removal procedure and replace all gaskets.

#### CYLINDER HEAD

1) Remove air cleaner, spark plug wire tube and valve cover. Disconnect battery ground cable and drain cooling system. Disconnect fuel line at fuel pump and accelerator linkage.

2) Disconnect all fuel and vacuum lines, along with all wiring from injection system and cylinder head. Disconnect accelerator linkage.

3) Remove upper front cover. See *Engine Front Cover & Oil Seal.* Bend back lock tabs and remove camshaft sprocket bolts and sprocket. Remove timing chain tensioner plug, spring and piston. Disconnect water hoses at base of intake manifolds.

4) Disconnect exhaust pipes. Remove cylinder head bolts and install aligning pins to keep rocker arm shafts from moving. Remove cylinder head.

**Fig. 1  Cylinder Head Tightening Sequence**

5) To install, reverse removal procedure. Thoroughly clean mating surfaces and install a new gasket with sealer. Tighten bolts to specifications in sequence shown in illustration.

**NOTE** – *Tighten bolts in 3 stages. See Tightening Specifications.* Never loosen bolts during tightening sequence; turn only in tightening direction.

## 530i, 633CSi & 733i 6 CYLINDER (Cont.)

6) Install camshaft sprocket and timing chain in correct position. *See Timing Chain Replacement.* Install valve cover and tighten nuts to specification.

7) After installation is complete and engine has run for a short time, shut off and allow to cool to approximately 100°F (38°C). Retighten cylinder head bolts to specification in same sequence.

## VALVES

### VALVE ARRANGEMENT

**Left Side** — Intake valves.
**Right Side** — Exhaust valves.

### ROCKER ARM ASSEMBLY

1) Remove camshaft. *See Camshaft Removal.* Push rocker arms and thrust rings against springs and remove circlips from front rocker arm shafts.

2) Remove two countersunk rocker arm shaft locking bolts next to number one bearing bore of camshaft. Install a suitable removing tool (No. 11 3 060) in shaft and pull out of cylinder head. Remove rocker arms, thrust rings, springs and disc.

**Fig. 2   Installed View of Rocker Arm Assembly**

3) Check rocker arms and shaft for excessive play. Normal shaft diameter should be at least .609″ (15.466 mm) and maximum bushing bore in rocker arms should not exceed .611″ (15.518 mm). Check cam follower pads on rocker arms for wear and security. If loose, replace rocker arms.

4) Install spring, disc, rocker arm and thrust ring. Install rocker arm shafts and adjust so that recesses in shafts are aligned with cylinder head bolt holes in cylinder head.

5) To disassemble rear rocker arm assemblies, remove rear cover on cylinder head. Use same procedure for rear shafts as used for front. Install self sealing discs on bolts for rear cover plate and use Cabritol sealer on plate gasket.

### VALVE GUIDE SERVICING

1) With valve removed, check inside diameter of valve guide. If size exceeds specifications, drive guide out through combustion chamber with a suitable driver (No. 11 1 100).

2) Check size of valve guide bore in cylinder head. If size exceeds .5519″ (14.018 mm), an oversize guide must be installed. If guide or bore condition warrant, the following sizes of guides are available for service replacement: .5551″ (14.10 mm), .5591″ (14.20 mm), and .5630″ (14.30 mm).

3) Guides require a .0006-.0019″ (.015-.044 mm) press fit in cylinder head with head heated to 430-480°F (220-250°C). Ream head bores according to guide size being installed.

4) Using suitable driver (No. 11 1 120), drive guide into cylinder head from top until top of guide protrudes .591″ (15.0 mm) for standard guide, or .531″ (13.5 mm) for modified guide. Ream valve guide until correct clearance with valve is obtained.

### VALVE SPRING

With rocker arms and shafts removed, compress valve spring with suitable tool (11 1 060) and remove keepers. Remove valve spring and retainer and check spring free length. Check compressed length and pressure in a suitable tester. Replace defective springs and assemble with paint stripe (tight coil end) against head. Install retainer and keepers.

### VALVE STEM OIL SEALS

To replace valve stem oil seals, use guide or tape over stem grooves to prevent damage to new seals. Lubricate seal and press into position with suitable tool (11 1 130).

### VALVE CLEARANCE ADJUSTMENT

Remove valve cover and turn crankshaft so that No. 1 cylinder is at TDC on firing stroke. Assure that engine temperature is cool (max. 95°F, 35°C) and use feeler gauge to check clearance between valve and adjusting eccentric. Clearance for both intake and exhaust valves should be .010-.012″ (.25-.30 mm). To adjust clearance, loosen nut on rocker arm and rotate eccentric.

**Fig. 3   Valve Clearance Adjustment Procedure**

## 530i, 633CSi & 733i 6 CYLINDER (Cont.)

### PISTONS, PINS & RINGS

#### OIL PAN

Drain engine oil and remove wires from oil level switch (if equipped). Remove power steering pump but do NOT disconnect hoses. Remove alternator and loosen mounting pad bolts enough to allow access to pan bolts. Remove bottom rear bolt of mounting pad and unscrew pan bolts. Turn crankshaft so that No. 6 connecting rod is above crankcase sealing surface and remove pan. On 733i, it may be necessary to detach engine mounts and lift engine slightly to completely remove pan. To install, use new gaskets and apply Atmosit sealer (or equivalent) to all junctions of block, pan and end covers. Continue in reverse order of removal.

#### PISTON & ROD ASSEMBLY

With cylinder head, oil pan and oil pump removed, remove connecting rod cap. Push piston and rod assembly up and out through top of block. To install, ensure that ring gaps are offset 120° to each other. Apply ring compressor and insert bearing halves in rod and cap. Install with arrow on piston top facing timing chain. Assemble cap to rod with numbers matching and tighten cap to specifications.

#### PISTON PIN REPLACEMENT

1) With piston and rod assembly removed, remove circlips from piston pin hole in piston. Drive out piston pin and separate piston from connecting rod. Thoroughly clean and inspect rod and piston.

2) Pistons and pins are installed as a matched set only. Pin class may be coded by white or black marking for standard or blue for oversize pins.

#### Piston Pin Class Designation

| Application | Pin Diameter In. (mm) |
| --- | --- |
| White ...................................... | .8660-.8661 (21.997-22.000) |
| Black ...................................... | .8659-.8661 (21.994-21.997) |
| Blue ........................................ | .8661-.8663 (22.000-22.005) |

**Fig. 4   View Showing Connecting Rod Cap Installation**

3) Classes of pins and pistons must not be interchanged. If piston or pin is replaced, it must be replaced with one of a corresponding class and weight. Weight classification is designated by a "+" or a "-" stamped in top of piston.

4) Check pin-to-piston clearance, if clearance exceeds that specified and pin is not worn, replace piston. Check pin-to-rod clearance, if clearance exceeds that specified, depending on pin class, new bushing must be installed.

5) Press out old bushing and install new one with split in bushing rotated 90° from oil hole in connecting rod. Drill through oil hole in connecting rod. Ream bushing to specified clearance with piston pin.

6) If connecting rod is replaced, replace with rod which is within 4 grams of rod being replaced. Position piston on connecting rod with arrow on piston facing in same direction as oil hole in connecting rod. Lubricate and install piston pin and circlips.

**Fig. 5   Piston & Connecting Rod Assembly & Markings**

#### FITTING PISTONS

1) With piston removed and disassembled from connecting rod, measure diameter of piston. Measure with micrometer positioned 90° from pin hole and at a point measured from bottom of piston skirt. (Distance "A" in illustration.)

**NOTE** – *Distance depends on engine and manufacturer of pistons.*

| Application | Manufacturer | Distance "A" |
| --- | --- | --- |
| 530i, 633CSi .................. | Mahle ............ | .630" (16.0 mm) |
| 530i, 633CSi .................. | KS .................... | .947" (24.05 mm) |
| 733i .............................. | Mahle .......... | 1.024" (26.0 mm) |
| 733i .............................. | KS ............ | 1.340" (34.05 mm) |

## 530i, 633CSi & 733i 6 CYLINDER (Cont.)

**Fig. 6    View Showing Correct Procedure to Measure Piston Diameter**

2) Measure inside diameter of bore in crankcase. If clearance exceeds specification, crankcase must be bored for next oversize piston. Pistons are available in .010" (.25 mm) and .020" (.50 mm) oversize.

3) Check piston ring side clearance and end gap. If new rings are installed, install with word "TOP" stamped in ring toward top of piston.

## CRANKSHAFT MAIN & CONNECTING ROD BEARINGS

### MAIN & CONNECTING ROD BEARING SERVICE

1) With engine removed, remove clutch, flywheel, cylinder head, oil pan and timing chain. See *Timing Chain Replacement*. Remove rear main bearing oil seal mount.

2) Remove pistons and connecting rods. Remove main bearing caps and lift out crankshaft. Thoroughly clean and inspect crankshaft. Blow out oil passages with compressed air.

3) Main bearings journals are manufactured in two standard sizes. Sizes are designated by a colored dot on crankshaft balance weight next to individual journal (see illustration).

4) Check main and connecting rod bearing clearance using Plastigage method. If clearance will not meet specifications when installing new bearings, it will be necessary to exchange crankshaft. Crankshaft is tenifer treated and may only be reground at the factory.

5) Install bearing halves in crankcase and bearing caps. Lubricate crankshaft bearing journals and install crankshaft in crankcase.

**NOTE** — *In the event of a crankshaft of a different colorcode than the crankcase, use one blue and one red bearing shell for each journal. Make sure that all red or all blue shells are installed facing up and the remaining color facing down.*

**Fig. 7    Crankshaft Color Code Markings**

6) Install bearing caps with numbers on caps running from one through six in order from front to rear. Install caps with bearing locks on same side as bearing locks in crankcase.

7) Tighten caps to specifications. Check crankshaft endplay. See *Thrust Bearing Alignment*. To install remaining components, reverse removal procedure.

**NOTE** — *Ground crankshafts are marked with painted stripes (See Fig. 8).*

**Fig. 8    View Showing Crankshaft Undersize Markings**

### Crankshaft Journal Sizes

| Connecting Rod | In. (mm) |
|---|---|
| Standard | 1.888-1.889 (47.97-47.99) |
| 1 paint stripe | 1.852-1.853 (47.72-47.74) |
| 2 paint stripes | 1.851-1.852 (47.48-47.49) |
| 3 paint stripes | 1.850-1.851 (47.22-47.24) |
| **Main Bearings Red Code** | **In. (mm)** |
| Standard | 2.361-2.362 (59.98-59.99) |
| 1 paint stripe | 2.324-2.325 (59.73-59.74) |
| 2 paint stripes | 2.323-2.324 (59.48-59.49) |
| 3 paint stripes | 2.322-2.323 (59.23-59.24) |
| **Main Bearings Blue Code** | **In. (mm)** |
| Standard | 2.361-2.362 (59.98-59.99) |
| 1 paint stripe | 2.324-2.325 (59.72-59.73) |
| 2 paint stripes | 2.323-2.324 (59.47-59.48) |
| 3 paint stripes | 2.322-2.323 (59.22-59.23) |

## 530i, 633CSi & 733i 6 CYLINDER (Cont.)

### THRUST BEARING ALIGNMENT

Check axial play prior to disassembly by attaching dial indicator to block and moving flywheel to front and rear. If play exceeds .007" (.174 mm), check and replace main bearings as required.

### REAR MAIN BEARING OIL SEAL REPLACEMENT

**NOTE** — *To replace rear main bearing oil seal in vehicle, transmission must be removed.*

**1)** Remove clutch and flywheel and drain engine oil. Remove bolts securing oil pan to rear main bearing oil seal mount.

**2)** Pry oil pan down at area around seal mount, taking care not to damage gasket. Remove bolts securing seal mount to crankcase and remove mount.

**Fig. 9   Installing Rear Main Bearing Oil Seal**

**3)** Pry old seal from mount and install new one using driver and adapter (00 5 500 and 11 1 260). Use guide (11 2 213) when replacing mount to prevent damage to seal. Pack seal lips with grease and apply Atmosit (or equivalent) sealer to junction of oil pan and seal mount. Reverse removal procedure to complete installation.

### ENGINE FRONT COVER AND OIL SEAL

**Upper Front Engine Cover — 1)** Remove distributor cap and valve cover. Remove thermostat housing and thermostat. Rotate crankshaft untill number one cylinder is at TDC of compression stroke. Distributor rotor should point at notch in distributor.

**2)** Disconnect vacuum lines to distributor. Loosen pinch bolt on distributor mounting and pull out distributor. Remove guard, EGR line and check valve. Remove upper timing cover bolts and take off cover with distributor drive gear.

**3)** To install, thoroughly clean all mating surfaces, fill bores of timing cover with Dirco (or equivalent) sealer, replace cord seal around distributor drive gear, and replace cover with new gasket and sealer. Turn distributor rotor counterclockwise so that rotor tip is about 1½" (3.5 cm) from notch in distributor housing and guide distributor into position. Note that vacuum advance unit is aligned approximately 90° to valve cover when installed properly.

**4)** Lightly tighten bolts one and two (see illustration), then tighten remaining bolts to specification in sequence shown in illustration. Tighten bolts one and two to specification. To install remaining components, reverse removal procedure.

**Fig. 10   Upper Front Cover Tightening Sequence**

**Lower Front Engine Cover — 1)** Remove upper front engine cover as previously outlined. Remove timing chain tensioner piston, fan clutch and crankshaft pulley. Remove lower front engine cover.

**2)** Replace oil seal. To install cover, reverse removal procedure. Thoroughly clean mating surfaces and use new gasket with sealer. Tighten bolts to specification.

**NOTE** — *Oil seal can be replaced without removing lower front engine cover.*

**Timing Case Cover Oil Seal — 1)** Remove lower flywheel cover and install suitable ring gear lock. Remove fan housing and all drive belts. Unscrew crankshaft nut and remove vibration damper with hub. Pry out radial seal.

**2)** Pack lips of new radial seal with grease. Press seal in with installing tool (11 1 280). Install components in reverse order of removal and remove lock on flywheel.

### CAMSHAFT

**Removal — 1)** With cylinder head removed, unscrew EGR valve nut with tool (11 7 000), detach EGR line and remove coolant hose. Loosen bolts attaching oil distribution line to rocker arm supports and remove line. Loosen all valve adjustments to maximum clearance position.

**2)** Rotate camshaft from TDC position of No. 1 cylinder toward intake approximately .59" (15 mm) and install compression tool (11 1 060). Tighten exhaust side nuts on tool to stop, then intake side nuts. Remove camshaft retaining bolts and pull out camshaft

## 530i, 633CSi & 733i 6 CYLINDER (Cont.)

**Installation** – 1) Install camshaft in head and tighten thrust plate bolts. Cam must turn easily without excess end play. Turn camshaft to No. 6 overlap position (See Fig. 11) and remove compression tool.

**2)** Install oil line so that oil bores will give off spray between rocker arms and cams of intake and exhaust valves. Ensure that seals are used between line and rocker supports as well as under head of attaching bolts. Continue assembly in reverse order of removal.

*Fig. 11   Position Camshaft as Shown Prior to Removing Compression Frame*

### CAMSHAFT ENDPLAY

Check camshaft endplay with a feeler gauge. If endplay exceeds .001-.007" (.03-.18 mm), replace camshaft thrust plate.

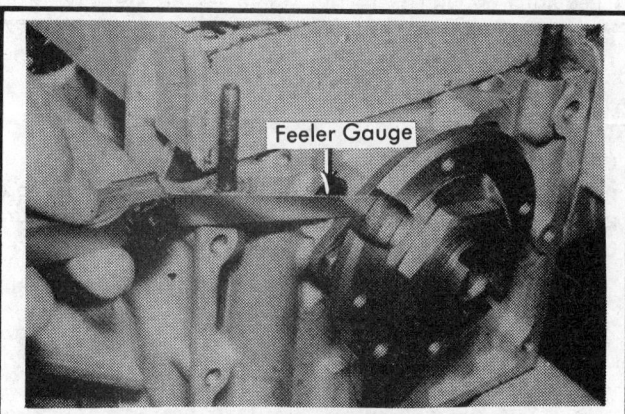

*Fig. 12   Using Feeler Gauge to Check Camshaft Endplay*

### TIMING CHAIN REPLACEMENT

**1)** Rotate crankshaft until number one cylinder is at TDC of compression stroke. Rotor should point to notch in distributor. Remove front engine covers as previously outlined. Mark front side of timing chain for installation.

**2)** Bend over lock tabs and remove camshaft sprocket with timing chain. If mileage of vehicle exceeds 30,000 miles, replace timing chain. Replace sprockets if worn or damaged.

**3)** To replace crankshaft sprocket, remove oil pan, oil pump chain and sprocket, and crankshaft Woodruff key. Pull off sprocket with puller (11 2 000). To install, reverse removal procedure and adjust oil pump chain tension.

**4)** To install timing chain, reverse removal procedure, making sure number one cylinder is at TDC of compression stroke. Line up tapped hole in sprocket hub with cast protrusion in cylinder head and install timing chain and sprocket.

*Fig. 13   Correct Alignment for Timing Chain Installation*

### TIMING CHAIN TENSIONER

**1)** Remove tensioner plug, spring and piston. Check length of spring and piston assembly. Length of spring should be 6.122" (155.5 mm). Piston assembly length should be 2.441" (62.0 mm)

**2)** Check piston with compressed air to see if air vent slots (see illustration) are plugged. Clean slots if air does not pass through. When assembling piston, do not block air vents with disc.

*Fig. 14   Exploded View of Timing Chain Tensioner Piston*

**3)** Install piston, spring with conical end toward plug and slightly tighten plug. Fill oil well full of oil and remove valve cover to vent air from piston. Move tensioning rail back and forth untill oil comes out at plug. Tighten plug and reverse removal procedure to install remaining components.

## ENGINE OILING

### ENGINE OILING SYSTEM

Full pressure oil system, utilizing a chain driven Eaton rotor type oil pump, a full flow oil filter and a pressure regulator valve.

**Crankcase Capacity** – 6 qts.

**Oil Filter** – Full-flow, paper element type.

**Normal Oil Pressure** – 7-28 psi (.5-2.0 kg/cm²) at idle and 71 psi (5.0 kg/cm²) at max. RPM.

**Pressure Regulator Valve** – Mounted in oil pump. See *Oil Pump Removal.*

## 530i, 633CSi & 733i 6 CYLINDER (Cont.)

### OIL PUMP

1) Remove oil pan, front engine covers and timing chain as previously outlined. Remove oil pump drive sprocket and chain. Remove oil pump.

2) Remove pressure regulator plug, spring and piston. Remove pump cover and thoroughly clean and inspect all components. Check clearance between inner and outer rotors. If clearance exceeds maximum specified, replace rotors.

3) Check clearance between outer rotor and pump body and clearance between rotor sealing face and mating surface of pump body and pump cover. If either clearance exceeds maximum specified, replace pump body.

**Fig. 15   View of Oil Pump Assembly**

4) To remove sprocket flange, pull with suitable tool. Install flange so that distance between sprocket side of flange and sealing side of inner rotor is 1.744±.004" (44.30±.10 mm).

5) Check free length of regulator spring, if less than specified, replace spring. To assemble pump, reverse removal procedure. Attach oil pump to crankcase and install sprocket and chain. Chain should slightly depress when pushed in with thumb.

6) If chain depresses more than recommended, remove pump and install shims between pump and crankcase mounting points. Make sure oil holes line up on front shim. Rear shim must be same thickness as front. To install remaining components, reverse removal procedure.

**Fig. 16   Checking Inner to Outer Rotor Clearance with Feeler Gauge**

| Oil Pump Specifications | |
| --- | --- |
| **Application** | **Measurement In. (mm)** |
| Rotor-to-Rotor Clearance ................. | .005-.008 (.12-.20 ) |
| Rotor-to-Housing Clearance | |
|    Radial ......................................... | .006-.011 (.150-.275) |
|    Axial ......................................... | .0014-.0037 (.035-.095) |
| Regulator Spring Free Length .................... | 2.677 (67.99) |

## ENGINE COOLING

### WATER PUMP

Remove clutch fan, pulley, side bar and connecting hose. Remove water pump. To install, reverse removal procedure. Use new gaskets and sealer.

**Thermostat** — Opens at 176°F (80°C).

**Cooling System Capacity** — 12.7 qts.

## ENGINE SPECIFICATIONS

| GENERAL SPECIFICATIONS | | | | | | | | | | |
| --- | --- | --- | --- | --- | --- | --- | --- | --- | --- | --- |
| **Year** | **Displ.** | | **Carburetor** | **HP at RPM** | **Torque (Ft. Lbs. at RPM)** | **Compr. Ratio** | **Bore** | | **Stroke** | |
| | **cu. ins.** | **cc** | | | | | **in.** | **mm** | **in.** | **mm** |
| 1978 530i | 182 | 2986 | Fuel Inj. | 175@5500 | 188@4500 | 8.1:1 | 3.504 | 89 | 3.150 | 80 |
| 633CSi & 733i | 196 | 3210 | Fuel Inj. | 177@5500 | 195@4000 | 8.4:1 | 3.504 | 89 | 3.386 | 86 |

## 530i, 633CSi & 733i 6 CYLINDER (Cont.)
### ENGINE SPECIFICATIONS (Cont.)

| VALVES | | | | | | | |
|---|---|---|---|---|---|---|---|
| Engine & Valve | Head Diam. In. (mm) | Face Angle | Seat Angle | Seat Width In. (mm) | Stem Diameter In. (mm) | Stem Clearance In. (mm) | Valve Lift In. (mm) |
| 2986 cc & 3210 cc | | | | | | | |
| Intake | 1.811 (46.0) | 45°30' | 45° | .063-.079 (1.6-2.0) | .3134-.3140 (7.960-7.975) | .0010-.0022 (.025-.055) | ..... |
| Exhaust | 1.496 (38.0) | 45°30' | 45° | .079-.095 (2.0-2.4) | .3128-.3134 (7.945-7.960) | .0016-.0027 (.040-.070) | ..... |

| VALVE SPRINGS | | | |
|---|---|---|---|
| Engine | Free Length In. (mm) | PRESSURE Lbs. @ In. (kg @ mm) | |
| | | Valve Closed | Valve Open |
| 2986 cc & 3210 cc | ① 1.712 (43.5) | 64±2.5@1.480 (29.0±1.2@37.6) | 154±6@1.122 (70.0±2.8@28.5) |

① — Some springs are 1.811" (46.0 mm), depending on manufacturer.

| PISTONS, PINS, RINGS | | | | | | |
|---|---|---|---|---|---|---|
| | PISTONS | PINS | | RINGS | | |
| Engine | Clearance In. (mm) | Piston Fit In. (mm) | Rod Fit In. (mm) | Rings | End Gap In. (mm) | Side Clearance In. (mm) |
| 2986 cc & 3210 cc | .0016-.0018 (.040-.045) | .0000-.0002 (.001-.005) | ① .0002-.0005 (.005-.013) ② .0003-.0006 (.008-.016) | No. 1 No. 2 Oil | .012-.020 (.30-.50) .008-.016 (.20-.40) .010-.016 (.25-.40) | ③ .002-.004 (.06-.09) ③ .001-.002 (.03-.06) ③ .0008-.002 (.02-.05) |

① — White color code.　② — Black color code.　③ — Mahle specifications shown; For KS, No. 1 .002-.004" (.06-.09 mm), No. 2 .002-.003" (.04-.07 mm), Oil .001-.002 (.03-.06 mm).

| CRANKSHAFT MAIN & CONNECTING ROD BEARINGS | | | | | | |
|---|---|---|---|---|---|---|
| | MAIN BEARINGS | | | | CONNECTING ROD BEARINGS | |
| Engine | Journal Diam. In. (mm) | Clearance In. (mm) | Thrust Bearing | Crankshaft End Play In. (mm) | Journal Diam. In. (mm) | Clearance In. (mm) | Side Play In. (mm) |
| 2986 cc & 3210 cc Red Code | 2.3614-2.3618 (59.98-59.99) | .0012-.0028 (.030-.070) | No. 4 | .0033-.0069 (.085-.174) | 1.8888-1.8894 (47.975-47.991) | .0009-.0027 (.023-.069) | ..... |
| Blue Code | 2.3610-2.3614 (59.97-59.98) | .0012-.0027 (.030-.068) | | | | | |

# BMW Engines

## 530i, 633CSi & 733i 6 CYLINDER (Cont.)

### ENGINE SPECIFICATIONS (Cont.)

| CAMSHAFT | | | |
|---|---|---|---|
| Engine | Journal Diam. In. (mm) | Clearance In. (mm) | Lobe Lift In. (mm) |
| 2986 cc & 3210 cc No. 1 | 1.3764-1.3770 (34.96-34.98) | .0013-.003 (.034-.075) | .2802 (7.12) |
| No. 2 | 1.7304-1.7310 (43.95-43.97) | | |
| No. 3 | 1.7704-1.7710 (44.97-44.98) | | |
| No. 4 | 1.8094-1.8100 (45.96-45.97) | | |

| VALVE TIMING | | | | |
|---|---|---|---|---|
| | INTAKE | | EXHAUST | |
| Engine | Open (BTDC) | Close (ALDC) | Open (BLDC) | Close (ATDC) |
| 2986 cc & ① | 14° | 54° | 54° | 14° |
| 3210 cc ② | 26° | 66° | 66° | 26° |

① — With .020″ (51 mm) clearance between heel of camshaft and rocker pad.

② — With .014″ (.37 mm) clearance between heel of camshaft and rocker pad.

| TIGHTENING SPECIFICATIONS | |
|---|---|
| Application | Ft. Lbs. (mkg) |
| Cylinder Head Bolts① | |
|   1st Stage | 26-32 (3.5-4.5) |
|   2nd Stage | 49-52 (6.8-7.2) |
|   3rd Stage | 56-59 (7.8-8.2) |
| Main Bearing Bolts | 42-45 (5.8-6.3) |
| Rod Cap Nuts | 38-41 (5.3-5.7) |
| Camshaft Thrust Plate | 101-108 (14.0-15.0) |
| Upper Front Engine Cover | 7-8 (0.9-1.1) |
| Lower Front Engine Cover | 7-8 (0.9-1.1) |
| Oil Pan Bolts | 7-8 (0.9-1.1) |
| Timing Chain Tensioner Plug | 22-29 (3.0-4.0) |
| Rocker Arm Clamp Bolt | 6.5-8.0 (0.8-1.1) |
| Flywheel Bolts ② | 72-84 (10.0-11.6) |
| Crankshaft Pulley Nut | 318-333 (44.0-46.0) |
| Oil Pump Regulator Plug | 26-30 (3.6-4.1) |
| Camshaft Oil Line Hollow Bolt | 8-9 (1.1-1.3) |

① — With engine cool — Max. 95°F (33°C).

② — Coat threads with Loctite

## 2300 cc 4 CYLINDER

### ENGINE CODING

#### ENGINE IDENTIFICATION

Vehicle identification plate is riveted to top right fender apron (Capri) or is located on body at right rear corner of engine compartment (Courier). Code is located in block labeled engine or engine model. Use table to identify code.

#### Engine Codes

| Application | Code |
|---|---|
| Capri 2300 cc | YA |
| Courier 2300 cc | WB |

### ENGINE, CYLINDER HEAD & MANIFOLDS

#### ENGINE

**Capri — 1)** Disconnect battery cables. Disconnect all hoses and connections to air cleaner assembly while noting positions to aid in reassembly, then remove air cleaner assembly. Mark hood hinge locations, then remove hood. Raise vehicle on a hoist and remove engine shield. Drain cooling system and crankcase.

**2)** Remove starter. Remove converter bolt access plug and three converter-to-flywheel bolts. Remove flywheel or converter housing cover and lower housing attaching bolts. Disconnect exhaust pipe from exhaust manifold. Disconnect transmission cooler lines from radiator on models with automatic transmission.

**3)** Remove engine mount nuts. Disconnect and plug fuel lines at fuel pump. Remove power steering pump pulley and lower power steering-to-bracket bolt. Lower vehicle. Remove fan shroud, radiator hoses, and radiator. Disconnect heater and vacuum hoses at engine. Disconnect power brake hose and oil pressure line.

**4)** Disconnect kickdown cable. Disconnect accelerator cable retaining clip at ball stud, then pull lightly on cable while depressing tangs one at a time on bracket clip and remove throttle cable. Disconnect idle solenoid. Disconnect water temperature wire, vacuum amplifier, alternator wires, and ground wire.

**5)** Disconnect vacuum hose and coil wire from distributor. Remove alternator adjusting arm bolt, power steering pump-to-bracket bolts and remove pump. Disconnect choke wire. Support transmission and housing with a floor jack, then remove housing-to-engine attaching bolts. Attach lifting hoist to engine, and carefully lift engine from vehicle.

**Courier — 1)** Remove hood, marking location of hinges. Disconnect battery, drain cooling system. Remove air cleaner and heat stove assembly. Disconnect radiator hoses at radiator. Remove radiator and shroud. Disconnect thermactor hoses at pump. Disconnect heater hoses, choke cable and accelerator linkage. Disconnect brake vacuum booster hose and vacuum amplifier.

**2)** Remove alternator and bracket, and move out of the way. Disconnect fuel line at carburetor. Raise vehicle and drain crankcase. Disconnect exhaust pipe from manifold and remove exhaust pipe hanger. Remove right engine mount bracket. Remove lower transmission-to-engine attaching bolts. Lower vehicle, support transmission with a jack and remove remaining transmission-to-engine attaching bolts.

**3)** Install a suitable engine lifting sling, to engine lifting hooks. Remove clutch slave cylinder from transmission. Pull engine forward until it clears transmission shaft. Lift engine from vehicle.

#### INTAKE MANIFOLD

**Removal & Installation —** Remove air cleaner and disconnect fuel line from carburetor. Disconnect distributor and crankcase ventilation hoses at intake manifold. Disconnect carburetor linkage from carburetor. Remove nuts and bolts, then remove intake manifold and carburetor as an assembly from engine. To install, reverse removal procedure while noting the following: Use a new gasket upon installation. Tighten manifold nuts and bolts, in two steps, using sequence as shown in illustration.

*Fig. 1   Intake Manifold Tightening Sequence*

#### EXHAUST MANIFOLD

**Removal & Installation —** Remove air cleaner and two attaching nuts from top of exhaust manifold shroud. Remove attaching nuts from muffler inlet pipe and manifold, then remove exhaust manifold. To install, apply a light film of graphite grease on exhaust manifold and install manifold. Tighten nuts to specification in sequence shown in illustration.

*Fig. 2   Exhaust Manifold Tightening Sequence*

#### CYLINDER HEAD

**Removal —** Drain cooling system, remove air cleaner and rocker arm cover. Remove exhaust manifold. Remove intake manifold and carburetor as an assembly. Disconnect spark plug wires from plugs. Remove all drive belts, fan, and pulley. Remove crankshaft pulley attaching bolt and crankshaft pulley. Remove camshaft drive belt cover, loosen drive belt

## 2300 cc 4 CYLINDER (Cont.)

tensioner and remove belt. Remove water outlet elbow from cylinder head. Remove timing belt inner cover-to-cylinder head attaching bolt. Remove cylinder head bolts, then remove cylinder head and camshaft as an assembly.

**Installation** — Clean gasket material from cylinder head and block. Install new gasket on block. Place cylinder head assembly on block and install head bolts. Tighten bolts, in two steps, using sequence shown in illustration. Reverse removal procedure for remaining components and adjust timing belt tension.

*Fig. 3   Cylinder Head Tightening Sequence*

## VALVES

### VALVE ARRANGEMENT

E-I-E-I-E-I-E-I (front to rear).

### VALVE GUIDES

If valve guides become worn they may be reamed to install a new valve with oversize stem. When going from a standard size stem to oversize, always use reamers in sequence to obtain final desired bore. The valve seat must be refaced after a guide has been reamed, and a suitable tool used to break sharp corner (ID) of guide.

### VALVE STEM OIL SEALS

With valve in head, place plastic installation cap over end of valve stem. Start stem seal carefully over cap and push seal down until jacket touches top of valve guide. Remove plastic cap and bottom seal on valve guide.

### VALVE SPRINGS

**Removal** — Remove valve rocker arm cover. Remove both rocker arms (cam followers) from cylinder being serviced. Remove spark plug from cylinder and install air line and adapter to cylinder with a minimum of 140 psi line pressure.

**NOTE** — *If air pressure does not hold valve shut, remove cylinder head for inspection. Use a suitable tool to compress valve spring, then remove retainer locks. Remove tool, spring retainer, spring, and valve stem seal.* **CAUTION** — *DO NOT remove air pressure.*

**Installation** — Install NEW valve stem oil seal, valve spring and retainer. Compress spring and install retainer locks. **CAUTION** — *Do not compress spring more than necessary to install locks. Remove compressor tool, turn off air and remove adapter. Apply Lubriplate to all contact surfaces of rocker arms and install in position.* **CAUTION** — *Make sure that the*

affected lash adjuster has been collapsed and released before rotating camshaft.

### VALVE SPRING INSTALLED HEIGHT

Measure assembled height of valve spring from surface of the spring pad to underside of spring retainer. If height is not within specifications, install .030" (.76 mm) spacer(s) between spring and pad to obtain recommended height. DO NOT install spacers unless necessary, as excess use of spacers will result in overstressing valve springs and overloading camshaft lobe.

#### Spring Height Specifications

| Engine | Installed Height |
|---|---|
| 2300 cc | 1.531-1.594 |

### HYDRAULIC LASH ADJUSTER ASSEMBLY

Two types of hydraulic lash adjusters are used in 2300 cc engines. Clean and inspect all parts of assembly. Replace the entire assembly if plunger is not free in body. Assemble lifter assembly and check for freeness of operation by pressing down on the cap. Lifters may also be checked with a hydraulic tester to check leakdown rate.

### HYDRAULIC LASH ADJUSTMENT

Position camshaft so high point of cam lobe is facing away from valve to be checked (valve closed). Remove coil spring holding cam follower arm to lash adjuster. Use special tool (T74P-6565-B) to slowly apply pressure to cam follower until lash adjuster is completely collapsed. Hold in this position and check clearance between follower and cam. If not within specifications, inspect cam follower, valve spring installed height, and cam.

#### Hydraulic Lash Adjustment

| Application | ①Clearance |
|---|---|
| Base of Lobe-to-Rocker Arm | |
| Desired | .040-.050" (1.0-1.3 mm) |
| Allowable | .035-.055" (.9-1.4 mm) |

① — Leak down rate is 2-8 seconds.

## PISTONS, PINS & RINGS

### OIL PAN

**Removal** — Remove dipstick and flywheel housing cover, then drain crankcase. Disconnect steering coupling from rack and pinion and unbolt rack and pinion from crossmember; move assembly forward for clearance. Withdraw oil pan mounting bolts and maneuver pan from vehicle.

*Fig. 4   Oil Pan Tightening Sequence*

## 2300 cc 4 CYLINDER (Cont.)

**Installation** – To install oil pan, reverse removal procedure refering to tightening sequence illustration.

## PISTON & ROD ASSEMBLY

**Removal** – Remove cylinder head, oil pan, and oil pump. Remove ridge at top of cylinder bores using a ridge reamer before removing pistons from block. **NOTE** – *Keep tops of pistons covered during this procedure.* Rotate crankshaft and inspect connecting rods and rod caps for cylinder identification. Identify them if necessary. Remove rod cap and push each piston and rod assembly out top of cylinder bore. **NOTE** – *Be careful not to nick crankshaft journals.* Install rod caps on mating rods.

**Installation** – Oil piston rings and cylinder walls with light engine oil. Install ring compressor on piston, then insert rod and piston assembly into cylinder bore and guide rod over crankshaft journal. **NOTE** – *Notch on piston head should point towards front of engine.* Tap piston into cylinder bore using a wooden handle, install rod cap and tighten nuts in two steps. Repeat procedure for each piston assembly.

**Fig. 5  Piston & Rod Assembly Installation Features**

## FITTING PISTONS

1) Check piston to cylinder bore clearance by measuring the piston and cylinder bore diameters. Measure outer diameter of piston at centerline of piston pin bore and at 90° to pin bore axis. Measure the diameter of each cylinder bore at the top, middle and bottom, with the gauge placed at right angles and parallel to the centerline of the engine.

2) Standard size pistons are color coded; red, blue or have .003" OS stamped on the dome. Select the piston to assure the proper clearance. When the bore diameter is in the lower one third of specified range, a red piston should be used. When the bore diameter is in the middle one third a blue piston should be used. When the bore diameter is in the upper one third, the .003" OS piston should be used.

3) If no piston can be fitted, refinish the cylinder to provide proper clearance. When a piston has been fitted, mark it for assembly in the cylinder to which it has been fitted.

| Piston Code | Diameter In. (mm) |
|---|---|
| Red | 3.7780-3.7786 (95.961-95.976) |
| Blue | 3.7792-3.7798 (95.991-96.006) |
| .003" O.S. | 3.7804-3.7810 (96.022-96.037) |

**Cylinder Bore Range** . 3.7795-3.7831" (95.999-96.090mm)
**Piston-to-Bore Clearance** .. .0014-.0022" (.0355-.0558mm)

## PISTON PINS

**Removal** – Remove bearing inserts from connecting rod and cap. Mark pistons and pins to assure assembly with same rod. Press piston pin from piston and connecting rod.

**Installation** – Apply light coat of engine oil to all parts. Assemble piston to connecting rod with oil squirt hole (in connecting rod) and notch (on piston head) positioned as shown in illustration. Start piston pin in piston and connecting rod, then press pin through piston and connecting rod until pin is centered in piston.

## CRANKSHAFT MAIN & CONNECTING ROD BEARINGS

### MAIN & CONNECTING ROD BEARINGS

**NOTE** – *Following procedures are with oil pan and oil pump removed.*

**Connecting Rod Bearings** – After ensuring rod caps are marked for cylinder identification, remove rod caps. Use Plastigage method to check for proper bearing clearance. If not within specifications, new bearings must be installed. New bearings are available in .001" (.025 mm) and .002" (.051 mm) undersizes. Selective fitting is required on each connecting rod. A standard bearing may be used in combination with either undersize bearing. **NOTE** – *Always replace bearings in pairs. Never use a new bearing in combination with a used bearing.* Coat bearing surfaces with oil, install rod cap and tighten nuts.

**Main Bearings** – 1) Position jack under counterweight adjoining bearing being checked so weight of crankshaft will not compress Plastigage and provide an erroneous reading. With all bearing caps (other than one being checked) tight, check clearances using Plastigage method.

2) If clearances are excessive, a .001" (.025 mm) or .002" (.051 mm) undersize bearing may be used in combination with a standard bearing. If .002" (.051 mm) undersize bearings are used on more than one journal, they must be positioned in cylinder block rather than bearing cap. **NOTE** – *Always replace bearings in pairs. Never use a new bearing in combination with a used bearing.* If standard and .002" (.051 mm) undersize combination do not bring bearing clearance within specified limits, crankshaft will have to be refinished and undersized bearings installed.

3) Remove all upper main bearings by inserting suitable tool in oil hole of crankshaft journal and rotating crankshaft clockwise to roll bearing from engine. Oil new upper bearing and insert plain (unnotched) end between crankshaft and indented (or notched) side of block. Rotate bearing into place. Install all main bearing caps with arrows pointing to front of engine.

### REAR MAIN BEARING OIL SEAL

**Removal & Installation** – 1) Split lip type seal is provided for service replacement. Remove oil pan and oil pump. Loosen

## 2300 cc 4 CYLINDER (Cont.)

all main bearing cap bolts, allowing crankshaft to drop (not more than ⅟₃₂") and remove rear main bearing cap. Remove oil seal from cap and clean oil seal groove. Remove upper seal half from block using seal removal tool or small metal screw in end of seal. CAUTION — *Extreme care should be taken not to scratch or mar crankshaft seal surface.*

2) Dip new split lip type seal halves in clean engine oil. Carefully install upper seal into its groove with undercut side of seal toward front of engine, by rotating it on seal journal of crankshaft until approximately ⅜" protrudes below parting surface. CAUTION — *Be sure no rubber has been shaved from outside diameter of seal.* Tighten remaining bearing caps. Install lower seal in rear main bearing cap with undercut side of seal toward front of engine.

3) Allow seal to protrude approximately ⅜" above parting surface to mate with upper seal. NOTE — *Locating tab must face rear of engine.* Apply suitable sealer to rear main bearing cap mating surfaces, taking care not to permit sealer on seal, install main bearing cap and tighten bolts.

### FRONT CRANKSHAFT OIL SEAL REPLACEMENT

**Removal & Installation** — Remove alternator drive belt and crankshaft pulley. Remove camshaft drive belt. *See Camshaft Drive Belt Replacement.* Slide camshaft drive belt sprocket and belt off crankshaft. NOTE — *It may be necessary to utilize a puller to withdraw sprocket.* Fit a suitable tool (T71P-6150-A) over end of crankshaft and remove seal. To install new seal, reverse removal procedure.

NOTE — *Cylinder front cover and auxiliary shaft seals are replaced using procedure outlined above.*

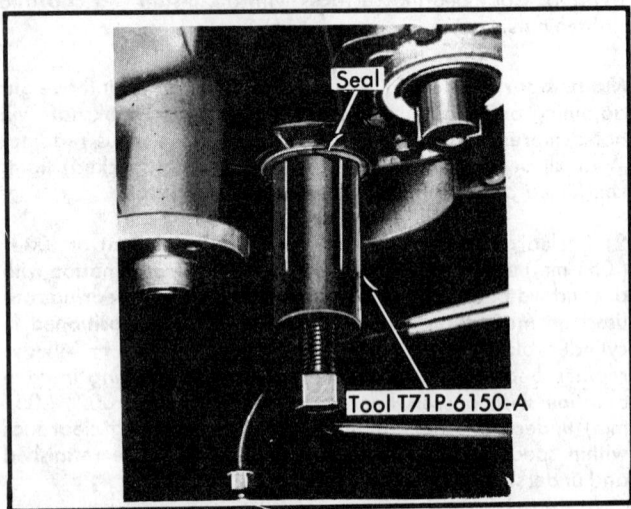

**Fig. 6   Removing Front Crankshaft Oil Seal**

## CAMSHAFT

### CAMSHAFT DRIVE BELT

**Removal & Installation** — *See Camshaft Timing.*

### CAMSHAFT

**Removal** — With cylinder head removed from engine, remove rocker arms. NOTE — *Keep rocker arms in order for*

reinstallation in original position. Remove camshaft sprocket attaching bolt. Slide sprocket and belt guide plate from camshaft. Remove camshaft thrust plate from rear of cylinder head and carefully slide camshaft out rear of cylinder block.

**Installation** — Oil camshaft with engine oil and apply Lubriplate to valve stem tips. Oil rocker arms and carefully install camshaft in cylinder head. Install thrust plate, bolts and tighten. Check camshaft endplay and replace thrust plate if endplay is not within specifications. NOTE — *Use new camshaft attaching bolt or use new Teflon tape on threads of old bolt.*

### CAMSHAFT BEARINGS

**Removal & Installation** — Use suitable tool (71P-6250A) to remove and install bearings. NOTE — *Lube hole in bearing must be aligned with oil hole in journal.*

### CAMSHAFT LOBE LIFT

Measure distance between major and minor diameters of each cam lobe with a micrometer. Difference in readings is lobe lift. If readings vary or do not meet specifications, replace camshaft.

### CAMSHAFT END PLAY

With camshaft drive belt cover removed, push camshaft toward rear of engine. Install dial indicator so indicator point is on camshaft sprocket attaching screw or gear hub and zero dial indicator. Using a large screwdriver between camshaft sprocket or gear and cylinder head, pull the camshaft forward and release it. Read dial indicator and if endplay is not within specifications, replace thrust plate at rear of cylinder head.

### CAMSHAFT TIMING

**Checking Timing** — Remove access plug from belt cover and position crankshaft to TDC by aligning pointer on cover with "O" mark on crankshaft damper. CAUTION — *Turn engine in direction of normal rotation only.* Look through access hole and check that timing mark on camshaft drive sprocket is aligned with pointer on inner belt cover. Remove distributor cap and check that rotor is facing number one position on cap.

**Adjusting Timing** — 1) If timing is incorrect or it is necessary to remove belt, remove timing belt outer cover and loosen belt tensioner adjustment screw. Position tension adjusting tool on tension spring roll pin and release belt tensioner. Tighten adjustment screw to hold tensioner in released position. Remove crankshaft damper, belt guide and drive belt.

2) Position crankshaft sprocket and camshaft sprocket as shown in illustration. Remove distributor cap and set rotor to No. 1 firing position by turning auxiliary shaft. Install drive belt over crankshaft sprocket and then counterclockwise over auxiliary and camshaft sprockets. Align belt fore and aft on sprockets.

3) Loosen tensioner adjustment screw and allow tensioner to move against drive belt. Remove spark plugs and rotate crankshaft two complete turns in direction of normal rotation to remove slack from belt. Tighten tensioner adjustment and pivot bolts. Recheck timing mark alignment.

## 2300 cc 4 CYLINDER (Cont.)

Fig. 7    Location of Timing Marks

### AUXILIARY SHAFT

**Removal** — Remove drive belt cover, drive belt and auxiliary sprocket retaining bolt and washer. Slide sprocket from auxiliary shaft. Remove distributor, fuel pump and auxiliary shaft cover. Remove thrust plate and carefully remove shaft from cylinder block. Remove bearing from block, if worn or damaged, using suitable tool.

**Installation** — Align oil holes in bearing with those in block and drive bearing into place using a suitable tool. Oil shaft with engine oil and slide into cylinder block. **CAUTION** — *Do not allow gear and fuel pump eccentric to touch bearing surfaces during installation.* Install thrust plate, gasket and shaft cover, fuel pump, distributor and sprocket. Install and adjust drive belt. Install drive belt cover.

## ENGINE OILING

### ENGINE OILING SYSTEM

Oiling system is force feed type using a full flow oil filter. Oil enters main oil gallery from oil filter and flows to main bearings and camshaft bearings. Connecting rod bearings are supplied from front and rear main bearings via inclined main oil gallery. Distributor shaft receives oil from passage drilled in auxiliary shaft. Cams and cam follower arms are passages. A squirt hole in each rod bearing end supplies oil to piston thrust side of cylinder. Auxiliary shaft is connected with supplied from camshaft bearings and valve lash adjusters are oiled from drilled oil passages in cylinder head.

**Crankcase Capacity** — 4 qts. with filter change

**Oil Filter Type** — Full flow.

**Normal Oil Pressure (Hot)** — 40-60 psi at 2000 RPM.

**Pressure Regulator Valve** — In pump body. Not adjustable.

Fig. 8    Engine Oiling System

### OIL PUMP

**NOTE** — *Remove oil pump and cover. Check clearances and if not within specifications, replace oil pump. Do not disassemble oil pump.*

**Removal** — Remove oil pan and separate pick-up tube and screen from body of pump. Remove oil pump attaching bolts. Remove three cover attaching screws and remove cover.

| Oil Pump Specifications | |
|---|---|
| **Application** | **Clearance In.(mm)** |
| Drive Shaft-to-Housing | .0015-.0029(.038-.074) |
| Rotor Assembly End Clearance | .001-.004(.025-.101) |
| Outer Rotor-to-Housing | |
|   Capri | .001-.007 (.025-.178) |
|   Courier | .001-.013 (.025-.330) |
| Relief Valve Spring | |
|   Tension | 15.2-17.2 lbs.@1.20" |
| | (6.9-7.8 kg@30.4 mm) |

# Capri & Courier Engines

## 2300 cc 4 CYLINDER (Cont.)

**Installation** — Clean and check pump clearances. Install pump cover and attaching screws. Position a new gasket and oil inlet tube on pump and install attaching bolts.

### ENGINE COOLING

**Thermostat** — Opens at 185-192°F (85-89°C). Full Open at 210-216°F (99-102°C).

**Cooling System Capacity**

Capri — 7½ qts.
Courier — 8½ qts.

**Radiator Cap** — 13 psi.

### ENGINE SPECIFICATIONS

| GENERAL SPECIFICATIONS | | | | | | | | | | |
|---|---|---|---|---|---|---|---|---|---|---|
| Year | Displ. | | Carburetor | HP at RPM | Torque (Ft. Lbs. at RPM) | Compr. Ratio | Bore | | Stroke | |
| | cu. ins. | cc | | | | | in. | mm | in. | mm |
| 1978 | 140 | 2300 | 2-Bbl. | ..... | ..... | 8.4:1 | 3.78 | 96.01 | 3.126 | 79.40 |

| VALVES | | | | | | | |
|---|---|---|---|---|---|---|---|
| Engine & Valve | Head Diam. In. (mm) | Face Angle | Seat Angle | Seat Width In. (mm) | Stem Diameter In. (mm) | Stem Clearance In. (mm) | Valve Lift In. (mm) |
| 2300 cc Intake | 1.728-1.744 (43.89-44.30) | 44° | 45° | .060-.080 (1.52-2.03) | .3416-.3423 (8.68-8.69) | .0010-.0027 (.025-.069) | .3997 (10.15) |
| Exhaust | 1.492-1.508 (37.90-38.30) | 44° | 45° | .070-.090 (1.78-2.29) | .3411-.3418 (8.66-8.68) | .0015-.0032 (.038-.081) | .3997 (10.15) |

| PISTONS, PINS, RINGS | | | | | | |
|---|---|---|---|---|---|---|
| Engine | PISTONS | PINS | | RINGS | | |
| | Clearance In. (mm) | Piston Fit In. (mm) | Rod Fit In. (mm) | Rings | End Gap In. (mm) | Side Clearance In. (mm) |
| 2300 cc | .0014-.0022 (.035-.056) | .0002-.0004 (.005-.010) | ① | Comp. | .010-.020 (.25-.51) | .002-.004 (.051-.102) |
| | | | | Oil | .015-.055 (.38-1.40) | Snug |

① — Interference Fit.

| CRANKSHAFT MAIN & CONNECTING ROD BEARINGS | | | | | | |
|---|---|---|---|---|---|---|
| Engine | MAIN BEARINGS | | | | CONNECTING ROD BEARINGS | |
| | Journal Diam. In. (mm) | Clearance In. (mm) | Thrust Bearing | Crankshaft End Play In. (mm) | Journal Diam. In. (mm) | Clearance In. (mm) | Side Play In. (mm) |
| 2300 cc | 2.3982-2.3990 (60.91-60.93) | .0008-.0015 (.020-.038) | No. 3 | .004-.008 (.10-.20) | 2.0464-2.0472 (51.979-51.999) | .0008-.0015 (.020-.038) | .0035-.0105 (.089-.267) |

# Capri & Courier Engines

## 2300 cc 4 CYLINDER (Cont.)
### ENGINE SPECIFICATIONS (Cont.)

### VALVE SPRINGS

| Engine | Free Length In. (mm) | PRESSURE Lbs. @ In. (kg @ mm) | |
|---|---|---|---|
| | | Valve Closed | Valve Open |
| 2300 cc | 1.824 (46.3) | 71-79@1.56 (32-36@39.6) | 180-198@1.16 (82-90@29.5) |

### CAMSHAFT

| Engine | Journal Diam. In. (mm) | Clearance In. (mm) | Lobe Lift In. (mm) |
|---|---|---|---|
| 2300 cc | 1.7713-1.7720 (44.991-45.009) | ① .001-.003 (.025-.076) | .2437 (6.19) |

① — Endplay is .001-.007″ (.025-.178 mm).

### TIGHTENING SPECIFICATIONS

| Application | Ft. Lbs.(mkg) |
|---|---|
| Auxiliary Shaft Gear | 28-40(3.9-5.5) |
| Auxiliary Shaft Thrust Plate | 6-9(.8-1.2) |
| Belt Tensioner Pivot | 28-40(3.9-5.5) |
| Belt Tensioner Adjuster | 14-21(1.9-2.9) |
| Camshaft Sprocket | 80-90(11.1-12.4) |
| Camshaft Thrust Plate | 6-9(.8-1.2) |
| Connecting Rod | |
| Step 1 | 25-30(3.5-4.1) |
| Step 2 | 30-36(4.1-5.0) |
| Crankshaft Pulley | 100-120(13.8-16.6) |
| Cylinder Head | |
| Step 1 | 60(8.3) |
| Step 2 | 80-90(11.1-12.4) |
| Exhaust Manifold-to-Cylinder Head | 16-23(2.2-3.2) |
| Flywheel-to-Crankshaft | 54-64(7.5-8.8) |
| Front Cover | 6-9(.8-1.2) |
| Intake Manifold-to-Cylinder Head | 14-21(1.9-2.9) |
| Main Bearing Cap | |
| Step 1 | 60(8.3) |
| Step 2 | 80-90(11.1-12.4) |
| Oil Pan-to-Block | |
| M6 Bolts | 7-9(1.0-1.2) |
| M8 Bolts | 11-13(1.5-1.8) |
| Rocker Arm Cover | 4-7(.6-1.0) |
| Timing Belt Cover | 6-9(.8-1.2) |
| Water Pump-to-Cylinder Block | 14-21(1.9-2.9) |

## 2800 cc V6

### ENGINE CODING

#### ENGINE IDENTIFICATION

The second series of digits of vehicle identification plate, located on top of right front fender apron, indicates engine type.

| Application | Engine Code |
|---|---|
| 2800 cc.............................................................. | PX |

### ENGINE, CYLINDER HEAD & MANIFOLDS

#### ENGINE

**1)** Disconnect battery cables. Disconnect all hoses and connections to air cleaner assembly while noting positions to aid in reassembly, then remove air cleaner assembly. Mark hood hinge locations, then remove hood. Raise vehicle on a hoist. Drain cooling system and crankcase.

**2)** Remove lower radiator hose and starter. Remove converter bolt access plug and three converter-to-flywheel bolts. Disconnect exhaust pipes from exhaust manifold. Remove converter housing-to-engine attaching bolts. Remove engine mount nuts.

**3)** Disconnect transmission cooler lines from radiator on models with automatic transmission. Disconnect and plug fuel lines at fuel pump. Loosen power steering pump idler, then remove power steering pump from bracket and position to one side. Disconnect oil pressure line and lower vehicle.

**4)** Remove downshift rod. Remove clutch linkage on models with manual transmission. Remove upper radiator hose, fan shroud, and radiator. Disconnect heater hoses at engine, remove hose retainer at rocker arm cover, and position hoses to one side.

**5)** Disconnect distributor vacuum line, connector and coil wire. Disconnect transmission vacuum line at intake manifold, and power brake vacuum hose. Disconnect accelerator cable retaining clip at ball stud, then pull lightly on cable while depressing tangs one at a time on bracket clip and remove throttle cable.

**6)** Disconnect rear ground wire and alternator connectors. Position a floor jack to support transmission. Attach lifting hoist to engine, and carefully lift engine from vehicle.

#### INTAKE MANIFOLD

**Removal — 1)** Remove air cleaner, disconnect battery negative cable, and throttle cables. Drain cooling system, disconnect hose from water outlet-to-radiator, and hoses and line from water outlet-to-water pump. Remove distributor cap and spark plug wires as an assembly.

**2)** Disconnect distributor wire and distributor vacuum line. Mark location of rotor and distributor housing, then remove distributor. Remove fuel line and filter between fuel pump and carburetor, then remove rocker arm covers. Remove intake manifold nuts and bolts, then remove intake manifold assembly.

**Installation —** Apply sealing compound to joining surfaces and position gasket on block. Tab on right bank cylinder head gasket must fit into cutout of manifold gasket. Install sealing compound to retaining bolt bosses on intake manifold. Install manifold on cylinder block. Install bolts and nuts, then tighten in sequence as shown in illustration. Install remaining components in reverse of removal procedure.

*Fig. 1    Intake Manifold Tightening Sequence*

#### CYLINDER HEAD

**Removal —** Remove intake manifold. Disconnect carburetor linkage and remove carburetor. Remove rocker arm shaft by loosening two bolts at a time. Remove oil baffles. Remove push rods while keeping in correct order for reinstallation into original position. Remove exhaust manifold. Remove cylinder head bolts and lift cylinder head from block.

**Installation —** Clean old gasket material from cylinder head and block. Install new cylinder head gaskets on block ensuring that "TOP" and "FRONT" markings on gasket are properly positioned. Position cylinder heads on block, install bolts and tighten in sequence as shown in illustration. Install remaining components in reverse of removal procedure.

*Fig. 2    Cylinder Head Tightening Sequence*

## VALVES

#### VALVE ARRANGEMENT

I-E-E-I-E-I (Left Side Front-to-Rear).

I-E-I-E-E-I (Right Side Front-to-Rear).

## 2800 cc V6 (Cont.)

### VALVE GUIDES

Worn valve guides can be reamed to .008" (.203 mm), .016" (.406 mm), or .032" (.813 mm) oversizes. When going from standard size valve to an oversize, always use reamers in sequence. After reaming, break sharp corner (ID) at top of valve guide. When valve guides are reamed, valve seats must be refaced to maintain proper valve seal.

### VALVE STEM OIL SEALS

Cup or umbrella type seals used on all valves. Install seals with cup side down.

### VALVE SPRINGS

**Removal** — Remove valve rocker arm cover. Remove rocker arm shaft and both push rods of cylinder to be serviced. Remove spark plug from cylinder and install air line and adapter to cylinder. **NOTE** — *If air pressure does not hold valve shut, remove cylinder head for inspection.* Use a suitable tool to compress valve, then remove retainer locks. Remove tool, spring retainer, spring, and valve stem seal. **CAUTION** — *DO NOT remove air pressure.*

**Installation** — Install NEW valve stem oil seal, valve spring and retainer. Compress spring and install retainer locks. **CAUTION** — *Do not compress spring more than necessary to install locks.* Remove compressor tool, turn off air and remove adapter. Install remaining components in reverse of removal procedure.

### VALVE SPRING INSTALLED HEIGHT

Install valve springs with open spaced coils away from head. Measure distance between cylinder head spring pad and valve spring retainer. Install spacers if necessary to bring spring to proper specifications. **CAUTION** — *Excess spacers will result in possible spring breakage and camshaft lobe wear.*

### Spring Height Specifications

| Application | Installed Height In. (mm) |
|---|---|
| All | 1.578-1.609 (40.08-40.86) |

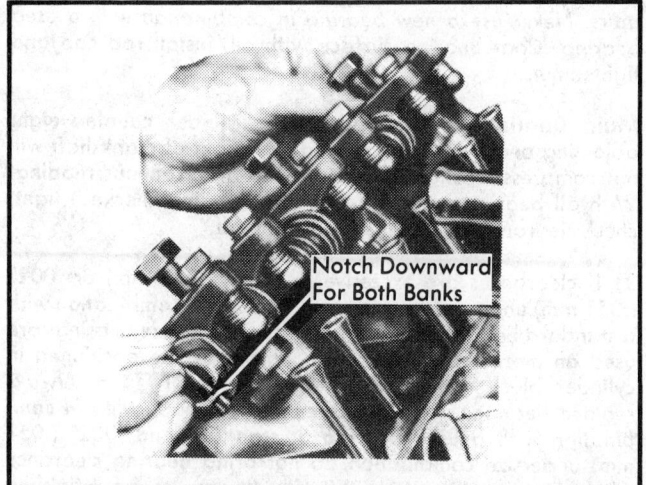

**Fig. 3   Rocker Arm Assembly Alignment**

### ROCKER ARM ASSEMBLY OVERHAUL

**Disassembly** — With rocker arm cover removed, remove rocker arm shaft stand bolts and lift off rocker arm assembly. Using a drift, drive lock sleeve (pin) out of rocker. Remove spring washers, rocker arms, springs and rocker shaft supports.

**Assembly** — Fit shaft supports, springs, rocker arms and spring washers. Install new drive lock sleeve (pin). Rocker arm shaft must be fitted to cylinder head with oil holes facing down toward head. Position notch on front of rocker shaft downward (see illustration).

### VALVE CLEARANCE ADJUSTMENT

**Preliminary (Cold) Adjustment** — 1) Before adjusting valves, torque rocker arm stand bolts to specifications.

2) Adjust valves at TDC on compression stroke in firing order sequence (1-4-2-5-3-6).

3) Rotate crankshaft clockwise, (viewed from front), until number one piston is at TDC. Using a step-type feeler gauge (go and no go), adjust intake to .014" and exhaust to .016".

4) Adjust remaining valves by rotating crankshaft a 1/3 of a turn for each cylinder until all valves have been adjusted. Two complete revolutions will adjust all valves.

**Final (Hot) Adjustment** — 1) Run engine until normal operating temperature is reached.

2) Using a step-type feeler gauge and engine at idle, adjust intake and exhaust valves to .014" intake and .016" exhaust.

## PISTONS, PINS & RINGS

### OIL PAN

**Removal** — Remove oil level dipstick and bolts attaching fan shroud to radiator. Position shroud over fan. Disconnect battery ground cable. Loosen alternator bracket and adjusting bolts. Raise vehicle, drain crankcase, remove splash shield, and starter. Remove engine front support nuts, raise engine, then place wood blocks between front supports and chassis. Remove clutch or converter housing cover, then withdraw oil pan bolts and oil pan.

**Fig. 4   Oil Pan Tightening Sequence**

# Capri Engines

## 2800 cc V6 ( Cont.)

**Installation** — Using a suitable sealing compound, coat contact surfaces and place two piece gasket on face of block. Position front and rear oil pan seals in place with tabs of seals lapping over oil pan gasket. Position oil pan on block and tighten bolts as shown in illustration.

### PISTON & ROD ASSEMBLY

NOTE — *New pistons must be installed in same cylinders for which they were fitted and used pistons in same cylinder from which they were removed.*

**Removal** — With cylinder head and oil pan removed, use a suitable ridge cutter to remove any ridge or deposits on upper end of cylinder bore. NOTE — *Piston must be at bottom of stroke and covered with cloth to collect cuttings.* Inspect connecting rods and caps for cylinder identification and mark as necessary. Remove rod cap and push piston and rod assembly out top of cylinder block taking care not to nick crankshaft journal or cylinder wall.

**Fig. 5   Piston & Rod Assembly Installation Features**

**Installation** — Lightly coat cylinder bores, pistons and rings with engine oil. Ensure that ring gaps are properly spaced (see illustration) and install ring compressor on piston. Install each piston and rod assembly (with notch on piston head facing front of engine) in its respective bore and guide connecting rod onto crankshaft journal while tapping piston head with hammer handle to seat connecting rod against crankshaft. Install rod caps and tighten.

**Fig. 6   Spacing of Piston Ring Gaps**

### FITTING PISTONS

Check piston to cylinder bore clearance by measuring piston and bore diameters. Measure OD of piston at centerline of piston pin bore and at 90° to pin bore axis. Refer to specifications for correct clearance. Oversize pistons are available in .020″ and .040″ oversizes.

### PISTON PIN REPLACEMENT

Piston pin bore and OD of piston pin must be within specifications. Remove old pin using an arbor press and suitable piston support and driver tool. Assemble piston to rod with notches on piston facing forward. Rod numbers face to left side of engine.

**Fig. 7   Piston Pin Installation Tools**

## CRANKSHAFT MAIN & CONNECTING ROD BEARINGS

### MAIN & CONNECTING ROD BEARINGS

NOTE — *Following procedures are with oil pan and oil pump removed.*

**Connecting Rod Bearings** — After ensuring rod caps are marked for cylinder identification, remove rod caps. Use Plastigage method to check for proper bearing clearance. If not within specifications, new bearings must be installed. New bearings are available in .001″ (.025 mm) and .002″ (.051 mm) undersizes. Selective fitting is required on each connecting rod. A standard bearing may be used in combination with either undersize bearing. NOTE — *Always replace bearings in pairs. Never use a new bearing in combination with a used bearing.* Coat bearing surface with oil, install rod cap and tighten nuts.

**Main Bearings** — 1) Position jack under counterweight adjoining bearing being checked so weight of crankshaft will not compress Plastigage and provide an erroneous reading. With all bearing caps (other than one being checked) tight, check clearances using Plastigage method.

2) If clearances are excessive, a .001″ (.025 mm) or .002″ (.051 mm) undersize bearing may be used in combination with a standard bearing. If .002″ (.051 mm) undersize bearings are used on more than one journal, they must be positioned in cylinder block rather than bearing cap. NOTE — *Always replace bearings in pairs. Never use a new bearing in combination with a used bearing.* If standard and .002″ (.051 mm) undersize combination do not bring bearing clearance within specified limits, crankshaft will have to be refinished and undersized bearings installed.

## 2800 cc V6 (Cont.)

**3)** Remove all upper main bearings (except rear main) by inserting suitable tool in oil hole of crankshaft journal and rotating crankshaft clockwise to roll bearing from engine. Oil new upper bearing and insert plain (unnotched) end between crankshaft and indented (or notched) side of block. Rotate bearing into place. Install all main bearing caps with arrows pointing to front of engine. **NOTE** — *If rear main bearing is to be replaced, engine must be removed from vehicle.*

### THRUST BEARING ALIGNMENT

Install all bearing caps except thrust bearing cap and tighten. Install thrust bearing cap with bolts finger tight. Pry crankshaft to front of engine and hold forward while prying thrust bearing cap to rear. Hold crankshaft forward and tighten bolts on thrust bearing cap. Check crankshaft endplay.

### REAR MAIN BEARING OIL SEAL

**Removal** — Remove transmission, clutch pressure plate and disc (if equipped), flywheel, flywheel housing and rear plate. Remove old seal using two sheet metal screws (see illustration) while taking care not to damage oil sealing surface.

*Fig. 8 Using Metal Screws to Remove Crankshaft Rear Oil Seal*

**Installation** — Coat seal-to-cylinder block surface of oil seal with oil. Coat seal contact surface of oil seal and crankshaft with Lubriplate. Start seal in recess and install with suitable tool (T72C-6165). Drive seal into position until firmly seated.

*Fig. 9 Installing Crankshaft Rear Oil Seal*

### ENGINE FRONT COVER

**Removal** — Remove oil pan, radiator, alternator, drive belts, water pump, and water hoses. Remove drive belt pulley and if necessary, remove guide sleeves from block. Remove front cover attaching bolts. Tap cover with a plastic hammer to break seal and remove cover.

**Installation** — Apply sealing compound to gasket surfaces on cylinder block and both sides of gasket. Position gasket and front cover, then install retaining bolts. Fit new seal rings to guide sleeve and insert guides in block with chamfered end toward front cover. Apply sealer to front cover and place gasket on cover. Using suitable alignment tool (T74P-6019) to center cover, then install and tighten bolts.

*Fig. 10 Using Tool to Align Engine Front Cover*

### FRONT COVER OIL SEAL

**Removal & Installation** — Remove radiator and crankshaft pulley. Using a suitable pulling tool (as shown in illustration), remove front cover oil seal. To install a new seal, coat seal with Lubriplate and slide installing tool (T74P-6700) and seal onto crankshaft. Seat seal until tool bottoms out on front cover. Reinstall crankshaft pulley, radiator and adjust drive belt.

*Fig. 11 Removing Front Oil Seal*

*Fig. 12 Installing Front Oil Seal*

## 2800 cc V6 (Cont.)

### CAMSHAFT

#### TIMING GEARS

Using a dial indicator, check that backlash between camshaft gear and crankshaft gear is .006-.010" (.15-.25 mm). If backlash exceeds specifications, replace both gears as follows:

**Removal** — Drain cooling system and crankcase. Remove radiator, oil pan, front cover and water pump. Remove camshaft gear retaining bolt and slide gear off camshaft. Use a suitable gear puller and remove crankshaft gear.

**Installation** — Turn camshaft and crankshaft as necessary to align timing marks (see illustration) and install camshaft gear. Install retaining washer and bolt, then tighten. Install crankshaft gear. Recheck that timing marks line up as shown in illustration. Install remaining components in reverse of removal procedure.

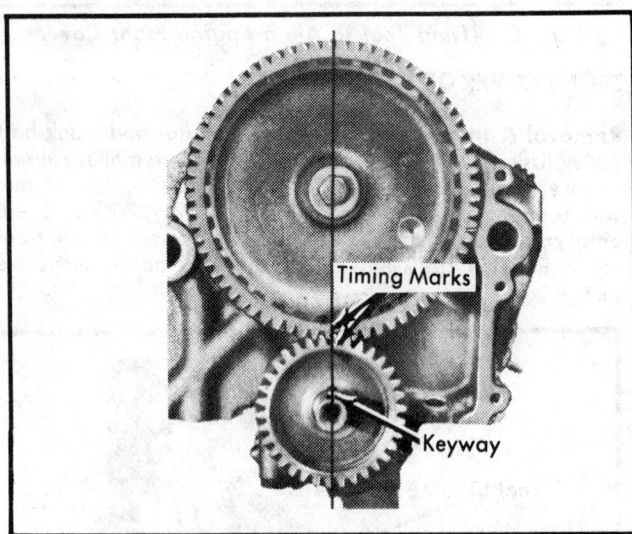

**Fig. 13   Aligning Camshaft Timing Marks**

### CAMSHAFT

**Removal** — Drain cooling system and remove radiator, fan, spacer, water pump pulley, and drive belt. Remove intake manifold, carburetor, and alternator. Drain crankcase and remove rocker arm and shaft assemblies. Remove push rods and mark for installation in original position. Remove oil pan, crankshaft pulley, front cover, and camshaft gear. Remove camshaft thrust plate and screws. Remove valve lifters. Carefully pull camshaft from cylinder block taking care not to damage bearings.

**Installation** — Oil camshaft journals with engine oil and apply Lubriplate to cam lobes. Carefully install camshaft in engine. Install spacer ring (chamfered side toward camshaft), camshaft key and thrust plate (covering main oil gallery). Reverse removal procedure for remaining parts.

### ENGINE OILING

#### ENGINE OILING SYSTEM

The V-6 engine is pressure feed by a rotor type oil pump, which filters all oil through a full flow filter before entering engine. An oil gallery supplies oil to crankshaft main bearings, from

there through slanted passages in crankshaft to connecting rod journals. Connecting rod big ends have a squirt hole which sprays oil on thrust side of cylinder bores. Oil from the oil gallery also feeds camshaft main bearings, which have grooves 180° of their circumference. From these grooves passages lead to distributor drive gear and rocker arm shafts.

**Crankcase Capacity** — 4.5 quarts. Add .5 quart with filter change.

**Oil Filter** — Full flow type.

### CAMSHAFT BEARINGS

**Removal** — With engine removed from vehicle, remove flywheel, camshaft and rear bearing bore plug. Use suitable collet and back-up nut assembled on expanding mandrel to remove bearings.

**Installation** — Position new bearings at bearing bores and press into place using correct size expanding collet being sure to center pulling plate and puller screw to avoid damage to bearing. Align oil holes in cylinder block when bearings are installed. Front edge of No. 1 bearing must be installed .040-.060" (1.0-1.5 mm) below front face of cylinder block.

### CAMSHAFT END THRUST

Rocker arm shaft assembly must be loosened sufficiently to free camshaft. Push camshaft toward rear of engine and install dial indicator so point is on camshaft sprocket bolt. Zero indicator. Position screwdriver between camshaft gear and block, pull camshaft forward and release. If endplay is excessive, replace thrust plate. CAUTION — *Do not attempt to pry camshaft back and forth with valve train load on camshaft.*

### CHECKING CAMSHAFT LOBE LIFT

Check lift of each camshaft lobe in consecutive order as follows:

1) Remove rocker arm shaft assemblies, making sure each push rod is in valve lifter socket. Install a dial indicator so that ball socket adapter of indicator rests on the end of push rod and in same plane as push rod movement.

2) With an auxiliary starter switch connected to starter solenoid and ignition switch "OFF", bump crankshaft until tappet is on base circle of camshaft lobe. This will be push rods lowest point.

3) Zero dial indicator and continue to rotate crankshaft until push rod is in fully raised position (highest indicator reading). Compare total lift from indicator readings with specifications.

4) To check accuracy of indicator readings, continue to rotate crankshaft until indicator reads zero. If lift on any lobe is .005" less than specifications, camshaft and tappet operating on worn lobe must be replaced.

**Normal Oil Pressure** — 40-55 psi @ 2000 RPM.

**Pressure Regulator Valve** — Non-adjustable.

### OIL PUMP

**Disassembly** — Remove pick-up tube and screen assembly from pump housing. Remove cover and lift out two-piece rotor assembly. Drill a small hole and insert self-threading sheet metal screw into oil pressure relief valve plug and remove plug. Remove spring and valve.

## 2800 cc V6 (Cont.)

**Reassembly** — Clean, inspect (see specifications) and oil all parts. Install relief valve, spring and new plug in oil pump housing. Install plug with flat side pointing out and spread plug in housing using a drift. Install inner and outer rotors and shaft assembly in housing with dot reference marks up. Install cover and pick-up tube assembly.

**Cooling System Capacity** — 8.5 quarts.

**Pressure Radiator Cap** — Opens at 13 psi.

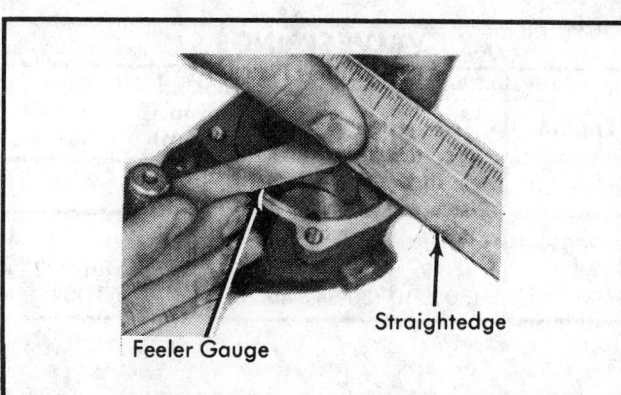

Fig. 14   Measuring Oil Pump Rotor End Play

| Oil Pump Specifications | |
|---|---|
| **Clearance** | **Specification In.(mm)** |
| Outer Race-to-Housing ......................... | .006-.012(.15-.30) |
| Rotor Endplay ........................... | .0011-.0041(.028-.104) |
| Shaft-to-Housing ......................... | .0014-.0029(.036-.074) |
| Relief Valve-to-Bore ....................... | .0015-.0030(.038-.076) |

**Relief Valve Spring Pressure** — 13.6-14.7 Lbs. @ 1.39" (6.17-6.67 kg @ 35.3 mm).

## ENGINE COOLING

### WATER PUMP

**Removal** — Drain cooling system. Remove lower radiator hose, and heater return hose. Loosen alternator mounting bolts and remove drive belt. Disconnect fan shroud from radiator and position behind fan. Remove fan, pulley and shroud. Remove attaching bolts, water pump, water inlet housing and thermostat from front cover.

**Installation** — Apply sealer to both sides of a new gasket and position gasket on water pump. Position water pump on front cover with two bolts finger tight. Install new water inlet housing gasket, with sealer on both sides, to water pump. Install thermostat, rubber gasket, and water inlet housing. Install and tighten remaining water pump attaching bolts while noting different length bolts. Reinstall, fan, pulley, shroud, drive belt and hoses. Fill cooling system.

**Thermostat** — Starts to Open at 185-192°F (85-89°C). Fully Open at 210-216°F (99-102°C).

| TIGHTENING SPECIFICATIONS | |
|---|---|
| **Application** | **Ft. Lbs.(mkg)** |
| Camshaft Gear ......................... | 32-36(4.4-5.0) |
| Camshaft Thrust Plate ............................ | 12-15(1.7-2.1) |
| Connecting Rod Bearing Cap ................. | 21-25(2.9-3.5) |
| Crankshaft Damper ......................... | 92-103(12.7-14.2) |
| Crankshaft Pulley-to-Damper .................. | 18-25(2.5-3.5) |
| Cylinder Head | |
|   Step One ......................... | 29-40(4.0-5.5) |
|   Step Two ......................... | 40-51(5.5-7.1) |
|   Step Three ......................... | 65-80(9.0-11.1) |
| Exhaust Manifold ......................... | 16-23(2.2-3.2) |
| Flywheel ......................... | 47-51(6.5-7.1) |
| Front Cover ......................... | 12-15(1.7-2.1) |
| Intake Manifold | |
|   Step One ......................... | 3-6(.4-.8) |
|   Step Two ......................... | 6-11(.8-1.5) |
|   Step Three ......................... | 11-16(1.5-2.2) |
|   Step Four ......................... | 15-18(2.1-2.5) |
| Main Bearing Cap ......................... | 65-75(9.0-10.4) |
| Oil Pan ......................... | 5-7(.7-1.0) |
| Oil Pump ......................... | 12-15(1.7-2.1) |
| Rocker Arm Cover ......................... | 3-5(.4-.7) |
| Rocker Shaft Supports ......................... | 43-49(5.9-6.8) |
| Water Pump ......................... | 7-9(1.0-1.2) |

## ENGINE SPECIFICATIONS

| GENERAL SPECIFICATIONS | | | | | | | | | | |
|---|---|---|---|---|---|---|---|---|---|---|
| **Year** | **Displ.** | | **Carburetor** | **HP at RPM** | **Torque (Ft. Lbs. at RPM)** | **Compr. Ratio** | **Bore** | | **Stroke** | |
| | cu. ins. | cc | | | | | in. | mm | in. | mm |
| 1978 | 170 | 2800 | 2-Bbl. | ..... | ..... | 8.2-1 | 3.66 | 92.964 | 2.79 | 70.866 |

# Capri Engines

## 2800 cc V6 (Cont.)

### ENGINE SPECIFICATIONS (Cont.)

### VALVE SPRINGS

| Engine | Free Length In. (mm) | PRESSURE Lbs. @ In. (kg @ mm) | |
|---|---|---|---|
| | | Valve Closed | Valve Open |
| 2800 cc All | 1.99 (50.55) | 67-75@1.585 (30-34@40.26) | 144-156@1.222 (65-71@31.04) |

### CAMSHAFT

| Engine | Journal Diam. In. (mm) | Clearance In. (mm) ① | Lobe Lift In. (mm) |
|---|---|---|---|
| 2800 cc Front | 1.6497-1.6505 (41.902-41.923) | .001-.0026 (.025-.066) | .2555 (6.49) |
| No. 2 | 1.6347-1.6355 (41.521-41.542) | | |
| No. 3 | 1.6197-1.6205 (41.140-41.161) | | |
| Rear | 1.6065-1.6073 (40.805-40.825) | | |

① — Endplay is .0008-.0040" (.02-.10 mm).

### VALVES

| Engine & Valve | Head Diam. In. (mm) | Face Angle | Seat Angle | Seat Width In. (mm) | Stem Diameter In. (mm) | Stem Clearance In. (mm) | Valve Lift In. (mm) |
|---|---|---|---|---|---|---|---|
| 2800 cc Intake | 1.570 (39.88) | 44° | 45° | .050-.079 (1.3-2.0) | .3158-.3167 (8.02-8.04) | .0008-.0025 (.02-.06) | .373 (9.47) |
| Exhaust | 1.269 (32.23) | 44° | 45° | .050-.079 (1.3-2.0) | .3149-.3156 (8.00-8.02) | .0018-.0035 (.046-.089) | .373 (9.47) |

### CRANKSHAFT MAIN & CONNECTING ROD BEARINGS

| Engine | MAIN BEARINGS | | | | CONNECTING ROD BEARINGS | | |
|---|---|---|---|---|---|---|---|
| | Journal Diam. In. (mm) | Clearance In. (mm) | Thrust Bearing | Crankshaft End Play In. (mm) | Journal Diam. In. (mm) | Clearance In. (mm) | Side Play In. (mm) |
| 2800 cc All | 2.2433-2.2441 (56.980-57.000) | 0005-.0019 (.013-.048) | No. 3 | .004-.008 (.10-.20) | 2.1252-2.1260 (53.980-54.000) | .0005-.0022 (.012-.056) | .004-.011 (.10-.28) |

### PISTONS, PINS, RINGS

| Engine | PISTONS | PINS | | RINGS | | |
|---|---|---|---|---|---|---|
| | Clearance In. (mm) | Piston Fit In. (mm) | Rod Fit In. (mm) | Rings | End Gap In. (mm) | Side Clearance In. (mm) |
| 2800 cc | .0011-.0019 (028-.048) | .0003-.0006 (.008-.015) | ① | Comp. | .015-.023 (.381-.584) | .0020-.0033 (.051-.084) |
| | | | | Oil | .015-.055 (.381-.584) | Snug |

① — Interference Fit.

## 1600, 2000 & 2600 cc 4 CYLINDER

### ENGINE CODING

#### ENGINE IDENTIFICATION

Engine model code and serial number is stamped on engine block just below number 1 spark plug on right side of block. Model codes are as follows:

| Application In. (cc) | Model Code |
|---|---|
| 97.5 (1600) ........................................... | G32B |
| 121.7 (2000) ........................................... | G52B |
| 155.9 (2600) ........................................... | G54B |

### ENGINE & CYLINDER HEAD

#### ENGINE

1) Drain cooling system, remove battery, disconnect ground strap, wiring from ignition coil, vacuum control solenoid valve, fuel cut-off solenoid valve, generator, starter, transmission switch, back-up light switch, water temperature gauge and oil pressure switch.

2) Remove air cleaner and disconnect attaching hoses. Disconnect accelerator linkage and heater hoses. Unbolt and separate exhaust pipe from manifold. Disconnect pipe mounting bracket at transmission.

3) Disconnect hose between fuel filter and fuel pump return pipe. Remove radiator and radiator shroud. If equipped with automatic transmission, remove oil cooler pipe and tie rod when removing radiator.

4) Remove console box, then detach control lever assembly from transmission. Remove hood. Disconnect speedometer cable and back-up light switch wiring from transmission. Disconnect clutch cable from shift lever and then disconnect cable from its bracket (if equipped with manual transmission). Drain transmission. If equipped with transmission dynamic vibration damper, remove damper, remove locking bolts for attaching flange yoke at rear of propeller shaft, then draw shaft out of transmission.

5) Support transmission on a suitable jack and remove front and rear mount bolts. Remove rear engine support bracket. Attach suitable lifting device to front and rear engine hangers. Lift engine-transmission assembly obliquely upward and out of engine compartment. NOTE — *Keep transmission lower than engine when removing.*

#### CYLINDER HEAD & INTAKE MANIFOLD

**Removal — 1)** Drain cooling system, disconnect water hoses at cylinder head, manifold and carburetor. Remove breather and purge hose, vacuum hose at distributor and purge control valve.

2) Disconnect accelerator linkage, spark plug wires, water temperature gauge unit and exhaust manifold flange. Remove air cleaner, fuel line, distributor and fuel pump. Remove ex-

haust manifold, then intake manifold and carburetor assembly.

3) Remove rocker cover and breather, and on 1600 cc engine, remove timing belt upper front cover. Turn crankshaft so number 1 piston is at TDC on compression stroke. Mark belt (1600 cc) or chain (2000 and 2600 cc) with suitable marker, in line with sprocket mark.

4) Remove camshaft sprocket from camshaft, and on 1600 cc engine, remove timing belt upper inner cover. Remove cylinder head bolts in two or three stages according to removal sequence shown in *Fig. 2* (loosen high numbers first). Lift off head using caution to avoid twisting sprocket and chain (belt).

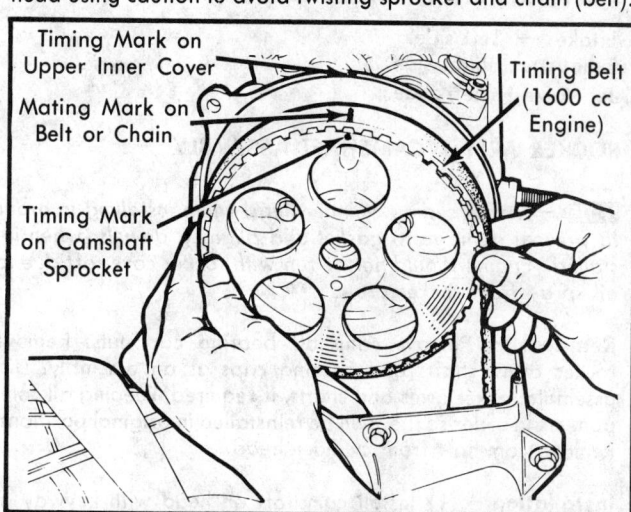

**Fig. 1   Aligning Timing Marks at TDC (1600 cc Engine Shown)**

**Installation — 1)** To install, reverse removal procedure. Gasket surfaces must be clean and NEW gaskets must be used. Use sealer ONLY at points where cylinder head joins front cover case (2000 and 2600 cc engines) and to intake manifold gasket around water passages (all models).

**Fig. 2   Cylinder Head Bolt Tightening Sequence (Remove in Reverse Order)**

## 1600, 2000 & 2600 cc 4 CYLINDER (Cont.)

**2)** Tighten cylinder head bolts to initial torque (25 ft. lbs. for 1600 cc, 35 ft. lbs. for others) according to sequence shown in *Fig. 2*. Repeat the procedure, retightening all cylinder head bolts to specified torque.

**3)** Temporarily set valve clearance to cold engine settings, then readjust to hot engine settings after engine is at normal operating temperature. Install rocker cover, air cleaner and breather hoses.

## VALVES

### VALVE ARRANGEMENT

Intake — Left side.
Exhaust — Right side.
Jet Valve — Left Side.

### ROCKER ARM & CAMSHAFT ASSEMBLY

**NOTE** — *Avoid sliding cylinder head when installing in order to prevent damage to gasket and aligning dowels (when installed). Engine should not be run with rocker cover off due to oil spray from rocker arms.*

**Removal** — Remove camshaft bearing cap nuts. Remove rocker arms, shafts and bearing caps as an assembly. Disassemble rocker arms and shafts, if required, keeping all components in order so they will be reinstalled in original positions. Remove camshaft from cylinder head.

**Installation — 1)** Install camshaft on head with keyway at 41° position (1600 cc engines) or dowel in 12 o'clock position (2000 and 2600 cc engines). See *Figs. 3 and 4*. Assemble rocker arm assembly, assuring that mating marks on bearing caps and rocker arm shafts face front of engine and are properly aligned with each other. Insert bolts through bearing caps and rocker arm shafts to keep assembly together during installation. See *Fig. 5*.

**2)** Install rocker arm assembly to cylinder head, assuring that camshaft is in proper position. Tighten bolts to 7 ft. lbs. in sequence of center, 2, 4, front and rear. Repeat sequence, tightening to final specified torque.

**Fig. 3   Camshaft Woodruff Key Position for Installation (1600 cc Engine)**

**Fig. 4   Camshaft Installation Position (2000 & 2600 cc Engine)**

**Fig. 5   Camshaft Bearing Cap & Rocker Shaft Mating Marks**

**Fig. 6   Exploded View of Rocker Arm and Shaft Assembly**

### JET VALVES

Using special Jet Valve Socket Wrench (MD998310), remove jet valves. Disassemble valve using spring pliers (MD998309) to compress spring and remove retainer lock. Check valve head and seat for damage and make sure jet valve slides smooth in body without play.

## 1600, 2000 & 2600 cc 4 CYLINDER (Cont.)

CAUTION — *Make certain that jet valve socket wrench is not tilted with respect to center of valve when used. If tool is tilted, stem may be bent resulting in defective valve operation and a broken wrench. Do not disturb jet valve and body combination. If defective, jet valve and body should be replaced as an assembly.*

### VALVE SPRINGS

With camshaft and rocker arm assembly removed, use valve lifter and remove retainer locks (keepers). Remove all retainers, springs, spring seats and valves, keeping in proper order for reassembly. Check valve spring free length and pressure. Standard spring squareness should be 1.5° or less. If beyond 3°, replace spring.

### VALVE GUIDE SERVICING

1) Check valve stem-to-guide clearance, and if clearance exceeds service limits as listed in table, replace valve guide with next oversize component. Guides are available in the following oversizes:

#### Valve Guide Oversizes

| Size Mark | Guide Size In. (mm) | Cyl. Head Bore In. (mm) |
|---|---|---|
| 5 | .002 (.05) | .5138-.5145 (13.05-13.07) |
| 25 | .010 (.25) | .5216-.5224 (13.25-13.27) |
| 50 | .020 (.50) | .5315-.5323 (13.50-13.52) |

.539-.563" (13.7-14.3 mm)

Valve Guide Tool

**Fig. 7    Valve Guide Installation and Height**

2) Heat cylinder head to approximately 480°F (249°C), and then use a suitable valve guide tool to drive out each guide toward the combustion chamber. Ream guide bore in cylinder head to specified size (after head has cooled to room temperature).

3) To install new guides, reheat head to same temperature, quickly insert and drive guides into head. Guide should protrude .539-.563" (13.69-14.30 mm) above head surface, as illustrated. Check guide I.D. and ream as necessary.

### VALVE STEM OIL SEALS

After installing valve spring seat, place stem seal on valve guide. Using suitable tool (MD998005), lightly hammer seal into proper position (see illustration). When installing, use care not to twist seal. Do not reuse old seals.

.579-.595" (14.7-15.1 mm)

Tool MD998005

**Fig. 8    Valve Stem Oil Seal Installation and Height**

### VALVE SEAT SERVICING

1) Check valve seat for damage or wear. Replace or rework seat, as necessary. If reworking seat, check valve guide first. Make proper replacement, if required, then check seat for necessary corrections.

2) Recondition valve seat with suitable grinder or cutter to specified contact width. After rework, valve and seat should be lapped with suitable compound.

3) Valve seat sink (wear of seat inward allowing valve to seat too deep in head) must be checked by measuring installed height of spring between the spring seat and retainer with all spring components installed. Standard dimension is 1.590" (40.4 mm) with additional wear limit of .039" (1.0 mm). Replace valve seat if beyond limit.

4) Remove valve seat by thinning down with a suitable cutter, then machine seat bore to proper size for replacement seat. Heat head to approximately 480°F (250°C) and press in oversize seat. Replacement seats are available in .012" (.305 mm) and .024" (.610 mm) oversizes, marked "30" and "60" respectively.

### VALVE CLEARANCE ADJUSTMENT

1) Ensure timing marks on camshaft sprocket and chain are aligned. With head assembly installed, temporarily adjust valves (sequence for adjustment; 1-3-4-2), according to following procedure: At compression stroke TDC, for cylinder being adjusted, loosen rocker arm nuts; then, turning adjusting screw, adjust valve clearance to specifications.

2) Complete engine assembly and temporarily install rocker cover. Warm engine until coolant temperature is 170 to 180°F. With piston at TDC on compression stroke, back intake valve adjusting screw off 2 or more turns. Adjust jet valve clearance, then adjust intake valve clearance. Adjust exhaust valve clearance and assure that all adjusting screw lock nuts are tightened securely.

## 1600, 2000 & 2600 cc 4 CYLINDER (Cont.)

**NOTE** — *Jet valve spring is comparatively weak and must not be forced in when making adjustment. Final valve clearance should be adjusted after cylinder head bolts have been tightened to final torque.*

### Valve Clearance

| Application | Cold In. (mm) | Hot In. (mm) |
|---|---|---|
| Intake | .003 (.07) | .006 (.15) |
| Exhaust | .007 (.17) | .010 (.25) |
| Jet Valve | .003 (.07) | .006 (.15) |

## PISTONS, PINS & RINGS

### PISTON & CONNECTING ROD ASSEMBLY

**Removal** — Remove cylinder head and oil pan. Check to ensure connecting rods and rod caps are marked to aid in assembling components to their original position. Remove carbon ridge from cylinder bores. Remove connecting rod caps. Remove connecting rod and piston assembly through top of cylinder block.

**Installation** — To reinstall, lubricate all internal surfaces with engine oil before installation. Make sure front mark on piston head faces front of engine. Use a ring compressor to compress rings (without changing their position) and install piston and connecting rod assembly in to cylinder block in their original position. Tap lightly on piston dome with wooden handle tool while guiding connecting rod onto crankshaft. Install rod cap onto proper piston and connecting rod assembly. Tighten attaching bolts. Install cylinder head and oil pan.

### FITTING PISTONS

1) After checking block for distortion, cracks, scratches or other abnormalities, measure bores at 3 levels. If any distortion exceeds .001" (.02 mm) from standard bore size, block must be rebored and oversize pistons installed.

### Oversize Pistons

| Application | Size Mark | Diam. In. (mm) |
|---|---|---|
| 1600 cc | | |
| .010" OS | 0.25 | 3.0374 (77.15) |
| .020" OS | 0.50 | 3.0472 (77.40) |
| .030" OS | 0.75 | 3.0571 (77.65) |
| .039" OS | 1.00 | 3.0669 (77.90) |
| 2000 cc | | |
| .010" OS | 0.25 | 3.3163 (84.23) |
| .020" OS | 0.50 | 3.3262 (84.49) |
| .030" OS | 0.75 | 3.3360 (84.73) |
| .039" OS | 1.00 | 3.3464 (85.00) |
| 2600 cc | | |
| .010" OS | 0.25 | 3.5964 (91.35) |
| .020" OS | 0.50 | 3.6063 (91.60) |
| .030" OS | 0.75 | 3.6161 (91.85) |
| .039" OS | 1.00 | 3.6260 (92.10) |

2) Check outside diameter of piston by measuring at a point .079" (2 mm) from bottom of skirt and at 90° to pin bore. Determine amount of cylinder reboring required to meet specified clearance.

### PISTON PINS

Check piston pin-to-bore fit; pin should press in smoothly by hand (at room temperature). When assembling, apply engine oil to outside of pin and to piston pin bore, position rod to piston ("FRONT" mark upward), align pin with pressing tool, and press pin into piston and rod.

### PISTON RINGS

Measure piston ring side and end clearance for all pistons and replace rings as necessary. When replacing a ring without correcting the cylinder bore, check ring end gap at lower part of cylinder that is less worn. When replacing a ring, be sure to use one of the same size. Install rings on piston with end gaps staggered at 120° intervals, but make sure no ring gap is in line with thrust face of pin bore. Also be sure the manufacturer's marks are facing upward when rings are installed.

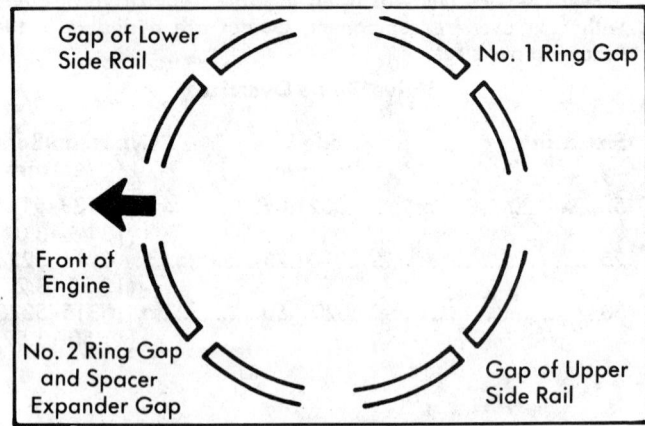

**Fig. 9  Piston Ring Gap Positions**

**CAUTION** — *Install oil ring first WITHOUT using a ring expander. Spacer expander gap should be installed more than 45° from side rail gaps, and rails should turn smoothly when installed.*

### Piston Ring Sizes

| Ring Size | Size Mark |
|---|---|
| 1600, 2000 & 2600 cc | |
| Standard | No Mark |
| .010" (.25 mm) OS | 25 |
| .020" (.50 mm) OS | 50 |
| .030" (.75 mm) OS | 75 |
| .039" (1.00 mm) OS | 100 |

## CRANKSHAFT MAIN & CONNECTING ROD BEARINGS

### MAIN & CONNECTING ROD BEARINGS

1) Inspect each bearing for peeling, melting, seizure or improper contact. Replace defective bearings. Measure outside diameter of crankshaft and connecting rod journals to determine if out-of-round or tapered.

2) Cut Plastigage to same length as width of bearing. Place it parallel with journal (not over oil holes). Install crankshaft

## 1600, 2000 & 2600 cc 4 CYLINDER (Cont.)

bearings and caps, tightening to specifications. Always install caps with arrow facing forward.

**NOTE** — *Do not turn crankshaft with Plastigage installed.*

3) Remove main bearing cap from crankshaft and measure Plastigage at widest part (using scale on Plastigage package). Repeat procedure for connecting rod bearings. If clearance exceeds limits, bearing should be replaced or undersize bearing installed. Undersize bearings are available in .010" (.25 mm), .020" (.50 mm), and .030" (.75 mm) undersizes.

### THRUST BEARING

With crankshaft bearing caps installed, check thrust clearance (end play) by inserting feeler gauge between center main bearing and crankshaft thrust face. If clearance exceeds specified limits, replace center main bearing.

## CAMSHAFT

### COUNTERBALANCE SHAFT & TIMING BELT

**1600 cc** — Timing belt drives camshaft, oil pump and (left) counterbalance shaft. A separate belt drives counterbalance shaft on the right side.

**Removal — 1)** With engine removed and timing belt marked. Remove crankshaft pulley, upper and lower timing belt front covers. Loosen belt tensioner mounting nut and bolt. Remove timing belt. Remove camshaft sprocket, crankshaft sprocket and flange, remove timing belt tensioner.

**2)** Remove plug at bottom of left side of cylinder block and insert a screwdriver, to keep left counterbalance shaft in position. Remove crankshaft sprocket and counterbalance shaft sprocket from right side. Remove timing belt covers from right side. Remove water pump and cylinder head assembly. Remove oil pan and oil pick-up screen. Remove oil pump cover.

**3)** With screwdriver through plug hole in cylinder block to hold counterbalance shaft, loosen oil pump driven gear bolt. Remove front case with left counterbalance shaft attached. Remove right counterbalance shaft from cylinder block.

**Installation — 1)** To install, reverse removal procedure. Check to ensure that all timing marks are in alignment. To adjust tension on right side. Lift tensioner toward belt; tighten nut and bolt. Make sure that the shaft of the tensioner does not rotate in the same direction as the bolt tightens. Correct adjustment is obtained when belt deflects .20-.27" (5-7 mm) with finger pressure.

**2)** To adjust counterbalance shaft and timing belt, start with timing belt installed on crankshaft sprocket, oil pump sprocket and camshaft sprocket, making sure that all timing marks are in alignment. With tensioner installed, lightly push up toward mounting nut, to make sure that timing belt comes into complete mesh with camshaft sprocket. Tighten mounting nut and bolt (tighten nut first).

**3)** Turn crankshaft through a complete rotation in normal direction. (Make sure that crankshaft is turned smoothly and in the correct direction.) Loosen tensioner mounting nut and bolt. At this time, the loose side of the belt will be given tension. Tighten nut and bolt (nut first).

### COUNTERBALANCE SHAFT & CHAIN

**2000 & 2600 cc** — Counterbalance shafts are driven by chains off crankshaft sprocket. Left shaft turns in same direction as crankshaft. Right counterbalance shaft turns counterclockwise, being driven by oil pump in the opposite direction of engine rotation.

### COUNTERBALANCE DRIVE CHAIN

**Removal** — Remove crankshaft pulley and timing chain case. Remove chain guides A, B and C, sprocket B locking bolts and crankshaft sprocket B. See Fig. 11. Remove both countershaft sprockets (B) and drive chain.

**Fig. 10   Counterbalance and Timing Belt Installation (1600 cc)**

**Fig. 11   Exploded View of Counterbalance Shafts and Drive Chain (2000 & 2600 cc)**

## 1600, 2000 & 2600 cc 4 CYLINDER (Cont.)

**Installation** – To install, reverse removal procedure, referring to *Fig. 12* for component location. Ensure that mating marks on sprockets align with plated links on counterbalance chain. Adjust tension by installing guides A and C, then shake counterbalance shaft sprockets to take slack from chain. Adjust guide B so that there will be .040-.140″ (1.0-3.5 mm) clearance between guide and chain at point P. Tighten guide mounting bolts and complete assembly.

stall, rotate crankshaft until number 1 piston is at TDC on compression stroke, align mating marks on sprockets and chain, then install chain on camshaft and crankshaft with keys and keyways aligned. Inspect chain tensioner and complete installation in reverse order of removal.

**Fig. 12   Installing and Adjusting Counterbalance Drive Chain (2000 & 2600 cc)**

**Fig. 13   Timing Chain Alignment and Installation (2000 & 2600 cc)**

### COUNTERBALANCE SHAFTS

**Removal & Installation – 1)** With counterbalance drive chain removed, remove oil pump mounting bolts. Remove bolt holding oil pump driven gear and counterbalance shaft together, then remove oil pump mounting bolts. Remove oil pump, then withdraw counterbalance shaft.

**NOTE** – *If bolt locking oil pump driven gear and counterbalance shaft is hard to loosen, remove oil pump and counterbalance shaft as an assembly. Then remove lock bolt to disassemble.*

**2)** Remove thrust plate supporting front of left counterbalance shaft. (Thrust plate is removed by threading bolts into plate holes at same time). Withdraw counterbalance shaft from cylinder block. To install, reverse removal procedure.

### TIMING CHAIN

**2000 & 2600 cc** – With counterbalance drive chain removed, take off chain tensioner and right and left chain guides. Remove camshaft sprocket, and timing chain. To in-

### CAMSHAFT

With camshaft removed, inspect bearings, journals and lobes for wear or damage. Bearing damage or excess wear requires cylinder head replacement. If journals or lobes are worn excessively or damaged, replace camshaft. End play when camshaft is installed in head should be .002-.006″ (.05-.15 mm) for 1600 cc, and .004-.008″ (.1-.2 mm) for 2000 and 2600 cc.

**Fig. 14   Camshaft Sprocket Alignment and Installation (2000 & 2600 cc)**

## 1600, 2000 & 2600 cc 4 CYLINDER (Cont.)

### ENGINE OILING

#### ENGINE OILING SYSTEM

Force-feed type system uses a trochoid type pump on 1600 cc WITHOUT silent shaft and gear type pump on all other engines WITH silent shaft (counterbalance). Driven gear of oil pump also drives counterbalance shaft on silent shaft engines.

| Crankcase Capacity (with Filter) | |
|---|---|
| **Application** | **Quantity** |
| 1600 cc engine ............................................. | 4.2 quarts |
| 2000 cc engine ............................................. | 4.5 quarts |
| 2600 cc engine ............................................. | 5.2 quarts |

**Oil Pressure @2000 RPM** — 1600 cc engine — 57-71 psi; 2000 and 2600 cc engine — 49-64 psi.

**Oil Filter** — Full-flow spin-on, throw-away type.

**Fig. 15 Cutaway View of Gear Type Oil Pump**

### OIL PUMP

**1600 cc Without Silent Shaft** — Mounted at lower left of engine, driven by camshaft drive belt. Cover and rotor assembly may be removed after removing drive sprocket by taking out cover bolts and lifting assembly out. May also be removed with engine front case as an assembly.

**1600 cc With Silent Shaft** — Gear type pump mounted at lower left front of engine. To remove, first insert screwdriver in plug hole at bottom left of block to prevent counterbalance from turning, then remove drive sprocket. Remove pump cover and bolt holding driven gear to counterbalance. Pump gears and left counterbalance shaft may be removed along with front case. Inspect and replace worn gears or cover. To install, assure that timing marks on pump are aligned, insert left

counterbalance shaft in driven gear, and temporarily tighten bolt. Install left counterbalance shaft with front case and oil pump as an assembly.

**2000 & 2600 cc** — Pump is mounted at lower right side of engine block, and driven by countershaft drive chain. For removal, see COUNTERBALANCE SHAFTS, 2000 & 2600 cc. To install, reverse removal procedure, assuring that oil pump gear mating marks are aligned and that woodruff key on counterbalance shaft fits in keyway of driven gear.

**CAUTION** — *Prior to installing oil pump (all models), fill with sufficient amount of engine oil to prime pump.*

| Oil Pump Specifications | |
|---|---|
| **Application** | **Clearance In. (mm)** |
| **1600 cc Trochoid Type** | |
| Side Clearance ............................ | .0024-.0047 (.06-.12) |
| Tip Clearance ............................... | .0016-.0047 (.04-.12) |
| Body Clearance ........................... | .0039-.0063 (.10-.16) |
| Drive Shaft-to-Cover Clearance .. | .0008-.0020 (.02-.05) |
| **1600 cc Gear Type** | |
| Gear End Play ............................. | .0024-.0047 (.06-.12) |
| Gear Shaft-to-Pump Cover ......... | .0008-.0019 (.02-.05) |
| Gear Tip-to-Body Clearance .......... | .0039-.0078 (.1-.2) |
| Tip Clearance Between Gears ......... | .0158-.0275 (.4-.7) |
| **2000 & 2600 cc Gear Type** | |
| Gear Tip-to-Body Clearance ... | .0041-.0059 (.105-.150) |
| Gear End Play ............................. | .0024-.0047 (.06-.12) |
| Drive Gear-to-Bearing .............. | .0008-.0018 (.02-.046) |
| Drive Gear-to-Rear Bearing .... | .0017-.0026 (.044-.066) |

**Fig. 16 Mating Marks of Oil Pump Gears**

# Chrysler Corp. Import Engines

## 1600, 2000 & 2600 cc 4 CYLINDER (Cont.)

### ENGINE COOLING

Thermostat — 180°F (82°C)

Radiator Cap — 12.8 psi (87.6 kPa)

| Cooling System Capacity | |
|---|---|
| 1600 cc | 7.7 qts. |
| 2000 cc | 9.5 qts. |
| 2600 cc | 9.7 qts. |

**WATER PUMP**

**1600 cc** — Drain cooling system, remove drive belt, fan and pulley. Assure that number 1 piston is at TDC on compression stroke, then remove camshaft pulley, timing belt covers, timing belt, camshaft sprocket, upper inner cover and timing belt tensioner. Remove 4 mounting bolts and remove water pump. To install, use new mounting gasket and reverse removal procedure.

**2000 & 2600 cc** — Pump may be removed after drive belt, fan and pulley are removed by taking out mounting bolts. To install, use new gasket and reverse removal procedure.

## ENGINE SPECIFICATIONS

### GENERAL SPECIFICATIONS

| Year | Displ. cu. ins. | Displ. cc | Carburetor | HP at RPM | Torque (Ft. Lbs. at RPM) | Compr. Ratio | Bore in. | Bore mm | Stroke in. | Stroke mm |
|---|---|---|---|---|---|---|---|---|---|---|
| 1978 | 97.5 | 1600 | 2-Bbl. | 77@5200 | 87@3000 | 8.5:1 | 3.03 | 77 | 3.39 | 86 |
| | 121.7 | 2000 | 2-Bbl. | 93@5200 | 108@3000 | 8.5:1 | 3.31 | 84 | 3.54 | 90 |
| | 155.9 | 2600 | 2-Bbl. | 105@5000 | 139@2500 | 8.2:1 | 3.59 | 91 | 3.86 | 98 |

### VALVES

| Engine & Valve ① | Head Diam. In. (mm) | Face Angle | Seat Angle | Seat Width In. (mm) | Stem Diameter In. (mm) | Stem Clearance In. (mm) | Valve Lift In. (mm) |
|---|---|---|---|---|---|---|---|
| 1600 cc Intake | 1.50 (38.1) | 45° | 45° | .035-.051 (.9-1.3) | .315 (8.0) | .001-.0022 (.025-.055) | ..... |
| Exhaust | 1.22 (31.0) | 45° | 45° | .035-.051 (.9-1.3) | .315 (8.0) | .002-.0033 (.05-.085) | ..... |
| 2000 & 2600 cc Intake | 1.65 (41.9) | 45° | 45° | .035-.051 (.9-1.3) | .315 (8.0) | .001-.0023 (.025-.058) | ..... |
| Exhaust | 1.34 (34.0) | 45° | 45° | .035-.051 (.9-1.3) | .315 (8.0) | .002-.0035 (.05-.088) | ..... |

① — Jet valve and body not individually serviceable. Replace as an assembly when defective.

### PISTONS, PINS, RINGS

| Engine | PISTONS Clearance In. (mm) | PINS Piston Fit In. (mm) | PINS Rod Fit In. (mm) | Rings | End Gap In. (mm) | Side Clearance In. (mm) |
|---|---|---|---|---|---|---|
| 1600 cc | .0008-.0016 (.02-.04) | ① | Press Fit | No. 1 | .008-.016 (.2-.4) | .0012-.0028 (.03-.07) |
| | | | | No. 2 | .008-.020 (.2-.4) | .0008-.0024 (.02-.06) |
| | | | | Oil | .008-.020 (.2-.4) | ..... |
| 2000 & 2600 cc | .0008-.0016 (.02-.04) | ① | Press Fit | No. 1 | .0098-.0177 (.25-.45) | .0024-.0039 (.06-.10) |
| | | | | No. 2 | .0078-.0359 (.2-.9) | .0008-.0024 (.02-.06) |
| | | | | Oil | .0078-.0359 (.2-.9) | ..... |

① — Thumb press fit without rod installed

## 1600, 2000 & 2600 cc 4 CYLINDER (Cont.)
### ENGINE SPECIFICATIONS (Cont.)

### CRANKSHAFT MAIN & CONNECTING ROD BEARINGS

| | MAIN BEARINGS | | | | CONNECTING ROD BEARINGS | | |
|---|---|---|---|---|---|---|---|
| Engine | Journal Diam. In. (mm) | Clearance In. (mm) | Thrust Bearing | Crankshaft End Play In. (mm) | Journal Diam. In. (mm) | Clearance In. (mm) | Side Play In. (mm) |
| 1600 cc | 2.244 (57) | .0008-.0028 (.02-.07) | No. 3 | .002-.007 (.05-.18) | 1.772 (45) | .0004-.0024 (.01-.06) | .004-.01 (.1-.25) |
| 2000 & 2600 cc | 2.598 (66) | .0008-.0028 (.02-.07) | No. 3 | .002-.007 (.05-.18) | 2.087 (53) | .0008-.0028 (.02-.06) | .004-.01 (.1-.25) |

### CAMSHAFT

| Engine | Cam Lobe Height In. (mm)① | Clearance In. (mm) | Lobe Lift In. (mm) |
|---|---|---|---|
| 1600 cc | | .002-.004 (.05-.09) | .359 (9.2) |
| Intake | 1.4316 (36.36) | | |
| Exhaust | 1.4397 (36.41) | | |
| 2000 & 2600 cc | | .002-.004 (.05-.09) | .393 (10.0) |
| Intake | 1.660 (42.18) | | |
| Exhaust | 1.663 (42.24) | | |

① — Maximum wear limit .020" (.5 mm).

### VALVE SPRINGS

| Engine | Free Length In. (mm)① | PRESSURE Lbs. @ In. (kg @ mm) | |
|---|---|---|---|
| | | Valve Closed | Valve Open |
| 1600 cc | 1.823 (46.3) | 61.7@1.469 (27.9@37.3) | ..... |
| 2000 & 2600 cc | 1.869 (47.5) | 61@1.59 (27.6@40.4) | ..... |

① — Jet Valve Spring (All models) — 1.165" (29.6 mm).

### TIGHTENING SPECIFICATIONS

| Application | Ft. Lbs. (mkg) |
|---|---|
| **Camshaft Bearing Cap** | |
| 1600 cc | 14-15 (19-20.5) |
| 2000 & 2600 cc | 13-14 (18-19) |
| **Camshaft Sprocket** | |
| 1600 cc | 44-58 (59-78) |
| 2000 & 2600 cc | 37-43 (49-58) |
| **Cylinder Head Bolts (Cold)** | |
| 1600 cc | 51-54 (69-73) |
| 2000 & 2600 cc | 65-72 (89-98) |
| **Main Bearing Caps** | |
| 1600 cc | 37-39 (50-53) |
| 2000 & 2600 cc | 55-61 (74-83) |
| **Connecting Rod Caps** | |
| 1600 cc | 24-25 (32-34) |
| 2000 & 2600 cc | 33-34 (45-47) |
| **Crank Pulley** | |
| 1600 cc | 8-9 (10-12) |
| 2000 & 2600 cc | 80-94 (108-127) |
| **Crankshaft Sprocket Bolt** | |
| 1600 cc only | 44-50 (59-68) |
| Flywheel-to-Crankshaft | 94-101 (128-137) |
| Drive Plate (A/T) to Crankshaft | 84-90 (113-122) |
| **Oil Pump/Cover** | |
| 1600 cc | 11-13 (15-17) |
| 2000 & 2600 cc | 6-7 (8-9) |
| Jet Valve | 13-15 (18-21) |

# Courier Engines

## 1800 cc 4 CYLINDER

### ENGINE CODING

#### ENGINE IDENTIFICATION

Vehicle engine information is stamped on a plate riveted to body at right rear of engine compartment.

| Application | Engine Code |
|---|---|
| All Models ................................................. | VB |

### ENGINE, CYLINDER HEAD & MANIFOLDS

#### ENGINE

1) Remove hood and drain cooling system. Remove air cleaner assembly. Disconnect upper radiator hose at engine and lower hose at radiator. Unbolt and remove radiator.

2) Disconnect accelerator linkage and fuel line at carburetor. Disconnect linkage from intake manifold, cable at air by-pass valve, choke cable, battery cables, coil wires at distributor and coil lead wires.

3) Remove fan, loosen alternator retaining bolts and remove alternator belt. If equipped with Thermactor (air pump), remove mounting bolts and pump drive belt. Remove alternator bracket and adjusting arm bolts and position alternator out of the way. Pull Thermactor hoses off pump, remove bracket and position pump aside. Disconnect heater hoses from intake manifold and Thermactor air hose from by-pass valve.

4) Disconnect lead wire and boot from oil pressure sending unit, battery cable from block and wires from starter solenoid. Raise vehicle and drain oil. Remove splash shield and separate exhaust pipe from manifold. Remove clutch housing and bottom starter bolts.

5) Lower vehicle, remove upper starter bolts and withdraw starter. Place a floor stand under transmission. Connect a lifting sling to engine hanger brackets. Disconnect engine mounts and pull engine forward until clear of transmission shaft. Lift engine from vehicle. To install, reverse removal procedures.

#### INTAKE MANIFOLD

**Removal** — 1) Disconnect and drain cooling system. Remove air cleaner assembly and accelerator linkage. Disconnect choke cable and fuel line at carburetor. Index mark and disconnect vacuum lines and any addition electrical wires at intake manifold.

2) Disconnect Thermactor hoses (if equipped), crankcase ventilation hose, heater return hose and by-pass hose. Remove attaching nuts and lift manifold, with carburetor, off studs.

**Installation** — To install, reverse removal procedure while noting the following: Clean all gasket surfaces and install a new gasket. Install intake manifold and tighten attaching bolts working from the center of manifold towards each end. Fill cooling system when all components are installed.

#### EXHAUST MANIFOLD

**Removal** — 1) Remove hot air ducting. Remove spark plug wires. Remove air injection from exhaust manifold. Remove upper and lower heat insulators.

2) Disconnect EGR line. Raise vehicle. Remove exhaust pipe hanger from bracket on transmission. Disconnect exhaust pipe at manifold. Remove manifold nuts and manifold.

**Installation** — To install, reverse removal procedure using new gaskets and applying a light coat of graphite grease on exhaust manifold mating surfaces.

#### CYLINDER HEAD

**Removal** — 1) Drain cooling system. Remove air cleaner assembly. Remove exhaust manifold. Disconnect throttle and choke. Disconnect fuel lines.

2) From cylinder head, disconnect the following:
- Carburetor solenoid.
- Heater hoses.
- By-pass hose.
- Thermac air hoses.
- Vacuum lines.
- EGR valve.

3) Remove water pump. Disconnect lead wire and vacuum line from distributor. Rotate crankshaft until No. 1 piston is TDC.

4) Remove valve cover. Remove distributor with plug wires. Remove timing chain tensioner cover (Fig. 6) and release chain tension. Refer to Timing Chain Tension in this article.

5) Remove nut, washer and distributor gear from crankshaft. Remove nut and washer from camshaft sprocket. Remove lower front head bolt located below camshaft sprocket on boss.

6) Remove cylinder head bolts. Remove rocker arm assembly. Separate camshaft and sprocket. Place camshaft sprocket and chain on top of chain guide strip and vibration damper. Make sure sprocket and chain are not moved. Remove cylinder head.

**NOTE** — After removing cylinder head, release all tension from timing chain.

**Installation** — To install, reverse removal procedure while noting the following: Clean all gasket surfaces and use new gaskets upon installation. Install cylinder head and tighten bolts to specifications in sequence as shown in illustration.

← FRONT

*Fig. 1  Cylinder Head Tightening Sequence*

## 1800 cc 4 CYLINDER (Cont.)

## VALVES

### VALVE ARRANGEMENT

**Intake** — Left side.
**Exhaust** — Right side.

### VALVE GUIDE SERVICING

Check guides for wear or damage, replace as necessary. With valves removed, using suitable tool (T72J-6510), drive valve guides out top of cylinder head. Install new guides, making sure exhaust and intake guides are in proper locations. Drive guide in until ring around guide touches head.

### VALVE STEM OIL SEALS

With valves and springs removed, pull oil seals off valve guides using suitable tools (T72J-6571 and T59L-100-B). Install new seals on valve guides with large diameter hole facing cylinder head.

### VALVE SPRINGS

**Removal** — With cylinder head removed from engine proceed as follows: Compress valve springs and remove retainer locks. Release springs and remove spring retainers, springs, and valves. **NOTE** — *Identify all valve components for installation into original positions. Exhaust and intake retainers must be installed in original position to prevent premature valve failure.*

**Inspection** — Check valve spring pressure at specified height, replace if not within specifications. Measure free length of spring, if not within 3% of specified value, replace spring. Using a square, check that springs are not more than $\frac{1}{16}$" out-of-square.

**Installation** — Lubricate valves, valve stems and valve guide with engine oil. Apply Lubriplate to valve tips. Install new valve oil seals on valve guides and install valves in guide from which it was removed. Install valve springs and retainer. Compress springs and install retainer locks. Release springs and install cylinder head.

### ROCKER ARM ASSEMBLY

1) Remove front bearing cap from rocker shafts. Slide rocker arms, springs, supports and bearing caps (with oil pipe) off both shafts, keeping parts in order for reassembly.

2) Remove oil pipe from bearing caps. Remove camshaft thrust plate from front bearing cap, if necessary. Prior to reassembly, lubricate arms and shafts with heavy (MS) motor oil. When installing shafts in intake side, ensure ends with longer length between oil hole and tip are turned inward, toward each other. Make sure "O" ring on oil pipe is centered in middle bearing cap passage.

### VALVE CLEARANCE ADJUSTMENT

1) With engine at normal operating temperature, rotate crankshaft until number one piston is at TDC of compression stroke. Check clearance with feeler gauge at either camshaft or valve.

2) Clearance must be .012" (.305 mm). If not within specifications, loosen adjusting screw lock nut and turn adjusting screw with feeler gauge in place. Hold screw in position and tighten lock nut. Adjust valves in firing order sequence; 1-3-4-2.

**Fig. 2   Exploded View of Rocker Arm & Shaft Assembly**

## PISTONS, PINS & RINGS

### OIL PAN

**Removal** — Raise vehicle on hoist and remove front splash shield. Drain crankcase, remove clutch release cylinder attaching nuts and position cylinder to one side. Remove the engine rear brace attaching bolts and loosen bolts on left side. Remove oil pan attaching nuts and bolts, and lower oil pan onto crossmember. Remove oil pump pick-up tube. Remove oil pan from vehicle.

**Installation** — To install, reverse removal procedure while noting the following: Clean all gasket surfaces and use new

## 1800 cc 4 CYLINDER (Cont.)

gaskets upon installation. Ensure that oil pump pick-up tube and screen are clean before installing.

### PISTON & ROD ASSEMBLY

**Removal** — **1)** With cylinder head and oil pan removed, remove oil pump. Rotate crankshaft until piston to be removed is at bottom of travel. Place a cloth on piston to collect cuttings, then using a ridge reamer, remove any ridge or deposits from upper end of cylinder. NOTE — *Do not cut into ring travel area in excess of 1/32".*

Fig. 3   *Piston & Rod Assembly Installation Features*

**2)** Make sure connecting rod caps are marked so they may be replaced in their original positions, then remove rod caps. Push piston and rod assembly out top of cylinder. Take care not to damage bearing journal.

**Installation** — Oil piston rings, pistons and cylinder walls with engine oil. With rings properly spaced, install ring compressor onto piston. Install piston and rod assembly into its original bore. Make sure connecting rod marks are facing left side of engine and "F" mark on piston is facing forward (see illustration). Install rod caps and tighten rod bolts.

### FITTING PISTONS

**1)** Determine piston-to-cylinder bore clearance. Check cylinder for out-of-round or taper. Fit new pistons if necessary. Pistons are available in .010", .020", .030" and .040" oversizes.

**2)** Place rings in cylinder near bottom of bore and measure end gaps. Place rings on piston and measure side clearance. If high steps have developed on lower back side of ring lands replace piston.

**3)** Place rings on piston with end gaps 120° apart so that no gap is located on thrust face or piston pin bore. Using suitable ring compressor, install piston in proper bore with "F" marking facing forward.

### PISTON PINS

Piston pins are removed using an arbor press, pilots and driver. Measure pin and connecting rod diameters to ensure proper fit.

Fig. 4   *Measuring Piston Ring Gap*

## CRANKSHAFT MAIN & CONNECTING ROD BEARINGS

### MAIN & CONNECTING ROD BEARINGS

**1)** Inspect each bearing for scored, chipped or worn surface and replace if condition exists. If copper base is visible through bearing overlay, replacement is not necessary, if within specifications.

**2)** When installing new bearings, fit bearings to minimum specified clearance. Use Plastigage method to determine bearing clearances. Inserts are available in .010", .020" and .030" undersizes.

### THRUST BEARING ALIGNMENT

Push crankshaft to one side to take up end play. Insert a feeler gauge between thrust washers and crankshaft. Replace thrust washers if measurement is not within specifications. Install new thrust washers with oil groove facing crankshaft thrust side.

### REAR MAIN BEARING OIL SEAL

NOTE — *If rear main bearing seal replacement is only operation being performed, it can be done in vehicle; however if it is being replaced in conjunction with rear main bearing, engine must be removed.*

Remove transmission and clutch assembly. Using an awl, punch two holes in seal and install sheet metal screws. Using a pair of levers, pry out old seal. Press in new seal, reinstall clutch and transmission.

### ENGINE FRONT COVER

**Removal** — **1)** Remove hood and drain cooling system. Disconnect upper radiator hose at engine and lower hose at radiator. Remove radiator, drive belts, crankshaft pulley, and water pump. Remove cylinder head to front cover bolt. Raise vehicle and remove front splash shield.

**2)** Disconnect emission line from oil pan. Remove oil pan. Lower vehicle, remove alternator bracket to block bolts and position alternator to one side. Remove thermactor pump to block bolts and position to one side. Remove steel tube bolts and tube from front of engine. Remove attaching bolts for front cover and remove front cover.

## 1800 cc 4 CYLINDER (Cont.)

**Installation** — To install engine front cover, reverse removal procedure.

### FRONT COVER OIL SEAL

Drain cooling system, disconnect radiator hoses and remove radiator. Loosen alternator and Thermactor attaching bolts (if equipped). Remove drive belts. Remove crankshaft pulley, then pull seal from shaft, using suitable tool (T72J-6700). Install new seal using suitable tool (T72J-6700-A). Reverse removal procedures for remaining components.

### TIMING CHAIN

**Removal** — 1) Remove cylinder head and front cover. Remove oil pump gear attaching nut, oil pump-to-block attaching bolts and loosen gear on the pump. Remove oil pump, gear and oil pump chain.

2) Remove timing chain tensioner and loosen timing chain guide strip screws. Remove oil slinger. Remove outer gear (for oil pump chain) from crankshaft. Remove timing chain and crankshaft gear.

**Installation** — 1) Position crankshaft inner sprocket into timing chain, then install sprocket and chain onto crankshaft. Install oil pump with gear onto cylinder block. Install oil pump chain and outer sprocket to crankshaft while positioning chain onto oil pump gear. Install timing chain tensioner. See *Timing Chain Tensioner*. Do not release snubber spring tension. Install cylinder head and camshaft to cylinder block.

**NOTE** — *Do not install rocker arm assembly at this time.*

2) Obtain correct timing chain alignment referring to *Timing Chain Alignment* illustration and using the following procedure: Rotate crankshaft to TDC of compression stroke on number one cylinder. This will place crankshaft with keyway facing straight up. Position camshaft with keyway facing straight up. Timing chain must now be positioned on camshaft sprocket so single plated link is aligned with timing mark on right-hand side of camshaft sprocket at rocker arm cover joint face, while facing engine. The two plate links on timing chain must straddle timing mark on BDC of crankshaft sprocket.

3) Install rocker arm shaft assembly, cylinder head bolts, and tighten all bolts to specifications. Adjust timing chain tension. See *Timing Chain Tension*. Release tensioner snubber and install front cover. Install remaining components in reverse of removal procedure and adjust valve clearance.

### TIMING CHAIN TENSION

1) Remove crankshaft pulley and water pump. Remove cover from tensioner. Rotate crankshaft slightly in direction of engine rotation. Lift release on tensioner and compress snubber spring fully. Install wedge in tensioner so it will not release.

2) Remove two access plugs and aluminum washers from holes in timing chain cover and side of head. Loosen guide strip attaching screws. Press top of strip with lever inserted through access hole in head.

3) Tighten guide strip attaching screws with screwdriver inserted through hole in cover. Remove wedge from tensioner, allowing snubber to take up chain slack.

*Fig. 5   Timing Chain & Sprocket Alignment*

4) Install access plugs and aluminum washers to their respective holes. Replace chain tensioner cover and gasket. Install water pump and crankshaft pulley. Tighten bolts and adjust belt tension.

*Fig. 6   Adjusting Timing Chain Tension*

## 1800 cc 4 CYLINDER (Cont.)

### OIL PUMP CHAIN

Check oil pump chain for excessive deflection as shown in illustration. If deflection is more than .157" (3.97 mm), install adjusting shims between cylinder block and oil pump body.

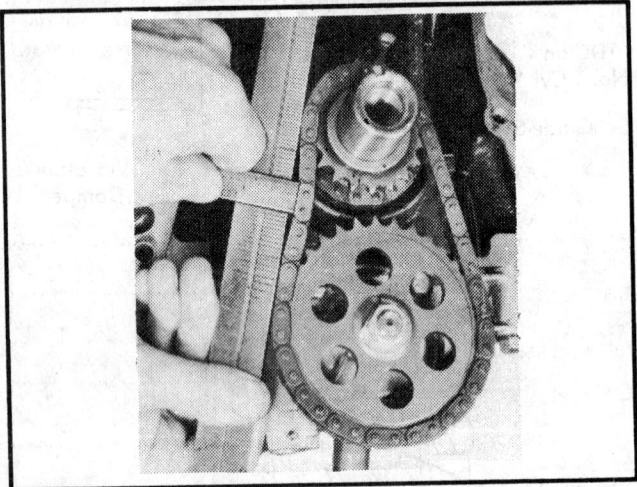

*Fig. 7   Measuring Oil Pump Chain Deflection*

## CAMSHAFT

### CAMSHAFT

**Removal** — 1) Remove hood and water pump. Disconnect vacuum line and lead wire from distributor. Rotate crankshaft to position number one cylinder on TDC of compression stroke. Remove plug wires and distributor cap as an assembly, then remove distributor from engine. Remove rocker arm cover.

2) Remove crankshaft pulley, then remove cover from timing chain tensioner. Lift release on tensioner and compress snubber spring fully. Wedge a screwdriver in the tensioner to keep spring compressed. Remove cylinder head bolts and rocker arm assembly.

3) Remove nut, washer, and distributor gear from camshaft. Remove camshaft gear attaching nut and washer. Carefully remove camshaft from gear and engine block. **NOTE** — *Do not remove camshaft gear from timing chain and ensure that gear teeth-to-chain relationship is not disturbed.*

**Installation** — To install, reverse removal procedure while noting the following: When installing camshaft to gear take care not to disturb gear-to-chain relationship. Adjust timing chain tension. Check camshaft end play. Adjust valve clearance.

### CAMSHAFT BEARINGS

Remove camshaft and inspect bearings for wear or damage. Use Plastigage method to determine clearance. Replace bearings which do not meet specifications.

### CAMSHAFT END THRUST

Check camshaft end play with a feeler gauge inserted between thrust plate and camshaft flange. End play should be checked at time of overhaul, before gear and sprocket are replaced.

### CAM LOBE LIFT

Remove rocker arm cover. Measure distance between major and minor diameters (see illustration) of each lobe with a Vernier caliper. Difference between diameters of each cam is lobe lift. If lobe lift loss exceeds .008" (.20 mm), replace camshaft. Check lift of each lobe in consecutive order and note each reading.

*Fig. 8   Measuring Camshaft Base Circle and Lobe Lift*

### VALVE TIMING

Rotate crankshaft and camshaft until keyways are straight up. Place timing chain on camshaft sprocket so single plated link is aligned with timing mark on right-hand side of camshaft sprocket at rocker arm cover joint face, while facing engine. The two plate links on timing chain must straddle timing mark on BDC of crankshaft sprocket. Crankshaft in this position will be TDC of number one cylinder.

## ENGINE OILING

**Crankcase Capacity** — 4 qts. (Add 1 qt. with filter change).
**Oil Filter** — Disposable type.
**Oil Pressure** — 50-64 psi @ 3000 RPM; 4.25 psi @ idle.

### ENGINE OIL SYSTEM

Rotor type oil pump is chain driven by crankshaft. Timing chain is lubricated by oil jet in cylinder block and oil holes in slipper head of adjuster. Oil holes in large end of connecting rods align with oil holes in crankshaft to lubricate pistons and components.

### OIL PUMP

1) Remove oil inlet tube from pump. Remove and discard gaskets. Remove cover, withdraw inner rotor and shaft assembly. Remove outer race. Remove cotter pin from body, pull cap out of chamber, and take out spring and plunger.

2) Assemble in reverse order. Rotor, shaft and outer race are serviced as an assembly. If one component is damaged, replace all three. Install new cotter pin and gasket. Prime pump with oil before installing unit in block.

| Oil Pump Specifications | |
|---|---|
| **Application** | **Clearance In. (mm)** |
| Lobe-to-Lobe | .002-.006 (.051-.152) |
| Rotor End Clearance | .002-.004 (.051-.102) |
| Outer Rotor-to-Housing | .006-.010 (.152-.254) |

# Courier Engines

## 1800 cc 4 CYLINDER (Cont.)

### ENGINE COOLING

Thermostat — Begins to open at 180°F; fully open 203°F.

Cooling System Capacity — 7½ qts. (includes heater).

Radiator Cap — 13 psi.

### WATER PUMP

Remove hood and drain cooling system. Remove lower hose from water pump, disconnect upper radiator hose at engine and lower hose at radiator. Remove radiator from vehicle. Loosen alternator and Thermactor pump (if equipped). Remove drive belt(s), fan, and pulley. Remove crankshaft pulley. Remove water pump. To install, reverse removal procedure.

## ENGINE SPECIFICATIONS

### GENERAL SPECIFICATIONS

| Year | Displ. | | Carburetor | HP at RPM | Torque (Ft. Lbs. at RPM) | Compr. Ratio | Bore | | Stroke | |
| | cu. ins. | cc | | | | | in. | mm | in. | mm |
|---|---|---|---|---|---|---|---|---|---|---|
| 1978 | 109.6 | 1796 | 2-Bbl. | ....... | ....... | 8.6-1 | 3.07 | 78 | 3.70 | 94 |

### VALVES

| Engine & Valve | Head Diam. In. (mm) | Face Angle | Seat Angle | Seat Width In. (mm) | Stem Diameter In. (mm) | Stem Clearance In. (mm) | Valve Lift In. (mm) |
|---|---|---|---|---|---|---|---|
| 1796 cc Int. | 1.6496-1.6575 (41.90-42.10) | 45° | 45° | .055 (1.397) | .3161-.3167 (8.029-8.044) | .0007-.0021 (.017-.053) | ..... |
| Exh. | 1.2953-1.3031 (32.90-33.09) | 45° | 45° | .055 (1.397) | .3159-.3167 (8.024-8.044) | .0007-.0023 (.017-.058) | ..... |

### VALVE SPRINGS

| Engine | Free Length In. (mm) | PRESSURE Lbs. @ In. (kg @ mm) | |
| | | Valve Closed | Valve Open |
|---|---|---|---|
| 1796 cc Inner | 1.438 (36.52) | 20.9@1.260 (9.5@32) | ..... |
| Outer | 1.469 (37.31) | 31.4@1.339 14.2@34 | ..... |

### VALVE TIMING

| Engine | INTAKE | | EXHAUST | |
| | Open (BTDC) | Close (ALDC) | Open (BLDC) | Close (ATDC) |
|---|---|---|---|---|
| 1796 cc | 18° | 49° | 62° | 5° |

### PISTONS, PINS, RINGS

| Engine | PISTONS | PINS | | RINGS | | |
| | Clearance In. (mm) | Piston Fit In. (mm) | Rod Fit In. (mm) | Rings | End Gap In. (mm) | Side Clearance In. (mm) |
|---|---|---|---|---|---|---|
| 1796 cc | .0022-.0028 (.056-.071) | .0002-.0006 (.005-.015) | .0004-.0012 (.010-.030) | 1 | .008-.016 (.203-.406) | .0014-.0028 (.036-.071) |
| | | | | 2 | .008-.016 (.203-.406) | .0012-.0025 (.030-.064) |
| | | | | Oil | .012-.035 (.304-.889) | ..... |

# Courier Engines

## 1800 cc 4 CYLINDER (Cont.)
### ENGINE SPECIFICATIONS (Cont.)

### CRANKSHAFT MAIN & CONNECTING ROD BEARINGS

| Engine | MAIN BEARINGS | | | | CONNECTING ROD BEARINGS | | |
| --- | --- | --- | --- | --- | --- | --- | --- |
| | Journal Diam. In. (mm) | Clearance In. (mm) | Thrust Bearing | Crankshaft End Play In. (mm) | Journal Diam. In. (mm) | Clearance In. (mm) | Side Play In. (mm) |
| 1796 cc | 2.4779-2.4785 (62.93-62.95) | ① .0005-.0015 (.013-.038) ② .0012-.0024 (.030-.061) | 5 | .003-.01 (.076-.254) | 2.0842-2.0848 (52.938-52.954) | ① .001-.0011 (.025-.028) ② .001-.003 (.025-.076) | .004-.008 (.102-.203) |

① — Desired.
② — Allowable.

### CAMSHAFT

| Engine | Journal Diam. In. (mm) | Clearance In. (mm) ① | Lobe Lift In. (mm) |
| --- | --- | --- | --- |
| 1796 cc Front | 1.7695-1.7701 (44.945-44.960) | .0007-.0027 (.018-.069) | ② |
| Center | 1.7691-1.7697 (44.935-44.950) | .0011-.0031 (.028-.079) | ② |
| Rear | 1.7695-1.7701 (44.945-44.960) | .0007-.0027 (.018-.069) | ② |

① — End play is .001-.007" (.025-.178 mm).
② — See Cam Lobe Lift procedure.

### TIGHTENING SPECIFICATIONS

| Application | Ft. Lbs.(mkg) |
| --- | --- |
| Main Bearing Caps | 60-65(8.3-9.0) |
| Connecting Rod Caps | 30-33(4.1-4.6) |
| Cylinder Head | |
|   Cold | 63-68(8.7-9.4) |
|   Hot | 69-73(9.5-10.1) |
| Oil Pan | 5-9(.7-1.2) |
| Flywheel | 112-118(15.5-16.3) |
| Distributor Drive Gear | 57(7.9) |
| Oil Pump-to-Block | 13-20(1.8-2.8) |
| Camshaft Sprocket | 51-64(7.1-8.8) |
| Rocker Arm Cover | 1-2(.1-.3) |
| Oil Pump Sprocket | 22-26(3.0-3.6) |
| Intake Manifold | 14-19(1.9-2.6) |
| Exhaust Manifold | 16-21(2.2-2.9) |

## B210 & F10 4 CYLINDER

### ENGINE CODING

#### ENGINE IDENTIFICATION

Engine serial and code number is stamped on right rear side of cylinder block, below mating surface of cylinder head and cylinder block. First three digits are engine code.

| Application | Code |
| --- | --- |
| 1397 cc | A14 |

### ENGINE, CYLINDER HEAD & MANIFOLDS

#### ENGINE

**NOTE** — *Manufacturer recommends that engine and transmission be removed as an assembly.*

**Removal (B210)** — **1)** Disconnect battery ground and fusible links. Mark hood location and remove hood. Remove engine protective undercover. Drain coolant and engine oil.

**2)** Remove radiator. Disconnect electrical wires and other lines attached to air cleaner, then remove air cleaner assembly. Disconnect accelerator cable from carburetor. Disconnect the following components:
- Automatic choke wire.
- Throttle solenoid or throttle switch.
- Fuel cut solenoid.
- Vacuum switching valve.
- Coil and distributor.
- Starter.
- Thermal transmitter.
- Alternator and oil pressure switch.
- Engine ground and coil at engine wiring harness.
- Fuel pump and necessary emission control hoses.

**3)** On models equipped with air conditioning, loosen system and lay out of way without disconnecting any hoses. Disconnect speedometer cable. Remove shift linkage. Disconnect exhaust at manifold. Index and remove propeller shaft.

**4)** Support transmission with jack. Remove crossmember mounting bolts. Attach hoist to engine and take up weight. Remove front engine mounts. Remove engine and transmission as one unit.

**Installation** — To install, reverse removal procedure.

**Removal (F10)** — **1)** Remove hood. Remove battery. Drain coolant. Disconnect necessary components from air cleaner and remove air cleaner assembly. Disconnect accelerator cable.

**2)** Disconnect following components so they are free when engine and transmission assembly is lifted out:
- Coil and distributor wires.
- Coil wires at block connector.
- Fusible links.
- Engine wiring harness.
- Fuel pump.
- Radiator and heater hoses.
- Master-Vac vacuum line.
- Air pump and carbon canister.

**3)** Remove carbon canister, auxiliary fan and washer tank. Remove radiator together with auxiliary fan motor. Remove

slave cylinder. Remove left and right damper rods. Disconnect speedometer cable.

**4)** On models equipped with air conditioning, loosen air conditioning equipment and lay components out of way. Do not discharge system. Disconnect shift linkage. Attach hoist to engine.

**5)** Disconnect exhaust system at manifold, rear engine mount and "U" clamp. Disconnect both axle drive shafts at transaxle case. Lower out shift linkage. Disconnect engine mounts and lift out engine.

**Installation** — Make sure there is .39-.47" (10-12 mm) between lower edge of clutch housing and sub-frame. If clearance is less than .28" (7 mm), add shims at each engine mount. Place shims between mount and sub-frame. Adjust right damper rod to 8.2-8.3" C209-211 mm) and left rod to 5.4-5.5" (137-139 mm).

#### INTAKE & EXHAUST MANIFOLDS

**Removal & Installation** — **1)** Remove air cleaner and disconnect accelerator cable and choke cable. Disconnect and plug fuel line at carburetor. Disconnect exhaust pipe at exhaust manifold.

**2)** Remove nuts retaining intake and exhaust manifold to cylinder head and remove intake and exhaust manifold as an assembly. Remove gasket and thoroughly clean mating surfaces. Remove bolts and separate intake and exhaust manifold. To install, reverse removal procedure and use new gasket. Tighten nuts and bolts to specifications.

#### CYLINDER HEAD

**Removal** — Remove any components necessary to take off manifold. Remove manifold. Remove rocker arm cover, rocker arm assembly, and push rods. Remove cylinder head retaining bolts and remove cylinder head.

**Installation** — Thoroughly clean mating surfaces. Use new gasket with no sealer and install cylinder head. Install cylinder head retaining bolts. **NOTE** — *One cylinder head bolt is smaller diameter and has a hollow head. Install this bolt on right side center of cylinder head.* Tighten cylinder head bolts in two or three steps to specifications in sequence as shown in illustration. Reverse removal procedure to install remaining components. Adjust valve clearance.

*Fig. 1  Tightening Sequence for Cylinder Head*

### VALVES

#### VALVE ARRANGEMENT

E-I-I-E-E-I-I-E (front to rear).

# Datsun Engines

## B210 & F10 4 CYLINDER (Cont.)

### VALVE GUIDE SERVICING

Check valve stem-to-guide clearance. If clearance is more than .0039" (.1 mm) and valve stem is not worn, valve guide must be replaced. Replace valve guide using the following procedure.

*Fig. 2   Installation of Valve Guides*

1) Using suitable tool (ST11320000), remove guide from cylinder head. Ream guide hole in cylinder head to .4803-.4807" (12.19-12.21 mm) to install replacement guide.

2) Heat cylinder head to approximately 302-392°F (150-200°C). Install guide using same driver as used for removal. Ream valve stem bore in guide to .3150-.3156" (8.00-8.015 mm) using a suitable reamer (ST110320000). Reface valve seat surface.

### VALVE STEM OIL SEALS

An oil seal is installed on all valve stems inside valve spring. Install seal with large end over valve guide.

*Fig. 3   Disassembled View of Valve Assemblies*

*Fig. 4   Removing the Valve Spring*

### VALVE SPRINGS

**Removal** — With cylinder head removed, compress valve spring using a suitable valve spring compressor (ST12070000) and remove valve keepers. Release spring compressor and remove spring retainer and spring.

**Installation** — Install valve spring with white painted end toward cylinder head. Install valve spring retainer. Compress valve spring using removal tool and install valve keepers. **NOTE** — *Make sure valve is properly seated on spring seat.*

### VALVE SPRING INSTALLED HEIGHT

Valve spring must be square within 1/16". Valve spring installed height is 1.52" (38.7 mm). Check valve spring by applying specified load and measuring spring height. If spring height and pressure, or squareness does not meet specifications, replace spring.

### ROCKER ARM ASSEMBLY

1) Remove valve cover and remove bolts securing rocker arm assembly to cylinder head. Remove rocker arm assembly.

2) Slide off support stands, rocker arms and springs. Thoroughly clean and inspect all components for signs of wear or seizure. Measure rocker arm-to-shaft clearance. Standard clearance is .0008-.0021" (.020-.054 mm). Replace as necessary.

*Fig. 5   Rocker Arm Assembly Components*

3) If valve contact surface of rocker arm is worn, resurface using a suitable grinder.

4) Reverse disassembly and removal procedures to assemble and install rocker arm assembly. Tighten bolts to specifications and adjust valve clearance.

### VALVE CLEARANCE

Run engine until normal operating temperature is reached. Shut down engine. Rotate crankshaft until No. 1 cylinder is TDC, compression stroke. Adjust:
- No. 1 Exhaust and Intake.
- No. 2 Intake.
- No. 3 Exhaust.

Rotate engine through 1 full turn, then adjust remaining valves.
- No. 2 Exhaust.
- No. 3 Intake.
- No. 4 Intake and Exhuast.

All valves must be set at .014" (.35 mm) hot or .010" (.25 mm) cold. The cold setting should be considered a preliminary adjustment.

## B210 & F10 4 CYLINDER (Cont.)

### PISTONS, PINS & RINGS

#### PISTON & ROD ASSEMBLY

1) Remove cylinder head and oil pan. Remove nuts from connecting rod and remove connecting rod cap with bearing half. Push piston and connecting rod assembly with bearing half up and out through top of crankcase.

2) To install piston and connecting rod assembly, thoroughly oil rings, piston and cylinder wall. Make sure ring gaps are situated approximately 180° apart and not on thrust side of piston. Make sure bearing halves are properly seated in connecting rod and cap.

3) Install a ring compressor and compress rings. Install piston in cylinder with number on top of piston toward front of engine. With piston installed in cylinder, and connecting rod and bearings seated against crankshaft journal, install rod cap with numbers on the same side as connecting rod. Tighten nuts to specification.

4) Install cylinder head and oil pan as previously outlined.

**Fig. 6   Position of Pistons After Being Installed in Block.**

### FITTING PISTONS

1) Check piston-to-cylinder clearance with a feeler gauge and spring tension gauge. With a .0016" (.04 mm) feeler gauge installed between piston and cylinder wall, a force of 1.1-3.3 lbs. (.5-1.5 kg) measured on spring tension gauge, should be needed to extract feeler gauge.

**Fig. 7   Position of Piston Rings in Relation to Piston Fitted Direction and Thrust Direction**

2) Measure piston diameter at top of skirt 90° to piston pin axis. Measure cylinder bore halfway down cylinder and 90° to crankshaft center line. Pistons and rings are available in standard and two oversizes.

#### Piston Specifications

| Application In.(mm) | Piston Size In.(mm) |
| --- | --- |
| Std. | 2.9908-2.9927(75.967-756.017) |
| .020(.50) O/S | 3.0105-3.0124(76.467-76.517) |
| .040(1.0) O/S | 3.0301-3.0321(76.967-77.017) |

### PISTON PIN REPLACEMENT

1) Remove piston and connecting rod assembly as previously outlined. Piston pin is press fit in connecting rod and is removed using a press and suitable pin press stand (ST13040000).

2) Check piston-to-pin clearance. If clearance is not within specifications, replace both piston and piston pin. Piston pin should push fit through piston by hand with both piston and pin at room temperature.

3) Piston pin should be press fit into connecting rod. If interference fit is not within specifications, replace connecting rod or piston pin as necessary. If connecting rod is replaced, insure that new rod is within .176 ounces (5 grams) of defective connecting rod.

4) To assemble piston and connecting rod assembly, use same mandral and driver used for disassembly. Thoroughly oil pin, piston and connecting rod. Install piston on connecting rod so that number on top of piston is pointing toward front of engine and oil squirt hole on connecting rod is toward right side of crankcase.

**Fig. 8   Removing and Installing Piston Pin**

### CRANKSHAFT MAIN & CONNECTING ROD BEARINGS

#### MAIN & CONNECTING ROD BEARINGS

**Removal** — With engine removed from vehicle, remove cylinder head, oil pan, and piston and connecting rod assemblies. Remove alternator and engine mounting bracket from left side. Remove water pump, crankshaft pulley, and timing chain cover. Remove oil thrower and chain tensioner.

## B210 & F10 4 CYLINDER (Cont.)

Remove camshaft sprocket bolt, and remove both sprockets and timing chain as an assembly. Remove clutch and flywheel. Loosen main bearing cap bolts in two or three steps, then remove caps. Remove rear oil seal and carefully lift out crankshaft.

**Inspection – 1)** Thoroughly clean and inspect crankshaft. Blow out oil passages with compressed air. Check crankshaft for runout on center main bearing journal. If runout is more than .002" (.05 mm), crankshaft is bent and must be replaced.

**2)** Check all main and connecting rod bearings using Plastigage method. Check main and connecting rod journals for out-of-round or taper. If more than .0012" (.03 mm), crankshaft must be ground to next undersize. Main and connecting rod journals may be ground to the undersizes indicated in tables.

### Main Bearing Journals

| Application In. (mm) | Diameter In. (mm) |
| --- | --- |
| Std. | 1.9666-1.9671 (49.951-49.964) |
| .001 (.02) | 1.9665-1.9670 (49.949-49.962) |
| .01 (.25) | 1.9567-1.9572 (49.701-49.714) |
| .02 (.50) | 1.9469-1.9474 (49.451-49.464) |
| .03 (.75) | 1.9370-1.9376 (49.201-49.214) |
| .04 (1.0) | 1.9272-1.9277 (48.951-48.964) |

### Connecting Rod Journals

| Application In. (mm) | Diameter In. (mm) |
| --- | --- |
| Std. | 1.7701-1.7706 (44.961-44.974) |
| .003 (.08) | 1.7670-1.7675 (44.881-44.894) |
| .005 (.12) | 1.7654-1.7659 (44.841-44.854) |
| .01 (.25) | 1.7603-1.7608 (44.711-44.724) |
| .02 (.50) | 1.7504-1.7509 (44.461-44.474) |
| .03 (.75) | 1.7406-1.7411 (44.211-44.224) |
| .04 (1.0) | 1.7307-1.7313 (43.961-43.974) |

**Installation – 1)** Install main bearing halves to engine block ensuring that all bearings are on correct journal. Bearings for journal No. 1 and No. 5 are the same. Bearings for journals No. 2 and No. 4 are the same. Journal No. 3 requires the thrust bearing. Upper and lower bearings are not interchangeable except for journals No. 2 and No. 4.

**2)** Apply oil to main bearing surface and install crankshaft. Install main bearing caps with arrow pointing toward front of engine. **NOTE** – *Apply sealer to main bearing caps at point where cap contacts cylinder block.* Tighten main bearing caps, in two or three steps, starting at center bearing and working outwards. Ensure crankshaft rotates smoothly.

*Fig. 9  Checking Bearings with Plastigage Method*

**3)** Check crankshaft end play. *See Thrust Bearing Alignment.* Install timing chain in correct position with crankshaft and camshaft sprockets. Install rear oil seal. Install clutch and flywheel. Install oil thrower and chain tensioner. Install timing chain cover, crankshaft pulley, and water pump. Install alternator and engine mounting bracket. Install piston and connecting rod assemblies, oil pan, and cylinder head.

### THRUST BEARING ALIGNMENT

Thrust bearing is installed on No. 3 main bearing journal. Check crankshaft end play by inserting a feeler gauge between flange of thrust bearing and crankshaft. End play should be .002-.006" (.05-.15 mm). Service limit is .012" (.30 mm).

*Fig. 10  Checking Crankshaft End Play*

### REAR MAIN BEARING OIL SEAL SERVICE

Apply sealer to corners of crankcase that holds rear main bearing cap. Apply light grease to sealing edge on seal and install seal. Install rear main bearing cap and tighten bolts to specifications.

Apply Lithium Grease

*Fig. 11  Installing Rear Main Bearing Oil Seal*

### ENGINE FRONT COVER & OIL SEAL

**Removal & Installation** – Remove drive belt, fan, and water pump pulley. Remove water pump and crankshaft pulley. Remove oil pan and front cover. Replace seal in front cover whenever cover is removed. Thoroughly clean mating surfaces and apply sealer to both sides of gasket. Install gasket and cover. Tighten bolts and nuts to specifications. Reverse removal procedure to install remaining components.

## CAMSHAFT

### TIMING CHAIN

**Removal** – Remove engine front cover as previously outlined. Remove timing chain tensioner and bolt securing camshaft sprocket to camshaft. Pull off sprocket with timing chain.

# Datsun Engines

## B210 & F10 4 CYLINDER (Cont.)

Fig. 12    Correct Alignment for Timing Chain Installation.

**Installation** — Install timing chain and camshaft sprocket with markings correctly aligned as shown in illustration. Oil sprocket teeth and chain with engine oil. Install and tighten camshaft sprocket bolt. Install chain tensioner and tighten attaching bolts. Check dimension "L" of tensioner, and if over .591" (15 mm), replace chain tensioner. Install oil thrower in front of camshaft sprocket. Install timing chain cover.

## CAMSHAFT

**Removal** — Remove engine front cover, and valve train components as previously outlined. Remove fuel pump and oil pump with filter. Remove timing chain tensioner and remove timing chain with sprockets. Remove two bolts from camshaft lock plate and carefully pull camshaft from engine block.

**Inspection** — Thoroughly clean and inspect camshaft for wear or scoring. Check runout of camshaft using a dial indicator on center bearing journal. If runout exceeds .002" (.05 mm), replace camshaft. Check journal diameter, and if diameter is more than .0039" (.10 mm) from standard, camshaft journals must be ground to next undersize. Bearings are available in standard and three undersizes.

**Installation** — Coat camshaft with light coat of engine oil and carefully install camshaft into engine. Install camshaft lock plate with word "LOWER" at bottom. Install valve train components. Install timing chain with sprockets and timing chain tensioner. Install engine front cover. Install fuel pump and oil pump.

Fig. 13    Checking the Timing Chain Tensioner

## CAMSHAFT BEARING REPLACEMENT

**1)** With camshaft removed, check journal diameter and bearing inside diameter. If journal measurement is within tolerance and clearance between camshaft journals and bearings exceeds .0059" (.15 mm), bearings must be replaced.

**2)** Remove and install appropriate bearings in crankcase using a suitable driver (ST16110000). Make sure oil holes in bearings align with oil holes in crankcase. Bearings must be line bored after installation. Install taper plug in crankcase using sealer. Install camshaft as previously outlined.

Fig. 14    Correct Camshaft Lock Plate Installation

## CAMSHAFT END THRUST

Check camshaft end thrust with camshaft, lock plate, and camshaft sprocket in position by using a dial indicator on camshaft sprocket bolt. If end play exceeds .0039" (.10 mm), replace lock plate.

# ENGINE OILING

**Crankcase Capacity** — $3\frac{1}{2}$ quarts for F10 models and $3\frac{7}{8}$ quarts for B210 models. Specifications include filter change.

**Oil Filter** — Full-flow, replaceable element.

**Oil Pressure** — More than 11 psi (.8 kg/cm²) at idle; 54-74 psi (3.8-5.2 kg/cm²) at 3000 RPM.

**Pressure Relief Valve** — Nonadjustable, located in oil pump cover.

## ENGINE OILING SYSTEM

Oil is circulated through engine by pressure provided by a trochoid rotor type pump. Oil pump is mounted on side of crankcase and driven by camshaft. Oil is drawn from oil pan by oil pump and into full flow oil filter mounted under oil pump. Oil is then pumped into main oil gallery of crankcase where it is distributed to crankshaft journals, timing chain tensioner and squirter that lubricates timing chain. Oil is circulated from crankshaft main bearing journals to camshaft journals and from center camshaft journal to rocker arm shaft to lubricate rocker arms and valves. Cylinder walls and piston pins are lubricated by oil squirted from squirt hole in connecting rod.

# Datsun Engines

## B210 & F10 4 CYLINDER (Cont.)

### OIL PUMP

Remove pump cover from pump body. Slide outer rotor from pump body. Remove pressure regulator plug, washer, shim, spring, and valve. Thoroughly clean and inspect all components for wear or scoring. Check side and tip clearance between rotors. Check clearance between outer rotor and pump body. If clearances are excessive, replace components as necessary.

| Oil Pump Specifications | |
|---|---|
| **Application** | **Wear Limit In. (mm)** |
| Rotor-to-Rotor Side Clearance ...................... | .0079 (.20) |
| Rotor-to-Tip Clearance ............................ | .0079 (.20) |
| Rotor-to-Pump Body .............................. | .0197 (.50) |
| Regulator Valve Spring | |
|   Free Length ................................. | 1.71 (43.49) |
|   Length at 8.09 lbs. (3.67 kg) ...................... | 1.19 (30.3) |

## ENGINE COOLING

### WATER PUMP

**Removal & Installation** — Drain cooling system and remove fan belt. Remove fan shroud, fan blade, spacer and pulley (or torque coupling). Remove water pump assembly and gasket from front cover. To install, reverse removal procedure.

**Thermostat** — Opens at 177-183°F.

*Fig. 15  Engine Oiling System*

| Cooling System Capacity | |
|---|---|
| **Application** | **Capacity** |
| B210 Auto. Trans. .............................. | 6 quarts |
| B210 Man. Trans. .............................. | 6¼ quarts |
| F10 .......................................... | 7 quarts |

## ENGINE SPECIFICATIONS

| GENERAL SPECIFICATIONS | | | | | | | | | | | |
|---|---|---|---|---|---|---|---|---|---|---|---|
| **Year** | **Displ.** | | **Carburetor** | **HP at RPM** | **Torque (Ft. Lbs. at RPM)** | **Compr. Ratio** | **Bore** | | **Stroke** | |
| | **cu. ins.** | **cc** | | | | | **in.** | **mm** | **in.** | **mm** |
| 1978 | 85.24 | 1397 | 1 x 2-Bbl. | ..... | ..... | 8.5-1① | 2.99 | 76 | 3.03 | 77 |

① — B210 federal models with CAT 9.0-1.

| VALVES | | | | | | | |
|---|---|---|---|---|---|---|---|
| **Engine & Valve** | **Head Diam. In. (mm)** | **Face Angle** | **Seat Angle** | **Seat Width In. (mm)** | **Stem Diameter In. (mm)** | **Stem Clearance In. (mm)** | **Valve Lift In. (mm)** |
| All Int. | 1.46 (37) | 45.5° | 45° | .071 (1.8) | .3138-.3144 (7.970-7.985) | .0006-.0018 (.015-.045) | .3114 (7.91) |
| Exh. | 1.18 (30) | 45.5° | 45° | .087 (2.2) | .3128-.3134 (7.945-7.960) | .0016-.0028 (.040-.070) | .3236 (8.22) |

## B210 & F10 4 CYLINDER (Cont.)

### ENGINE SPECIFICATIONS (Cont.)

| VALVE SPRINGS | | | |
|---|---|---|---|
| Engine | Free Length In. (mm) | PRESSURE Lbs. @ In. (kg @ mm) | |
| | | Valve Closed | Valve Open |
| All | 1.831 (46.5) | 52.7 @ 1.52 (23.9 @ 38.7) | 129 @ 1.189 (58.5 @ 30.2) |

| VALVE TIMING | | | | |
|---|---|---|---|---|
| Engine | INTAKE | | EXHAUST | |
| | Open (BTDC) | Close (ALDC) | Open (BLDC) | Close (ATDC) |
| All | 14° | 54° | 56° | 20° |

| In. (mm) | PISTONS, PINS, RINGS | | | | | |
|---|---|---|---|---|---|---|
| Engine | PISTONS | PINS | | RINGS | | |
| | Clearance In. (mm) | Piston Fit In. (mm) | Rod Fit In. (mm) | Rings | End Gap In. (mm) | Side Clearance In. (mm) |
| All | .0009-.0017 (.023-.043) | .0003-.0005 (.008-.012) | .0007-.0014① (.017-.035) | 1 | .0079-.0138 (.20-.35) | .0016-.0028 (.04-.07) |
| | | | | 2 | .0059-.0118 (.15-.30) | .0011-.0024 (.03-.06) |
| | | | | Oil | .0118-.0354 (.30-.90) | snug |

① — Interference fit.

| CRANKSHAFT MAIN & CONNECTING ROD BEARINGS | | | | | | |
|---|---|---|---|---|---|---|
| Engine | MAIN BEARINGS | | | | CONNECTING ROD BEARINGS | | |
| | Journal Diam. In. (mm) | Clearance In. (mm) | Thrust Bearing | Crankshaft End Play In. (mm) | Journal Diam. In. (mm) | Clearance In. (mm) | Side Play In. (mm) |
| All | 1.9666-1.9671 (49.95-49.96) | .0008-.0024 (.020-.062) | No. 3 | .0020-.0059 (.050-.150) | 1.7701-1.7706 (44.96-44.97) | .0008-.0020① (.020-.050) | .004-.008 (.1-.2) |

① — For F10 models, .0004-.0024" (.010-.060 mm)

| CAMSHAFT | | | |
|---|---|---|---|
| Engine | Journal Diam. In. (mm) | Clearance In. (mm) | Lobe Lift In. (mm) |
| All No. 1 | 1.7237-1.7242 (43.78-43.80) | .0015-.0024 (.037-.060) | Int. .222 (5.65) |
| 2 | 1.7041-1.7046 (43.28-43.30) | .0011-.0020 (.027-.050) | Exh. .233 (5.92) |
| 3 | 1.6844-1.6849 (42.78-42.80) | .0016-.0025 (.040-.063) | |
| 4 | 1.6647-1.6652 (42.28-42.30) | .0011-.0020 (.029-.050) | |
| 5 | 1.6224-1.6229 (41.21-41.22) | .0015-.0024 (.037-.060) | |

| TIGHTENING SPECIFICATIONS | |
|---|---|
| Application | Ft. Lbs. (mkg) |
| Cylinder Head | 51-54 (7.0-7.5) |
| Connecting Rod | 23-27 (3.2-3.8) |
| Main Bearing Caps | 36-43 (5.0-6.0) |
| Camshaft Sprocket | 29-35 (4.0-4.8) |
| Camshaft Lock Plate | 3.6-5.8 (.5-.8) |
| Timing Chain Tensioner | 4.3-5.8 (0.6-0.8) |
| Front Cover | 3.6-5.1 (.5-.7) |
| Oil Pan | 2.9-4.3 (.4-.6) |
| Oil Pump | 6.5-10.1 (.9-1.4) |
| Rocker Arm Shaft | 14-18 (2.0-2.5) |
| Manifolds | 10.8-14.5 (1.5-2.0) |
| Crankshaft Pulley | 108-145 (15-20) |
| Flywheel | 58-65 (8.0-9.0) |
| Oil Strainer | 6.5-10 (.9-1.4) |
| Engine Mounts | 14-18 (1.9-2.5) |
| Water Pump | 6.5-10.0 (.9-1.4) |

## 200SX, 510 & PICKUP 4 CYLINDER

### ENGINE CODING

#### ENGINE IDENTIFICATION

Engine number is stamped on right rear side of cylinder block at cylinder head contact surface. The number is preceded by engine model L20B.

### ENGINE, CYLINDER HEAD & MANIFOLD

#### ENGINE

**NOTE** — *It is recommended that engine and transmission be removed as a unit. Engine can then be separated from transmission.*

**Model 620 (Pickup) — 1)** Remove battery, scribe alignment marks on hood and hinges, then remove hood. Disconnect all hoses and ducts from air cleaner, loosen air cleaner supporting attachments and remove air cleaner.

**2)** Drain cooling system and remove radiator hoses and oil cooler lines (if equipped). Remove radiator shroud, then remove radiator. Disconnect fuel pump-to-filter and return hoses. Disconnect carbon canister hose on engine side.

**3)** Disconnect wires to following components: Accelerator wire at carburetor, oil pressure switch, auto choke heater, vacuum control solenoid, coil lead, distributor, thermal transmitter, anti-dieseling solenoid, alternator, starter, and back-up lamp switch.

**4)** Disconnect power brake unit vacuum hose at intake manifold. Disconnect speedometer cable from rear extension housing. On manual transmissions, remove floor cover, detach rubber boot, remove "E" ring and control lever pin from transmission striking rod guide, remove lever. On automatic transmissions remove screws to disconnect control knob from lever, remove selector rod, range lever and control lever assembly with bracket.

**5)** On models with air conditioning, remove flexible hose support, remove four compressor bolts, move compressor to battery support. Remove hoses to fast idle control device solenoid valve, remove fast idle control device actuator.

**6)** Remove attaching screws, disconnect clutch operating cylinder and flexible tube as an assembly. Disconnect exhaust pipe from exhaust manifold. Disconnect center bearing bracket from crossmenber and propeller shaft from flange at rear axle. Remove propeller shaft and plug rear end of transmission to prevent oil leakage.

**7)** Attach a lifting hoist to engine and remove front mount bolts at support. Support transmission with a floor jack and loosen two rear mounting bolts. Remove rear mount to side member bolts, remove rear mount. Remove steering idler arm and push down cross rod. Pull engine forward and carefully remove engine and transmission as an assembly.

**Model 200SX, 510 — 1)** Mark hood and hinges for alignment on reassembly, then remove hood. Disconnect battery ground cable. Drain cooling system and crankcase. Disconnect transmission oil cooler lines and remove splash board on automatic transmission models.

**2)** Remove all hoses and tubes to air cleaner, then remove air cleaner. Disconnect the following wires, cables and hoses: Fuel line to fuel pump, carbon canister hoses, high and low tension coil wires, air pump-to-air pump cleaner hose, distributor wires at top of radiator or at connectors, power brake vacuum hose at manifold, accelerator at carburetor, heater inlet and outlet hoses, fast idle control device vacuum hose.

**3)** On air conditioned models, dismount compressor by removing mounting bolts and moving compressor aside toward fender. DO NOT discharge gas from compressor or system or separate refrigerant lines. Hold compressor out of way with wire to prevent interference with engine removal.

**4)** Remove accelerator linkage from carburetor. Disconnect heater hoses, remove radiator hoses, shroud, grille and radiator. On manual transmission models, detach rubber boot, remove nut from shift lever, remove shift lever. On automatic transmissions, disconnect joint between control lever and selector rod.

**5)** Disconnect speedometer cable from extension housing. Remove clutch operating cylinder from clutch housing. On California models, remove heat shield insulators on front exhaust pipe and catalytic converter, then separate front exhaust pipe from converter. All other models, disconnect front pipe from rear pipe.

**6)** Remove front exhaust pipe mounting and separate pipe from exhaust manifold. Disconnect center bearing bracket from crossmember and propeller shaft from flange at rear axle. Remove propeller shaft and plug end of transmission to prevent oil leakage. Support transmission with a floor jack.

**7)** Remove rear engine mounts and connect a lifting hoist to engine. Remove front engine mounts. Pull engine forward and carefully remove engine and transmission as an assembly.

#### CYLINDER HEAD

**Removal — 1)** Drain cooling system. Remove air cleaner after disconnecting hoses and ducts. Disconnect spark plug wires from spark plugs and valve cover. Disconnect fuel hose from carburetor and remove fuel pump. Remove PCV hose and anti-backfire valve-to-EGR passage hose. Disconnect vacuum hoses and linkage to carburetor, then remove carburetor.

ST17420001

*Fig. 1  Holding Timing Chain with Special Support Tool*

## 200SX, 510 & PICKUP 4 CYLINDER (Cont.)

2) Disconnect all hoses and vacuum lines from intake manifold to cylinder head or block. Remove intake and exhaust manifold as an assembly. Remove rocker cover and fuel pump drive cam. Turn crankshaft so No. 1 piston is at TDC on compression stroke. Paint alignment marks on timing chain and camshaft sprocket to aid in installation. Remove camshaft sprocket, and use suitable retainer tool (ST17420001) to support timing chain as shown in *Fig.1.* Remove cylinder head attaching bolts and remove cylinder head.

**Installation** — 1) Ensure that mating surfaces of cylinder head and block are clean, then install cylinder head and gasket without sealer. Number 1 piston should be at TDC on compression stroke and camshaft sprocket location notch and plate oblong groove aligned.

2) Insert head bolts and tighten ① and ② to 14 ft. lbs. (2.0 mkg). Install and align sprockets and timing chain. Install remaining components in reverse order of removal, using new seals, gaskets and sealant where required.

3) Tighten head bolts in several steps in the sequence illustrated in *Fig. 2* to final specified torque. Recheck torque after engine has been running for several minutes.

*Fig. 2    Cylinder Head Tightening Sequence*

## VALVES

### VALVE ARRANGEMENT

E-I-I-E-E-I-I-E (front to rear)

**NOTE** — *Camshaft MUST be removed to take out valves. See Camshaft Removal & Installation in this Section.*

### VALVES

**Removal** — With camshaft removed. Remove valves using suitable valve spring compressor (ST12070000). Take care not to lose valve spring, seat, oil seal, valve collet, and rocker guide. Check each valve for worn, damaged or deformed heads or stems.

**Installation** — Install oil seal on valve guide. Assemble order, valve, inner and outer valve spring, spring retainer, valve collet and valve rocker guide. Install with suitable valve spring compressor (ST12070000). Make sure that components are clean.

### VALVE GUIDE SERVICE

1) Measure clearance between valve stem and valve guide, with aid of micrometer and hole gauge. Check diameter of valve stem in three places: top, center, and bottom.

2) Insert hole gauge in valve guide bore and measure at center. Subtract highest reading of valve stem diameter from valve guide bore to obtain clearance.

**NOTE** — *As a quick check, a valve may be inserted into valve guide and moved either left or right, (parallel with rocker arm). If tip moves .0079" or more, clearance is beyond maximum limit, of .0039".*

*Fig. 3    Intake & Exhaust Valve Guides*

### VALVE SEAT INSERTS

1) Check valve seats for pitting at valve contact surface. Valve seat inserts of .0197" oversize are available if necessary. To remove old inserts machine should be set so that boring cannot continue beyond bottom face of insert recess in cylinder head.

2) Machine cylinder head recess diameter to concentric circles to valve guide center so that insert will have correct fit. Heat cylinder head to 302-392° F and install insert making sure that it beds on bottom face of recess.

3) Valve seats should be cut or ground to correct face angle and seat width and to head diameter of valve to be installed.

### VALVE SPRING INSTALLED HEIGHT

With valves closed, inner spring should have a height of 1.378" (35.0 mm) and outer spring should have a height of 1.575" (40.0 mm). See specification for pressure with valves opened or closed.

### VALVE ADJUSTMENT

Loosen pivot locking nut and turn pivot screw until specified clearance is obtained with engine cold. Tighten pivot locking nut after adjustment and recheck clearance. Warm up engine. With engine stopped, measure valve clearance and reset to hot clearances if necessary.

#### Valve Adjustment Specifications

| Valve | Hot | Cold |
|---|---|---|
| Intake | .010" (.25 mm) | .008" (.20 mm) |
| Exhaust | .012" (.30 mm) | .010" (.25 mm) |

## 200SX, 510 & PICKUP 4 CYLINDER (Cont.)

### PISTONS, PINS & RINGS

#### PISTON & ROD ASSEMBLY

**Removal** — Remove connecting rod nuts and bearing caps. Push piston and rod assembly out top of cylinder, using care not to damage any bearing surface. Retain all components in proper order for reassembly.

*Fig. 4   Piston & Rod Assembly Installation Features*

**Installation** — Reassemble piston and rod so that oil hole in connecting rod is facing right side of engine and notch on top of piston is facing forward. Install connecting rod on original journal with rod and cap marks on same side. Tighten connecting rod nuts and check rod side play.

#### FITTING PISTONS

1) Measure cylinder bores for wear or taper at top, bottom and middle on thrust face and at 90° to thrust face. If excessive wear is found rebore cylinder and install oversize pistons. Oversize pistons are available as shown in table.

2) When boring cylinders, use cylinder order of 2-4-1-3 to prevent heat distortion. After honing cylinder to final fit, check piston fit using spring tension pull scale. A force of .44-3.31 lbs. (.2-1.5 kg.) should be obtained extracting a .0016" (.04 mm) feeler gauge.

*Fig. 5   Installation Order of Piston Rings*

3) Measure piston ring end gap and side clearance and replace as necessary. Install rings on pistons with end gaps 180° apart and so no end gap is in line with thrust face. Install rings with top mark facing upward.

**NOTE** — *If only piston ring is to be replaced, measure gap at bottom of bore. Oversize rings are available in .020" (1.00 mm).*

*Fig. 6   Exploded View of Piston and Rod Assy.*

#### PISTON PINS

Pin must be a tight press fit in connecting rod, pressing force is from one to one and a half tons. When pressing pin into connecting rod, oil pin and press pin so that oil jet of connecting rod large end is directed toward right side of cylinder block.

#### Piston Specifications

| Application In. (mm) | Piston Size In. (mm) |
|---|---|
| Standard | 3.3459-3.3478 (84.985-85.035) |
| .020 (.50) OS | 3.3648-3.3667 (85.465-85.515) |
| .040 (1.00) OS | 3.3844-3.3864 (85.965-86.015) |

## CRANKSHAFT MAIN & CONNECTING ROD BEARINGS

### CRANKSHAFT

**Removal** — With engine removed from vehicle, remove cylinder head and oil pan. Remove flywheel and rear plate. Remove oil strainer, oil pump and drive spindle. Remove front cover, chain tensioner, chain slack side guide, and timing chain. Remove oil thrower, crankcase worm gear, and timing drive sprocket. Remove piston and rod assemblies. Remove main bearing caps using suitable puller (KV101041SO) to remove center and rear main bearing caps.

**NOTE** — *Keep all main bearing caps in order to aid in reassembly. Remove rear oil seal, remove crankshaft.*

**Inspection** — Check all crankshaft journals for scoring, wear or cracks. Taper and out-of-round on all journals must not exceed .001" (.025 mm). Check crankshaft for bend using dial indicator at center journal of crankshaft. If bend exceeds .004" (.10 mm), which is one-half of indicator reading, replace crankshaft. Check main driveshaft pilot bearing at rear of crankshaft for wear or damage and replace if necessary.

## 200SX, 510 & PICKUP 4 CYLINDER (Cont.)

*Fig. 7   Rear Main Bearing Cap Removal*

KV101041SO

Slowly Remove Bearing Caps

**Installation** — 1) Install main bearing halves to engine block ensuring that all bearings are on correct journal. Journal No. 3 requires a thrust bearing. Bearing for No. 1 is the same as for journal No. 5 except that an oil hole is provided in No. 1. Upper and lower bearings are interchangeable.

2) Apply oil to main bearing surface and install crankshaft. Install main bearing caps with arrow pointing toward front of engine. Shift crankshaft toward front of engine, tighten main bearing caps, in two or three steps, starting at center bearing and working outwards. Ensure crankshaft rotates smoothly.

**NOTE** — *Apply sealer to rear main bearing cap at point where cap contacts cylinder block.*

*Fig. 8   Rear Oil Seal Removal*

Seal

Crankshaft

3) Check crankshaft end play, and if not within specifications replace center thrust bearing. Install side seals in rear main bearing cap, after applying sealer to seals. Install rear oil seal. Install rear end plate and flywheel. Install piston and rod assemblies. Install remaining components in reverse of removal procedure

### MAIN BEARINGS

1) Check all bearings for scoring or wear and replace if damage is found. Clean oil from crankshaft and place a strip of Plastigage on crankshaft journal. Install main bearing cap, with bearing installed, and tighten to 33-40 ft.lbs. (4.5-5.5 mkg).

**NOTE** — *Plastigage should run parallel with crankshaft and not block oil hole. Do not turn crankshaft while Plastigage is inserted.*

2) Remove cap and measure width of Plastigage at widest point using gauge provided. If clearance is not to specifications, replace bearings. Bearings are available in undersizes of .01" (.25 mm), .02" (.50 mm); and .03" (.75 mm).

### CONNECTING RODS

Check connecting rod bearings in same manner as main bearings using Plastigage. Tighten connecting rod caps to 33-40 ft. lbs. (4.5-5.5 mkg) Bearings are available in undersizes of .01" (.25 mm), .02" (.50 mm) and .03" (.75 mm). Check for clearance of .001-.002" (.025-.055 mm) when installing new bearings. Maximum wear limit for old bearings is .005" (.12 mm).

### ENGINE FRONT COVER

**Removal** — With engine removed from vehicle and mounted on engine stand, remove oil pump and drive spindle. Remove front cover attaching bolts and front cover.

**Installation** — Apply sealant at mating corners of oil pan, cylinder head and front cover. Oil seal should be coated with engine oil before installation in cover and before cover is installed. Use new gasket and install cover.

**NOTE** — *Check height difference between cylinder block and front cover upper face. Difference must not exceed .006" (.15 mm).*

## CAMSHAFT

### CAMSHAFT

**Removal** — With cylinder head removed, remove valve rocker springs. Loosen valve rocker pivot lock nuts and remove rocker arms by pressing down on spring. Use care not to lose valve rocker guide. Carefully remove camshaft from cylinder head.

**Installation** — Carefully install camshaft into cylinder head taking care not to damage bearing. Install camshaft locating plate with oblong groove of plate, facing front of cylinder head. Install camshaft sprocket and tighten attaching bolts. Install remaining components in reverse of removal procedure and tighten all nuts and bolts.

Carefully Withdraw Camshaft

*Fig. 9   Withdrawing Camshaft from Cylinder Head*

# Datsun Engines

## 200SX, 510 & PICKUP 4 CYLINDER (Cont.)

### CAMSHAFT BEARINGS

Measure inner diameter of camshaft bearing and outer diameter of camshaft journal. If wear or damage is excessive, replace cylinder head assembly.

**NOTE** — *Do not remove camshaft bearings. If bearings are removed, bearing centers will be out of alignment and proper reassembly will be difficult without center boring.*

### TIMING CHAIN & GEARS

Remove engine front cover and camshaft drive sprocket and fuel pump cam. Remove timing chain, tensioner and chain guide. Remove oil thrower, crankshaft worm gear and crankshaft chain drive gear. To install, reverse removal procedure.

**NOTE** — *When Installing timing chain, camshaft key points upward. Set timing chain so that mating marks align with crankshaft and camshaft sprockets There are 44 chain links between the two timing marks.*

Fig. 11   Cutaway View of Engine Oiling System

Fig. 10   Timing Chain & Sprocket Alignment

## ENGINE OILING

**Crankcase Capacity** — 4.5 Quarts with filter change.

**Oil Filter** — Full-flow, disposable cartridge.

**Oil Pressure** — 11-40 psi. (.8-2.8 kg/cm²) at idle, 50-70 psi. (3.5-5.0 kg/cm²) at maximum.

**Pressure Relief Valve** — Non-adjustable.

### ENGINE OILING SYSTEM

Oil drawn from pan passes through screen to oil pump and is delivered to oil filter and to main oil gallery. Main oil gallery supplies oil to crankshaft main bearings and drilled passages in crankshaft. Oil sprayed from jet holes on connecting rods lubricates cylinders and piston pins. Oil from main gallery lubricates chain tensioner and timing chain. Center hole in crankshaft, center bearing feeds camshaft bearings on cylinder head. Valve rocker mechanism is lubricated through oil gallery in camshaft and through a small channel at base circle portion of each cam. Rocker arms and valves are lubricated intermittently through small holes or oil pipe.

Fig. 12   Aligning Oil Pump Timing Marks

### OIL PUMP

**Removal** — Pump assembly is installed at bottom right of front cover and held in place by four bolts. Pump is driven by helical gear on crankshaft and in turn drives distributor shaft. Remove distributor, splash shield board and pump mounting bolts. Remove oil pump and drive spindle assembly.

## 200SX, 510 & PICKUP 4 CYLINDER (Cont.)

**Inspection** — Remove cover from oil pump body, remove gears. Wash parts with cleaning solvent, inspect for wear or damage. Make sure clearances are to specification. Pump is serviced as an assembly only. Replace pump if any part is worn or damaged.

*Fig. 13   Position of Distributor and Oil Pump Drive in Engine*

*Fig. 14   Exploded View of Oil Pump & Pickup Tube*

**Installation** — Rotate engine until number one piston is at TDC. Fill pump housing with oil and align punch mark on shaft with hole in pump (*Fig. 12*). Using a new gasket, install oil pump and drive shaft assembly so that tongue is positioned at 11:25 o'clock position. Small crescent will be facing forward (*Fig. 13*). Check drive gear engagement through distributor mounting hole.

### Oil Pump Specifications

| Application | ①Clearance In. (mm) |
|---|---|
| Rotor Side Clearance (Rotor to Bottom Cover) | 0.20 (0.0079) |
| Rotor Tip Clearance | 0.20 (0.0079) |
| Outer Rotor to Body | 0.5 (0.0197) |

① — Wear limit specifications given.

## ENGINE COOLING

**Thermostat** — Opens at 180° F (82° C). Full open at 203° F (95° C).

**Radiator Cap** — 13 psi.

**Cooling System Capacity** — 200SX — 8 qts.; 510 and Pickup 9 qts.

### WATER PUMP

Centrifugal type pump with aluminum body. To remove drain cooling system and remove upper and lower radiator hoses, shroud, fan, belts and pulley. Remove pump attaching bolts and remove water pump.

## ENGINE SPECIFICATIONS

### GENERAL SPECIFICATIONS

| Year | Displ. | | Carburetor | HP at RPM | Torque (Ft. Lbs. at RPM) | Compr. Ratio | Bore | | Stroke | |
|---|---|---|---|---|---|---|---|---|---|---|
| | cu. ins. | cc | | | | | in. | mm | in. | mm |
| 1978 L20B | 119.1 | 1952 | 2Bbl. | ..... | ..... | 8.5-1 | 3.35 | 85 | 3.39 | 86 |

### VALVES

| Engine & Valve | Head Diam. In. (mm) | Face Angle | Seat Angle | Seat Width In. (mm) | Stem Diameter In. (mm) | Stem Clearance In. (mm) | Valve Lift In. (mm) |
|---|---|---|---|---|---|---|---|
| L20B Intake | 1.654-1.661 (42.0-42.2) | 45° | 45° | .0551-.0630 (1.4-1.6) | .3136-.3142 (7.965-7.980) | .0008-.0021 (.020-.053) | .413 (10.5) |
| Exhaust | 1.378-1.386 (.35.0-35.2) | 45° | 45° | .0709-.0866 (1.8-2.2) | .3128-.3134 (7.945-7.960) | .0016-.0029 (.040-.073) | .413 (10.5) |

# Datsun Engines

## 200SX, 510 & PICKUP 4 CYLINDER (Cont.)

### ENGINE SPECIFICATIONS (Cont.)

#### PISTONS, PINS, RINGS

| Engine | PISTONS | PINS | | RINGS | | |
| --- | --- | --- | --- | --- | --- | --- |
| | Clearance In. (mm) | Piston Fit In. (mm) | ①Rod Fit In. (mm) | Rings | End Gap In. (mm) | Side Clearance In. (mm) |
| L20B | .0010-.0018 (.025-.045) | .0001-.0006 (.003-.015) | .0006-.0013 (.015-.033) | No.1 | .010-.016 (.25-.40) | .0016-.0029 (.040-.073) |
| | | | | No. 2 | .012-.020 (.30-.50) | .0012-.0028 (.030-.070) |
| | | | | Oil | .012-.035 (.30-.90) | ..... |

① — Interference fit.

#### CRANKSHAFT MAIN & CONNECTING ROD BEARINGS

| Engine | MAIN BEARINGS | | | | CONNECTING ROD BEARINGS | | |
| --- | --- | --- | --- | --- | --- | --- | --- |
| | Journal Diam. In. (mm) | Clearance In. (mm) | Thrust Bearing | Crankshaft End Play In. (mm) | Journal Diam. In. (mm) | Clearance In. (mm) | Side Play In. (mm) |
| L20B | 2.3599-2.3604 (59.942-59.955) | .0008-.0024 (.020-.062) | No. 3 | .002-.007 (.05-.18) | 1.9670-1.9675 (49.961-49.974) | .001-.002 (.025-.055) | .0079-.0118 (.20-.30) |

#### VALVE SPRINGS

| Engine | ①Free Length In. (mm) | PRESSURE Lbs. @ In. (kg @ mm) | |
| --- | --- | --- | --- |
| | | Valve Closed | Valve Open |
| Inner | 1.766 (44.85) | 27.1@1.378 (12.3@35) | 56.2@.965 (25.5@24.5) |
| Outer | 1.968 (49.98) | 47@1.575 (21.3@40) | 108@1.161 (49@29.5) |

① — If valve spring is out-of-square more than .063" (1.6 mm) replace spring.

#### CAMSHAFT

| Engine | Journal Diam. In. (mm) | ①Clearance In. (mm) | Lobe Lift In. (mm) |
| --- | --- | --- | --- |
| L20B | 1.8877-1.8883 (47.948-47.963) | .0015-.0026 (.038-.067) | .276 (7.0) |

① — End play is .003-.015" (.08-.38 mm).

#### TIGHTENING SPECIFICATIONS

| Application | Ft. Lbs. (mkg) |
| --- | --- |
| Cylinder Head | 47-61 (6.5-8.5) |
| Front Cover | |
|   8 mm bolts | 7-9 (1.0-1.3) |
|   6 mm bolts | 3-4.3 (.4-.6) |
| Connecting Rods | 33-40 (4.6-5.5) |
| Flywheel | 101-116 (14-16) |
| Main Bearings | 33-40 (4.6-5.5) |
| Camshaft Sprocket | 86-116 (12-16) |
| Oil Pan | 4-7 (.6-.9) |
| Crankshaft Pulley | 86-116 (12-16) |
| Manifolds | 9-12 (1.2-1.7) |
| Rocker Pivot Lock Nuts | 36-43 (5-6) |

## 810 & 280Z 6 CYLINDER

### ENGINE CODING

#### ENGINE IDENTIFICATION

Engine serial number is stamped on right rear side of cylinder block where cylinder head contacts block. Number is preceeded by engine model designation, L28 (280Z), L24 (810).

### ENGINE & CYLINDER HEAD

#### ENGINE

**NOTE** — *It is recommended that engine and transmission be removed as a unit. Engine can then be separated from transmission assembly.*

1) Fuel hose pressure must be decreased to zero, before engine removal. Disconnect battery ground cable, ground lead wire (black) from fuel pump, and lead wire from "S" terminal of starter. Remove cold start valve attaching bolts and valve. Connect a ground cable to battery. Place cold start valve in a container, turn ignition switch to "START" position, and release fuel hose pressure.

**NOTE** — *280Z Disconnect cold start valve harness connector. Using two jumper wires, connect each terminal to the battery, positive and negative terminals. Connect other terminals of jumpers to cold start valve, for two or three seconds.*

2) Scribe alignment marks around hood hinges and remove hood. Drain cooling system and engine crankcase. Disconnect battery cables. Remove radiator hoses. Remove air flow meter and air duct clamps with rubber hoses. Remove air cleaner and disconnect hoses from canister, then remove canister. Disconnect transmission cooler lines (automatic transmission models), and remove radiator and shroud.

3) Disconnect accelerator linkage. Disconnect the wiring to starter, alternator, oil pressure switch, neutral switch, back-up lamp switch, EGR solenoid valve, electric fuel injector, throttle valve switch, cold start valve, air regulator, vacuum cutting solenoid (manual transmission models), and all wiring to thermostat housing.

4) Disconnect wiring to boost controlled deceleration solenoid valve. Disconnect engine ground cable to engine, and high tension cable between coil and distributor. Disconnect wire for block terminal. Disconnect fuel return hose and fuel charge hose, heater hoses, and all vacuum hoses. On models with automatic transmission, disconnect wire to inhibitor switch and downshift solenoid.

5) Remove clutch operating cylinder on models with manual transmission. Disconnect speedometer cable from rear extension housing. Remove center console, "C" ring, and control lever pin from transmission striking rod guide, then remove control lever on models with manual transmission. On models with automatic transmission, disconnect shift control lever.

6) Disconnect exhaust pipe from exhaust manifold. Disconnect exhaust pipe bracket from rear extension housing and tie exhaust pipe out of the way. Mark propeller shaft and pinion flange to aid in reassembly, then remove propeller shaft from vehicle. Plug rear of extension housing to prevent oil leakage. Support transmission with a jack and remove rear engine mount. Use a hoist to raise engine and remove front engine mount attaching bolts. Raise engine and transmission and remove from vehicle as a unit.

### CYLINDER HEAD

**Removal** — 1) Drain cooling system and disconnect upper radiator hose and heater hoses. Dissipate fuel hose pressure to zero. *See step 1) under Engine Removal.* Remove air regulator and all connecting hoses as an assembly. Remove spark plug wires at plug end. Remove EGR control valve, vacuum switching valve and hoses as an assembly. Remove throttle chamber with dash pot and boost controlled deceleration device.

2) Remove fuel lines, vacuum hoses, and canister purge hose pressure regulator. **NOTE** — *Remove clip attaching fuel inlet hose to injector and take care not to twist or bend fuel inlet hose during removal.* Remove thermostat housing and all attached switches as an assembly. Remove PCV valve hose, sub-heat shield plate, and EGR tube.

3) Remove intake manifold and heat shield plate. Remove exhaust manifold. Remove all drive belts. Remove camshaft sprocket attaching bolt and remove sprocket from timing chain. **NOTE** — *Use special tool ST17420001 to support timing chain so timing marks on crankshaft sprocket and timing chain will remain unchanged to simplify timing mark alignment upon reassembly.* Remove oil pipe. Remove cylinder head attaching bolts working from the ends towards center of cylinder head. Remove cylinder head from engine block.

**Installation** — 1) Ensure that mating surfaces of cylinder head and block are clean, then install cylinder head and gasket without sealer. Number 1 piston should be at TDC on compression stroke and camshaft sprocket location notch and plate oblong groove aligned.

**CAUTION** — *Do not rotate crankshaft and camshaft separately or valves may hit head of pistons.*

2) Insert head bolts and tighten ① and ② to 7-12 ft. lbs. (1.0-1.6 mkg). Install and align sprockets and timing chain. Install remaining components in reverse order of removal, using new seals, gaskets and sealant where required.

3) Tighten head bolts in several steps in the sequence illustrated in *Fig. 1* to final specified torque. Recheck torque after engine has been running for several minutes.

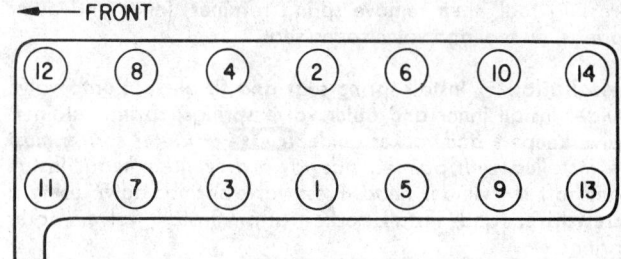

*Fig. 1  Cylinder Head Tightening Sequence.*

### VALVES

#### VALVE ARRANGEMENT

E-I-I-E-I-E-E-I-E-I-I-E (front to rear).

#### VALVE GUIDES CHECKING

1) Measure clearance between valve stem and valve guide with aid of micrometer and hole gauge. Check diameter of valve stem in three places: top, center and bottom.

## 810 & 280Z 6 CYLINDER (Cont.)

2) Insert hole gauge in valve guide bore and measure at center. Subtract highest reading of valve stem diameter from valve guide bore to obtain clearance.

**NOTE** — *As a quick check, a valve may be inserted into valve guide and moved either left or right (parallel with rocker arm). If its tip moves about .0079" or more, the clearance is beyond maximum limit of .0039".*

### VALVE GUIDE REPLACEMENT

1) Using a press and drift pin, force worn guide from cylinder head working from combustion cylinder side. Although this procedure may be carried out at room temperature, higher temperatures will aid removal.

2) Ream cylinder head side guide hole to provide interference fit of .0011-.0019" (.027-.049 mm). Press new valve guide into cylinder head so that it will fit smoothly when cylinder head is heated to 302-392°F (150-200°C).

3) Ream bore of valve guides to .3150-.3157" (8.000-8.018 mm). Correct valve seat surface using new valve guide as axis.

### VALVE SEAT INSERTS

Check valve seats for pitting at valve contact surface. Valve seat inserts of .020" (.5 mm) oversize are available if necessary.

### VALVE STEM OIL SEALS

An oil seal is installed on all intake and exhaust valve stems inside of valve spring.

### VALVE SPRINGS

**Removal** — With cylinder head removed, loosen pivot lock nut and remove rocker arm by pressing valve spring down, taking care not to lose valve rocker guide. Remove camshaft taking care not to damage camshaft bearings and cam lobes. Compress valves and remove valve keepers. Remove compressing tool, then remove spring retainer, inner and outer springs, oil seal and valve spring seat.

**Installation** — Install spring seat and fit oil seal onto valve guide. Install inner and outer valve springs, spring retainer, valve keepers and rocker guide. **NOTE** — *Outer spring must be installed with painted side toward cylinder head.* Install camshaft to cylinder head. Press valve springs down using a screwdriver and install rocker arms. Install valve rocker springs.

### VALVE SPRING INSTALLED HEIGHT

Valve spring must be square within 1/16". Valve spring installed height is 1.38" (35 mm) for inner spring and 1.57" (40 mm) for outer spring. If spring height and pressure, or squareness does not meet specifications, replace spring.

### VALVE ADJUSTMENT

Loosen pivot locking nut and turn pivot screw until specified clearance is obtained with engine cold. Tighten pivot locking nut after adjustment and recheck clearance. Warm up engine. With engine stopped, measure valve clearance and reset to hot clearances if necessary.

### Valve Adjustment Clearances

| Valve | Hot | Cold |
|-------|-----|------|
| Intake | .010"(.25 mm) | .008"(.20 mm) |
| Exhaust | .012"(.30 mm) | .010"(.25 mm) |

## PISTONS, PINS & RINGS

### PISTON & ROD ASSEMBLY

1) Remove cylinder head and oil pan. Remove nuts from connecting rod and remove connecting rod cap with bearing half. Push piston and connecting rod assembly with bearing half up and out through top of crankcase. **NOTE** — *Keep connecting rod caps with their respective piston and rod assembly as caps are not interchangeable.*

2) To install piston and connecting rod assembly, thoroughly oil rings, piston and cylinder wall. Make sure ring gaps are situated approximately 180° apart and not on thrust side of piston or in line with piston pin. Make sure bearing halves are properly seated in connecting rod and cap.

3) Install a ring compressor and compress rings. Install piston in cylinder with notch mark on piston head toward front of engine. With piston installed in cylinder, and connecting rod and bearings seated against crankshaft journal, install rod caps to their respective piston and rod assembly. Oil jet of connecting rod should face right side of cylinder block. Install cylinder head and oil pan.

### FITTING PISTONS

1) Visually inspect cylinder block for cracks or flaws. Using a suitable bore gauge, measure cylinder for out-of-round or taper. If cylinder bore out-of-round or taper exceeds .0006" (.015 mm), refinish cylinder bore. When any one cylinder is bored, all cylinders must be bored.

2) Determine piston oversize according to amount of wear in cylinder (see specifications). By measuring piston at thrust face and adding mean of piston-to-cylinder clearance, finish hone of cylinder may be determined.

3) After honing cylinder to final fit, measure piston-to-cylinder clearance using pull scale and feeler gauge. Extracting force to pull scale should be .44-3.31 lbs. (.2-1.5 kg) using a .0016" (.04 mm) feeler gauge. If cylinder bores are worn beyond limits, undersize cylinder liners are available. Liners should have an interference fit of .0031-.0035" (.08-.09 mm) in cylinder block.

### Piston Specifications

| Piston Size In. (mm) | Piston Diameter In. (mm) |
|----------------------|--------------------------|
| Standard | 3.3852-3.3872(85.985-86.035) |
| .020 (.50) O/S | 3.4041-3.4061(86.465-86.515) |
| .040 (1.0) O/S | 3.4238-3.4258(86.965-87.015) |

## 810 & 280Z 6 CYLINDER (Cont.)

### PISTON PINS

Using suitable press and related adaptors, remove piston pin from piston and connecting rod. Measure pin bore diameter in piston and connecting rod. If wear exceeds specifications, replace both piston and pin. Pin must fit piston with light thumb pressure at room temperature. Piston pin is a press fit (interference) in connecting rod. If connecting rod is replaced, insure that new rod is within .247 ounce (7 grams) of the defective connecting rod. Install piston pin to piston and connecting rod so oil hole on connecting rod will face right side of engine and notch on piston head will face forward when assembly is installed.

Piston Notch — MUST Face Forward

Oil Hole — MUST Face Right Side of Block

*Fig. 2 Piston and Connecting Rod Alignment.*

## CRANKSHAFT MAIN & CONNECTING ROD BEARINGS

### CRANKSHAFT

**Removal** — With engine removed from vehicle, remove cylinder head and oil pan. Remove flywheel and end plate. Remove oil pump, front cover, chain tensioner and chain guides. Remove timing chain, oil thrower, crankshaft worm gear, and chain drive sprocket. Remove piston and rod assemblies. Remove main bearing caps using a special puller (ST1651S000) to remove center and rear main bearing caps. **NOTE** — *Keep all main bearing caps in order to aid in reassembly.* Remove rear oil seal, then remove crankshaft.

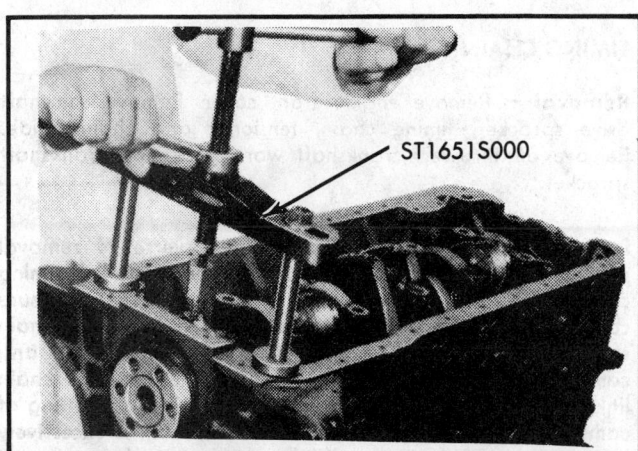

ST1651S000

*Fig. 3 Rear Main Bearing Cap Removal.*

**Inspection** — Check shaft journals and crankpins for scoring, wear, or cracks. Taper and out-of-round of journals and crankpins must not exceed .0012" (.03 mm). Check crankshaft for bend using a dial indicator at center journal of crankshaft. If bend exceeds .004" (.10 mm), which is one-half of indicator reading, replace crankshaft. Check main drive shaft pilot bearing at rear of crankshaft for wear or damage and replace if necessary.

**Installation** — 1) Install main bearing halves to engine block ensuring that all bearings are on correct journal. Journal No. 4 requires a thrust bearing. Bearing for journal No. 1 is the same as for journal No. 7. Upper and lower bearings are not interchangeable.

2) Apply oil to main bearing surface and install crankshaft. Install main bearing caps with arrow pointing toward front of engine. **NOTE** — *Apply sealer to main bearing caps at point where cap contacts cylinder block.* Shift crankshaft toward front of engine, then tighten main bearing caps, in two or three steps, starting at center bearing and working outwards. Ensure crankshaft rotates smoothly.

3) Check crankshaft end play, and if not within specifications, replace center thrust bearing. Install side seals in rear main bearing cap after applying sealer to seals. Install rear oil seal. Install rear end plate and flywheel. Install piston and rod assemblies. Install cylinder head, crankshaft sprocket, worm gear, chain drive sprocket, oil thrower, and timing chain. Install chain guides and tensioner, front cover, oil pump and oil pan. Install remaining components in reverse of removal procedure.

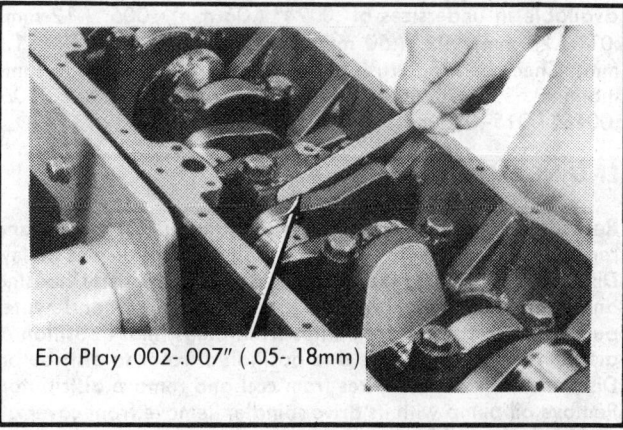

End Play .002-.007" (.05-.18mm)

*Fig. 4 Measuring End Play at No.4 Main Bearing.*

### MAIN BEARING CLEARANCE

1) Check all bearings for scoring or wear and replace if damage is found. Clean oil from crankshaft and place a strip of Plastigage on crankshaft journal. **NOTE** — *Plastigage should run parallel with crankshaft journal and should not block oil hole.* Install main bearing cap, with bearing installed, and tighten to 33-40 ft. lbs. (4.5-5.5 mkg). **NOTE** — *Do not turn crankshaft while Plastigage is inserted.*

2) Remove cap and measure width of Plastigage at widest point using gauge provided with Plastigage. If clearance is not to specifications, replace bearings. Bearings are available in undersizes of .01" (.25 mm), .02" (.50 mm), .03" (.75 mm), and .04" (1.0 mm).

## 810 & 280Z 6 CYLINDER (Cont.)

3) Bearings are manufactured with crush to cause bearing to snug down into bore. To measure, set bearing in cap or cylinder block and lock one side end of bearing. Press other side of bearing until back surface touches bore. Measure bearing crush, as shown in illustration, using a feeler gauge. Measurement must be 0-.0012" (0-.03 mm).

*Fig. 5   Measuring Bearing Crush in Cylinder Block.*

### CONNECTING ROD BEARING CLEARANCE

Check connecting rod bearing clearance in same manner as main bearing clearance using Plastigage. Tighten connecting rod caps to 33-40 ft. lbs. (4.5-5.5 mkg). Bearings are available in undersizes of .0024" (.06 mm), .005" (.12 mm), .01" (.25 mm), .02" (.50 mm), .03" (.75 mm), and .04" (1.0 mm). Check bearing crush of connecting rod bearings in same manner as for main bearings. Clearance must be .0006-.0018" (.015-.045 mm).

### ENGINE FRONT COVER

**Removal** — Drain cooling system, disconnect hoses and remove radiator. Remove all drive belts, fan blade and pulley. Disconnect all wiring and connections to thermostat housing and remove housing. Remove crankshaft pulley and water pump. Remove spark plug wires from plugs, mark position of distributor base to engine and position of rotor to distributor. Disconnect distributor wires from coil and remove distributor. Remove oil pump with its drive spindle. Remove front cover attaching bolts and front cover.

**Installation** — Apply sealer to four corners of front cover and gasket, then install cover onto cylinder block. Tighten front cover attaching bolts. Install oil pump with drive spindle. Install distributor while aligning matching marks. Reconnect spark plug wires and all distributor connections. Install water pump and crankshaft pulley. Install thermostat housing and reconnect all wiring. Install fan blade and pulley. Install drive belts, radiator, hoses, and fill cooling system.

## CAMSHAFT

### CAMSHAFT

**Removal** — Remove cylinder head. Remove valve rocker springs. Loosen valve rocker pivot lock nuts and remove rocker arms by pressing down on spring. Use care not to lose valve rocker guide. Carefully remove camshaft from front of cylinder head.

*Fig. 6   Withdrawing Camshaft From Cylinder Head.*

**Installation** — Carefully install camshaft into cylinder head taking care not to damage bearings. Install camshaft locating plate with oblong groove of plate facing front of cylinder head. Install camshaft sprocket and tighten attaching bolt. Install remaining components in reverse of removal procedure, and tighten all nuts and bolts.

### CAMSHAFT BEARINGS

NOTE — *Do not remove camshaft bearings. If bearings are removed, bearing centers will be out of alignment and proper reassembly will be difficult without center boring.*

Measure inner diameter of camshaft bearing and outer diameter of camshaft journal. If wear or damage is excessive, replace cylinder head assembly.

### TIMING CHAIN

**Removal** — Remove engine front cover. Remove camshaft drive sprocket, timing chain, tensioner and chain guide. Remove oil thrower, crankshaft worn gear and crankshaft sprocket.

**Installation** — Install components in reverse of removal procedure while noting the following: When installing timing chain, camshaft sprocket or crankshaft sprocket, make sure camshaft and crankshaft keys point upward. Set timing chain so that its mating marks match marks on crankshaft and camshaft sprockets on right-hand side. There are 42 chain links between the two timing chain marks. Factory setting of camshaft sprocket is number one hole, if chain is excessively stretched use number two or three hole to achieve correct valve timing.

## 810 & 280Z 6 CYLINDER (Cont.)

Fig. 7 Timing Chain and Sprocket Installation.

## ENGINE OILING

### ENGINE OILING SYSTEM

Oil drawn from oil pan passes through a screen to oil pump. Oil is delivered to full flow oil filter and to main oil gallery. Main oil gallery supplies oil to crankshaft main bearings and drilled passages in crankshaft. Oil sprayed from jet holes on connecting rods lubricates cylinders and piston pins. Oil from main gallery lubricates chain tensioner and timing chain. A center oil hole in the crankshaft center bearing feeds camshaft bearings on cylinder head. Valve rocker mechanism is lubricated through oil gallery in camshaft and through a small channel at base circle portion of each cam. Rocker arms and valves are lubricated intermittently through small holes or oil pipe.

**Crankcase Capacity** — 280Z — 5 qts.; 810 — 6 qts. (including filter change).

**Oil Filter** — Full-flow, with disposable cartridge.

**Oil Pressure** — 50-57 psi (3.5-4.0 kg/cm²) @ 2000 RPM.

### OIL PUMP

Oil pump assembly is installed to bottom of front cover by four bolts. Pump is driven by oil pump drive spindle assembly which is in turn driven by gear on crankshaft. To remove oil pump, first remove distributor. Drain engine oil and remove oil pump body together with drive spindle. To disassemble, proceed as follows:

**1)** Remove pump cover and gasket. Slide pump rotors from pump body. Remove regulator cap, valve and spring. Clean all components with cleaning solvent, and inspect for wear or damage. Check the clearances indicated in the following table and ensure clearances are to specifications. If components are not to specifications, replace entire pump assembly.

**2)** Assemble pump in reverse of disassembly while making sure mark dotted on rotors faces oil pump body. Fill pump housing with engine oil before installing to front cover.

| Oil Pump Specifications | |
|---|---|
| Application | Clearance In. (mm) |
| Inner-to-Outer Rotor | |
| Side Clearance | .0016-.0032"(.04-.08 mm) |
| Rotor Tip Clearance | Less Than .0047 (.12) |
| Outer Rotor-to-Body | .0059-.0083 (.15-.21) |
| Rotor-to-Cover | .0012-.0051 (.03-.13) |

Fig. 8 Location of Oil Pump Assembly.

## ENGINE COOLING

### WATER PUMP

Centrifugal type pump with aluminum body. To remove, drain cooling system and remove fan shroud. Remove fan belts, fan, and pulley. Remove pump attaching bolts and remove water pump from front cover.

**Thermostat** — Opens at 180°F (82°C).

**Cooling System Capacity** — 11 qts.

**Radiator Cap** — 13 psi.

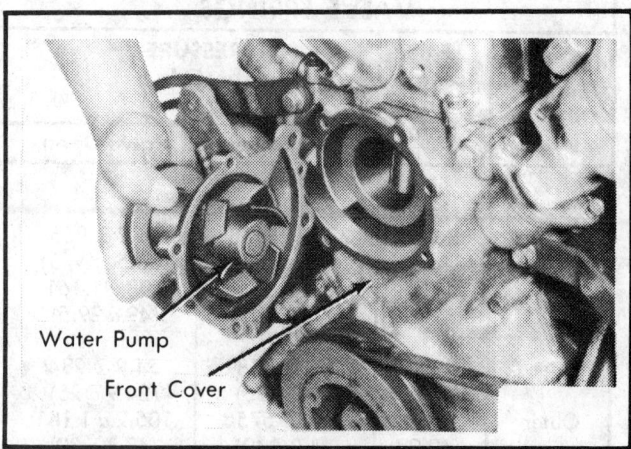

Fig. 9 Installing Water Pump to Front Cover.

# Datsun Engines

## 810 & 280Z 6 CYLINDER (Cont.)

### ENGINE SPECIFICATIONS

| GENERAL SPECIFICATIONS | | | | | | | | | | |
|---|---|---|---|---|---|---|---|---|---|---|
| Year | Displ. | | Carburetor | HP at RPM | Torque (Ft. Lbs. at RPM) | Compr. Ratio | Bore | | Stroke | |
| | cu. ins. | cc | | | | | in. | mm | in. | mm |
| 1977 | | | | | | | | | | |
| L28 | 168.0 | 2753 | Fuel Inj. | ..... | ..... | 8.3-1 | 3.390 | 86 | 3.110 | 79 |
| L24 | 146.0 | 2393 | Fuel Inj. | ..... | ..... | 8.6-1 | 3.270 | 83 | 2.90 | 73.7 |

| VALVES | | | | | | | |
|---|---|---|---|---|---|---|---|
| Engine & Valve | Head Diam. In. (mm) | Face Angle | Seat Angle | Seat Width In. (mm) | Stem Diameter In. (mm) | Stem Clearance In. (mm) | Valve Lift In. (mm) |
| L28 | | | | | | | |
| Int. | 1.73 (44.0) | 45.5 | 45.5 | .055-.063 (1.4-1.6) | .3136-.3142 (7.965-7.980) | .0008-.0021 (.020-.053) | .433 (11) |
| Exh. | 1.38 (35.0) | 45.5° | 45.5° | .071-.087 (1.8-2.2) | .3128-.3134 (7.945-7.960) | .0016-.0029 (.040-.073) | .433 (11) |
| L24 | | | | | | | |
| Int. | 1.64 (42.0) | 45.5° | 45.5° | .055-.063 (1.4-1.6) | .3136-.3142 (7.965-7.980) | .0008-.0021 (.020-.053) | .394 (10) |
| Exh. | 1.38 (35.0) | 45.5° | 45.5° | .071-.087 (1.8-2.2) | .3128-.3134 (7.945-7.960) | .0016-.0029 (.040-.073) | .413 (10.5) |

| VALVE SPRINGS | | | |
|---|---|---|---|
| Engine | Free Length In. (mm) | PRESSURE Lbs. @ In. (kg @ mm) | |
| | | Valve Closed | Valve Open |
| L28 | | | |
| Inner | 1.766 (44.85) | 27.1@1.378 (12.3@35) | 56.2@.965 (25.5@24.5) |
| Outer | 1.968 (49.98) | 47@1.575 (21.3@40) | 108@1.161 (49@29.5) |
| L24 | | | |
| Inner | 1.766 (44.85) | 27@1.378 (12.3@35) | 54.9@.984 (24.9@25) |
| Outer | 1.968 (49.98) | 47@1.575 (21.3@40) | 105.2@1.181 (47.7@30) |

| CAMSHAFT | | | |
|---|---|---|---|
| Engine | Journal Diam. In. (mm) | Clearance In. (mm) | Lobe Lift In. (mm) |
| L28 | 1.8878-1.8883 (47.949-47.962) | .0015-.0026 (.038-.067) | In.&Exh. .275 (7.00) |
| L24 | 1.8878-1.8883 (47.949-47.962) | .0015-.0026 (.038-.067) | In. .261 (6.65) Exh. .275 (7.00) |

## 810 & 280Z 6 CYLINDER (Cont.)

### ENGINE SPECIFICATIONS (Cont.)

| PISTONS, PINS, RINGS | | | | | | | |
|---|---|---|---|---|---|---|---|
| | PISTONS | PINS | | RINGS | | | |
| Engine | Clearance In. (mm) | Piston Fit In. (mm) | Rod Fit In. (mm) | Rings | End Gap In. (mm) | Side Clearance In. (mm) | |
| L28 | .0010-.0018 (.025-.045) | .0002-.0005 (.006-.013) | ① .0006-.0013 (.015-.033) | No.1 | .0098-.0157 (.25-.40) | .0016-.0029 (.040-.073) | |
| | | | | No.2 | .0118-.0197 (.30-.50) | .0012-.0028 (.030-.070) | |
| | | | | Oil | .0118-.0354 (.30-.90) | Snug | |
| L24 | .0010-.0018 (.025-.045) | .0002-.0005 (.006-.013) | ① .0006-.0013 (.015-.033) | No.1 | .0098-.0157 (.25-.40) | .0016-.0029 (.040-.073) | |
| | | | | No.2 | .0118-.0197 (.30-.50) | .0012-.0028 (.030-.070) | |
| | | | | Oil | .006-.012 (.15-.30) | Snug | |

① — Interference fit.

| CRANKSHAFT MAIN & CONNECTING ROD BEARINGS | | | | | | |
|---|---|---|---|---|---|---|
| | MAIN BEARINGS | | | | CONNECTING ROD BEARINGS | |
| Engine | Journal Diam. In. (mm) | Clearance In. (mm) | Thrust Bearing | Crankshaft End Play In. (mm) | Journal Diam. In. (mm) | Clearance In. (mm) | Side Play In. (mm) |
| L28&L24 | 2.1631-2.1636 (54.942-54.955) | .0008-.0028 (.022-.071) | Center | .002-.007 (.05-.18) | 1.9670-1.9675 (49.961-49.974) | .0010-.0022 (.025-.056) | .0079-.0118 (.20-.30) |

### TIGHTENING SPECIFICATIONS

| Application | Ft. Lbs.(mkg) |
|---|---|
| Cylinder Head | 51-61 (7.0-8.5) |
| Connecting Rod | 33-40(4.5-5.5) |
| Flywheel | 94-108(13-15) |
| Camshaft Gear | 94-108(13-15) |
| Oil Pan | 4.3-7.2(.6-1.0) |
| Oil Pump-to-Front Cover | 8-11(1.1-2.1) |
| Oil Pump Cover | 5-7(.7-1.0) |
| Camshaft Lock Plate | 3.6-5.8(.5-.8) |
| Crankshaft Pulley | 94-108(13-15) |
| Main Bearing Cap | 33-40(4.5-5.5) |
| Front Cover | |
| 6M Bolt | 2.9-5.8(.4-.8) |
| 8M Bolt | 7.2-11.6(1.0-1.6) |
| Rocker Pivot Lock Nuts | 36-43(5-6) |
| Intake & Exhaust Manifolds | |
| 8M Bolt | 1-13(1.4-1.8) |
| 10M Bolt | 29-40(4.0-5.5) |

## 128 & X1/9 4 CYLINDER

### ENGINE CODING

#### ENGINE IDENTIFICATION

Engine identification and serial numbers are stamped in crankcase on flywheel side of engine next to union for radiator hoses. Engine code is stamped above serial number.

| Application | Engine Code |
| --- | --- |
| 128 (Calif.) | 128A1.031.6 |
| 128 (Federal) | 128A1.040.6 |
| X1/9 (Calif.) | 128AS.031.6 |
| X1/9 (Federal) | 128AS.031.5 |

### ENGINE, CYLINDER HEAD & MANIFOLDS

#### ENGINE

**NOTE** – Engine and transmission are removed as one unit.

**Model 128 – 1)** Raise and support vehicle with safety stands. Raise hood and disconnect stay rod. Remove spare tire from engine compartment. Remove lower protective guard. Disconnect both battery cables.

**2)** Drain complete cooling system. Lower heater lever inside vehicle. Remove radiator cap and supply tank cap. Open drain on bottom of radiator and on inner side of crankcase.

**3)** Disconnect wires from coil to distributor. Disconnect wires at generator, starter, oil pressure switch and water temperature sending unit. Remove air cleaner housing and cartridge.

**4)** Disconnect accelerator linkage and choke cable at carburetor. Disconnect fuel inlet line at fuel pump. Disconnect exhaust pipe at exhaust manifold.

**5)** Remove radiator hoses from union at left side of engine. Remove heater hoses from engine. Remove speedometer cable from transmission. Remove adjustable rod from clutch release lever by removing nut and lock-nut.

**6)** From underneath vehicle, remove stabilizer bar from body and lower suspension control arms. Remove exhaust pipe support bracket from transmission. Disconnect rod from gear shift control lever.

**7)** Remove left wheel and tire. Remove left tie-rod nut and separate tie-rod from steering arm using a suitable puller (A.47044). Disconnect shock absorber at lower mount. Remove outer axle nuts from both sides.

**8)** Remove strut connecting engine to body. Attach a suitable lifting fixture (A.60559) to engine. Connect lifting fixture to a hoist and raise engine slightly. Remove bolt from clamp securing engine to body. Remove engine support crossmember from under engine.

**9)** Pull shafts of axle joints from bearing housings. Secure axle shafts to differential with wire to prevent working loose from seats. Remove engine and transmission assembly from bottom of vehicle. Separate transmission and differential assembly from engine.

**Model X1/9 – 1)** Disconnect battery cables and loosen fuel cap to vent fuel tank. Drain complete cooling system. Disconnect hoses from air injection valve and air cleaner, then disconnect fresh air duct from fan. Remove air cleaner assembly with fresh air duct.

**2)** Disconnect hoses from air pump, then separate heater return hose at coupling joint and heater hose at pump. Disconnect wires from alternators. Remove bolts holding louvered protection panel below carbon trap in rear firewall.

**3)** Disconnect choke linkage, hoses and wires from carburetor. Disconnect electrical leads from distributor, oil pressure switch, water temperature sending unit and starter.

**4)** Remove clamp holding fuel lines to firewall and disconnect fuel lines from firewall. Disconnect accelerator cable from support. Remove cooling system expansion tank and disconnect hoses from thermostat. Disconnect clutch master cylinder from transmission and swing out of way.

**5)** Raise and support vehicle with safety stands. Remove remaining bolt attaching louvered panel in rear firewall, then remove panel. Remove alternator heat shield, engine panels and wheel panels. Drain transmission and differential assembly. Disconnect back-up light and seat belt interlock connectors, then remove clamps to allow wires to come out with engine. Disconnect speedometer cable and gearshift linkage from transmission.

**6)** Disconnect ground strap at engine, then remove muffler and muffler upper bracket. Remove axle boot retaining bolts and slide boots away from differential.

**7)** Remove nuts securing hand brake cable brackets to control arms. Remove bolts attaching control arms to body and swing arms down out of brackets. **NOTE** – Record number of shims at control arm mounting points for installation purpose. Move control arms away from differential until axles are free of differential.

**8)** Remove lower crossmember attaching bolts and remove crossmember. From above engine, disconnect reaction arm from bracket on engine, then remove front engine mount through bolt. Remove engine and transmission assembly from bottom of vehicle. Separate transmission and differential from engine.

#### INTAKE & EXHAUST MANIFOLD

**1)** Drain cooling system. Remove spare tire from engine compartment. Remove air cleaner and cartridge. Disconnect accelerator linkage and choke cable from carburetor. Remove carburetor pre-heating water hoses.

**2)** Remove carburetor with guard and gaskets. Remove shroud from intake and exhaust manifold. Remove intake and exhaust manifold from engine.

**3)** To install, use new gaskets and reverse removal procedure.

# Fiat Engines

## 128 & X1/9  4 CYLINDER (Cont.)

### CYLINDER HEAD

**NOTE** – *This procedure is with engine in vehicle.*

1) Drain engine cooling system and remove spare tire from engine compartment. Remove air cleaner housing and cartridge. Disconnect spark plug wires at spark plugs.

2) Disconnect accelerator linkage and choke cable at carburetor. Disconnect fuel line at carburetor. Disconnect wire from temperature sending unit.

3) Disconnect heater hose at cylinder head. Disconnect all water hoses at union on left side of engine. Disconnect exhaust pipe from exhaust manifold.

4) Disconnect reaction rod from engine bracket and hose from exhaust shroud. Remove timing cover, then remove alternator and water pump drive belt. Remove air pump drive belt, then loosen nut on tensioner pulley and remove timing belt. Remove cylinder head nuts and bolts, then remove head and manifolds as an assembly.

5) Thoroughly clean all gasket surfaces on cylinder head and block. Use new gasket with word "ALTO" facing up when installing head. Tighten bolts and nuts in sequence shown in *Fig. 1* in two steps: first to about 29 ft.lbs. (4.0 mkg), and then to final torque of 69 ft.lbs. (9.5 mkg). Complete assembly in reverse order of removal. *See Timing Belt Replacement.*

**Fig. 1  Cylinder Head Tightening Sequence**

### VALVES

#### VALVE ARRANGEMENT

E-I-I-E-E-I-I-E

#### VALVE GUIDE SERVICING

1) With cylinder head removed and disassembled, check clearance between valve stem and valve guide. If clearance is more than .006", and valve stem is not worn, valve guide must be replaced.

2) Drive guide from cylinder head using a suitable driver (A.60153). Use same driver to install guides with a suitable spacer installed (6A intake and 6S exhaust).

#### VALVE STEM OIL SEALS

Use new seals when assembling cylinder head. Use a suitable guide (A.60313) to install seals on valve guides.

**Fig. 2  Using Special Driver to Remove Valve Guide**

### VALVE SPRING REMOVAL

1) Remove cylinder head as previously outlined. Remove camshaft housing cover, carburetor, intake and exhaust manifolds. Remove camshaft housing with camshaft.

**Fig. 3  Using Special Valve Spring Compressor to Remove Valve Springs**

2) Using a suitable valve spring compressor (A.60311) compress valve spring. Remove valve keepers and release compressor. Remove spring retainer, inner spring, outer spring, lower spring seat and washer.

3) Inspect valve springs for wear or cracking. Using a suitable spring tester (AP.5049) check inner and outer springs against specifications with specified load applied.

4) To install valve spring, reverse removal procedure. Install cylinder head as previously outlined.

## 128 & X1/9  4 CYLINDER (Cont.)

**Fig. 4  Expanded View of Valve Train Components**

## VALVE CLEARANCE ADJUSTMENT

**NOTE** — *Valve clearance is checked and adjusted with engine cold.*

1) Remove camshaft cover. Rotate engine until lobe on camshaft of valve being checked is pointing straight up. Using a feeler gauge, check clearance between camshaft lobe and valve tappet plate.

**Fig. 5  Showing Where to Make Valve Clearance Check**

2) If clearance is not as specified, insert a suitable spring compressor (A.60421) under camshaft to release spring tension against camshaft lobe. Remove tappet plate with a suitable removing tool (A.87001). With plate removed, measure thickness to determine size of plate to be installed.

### Valve Clearance Specifications

| Application | Intake Valve | Exhaust Valve |
| --- | --- | --- |
| All | .012" (.3mm) | .016" (.4mm) |

3) Valve tappet plates are available in various thicknesses: .1280-.1850" (3.251-4.699 mm) in increments of .0019" (.048 mm). Plate size is shown on face, install this side toward tappet. Use same procedure on both intake and exhaust valves. Recheck clearance and install camshaft cover.

**Fig. 6  Using Special Tool to Remove Valve Tappet Plate**

## PISTONS, PINS & RINGS

### OIL PAN

**NOTE** — *This procedure is with engine in vehicle.*

1) Attach a suitable engine support (A.70526) to top of engine. Remove protective shields and engine crossmember.

2) Drain oil and remove oil pan retaining screws and oil pan. To install, clean all gasket surfaces, use new gasket and reverse removal procedure.

### PISTON & ROD ASSEMBLY

1) Remove oil pan and cylinder head as previously outlined. Remove oil pump. See *Oil Pump.* Remove nuts from connecting rods and remove rod caps. Push piston and rod assembly up and out through top.

2) To install, compress piston rings with a suitable ring compressor. Pistons must be installed with number stamped on connecting rod and rod cap facing away from auxiliary shaft on 128 models and with number facing towards auxiliary shaft on model X1/9.

3) Tighten rod nuts to specifications. Install remaining components as previously outlined.

## 128 & X1/9   4 CYLINDER (Cont.)

**Fig. 7   Piston & Connecting Rod Assembly Showing Identification Class Numbers**

### FITTING PISTONS

**1)** With piston and rod assembly removed and disassembled as previously outlined, thoroughly clean piston. Check ring side clearance, side clearance should be no more than .006" (.15mm). Check ring end gap in cylinder against specifications.

**2)** Check fit of piston in cylinders with rings removed. There should be no more than .006" (.15mm) clearance. Pistons are available in .0079" (.2mm), .0157" (.4mm) and .0236" (.6mm) oversizes. There are three classes of standard size pistons. If piston is replaced, one of the same class must be installed. Class of piston is stamped on bottom of piston.

**Fig. 8   Using a Feeler Gauge to Check Piston-to-Cylinder Wall Clearance**

### Piston Class Specification

| Application | ①Size |
| --- | --- |
| X1/9 | |
| Class A | 3.3827-3.3831" (85.92-85.93 mm) |
| Class C | 3.3842-3.3846" (85.96-85.97 mm) |
| Class E | 3.3850-3.3854" (85.98-85.99 mm) |

① — Measured at 1.35" (34.3 mm) from piston skirt edge.

### Piston Class Specification

| Application | ①Size |
| --- | --- |
| 128 | |
| Class A | 3.3827-3.3831" (85.92-85.93 mm) |
| Class C | 3.3835-3.3839" (85.94-85.95 mm) |
| Class E | 3.3842-3.3846" (85.96-85.97 mm) |

① — Measured at 1.35" (34.3 mm) from piston skirt edge.

**3)** When installing rings, make sure gaps are spaced approximately 120° apart. Assemble piston and connecting rod and install in vehicle as previously outlined.

### PISTON PIN REPLACEMENT

**1)** Remove piston and rod assembly as previously outlined. Remove circlips and drive out piston pin using a suitable driver (A.60251).

**2)** Check fit of pin in piston. Pin should be push fit in piston and should not fall through under its own weight. There are two classes of piston pin and piston bore sizes. If piston pin is replaced it must be replaced with a pin of the same class. Class of piston is stamped on bottom and class of pin is stamped on face of pin.

### Piston Pin & Bore Class Specifications

| Application | Size |
| --- | --- |
| Piston Pin | |
| Class 1 | .8658-.8659" (21.991-21.994mm) |
| Class 2 | .8659-.8660" (21.994-21.996mm) |
| Piston Pin Bore | |
| Class 1 | .8660-.8661" (21.996-21.999mm) |
| Class 2 | .8661-.8662" (21.999-22.002mm) |

**3)** Check piston pin clearance in connecting rod. If clearance is more than specified, drive bushing from connecting rod using a suitable driver (A.60054). Install a new bushing with same driver and ream to size with a new piston pin.

**4)** Piston pin bore in piston is offset .08". Install connecting rod with numbered side on same side as offset. Lubricate piston pin and secure connecting rod big end in a vise. Place piston in proper position with connecting rod and push in piston pin using a sutable driver (A.60251). Install circlips.

**5)** Install piston and connecting rod assembly as previously outlined.

# Fiat Engines

## 128 & X1/9  4 CYLINDER (Cont.)

### CRANKSHAFT MAIN & CONNECTING ROD BEARINGS

#### MAIN & CONNECTING ROD BEARING SERVICE

1) Remove engine as previously outlined. Remove cylinder head, oil pan, clutch and flywheel as previously outlined. Remove oil pump. See *Oil Pump*. Remove all sprockets and timing belt. See *Timing Belt Replacement*.

2) Remove cover plates and seals from both ends of engine. Remove all piston and connecting rod assemblies. Remove main bearing caps with lower bearing halves.

3) Remove crankshaft and upper bearing halves. Remove thrust bearings from flywheel end main bearing saddle. Thoroughly clean and inspect crankshaft and crankcase.

4) Check crankshaft journals for out-of-round, if more than .0002", crankshaft must be ground to next undersize. Bearings for undersize crankshafts are available in .010", .020", .030" and .040" undersize.

5) Use the Plastigage method to check main bearing clearances. Install upper bearing halves in crankcase and install crankshaft. Place a piece of Plastigage on journal and install main bearing cap with bearing. Tighten bolts to specifications and then remove main bearing cap.

6) With cap removed, check flattened Plastigage against scale on back of package to determine if clearance is as specified. Check connecting rod bearing clearance using same procedure. If clearance is incorrect, crankshaft must be ground to next undersize and bearings of corresponding undersize installed.

7) With correct clearance obtained, install upper bearing halves in crankcase. Lubricate bearings and install crankshaft. Install main bearing caps with bearings and tighten bolts to specifications. Rotate crankshaft to check for freedom of movement.

8) Check crankshaft endplay. See *Thrust Bearing Alignment*. Install remaining components in reverse of removal order or as previously outlined. Install engine as previously outlined.

#### THRUST BEARING ALIGNMENT

1) With crankshaft installed and main bearing caps tightened to specifications. Attach a dial indicator to crankcase with arm against flywheel end of crankshaft. Pry crankshaft back and forth to measure endplay.

2) If endplay is more than .0104", remove flywheel end main bearing cap and install oversize thrust rings. Thrust rings are available in .005" oversize. Install a suitable size thrust ring to obtain correct endplay.

#### FRONT & REAR MAIN BEARING OIL SEAL SERVICE

1) Front and rear main bearing oil seals are secured in end plates mounted to both ends of crankcase. Both seals should be replaced when crankshaft has been removed.

2) Drive seals from end plates and install new ones. Lubricate sealing lip of seal and use new gaskets when installing end plates.

### CAMSHAFT

#### TIMING BELT REPLACEMENT

**NOTE** — *This procedure is with engine in vehicle. If a timing belt is loosened or removed to perform repair work, it should always be replaced.*

**Removal 128 — 1)** Remove right guard and loosen timing chain cover retaining screws, from under vehicle. Remove timing chain cover. Check timing by aligning index marks on top and bottom of camshaft sprocket with index marks on engine mounting and upper case. Index on crankshaft sprocket should be in alignment with index on crankshaft seal case.

2) Put vehicle in low gear and apply hand brake to prevent crankshaft from turning. Remove fan belt, loosen tensioner pulley retaining nut and relieve tension. Remove timing belt.

**Installation** — Install new belt, making sure belt and sprocket teeth engage correctly. Tighten pulley support nut. Recheck timing. Install remaining components.

**Fig. 9    Fitting Crankshaft Thrust Washer to Block**

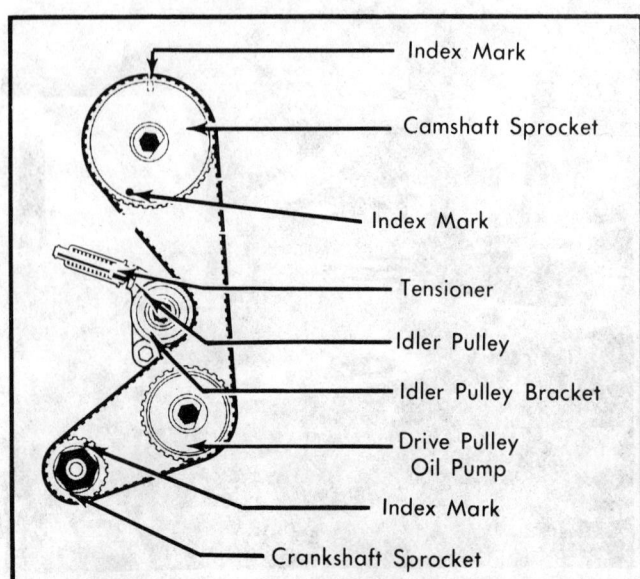

Index Mark

Camshaft Sprocket

Index Mark

Tensioner

Idler Pulley

Idler Pulley Bracket

Drive Pulley Oil Pump

Index Mark

Crankshaft Sprocket

**Fig. 10    Front View of Engine Showing Timing Belt Installed**

## 128 & X1/9   4 CYLINDER (Cont.)

**Removal X1/9 — 1)** Rotate No. 4 cylinder into firing position at top dead center. Position transmission into 4th gear, to prevent crankshaft from turning. Apply parking brake.

**NOTE** — *If camshaft is turned independently of engine, valves may hit pistons causing engine damage.*

**2)** Remove right guard from under engine. Remove timing bolts and cover. Loosen alternator and remove alternator/water pump drive belt. Loosen air pump and remove drive belt.

**3)** Remove valve cover and check that camshaft lobes of No. 4 cylinder are pointing up. Remove distributor. Loosen idler pulley lock nut. Remove timing belt starting at idler pulley.

**Installation — 1)** Install timing belt making sure that teeth are properly engaged in sprockets. Start installation of timing belt at crankshaft pulley. Release idler pulley lock nut and retighten after tension is on belt.

**NOTE** — *Never allow engine to rotate backwards, or slack will develop in belt and belt will jump timing.*

**2)** Rotate engine one-half turn. Loosen idler pulley lock nut to ensure all slack is removed. Retighten lock nut. Rotate engine until No. 4 cylinder is in firing position (cam lobe up). Install remaining components in reverse of removal order.

## CAMSHAFT

**1)** Remove timing belt protective cover and loosen belt tensioner. Remove timing belt from camshaft sprocket and remove sprocket from camshaft. Remove camshaft cover, camshaft and housing. Remove camshaft from housing and thoroughly clean and inspect both.

**2)** If camshaft housing bores show signs of wear or scoring and are out of round, replace housing. Check camshaft for signs of seizure or scoring. If scoring or seizure marks cannot be removed with a fine abrasive stone, replace camshaft.

**3)** Check camshaft for out-of-round conditions. Center camshaft journal should not vary more than .008" out-of-round. Check lobe lift.

**4)** Install camshaft in housing using new drive end seal. Install sprocket and place housing and camshaft on cylinder head. Tighten nuts to specifications. Install timing belt correctly. See *Valve Timing.* Check valve clearance. See *Valve Clearance Adjustment.* Install camshaft cover.

## AUXILIARY SHAFT

**1)** Auxiliary shaft drives; distributor, oil pump and fuel pump. Shaft is driven by timing belt. Remove oil pump. See *Oil Pump Removal.* Remove fuel pump and distributor. Inspect drive gears of distributor and oil pump, if gears are chipped or worn, auxiliary shaft must be replaced.

**2)** Remove timing belt as previously outlined. With fuel pump, oil pump and distributor removed, remove auxiliary shaft sprocket. Remove lock plate and auxiliary shaft. Thoroughly clean and inspect shaft.

**3)** Check inner and outer journals of shaft. If journal size is less than specified, replace shaft. Check inside diameter of inner and outer bushings, if more than specified, replace bushings.

**4)** To replace bushings, drive out of crankcase using a suitable driver (A.60372/1/2 outer journal and A.660372/1 inner journal). Install new bushings using same drivers as used for removal. Make sure oil holes in bushings align with oil holes in crankcase. Ream bushings to specified clearance with shaft using a suitable reamer (A.90365).

**5)** Install auxiliary shaft and lock plate. Install sprocket and secure with lock plate and screw. Install remaining components as previously outlined or in reverse of removal order.

### Auxiliary Shaft Specifications

| Application | Size |
|---|---|
| **Auxiliary Shaft** | |
| Outer Journal | 1.4013-1.4023" (35.59-35.62mm) |
| Inner Journal | 1.2575-1.2583" (31.94-31.96mm) |
| **Bushings (Reamed)** | |
| Outer Journal | 1.4041-1.4049" (35.66-35.68mm) |
| Inner Journal | 1.2598-1.2606" (32.00-32.02mm) |
| **Clearance** | |
| Outer Journal | .0018-.0036" (.046-.091mm) |
| Inner Journal | .0016-.0031" (.04-.08mm) |

### VALVE TIMING

**1)** With timing belt removed, rotate camshaft sprocket until marks on sprocket are in alignment with index marks on engine.

**2)** Rotate crankshaft sprocket until mark on sprocket aligns with index on end plate. Install timing belt as previously outlined, making sure camshaft or crankshaft are not rotated.

## ENGINE OILING

**Crankcase Capacity** — Total capacity of entire system is 5.3 quarts. Normal drain and refill capacity (with filter) is 4.5 quarts.

**Oil Filter** — Full flow, mounted on front side of engine.

**Normal Oil Pressure** — 64-85 psi. with engine @212°F.

**Pressure Relief Valve** — Mounted in oil pump. *See Oil Pump.*

### ENGINE OILING SYSTEM

Oil is circulated through engine by pressure provided by a gear type oil pump. Pump is mounted on bottom of crankcase and driven by the auxiliary shaft. Oil is drawn from oil pan by oil pump and circulated through a full flow oil filter. Oil is then pumped into main oil gallery of crankcase where it is distributed to crankshaft and camshaft. Oil flows through crankshaft to lubricate main and connecting rod bearings. Cylinders, pistons and piston pins are lubricated by oil squirted from hole in connecting rod. Oil flows through camshaft to journals. Oil is squirted from number two and four journal to lubricate valve tappets and valves. Auxiliary shaft is lubricated by oil from main oil gallery. Excess oil flows back into oil pan.

# Fiat Engines

## 128 & X1/9  4 CYLINDER (Cont.)

**Fig. 11  Diagram Showing Engine Lubrication Flow**

### OIL PUMP

1) Remove oil pan as previously outlined. Remove retaining screws and slide out oil pump with suction tube.

2) Clamp pump housing in a vise and remove suction pipe with filter screen and relief valve. Remove pump cover and gears. Thoroughly clean all components.

3) Check both gears for excess wear and replace if necessary. Check clearance between gears, if more than .010", replace both gears. Check gear-to-pump housing clearance, if more than .010", replace gears or housing as necessary.

4) Check gear endplay by placing a straight edge on mating surface of pump and inserting a feeler gauge between straight edge and gears. If clearance is more than .006", replace gears or housing as necessary. Check clearance between drive gear shaft and housing, if more than .004", replace gear or housing as necessary.

5) Inspect pressure relief spring for cracking or wear. Inspect valve for wear or scoring. Check spring against specifications. Spring should not collapse below given length under given load. Replace spring if length is less than specified.

6) Assemble oil pump in reverse of disassembly order. To install, reverse removal procedure.

### Oil Pump Specifications

| Application | Clearance |
|---|---|
| Gear-to-Gear | .006" (.15mm) |
| Gear-to-Housing | .004-.007" (.11-.18mm) |
| Gear Endplay | .0008-.0041" (.02-.11mm) |

## ENGINE COOLING

**Thermostat** — Fully open @176-183° F.

### Cooling System Capacity
128 — 6.8 quarts.
128 3P — 7.4 quarts.
X1/9 — 11.4 quarts.

### WATER PUMP

1) Remove protective panels from bottom of engine and drain cooling system. Remove alternator and drive belt. Disconnect hoses from water pump, then remove nuts attaching water pipe to pump and disconnect pipe. Remove bolts holding water pump to engine and remove pump.

2) Clean all gasket surfaces and install new gasket. To install, reverse removal procedure and refill cooling system. Run engine and check for leaks.

## ENGINE SPECIFICATIONS

### GENERAL SPECIFICATIONS

| Year | Displ. | | Carburetor | HP at RPM | Torque (Ft. Lbs. at RPM) | Compr. Ratio | Bore | | Stroke | |
|---|---|---|---|---|---|---|---|---|---|---|
| | cu. ins. | cc | | | | | in. | mm | in. | mm |
| 1978 | | | | | | | | | | |
| 128 | 78.7 | 1290 | 1-Bbl. | 62@6000 | 67@4000 | 8.5-1 | 3.39 | 86 | 2.19 | 55.5 |
| X1/9 | 78.7 | 1290 | 1-Bbl. | 61@5800 | 76@4000 | 8.5-1 | 3.39 | 86 | 2.19 | 55.5 |

### VALVES

| Engine & Valve | Head Diam. In. (mm) | Face Angle | Seat Angle | Seat Width In. (mm) | Stem Diameter In. (mm) | Stem Clearance In. (mm) | Valve Lift In. (mm) |
|---|---|---|---|---|---|---|---|
| 1290cc | | | | | | | |
| Intake | 1.4173 (36) | 45° | 45° | .0787 (2) | .3139-.3146 (7.974-7.992) | .0012-.0026 (.030-.066) | .3839 (9.75) |
| Exhaust | 1.2205 (31) | 45° | 45° | .0787 (2) | .3139-.3146 (7.974-7.992) | .0012-.0026 (.030-.066) | .3839 (9.75) |

# Fiat Engines

## 128 & X1/9  4 CYLINDER (Cont.)

### ENGINE SPECIFICATIONS (Cont.)

#### VALVE SPRINGS

| Engine | Free Length | PRESSURE (LBS.) | |
| --- | --- | --- | --- |
| | | Valve Closed | Valve Open |
| 1290 cc Inner | 1.646 (41.81) | 33@1.220 (15@31.00) | 62@.846 (28@21.49) |
| Outer | 2.122 (53.90) | 86@1.417 (39@36.00) | 131@1.043 (60@26.49) |

#### VALVE TIMING

| Engine | INTAKE | | EXHAUST | |
| --- | --- | --- | --- | --- |
| | Open (BTDC) | Close (ABDC) | Open (BBDC) | Close (ATDC) |
| 1290 cc① | 10° | 54° | 54° | 10° |

① — Valve timing checked with all valves adjusted to .020".

#### PISTONS, PINS, RINGS

| Engine | PISTONS | PINS | | RINGS | | |
| --- | --- | --- | --- | --- | --- | --- |
| | Clearance In. (mm) | Piston Fit In. (mm) | Rod Fit In. (mm) | Rings | End Gap In. (mm) | Side Clearance In. (mm) |
| 1290cc | .0020-.0028① (.05-.07) | .0001-.0003 (.002-.008) | .0004-.0006 (.010-.016) | No. 1 | .0118-.0177 (.30-.45) | .0018-.0030 (.045-.077) |
| | | | | No. 2 | .0118-.0177 (.30-.45) | .0016-.0028 (.040-.072) |
| | | | | No. 3 | .0098-.0157 (.25-.40) | .0012-.0024 (.030-.062) |

① — 128 models .0028-.0035" (.07-.09 mm).

#### CRANKSHAFT MAIN & CONNECTING ROD BEARINGS

| Engine | MAIN BEARINGS | | | | CONNECTING ROD BEARINGS | | |
| --- | --- | --- | --- | --- | --- | --- | --- |
| | Journal Diam. In. (mm) | Clearance In. (mm) | Thrust Bearing | Crankshaft End Play In. (mm) | Journal Diam. In. (mm) | Clearance In. (mm) | Side Play In. (mm) |
| 1290cc | 1.9994-2.0002 (50.785-50.805) | .0016-.0033 (.040-.085) | ① | .0021-.0104 (.055-.265) | 1.7913-1.7920 (45.498-45.518) | .0014-.0034 (.036-.086) | ......... |

① — Thrust ring is installed at flywheel end main bearing cap.

#### CAMSHAFT

| Engine | Journal Diam. In. (mm) | Clearance In. (mm) | Lobe Lift In. (mm) |
| --- | --- | --- | --- |
| 1290cc | | | |
| No. 1 | 1.1789-1.1795 (29.944-29.960) | .0011-.0028 (.029-.070) | .... |
| No. 2 | 1.8872-1.8878 (47.935-47.950) | .0012-.0028 (.030-.070) | .... |
| No. 3 | 1.8951-1.8957 (48.135-48.150) | .0012-.0028 (.030-.070) | .... |
| No. 4 | 1.9030-1.9035 (48.335-48.350) | .0012-.0028 (.030-.070) | .... |
| No. 5 | 1.9108-1.9114 (48.535-48.550) | .0012-.0028 (.030-.070) | .... |

#### TIGHTENING SPECIFICATIONS

| Application | Ft. Lbs. (mkg) |
| --- | --- |
| Cylinder Head Bolts | 69 (9.5) |
| Cylinder Head Nuts | 69 (9.5) |
| Main Bearing Cap Bolts | 58 (8.0) |
| Connecting Rod Cap Bolts | 36 (5.0) |
| Intake and Exhaust Manifold Nuts | 22 (3.0) |
| Camshaft Sprocket Bolt | 61 (8.5) |
| Timing Belt Tensioner Pulley Nut | 33 (4.5) |
| Crankshaft Pulley and Sprocket Nut | 101 (14.0) |
| Flywheel-to-Crankshaft Bolts | 61 (8.5) |

## 124 & 131 4 CYLINDER

### ENGINE CODING

#### ENGINE IDENTIFICATION

Engine identification number is stamped in pad above oil filter mount on left side of engine.

| Application | Engine Code |
|---|---|
| 124 Spider & 131 Models with Catalytic Converter ............................. | 132 A1.031.6 |
| 124 Spider & 131 Models without Catalytic Converter ......................... | 132 A1.040.6 |

### ENGINE & CYLINDER HEAD

#### ENGINE

**Removal — 1)** Remove hood and air cleaner. Loosen fuel tank cap to relieve pressure. Disconnect battery. Mark for identification and disconnect vacuum and fuel lines and electrical leads. Disconnect accelerator and remove linkage from cam housing cover.

**NOTE** — *On A/C equipped cars, it will be necessary to discharge system and remove condenser and fan assembly prior to removal of engine. When installing, system will require evacuation and charging.*

**2)** Drain cooling system and disconnect hoses. Disconnect automatic transmission cooling lines (if equipped). Remove radiator and cooling fan assembly.

**3)** Disconnect remaining hoses and wires from chassis to engine at engine. Disconnect exhaust pipe at manifold. Disconnect A/T fluid dipstick from support bracket (if equipped).

**4)** From underneath vehicle, remove oil filter, engine splash pans and any remaining electrical connections. Remove starter by passing through oil filter opening. (On A/C equipped vehicles, pull starter from mounted position and tie to engine until engine is removed.) Remove speedometer cable support bracket from engine mount.

**5)** Remove fuel inlet line from pump. Remove nuts and washers holding engine mount isolators to crossmembers, and ground strap to engine mount. Install transmission support and remove bolts securing transmission to engine. If A/T equipped, remove bolts attaching flywheel to torque converter.

**6)** Attach engine sling and hoist engine until mount clears cross members. Move engine forward until clear and lift from engine compartment.

**Installation —** To install, reverse removal procedure. Ensure that pilot shaft engages clutch properly (manual transmission).

#### CYLINDER HEAD

**Removal — 1)** Disconnect battery, drain cooling system and remove air cleaner. Disconnect water temperature sending unit connection and spark plug wires. Disconnect water hoses.

**2)** Remove timing belt cover and oil dipstick tube. Rotate crankshaft by hand until timing marks on rear of camshaft sprockets align with pointers on cam housing. Remove timing belt. See *Timing Belt Replacement.* From engine left side, remove vacuum and fuel lines and electrical connections.

**3)** Disconnect accelerator rod from carburetor, then remove linkage from cam housing cover. Disconnect exhaust pipe from manifold. Disconnect transmission fluid dipstick from support bracket (A/T only). Remove cylinder head bolts and lift off head with gasket.

**Installation — 1)** Before installation of cylinder head, position camshafts so that reference marks on sprockets are aligned with fixed pointers on front of cylinder head.

**2)** When installing cylinder head, camshafts must not be moved in either direction. Rotate crankshaft and bring pistons number 1 and 4 to TDC.

**3)** Install two dummy studs in one cylinder head bolt hole at front and rear of engine. Install new cylinder head gasket on block and carefully install cylinder head, making sure any valves in open position do not contact block.

**4)** Install a few head bolts and tighten manually and remove dummy studs. Install remaining head bolts and tighten to specification in sequence shown in illustration.

**Fig. 1  Cylinder Head Tightening Sequence**

### VALVES

#### VALVE ARRANGEMENT

**Left Side —** All Intake
**Right Side —** All Exhaust

#### VALVE GUIDE SERVICING

**1)** Measure clearance of valve stem in guide with a dial indicator. If clearance exceeds specifications, valve guide must be replaced.

**2)** With driver (A.60153/60395), remove defective guides from head, driving from combustion chamber side. Press new guide in place from camshaft side with drift (A.60462). Guides are prefinished to size, however minor faults caused during replacement may be hand reamed if necessary.

#### VALVE SPRING REMOVAL

**1)** With cylinder head removed, remove camshaft carriers with camshafts. Compress valve spring with a spring compressor and remove both valve keepers.

## 124 & 131 4 CYLINDER (Cont.)

2) Release spring compressor, remove upper spring retainer, inner and outer springs and lower spring retainer. To assemble cylinder head, reverse disassembly procedure.

### VALVE CLEARANCE ADJUSTMENT

1) Valve clearance is checked and/or adjusted with engine cold. Intake valve clearance is .018" (.457 mm). Exhaust valve clearance is .020" (.508 mm).

2) To adjust valves, remove camshaft covers from cylinder head. Rotate crankshaft until camshaft lobe of valve being adjusted is pointing away from valve (valve will be closed).

3) Using a feeler gauge, measure valve clearance. If clearance is not as specified, a thicker or thinner tappet plate must be installed to obtain specified clearance.

4) Tappet plates are available in service thicknesses of .128" (3.25 mm) and from .130" to .185" (3.30 mm to 4.70 mm) in increments of .004" (.10 mm).

5) To replace tappet plate, rotate camshaft until valve is fully open. Insert a suitable tappet hold down tool (A 60422) over lobe of valve being adjusted. Rotate camshaft and remove tappet plate by means of scribe through notch in tappet. Alternately, tappet may be pried down using suitable pry tool (A 60443) and tappet plate may then be removed using scribe.

6) Insert correct thickness tappet plate, rotate camshaft until lobe is resting on tappet plate and remove tool. Use this same procedure for adjusting both intake and exhaust valve clearances.

**Fig. 2   Correct Procedure to Adjust Valve Clearance**

## PISTONS, PINS & RINGS

### OIL PAN

Raise vehicle and drain crankcase. Remove engine splash shields. Remove pan bolts and strike pan firmly with rubber mallet to free from block assembly. To install, clean all mating surfaces and install gasket with sealer applied to BOTH sides. Reverse removal procedure and tighten bolts evenly to specification.

**NOTE** — *It may be necessary to disconnect motor mounts and raise engine in order to provide enough clearance to remove pan.*

### PISTON & ROD ASSEMBLY

1) When installing piston and rod assembly, thoroughly oil piston pin in piston boss. Make sure ring gaps are spaced approximately 120° apart.

2) Lubricate rings and cylinder bore. Compress rings with a ring compressor and install assembly in cylinder block so that numbers on connecting rod and cap are facing away from auxiliary shaft. Tighten connecting rod nuts to specification.

### FITTING PISTONS

1) Standard pistons are manufactured in three size classes and cylinder bores are machined according to piston class. Class of piston and bore is designated by a letter code.

2) Class code of piston is stamped on bottom of piston pin boss. Class of cylinder bore is stamped next to appropriate cylinder on oil pan flange on bottom of cylinder block.

3) Measure piston size at right angles to piston pin and 1.181" (30 mm) from piston skirt. If piston is replaced for any reason, one of the same class must be installed.

**NOTE** — *Refer to class designation letter on bottom of piston pin boss and mating surface of crankcase. (See Figs. 3 and 4).*

### Std. Piston Class Designation & Size

| Class | In. (mm) |
| --- | --- |
| A | 3.3051-3.3055 (83.95-83.96) |
| C | 3.3059-3.3063 (83.97-83.98) |
| E | 3.3066-3.3070 (83.99-84.00) |

4) Measure cylinder bore lengthwise and crosswise near top, center and bottom of bore. Check piston fit in bore at right angles to pin 1.876" (47.65 mm) below piston head using a feeler gauge. If clearance exceeds .0059" (.15 mm), cylinders must be rebored and oversized pistons installed.

### Oversize Pistons

| Application | Amt. of Oversize In. (mm) |
| --- | --- |
| 1st Oversize | .0079 (0.2) |
| 2nd Oversize | .0157 (0.4) |
| 3rd Oversize | .0236 (0.6) |

**NOTE** — *If replacement pistons are used, ensure that the four pistons are the same weight within ±.18 oz. (±5g).*

## 124 & 131 4 CYLINDER (Cont.)

**5)** Check ring side clearance in piston grooves prior to intallation on piston. Push rings squarely into cylinder bores and check ring gaps with feeler gauge. Install rings on pistons with gaps 120° apart.

**Fig. 3   Piston & Rod Assembly Markings**

**Fig. 4   Piston Bore Class Designation Marks**

### PISTON PIN REPLACEMENT

**1)** Remove circlips from piston and push piston pin out of piston and connecting rod. Separate piston from connecting rod.

**2)** Check clearance of piston pin in piston and connecting rod. If clearance is excessive, piston and connecting rod must be rebored for a .0079" (.2 mm) oversize pin.

**3)** Bushing in small end of connecting rod is replaceable and requires a .0017-.0040" (.043-.102 mm) interference fit.

**4)** To assemble piston and rod assembly, position piston on connecting rod with side of piston having offset portion of piston pin bore on same side as connecting rod numbers.

**5)** Oil piston pin and insert in piston and connecting rod. Install circlips and check piston for freedom of movement on pin. Check alignment.

## CRANKSHAFT MAIN & CONNECTING ROD BEARINGS

### MAIN & CONNECTING ROD BEARINGS

**1)** With crankshaft removed, thoroughly clean and inspect for cracks or scoring on journals. Check all journals for out-of-round condition, using a micrometer. If journal is out-of-round or tapers more than .0002" (.005 mm), crankshaft must be reground for undersize bearings.

**2)** Bearing-to-journal clearance is checked by the Plastigage method. If clearance exceeds specifications, crankshaft must be ground for undersize bearings.

**3)** Main and connecting rod bearings are available in .010" (.25 mm), .020" (.51 mm), .030" (.76 mm), and .040" (1.02 mm) undersizes.

**NOTE** – *Main bearing caps are stamped with a number that must correspond to the number stamped on crankcase near flywheel. Notches on caps face auxiliary shaft side and coincide with position. Front main bearing cap has no notch, however 2nd, center 4th and rear caps have 1, 2, 3, and 4 notches respectively.*

### CRANKSHAFT END PLAY

**1)** Mount a dial indicator on front of engine and pry crankshaft back and forth to measure crankshaft end play.

**2)** If end play exceeds specifications, adjustment may be made by installing new thrust washers to bring end play within specification.

### ENGINE FRONT COVER & OIL SEAL

Engine front cover oil seal should be replaced whenever front cover is removed. Make sure new seal is squarely seated in cover. Lubricate seal contact lip before installing cover.

### TIMING BELT REPLACEMENT

**1)** Drain cooling system and remove upper radiator hose. Remove upper section of air duct. Rotate crankshaft until marks on both camshaft sprockets are aligned with fixed pointer on front of engine. Number 4 piston should now be at TDC firing position.

**2)** Place transmission in fourth gear and apply parking brake to prevent crankshaft from turning. **CAUTION** – *Do not turn crankshaft or camshafts independent of each other as valves may hit pistons.*

## 124 & 131 4 CYLINDER (Cont.)

**Fig. 5   Camshaft Sprocket Timing Marks**

**3)** Remove lower engine protection plate and all drive belts. Loosen belt idler pulley nut and mounting bracket bolt, release tension on timing belt, tighten pulley nut and bracket bolt and remove belt. **NOTE** — *Anytime tension is relieved from timing belt, it must be replaced.* Install belt making sure not to move sprockets. Make sure that hole in auxiliary shaft pulley is lined up with tensioner pulley bolt.

**4)** To adjust timing belt tension, loosen idler pulley tensioner nut and allow pulley to take out play. Rotate crankshaft pulley 2 full turns and recheck timing marks. Tighten tensioner nut and bracket bolt.

## CAMSHAFT

### CAMSHAFT

With cylinder head removed from engine, remove distributor, manifolds and carburetor assembly. Install pulley holder (A.60446) at front of cam housing and remove bolt, washer and pulley from camshaft. Remove attaching bolts and lift off cam housing with cam. Remove cap from rear of housing and pull out camshaft. Repeat for other side. To install, reverse removal procedure, noting that distributor drive gear is on exhaust camshaft.

### AUXILIARY SHAFT

Auxiliary shaft is driven by timing belt and drives oil pump and fuel pump. With engine out of vehicle and front crankshaft pulley removed, take off auxiliary drive pulley. Remove auxiliary shaft cover and gasket. Remove spacer and gasket. Rotate auxiliary shaft to raise oil pump gear and lift gear out with long nose pliers. Remove bolts holding retainer at front of block and pull out shaft along with retainer. To install, reverse removal procedure.

## ENGINE OILING

**Crankcase Capacity** — Total capacity of entire system is 5.2 quarts. Normal drain and refill capacity (with filter) is 4 quarts.

**Oil Filter** — Full-flow, cartridge type.

**Normal Oil Pressure** — 64-85 psi (4.5-6 kg/cm²) at idle.

**Pressure Regulator Valve** — Installed in pump cover.

**NOTE** — *On air conditioned models, oil filter support mounts A/C compressor. Filter screws on from side rather than from bottom.*

### ENGINE OILING SYSTEM

Engine oiling system is full pressure lubrication utilizing a gear type oil pump driven by auxiliary shaft. A full-flow oil filter and a pressure regulator valve is also employed.

### OIL PUMP

**1)** To remove oil pump, drain oil and remove oil pan. Remove two bolts and washers holding oil pump to engine and remove pump and gasket. Visually inspect all parts for wear or damage.

**2)** Check gears for tooth-to-housing clearance. Clearance should be .004-.007" (.11-.18 mm). Place straightedge across pump body and measure gear end play. End play should be .0012-.0045" (.031-.116 mm).

**Fig. 6   Checking Oil Pump Gear End Play**

**3)** Check relief valve spring for pressure of at least 9.5 lbs. (4.3 kg) at .886" (22.5 mm). To install, reverse removal procedure and mount pump using a new gasket. Make sure pump is seated before tightening mounting bolts.

# Fiat Engines

## 124 & 131 4 CYLINDER (Cont.)

### ENGINE COOLING

Thermostat Opening Temperature — 178-185°F (81-85°C).

Cooling System Capacity — 8.5 qts.

Radiator Cap — 11 psi.

### WATER PUMP

To remove water pump, remove alternator and drive belt. Disconnect water hoses from pump and remove three bolts securing pulley on pump. Remove four bolts securing pump to engine and remove pump and gasket. To install, reverse removal procedure and use new gasket.

## ENGINE SPECIFICATIONS

### GENERAL SPECIFICATIONS

| Year | Displ. cu. ins. | Displ. cc | Carburetor | HP at RPM | Torque (Ft. Lbs. at RPM) | Compr. Ratio | Bore in. | Bore mm | Stroke in. | Stroke mm |
|------|-----------------|-----------|------------|-----------|--------------------------|--------------|----------|---------|------------|-----------|
| 1978 | 107.13 | 1756 | 1x2-Bbl. | ①86@6200 | ②90@2800 | 8.0-1 | 3.31 | 84 | 3.12 | 79.2 |

① — 83@5800 when equipped with catalytic converter.
② — 86@2800 on 131 models or 89@2800 on 124 models when equipped with catalytic converter.

### VALVES

| Engine & Valve | Head Diam. In. (mm) | Face Angle | Seat Angle | Seat Width In. (mm) | Stem Diameter In. (mm) | Stem Clearance In. (mm) | Valve Lift In. (mm) |
|----------------|---------------------|------------|------------|---------------------|------------------------|-------------------------|---------------------|
| 1756 cc Int. | 1.622-1.638 (41.2-41.6) | 45° | 45° | .079 (2.0) | .3139-.3146 (7.974-7.992) | .0012-.0026 (.030-.066) | .3765 (9.564) |
| Exh. | 1.412-1.435 (35.85-36.45) | 45° | 45° | .079 (2.0) | .3139-.3146 (7.974-7.992) | .0012-.0026 (.030-.066) | .3765 (9.564) |

### VALVE SPRINGS

| Engine | Free Length In. (mm) | PRESSURE Lbs. @ In. (kg @ mm) Valve Closed | PRESSURE Lbs. @ In. (kg @ mm) Valve Open |
|--------|----------------------|--------------------------------------------|------------------------------------------|
| 1756 cc Inner Spring | 1.646 (41.8) | 33@1.220 (14.9@31) | 62@.846 (28.1@21.5) |
| Outer Spring | 2.122 (53.9) | 86@1.417 (38.9@36) | 131@1.043 (59.5@26.5) |

### VALVE TIMING

| Engine | INTAKE Open (BTDC) | INTAKE Close (ALDC) | EXHAUST Open (BLDC) | EXHAUST Close (ATDC) |
|--------|--------------------|--------------------|--------------------|---------------------|
| 1756 cc | 5° | 53° | 53° | 5° |

### PISTONS, PINS, RINGS

| Engine | PISTONS Clearance In. (mm) | PINS Piston Fit In. (mm) | PINS Rod Fit In. (mm) | Rings | RINGS End Gap In. (mm) | RINGS Side Clearance In. (mm) |
|--------|----------------------------|--------------------------|-----------------------|-------|------------------------|-------------------------------|
| 1756 cc | .0016-.0024 (.040-.060) | .0001-.0003 (.002-.008) | .0004-.0006 (.010-.016) | No. 1 | .0118-.0177 (.30-.45) | .0018-.0030 (.045-.077) |
| | | | | No. 2 | .0078-.0139 (.20-.35) | .0011-.0027 (.030-.070) |
| | | | | Oil | .0078-.0139 (.20-.35) | .0011-.0024 (.030-.062) |

## 124 & 131 4 CYLINDER (Cont.)
### ENGINE SPECIFICATIONS (Cont.)

| CRANKSHAFT MAIN & CONNECTING ROD BEARINGS | | | | | | | |
|---|---|---|---|---|---|---|---|
| | MAIN BEARINGS | | | | CONNECTING ROD BEARINGS | | |
| Engine | Journal Diam. In. (mm) | Clearance In. (mm) | Thrust Bearing | Crankshaft End Play In. (mm) | Journal Diam. ① In. (mm) | Clearance ② In. (mm) | Side Play In. (mm) |
| 1756 cc | 2.0860-2.0868 (52.99-53.00) | 0020-.0037 (.050-.095) | No. 5 | .002-.012 (.05-.30) | 1.9997-2.0001 (50.79-50.80) | .0018-.0031 (.045-.079) | .... |

① — Journal diameter is machined in two sizes designated by class codes. Specification given is class "A". Class "B" is smaller by .0004" (.010 mm).

② — Clearance varies according to class of connecting rod journal. Specification given is class "A". Class "B" clearance is larger by .0001" (.002 mm).

| CAMSHAFT | | | |
|---|---|---|---|
| Engine | Journal Diam. In. (mm) | Clearance In. (mm) | Lobe Lift In. (mm) |
| 1756 cc Front | 1.1788-1.1795 (29.94-29.96) | .0019-.0035 (.049-.090) | .3824 (9.71) |
| Middle | 1.8013-1.8020 (45.75-45.77) | .0011-.0027 (.029-.070) | .3824 (9.71) |
| Rear | 1.8171-1.8178 (46.15-46.17) | .0011-.0027 (.029-.070) | .3824 (9.71) |

### TIGHTENING SPECIFICATIONS

| Application | Ft. Lbs. (mkg) |
|---|---|
| Cylinder Head Bolts | 61 (8.5) |
| Front Main Bearing Cap Bolts | 59 (8.2) |
| Intake & Exhaust Manifold Nuts | 18 (2.5) |
| Intake Manifold Bolts | 18 (2.5) |
| Connecting Rod Nuts | 37 (5.1) |
| Flywheel-to-Crankshaft Bolt | 105 (14.5) |
| Camshaft Sprocket Bolt | 87 (12) |
| Oil Pump Mounting Bolt | 14 (2.0) |
| Tensioner Nut | 33 (4.5) |

## 1600 cc 4 CYLINDER

### ENGINE CODING

#### ENGINE IDENTIFICATION

Push-rod operated overhead valve, 4-cylinder in-line engine is transversely mounted at front of car. Engine identification is stamped on number plate attached to panel under hood just above right headlight. Engine code is L4.

### ENGINE, CYLINDER HEAD & MANIFOLDS

#### ENGINE

NOTE — *Engine and transmission assembly are removed from vehicle as a unit. Removal and installation of assembly is accomplished with transmission in 4th gear to aid in subsequent assembly adjustment.*

**Removal 1)** Disconnect and remove battery. Drain coolant by removing radiator and heater hoses. (No petcock radiator drain is provided.) Remove air cleaner and breather hose.

**2)** Disconnect and remove accelerator cable and bracket from carburetor and intake manifold. Remove fuel line from pump to carburetor. Disconnect carburetor fuel vent hoses, and remove emission and servo vacuum hoses.

**3)** Disconnect the following electrical leads: temperature sending unit, oil pressure switch, distributor and coil wires, choke wire, fan switch, air pump ground wire and engine grounding strap. Disconnect speedometer cable at drive fitting. Unhook clutch cable. Remove exhaust manifold heat stove and inlet pipe from exhaust manifold.

**4)** Raise vehicle on hoist. Loosen clamp bolt and remove gear selector rod. Unhook spring between selector rod and longitudinal member. Back off mounting nuts on stabilizer rubber insulators and engine mounts. Loosen stud locknut and remove stud from transmission with an Allen wrench. Disconnect mounting rubbers and remove complete exhaust assembly.

**5)** Remove 4 bolts holding shift tower to floor pan, then remove shift tower. Rotate gear selector rod with stabilizer halfway around and hang from wire. Disconnect alternator and starter leads. Remove 6 Allen head bolts from right and left driveshaft couplings and disconnect couplings.

**6)** Support engine and transmission assembly on suitable jack. Remove engine mountings as follows: right front upper engine mounting rubber insulator, engine-to-body bracket in engine compartment, left engine mounting bolt, and bottom engine mounting strap. Raise hoist to lift vehicle away from transmission-engine assembly, then lower jack to remove assembly from beneath vehicle.

**Installation — 1)** Reverse removal procedure, using caution that front engine insulator stud engages right apron bracket. Front engine mount rubber insulators must be parallel to front of engine. Do NOT distort when nut is tightened.

**2)** Lower and remove jack. Assure that shift shaft is in 4th gear to position and slide selector rod onto shaft. Adjust as follows: pull gear selector rod and shift lever downward, lock shift lever in 4th gear position with suitable .16" (4 mm) arbor, insert 2.76" (70 mm) spacer between floor pan and selector rod, turn shift shaft CLOCKWISE against stop using arbor, then tighten selector rod locating bolt. Remove spacer and arbor.

**3)** Complete installation noting that accelerator cable must be routed OVER air cleaner snorkel to prevent damage to cable from EGR pipe and to avoid interference with ignition system. Adjust cable so that clearance between throttle stop and pedal lever does not exceed .015" (.38 mm) with throttle fully open. Refill all fluids and check for leaks.

#### INTAKE MANIFOLD

**Removal & Installation — 1)** Partially drain cooling system, remove air cleaner and thermostat housing. Disconnect accelerator cable from throttle lever, fuel and vacuum lines from carburetor, and water outlet hose and crankcase ventilation hose from intake manifold.

**2)** Disconnect decel valve-to-carburetor pipe (if equipped) and fan switch. Remove attaching bolts and nuts and lift out manifold with old gasket. To install, reverse removal procedure, noting that if installing a new manifold, decel valve must be placed over adapter and installed with special tool.

#### EXHAUST MANIFOLD

**Removal & Installation —** Remove exhaust pipe flange nuts and separate the joint. (If necessary, remove air pump and mounting bracket before removing pipe.) Disconnect hot air pipe from air cleaner at exhaust manifold. Remove attaching bolts and nuts and lift off manifold. To install, reverse removal procedure using new gaskets.

#### CYLINDER HEAD

**Removal — 1)** Drain engine coolant, remove air cleaner assembly and fuel line from fuel pump to carburetor. Disconnect wires from spark plugs and tie out of way.

**2)** Disconnect the following: radiator fan switch, heater and vacuum hoses at intake manifold, hoses at choke housing, temperature sending unit wire, exhaust pipe, throttle linkage, and distributor vacuum advance hose from carburetor.

**3)** Remove thermostat and housing, rocker arm cover and gasket, rocker arm shaft assembly, and push rods. Remove head bolts and lift off cylinder head.

CAUTION — *Maintain push rods in order removed for installation in original location. Do not lay head flat as spark plugs or gasket surface may be damaged.*

**Installation —** To install, reverse removal procedure and tighten head bolts in increments in sequence shown in *Fig 1.* Adjust valve clearance to specifications.

*Fig. 1  Cylinder Head Bolt Tightening Sequence*

## 1600 cc 4 CYLINDER (Cont.)

## VALVES

### VALVE ARRANGEMENT

E-I-I-E-E-I-I-E

### VALVE GUIDES

If valve guides become worn they may be reamed to install valves with .015" (.39 mm) oversize stems.

### VALVE STEM OIL SEALS

Valve stem oil seals should be replaced any time cylinder head is disassembled. Install new stem seal over valve stem with open end toward head. Replace spring and retainer.

### VALVE SPRINGS

Use suitable spring compressor tool to remove locks and retainers. Spring may be removed with head installed on engine if rocker arms and push rods are removed. It will be necessary to hold the valves closed with compressed air during the operation.

### VALVE SPRING INSTALLED HEIGHT

Measure spring installed height from surface of spring pad to bottom of retainer. If height is greater than specified, install .030" (.76 mm) spacers between spring pad and valve spring to bring within limits. Do NOT install spacers unless necessary due to excess strain on valve train.

### ROCKER ARM ASSEMBLY OVERHAUL

**Disassembly —** With rocker arm assembly removed from head, remove cotter pin from one end of rocker shaft and slip flat washers and crimped washer from shaft. Remove shaft supports, rocker arms and springs, keeping them in proper order for reassembly. Remove plugs from rocker arm shafts in order to clean hollow of shaft.

**Assembly —** Drive new plugs in ends of rocker shaft. Assemble rocker arm shaft so that bolt hole in rocker arm shaft support is on same side as rocker arm adjusting screw. Rocker arms are right-hand and left-hand, with pads inclined toward support. Install washers and cotter pins.

### VALVE CLEARANCE ADJUSTMENT

**Preliminary (Cold) Adjustment —** With valve cover off, rotate crankshaft until number 1 and number 6 valves are fully open and check clearance on number 3 and 8 valve. Use feeler gauge inserted from front to rear (parallel to crankshaft centerline). Do NOT use go, no-go feeler gauge and do NOT insert perpendicular to centerline of crankshaft since an erroneous feel will result in excessively tight valves. Check remaining valves by rotating crankshaft until desired sequence shown in following table is completed:

| Valves Fully Open | 1 & 6 | 2 & 4 | 3 & 8 | 5 & 7 |
|---|---|---|---|---|
| Check Clearance on | 3 & 8 | 5 & 7 | 1 & 6 | 2 & 4 |

**Final Adjustment —** Start and warm engine to normal operating temperature. Reposition or remove components as necessary to remove rocker arm cover, then recheck torque on cylinder head bolts and rocker arm shaft attaching bolts. Recheck valve clearance as in *Preliminary Adjustment*.

## PISTONS, PINS & RINGS

### OIL PAN

**Removal —** Drain crankcase, remove oil dipstick and remove battery. Disconnect throttle linkage from carburetor and steering cable from rack and pinion. Disconnect rack and pinion from crossmember and move forward to provide clearance for removing pan. Remove starter motor and lower rear cover. Disassemble engine rear plate from rear plate assembly. Remove oil pan bolts, oil pan and oil pump inlet tube

**Installation —** Use new gaskets with sealer on engine block side and place on block. Place pan in position and tighten bolts evenly to specifications. Follow *Alphabetical* and then *Numerical* sequence shown in *Fig. 2*. Continue installation in reverse order of removal and replenish crankcase oil supply.

*Fig. 2 Oil Pan Bolt Tightening Sequence*

### PISTON & ROD ASSEMBLY

**Removal —** With cylinder head and pan removed, partially loosen bearing cap bolts several turns, then tap them to release the cap. Completely remove bolts and bearing caps, keeping them in order so they can be installed in original positions. Push piston and connecting rod out of bore from bottom.

**Installation —** Place bearing liners in connecting rods and caps. Turn crankshaft to fit each rod to crankpin and install previously fitted bearing and cap. If bearings have not been previously fitted, use Plastigage method, then tighten caps to specified torque.

### FITTING PISTONS

Determine piston-to-cylinder bore clearance by measuring bore at a point $2\frac{11}{32}$" from top, across the axis of the crankshaft, and piston diameter at a point $2\frac{1}{4}$" below dome at 90° to pin bore. If beyond service limits, oversize pistons are available in .0025" (.064 mm), .015" (.381 mm), and .030" (.762 mm).

### PISTON PIN REPLACEMENT

Full floating wrist pins are retained by snap rings in piston pin bore. Pin may be pushed from assembly after removing retainers. Pistons are only supplied in service complete with pin to ensure correct fit and pins must not be interchanged. When assembling, make sure that FRONT marking on connecting rod is on same side of the assembly as the arrow in the piston crown. Heat piston in oil or water prior to inserting pin and retain with snap rings.

## 1600 cc 4 CYLINDER (Cont.)

### CRANKSHAFT MAIN & CONNECTING ROD BEARINGS

**Connecting Rod Bearings —** Bearing inserts are fitted in rod and cap in conventional manner, using Plastigage method to determine clearance. When installing, ensure that arrow on piston points to front of engine and that number on connecting rod and cap is on camshaft side.

**Main Bearings —** Conventional replaceable inserts are used in all 5 main bearings. Number 3 (center) main bearing controls end play by means of half-circle thrust bearings inserted between thrust faces of crankshaft and block. Bearing caps are marked in order F, R2, C, R4 and R for proper installation. Use Plastigage method to determine clearance and select undersize bearings as required. Check end play with feeler gauge and install thrust bearings of correct thickness to establish specified end play.

### MAIN BEARING OIL SEALS

**Rear —** With engine out of car, remove pressure plate and clutch disc, then remove flywheel. Remove oil pan and rear oil seal carrier. Install 2 metal screws in seal above center line (do NOT let them bottom against crankshaft or block). Pry against screws and remove seal and carrier. Ensure that seal surfaces are free of burrs, then use tool (T70P-6165) to install new seal in carrier. Use oil resistant sealer at ends of new gasket positioned on carrier and install on block face using tool (T70P-6165) to align. Install remaining components in reverse order of removal.

**Front —** Front oil seal is pressed in front cover and seals against pulley hub. With cover off engine, support around oil seal and drive seal out from rear using installation/removal tool (T70P-6150). To install, turn cover over and support from rear. Use tool to drive new seal in position.

### CAMSHAFT

**Timing Chain —** With front cover off, remove crankshaft oil slinger. Remove camshaft sprocket retainer and bolts, then remove chain tensioner and bolts. Remove camshaft sprocket and timing chain. To install, place timing chain over sprockets so that timing marks on camshaft gear and crankshaft gear are aligned. Install remaining components, then bend up locking tabs after bolts have been tightened to specifications.

**Camshaft —** Proceed as in *Timing Chain*, then remove oil pump and fuel pump. Remove rocker arm cover, rocker arm assembly, distributor, and push rods. Remove camshaft thrust plate and pull out camshaft. Valve lifters may be removed if desired. To install, reverse removal procedures assuring that timing marks are aligned when installing timing chain.

**Fig. 3  Exploded View of Fiesta Oil Pump Assembly**

**Fig. 4  Exploded View of Engine Internal Components**

## 1600 cc 4 CYLINDER (Cont.)

### ENGINE OILING

#### OIL PUMP

Oil pump and filter assembly is bolted to right side of cylinder block. Assembly is removable with engine in place. Pump is driven by a gear on the engine camshaft. The full flow element type filter is bolted to a mounting flange integral with the oil pump body.

| Engine Oiling System Specifications | |
|---|---|
| Application | Specification |
| Oil Pressure @ 2000 RPM ① | 24-45 psi. |
| Oil Filter Type | Full Flow Element |
| Inner-to-Outer Rotor Clearance | .005″ (.127 mm) |
| Outer Rotor-to-Housing Clearance | .010″ (.254 mm) |
| Housing-to-Rotor Face Clearance | .0025″ (.064 mm) |
| Relief Valve Spring Tension | 7.5-8.5 lbs. @ 1.04″ |
| Relief Valve Clearance | .001-.003″ (.025-.076 mm) |

① — Engine hot.

**Crankcase Capacity** — 3.5 quarts including filter.

**Oil Filter** — Disposable spin-on type.

### ENGINE COOLING

**Thermostat** — Begins to open at 185°F; fully open at 216°F.

**Cooling System Capacity** — 6.6 qts. (includes heater).

**Radiator Cap** — 14.5 psi pressure cap.

**Radiator** — Cross-flow with electric cooling fan.

#### WATER PUMP

Disconnect battery and drain radiator. Loosen pump pulley bolts, then remove air pump and alternator drive belts. Remove lower radiator hose from pump. Remove pump pulley bolts and take pulley off shaft. Remove pump retaining bolts and lift pump from engine. To install, position pump on connecting hose and reverse removal procedures.

## ENGINE SPECIFICATIONS

### GENERAL SPECIFICATIONS

| Year | Displ. cu. ins. | cc | Carburetor | HP at RPM | Torque (Ft. Lbs. at RPM) | Compr. Ratio | Bore in. | mm | Stroke in. | mm |
|---|---|---|---|---|---|---|---|---|---|---|
| 1978 | 94 | 1600 | 2-Bbl. | ..... | ..... | 8.6:1 | 3.188 | 80.97 | 3.056 | 77.62 |

### VALVES

| Engine & Valve | Head Diam. In. (mm) | Face Angle | Seat Angle | Seat Width In. (mm) | Stem Diameter In. (mm) | Stem Clearance In. (mm) | Valve Lift In. (mm) |
|---|---|---|---|---|---|---|---|
| 1600 cc Intake | 1.410 (35.8) | 45° | 45° | .050-.065 (1.27-1.65) | .3098-.3105① (7.868-7.886) | .0008-.0027② (.020-.069) | .3536③ (8.98) |
| Exhaust | 1.239 (31.47) | 45° | 45° | .070-.085 (1.78-2.16) | .3089-.3096① (7.846-7.863) | .0017-.0036② (.043-.091) | .3553③ (9.02) |

① — .015″ (.381 mm) oversize limits are:
Intake — .3248-.3255″ (8.25-8.26 mm)
Exhaust — .3239-.3246″ (8.22-8.24 mm)
② — Wear limit — .0055″ (.139 mm)
③ — At ZERO valve lash

| VALVE SPRINGS | | | |
|---|---|---|---|
| Engine | Free Length In. (mm) | PRESSURE Lbs. @ In. (kg @ mm) Valve Closed | Valve Open |
| 1600 cc | 1.48 (37.6) | 47.5-52.5@1.263① (3.34-3.69@32) | 122.5@.953② (8.61@24.2) |

① — Wear Limit — 42 lbs.@1.263″ (2.95 kg/cm²@32.08 mm)
② — Wear Limit — 104 lbs.@.953″ (7.31 kg/cm²@24.2 mm)

| CAMSHAFT | | | |
|---|---|---|---|
| Engine | Journal Diam. In. (mm) | Clearance① In. (mm) | Lobe Lift In. (mm) |
| 1600 cc | 1.5597-1.5605 (39.62-39.64) | .0010-.0023 (.025-.058) | .2309② (5.865) .2320③ (5.893) |

① — End play is .0025-.0075″ (.064-.191 mm).
② — Intake lobe
③ — Exhaust lobe

# Fiesta Engines

## 1600 cc 4 CYLINDER (Cont.)
### ENGINE SPECIFICATIONS (Cont.)

### CRANKSHAFT MAIN & CONNECTING ROD BEARINGS

| Engine | MAIN BEARINGS | | | | CONNECTING ROD BEARINGS | | |
|---|---|---|---|---|---|---|---|
| | Journal Diam. In. (mm) | Clearance In. (mm) | Thrust Bearing | Crankshaft End Play In. (mm) | Journal Diam. In. (mm) | Clearance In. (mm) | Side Play In. (mm) |
| 1600 cc | 2.1253-2.1261① (53.98-54.00) | .0005-.0015 (.013-.038) | No. 3② | .003-.011 (.076-.279) | 1.9368-1.9376① (49.19-49.22) | .0004-.0015③ (.010-.038) | .004-.010④ (.102-.254) |

① — Maximum out of round — .0004″ (.010 mm)  
② — Thrust washers  
③ — Allowable limit — .0004-.0024″ (.010-.061 mm)  
④ — Maximum limit — .014″ (.356 mm)

### PISTONS, PINS, RINGS

| Engine | PISTONS | PINS | | RINGS | | |
|---|---|---|---|---|---|---|
| | Clearance In. (mm) | Piston Fit In. (mm) | Rod Fit In. (mm) | Rings | End Gap In. (mm) | Side Clearance In. (mm) |
| 1600 cc | .0009-.0017 (.023-.431) | .0001-.0003① (.002-.008) | .0001-.0004② (.002-.010) | Comp. | .009-.014 (.228-.356) | .0016-.0036 (.041-.091) |
| | | | | Oil | .009-.014 (.228-.356) | .0018-.0038 (.046-.097) |

① — Tight  
② — Loose

### TIGHTENING SPECIFICATIONS

| Application | Ft. Lbs. (mkg) |
|---|---|
| Cam Sprocket-to-Cam Bolt | 12-15 (1.7-2.1) |
| Cam Thrust Plate Bolts | 25-35 (3.5-4.8) |
| Connecting Rod Bolts | 30-35 (4.1-4.8) |
| Cylinder Head Bolts | |
| 1st Increment | 5 (.7) |
| 2nd Increment | 20-30 (2.8-4.1) |
| 3rd Increment | 50-55 (6.9-7.6) |
| Final Torque | 65-70 (9.0-9.7) |
| Crankshaft Pulley Bolt | 24-28 (3.3-3.9) |
| Cylinder Front Cover | 5-7 (.7-1.0) |
| Clutch Pressure Plate | |
| To Flywheel | 12-15 (1.7-2.1) |
| Carburetor Nuts | 12-15 (1.7-2.1) |
| Exhaust Manifold-to-Head Studs | 9-12 (1.2-1.7) |
| Exhaust Manifold-to-Head Nuts | 15-18 (2.1-2.5) |
| Pulley-to-Hub | |
| Metal | 5-7 (.7-1.0) |
| Plastic | 7-9 (1.0-1.2) |
| Flywheel-to-Crankshaft Bolts | 50-55 (6.9-7.6) |
| Intake Manifold-to-Head Bolts | 12-15 (1.7-2.1) |
| Intake Manifold-to-Head Nuts | 12-15 (1.7-2.1) |
| Intake Manifold-to-Head Studs | 9-12 (1.2-1.7) |
| Main Bearing Cap Bolts | 55-60 (7.6-8.3) |
| Oil Pump-to-Block | 12-15 (1.7-2.1) |
| Oil Drain Plug | 20-25 (2.8-3.5) |
| Oil Pan Bolts | |
| Step 1 | Finger Tight Corner Bolts |
| Step 2 | Snug All Bolts |
| Step 3 | 6.8 (.94) |
| Rear Oil Seal Retainer-to-Block | 12-15 (1.7-2.1) |
| Rocker Shaft Support Bolt | 25-30 (3.46-4.15) |
| Spark Plug | 10-15 (1.38-2.1) |
| Water Pump-to-Block | |
| ¼″ Bolts | 5-7 (.7-1.0) |
| 5⁄16″ Bolt | 12-15 (1.7-2.1) |
| Timing Pointer | 8-10 (1.1-1.4) |

# Honda Engines

## CIVIC 4 CYLINDER

### ENGINE CODING

#### ENGINE IDENTIFICATION

Engine serial number is stamped on a machined surface at rear of engine, near starter. Engine serial number is preceded by engine model number. Model number is EB3.

### ENGINE & CYLINDER HEAD

#### ENGINE

**Removal** — 1) Disconnect battery ground cable. Remove hood after scribing location marks for reinstallation. Drain radiator and disconnect hoses from engine. Drain lubricant from transmission. Remove air cleaner and air intake pipe.

2) Remove fan shroud. Disconnect hoses from canister fitting being careful not to bend fittings. Disconnect fuel pump inlet line. Disconnect and place out of way the following wires, hoses or cables: Throttle and choke cable from carburetor. Clutch cable from release arm. Ignition coil wires at distributor. Back-up light wires. TCS wires. Alternator harness wires. Water temperature and oil pressure switch wires. Throttle opener hose and carburetor insulator to throttle opener vacuum hose.

3) Remove by-pass valve assembly and bracket. Disconnect heater hoses at firewall. Remove engine torque rod, starter and front wheels. Remove exhaust pipe flange nuts, then lower pipe. Disconnect both lower control arm ball joints.

4) Hold brake disc and pull left and right axle drive shafts out of differential case. Drive out gear shift 8 mm pin and disconnect rod at transmission case. Disconnect gearshift extension at engine (not at shift lever). On automatic transmission models only, disconnect shift cable at console, then disconnect cooler lines at transmission.

5) Attach an engine hoist to motor and take up slack allowing load to be lifted from mounts. With engine supported, remove two center mount bracket nuts. Remove left engine mount. Lift engine from vehicle being careful not to allow auxiliary components to bang against vehicle.

**Installation** — To install engine, reverse removal procedure and note the following: Use new shift rod pin. After installing drive shafts attempt to move inner joint housing in and out of differential housing. If movement is easy, drive shaft end clips should be replaced. When connecting heater hoses, upper hose goes to water pump connecting pipe.

#### CYLINDER HEAD

**NOTE** — *To minimize the chances of warping cylinder head, remove head after engine has been allowed to cool.*

**Removal** — 1) Scribe index marks on hood, then take hood off. Drain coolant from radiator. Remove air cleaner hardware. Disconnect upper radiator hose. Disconnect tubing between canister and idle cut-off valve. Disconnect throttle linkage.

2) Disconnect the following items: heater hoses at intake manifold. Temperature sensor wires. Fuel line to carburetor. Engine torque rod.

3) Remove air pump to exhaust manifold hose. Disconnect exhaust pipe at manifold. Remove valve cover. Remove upper timing belt cover. Bring No. 1 piston to TDC.

4) Loosen timing belt adjusting and pivot bolt, then remove camshaft pulley bolt and remove pulley. Take off fuel pump and take out distributor. Remove the oil pump gear holder and the pump gear and shaft. Loosen bolts evenly and lift off cylinder head.

**Installation** — To install cylinder head, reverse removal procedure and tighten bolts in sequence shown in *Fig. 1.*

**Fig. 1  Cylinder Head Tightening Sequence
(Loosen in Reverse Sequence)**

### VALVES

#### VALVE ARRANGEMENT

**Front Side** —  All Exhaust
**Rear Side** —  All Intake

#### ROCKER ARM ASSEMBLY

**Removal** — Loosen rocker arm shaft bolts in criss-cross pattern starting with end supports. Starting with number four cylinder support, pull out 4 mm pin and remove supports, rocker collars, rocker arms and springs. Retain components in proper order for reassembly.

**Installation** — When reinstalling rocker arms, place intake rocker arm shaft so that notch faces rear of vehicle and oil holes are on the bottom. Exhaust rocker arm shaft is installed with oil holes facing down and dowel pin hole on left-hand side of engine. After assembly check rocker arms for freedom of movement.

#### VALVE SPRINGS

Using a suitable valve spring compressor, remove valve keepers, collars and springs. Check valve springs for squareness, they should be within 2° of true. Measure free length of spring. Minimum length for inner and outer intake springs is 1.6063" (40.8 mm). Inner exhaust valve spring should be at least 1.9291" (49.0 mm), and outer spring should be at least 2.0591" (52.3 mm).

#### VALVE GUIDE SERVICING

Using a suitable drift, drive valve guides out top side of head. Install new guides and ream to provide proper clearance. Install new intake valve guide seals.

#### VALVE CLEARANCE ADJUSTMENT

1) Rotate engine until number 1 piston is at TDC on compression stroke. Check intake valves of number 1 and 2 cylinders

## CIVIC 4 CYLINDER (Cont.)

and exhaust valves of number 1 and 3 cylinders. Rotate crankshaft 360° and check intake valves of number 3 and 4 cylinders and exhaust valves of number 2 and 4 cylinders.

**2)** Loosen lock nut of valve to be adjusted. Insert a feeler gauge between rocker arm and valve stem to measure clearance. Turn adjuster until proper clearance is obtained. This procedure is performed with engine cold, and proper valve clearance is .004-.006" (.10-.16 mm).

### PISTONS, PINS & RINGS

#### OIL PAN

**1)** Raise front of vehicle and support with floor stands. Attach a hoist to clutch cable bracket on transmission and raise just enough to take load off center mount.

**2)** Remove center beam and lower engine mount. Loosen and remove oil pan bolts in a criss-cross pattern, starting from outside bolts. Tap corners lightly with a mallet to break seal and remove oil pan.

#### PISTON & ROD ASSEMBLY

**1)** With oil pan and cylinder head removed, ream any ridge from top of cylinders. Mark piston and rod assemblies for proper reinstallation. Remove rod caps and push piston and rod assemblies out top of cylinder with a hammer handle.

**2)** Assemble piston and connecting rod with piston front mark and connecting rod oil jet hole on same side and facing intake manifold. Using a ring compressor, install piston and rod assemblies in proper cylinder.

#### FITTING PISTONS

Measure cylinder bore for wear and taper. Measure piston diameter, then determine if piston-to-cylinder clearance is within specification. If not, two different oversize pistons (and rings) are available. Oversizes are .010" (.25 mm) and .020" (.50 mm). Oversize pistons are stamped on the crown with a number corresponding to the metric equivalent of oversize. Similarly, oversize rings are also stamped on their top side to correspond to amount to oversize. Match pistons and rings according to these oversize markings.

**Fig. 2 View of Piston Rings Showing Ring End Gap Locations**

Top Ring
(Chamfered and Chromed)

Oil Ring

.8-1.2" (2-3 cm)

.8-1.2" (2-3 cm)

Second Ring
(Tapered)

**Fig. 3 Showing Piston and Ring Size Stamped on Component**

#### PISTON PINS

Using a press and suitable tool (07973-6570001), press piston pin out of piston and connecting rod. Install new pin by placing pilot through piston and connecting rod. Lightly oil piston pin and place piston, rod, pin and ram on the base. Press in pin until it is centered in connecting rod.

## CRANKSHAFT MAIN & CONNECTING ROD BEARINGS

### MAIN & CONNECTING ROD BEARINGS

**1)** Loosen main bearing cradle bolts in a criss-cross sequence beginning at ends of cradle. Mark connecting rods, caps and pistons for reassembly in original positions, then remove main bearing cradle and rod caps. Remove and measure crankshaft for bend, out-of-round, or taper.

**NOTE** – Bearing journals are specially heat-treated and should not be reground. Do not attempt to adjust bearing clearances by filing or shimming bearing caps.

**2)** Using Plastigage method, determine bearing clearances. If bearing replacement is necessary use following procedure to determine bearing size required.

**3)** Referring to illustration, note that all **letters** stamped on crankshaft counterweight pads apply to connecting rods and all **numbers** apply to main bearing journals. Both connecting rods and main bearing journals have mating numbers (stamped on connecting rod) or letters (stamped on block) which when paired are used to determine color of bearing insert to be used. See Engine Specifications

### THRUST BEARING ALIGNMENT

Measure thrust bearing clearance and replace thrust washers if necessary. Install thrust washers with oil grooves facing toward crankshaft.

## CAMSHAFT

### TIMING BELT

**1)** Remove water pump drive belt, water pump pulley and crankshaft pulley. Remove upper timing belt cover from cylinder head.

**2)** Remove lower timing belt cover from engine block. Loosen (do not remove) timing belt adjusting and pivot bolts. Slide belt off pulleys. To install, reverse removal procedure using care not to excessively bend or twist timing belt. Do not expose belt to engine oil as this will cause belt rubber to swell. Install belt in same direction of rotation to prevent premature wear or failure.

## CIVIC 4 CYLINDER (Cont.)

### CAMSHAFT

**1)** With cylinder head removed, loosen rocker shaft support bolts in a criss-cross pattern beginning with outside support. Lift rocker shaft assembly from head. Remove camshaft and right head seal or tachometer drive body (if equipped).

**2)** Inspect camshaft and cylinder head bearing surfaces for wear or damage. Check camshaft maximum runout of .002" (.05 mm). Measure cam lobes for no more than .0118" (0.3 mm) wear from standard dimension of 1.4477-1.4363" (36.77-36.48 mm) for intake lobes and 1.4429-1.4311" (36.65-36.35 mm) for exhaust lobes. End play of camshaft when installed in head should not exceed .0197" (.50 mm). Standard oil clearance between camshaft and head is from .0020-.0035" (.05-.09 mm).

**3)** Oil camshaft bearing journals. Install camshaft and seal or tachometer drive body (if equipped). Loosen rocker arm adjusting screws, and apply silicone seal to mating surfaces on end camshaft supports and cylinder head. Install rocker arm assembly and tighten support bolts in reverse of removal.

### VALVE TIMING

Rotate crankshaft pulley until TDC mark is aligned with index mark on timing belt cover. Rotate camshaft pulley until Woodruff key is facing up and timing marks on pulley are parallel with top of cylinder head. Without disturbing pulley position, slide on timing belt. Rotate engine a quarter of a turn in the normal direction (counterclockwise when viewed from timing belt end) and tighten adjusting bolt, then pivot bolt. Do not apply pressure to timing belt; use only tension of adjusting spring.

Timing Marks

Timing Marks

*Fig. 5  Camshaft Alignment Marks in Position for Installing Camshaft Belt*

Connecting Rod Journal Letters

Main Bearing Journal Size Indicator Numbers

Connecting Rod Fit Marking

Identification Color

Main Bearing Number Sequence

Bearing Cradle

Main Bearing Bore Size Identification Letters

*Fig. 4  Crankshaft and Connecting Rod Bearing Identification with Detail for Each Component*

# Honda Engines

## CIVIC 4 CYLINDER (Cont.)

### ENGINE OILING

**Crankcase Capacity** — 3.2 qts.
**Oil Filter** — Disposable with built-in by-pass valve.
**Normal Oil Pressure** — 48-58 psi, 21 psi minimum at idle.
**Pressure Regulator Valve** — Non-adjustable.

### ENGINE OILING SYSTEM

A trochoid type oil pump draws oil from oil pan and delivers it under pressure through main bearing cradle to main and connecting rod bearings. Oil passes through rods to an oil jet which lubricates pistons and cylinder walls. An oil passage carries oil to camshaft bearings and rocker arms. Oil mist lubricates valve stems.

### OIL PUMP

1) Remove oil pan, oil passage block and oil pump assembly. Pull oil relief valve cotter pin and remove seat, spring and valve.

2) Remove two pump body bolts and disassemble pump. Inspect pump for wear or damage. Measure pump operating clearances. Reassemble pump and place strainer in container of engine oil. Rotate pump with a screwdriver and check that oil comes out of delivery side. Place finger over hole and see if pressure develops as pump is turned.

### ENGINE COOLING

**Thermostat** — Opens at 178-183°F (80-84°C).

**Thermoswitch** — On: 191-197°F (88-92°C); Off: 182-188°F (83-87°C).

**Cooling System Capacity** — 4.2 qts.

Bleed Screw

*Fig. 6   Coolant Bleed Valve in Intake Manifold*

### WATER PUMP

**Removal** — Drain radiator and loosen alternator adjusting bolts. Push alternator toward engine and remove drive belt. Remove pump and "O" ring seal.

**Installation** — 1) Reinstall water pump. Loosen cooling system bleed valve located on intake manifold, see *Fig. 6*. Fill radiator with coolant. When air bubbles no longer appear in coolant draining from bleed valve, close valve.

2) Start engine and place heater temperature control lever in high position. Run engine approximately ten minutes. Again bleed system until there are no air bubbles in coolant draining from bleed valve. Refill radiator.

| Oil Pump Specifications | | |
|---|---|---|
| **Application** | **Std. Clearance In. (mm)** | **Service Limit In. (mm)** |
| Inner-to-Outer Rotor | .0059 (.15) | .0079 (.20) |
| Rotor-to-Body | .0012-.0039 (.03-.10) | .0059 (.15) |
| Rotor Side-to-Body | .0039-.0071 (.10-.18) | .0079 (.20) |

## ENGINE SPECIFICATIONS

| GENERAL SPECIFICATIONS | | | | | | | | | | |
|---|---|---|---|---|---|---|---|---|---|---|
| Year | Displ. | | Carburetor | HP at RPM | Torque (Ft. Lbs. at RPM) | Compr. Ratio | Bore | | Stroke | |
| | cu. ins. | cc | | | | | in. | mm | in. | mm |
| 1978 | 75.48 | 1237 | 2-Bbl. | .... | .... | 8.1:1 | 2.83 | 72 | 2.99 | 76 |

| VALVES | | | | | | | |
|---|---|---|---|---|---|---|---|
| Engine & Valve | Head Diam. In. (mm) | Face Angle | Seat Angle | Seat Width In. (mm) | Stem Diameter In. (mm) | Stem Clearance In. (mm) | Valve Lift In. (mm) |
| 1237 cc Intake | 1.335-1.342 (33.9-34.1) | 45° | 45° | .0551 (1.4) | .2591-.2594 (6.58-6.59) | .0008-.0020 (.02-.05) | ..... |
| Exhaust | 1.177-1.185 (29.9-30.1) | 45° | 45° | .0551 (1.4) | .2579-.2583 (6.55-6.56) | .0020-.0031 (.05-.08) | ..... |

## CIVIC 4 CYLINDER (Cont.)
### ENGINE SPECIFICATIONS (Cont.)

| VALVE TIMING | | | | |
|---|---|---|---|---|
| | INTAKE | | EXHAUST | |
| Engine | Open (ATDC) | Close (ALDC) | Open (BLDC) | Close (BTDC) |
| 1237 cc | 10° | 20° | 30° | 10° |

| PISTONS, PINS, RINGS | | | | | | |
|---|---|---|---|---|---|---|
| | PISTONS | PINS | | RINGS | | |
| Engine | Clearance In. (mm) | Piston Fit In. (mm) | Rod Fit In. (mm) | Rings | End Gap In. (mm) | Side Clearance In. (mm) |
| 1237 cc | 0-.0016 (0-.04) | .0003-.0007 (.007-.014) | ① .0006-.0015 (.016-.039) | No. 1 | .008-.016 (.20-.40) | .0008-.0018 (.020-.045) |
| | | | | No. 2 | .008-.016 (.20-.40) | .0008-.0018 (.020-.045) |
| | | | | Oil | .011-.039 (.3-.9) | ..... |

① — Interference fit.

| Main Bearing Journals | | | | In. (mm) |
|---|---|---|---|---|
| Crankcase Counterbore Dia.2.13 (54) / Journal Dia. 1.97 (50) | A 0 to .0002 (0 to .006) | B .0002 to .0005 (.006 to .012) | C .0005 to .0007 (.012 to .018) | D .0007 to .0009 (.018 to .024) |
| 1 0 to −.0002 (0 to −.006) | Red −.0001 to −.0002 (−.002 to −.005) | Pink .00004 to −.0001 (.001 to −.002) | Yellow .0002 to .00004 (.004 to .001) | Green .0003 to .0002 (.007 to .004) |
| 2 −.0002 to −.0005 (−.006 to −.012) | Pink .00004 to −.0001 (.001 to −.002) | Yellow .0002 to .00004 (.004 to .001) | Green .0003 to .0002 (.007 to .004) | Brown .0004 to .0003 (.010 to .007) |
| 3 −.0005 to −.0007 (−.012 to −.018) | Yellow .0002 to .00004 (.004 to .001) | Green .0003 to .0002 (.007 to .004) | Brown .0004 to .0003 (.010 to .007) | Black .0005 to .0004 (.013 to .010) |
| 4 −.0007 to −.0009 (−.018 to −.024) | Green .0003 to .0002 (.007 to .004) | Brown .0004 to .0003 (.010 to .007) | Black .0005 to .0004 (.013 to .010) | Blue .0006 to .0005 (.016 to .013) |

| CRANKSHAFT MAIN & CONNECTING ROD BEARINGS | | | | | | | |
|---|---|---|---|---|---|---|---|
| | MAIN BEARINGS | | | | CONNECTING ROD BEARINGS | | |
| Engine | Journal Diam. In. (mm) | Clearance In. (mm) | Thrust Bearing | Crankshaft End Play In. (mm) | Journal Diam. In. (mm) | Clearance In. (mm) | Side Play In. (mm) |
| 1237 cc | 1.969-1.970 (49.9-50.0) | .0009-.0017 (.024-.042) | No. 2 | .004-.014 (.10-.35) | 1.575-1.576 (39.9-40.0) | .0008-.0015 (.020-.038) | .0059-.0118 (.15-.30) |

# Honda Engines

## CIVIC 4 CYLINDER (Cont.)
### ENGINE SPECIFICATIONS (Cont.)

| Connecting Rod Bearing Journals | | | | In. (mm) |
|---|---|---|---|---|
| Connecting Rod Dia. 1.69 (43) / Crankpin Dia. 1.57 (40) | **1**<br>0 to .0002<br>(0 to .006) | **2**<br>.0002 to .0005<br>(.006 to .012) | **3**<br>.0005 to .0007<br>(.012 to .018) | **4**<br>.0007 to .0009<br>(.018 to .024) |
| **A**<br>0 to −.0002<br>(0 to −.006) | Red<br>−.0002 to −.0003<br>(−.005 to −.008) | Pink<br>−.0001 to −.0002<br>(−.002 to −.005) | Yellow<br>.00004 to −.0001<br>(.001 to −.002) | Green<br>.0002 to .00004<br>(.004 to .001) |
| **B**<br>−.0002 to −.0005<br>(−.006 to −.012) | Pink<br>−.0001 to −.0002<br>(−.002 to −.005) | Yellow<br>.00004 to −.0001<br>(.001 to −.002) | Green<br>.0002 to .00004<br>(.004 to .001) | Brown<br>.0003 to .0002<br>(.007 to .004) |
| **C**<br>−.0005 to −.0007<br>(−.012 to −.018) | Yellow<br>.00004 to −.0001<br>(.001 to −.002) | Green<br>.0002 to .00004<br>(.004 to .001) | Brown<br>.0003 to .0002<br>(.007 to .004) | Black<br>.0004 to .0003<br>(.010 to .007) |
| **D**<br>−.0007 to −.0009<br>(−.018 to −.024) | Green<br>.0002 to .00004<br>(.004 to .001) | Brown<br>.0003 to .0002<br>(.007 to .004) | Black<br>.0004 to .0003<br>(.010 to .007) | Blue<br>.0005 to .0004<br>(.013 to .010) |

## TIGHTENING SPECIFICATIONS

| Application | Ft. Lbs. (mkg) |
|---|---|
| Main Bearing Cap | 27-31 (3.7-4.3) |
| Connecting Rod Cap | 18-21 (2.6-3.0) |
| Camshaft Support | 13-16 (1.8-2.4) |
| Flywheel | 34-38 (4.7-5.3) |
| Cylinder Head Bolts | 37-42 (5.1-5.8) |
| Crankshaft Pulley | 34-38 (4.7-5.3) |
| Timing Belt Pulley | 18-25 (2.5-3.5) |
| Intake & Exhaust Manifolds | 13-17 (2.0-2.5) |

## CIVIC CVCC & ACCORD 4 CYLINDER

### ENGINE CODING

#### ENGINE IDENTIFICATION

Engine serial number is stamped at right, rear of engine. Serial number is preceded by engine model number.

| Application | Code |
|---|---|
| CVCC | |
| Sedan | ED3-4 |
| Station Wagon | ED4-4 |
| Accord | |
| Fed. | KA |
| Calif. | KL |
| High Alt. | KH |

### ENGINE & CYLINDER HEAD

#### ENGINE

**Removal — 1)** Remove grill to gain access to hood screws and remove hood after scribing location marks for reinstallation. Disconnect battery ground cable from battery and transmission. Completely remove engine torque arm. Disconnect all wiring and vacuum hoses to engine.

**2)** Drain radiator and disconnect coolant lines. Remove radiator. On automatic transmission models, remove transmission oil cooler lines. Remove starter motor and distributor cap. Disconnect clutch cable from clutch arm. Remove cooling fan housing with fan. Remove emission control box from firewall. Remove complete air cleaner assembly and engine mount heat shield.

**3)** On Accord models only, remove clutch slave cylinder with hose. Disconnect throttle and choke cables from carburetor. On automatic transmission models only, remove center console and remove shift control from shift lever. Raise front of vehicle and remove both front wheels. Drain crankcase and transmission fluid. Disconnect speedometer cable from transmission complete with drive gear.

**4)** Remove lower ball joints and tie rod ends on Accord using ball joint remover (07941-6710000). On Civic CVCC, remove lower control arm at stub frame. Pull stub axles from transmission case and protect splines. Remove front crossmember and lower engine mount bolt. Drive out pin securing shift linkage on manual transmission models.

**5)** Disconnect lower torque arm from transmission. On automatic transmission models, pull shift control cable out of housing. Disconnect exhaust pipe. Attach chain hoist to engine and position lifting hook 7 chain links from left side of engine and 14 links from right side of engine on Civic CVCC, and 17 links from left, 13 links from right on Accord. Raise hoist slightly to place tension on lifting sling. Install protective shield between engine and radiator.

**6)** Disconnect nut from rear engine mount and remove complete front engine mount assembly. Remove three bolts from left shock absorber mount assembly and push left engine mount into shock absorber mount bracket as far as it will go. Lift engine and remove from vehicle.

**Installation —** To install, reverse removal procedure and note following: Use new shift rod pin. Make sure sub-axles bottom

in transmission, and spring clip holds sub-axle securely. Arrows on combination lights point outward. Adjust all control cables after installation is completed.

#### CYLINDER HEAD

**NOTE** — *To minimize the chances of warping cylinder head, remove head after engine has been allowed to cool.*

**Removal — 1)** Scribe index marks on hood, then remove hood. Drain radiator and remove complete air cleaner assembly. Disconnect upper radiator hose and all vacuum lines to cylinder head and intake manifold. Disconnect throttle and choke cables.

**2)** Disconnect all wiring and hoses to intake manifold and cylinder head. Remove engine torque rod. Disconnect exhaust pipe from manifold. Remove valve cover and upper timing belt cover. Rotate engine until number one piston is at top dead center position.

**3)** Loosen timing belt adjusting and pivot bolt, then remove camshaft pulley bolt and remove pulley. Take off fuel pump and remove distributor. Remove oil pump gear holder and pump gear and shaft. Loosen bolts in reverse of tightening sequence (See Fig. 1), a little at a time and lift off cylinder head.

**Installation —** To install cylinder head, reverse removal procedure and tighten bolts in sequence shown in *Fig. 1*.

*Fig. 1  Cylinder Head Tightening Sequence*

### VALVES

#### VALVE ARRANGEMENT

**Rear Side —** I-E-E-I-I-E-E-I (left to right).
**Front Side —** All Auxiliary.

#### ROCKER ARM ASSEMBLY

**Removal —** Loosen rocker arm shaft support bolts in crisscross pattern starting with end supports. Pull out roll pins from both end shaft supports and remove supports, rocker collars, rocker arms and springs. Retain components in proper order for reassembly.

# Honda Engines

## CIVIC CVCC & ACCORD 4 CYLINDER (Cont.)

**Installation** — Measure all rocker arms for arm-to-shaft clearance. If clearance exceeds .0035" (.08 mm), replace rocker shaft and/or arms. Assemble in reverse of disassembly and install rocker arm assembly on engine. Tighten support bolts in a criss-cross pattern starting with center support.

### VALVE SPRINGS

**Intake & Exhaust Valves** — Using valve spring compressor, remove valve keepers, collars and springs. Check valve springs for squareness, free length and tension. Install in reverse of removal procedure, making sure closely wound coils are nearest cylinder head.

### AUXILIARY VALVES

1) Remove valve holder nut using special tool (07907-6570001) and pull valve holder assembly out of head. Auxiliary chamber collar may be removed using special puller (07940-6590000).

2) Compress spring and remove keepers. Disassemble and inspect valve assembly. Valve seat may be reconditioned, however entire assembly should be replaced if any component exceeds service limit.

3) Install chamber collar in each auxiliary valve hole with 2 new gaskets. Use alignment tool (07944-6590000) inserted in round hole toward spark plug opening with oval hole of collar towards combustion chamber. Leave alignment tool in place and insert auxiliary valve with new "O" ring, torquing to final specification with same tool used for removal.

### VALVE GUIDE SERVICING

**NOTE** — *For best results, heat cylinder head to 300°F (150°C) to remove or replace valve guides.*

Using driver (07942-6110000), drive valve guides out of cylinder head from port side. Install new guides from top of head using driver and attachment (07943-6710000). Drive guide in until tool bottoms on cylinder head. Ream valve guides to provide proper clearance.

### VALVE CLEARANCE ADJUSTMENT

1) Rotate engine until number one piston is at TDC on compression stroke, check and adjust intake valves of cylinder 1 and 2, exhaust valves of cylinders 1 and 3 and auxiliary valves of cylinders 1 and 2. Rotate crankshaft 360° and check and adjust intake valves of cylinder 3 and 4, exhaust valves of cylinders 2 and 4 and auxiliary valves of cylinders 3 and 4.

**NOTE** — *Cylinder head temperature should be below 100°F when adjusting valves.*

2) To adjust all valves, loosen lock nut and insert feeler gauge between rocker arm and valve stem. Turn adjuster to obtain proper clearance and tighten lock nut, then recheck clearance. On 1500 cc engines, intake and auxiliary valve clearance should be .006" (.15 mm), exhaust clearance should be .008" (.20 mm). Specified clearance for 1600 cc engines is .005" (.12 mm) for intake and auxiliary valves, .007" (.17 mm) for exhaust valves.

## PISTONS, PINS & RINGS

### PISTON & ROD ASSEMBLY

1) With oil pan and cylinder head removed, ream any ridge from top of cylinders. Mark piston and rod assemblies for proper reinstallation. Remove rod caps and push piston and rod assemblies out top of cylinder with a hammer handle.

2) Assemble piston and connecting rod with piston front mark and connecting rod oil jet hole on same side and facing intake manifold. Using a ring compressor, install piston and rod assemblies in proper cylinder.

**NOTE** — *Do NOT confuse reference number stamped across bearing cap and connecting rod with number indicating position of assembly in engine. This number indicates rod bore diameter only.*

### FITTING PISTONS

1) Measure cylinder bore for taper and out-of-round. If taper exceeds .004" (.1 mm) or out-of-round exceeds .002" (.05 mm), rebore cylinder for oversize pistons. Determine piston-to-cylinder clearance. If not within specifications, rebore cylinder for oversize pistons. An oversize piston of 2.923" (74.25 mm) diameter is available.

**Fig. 2   Piston Ring Installation**

2) Install three piece oil ring on piston with end gaps of rails and spacer staggered about 15°. Install top ring about 90° from oil spacer and second ring about 180° from spacer. Make sure no end gaps are in line with piston pin hole or thrust face of piston. Install all rings with markings facing upward.

### PISTON PINS

Using a press and piston pin removal tool set (07973-6570000), press piston pin out of piston and connecting rod. Install new pin by placing pilot through piston and connecting rod. Lightly oil piston pin and place piston, rod, pin and ram on press base. Press in pin until centered in connecting rod.

## CIVIC CVCC & ACCORD 4 CYLINDER (Cont.)

### CRANKSHAFT MAIN & CONNECTING ROD BEARINGS

#### MAIN & CONNECTING ROD BEARINGS

**1)** Prior to disassembly, mark main and connecting rod bearings caps for reassembly in their original positions and check crankshaft endplay and connecting rod side play. Remove piston and connecting rod assemblies, remove main bearing caps and remove crankshaft.

**2)** Measure crankshaft for bend, out-of-round and taper *(See Specifications)*. If any measurement exceeds specifications, crankshaft must be replaced. Do not attempt to regrind crankshaft as bearing journals are specifically heat-treated.

#### Crankshaft Wear Specifications

| Application | Standard In. (mm) | Service Limit In. (mm) |
|---|---|---|
| Bend | .0024 (.06) | .0118 (.30) |
| Taper | .0002 (.005) | .0004 (.010) |
| Out-Of-Round | .0002 (.005) | .0004 (.010) |

**3)** Using Plastigage method, determine bearing clearances. If bearing replacement is necessary, use following procedure to determine bearing size to use.

**4)** Referring to *Fig. 3* and *Fig. 4*, note that all **letters** stamped on crankshaft counterweight pads apply to connecting rod journal nearest letter. All **numbers** stamped on crankshaft apply to nearest main bearing journal. Connecting rod caps have numbers stamped on cap and cylinder block has Roman numerals stamped on pad at flywheel end of block.

**5)** To determine color (size) of bearing insert to use, pair up numbers and/or letters on tables and where the column and row intersect, this will be bearing insert to use. Example: For a main bearing, use "Main Bearing Journals" table. If number stamped on crankshaft is "2" and roman numeral stamped on block for corresponding journal is "III", you would use a "Green" bearing insert

**Fig. 3   Crankshaft Identification Locations (All Engines)**

#### THRUST BEARING ALIGNMENT

Measure thrust bearing clearance and replace thrust washers or crankshaft as necessary. Do not change thrust washer thickness either by grinding or shimming. Install thrust washers with oil grooves facing toward crankshaft.

**NOTE** — *Main Bearing Caps ONLY are Marked with Number for Position.*

**Fig. 4   Connecting Rod Bearing & Cylinder Block Identification Locations**

# Honda Engines

## CIVIC CVCC & ACCORD 4 CYLINDER (Cont.)

### CVCC 1487cc Main Bearing Journals    In. (mm)

| Journal Dia. 1.97 (50) / Crankcase Bore Dia. 2.13 (54) | I | II | III | IIII |
|---|---|---|---|---|
| | +.0021 to +.0023 (+.052 to +.058) | +.0023 to +.0025 (+.058 to +.064) | +.0025 to +.0027 (+.064 to +.070) | +.0027 to +.0030 (+.070 to +.076) |
| **1** +.0013 to +.0016 (+.033 to +.041) | Red −.0001 to −.0002 (−.002 to −.005) | Pink −.0001 to +.00004 (−.002 to +.001) | Yellow +.00004 to +.0002 (+.001 to +.005) | Green +.0002 to +.0003 (+.004 to +.007) |
| **2** +.0011 to +.0013 (+.028 to +.033) | Pink −.0001 to +.00004 (−.002 to +.001) | Yellow +.00004 to +.0002 (+.001 to +.025) | Green +.0002 to +.0003 (+.005 to +.007) | Brown +.00004 to +.0003 (+.001 to +.007) |
| **3** +.0009 to +.0011 (+.023 to +.028) | Yellow +.00004 to +.0002 (+.001 to +.005) | Green +.0002 to +.0003 (+.005 to +.007) | Brown +.00004 to +.0003 (+.001 to +.007) | Black +.0004 to +.0005 (+.010 to +.013) |
| **4** +.0006 to +.0009 (+.016 to +.023) | Green +.0002 to +.0003 (+.005 to +.007) | Brown +.00004 to +.0003 (+.001 to +.007) | Black +.0004 to +.0005 (+.010 to +.013) | Blue +.0005 to +.0006 (+.013 to +.016) |

### Accord 1600cc Main Bearing Journals    In. (mm)

| Journal Dia. 1.97 (50) / Crankcase Bore Dia. 2.13 (54) | I | II | III | IIII |
|---|---|---|---|---|
| | +.0016 to +.0018 (+.041 to +.046) | +.0018 to +.0020 (+.046 to +.051) | +.0020 to +.0023 (+.051 to +.058) | +.0023 to +.0025 (+.058 to +.064) |
| **1** +.0009 to +.0012 (+.023 to +.030) | Red −.0001 to −.0002 (−.002 to −.005) | Pink −.0001 to +.00004 (−.002 to +.001) | Yellow +.0002 to +.00004 (+.005 to +.001) | Green +.0002 to +.0003 (+.005 to +.007) |
| **2** +.0007 to +.0009 (+.018 to +.023) | Pink −.0001 to +.00004 (−.002 to +.001) | Yellow +.0002 to +.00004 (+.005 to +.001) | Green +.0002 to +.0003 (+.005 to +.007) | Brown +.00004 to +.0003 (+.001 to +.007) |
| **3** +.0005 to +.0007 (+.013 to +.018) | Yellow +.0002 to +.00004 (+.005 to +.001) | Green +.0002 to +.0003 (+.005 to +.007) | Brown +.00004 to +.0003 (+.001 to +.007) | Black +.0004 to +.0005 (+.010 to +.013) |
| **4** +.0002 to +.0005 (+.005 to +.013) | Green +.0002 to +.0003 (+.005 to +.007) | Brown +.00004 to +.0003 (+.001 to +.007) | Black +.0004 to +.0005 (+.010 to +.013) | Blue +.0005 to +.0006 (+.013 to +.015) |

## CIVIC CVCC & ACCORD 4 CYLINDER (Cont.)

| Connecting Rod Bearing Journals | | | In. (mm) | |
|---|---|---|---|---|
| Connecting Rod Dia. 1.69 (43) <br><br> Journal Dia. 1.654 (42) | 1 <br><br> 0 to +.0002 <br> (0 to +.006) | 2 <br><br> +.0002 to +.0005 <br> (+.006 to +.012) | 3 <br><br> +.0005 to +.0007 <br> (+.012 to +.018) | 4 <br><br> +.0007 to +.0009 <br> (+.018 to +.024) |
| A <br> 0 to −.0002 <br> (0 to −.006) | Red <br> −.0002 to −.0003 <br> (−.005 to −.008) | Pink <br> −.0001 to −.0002 <br> (−.002 to −.005) | Yellow <br> −.0001 to +.00004 <br> (−.002 to +.001) | Green <br> +.00004 to +.0002 <br> (+.001 to +.004) |
| B <br> −.0002 to −.0005 <br> (−.006 to −.012) | Pink <br> −.0001 to −.0002 <br> (−.002 to −.005) | Yellow <br> −.0001 to +.00004 <br> (−.002 to +.001) | Green <br> +.00004 to +.0002 <br> (+.001 to +.004) | Brown <br> +.0002 to +.0003 <br> (+.004 to +.007) |
| C <br> −.0005 to −.0007 <br> (−.012 to −.018) | Yellow <br> −.0001 to +.00004 <br> (−.002 to +.001) | Green <br> +.00004 to +.0002 <br> (+.001 to +.004) | Brown <br> +.0002 to +.0003 <br> (+.004 to +.007) | Black <br> +.0003 to +.0004 <br> (+.007 to +.010) |
| D <br> −.0007 to −.0009 <br> (−.018 to −.024) | Green <br> +.00004 to +.0002 <br> (+.001 to +.004) | Brown <br> +.0002 to +.0003 <br> (+.004 to +.007) | Black <br> +.0003 to +.0004 <br> (+.007 to +.010) | Blue <br> +.0004 to +.0005 <br> (+.010 to +.013) |

## CAMSHAFT

| Camshaft Lobe Height | |
|---|---|
| Application | In. (mm) |
| 1487 cc | |
| Intake.......................... | 1.4966-1.5029 (38.01-38.17) |
| Exhaust........................ | 1.4789-1.4851 (37.56-37.72) |
| Auxiliary...................... | 1.6475-1.6537 (41.85-42.01) |
| 1600 cc | |
| Intake.......................... | 1.4856-1.4951 (37.74-37.98) |
| Exhaust........................ | 1.4856-1.4951 (37.74-37.98) |
| Auxiliary...................... | 1.7316-1.7410 (43.98-44.22) |

### TIMING BELT

1) Remove water pump drive belt, water pump pulley and crankshaft pulley. Remove upper timing belt cover from cylinder head and remove lower timing belt cover from engine block.

2) Loosen, do not remove, timing belt adjusting and pivot bolts. Slide belt off pulleys. To install, reverse removal procedure using care not to excessively bend or twist belt. Do not expose belt to engine oil or grease as this will damage belt. Install belt so same direction of rotation will be maintained to prevent excessive belt wear.

### CAMSHAFT

1) Remove rocker arm assembly, then lift out camshaft. Inspect camshaft and cylinder head bearing surfaces for wear or damage. Check camshaft runout. If runout exceeds .004" (.10 mm), replace camshaft. Measure total camshaft lobe height. If total height of lobes is not to specifications, replace camshaft.

2) Oil camshaft bearing journals and install camshaft and seal or tachometer drive body. Apply silicone seal to mating surfaces on end camshaft supports and cylinder head. Install rocker arm assembly and tighten to specifications.

### VALVE TIMING

Rotate crankshaft until TDC mark on flywheel or automatic transmission drive plate is aligned with index mark. Rotate camshaft until woodruff key is pointing straight up and timing marks on pulley are parallel with top of cylinder head (See Fig. 5). Without disturbing pulley positions, slide on timing belt and adjust belt tension.

**Fig. 5 Camshaft Alignment Marks in Position for Installing Camshaft Belt**

### TIMING BELT TENSION

Loosen timing belt pivot and adjustment bolts on lower timing belt cover. **NOTE** – *Upper bolt is pivot bolt and lower bolt is adjusting bolt.* Rotate engine a quarter of a turn counterclockwise and tighten adjusting bolt, then tighten pivot bolt. Do not apply pressure to timing belt while adjusting tension.

# Honda Engines

## CIVIC CVCC & ACCORD 4 CYLINDER (Cont.)

### ENGINE OILING

#### ENGINE OILING SYSTEM

A rotor type oil pump draws oil from oil pan and delivers it under pressure through main bearing cradle to main and connecting rod bearings. Oil passes through rods to an oil jet which lubricates pistons and cylinder walls. An oil passage carries oil to camshaft bearings and rocker arms. Oil mist lubricates valve stems.

#### OIL PUMP

1) Remove oil pan, then oil pump assembly may be removed by removing four long bolts (one bolt under strainer). Pull out relief valve cotter pin and remove seat, spring and valve.

2) Remove two pump body bolts and disassemble pump. Inspect pump for wear or damage. Measure pump operating clearances and relief valve spring free length. Reassemble pump making sure marks on rotors face outward and are adjacent to each other. Place oil pickup in container of oil and operate pump with screwdriver to ensure that it is operating. Place finger over outlet hole and check the pressure is created as pump is turned.

**NOTE** — If oil pump driven gear is to be replaced, camshaft must also be replaced.

#### Oil Pump Specifications

| Application | Standard In. (mm) | Service Limit In. (mm) |
|---|---|---|
| Inner-to-Outer Rotor | .0059 (.15) | .0079 (.20) |
| Rotor-to-Body | .0039-.0071 (.10-.18) | .0079 (.20) |
| Rotor End Clearance | .0012-.0039 (.03-.10) | .0059 (.15) |

**Crankcase Capacity** — 3.2 qts. (includes filter)

**Oil Filter** — Disposable with built-in by-pass valve.

**Pressure Regulator Valve** — Non-adjustable.

**1487 cc Normal Oil Pressure** — 48-58 psi (3.4-4.2 kg/cm) at 3000 RPM. 20 psi (1.4 kg/cm$^2$) minimum at idle speed.

**1600 cc Normal Oil Pressure** — 54-60 psi (3.8-4.2 kg/cm$^2$) at 3000 RPM. 21 psi (1.5 kg/cm$^2$) minimum at idle speed.

### ENGINE COOLING

**Thermostat** — Starts to open at 176-183°F (80-84°C) and is fully open at 203°F (95°C).

**Thermoswitch** — Operates at 191-197°F (88.5-91.5°C).

**Cooling System Capacity** — 4.2 quarts on 1487 cc, and 5.3 quarts on 1600 cc.

#### WATER PUMP

**Removal** — Drain radiator and loosen alternator adjusting bolts. Push alternator toward engine and remove drive belt. Remove water pump and "O" ring seal.

**Installation** — 1) Reinstall water pump. Loosen cooling system bleed valve located on thermostat housing. Fill radiator with coolant. When air bubbles no longer appear in coolant draining from bleed valve, close valve.

2) Start engine and place heater temperature control lever in high position. Run engine about ten minutes. Again open bleed valve and bleed system until there are no air bubbles in coolant draining from bleed valve. Refill radiator.

## ENGINE SPECIFICATIONS

### GENERAL SPECIFICATIONS

| Year | Displ. | | Carburetor | HP at RPM | Torque (Ft. Lbs. at RPM) | Compr. Ratio | Bore | | Stroke | |
|---|---|---|---|---|---|---|---|---|---|---|
| | cu. ins. | cc | | | | | in. | mm | in. | mm |
| 1978 CVCC | 90.80 | 1487 | 1x3-Bbl. | 63@5000 | 77@3000 | 7.9:1 | 2.91 | 74.0 | 3.41 | 86.5 |
| Accord | 97.63 | 1600 | 1x3-Bbl. | ..... | ..... | 8.0:1 | 2.91 | 74.0 | 3.66 | 93.0 |

## CIVIC CVCC & ACCORD 4 CYLINDER (Cont.)
### ENGINE SPECIFICATIONS (Cont.)

| VALVES | | | | | | | |
|---|---|---|---|---|---|---|---|
| Engine & Valve | Head Diam. In. (mm) | Face Angle | Seat Angle | Seat Width In. (mm) | Stem Diameter In. (mm) | Stem Clearance In. (mm) | Valve Lift In. (mm) |
| 1487 cc | | | | | | | |
| Intake | 1.374-1.382 (34.9-35.1) | 46° | 46° | .055 (1.4) | .259-.260 (6.58-6.59) | .0004-.0016 (.01-.04) | ..... |
| Exhaust | 1.098-1.106 (27.9-28.1) | 46° | 46° | .055 (1.4) | .258-.259 (6.55-6.56) | .002-.003 (.05-.08) | ..... |
| Auxiliary | .469-.476 (11.9-12.1) | 45° | 45° | .022 (.56) | .216-.217 (5.48-5.49) | .0008-.002 (.02-.05) | ..... |
| 1600 cc | | | | | | | |
| Intake | 1.374-1.382 (34.9-35.1) | 46° | 46° | .055 (1.4) | .259-.260 (6.58-6.59) | .0008-.002 (.02-.05) | ..... |
| Exhaust | 1.098-1.106 (27.9-28.1) | 46° | 46° | .055 (1.4) | .258-.259 (6.55-6.56) | .002-.003 (.05-.08) | ..... |
| Auxiliary | .469-.476 (11.9-12.1) | 45° | 45° | .022 (.56) | .216-.217 (5.48-5.49) | .001-.002 (.02-.05) | ..... |

| PISTONS, PINS, RINGS | | | | | | |
|---|---|---|---|---|---|---|
| | PISTONS | PINS | | RINGS | | |
| Engine | Clearance In. (mm) | Piston Fit In. (mm) | Rod Fit In. (mm) | Rings | End Gap In. (mm) | Side Clearance In. (mm) |
| 1487 cc & 1600 cc | .0012 (.03) | .0004-.0009 (.010-.022) | ①0-.0007 (0-.019) | No. 1 | .008-.016 (.2-.4) | .0008-.0018 (.020-.045) |
| | | | | No. 2 | .008-.016 (.2-.4) | .0008-.0018 (.020-.045) |
| | | | | Oil | ②.008-.035 (.2-.9) | ..... |

① — Interference fit.
② — .012-.035" (0.3-0.9 mm) on 1600 cc.

| CRANKSHAFT MAIN & CONNECTING ROD BEARINGS | | | | | | | |
|---|---|---|---|---|---|---|---|
| | MAIN BEARINGS | | | | CONNECTING ROD BEARINGS | | |
| Engine | Journal Diam. In. (mm) | Clearance In. (mm) | Thrust Bearing | Crankshaft End Play In. (mm) | Journal Diam. In. (mm) | Clearance In. (mm) | Side Play In. (mm) |
| 1487 cc & 1600 cc | 1.9687-1.9697 (50.006-50.030) | ①.0010-.0022 (.026-.055) | No. 4 | .0039-.0138 (.10-.35) | 1.6526-1.6535 (41.976-42.000) | .0008-.0015 (.020-.038) | .0059-.0118 (.15-.30) |

① — .0010-.0017" (.026-.044 mm) on 1600 cc.

| CAMSHAFT | | | |
|---|---|---|---|
| Engine | Journal Diam. In. (mm) | Clearance In. (mm) | End Play In. (mm) |
| 1487 cc & 1600 cc | ..... | .0020-.0059 (.050-.150) | .002-.006 (.050-.150) |

# Honda Engines

## CIVIC CVCC & ACCORD 4 CYLINDER (Cont.)
### ENGINE SPECIFICATIONS (Cont.)

| Engine | Free Length In. (mm) | PRESSURE Lbs. @ In. (kg @ mm) | |
|---|---|---|---|
| | | Valve Closed | Valve Open |
| **1487 cc** | | | |
| **Intake** | | | |
| Inner | 1.665 (42.3) | 8@1.401 (4@35.6) | 30@1.008 (14@25.6) |
| Outer | 1.665 (42.3) | 28@1.488 (13@37.8) | 108@1.094 (49@27.8) |
| **Exhaust** | | | |
| Inner | 1.988 (50.5) | 27.5@1.331 (12.5@33.8) | 44@1.024 (20@26) |
| Outer | 2.118 (53.8) | 51@1.437 (23.3@36.5) | 85@1.102 (39@28) |
| Auxiliary | 1.146 (29.1) | 15@.906 (7@23) | 23@.787 (11@20) |
| **1600 cc** | | | |
| **Intake** | | | |
| Inner | 1.583 (40.2) | 22@1.358 (10@34.5) | 64@1.024 (29@26) |
| Outer | 1.573 (39.95) | 19@1.437 (8.5@36.5) | 78@1.094 (35@27.8) |
| **Exhaust** | | | |
| Inner | 2.0 (52.0) | 28@1.358 (13@34.5) | 44@1.024 (20@26) |
| Outer | 2.118 (53.8) | 57@1.437 (25@36.5) | 85@1.108 (39@28) |
| Auxiliary | 1.146 (29.1) | 15@.906 (7@23) | 24@.787 (11@20) |

**VALVE SPRINGS** (table title)

## TIGHTENING SPECIFICATIONS

| Application | Ft. Lbs. (mkg) |
|---|---|
| **1487cc** | |
| Connecting Rod Bolts | 20 (2.7) |
| Main Bearing Bolts | 33 (4.7) |
| Cylinder Head Bolts | 44 (6.0) |
| Aux. Valve Holder Nut | 50 (7.0) |
| Camshaft Sprocket Bolt | 22 (3.0) |
| Intake/Exhaust Manifold Bolts | 16 (2.2) |
| Rocker Arm Support | |
|   6 mm Bolts | 10 (1.4) |
|   8 mm Bolts | 16 (2.2) |
| Lower Torque Arm | 5-9 (.7-1.2) |
| Upper Torque Arm | 25-31 (3.5-4.3) |
| **1600 cc** | |
| Connecting Rod Bolts | 18-21 (2.5-2.9) |
| Main Bearing Bolts | 30-35 (4.2-4.8) |
| Cylinder Head Bolts | 40-47 (5.5-6.5) |
| Aux. Valve Holder Nut | 54-61 (7.5-8.5) |
| Camshaft Sprocket Bolt | 18-22 (2.5-3.0) |
| Intake/Exhaust Manifold Bolts | 14-17 (2.0-2.4) |
| Rocker Arm Support | |
|   6 mm Bolts | 7-10 (1.0-1.4) |
|   8 mm Bolts | 14-17 (2.0-2.4) |
| Upper Torque Arm | 25-31 (3.5-4.3) |

## XJ6 4.2 LITER 6 CYLINDER

### ENGINE CODING

#### ENGINE IDENTIFICATION

Engine can be identified by the number stamped on top of cylinder block at rear of engine and on identification plate in engine compartment.

### ENGINE & CYLINDER HEAD

#### ENGINE

1) Remove hood and disconnect battery. Discharge air conditioning system. Disconnect and cap refrigerant lines. Remove fuel pipes at heat exchanger. Plug inlet pipe and move clear of engine. Remove heat exchanger mounting screws. Secure A/C hoses away from engine. From right fender well, remove receiver-drier retaining screws. Fasten receiver-drier and hoses clear of engine.

2) Remove wing valance stays. Remove air cleaner. Detach and remove radiator. Disconnect coolant hoses to expansion tank. Remove both engine mount-to-bracket nuts. Drain power steering fluid. Disconnect power steering lines. Slacken pump mounting bolts and push pump as close as possible to engine.

3) Pull connectors from alternator. Separate connector plug from engine harness. Disconnect brake vacuum pipe at manifold, and secure pipe out of way. Release pipe clip and pull heater-A/C operating vacuum pipe from non-return valves; secure away from engine. Remove exhaust manifolds.

4) Remove starter cable and solenoid cable. Disconnect heater hoses at firewall connectors. Detach inner and outer throttle cables and secure away from engine. Remove choke cables from carburetors and position out of way. Disconnect hoses from charcoal canister.

5) Position suitable lifting device and attach to rear lifting eye on engine. Remove nut at center of rear transmission mounting. Unscrew nuts securing bracket on transmission. Remove heat shield. Position jack to support mounting plate of transmission and unscrew mounting bolts. Lower jack and remove mounting plate along with spring washers and rubber rings.

6) Remove special nuts securing propeller shaft to output flange. From transmission unit selector lever, remove nut to release ball peg on inner selector cable. Remove setscrew and spring washer securing outer selector cable clamp. Disconnect speedometer cable from transmission.

7) From front of vehicle, position jack to support transmission assembly below oil sump. Support engine on lifting assembly. Lift front of engine while lowering rear and withdraw engine forward and upward.

**CAUTION** — *Use extreme care when withdrawing engine to prevent damage to air conditioning expansion valve.*

#### CYLINDER HEAD

**Removal — 1)** Disconnect battery and drain cooling system. Remove both wing valance stays (firewall-to-fender support rods), removing Pressure line from support rod. Remove air cleaner. Detach inner and outer throttle cables from abutment and linkage brackets. Separate kickdown cable from linkage and retainers.

2) Release inlet and outlet fuel line union nuts at heat exchanger. Plug line. Remove clips securing A/C suction line to engine. Remove screws and lay heat exchanger at left side of engine compartment.

3) Release union nut at EGR "Y" connector. Remove four screws and carefully separate cover from secondary throttle housing. Pull vacuum line from EGR valve. **NOTE** — *Completion of this step will depend upon whether vehicle is equipped with a fixed orifice EGR valve or a variable orifice EGR valve.*

**Fig. 1    Retaining Bolts Installed to Hold Camshaft During Cylinder Head Installation**

4) Pull anti-diesel system vacuum line "H" fitting from "T" connector at gulp valve. Detach air line from fresh air injection manifold. Remove float chamber and carburetor breather crossover pipes from rubber connectors and plastic clips; lay these to left side of engine compartment.

5) Slacken pipe clip at air injection manifold check valve, then remove air injection pipe. Remove air pump and bracket. Detach setscrew at rear of cylinder block securing EGR system supply line. Unscrew EGR pipe from exhaust manifold adaptor. Remove adaptor.

6) Remove heat shield from exhaust manifold. Remove steering pump drive belt and swing pump away from engine. Detach top hose from radiator. Pull remote header and radiator bleed lines from header tank. Release coolant hose from water pump. Remove secondary throttle heater hose. Note connections and remove all vacuum lines and wires from beneath intake manifold.

# Jaguar Engines

## XJ6 4.2 LITER 6 CYLINDER (Cont.)

**7)** Remove exhaust manifolds from cylinder head. Disconnect two camshaft oil lines from rear of head. Remove distributor cap, spark plugs, and plug wires. Unbolt and remove camshaft covers. Detach breather housing from front of head.

**Fig. 2   Jaguar XJ6 Cylinder Head Tightening Sequence**

**8)** Remove camshaft sprocket retaining bolt (from both camshafts), then rotate engine until remaining two bolts are accessible and remove both bolts. **CAUTION** — *The engine must not be rotated after camshaft sprockets are disconnected and cylinder head is still in place.* Withdraw camshaft sprockets. Mark aligning holes in adjuster plates.

**9)** Working from center outward, remove cylinder head retaining bolts and nuts, and lift head from engine. **CAUTION** — *Do not rest cylinder head on flat surface. Support head with wooden blocks at each end of mounting face to protect open valves which protrude.*

**Installation** — **1)** Install new head gasket (ensuring "TOP" mark is upward). Rotate crankshaft until No. 6 cylinder (front) is at TDC, with rotor pointing approximately forward along engine.

**2)** Rotate camshafts until suitable timing gauge (C.3993) can be located in front flange slots *(Fig. 1)*. Lower cylinder head into position, attach spark plug wire brackets and lifting brackets to appropriate head studs, then place washers and 14 large domed nuts on stud. Affix nuts and washers at forward end of head, then tighten all nuts *(Fig. 2)*.

**3)** Locate sprockets on camshaft flanges and ensure both holes in each flange are positioned with aligning holes marked during removal. If necessary, remove circlip and reposition adjuster plate. Make sure engine is not rotated until camshaft sprockets are fully seated and chain installed.

**4)** Secure each adjuster plate to camshaft, then rotate engine until remaining attachment holes are accessible. Install bolts and bend up lock plate tabs. Set timing chain tension using a suitable adjusting tool (JD2B). Tighten lock nut.

**5)** Ensure No. 6 (front) cylinder is at TDC and recheck position of camshafts using timing gauge (C.3993). Complete installation by reversing remainder of removal procedures. Recheck ignition timing and perform exhaust emission check.

## VALVES

### VALVE ARRANGEMENT
**Left Side** — All exhaust.
**Right Side** — All intake.

### VALVE GUIDE SERVICING

Check valve guide for wear and proper guide-to-valve stem clearance. If guide is worn beyond specifications, replace guide by heating head in boiling water for approximately 30 minutes (or by other suitable method), then drive guide(s) out of head from combustion chamber end. Coat new guide with graphite grease and refit circlip. Reheat head and drive new guide in from top until circlip is seated in groove. **NOTE** — *When installing oversize replacement guides, check O.D. of guide to be used, and if necessary, ream cylinder head bore to obtain proper interference fit.*

#### Replacement Valve Guides

| Application | Size Mark | Dimension In. (mm) |
|---|---|---|
| Standard | No Mark | .501-.502 (12.73-12.75) |
| 1st Oversize | 1 Groove | .503-.504 (12.78-12.80) |
| 2nd Oversize | 2 Grooves | .506-.507 (12.85-12.87) |
| 3rd Oversize | 3 Grooves | .511-.512 (12.98-13.00) |

### VALVE SPRING SERVICING

**CAUTION** — *Support ends of cylinder head with wooden blocks to prevent damage to valves. Opened valves protrude below face of cylinder head.*

**1)** Remove camshaft bearing caps, note markings for reassembly. Remove camshaft, tappets and adjusting pads. Retain tappets and pads in proper order for reassembly.

**Fig. 3   Using Special Valve Spring Compressor Tool No. JD.6118C to Remove Spring**

**2)** Install suitable spring compressor (Churchill No. JD.6118C) and a block of wood between valve and work table. Compress springs and remove valve keepers. Compare old spring

## XJ6 4.2 LITER 6 CYLINDER (Cont.)

with new spring or with specification table. Replace springs as necessary. To install, reverse procedure.

### VALVE TAPPET SERVICE

Remove tappets and adjusting pads, keeping components in order. **NOTE** — *Valves are numbered and must be kept in order (if removed). No. 1 is at flywheel end of engine.* Inspect all tappets, guides, and adjusting pads for wear. If tappet guide is to be replaced, bore out old guide until it collapses (taking care not to damage head bore). Ensure head is at room temperature and measure tappet guide bore, then grind replacement guide to obtain a .003" (.076 mm) interference fit. Also grind the same amount from the "lead in" at the bottom end of guide. Heat head and drive in tappet guide, then ream guide to 1.75" (44.5 mm). Replace other necessary parts.

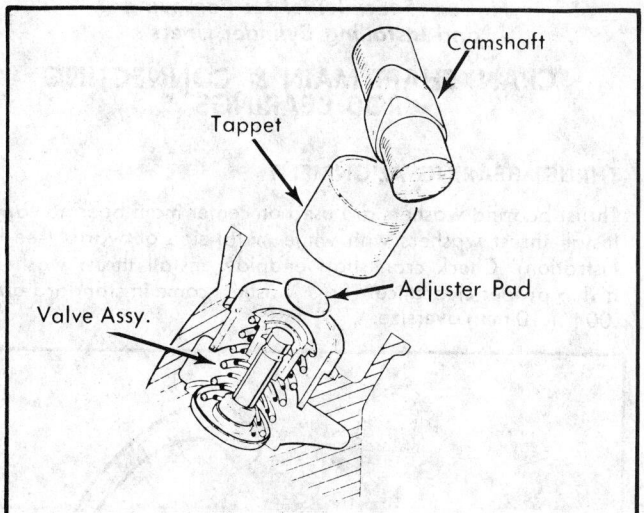

**Fig. 4    Expanded View of Valve Tappet Assemblies**

Camshaft

Tappet

Adjuster Pad

Valve Assy.

### VALVE TAPPET CLEARANCE

**NOTE** — *If checking valve clearances with cylinder head removed, the camshafts must be installed and checked one at a time. It is imperative that this be followed, as position fouling is likely if camshafts are rotated independently while both are installed.*

**1)** If not already done, remove camshaft covers. Rotate camshaft and record clearance between heel of each cam and its respective tappet. If head is installed, and adjustment is to be made, rotate camshaft and install valve timing gauge (C.3993) before removing final camshaft retaining bolt. If required, disconnect sprockets from camshafts. *See Valve Timing.*

**2)** Remove camshaft bearing caps and lift off camshaft. Remove each tappet taking note of its location. Remove adjusting pad. Subtract appropriate valve clearance of .012-.014" (.305-.356 mm) from initial clearance measured. Select appropriate adjusting shim which will equal this measurement. Adjusting pads are available in increments of .001" (.03 mm)

from .085" (2.16 mm) to .110" (2.79 mm) and are marked with letters from "A" to "Z" respectively.

**3)** Insert adjusting pads and install tappets. Attach camshafts (using timing gauge if head is installed). Torque camshaft bearing cap nuts, connect camshaft sprockets, and install camshaft covers.

## PISTONS, PINS & RINGS

### OIL PAN REMOVAL (ENGINE INSTALLED)

**1)** Remove front suspension components to gain access and suitable clearance. Drain engine oil. Remove nuts securing oil return pipe. Unscrew nuts, bolts, and washers securing transmission oil cooler pipe clips (Auto. Trans.).

**2)** Remove setscrews and nuts retaining oil pan to block (note location of short screw at right front). Unbolt and remove intake strainer box.

**3)** When installing, ensure "O" ring is properly positioned on oil return pipe. Lightly coat new oil seal with grease and locate in oil pan groove (DO NOT trim seal ends, press into groove until flush). Lightly coat new pan gasket and install pan. Reverse remaining procedures.

**Fig. 5    Position of Short Screw in Oil Pan**

### PISTON & ROD ASSEMBLY

**1)** With cylinder head and oil pan removed, unscrew nuts from connecting rod caps, and remove caps, keeping in order for reassembly. **NOTE** — *Rod caps and rods are numbered to correspond to their positions (No. 1 is at flywheel end). Remove connecting rod bolt and withdraw piston and rod assembly out top of cylinder.*

**2)** If installing original assemblies, ensure they are replaced in original cylinders. If installing new assemblies, stamp-mark assemblies with numbers "1" through "6". Position pistons in cylinders with "FRONT" mark forward.

# Jaguar Engines

## XJ6 4.2 LITER 6 CYLINDER (Cont.)

### PISTON RINGS

After checking ring end gap and side play, install compression rings in top two grooves and oil ring in bottom groove. Both compression rings have tapered peripheries and are marked with "TOP" to ensure correct installation. The top ring is also chrome-plated and cargraph (red) coated; the red coating must NOT be removed. When fitting oil ring, ensure expander ends do not overlap.

### PISTON PINS

When removing and replacing piston pins, immerse assembly in hot oil bath (or use other suitable method) to bring piston end of assembly to approximately 230°F (110°C). When installing pins, always use new pin circlips. Note that pins are color coded for grading purposes. Always select proper color pin for replacement.

### FITTING PISTONS

Check piston and cylinder bore to determine if proper clearance exists. If necessary to rebore cylinder for installation of oversize piston, note that reboring is not to exceed .030" (.76 mm). Oversize pistons are available in .010", .020", and .030" (.25 mm, .51 mm, and .76 mm) oversizes. If replacing pistons with standard sizes (no reboring), note the following list of piston grades and select replacement piston of same grade. Piston grade is stamped in piston crown and on top face of block adjacent to cylinder.

#### Standard Piston Grading

| Stamp Mark | Cylinder Diameter In. (mm) |
|---|---|
| F | 3.6250-3.6253 (92.075-92.083) |
| G | 3.6254-3.6257 (92.085-92.093) |
| H | 3.6258-3.6261 (92.095-92.103) |
| J | 3.6262-3.6265 (92.106-92.113) |
| K | 3.6266-3.6269 (92.116-92.123) |

### CYLINDER LINERS

1) Should piston-to-cylinder clearance be excessive and reboring requires more than .030" (.76 mm) to clean up cylinders, new cylinder liners must be installed.

2) Press out the worn liners from below, using a suitable block. Lightly coat outer top half of new liner with a jointing compound, then press in new liner until flush with top of block. Smear more jointing compound around area of liner-to-block mating surface.

3) Bore out liner to correspond with grade of piston to be installed. Following reboring process, the blanking plugs in the main oil gallery should be removed and cylinder block oilways thoroughly cleaned. When dry, coat interior of crankcase with an oil and heat resistant paint.

**Fig. 6** *Special Tool for Removing and Installing Cylinder Liners*

## CRANKSHAFT MAIN & CONNECTING ROD BEARINGS

### THRUST BEARING ALIGNMENT

Thrust bearing washers are used on center main bearing caps. Install thrust washers with white metal side outwards (see illustration). Check crankshaft endplay, install thrust washers giving proper clearance. Thrust washers come in standard and .004" (.10 mm) oversize.

**Fig. 7** *Position of Thrust Washers on Crankshaft*

### MAIN BEARING SERVICE

Remove connecting rod and main bearing caps, retaining all parts in exact order for reassembly. Note that all caps are numbered for reassembly reference. When wear or out-of-roundness exceeds .003" (.08 mm), regrind crankshaft and install undersize bearings. Bearings are available in .010", .020", .030", and .040" (.25 mm, .51 mm, .76 mm, and 1.02 mm) undersizes. If regrinding must exceed .040" (1.02 mm), replace crankshaft.

## XJ6 4.2 LITER 6 CYLINDER (Cont.)

### REAR MAIN BEARING OIL SEAL

**NOTE** – *The following procedure must be performed before crankshaft is reinstalled.*

*Fig. 8   Expanded View of Crankshaft Rear Oil Seal*

*Fig. 9   Using Special Tool to Size Rear Oil Seal*

**1)** Carefully tap new rear oil seal halves into position, then roll seal into housing (with a hammer handle) until ends do not protrude. **NOTE** – *DO NOT cut seal ends.* When both halves are properly in place, secure them with Allen screws.

**2)** Attach rear main bearing cap without bearings and torque to 72 ft. lbs. (10 mkg). Assemble rear oil seal housing to cylinder block, using three Allen screws. Lightly coat inside surface of oil seal with graphite grease and insert a suitable sizing tool (JD.17B) as shown in illustration. Press tool inward and turn until it is fully seated; this should properly size the oil seal. Remove sizing tool by pulling and twisting in opposite direction. Remove oil seal housing and install crankshaft.

## CAMSHAFT

### ENGINE FRONT COVER & OIL SEAL

**Removal** – **1)** Remove radiator and fan belt. Mark position of vibration damper for reassembly. Remove pulley. Using a pair of levers, pry damper off of split cone. Remove split cone.

**2)** Remove oil pan and water pump. Unscrew screws attaching timing cover and slide timing cover and oil seal off of crankshaft.

**Installation** – **1)** Place new seal in groove in timing cover. Using a new gasket and sealing compound, intall timing cover and seal. Reinstall oil pan with a new gasket. Install short screw in front right hand corner of oil pan.

**2)** Reinstall split cone on crankshaft. Position crankshaft damper to mark, install pulley and torque attaching bolts to specifications. Reinstall remaining components in reverse of removal procedures.

### CAMSHAFT

**1)** After removing necessary components to gain access to camshaft covers, unscrew ten dome head nuts and two cross head screws which retain each camshaft cover. Detach crankcase breather from front of head. Use a suitable tool (JD.2B) to slacken timing chain (rotate tool in clockwise direction).

**2)** Bend back tabs from camshaft sprockets and remove two top bolts from each camshaft sprocket, then rotate engine to

Front Oil Seal

*Fig. 10   Exploded View of Crankshaft Damper with Detail of Oil Seal*

# Jaguar Engines

## XJ6 4.2 LITER 6 CYLINDER (Cont.)

gain access to other two screws. Rotate engine further until valve timing gauge (C.3993) can be installed. **CAUTION** — *Engine is not to be rotated once sprockets are removed from camshafts.* Draw sprockets from camshafts and slide sprockets up support brackets. Mark attachment holes in adjuster plate for reassembly reference. Remove camshaft bearing cap retaining nuts and withdraw camshaft. Keep all components in proper order for reassembly.

### TIMING CHAIN REPLACEMENT

**Removal — 1)** Remove cylinder head, oil pan, water pump, crankcase breather, vibration damper (including cone and Woodruff key), and timing gear cover. Withdraw timing pointer, distance piece, and front oil seal.

**2)** Remove oil slinger from crankshaft. Unscrew two bottom timing chain tensioner and chain guides retaining screws. Withdraw conical filter behind tensioner. Slacken four setscrews securing top timing chain assembly (do not remove setscrews at this point).

**3)** Withdraw crankshaft timing sprocket and chain assembly. Be sure to remove spacers, top timing chain damper, and top timing chain retainer. Disengage camshaft sprockets from top chain. Remove nut and serrated washer from idler shaft and withdraw serrated plate, plunger, and spring.

**4)** Remove nuts retaining front mounting bracket to rear mounting bracket. Remove timing chains from intermediate and idler sprockets. Draw idler shaft, idler sprocket, and bushing from rear mounting bracket. Remove circlip and press intermediate shaft from rear mounting bracket. Note location of bushing and shim under intermediate sprocket.

**Installation — 1)** Position eccentric idler shaft to hole in front mounting bracket. Position spring and plunger in bracket and locate serrated plate on shaft. Loosely secure plate using washer and nut.

**2)** Attach idler sprocket (21 teeth) to idler shaft. Replace intermediate sprocket (large gear forward) onto intermediate shaft, placing shim in position. Install shaft assembly in rear mounting bracket, ensuring roll pin engages in slot; retain with circlip.

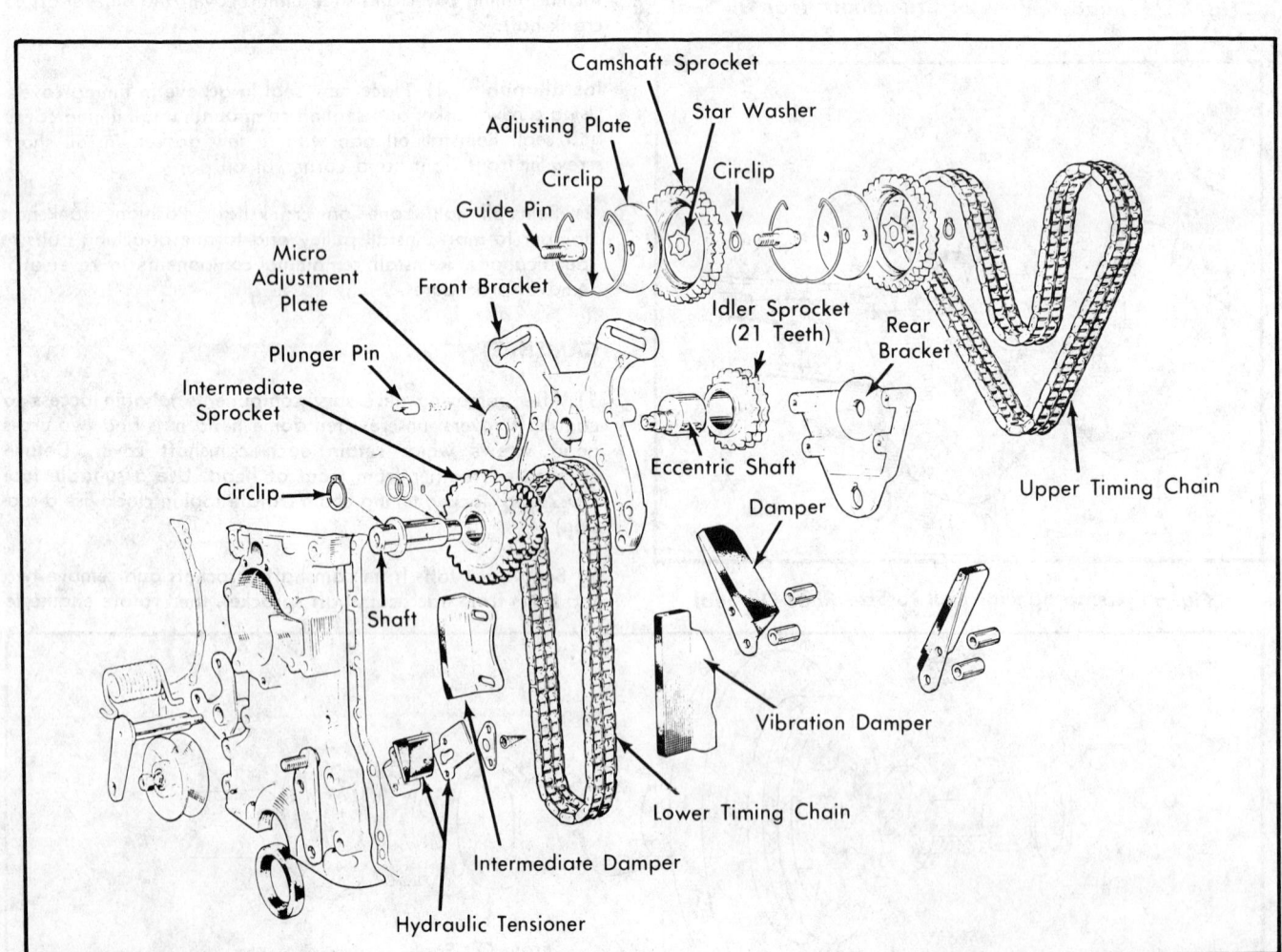

*Fig. 11  Exploded View of Timing Gear Assembly*

## XJ6 4.2 LITER 6 CYLINDER (Cont.)

3) Locate top timing chain (longer) on small intermediate sprocket, and lower timing chain on large sprocket. Loop top chain beneath idler sprocket and secure top mounting bracket to rear bracket.

4) Install four long setscrews and spring washers to front mounting bracket and attach dampers, chain support plate, and spacers to setscrews. Equalize loops of top timing chain and locate camshaft sprockets in loops. Rotate eccentric idler shaft to lift idler sprocket to its highest position between camshaft sprockets.

5) Ensure Woodruff key is positioned in crankshaft. Locate crankshaft sprocket, but do not fully seat at this time. Loop bottom timing chain beneath crankshaft sprocket, then tap sprocket until it is fully seated. Position and secure crankshaft sprocket assembly.

6) Install, but do not tighten, bottom timing chain guides. Insert conical filter into its hole in cylinder block. Screw slipper into tensioner until .125" (3.17 mm) exists between slipper and body. Locate tensioner on shims as necessary to ensure slipper runs central on chain, and secure using two setscrews and lock plate.

7) Place slip gauge or spacer card supplied with new tensioner between slipper and body of tensioner to maintain dimension set earlier, then adjust intermediate damper to touch chain. Tighten setscrews and bend up tabs of lock plate. Remove slip gauge and top chain or tensioner slipper to release ratchet. Position oil slinger on crankshaft. Replace timing cover.

**Fig. 13   Making Upper Timing Chain Adjustment**

### VALVE TIMING

1) Rotate engine so that No. 6 (front) piston is at TDC on compression stroke, and distributor rotor arm points at No. 6 segment. Check that timing chains are properly adjusted. *See Timing Chain Replacement.*

**Fig. 14   View Showing Camshaft Sprockets in Disconnected Position**

2) Remove lock wire from camshaft sprocket screws. Rotate engine until inaccessible screws can be removed. Return engine to TDC of No. 6 piston and remove remaining screws. Tap camshaft sprockets off camshaft flanges.

3) Accurately position camshafts with valve timing gauge (Fig. 14), and check that TDC marks are in exact alignment. Withdraw circlips from camshaft sprocket assembly and press adjusting plates forward until serrations disengage (Fig. 14).

Intermediate Damper Chain Guide

.125" (3.17 mm)

Vibration Damper Chain Guide

**Fig. 12   Lower Timing Chain Adjustment Measurement Point**

## XJ6 4.2 LITER 6 CYLINDER (Cont.)

**Fig. 15 Expanded View of Camshaft Sprocket Assembly**

4) Replace sprockets on flanges of camshaft and align two holes in adjuster plate with holes in flanges. Engage serrations of adjuster plates with serrations in sprocket.

**NOTE** — *Screw holes must be in exact alignment. If difficulty is experienced in aligning holes turn adjuster plates 180° and realign holes.*

## ENGINE OILING

### ENGINE OILING SYSTEM

Lubrication is provided by a gear driven eccentric rotor type pump. Oil from pump goes through a full-flow oil filter to all moving engine components.

**Crankcase Capacity** — 8.75 quarts.

**Oil Filter** — Replace every 3,000 miles.

**Normal Oil Pressure (Hot)** — 40 psi @ 3,000 RPM.

### OIL PUMP

**Removal** — Remove oil pan, suction and delivery pipes. Remove bolts attaching oil pump to front main bearing cap. Withdraw pump and coupling sleeve at top of drive shaft.

**Disassembly — 1)** Remove bolts and take off bottom cover. Remove inner and outer rotors. Inner rotor is pinned to drive shaft and cannot be disassembled.

**2)** Check clearances of inner and outer rotor lobes, outer rotor-to-body and rotor-to-cover plate. Place drive shaft in a soft jawed vise and check that rotor is tight on pin.

**NOTE** — *Drive shaft, inner and outer rotors are supplied as an assembly only.*

**Assembly** — Reassemble in reverse order of disassembly. Install outer rotor to pump body with chamfered end forward. Use new "O" rings on suction and delivery pipes. To install, reverse removal procedures.

### Oil Pump Specifications

| Application | Clearance In. (mm) |
|---|---|
| Inner-to-Outer Rotor | .006 (.15) |
| Outer Rotor-to-Body | .010 (.25) |
| Rotor-to-Cover (End Play) | .0025 (.06) |

**Fig. 16 Valve Timing Guide Inserted in Place**

5) Replace circlips in camshaft sprockets. Replace camshaft sprocket screws and lock wire. Recheck valve timing.

**Fig. 17 Exploded View of Jaguar Oil Pump**

## XJ6 4.2 LITER 6 CYLINDER (Cont.)

### ENGINE COOLING

**WATER PUMP**

**Disassembly – 1)** Remove water pump and gasket from timing cover. Pull fan hub from shaft with a puller. Loosen lock nut and remove Allen locating screw.

**2)** Using an arbor press and a tube measuring 1 3/32" O.D. and 31/32" I.D., press shaft and impeller assembly out of pump body. Do not press on shaft or bearing will be damaged.

**3)** Press shaft from impeller and remove seal and rubber thrower. Spindle and bearing assembly cannot be further disassembled.

**4)** Clean and inspect all parts for wear or damage. Bearing is sealed and lubricated, therefore do not wash in solvents.

**Assembly – 1)** Install shaft and bearing assembly into pump body from rear. Align and install locating screw and lock nut. Place rubber thrower in its groove on shaft in front of seal.

**2)** Coat outside of brass seal housing with suitable water resistant sealer and install into recess in pump housing. Push seal into its housing with carbon face towards rear of pump.

**3)** Press impeller onto shaft until rear face of impeller is flush with end of shaft. Press fan hub onto shaft until it is flush with end of shaft.

**Cooling System Capacity –** 19.25 qts.

### TIGHTENING SPECIFICATIONS

| Application | Ft. Lbs. (mkg) |
|---|---|
| Cylinder Head Nuts | 54 (7.5) |
| Main Bearing Caps | 72 (10) |
| Connecting Rod Caps | 41 (5.7) |
| Flywheel | 67 (9.2) |
| Camshaft Cap | 9 (1.2) |
| Torque Converter | 35 (4.8) |
| Camshaft Cover | 5-6 (.7-.8) |
| Rear Engine Mount-to-Body | |
| 5/16" Bolt | 14-18 (1.9-2.5) |
| 3/8" Bolt | 27-32 (3.7-4.4) |
| Front Engine Bracket-to-Beam | 14-18 (1.9-2.5) |

### ENGINE SPECIFICATIONS

#### GENERAL SPECIFICATIONS

| Year | Displ. | | Carburetor | HP at RPM | Torque (Ft. Lbs. at RPM) | Compr. Ratio | Bore | | Stroke | |
|---|---|---|---|---|---|---|---|---|---|---|
| | cu. ins. | cc | | | | | in. | mm | in. | mm |
| 1978 | 258.4 | 4235 | Fuel Inj. | 195 @ 4750 | ..... | 7.8:1 | 3.625 | 92.07 | 4.173 | 106 |

#### VALVES

| Engine & Valve | Head Diam. In. (mm) | Face Angle | Seat Angle | Seat Width In. (mm) | Stem Diameter In. (mm) | Stem Clearance In. (mm) | Valve Lift In. (mm) |
|---|---|---|---|---|---|---|---|
| 4235 cc Intake | 1.75 (44.45) | 45° | 45° | ..... | .310-.3125 (7.87-7.94) | .001-.004 (.025-.10) | .375 (9.525) |
| Exhaust | 1.625 (41.28) | 45° | 45° | ..... | .310-.3125 (7.87-7.94) | .001-.004 (.025-.10) | .375 (9.525) |

#### CAMSHAFT

| Engine | Journal Diam. In. (mm) | Clearance In. (mm) | Lobe Lift In. (mm) |
|---|---|---|---|
| 4235 cc | .9990-.9995 (25.375-25.387) | .0005-.002 (.013-.05) | ..... |

#### VALVE TIMING

| Engine | INTAKE | | EXHAUST | |
|---|---|---|---|---|
| | Open (BTDC) | Close (ABDC) | Open (BBDC) | Close (ATDC) |
| 4235cc | 15° | 57° | 57° | 15° |

# Jaguar Engines

## XJ6 4.2 LITER 6 CYLINDER (Cont.)

### ENGINE SPECIFICATIONS (Cont.)

| PISTONS, PINS, RINGS | | | | | | |
|---|---|---|---|---|---|---|
| | PISTONS | PINS | | RINGS | | |
| Engine | Clearance In. (mm) | Piston Fit In. (mm) | Rod Fit In. (mm) | Rings | End Gap In. (mm) | Side Clearance In. (mm) |
| 4235 cc | .0007-.0013 (.018-.033) | ① Press Fit | ② Push Fit | No. 1 | .015-.020 (.38-.51) | .0015-.0035 (.038-.089) |
| | | | | No. 2 | .009-.014 (.23-.35) | .0015-.0035 (.038-.089) |
| | | | | Oil | .015-.045 (.38-1.14) | ③ |

① — When heated to 230°F (110°C).　② — At room temperature, without piston.　③ — Self-expanding.

| CRANKSHAFT MAIN & CONNECTING ROD BEARINGS | | | | | | | |
|---|---|---|---|---|---|---|---|
| | MAIN BEARINGS | | | | CONNECTING ROD BEARINGS | | |
| Engine | Journal Diam. In. (mm) | Clearance In. (mm) | Thrust Bearing | Crankshaft End Play In. (mm) | Journal Diam. In. (mm) | Clearance In. (mm) | Side Play In. (mm) |
| 4235 cc | 2.749-2.750 (69.85-69.86) | .0008-.0025 (.020-.063) | Center | .004-.006 (.10-.15) | 2.086-2.0866 (52.98-53.00) | .001-.0027 (.025-.069) | .0058-.0087 (.147-.221) |

| VALVE SPRINGS | | | |
|---|---|---|---|
| | Free Length In. (mm) | PRESSURE Lbs. @ In. (kg @ mm) | |
| Engine | | Valve Closed | Valve Open |
| 4235 cc Inner | 1.734 (44.04) | ..... | ..... |
| Outer | 2.103 (53.42) | ..... | ..... |

## XJ S & XJ12 SERIES 2 V12

### ENGINE CODING

#### ENGINE IDENTIFICATION

Engine number is stamped on cylinder block at rear of engine, between cylinder heads.

### ENGINE, CYLINDER HEAD & MANIFOLDS

#### ENGINE

**NOTE** — *It is necessary to remove entire power unit (engine and transmission assembly) as an assembly. Engine and transmission may then be separated.*

1) Remove hood, lower grill and battery. Depressurize fuel system. Drain engine and cooling system.

**NOTE** — *Only qualified air conditioning personnel should loosen or remove air conditioning hoses or fittings to prevent personal injury. All hoses or fittings which are removed should be immediately sealed with clean dry plugs.*

2) On air conditioned models, discharge air conditioning system. Disconnect suction and pressure hoses. Remove pressure and suction unions from rear of compressor and plug openings. Tie hoses back away from engine.

3) Remove fender well straps and air cleaners. Disconnect oil pump-to-cooler lines and remove radiator complete with oil cooler.

4) On air conditioned models, remove compressor delivery hose from vehicle. Tie condenser/evaporator hose back away from engine.

5) Disconnect coolant hoses to remote header tank at engine. Remove nut and lock washer attaching engine mount to engine bracket. Remove oil from power steering reservoir. Disconnect lines from power steering pump.

6) Disconnect connectors from alternator and separate engine harness connector. Remove hose between servo unit and vacuum reservoir. Disconnect clips securing fuel pipes to filter, plug pipes.

7) Disconnect operating line from heater vacuum reservoir non-return valve at manifold stub and heater water valve at valve inlet. Disconnect heater return line from water rail at firewall union. Remove coil and ballast resistor assembly.

8) Disconnect clips securing cold start relay harness from left hand fuel rail and cross over pipe. Remove remaining clips on harness. Remove cover of cold start relay, disconnect cables. Remove harness from engine.

9) Disconnect cable from throttle switch and trigger unit. Remove connectors from kickdown switch. Remove starter cable from firewall terminal.

10) Install suitable engine support tool (MS.53A) into drip channel directly above rear lifting eyes and tighten supporting screws. Disconnect both exhaust pipes at manifolds. Remove front exhaust pipe which is not trapped by steering pinion housing. Lower trapped front pipe and move rear end of pipe toward center line of vehicle. Slide pipe towards front of vehicle and draw flanges down past steering housing.

11) Remove attaching hardware from heat shields. Remove four screws, washers and spacers from engine mounting plate. Place a jack and suitably formed block of wood beneath mounting plate and remove nut attaching rear engine mount.

12) Lower jack and remove mounting plate. Disconnect propeller shaft and speedometer cable. Remove pinch bolt attaching transmission outer selector cable and disconnect inner cable from selector lever at transmission by removing nut and lock washer.

13) Remove ground strap from frame member. Place a jack beneath front suspension crossmember and remove engine support tool. Attach suitable lifting sling to engine eyes.

**NOTE** — *Chains of engine hoist must be of sufficient length to ensure that distance between lifting eyes and hook of hoist is 34.5" (876 mm) from front eyes to hook and 41" (1041 mm) from rear eyes to hook.*

14) Carefully lift engine with hoist, simultaneously raising jack to keep engine level. Lift only 2-3" (51-76 mm).

**CAUTION** — *Throughout lift, rear of engine must be kept as high as possible until oil pan is clear of steering housing.*

15) Lift engine level, while observing forward corner of oil pan and steering housing. Apply side pressure to engine until it has been lifted clear of steering assembly and lines. Pull engine from subframe, allowing angle of tilt to increase until drive flange is clear of firewall. Lift engine to clear bumper.

#### INTAKE MANIFOLDS (LEFT & RIGHT)

1) Remove air cleaner and drain cooling system. Depressurize fuel system (remove connector from fuel pump relay switch, crank engine for a few seconds). Remove fuel pipe from overrun valves. Remove hose clip securing pressure regulator return hose from fuel rail.

2) Disconnect manifold pressure hose and electrical connectors from kickdown switch. Disconnect throttle cable from pedestal. Release throttle cross-rod from bell-crank. Disconnect electrical connectors from injectors and cold start injector. Disconnect brake vacuum hose.

3) Remove nuts securing manifold to cylinder head. Remove screws securing air rail clips to manifold ram tubes. Remove EGR valve from throttle housing flange. Remove manifold stud spacers. Remove intake manifold, carefully moving air balance pipe and fuel pipes out of the way. Plug intake ports.

#### CYLINDER HEAD

**NOTE** — *The following procedure may be used for removal of either right or left cylinder head.*

**Removal** — 1) Disconnect battery and drain cooling system. Remove right camshaft cover (required when either right or left cylinder head is removed). Remove rubber grommet from front of timing cover.

## XJ S & XJ12 SERIES 2 V12 (Cont.)

**2)** Rotate crankshaft until valve timing gauge (C.3993) can be fitted in slot in camshaft front flange. Insert blade of release tool through timing cover grommet hole and release locking catch on timing chain tensioner. Using suitable tool (JD.50), retract timing chain tensioner.

**Fig. 1    Valve Timing Gauge in Position for Timing Chain Removal or Installation**

**3)** If left cylinder head is to be removed, remove left camshaft cover. Disconnect camshaft sprocket from camshaft and attach a suitable retaining tool (Special Tool JD.40).

**4)** Remove heat shield from exhaust manifold and solenoid heat shield (right-hand head). Loosen screw clamp attaching heater return pipe-to-hose and ease cross pipe forward. Remove clamps attaching manifold coolant bleed pipe to front of cylinder head.

**5)** Remove camshaft oil feed banjo nut. Remove three nuts holding front of cylinder head to timing cover. Progressively loosen cylinder head nuts working from center outward. Remove cylinder head and place on wood blocks to prevent damage to valves. Discard old gasket.

**NOTE** — *Do not rotate engine until suitable cylinder liner retaining tools (Special Tool JD.41) have been attached to cylinder head studs.*

**Fig. 2    Retracting Timing Chain Tensioner**

**Installation — 1)** Attach dial indicator to a cylinder head stud and rotate crankshaft to set No. 1 piston on right bank at TDC. Turn camshaft until valve timing gauge (C.3993) can be attached to slot in camshaft front flange. Repeat for camshaft on left cylinder head. Remove cylinder liner retaining tool.

**NOTE** — *Do not rotate crankshaft until cylinder head(s) are installed.*

**2)** Install gasket making sure side marked "TOP" is up. Do not use jointing compound or grease. Install right cylinder head and nuts. Tighten nuts to specifications in order shown in illustration.

**3)** Tighten cylinder head-to-timing cover nuts to specifications. If camshaft and sprocket holes are not in alignment, remove circlip which holds camshaft coupling to sprocket and disengage coupling from splines.

**4)** Rotate coupling until access to retaining bolt holes can be obtained. Remove sprocket retaining tool (JD.40) and bolt coupling to camshaft.

**5)** Engage sprocket with coupling, then replace circlip and remove valve timing gauge (C.3993). Repeat procedures as outlined in steps **2)** through **6)** for left cylinder head.

**6)** Rotate engine until remaining camshaft sprocket retaining bolts can be installed; secure bolts with tab washers. Remove timing chain tensioner retracting tool (Special Tool JD.42 and Support Plate JD.42-1).

**7)** Insert blade of release tool through hole in timing cover and trip locking catch. Reinstall rubber grommet. Install exhaust pipes and camshaft covers. Refill cooling system and connect battery.

**Fig. 3    Cylinder Head Tightening Sequence**

## VALVES

### VALVE ARRANGMENT

**Right Side** — E-I-I-E-E-I-I-E-E-I-I-E (front to rear).
**Left Side** — E-I-I-E-E-I-I-E-E-I-I-E (front to rear).

### VALVE GUIDE SERVICING

**1)** With valves and valve springs removed, check clearance between valve guide and stem. Clearance should be to specification.

## XJ S & XJ12 SERIES 2 V12 (Cont.)

**2)** To replace guides, immerse head in boiling water for 30 minutes. Using piloted drift, drive guide out of head from combustion chamber side. Coat new guide with graphite grease and attach circlip.

**3)** Heat cylinder head once again and drive guide in from top until circlip is seated in groove.

### Replacement Guides

| Application | Marking | Size In. (mm) |
|---|---|---|
| 1st Oversize | 2 Grooves | .506-.507 (12.85-12.88) |
| 2nd Oversize | 3 Grooves | .511-.512 (12.98-13.00) |

**4)** When new guides are installed, always use next size larger than old guide. Ream guides to obtain proper valve stem clearance.

*Fig. 4   View Showing Correct Valve Guide Installation*

### VALVE STEM OIL SEALS

Install valves and place cylinder head on wooden blocks. Install valve spring seats, intake valve oil seals, springs and collars. Compress springs using suitable tool (Special Tool J.6118B and Adaptor J.6118C-2) and install keepers.

**NOTE** — *Oil seals used on intake valves only.*

### VALVE TAPPET CLEARANCE ADJUSTMENT

**1)** With intake manifolds and camshaft covers removed, check clearance between each tappet and heel of each cam. Record clearance for each and then subtract appropriate valve clearance from clearances obtained. Select suitable adjusting pads which equal this new measurement. Corrected clearance should be .012-.014" (.305-.356 mm) with engine cold.

**2)** To install new adjusting pads, proceed as follows to remove camshaft and tappets: Bend back locking tabs and remove two camshaft sprocket retaining bolts. Rotate engine until access to remaining bolts is obtained. Bend back locking tabs, mark position of camshaft to sprocket, and remove bolts.

**3)** Using suitable tool (Jaguar Sprocket Retaining Tool JD.40), hold sprocket in place. Lift camshaft out of tappet block. Remove tappets and install adjusting pads.

**NOTE** — *Do not rotate engine with camshaft disconnected.*

**4)** Reinstall tappets, camshaft, bearing caps, washers and nuts. Tighten bearing cap nuts evenly and torque to 9 ft. lbs. Recheck clearance, reassemble, replace camshaft cover and manifolds.

**NOTE** — *Adjusting pads are available in .001" (.03 mm) increment sizes from .085-.110" (2.16-2.79 mm). Pads have a letter stamped on surface which indicates size: "A" through "Z" respectively.*

*Fig. 5   Correct Valve Tappet Clearance Adjustment Procedure*

## PISTONS, PINS & RINGS

### OIL PAN REMOVAL

**NOTE** — *Complete oil pan removal is best accomplished with engine out of vehicle. Lower oil sump pan removal and replacement procedures follow.*

To remove oil sump pan, drain engine oil and remove pan retaining screws. Remove sump pan and clean gasket surfaces. Coat new gasket lightly with suitable sealant and replace pan. Due to the different lengths of pan retaining screws, it is essential that they be replaced in their proper location.

# Jaguar Engines

## XJ S & XJ12 SERIES 2 V12 (Cont.)

### PISTON & ROD REMOVAL & INSTALLATION

1) With cylinder head and oil pan removed, remove crankcase baffle plate. Remove nuts, bearing cap and bearing. Push connecting rod up cylinder bore, remove piston together with connecting rod.

**NOTE** — *Cylinder liner retaining tools (JD.41) must be installed prior to disassembly or any movement of engine parts due to wet liner type cylinder sleeve.*

2) Coat all parts with engine oil and make sure that piston ring gaps are evenly spaced around circumference of piston. Place piston into bore with word "FRONT" facing forward and chamber on rod big-end facing crank pin radius. Push piston and rod assembly down into bore, locate bearings, install bearing caps and nuts and tighten to specifications.

### PISTON PIN REPLACEMENT

**NOTE** — *Pistons are supplied complete with pin. As pins and pistons are matched assemblies, it is not permissible to interchange component parts.*

Remove circlip, push pin out of piston. When installing pin, piston should be fitted so the word FRONT faces towards front of engine.

### FITTING PISTONS

No oversize pistons are available due to use of wet liner type cylinder sleeves. If liner or piston is damaged or worn, replacement must be of standard size.

**NOTE** — *Bearings are available in only standard size. Due to extremely hard surface of crankshaft journals, it is not possible to grind crankshafts satisfactory. Crankshafts are available on exchange basis and are supplied complete with matching bearings.*

### CRANKSHAFT MAIN & CONNECTING ROD BEARINGS

#### MAIN BEARING SERVICE

**NOTE** — *While it is possible to replace main bearing shells with engine in vehicle, this should only be accomplished when it is certain that crankshaft is not damaged.*

1) With engine out of vehicle and piston and rod assemblies removed, remove drive plate from crankshaft. Timing cover must be removed and timing chain disengaged from sprocket. Remove oil pump assembly.

2) Remove small nuts from main bearing caps, starting from center bearing. Remove pillar nuts and large nuts from caps in same sequence. Remove bearing caps and shells. Lift crankshaft from block and remove upper half of main bearing shells.

3) Ensure that all components are scrupulously clean and replace all seals. Oil bearing shells liberally and place upper halves in block. Replace crankshaft and lower bearing caps with shells. Beginning at center, tighten bearing caps one at a time to specified torque.

#### CYLINDER LINER REPLACEMENT

**NOTE** — *If liners are to be replaced after removal, they should be marked and reinstalled in their original bore.*

1) With crankshaft and pistons removed, remove cylinder liner retaining tools (Special Tools JD.41). Position a suitable mandrel between cylinder liner and arbor press.

2) Press out cylinder liners from below. To install, smear liners with Hylomar and slip liners into cylinder block. Remove excessive sealant. Make sure liners are correctly seated and install retaining tools.

**NOTE** — *If cylinder liners are replaced. New liners must be of the same grade as the old liners.*

*Fig. 6   Exploded View of Piston Assembly*

*Fig. 7   Exploded View of Main Bearing & Rear Oil Seal Assemblies*

## XJ S & XJ12 SERIES 2 V12 (Cont.)

### Cylinder Liners

| Bore Grade | In. (mm) |
|---|---|
| A-Red | 3.543 (89.98) |
| B-Green | 3.544 (90.01) |

### REAR MAIN BEARING OIL SEAL SERVICE

1) With crankshaft out of cylinder block and rear main bearing casting removed, install new sealing strips in grooves of rear main bearing casting. Install new rear oil seal. Install bearing casting on cylinder block and tighten nuts. Seat rear oil seal using suitable tool (Special Tool JD.17B & Adaptor JD.17B-1). Remove rear main bearing casting.

2) Coat upper main bearings with oil and install in cylinder block. Smear rear oil seal with Dag Colloidal Graphite. Oil upper main bearings and install in cylinder block, position crankshaft, install bearings in caps and install caps. Tighten to specifications.

### THRUST WASHER ALIGNMENT

Measure crankshaft end play. Remove bearing caps and install thrust washer(s) in groove in block; select washers as necessary to bring end play within specifications. Grooved side of washer must face outward.

### ENGINE FRONT COVER & OIL SEAL

1) Drain cooling system and remove front sub-frame crossmember complete with expansion tank. Remove both cylinder heads and oil pan. Remove alternator and power steering pump. Remove air injection pump and water pump.

2) Remove bolts holding pulley to damper and remove pulley. Remove crankshaft damper bolt and strike damper sharply with leather mallet. Remove damper and cone.

3) Pry seal out of timing cover and discard. Remove spacer. Smear new oil seal with engine oil and install oil seal in recess. Tap into place using leather mallet. Reinstall spacer and reverse removal procedure.

4) If entire front cover is to be removed, remove alternator and air pump mounting brackets and remove bolt and serrated washers which hold timing cover to cylinder block. Note positions of bolts and dowel bolts. Remove timing cover.

**NOTE** — *If entire front cover is removed, oil seal may be replaced with front cover removed from engine.*

## CAMSHAFT

### CAMSHAFT REMOVAL

1) With camshaft covers removed, bend back locking tabs and remove two camshaft sprocket retaining bolts. Rotate engine until valve timing gauge can be installed in slot in camshaft. Bend back locking tabs and mark relative position of camshaft to sprocket.

2) Remove bolts. Attach sprocket retaining tool (Special Tool JD.40). Do not rotate engine with camshaft disconnected. Progressively loosen camshaft bearing caps nuts starting with center cap and working towards ends. Remove bearing caps, lift camshaft out of tappet block.

### TIMING CHAIN REMOVAL

With timing cover removed, install suitable tool to retain intermediate shaft (jackshaft). Retaining tool (Special Tool JD.39) available for this purpose. Disconnect timing chain from camshaft and intermediate shaft (jackshaft) sprockets. Remove crankshaft sprocket and chain.

**NOTE** — *Do not rotate engine with chain removed.*

Fig. 9  *View of Timing Chain Installation*

**Fig. 8**  *Detail of Front Cover Oil Seal*

## ENGINE OILING

**Crankcase Capacity** — 12 quarts (includes filter).

**Oil Filter** — Full-flow, replaceable element.

## XJS & XJ12 SERIES 2 V12 (Cont.)

### OIL PUMP

Pump is of "Epicyclic" type with internal and external gears and crescent type cut off. Drive gear is concentric around crankshaft nose.

**Removal** — Remove timing cover and timing chain tensioner. Remove spacer from crankshaft and remove timing chain and sprocket from crankshaft. Remove Woodruff key. To install, reverse removal procedure.

**Fig. 10  Correct Procedure to Measure Oil Pump Clearances**

**Overhaul** — **1)** Remove eight bolts and lockwashers and remove pump cover from gear housing. Mark drive and driven gear faces to make sure gears are replaced in same position as removed.

**2)** Remove both gears, and clean thoroughly. Check condition of all gears. Remove burrs with file. Reinstall driven gear and check radial clearance between gear and housing. Checks should not be taken at any of the six radial flats on the gear.

**3)** Reinstall drive gear and check radial clearance between gear and crescent. Check gear end play by placing straight edge across joint face of housing and measure clearance between straight edge and gear.

**4)** To reassemble, lubricate all gears with clean oil, check that surfaces are clean, and reverse disassembly procedure.

### Oil Pump Specifications

| Application | Clearance ①In. (mm) |
|---|---|
| Driven Gear-to-Housing | .005 (.127) |
| Drive Gear-to-Crescent | .006 (.152) |
| Gear End Play | .005 (.127) |

① — Specifications given are maximum allowable.

## ENGINE COOLING

### WATER PUMP REMOVAL

**NOTE** — Water pump is sealed unit and no overhaul is possible. Exchange pumps do not come with pulley, therefore pulley must be removed before sending in defective pump. Pulley must then be installed on pump before placing on engine.

**1)** Drain and remove radiator. Remove lower cowl and mounting bracket and lay aside. Remove fan and fan drive unit. Remove fan belt.

**2)** Remove trunnion adjusting bolt and hardware attaching idler pulley housing. Unscrew two studs. Remove air pump and compressor pump belts.

**3)** Loosen steering pump pivot bolts enough to draw adjustment bolt from special stud. Remove special stud. Remove thermostat switch housing and bottom hose complete as an assembly. Remove crankshaft pulley and damper assembly.

**NOTE** — Tap damper with a rawhide mallet to break taper. Do not mislay Woodruff key.

**4)** Loosen upper hose clamp on engine cross pipe. Remove screw and washers attaching water pump. Pull pump out and downwards to clear cross pipe hose. To install, reverse removal procedure.

**Thermostats** — Two thermostats are used. Opening temperature is 174-181F (79-83C).

**Cooling System Capacity** — 22 quarts.
**Radiator Cap** — 13 psi.

## ENGINE SPECIFICATIONS

### GENERAL SPECIFICATIONS

| Year | Displ. | | Carburetor | HP at RPM | Torque (Ft. Lbs. at RPM) | Compr. Ratio | Bore | | Stroke | |
|---|---|---|---|---|---|---|---|---|---|---|
| | cu. ins. | cc | | | | | in. | mm | in. | mm |
| 1978 | 326 | 5343 | Fuel Inj. | 244 @ 5250 | 269 @ 4500 | 7.8:1 | 3.543 | 90 | 2.756 | 70 |

## XJS & XJ12 SERIES 2 V12 (Cont.)
### ENGINE SPECIFICATIONS (Cont.)

| Engine & Valve | Head Diam. In. (mm) | Face Angle | Seat Angle | Seat Width In. (mm) | Stem Diameter In. (mm) | Stem Clearance In. (mm) | Valve Lift In. (mm) |
|---|---|---|---|---|---|---|---|
| **VALVES** | | | | | | | |
| V12 | | | | | | | |
| Intake | ① 1.623-1.627 (41.22-41.32) | 45° | 44.5° | .... | .3092-.3093 (7.854-7.856) | .001-.004 (.03-.10) | .375 (9.5) |
| Exhaust | ① 1.358-1.362 (34.50-34.60) | 45° | 44.5° | .... | .3092-.3093 (7.854-7.856) | .001-.004 (.03-.10) | .375 (9.5) |

① — XJ-S models; Intake 1.620-1.630" (41.15-41-40 mm), Exhaust 1.355-1.365" (34.42-34.67 mm).

| Engine | Free Length In. (mm) | PRESSURE Lbs. @ In. (kg @ mm) | |
|---|---|---|---|
| **VALVE SPRINGS** | | | |
| | | Valve Closed | Valve Open |
| V12 | | | |
| Inner | 1.734 (44) | .... | .... |
| Outer | 2.103 (53.4) | .... | .... |

| Engine | PISTONS Clearance In. (mm) | PINS Piston Fit In. (mm) | PINS Rod Fit In. (mm) | Rings | RINGS End Gap In. (mm) | RINGS Side Clearance In. (mm) |
|---|---|---|---|---|---|---|
| **PISTONS, PINS, RINGS** | | | | | | |
| V12 | .0012-.0017 (.03-.04) | Push Fit | .0000-.0002 (.000-.005) | 1 | .014-.020 (.36-.51) | .0029 (.07) |
| | | | | 2 | .010-.015 (.25-.38) | .0034 (.09) |
| | | | | Oil | .015-.045 (.38-1.14) | ① .0055-.0065 (.14-.17) |

① — XJ-S models have a self expanding oil ring.

| Engine | MAIN BEARINGS Journal Diam. In. (mm) | Clearance In. (mm) | Thrust Bearing | Crankshaft End Play In. (mm) | CONNECTING ROD BEARINGS Journal Diam. In. (mm) | Clearance In. (mm) | Side Play In. (mm) |
|---|---|---|---|---|---|---|---|
| **CRANKSHAFT MAIN & CONNECTING ROD BEARINGS** | | | | | | | |
| V12 | 3.0007-3.0012 (76.218-76.231) | .0015-.003 (.04-.07) | Center | .004-.006 (.10-.15) | 2.2994-2.3000 (58.40-58.42) | .0015-.003 (.04-.07) | .007-.013 (.17-.33) |

# Jaguar Engines

## XJS & XJ 12 SERIES 2 V12 (Cont.)

### ENGINE SPECIFICATIONS (Cont.)

| CAMSHAFT | | | |
|---|---|---|---|
| Engine | Journal Diam. In. (mm) | Clearance In. (mm) | Lobe Lift In. (mm) |
| V12 | 1.0615-1.0620 (26.96-26.97) | .001-.003 (.03-.07) | .... |

| VALVE TIMING | | | | |
|---|---|---|---|---|
| | INTAKE | | EXHAUST | |
| Engine | Open (BTDC) | Close (ABDC) | Open (BBDC) | Close (ATDC) |
| V12 | 17° | 59° | 59° | 17° |

### TIGHTENING SPECIFICATIONS

| Application | Ft. Lbs. (mkg) |
|---|---|
| Cylinder Head | |
| 7/16" Nuts | 52 (7.2) |
| 3/8" Nuts | 27-28 (3.7-3.9) |
| Main Bearing Cap | |
| 1/2" Nuts | 63 (8.7) |
| 3/8" Nuts | 27-28 (3.7-3.9) |
| Connecting Rod Caps | 40-41 (5.5-5.7) |
| Flywheel | 67 (9.3) |
| Crankshaft Bolt | 125-150 (17.3-20.7) |
| Camshaft Cap Nuts | 9 (1.2) |
| Camshaft Cover Screws | 8 (1.1) |
| Union Block-to-Compressor | 10-25 (1.4-3.5) |

## 1800 cc 4 CYLINDER

### ENGINE CODING

#### ENGINE IDENTIFICATION

Engine number is stamped on cylinder block. Further identification data is found below windshield inside engine compartment, on upper left hand side of instrument panel by windshield, and inside door closing areas.

#### Engine Identification Numbers①

| Body Style | Chassis No. | Engine No. |
|---|---|---|
| Beta Sedan | 828 CB.6 | 828 A1.040.6 |
| Beta HPE | 828 AF.1 | 828 A1.040.6 |
| Beta Coupe | 828 AC.1 | 828 A1.040.6 |

① — Engines equipped with catalytic converters are numbered 828 A1.031.6.

### ENGINE & CYLINDER HEAD

#### ENGINE

**1)** Remove the alternator and slacken front wheel retaining bolts. Raise vehicle and drain coolant from engine and radiator. Take off front wheels and splash guards. Remove all flexible hoses from carburetor and electrical lead from slow-running cut-out switch.

**2)** Remove low pressure hose for servo-brake, fast idling and diverter valve from induction manifold. Disconnect leads from the distributor and diverter valve thermo-switches.

**3)** On vehicles with air conditioning, slacken mounting bolts and drop compressor downward. Remove drive belt. Disconnect electric cables from the isobaric valve and compressor ground cable. Remove compressor and position it on its side so oil does not enter conditioner circuit. Remove leads from thermistor and engine oil pressure switch and take off oil filter base.

**4)** Lift out battery. Remove line from recovery tank, and remove tank. Slide line from diverter valve and disconnect drive belt from air pump. Remove air pump complete with support and line. Detach pipe from air pipe leading to exhaust ducts on the cylinder head. Remove distributor assembly.

**5)** Unscrew the constant velocity joints from their flanges by the wheel well. Take off support brackets and disconnect the exhaust pipe from the manifold. Remove flywheel guard and bolts holding transmission and engine mounts. Remove the gear front control shaft from the idler lever and selector rod.

**6)** Detach heater hoses from cylinder head and water pump inlet hose. Remove hoses from radiator. Remove speedometer drive shaft from transmission and cables from 1st and 2nd gear switch, 3rd and 4th gear switch and 5th gear commutator switch. Mark electrical connections for later installation.

**7)** Disconnect ground wire from transmission and leads from starter motor. Remove clutch release lever return spring. Release the control cable from the clutch release lever and slip the cable sheath from stop bracket.

**8)** Remove circlip and detach the release lever from the shaft. Remove clutch stop bracket. Remove engine-to-body anchoring rod. Disconnect fan leads and remove the fan from the radiator. Mount brackets (88017363) on cylinder block stud bolts for use in hoisting engine and transmission from vehicle.

**9)** Mount a hoist above vehicle and attach hook (88017362). Raise engine and transmission and remove from vehicle. Set on support stand (88017364) and attach support (88027068A) to transmission. Remove starter motor and transmission from engine. Lock the crankshaft with locking tool (88013347), and remove the clutch assembly.

**10)** To install engine, reverse removal procedure. Be sure to tighten constant velocity flange bolts to proper torque. Start engine and check for leaks.

#### CYLINDER HEAD

**1)** Disconnect positive battery cable. Drain coolant from radiator and engine. Remove exhaust pipe from manifold. Remove right-hand brace from engine compartment opening and take off air cleaner. Disconnect choke control cable and fuel supply and leak-off hoses from carburetor.

*Fig. 1 Align Camshaft Timing Marks with Bearing Reference Marks When Installing Timing Belt*

**2)** Disconnect brake servo unit vacuum hose from intake manifold. Disconnect cables from spark plugs, coolant temperature gauge transmitter and engine overheating warning light switch. Disconnect throttle control rod from carburetor and set it aside. Remove splash guard from right hand wheel well. Remove timing gear cover.

**3)** Using a spanner wrench (88011321) on crankshaft nut, turn crankshaft in direction of rotation until the camshaft bearing timing marks (See Fig. 1) line up with holes in camshaft drive gears. Remove the timing reference pointers fitted bracket. Disconnect coolant outlet pipe from both the cylinder head and rubber hoses.

## 1800 cc 4 CYLINDER (Cont.)

**4)** Remove engine-to-body anchoring rod. Lift off engine coolant outlet and inlet pipes. Disconnect heater hose with mounting bracket from cylinder head. Remove alternator upper mounting link.

**5)** Loosen timing belt stretcher and remove timing belt from gears and stretcher. Remove bolts and lift off cylinder head complete with manifolds.

**Fig. 2   Tighten Cylinder Head Bolts in Sequence Shown**

**6)** To install cylinder heads, reverse removal procedure, noting the following: Clean block and head mating surfaces. Install new head gasket to block. Tighten cylinder head bolts to a final torque of 61.5 ft. lbs. (8.5 mkg) in proper sequence and in two stages. See Fig. 2. Refit timing belt and set valve timing. Check valve clearance and install remaining parts in reverse order.

## VALVES

### VALVE ARRANGEMENT

Intake — Left side (Viewed from flywheel end).
Exhaust — Right side (Viewed from flywheel end).

### VALVE SPRINGS

**1)** Remove cylinder head. Remove both intake and exhaust manifolds and carburetor. Use spring compressor (88012041) to load valve springs. Remove split collets and remove upper collars, inner and outer springs, lower cups and washers.

**2)** Test springs for proper strength, using a suitable tester (88095021).

### VALVE GUIDE SERVICING

**1)** Visually check inner diameter of valve guides for scoring or signs of seizure. Use gauges (88015018 and 88015019) to measure valve guide bores.

**2)** If guides need servicing, remove guide seals. Using a remover-installer tool (88012042), remove guides from cylinder head. Check guides to determine class, by measuring external diameter. New valve guides should belong to same class as those removed.

### Available Valve Guide Diameters

| Measurement | Inches (mm) |
|---|---|
| Standard Guide O.D. ................ | .590-.591 (14.998-15.016) |
| 1st Oversize Guide O.D. ............ | .591-.592 (15.018-15.036) |
| 2nd Oversize Guide O.D. ............ | .598-.599 (15.198-15.216) |

**3)** Heat cylinder head (manufacturer recommends in an electric furnace) to 212° F (100° C). Install the new guides using the installer tool (88012042) and spacer (88012042B).

**NOTE** — *Replacement valve guides feature an inner diameter bored to specifications. Reaming may be necessary, however, in isolated cases.*

**4)** After the cylinder head has cooled, check inner diameter and if necessary ream to proper size. With guides fitted in cylinder head, inner diameter should measure .3158-.3165" (8.022-8.040 mm). Use gauge 88015018 to check for inner diameter of .3153-3157" (8.01-8.02 mm) and 88015019 to check for inner diameter of .3161-.3165" (8.03-8.04 mm).

**Fig. 3   Measure Valve Clearance (COLD) Between Heel of Cam and Tappet Shim**

### VALVE CLEARANCE ADJUSTMENT

**1)** The Lancia 1800 cc engine has two camshafts, one operating directly upon the exhaust valves, the other on the intake valves. No rocker arms or shafts are necessary.

**2)** Check valve clearance in order of firing sequence (1-3-4-2). Using a spanner wrench (88011321), turn crankshaft so that cylinder to be checked is in the expansion stroke (cam lobe pointing vertically for that cylinder). See Fig. 3.

**3)** Measure clearance of each valve, using a feeler gauge between the base of the cam lobe and the tappet shim. Make a note of each valve's clearance.

### Valve Clearance Specifications

| Valve | Inches (mm) |
|---|---|
| Intake ................................................ | .0161-.0193 (.41-.49) |
| Exhaust ............................................ | .0181-.0213 (.46-.54) |

## 1800 cc 4 CYLINDER (Cont.)

Fig. 4  Insert Tool to Remove Shims
When Adjusting Valve Clearance

Fig. 5  Apply Air to Slot to Remove Adjusting Shims

4) To adjust valves, turn crankshaft until piston of cylinder to be adjusted is in expansion stroke (cam lobe vertical). Turn tappets so slot (See Fig. 4) is toward side of engine. Turn crankshaft further so that valve to be adjusted is fully open. Attach suitable tool (88013036) between camshaft and tappet and secure against housing.

5) Turn the crankshaft (turning camshafts) until camshaft lobe does not depress the tappet any longer, while the tool keeps the tappet locked in the open valve position. Apply air pressure to tappet slot, and remove the adjusting shim (See Fig. 5) using pliers (88013038).

6) Measure the thickness of the adjusting shim removed. Add the previously measured valve clearance for valve being adjusted. Subtract from this total the recommended valve clearance. Replace the previously removed adjusting shim with one having the thickness of the difference obtained by your subtraction.

**Example:**

| | |
|---|---|
| Measured intake valve clearance | = .015" (0.38mm) |
| Add measured shim thickness | = .142" (3.60mm) |
| | |
| Total of shim thickness and clearance | = .157" (3.98mm) |
| Subtract recommended clearance | = .017" (0.43mm) |
| | |
| Difference is required shim thickness① | = .140" (3.55mm) |

① — Shims for adjusting valve clearance are available in thicknesses ranging from .1280-.1850" (3.25-4.70 mm) in .0020" (.05 mm) increments. Thickness of shim is stamped on its face, and stamped side must be installed facing downward. To be on safe side, always check shim thickness with a micrometer before installing it.

7) Fit the shim in place, using pliers (88013038). Turn crankshaft until camshaft fully depresses the tappet. Remove tool (88013036). When all valves have been set, recheck for proper clearance and reinstall parts previously removed.

## PISTONS, PINS & RINGS

### OIL PAN

1) Remove bracket securing exhaust pipe to engine block. Remove right-hand constant velocity joint from drive flange and set drive shaft aside. Remove exhaust pipe from manifold. Take off flywheel guard and remove bolts from right-hand engine mount. Loosen left-hand engine mount.

2) Remove the gear control selector rod from the front control shaft. Drain coolant and oil from engine. Disconnect speedometer drive cable, and remove gear front control shaft from idler lever. Disconnect speedometer drive cable from EGR valve. Remove battery cables and lift out battery.

3) Remove ignition coil and hose clip. Remove clutch control cable support bracket. Disconnect inlet hose from the radiator. Detach anchoring rod from cylinder head and frame. Remove heater hose support bracket from exhaust camshaft housing and remove air cleaner assembly.

4) Remove engine compartment opening right-hand brace. Turn front wheels to full right and remove splash guard from right-hand wheel well. Disconnect outlet hoses from radiator.

5) Attach lifting cable (88017362) to engine and using a hoist, lift engine slowly upward only enough to permit oil pan bolt removal. Then, lift engine further until oil pan can be removed. To install, reverse removal procedures.

### PISTON & ROD ASSEMBLY

1) Place engine on stand, remove timing belt, cylinder head and oil pan. Remove oil pump from crankcase. Turn ancillary units drive shaft until the fuel pump control cam points towards the fuel pump itself. Remove connecting rod caps and slide pistons and rods out top of block as an assembly. Inspect connecting rods, bearing shells and crankshaft surfaces for scoring and wear. Check that crankpin surfaces do not show signs of scoring or seizure.

2) Always keep connecting rods and caps together so that they are not interchanged before or during assembly. To install piston and rod assemblies, turn flywheel so crankpins of No. 1 and No. 4 cylinders are at bottom dead center. Stagger piston rings at 120° intervals (gaps not aligned). Lubricate pistons for No. 1 and No. 4 cylinders and slide them part way into bores.

# Lancia Engines

## 1800 cc 4 CYLINDER (Cont.)

**3)** Use a ring compressor (88013200) to complete installation of pistons, pushing lubricated connecting rod bearings down onto crankpins.

**NOTE** — *The numbers stamped on the connecting rod side must face the side of the engine block opposite from the fuel pump.*

**4)** Using Plastigage method, check clearance between crankpins and bearing shells. To do so, remove oil marks from connecting rod bearing shell. Place a piece of Plastigage lengthwise on crankpin at center of connecting rod cap bearing shell. Lightly grease ends of string to stick it to crankpin.

**5)** Attach connecting rod cap with bearing shell and torque to 38 ft. lbs. (5.2 mkg). **NOTE** — *Be sure you do not turn crankshaft in process, or Plastigage may be damaged and give incorrect reading.* Remove connecting rod cap and measure width of the flattened Plastigage at its widest point. Use scale stamped on envelope for reading clearance between connecting rod bearing shells and crankpin. Clearance should match specifications.

**6)** Remove Plastigage from crankpins and lubricate and fit caps of No. 1 and No. 4 connecting rods. Tighten to proper torque. Install piston and rod assemblies in cylinders No. 2 and No. 3 and check for clearance in same manner. When proper, torque connecting rod cap nuts. Reinstall oil pump, oil pan, oil filter base and other parts previously removed.

Fig. 6   Measure Piston Diameter at Points Shown

### FITTING PISTONS

**1)** Visually inspect pistons for signs of seizure or scoring. Remove rings and set aside in proper location for later installation (if not to be replaced). Measure outside diameter of pistons at a point 1.86" (47.25 mm) below piston crown and at right angles with piston pin bore. See Fig. 6.

**2)** Measure cylinder diameters at points .394" (10 mm), 2.166" (55 mm), and 3.94" (100 mm) below surface of block and parallel and at right angles to crankshaft. See Fig. 7.

**3)** Subtract the diameter of each piston from the diameter of its cylinder. Clearance should be .0157–.0236" (.40–.60 mm). Pistons, piston pins and bores vary by class as to size. Class identification numbers and letters for pistons and pins are found inside the piston on piston pin bore casting (underneath side of piston). See Fig. 8. Cylinder blocks are also stamped as to cylinder bore class.

Fig. 7   Measuring Cylinder Bore Diameters

Fig. 8   Identifying Marks for Piston & Pin Classes

### Piston Sizes Available①

| Class | Inches (mm) |
|---|---|
| Class A | 3.3051-3.3055 (83.95-83.96) |
| Class B | 3.3055-3.3059 (83.96-83.97) |
| Class C | 3.3059-3.3063 (83.97-83.98) |
| Class D | 3.3063-3.3067 (83.98-83.99) |
| Class E | 3.3067-3.3070 (83.99-84.00) |

① — Standard pistons for Classes A, C, and E and pistons and rings .0078" (.2 mm), .0157" (.4 mm), and .0235" (.6 mm) oversize are furnished for repairs.

### Cylinder Bore Classes

| Class | Inches (mm) |
|---|---|
| Class A | 3.3070-3.3074 (84.00-84.01) |
| Class B | 3.3074-3.3079 (84.01-84.02) |
| Class C | 3.3079-3.3083 (84.02-84.03) |
| Class D | 3.3083-3.3087 (84.03-84.04) |
| Class E | 3.3087-3.3091 (84.04-84.05) |

# Lancia Engines

## 1800 cc 4 CYLINDER (Cont.)

### Piston Pin Sizes①

| Class | Inches (mm) |
|---|---|
| Class 1 ................................. | .8658-.8659 (21.991-21.994) |
| Class 2 ................................. | .8659-.8660 (21.994-21.997) |

① — Piston pin bore sizes for each class pin should be .0002"
(.005 mm) larger than above pin sizes.

**Fig. 9   Piston Crown Viewed From Top**

**4)** When installing pistons on connecting rods, be sure the intake valve recess (See Fig. 9) in the piston crown is on the side of the connecting rod with the lubrication hole. Use suitable tool (88012211) to install circlips securing piston pins.

**Fig. 10   Install Piston Rings as Shown**

**5)** Fit the rings to the piston using pliers (88012202), making sure all "Top" markings are facing upwards and gaps are staggered 120° from each other. See Fig. 10.

## CRANKSHAFT MAIN & CONNECTING ROD BEARINGS

### MAIN & CONNECTING ROD BEARINGS

**1)** With crankshaft removed, check main journal and connecting rod journal diameters. Oversize bearing shells are available if journals require grinding. Check clearance of both crankpin and main bearing journals, using Plastigage method outlined under PISTON & ROD ASSEMBLY.

**2)** When reassembling, be sure to align connecting rod caps and rods so that matching numbers align. When installing main bearing caps, front cap is of different shape and caps are numbered for proper installation.

**3)** Check crankshaft end play. End play is controlled by two half thrust washers in the cap of the rear main journal. Standard width of thrust washers is .0909-.0929" (2.310-2.360 mm). Oversize thrust washers are .0960-.0979" (2.437-2.487 mm) thick.

### Main Bearing Shell Thickness

| Journal Status | Journal Diameter Inches (mm) | Bearing Shell Thickness Inches (mm) |
|---|---|---|
| Standard ................ | 2.0860-2.0868 (52.985-53.005) | .0718-.0721 (1.825-1.831) |
| 1st Undersize .......... | 2.0810-2.0818 (52.858-52.878) | .0743-.0746 (1.888-1.894) |
| 2nd Undersize ......... | 2.0760-2.0768 (52.731-52.751) | .0769-.0771 (1.952-1.958) |
| 3rd Undersize ......... | 2.0660-2.0668 (52.477-52.497) | .0819-.0821 (2.079-2.085) |
| 4th Undersize .......... | 2.0560-2.0568 (52.223-52.243) | .0869-.0871 (2.206-2.212) |
| 5th Undersize .......... | 2.0460-2.0468 (51.969-51.989) | .0919-.0921 (2.333-2.339) |

### Crankpin Bearing Shell Thickness

| Journal Status | Journal Diameter Inches (mm) | Bearing Shell Thickness Inches (mm) |
|---|---|---|
| Standard ................ (Class A - Red) ........ | 2.0000-2.0001 (50.792-50.802) | .0600-.0601 (1.523-1.527) |
| Standard ................ (Class B - Blue) ........ | 1.9993-1.9996 (50.782-50.792) | .0601-.0602 (1.527-1.531) |
| 1st Undersize .......... (Class A - Red) ........ | 1.9943-1.9951 (50.655-50.675) | .0624-.0626 (1.586-1.590) |
| 1st Undersize .......... (Class B - Blue) ........ | 1.9942-1.9951 (50.655-50.675) | .0650-.0653 (1.590-1.594) |
| 2nd Undersize ......... | 1.9893-1.9900 (50.528-50.548) | .0650-.0653 (1.650-1.658) |
| 3rd Undersize ......... | 1.9793-1.9801 (50.274-50.294) | .0700-.0703 (1.777-1.785) |
| 4th Undersize .......... | 1.9693-1.9701 (50.020-50.040) | .0750-.0753 (1.904-1.912) |
| 5th Undersize .......... | 1.9597-1.9605 (49.776-49.796) | .0800-.0803 (2.031-2.039) |

**4)** When installing piston on connecting rod, use suitable tool (88012210). The following size connecting rods (bushing inner diameters) are available:

### Connecting Rod Bushing Diameters①

| Pin Class | Bushing I.D. Inches (mm) |
|---|---|
| Class 1 ................................. | .8663-.8664 (22.004-22.007) |
| Class 2 ................................. | .8664-.8665 (22.007-22.009) |

① — Inner diameters for clearance purposes should be measured with bushing installed in rod.

### FRONT OIL SEAL

Fit the crankshaft front oil seal cover on new gasket. Do not tighten bolts. Place new oil seal in cover and using suitable installing tool (88012313), drive oil seal in by screwing the sheave mounting nut to the crankshaft. Remove the tool, fit the timing belt drive gear to the crankshaft and tighten bolts to secure the oil seal cover.

# Lancia Engines

## 1800 cc 4 CYLINDER (Cont.)

### REAR OIL SEAL & FLYWHEEL

Fit the crankshaft rear oil seal cover on new gasket. Position crankshaft with crankpins for No. 1 and No. 4 cylinders at TDC. Fit flywheel so timing mark registers with TDC for crankpins No. 1 and No. 4. Install flywheel mounting bolts. Install flywheel locking tool (88013347) and torque bolts to 61 ft. lbs. (8.5 mkg).

### ANCILLARY DRIVE SHAFT

1) Using installing-removing tool (88012455), drive off crankcase-mounted bearings of ancillary drive shaft. See Fig. 11. Tool features a front end divided in two sections of different diameters to match each bearing's inner diameter.

2) Clean bearing seats and be sure crankcase oilways are not clogged. Using same tool, install smaller diameter inner bearing into its housing. Then install front bearing. Make sure oilways coincide with those present on crankcase.

3) Ream the bearing inner diameter using suitable reamer (88014325). Clean bearings with compressed air through the oilways.

**Fig. 11  Ancillary Drive Shaft Components**

4) Using similar procedure and removing-installer tool (88012456) drive out oil pump and ignition distributor drive gear bushing. Clean and inspect oilways and bushing seat. If reaming is necessary, use an adjustable reamer (88094053).

**NOTE** – *Front and rear journal clearance should be .0018-.0036" (.046-.091 mm) with an end play of .0028-.0087" (.070-.220 mm).*

### TIMING BELT

**Removal** – 1) Remove timing gear cover, spark plugs, and valve covers. Install handles (88013344) on flywheel. Turn crankshaft in direction of rotation until holes in camshaft drive gears (See Fig. 1) align with timing reference pointers. Remove reference pointers bracket. Attach locking fixture (88013039), by engaging dowel pins in camshaft gear timing holes. Attach fixture to cylinder head.

2) Remove belt stretcher nut and bolt and release tension from belt. Slip belt off gears and install new belt every 25,000 miles. Check belt stretcher spring strength using a suitable tool (80015052). Torque spanner (88091134) set at 10 ft. lbs. (1.4 mkg) must yield when reference marks on tool and spring are aligned.

**Installation** – 1) Align reference mark on crankshaft pulley with timing mark on fixture (88013039). When both marks correspond exactly, pistons No. 1 and No. 4 will be at TDC. Fixture reference hole should also line up with ancillary drive shaft reference hole. Check alignment by inserting dowel pin.

2) Install timing belt. Unlock the belt stretcher bolt applying pressure to the belt. Tighten bolt and nut to 32.5 ft. lbs. (4.5 mkg). Once tensioning bolt is torqued, remove fixture (88013039). Turn the crankshaft a few times, partially release the belt stretcher and finally relock it properly. Install timing reference pointers bracket.

## CAMSHAFT

### CAMSHAFTS

1) With timing belt removed, remove camshaft gears. Attach retainer (88013151) to camshaft drive gears and tighten bolt which clamps the two halves of retainer together. Knock down tab of lock plates and partly unscrew gear securing bolts. Lift off retainer and gears with respective bolts and lock plates.

2) Remove rear cover plate from camshaft housing and remove camshaft. Using tool (88012315) remove oil seal. Examine camshaft journals and lobes for signs of seizure or scoring. Check camshaft housing bearings for scoring and excessive wear. Check clearances between journals and bearings. See charts for proper clearance. End play should be .0039-.0077" (.100-.195 mm).

3) When installing camshaft gears, reverse procedure and torque camshaft gear bolts to 87 ft. lbs. (12 mkg).

### VALVE TIMING

To check valve timing, turn crankshaft until reference mark on sheave aligns with long mark on timing gear cover. See Fig. 12. Check that the two holes in camshaft gears (one in each) are aligned with reference marks on front camshaft bearings. See Fig. 12. If adjustment is necessary, use tool (88013039) as instructed under TIMING BELT.

## ENGINE OILING

**Crankcase Capacity** – 4.25 qts. (4 ltr) without filter; 5.25 qts. (5 ltr) with filter.

**Oil Filter** – Full-flow, quick-change. Gauze-type filter in pump strainer.

**Normal Oil Pressure** – 57-87 psi. (4-6 kg/cm²) at 6000 RPM at 185°F (85°C).

## 1800 cc 4 CYLINDER (Cont.)

### ENGINE OILING SYSTEM

The gear-type oil pump is driven off the ancillary drive shaft and provides pressure lubrication to all engine parts. A full-flow type oil filter is used along with an oil pressure regulating valve.

### OIL PUMP

**1)** Remove oil pan. Loosen mounting bolts and remove oil pump. Place pump in soft-jawed vise and remove strainer assembly. Remove spring, pressure regulating valve and pump body plate.

*Fig. 12   Valve Timing Reference Marks*

**2)** Remove pump from vise and remove gears from pump body. See *Fig. 13*. Inspect gears for scoring or "steps" and replace if necessary. Check side clearance between gears and pump body. See *Fig. 14*. Excessive clearance indicates wear to drive gear shaft in the pump body or between the driven gear and its shaft.

*Fig. 13   Oil Pump Components*

**3)** Using "V" blocks and surface plate, check end play with a dial indicator, measuring play between gears and face of pump body. Excessive end play could be due to excessive wear to pump body inner surface, requiring a new pump body, or wear to gear faces, requiring only new gears.

**4)** Check that face of the pump body plate contacting gears is not scored and that pressure regulator valve seating area is not scored, worn out or otherwise impairing proper valve operation.

**5)** Check sealing face of the pressure regulating valve. Test spring for strength. It should have a free length of 1.00" (25.2 mm). Under static load of 5.40-6.06 lbs. (2.45-2.75 kg) spring should compress to .59" (15 mm) length. Under dynamic load of 7.65-8.31 lbs. (3.47-3.77 kg), spring should compress to .43" (11 mm).

**6)** Reassemble pump and insure free movement of gears. Reinstall oil pump, tightening bolts by stages using a criss-cross pattern.

**7)** Install a new gasket and complete installation of oil pan and parts previously removed. Use tool (88013039) for retiming camshafts and ancillary drive shaft. Lower engine into place on mounting buffers and complete installation.

### Oil Pump Specifications

| Measurement | Inches (mm) |
| --- | --- |
| Drive Shaft Bushing, I.D. | .6305-.6314 (16.016-16.037) |
| Diameter, Gear Shank | .6287-.6293 (15.970-15.985) |
| Clearance, Bushing-to-Shaft | .0012-.0026 (.031-.067) |
| Pump Gear Housing Depth | 1.819-1.839 (30.020-30.072) |
| Pump Gear Thickness | 1.1794-1.1807 (29.956-29.989) |
| Gear End Play | .0012-.0046 (.031-.116) |
| Clearance, Gear-to-Housing | .0010-.0032 (.026-.080) |
| Clearance, Gear-to-Gear | .0059 (.15 ) |

*Fig. 14   Checking Oil Pump Gear Side Clearance*

### ENGINE COOLING

**Cooling System Capacity** — 9 quarts (8.5 ltr).

**Thermostat** — Coolant blending thermostat device in water pump inlet pipe. Also equipped with fan thermoswitch, which turns on cooling fan at 194-201°F (90-94°C); turns fan off at 185-192°F (85-89°C). Engine overheating warning light switch comes on at 233-244°F (112-118°C).

### COOLING SYSTEM

Cooling system features forced coolant circulation with a water pump, radiator, filling and overflow tank, and thermo-electrically controlled cooling fan.

### WATER PUMP

**1)** To remove water pump, remove hub cap and loosen bolts on front right-hand wheel. Lift front end of car and rest it on stands. Drain coolant from radiator and engine block and remove nuts which secure inlet pipe assembly to water pump (from beneath vehicle).

# Lancia Engines

## 1800 cc 4 CYLINDER (Cont.)

**2)** Remove right-hand wheel and engine guard. Loosen retaining bolts on water pump sheave and slacken drive belt. Remove drive sheave. Remove timing gear cover, bolts securing pump inlet pipe to mounting bracket of engine anchoring rod, and inlet pipe from water pump.

**3)** Remove bolts securing pump to the crankcase and lift off pump. Pump assembly is supplied only as a complete unit and cannot be repaired. When installing new pump, use new seal between pipe and water pump. Fill with coolant and check for leaks.

## ENGINE SPECIFICATIONS

### GENERAL SPECIFICATIONS

| Year | Displ. | | Carburetor | HP at RPM ① | Torque (Ft. Lbs. at RPM) ① | Compr. Ratio | Bore | | Stroke | |
|---|---|---|---|---|---|---|---|---|---|---|
| | cu. ins. | cc | | | | | in. | mm | in. | mm |
| 1978 | 107.13 | 1756 | 2-Bbl | 86@6200 | 90@2800 | 8.0-1 | 3.31 | 84 | 3.12 | 79.2 |

① — Models with catalytic converters — 83 HP at 5800 RPM; 89 Ft. Lbs. at 3200 PM.

### VALVES

| Engine & Valve | Head Diam. In. (mm) | Face Angle | Seat Angle | Seat Width In. (mm) | Stem Diameter In. (mm) | Stem Clearance In. (mm) | Valve Lift In. (mm) |
|---|---|---|---|---|---|---|---|
| 1800 cc Intake | 1.622-1.638 (41.2-41.6) | 45° | 45° | .083 (2.1) | .314-.315 (7.974-7.992) | .001-.003 (.030-.066) | ..... |
| Exhaust | 1.411-.435 (35.85-36.45) | 45° | 45° | .067 (1.7) | .314-.315 (7.974-7.992) | .001-.003 (.030-.066) | ..... |

### VALVE SPRINGS

| Engine | Free Length In. (mm) | PRESSURE Lbs. @ In. (kg @ mm) | |
|---|---|---|---|
| | | Valve Closed | Valve Open |
| 1800 cc Inner | 1.666 (42.32) | 31.7-34.0@1.22 (14.4-15.4@31) | 59.3-64.6@.85 (269-29.3@21.5) |
| Outer | 2.122 (53.9) | 82.5-89.1@1.42 (37.4-40.4@36) | 125.7-136.7@1.02 (57-62@26) |

### CAMSHAFT

| Engine | Journal Diam. In. (mm) | Clearance In. (mm) | Lobe Lift In. (mm) |
|---|---|---|---|
| 1800 cc Front | 1.1789-1.1795 (29.944-29.960) | .0019-.0035 (.049-.090) | ..... |
| Center | 1.801-1.802 (45.755-45.771) | .0011-.0028 (.029-.070) | ..... |
| Rear | 1.8171-1.8178 (46.155-46.171) | .0011-.0028 (.029-.070) | ..... |

### PISTONS, PINS, RINGS

| Engine | PISTONS | PINS | | RINGS | | |
|---|---|---|---|---|---|---|
| | Clearance In. (mm) | Piston Fit In. (mm) | Rod Fit In. (mm) | Rings | End Gap In. (mm) | Side Clearance In. (mm) |
| 1800 cc | .0157-.0236 (.40-.60) | .0001-.0003 (.002-.008) | .0004-.0006 (.010-.016) | No. 1 | .012-.018 (.30-.45) | 0018-.0030 (.045-.077) |
| | | | | No. 2 | .008-.014 (.20-.35) | .0012-.0028 (.030-.070) |
| | | | | No. 3 (Oil) | .008-.014 (.20-.35) | .0012-.0024 (.030-.062) |

## 1800 cc 4 CYLINDER (Cont.)
### ENGINE SPECIFICATIONS (Cont.)

### CRANKSHAFT MAIN & CONNECTING ROD BEARINGS

| Engine | MAIN BEARINGS | | | | CONNECTING ROD BEARINGS | | |
|---|---|---|---|---|---|---|---|
| | Journal Diam. In. (mm) | Clearance In. (mm) | Thrust Bearing | Crankshaft End Play In. (mm) | Journal Diam. In. (mm) | Clearance In. (mm) ① | Side Play In. (mm) |
| 1800 cc | 2.086-2.087 (52.985-53.005) | .002-.003 (.050-.094) | Center | .002.012 (.055-.305) | 2.000-2.001 (50.792-50.802) | .0016..0030 (.041-.075) | .005-.018 (.127-.457) |

① — Dimensions given are for Class A Bearing Shells. With Class B Bearing Shells, clearance would be .0017-.0030" (.043-.077 mm) for crankpin journals of 1.999-2.000" (50.782-50.792 mm).

### VALVE TIMING

| Engine | INTAKE | | EXHAUST | |
|---|---|---|---|---|
| | Open (BTDC) | Close (ALDC) | Open (BLDC) | Close (ATDC) |
| 1800 cc | 5° | 53° | 53° | 5° |

### TIGHTENING SPECIFICATIONS

| Application | Ft. Lbs. (mkg) |
|---|---|
| Front Main Bearing Cap Nuts | 59.3 (8.2) |
| Other Main Bearing Cap Nuts | 83.2 (11.5) |
| Flywheel Bolts | 61.5 (8.5) |
| Connecting Rod Cap Nuts | 37.6 (5.2) |
| Cylinder Head Bolts | ①61.5 (8.5) |
| Camshaft Housing Nuts | 16 (2.2) |
| Exhaust Pipe Nuts | 17.4 (2.4) |
| Manifold Nuts | 18 (2.5) |
| Crankshaft Nut | 181 (25) |
| Camshaft Gear Bolts | 87 (12) |
| Spark Plugs | 27.5 (3.8) |
| Temperature Gauge Transmitter | 36 (5) |
| Timing Belt Tensioner Nut | 32.5 (4.5) |

① — Tighten in two stages to final torque setting.

## LUV PICKUP 4 CYLINDER

### ENGINE CODING

#### ENGINE IDENTIFICATION

Engine number is located in casting on right upper center portion of cylinder head.

### ENGINE, CYLINDER HEAD & MANIFOLDS

#### ENGINE

**Removal** — **1)** Disconnect battery cables, drain crankcase and cooling system. Disconnect carburetor linkage, all necessary water and fuel hoses. Disconnect all necessary vacuum lines and electrical leads. Disconnect exhaust pipe at manifold flange.

**2)** Disconnect drive shaft, slave cylinder and speedometer-cable. Remove starter. Remove flywheel inspection cover and bell housing bolts. Support transmission. Attach hoist and take up vehicle weight. Remove front and rear engine mount nuts. Pull engine forward and lift out of vehicle.

**Installation** — To install engine, reverse removal procedure.

#### INTAKE & EXHAUST MANIFOLD

**1)** Remove air cleaner and carburetor. Disconnect PCV valve, power brake vacuum line and exhaust pipe from exhaust manifold. Note for reinstallation position of lifting hanger.

**2)** Remove nuts, lock washers and flat washers holding manifolds to cylinder head. Slide manifolds off together. Once off, manifolds can be separated by removing exhaust manifold mounting studs. To install, reverse removal procedure.

**NOTE** — *Torque manifold stud in sequence, working from inner nuts outward.*

#### CYLINDER HEAD

**1)** Drain cooling system. Disconnect exhaust pipe from manifold. Disconnect all necessary water hoses, vacuum lines, carburetor linkage, and electrical leads. Remove air cleaner assembly and valve cover. Rotate number four cylinder into firing position. Lock timing chain adjuster by depressing and turning automatic adjuster slide pin 90° clockwise (See Fig. 6).

**NOTE** — *Do not remove the timing chain from camshaft sprocket.*

**2)** Remove timing chain sprocket from camshaft. Remove front cover. Using suitable tool (J-24239), remove cylinder head bolts in progressional sequence starting with outer bolts. Remove cylinder head, intake and exhaust manifolds as an assembly. To install, reverse removal procedure.

**Fig. 1  Cylinder Head Tightening Sequence**

### VALVES

#### VALVE ARRANGEMENT

E-I-I-E-E-I-I-E

#### VALVE GUIDES

**Removal & Installation** — **1)** Inspect inside diameter of valve guide for grooves or uneven wear. Measure inside diameter of valve guides with caliper gauge. Measure diameter of valve stem and compare measured values to determine clearance. If clearance is greater than .008" (.20 mm) for intake, or .010" (.25 mm) for exhaust, replace both valve and valve guide.

**2)** Drive valve guides toward upper face of cylinder head, using suitable valve guide replacer tool (J-26512). Valve guides cannot be driven downward. Valve guides are held in position by snap rings.

**NOTE** — *Before installation of valve guide, remove lower spring seat.*

**3)** To install, apply engine oil to outer circumference of valve guide, and install into position in cylinder head. Holding valve guide installer tool (J-26512-1) and (J-26512-2) against valve guide, drive valve guide into cylinder head until tool bottoms on cylinder head.

**NOTE** — *Replace valve whenever valve guide is replaced.*

#### VALVE STEM OIL SEALS

Inspect intake and exhaust valve stem oil seal lips and inner face. Replace valve stem oil seals at time of reassembly, if wear is noticable.

#### VALVE SPRINGS

Remove rocker arm shaft and bracket assembly. Remove spark plug, and connect compressed air to cylinder at spark plug opening. Using spring compressor tool (J-26513), compress valve spring and remove retainers, spring, and spring cap. Remove valve stem oil seal and lower spring seat. To install, reverse removal procedure.

#### VALVE SPRING INSTALLED HEIGHT

Visually check valve springs for damage and replace as necessary. Measure free length of valve springs using suitable calipers and replace if measured value is beyond limit. With a valve spring tester check valve spring tension and compare it with values in chart, replace as necessary.

**NOTE** — *Install springs with close wound coils next to cylinder head.*

#### ROCKER ARM ASSEMBLY

**1)** Loosen rocker shaft bracket nuts in sequence, starting with outer brackets. Remove the spring from the shaft, and then remove rocker arm brackets and arms keeping parts in order for reassembly.

## LUV PICKUP 4 CYLINDER (Cont.)

**2)** Inspect rocker arm shaft for wear damage or excessive runout. If runout is greater than .0156" (.396 mm), replace shaft. Diameter of shaft is .8071" (20.5 mm). Replace shaft if diameter is less than .8012" (20.35 mm).

**3)** To install, apply engine oil to rocker arm shaft, rocker arms, and valve stems. Install longer shaft on exhaust side and shorter shaft on intake side. Aligning marks on shafts are turned to front side.

**4)** Assemble brackets and arms to shafts, so cylinder number (on upper face of bracket) is pointed to front of engine. Align No. 1 shaft bracket with mark on the intake and exhaust valve side rocker arm shafts. Place springs between shaft bracket and rocker arm. Punch mark on rocker arm shafts must be turned upward. Tighten shaft bracket nuts.

**NOTE** — *Hold rocker arm springs with a wrench while torquing nuts, to prevent damage to spring. Torque nuts in sequence, starting with center bracket and working outward.*

### VALVE CLEARANCE

With No. 1 or No. 4 cylinder piston at top dead center, loosen lock nut and adjust intake valves to .006" (.15 mm), and exhaust valves to .010" (.25 mm). When valves are correctly adjusted reset lock nut.

**Valve Adjustment Sequence**

| Application | Intake/Cylinder | Exhaust/Cylinder |
|---|---|---|
| No. 1 @ TDC | 1,2 | 1,3 |
| No. 4 @ TDC | 3,4 | 2,4 |

## PISTONS, PINS & RINGS

### OIL PAN

Raise vehicle. Drain crankcase and remove front splash shield. Remove crossmember. Disconnect relay rod at idler arm and lower relay rod. Remove left hand bell housing brace. Remove oil pan bolts and pan. To install, reverse removal procedure.

### PISTON & ROD ASSEMBLY

**1)** Position cylinder body so flywheel side is down. Using suitable tool, scrape carbon from upper part of cylinder wall.

**2)** Remove connecting rod bearing cap nuts and bearing cap. Using a wood rod, push piston, together with connecting rod, upward. Removal sequence is 1, 4, 2, & 3. **NOTE** — *Ensure piston and connecting rod are pulled parallel to cylinder wall.*

**3)** To install piston and rod assembly, position piston so notch mark on crown of piston is facing front of engine. Align cylinder number marks on connecting rods so they will be on right-hand side of front mark on piston.

### PISTON PIN

**Removal** — Using a press and piston pin removal tool set (J-25270), press piston pin out of piston and connecting rod assembly.

**NOTE** — *Manufacturer recommends replacing with NEW piston pins.*

**Installation** — Install new pin by placing pilot through piston and connecting rod. Lightly oil piston pin and place piston, rod, pin, and ram on press base. Press in pin until its centered in connecting rod.

Fig. 2  Exploded View of Piston & Connecting Rod

Fig. 3  Position of Piston Rings

### PISTON RINGS

**1)** Assemble piston rings to piston with a piston ring expander. When replacing piston rings, position compression rings so that "NPR" or "TOP" mark is turned up. The expander ring and side rail is not marked.

**2)** Install oil control ring in this order; expander ring, lower side rail, and upper side rail. After installing all rings, apply clean engine oil to the entire rings. Check that rings turn smoothly in their ring grooves.

## LUV PICKUP 4 CYLINDER (Cont.)

### FITTING PISTONS

1) Check piston clearance by inserting piston pull-scale with .0018-.0026" feeler gauge, one inch long, into cylinder. Fit piston, crown first, into cylinder so feeler gauge is wedged by piston.

2) Holding piston to prevent side thrust, withdraw gauge with a steady pull on scale. Clearance is correct when gauge reads 1.1-2.2 lbs. **NOTE** – *It is advisable to take several readings.*

3) Measure weight of assembled pistons and compare the values. Ensure values between pistons are within .2 ozs. If value is exceeded, make necessary adjustments by selecting a connecting rod of suitable weight or by grinding.

#### Piston Class

| Piston Size | Piston Grade | Piston Diameter In. (mm) |
| --- | --- | --- |
| Standard | A | 3.3049-3.3053 (83.944-83.955) |
| Standard | B | 3.3053-3.3057 (83.955-83.965) |
| Standard | C | 3.3057-3.3061 (83.965-83.975) |
| Standard | D | 3.3061-3.3065 (83.975-83.985) |

**NOTE** – *Pistons are available in .020" (0.5mm) and .040" (1.0mm) oversize.*

## CRANKSHAFT MAIN & CONNECTING ROD BEARINGS

### MAIN & CONNECTING ROD BEARING SERVICE

**NOTE** – *The following procedure is with engine, cylinder head, timing cover, oil pan, and timing chain removed.*

**Connecting Rod Bearings** – After ensuring rod caps are marked for cylinder identification, remove rod caps. Use Plastigage method to check for proper clearance. If not within specifications, new bearings must be installed. New bearings are available in standard, .010", and .020".

**NOTE** – *Always replace bearings in pairs. Never use a new bearing in combination with a used bearing.*

**Main Bearings** – 1) With all bearing caps (except one being checked) tight, check clearances using Plastigage method. If clearances are excessive, undersized bearings will have to be installed. Remove upper bearings by inserting tool into oil hole of crankshaft and rotating crankshaft clockwise to roll bearing from engine.

2) To check crankshaft out of round place crankshaft on two "V" shaped blocks at No. 1 and No. 5 journals. Hold dial indicator in contact with No. 3 journal and slowly turn crankshaft, recording highest point on journal. Replace crankshaft if bend exceeds .0038" (.097 mm). Standard assembly value is .0012" (.030 mm) or less.

3) To check crankshaft end play, place bearings and crankshaft in crankcase. Install thrust bearing on both sides of No. 3 crankshaft journal. Shift crankshaft endwise and measure clearance between thrust bearing and journal side

face. If clearance is greater than .0117" (.297 mm), install oversize thrust bearings. Standard value is .0024-.0094" (.061-.239 mm).

**NOTE** – *Main bearing caps are installed with marks on bottom of caps facing forward. Number two and three bearing caps can be distinguished by an "A" stamped on caps.*

*Fig. 4  Installing Thrust Bearing*

### REAR MAIN OIL SEAL

**Removal** – Remove oil pan and transmission. Remove clutch (if equipped). Remove starter and flywheel assembly. Remove seal retainer bolts and pry seal out of retainer.

**Installation** – To install, reverse removal procedure noting the following: Fill clearance between lips of seal with grease, and coat lips of seal with engine oil. Place retainer on flat surface and drive seal into place using suitable seal installer tool (J-22354).

*Fig. 5  Installing Timing Cover Oil Seal*

### FRONT COVER & OIL SEAL

**Removal** – Remove cylinder head and oil pan as previously outlined. Remove oil pump pickup tube. Remove harmonic balancer and AIR belt. If equipped with air conditioning, remove compressor and mounting brackets. Remove distributor cap (wires attached), then remove distributor. Remove front cover.

## LUV PICKUP 4 CYLINDER (Cont.)

**Installation** — Align oil pump drive gear punch mark with oil filter side of cover. Align center of dowel pin with alignment mark on oil pump case. Rotate No. 1 and 4 cylinders to top dead center. Install front cover by engaging pinion gear with oil pump drive gear on crankshaft (See Fig. 5). Install front cover and reverse removal procedure.

## CAMSHAFT

### CAMSHAFT

1) Remove valve cover. Position No. 4 cylinder in firing position. Remove distributor cap and mark rotor position. Lock timing chain adjuster by depressing and turning automatic adjuster slide pin 90° in a clockwise direction. See Fig. 6.

**Fig. 6   Locking Timing Chain Adjuster**

**NOTE** — After locking chain adjuster, check that chain is in free state.

2) Remove timing sprocket from camshaft, keeping sprocket on chain damper and tensioner without removing sprocket from chain. Remove rocker arm shaft and bracket assembly. Remove camshaft.

3) Check camshaft journals and cams for wear or damage. Measure height of cams with a micrometer, and replace camshaft if height is less than 1.4311" (36.3 mm). If working faces of cams have slight scores or steps, eliminate them by honing. Measure outside diameter of camshaft journals, replace camshaft if diameter is less than 1.3307" (33.8 mm). To install, reverse removal procedure.

### CAMSHAFT END PLAY

Measure camshaft end play with thrust plate installed in thrust groove. Replace thrust plate if end play is found to exceed .0078" (.198 mm). Standard end play is .002-.006" (.05-.15 mm).

### CAMSHAFT BEARING REPLACEMENT

Camshaft bearings are not replaceable. Camshaft rides in a carrier. If clearance is beyond limits, replace camshaft carrier.

### TIMING CHAIN REPLACEMENT

1) Remove front cover as outlined previously. Remove camshaft sprocket and timing chain. All other parts can now be inspected for wear, replace as necessary. If crankshaft sprocket needs replacement, remove with suitable gear puller (J-25031).

2) Install timing sprocket and pinion gear, groove side toward front cover. Align key grooves with key on crankshaft, then drive into position with suitable installing tool (J-26587). Turn crankshaft so that key is turned toward cylinder head side and No. 1 and 4 cylinders are at top dead center.

**NOTE** — Keep timing chain engaged with camshaft sprocket until sprocket is installed on camshaft.

3) Align mark plate on timing chain with mark on crankshaft timing sprocket. Side of chain with mark plate is on front side, and side of chain with most links between mark plates is on chain guide side. Camshaft timing sprocket marked side, faces forward and marks align with timing chain mark plate. Install front cover.

**Fig. 7   Camshaft, Timing Chain & Components**

### ENGINE OILING SYSTEM

Trochoid type oil pump is designed to deliver 3.7 gallons of oil per minute through the engine at a pump speed of 1400 RPM. Lubricating system is designed to deliver oil at a rate of 57 psi.

**Crankcase Capacity** — 5.7 quarts with filter.

## LUV PICKUP 4 CYLINDER (Cont.)

### ENGINE OILING

**Oil Filter** — Full-flow disposable canister type.

**Normal Oil Pressure** — 57 psi.

**Relief Valve** — Located on side of cylinder block near oil filter. Opening pressure of relief valve is 57-71 psi.

### OIL PUMP

**NOTE** — *Oil pump can be serviced with engine in or out of vehicle. Procedure given is with engine in vehicle.*

**Removal** — Remove front cover, distributor, and oil pan as outlined previously. Remove oil pickup tube. Remove oil pump mounting bolts and remove pump assembly.

**Inspection** — 1) Measure tip clearance with a feeler gauge, between drive rotor and driven rotor. Replace entire pump assembly if clearance is greater than .0079" (.2 mm).

**Fig. 8   Exploded View of Oil Pump Assembly**

2) Measure clearance between driven rotor and inner wall of pump body. Replace entire pump assembly if clearance is greater than .0098" (.249 mm).

3) Using a square and a feeler gauge, measure clearance between drive rotor, driven rotor, and oil pump cover. Replace entire pump assembly if clearance is greater than .0079" (.2 mm). Inspect all parts wear or damage.

**Installation** — 1) Align mark on camshaft with mark on No. 1 rocker arm shaft bracket. Align notch on crankshaft pulley with "O" mark on front cover. When the two sets of marks are

aligned, No. 4 cylinder is at top dead center on **compression** stroke.

2) Install driven rotor so that alignment mark aligns with **mark** on the drive rotor. Engage drive gear with pinion **gear** on crankshaft so alignment mark is turned rearward and is **away** from crankshaft by approximately 20° in clockwise rotation *(See Fig. 9).*

3) When oil pump is installed; make sure mark on drive **gear** is turned to rear side as viewed from the clearance **between** front cover and cylinder block. Slit at end of shaft **must be** parallel with front face of cylinder block, and is offset as viewed through distributor fitting hole.

4) Install pump cover by fitting it to the dowel pins, then **install** mounting bolts. Install relief valve assembly and rubber **hose** on cover. Reverse removal procedure.

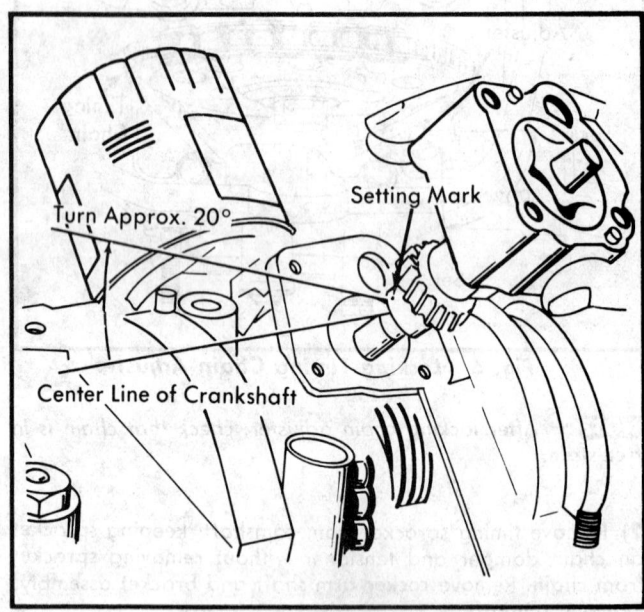

**Fig. 9   Installing Oil Pump**

### ENGINE COOLING

#### WATER PUMP

Disconnect negative battery cable. Remove lower cover. **Drain** cooling system. If equipped with air conditioning, remove **fan** and air pump drive belt. Remove fan, fan pulley, and **air** pump drive pulley. Remove set plate and pulley. On all other models remove fan nuts and fan. On all models, remove at-taching bolts and water pump from vehicle.

**Thermostat** — Opens at about 180°F (82°C).

**Cooling System Capacity** — 6.4 qts.

**Pressure Cap** — 15 psi.

## LUV PICKUP 4 CYLINDER (Cont.)

### ENGINE SPECIFICATIONS

#### GENERAL SPECIFICATIONS

| Year | Displ. cu. ins. | Displ. cc | Carburetor | HP at RPM | Torque (Ft. Lbs. at RPM) | Compr. Ratio | Bore in. | Bore mm | Stroke in. | Stroke mm |
|---|---|---|---|---|---|---|---|---|---|---|
| 1978 | 110.8 | 1816 | 1x2-Bbl. | 80 @4800 | 95 @3000 | 8.5:1 | 3.31 | 84 | 3.23 | 82 |

#### VALVES

| Engine & Valve | Head Diam. In. (mm) | Face Angle | Seat Angle | Seat Width In. (mm) | Stem Diameter In. (mm) | Stem Clearance In. (mm) | Valve Lift In. (mm) |
|---|---|---|---|---|---|---|---|
| 1816 cc Int. | 1.67 (42.4) | 45° | 45° | .047-.063 (1.19-1.60) | ..... | .0009-.0022 (.023-.056) | ..... |
| Exh. | 1.34 (34.0) | 45° | 45° | .047-.063 (1.19-1.60) | ..... | .0015-.0031 (.038-.079) | ..... |

#### PISTONS, PINS, RINGS

| Engine | PISTONS Clearance In. (mm) | PINS Piston Fit In. (mm) | PINS Rod Fit In. (mm) | Rings | End Gap In. (mm) | Side Clearance In. (mm) |
|---|---|---|---|---|---|---|
| 1816 cc | .0018-.0026 (.046-.066) | ① | .0024 (.061) | 1 | .008-.016 (.20-.41) | ..... |
| | | | | 2 | .008-.016 (.20-.41) | ..... |
| | | | | Oil | .008-.035 (.20-.89) | ..... |

① — Press fit.

#### CRANKSHAFT MAIN & CONNECTING ROD BEARINGS

| Engine | MAIN BEARINGS Journal Diam. In. (mm) | MAIN BEARINGS Clearance In. (mm) | Thrust Bearing | Crankshaft End Play In. (mm) | CONNECTING ROD BEARINGS Journal Diam. In. (mm) | CONNECTING ROD BEARINGS Clearance In. (mm) | Side Play In. (mm) |
|---|---|---|---|---|---|---|---|
| 1816 cc | 2.205 (56.01) | .0016 (.041) | No. 3 | .118 (.3) | 1.929 (48.99) | .0020 (.051) | .011 (.28) |

#### CAMSHAFT

| Engine | Journal Diam. In. (mm) | Clearance In. (mm) | Lobe Lift In. (mm) |
|---|---|---|---|
| 1816 cc | 1.3362-1.3370 (33.94-33.96) | .0024 ① (.061) | ..... |

① — End Play .002-.006" (.05-.15 mm)

#### VALVE TIMING

| Engine | INTAKE Open (BTDC) | INTAKE Close (ALDC) | EXHAUST Open (BLDC) | EXHAUST Close (ATDC) |
|---|---|---|---|---|
| 1816 cc | 21° | 65° | 55° | 20° |

# LUV Engines

## VALVE SPRINGS

| Engine | Free Length In. (mm) | PRESSURE Lbs. @ In. (kg @ mm) | |
|---|---|---|---|
| | | Valve Closed | Valve Open |
| 1816 cc Inner | 1.78 (45.2) | 21.5 @ 1.52 (9.7 @ 38.6) | ..... |
| Outer | 1.85 (47.0) | 37.0 @ 1.61 (16.8 @ 40.9) | ..... |

## TIGHTENING SPECIFICATIONS

| Application | Ft. Lbs. (mkg) |
|---|---|
| Cylinder Head | |
| Step 1 | 61 (8.43) |
| Step 2 | 72 (9.95) |
| Main Bearings | 72 (9.95) |
| Connecting Rod Bearings | 43 (5.95) |
| Flywheel | 69 (9.54) |
| Camshaft Sprocket | 58 (8.02) |
| Rocker Arm Shaft Bracket Nuts | 16 (2.21) |

## B1800 & GLC 4 CYLINDER

## ENGINE CODING

### ENGINE IDENTIFICATION

Engine number on 1796 cc engine is stamped on cylinder block next to dipstick. Engine number on 1272 cc engine is stamped on cylinder block just above fuel pump.

#### Engine Identification

| Application | Code |
|---|---|
| GLC (1272 cc) ................................................ | TC |
| B1800 (1796 cc) ............................................. | VB |

## ENGINE & CYLINDER HEAD

### ENGINE

**Removal** — **1)** Remove hood after marking hood hinge location. Drain cooling system and crankcase. Remove battery and air cleaner. Disconnect accelerator and choke cable from carburetor. Disconnect fuel lines at fuel pump and carburetor (if necessary).

**2)** Disconnect wires from temperature sending unit, oil pressure switch, alternator, distributor, reverse lamp switch and starter. Disconnect exhaust pipe from manifold. Remove cover plate from clutch housing. Support transmission with a jack and remove nuts and bolts attaching transmission to engine.

**3)** Remove engine mount attaching nuts and bolts. Install a lifting sling to engine lifting brackets, attach a lifting hoist and raise slightly. Pull engine forward until clear of clutch shaft. Lift engine from vehicle.

**Installation** — To install, reverse removal procedure.

**NOTE** — *Additional engine component disassembly (with engine removed).*

### CYLINDER HEAD

**Removal** — **1)** Remove engine lifting brackets from cylinder head. Remove exhaust manifold or thermal reactor along with port liners and gaskets. Disconnect ignition wires at spark plugs and vacuum control tube at distributor. Remove lock nut, then remove distributor from cylinder head.

**2)** Disconnect hoses and remove air pump with bracket. Remove water pump fan and pulley. Disconnect hose from ventilation valve at intake manifold. Disconnect anti-afterburn valve hose on 808 models. Remove attaching bolts, then remove intake manifold and carburetor as an assembly.

**3)** Remove rocker arm cover, gasket, and oil seals. Install ring gear brake tool (49 0118 271A) to flywheel to prevent flywheel from rotating. Remove lock nut and washer, then slide distributor drive gear from camshaft. Remove camshaft sprocket lock nut. Remove cylinder head-to-front cover attaching bolt.

**4)** Loosen, in steps, cylinder head bolts in the reverse of tightening sequence and then remove bolts. Remove rocker arm assembly. Carefully pull camshaft to rear and remove from sprocket and cylinder head.

**5)** Remove camshaft sprocket. **CAUTION** — *Timing chain should be lifted up to prevent chain tensioner slipper head from disengaging which will cause difficulty in chain tension adjustment upon reassembly.* Remove camshaft bearings from cylinder head. Remove cylinder head and gasket.

**Installation** — **1)** Install camshaft sprocket to timing chain and position on top of chain guide strip and chain vibration damper. **NOTE** — *Ensure matching marks on chain and sprocket are aligned.* Install new cylinder head gasket, then position cylinder head while aligning dowels.

**2)** Install camshaft bearings to cylinder head and to bearing caps. Lubricate bearing surfaces with engine oil. Carefully install camshaft to sprocket while aligning keyway and fit journals to respective bearings. Position rocker arm assembly on cylinder head. **NOTE** — *Ensure that the flat surface of ball on each rocker arm is facing down.*

**3)** Install cylinder head bolts and tighten, in steps, according to sequence shown in *Fig. 1.* Install cylinder head-to-front cover bolt. Install and tighten camshaft lock nut, then bend tab of lock washer. Install distributor drive gear, tighten nut and bend lock washer.

**Fig. 1  Tightening Sequence for Cylinder Head**

**4)** Carefully press top of chain guide strip, using a lever, through opening of cylinder head. Tighten guide strip attaching screws. Adjust timing chain tension. *See Timing Chain Adjustment.* Install remaining components in reverse of removal procedure.

## VALVES

### VALVE ARRANGEMENT

**Right Side** — All Intake.
**Left Side** — All Exhaust.

### VALVE GUIDE SERVICING

Remove worn valve guide, using valve guide removal/installation tool and hammer. Install new guide until ring on guide just touches cylinder head. Install new valve seal onto valve guide using a seal pusher tool (42 0223 160B).

## B1800 & GLC 4 CYLINDER (Cont.)

*Fig. 2   Setting Rocker Arm Supports so Intake
and Exhaust Rocker Arms are Offset from
Valve Stem Center*

*Fig. 4 1796 cc Rocker Arm Assembly*

### VALVE SPRINGS

1) Remove all carbon from inside combustion chamber. Using a suitable valve spring compressor, collapse springs and remove tapered sleeves, upper spring seat, valve springs and lower spring seat. If necessary, valve can now be removed.

2) With valve springs removed, inspect for corrosion or obvious signs of damage. Use a valve spring tester to determine valve spring condition under a load. Measure valve spring free length and compare findings with specification table.

### ROCKER ARM ASSEMBLY

1) With rocker arm assembly removed and disassembled, inspect all components for wear or damage. The standard clearance between rocker arm bore and shaft on 1272 cc is, .0008-.0029″ (.020-.074 mm), and on 1796 cc is, .0011-.0032″ (.028-.081 mm). If measured clearance is beyond .004″ (.102 mm), replace rocker arm or shaft.

*Fig. 3   1272 cc Rocker Arm Assembly*

2) Reassemble and install rocker shaft while noting the following: Intake and exhaust rocker arm shaft supports are interchangeable. Intake side uses two rocker shafts. On intake side, end of shaft with longer distance between oil hole and shaft end face each other. Center bearing cap oil hole faces toward intake side.

3) When installing the oil distribution pipe make sure the oil ejection hole faces camshaft. After pipe is installed press "O" ring into hole for pipe on center bearing cap. When installing rocker arm assembly make sure flat surface on ball of each rocker arm faces downward. Align dowels and install assembly to cylinder head. Before tightening cylinder head bolts, offset each exhaust rocker arm .040″ (1 mm) from valve stem center.

### VALVE CLEARANCE

With engine warmed to operating temperature, adjust clearance. Loosen lock nut and insert feeler gauge between rocker arm and valve stem. Turn adjusting screw until proper clearance is obtained.

**NOTE** — *Before adjusting, ensure flat surface of ball on rocker arm is facing downward.*

**Valve Clearance Specifications**

| Application | Intake In.(mm) | Exhaust In.(mm) |
|---|---|---|
| **1272cc** | | |
| Valve side | .010 (.25) | .012 (.30) |
| Camshaft side | .007 (.18) | .009 (.22) |
| **1796 cc** | | |
| Valve side | .012 (.30) | .012 (.30) |
| Camshaft side | .009 (.22) | .009 (.22) |

## PISTONS, PINS & RINGS

### PISTON & ROD ASSEMBLY

**Removal** — Remove oil pan, cylinder head, and oil pump. Make sure connecting rod caps are marked so they may be replaced in their original positions, then remove rod caps. Push piston and rod assembly out top of cylinder. Take care not to damage bearing journal.

# Mazda Engines

## B1800 & GLC 4 CYLINDER (Cont.)

**Installation** – Oil piston rings, pistons, and cylinder walls with engine oil. Place piston rings approximately 120° apart so gap is not on thrust side or piston pin side. Install a ring compressor onto piston without disturbing position of rings. Install piston and rod assembly into its original bore. Make sure "F" mark on piston is facing front of engine. Install rod caps and tighten rod bolts. Install oil pump, oil pan, and cylinder head.

### FITTING PISTONS

**1)** Cylinder bore can be measured using a cylinder gauge. Measurement must be taken at three depths and two angles as shown in illustration. Difference between maximum and minimum values is actual wear. If cylinder bore wear is .006" (.15 mm) or more, all cylinders must be honed or rebored. If cylinder is honed or rebored, oversize pistons and rings are available in .010" (.25 mm), .020" (.50 mm), .030" (.75 mm), and .040" (1.00 mm) oversizes.

**Fig. 5   Points for Measuring Cylinder Bore**

### Standard Piston Specifications

| Application | Diameter In. (mm) |
|---|---|
| 1272 cc | |
| A | 2.8718-2.8726 (72.948-72.956) |
| B | 2.8722-2.8730 (72.959-72.967) |
| C | 2.8590-2.8598 (72.649-72.657) |
| 1796 cc | |
| A | 3.0683-3.0691 (77.935-77.955) |
| B | 3.0705-3.0713 (77.991-78.011) |
| C | 3.0583-3.0591 (77.681-77.701) |

**2)** Carefully inspect pistons and replace those severely damaged due to scoring, scratching or burning. Measure pistons at points A, B & C, as shown in *Fig. 6* using a micrometer. If piston is not within specifications, replace piston and rebore cylinder.

**Fig. 6   Points for Measuring Piston**

### PISTON PIN REPLACEMENT

**1)** Remove piston pin circlips. Using suitable piston pin removal tool, extract piston pin. If pin is hard to remove, heat piston assembly.

**2)** Check fit of piston pin in connecting rod bushing. Fit should be .0004-.0012". If tolerance is exceeded, replace bushing.

**3)** To replace connecting rod bushing, press out worn bushing and install new one; ensure connecting rod and bushing oil holes align. Using suitable tool, finish ream new bushing. Correct fit is hand push, light resistance.

**4)** Begin reassembly by replacing piston pin circlip. Place connecting rod in piston so oil hole on connecting rod and piston index mark "F" are in relation. See *Fig. 7*. Using suitable piston pin installation tool, seat piston pin. Install second circlip.

**Fig. 7   Installing Piston Pin**

## B1800 & GLC 4 CYLINDER (Cont.)

### CRANKSHAFT MAIN & CONNECTING ROD BEARINGS

#### MAIN & CONNECTING ROD BEARINGS

1) Remove engine and oil pan. Check main and connecting rod bearing clearances using Plastigage method. If measured value exceeds correct clearance, bearing must be replaced.

2) Using a micrometer, measure diameter of connecting rod and main bearing journals. If wear is more than .0020" at any journal, crankshaft must be ground to fit .010", .020" or .030" undersize bearings.

3) Using a dial indicator, check crankshaft for out-of-round. Maximum allowable out-of-round is .0012" (.030 mm).

4) Fit five upper main bearings to cylinder block and lower bearings to caps. Install thrust washer halves to cylinder block with oil grooved surface facing crankshaft thrust side. Fit new oil seal at rear of crankshaft. Insert side seals on both sides of rear main bearing cap. Install main bearing caps. No. 1 through No. 4 bearing caps are marked for correct installation, No.5 may or may not be indexed.

5) Insert connecting rod assembly into cylinder as previously described. Fit upper bearing to rod and over crankshaft. Fit lower bearing to rod cap and install cap. Tighten all bolts to specifications.

NOTE — Ensure engine is free to turn.

6) End play is compensated for by thrust washers placed at No. 5 main bearing. Check crankshaft end play using a dial indicator. End play must not exceed .012", if it does thrust washers must be replaced. Thrust washers are available in .010", .020" & .030" oversizes.

### CAMSHAFT

#### CAMSHAFT

NOTE — Lift timing chain upward to prevent the slipper head of chain tensioner from coming out, and causing difficulty in adjusting the timing chain.

1) Remove valve cover. Install ring gear brake tool (49 0118 271A) to the flywheel. Remove lock nut and washer, and slide distributor drive gear from camshaft. Remove lock nut from camshaft sprocket.

2) Remove the bolt that attaches timing chain cover to cylinder head. Remove cylinder head bolts in reverse of tightening sequence. Lift out rocker arm assembly. Pull camshaft rearward and remove sprocket. Carefully remove camshaft. If necessary camshaft bearings can be removed at this time.

#### CAMSHAFT BEARING REPLACEMENT

1) Inspect cam face and journals, ensuring they are not worn or scored. Using a micrometer, measure cam height. Standard cam height for 1272 cc intake and exhaust is 1.7369" (44.116 mm). Standard cam height for 1796 cc intake is 1.773" (45.037 mm) and for 1796 cc exhaust is 1.778" (45.004 mm). On 1272 cc, measured values must not exceed standard value by more than .008" (.20 mm). Replace components as required.

2) Measure diameter of camshaft bearing journals. If wear is more than .002" (.051 mm) above maximum standard diameter, camshaft must be ground to accept .010", .020" or .030" undersize bearings.

3) Inspect camshaft bearing clearances using Plastigage method. If standard clearances are exceeded, replace bearings. If new bearings are properly fitted, correct clearance can be obtained without filing, shimming or scraping.

4) Using a dial indicator, check camshaft out-of-round. Camshaft must not exceed .0012" (.030 mm) out-of-round.

5) Check camshaft end play using a feeler gauge. Standard clearance is .001-.007" (.025-.178 mm). If wear limit of .008" (.20 mm) is exceeded, replace thrust plate.

### TIMING CHAIN

**Removal — 1)** Remove cylinder head and oil pan with engine removed from vehicle. Remove front cover and gaskets, then remove oil thrower from crankshaft. Remove chain tensioner, guide strip, and vibration damper.

2) Remove oil pump sprocket lock nut and washer. Remove crankshaft sprocket, oil pump drive chain, and oil pump sprocket. Remove crankshaft spacer, timing chain and crankshaft sprocket. Remove key and spacer from crankshaft.

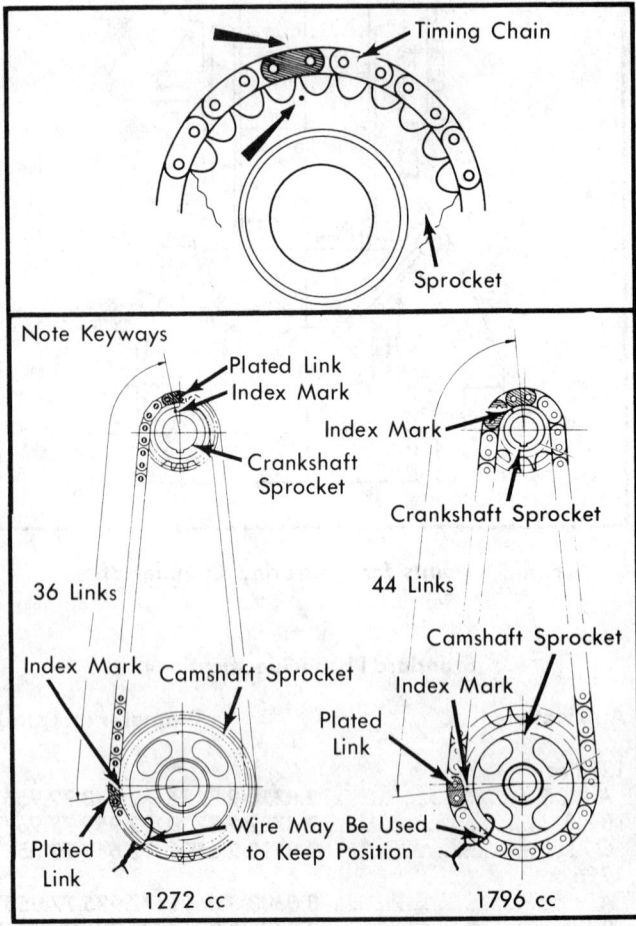

*Fig. 8   Alignment Marks of Timing Chain & Sprockets*

## B1800 & GLC 4 CYLINDER (Cont.)

**Installation** — 1) On 1272 cc models, install timing chain guide strip, but do not tighten attaching screws. Install vibration damper. On all models, install spacer and key onto crankshaft. Place timing chain on crankshaft and camshaft sprockets with index marks aligned.

**2)** Align crankshaft and its sprocket keyway, then fit sprocket onto crankshaft. Install crankshaft spacer. Fit key on oil pump shaft. Install oil pump drive chain onto oil pump and crankshaft sprockets, align keyway and install assembly onto crankshaft and oil pump shafts.

**3)** On 1272 cc models, tighten oil pump sprocket nut and bend tab of lockwasher. Install oil baffle plate a spacer onto crankshaft. On all other models, check the slack of oil pump drive chain. If slack exceeds .157" (4 mm), install adjusting shims between cylinder block and oil pump body. Tighten oil pump sprocket nut and bend tab of lockwasher.

*Fig. 9   Checking Oil Pump Chain Slack (1796 cc Engines Only)*

**4)** Compress snubber spring of chain tensioner fully and insert a plate to retain tension in this position. Install chain tensioner to cylinder block. On 1796 cc engines, install chain vibration damper and tighten attaching screws. Install chain guide strip, but do not tighten attaching screws at this time. Install oil deflector and seal into front cover. Install oil thrower on crankshaft with the edge facing forward.

**5)** On all models, fill oil seal lip with grease and install front cover. Install oil pan and gasket. Position camshaft sprocket and chain on top of chain guide strip and chain vibration damper. Install gasket and cylinder head to block. **NOTE** — *Make sure matching marks on chain and sprockets are aligned. Install camshaft and bearings to cylinder head.*

**6)** Install rocker arm assembly. Tighten cylinder head bolts. Rotate crankshaft in direction of rotation slightly. Press top of chain guide strip with a lever through opening in cylinder head, then tighten guide strip attaching screws through holes in front cover. Remove plate installed in chain tensioner and tensioner will be properly set. Install remaining components in reverse of removal procedure.

## ENGINE OILING

### ENGINE OILING SYSTEM

Oil is circulated under pressure by a rotor type pump. The pump is mounted on cylinder block inside the oil pan and is driven by crankshaft.

**Crankcase Capacity** — 3.2 quarts for 1272 cc engines and 3.8 quarts for 1796 cc engines.

**Oil Pressure** — 50-64 psi (3.5-4.5 kg/cm²) @ 3000 RPM.

**Oil Filter** — Full flow cartridge.

**Pressure Regulator Valve** — Nonadjustable.

### OIL PUMP

1) Check clearance between lobes of rotors with a feeler gauge. If clearance exceeds .010", replace both rotors.

*Fig. 10   1976 cc Oil Pump Assembly*

*Fig. 11   1272 cc Oil Pump Assembly*

# Mazda Engines

## B1800 & GLC 4 CYLINDER (Cont.)

**2)** Inspect clearance between outer rotor and pump body, using a feeler gauge. Maximum clearance is .012".

**3)** To check rotor ends, place a straightedge across pump body and measure clearance between rotor and straight edge, using a feeler gauge. Then place straightedge across cover and measure clearance between straight edge and cover.

### Oil Pump Specifications

| Application | Clearance In. (mm) |
|---|---|
| Rotor-to-Rotor | .002-.006 (.051-.152) |
| Rotor-to-Body | .006-.010 (.152-.254) |
| End Play | .002-.004 (.051-.102) |

## ENGINE COOLING

### WATER PUMP

**NOTE** — *It may be necessary to remove radiator.*

Remove bolts mounting fan and pulley to water pump. Remove nuts and bolts holding water pump to timing chain cover. Remove alternator bracket and water pump.

**Cooling System Capacity** — 5.9 quarts for 1272 cc models and 7.6 quarts for 1796 cc models.

**Thermostat** — Begins to open at 180°F (82°C) and is fully open at 203°F (95°C).

**Radiator Cap** — 13 psi.

## ENGINE SPECIFICATIONS

### GENERAL SPECIFICATIONS

| Year | Displ. cu. ins. | Displ. cc | Carburetor | HP at RPM | Torque (Ft. Lbs. at RPM) | Compr. Ratio | Bore in. | Bore mm | Stroke in. | Stroke mm |
|---|---|---|---|---|---|---|---|---|---|---|
| 1978 GLC | 77.6 | 1272 | 1x2-Bbl. | ..... | ..... | 9.2:1 | 2.87 | 73 | 2.99 | 76 |
| B1800 | 109.6 | 1796 | 1x2-Bbl. | ..... | ..... | 8.6:1 | 3.07 | 78 | 3.70 | 94 |

### VALVES

| Engine & Valve | Head Diam. ① In. (mm) | Face Angle | Seat Angle | Seat Width In. (mm) | Stem Diameter In. (mm) | Stem Clearance In. (mm) | Valve Lift In. (mm) |
|---|---|---|---|---|---|---|---|
| 1272 cc Intake | 1.4173 (35.99) | 45° | 45° | .055 (1.4) | .3162-.3168 (8.03-8.05) | .0007-.0021 (.018-.053) | ..... |
| Exhaust | 1.2205 (31.00) | 45° | 45° | .055 (1.4) | .3162-.3168 (8.03-8.05) | .0007-.0023 (.018-.058) | ..... |
| 1796 cc Intake | 1.6536 (42.00) | 45° | 45° | .055 (1.4) | .3162-.3168 (8.03-8.05) | .0007-.0021 (.018-.053) | ..... |
| Exhaust | 1.2992 (32.99) | 45° | 45° | .055 (1.4) | .3162-.3168 (8.03-8.05) | .0007-.0023 (.018-.058) | ..... |

① — Specification is ± .0039" (.099 mm).

### PISTONS, PINS, RINGS

| Engine | PISTONS Clearance In. (mm) | PINS ① Piston Fit In. (mm) | PINS Rod Fit In. (mm) | RINGS Rings | RINGS End Gap In. (mm) | RINGS Side Clearance In. (mm) |
|---|---|---|---|---|---|---|
| 1272 cc & 1796 cc | .0021-.0026 (.057-.066) ② | -.0006 to +.0002 (-.014 to +.005) | .0004-.0012 (.01-.03) | No. 1 | .008-.016 (.2-.4) | .0014-.0028 (.035-.070) |
| | | | | No. 2 | .008-.016 (.2-.4) | .0012-.0025 (.030-.064) |
| | | | | Oil | .008-.016③ (.2-.4) | .0012-.0024④ (.030-.062) |

① — In some instances it may be necessary to heat piston to insert pin.  ② — 1796 cc should be .0022-.0028" (.056-.071 mm).
③ — 1796 cc should be .012-.035" (.3-.9 mm).  ④ — 1272 cc only.

## B1800 & GLC 4 CYLINDER (Cont.)
### ENGINE SPECIFICATIONS (Cont.)

### CRANKSHAFT MAIN & CONNECTING ROD BEARINGS

| | MAIN BEARINGS | | | | CONNECTING ROD BEARINGS | | |
|---|---|---|---|---|---|---|---|
| Engine | Journal Diam. In. (mm) | Clearance In. (mm) | Thrust Bearing | Crankshaft End Play In. (mm) | Journal Diam. In. (mm) | Clearance In. (mm) | Side Play In. (mm) |
| 1272 cc | 2.4780-2.4786 (62.941-62.956) | .0012-.0024 (.030-.061) | No. 5 | .003-.009 (.08-.23) | 1.7693-1.7699 (44.940-44.955) | .0011-.0029 (.028-.074) | .004-.008 (.10-.20) |
| 1796 cc | 2.4780-2.4786 (62.939-62.954) | .0012-.0019 (.030-.050) | No. 5 | .003-.009 (.08-.23) | 2.0842-2.0848 (52.939-52.954) | .0011-.0030 (.028-.074) | .004-.008 (.10-.20) |

### VALVE SPRINGS

| Engine | Free Length In. (mm) | PRESSURE Lbs. @ In. (kg @ mm) | |
|---|---|---|---|
| | | Valve Closed | Valve Open |
| 1272 cc Inner | 1.449 (36.8) | 20.9 @ 1.26 (9.5 @ 32.0) | ..... |
| Outer | 1.587 (40.3) | 43.7 @ 1.319 (19.8 @ 33.5) | ..... |
| 1796 cc Inner | 1.449 (36.8) | 20.9 @ 1.26 (9.5 @ 32.0) | ..... |
| Outer | 1.469 (37.3) | 31.4 @ 1.339 (14.25 @ 34.0) | ..... |

### VALVE TIMING

| Engine | INTAKE | | EXHAUST | |
|---|---|---|---|---|
| | Open (BTDC) | Close (ALDC) | Open (BLDC) | Close (ATDC) |
| 1272 cc | 13° | 50° | 57° | 6° |
| 1796 cc | 18° | 49° | 62° | 5° |

### CAMSHAFT

| Engine | Journal Diam. In. (mm) | Clearance In. (mm)① | Lobe Lift In. (mm) |
|---|---|---|---|
| 1272 cc Front | 1.6516-1.6522 (41.950-41.966) | .0014-.0030 (.035-.076) | ..... |
| Center | 1.6504-1.6510 (41.920-41.936) | .0026-.0042 (.065-.106) | ..... |
| Rear | 1.6516-1.6522 (41.950-41.966) | .0014-.0030 (.035-.076) | ..... |
| 1796 cc Front | 1.7695-1.7701 (44.946-44.961) | .0007-.0027 (.019-.069) | ..... |
| Center | 1.7691-1.7697 (44.936-44.951) | .0011-.0031 (.029-.079) | ..... |
| Rear | 1.7695-1.7701 (44.946-44.961) | .0007-.0027 (.019-.069) | ..... |

① — End play is .001-.007" (.025-.178 mm).

### TIGHTENING SPECIFICATIONS

| Application | Ft. Lbs. (mkg) |
|---|---|
| **1272 cc** | |
| Cylinder Head | |
|   Cold | 47-51 (6.5-7.0) |
|   Hot | 51-54 (7.0-7.5) |
| Main Bearing Cap | 43-47 (6.0-6.5) |
| Connecting Rod Cap | 29-33 (4.0-4.5) |
| Oil Pump Sprocket | 22-25 (3.0-3.5) |
| Camshaft Sprocket | 51-58 (7.0-8.0) |
| Crankshaft Pulley | 80-87 (11.0-12.0) |
| Distributor Drive Gear | 51-58 (7.0-8.0) |
| Intake Manifold | 14-19 (1.9-2.6) |
| Exhaust Manifold | 12-17 (1.6-2.3) |
| **1796 cc** | |
| Cylinder Head | |
|   Cold | 56-60 (7.7-8.3) |
|   Hot | 69-72 (9.5-10.0) |
| Main Bearing Cap | 61-65 (8.4-9.0) |
| Connecting Rod Cap | 36-40 (5.0-5.5) |
| Oil Pump Sprocket | 22-25 (3.0-3.5) |
| Camshaft Sprocket | 51-58 (7.0-8.0) |
| Crankshaft Pulley | 101-108 (14.0-14.9) |
| Distributor Drive Gear | 51-58 (7.0-8.0) |
| Intake Manifold | 14-19 (1.9-2.6) |
| Exhaust Manifold | 16-21 (2.2-2.9) |

## RX-4 & COSMO ROTARY ENGINE

### ENGINE CODING

**ENGINE IDENTIFICATION**

Engine identification number is stamped on the front engine housing behind the distributor. Engines are identified with code numbers as follows:

**Engine Codes**

| Application | Code |
|---|---|
| RX-4 & Cosmo | 13B |

### ENGINE REMOVAL

**ENGINE REMOVAL**

1) Disconnect negative battery cable and drain cooling system and engine oil. Disconnect primary wiring coupler and high tension wires from ignition coils. Disconnect wire at "B" terminal of alternator and remove coupler from rear of alternator. Disconnect coupler from vacuum control valve (manual transmission).

2) Disconnect bullet connector from choke heater lead of carburetor. Remove couplers from water temperature switch,

*Fig. 1  Exploded View of Rotors & Eccentric Shaft Assembly*

## RX-4 & COSMO ROTARY ENGINE (Cont.)

vacuum switch (automatic transmission), A/C solenoid valve, and from deceleration control valve.

3) Remove connector from EGR solenoid (California). Disconnect couplers to transmission at rear of engine, from oil thermo sensor (except California), and from oil level sensor lead. Disconnect connector from water temperature gauge unit.

4) Remove positive cable from "B" terminal and ignition switch wire from "S" terminal of starting motor. Disconnect vacuum sensing hose from No. 2 vacuum switch (California). Remove air cleaner assembly. Pull couplers from idle switch and air control valve. Disconnect coupler from richer solenoid (manual transmission) and from power valve solenoid

5) Remove fuel line and fuel return line from carburetor. Disconnect accelerator and choke cables from carburetor. Remove sub-zero starting assist hose (except California). Disconnect vacuum sensing hose from vacuum line (automatic transmission), and vacuum sensing line for power brakes from inlet manifold.

6) Disconnect air hose to heat exchanger at inlet manifold. Remove A/C compressor, cooling fan and fan drive assembly. Remove upper and lower radiator hoses. Disconnect automatic transmission fluid lines at radiator. Disconnect heater hoses from radiator and rear housing and hoses from oil cooler. Remove expansion tank cap and radiator.

7) Remove secondary air line from heat exchanger to thermal reactor and pipe from exchanger to inlet manifold. Disconnect exhaust pipe from thermal reactor and remove gasket. Remove exhaust pipe hanger from transmission bracket. Remove clutch release cylinder from clutch housing. Remove starting motor. Remove transmission-to-engine bolts, while supporting transmission with suitable jack.

8) Remove nuts from right and left engine mounts. Install lifting sling on engine hanger brackets and hoist slightly to take up slack. Pull engine forward until it clears clutch shaft. Lift engine from vehicle.

9) To install engine, reverse removal procedure.

### ENGINE DISASSEMBLY

**NOTE** — *To simplify engine disassembly, manufacturer recommends use of a special engine stand (49 0839 000 or 49 0107 680A) and special hanger (49 1114 005) for supporting the front housing. See Fig. 2. Also note that this front housing support may be used on previous engines (where rear housing support units were previously used).*

1) Remove oil hose support bracket from front housing, then mount engine on stand and front housing support. Remove engine hanger bracket from front cover. Disconnect vacuum hoses, air hoses and wiring. Remove deceleration valve and vacuum control valve. Remove air pump and drive belt. Remove alternator and belt.

2) Disconnect metering oil pump connecting rod and oil tubes. Remove inlet manifold and carburetor as an assembly. Remove manifold gasket and "O" rings. Remove thermal reac-

tor (exhaust manifold), distributor, engine mounts and oil filter assembly. Remove eccentric shaft pulley for compressor.

**NOTE** — *Further disassembly requires attachment of braking tool (49 1881 060) to flywheel of manual transmission equipped vehicles or stopping tool (49 1881 055) to counterweight of automatic transmission equipped vehicles.*

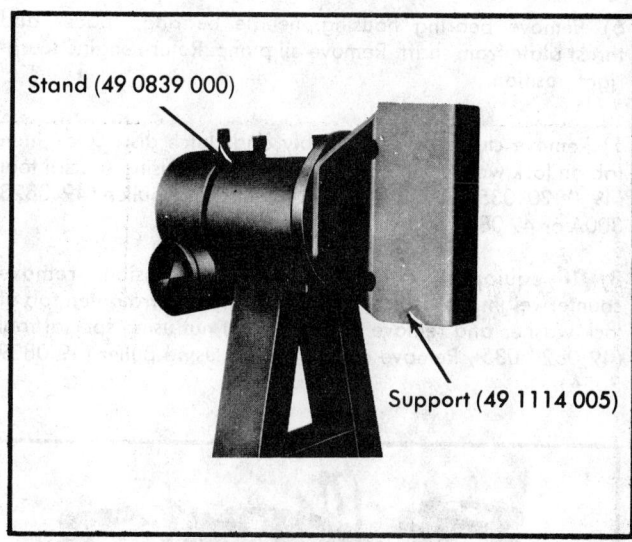

Stand (49 0839 000)

Support (49 1114 005)

**Fig. 2   Engine Stand & Hanger Support**

3) Remove water pump and gasket. Invert engine on stand and remove oil pan, gasket and strainer with gasket.

**NOTE** — *When removing oil pan, pry upward using two screwdrivers, one on each side of oil pan and just in front of tapered corners on flywheel end.*

4) Mark front and rear housings for installation in their original positions. Return engine to upright position. Unscrew eccentric shaft pulley bolt and remove pulley.

**Fig. 3   Removing Sprocket & Chain from Engine**

## RX-4 & COSMO ROTARY ENGINE (Cont.)

5) Turn engine so that front end is up. Remove front cover with gasket. Remove "O" ring from oil passage on front housing. Slide distributor drive gear off shaft. Remove chain adjuster. Remove oil pump sprocket lock washer and nut. Slide oil pump sprocket and eccentric shaft sprocket and drive chain off shafts simultaneously. See Fig. 3. Remove keys from shafts. Slide balance weight, thrust washer and needle bearing off shaft.

6) Remove bearing housing, needle bearing, spacer and thrust plate from shaft. Remove oil pump. Return engine to upright position.

7) Remove clutch cover assembly and clutch disc. Straighten tab on lock washer and remove flywheel nut using special tool (49 0820 035). Remove the flywheel using puller (49 0823 300A or 49 0839 305A).

8) If equipped with automatic transmission, remove counterweight. To do so, remove drive plate. Straighten tab of lock washer and remove counterweight nut using special tool (49 0820 035). Remove counterweight, using puller (49 0839 305A).

**Fig. 4    Loosening Sequence of Tension Bolts**

9) Turn rear of engine upward. Loosen tension bolts in sequence shown in Fig. 4, doing so in two or three steps. Remove bolts and lift rear housing off shaft. Remove any seals stuck to rotor sliding surface of rear housing, and replace them in original positions. Remove and discard two sealing rubbers and two "O" rings from rear side of rear rotor housing.

10) Attach dowel puller (49 0813 215A). Pull tubular dowels (See Fig. 5) from rear rotor housing. Hold housing with hand to prevent it from turning or pulling upward. Lift rear rotor housing away from rotor, being careful not to drop apex seals off rear rotor. Remove and discard two sealing rubbers and two "O" rings from front side of rear rotor housing.

**Fig. 5    Extracting Tubular Dowels from Engine**

11) Remove side pieces, apex seals and springs from rear rotor and store in order for reassembly. Remove all corner seals, corner seal springs, side seals and side seal springs and store in order for later reassembly.

12) Remove rear rotor from eccentric shaft and place it upside down on a clean sheet of cloth. Remove seals and springs from remaining side of rear rotor and store in order for reassembly.

**Fig. 6    Prying Oil Seal from Rotor**

13) Mark each rotor as to front or rear. Remove oil seals from rear rotor using suitable prying tool (49 0813 225), Fig. 6, being careful not to damage oil seal lip.

**NOTE** — Do not exert strong force at any one point in removing seal. Mark rear oil seal springs of each rotor to aid in repositioning them upon reassembly.

14) Holding intermediate housing down by hand, pull tubular dowel from intermediate housing, using dowel puller (49 0813 215A). See Fig. 5. Lift intermediate housing from shaft. To do so, hold housing up off front housing, while helper pushes upward on eccentric shaft. Lift out eccentric shaft.

15) Repeat procedures 10) through 14) to remove front rotor housing and rotor assembly.

## RX-4 & COSMO ROTARY ENGINE (Cont.)

### INSPECTION & OVERHAUL

#### FRONT, INTERMEDIATE & REAR HOUSINGS

**1)** To clean front housing, use extra fine emery paper to remove carbon deposits from rotor running surface. Use ketone or thinner to remove sealing agent.

**2)** Inspect housing for signs of water or gas leakage. Check for wear or damage to rotor running surface or stationary gear. Check main bearings for signs of scoring or flaking.

**3)** Place a straightedge across housing surface in positions shown in illustration. Using a feeler gauge, measure distortion of front housing. Replace or reface housing if distortion limit of .0016" (.04 mm) is exceeded, (Fig. 7).

**Fig. 7   Straightedge Positions for Checking Housing Distortion**

**4)** Check for wear on rotor sliding surfaces of housing and joint surfaces with rotor housing. Measurements are made us-

**Fig. 8   Measuring Housing Wear with a Dial Indicator**

ing a dial indicator, *Fig. 8.* If wear exceeds .0039" (.10 mm), reface or replace housing.

**NOTE** — *Side housings (front, intermediate and rear housings) can be reused by grinding them, if the required finish can be maintained.*

**5)** Measure inner diameter of main bearing and outer diameter of bearing journal on eccentric shaft. Standard clearance is .0016-.0028" (.04-.07 mm). If clearance exceeds .0039" (.10 mm), replace bearing or eccentric shaft.

**6)** To replace main bearing, remove stationary gear retaining bolts. Drive stationary gear, with bearing, out of housing using a suitable mandrel (49 0813 235).

**7)** Place stationary gear in a press, use same mandrel and press main bearing out of stationary gear. Install new bearing while aligning tang of bearing with slot of stationary gear. Press bearing into gear until adapter of mandrel just contacts stationary gear flange. Drive stationary gear into housing with same mandrel. Align dowel pin on housing with slot in gear flange, (Fig. 9). Tighten stationary gear retaining bolts.

**NOTE** — *When installing rear main bearing, check condition of "O" ring and replace if necessary. Apply sealing agent on stationary gear flange prior to installing it on rear housing. Align pin and slot.*

**Fig. 9   Stationary Gear Slot & Dowel Alignment**

### ROTOR HOUSING, INTERMEDIATE HOUSING, & ROTOR

#### ROTOR HOUSINGS

**1)** To clean housing, wipe off sealing agent or carbon in rotor running surface with a rag and ketone or thinner. Remove rust deposits in water cooling passages.

**2)** Inspect for cracks or damage to chromium plated surface. Check for signs of gas or water leakage. Housing must be replaced if any of these conditions exist.

**3)** Place a straightedge across sealing surface of rotor housing and check for distortion, using a feeler gauge. If distortion exceeds .0016" (.04 mm), replace housing. See Fig. 10.

# Mazda Engines

## RX-4 & COSMO ROTARY ENGINE (Cont.)

*Fig. 10  Measuring Rotor Housing for Distortion*

4) Check rotor housing thickness at points A, B, C, and D in *Fig. 11*. If micrometer readings vary between point A and minimum value for B, C, and D by more than .0024" (.06 mm), replace rotor housing.

**NOTE** — *This excessive clearance would indicate a possibility of gas or water leakage.*

### ROTORS

1) Combustion condition of rotor can be determined by analyzing color of combustion area before cleaning. General color of combustion area should be brown.

2) Combustion is correct if leading side area of rotor combustion area is brown and trailing side is a blackish color. Check side surface of rotor for signs of gas leakage.

3) Inspect oil seals and replace if necessary. Remove carbon from rotor with fine emery paper. Remove carbon from seal grooves with a carbon remover. Wash rotor in a cleaning solution and blow dry, with compressed air. Inspect rotor for wear or damage and check internal gear for cracking or chipped teeth.

*Fig. 11  Rotor Housing Thickness Check Points*

4) Measure width of rotor at three points around edge. Subtract maximum rotor width from width of rotor housing at point A, *(Fig. 11)*. Difference should be within .0039-.0083" (.10-.21 mm). If clearance is excessive, replace rotor assembly. If less than specified, internal gear has probably come out. Strike internal gear lightly with plastic hammer and remeasure clearance.

5) Measure inner diameter of rotor bearing and outside diameter of rotor bearing journal on eccentric shaft. Replace rotor bearing if clearance exceeds .0039" (.10 mm). *See Rotor Bearing Replacement.*

## OIL SEALS

### ROTOR OIL SEAL

With oil seal installed in rotor, measure contact lip width of seal. Seal must be replaced if contact width exceeds .031" (.8 mm). Measure seal protrusion *(See Fig. 12)* and replace seal spring if protrusion is less than .020" (.5 mm).

*Fig. 12  Measuring Point of Oil Seal Protrusion*

### ROTOR BEARING REPLACEMENT

Place rotor bearing on support so internal gear is facing downward. Using rotor bearing replacer (49 0813 240) without adapter ring, press bearing out of rotor, *(Fig. 13)*. Clean bearing bore with emery paper if necessary. Place rotor on support with internal gear upward. Place a new rotor bearing so slot in rotor bore is in line with bearing lug. Press new bearing (using tool without adaptor), until bearing is flush with rotor boss.

*Fig. 13  Pressing Rotor Bearing from Rotor*

## RX-4 & COSMO ROTARY ENGINE (Cont.)

### APEX SEAL

1) Clean all carbon from apex seal and spring with a cleaning solution (not emery paper). Measure height of apex seal with a micrometer (see illustration). Replace seal if height is less than .275" (7.0 mm).

**Fig. 14   Measuring Apex Seal Height**

2) Check gap between apex seal and groove. To check gap, place apex seal in its respective groove on rotor and measure gap between apex seal and groove with a feeler gauge. Feeler gauge should be inserted until tip of gauge reaches bottom of groove. Standard clearance is .0020-.0035" (.05-.09 mm). If gap exceeds wear limit of .0059" (.15 mm), replace apex seal.

3) When installing new apex seal, check gap between seal and side housing. Measure length of seal with micrometer and subtract length from rotor housing width at point A, (Fig. 11). Clearance should be .0051-.0067" (.13-.17 mm). If seal length is excessive, correct with emery paper.

4) Be sure free height of apex seal spring (Fig. 15), is at least .22" (5.5 mm) on RX-3 models and .15" (3.8 mm) on other models.

**Fig. 15   Measuring Free Height of Apex Seal Spring**

### SIDE SEAL

1) Remove all carbon from side seal and spring. Check side seal protrusion from rotor surface, and confirm free movement by pressing with finger. Protrusion should be more than .02" (.5 mm). Check gap between side seal and groove with a feeler gauge. Standard gap is .0016-.0028" (.04-.07 mm). If wear limit of .004" (.10 mm) is measured, replace side seal.

2) Check gap between side seal and corner seal with seals installed on rotor. Insert feeler gauge between end of side seal (against rotating direction of rotor) and the corner seal. If gap exceeds .016" (.4 mm), replace side seal.

3) When side seal is replaced, adjust gap between side seal and corner seal by grinding one end of side seal along round shape of corner seal, using a fine file. Make gap .002-.006" (.05-.15 mm).

### CORNER SEAL

1) Clean carbon from corner seal. Check corner seal protrusion from rotor surface, and check free movement by pressing with finger. Protrusion should be more than .02" (.5 mm).

2) Check gap between corner seal and seal groove. Gap limit is .0031" (.08 mm). A gap this large indicates uneven wear of corner seal groove caused by dirt entering engine (due to damaged or clogged air cleaner).

**Fig. 17   Checking Corner Seal Groove Measurement**

**Fig. 16   Measuring Clearance of Apex, Side & Corner Seals**

# Mazda Engines

## RX-4 & COSMO ROTARY ENGINE (Cont.)

**3)** Extent of corner seal groove wear is determined by using special Bar Limit Gauge (49 0839 165), and is classified according to the following:

**Neither End of Gauge Goes Into Groove** — Indicates that gap conforms to specifications.

**"Go" End of Gauge Goes Into Groove** — Indicates that gap is more than standard, but less than wear limit. In this case replace corner seal, (Fig. 17).

**Both Ends of Gauge ("Go" and "No Go") Go in Groove** — Indicates gap exceeds wear limit of .0031" (.8 mm). Replace rotor.

## ECCENTRIC SHAFT MAIN & ROTOR BEARINGS

### ECCENTRIC SHAFT

**1)** Thoroughly clean eccentric shaft in a suitable cleaning solution and blow out oil passages with compressed air. Inspect shaft for scratching or scoring of bearing journals and possible blocked oil passages.

**2)** Check rotor bearing clearance by measuring inner diameter of the rotor bearing and outer diameter of the eccentric shaft rotor journal. Clearance should be .0016-.0031" (.04-.08 mm). Replace the bearing if clearance exceeds .0039" (.10 mm). Replace eccentric shaft if journal diameters are under specified limits.

**3)** Place eccentric shaft in two "V" blocks. Mount a dial indicator and check runout of both ends by rotating shaft slowly. If runout exceeds .0024" (.06 mm), replace shaft.

**4)** Oil passages in eccentric shaft are sealed by a blind plug in rear of shaft. Inspect plug for possible oil leakage. If leakage is detected, remove plug with an Allen wrench and install new "O" ring. Tighten plug.

**5)** Inspect needle bearings in end of shaft for wear or damage. Check for spring weakness, stuck, or damaged steel ball at the oil jets. Inspect front needle bearing, bearing housing, and thrust plate for wear or damage. Inspect front and rear oil seals for leaks, replace as necessary.

## ENGINE ASSEMBLY

### OIL SEALS

**1)** Place rotor on rubber pad or cloth. Install oil seal springs in their respective grooves on rotors, with each edge of spring fitted in stopper hole. Ensure oil seal springs have been painted in cream or blue color: cream colored springs must be placed on front faces of both rotors and blue springs on rear faces of rotors. When installing, painted side of spring must face oil seal (upward), Fig. 18.

**2)** Insert new "O" ring in each oil seal. Install inner oil seal to each side of rotor as follows: Position oil seal to groove so square edge of spring fits in stopper notch of oil seal. Press into position by using a used inner oil seal so lip of inner oil

seal sinks into position approximately .016" (.4 mm) below surface of rotor.

**Fig. 18   Installing Oil Seal Spring on Rotor**

**3)** Install outer oil seal so square edge of spring fits in stopper notch of oil seal. Push head of oil seal in position slowly with fingers. **NOTE** — *Take care not to deform lip of oil seal.* Apply sufficient lubricant to each oil seal and groove, and confirm smooth movement of each seal by pressing head of seals. Check oil seal protrusion. *See Rotor Oil Seal Replacement.*

### APEX, CORNER & SIDE SEALS

**NOTE** — *Before installing apex seal, cut the assist piece with a knife to a length of .08-.10" (2.0-2.8 mm). Peel off paper and install assist piece on apex seal, Fig. 19.*

**Fig. 19   Installing Assist Piece on Apex Seal**

**1)** Position apex seals, without springs, and side pieces into their respective grooves so that each side piece rests on rear side of each rotor. Place corner seals and springs into their respective grooves, then position side seals and springs in proper grooves.

## RX-4 & COSMO ROTARY ENGINE (Cont.)

**2)** Apply engine lubricant to each spring. Ensure smooth movement of each spring. Check seal protusion, as described previously. Invert rotor and install seals on other side of rotor.

### INSTALLING FRONT ROTOR

**1)** Mount front housing on work stand (49 0839 000) and special hanger (49 1114 005). Turn front housing on stand so that top of housing is upward. Apply engine lubricant to internal gear of rotor. Hold apex seals in place by using the old "O" ring and position rotor assembly on front housing. Turn housing so that sliding surface of front housing faces upward.

**Fig. 20   Positioning Rotor Apex for Reassembly**

**2)** Mesh internal gear and stationary gear so that one of the rotor apexes is set to any one of the four positions as illustrated. Remove old "O" ring. See Fig. 20.

**NOTE** — *Take care not to drop corner seals into ports.*

### INSTALLING ECCENTRIC SHAFT

Lubricate front rotor journal and main journal on shaft with engine lubricant. Insert eccentric shaft being careful not to damage rotor bearing and main bearing.

### INSTALLING FRONT ROTOR HOUSING

**NOTE** — *Front and rear rotor housings are not interchangeable. Be sure they are installed in correct sequence.*

**Fig. 21   Applying Sealing Agent to Rotor Assembly**

**1)** Apply sealing agent to front side of front rotor housing in areas shown in *Fig. 21*. Do not use cooling system sealers.

**Fig. 22   Installing Protectors for Inner Sealing Rubbers**

**2)** To provide greater durability to sealing rubbers, install a protector behind each inner sealing rubber, *(Fig. 22)*. Install new "O" ring, sealing rubbers and protector in front side of rotor housing. Apply a light coating of petroleum jelly to hold them in place.

**Fig. 23   Positioning Inner Sealing Rubber**

**NOTE** — *Inner sealing rubber is square type. The wider white line of sealing rubber should face toward combustion chamber and seam of rubber should be placed as shown in Fig. 23. Do not stretch sealing rubbers.*

**3)** Invert front rotor housing, being careful of seals, and install it on front housing. Apply engine lubricant to dowels and insert them through front rotor housing into front housing. Install new "O" rings, sealing rubbers and protector to rear side of front housing.

**4)** Insert apex seal springs, confirming spring direction, *Fig 16*. Install corner seal springs and corner seals in their respective grooves. Install side seal springs and side seals. Fit side pieces to their original positions. Apply engine oil to all seals. Apply sealant to rear side of front rotor housing in areas shown in *Fig. 21*. Apply engine oil to sliding surfaces of front rotor housing.

## RX-4 & COSMO ROTARY ENGINE (Cont.)

### INSTALLING INTERMEDIATE HOUSING

Turn front housing and rotor assembly so that top of housing is upward. Pull eccentric shaft outward approximately 1.0" (25 mm), but not more than 1.5" (38 mm). Rotate eccentric shaft until eccentric portion points to 2 o'clock position. Install intermediate housing over eccentric shaft and turn engine so that rear of engine is upward.

### INSTALLING REAR ROTOR & HOUSING

Use same procedures up to *Intermediate Housing* when installing rear rotor and rotor housing.

### INSTALLING REAR HOUSING

Position engine with rear end upward. Apply sufficient lubricant onto stationary gear and main bearing. Install rear housing onto rear rotor housing, and turn rear rotor slightly to engage rear housing stationary gear with rear rotor internal gear.

### TIGHTENING TENSION BOLTS

Place a new sealing washer on each tension bolt and oil threads of each bolt. Refer to illustration and tighten bolts in sequence shown in *Fig. 24*. Tighten bolts in steps until final torque setting of 23-27 ft. lbs. (3.2-3.8 mkg) is reached. After tightening, turn eccentric shaft and make sure rotation is light and smooth.

**Fig. 24  Tightening Sequence of Tension Bolts**

### FLYWHEEL COUNTERWEIGHT INSTALLATION

**With Man. Trans. — 1)** Apply lubricant to oil seal in rear housing. Mount flywheel to rear end of eccentric shaft so that key fits into flywheel keyway. Apply sealing agent to both sides of flywheel lock washer, and place washer in position. Fit lock nut by fingers. Hold flywheel with suitable ring gear brake tool (49 1881 060) and tighten lock nut to 289-362 ft. lbs. (40-50 mkg). Bend up lock tabs on washer.

**2)** Hold clutch disc in position with clutch disc centering tool (49 0813 310). Mount clutch cover and pressure plate assembly on flywheel and align the "0" marks of clutch cover and flywheel. Install 4 standard and 2 reamer bolts finger tight. To avoid distortion of pressure plate cover, tighten bolts in steps, a few turns at a time, until all are tight. Torque bolts to 13-20 ft. lbs. (1.8-2.7 mkg).

**With Auto. Trans. —** Fit key, lock washer and lock nut on eccentric shaft as described for Man. Trans. vehicles. Hold counterweight with suitable tool (49 1881 055) and tighten lock nut to 289-362 ft. lbs. (40-50 mkg). Bend tab of lock washer and attach drive plate on counterweight.

### ECCENTRIC SHAFT END-THRUST ADJUSTMENT

**1)** Turn engine so front is up. Install thrust plate with chamfer downward, and slide spacer and needle bearing on eccentric shaft. Lubricate shaft and bearings and install bearing housing.

**NOTE** — *If bearing housing has not been removed, use care that center of needle bearing in bearing housing comes to center of eccentric shaft and that spacer is seated to thrust plate.*

**2)** Lubricate and install needle bearing, thrust washer, and balance weight on shaft. Install keys in oil pump and eccentric shaft keyways. Place oil pump drive chain on oil pump sprocket and eccentric shaft sprocket, and install sprockets on shafts.

**3)** Install key in eccentric shaft. Install distributor drive gear, with "F" mark on gear, facing front of engine. Install eccentric shaft pulley on shaft. Use new washer and tighten pulley bolt to 54-69 ft. lbs. (7.5-9.5 mkg).

**Fig. 25  Measuring Eccentric Shaft End Play with a Dial Indicator**

**4)** Turn engine so top is upward. Attach a dial indicator on the flywheel or counterweight so it contacts rear housing. Move flywheel or counterweight back and forth. Standard end play is .0016-.0028" (.04-.07 mm). If end play is more than .0035" (.09 mm) grind spacer on surface plate with

## RX-4 & COSMO ROTARY ENGINE (Cont.)

emery paper or install thinner spacer. If end play is less than .0016" (.04 mm), install thicker spacer.

5) Oversize spacers are available in four oversizes from .3181" to .3150" (8.08 mm to 8.00 mm) and are identified by stamped letter "X", "Y", "V", and "Z" respectively. When spacer has been installed, recheck end play.

**NOTE** — *If end play is below specified amount, spacer thickness is too small; if end play is beyond specifications, spacer is too thick.*

6) When end play is within specifications, remove eccentric shaft pulley and proceed with engine assembly.

### INSTALLING FRONT COVER & ECCENTRIC SHAFT PULLEY

Turn engine so front is upward. Remove eccentric shaft pulley. Tighten oil pump sprocket nut and bend tab of lock washer. Place chain adjuster in position and tighten attaching nuts. Check that plunger extends .47" (12 mm). *(See Fig. 27).* If measurement is less, replace adjuster or chain. Install new "O" ring on front housing oil passage and install guide plate over chain adjuster. Install front cover and gasket on front housing. Lubricate oil seal in front cover. Install eccentric shaft pulley, using a new washer. Torque to 54-69 ft. lbs. (7.5-9.5 mkg).

### INSTALLING OIL STRAINER & OIL PAN

Invert engine so bottom of engine is up. Install oil strainer gasket and strainer on front housing. Cut off excess gaskets along mounting surface of oil pan. Apply sealant to joints of each housing. Place gasket and oil pan in position and torque bolts to 5-7 ft. lbs. (.7-1.0 mkg) evenly.

### INSTALLING WATER PUMP

Turn engine upright, position gasket and water pump on front housing and tighten attaching bolts. **NOTE** — *For further information on cooling system components, see Cooling System in this article.*

### INSTALLING DISTRIBUTOR

Rotate eccentric shaft until yellow mark (leading timing mark) on pulley aligns with indicator pin on front cover. Align notch on distributor housing with punch mark on driven gear. Insert distributor so that lock bolt is located in center of its slot; then engage distributor gears. Rotate distributor to the right until contact points close. Then, turn left and stop when contact points just begin to separate. Tighten lock nut and install rotor and cap.

### INSTALLING EXTERNAL COMPONENTS

Install thermal reactor, inlet manifold with carburetor, alternator and drive belt, air pump and drive belt, oil filter assembly and all other external components. Before removing engine from stand, install engine hanger bracket to front cover.

## ENGINE OILING

**Crankcase Capacity**
RX-4 and Cosmo — 5.3 quarts without filter change.

**Oil Filter** — Full-flow, disposable cartridge-type filter mounted on rear housing.

**Normal Oil Pressure** — 14-54 psi at engine idle speed; 64-79 psi at 3000 RPM.

**Pressure Regulator Valve** — Mounted in rear housing, valve regulates oil pressure at high RPM. Valve opens to release oil pressure. If oil pressure is less than normal, check regulator valve piston for wear and ensure that spring free length is 1.83" (46.4 mm).

## ENGINE OILING SYSTEM

Engine oiling system is forced circulation utilizing a two rotor type oil pump. Oil pump is mounted on front housing and is chain driven through eccentric shaft. A full-flow oil filter is mounted on rear housing. An oil metering pump, pressure regulator valve and an oil cooler in radiator are also employed.

*Fig. 26  Cutaway View of Engine Oiling System*

## OIL PUMP

**NOTE** — *Oil pump is mounted on front engine housing and must be checked or overhauled with front engine cover removed.*

1) With front engine cover removed, check chain adjuster. If it extends more than .47" (12 mm) from housing, replace chain or adjuster *Fig. 27.*

# Mazda Engines

## RX-4 & COSMO ROTARY ENGINE (Cont.)

**Fig. 27 Measuring Oil Pump Drive Chain Tensioner Extension**

.47"
(12mm)

2) With oil pump removed, remove snap ring, rear rotors and key from shaft. Remove middle plate lock screw and middle plate.

**Fig. 28 Measuring Rotor Lobe Clearance**

3) Insert a feeler gauge between lobes of inner and outer rotors and check clearance (Fig. 28). If beyond .006" (.15 mm), replace both rotors.

Oil Pump Chain
Chain Adjuster Assembly
Outer Rotor
Snap Ring
Keys
Middle Plate
Shaft
Inner Rotor
Pump Body
Lock Screw
Oil Pump Driven Sprocket

**Fig. 29 Exploded View of Oil Pump Assembly**

4) Check clearance between outer rotor and pump housing with a feeler gauge. If clearance exceeds .012" (.30 mm), replace rotors or housing.

5) Place a straightedge across pump mounting surface and check rotor end play with a feeler gauge. If beyond .006" (.15 mm), correct pump body or replace rotors.

6) To assemble oil pump, reverse disassembly procedure. Install oil pump and tighten bolts. Install sprockets and chain as previously outlined. *See Eccentric Shaft Endthrust Adjustment.*

### METERING OIL PUMP

Metering oil pump regulates amount of oil pumped to float chamber of carburetor. The oil enters combustion chamber with air/fuel mixture to lubricate seals within chamber. Amount of oil increases as engine RPM increases and the control lever on metering pump is actuated by a rod connected to throttle lever. To check amount of oil discharge proceed as follows:

1) Disconnect connecting rod, then disconnect oil lines at carburetor. Start engine and adjust idle to 2000 RPM. Once oil flow from hoses becomes steady, measure volume discharged. Pump should discharge .068-.085 oz. (2.0-2.5 cc) in six minutes.

**NOTE** — *As carburetor will not be receiving oil during test, add a small amount of clean oil to carburetor to provide proper lubrication during testing.*

2) To adjust oil metering pump, turn the adjusting screw clockwise to increase flow or counterclockwise to decrease flow. One complete turn will change oil discharge flow by .0068 ounces for six minutes of operation. Make sure lock nut of adjustment screw is locked, then recheck metering oil pump discharge rate.

### ENGINE COOLING

**Thermostat** — Wax Pellet Type

**RX-4 and Cosmo** — 180°F (82°C).

**Cooling System Capacity** — 10.6 quarts.

**Pressure Cap** — 13 psi.

### WATER PUMP

1) Drain cooling system and remove air cleaner. Remove attaching bolts and drive fan. Loosen water pump pulley bolts. Remove air pump and drive belt.

2) Remove alternator and drive belt. Remove water pump pulley bolts and pulley. Remove water pump attaching nuts and bolts, then remove water pump. To install, reverse removal procedure.

# Mazda Engines

## RX-4 & COSMO ROTARY ENGINE (Cont.)
### ENGINE SPECIFICATIONS

### GENERAL SPECIFICATIONS

| Engine | cu. ins. | cc | Carburetor | HP at RPM | Torque (Ft. Lbs. at RPM) | Compr. Ratio | Rotor Housing Width in. | mm |
|---|---|---|---|---|---|---|---|---|
| Rotary | 40 | 654 | 4-Bbl. | ..... | ..... | 9.2-1 | 3.150 | 80 |

### ROTOR HOUSING, INTERMEDIATE HOUSING & ROTOR

| Engine | ROTOR HOUSING Width In. (mm) | Distortion Limit In. (mm) | INTERMEDIATE HOUSING Width In. (mm) | Distortion Limit In. (mm) | Inside Diameter In.(mm) | ROTOR Housing-to-Rotor Clearance In. mm) | Land Protrusion In. (mm) |
|---|---|---|---|---|---|---|---|
| Rotary | 3.150 (80) | .0024 (.06) | ..... | .0024 (.06) | ..... | 0039-.0083 (.10-.21) | ..... |

### OIL SEAL

| Height In. (mm) | Seal Lip Contact Width Standard In. (mm) | Limit In. (mm) |
|---|---|---|
| .220 (5.6) | .008 (.2) | .031 (.8) |

### SEAL SPRINGS

| Engine | Spring | Free Height In. (mm) |
|---|---|---|
| Rotary | Apex | .185 (4.7) |
| | Side | .075 (1.9) |
| | Corner | .098 (2.5) |
| | Inner Oil | .110 (2.8) |
| | Outer Oil | .102 (2.6) |

### ① APEX SEAL

| Engine | Length | Seal Width | Height | Seal-to-Housing Clearance | Wear Limit | Seal-to-Rotor Groove Clearance | Wear Limit |
|---|---|---|---|---|---|---|---|
| Rotary | 3.1438 (79.85) | .118 (3) | .335 (8.5) | .0051-.0067 (.13-.17) | .0012 (.30) | .0020-.0035 (.051-.089) | .006 (.15) |

① – In. (mm)

### SIDE SEAL

| Engine | Thickness In. (mm) | Width In. (mm) | Seal-to-Groove Clearance In. (mm) | Limit In. (mm) | Side Seal-to-Corner Seal Clearance In. (mm) | Limit In. (mm) |
|---|---|---|---|---|---|---|
| All | .039 (1) | .138 (3.5) | .0012-.0028 (.04-.07) | .004 (.10) | .0020-.0059 (.05-.15) | .016 (.40) |

### CORNER SEAL

| Engine | Diameter In. (mm) | Width In. (mm) | Seal-to-Groove Clearance In. (mm) | Limit In. (mm) | Side Seal-to-Corner Seal Clearance In. (mm) | Limit In. (mm) |
|---|---|---|---|---|---|---|
| All | .433 (11) | .276 (7) | .0008-.0019 (.020-.048) | .0031 (.08) | .0020-.0059 (.05-.15) | .016 (.40) |

# Mazda Engines

## RX-4 & COSMO ROTARY ENGINE (Cont.)

### ENGINE SPECIFICATIONS (Cont.)

| ECCENTRIC SHAFT MAIN & ROTOR BEARINGS | | | | | |
|---|---|---|---|---|---|
| | MAIN BEARINGS | | | ROTOR BEARINGS | |
| Engine | Journal Diameter In. (mm) | Clearance In. (mm) | Eccentric Shaft Endplay In. (mm) | Journal Diameter In. (mm) | Clearance In. (mm) |
| All | 1.6929 (43) | .0016-.0028 (.04-.07) | .0016-.0028 (.04-.07) | 2.9134 (74) | .0016-.0031 (.04-.08) |

| PORT TIMING | | | | |
|---|---|---|---|---|
| | INTAKE | | EXHAUST | |
| Engine | Open (ATDC) | Close (ABDC) | Open (BBDC) | Close (ATDC) |
| All | 32° | 40° | 75° | 38° |

| TIGHTENING SPECIFICATIONS | |
|---|---|
| Application | Ft. Lbs. (mkg) |
| Oil Pump Sprocket | 22-25 (3.0-3.5) |
| Oil Pan | 5-7 (0.7-1.0) |
| Eccentric Shaft Pulley | 72-87 (10-12) |
| Intake Manifold | 12-17 (1.6-2.3) |
| Thermal Reactor | 22-40 (3.0-5.5) |
| Flywheel Lock Nut | 289-362 (40-50) |
| Crankshaft Pulley | 72-87 (10-12) |
| Water Pump | 13-20 (1.8-2.7) |
| Clutch Cover | 13-20 (1.8-2.7) |

## 230 4 CYLINDER

### ENGINE CODING

#### ENGINE IDENTIFICATION

Engine code is determined by first six digits of engine identification number, stamped on left side of engine block.

| Model | Type | Engine Code |
|---|---|---|
| 230 | 123.023 | 115.954 |

### ENGINE & CYLINDER HEAD

#### ENGINE

**NOTE** — *The hood no longer has to be removed, to remove the engine. The hood can be opened to a 90° position and held in place by a locking mechanism located on the left hinge.*

**Removal** — **1)** Disconnect battery ground cable. Drain cooling system and remove engine oil cooler lines. Remove radiator guard and radiator, disconnect heater hoses.

**2)** Disconnect all vacuum, fuel and oil lines from engine and transmission. On vehicles with air conditioning, remove compressor from engine and set aside with hoses connected. Disconnect all electrical leads and cables from engine and transmission.

**3)** Disconnect linkage and choke cable from carburetor, gearshift linkage from transmission, and exhaust pipe from manifold. Loosen steering relay arm and move it downward together with center tie rod and steering shock absorber.

**4)** Disconnect engine shock absorber from support and exhaust pipe bracket from transmission. Attach suitable lifting sling to engine. Mark position of transmission crossmember in relation to chassis base panel, disconnect rubber mount and remove crossmember.

**5)** Disconnect speedometer cable from transmission. Disconnect propeller shaft and shaft plate from transmission, loosen clamping nut and slide shaft and plate to the rear. Loosen power steering pump bracket and push reservoir towards engine.

**6)** Remove front engine mount bolts and front limit stop. Raise engine slightly, tilt it at a 45° angle and lift out engine and transmission assembly. Separate engine from transmission. To install, reverse removal procedure.

#### CYLINDER HEAD

**Removal** — **1)** Drain cooling system. Disconnect all water hoses attached to cylinder head. Remove vent line, air cleaner and rocker cover.

**2)** Disconnect vacuum and fuel line from carburetor. Loosen fuel filter screws and move filter out of way. Disconnect exhaust pipe at manifold.

**3)** Disconnect spark plug wires from spark plugs and heat sensor from thermostat. Rotate crankshaft so that No. 1 cylinder is in TDC firing position. Mark chain and sprocket position and remove distributor.

**4)** Remove top chain guide. Counterhold camshaft sprocket with screwdriver or small bar and remove sprocket bolt. Remove chain tensioner and camshaft sprocket. Loosen fuel line holder and swivel out of way.

**5)** Loosen and remove head bolts, working from outside toward inside of head. Remove four socket screws at front of head. Lift off head and gasket.

**NOTE** — *Engine must be cooled down prior to loosening bolts and lifting head from engine. Head is removed with intake and exhaust manifold attached.*

**Fig. 1  Cylinder Head Tightening Sequence**

**Installation** — **1)** Rotate engine until No. 1 piston is at TDC on compression stroke. Install head gasket and cylinder head. Torque head bolt in sequence shown in illustration to required specifications.

**2)** Complete installation in reverse order of removal and adjust valve clearance. Run engine until has reached 176°F (80°C). Recheck cylinder head bolts by loosening 1/4 turn at a time in tightening sequence, then tighten to final torque.

**NOTE** — *No check of valve clearance is required after retightening head bolts.*

### VALVES

#### VALVE ARRANGEMENT

E-I-I-E-E-I-I-E (front to rear).

#### VALVE GUIDE SERVICING

**1)** Thoroughly clean carbon from guide bore and measure inside diameter. If measurement exceeds .3553" (9.03 mm) on intake guides or .4343" (11.03 mm) on exhaust guides, guide must be replaced.

**2)** Drive guides out through top of head with a suitable driver. Drive new guides into cylinder head from top until snap ring contacts top of head. Guide bores might require reaming to obtain correct fit with valve stem.

**NOTE** — *Valve guide must be chilled or cylinder head heated when replacing valve guides.*

## 230 4 CYLINDER (Cont.)

**3)** Valve guides require a .0004-.0012" (.01-.03 mm) press fit in cylinder head. If fit is too loose, two oversize valve guides are available. Size of oversize guides is determined by a color code. Standard guide outside diameter is .5523-.5531" (14.03-14.05 mm) for intake guides and .5917-5925" (15.03-15.05 mm) for exhaust guides.

**Fig. 2 Sectional View of Valve Train Components**

Labels: Camshaft, Rocker Arm, Adjusting Screw, Valve Clearance Measuring Point, Pressure Plate, Valve Keepers, Spring Retainer, Valve Stem Oil Seal, Outer Spring, Inner Spring, Valve Rotator, Valve Stem, Valve Guide

### Valve Guide Specifications

| Application | In. (mm) |
|---|---|
| Intake Guide | |
| Red Code | .5594-.5602 (14.21-14.23) |
| White Code | .5673-.5681 (14.41-14.43) |
| Exhaust Guide | |
| Red Code | .5988-.5996 (15.21-15.23) |
| White Code | .6066-.6075 (15.41-15.43) |

### VALVE STEM OIL SEALS

Valve seals are used on both intake and exhaust valves. Seal is teflon-type material utilizing lock ring mounted around seal to secure unit to valve guide. Valve spring must be removed to replace seal.

### VALVE SPRING REMOVAL

Compress valve spring with a suitable spring compressor. Remove valve keepers and release spring compressor. Remove upper spring seat, both valve springs and valve rotator. Check spring for wear or fatigue and replace as necessary. To install valve springs, reverse removal procedure.

### ROCKER ARM ASSEMBLY

**1)** Remove valve cover. Remove spring clamp from notch in top of rocker arm and push outward over ball cup of rocker arm. Rotate camshaft until there is no load on rocker arm being removed.

**CAUTION** — *Rotate engine in correct direction of rotation by cranking collar bolt on crankshaft. Do not rotate by turning bolt on camshaft. If these procedures are not followed, drive chain tensioning rail could be distorted or damaged.*

**2)** Insert suitable spring compressor (123 589 03 61 00) with bracket (02 for No. 1 exhaust, 01 for others) between camshaft and valve spring. Push valve spring down to relieve pressure from rocker arm and remove arm by lifting off of ball pin.

**3)** To install rocker arm, reverse removal procedure. Check and, if necessary, adjust valve clearance.

### MECHANICAL VALVE LIFTER ADJUSTMENT

**1)** Valve clearance can be checked or adjusted with engine either cold or warm. Clearance is measured between sliding surface of rocker arm and heel of camshaft. Remove breather line from valve cover and remove valve cover.

**2)** Rotate crankshaft until camshaft lobe is pointing away from sliding surface of rocker arm to be checked.

**CAUTION** — *Rotate engine in correct direction of rotation by use of collar bolt on crankshaft. Do not try to turn engine using bolt on camshaft end as drive chain tensioning rail could be distorted or damaged by not following correct procedure.*

**3)** Measure valve clearance. If clearance is too tight, turn rocker arm adjusting screw clockwise using suitable adjusting wrench (110 589 00 01 00) and a torque wrench. If clearance is excessive, turn adjusting screw counterclockwise.

**4)** A required torque of 14.5-28.8 ft. lbs. (2-4 mkg) is needed when screwing adjusting screw in or out of cylinder head. If torque is less, adjusting screw, base plate or both must be replaced.

**5)** If clearance is too small and adjusting screw cannot be screwed into cylinder head any further, a thinner pressure plate must be installed in valve spring retainer. Standard thickness of pressure plate is .177" (4.5 mm). Undersize plates are available .138" (3.5 mm) and .098" (2.5 mm) thick.

### Valve Clearance Specifications

| Application | Clearance |
|---|---|
| Intake | |
| Cold | .004" (.10 mm) |
| Warm | .006" (.15 mm) |
| Exhaust | |
| Cold | .008" (.20 mm) |
| Warm | .010" (.25 mm) |

## PISTONS, PINS & RINGS

### OIL PAN

**NOTE** — *Oil pan is comprised of upper and lower half. Upper half is best removed with engine out of vehicle due to complexity of operation.*

To remove oil pan (lower half), drain oil and remove cap screws. Remove old gasket and clean mating surfaces. Install new gasket with lower pan and tighten cap screws evenly to specifications.

## 230 4 CYLINDER (Cont.)

### PISTON & ROD ASSEMBLY

**Removal** — With cylinder head and oil pan completely removed, unscrew connecting rod nuts. Tap bolts with plastic mallet to loosen rod on crankshaft. Ensure that bearing caps are properly marked and push piston and rod assembly out top of block. Remove piston pin circlips and force pin out.

**Installation 1)** — Assemble piston to rod so that arrow on piston points to front of engine and offset oil hole in small end of rod points to right side. Piston pin should be oiled and pushed in manually. Install pin locks in grooves and assemble rings on piston.

**NOTE** — *Do NOT heat piston when fitting or installing wrist pin.*

**2)** Install previously fitted rings on pistons with gaps staggered. Lubricate cylinder walls and crankshaft journals. Lubricate piston/rod assembly and install ring compressor. Install asssembly with arrow on piston crown facing forward.

**3)** Connecting rod bolts must be replaced if, after several tightenings, expansion has reached minimum diameter of .2834" (7.2 mm). Normal diameter of connecting rod bolts is .3307" (8.4 mm). Drive out old bolts and insert new bolts using same spline face position.

**NOTE** — *First tightening after new bolts are installed is 50 ft. lbs. (7 mkg). Subsequent tightenings are 36 ft. lbs. (5 mkg).*

**4)** Rotate crankshaft until piston is at TDC. Measure distance between top of cylinder block and piston crown. Piston must not recess more than .024-.043" (.6-1.1 mm) below block surface.

### FITTING PISTONS

Measure piston and cylinder diameters to determine running clearance. Piston diameter is measured at 90° to piston pin bore near bottom of piston skirt. Install rings with marking "TOP", "F" or "GOE" up.

#### Piston Specifications

| Application | In. (mm) |
| --- | --- |
| Standard | 3.6902-3.6910 (93.73-93.75) |
| 1st Oversize | 3.7059-3.7067 (94.13-94.15) |
| 2nd Oversize | 3.7216-3.7224 (94.53-94.55) |

### PISTON PINS

Piston pins are removed by taking out circlips and forcing pin out of piston/rod assembly. Piston pin diameter should be .9039-.9055" (22.996-23.000 mm). Do NOT heat piston to install wrist pin. Coat pin with oil and push in manually. Place locks (circlips) in grooves of piston.

## CRANKSHAFT MAIN & CONNECTING ROD BEARINGS

### MAIN & CONNECTING ROD BEARINGS

Measure main bearing and connecting rod journals for out-of-round and taper. Out-of-round must not exceed .0002-.0004"

(.005-.010 mm) and taper .0004-.0006" (.010-.015 mm). Select proper undersize and grind crankshaft to following diameters:

#### Crankshaft Journal Diameters

| Application | Main In. (mm) | Connecting Rod In. (mm) |
| --- | --- | --- |
| Standard | 2.7541-2.7545 (69.95-69.96) | 2.0454-2.0458 (51.95-51.96) |
| 1st Undersize | 2.7442-2.7446 (69.70-69.71) | 2.0356-2.0360 (51.70-51.71) |
| 2nd Undersize | 2.7344-2.7348 (69.45-69.46) | 2.0257-2.0261 (51.45-51.46) |
| 3rd Undersize | 2.7246-2.7249 (69.20-69.21) | 2.0159-2.0163 (51.20-51.21) |
| 4th Undersize | 2.7147-2.7151 (68.95-68.96) | 2.0060-2.0064 (50.95-50.96) |

### THRUST BEARING ALIGNMENT

Measure crankshaft end play. Wear limit is .012" (.30 mm). End play is adjusted by machining collars of No. 3 (center) main bearing shells to minimal clearance value.

### REAR MAIN BEARING OIL SEAL

**1)** With oil pan and crankshaft removed, insert fabric oil seal in crankcase groove behind rear main bearing. Cut seal so that seal protrudes slightly above parting face.

**2)** Install other seal half in oil pan groove, coat lubricant on seal halves. Reinstall crankshaft and oil pan. Rotate crankshaft to check tightness of seal, if too tight, remove oil pan and crankshaft, tamp down high spots using suitable tool to roll down material. Reinstall all related parts.

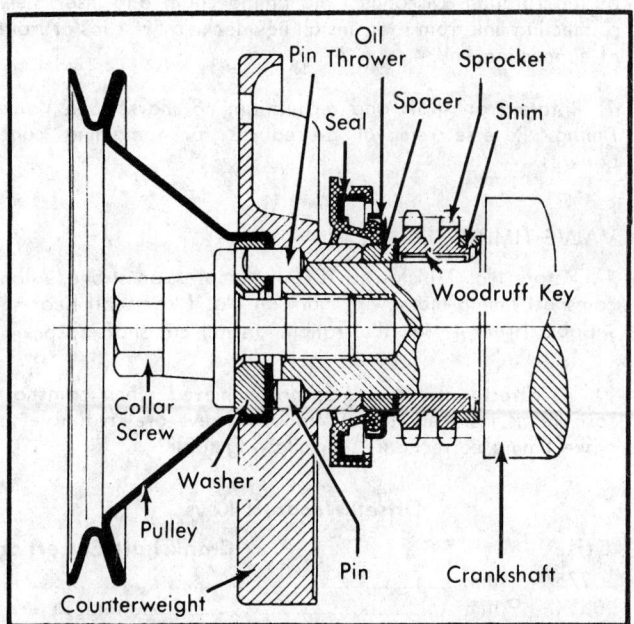

*Fig. 3 Sectional View of Crankshaft Front Oil Seal*

# Mercedes-Benz Engines

## 230 4 CYLINDER (Cont.)

### FRONT OIL SEAL

**Removal** — 1) Remove attaching bolt and crankshaft pulley. Attach a suitable puller and remove counterweight.

2) Press out seal ring and remove spacer from crankshaft.

**Installation** — 1) Beginning with chassis number 018206, a new seal ring with a 360° shoulder replaced the previous ring with a 180° shoulder. These engines also have the face of the oil seal bore on the oil pan machined, so that the crankcase and oil pan have a flat surface. Rings with the 180° shoulder may still be used in repairing older models.

**NOTE** — *Radial seal rings with the 360° shoulders must be used in repairing engines with oil pans having the machined oil seal bores.*

2) Install new spacing ring (614 031 01 51) on crankshaft. Lubricate seal lips and install with tool (130 589 00 61 00) ensuring that seal lips are square with crankshaft journal. Install balancing disc and pulley. Install remaining components in reverse of removal order.

## CAMSHAFT

### TIMING CHAIN REPLACEMENT

1) Remove rocker cover and disconnect spark plug wires at spark plugs. Remove all four spark plugs to allow engine to turn over freely.

2) Grind off pins on a link of old chain and remove link. Using a master link, connect new chain to old chain on driving side of old chain.

3) Slowly turn engine in direction of normal rotation with tool at crankshaft hub until connecting link is at top of sprocket. Ensure that timing chain remains in mesh with camshaft sprocket during rotation. Disconnect old timing chain and insert new connecting link from rear. Install new locking "E" clips at front of connecting link.

4) Rotate crankshaft and recheck timing marks. See *Valve Timing*. Reverse removal procedures for remaining components.

### VALVE TIMING

1) Rotate No. 1 piston to TDC of compression stroke. Align camshaft timing mark with mark on No. 1 camshaft bearing support bracket (see illustration). Install camshaft sprocket.

2) If correct valve timing is not achieved when camshaft sprocket is installed, offset Woodruff keys are available to make timing corrections, see following table:

#### Offset Woodruff Keys

| Offset | Crankshaft Correction |
| --- | --- |
| .0275" (.7 mm) | 4° |
| .0354" (.9 mm) | 6 1/2° |
| .0433" (1.1 mm) | 8° |
| .0511" (1.3 mm) | 10° |

**Fig. 4 Camshaft Timing Marks with Master Timing Chain Link and "E" Locks**

## ENGINE OILING

**Crankcase Capacity** — 5.8 qts. with filter.

**Oil Filter** — Full-flow, clean main element 3,000 miles. Replace by-pass element 3,000 miles.

**Normal Oil Pressure** — 7.1 psi (.5 kg/cm²) at idle speed; 42 psi (3.07 kg/cm²) at 3000 RPM.

**Pressure Regulator Valve** — Non-adjustable.

### ENGINE OILING SYSTEM

Engine lubrication is provided by a gear type oil pump, which force feeds oil through an oil filter to oil gallery. From oil gallery, oil flows to main and connecting rod bearings. Pistons, wrist pins and connecting rod bushings are splash lubricated. A vertical oil passage from oil gallery has a transverse passage which supplies oil to intermediate sprocket shaft and bearings. Another oil passage supplies oil to oil pump drive shaft and helical gear. Vertical passage also supplies oil to No. 1 camshaft bearing. An external oil tube attached to No. 1 camshaft bearing support lubricates other camshaft bearings and rocker arms.

### OIL PUMP

To remove oil pump, first remove fuel pump, then remove oil pan lower half. Remove mounting screws on crankcase and bearing half, and pull out oil pump. To install, reverse removal procedures. Use new oil pan gasket and mount oil pan lower half.

## ENGINE COOLING

**Cooling System Capacity** — 10.6 qts. with heater.

**Thermostat** — Wax Pellet Type, opens at 170-179°F (77-81°C).

## 230 4 CYLINDER (Cont.)

### WATER PUMP

**Removal** – Completely drain cooling system. Remove fan, belts and pulley. On A/C models, remove compressor and carrier without disconnecting refrigerant lines. Remove water pump mounting bolts and take off pump.

**Installation** – Use new gasket and install water pump. Replace remaining components in reverse order of removal. Fill cooling system and pressure-test with tester.

**NOTE** – *Late model pumps use shaft with compact bearing instead of spacer and 2 bearings.*

**Fig. 5  Sectional View of Water Pump**
*(Early Model Shown – Specifications are for Late Model)*

## ENGINE SPECIFICATIONS

### GENERAL SPECIFICATIONS

| Year | Displ. cu. ins. | Displ. cc | Carburetor | HP at RPM | Torque (Ft. Lbs. at RPM) | Compr. Ratio | Bore in. | Bore mm | Stroke in. | Stroke mm |
|---|---|---|---|---|---|---|---|---|---|---|
| 1978 | 140.8 | 2307 | 1x1 Bbl. | 86@4800 | 116@3000 | 8-1 | 3.69 | 93.75 | 3.29 | 83.6 |

### VALVES

| Engine & Valve | Head Diam. In. (mm) | Face Angle | Seat Angle | Seat Width In. (mm) | Stem Diameter In. (mm) | Stem Clearance In. (mm) | Valve Lift In. (mm) |
|---|---|---|---|---|---|---|---|
| 2307 cc Intake | 1.846-1.854 (46.9-47.1) | 45° | 45° | .071-.099 (1.8-2.5) | .352-.353 (8.95-8.97) | ..... | ..... |
| Exhaust | 1.455-1.467 (36.95-37.25) | 45° | 45° | .059-.099 (1.5-2.5) | .430-.431 (10.93-10.95) | ..... | ..... |

### PISTONS, PINS, RINGS

| Engine | PISTONS Clearance In. (mm) | PINS Piston Fit In. (mm) | PINS Rod Fit In. (mm) | RINGS Rings | RINGS End Gap In. (mm) | RINGS Side Clearance In. (mm) |
|---|---|---|---|---|---|---|
| 2307 cc | .0006-.0014 (.015-.035) Wear Limit .0031 (.08) | .00008-.0004 (002-.011) | .0004-.0009 (.012-.022) | No. 1 | .014-.022 (.35-.55) | .0020-.0032 (.050-.080) |
| | | | | No. 2 | .014-.022 (.35-.55) | .0011-.0024 (.030-.060) |
| | | | | No. 3 | .010-.016 (.25-.50) | .0012-.0024 (.030-.062) |

### CRANKSHAFT MAIN & CONNECTING ROD BEARINGS

| Engine | MAIN BEARINGS Journal Diam. In. (mm) | MAIN BEARINGS Clearance In. (mm)① | Thrust Bearing | Crankshaft End Play In. (mm)② | CONNECTING ROD BEARINGS Journal Diam. In. (mm) | CONNECTING ROD BEARINGS Clearance In. (mm)① | Side Play In. (mm)③ |
|---|---|---|---|---|---|---|---|
| 2307 cc | 2.7541-2.7545 (69.95-69.96) | .0012-.0028 (.031-.068) | Center | .004-.009 (.10-.22) | 2.045-2.046 (51.94-51.97) | .0012-.0027 (.031-.068) | .005-.010 (.12-.26) |

① – Limit .0031″ (.08 mm).　　② – Limit .0118″ (.30 mm).　　③ – Limit .01969″ (.50 mm).

# Mercedes-Benz Engines

## 230 4 CYLINDER (Cont.)

### ENGINE SPECIFICATIONS (Cont.)

### VALVE SPRINGS

| Engine | Free Length In. (mm) | PRESSURE Lbs. @ In. (kg @ mm) | |
|---|---|---|---|
| | | Valve Closed | Valve Open |
| 2307 cc Inner | 1.77 (44.9) | 28.2-33.5@1.22 (12.8-15.2@31) | 50.3-55.6@.827 (22.8-25.2@21) |
| Outer | 1.97 (50) | 79.4@1.54 (36@39) | 149.3-168.2@1.18 (67.7-76.3@30) |

### VALVE TIMING

| Engine | INTAKE | | EXHAUST | |
|---|---|---|---|---|
| | Open (ATDC) | Close (ALDC) | Open (BLDC) | Close (BTDC) |
| 2307 cc | 14° | 20° | 22° | 12° |

### TIGHTENING SPECIFICATIONS

| Application | Ft. Lbs. (mkg) |
|---|---|
| Cylinder Head Bolts | |
| 10 mm Bolts① | |
| Stage 1 | 22 (3.0) |
| Stage 2 | 40 (5.5) |
| Stage 3 (Warm) | 40 (5.5) |
| 12 mm Bolts① | |
| Stage 1 | 51 (7.0) |
| Stage 2 | 72 (10) |
| Stage 3 (Warm) | 72 (10) |
| Timing Chain Cover Bolts | 11 (1.5) |
| Connecting Rod Bolts | ②29-36 (4.0-5.0) |
| Main Bearing Cap Bolts | 65 (9.0) |
| Crankshaft Sprocket Bolt | 195-239 (27-33) |
| Oil Pan Bolts | 6 (1.1) |
| Flywheel Bolts | 22-29 (3.0-4.0) |
| Camshaft Bearing Bolts | 18 (2.5) |
| Camshaft Sprocket Bolt | 58 (8.0) |

① — Final step with engine warm, 10 mm bolts 40 ft lbs. (5.5 mkg), 12 mm bolts 72 ft lbs. (10 mkg).

② — Plus 90-100° rotation.

## 240D DIESEL 4 CYLINDER

### ENGINE CODING

#### ENGINE IDENTIFICATION

Engine identification number is stamped on left side of cylinder block. First six digits of this number are used for engine identification purposes.

| Application | Type | Engine Coding |
|---|---|---|
| 240D | 123.123 | 616.912 |

**NOTE** — *If vehicle is equipped with air conditioning, it is not necessary to disconnect refrigerant hoses. Only detach compressor from its mounting and position compressor and hoses out of way.*

### ENGINE CYLINDER HEAD & MANIFOLDS

#### ENGINE

**NOTE** — *The hood no longer has to be removed, to remove the engine. The hood can be opened to a 90° position and held in place by a locking mechanism located on the left hinge.*

**Removal** — 1) Disconnect battery ground cable. Drain cooling system and remove engine oil cooler lines. Remove radiator guard and radiator, disconnect heater hoses.

2) Remove air intake silencer. Disconnect fuel hoses and vacuum hose to power brake. On models with power steering and level control, disconnect and plug oil lines.

3) Disconnect oil pressure gauge hose. Disconnect idle control cable and stop-start cable. Remove accelerator linkage.

4) Disconnect ground cable from engine to chassis and all other electrical leads. Disconnect gearshift linkage and exhaust pipe at manifold.

5) Loosen steering relay arm and move downward together with center tie rod and steering shock absorber. Disconnect hydraulic line from clutch slave cylinder.

6) On Auto. Trans. models, disconnect oil cooler lines between transmission and oil cooler.

7) Disconnect exhaust pipe support bracket at transmission, loosen clamp on exhaust pipe and push downward.

8) Attach suitable lifting sling to engine. Mark position of rear engine crossmember in relation to chassis base panel, disconnect rubber mount at transmission and remove crossmember.

9) Disconnect speedometer cable. Disconnect propeller shaft and shaft plate from transmission. Push propeller shaft to rear after loosening clamping nut.

10) Disconnect plug from automatic transmission.

11) Remove bolts at both front engine mounts. Remove front limit stop. Loosen one screw and move power steering reservoir to one side.

12) Lift out engine at a 45° angle.

**Installation** — To install, reverse removal procedures.

### INTAKE & EXHAUST MANIFOLD

**Intake Manifold** — Remove air cleaner. Disconnect throttle linkage and bowden cable for idling control on throttle duct. Unscrew vacuum line. Remove attaching nuts and intake manifold from cylinder head.

**Exhaust Manifold** — Disconnect exhaust pipe from manifold. Remove attaching nuts and lift off exhaust manifold.

### CYLINDER HEAD

**Removal** — 1) Drain cooling system. Disconnect all water hoses attached to cylinder head. Remove vent line, air cleaner and rocker cover.

2) Disconnect vacuum line, injection lines and leakage oil line. Loosen fuel filter screws and move filter out of the way. Remove exhaust pipe from manifold.

3) Disconnect cable to glow plugs and heat sensor from water thermometer. Rotate engine until there is no load on rocker arms and remove rocker arm assembly.

4) Remove top chain guide. Unscrew camshaft sprocket screw. Remove chain tensioner and camshaft sprocket.

5) Loosen and remove head bolts, working from outside toward inside of head. Remove four socket screws at front of head. Lift off head and gasket.

*Fig. 1   Cylinder Head Tightening Sequence*

**Installation** — 1) Rotate engine until No. 1 piston is at TDC of compression stroke. Install head gasket and cylinder head, torque head bolts to specifications (see illustration).

2) Install four socket screws in front of head. Connect ground lead for glow plugs to screw under main fuel filter. Insert Woodruff key in camshaft. Place shim on camshaft so mark aligns with mark of first camshaft bearing support.

3) Install camshaft sprocket and chain with tension on driving side of chain, using care not to move camshaft or crankshaft.

4) Check endplay of camshaft. *See Camshaft Bearing Replacement.* Install upper chain guide. Using a new seal, install chain tensioner filled with oil.

5) Install rocker arm assembly, rotating camshaft so there is no load on rocker arms while tightening. Adjust tappets with engine cold. *See Valve Clearance Adjustment.*

6) Reinstall remaining components in reverse of removal. Run engine until it has reached 176°F (80°C) and retighten cylinder head bolts, check tappet clearance. (Loosen each head bolt slightly, a bolt at a time, then retorque to specifications).

## 240D DIESEL 4 CYLINDER (Cont.)

### VALVES

**VALVE ARRANGEMENT**

E-I-I-E-E-I-I-E (front to rear).

**VALVE GUIDE SERVICING**

**1)** Check valve guide bores and ensure they are not less than .3937" (10.00 mm) or larger than .3947" (10.025 mm). Remove all carbon before measuring guides.

**2)** Using a suitable drift, drive intake guide out toward top of head and exhaust guide toward combustion chamber.

**3)** Press in new guides from combustion side until specified distance is achieved. See Fig. 2. Check guide bores and remove any tight spots.

Fig. 2 Installed View of Valve Assemblies

**4)** Valve guides are available in standard and one oversize (coded red). An interference fit of .0004-.0015" (.010-.040 mm) is used. If guide does not meet specifications, install oversize part. Note that intake guides are 2.40" (60.96 mm) long and exhaust guides are 1.95" (49.53 mm) long.

#### Valve Guide Specification

| Application | Guide O.D.<br>In. (mm) | Cyl. Head Bore<br>In. (mm) |
|---|---|---|
| Standard | .5522-.5527<br>(14.03-14.04) | .5511-.5518<br>(14.00-14.02) |
| Oversize (Red) | .5601-.5605<br>(14.23-14.24) | .5590-.5597<br>(14.20-14.22) |

**VALVE STEM OIL SEALS**

**1)** Using a spring compressor, unscrew cap nut and lock nut from valve stem. Remove valve collar and spring.

**2)** Prepare a tool for removing oil seal. See Fig. 3. Using oil seal tool, lever oil seal off of guide and stem.

Fig. 3 Valve Stem Oil Seal Tool

**3)** Place plastic sleeve over threaded end of valve stem. Slide new oil seal in place, using oil seal tool. Install spring and collar. Screw lock nut and cap nut on end of valve stem.

**VALVE SPRING**

Remove rocker arms. Using a spring compressor, unscrew cap nut and lock nut. Remove valve spring collar and lift out spring. Check spring for wear or fatigue, replace as necessary. To install, reverse removal procedures with close wound coils next to cylinder head.

**ROCKER ARM ASSEMBLY**

**1)** Remove air cleaner and tappet cover. Loosen rocker arm bracket bolts, rotate camshaft so there is no load on rocker arms being removed.

Fig. 4 Detail of Rocker Arm Assembly

**2)** Slide rocker arm brackets, rocker arms tightening clamp and spacer off of shaft. Inspect all parts for wear. Replace shaft, rocker bushing or rocker bracket if necessary. To install, reverse removal procedures.

## 240D DIESEL 4 CYLINDER (Cont.)

### VALVE CLEARANCE ADJUSTMENT

1) Adjust valves according to firing sequence (1-3-4-2). Rotate crankshaft until piston of valves to be adjusted is at TDC of compression stroke. Measure clearance between slide surface of rocker arm and cam base circle of camshaft. Cam lobe should be vertical to cam base circle.

2) To adjust, fit holding wrench on valve retainer. Loosen cap nut while holding hex nut. Adjust clearance by turning cap nut. After adjustment, lock cap nut by tightening hex nut. Recheck valve clearance:

### Valve Clearance Specifications

| Valve | Inches (mm) |
|---|---|
| Intake | |
|   Cold | ① .0039 (.10) |
|   Warm | ① .0059 (.l5) |
| Exhaust | |
|   Cold | .012 (.30) |
|   Warm | .014 (.35) |

① — Add .002" (.05 mm) additional clearance if ambient temperatures are below -4° F (-20° C) for extended periods.

## PISTONS, PINS & RINGS

### OIL PAN

1) Remove oil pan cover, if equipped. Drain engine oil. Remove dipstick and tube. Detach cover plate from clutch housing. Remove oil pan bolts.

2) Loosen steering shock absorber and drag link and turn to one side. Unscrew drag link on intermediate steering and turn aside. Remove oil pan.

**NOTE** - *Beginning at chassis number 033886, two studs are provided at the front to make it easier to center oil pan on crankcase. At same time, oil seal bore on the oil pan began to be machined.*

### PISTON & ROD ASSEMBLY

**Removal — 1)** Remove cylinder head and oil pan. Unscrew connecting rod nuts. Tap rod bolts with a plastic mallet to loosen rod on crankshaft. Push piston and connecting rod assembly out top of cylinder block.

2) Remove piston pin circlips. Heat piston to 104-140° (40-60°C) and press out piston pins.

**Installation — 1)** Heat piston and reinstall wrist pin and circlips. Piston and wrist pin must be matched.

2) Install connecting rod and cap so cylinder numbers face left side of engine and arrow on piston crown faces forward.

**NOTE** — *Piston must be installed facing proper direction or damage to the engine will occur.*

3) Connecting rod bolts are of a special design, having an expansion shank which is used to measure bolt stress. If, after several tightenings, the expansion section of the bolt has reached a minimum diameter of .2834" (7.2 mm), the bolt must be replaced. When new, this shank portion should be

.3307" (8.4 mm). When replacing, drive out old bolts and insert new ones into same spline pattern in rod cap. **NOTE** — *First tightening of NEW bolts is to 50.6 ft. lbs. (7.0 mkg); subsequent tightenings should be to 36 ft. lbs. (5.0 mkg).*

4) Rotate crankshaft until piston to be measured is at TDC. Measure distance from top of cylinder block to piston crown. Piston must not protrude more than .035" (.90 mm) nor less than .004" (.10 mm) above block surface.

### FITTING PISTONS

Measure piston and cylinder diameters to determine running clearance. Piston diameter is measured at 90° to piston pin bore near bottom of piston skirt. There are two compression rings and one oil ring. Install compression rings with markings "top" or "F" and oil ring with marking "GOE" or "F" facing upward.

## CRANKSHAFT MAIN & CONNECTING ROD BEARINGS

### MAIN BEARING SERVICE

Measure main bearing and connecting rod journals for out-of-round and taper. Out-of-round must not exceed .0002-.0004" (.005-.010 mm) and taper must not exceed .0004-.0006" (.010-.015 mm). Select proper undersize, if required, and grind crankshaft to following diameters:

### Crankshaft Journal Diameters

| Application | Main In. (mm) | Con. Rod In. (mm) |
|---|---|---|
| Standard | 2.7541-2.7545 (69.95-69.96) | 2.0454-2.0458 (51.95-51.96) |
| 1st Undersize | 2.7442-2.7446 (69.70-69.71) | 2.0356-2.0360 (51.70-51.71) |
| 2nd Undersize | 2.7344-2.7348 (69.45-69.46) | 2.0257-2.0261 (51.45-51.46) |
| 3rd Undersize | 2.7246-2.7249 (69.20-69.21) | 2.0159-2.0163 (51.20-51.21) |
| 4th Undersize | 2.7147-2.7151 (68.95-68.96) | 2.0060-2.0064 (50.95-50.96) |

*Fig. 5  Detail of Center Main Bearing Cap*

## 240D DIESEL 4 CYLINDER (Cont.)

### THRUST BEARING ALIGNMENT

Center main bearing cap has pin located thrust washers to adjust crankshaft end play. Measure end play and install thrust washer(s) required to give proper end play. Measure pin protrusion from main bearing cap to ensure it does not exceed .062" (1.57 mm) as illustrated. Standard and oversize thrust washers are available in the following sizes:

### Thrust Washer Thicknesses

| Application | In. (mm) |
|---|---|
| Standard | .078 (1.98) |
| 1st Oversize | .080 (2.03) |
| 2nd Oversize | .082 (2.08) |
| 3rd Oversize | .084 (2.13) |
| 4th Oversize | .086 (2.18) |
| 5th Oversize | .088 (2.23) |
| 6th Oversize | .090 (2.28) |
| 7th Oversize | .092 (2.33) |

### REAR MAIN BEARING OIL SEAL SERVICE

1) With oil pan and crankshaft removed, insert fabric oil seal in groove in crankcase behind rear main bearing. Cut seal at parting face so that it protrudes slightly above parting face.

2) Install other half in oil pan groove, using tallow on seal halves. Reinstall crankshaft and oil pan. Rotate crankshaft to check tightness of seal. If seal is too tight, remove oil pan and crankshaft and roll down high spots with a hammer handle.

### FRONT OIL SEAL

Removal — 1) Remove attaching bolt and crankshaft pulley. Attach a suitable puller and remove counterweight. Remove oil pan.

2) Press out seal ring and remove spacer from crankshaft.

Fig. 6  Sectional View of Crankshaft Front Oil Seal

Installation — 1) Beginning with chassis number 033886, a new seal ring with a 360° shoulder replaced the previous ring with a 180° shoulder. The face of the oil seal bore on the oil pan also became machined, so that the crankcase and oil pan have a flat surface. Rings with the 180° shoulder may still be used in repairing previous models.

NOTE — Radial seal rings with the 360° shoulders must be used in repairing engines with oil pans having the machined oil seal bore.

2) Lubricate seal lip with oil. Slide oil thrower ring onto crankshaft. Slip radial seal ring onto installation sleeve (130 589 00 61 00) and press seal in until it touches the crankcase face. Install a new hard-chromium plated spacer washer (615 031 01 51) on crankshaft.

3) Place oil pan on two centering studs at front of crankcase and complete installation, by installing components in reverse of removal procedures.

## CAMSHAFT

### CAMSHAFT

1) Remove camshaft sprocket and rocker arm assembly. Disconnect external camshaft oiling tube.

2) Remove camshaft bearing supports. Slide camshaft bearing supports off of camshaft. To install, reverse removal procedures.

### CAMSHAFT BEARING REPLACEMENT

1) Inspect camshaft bearing journals for wear. If worn, grind bearing journals and fit undersize bearings.

Fig. 7  Detail of Camshaft

2) Bearing on No. 1 journal controls camshaft end play. Width of journal is 1.3385-1.3401" (34.0-34.03 mm). Place bearing on camshaft and install retaining ring. Using a feeler gauge, measure clearance between camshaft flange and bearing. See Fig. 8. Lap bearing to proper fit. The following table lists camshaft bearing journal diameters for standard and undersize bearings:

### Camshaft Journal Diameters

| Application | Journal No. 1 In. (mm) | Journal No. 2 & 3 In. (mm) |
|---|---|---|
| Standard | 1.3763-1.3769 (34.96-34.97) | 1.8290-1.8297 (6.46-46.47) |
| Intermediate (Grey) | 1.3723-1.3730 (34.86-34.87) | 1.8251-1.8257 (46.36-46.37) |
| 1st Undersize (Red) | 1.3664-1.3671 (34.71-34.72) | 1.8192-1.8198 (46.21-46.22) |

## 240D DIESEL 4 CYLINDER (Cont.)

Fig. 8   Measuring Camshaft End Play

Fig. 9   Camshaft Timing Marks Location

### TIMING CHAIN REPLACEMENT

1) Remove rocker cover and glow plugs so that engine turns easily. Remove chain tensioner and rocker arm brackets.

**NOTE** — *Removal of rocker arm brackets is not imperative, but is recommended in order to avoid damage to valves or pistons, if, while turning engine, chain jumps over camshaft sprocket.*

2) Grind off pins on a link of old chain and remove link. Using a master link, connect new chain to old chain on driving side of old chain.

**NOTE** — *Install master link facing camshaft side of chain with spring lock closed end facing direction of rotation (see illustration).*

3) Slowly turn engine in direction of rotation, feeding new chain in and old chain out uniformly. After chain threading is complete join ends of new chain with master link and make sure spring lock closed end is facing direction of rotation. Check that valve timing is correct. *See Valve Timing.* Reverse removal procedures for remaining components.

### VALVE TIMING

1) Rotate No. 1 piston to TDC of compression stroke. Align camshaft timing mark with mark on No. 1 camshaft bearing support bracket (see illustration). Install camshaft sprocket.

2) If correct valve timing is not achieved when camshaft sprocket is installed, offset Woodruff keys are available to make timing corrections, see following table:

#### Offset Woodruff Keys

| Offset | Crankshaft Correction |
|---|---|
| .0275" (.7 mm) | 4° |
| .0354" (.9 mm) | 6 1/2° |
| .0433" (1.1 mm) | 8° |
| .0511" (1.3 mm) | 10° |

### ENGINE OILING

#### ENGINE OILING SYSTEM

Engine lubrication is provided by a gear type oil pump, which force feeds oil through an oil filter to oil gallery. From oil gallery, oil flows to main and connecting rod bearings. Pistons, wrist pins and connecting rod bushings are splash lubricated. A vertical oil passage from oil gallery has a transverse passage which supplies oil to intermediate sprocket shaft and bearings. Another oil passage supplies oil to oil pump drive shaft and helical gear. Vertical passage also supplies oil to No. 1 camshaft bearing. An external oil tube attached to No. 1 camshaft bearing support lubricates other camshaft bearings and rocker arms.

**Crankcase Capacity** — 6.9 qts.

**Normal Oil Pressure** — 7.1 psi. (.5 kg/cm²) at 700-780 RPM idle speed; 42 psi. (3 kg/cm²) at 3000 RPM.

**Oil Filter** — Full-flow, clean main element 3,000 miles. Replace by-pass element 3,000 miles.

**Pressure Regulator Valve** — Non-adjustable.

#### OIL PUMP

**Removal** — Remove oil pan. Remove two attaching screws and lift out pump.

**Disassembly** — 1) Remove oil strainer. Unscrew lower pump body, and remove pump gears and shafts. Measure clearances between gear-to-body and gear-to-cover (see specifications).

## 240D DIESEL 4 CYLINDER (Cont.)

**2)** If cast-in bushings in housing are worn, replace complete housing. Worn gears are replaced as an assembly. Assemble upper and lower housing without a gasket. Install strainer with a new gasket. Check that pump turns freely.

**Installation — 1)** Align drive shaft follower with helical gear and follower faces with respect to one another.

**2)** Insert oil pump with bracket and tighten mounting screws. Install oil pan.

### Oil Pump Specifications

| Application | In. (mm) |
|---|---|
| Gear-to-Body ...................................... | .0009-.0022 (.023-.056) |
| Gear-to-Cover ..................................... | .0018-.0029 (.046-.074) |
| Gear Backlash ..................................... | .0019-.0059 (.048-.15) |

## ENGINE COOLING

**Thermostat —** Open at 172-180° F (78-82° C).

**Cooling System Capacity —** 10.5 qts.

### WATER PUMP

**Removal — 1)** Drain cooling system below level of pump. Loosen hose clamps on top radiator hose. Remove radiator mounting bolts and push radiator forward.

**2)** Remove fan from drive pulley. Loosen nuts and adjusters on generator enough so fan belt may be removed. Unscrew and remove venting line between pump and cylinder head.

**3)** Water pump is a maintenance free type. When installing pump, check hub-to-flange and impeller-to-flange distance, (see illustration).

*Fig. 10  Sectional View of Water Pump*

## ENGINE SPECIFICATIONS

### GENERAL SPECIFICATIONS

| Year | Displ. | | Carburetor | HP at RPM | Torque (Ft. Lbs. at RPM) | Compr. Ratio | Bore | | Stroke | |
|---|---|---|---|---|---|---|---|---|---|---|
| | cu. ins. | cc | | | | | in. | mm | in. | mm |
| 1978 | 146.7 | 2404 | Fuel Inj. | 62@4200 | 97@2400 | 21.0-1 | 3.58 | 91 | 3.64 | 92.4 |

### VALVES

| Engine & Valve | Head Diam. In. (mm) | Face Angle | Seat Angle | Seat Width In. (mm) | Stem Diameter In. (mm) | Stem Clearance In. (mm) | Valve Lift In. (mm) |
|---|---|---|---|---|---|---|---|
| 2404 cc Intake | 1.563-1.571 (39.70-39.90) | 30° | 30° | .051-.063 (1.3-1.6) | .3906-.3913 (9.92-9.94) | .0030 (.075) | ..... |
| Exhaust | 1.343-1.350 (34.10-34.30) | 30° | 30° | .098-.114 (2.5-2.9) | .3906-.3913 (9.92-9.94) | .0030 (.075) | ..... |

## 240D DIESEL 4 CYLINDER (Cont.)

### ENGINE SPECIFICATIONS (Cont.)

### PISTONS, PINS, RINGS

| Engine | PISTONS | PINS | | RINGS | | |
| | Clearance In. (mm) | Piston Fit In. (mm) | Rod Fit In. (mm) | Rings | End Gap In. (mm) | Side Clearance In. (mm) |
|---|---|---|---|---|---|---|
| 2404 cc | .0007-.0015 (.018-.038) | ① | Push Fit | No. 1 | .0079-.0138 (.20-.35) | .004-.005 (.100-.132) |
| | | | | No. 2 | .0079-.0138 (.20-.35) | .003-.004 (.070-.102) |
| | | | | No. 3 | .0098-.0157 (.25-.40) | .001-.002 (.030-.062) |

① — Interference fit. See *Piston & Rod Assembly* in this article.

### CRANKSHAFT MAIN & CONNECTING ROD BEARINGS

| Engine | MAIN BEARINGS | | | | CONNECTING ROD BEARINGS | | |
| | Journal Diam. In. (mm) | Clearance In. (mm) | Thrust Bearing | Crankshaft End Play In. (mm) | Journal Diam. In. (mm) | Clearance In. (mm) | Side Play In. (mm) |
|---|---|---|---|---|---|---|---|
| 2404 cc | 2.7541-2.7545 (69.95-69.96) | .0012-.0027 (.031-.068) | Center | .0039-.0090 (.10-.22) | 2.0454-2.0458 (51.95-51.96) | .0012-.0027 (.031-.068) | .005-.010 (.12-.26) |

### VALVE SPRINGS

| Engine | Free Length In. (mm) | PRESSURE Lbs. @ In. (kg @ mm) | |
| | | Valve Closed | Valve Open |
|---|---|---|---|
| 2404 cc | 1.988 (50.5) | 58.2@1.512 (26.4@38.41) | 116.8@1.177 (53.0@29.9) |

### VALVE TIMING

| Engine | INTAKE | | EXHAUST | |
| | Open (ATDC) | Close (ALDC) | Open (BLDC) | Close (BTDC) |
|---|---|---|---|---|
| 2404 cc | 13.5° | 15.5° | 19° | 17° |

### CAMSHAFT ①

| Engine | Journal Diam. In. (mm) | Clearance In. (mm) | Lobe Lift In. (mm) |
|---|---|---|---|
| 2404 cc No. 1 | 1.3763-1.3769 (34.96-34.97) | .0010-.0026 (.025-.066) | ..... |
| No. 2 & 3 | 1.8290-1.8297 (46.46-46.47) | .0010-.0026 (.025-.066) | ..... |

① — End play should be .003-.006" (.070-.149 mm)

### TIGHTENING SPECIFICATIONS

| Application | Ft. Lbs. (mkg) |
|---|---|
| Cylinder Head | |
| Step 1 | 29 (4) |
| Step 2 | 43 (6) |
| Step 3① | 65 (9) |
| Camshaft Bearing Caps | 18 (2.5) |
| Glow Plugs | 36 (5) |
| Prechamber in Cyl. Head | 108-130 (15-18) |
| Connecting Rod Caps | 29-36 (4-5) |
| Main Bearing Caps | 65 (9) |
| Crankshaft Front Hex Bolt | 195-239 (27-33) |
| Oil Pan Bolts | 8 (1.1) |
| Camshaft Sprocket Bolt | 58 (8) |

① — With engine warm.

# Mercedes-Benz Engines

## 300D DIESEL 5 CYLINDER

### ENGINE CODING

#### ENGINE IDENTIFICATION

Engine identification number is stamped on left side of cylinder block. First six digits of this number are used for engine identification purposes.

| Application | Chassis Type | Engine Code |
|---|---|---|
| 300D | 123.130 | 617.912 |

**NOTE** — *If vehicle is equipped with air conditioning, it is not necessary to disconnect refrigerant hoses. Only detach compressor from its mounting and position compressor and hoses out of way.*

### ENGINE & CYLINDER HEAD

#### ENGINE

**NOTE** — *The hood no longer has to be removed, to remove the engine. The hood can be opened to a 90° position and held in place by a locking mechanism located on the left hinge.*

**Removal — 1)** Disconnect battery ground cable. Drain cooling system and remove engine oil cooler lines. Remove radiator guard and radiator, disconnect heater hoses.

**2)** Remove air intake silencer. Disconnect fuel hoses and vacuum hose to power brake. On models with power steering and level control, disconnect and plug oil lines.

**3)** Disconnect oil pressure gauge hose. Disconnect idle control cable and stop-start cable. Remove accelerator linkage.

**4)** Disconnect ground cable from engine to chassis and all other electrical leads. Disconnect gearshift linkage and exhaust pipe at manifold.

**5)** Loosen steering relay arm and move downward together with center tie rod and steering shock absorber. Disconnect hydraulic line from clutch slave cylinder.

**6)** Disconnect oil cooler lines between transmission and oil cooler.

**7)** Disconnect exhaust pipe support bracket at transmission. Loosen clamp on exhaust pipe and push downward.

**8)** Attach suitable lifting sling to engine. Mark position of rear engine crossmember in relation to chassis base panel, disconnect rubber mount at transmission and remove crossmember.

**9)** Disconnect speedometer cable. Disconnect propeller shaft and shaft plate from transmission. Push propeller shaft to rear after loosening clamping nut.

**10)** Disconnect plug from automatic transmission.

**11)** Remove bolts at both front engine mounts. Remove front limit stop. Loosen one screw and move power steering reservoir to one side.

**12)** Lift out engine at a 45° angle. To install, reverse removal procedures.

#### INTAKE & EXHAUST MANIFOLD

**Intake Manifold** — Remove air cleaner. Disconnect throttle linkage and bowden cable for idling control on throttle duct.

Unscrew vacuum line. Remove attaching nuts and intake manifold from cylinder head.

**Exhaust Manifold** — Disconnect exhaust pipe from manifold. Remove attaching nuts and lift off exhaust manifold.

#### CYLINDER HEAD

**Removal — 1)** Drain cooling system. Disconnect all water hoses attached to cylinder head. Remove vent line, air cleaner and rocker cover.

**2)** Disconnect vacuum line, injection lines and leakage oil line. Loosen fuel filter screws and move filter out of the way. Remove exhaust pipe from manifold.

**3)** Disconnect cable to glow plugs and heat sensor from water thermometer. Rotate camshaft until there is no load on rocker arms, and remove rocker arm assemblies (rear assembly for three cylinders; front assembly for two).

**4)** Remove top chain guide. Unscrew camshaft sprocket screw. Remove chain tensioner and camshaft sprocket.

**5)** Loosen and remove head bolts, working from outside toward inside of head. Remove four socket screws at front of head. Lift off head and gasket.

*Fig. 1  Cylinder Head Tightening Sequence*

**Installation — 1)** Rotate engine until No. 1 piston is at TDC of compression stroke. Install head gasket and cylinder head, torque head bolts to specifications (see illustration).

**2)** Install four socket screws in front of head. Connect ground lead for glow plugs to screw under main fuel filter. Insert Woodruff key in camshaft. Place shim on camshaft so mark aligns with mark of first camshaft bearing support.

**3)** Install camshaft sprocket and chain with tension on driving side of chain, using care not to move camshaft or crankshaft.

**4)** Check endplay of camshaft. *See Camshaft Bearing Replacement.* Install upper chain guide. Using a new seal, install chain tensioner filled with oil.

**5)** Install rocker arm assemblies (rear assembly for three cylinders; front for two). Rotate camshaft so there is no load on rocker arms while tightening. Adjust valve clearance with engine cold. See *Valve Clearance Adjustment.*

**6)** Reinstall remaining components in reverse of removal. Run engine until it has reached 176°F (80°C) and retighten cylinder head bolts, check tappet clearance. (Loosen each head bolt slightly, a bolt at a time, then retorque to specifications).

## 300D DIESEL 5 CYLINDER (Cont.)

## VALVES

### VALVE ARRANGEMENT

E-I-I-E-E-I-I-E-E-I (front to rear).

### VALVE GUIDE SERVICING

1) Check valve guide bores and ensure they are not less than .3937" (10.00 mm) or larger than .3947" (10.025 mm). Remove all carbon before measuring guides.

2) Using a suitable drift, drive intake guide out toward top of head and exhaust guide toward combustion chamber.

3) Press in new guides from combustion side until specified distance is achieved. See Fig. 2. Check guide bores for free movement of valves, and remove any tight spots.

Fig. 2   Installed View of Valve Assemblies

4) Valve guides are available in standard and one oversize (coded red). An interference fit of .0004-.0015" (.010-.040 mm) is used. If guide does not meet specifications, install oversize part. Note that intake guides are 2.40" (60.96 mm) long and exhaust guides are 1.95" (49.53 mm) long.

#### Valve Guide Specification

| Application | Guide O.D. In. (mm) | Cyl. Head Bore In. (mm) |
|---|---|---|
| Standard | .5522-.5527 (14.03-14.04) | .5511-.5518 (14.00-14.02) |
| Oversize (Red) | .5601-.5605 (14.23-14.24) | .5590-.5597 (14.20-14.22) |

### VALVE STEM OIL SEALS

1) Using a spring compressor, unscrew cap nut and lock nut from valve stem. Remove valve collar and spring.

2) Prepare a tool for removing oil seal. See Fig. 3. Using oil seal tool, lever oil seal off guide and stem.

3) Place plastic sleeve over threaded end of valve stem. Slide new oil seal in place, using oil seal tool. Install spring and collar. Screw lock nut and cap nut on end of valve stem.

Fig. 3   Valve Stem Oil Seal Tool

Remove rocker arms. Using a spring compressor, unscrew cap nut and lock nut. Remove valve spring collar and lift out spring. Check spring for wear or fatigue, replace as necessary. To install, reverse removal procedures with close wound coils next to cylinder head.

### ROCKER ARM ASSEMBLIES

**NOTE** — Rocker arms are mounted in two groups. Rear group serves three cylinders; front group, two cylinders.

1) Remove air cleaner and tappet cover. Loosen rocker arm bracket bolts, rotate camshaft so there is no load on rocker arms being removed.

Fig. 4   Detailed View of Front Rocker Arm Assembly

2) Slide rocker arm brackets, rocker arms tightening clamp and spacer off of shaft. Inspect all parts for wear. Replace shaft, rocker bushing or rocker bracket if necessary. To install, reverse removal procedures.

### VALVE CLEARANCE ADJUSTMENT

1) Adjust valves according to firing sequence (1-2-4-5-3). Rotate crankshaft until piston of valves to be adjusted is at

## 300D DIESEL 5 CYLINDER (Cont.)

TDC of compression stroke. Measure clearance between slide surface of rocker arm and cam base circle of camshaft. Cam lobe should be vertical to cam base circle.

**2)** To adjust, fit holding wrench on valve retainer. Loosen cap nut while holding hex nut. Adjust clearance by turning cap nut. After adjustment, lock the cap nut by tightening hex nut against it. Recheck valve clearance:

### Valve Clearance Specifications

| Valve | Inches(mm) |
|---|---|
| Intake | |
| Cold | ① .0039 (.10) |
| Warm | ① .0059 (.15) |
| Exhaust | |
| Cold | .012 (.30) |
| Warm | .014 (.35) |

① — Add .002" (.05 mm) additional clearance if ambient temperatures are below -4°F (-20°C) for extended periods.

## PISTONS, PINS & RINGS

### OIL PAN

**NOTE** — *Two studs are provided at the front to make it easier to center oil pan on crankcase. Oil seal bore on oil pan is also machined to provide a common flat surface.*

**1)** Remove oil pan cover, if equipped. Drain engine oil. Remove dipstick and tube. Detach cover plate from clutch housing. Remove oil pan bolts.

**2)** Loosen steering shock absorber and drag link and turn to one side. Unscrew drag link on intermediate steering and turn aside. Remove oil pan.

### PISTON & ROD ASSEMBLY

**Removal — 1)** Remove cylinder head and oil pan. Unscrew connecting rod nuts. Tap rod bolts with a plastic mallet to loosen rod on crankshaft. Push piston and connecting rod assembly out top of cylinder block.

**2)** Remove piston pin circlips. Heat piston to 104-140° (40-60°C) and press out piston pins.

**Installation — 1)** Heat piston and reinstall wrist pin and circlips. Piston and wrist pin must be matched.

**2)** Install connecting rod and cap so cylinder numbers face left side of engine and arrow on piston crown faces forward.

**NOTE** — *Piston must be installed facing proper direction or damage to the engine will occur.*

**3)** Connecting rod bolts are of a special design, having an expansion shank which is used to measure bolt stress. If, after several tightenings, the expansion section of the bolt has reached a minimum diameter of .2834" (7.2 mm), the bolt must be replaced. When new, this shank portion should be .3307" (8.4 mm). When replacing, drive out old bolts and insert new ones into same spline pattern in rod cap. **NOTE** —

*First tightening of NEW bolts is to 50.6 ft. lbs. (7.0 mkg); subsequent tightenings should be to 36 ft. lbs. (5.0 mkg).*

**4)** Rotate crankshaft until piston to be measured is at TDC. Measure distance from top of cylinder block to piston crown. Piston must not protrude more than .035" (.90 mm), nor less than .004" (.10 mm) above block surface.

### FITTING PISTONS

Measure piston and cylinder diameters to determine running clearance. Piston diameter is measured at 90° to piston pin bore near bottom of piston skirt. There are two compression rings and one oil ring. Install compression rings with marking, "top" or "F", and oil ring with marking, "GOE" or "F", facing upward.

## CRANKSHAFT MAIN & CONNECTING ROD BEARINGS

### MAIN BEARING SERVICE

**NOTE** — *The 300D crankshaft has four counterweights and six main bearings.*

Measure main bearing and connecting rod journals for out-of-round and taper. Out-of-round must not exceed .0002-.0004" (.005-.010 mm) and taper must not exceed .0004-.0006" (.010-.015 mm). Select proper undersize, if required, and grind crankshaft to following diameters:

### Crankshaft Journal Diameters

| Application | Main In. (mm) | Con. Rod In. (mm) |
|---|---|---|
| Standard | 2.7541-2.7545 (69.95-69.96) | 2.0454-2.0458 (51.95-51.96) |
| 1st Undersize | 2.7442-2.7446 (69.70-69.71) | 2.0356-2.0360 (51.70-51.71) |
| 2nd Undersize | 2.7344-2.7348 (69.45-69.46) | 2.0257-2.0261 (51.45-51.46) |
| 3rd Undersize | 2.7246-2.7249 (69.20-69.21) | 2.0159-2.0163 (51.20-51.21) |
| 4th Undersize | 2.7147-2.7151 (68.95-68.96) | 2.0060-2.0064 (50.95-50.96) |

.062"

*Fig. 5   Detail of Third Main Bearing Cap*

## 300D DIESEL 5 CYLINDER (Cont.)

### THRUST BEARING ALIGNMENT

Third main bearing cap has pin located thrust washers to adjust crankshaft end play. Measure end play and install thrust washer(s) required to give proper end play. Measure pin protrusion from main bearing cap to ensure it does not exceed .062" (1.57 mm) as illustrated (See Fig. 5). Standard and oversize thrust washers are available in the following sizes:

#### Thrust Washer Thicknesses

| Application | In. (mm) |
| --- | --- |
| Standard | .078 (1.98) |
| 1st Oversize | .080 (2.03) |
| 2nd Oversize | .082 (2.08) |
| 3rd Oversize | .084 (2.13) |
| 4th Oversize | .086 (2.18) |
| 5th Oversize | .088 (2.23) |
| 6th Oversize | .090 (2.28) |
| 7th Oversize | .092 (2.33) |

### REAR MAIN BEARING OIL SEAL SERVICE

1) With oil pan and crankshaft removed, insert fabric oil seal in groove in crankcase behind rear main bearing. Cut seal at parting face so that it protrudes slightly above parting face.

2) Install other half in oil pan groove, using tallow on seal halves. Reinstall crankshaft and oil pan. Rotate crankshaft to check tightness of seal. If seal is too tight, remove oil pan and crankshaft and roll down high spots with a hammer handle.

### FRONT OIL SEAL

**Removal** — 1) Remove attaching bolt and crankshaft pulley. Attach a suitable puller and remove counterweight. Remove oil pan.

2) Press out seal ring and remove spacer from crankshaft.

**Fig. 6   Sectional View of Crankshaft Front Oil Seal**

**Installation** — 1) The 300D Diesel features a radial seal ring with a 360° shoulder and an oil pan with a machined oil seal bore area. Always use the 360° shouldered seal ring.

2) Lubricate seal lip with oil. Slide oil thrower ring onto crankshaft. Slip radial seal ring onto installation sleeve (130 589 00 61 00) and press seal in until it touches the crankcase face. Install a new hard-chromium plated spacer washer (615 031 01 51) on crankshaft.

3) Place oil pan on two centering studs at front of crankcase and complete installation, by installing components in reverse of removal procedures.

4) When installing vibration damper, use the collar screw (000 961 018 019) with three conical spring washers (127 993 00 26) instead of the collar screw with conical sleeve, used on the 300D models through Chassis No. 000984. See Fig. 6.

5) To install collar screw with spring washers on vehicles equipped with the old vibration damper and conical sleeve, either install a new vibration damper (617 030 01 03) or bore out old damper to accept spring washers. See Fig. 7 for dimensions when reboring damper.

#### Vibration Damper Boring Dimensions

| Location | Inches (mm) |
| --- | --- |
| Diameter of Bore | 1.922-1.938 (48.8-49.2) |
| Depth of Bore | .55 (14.0) |

**Fig. 7   Instructions for Reboring Vibration Damper**

## CAMSHAFT

### CAMSHAFT

1) Remove camshaft sprocket and rocker arm assemblies. See Fig. 8. Disconnect external camshaft oiling tube.

**Fig. 8   Rocker Arm Assemblies and Camshaft Bearings**

# Mercedes-Benz Engines

## 300D DIESEL 5 CYLINDER (Cont.)

2) Remove camshaft bearing supports. Slide bearing supports off of camshaft. To install, reverse removal procedures.

### CAMSHAFT BEARING REPLACEMENT

1) Inspect camshaft bearing journals for wear. If worn, grind bearing journals and fit undersize bearings.

Fig. 9   Detailed View of Camshaft

Fig. 10   Measuring Camshaft End Play

2) Bearing on No. 1 journal controls camshaft end play. Width of journal is 1.3385-1.3401" (34.0-34.03 mm). Place bearing on camshaft and install retaining ring. Using a feeler gauge, measure clearance between camshaft flange and bearing (see illustation). Lap bearing to proper fit. The following table lists camshaft bearing journal diameters for standard and undersize bearings:

### Camshaft Journal Diameters

| Application | Journal No. 1 In. (mm) | Journal No. 2, 3, & 4 In. (mm) |
|---|---|---|
| Standard | 1.3763-1.3769 (34.96-34.97) | 1.8290-1.8297 (6.46-46.47) |
| Intermediate (Grey) | 1.3723-1.3730 (34.86-34.87) | 1.8251-1.8257 (46.36-46.37) |
| 1st Undersize (Red) | 1.3664-1.3671 (34.71-34.72) | 1.8192-1.8198 (46.21-46.22) |

### TIMING CHAIN REPLACEMENT

1) Remove rocker cover and glow plugs so that engine turns easily. Remove chain tensioner and rocker arm brackets.

Fig. 11   Timing Chain & Related Components

**NOTE** – *Removal of rocker arm brackets is not imperative, but is recommended in order to avoid damage to valves or pistons, if, while turning engine, chain jumps over camshaft sprocket.*

2) Grind off pins on a link of old chain and remove link. Using a master link, connect new chain to old chain on driving side of old chain.

**NOTE** – *Install master link facing camshaft side of chain with spring lock closed end facing direction of rotation (see illustration).*

3) Slowly turn engine in direction of rotation, feeding new chain in and old chain out uniformly. After chain threading is complete join ends of new chain with master link and make sure spring lock closed end is facing direction of rotation. Check that valve timing is correct. See Valve Timing. Reverse removal procedures for remaining components.

### VALVE TIMING

1) Rotate No. 1 piston to TDC of compression stroke. Align camshaft timing mark with mark on No. 1 camshaft bearing support bracket (see illustration). Install camshaft sprocket.

2) If correct valve timing is not achieved when camshaft sprocket is installed, offset Woodruff keys are available to make timing corrections, see following table:

### Offset Woodruff Keys

| Offset | Crankshaft Correction |
|---|---|
| .0275" (.7 mm) | 4° |
| .0354" (.9 mm) | 6 1/2° |
| .0433" (1.1 mm) | 8° |
| .0511" (1.3 mm) | 10° |

## 300D DIESEL 5 CYLINDER (Cont.)

Fig. 12   Camshaft Timing Mark Locations

Spring Lock — Sprocket Mark — Cam Bearing Support Mark — Master Link

## ENGINE OILING

### ENGINE OILING SYSTEM

Engine lubrication is provided by a gear type oil pump, which force feeds oil through an oil filter to oil gallery. From oil gallery, oil flows to main and connecting rod bearings. Pistons, wrist pins and connecting rod bushings are splash lubricated.

A vertical oil passage from oil gallery has a transverse passage which supplies oil to intermediate sprocket shaft and bearings. Another oil passage supplies oil to oil pump drive shaft and helical gear. Vertical passage also supplies oil to No. 1 camshaft bearing. An external oil tube attached to No. 1 camshaft bearing support lubricates other camshaft bearings and rocker arms.

**Crankcase Capacity** — 7.0 quarts including filter.

**Oil Filter** — Full-flow. Thermostat opens to oil cooler at 203°F (95°C). Clean main element every 3,000 miles. Replace by-pass element every 3,000 miles.

**Normal Oil Pressure** — 7.1 psi (.5 kg/cm²) at 700-800 RPM; 42 psi (3 kg/cm²) at 3000 RPM.

**Pressure Regulator Valve** — Non-adjustable.

### OIL PUMP

**Removal** — Remove oil pan. Remove two attaching screws and lift out pump.

**NOTE** — *Beginning at Chassis No. 31200 (Engine No. 012967), the yellow lock screw (M8) securing the thrust bushing in the oil pump drive was replaced with a black lock screw (M10). To improve the secure positioning of thrust bushing, the black screw (615 990 01 15) should be substituted at the earliest possible opportunity. Tighten lock screw to 11-19 ft. lbs. (1.5-2.5 mkg). See Fig. 13.*

**Disassembly** — 1) Remove oil strainer. Unscrew lower pump body, and remove pump gears and shafts. Check clearances between gear-to-body and gear-to-cover.

2) If cast-in bushings in housing are worn, replace complete housing. Worn gears are replaced as an assembly. Assemble

upper and lower housing without a gasket. Install strainer with a new gasket. Check that pump turns freely.

**NOTE** — *Beginning at Engine No. 027648, a new thrust bushing (615 180 00 44) with a thicker wall was adapted. The cover disc under the screw plug has been eliminated, and the "O" ring formerly located under the cover disc has been moved down onto the side of the thrust bushing. Parts are not interchangeable. Always use the black locking screw (615 990 01 15).*

**Installation** — 1) Align drive shaft follower with helical gear and follower faces with respect to one another.

2) Insert oil pump with bracket and tighten mounting screws. Install oil pan.

"O" Ring — Screw Plug — M 10 Lock Screw — Thrust Bushing — Bearing Bushing — Helical Gear — Int. Gear Shaft — Bearing Bushing — Oil Pump Shaft

Fig. 13   Location of Thrust Bushing Lock Screw

## ENGINE COOLING

**Thermostat** — Opens at 78-82°F (26-28°C).

Vent Screw

Fig. 14   Thermostat Housing Vent Screw

# Mercedes-Benz Engines

## 300D DIESEL 5 CYLINDER (Cont.)

**Cooling System Capacity** – 11.6 quarts.

**NOTE** – *When filling engine with water, vent screw on thermostat housing must be removed until water flows from it. See Fig. 14.*

### WATER PUMP

**Removal** – 1) Drain cooling system below level of pump. Loosen hose clamps on top radiator hose. Remove radiator mounting bolts and push radiator forward.

2) Remove fan from drive pulley. Loosen nuts and adjusters on generator enough so fan belt may be removed. Unscrew and remove venting line between pump and cylinder head.

3) Water pump is a maintenance free type. When installing pump, check hub-to-flange and impeller-to-flange distance. See Fig. 15.

Fig. 15   Sectional View of Water Pump

## ENGINE SPECIFICATIONS

### GENERAL SPECIFICATIONS

| Year | Displ. | | Carburetor | HP at RPM | Torque (Ft. Lbs. at RPM) | Compr. Ratio | Bore | | Stroke | |
| | cu. ins. | cc | | | | | in. | mm | in. | mm |
|---|---|---|---|---|---|---|---|---|---|---|
| 1978 | 183.4 | 3005 | Fuel Inj. | 77@4000 | 115@2400 | 21.0-1 | 3.58 | 91 | 3.64 | 92.4 |

### VALVES

| Engine & Valve | Head Diam. In. (mm) | Face Angle | Seat Angle | Seat Width In. (mm) | Stem Diameter In. (mm) | Stem Clearance In. (mm) | Valve Lift In. (mm) |
|---|---|---|---|---|---|---|---|
| 3005 cc Intake | 1.563-1.571 (39.70-39.90) | 30° | 30° | .051-.063 (1.3-1.6) | .3906-.3913 (9.92-9.94) | .0030 (.075) | ..... |
| Exhaust | 1.343-1.350 (34.10-34.30) | 30° | 30° | .098-.114 (2.5-2.9) | .3906-.3913 (9.92-9.94) | .0030 (.075) | ..... |

### VALVE SPRINGS

| Engine | Free Length In. (mm) | PRESSURE Lbs. @ In. (kg @ mm) | |
| | | Valve Closed | Valve Open |
|---|---|---|---|
| 3005 cc | 1.988 (50.5) | 58.2@1.512 (26.4@38.41) | 116.8@1.177 (53.0@29.9) |

### CAMSHAFT ①

| Engine | Journal Diam. In. (mm) | Clearance In. (mm) | Lobe Lift In. (mm) |
|---|---|---|---|
| 3005 cc No. 1 | 1.3763-1.3769 (34.96-34.97) | .0010-.0026 (.025-.066) | ..... |
| No. 2, 3, & 4 | 1.8290-1.8297 (46.46-46.47) | .0010-.0026 (.025-.066) | ..... |

① – End play is .003-.006" (.070-.149)

## 300D DIESEL 5 CYLINDER (Cont.)

### ENGINE SPECIFICATIONS (Cont.)

### PISTONS, PINS, RINGS

| Engine | PISTONS | PINS | | RINGS | | |
| --- | --- | --- | --- | --- | --- | --- |
| | Clearance In. (mm) | Piston Fit In. (mm) | Rod Fit In. (mm) | Rings | End Gap In. (mm) | Side Clearance In. (mm) |
| 3005 cc | .0007-.0015 (.018-.038) | ① | Push Fit | No. 1 | .0079-.0138 (.20-.35) | .004-.005 (.100-.132) |
| | | | | No. 2 | .0079-.0138 (.20-.35) | .003-.004 (.070-.102) |
| | | | | No. 3 | .0098-.0157 (.25-.40) | .001-.002 (.030-.062) |

① — Interference fit. See Piston & Rod Assembly in this article.

### CRANKSHAFT MAIN & CONNECTING ROD BEARINGS

| Engine | MAIN BEARINGS | | | | CONNECTING ROD BEARINGS | | |
| --- | --- | --- | --- | --- | --- | --- | --- |
| | Journal Diam. In. (mm) | Clearance In. (mm) | Thrust Bearing | Crankshaft End Play In. (mm) | Journal Diam. In. (mm) | Clearance In. (mm) | Side Play In. (mm) |
| 3005 cc | 2.7541-2.7545 (69.95-69.96) | .0012-.0029 (.031-.073) | No. 3 | .0039-.0090 (.10-.22) | 2.0454-2.0458 (51.95-51.96) | .0012-.0029 (.031-.073) | .005-.010 (.12-.26) |

### VALVE TIMING

| Engine | INTAKE | | EXHAUST | |
| --- | --- | --- | --- | --- |
| | Open (ATDC) | Close (ALDC) | Open (BLDC) | Close (BTDC) |
| 3005 cc | 13.5° | 15.5° | 19° | 17° |

### TIGHTENING SPECIFICATIONS

| Application | Ft. Lbs. (mkg) |
| --- | --- |
| Cylinder Head | |
| Step 1 | 29 (4) |
| Step 2 | 43 (6) |
| Step 3① | 65 (9) |
| Camshaft Bearing Caps | 18 (2.5) |
| Glow Plugs | 36 (5) |
| Prechamber in Cyl. Head | 108-130 (15-18) |
| Connecting Rod Caps | 29-36 (4-5) |
| Main Bearing Caps | 65 (9) |
| Crankshaft Front Hex Bolt | 195-239 (27-33) |
| Oil Pan Bolts | 8 (1.1) |
| Oil Pump Lock Screw (M10) | 11-19 (1.5-2.5) |
| Oil Pump Screw Plug | 32-40 (4.5-5.5) |
| Camshaft Sprocket Bolt | 58 (8) |

① — After engine is warm, recheck for 65 ft. lbs. (9 mkg) torque.

# Mercedes-Benz Engines

## 280 6 CYLINDER

### ENGINE CODING

#### ENGINE IDENTIFICATION

Engine number is stamped on front left side of cylinder block. Engine is a six cylinder double overhead cam type referred to as an M110.

| Application | Chassis Type | Engine Coding |
|---|---|---|
| 280E | 123.033 | 110.984 |
| 280CE | 123.053 | 110.984 |
| 280SE | 116.024 | 110.985 |

### ENGINE, CYLINDER HEAD & MANIFOLDS

#### ENGINE

**NOTE** — *Engine and transmission must be removed as a unit. On 123 series vehicles, engine hood does not have to be removed. The hood can be opened to a 90° position and held in place by a locking mechanism on the left hinge.*

**Removal & Installation** — **1)** Remove radiator and fan. On vehicles with level control, remove pump from engine and set aside with hoses connected. On vehicles with air conditioning, remove compressor and set aside without disconnecting refrigerant hoses.

**2)** Drain oil supply tank and disconnect power steering hoses from pump. Remove retaining ring from longitudinal accelerator shaft and push toward firewall to remove.

**3)** Disconnect all water, vacuum, oil and electrical lines leading to engine. Disconnect exhaust pipes from manifold and strut on transmission. Attach suitable lifting sling and remove engine mounting hardware. Lift engine from vehicle at a 45° angle. To install, reverse removal procedures.

#### INTAKE MANIFOLD

**Removal** — Partially drain radiator and remove air cleaner. Disconnect electrical wires, water hoses and vacuum lines. Disconnect cold start valve and remove linkage. Remove attaching screws and remove intake manifold.

**Installation** — To install, reverse removal procedure, using a new gasket.

#### CYLINDER HEAD

**NOTE** — *Cylinder head may only be removed after engine has cooled down. Head is removed complete with manifolds and camshaft housing.*

**Removal** — **1)** Drain cooling system. Remove A/C compressor (leave lines connected) and level control oil pump for models so equipped. Remove both camshaft housing front covers.

**2)** Remove cover and vacuum pump from front of camshaft housing. Disconnect all electrical leads, water hoses and vacuum lines from cylinder head and manifold.

**3)** Remove longitudinal regulating linkage and EGR line. Disconnect oil return line at cylinder head. Loosen hose between water pump and thermostat housing. Disconnect bypass line at water pump.

**4)** Loosen dipstick guide tube at cylinder head and bend slightly to the side. Disconnect exhaust pipes at manifold and transmission. Remove preheater scoop. Using a screwdriver,

force out rocker arm tension springs. Using suitable tool (110 589 04 61 00), remove all rocker arms.

**5)** Rotate crankshaft until both camshaft timing marks are correctly aligned with crankshaft at TDC on firing stroke. Using suitable holding wrench (116 589 01 01 00), remove both camshaft sprocket bolts.

**6)** Remove upper slide rail and pull out bearing bolts with suitable extractor (116 589 20 33 00). Remove chain tensioner. Push both camshafts to rear and remove sprockets.

**7)** Using suitable extractor, pull out bearing pins and remove idler pulley. Extract guide rail bearing pins and remove guide rail.

**8)** Loosen head bolts in reverse of tightening order. Remove two 8mm bolts in chain box with a magnet, do not drop washers into timing cover. Pull up timing chain and force tension rail toward center of engine. Using two men, lift cylinder head vertically from cylinder block.

**Installation** — **1)** Place head gasket on cylinder block. Lay two pieces of wood, ½"x1¾"x9½" long, upright between cylinders one and two and flat between cylinders five and six. Mount cylinder head at an inclined position, so that timing chain and tensioner rail can be installed.

**2)** Lift cylinder head and carefully remove wooden pieces. Lower head carefully, ensuring that front and rear dowels are properly engaged. Insert lubricated head bolts and tighten in 2 stages according to sequence shown in *Fig. 1*. Insert and tighten 8 mm bolts in chain box with Allen wrench.

**NOTE** — *After tightening all head bolts, camshaft should be free to turn by hand.*

**3)** Install lower slide rail and idler sprocket. Place spacer on intake camshaft journal. With engine at TDC, install camshaft sprockets with timing marks aligned.

**NOTE** — *TDC mark on vibration damper is next to dowel pin.*

**4)** Place spacers in front camshaft bearing of both camshafts. Install camshaft sprockets bolts, but do not tighten. Install upper slide rail and rigid chain tensioner. Using suitable holder tool (116 589 01 01 00), tighten expansion bolts.

**NOTE** — *If early type camshaft sprocket bolts with two spring washers were installed, replace with new expansion bolts (110 990 02 19) and a single washer (110 990 23 40).*

**5)** Rotate engine two revolutions and recheck camshaft timing marks. Install swing lever and tensioner springs. Install chain tensioner and adjust valve clearances. Retighten head bolts after engine has been warmed to 176°F (water temperature). Tighten by first loosening head bolts a ¼ of a turn, one at a time and tighten in tightening order. Retighten 8mm bolts in chain box.

**NOTE** — *Further tightening of head bolts after 300-500 miles is no longer required. It is not necessary to recheck valve clearances after final tightening of head bolts.*

## 280 6 CYLINDER (Cont.)

**Fig. 1  Cylinder Head Tightening Sequence
(Remove in Reverse Sequence)**

## VALVES

### VALVE ARRANGEMENT

**Right Side** — All exhaust.
**Left Side** — All intake.

### VALVE GUIDE SERVICING

1) Using a suitable drift, drive valve guide out top of cylinder head. Inspect guide bore in cylinder head, drive new standard guide in until lock ring touches head, if head condition permits.

2) If standard valve guide is not tight in head, ream cylinder head and install oversize valve guide. Heat cylinder head to 194°F and chill valve guide. Drive new guide in until lock ring touches head.

### Valve Guide Specifications

| Application | Guide O.D. In. (mm) | Head I.D. In. (mm) |
|---|---|---|
| Intake | | |
| Std. .......................... | .5523-.5331 (14.03-14.05) | .5519-.5527 (14.02-14.04) |
| 1st O.S. (red) ............. | .5594-.5602 (14.21-14.23) | .5590-.5598 (14.20-14.22) |
| 2nd O.S. (white) ......... | .5673-.5681 (14.41-14.43) | .5669-.5677 (14.40-14.42) |
| Exhaust | | |
| Std. .......................... | .5917-.5925 (15.03-15.05) | .5913-.5921 (15.02-15.04) |
| 1st O.S. (red) ............. | .5988-.5996 (15.21-15.23) | .5984-.5992 (15.20-15.22) |
| 2nd O.S. (white) ......... | .6066-.6074 (15.41-15.43) | .6062-.6070 (15.40-15.42) |

### VALVE STEM OIL SEALS

With valve springs removed, pull off old seal. Place assembly sleeves over intake valve stems and slide new valve stem seal over valve stems. Remove assembly sleeve and force seal over end of valve guide with installation mandrel.

### VALVE SPRINGS

1) With camshaft housing removed, place piston on TDC of cylinder from which springs are to be removed. Install a compressed air line to spark plug hole to pressurize valves.

2) Remove valve thrust pieces. Attach suitable holding rail (110 589 06 62 00) to cylinder head. Lightly tap valve collars to loosen keepers. Install suitable spring compressor and press down on springs. Remove valve keepers and release pressure on springs. Remove inner and outer springs and check for wear or fatigue. To install, reverse removal procedures with close wound coils (color coding) next to cylinder head.

### ROCKER ARM & STUD ASSEMBLY

1) With a screwdriver, pry out rocker arm tensioner springs. Using crankshaft, rotate engine until heel of cam lobe is next to rocker arm. Using suitable tool (110 589 04 61 00), remove rocker arm.

2) Unscrew threaded bushing with valve adjusting screw. Lubricate threads of adjusting screw with tallow and check that screw has at least 14.5 ft. lbs. of turning torque in bushing.

3) Install threaded bushing and adjusting screw in cylinder head. Lubricate rocker arm and pivot. Using suitable tool (110 589 04 61 00), install rocker arms and tensioner springs. Readjust valve clearances.

**CAUTION** — *Do not rotate engine by camshaft sprocket bolts. Do not rotate engine in reverse as camshaft sprocket may jump time.*

**Fig. 2  Sectional View of Rocker Arm
and Valve Assembly**

### VALVE CLEARANCE ADJUSTMENT

Rotate crankshaft until heel of camshaft lobe is next to rocker arm. Insert a feeler gauge between camshaft and rocker arm. Turn adjusting screw until proper clearance is achieved.

# Mercedes-Benz Engines

## 280 6 CYLINDER (Cont.)

### Valve Clearance

| Application | In. (mm) |
|---|---|
| Intake | |
| Hot | ①.006 (.15) |
| Cold | ①.004 (.10) |
| Exhaust | |
| Hot | .012 (.30) |
| Cold | .010 (.25) |

① — Winter Clearance, add .002" (.05mm).

## PISTONS, PINS & RINGS

### OIL PAN

**NOTE** — *A 2 piece oil pan is used. Due to complexity of operation, engine assembly must be removed to remove complete oil pan.*

To remove lower oil pan, remove fuel pump (carburetor engines), drain engine oil, remove mounting bolts and separate lower pan from upper section. To install, use suitable sealant on clean mating surface, use new gasket and reverse removal procedure.

### PISTON & ROD ASSEMBLY

**Removal** — With oil pan and cylinder head removed, remove rod caps and push piston and rod assembly out top of cylinder. Remove wrist pin locks and push out wrist pins. Clean and inspect all parts.

**Installation — 1)** Place piston on connecting rod so that arrow faces forward and recess for bearing insert is facing rear of engine. Install piston and rod assembly in cylinder. Install rod cap with code numbers facing rod numbers.

**2)** Rod bolts should be checked for minimum diameter with a pair of sharp edged calipers. If diameter is less than .283", replace rod bolts. Tighten rod bolts to 36 ft. lbs. and then tighten an additional 100° of rotation.

### FITTING PISTONS

Measure cylinder bores near top, bottom, and center in at least 2 directions. If greater than .004" (.10 mm) from standard, cylinders must be bored and new pistons fitted.

### Cylinder Bore Specifications

| Application | In. (mm) |
|---|---|
| Standard | 3.3858-3.3866 (86.0-86.02) |
| 1st Oversize | 3.4055-3.4063 (86.50-86.52) |
| 2nd Oversize | 3.4252-3.4260 (87.0-87.02) |

### PISTON PINS

Piston pins are retained with circlips in pistons. To remove pins, remove circlips and press out piston pins. To install, ensure that arrow on piston crown faces front (timing chain end) and that bearing retaining notch in connecting rod faces left (intake manifold) side of engine. Lubricate pin and press into piston rod assembly by hand.

**NOTE** — *Do NOT heat piston to install piston pin.*

## CRANKSHAFT MAIN & CONNECTING ROD BEARINGS

### MAIN & CONNECTING ROD BEARINGS

**1)** Remove connecting rod and main bearing caps. Check all bearing journals for wear, taper or out-of-round. The following table gives maximum dimensions which are permissible without repair or new bearings.

### Crankshaft Specifications

| Application | In. (mm) |
|---|---|
| Out-of Round | .0002 (.005) |
| Journal Taper | .0004 (.010) |
| Journal Flatness | .0006 (.015) |
| Bearing Bore Out-of-Round | .0004 (.010) |
| Bearing Bore Taper | .0004 (.010) |

**2)** Bearing inserts for both main and connecting rod journals are color coded. Main bearing inserts with no color are thicker than ones which are blue. Connecting rod inserts with red color are thicker than ones with blue color. Select inserts which will give the mean of clearance range.

### Crankshaft Journal Diameters

| Application | Main Bearing In. (mm) | Connecting Rod In. (mm) |
|---|---|---|
| Std. | 2.3602-2.3606 (59.95-59.96) | 1.8878-1.8882 (47.95-47.96) |
| 1st U.S. | 2.3504-2.3508 (58.70-59.71) | 1.8779-1.8783 (47.70-47.71) |
| 2nd U.S. | 2.3405-2.3409 (59.45-59.46) | 1.8681-1.8685 (47.45-47.46) |
| 3rd U.S. | 2.3307-2.3311 (59.20-59.21) | 1.8583-1.8587 (47.20-47.21) |
| 4th U.S. | 2.3209-2.3213 (58.95-58.96) | 1.8484-1.8488 (46.95-46.96) |

### Bearing Insert Wall Thickness

| Application ① | Main Bearing In. (mm) | Connecting Rod In. (mm) |
|---|---|---|
| Std. | .1378 (3.50) | .0713 (1.81) |
| 1st U.S. | .1429 (3.63) | .0764 (1.94) |
| 2nd U.S. | .1476 (3.75) | .0811 (2.06) |
| 3rd U.S. | .1528 (3.88) | .0858 (2.18) |
| 4th U.S. | .1575 (4.00) | .0909 (2.31) |

① — Late models use bearings with 360° groove on both halves of all main bearings except for No. 4, which is smooth on both halves. Number 3 main bearing requires machining to establish proper end play. See *Thrust Bearing Alignment.*

### THRUST BEARING ALIGNMENT

Install number three main bearing and measure clearance between bearing and crankshaft sides. If clearance is excessive, install new bearing. New bearings are supplied in oversize widths and must be lapped on non-thrust side to achieve proper clearance. Lap only side away from flywheel.

### REAR MAIN BEARING OIL SEAL

Press pieces of seal into cylinder block and oil pan with a wooden hammer handle. Cut ends of seal so they protrude .020" (.5 mm) above parting surfaces. Oil seal halves liberally and install crankshaft and oil pan. Check for easy rotation of crankshaft and reassemble engine.

## 280 6 CYLINDER (Cont.)

### FRONT COVER OIL SEAL

**1)** Remove radiator and fan, pulley and vibration damper. Mark balance disc and crankshaft with punch for assembly purposes. Use suitable puller and remove balance disc.

**2)** Pry old seal out with screwdriver, using caution not to damage seal bore or crankshaft journal. Clean and inspect seal bore and apply oil to new seal (do NOT use sealing compound). Press seal into position with installing tool (110 589 07 61 00).

**3)** Install new spacing ring or turn used ring around so that worn groove is at rear. Install remaining components in reverse order of assembly.

**Fig. 3   Cut-Away View of Vibration Damper**

## CAMSHAFT

### TIMING CHAIN

**1)** Remove spark plugs and cylinder head cover. Remove rocker arms of right hand (exhaust) camshaft. Remove chain tensioner and install rigid chain tensioner (110 589 03 31 00).

**2)** Cover chain box with a rag, using a chain breaker, separate chain. Join ends of new and old chains together with a master link. Rotate crankshaft in direction of rotation and pull old chain out of engine. Use care that chain does not jump a tooth on sprockets.

**CAUTION** — *Do not turn engine by camshaft bolts. Do not rotate crankshaft in reverse.*

**3)** Join ends of new chain. Rotate crankshaft and check timing marks. Replace rigid chain tensioner with normal chain tensioner. Install rocker arms and adjust exhaust valve clearance. Install camshaft cover and spark plugs.

**Fig. 4   Front View of Timing Chain and Sprockets**

### CAMSHAFT & CAMSHAFT HOUSING

**Removal — 1)** Remove battery and A.I.R. pump. Disconnect air conditioning compressor and set aside with hoses connected. Drain radiator and remove hose between radiator and engine. Remove camshaft cover.

**2)** Remove camshaft sprocket covers from front of housing. Pry all rocker arm tension springs from rocker arms. Using a suitable tool (110 589 04 61 00), remove all rocker arms.

**3)** Using suitable holding tool (116 589 01 01 00), remove right-hand camshaft sprocket bolt. Set number one piston to TDC on firing stroke with both camshaft timing marks aligned. Remove chain tensioner.

**4)** Remove slide rail in camshaft housing, using suitable puller (115 589 19 33 00). Remove rear right-hand camshaft cover. Push camshaft to the rear, using suitable tool (110 589 03 33 00), while holding camshaft sprocket in place. Remove sprocket and slide camshaft back in place.

**5)** Remove head bolts, shown in illustration, in reverse of tightening sequence. Do not remove bolts marked with an "x" in illustration. Remove camshaft housing and camshafts.

**NOTE** — *Camshaft housing may only be removed after engine has cooled down.*

# Mercedes-Benz Engines

## 280 6 CYLINDER (Cont.)

*Fig. 5 Camshaft Housing Tightening Sequence (Remove ONLY Numbered Bolts in Reverse Sequence)*

*Fig. 6 Camshaft Timing Marks with No. 1 Piston at TDC on Firing Stroke*

6) Remove left-hand camshaft sprocket in same manner as right-hand sprocket. Remove spacer ring at intake camshaft and slide both camshafts out rear of housing.

**Installation** — Install steel gasket on cylinder head without sealing compound. Place camshaft housing on head. Oil head bolts and tighten to 29 ft. lbs. (4.0 mkg), then to 51 ft. lbs. (7.0 mkg). Loosen 5 deeper head bolts slightly, then tighten all head bolts to final torque in sequence shown in *Fig. 1*. Tighten the 8 mm bolts to 18 ft. lbs. (2.5 mkg) working from center outward.

**NOTE** — *If early type camshaft sprocket bolts with two spring washers were installed, replace with new expansion bolts (110 990 02 19) and a single washer (110 990 23 40).*

## CAMSHAFT BEARINGS

If camshaft bearing journals are worn, damaged or have excessive clearance in camshaft housing bearings, camshaft journals may be ground undersize and a repair housing installed.

Front bearing journal (See "a" in *Fig. 6*) is not ground and remains standard. Journal should be fitted with a spacer sleeve. Camshafts do not have to be ground or replaced because of rough surfaces or bearings.

## VALVE TIMING

Rotate crankshaft until number one piston is at TDC on firing stroke. Both camshaft timing marks should be aligned with marks on camshaft housing. Offset woodruff keys are available to make corrections to timing. Remember that camshaft sprockets rotate in opposite directions, they rotate toward each other.

**NOTE** — *Some balance discs have two "O" degree marks. TDC is next to a dowel pin.*

### Offset Woodruff Keys

| Offset | Part No. | Correction |
|---|---|---|
| .0275" (.7 mm) | 621 991 04 67 | 4° |
| .0354" (.9 mm) | 621 991 02 67 | 6.5° |
| .0433" (1.1 mm) | 621 991 01 67 | 8° |
| .0511" (1.3 mm) | 621 991 00 67 | 10° |

## ENGINE OILING

**Crankcase Capacity** — 7.5 quarts (including filter).

**Oil Filter** — 1.5 pts. (Full-flow).

**Normal Oil Pressure** — 7.1 psi (.5 kg/cm²) at 800-900 RPM; 42 psi (3 kg/cm²) at 3000 RPM.

**Pressure Regulator Valve** — Nonadjustable.

## ENGINE OILING SYSTEM

Oil is drawn from the oil pan by a gear type oil pump and pressure fed through a full-flow oil filter to crankshaft main bearings. Passages drilled in crankshaft carry oil to connecting rod bearings. A passageway drilled longitudinally through the connecting rod carries oil from connecting rod bearing to wrist pin bushing. A further passageway carries oil to intermediate shaft, oil pump, and distributor drive gears. This passageway also lubricates camshaft bearings, cam lobes, rocker arms, idler sprocket, and chain tensioner.

## OIL PUMP

Remove fuel pump and lower half of oil pan. Remove screws from crankcase and main bearing cap. Pull out oil pump. Disassemble, clean and inspect oil pump. To install, reverse removal procedure.

## ENGINE COOLING

**Cooling System Capacity** — 280E, 280CE — 10.6 qts. 280SE — 11.6 qts.

**Cooling System Capacity** — 280E, 10.5 qts. 280SE, 11.5 qts.

**Thermostat** — Opens at 185-193°F (85-89°C).

## WATER PUMP

Drain radiator and disconnect water hoses. Loosen radiator shell and remove radiator. Remove fan and fan clutch (store in upright position). Remove all drive belts. Remove six Allen screws attaching pulley and vibration damper. Withdraw pulley and damper. Remove water pump. To install, reverse removal procedure.

## 280 6 CYLINDER (Cont.)
### ENGINE SPECIFICATIONS

### GENERAL SPECIFICATIONS

| Year | Displ. cu. ins. | Displ. cc | Carburetor | HP at RPM | Torque (Ft. Lbs. at RPM) | Compr. Ratio | Bore in. | Bore mm | Stroke in. | Stroke mm |
|---|---|---|---|---|---|---|---|---|---|---|
| 1978 | 167.6 | 2746 | Fuel Inj. | 142@5750① | 149@4600② | 8.0-1 | 3.39 | 86 | 3.10 | 78.8 |

① — Calif. 137@5750    ② — Calif. 142@4600

### VALVES

| Engine & Valve | Head Diam. In. (mm) | Face Angle | Seat Angle | Seat Width In. (mm) | Stem Diameter In. (mm) | Stem Clearance In. (mm) | Valve Lift In. (mm) |
|---|---|---|---|---|---|---|---|
| 2746 cc Intake | 1.775-1.783 (45.1-45.3) | 45° | 45° | .071-.098 (1.8-2.5) | .3524-.3531 (8.95-8.97) | .0019 (.05) | ..... |
| Exhaust | 1.4567-1.4645 (37.0-37.2) | 45° | 45° | .059-.079 (1.5-2.0) | .4307-.4315 (10.94-10.96) | .0023 (.06) | ..... |

### PISTONS, PINS, RINGS

| Engine | PISTONS Clearance In. (mm) | PINS Piston Fit In. (mm) | PINS Rod Fit In. (mm) | Rings | End Gap In. (mm) | Side Clearance In. (mm) |
|---|---|---|---|---|---|---|
| 2746 cc | .0010-.0013 (.025-.035) Limit .03 (.08) | .00008-.0004 (.002-.011) | .0003-.0007 (.007-.017) | No. 1 | .012-.018 (.30-.45) | .0019-.0032 (.050-.082) |
| | | | | No. 2 | .012-.018 (.30-.45) | .0011-.0024 (.030-.062) |
| | | | | No. 3 | .010-.016 (.25-.40) | .0004-.0016 (.010-.042) |

### CAMSHAFT①

| Engine | Journal Diam. In. (mm) | Clearance In. (mm) | Lobe Lift In. (mm) |
|---|---|---|---|
| 2746 cc | | | |
| a | .9441-.9445 (23.98-23.99) | .002-.005 (.06-.12) | ..... |
| b | 1.9654-1.9661 (49.92-49.94) | .003-.006 (.10-.14) | ..... |
| c | 1.9657-1.9665 (49.93-49.95) | .002-.004 (.06-.09) | ..... |
| d | 2.0244-2.0252 (51.42-51.44) | .002-.004 (.06-.10) | ..... |
| e | 2.0835-2.0842 (52.92-52.94) | .002-.004 (.06-.10) | ..... |
| f | 2.1228-2.1236 (53.92-53.94) | .002-.004 (.06-.10) | ..... |

① — Journal diameters vary, with steps from smaller to larger going from front to rear. Later or exchange camshafts and housings may have only 10 bearing points. End play is .002-.005" (.050-.128 mm). See Fig. 7.

NOTE — Late model or exchange housings may not have bearing points indicated by ①. Earlier camshafts may nevertheless be used in these housings.

**Fig. 7  Camshaft Housing Bearing Identification**

# Mercedes-Benz Engines

## 280 6 CYLINDER (Cont.)
### ENGINE SPECIFICATIONS (Cont.)

### CRANKSHAFT MAIN & CONNECTING ROD BEARINGS

| Engine | MAIN BEARINGS | | | | CONNECTING ROD BEARINGS | | |
| | Journal Diam. In. (mm) | Clearance In. (mm) | Thrust Bearing | Crankshaft End Play In. (mm) | Journal Diam. In. (mm) | Clearance In. (mm) | Side Play In. (mm) |
|---|---|---|---|---|---|---|---|
| 2746 cc | 2.3602-2.3606 (59.95-59.96) | .001-.003 (.03-.05) | No. 3 | .004-.009 (.10-.24) | 1.8878-1.8882 (47.95-47.96) | .0005-.0020 (.013-.050) | .004-.009 (.11-.23) |

### VALVE SPRINGS

| Engine | Free Length In. (mm) | PRESSURE Lbs. @ In. (kg @ mm) | |
| | | Valve Closed | Valve Open |
|---|---|---|---|
| 2746 cc Inner | 1.772 (45) | 26.01@1.299 (11.8@33) | 50.7@.846 (23@21.5) |
| Outer | 1.949 (49.5) | 67.24@1.6535 (30.5@42) | 194@1.20 (88@30.5) |

### VALVE TIMING

| Engine | INTAKE | | EXHAUST | |
| | Open (ATDC) | Close (ALDC) | Open (BLDC) | Close (BTDC) |
|---|---|---|---|---|
| 2746 cc | 7° | 21° | 30° | 12° |

### TIGHTENING SPECIFICATIONS

| Application | Ft. Lbs. (mkg) |
|---|---|
| Main Bearings | 58 (8.0) |
| Connecting Rods | ①36 (5.0) |
| Crankshaft Bolt | 289-325 (40-45) |
| Camshaft Cover | 4 (.5) |
| Cylinder Head Bolts | |
| Stage 1 | 51 (7.0) |
| Stage 2 | 72 (10) |
| Stage 3② | 72 (10) |
| Camshaft Bolt | 72 (10) |
| Oil Pump | 21 (3.0) |
| Chain Tensioner Nut | 36 (5.0) |

① — Tighten bolts to 36 ft. lbs. (5 mkg) and then turn bolts an additional 100° of rotation.

② — With engine warm (176°F or 80°C), loosen all head bolts ¼ turn in tightening sequence, then tighten to final torque.

## 4.5 LITER V8

## ENGINE CODING

### ENGINE IDENTIFICATION

Identification number is located on tag attached to engine crankcase. First six digits of code are used to identify engine, as follows:

| Application | Chassis Type | Engine Code |
|---|---|---|
| 450 SLC | 107.024 | 117.985 |
| 450 SL | 107.044 | 117.985 |
| 450 SEL | 116.033 | 117.986 |

## ENGINE, CYLINDER HEAD & MANIFOLD

### ENGINE

**Removal** — **1)** Remove head and drain cooling system. Note that there are both left and right engine block drains. Disconnect and remove battery and remove battery frame. Evacuate air conditioning system and remove pipe set at compressor. Disconnect and remove all water, vacuum, oil, fuel and electric lines leading to engine.

**2)** On 450 SEL, disconnect exhaust system and remove right drag link end from ball head. On 450 SL and 450 SLC, completely remove exhaust system. On all models, drain power steering reservoir and disconnect hoses. Unscrew TDC test socket and remove cable for TDC transmitter.

**3)** Remove left and right engine shock absorbers. Attach engine sling and hoist to engine and remove engine mount bolts. Remove rear engine carrier with engine mount. Loosen and disconnect driveshaft from transmission. Remove linkages connecting transmission to chassis and lift engine out (with transmission attached) at a 45° angle.

**Installation** — Ensure that oil cooler and all hoses have been flushed and are free from contamination. Renew engine mounts and components as required and reverse removal procedure. Evacuate and charge air conditioning system and check entire installation for leaks.

### INTAKE MANIFOLD

Drain cooling system and remove air cleaner. Disconnect fuel injection linkage and fuel lines on pressure regulator. Disconnect fuel start valve. Remove ignition valves. Extract intake manifold bolts and lift manifold off in rearward direction. To install, reverse removal procedure.

### CYLINDER HEAD

**NOTE** — Cylinder head removal should not be attempted until engine has cooled down. Several specially shaped Allen wrenches are required for cylinder head bolt removal and replacement.

**Removal** — **1)** Remove left and right drain plugs and drain cooling system. Remove air cleaner and battery. Remove fuel line and injection valves. Disconnect fuel injection linkage.

**2)** Disconnect and remove intake pipe (manifold). Remove A/T fluid filler pipe from attachment to cylinder head. Remove alternator and mounting bracket. Remove distributor and power steering pump with mounting bracket.

**3)** Disconnect exhaust pipe from manifold and exhaust gas return line at 90° fitting. Remove chain tensioner and slide rails. Mark camshaft sprocket and timing chain position for assembly reference. Remove sprocket from camshaft. Using specially shaped Allen wrenches, remove head bolts and lift off head.

**Installation** — **1)** Ensure that all mating surfaces are clean and install new cylinder head gasket. Tighten cylinder head bolts in sequence shown to 22 ft. lbs. (3 mkg), and then to 43 ft. lbs. (6 mkg). Tighten 8 mm bolts to 18 ft. lbs. (2.5 mkg).

**2)** Complete assembly in reverse order of removal and run engine until normal operating temperature is reached. Slightly loosen head bolts individually, then retighten in sequence shown to final warm torque of 43 ft. lbs. (6 mkg).

**Fig. 1  Cylinder Head Tightening Sequence
(Loosen in Reverse Order)**

## VALVES

### VALVE ARRANGEMENT

**Right Bank** — E-I-E-I-E-I-I-E (front to rear).
**Left Bank** — E-I-I-E-I-E-I-E (front to rear).

### HYDRAULIC VALVE LIFTERS

**1)** Hydraulic valve lifters eliminate the need to adjust for valve clearance. See Fig. 2. Constant contact of rocker arms with camshaft, valves and lifters not only reduces noise, but also compensates for wear or temperature changes.

**2)** Oil pressure to operate the lifters is supplied by the oil pump, through a lateral passage in the cylinder head (with connecting bores to each lifter) and an oil passage in the fifth camshaft bearing. The spherical head plunger contains an oil reservoir, which is separated from the pressure chamber by a ball valve. See Fig. 2.

# Mercedes-Benz Engines

## 4.5 LITER V8 (Cont.)

**Camshaft**

**Rocker Arm**

**Thrust Piece**

**Valve Spring Retainer**

**Conical Valve Key Halves**

**Outer Valve Spring**

**Inner Valve Spring**

**Valve Stem Seal**

**Rotocap**

**Valve Guide**

**Intake Valve**

**Valve Seat Insert**

**Snap Ring**

**Hydraulic Valve Lifter**

**Spherical Head Plunger**

**Retaining Cap**

**Lifter Body**

**Reservoir**

**Ball**

**Compression Spring**

**Ball Guide**

**Compression Spring**

**Pressure Chamber**

*Fig. 2   Cutaway View of Valve System and Lifter*

**3)** When engine is stopped and cam lobe exerts pressure on the valve lifter, the plunger can be completely depressed. Oil from pressure chamber flows to reservoir. Turning cam lobe away from rocker arm releases plunger and compression spring pushes it upward until rocker arm rests against cam. Upward plunger movement causes a suction in the pressure chamber, causing oil to flow from reservoir to chamber.

**4)** The ball valve closes when the cam lobe exerts pressure on rocker arm. Trapped oil in pressure chamber forms a solid hydraulic connection which prevents the plunger from moving fully downward. Leak-off vents permit air and excess oil to escape.

**5)** To check hydraulic compensating element (lifter) performance, press on rocker arm at lifter end with valve in closed position. If pressure bleeds off too rapidly in comparison with other elements, replacement is required. If lifters are removed, they should be stored in an upright position and reinstalled in original location.

### VALVE GUIDE SERVICING

**1)** With cylinder head removed and suitably supported, clean bores of valve guides. Hard oil carbon deposits can be eliminated with a honing needle.

**2)** Using a suitable plug gauge, inspect valve guides. Inner diameter of new inlet guides should be .354-.355" (9.000-9.015 mm); exhaust guides should be .433-.434" (11.000-11.018 mm). If guide is beyond this tolerance, replace with new guide. See *Fig. 2.*

**3)** With suitable reamer/installer mandrel, drive worn guide from its bore. Inspect valve guide bore in cylinder head and ream to accept next oversize guide.

**NOTE** — *Replacement Inlet valve guides are available in overlapping sizes, ranging from .552-.568" (14.014-14.431 mm) outside diameter. Exhaust valve guides are available with outside diameters of .591-.608" (15.014-15.431 mm).*

**4)** Heat cylinder head to approximately 194° F (90° C) and cool valve guides (if possible). Coat guide bore with oil and, using remover/installer mandrel, seat new guide in bore.

**NOTE** — *Be sure snap ring is properly installed. Recheck valve guide clearance and that valve moves freely in guide.*

123 589 03 61 00

116 589 06 63 00

*Fig. 3   Removing Conical Valve Key Halves*

## 4.5 LITER V8 (Cont.)

### VALVE STEM SEALS

**Removal** — Using spring compressor (116 589 00 61 00), remove rocker arms. See Fig. 3. Lift out thrust plate, and using special magnet (116 589 06 63 00), remove conical valve key halves (keepers). Remove spring retainer, inner and outer valve springs, valve stem seals and rotocaps.

**Installation** — Replacement valve stem seals are supplied in a kit which includes assembly sleeves. Place sleeve over stem and install lubricated seal with installing tool. See Fig. 4. Install remaining components in reverse order of removal.

**Fig. 4  Installing Valve Stem Seal**

### VALVE SEAT RING

1) Check valve guide prior to removing seat ring. See Valve Guide Servicing. If seat ring is worn, carefully remove it by machining with a valve seat ring turning tool.

2) Thoroughly clean the receiving bore and check its diameter. If diameter is within specifications, install a new valve seat ring of the same size. If diameter is not within specification, 1.811-1.812" (46.0-46.02 mm) for intake or 1.575-1.576" (40.0-40.01 mm), machine bore to next oversize.

3) To install, heat cylinder head in water to approximately 140° F (60° C). Place pre-cooled seat ring into bore. To position seat ring, lightly tap ring, using a suitable mandrel and hammer. Machine valve seat to correct width and correct for runout. Do NOT machine rounded bead on lower part of valve seat. Valve seat runout should not exceed .0016" (.04 mm).

### ROCKER ARMS

1) Rocker arms are individually-mounted on the 16 valves, without use of a shaft. They are in constant contact with the camshaft, thrust plates above the valve stems, and hydraulic valve lifters. To remove, compress spring on each valve using compressor (123 589 03 61 00). Mark each arm for installation in original position.

2) Rocker arms have a chamfer behind ball socket (lifter end). This prevents rocker arm from striking retaining cap of lifters in extreme cases. Do not use rocker arms unless they have this chamfer.

3) Whenever camshaft is replaced, new rocker arms must also be installed. Likewise, when new rocker arms are installed, replace the camshaft, as well. When making replacements, check base setting of hydraulic valve lifters using test gauge (100 589 04 23 00). Correct, as required, using new thrust piece. Thrust pieces are available in steps of .0014" (.35 mm) from .147" (3.7 mm) to .228" (5.8 mm). See Adjusting Lifters to Base Setting.

### ADJUSTING LIFTERS TO BASE SETTING

**NOTE** — Always keep hydraulic valve lifters in an upright position. Rocker arms and valve lifters should always be reinstalled in original locations. When checking and adjusting lifter settings, crank engine for 30 seconds with starter contact switch.

1) When replacing compensating element (hydraulic lifters) or camshaft and rocker arms, basic position of compensating element must be checked. Rotate engine so that cam lobe of element to be checked is in the upright position and install test gauge (100 589 04 23 00).

2) Set measuring pin of gauge through rocker arm hole so that it rests on ball pin of lifter. Basic position is correct when red groove of pin is aligned with measuring edge of tool. If groove is below measuring edge, a plus (+) deviation is indicated, requiring a thinner thrust piece. Entire groove showing above measuring edge indicates a minus (−) deviation and requires a thicker thrust piece.

3) To correct setting, remove rocker arm and thrust piece. Install thinner or thicker thrust piece as required and reinstall rocker arm. Repeat measuring procedure. Position is correct when center of measuring groove aligns with edge of gauge.

## PISTONS, PINS & RINGS

### OIL PAN

**450 SL and 450 SLC** — 1) Remove radiator shell and shroud. Remove front axle assembly. Remove A/C compressor and mounting bracket. Remove supporting angle bracket between pan and transmission.

2) Remove oil pan bolts and lower oil pan along with dip stick guide tube from engine. To install, apply grease to clean mating surfaces and install new gasket. Place pan in position and reverse removal procedure.

**450 SEL** — 1) Remove A/C compressor and mounting bracket from engine. Remove drive belt tensioning pulley. Unbolt and remove oil pan lower half. Remove oil pump drive sprocket and mounting bolts. Remove oil pump.

2) Remove cooling fan pulley and thermostat housing cover. Knock oil pan dip stick guide tube from pan and disconnect transmission oil lines. Remove supporting angle bracket on transmission. Remove oil pan bolts and rotate crankshaft so that oil pan can be removed in a down and forward direction.

3) To install, ensure that all mating surfaces are clean and apply thin layer of grease. Use new gasket and install oil pan upper half. Continue assembly in reverse order of removal.

## 4.5 LITER V8 (Cont.)

### CRANKSHAFT MAIN & CONNECTING ROD BEARINGS

#### MAIN & CONNECTING ROD BEARINGS

1) Mount main bearing cap to cylinder block (without bearings in place). Measure inside diameter at three locations. See Fig. 5. Be sure cap is properly positioned when taking reading. Offset bearing caps can be moved into center position by lightly tapping them with a plastic hammer.

**Fig. 5   Location for Measuring Main Bearing Bore Diameter**

2) All three measurements should agree. If basic bores exceed specifications and the required overlap of bearing shell halves is not assured, remove .008″ (.02 mm) from contact surfaces, using a surface plate.

3) Measure main bearing and connecting rod bearings at front and rear to check for taper. If beyond .0006″ (.015 mm), remove excess material from one side of bearing cap, using surface plate.

4 Use proper bearing shells to match measurements obtained. Several overlapping bearing sizes are available. Fit bearing halves into bearing bore and tighten bolts to proper torque. Measure inner diameter of bearings and outer diameter of journals. Difference in measurements should be within bearing clearance specifications. If not, change bearing shell halves.

**Fig. 6   Crankshaft Main Bearing Tightening Sequence**

5) When proper clearance is calculated, clean and oil all parts and install crankshaft. Torque to specifications according to sequence. See Fig. 6.

6) With crankshaft properly installed, check for free rotation and for proper end play. Install connecting rods.

### REAR CRANKSHAFT SEALING RING

1) With engine removed from vehicle, unbolt and remove rear cover. Force out old sealing ring. Clean cover and sealing surfaces.

2) Check crankshaft running surface for scoring. Sealing ring with sealing lip offset inward is available in case of scored crankshaft. Press new seal into cover with suitable tool.

**Fig. 7   Removing Rear Cover and Seal**

3) Lubricate lip of seal and coat cover with sealing compound. Place conical sleeve (116 589 03 43 00) over crankshaft end and place cover in position. Use care so that pan gasket is not damaged. Tighten cover bolts evenly and install drive plate.

**NOTE** — Drive plate (flywheel) can only be mounted in one position due to offset of 1 of the 8 fastening bolts.

Conical Sleeve (116 589 03 43 00)

**Fig. 8   Installing Rear Cover and Seal**

## 4.5 LITER V8 (Cont.)

### FRONT CRANKSHAFT SEALING RING

**Removal** – With engine removed from vehicle. Remove all V-belts, mark hub and crankshaft with paint or chalk. Remove vibration damper, pulley and hub. Remove sealing ring, making sure that crankshaft and receiving bore are not damaged.

**Installation** – Deburr edge of receiving bore before installing new seal. Lubricate receiving bore and seal lip with oil. Install sealing ring with installation sleeve (110 589 07 61 00). Reassemble remaining components in reverse of removal procedure.

### CAMSHAFT

**Removal** – With cylinder head covers removed, set No. 1 piston at TDC firing position and remove rocker arms. Mark sprockets and timing chain for reassembly. Remove camshaft sprockets. Unbolt and remove camshaft bearings, oil tube and camshaft as an assembly.

**Installation** – 1) Assemble bearings on camshaft. Note that smooth bearing journals must fit in bearings with an oil groove, and camshaft journals with an oil groove fit only in bearings WITHOUT an oil groove.

2) Place camshaft and bearing assembly on head. Note that outer screw of left camshaft rear bearing must be inserted in bearing prior to mounting due to interference from brake unit. Oil pipe connections on bearings must be renewed to ensure proper oil pressure.

3) Tighten camshaft bearing mounting screws and check that camshaft rotates freely. Mount compensating washer so that both inner and outer notches align with Woodruff key in camshaft. Assmble sprockets to camshaft so that white color faces camshaft and timing marks are aligned.

**Fig. 9   Timing Chains & Sprockets**

4) Install rocker arms and check basic clearance of lifters. Complete assembly in reverse order of removal.

**NOTE** – *Whenever it is necessary to install either new rocker arms or camshaft, both rocker arms and camshaft must be replaced. Camshaft journals may be reground and undersize bearings installed.*

### DISTRIBUTOR DRIVE GEAR

1) With timing and crankshaft chains exposed, disconnect all chain dampers (slide rails) and timing chain tensioner. Remove chain from intermediate sprocket and pull sprocket from engine.

2) Use suitable puller to extract bushing from crankcase and cover. Press new bushings in position so that lubricating groove is at bottom. Lubricate bushings and install intermediate sprocket. Note that mark on sprocket must align with mark on crankcase with engine at TDC position. Continue assembly in reverse order of removal.

### CHAIN TENSIONER

**NOTE** – *In all instances chain tensioner is lubricated and connected to oiling circuit.*

1) Remove air injector pipe and 3 screws fastening tensioner. Remove chain tensioner.

2) To check tensioner, place in container of oil vertically so that oil covers flange. Actuate plunger to fill tensioner with oil. After filling and venting, plunger should allow compression very slowly and evenly, and with considerable force.

3) To install, use new gasket and tighten screws evenly. Pressure pin of tensioner must press against lug of tensioning rail.

### VALVE TIMING

1) Measure timing periods on inlet valves of cylinder 1 and 6. Remove hydraulic valve lifters and replace with adjusting screws (116 050 11 20). Adjust each screw so rocker arm just touches the base circle of the cam.

2) Attach dial indicator so that pointer rests vertically on valve spring retainer. Pin should have .118" (3 mm) preload and dial should be set to zero.

3) Turn engine in direction of normal rotation until pointer moves .0787" (2 mm), leaving a preload of .039" (1 mm). Readings should be in accordance with valve timing chart. Repeat for No. 6 intake valve.

4) If timing requires correction, install an offset Woodruff Key or new chain. Keys are available in four offsets providing corrections of 4°, 6½°, 8°, and 10°.

5) After checking and adjusting valve timing, reinstall hydraulic lifters and adjust for proper base setting. See *ADJUSTING LIFTERS TO BASE SETTING.*

# Mercedes-Benz Engines

## 4.5 LITER V8 (Cont.)

### ENGINE OILING

#### ENGINE OILING SYSTEM

Lubrication is provided by a gear type oil pump directly driven by crankshaft. Oil is picked up through a strainer from lower portion of oil pan and forced to oil filter through a duct in timing casing. After passing through filter, oil flows to center main duct, to crankshaft and through rod bearings up rods to piston pin bushing. Oil galleries run to cylinder head, valve assemblies and to camshafts. Circuit also includes chain tensioner, ignition and, if applicable, air compressor.

**Oil Filter** — Disposable cartridge type. Located near front of engine.

**Normal Oil Pressure** — 7.1 psi@idle; 42.6 psi@3000 RPM.

**Over Flow Valve** — Valve is located in crankcase and enters into main oil gallery. When filter becomes severely contaminated valve will open and oil will enter in an unfiltered state.

**Crankcase Capacity** — 8.4 quarts with filter.

### ENGINE COOLING

#### WATER PUMP

Disconnect all necessary water hoses and any remaining components from water pump housing. Remove distributor and all mounting bolts. Remove pump from vehicle. To install, reverse removal procedure.

**Thermostat** — Located in water pump housing, as shown in illustration. To remove drain cooling system, remove air cleaner, disconnect battery and alternator. Remove housing and thermostat. When installing ensure ball valve is mounted at highest point.

**Cooling System Capacity** — 15.8 quarts.

**Thermostat** — Opens at 162-169° F (72-76° C).

**Radiator Cap** — 13-15 psi.

*Fig. 10   Water Pump Assembly*

*Fig. 11   Water Pump Assembly*

## ENGINE SPECIFICATIONS

### GENERAL SPECIFICATIONS

| Year | Displ. | | Carburetor | HP at RPM | Torque (Ft. Lbs. at RPM) | Compr. Ratio | Bore | | Stroke | |
|---|---|---|---|---|---|---|---|---|---|---|
| | cu. ins. | cc | | | | | in. | mm | in. | mm |
| 1978 | 275.8 | 4520 | Fuel Inj. | 180@4750 | 220@3000 | 8.1-1 | 3.62 | 92 | 3.35 | 85 |

### VALVES

| Engine & Valve | Head Diam. In. (mm) | Face Angle | Seat Angle | Seat Width In. (mm) | Stem Diameter In. (mm) | Stem Clearance In. (mm) | Valve Lift In. (mm) |
|---|---|---|---|---|---|---|---|
| Int. | 1.7362-1.7440 (44.10-44.30) | 45° | 45° | .051-.078 (1.3-2.0) | .3523-.3531 (8.95-8.97) | Limit .003 (.075) | ..... |
| Exh. | 1.4547-1.4665 (36.95-37.25) | 45° | 45° | .059-.079 (1.5-2.0) | .4303-.4311 (10.93-10.95) | | ..... |

## 4.5 LITER V8 (Cont.)
### ENGINE SPECIFICATIONS (Cont.)

### PISTONS, PINS, RINGS

| Engine | PISTONS | PINS | | RINGS | | |
| --- | --- | --- | --- | --- | --- | --- |
| | Clearance In. (mm) | Piston Fit In. (mm) | Rod Fit In. (mm) | Rings | End Gap In. (mm) | Side Clearance In. (mm) |
| 4520 cc | .0005-.0015 (.012-.037) | ..... | .0002-.0007 (.005-.018) | No. 1 | .014-.022 (.35-.55) | .002-.0036 (.050-.092) |
| | | | | No. 2 | .014-.022 (.35-.55) | .0016-.0030 (.040-.082) |
| | | | | Oil | .010-.016 (.25-.40) | .0012-.0030 (.030-.072) |

### CRANKSHAFT MAIN & CONNECTING ROD BEARINGS

| Engine | MAIN BEARINGS | | | | CONNECTING ROD BEARINGS | | |
| --- | --- | --- | --- | --- | --- | --- | --- |
| | Journal Diam. In. (mm) | Clearance In. (mm) | Thrust Bearing | Crankshaft End Play In. (mm) | Journal Diam. In. (mm) | Clearance In. (mm) | Side Play In. (mm) |
| 4520 cc | 2.517-2.519 (63.93-63.98) | .0018-.0033 (.045-.084) | ..... | .004-.009 (.10-.23) | 2.044-2.047 (51.93-52.00) | .0008-.0027 (021-.068) | .009-.015 (.22-.39) |

### VALVE SPRINGS

| Engine | Free Length In. (mm) | PRESSURE Lbs. @ In. (kg @ mm) | |
| --- | --- | --- | --- |
| | | Valve Closed | Valve Open |
| 4520 cc Inner | 1.77 (45) | 24.7@1.3 (11.2@33) | 50.7@.846 (23@21.5) |
| Outer | 1.95 (49.5) | 67.24@1.65 30.5@42 | 194@1.2 (88@30.5) |

### VALVE TIMING

| Engine | INTAKE | | EXHAUST | |
| --- | --- | --- | --- | --- |
| | Open ATDC | Close ALDC | Open BLDC | Close BTDC |
| 4520 cc | 6.5° | 18.5° | 23° | 8° |

### CAMSHAFT ①

| Engine | Journal Diam. In. (mm) | Clearance In. (mm) | Lobe Lift In. (mm) |
| --- | --- | --- | --- |
| 4520 cc No. 1 | 1.363-1.364 (34.96-34.98) | .0004-.0023 (.02-.06) | ..... |
| No. 2 & 3 | 1.918-1.919 (49.20-49.22) | .011-.027 (.03-.07) | |
| No. 4 & 5 | 1.926-1.927 (49.40-49.42) | .0011-.0027 (.03-.07) | |

① End play should be .003-.006" (.07-.14 mm).

### TIGHTENING SPECIFICATIONS

| Application | Ft. Lbs. (mkg) |
| --- | --- |
| Cylinder Head Bolts | |
| Cold, First Stage | 22 (3) |
| Cold, Second Stage | 43 (6) |
| Warm, Third Stage | 43 (6) |
| Rocker Cover Bolts | 4 (.5) |
| Camshaft Bearing Bracket Bolts | 36 (5) |
| Camshaft Sprocket Bolts | 72 (10) |
| Injection Nozzle-to-Injection Valve | 7 (1) |
| Connecting Rod Bolts | ①33 (4.5) |
| Main Bearing Caps | |
| Large Bolt | 72 (10) |
| Small Bolt | 47 (6.5) |
| Crankshaft Bolt | 195-239 (27-33) |
| Oil Pan | 8 (1.1) |
| Oil Filter-to-Case | 29 (4) |
| Oil Drain Plug | 22 (3) |
| Oil Pressure Relief Valve | 29 (4) |
| Flywheel or Driven Plate | ①25 (3.5) |
| Hydraulic Valve Lifters | 36 (5) |
| Chain Tensioner Nut | 80 (11) |
| Spark Plugs | 22 (3) |

① — After torque values are achieved, torque an additional 90-100°.

# Mercedes-Benz Engines

## 6.9 LITER V8

### ENGINE CODING

#### ENGINE IDENTIFICATION

Engine identification number is located on tag attached to engine crankcase. First six digits of code are used to identify engine.

| Application | Chassis Type | Engine Code |
|---|---|---|
| 6.9 Liter | 116.036 | 100.985 |

### ENGINE & CYLINDER HEAD

#### ENGINE

**NOTE** — *Engine and transmission must be removed as a unit.*

**Removal — 1)** Remove hood, fan, fan shroud and radiator. Remove air cleaner, battery and battery frame. Remove hydraulic lines from hydropneumatic suspension pump. Discharge air-conditioning system.

**2)** Drain power steering reservoir and remove hoses. Remove all water, vacuum, oil, fuel and electrical lines leading to engine. Remove throttle control shaft.

**3)** Remove shield between oil pan and reservoir. Remove oil feed and return lines. Remove exhaust pipes and exhaust heat shield. Loosen locknut on drive shaft. Unbolt drive shaft at transmission and push toward the rear. Loosen all connections on transmission. Remove both engine shock absorbers, at frame crossmember.

**4)** Attach a engine hoist to lifting eyes on engine. Remove rear engine carrier with engine mount. Remove front engine mount. Remove engine and transmission.

**Installation —** To install reverse removal procedure.

#### CYLINDER HEAD

**NOTE** — *Cylinder head can only be removed when engine is cold.*

**Removal — 1)** Drain cooling system and crankcase. Remove battery, fan and fan shroud. Disconnect hydraulic oil pump lines. Remove alternator and bracket. Remove windshield washer reservoir and bracket. Disconnect injection lines at injector nozzles, and warm-up compensator.

**2)** Disconnect fuel supply and return from fuel distributor. Disconnect control linkage, remove mixture regulator assembly with lower housing. Remove throttle control shaft. Remove injection nozzles. Remove bracket for oil lines. Disconnect all electrical lines and vacuum lines. Remove intake manifold.

**3)** Unbolt exhaust pipe at manifold. Remove timing chain tensioner. Remove timing chain guide rails. Mark camshaft sprocket and timing chain. Carefully remove camshaft sprocket, letting timing chain fall down. Remove cylinder head bolts in reverse of tightening sequence. (*Fig. 1*).

**Fig. 1  Cylinder Head Tightening Sequence**

**NOTE** — *To remove cylinder head bolts at rear of left cylinder bank, raise engine at transmission mount. Level adjusting switch must be pulled out to first notch.*

**Installation —** To install, reverse removal procedure.

**NOTE** — *Place cylinder head on crankcase and lift, insert new cylinder head gasket.*

### VALVES

#### VALVE GUIDE SERVICING

**1)** Clean valve guide and remove all hard carbon. Using suitable go no-go plug gauges, check valve guide clearance. Drift out old guide using a suitable drift. Check bore in cylinder head and ream to oversize if necessary.

**2)** Heat cylinder head to 176-194°F (80-90°C) and chill valve guide. Drive valve guide in until lock ring is seated against cylinder head. Allow cylinder head to cool and check guide fit in head.

#### VALVE STEM OIL SEALS

**Removal — 1)** Remove camshaft cover. Remove rocker arm. Rotate engine until both valves are closed and supply compressed air to spark plug hole to hold valves closed.

**2)** Compress valve springs, using suitable valve spring compressor. Remove valve keepers, collar, springs and valve stem oil seal.

**Installation — 1)** Install valve stem oil seal. On intake guide, position coil spring at top and clamping strap at bottom. On exhaust, place installation bead on bottom next to valve guide.

**2)** Install springs, collars and keepers, using a suitable valve spring compressor. Install rocker arm and check tappet clearance. Replace camshaft cover and tighten nuts.

#### VALVE SPRING

With cylinder head and rocker arms removed, compress valve springs with a suitable valve spring compressor. Remove valve keepers, collar and springs.

## 6.9 LITER V8 (Cont.)

*Fig. 2   Valve Assembly*

*Fig. 4   Checking Hydraulic Lifter Base Setting*

## HYDRAULIC VALVE LIFTERS

**Removal** — Remove camshaft cover and rocker arms. Unscrew hydraulic valve lifters.

**Installation** — Moisten threads of valve lifter with engine oil and screw into cylinder head. Install rocker arms and camshaft cover. When installing new valve lifters the base setting must be adjusted.

## BASE SETTING ADJUSTMENT

**NOTE** — *With new hydraulic valve lifters installed; crank engine for 30 seconds with remote starter switch, before making adjustment.*

1) Remove tension from rocker arm by cranking engine until cam lobe points up. Set test gauge (100 58 04 23 00) over lifter so that measuring pin rests on ball pin of lifter. Basic position is correct when red groove of pin is aligned with measuring edge of tool.

2) If groove of pin is below measuring edge, a plus (+) deviation is indicated, requiring a thinner thrust piece (pressure pad). Entire groove showing above measuring edge indicates a minus (−) deviation and requires a thicker thrust piece.

3) To correct base setting, remove rocker arm. Remove thrust piece and measure thickness. Thrust pieces are available in steps of .0014 (.25 mm) from .147" (3.7 mm) to .228" (5.8 mm). Install thinner or thicker thrust piece as required and reinstall rocker arm. Repeat measuring procedure.

*Fig. 3   Thrust Piece (Pressure Pad)*

## ROCKER ARM ASSEMBLY

**Removal** — Remove battery and camshaft cover. Rotate camshaft (by remote starter switch) until camshaft lobe is pointed up. Using a suitable valve spring compressor (100 589 06 61 00), position compressor between camshaft and valve spring collar, lever valve downward until rocker arm can be removed.

**Installation** — Reverse removal procedure.

**NOTE** — *When installing new rocker arms, replace camshaft and check base setting of hydraulic valve lifters.*

## PISTONS, PINS & RINGS

### OIL PAN

**Removal** — 1) Remove hood, drain cooling system and engine oil. Remove upper radiator hose and air filter. Remove throttle control shaft. Loosen lines on oil cooler and loosen cooler frame.

2) Remove guard plate between oil pan and reservoir. Unscrew hoses from fittings on pan and remove upper 2 fittings from pan by removing mounting bolts. Remove A/C compressor with hoses, and gear oil pump with holder.

3) Loosen front engine mounting bolts and engine damper on cross member. Remove oil pan attaching bolts. Lift engine at front eye until oil pan can be removed.

**Installation** — Clean mating surfaces and coat with suitable sealer. Install new gasket on pan. Install new "O" rings and gaskets on connecting flanges and install in original position. Continue in reverse order of removal.

# Mercedes-Benz Engines

## 6.9 LITER V8 (Cont.)

### FITTING PISTONS

Measure pistons and cylinder diameters to determine if pistons or cylinders are worn. Oversize pistons are available.

Thrust Face

Retaining Groove
for Bearing Shells

**Fig. 5   Piston & Connecting Rod Alignment**

### PISTON PINS

Piston pins are retained by circlips in grooves of piston. To remove, take out circlips and force pin from assembly. When installing, ensure that arrow on piston crown faces forward and lock grooves for bearing tabs face center of engine.

**NOTE** – *Do NOT heat piston when removing or replacing piston pin.*

## CRANKSHAFT MAIN & CONNECTING ROD BEARINGS

### MAIN & CONNECTING ROD BEARINGS

Inspect main and connecting rod journal for wear or damage. Maximum wear or out of round is .0004" (.01 mm). Crankshaft may be reground for up to 4 repair stages, and hardness checked prior to reassembly.

### REAR MAIN BEARING OIL SEAL

With engine out of car and crankshaft removed, pull old seal and rubber strip from crankcase and end cover. Place rubber strip in crankcase, then radial seal half. Preload in position with piece of 2¾" (70 mm) pipe, then cut seal and strip off so that .004" (.1 mm) extends from ends of seal. Repeat in end cover. Lubricate seal and install crankshaft. Install end cover with new sealing pins and continue in reverse of removal procedure.

### FRONT MAIN BEARING OIL SEAL

**Removal** – Using suitable hub extractor (100 589 12 33 00), remove hub, vibration damper and pulley. Pry seal from end

cover with screwdriver, using care not to damage seal bore or crankshaft.

**Installation** – Lubricate seal and press into position with installer (100 589 07 61 00). If hub shows wear from old seal, hub must be replaced. Install hub, vibration damper and pulley.

## CAMSHAFT

**NOTE** – *If camshaft is replaced, install new rocker arms. Camshaft code is located at rear of shaft.*

### CAMSHAFT

**Removal** – **1)** Place No. 1 piston at TDC of compression stroke. Remove rocker arms. Remove compression spring of the timing chain tensioner by unscrewing plug (See Fig. 6).

**Fig. 6   Timing Chain Tensioner Spring Plug**

**2)** Mark both camshaft sprockets and timing chain. Remove camshaft sprockets and mounting bolts for camshaft bearings. Remove camshafts.

**NOTE** – *Camshaft bearing bolts for 4th and 5th bearing can only be removed by raising left side of engine. If not replacing these bearings, they may be left installed and camshaft pulled out from front of engine.*

**Installation** – **1)** Oil camshaft bearings, mount bearings with camshaft. Tighten mounting bolts (in steps) from the inside to the outside. Camshaft should turn freely.

**2)** Install compensating washer (V-notch in washer on top of woodruff key). Install camshaft sprockets and timing chain checking alignment of marks. Turn crankshaft one full revolution and place the piston of No. 1 cylinder at TDC of compression stroke.

## 6.9 LITER V8 (Cont.)

**3)** With No. 1 piston at TDC the marks on both camshafts must be in alignment (See *Fig. 7*). Install oil pipe. Reverse removal procedure to install remaining components.

**Fig. 7  Camshaft Aligning Marks**

### TIMING CHAIN

**1)** Remove spark plugs and right hand cylinder head cover. Remove rocker arms on righthand side, marking them for installation in same spot as they were originally. Remove chain tensioner.

**2)** Cover chain box with rag and break chain with separating tool or grind pin ends off one link. Attach new chain to original with master link and rotate crankshaft in normal direction with socket and ratchet applied to front hub. Keep chain engaged with sprocket while turning, and pull old chain until master link is in position at top of righthand camshaft sprocket.

**3)** Fasten ends of new chain with master link. Insert from front so that "E" locks are on rear side of chain. Set engine to TDC position and check that camshaft/bearing marks are properly aligned. *See Valve Timing.* Complete assembly in reverse order of removal.

### VALVE TIMING

NOTE — *For routine assembly jobs, ensuring that camshaft marks and crankshaft TDC marks align is sufficient.*

**1)** Camshafts should have code "36" stamped on rear end of left camshaft and "37" stamped on rear of right camshaft. To check valve timing, remove rocker arm and hydraulic valve lifter of intake valves on No. 1 and No. 6 cylinders. Install solid adjusting bolts (116 050 11 20) where valve lifters were removed.

**2)** Install rocker arms and adjust bolts for zero clearance when cam lobes point up. Mount dial indicator on head so that gauge pin rests on spring retainer with .118" (3 mm) preload. Zero indicator dial and rotate crankshaft until dial indicator needle moves .078"(2 mm). Value on vibration damper must agree with *Intake Open* value on *Valve Timing* chart.

**3)** Offset Woodruff keys are available for corrections of approximately 4°, 6½°, 8°, and 10°. Each tooth on the camshaft sprocket will change timing by about 18°. After checking and correcting valve timing, install original lifters and rocker arms in correct position.

**Fig. 8 Engine Oiling System**

## 6.9 LITER V8 (Cont.)

### ENGINE OILING

**Crankcase Capacity** — 12 quarts with filter.

**Oil Filter** — Full-flow paper cartridge with 50 psi (3.5 kg/cm²) relief valve built in.

**Pressure Regulator Valve** — Non-adjustable relief valve opens at 115 psi (8 kg/cm²).

**Normal Oil Pressure** — At least 7 psi at idle and 50 psi (3.5 kg/cm²) at 3000 RPM.

### OIL PUMP

A gear type oil pump consisting of a oil feed and oil return pump. The pump is attached to the crankcase and is driven by a duplex roller chain. The oil return pump is larger than the oil feed pump, to limit oil foaming.

### ENGINE COOLING SYSTEM

**Thermostat** — Opens at 189°F (87°C)

**Cooling System Capacity** — 17 qts.

**Radiator Cap** — 14 psi

### WATER PUMP

**Removal** — **1)** Drain coolant and detach upper radiator hose. Loosen "V" drive belts. Remove radiator shroud and visco fan clutch. Take off water pump pulley.

**2)** Remove heater hose and lower hose from pump. Remove thermostat housing from water pump. Unscrew mounting bolts and remove water pump.

**Installation** — Replace gaskets and seals and reverse removal sequence.

**Fig. 9   Water Pump Assembly**

## ENGINE SPECIFICATIONS

### GENERAL SPECIFICATIONS

| Year | Displ. | | Carburetor | HP at RPM | Torque (Ft. Lbs. at RPM) | Compr. Ratio | Bore | | Stroke | |
| --- | --- | --- | --- | --- | --- | --- | --- | --- | --- | --- |
| | cu. ins. | cc | | | | | in. | mm | in. | mm |
| 1978 | 417.1 | 6834 | Fuel Inj. | 250@4000 | 360@2500 | 8.0:1 | 4.21 | 107 | 3.74 | 95 |

### VALVES

| Engine & Valve | Head Diam. In. (mm) | Face Angle | Seat Angle | Seat Width In. (mm) | Stem Diameter In. (mm) | Stem Clearance In. (mm) | Valve Lift In. (mm) |
| --- | --- | --- | --- | --- | --- | --- | --- |
| 6834<br>Intake | 1.985-1.989<br>(50.9-51.0) | 45° | 45° | .05-.08<br>(1.3-2.0) | .3525-.3531<br>(8.955-8.970) | ..... | ..... |
| Exhaust | 1.673-1.681<br>(42.9-43.1) | 45° | 45° | .06-.08<br>(1.5-2.0) | .4303-.4311<br>(10.93-10.95) | ..... | ..... |

## 6.9 LITER V8 (Cont.)

### ENGINE SPECIFICATIONS (Cont.)

#### VALVE TIMING

| Engine | INTAKE | | EXHAUST | |
|---|---|---|---|---|
| | Open (ATDC) | Close (ALDC) | Open (BLDC) | Close (ATDC) |
| 6384 | | | | |
| New① | | | | |
| Left (36) | 12° | 25° | 32° | 19° |
| Right (37) | 10° | 23° | 34° | 21° |
| | | | | |
| In Service② | | | | |
| Left & Right | 14° | 27° | 30° | 17° |

① — New engine or timing chain.
② — More than 12,500 miles.

#### CAMSHAFT

| Engine | Journal Diam. In. (mm) | Clearance In. (mm) | Lobe Lift In. (mm) |
|---|---|---|---|
| 6384 | | | |
| No. 1 | 1.364-1.363 (34.97-34.95) | .0008-.0023 (.02-.06) | ..... |
| No. 2 & 3 | 1.968-1967 (50.47-50.45) | .0012-.0027 (.03-.07) | |
| No. 4 & 5 | 1.988-1.987 (50.97-50.95) | .0012-.0027 (.03-.07) | |

#### PISTONS, PINS, RINGS

| Engine | PISTONS | PINS | | RINGS | | |
|---|---|---|---|---|---|---|
| | Clearance In. (mm) | Piston Fit In. (mm) | Rod Fit In. (mm) | Rings | End Gap In. (mm) | Side Clearance In. (mm) |
| 6384 cc | .0006-.0010 (.015-.025) | .0001-.0004 (.003-.011) | .0002-.0006 (.007-.017) | No. 1 | .016-.023 (.40-.60) | .0078-.0023 (.04-.06) |
| | | | | No. 2 | .016-.023 (.40-.60) | .0008-.0016 (.02-.04) |
| | | | | No. 3 | .012-.018 (.30-.45) | .0008-.0016 (.02-.04) |

#### CRANKSHAFT MAIN & CONNECTING ROD BEARINGS

| Engine | MAIN BEARINGS | | | | CONNECTING ROD BEARINGS | | |
|---|---|---|---|---|---|---|---|
| | Journal Diam. In. (mm) | Clearance In. (mm) | Thrust Bearing | Crankshaft End Play In. (mm) | Journal Diam. In. (mm) | Clearance In. (mm) | Side Play In. (mm) |
| 6834 cc | 2.728 (69.96) | .0011-.0031 (.03-.08) | No. 3 | .004-.009 (.10-.24) | 2.143 (54.96) | .0008-.0027 (.03-.08) | .009-.015 (.22-.39) |

#### TIGHTENING SPECIFICATIONS

| Application | Ft.Lbs (mkg) |
|---|---|
| Cylinder Head Bolts | |
| Stage 1 | 29 (4.0) |
| Stage 2 | ①65 (9.0) |
| Main Bearing Caps | 58 (8.0) |
| Connecting Rod Caps② | 36 (5.0) |
| Flywheel | 36 (5.0) |
| Crankshaft Pulley | 290 (30) |
| Camshaft Bearing | 36 (5.0) |
| Camshaft Sprocket | 72 (10) |
| Chain Tensioner Plug | 36 (5.0) |
| Hydraulic Valve Lifters | 36 (5.0) |

① — Retorque with warm engine to 65 ft. lbs. (9mkg)
② — Turn 90° after reaching final torque.

## MGB 4 CYLINDER

### ENGINE CODING

#### ENGINE IDENTIFICATION

Engine identification and serial number are stamped on a plate secured to right side of engine just below spark plugs. Engine can also be identified by the second digit of the VIN code. Second digit should be an H.

| Engine Identification | |
|---|---|
| Application | Code |
| Federal W/Overdrive | 18V 883 AE |
| Federal W/O Overdrive | 18V 884 AE |
| California W/Overdrive | 18V 891 AE |
| California W/O Overdrive | 18V 890 AE |

**NOTE** – *Starting VIN number for 1978 MGB is GHN5U-J447001G.*

### ENGINE, CYLINDER HEAD & MANIFOLD

#### ENGINE

**NOTE** – *Remove engine and transmission as an assembly.*

**Removal** – **1)** Disconnect battery. Remove hood. Drain engine oil and cooling system. Disconnect oil pressure line at block. Disconnect oil cooler lines from engine at filter. Disconnect all coolant hoses and remove radiator.

**2)** Disconnect alternator and distributor wires, then remove distributor cap. Place heater valve out-of-way. Disconnect preheater and temperature sender wires. Remove air cleaner.

**3)** Disconnect throttle cable and fuel inlet line at carburetor. Take off purge hose at rocker cover. Disconnect fuel evaporation canister lines. Disconnect both power brake vacuum and anti-diesel vacuum lines. Remove shifter lever.

**4)** Disconnect back-up lights, overdrive, and starter wiring. Remove wiring from clips. Separate clutch slave cylinder from clutch housing. Disconnect speedometer cable. Disconnect exhaust at manifold. Remove propeller shaft. Remove engine restraint rod.

**5)** Remove 4 bolts holding rear mounting crossmember to chassis and allow transmission to drop to fixed crossmember. Remove bolts mounting bracket (in middle of crossmember) to crossmember. Remove nuts holding rear mounts to crossmember; then remove crossmember. Take up weight of vehicle, free front motor mounts, and lift out engine/transmission assembly.

**Installation** – To install engine/transmission assembly, reverse removal procedure.

#### INTAKE & EXHAUST MANIFOLDS

**Removal** – **1)** Drain cooling system. Remove air cleaner. Disconnect fuel evaporation hose at carburetor. Disconnect heater line from bottom radiator hose. Disconnect wire from preheater.

**2)** Remove carburetor (4 nuts) with pre-heater components. Disconnect brake unit vacuum hose, anti-diesel valve hose, and gulp valve hose. Remove gulp valve and swing out-of-way.

**3)** Remove hot air shroud. Separate exhaust pipe from bracket at front mount. Separate pipe at manifold. Remove manifold mounting nuts and bolts and lift off manifold assembly.

**Installation** – To install, reverse removal procedure and note: Attach exhaust pipe to manifold before tightening to mounting bracket.

#### CYLINDER HEAD

**Removal** – **1)** Drain cooling system. Disconnect radiator hose at thermostat housing. Disconnect carburetor vent line and anti-diesel line. Remove hose secured to thermostat housing. Disconnect purge hose at rocker cover.

**2)** Free automatic choke water hose. Disconnect gulp valve, air pump, and check valve hoses. Remove necessary air pump bolts. Disconnect spark plug, temperature sender, and pre-heater wires.

**3)** Place heater valve out-of-way. Remove hose from water pump. Remove air cleaner assembly. Free hot air shroud. Slide shroud back and remove manifold.

**4)** Remove rocker shaft and withdraw push rods. Remove AIR manifold rail. Do not remove check valve. Remove cylinder head nuts making note of nut mounting AIR manifold. Lift off head.

**Installation** – To install, reverse removal procedure and note: New gasket is marked "TOP" and "FRONT". Top must face up and front must face water pump.

*Fig. 1  MGB Cylinder Head Tightening Sequence*

### VALVES

#### VALVE ARRANGEMENT

E-I-I-E-E-I-I-E (front-to-rear).

#### VALVE GUIDE SERVICING

**1)** Remove cylinder head and valves. Rest cylinder head with machined face downward on a clean surface. Drive valve guide downwards into combustion chamber space with a suitable drift. When installing new guides, they must be driven in from top of cylinder head.

**2)** Guides must be inserted with end having largest chamfer at top. Guides should be driven into combustion chamber until exhaust valve guides are $\frac{5}{8}$" and intake valve guides are $\frac{3}{4}$" above machined surface of valve spring seating.

## MGB 4 CYLINDER (Cont.)

Exhaust .625" (15.86 mm)    Intake .750" (19.05 mm)

**Fig. 2   Cross Sectional View of Installed Valve Guide**

## VALVE SPRINGS

**Removal** — Remove cylinder head and rocker arm assembly. Compress springs using suitable tool (18G45). Remove two valve keepers. Release valve springs and remove compressor. Take out valve spring retainer, spring, and bottom retainer. Remove "O" ring seal from groove and remove valve from guide.

**Installation** — Reverse removal procedure using new valve "O" ring seals. Soak rings in clean engine oil for a short time before use to ease installation.

## ROCKER ARM ASSEMBLY

**Removal** — 1) Drain cooling system and disconnect breather pipe from rocker cover. Remove throttle cable, remove two rocker cover attaching nuts and lift off rocker cover. Take care not to damage cork gasket or lose washers or rubber seals.

2) Notice that under the right rear rocker stud nut there is a locking plate. Unscrew eight rocker shaft bracket nuts and external cylinder head nuts gradually, one turn at a time, until all load is released.

**NOTE** — *It is important that external cylinder head nuts are loosened at same time to avoid possibility of head distortion and water entering cylinders.*

3) Remove all rocker shaft bracket nuts and remove rocker assembly, complete with brackets and rockers. Remove push rods, arranging them so that they may be replaced in same positions.

**Disassembly 1)** — Remove set screw locating rocker shaft in rear rocker mounting bracket, then remove cotter pins, flat washers and spring washers. Slide rockers, brackets, and springs off shaft. Make sure to note how components come off so they can be reassembled accurately.

**2)** Using suitable tool (18G226), place rocker on anvil and drive out worn bushing. Place new bushing on driver and position bushing with butt joint at top of rocker bore and oil groove in bushing at bottom of rocker bore.

3) It is necessary to drill oil holes in bushing to coincide with oilways in rocker. Holes may be drilled either before or after installation.

4) If holes are drilled after installation, remove adjuster screw and use .093" (2.36 mm) drill to extract end plug and to continue oilway through bushing.

Oilway    Joint In Bushing    Oilway

Oil Groove

**Fig. 3   Rocker Arm Bushing with Detail of Oil Holes**

5) Replug end after operation using a rivet and weld rivet into position. Oil hole in top of rocker barrel must continue through the bushing with a No. 47 drill. Finally, burnish ream bushing to .6255-.6260" (15.89-15.90 mm).

**Reassembly** — Reverse disassembly procedure. Remember to replace rocker shaft locating screw lock plate.

**Installation** — To install rocker assembly on cylinder head, reverse removal procedure. Make sure cylinder head bolts are retorqued before installing rocker cover.

## VALVE TAPPETS

**Removal** — Remove manifolds. Remove rocker shaft. Withdraw push rods and keep in order. Loosen clamp and separate hose from neck attached to tappet cover. Remove side covers and gaskets. Take out tappets keeping them in order.

**Installation** — To install valve tappets, reverse removal procedure and note: Tappets should seat without forcing.

## VALVE CLEARANCE ADJUSTMENT

Remove valve cover and observe opening and closing of valves. To check clearances, turn crankshaft until valves in first column are fully open, then valves in second column may be checked and adjust to .013" (.33 mm). Set clearance with engine warm.

### Valve Adjustment Sequence

| Valves Open | Valves to Adjust |
|---|---|
| 1 | 8 |
| 3 | 6 |
| 5 | 4 |
| 2 | 7 |
| 8 | 1 |
| 6 | 3 |
| 4 | 5 |
| 7 | 2 |

## MGB 4 CYLINDER (Cont.)

### PISTONS, PINS & RINGS

#### OIL PAN

1) Drain engine oil and drain coolant. Disconnect radiator hoses and remove engine front mounting bolts. Lift engine enough to gain access to front oil pan bolts.

2) Remove all oil pan bolts and remove oil pan from engine. To install, reverse removal procedure using new oil pan gasket.

#### PISTON & ROD

1) Remove cylinder head and oil pan. Pistons and rods must be removed from top of cylinder block. Unlock and remove big-end bolts and remove bearing caps. Release connecting rods from crankshaft.

2) Remove piston and rod assembly out top of cylinder block and reinstall bearing cap. Connecting rod bearing caps are offset. Make sure that parts are marked so reassembly will be in original position.

#### PISTON RINGS

1) Place rings in top of cylinder bore. Check ring gaps. Check oil ring to groove clearance. Fit oil control expander. Make sure ends of expander are butting, but not overlapping. Set gaps of rails and expander 90° to each other.

2) Fit stepped compression rings into SECOND groove with face marked "TOP" up. Fit top ring. Place ring gaps 90° to each other away from thrust side of piston.

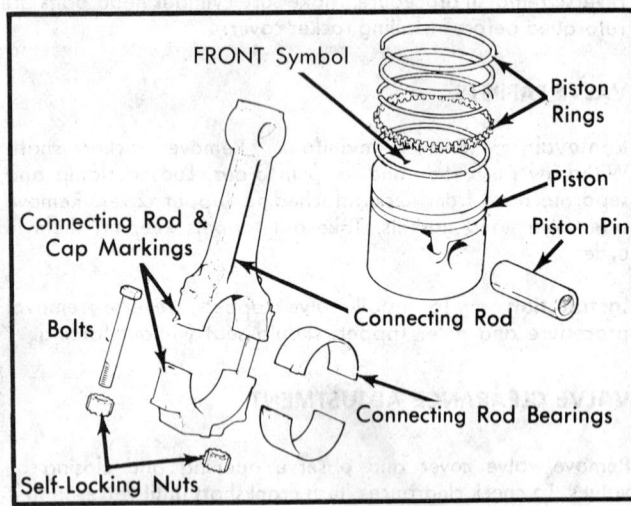

**Fig. 4  Exploded View of Piston and Rod Assembly**

#### PISTON PINS

Piston pins are press fit and are fully interchangeable in complete sets with earlier assemblies which have full floating pin. Use suitable tool or press to remove or install pins.

### CRANKSHAFT MAIN & CONNECTING ROD BEARINGS

#### CRANKSHAFT

**Removal — 1)** Drain cooling system. Remove engine as previously outlined. Separate transmission from engine.

2) Remove following components from engine:
- Oil pan and oil pump.
- Clutch assembly, flywheel, and transmission adaptor plate.
- Timing cover, tensioner, chain and sprockets.
- Camshaft lock plate.

3) Remove main bearing and connecting rod caps, then take out bearing halves. Remove thrust washers and lift out crankshaft.

**Installation — 1)** Thoroughly clean out all crankshaft oil passages. Insert top bearing halves in block. Slide crankshaft into bearings.

2) Install thrust washers at rear main bearing with oilways facing away from bearing. Make sure thrust washer tabs locate in slot in main bearing cap.

3) Install bottom bearing halves and main bearing caps. Torque cap bolts.

4) Check crankshaft end play and adjust if necessary with selective fit washers. End play should be as specified in table.

5) Install remaining components in reverse of removal procedure.

#### CONNECTING ROD BEARINGS

To remove bearings, bend down locking strips so that bolts may be removed. Remove connecting rod caps and extract bearings. No scraping of bearings is required as bearings are machined to give correct clearance of .001-.0027" (.03-.07 mm).

#### MAIN BEARINGS

1) Remove engine from car and remove flywheel and clutch, timing chain, oil pan and oil strainer. Remove rear engine mounting plate. Remove two bolts and locking plate holding front main bearing cap to engine front plate. Remove main bearing cap retaining nuts and remove caps and bearings.

2) Bearings are machined to give correct clearance of .001-.0027". When replacing bearings that have been used but are not damaged or worn, make sure that bearing and all surfaces are thoroughly cleaned. Rear main bearing cap horizontal joint surface should be lightly covered with Hylomar Jointing Compound or equivalent before cap is fitted to cylinder block. Tighten bearing cap nuts.

#### THRUST BEARINGS

A thrust washer is fitted on each side of center main bearing to take crankshaft end thrust. Washers each consist of two semicircular halves, one having a lug located in recess in removable half of bearing and other one being plain.

### CAMSHAFT

#### FRONT COVER & OIL SEAL

**Removal —** Drain cooling system. Remove radiator. Remove alternator belt and A.I.R. pump belt. Remove fan and pulley from crankshaft. Remove front cover bolts and remove from vehicle. Pry or drive out crankshaft oil seal.

## MGB 4 CYLINDER (Cont.)

**Installation** — Dip new oil seal in engine oil. Use installing tool 18G 134 and adapter 18G 134BD to fit seal. Be sure lip of seal is facing inward. Position oil thrower with "F" mark showing. Smear sealing compound on cover and seal. Tighten bolts evenly. Lubricate crankshaft hub and slide pulley on to crankshaft, engaging keyway. Put on new lock nut and tighten bolt.

### TIMING CHAIN & TENSIONER

**Removal** — Remove front cover as previously outlined. Remove oil thrower. Bend back tensioner lock tabs. Remove tensioner bolts. Pry tensioner mechanism out of front plate. Slipper head (piece that rides against chain) is under spring tension. Remove all tensioner components and disassemble any that are not apart. Unlock and remove camshaft nut. Pull off camshaft and crankshaft sprockets.

**Fig. 5 Exploded View of Timing Chain Tensioner**

**NOTE** — *Use care not to lose sprocket packing washers behind crankshaft sprocket. Make sure to replace the same number of washers as removed. To determine correct thickness of washers to be used if new camshaft or crankshaft components have been installed, place straightedge across sides of crankshaft sprocket and measure gap between straightedge and crankshaft sprocket. Select and fit washers as required.*

**Installation** — 1) When replacing timing chain and sprockets, set crankshaft keyway at TDC and camshaft keyway at 2 o'clock position. Assemble sprockets to timing chain with index marks in sprockets (if equipped) opposite each other.

**Fig. 6 Camshaft and Crankshaft Sprocket Alignment**

2) Keep sprockets in this position and engage crankshaft sprocket keyway with key on crankshaft and rotate camshaft until camshaft sprocket keyway and key are aligned. Push sprockets onto shafts as far as possible and tighten with lock washer and nut.

3) Refit chain tensioner inner cylinder and spring into cylinder of slipper head. Make sure serrated seat in inner cylinder engages peg in slipper cylinder. Turn inner cylinder clockwise against tension until cover serrations in seat engage peg and retains inner cylinder in slipper cylinder. Refit tensioner with mounting bolts. Fit oil thrower with face marked "F" to front. Reverse removal procedure to install remaining components.

### CAMSHAFT

**Removal & Installation** — 1) Disconnect battery and remove intake and exhaust manifolds (if necessary). Remove push rods and tappets. Remove timing cover, timing chain and timing sprockets.

2) Disconnect distributor vacuum line at distributor and remove two bolts with flat washers which hold distributor to housing. Do not loosen clamping plate bolt or ignition timing will be disturbed. Remove distributor assembly.

3) Remove oil pan, oil pump, and oil pump drive shaft. Remove 3 set screws and lock washers holding camshaft locating plate to cylinder block. Remove camshaft.

4) Before reassembly, fix camshaft thrust plate and sprocket to camshaft, then check end play. Specifications should not exceed .003-.007" (.076-.178 mm). Make measurement between retaining plate and thrust face of camshaft front journal.

**Fig. 7 Using a Feeler Gauge to Measure Camshaft End Play**

### CAMSHAFT BEARINGS

**NOTE** — *Follow manufacturers instructions for proper adapter and washer use on each bearing for removal and installation.*

## MGB 4 CYLINDER (Cont.)

**Removal** — Use bearing removal/installation tool 18G 124A and adapters to remove camshaft front bearing. Remove rear bearing in same manner as front bearing, then index tool through front bearing bore to remove center bearing.

**NOTE** — *Be sure oil holes in new bearings are aligned with lubrication ports in block. The holes must not move once they have been located.*

**Installation** — Fit new bearings into bore in reverse order of removal. After bearings have been installed, use camshaft bearing bore tool 18G 123A to line bore new bearings.

**NOTE** — *Cutting edge of boreing tool must be kept dry and free of cuttings at all times.*

### VALVE TIMING

1) Set No. 1 cylinder intake valve clearance to .055" with engine cold. Turn crankshaft until valve is about to open. Indicator groove in flange of crankshaft pulley should be opposite longest pointer on indicator bracket beneath crankshaft pulley, indicating TDC.

2) After timing has been checked, valve clearance should be reset. See *Valve Clearance Adjustment.*

## ENGINE OILING

**Crankcase Capacity** — 7¼ pints with filter change.

**Oil Filter** — Full flow type with disposable cartridge.

**Oil Pressure** — 10-25 psi (.7-1.7 kg/cm²) @idle: 50-80 psi (3.5-5.6 kg/cm²) @2000 RPM.

**Oil Pump Relief Valve** — Free length is 3" (76.2 mm). Installed length is 2.156" (54.77 mm).

### ENGINE OILING SYSTEM

Force feed type with Hobourn-Eaton rotor type oil pump. A full-flow filter is used. An oil pressure relief valve is used to enable oil to by-pass filter if oil filter becomes blocked.

### OIL PUMP

Two bolts hold on oil pump cover and three studs hold pump to crankcase. To remove pump, remove stud nuts and remove pump and drive shaft. To disassemble, proceed as follows:

1) Remove cover, located at base of oil pump by two dowels. Remove outer rotor complete with oil pump shaft. Clean all parts in kerosene and inspect for wear.

2) Rotor end play should be checked as follows: Install rotors in pump body and place straightedge across joint face of pump body. Measure clearance between top face of rotors and underside of straightedge. Clearance should not exceed .005" (.13 mm). If clearance is excessive, remove two cover locating dowels and tap the joint face of pump body.

Straightedge

Feeler Gauge

Clearance: .005" (.13 mm)

**Fig. 8 Measuring Oil Pump Rotor End Play**

3) Check clearance between outer rotor and rotor pocket in pump body. If clearance exceeds .010" (.25 mm), pump rotor, pump body, or complete pump assembly should be replaced.

4) Measure clearance of rotor lobes with rotors installed in pump body. If clearance exceeds .006" (.15 mm), rotors must be replaced.

.006" (.15 mm)

Feeler Gauge

.006" (.15 mm)

**Fig. 9 Measuring Oil Pump Rotor Lobe Clearance**

5) Reassemble pump and lubricate all parts with clean engine oil. Make sure outer rotor is installed in pump body with chamfered end at drive end of rotor pocket in pump body.

## ENGINE COOLING

**Cooling System Capacity** — 7.2 quarts with heater.

**Thermostat** — 180°F (82°C) thermostat is standard. A 190 F (88°C) thermostat is available for use in cold climates.

**Pressure Cap** — Maintains pressure at 15 psi (1.05 kg)

### WATER PUMP

**Removal** — Drain cooling system. Remove AIR pump and alternator drive belts, then pivot units out-of-way. Remove water pump bottom hose. Remove belt pulleys. Remove mounting bolts. Withdraw AIR brackets and water pump.

**Installation** — To install, reverse removal procedure and adjust both belts.

## MGB 4 CYLINDER (Cont.)

### ENGINE SPECIFICATIONS

#### GENERAL SPECIFICATIONS

| Year | Displ. | | Carburetor | HP at RPM | Torque (Ft. Lbs. at RPM) | Compr. Ratio | Bore | | Stroke | |
| --- | --- | --- | --- | --- | --- | --- | --- | --- | --- | --- |
| | cu. ins. | cc | | | | | in. | mm | in. | mm |
| 1978 | 110 | 1798 | 2x1-Bbl. | ..... | ..... | 8.0-1 | 3.16 | 80.26 | 3.5 | 88.9 |

#### VALVES

| Engine & Valve | Head Diam. In. (mm) | Face Angle | Seat Angle | Seat Width In. (mm) | Stem Diameter In. (mm) | Stem Clearance In. (mm) | Valve Lift In. (mm) |
| --- | --- | --- | --- | --- | --- | --- | --- |
| 1798 cc Int. | 1.562-1.567 (39.67-39.80) | 45° | 45.5° | ... | .3429-.3434 (8.70-8.72) | .0007-.0019 (.02-.05) | .3645 (9.25) |
| Exh. | 1.343-1.348 (34.11-34.23) | 45° | 45.5° | ... | .3423-.3428 (8.69-8.70) | .0013-.0025 (.03-.06) | .3645 (9.25) |

#### PISTONS, PINS, RINGS

| Engine | PISTONS | PINS | | RINGS | | |
| --- | --- | --- | --- | --- | --- | --- |
| | Clearance In. (mm) | Piston Fit In. (mm) | Rod Fit In. (mm) | Rings | End Gap In. (mm) | Side Clearance In. (mm) |
| 1798 cc | ① .0021-.0033 (.053-.084) ② .0006-.0012 (.015-.030) | ③ | Press Fit | No. 1 | .012-.022 (.30-.56) | .0015-.0035 (.038-.088) |
| | | | | No. 2 | .012-.022 (.30-.56) | .0015-.0035 (.038-.088) |
| | | | | Oil | .015-.045 (.38-1.14) | .0016-.0036 (.04-.09) |

① — Top.
② — Bottom.
③ — Hand Push Fit at 60°F (15.6°C).

#### CRANKSHAFT MAIN & CONNECTING ROD BEARINGS

| Engine | MAIN BEARINGS | | | | CONNECTING ROD BEARINGS | | |
| --- | --- | --- | --- | --- | --- | --- | --- |
| | Journal Diam. In. (mm) | Clearance In. (mm) | Thrust Bearing | Crankshaft End Play In. (mm) | Journal Diam. In. (mm) | Clearance In. (mm) | Side Play In. (mm) |
| 1798 cc | 2.1262-2.1270 (54.01-54.02) | .001-.0027 (.03-.07) | Center | .004-.005 (.10-.13) | 1.8759-1.8764 (47.64-47.66) | .001-.0027 (.03-.07) | ..... |

#### CAMSHAFT

| Engine | Journal Diam. In. (mm) | Clearance In. (mm) | Lobe Lift In. (mm) |
| --- | --- | --- | --- |
| 1798 cc Front | 1.7888-1.7893 (45.42-45.44) | .001-.002 (.025-.051) | .250 (6.35) |
| Center | 1.7288-1.7293 (43.91-43.92) | | |
| Rear | 1.6228-1.6233 (41.22-41.23) | | |

# MG Engines

## MGB 4 CYLINDER (Cont.)

### ENGINE SPECIFICATIONS (Cont.)

#### VALVE SPRINGS

| Engine | Free Length In. (mm) | PRESSURE Lbs. @ In. (kg @ mm) | |
|---|---|---|---|
| | | Valve Closed | Valve Open |
| 1798 cc | 1.92 (48.8) | ..... | ..... |

#### VALVE TIMING

| Engine | INTAKE | | EXHAUST | |
|---|---|---|---|---|
| | Open (BTDC) | Close (ALDC) | Open (BLDC) | Close (ATDC) |
| 1798 cc | 8° | 42° | 54° | 18° |

#### TIGHTENING SPECIFICATIONS

| Application | Ft. Lbs. (mkg) |
|---|---|
| Main Bearing Nuts | 70 (9.7) |
| Flywheel Set Screws | 40 (5.5) |
| Connecting Rod Bolts | 31-35 (4.2) |
| Rocker Bracket Nuts | 25 (3.5) |
| Oil Pump-to-Crankcase | 14 (.8) |
| Oil Pan Bolts | 6 (.8) |
| Side Covers | 3-4 (.4-.5) |
| Timing Cover | |
| ¼" Screws | 6 (.8) |
| 5/16" Screws | 14 (1.9) |
| Rear Plate | |
| 5/16" Screws | 20 (2.8) |
| 3/8" Screws | 30 (4.1) |
| Water Pump | 17 (2.3) |
| Thermostat Housing | 8 (1.1) |
| Rocker Cover Nuts | 4 (.56) |
| Manifold Nuts | 16 (2.2) |
| Clutch-to-Flywheel | 25-30 (3.5-4.1) |
| Carburetor Stud Nuts | 15 (2.1) |
| Cylinder Head | 45-50 (6.2-6.9) |

## MIDGET 4 CYLINDER

### ENGINE CODING

#### ENGINE IDENTIFICATION

Number is stamped on a plate secured to left side of cylinder block or stamped directly into block. Engine can also be identified by the second digit in the VIN. Second digit should be an "A". The beginning identification number for 1978 Midget is GAN6UJ200001G.

### ENGINE, CYLINDER HEAD & MANIFOLD

#### ENGINE

**Removal — 1)** Disconnect battery, remove hood, drain cooling system and remove radiator. Disconnect heater air intake hose. Remove fan, drain engine oil, and remove CAT.

**2)** Disconnect anti-diesel valve vacuum line. Disconnect heater hoses and temperature sender unit. Disconnect diverter valve hose from check valve. Disconnect electrical lead from alternator.

**3)** Disconnect distributor and coil wires and remove distributor cap. Remove air pump. Remove oil pressure switch wire. Separate ground cable from engine. Disconnect starter wires.

**4)** Disconnect fuel line from union in transmission tunnel. Disconnect back-up light lead. Remove speedometer cable, then refit clamp and bolt. Remove slave cylinder and wire out of way.

**5)** Remove transmission restraint cable. Disconnect propeller shaft from transmission. Remove 2 rear mounting bracket bolts that go into floor panel. Working inside vehicle, remove gear shaft lever assembly.

**6)** Remove 2 bolts securing rear mounting bracket to transmission tunnel. Remove nuts from front engine mounts. Attach hoist to engine so as to keep engine at about 70° during removal.

**7)** Take up engine weight, knock out front engine mount bolts and lift engine from vehicle.

**Installation —** To install, reverse removal procedure.

#### INTAKE MANIFOLD

**Removal — 1)** Drain cooling system. Remove carburetor. Disconnect heater hose and remove anti-diesel solenoid vacuum line.

**2)** Disconnect EGR valve. Remove 2 bolts mounting exhaust manifold to intake manifold. Disconnect thermostat hose.

**3)** Remove 6 nuts retaining intake manifold to cylinder head. Pull off manifold while removing both anti-diesel solenoid vacuum adaptor and EGR valve hose adaptor.

**Installation —** To install cylinder head, reverse removal procedure and note: 2 larger clamps and 2 washers go on inner lower cylinder head studs BEFORE installing cylinder head.

### CYLINDER HEAD

**Removal — 1)** Disconnect battery. Drain cooling system. Remove carburetor. Disconnect temperature sender. Remove hose to thermostat. Remove fan shroud. Remove 3 water pump housing bolts.

**2)** Remove flame trap mounting bracket located on manifold, then place bracket to one side. Disconnect heater hoses at manifold. Disconnect anti-diesel solenoid. Disconnect EGR line at exhaust manifold and at clip on transmission. Remove preheater ducting. Separate CAT from exhaust manifold (6 nuts).

**3)** Remove nut and washer mounting heater return to cylinder head at stud. Remove rocker cover and place temperature unit to one side.

**4)** Remove rocker arm shaft. Remove push rods and keep them in order. Disconnect spark plug wires. Remove 10 mounting nuts and withdraw cylinder head.

**Installation —** To install cylinder head, reverse removal procedure and note: Make sure head gasket is installed with "Top" facing up.

*Fig. 1   Midget Cylinder Head Tightening Sequence*

### VALVES

#### VALVE ARRANGEMENT

E-I-I-E-E-I-I-E

#### VALVE GUIDE SERVICING

**Removal & Installation —** With cylinder head removed, remove valve, spring and retainer. Using suitable tool (60A) and adapter (S 60A-2A), position tool on combustion chamber face of cylinder head, pull replacement guide in driving old guide out. Insure that guide protrusion above cylinder head top face is correct.

#### ROCKER ARM ASSEMBLY

**Removal —** Disconnect breather pipe from rocker cover and remove cover. Remove nuts and washers securing rocker arm shaft and remove rocker arm assembly.

**Disassembly —** Remove cotter key from front end of rocker shaft. Slide off rockers, pedestals, springs and spacers from shaft noting the order for reassembly. Remove screw securing rear pedestal to shaft and remove pedestal and rocker arm.

**Reassembly —** Reverse disassembly procedure, applying Loctite to rear pedestal locating screw.

## MIDGET 4 CYLINDER (Cont.)

**Installation** — To install rocker arm assembly, reverse removal procedure. Adjust valve clearance.

**Fig. 2   Disassembled View of Rocker Arm & Shaft**

### VALVE CLEARANCE ADJUSTMENT

With engine cold, set valve clearance to .010" (.25 mm). To check valve clearance, turn crankshaft until valves in first column are fully open, then valves in the second column may be checked and adjusted as necessary.

| Valves Open | Valves to Adjust |
|---|---|
| 1 | 8 |
| 3 | 6 |
| 5 | 4 |
| 2 | 7 |
| 8 | 1 |
| 6 | 3 |
| 4 | 5 |
| 7 | 2 |

## PISTON, PINS & RINGS

### OIL PAN

Drain engine oil, remove oil pan screws and lower oil pan.

### PISTON & ROD ASSEMBLY

**Removal** — Remove cylinder head, drain oil and remove pan. Remove bearing caps and move connecting rods off of crankshaft. Remove piston and rod assembly from cylinder head side of block.

**Installation** — Lubricate pistons, cylinder bores, and crankshaft with clean oil. Fit pistons and connecting rods to their original bores. Make sure that arrow on piston is pointing towards front of engine and that ring gaps are staggered. To complete installation, reverse removal procedure.

### PISTON PINS

**Removal & Installation** — Piston pin is hand press fit in connecting rod. To remove pin, remove circlips then press out

pin. Separate piston from connecting rod. To install, reverse removal procedure and note the following: Install new bushing and ream to proper size. Ensure piston is fitted correctly on connecting rod; arrow on top of piston facing front and cylinder number stamped on connecting rod and cap facing camshaft.

## CRANKSHAFT MAIN & CONNECTING ROD BEARINGS

### CRANKSHAFT & MAIN BEARING

**Removal** — 1) Remove engine from vehicle, then remove clutch assembly, and remove flywheel. Remove engine rear adapter plate, water pump and thermostat housing, then remove timing chain and gears. Remove camshaft locating plate and front mounting plate.

**2)** Remove dipstick, oil pan, crankshaft pulley and drive key. Remove shims if fitted, and two screws securing front sealing block. Remove crankshaft rear oil seal housing. Remove connecting rod and main bearing caps and remove crankshaft.

**Installation** — 1) Coat pilot bushing with zinc oxide grease and install in crankshaft. Install main bearings, crankshaft, and main bearing caps. Tighten caps to specification. Check crankshaft end play; adjust with selective thrust washers.

**2)** Install connecting rods, bearings, and caps. Use new bolts and tighten to specification. Install front sealing block using suitable sealing compound, then drive new wedges into slots. Cut protruding edges from wedges. To complete installation, reverse removal procedure.

## CAMSHAFT

### TIMING SPROCKET COVER & OIL SEAL

**Removal** — 1) Drain cooling system and remove radiator. Remove drive belts. Remove carburetor. Remove pre-heater ducting. Remove 6 CAT-to-exhaust manifold nuts.

**2)** Support engine with jack. Remove nuts, bolts and washers mounting both front motor mounts. Raise engine enough to remove crankshaft pulley and nut.

**3)** Remove 8 screws, 1 bolt, and 3 nuts keeping timing sprocket cover to block. Pull off cover. Remove oil seal from cover.

**Installation** — Dip new seal in oil and fit to cover using suitable tools (18 G 134 & 18 G 134BM). Complete installation by reversing removal procedure.

### TIMING CHAIN

**Removal** — 1) Remove engine front cover as previously outlined. Remove oil thrower. Turn crankshaft until chain sprocket index marks are aligned.

**NOTE** — When sprockets are aligned the punch marks in center of camshaft sprocket and on camshaft will be aligned as shown in Fig. 3. Camshaft punch mark is visible through hole in camshaft sprocket.

**2)** Bend back camshaft sprocket lock plate tabs and remove 2 bolts mounting sprocket. While making sure neither camshaft or crankshaft is moved, remove both sprockets and chain.

## MIDGET 4 CYLINDER (Cont.)

**Installation** — 1) Remove crankshaft key. Temporarily install both sprockets. Check fit of sprockets by placing a metal straightedge across teeth of both sprockets. If necessary, shim crankshaft behind sprocket.

2) Remove sprockets. Refit key to crankshaft. Fit chain and sprockets making sure alignment marks are indexed. Install camshaft mounting bolts.

3) Place a straightedge along the left side (facing) chain run. If deflection at mid point exceeds .4" (10 mm), replace chain. Remove camshaft mount bolts, insert new lock plate and refit bolts. Reverse removal procedure to install remaining components.

**Fig. 3   Timing Chain Sprocket Alignment**

### CAMSHAFT

**Removal** — 1) Remove radiator, air pump drive belt and fan belt. Remove thermostat, water pump and fan. Remove crankshaft pulley, and engine front cover. Remove timing chain and gears.

2) Remove bolt securing cam locating plate and remove plate then remove cylinder head. Remove lifters and identify for reassembly. Remove distributor drive shaft and fuel pump. Withdraw camshaft from block.

**NOTE** — Water pump housing removal is not required.

**Installation** — To install camshaft, reverse removal procedure and note the following: Mark new camshaft with a punch mark in the position corresponding to that of the camshaft being removed. Check camshaft end play; if end play is beyond standard value of .0045-.0085" (.120-.216 mm), install new lock plate.

### VALVE TIMING

1) Adjust valve clearance of number 7 and number 8 valves to .050" (1.27 mm). Rotate crankshaft to bring number 1 piston to TDC on compression stroke. Check that number 1 and 2 valves are fully closed and number 7 and 8 valves have the same clearance.

2) After valve timing has been checked, valve clearance should be set to specification.

### ENGINE OILING

**Crankcase Capacity** — 4.8 qts. including filter.

**Oil Filter** — Full flow type with disposable cartridge.

**Normal Oil Pressure** — 40-60 psi; at idle 20 psi.

### ENGINE OILING SYSTEM

Force feed system with rotor type oiling pump. A full-flow type oil filter is used. An oil pressure relief valve is used to enable oil to by-pass filter if oil becomes blocked .

### OIL PUMP

**Removal** — Drain crankcase oil and remove oil pan. Loosen oil strainer locknut and unscrew oil strainer from oil pump cover plate. Remove three bolts securing oil pump to crankcase and remove pump.

**Disassembly & Inspection** — Remove inner rotor and shaft assembly. Remove outer rotor. Clean all components then reinstall rotors in pump body with chamfered edge of outer rotor at driving end of pump body. Place straightedge across face of pump body and check clearance between straightedge and rotors. Clearance should not exceed .0004" (0.1 mm). Check clearance between inner and outer rotors and pump body. Clearance between the inner and outer rotors, measured at the rotor lobes should not exceed .010" (.25 mm). Clearance between outer rotor and pump body should not exceed .008" (0.2 mm). If clearance is excessive at any location, pump should be replaced.

**Reassembly** — To reassemble, reverse disassembly procedure and ensure that outer rotor is installed in pump body with chamfered end at driving end of pump body.

**NOTE** — Oil pressure relief valve is located in front of block behind hex head plug bolt. Spring free length should be 1.53" (38.8 mm).

**Fig. 4   Engine Oil Pump Disassembled View**

# MG Engines

## MIDGET 4 CYLINDER (Cont.)

**Installation** — To install oil pump, reverse removal procedure.

### ENGINE COOLING

**Cooling System Capacity** — 5.7 quarts including heater.

**Thermostat** — Opening temperature, 190°F (88°C)

**Radiator Cap** — 15 psi (1.5 kg)

### WATER PUMP

**Removal** — Remove radiator, loosen alternator adjusting bracket and remove fan belt. Remove nuts and bolts securing fan and remove fan from coupling assembly. Remove nuts securing water pump to thermostat housing and remove water pump, fan coupling, and tolerance ring.

**Installation** — To install water pump, reverse removal procedure and refill cooling system.

## ENGINE SPECIFICATIONS

### GENERAL SPECIFICATIONS

| Year | Displ. | | Carburetor | HP at RPM | Torque (Ft. Lbs. at RPM) | Compr. Ratio | Bore | | Stroke | |
| --- | --- | --- | --- | --- | --- | --- | --- | --- | --- | --- |
| | cu. ins. | cc | | | | | in. | mm | in. | mm |
| 1977 | 91.0 | 1493 | 1x1-Bbl. | ..... | ..... | 7.5-1 | 2.9 | 73.7 | 3.44 | 87.5 |

### VALVES

| Engine & Valve | Head Diam. In. (mm) | Face Angle | Seat Angle | Seat Width In. (mm) | Stem Diameter In. (mm) | Stem Clearance In. (mm) | Valve Lift In. (mm) |
| --- | --- | --- | --- | --- | --- | --- | --- |
| 1493 cc Int. | 1.380 (34.99) | 45° | 45.5° | ..... | .3107-.3113 (7.89-7.91) | .0007-.0023 (.02-.06) | ..... |
| Exh. | 1.170 (29.71) | 45° | 45.5° | ..... | .3100-.3105 (7.874-7.887) | .0015-.0030 (.04-.07) | ..... |

### PISTONS, PINS, RINGS

| Engine | PISTONS Clearance in. (mm) | PINS Piston Fit in. (mm) | Rod Fit in. (mm) | RINGS Rings | End Gap in. (mm) | Side Clearance in. (mm) |
| --- | --- | --- | --- | --- | --- | --- |
| 1493 cc | ①.002-.003 (.051-.076) ②.0002-.0016 (.005-.041) | ③ | ④ | 1 | .012-.022 (.305-.559) | .0015-.0035 (.038-.089) |
| | | | | 2 | .012-.022 (.305-.559) | .0015-.0035 (.038-.089) |
| | | | | Oil | .015-.055 (.38-1.40) | ..... |

① — At top of skirt.  ③ — Hand push fit.
② — At bottom of skirt.  ④ — Interference fit.

### CRANKSHAFT MAIN & CONNECTING ROD BEARINGS

| Engine | MAIN BEARINGS Journal Diam. In. (mm) | Clearance In. (mm) | Thrust Bearing | Crankshaft End Play In. (mm) | CONNECTING ROD BEARINGS Journal Diam. In. (mm) | Clearance In. (mm) | Side Play In. (mm) |
| --- | --- | --- | --- | --- | --- | --- | --- |
| 1493 cc | 2.3115-2.3120 (58.713-58.725) | .0005-.002 (.013-.050) | Rear | .006-.014 (.15-.36) | 1.8750-1.8755 (47.625-47.638) | .001-.003 (.03-.08) | ..... |

# MG Engines

## MIDGET 4 CYLINDER (Cont.)

### ENGINE SPECIFICATIONS (Cont.)

#### VALVE SPRINGS

| Engine | Free Length In. (mm) | PRESSURE (LBS.) | |
| --- | --- | --- | --- |
| | | Valve Closed | Valve Open |
| 1493 cc | 1.52 (38.6) | ..... | ..... |

#### VALVE TIMING

| Engine | INTAKE | | EXHAUST | |
| --- | --- | --- | --- | --- |
| | Open (BTDC) | Close (ALDC) | Open (BLDC) | Close (ATDC) |
| 1493 cc | 18° | 58° | 58° | 18° |

#### CAMSHAFT

| Engine | Journal Diam. in. (mm) | Clearance in. (mm) | Lobe Lift in. (mm) |
| --- | --- | --- | --- |
| 1493 cc | | | |
| No. 1 | 1.9659-1.9664 (49.93-49.95) | .0016-.0036 (.04-.09) | ..... |
| No. 2 | 1.9649-1.9654 (49.90-49.92) | .0026-.0046 (.07-.12) | ..... |
| No. 3 | 1.9659-1.9664 (49.93-49.95) | .0016-.0036 (.04-.09) | ..... |

#### TIGHTENING SPECIFICATIONS

| Application | Ft. Lbs. (mkg) |
| --- | --- |
| Cylinder Head | 46 (6.4) |
| Connecting Rod Bolt | 40-45 (5.5-6.2) |
| Rocker Shaft | 32 (4.4) |
| Oil Pan | 20 (2.8) |
| Engine Front Cover | |
| Small Bolt | 10 (1.4) |
| Large Bolt | 20 (2.8) |
| Water Pump | 20 (2.8) |
| Manifold | 25 (3.5) |
| Crankshaft Pulley | 150 (20.7) |
| Rocker Cover | 2 (.03) |
| Main Bearing Cap Bolts | 65 (9.0) |

## 1800 cc 4 CYLINDER

### ENGINE CODING

#### ENGINE IDENTIFICATION

Engine serial number is stamped on a machined pad on right side of cylinder block. 5th digit of VIN (located at top left of instrument panel) also identifies engine.

### ENGINE, CYLINDER HEAD & MANIFOLD

#### ENGINE

**Removal — 1)** Remove battery cables and hood. Drain cooling system and crankcase. Remove air cleaner by disconnecting PCV, ECS, AIR and CCS hoses.

**2)** Disconnect the CCS hot air hose, remove manifold cover and disconnect alternator wiring at connector. Remove exhaust pipe from manifold. Free clutch control cable by turning adjusting nut. Disconnect heater hose at engine and from heater and joint. Disconnect control cable and remove water cock assembly with heater hose. Remove left engine mounting nut and install engine hanger (J-26555) on exhaust manifold stud bolts.

**3)** Disconnect ground cable from engine, fuel hoses from carburetor and high tension cable from coil. Disconnect vacuum hose at rear of manifold, accelerator control cable from carburetor, and starter motor connections. Disconnect the thermo unit, oil pressure switch, and distributor wiring at connector.

**4)** Disconnect carburetor solenoid valve lead and automatic choke wiring at connector. Disconnect backup light switch at rear of engine. Disconnect ECS hose from oil pan. Remove right engine mounting nut and stopper plate.

**5)** Disconnect water hoses from engine and radiator. Remove fan shroud and radiator assembly. Remove gearshift lever assembly. Remove parking brake return spring and disconnect brake cable. Disconnect propeller shaft from transmission.

**6)** Remove clutch cable heat protector, clutch return spring, and clutch control cable. Remove exhaust pipe bracket from transmission. Remove front side exhaust pipe. Disconnect speedometer cable. Remove four rear engine mounting bolts after lifting engine slightly.

**7)** Check that all parts have been properly disconnected or removed, and remove engine toward front of vehicle.

**Installation** — Install all components in reverse order of removal. Check that crankcase and cooling system are refilled. Adjust clutch pedal free play. Check engine for leaks after running at idle. Adjust fan belt tension, distributor breaker point gap, valve clearances, ignition timing and engine idle.

#### EXHAUST MANIFOLD

Remove air cleaner and hot air hose. Remove manifold cover, EGR pipe and exhaust pipe from manifold, and exhaust manifold from engine. To install, reverse removal procedure, using new gaskets.

### INTAKE MANIFOLD

**Removal — 1)** Drain cooling system completely. Remove air cleaner (See *Engine Removal*).

**NOTE** — *Incomplete draining will permit coolant to enter cylinders when intake manifold is removed.*

**2)** Remove the following parts from intake manifold: water top hose, fuel hose, vacuum hose, heater hose (also from connector under instrument panel). Disconnect accelerator control cable and vacuum hose from carburetor. Disconnect automatic choke and solenoid wiring at connectors, PCV hose from cylinder head cover, and EGR pipe from EGR valve. Disconnect AIR vacuum hose from manifold. Remove intake manifold from engine.

**Installation** — Reverse removal procedure. Use new gaskets and fill cooling system with equal amounts of water and antifreeze.

### CYLINDER HEAD

**Removal — 1)** Drain cooling system, remove air cleaner, and all parts attached to intake manifold. Remove manifold cover.

**Fig. 1 Locking Timing Chain Adjuster**

**2)** Remove EGR pipe clip from rear of cylinder block, and disconnect exhaust pipe from manifold. Remove cylinder head cover, lock timing chain in place (See *Fig. 1*), and separate sprocket from camshaft. Disconnect air hoses from check valve and AIR pump. Remove air bypass valve and bracket, and remove two bolts securing front cover and cylinder head. Loosen cylinder head bolts in sequence shown in *Fig. 2*. Remove cylinder head with exhaust and intake manifolds.

## 1800 cc 4 CYLINDER (Cont.)

*Fig. 2  Cylinder Head Bolt Loosening & Tightening Sequence*

**NOTE** — *Do not separate camshaft timing sprocket from chain. Keep sprocket in chain, and chain between guide and tensioner.*

**Installation** — 1) Install components in reverse order of removal. Apply a thin coat of liquid gasket evenly on clean block face around sprocket hole. Install a new cylinder head gasket with "TOP" mark up, using dowels for proper alignment. See *Fig. 3*.

Apply Sealer

Dowel

"TOP" Mark

TOP

*Fig. 3  Installing Liquid Gasket & Head Gasket*

2) Align cylinder head over dowels, oil cylinder head bolt threads and install bolts. Install two bolts securing front cover to cylinder head. Tighten cylinder head bolts in sequence (See *Fig. 2*) in two stages. Tighten securely front cover-to-cylinder head bolts.

### Cylinder Head Bolt Tightening Specifications

|  | Ft. Lbs. (mkg) |
| --- | --- |
| Step One | 61 (8.4) |
| Step Two | 72 (9.9) |

## VALVES

### VALVE ARRANGEMENT

E-I-I-E-I-I-E

### ROCKER ARM ASSEMBLY & CAMSHAFT

**Removal** — 1) Remove air cleaner and disconnect accelerator control cable from carburetor. Pull out three clips and high tension cables from head cover. Disconnect AIR vacuum hose and PCV hose. Remove head cover.

2) Align mark on camshaft with mark on No. 1 rocker arm shaft bracket by turning crankshaft, *Fig. 4*. Lock the automatic chain adjuster in free state, by pressing downward on pin while turning it 90 degrees clockwise (See *Fig. 1*).

3) Remove bolt and slip timing sprocket off camshaft. Keep chain on sprocket and support sprocket on chain guide and tensioner. Loosen nuts on rocker arm shaft brackets in stages, starting with the outer brackets. Remove rocker arm assembly and camshaft from cylinder head.

Punch Marks On Rocker Arm Shafts Up

Align Setting Mark

Thrust Grooves

*Fig. 4  Installing Camshaft & Rocker Arm Assembly*

**Installation** — 1) Lubricate camshaft and rocker arm assemblies well prior to installation. Install camshaft, aligning thrust grooves, *Fig. 4*. Be sure punch marks on rocker arm shafts are in upward position.

2) Install rocker arm shaft bracket assembly and align camshaft mark with mark on No. 1 rocker arm shaft bracket. See *Fig. 4*. Tighten rocker arm shaft bracket nuts to 16 ft. lbs. (2.2 mkg) torque, while holding rocker arm springs with an adjustable wrench.

3) Align crankshaft pulley groove with TDC mark ("O" mark) on front cover. Be sure No. 4 cylinder (rear) is at TDC. Align sprocket hole with camshaft pin. Install sprocket and tighten bolt to 58 ft. lbs. (8.02 mkg). Set automatic chain adjuster by turning pin 90 degrees counterclockwise (See *Fig. 1*). Be sure chain is tensioned.

# Opel Engines

## 1800 cc 4 CYLINDER (Cont.)

### VALVE GUIDE SERVICING

1) Using valve spring compressor (J-26513), remove valve collets, upper seats, and outer and inner springs. Remove seals and lower seat springs. Check stems and guides for wear and clearance. Do not remove guides unless they are to be replaced.

2) To remove guides, use driver (J-26512) to drive guide upward. Drive new guide in until it extends 0.6378" (16.2 mm) above cylinder head, (See Fig. 5). Be sure valve moves freely in guide. Install seals over guides and reassemble.

**Fig. 5   Installing Valve Guide to Proper Depth**

### VALVE FACE AND SEAT

1) To replace valve seat insert, weld end of welding rods to several portions of inner face of insert. Allow cylinder head to cool. Apply shock load to welding rods and pull out inserts. Clean insert face area of cylinder head and heat with steam. Chill new insert on dry ice and install in cylinder head.

2) Cut valve seat face with 15°, 45°, and 75°cutters to achieve specified valve seat contact width. Grind valves to an angle of 45° and lap valve and seat to specified width.

### VALVE CLEARANCE ADJUSTMENT

1) Check rocker arm shaft bracket nuts for 16 ft. lbs. (2.2 mkg) torque. Bring No. 1 piston (front) to TDC on compression stroke (notched line on crankshaft pulley aligns with "0" mark on front cover). Check clearances of No. 1 and 2 intake valves and No. 1 and 3 exhaust valves.

2) Turn crankshaft one full turn until No. 4 piston (rear) is at TDC on compression stroke, and check clearances of No. 3 and 4 intake valves and No. 2 and 4 exhaust valves.

3) Adjust intake valves to .006"C (.15 mm) and exhaust valves to .010"C (.25 mm).

### PISTONS, PINS & RINGS

#### OIL PAN

**Removal** — Remove oil pressure switch from block and remove 14 bolts and 6 nuts holding pan to block. Remove dust cover.

**Installation** — Apply liquid gasket to points shown in Fig. 6. Place oil pan gasket on cylinder block, aligning bolt holes. Install and tighten bolts and nuts to 3.6 ft. lbs. (.5 mkg). Check gasket position and install dust cover on the rear plate.

**Fig. 6   Installing Oil Pan & Gasket**

#### PISTON & ROD ASSEMBLY

**Removal** — Remove cylinder head and oil pan. Remove carbon ridge from cylinder bore. Remove bearing and cap from connecting rod. Remove piston and rod assembly by pushing upward with wooden handle of hammer.

**NOTE** — *Remove one piston at a time and mark piston, rod, and bearings with their cylinder numbers.*

**Installation** — 1) Turn crankshaft so that the crankpin of No. 1 cylinder (front) is in uppermost position. Install bearings with tangs inserted in notches in rod and cap. Oil bearing surfaces and outer contact areas of piston and rings.

2) Arrange ring gaps as shown in Fig. 7. Mark on head of piston should point toward front of engine. Using ring compressor, push piston head in until connecting rod contacts crankpin. Head of piston should be approximately .016" (.4 mm) below face of block when at TDC.

3) Face of connecting rod with cylinder number mark should be toward starter side of engine. Align number marks on connecting rod cap and rod and torque nuts to 33 ft. lbs. (4.6 mkg).

## 1800 cc 4 CYLINDER (Cont.)

*Fig. 7  Piston Ring Position & Piston Marking*

**4)** After piston and rod assembly is installed in No. 1 cylinder, proceed with No. 4, No. 2, and No. 3 cylinders in sequence. After bearing nuts are tightened, check that crankshaft turns smoothly.

## PISTON PINS

Do not remove piston from connecting rod unless replacing parts. Always use new piston pin. Check piston pin hole in piston and connecting rod for damage. If pin is to be removed, remove rings and use pin remover (J-25270-45) to press pin from rod. Position piston so that marks on head and notches in connecting rod point upward. Use same position and tool for removal and installation.

## FITTING PISTONS

**1)** Measure cylinder bores .32" (8.1 mm) and 2.76" (70.1 mm) below cylinder block face. Measure both in line and at right angles to crankshaft. If diameter varies more than .0079" (.2 mm), reboring is indicated. Variance of bore diameter after reboring and honing should be less than .0008" (.02 mm).

**2)** Cylinder bores for various pistons available include:

### Cylinder Bore Sizes

| Piston Size | Bore Diameter Inches (mm) |
| --- | --- |
| Standard | 3.3071-3.3087 (84.00-84.04) |
| .020" Oversize | 3.3268-3.3276 (84.50-84.52) |
| .040" Oversize | 3.3465-3.3472 (85.00-85.02) |

**3)** Cylinder blocks are stamped on the upper face to show cylinder bore grade or size:

### Cylinder Bore Grades

| Bore Size | Bore Grade | Bore Diameter Inches (mm) |
| --- | --- | --- |
| Standard | A | 3.3071-3.3075 (84.00-84.01) |
| | B | 3.3075-3.3079 (84.01-84.02) |
| | C | 3.3079-3.3083 (84.02-84.03) |
| | D | 3.3083-3.3087 (84.03-84.04) |

**4)** Pistons are also stamped with a grade on their heads to show their diameter at a point 1.575" (40 mm) below piston head and at right angles to piston pin.

### Piston Grades and Diameters

| Piston Size | Piston Grade | Diameter Inches (mm) |
| --- | --- | --- |
| Standard Size | A | 3.3049-3.3053 (83.94-83.95) |
| | B | 3.3053-3.3057 (83.95-83.96) |
| | C | 3.3057-3.3061 (83.96-83.97) |
| | D | 3.3061-3.3065 (83.97-83.98) |
| .020" Oversize | A.B | 3.3246-3.3254 (84.44-84.47) |
| .040" Oversize | A.B | 3.3443-3.3451 (84.95-84.97) |

**5)** Check cylinder-to-piston clearance by measuring piston diameter 1.575" (40 mm) below piston head and at right angles with piston pin. Subtract this measurement from cylinder bore diameter, measured 4.724" (120 mm) below face of cylinder block. If clearance is excessive, install oversize pistons.

**6)** Check end gap and groove clearance. Install rings on pistons using a ring expander. Compression rings should be installed with "NPR" or "TOP" mark turned up. When installing oil control ring, install expander ring, followed by lower side rail and upper side rail. Oil rings are not marked.

**7)** When all rings are installed, apply engine oil and see that rings move freely in grooves. Weigh piston and rod assemblies. Variation in weight should be less than .42 oz. (12 gms). Adjust gaps as shown in *Fig. 7* and install pistons in block.

## CRANKSHAFT MAIN & CONNECTING ROD BEARINGS

### MAIN & CONNECTING ROD BEARINGS

**Removal — 1)** Remove oil pan and pipe from oil pump. Remove crankshaft pulley and front cover assembly. Remove cylinder head, sprockets and timing chain. Remove flywheel assembly, rear plate and oil seal retainer. Remove connecting rod and piston assemblies.

**2)** Loosen main bearing cap bolts in sequence, beginning with outer bolts. Remove bolts, bearing caps and bearings.

## 1800 cc 4 CYLINDER (Cont.)

**NOTE** – *Check each connecting rod and main bearing cap for identification, so that it can be reinstalled in its original location and position.*

**3)** Lift out crankshaft. Remove thrust bearings and crankshaft bearings from cylinder block.

**Inspection** – **1)** Using an outside micrometer, measure crankshaft and crankpin journals at front and rear of each journal, (1 and 2). See Fig. 8. Take both vertical and horizontal measurements (A and B). If wear exceeds .002" (.05 mm), grind crankshaft and install undersize bearings.

**Fig. 8   Measuring Crankshaft & Crankpin Journals**

**2)** Install crankshaft bearings in block and install bearing caps and bolt. Torque to 72 ft. lbs (10 mkg) and measure inside diameter of bearings. Measure inside diameter of connecting rod bearings in same manner, torquing to 33 ft. lbs. (4.6 mkg). Compare outside diameters of journals with inside diameter of bearings to determine oil clearance. Plastigage method may also be used to determine clearance.

**3)** When installing undersize bearings, grind crankshaft and crankpin journals to match bearing size:

### Crankshaft & Crankpin Journal Diameters

| Bearing Size | Crankshaft Journal Inches (mm) | Crankpin Journal Inches (mm) |
|---|---|---|
| Standard | 2.2016-2.2022 (55.92-55.94) | 1.9262-1.9268 (48.92-48.94) |
| .010" Undersize | 2.1917-2.1923 (55.67-55.68) | 1.9163-1.9169 (48.67-48.69) |
| .020" Undersize | 2.1819-2.1825 (55.42-55.44) | 1.9065-1.9071 (48.42-48.44) |

**4)** Check crankshaft end play, and install new thrust bearings on each side of No. 3 journal if excessive.

**Installation** – **1)** Install bearings in cylinder block and oil generously. Install crankshaft over bearings. Install thrust bearings with oil grooves outward. Clean surfaces and install bearings in caps.

**2)** Install main bearing caps so cast arrows point toward engine front and numbers on caps and journals align. Tighten bolts in sequence: Cap No. 3, No. 4, No. 2, No. 5, and No. 1. Torque to 72 ft. lbs. (10 mkg). Be sure crankshaft turns easily.

**3)** Install piston and connecting rod assemblies and other components previously removed.

### REAR MAIN BEARING OIL SEAL

**Removal** – Remove clutch pressure plate assembly. Flatten flywheel bolt lock plates and remove flywheel assembly. Pry off oil seal from retainer.

**Installation** – Apply grease between lips of oil seal and engine oil to crankshaft. Install oil seal in retainer using setting tool (J-22928-2). Be sure flanged part of oil seal is properly seated on retainer. Reverse removal procedure to complete installation. Use new flywheel bolt lock plates and torque to 69 ft. lbs. (9.5 mkg).

## CAMSHAFT

### FRONT COVER

**Removal** – Remove crankshaft pulley, oil filter and distributor from cover. Remove front cover with water pump and oil pump.

**Fig. 9   Aligning Oil Pump in Front Cover**

**Installation** – **1)** Install gasket on block. Be sure oil pump, water pump and oil seal are installed properly. Punch mark on oil pump drive gear face should be turned to oil filter side. Align center of dowel pin with setting mark on oil pump case. See Fig. 9.

**2)** Set No. 1 and No. 4 pistons at TDC. Install cover assembly, engaging pinion gear with oil pump drive gear. Punch mark on oil pump gear should be pointing toward cylinder block. Slot in end of oil pump shaft should be parallel with front of block and offset forward.

## 1800 cc 4 CYLINDER (Cont.)

### FRONT COVER OIL SEAL

**Removal & Installation** — Remove fan assembly, A/C compressor drive belt, fan belts, crankshaft pulley and pulley boss. Pry out oil seal. To install, fill space between oil seal lips with bearing grease and use setting tool (J-26587). Install crankshaft pulley and torque bolt to 87 ft. lbs. (12 mkg).

### TIMING CHAIN

**1)** To install, turn crankshaft so key points to cylinder head (piston for No. 1 and 4 cylinders at TDC). Place timing chain on crankshaft sprocket, so that mark plate on chain faces forward and aligns with sprocket timing mark.

**Fig. 10   Installing Timing Chain on Sprockets**

**NOTE** — *Chain has two mark plates. Be sure side of chain with most links between mark plates is toward chain guide side.*

**2)** Place camshaft timing sprocket in chain so that mark plate on chain aligns with triangular mark on camshaft sprocket. Install camshaft sprocket on camshaft as instructed under *Rocker Arm Assembly & Camshaft.*

### VALVE TIMING

Valve timing will be correct if chain is properly installed and if camshaft is installed as instructed under *Rocker Arm Assembly & Camshaft.*

### ENGINE OILING

**Crankcase Capacity** — 5 quarts.

**Relief Valve** — A relief valve built into oil pump cover bypasses oil to oil pan at 57-71 psi.

**Oil Filter** — Full-flow type, disposable cartridge. Filter has built-in bypass valve to permit engine oiling in event filter becomes restricted.

### ENGINE OILING SYSTEM

A trochoid type pump feeds oil under pressure through the full-flow filter into the oil gallery, which supplies oil to crankshaft journals through drilled passages and ports. Oil is fed to crankpins, piston rings and pins as well as cylinder bore. Pressurized oil is also delivered through the No. 3 crankshaft oil port into the cylinder head to rocker arms, rocker arm shafts and camshaft. Timing chain and sprockets are lubricated by oil fed through No. 1 crankshaft journal to the oil jet on chain guide. Oil splashed by crankshaft lubricates cylinder walls.

### OIL PUMP

**Removal** — **1)** Remove engine from vehicle. Remove cylinder head cover, distributor assembly, engine stiffeners and oil pan. Remove oil pipe from pump and remove pump assembly. Remove rubber hose and relief valve assembly.

**2)** Inspect parts for wear and for clearance between drive rotor and driven rotor and between driven rotor and pump body. Check pump cover gear end clearance and clearance between drive shaft and pump cover hole.

**Fig. 11   Aligning Rotor Timing Marks**

**Installation** — **1)** Align timing marks on camshaft and rocker arm shaft support. Align notched line on crankshaft pulley with "0" mark on front cover (piston in No. 4 cylinder at TDC on compression stroke).

## 1800 cc 4 CYLINDER (Cont.)

**2)** Install driven rotor so timing marks align with drive rotor, *Fig 11.* Install oil pump, engaging drive gear with crankshaft pinion gear. Setting mark on drive gear should be rearward and approximately 20 degrees clockwise from crankshaft centerline. *(See Fig. 12).*

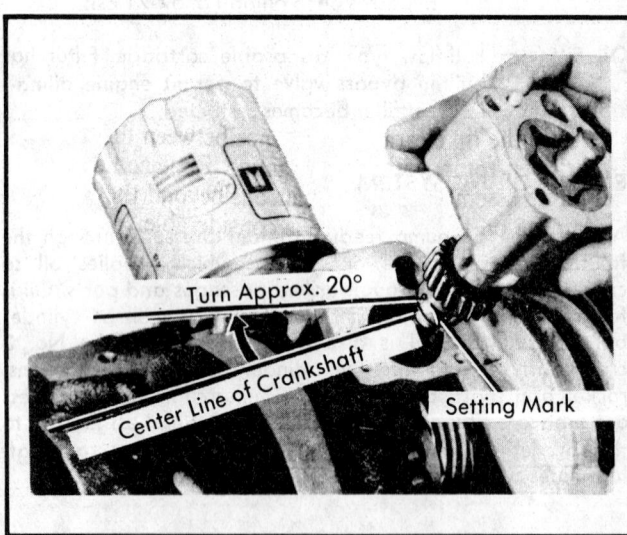

**Fig. 12   Installing Oil Pump**

**3)** After installation, check that setting mark is rearward (in clearance between front cover and block). Check that slot in end of pump drive shaft is parallel with front cylinder block face and offset forward, when viewed through distributor hole.

**4)** Install oil pump cover on dowels, install bolts, relief valve assembly, rubber hose and oil pipe assembly. Install parts previously removed.

### Oil Pump Specifications

| Measurement Point | Inches (mm) |
|---|---|
| Drive Rotor-to-Driven Rotor .............. | .0005-.0059 (.012-.150) |
| Driven Rotor-to-Pump Body ............. | .0063-.0087 (.160-.220) |
| Rotors-to-Pump Body ...................... | .0012-.0035 (.030-.088) |
| Drive Shaft-to-Pump Cover Hole ..... | .0028-.0043 (.071-.109) |

## ENGINE COOLING

**Thermostat** — Wax pellet-type. Begins to open at 177-182° F (81-83° C); fully open at 203° F (95° C).

**Cooling System Capacity** — 6.8 quarts.

### WATER PUMP

**Removal** — Disconnect battery ground cable, remove radiator shroud and drain coolant from radiator. Remove drive belts. Remove cooling fan and pulley. Remove water pump from front cover.

**Installation** — If pump body is cracked, water is leaking from seal unit, bearing is noisy or has play, or impellers or front cover assembly are cracked or corroded, replace entire pump. Install new pump by reversing removal procedure.

## ENGINE SPECIFICATIONS

### GENERAL SPECIFICATIONS

| Year | Displ. | | Carburetor | HP at RPM | Torque (Ft. Lbs. at RPM) | Compr. Ratio | Bore | | Stroke | |
|---|---|---|---|---|---|---|---|---|---|---|
| | cu. ins. | cc | | | | | in. | mm | in. | mm |
| 1978 | 110.8 | 1800 | 2-Bbl | ..... | 95@3000 | 8.5-1 | 3.31 | 84.1 | 3.23 | 82.0 |

### VALVES

| Engine & Valve | Head Diam. In. (mm) | Face Angle | Seat Angle | Seat Width In. (mm) | Stem Diameter In. (mm) | Stem Clearance In. (mm) | Valve Lift In. (mm) |
|---|---|---|---|---|---|---|---|
| 1800 cc Intake | ..... | 45° | ①45° | .0472-.0630 (1.20-1.60) | .315 (8.0) | .0009-.0022 (.022-.056) | ..... |
| Exhaust | ..... | 45° | ①45° | .0472-.0630 (1.20-1.60) | .315 (8.0) | .0015-.0031 (.038-.079) | ..... |

① — Grind seat to obtain proper width.

## 1800 cc 4 CYLINDER (Cont.)

### ENGINE SPECIFICATIONS (Cont.)

#### PISTONS, PINS, RINGS

| Engine | PISTONS | PINS | | RINGS | | |
| | Clearance In. (mm) ① | Piston Fit In. (mm) | Rod Fit In. (mm) | Rings | End Gap In. (mm) ② | Side Clearance In. (mm) |
|---|---|---|---|---|---|---|
| 1800 cc | .0018-.0026 (.046-.066) | Push Fit | Press Fit | No. 1 & 2 <br><br> Oil | .008-.016 (.203-.406) <br> .008-.035 (.203-.890) | .0010-.0024 (.025-.061) <br> .0008 (.020) |

① — Piston diameter measured 1.575" (40 mm) below piston head and at right angles to piston pin.

② — End gap is measured with ring in cylinder.

#### CRANKSHAFT MAIN & CONNECTING ROD BEARINGS

| Engine | MAIN BEARINGS | | | | CONNECTING ROD BEARINGS | | |
| | Journal Diam. In. (mm) | Clearance In. (mm) | Thrust Bearing | Crankshaft End Play In. (mm) | Journal Diam. In. (mm) | Clearance In. (mm) | Side Play In. (mm) |
|---|---|---|---|---|---|---|---|
| 1800 cc | 2.2016-2.2022 (55.92-55.94) | .0008-.0025 (.020-.063) | No. 3 | .0024-.0094 (.061-.239) | 1.9262-1.9268 (48.93-48.94) | .0007-.0030 (.018-.076) | .0079-.0130 (.201-.330) |

#### VALVE SPRINGS

| Engine | Free Length In. (mm) | PRESSURE Lbs. @ In. (kg @ mm) | |
| | | Valve Closed | Valve Open |
|---|---|---|---|
| 1800 cc <br> Outer | 1.8465 (46.9) | ..... | 32.2-37@1.614 (14.6-16.8@41.0) |
| Inner | 1.7835 (45.3) | ..... | 18.7-21.5@1.516 (8.5-9.8@38.5) |

#### CAMSHAFT

| Engine | Journal Diam. In. (mm) | Clearance ① In. (mm) | Lobe Lift In. (mm) |
|---|---|---|---|
| 1800 cc | 1.3362-1.3370 (33.94-33.96) | .0016-.0035 (.041-.089) | ..... |

① — End play is .0020-.0059" (.051-.150 mm).

#### TIGHTENING SPECIFICATIONS

| Application | Ft. Lbs. (mkg) |
|---|---|
| Cylinder Head Cover Bolts | 3.6 (.50) |
| Cylinder Head Bolts | 72 (9.95) |
| Oil Pan Bolts | 3.6 (.50) |
| Crankshaft Bearing Cap Bolts | 72 (9.95) |
| Connecting Rod Bearing Cap Bolts | 33 (4.56) |
| Rocker Arm Shaft Bracket Nuts | 16 (2.21) |
| Timing Sprocket Bolt | 58 (8.02) |
| Crankshaft Pulley Bolt | 87 (12.03) |
| Flywheel Bolts | 69 (9.45) |

# Porsche Engines

## 911 SC & TURBO 6 CYLINDER

### ENGINE CODING

#### ENGINE IDENTIFICATION

Engine identification number is die stamped on blower fan support near oil temperature sensor. Second digit of number identifies engines as follows:

| Application | Engine Code |
|---|---|
| 911 SC | |
|   Federal | 2 |
|   California | 5 |
| Turbo | 8 |

### ENGINE & CYLINDER HEAD

#### ENGINE

1) Place vehicle on jack stands. Disconnect negative battery cable. Remove air cleaner. Loosen engine block vent hose at engine and plug vent cover hole. If equipped with air conditioning, detach compressor at console but leave hoses attached.

**NOTE** — *Air conditioning system is under pressure, DO NOT disconnect hoses until pressure is released.*

2) Remove relay plate cover and disconnect the engine wires at; relay plate, adapter plug, relay plate socket, and ignition control unit. Remove fuel hoses at filter and return line. Disconnect accelerator linkage.

3) Remove rear center tunnel cover in passenger compartment. Remove rubber boot in tunnel by pulling forward over the selector rod. Loosen shift rod coupling and pull coupling off of transmission inner shift rod.

4) Disconnect speedometer sensor wires in tunnel. Remove rubber plug with wire plug. Drain crankcase and plug hoses on engine and oil tank. Remove heater hoses at exchangers. Remove rear stabilizer.

5) Disconnect ground strap at body and battery wires at starter. Disconnect accelerator linkage from pedal and clutch cable from transmission. Loosen drive shaft flange socket head screws at transmission.

**CAUTION** — *Be careful when jacking assembly upward not to damage the secondary air injection pipes.*

6) Place a suitable jack under engine/transmission assembly and apply a little upward pressure to relieve tension on motor mounts. Remove transmission and engine mount bolts. Lower engine/transmission assembly out of vehicle.

**CAUTION** — *Do not move vehicle unless drive shafts are suspended horizontally, to prevent damage to dust covers.*

**Installation** — Reverse removal procedure and note the following: Do not clamp heater hoses, slide them onto the exchangers just before the engine/transmission assembly is in final installation position.

#### CYLINDER HEAD

**Removal** — 1) With fuel injection system removed, remove distributor cap and spark plug wires. Remove all cool air ducts and cover shrouds.

2) Remove air ducts connecting air blower outlets and heat exchanger inlets, together with cover shrouds. Remove rear engine mount (transverse leaf spring) from holder.

3) Remove fuel pump and hoses. Remove exhaust pipes and engine mounting bracket. Remove blower pulley and drive belt.

4) Loosen both screws of band strap which attaches alternator to blower housing. Pull blower housing rearward. Disconnect alternator cables and remove blower housing with alternator.

5) Remove heat exchanger using suitable wrenches (No. P 205 & P 217). Disconnect camshaft oil lines between crankcase and chain housing covers. Remove covers.

6) Remove chain tensioner, pivot lever and chain sprocket as an assembly. Remove camshaft sprocket nuts using suitable tools (No. P 202 & P 203). Withdraw sprocket dowel pin, using suitable tool (No. P 212).

7) With a screwdriver lift spring retainers from groove and remove chain guides. Remove camshaft sprockets and flanges. Pry Woodruff keys from camshafts.

**NOTE** — *Each cylinder has a separate cylinder head. If camshaft housing is removed, any single head may be removed. If camshaft housing is left attached to cylinder heads, cylinder heads and camshaft housing may be removed as an assembly.*

8) To remove a single head, rotate camshaft to take load off of rocker arm shaft to be removed. Loosen rocker arm shafts and push out shafts. Remove camshaft housing.

9) Using a suitable tool (No. P 119), remove cylinder head nuts and lift off cylinder head.

**NOTE** — *Mark cylinder heads, cylinders and camshaft housings so they will be reassembled in their original positions.*

10) To remove all three cylinder heads and camshaft housing as an assembly, evenly loosen and unscrew cylinder head nuts using suitable tool (No. P 119).

# Porsche Engines

## 911 SC & TURBO 6 CYLINDER (Cont.)

**Installation** — 1) Place cylinder head gaskets on cylinders with perforated side of steel insert facing cylinder. Install cylinder heads and oil return tubes at same time. Coat oil return tubes with engine oil for easier installation. Lightly tighten cylinder head nuts.

**NOTE** — *Split (2 piece) oil return pipes may be installed without removing and disassembling the engine. If using this type, all "O" rings and seals must be lightly oiled and pipe telescoped. Extend pipe until end seals are seated and place retaining ring in its groove. Short pipe must be installed in crankshaft housing.*

2) Install cool air shrouds and attach with clamps. Thinly coat camshaft housing gasket with gasket compound. Slide camshaft housing onto mounting studs. Tighten camshaft housing nuts down a few turns to ensure gasket seal. Install Allen screws in proper location and tighten camshaft housing in a crosswise pattern.

**Fig. 2    Cross Sectional View of Rocker Arm Shaft Assembly**

**Fig. 1    View of Porsche 6 Cylinder Engine (Turbo Shown)**

**NOTE** — *Camshaft housings are interchangeable, but camshafts are not. Camshafts must be positioned on their proper side; see Fig. 4.*

3) Tighten cylinder head nuts in a crosswise pattern, checking that camshaft does not bind in housing. If camshaft binds, loosen cylinder head nuts and tighten in a different sequence. With cylinder head nuts tight, camshaft must be free to rotate.

4) Install rocker arms and shafts. Install rocker arm shaft with approximately .060" (1.52 mm) clearance between shaft grooves and mounting face; see *Fig. 2*. Tighten Allen bolts to 13 ft. lbs. (1.8 mkg), using suitable tools (P 210 & P 211).

5) Install gasket, "O" ring, sealing flange, thrust plate, spacer, Woodruff key and camshaft sprocket flange as shown in *Fig. 3*. No provision is made to adjust camshaft end play, if sealing flange is worn, replace it.

**Fig. 3    Assembling Components to Install Camshaft Sprocket Flange and Sprocket**

6) Install camshaft sprockets. Check chain alignment; see *Fig. 11*.

7) Install heat exchanger before chain tensioner. Slide chain guides on mounting studs. With a screwdriver lift retaining spring and slide chain guide into place. Install chain tension pivot lever and sprocket. Check that oil holes in pivot stud face upward.

8) Fill and bleed chain tensioners, depress chain tensioners and install. Left chain tensioner may be positioned in only as far as to let camshaft nut to be installed after valve timing. See *Valve Timing.*

# Porsche Engines

## 911 SC & TURBO 6 CYLINDER (Cont.)

**Fig. 4  Camshaft Sprocket Position (Viewed from Blower End of Engine)**

9) Install chain housing covers and camshaft oil lines. Reverse removal procedures for remaining components.

## VALVES

### VALVE ARRANGEMENT

All upper valves are intake.

All lower valves are exhaust.

### VALVE GUIDE SERVICING

1) In order to avoid spreading the end of the valve guide when removing it, mill the guide down to the head on the camshaft side. A .433" (11 mm) drill bit may be used if milling tool not available. Drive valve guide out into combustion chamber.

2) Using a hole gauge, measure bore in cylinder head. Turn oversize guide down in a lathe so that O.D. gives an interference fit of .0024"-.0035" (.060-.090 mm).

3) Press valve guide into head from camshaft side until a measurement of .5196" (13.2 mm) is reached. (See Fig. 5). Use suitable grease as a lubricant when pressing in valve guides. Bore or ream valve guide I.D. to .3543-.3549" (8.99-9.01 mm).

**Fig. 5  Cross Sectional View of Valve Guide for Replacement**

### VALVE STEM OIL SEALS

1) Using a suitable spring compressor, remove valve keepers. Withdraw collar and springs. Remove valve stem oil seal from end of valve guide.

2) Slide a new oil seal over valve stem, using care not to damage seal as it passes over keeper grooves. Force seal over end of valve guide. Reverse removal procedure for springs, collar and keepers.

**Fig. 6  Arrows Indicate Measurement Location Points for Valve Spring Installed Height**

### VALVE SPRING SERVICING

1) Using a suitable spring compressor, remove valve keepers and collar. Check springs for wear or fatigue, replace as necessary.

2) Install outer sping with closely wound coils next to cylinder head. Measure installed height of springs; add or remove spacers under valve spring to attain specified installed height.

### ROCKER ARM ASSEMBLY

1) Using an Allen wrench, loosen rocker arm shaft bolt. Slide rocker shaft out of cylinder head and remove arm.

2) Check rocker arm shaft and rocker bushing for wear.

### Rocker Arm Specifications (In.)

| Application | Diameter | Wear Limit |
|---|---|---|
| Rocker Arm Bushing | .7090-.7094 | .7106 |
| Rocker Arm Shaft | .7080-.7084 | .7074 |
| Rocker Arm Width | 1.015-1.019 | 1.011 |
| Housing Width | 1.023-1.029 | 1.033 |

## 911 SC & TURBO 6 CYLINDER (Cont.)

**3)** Install rocker arm shaft. Center rocker arm shaft in housing; see *Fig. 2*. Tighten rocker arm Allen bolt.

**NOTE** — *Install outside rocker arm shafts with Allen bolt facing either cylinder two or five.*

### VALVE CLEARANCE ADJUSTMENT

**1)** Valve clearance should be set to .004" (.10 mm) with engine cold. If valves or seats have been reground, set clearances to .010" (.25 mm), run engine for one-half hour, then reset valves to original cold clearance.

**2)** Adjust valves in firing order sequence 1, 6, 2, 4, 3 and 5. Rotate to TDC of firing stroke on No. 1 cylinder and adjust clearance.

**3)** Rotate engine 120° until No. 6 cylinder is at TDC and adjust. Rotate engine 120° for each cylinder to be adjusted.

## PISTONS, PINS & RINGS

### OIL PAN

Remove nuts attaching oil pan (strainer cover plate). Remove strainer plate, gaskets and strainer. Clean strainer and cover plate. Using new gaskets, replace strainer and cover plate, making sure oil strainer hole slides over pickup tube.

### PISTON ASSEMBLY

Mark piston and cylinder for proper relocation upon reassembly. Remove cylinders. Extract piston pin circlip, heat piston to approximately 176°F (80°C), and press out pin. Clean and inspect piston, rings, and pin for each cylinder. **NOTE** — *See measurement procedures in Fitting Pistons. Replace parts as necessary.*

### FITTING PISTONS

The Turbo Carrera model uses a light alloy forged and lead coated piston. Piston crown is nearly flat and is marked with a symbol indicating flywheel direction. Pistons may only be installed one way due to .051" (1.5 mm) offset of pin from center.

The 911 SC piston has a depressed dome shape, and this depression must face the exhaust valve when installed. Pistons must be of same weight class and cylinders of same size in order to prevent unbalance of the engine.

**1)** Measure cylinder for wear and out-of-round. Cylinders and pistons are marked according to size. "0" indicates standard, while "1" or "2" indicates first or second oversize. Measure cylinder diameter 1.18" (30 mm) below top edge of cylinder.

**2)** Take one measurement in line with thrust face and another at 90° to this measurement. Cylinder is worn if diameter measurement is more than .004" (0.1 mm) beyond diameter

specification. If difference in the two measurements is more than .0016" (.04 mm), then cylinder has exceeded its ovality limit.

Depressed Portion of Dome Faces Exhaust Valve

**Fig. 7   911 SC Model Type Piston Head Shape**

Marking Faces Flywheel End

**Fig. 8   Turbo Carrera Piston Shape**

**3)** Position piston rings in bottom of cylinder and measure ring gap. Check side clearance in piston ring grooves. Install rings on piston with marking "TOP" facing upward as shown in *Fig. 9*.

**Fig. 9   Sectional View of Piston Ring Installation**

## 911 SC & TURBO 6 CYLINDER (Cont.)

### CRANKSHAFT MAIN & CONNECTING ROD BEARINGS

#### MAIN BEARING SERVICE

1) Separate crankcase halves. Lift out crankshaft and connecting rods. Place crankshaft on a suitable stand and remove connecting rods.

**NOTE** — *Replace connecting bolts whenever rods are disassembled. Connecting rod bolts are stretch bolts and should never be reused.*

2) Inspect crankshaft and connecting rods for wear, damage or out-of-true. Crankshaft main journals one through seven and all connecting rod journals have the same diameter. Replace bearings or fit undersize bearings as required.

3) Main bearing number eight is a special bearing with an external "O" ring and internal oil seal. A steel dowel pressed in crankcase is used to locate number eight bearing and prevent it from turning. Use care when installing bearing that dowel engages hole and not groove in bearing.

#### THRUST BEARING ALIGNMENT

Check end play at No. 1 main bearing. Width of No. 1 bearing is 1.1024-1.1044" (28.0-28.05 mm). Maximum wear limit is .011" (.28 mm) beyond specifications. Replace main bearing or crankshaft if excessive wear is present.

#### MAIN BEARING OIL SEALS (BLOWER END)

Remove belt pulley. Using a screwdriver, pry out old seal. Coat new seal with oil and press in place using suitable tool (No. P 216).

**NOTE** — *Distributor drive gear now turns distributor Counterclockwise and is marked with Porsche emblem. Old style gear (clockwise drive) is marked with VW emblem.*

#### MAIN BEARING OIL SEAL SERVICE (FLYWHEEL END)

Remove flywheel. With a chisel or drift, displace oil seal. With a screwdriver pry out seal. Coat outer seal edges with sealing compound and press into crankcase until seal is flush with face of crankcase, using suitable tool (P 215).

#### INTERMEDIATE SHAFT BEARING SERVICE

With crankcase halves separated, lift out intermediate shaft and bearings. Inspect shaft and bearings for wear or damage. Replace shaft and bearings as necessary. No undersize bearings are available.

### CAMSHAFT

#### TIMING CHAIN

Remove timing chain housing covers. Remove chain tensioner and chain tensioner sprocket. Remove timing chains. Install

*Fig. 10 Crankshaft Assembly with Component Locations*

## 911 SC & TURBO 6 CYLINDER (Cont.)

**Fig. 11    Top View Showing Timing Chain Alignment**

new timing chains. Reverse removal procedure to reassemble. Check valve timing and chain alignment; *see Fig. 11 & 13.*

## CAMSHAFT

1) Remove rocker covers and rocker arm assemblies. Disconnect exhaust muffler. Remove oil hose from crankcase to chain housing cover. Remove chain tensioner and chain tensioner sprocket.

2) On 911S models, remove belt pulley from left camshaft. Remove bearing and chain housing covers. With a puller, remove ball bearing from camshaft.

3) Unscrew nuts attaching camshaft sprocket, using suitable tools (No. P 202 & P 203). Using suitable tool (No. P 212), remove dowel pin from camshaft sprocket.

4) Pull sprocket and sprocket flange. Remove Woodruff key from camshaft. Remove three attaching screws, "O" ring and withdraw camshafts rearward.

**NOTE** – *Camshafts are not symmetrical and must be replaced on side they were removed from during disassembly.*

## CAMSHAFT END THRUST

With a dial indicator measure camshaft end play. If end play is excessive replace aluminum thrust washer located behind camshaft sprocket flange.

**Fig. 12    Camshaft and Housing Location
(Viewed from Blower End of Engine)**

## VALVE TIMING

1) Rotate crankshaft until mark "Z 1" on crankshaft pulley aligns with mark on crankcase.

**NOTE** – *Use care when rotating crankshaft or camshafts so that valve and piston do not collide. If resistance is felt, backoff a little and rotate camshaft until you are free to continue.*

2) Use suitable tool (No. P 202) to rotate camshaft until dot on end of shaft is on top of camshaft vertical center line (see Fig. 13). Find hole in camshaft sprocket which exactly lines-up with camshaft flange and insert dowel pin. Install lock washer and nut.

# Porsche Engines

## 911 SC & TURBO 6 CYLINDER (Cont.)

*Fig. 13   Head on View of Engine Showing Valve Timing Marks*

**3)** Adjust cylinder No. 1 intake valve clearance to .04" (1 mm). Install a dial indicator with pressure foot resting squarely on valve spring collar. Preload dial indicator to .4" (10 mm) to provide for valve movement.

**4)** Using a screwdriver, depress chain tensioner on side to be measured and block it with piece of metal. Rotate crankshaft 360° until "Z 1" (TDC) mark is aligned with mark on crankcase. Read dial indicator and compare with measurement given in *Intake Valve Lift Table*.

**5)** If correct valve opening measurement is not achieved, loosen camshaft nut, remove dowel pin and rotate camshaft until valve is open correct amount. Locate holes which align exactly and install dowel pin. Make sure crankshaft remains on TDC. Rotate crankshaft 2 complete revolutions and recheck valve lift. Repeat timing procedure if necessary. Repeat procedure on No. 4 cylinder for other side of engine.

### Intake Valve Lift

| Application | In. (mm) |
|---|---|
| 911 SC & Turbo ......................................... | .035-.423" (.9-1.1) |

## ENGINE OILING

**Oil Capacity** — Total system capacity for both 911 SC and Turbo Carrera is 13.7 quarts. Oil change requires 10.6 quarts. Check oil level with dipstick while engine is idling at operating temperature.

**Oil Filter** — Disposable spin-on type.

**Normal Oil Pressure** — 911 SC and Turbo Carrera at 5000 RPM with 165°F (80°C) oil temperature should have 65 psi oil pressure.

**Pressure Relief and Safety Valves** — Identically constructed coil spring operated valves. Safety valve is set to operate at a higher pressure than relief valve.

## ENGINE OILING SYSTEM

Lubrication is dry sump type. Two independent oil pumps provided for pressure and suction in system. Pressure pump takes oil from an externally mounted oil tank and forces oil to individual oil passages for all main bearings. From main bearings a drilled passage in crankshaft carries oil to connecting rod bearings. Another passage leads to front bearing of intermediate shaft. A passage in intermediate shaft takes oil to rear bearing of shaft.

Camshaft oiling is accomplished by external oil lines leading to camshaft housings. Camshaft housings contain aluminum tubes with holes; three holes of .12" (3.0 mm) diameter carry oil to lubricate camshaft. Six holes of .04" (1.0 mm) diameter splash oil on camshaft lobes. Remaining three holes allow oil to splash against intake valve cover in such a manner that it will drip on rocker arms and valve stems.

Suction pump takes oil from engine sump through a strainer and forces it through oil filter to oil tank. Oil collected in lower part of camshaft housing is returned to crankcase by oil return pipes. Suction pump then returns oil to oil tank. A tube in oil tank carries oil to base of oil tank and filter. The turbo charger is lubricated from a branch off of oil pressure indicator or oil temperature indicator.

Oil pressure regulation is controlled by means of four separate valves. A thermostatically controlled valve directs oil directly to engine when temperature is below 176°F. When temperature

## 911 SC & TURBO 6 CYLINDER (Cont.)

is above 176°F, oil flows through oil cooler and then to main bearings. A pressure relief and safety valve located in right crankcase half opens if oil pressure rises above 76.9-99.6 psi and oil is passed directly into crankcase. A safety valve is mounted in left crankcase half immediately after oil pump. It operates in event of a defective pressure relief valve to prevent damage to oil cooler or oil lines. As a safety measure, by-pass valves are built into filter base and filter body. If oil pressure exceeds 28.4 psi, oil by-passes oil filter and flows directly into oil tank.

### OIL PUMP

Oil pump may be removed when crankcase halves are separated. No repair of pump is possible, replace if defective.

### ENGINE COOLING

Cooling is accomplished by means of a blower, consisting of an impeller and blower housing. Center of blower housing holds support for alternator. Impeller and belt pulley are attached to alternator shaft. Blower delivers air required for cooling engine, oil cooler, alternator as well as fresh air for heating system. Cooling air flows through upper molded plastic air guides to cylinders and heads. Baffle plates provide uniform distribution of air. A duct incorporated into upper air guide leads air flow directly to oil cooler. Ducting for air delivery to heat exchangers is on both sides of blower housing. Adjustment of blower drive belt is done by adding or removing spacers between impeller housing and pulley half. This will cause belt to ride higher of lower on pulley, thereby loosening or tightening drive belt.

## ENGINE SPECIFICATIONS

### GENERAL SPECIFICATIONS

| Year | Displ. | | Carburetor | HP at RPM | Torque (Ft. Lbs. at RPM) | Compr. Ratio | Bore | | Stroke | |
| | cu. ins. | cc | | | | | in. | mm | in. | mm |
|---|---|---|---|---|---|---|---|---|---|---|
| 1978 911 SC | 182.7 | 2944 | Fuel Inj. | 172@5500 | 180@4200 | 8.5:1 | 3.74 | 95 | 2.77 | 70.4 |
| Turbo | 201.3 | 3299 | Fuel Inj. | 261@5500 | 291@4000 | 7.0:1 | 3.82 | 97 | 2.93 | 74.4 |

### VALVES

| Engine & Valve | Head Diam. In. (mm) | Face Angle | Seat Angle | Seat Width In. (mm) | Stem Diameter In. (mm) | Stem Clearance In. (mm) | Valve Lift In. (mm) |
|---|---|---|---|---|---|---|---|
| 2944 cc Intake | ..... | 45° | 45° | ..... | ..... | ..... | ..... |
| Exhaust | ..... | 45° | 45° | ..... | ..... | ..... | ..... |
| 3299 cc Intake | ..... | 45° | 45° | ..... | ..... | ..... | ..... |
| Exhaust | ..... | 45° | 45° | ..... | ..... | ..... | ..... |

### PISTONS, PINS, RINGS

| Engine | PISTONS | PINS | | RINGS | | |
| | Clearance In. (mm) | Piston Fit In. (mm) | Rod Fit In. (mm) | Rings | End Gap In. (mm) | Side Clearance In. (mm) |
|---|---|---|---|---|---|---|
| 2944 cc & 3299 cc | .001-.002 (.025-.052) | Press Fit | .0007-.0015 (.018-.038) | No. 1 | .004-.008 (.10-.20) | .003-.004 (.07-.10) |
| | | | | No. 2 | .004-.008 (.10-.20) | .001-.003 (.04-.07) |
| | | | | Oil | .006-.012 (.15-.30) | .0008-.002 (.02-.05) |

① — Limit .006" (.15 mm).

# Porsche Engines

## 911 SC & TURBO 6 CYLINDER (Cont.)
### ENGINE SPECIFICATIONS (Cont.)

### CRANKSHAFT MAIN & CONNECTING ROD BEARINGS

| Engine | MAIN BEARINGS | | | | CONNECTING ROD BEARINGS | | |
| --- | --- | --- | --- | --- | --- | --- | --- |
| | Journal Diam. In. (mm) | Clearance In. (mm) | Thrust Bearing | Crankshaft End Play In. (mm) | Journal Diam. In. (mm) | Clearance In. (mm) | Side Play In. (mm) |
| 2994 | | | | | | | |
| Jrnls 1-7 | 2.362 (60) | .0003-.0028 (.008-.07) | No. 1 | .0043-.0076 (.11-.19) | 2.085 (53) | .0011-.0034 (.028-.086) | ..... |
| Jrnl 8 | 1.220 (31) | .004 (.10) | | | | | |
| 3299 | | | | | | | |
| Jrnls 1-7 | 2.362 (60) | .0003-.0028 (.008-.07) | No. 1 | .0043-.0076 (.11-.19) | 2.165 (55) | .0011-.0034 (.0028-.086) | ..... |
| Jrnl 8① | 1.220 (31) | .004 (.10) | | | | | |

① — Some models may have 1.575" (40 mm) diameter journal.

### VALVE SPRINGS

| Engine | Free Length In. (mm) | PRESSURE ① Lbs. @ In. (kg @ mm) | |
| --- | --- | --- | --- |
| | | Valve Closed | Valve Open |
| 2994 cc | | | |
| Intake | ..... | 1.358 (34.5) | ..... |
| Exhaust | ..... | 1.358 (34.5) | ..... |
| 3299 cc | | | |
| Intake | ..... | 1.319 (33.5) | ..... |
| Exhaust | ..... | 1.319 (33.5) | ..... |

① — Measurement given is spring height; no pressure specification is provided. See *Valve Spring Servicing.*

### VALVE TIMING

| Engine | INTAKE | | EXHAUST | |
| --- | --- | --- | --- | --- |
| | Open (BTDC) | Close (ALDC) | Open (BLDC) | Close (ATDC) |
| 2994 cc | 1° | 53° | 43° | 3° |
| 3299 cc | 3° | 37° | 29° | 3° |

### TIGHTENING SPECIFICATIONS

| Application | Ft. Lbs. (mkg) |
| --- | --- |
| Crankcase Joining Bolts | 25 (3.5) |
| Camshaft Housing | 18 (2.5) |
| Main Bearing Caps | 25 (3.5) |
| Flywheel (9 Bolt) | 65 (90) |
| Connecting Rod Caps | 36 (5.0) |
| Cylinder Head | 22 (3.3) |
| Crankshaft Pulley | 58 (8.0) |
| Camshaft Nut | 101 (14) |
| Rocker Arm Shafts | 13 (1.8) |

# Porsche Engines

## 924 4 CYLINDER

### ENGINE CODING

#### ENGINE IDENTIFICATION

Engine number is located on left side of crankcase next to the clutch housing. Engine number is coded as follows:

**Engine Code Number**

| Application | Codes |
|---|---|
| 924 Federal | XG |
| 924 California | XE |

### ENGINE, CYLINDER HEAD

#### ENGINE

**Removal — 1)** Disconnect battery cable and remove engine protection plate. Scribe hood at hinges and remove hood. Drain cooling system, remove hoses and expansion tank. Remove fan motors with shroud and alternator cooling hose.

**NOTE** — *Remove A/C compressor without disconnecting hoses and lay aside.*

**2)** Disconnect all wiring, hoses, lines, linkage and brackets from engine. Disconnect exhaust pipe at manifold. Support drive line at front brace with wooden block. *See Fig. 1.*

**Fig. 1  Drive Line Support Block**

**3)** Disconnect universal joint at steering rack. Disconnect stabilizer bar at frame on both sides and remove crossmember. Attach hoist and lift engine slightly. Remove bellhousing bolts and engine mounts. On vehicles equipped with automatic transmissions, remove bolts from metal/rubber damper. Lift engine carefully and turn at same time.

**Installation** — To install engine, reverse removal procedure.

#### CYLINDER HEAD

**Removal & Installation — 1)** Disconnect battery ground strap and drain cooling system. Remove hoses and wiring con-

nected to cylinder head. Remove exhaust pipe at manifold and remove camshaft timing belt and "V" belt.

**2)** Remove cylinder head cover and head bolts in sequence. To install, reverse removal procedures.

**NOTE** — *Retorque head bolts after 1000 miles (1600 km). Loosen bolts in sequence and retorque to 86 ft. lbs. (12 mkg).*

**Fig. 2  Cylinder Head Tightening Sequence (Loosen in Reverse Order)**

### VALVES

#### VALVE ARRANGEMENT

I-E-I-E-I-E-I-E (Front to rear).

#### VALVE GUIDE SERVICING

**1)** With dial indicator, measure amount of clearance between valve and guide with end of stem flush with guide. If wear exceeds limits of .032" (0.8 mm) for intake, or .039" (1.0 mm) for exhaust, replace valve guides.

**Fig. 3  Measuring Valve Guide Clearance**

## 924 4 CYLINDER (Cont.)

**2)** Press worn guide out from combustion chamber side. Place circlip into groove of replacement guide and press new guide in from camshaft side. Production guides do not have circlips and may be smooth or have one groove. Replacement guides have a circlip in addition to 1 or 2 grooves on camshaft end.

**3)** Ream replacement guide by hand with dry reamer for proper clearance. Change valve spring retainer resting on head to replacement type with groove.

### Valve Guides

| Identification | Circlip | Outside Diameter In. (mm) |
|---|---|---|
| Original Smooth | W/O Circlip | .548 (14.06) |
| Original 1 Groove | W/O Circlip | .556 (14.26) |
| Replacement 1 Groove | With Circlip | .556 (14.26) |
| Replacement 2 Groove | With Circlip | .564 (14.46) |

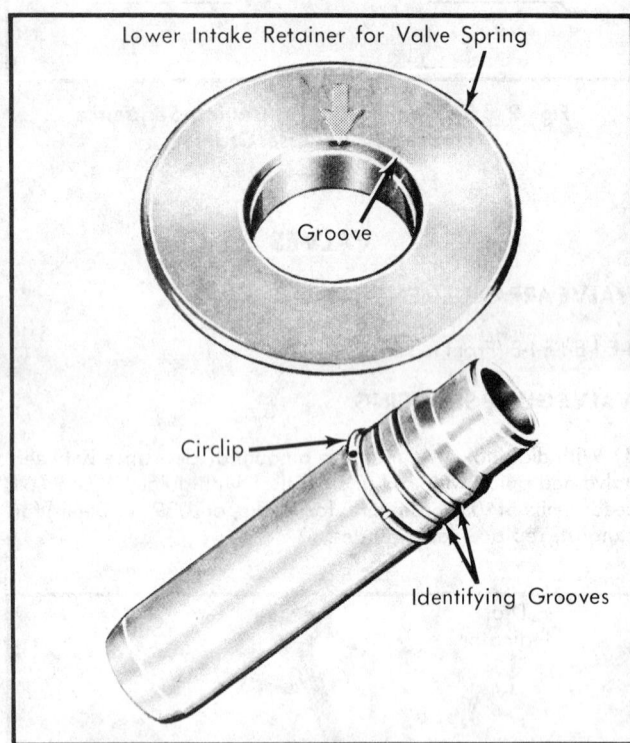

**Fig. 4    Replacement Valve Guide and Intake Spring Retainer**

### VALVE STEM OIL SEALS

**NOTE** — *Valve stem oil seal may be replaced with cylinder head installed.*

Remove spark plug on cylinder being serviced, install air hose and adapter to maintain constant pressure in cylinder. Remove camshaft, tappets, valve stem keepers and valve spring. Remove oil seal and discard. To install, reverse removal procedures while noting the following; Be sure plastic sleeve is installed prior to seal installation. Place sleeve on valve stem, lubricate seal and install onto valve stem.

### MECHANICAL VALVE LIFTERS

With camshaft removed, lift out tappet and inspect for wear or damage. Oil tappets lightly and replace in original position.

### VALVE CLEARANCE ADJUSTMENT

**1)** Remove cylinder head cover and turn crankshaft until cam lobes of cylinder to be adjusted are pointing upward. Check valve clearance with feeler gauge between tappet and lobe.

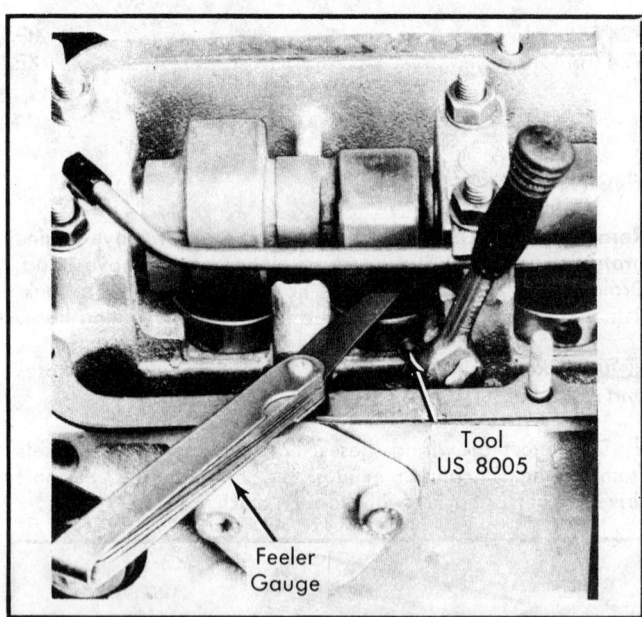

**Fig. 5    Checking and Adjusting Valve Clearance (Note Cam Lobes Pointing Upward)**

**2)** Basic valve clearance with engine cold (when reconditioning engine) is .004" (.10 mm) for intake valve and .016" (.40 mm) for exhaust valve. Valve clearance should be checked with engine warmed to 176°F (80°C) oil temperature. Intake valve clearance is .008" (.20 mm) and exhaust clearance is .018" (.45 mm).

**3)** Adjust clearance by turning screw mounted in tappet with adjusting tool US 8005. Adjustment must be in complete turns only. One turn of screw changes clearance by .002" (.05 mm). After adjusting valve, be sure edge of tappet is in line with green area of tool.

**Fig. 6    Valve Lifter (Tappet) with Adjusting Screw and Tool**

## 924 4 CYLINDER (Cont.)

### PISTONS, PINS & RINGS

#### OIL PAN

Drain engine oil and loosen left engine mount slightly. Disconnect steering at crossmember and remove crossmember. Remove oil pan bolts and lower oil pan. To install, reverse removal procedure and tighten pan bolts to specifications.

#### PISTONS & ROD ASSEMBLY

**1)** Before removing connecting rods, mark rod and cap for installation in original position. Remove rod caps and carefully push piston and rod assembly out top of block.

**2)** On reassembly of piston and rod assembly, cast bosses on rod and cap must face pulley end of engine. Code numbers must be on same side. Using a suitable ring compressor, install piston and rod assembly with arrow on crown of piston facing front of engine.

#### FITTING PISTONS

**1)** Measure cylinder bore .39" (9.9 mm) down from top and up same distance from bottom, also in the center. Take two measurements, one in line with crankshaft and again 90° to crankshaft.

**Fig. 7    Measuring Piston Diameter at Skirt**

**2)** Measure piston .63" (16 mm) from bottom of skirt 90° to pin bore. Combine measurements with those taken from cylinder bore. If piston-to-cylinder measurement exceeds .0016" (.04 mm), oversized pistons must be installed.

**Fig. 8    Measuring Ring Gap in Cylinder Bore**

**3)** Place piston rings squarely in bottom of cylinder bore approximately .59" (15 mm) from surface and measure ring gap. Wear limit is .039" (1.0 mm). Measure ring side clearance in piston. Wear limit is .004" (0.1 mm). Install rings with "TOP" mark facing piston crown and gaps offset 120° from each other.

#### PISTON PINS

Remove circlip and using piston pin remover VW 207c, remove pins. To install, reverse removal procedure.

**NOTE** — *If pin is hard to install, heat piston to approximately 140°F (60°C).*

Tool VW207c

**Fig. 9    Piston Pin Removal and Installation**

Feeler Gauge

**Fig. 10    Checking Piston Ring Side Clearance**

## 924 4 CYLINDER (Cont.)

### CRANKSHAFT MAIN & CONNECTING ROD BEARINGS

#### MAIN & CONNECTING ROD BEARINGS

1) Push crankshaft toward one end and measure end play at No. 3 thrust bearing. Be sure main bearing caps are marked for reinstallation. Measure connecting rod side play. Remove rod and main bearing caps and check bearing clearance using Plastigage method.

**Fig. 11    Measure Crankshaft End Play as Shown (Check Connecting Rod Side Clearance Using Same Method)**

2) Install plain bearing shell into bearing cap. Place grooved shell in block. Do not mix shells. Lubricate bearings and install caps.

**NOTE** — *On No. 5. bearing, coat mating surface of bearing with sealing compound.*

### CAMSHAFT

#### FRONT MAIN BEARING OIL SEAL

Remove pulley bolt and using oil seal removing tool 10-221 (or equivalent), pry oil seal out of oil pump. Use installing tool 2033 to install new seal.

#### TIMING BELT

Remove belt cover and loosen drive belt tensioner. Remove crankshaft pulley and drive belt pulley. Remove drive belt. To install, reverse removal procedure.

**NOTE** — *Belt must be tightened until belt can be turned 90° with thumb and index finger at a point midway between crankshaft and camshaft.*

#### CAMSHAFT

1) Remove cylinder head cover and timing belt cover. Rotate crankshaft so marks on crankshaft pulley and camshaft sprocket are in No. 1 TDC position. Remove camshaft sprocket, distributor and distributor drive housing.

2) Remove camshaft lubrication tube, then replace nuts (hand tight) on bearing caps 2 and 4. Remove bearing caps 5, 1 and 3. Loosen bearing caps 2 and 4 evenly in a crosswise pattern and lift out camshaft.

**NOTE** — *Ensure that bearing caps are replaced in original position. Note the correct off-center position of bearing caps.*

3) To install camshaft, reverse removal procedure and note the following; Place camshaft into position and install caps 2 and 4 again using a crosswise pattern. Install caps 1, 3 and 5 and tighten all nuts to specifications. Loosen nuts 2 and 4 to install lubrication tube.

### VALVE TIMING

Using either TDC mark on flywheel and casting in bell housing, or crankshaft pulley TDC mark, rotate crankshaft to TDC position. Mark on rear of camshaft sprocket and indicator on cylinder head cover must be in line. Ensure that Woodruff key is installed and camshaft sprocket bolt is tightened properly. Install timing belt and adjust tension.

**Fig. 12    Camshaft Sprocket Alignment**

### ENGINE OILING

**Crankcase Capacity** — 4.7 qts. Add approximately 1 pt. with filter.

**Oil Filter** — Spin-on type. Change at first oil change and every other one thereafter.

**Oil Pressure** — 73-101 @ 5000 RPM.

#### ENGINE OILING SYSTEM

The engine oiling system is full pressure with rotary (sickle) type pump. Oil is picked up by pump through strainer and suction tube. Oil passes through pump and pressure control valve to oil filter and main oil channels. It is then distributed to main

## 924 4 CYLINDER (Cont.)

**Fig. 13   Engine Oiling System**

bearings, connecting rods and crankshaft. Camshaft lubrication is provided by spray tube at No. 1 cam bearing. Oil pressure switch is located at end of camshaft lubrication passage. A temperature sensor is located in oil pan.

### OIL PUMP

Oil pump is gear driven sickle type. Pump is mounted at front of engine and driven directly by crankshaft. Gear replacement is in pairs only.

### ENGINE COOLING

**Cooling System Capacity** — 8.4 quarts with heater.

**Thermostat** — Opens at approximately 180°F.

**Radiator Cap** — 12.8-16.4 psi.

**Cooling Fan** — Comes on at 198°F, goes off at 189°F.

### ENGINE SPECIFICATIONS

| GENERAL SPECIFICATIONS | | | | | | | | | | |
|---|---|---|---|---|---|---|---|---|---|---|
| Year | Displ. | | Carburetor | HP at RPM | Torque (Ft. Lbs. at RPM) | Compr. Ratio | Bore | | Stroke | |
| | cu. ins. | cc | | | | | in. | mm | in. | mm |
| 1978 | 121 | 1984 | Fuel Inj. | 110 @ 5750 | 111 @ 3500 | 8.5:1 | 3.41 | 86.5 | 3.32 | 84.4 |

| VALVES | | | | | | | |
|---|---|---|---|---|---|---|---|
| Engine & Valve | Head Diam. In. (mm) | Face Angle | Seat Angle | Seat ① Width In. (mm) | Stem Diameter In. (mm) | Stem Clearance In. (mm) | Valve Lift In. (mm) |
| 1984 cc<br>Int. | 1.575<br>(40) | 45° | 45° | .087-.118<br>(2.2-3.0) | .3532<br>(8.97) | .0157<br>(0.4) | ..... |
| Exh. | 1.299<br>(33) | 45° | 45° | .087-.118<br>(2.2-3.0) | .3524<br>(8.95) | .020<br>(0.5) | ..... |

① — Maximum seat width .138″ (3.5 mm).

| PISTONS, PINS, RINGS | | | | | | |
|---|---|---|---|---|---|---|
| Engine | PISTONS | PINS | | | RINGS | |
| | Clearance In. (mm) | Piston Fit In. (mm) | Rod Fit In. (mm) | Rings | End Gap In. (mm) | Side Clearance In. (mm) |
| 1984 cc | .0012<br>(.03) | ..... | .0004-.0008<br>(.01-.02) | ..... | .012-.020<br>(.3-.5) | .0016-.0028<br>(.04-.07) |

# Porsche Engines

## 924 4 CYLINDER (Cont.)

### ENGINE SPECIFICATIONS (Cont.)

| CRANKSHAFT MAIN & CONNECTING ROD BEARINGS | | | | | | | |
|---|---|---|---|---|---|---|---|
| | MAIN BEARINGS | | | | CONNECTING ROD BEARINGS | | |
| Engine | Journal Diam. In. (mm) | Clearance In. (mm) | Thrust Bearing | Crankshaft End Play In. (mm) | Journal Diam. In. (mm) | Clearance In. (mm) | Side Play In. (mm) |
| 1984 cc | 2.518-2.519 (63.95-63.97) | .0008-.0031 (.02-.08) | 3 | .0020-.0031 (.05-.08) | 1.888-1.889 (47.95-47.97) | .0008-.0027 (.02-.07) | .004-.007 (.1-.19) |

| CAMSHAFT | | | |
|---|---|---|---|
| Engine | Journal Diam. In. (mm) | Clearance In. (mm) | Lobe Lift In. (mm) |
| 1984 cc | 1.0236-1.0245 (26.00-26.02) | .002-.006 (.06-.061) | ..... |

| VALVE TIMING | | | | |
|---|---|---|---|---|
| | INTAKE | | EXHAUST | |
| Engine | Open (BTDC) | Close (ALDC) | Open (BLDC) | Close (ATDC) |
| 1984 cc ① | 6° | 42° | 47° | 2° |

① — With .039" (1 mm) valve clearance.

### TIGHTENING SPECIFICATIONS

| Application | Ft. Lbs. (mkg) |
|---|---|
| Cylinder Head Bolts | ① |
|   Cold | 72 (10) |
|   Warm | 86 (12) |
| Main Bearing Caps | 58 (8) |
|   No. 5 Allen Head Bolt | 47 (6.5) |
| Connecting Rod Nuts | 43 (6) |
| Flywheel | 65 (9) |
| Crankshaft Pulley | 180 (25) |
| Oil Pan Bolts | |
|   (M 6) | 6 (.8) |
|   (M 8) | 11 (1.5) |
| Exhaust Manifold | 18 (2.5) |
| Intake Manifold | 17 (2.4) |
| Camshaft Bearing Cap Nuts | 12-15 (1.6-2.1) |
| Camshaft Bearing Cap Bolts | 7 (1) |
| Camshaft Sprocket Bolt | 58 (8) |
| Oil Pump Mounting Bolts | 7 (1) |

① — Bolts must be retorqued after 1000 miles (1600 Km). Loosen bolts in sequence about 30° and retorque to 86 ft. lbs. (12 mkg).

## 4.5 LITER V8

### ENGINE CODING

#### ENGINE IDENTIFICATION

Dual overhead camshaft V8 engine is coded M 28. Engine code and identification number is stamped on the front reinforcing rib in the top half of the crankcase.

### ENGINE & CYLINDER HEADS

#### ENGINE

**Removal — 1)** With car standing on all 4 wheels, loosen engine compartment cross braces. Disconnect battery ground cable at spare wheel well. Detach windshield washer hoses and engine compartment light wires. Remove engine hood. Remove cap from coolant expansion tank. Remove air intake hoses and entire air cleaner assembly.

**2)** Raise car on hoist at specified pick up points. Place wooden block between central tube and rear tunnel brace. Detach splash shield at bottom and drain radiator. Remove left and right water drain plugs from crankcase. Drain engine oil and remove lower body brace. Disconnect exhaust pipes at manifolds and remove left and right heat shields. Detach ground cable at body. Install and tighten drain plugs.

**3)** Unscrew clutch slave cylinder at clutch housing and remove with line connected. Remove mounting strap for pressure line to slave cylinder. Disconnect wires at starter and remove clutch housing with starter.

**4)** Disconnect clutch lever by pressing down in direction of clutch. Release starter wire from clamps on steering cross member. Remove socket head bolts and push drive shaft coupling back on drive shaft. Unscrew throwout bearing sleeve mounting bolts and push sleeve toward flywheel.

**5)** Detach left and right engine shock absorbers at control arms, then at upper mountings. Disconnect air conditioner temperature switch wires on radiator and compressor clutch at connector plug. Loosen compressor and remove from console but do not disconnect hoses. Suspend compressor with wire.

**6)** Remove air pump filter housing and alternator cooling hose. Remove lower fan shroud. Disconnect all coolant hoses and bottom oil hose at radiator. Remove engine mounts separately by lifting with hydraulic jack and wooden block on oil pan. Lower engine to front cross member carefully. Move jack and pad to second side and remove mount in same manner.

**7)** Remove clutch/engine mounting bolts and lower car. Remove remaining coolant/heater hoses between engine and radiator/chassis. Disconnect upper oil hose at radiator. Remove radiator mounting bolts and lift out radiator. Disconnect engine wire harness and distributor wire transmitter plugs. Disconnect B+ wire and remove control unit. Detach and place ignition coil aside.

**8)** Disconnect fuel feed and return lines. Detach power steering pump lines at pump and supply tank. Drain oil and remove tank. Disconnect brake booster vacuum hose at manifold. Disconnect accelerator and cruise control cable, remove holder and clamp and place cables outside. Cover A/C condenser with a thin board to prevent damage when removing engine.

**9)** With engine adapter (9137) in eyelets provided, lift until snug with car resting on its wheels. Remove upper engine block/clutch housing mounting bolts. Pull engine forward carefully and remove short drive shaft with guide tube. Lift engine out of car.

**Installation —** To install, reverse removal procedures noting that heater lever should be in "warm" position when filling cooling system. Coolant level must reach center of expansion tank with engine warm.

#### CYLINDER HEADS

**NOTE** — *Manufacturer does not furnish removal and replacement procedures for cylinder heads. Heads may be removed with engine in vehicle. Following items must be noted when performing cylinder head operations:*

**1)** Allow engine to cool prior to draining coolant. Heads must not be removed while engine is still hot. Remove camshaft housing, then loosen cylinder head nuts in reverse of tightening sequence.

**2)** Left and right cylinder head gaskets are different. Arrow must face forward and word "TOP/OBEN" must face up. Tighten head in 3 steps according to the sequence shown in *Fig.1*. Tighten to final torque and allow to stand at least 30 minutes. Loosen nuts by ¼ turn, then tighten to final torque of 61 ft. lbs. (8.5 mkg).

**3)** Flat gasket between cylinder head and camshaft housing must be placed properly to ensure that oil supply bore to camshaft is not blocked. Camshaft housing must be completely assembled prior to installation. Housing is located on heads with 2 dowel pins and mounted with Allen head bolts.

**Fig. 1  Cylinder Head Tightening Sequence
(Loosen in Reverse Order)**

### VALVES

#### VALVE ARRANGEMENT

Valves are arranged in-line with the larger, intake valve at the front of each cylinder.

## 4.5 LITER V8 (Cont.)

### HYDRAULIC VALVE LIFTERS

Bucket type hydraulic lifters operate in sintered metal sleeves. Cam lobes depress the lifters which are filled with engine oil under pressure through internal passages. With hydraulic lifters, no further valve clearance adjustment is necessary.

**NOTE** – *Use caution that lifters and sleeves are installed in original positions. Do NOT mix up lifters and sleeves.*

*Fig. 2   Cross Sectional View of Cylinder Head with Valve Lifter and Camshaft*

### VALVE SPRINGS

Valve springs may be removed using conventional overhead valve type compressor. Remove keepers and lift off retainer and spring. To install, reverse removal procedures.

**CAUTION** – *Note number of shims between valve spring and cylinder head and replace in same position.*

*Fig. 3   Measuring Installed Valve Spring Length*

### VALVE SPRING INSTALLED LENGTH

To check valve spring installed length, install tool (9138) with shims for applicable valve, spring retainer and keepers. Read distance from tool and correct, if required, by adding or removing shims. Correct intake spring length is 1.544+ .020" (39.6+.5 mm) and exhaust length should be 1.505+.020" (38.6+.5 mm).

### VALVE STEM OIL SEALS

With valve springs removed, pry off old seal using caution to prevent marring guide. Place plastic sleeve on valve stem, lubricate seal and push into place using "mushroom" type installing tool.

## PISTONS, PINS & RINGS

### OIL PAN

Oil pan is of cast aluminum design with ribs for reinforcing and cooling. Pan attaches to lower crankcase section with gasket and cap screws. Manufacturer does not provide specific removal and replacement instructions.

### PISTONS

Pistons and bore diameters come in 3 tolerance groups. Piston crown is stamped "0", "1" or "2" to correspond with similar marking stamped on cylinder block.

| Tolerance Group | Cylinder Bore In. (mm) | Piston Diameter① In. (mm) |
|---|---|---|
| 0 | 3.7050 (95.000) | 3.7036 (94.964) |
| 1 | 3.7054 (95.010) | 3.7040 (94.974) |
| 2 | 3.7058 (95.020) | 3.7044 (94.984) |

① – ±.0003" (.007 mm).

Piston pin bore is offset from center of piston by .0058" (1.5 mm). Depressions for valves are cast into piston crown at an angle of 20°. Piston and rod must be properly assembled and installed with valve pockets facing EXHAUST manifold.

## CRANKSHAFT MAIN & CONNECTING ROD BEARINGS

### CRANKCASE LOWER SECTION

Crankcase lower section provides saddles for main bearings. When replacing, it is not necessary to remove old sealant. Clean grease from surfaces and apply Loctite 573 (green) with a short-pile roller. Install lower section and tighten mounting bolts by hand. Install oil pump, then tighten lower section mounting nuts to final torque in sequence illustrated.

### MAIN & CONNECTING ROD BEARINGS

Use Plastigage method to determine main and connecting rod bearing clearance. Check crankshaft end play using dial indicator. Main bearing radial wear limit is .0062" (.16 mm) and end play limit is .0156" (.40 mm). Connecting rod bearing wear limit is .0039" (.10 mm). Ensure that connecting rods are installed to piston correctly. With piston indentations facing

## 4.5 LITER V8 (Cont.)

away from centerline (down), small chamfer on rod faces rod on same journal. Larger chamfer faces web of crankshaft.

**Fig. 4    Crankcase Lower Section Tightening Sequence**

### CRANKSHAFT OIL SEALS

Crankshaft oil seals are installed with crankcase lower half removed. Use tool (9126) to align flywheel end seal, and tool (9125) to install pulley end oil seal.

## CAMSHAFT

### TIMING BELT

Toothed timing belt drives camshafts, distributor, oil pump and water pump. As the engine assembly heats and cools, belt tension varies, so a multiple disc belt tensioner is installed to compensate for these changes. To adjust tension, remove right hand camshaft drive belt upper cover. Turn engine in normal direction through two revolutions and check belt for damage or wear. Continue turning until TDC mark on crankshaft and camshaft align with markers. Using tester (9138), check belt tightness between tension roller and camshaft sprocket. Set adjustment screw on tensioner as required and recheck tension.

**Fig. 5    Front View of Engine with Belt Covers Removed**

### CAMSHAFT TIMING ADJUSTMENT

With timing belt and tensioner removed, turn both camshafts until notches in drive sprockets align with marks on camshaft housings. Rotate crankshaft so that TDC mark on vibration damper aligns with indicator. Install belt and tensioner. Rotate crankshaft and recheck tension as in previous step.

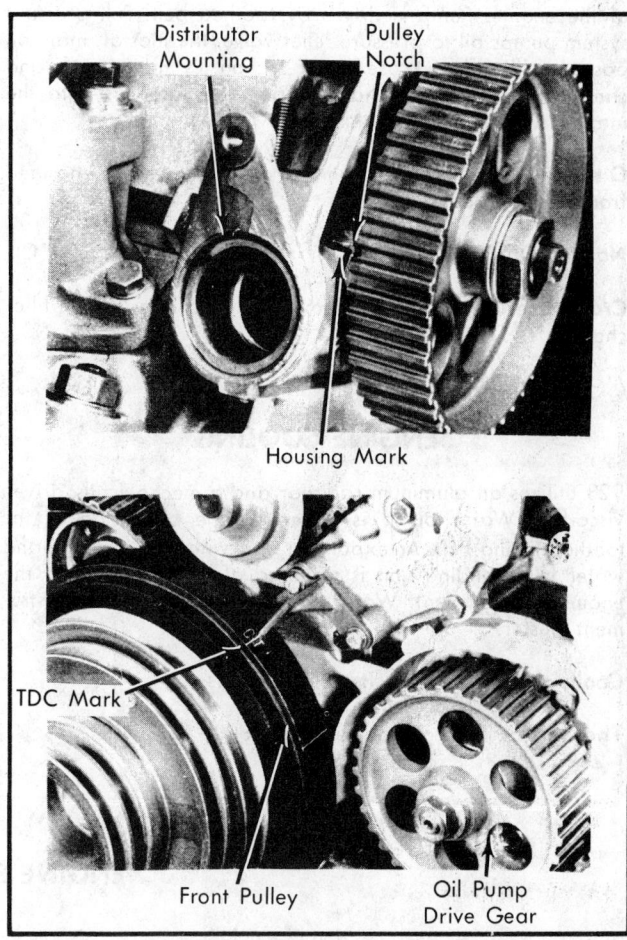

**Fig. 6    View of Left Camshaft Sprocket and Front Pulley with Timing Marks Aligned**

### DRIVE BELT TENSIONER

Tensioner consists of 8 packets of 5 bimetal discs stacked alternately. If service is required, remove housing from engine and disassemble, noting that housing contains transmission fluid. Clean and reassemble, ensuring that packs of 5 discs are installed alternately. Fill housing $\frac{1}{3}$ full with SAE 90 transmission fluid. Slide in piston assembly and install circlip. Add transmission oil, if necessary, until oil level reaches circlip. Replace dust cover, clamp and pressure rod. Install on engine.

### CAMSHAFTS

Camshafts run in 5 bearings without shells in camshaft housing. Housing cover plates must be removed in order to remove rubber plugs covering top row of bolts. Camshaft housing assembly must be completely assembled before installation. Housing is located on heads with 2 dowel pins and mounted with Allen head bolts.

## 4.5 LITER V8 (Cont.)

### ENGINE OILING

#### ENGINE OILING SYSTEM

Engine utilizes a wet sump with an oil cooler integrated in the car radiator as a heat exchanger. Sickle type oil pump is located in a separate cast iron housing bolted to the left front of the engine. Pump is driven by toothed belt. Full pressure system pumps oil to pressure relief valve, thermostat, main oil passage, filter, crankcase upper section, cylinder heads and camshaft housings. All main oil passages are cast into the mating surface of the crankcase lower section.

**Oil Filter** — Full-flow spin-on type oil filter is easily changed from beneath left side of car.

**Normal Oil Pressure** — 72 psi at 5000 RPM, 178°F (80°C).

**Crankcase Capacity** — Approximately 8.5 quarts, with filter change.

### ENGINE COOLING

928 utilizes an aluminum radiator and a mechanically driven visco-fan. Water pump is driven by the back side of the toothed timing belt. An expansion tank with filler opening and water level sending unit is mounted at the right rear of the engine compartment. Water level is indicated on the instrument cluster.

**Cooling System Capacity** — 17 quarts.

**Thermostat** — Begins to open at 180°F (83°C).

Fig. 7   Porsche 928 Engine Lubrication System

## ENGINE SPECIFICATIONS

| GENERAL SPECIFICATIONS | | | | | | | | | | | |
|---|---|---|---|---|---|---|---|---|---|---|---|
| Year | Displ. | | Carburetor | HP at RPM | Torque (Ft. Lbs. at RPM) | Compr. Ratio | Bore | | Stroke | |
| | cu. ins. | cc | | | | | in. | mm | in. | mm |
| 1978 | 273 | 4474 | Fuel Inj. | 219@5250 | 245@3600 | 8.5:1 | 3.74 | 95.0 | 3.11 | 78.9 |

| VALVES | | | | | | | |
|---|---|---|---|---|---|---|---|
| Engine & Valve | Head Diam. In. (mm) | Face Angle | Seat Angle | Seat Width In. (mm) | Stem Diameter In. (mm) | Stem Clearance In. (mm) | Valve Lift In. (mm) |
| 4474 cc Intake | 1.677 (43) | 45° | 45° | ..... | .3498 (8.97) | ..... | ..... |
| Exhaust | 1.482 (38) | 45° | 45° | ..... | .3490 (8.95) | ..... | ..... |

# Porsche Engines

## 4.5 LITER V8 (Cont.)
### ENGINE SPECIFICATIONS (Cont.)

| | PISTONS, PINS, RINGS | | | | | | |
|---|---|---|---|---|---|---|---|
| | PISTONS | PINS | | RINGS | | | |
| Engine | Clearance In. (mm) | Piston Fit In. (mm) | Rod Fit In. (mm) | Rings | End Gap In. (mm) | Side Clearance In. (mm) | |
| 4474 cc | .0014 (.036) | Interference | Interference | ..... | ..... | ..... | |

| | CRANKSHAFT MAIN & CONNECTING ROD BEARINGS | | | | | | |
|---|---|---|---|---|---|---|---|
| | MAIN BEARINGS | | | | CONNECTING ROD BEARINGS | | |
| Engine | Journal Diam. In. (mm) | Clearance In. (mm) | Thrust Bearing | Crankshaft End Play In. (mm) | Journal Diam. In. (mm) | Clearance In. (mm) | Side Play In. (mm) |
| 4474 cc | 2.730 (70.0) | .0008-.0038 (.070-.098) | No. 3 | .0042-.0121 (.110-.312) | 2.028 (52.0) | .0008-.0027 (.02-.07) | ..... |

### VALVE TIMING

| | INTAKE | | EXHAUST | |
|---|---|---|---|---|
| Engine | Open (ATDC) | Close (ALDC) | Open (BLDC) | Close (BTDC) |
| 4474 cc | 8° | 55° | 38° | 2° |

## TIGHTENING SPECIFICATIONS

| Application | Ft. Lbs. (mkg) |
|---|---|
| Cylinder Head Bolts | |
| Step 1 | 14 (2.0) |
| Step 2 | 36 (5.0) |
| Step 3① | 61 (8.5) |
| Main Bearing Carrier | |
| Step 1 | 14 (2.0) |
| Step 2 | 29 (4.0) |
| Step 3 | |
| 10 mm | 38-41 (5.2-5.7) |
| 12 mm | 43-47 (6.0-6.5) |
| Connecting Rod Nuts | 42-46 (5.8-6.3) |
| Camshaft Housing | 33 (4.5) |
| Flywheel | 69-73 (9.5-10.0) |
| Front Pulley | 181-188 (25.0-26.0) |
| Camshaft Pulley | 29-33 (4.0-4.5) |
| Oil Pump | |
| Step 1 | 11 (1.5) |
| Step 2 | 14-16 (2.0-2.2) |
| Spark Plugs | 18-25 (2.5-3.5) |

① — Allow to stand for 30 min. after setting Step 3 torque, then loosen ¼ turn each. Retighten to 61 ft. lbs. (8.5 mkg).

# Renault Engines

## R-5 4 CYLINDER

### ENGINE CODING

#### ENGINE IDENTIFICATION

Type of vehicle and engine number is marked on a number plate riveted to the left rear side of the engine block. Plate is located just below cylinder head mating surface. First five digits indicate engine type.

#### Engine Identification

| Application | Engine Code |
|---|---|
| R-5 (1228) ............................................................ | 810-28 |

### ENGINE, CYLINDER HEAD & MANIFOLDS

#### ENGINE

**NOTE** — *Engine and transaxle are removed as an assembly.*

**Removal — 1)** Remove battery. Drain coolant from engine and radiator. Drain oil. Take out grille. Remove hood and inner fender support. Remove air cleaner.

**2)** Disconnect all electrical leads, control cables, vacuum lines and coolant hoses that might interfere with engine removal. Mark each item as it is disconnected. Remove transaxle cover.

**3)** Remove exhaust pipe flange. Remove radiator mounting nuts. Lift out radiator, cooling fan, and expansion tank. Disconnect steering shaft at flexible coupling. Do not lose rubber bushing.

**4)** Remove front wheels and place calipers out of way. Disconnect tie rods at rack. Use suitable tool and separate upper ball joints. Remove steering gear box. Be sure to index steering box shims.

**5)** Remove air pump complete with bracket. Remove top transaxle bolts on bell housing. Attach hydraulic hoist to engine. Remove nuts from engine mounts. Remove shift rod support bolts.

**6)** Disconnect clutch cable. Remove front transaxle mounting bracket. Slide transaxle to left, then to right to free axle drive shafts. Remove engine assembly from vehicle.

**Installation** — To install, reverse removal procedure and note: Grease transaxle input shaft and axle drive shafts. Do not damage oil seals on axle drive shafts. Make sure axle drive shafts fully seat. Adjust clutch. Refit steering rubber bushing. Bleed cooling system.

No. 1 Cylinder on Flywheel End

*Fig. 1 Cylinder Head Tightening Sequence*

#### INTAKE/EXHAUST MANIFOLD

**Removal** — Disconnect battery. Remove air filter hose. Disconnect and plug carburetor heating hose. Disconnect choke, accelerator, fuel lines and vacuum lines. Take off carburetor. Separate exhaust pipe. Remove manifold nuts and starter heat shield. Pull manifold from engine.

**NOTE** — *It may be necessary to remove nut on left engine mount and tilt engine to right to gain enough clearance for removal.*

**Installation** — To install, reverse removal procedure and replace all gaskets.

#### CYLINDER HEAD

**Removal — 1)** Disconnect battery. Drain cooling system. Remove air cleaner. Disconnect all hoses, vacuum lines, wires, and cables from cylinder head. Loosen air pump and take off belt. Disconnect exhaust pipe at manifold.

**2)** Disconnect hood lock control cable, place out of way. Take off valve cover. Remove cylinder head bolts; only loosen bolt next to distributor ½ turn. Tap head until free. Remove bolt and head.

**Installation** — To install cylinder head, reverse removal procedure and note: Make sure new head gasket is installed with "HAUT-TOP" facing up.

### VALVES

#### VALVE ARRANGEMENT

E-I-I-E-E-I-I-E

#### VALVE GUIDE SERVICING

**1)** Measure worn guide and replace with nearest oversize. Standard valve guide diameter is .433" (11 mm). First oversize is .437" (11.10 mm) and is identified by one groove mark. Second oversize is .443" (11.25 mm) and is identified by two groove marks.

**2)** Ream valve guide hole in head to accept new guide. Size of reamer must be equal to outside diameter of new valve guide. To install new guide, lightly lubricate with oil. Fit guide to press with chamfer facing out. Seat guide completely in head. Finish ream valve guide bore to accept valve.

#### VALVE SPRINGS

**Removal, Cylinder Head Installed** — Remove valve cover. Remove spark plug of cylinder requiring work. Loosen rocker arm as far as possible and remove push rod. Fit valve retaining tool in spark plug hole. Compress valve spring. Remove keepers, top cup, spring, and base washer. Check spring at free length and under a load.

**Installation** — Reverse removal procedure and note: Make sure valve spring is installed with closest coil spacing toward cylinder head.

## R-5 4 CYLINDER (Cont.)

### ROCKER SHAFT

After cleaning rocker shaft components, remove clips and take off springs, rocker arms, and support bearings. End plugs are press fit and cannot be removed. For correct reassembly sequence refer to *Fig. 2*.

**Fig. 2  Rocker Arm Assembly. Illustration Shows Detail of Rocker Shaft Reassembly Sequence**

### VALVE CLEARANCE

Set intake valve clearance to .006" (.15 mm) cold or .007" (.18 mm) hot. Set exhaust valve clearance to .008" (.20 mm) cold or .010" (.25 mm) hot. Hot refers to an engine that has been operated at normal engine temperature and allowed to cool for 50 minutes.

| Valve Adjusting Sequence | |
|---|---|
| **Valve Open** | **Valve to Adjust** |
| No. 1 Exhaust | No. 3 Int. & No. 4 Exh. |
| No. 3 Exhaust | No. 4 Int. & No. 2 Exh. |
| No. 4 Exhaust | No. 2 Int. & No. 1 Exh. |
| No. 2 Exhaust | No. 1 Int. & No. 3 Exh. |

## PISTONS, PINS & RINGS

### OIL PAN

**Removal — 1)** Drain oil. Remove sway bar "U" brackets and pull bar down. Remove lower transaxle metal cover. Remove transaxle bolts that mount through gear shift bracket. Clutch protective cover must be removed.

**2)** Place a jack under front of transaxle to support it. Remove front pad. Raise transaxle front. Remove mounting bolts and tilt pan toward back of vehicle. Rotate crankshaft to provide clearance. Clean gasket surfaces.

**Installation —** To install, reverse removal procedure and note: Apply gasket sealer to rubber gaskets. Make sure pan side gaskets overlap bearing gaskets.

### CYLINDER LINERS

**Removal — 1)** Disconnect battery. Drain cooling system and oil pan. Remove air cleaner, cylinder head, oil pan, and oil pump. Fit liner clamp on head.

**2)** Index connecting rods and bearing caps. Remove connecting rod caps and bearings. Remove liner clamp and liner-piston-rod assembly.

**NOTE** — *Before installing pistons in liners, protrusion of liner above cylinder block must be measured without seal.*

**Installation — 1)** Check liner protrusion with special tools (Mot. 252 and 251). See *Fig. 3*. Make measurement at two points. Subtract the larger measurement from .005" (.12 mm) to determine correct seal thickness.

**Fig. 3  Using Special Tool Mot. 251 and 252 to Check Cylinder Liner Protrusion. Make Sure Measurement is Made in TWO Places.**

**2)** Seals are available in .003" (.08 mm), .004" (.10 mm), and .005" (.12 mm). Each liner may require a different seal thickness. Fit seal, install liner assembly and recheck measurement.

**3)** Lubricate bearings and replace connecting rod caps. Place liner-piston-connecting rod assemblies into block. Make sure No. 1 is at clutch end. Number on connecting rod bearing end is on opposite side of camshaft. Arrow on piston must face flywheel. Reverse removal procedure for remaining components.

### PISTON & ROD ASSEMBLY

**Removal —** Remove piston and rod assembly from block with cylinder liners. *See Cylinder Liners*. Remove piston out bottom of liner. Take off rings, piston pin, and connecting rod. *See Piston Pins*.

## R-5 4 CYLINDER (Cont.)

**Installation** — Fit piston pin. Fit rings. Piston rings are pregapped. Assemble with "O" mark or "TOP" facing up. Lubricate connecting rod assemblies with oil and fit to liner. Make sure machined side of connecting rod bearing is parallel with flat edge on liner top.

**Fig. 4** *Piston Mounting and Identification Marks. Reassemble Piston and Connecting Rod Assemblies According to Illustration*

### PISTON PIN

**Removal** — Remove piston assembly from liner. Remove rings. Using suitable tool (Mot. 574), extract piston pin.

**Installation** — **1)** Position piston with arrow facing flywheel. Index mark made during removal on connecting rod must face away from camshaft.

**2)** Heat connecting rod to 482° F (250° C). Slide new piston over installing mandrel and screw in locating plug (part of tool kit Mot. 574). Lightly oil piston pin. Push mandrel, pin guide, and pin assembly through piston by hand, until piston pin makes contact with rod. This procedure will automatically center and correctly space pin.

## CRANKSHAFT MAIN & CONNECTING ROD BEARINGS

### MAIN BEARING SERVICE

**1)** Remove cylinder head and oil pan. Invert engine. Remove connecting rod bearing caps. Mark position of main bearing to block. Remove main bearing caps. Remove crankshaft, upper main bearings, and thrust washers.

**2)** Use a micrometer and measure crankshaft journals. If any main bearing journal is worn beyond 2.148" (54.56 mm) or any connecting rod journal beyond 1.721" (43.71 mm), crankshaft must be reground and fitted with new bearings.

**NOTE** — *Connecting rod journals are roll hardened. Make sure roll hardening remains intact over a 140° section facing rotational centerline of crankshaft.*

**Fig. 5** *Crankshaft MUST Maintain Roll Hardened Surfaces as Shown in Illustration*

**3)** Fit upper main bearings. Nos. 1 and 3 are same. Nos. 2, 4, and 5 have two oil holes. Lubricate main bearing journals and fit crankshaft into position. Fit thrust washers, white metal toward crankshaft. Fit bearing to main bearing caps (those with no oil holes). Fit caps being sure to align with previously made reference marks.

**4)** Fit upper connecting rod bearings and slide over crankshaft. Fit lower half of bearing in cap, then tighten cap. Make sure crankshaft is free to turn.

**5)** Use a dial indicator and check crankshaft end play. Crankshaft should not have more than .002-.009" (.05-.23 mm) end play. Replace thrust washers if end play is beyond specification.

### REAR MAIN BEARING OIL SEAL

**With New Crankshaft** — Fit new seal to tool Mot. 259-01 (or equivalent). Lubricate outer seal lip. Install seal in original position, seating it until tool lip just contacts cylinder block.

**With Original Crankshaft** — Offset new seal approximately ⅛" (3 mm) to position seal so it does not rest in same place original seal did. Drive seal into place with tool Mot 259-01 (or equivalent). Seal is seated when tool edge just touches block. Remove tool, insert ⅛" thick spacer, and repeat seating process. This will correctly seat seal into position.

## CAMSHAFT

### TIMING CHAIN

**Removal** — With engine removed and suitably supported, remove timing cover and chain tensioner. *NOTE — Tensioner does not have to be removed, it can be wired out of way.* Remove camshaft sprocket lock bolt. Use puller (B. Vi. 28) and remove camshaft sprocket with timing chain. Chain will come off without disturbing crankshaft sprocket.

# Renault Engines

## R-5 4 CYLINDER (Cont.)

**Fig. 6** *Installing Timing Chain Keeping Camshaft and Crankshaft Reference Marks Properly Aligned. Also, Note Positions of Crankshaft and Camshaft Keyways. Illustration Does Not Show Timing Chain Tensioner, See Figure 7*

**Installation** — 1) Position chain on camshaft sprocket. Align camshaft reference mark with one on crankshaft. Note position of of camshaft and crankshaft keyway shown in *Fig. 6*. Using a small Allen wrench, activate tensioner mechanism.

2) Refit chain tensioner with thrust plate. Tighten mounting bolts and release load on automatic wear compensator tensioner. Release load by pressing down on bottom of tensioner body. Install new timing chain tensioner.

**Fig. 7** *Sequence of Automotive Wear Compensator Timing Chain Tensioner*

## CAMSHAFT

**Removal** — Remove engine and suitably support on stand. Remove cylinder head, distributor drive gear, oil pan, timing chain cover, and timing chain. Work through access slots in camshaft sprocket and remove two flange bolts. Carefully slide camshaft from engine.

**Installation** — Check clearance between camshaft sprocket and flange. Clearance must not exceed .002-.005" (.05-.12 mm). Lubricate camshaft journals and lobes, then refit camshaft. Install flange and tighten. Refit sprocket and tighten mounting bolt. Make sure all camshaft and crankshaft alignment marks are matched. See *Fig. 6*. Reverse removal procedure for remaining components.

## CAMSHAFT OIL SEAL

**NOTE** — *Camshaft oil seal can be changed without removing engine.*

**Removal** — Remove air cleaner, air pump, pump support, and drive belt. Remove serrated pulley from camshaft. Insert tool Mot. 500-01 (or equivalent) until lip of oil seal slips over shoulder of tool. Push tool sleeve in. Tighten tool bolt clockwise until seal is removed.

**Installation** — Slip sleeve of tool over end of camshaft to spread lip of seal. Lubricate seal and slide over sleeve. Using oil seal inserting tool (part of tool Mot. 500-01), press seal inward until it just touches block. Remove sleeve. Screw threaded rod into camshaft with nut and washer at rod end. Tighten nut until tool just meets clutch housing. Replace remaining components in reverse of removal procedure.

## ENGINE OILING

**Crankcase Capacity** — 3¼ quarts without filter change. 3½ quarts with filter change.

**Oil Filter** — Disposable canister type.

**Normal Oil Pressure** — 10 psi at idle speed. 50 psi at 4000 RPM.

## OIL PUMP

**Removal** — Drain oil. Remove oil pan. Take out three bolts mounting oil pump and remove pump.

**Disassembly** — Remove four pump cover bolts. Remove cover slowly; relief valve is under spring tension. Remove driven gear, drive gear, and drive gear shaft.

**Inspection** — Examine splines on drive shaft. Check ball seat for damage. Check pressure relief spring for fatigue. Check clearance between gears and body. Replace gears if clearance exceeds .008" (.2 mm).

**Reassembly** — Reverse disassembly procedure.

**Installation** — Install pump, do not use gasket between oil pump and block. Tighten mounting bolts.

# Renault Engines

## R-5 4 CYLINDER (Cont.)

**Fig. 8 Exploded View of Oil Pump Assembly**

Splines

Drive Shaft

Cover

Relief Valve Assy.

Driven Gear

### ENGINE COOLING

**WATER PUMP**

**Removal** — Disconnect battery. Disconnect hoses. Drain block at plug near timing cover. Loosen alternator. Remove water pump drive belt. Remove A.I.R. pump, water pump pulley, grooved belt, and temperature sending unit. Remove mounting bolts and tap pump free.

**Installation** — To install, reverse removal procedure and be sure to bleed air from cooling system.

**Cooling System Capacity** — Approximately 6.5 quarts, including heater.

### TIGHTENING SPECIFICATIONS

| Application | Ft. Lbs. (mkg) |
|---|---|
| Cylinder Head Bolts | |
| Cold | 40 (5.5) |
| Hot (After cooling 50 minutes) | 45 (6.2) |
| Connecting Rods | 35 (4.8) |
| Main Bearings | 40-50 (5.5-6.9) |
| Manifolds | 10 (1.4) |
| Rocker Arm Shaft | 10-15 (1.4-2.1) |
| Timing Sprocket-to-Camshaft | 20 (2.8) |

## ENGINE SPECIFICATIONS

### GENERAL SPECIFICATIONS

| Year | Displ. | | Carburetor | HP at RPM | Torque (Ft. Lbs. at RPM) | Compr. Ratio | Bore | | Stroke | |
|---|---|---|---|---|---|---|---|---|---|---|
| | cu. ins. | cc | | | | | in. | mm | in. | mm |
| 1978 | 78.66 | 1289 | 1x2-Bbl. | ..... | 60 a 6000 | 9.5-1① | 2.87 | 73 | 3.03 | 77 |

① — Calif. 8.5-1.

### VALVES

| Engine & Valve | Head Diam. In. (mm) | Face Angle | Seat Angle | Seat Width In. (mm) | Stem Diameter In. (mm) | Stem Clearance In. (mm) | Valve Lift In. (mm) |
|---|---|---|---|---|---|---|---|
| 1289 | | | | | | | |
| Int. | 1.319 (33.5) | 45° | 45° | .043-.055 (1.1-1.4) | .276 (7) | ..... | ..... |
| Exh. | 1.193 (30.3) | 45° | 45° | .055-.067 (1.4-1.7) | .276 (7) | ..... | ..... |

### PISTONS, PINS, RINGS

| Engine | PISTONS | PINS | | RINGS | | |
|---|---|---|---|---|---|---|
| | Clearance In. (mm) | Piston Fit In. (mm) | Rod Fit In. (mm) | Rings | End Gap In. (mm) | Side Clearance In. (mm) |
| 1289 | ..... | Free Fit | Press Fit | ..... | ① | ..... |

① — Pre-set gap; do not alter.

## R-5 4 CYLINDER (Cont.)

### ENGINE SPECIFICATIONS (Cont.)

| CRANKSHAFT MAIN & CONNECTING ROD BEARINGS | | | | | | | |
|---|---|---|---|---|---|---|---|
| | MAIN BEARINGS | | | | CONNECTING ROD BEARINGS | | |
| Engine | Journal Diam. In. (mm) | Clearance In. (mm) | Thrust Bearing | Crankshaft End Play In. (mm) | Journal Diam. In. (mm) | Clearance In. (mm) | Side Play In. (mm) |
| 1289 | 2.157 (54.80) | ..... | No. 3 | .002-.009 (.05-.23) | 1.731 (43.97) | ..... | .012-.022 (.30-.56) |

| CAMSHAFT | | | |
|---|---|---|---|
| Engine | Journal Diam. In. (mm) | Clearance In. (mm) | Lobe Lift In. (mm) |
| 1289 | ..... | ① | ..... |

① — End play .002-.005" (.05-.12 mm).

| VALVE TIMING | | | | |
|---|---|---|---|---|
| | INTAKE | | EXHAUST | |
| Engine | Open (BTDC) | Close (ALDC) | Open (BLDC) | Close (ATDC) |
| 1289 | 22° | 62° | 65° | 25° |

| VALVE SPRINGS | | | |
|---|---|---|---|
| Engine | Free Length In. (mm) | PRESSURE Lbs. @ In. (kg @ mm) | |
| | | Valve Closed | Valve Open |
| 1289 | 1.65 (42) | ..... | 80@1.0 (36@25) |

# Saab Engines

## 99 – 4 CYLINDER

### ENGINE CODING

#### ENGINE IDENTIFICATION

Engine number is stamped on block and is located near the summer setting on air cleaner.

#### Engine Identification

| Application | ①Engine Code |
|---|---|
| Federal | |
| Man. Trans. ...................................... | BI20-P06 |
| Auto. Trans. ...................................... | BI20-P03 |
| Calif. | |
| Man. Trans. ...................................... | BI20-P04 |
| Auto. Trans. ...................................... | BI20-P05 |

① – Engine code number is followed by 6 digit serial number.

### ENGINE & CYLINDER HEAD

#### ENGINE

**NOTE** – *It is not recommended to remove engine without transmission. Remove engine and transmission as an assembly.*

1) Remove hood attaching bolts and lift off hood. Disconnect battery cables. Unclamp and remove battery. Drain coolant from radiator, engine block and heater core by opening all petcocks.

2) Disconnect vacuum hoses from power assist cylinder and air flow sensor. Disconnect fuel lines from injector tubes. Disconnect EGR system. Remove air cleaner and mixture control unit.

3) Disconnect electrical wires from following components: coil, temperature sender, radiator fan, headlights, and automatic transmission switch.

4) Disconnect wires at fuel injection warm-up regulator, auxiliary air valve, cold start valve and thermo-time switch.

5) Disconnect throttle control cable. Disconnect coolant hoses at thermostat housing, radiator, water pump and intake manifold.

6) Remove hood lock operating cable at both firewall and fender panel. Remove 2 front panel metal screws and the 4 other screws mounting headlights to body. Lift out entire front panel (radiator and electric fan will come out with panel).

7) On Man. Trans., remove clutch slave cylinder and hang it out of the way.

8) On Auto. Trans., remove heat shield on exhaust manifold at exhaust manifold and exhaust pipe.

9) On all models, remove exhaust pipe from manifold. Disconnect ground strap at transmission. Remove air pump. Raise front of vehicle and place blocks under chassis.

10) On Man. Trans., place transmission in neutral. Knock out front taper pin from gear shift rod. Pull rubber bellows free of groove in gear selector rod, if so equipped. Separate gear selector rod and arm.

11) On Auto. Trans., remove screw for gear selector wire at transmission. Move gear selector lever to position No. 1 and pull outer cable housing back. Using Saab tool 8790388 (or equivalent) on wire, turn tool a small amount and pull out wire.

12) Disconnect speedometer cable from transmission. Remove nuts from engine mounts. Unclamp larger clamps around rubber bellows on inner universal joints. Attach suitable lifting sling to engine.

13) Remove attaching hardware from lower end piece of control arm on right-hand side. Turn steering wheel to left and raise engine slightly. Move engine to right and withdraw left universal joint, then move it to left and remove right universal joint.

14) Raise engine to gain access to starter and alternator, disconnect cables. Lift engine clear of vehicle and place on an engine stand. To install, reverse removal procedures.

#### CYLINDER HEAD

**Removal** – 1) Disconnect battery cables. Drain coolant (including block). Disconnect throttle cable at housing. Disconnect electrical lead from temperature sender. Remove brake vacuum hose from intake manifold.

2) Disconnect and plug fuel lines from fuel distributor. Disconnect all necessary coolant hoses. Separate exhaust pipe from manifold. Take off ignition wires and cap. Thread a nut on center stud of camshaft sprocket. Clamp stud against mounting plate.

**NOTE** – *Make sure nut is securely tightened so center stud will not move.*

3) Unbolt retaining bolts from camshaft sprocket. Separate sprocket from camshaft plate. Let sprocket hang in mounting plate by center stud. Remove cylinder head bolts. Support rear of engine. Remove engine mount bolt from head. Take out screws at transmission cover. Remove head.

**Installation** – To install reverse removal procedures and note the following: Make sure camshaft and bearing cap index marks are aligned. Align flywheel mark with mark on cylinder block. Set ignition with No. 1 piston at TDC. Retorque head bolts after engine has run and allowed to cool.

*Fig. 1  Cylinder Head Tightening Sequence*

## 99 – 4 CYLINDER (Cont.)

## VALVES

### VALVE ARRANGEMENT

E-I-I-E-E-I-I-E (front to rear).

### VALVE GUIDE SERVICING

1) Check valve guide and valve stem for wear or damage. Using tool 8390437 (or equivalent), withdraw valve guide from camshaft side of head.

2) Install guide from cylinder side of head, using valve guide removal/installation tool 8390437 and adapters. Ream guide to standard size, using a suitable reamer. Check valve seat for true, reface if necessary.

### VALVE SPRINGS

1) With cylinder head removed, remove camshaft bearing caps and camshaft.

2) Using a magnet, lift out cam followers along with adjusting pallets and retain in proper order for reassembly.

3) With spring compressor, depress spring and remove valve keepers. Release spring and valve collar.

4) Replace spring and reverse removal procedure.

### VALVE CLEARANCE ADJUSTMENT

1) With valve cover removed, rotate engine until valve to be adjusted or checked has heel of cam opposite cam follower. Measure clearance with feeler gauge. If clearance is not within specifications, intake .006-.012" (.152-.305 mm) and .014-.020" (.356-.508 mm) for exhaust, a direct measurement will be required.

2) Install valve measuring tool 8391450 and dial indicator. Measure clearance of all valves and note reading. Proceed to adjust any valve which does not come within the following limits: .008-.010" (.20-.25 mm) intake and .016-.018" (.40-.45 mm) exhaust.

3) Remove camshaft, cam followers and adjusting pallets of any valve needing adjustment.

4) Measure pallet thickness and add noted valve clearance to arrive at total clearance. Subtract proper valve clearance from total clearance to determine needed pallet thickness.

5) Install new adjusting pallets and recheck valve clearance.

## PISTONS, PINS & RINGS

### PISTON & ROD ASSEMBLY

Connecting rods and rod caps are numbered. Note positioning and location before disassembly.

**Removal** — With oil pan and cylinder head removed, unscrew rod nuts and withdraw bearing caps. Place plastic sleeves over rod bolts and push out rod and piston.

**Installation** — Use a ring compressor over piston and fit piston to bore. Make sure notch in piston faces engine/transmission. Install rod cap in position and tighten bolts.

### PISTON PIN REPLACEMENT

Piston pins are retained by circlips. Remove circlips and press out piston pins. Check pins and bearings for wear or damage, replace if necessary.

### FITTING PISTONS

1) To fit pistons to cylinder bores, use a feeler gauge .500" (12.7 mm) wide and .0005-.0016" (.014-.040 mm) thick. Oil cylinder lightly and insert piston without rings.

2) Attach feeler gauge to a spring scale. Insert feeler gauge between piston and cylinder wall at right angles to piston pin. When feeler gauge can be pulled out of cylinder with a force of 1.8-2.6 lbs. (.816-1.18 kg), piston clearance has been determined.

3) Repeat test at several different depths in cylinder bore. Graded standard and non-graded oversize pistons are available.

#### Piston Specifications

| Application | Diameter In. (mm) |
| --- | --- |
| Std. (AB) | 3.5425-3.5427 (89.980-89.986) |
| Std. (C) | 3.5433-3.5437 (89.999-90.010) |
| 1st Oversize | 3.5619-3.5625 (90.472-90.487) |
| 2nd Oversize | 3.5816-3.5822 (90.972-90.987) |

4) Check piston rings for end gap and side clearance, using an inverted piston to position ring in bore. On worn bores, measure at lower end of bore.

5) Install rings on piston, making sure gaps of compression rings are 180° apart with lower compression ring mark "TOP" facing up. On three piece oil ring make sure ends are staggered.

## CRANKSHAFT MAIN & CONNECTING ROD BEARINGS

### MAIN BEARING SERVICE

1) Remove connecting rods and main bearing caps. Measure journals with a micrometer. Out-of-round should not exceed .002" (.051 mm). If crankshaft is near or over stated limit of wear, regrind journals and fit undersize bearings.

2) Using "V" blocks and a dial indicator check crankshaft for bend. If bend exceeds .002" (.051 mm), replace or repair crankshaft.

3) Using Plastigage method, check main bearing and connecting rod bearing journals. If clearance is found excessive, combine suitable undersize bearings to correct clearance. Undersize bearings are available in various thicknesses.

## 99 – 4 CYLINDER (Cont.)

### THRUST BEARING ALIGNMENT

Center main bearing is thrust bearing. Check crankshaft endplay. If it exceeds specifications, replace thrust washers with oil grooves facing crankshaft.

## CAMSHAFT

### FRONT OIL SEAL SERVICE

**NOTE** – *Seal may be replaced with engine in vehicle if clutch and flywheel are removed.*

Remove seal ring with a screwdriver. Oil ring surface before installing. Fit new seal with spring ring facing crankshaft.

### TIMING COVER & OIL SEAL

Remove pulley using a puller. Pry out old seal. Grease seal with silicone. Install new seal.

### CAMSHAFT

**Removal** – 1) Remove camshaft cover and gaskets. Rotate crankshaft until number one piston is at TDC of compression stroke.

2) Remove camshaft sprocket by screwing a nut onto center stud of camshaft sprocket and clamp center stud against mounting bracket.

**CAUTION** – *Tighten nut securely, so sprocket and chain can not move. Otherwise chain tensioner will tighten chain, and tensioner can not be reset without lifting engine out of vehicle.*

3) Bend back locks and remove attaching screws from camshaft sprocket. Separate sprocket from camshaft plate until it hangs free with bracket.

4) Remove camshaft bearing caps. Lift off camshaft, inspect camshaft and bearings for wear or damage.

*Fig. 2   Camshaft Timing Marks*

5) Replace camshaft bearings and caps, then tighten cap nuts. Align camshaft timing mark with mark on cylinder head as shown in *Fig. 3*.

6) Install camshaft sprocket on camshaft. Unscrew nut from center stud on camshaft sprocket and lock both attaching screws. Replace camshaft cover and gaskets.

**CAUTION** – *Nut on camshaft sprocket center stud must not on any account be unscrewed before sprocket is tightly screwed to camshaft.*

### CHAIN TENSIONER MECHANISM

If chain tensioner mechanism has been dismantled or came apart, follow porcedure outlined for reassembly before fitting to engine:
- Place lock washer with ratchet sleeve into tensioner housing, large diameter end first.
- Fit spring against ratchet sleeve.
- Push neck of tensioner and spring into housing, simultaneously pressing and turning tensioner neck until seated.

**NOTE** – *Tensioner neck must be kept depressed while tensioner mechanism is being fitted.*

### VALVE TIMING & CHAIN REPLACEMENT

**Removal** – 1) Remove timing cover and camshaft cover. Separate camshaft from camshaft sprocket. *See Camshaft Removal.*

2) Mount pinion sprocket on crankshaft. Align "O" degree mark on flywheel with mark on cylinder block. *See Fig. 3.*

3) Remove chain guides, oil thrower ring and pull sprocket off crankshaft, using a suitable puller.

4) Remove idler shaft keeper plate and withdraw idler shaft.

**Installation** – 1) Reinstall idler shaft. Install keeper plate and attaching bolts. Position idler sprocket so marked line is horizontal.

2) Mount pinion sprocket on crankshaft. Align "O" degree mark on flywheel with mark on cylinder block (see illustration).

*Fig. 3   Aligning "O" Degree Mark on Flywheel with Mark on Cylinder Block.*

3) Align camshaft mark with mark on cylinder head. Install straight chain guide with long screw in bottom hole.

4) Loosely mount curved chain guide with short screw in hole nearest idler shaft.

## 99 – 4 CYLINDER (Cont.)

**5)** Place camshaft chain over camshaft sprocket and mounting bracket. Lower chain and sprocket past camshaft flange until center stud of sprocket is lined up with camshaft.

**6)** Rotate camshaft sprocket until screw holes match threaded holes in camshaft flange.

**7)** Place timing chain over crankshaft and idler sprockets so chain will be in a straight line between camshaft and crankshaft as shown in *Fig. 4*. Do not change any of the sprocket settings while installing chain.

*Fig. 4    Front View of Timing Chain Installed and Tightened*

**8)** Guide center stud of camshaft sprocket into camshaft. Install locking plate and one screw. Install screws for chain guides and camshaft sprocket mounting bracket.

**9)** Rotate crankshaft one revolution. Install and tighten camshaft sprocket screws. Lock screws with locking plate. Check timing marks to see they are properly aligned.

**10)** Install chain tensioner as follows: Relieve spring pressure on tensioner by turning clamping sleeve clockwise to mounting position. Fit a spacer on neck of tensioner and push neck into body of tensioner.

**11)** Mount chain tensioner and guide plate block. Press curved chain guide against chain to stretch it and push tensioner neck into housing. Remove spacer. Adjust to leave a clearance of .020" (.5 mm) between housing and tensioner neck, then tighten chain guide.

**12)** Rotate crankshaft 1 full turn and check that tensioner has not less than .020" (.5 mm) and not more than .060" (1.5 mm) of clearance. Remove nut from camshaft center stud. Reinstall remaining components in reverse order of removal.

### IDLER SHAFT

**Removal — 1)** Remove alternator drive belt. Remove cover screws, then tap cover forward to unseat from dowels. Rotate crankshaft until No. 1 piston is at TDC. Remove distributor.

**2)** Hold idler shaft sprocket and take off lock plate. Make sure crankshaft is not moved from this point on. Loosen tensioner mounting screws and move tensioner out-of-way. Remove idler shaft.

**Installation — 1)** Install idler shaft with mounting plate. Tighten countersunk screws. Install a new locating pin. Align chain and sprocket as shown in *Fig. 5*. Fit locating plate with new retaining bolt. Hold sprocket and tighten retaining bolt.

**2)** Set chain tensioner self-adjuster so it is in seated position. Reposition chain tensioner. Set clearance between tensioner and pad to .020-.040" (.5-1 mm). Slightly tap in cover dowels. Install cover and new gasket (if necessary). Reverse removal procedure for remaining components.

*Fig. 5    Idler Shaft Index Marks. Bow in Cutout on Idler Shaft Sprocket Must Line Up with Small Hole in Mounting Plate.*

## ENGINE OILING

**Crankcase Capacity —** 4.0 qts. including filter.

**Oil Filter —** Full-flow type.

**Normal Oil Pressure —** 43 psi (3.0 kg/cm$^2$) @2000 RPM.

**Pressure Regulator Valve —** Non-adjustable, opens at 57-71 psi (4.0-5.0 kg/cm$^2$).

### ENGINE OILING SYSTEM

Oil pressure is generated by a dual-rotor pump driven from idler shaft. Pump is located on outside of engine. Oil is forced through a full-flow filter and oil channels to various lubrication points. Each connecting rod bearing has a separate oil passage from main bearings.

### OIL PUMP

**Removal — 1)** Remove four screws attaching pump to engine. Withdraw pump and "O" ring from engine. Remove two screws attaching pump cover to housing. Remove rotors and "O" ring from housing.

**2)** Pull cotter pin from cover and remove plug, "O" ring, spring and pressure relief valve piston. Using a straightedge and feeler gauge, measure clearance between rotors and housing face. If clearance exceeds .002-.0035" (0.05-0.09 mm), use fine emery paper to resurface housing or sides of rotors.

# Saab Engines

## 99 – 4 CYLINDER (Cont.)

**Installation** – 1) Clean and oil all parts. Install outer rotor with chamfered edge inward facing toward drive shaft. Install valve piston, spring plug, "O" ring and cotter pin in pump cover.

2) Place "O" ring in pump housing groove. Install cover and tighten screws. Rotate pump up until drive shaft engages in engine. Slide pump up against engine and install four attaching bolts.

## ENGINE COOLING

**Cooling System Capacity** – 8.5 quarts.

**Thermostat** – Thermostat begins to open at approximately 190°F (88°C).

**Radiator Cap** – Radiator pressure cap opens at approximately 14.2 psi.

## WATER PUMP

**Removal** – 1) Drain coolant. Disconnect battery. Remove intake manifold. Remove alternator. Remove bolt mounting bracket to pump cover. Unbolt rear engine mounts. Raise rear of engine. Remove bolt mounting alternator bracket to transmission cover. Loosen lower bolt and twist bracket away from engine. Remove last two bolts from cover and remove.

2) Position special tool 8392441 (or equivalent) over water pump and fit two bolts (DO NOT TIGHTEN). Turn tool counterclockwise so peg engages a fin on impeller. Loosen center impeller nut (left hand threads). Remove water pump. DO NOT tap out with hammer.

**Installation** – To install, reverse removal procedure and note: It may be necessary to use sleeve 8392490 (or equivalent) to seat bearing housing.

## ENGINE SPECIFICATIONS

### GENERAL SPECIFICATIONS

| Year | Displ. cu. ins. | Displ. cc | Carburetor | HP at RPM | Torque (Ft. Lbs. at RPM) | Compr. Ratio | Bore in. | Bore mm | Stroke in. | Stroke mm |
|---|---|---|---|---|---|---|---|---|---|---|
| 1978 | 121 | 1985 | Fuel Inj. | ..... | ..... | 9.25-1① | 3.543 | 90 | 3.071 | 78 |

① – Calif. 8.7-1

### VALVES

| Engine & Valve | Head Diam. In. (mm) | Face Angle | Seat Angle | Seat Width In. (mm) | Stem Diameter In. (mm) | Stem Clearance In. (mm) | Valve Lift In. (mm) |
|---|---|---|---|---|---|---|---|
| 1985 cc Int. | 1.654 (42.9) | 44.5° | 45° | .004-.008 (1-2) | .313-.314 (7.950-7.976) | 0.02 (0.5) | ..... |
| Exh. | 1.398 (35.5) | 44.5° | 45° | .004-.008 (1-2) | .313-.314 (7.950-7.976) | 0.02 (0.5) | ..... |

### PISTONS, PINS, RINGS

| Engine | PISTONS Clearance In. (mm) | PINS Piston Fit In. (mm) | PINS Rod Fit In. (mm) | RINGS Rings | RINGS End Gap In. (mm) | RINGS Side Clearance In. (mm) |
|---|---|---|---|---|---|---|
| 1985 cc | .0006-.0016 (.014-.040) | .0002-.0006 (.005-.014) | ① | No. 1 | .014-.021 (.35-.55) | .002-.003 (.050-.082) |
| | | | | No. 2 | .012-.018 (.30-.45) | .0016-.003 (.040-.072) |
| | | | | Oil | .015-.055 (.38-1.40) | ..... |

① – Interference fit.

## 99 - 4 CYLINDER (Cont.)

### ENGINE SPECIFICATIONS (Cont.)

| CRANKSHAFT MAIN & CONNECTING ROD BEARINGS | | | | | | | |
|---|---|---|---|---|---|---|---|
| | MAIN BEARINGS | | | | CONNECTING ROD BEARINGS | | |
| Engine | Journal Diam. In. (mm) | Clearance In. (mm) | Thrust Bearing | Crankshaft End Play In. (mm) | Journal Diam. In. (mm) | Clearance In. (mm) | Side Play In. (mm) |
| 1985 cc | 2.283-2.284 (57.981-58.000) | .001-.002 (.026-.062) | Center | .003-.0011 (0.08-0.28) | 2.046-2.047 (51.981-52.000) | .001-.002 (.026-.062) | ..... |

### VALVE SPRINGS

| Engine | Free Length In. (mm) | PRESSURE Lbs. @ In. (kg @ mm) | |
|---|---|---|---|
| | | Valve Closed | Valve Open |
| 1985 cc | 1.700 (43.1) | ..... | 170-183@1.161 (77.1-83.0@29.5) |

### CAMSHAFT

| Engine | Journal Diam. In. (mm) | Clearance In. (mm) ① | Lobe Lift In. (mm) |
|---|---|---|---|
| 1985 cc | 1.139 (28.94) | ..... | Int. .421 (10.7) Exh. .433 (11.0) |

① — End play is .003-.010″ (.08-.25 mm)

### VALVE TIMING

| Engine | INTAKE ① | | EXHAUST ② | |
|---|---|---|---|---|
| | Open (BTDC) | Close (ALDC) | Open (BLDC) | Close (ATDC) |
| 1985cc | 10° | 54° | 46° | 18° |

① — With .014″ (.35 mm) valve clearance.
② — With .022 (.55 mm) valve clearance.

### TIGHTENING SPECIFICATIONS

| Application | Ft. Lbs. (mkg) |
|---|---|
| Main Bearings | 79 (10.9) |
| Rod Bearings | 40 (5.5) |
| Camshaft Bearing Caps | 13 (1.8) |
| Camshaft Cover | 1 (.14) |
| Crankshaft Pulley | 137 (19.00) |
| Rear Crankshaft Seal | 14 (1.9) |
| Cylinder Head | |
|   Step One | 43 (6.0) |
|   Step Two | 69 (9.5) |
| Flywheel | 43 (6.0) |
| Water Pump Impeller | 11 (1.5) |
| Oil Pump | 13 (1.8) |
| Idler Shaft Plate | 14 (1.9) |
| Idler Sprocket | 18 (2.5) |
| Camshaft Sprocket | 14 (1.9) |
| Intake Manifold | 13 (1.8) |
| Exhaust Manifold | 14 (1.9) |
| Thermostat Housing | 13 (1.8) |

# Subaru Engines

## 1600 4 CYLINDER

### ENGINE CODING

#### ENGINE IDENTIFICATION

Engine number is stamped on a machined pad near distributor. See table below for engine codes.

**Engine Codes**

| Application | Calif. | Federal |
|---|---|---|
| 1600 cc | | |
| 4-Speed | EA71AC | EA71AA, EA71AH EA71AK |
| 4-Speed, 4WD | EA71WC | EA71WA, EA71WH EA71WK |
| 5-Speed | EA71GC | EA71GA, EA71GH EA71GK |
| Auto. Trans. | EA71TC | EA71TA, EA71TH EA71TK |

### ENGINE

#### ENGINE

**NOTE** — *It is possible to remove engine with transmission fitted. Removal procedure given is with transmission remaining in vehicle.*

#### REMOVAL & INSTALLATION

**Removal** — **1)** Disconnect battery cable. Remove spare wheel from engine compartment. Remove air cleaner assembly.

**2)** Disconnect fuel line from fuel pump intake, allow fuel to drain into a suitable container. Drain radiator and engine block. Disconnect radiator hoses at engine.

**3)** Disconnect all wiring to engine and accessories. On 4-WD models remove engine fan from pulley. On Automatic Transmission models disconnect oil cooler pipes.

**4)** Remove two upper radiator bolts and lift out radiator. Remove nuts on each end of engine-to-firewall strut and remove strut by moving to rear to clear engine hanger. Remove starter from transmission housing.

**5)** Remove all control cables and vacuum hoses from engine. On Automatic Transmission models disconnect torque converter from engine by rotating crankshaft to remove four bolts through timing hole. Use care that bolts do not drop into housing.

**6)** Remove engine-to-transmission bolts and nuts and disconnect exhaust pipe. Remove bolts securing front engine mounts-to-engine. Slightly hoist engine with chain hoist attached to front to rear hangers and separate engine from transmission.

**7)** When separating engine from transmission, ensure that torque converter remains with transmission (Automatic Transmission only). Also, it may be helpful to slightly jack up transmission during removal procedure. Remove engine completely and place on engine stand.

**Installation** — To install, reverse removal procedure and tighten all bolts and nuts. Adjust all controls and fill engine with suitable coolant.

### ENGINE DISASSEMBLY & REASSEMBLY

**NOTE** — *Remove engine, place on engine stand (399814300X2 or equivalent). Remove starter and proceed as follows:*

**Disassembly** — **1)** Separate engine from transmission if necessary. Ensure that converter remains attached to automatic transmission (if equipped). Drain oil and coolant. Make sure that liquid does not run over clutch cover. On manual transmission models, remove clutch cover and disc.

**2)** Remove silencer with tapered sleeve. Remove fan and pulley. Remove intake manifold assembly with carburetors, vacuum control valve and modulator. Remove EGR valve, thermostat and sending unit. Remove air cleaner, distributor, EGR pipe and air suction system.

**3)** Remove oil filter duct. 4WD models have a bracket. Use a puller and remove crankshaft pulley. Remove oil pump and filter as an assembly. Remove water pump with hoses and tubes attached.

**4)** Turn engine over on stand and remove oil pan, crankcase, gasket and transmission cover (if necessary). Remove oil strainer and brackets. Remove either flywheel or converter drive plate. Take off flywheel housing.

**5)** Remove spark plugs and valve cover. Remove rocker assembly and push rods. Remove cylinder head bolts in sequence See Fig. 1. Remove cylinder head and gasket. Use Allen wrench and remove crankcase plug.

**6)** Position pistons at bottom dead center and remove circlip with long nosed pliers. Access to No. 1 and No. 2 pins is through front crankcase plug holes. Access to No. 3 and No. 4 pins is through rear service holes. Remove pins and pistons, marking for reassembly.

**7)** Work through hole in camshaft gear and straighten lockwasher, then remove nut. Remove nuts and washers and separate cases. Use valve lifter clips (899804100 or equivalent), to prevent upper crankcase lifters from falling off.

*Fig. 1  Cylinder Head Nut Loosening Sequence (Rocker Arm Assembly Removed)*

## 1600 4 CYLINDER (Cont.)

**NOTE** — *Pull camshaft to rear for crankcase clearance.*

8) Remove oil seal. Lift out crankshaft, distributor gear, and connecting rods. Keep crankshaft bearings in order for reassembly. Remove camshaft and gear. Remove oil pressure switch and valve lifters.

**Reassembly** — Lubricate all friction surfaces with engine oil prior to reassembly. Install crankshaft and camshaft with bearings in left half (No. 2 & 4 Cyl.) of crankcase. Apply liquid gasket to mating surfaces of crankcase and continue in reverse order of disassembly. Tighten crankcase halves and cylinder heads in sequence shown.

**NOTE** — *Use spacers (899848600) in place of rocker arm supports when tightening head nuts.*

Spacers
(899848600)

*Fig. 2  Cylinder Head Tightening Sequence*

*Fig. 3  Tightening Sequence for Crankcase*

## VALVES

### VALVE ARRANGEMENT

I-E-E-I (both banks, front to rear).

### VALVE GUIDE SERVICING

1) Check valve guide for wear or damage. Replace defective guides by using a drift and driving out guide through top of head. Press in new guide from top of head until correct projection of guide above head is achieved. See Fig. 3.

2) Ream valve guide to provide correct clearance. Inspect valve seat to make sure it is true with guide. Reface valve seat if necessary.

*Fig. 4  Correct Projection of Valve Guides*

### VALVE STEM OIL SEALS

Valve stem oil seals are found only on intake valves. Slide seal off of valve guide and replace with a new seal. Use care when inserting valve stem not to damage seal.

### VALVE SPRING

Use a spring compressor, remove "O" ring, valve keepers and spring retainer. Check spring under pressure and at free length. Replace if necessary. Install spring with wide spaced coils (paint mark) facing valve spring retainer.

### ROCKER ARM ASSEMBLY

Check rocker shaft, rocker arm and bushing for wear or damage. Replace any worn parts. Press in new bushing and ream until a clearance of .0006-.002" (.016-.052 mm) is achieved between bushing and shaft.

### VALVE TAPPET SERVICE

Remove lifters from crankcase. Inspect tappet for wear or clogged oil hole. Replace lifter if lifter-to-crankcase clearance exceeds .004" (.100 mm). Standard lifter clearance is .0012-.0028" (.030-.072 mm).

### VALVE CLEARANCE ADJUSTMENT

With engine cold, rotate engine to TDC of firing stroke. Insert feeler gauge between rocker arm and valve stem. Clearances should be as follows:

| Application | Intake In. (mm) | Exhaust In. (mm) |
|---|---|---|
| 1600 | .009-.011 (.23-.27) | .013-.015 (.33-.37) |

## PISTON, PINS & RINGS

### FITTING PISTONS

1) Measure piston bore .028" (7 mm) from top of cylinder in line with crankshaft and again 90° from centerline of crankshaft. Make same measurements 1.48" (37 mm) from top and 2.64" (67 mm) from top of cylinder bore.

## 1600 4 CYLINDER (Cont.)

**2)** Measure piston at bottom of skirt 90° from piston pin hole. Measurements should be performed at temperature of 68°F (20°C).

**3)** Check piston ring end gap and side clearance. Check gap at bottom of cylinder bore. Fit piston rings with "R" or "N" facing up.

*Fig. 5   Piston Ring Gap Position*

### PISTON PIN

Check piston pin for damage, cracks, wear or distortion. Check connecting rod bushing for wear. If pin or bushing are worn beyond specification, replace bushing in connecting rod and ream to fit standard pin. Piston pin is a thumb push fit at 68°F.

## CRANKSHAFT MAIN & CONNECTING ROD BEARINGS

### MAIN & CONNECTING ROD BEARINGS

**1)** Check connecting rod side play with a feeler gauge. If side play exceeds specifications, replace connecting rod.

**2)** Use Plastigage method to measure both connecting rod and main bearing clearances. Bearing inserts are available in standard, .002" (.05 mm) and .010" (.25 mm) undersize.

**3)** Check crankshaft for bend by placing front and rear main journals on "V" blocks and fitting a dial indicator on center journal. Correct or replace crankshaft if bend exceeds .0014" (.035 mm).

### REAR MAIN BEARING OIL SEAL SERVICE

Seal is replaced when crankcase halves are split. After crankcase halves have been reassembled, install new seal.

## CAMSHAFT

### ENGINE FRONT COVER OIL SEAL

With front cover removed drive out old seal. Install new seal using suitable tool (899064110) with or without front cover on engine.

### CAMSHAFT

**1)** Camshaft may be removed when crankcase has been split. Check for wear or damage, replace camshaft if necessary. Using a dial indicator, check that bend does not exceed .002" (.051 mm).

**2)** Measure end play, if it exceeds .0018-.0045" (.045-.115 mm), remove cam gear and replace thrust plate. Measure camshaft lobe height. If wear exceeds .012" (.3 mm), replace camshaft.

**3)** Measure camshaft gear runout with dial indicator. Replace camshaft gear if runout exceeds .010" (.25 mm). Measure backlash between camshaft gear and crankshaft gear, if backlash exceeds .006" (.015 mm), replace camshaft gear. Standard value of backlash is .0008-.0020" (.020-.050 mm).

*Fig. 6   Align Camshaft with Crankshaft as Shown*

### VALVE TIMING

With crankcase halves split, install crankshaft and camshaft so punch mark on camshaft gear is visible through chamfered hole in crankshaft gear.

## ENGINE OILING

**Crankcase Capacity** — 3.8 quarts with filter change.

**Oil Filter** — Full-flow.

**Normal Oil Pressure** — 35 psi (2.5 kg/cm²) @500 RPM; 57 psi (4.0 kg/cm²) @2500 RPM.

**Pressure Regulator Valve** — Non-adjustable, opens at 57-64 psi (4.0-4.5 kg/cm²).

### ENGINE OILING SYSTEM

Oil is pressure fed by a camshaft driven trochoid type oil pump. Pump incorporates an oil relief and by-pass valve in its body. Oil pump is located externally on engine. Oil from pump passes from main oil gallery to journals of camshaft and crankshaft. From there, oil goes to main bearings, pistons pin bearings and cylinder walls. Oil passes through valve lifters and push rods to oil rocker arms.

### OIL PUMP

**Removal** — Remove four attaching bolts and pull pump and filter forward. Remove oil filter from pump.

## 1600 4 CYLINDER (Cont.)

**Disassembly** — 1) Remove screws, lift cover and rotor from pump body. Remove "O" ring. Remove by-pass spring and ball. Unscrew plug and remove washers, spring and pressure relief valve.

2) Measure rotor-to-rotor and outer rotor-to-body clearance, replace any component which exceeds wear limits. Measure rotor side clearance.

3) Inspect relief valve spring, valve and pump body for wear or damage.

**NOTE** — Make sure oil pump shaft is aligned with slot in camshaft when reassembling.

**Reassembly** — Reassemble in reverse order, using all new gaskets and "O" rings.

**Installation** — Install oil filter on pump. Using rearward movement reinstall oil pump and four attaching bolts.

### Oil Pump Specifications

| Application | Std. Clearance In. (mm) |
|---|---|
| Inner-to-Outer Rotor | .0008-.005 (.02-.12) |
| Outer Rotor-to-Body | .006-.008 (.15-.21) |
| Rotor Side Clearance | .002-.005 (.05-.12) |
| Relief Valve Spring Free Length | 1.85 (47.1) |

## ENGINE COOLING

### THERMOSTAT

**Thermostat** — Begins to open at 190°F (88°C) and is fully open at approximately 212°F (100°C).

**Coolant Capacity** — All models approximately 6.3 quarts.

**Radiator** — Cross flow with electric cooling fan. (Station Wagon with 4WD also has engine driven fan.)

### WATER PUMP

**Removal** — Drain coolant and disconnect main radiator outlet hose. Remove drive belt and attaching bolts, remove water pump.

**Disassembly** — 1) Remove four screws attaching cover plate and gasket. Remove pulley and locking clip.

2) Withdraw shaft, impeller and mechanical seal from pump body. Press pump shaft from impeller.

Pulley  Shaft  Mechanical Seal  Impeller  Gasket  Plate

**Fig. 7  Exploded View of Water Pump**

**Reassembly** — 1) Using an arbor press, press pump shaft into pump body until locking clip may be installed. Apply sealing compound to edge of mechanical seal and in housing with carbon ring facing toward impeller.

2) Press impeller onto shaft until impeller-to-body clearance is .020-.028" (.5-.7 mm). Support impeller side of pump shaft and press on pulley until distance between center of pulley groove and rear face of pump housing is 2.34-2.37" (59.5-60.1 mm).

**Installation** — Install water pump together with slotted clip, water pipe, and water by-pass pipe as a unit. Gradually tighten bolts alternately and evenly in several steps to prevent leakage. The clamps for the water hose should be positioned low to prevent interference with the EGR pipe.

Wear Limit .06" (1.52 mm)  Spring  Spring Retainer  Packing  Seal Ring

**Fig. 8  Detail of Water Pump Seal**

### ELECTRIC COOLING FAN

All models are equipped with an electric cooling fan motor. 4WD models use a combination of electric fan, engine drive fan and forced cooling (water cooling). All other models utilize electric fan and forced cooling (water cooling).

# Subaru Engines

## 1600 4 CYLINDER (Cont.)

### ENGINE SPECIFICATIONS

| GENERAL SPECIFICATIONS | | | | | | | | | | |
|---|---|---|---|---|---|---|---|---|---|---|
| Year | Displ. | | Carburetor | HP at RPM | Torque (Ft. Lbs. at RPM) | Compr. Ratio | Bore | | Stroke | |
| | cu. ins. | cc | | | | | in. | mm | in. | mm |
| 1978 | 97 | 1595 | 2-Bbl. | 67@5200① | 81@2400 | 8.5-1 | 3.62 | 92 | 2.36 | 60 |

① — 4-Wheel drive vehicles — 65@5200.

| VALVES | | | | | | | |
|---|---|---|---|---|---|---|---|
| Engine & Valve | Head Diam. In. (mm) | Face Angle | Seat Angle | Seat Width In. (mm) | Stem Diameter In. (mm) | Stem Clearance In. (mm) | Valve Lift In. (mm) |
| 1600 cc Int. | ..... | 45° | 45° | .028-.051 (.7-1.3) | .3130-.3136 (7.950-7.965) | .0014-.0026 (.035-.065) | ..... |
| Exh. | ..... | 45° | 45° | .039-.071 (1.0-1.8) | .3128-.3134 (7.945-7.960) | .0016-.0028 (.040-.070) | ..... |

| PISTONS, PINS, RINGS | | | | | | |
|---|---|---|---|---|---|---|
| | PISTONS | PINS | | RINGS | | |
| Engine | Clearance In. (mm) | Piston Fit In. (mm) | Rod Fit In. (mm) | Rings | End Gap In. (mm) | Side Clearance In. (mm) |
| 1600 cc | .0004-.0016 (.010-.040) | .00004-.00067 (.001-.017) | .0002-.0016 (.005-.040) | No.1 | .012-.020 (0.3-0.5) | .0016-.0031 (.04-.08) |
| | | | | No.2 | .012-.020 (0.3-0.5) | .0012-.0028 (.03-.07) |
| | | | | No.3 | ①.012-.035 (0.3-0.9) | ..... |

① — Riken piston ring. For Nippon piston ring, .008-.035" (.20-.89 mm)

| CRANKSHAFT MAIN & CONNECTING ROD BEARINGS | | | | | | | |
|---|---|---|---|---|---|---|---|
| | MAIN BEARINGS | | | | CONNECTING ROD BEARINGS | | |
| Engine | Journal Diam. | Clearance | Thrust Bearing | Crankshaft End Play | Journal Diam. | Clearance | Side Play |
| 1600 cc Front & Rear | 1.9667-1.9673 (49.955-49.970) | ①.0004-.0016 (.010-.040) | Center | .0016-.0054 (.040-.137) ③ | 1.7715-1.7720 (44.995-45.010) | .0008-.0025 (.020-.064) | .0028-.013 (.07-.33) ④ |
| Center | 1.9671-1.9677 (49.965-49.980) | ②.0-.0008 (.0-.020) | | | | | |

① — Limit — .0022" (.055 mm).
② — Limit — .0018" (.045 mm).
③ — Limit — .012" (.3 mm).
④ — Limit — .016" (.4 mm).

## 1600 4 CYLINDER (Cont.)
### ENGINE SPECIFICATIONS (Cont.)

### CAMSHAFT

| Engine | Journal Diam. In. (mm) | Clearance In. (mm)① | Lobe Lift In. (mm) |
|---|---|---|---|
| 1600 cc Front & Center | 1.0218-1.0226 (25.954-25.975) | .0010-.0025 (.025-.064) | ..... |
| Rear | 1.4155-1.4163 (35.954-35.975) | .0010-.0025 (.025-.064) | |

① — Limit — .0039" (.100 mm).

### VALVE SPRINGS

| Engine | Free Length In. (mm) | PRESSURE Lbs. @ In. (kg @ mm) | |
|---|---|---|---|
| | | Valve Closed | Valve Open |
| 1600 cc Inner | 1.92 (48.7) | 19.7-22.6@1.46 (8.93-10.3@37) | 43.1-49.5@1.10 (19.5-22.5@28) |
| Outer | 1.90 (48.2) | 40.0-46.0@1.54 (18.1-21.0@39) | 91.1-104.7@1.22 (41.3-44.5@31) |

### TIGHTENING SPECIFICATIONS

| Application | Ft. Lbs. (mkg) |
|---|---|
| Cylinder Head | |
| Step 1 | 14 (2.0) |
| Step 2 | 25-29 (3.5-4.0) |
| Step 3 | 37-43 (5.1-5.9) |
| Connecting Rod Nuts | 29-31 (4.0-4.3) |
| Crankshaft Pulley | 39-42 (5.4-5.8) |
| Flywheel Housing | 17-20 (2.3-2.7) |
| Crankcase Plug | 51 (7.0) |
| Crankcase Halves   10 mm Bolts | 29-35 (4.0-4.8) |
| 8 mm Bolts | 17-20 (2.3-2.7) |
| 6 mm Bolts | 3.3-4 (.45-.55) |
| Intake Manifold | 13-16 (1.8-2.2) |
| Rocker Arm Cover | 2.2-2.9 (.30-.40) |
| Flywheel | 30-33 (.42-4.6) |
| Rocker Arms | 37-43 (5.1-5.9) |
| Oil Pan | 3.3-4.0 (.45-.55) |

## 3K-C 4 CYLINDER

### ENGINE CODING

#### ENGINE IDENTIFICATION

Engine serial number and code is stamped on right side of block above oil filter. First series of digits (3K) indicates engine code.

| Application | Code |
|---|---|
| 1166cc Engine (1200 Model) ....................................... | 3K-C |

### ENGINE, CYLINDER HEAD & MANIFOLDS

**NOTE** — *Following general procedures may not apply to all vehicles with 3K-C engine installed.*

#### ENGINE

**Removal — 1)** Disconnect and remove battery. Drain cooling system and remove radiator with cooling fan assembly. Hood may be removed to provide greater access to engine and increased clearance when removing engine. Remove air cleaner and disconnect carburetor linkage. Disconnect fuel line at pump.

**2)** Disconnect exhaust pipe from manifold. Disconnect all engine-to-chassis electrical connections at engine. Remove drive shaft and insert suitable plug in rear of transmission to prevent fluid loss. Disconnect transmission linkage, wiring and speedometer cable.

**3)** Attach suitable hoist to engine hangers. Support transmission and remove crossmember. With hoist supporting engine, remove engine mounting bolts and/or nuts. Lift engine and transmission assembly up and out toward front of vehicle.

**Installation** — To install, reverse removal procedure, assuring that all fluid levels and adjustments are checked prior to starting engine.

#### MANIFOLDS

**NOTE** — *Aluminum intake and cast iron exhaust manifolds are removed as an assembly.*

**Removal & Installation — 1)** Remove air cleaner. Disconnect fuel and vacuum lines at carbureter. Disconnect choke and throttle linkage at carburetor.

**2)** Remove heat insulator, PCV valve and PCV hose. Disconnect exhaust pipe at manifold. Remove manifold retaining nuts and take off manifold. To install, reverse removal procedure, assuring that mating surfaces are clean and new gaskets are used. Front engine hanger is installed on stud between number 1 intake and exhaust manifold.

#### CYLINDER HEAD

**Removal — 1)** Drain cooling system and remove upper radiator hose. Remove manifold and carburetor assembly. See *MANIFOLDS* in this article. Disconnect heater hose at rear of head. Remove rocker arm cover.

**2)** Remove rocker shaft assembly. Remove push rods and keep them in order for reassembly in original positions. Disconnect spark plug wires. Remove head bolts beginning with ends. See *Fig. 1* Lift head from engine.

**Installation** — Ensure that mating surfaces are clean, then install new gasket with "front" side facing up. Continue assembly in reverse order of removal. Tighten head bolts gradually in 2 or 3 steps as shown in *Fig. 1*. Install push rods and rocker shaft assembly, then adjust valves.

**NOTE** — *When installing rocker shaft assembly, assure that adjusting screws are backed off about 2 turns.*

**Fig. 1   Tighten Cylinder Head in Sequence Shown (Remove in Reverse Order ①Through ⑩)**

**Fig. 2   Install Cylinder Head Gasket with Metal Bridge Down (Toward Block)**

### VALVES

#### VALVE ARRANGEMENT

E-I-I-E-E-I-I-E

#### VALVE GUIDE SERVICING

**1)** Check clearance between valve stem and guide. If intake clearance exceeds .003" (.08 mm) or exhaust clearance exceeds .005" (.10 mm), replace valve guide.

## 3K-C 4 CYLINDER (Cont.)

2) To replace valve guide, break off upper portion of guide at snap ring. Drive remaining portion of guide out of head through combustion chamber with suitable driver (09201-60010).

**NOTE** — *Cylinder head should be heated to about 212-264°F before removal or replacement of valve guide.*

3) Install snap ring on guide and install from top with suitable driver (09201-60010). Drive guide in until snap ring contacts head and ream for proper stem clearance.

### VALVE STEM OIL SEALS

Valve stem oil seal fits over guide and stem, under spring assembly.

### VALVE SPRINGS

**Removal** — Use suitable compressor (09202-43011) to compress springs and retainers. Remove valve spring retainer locks (keepers), then remove retainer, spring, seal and washer. Mark and remove valves and components for reassembly.

**Installation** — Install components in original location and order. Use new seals on valve stems. Compress springs and install keepers.

**NOTE** — *Some engines may have a spring shield under retainer and "O" ring seal on valve stem above keepers.*

*Fig. 3   View of Valve Train Components*

### VALVE SPRING INSTALLED HEIGHT

1) With valve spring removed, check length under specified load (see specifications) in a spring tester. Check valve spring free length, if less than 1.83", replace spring.

2) Check valve spring squareness with a steel square. If spring is out of square more than .063" (1.6 mm), replace spring.

### ROCKER ARM ASSEMBLY

1) Remove valve cover and rocker arm assembly retaining bolts. Remove rocker arm assembly. Remove retaining clips from both ends of rocker arm shaft. Remove conical springs, rocker arms, springs and support stands.

2) Thoroughly clean and inspect all components. Check rocker arm-to-shaft clearance. If clearance exceeds .003", replace rocker arms or shafts as necessary. Reface valve end of rocker arm if worn. Lubricate all components before assembly.

3) Assemble rocker arm assembly in reverse of removal order. There are two types of rocker arms used, install rocker arm so that protruding side of valve end of rocker arm faces support stand. Install rocker stand so that when rocker assembly is installed, "F" mark on rocker stand faces front of engine.

*Fig. 4   Rocker Arms and Support Assembly Order*

### VALVE TAPPET SERVICE

1) Check clearance between valve tappet and tappet bore in crankcase. If clearance exceeds .004", replace tappet with oversize tappet and ream bore in crankcase to appropriate clearance.

2) Oversize tappet available is .002" over standard. Crankcase must be reamed .002" over standard or until correct clearance is obtained. Correct clearance is .0006-.0011".

### VALVE CLEARANCE ADJUSTMENT

With number 1 cylinder at TDC on firing stroke, adjust clearance on valves number 1, 2, 3, and 5. Rotate crankshaft one revolution (360°) and set valves number 4, 6, 7, and 8. Set clearances COLD to: Intake — .005" (.13 mm), Exhaust — .009" (.23 mm). If setting HOT, use following clearances: Intake — .008" (.20 mm), Exhaust — .012" (.30 mm).

*Fig. 5   Adjust Valve Clearance in Order Shown*

## 3K-C 4 CYLINDER (Cont.)

### PISTONS, PINS & RINGS

#### OIL PAN

**NOTE** — *Engine must be removed to remove oil pan.*

**1)** Remove engine as previously outlined. Drain oil from oil pan and remove oil pan retaining nuts and bolts. Remove oil pan.

**2)** Clean mating surfaces. Apply sealer to new gasket and install gasket and oil pan. Tighten retaining nuts and screws to specifications. Install engine as previously outlined.

#### PISTON & ROD ASSEMBLY

**1)** Remove engine as previously outlined. Remove cylinder head and oil pan as previously outlined. Remove connecting rod cap with bearing half and push piston and connecting rod assembly up and out through top of engine. Mark connecting rod cap to insure that it is installed on same rod and in same position.

**2)** Mark piston to insure that it is installed in same cylinder. To install piston and rod assembly, make sure ring gaps are in correct position (see illustration). Coat piston and rings with oil.

**3)** Compress piston rings with a ring compressor and install piston and rod assembly in crankcase with notch in piston facing front of engine. Make sure bearings are properly seated in connecting rod and cap and apply oil to crankshaft journal.

**4)** Make sure bearing in connecting rod is properly seated against crankshaft journal. Install connecting rod cap in correct position and tighten nuts to specifications. Install cylinder head, oil pan and engine as previously outlined.

*Fig. 6   Arrange Piston Ring Gaps as Shown*

#### PISTON PIN REPLACEMENT

**1)** Remove circlips from pin hole in piston, heat piston to approximately 158-176°F and drive out piston pin. Make sure piston, pin and connecting rod are marked for assembly with each other.

**2)** Thoroughly clean and inspect all components. Piston pin should push fit through piston with piston heated to approximately 158-176°F. If pin falls through piston or fit is to loose, replace piston and pin.

**3)** Check piston pin-to-connecting rod clearance, if more than .002", bushing must be replaced. Press bushing out and install new bushing using a press and a suitable driver (09222-30010). With new bushing installed, ream to correct clearance with piston pin.

**4)** Thoroughly lubricate all components before assembly. Position piston on connecting rod with notch in piston facing in same direction as mark on lower part of connecting rod (see illustration). Heat piston to 158-176°F and install piston pin and circlips.

#### FITTING PISTONS

**1)** Check size of cylinder bore in crankcase, if size is more than .008" over standard, cylinders must be bored to next oversize piston. Pistons and rings are available in .010", .020", .030" and .040" oversize.

**2)** Check fit of piston in the cylinder with a feeler gauge and a spring tension gauge. A .001" to .002" feeler gauge should require 2.2-2.5 lbs., measured on spring tension gauge, to withdraw feeler gauge from between piston and cylinder bore.

**3)** Check piston rings for wear or damage and replace as necessary. Check piston ring gap in cylinders and piston ring side clearance in pistons (see specifications). Install rings on pistons with marks on rings up and make sure ring grooves in pistons are clean.

*Fig. 7   Piston & Rod Assembly Markings*

### CRANKSHAFT MAIN & CONNECTING ROD BEARINGS

#### MAIN & CONNECTING ROD BEARING SERVICE

**1)** With engine mounted on suitable workstand, remove piston and rod assemblies as previously outlined. Remove crankshaft pulley bolt and take off crankshaft pulley with suitable puller (09213-31021). Remove timing chain cover and rear oil seal retainer. Remove camshaft sprocket and timing chain.

**2)** Remove oil pump. Remove main bearing caps with bearing halves and remove crankshaft. Crankshaft timing sprocket and pilot bearing in rear of crankshaft may be removed if desired.

**3)** Thoroughly clean and inspect crankshaft. Blow out all oil passages with compressed air. Check crankshaft for runout by

## 3K-C 4 CYLINDER (Cont.)

checking center main bearing journal with a dial indicator. If crankshaft is bent more than .0012", replace or repair crankshaft.

**Fig. 8   Checking Crankshaft Runout at Center**

**4)** Check main and connecting rod bearing journals with a micrometer. If journals are more than .0003" out-of-round or undersize, crankshaft must be ground to next undersize. Undersize main and connecting rod bearings for ground crankshafts are available in .010", .020" and .030" undersizes.

**5)** Main and connecting rod bearing clearance is checked by the Plastigage method. To check connecting rod bearing clearance, make sure bearing halves and crankshaft journal are thoroughly clean. Place a piece of Plastigage wire on journal being checked. Install connecting rod cap on connecting rod and tighten nuts to specifications.

**6)** Remove connecting rod cap and check flattened wire against scale on back of Plastigage package to determine clearance. Main bearing clearance is checked in same manner. If rod bearing clearance is more than standard, a .002" undersize bearing is available. If clearance with this bearing will still exceed standard clearance, crankshaft must be ground to next undersize. The limit of bearing clearance on both main and rod bearings is .004".

**7)** Check crankshaft end play with number 3 main bearing cap and original thrust washers installed. Pry crankshaft back and forth and measure clearance with a feeler gauge. Standard clearance is .002-.009" (.04-.22 mm) with a maximum limit of .012" (.3 mm). Excessive clearance may be reduced with washers .002" (.125 mm) or .004" (.250 mm) oversize. Install thrust washers with grooves toward crankshaft.

**8)** Install bearing halves in crankcase and main bearing caps. Lubricate bearings and install crankshaft. Install main bearing caps with arrows toward front and tighten cap bolts in 3, 2, 4, 5, 1 order.

**NOTE** — *Tighten bolts in 2 or 3 steps, checking crankshaft turning resistance after each step.*

**9)** Install remaining components in reverse order of removal, noting proper alignment of timing marks. See *TIMING CHAIN REPLACEMENT*.

## CAMSHAFT

### ENGINE FRONT COVER OIL SEAL

To replace front cover oil seal, remove crankshaft pulley, then pull out old seal with suitable tool (09308-10010). Install new seal with driver (09223-22010). Lubricate seal lips and install crankshaft pulley.

### TIMING CHAIN REPLACEMENT

**1)** With timing chain installed on engine, attach a spring tension gauge to chain and pull out on chain with a pressure of 22 lbs. and check distance between chain tensioner plunger and tensioner body.

**Fig. 9   Checking Timing Chain Elongation**

**2)** If clearance exceeds .532", chain and sprockets must be removed and checked. Remove camshaft sprocket bolt and remove sprocket and chain. Pull crankshaft sprocket from crankshaft.

**3)** Secure one link of timing chain and attach spring tension gauge to opposite end (see illustration). With 11 lbs. tension applied to chain, distance "A" should be no more than 10.7". Replace chain if distance is more.

**4)** Place timing chain on crankshaft sprocket and measure diameter, if less than 2.34", replace sprocket. Measure camshaft sprocket in same manner, if less than 4.48", replace camshaft sprocket.

**5)** To correctly install sprockets and timing chain, install crankshaft sprocket with "O" mark in line with dowel pin on camshaft (see illustration). Place timing chain on sprocket with mark on chain aligned with mark on sprocket.

**6)** Align camshaft sprocket "O" mark with mark on timing chain and install camshaft sprocket on camshaft. Tighten camshaft sprocket bolt to specification. Install chain tensioner and vibration damper. Install timing chain cover as previously outlined.

**Fig. 10   Aligning Marks for Timing Chain & Sprocket Installation**

## 3K-C 4 CYLINDER (Cont.)

### TIMING CHAIN TENSIONER & DAMPER

1) Inspect surfaces of tensioner plunger and bore of tensioner body. To test clearance, lubricate plunger and insert it into plunger body. Cover two oil passages with fingers and pull plunger about half way out. Vacuum strong enough to return plunger should be felt.

2) Measure thickness of tensioner head and chain damper wall. Head should be minimum .47" (12 mm) and chain damper should be minimum .28" (7 mm).

### CAMSHAFT

With camshaft sprocket and timing chain removed, take off camshaft thrust plate. Remove front end plate from engine block. Remove tappets (valve lifters) and distributor if not previously removed. Pull camshaft straight out, using care not to damage bearings or journals.

**NOTE** — A head bolt may be screwed into end of camshaft to provide gripping surface for removal.

Check camshaft runout at number 2 journal by using ½ of the largest difference shown by dial indicator. Maximum runout limit is .0012" (.03 mm), and maximum journal out-of-round or taper is .0008" (.02 mm).

### CAMSHAFT BEARINGS

Measure camshaft journal diameter and subtract from measured diameter of bearing bore to determine clearance. Bearings should be replaced if clearance exceeds .004" (.1 mm). Journals may be ground and .005" (.125 mm) or .010" (.250 mm) undersized bearings installed if necessary. To replace bearings, remove expansion plug from rear of engine. Use bearing replacement tool (09215-22010) to remove old bearings and insert new ones.

**CAUTION** — Oil holes in bearings must be aligned with oil holes in cylinder block. Install new expansion plug, coated with sealer, when all bearings have been installed.

### CAMSHAFT END THRUST

Check clearance between thrust plate and first bearing journal, if clearance exceeds .012", replace thrust plate.

*Fig. 11  Measure Camshaft Thrust Clearance with Camshaft Sprocket Installed*

**NOTE** — If clearance is still excessive after replacing thrust plate and installing sprocket, it will be necessary to replace the camshaft.

### CAM LOBE LIFT

Total height of camshaft lobe is 1.436-1.440" (intake) and 1.432-1.436" (exhaust). Check total lobe height, if less than 1.424" (intake) and 1.420" (exhaust), replace camshaft.

## ENGINE OILING

**Crankcase Capacity** — Approximately 3.7 qts. (3.5 ltr) with filter.

**Oil Filter** — Full flow, mounted on outside of crankcase next to distributor.

**Normal Oil Pressure** — With engine at 212°F, 28.4 psi @ 300 RPM, 42.6 psi @ 3000 RPM.

**Pressure Regulator Valve** — Mounted in oil pump. *See Oil Pump.*

### ENGINE OILING SYSTEM

Oil is circulated through engine by pressure provided by a trochoid rotor type oil pump. Pump is mounted on bottom of crankcase and driven by camshaft via distributor drive. Oil is drawn from oil pan and circulated through a full flow oil filter into main oil gallery. Oil is then distributed to main and connecting rod bearing journals and camshaft bearing journals. Cylinders and piston pins are lubricated by oil squirting from hole in connecting rod. Oil is supplied to timing chain by oil from timing chain tensioner. Oil flows from number two cam bearing journal to rocker arm shaft to lubricate rocker arms. Excess oil from rocker arm shaft lubricates valves and valve stems.

*Fig. 12  Engine Oiling System*

## 3K-C 4 CYLINDER (Cont.)

### OIL PUMP

1) Remove oil pan as previously outlined and remove oil pump. Remove oil strainer, pump cover and pressure regulator plug from side of pump body. Remove spring, piston and rotors from pump body.

2) Thoroughly clean and inspect all components. Check rotor tip clearance, if more than .0079", replace rotors. Check clearance between drive rotor and cover. Place a straight edge on mating surface of pump body and insert a feeler gauge between straight edge and drive rotor. If clearance exceeds .0059", replace cover, pump body or rotors.

**Fig. 13   Checking Oil Pump Rotor Tip Clearance**

3) Check clearance between outer rotor and pump body with a feeler gauge. If clearance exceed .0079", replace pump body or rotors. Check pressure regulator spring and piston for wear or signs of seizure. Replace as necessary.

4) To assemble pump, reverse disassembly procedure. Install rotors with punch marks to cover. With pump assembled, submerge in clean motor oil and rotate drive shaft to check flow of oil from outlet port. To install pump, reverse removal procedure and install oil pan as previously outlined.

### Oil Pump Specifications

| Application | In. (mm) |
| --- | --- |
| Rotor Tip Clearance | .002-.006 (.04-.16) |
| | Limit .008 (.2) |
| Rotor Side Clearance | .001-.004 (.03-.09) |
| | Limit .006 (.15) |
| Rotor-to-Body Clearance | .004-.006 (.10-.16) |
| | Limit .008 (.2) |

### ENGINE COOLING

**Coolant Capacity** — 5.5 quarts.

**Thermostat** — Begins to open as low as 177°F (80°C) and must be fully open at 212°F (100°C).

**Radiator Cap** — 13-15 psi.

### WATER PUMP

Drain cooling system and loosen drive belt. Disconnect radiator and heater hoses at pump. Remove mounting bolts and take off water pump. Clean mating surfaces, coat new gasket with sealant and install water pump.

**NOTE** — *Cooling fan is electrically driven and may run at any time the ignition is on if coolant temperature is high. It may be necessary to remove fan and shroud to provide greater access to the water pump.*

## ENGINE SPECIFICATIONS

### GENERAL SPECIFICATIONS

| Year | Displ. | | Carburetor | HP at RPM | Torque (Ft. Lbs. at RPM) | Compr. Ratio | Bore | | Stroke | |
| --- | --- | --- | --- | --- | --- | --- | --- | --- | --- | --- |
| | cu. ins. | cc | | | | | in. | mm | in. | mm |
| 1978 | 71.1 | 1166 | 2-Bbl. | 58 @ 5800 | 63 @ 3800 | 9.0-1 | 2.953 | 75 | 2.598 | 66 |

### VALVES

| Engine & Valve | Head Diam. In. (mm) | Face Angle | Seat Angle | Seat Width In. (mm) | Stem Diameter In. (mm) | Stem Clearance In. (mm) | Valve Lift In. (mm) |
| --- | --- | --- | --- | --- | --- | --- | --- |
| 3K-C Intake | ..... | 45° | 45° | .047-.063 (1.2-1.6) | .3136-.3140 (7.965-7.975) | .0014-.0026 (.035-.065) | ..... |
| Exhaust | ..... | 45° | 45° | .047-.063 (1.2-1.6) | .3134-.3140 (7.960-7.975) | .0014-.0028 (.040-.071) | ..... |

## 3K-C 4 CYLINDER (Cont.)

### ENGINE SPECIFICATIONS (Cont.)

| PISTONS, PINS, RINGS | | | | | | |
|---|---|---|---|---|---|---|
| | PISTONS | PINS | | RINGS | | |
| Engine | Clearance In. (mm) | Piston Fit In. (mm) | Rod Fit In. (mm) | Rings | End Gap In. (mm) | Side Clearance In. (mm) |
| 3K-C | .001-.002 (.03-.05) | ① | .0002-.0003 (.004-.008) | No. 1 | .004-.011 (.10-.28) | .0012-.0028 (.03-.04) |
| | | | | No. 2 | .004-.011 (.10-.28) | .0008-.0024 (.02-.06) |
| | | | | Oil. | .008-.035 (.2-.9) | ..... |

① — Push fit with piston and pin heated to 158-175°F.

| CRANKSHAFT MAIN & CONNECTING ROD BEARINGS | | | | | | |
|---|---|---|---|---|---|---|
| | MAIN BEARINGS | | | | CONNECTING ROD BEARINGS | |
| Engine | Journal Diam. In. (mm) | Clearance In. (mm) | Thrust Bearing | Crankshaft End Play In. (mm) | Journal Diam. In. (mm) | Clearance In. (mm) | Side Play In. (mm) |
| 3K-C | 1.968-1.969 (49.976-50.000) | .0006-.0016 (.016-.040) | No. 3 | .002-.009 (.04-.22) | 1.653-1.654 (41.976-42.000) | .0009-.0019 (.024-.048) | .004-.008 (.11-.21) |

| VALVE SPRINGS | | | |
|---|---|---|---|
| Engine | Free Length In. (mm) | PRESSURE Lbs. @ In. (kg @ mm) | |
| | | Valve Closed | Valve Open |
| 3K-C | 1.831 (46.5) | 70.1@1.512 (31.8@38.4) | ..... |

| CAMSHAFT | | | |
|---|---|---|---|
| Engine | Journal Diam. In. (mm) | Clearance In. (mm) | Lobe Lift In. (mm) |
| 3K-C Journal | | .001-.003 (.03-.07) | ..... |
| No. 1 | 1.701-1.702 (43.21-43.23) | | |
| No. 2 | 1.691-1.692 (42.96-42.98) | | |
| No. 3 | 1.681-1.682 (42.71-42.73) | | |
| No. 4 | 1.671-1.672 (42.46-42.48) | | |

### TIGHTENING SPECIFICATIONS

| Application | Ft. Lbs. (mkg) |
|---|---|
| Cylinder Head Bolts | 39-48 (5.4-6.6) |
| Manifold Nuts | 14-22 (2.0-3.0) |
| Main Bearing Cap Bolts | 39-48 (5.4-6.6) |
| Connecting Rod Cap Nuts | 29-38 (4.0-5.2) |
| Oil Pan Bolts | 2-3 (.3-.4) |
| Camshaft Thrust Plate Bolts | 4-7 (.6-.9) |
| Camshaft Sprocket Bolt | 39-48 (5.4-6.6) |
| Crankshaft Pulley Bolt | 33-40 (4.5-6.5) |
| Flywheel Bolts | 39-48 (5.4-6.6) |

## 2T-C 4 CYLINDER

### ENGINE CODING

#### ENGINE IDENTIFICATION

Engine can be identified by first group of numbers and letters in engine serial number. Engine serial number is located on left side of cylinder block behind dipstick. Engine codes are as follows:

**Engine Identification**

| Application | Code |
| --- | --- |
| Corolla | 2T-C |

### ENGINE, CYLINDER HEAD & MANIFOLD

#### ENGINE

**NOTE** — Following general procedures may not apply to all vehicles equipped with 2T-C engine.

1) Disconnect battery and drain cooling system. Remove hood support from body, scribe alignment marks on hood and hinges, and remove hood. Remove right headlight door and remove radiator grille, lower grille moulding, radiator baffle (if equipped), hood lock base, and lock brace.

2) On vehicles with automatic transmission, disconnect oil hoses from radiator. On all vehicles, remove radiator hoses and radiator. Disconnect heater hoses from engine and disconnect water temperature gauge wiring.

3) Remove air cleaner, accelerator torque rod, bond cable and clutch hose bracket. Disconnect right front engine mount. Remove distributor wiring, fuel hose, and disconnect exhaust pipe from manifold. Disconnect left front engine mount.

4) Remove shift lever from inside of vehicle and jack up rear end of vehicle and support on stands. Remove exhaust pipe support bracket, propeller shaft, and disconnect speedometer cable. Remove engine rear support member and lightly support transmission with jack and remove engine rear support.

5) With suitable engine hoist, lift up engine, remove jack and move engine to front and remove from vehicle. To install, reverse removal procedure.

#### INTAKE MANIFOLD

**Removal** — Drain cooling system, remove air cleaner and carburetor. Disconnect water hose under manifold. Disconnect ventilation hose from manifold, remove manifold bolts and remove manifold.

**Installation** — Clean all mating surfaces and use new gaskets. Reverse removal procedure to complete installation.

#### CYLINDER HEAD

1) Drain cooling system and remove air cleaner assembly. Disconnect radiator hoses, heater hoses, and water temperature sending unit wiring.

2) Remove carburetor torque rod and disconnect choke stove pipe and intake pipe. Disconnect PCV valve hose at intake manifold. Disconnect fuel line and vacuum hose at carburetor.

3) Remove clutch flexible hose bracket at cylinder head and jack up vehicle. Remove exhaust pipe clamp and disconnect exhaust manifold from cylinder head. Remove rocker arm cover.

4) Remove cylinder head bolts in sequence, taking two or three steps. Remove rocker arm assembly and push rods. Remove cylinder head with intake manifold attached. To install, reverse removal procedure.

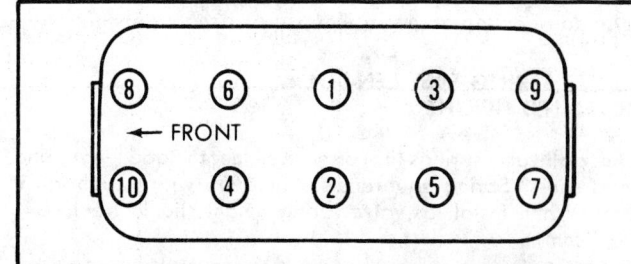

**Fig. 1  Cylinder Head Tightening Sequence (Loosen in Reverse Order)**

### VALVES

#### VALVE ARRANGEMENT

**Right Side** — All intake.
**Left Side** — All exhaust.

#### VALVE GUIDE SERVICING

**NOTE** — Manufacturer recommends using new valve guides whenever valves are replaced.

1) Measure clearance between valve stem and valve guide bushing. If clearance is greater than .003" (.08 mm) for intake or .004" (.10 mm) for exhaust, replace valve and/or guide bushing.

2) Break off upper half of valve guide and heat cylinder head to 176-212°F (80-100°C). Using guide replacement tool (09201-60011), drive out guide bushing toward combustion chamber.

3) Drive in new guide bushing in same direction it was removed. Valve guide should protrude .67" (17 mm) above cylinder head for both intake and exhaust. If necessary, finish bore of valve guide with reamer, to achieve proper clearance.

**Fig. 2  Removing Valve Guide Bushing and Reaming to Proper Clearance**

# Toyota Engines

## 2T-C 4 CYLINDER (Cont.)

### VALVE STEM OIL SEALS

Cup type oil seals are used on all valves. Do not use old seals when valves have been removed. To install, lubricate valve stem and insert in cylinder head. Again lubricate valve stem and carefully push oil seal over valve guide. **NOTE** — *Do not push down on top of seal, use pressure on seal sides only.*

### VALVE SPRING FREE LENGTH & INSTALLED HEIGHT

Check all valve springs for correct free length, load length and squareness. Spring squareness should be within .075" (1.9 mm). When installed, valve spring height should be 1.484" (37.7 mm).

### ROCKER ARM ASSEMBLY

**NOTE** — *There are three kinds of valve rocker shaft supports and two kinds of valve rocker shafts and rocker arms. Do not mix them up.*

**Fig. 3   Using a Straightedge to Check Valve Spring Squareness Limit**

Remove cylinder head and remove rocker assembly. To disassemble, remove retainer springs, valve rocker support No. 1, compression springs, valve rocker arms for intake valves, valve rocker arms for exhaust valves and rocker supports No. 3 and No. 2. Clearance between rocker arms and shaft should be .001-.002" (.02-.04 mm). Rocker arm shaft for exhaust valves can be identified by oil hole in end of shaft.

**NOTE** — *Mark all parts to reassemble in order. Place washer between rocker arm and support number three (center).*

**Fig. 4   Partially Disassembled View of Rocker Arm Assembly**

### VALVE LIFTERS

Inspect lifters and check clearance in bore. If clearance exceeds .004" (.10 mm), select oversize lifter and ream lifter bore to obtain clearance of .001-.002" (.02-.05 mm).

**Fig. 5   Measurement Point for Valve Lifter**

### VALVE CLEARANCE ADJUSTMENT

Set number 1 cylinder to TDC on compression stroke. Adjust intake valves on number 1 and 2 cylinders, exhaust valves on number 1 and 3 cylinders. Turn crankshaft one revolution (360°) and adjust intake valves on number 3 and 4, exhaust valves on number 2 and 4 cylinders.

#### Valve Clearance Adjustment

| Valve | Cold In. (mm) | Hot In. (mm) |
|---|---|---|
| Intake | .007 (.18) | .008 (.20) |
| Exhaust | .012 (.30) | .013 (.33) |

## PISTONS, PINS & RINGS

### OIL PAN

**1)** Disconnect left and right engine front mounts. Jack up vehicle and support on stands. Remove engine front undercover and right hand stiffener plate. Remove stabilizer bar and oil pan bolts.

**2)** Place jack under clutch housing and raise slightly taking care not to pull lower radiator hose. Lower oil pan and remove oil pump bolts. Pull oil pan and oil pump forward and outward.

**NOTE** — *Apply liquid sealer to four corners of oil pan gasket.*

### PISTON & ROD ASSEMBLY

**Removal** — Drain engine coolant system and crankcase. Remove cylinder head, oil pan and oil pump. Remove connecting rod caps and using a wood bar or hammer handle, drive out pistons through top of cylinder block.

## 2T-C 4 CYLINDER (Cont.)

**Installation** — Install piston rings on piston with ring gaps spaced and positioned as shown in *Fig. 6*. Code letter and number on ring outside surface should face up. Lubricate piston, crankshaft and cylinder. Using suitable piston ring compressor, insert pistons in cylinders, making sure that notch on piston top is toward front of engine. Install connecting rod bearing caps and tighten bolts.

**Fig. 6   Installed Position of Piston Rings**

**NOTE** — *Keep pistons arranged so that they will be replaced in the correct bores.*

### FITTING PISTONS

**1)**  With piston pin removed and pistons at 68°F, measure diameter of pistons $\frac{7}{16}$" (11 mm) below lowest ring groove in direction of thrust. Pistons are available .010", .020", .030" and .040" (.25, .50, .75 and 1.00 mm) oversizes.

**2)**  Measure cylinders at top, center and bottom of bore in two directions. If wear exceeds .008" (.20 mm) on any one cylinder, rebore all cylinders for oversize pistons.

**3)**  Insert piston rings into cylinders and measure end gap at lower part of cylinder where wear is smallest. Measure clearance between ring and ring groove.

**Fig. 7   Diagram Showing Necessary Piston and Cylinder Index Marks**

### PISTON PIN REPLACEMENT

Using suitable tool and press, press out pin from connecting rod and piston assembly. When installing connecting rod to piston, position so that notch at piston top will be on same side as mark on rod center.

**Fig. 8   Using a Press to Remove and Install Piston Pin**

## CRANKSHAFT MAIN & CONNECTING ROD BEARINGS

### MAIN & CONNECTING ROD BEARINGS

**1)**  Using Plastigage method, measure clearance of bearings. Clearance limit is .004" (.10 mm). If proper clearance cannot be obtained with .002" (.05 mm) undersize bearings, grind crankshaft. Bearings are available .002", .010", .020" and .030" (.05, .25, .50, .75 mm) undersizes.

**2)**  Crankshaft bend limit is .001" (.03 mm). Oval and taper wear limit is .0004" (.01 mm). If limits are exceeded, crankshaft must be ground for undersize bearings.

**Fig. 9   Crankshaft Bearings**

**Fig. 10   Connecting Rod Bearings**

# Toyota Engines

## 2T-C 4 CYLINDER (Cont.)

### THRUST BEARING ALIGNMENT

Measure crankshaft end play at center bearing. If end play exceeds limit of .012" (.30 mm), install replacement thrust bearings. Bearings are available in standard and oversizes of .005" and .010" (.125 and .25 mm). **NOTE** – *Oil groove on bearing faces toward center.*

### REAR MAIN BEARING OIL SEAL

Remove oil seal retainer and drive out old oil seal. Apply grease to seal inner lip and take care not to damage this surface. Using suitable tool (09250-10011), drive new seal into place. Replace oil seal retainer with new gasket.

### ENGINE FRONT COVER

1) Jack up vehicle and remove headlamp door and radiator grille. Remove grille lower molding, hood lock base and lock brace. Remove radiator grille and radiator upper baffle. Drain cooling system, disconnect hoses and remove radiator.

**Fig. 11    Rear Oil Seal and Retainer with Related Components**

2) If equipped with Auto. Trans., remove oil cooler hose from radiator. Remove fan belt and water pump assembly. Remove crankshaft pulley. Drain engine oil and remove engine undercover. Remove right hand stiffener plate, and remove oil pan bolts.

3) Timing chain cover may now be removed. To install, reverse removal procedure and tighten components to specifications.

## CAMSHAFT

### FRONT COVER OIL SEAL

Special Tool 09308-10010 is recommended to pull out oil seal. To install, drive new oil seal into recess in timing cover by using Special Tool 09223-22010.

**Fig. 12    Using Special Tool to Install Oil Seal in Front Cover**

### TIMING CHAIN AND GEAR INSTALLATION

1) After camshaft has been replaced, rotate crankshaft so that key is pointing up with pistons No. 1 and No. 4 at TDC. Turn camshaft and position key so that it lines up with timing mark in thrust plate.

**Fig. 13    Timing Chain and Timing Sprocket Marks**

2) Assemble crankshaft timing gear and camshaft timing gear to chain so that Toyota marks on each gear line up with chain timing marks. Install gears and chain onto crankshaft and camshaft. Install chain tensioner, chain damper and timing cover.

3) Inspect camshaft for bending and wear. Maximum bend limit is .0012" (.03 mm).

### TIMING CHAIN TENSIONER & DAMPER

1) Inspect surfaces of tensioner plunger and bore of tensioner body. To test clearance, lubricate plunger and insert it into

## 2T-C 4 CYLINDER (Cont.)

plunger body. Cover two oil passages with fingers and pull plunger. Vacuum strong enough to return plunger should be felt.

2) Measure thickness of tensioner head and chain damper wall. Head should be minimum .492" (12.5 mm) and chain damper should be minimum .20" (5.0 mm).

3) To measure chain deflection, pull chain tensioner head with spring scale at 22 lbs. (10 kg). Clearance between tensioner head and body must not exceed .532" (13.5 mm). If limit is exceeded, replace chain, gear or tensioner plunger.

**NOTE** — *Chain tensioner must be filled with oil after replacing tensioner or timing chain.*

### CAMSHAFT

1) Remove timing chain cover. *See Timing Chain Cover Removal.* Remove cam timing gear bolt and timing chain tensioner. Remove timing chain and gears, from camshaft and crankshaft, as a unit. Remove cylinder head, distributor and fuel pump.

2) Remove shift lever and support transmission lightly on jack and remove engine rear support member. Then carefully lower jack. Remove camshaft thrust plate and pull out camshaft, being careful not to damage bearings.

### CAMSHAFT BEARINGS

Using suitable bearing remover tool (09215-25010), pull out bearings one, two and five toward front and bearings three and four toward rear. Using same tool, install new bearings in order one through five, taking care to line up oil holes in bearings with oil holes in block. Bearings are available .005" and .010" (.125 and .250 mm) undersize.

**NOTE** — *Apply liquid sealer to plug at rear of block.*

### CAMSHAFT END THRUST

To measure end thrust, install thrust plate and timing gear. Tighten timing gear bolt and use feeler gauge to measure end thrust. Standard clearance is .003-.009" (.07-.22 mm) and limit is .012" (.30 mm). If thrust clearance maximum is exceeded, replace camshaft.

## ENGINE OILING

**Crankcase Capacity** — 4.4 qts. (Includes filter).

**Oil Filter** — Full flow type with integral relief valve.

**Normal Oil Pressure** — 28 psi (2 kg/cm²) at idle; 43 psi (3 kg/cm²) running (minimum values).

**Oil Pressure Regulator Valve** — Begins to open at 51-63 psi (3.6-4.4 kg/cm²).

### OIL PUMP

Oil pan must be removed to gain access to oil pump. If oil pump assembly is tight, tap it out lightly from distributor side. Both drive and driven rotors have punch marks on upper side of rotors, which should be matched when assembling oil pump.

| Oil Pump Specifications | |
|---|---|
| **Application** | **In. (mm)** |
| Rotor Tip Clearance | .002-.006 (.04-.16) |
| | Limit .010 (.25) |
| Rotor Side Clearance | .001-.004 (.03-.09) |
| | Limit .006 (.15) |
| Rotor-to-Body Clearance | .004-.006 (.10-.16) |
| | Limit .010 (.25) |

**Fig. 14  Exploded View of Oil Pump & Pressure Relief Valve Assembly**

## ENGINE COOLING

**Thermostat** — Wax pellet type thermostat with opening temperature of 187-194°F (80-90°C). Fully opened at 212°F (100°C).

**Coolant Capacity** — Approximately 8 qts.

### WATER PUMP

Drain cooling system, remove radiator hoses and by-pass and heater hoses. Remove fan belt. Remove attaching bolts and remove water pump. Separate fan and pulley. To install, reverse removal procedure.

### COOLANT DRAINING

Engine must be cool, then remove radiator cap. Loosen drain plugs at bottom of radiator and left side of engine block and drain coolant. To refill, make sure both drains are closed and fill radiator wth coolant. Start and run engine until warm, then top off radiator with coolant. Fill reservoir half full, then install radiator and reservoir caps.

# Toyota Engines

## 2T-C 4 CYLINDER (Cont.)

### ENGINE SPECIFICATIONS

| GENERAL SPECIFICATIONS | | | | | | | | | | |
|---|---|---|---|---|---|---|---|---|---|---|
| Year | Displ. | | Carburetor | HP at RPM | Torque (Ft. Lbs. at RPM) | Compr. Ratio | Bore | | Stroke | |
| | cu. ins. | cc | | | | | in. | mm | in. | mm |
| 1978 | 96.9 | 1588 | 1x2-Bbl. | 75 @ 5400① | 85 @ 2800② | 9.0:1③ | 3.35 | 85 | 2.76 | 70 |

① — California — 73 @ 5800.
② — California — 83 @ 3800.
③ — California — 8.5:1.

| VALVES | | | | | | | |
|---|---|---|---|---|---|---|---|
| Engine & Valve | Head Diam. In. (mm) | Face Angle | Seat Angle | Seat Width In. (mm) | Stem Diameter In. (mm) | Stem Clearance In. (mm) | Valve Lift In. (mm) |
| 2T-C Intake | 1.61 (41) | 45° | 45° | .055 (1.4) | .3137-.3143 (7.97-7.99) | .0010-.0024 (.025-.061) | ..... |
| Exhaust | 1.42 (36) | 45° | 45° | .055 (1.4) | .3135-.3141 (7.96-7.98) | .0012-.0026 (.030-.066) | ..... |

| PISTONS, PINS, RINGS | | | | | | |
|---|---|---|---|---|---|---|
| Engine | PISTONS | PINS | | RINGS | | |
| | Clearance In. (mm) | Piston Fit In. (mm) | Rod Fit In. (mm) | Rings | End Gap In. (mm) | Side Clearance In. (mm) |
| 2T-C | .002-.003 (.05-.07) | Press Fit | Press Fit | No. 1 | .008-.016 (.20-.40) | .0008-.0024 (.02-.06) |
| | | | | No. 2 | .004-.012 (.10-.30) | .002-.0022 (.05-.055) |
| | | | | Oil | .008-.020 (.20-.51) | ..... |

| CRANKSHAFT MAIN & CONNECTING ROD BEARINGS | | | | | | | |
|---|---|---|---|---|---|---|---|
| Engine | MAIN BEARINGS | | | | CONNECTING ROD BEARINGS | | |
| | Journal Diam. In. (mm) | Clearance In. (mm) | Thrust Bearing | Crankshaft End Play In. (mm) | Journal Diam. In. (mm) | Clearance In. (mm) | Side Play In. (mm) |
| 2T-C | 2.282-2.284 (57.976-58.000) | .0009-.0019 (.024-.048) | Center | .003-.007 (.07-.18) | 1.8888-1.8898 (47.976-48.000) | .0009-.0019 (.024-.048) | .006-.010 (.16-.26) |

## 2T-C 4 CYLINDER (Cont.)

## ENGINE SPECIFICATIONS (Cont.)

### TIGHTENING SPECIFICATIONS

| Application | Ft. Lbs. (mkg) |
|---|---|
| Cylinder Head Bolts | 61.5-68.7 (8.5-9.5) |
| Rocker Arm Support | 52-64 (7.2-8.8) |
| Manifold Bolts | 7-12 (1.0-2.0) |
| Camshaft Thrust Plate | 7-12 (1.0-2.0) |
| Timing Gear Bolt | 51-80 (7.0-11.0) |
| Crankshaft Pulley Bolt | 29-43 (4.0-6.0) |
| Connecting Rod Cap Bolts | 29-36 (4.0-5.0) |
| Main Bearing Cap Bolts | 52-64 (7.2-8.8) |
| Flywheel Bolts | 42-43 (5.8-6.0) |
| Oil Pan Bolts | 2-3 (.3-.4) |
| Radiator Thermo Switch | 22-29 (3.0-4.0) |

### CAMSHAFT

| Engine | Journal Diam. In. (mm) | Clearance In. (mm) | Lobe Lift In. (mm) |
|---|---|---|---|
| 2T-C | | .0010-.0026 (.025-.066) | Int. .252 (6.39) |
| No.1 | 1.829-1.830 (46.46-46.48) | | |
| No. 2 | 1.819-1.820 (46.21-46.23) | | Exh. .258 (6.55) |
| No. 3 | 1.809-1.810 (45.96-45.98) | | |
| No. 4 | 1.800-1.801 (45.71-45.73) | | |
| No. 5 | 1.790-1.791 (45.46-45.48) | | |

### VALVE SPRINGS

| Engine | Free Length In. (mm) | PRESSURE (LBS.) Lbs. @ In. (kg @ mm) | |
|---|---|---|---|
| | | Valve Closed | Valve Open |
| 2T-C | 1.657 (42.1) | 58.4 @ 1.484 (26.3 @ 37.7) | ..... |

# Toyota Engines

## 20 R 4 CYLINDER

## ENGINE CODING

### ENGINE IDENTIFICATION

Engine serial number is stamped on left side of cylinder block, behind the alternator. Last group of numerals and letters designates engine type.

| Application | Engine Code |
|---|---|
| 2189 cc.................................................................... | 20R |

## ENGINE & CYLINDER HEAD

**NOTE** — *Following general procedures may not apply to all vehicles equipped with 20 R engine.*

### ENGINE

1) Drain coolant and engine oil. Disconnect battery cables. If equipped with automatic transmission, drain fluid. Unscrew hinge bolts and remove hood.

2) Remove air cleaner and disconnect heater hoses, fuel lines and all engine wiring. Disconnect flexible cable to carburetor and remove bracket holding cable to cylinder head cover. Disconnect vacuum hoses to emission control and mark them for reinstallation. Make sure to disconnect throttle retard hose connection at base of carburetor.

3) Disconnect vacuum line for brake booster at intake manifold. If equipped with air conditioning, disconnect lines at compressor. Disconnect plug-in for electric clutch.

4) Remove baffle between radiator and front suspension to gain access to lower radiator hose and A/T hoses. Remove radiator and A/T cooler hoses. Remove fan shrouds and grill, radiator baffle and radiator. Remove condenser lines and condenser.

5) Remove hood lock support. Disconnect clutch hose bracket (if equipped). Remove front engine mount attaching bolts. Engine will rest on mounts.

6) Disconnect exhaust pipe from exhaust manifold and disconnect support bracket from side of transmission. Remove clutch cylinder (if equipped). Remove support bracket for parking brake equalizer.

7) Disconnect speedometer drive cable, transmission linkage and driveshaft. Remove rear engine support after placing jack under engine and removing engine mounting bolts and crossmember. Engine will rest on jack. Remove engine using engine hoist. To install, reverse removal procedure.

### CYLINDER HEAD

1) Disconnect battery and exhaust pipe and drain coolant. Remove air cleaner and cover carburetor. Remove all hoses and linkages to intake manifold, carburetor and cylinder head. Remove spark plug wires and distributor. Remove valve cover and set number one piston to TDC on compression stroke.

2) Paint mating marks on camshaft sprocket and timing chain. Remove rubber half circle seal, distributor drive seal and cam

sprocket retaining bolt and remove sprocket from camshaft, allowing sprocket and chain to rest in cylinder head. Remove chain cover bolt, then remove cylinder head bolts in reverse of tightening sequence (See Fig. 1).

3) Pry equally on front and rear of rocker arm assembly and remove same. Lift off cylinder head using care to clear locating dowels. Do not pry between cylinder head and block. To install, reverse removal procedure and note the following: Apply liquid sealer at two front corners of block. Make sure valve timing and clearance is correctly set. Tighten cylinder head bolts in three steps to specified torque and in sequence indicated (See Fig. 1). Set ignition timing statically at 8°BTDC, then reset with timing light.

**Fig. 1  Cylinder Head Tightening Sequence
(Remove in Reverse Sequence)**

## VALVES

### VALVE ARRANGEMENT

**Left Side** — All exhaust.

**Right Side** — All intake.

### VALVE GUIDE SERVICING

1) Measure clearance between valve stem and guide. If clearance exceeds specifications, valve guides must be replaced. If valve guide being replaced has a snap ring installed, break guide using brass punch and hammer. Using driver tool (09201-60011), drive old guide down through combustion chamber.

**NOTE** — *Only replacement valve guides have snap rings.*

2) Drive in new valve guide from top of head until snap ring contacts cylinder head. Guide should have .75" (19 mm) protrusion above cylinder head. Ream new valve guide to provide proper stem clearance.

### VALVE STEM OIL SEALS

1) Using a suitable spring compressor, remove valve keepers. Withdraw spring retainer and springs. Remove valve stem oil seal from end of valve guide.

## 20 R 4 CYLINDER (Cont.)

**2)** Slide a new oil seal over valve stem, using care not to damage seal as it passes over keeper grooves. Force seal over end of valve guide. Reverse removal procedure for remaining components.

### VALVE SPRING INSTALLED HEIGHT

**1)** With valve spring removed, check length under specified load in a spring tester. Check valve spring free length, if less than specified, replace spring.

**2)** Check valve spring squareness with a steel square. If spring is out of square more than specified, replace spring.

Limit: .075" (1.9 mm)

Square

*Fig. 2   Checking Valve Spring Squareness*

### ROCKER ARM ASSEMBLY

If rocker arms appear loose, disassemble rocker arm assembly and measure rocker arm-to-shaft clearance. Clearance should be .0004-.0020" (.01-.05 mm). If clearance is greater than specifications, replace rocker arm and/or shafts. Reassemble in reverse of disassembly noting that all rocker arms are identical but that all rocker stands are different (See Fig. 3).

Front

Hole

*Fig. 3   Disassembled View of Rocker Arm Assembly*

### VALVE CLEARANCE ADJUSTMENT

Set No. 1 piston to TDC compression stroke. Sprocket timing mark should be slightly left of top. Valve clearance is measured between valve stem and rocker arm. Adjust intake

valves 1 and 2 to .008" (.2 mm) and exhaust valves 1 and 3 to .012" (.3 mm). Rotate crankshaft one complete revolution and align timing marks at pulley. Adjust intake valves 3 and 4 to .008" (.2 mm) and exhaust valves 2 and 4 to .012" (.3 mm).

## PISTONS, PINS & RINGS

### OIL PAN

Drain engine oil. Remove pan bolts and pan. When installing, apply liquid sealer to 4 corners of gasket where front cover and rear seal retainer join cylinder block. Use studs to guide pan into position and install pan bolts.

### PISTON & ROD ASSEMBLY

**Removal** — Remove connecting rod caps and remove bearings. Push piston and rod assembly up through cylinder head side. Mark all components with cylinder numbers for correct reassembly.

**Installation** — Apply oil to piston and piston rings. Install compression rings so stamped code on ring faces upward. Position piston ring gaps as shown in *Fig. 4*. Using suitable ring compressor, install piston and rod assembly in cylinder. Make sure indent on piston faces forward.

Comp. Ring #2

Front

Comp. Ring #1

Oil Ring Side Rail    45°    45°    Oil Ring Side Rail

*Fig. 4   Correct Piston Ring Gap Arrangement*

### FITTING PISTONS

**1)** Measure clearance of piston in cylinder. When measuring piston diameter, measure 90° to pin bore .83" (21 mm) from piston skirt. If clearance exceeds specifications, cylinders must be bored for oversize piston.

Measuring Point
.83" (21 mm)

*Fig. 5   Piston Diameter Measuring Point*

## 20 R 4 CYLINDER (Cont.)

2) Measure piston ring end gaps in cylinder. If cylinder has not been bored, check gap with ring in lowest part of cylinder. Check clearance of piston ring in ring groove.

**Fig. 6   Measuring Ring Groove Clearance**

### PISTON PINS

**Removal** — Heat piston to 176°F (80°C) and push piston pin out of piston and connecting rod. Piston pin should push through connecting rod with thumb pressure when rod is at 68°F (20°C). If pin is too loose in rod, press out bushing from connecting rod using press tool (09222-30010). Install and hone new bushing.

**NOTE** — *Piston and pin are a matched set.*

**Installation** — Heat piston to 176°F (80°C) and position piston and connecting rod so mark on rod and indent on piston crown face same direction. Push piston pin into piston and rod assembly.

**Fig. 7   Correct Alignment of Piston & Rod Assembly**

## CRANKSHAFT MAIN & CONNECTING ROD BEARINGS

### MAIN & CONNECTING ROD BEARINGS

1) Measure crankshaft runout at center bearing journal. If runout exceeds .004" (.1 mm), replace crankshaft. Inspect all journals for wear or scoring. Check for out-of-round or taper. If crankshaft is worn excessively, grind journals for undersize bearings.

2) Measure bearing clearances using Plastigage method. If clearance exceeds specifications, grind journals for undersize bearings. Both main and connecting rod bearings are available .010" (.25 mm) undersize.

### THRUST BEARING ALIGNMENT

Check crankshaft thrust clearance at thrust bearing using a feeler gauge. If end play exceeds limit of .012" (.3 mm), replace thrust washers. Thrust washers are available in two oversizes, .005" (.13 mm) and .010" (.25 mm).

### REAR MAIN BEARING OIL SEAL

With rear main bearing oil seal retainer removed, pry out old seal. Using suitable tool (09223-41010) drive oil seal in place. After installing new seal, coat seal lip lightly with multi-purpose grease.

**Fig. 8   Installed View of Rear Seal & Retainer**

## CAMSHAFT

### ENGINE FRONT COVER OIL SEAL

With engine front cover removed, pry out old seal toward front side. Using suitable tool (09223-50010), drive seal into place. After installing new seal, coat seal lip lightly with multi-purpose grease.

### TIMING CHAIN

**Removal** — 1) Remove cylinder head and oil pan. Remove radiator, drive belts, air pump and alternator bracket. Remove crankshaft pulley and timing chain cover assembly.

2) Remove chain from damper sprocket and remove cam sprocket and chain. Using puller (09213-36010), remove both oil pump drive and chain sprocket. Check chain, sprockets, tensioner and chain dampers for wear and replace as necessary.

**Installation** — 1) Turn crankshaft until shaft key is at TDC and slide sprocket over key. Position chain with chromed link over sprocket and aligned with mark on sprocket (See Fig. 9).

## 20 R 4 CYLINDER (Cont.)

Shaft Key at TDC

Chromed Link       Sprocket Mark

**Fig. 9    Aligning Crankshaft Sprocket & Timing Chain**

2) Install cam sprocket in chain so that timing mark on sprocket is located between two chromed links on chain (See Fig. 10). Slide oil pump drive spline over crankshaft key. Install new timing cover gasket after first cleaning mounting surface. Turn cam sprocket counterclockwise to remove slack from chain and install timing chain cover.

Two Chromed Links

Sprocket Mark

**Fig. 10    Aligning Camshaft Sprocket & Timing Chain**

3) Continue installation in reverse of removal procedure and set camshaft timing as follows: With No. 1 cylinder at TDC on compression stroke, position camshaft so that dowel on sprocket flange is at 12 o'clock position. Complete assembly procedure.

## CAMSHAFT

With cylinder head and rocker arm assembly removed, remove camshaft bearing caps and lift out camshaft. Camshaft bearing clearance may be checked using Plastigage method. If clearance exceeds specifications, replace cylinder head and/or camshaft. To install, reverse removal procedure. Install bearing caps in numbered order with arrows pointing toward the front. Adjust valve timing.

## VALVE TIMING

Valve timing is determined by the relationship between the camshaft and the crankshaft. Turn crankshaft to position No. 1 piston at TDC (align mark on crankshaft with pointer on chain cover). Turn camshaft to locate dowel pin and stamped mark on camshaft at 12 o'clock position. Install timing gear and chain on camshaft. A locating pin may be needed to stretch chain and a hammer may be needed to drive on gear. Tighten timing gear bolts to specifications.

## ENGINE OILING

**Crankcase Capacity** — 3.9 qts. on Pickup, 4.4 qts. on Celica and Corona. Add .9 qts. with filter change on all models.

**Pressure Relief Valve** — 64 psi (4.5 kg/cm²) operating pressure.

**Oil Filter** — Full-flow type with paper elements. Located at right side of engine.

## ENGINE OILING SYSTEM

Forced feed oiling system utilizing a gear and crescent type oil pump driven from front of crankshaft. Oil from oil pan is pumped through a full flow oil filter and then to oil galleries in cylinder block. Oil is fed to crankshaft bearings, timing chain assembly, camshaft and rocker arm assembly.

**Fig. 11    Engine Oiling System**

## OIL PUMP

1) Remove oil pan and strainer. Remove drive belts and crankshaft pulley. Unbolt and remove oil pump assembly. Remove oil pump drive spline from crankshaft and "O" ring

## 20 R 4 CYLINDER (Cont.)

from engine block. Remove relief valve plug, spring and piston from pump body. Remove driven and drive gear from pump body.

2) Inspect pump visually for wear or damage and replace parts as necessary. Place gears in pump body and with feeler gauges measure clearance between driven gear and pump body, driven gear-to-crescent tip clearance, drive gear-to-crescent tip clearance. Measure end clearance by placing straight edge across pump body and measuring clearance between gears and straightedge. To reassemble and install, reverse disassembly and removal procedure.

**Fig. 12   Exploded View of Oil Pump**

| Oil Pump Specifications | |
|---|---|
| **Application** | **In. (mm)** |
| Driven Gear-to-Pump Body | .0024-.0059 (.06-.15) |
| Driven Gear-to-Crescent | .0059-.0083 (.15-.21) |
| Drive Gear-to-Crescent | .0087-.0098 (.22-.25) |
| End Clearance | .0012-.0034 (.03-.09) |

## ENGINE COOLING

**Thermostat** — Starts to open at 187-194°F (86-90°C) and is fully open at 212°F (100°C).

**Cooling System Capacity** — 7.4 qts. on Celica and Pickup, 8.5 qts. on Corona.

**Radiator Cap** — 13 psi (.9 kg/cm²).

## WATER PUMP

Loosen fan belt and remove fluid coupling assembly, water pump pully and fan belt. Remove fan from fluid coupling. Remove water pump assembly. To install, reverse removal procedure and use a new gasket.

## ENGINE SPECIFICATIONS

### GENERAL SPECIFICATIONS

| Year | Displ. | | Carburetor | HP at RPM | Torque (Ft. Lbs. at RPM) | Compr. Ratio | Bore | | Stroke | |
|---|---|---|---|---|---|---|---|---|---|---|
| | cu. ins. | cc | | | | | in. | mm | in. | mm |
| 1978 | 133.6 | 2189 | 1x2-Bbl. | ①95 @ 4800 | 122 @ 2400 | 8.4:1 | 3.48 | 88.5 | 3.50 | 89.0 |

① — Horsepower is 90@4800 RPM on California models.

### PISTONS, PINS, RINGS

| Engine | PISTONS | PINS | | RINGS | | |
|---|---|---|---|---|---|---|
| | Clearance In. (mm) | Piston Fit In. (mm) | Rod Fit In. (mm) | Rings | End Gap In. (mm) | Side Clearance In. (mm) |
| 20R | .0012-.0020 (.03-.05) | Press Fit ① | .0002-.0004 (.005-.011) ② | No. 1 | .004-.012 (.10-.30) | .008 (.2) |
| | | | | No. 2 | .004-.12 (.10-.30) | .008 (.2) |
| | | | | Oil | ..... | ..... |

① — Push fit with piston heated to 176°F (80°C).          ② — Push fit with piston at room temperature.

# Toyota Engines

## 20 R 4 CYLINDER (Cont.)

### ENGINE SPECIFICATIONS (Cont.)

### CRANKSHAFT MAIN & CONNECTING ROD BEARINGS

| Engine | MAIN BEARINGS | | | | CONNECTING ROD BEARINGS | | |
| | Journal Diam. In. (mm) | Clearance In. (mm) | Thrust Bearing | Crankshaft End Play In. (mm) | Journal Diam. In. (mm) | Clearance In. (mm) | Side Play In. (mm) |
|---|---|---|---|---|---|---|---|
| 20R | 2.3614-2.3622 (59.98-60.00) | .0010-.0022 (.025-.055) | Center | .0008-.0079 (.02-.20) | 2.0862-2.0866 (52.99-53.00) | .0010-.0022 (.03-.06) | .0063-.0102 (.16-.26) |

### VALVES

| Engine & Valve | Head Diam. In. (mm) | Face Angle | Seat Angle | Seat Width In. (mm) | Stem Diameter In. (mm) | Stem Clearance In. (mm) | Valve Lift In. (mm) |
|---|---|---|---|---|---|---|---|
| 20R | | | | | | | |
| Intake | ..... | 45° | 45° | .047-.063 (1.2-1.6) | .3138-.3144 (7.97-7.99) | .0008-.0024 (.02-.06) | ..... |
| Exhaust | ..... | 45° | 45° | .047-.063 (1.2-1.6) | .3136-.3142 (7.97-7.98) | .0012-.0028 (.03-.07) | ..... |

### VALVE SPRINGS

| Engine | Free Length In. (mm) | PRESSURE Lbs. @ In. (kg @ mm) | |
| | | Valve Closed | Valve Open |
|---|---|---|---|
| 20R | 1.79 (45.4) | 60@1.594 (27.2@40.5) | ..... |

### CAMSHAFT

| Engine | Journal Diam. In. (mm) | Clearance In. (mm) | ①Lobe Lift In. (mm) |
|---|---|---|---|
| 20R | 1.2984-1.2990 (32.98-33.00) | ②.0004-.0020 (.01-.05) | Int. 1.680 (42.68) Exh. 1.682 (42.74) |

① — Total Lobe Height.
② — End play is .0031-.0071" (.08-.18 mm)

### TIGHTENING SPECIFICATIONS

| Application | Ft. Lbs. (mkg) |
|---|---|
| Cylinder Head Bolts | 52-64 (7.2-8.8) |
| Main Bearing Cap Bolts | 69-83 (9.5-11.5) |
| Connecting Rod Cap Bolts | 39-48 (5.4-6.6) |
| Camshaft Bearing Cap Bolts | 12-17 (1.7-2.3) |
| Timing Chain Cover | 7-12 (1.0-1.6) |
| Crankshaft Pulley Bolt | 80-94 (11-13) |
| Camshaft Sprocket Bolt | 51-65 (7.0-9.0) |
| Intake Manifold | 11-15 (1.5-2.1) |
| Exhaust Manifold | 29-36 (4.0-5.0) |
| Oil Pan | 2-3 (.3-.4) |
| Flywheel Bolts | 61-69 (8.5-9.5) |

# Toyota Engines

## 4M 6 CYLINDER

### ENGINE CODING

#### ENGINE IDENTIFICATION

Engine number is stamped into a machined surface on left side of engine block just above oil dipstick.

## ENGINE, CYLINDER HEAD & MANIFOLDS

**NOTE** — *Following general procedures may not apply to all vehicles equipped with 4M engine.*

### ENGINE

1) Disconnect battery and drain cooling system. Remove hood and fan shroud. Remove radiator hoses, radiator, heater hoses, and all oil cooler hoses. Remove oil pressure gauge sending wire, and alternator wiring.

2) Remove air cleaner and disconnect brake booster vacuum hose. Disconnect distributor primary wiring, coil secondary wiring, and water temperature gauge sending wire. Disconnect fuel line and vacuum hose.

3) Disconnect starter wiring and accelerator connecting rod. Disconnect clutch flexible hose from master cylinder tube (if equipped). **NOTE** — *To prevent spillage of fluid, install bleeder plug cap onto master cylinder tube end.* Disconnect power steering feed hose (if equipped).

4) Raise front and rear of vehicle with jack and support on stands. Disconnect exhaust pipe from manifold and remove exhaust pipe supports and insulator. Disconnect speedometer drive cable and back-up light wiring.

5) On manual transmission cars with column shift, remove low speed connecting rod, cross shaft, and gear shift rod. On automatic transmission cars with column shift, remove control rod and cross shaft and remove throttle link connecting firs rod and second rod.

6) On manual transmission cars with floor shift, remove console box and gear shift lever. On automatic transmission cars with floor shift, remove connecting rod swivel nut and disconnect control rod from shift lever.

7) Remove propeller shaft and plug rear of transmission to prevent oil leakage. Remove rear engine undercover and remove front engine mounts. Support transmission with jack and remove rear engine mount and crossmember.

8) Lower jack supporting transmission and remove stands. Using suitable engine hoist, remove engine and transmission assembly from vehicle.

9) To install, reverse removal procedure. Check all fluid levels and linkage adjustments prior to starting engine.

### INTAKE MANIFOLD

**Removal** — 1) Disconnect battery and drain coolant. Remove air cleaner and distributor cap. Remove radiator inlet hose and heater hoses. Disconnect temperature gauge sending wire and fuel line.

2) Disconnect vacuum hoses at carburetor and manifold, and remove accelerator connecting rod. Remove automatic choke stove inlet hose and outlet pipe. Remove water by-pass hose under manifolds, and remove manifold with carburetor attached.

**Installation** — Thoroughly clean all gasket surfaces and install new gaskets. Install manifold assembly and gradually tighten bolts working from center out. Install remaining components in reverse of removal procedure.

### CYLINDER HEAD

**Removal** — 1) Remove intake and exhaust manifolds. Remove heater and by pass hoses attached to head. Remove spark plugs and cylinder head cover. Turn crankshaft so that number 1 piston is at TDC on firing stroke and note that mating marks are aligned on timing gear and timing chain.

2) Remove chain tensioner, then remove timing gear bolt noting that bolt has *LEFT* hand threads. Loosen head/rocker shaft bolts a little at a time in reverse of tightening sequence shown in *Fig. 1*. Lift off rocker arm assembly, then lift head straight up from block.

**Installation** — Clean all gasket surfaces and apply sealer to cylinder head, around oil holes in the block, and in area of timing chain cover and block. Install new gasket. Clean all foreign matter from bolt holes and place cylinder head on block. Make sure valve adjusting screws have been loosened and install rocker shaft assembly. Install bolts and tighten in several steps according to the sequence in *Fig. 1*. Align timing marks and install remaining components in reverse of removal procedure.

*Fig. 1  Cylinder Head Bolt Tightening Sequence (Loosen in Reverse Order)*

## VALVES

### VALVE ARRANGEMENT

**Left Side** — All Intake.

**Right Side** — All Exhaust.

### VALVE GUIDE SERVICING

1) Break off valve guide bushing at snap ring and remove snap ring. Heat cylinder head to approximately 176-212°F (80-100°C) and drive out bushing toward combustion chamber.

2) Allow head to cool and measure cylinder head bushing bore. Install oversize bushing if bore exceeds .5118-.5129" (13.000-13.027 mm). Machine cylinder head to .5138-.5148" (13.050-13.077 mm) and fit .05 mm bushing. Ensure valve guide bushing length is 1.97" (50.0 mm) intake and 2.34" (59.5 mm) exhaust. Make sure that proper valve guide bushing to valve stem clearance is obtained.

## 4M 6 CYLINDER (Cont.)

**2)** Allow head to cool and measure cylinder head bushing bore. If bore exceeds .5125" (13.018 mm), machine bore to .514" (13.054 mm) and insert .002" (.05 mm) oversize bushing. Head should be heated to 176-212°F (80-100°C) and bushing driven in with drift (09201-60011) until snap ring contacts head.

**3)** Measure installed height of .650" (16.5 mm) for intake guide and .551 (14 mm) for exhaust guide. Hand ream guide bore to provide specified stem clearance.

**NOTE** — *Valve guide replacement is recommended whenever new valves are installed.*

**Fig. 2  Disassembled View of Valve with Detail of Components**

### VALVE STEM OIL SEALS

Intake seals are slightly longer than exhaust valve seals and must not be switched. To install, assemble in order: plate washer, oil seal, inner and outer springs, and valve spring retainer. With suitable tool (09202-43011), install retainer locks.

### VALVE & VALVE SPRING

Mark each valve and using valve spring compressor, remove valves, valve retainers, retainer locks, springs and valve stem oil seals. When replacing valve springs, closed coil ends face toward cylinder head.

### VALVE SPRING HEIGHT

Measure valve spring free length with caliper type ruler and check for squareness within .063" (1.6 mm). Using a spring tester, check load when spring is compressed to installed height. Check installed height with valve in closed position by measuring distance from upper edge of washer to lower edge of spring retainer.

**Fig. 3   Measure Installed Valve Spring Height as Shown**

### ROCKER ARM ASSEMBLY

Check arm-to-shaft clearance by twisting on shaft. Little or no movement should be felt. If movement is felt, disassemble and inspect. Bushings may be replaced and finished to give standard clearance of .0005-.0013" (.012-.033 mm) using pin hole grinder. Assemble rocker arm assembly, starting with rocker support number 1. Install on head and tighten bolts in sequence shown in *Fig. 1*.

**NOTE** — *Disassemble and mark all parts for reassembly in proper order. Loosen adjusting screws and nuts prior to installing rocker arm assembly.*

**Fig. 4   Assemble Rocker Arm Assembly as Shown (Start with Rocker Support No. 1)**

### VALVE CLEARANCE ADJUSTMENT

**1)** With No. 1 piston at TDC of compression stroke, adjust intake valves 1, 2, and 4 and exhaust valves 1, 3, and 5 to specified clearance.

**2)** Rotate crankshaft one turn (360°) clockwise and adjust intake valves 3,5 and 6, and exhaust valves 2,4 and 6.

#### Valve Clearance Specifications

| Valve | Hot In. (mm) | Cold In. (mm) |
|---|---|---|
| Intake | .011 (.28) | .010 (.25) |
| Exhaust | .014 (.35) | .013 (.33) |

### PISTON & ROD ASSEMBLY

**Removal** — With cylinder head and oil pan removed, remove connecting rod caps and remove bearings. Push piston and rod assembly up through cylinder head side. Mark all components with cylinder numbers for correct reassembly.

**Fig. 5   Position Ring Gaps as Shown for Installation**

## 4M 6 CYLINDER (Cont.)

**Installation** — 1) Apply oil to piston and piston rings. Install rings with mark on side of ring facing upwards. Position piston ring gaps shown in illustration. Using suitable ring compressor, install piston and rod assembly in cylinder block. Make sure mark on piston faces front.

2) Replace connecting rod caps with mating marks aligned. Tighten nuts evenly in 2 or 3 steps and check connecting rod side play.

### FITTING PISTONS

Measure top, center and bottom of cylinder bore with dial indicator. If wear exceeds .008" (.2 mm) or taper and out-of-round exceeds .0008" (.02 mm), cylinders must be rebored. Bore in sequence number 1, 3, 6, 4, 2 and 5 cylinders. Last cut of boring bar should not remove more than .0020" (.05 mm). Finish to final dimension by honing the last .0008" (.02 mm).

**NOTE** — *Allow bore to cool after boring and honing to avoid erroneous readings while measuring. Cool measurement of piston and bore should provide .0020-.0028" (.05-.07 mm) for proper clearance.*

### Piston Table

| Application | Piston O.D. In. (mm) |
| --- | --- |
| Standard | 3.146-3.148 (79.93-79.98) |
| .50 Oversize | 3.166-3.168 (80.43-80.48) |
| .75 Oversize | 3.176-3.178 (80.68-80.73) |
| 1.00 Oversize | 3.186-3.188 (80.93-80.98) |

Make Measurement .059" (1.5 mm) Below Oil Ring Groove

**Fig. 6   Measure Piston as Shown at 68°F (20°C)**

Piston Pin Fitting Mark
Piston Size Mark
All Marks May Not Appear On All Pistons
Piston Fitting Mark
Front Mark

**Fig. 7   Typical Reference Marks on Piston Head**

### PISTON PINS

**Removal** — Remove circlips in piston pin hole with needle nose pliers. Heat piston to about 140°F (60°C) and remove pin by tapping lightly with plastic hammer. Keep piston, pin and rod together as a set.

**Installation** — Install one circlip in piston and heat to about 140°F (60°C). Align piston notch with rod mark and push pin in with thumb. Install remaining circlip.

Notch (Front)
Toyota Mark

**Fig. 8   Notch on Piston and Mark on Rod Must Face Same Direction When Installing Wrist Pin**

### MAIN & CONNECTING ROD BEARINGS

1) Measure connecting rod side play with dial indicator. If greater than .012" (.3 mm), rod must be replaced. Wipe off bearing and journal, then check clearance with Plastigage. If clearance exceeds .003" (.08 mm) and cannot be corrected with .002" (.05 mm) undersize bearings, or if taper or out-of-round exceeds .0008" (.02 mm), crankshaft must be ground to next undersize.

2) Check crankshaft runout with dial indicator. If runout exceeds .0012" (.03 mm), correct or replace crankshaft. Check main bearing journal for taper and out-of-round. Check main bearing clearance using Plastigage. If required, crankshaft may be reground for undersize bearings. Undersize bearings for main and connecting rods are available in .002" (.05 mm), .010" (.25 mm) and .020" (.50 mm) as well as standard.

### THRUST BEARING

Measure crankshaft end play with center (number 4) main bearing and cap installed. If clearance exceeds .012" (.3 mm), replace thrust washers to achieve standard clearance of .002-.010" (.05-.25 mm). Standard thickness of thrust washer is .115" (2.92 mm) with .005" (.125 mm) and .010" (250 mm) oversizes available.

**NOTE** — *Install thrust washers with oil grooves facing outward*

09223-41010

**Fig. 9   Using Special Tool to Install Rear Seal**

## 4M 6 CYLINDER (Cont.)

### REAR MAIN OIL SEAL

Inspect oil seal lip and replace if worn or damaged. Pry old seal out without damaging cover or retainer. Install seal using replacer tool (09223-41010). Apply multipurpose lubricant to seal lip.

### ENGINE FRONT COVER

Remove crankshaft damper attaching bolt and remove damper using suitable puller (09213-41013). Remove oil pan and remove front cover bolts and front cover. Use liquid sealer on front cover gaskets when assembling.

### ENGINE FRONT COVER OIL SEAL

Inspect oil seal lip and replace if worn or damaged. Pry old seal out without damaging cover or retainer. Install seal using replacer tool (09223-50010). Apply multipurpose lubricant to seal lip.

**Fig. 10   Using Special Seal Installing Tool to Drive in Front Oil Seal**

### TIMING CHAIN

**Removal** — See *Valve Timing.* Remove cylinder head cover, rocker arm shafts and camshaft. Remove cylinder head. Remove crankshaft damper attaching bolt and remove damper using suitable puller (09213-41013). Remove oil pan, timing chain cover and timing chain.

**Fig. 11   Front View of Timing Chain and Gears**

**Installation** — 1) Inspect chain, sprockets and tensioner. Position crankshaft sprocket so that key is pointed straight toward cylinder head and Toyota mark is in line with pump sprocket shaft. Install timing chain with white links aligned with punch marks on crankshaft gear and pump gear. See *Fig. 12.*

**NOTE** — *Do NOT confuse index marks. Plated or white links align with punch marks on gears. Toyota symbol marks align with each other.*

2) Insert bolt in collar and install both chain vibration dampers and guide. With head and camshaft in position, assure that camshaft flange pin is aligned with embossed mark on rocker support number 1. Align mating link on chain with punch mark on camshaft drive gear and install drive gear on camshaft. Note that attaching bolt has LEFT hand threads.

3) Adjust timing chain tension by first rotating engine in normal direction (clockwise) until chain is at most slack position. Loosen tensioner locknut, then turn adjusting screw clockwise until resistance is felt. Loosen screw 2 full turns and tighten lock nut. If chain is noisy after starting engine, loosen adjusting screw ½ turn more. See *Valve Timing.*

**Fig. 12   Timing Chain with Pump Sprocket and Crankshaft Marks Aligned**

## CAMSHAFT

### CAMSHAFT

**Removal** — Remove rocker arm assembly. *See Cylinder Head.* Remove camshaft sprocket bolt (LEFT hand threads) and separate sprocket from camshaft. Remove camshaft bearing caps and keep in order for assembly. Remove camshaft from head and check for maximum runout of .0012" (.03 mm).

**Installation** — Lubricate camshaft bearing journals and place camshaft in position. Assemble bearing caps in original positions with arrow marks toward front. Complete assembly in reverse of removal procedure.

### CAMSHAFT BEARINGS

Inspect bearings for wear or damage. Check that oil clearance does not exceed .004" (.10 mm). When checking clearance, use Plastigage method. Bearings are available in standard, .002", .010" and .020" (.05, .25 and .50 mm) oversizes.

### CAMSHAFT END THRUST

Install camshaft in cylinder head and tighten all bearing caps. Attach dial indicator and check end thrust at flange end. Maximum clearance is .012" (.3 mm). Specified standard clearance is .003-.007" (.08-.18 mm).

# Toyota Engines

## 4M 6 CYLINDER (Cont.)

### CAM HEIGHT

Measure cam height. Minimum for intake is 1.664" (42.46 mm) and for exhaust is 1.666" (42.32 mm). If less than specified, replace camshaft.

### PUMP SHAFT

**1)** With front cover and timing chain removed, use puller (09213-36010) to remove pump shaft sprocket. Remove thrust plate bolt and pull pump shaft from cylinder block. Replace and tighten sprocket on shaft, then check end play between gear and plate with feeler gauge. If beyond limits, replace thrust plate.

**2)** Check bearing bore diameter with inside micrometer and journal diameter with outside micrometer. Standard clearance is .0010-.0026" (.025-.066 mm). If clearance exceeds .0031" (.08 mm), replace bearings with special tool (09233-41010).

### Pump Shaft Specifications

| Application | In. (mm) |
|---|---|
| Out-of-Round & Taper Limit | .0004 (.01) |
| Thrust Clearance | .002-.005 (.06-.13) |
| | Limit .012 (.30) |
| Bearing Clearance | .001-.0025 (.025-.066) |
| | Limit .003 (.08) |

### VALVE TIMING

**1)** Rotate crankshaft in normal direction (clockwise) so that number 1 piston is at TDC on compression stroke. Check that camshaft flange timing pin is aligned with embossed mark on rocker support. (Timing chain cover graduation should indicate 0° mark aligned with notch in pulley.)

**Fig. 13   Camshaft Flange Straight Pin Aligned with Support for Installation of Camshaft Gear**

**Fig. 14   Front View of Camshaft Gear with Alignment Marks and Straight Pin Holes**

**2)** If marks are not as described, turn crankshaft until timing pin is in line with embossed mark and note timing cover graduation. Remove chain tensioner and timing gear set bolt. If timing was retarded 3 to 9 degrees, remove gear and install to second straight pin hole with piston at TDC. Install and adjust chain tensioner and recheck valve timing.

**NOTE** – *Movement of straight pin to No. 2 hole and No. 3 hole advances valve timing in steps of 6° each.*

**Fig. 15   Diagram of Engine Lubrication System (Oil Cooler Not Shown)**

### ENGINE OILING

**Crankcase Capacity** – 5.7 quarts with filter, 4.7 quarts WITHOUT filter.

**Pressure Relief Valves** – There are 3 relief valves in the engine oiling system. The pressure relief valve in the oil pump opens at 71-85 psi (5.0-6.0 kg/cm²), the oil regulator valve-to-cooler opens at 38-50 psi (2.7-3.5 kg/cm²), and the relief valve in the filter opens with a pressure difference of 1-17 psi (.8-1.2 kg/cm²).

**Oil Filter** – Full flow spin-on type.

### ENGINE OILING SYSTEM

System is force feed with full-flow filtering unit. Pressure is delivered by a gear-driven oil pump. From filter oil travels through cylinder block passages by which internal components are lubricated. An external oil cooler is mounted at the upper left front of the radiator. It receives oil from the regulator mounted on the block, cools and returns the oil to the pan.

### OIL PUMP

With pan off engine, remove oil pump mounting bolts and take out oil pump. Disassemble pump by removing (in order) snap ring, spacer, driveshaft gear, Woodruff key, pump cover, pump shaft sub-assembly, driven gear, relief valve plug, gasket, spring and relief valve. Check side clearance between gear and cover for maximum of .006" (.15 mm). Check clearance between gear teeth and body for not more than .008" (.2 mm). Measure backlash between gear teeth with feeler gauge for no more than .035" (.9 mm). Clean and inspect components and reverse disassembly procedure. Pump may be checked for operation by immersing screen in oil and turning shaft clockwise. Oil should discharge from pump outlet.

# Toyota Engines

## 4M 6 CYLINDER (Cont.)

Fig. 16   Exploded View of Gear Driven Oil Pump

### ENGINE COOLING

**Thermostat** — Wax pellet type, begins to open at 176-183°F (80-84°C) and should open to more than .32" (8 mm) at 203°F.

### WATER PUMP

**NOTE** — *It is not necessary to remove complete water pump housing to service water pump. Pump cover may be removed from housing and housing may be left on cylinder block.*

Remove fluid coupling and fan assembly. Remove fan belt and pulley. Remove 5 cover bolts and take off cover assembly. Replaces seals and bearings as required. Use new gasket and reverse removal procedure.

## ENGINE SPECIFICATIONS

### GENERAL SPECIFICATIONS

| Year | Displ. | | Carburetor | HP at RPM | Torque (Ft. Lbs. at RPM) | Compr. Ratio | Bore | | Stroke | |
|---|---|---|---|---|---|---|---|---|---|---|
| | cu. ins. | cc | | | | | in. | mm | in. | mm |
| 1978 4M | 156.4 | 2563 | 2-Bbl. | 108@5000 | 134@2800 | 8.5-1 | 3.15 | 80 | 3.35 | 85 |

### VALVES

| Engine & Valve | Head Diam. In. (mm) | Face Angle | Seat Angle | Seat Width In. (mm) | Stem Diameter In. (mm) | Stem Clearance In. (mm) | Valve Lift In. (mm) |
|---|---|---|---|---|---|---|---|
| 4M Int. | ..... | 45.5° | 45° | .047-.063 (1.2-1.6) | .3138-.3144 (7.970-7.985) | .0010-.0024 (.025-.060) | ..... |
| Exh. | ..... | 45.5° | 45° | .047-.063 (1.2-1.6) | .3134-.3140 (7.960-7.975) | .0014-.0028 (.035-.070) | ..... |

① — Wear limit for intake — .004" (.10 mm), exhaust — .005" (.13 mm).

### VALVE SPRINGS

| Engine | Free Length In. (mm) | PRESSURE Lbs. @ In. (kg @ mm) | |
|---|---|---|---|
| | | Valve Closed | Valve Open |
| 4M Inner | 1.768 (44.9) | 14.1-17.2@1.492 (6.4-7.8@37.9) | ..... |
| Outer | 1.846 (46.9) | 37.3-46.5@1.630 (17.1-21.1@41.4) | ..... |

① — If valve spring is out of square more than .063" (1.6 mm), replace spring.

### CAMSHAFT

| Engine | Journal Diam. In. (mm) | Clearance In. (mm) | Runout In. (mm) |
|---|---|---|---|
| 4M | 1.3378-1.3384 (33.979-33.995) | .0007-.0022 (.017-.057) | .0012 (.03) |

# Toyota Engines

## 4M 6 CYLINDER (Cont.)
### ENGINE SPECIFICATIONS (Cont.)

### PISTONS, PINS, RINGS

| Engine | PISTONS | PINS | | RINGS | | |
| | Clearance In. (mm) | Piston Fit In. (mm) | Rod Fit In. (mm) | Rings | End Gap In. (mm) | Side Clearance In. (mm) |
|---|---|---|---|---|---|---|
| 4M | .0019-.0027 (.05-07) | ..... | .0002-.0004 (.005-.011) Limit .0006 (.015) | No. 1<br>No. 2<br>Oil | .0039-.0110 (.10-.28)<br>.0059-.0110 (.15-.28)<br>.0079-.0354 (.20-.90) | .0012-.0028 (.03-.07)<br>.0008-.0024 (.02-.09) |

### CRANKSHAFT MAIN & CONNECTING ROD BEARINGS

| Engine | MAIN BEARINGS | | | | CONNECTING ROD BEARINGS | | |
| | Journal Diam. In. (mm) | Clearance In. (mm) | Thrust Bearing | Crankshaft End Play In. (mm) | Journal Diam. In. (mm) | Clearance In. (mm) | Side Play In. (mm) |
|---|---|---|---|---|---|---|---|
| 4M | 2.3617-2.3627 (59.988-60.012) | .0008-.0021 (.021-.053) | No. 4 | .002-.010 (.05-.25) | 2.0463-2.0472 (51.976-52.000) | .0008-.0021 (.021-.053) | .006-.012 (.16-.30) |

### OIL PUMP SPECIFICATIONS

| Application | Specification |
|---|---|
| Side Clearance | .0012-.0035" (.03-.09 mm) |
| Body Clearance | .0012-.0024" (.03-.06 mm) |
| Gear Backlash | .020-.024" (.5-.6 mm) |
| Driven Shaft Diameter | .5496-.5501" (13.96-13.97 mm) |
| Relief Valve Opening Psi | 71.1-83.3 psi (5.0-6.0 kg/cm²) |

### TIGHTENING SPECIFICATIONS

| Application | Ft.Lbs. (mkg) |
|---|---|
| Cylinder Head | |
| 12 mm bolts | 54-62 (7.5-8.5) |
| 8 mm bolts | 11-16 (1.5-2.2) |
| Intake Manifold | 11-15 (1.5-2.1) |
| Exhaust Manifold | 18-22 (2.5-3.1) |
| Camshaft Bearing Cap | 12-17 (1.7-2.3) |
| Camshaft Timing Gear (L.H. Thread) | 47-54 (6.5-7.5) |
| Pump Drive Shaft Gear | 7-12 (1.0-1.6) |
| Crankshaft Bearing Caps | 72-79 (9.9-10.9) |
| Connecting Rod Cap | 30-35 (4.2-4.8) |
| Oil Pan | 5-7 (.65-.95) |
| Crankshaft Pulley | 69-76 (9.5-10.5) |
| Flywheel | 51-58 (7.0-8.0) |
| Chain Tensioner | 22-29 (3.0-4.0) |
| Timing Cover | |
| 8 mm Bolt | 7-12 (1.0-1.6) |
| 8 mm Nut | 11-16 (1.5-2.2) |
| 10 mm Bolt | 14-22 (1.9-3.1) |
| 10 mm Nut | 14-22 (1.9-3.1) |

## 2F 6 CYLINDER

## ENGINE CODING

### ENGINE IDENTIFICATION

Engine number is stamped on right side of cylinder block above starter motor. First two digits indicate engine type.

| Application | Engine Code |
|---|---|
| 4230 cc | 2F |

## ENGINE, CYLINDER HEAD & MANIFOLD

### ENGINE

1) Disconnect battery and drain cooling system. Remove hood, radiator grille and hood lock support rod. Disconnect hood lock from radiator support and remove radiator support. Disconnect heater and radiator hoses and remove radiator.

2) Disconnect all necessary wiring and fuel lines. Remove fuel filter assembly and air cleaner. Disconnect rod end of high and low shift rod from shift link lever. Disconnect throttle rod, choke rod, and accelerator rod from carburetor.

3) Remove vacuum hose connection on intake manifold and remove check valve of transfer front drive controller. Disconnect exhaust pipe from manifold and parking brake cable from intermediate lever. Disconnect front propeller shaft from transfer output front shaft flange.

4) Remove engine and transmission undercovers. Disconnect high and low shift rod from transfer high and low shift inner lever. Remove high and low shift link lever and high and low shift rod. Remove clutch release cylinder assembly from engine mount rear bracket.

5) Loosen clamp screws and disconnect vacuum hoses from transfer diaphragm cylinder. Remove front drive indicator switch and disconnect speedometer drive cable from transmission. Disconnect rear propeller shaft from transmission.

6) Disconnect gear shifting rod and gear selecting rod from gear shift outer lever and gear select outer lever. Remove nuts at front and rear engine mounts. Using suitable hoist, move engine up and forward to remove. To install, reverse removal procedure.

### INTAKE & EXHAUST MANIFOLDS

**Removal** — 1) Disconnect battery and remove air cleaner. Disconnect throttle rod, choke rod, accelerator wire, vacuum line, and fuel line from carburetor.

2) Disconnect magnetic valve wire from ignition coil terminal and remove carburetor assembly. Disconnect exhaust pipe from exhaust manifold. Remove manifold nuts, manifolds and gaskets.

**Installation** — Thoroughly clean all gasket surfaces and install new gaskets. Install manifold assembly and gradually tighten bolts working from center out. Install remaining components in reverse of removal procedure.

**Fig. 1   Manifold Tightening Sequence**

### CYLINDER HEAD

**Removal** — 1) Disconnect battery, drain cooling system and remove air cleaner. Remove intake and exhaust manifolds. See Intake & Exhaust Manifolds. Remove bolts attaching oil filler tube to rocker arm cover and remove rocker arm cover.

2) Disconnect all necessary wiring, radiator and heater hoses. Remove ignition coil from cylinder head. Remove rocker arm assembly support retaining nuts and bolts and remove rocker arm assembly.

3) Remove push rods and keep in order for proper installation. Loosen cylinder head bolts gradually in sequence shown and remove cylinder head.

**Fig. 2   Cylinder Head Loosening Sequence**

**Installation** — Clean all gasket surfaces and install new gasket. Install cylinder head and tighten bolts gradually in sequence shown. Reverse removal procedure for remaining components.

**Fig. 3   Cylinder Head Tightening Sequence**

## 2F 6 CYLINDER (Cont.)

### VALVES

#### VALVE ARRANGEMENT

E-I-I-E-E-I-I-E-E-I-I-E (front to rear).

#### VALVE GUIDE SERVICING

1) Check clearance between valve stems and valve guides. If clearance exceeds .004" (.10 mm) for intake or .005" (.12 mm) for exhaust, replace valve and/or valve guide.

*Fig. 4    Intake Valve Guide Installation*

2) To replace valve guide, drive guide toward combustion chamber using suitable driver (09201-60011). Using same tool, install new guide from top of cylinder head. Valve guide should extend .67" (17 mm) from top of cylinder head *(See Fig. 4 & 5)*. Intake valve guide length is 2.13" (54 mm) and exhaust guide is 2.32" (59 mm) long. After installing new guide, ream for proper clearance.

*Fig. 5    Exhaust Valve Guide Installation*

#### VALVE SPRINGS

**Removal** — Using suitable valve spring compressor, compress valve spring and remove valve spring retainer locks. Release compressor and remove spring retainer, spring, valve stem oil seal and spring seat. Remove valve.

**Installation** — Insert valve into valve stem guide, and install valve spring seat, valve spring, valve stem oil seal and valve spring retainer onto valve stem. Compress valve spring using suitable valve spring compressor and install valve spring retainer locks. Make sure retainer locks seat properly in valve stem groove.

*Fig. 6    Removing Valve Springs*

#### VALVE SPRING INSTALLED HEIGHT

After assembling valve, check installed height of valve spring by measuring from spring seat to point where spring contacts oil shield or spacer. Installed height of both intake and exhaust valve springs should be 1.693" (43.0 mm). Check squareness of springs by placing spring on flat surface next to steel square. Squareness should be within .071" (1.8 mm).

#### ROCKER ARM ASSEMBLY

1) Check rocker arms and shaft for damage or wear. If clearance is excessive, replace bushing and ream to provide a clearance of .0007-.0015" (.017-.037 mm). When replacing bushing make sure oil hole in bushing lines up with oil hole in rocker arm.

2) Install rocker arms, springs and rocker shaft supports onto valve rocker shaft, then install valve rocker shaft lock springs. **NOTE** — *There are two types of rocker arms and two types of rocker supports. Rocker support with oil hole is installed in the fourth position. Boss of rocker supports should face forward.*

*Fig. 7    Rocker Shaft Bushing Alignment*

#### VALVE CLEARANCE ADJUSTMENT

1) Set No. 1 piston at TDC of compression stroke and align timing mark with pointer. Adjust valves 1,2,3,5,7 and 9 (as numbered from front).

## 2F 6 CYLINDER (Cont.)

**2)** Rotate crankshaft one complete turn and again align timing mark with pointer. Adjust remaining valves 4,6,8,10,11 and 12.

### Valve Clearance Specifications

| Valve | Clearance (Hot) In. (mm) |
|---|---|
| Intake | .008 (.20) |
| Exhaust | .014 (.35) |

## PISTONS, PINS & RINGS

### OIL PAN

**Removal** — Remove engine undercovers, and remove flywheel side and undercover. Remove front propeller shaft. Drain oil, remove oil pan attaching bolts and oil pan.

**Installation** — Thoroughly clean all gasket mating surfaces. Apply liquid sealer onto both oil pan gasket surfaces, install oil pan and tighten bolts. Reverse removal procedure for remaining components.

### PISTON & ROD ASSEMBLY

**Removal** — With cylinder head and oil pan removed, remove connecting rod caps and remove bearings. Push piston and rod assembly up through cylinder block. Mark all components with cylinder numbers for correct reassembly.

*Fig. 8    Piston Ring Gap Spacing*

**Installation** — **1)** Apply oil to piston and rings. Position ring gaps as shown in *Fig. 8*. Use a ring compressor and install piston assemblies through top of cylinder. Notch on piston MUST face FORWARD and index mark (symbol) on connecting rod MUST face REAR.

**2)** Replace connecting rod bearings and connecting rod caps. Tighten connecting rod bearing cap nuts. Rotate crankshaft to make sure bearings are not too tight.

### FITTING PISTONS

**1)** Measure cylinder bores and pistons to be fitted. Measure piston with micrometer at bottom of skirt at right angles to piston pin. If clearance exceeds specifications, replace piston.

**2)** If cylinder bore is worn or tapered beyond specifications, cylinder must be bored and oversize pistons installed. Oversize pistons are available in .020" .040" and .060" (.50, 1.00 and 1.50 mm).

### Cylinder Bore Specifications

| Application | Wear Limits |
|---|---|
| Bore Wear Limit | .008" (.2 mm) |
| Taper | .0008" (.02 mm) |
| Difference Between Cylinders | .002" (.05 mm) |

*Fig. 9    Measuring Piston Ring Gap*

**3)** Use .001-.002" (.03-.05 mm) feeler gauge with pull scale to check clearance of oversize pistons. Force of 2.2-5.5 lbs. (1.0-2.5 kg) must not be exceeded when pulling feeler gauge from cylinder.

**4)** Measure piston ring gaps in cylinder. If cylinder has not been bored, check gap with ring in lowest part of cylinder. Check clearance of piston ring in ring groove. Always install rings with marks facing upward.

### PISTON PINS

**Removal** — Remove piston pin bolt and push out piston pin from piston and connecting rod. Mark all parts for correct reassembly.

*Fig. 10    Piston and Rod Assembly*

## 2F 6 CYLINDER (Cont.)

**Installation** — Position piston and connecting rod so that when notch on top of piston faces forward, oil hole in connecting rod faces camshaft side. Push pin into assembly and center pin in piston. Center connecting rod between piston pin bosses and tighten piston pin bolt.

## CRANKSHAFT MAIN & CONNECTING ROD BEARING

### MAIN & CONNECTING ROD BEARINGS

1) Thoroughly clean crankshaft and blow out oil passages with compressed air. Check crankshaft for runout with a dial indicator on second or third main bearing journal. If runout exceeds .004" (.10 mm), straighten or replace crankshaft.

2) Check main and connecting rod bearing journals for taper or out-of-round. If taper or out-of-round exceeds .0004" (.01 mm), crankshaft must be ground to next undersize.

3) Main and connecting rod bearing clearance is checked by the Plastigage method. If clearance exceeds specifications, replace bearings. If crankshaft wear is excessive and clearance cannot be brought to specifications by use of new standard size bearings, crankshaft must be reground to next undersize. Bearings are available in .002", .010", and .020" (.05, .25, and .50 mm) undersize.

**NOTE** — *All main bearing configurations are different.*

4) Make sure oil hole in No. 1 and No. 4 main bearing is installed toward block. Arrow on connecting rod cap MUST face FRONT.

### THRUST BEARING

Check crankshaft end play at No. 3 main bearing. If clearance exceeds .012" (.3 mm), replace crankshaft bearings.

### REAR MAIN BEARING OIL SEAL

To install oil seal without disassembling crankshaft, pry out oil seal with a screwdriver. Use crankshaft rear oil seal replacer tool (Tool 09223-60010) to drive new oil seal into place.

09223-60010

**Fig. 11    Rear Oil Seal Installation**

## CAMSHAFT

### ENGINE FRONT COVER

1) Drain cooling system and remove upper and lower radiator hoses. Remove bolts holding radiator to radiator support. Remove radiator upward using care not to damage radiator.

09213-60015

**Fig. 12    Crankshaft Pulley Removal**

2) Remove fan belt. Remove crankshaft pulley using suitable puller (09213-60015). Remove bolts and remove timing gear cover and gasket. To install, reverse removal procedure.

### FRONT COVER OIL SEAL

Pry old oil seal out using screwdriver. Install new oil seal so that open end of seal is towards inside of timing gear cover. Drive seal in place with suitable tool (09515-35010).

**Fig. 13    Front Oil Seal Installation**

### CAMSHAFT

Remove timing gear cover and gasket. Slide out oil slinger from crankshaft. Remove two bolts retaining camshaft thrust plate onto cylinder block by working through holes in camshaft timing gear. Remove camshaft by pulling out through front of block. Use care not to damage camshaft bearings or journals. To install, reverse removal procedure and set valve timing.

**NOTE** — *Ensure timing gear oil nozzle is positioned to direct oil onto timing gears. Stake into place with a punch.*

## 2F 6 CYLINDER (Cont.)

Fig. 14   Removing Camshaft Thrust Plate Bolts

### CAM LOBE HEIGHT

Measure height of cam lobe. If wear exceeds specification limit, replace camshaft. Intake lobe limit, 1.496" (38 mm); Exhaust lobe limit, 1.492" (37.9 mm).

### CAMSHAFT BEARING

1) Inspect camshaft for runout. If runout exceeds .0059" (.15 mm), replace camshaft. Inspect camshaft journals and bearings for wear or damage. If clearance exceeds specifications, replace camshaft bearings and/or regrind camshaft. Bearings are available in standard .010" and .020" (.25 and .50 mm) oversizes.

2) Drive out camshaft rear expansion plug from cylinder block. Remove front and No. 2 bearing using Camshaft Bearing Remover (Tool 09215-60010). Place front and second bearing adapters against rear of respective bearing, and place replacer against front part of cylinder block.

3) Insert replacer shaft into the three parts, and screw in retainer nut onto replacer shaft. Hold slotted part of shaft with wrench to prevent shaft from turning. By screwing in retainer nut with another wrench, the front and No. 1 bearing will be pulled out to the front.

Fig. 15   Typical Camshaft Bearing Removal Procedure (No. 3 & Rear Bearings Shown)

4) Remove No. 3 and rear bearing towards rear of block using tool in same manner as for front and No. 3 bearing. When installing new bearings, make sure that oil holes of bearing match up with oil holes in cylinder block.

5) When new bearings have been installed, measure to obtain proper clearance. Only a very light cut is required to ream bearings to proper size. Coat rear expansion plug with sealer and reinstall plug in block.

### CAMSHAFT END THRUST

Measure end thrust with feeler gauge. Thrust should be .0035-.0059" (.09-.15 mm). If thrust exceeds .008" (.2 mm), replace camshaft thrust plate.

Fig. 16   Measuring Camshaft End Thrust

### CRANKSHAFT TIMING GEAR

Remove pulley key from crankshaft. Using suitable puller (09213-60015), pull off crankshaft gear. To reinstall, drive on gear using suitable driver (09214-60010). Make sure timing mark on gear faces outward.

### VALVE TIMING

1) With crankshaft timing gear installed on crankshaft, oil camshaft journals and bearings and insert camshaft. Align mating mark on camshaft timing gear with mark on crankshaft timing gear and push camshaft into position. No. 6 cylinder should be at TDC, compression stroke. If oil nozzle was removed, refit with oil hole facing down (toward gears).

Fig. 17   Crankshaft Timing Gear Removal

## 2F 6 CYLINDER (Cont.)

2) Tighten camshaft thrust plate retaining bolts to specifications. Check that timing gear backlash does not exceed .008" (.2 mm). Standard backlash is .0020-.0051" (.05-.13 mm). If backlash exceeds specifications, replace both camshaft and crankshaft gears.

*Fig. 18   Timing Mark Alignment*

## ENGINE OILING

**Crankcase Capacity** — 7.4 qts. Add 1.0 qts. with filter.

**Oil Filter** — Full flow cartridge type with integral relief valve.

**Normal Oil Pressure** — Pressure maintained at 50-64 psi (3.5-4.5 kg/cm²) by safety valve in oil pressure regulator.

*Fig. 19   Exploded View of Oil Pump Assembly*

**Pressure Regulator** — Located in oil pump, non-adjustable.

## ENGINE OILING SYSTEM

Forced feed system insures positive lubrication through oil holes and galleries in engine block.

### OIL PUMP

1) Remove engine front undercover, engine floor pan. Remove flywheel side cover and flywheel housing undercover. Remove front propeller shaft. Drain engine oil.

2) Remove oil pan. Remove oil strainer and loosen union nuts on oil pump pipe. Remove lock wire and oil pump retaining bolt and remove oil pump and pipe.

3) Straighten union bolt lock washer and remove union bolt, lock washer, gasket, and oil pump inlet pipe from oil pump cover. Remove cover and slide out oil pump driven gear and oil pump drive gear together with oil pump shaft.

4) Inspect gears and housing and check clearance between gear tip and pump body. Measure gear backlash. Place straightedge across pump housing and measure clearance between gear side and straightedge. Place straight edge across pump cover and measure wear. If any parts show wear exceeding specifications or other damage, replace parts as necessary.

### Oil Pump Specifications

| Application | Standard In. (mm) | Wear Limit In. (mm) |
|---|---|---|
| Gear-to-Housing Clearance | .0012-.0043 (.03-.11) | .008 (.2) |
| Gear Backlash | .0020-.0028 (.05-.07) | .0374 (.95) |
| Gear Side Clearance | .0012-.0035 (.03-.09) | .0059 (.15) |
| Cover Wear | | .0059 (.15) |

## ENGINE COOLING

**Thermostat** — Wax pellet type. Begins to open at 180°F (82°C) and is fully opened at 203°F (95°C).

**Coolant Capacity** — All models, 4.5 gallons.

### WATER PUMP

1) Drain cooling system and remove alternator adjusting bar. Remove fan, fan pulley and fan belt. Loosen hose clamps, disconnect radiator lower hose and by-pass hose from water pump.

2) Remove water pump retaining bolts, and remove water pump and gasket. To install, reverse removal procedure using new water pump gasket. Adjust fan/alternator belt tension to provide .5-.6" (13-15 mm) deflection and fan/air pump belt to provide .3-.4" (7-10 mm) deflection.

## 2F 6 CYLINDER (Cont.)

### ENGINE SPECIFICATIONS

| GENERAL SPECIFICATIONS | | | | | | | | | | |
|---|---|---|---|---|---|---|---|---|---|---|
| Year | Displ. | | Carburetor | HP at RPM | Torque (Ft. Lbs. at RPM) | Compr. Ratio | Bore | | Stroke | |
| | cu. ins. | cc | | | | | in. | mm | in. | mm |
| 1978 | 257.9 | 4230 | 1x2-Bbl. | ......... | ......... | 7.8-1 | 3.70 | 94 | 4.00 | 101.6 |

| VALVES | | | | | | | |
|---|---|---|---|---|---|---|---|
| Engine & Valve | Head Diam. In. (mm) | Face Angle | Seat Angle | Seat Width In. (mm) | Stem Diameter In. (mm) | Stem Clearance In. (mm) | Valve Lift In. (mm) |
| 2F Engine Intake | 1.81 (46.0) | 45° | 45° | .055 (1.4) | .3138-.3144 (7.970-7.985) | .0012-.0024 (.03-.06) | ..... |
| Exhaust | 1.48 (37.5) | 45° | 45° | .067 (1.7) | .3134-.3140 (7.960-7.975) | .0016-.0028 (.04-.07) | ..... |

| PISTONS, PINS, RINGS | | | | | | |
|---|---|---|---|---|---|---|
| | PISTONS | PINS | | RINGS | | |
| Engine | Clearance In. (mm) | Piston Fit In. (mm) | Rod Fit In. (mm) | Rings | End Gap In. (mm) | Side Clearance In. (mm) |
| 2F Engine | .0012-.0020 (.03-.05) | .0003-.0005 (.008-.012) | ① | No. 1 | .008-.016 (.20-.40) | .0012-.0024 (.03-.06) |
| | | | | No. 2 | .008-.016 (.20-.40) | .0008-.0024 (.02-.06) |
| | | | | Oil | ..... | ..... |

① — No clearance.

| CRANKSHAFT MAIN & CONNECTING ROD BEARINGS | | | | | | |
|---|---|---|---|---|---|---|
| | MAIN BEARINGS | | | | CONNECTING ROD BEARINGS | |
| Engine | Journal Diam. In. (mm) | Clearance In. (mm) | Thrust Bearing | Crankshaft End Play In. (mm) | Journal Diam. In. (mm) | Clearance In. (mm) | Side Play In. (mm) |
| 2F Engine No. 1 | 2.6367-2.6376 (66.972-66.996) | .0008-.0017 (.020-.044) | No. 3 | .002-.006 (.06-.16) | 2.1252-2.1260 (53.98-54.00) | .0008-.0024 (.020-.060) | .004-.009 (.11-.23) |
| No. 2 | 2.6957-2.6967 (68.472-68.496) | | | | | | |
| No. 3 | 2.7548-2.7557 (69.972-69.996) | | | | | | |
| No. 4 | 2.8139-2.8148 (71.472-71.496) | | | | | | |

## 2F 6 CYLINDER (Cont.)

### ENGINE SPECIFICATIONS (Cont.)

### VALVE SPRINGS

| Engine | Free Length In. (mm) | PRESSURE (LBS.) Lbs. @ In. (kg @ mm) | |
| --- | --- | --- | --- |
| | | Valve Closed | Valve Open |
| 2F Engine | 2.028 (51.5) | 71.7 @ 1.693 (32.5 @ 43.0) | ..... |

### CAMSHAFT

| Engine | Journal Diam. In. (mm) | Clearance In. (mm) | Lobe Lift In. (mm) |
| --- | --- | --- | --- |
| 2F Engine No. 1 | 1.8880-1.8888 (47.955-47.975) | .001-.003 (.025-.075) | ..... |
| No. 2 | 1.8289-1.8297 (46.455-46.475) | | |
| No. 3 | 1.7699-1.7707 (44.955-44.975) | | |
| No. 4 | 1.7108-1.7116 (43.455-43.475) | | |

### TIGHTENING SPECIFICATIONS

| Application | Ft. Lbs. (mkg) |
| --- | --- |
| Cylinder Head | 83-98 (11.5-13.5) |
| Piston Pin Bolt | 39-51 (5.4-7.0) |
| Connecting Rod Bearing Caps | 35-55 (4.8-7.6) |
| Crankshaft Main Bearing Caps | |
| Front, No. 2 & No. 3 | 90-108 (12.5-15) |
| Rear | 76-94 (10.5-13) |
| Camshaft Thrust Plate Bolts | 7-12 (1.0-1.6) |
| Manifold Nuts | |
| Federal | 28-37 (3.5-5.1) |
| California | 36-51 (5.0-7.0) |
| Flywheel Bolts | 59-62 (8.1-8.5) |
| Crankshaft Pulley | 116-145 (16-20) |

## SPITFIRE 4 CYLINDER

### ENGINE CODING

#### ENGINE IDENTIFICATION

Engine number is stamped on a machined flange on left side of cylinder block. Number can be broken down as follows:

**FM1234UCE**

**1st & 2nd Digits** — Model range.
**3rd through 6th Digits** — Sequence build number.
**7th Digit** — USA market.
**8th Digit** — Calif. market (Catalytic Converter).
**9th Digit** — Engine unit.

### ENGINE, CYLINDER HEAD & MANIFOLD

#### ENGINE

**Removal** — 1) Disconnect battery. Drain coolant and engine oil. Remove hood. Remove air cleaner and disconnect emission control lines. From exhaust manifold, separate converter or pipe.

2) Disconnect all necessary water hoses, carburetor throttle linkage, and engine electrical leads. Disconnect and plug fuel lines.

3) Raise vehicle and place on safety stands. Separate exhaust pipe from bracket at transmission, then pull pipe downward past chassis. Take off engine restraint cable located near lower edge of bell housing. Remove lower bell housing nuts and bolts. Place a jack under bell housing.

4) Lower vehicle to ground. Attach hoist to engine. Remove remaining bell housing bolts, then take out starter. Remove motor mount bolts. Remove engine with hoist.

**Installation** — Reverse removal procedures to install engine.

#### INTAKE MANIFOLD

1) Remove air cleaner and disconnect fuel line. Disconnect hose to rocker cover. Unhook throttle return spring. Disconnect and remove throttle cable. Disconnect choke cable, ignition vacuum line and water hoses.

2) Unscrew manifold bolts connecting intake to exhaust manifold. Remove manifold-to-engine bolts and lift out manifold assembly.

#### CYLINDER HEAD

**Removal** — 1) Disconnect battery. Drain coolant. Disconnect emission control hoses and vacuum lines; mark for reinstallation. Loosen alternator belt. Disconnect heater hoses. On federal vehicles, disconnect mixture cable attached at back carburetor. Disconnect fuel evaporation hoses. Separate throttle linkage from carburetors. Remove valve cover. Disconnect heater return line.

2) Remove heat shield from between carburetor and air cleaner. Disconnect exhaust (CAT, if equipped) at manifold flange. Remove water pump. Remove rocker arm assembly. Take out push rods. Disconnect fuel line and remove cylinder head.

**NOTE** — *It may be necessary to remove intake and exhaust manifolds.*

**Installation** — Note following during installation. Make sure "TOP" tag on rear of gasket faces up.

*Fig. 1   Cylinder Head Tightening Sequence*

### VALVES

#### VALVE ARRANGEMENT

E-I-I-E-E-I-I-E (front to rear)

#### VALVE GUIDE SERVICING

1) Inspect valve guide wear by inserting a new valve, lifting it slightly off its seat, and rocking sideways. Movement of valve head across seat should not exceed .020″ (.51 mm).

2) If replacement is required, use valve guide removal tool 60A and adapters to remove and replace valve guide. Guide protrusion above top face of cylinder head must be between .749-.751″ (19.02-19.08 mm).

#### VALVE SPRINGS

Using suitable valve spring compressor, remove valve retainers. Withdraw collars and valves. Check valve springs for cracks, distortion and load length. When any one spring is defective, it is advisable to replace all springs.

**NOTE** — *Valve springs can be removed with cylinder head installed in vehicle. Apply air pressure to spark plug hole of spring (valve) to be removed. Air pressure will prevent valve from dropping.*

#### ROCKER ARM ASSEMBLY

Remove rocker arm cover. Progressively and evenly remove rocker arm pedestal nuts. Lift off rocker arm assembly. Pull cotter pin from front end of rocker shaft. Slide rockers, pedestals, springs and spacers from shaft, noting order for reassembly. Remove screw locating rear pedestal to shaft. Inspect and replace excessively worn parts. To install, reverse removal procedure making sure rear pedestal screw correctly engages rocker shaft.

#### VALVE TAPPETS

Check valve tappets for chips, score marks, ridges or excessive wear. Replace as necessary and ensure tappets are free to slide and rotate.

## SPITFIRE 4 CYLINDER (Cont.)

Fig. 2 Detailed View of Rocker Arm Assembly

Fig. 3 Assembled View of Piston and Connecting Rod

### VALVE CLEARANCE ADJUSTMENT

Disconnect battery, then remove rocker cover and spark plugs. Make necessary adjustment in sequence as indicated in chart below. Turning adjustment screw clockwise will decrease clearance, and turning screw counterclockwise will increase clearance. Proper clearance for intake and exhaust valves is .010" (.25 mm).

| Valves Open① | Valves to Adjust |
|---|---|
| No. 8 & 6 | No. 1 & 3 |
| No. 4 & 7 | No. 5 & 2 |
| No. 1 & 3 | No. 8 & 6 |
| No. 5 & 2 | No. 4 & 7 |

① — Counting from front.

## PISTONS, PINS & RINGS

### OIL PAN

**Removal** — Drain oil pan (Calif. models have a bolt with a banjo and two washers instead of the regular sump plug). Remove the 16 bolts mounting oil pan to engine. Drop out oil pan and remove gasket.

**Installation** — Clean mating surfaces. Lightly coat both sides of gasket with grease or sealer. Refit pan. Make sure longer bolts are fitted to rear of pan.

### PISTON & ROD ASSEMBLY

1) Disconnect battery ground cable and drain engine oil. Remove oil pan and cylinder head as previously described.

2) Remove pickup strainer and bring No. 1 & No. 4 connecting rods to accessible position. Index bearing caps and connecting rods.

3) Remove connecting rod bolts and withdraw bearing caps. Push pistons and connecting rods upward, withdrawing them out top of cylinder. Attach bearing cap to respective connecting rod.

4) To install, position No. 1 and No. 4 connecting rods at bottom dead center. Lube journals and connecting rod assemblies with engine oil. Insert connecting rod assembly into cylinder. Make sure arrow on piston head faces engine FRONT. Stagger piston rings away from thrust side of piston. Make sure connecting rod bearing is away from thrust side of cylinder bore.

5) Fit upper bearing and pull connecting rod over crankshaft. Install lower bearing cap and torque bolts to specifications.

### PISTON PIN REPLACEMENT

1) Remove circlips from pistons and extract piston pin. Separate piston from connecting rod. Inspect connecting rod bushing for wear and replace if necessary.

2) Using suitable press, remove worn bushing and install replacement. Ensure oil hole in new bushing is aligned with hole in connecting rod. Ream bushing to fit piston pin. Piston pin diameter is .8123-.8125" (20.63-20.64 mm) and is a thumb push fit at 68°F (20°C).

### FITTING PISTONS

1) Measure piston across skirt. Check piston for scoring or cracks. Measure cylinder bore and determine if clearance is excessive.

2) Two grades of standard pistons are used; F and G. Identification mark is on piston head and block. One oversize piston is available; .001" (.025 mm). It will be necessary to hone cylinder to insert oversize piston.

3) Install expanding ring in bottom groove of piston with end butting, but not overlapping. Work from bottom of piston and fit bottom rail. Fit top rail into position going over head of piston. Install middle ring with "TOP" facing up. Put on upper compression ring. Stagger rings.

## SPITFIRE 4 CYLINDER (Cont.)

Fig. 4  Order and Detail of Piston Ring Installation

## CRANKSHAFT MAIN & CONNECTING ROD BEARINGS

### MAIN & CONNECTING ROD BEARINGS

1)  Remove engine, cylinder head and oil pan. Remove main and rod bearing caps. Slightly push up connecting rod assembly but do not dislodge it from cylinder. Remove upper connecting rod bearings.

2)  Remove crankshaft and upper main bearings. Remove thrust washers from rear main bearing. Examine all bearing journals and determine if regrinding is necessary.

3)  Examine each bearing and replace as required. Bearings are available in .010", .020", and .030" (.25, .51, and .76 mm) undersizes. Any undersize crankshaft which is installed or has been installed in service should have a size marking stamped in which corresponds to similar marking on bearings.

4)  To install main and connecting rod bearings, reverse removal procedure, noting the following: bend over locking tabs, if equipped.

### CRANKSHAFT END PLAY

NOTE — End play can be adjusted with engine installed in vehicle. Procedure given is with engine removed. Difference occurs as to where dial indicator is mounted.

Use a dial indicator and set it up as shown in Fig. 5. Measure end play by prying against crankshaft and reading dial indicator. Obtained value must lie within specifications. If end play is exceeded, fit oversize thrust washers to rear main bearing.

### REAR MAIN BEARING OIL SEAL

1)  Remove rear transmission adaptor plate. Remove two bolts attaching oil pan to seal housing and seven bolts attaching seal housing to crankcase. Remove seal housing and press out old seal.

Fig. 5  Using Dial Indicator to Check Crankshaft End Play

2)  Coat O.D. of seal with grease and press seal into housing with lip facing crankshaft. Install a new gasket coated with sealing compound. Carefully install seal housing with a plain copper washer on top bolt.

Fig. 6  Fitting Rear Main Bearing Seal Housing into Place

## CAMSHAFT

### ENGINE FRONT COVER & OIL SEAL

**Removal** — Remove radiator. Remove left side inner fender panel. Remove air pump, alternator, fan, and crankshaft pulley. Remove air pump/alternator brackets, adjusting links and spacer. Take out timing cover mounting hardware. Loosen and remove cover. Press out old seal. Refit new seal with open side facing engine.

**Installation** — Note for installation that chain tensioner is inside cover. To facilitate cover installation, use a short piece of welding rod bent 90° to hold tensioner off chain.

## SPITFIRE 4 CYLINDER (Cont.)

### CAMSHAFT

**Removal – 1)** Disconnect battery. Remove radiator. Remove cylinder head. Remove water pump and fan. Remove alternator, air pump, crankshaft pulley, timing cover and chain.

**2)** Remove two bolts mounting camshaft keeper plate, then withdraw plate. Remove cam followers and index mark for reinstallation. Take out distributor drive shaft and gear. Remove fuel pump. Withdraw camshaft.

**Installation –** To install, reverse removal procedure and note the following: Lube camshaft bearing journals. Fit keeper plate with two bolts. Check camshaft end play. Pull camshaft against keeper plate and insert feeler gauge between camshaft and plate. End play must not exceed .004-.008" (.110-.216 mm). Oversize thrust plates are available to bring end play within specifications.

**Fig. 7   Positioning Camshaft Thrust Plate**

### TIMING CHAIN

**Removal – 1)** Disconnect battery. Remove timing chain cover. Take off oil thrower. Rotate crankshaft until index marks on crankshaft and camshaft sprockets align. Make sure crankshaft keyway is at 12 o'clock and that camshaft punch mark aligns with crankshaft keyway.

**2)** Bend back camshaft nut lock tabs and remove bolts mounting camshaft sprocket to camshaft. Remove camshaft sprocket and timing chain.

**NOTE –** *DO NOT rotate camshaft or crankshaft while chain is off sprockets.*

**Installation – 1)** Remove crankshaft key. Refit both sprockets. Check alignment with straightedge. Install selective fit shims to crankshaft if misalignment occurs. Install key.

**2)** Fit chain to sprockets. Install sprocket, keep index marks aligned. Slightly secure camshaft sprocket. Measure chain deflection along slack run of chain. ⅜" (9.53 mm) slack should not be exceeded. Reverse removal procedure for remaining components.

### VALVE TIMING

**1)** Remove valve cover. Adjust No. 7 and No. 8 valves to .080" (2.03 mm) clearance. Turn crankshaft until No. 1 piston is at TDC, compression stroke (pulley "V" aligned with zero line on timing cover scale).

**2)** Insert feeler gauge between valve tip and rocker pad to make sure No. 1 and No. 2 valves are fully closed. Make sure No. 7 and No. 8 valve clearances are unchanged (use two feeler gauges). Move crankshaft as necessary to maintain equality.

**3)** Readjust No. 7 and No. 8 valves to and all other valves to .010" (.25 mm). Replace rocker cover.

**NOTE –** *If chain or sprockets were removed, make sure timing marks are aligned when sprockets are reinstalled. See Timing Chain Removal and Installation.*

**Fig. 8   Camshaft and Crankshaft Alignment**

### ENGINE OILING

### ENGINE OILING SYSTEM

Oil is drawn from engine by a rotor type pump which discharges via a nonadjustable relief valve to a full-flow filter. Cylinder bores, pistons and piston pins are splash lubricated all other components are oiled through drilled passages.

**Crankcase Capacity (Drain and Refill) –** 4.2 quarts.

**Oil Filter –** Full-flow type. Disposable cannister.

**Oil Pressure Relief Valve –** Located in cylinder block beneath oil filter. Check relief valve spring free length; it should be 1.53" (38.8 mm).

## SPITFIRE 4 CYLINDER (Cont.)

### OIL PUMP

1) Remove oil pan previously described. Remove three bolts securing oil pump to crankcase. Lift from vehicle and place in a vise.

2) Place a straightedge across pump body, then use a feeler gauge to check clearance between rotor face and straight edge; it should be .004" (.10 mm).

3) Check clearance between inner rotor and outer rotor. Clearance must not exceed .010" (.25 mm).

4) Check clearance between outer rotor and body; it must not exceed .008" (.20 mm).

5) Check cover plate for scoring, and test on a surface plate for distortion. Examine pump spindle bearing surface in body for excessive wear.

6) Reassembly oil pump installing any new parts as necessary to satisfy specifications. To install oil pump, reverse removal procedure.

### ENGINE COOLING

**Cooling System Capacity** — 4.8 qts.

### WATER PUMP

Drain cooling system. Remove radiator hoses, then unbolt and remove radiator. Detach fan belt. Unscrew three nuts securing water pump flange to thermostat and pump housing. Withdraw water pump. Remove fan. To install, reverse procedure.

## ENGINE SPECIFICATIONS

| GENERAL SPECIFICATIONS | | | | | | | | | | | |
|---|---|---|---|---|---|---|---|---|---|---|---|
| Year | Displ. | | Carburetor | HP at RPM | Torque (Ft. Lbs. at RPM) | Compr. Ratio | Bore | | Stroke | |
| | cu. ins. | cc | | | | | in. | mm | in. | mm |
| 1978 | 91 | 1493 | 1x1-Bbl. | .... | .... | 7.5-1 | 2.90 | 73.7 | 3.44 | 87.5 |

| VALVES In. (mm) | | | | | | | |
|---|---|---|---|---|---|---|---|
| Engine & Valve | Head Diam. | Face Angle | Seat Angle | Seat Width | Stem Diameter | Stem Clearance | Valve Lift |
| 1493 cc Intake | 1.375-1.385 (34.97-35.01) | 45° | 45° | .248-.250① (6.29-6.35) | .3107-3113 (8.05-8.12) | .0008-.0023 (.020-.060) | ... |
| Exhaust | 1.168-1.172 (29.66-29.76) | 45° | 45° | .248-.250① (6.29-6.35) | .3100-.3105 (7.874-7.887) | .0015-.0030 (.038-.076) | ... |

① — With catalytic converter .258-.260" (31.95-31.00 mm).

| PISTONS, PINS, RINGS In. (mm) | | | | | | |
|---|---|---|---|---|---|---|
| | PISTONS | PINS | | RINGS | | |
| Engine | Clearance | Piston Fit | Rod Fit | Rings | End Gap | Side Clearance |
| 1493 cc | .002-.003 (.05-.07) | Push Fit | Push Fit | No. 1 & 2 | .012-.022 (.30-.55) ① | .002-.0025 (.051-.063) |
| | | | | Oil | | .0025-.0035 (.063-.088) |

① — Ends butt.

# Triumph Engines

## SPITFIRE 4 CYLINDER (Cont.)
### ENGINE SPECIFICATIONS (Cont.)

### CRANKSHAFT MAIN & CONNECTING ROD BEARINGS

| Engine | MAIN BEARINGS | | | | CONNECTING ROD BEARINGS | | |
| | Journal Diam. In. (mm) | Clearance In. (mm) | Thrust Bearing | Crankshaft End Play In. (mm) | Journal Diam. In. (mm) | Clearance In. (mm) | Side Play In. (mm) |
|---|---|---|---|---|---|---|---|
| 1493 cc | 2.3115-2.3120 (58.713-58.725) | ... | Rear | .004-.008 (.10-.20) | 1.8750-1.8755 (47.625-47.638) | .... | .... |

### VALVE SPRINGS

| Engine | Free Length In. (mm) | PRESSURE Lbs. @ In. (kg @ mm) | |
| | | Valve Closed | Valve Open |
|---|---|---|---|
| 1493 cc | 1.52 (38.6) | ...@1.342 ...@(34.1) | 20 @ .875 (2.8 @ 22.2) |

### VALVE TIMING

| Engine | INTAKE | | EXHAUST | |
| | Open (BTDC) | Close (ABDC) | Open (BBDC) | Close (ATDC) |
|---|---|---|---|---|
| 1493cc | 18° | 58° | 58° | 18° |

### CAMSHAFT In. (mm)

| Engine | Journal Diam. | Clearance | Lobe Lift |
|---|---|---|---|
| 1493 cc | 1.9659-1.9664① (49.934-49.947) | ② | ... |

① — Intermediate Journal 1.9649-1.9654″ (49.908-49.921).

② — End play should be .004-.008″ (.11-.21 mm).

### TIGHTENING SPECIFICATIONS

| Application | Ft. Lbs. (mkg) |
|---|---|
| Connecting Rod Bolts | |
|   Color Dyed | 45 (6.2) |
|   Phosphated | 46 (6.4) |
| Sprocket-to-Camshaft | 24 (3.3) |
| Crankshaft Pulley Nut | 150 (20.7) |
| Cylinder Head Bolts | 46 (6.4) |
| Flywheel-to-Crankshaft | |
|   Cadmium Plated Bolt | 40 (5.5) |
|   Parkarised Bolt | 45 (6.2) |
| Intake-to-Exhaust Manifold | 14 (1.9) |
| Manifold-to-Head | 25 (3.5) |
| Main Bearing Cap Bolts | 65 (9.0) |
| Oil Pan Bolts | 20 (2.8) |
| Oil Seal Block Screw | 14 (1.9) |
| Rocker Cover-to-Head | 2 (0.3) |
| Rocker Shaft-to-Head | 34 (4.7) |
| Rear Crankshaft Seal | 20 (2.8) |
| Spark Plugs | 20 (2.8) |
| Timing Cover-to-Front Plate | |
|   3/8 ″ Screw | 10 (1.4) |
|   7/8 ″ Screw | 20 (2.8) |
|   Stud | 16 (2.2) |
|   Bolt | 20 (2.8) |
| Water Pump-to-Head | 20 (2.8) |

## TRIUMPH TR7 4 CYLINDER

## ENGINE CODING

### ENGINE IDENTIFICATION

Engine number is stamped on cylinder head and may be seen by looking down between intake manifold branches.

### CL(CV)12345UE

**1st & 2nd Digits** — Model.
**3rd through 7th Digits** — Serial number.
**8th Digit** — "U" denotes USA specification engine.
**9th Digit** — "E" denotes engine unit (may not be in all codes).

Starting serial number of 1978 TR7 is ACW40000U.

## ENGINE, CYLINDER HEAD & MANIFOLD

### ENGINE

1) Disconnect battery and bottom radiator hose, allow coolant to drain. Remove hood, radiator, air cleaner duct and air cleaner hot air hose. Disconnect heater hoses at firewall and brake booster vacuum hose at intake manifold. Disconnect vapor canister hoses from canister, cooling system expansion hose from thermostat housing and vacuum hose from intake manifold to anti-runon valve.

2) Disconnect all electrical leads to engine, fuel line at carburetor(s), choke cable from rear carburetor and throttle cable from throttle linkage. Remove gearshift lever by first removing shift boot, then releasing bayonet cap securing lever to transmission extension. Raise front and rear of vehicle and place on stands. Disconnect propeller shaft from transmission.

3) Disconnect wiring from transmission and remove exhaust downpipe from manifold. Disconnect speedometer cable and remove clutch slave cylinder. Remove complete engine torque strap assembly (if equipped) and disconnect wiring from starter. Release wiring harness from clutch housing clips. Remove clutch housing bolts necessary to remove clips and release clutch hydraulic line.

4) Remove engine ground strap and hood lock from firewall. Relieve pressure from air conditioning system (if equipped) and disconnect hoses from compressor. Using a lifting sling with a 23" (58.4 cm) leg to rear lift eye and a 18" (45.7 cm) leg to front eye, raise hoist to remove weight of engine.

5) Disconnect right side engine mount and remove five bolts securing rear crossmember to body. Raise rear of vehicle. Hoist engine and remove left side engine mount. Continue raising engine and work it away from vehicle. To install, reverse removal procedure.

### INTAKE MANIFOLD

Disconnect battery and drain cooling system, including cylinder block. Remove ducts and air cleaner. Disconnect all hoses, wiring and control cables from manifold and carburetor(s). Remove distributor cap and six manifold bolts. Lift out manifold complete with carburetor(s). To install manifold, reverse removal procedure.

**Fig. 1  Cylinder Head Tightening Sequence**

### CYLINDER HEAD

1) Remove intake manifold as previously described. Remove camshaft cover and semi-circular grommet to gain access to camshaft sprocket nut. Crank engine until camshaft sprocket bottom bolt is accessible and remove bottom bolt. Anchor camshaft sprocket to support bracket. Crank engine so that timing mark on camshaft flange is in line with groove in camshaft front bearing cap and distributor rotor points to manifold rear attachment bolt hole in cylinder head.

2) Unlock and remove top sprocket retaining bolt. Disconnect air hose from air injection check valve and disconnect water pipe from thermostat housing. Disconnect exhaust pipe from manifold. Remove the two cylinder head to timing cover nuts and bolts and loosen cylinder head nuts and bolts in reverse of tightening sequence (See Fig. 1). Remove cylinder head complete with exhaust manifold. To install, reverse removal procedure and tighten bolts to specifications in sequence shown in Fig. 1.

## VALVES

### VALVE ARRANGEMENT

E-I-I-E-E-I-I-E (front to rear).

### VALVE GUIDE SERVICING

1) Inspect valve guide wear by inserting a new valve, lifting it slightly from its seat, and rocking sideways. Movement of valve head across seat should not exceed .020" (.508 mm).

2) If replacement is required, use valve guide removal and installation tool S-60A and adapters to remove and replace valve guide. After guides are installed, ream out guide using a .3130" (7.95 mm) reamer.

### VALVE SEAT INSERT SERVICING

1) If valve seat inserts are too badly damaged to be refaced, replace inserts as follows: Machine-out existing inserts taking care not to damage insert bores in cylinder head. Machine in-

## TRIUMPH TR7 4 CYLINDER (Cont.)

take valve seat bore to a diameter of 1.665-1.666" (42.29-42.32 mm) or exhaust valve seat bore to a diameter of 1.329-1.330" (33.75-33.78 mm).

2) Heat cylinder head uniformly to a temperature of 356°F (180°C) and immediately install new valve seats squarely into cylinder head. Allow cylinder head to cool and machine valve seats to an inclusive angle of 89°.

### VALVE SPRINGS

With cylinder head removed, remove camshaft bearing caps (check that caps are numbered for reassembly in same position) and camshaft. Remove tappets and adjusting shims keeping them in correct order for reassembly. With spring compressor, depress spring and remove valve keepers. Release spring and remove spring and valve collar. To install, reverse removal procedure.

### VALVE CLEARANCE ADJUSTMENT

**NOTE** — This operation may be performed with cylinder head on the bench. When on the bench, turn camshaft using a wrench on hexagon at rear of camshaft.

1) Disconnect battery and remove camshaft cover if cylinder head is installed on engine. Loosen camshaft bearing caps and retighten to specifications. Rotate camshaft or engine and check and record clearance of each valve using a feeler gauge between cam heel and tappet. Maximum clearance exists when cam is straight up.

2) If all clearances are correct, adjustment procedure is completed. If any clearances are incorrect, proceed as follows: Remove camshaft and withdraw each tappet and adjusting shim where clearance requires adjustment, keeping tappets and shims in sequence.

3) Measure shim thickness and add measured valve clearance to arrive at total clearance. Subtract proper valve clearance from total clearance to determine needed shim thickness. Install tappets with correct shims then install camshaft. Recheck valve clearance and install camshaft cover.

| Application | Valve Clearance |
|---|---|
| Intake | .008" (.2 mm) |
| Exhaust | .018" (.5 mm) |

## PISTONS, PINS & RINGS

### OIL PAN

1) Disconnect battery and remove fresh air duct and fan shroud. Raise vehicle and drain engine oil. Remove two bolts securing coupling plate on bottom of oil pan to clutch housing. Remove engine torque strap assembly. Support front of engine using hoist or jack. **NOTE** — A bracket, made of angle iron, may be fabricated to bolt into lower timing cover bolt holes. Engine may then be supported by a jack via the fabricated bracket.

2) Remove two engine right side mounting bolts, then remove left side engine mounting to sub-frame nut. Remove oil pan nuts and bolts. Raise engine sufficiently to enable oil pan,

complete with left side engine mounting and cross-member to be removed. To install, reverse removal procedure.

### PISTON & ROD ASSEMBLY

Connecting rods and rod caps are numbered. Note positioning and location before disassembly.

**Removal** — With oil pan and cylinder head removed, unscrew rod nuts and withdraw bearing caps. Place protective sleeves over rod bolts and push out rod and piston. Rotate crankshaft as necessary to gain access to piston and rod assemblies.

**Installation** — 1) Stager piston ring gaps, lubricate pistons and rings and, using a ring compressor, place piston in cylinder bore ensuring that raised flat portion of piston crown is towards right side of engine.

**NOTE** — Some pistons may have arrows stamped on both sides of skirt, on the piston pin bore side, to indicate direction of pin off-set. Ensure that these arrows point to right side of engine also. Alternatively some pistons may have an arrow on the crown. These piston assemblies must be installed with arrow pointing to front of engine.

2) Install bearing halves in connecting rod and cap and pull connecting rod onto crankpins. Install bearing caps to their respective numbered connecting rod making sure the bearing keeper recesses in connecting rods and caps are on the same side. Install new nuts and tighten.

### PISTON PIN REPLACEMENT

1) Remove circlips from pistons and extract piston pin. Separate piston from connecting rod. Inspect connecting rod bushing for wear and replace if necessary.

Should be Butted, Not Overlapping

**Fig. 2   View Showing Correct Piston Ring Installation**

## TRIUMPH TR7 4 CYLINDER (Cont.)

**2)** Using a press, remove worn bushing and install replacement. Ensure oil hole in new bushing is aligned with hole in connecting rod. Ream bushing to fit piston pin. Piston pin diameter is .9374-.9376" (23.810-23.815 mm).

### FITTING PISTONS

Inspect and measure cylinder for wear or taper. Measure piston diameter and determine if clearance is correct. Install expanding ring in bottom groove of piston with ends butting but not overlapping. From bottom of piston install bottom rail and from top, upper rail. Install middle ring with word "TOP" facing upward (see Fig. 2). Install upper compression ring and stagger ring gaps.

**NOTE** — Oversize rings are available in .010 and .020" (.254 and .508 mm) oversizes.

## CRANKSHAFT MAIN & CONNECTING ROD BEARINGS

### MAIN & CONNECTING ROD BEARINGS

**1)** Remove engine and separate engine and transmission. Remove clutch, flywheel, engine rear adapter plate, oil pan and dipstick. Remove rear main bearing oil seal, timing chain cover, oil pickup screen and oil slinger. Remove crankshaft sprocket, drive key and shims.

**2)** Remove connecting rod bearing caps and slightly push up connecting rod assembly but do not dislodge it from cylinder. Remove upper and lower connecting rod bearings and install protectors over connecting rod bolts. Remove timing chain and main bearing caps. Lift out crankshaft. Remove pilot bushing, upper and lower main bearing inserts and thrust washers.

**3)** Examine all bearing journals and determine if regrinding is necessary. When regrinding crankshaft, do not grind journal diameter to less than specified minimum diameter. Examine each bearing half and replace any damaged bearings. Bearings are available in various oversizes. To install, reverse removal procedure making sure that grooves in thrust washers face outward.

### Minimum Crankshaft Regrind Diameters

| Application | In. (mm) |
|---|---|
| Main Journal | 2.0860-2.0865 (52.984-52.997) |
| Connecting Rod | 1.7100-1.7105 (43.434-43.447) |

### CRANKSHAFT END PLAY

Using a feeler gauge or dial indicator, measure crankshaft end play by levering crankshaft back and forth. Value must be within specifications. If not, thrust washers are available in various oversizes.

### REAR MAIN BEARING OIL SEAL

**1)** Disconnect battery and remove transmission, clutch and flywheel. Remove two rear oil pan bolts, loosen two right side

rear and one left side rear oil pan bolts. Remove six bolts securing rear main bearing oil seal housing to crankcase. Press oil seal out of housing.

Fig. 3   **Exploded View of Rear Main Bearing Oil Seal**

**2)** Lubricate outer diameter of new seal and press it squarely into housing with lip facing crankshaft. Clean gasket area and install new gasket using sealing compound. Lubricate crankshaft and carefully ease seal housing into position on two dowels. Install six retaining bolts noting that two lower bolts are longer. Evenly tighten bolts then install two pan bolts removed previously. Tighten all oil pan bolts and continue assembly in reverse of disassembly.

## CAMSHAFT

### ENGINE FRONT COVER & OIL SEAL

**1)** Disconnect battery and remove crankshaft pulleys after first loosening drive belts and removing cooling fan. Remove alternator and mounting brackets. Remove air pump and bracket, and diverter valve and bracket. Remove air conditioning compressor strut (if equipped).

**2)** Remove two bolts and nuts securing front cover to cylinder head. Remove four bolts securing compressor to engine and three compressor adjusting bolts (if equipped). Remove two front oil pan bolts. Remove front cover center attachment bolt and bottom left side bolt. Remove front cover and gaskets and pry out old seal.

**3)** Dip new seal in engine oil and with lip facing inward, tap in squarely into front cover until flush with cover. Install front cover on engine in reverse of removal procedure using new gaskets. **NOTE** — Front oil seal may be replaced with front cover installed by first removing crankshaft pulleys and prying out old seal.

## TRIUMPH TR7 4 CYLINDER (Cont.)

### CAMSHAFT

1) Disconnect battery and remove camshaft cover. Crank engine until camshaft timing mark is 180° from groove in camshaft front bearing cap. Unlock and remove exposed camshaft sprocket retaining bolt. Crank engine so that timing mark on camshaft flange is exactly in line with groove in camshaft front bearing cap. Secure sprocket to support bracket with a suitable nut.

2) Unlock and remove remaining sprocket retaining bolt. Evenly loosen camshaft bearing cap nuts and remove bolts and washers. Check that bearing caps are numbered for identification and remove caps. Remove camshaft. To install, reverse removal procedure making sure timing marks are correctly aligned.

### INTERMEDIATE SHAFT

1) Disconnect battery and remove fresh air duct, radiator, air conditioning condenser (if equipped), engine front cover, intake manifold, water pump cover and impeller, fuel pump, and camshaft cover. Crank engine so that timing mark on camshaft flange is in line with groove on front bearing cap. Remove distributor cap and check that rotor points to last intake manifold bolt hole in cylinder head, which indicates number one cylinder TDC.

2) Remove the distributor, hydraulic chain tensioner and adjustable timing chain guide. Remove two Allen head screws and withdraw intermediate shaft keeper plate. Lift timing chain clear of sprocket and pull out intermediate shaft (complete with sprocket). Clamp intermediate shaft in a vise and remove sprocket retaining bolt, tab washer and sprocket. To install, reverse removal procedure, making sure valve timing is set correctly and adjusting timing chain tension.

### TIMING CHAIN

1) Remove engine front cover, camshaft cover and distributor cap. Disconnect camshaft sprocket as described under *Camshaft Removal.* Make sure that camshaft timing marks are aligned when engine is TDC, No. 1 cylinder compression stroke. Remove hydraulic chain tensioner and guide plate.

2) Remove locking bolt from adjustable chain guide and common bolt securing adjustable guide and camshaft sprocket support bracket. Remove adjustable guide. Remove bolt securing camshaft support bracket and fixed guide while holding camshaft sprocket. Remove fixed guide and release chain from intermediate shaft and camshaft sprockets. Remove (upward) camshaft sprocket and bracket along with timing chain. To install, reverse removal procedure and check valve and intermediate shaft timing.

3) Set chain tension as follows: Insert a .100" (2.54 mm) feeler gauge between chain slipper and tensioner body (see Fig. 4). Loosen three chain guide retainer bolts and press down on timing chain guide between camshaft and intermediate shaft sprockets until feeler gauge is a sliding fit. Hold guide in this position and tighten adjustable guide bolt first, then two remaining bolts. Remove feeler gauge and continue reassembly.

### VALVE TIMING

Crank engine until timing mark on crankshaft pulley coincides with zero mark on front cover scale. At this time, distributor

rotor should point to rear bolt securing intake manifold to cylinder head and timing mark on camshaft flange is in line with groove in camshaft front bearing cap. To adjust timing it is necessary to remove timing chain.

**Fig. 4    Adjusting Timing Chain Tension**

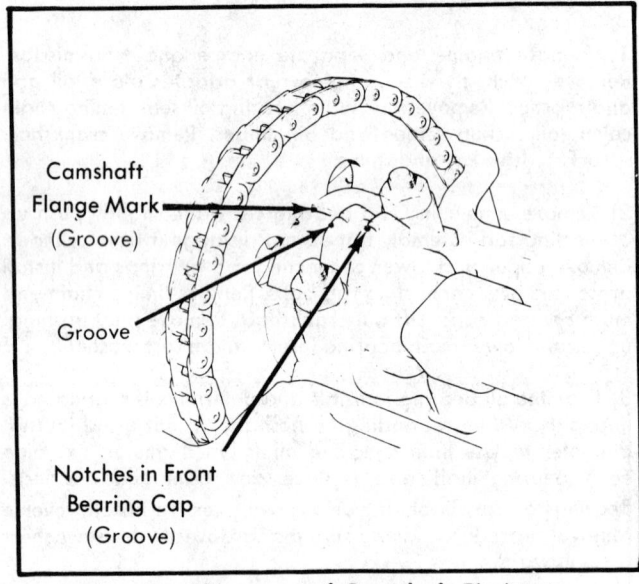

**Fig. 5    Alignment of Camshaft Timing**

## ENGINE OILING

### ENGINE OILING SYSTEM

Oil is drawn from engine by a rotor type pump which discharges via a nonadjustable relief valve to a full-flow filter. Cylinder bores, pistons and piston pins are splash lubricated. All other components are oiled through drilled passages.

**Crankcase Capacity** — 9.5 pts. (including filter).

**Oil Filter** — Full-flow, paper element type filter.

**Oil Pressure Relief Valve** — Nonadjustable.

## TRIUMPH TR7 4 CYLINDER (Cont.)

### OIL PUMP

1) Disconnect battery and raise vehicle. Remove two bolts securing clutch slave cylinder to clutch housing. **NOTE** — *Use care when removing slave cylinder that clutch release mechanism doesn't become dislodged. If mechanism does dislodge, transmission will have to be removed to repair it.* Leave hydraulic line attached and wire slave cylinder out of way.

2) Remove clutch housing nut and bolt, then remove four oil pump retaining bolts and washers. Remove pump from engine complete with hexagonal drive shaft. Remove "O" ring. To disassemble pump, first remove drive shaft. Remove two screws and lift off pump cover from body. Remove pump rotors and "O" ring. Remove cotter pin from pump body and pull out relief valve plug, spring and valve. Remove "O" ring from relief valve plug.

3) Clean all components and install rotors in pump body, ensuring that chamfered edge of outer rotor is at driving end of rotor pocket. Place a straight edge across pump body and with a feeler gauge check clearance between rotor and straight edge. This clearance should be .004" (.1 mm)

4) With a feeler gauge, check clearance between outer rotor and pump body. Clearance must not exceed .008" (.2 mm). Now check the clearance between the inner and outer rotors with a feeler gauge. This clearance must not exceed .010" (.25 mm).

5) Reassemble and install oil pump in reverse of disassembly, using new "O" rings and making sure large end of relief valve is installed inward so spring will engage small end of valve.

**Fig. 6   View Showing Oil Pump Checking Points**

### ENGINE COOLING

#### WATER PUMP

1) Disconnect battery and remove intake manifold. Disconnect hoses from water pump cover and remove three bolts securing pump cover to engine. Lift off cover and gaskets. Turn impeller center bolt clockwise until either water pump is released from intermediate shaft drive gear and can be removed, or center bolt is removed. If center bolt comes out, use impact tool (4235A) and adapter (S4235A/10) to remove pump.

2) To overhaul pump, remove center bolt if not previously removed. Use a drift and support tool to remove impeller from shaft. Invert pump assembly (drive gear up) and drift shaft from housing. Remove "O" ring, graphite seal, water slinger, oil seal and circlip from pump shaft. Again invert shaft and drift shaft from bearing. Remove oil slinger. Remove "O" rings from housing.

3) To assemble, reverse disassembly procedure using new seals and "O" rings and noting the following: Make sure oil slinger dish is towards gear. Flat face of oil seal should face bearing. Dish of water slinger should be towards bearing. Install graphite seal with flat face towards bearing.

4) Place pump in housing ensuring that pump and jackshaft gear, mesh correctly and that pump is properly seated. **CAUTION** — *Use of force or impact to seat pump will damage pump.* Ensure gasket surfaces are clean and temporarily install pump cover. Using feeler gauges, check that gap between pump cover and engine is equal, equalize gap by adjusting bolts.

5) Select water pump cover gaskets to equal the gap noted in step 4) plus .010-.020" (.25-.5 mm) to provide running clearance. Remove pump cover, install selected gaskets, reinstall cover and tighten bolts to specifications. Complete installation in reverse of removal procedure.

**Thermostat** — Begins to open at about 190°F (88°C).

**Cooling System Capacity** — 15.5 pts. (including heater).

**Radiator Cap** — 15 psi (1.05 kg/cm²).

**Fig. 7   Exploded View of Water Pump Assembly**

# Triumph Engines

## TR7 4 CYLINDER (Cont.)

### ENGINE SPECIFICATIONS

| | GENERAL SPECIFICATIONS | | | | | | | | | |
|---|---|---|---|---|---|---|---|---|---|---|
| Year | Displ. | | Carburetor | HP at RPM | Torque (Ft. Lbs. at RPM) | Compr. Ratio | Bore | | Stroke | |
| | cu. ins. | cc | | | | | in. | mm | in. | mm |
| 1978 | 122 | 1998 | 2x1-Bbl. | ..... | ..... | 8.0-1 | 3.56 | 90.3 | 3.07 | 78.0 |

| | VALVES | | | | | | |
|---|---|---|---|---|---|---|---|
| Engine & Valve | Head Diam. In. (mm) | Face Angle | Seat Angle | Seat Width In. (mm) | Stem Diameter In. (mm) | Stem Clearance In. (mm) | Valve Lift In. (mm) |
| 1998 cc Intake | 1.560 (39.62) | 45° | 44.5° | ..... | .3103-.3113 (7.881-7.907) | .0017-.0023 (.043-.058) | ..... |
| Exhaust | 1.280 (32.51) | 45° | 44.5° | ..... | .3098-.3106 (7.87-7.89) | .0014-.0030 (.035-.076) | ..... |

| | PISTONS, PINS, RINGS | | | | | |
|---|---|---|---|---|---|---|
| | PISTONS | PINS | | RINGS | | |
| Engine | Clearance In. (mm) | Piston Fit In. (mm) | Rod Fit In. (mm) | Rings | End Gap In. (mm) | Side Clearance In. (mm) |
| 1998 cc | .0005-.0015 (.013-.038) | 0-.0004 (0-.010) | .0001-.0006 (.003-.015) | No. 1 | .015-.025 (.39-.64) | .0019-.0039 (.048-.099) |
| | | | | No. 2 | .015-.025 (.39-.64) | .0015-.0025 (.038-.064) |
| | | | | Oil | .015-.055 (.39-1.40) | Ends Butted |

| | CRANKSHAFT MAIN & CONNECTING ROD BEARINGS | | | | | | |
|---|---|---|---|---|---|---|---|
| | MAIN BEARINGS | | | | CONNECTING ROD BEARINGS | | |
| Engine | Journal Diam. In. (mm) | Clearance In. (mm) | Thrust Bearing | Crankshaft End Play In. (mm) | Journal Diam. In. (mm) | Clearance In. (mm) | Side Play In. (mm) |
| 1998 cc | 2.1260-2.1265 (54.000-54.013) | .0012-.0022 (.030-.055) | Center | .003-.011 (.08-.28) | 1.7500-1.7505 (44.450-44.463) | .0008-.0023 (.020-.058) | .006-.013 (.15-.33) |

## TRIUMPH TR7 4 CYLINDER (Cont.)
### ENGINE SPECIFICATIONS (Cont.)

| VALVE SPRINGS | | | |
|---|---|---|---|
| Engine | Free Length In. (mm) | PRESSURE Lbs. @ In. (kg @ mm) | |
| | | Valve Closed | Valve Open |
| 1998 cc | 1.60 (40.64) | ..... | ..... |

| VALVE TIMING | | | | |
|---|---|---|---|---|
| | INTAKE | | EXHAUST | |
| Engine | Open (BTDC) | Close (ALDC) | Open (BLDC) | Close (ATDC) |
| 1998 cc | 16° | 56° | 56° | 16° |

### TIGHTENING SPECIFICATIONS

| Application | Ft. Lbs. (mkg) |
|---|---|
| Main Bearing Caps | 65 (9.0) |
| Camshaft Sprocket Bolt | 10 (1.4) |
| Camshaft Bearing Caps | 14 (1.9) |
| Connecting Rod Bolts | 45 (6.2) |
| Crankshaft Pulley Bolt | 120 (16.5) |
| Cylinder Head Bolts (Nuts) | 55 (7.6) |
| Idler Shaft Sprocket Bolt | 38 (5.3) |
| Timing Chain Tensioner-to-Block | 7 (.9) |
| Timing Chain Support Brackets & Guides | 20 (2.8) |
| Flywheel-to-Crankshaft | 45 (6.2) |

# Volkswagen Engines

## TYPE 1 1600 cc 4 CYLINDER

### ENGINE CODING

#### ENGINE IDENTIFICATION

Engine identification is determined by first digits of serial number. Engine serial number is stamped on crankcase under generator support flange

| Application | Engine Code |
|---|---|
| Type 1 | |
| Fuel Injected .................................................................. AJ | |

### ENGINE, CYLINDER HEAD & MANIOLD

#### ENGINE

**Removal — 1)** Remove air cleaner. Drain oil. Disconnect hoses between fan housing and heat exchangers. Disconnect battery ground, coil wires, alternator, and oil pressure switch.

**2)** Disconnect fuel injection wiring harness from coil, injectors, crankcase, temperature sensors, air intake distributor and other related parts. Make sure to index mark each wire for reinstallation.

**3)** From under vehicle, disconnect starter electrical wires. Disconnect fuel line from pressure regulator and plug hose. Unhook back-up lights.

**4)** Disconnect throttle cable. Remove small cover plates over preheater pipe connections. On models equipped with automatic stick shift, disconnect lead and vacuum hose from control valve. Disconnect transmission lines and plug. Disconnect heater control cables. Disconnect heater ducting at front of heat exchangers.

**5)** On models equipped with automatic stick shift, remove four converter to drive plate bolts. Remove nuts from lower engine mounting studs. Place a jack under engine and raise until squarely seated against crankcase. Remove left side upper mounting bolt and right side nut and bolt. Slide engine rearward until clear. Lower jack and continue to pull engine to rear.

**NOTE** — *After engine has been removed, install a retainer to bell housing to keep torque converter in place.*

**Installation** — To install, reverse removal procedure and note: Lubricate transmission input shaft and clutch release bearing. Also, lightly lubricate starter (Bosch only) drive bushing with multi-purpose grease. Adjust clutch free play. Make sure ignition timing and accelerator control linkage are properly adjusted.

#### INTAKE MANIFOLD

**Removal — 1)** Remove fan housing. Disconnect preheating pipes at flanges. Remove injectors, intake air sensor and air intake distributor from crankcase.

**2)** Remove nuts holding manifold. Disconnect all air and vacuum hoses from air intake distributor. Be sure to index each item for reinstallation.

**3)** Disconnect exhaust line from EGR valve by removing mounting nuts. Lift off manifold with intake air distributor.

**Installation** — To install, reverse removal procedure and replace gaskets where necessary.

#### CYLINDER HEAD

**NOTE** — *Engine must be removed from vehicle, and manifolds removed, before removing cylinder heads. If cylinders are not to be removed, use retaining device to keep cylinders from pulling free.*

*Fig. 1  Push Rod Tube Installation with Detail of Seal Fit*

**Removal — 1)** Remove engine and intake manifold as previously outlined. Remove muffler and heat exchangers. Disconnect spark plug wires at spark plugs. Remove deflector cover plates from under cylinder cover plates and remove cylinder cover plates.

**2)** On fuel injected engines remove lower left side warm air duct. Remove bolt securing thermostat to bracket and unscrew thermostat from control rod. Disconnect rod from control lever at top.

**3)** Remove rocker arm cover with gasket and remove rocker arm assemblies. Remove push rods, keeping in order for reassembly. Loosen cylinder head nuts gradually working in sequence from outside toward center and remove cylinder head.

**Installation — 1)** Install new seals on pushrod tubes. Install cylinder head with new cylinder seals and position pushrod tubes with seams facing upward. Push head onto cylinders to hold pushrod tubes.

**2)** Install cylinder head washers and nuts to studs and tighten just enough to hold head and pushrod tubes in place. Uniformly tighten nuts in sequence shown in illustration "A" to 7 ft. lbs., then tighten in sequence shown in illustration "B" to required torque. Reverse removal procedure for remaining components. Adjust valves.

## TYPE 1 1600 cc 4 CYLINDER (Cont.)

Fig. 2   Tighten to 7 Ft.Lbs. in Step "A" Sequence, and to Final Torque in Step "B" Sequence

## VALVES

### VALVE ARRANGEMENT

E-I-I-E (front to rear), both banks.

### VALVE GUIDE SERVICING

1) Place valve in valve guide with stem flush with end of guide. With dial indicator, measure valve rock at valve head. If rock exceeds .031" replace valve guide or valve. Valve guide with inside machined shoulder is exhaust.

2) To replace valve guide, drill guide with shouldered drill to depth of 1½ -2" using slow speed drill. Drive guides down through cylinder head with suitable tool. Drive oversize guide from top of cylinder head using press. Pressure required should be 2000-4000 lbs. Ream guides to proper fit.

### VALVE STEM OIL SEALS

Coat valve stems with molybdenum-disulfide paste and insert in cylinder head. Slide valve stem seal ring over valve stem and install spring, retainer and keeper.

### VALVE SPRINGS

NOTE — *Valve spring may be removed with cylinder head installed. Apply constant air pressure (minimum 85 psi) to cylinder through spark plug hole to hold valve in place while compressing spring.*

Removal — Remove cylinder head cover and rocker arm shaft. Install suitable valve spring compressor tool (VW311H with cylinder head removed, VW653/2 with cylinder head installed). Compress spring retainer and spring and remove valve keepers. Release compressor and remove spring retainer and spring.

Installation — Install valve, valve spring, valve stem seal ring and spring retainer.

NOTE — *Install spring with closely spaced coils against cylinder head.*

2) Compress spring with suitable compressor and install valve keepers.

### ROCKER ARM ASSEMBLY

1) Remove valve cover. Remove nuts from rocker arm studs and remove rocker arm assembly. Remove clips from end of shaft and remove washers, rocker arms and shaft supports.

2) Inspect shaft, supports and rocker arms for wear. Inspect sides of rocker arms and supports for wear. Smooth sides with emery paper before installing if worn.

3) To assemble reverse removal procedure. Install new seals on rocker arm studs, and reverse removal procedure to install. Adjust valve clearance.

Fig. 3   Sectional View of Valve with Related Parts

### VALVE CLEARANCE ADJUSTMENT

Perform adjustment with engine cold. Turn crankshaft until No. 1 cylinder is at TDC position and distributor rotor points to No. 1 cylinder position. Loosen lock-nut and adjust rocker arm adjusting screw until valve clearance is .006". Check clearance between adjusting screw and valve stem of both valves. Tighten lock nut. Turn crankshaft 90° while noting rotor travel. Adjust valves of Nos. 2, 3 and 4 in turn.

# Volkswagen Engines

## TYPE 1 1600 cc 4 CYLINDER (Cont.)

Fig. 4    *Expanded View of 1600 cc Rocker Arm Assembly*

Rocker Shaft

Rocker Arm

Support

## PISTONS, PINS & RINGS

### CYLINDERS

**Removal** — Remove engine and remove cylinder head. **NOTE** — *Mark cylinders to insure they are reinstalled in original position. Remove deflector plates from bottom of cylinders and pull cylinders from pistons.*

**Installation** — 1) Check seating surfaces of cylinders on both ends. Make sure seating areas are perfectly clean and true before installing cylinders. Stagger ring gaps 90° apart so that oil ring gap faces upward when cylinder is installed.

Fig. 5    *Shows Correct Position of Cylinder Seal*

2) Apply oil to cylinder, piston, rings and piston pin. Compress rings with suitable ring compressor (VW123). Install new sealing gasket on crankcase side and slide cylinder over piston.

Fig. 6    *Installation of Compression Rings 1 and 2*

3) Make sure studs do not contact cooling fins when cylinder is completely seated against crankcase. Install cylinder deflector plates and remaining components in reverse of removal.

Fig. 7    *Cylinder Installation*

### FITTING PISTONS

1) With piston and cylinder removed, measure clearance between piston and cylinder. Check piston size at bottom of skirt and 90° to piston pin. Check cylinder size at several points throughout cylinder, using largest reading to determine clearance.

Front (Flywheel End) Mark

Index Letter

Weight Grade

Paint Spot Weight Grading

Paint Spot Size Grading

Piston Size

85.5

Fig. 8    *Top View of Piston with Detail of Piston Markings*

## TYPE 1 1600 cc 4 CYLINDER (Cont.)

**2)** If clearance exceeds .008" (.20 mm) replace piston and cylinder as a set. New piston must be of same weight grade as original or within 10 g of original piston weight. Piston size, weight and installation position are marked on top of piston.

**NOTE** — *Piston alone may be replaced with one of matching size. Only pistons of same size and weight grade should be installed in same engine.*

**3)** New piston rings are size graded to match piston-cylinder sets. Measure ring gap with ring installed approximately ¼" from bottom of cylinder.

*Fig. 9   Using a Feeler Gauge to Measure Ring Gap*

**4)** Install rings on piston and measure ring side clearance using feeler gauge. If clearance exceeds .005" (.12 mm) on top ring or .004" (.10 mm) on second or oil ring, piston must be replaced.

### PISTON PINS

**Removal** — Remove cylinders and mark pistons before removing for proper installation. Using suitable pliers (VW122b), remove piston pin circlips and push piston pin out of piston using suitable tool (VW207).

**Installation** — **1)** Check fit of pin in piston. Piston pin should be light push fit with piston 68-167°F. If pin is too loose, both pin and piston must be replaced. Check clearance of pin in rod. If clearance exceeds .0016" (.04 mm) replace piston pin and rod bushing. See Piston Pin Bushing Replacement.

*Fig. 10   Using a Feeler Gauge to Measure Ring Clearance*

**2)** Install one circlip in piston on side facing flywheel. Position piston on connecting rod and push piston pin through piston. Replace remaining circlip. **NOTE** — *Piston may be heated to ease pin installation. Replace remaining components in reverse of removal.*

### PISTON PIN BUSHING REPLACEMENT

**1)** At normal temperature, piston pin should push fit in connecting rod. If side clearance is felt with a new pin installed, bushing must be replaced and reamed to correct fit with a new piston pin.

**2)** Press bushing out using a suitable mandrel and components. Install new bushing using same procedure and tools used for removal.

**3)** Drill through oil holes in connecting rod. Use handreamer to fit pin into bushing. Bushing should be free of chatter marks when reaming is completed. Piston pin should push fit into bushing without oil. Clearance must be .0004-.0008" (.01-.02 mm).

## CRANKSHAFT MAIN & CONNECTING ROD BEARINGS

### CRANKCASE DISASSEMBLY

**NOTE** — *Crankcase must be taken apart to replace connecting rods, connecting rod bearings and main bearings. It is also necessary to disassemble crankcase to remove crankshaft, camshaft and camshaft bearings.*

*Fig. 11   Bottom View Showing Oil Strainer and Components*

**1)** Remove engine from vehicle and remove cylinder heads, cylinders and pistons as previously outlined. Remove flywheel or drive plate, distributor, fuel pump, distributor drive, distributor drive washer and oil cooler.

**2)** Remove front pulley nut and remove pulley using suitable puller (VW203). Remove generator support housing and metal shroud from front of engine.

## TYPE 1 1600 cc 4 CYLINDER (Cont.)

**3)** On all models remove oil pump cover and pull oil pump from crankcase using a suitable puller (VW201). Remove retaining plate and screen from bottom of motor. Remove nuts and bolts securing crankcase halves and separate.

**CAUTION** — *Use a rubber hammer to separate crankcase halves, do not insert any kind of tool between sealing edges.*

**4)** Remove camshaft and crankshaft. Remove crankshaft oil seal and cam plug. Remove number two bearing halves from both sides of crankcase and remove bearing dowel pins. Remove cam bearings if equipped. Remove oil pressure relief valve.

### CRANKCASE ASSEMBLY

**1)** Thoroughly clean and inspect crankcase halves for wear or cracking. Assemble empty crankcase halves and tighten nuts to specifications. Measure crankshaft bearing bores with an inside micrometer. Specified diameter for bearing bores 1 through 3 is 2.1641-2.1649" (54.97-54.99 mm). Diameter for number 4 bearing bore is 1.5740-1.5748" (40.00-40.01 mm).

**2)** Flush out all oil passages and blow out with compressed air. Make sure oil suction tube and all studs are tight in crankcase halves.

**3)** Insert valve tappets and crankshaft bearing dowel pins. Install camshaft bearings if equipped. Install No. 2 bearing halves. Install crankshaft and connecting rod assembly, making sure bearings line up with dowel pins.

**4)** Install camshaft with "O" on cam gear centered between two teeth with punch marks on crankshaft gear. Install cam plug using sealer. Spread a thin coat of sealer on sealing edges of crankcase halves, making sure sealer does not enter oil passages.

**5)** Install "O" ring on large crankcase studs and push "O" ring into beveled portion of crankcase. Join crankcase halves together and lightly tighten nuts. Tighten M8 nut next to M12 nut near number 1 bearing then tighten all M12 nuts. Tighten remaining nuts and bolts.

**6)** Check crankshaft for freedom of movement. Install oil pressure relief valve. Install pistons, cylinders and cylinder heads as previously outlined.

**7)** On all models install all components except distributor and distributor drive in reverse of removal order. Set engine on number one firing position. Place distributor drive washer on a long screwdriver. Insert screwdriver into bottom of distributor hole, drop washer and center in bottom of hole with screwdriver.

**8)** Insert distributor drive with slot at 90° with crankshaft and small segment of slot toward pulley.

### MAIN & CONNECTING ROD BEARING SERVICE

**1)** Split crankcase and remove crankshaft and connecting rod assembly as previously outlined. Attach crankshaft to a suitable holding fixture (VW310A).

**2)** Remove Woodruff key, oil thrower and number 4 bearing. Remove connecting rods and bearings. Remove snapring from end of crankshaft.

**3)** Press distributor drive gear, spacer and crankshaft gear from crankshaft. Remove number 3 bearing. Thoroughly clean crankshaft and blow out all oil passages with compressed air.

**4)** Check crankshaft for runout, maximum runout is .0011". Check crankshaft journals for out-of-round, maximum out-of-round is .0011". If excessive out-of-round conditions exist, crankshaft must be ground to next undersize.

**5)** Bearings for undersize crankshafts are available in .010, .020 and .030" undersize. Connecting rod bearing journals are also available in same undersizes.

**6)** Clean and inspect connecting rods. If bushing has been determined to be worn excessively, install new bushing. See *Piston Pin and Piston Pin Bushing Replacement*. Check connecting rod for twist and bending.

**7)** If connecting rod is replaced, make sure there is no more than 10 grams difference in weight between new and old connecting rods.

*Fig. 12  1600 cc Distributor Drive Installation*

*Fig. 13  Using a Feeler Gauge to Check Connecting Rod Side Clearance*

## TYPE 1 1600 cc 4 CYLINDER (Cont.)

**8)** Main bearing clearance is checked by the Plastigage method. Place a piece of Plastigage wire across crankshaft journal. Install bearings on crankshaft and install crankshaft in empty crankcase halves. Bolt crankcase together at specified torque. Do not turn crankshaft. Separate crankcase and remove crankshaft. Remove bearings and compare flattened wire to scale on Plastigage package. Compare to specified clearance.

**9)** If clearance is more than specified, crankshaft can be ground to .010", .020" and .030" undersize. Replacement bearings of appropriate size must be used. This same procedure is used when determining connecting rod bearing clearance.

**10)** Install bearing halves in rod and rod cap. Install on crankshaft with numbers on rod and rod cap together and with forged mark on rod up when crankshaft is installed. Tighten rod bolts or nuts to specifications. Check rod side clearance.

**11)** Oil and install number 3 bearing on crankshaft with dowel pin hole toward flywheel. Press on crank gear, spacer and distributor drive gear. Install snap ring. Oil and install number 4 bearing with groove toward oil thrower. Install oil thrower and Woodruff key.

**12)** Oil and install number 1 bearing and install crankshaft in crankcase as previously outlined.

### THRUST BEARING ALIGNMENT

**1)** Crankshaft endplay must be adjusted with crankshaft oil seal removed. Install two shims, flywheel gasket (paper or metal) and flywheel.

**Fig. 14   Checking Crankshaft End Play with Dial Gauge**

**2)** Correct end play is .0028-.0051" and must not exceed .006". Mount dial indicator to crankcase so back and forth movement of crankshaft can be determined. Rock crankshaft back and forth and determine thickness of third shim.

**3)** Install third shim, oil seal, and flywheel with gasket. Recheck end play. Following shim sizes are available:

| Millimeter Marking (Etched in Shim) | Inch Equivalent |
|---|---|
| 0.24 mm | .0094" |
| 0.30 mm | .0118" |
| 0.32 mm | .0126" |
| 0.34 mm | .0133" |
| 0.36 mm | .0142" |

### MAIN BEARING OIL SEAL SERVICE

**1)** Remove flywheel and pry out old seal. Clean recess in crankcase and coat with a thin film of sealer.

**2)** Install a new seal using a suitable installer (VW240D). Make sure seal is squarely seated in recess.

**Fig. 15   Crankshaft Oil Seal Installation with Special Tool**

**3)** Lubricate contact surface or seal and install flywheel. Tighten flywheel retaining nut to specification.

## CAMSHAFT

### CAMSHAFT

**1)** Split crankcase and remove camshaft as previously outlined. Clean camshaft and inspect riveted joint between camshaft and gear.

**2)** Inspect camshaft lobes and bearing journals for excessive wear. Maximum wear for bearing journals is .0015". Check camshaft runout on number 2 bearing journal. Maximum runout is .0016".

**3)** Check backlash between camshaft and crankshaft gears. Correct backlash is 0-.002". If backlash is incorrect, camshafts with different pitch radius are available. Pitch radius is stamped on inner face of gear.

**Fig. 16   Correct Position of Camshaft Timing Gear**

# Volkswagen Engines

## TYPE 1 1600 cc 4 CYLINDER (Cont.)

### CAMSHAFT END THRUST

Camshaft end play is checked with camshaft installed in crankcase half. Measure back and forth movement of camshaft with a dial indicator. If end play exceeds .0062", replace camshaft or camshaft bearings. Correct end play is .0016-.0051".

### VALVE TIMING

Install camshaft with "O" stamped in tooth on outside of camshaft gear between two teeth with punch marks on crankshaft gear.

## ENGINE OILING

**Oil Capacity** — 2.6 qts.

**Normal Oil Pressure** — 28 psi at 2500 RPM

Fig. 17   Oil Pressure Regulator Valves Location

**Pressure Regulator Valves** — Oil pressure relief valve, used to protect oil cooler from excessive pressure, is located in crankcase to rear of oil pan. Oil pressure control valve, used to control oil pressure to bearings, is located in crankcase forward of oil pan. Oil pressure relief spring should have length of 1.73" at 12.3-16.0 lbs. load. Oil pressure control spring should have length of .795" at 6.8-8.4 lbs. load.

Fig. 18   Engine Lubrication Circulation Diagram

### ENGINE OILING SYSTEM

Full pressure lubrication system with gear type oil pump. Oil pump is mounted at front of engine and driven by the camshaft. Oil is pumped through oil cooler into oil passages. Crankshaft main and connecting rod journals oil through cross drilled holes in crankshaft. Oil is pumped to camshaft through oil passages that also lubricate valve tappets. Oil flows through tappets and into push rods to lubricate rocker arms and shafts. Valves and valve stems are lubricated by splash oil. Excess oil flows back into crankcase through push rod tubes. Cylinder walls, pistons and piston pins are oiled by splash oil.

### OIL PUMP REPLACEMENT

**W/Man. Trans.** — **1)** Remove crankshaft pulley and metal shroud from behind pulley.

**2)** Remove oil pump cover and gears. Pull pump housing from crankcase using a suitable puller (VW201). Check gear backlash and endplay.

Fig. 19   Removing Oil Pump with Puller Tool

**3)** Inspect pump body mating surfaces for wear or damage. Install pump body and gasket (without sealer) in crankcase. Insert a suitable pilot in housing in place of gear.

Fig. 20   View of Partially Disassembled Oil Pump

**4)** Rotate crankshaft 360° twice to center pump body with slot in camshaft. Remove pilot and install gears. Inspect cover and machine flat if necessary. Use new gasket (without sealer) and install cover. Tighten bolts and install remaining components as previously outlined.

## TYPE 1 1600 cc 4 CYLINDER (Cont.)

**W/Auto Stick Shift** — Apply same procedures as outlined above, noting the following: Remove Woodruff keys to avoid damage to intermediate plate seals. If intermediate plate or front cover are damaged, replace complete oil pump.

### Oil Pump Specifications

| Application | Measurement |
|---|---|
| Gear Backlash | 0-.008" (0-.20 mm) |
| End Play Without Gasket (Max.) | .004" (.10 mm) |

## ENGINE COOLING

### COOLING SYSTEM

Engine is cooled by a radial fan mounted on end of generator and inside of upright shroud. Fan draws air in through large hole in fan shroud. Air is then directed over finned cylinders and cylinder heads by deflector plates. A thermostat is mounted under cylinders number one and two. Thermostat operates by opening and closing deflector plates in fan shroud.

### AIR DUCTS, FAN HOUSING & CONTROL FLAPS

**Partical Removal** — 1) Remove alternator drive belt. Remove air cleaner and intake air sensor. Remove accelerator cable from guide tube. Remove alternator mounting bracket.

Disconnect ignition cables, any hoses, air ducts, or wires that might prevent fan housing upward movement.

2) Remove oil cooler cover bolt and bolt holding fan housing to oil cooler flange. Take off cover and air duct. Remove screws from each end of fan housing. Remove thermostat. Pry off spring clip, separate connecting link from left control flap. Raise fan housing and remove intake manifold and alternator.

**NOTE** — *For complete removal of components, continue with remaining procedures. It is easier to remove remaining components with engine removed.*

3) Remove fresh air to heat exchangers distributing hoses. Remove crankshaft pulley cover plate and preheater rear cover plates. Free lower air ducting from crankcase and heat exchangers.

4) Slide alternator mounting bracket off support stand. Remove fan housing screws, lift up fan housing and remove. Both control flaps can be removed by unhooking return spring and removing mounting screws in lower part of fan housing.

**Installation** — To install components, reverse removal procedure.

## ENGINE SPECIFICATIONS

### GENERAL SPECIFICATIONS

| Year | Displ. cu. ins. | Displ. cc | Carburetor | HP at RPM | Torque (Ft. Lbs. at RPM) | Compr. Ratio | Bore in. | Bore mm | Stroke in. | Stroke mm |
|---|---|---|---|---|---|---|---|---|---|---|
| 1978 Type 1 AJ | 96.9 | 1584 | Fuel Inj. | 48@4200 | 73@2800 | 7.3-1 | 3.36 | 85.5 | 2.72 | 69 |

### VALVES

| Engine & Valve | Head Diam. In. (mm) | Face Angle | Seat Angle | Seat Width In. (mm) | Stem Diameter In. (mm) | Stem Clearance In. (mm) | Valve Lift In. (mm) |
|---|---|---|---|---|---|---|---|
| 1600 cc Int. | 1.40 (35.6) | 44° | 45° | .051-.063 (1.3-1.6) | .3126-.3130 (7.94-7.95) | .009-.011 (.23-.27) | ..... |
| Exh. | 1.19 (30.2) | 45° | 45° | .067-.079 (1.70-2.00) | .3508-.3512 (8.91-8.92) | .009-.011 (.23-.27) | ..... |

# Volkswagen Engines

## TYPE 1 1600 cc 4 CYLINDER (Cont.)
### ENGINE SPECIFICATIONS (Cont.)

| PISTONS, PINS, RINGS | | | | | | |
|---|---|---|---|---|---|---|
| | PISTONS | PINS | | RINGS | | |
| Engine | Clearance In. (mm) | Piston Fit In. (mm) | Rod Fit In. (mm) | Rings | End Gap In. (mm) | Side Clearance In. (mm) |
| 1600 cc | .0016-.0024 (.041-.061) | ① | .0004-.0008 (.010-.020) | 1 | .012-.018 (.20-.45) | .0028-.0039 (.07-.10) |
| | | | | 2 | .012-.018 (.30-.45) | .0020-.0028 (.05-.07) |
| | | | | 3 | .010-.016 (.25-.40) | .0012-.0020 (.030-.050) |

① — Push fit with piston heated to approximately 176°F.

| CRANKSHAFT MAIN & CONNECTING ROD BEARINGS | | | | | | | |
|---|---|---|---|---|---|---|---|
| | MAIN BEARINGS | | | | CONNECTING ROD BEARINGS | | |
| Engine | Journal Diam. In. (mm) | Clearance In. (mm) | Thrust Bearing | Crankshaft End Play In. (mm) | Journal Diam. In. (mm) | Clearance In. (mm) | Side Play In. (mm) |
| 1600 cc Journal No. 1 | 2.1641-2.1649 (54.97-54.99) | .0016-.004 (.04-.10) | No. 1 | .003-.005 (.069-.131) | 2.1646-2.1654 (54.98-55.00) | .0008-.0028 (.02-.07) | .004-.016 (.10-.40) |
| 2 | 2.1641-2.1649 (54.97-54.99) | .001-.0035 (.03-.09) | | | | | |
| 3 | 2.1641-2.1649 (54.97-54.99) | .0016-.004 (.04-.10) | | | | | |
| 4 | 1.5740-1.5748 (39.98-40.00) | .002-.004 (.05-.10) | | | | | |

| VALVE SPRINGS | | | |
|---|---|---|---|
| | Free Length In. (mm) | PRESSURE Lbs. @ In. (kg @ mm) | |
| Engine | | Valve Closed | Valve Open |
| 1600 cc Int. & Exh. | ..... | 117-135@1.22 (53-61@31.0) | ..... |

| CAMSHAFT | | | |
|---|---|---|---|
| Engine | Journal Diam. In. (mm) | Clearance In. (mm) | Lobe Lift In. (mm) |
| 1600 cc | .9839-.9843 (24.99-25.00) | .0008-.002 (.02-.05) | ..... |

## TIGHTENING SPECIFICATIONS

| Application | Ft. Lbs. (mkg) |
|---|---|
| Cylinder Head | 23 (3.2) |
| Connecting Rod | 22-25 (3.0-3.5) |
| Crankcase Halves (8 mm) | 14 (2.0) |
| Crankcase Halves (12 mm) | 18 (2.5) |
| Rocker Shaft-to-Cylinder Head | 14-18 (2.0-2.5) |
| Oil Pump-to-Crankcase | 14 (2.0) |
| Oil Drain Plug | 25 (3.5) |
| Oil Strainer-to-Crankcase | 5 (.7) |
| Flywheel-to-Crankshaft | 253 (35.0) |
| Clutch-to-Flywheel | 18 (2.5) |
| Converter-to-Driveplate | 18 (2.5) |
| Engine-to-Transmission | 22 (3.0) |
| Generator Pulley | 40-47 (5.5-6.5) |
| Crankshaft Pulley | 29-36 (4.0-5.0) |
| Fan Nut | 40-47 (5.5-6.5) |

# Volkswagen Engines

## TYPE 2 2000 cc 4 CYLINDER

### ENGINE CODING

#### ENGINE IDENTIFICATION

Engine code number is stamped on crankcase below breather, near coil. First two digits of cast number are engine code.

**Engine Identification**

| Application | Engine Code |
|---|---|
| Type 2 ............................................................ | GD |

### ENGINE, CYLINDER HEAD & MANIFOLD

#### ENGINE

**Removal** — 1) Remove air cleaner. Disconnect battery. Disconnect electrical wiring from the following components: distributor, regulator, oil pressure sending unit, and transmission switch. Make sure to tag each wire for reinstallation. Disconnect back-up light lead at in-line fuse. Fuse is located near coil. Disconnect wire from temperature sensor, if equipped.

2) Disconnect fuel injection wiring harness from coil, injectors, intake air distributors, crankcase, temperature sensors. Disconnect evaporation canister hoses. Remove coil. Remove ducting between warm air blower and heat exchanger. Disconnect accelerator cable from lever on throttle valve shaft.

3) Remove oil filler neck and dipstick. Remove rear side engine cover plates. On automatic transmission models, remove transmission filler pipe by rotating counterclockwise. Also, disconnect vacuum line from intake air distributor. On automatic transmission models, remove converter bolts through opening in lower left side of bell housing. Disconnect starter electrical wires.

4) Disconnect heater control cables. Remove ducting connecting heat exchangers with inside of vehicle. Remove both upper engine to transmission mounting bolts. Place a support (VW785) under transmission. Pull accelerator from guide tube. Disconnect fuel line from pressure regulator and plug opening. Remove both lower engine to transmission mounting bolts.

5) Place a floor jack (or equivalent) under engine. Raise jack until engine is just supported. Remove bolts mounting engine brackets to frame. Slide engine assembly slightly to rear to free input shaft. Lower engine to floor.

**NOTE** — *On vehicles equipped with automatic transmissions, install strap across converter to prevent torque converter from sliding off support tube.*

**Installation** — To install, reverse removal procedure and note following: When lining up engine and transmission, place transmission in gear, set parking brake and hand turn crankshaft until splines line up. Make sure rubber seal between engine cover and body is properly positioned. Lubricate clutch release bearing, transmission drive shaft and starter drive bushing (Bosch starters).

### INTAKE MANIFOLD

**Removal** — 1) Fuel injection manifold can be removed with engine in vehicle. Remove air cleaner, hoses, and pressure switch.

2) Disconnect wires on fuel injectors and remove two screws. Pull injectors off with plate and retainer. Make sure locating bushings are removed from manifold. Disconnect hoses on injectors and remove.

3) Remove intake manifold cover plate. Remove nuts and washers securing manifold to cylinder heads. Lift up on manifold and pull from tubes on air distributor.

**Installation** — To install manifold, reverse removal procedure and note the following: Use new gaskets and tighten intake manifold mounting nuts uniformly. Make sure gray protective cap on injector is to rear and cap is to front.

### CYLINDER HEAD

**NOTE** — *Engine must be removed from vehicle and manifolds removed, before removing cylinder heads. If cylinders are not to be removed, use retaining device to keep cylinders from pulling free.*

**Removal** — 1) Remove rocker arm cover and gasket. Remove rocker arm shaft retaining nuts, loosening gradually one at a time to relieve spring tension evenly. Remove rocker arm assemblies.

2) Remove push rods, keeping in order for reassembly. Loosen cylinder head nuts gradually working in sequence from outside toward center.

*Fig. 1     2000 cc Engine, Cylinder Head Bolt Tightening Sequence*

**Installation** — Install new seal on push rod tubes. Install cylinder head with new gasket over studs. Loosely attach head nuts and washers. Torque cylinder head according to sequence shown in *Fig. 1*. Install push rod tube in place by sliding through top of cylinder head. Reverse removal procedure for remaining components.

## VALVES

### VALVE ARRANGEMENT

E-I-I-E (both banks)

# Volkswagen Engines

## TYPE 2 2000 cc 4 CYLINDER ( Cont.)

### VALVE GUIDE SERVICING

**1)** Place valve in valve guide with stem flush with end of guide. With dial indicator, measure valve rock at valve head. If rock exceeds .047" (1.2 mm), replace valve guide or valve. Valve guide with inside machined shoulder is exhaust.

**2)** To replace valve guide, drill guide with shouldered drill to depth of 1⁹/₁₆ - 1⁶¹/₆₄" using slow speed drill. Drive guides down through cylinder head with suitable tool. Drive oversize guide from top of cylinder head using press. Pressure required should be 1000-2000 lbs. Ream guides to proper fit.

### VALVE SPRINGS

**NOTE** — *Valve spring may be removed with cylinder head installed. Apply constant air pressure (minimum 85 psi) to cylinder through spark plug hole to hold valve in place while compressing spring.*

**Removal** — Remove cylinder head cover and rocker arm shaft. Install suitable valve spring compressor tool (VW311s with cylinder head removed, VW653/2 with cylinder head installed). Compress spring retainer and spring and remove valve keepers. Release compressor and remove spring retainer and spring.

Fig. 2   Using Special Tool VW311s
to Remove Valve Spring

**Installation** — Install valve, valve spring, and valve spring retainer. **NOTE** — *Install spring with closely spaced coils against cylinder head.* Compress spring with suitable compressor and install valve keepers.

### ROCKER ARM ASSEMBLY

**Removal** — Disengage wire valve cover clip. Remove valve cover. Remove 4 rocker shaft retaining nuts. Each side has two separate shafts. Make sure mounting nuts are gradually and evenly loosened until spring tension is relieved.

**Inspection** — Check rocker arms and shafts for wear. If inside diameter of rocker arm is worn more than .789" (20.0 mm), replace rocker arm. If diameter of rocker shaft is worn to less than .783" (19.9 mm), replace rocker shaft.

**Installation** — To install, reverse removal procedure and note: Make sure push rod tube retaining wire is reinstalled. Adjust valve clearance.

Fig. 3   Sectional View of Valve with Related Parts

### VALVE CLEARANCE ADJUSTMENT

Perform adjustment with engine cold. Turn crankshaft until No. 1 cylinder is at TDC position and distributor rotor points to No. 1 cylinder position. Loosen lock nut and adjust rocker arm adjusting screw until valve clearance is .006". Check clearance between adjusting screw and valve stem of both valves. Tighten lock nut. Turn crankshaft 90° while noting rotor travel. Adjust valves of Nos. 2, 3 and 4 in turn.

## PISTONS, PINS & RINGS

### CYLINDERS

**Removal** — Remove engine and remove cylinder head. **NOTE** — *Mark cylinders to insure they are reinstalled in original position.* Remove deflector plates from bottom of cylinders and pull cylinders from pistons.

Fig. 4   Location and Seating of Cylinder Seal

Fig. 5   Installing Cylinder Assembly into Case

## TYPE 2 2000 cc 4 CYLINDER (Cont.)

**Installation** — 1) Check seating surfaces of cylinders on both ends. Make sure seating areas are perfectly clean and true before installing cylinders. Stagger ring gaps 90° apart so that oil ring gap faces upward when cylinder is installed.

2) Apply oil to cylinder, piston, rings and piston pin. Compress rings with suitable ring compressor (VW123). Install new sealing gasket on crankcase side and slide cylinder over piston.

3) Make sure studs do not contact cooling fins when cylinder is completely seated against crankcase. Install cylinder deflector plates and remaining components in reverse of removal.

### FITTING PISTONS

1) With piston and cylinder removed, measure clearance between piston and cylinder. Check piston size at bottom of skirt and 90° to piston pin. Check cylinder size at several points throughout cylinder, using largest reading to determine clearance.

2) If clearance exceeds .008" (.20 mm), replace piston and cylinder as a set. New piston must be of same weight grade as original or within 10 g of original piston weight. Piston size, weight and installation position are marked on top of piston (See Fig. 6). Piston and cylinders are available in two oversizes .020" and .040".

NOTE — *Piston alone may be replaced with one of matching size. Only pistons of same size and weight grade should be installed in same engine.*

**Fig. 6   Top View of Piston with Detail of Piston Markings**

3) New piston rings are size graded to match piston/cylinder sets. Measure ring gap with ring installed approximately 3/16 in cylinder. If ring end gap exceeds .035" (.90 mm) for compression rings or .037" (.95 mm) for oil scraper, replace.

4) Install rings on piston and measure ring side clearance using feeler gauge. If clearance exceeds .005" (.12 mm) on top ring or .004" (.10 mm) on second or oil ring, piston must be replaced.

**Fig. 7   Measuring Piston Ring Side Clearance with Feeler Gauge**

### PISTON PINS

**Removal** — Remove cylinders and mark pistons before removing for proper installation. Using suitable pliers (VW122b), remove piston pin circlips and push piston pin out of piston.

**Installation** — 1) Check fit of pin in piston. Piston pin should be light push fit with piston at 68-167°F. If pin is too loose, both pin and piston must be replaced. Check clearance of pin in rod. It clearance exceeds .0016" (.041 mm), replace piston pin and rod bushing. See *Piston Pin Bushing Replacement.*

NOTE — *During manufacturing some pistons were made with oversize bores. Oversize pins are supplied for these pistons and are identified by a green paint spot. No attempt should be made to compensate pin or bushing wear with oversize pin.*

2) Install one circlip in piston on side facing flywheel. Position piston on connecting rod and push piston pin through piston. Replace remaining circlip. NOTE — *Piston may be heated to ease pin installation.* Replace remaining components in reverse of removal.

### PISTON PIN BUSHING REPLACEMENT

1) At normal temperature, piston pin should push fit in connecting rod. If side clearance is felt with a new pin installed, bushing must be replaced and reamed to correct fit with a new piston pin.

2) Press bushing out using a suitable mandrel and components (VW402, 409, 421 and 416B). Install new bushing using same procedure and tools as used for removal.

3) Drill through oil holes in connecting rod. Ream bushing to provide a .0004-.0012" (.01-.03 mm) clearance. Bushing should be free of chatter marks when reaming is completed. Piston pin should be a push fit into bushing without oil.

## CRANKSHAFT MAIN & CONNECTING ROD BEARINGS

### CRANKCASE

Crankcase must be taken apart to replace connecting rods, connecting rod bearings and main bearings. It is also necessary to disassemble crankcase to remove crankshaft, camshaft, and camshaft bearings.

## TYPE 2 2000 cc 4 CYLINDER (Cont.)

**Disassembly** — 1) Remove engine from vehicle and remove cylinder heads, cylinders, and pistons. Remove flywheel or drive plate, and crankshaft pulley. Remove distributor, distributor drive shaft and fuel pump.

2) Remove oil cooler, oil filter and bracket, and oil pump assembly. *See Oil Pump Removal.* Remove rear engine carrier crossmember, bonded rubber mountings, and fan hub. Remove oil pan and oil filler pipe mounting bracket bolt.

3) Remove six 10 mm nuts and five 8 mm bolts and nuts. Using spring clips, clamp tappets in right hand crankcase half and lift off right hand crankcase half. **CAUTION** — *Never use sharp tool to pry crankcase halves apart. Smallest scratches will cause oil leak. Use rubber hammer to loosen crankcase halves.*

**Assembly** — 1) Thoroughly clean and inspect both crankcase halves. Remove old sealing compound from mating surfaces and from all bolts, studs and washers. Blow out oil passages with compressed air. Check studs for tightness and check oil suction pipe for tightness.

2) Install crankshaft with connecting rods, in left side crankcase half, making sure dowel pins are properly seated in bearings. Install camshaft. *See Camshaft Installation.* Install camshaft plug using liquid sealer all around plug. Spread liquid sealer over mating surfaces of crankcase halves.

3) Using spring clips, clamp tappets in right hand half of crankcase and join crankcase halves. Coat main bearing bolt heads (10 mm) with sealer and install in crankcase. **NOTE** — *Install plastic dampers (part No. 021 101 107) on shank of main bearing bolts whether or not originally equipped.*

4) Coat the sealing nuts for main bearing bolts with sealer and install nuts with sealing rings outward. Tighten main bearing nuts and bolts and hand turn crankshaft to check for free movement. Coat bolt heads and nuts of 8 mm bolts with sealer, then install and tighten.

5) Check crankshaft end play. *See Thrust Bearing Alignment.* Install new crankshaft oil seals. *See Front Crankshaft Oil Seal Replacement and Rear Crankshaft Oil Seal Replacement.* Install remaining components in reverse of removal procedure.

### MAIN & CONNECTING ROD BEARING SERVICE

1) With crankshaft and connecting rod assembly removed, remove snap ring securing distributor drive gear and crankshaft gear to crankshaft. Remove distributor drive gear and crankshaft gear by pressing or using a suitable mandrel (VW457). Remove number three bearing. Remove connecting rods.

2) Thoroughly clean and inspect crankshaft. Blow out oil passages with compressed air. Check runout of crankshaft, if runout is more than .0008" (.020 mm), regrind crankshaft to next undersize.

3) Check crankshaft journals for wear, if journals are worn more than .0012" (.030 mm), regrind crankshaft to next undersize. Main and connecting rod bearings are available in .010", .020" and .030" undersize.

4) Lubricate and install number three bearing. Heat crankshaft to approximately 176°F in an oil bath and install

crankshaft and distributor drive gears using suitable drivers (VW427, VW428 and VW415a). Install snap ring.

5) Using Plastigage method, check main and connecting rod bearings. If main bearing clearance on Nos. 1 and 3 exceeds .007" (.18 mm), .0067" (.17 mm) on No. 2, or .0075" (.19 mm) on No. 3; replace bearing. If clearance on any connecting rod bearing exceeds .007" (.15 mm), replace bearing.

6) Install Nos. 1, 3, and 4 main bearings on crankshaft. *See Step 4 for No. 3 main bearing installation.* Install lower bearing half of No. 2 bearing in crankcase. Make sure bearing engages hole in bearing half. Turn bearings on crankshaft to align oil holes. Install connecting rod bearing halves in rod cap and rod. Fit to crankshaft with numbers on rod and cap on same side. Forged mark on connecting rod must face up when crankshaft is installed.

7) Check connecting rod side play with feeler gauge. If side play exceeds .0275" (.70 mm), replace connecting rod. Install crankshaft and connecting rod assembly as previously outlined. Check crankshaft end play. *See Thrust Bearing Alignment.*

*Fig. 8   Using a Feeler Gauge to Check Connecting Rod Side Clearance*

### THRUST BEARING ALIGNMENT

**NOTE** — *Crankshaft end play is checked with engine assembled.*

1) Install flywheel with two shims, but do not install crankshaft oil seal. Attach dial indicator to crankcase and measure back and forth movement of crankshaft.

2) Calculate necessary thickness of third shim. Install third shim and recheck end play. Thickness of shim is etched on face of shim, always use three shims to obtain correct end play.

## TYPE 2 2000 cc 4 CYLINDER (Cont.)

**Fig. 9   Using a Dial Indicator to Check Crankshaft End Play**

### Thrust Bearing Shims

| MM Markings On Shim | Inch Equivalent |
| --- | --- |
| .24 mm | .0094″ |
| .30 mm | .0118″ |
| .32 mm | .0126″ |
| .34 mm | .0134″ |
| .36 mm | .0142″ |
| .38 mm | .0150″ |

3) With correct shim thickness determined, install crankshaft oil seal. *See Front Crankshaft Oil Seal.* Install flywheel, tighten bolts as required, and recheck crankshaft end play.

## CAMSHAFT

### FRONT CRANKSHAFT OIL SEAL

1) Remove flywheel and pry out crankshaft oil seal. Make sure seal seat in crankcase is clean. If necessary, chamfer edges of seal seat.

2) Press seal into crankcase, using a suitable seal installer (VW191). Make sure seal is seated in bottom of crankcase. Lubricate sealing edge of seal, install flywheel, and tighten bolts.

### REAR CRANKSHAFT OIL SEAL

1) Remove cooling blower impeller from rear of engine. Remove impeller hub, using a suitable puller (VW185).

2) Pry out old seal and thoroughly clean seal seat in crankcase. Chamfer edges of seal seat, if necessary. Press new seal into crankcase, using a suitable seal installer (VW190). Make sure seal is seated in bottom of crankcase. Lubricate sealing edge of seal and install cooling blower impeller.

### DISTRIBUTOR DRIVE INSTALLATION

When crankcase has been assembled, and remaining components installed, distributor drive must be installed. Rotate crankshaft until No. 1 piston is at TDC, compression stroke. Align timing mark on pulley with 0° mark on ignition timing scale. Insert distributor drive with slot at a 12° angle to center line of engine. Small segment of slot must face toward outside of vehicle (*See Fig. 10*).

**Fig. 10   Engine Distributor Drive Installation Position**

### CAMSHAFT INSTALLATION

1) With camshaft removed, check riveting of camshaft gear to camshaft. Check camshaft for runout, if runout exceeds .0016″ (.041 mm), replace camshaft.

2) Check gear backlash with camshaft and crankshaft installed in crankcase half. Correct backlash is .002″ (.05 mm). Gears have correct fit when crankshaft is rotated backwards and camshaft does not try to lift out of bearings.

**Fig. 11   Measuring Camshaft End Play with a Dial Indicator**

3) If camshaft rises out of bearings, teeth on camshaft gear have the wrong pitch radius for crankshaft gear. Camshafts with gears that have various pitch radii are available. Pitch radius is stamped on back of gear facing number three bearing journal of camshaft.

4) Install camshaft with "O" stamped in tooth on outside of camshaft gear between two teeth with punch marks on crankshaft gear. Assemble crankcase halves as previously outlined (*See Fig. 12*).

### CAMSHAFT END PLAY

Camshaft end play is checked with camshaft installed in crankcase half. Measure back and forth movement of

## TYPE 2 2000 cc 4 CYLINDER (Cont.)

camshaft with a dial indicator. If end play exceeds .006" (.16 mm), replace camshaft or bearings.

### VALVE TIMING

Install camshaft with "O" stamped in tooth on outside of camshaft gear between two teeth with punch marks on crankshaft gear.

*Fig. 12   Position of Camshaft Timing Gear*

### ENGINE OILING

**Oil Capacity** — 3.15 qts. Add .5 qt. with filter change.

**Oil Pressure** — 42 psi at 2500 RPM with engine at 158°F.

**Oil Filter** — Full-flow, throw-away type oil filter.

**Pressure Regulator Valves** — Oil pressure relief valve, used to protect oil cooler from excessive pressure, is located in crankcase under oil filter. Oil pressure control valve, used to control oil pressure to bearings, is located in crankcase below oil breather. Oil pressure relief spring should have length of 1.54" (39 mm) at 15-19 lbs. (6.8-8.8 kg) load. Oil pressure control valve spring should have a length of 1.02" (26 mm) at 3¾-4⅜ lbs. (1.7-2.0 kg) load.

*Fig. 13   Expanded View of Relief Valve Components*

### ENGINE OILING SYSTEM

Full pressure lubrication system utilizing a gear-type oil pump and installed in rear of engine and driven by camshaft. Oil is pumped through oil filter, oil cooler and into main oil passages in crankcase. Crankshaft main and connecting rod journals are oiled through cross-drilled oil passages in the crankcase. Oil is pumped to camshaft through oil passages that also lubricate valve tappets. Oil flows through push rods to lubricate rocker arms and shafts. Valve stems are lubricated by splash oil from rocker arms. Excess oil flows back into crankcase through push rod tubes. Cylinder walls and piston pins are lubricated by splash oil.

*Fig. 14   Distribution of Oil for Engine Lubrication*

### OIL COOLER

To remove oil cooler, remove cooling air fan housing, three 6 mm nuts with washers attaching oil cooler to rear of crankcase, and bolts attaching oil cooler support strap. Remove support strap and oil cooler as unit. Always use new rubber seals when installing oil cooler.

### OIL PUMP

**Removal** — Remove engine. Remove 4 nuts holding oil pump. Using puller VW803 (or equivalent) as shown in *Fig. 15*, pry oil pump out of crankcase.

**Inspection** — Check housing for excessive wear, mainly in gear seating portions. Measure gear backlash for wear. Backlash must not exceed .008" (.20 mm). Replace bearing plate if scored.

**Installation** — Hand turn oil pump drive shaft until fully engaged in camshaft. Rotate crankshaft two revolutions. Pump plate should now be aligned with camshaft. Refit new gasket and reverse removal procedure for remaining components.

## TYPE 2 2000 cc 4 CYLINDER (Cont.)

**Fig. 15    Using Special Tool (Puller) to Remove Oil Pump**

### ENGINE COOLING

**Thermostat** — At 149-158°F (65-70°C), thermostat length should be at least 1 13/16" (46 mm) measured from shoulders on bellows shaft.

### COOLING SYSTEM

Engine is cooled by a radial blower mounted to rear end of crankshaft. Blower draws air through opening in blower shroud at rear of engine. Blower shroud is two-piece unit, mounted around blower and attached to crankcase. As air is drawn in, it is directed over finned cylinders and cylinder heads by deflector plates. A thermostat is mounted under No. 1 and No. 2 cylinders and actuates flaps mounted in shroud to control volume of air directed in deflector plates.  As engine warms up, thermostat opens flaps completely to allow total flow of air.

### BLOWER SHROUD REMOVAL

**1)**  Remove engine as previously outlined. Remove air injection pump, belt, and adjusting bracket. Remove extension shaft with pulley, ignition timing scale, fan with crankshaft pulley and alternator belt.

**2)**  Disconnect cooling air control cable from control flap shaft. Pull rubber elbow for alternator out of front half of blower shroud. Remove four nuts attaching blower shroud to crankcase and pull assembly to rear and off engine. To install, reverse removal procedure. Adjust air flap control cable by pushing flaps into closed position and tighten cable.

**3)**  Disconnect flap actuating cable from control shaft. Remove nuts securing shroud to crankcase and remove both halves of blower shroud.

**4)**  To install, reverse removal procedure. Adjust air flap control by pushing flaps into closed position and tighten cable control. Attach elbow for cooling alternator to fan shroud front half.

**5)**  Install drive belt and tighten alternator into proper belt tensioning position (maximum 0.6" deflection). Install cover plates and engine as previously outlined.

## ENGINE SPECIFICATIONS

### GENERAL SPECIFICATIONS

| Year | Displ. | | Carburetor | HP at RPM | Torque (Ft. Lbs. at RPM) | Compr. Ratio | Bore | | Stroke | |
| | cu. ins. | cc | | | | | in. | mm | in. | mm |
|---|---|---|---|---|---|---|---|---|---|---|
| 1978 | 120 | 1970 | Fuel Injection | 67@4200 | 101@3000 | 7.3-1 | 3.70 | 94 | 2.795 | 71 |

### VALVES

| Engine & Valve | Head Diam. In. (mm) | Face Angle | Seat Angle | Seat Width In. (mm) | Stem Diameter In. (mm) | Stem Clearance In. (mm) | Valve Lift In. (mm) |
|---|---|---|---|---|---|---|---|
| 2000 cc Int. | 1.476 (37.5) | 29.5 | 30° | .071-.087 (1.80-2.21) | .3125-.3129 (7.936-7.948) | .018 (.46) | ..... |
| Exh. | 1.299 (33.0) | 45° | 45° | .079-.098 (2.01-2.49) | .3508-.3512 (8.910-8.920) | .014 (.35) | ..... |

### VALVE SPRINGS

| Engine | Free Length In. (mm) | PRESSURE Lbs. @ In. (kg @ mm) | |
| | | Valve Closed | Valve Open |
|---|---|---|---|
| 2000 cc Int. & Exh. | ..... | 168-186@1.14 (76.20-84.37@28.96) | |

### CAMSHAFT

| Engine | Journal Diam. In. (mm) | Clearance In. (mm) | Lobe Lift In. (mm) |
|---|---|---|---|
| 2000 cc | .9839-.9843 (24.991-25.001) | .0008-.0020 (.020-.051) | ..... |

# Volkswagen Engines

## TYPE 2 2000 cc 4 CYLINDER (Cont.)
### ENGINE SPECIFICATIONS (Cont.)

### PISTONS, PINS, RINGS

| Engine | PISTONS | PINS | | RINGS | | |
|---|---|---|---|---|---|---|
| | Clearance In. (mm) | Piston Fit In. (mm) | Rod Fit In. (mm) | Rings | End Gap In. (mm) | Side Clearance In. (mm) |
| 2000 cc | .0016-.0024 (.04-.06) | ① | .0004-.0012 (.010-.030) | 1 | .014-.021 (.35-.55) | .002-.003 (.06-.09) |
| | | | | 2 | .014-.021 (.35-.55) | .0016-.0028 (.04-.07) |
| | | | | 3 | .010-.016 (.25-.40) | .0008-.0019 (.02-.05) |

① — Push fit with light thumb pressure.

### CRANKSHAFT MAIN & CONNECTING ROD BEARINGS

| Engine | MAIN BEARINGS | | | | CONNECTING ROD BEARINGS | | |
|---|---|---|---|---|---|---|---|
| | Journal Diam. In. (mm) | Clearance In. (mm) | Thrust Bearing | Crankshaft End Play In. (mm) | Journal Diam. In. (mm) | Clearance In. (mm) | Side Play In. (mm) |
| 2000 cc No. 1 | 2.3609-2.3617 (59.967-59.987) | .0016-.0039 (.041-.099) | No. 1 | .0027-.0050 (.069-.127) | 1.9677-1.9685 (49.98-50.00) | .0008-.0027 (.020-.069) | .004-.016 (.10-.41) |
| 2 | 2.3609-2.3617 (59.967-59.987) | .0012-.0035 (.030-.089) | | | | | |
| 3 | 2.3609-2.3617 (59.967-59.987) | .0016-.0039 (.041-.099) | | | | | |
| 4 | 1.5739-1.5748 (39.977-40.025) | .0020-.0039 (.051-.099) | | | | | |

### TIGHTENING SPECIFICATIONS

| Application | Ft. Lbs. (mkg) |
|---|---|
| Connecting Rod Nut | 24 (3.32) |
| Crankcase Half Nuts (8 mm) | 14 (1.94) |
| Crankcase Half Sealing Nuts (10 mm) | 25 (3.46) |
| Cylinder Head Nuts | 23 (3.2) |
| Rocker Shaft-to-Cylinder Head Nuts | 10 (1.4) |
| Heat Exchanger-to-Cylinder Head | 16 (2.21) |
| Oil Pan-to-Crankcase Nuts | 9 (1.24) |
| Drive Plate-to-Crankshaft | 65 (8.99) |
| Hub-to-Crankshaft Bolt | 23 (3.18) |
| Fan-to-Hub | 14 (1.94) |
| Extension Shaft & Pulley-to-Fan | 14 (1.94) |
| Engine-to-Transmission | 22 (3.04) |
| Oil Pump-to-Crankcase | 14 (1.94) |
| Oil Cooler-to-Crankcase | 14 (1.94) |
| Flywheel-to-Crankshaft | 80 (11.06) |
| Clutch-to-Flywheel | 18 (2.5) |
| Torque Converter-to-Driveplate | 14 (2.0) |

## RABBIT (GASOLINE), SCIROCCO & DASHER 4 CYLINDER

### ENGINE CODING

#### ENGINE IDENTIFICATION

Engine identification number is stamped on left side of engine block near ignition distributor.

#### Engine Codes

| Application | Code |
| --- | --- |
| Rabbit/Scirocco with Fuel Injection | EH |
| Rabbit with Carburetor | FX |
| Dasher | |
|   Man. Trans. | YG, YK |
|   Auto. Trans. | YH |

### ENGINE, CYLINDER HEAD & MANIFOLDS

#### ENGINE

**NOTE** — *On Rabbit and Scirocco models only, engine and transaxle must be removed as an assembly.*

**Removal, Rabbit & Scirocco with Man. Trans. — 1)** Disconnect battery ground cable. Drain coolant and remove radiator with air ducts and fan. If equipped with A/C, remove compressor and condenser and set aside without disconnecting hoses.

**2)** On carburetor equipped cars, remove fuel hose. On fuel injection models, remove injectors from manifold tubes of intake distributor. Disconnect all fuel lines except injector lines from fuel distributor. Remove injection control unit, air ducting and air cleaner.

**3)** Disconnect electrical wiring from the following: Ignition coil, oil pressure switch, distributor, temperature sending unit, alternator, fuel injection, starter and transmission.

**4)** Disconnect coolant hoses, accelerator cable, speedometer cable and clutch cable. Remove engine/transaxle front mount. Remove right side headlight cap.

**5)** Disconnect axle drive shafts and support with wire. Disconnect exhaust pipe from manifold and remove exhaust pipe support. Remove transmission rear mount and ground strap from body to transmission. Remove gear shift linkage.

**6)** Attach hoist to mount, cast at rear of cylinder head and lower alternator mount in front of engine. Disconnect engine carrier from body and remove left transmission mount. Lift engine and transmission out of vehicle.

**7)** Using suitable wrench (US 4463), remove TDC sensor (part of analysis system) from clutch housing. To separate transaxle from engine, turn flywheel until mark on flywheel aligns with mark on clutch housing. Remove drive shaft flange cover plate. Then, remove engine-to-transaxle bolts.

**Installation** — To install engine/transaxle assembly, reverse removal procedure and note the following: When attaching engine to transaxle, align recess (window) in flywheel level with drive shaft flange. Lift assembly into vehicle. Loosely install right engine mount bolt and loosely attach left transaxle mount to transaxle. Align assembly and loosely attach remaining mounts. Tighten mounts.

**NOTE** — *Mounts must be properly aligned and free of tension before tightening.*

**Removal, Rabbit & Scirocco with Auto. Trans. — 1)** Disconnect battery. Drain coolant and remove radiator with air ducts and fan. If equipped with A/C, remove compressor and condenser and set aside without disconnecting hoses. On fuel injection models, remove injectors from manifold tubes of intake distributor. Disconnect all fuel lines except injector lines from fuel distributor. Remove mixture control unit, air cleaner, and intake air duct. Disconnect fuel return line and electrical plug from regulator. Disconnect accelerator cable from throttle housing assembly and wiring plug from auxiliary air regulator.

**2)** On carburetor equipped models, remove air cleaner and ducting. Disconnect fuel tank-to-engine fuel hose from fuel pump. Remove accelerator cable bracket screws from carburetor. Do NOT change settings when removing bracket. On all models, disconnect all engine electrical wiring.

**3)** Disconnect speedometer cable. Disconnect selector lever cable at transaxle. Disconnect throttle cable ball socket from lever and unhook accelerator cable from lever. On Scirocco models, remove right side headlight cap.

**4)** Disconnect axle drive shafts and support with wire. Disconnect exhaust pipe at manifold flange. Remove engine/transaxle rear mount. Remove cover from engine end of clutch housing. Remove torque converter from drive plate.

**5)** Fit engine hoist to eyes on cylinder head and slightly raise engine. Remove alternator if necessary. Remove front and left transaxle mounts. Remove right engine mount. Engine is free for removal.

**6)** Separate engine and transaxle. Make sure drive plate pulls cleanly away from converter and does not move cover off support.

**Installation** — To install engine/transaxle assembly, reverse removal procedure and note the following: After lifting assembly into vehicle, loosely install right engine mount bolt and attach left transaxle mount to transaxle. Install all other components while assembly is aligned prior to tightening to final torque.

**NOTE** — *Mounts must be properly aligned and free of tension before tightening.*

**Removal, Dasher — 1)** Disconnect battery and, if equipped with A/C, remove battery from car. Drain oil. Remove air cleaner. Disconnect clutch operating lever then disengage cable housing from bracket on engine mount. Disconnect and plug fuel inlet hose.

**2)** Remove fuse block mounting screws and bend open wiring harness clip. Tie fuel hose, clutch cable and fuse block out of way. Disconnect heater control cable. Remove front engine mount and mount support.

## RABBIT (GASOLINE), SCIROCCO & DASHER 4 CYLINDER (Cont.)

3) Disconnect coil and any engine electrical items that might hinder engine removal. Disconnect all wires from fuel injection components. If equipped with A/C, remove compressor and condenser and set aside without disconnecting hoses. Drain coolant. Remove radiator.

4) Work under vehicle and disconnect electrical wires from starter. Remove starter. Disconnect exhaust pipe at manifold. Remove converter bolts through hole left by starter removal. Remove lower bolts that mount engine to transaxle.

5) Attach engine hoist. Raise engine until assembly hits steering rack housing. Support transaxle. Remove upper bolts mounting engine to transaxle. Pry engine from transaxle. Remove intermediate plate. Make sure torque converter is supported.

**Installation** — To install engine, reverse removal procedure. Make sure all fluid levels are correct. Adjust any cables removed.

### CYLINDER HEAD & MANIFOLDS

**Removal** — 1) On cars with carburetors, remove air cleaner and ducting. On fuel injection models, disconnect duct connecting throttle valve housing with mixture control unit. On all models, remove camshaft drive belt and drain engine coolant. If equipped with A.I.R. (California models), disconnect air lines from connections on exhaust manifold.

**CAUTION** — *Never drain coolant while engine is hot. Doing so could cause engine block or cylinder head to warp.*

2) Disconnect exhaust pipe. Remove nuts and bolts that hold exhaust manifold and intake manifold (air intake distributor) to head. Remove manifolds. Remove upper alternator bolt and adjusting bracket. Disconnect all coolant hoses and temperature gauge wire. Remove spark plugs.

3) Remove valve cover. Remove head bolts. Start at either end and work toward center. If head is stuck, insert block of wood in each outboard exhaust port and pry head free.

**Installation** — To install, reverse removal procedure and note the following: Make sure head gasket is positioned with "OBEN" mark facing up. Tighten head bolts in sequence and steps shown.

### Cylinder Head Tightening Steps

| Application | Ft. Lbs. (mkg) |
| --- | --- |
| Step One | 22 (3.0) |
| Step Two | 43 (6.0) |
| Step Three | 54 (7.5) |

**NOTE** — *Polygon (12 point) socket head bolts are set to final torque while cold and do not need to be retorqued when hot. Tighten in sequence to 54 ft. lbs. (7.5 mkg) plus an additional ¼ turn.*

***Fig. 1  Cylinder Head Tightening Sequence
(Loosen in Reverse Order)***

## VALVES

### VALVE ARRANGEMENT

E-I-E-I-I-E-I-E (front to rear).

### VALVE GUIDE SERVICING

1) Clean valve guides before making measurements. To measure guide, attach a suitable mounting device with a dial gauge (VW689/1) to mounting surface of cylinder head. Insert a new valve until end of stem is flush with end of valve guide.

2) Rock valve head against dial indicator and check amount of rock recorded. Maximum allowable rock is .039" (1 mm) for intake valves and .051" (1.3 mm) for exhaust valves. Proper valve guide diameter is .315"-.316" (8.01-8.04 mm).

3) Use a press and suitable adaptor (10-206) to remove and install valve guides. To remove guides, press out from combustion chamber side of head.

4) Coat new valve guides with engine oil. Press new guides into cold head from camshaft side. Make sure shoulder of guide meets firmly with top of cylinder head. Ream guides to uniform inside diameter.

**CAUTION** — *Do not use more than 1 ton pressure once guide shoulder is seated or shoulder may break.*

### VALVE SPRINGS

**NOTE** — *Although normal maintenance on valve system is performed with head removed, it is possible to replace stem seals, keepers, retainers or broken springs with cylinder head installed.*

**Removal (Head Installed)** — With camshaft and tappets removed, turn crankshaft until piston of cylinder you are working on is at BDC. Apply steady air pressure of at least 85 psi through spark plug hole adapter to keep valves seated. Compress spring with suitable tool (VW 541) and remove valve keepers. Remove and replace damaged or worn parts.

**Removal (Head Removed)** — With camshaft and tappets removed, use suitable compressor (VW 541) to depress retainer and remove keepers. Take out retainer and springs.

**Installation** — Check springs on spring tester and inspect for cracks or distortion. Reverse removal procedure and note the following: Lower edge of valve spring retainer should be chamfered to prevent valve stem scoring. If necessary, grind a

## RABBIT (GASOLINE), SCIROCCO & DASHER 4 CYLINDER (Cont.)

chamfer using stone or other suitable tool. When installing the springs, make sure closely spaced coils of outer springs are against spring seats.

### VALVE STEM OIL SEALS

With tappet, adjuster pad, keepers, springs, and spring seats removed, extract valve stem oil seal. When installing new seal, first position protective plastic sleeve on valve stem, lubricate seal, and use a suitable mandrel (10-204) to push seal onto valve guide.

### VALVE CLEARANCE ADJUSTMENT

1) Adjust valves with engine at normal operating temperature. Clearance adjustments are to be checked and made according to firing sequence (1-3-4-2). Rotate crankshaft until No. 4 cylinder valves overlap, then measure valve clearances of No. 1 cylinder.

2) If adjustment is necessary, use special tools 10-208 (disc removal tool) and VW546 (tappet depressing tool) to remove and install adjusting discs. Rotate camshaft until cam lobes no longer rest on adjusting discs of cylinder to be adjusted. Turn tappet until notches are at 90° to camshaft. Insert tool VW546 and depress tappet. Using tool 10-208, grasp tappet disc and rotate it out from under camshaft.

3) Thickness is stamped on bottom side of dics. Using clearance measurement, determine thickness of adjusting disc necessary to bring valve clearances within specifications. Discs are available in .0019" (.05 mm) increments from .1181" (3.0 mm) to .1673" (4.25 mm). Reverse removal procedure to install proper disc. Repeat procedure as required for remaining valves.

**Fig. 2  Assembled View of Valve and Camshaft**

### Valve Clearance Specifications

| Application | In. (mm) |
|---|---|
| Intake | |
| Hot | .008-.012 (.20-.30) |
| Cold | .006-.010 (.15-.25) |
| Exhaust | |
| Hot | .016-.020 (.40-.50) |
| Cold | .014-.018 (.35-.45) |

**NOTE** — Cold settings are given for reference as initial settings to be used during cylinder head rework. Final adjustments are to be made with engine at normal operating temperature. After head repairs, recheck valve clearances after 600 miles.

## PISTONS, PINS & RINGS

### OIL PAN

**Removal** — On Rabbit and Scirocco, drain oil, remove bolts and remove oil pan. On Dasher, support engine from above with support bar and threaded rod. Remove nuts holding engine mounts on subframe and bolts holding subframe to body. Pull subframe downward to separate engine mounts and body. Drain oil, remove mounting bolts and remove oil pan.

**Installation** — To install, reverse removal procedure. Make sure gasket surfaces are clean before installing new gaskets.

### PISTON & ROD ASSEMBLY

**NOTE** — Piston and rod assemblies can be removed with engine in vehicle. Manufacturer recommends engine removal for extensive overhaul work.

**Removal** — Mark cylinder number on crown of each piston. If necessary, mark arrows pointing toward front of block on piston crowns. Remove rod cap bolts and force piston out top of cylinder. Use wooden hammer handle for this operation. Mark connecting rods and bearing caps for proper reinstallation.

**NOTE** — If a ridge at top of cylinder prevents piston removal, use a ridge reamer to cut down the ridge. DO NOT force piston out of cylinder.

**Installation** — Turn crankshaft so No. 1 journal is at BDC. Install piston connecting rod assembly until ring compressor contacts block. Use a wood handle to push piston into cylinder. Install No. 4 Piston and rod assembly. Ensure tabs on bearing halves engage notch in rod and cap. Install and tighten caps on rods 1 and 4. Turn crankshaft 180° and install No. 2 and 3 rod assemblies and rod caps.

### PISTON PINS

**Removal** — Use needle-nosed pliers to remove pin circlips. Press out pin and remove piston from rod. For installation purposes, note direction piston is fitted to rod.

## RABBIT (GASOLINE), SCIROCCO & DASHER 4 CYLINDER (Cont.)

**Installation — 1)** Check pin fit in each piston. Piston pin must be a thumb-push fit in piston. If correct fit is not obtained, replace both pin and piston.

**2)** Check pin fit in connecting rod. Wear limit is .0015" (.04 mm). Rebush connecting rod and hone bushing to obtain correct clearance.

### FITTING PISTONS

**1)** Measure cylinder at three points: .39" (10 mm) from top and bottom, and at center of bore. Take measurements in line with thrust face and also at 90° to thrust face. Cylinder wear limit is .0028" (.07 mm) beyond standard dimensions; if this is exceeded, rebore cylinder and install oversize pistons.

**2)** Measure pistons at .63" (16 mm) from bottom of piston skirt (measuring 90° to pin bore). Combining this measurement with measurement of corresponding cylinder bore, note piston-to-cylinder clearance. If this exceeds .0028" (.07 mm), oversize pistons must be installed.

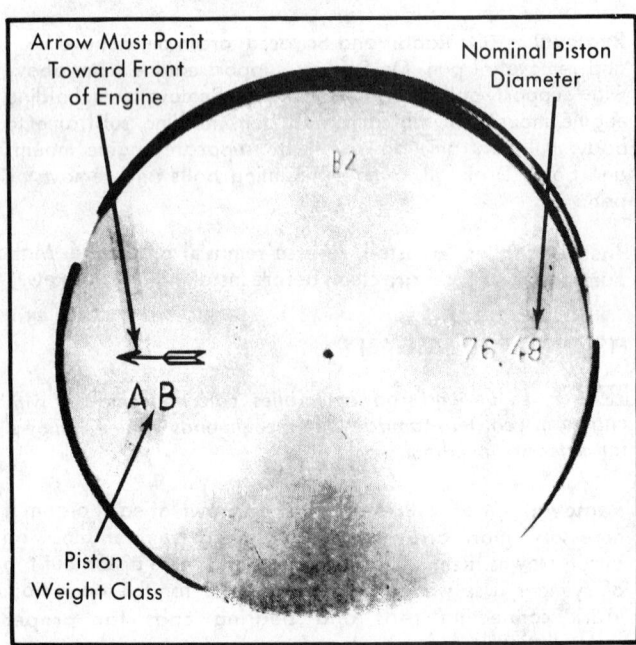

Fig. 3   Codes Stamped on Piston Head

Fig. 4   Piston Ring Installation — Word TOP Must Face Piston Crown

**3)** Place piston rings squarely in top of cylinder bore (above ring ridge) and measure end gap. Measure ring side clearance. Install rings on piston with end gaps 120° offset to each other (start with oil ring gap directly to the rear). Ensure stamp mark "TOP" on rings is facing upward.

## CRANKSHAFT MAIN & CONNECTING ROD BEARINGS

### MAIN & CONNECTING ROD BEARINGS

**1)** Push crankshaft toward one end and measure crankshaft end play at No. 3 (thrust) bearing. Main bearing caps are stamped "1" to "5" (front to rear), and must be returned to original positions upon reassembly. Measure end play (side play) of connecting rods. Remove all bearing caps and check bearing clearance using Plastigage method.

**2)** Measure crankshaft journals with a micrometer to determine if crankshaft is out-of-round. Maximum ovality permissible is .0012" (.03 mm). Install main inserts with bearing half having oil groove into block. Lubricate bearings and install caps.

### Crankshaft Journal Diameters

| Size | Main Bearing In. (mm) | Con. Rod Bearing In. (mm) |
|---|---|---|
| Standard | 2.126 (54.00) | 1.81 (46.00) |
| 1st US | 2.116 (53.75) | 1.80 (45.75) |
| 2nd US | 2.106 (53.50) | 1.79 (45.50) |
| 3rd US | 2.096 (53.25) | 1.78 (45.25) |

### REAR MAIN BEARING OIL SEAL

**NOTE** — *Rear main bearing oil seal may be replaced with engine in vehicle. Transmission and flywheel must be removed.*

Insert screwdriver between crankshaft flywheel flange and inside lip of oil seal. Pry oil seal out. Install seal guide sleeve tool 2003 (or equivalent) over crankshaft flange. Start new seal over guide and into recess in seal carrier. Pull out guide tool and fit drive PLATE 2003 (or equivalent) with bolts to flywheel mounting flange. Tighten bolts evenly to seat seal.

Fig. 5   Using Special Tool to Install Rear Main Oil Seal

## RABBIT (GASOLINE), SCIROCCO & DASHER 4 CYLINDER (Cont.)

### FRONT MAIN BEARING OIL SEAL AND INTERMEDIATE SHAFT OIL SEAL

Remove camshaft belt. Remove crankshaft sprocket. Pry seal from seal carrier, being careful not to damage carrier. Use tool 10-219 (or equivalent) to remove seal (*Fig. 6*). Using suitable tool (10-203), press in new seal until flush with seal carrier. If tool 10-203 was used, remove it and use aluminum part of tool (or equivalent) to press seal in until recessed .080" (2 mm) from front of seal carrier.

**NOTE** — *Same procedure applies to intermediate shaft oil seal except: Remove intermediate shaft sprocket. Only press new seal in until flush with seal carrier.*

### CAMSHAFT

#### TIMING BELT

**NOTE** — *Sprockets DO NOT have to be removed to replace camshaft drive belt.*

**Removal** — Remove A.I.R. pump belt and alternator belt. Remove water pump pulley. Remove camshaft belt cover. Loosen camshaft drive belt tensioner lock nut. Turn adjuster counterclockwise to release tension on belt. Work belt off sprockets.

10-219

**Fig. 6   Using Special Tool to Remove Front Oil Seal**

**Installation** — 1) Rotate camshaft sprocket until index mark (punch mark) on camshaft sprocket is lined up with top surface of valve cover mounting flange. Make sure to align index marks on spark plug side.

2) Rotate crankshaft and intermediate shafts until index mark (punch mark) on intermediate shaft sprocket is positioned in "V" notch on crankshaft pulley.

**NOTE** — *Make sure sprockets are not moved after belt has been removed.*

3) Being careful not to move sprockets, fit belt from bottom first. Make sure there is no slack between sprockets. Tighten belt tensioner until belt can just be twisted 90°. Make twist half way between camshaft and intermediate sprockets. Tighten lock nut. Reverse removal procedure for remaining components.

Intermediate Shaft Sprocket

Align Dot on Sprocket with "V" on Pulley

Crankshaft Pulley

**Fig. 7   Crankshaft and Intermediate Shaft Index Marks Aligned with Notch on Crankshaft Pulley**

### CAMSHAFT

**Removal** — 1) Remove camshaft cover. Loosen and remove bearing caps in following sequence: 5, 1, and 3, then loosen bearing caps 2 and 4 diagonally. Bearing caps are numbered front to rear.

2) Check camshaft end play. Remove camshaft and lift out cam followers. Install camshaft using only bearing caps 1 and 5. Fit dial indicator so tip of gauge touches front of camshaft. Pry camshaft back and forth. Reading should not exceed .006" (.15 mm). If end play is beyond limits, replace either camshaft or cylinder head.

3) Check camshaft runout. Fit dial indicator so gauge pin is against camshaft center journal. Turn camshaft and record runout range. Runout must not exceed .0004" (.01 mm). Replace camshaft as necessary.

4) Inspect camshaft lobes for wear. Worn lobes usually indicate lack of lubrication. Check engine oiling passages to make sure they are not restricted. Replace worn camshafts and worn discs.

5) Inspect cam followers for signs of seizure or lack of lubrication. If any aluminum particles from head are found on cam followers, replace followers. Cylinder head must be replaced if any follower bores are worn or excessively rough.

**Installation** — Lightly lube cam follower bores, then fit followers in their original bores. Install adjusting discs. Place camshaft on cylinder head. Loosely attach No. 2 and No. 4 bearing caps. Gradually tighten caps. Fit No. 5 and No. 3 bearing caps. Install new oil seal in front of camshaft. Install No. 1 bearing cap. Make sure all caps are torqued to proper specifications.

### VALVE TIMING

With timing belt removed as previously described, rotate crankshaft and intermediate shaft until index mark (punch mark) on intermediate shaft is positioned in "V" notch on crankshaft pulley (*Fig. 7*). This is firing point of No. 1 cylinder. Next, turn camshaft until marking on rear of camshaft sprocket is in line with cylinder head cover (*Fig. 8*). Replace timing belt.

## RABBIT (GASOLINE), SCIROCCO & DASHER 4 CYLINDER (Cont.)

**Fig. 8　Index Mark on Camshaft Sprocket Aligned with Cylinder Head Flange**

*(labels within figure: Camshaft Sprocket Mark Align Dot on Sprocket with Cylinder Head Flange)*

### ENGINE OILING

**Crankcase Capacity** — On Rabbit and Scirocco models, 3.7 quarts with filter change. On Dasher models, 3.2 quarts with filter change.

**Oil Filter** — Replaceable spin-on type.

**Normal Oil Pressure** — 28 psi@2000 RPM (normal operating temperature).

### ENGINE OILING SYSTEM

Oiling system is a pressure feed type. A gear oil pump lifts oil from pan and pressure feeds it to crankshaft journals, camshaft bearings, and intermediate shaft. Other parts of system receive oil mist or splash for lubrication.

### OIL PUMP

**Removal** — 1) With oil pan removed (see *OIL PAN* in this article), remove pump mounting bolts. Remove oil pump, leaving pickup tube attached.

2) Separate pickup tube from pump. Check oil pump gear backlash. Clearance should be between .002-.008" (.05-.20 mm). If specification is exceeded, replace gears or pump.

3) Measure oil pump gear end play. If end play exceeds .006" (.15 mm), replace pump.

**Installation** — To install, reverse removal procedure. Make sure all mating surfaces are clean before installing gaskets. Oil pump drive shaft must align with distributor drive gear.

### ENGINE COOLING

#### Cooling System Capacity

| Application | Capacity |
|---|---|
| Rabbit/Scirocco | 4.9 qts. |
| Dasher | |
|   With Expansion Tank | 6.9 qts. |
|   Without Expansion Tank | 6.4 qts. |

**Thermostat** — Begins to open at 176° F (80° C) and is fully open at 200° F (94° C).

### WATER PUMP

**NOTE** — *The front portion of water pump (shaft, seals, bearing, and housing) can be replaced separately. To do this camshaft drive belt and sprockets must be removed. To avoid removing drive belt, remove water pump as an assembly.*

**Removal** — Drain coolant. Remove alternator belt and alternator. On some Calif. models A.I.R. pump must be removed. Remove bolt holding camshaft belt cover to pump. Disconnect hoses from water pump. Remove water pump bolts.

**Installation** — To install, reverse removal procedure and make sure to use new "O" ring in recess in pump mounting flange.

**NOTE** — *Do not use sealer between water pump mounting flange and engine block.*

### ENGINE SPECIFICATIONS

| GENERAL SPECIFICATIONS | | | | | | | | | | | |
|---|---|---|---|---|---|---|---|---|---|---|---|
| Year | Displ. | | Carburetor | HP at RPM | Torque (Ft. Lbs. at RPM) | Compr. Ratio | Bore | | Stroke | |
| | cu. ins. | cc | | | | | in. | mm | in. | mm |
| 1978 Rabbit & Scirocco | 88.9 | 1457 | Fuel Inj.① | ②71@5800 | ③73@3500 | 8.0:1 | 3.13 | 79.5 | 2.89 | 73.4 |
| Dasher | 96.9 | 1588 | Fuel Inj. | ④78@5500 | ③83@3200 | 8.0:1 | 3.13 | 79.5 | 3.15 | 80 |

① — 34 PICT-5 carburetor on some Rabbits.
② — Calif. Models 70@5800 RPM.
③ — Calif. Models slightly less.
④ — Calif. Models 76@5500 RPM.

## RABBIT (GASOLINE), SCIROCCO & DASHER 4 CYLINDER (Cont.)
### ENGINE SPECIFICATIONS (Cont.)

### VALVES

| Engine & Valve | Head Diam. In. (mm) | Face Angle | Seat Angle | Seat Width In. (mm) | Stem Diameter In. (mm) | Stem Clearance In. (mm) | Valve Lift In. (mm) |
|---|---|---|---|---|---|---|---|
| All Models Intake | 1.338 (33.9) | 45° | 45° | .079 (2.0) | .314 (7.98) | .001-.002 (.03-.05) | .... |
| Exhaust | 1.220 (31.0) | 45° | 45° | .095 (2.4) | .313 (7.95) | .002-.003 (.05-.07) | .... |

### PISTONS, PINS, RINGS

| Engine | PISTONS | PINS | | RINGS | | |
|---|---|---|---|---|---|---|
| | Clearance In. (mm) | Piston Fit In. (mm) | Rod Fit In. (mm) | Rings | End Gap In. (mm) | Side Clearance In. (mm) |
| All Models | .0012 (.03) | Push Fit | .0004-.0008 (.01-.02) | Comp. | .012-.018 (.30-.45) | .0008-.002 (.02-.05) |
| | | | | Oil | .010-.016 (.25-.40) | .0008-.002 (.02-.05) |

### CRANKSHAFT MAIN & CONNECTING ROD BEARINGS

| Engine | MAIN BEARINGS | | | | CONNECTING ROD BEARINGS | | |
|---|---|---|---|---|---|---|---|
| | Journal Diam. In. (mm) | Clearance In. (mm) | Thrust Bearing | Crankshaft End Play In. (mm) | Journal Diam. In. (mm) | Clearance In. (mm) | Side Play In. (mm) |
| All Models | 2.126 (54) | .0011-.0033 (.028-.088) | No. 3 | .003-.007 (.07-.17) | 1.81 (46) | .0011-.0033 (.028-.088) | ① .010 (.25) |

① — Wear Limit.

### CAMSHAFT

| Engine | Journal Diam. In. (mm) | Clearance In. (mm)① | Lobe Lift In. (mm) |
|---|---|---|---|
| All Models | ..... | .0008-.002 (.02-.05) | ..... |

① — End play .006" (.15 mm)

### VALVE SPRINGS

| Engine | Free Length In. (mm) | PRESSURE Lbs. @ In. (kg @ mm) | |
|---|---|---|---|
| | | Valve Closed | Valve Open |
| All Models Inner | .... | 46-51@.719 (21-23@18.3) | .... |
| Outer | .... | 96-106@.916 (43.5-48@22.3) | .... |

### TIGHTENING SPECIFICATIONS

| Application | Ft. Lbs. (mkg) |
|---|---|
| Timing Belt Tensioner Lock Nut | 33 (4.5) |
| Intermediate Sprocket Bolt | 58 (8.0) |
| Crankshaft Sprocket Bolt | 58 (8.0) |
| Water Pump Pulley Bolts | 14 (2.0) |
| Crankshaft Pulley Bolts | 14 (2.0) |
| Main Bearing Cap Bolts | 47 (6.5) |
| Flywheel-to-Crankshaft Bolts | 54 (7.5) |
| Connecting Rod Cap Bolts | 33 (4.5) |
| Camshaft Sprocket Bolt | 58 (8.0) |
| Camshaft Bearing Cap Nuts | 14 (2.0) |
| Cylinder Head Bolts ① | |
| Cold | 54 (7.5) |
| Hot | 61 (8.5) |
| Manifolds-to-Cylinder Head | 18 (2.5) |
| Oil Pump Mounting Bolts | |
| Socket Head Bolt | 14 (2.0) |
| Hex Head Bolt | 7 (1.0) |
| Oil Pan Bolts | 7 (1.0) |

① — For 12-point socket bolts, tighten COLD only to 54 ft. lbs. (7.5 mkg), then ¼ turn tighter.

## RABBIT (DIESEL) 4 CYLINDER

### ENGINE CODING

#### ENGINE IDENTIFICATION

Engine coding for Volkswagen Diesel engines is CK. Engine identification is stamped on left side of block on machined pad near number three cylinder.

### ENGINE, CYLINDER HEAD & MANIFOLDS

#### ENGINE

**NOTE** — *Manufacturer recommends removal of engine-transaxle as a unit.*

**Fig. 1   End View of VW Diesel Engine**

**Removal** — **1)** Disconnect battery ground strap, open heater valve and drain all coolant. Remove radiator with fan, remove alternator and detach fuel filter from body.

**2)** Detach fuel supply and return lines from injection pump. Disconnect cold start cable, accelerator cable, and cable bracket from pump. Disconnect wires from oil pressure switch, temperature sensor, stop control, glow plugs, starter and back-up light switch.

**3)** Remove entire front transaxle mounting. Detach clutch cable and conduit from transaxle. Remove shift linkage relay shaft and detach from lever at rear. From underneath car, remove exhaust pipe supports, then remove nuts holding exhaust pipe to manifold. Remove rear transaxle mount.

**4)** Attach suitable sling to engine and lift slightly. Remove drive shafts at flanges from transaxle. Remove right engine mounting, then lift engine carefully to avoid damage to body, wires and cables.

**5)** Rotate crankshaft so that disassembly mark on flywheel is aligned with timing pointer. Remove cover plate over drive shaft flange. Remove engine/transmission mounting bolts and separate engine from transaxle.

**NOTE** — *Do not allow either engine or transaxle to be supported by transmission mainshaft. Damage could result to clutch, push rod or mainshaft if a strain is placed on them.*

**Installation** — To install, reverse removal procedures noting that recess in flywheel is level with clutch hub and drive shaft flange. Install left transaxle mounting loosely first, then complete alignment and assembly procedure.

#### CYLINDER HEAD & MANIFOLDS

**NOTE** — *Cylinder head may be removed and installed with engine in car.*

**Removal** — **1)** Remove air cleaner and ducting, then drain cooling system. Remove camshaft drive belt. Unbolt thermostat housing from water pump. Disconnect battery ground strap.

**2)** Disconnect accelerator cable from injection pump. Detach fuel lines at injectors by unscrewing unions. Disconnect wire from glow plug bus, temperature sending wire and any other wires which could interfere with removal of cylinder head.

**3)** Remove nuts holding exhaust pipe to manifold and unbolt exhaust pipe support from engine/transaxle assembly. From underneath car, remove bolts and nuts holding exhaust manifold to cylinder head, then remove manifold from head. Disconnect coolant hoses from head and remove any other hoses which may interfere with head removal.

**4)** Remove cylinder head cover bolts and retaining plates. Carefully lift off cover and gasket. Loosen head bolts beginning at outer ends and work toward center. Lift off head and remove injectors and glow plugs to prevent damage while working on head.

**5)** Remove combustion chamber inserts by placing drift through injector hole and tapping out with hammer. Prior to installation, pre-chamber inserts must be reinstalled. When replacing injectors, new heat shields must be used between each injector and cylinder head. Remove old heat shield and place new shield in position with recess upward, towards injector. Tighten injector to 50 ft. lbs. (7.0 mkg).

**Installation** — **1)** Clean gasket surface and ensure that cylinder head and block are not warped. Maximum distortion of .004" (.010 mm) is allowed. If installing on original piston and block assembly select a new head gasket that has the same marks as the original.

**2)** To determine proper gasket, measure projection of piston above block when at TDC. Select proper gasket from following table:

### Available Cylinder Head Gaskets

| Piston Projection in Inches (mm) | Gasket Thickness in Inches (mm) | Identification Notches |
|---|---|---|
| .017-.025 (.43-.63) | .051 (1.30) | 2 |
| .025-.032 (.63-.82) | .055 (1.40) | 3 |
| .032-.036 (.82-.92) | .059 (1.50) | 4 |
| .036-.040 (.92-1.02) | .063 (1.60) | 5 |

Gasket must be installed with word "OBEN" facing up.

## RABBIT (DIESEL) 4 CYLINDER (Cont.)

*Fig. 2  Measuring Piston Projection*

**CAUTION** — *Due to the aluminum construction of the head, do not use metal brushes or scrapers to clean gasket sealing surface or combustion chambers. Use solvent and wooden or plastic scrapers to remove foreign material. Do not mar piston tops when cleaning cylinder block. Ensure that all bolt holes and cylinder bores are absolutely free of debris prior to installing head or bolts.*

**3)** Lower head carefully onto gasket using two of the outermost bolts and washers to keep gasket and head aligned with block. Tighten head bolts in the sequence shown, first to 22 ft. lbs. (3.0 mkg), then to 43 ft. lbs. (6.0 mkg) and finally to 61 ft. lbs. (8.5 mkg). Complete installation in reverse order of removal.

*Fig. 3  Cylinder Head Tightening Sequence*

## VALVES

### VALVE ARRANGEMENT

E-I-E-I-I-E-I-E (front to rear).

### VALVE GUIDE SERVICING

**1)** To check for wear, insert NEW valve in clean valve guide until stem end is flush with spring end of guide. Use dial indicator to check that no more than .051" (1.3 mm) lateral (rocking) movement is indicated at valve head when moved back and forth against indicator.

**2)** Prior to replacing worn guides, check that head is not cracked and that valve seats can be refaced. Press out old guides and coat new guides with oil. Press new guides in up to shoulder but do not use more than one ton of pressure once shoulder is seated. Hand ream guides to proper uniform diameter of .315-.316" (8.013-8.035 mm).

### VALVE STEM SEALS AND SPRINGS

**NOTE** — *It is possible to replace valve springs and seals with head installed provided camshaft and tappets are removed. Piston of cylinder concerned must be at top dead center position.*

Use suitable spring compressor to depress spring and retainer. Remove keepers, then remove retainer and springs. Remove stem seal. Use protective sleeve over valve stem and install new seal. Complete assembly in reverse order of disassembly.

*Fig. 4  View of Valve and Camshaft*

### VALVE CLEARANCE ADJUSTMENT

**1)** Engine should be near operating temperature (coolant at about 95°F (35°C). Rotate crankshaft so that cam lobes for No. 1 cylinder (curb side) point upward. Check intake and exhaust clearance between heel of cam lobe and follower.

**2)** Use crankshaft pulley to rotate crankshaft 180° at a time and check No. 3, No. 4, and No. 2 clearance. If clearances are not within specifications, use thinner or thicker adjusting discs to increase or decrease clearance.

**NOTE** — *Do not turn engine by camshaft pulley. Use crankshaft pulley with wrench or put vehicle in 4th gear and push to move crankshaft/valve train.*

**3)** Twenty-six different thicknesses of discs are available in increments of .0019" (.05 mm) from .1181" (3.0 mm) to .1673" (4.25 mm). To install, turn crankshaft about ¼ turn past TDC and press cam follower down with suitable tool (VW 546). Remove old disc with special pliers (VW 10-208) and insert new disc with etched thickness marking toward cam follower.

## RABBIT (DIESEL) 4 CYLINDER (Cont.)

### Valve Clearance Specifications

| Application | In. (mm) |
|---|---|
| **Intake** | |
| Hot .................................................. | .008-.012 (.20-.30) |
| Cold .................................................. | .006-.010 (.15-.25) |
| **Exhaust** | |
| Hot .................................................. | .016-.020 (.40-.50) |
| Cold .................................................. | .014-.018 (.35-.45) |

**NOTE** — *Cold settings are given for reference as initial settings to be used during cylinder head rework. Final adjustments are made at normal operating temperatures and should be checked after 600 miles of operation.*

## PISTONS, PINS & RINGS

### OIL PAN

Due to transverse suspension of engine ahead of front suspension, oil pan may be removed simply by removing mounting bolts. Oil pump may inspected or removed and replaced with pan off. It is recommended that any further repairs be accomplished with engine removed from car.

### PISTON & ROD ASSEMBLY

**Removal** — Mark cylinder number on crown of each piston. If necessary, mark arrows pointing toward front of block on piston crowns. Remove rod cap bolts and force piston out top of cylinder using wooden hammer handle. Mark rods and bearing caps for proper installation.

**NOTE** — *If ridge at top of cylinder prevents piston removal, use ridge reamer prior to further disassembly. DO NOT force piston out of cylinder.*

**Installation** — Turn crankshaft so No. 1 journal is at BDC. Install piston/rod assembly until ring compressor contacts block. Guide rod over journal and use wooden handle of hammer to push piston into cylinder. Repeat with No. 4 piston and rod assembly ensuring that tabs on bearing halves engage notches in respective rod and cap. Tighten caps on rods 1 and 4, then rotate crankshaft 180° and install No. 2 and No. 3 piston/rod assemblies.

### PISTON PINS

**Removal** — Use needle-nose pliers to remove circlips. Press out pin and remove piston, noting direction piston is fitted to rod.

**Installation** — Check piston/pin fit for thumb push fit. Connecting rod/pin wear limit is .0015" (.04 mm). Connecting rod may be rebushed and honed to proper size if required. If pin is too loose in piston, replace both pin and piston.

### FITTING PISTONS

**1)** Measure cylinder at three points: 3/8" (10 mm) from top and bottom, and at center of bore. Measure in line with and at 90° to thrust face. Cylinder wear limit is .0015" (.04 mm) beyond standard dimensions and/or out of round. If limits are exceeded, cylinders must be honed and new pistons fitted.

**2)** Measure pistons 5/8" (15 mm) from bottom of skirt 90° to pin bore. Subtract this measurement from that of corresponding cylinder bore and note piston-to-cylinder clearance. If clearance exceeds .0028" (.07 mm), oversize pistons must be installed.

**3)** Place each piston ring squarely into bottom of cylinder about 5/8" (15 mm) and measure end gap. Measure ring side gap in pistons. Install properly fitted rings on pistons with end gaps offset 120° from each other (start with oil ring gap to rear). The word "TOP" on each ring must face upward.

*Fig. 5   Side and Top View of Diesel Piston*

**NOTE** — *In case any pistons require replacement, new pistons must be of same weight class. Unmarked pistons must be within 10 grams of weight of other installed pistons. Replacement piston rods must also be installed in sets of four from the same weight group.*

## CRANKSHAFT MAIN & CONNECTING ROD BEARINGS

### MAIN & CONNECTING ROD BEARINGS

**1)** Push crankshaft toward one end and measure end play at No. 3 (thrust) bearing. Main bearing caps are numbered "1" to "5" with "1" at drive belt end and "5" at flywheel end. Measure connecting rod end play (side play). Check all bearing clearances by the Plastigage method.

**2)** Measure crankshaft journals to determine size and any out-of-round. Maximum allowable out of round is .0012" (.03 mm). Install main inserts with bearing half having oil groove into block. Lubricate bearings and install caps in original positions.

### Crankshaft Journal Diameters

| Size | Main Bearing In. (mm) | Con. Rod. Bearing In. (mm) |
|---|---|---|
| Standard .................. | 2.126 (54.00) | 1.81 (46.00) |
| 1st US .................... | 2.116 (53.75) | 1.80 (45.75) |
| 2nd US .................... | 2.106 (53.50) | 1.79 (45.50) |
| 3rd US .................... | 2.096 (53.25) | 1.78 (45.25) |

## RABBIT (DIESEL) 4 CYLINDER (Cont.)

### REAR MAIN BEARING OIL SEAL

**NOTE** — *Rear main bearing oil seal may be replaced with engine in vehicle. Transmission and flywheel must be removed.*

Insert screwdriver between crankshaft flywheel flange and inside lip of oil seal. Pry oil seal out. Install guide sleeve tool 2003/2A (or equivalent) over crankshaft flange. Start new oil seal into recess in carrier. Remove guide sleeve then fit drive plate 2003/1 (or equivalent) and seat seal by tightening flywheel bolts in plate.

### FRONT MAIN BEARING OIL SEAL AND INTERMEDIATE SHAFT OIL SEAL

**NOTE** — *Diesel engine intermediate shaft rotates counterclockwise and utilizes a different seal than the gas engine. Arrow pointing counterclockwise on seal indicates correct application for Diesel model.*

Remove camshaft belt and crankshaft sprocket. Pry seal from carrier carefully to avoid damage to carrier. Use tool 10-219 or equivalent to remove seal. Use suitable installing tool (10-203 or equivalent) and press new seal into carrier until flush with front of carrier. Remove steel driving sleeve from carrier and use aluminum part of tool to drive seal further in until it is recessed .080" (2 mm) from front of seal carrier.

**NOTE** — *Same procedures are used for intermediate shaft seal except that intermediate shaft sprocket is removed. Seal is pressed in only until flush with carrier.*

## CAMSHAFT

### TIMING BELT

**NOTE** — *Sprockets do not have to be removed to replace drive belt.*

**Removal** — Loosen alternator and remove V-belt, then remove crankshaft V-belt pulley. Remove air cleaner and ducting. Remove drive belt cover and cylinder head cover. Remove timing plug on top of bell housing and rotate crankshaft to No. 1 cylinder at TDC with both No. 1 cam lobes pointed upward. Using tool 2065 (or equivalent), lock camshaft in position. Lock injection pump in position with special pin (2064) and loosen tensioner. Remove drive belt toward right side of car.

**Installation** — Assure that flywheel is aligned with TDC mark. Loosen camshaft bolt ½ turn and tap camshaft gear loose from camshaft. Ensure that injection pump marks are aligned and install drive belt. Tension belt by turning tensioner to right until scale reads 12 to 13 on VW 210 tool. Tighten camshaft sprocket bolt to 32 ft. lbs. (4.5 mkg). Turn crankshaft two turns in direction of engine rotation, strike belt with rubber hammer between camshaft sprocket and injection pump sprocket. Recheck belt tension and replace remaining components.

### CAMSHAFT

**Removal** — With camshaft drive sprocket and cylinder head cover removed, loosen bearing caps in following sequence: 5, 1, and 3, then loosen caps 2 and 4 diagonally. Bearing caps are numbered front (sprocket end) to rear (flywheel end).

**Inspection** — **1)** Number and remove cam followers, then reinstall camshaft using only end (1 and 5) bearing caps. Check axial play of camshaft with dial indicator. If play exceeds .006" (.15 mm), either head or camshaft is worn and must be replaced.

**2)** To measure camshaft bearing clearance, install caps one at a time and check with either a dial indicator or Plastigage. Check camshaft runout by installing shaft between centers and applying dial indicator at center bearing journal. Runout must not exceed .0004" (.01 mm) when camshaft is rotated.

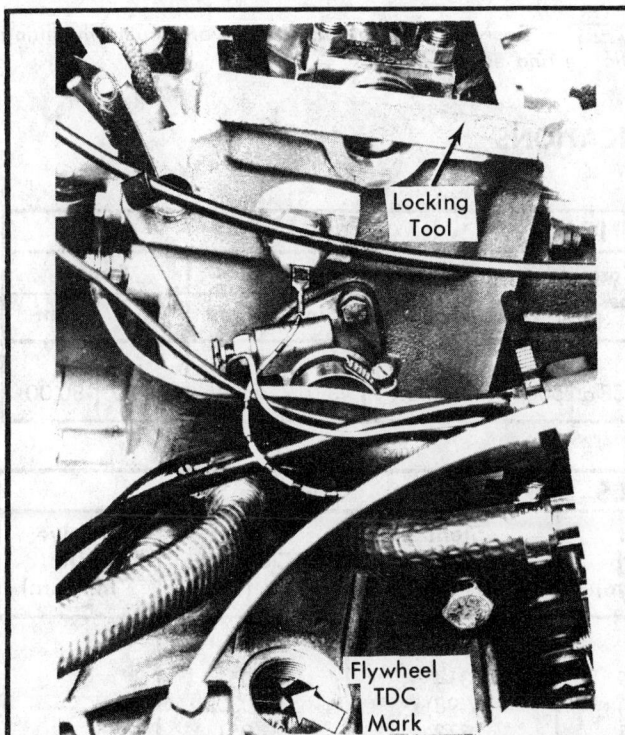

**Fig. 6  Flywheel TDC Mark and Camshaft Locking Tool**

**Fig. 7  Measuring Camshaft Endplay**

**3)** Inspect cam lobes, followers, and all bearing surfaces. Ensure that all oil passages are clean. Replace any components showing signs of pitting, galling or signs of seizure.

# Volkswagen Engines

## RABBIT (DIESEL) 4 CYLINDER (Cont.)

**Installation** — Lightly lubricate all components for assembly. Install cam followers in original bores with matching adjusting discs. Place camshaft and number 2 and 4 bearing caps in position. Gradually tighten all four bearing cap nuts until camshaft is fully seated, then install caps 5, 3, and 1. Use tool 10-203 (or equivalent) to install front oil seal and complete installation in reverse order of removal.

### VALVE TIMING

See *TIMING BELT* procedures in this article.

### INJECTION PUMP TIMING

See *ADJUSTING INJECTION PUMP TIMING* in *BOSCH DIESEL INJECTION* section.

## ENGINE OILING

**Crankcase Capacity** — 3.7 quarts with filter change; 3.2 quarts without filter change.

**Oil Filter** — Replaceable spin-on type.

**Normal Oil Pressure** — 28 psi @2000 RPM (normal operating temperature).

### ENGINE OILING SYSTEM

Gear type oil pump provides oil for pressure feed to crankshaft journals, camshaft bearings, and intermediate shaft. A larger, heavy-duty oil filter and revised oil pump drive are used in the Diesel. Other lubrication characteristics are similar to the spark ignition engines.

### OIL PUMP

**Removal** — Drain oil and remove oil pan. Remove pump mounting bolts and pump along with pick-up tube. Install in vise and remove pick-up tube.

**Inspection** — Check oil pump gear backlash with feeler gauge. Clearance should be between .002-.008" (.05-.20 mm). Measure pump gear end play using machinist's square and feeler gauge for .006" (.15 mm) clearance or less. If specifications are exceeded, replace gears or pump.

**Installation** — To install, assure that all mating surfaces are clean, install gaskets and reverse removal procedure.

## ENGINE COOLING

**Cooling System Capacity** — 6.8 U.S. quarts.

**Thermostat** — Begins to open at 176°F (80°C) and is fully open at 200°F (94°C). Radiator fan thermo switch causes fan to operate above 194°-203°F (90°-95°C) and switch off at 185°-194°F (85°-90°C) and below. Radiator relief pressure should be 13-15 psi.

**CAUTION** — *Never drain the coolant while the engine is hot. Cylinder head or engine block could warp if not allowed to cool prior to draining.*

### WATER PUMP

**NOTE** — *Front portion of water pump (shaft, seals, bearing, and housing) can be replaced separately. To do this, camshaft drive belt and sprockets must be removed. To avoid removing drive belt, remove water pump as an assembly.*

**Removal** — Drain cooling system. Disconnect battery ground strap and unplug alternator wires. Remove alternator. Disconnect thermostat housing and hoses from water pump. Remove bolts holding pump to engine block and remove pump.

**Installation** — To install, reverse removal procedure and use new "O" ring in recess in pump mounting flange.

**NOTE** — *Do NOT use sealer between water pump mounting flange and engine block.*

## ENGINE SPECIFICATIONS

| GENERAL SPECIFICATIONS | | | | | | | | | | |
|---|---|---|---|---|---|---|---|---|---|---|
| Year | Displ. | | Carburetor | HP at RPM | Torque (Ft. Lbs. at RPM) | Compr. Ratio | Bore | | Stroke | |
| | cu. ins. | cc | | | | | in. | mm | in. | mm |
| 1978 Diesel | 89.7 | 1471 | Fuel Inj. | 48@5000 | 58@2500 | 23.5:1 | 3.012 | 76.5 | 3.150 | 80.00 |

| VALVES | | | | | | | |
|---|---|---|---|---|---|---|---|
| Engine & Valve | Head Diam. In. (mm) | Face Angle | Seat Angle | Seat Width In. (mm) | Stem Diameter In. (mm) | Stem Clearance In. (mm) | Valve Lift In. (mm) |
| Diesel Intake | 1.338 (33.9) | 45° | 45° | .079 (2.0) | .314 (7.98) | .051 (1.30) | ..... |
| Exhaust | 1.220 (31.0) | 45° | 45° | .095 (2.4) | .313 (7.95) | .051 (1.30) | ..... |

# Volkswagen Engines

## RABBIT (DIESEL) 4 CYLINDER (Cont.)

### ENGINE SPECIFICATIONS (Cont.)

#### PISTONS, PINS, RINGS

| Engine | PISTONS | PINS | | RINGS | | |
| | Clearance In. (mm) | Piston Fit In. (mm) | Rod Fit In. (mm) | Rings | End Gap In. (mm) | Side Clearance In. (mm) |
|---|---|---|---|---|---|---|
| Diesel | .001 (.03) | Push Fit | .0004-.0008 (.01-.02) | Comp. | .012-.018 (.30-.45) | .0008-.002 (.02-.05) |
| | | | | Oil | .010-.016 (.25-.40) | .0008-.002 (.02-.05) |

#### CRANKSHAFT MAIN & CONNECTING ROD BEARINGS

| Engine | MAIN BEARINGS | | | | CONNECTING ROD BEARINGS | | |
| | Journal Diam. In. (mm) | Clearance In. (mm) | Thrust Bearing | Crankshaft End Play In. (mm) | Journal Diam. In. (mm) | Clearance In. (mm) | Side Play In. (mm) |
|---|---|---|---|---|---|---|---|
| Diesel | 2.126 (54) | .0011-.0033 (.02-.088) | No. 3 | .014 (.37) | 1.81 (46) | .0011-.0035 (.028-.088) | ① .014 (.37) |

① — Wear Limit

#### VALVE SPRINGS

| Engine | Free Length In. (mm) | PRESSURE Lbs. @ In. (kg @ mm) | |
| | | Valve Closed | Valve Open |
|---|---|---|---|
| Diesel Inner | ..... | 46-51@.719 (21-23@18.3) | ..... |
| Outer | ..... | 96-106 @ .875 43.5-48@22.3 | ..... |

#### CAMSHAFT

| Engine | Journal Diam. In. (mm) | Clearance In. (mm)① | Lobe Lift In. (mm) |
|---|---|---|---|
| Diesel | ..... | .0008-.002 (.02-.05) | ..... |

① — End play .006" (.1 mm)

#### TIGHTENING SPECIFICATIONS

| Application | Ft. Lbs. (mkg) |
|---|---|
| Timing Belt Tensioner Lock Nut | 32 (4.5) |
| Intermediate Sprocket Bolt | 32 (4.5) |
| Crankshaft Sprocket Bolt | 58 (8.0) |
| Water Pump Pulley Bolts | 14 (2.0) |
| Crankshaft Pulley Bolts | 14 (2.0) |
| Main Bearing Cap Bolts | 47 (6.5) |
| Flywheel-to-Crankshaft Bolts | 54 (7.5) |
| Connecting Rod Cap Bolts | 32 (4.5) |
| Camshaft Sprocket Bolt | 32 (4.5) |
| Camshaft Bearing Cap Nuts | 14 (2.0) |
| Cylinder Head Bolts | |
|   Cold | 61 (8.5) |
|   Hot | 68 (9.5) |
| Manifolds-to-Cylinder Head | 18 (2.5) |
| Oil Pump Mounting Bolts | 14 (2.0) |
| Oil Pan Bolts | 14 (2.0) |
| Fuel Injectors in Head | 50 (7.0) |
| Fue Injector Line Unions | 18 (2.5) |
| Fuel Injection Pump Mounting Bolts | 18 (2.5) |

# Volvo Engines

## 240 SERIES 4 CYLINDER

### ENGINE CODING

#### ENGINE IDENTIFICATION

Engine identification number is located on camshaft timing belt cover. Last 3 digits identify engine.

| Engine Identification Numbers | | |
|---|---|---|
| Application | Man. Trans. | Auto. Trans. |
| B21F Engines | | |
| Federal .................. | 498578 .................. | 498579 |
| Calif. .................... | 498580 .................. | 498581 |

**Last 6 Digits** — Chassis Number. Starting 1978 Chassis numbers are: 242, 122895; 244, 274965; 245, 123835.

### ENGINE, CYLINDER HEAD & MANIFOLD

#### ENGINE

1) Disconnect rubber boot and lock ring at base of gearshift lever (manual transmission). Remove battery. Disconnect windshield washer hose and engine compartment lamp. Remove hood.

2) Remove cap from expansion tank. Open radiator drain cock and drain coolant. Disconnect lower radiator hose at radiator, crankcase ventilation hose at cylinder head, and upper radiator hose at engine. Detach expansion tank hoses from radiator. Disconnect oil cooler pipes for automatic transmission at radiator. Remove fan shroud screws, disconnect radiator, and lift radiator and fan shroud from car.

3) Remove air cleaner and hose assembly. Loosen tensioner nut and remove belt from air pump. Disconnect hoses at pump and remove pump and bracket assembly. Remove vacuum pump after disconnecting hoses, including hose to brake power cylinder. Remove tensioner bar bolts, drive belt and power steering pump.

4) If equipped with air conditioning, remove crankshaft pulley and A/C drive belt. Reinstall pulley loosely. Disconnect and remove compressor and bracket.

5) Mark and disconnect four vacuum hoses at engine and two carbon filter hoses. Remove wire or connector from distributor, high tension lead from coil, and starter motor cables and clutch cable clamp from starter.

6) Detach wiring harness from voltage regulator. Disconnect throttle cable at pulley and A/C wire at solenoid on intake manifold.

7) Remove fuel cap to relieve pressure, and remove fuel hoses from filter and return pipe. Remove guard plate for ballast resistor, and disconnect two wire connectors from intake manifold micro switch, four in wiring harness, and two at ballast resistor.

8) Disconnect heater hoses at firewall and drain oil from engine. Remove exhaust pipe flange nuts and gasket. Remove front engine mounting bolts and front exhaust pipe mounting bracket. Disconnect gearshift control rod (automatic transmission) or clutch cable (manual transmission).

9) Disconnect speedometer cable, propeller shaft U-joint, and gearshift selector from control rod. If manual transmission has overdrive, disconnect wire to gearshift selector. Using a wooden block, place jack under transmission. Remove transmission support member.

10) Attach lifting yoke assembly (5035) to three engine lifting eyes, and adjust lifting beam (2810) to its rearmost position. Hoist slightly to release front engine mount dowels. Check for wires or hoses, and disconnect as necessary. Adjust lifting beam to forward position and lift engine from car.

#### INTAKE & EXHAUST MANIFOLDS

**Removal** — 1) Disconnect battery ground cable, then remove air bellows from CI unit to intake manifold. Disconnect PCV hoses at intake manifold and flame arrester. Disconnect vacuum pump hose at intake manifold. Disconnect diverter valve hoses. Disconnect air pump with tensioner and position to one side.

2) Disconnect the following fuel lines: control pressure regulator (one hose), cold start injector (one hose), distributor pipe to engine (two hoses) front fuel filter to engine (two hoses), and injector hoses (four hoses). Disconnect wiring at control pressure regulator, cold start injector, and auxiliary air valve.

3) Remove air injection pipe. Disconnect throttle cable from intake manifold. Disconnect charcoal canister hoses and EGR valve hose from intake manifold. Remove intake manifold brace, attaching nuts, and intake manifold. Disconnect transmission fill pipe from flywheel housing (automatic transmissions only). Remove attaching nuts and exhaust manifold.

**Installation** — To install, reverse removal procedure and use new manifold gaskets. Tighten nuts and bolts to specifications.

#### CYLINDER HEAD

**Removal** — 1) Drain cooling system at radiator and cylinder block. Disconnect battery ground cable. Disconnect upper radiator hose at engine. Disconnect air bellows between CI unit and air cleaner. Remove PCV hoses from intake manifold and oil trap on block. Disconnect vacuum pump hose at intake manifold.

2) Disconnect diverter valve hoses. Remove air pump and bracket. Disconnect the following fuel lines: control pressure regulator (one hose), cold start injector (one hose), distributor pipe to engine (two hoses), front fuel filter to engine (two hoses), and injector hoses (four hoses).

## 240 SERIES 4 CYLINDER (Cont.)

**3)** Disconnect wires at following components: control pressure regulator, cold start injector, auxiliary air valve, and temperature sender. Disconnect throttle cable from intake manifold. Disconnect charcoal canister hoses and EGR valve hose from intake manifold. Disconnect transmission fill pipe from transmission housing (automatic transmissions only).

**4)** Remove water pipe rear clamp from manifold. Remove exhaust manifold to exhaust pipe attaching nuts. Remove intake manifold brace. Disconnect spark plug cables at plugs, then disconnect upper water hose at firewall. Remove valve cover and cylinder head bolts. Lift cylinder head from engine.

**Installation** – **1)** Install new head gasket with "TOP" mark upward. Be sure all contact surfaces are clean. Position cylinder head over gasket.

**2)** Dip head bolts and washers in engine oil before installation. Install and torque, in two steps, to specifications shown in table, and according to sequence shown in *Fig. 1*.

**3)** Adjust valves to .014-.016" (.35-.40 mm) with engine cold. **NOTE** – *See Valve Clearance Adjustment for procedure.* Reverse remainder of removal procedure, and then make final valve adjustment after running engine for 10 minutes. Adjust to .016-.018" (.40-.45 mm). Retorque cylinder head bolts.

### Cylinder Head Tightening Specifications

| Sequence | Ft.Lbs (mkg) |
|---|---|
| Step One | 44 (6.0) |
| Step Two | ①76-83 C10.5-11.5) |

① – Run engine for 10 minutes until hot, allow engine to cool 30 minutes, and retorque.

**Fig. 1  Cylinder Head Tightening Sequence**

## VALVES

### VALVE ARRANGEMENT

E-I-E-I-E-I-E-I – Front to Rear.

### VALVE GUIDE SERVICING

**Removal** – Heat cylinder head to 212° ± 18°F (100° ± 10°C). Use drift 9992818-6 (or equivalent) to press out old guide. Make sure guide is not scored when being pressed out. If it is, the hole must be machined oversize.

**Valve Guide Identification** – New guides are grooved for identification. Guide must be same size as old guide. Guides are marked as follows:

| No. of Grooves | Std. |
|---|---|
| 1 | Os 1 |
| 2 | Os 2 |
| 3 | Os 3 |

**Installation** – With cylinder head heated, use drift 9995027-1 or equivalent)) to press in intake valve guide. Use drift 9995028-9 for exhaust valve guide. Press guide down until drift touches cylinder head. This establishes correct location. Force required to press in guide should be at least 2023 lbs. If force used does not reach this figure, guide seat must be reamed to nearest oversize.

### VALVE SPRINGS

**Removal & Installation** – With cylinder head removed, compress valve springs using suitable valve spring compression tool, and remove valve retainers. Disassemble valve spring components and place valves in order in suitable valve rack. To install, place valves in position, fit valve guide seal, valve spring, upper washer and retainer.

**Fig. 2  Valve & Guide Assembly**

### VALVE SPRING INSTALLED HEIGHT

Valve spring ends must be square. Installed height of valve spring cannot exceed specifications. Measure spring height from base of spring pad on cylinder head to underside of spring retainer.

### VALVE CLEARANCE ADJUSTMENT

**1)** Valve clearance is adjusted with engine off, and may be done either warm or cold. Remove valve cover. Turn crankshaft center bolt until camshaft is in position for firing No. 1 cylinder. Both cam lobes should point up at equally large angles. Pulley timing mark should be on 0°.

## 240 SERIES 4 CYLINDER (Cont.)

**2)** Using feeler gauge, check valve clearance of No. 1 cylinder, measuring between camshaft lobe and discs. Intake and exhaust valves should have same clearances:

### Valve Clearances

| When Checking | In. (mm) |
|---|---|
| Cold engine | .012-.018" (.30-.45 mm) |

| When Setting | In. (mm) |
|---|---|
| Cold Engine | .014-.016" (.35-.40 mm) |
| Hot Engine | .016-.018" (.40-.45 mm) |

**3)** If clearance is incorrect, line up notches in valve depressors, so they are at right angles to engine center line. Install valve adjustment tool (5022) and turn handle downward until depressor groove is just above edge of cylinder head. Remove adjusting disc with special pliers (5026).

**4)** Using micrometer, measure thickness of disc. Then determine proper thickness required of new disc to bring clearance within specifications. For example: Measure existing clearance and subtract correct clearance. Difference should be added to thickness of old disc to determine thickness of new disc required. Discs are available in thicknesses ranging from 3.30 to 4.50 mm in increments of .05 mm.

**5)** Discs should be oiled and installed with marks down. Remove valve adjustment tool (5022), rotate crankshaft to correct firing position for No. 3 cylinder and repeat procedure. Then adjust valve clearance for No. 4 and No. 2 cylinders. When all four cylinders have been adjusted, turn camshaft a few turns and recheck valve clearance at all cylinders.

**6)** Position gasket on cylinder head and install valve cover.

Adjusting Discs

*Fig. 3   Removing Valve Adjusting Discs*

## PISTONS, PINS & RINGS

### OIL PAN

**Removal** — Position lifting tools (5006, 5033 & 5115) as shown in *Fig. 4*. Disconnect A/C compressor (if equipped). Remove bolts from left engine mount. Lift engine slightly and drain oil. Remove splash guard, left engine mount, and brace. Remove bolts from oil pan and tap to loosen.

*Fig. 4   Removing Oil Pan*

**Installation** — Place new gasket on oil pan. Turn and lift into position. Install bolts, brace, left engine mount, and splash guard. Lower engine and install bolts in left engine mount. Remove tools and connect A/C compressor. Fill engine with oil.

### PISTON & ROD ASSEMBLY

**Removal** — Remove cylinder head, oil pan and oil pump. Be sure connecting rods and caps are properly marked, so they may be reinstalled in original location. Remove carbon ridge from cylinder bores. Remove rod cap, and using wooden hammer handle, push piston out top of cylinder bore. Reinstall rod cap on piston and rod from which removed.

**Installation** — **1)** Remove rod cap from connecting rod. Secure piston pin with retaining rings. Be sure "TOP" mark on rings is facing top of piston and end gaps are 120 degrees from each other and rings are properly installed. Install bearings in connecting rods and caps. Lubricate cylinder bores, pistons and bearings.

**2)** Using piston ring compressor (5031), insert rod and piston into bore, with mark on top of piston and on connecting rod toward front of engine.

**3)** Using wooden hammer handle, tap lightly on top of piston. Align marks and torque end caps to 43 ft. lbs. Install oil pump, oil pan and cylinder head.

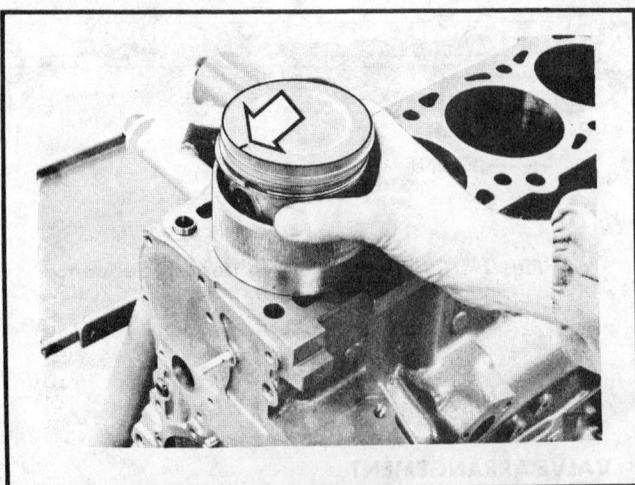

*Fig. 5   Installation of Piston in Cylinder Block*

# Volvo Engines

## 240 SERIES 4 CYLINDER (Cont.)

### FITTING PISTONS

Measure piston diameter at right angle to piston pin bore and .25" (7 mm) from lower edge. Measure cylinder bore at several positions. If difference exceeds clearance specifications, oversize pistons are available.

### PISTON PINS

Piston pins are available in .002" (.05 mm) oversize from standard diameter. If replacement oversize pins are needed, piston pin hole should be reamed out to correct measurement using suitable reaming tool. Use reamer fitted with pilot guide, take only small cuts at a time. Pin fit is correct when pin can be pushed through connecting rod hole by hand, with only light resistance.

Pin

Connecting Rod

*Fig. 6   Thumb Pressure Piston Pin Fit*

## CRANKSHAFT MAIN & CONNECTING ROD BEARINGS

### MAIN & CONNECTING ROD BEARINGS

**Removal & Installation** — 1) Remove oil pan and related parts. *See Oil Pan Removal.* Identify and mark connecting rod caps and main bearing caps to ensure correct replacement.

**2)** Remove connecting rod caps and push pistons towards top of cylinders. Remove main bearing caps (one at a time) and thoroughly clean all bearing surfaces.

**3)** Measure all journals, using a micrometer. Out-of-roundness on connecting rod bearings should not exceed .003" (.07 mm)

and on main bearings, it should not exceed .002" (.05 mm). If values obtained are close to, or in excess of wear limits, crankshaft must be reground to next suitable undersize.

**4)** If all journals check out to standard size, refit with replacement bearings. Reinstall main bearing caps, refit connecting rods to crankshaft and tighten all nuts and bolts to specifications. Reassemble engine in reverse order of removal.

### REAR MAIN BEARING OIL SEAL

**Removal & Installation** — 1) Remove transmission, clutch, and flywheel from engine. Remove two bolts from oil pan (into rear flange). Slacken two bolts on each side of flange, and remove flange. Use a suitable drift (2817) to remove oil seal.

**2)** Clean flange area thoroughly and inspect seal mating surface of crankshaft. Install new seal to flange using drift (2817). **NOTE** — *If a new crankshaft has been installed, screw center bolt of tool in fully and install seal to its outer position in flange. If crankshaft has not been replaced, install seal with center bolt of tool screwed out a couple of turns.*

**3)** Oil new seal and install flange with new gasket to cylinder block. Install attaching bolts and tighten. Install oil pan attaching bolts and tighten. Install flywheel, clutch, and transmission.

## CAMSHAFT

### ENGINE FRONT COVER

**Removal** — 1) Remove fan shroud, fan belt and fan pulley. Remove water pump pulley and camshaft drive belt cover. Remove crankshaft hub, sprocket and belt guide. Remove sprocket from intermediate shaft. Detach wiring harness across front of engine. Remove two oil pan bolts from base of front cover and loosen two on each side of them. Remove drive belt guard plate and front cover.

**2)** Using suitable tool (5025) press out intermediate shaft seal from front cover. Using similar tool (5024) press out crankshaft seal. Use same tools to install new seals.

**Installation** — 1) Using new gasket, install front cover. Install oil pan, drive belt guard plate, and wiring harness.

**2)** Using tool (5024), install crankshaft seal. Using similar tool (5025), install intermediate shaft seal in front cover. **NOTE** — *Oil seals prior to installation.* Install inner belt guide on camshaft (collar facing away from belt). Install camshaft sprocket, aligning notch with dowel on camshaft. Install outer belt guide, washer and center bolt. Use suitable tool (5034) to hold sprocket and torque to 37 ft. lbs.

**3)** Install sprocket on intermediate shaft, aligning notch with dowel on shaft. Use tool (5034) to hold shaft while tightening center bolt to 37 ft. lbs.

**4)** Install belt guide and sprocket on crankshaft. Install front hub and torque center bolt to 122 ft. lbs. Install drive belt and complete installation of previously removed parts.

## 240 SERIES 4 CYLINDER (Cont.)

Fig. 7   Timing Marks for Crankshaft, Intermediate Shaft & Camshaft

### INSTALLING DRIVE BELT

1) Install belt tensioner if previously removed. Align notch in crankshaft belt guide with timing mark on front cover. Rotate intermediate shaft so timing mark on sprocket aligns with mark on belt guard. Align marks on camshaft belt guide with timing mark on valve cover.

2) New drive belts have yellow markings. Two lines should fit toward crankshaft marks and next mark toward intermediate shaft mark. Place belt over crankshaft sprocket first, then intermediate shaft. Stretch belt on tension side and fit over camshaft sprocket. Slide back of belt inside tension roller.

3) Loosen nut on belt tensioner to permit spring tension to act against drive belt. Recheck timing marks for proper location and torque nut on tensioner to 37 ft. lbs. Attach pulley to front hub on crankshaft.

## ENGINE OILING

**Crankcase Capacity** — 4 qts. including filter.
**Oil Filter** — Full-flow canister, disposable type.
**Normal Oil Pressure** — 35-85 psi @2000 RPM with engine hot.

### ENGINE OILING SYSTEM

Engine utilizes a force-feed lubricating system. Oil circulates through oil pump to oil filter on outside of engine block assembly. From filter, oil is forced to drilled gallery in center of block, where it moves under pressure to main bearings. Main bearings are drilled to permit lubricant to pass on to connecting rod and camshaft bearings.

Oil from camshaft bearings is used to lubricate discs, valves, and cylinder head assembly. Cylinder walls and rings are lubricated by the splash from connecting rods. Excess oil from all areas returns to sump through drain holes in block assembly.

Fig. 8   Oiling System Components

### OIL PUMP

1) Remove oil pan and related parts. *See Oil Pan Removal.* Pull oil pump out of engine, disassemble and clean all parts thoroughly. Check all parts for excessive wear or signs of fatigue.

## 240 SERIES 4 CYLINDER (Cont.)

Drive Shaft

Pump Body

Bushes

Driving Gear

Valve Ball

Spring for Relief Valve

Drive Gear

Cover

Retainer Clip

Strainer

**Fig. 9  Cutaway & Operational View of Oil Pump Assembly**

**2)** Measure backlash (clearance) between pump gears. It should be .006-.014" (.15-.35 mm). Also measure end play of gears. Allowable end play is .0008-.0048" (.02-.12 mm). If any parts show excessive wear or play, replace necessary components. Drive shaft and gear are matched set and must be replaced as an assembly.

**3)** Reinstall oil pump, making sure that sealing rings on oil delivery pipe are securely in place. Be sure oil pump properly engages pump drive shaft. Replace oil pan and related components.

### ENGINE COOLING

**WATER PUMP**

**Removal & Installation** — **1)** Remove expansion tank cap, open engine block drain cock, and disconnect lower radiator hose at radiator. Remove fan shroud and fan. Loosen alternator and air pump and remove drive belts.

**2)** Remove water pump pulley, timing gear cover, and lower radiator hose. Remove retaining bolt and slide coolant pipe rearward. Remove pump.

**3)** Clean all surfaces. Place new sealing ring on coolant pipe. Install new gasket when mounting pump. Install other components previously removed. Fill with coolant.

**Thermostat** — Standard wax-type (marked 87°) opens at 189° F (87° C); fully open at 207° F (97° C).

**Cooling System Capacity** — All models, 10 quarts.

### ENGINE SPECIFICATIONS

| GENERAL SPECIFICATIONS | | | | | | | | | | |
|---|---|---|---|---|---|---|---|---|---|---|
| Year | Displ. | | Carburetor | HP at RPM | Torque (Ft. Lbs. at RPM) | Compr. Ratio | Bore | | Stroke | |
| | cu. ins. | cc | | | | | in. | mm | in. | mm |
| 1978 B21F | 130.0 | 2130 | F.I. | ..... | ..... | 8.5-1 | 3.623 | 92 | 3.150 | 80 |

| VALVES | | | | | | | |
|---|---|---|---|---|---|---|---|
| Engine & Valve | Head Diam. In. (mm) | Face Angle | Seat Angle | Seat Width In. (mm) | Stem Diameter In. (mm) | Stem Clearance In. (mm) | Valve Lift In. (mm) |
| B21F Intake | 1.732 (44) | 45.5° | 44.75° | .068-.092 (1.7-2.3) | .3134-.3138 (7.96-7.97) | .0012-.0024 (.030-.060) | .44 (11.2) |
| Exhaust | 1.278 (35) | 45.5° | 44.75° | .068-.092 (1.7-2.3) | .3122-.3126 (7.93-7.94) | .0024-.0035 (.060-.090) | .44 (11.2) |

# Volvo Engines

## 240 SERIES 4 CYLINDER (Cont.)

### ENGINE SPECIFICATIONS (Cont.)

#### PISTONS, PINS, RINGS

| Engine | PISTONS | PINS | | RINGS | | |
|--------|---------|------|---|-------|---|---|
| | Clearance In. (mm) | Piston Fit In. (mm) | Rod Fit In. (mm) | Rings | End Gap In. (mm) | Side Clearance In. (mm) |
| B21F | .0004-.0012 (.010-.030) | Push Fit | Push Fit | 2 Comp. | .0138-.0217 (.35-.55) | .0016-.0028 (.040-.072) |
| | | | | Oil | .010-.016 (.25-.40) | .0012-.0024 (.030-.062) |

#### CRANKSHAFT MAIN & CONNECTING ROD BEARINGS

| Engine | MAIN BEARINGS | | | | CONNECTING ROD BEARINGS | | |
|--------|---------------|---|---|---|-------------------------|---|---|
| | Journal Diam. In. (mm) | Clearance In. (mm) | Thrust Bearing | Crankshaft End Play In. (mm) | Journal Diam. In. (mm) | Clearance In. (mm) | Side Play In. (mm) |
| B21F | 2.4981-2.4986 (63.451-63.464) | .0011-.0033 (.028-.083) | ..... | .0015-.0058 (.037-.147) | 2.1255-2.1260 (53.987-54.000) | .0009-.0028 (.024-.070) | .006-.014 (.15-.35) |

#### VALVE SPRINGS

| Engine | Free Length In. (mm) | PRESSURE Lbs. @ In. (kg @ mm) | |
|--------|----------------------|-------------------------------|---|
| | | Valve Closed | Valve Open |
| B21F | 1.77 (45) | 63-72@1.50 (29-33@38) | 160-178@1.06 (73-81@27) |

#### CAMSHAFT

| Engine | Journal Diam. In. (mm) | Clearance In. (mm) | Lobe Lift In. (mm) |
|--------|------------------------|--------------------|--------------------|
| B21F | 1.1437-1.1445 (29.050-29.070) | .0012-.0028 (.030-.071) | ..... |

#### TIGHTENING SPECIFICATIONS

| Application | Ft. Lbs (mkg) |
|------------|---------------|
| Cylinder Head Bolts | |
|   Step One | 44 (6.0) |
|   Step Two | ①76-83 (10.5-11.5) |
| Main Bearing Caps | 85-91 (11.8-12.6) |
| Connecting Rod Caps | 43-48 (6.0-6.6) |
| Camshaft Bearing Caps | 13-16 (1.8-2.2) |
| Exhaust & Intake Manifold Bolts | 15 (2.0) |
| Flywheel Bolts | 47-54 (6.5-7.5) |
| Engine Mount Bolts | 15 (2.0) |
| Spark Plugs | 25-29 (3.5-4.0) |
| Sprockets | |
|   Camshaft | 37 (5.1) |
|   Intermediate Shaft | 37 (5.1) |
|   Crankshaft | 122 (16.9) |
| Fan Bolt | 33 (4.6) |
| Drive Belt Tensioner Nut | 37 (5.1) |
| Oil Pan Bolts | 8 (1.1) |

① Run engine for 10 minutes, until hot, allow engine to cool 30 minutes, and retorque.

## 260 SERIES V6

### ENGINE CODING

#### ENGINE IDENTIFICATION

Engine identification number is located just below manifold on driver's side of engine. Last 3 digits identify engine.

| Engine Identification Numbers | | |
|---|---|---|
| **Application** | **Man. Trans.** | **Auto. Trans.** |
| B27F Engines | | |
| Federal ..................... 498608 | ..................... | 498609 |
| Calif. ....................... 498606 | ..................... | 498607 |

**Last 6 Digits** — Chassis Number. Starting chassis numbers for 1978 are: 262, 2660; 264,46515; 265, 10920.

### ENGINE, CYLINDER HEADS & MANIFOLDS

#### ENGINE

**1)** Remove gearshift lever (manual) or place lever in "Park" (automatic). Remove battery, hood, air cleaner and engine splash guard.

**2)** Drain cooling system (each side of block), and disconnect all coolant hoses. Disconnect automatic transmission oil cooler pipes at radiator. Remove radiator and fan shroud. Disconnect heater hose at intake pipe, power brake hose at intake manifold, and vacuum pump hose at pump. Remove vacuum pump.

**3)** Disconnect fuel hoses at filter and return pipe. Disconnect wiring harness and relay connectors. Remove high tension lead from distributor and heater hoses at fire wall. Disconnect carbon filter hose at filter, and hose from EGR valve. Remove connector at voltage regulator and wire clamp. Disconnect connector for distributor, throttle cable, vacuum amplifier hose at T-pipe, and wax thermostat hoses.

**4)** Remove hose from air pump to backfire valve and wires from solenoid valve and micro switch. Remove nuts from both exhaust manifold flanges. Remove A/C compressor and drive belt without disconnecting hoses. Drain engine oil. Remove power steering pump and belt.

**5)** Remove nuts from front engine mounts. Remove exhaust pipe clamps (front exhaust pipe with catalytic converter). Disconnect shift control lever at automatic transmission.

**6)** Disconnect slave cylinder from clutch (manual transmission) and detach speedometer cable. Disconnect propeller shaft. Put stands under front of car, and using wooden block, place jack under oil pan. Remove transmission attachment member.

**7)** Using safe hoisting equipment, lift engine from car.

**NOTE** — *When removing engine, check for hoses and wires not previously removed.*

#### CYLINDER HEAD (ENGINE IN VEHICLE)

**Removal — 1)** Disconnect battery ground cable. Remove air cleaner and disconnect throttle cable. Disconnect kick-down cable (automatic transmission) and remove pipe from EGR valve and intake manifold. Disconnect vacuum hose at EGR valve. Remove oil filler cap and stuff rag in filler hole. Disconnect crankcase ventilation pipe from intake manifold and remove intake manifold front, gaskets, and rubber rings.

**2)** Disconnect fuel line and connector from cold start injector. Disconnect vacuum hose, connector and two fuel lines from control pressure regulator. Disconnect hoses, pipes and electrical connectors, and remove auxiliary air valve. Remove connector at fuel distributor and wiring harness. Disconnect high tension leads from spark plugs and injectors from holders in both banks.

**3)** Disconnect vacuum hose at distributor, and remove vacuum, carbon filter, diverter valve, power brake, and heater hoses at intake manifold. Disconnect wires at throttle micro switch and solenoid valve, and fuel lines from filter and return pipe. Remove fuel distributor.

**4)** Disconnect EGR valve hose from throttle housing. Remove cold start injector and pipe. Remove intake manifold and rubber rings. Remove splash guard under engine and drain coolant from both sides of block. Remove air pump, vacuum pump and vacuum hoses at thermostat. Disconnect upper radiator hose and remove A/C compressor (do not remove hoses).

**5)** Remove distributor and EGR valve and bracket. Disconnect relay connectors and remove rear A/C bracket. Remove lower radiator hose at water pump and hoses from pump to cylinder heads. Disconnect supply hose from cylinder heads, and separate air manifold at rear of engine. Remove backfire valve and air hose. Remove valve covers.

**6)** On left side, remove four upper timing gear cover bolts and Allen head screw (not camshaft center bolt). On right side, remove four upper timing gear cover bolts and cover plate. Remove exhaust pipe clamps under vehicle and oil dipstick and pipe. Remove exhaust pipe flange and exhaust manifold. Remove cover plates at rear of cylinder heads.

***Fig. 1  Sequence for Removing and Installing Cylinder Head Bolts***

## 260 SERIES V6 ( Cont.)

Rods

*Fig. 2   Special Tools for Removing Cylinder Heads*

**7)** Rotate each camshaft until large hole in sprocket aligns with rocker arm shaft. Remove rocker arm and shaft assembly by removing bolts in sequence shown in *Fig. 1.* Loosen bolt and push camshaft lock fork to one side.

**8)** Install tool to hold camshaft sprocket in place (5104). With tool installed, remove camshaft center bolt and slide camshaft to rear. Be sure camshaft stud is free from sprocket.

**NOTE** — *If tool is not used, camshaft chain will slacken and be held by chain tensioner. Sprocket then cannot be pulled upward when installing camshaft. If this should occur, timing gear cover must be removed for access to chain tensioner.*

**9)** Insert two 12" long rods into cylinder head bolt holes, *Fig. 2,* and push downward to loosen cylinder head from block. Do not attempt to remove cylinder head by lifting straight upward. If liners are not to be removed, be sure they do not separate from their seals in lower liner seat. If seals are damaged, coolant will enter crankcase. Lift out cylinder head carefully.

**10)** Tap guide sleeves flush with block face and remove gasket. Install liner holders (5093) to secure liners against seat seals. Clean gasket surfaces and install camshaft retaining tool (5105). After tool is securely in place, remove fixing bolt from previously installed tool (5l04). *See Fig. 2.*

**NOTE** — *Sprocket retaining tool (5105) should be kept securely in place while cylinder heads are removed. This prevents camshaft chains from slackening, yet permits turning of crankshaft.*

**Installation** — **1)** Insert fixing bolt into camshaft sprocket retainer (5104) and remove other retainer (5105) from cylinder block face. Pull up on guide sleeves and insert a 1/8" drill bit under each sleeve. Remove liner holders (5093) and position cylinder head gasket on block face (left and right gaskets differ). Install cylinder head with one bolt and push camshaft into camshaft sprocket. Install camshaft center bolt, but do not torque. Remove drill bits from under guide sleeves

**2)** Position rocker arm and shaft assembly and install cylinder head bolts. Tighten all bolts in sequence shown in *Fig. 1* in three stages:

**Cylinder Head Tightening Specifications**

| Sequence | Ft. Lbs. (mkg) |
| --- | --- |
| Step One | 7 (1.0) |
| Step Two | 22 (3.0) |
| Step Three | ①44 (6.1) |

① — After 10-15 minutes retorque with protractor (5098).

**3)** Torque camshaft center bolt and remove sprocket retainer (5104). Center lock fork over camshaft and tighten. Back off all cylinder head bolts in sequence, *Fig. 1.* Tighten to 11-14 ft. lbs. Using protractor (5098) on standard socket, torque head bolts as follows:

1. Use rocker arm and shaft as a guide line for protractor.
2. Fit socket over bolt 1 and take up slack of tool. Rotate protractor so that "0" mark aligns with rocker arm and shaft assembly.
3. Tighten bolt until protractor angle of 116-120° aligns with rocker arm guide line.
4. Repeat procedure in proper tightening sequence for other head bolts.
5. After engine is assembled, run at operating temperature for 15 minutes and cool for 30 minutes. Back off head bolts once more and torque to 11-14 ft. lbs. Then use protractor to torque bolts in sequence shown (*Fig. 3*) to 113-117°.

11-14 ft. lbs. +113-117°

*Fig. 3   Final Torquing of Cylinder Head Bolts After Running and Cooling Engine*

## 260 SERIES V6 ( Cont.)

**4)** Install remainder of components in reverse order of removal procedure, noting the following:

1. Before installing valve cover, adjust valves (cold setting).
2. When installing distributor, rotor should initially point to clamp clockwise from mark on distributor housing. Crankshaft should still be in position for firing No. 1 cylinder following valve adjustment. When distributor is pushed into place, rotor will point to mark on housing. *Fig. 4 and 5.*
3. Use new gaskets and rubber sealing rings.
4. When installing spark plug wires, firing order is 1-6-3-5-2-4.
5. Be sure to fill engine with oil and coolant. Retorque cylinder head bolts after assembly is completed.

**Fig. 4    Distributor Rotor Position Prior to Final Positioning**

## VALVES

### VALVE ARRANGEMENT

Right Bank ..................................... E-I-E-I-E-I (Front-to-Rear)
Left Bank ..................................... I-E-I-E-I-E (Front-to-Rear)

### ROCKER ARM ASSEMBLY

**1)** Mark rocker arm assemblies for right and left bank. Disassemble, keeping parts in same order as removed from shaft. Shaft-to-arm clearance should be .00047-.00213" (.012-.054 mm). Shaft diameter (new) is .7858-.7866" (19.96-19.98 mm). Replace parts as necessary.

**2)** Install rocker shaft support on shaft with lubricating holes downward and flat top surface of support pointing toward ring groove end of shaft. Tighten lock bolt. Install thick spacer, exhaust valve arm, thin spacer, intake valve arm, spring and rocker arm support in order. After installing three such sets, install lock ring in shaft groove.

### VALVE STEM OIL SEALS AND VALVE SPRINGS

With cylinder head removed from engine, remove spark plugs, injectors, rear cover plate, lock fork and camshaft. Using valve

spring compressor, remove valve collets, spring retainer, spring, lower spring seat and valve. Remove valve guide seal from guide. Place valves in order in suitable rack.

### VALVE GUIDE SERVICING

**1)** Check valve guides for wear. If replacement is necessary, press out old guide using drift (2818). Ream hole in cylinder head to oversize class 1 or 2:

#### Valve Guide Specifications

| Application | Diameter In. (mm) |
|---|---|
| Cylinder Head Hole, Class 1 ....... | .5193-.5209 (13.19-13.23) |
| Cylinder Head Hole, Class 2 ........ | 5311-.5327 (13.49-13.53) |
| Valve Guide, Class 1 ................ | ①.5228-.5232 (13.28-13.29) |
| Valve Guide Class 2 ................ | ①.5346-.5350 (13.58-13.59) |

① — Oversize Valve Guides Shown

**2)** Using drifts (5108 for intake; 5109 for exhaust), press in new guides. Ream guides to .3150-.3158" (8.00-8.02 mm). Check for burrs and be sure valves move freely in guides.

### RECONDITIONING VALVES

After inspection, grind valves, mill or grind valve seats, and lap valves with grinding paste, as necessary. Check valve springs for proper length and tension. Install seals, valves, spring seats, spring, and spring retainers. Compress spring and install collets. Remove tool, and reinstall all parts previously removed from cylinder head.

**Fig. 5    Adjusting Crankshaft to Firing Position for No. 1 Cylinder**

### VALVE CLEARANCE ADJUSTMENT

**1)** Rotate crankshaft to firing position for No. 1 cylinder. See *Fig.5.* In this position, both rocker arms should have clearance. Check and adjust the following cylinders for clearance: Intake

## 260 SERIES V6 (Cont.)

valves on cylinders 1, 2, and 4; exhaust valves on cylinders 1, 3, and 6 (White valves in *Fig. 6*).

**Fig. 6   Valve Clearance Adjustment Sequence**

### Valve Clearance Specifications①

| Valve | In. (mm) |
|---|---|
| Intake ................................................ | .004-.006 (.10-.15) |
| Exhaust ............................................. | .010-.012 (.25-.30) |

① — Specifications are for cold engine.

**2)** Rotate crankshaft one full turn so marking is again opposite 0° mark. Rocker arms for No. 1 cylinder will now rock. Check and adjust the following cylinders for clearance: Intake valves on cylinders 3, 5, and 6; exhaust valves on cylinders 2, 4, and 5 (Grey valves in *Fig. 6*).

## PISTONS, PINS & RINGS

### LOWER CRANKCASE

**Removal** — Remove oil pan and gasket, oil strainer and baffle plate. Remove 14 crankcase bolts and 8 main bearing nuts. Lift off lower crankcase. Install main bearing cap retainers (5096) on two outer bearings.

**Installation — 1)** Install rubber ring for oil channel. Clean and apply sealing compound to crankcase and block surfaces. Remove main bearing cap retainers and install lower crankcase.

**2)** Be sure crankcase and block are flush at rear end, and tighten main bearing nuts to 22 ft. lbs. torque. Use sequence shown in *Fig. 7*. Then back off No. 1 nut and retorque to 22-25 ft. lbs. Using a protractor tool (5098), tighten nut an additional 73-77°. Continue in sequence retorquing one nut at a time.

**3)** Tighten 14 lower crankcase bolts to 11-15 ft. lbs. Install baffle plate, oil strainer, gasket and oil pan.

**Fig. 7   Tightening Sequence for Main Bearing Nuts**

## PISTON & ROD ASSEMBLIES

**Removal** — Remove cylinder heads and lower crankcase. Check connecting rod and crankshaft markings so piston assemblies can be reinstalled in original location. Connecting rods are marked "A" through "F" from rear to front. Remove nuts and bearing cap and press connecting rod and piston out of cylinder liner after removing carbon ridge from bore. Remove big-end bearing.

**Fig. 8   Piston Ring Location & Markings**

**Installation** — Install piston & rod assemblies one cylinder at a time. Connecting rods and caps are marked "A" through "F" from rear to front for cylinders 1-4-2-5-3-6. Adjust rings so end gaps are not aligned. Oil rings and install piston with arrow marking on top pointing toward front of engine. Using installation tool (5106) press piston into liner. Install connecting rod cap after oiling the bearing. Tighten cap to 33-37 ft. lbs.

### PISTONS AND LINERS

**1)** Pistons and liners are matched. Pistons are marked "A", "B", or "C" according to diameter and correspond to liners "1", "2", or "3" (marked in recesses at top of liners). Pistons and piston pins are also marked blue, white or red for proper matching.

## 260 SERIES V6 (Cont.)

**2)** Two types of pistons are used, Demolin (overall height 2.695" or 68.45 mm) and Mahle (overall height of 2.474" or 62.85 mm). Measure piston diameter at right angles to pin bore. Measure Demolin pistons .433" (11 mm) above lower edge of piston; Mahle pistons .236" (6 mm) above lower edge.

### Piston and Liner Diameters①

| Piston | In. (mm) |
|---|---|
| Demolin A | 3.4610-3.4614 (87.910-87.920) |
| Demolin B | 3.4617-3.4618 (87.928-87.930) |
| Demolin C | 3.4618-3.4622 (87.930-87.940) |
| Mahle A | 3.4634-3.4638 (87.970-87.980) |
| Mahle B | 3.4638-3.4642 (87.980-87.990) |
| Mahle C | 3.4642-3.4646 (87.990-88.000) |

| Liner | In. (mm) |
|---|---|
| No. 1 for A Piston | 3.4646-3.4650 (88.00-88.01) |
| No. 2 for B Piston | 3.4650-3.4653 (88.01-88.02) |
| No. 3 for C Piston | 3.4653-3.4657 (88.02-88.03) |

① — Measurements for new parts.

**3)** To determine piston-to-cylinder clearance, subtract piston diameter from maximum and minimum bore diameters. Do not remove pistons from connecting rods, unless piston and liner replacement is necessary.

**4)** If liner is to be removed for cleaning or inspection, mark liner and block with colored pen. Do not damage gasket surface. Remove liner holders and pull up liners. When installing liners, be sure contact surfaces on block and liner are clean and without defect. Install No. 1 liner first (without shims) using previous pen markings for alignment. Tighten liner by hand, using two liner holders (5093). Using dial indicator, measure liner height above block at three points. Largest measurement should not exceed smallest measurement by more than .002" (.05 mm). Liner should be as close to .0091" (.23 mm) above block face as possible. Use correct shims to achieve dimension:

### Liner Shim Thicknesses①

| Color | Thickness - In. (mm) |
|---|---|
| Blue | .0028-.0041 (.070-.105) |
| White | .0033-.0047 (.085-.120) |
| Red | .0041-.0055 (.105-.140) |
| Yellow | .0051-.0065 (.130-.165) |

① — Use same thickness shims for all liners.

**5)** Install shims with color marking up and positioned as shown in *Fig. 9.* Inner tabs on shims should be in liner groove.

*Fig. 9    Positioning Shims on Liners*

**6)** After shimming, install four liner holders (5093) for each bank. Again measure each liner at three points. Largest and smallest dimensions should be within .002" (.05 mm). Measure three liners at points shown in *Fig. 10.* Difference in measurements between points "1" and "2" and between "3" and "4" should not exceed .0016" (.04 mm). If height difference is excessive, change shims.

*Fig. 10    Checking Liner Height Above Block Face*

## CRANKSHAFT MAIN & CONNECTING ROD BEARINGS

### CRANKSHAFT

**Removal — 1)** Remove oil pan, lower crankcase, cylinder heads, clutch, drive plate or flywheel, spacer (automatic transmission) and input shaft pilot bearing (manual transmission). Remove seal holder and use drift (5107) to press out seal. Press new seal in flush with retainer.

**2)** Check main bearing cap markings (marked 1 through 4, from rear-to-front). Remove main bearing retainers and caps. Remove upper and lower thrust bearings and lift out crankshaft. Remove main bearings from block and caps.

**Installation — 1)** Oil and install main bearings (with lubricating holes) in block. Place crankshaft in block. Oil and install "hooked" thrust bearings in block groove. Oil and install "non-hooked" thrust bearings on crankshaft.

## 260 SERIES V6 (Cont.)

**2)** Oil bearing and install in main bearing cap. Position cap with "1" marking toward front of engine. Install main bearing retainers (5096). Check crankshaft end play and install thrust bearing washers as necessary.

**3)** Install other three main bearing caps and main bearing retainers (5096) on front cap. Install caps with "2", "3", and "4" marks toward front of engine. Position gasket on seal retainer, align flush with block and torque to 7-11 ft. lbs. Install other components previously removed.

## CAMSHAFT

### TIMING GEAR COVER

**Removal** — Remove both valve covers, lock flywheel (5112), and remove crankshaft nut. Remove pulley while key is on top of shaft (prevents dropping key in crankcase). Use puller (5069) to remove crankshaft seal. Remove timing gear cover.

**Installation** — Clean surfaces and place gaskets on block and timing gear cover. Install cover and tighten bolts to 7-11 ft. lbs. Install crankshaft seal (drift 5103). Block flywheel with locking tool (5112), install pulley and tighten crankshaft nut to 118-132 ft. lbs.

### CHAINS & SPROCKETS

**Removal** — **1)** Remove timing gear cover, oil pump chain, sprocket, oil pump and gears. Turn each tensioner lock ¼ turn counterclockwise and push in piston to slacken camshaft chains. Remove both tensioners, strainers, and curved and straight dampers. Remove camshaft sprockets and chains.

**2)** Stuff rag in holes near crankcase to keep key from falling in crankcase. Remove outer sprocket and inner double sprocket from crankshaft (either by hand or with puller).

**Installation** — **1)** Place key in crankshaft. Oil sprocket and shaft. Install double sprocket (drift 4028) with mark outward. Install spacer ring and outer key. Install oil pump sprocket, strainers and chain tensioners, and curved and straight dampers.

**2)** Rotate crankshaft so key aligns with camshaft in left bank (No. 1 cylinder at TDC). Position camshaft so key points upward (rocker arms for No. 1 cylinder rock). Place chain on camshaft sprocket so that link between two white lines is centered over camshaft sprocket timing mark. Place chain on inner crankshaft sprocket so timing mark on sprocket is aligned with white mark on chain. Install left camshaft sprocket onto camshaft so that pin on sprocket slips into recess in camshaft. Chain should be stretched on tension side. Use screwdriver to hold sprocket and tighten center bolt to 51-59 ft. lbs.

**3)** Rotate crankshaft clockwise 150° so that key points straight downward. Set right camshaft so keyway is in position shown in *Fig. 11*. Place chain on sprocket so link between white lines on chain aligns with sprocket timing mark. Place chain on crankshaft center sprocket so that chain and sprocket timing marks align. Fit sprocket on camshaft with chain stretched on tension side. Pin on sprocket should slip into camshaft recess. Use screwdriver to hold sprocket and torque center bolt to 51-59 ft. lbs.

**Fig. 11    Right Camshaft Keyway and Timing Marks**

**4)** Turn lock on each chain tensioner ¼ turn clockwise. Tension chains by rotating crankshaft 2 full turns in direction of rotation (clockwise). Remove crankshaft nut. Markings on chains and sprockets will no longer align. Reassemble oil pump, install chain and chain sprocket. Install timing gear cover after removing rag from crankcase holes.

**Fig. 12    Locating Top Dead Center for No. 1 Cylinder**

### IGNITION TIMING PLATE

**1)** Rotate crankshaft so that mark No. 1 (See *Fig. 5*) is at 20° mark on ignition timing plate. Remove plug and insert ⁵⁄₁₆" drill bit or similar rod into hole and against crankshaft counterweight, See *Fig. 12*. Rotate crankshaft in direction of rotation until drill bit can be pressed into recess in counterweight (TDC for No. 1 cylinder).

**NOTE** — *Do not drop drill bit into engine. Use drill or pin up to 10" long.*

## 260 SERIES V6 (Cont.)

2) Loosen two bolts and adjust ignition timing plate so that "0" mark is aligned with pulley mark. Tighten two bolts, remove drill bit or rod and install plug. Check camshaft setting. Valve clearance should be .28" (.7 mm). Intake valve should open at:

### Intake Valve Opening

| Valve | Crankshaft Degrees |
|---|---|
| Left bank | 9°±3°BTDC |
| Right bank | 7°±3°BTDC |

## ENGINE OILING

**Crankcase Capacity** — 6.9 quarts including filter.

**Oil Filter** — Full-flow type, disposable spin-on element.

**Oil Pressure** — 26 psi @900 RPM; 58 psi @3000 RPM with engine warm and new filter.

### ENGINE OILING SYSTEM

Engine utilizes a force-feed lubrication system. Oil moves from oil pan through strainer to oil pump and full-flow oil filter mounted outside of engine block assembly. Oil is pressure fed from filter to drilled galleries in block.

Lubricant moves under pressure to main bearings, which are drilled to pass oil on to connecting rod and camshaft bearings, upward in block to rocker arm shafts. Excess or run-off oil drains back down into oil pan through drain holes in cylinder head. Cylinder walls and piston rings are lubricated by splash from connecting rods.

### OIL PUMP

**Removal & Installation** — 1) *See Chains and Sprockets.* Inspect housing, cover and gears for damage or wear. Replace if necessary.

2) Oil pumps are serviced as complete units (pump cover with impeller and relief valve).

### Oil Pump Specifications ①

| Application | Dimension  In. (mm) |
|---|---|
| Pump Gear Width, Class I | 1.2167-1.2175 (30.905-30.925) |
| Pump Gear Width, Class II | 1.2175-1.2183 (30.925-30.945) |
| Pump Housing Width, Class I | 1.2185-1.2195 (30.950-30.975) |
| Pump Housing Width, Class II | 1.2195-1.2209 (30.975-31.010) |
| End Play | .0010-.0033 (.025-.084) |
| Clearance (Tooth-to-Housing) | ①.0043-.0073 (.11-.185) |
| Backlash | ①.0067-.0106 (.17-.27) |
| Bearing Clearance, Driving Shaft | .0006-.0021 (.015-.053) |
| Bearing Clearance, Trailing Shaft | .0006-.0020 (.015-.051) |
| Relief Valve Spring Length, No Load | 3.52 (89.5) |
| Relief Valve Spring Length, 19.8 lbs. | 2.22-2.38 (56.5-60.5) |

① — Excluding bearing clearance.

## ENGINE COOLING

**Thermostat** — Wax-type. Begins to open at 176-181° F (80-83° C); fully open at 194-201° F (90-94° C). Marking, 180° F (82° C).

**Cooling System Capacity** — All models, 11.5 quarts.

**Radiator Cap** — 9-12 psi.

### WATER PUMP

1) Drain coolant from both sides of block. Remove intake manifold, two expansion tank hoses from radiator, upper radiator hose and automatic transmission oil cooler pipes. Remove fan shroud, radiator and fan.

2) Remove hoses from pump to block. Remove fan belts, water pump pulley, and remaining hose clamps. Remove senders from water pump, and pump from block. Remove cover and thermostat and cover from body. Install in reverse order.

## ENGINE SPECIFICATIONS

### GENERAL SPECIFICATIONS

| Year | Displ. | | Carburetor | HP at RPM | Torque (Ft. Lbs. at RPM) | Compr. Ratio | Bore | | Stroke | |
|---|---|---|---|---|---|---|---|---|---|---|
| | cu. ins. | cc | | | | | in. | mm | in. | mm |
| 1978 B27F | 162.3 | 2660 | F.I. | ..... | ..... | 8.2-1 | 3.4646 | 88 | 2.8740 | 73 |

# Volvo Engines

## 260 SERIES V6 (Cont.)

### ENGINE SPECIFICATIONS (Cont.)

| VALVES | | | | | | | |
|---|---|---|---|---|---|---|---|
| Engine & Valve | Head Diam. In. (mm) | Face Angle | Seat Angle | Seat Width In. (mm) | ① Stem Diameter In. (mm) | ① Stem Clearance In. (mm) | ② Valve Lift In. (mm) |
| B27F Intake | 1.73 (44) | 30° | 30° | .067-.083 (1.7-2.1) | .3140-.3146 (7.97-7.99) | .0004-.0018 (.010-.046) | LB .327 (8.3) |
| Exhaust | 1.46 (37) | 30° | 30° | .079-.094 (2.0-2.4) | .3136-.3142 (7.96-7.98) | .0008-.0022 (.020-.056) | RB .321 (8.1) |

① — Stem diameter gets larger from disc toward collet end of valve, where measurement above is taken.

② — Exhaust and intake valves have same lift, but valves in right bank (RB) vary from those in left bank (LB).

| PISTONS, PINS, RINGS | | | | | | |
|---|---|---|---|---|---|---|
| | PISTONS | PINS | | RINGS | | |
| Engine | Clearance In. (mm) | Piston Fit In. (mm) | Rod Fit In. (mm) | Rings | End Gap In. (mm) | Side Clearance In. (mm) |
| B27F | Demolin .0035-.0043 (.090-.110) Mahle .0008-.0016 (.020-.040) | Push Fit .0005-.0008 (.013-.020) Push Fit .0004-.0006 (.010-.015) | Press Fit .0008-.0016 (.020-.041) Press Fit .0008-.0016 (.020-.041) | Comp. 1 Comp. 2 Oil | .016-.022 (.40-55) .016-.022 (.40-.55) .015-.055 (.38-1.4) | .0018-.0029 (.045-.074) .0010-.0021 (.025-.054) .0004.0092 (.009-.233) |

| CRANKSHAFT MAIN & CONNECTING ROD BEARINGS | | | | | | |
|---|---|---|---|---|---|---|
| | MAIN BEARINGS | | | | CONNECTING ROD BEARINGS | |
| Engine | Journal Diam. In. (mm) | Clearance In. (mm) | Thrust Bearing | Crankshaft End Play In. (mm) | Journal Diam. In. (mm) | Clearance In. (mm) | Side Play In. (mm) |
| B27F | 2.7576-2.7583 (70.043-70.062) | .0015-.0035 (.038-.088) | ..... | .0028-.0106 (.070-.270) | 2.0578-2.0585 (52.267-52.286) | .0012-.0031 (.030-.080) | .008-.015 (.20-.38) |

| CAMSHAFT | | | |
|---|---|---|---|
| Engine | Journal Diam. In. (mm) | Clearance In. (mm) | Lobe Lift In. (mm) |
| B27F Front | 1.5921-1.5931 (40.440-40.465) | ① .0014-.0033 (.035-.085) | ..... |
| 2nd | 1.6157-1.6173 (41.040-41.065) | | |
| 3rd | 1.6394-1.6404 (41.640-41.665) | | |
| 4th | 1.6630-1.6640 (42.240-42.265) | | |

① — End play should be .0028-.0057" (.070-.144 mm).

| VALVE SPRINGS | | | |
|---|---|---|---|
| Engine | Free Length In. (mm) | PRESSURE Lbs. @ In. (kg @ mm) | |
| | | Valve Closed | Valve Open |
| B27F | 1.81 (47.2) | 52-60@1.57 (24-27@40) | 117-132@1.27 (53-60@32) |

## 260 SERIES V6

### ENGINE SPECIFICATIONS (Cont.)

---

### TIGHTENING SPECIFICATIONS

| Application | Ft. Lbs. (mkg) |
|---|---|
| Cylinder Head Bolts | |
| Step One | 7 (1.0) |
| Step Two | 22 (3.1) |
| Step Three | ①44 (6.1) |
| Main Bearing Cap Nuts | ②22-25 (3.1-3.5) |
| Connecting Rod Cap Nuts | 33-37 (4.6-5.1) |
| Flywheel Bolts | 33-37 (4.6-5.1) |
| Clutch-to-Flywheel Bolts | 15-18 (2.1-2.5) |
| Camshaft Center Bolts | 51-59 (7.1-8.2) |
| Crankshaft Pulley Nut | 175-200 (24.2-27.6) |
| Alternator Attaching Bolts | 29-37 (4.0-5.1) |
| Fan Hub | 22-37 (3.1-5.1) |
| Spark Plugs | 13-15 (1.8-2.1) |
| Oil Pressure Sensor | 26-37 (3.6-5.1) |
| Temperature Sensor | 18-22 (2.5-3.1) |
| Transmission-to-Engine | 30-36 (4.2-5.0) |
| Front Engine Mounts | 11-18 (1.5-2.5) |
| Oil Pan Plug | 18-25 (2.5-3.5) |
| Exhaust & Intake Manifolds | 7-11 (1.0-1.5) |
| Valve Covers | 7-11 (1.0-1.5) |
| Water Pump-to-Block | 11-15 (1.5-2.1) |

① — After step 3, wait 10-15 minutes, slacken bolts and retorque to 11-14 ft. lbs. (1.5-1.9 mkg). Protractor torque to 116-120°. Run engine until hot and cool for 30 minutes. Slacken and retorque each individual bolt in stages again to 11-14 ft. lbs. (1.5-1.9 mkg) and protractor torque 113-117°.

② — Torque all nuts to 22 ft. lbs. (3.1 mkg). Slacken No. 1 nut, retorque to 22-25 ft. lbs. (3.1-3.5 mkg), and protractor torque 73-77°. Repeat procedure for other seven nuts in sequence.

# Section 6
# CLUTCHES

# Contents

*NOTE — ALSO SEE GENERAL INDEX*

# Clutches

## CLUTCH TROUBLE SHOOTING

| CONDITION | POSSIBLE CAUSE | CORRECTION |
|---|---|---|
| ▶ Chattering or Grabbing | 1) Incorrect Lever Adjustment | 1) Adjust Clutch |
| | 2) Oil or Grease on Facings | 2) Check for Oil Leaks |
| | 3) Loose "U" Joint Flange | 3) Check "U" Joint Flange and Tighten |
| | 4) Worn Input Shaft Spline | 4) Replace Shaft |
| | 5) Binding Pressure Plate | 5) Check for Binding, Replace as Necessary |
| | 6) Binding Release Lever | 6) Free Binding Levers or Replace |
| | 7) Binding Disc Hub | 7) Replace Disc and Adjust Clutch |
| | 8) Glazed Facings | 8) Replace Disc After Checking Pressure Plate and Flywheel for Scoring. Replace as Necessary |
| | 9) Unequal Pressure Plate Contact | 9) Check Release Lever Clearance, Disc Thickness, and Pressure Plate for Paralleism with Flywheel |
| | 10) Bent Clutch Disc | 10) Replace Clutch Disc |
| | 11) Uneven Spring Pressure | 11) Adjust Spring Tension |
| | 12) Incorrect Transmission Alignment. | 12) Check Clutch Housing Alignment |
| | 13) Loose Facings | 13) Replace Clutch Disc |
| | 14) Scored Pressure Plate | 14) Replace Pressure Plate if Warped More Than .015" |
| | 15) Worn Pressure Plate, Disc or Flywheel | 15) Replace When There are Signs of Excessive Wear, Heat Checking or Scoring |
| | 16) Clutch Disc Hub Sticking on Shaft | 16) Check Shaft for Excessive Wear or Burrs, Check Shaft for Distortion and Replace as Necessary |
| | 17) Worn or Binding Release Levers | 17) Replace Levers and Release Bearing |
| | 18) Broken or Weak Pressure Springs | 18) Replace Springs |
| | 19) Sticking Clutch Pedal | 19) Check for Worn or Misaligned Components |
| | 20) Incorrect Disc Facing | 20) Replace Clutch Disc |
| | 21) Engine Loose in Chassis | 21) Check Motor Mounts and Replace or Tighten |
| ▶ Spinning | 1) Dry or Worn Bushings | 1) Replace Bushings |
| | 2) Misaligned Clutch Housing | 2) Check Clutch Housing Alignment |
| | 3) Bent or Distorted Clutch Disc. | 3) Replace Clutch Disc |
| | 4) Warped Pressure Plate | 4) Replace Pressure Plate |
| | 5) Excessive Pedal Free Play | 5) Readjust Pedal Free Play |

# Clutches

## CLUTCH TROUBLE SHOOTING

| CONDITION | POSSIBLE CAUSE | CORRECTION |
|---|---|---|
| ▶ Dragging | 1) Oil or Grease on Facings | 1) Free Release Levers |
| | 2) Incorrect Lever Adjustment | 2) Check for Damage and Readjust Lever |
| | 3) Incorrect Pedal Adjustment | 3) Adjust Pedal |
| | 4) Dust or Dirt on Clutch | 4) Disassemble Clutch and Clean Throughly |
| | 5) Worn or Broken Facings | 5) Replace Clutch Disc |
| | 6) Bent Clutch Disc | 6) Replace Clutch Disc, Check for Cause |
| | 7) Clutch Disc Hub Binding on Shaft | 7) Check Shaft for Burrs or Gummed Splines |
| | 8) Binding Pilot Bushing | 8) Replace Pilot Bushing |
| | 9) Sticking Release Bearing Sleeve | 9) Free Sleeve, Check for Scoring or Rough Spots |
| | 10) Warped Pressure Plate | 10) Replace Pressure Plate if Worn More Than .015" |
| ▶ Rattling | 1) Weak or Broken Release Lever Spring | 1) Replace Spring |
| | 2) Damaged Pressure Plate | 2) Replace Pressure Plate and Adjust Clutch |
| | 3) Broken Clutch Return Spring | 3) Replace Return Spring |
| | 4) Worn Splines in Clutch Disc Hub or Transmission Input Shaft | 4) Replace Clutch Disc or Transmission Input Shaft |
| | 5) Worn Clutch Release Bearings | 5) Replace Release Bearing, Check Tips of Release Levers for Wear, Replace as Necessary |
| | 6) Dry or Worn Pilot Bushing | 6) Lubricate or Replace Pilot Bushing |
| | 7) Unequal Release Lever Contact | 7) Readjust Release Levers |
| | 8) Incorrect Pedal Freeplay | 8) Adjust Pedal Free Play |
| | 9) Warped Clutch Disc | 9) Replace Clutch Disc, Check Pressure Plate for Wear and Replace as Necessary |
| ▶ Slipping | 1) Pressure Springs Worn or Broken | 1) Replace Springs |
| | 2) Worn Facing | 2) Replace Clutch Disc |
| | 3) Incorrect Clutch Alignment | 3) Adjust Clutch |
| | 4) Oil or Grease on Facings | 4) Replace Clutch Disc, Fix Oil Leaks |
| | 5) Warped Clutch Disc | 5) Replace Clutch Disc |
| | 6) Warped or Scored Pressure Plate | 6) Replace Pressure Plate if Scored, Heat Checked, or Warped More Than .015", Test Spring Tension and Replace Clutch Disc |
| | 7) Binding Release Levers | 7) Free Release Lever |
| | 8) Binding Clutch Pedal | 8) Check for Worn or Misaligned Parts |

# Clutches

## CLUTCH TROUBLE SHOOTING

| CONDITION | POSSIBLE CAUSE | CORRECTION |
|---|---|---|
| ► Squeaking | 1) No Lubrication in Release Bearing | 1) Lubricate |
| | 2) Worn Release Bearing | 2) Replace Release Bearing |
| | 3) Dry or Worn Pilot Bushing | 3) Lubricate or Replace Pilot Bushing |
| | 4) Pilot Bearing Turning in Crankshaft | 4) Replace Pilot Bearing |
| | 5) Worn Input Shaft Bearing | 5) Replace Input Shaft Bearing |
| | 6) Incorrect Transmission Alignment | 6) Check Clutch Housing Alignment |
| | 7) No Lubrication Between Clutch Fork and Pivot | 7) Lubricate |
| | 8) No Lubrication in Torque Shaft | 8) Lubricate |
| ► Heavy, Stiff Pedal | 1) Dry or Binding Linkage Components | 1) Lubricate Linkage Components |
| | 2) Sticking Release Bearing Sleeve | 2) Check Release Bearing Sleeve for Wear, Burrs or Roughness on Mating Surface |
| | 3) Dry or Binding Pedal Hub | 3) Replace Bushing or Bearings in Pedal Hub and Lubricate |
| | 4) Pedal Interference With Floorboard or Mat | 4) Check for Pedal Interference |
| | 5) Rough, Dry or Binding Pivot Ball, or Fork Pivots | 5) Lubricate All Moving Points |
| ► Grinding | 1) Dry Release Bearing | 1) Replace Release Bearing |
| | 2) Worn or Dry Pilot Bearing | 2) Lubricate or Replace Pilot Bearing |
| | 3) Worn Input Shaft Bearing | 3) Replace Input Shaft Bearing |
| ► Whirring | 1) Incorrect Pedal Free Play | 1) Adjust Pedal Free Play |
| | 2) Incorrect Transmission Alignment | 2) Check Clutch Housing Alignment |

# Clutches

## ARROW, CHALLENGER, COLT & SAPPORO

Arrow
Challenger
Colt
Sapporo

## DESCRIPTION

Clutch is a diaphragm spring, single disc type. Operation is controlled mechanically by a cable. Clutch release bearing is sealed and permanently lubricated.

*Fig. 1   Exploded View of Clutch Assembly*

## REMOVAL & INSTALLATION

### CLUTCH ASSEMBLY

1) With battery disconnected, air cleaners removed and battery cables disconnected from starter, remove starter. Remove two bolts from top of transmission.

2) Inside vehicle, remove dust cover retaining plate and four bolts securing gearshift lever assembly to vehicle. **NOTE** — *Lever should be in 2nd gear on 4-speed transmission models and in 1st gear on 5-speed transmission models.*

3) With car raised and supported on jack stands, drain transmission fluid. Remove speedometer cable and electrical leads from transmission, then remove bolts from rear of propeller shaft and remove shaft from transmission.

4) Disconnect exhaust system from brackets, then disconnect clutch cables. With transmission supported by a jack, remove insulators from crossmembers by removing attaching bolts.

**NOTE** — *Jack should be placed under transmission oil pan, making sure support area is as wide as possible.*

5) Remove each crossmember from frame by pulling off sideways. Remove clutch inspection cover, then remove remaining transmission to engine attaching bolts. Pull transmission to rear and remove from vehicle. **NOTE** — *Use care not to twist front end of main drive gear.*

6) Insert a suitable clutch centering tool (MD998017) into center of clutch to prevent clutch disc from falling. Loosen

clutch attaching bolts alternately and evenly until pressure plate can be removed. Remove pressure plate and clutch disc.

7) To install, reverse removal procedure and note the following: Use a suitable clutch centering tool (MD998017) to center clutch disc on flywheel. Adjust clutch cable and clutch pedal.

### CLUTCH CABLE

**Removal** — Loosen cable adjusting wheel inside engine compartment, then loosen clutch pedal lock nut. Remove clutch cable from pedal lever, then remove cable from clutch shift lever and remove.

**Installation** — To install clutch cable, reverse the removal procedure and note following: Apply engine oil as necessary to install cable. Some models are equipped with insulating pads. Fit pads where cable routes near intake manifold and at rear side of engine mount.

### CLUTCH RELEASE BEARING & SHIFT ARM

**Removal** — With transmission removed, remove return clip on transmission side, then slide off release bearing carrier and release bearing. Using a ³⁄₁₆" punch, remove shift arm spring pin and control lever assembly, then remove the shift arm and return springs.

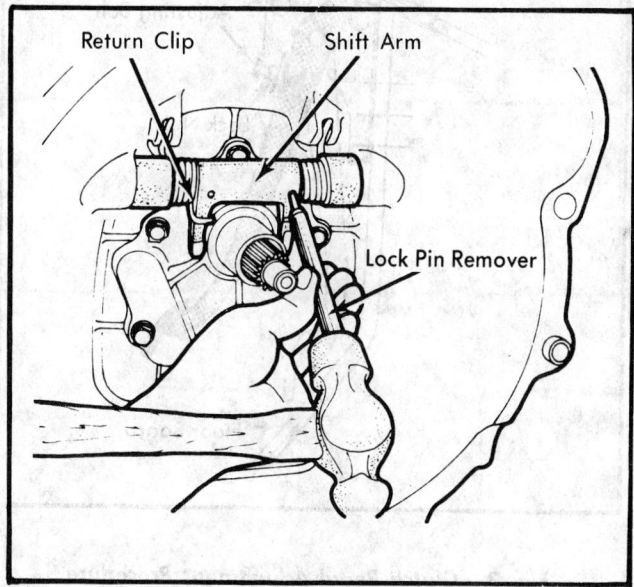

*Fig. 2   Using a ³⁄₁₆" Punch to Remove Shift Arm Spring Pin*

**Installation** — 1) Insert lever and shaft into transmission case from left side.

2) Install onto shaft:
- Shift arm
- 2 felt packings
- Return springs

3) Apply grease to inside of bushing. Oil seal lips.

4) Oil felt packings.

## ARROW, CHALLENGER, COLT & SAPPORO (Cont.)

**5)** Drive in 2 shift arm springs pins. Face spring pin slots UP. See *Fig. 2*.

## ADJUSTMENT

### PEDAL HEIGHT ADJUSTMENT

Rotate clutch pedal adjusting bolt (at top of clutch pedal) so that height is as indicated in table. Height is measured between toe board and top of clutch pedal pad.

| Clutch Pedal Height | |
|---|---|
| Application | Height In. (mm) |
| 1600 cc & 2000 cc ........................................... | 6.8 (175) |
| 2600 cc .......................................................... | 7.2 (185) |

**NOTE** — *With clutch pedal and cable properly adjusted, clutch pedal travel should be 5.5" (140 mm) on 1600 cc and 2000 cc models, or 5.7" (150 mm) on 2600 cc models.*

*Fig. 3   Clutch Pedal Adjustment Procedure*

### CABLE ADJUSTMENT

Pull outer cable out toward engine compartment. Rotate cable adjusting nut until specified clearance is obtained between nut and holder (1600 cc & 2000 cc) or between nut and insulator (2600 cc)

| Clutch Cable Adjustment | |
|---|---|
| Application | Clearance In. (mm) |
| 1600 cc ....................................................... | .20-.24 (5-6) |
| 2000 cc .................................................. | .14-.18 (3.5-4.5) |
| 2600 cc ..................................................... | .12-.16 (3-4) |

**NOTE** — *With clutch cable properly adjusted, clutch pedal free play should be .8-1.2" (20-30 mm) for Arrow and Colt (except Colt Station Wagon) or .4-.6" (10-15 mm) for all other models.*

*Fig. 4   Clutch Cable Adjustment Points*

| TIGHTENING SPECIFICATIONS | |
|---|---|
| Application | Ft. Lbs. (mkg) |
| Transmission-to-Engine ......................... | 22-30 (3.0-4.15) |
| Transmission-to-Engine | |
|   Flange Bolts............................................ | 32-39 (4.4-5.4) |
|   Starter Bolts............................................. | 16-23 (2.2-3.2) |

# Clutches

## AUDI FOX

### Fox

## DESCRIPTION

Clutch is single plate dry disc type, using a diaphragm type pressure plate and a pre-lubricated clutch release bearing. Clutch is cable actuated.

Fig. 1 Exploded View of Clutch Assembly

Labels: Release Bearing Guide Sleeve, Clutch Fork, Release Bearing, Clip, Clutch Disc, Pressure Plate, Clutch Fork Lever

## REMOVAL & INSTALLATION

### CLUTCH ASSEMBLY

**Removal — 1)** Disconnect battery ground cable at battery. Disconnect exhaust head pipe at manifold and bracket on transmission.

**2)** Remove bolt mounting shift assembly coupling to rear of transmission shifting shaft and separate assemblies. Unhook clutch cable at release lever. Disconnect speedometer.

**3)** Disconnect axle drive shafts at inner drive flanges. Remove starter. Take out front clutch housing cover plate. Remove transmission-to-engine mounting bolts.

**4)** Suitably support transmission with jack. Remove transmission rear mounts and brackets. Pry transmission away from engine and slide it out of vehicle.

**5)** Index mark pressure plate and flywheel. Loosen pressure plate bolts ¼ turn at a time. Work bolts loose in criss-cross pattern. Slide pressure plate off dowels on flywheel.

**Installation —** To install, reverse removal procedure and note: Use clutch alignment tool to fit pressure plate and clutch. Make sure alignment marks are observed.

Fig. 2 Aligning Clutch Assembly Reference Marks for Reinstallation

Labels: Dowel Pin, Flywheel Index Marks, Dowel Pin, Clutch Alignment Tool US 219

### CLUTCH RELEASE BEARING

**1)** With transmission separated from engine, remove spring clips securing release bearing to clutch fork. Bearing is pre-lubricated; do not wash in any cleaning solution.

**2)** Rotate bearing and check for roughness or noise, replace as necessary. Apply Molykote paste to bearing contact points on clutch fork. To install, reverse removal procedure.

### PILOT BEARING

**1)** To remove bearing, install a suitable remover tool (10-202) into pilot bearing, then remove bearing by tightening tool.

**2)** Install bearing so that lettering is facing out. Drive bearing into crankshaft using a suitable driver tool (US 219) until it is flush, then lubricate bearing.

## ADJUSTMENT

### CLUTCH PEDAL FREE PLAY

To obtain correct free play between clutch release bearing and clutch, clutch pedal free play must be correct. Free play can be adjusted by loosening and adjusting both counternuts at clutch cable to obtain .590" (15 mm) free play at pedal.

### TIGHTENING SPECIFICATIONS

| Application | Ft. Lbs. (mkg) |
|---|---|
| Clutch Assembly-to-Flywheel | 18 (2.5) |
| Transmission-to-Engine | 40 (5.5) |
| Clutch Lever-to-Transmission | 12-18 (1.7-2.5) |
| Drive Shaft-to-Transmission | 25.5 (3.5) |

## AUDI 5000

**5000**

### DESCRIPTION

Clutch is a single plate, dry disc type. Pressure plate is a diaphragm spring type. A pre-lubricated release bearing is used. Bearing is operated by slave cylinder push rod and release lever. Slave cylinder is mounted to top of clutch housing and extends to inside of housing. Clutch pedal is hooked directly to clutch master cylinder push rod fork via a clevis pin. Master cylinder is secured to clutch/brake pedal mounting brace.

### REMOVAL & INSTALLATION

#### CLUTCH ASSEMBLY

**Removal** — 1) Disconnect battery ground cable. Remove windshield washer bottle. Remove upper engine-to-transmission mounting bolts. Disconnect speedometer cable.

2) Using a punch, drive out slave cylinder lock pin. Remove cylinder with fluid line connected. Suitably support weight of engine. Remove exhaust heat shield. Disconnect exhaust pipe at manifold.

3) Disconnect axle drive shafts at transaxle and hang out of way. Disconnect back-up light wire. Pry off both shifting and adjusting rods. Remove lower engine-to-transmission mounting bolts.

4) Take out starter. Remove subframe cover shield. Slightly raise transmission. Remove transmission support bolts and bushings from both sides of subframe, then loosen both rear subframe mounting bolts. Remove right side transmission bracket. Remove transmission off dowels and take out of vehicle.

5) Index mark position of pressure plate in relation to flywheel. Insert flywheel retainer tool. Loosen pressure plate mounting bolt evenly in a diagonal pattern until pressure is relieved. Remove pressure plate and clutch disc.

**Installation** — To install, reverse removal procedure and note following: Clutch disc spring cage must face pressure plate. Clutch disc must slide freely with no radial play on input shaft. Lubricate input shaft splines with appropriate grease. Align pressure plate index marks. Use clutch disc alignment tool to center disc.

#### RELEASE BEARING & LEVER

**Removal** — Remove transmission. Remove cap bolt (attaching 2 retainer pieces) at lower edge of release lever. Slide release lever and bearing out of slave cylinder push rod and off guide sleeve. Disengage circlip and retainer clips keeping release bearing to lever. Separate bearing from lever. If necessary, guide sleeve can also be removed.

**Inspection** — Check clutch release bearing for wear or unusual noise. Do not wash bearing in solvent. If bearing is excessively noisy, replace.

**Installation** — To install, reverse removal procedure and note: Lubricate ball cap located in clutch housing with appropriate grease. Make sure clutch release lever locates directly into slave cylinder push rod tip. Push rod tip should be lubricated.

**Fig. 1  Clutch Release Bearing with Related Components**

#### MASTER CYLINDER

**Removal** — Disconnect and plug fluid lines. Separate cylinder from clutch pedal by removing clevis pin. Remove 2 bolts mounting master cylinder to pedal bracket and take out cylinder.

**Fig. 2  Exploded View of Master Cylinder**

## AUDI 5000 (Cont.)

**Installation** — Reverse removal procedure and bleed air from fluid line.

### SLAVE CYLINDER

**Removal** — Working from under vehicle, drive out slave cylinder lock pin located on top of transmission. Slide cylinder back until push rod clears, then maneuver cylinder until fluid line can be disconnected and plugged.

**Fig. 3   Exploded View of Slave Cylinder**

**Installation** — To install, reverse removal procedure. Coat outer surface of cylinder with oil before inserting into place. Bleed air from fluid line.

## ADJUSTMENTS

### CLUTCH PEDAL

Adjust master cylinder push rod so that in the rest position clutch pedal stands 3/8" (10 mm) above brake pedal.

**NOTE** — *If clutch pedal is correctly adjusted but fails to properly return, check hydraulic system for air.*

### TIGHTENING SPECIFICATIONS

| Application | Ft. Lbs. (mkg) |
|---|---|
| Pressure Plate Bolts | 18 (2.5) |
| Axle Drive Shaft-to-Transaxle Bolts | 25 (3.5) |
| Transmission Bracket | 29 (4.0) |
| Transmission Support Bolts on Subframe | 29 (4.0) |
| Subframe-to-Body | 80 (11.0) |
| Master Cylinder-to-Pedal Bracket | 14 (2.0) |

## BMW

320i
530i
633CSi
733i

### DESCRIPTION

BMW clutch system consists of the following major components:

- Dry, single plate disc
- Diaphragm spring pressure plate
- Pre-lubricated clutch release bearing with release lever

Clutch is hydraulically operated. Clutch master cylinder is mounted to fire wall and provides hydraulic fluid to slave cylinder. Slave cylinder is mounted off the clutch housing. Release portion of system is self-adjusting. Pedal travel is the only adjustment that may have to be made.

**Fig. 1  Sectional View of Clutch Assembly for Part Identification and Component Relationship (633 CSi Shown — All Models Similar)**

### REMOVAL & INSTALLATION

#### CLUTCH ASSEMBLY

**Removal, 320i — 1)** Remove console.

**2)** Disengage circlip, remove washer, and pull out gear shift selector rod. Gear shift lever will remain in vehicle.

**3)** Remove all upper clutch housing mounting bolts.

**4)** Remove exhaust pipe support bracket. Separate exhaust pipe at manifold.

**NOTE** — *A special clamp tool designed to hold Giubo coupling while mounting nuts and bolts are being removed has been released. Special tool number is 26 1 012.*

**5)** Remove bolts mounting propeller shaft to transmission.

**NOTE** — *Coupling remains on propeller shaft.*

**6)** Remove heat shield. Separate center support bearing. Maneuver propeller shaft downward and pull it from center support journal. Place shaft out of way.

**7)** Disconnect speedometer cable.

**8)** Disconnect back-up light wires. Separate wiring harness from mounting clips.

**9)** Remove 2 clutch slave cylinder bolts and hydraulic line mounting bracket (located on clutch housing).

**10)** Remove flywheel inspection cover.

**11)** Place support under engine and an adjustable jack under transmission.

**12)** Unbolt remaining clutch housing bolts. Slide transmission rearward until free.

**13)** Retain flywheel. Loosen clutch assembly mounting bolts alternately and evenly. Remove clutch assembly.

**Installation** — Make the following notes during installation:
- Slide clutch disc into place. Fit pressure plate over flywheel dowels.
- Center the clutch assembly with alignment tool 21 2 100 (or equivalent).
- Tighten mounting bolts evenly.
- Make sure exhaust pipe support bracket is loose when pipe-to-manifold nuts are tightened.
- Preload center bearing on propeller shaft by moving bracket .078" (2 mm) forward. Slots are provided for adjustment.
- Slave cylinder bleed screw must face down.

**Removal, Except 320i — 1)** From under vehicle, remove circlip and washer from selector rod. Disengage rod from control arm. From inside vehicle, force up shifter dust boot and remove retainer circlip. Pull up on gear shift lever to remove.

**2)** Remove any exhaust system parts that may interfere with transmission removal.

**NOTE** — *A special clamp tool designed to hold Giubo coupling while mounting nuts and bolts are being removed has been released. Special tool number is 26 1 012.*

**3)** Separate propeller shaft from transmission.

**NOTE** — *Special propeller shaft coupler remains on propeller shaft.*

**4)** Remove heat shield. On 733i models only, remove crossbracket that runs under propeller shaft and attaches to underbody with 4 bolts.

**5)** Remove center support bearing.

**6)** Maneuver propeller shaft out of center bearing housing and place out of way.

**7)** Support engine. Place an adjustable jack under transmission.

## BMW (Cont.)

8) Disconnect speedometer from transmission.

9) Remove 2 crossmember-to-body nuts and bolts. Slightly lower transmission.

10) Separate clip on clutch housing. Clip is bolted to driver's side.

11) Remove slave cylinder. Hydraulic line does not have to be disconnected.

12) Disconnect brake back-up light wires.

13) Remove bolts holding transmission to clutch housing. Slide transmission back until clear, then remove from vehicle.

14) Remove clutch housing mounting bolts. Take off flywheel inspection cover. Slide clutch housing off.

15) Retain flywheel from rotating. Loosen pressure plate mounting bolts alternately and evenly. Slide out clutch assembly.

**Installation** — Note the following when reinstalling transmission and clutch assembly:
- Place pressure plate over dowels. Center entire clutch assembly on flywheel using tool 21 2 100 (or equivalent).
- Temporarily fit slave cylinder. Face cylinder face down.
- Align release lever and slave cylinder.
- Fill lubricating groove in release bearing with Molykote BR 2-750 (or equivalent).
- Make sure transmission is in gear before inserting into clutch assembly.
- Carefully slide transmission guide sleeve into release bearing and clutch assembly.
- Rotate output flange until input shaft is fitted into clutch.
- Remove slave cylinder.
- Tighten transmission mounting bolts.
- Tighten from nut side when installing propeller shaft.
- Preload center bearing by sliding bracket .078" (2 mm) forward. Adjustment slots are provided.

## RELEASE BEARING & RELEASE BEARING LEVER

**Removal** — 1) Remove transmission.

2) On 320i models, remove clutch housing.

3) Remove spring clip from mounting holes in clutch housing.

4) Slide off release lever and separate lever from bearing.

**Inspection** — Measure bearing at points shown in *Fig. 2*. If bearing is not within specifications it should be replaced.

**Installation** — To install, reverse removal procedure.

## CLUTCH MASTER CYLINDER

**Removal** — 1) Remove trim from under left side of instrument panel.

**NOTE** — *On 733i models only, it is necessary to detach windshield wiper fluid reservoir for access.*

**Fig. 2   Make Measurements Shown to Determine Serviceability of Clutch Release Bearing**

1.00" ± .010"
(25.5 mm ± .25 mm)

1.949" ± .016"
(49.5 mm ± .4 mm)

2) Remove bolt and separate master cylinder push rod from pedal. On 733i models only, once master cylinder push rod is released, pedal spring may become dislodged.

3) Siphon off most of hydraulic fluid from master cylinder reservoir.

4) Separate reservoir line.

5) Separate slave cylinder line.

6) Remove mounting bolts. Pull master cylinder forward and out of vehicle.

**Installation** — To install, reverse removal procedure. Bleed hydraulic system. Make sure 733i pedal spring is engaged in guide before piston rod is attached.

## CLUTCH SLAVE CYLINDER

**Removal** — 1) Siphon off as much hydraulic fluid as possible.

2) Remove slave cylinder mounting bolts located on clutch housing.

3) Once slave cylinder is pulled back, disconnect hydraulic line.

**Installation** — Reverse removal procedure and note:
- Bleed screw faces DOWN.
- Push rod must be coated with Molykote 2 (or equivalent).
- Bleed hydraulic system.

## OVERHAUL

### CLUTCH MASTER CYLINDER

**Disassembly** — 1) Remove push rod, if necessary.

2) Side back dust boot.

3) Remove circlip.

4) Extract internal components.

## BMW (Cont.)

**Cleaning & Inspection — 1)** Clean all internal components with alcohol.

**2)** If master cylinder bore is badly scored or has excessive corrosion, replace cylinder.

**Reassembly — 1)** Replace following parts with new ones provided in overhaul kit:
- Cap
- Circlip
- Seals
- Seal Plug
- Plain Washer
- Dust Boot

**2)** Insert master cylinder push rod and adjust length to approximately 5.5" (140 mm). See *Fig. 3*.

**Fig. 3   Sectional View of Clutch Master Cylinder**

## CLUTCH SLAVE CYLINDER

**Disassembly — 1)** Remove push rod.

**2)** Remove retainer ring.

**3)** Tip slave cylinder in a manner that will allow internal components to fall out.

**Cleaning & Inspection — 1)** Clean all internal components with alcohol.

**2)** If slave cylinder bore is badly scored or has excessive corrosion, replace cylinder.

**Reassembly —** Replace following parts with new ones provided in overhaul kit:
- Retainer ring
- Dust Cap
- Sleeve

**Fig. 4   Sectional View of Clutch Slave Cylinder**

## ADJUSTMENT

**320i & 530i Only —** Adjust pedal at master cylinder push rod. Vary rod length by loosening lock nut and turning rod in or out to obtain a total pedal travel of approximately 6.1" (155 mm).

### HYDRAULIC BLEEDING

**1)** Fill fluid reservoir.

**2)** Attach bleeder hose to slave cylinder bleed screw. Submerge the free end of hose into a container part full with brake fluid.

**3)** Pump clutch pedal about 10 times. Hold pedal down on last pump stroke.

**4)** Loosen bleed screw and allow air to escape.

**5)** Close bleed screw.

**6)** Repeat steps **3-5** until all air is bled from clutch hydraulic system.

| TIGHTENING SPECIFICATIONS | |
| --- | --- |
| **Application** | **Ft. Lbs. (mkg)** |
| Clutch-to-Flywheel ................................... | 16-17 (2.2-2.4) |
| Master Cylinder Mounting Bolt | |
|   Except 733i ..................................... | 16-17 (2.2-2.4) |
|   Except 530i and 733i ......................... | 18-20 (2.5-2.8) |
| Clutch Housing-to-Engine | |
| 530i | |
|   8 mm Bolts ...................................... | 16-17 (2.2-2.4) |
|   10 mm Bolts .................................... | 31-35 (4.3-4.8) |
| 320i, 633CSi, 733i | |
|   8 mm Bolts ...................................... | 18-19 (2.5-2.7) |
|   10 mm Bolts .................................... | 34-37 (4.7-5.1) |
| Transmission-to-Clutch Housing | |
| 633CSi ................................................. | 52-57 (7.2-8.0) |
| 733i .................................................... | 54-59 (7.5-8.2) |

## CAPRI

**2300 cc**
**2800 cc**

## DESCRIPTION

Clutch disc is of single plate, dry type with a spring cushioned hub. A diaphragm type pressure plate is used. Clutch operation is mechanical through cable actuation.

**Fig. 1  Exploded View of Clutch Assembly & Linkage**

*Labels:* Pressure Plate Assy. — Release Lever — Clutch Release Bearing — Release Cable — Clutch Disc Assy. — Spring Washers — Pin — Ring Gear — Flywheel — Clutch Pedal

## REMOVAL & INSTALLATION

### CLUTCH ASSEMBLY

**Removal — 1)** With battery disconnected, raise vehicle on a hoist. Remove four bolts securing drive shaft to rear axle pinion flange. Remove two bolts securing center bearing carrier to bracket, then lower rear of shaft down and slide front yoke from transmission. Install a dummy yoke in transmission to prevent oil leakage.

**2)** Remove speedometer cable from extension housing, then disconnect exhaust pipe from transmission bracket and secure out of way. Lift up clutch release lever boot and disconnect clutch cable from lever. Unclip spring retainers and disconnect shift rods from transmission.

**3)** Remove starter attaching bolts, then place starter out of way. Remove clutch housing-to-engine attaching bolts and bolts securing engine rear plate to front lower part of flywheel housing.

**4)** Place a suitable transmission jack under transmission, remove four bolts securing crossmember to body, then slide transmission assembly rearward and detach from engine. Loosen clutch attaching bolts working diagonally across clutch, then remove clutch assembly.

**Installation —** To install, reverse removal procedure noting the following: Apply a light coat of molybdenum-based grease to clutch disc splines. Insure input shaft fully extends into crankshaft pilot bearing.

### CLUTCH RELEASE BEARING

With transmission and clutch assembly removed, withdraw release lever and bearing assembly from clutch housing.

Remove release lever from hub and bearing assembly. Before installing, apply molybdenum-based grease to hub and release lever. To install, reverse removal procedure.

### PILOT BEARING

With transmission and clutch assembly removed, insert a suitable puller behind bearing, then screw puller attachment (T69L-1102-A) into puller. Tighten thrust nut on center shaft to remove bearing. Install bearing into end of crankshaft using a suitable driver, making sure that bearing is .156-.175" (3.96-4.44 mm) below crankshaft flange.

### CLUTCH CABLE

**Removal —** Raise vehicle on a hoist. Loosen clutch cable at adjuster on clutch housing, then remove spring clip securing clutch cable to top of pedal. Remove pivot pin *(Fig. 1)* and pull top of cable into engine compartment. Move clutch release lever boot on clutch housing and free cable from lever, then remove cable from vehicle.

**Installation — 1)** Pass top end of clutch cable through dash panel so that it is near clutch pedal. Assemble cable to pedal and install pivot pin (lubricate prior to assembly). Secure cable in position with spring clip.

**2)** Install clutch cable lower end to clutch release lever. Coat ball end of cable with ball joint lubricant. Locate rubber boot in opening and adjust clutch pedal free play.

## ADJUSTMENT

### CLUTCH PEDAL & CABLE ADJUSTMENT

**2300 cc — 1)** Pull clutch pedal against back stop and retain with a wood block. Loosen adjustment lock nut. Pull cable forward taking up slack. Hold cable forward and turn adjusting nut until a clearance of .124-.144" (3.15-3.65 mm) is obtained between nut and clutch housing cable bushing. Tighten lock nut.

**2)** Press clutch pedal to floor twice. Hold pedal up against stop, and measure distance to floor. Depress pedal to floor and release easily; then measure from pedal to floor. The difference between these two measurements (free play) should be .866-1.02" (22-26 mm).

**2800 cc — 1)** Pull clutch pedal against back stop and retain with a wood block. Pull cable forward until adjusting nut is accessible. Apply enough pressure to clutch cable to eliminate free play in release lever. Rotate adjusting nut until it just contacts recess. Release cable and allow adjusting nut to re-enter recess.

**2)** Before making further adjustments, depress clutch pedal to floor twice. With clutch pedal retained in position against stop, measure distance to floor. Depress pedal to floor and release easily; then measure from pedal to floor. The difference between these two measurements (free play) should be 1.06-1.22" (27-31 mm).

### TIGHTENING SPECIFICATIONS

| Application | Ft. Lbs. (mkg) |
| --- | --- |
| Pressure Plate-to-Flywheel | 11-14 (1.5-1.9) |
| Clutch Housing-to-Transmission | 40-47 (5.5-6.5) |
| Clutch Housing-to-Engine | 22-27 (3.0-3.7) |

## COURIER

**Courier**

### DESCRIPTION

Clutch is of single dry disc type. Clutch assembly consists of clutch disc, clutch cover and pressure plate assembly, and clutch release mechanism. Clutch housing also acts as the transmission input shaft bearing retainer, and contains the input shaft bearing oil seal and a selective fit thrust washer for controlling input shaft end play. Clutch release mechanism is hydraulic, consisting of a firewall mounted master cylinder and a slave cylinder mounted on flywheel housing. To control clutch engagement, a one-way valve mounted on master cylinder controls flow of return fluid when pressure on clutch pedal is released.

**Fig. 1  Exploded View of Courier Clutch Assembly with Detail of Internal Components – Note That Fork Return Spring and Release Bearing Retainer Spring are No Longer Used**

### REMOVAL & INSTALLATION

#### CLUTCH ASSEMBLY

1) Place gear shift lever in neutral and remove shift lever, tower and boots as an assembly. Raise vehicle, disconnect drive shaft at rear axle and at center bearing support and remove from transmission.

2) Disconnect exhaust pipe brackets from transmission case and clutch housing. Remove exhaust pipe and resonator assembly. Disconnect clutch release lever return spring. Remove clutch slave cylinder and secure to one side.

3) Remove speedometer cable from extension housing and disconnect wiring from starter and transmission. Using a suitable jack, support engine and remove starter. Support transmission and remove transmission-to-engine rear plate attaching bolts.

4) Remove crossmember attaching bolts at transmission and frame side rails, and remove crossmember. Lower jack supporting engine and remove transmission by sliding rearward and downward. Mark location of two pilot bolt holes on flywheel and pressure plate and remove clutch attaching bolts and clutch assembly.

5) To install, reverse removal procedure noting the following: Use a suitable centering tool to align clutch disc to flywheel. Install pressure plate, four standard, and two pilot bolts finger tight. To avoid distorting pressure plate, tighten bolts a few turns at a time until tight, using a criss-cross pattern. Bleed hydraulic system and adjust clutch pedal free play.

### RELEASE LEVER & BEARING

1) With transmission removed, disconnect release collar spring and slide out release lever, boot and release bearing. Inspect all parts for wear or damage.

2) To install, apply lubricant to input shaft bearing retainer portion of clutch housing and pivot bolt. Drive release lever onto pivot. Apply lubricant to bearing contact surface of lever and install release bearing and hook release collar spring. Apply lubricant to face of release bearing. Check to see that lever and bearing operate freely.

### CLUTCH MASTER CYLINDER

1) Disconnect fluid outlet line at master cylinder one-way valve. Remove nuts and bolts attaching master cylinder to firewall and pull cylinder out and away.

2) To install, start pedal push rod into master cylinder, then position cylinder against firewall. Install and tighten attaching bolts and connect fluid outlet line. Bleed hydraulic system and check pedal free play.

### CLUTCH SLAVE CYLINDER

**Removal** – 1) Disconnect brake fluid inlet hose at slave cylinder.

2) Unhook release lever from push rod.

3) Remove nuts attaching slave cylinder to clutch housing. Remove cylinder.

**Installation** – 1) Locate cylinder on studs in housing. Tighten nuts.

2) Connect fluid inlet hose.

3) Fill master cylinder. Bleed hydraulic system.

4) Hook clutch release lever into slave cylinder push rod.

### OVERHAUL

#### CLUTCH MASTER CYLINDER

1) Clean outside of cylinder, drain fluid, and remove dust boot. Using a screwdriver, remove piston stop ring and washer. Remove piston, piston cup and return spring from cylinder, then carefully remove and disassemble one-way valve.

2) Wash all parts in clean alcohol or brake fluid. Check all rubber components and replace if damaged, worn, softened or swollen. Check cylinder bore for wear or damage, and check clearance between cylinder bore and piston. Replace cylinder or piston if clearance is more than .004" (.102 mm)

3) To assemble, dip all parts in clean brake fluid and reverse disassembly procedure. When assembled, fill reservoir with fluid and operate piston with a screwdriver until fluid is ejected at outlet fitting.

## COURIER (Cont.)

### CLUTCH MASTER CYLINDER ONE-WAY VALVE

**Disassembly** — Remove cap from side of clutch master cylinder. See Fig. 2. Slide out washer, one-way valve and spring.

**Reassembly** — Position spring along with one-way valve into cylinder housing. Fit cap and washer.

Fig. 3   Exploded View of Courier Slave Cylinder

Fig. 2   Exploded View of Clutch Master Cylinder Assembly with Detail of One-Way Valve Used on Models Equipped with 2300 cc Engine

### SLAVE CYLINDER

1) Clean outside of housing.

2) Remove dust boot and clutch release rod.

3) Remove piston assembly and return spring.

4) From slave cylinder, remove:
   - Bleeder screw cap
   - Bleeder screw
   - Steel ball

**Inspection** — 1) Check cylinder bore and piston for:
   - Wear
   - Roughness
   - Scoring

2) Clearance between cylinder bore and piston should be .004" (.102 mm). Replace piston or cylinder if specification is exceeded.

**Reassembly** — 1) Lightly coat piston and cups with brake fluid.

2) Fit cups to piston.

3) Install piston into cylinder.

4) Install release rod and boot.

5) Put steel ball into cylinder.

6) Screw in bleeder. Fit dust cap.

## ADJUSTMENT

### CLUTCH PEDAL

Pedal free play is adjusted by loosening lock nut on push rod and rotating rod until .025-.121" (.64-3.07 mm) free travel is obtained at pedal pad. See Fig. 4. Tighten lock nut when adjustment is completed.

Fig. 4   Clutch Pedal Adjustment Procedure

### HYDRAULIC SYSTEM BLEEDING

Remove rubber cap from bleeder valve and attach a bleeder tube and fixture to bleeder screw. Place other end of tube in a glass jar of brake fluid and open bleeder screw. Depress clutch pedal and allow to return slowly. Continue pumping action until air bubbles cease to appear in glass jar, then close bleeder screw. Install rubber cap on bleeder screw and fill master cylinder. **NOTE** — *During bleeding, master cylinder must be kept ¾ full of brake fluid.*

### TIGHTENING SPECIFICATIONS

| Application | Ft. Lbs. (mkg) |
| --- | --- |
| Clutch Housing-to-Engine | |
| 1800 cc Engine | 34-45 (4.7-6.2) |
| 2300 cc Engine | 28-40 (3.9-5.5) |
| Pressure Plate-to-Flywheel | 13-20 (1.8-2.8) |
| Slave Cylinder-to-Clutch Housing | 12-17 (1.7-2.4) |
| Pivot Pin | 23-34 (3.2-4.7) |

# Clutches

## DATSUN EXCEPT F10

B210
200SX
280Z
510
810
Pickup

### DESCRIPTION

Clutch is dry, single disc type. All models use a diaphragm spring type pressure plate and pre-lubricated clutch release bearing. Clutch is operated by a firewall mounted master cylinder and a clutch housing mounted slave cylinder. All models except B210 with 5-speed transmission have non-adjustable slave cylinder assembly.

**Fig. 1  View of Typical Datsun Clutch System —
Note Some Models have Different Clutch Release
Forks and Others Have Different Slave
Cylinder Configurations**

### REMOVAL & INSTALLATION

#### CLUTCH ASSEMBLY

**NOTE** — *Removal procedure is general. Not all steps apply to each model.*

**Removal — 1)** Disconnect ground cable at battery.

**2)** Remove console box.

**3)** Place transmission shift lever in Neutral.

**4)** On 280Z, disconnect accelerator linkage.

**5)** Remove snap ring (nut on B210) and shift lever pin, then pull out lever.

**6)** Raise vehicle and support on safety stands.

**7)** Disconnect exhaust pipe at manifold.

**8)** On 280Z and 200SX, remove bolts mounting exhaust pipe bracket to extension housing (280Z) or engine rear crossmember (200SX).

**9)** Disconnect back-up lights, transmission controlled spark (200SX), and speedometer cable.

**10)** Remove slave cylinder.

**11)** Remove exhaust pipe insulator and lay over on exhaust pipe.

**12)** On models so equipped, separate center support bearing from crossmember.

**13)** Index mark, disconnect, and remove propeller shaft.

**14)** Support engine.

**15)** Place appropriate jack under transmission.

**16)** Remove transmission rear crossmember.

**17)** Remove starter. Remove bolts mounting transmission to engine. With transmission supported, slide rearward until input shaft is cleared, then remove from vehicle.

**18)** Loosen bolts attaching pressure plate to flywheel. Use a criss-cross pattern to loosen bolts. Also, loosen bolts evenly until spring pressure is relieved.

**Installation** — To install, reverse removal procedure and note:
- Lubricate clutch disc splines with small amount of multipurpose grease.
- Slip clutch assembly over guide dowels.
- Use clutch aligning tool to center disc and pressure plate.
- Adjust linkage.
- Refill transmission, if necessary.
- Bleed clutch hydraulic system if it was opened.

### CLUTCH MASTER CYLINDER

**Removal & Installation** — Disconnect master cylinder push rod at clevis. Disconnect hydraulic line to slave cylinder. Remove cylinder attaching bolts and remove cylinder from firewall. To install, reverse removal procedure, bleed hydraulic system and adjust clutch pedal height.

### CLUTCH SLAVE CYLINDER

**Removal & Installation** — Remove clutch fork return spring (if equipped). Disconnect hydraulic line from cylinder, remove bolts attaching cylinder to clutch housing, and remove slave cylinder. To install, reverse removal procedure and bleed hydraulic system.

### CLUTCH RELEASE BEARING & LEVER

**Removal** — With transmission removed from vehicle, remove dust boot from clutch housing. Disconnect release lever retaining spring or return spring, as required, and retaining clips holding release bearing to lever. Remove bearing and lever through front of clutch housing. Remove bearing from collar using a puller.

## DATSUN EXCEPT F10 (Cont.)

**Installation** — To install, reverse removal procedure and note the following: Apply multi-purpose grease to inside surface of bearing collar, release bearing contact points, release bearing, ball pin in clutch housing, and ball contact points on release lever.

## OVERHAUL

### CLUTCH MASTER CYLINDER

1) With master cylinder removed, remove filler cap and drain brake fluid. Pull back dust boot and remove snap ring. Remove stopper, push rod and piston assembly. Remove spring seat from piston and take off piston cup. Thoroughly clean all components in brake fluid.

**Fig. 2  Exploded View of Clutch Master Cylinder**

2) Inspect all parts for wear or damage. If clearance between cylinder and piston exceeds .006", replace master cylinder. Replace piston cup any time master cylinder is disassembled.

3) Lubricate all parts with clean brake fluid before assembly. To assemble, reverse disassembly procedures.

**Fig. 3  Exploded View of Clutch Slave Cylinder Assembly — (Except B210 4-Speed)**

### CLUTCH SLAVE CYLINDER

1) With slave cylinder removed, take out push rod along with dust boot. Remove entire piston assembly and piston spring. Remove bleed screw.

2) Visually inspect all parts and replace those determined unuseable. To assemble, reverse disassembly procedure noting the following: Dip all components in clean brake fluid and ensure cup is installed in correct direction.

**Fig. 4  Exploded View of Clutch Slave Cylinder (B210 Models Shown)**

## ADJUSTMENT

### PEDAL HEIGHT & FREE PLAY

Adjust clutch pedal height to specification by turning pedal stopper adjusting nut in or out. Tighten lock nut. Adjust pedal free play to .039-.197" (1-5 mm) by turning clutch master cylinder push rod in or out.

### Pedal Height Specifications

| Application | Height In. (mm) |
| --- | --- |
| B210 | 6.02-6.26 (153-159) |
| 200SX | 7.36-7.59 (187-193) |
| 280Z | 8.78 (223) |
| 510 | 6.34-6.57 (161-167) |
| 810 | 6.90 (175.5) |
| Pickup | 6.42 (163) |

## DATSUN EXCEPT F10 (Cont.)

Push Rod Adjusting Screw

Pedal Stopper

Lubrication Points

Pedal Height Measurement Point

*Fig. 5   Clutch Pedal Height and Free Play Adjustment
Locations — All Models Similar*

### CLUTCH FORK FREE PLAY

1) Loosen lock nut and push nut. See *Fig. 6*.

2) Turn push rod until release bearing lightly touches clutch diaphragm spring.

3) Turn rod back (opposite direction) about 1¼ turns. This provides about .039-.079" (1-2 mm) clearance between push nut and lever.

4) Tighten lock nut.

5) Work clutch pedal several times. Recheck pedal free play.

Boot

Clutch Release
Lever (Fork)

Slave
Cylinder

Lock Nut

.039-.079"
(1-2 mm)

Push Nut

*Fig. 6   Clutch Fork Free Play Adjustment Locations
for Datsun B210*

### HYDRAULIC SYSTEM BLEEDING

1) Remove dust cap from slave cylinder bleed plug. Check fluid level in master cylinder, fill as necessary. Open bleed plug approximately ¾ turn.

2) Attach a tube to slave cylinder bleed plug, and place opposite end of tube in a container half-full of brake fluid. Push clutch pedal to bottom of travel.

3) With pedal down, tighten bleed plug. Continue operation until air bubbles are no longer seen in container. Close bleed plug on a downward stroke of pedal. Install dust cap and adjust fluid level in master cylinder.

### TIGHTENING SPECIFICATIONS

| Application | Ft. Lbs. (mkg) |
|---|---|
| Clutch-to-Flywheel | 11-16 (1.5-2.2) |
| Engine-to-Transmission | |
| B210 | |
|   4-Speed | 12-16 (1.6-2.2) |
|   5-Speed & 200SX | 27-36 (3.7-5.0) |
| 280Z, 810, Pickup | 32-43 (4.4-5.9) |
| All Others | 32-43 (4.4-5.9) |
| Salve Cylinder-to-Clutch Housing | |
| 280Z & 510 | 18-25 (2.5-3.5) |
| Pickup | 18-22 (2.5-3.0) |
| All Others | 22-30 (3.1-4.1) |

## DATSUN F10

### Datsun F10

## DESCRIPTION

Clutch is a single, dry disc, diaphragm spring type. Main components consist of: clutch cover, pressure plate, and diaphragm spring. Clutch plates are riveted together. A release bearing and fork control clutch engagement and disengagement. Clutch is hydraulic type with a firewall mounted master cylinder and clutch housing mounted slave cylinder.

**Fig. 1  Exploded View of Clutch Components**

## REMOVAL & INSTALLATION

### CLUTCH ASSEMBLY

**NOTE** — *Clutch assembly can be serviced, removed, or overhauled while transmission and engine remain in vehicle. Also, transmission cannot be removed without removing engine.*

**Removal** — 1) Disconnect the following: Battery ground cable, fresh air duct, electrical connectors on clutch housing and carbon cannister hoses. Remove upper portion of clutch housing inspection cover, then take out six bolts mounting clutch cover.

**NOTE** — *To gain access to mounting bolts, raise right front wheel and rotate by hand until bolts are visible.*

2) Turn wheels to left stop, then remove right side inspection cover and disconnect clutch release fork. Remove six bolts on bearing housing. Pull out primary drive gear assembly. (See Fig. 2). Lift out clutch cover and disc through inspection opening. Remove strap securing pressure plate to clutch cover. Keep strap in relative position since it is part of dynamic balance.

**Fig. 2  Removing Primary Drive Gear Assembly**

**Installation** — To install, reverse removal procedure and note the following: Make sure all alignment marks are positioned before tightening.

### RELEASE BEARING

**Removal** — Separate release lever by removing pivot pin and removing bearing housing. Remove "O" ring and bearing. Hold bearing and rotate outer race, replace if operation is rough or noisy.

**Installation** — To install, reverse removal procedure and apply multi-purpose grease to sliding parts of release lever.

### CLUTCH MASTER CYLINDER

**Removal** — Remove lock ring from clevis pin and pull out clevis pin. Disconnect and plug clutch line from master cylinder. Remove nuts mounting master cylinder to insturment panel.

**Installation** — To install, reverse removal procedure and note the following: Adjust pedal play and bleed air from hydraulic system.

### SLAVE CYLINDER

**Removal** — Disconnect clutch hose from slave cylinder. Remove two bolts mounting slave cylinder to clutch housing.

**Installation** — To install, reverse removal procedure and note the following: Bleed air from hydraulic system.

## OVERHAUL

### MASTER CYLINDER

**Disassembly** — Remove dust cover and pull stopper ring from cylinder body. Remove push rod, then take out entire piston assembly.

**Inspection** — Wash all internal parts in clean brake fluid. Check cylinder bore and piston for burrs or score marks. Check bore for wear. If clearance between bore and piston is more than .006" (.15 mm), piston must be replaced. Check all passages to make sure they are clear.

## DATSUN F10 (Cont.)

**Fig. 3   Exploded View of Master Cylinder**

**Reassembly** — To reassemble, reverse disassembly procedure and note the following: Make sure piston cup is correctly positioned. Apply a light coat of brake fluid to cylinder and piston.

### SLAVE CYLINDER

**Disassembly** — Remove dust boot. Separate remaining components as shown in *Fig. 4.*

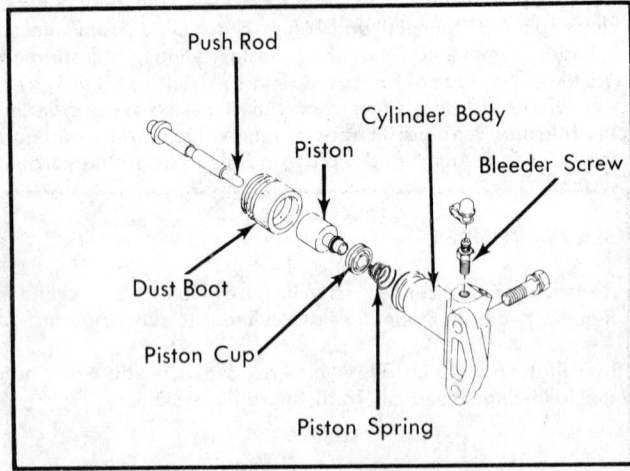

**Fig. 4   Exploded View of Clutch Slave Cylinder**

**Inspection** — Visually inspect all components and replace those which indicate signs of damage or wear. Clean all components in brake fluid. Check cylinder piston and bore for score marks and rust. Inspect cylinder bore and piston for wear. If clearance is more than .006" (.15 mm), replace piston. Make sure bleed hole is dirt free.

**Reassembly** — To reassemble, reverse disassembly procedure and note the following: Apply a light coat of brake fluid to cylinder and piston before reassembly.

**NOTE** — *When pressure plate and clutch disc are replaced, or if any components of release mechanism is replaced, a new push rod may have to be installed.*

## ADJUSTMENTS

### CLUTCH PEDAL HEIGHT & FREE PLAY

Adjust clutch pedal height by turning master cylinder push rod. Correct height is 6.65-6.9" (169-175 mm). Tighten lock nut. Adjust stopper nut so pedal free play is .236-.551" (6-14 mm). Tighten lock nut. *Fig. 5.*

**Fig. 5   Pedal Height and Free Play Adjustment**

### HYDRAULIC SYSTEM BLEEDING

Fit bleeder hose to bleeder valve. Place opposite end into a clear container partially filled with brake fluid. Pump clutch pedal two or three times and hold to floor. Break bleeder valve loose and allow air to vent. Close bleeder screw and allow pedal to return. Repeat procedure several times.

## TIGHTENING SPECIFICATIONS

| Application | Ft. Lbs. (mkg) |
|---|---|
| Clutch Cover Assembly | 5.1-7.2 (.7-1.0) |
| Pressure Plate Strap | 5.1-5.8 (.7-.8) |
| Bleeder Screw | 5.1-6.5 (.7-.9) |
| Push Rod Lock Nut | 5.8-8.0 (.8-1.1) |
| Master Cylinder-to-Instrument Panel | 5.8-8.0 (.8-1.1) |
| Slave Cylinder Bolts | 12-15 (1.6-2.1) |

# Clutches

## FIAT X1/9

### X1/9

## DESCRIPTION

Clutch is a dry, single plate, diaphragm spring type. Clutch actuation is hydraulic, using a firewall mounted master cylinder and a clutch housing mounted slave cylinder. A prelubricated clutch release bearing is also used.

## REMOVAL & INSTALLATION

### CLUTCH ASSEMBLY

**Removal — 1)** Disconnect positive battery cable. Remove air cleaner and carburetor duct cooling. From inside engine compartment, separate slave cylinder from transmission case. Install engine support. Remove upper transmission-to-cranckcase mounting bolts.

**2)** Working from under the vehicle, disconnect and swing out-of-way shifting flexible link. Disconnect back-up lights and seat belt warning system wire. Remove starter. Disconnect and remove exhaust pipe.

**3)** Remove nuts from the hub end of half shaft. Remove attaching hardware mounting suspension control arm to supports. Free half shaft from hub end and fix other end to transmission to prevent premature disconnection.

**4)** Remove the following items: Flywheel cover, engine cross-member support, and lower engine-to-transmission bolts. Remove transmission/differential from below vehicle. Mark clutch position on flywheel and remove clutch.

**Installation —** To install, reverse removal procedure using suitable tool (A. 70210) to center clutch assembly.

### CLUTCH MASTER CYLINDER

**Removal —** Steering column must be removed to gain access to clutch master cylinder. Disconnect and cap master cylinder hydraulic line. Remove two bolts attaching cylinder to support plate. Withdraw cylinder from actuating rod and remove from vehicle.

**Installation —** To install, reverse removal procedure and bleed hydraulic system.

### CLUTCH SLAVE CYLINDER

**Removal —** Remove slave cylinder hydraulic hose and union. Disconnect cylinder push rod from clutch release bearing fork. Slightly compress return spring and remove two mounting bolts; slowly withdraw cylinder from support plate.

**Installation —** To install, reverse removal procedure ensuring slave cylinder snugly fits against support and that hydraulic system is bled.

*Fig. 1  Clutch Slave Cylinder Location*

## ADJUSTMENT

### CLUTCH PEDAL HEIGHT & FREE PLAY ADJUSTMENT

**1)** Check clutch pedal travel, it should be approximately 6.7" (170 mm). If specification is not met, adjust screw on top of clutch pedal assembly until travel is correct. Turn screw out to reduce travel and in to increase it.

**2)** Check clutch pedal for approximately 1.25" (31.8 mm) free play. If specification is incorrect, adjust nut on slave cylinder until free play is to specification.

*Fig. 2  Exploded View of Clutch Master Cylinder*

# Clutches

## FIAT X1/9 (Cont.)

### OVERHAUL

#### CLUTCH MASTER CYLINDER

**Disassembly** — Ease rubber dust boot back and remove snap ring, using long nosed pliers. Remove seal and complete plunger assembly. Pull out remaining gasket, seal and spring.

**Reassembly** — Lightly coat all components with brake fluid. Insert spring and seal into position. Fit piston assembly and seal, then install snap ring. Slip boot over cylinder housing.

#### CLUTCH SLAVE CYLINDER

**Disassembly** — Pull push rod from slave cylinder. Slide dust boot off housing. Remove lock ring, washer, and spring, then shake out piston assembly. Seal at rear of cylinder bore may not come out with piston assembly.

**Reassembly** — Lightly coat all components with brake fluid before reassembly. Insert rear seal, and piston assembly. Refit spring, washer, and lock ring. Install dust boot and push rod.

**Fig. 3   Exploded View of Clutch Slave Cylinder**

## TIGHTENING SPECIFICATIONS

| Application | Ft. Lbs. (mkg) |
| --- | --- |
| Clutch Flywheel Bolts | 10.8 (1.5) |
| Clutch Release Fork Bolt | 18 (2.5) |
| Slave Cylinder Piston Adjusting Nut | 18 (2.5) |
| Slave Cylinder Support Plate-to-Transmission Case | 18 (2.5) |
| Support Plate-to-Transmission Case Stud Nut | 18 (2.5) |

## FIAT 124

**124 Spider**

### DESCRIPTION

Clutch is a dry, single-disc, diaphragm spring type. Clutch is engaged or disengaged through a cable which is actuated by the clutch pedal.

### REMOVAL & INSTALLATION

#### CLUTCH

1) Raise and suitably support vehicle. From inside drivers compartment, press down on gearshift lever and pry out retaining ring with screwdriver. Remove transmission cover.

2) From under vehicle, disconnect drive shaft from transmission and remove drive shaft safety cross strap. Remove drive shaft center pillow block. Disconnect speedometer drive from transmission. Disconnect back-up light switch (if equipped). Disconnect clutch fork return spring and remove adjusting rod.

3) Remove inspection cover from bottom of clutch housing. Disconnect exhaust pipe support bracket from rear of transmission and remove starter from clutch housing. Position a suitable transmission holding fixture (A. 70509) to a floor jack and position under transmission.

4) Remove bolts securing transmission to engine and remove rear crossmember. With transmission supported by jack, pull to rear until input shaft clears release bearing. Lower jack when transmission is clear and remove from under vehicle. Remove clutch assembly from flywheel after marking their relationship for reinstallation.

5) To install transmission and clutch assembly, reverse removal procedures noting the following: Lightly lubricate transmission input shaft splines. Ensure clutch and flywheel are properly aligned.

### ADJUSTMENT

#### CLUTCH PEDAL

Clutch pedal should have approximately 1" (25 mm) free play. If specification is not met, loosen lock nut and rotate adjust-

ment nut *(Fig. 1)* until clutch pedal free play is to specification. When free play is correctly adjusted maximum pedal travel (measured from first resistance) should be about 4.72" (120 mm).

**Fig. 1  Clutch Actuating Components Showing Cable Adjustment Point**

## TIGHTENING SPECIFICATIONS

| Application | Ft. Lbs. (mkg) |
| --- | --- |
| Clutch-to-Flywheel ................................................ | 22 (3.0) |
| Transmission Case-to-Bell Housing Bolts ............... | 36 (5.0) |
| Transmission Case-to-Bell Housing Nut.................. | 18 (2.5) |
| Bell Housing-to-Engine Mounts............................ | 61 (8.4) |

## FIAT 128

128
Sedan
Station Wagon
3P

### DESCRIPTION

Clutch is a dry, single disc, diaphragm spring type. Clutch is engaged or disengaged through a cable, actuated by clutch pedal.

### REMOVAL & INSTALLATION

#### CLUTCH

**1)** Disconnect positive battery cable and remove spare tire. Disconnect speedometer cable from transaxle housing. Remove engine protective cover from engine and front of body.

**2)** Disconnect clutch fork return spring and disconnect cable from clutch fork. Remove all bolts securing engine to transaxle accessible from inside engine compartment.

**3)** Attach a suitable support to engine (A. 70526) to secure engine when separated from transaxle. Remove hub caps and separate drive axles from hubs and remove left front wheel.

**4)** Disconnect tie rod from steering arm using a suitable puller (A. 47035). Remove stabilizer bar and disconnect left side strut assembly from steering knuckle.

**5)** From under vehicle, remove lower guards and disconnect exhaust pipe bracket from transaxle. Disconnect gear shift linkage from transaxle and remove starter.

**6)** Remove engine support crossmember and flywheel cover. Remove remaining bolts securing transaxle to engine. Disconnect ground cable from transaxle.

**7)** Secure drive axles to transaxle with wire to prevent axles from slipping out of transaxle during removal. Secure a suitable lifting fixture (A. 70547) to a floor jack.

**8)** Position floor jack and lifting fixture to transaxle and remove transaxle from vehicle. Mark position of clutch on flywheel and remove clutch assembly.

**9)** To install clutch assembly, reverse removal procedure. Align clutch and flywheel marks and tighten evenly on flywheel. Drive axle to hub nuts must be tightened to specification.

**Fig. 1  Clutch Actuating Components Showing Cable Adjustment Point**

### ADJUSTMENT

#### CLUTCH PEDAL

**1)** Clutch pedal should have about 1" (25 mm) free play. If specification is not met, loosen adjustment lock nut and rotate adjusting nut until pedal free play is within specification.

**2)** When free play is correctly adjusted maximum pedal travel (measured from first resistance) should be about 4.72" (120 mm) for sedan and station wagon models or 4.02" (102 mm) for 3P models.

### TIGHTENING SPECIFICATIONS

| Application | Ft. Lbs. (mkg) |
| --- | --- |
| Clutch Assembly-to-Flywheel | 11 (1.5) |
| Transmission-to-Clutch Housing | 18 (2.5) |
| Clutch Housing-to-Engine | 58 (8.0) |

## FIAT 131

131

### DESCRIPTION

Clutch is a dry, single disc type using a diaphragm spring pressure plate. Clutch disc is a conventional friction lining kind. Clutch operation is accomplished by a control cable attached at upper end directly to clutch pedal and lower end to clutch release fork.

### REMOVAL & INSTALLATION

#### CLUTCH ASSEMBLY

**1)** Disconnect battery ground cable. Remove exhaust pipe-to-manifold bracket. From inside vehicle, remove transmission cover, then pry snap ring from gear shift lever. Disconnect electrical lead on fast idle switch and pull wire through tunnel.

**2)** Disconnect drive shaft at flexible coupler. Remove protection shield and bracket (if necessary) and secure drive shaft out of way. Disconnect remaining electrical leads from transmission.

**3)** Fit a hydraulic jack with necessary adaptors (if any) under transmission, then suitably support the engine. Take out starter bolts. Disconnect clutch linkage and speedometer cable.

**4)** Remove flywheel cover bolts, then remove exhaust pipe support and place out of way. Remove transmission support mount. Pull transmission rearward, tilting to slide input shaft out of clutch. Lower transmission to floor. Index mark clutch position on flywheel, then remove clutch.

**5)** To install clutch and transmission assembly, reverse removal procedure noting the following: Clutch disc must be installed with protrusion on hub facing transmission. Lightly coat input shaft splines with oil and use centering tool to align clutch disc.

### ADJUSTMENT

#### CLUTCH PEDAL

Clutch pedal free play should be approximately 1" (25 mm). If pedal is out of adjustment, loosen lock nut (near firewall) and rotate adjustment nut until free play is to specification.

*Fig. 2   Exploded View of Clutch Cable & Pedal Components*

*Fig. 1   Clutch Actuating Components Showing Cable Adjustment Point*

### TIGHTENING SPECIFICATIONS

| Application | Ft. Lbs. (mkg) |
| --- | --- |
| Clutch-to-Flywheel | 22 (3.0) |

## FIESTA

### Fiesta

## DESCRIPTION

The Fiesta clutch consists of a single dry plate clutch disc and a diaphragm spring pressure plate. The disc has 4 torsion springs. The clutch assembly is operated by an automatic self-adjusting device with a release shaft and thrust bearing inside the clutch housing.

**Fig. 1   Fiesta Clutch System Components**

## REMOVAL & INSTALLATION

### CLUTCH ASSEMBLY

**Removal — 1)** Engage transmission in 4th gear position to ensure correct adjustment after installation.

**2)** Disconnect battery ground cable.

**3)** Insert engine support bar and clamp. See Fig. 2. Engine must be supported with transmission removed.

**Fig. 2   Engine Support Bar Assembly**

**4)** Unscrew speedometer driven gear.

**5)** Unhook clutch cable from release lever by pulling cable through between lever and support.

**6)** Remove (4) upper transmission flange bolts.

**7)** Jack up vehicle and drain transmission fluid.

**NOTE** — *Remove plunger retainer and drain fluid out through plunger retainer hole.*

**8)** Remove shift rod bias spring and shift rod from selector shaft gear. Loosen clamping screw and withdraw shift rod.

**9)** Unhook spring between shift rod and selector rail.

**10)** Remove stabilizer shift assembly from transmission.

**11)** Unscrew and reposition (2) inner nuts on rubber coupling and engine support.

**12)** Loosen lock nut on stud, and remove stud from transmission housing with Allen wrench.

**NOTE** — *Allow stabilizer and screw to hang on engine support bar.*

**13)** Remove left driveshaft by removing (6) Allen bolts at coupling of inner constant velocity joint and stubshaft.

**14)** Remove front axle shaft by removing (6) Allen bolts at inner constant velocity joint.

**15)** Remove starter.

**16)** Remove (2) lower flange bolts from transmission.

**17)** Remove (3) bolts from engine mounting.

**18)** Lift out transmission.

**19)** Remove screws from clutch pressure plate evenly (one turn at a time) and remove clutch assembly from flywheel.

**Installation** — Reverse removal procedure making note of the following:

**1)** Apply light coating of grease on splines of driveshaft and differential gear.

**2)** Be sure engine adaptor plate is properly seated on engine guide bushings.

**3)** Install transmission. Insert (2) flange bolts and snug.

**4)** Align engine adaptor plate and secure with two drivers.

**5)** Mount transmission and clutch adaptor plate to engine mounting using (3) new self-locking bolts. Lower engine and torque these 3 bolts. Torque 2 flange bolts now also.

**NOTE** — *It is absolutely essential to use NEW self-locking bolts. It is extremely important to use the proper torque values on all bolts and nuts.*

## FIESTA (Cont.)

**6)** Install control shaft plunger with spring and retainer.

**NOTE** — *Lightly coat retainer threads with "Omnifit" type lubricant.*

**7)** Install starter and connect cable.

**8)** When installing stabilizer gear to transmission, gently turn Allen screw as far as stop in transmission housing. Lock with nut on rubber coupling of stabilizer. Bring inner nuts on engine mount into contact, and torque outer engine mount nuts.

**9)** Adjust gearshift as follows:
   **a.** Be sure gearshift is in 4th gear position. Slide selector rod onto shaft.
   **b.** Pull selector rod and gear lever down until holes in end of gear lever and selector housing line up. Lock in position with .16" (4 mm) arbor or pin.

**NOTE** — *Remember to wedge a spacer between selector rod and floor pan. Spacer height should be 2.75" (70 mm).*

   **c.** Using a suitable mandrel, turn shift shaft clockwise to stop. Push shaft into transmission case and hold.
   **d.** Lock selector rod clamp bolt. Remove spacer, mandrel and pin. Check gear shift operation.

**10)** Hook selector rod spring into frame member.

**11)** Remove engine support assembly.

**Fig. 3   Automatic Clutch Cable Adjuster**

### AUTOMATIC CLUTCH CABLE ADJUSTER

Fiesta is equipped with an automatic clutch cable adjuster, and no manual adjustment is required. Automatic adjuster is located at upper end of clutch pedal. Cable tension is set whenever clutch pedal is depressed as pawl engages with nearest adjusting segment.

### CLUTCH CABLE

**Removal** — **1)** Push cable between lever and support forward and release. Unhook cable from release lever.

**2)** Remove lower insulating panel on left side of dash. Bend retaining tabs upward. Remove screws and lift off.

**3)** Unhook clutch cable from pedal. Pull pedal to rear to release pawl from toothed segment.

**4)** Rotate segment forwards, and unhook cable from segment.

**5)** Let toothed segment swivel backwards.

**6)** Pull cable out through recess between pedal and automatic adjuster.

**Installation** — Reverse removal procedure.

### ADJUSTMENT

**NOTE** — *Fiesta is equipped with automatic clutch cable adjuster. No manual adjustment is required.*

| TIGHTENING SPECIFICATIONS | |
|---|---|
| **Application** | **Ft. Lbs. ( mkg)** |
| Gearbox-to-Engine Flange Bolts | 30 (4.1) |
| Gearbox-to-Engine Brace | |
| Self-Locking Bolts | 65 (9.0) |
| Small Housing-to-Large Housing | 18 (2.5) |
| Gearshift Lock Cap Nut-to-Housing | 21.7 (3.0) |
| Gear/Differential Housing | 60 (8.3) |
| Shift Housing-to-Floor Pan | 11.6 (1.6) |
| Cover-to-Housing | 7.2 (1.0) |
| Pressure Plate-to-Flywheel | 13 (1.8) |
| Selector Rod Mechanism-to- | |
| -Stabilizer Allen Bolt | 40 (5.5) |

## HONDA ACCORD

**Accord**

## DESCRIPTION

Clutch is a single plate, dry disc type. Clutch assembly consists of clutch disc, clutch cover and pressure plate assembly, and clutch release mechanism. Clutch release mechanism is hydraulic, consisting of a firewall mounted master cylinder and a slave cylinder mounted to clutch housing. Clutch release fork free play is adjustable.

## REMOVAL & INSTALLATION

### CLUTCH

**Removal** — 1) Disconnect battery ground at transmission. Put gear shift in Neutral. Disconnect following electrical wiring.

- Positive battery cable at starter.
- Black/White wire from starter solenoid.
- Yellow/Green wire from temperature sending unit.
- Black/Yellow and Yellow wires from temperature sensor A.
- Black/White and Red wires from temperature sensor B
- Black/Green and Yellow wires from back-up light switch.

**2)** Disconnect clutch control cable at firewall and release fork. Remove the right side starter bolt and two upper transmission mounting bolts.

**3)** Raise vehicle. Drain transmission fluid. Remove front wheels. Fit transmission jack squarely under transmission. Remove rightside inner fender panel. Remove speedometer from transmission. Take off sub-frame center support.

**4)** Remove stop bracket from front of clutch housing. Disconnect lower torque rod at transmission. Use suitable driver and force out shift linkage spring pin at transmission. Disconnect stabilizer bar from both radius rods.

**5)** Remove lower control arm bolt at rear of arm. Disconnect tie rods at steering knuckle. With steering knuckle at outer most position, pry constant velocity (CV) joint outward approximately ½". Pull stub axle from transmission housing. Remove clutch cover. Remove left starter bolt and starter.

**6)** Remove engine mounting bolts (3 rear) from transmission housing. Remove single front transmission mounting bolt. Remove transmission. Fit suitable flywheel holding device into flywheel. Remove eight (8) pressure plate mounting bolts. Separate pressure plate from diaphragm spring by removing retainers. Remove clutch disc. Remove six (6) flywheel mounting bolts and slide off flywheel.

**Installation** — To install reverse removal procedure and note: Make sure flywheel and pressure plate alignment marks are matched. **NOTE** — *New pressure plates are not indexed.* Use clutch disc alignment tool to ensure all components are properly set. Torque pressure plate bolts in criss-cross pattern. Refill transmission with SAE 10W-40 oil.

### CLUTCH MASTER CYLINDER

**Removal** — Separate clutch pedal operating rod from master cylinder push rod by removing through pin at clevis. Disconnect and plug hydraulic lines. Remove nuts mounting master cylinder to firewall. Make sure brake fluid does not spill on painted surfaces.

**Installation** — To install master cylinder, reverse removal procedure and note: Bleed hydraulic system.

### CLUTCH SLAVE CYLINDER

**Removal** — Disconnect hydraulic line from slave cylinder. Unhook return spring. Separate threaded rod from end of slave cylinder. Remove slave cylinder mounting bolts and take cylinder off clutch housing.

**Installation** — To install, reverse removal procedure and note: Bleed hydraulic system.

### CLUTCH RELEASE FORK AND BEARING

**Removal** — With transmission removed, separate slave cylinder push rod from release fork. Slide release fork through slot in clutch housing (inward) and remove fork. Release fork bolt can now be removed, if necessary. Slide bearing out of release fork. Using a driver, release bearing can be separated from holder, if necessary.

**Installation** — To install, reverse removal procedure and lightly coat all moving parts and contact areas with grease.

## OVERHAUL

### MASTER CYLINDER

**Disassembly** — Remove boot and take off snap ring. Use compressed air and force piston assembly from master cylinder. Separate piston, cups, spring retainer, return spring and valve assembly.

**Inspection** — Check all components for damage or excessive wear. Check cylinder to piston for wear. Clearance should not exceed .006" (.15 mm). Make sure all rubber components are replaced.

**Reassembly** — To reassemble, reverse disassembly procedure.

# Clutches

## HONDA ACCORD (Cont.)

Fig. 1  Exploded View of Master Cylinder

### CLUTCH SLAVE CYLINDER

**Disassembly** — Remove air bleed screw. Pull off dust boot. Force piston out of slave cylinder using compressed air. Take off piston rubber cup. Remove union plug with metal gasket. Carefully lift off valve plate. Remove spring.

**Inspection** — Check cylinder to piston wear. Clearance should not exceed .006" (.15 mm). Inspect all components for excessive wear or damage. Replace all rubber components with new parts.

Fig. 2  Exploded View of Slave Cylinder

**Reassembly** — Reverse disassembly procedure. Lightly coat all components with brake fluid before reassembly.

## ADJUSTMENT

### CLUTCH PEDAL HEIGHT AND FREE PLAY

Adjust clutch pedal height to 7.24" (184 mm) using pedal stopper bolt. Rotate bolt in direction necessary to bring pedal height into specifications. Adjust pedal free play (clearance between clutch pedal push rod and master cylinder) using nut on master cylinder push rod. Pedal free play should be approximately .04-.12" (1-3 mm).

### CLUTCH RELEASE FORK FREE PLAY

Loosen lock nut. Hold push rod end nut stationary and rotate Push rod with screw driver. Rotate counterclockwise to increase free play. After eliminating free play, back out rod 1¾ to 2 turns. Final free play should be .08-.1" (2.0-2.6 mm).

Fig. 3  Clutch Release Fork Adjustment Locations

### TIGHTENING SPECIFICATIONS

| Application | Ft. Lbs. (mkg) |
|---|---|
| Master Cylinder-to-Firewall | 5-9 (.7-1.2) |
| Slave Cylinder-to-Clutch Housing | 14-18 (1.9-2.5) |
| Slave Cylinder Hydraulic Line | 11-18 (1.5-2.5) |
| Flywheel | 34-38 (4.7-5.3) |
| Master Cylinder Push Rod Lock Nut | 22-29 (3.0-4.0) |

## HONDA CIVIC & CIVIC CVCC

Civic
Civic CVCC

### DESCRIPTION

Clutch is single plate dry disc type, using a diaphragm spring to engage pressure plate. Clutch has a mechanical release system consisting of clutch pedal, cable, clutch release lever, and release bearing.

### REMOVAL & INSTALLATION

#### CLUTCH ASSEMBLY

1) Raise and support vehicle, then remove front wheels. Disconnect battery ground cable at battery and transmission case. Disconnect electrical leads from starter and separate connections for back-up lights. On CVCC models, disconnect leads to temperature sending units. Disconnect clutch cable and on Civic models, remove speedometer cable.

2) On CVCC models, remove right starter motor bolt and two upper transmission mounting bolts. Drain transmission. Place jack under transmission. Remove fender well shield on right side. Remove speedometer drive holder and pull assembly from transmission. Remove subframe crossmember and support bracket from clutch housing front.

3) On Civic models, disconnect lower arm ball joints at knuckles with suitable ball joint remover tool (07941-6340000). Pull drive shafts out of differential case. Drive gear shift rod retainer pin out with a pin driver, then disconnect rod at transmission case. Disconnect gear shift extension at clutch housing.

4) On CVCC models, disconnect torque rod from mounting at transmission. Disconnect gear shift by removing pin, then disconnect stabilizer spring from both radius rods. Separate ball joint from steering knuckle. Separate stub axle of transmission housing.

5) On Civic models, raise and support engine to take load off engine mounts. Remove the two center beam-to-lower engine mount nuts. Remove center beam and engine mount. Reinstall center beam (less mount) and lower engine until it rests on beam.

6) On CVCC models, remove clutch cover, left starter bolt, then remove starter. Remove three rear engine mounting bolts from transmission housing. Remove front transmission bolts and pull transmission rearward off dowels.

7) On Civic models, place a jack under transmission and remove four attaching bolts. Slide transmission away from engine and lower jack until transmission clears vehicle. On all models, loosen pressure plate retaining bolts two turns at a time in a circular pattern, and remove clutch assembly.

8) To install, reverse removal procedure and note the following: Use a suitable aligning pin to center clutch disc on flywheel. When installing pressure plate, align mark on outer edge of flywheel with alignment mark on pressure plate. Tighten pressure plate retaining bolts 2 turns at a time in a circular (Civic) or criss-cross (Civic CVCC) pattern to prevent distorting diaphragm spring.

#### CLUTCH RELEASE LEVER & BEARING

1) With transmission removed, unbend locking tab and remove the 8 mm release arm retaining bolt. Slide release shaft out of transmission case. Slide release arm and release bearing off transmission input shaft as an assembly.

2) Separate release bearing from arm taking care not to damage retaining clip. **NOTE** — *Attempting to remove or install release bearing with release arm in case will damage retaining clip. Using a suitable bearing driver, separate release bearing from holder.*

3) **NOTE** — *Bearing is filled with grease and should not be immersed in cleaning solvent.* To install, reverse removal procedure and note the following: Install release bearing with radiused (rounded) side opposite holder. When installing release shaft and arm, place a lock tab washer under retaining bolt.

*Fig. 1  Exploded View of Clutch Assembly with Bell Housing*

## HONDA CIVIC & CIVIC CVCC (Cont.)

### ADJUSTMENT

#### CLUTCH PEDAL

**NOTE** — *Before adjusting clutch pedal height, make sure brake pedal free play is properly adjusted.*

1) Check clutch pedal height and if necessary, adjust upper stop so that clutch and brake pedals rest at approximately same height from floor.

**Fig. 2   Clutch Adjustment Point for Civic**

2) On Civic models, adjust clutch release lever to .12-.16" (3-4 mm) free play, measured at release lever. Adjustment is made at outer cable housing adjuster near release lever.

**NOTE** — *Insure upper and lower adjusting nuts are tightened after adjustment has been made.*

3) On Civic CVCC models, adjust clutch cable clip (near firewall) until pedal free play is approximately .6-.8" (15-20 mm).

4) Check clutch pedal release height as follows: Raise front wheels off ground and place transmission in fourth gear. Depress clutch pedal and start engine. Release pedal until wheels start to turn, and measure pedal height at this point. Pedal release height should be greater than 1.18" (30 mm).

**NOTE** — *If release lever free play and pedal height are properly adjusted, but pedal release height is not within specifications, clutch components are damaged.*

**Fig. 3   Clutch Pedal Adjustment Point for CVCC**

### TIGHTENING SPECIFICATIONS

| Application | Ft. Lbs (mkg) |
|---|---|
| Clutch-to-Flywheel | 7-10 (.97-1.3) |
| Flywheel-to-Crankshaft | 34-38 (4.7-5.2) |
| Release Arm Bracket Bolt | 14-20 (1.9-2.7) |
| Clutch Case-to-Engine (Civic) | 29-36 (4.0-4.9) |

## LANCIA

Lancia
(Except Scorpion)

### DESCRIPTION

Clutch is a dry, single disc, diaphragm spring type. Clutch is engaged and disengaged through a control cable. Cable is actuated by the clutch pedal.

### REMOVAL & INSTALLATION

#### CLUTCH ASSEMBLY

**Removal** — **NOTE** — *Engine and Transaxle assembly must be removed to gain access to clutch assembly.* Separate clutch housing (with transaxle) from engine. Set flywheel so index mark is facing top. Hold flywheel from turning. Index mark clutch and flywheel assembly before removing. Loosen clutch mounting bolts alternately and evenly, then remove clutch.

**Installation** — To install, reverse removal procedure and note following: Use suitable tool (88023030) to align clutch assembly.

#### CLUTCH CABLE

**Removal** — Disconnect and remove battery. Remove control cable lock and adjustment nut. Slip cable from release lever. Separate cable from clutch pedal by removing clevis pin on pedal arm. Remove cable out through engine compartment.

**Installation** — To install, reverse removal procedure. Make clutch pedal adjustment.

#### CLUTCH PEDAL

**Removal** — Loosen lock and adjustment nut on clutch cable. Unhook pedal spring from upper pin. Remove pedal mounting bolt. Pull clutch pedal downward, disconnect cable, remove hook and spring. Remove pedal.

**Installation** — To install pedal, reverse removal procedure and adjust pedal free play.

#### RELEASE BEARING

**Removal** — With transaxle removed or slid back, slide bearing off input shaft. Remove clutch operating lever and bushings. Inspect bushings and replace if excessively worn. Inspect bearing and replace if found worn or defective.

**Installation** — To install, reverse removal procedure. Make sure to lightly grease the support.

### ADJUSTMENT

#### CLUTCH PEDAL

Clutch pedal should have approximately .590" (15 mm) free play. If specification is not met, loosen lock nut on control cable and rotate adjustment nut until free play is correct. When pedal free play is correct, clutch release lever will have approximately .118-.196" (3-5 mm) free play.

*Fig. 1  Clutch Free Play Adjustment Location*

## LUV

### LUV

## DESCRIPTION

Clutch assembly is a single dry disc type using a diaphragm spring pressure plate with a pre-lubricated release bearing. Clutch release lever is cable actuated. Cable is hooked to release lever and clutch pedal.

**Fig. 1   Exploded View of LUV Clutch Assembly**

## REMOVAL & INSTALLATION

### CLUTCH ASSEMBLY

**1)** Disconnect negative battery terminal and remove air cleaner assembly. Slide gearshift lever boot upwards on lever, remove gearshift lever attaching bolts, and remove lever assembly. Remove starter attaching bolts, and lay starter aside.

**2)** Raise vehicle on hoist and disconnect exhaust pipe hanger at transmission. Disconnect speedometer cable at transmission. Remove propeller shaft.

**3)** Remove clutch release lever return spring. Remove flywheel inspection cover. Remove 3 bolts mounting frame bracket to rear mount. Using a jack slightly raise transmission and remove 4 crossmember-to-frame bracket bolts. Remove 2 bolts mounting transmission extension housing. Lower engine/transmission assembly and support rear of engine.

**4)** Disconnect electrical leads at transmission. Remove transmission to engine attaching bolts and remove transmission.

**5)** Mark pressure plate and flywheel for reassembly reference. Loosen clutch to flywheel attaching bolts one turn at a time until spring pressure is released. Support clutch assembly with a suitable clutch aligning tool, remove bolts, and remove clutch.

**6)** To install, apply a thin coat of Lubriplate or equivalent to clutch disc splines. Install clutch assembly to flywheel, matching alignment marks made at disassembly. Use a suitable clutch alignment tool to center clutch assembly on flywheel, then install and tighten attaching bolts. To complete installation, reverse removal procedure.

### RELEASE BEARING, SHIFT BLOCK & RELEASE LEVER

**Removal** — Remove release lever from transmission case. Disengage release bearing to lever retaining springs. Slide out release bearing with shift block. Remove release lever from transmission ball stud.

**Inspection — 1)** Check release bearing for noise or lubricant loss by spinning bearing. Replace bearing if either condition exists.

**2)** Inspect release lever ball socket and lever contact surface for signs of excessive wear. Also, check retaining spring for signs of weakening. Make sure spring will hold lever tightly to ball stud.

**Installation** — Install release lever ball stud in cover. Lube shift block inner groove, ball seat and release bearing contact surface. Install release lever and bearing assembly. Attach release bearing spring to lever and spring clip to ball stud.

### PILOT BEARING

Check pilot bearing for seizing, sticking, abnormal noise or wear. If replacement is required, use a suitable tool (J-23907) to remove bearing.

### CLUTCH CABLE

**Removal — 1)** Loosen clutch cable lock nut and adjusting nut. Free cable from various routing clips in engine compartment. Working under vehicle, disengage return spring from release lever.

**2)** Disconnect cable from release lever and pull cable forward through bracket. Separate cable from clutch pedal and pull cable into engine compartment. Remove cable out of engine compartment. Make sure boots are not damaged.

**Installation** — To install, reverse removal procedure and note: Make sure cable is not kinked or bent sharply.

## ADJUSTMENT

### CLUTCH CABLE

Pull cable into engine compartment. Rotate adjuster nut until washer damper assembly is brought back into contact with firewall. Work clutch pedal several times. Pull cable out again and fully tighten nut. Back adjusting nut off until there is about .196" (5 mm) between adjusting nut and boot. See Fig. 2. Tighten lock nut.

**Fig. 2   Clutch Cable Adjustment Gap**

## MAZDA COSMO, RX4 & B1800 PICKUP (Cont.)

Cosmo
RX4
B1800 Pickup

### DESCRIPTION

Clutch is a dry, single disc, diaphragm spring type. Clutch system is hydraulic using a firewall mounted master cylinder and a slave cylinder attached to clutch housing. Release bearing is pre-lubricated and sealed.

**Fig. I  Exploded View of Mazda Clutch Assembly (Cosmo and RX4 Shown)**

### REMOVAL & INSTALLATION

#### CLUTCH ASSEMBLY

**Removal (Cosmo & RX4 5-Speed) —** 1) Disconnect ground at battery. Remove gear shift knob. Remove console. Put shift lever in neutral. Remove boot. Remove shift retainer cover. Lift up on shifter and remove shifter, wave washer, shim and bushing from retainer.

2) Remove slave cylinder. Disconnect back-up lights. Remove upper starter mounting bolt and 3 upper bolts mounting transmission to engine. Raise vehicle and support with stands.

3) Drain transmission. Disconnect or remove any exhaust components that might interfer with removal of transmission. Disconnect and remove propeller shaft. Disconnect speedometer cable. Remove starter-to-clutch housing lower bolt and remove starter.

4) Place a jack under front side of transmission. Remove bolt mounting transmission support-to-body. Remove lower transmission-to-engine bolts and slide out transmission.

5) Fit flywheel holding tool. Loosen pressure plate mounting bolts evenly until entire assembly can be removed. Note location of "O" index marks.

**Installation —** To install clutch and transmission, reverse removal procedure and note: Lightly coat input shaft splines with grease. Use clutch alignment tool to center clutch assembly. Make sure gear shift lever has adequate tension by inserting adjusting shim between wave washer and bushing. Shims are available in .004" (.1 mm) and .012" (.3 mm).

**Removal (B1800 Pickup 4 and 5-Speed) —** 1) Disconnect ground cable at battery. Put shift lever in neutral. Remove lever boot, retainer cover and gasket from gear shift retainer. Pull following from gear shift retainer: lever, wave washer, shim, and bushing.

2) Raise and support vehicle. Drain transmission. Disconnect and remove propeller shaft. Disconnect exhaust pipe hanger from clutch housing. Remove release cylinder leaving fluid line connected.

3) Disconnect back-up lights, speedometer cable and starter wiring. Remove starter. Place jack (with wood block) under rear portion of oil pan. Remove bolts mounting transmission-to-engine.

4) Place appropriate jack under transmission. Remove crossmember. Slide transmission back until input shaft is cleared and remove from vehicle.

5) Fit flywheel holding tool. Loosen pressure plate mounting bolts evenly until assembly can be removed. Note location of "O" index marks.

**Installation —** To install clutch and transmission, reverse removal procedure and note: Lightly coat input shaft splines with grease. Use clutch alignment tool to center clutch assembly. Make sure gear shift lever has adequate tension by inserting adjusting shim between wave washer and bushing. Shims are available in .004" (.1 mm) and .012" (.3 mm).

#### CLUTCH MASTER CYLINDER

**Removal & Installation —** Disconnect hydraulic line from master cylinder. Remove nuts mounting cylinder to firewall. Unhook clutch pedal from cylinder push rod. Remove cylinder. To install, reverse removal procedure and bleed hydraulic system.

#### CLUTCH SLAVE CYLINDER

**Removal & Installation —** Raise vehicle and support. Disconnect fluid hose. Remove nuts mounting slave cylinder to clutch housing and slide off cylinder. To install, reverse removal procedure and bleed clutch.

#### PILOT BEARING

**Rotary Engine Models —** Remove nut mounting flywheel to eccentric shaft. Free flywheel from shaft. It may be necessary to use puller to remove flywheel. Use a slide hammer (49 1285 071) to remove bearing and seals. Use installer tool 49 0823 72A (or equivalent) to seat new bearing into place. Install seal.

**Piston Engine Models —** Pilot bearing is pressed into flywheel. If replacement is required, remove using a suitable puller. To install lubricate bearing with grease and install into flywheel using a driver.

## MAZDA COSMO, RX4 & B1800 PICKUP (Cont.)

### OVERHAUL

#### CLUTCH MASTER CYLINDER

1) Clean outside of master cylinder thoroughly and drain brake fluid. Remove dust boot, retaining clip, and retaining washer. Remove piston assembly, primary cup and return spring from cylinder. Remove reservoir from cylinder.

2) Wash all parts in clean alcohol or brake fluid. **CAUTION** — *Do not use gasoline or kerosene.* Check all parts for wear or damage, replace as necessary. Check clearance between piston and cylinder bore. If clearance exceeds .006", replace piston or cylinder as necessary. Ensure that compensating port on cylinder is open.

3) To assemble, reverse disassembly procedure and note the following: Before assembly, dip piston and cups in clean brake fluid. Install primary cup so that flat side of cup is against piston. When assembled, fill reservoir with brake fluid and operate piston with a screwdriver until fluid is ejected at outlet port.

**Fig. 2  Exploded View of Clutch Master Cylinder**

#### CLUTCH SLAVE CYLINDER

1) Clean outside of slave cylinder. Remove dust boot and release rod. Remove piston and cup assembly with compressed air, if necessary. Remove spring and bleeder screw/valve assembly.

2) Inspect all parts for damage or wear. Wash all components in clean alcohol or brake fluid. **CAUTION** — *Do not use gasoline or kerosene.* Check clearance between piston and cylinder bore. If clearance exceeds .006" (.15 mm), replace cylinder or piston as necessary.

3) Install spring into cylinder. Fit piston cup to piston and slip them into cylinder. Install release rod into cylinder and fit dust boot. Install valve and bleeder screw.

**Fig. 3  Exploded View of Slave Cylinder**

### ADJUSTMENT

#### CLUTCH PEDAL FREE PLAY

1) Loosen lock nut.
2) Turn push rod.

**Fig. 4  Clutch Pedal Free Play Adjustment Location**

#### HYDRAULIC SYSTEM BLEEDING

1) Clutch hydraulic system must be bled whenever a fluid line has been disconnected or air has entered system. To bleed system, remove rubber cap on slave cylinder bleeder screw and attach a hose.

2) Place opposite end of hose into a jar partially filled with brake fluid. Open bleeder screw, depress clutch pedal, and allow pedal to return slowly. Continue operation until air bubbles cease to appear in discharged fluid, then close bleeder screw. **NOTE** — *During bleeding operation, master cylinder reservoir must be kept at least ¾ full of brake fluid.*

### TIGHTENING SPECIFICATIONS

| Application | Ft. Lbs. (mkg) |
| --- | --- |
| Flywheel-to-Crankshaft (Piston Engines) | 112-118 (15.5-16.3) |
| Flywheel-to-Eccentric Shaft (Rotary Engines) | 289-362 (40-50) |
| Clutch-to-Flywheel | 13-20 (1.8-2.7) |

# MAZDA GLC

**Mazda GLC**

## DESCRIPTION

Clutch is a dry, single disc, diaphragm type, and cable actuated. A prelubricated clutch release bearing is used and is located in the transmission housing.

**Fig. 1  Exploded View of Clutch Assembly**

## REMOVAL & INSTALLATION

### CLUTCH ASSEMBLY

**Removal** — 1) Disconnect battery ground cable. Remove gear shift lever from inside of driver's compartment.

2) Raise vehicle and then support engine and transmission. Disconnect electrical wires from transmission. Remove electrical wires from starter then remove starter.

3) Disconnect exhaust pipe from exhaust manifold and speedometer cable from extension housing on transmission. Disconnect propeller shaft at rear axle and slide shaft from transmission.

**NOTE** — *Insert a suitable plug into transmission tail housing to prevent fluid leakage.*

4) Support transmission with a jack, disconnect crossmember at transmission and at side supports. Remove crossmember.

5) Remove transmission attaching bolts and slide transmission rearward until input shaft clears clutch splines. Remove transmission.

6) Note flywheel and pressure plate index mark for reassembly reference. Install a flywheel holding tool and loosen clutch attaching bolts one turn at a time until spring pressure is released. Remove clutch assembly.

**Installation** — To install, reverse removal procedure while noting the following:
Lubricate clutch pilot bearing in crankshaft with grease prior to installing clutch.
Use a clutch aligning tool to center disc on flywheel.
Adjust clutch pedal free play.

## CLUTCH RELEASE BEARING & FORK

**Removal** — 1) With transmission removed, disconnect return spring for release bearing.

2) Slide bearing off transmission front cover. Pull release fork outward until spring clip releases from ball pivot.

3) Remove fork from clutch housing.

**Installation** — To install, apply a light coat of grease to all contact surfaces and reverse removal procedure.

**NOTE** — *Bearing is prelubricated and should not be washed in any solvent or cleaning solution.*

## CLUTCH CABLE

**Removal** — 1) Loosen cable lock nut and adjustment nut. Pull cable toward clutch pedal and disconnect from pedal.

2) Push cable through stop ring into engine compartment. Disconnect cable at clutch lever. See *Fig. 2*. Remove retainer ring at bracket. Pull cable housing from bracket and remove.

**Installation** — To install, reverse removal procedure.

**Fig. 2  Installed View of Clutch Cable
with Detail of Items to Disconnect for Cable Removal.
Illustration Also Shows Pedal Height Location.**

## MAZDA GLC (Cont.)

### PILOT BEARING

Pilot bearing is pressed into flywheel. If replacement is required, remove using a puller. To install, lubricate bearing with grease and install into flywheel using a driver.

## ADJUSTMENT

### CLUTCH PEDAL HEIGHT

Loosen lock nut (Fig. 2) and turn adjusting bolt until pedal height is approximately 7.48" (190 mm). Tighten lock nut. Check clutch pedal free play.

### CLUTCH PEDAL

**Pedal Free Play — 1)** Loosen lock nut on clutch cable (engine compartment side of firewall).

**2)** Pull outer clutch cable (housing) away from firewall and measure distance from adjusting nut to cable housing protruding through firewall.

**3)** Measurement should be .06-.09" (1.5-2.25 mm). If not, turn adjusting nut until correct specification is obtained.

**4)** Tighten lock nut then check clutch pedal free play. Free play should now be .39-.59" (10-15 mm). If not, readjust clutch cable.

### TIGHTENING SPECIFICATIONS

| Application | Ft. Lbs. (mkg) |
|---|---|
| Flywheel-to-Engine | 112-118 (15.5-16.3) |
| Pressure Plate Assembly-to-Flywheel | 13-20 (1.8-2.7) |

## MERCEDES-BENZ

**240D**

### DESCRIPTION

Dry single disc type clutch uses a diaphragm spring type pressure plate. Clutch actuation is hydraulic, using a clutch pedal mounted master cylinder and a clutch housing mounted slave cylinder. A pedal mounted over-center spring assists in clutch pedal actuation. A sealed prelubricated clutch release bearing is also used.

### REMOVAL & INSTALLATION

**Removal — 1)** Disconnect battery ground cable, support transmission with suitable jack, then remove rear crossmember, exhaust support bracket, exhaust pipe and clamp. Loosen, DO NOT remove, propeller shaft center bearing, remove propeller shaft-to-transmission bolts, and ensuring that companion plate remains attached to propeller shaft, push propeller shaft towards rear.

**2)** Remove tachometer drive from rear of transmission. Remove clutch slave cylinder and pull towards the rear with lines connected, until rod is released from clutch housing. Remove shift linkage from transmission shift levers. Remove starter.

**3)** Remove transmission-to-intermediate flange attaching bolts (removing two upper bolts last). Pull transmission out horizontally, until input shaft is clear of clutch. Then remove in a downward direction.

**4)** Loosen pressure plate attaching bolts 1 to 1½ turns at a time until tension is released, then remove all bolts, pressure plate and clutch disc.

**Installation — 1)** To install, place slave cylinder and line above transmission, then, using an aligning tool, center clutch disc on flywheel and install pressure plate. Tighten bolts 1 to 1½ turns at a time until tight.

**NOTE** — *When installing propeller shaft to transmission, raise engine and transmission with suitable jack. Tighten propeller shaft center bearing clamp nut to 22-29 ft. lbs. (3-4 mkg).*

**CAUTION** — *During installation, make sure that clutch is fully pulled into recess in flywheel.*

**2)** To complete installation, reverse removal procedure. Bleed slave cylinder and check hydraulic fluid level. Check clutch adjustment and shift linkage adjustment.

### RELEASE BEARING & LEVER

**Removal** — Remove release bearing from bearing tube on front transmission cover. Move release lever down and to the left, then pull from ball pin on clutch housing.

**Installation** — To install, apply suitable lubricant to all bearing and lever contact surfaces, and reverse removal procedure.

### CLUTCH MASTER CYLINDER

**Removal — 1)** Remove floor mats and lining from driver compartment, then remove cover under instrument panel. Siphon fluid from reservoir to below minimum mark and loosen input line by pulling elbow out of rubber clamping ring on master cylinder.

**2)** Disconnect pressure line from master cylinder and unscrew master cylinder from pedal assembly. Remove master cylinder and connecting hose, leaving push rod on clutch pedal.

**Installation** — To install, reverse removal procedure, adjust fluid level in reservoir, adjust master cylinder push rod length to a clearance of .008" (.2 mm) by loosening hex nut of eccentric adjusting screw and turning screw. Bleed hydraulic system.

*Fig. 1   Mercedes 240D Clutch Components*

## MERCEDES-BENZ (Cont.)

### CLUTCH SLAVE CYLINDER

**Removal** – Disconnect hydraulic line from slave cylinder, then plug line with a rubber cap to prevent loss of fluid. Remove bolts attaching cylinder to clutch housing, then remove slave cylinder and push rod from housing as an assembly.

**NOTE** – *Take care not to lose plastic shim installed between cylinder and housing. Shim is recessed to accommodate inspection gauge.*

**Installation** – To install, place shim with grooved end against clutch housing and hold in position. Insert slave cylinder with push rod into clutch housing, and install and tighten mounting bolts. Connect hydraulic line to cylinder and bleed hydraulic system.

**NOTE** – *Wear on clutch disc may only be checked using special inspection gauge inserted in groove of plastic shim. Disc is serviceable if notches on gauge disappear in flange. If notches remain visible, wear limit is exceeded and disc must be replaced. See illustration.*

**Fig. 2  Clutch Pedal Assembly with Master Cylinder and Over Center Spring**

### ADJUSTMENT

#### OVER CENTER SPRING

Adjust nuts at bottom of over center spring so that spring length measured across retainers is 2.05" (52.5 mm). Improper adjustment will result in failure of pedal to return when released or excessive pressure required to depress pedal.

#### HYDRAULIC SYSTEM BLEEDING

**With Pressure Bleeder** – 1 Connect pressure line of bleeder to opened bleeder screw of slave cylinder. Fluid reservoir of vehicle should be almost empty so that brake fluid can flow from bottom upward through system, allowing air to escape in upward direction.

2) Make sure bleeder is set at lowest possible pressure, and watch reservoir to prevent overflow of fluid. When fluid approaches maximum level in reservoir, remove bleeder and close bleeder screw. Adjust fluid level in reservoir, if necessary, to maximum level in reservoir.

**With Assistance of Brake System** – 1) Check fluid level in reservoir and make sure it is at maximum level. Place a hose on bleeder screw of right front brake caliper and open screw. Press down on brake pedal until hose is filled with brake fluid and no more air bubbles are showing.

2) Place opposite end of hose on clutch slave cylinder bleeder screw, and open screw. Keep pressure on brake pedal. Close bleeder screw on caliper and release brake pedal. Repeat operation until no more air bubbles appear at fluid reservoir.

**Fig. 3  Checking for Clutch Disc Wear**

# Clutches

## MGB

MGB

### DESCRIPTION

Clutch is single dry disc type, using a diaphragm spring type pressure plate. Clutch actuation is hydraulic, using a firewall mounted master cylinder and a bell housing mounted slave cylinder. Release bearing is graphite type, and is mounted in a cup which fits into fork of clutch release lever.

*Fig. 1   Exploded View of Clutch Assembly*

## REMOVAL & INSTALLATION

### CLUTCH ASSEMBLY

1) Remove engine. *See Engine Removal in ENGINE Section.*

2) Remove bolts securing clutch assembly to flywheel by extracting evenly. Pressure plate assembly can now be withdrawn off dowels and further disassembled.

**NOTE** – *Flywheel side of clutch disc is marked.*

**Installation** – To install, reverse removal procedure and note the following: Use suitable aligning tool to center clutch disc on flywheel. Tighten clutch attaching bolts one turn at a time in a diagonal sequence. Remove aligning tool only after bolts have been tightened.

### CLUTCH MASTER CYLINDER

**Removal** – 1) Drain fluid from master cylinder through slave cylinder bleeder. Remove facia panel below left side of steering wheel, then remove rubber plug in bulkhead. *See Fig. 2.*

2) Remove 8 screws holding cover plate and seal to pedal box. Separate push rod from clutch pedal at clevis pin. Disconnect hydraulic outlet line and remove master cylinder.

**NOTE** – *Access to lower bolt is achieved inside car through hole in bulkhead.*

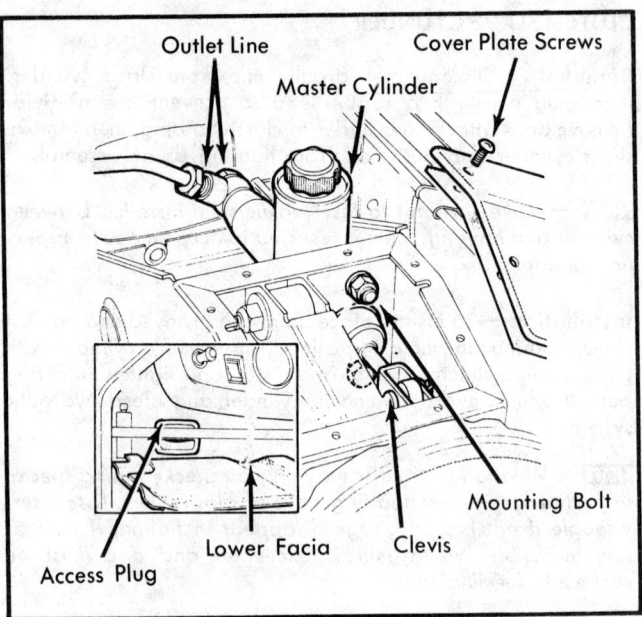

*Fig. 2   Items to Take Off in Order to Free Master Cylinder for Removal*

**Installation** – Reverse removal procedure and bleed hydraulic system.

### CLUTCH SLAVE CYLINDER

**Removal** – Remove bolts and washers holding slave cylinder. Slide cylinder from push rod. Remove fluid hose from cylinder being careful not to lose copper sealing washer. Plug open end of hose.

**Installation** – Reverse removal procedure and bleed hydraulic system.

### CLUTCH RELEASE BEARING

**Removal** – Remove transmission and separate clutch assembly. Release clips which retain release bearing by rotating clips forward. Slide out bearing and remove clips.

**Installation** – Reverse removal procedure and note: Make sure clips are installed with spring arm of clip facing AWAY from release bearing.

## OVERHAUL

### CLUTCH MASTER CYLINDER

**Disassembly** – 1) Drain fluid and pull dust boot back. Remove circlip from push rod, then withdraw rod, washer, clip, and boot.

2) Remove piston with secondary cup seal. Remove piston washer, main cup, seal spring retainer, and spring. Remove secondary cup seal from piston by stretching over end of piston.

## MGB (Cont.)

**Fig. 3   Exploded View of MGB Clutch Master Cylinder**

**Inspection** — 1) Wash master cylinder body in alcohol and dry.

2) Clean internal parts in brake fluid.

3) Check cylinder bore for score marks or deep ridges. New seal will hold if damage is slight.

**Reassembly** — Coat all components with brake fluid. reverse removal procedure and note the following: Be sure secondary cup seal lip faces toward rear of piston. Insert spring into cylinder bore, large end first. Install circlip, then dust boot.

### CLUTCH SLAVE CYLINDER

**Disassembly** — Remove retaining ring, pull back dust cover and remove small internal retaining ring. Apply air pressure to fluid port and remove piston, cup, spring retainer, and spring. Remove bleeder screw.

**Inspection** — 1) Wash cylinder body in alcohol.

2) Clean internal parts with brake fluid.

**Fig. 4   Exploded View of MGB Clutch Slave Cylinder**

3) Check bore for scoring or ridge marks, replace as necessary.

**Reassembly** — Reverse removal procedure, noting the following: Install bleeder screw last, after checking that orifice is not blocked. Use a new cup seal.

## ADJUSTMENT

### HYDRAULIC BLEEDING

1) Fill master cylinder. Attach bleed tube to bleed valve on slave cylinder. Submerge free end of tube in container of brake fluid.

2) Slowly depress pedal to force air out. Close bleed valve and let pedal rise unassisted. Check that fluid level does not drop too low, and repeat until no more bubbles of air are visible.

## MG MIDGET

### Midget

### DESCRIPTION

The clutch is a single, dry-disc type, using a diaphragm spring type pressure plate. Clutch actuation is hydraulic. Hydraulic components are a firewall-mounted master cylinder and a clutch housing-mounted slave cylinder. The hydraulic design of the clutch control eliminates the necessity of pedal adjustment.

### REMOVAL & INSTALLATION

#### CLUTCH ASSEMBLY

**Removal** — Remove engine. See *Engine Removal in ENGINE Section.* If engine and transmission are removed as an assembly, separate and remove transmission. Mark parts for reassembly and loosen clutch bolts one at a time until pressure plate tension is released.

**Installation** — Reverse removal procedure and use aligning tool to center disc on flywheel.

#### CLUTCH MASTER CYLINDER

**Removal** — Remove the high tension lead from ignition coil and white/blue lead from ballast resistor. Remove the four screws mounting cover plate and remove with ignition coil. Remove cotter pin and separate clevis pin. Disconnect and plug hydraulic line at master cylinder. Remove bolts mounting master cylinder and lift from pedal box.

**Installation** — To install master cylinder, reverse removal procedure and note the following: Bleed clutch hydraulic system.

#### CLUTCH SLAVE CYLINDER

**Removal** — Disconnect hydraulic line from slave cylinder and plug open line. Remove mounting hardware and withdraw slave cylinder from housing.

**Installation** — Center push rod in cylinder housing. Align groove in slave cylinder with bolt hole in housing. Attach mounting hardware, reconnect hydraulic line and bleed slave cylinder.

**Fig. 1  Installed View of Clutch Slave Cylinder**

#### CLUTCH RELEASE LEVER & RELEASE BEARING

**Removal** — With transmission and clutch housing removed, drive out pin retaining clutch release bearing lever in clutch housing. Press out pins from release lever. Remove both bearing sleeve plugs and separate bearing from release lever. Sleeve can now be pressed from bearing.

**Installation** — Grease sleeve and bearing, then press bearing onto sleeve. **NOTE** — *Do not apply pressure to outer race.* Fit bearing in release lever and insert sleeve locating plugs. Press in both pins to retain plugs. Reinstall release lever.

**Fig. 2  Exploded View of Clutch Release Bearing & Lever**

### OVERHAUL

#### CLUTCH MASTER CYLINDER

**Disassembly** — Drain fluid from reservoir. Separate rubber boot from housing and slide off push rod. Disengage snap ring holding push rod, then pull out push rod with snap ring, dished washer, and rubber boot. Extract piston with secon-

**Fig. 3  Exploded View of Clutch Master Cylinder**

## MG MIDGET (Cont.)

dary cup seal. Remove piston washer, primary cup seal spring retainer, and spring. Separate secondary cup seal from piston; it must be stretched over end of piston.

**Inspection** — Wash master cylinder in suitable cleaner and clean internal components with brake fluid. Check cylinder for ridges or score marks. Cylinder bore diameter (new) should be approximately .704" (17.88 mm). New seals can be used if cylinder is not damaged.

**Reassembly** — Fit new secondary cup seal over piston with lip of seal facing piston head. Insert spring retainer into small end of spring and fit spring into body, large end first. Install the following: primary cup seal, washer, piston, and push rod. **NOTE** — *When fitting cup seals, install lip edge of cup seals into bore first.* Engage snap ring and pull over boot.

## CLUTCH SLAVE CYLINDER

**Disassembly** — Remove bleed valve, dust boot, plunger (piston), spring, then separate seal from plunger.

**Inspection** — Wash slave cylinder in suitable cleaner and clean all internal components in brake fluid. Install new seals if cylinder bore is not damaged. Replace cylinder if bore is excessively worn or damaged. Cylinder diameter (new) should be .875" (22.2 mm).

**Fig. 4  Exploded View of Clutch Slave Cylinder**

**Reassembly** — Fit seal to plunger. Refit spring and plunger into cylinder bore. Install bleed valve. Slip dust boot into position, install slave cylinder, and bleed hydraulic system.

## ADJUSTMENT

### HYDRAULIC SYSTEM BLEEDING

Fill master cylinder and attach a bleed hose to slave cylinder bleed valve; submerge free end of hose in a half-full container of brake fluid. Pump clutch pedal, open bleed valve approximately three-quarters turn; at end of down stroke close bleed valve. Continue procedure until air bubbles stop.

## OPEL

### All Models

## DESCRIPTION

Clutch is a dry, single disc diaphragm spring type. Clutch operation is mechanical by cable. Release lever holds throw-out bearing and support in place with spring clip.

**Fig. 1  Exploded View of Clutch Components**

## REMOVAL & INSTALLATION

### CLUTCH ASSEMBLY

**Removal** — **1)** Disconnect battery ground cable. Remove gearshift assembly. From left side of engine, loosen clutch cable adjusting nuts. Disconnect starter wiring and remove upper starter mounting bolt.

**2)** Raise and support vehicle at front and rear. Remove propeller shaft. Disconnect speedometer cable. Remove clutch heat shield and cable.

**3)** Remove lower starter bolt and take out starter. Disconnect exhaust pipe at manifold. Take off flywheel inspection cover.

**4)** Remove rear crossmember support bolt. With jack placed under transmission, remove crossmember from frame. Slightly lower transmission and disconnect back-up light and CRS switches. Remove transmission-to-engine mounting bolts and pull straight back.

**5)** Index mark clutch assembly. Insert clutch alignment tool, then remove six mounting bolts and pull out clutch assembly.

**Installation** — To install, reverse removal procedure noting the following: Use alignment tool to center clutch assembly while tightening mounting bolts. Lightly lubricate transmission input shaft before installing. Refill transmission with SAE 30 engine oil. Adjust clutch.

### CLUTCH CABLE

**Removal** — Loosen clutch lock and adjusting nuts. Raise vehicle and support. Remove heat shield, then separate return spring from release fork. Remove clutch cable from release fork and slide cable through mounting bracket.

**Installation** — To install, reverse removal procedure and make sure cable is properly fitted to clutch pedal.

### PILOT BEARING

**Replacement** — With clutch and pressure plate removed, use pilot bearing remover tool J-23907 (or equivalent) and remove bearing. To fit new pilot bearing in crankshaft use installer tool J-26516 (or equivalent). Drive bearing in until bottom face of bearing is seated into place. Install all remaining components in reverse of removal procedure.

## ADJUSTMENT

### CLUTCH PEDAL HEIGHT

Adjust clutch pedal height, measured from floor, to 6.2" (153 mm) by rotating clutch switch located behind pedal. When correct height is reached, tighten lock nut. Check and adjust clutch pedal free play.

### CLUTCH FREE PLAY

Loosen both locking nut and adjusting nut on clutch cable. See Fig. 2. Take up cable slack by pulling cable forward. Turn adjustment nut until pedal free play is about 5/8" (.625 mm). Tighten lock nut.

**Fig. 2  Clutch Free Play Adjustment Location — Adjustment Nut Moves Along Threaded Rod**

### TIGHTENING SPECIFICATIONS

| Application | Ft. Lbs. (mkg) |
| --- | --- |
| Clutch Assembly-to-Flywheel | 13 (1.8) |
| Release Fork Ball Stud | 30 (4.2) |

## PORSCHE

911SC
924
928
930 Turbo

### DESCRIPTION

All models use a dry, single disc, diaphragm spring type of clutch system. Clutch operation is mechanical. Pedal is connected to release lever by cables. All models have similar clutch disc designs: 930 models have thicker clutch lining, stronger springs, and larger diameter hubs. 930 models also have release lever mounted so a shorter, thicker cable can be used.

### REMOVAL & INSTALLATION

#### CLUTCH ASSEMBLY

**Removal (911SC, Turbo & 924) 1)** — On all vehicles, remove engine and transaxle as described in *Engine Section*. On 924 after detatching transmission mounts, move the central tube with the transmission back about 4" to remove clutch disc and pressure plate.

**2)** Index mark pressure plate and flywheel for reassembly. Insert clutch alignment tool. Loosen clutch mouting bolts alternately and evenly until spring pressure is released. Slip clutch assembly from vehicle.

**Removal (928) 1)** — Remove lower body brace and slave cylinder with line connected. Remove clutch housing cover with starter and suspend from stabilizer bar. Remove coupling screws and push coupling back onto drive shaft.

**2)** Remove release bearing bolts and push bearing sleeve toward flywheel. Mark position of pressure plate, intermediate ring and flywheel as they are a balanced unit. Loosen mounting bolts evenly and alternately until pressure is off clutch. Remove bolts, disconnect release lever and push clutch assembly back and remove downward.

**Inspection** — **1)** Check pressure plate and disc for wear, cracks, burning or loose rivets. Replace any part found defective. Check ends of diaphragm spring for wear marks from release bearing.

**2)** Lay a straightedge across pressure plate face and check for distortion; up to .011" (.3 mm) is permissible. Place clutch disc on input shaft and see that it moves freely on splines. Check disc for maximum allowable runout of .24" (.6 mm).

**3)** Check clutch release bearing for noise or rough operation. Do not wash bearing in any cleaning solution; clean with a lint free cloth only. Replace bearing if contaminated or loud. Check pilot bearing in crankshaft for rough operation, replace as necessary.

**Installation** — **1)** Place graphite grease or molybdenum disulphide grease in crankshaft pilot bearing, and moisten felt seal with engine oil. Install clutch disc on flywheel using a suitable aligning tool to center disc. Coat diaphragm spring of pressure plate with a thin coat of molybdenum disulphide grease. See Fig. 1.

*Fig. 2   View of Clutch Adjusting Mechanism (911SC & 930 Turbo)*

*Fig. 1   Sectional View of Clutch Assembly*

## PORSCHE (Cont.)

2) Install pressure plate to flywheel, aligning marks made at disassembly. **NOTE** — *If a new clutch is installed, balancing marks on clutch and flywheel should be offset 180°.* Install and tighten clutch attaching bolts one turn at a time in a diagonal sequence to prevent distorting pressure plate.

3) On 911SC models, when transmission is installed on engine, pull release lever in a direction opposite engine. There must be a distance of at least .787" between release lever and transmission housing.

### CLUTCH RELEASE BEARING

**Removal (911SC, 928 & 930)** — Bearing is removed with pressure plate and must be removed by laying pressure plate on bearing. Remove snap ring and take out bearing together with washers.

**Removal (924)** — With clutch removed, detach bearing spring clips from release lever. Move lever forward and take release bearing off of guide tube.

**Installation** — Apply thin coat of suitable lubricant to guide tube and reverse removal procedures.

**NOTE** — *Do not wash clutch release bearing in cleaning solvent. Bearing is pre-packed and requires no lubrication.*

## ADJUSTMENT

### CLUTCH ADJUSTMENT

**911SC & 930 Turbo** — Clutch free play must be checked at transmission adjusting lever due to auxiliary clutch spring. With cable snug, adjust play at lever to .004" (1.0 mm). Clutch pedal travel may be adjusted at stop on floor plate. Release travel for 911SC should be .982-.986" (24.5-25.5 mm), and for 930 Turbo should be 1.061-1.065" (26.5-27.5 mm) when measured at cable end.

**924** — Lower end of clutch cable should measure 5.36-5.52" (136-140 mm) when measured from lower edge of cable holder to pin at release lever with release bearing against diaphragm spring. To adjust, turn outboard release lever on shaft and tighten in position. Adjust cable with counternuts on holder to give .8-1" (20-25 mm) free play at clutch pedal.

| Clutch Pedal Free Play | |
|---|---|
| **Application** | **Free Play** |
| 911SC & 924 | .8-1.0" (20-25 mm) |
| 930 Turbo | .9" (23 mm) |

**928** — No adjustment is necessary because of auotmatic adjustment of slave cylinder. There must however, be .5 mm (.05") play between the push rod and master cylinder piston. This cannot be measured directly, but can be felt at the pedal. Play can be corrected by adjusting the push rod (*See Fig. 3*).

**Fig. 3   928 Clutch Push Rod Adjustment**

### PEDAL ADJUSTMENT

**All Models** — 1) With engine and transmission warm, depress clutch pedal to stop. In this position reverse gear must just be able to be engaged silently.

2) When clutch pedal is fully depressed, clutch release lever should move .6" (15mm) to completely disengage clutch. If cable housing rests on bottom of guide clamp when pedal is fully depressed, inner cable must be adjusted at yoke end.

3) Measure from threaded cable end of yoke to outer edge of lock nut. Measurement should be .7-.9" (17-22mm), adjust if necessary. If cable housing rests on bottom of guide clamp when clutch pedal is fully depressed, inner cable must be lengthened at yoke end.

4) If arc of cable is too large, allowing cable to come out of guide clamp when pedal is released, inner cable must be shortened at yoke end.

## TIGHTENING SPECIFICATIONS

| Application | Ft. Lbs. (mkg) |
|---|---|
| Flywheel (All Models) | 108 (15) |
| Clutch | |
| 911SC | 25 (3.5) |
| 924 | 23 (3.2) |
| 928 | 14-17 (1.9-2.3) |
| 930 Turbo | 14-18 (1.9-2.5) |

## RENAULT

**R-5**

### DESCRIPTION

Clutch system is single disc dry plate type. Main components are: Disc, diaphragm spring operated pressure plate, ball bearing type clutch release bearing, release fork, and pilot bearing. Clutch operation is mechanical through cable actuation.

### REMOVAL & INSTALLATION

#### CLUTCH ASSEMBLY

**Removal** — **1)** Disconnnect battery. Separate speedometer. Remove water pump belt, camshaft belt, and air injection components. Remove both upper starter bolts (it may be necessary to use special wrench Ele. 565).

**2)** Remove clutch housing mounting bolts. Take off calipers and support out of way. Disconnect tie rods at steering rack end. Disconnect upper ball joints. Separate axle drive shafts by pulling stub axle out and down. **NOTE** — *Be careful not to damage oil seal lips on differential adjusting ring nuts.*

**3)** Remove bolts from support tab on underside of transaxle. Disconnect and free clutch cable lever. Remove tubular crossmember bolts and slide crossmember out rearward. Use a jack and support front of transaxle. Remove front mount. Remove lower starter bolt. Remove clutch cover and any side reinforcement bolts. Remove transaxle from vehicle. Mark pressure plate assembly for installation reference and remove entire clutch assembly.

**Installation** — To install, reverse removal procedure and note following: Larger end of clutch disc hub should face engine. Use centering tool to align pressure plate and disc. Lightly grease input shaft and axle drive shaft splines. Make sure axle drive shafts fully seat into side gears.

#### CLUTCH CABLE

**Removal** — **1)** Disconnect cable from lever on transmission. Remove the bolt securing mounting pad (if equipped). From inside vehicle, remove pedal shaft retaining clip, push shaft to the right, and disconnect clutch pedal.

**2)** Disconnect clutch pedal return spring from pin retaining cable end-to-pedal, remove pin, and disconnect cable end from pedal. Free cable from sleeve stop on pedal assembly bracket, and remove cable.

**Installation** — To install, reverse removal procedure and note the following: Lubricate pedal bores and retaining pins with Molykote BR 2 lubricant. Adjust clutch free play.

#### CLUTCH RELEASE BEARING & FORK

**Removal** — With transmission removed, disconnect return spring from release bearing and fork, and slide bearing off transmission input shaft. Using a suitable tool (Emb. 384), extract fork retaining roll pins. Remove fork shaft, fork, and return spring.

**Installation** — **1)** Lubricate fork shaft with Molykote BR 2 grease, and slide shaft into transmission housing (fitted with rubber seal), and through release fork and return spring.

**2)** Align holes in shaft with those in fork and install roll pins, making sure that pins protrude $\frac{1}{32}$" on forward side of fork. Lubricate bearing sleeve and fork fingers with Molykote BR 2 grease, and slide bearing onto transmission input shaft.

**3)** Install return spring, placing ends in holes of release bearing support and in fork. Lubricate bearing face and portion of clutch diaphragm spring which bearing contacts with Molykote BR 2 grease. Install transmission and adjust clutch free play.

#### PILOT BEARING

**Removal** — Remove transmission, clutch assembly, and flywheel. Using a suitable tool (Mot. 11), extract bearing from crankshaft.

**Installation** — Using a suitable driver, install pilot bearing into crankshaft. **NOTE** — *Bearing is pre-greased, do not clean.* Install flywheel, clutch assembly, and transmission. Adjust clutch free play.

#### OIL SEAL

**Removal** — Remove transmission from vehicle. Remove clutch housing attaching bolts and separate clutch housing from transmission. Using a suitable tool, remove oil seal from clutch housing.

**Installation** — Fit oil seal into place over special tool B. Vi. 526 or 488. Coat paper gasket with sealer. Place tool inside clutch release bearing guide to spread seal lip. Refit clutch housing on transaxle and slide tool along clutch shaft, then remove tool. Tighten clutch housing nuts.

### ADJUSTMENT

#### CLUTCH FREE PLAY

Loosen lock nut. Turn adjusting nut to obtain free travel at end of release lever of $\frac{1}{8}$ -$\frac{5}{32}$" (3-4 mm).

| TIGHTENING SPECIFICATIONS | |
|---|---|
| **Application** | **Ft. Lbs. (mkg)** |
| Flywheel-to-Crankshaft | 35 (4.8) |
| Clutch Housing-to-Transmission | |
|   8 mm Bolts | 15 (2.0) |
|   10 mm Bolts | 30 (4.1) |

## SAAB

99
### DESCRIPTION

Clutch is dry, single plate, diaphragm spring type. Primary components are: Disc, pressure plate assembly, and release bearing. Release bearing is a special design ball bearing with elongated outer ring which presses directly against diaphragm when clutch pedal is let out. Clutch operation is hydraulic. Clutch pedal operates on a master cylinder which is connected to slave cylinder. Slave cylinder is located inside clutch cover around input shaft. Slave cylinder acts directly on release bearing. Clutch adjustment is automatic.

### REMOVAL & INSTALLATION

#### CLUTCH ASSEMBLY

**Removal — 1)** Drain coolant.

**2)** Remove hood.

**3)** Disconnect battery ground cable.

**4)** Disconnect wiring harness from fan housing and disconnect following electrical leads:
- Ignition coil.
- Oil pressure switch.
- Temperature switch.
- Headlight wiper motor.
- Thermal fan switch (located on radiator).

**5)** Disconnect radiator hoses.

**6)** Remove grille.

**7)** Remove radiator.

**8)** Remove clutch cover assembly (bell housing).

**9)** Fit special spacer 8390023 (or equivalent) between cover and diaphragm spring.

**NOTE** — *Clutch pedal may need to be depressed during this operation.*

**10)** Dislodge lock ring. Remove seal cap from input shaft.

**11)** Remove plastic propeller "O" ring from input shaft.

**12)** Pull out input shaft using slide hammer (8390270) and universal adaptor (8390015).

Tool 8390270          Tool 8390015

*Fig. 1   Pulling Input Shaft Using Special Tools*

**13)** Remove 3 bolts securing slave cylinder guide sleeve to primary gear case.

**14)** Remove bolts mounting clutch pressure plate and remove together:
- Pressure plate.
- Disc.
- Slave cylinder (guide sleeve).
- Release bearing.

**NOTE** — *Slave cylinder does not need to be disconnected.*

*Fig. 2   Lifting Out Clutch Assembly — Illustration Shows Relationship of Clutch Assembly to Surrounding Engine Components*

**NOTE** — *Before beginning clutch installation make sure input shaft seal is in good condition. Seal is located inside slave cylinder in primary gear case. Seal forms a direct bond with sealing surface of input shaft.*

**Installation — 1)** Install collective clutch parts and loosely install two clutch pressure plate bolts.

**NOTE** — *Make sure:*
- *Diaphragm spring does not damage slave cylinder sleeve because piston may sieze.*
- *Hardened side of release bearing faces diaphragm spring.*

**2)** Bolt slave cylinder to primary gear casing.

**3)** Install input shaft.

**4)** Fit plastic propeller and "O" ring to input shaft.

**5)** Fit sealing cap and "O" ring at input shaft.

**6)** Tighten clutch assembly (pressure plate) to flywheel.

**7)** Depress clutch pedal and remove spacer.

**NOTE** — *DO NOT depress clutch pedal further than necessary. Seal lip may be pressed too far, causing a hydraulic leak.*

**8)** Install remaining components in reverse of removal procedure.

#### CLUTCH MASTER CYLINDER

**Removal — 1)** Separate cylinder hydraulic line.

# Clutches

## SAAB (Cont.)

2) On left side, remove screen under instrument panel. This provides access to master cylinder push rod and mounting nuts.

3) Remove clevis pin holding push rod to clutch pedal.

4) Remove mounting nuts under instrument panel. These nuts hold master cylinder to bulkhead.

5) Pull off master cylinder inlet hose (from reservoir) and position so fluid does not leak.

**Installation** — Reverse removal procedure and bleed hydraulic system.

### CLUTCH SLAVE CYLINDER

**NOTE** — *Slave cylinder removal is accomplished during clutch assembly removal. See Clutch Assembly Removal in this article.*

## OVERHAUL

### CLUTCH MASTER CYLINDER

**Disassembly** — Pull back sealing bellows and remove retaining ring. Remove push rod and washer. Remove piston, convex washer, piston seal, and spring. Inspect cylinder bore for wear or damage. Replace complete assembly if cylinder is worn or damaged. Replace seal if worn or swollen.

Fig. 3   Exploded View of Clutch Master Cylinder

**Reassembly** — Install return spring and spring retainer. Lubricate piston and seals with Girling Rubber Grease No. 3 .

Fig. 4   Cut-Away View of Clutch Master Cylinder Bore Showing Convex Washer Correctly Installed. Convex Side MUST Face Master Cylinder Piston

Install seals, convex washer and piston. Install push rod followed by washer and retaining ring. Install sealing bellows.

### CLUTCH SLAVE CYLINDER

**Disassembly** — 1) Remove clutch release bearing from slave cylinder.

2) Set slave cylinder with release bearing end facing up. Press cylinder sleeve out.

3) Remove "O" ring from sleeve.

4) Remove piston and lip seal.

Fig. 5   Exploded View of Clutch Slave Cylinder

**NOTE** — *Before beginning reassembly, lightly coat lip seal and piston (not "O" ring) with Caster Rubber Grease (or equivalent).*

**Reassembly** — 1) Fit "O" ring to sleeve flange.

2) Slide seal lip on sleeve.

3) Coat sleeve flange with brake fluid. Insert sleeve into cylinder. Push seal lip part way into cylinder.

4) Guide sleeve and cylinder together by pushing on piston until lock rings and "O" ring are fitted.

5) Place slave cylinder on support and seat sleeve into cylinder.

6) Fit release bearing to piston.

## ADJUSTMENT

### HYDRAULIC SYSTEM BLEEDING

1) Connect a ¼" hose to slave cylinder bleeder screw, and place opposite end in a container partially filled with hydraulic fluid. Fill master cylinder reservoir with hydraulic fluid. Open bleeder screw on slave cylinder ½ turn.

2) Place a coolant system tester over filler opening of master cylinder. Pump tester until all air has been removed from system. Close slave cylinder bleeder screw and check to see that all air has been expelled by depressing clutch pedal.

## SUBARU

**Subaru
1600
BRAT**

### DESCRIPTION

Clutch is a diaphragm spring, single dry disc type, with mechanical actuation through a clutch cable. Release bearing is a sealed unit and requires no lubrication.

**Fig. 1  Exploded View of Subaru
Clutch Assembly**

### REMOVAL & INSTALLATION

#### CLUTCH ASSEMBLY

**Removal — 1)** Remove spare tire. Disconnect and remove battery ground cable. Remove air cleaner leaving vacuum hoses attached to ports on air cleaner assembly.

**2)** Disconnect fuel line at pump. Disconnect vacuum hose for power brake unit at intake manifold. Disconnect following:
- Alternator.
- Fan motor and thermoswitch.
- Starter.
- Engine wiring harness. On Calif. models only, disconnect distributor lead at harness connector.
- Back-up lights.
- On automatic transmission models only disconnect electrical wires for inhibitor switch, downshift solenoid, and governor cover ground wire.
- On 4WD models only, disconnect 2 drive selector switch wires.

**3)** Drain coolant. Disconnect heater hoses and automatic transmission cooling lines. Remove radiator. Remove engine torque rod stopper.

**4)** Disconnect all necessary control cables (speedometer, etc.). Disconnect clutch cable at fork. On 4WD models only, remove engine shield. Drain automatic transmission and disconnect fluid lines.

**5)** Disconnect exhaust system at intake manifold, pre-muffler, and 2 bolts on transmission bracket. On 4WD models only, remove drive lever and gear selector lever into passenger compartment.

**6)** On manual transmission models (except 4WD), remove gear shift as follows:
- Remove through bolt mounting engine brace to engine rear mounting bracket.
- Remove through bolt connecting control rod to joint.

**7)** On automatic transmission models only, disconnect control rod from selector arm at clevis pin. On 4WD models only, disconnect propeller shaft. Also, disconnect parking brake hardware at crossmember and transverse link.

**8)** Drive out pins from axle drive shaft. Remove inner end of transverse link from crossmember. Support axle drive shaft by pushing outward on assembly. Remove nuts mounting engine front insulators to front crossmember. Support engine weight.

**9)** On 4WD models only, install stabilizer bar mounting brackets. Remove engine rear insulators from crossmember. Support transmission with jack and remove crossmember. On all models remove engine.

**10)** Remove 6 bolts mounting pressure plate and disc to flywheel.

**Installation —** To install, reverse removal procedure and note the following: Use alignment tool (399740100) to center clutch disc and pressure plate against flywheel. Make sure there is at least 120° between "O" mark on pressure plate and flywheel.

### CLUTCH RELEASE BEARING & HOLDER

**Removal — 1)** Remove transmission from engine.

**2)** Disconnect return springs from release bearing holder.

**3)** Remove release bearing and holder from bearing guide.

**4)** Remove clutch release fork and fork seal.

**Disassembly, Release Bearing — 1)** Fit bearing to suitable press (899754112).

**2)** Apply enough pressure to force guide off of bearing.

**Inspection — 1)** Rotate bearing with pressure against thrust side to make sure of smooth operation.

**2)** Check bearing holder surface where it contacts fork. There should be no evidence of wear or damage.

**3)** Do not wash bearing in solvent. Bearing is sealed and prelubricated.

**4)** Check release fork for wear at fork pivot and guide flange.

**Reassembly —** Reverse disassembly procedure.

**NOTE** — *Before beginning installation, lubricate following locations with multipurpose grease:*
- *Inner release bearing sleeve groove.*

## SUBARU (Cont.)

- Fork, fork ball pin, and guide contact surfaces.
- Transmission input shaft.

**Installation — 1)** Fit release fork seal.

**2)** Insert release fork.

**3)** Slide on release bearing holder and hook 2 return springs.

**4)** Refit transmission.

**5)** Check clutch release bearing fork free play.

### PILOT BEARING

**Removal — 1)** Remove transmission.

**2)** Remove pressure plate and clutch disc.

**3)** Remove oil seal and pilot bearing seated in crankshaft.

**Inspection — 1)** Check bearing fit in crankshaft.

**2)** Check inner surface of pilot bearing for wear. Replace bearing if excessively worn.

**3)** If pilot bushing is worn, also check transmission input shaft for wear.

**Installation — 1)** Thoroughly clean bearing location in crankshaft.

**2)** Use an aluminum rod and plastic mallet to seat bearing in crankshaft.

**3)** Insert oil seal in crankshaft.

**4)** Install clutch and pressure plate.

**5)** Install transmission.

## ADJUSTMENT

### CLUTCH FREE PLAY

**1)** Remove release fork spring.

**2)** Loosen lock nut.

**3)** Rotate adjustment nut to obtain .14-.18" (3.6-4.6 mm) play measured at fork end (center of adjustment nut).

**NOTE** — *When adjustment is correct pedal free play will be approximately .94-1.18" (24-30 mm).*

**4)** Tighten lock nut.

| Clutch Adjustment Specifications | |
|---|---|
| **Application** | **In. (mm)** |
| Clutch Pedal Stroke | 5.12 (130) |
| Release Fork Stroke | .67-.71 (17-18) |
| Release Fork Free Play | .14-.18 (3.6-4.6) |
| Pedal Free Play | .94-1.2 (24-30) |

**Fig. 2  Clutch Cable Adjustment Locations and Specifications**

| TIGHTENING SPECIFICATIONS | |
|---|---|
| **Application** | **Ft. Lbs. (mkg)** |
| Clutch-to-Flywheel Bolts | 12 (1.6) |
| Engine Mounts | 15-22 (2.0-3.0) |
| Transmission Stablizer Bar | 5-9 (.69-1.2) |

## TOYOTA CELICA, COROLLA, CORONA, & PICKUP

Celica
Corolla 1600
Corona
Pickup

### DESCRIPTION

Clutch is a dry, single plate, diaphragm spring type. Clutch is hydraulic using a firewall mounted master cylinder (all models similar) and a clutch housing mounted slave cylinder. Pickup slave cylinders are adjustable type similar to those used in past years. Other models use a new, non-adjustable slave cylinder. As the clutch disc wears, clearance is automatically compensated for by slave cylinder internal design.

**Fig. 1  Exploded View of Typical Clutch Arrangement. Some Models Have Different Pressure Plate Assy. and Others Have Different Hub/Sleeve Retainer Springs.**

### REMOVAL & INSTALLATION

#### CLUTCH ASSEMBLY

**NOTE** — *Clutch removal procedures are of a general nature written to cover all Toyota models.*

**Removal** — **1)** Disconnect battery cable. Remove air cleaner and drain cooling system, then disconnect top radiator hose. Disconnect accelerator control rod linkage. Remove shift lever boot and shifter assembly. Remove starter.

**2)** Raise vehicle and support at front and rear with jack stands. If equipped, remove protective cover from under engine.

**3)** Remove clutch slave cylinder, but only disconnect hydraulic line if necessary. Disconnect exhaust pipe support bracket from mounting and separate exhaust pipe from manifold. Disconnect speedometer cable and electrical leads from transmission.

**4)** Scribe index marks on drive shaft and coupling for reinstallation reference, then remove drive shaft. Insert suitable plug into extension housing to prevent oil spillage.

**5)** Support transmission using a floor jack and remove rear support crossmember. Lower jack and remove bolts mounting transmission to engine. Index mark clutch assembly and flywheel for reassembly. Loosen bolts securing clutch assembly alternately and evenly until pressure is released from clutch. Lift out clutch assembly.

**Installation** — To install, reverse removal procedure and note the following: Use a suitable aligning tool to center clutch disc on flywheel. Tighten clutch pressure plate attaching bolts alternately and evenly in a diagonal progression. With transmission installed, adjust clutch.

### CLUTCH MASTER CYLINDER

**Removal** — Remove cotter pin and clevis pin connecting master cylinder push rod to clutch pedal, then disconnect push rod. Disconnect hydraulic line from cylinder, remove cylinder attaching nuts at firewall, and remove cylinder from vehicle.

**Installation** — To install, reverse removal procedure and note the following: When installing master cylinder, make sure rubber boot hole faces downward. Adjust pedal height and free play, and bleed hydraulic system.

### CLUTCH SLAVE CYLINDER

**Removal** — Raise and support vehicle with safety stands. If equipped, remove protective cover under engine. Disconnect hydraulic line. Back off push rod (if necessary) and remove slave cylinder attaching nut with slave cylinder.

**Installation** — To install, reverse removal procedure and bleed hydraulic system.

### CLUTCH RELEASE BEARING

**Removal** — With transmission removed, check release bearing for freedom of rotation with bearing still installed on hub. To remove, disconnect spring clips from bearing collar and slide bearing off transmission input shaft. Use a press to remove and install bearing on sleeve.

**Installation** — Slide bearing and collar over transmission input shaft and secure to release lever with new retaining clips. Apply grease to diaphragm spring contact points before installing transmission.

### OVERHAUL

#### CLUTCH MASTER CYLINDER

**Disassembly** — **1)** With cylinder removed from vehicle, clamp it into a soft jawed vise. Remove reservoir, snap ring, and push rod. Pull out piston, cup, and remaining internal components. Further disassemble piston by prying up spring retainer and separating retainer from piston.

## TOYOTA CELICA, COROLLA, CORONA, & PICKUP (Cont.)

NOTE: Later Models May Have Different Piston Configuration

**Fig. 2   Exploded View of Clutch Master Cylinder Corolla Shown – All Similar**

**Inspection** – Wash all parts in clean brake fluid. Check master cylinder piston to bore for a clearance of .006" (.15 mm); replace components as necessary. Check compression spring for distortion or weakening and reservoir for damage. Make sure vent hole in reservoir is open.

**Reassembly** – Dip cylinder cups into clean brake fluid or coat with rubber grease before assembly. Assemble piston components in reverse order of disassembly. Install piston assembly, push rod, and reservoir into master cylinder.

### CLUTCH SLAVE CYLINDER

**Disassembly** – On all cylinders, remove rubber boot and push rod. On Pickup models, remove piston and cup. On all other models, remove piston assembly and spring. On all models, remove bleeder screw, if necessary.

**Inspection** – Thoroughly clean all parts with clean brake fluid and inspect for wear or damage. **NOTE** – *Manufacturer recommends replacing seals each time slave cylinder is disassembled.*

**Fig. 3   Exploded View of Slave Cylinder Celica, Corolla, Corona Shown**

**Reassembly** – Soak all parts in clean brake fluid before assembly. Install seals on piston. On all models except Pickup, fit spring into cylinder followed by piston assembly. On Pickup models, fit piston assembly into cylinder. On all models, install rubber boot and push rod. Put bleeder screw back in place and fit cap.

**Fig. 4   Exploded View of Slave Cylinder Pickup Models Only**

## ADJUSTMENT

### PEDAL HEIGHT

Adjust pedal stop bolt at top of pedal assembly until specified pedal height is obtained. Height is measured from floor mat to top of pedal pad.

**Fig. 5   Pedal Height and Free Play Measuring Points**

## TOYOTA CELICA, COROLLA, CORONA, & PICKUP (Cont.)

| Pedal Height Specifications | |
|---|---|
| **Application** | **Height** |
| Celica ............................................. | 6.48" (164.5 mm) |
| Corolla ........................................... | 6.65" (169 mm) |
| Corona ................................. | 6.29-6.69" (160-170 mm) |
| Pickup .................................................. | 6.29" (160 mm) |

| Pedal Free Play Specifications | |
|---|---|
| **Application** | **Free Play** |
| Pickup ...................................... | 1-2" 2&-50 mm) |
| All Others ............................. | .197-.591" (25-50 mm) |

### PEDAL FREE PLAY

**Except Pickup** — To obtain specified free play (measured at pedal) loosen lock nut (See Fig. 5) on push rod and adjust rod in or out as necessary.

**Pickup** — Prior to performing free play adjustment outlined above, clutch fork free play must be adjusted. Fork free play determines amount of clearance between clutch release bearing and clutch. Loosen lock nut on slave cylinder push rod and screw push rod in or out until .08-.12" (2.0-3.0 mm) free play is obtained. After performing both adjustments pedal free play should be accurate.

**Fig. 6 Clutch Fork Free Play Measurement. Only Pickup Models Still Use This Slave Cylinder**

### HYDRAULIC SYSTEM BLEEDING

1) Raise vehicle and support with safety stands. Make sure clutch master cylinder reservoir is full of fluid. Remove bleeder screw cap and loosen bleeder screw. Place a finger on vent hole of bleeder screw and push clutch pedal to bottom of stroke three or four times.

2) With pedal fully depressed, remove finger and allow air to vent out. Repeat procedure three or four times or until pressure is felt. Install a flexible hose on bleeder screw and insert free end into a container partially full of brake fluid.

3) Push pedal to bottom of stroke, loosen bleeder screw, and allow fluid to bleed into container. Tighten bleeder screw and release clutch pedal. Repeat procedure until air bubbles are no longer seen in container, then close screw on a down stroke of pedal. Check system for leaks and fill master cylinder.

## TIGHTENING SPECIFICATIONS

| Application | Ft. Lbs. (mkg) |
|---|---|
| Pressure Plate-to-Flywheel ...................... | 11-16 (1.5-2.2) |
| Clutch Housing-to-Engine ...................... | 36-58 (5.0-8.0) |

## TOYOTA COROLLA 1200

### Corolla 1200

### DESCRIPTION

Clutch is dry, single plate diaphragm spring type. Clutch actuation is mechanical, using a cable connected to clutch pedal. A pre-lubricated clutch release bearing is also used.

**Fig. 1   Clutch System Layout. Use Figure for Component Identification**

### REMOVAL & INSTALLATION

#### CLUTCH ASSEMBLY

**NOTE** — Clutch removal procedure outlined is of a general nature.

**Removal** — 1) From inside vehicle, remove shift lever boot, cap boot, snap ring, conical spring and shift lever. Cover open hole in transmission with a clean shop towel to prevent entry of dirt.

2) From engine compartment, disconnect positive battery cable and drain engine coolant. Disconnect back-up light switch wiring connector and radiator inlet hose. Position cooling fan horizontally.

3) Raise vehicle and support with safety stands. Disconnect drive shaft at differential and slide from transmission. Install a suitable plug (09325-12010) in transmission to prevent loss of lubricant.

4) Disconnect exhaust pipe at exhaust manifold, and exhaust pipe support bracket at transmission. Disconnect speedometer cable from transmission. Support front of transmission with a jack and remove transmission support crossmember.

5) Remove cotter pin from clutch fork and disconnect cable. Drop rear of transmission down, remove retaining bolts, slide transmission to rear, and lower out of vehicle. Remove clutch attaching bolts and remove pressure plate and disc assembly.

**Installation** — To install, reverse removal procedure and note the following: Long end of clutch disc hub must face transmission. Use a suitable aligning tool (09301-12020) to center disc on flywheel. Alternately tighten clutch attaching bolts evenly.

#### CLUTCH CABLE

**Removal** — From inside engine compartment, remove lock clip from clutch cable at firewall. Remove cotter pin from clutch fork and disconnect clutch cable. Disconnect cable from transmission case, and from actuating lever at clutch pedal, and remove from vehicle.

**Installation** — To install, reverse removal procedure and note the following: Apply grease to cable contacting points on clutch fork. Adjust pedal height and pedal free play.

#### CLUTCH RELEASE BEARING

**Removal** — With transmission removed, remove retaining clips from bearing collar and clutch fork. Slide release bearing and collar off transmission input shaft.

**Installation** — To install, apply grease to all bearing contact points of clutch fork, bearing collar, and transmission front bearing retainer, and reverse removal procedure.

#### PILOT BEARING

**Removal & Installation** — With transmission and clutch assembly removed, check bearing in end of crankshaft for roughness or noise during rotation. If defective, remove using a suitable puller (09303-35010). Apply grease to new bearing and install using a suitable driver (09304-12011).

### ADJUSTMENT

#### PEDAL HEIGHT

By turning stop bolt on clutch pedal, adjust pedal height to 6.65" (169 mm). Make height measurement between floor mat and top of pedal pad.

#### CLUTCH PEDAL FREE PLAY

From inside engine compartment, pull clutch cable out from firewall and remove lock clip. While holding cable out, insert lock clip on cable so that 5 or 6 protrusions and grooves are visible on cable between lock clip and firewall. See Fig. 1. If adjustment is correct, clutch pedal free play will be 0.8-1.4" (20-35 mm).

### TIGHTENING SPECIFICATIONS

| Application | Ft. Lbs. (mkg) |
| --- | --- |
| Pressure Plate-to-Flywheel | 11-16 (1.5-2.2) |
| Clutch Housing-to-Engine | 36-58 (5.0-8.0) |

## TOYOTA LAND CRUISER

**FJ40 Series**
**FJ55 Series**

### DESCRIPTION

Clutch is dry, single plate, coil spring type. Clutch actuation is hydraulic, using a master cylinder mounted at pedal bracket on firewall and a slave cylinder attached to the engine mounting rear bracket. A prelubricated clutch release bearing is also used.

### REMOVAL & INSTALLATION

#### CLUTCH ASSEMBLY

**Removal — 1)** Remove protective cover under transmission, and disconnect front and rear drive shafts from transfer case. Drain lubricant from transmission and transfer case. Disconnect parking brake cable from link lever. On FJ40 Series, drain fuel tank.

**2)** On FJ40 Series only, remove front seats, seat frames and console. Separate rear heater line clamp from tunnel. Remove fuel tank cover and fuel tank. On all series, remove shift lever boot and shift lever. Remove transmission cover.

**3)** Disconnect all electrical wires and vacuum lines from transfer case and transmission. Support transmission/transfer case assembly and remove mounting bolts.

**4)** Disconnect clutch fork return spring and remove slave cylinder, but do not disconnect hydraulic line unless necessary. Remove release bearing retaining clips, and release bearing with collar. Remove clutch lever assembly.

**5)** Mark pressure plate and flywheel for reassembly reference. Loosen clutch attaching bolts one turn at a time until spring pressure is released, then remove bolts and clutch assembly

**Installation —** To install, reverse removal procedure and note the following: Use suitable aligning tool to center disc on flywheel. Tighten clutch attaching bolts alternately and evenly. After reinstallation, adjust clutch fork free play and bleed hydraulic system if necessary.

#### CLUTCH MASTER CYLINDER

**Removal —** Remove clevis pin connecting master cylinder push rod to clutch pedal. Disconnect hydraulic line from cylinder body and plug opening. Remove cylinder attaching bolts at firewall and remove master cylinder. **CAUTION** — *Do not allow fluid to spill on painted surfaces.*

**Installation —** To install, reverse removal procedure, adjust pedal height and clutch pedal free play, and bleed hydraulic system. Check hydraulic system for leaks.

#### CLUTCH SLAVE CYLINDER

**Removal —** Plug master cylinder reservoir cap. Disconnect clutch return spring from hanger. Disconnect flexible hose from metal line and remove clip. Remove slave cylinder retaining bolts and remove slave cylinder.

**Installation —** To install, reverse removal procedure, adjust clutch fork free play and bleed hydraulic system.

#### CLUTCH RELEASE BEARING

**NOTE** — *Procedure for removal and installation of clutch release bearing is identical to that of clutch assembly. See Clutch Assembly Removal & Installation.*

#### PILOT BEARING

**Removal & Installation —** With clutch assembly removed, check pilot bearing in end of crankshaft for roughness or noise during rotation. If defective, remove using a suitable puller (0930355011). To install, lubricate bearing with multi-purpose grease and insert into crankshaft using suitable driver (0930447010).

### OVERHAUL

#### CLUTCH MASTER CYLINDER

**Disassembly —** Remove reservoir cap, drain fluid, and remove float. Remove reservoir and rubber boot from cylinder body. Remove snap ring, push rod, piston stop plate and boot. Remove piston and return spring from cylinder, then remove cylinder cup from piston. Clamp cylinder cap in a vise and, using a pipe wrench on cylinder body, remove body from cap. Remove cylinder cup spacer from cylinder.

**Inspection —** Clean all parts in clean brake fluid or alcohol and inspect for wear or damage. Check clearance between master cylinder bore and piston; if clearance exceeds .006", replace parts as necessary. Check return spring for wear or distortion. Replace spring if length is less than 3.31" with 4.5 lbs. load applied.

Reservoir · Boot · Push Rod · Snap Ring · Piston · Spring

*Fig. 1 Exploded View of Clutch Master Cylinder*

**Reassembly — 1)** **NOTE** — *Manufacturer recommends replacing cylinder cups each time cylinder is disassembled.* Soak all parts in clean brake fluid before assembly. Install piston stop plate, push rod, boot and snap ring into cylinder body.

## TOYOTA LAND CRUISER (Cont.)

2) Install a new cylinder cup onto piston, and insert piston into cylinder through front of bore. Install cup spacer and cylinder cup into cylinder bore. Install return spring with spring seat into cylinder and onto piston, then install cylinder cap with a new gasket.

3) Install reservoir onto master cylinder, install bolt and washer and tighten securely. Install float into fluid reservoir, and install reservoir cap.

### CLUTCH SLAVE CYLINDER

**Disassembly** — Remove push rod assembly and rubber boot from cylinder body. Withdraw cylinder piston and cup seal. Loosen and remove bleeder screw.

**Inspection** — Clean all parts thoroughly and inspect for wear or damage. Check clearance between slave cylinder bore and piston; if clearance exceeds .006", replace parts as necessary. Inspect spring for wear or distortion, and check bleeder screw and its seat in cylinder body for damage or distortion.

**Fig. 2 Exploded View of Clutch Slave Cylinder**

**Reassembly** — Soak all parts in clean brake fluid and reverse disassembly procedures. **NOTE** — *Manufacturer recommends that cylinder cups be replaced whenever cylinder has been disassembled.*

## ADJUSTMENT

### PEDAL HEIGHT

Pedal height is measured from floor mat to top of pedal pad as shown in *Fig. 3*. Loosen lock nut and push rod. Adjust stop bolt until specified pedal height is obtained.

#### Pedal Height

| Application | Height |
| --- | --- |
| FJ40 Series | |
| With Power Brake Unit | 8.47" (215 mm) |
| Without Power Brake Unit | 7.80" (198 mm) |
| FJ55 Series | |
| With Power Brake Unit | 7.28" (185 mm) |
| Without Power Brake Unit | 6.77" (172 mm) |

### PEDAL FREE PLAY

Clutch pedal free play is measured from a point where pedal is in fully up position to a point where master cylinder push rod

just contacts piston. Adjust free play by loosening lock nut and turning push rod to obtain specified pedal free play.

**Fig. 3 Pedal Height Measuring and Adjustment Points**

#### Pedal Free Play

| Application | Free Play |
| --- | --- |
| All Models | .79-1.57" (20-40 mm) |

### CLUTCH FORK FREE PLAY

To obtain correct amount of clearance between release bearing and pressure plate, adjust push rod tip to specifications.

#### Clutch Fork Free Play

| Application | Free Play |
| --- | --- |
| All Models | .12-.16 (3-4 mm) |

### HYDRAULIC SYSTEM BLEEDING

1) Connect a flexible tube to slave cylinder bleeder screw, and place opposite end in a container partially filled with brake fluid.

2) Pump clutch pedal several times. With pedal depressed, loosen bleeder screw one-third to one-half turn and allow air to bleed out. Tighten bleeder screw.

3) Continue operation until air bubbles are no longer seen in fluid being discharged into container. Tighten bleeder screw securely and install cap. Check fluid level in master cylinder reservoir, and check system for leaks.

### TIGHTENING SPECIFICATIONS

| Application | Ft. Lbs. (mkg) |
| --- | --- |
| Engine-to-Clutch Housing | 36-58 (5.0-8.0) |
| Pressure Plate-to-Flywheel | 11-16 (1.5-2.2) |
| Reservoir | 15-22 (2.0-3.0) |

## TRIUMPH

**Spitfire
TR7**

### DESCRIPTION

Clutch is dry, single plate, diaphragm spring type. Clutch actuation is hydraulic, using a firewall mounted master cylinder and a clutch housing-mounted slave cylinder. Due to self-adjusting feature of clutch assembly, no adjustment, with the exception of bleeding hydraulic system, is necessary.

### REMOVAL & INSTALLATION

#### CLUTCH ASSEMBLY

**Removal (Spitfire)** — **1)** Disconnect battery. Remove gear shift lever. On models equipped with overdrive, pry off knob cap and disconnect wires. Remove knob.

**2)** Remove transmission tunnel cover and propeller shaft cover. Disconnect propeller shaft and speedometer cable. Remove clutch slave cylinder, raise vehicle, and drain transmission.

**3)** Support engine. Disconnect exhaust pipe bracket and remove rear mounting nuts from transmission. Remove cable from clutch housing, remove lower housing bolts, and lower vehicle.

**4)** Remove starter bolts. Disconnect wires from transmission. Remove upper clutch housing bolts and remove transmission. Separate transmission and clutch housing.

**Installation** — Reverse removal procedure and note the following: Use clutch alignment tool to center clutch assembly. Tighten clutch bolts evenly and gradually.

**Removal (TR7)** — **1)** Raise and support vehicle. Disconnect battery ground cable. Remove gear shift lever assembly. Index mark and separate propeller shaft from transmission. Disconnect exhaust pipe at intake manifold (pipe may have to be comoletely removed).

**2)** Disconnect speedometer cable and all electrical wires attached to transmission. Remove starter heat shroud. Place a jack (with wood block) under oil pan. Remove slave cylinder without disconnecting fluid line. Hang cylinder out of way.

**3)** Remove 2 bolts holding oil pan plate to clutch housing. Remove 4 nuts keeping transmission rear crossmember to body. Slightly lower engine. Remove starter.

**4)** Remove nuts and bolts mounting clutch housing to engine. Support transmission with appropriate jack. Slide back transmission/clutch housing assembly and remove from vehicle.

**5)** Index mark pressure plate with flywheel. Loosen 6 pressure plate mounting bolts evenly (a few turns at a time). Slide out pressure plate with clutch disc.

**Installation** — To install, reverse removal procedure and note following: Ensure index marks on pressure plate align with those on flywheel. Use clutch aligning tool to center clutch disc.

#### CLUTCH MASTER CYLINDER

**Removal** — **1)** Disconnect hydraulic line and drain fluid. Plug open port and line.

**2)** Disconnect clevis mounting push rod to clutch pedal.

**3)** Remove 2 bolts (Spitfire) or 2 nuts (TR7) mounting master cylinder to bracket (Spitfire) or bulkhead (TR7).

**Installation** — Reverse removal procedure and bleed hydraulic system.

***Fig. 1  Exploded View of Spitfire Clutch
Master Cylinder — Note How Master Cylinder is Mounted***

#### CLUTCH SLAVE CYLINDER

**Removal** — Raise and support vehicle. Disconnect and plug hydraulic line and remove slave cylinder.

**NOTE** — *On TR7 models, do not move operating rod in a forward direction. Forward movement may cause release lever to dislodge. Transmission removal would then become necessary for installation of release lever.*

**Installation** — Reverse removal procedure and note:
- On Spitfire models, centralize push rod in housing before sliding slave cylinder in position.
- On TR7 models, slave cylinder must be mounted with bleed screw ABOVE fluid pipe.
- Bleed hydraulic line.

#### CLUTCH RELEASE BEARING

**Spitfire** — With transmission assembly removed, remove clutch fork pivot pin and remove fork and bearing assembly. Drive pins from fork and remove bearing and sleeve. Using a suitable press, remove bearing from sleeve. To install, reverse removal procedure. Lubricate all bearing contact points with multi-purpose grease.

# Clutches

## TRIUMPH (Cont.)

**TR7** — With transmission removed, use suitable tool (ST 1136) and unscrew clutch release lever pivot bolt from clutch housing. Pull release lever, complete with pivot bolt and release bearing. To install, reverse removal procedure making sure fork and collar engage evenly.

## OVERHAUL

### CLUTCH MASTER CYLINDER

**Disassembly, Spitfire** — 1) Drain fluid and remove master cylinder. Pull back rubber boot and release circlip, then pull out push rod and washer.

2) Apply compressed air to fluid inlet to remove piston and spring assembly. Remove thimble and spring from piston assembly, then disengage valve stem from slot in thimble. Remove seal spacer from valve stem and seals from valve and piston.

**Reassembly** — Reverse removal procedure, using new rubber seals and lubricating parts with brake fluid.

**Disassembly (TR7)** — 1) Remove master cylinder. Pull up rubber boot and remove snap ring. Slide out push rod and washer.

2) Pull out piston, spring, and seal as an assembly. It may be necessary to use air pressure to force out assembly.

3) Straighten spring thimble prong, then remove thimble and spring from piston. Disengage valve stem from slot in thimble. Slip spacer off valve stem. Remove valve seal.

**Fig. 2  Exploded View of TR7 Master Cylinder**

**Reassembly** — 1) Fit spacer, spring and thimble to valve stem. Fit new seal to piston with lip facing spring. Put spring thimble on piston and depress thimble prong.

2) Lubricate master cylinder bore with brake fluid and slide seal assembly, spring and piston into place. Reverse disassembly procedure to assemble remaining components.

### CLUTCH SLAVE CYLINDER

**Disassembly** — Remove slave cylinder and pull off dust cover. Remove circlip, then take out piston, seal and spring.

**Inspection** — Look at cylinder bore and piston for signs of damage. Replace either or both parts if wear is excessive.

**Reassembly** — Reverse removal procedure, lubricating parts with brake fluid and fitting small end of spring to piston.

**Fig. 3  Exploded View of Clutch Slave Cylinder (TR7 Shown, Spitfire Similar)**

## ADJUSTMENT

### HYDRAULIC SYSTEM BLEEDING

1) Fill master cylinder. Attach bleed tube to bleed valve on slave cylinder. Submerge free end of tube in container of brake fluid.

2) Slowly depress pedal to force air out. Close bleed valve and let pedal rise unassisted. Check that fluid level does not drop too low, and repeat until no more air bubbles are visible.

## TIGHTENING SPECIFICATIONS

| Application | Ft. Lbs. (mkg) |
|---|---|
| Clutch Assembly-to-Flywheel | 22 (3.0) |
| Clutch Housing-to-Transmission | 32 (4.4) |
| Slave Cylinder-to-Clutch Housing | 21 (2.9) |

## VOLKSWAGEN TYPE 1 & 2

Type 1
Type 2

## DESCRIPTION

Clutch is dry, single disc, diaphragm spring type. Clutch operation is mechanical through cable actuation. A prelubricated clutch release bearing is also used.

## REMOVAL & INSTALLATION

### CLUTCH ASSEMBLY

**Removal** — Remove engine. See *Engine Removal in ENGINE Section.* Install suitable holding tool to prevent flywheel from turning. Index mark pressure plate and flywheel for reassembly. Loosen pressure plate mounting bolts alternately and evenly. Remove assembly.

**Installation** — Apply multi-purpose grease to pilot bearing and light oil to felt ring. Lubricate transmission input shaft with molybdenum disulphide powder. Position clutch disc against flywheel and align using a suitable centering tool. Install pressure plate and mounting bolts, tightening alternately and evenly.

### CLUTCH CABLE

**Removal (Type 1)** — Disconnect clutch cable from clutch operating lever, then withdraw rubber sleeve from guide tube and cable. Remove accelerator pedal and disconnect accelerator cable. Remove push rod lock plate and disconnect brake pedal return spring at push rod pin. Remove pedal cluster mounting bolts, pull back pedal cluster and remove clutch cable by pulling toward front of vehicle.

**Installation** — Lubricate cable with multi-purpose grease. Insert threaded end of cable in guide tube and push completely through. Install pedal assembly with cable connected. Ensure rubber boot is seated correctly on rear of guide tube, connect clutch cable lever, then lubricate and install wing nut. Reverse removal procedure to install remaining components. Adjust free play.

**Removal (Type 2)** — Disconnect cable from clutch operating lever on transmission. Pull rubber boot from guide tube and rear of cable. Pull guide tube and cable out of bracket on transmission. From under vehicle, remove pedal cover plate. Unbolt clutch pedal and remove pedal lever assembly from frame. Disconnect cable, bend up lock plate and pull out cable toward front of vehicle.

**Installation** — Lubricate cable with multi-purpose grease and install into guide tube. Connect cable to pedal, push cable through boot, and install boot onto cable guide. Lubricate and install wing nut. Reverse removal procedure to install remaining components. Adjust free play.

### CLUTCH RELEASE BEARING

**Removal** — Remove engine. On Type 2 models, pry off spring clip retainers. On all models, disengage spring clips. Remove release bearing by sliding off guide tube.

**NOTE** — *Do not wash bearing in solvent or any cleaning solution.*

Clutch Release Bearing

Spring Clip Retainer

Spring Clip

Release Bearing Guide Sleeve

Nut

Lock Washer

Clutch Housing

Clutch Operating Shaft

**Fig. 1  Clutch Release Bearing Assembly (Type 2 Shown)**

**Installation** — Roughen plastic ring with coarse emery paper and apply a light coating of molybdenum disulphide paste. Coat pivoting points between bearing and operating shaft with multi-purpose grease. Position bearing to shaft and install spring clips and retainers (Type 2). Make sure clips are correctly positioned. With engine installed, check and adjust clutch free play.

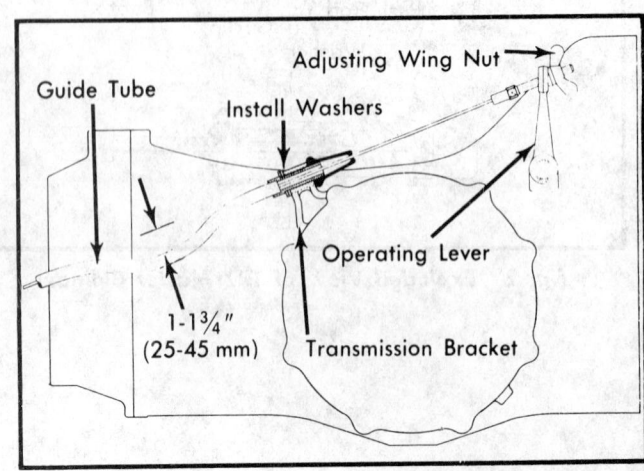

Adjusting Wing Nut

Guide Tube

Install Washers

Operating Lever

1-1¾"
(25-45 mm)

Transmission Bracket

**Fig. 2  Clutch Cable Measuring and Adjustment Points**

## VOLKSWAGEN TYPE 1 & 2 (Cont.)

### ADJUSTMENT

#### CLUTCH ADJUSTMENT

**Guide Tube** — Clutch cable guide tube should sag approximately 1-1¾" (25-45 mm). See *Fig. 2*. This preload is obtained by inserting or removing washers between bracket on transmission and end piece of guide tube.

**NOTE** — *If sag is greater than 1¾" (45 mm), stiff operation and/or damage may result.*

**Clutch Pedal Free Play — 1)** Clutch pedal free play should be about ⅜-¾" (10-20 mm) for Type 1 and ⅝-1" (15-25 mm) for Type 2 models.

**2)** Adjust clutch free play as follows: Raise and support vehicle. Adjust wing nut located on end of clutch cable where cable attaches to release lever until there is about .063" (1.6 mm) for Type 1 or about .031" (.79 mm), for Type 2 between operating lever and wing nut. See *Fig. 3*. After adjustment make sure 2 lugs of wing nut engage cutouts in lever.

**NOTE** — *On some replacement clutches, a white paint spot is used for a balance mark. Position mark 180° from ³⁄₁₆" (5 mm) countersunk hole or 180° from white paint balance mark on flywheel.*

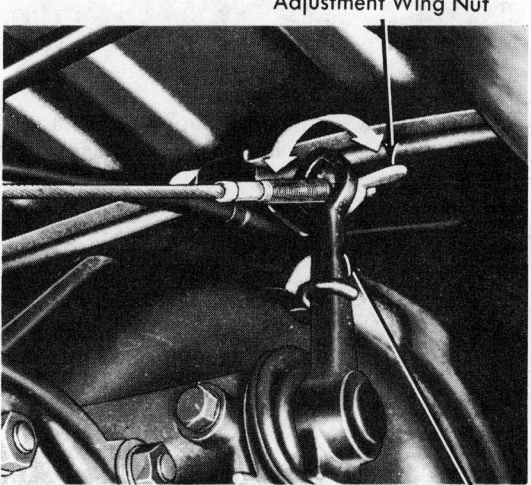

Adjustment Wing Nut

Release Lever Arm

*Fig. 3    Clutch Free Play Adjustment Point*

### TIGHTENING SPECIFICATIONS

| Application | Ft. Lbs. (mkg) |
| --- | --- |
| Engine-to-Transmission Nuts | 22 (3.0) |
| Flywheel-to-Crankshaft Bolt | 80 (11.0) |
| Clutch-to-Flywheel Bolts | 18 (2.5) |

## VOLKSWAGEN DASHER

**Dasher**

### DESCRIPTION

Clutch is single plate dry disc type, using a diaphragm type pressure plate and a pre-lubricated clutch release bearing. Clutch is cable actuated.

**Fig. 1   Exploded View of Clutch Assembly**

### REMOVAL & INSTALLATION

#### TRANSAXLE & CLUTCH ASSEMBLIES

**Removal** — **1)** Disconnect battery ground cable from battery. Disconnect exhaust pipe at manifold. Disconnect exhaust pipe bracket from rear of transaxle.

**2)** Disconnect gear shift lever and shift linkage. Disconnect back-up light wires. On some models there is a bolt mounting gear shift linkage to transaxle that must be removed.

**3)** Loosen clutch cable adjustment nut and disengage clutch housing from left side engine mount. Separate clutch cable from operating lever. Disconnect speedometer cable.

**4)** Disconnect front wheel axle drive shafts at transaxle. Suspend drive shafts with wire out of way. Remove starter.

**5)** Remove clutch housing front cover plate. Remove bolts mounting transaxle-to-engine. Place a jack under transaxle for support. Unbolt transaxle carrier from body. Slide transaxle to rear until input shaft is clear of clutch assembly. Lower out transaxle.

**6)** Index mark pressure plate and flywheel. Loosen pressure plate bolts ¼ turn at a time. Work in a criss-cross pattern. Slide pressure plate off dowels on flywheel.

**Installation** — **1)** Using a clutch alignment tool, fit pressure plate with clutch. Make sure alignment marks are observed. Loosely attach assembly with 6 bolts.

**NOTE** — *If replacement pressure plate has white paint spot, it is a balance mark and should be 180° from countersunk hole or 180° from white paint mark on flywheel.*

**2)** Tighten pressure plate bolts in criss-cross pattern about 2 turns at a time.

**3)** Position transaxle to engine. Loosely fit bolts holding transaxle carrier to body. Reverse removal procedure to install remaining components.

**Fig. 2   View Showing Clutch Assembly Alignment on Flywheel**

### CLUTCH RELEASE BEARING

**Removal** — **1)** Remove transmission.

**2)** Remove spring clips keeping release bearing to release bearing shaft.

**3)** Slide release bearing off release bearing guide sleeve.

**Inspection** — **1)** Rotate bearing and check for roughness or noise.

**2)** Bearing is pre-lubricated, DO NOT wash in solvent.

**3)** Apply Molykote paste to bearing contact points on clutch release shaft.

**Installation** — **1)** Slide release bearing into bearing guide sleeve.

**2)** Fit spring clips keeping release bearing in position on shaft.

**3)** Check fit closely.

**4)** Install transmission.

### CLUTCH CABLE

**Removal** — **1)** Loosen clutch cable adjusting nuts.

**2)** Free clutch cable housing from support bracket.

**3)** Separate end of cable from clutch operating lever. Operating lever is mounted to side of clutch housing.

# Clutches

## VOLKSWAGEN DASHER (Cont.)

**4)** Disconnect clutch cable from clutch pedal.

**5)** Force cable and housing through bulkhead into passenger compartment.

**Installation** — Refit new cable in reverse of removal procedure. Readjust clutch pedal free play.

**NOTE** — *If new clutch cable has been installed, make sure to recheck clutch pedal free play after 300 miles.*

### PILOT BEARING

**1)** To remove bearing, install a suitable remover tool (10-202) into pilot bearing, then remove bearing by tightening tool.

**2)** Install bearing so that lettering is facing out. Drive bearing into crankshaft using a suitable driver tool (US 219) until it is flush, then lubricate bearing.

## ADJUSTMENT

### CLUTCH PEDAL FREE PLAY

**1)** Raise hood and find adjusting nuts located just ahead of oil filter.

- **To Increase Free Play** — Loosen top adjusting nut 2 or 3 turns. Tighten bottom nut until locked against bracket. Pedal free play should be ⅝" (15.87 mm).

- **To Decrease Free Play** — Loosen nut under bracket 2 or 3 turns. Tighten top nut until locked against bracket. Pedal free play should be ⅝" (15.87 mm).

**2)** Check clutch pedal operation. Repeat adjustment procedure until clutch pedal free play is within specifications.

### TIGHTENING SPECIFICATIONS

| Application | Ft. Lbs. (mkg) |
|---|---|
| Clutch Assembly-to-Flywheel | 18 (2.5) |
| Transmission-to-Engine | 40 (5.5) |
| Clutch Lever-to-Transmission | 12-18 (1.7-2.5) |
| Drive Shaft-to-Transmission | 25.5 (3.5) |

# Clutches

## VOLKSWAGEN RABBIT/SCIROCCO

Scirocco

### DESCRIPTION

Clutch is a single plate dry disc type, using a diaphragm type pressure plate and a transmission mounted clutch release bearing. Clutch is cable operated.

**Fig. 1   Exploded View of Clutch and Flywheel Assembly**

### REMOVAL & INSTALLATION

#### TRANSMISSION

**1)** Disconnect battery ground strap and attach an engine support assembly. Remove 4 attaching bolts and left transmission mount. Remove TDC plug. Rotate flywheel until flywheel lug appears in hole.

**NOTE** — *Engine and transmission can be separated only when flywheel is in this position.*

**Fig. 2   Top View of Transmission and Clutch Housing Note Where Clutch Cable Mounts on Transmission Case**

**2)** Disconnect speedometer drive cable and plug hole in transmission with a rubber cap. Disconnect back-up light wires and clutch cable. Remove two upper clutch housing-to-engine bolts. Disconnect shift linkage from rod lever and relay lever.

**3)** Disconnect ground strap from transmission. Remove starter. Remove transaxle-to-engine bolts accessible once starter is removed.

**4)** Support transaxle with jack. Remove transaxle rear mount. Disconnect left and right axle drive shafts at transaxle.

**5)** Remove large plate cover bolts (large plate stays on engine). Remove small cover bolts and cover. Remove transaxle-to-engine mounting bolt that is now accessible. Remove nut near small cover plate. Rotate transaxle to left and remove from vehicle.

#### CLUTCH ASSEMBLY

**1)** Using a diagonal loosening pattern, gradually loosen and remove flywheel bolts and flywheel. Pry retaining ring from release plate and lift release plate from pressure plate.

**NOTE** — *A special dual purpose holding tool (VW558) may be used to lock either flywheel or pressure plate for removal purposes.*

**2)** Remove bolts attaching pressure plate to engine. Use Loctite 270 or 271 when installing pressure plate bolts. If a new flywheel is to be installed a new timing mark must be cut into flywheel ¼" (6 mm) to right of TDC mark. Install clutch assembly in reverse of disassembly with ends of retaining ring between two slots in release plate. Use a centering disc (VW 547) to center clutch disc in flywheel.

#### CLUTCH RELEASE BEARING & OPERATING LEVER ASSEMBLY

**Removal — 1)** Remove 4 bolts and washers mounting clutch release cover to the far left end of transaxle case. Cover is waffle patterned. Remove 2 circlips located at each side of clutch lever.

**2)** Pull operating lever and release shaft assembly out of case. Lift return spring along with clutch lever out of transaxle case. Take out release bearing, guide sleeve, and push rod.

**Inspection —** Check release bearing by hand. Make sure there is no apparent roughness or noise. Make sure push rod seal is good. Check push rod bushing for wear. Replace any unserviceable parts. Check clutch lever oil seal. If seal is bad, pry out and drive in a new one.

**Installation — 1)** Coat push rod with multipurpose grease and insert back into position. Grease sliding surface of bearing and guide sleeve.

**2)** Position return spring and clutch lever inside transaxle case. Return spring center hook should fit on top of clutch lever lug. Spring end hooks must point down to hold clutch lever away from release bearing.

**3)** Lightly coat release shaft with multipurpose grease. Fit shaft. Work operating lever until splines on release shaft mesh with those in clutch lever.

## VOLKSWAGEN RABBIT/SCIROCCO (Cont.)

**4)** Install circlips. Make sure when operating lever is in normal position that return spring has tension. Fit gasket and cover.

## ADJUSTMENT

**CLUTCH PEDAL FREE PLAY**

**1)** Locate adjusting nut in engine compartment. Nut is on cable conduit. To adjust, loosen lock nut and turn adjuster until cable conduit can be pulled up out of bracket about .125" (3 mm).

**2)** Check pedal free play. If there is about .625" (15.9 mm) free play at this time, tighten lock nut. If necessary, continue adjustment process.

## TIGHTENING SPECIFICATIONS

| Application | Ft. Lbs. (mkg) |
|---|---|
| Transmission-to-Engine | 47 (5.5) |
| Drive Shaft-to-Transmission | 32 (4.5) |
| Pressure Plate Bolts | 54 (7.5) |
| Flywheel Bolts | 14 (2.0) |
| Cover Plate | 11 (1.5) |

## VOLVO

**240
260**

## DESCRIPTION

Clutch is diaphragm spring type. Clutch assembly consists of the following components:

- Pressure plate
- Diaphragm spring
- Sheet metal clutch housing
- Clutch disc
- Clutch release bearing

Clutch actuation is mechanical on 240 series and hydraulic on 260 series. On 240, a cable provides linkage between clutch pedal and release fork. On 260 models, linkage on clutch pedal actuates clutch master cylinder which in turn supplies hydraulic pressure to clutch slave cylinder. Clutch release fork is actuated by slave cylinder piston and pin.

## REMOVAL & INSTALLATION

### CLUTCH ASSEMBLY

**Removal, M45 & M46 Transmission — 1)** Disconnect battery ground cable. Pull back-up light wiring harness connector. Working from under vehicle, disconnect gear shift lever from gear shift rod.

**2)** Separate gear shift boot from carpet. Using a 4 mm Allen wrench, remove reverse gear detent fork. With snap ring pliers, remove lock ring and pull up lever. Unhook clutch fork return spring and separate cable from housing.

**3)** Remove bolts at clutch housing and nut at exhaust pipe, then remove front exhaust pipe bracket. Position a support under engine. Remove transmission crossmember. Index mark and disconnect drive shaft. Separate speedometer cable from transmission.

**4)** Slightly lower rear of engine and take out all clutch housing bolts except top right. Fit jack to transmission for support and remove last clutch housing bolt. Pull transmission from vehicle. Remove upper starter mounting bolt. Remove bolts mounting clutch assembly, loosening in a criss-cross pattern. Make sure bolts are loosened evenly.

**Installation —** To install transmission and clutch assembly, reverse removal procedure and note the following: Insert clutch plate with long side of hub facing backward. Use aligning tool (2484 or equivalent) to center clutch assembly. Tighten clutch mounting bolts in a criss-cross pattern. Adjust clutch pedal free play.

**NOTE** — *Two different types of pressure plates and release bearings are used in 240 and 260 models. The 240 plate fingers are straight, requiring a longer $1^{11}/_{16}$" (43 mm) throwout bearing. The 260 pressure plate fingers are raised at the center by approximately $9/_{32}$" (7 mm), requiring use of a shorter $1^7/_{16}$" (36.5 mm) release bearing. Pressure plates and release bearings must never be mixed.*

## CLUTCH CABLE (240 Series)

**Removal —** Remove return spring and disconnect clutch cable at clutch fork; extract cable. Remove cover panel under instrument cluster. Remove clevis pin at upper end of cable. Separate clutch fork adjustment mechanism from clutch housing, if necessary. Force cable out of rubber grommet located in firewall.

**Installation —** Insert new cable into rubber grommet, feed it through cable guide and attach at upper end with clevis pin. Position adjustment mechanism into clutch housing. Attach cable to clutch fork, then refit return spring.

Clevis Pin

Pedal

Clutch Release Fork

Clutch Release Bearing

Clutch Cable

Support

Boot

Gasket

Return Spring

Adjuster Mechanism

Disc

Pressure Plate

**Fig. 1  Exploded View of Clutch System
(240 Mechanical Linkage Shown)**

### HYDRAULIC CLUTCH ACTUATION

Manufacturer does not provide maintenance instructions for hydraulically operated clutch linkage. There should be no free play in this type linkage.

### PILOT BEARING

Remove retaining clip and remove bearing using puller (SVO 4090). Pack bearing with heat resistant grease and install into crankshaft using a driver. Install retaining clip.

## VOLVO (Cont.)

Fig. 2  Measuring Clutch Fork Free Play
(240 with Mechanical Linkage Shown)

### ADJUSTMENT

#### CLUTCH FREE PLAY (240)

Using adjustment mechanism attached to clutch housing, set free play. Adjustment is correct when approximately ⅛" (3-5 mm) clutch fork free play is obtained.

| TIGHTENING SPECIFICATIONS | |
|---|---|
| Application | Ft.Lbs. (mkg) |
| Bell Housing Bolts ..................................... | 25-35 (3.5-4.8) |
| Output Shaft Flange Nuts ..................... | 67-88 (9.2-12.2) |
| Gearshift Assembly ................................ | 15-18 (2.0-2.5) |

# Contents

# Section 7
# BRAKES

*NOTE — ALSO SEE GENERAL INDEX.*

# Brakes

## BRAKE SYSTEM TROUBLE SHOOTING

**NOTE** — *This is a general trouble shooting guide. Not all steps will apply to all brake systems. When using this guide, locate the condition in column one that corresponds to your problem and determine the possible causes in column two. Match the number of the possible causes with the same number in column three.*

| CONDITION | POSSIBLE CAUSE | CORRECTION |
|---|---|---|
| ▶ Brake chatter, squeal, squeak | 1) Dust on drums/rotors, oil stained linings<br>2) Weak shoe return spring<br>3) Drum out of round<br>4) Excessively worn pads or shoes<br>5) Uneven rotor surface<br><br>6) Excessive lateral rotor runout<br><br>7) Excessive wheel bearing play | 1) Remove drum/rotor, clean<br><br>2) Check, replace springs<br>3) Turn drum on lathe<br>4) Replace pads or shoes<br>5) Check rotor surface in various locations with micrometer<br>6) Check runout with dial indicator, resurface or replace rotor<br>7) Readjust or replace bearings |
| ▶ Excessive pedal travel | 1) Excessive rotor runout<br><br>2) Brake fluid boil<br><br>3) Warped or excessively worn pads or shoes<br>4) Rear brakes out of adjustment<br>5) Power brake unit malfunction | 1) Check rotor with dial gauge, resurface or replace<br>2) Drain system, refill with fluid of correct specification<br>3) Check and replace pads or shoes<br>4) Adjust shoe to drum clearance<br>5) Check and either overhaul or replace unit |
| ▶ Poor brake operation | 1) Too long brake lever stroke<br>2) Brake cable sticking<br><br>3) Excessive shoe to drum clearance | 1) Readjust brake pedal lever<br>2) Check brake cable routing and lubricate<br>3) Check self-adjuster mechanism; readjust or replace components |
| ▶ Shock when pedal applied | 1) Brake durm cracked or distorted<br>2) Uneven brake drum wear<br>3) Broken return spring | 1) Replace drum<br>2) Resurface drum or replace<br>3) Replace springs |
| ▶ Leaks in caliper piston cylinder | 1) Damaged or excessively worn caliper piston seal<br>2) Deep scores or corrosion on surface of cylinder bore | 1) Overhaul caliper and install new seals<br>2) Overhaul caliper and hone (unless not recommended by manufacturer); install new seals |
| ▶ Rattling in front brakes | 1) Pad anti-rattle spring clip broken or missing<br>2) Excessive clearance between pads and caliper | 1) Install new part or reposition existing one<br>2) Fit caliper with new pads |
| ▶ Pull when brake applied | 1) Incorrect tire pressure<br><br>2) Front end out of alignment<br>3) Unmatched tires<br><br><br>4) Restricted brake lines or hoses | 1) Inflate tires evenly as indicated in owners manual<br>2) Check and align front end<br>3) Make sure all tires have approximately equal amounts of tred and pressure<br>4) Inspect for soft hoses or damaged lines. Replace with new hoses or brake tubing |

# Brakes

## BRAKE SYSTEM TROUBLE SHOOTING (Cont.)

| CONDITION | POSSIBLE CAUSE | CORRECTION |
|---|---|---|
| ▶ Excessive pedal pressure required | 1) Linings coated with brake fluid, oil or grease<br>2) Entire pad not contacting rotor<br>3) Scored brake rotors<br>4) Incorrect pads<br>5) Seized piston<br>6) Power brake failing | 1) Fit new pads or shoes<br>2) Replace pads<br>3) Resurface rotor according to specs.<br>4) Check pads<br>5) Overhaul caliper, check piston<br>6) Check power unit and replace |
| ▶ Low pedal effect | 1) Air in hydraulic system, brakes not properly bled<br>2) Hydraulic fluid leaking past primary cup in master cylinder<br>3) Bleeder screw not tight | 1) Check for air leaks and bleed hydraulic system<br>2) Overhaul master cylinder making sure to replace cups<br>3) Tighten bleeder screw |
| ▶ Uneven braking | 1) Linings contaminated<br>2) Unmatched disc pads<br><br>3) One or more seized pistons<br>4) Incorrect tire pressure<br><br>5) Front wheel out of alignment<br>6) Brake hose or line clogged<br>7) Caliper alignment improper | 1) Clean or refit with new pads/shoes<br>2) Ensure all pads on any axle are same quality<br>3) Overhaul caliper to free piston<br>4) Inflate tires according to manufacturers recommendations<br>5) Align front wheels<br>6) Free restriction<br>7) Remove and realign caliper |
| ▶ Brake pedal pulsation | 1) Excessive rotor lateral runout<br>2) Rotor not parallel<br>3) Wheel bearings out of adjustment<br>4) Rear drums out of round | 1) Check rotor runout with dial gauge<br>2) Check rotor and replace<br>3) Adjust<br>4) Check drums and turn or replace |
| ▶ Spongy pedal | 1) Air in brake system<br>2) Swollen brake hose(s)<br>3) Brake fluid boiling point too low<br><br>4) Filler cap vent hole plugged | 1) Bleed system<br>2) Replace hose and bleed system<br>3) Drain, flush and refill with fluid of proper specifications<br>4) Clean, then bleed system |
| ▶ Pedal yield under slight pressure | 1) Deteriorated check valve<br>2) External brake fluid leaks<br><br>3) Internal leak in master cylinder | 1) Replace valve, bleed system<br>2) Check master cylinder, lines, and wheel cylinders; replace<br>3) Overhaul master cylinder |
| ▶ Brake failure or heavy pedal | 1) Power unit diaphragm damaged<br>2) Check valve malfunctioning<br>3) Defective vacuum hose<br>4) Twisted air valve and valve rod plunger | 1) Check and/or replace diaphragm<br>2) Replace valve<br>3) Replace hose<br>4) Disassemble and repair |
| ▶ Brakes react slowly | 1) Check valve malfunction<br>2) Vacuum hose blocked or broke<br>3) Air cleaner clogged or restricted | 1) Clean or replace check valve<br>2) Replace hose<br>3) Clean or replace air cleaner |
| ▶ Brake drag or slow return | 1) Push rod out of alignment<br>2) Operating rod out of adjustment<br>3) Air valve and push rod plunger twisted | 1) Disassemble and repair<br>2) Adjust<br><br>3) Adjust |

# Brakes

## ARROW, CHALLENGER, COLT & SAPPORO

Arrow
Challenger
Colt
Sapporo

### DESCRIPTION

Brake system is hydraulically operated using a tandem master cylinder and, in some instances, a power brake unit. All models are equipped with front disc brakes. Challenger and Sapporo models equipped with 2600 cc engine use disc brakes on rear wheels. All other models are fitted with leading/trailing drum brakes. Rear brakes are self-adjusting and incorporate a dual-piston wheel cylinder. Parking brake is cable actuated and operates on rear brakes.

### ADJUSTMENT

#### DISC BRAKES

No adjustment required.

#### DRUM BRAKES

Self-adjusting

#### PEDAL HEIGHT & FREE PLAY

1) Back off stop light switch. Adjust pedal height (distance from top of pedal to floor board) to specifications by rotating master cylinder push rod.

**NOTE** — *Make sure push rod is not depressed during this procedure.*

2) Adjust stop light switch until it just contacts brake pedal lever. After making both adjustments, brake pedal free play should be as indicated in table.

| Pedal Height & Free Play Specifications | | |
|---|---|---|
| Application | Pedal Height In. (mm) | Free Play In. (mm) |
| Arrow & Colt | | |
| Man. Trans. | 6.4 (163) | .4-.6 (10-15) |
| Auto. Trans. | 6.5 (165) | .4-.6 (10-15) |
| Colt St. Wgn. | 6.9 (175) | .4-.6 (10-15) |
| Challenger & Sapporo | 6.9 (175) | .4-.6 (10-15) |

#### PARKING BRAKE

**Arrow & Colt (Exc. Colt St. Wgn.)** — Fully release parking brake. Remove parking lever cover to gain access to adjustment nut. Adjust nut until clearance between lever and stop is about .003-.08″ (.2-2 mm).

**Challenger, Sapporo & Colt St. Wgn. (Exc. Rear Disc)** — 1) Release parking brake lever. Loosen cable attaching bolt and adjusting nut. Move cable lever to the right and adjust clearance between extension lever and stopper on left rear wheel to .10″ (2.5 mm) or less.

Fig. 1  *Adjusting Parking Brake on Challenger, Sapporo and Colt St. Wgn.*

2) With left cable adjusted, turn adjusting nut until the same clearance is obtained on right wheel extension lever. With parking brake properly adjusted lever stroke should be 5-7 notches.

**Challenger & Sapporo (W/Rear Disc)** — Fully release parking brake lever. Depress brake pedal to floor 2 times. Loosen parking brake cable adjusting nut at center of rear axle housing. Adjust cable so rear wheel drag is 23 lbs. (10.5 kg) or less after brake rotors have been turned several revolutions. Use spring pull scale to measure drag.

### COMBINATION VALVE

**NOTE** — *Valve accomplishes three functions: Pressure control of rear service brakes; trouble warning; deactivating rear brake pressure control when front service brakes fail.*

**Pressure Test** — Use two pressure gauges that will measure at least 1,500 psi. Hook one gauge to master cylinder rear side and one to rear wheel cylinder. Pressure reading should be as shown in chart. Replace defective as required.

#### Brake Hydraulic Pressure Chart

| Application | Pressure |
|---|---|
| Wheel Cylinder | $460 \pm 28.4$ psi |
| Master Cylinder | 640 psi |

**Warning Light Test** — Slightly loosen bleeder screw of one wheel cylinder and depress brake pedal. At this time warning light should come on. If light doesn't work, check switch and wire connector.

**Combination Valve Reset** — After performing necessary repairs on brake system, bleed brake lines. After lines are bled and all bleeder valves are secure, press hard on brake pedal. This will force valve to return to center position. Warning light should go out.

## ARROW, CHALLENGER, COLT & SAPPORO (Cont.)

Fig. 2  Sectional View of Combination Valve Showing Detail of Internal Components. Valve Shown is for Models with Rear Drum Brakes

Fig. 3  Installation Direction of Spring and Clip on Brake Pads. Also, Installation Position of Retaining Pins. Caliper Shown is Used on Arrow & Colt Except Colt St. Wgn.

### HYDRAULIC SYSTEM BLEEDING

Attach a bleed tube to wheel cylinder bleeder screw and immerse opposite end of tube in a container partially filled with brake fluid. Depress and release pedal several times, hold in applied position, loosen bleeder screw, allow air to escape, and tighten bleeder screw. Continue operation until air bubbles are no longer seen in discharged fluid. Repeat procedure at remaining brake lines until all air is bled from system.

**Removal (Challenger, Sapporo & Colt St. Wgn.) — 1)** Raise and support vehicle. Remove front wheels. Remove retaining clip and pull out stopper plug.

**2)** Loosen caliper assembly mounting bolts. Slide caliper off rotor. Remove inner and outer pad clips, then pull pads and caliper support from caliper.

**Installation —** To install, reverse removal procedure and note the following: Press piston to bottom of caliper bore prior to pad installation. Ensure pad retaining clips are installed as shown in *Fig. 4*.

## REMOVAL & INSTALLATION

### FRONT DISC BRAKE PADS

**Removal (Arrow & Colt Exc. Colt St. Wgn.) —** Raise and support vehicle. Remove front wheel. Remove protector by prying up edge of clip at center of protector. Hold center of "M" clip, detach "M" clip from pad and its ends from retaining pins; remove clip. Remove retaining pins from caliper and remove "K" spring. Remove pads from caliper by grasping backing plate area of pads with pliers.

**NOTE** — *Replace all pads (left and right side) at same time.*

**Installation —** Press piston to bottom of bore using a suitable tool, install disc pads and retaining pins. Install "K" spring and "M" clip, making sure positions are not reversed. *See Fig. 2*. Install pad protector, making sure clips face outward.

Fig. 4  Installing Pad Retaining Clips on Front Disc Brakes of Challenger, Sapporo and Colt St. Wgn.

### FRONT DISC BRAKE CALIPER

**Removal (Arrow & Colt Exc. Colt St. Wgn.) —** Remove disc pads. Disconnect hydraulic line and remove bolts attaching caliper assembly to steering knuckle. Remove caliper assembly.

## ARROW, CHALLENGER, COLT & SAPPORO (Cont.)

**Installation** — Reverse removal procedure, tighten caliper mounting bolts evenly, and bleed hydraulic system.

**Removal (Challenger, Sapporo & Colt St. Wgn.)** — Remove disc pads. Pull out hose clip from strut area, then disconnect brake hose from caliper. Remove caliper.

**Installation** — To install, reverse removal procedure, tighten caliper mounting bolts evenly and bleed brake system.

### FRONT DISC BRAKE ROTOR

**Removal** — With caliper assembly removed, remove hub dust cap, cotter pin, lock nut, and adjustment nut. Pull hub and rotor assembly from spindle, taking care not to drop outer wheel bearing. Remove bolts attaching rotor to hub, then separate.

**Installation** — 1) To install, reverse removal procedure and tighten hub-to-rotor bolts evenly. Adjust wheel bearings.

**2)** Begin wheel bearing adjustment by tightening adjusting nut to 14.5 lbs. (.2 mkg) to seat all parts. Back off nut completely. Tighten adjusting nut again, this time to 3.6 ft. lbs. (.5 mkg). Install lock cap and cotter pin.

**NOTE** — *If cotter pin cannot be installed with nut properly adjusted, loosen nut until pin can be inserted. Nut should not be loosened more than 15°.*

### REAR DISC BRAKE PADS

**Removal (Challenger & Sapporo W/2600 cc Eng. & Colt St. Wgn.)** — 1) Raise and support vehicle. Remove rear wheels. Remove caliper assembly dust cover. Disconnect parking brake cable from caliper.

**2)** Remove retaining pin and pull out stopper plug. Remove caliper assembly from rotor. Pull pads from caliper support.

Groove Must be Positioned Here to Properly Install Pads

**Fig. 5   Positioning of Piston Stopper Groove on Rear Disc Brakes**

**Installation** — To install, reverse removal procedure and note the following: Press piston fully into caliper bore prior to pad installation. Ensure that groove in piston is positioned as shown in *Fig. 5* so that projection on back of pad will properly fit in groove. Ensure pad retaining clips are properly engaged.

### REAR DISC BRAKE CALIPER

**Removal (Challenger, Sapporo & Colt St. Wgn.)** — Remove disc pads. Pull out hose lip from axle housing and disconnect brake hose from caliper assembly. Remove clevis pin connecting lever assembly to parking brake cable. Remove caliper assembly.

**Installation** — To install, reverse removal procedure and bleed brake system.

### REAR DISC BRAKE ROTOR

**Removal (Challenger, Sapporo & Colt St. Wgn.)** — Remove disc pads. Remove caliper support-to-axle housing bolts. Remove caliper support. Remove rotor from axle shaft.

**Fig. 6   Exploded View of Rear Brake Assembly for Component Relationship**

# Brakes

B R A K E S

## ARROW, CHALLENGER, COLT & SAPPORO (Cont.)

**Installation** — To install, reverse removal procedure and tighten bolts evenly.

### REAR BRAKE SHOES

**Removal (Except Challenger, Sapporo & Colt St. Wgn.)** — 
**1)** Raise and support vehicle. Remove brake drum. Remove shoe hold-down springs. Disconnect strut-to-shoe spring and upper shoe return spring end from trailing shoe. Remove trailing shoe and lower return spring.

**2)** Hold adjuster latch down, Pull adjusting lever toward center of brake, and remove leading shoe assembly. Remove upper shoe return spring and strut-to-shoe spring.

**Installation** — Reverse removal procedure and note the following: Apply brake grease to all shoe contact points of backing plate, adjuster assembly, and wheel cylinder. Adjust amount of engagement of adjusting lever with strut only after pulling lever fully toward center of brake. Note that adjusting lever and latch spring differ between right and left sides.

### REAR WHEEL CYLINDER

**Removal** — With rear drum and brake shoes removed, disconnect hydraulic line from wheel cylinder at rear of backing plate, remove bolts attaching cylinder, and remove wheel cylinder.

**Installation** — Reverse removal procedure, tighten mounting bolts evenly, and bleed hydraulic system.

### MASTER CYLINDER

**Removal** — Disconnect brake lines from master cylinder. Depress brake pedal slowly several times to empty master cylinder housing of brake fluid. Separate master cylinder reservoir hoses from cylinder body. On models not equipped with power brakes, remove clevis bolt retaining master cylinder push rod to brake pedal. On all models, remove mounting hardware and lift off cylinder.

**Installation** — Reverse removal procedure, check and adjust pedal height, and bleed hydraulic system.

### POWER BRAKE UNIT

**NOTE** — *Before removal or overhaul test check valve. Pull off vacuum hose, place finger over check valve and crank engine; vacuum should be created.*

**Removal** — With master cylinder removed, disconnect vacuum hose from power brake unit. Remove clevis bolt retaining power unit operating rod to brake pedal. Remove mounting hardware and lift off power unit.

**Installation** — Reverse removal procedure and note the following: Apply a suitable sealer to power unit mounting surface and vacuum line connections. Adjust pedal height and bleed hydraulic system.

## OVERHAUL

### FRONT DISC BRAKE CALIPER

**Disassembly (Arrow & Colt Exc. Colt St. Wgn.)** — Remove caliper attaching bridge bolts. Separate outer and inner halves. Remove retaining ring and dust seal. Apply compressed air to fluid inlet to remove piston. Remove piston seal, but be careful not to damage caliper bore or seal groove.

*Fig. 7   Disassembled View of Disc Brake Caliper Used on Arrow and Colt (Exc. Colt St. Wgn.)*

**Cleaning & Inspection** — Clean all metal parts in trichloroethylene, alcohol, or brake fluid; clean piston seal in brake fluid or alcohol; clean dust seal and other rubber parts in alcohol only. Inspect caliper bore and piston for wear, damage or rust; replace parts as necessary.

**NOTE** — *Manufacturer recommends replacing piston seal and dust seal whenever piston has been removed.*

**Reassembly** — Reverse disassembly procedure and note the following: Apply rubber grease to piston seal and brake fluid to piston when reassembling. If torque plate was removed from inner caliper half, clean torque plate shaft and shaft bore in caliper, then apply special rubber grease to rubber bushing, wiper seal inner surface, and torque plate shaft before reassembly. Tighten bridge bolts of caliper halves evenly.

**NOTE** — *Possible cause of increased pedal stroke is: Insufficient fit between piston and piston seal. Correct by manually levering piston to seat several times. This will create a better fit between piston and seal. Make sure brake pad is removed during this procedure.*

**Disassembly (Challenger, Sapporo & Colt St. Wgn.)** — Remove dust boot. Force compressed air into fluid inlet to expel piston. Dig out piston seal, being careful not to gouge cylinder bore or caliper groove.

**Inspection** — Wash all components in suitable solution (clean brake fluid). Inspect cylinder and piston for obvious signs of

# Brakes

## ARROW, CHALLENGER, COLT & SAPPORO (Cont.)

wear or rust; replace worn parts. Always replace piston seal and dust boot.

**Reassembly** — Coat piston seal with suitable rubber grease. Slide seal into groove in cylinder bore. Slip piston into bore making sure seal is not twisted. Lightly coat dust seal groove with recommended rubber grease. Fit dust boot into place. Refit cylinder to caliper.

### REAR DISC BRAKE CALIPER

**Disassembly (Challenger & Sapporo W/2600 cc Eng.)** — 1) Remove cap ring and take off lever cap. See Fig. 9. Remove retaining ring and spring, then pull out lever assembly. Slightly rotate automatic adjuster spindle and pull out assembly.

**NOTE** — It may be necessary to use pliers to remove spindle.

**2)** Using suitable bearing remover tool (MB990665), pull bearings from caliper. Take off piston boot. Working through vacant area where automatic adjuster spindle has been removed, force piston out of caliper. Use a blunt tool to push out piston.

**3)** Dig out piston seal using a pointed tool. Be careful not to mar the cylinder bore or seal groove.

**Inspection** — 1) Wash all components in suitable solution (clean brake fluid). Inspect cylinder and piston for obvious signs of wear or rust; replace worn parts. Always replace piston seal, adjuster seal, and piston boot.

**Fig. 8   Exploded View of Front Disc Brake Caliper Used on Challenger, Sapporo & Colt St. Wgn.**

**Fig. 9   Exploded View of Rear Disc Brake Caliper Assembly Used on Challenger and Sapporo Models with 2600 cc Engine**

## ARROW, CHALLENGER, COLT & SAPPORO (Cont.)

**2)** Check bearings, connecting link, automatic adjuster spindle, and lever assembly for wear damage or rust. Make sure lever assembly does not have excessive play between shaft and bearing. Ensure clearance between automatic adjuster spindle and piston. Clearance should be .013-.017" (.33-.42 mm).

**Reassembly — 1)** Lightly coat piston seal and piston with lubricant. Slide piston and seal into place, ensuring seal does not twist in groove. Lubricate boot and slide boot into position making sure it engages groove in cylinder bore.

**2)** Using suitable bearing installation tool (MB990665), press in bearings until ends are flush with caliper body. Make sure mark on end of bearing faces out.

**3)** Coat automatic adjuster seal with recommended grease. Fit adjuster spindle and hardware in place until spindle turns freely. Make sure spring faces proper direction.

**4)** Press in connecting link spring washers. Special tool MB990666 may be helpful. Fit automatic adjuster spindle into place (spindle is not a press fit). Insert connecting link and lever assembly.

**5)** Fill lever cap with Niglube RX-2 (or equivalent), making sure all areas have significant amount of grease. Lightly grease stopper plug and caliper sliding surface. Assembly is ready for installation.

### MASTER CYLINDER

**Disassembly —** Remove dust boot, retaining ring, stop washer, and piston stop bolt, and withdraw primary piston assembly, secondary piston assembly, and secondary return spring from master cylinder. **NOTE** — *Do not disassemble primary piston assembly.* Remove check valve caps, tube seats, check valves, and check valve springs.

**Fig. 10 Disassembled View of Master Cylinder**

**Inspection —** Check master cylinder bore and piston for wear or other damage and replace as necessary. Check clearance between cylinder bore and piston; if clearance exceeds .006", replace parts as necessary. Check all parts of

secondary piston assembly; if any parts are found defective, replace complete secondary piston assembly.

**Reassembly —** Reverse disassembly procedure and note the following: Apply rubber grease to all parts (except boots) before reassembly. When assembled, check that return port is not blocked by piston cup when piston is located at return position.

### POWER BRAKE UNIT

**Disassembly — 1)** Hold front shell flange (master cylinder end of power unit) in a vice and remove clevis and lock nut. Scribe alignment mark on front and rear shells for reassembly reference. Holding neck of rear shell on both sides with pipes, remove rear shell by turning it counterclockwise. **NOTE** — *The diaphragm spring can be removed at the same time.* Remove diaphragm plate assembly from rear shell.

**2)** Using suitable driver, remove rear shell retainer and lift out bearing and valve body seal. Pull diaphragm from diaphragm plate assembly, then using a screwdriver, remove silencer retainer and lift out silencer and filter. Hold valve plunger, with key hole facing down and remove stop key by lightly pushing valve rod while shaking unit, then remove valve rod and plunger assembly. Remove reaction disc. **NOTE** — *Valve rod plunger assembly can not be disassembled.* Remove flange from front shell, then pull off plate and seal assembly.

**Cleaning & Inspection —** Thoroughly clean and dry each part. **NOTE** — *Cups and plastic parts must be wiped off only.* Inspect diaphragm plate for damage and cracks. **NOTE** — *Diaphragm plate is made of plastic and should be handled carefully at all times.* Check push rod for damage and straightness. Check front and rear shells for cracks, damage and deformation. Repair or replace any defective part.

**Reassembly — 1)** Apply a sufficient amount of silicone grease to the following parts (see illustration): Front shell seal and push rod sliding surfaces (A); push rod and seal contact surfaces (B); diaphragm lug-to-rear shell contacting surface (C); outside surface of reaction disc (D); reaction disc inserting part of diaphragm plate (E); rear shell seal and diaphragm plate sliding surfaces (F); interior of piston plate into which plunger assembly is inserted and seal sliding surfaces (G).

**Fig. 11 Lubricate at Points Indicated in Illustration**

# Brakes

## ARROW, CHALLENGER, COLT & SAPPORO (Cont.)

**2)** Install seal and bearing into rear shell, then press in retainer. Gently install valve rod and plunger, then install stop key with chamfered end toward piston side. **NOTE** — *After installing stop key, pull plunger assembly to ensure plunger is securely locked by stop key.* Install reaction disc and diaphragm in diaphragm plate assembly, then install silencer filter and silencer into rear of diaphragm plate and press in retainer.

**3)** Install diaphragm plate assembly into rear shell, then install valve body guard (rear end first) into end of seal retainer. Install rear shell into front shell, then install push rod and front shell flange. Align marks made at disassembly, then turn rear shell until its notch touches stopper fully. Check clearance between power unit push rod and master cylinder piston (see illustration); clearance should be .30" (7.6 mm) or less. If clearance is not to specifications, correct by adjusting push rod length. Install yoke onto threaded end of power unit operating rod.

Fig. 12  *Locations for Measuring Master Cylinder Rod-to-Piston Clearance*

### TIGHTENING SPECIFICATIONS

| Application | Ft. Lbs (mkg) |
|---|---|
| Master Cylinder | |
|   Check Valve Caps | 18-25 (2.5-3.5) |
|   Piston Stop Bolt | 1-2 (.14-.28) |
|   Retaining Nuts | 6-9 (.83-1.2) |
|   Hydraulic Lines | 9-12 (1.2-1.7) |
| Rotor-to-Hub Bolts | 25-29 (3.5-4.0) |
| Hydraulic Line-to-Caliper | 9-12 (1.2-1.7) |
| Wheel Cylinders & Bleeders | 4-7 (.55-.97) |
| Caliper | |
|   Adaptor (Front) | 29-36 (4.0-5.0) |
|   Torque Plate (Front) | 50-65 (8.0-9.0) |
|   Caliper Assembly (Rear) | 29-36 (4.0-5.0) |
|   Bridge Bolts (Caliper Halves, Front) | 58-69 (8.0-9.5) |

### BRAKE SYSTEM SPECIFICATIONS

| Application | Drum Diam. In. (mm) | Wheel Cylinder Diameter | | Master Cylinder Diameter In. (mm) |
|---|---|---|---|---|
| | | Front In. (mm) | Rear In. (mm) | |
| Arrow & Colt (Exc. Colt St. Wgn.) | 9 (229) | 2.012① (51.5) | .750 (19.1) | .815 (20.70) |
| Challenger & Sapporo Exc. with 2600 cc Eng. | 9 (229) | 2.000① (50.8) | .811 (20.59) | .813 (20.65) |
| All Others | ..... | 2.000① (50.8) | 1.375① (34.9) | .875 (22.2) |

① — Caliper bore diameter.

### BRAKE DRUM SPECIFICATIONS

| Application | Drum Diameter In. (mm) | Original Diameter In. (mm) | Maximum Refinish Diameter In. (mm) | Discard Diameter In. (mm) |
|---|---|---|---|---|
| All Models | 9 (229) | 9.000 (229) | ..... | 9.079 (230.6) |

## ARROW, CHALLENGER, COLT & SAPPORO (Cont.)

### DISC BRAKE ROTOR SPECIFICATIONS

| Application | Disc Diameter In. (mm) | Lateral Runout In. (mm) | Parallelism In. (mm) | Original Thickness In. (mm) | Minimum Refinish Thickness In. (mm) | Discard Thickness In. (mm) |
|---|---|---|---|---|---|---|
| Arrow & Colt (Exc. Colt St. Wgn.) | ..... | .006 (.15) | ..... | .507 (12.9) | ..... | .448 (11) |
| Challenger & Sapporo Exc. with 2600 cc Eng. | 7.87 (200) | .006 (.15) | ..... | .492 (12.5) | ..... | .433 (11) |
| All Others Front | .787 (200) | .006 (.15) | ..... | .492 (12.5) | ..... | .433 (11) |
| Rear | 8.07 (205) | .006 (.15) | ..... | .393 (10) | ..... | .330 (8.4) |

## AUDI 5000

**5000**

### DESCRIPTION

Brake system is hydraulically operated, utilizing a tandem master cylinder and dual diaphragm power brake unit. Front brakes consist of rotors attached to wheel hub and single piston floating calipers. A wear indicator mounts in the outboard brake pad and signals the need for pad replacement via a dashboard light. A pressure regulator mounted under the body is operated by a spring attached to the rear axle. Rear brakes are leading-trailing shoe/drum type, using a dual piston wheel cylinder. Parking brake is cable actuated, operating rear brake assembly.

### ADJUSTMENT

#### FRONT DISC BRAKES

Front disc brakes are self-adjusting, therefore, no adjustment is necessary.

#### REAR DRUM BRAKES

Raise and support rear of vehicle and release parking brake. Remove plug near wheel cylinder and tighten star adjuster with screwdriver until lining hits drum. Back off 6-8 teeth. Ensure that wheel can be turned by hand.

**NOTE** — *Due to residual pressure in brake regulator, right rear brake shoes might not fully release from drum. Before adjustments or brake drum removal, move lever on regulator toward rear axle to release pressure.*

#### PARKING BRAKE

Raise and support rear of vehicle and adjust rear brakes. Loosen adjusting nut at compensator bar. Lift lever to first ratchet stop, then tighten nut until neither wheel can be turned by hand. Release lever and ensure that both wheels rotate freely. Check operation of brake warning light.

#### BRAKE PRESSURE REGULATOR

**Checking & Adjusting** — **1)** If car is to be adjusted with weight off wheels, bounce rear of car several times and measure from top of rim to fender lip on both sides. Measurement must be made with trunk empty, gas tank full, and driver in car. Install spring tensioners and lift car. Remeasure to ensure rim-to-fender distance has not changed. Adjust tensioners if necessary.

**2)** If adjustment is made with weight on wheels, spring tensioners are not necessary. Press brake pedal firmly and release suddenly, checking that lever on brake pressure regulator moves.

**3)** Connect pressure gauges to left front and right rear wheels. Bleed pressure gauges. Apply pressure to pedal until front gauge reaches level indicated in specifications. Check rear pressure. Increase pressure and recheck readings.

**Brake Pressure Values**

| Front | Rear |
|---|---|
| 710 psi | 485-550 psi |
| 1420 psi | 810-880 psi |

**NOTE** — *DO NOT adjust brake pressure regulator when pressure is applied to brake pedal.*

**4)** If pressure is too high at rear axle, release spring tension by loosening bolt and moving toward front of car. If pressure is too low, loosen and move toward rear of car. Tighten bolt and recheck pressures. *See Fig. 1.*

**Fig. 1  Brake Pressure Regulator Adjustment**

#### HYDRAULIC SYSTEM BLEEDING

Fill master cylinder reservoir with brake fluid and maintain level throughout bleeding operation. Attach a hose to bleeder screw, and immerse opposite end in a container partially full of brake fluid. Open bleeder screw approximately one-half turn, depress brake pedal, close bleeder screw, and slowly return pedal. Continue operation until bubbles are no longer seen in discharged fluid. Bleeding sequence is right-rear, left-rear, right-front, left-front. When bleeding, push lever on regulator rearward.

### REMOVAL & INSTALLATION

#### FRONT DISC BRAKE PADS

**Removal** — **1)** Detach wear indicator wire at connector. Remove retaining clip and drive out retaining pins.

**2)** Pull out inner brake pad. Press floating frame and cylinder outward and remove outer brake pad. Remove wear indicator from hole in pad.

**Installation** — **1)** Press piston into caliper bore.

**NOTE** — *Fluid will rise in master cylinder reservoir. Siphon sufficient fluid to prevent overflowing.*

**2)** Position piston using 20° gauge (VW P84 or equiv.). Insert brake wear indicator in outboard pad and install pads.

## AUDI 5000 (Cont.)

**3)** Slide in retaining pins and install clip. Connect wear indicator wire. Pump brake pedal several times to position pads. Bleed hydraulic system if necessary.

### FRONT DISC BRAKE CALIPER

**Removal** – With wheel and tire removed, take out disc brake pads. Disconnect hydraulic line from caliper, Remove mounting bolts and take off caliper.

**Installation** –Reverse removal procedure to complete installation. Bleed hydraulic system.

### FRONT DISC BRAKE ROTOR

**Removal** – With wheel and tire removed, take off caliper. Do not disconnect hydraulic line unless necessary. Remove rotor carefully.

**Installation** – To install rotor assembly, reverse removal procedure. Bleed hydraulic system if necessary.

### REAR BRAKE DRUM

**Removal** – Raise and support vehicle. Remove wheel and tire assembly. Loosen brake adjuster and move brake pressure regulator lever toward rear axle. Pry off dust cap, remove cotter pin and hex nut. Remove drum, making sure retaining washer and bearing do not fall out.

**Installation** – To install, reverse removal procedure, adjust brakes and adjust wheel bearings.See *Wheel Bearing Adjustment* in *WHEEL ALIGNMENT Section.*

### REAR BRAKE SHOES

**Removal** – With brake drums removed, loosen parking brake cable adjusting nut. Remove return springs, shoe hold down

*Fig. 2  Front Disc Brake Assembly*

## AUDI 5000 (Cont.)

pins, springs and retainers. Remove brake shoes and disconnect parking brake cable.

**Installation** — To install, reverse removal procedure, noting the following: Grease adjuster threads. Ensure that brake shoes are correctly positioned on brake cylinder pistons.

### REAR BRAKE WHEEL CYLINDER

**Removal** — With drum and shoes removed, disconnect hydraulic line. Plug to prevent loss of fluid. Remove retaining screws and wheel cylinder.

**Installation** — Reverse removal procedure, adjust brakes and bleed hydraulic system.

### MASTER CYLINDER

**Removal** — Siphon fluid from master cylinder reservoir and remove hydraulic lines. Disconnect cylinder mounting nuts. Separate master cylinder from power unit.

### POWER BRAKE UNIT

**Removal** — Siphon fluid from master cylinder reservoir and remove hydraulic lines. Disconnect cylinder mounting nuts. Separate master cylinder from power unit.

**Installation** — To install, reverse removal procedure and note the following: Replace "O" ring between master cylinder and power unit. Replace filter on power unit before inserting into firewall. Bleed hydraulic system.

**NOTE** — *Clevis and brake lever each have two holes. Install clevis pin only in holes closest to front of car.*

**Check Valve** — Large diameter side fits into power unit. To test, remove vacuum line and check valve. Blow into large diameter hole — valve should open. In the other direction, valve must close. Replace as necessary.

**Installation** — Replace "O" ring seal between master cylinder and power brake unit. Reverse removal procedure and bleed hydraulic system.

*Fig. 3   Rear Drum Brake Assembly*

# Brakes

## AUDI 5000 (Cont.)

### OVERHAUL

#### FRONT DISC BRAKE CALIPER

**Disassembly** — Remove disc brake pads and wear indicator. Push brake caliper mounting frame off floating frame. Pry out circlip and remove dust seal by hand. Place a small block of wood in floating frame and remove piston by applying compressed air to fluid inlet. Remove seal from caliper bore using plastic or wood rod.

**Cleaning & Inspection** — Clean all parts in alcohol only. Check cylinder bore and piston for damage. Parts are serviced by replacement only.

**Reassembly** — Coat all parts with ATE brake cylinder paste (or equivalent), reverse disassembly procedure and note the following: Use new seals, dust boots and retaining rings when reassembling. Make sure machined surface of piston face makes a 20° angle to wall of caliper bore. Install disc pads after caliper has been installed on vehicle.

*Fig. 4  Master Cylinder Component Relationship*

## AUDI 5000 (Cont.)

### REAR WHEEL CYLINDER

**Disassembly** — Thoroughly clean outside of cylinder. Remove end boots, piston and seal assemblies and spring. Remove dust cap and bleeder screw.

**Cleaning & Inspection** — Clean all parts in alcohol only. Check all parts for rust, corrosion or wear. If necessary, replace complete cylinder.

**Reassembly** — Reverse disassembly procedure and note the following: Use all new rubber parts. Apply a thin coat of brake cylinder paste to all parts during assembly.

### MASTER CYLINDER

**Disassembly** — Thoroughly clean outside of master cylinder. Remove hydraulic fluid reservoir, stop screw and circlip. Withdraw primary and secondary piston assemblies. Disassemble piston assemblies.

**Cleaning & Inspection** — Clean all parts in alcohol only. Dry with compressed air and check that all passages are free from obstruction. Check cylinder bore for rust, corrosion or other damage. Inspect bore and piston for wear. Replace complete if necessary.

**Reassembly** — Reverse disassembly procedure and note the following: Lubricate primary piston shaft with silicone grease supplied with kit. Replace all rubber parts. Coat all other parts with brake cylinder paste. See Fig. 4.

### POWER BRAKE UNIT

Manufacturer does not recommend overhaul of power brake unit.

| TIGHTENING SPECIFICATIONS | |
|---|---|
| **Application** | **Ft. Lbs. (mkg)** |
| Caliper-to-Frame | 68-75 (9.5-10.5) |
| Master Cylinder-to-Power Unit | 18 (2.5) |
| Power Unit-to-Firewall | 18 (2.5) |

| BRAKE DRUM SPECIFICATIONS | | | | |
|---|---|---|---|---|
| Application | Drum Diameter In. (mm) | Original Diameter In. (mm) | Maximum Refinish Diameter In. (mm) | Discard Diameter In. (mm) |
| Audi 5000 | 9.005 (230) | 9.005 (230) | 9.094 (231) | 9.135 (232) |

| DISC BRAKE ROTOR SPECIFICATIONS | | | | | | |
|---|---|---|---|---|---|---|
| Application | Disc Diameter In. (mm) | Lateral Runout In. (mm) | Parallelism In. (mm) | Original Thickness In. (mm) | Minimum Refinish Thickness In. (mm) | Discard Thickness In. (mm) |
| Audi 5000 | 10.157 (258) | .004 (.1) | .0008 (.02) | .866 (22) | ..... | .807 (20.5) |

## AUDI FOX

Fox

# DESCRIPTION

Brake system is hydraulically operated using a tandem master cylinder in conjunction with a power booster unit. This year the booster diameter has been increased to 9". Front disc brakes have been changed to Girling type. Rear brakes are leading-trailing, shoe/drum type. Rear brakes use dual piston wheel cylinders. Parking brake is cable operated and works on secondary shoes of rear brakes. A pressure regulator valve is used in the hydraulic circuit to prevent premature rear wheel lock-up.

# ADJUSTMENT

## FRONT DISC BRAKE PADS

Front disc brakes are self-adjusting, therefore, no adjustment in service is required.

## REAR DRUM BRAKE SHOES

NOTE — *In order to rotate right rear wheel it may be necessary to relieve residual brake pressure. Push lever on brake pressure regulator in direction of rear axle.*

Raise and support rear of vehicle, release parking brake. Use a brake spoon, tighten rear star adjuster until wheel can no longer be turned by hand. Loosen star until wheels are just free to turn.

## PARKING BRAKE

With rear brake shoes properly adjusted, pull parking brake handle to second notch. Tighten parking brake adjusting nut until rear wheels can just be turned by hand, then tighten lock nut. Release handle and ensure both rear wheels rotate freely.

## PRESSURE REGULATOR VALVE

1) Remove everything from luggage compartment. Fill fuel tank. Load drivers seat with about 165 lbs. Bounce vehicle several times and allow to settle normally.

2) Measure distance from top of tire to lower edge of fender lip. Make measurement on both sides. If a hoist type lift is being used, install spring tensioners under shock absorbers and at top to frame. Tensioners will hold vehicle in settled position.

3) Connect 1 1500 psi minimum pressure gauge to right rear wheel cylinder and connect another to left front brake caliper. Bleed gauges.

4) Pump pedal several times. Depress pedal until front wheel gauge reads 710 psi. Check rear wheel gauge for pressure or 440-497 psi.

5) Continue to depress pedal until front gauge reads 1400 psi. Rear gauge must read 753-810 psi.

NOTE — *Do not adjust spring tension with brake pedal depressed.*

6) If both pressures in test were too high on rear wheel, loosen regulator clamp bolt and REDUCE spring tension. If both pressures were consistently low, INCREASE spring tension. If correct specifications cannot be obtained by adjusting spring tension, replace pressure regulator.

## HYDRAULIC SYSTEM BLEEDING

NOTE — *When bleeding brake system push lever on brake pressure regulator in direction of rear axle to relieve residual pressure.*

Fill master cylinder reservoir with brake fluid and maintain level throughout bleeding operation. Attach a hose to bleeder screw, and immerse opposite end in a container partially full of brake fluid. Open bleeder screw approximately one-half turn, depress brake pedal, close bleeder screw, and slowly return pedal. Continue operation until air bubbles are no longer seen in discharged fluid. Bleeding sequence is right-rear, left-rear, right-front, left-front.

# REMOVAL & INSTALLATION

## FRONT DISC BRAKE PADS

**Removal** — 1) Raise vehicle and place on safety stands. Remove front wheel. Using hand pressure force caliper to slide outward (toward outer wheel bearing). This forces piston into cylinder housing. Some brake fluid may need to be syphoned out of reservoir during this procedure.

2) Take an open end wrench and hold guide pin head while removing lower mounting bolt. See *Fig. 2*. Rotate caliper cylinder upward. Take out disc pads.

**Installation** — 1) Clean area where pads rest. Make sure grommets on guide pins are not damaged. Guide pins must slide smoothly in housing. Install brake pads. Swing caliper housing down.

2) Make sure pads do not hit piston; force piston deeper into housing if necessary. Tighten lower mounting bolt. Depress brake pedal several times to seat pads against rotor.

## FRONT DISC BRAKE CALIPER

**Removal** — Raise and support vehicle. Remove wheel. Disconnect brake line from caliper and plug opening to prevent entry of dirt and foreign matter. Bend back locking tabs (if equipped) on mounting bolts. Remove caliper mounting bolts and take off caliper assembly.

**Installation** — Reverse removal procedure and bleed hydraulic system.

## FRONT DISC BRAKE ROTOR

**Removal** — With wheel and tire assembly removed, remove caliper. NOTE — *Do not disconnect hydraulic line unless necessary.* Remove screw securing rotor to wheel hub and withdraw rotor.

**Installation** — Reverse removal procedure and bleed hydraulic system if necessary.

## REAR BRAKE DRUM

**Removal** — Pry off grease cap. Remove cotter pin, castle nut, hex nut, and washer. Pull off brake drum making sure that inner race of outer bearing is not lost.

**Installation** — Reverse removal procedure, adjust brake shoes, and adjust wheel bearings. See *Wheel Bearing Adjustment in WHEEL ALIGNMENT Section.*

## REAR BRAKE SHOES

**Removal** — 1) With brake drum removed, disconnect lower return spring by disengaging it from primary shoe. Remove primary shoe upper return spring. Remove hold-down clip and

# Brakes

## AUDI FOX (Cont.)

pin and take off primary shoe. Slide out brake shoe adjustment mechanism.

**2)** Disconnect parking brake cable from secondary shoe. Disengage upper and lower return springs. Take off hold-down clip and pin. Slide off secondary shoe.

**Installation** — To install, reverse removal procedure. Make sure brake shoes fully engage wheel cylinder and that all return springs lock into place.

**Fig. 1  Exploded View of Rear Brake Assy.**

### REAR BRAKE WHEEL CYLINDER

**Removal** — Remove brake shoes as previously outlined. Disconnect brake fluid line. Plug opening in line. Remove bolts attaching wheel cylinder to backing plate.

**Installation** — To install, reverse removal procedure and bleed brake system.

### MASTER CYLINDER

**Removal** — Siphon brake fluid from master cylinder reservoir. Disconnect hydraulic lines at cylinder, remove nuts attaching master cylinder to power unit, and remove master cylinder.

**Installation** — Reverse removal procedure and note the following: Make sure "O" ring is installed between master cylinder and power unit. After installing master cylinder, bleed hydraulic system.

## OVERHAUL

### FRONT DISC BRAKE CALIPER

**Disassembly** — **1)** Remove caliper and clean outside surfaces. Remove both cylinder housing mounting bolts. Place a block of wood between piston and housing. Blow compressed air into cylinder housing to dislodge piston.

**2)** Remove dust seal. Using a plastic instrument, carefully dig piston seal from groove in cylinder housing.

**Inspection** — Check housing and piston. Housing can not be honed. Replace housing and cylinder in sets. Boots, guide pins, and miscellaneous pieces are only available with new pad carrier.

**Reassembly** — Coat piston, cylinder bore, and new seal with suitable brake paste. Fit seal into cylinder. Slide dust seal onto piston. Slowly insert piston into cylinder fitting inner lip of dust seal into cylinder housing groove. Fully seat piston into cylinder. Engage outer lip of dust seal into groove of piston.

**Fig. 2  Audi Fox Disc Brake Caliper Assy.**

### REAR BRAKE WHEEL CYLINDER

**Disassembly** — Remove rubber dust caps, then withdraw front and rear piston and seal assemblies. Remove seals from pistons. Remove bleeder screw and dust cap.

**Cleaning & Inspection** — Thoroughly clean all components in alcohol. Inspect cylinder and pistons for rust, corrosion, or scoring; replace parts as necessary. **NOTE** — *Manufacturer recommends replacing all rubber parts whenever cylinder has been disassembled.*

**Reassembly** — Reverse disassembly procedure and note the following: Refer to *Fig. 3* for correct installation position of wheel cylinder pistons.

**Fig. 3  Exploded View of Rear Wheel Cylinder**

## AUDI FOX (Cont.)

Plug
Coat With Brake Fluid

Stop Screw
Remove Before Detaching Circlip

Brake Master Cylinder Housing

Seal

Seal

Brake Light Switch

Pressure Valves

Return Spring
Do Not Interchange
With Primary Return Spring

Spring Seat

Primary Cup

Washer

Secondary Piston

Secondary Cups
Insert With Sealing Lips
Facing Opposite Directions

Stop Sleeve

Stroke Limiting Screw

Primary Return Spring

Spring Seat

Primary Cup

Washer

Primary Piston

Plastic Washer

Washer

Secondary Cups
Always Replace With Sealing
Lip Pointing Toward Cylinder

Circlip

*Fig. 4  Exploded View of Fox Master Cylinder*

## MASTER CYLINDER

**Disassembly** — Remove "O" ring from master cylinder housing. Remove retaining ring and loosen piston stop screw, then remove both pistons from housing. Remove pressure valves and reservoir from master cylinder housing. Disassemble piston assemblies as necessary.

**Cleaning & Inspection** — Clean all parts in alcohol and check for rust, corrosion, or other damage; replace parts as necessary. Make sure compensating and filler holes are not plugged.

**Reassembly** — Reverse disassembly procedure and note the following: Make sure pressure and intermediate piston cups are installed correctly. *See Fig. 4.* Use new "O" ring on master cylinder between cylinder and power unit.

## POWER BRAKE UNIT

**NOTE** — *No information available for Overhaul of power brake unit.*

## TIGHTENING SPECIFICATIONS

| Application | Ft. Lbs. (mkg) |
| --- | --- |
| Caliper Mounting Bolts | 25 (3.5) |
| Backing Plate Mounting Bolts | 47 (6.5) |

# Brakes

## AUDI FOX (Cont.)

### DISC BRAKE ROTOR SPECIFICATIONS

| Application | Disc Diameter In. (mm) | Lateral Runout In. (mm) | Parallelism In. (mm) | Original Thickness In. (mm) | Minimum Refinish Thickness In. (mm) | Discard Thickness In. (mm) |
|---|---|---|---|---|---|---|
| Fox (Front) | ..... | .0023 (.06) | .0008 (.02) | .470 (12) | .413 (10.5) | .393 (10) |

### BRAKE DRUM SPECIFICATIONS

| Application | Drum Diameter In. (mm) | Original Diameter In. (mm) | Maximum Refinish Diameter In. (mm) | Discard Diameter In. (mm) |
|---|---|---|---|---|
| Fox (Rear) | 7.87 (200) | 7.87 (200) | 7.89 (200.5) | 7.91 (201) |

## BMW

320i
530i
633CSi
733i

## DESCRIPTION

Brake system is hydraulically operated. System uses both a tandem master cylinder and a power brake unit. 530i, 633CSi, and 733i models have 4 piston ATE front disc brake calipers and 2 piston ATE rear disc brake calipers. 320i models are equipped with 2 piston ATE front disc brake calipers and drum rear brakes. Parking brake is lever actuated and cable operated. On 530i, 633CSi, and 733i models only, parking brake shoes work against a drum machined in rear disc brake rotor. Some models are equipped with pressure regulator to reduce line pressure to rear brakes. All models are also fitted with disc pad wear indicators.

## ADJUSTMENT

### DISC PADS

Front and rear disc brake assemblies are self-adjusting; therefore, no adjustment in service is required.

### REAR DRUM BRAKES

**320i** — Raise vehicle. Release parking brake. Using special tool 34 2 000 (or equivalent wrench), tighten brake shoes by turning left cam counterclockwise and right cam clockwise. Loosen cam ⅛ turn or until wheel is just free to turn.

### PARKING BRAKE

**Except 320i** — 1) Release parking brake lever. Raise and support vehicle. Remove rear wheels. Insert a brake adjusting tool through inspection hole in rotor. Turn adjuster until rotor can no longer be turned by hand. Back off adjuster 2 or 3 teeth.

2) Work inside driver compartment, tighten adjustment nuts on lever until parking brake holds vehicle securely before fifth ratchet stop is reached.

**320i** — 1) Raise and support rear of vehicle. Fully release parking brake. Tighten brake shoes until wheel is locked. Back off adjusters about ⅛ turn or until wheel can just barely turn.

2) Work inside drivers compartment and tighten nuts on lever until parking brake holds vehicle securely before fifth ratchet stop is reached.

### BRAKE SYSTEM BLEEDING

**NOTE** — *BMW recommends replacing brake fluid in entire system once a year to avoid moisture build-up.*

**CAUTION** — *Follow tool manufacturer's instructions when using pressure bleeder.*

Raise and support vehicle. Remove wheels. Attach a bleeder hose to bleeder screw and immerse opposite end of hose in a container. Open bleeder screw and allow air to escape from system, then close bleeder. Continue operation until all air is bled from system.

**NOTE** — *On 530i and 633CSi models only, bleed lower inboard screw before bleeding lower outboard screw on front brakes.*

## REMOVAL & INSTALLATION

### DISC PADS

**Removal** — Raise and support vehicle. Remove wheels. Disconnect pad wear sensors. Drive out retaining pin toward inside of vehicle. Remove cross spring. Using an extractor tool, remove disc pads from caliper. If disc pad thickness has worn to .080" (2 mm), replace pads. Only replace pads in matched sets.

**Installation** — 1) Using a cylinder brush, clean guide surface and support surface in caliper. Siphon sufficient fluid from master cylinder reservoir to prevent overflowing, then press pistons to bottom of bores.

2) On rear two piston calipers, ensure machined postion of piston face makes a 20° angle to lower caliper wall. Install disc pads, cross spring, and retaining pins. After installation, depress brake pedal several times to position pads against rotor.

*Fig. 1  Piston Alignment for Dual Piston Calipers*

### CALIPER ASSEMBLY

**Removal** — Drain brake fluid from master cylinder reservoir. Remove caliper mounting bolts. Disconnect disc pad wear indicator electrical lead. Disconnect brake fluid inlet lines. Lift caliper off rotor.

**Installation** — Reverse removal procedure and bleed hydraulic system.

### ROTOR

**Removal: 530i; Front with Wheel Nuts** — With caliper assembly removed, remove hub grease cap, cotter pin, and nut. Remove hub and rotor assembly. Remove Allen head bolts retaining rotor to hub, then remove rotor.

**NOTE** — *Both brake rotors must be replaced at same time.*

## BMW (Cont.)

**Installation** — To install, reverse removal procedure. Tighten all bolts and fittings evenly. Bleed hydraulic system if necessary. Adjust front wheel bearings. *See Wheel Bearing Adjustment in WHEEL ALIGNMENT Section.*

**Removal: 320i, 530i with Wheel Bolts, 633CSi, 733i; Front** — Raise and support front of vehicle. Separate bracket from strut. Remove caliper and tie out of way with brake line still connected. Remove mounting bolt from hub and take off rotor.

**NOTE** — *Inboard vented brake discs are balanced, DO NOT move or replace balance clips.*

**Installation** — To install, reverse removal procedure.

**Removal: 503i, 633CSi, 733i; Rear** — Raise and support vehicle on safety stands. Remove tire and wheel. Remove caliper and support out of way. Brake line can stay connected. Slip brake line out of clamp. Take out mounting bolt and remove brake rotor.

**NOTE** — *Both rotors must be replaced at same time. Also, inboard vented brake discs are balanced, DO NOT move or replace balance clips.*

**Installation** — To install, reverse removal procedure.

### PARKING BRAKE SHOES

**Removal** — With rear caliper and rotor removed, disconnect lower return spring using brake spring pliers. Turn retaining springs 90° using removal tool, then set spring aside. Pull brake shoes apart at bottom and lift upward.

**Installation** — Reverse removal procedure and adjust parking brake shoes and cables.

### BRAKE DRUM

**Removal & Installation: 320i; Rear** — Loosen brake adjuster cams. Remove countersunk Allen bolt and slide off brake drum. To install, reverse removal procedure and note: If one brake drum is reground, drum on other side must also be machined.

### BRAKE SHOES

**Removal: 320i; Rear** — Remove brake drum. Disengage mounting spring, retainer, and pin from each shoe. Disconnect bottom return spring. Pull shoes apart and out of wheel cylinder. Disconnect parking brake cable and remove brake shoes. If brake shoe lining has worn to .118" (3.0 mm) or less, replace brake shoes.

**Installation** — Reverse removal procedure and note: Connect long end of spring between parking brake lever and brake shoe.

### WHEEL CYLINDER

**Removal: 320i; Rear** — Remove brake drum. Disconnect brake fluid inlet line. Remove wheel cylinder bleeder valve. Remove cylinder mounting bolts and take off cylinder being careful not to drop brake fluid on brake shoes.

*Fig. 2   Exploded View of 320i Rear Wheel Cylinder*

**Installation** — To install, reverse removal procedure and make sure to bleed brake system.

### MASTER CYLINDER

**NOTE** — *On 320i models only, mixture control unit must be removed to take off master cylinder.*

**Removal** — 1) Siphon off brake fluid from reservoir. On 320i models, disconnect clutch hose connection. On 633CSi models, remove air cleaner. On 530i models there is a relay holder that must be freed and layed out of way with components still attached.

2) Disconnect all hydraulic lines from master cylinder. Remove nuts mounting master cylinder to power booster. On 320i models, remove nuts mounting master cylinder support to inner fender panel. Remove support and master cylinder.

**Installation** — To install, reverse removal procedure and note: Make sure "O" ring on master cylinder is not damaged. An imperfect fit will not allow correct vacuum build-up.

### POWER BRAKE UNIT

**NOTE** — *Mixture control unit must be removed to take off power brake unit (with master cylinder).*

**Removal: 320i** — 1) Remove air intake ducting. Remove 3 screws located in top of control unit. Spread open cable clips. Remove wire holder. Lift up mixture control unit and retain piston with fingers until it can be tapped into place. Disconnect remaining vacuum lines. Remove unit mounting nuts and lift off unit.

# Brakes

7-23

## BMW (Cont.)

**2)** Siphon out brake fluid from reservoir. Disconnect push rod from brake pedal. Separate hydraulic lines from master cylinder. Also, disconnect clutch hose.

**3)** Disconnect vacuum hose from brake unit. Remove brake unit mounting nuts and bolts. Separate master cylinder support from inner fender panel. Slide master cylinder and power brake assembly from vehicle.

**Installation** – To install master cylinder and power brake assembly as a unit, reverse removal procedure.

**NOTE** – *On 733i models only, power steering pump also supplies hydraulic pressure through hydraulic accumulator to the power brake unit. If power steering fails, there will be sufficient pressure in the hydraulic accumulator to provide a few brake applications with full power.*

**Removal: 530i, 633CSi, 733i** – **1)** Drain off brake fluid from master cylinder reservoir and/or cylinder body. On 530i and 733i models, remove lower left trim panel. On all models, disconnect push rod from brake pedal.

**2)** On 530i models only, there is a relay holder that must be freeded and layed out of way with components still attached. Disconnect and plug master cylinder hydraulic lines. On 733i models only, disconnect hydraulic lines from power unit. Remove master cylinder/power brake unit as an assembly after removing power unit mounting bolts.

**Fig. 3   Disassembled View of Dual Piston Rear Disc Brake Caliper Used on 530i, 633CSi and 733i Models. Front Caliper for 320i Models is Similar**

**Fig. 4   Exploded View of Rear Drum Brake Assembly Used on BMW 320i Models. See Note on Illustration.**

## BMW (Cont.)

**Installation** — To install brake unit with master cylinder connected, reverse removal procedure. Bleed brake system after assembly is installed.

**Check Valve Replacement (Exc. 733i)** — Check valve is located in power unit vacuum line at intake manifold. To remove, loosen hose clamps, remove vacuum lines, and remove valve. To install, reverse removal procedure. Make sure arrow or black portion of valve faces intake manifold.

**Filter Replacement (Exc. 733i)** — With power brake unit removed from vehicle, pull back rubber dust boot. Remove retaining ring. Remove silencer and filter. To install, reverse removal procedure.

# OVERHAUL

## BRAKE CALIPER

**Disassembly** — With caliper removed from vehicle and disc pads removed from caliper, remove clamping rings and rubber protecting caps. Hold one piston in place using a suitable clamp, insert a piece of wood in caliper cavity, then apply

**Reassembly** — Reassemble caliper (if separated) using new seals and expansion bolts. Tighten expansion bolts from inside out. Coat pistons and caliper bores with ATE brake cylinder paste (or equivalent), install sealing rings, then install pistons into bores. Make sure pistons are not tilted when inserting. On two piston calipers, make sure machined surface of piston face makes a 20° angle to lower caliper wall. Install rubber protecting caps and clamp rings.

## MASTER CYLINDER

**NOTE** — All master cylinders are similar, procedures outlined are general.

**Disassembly** — Push in on primary piston and remove secondary piston stop screw. Remove snap ring from end of cylinder and remove primary and secondary piston assemblies and return spring. Disassemble piston assemblies noting number and position of parts used.

**Cleaning & Inspection** — Clean all parts in alcohol and inspect for wear or damage. **NOTE** — Cylinders with surface defects in bores must be replaced; do not overhaul.

*Fig. 6   Master Cylinder Primary Piston Assembly*

**Reassembly** — Reassemble piston assemblies using thin coating of ATE brake paste. Install piston assemblies into cylinder bore using a suitable guide sleeve (BMW 34 3 000) to prevent damaging seals. Install secondary piston stop screw, making sure that piston is pushed fully forward before screw is installed and tightened. Install retaining ring in end of master cylinder bore.

*Fig. 5   4 Piston Front Disc Brake Caliper Assy.
Used on 530i, 633CSi, and 733i Models*

*Fig. 7   Master Cylinder Secondary (Front) Piston Assy.*

## BMW (Cont.)

### TIGHTENING SPECIFICATIONS

| Application | Ft. Lbs. (mkg) |
|---|---|
| Caliper Mounting Bolts | |
| Front | 58-69 (8.0-9.5) |
| Rear | 43-48 (6.0-6.7) |
| Rotor-to-Wheel Hub | |
| 320i & 633CSi | 3.0-3.5 (.4-.5) |
| 530i | |
| 6 mm Bolts | 3.0-3.5 (.4-.5) |
| 8mm Bolts | 11-13 (1.5-1.8) |
| 733i | 23-24 (3.2-3.3) |
| Brake Line-to-Caliper | 9-12 (1.3-1.6) |
| Master Cylinder-to-Power Unit | |
| 320i | 12-14 (.16-2.0) |
| 530i | 15-18 (2.1-2.5) |
| 633CSi | 16-21 (2.1-2.9) |
| 733i | 12-18 (1.7-2.5) |
| Power Brake Unit-to-Mounting | 16-17 (2.2-2.4) |

### DISC BRAKE ROTOR SPECIFICATIONS

| Application | Disc Diameter In. (mm) | Lateral Runout In. (mm) | Parallelism In. (mm) | ③ Original Thickness In. (mm) | Minimum Refinish Thickness In. (mm) | Discard Thickness In. (mm) |
|---|---|---|---|---|---|---|
| 320i | | | | | | |
| Front | 10.040① (255) | .008② (.2) | .0008 (.02) | .866 (22) | ..... | .827 (21) |
| 530i | | | | | | |
| Front | 11.024① (280) | .008② (.2) | .0008 (.02) | .866 (22) | ..... | .827 (21) |
| Rear | 10.708① (272) | .008② (.2) | .0008 (.02) | .374 (9.5) | ..... | .334 (8.5) |
| 633CSi | | | | | | |
| Front | 11.024① (280) | .008② (.2) | ..... | .866 (22) | ..... | .827 (21) |
| Rear | 10.708① (272) | .008② (.2) | ..... | .748 (19) | ..... | .709 (18) |
| 733i | | | | | | |
| Front | 11.024① (280) | .006② (1.5) | ..... | .866 (22) | ..... | .827 (21) |
| Rear | 11.024① (280) | .006② (1.5) | ..... | .394 (10) | ..... | .354 (9) |

① − ±.008" (.2 mm).
② − Installed on vehicle.
③ − Machining of each braking surface is .020" (.5 mm). Minimum rotor thickness must be observed.

### BRAKE SYSTEM SPECIFICATIONS

| Application | Drum Diam. In. (mm) | Wheel Cylinder Diameter | | Master Cylinder Diameter In. (mm) |
|---|---|---|---|---|
| | | Front In. (mm) | Rear In. (mm) | |
| 320i | 9.842① (250) | 1.890② (48) | .750 (19.05) | ..... |
| 530i & 630CSi | 6.300③ (16) | 1.575② (40) | 1.652② (42) | ....... |
| 733i | 6.300③ (160) | 1.575 (40) | 1.29 (33) | ..... |

① − Rear
② − Piston Diameter
③ − Parking brake inside diameter.

## CAPRI

**Capri**

### DESCRIPTION

The brake system is hydraulically operated, utilizing a tandem master cylinder and a power brake unit. Front disc brakes consist of rotors attached to wheel hubs, and dual piston floating caliper assemblies. Rear brakes are leading-trailing shoe/drum type, using dual piston wheel cylinders. A combination valve is used to distribute correct pressure to each rear brake wheel cylinder. Parking brake system is cable and rod operated, acting on rear brake assemblies.

### ADJUSTMENT

#### FRONT DISC BRAKE PADS

Front disc brakes are self-adjusting; therefore, no adjustment in service is required.

#### REAR BRAKE SHOES

Rear drum brakes are self-adjusting (actuated by parking brake linkage); therefore, no adjustment in service is required.

#### PARKING BRAKE LINKAGE

**NOTE** — *It should only be necessary to adjust parking brake system in the event of wear on linkage components or replacement of parts. DO NOT adjust for rear brake wear.*

Ensure parking brake is fully released, then raise and support vehicle. To adjust primary cable, engage keyed sleeve (A) into abutment slot (B), then turn adjuster nut (C) until all slack is removed from cable. Parking brake is properly adjusted when clearance between parking brake lever stop and brake backing plate is .039-.059" (1.0-1.5 mm).

#### COMBINATION VALVE

**Warning Light Test** — 1) Turn ignition switch to on position and set parking brake, warning light should be on. If there is no light, electrical problem is indicated.

2) Release parking brake and operate pedal a few times; light should not work. If light comes on, hydraulic problem is indicated.

**NOTE** — *Piston in combination valve is self-centering.*

#### BLEEDING HYDRAULIC SYSTEM

1) Fill master cylinder reservoir with brake fluid and maintain level throughout bleeding operation. **NOTE** — *Piston in combination valve is self-centering and does not need to be held in central position while brakes are being bled.* Attach a hose to right front brake bleeder screw and immerse opposite end in a container partially full of brake fluid.

2) Open bleeder screw approximately one-half turn, depress brake pedal fully, then allow it to return to its off position. Continue depressing brake pedal, pausing after each return stroke to allow full recuperation of master cylinder, until fluid entering container is clean and free from air bubbles. Press brake pedal to the floor and hold it there while bleeder screw is tightened. Repeat operation on remaining brakes in the following sequence: left front, left rear and right rear.

**Fig. 1  Parking Brake Adjustment Points**

### REMOVAL & INSTALLATION

#### FRONT DISC BRAKE PADS

**Removal** — Remove retaining pin clips and pins. Lift-out brake pads, tension springs and shim, (if equipped). **NOTE** — *Clean any foreign matter from rotor. Ensure new pads are correct.*

**Fig. 2  Exploded View of Front Disc Brake Assy.**

## CAPRI (Cont.)

**Installation** — Press pistons to bottom of caliper bores. **NOTE** — *Siphon sufficient fluid from master cylinder to prevent overflowing when pistons are pressed back into bores.* Place tension springs on brake pads and shims, then install pads and shims into caliper assembly with arrow on shims pointing up. Install retaining pins and secure with pin clips. Pump brake pedal several times to position pads against rotor.

### FRONT DISC BRAKE CALIPER

**Removal** — With disc pads removed from caliper, disconnect hydraulic line from caliper and plug openings. Bend up lock tabs, remove caliper retaining bolts, and detach caliper assembly.

**Installation** — Position caliper on steering knuckle, install new lock tabs, then install and tighten retaining bolts. Install disc pads and bleed hydraulic system.

### FRONT DISC BRAKE ROTOR

**Removal** — With caliper assembly removed, remove dust cap, cotter pin, adjusting nut, thrust washer, and outer bearing. Remove hub and rotor assembly, bend back lock tabs, remove attaching bolts, and separate rotor from hub. Discard lock tabs and bolts.

**Installation** — Thoroughly clean mating surfaces of hub and rotor, position rotor on hub aligning mating marks, and install and tighten lock tabs and retaining bolts. To complete installation, reverse removal procedure, tighten all bolts evenly and adjust wheel bearings. *See Wheel Bearing Adjustment in WHEEL ALIGNMENT Section.*

### REAR BRAKE SHOES

**Removal** — Raise and support vehicle and remove rear wheels. Ensure parking brake is fully released, then remove brake drum. Remove brake shoe hold down springs and pins, then pull shoes from bottom guides and remove lower spring. Pull primary shoe from wheel cylinder slot and self-adjuster arm, then undo spring and remove shoe. Unhook secondary shoe from parking brake lever, disconnect spring and remove shoe.

**Installation** — Hook spring and parking brake lever to secondary shoe. Connect upper spring to both shoes and position primary shoe over self-adjuster arm. Connect lower spring to shoes, then install lower end of shoes into guides. Install hold down springs and pins. Ensure brakes are centered and install brake drum.

### REAR BRAKE WHEEL CYLINDER

**Removal** — Remove wheel, drum and brake shoe assemblies. Ensure there is no vacuum in booster system, then disconnect brake line from wheel cylinder. Remove wheel cylinder attaching bolts and lock washers and remove cylinder.

**Installation** — Place wheel cylinder into position, then connect brake line to cylinder and tighten fitting finger tight. Install and tighten cylinder attaching bolts with lock washers,

then tighten brake line fitting. Install links in ends of cylinder, then install shoe and adjuster assemblies. Install brake drum and bleed hydraulic system.

**Fig. 3   Assembled View of Rear Drum Brake Components**

### MASTER CYLINDER

**Removal** — Siphon fluid from reservoir, then disconnect hydraulic lines from master cylinder. Remove master cylinder-to-booster attachings nuts, then lift master cylinder from booster using care not to damage vacuum seal.

**Installation** — Position master cylinder and fluid seal onto push rod and start all brake line union nuts. Connect master cylinder to booster and tighten attaching nuts. Tighten brake line union nuts and fill master cylinder with brake fluid. Bleed hydraulic system and check operation of brakes.

### POWER BRAKE UNIT

**Removal** — Disconnect power unit push rod from brake pedal. Remove nuts retaining master cylinder to power unit and position master cylinder out of way. Remove vacuum hose from power unit, power unit-to-firewall retaining screws, and remove power unit from vehicle. Remove retaining bracket and gasket from power unit.

**Installation** — Reverse removal procedure and note the following: Assemble retaining bracket to power unit using a new gasket. Make sure seal ring is installed on master cylinder between cylinder and power unit.

## CAPRI (Cont.)

Fig. 4  *Exploded View of Master Cylinder and Related Components*

### COMBINATION VALVE

**Removal** — Disconnect the five brake fluid lines from ports on valve and plug ends of the two lines from master cylinder. Disconnect electrical wiring from warning switch. Remove bolt attaching valve to left side of engine compartment and lift out valve.

**Installation** — Position valve in place in engine compartment and loosely install attaching bolt. Reconnect brake lines, then tighten attaching bolt. Fill master cylinder reservoir with brake fluid and bleed hydraulic system.

## OVERHAUL

### FRONT DISC BRAKE CALIPER

**Disassembly** — Partially remove one piston from cylinder bore, remove snap ring, and remove sealing bellows from piston skirt. Remove piston by appling air pressure or hydraulic pressure to fluid inlet in caliper. Remove sealing bellows from annular ring in cylinder bore, and remove piston sealing ring. Repeat operation for remaining piston. **NOTE** — *DO NOT separate caliper halves.*

**Cleaning & Inspection** — Clean pistons and cylinder bores in alcohol or brake fluid. **CAUTION** — *DO NOT use mineral based solvents.* Check all parts for wear, scoring, or other damage; replace parts as necessary.

**Reassembly** — Install piston seal and sealing bellows into caliper bore. Lubricate piston with brake fluid and install through sealing bellows (crown first). Install inner edge of bellows in piston skirt, push piston to bottom of cylinder, and install snap ring. Repeat operation for remaining piston.

### REAR WHEEL CYLINDER

**Disassembly** — Remove dust boots and slide out piston assemblies. Remove seal from piston and spring from cylinder bore. Remove bleeder screw.

**Cleaning & Inspection** — Ensure pistons and cylinder are free of dirt, burrs and scratches. Thoroughly clean and dry all parts with a lint free cloth. Replace parts as necessary.

Fig. 5  *Expanded View of Rear Wheel Cylinder Assy.*

**Reassembly** — Install bleeder screw and tighten to specifications. Install new seals on pistons. Slide one piston into cylinder bore, then insert spring and remaining piston from opposite end and install dust boots.

### MASTER CYLINDER

**Disassembly** — Remove reservoir from body. Loosen stop screw and push piston inward; remove snap ring. From primary chamber remove stop washer and primary piston assembly. With compressed air, force secondary piston assembly from its chamber.

**Cleaning & Inspecting** — While apart clean master cylinder and inner components with alcohol. Thoroughly dry all parts before reassembly.

## CAPRI (Cont.)

**Reassembly** — Install secondary piston and replacement parts together in secondary chamber. Press piston inward and install stop screw. Release piston and let it contact stop screw. **NOTE** — *Length of stop screw must not change with new seal.* Reassemble primary piston and insert it into chamber. Position stop screw. **NOTE** — *Prevent burrs on secondary piston face by filling chambers with fluid before moving piston.* Install reservoir.

### COMBINATION VALVE

**Disassembly** — Unscrew and remove warning switch. Remove retaining bolt, then using a small screwdriver, gently push piston assembly out of valve bore. Remove two rubber seals from piston and slide off sleeves.

**Cleaning & Inspection** — Thoroughly clean all parts and dry with a lint free cloth. Inspect all parts for wear or damage and replace as necessary. Inspect retaining clips on piston for wear and tightness and replace if necessary.

**Reassembly** — Slide sleeves on piston and install new rubber seals. Slide piston assembly into cylinder, then install retaining bolt. Install warning switch.

**Fig. 6   Exploded View of Combination Valve Parts**

### TIGHTENING SPECIFICATIONS

| Application | Ft. Lbs. (mkg) |
|---|---|
| Caliper Mounting Bolts | 45-50 (6.2-6.9) |
| Rotor-to-Hub Bolts | 30-34 (4.2-4.7) |
| Rear Backing Plate Bolts | 15-18 (2.1-2.5) |
| Hydraulic Line Union Nuts | 5-7 (.7-1.0) |
| Bleeder Screws | 5-7 (.7-1.0) |

### BRAKE SYSTEM SPECIFICATIONS

| Application | Drum Diam. In. (mm) | Wheel Cylinder Diameter | | Master Cylinder |
|---|---|---|---|---|
| | | Front In. (mm) | Rear In. (mm) | Diameter In. (mm) |
| Capri | 9 (229) | 2.125 ① (53.9) | .700 (17.8) | ....... |

① — Caliper bore diameter.

### DISC BRAKE ROTOR SPECIFICATIONS

| Application | Disc Diameter In. (mm) | Lateral Runout In. (mm) | Parallelism In. (mm) | Original Thickness In. (mm) | Minimum Refinish Thickness In. (mm) | Discard Thickness In. (mm) |
|---|---|---|---|---|---|---|
| Capri | 9.625 (244.4) | .0035 (.089) | .0004 (.010) | .500 (12.7) | .460 (11.6) | .450 (11.3) |

## COURIER

**Courier**

### DESCRIPTION

Courier brake system consists of front disc brakes (New for 1977), rear drum brakes, dual piston master cylinder and power brake unit (New for 1977). Brake system is protected by a pressure differential valve and warning light. Differential valve indicates when there is a pressure loss by a warning light on dash board. Light will stay on until problem is corrected. Disc brakes consist of a single piston cylinder mounted in a caliper retaining bracket. Rear brakes are fitted with dual piston wheel cylinders.

### ADJUSTMENT

#### PEDAL FREE PLAY

Loosen lock nut on master cylinder push rod at clevis. Turn push rod in or out to obtain .33-.39" (8.5-10.0 mm) free play, measured at pedal pad. When clearance is correct, tighten lock nut.

#### FRONT DISC BRAKES

No adjustment is necessary.

#### REAR DRUM BRAKES

All shoe to drum adjustments must be made with brake shoes at normal room temperature. Turn lower wheel cylinder rachet to expand brake shoe locking it against drum. Back-off rachet 5 notches or until drum rotates freely. Repeat procedure for upper wheel cylinder.

#### PARKING BRAKE CABLE

**NOTE** — *Service brakes must be properly adjusted before adjusting parking brake.* Adjust length of cable at equalizer so that rear brakes are locked when parking brake lever is pulled out five to ten ratchet clicks (1 ⅝ -3 ⅛ "). After adjustment, apply and release parking brake several times, and make sure wheels rotate freely when parking brake is released.

#### COMBINATION VALVE

**Combination Valve Reset** — Place ignition switch in the on position. Depress brake pedal and piston will center itself. This will cause brake warning light to go out.

#### HYDRAULIC SYSTEM BLEEDING

**NOTE** — *Front and rear hydraulic systems are individual systems and are bled separately. Bleed longest line first on individual system being serviced.*

**CAUTION** — Do not bleed hydraulic system through master cylinder stop screw.

**Manual Bleeding-1)** Attach a bleeder tube to right rear lower brake cylinder, and immerse opposite end of tube in a container partially filled with brake fluid. Open bleeder screw ¾ turn, push brake pedal through full travel, close bleeder screw, and return pedal. Continue operation until air bubbles are no longer seen in discharged fluid.

**2)** Repeat procedure at upper right rear wheel cylinder, and at wheel cylinders on left rear brake. If primary system is to be bled, repeat procedure at each right front wheel cylinder and each left front wheel cylinder. When bleeding operation is completed, fill master cylinder reservoirs to within ¼" of top of reservoirs. Centralize pressure differential valve.

### REMOVAL & INSTALLATION

#### DISC BRAKE PADS

**Removal — 1)** Raise vehicle and place on safety stands. Remove front wheel. Remove 4 locking spring clips. Drift out both stopper plates.

**2)** Remove caliper piston and anti-rattle spring from pad bracket. Support caliper piston out of way. Pull out disc pads and shims (if any). Note position of shims.

**NOTE** — *All pads must be replaced at one time.*

**Installation — 1)** Pull bleeder cap off caliper and attach a tube over bleed screw. Open bleed screw and seat piston in cylinder with "C" clamp. Tighten bleed screw and remove "C" clamp.

**2)** Install new pads and shims if thickness of pads (including shoe) has worn to .315" (8 mm). Fit anti-rattle spring and caliper piston. Apply a light coat of grease to stopper plates. Install plates and spring clips.

#### FRONT DISC BRAKE CALIPER

**Removal** — Raise vehicle and support with safety stands. Remove front wheel. Disconnect hydraulic line at flexible hose. Remove "U" clip to free hose. Take out 2 mounting bolts holding caliper bracket, then remove entire assembly.

**Installation** — To install, reverse removal procedure and note: Bleed brake system.

#### BRAKE ROTOR

**Removal** — Remove caliper. Remove dust cap, cotter pin, adjustment nut, thrust washer and outer bearing. Slide out hub and rotor assembly. Index mark and separate hub from rotor.

**Installation** — Thoroughly clean mating surface of hub and rotor. Position rotor on hub aligning index marks. Tighten mounting bolts. To complete installation, reverse removal procedure. See *Wheel Bearing Adjustment* in WHEEL ALIGNMENT Section.

#### BRAKE DRUM

**Removal** — Remove tire and wheel. Remove brake drum attaching screws and install them in tapered holes in brake drum. Turn screws in evenly to force drum away from wheel hub. Lift off drum.

**Installation** — Align attaching screw holes with ones in wheel hub. Transfer screws to retaining position and tighten evenly. Install tire and wheel.

# Brakes

## COURIER (Cont.)

### BRAKE SHOES

**Removal** — Remove tire, wheel and brake drum. Remove brake shoe return springs, withdraw shoe retaining pin and spring. Disconnect handbrake link and cable from lever. Lift out brake shoes.

**Installation** — Reassemble handbrake. Position new brake shoes to backing plate with slots toward wheel cylinders. Install retaining springs and clips. Replace brake drum and adjust brakes.

**Fig. 1    Rear Brake Assembly Showing Relationship of Internal Components**

### WHEEL CYLINDER

**Removal** — With brake drum and shoes removed, disconnect hydraulic line from cylinder. Remove stud nuts and bolt which retain  cylinder to backing plate and remove cylinder.

**Installation** — Reverse removal procedure, adjust brake shoes and bleed hydraulic system.

### MASTER CYLINDER

**Removal & Installation** — Disconnect brake hydraulic lines at master cylinder outlets and inlet ports from cylinder reservoir. Remove 2 nuts mounting master cylinder to power brake booster. Lift assembly outward and upward away from booster push rod. To install reverse removal procedure and make sure to guide power brake booster push rod into master cylinder piston.

### COMBINATION VALVE

**Removal** — Disconnect warning light wire. Disconnect hydraulic lines from combination valve. Remove bolt mounting valve assembly and take off combination valve.

**Installation** — To install combination valve, reverse removal procedure and note the following: Bleed hydraulic system and reset piston in valve.

### POWER BRAKE BOOSTER

**Removal** — Remove master cylinder as previously outlined. Disconnect vacuum hose for power booster. Disconnect push rod from brake pedal. Work under instrument panel and remove 4 nuts mounting power brake booster.

**Installation** — Slide booster into position. Fit 4 mounting nuts. Install push rod to brake pedal. Connect vacuum line from intake manifold. Refit master cylinder to booster. Bleed brake system.

## OVERHAUL

### FRONT DISC BRAKE CALIPER

**Disassembly** — 1) Clean outside of caliper. Separate cylinder from bracket. Remove boot retainer and slide off dust boot. Force compressed air into brake line hole to remove piston from caliper.

2) It may be necessary to tap outside of piston housing with plastic hammer while applying air pressure to unseat piston. Dig out piston seal from inside caliper bore.

**Cleaning and Inspection** — Wash all disassembled parts in clean brake fluid and completely dry with compressed air. Inspect caliper bore and piston for scratches, grooves or rust. Minor imprefections can be eliminated with crocus cloth. Piston seal and dust boot must be replaced during each overhaul.

**Reassembly** — Lightly coat piston seal with brake fluid and insert into groove in caliper bore. Make sure seal is not twisted in groove. Lubricate piston and bore with brake fluid, then slide piston into place. Fit dust boot with flange seated in inner groove of caliper. Fit dust boot retainer.

**Fig. 2    Exploded View of Front Disc Brake**

### REAR WHEEL CYLINDER

**Disassembly** — Remove piston, adjusting screw, and boot assemblies from each end of cylinder and separate parts. Press in on either piston cup and force out piston cups, expanders, and return spring.

**Cleaning & Inspection** — Wash all parts in isopropyl alcohol. Examine cylinder bore, pistons, and adjuster for wear or damage. Check clearance between cylinder bore and pistons; if greater than .006" (.15 mm), replace parts as necessary.

## COURIER (Cont.)

**Fig. 3   Disassembled View of Courier Rear Wheel Cylinder**

**Reassembly** — Apply brake fluid to cylinder bore, adjuster, and cylinder cups. Position return spring in cup expanders, place cups against expanders, and install into cylinder bore with flat side of cups facing outward. Install boot to piston with smaller lip of boot in groove of piston, install piston into cylinder, and install larger lip of boot into cylinder groove. Install adjusting screw into adjuster.

## MASTER CYLINDER

**Disassembly** — 1) Drain brake fluid from reservoir and separate reservoir from master clyinder inlet ports.

**2)** Remove primary piston snap ring and stop washer. Slide out piston, return spring and cup from bore.

**3)** Remove secondary piston stop screw with "O" ring. Remove secondary pistion and return spring. If necessary, piston can be blown out with air pressure. Remove brake line fittings, gaskets, check valves and springs.

**Cleaning and Inspection** — Clean all parts in brake fluid and dry with compressed air. Check cups for wear, cracks or softening. Inspect piston and cylinder bore for wear, roughness, or scoring. Check clearance between cylinder bore and pistons. If clearance exceeds .006" (.15 mm), replace piston.

**Reassembly** — 1) Lightly coat all components with brake fluid. Install check valve springs and valves into outlet ports. Install gasket and brake line fittings.

**NOTE** — *Make sure check valve with hole is installed in hole on side of master cylinder.*

**2)** Insert secondary and primary cup onto secondary piston. Fit piston assembly and spring into cylinder. Seat piston with a screwdriver and install stop screw with washer.

**3)** Fit cup to primary piston. Insert primary piston assembly with return spring into cylinder. Install washer and snap ring.

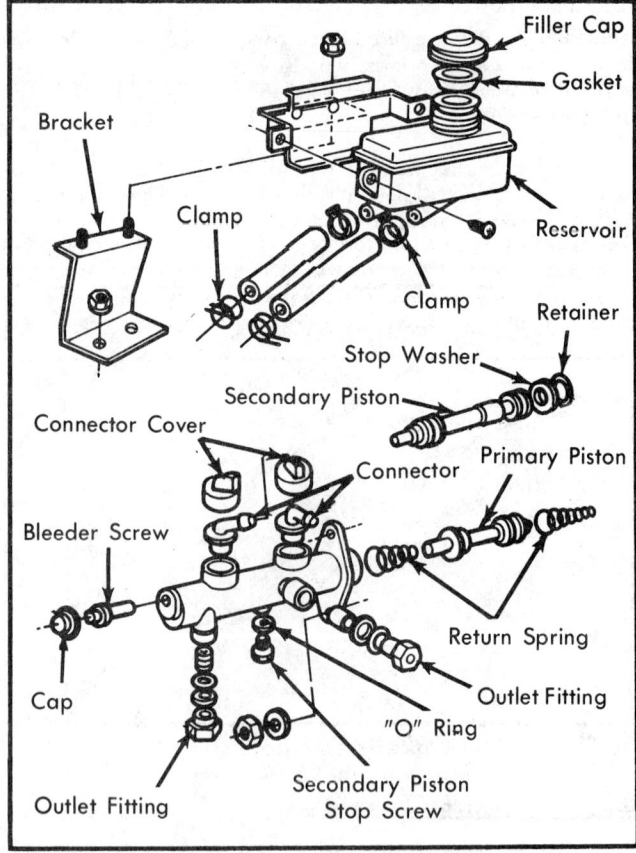

**Fig 4   Exploded View of Master Cylinder and Related Components**

## POWER BRAKE BOOSTER

**Disassembly** — 1) Fit booster in vise with rod facing up. Index mark shell sides with a scribe. Remove lock nut and boot. Rotate rear shell clockwise to unlocked position and lift off shell complete with:
- Diaphragm
- Power Piston Assembly
- Valve Rod
- Plunger Assembly

**2)** Remove spring from front shell. From inside rear shell remove:
- Diaphragm
- Power Piston Assembly
- Valve Rod
- Plunger Assembly

**3)** Remove rear seal, with punch, from rear shell only if seal needs replacing. Take out air silencer retainer and air filter from power piston. DO NOT damage piston.

**4)** Press in valve rod and remove retainer key. Take valverod and plunger assembly off power piston. Press out reaction disc. Slide push rod out of front shell.

**Cleaning** — 1) Wipe down all components. Carefully inspect all components for damage. Especially look at rubber parts for cuts, nicks or deformation.

## COURIER (Cont.)

**2)** Check power piston for cracks, distortion, chipping or damage.

**3)** Inspect reaction disc, valve rod and plunger. Replace components as necessary.

**Reassembly – 1)** Apply brake fluid to inside of power piston bore and to surface of valve rod plunger assembly. Insert valve rod and plunger assembly into power piston. Press in valve rod and align plunger groove with slot in power piston. Insert key.

**2)** Install diaphragm on power piston. Be sure diaphragm is squarely seated on piston groove. Fit air silencer retainer and filter and fit over rod, then place in power piston. Coat surface of reaction disc with brake fluid and install in power piston.

**3)** Lightly coat outer edge of diaphragm and rear shell seal with brake fluid. Carefully guide tube end of power piston through seal in real shell. Fit push rod to front of power piston.

**4)** Put return spring in front shell. Position complete rear shell assembly over front half, press down and rotate counterclockwise until scribe marks align. Install dust boot, fork end and lock nut.

*Fig. 5   Exploded View of Power Brake Booster*

### BRAKE DRUM SPECIFICATIONS

| Application | Drum Diameter In. (mm) | Original Diameter In. (mm) | Maximum Refinish Diameter In. (mm) | Discard Diameter In. (mm) |
|---|---|---|---|---|
| Courier | 10.236 (260) | 10.236 (260) | 10.2756 (261) | |

### DISC BRAKE ROTOR SPECIFICATIONS

| Application | Disc Diameter In. (mm) | Lateral Runout In. (mm) | Parallelism In. (mm) | Original Thickness In. (mm) | Minimum Refinish Thickness In. (mm) | Discard Thickness In. (mm) |
|---|---|---|---|---|---|---|
| Courier | 10.079 (256) | .004 (.10) | ..... | .472 (12) | .433 (11) | ..... |

### BRAKE SYSTEM SPECIFICATIONS

| Application | Drum Diam. In. (mm) | Wheel Cylinder Diameter | | Master Cylinder Diameter In. (mm) |
|---|---|---|---|---|
| | | Front In. (mm) | Rear In. (mm) | |
| Courier | 10.236 (260) | ① | .750 (19) | .875 (22.2) |

① — Front disc brake cylinder bore 2.12" (53.8 mm).

# Brakes

## DATSUN F10, 200SX, B210

F10
200SX
B210

## DESCRIPTION

Brake system is hydraulically operated, utilizing a tandem master cylinder and a Master-Vac power brake unit. Front disc brakes consist of rotors attached to wheel hubs, and single cylinder, dual-piston, floating-calipers attached to steering knuckles. Rear brakes are leading-trailing shoe/drum type, using a single piston sliding wheel cylinder. Parking brake is cable actuated, operating wheel cylinders of rear brake assemblies.

## ADJUSTMENT

### PEDAL HEIGHT & FREE PLAY

**F10** — Adjust pedal height to 6.8-7.0" (172-178 mm) by turning nut on master cylinder push rod. Adjust stop light switch so pedal just touches end of stop light switch; tighten lock nut. **NOTE** — *Brake pedal should be checked for travel and smooth operation. Travel should be 5-5.25" (127-133 mm).*

**200SX** — Adjust pedal height to about 6.9" (175.5 mm) using stop light switch. Lock switch in place with retaining nut. After pedal height is adjusted, loosen push rod lock nut and adjust pedal free play to .039-.118" ( 1-3 mm).

**B210** — Adjust pedal height to specifications by moving stop lamp switch. Pedal height should be 6.14" (156 mm) on vehicles equipped with manual transmission and 6.22" (158 mm) on vehicles with automatic transmission. After pedal height is adjusted, loosen push rod lock nut and adjust pedal free play to .039-.197" (1-5 mm).

### FRONT DISC BRAKE PADS

Front disc brakes are self-adjusting, therefore, no adjustment in service is required.

### REAR BRAKE SHOES

**F10** — Raise and support vehicle. Pump brake pedal several times to center brake shoes. Using a screwdriver, turn adjuster star until considerable drag is evident. Back off adjuster five or six notches and make sure drum rotates freely.

**200SX** — No adjustment required.

**B210** — Raise and support vehicle. Using a suitable brake adjusting tool, tighten adjuster eccentric clockwise until brake shoe contacts drum. Return adjuster eccentric until shoe is slightly separated from drum. Check operation by turning drum and applying brakes; if shoe interferes with drum rotation, readjust.

## PARKING BRAKE

With rear brakes properly adjusted, adjust parking brake cable turnbuckle until rear brakes are locked when parking brake lever is pulled to sixth or seventh ratchet stop. Release parking brake lever and ensure rear wheels turn freely and that all parts are returned to their original position.

## COMBINATION VALVE

**Function Test, All Models** — Accelerate engine to 30 mph and rapidly apply brakes. If rear wheels lock before front wheels, malfunction of combination valve assembly (200SX & B210), or of separate proportioning valve (F10) is indicated.

## HYDRAULIC SYSTEM BLEEDING

Attach a bleed tube to bleeder screw and immerse opposite end of tube in a container partially filled with brake fluid. Pump brake pedal two or three times, keep pedal fully depressed, open bleeder screw and exhaust air, close bleeder screw, and return brake pedal. Repeat operation until air bubbles are no longer seen in discharged fluid. Repeat procedure on remaining brake lines. Bleed rear wheels first, then front wheels.

## REMOVAL & INSTALLATION

### FRONT DISC BRAKE PADS

**Removal** — Raise front of vehicle and support in place, then remove front wheels. Remove clips from retaining pins and pull out pins, coil springs and pad springs. Remove pads from caliper assembly using a suitable pair of pliers.

**Inspection** — With friction pads removed, measure their thickness. Replace any pad that is worn to less than .063" (1.6 mm) in thickness (not including metal backing plate). It is recommended that friction pads be replaced as a set to prevent any possibility of uneven braking.

**NOTE** — *Replace all pads at same time.*

**Installation** — Clean and apply P.B.C. grease (or equivalent) on yoke guide groove of cylinder body, sliding contact portions of yoke and end surface of piston. Loosen bleeder screw and push outer piston in cylinder until end surface of piston coinsides with end surface of retaining ring on boot. Install inner brake pad. Push inner piston in cylinder by pulling on yoke, then install outer brake pad. After installing pads, depress brake pedal several times to seat pads.

### FRONT DISC BRAKE CALIPER

**Removal** — Raise vehicle and suitably support on safety stands; remove tire and wheel. Remove brake friction pads as previously described. Disconnect brake line from wheel cylinder. To ease removal of caliper, remove strut assembly and knuckle arm mounting bolt. Withdraw caliper mounting bolt and separate it from strut assembly.

## DATSUN F10, 200SX, B210 (Cont.)

**Installation** — To install brake caliper assembly, reverse removal procedures, noting the following: Bleed hydraulic system.

### FRONT DISC BRAKE ROTOR

**Removal (200SX & B210)** — With caliper removed, remove hub dust cap, cotter pin and nut. Remove hub and rotor assembly with wheel bearing and washer in place. Remove bolts attaching rotor to wheel hub and separate rotor from hub.

**Installation** — Reverse removal procedure, tighten rotor-to-hub bolts securely, and adjust wheel bearings. *See Wheel Bearing Adjustment in WHEEL ALIGNMENT Section.* Use a dial indicator to measure rotor runout. Resurface rotor if runout exceeds .0047" (.12 mm)

**Removal (F10)** — With caliper removed, remove stub axle cotter pin, washer and mounting nut. Using a puller, withdraw stub axle and brake rotor as an assembly. Rotor can now be separated from stub axle.

**Installation** — To install stub axle and rotor assembly, reverse removal procedure and tighten stub axle mounting nut to 87-145 ft. lbs. (12-20 mkg).

**Fig. 1   Exploded View of Datsun 200SX Rear Brake Assembly**

### REAR BRAKE ASSEMBLY

**Removal (Rear)** — Raise vehicle and suitably support on safety stands; remove tire and wheel. Loosen parking brake linkage at clevis pin and place out of way. Remove brake drum. Remove shoe retainer and return spring, then lift off shoe assembly. Disconnect brake line from wheel cylinder. If necessary, wheel cylinder can now be removed by taking out mounting bolt.

**Inspecting** — Inspect all brake components for damage or excessive wear and replace those found defective. Replace brake lining if it is oil soaked or lining is less than .059" (1.5mm) thick.

**Installation** — To install rear brake lining, reverse removal procedures, noting the following: Readjust shoe-to-drum clearance and, if necessary, bleed hydraulic system.

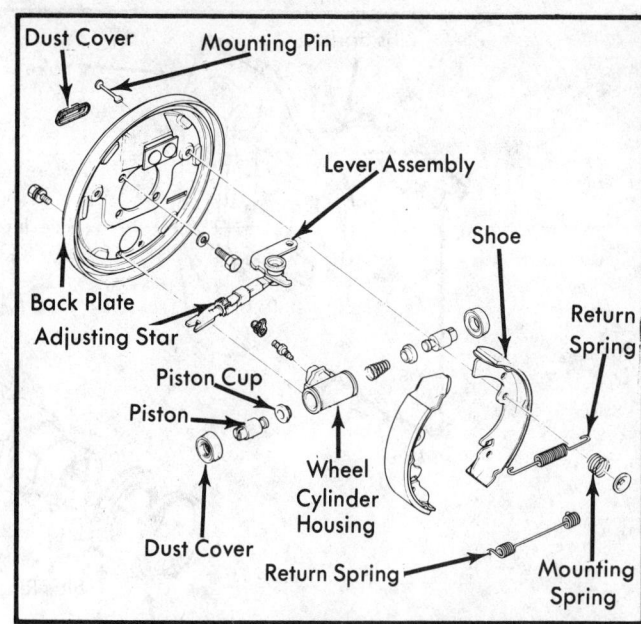

**Fig. 2   Exploded View of F10 and B210 Rear Brake Assembly**

### MASTER CYLINDER

**Removal** — Disconnect any electrical leads attached to cylinder reservoir. Disconnect front and rear brake lines from master cylinder outlet ports. On models equipped without power brakes, separate master cylinder push rod from pedal. Remove cylinder mounting nuts and slide unit off studs. Make sure brake fluid does not drop on paint.

**NOTE** — *On F10 models, fluid reservoir can be removed attached to cylinder.*

**Installation** — To install master cylinder, reverse removal procedures, noting the following: Bleed hydraulic system and check pedal height.

### POWER BRAKE UNIT

**Removal** — Disconnect power unit push rod from brake pedal by removing clevis pin. Disconnect hydraulic lines from master cylinder and vacuum line from power unit, remove master cylinder attaching nuts, and remove master cylinder. Remove nuts attaching power unit to firewall, and remove power unit from engine compartment.

**Installation** — Reverse removal procedure, adjust brake pedal height, and bleed hydraulic system.

**Check Valve Removal** — Check valve is located in vacuum line between intake manifold and power unit on firewall. To remove, disconnect retaining clip from firewall, remove hose clamps, separate hoses from valve, and remove check valve. To install, reverse removal procedure.

## OVERHAUL

### FRONT DISC BRAKE CALIPER

**Disassembly** — With caliper removed, drain brake fluid and remove bleeder screw. Push both pistons into cylinder bore, then place yoke in a vise and tap the top of yoke lightly with a

# Brakes

## DATSUN F10, 200SX, B210 (Cont.)

**Fig. 3   Exploded View of Front Disc Brake Caliper**

hammer to separate cylinder from yoke. Remove bias ring from outer piston, then remove retaining rings and boots. Push both pistons out in one direction. Remove piston seals from cylinder and yoke spring from yoke.

**Inspecting** — Thoroughly clean all internal parts and check each component for excessive wear or damage. If caliper bore is damaged or excessively rusted, it must be replaced. If, however, slight imperfections are evident, honing will eliminate them. It is recommended to replace all seals when overhauling.

**Reassembly** — Before assembling components, lightly coat with suitable brake grease. Insert bias ring into piston so round portion of ring fits to bottom of piston. Insert piston into cylinder. Do not fully seat piston. Install dust boot and retaining ring. Install yoke bias ring so it coincides with yoke groove of cylinder. Fit bias spring to yoke so bias spring faces bleeder side of cylinder. With yoke spring inserted in cylinder groove, properly align position of bias spring so groove of spring aligns with yoke. Assemble body-to-yoke, tapping lightly if necessary.

## MASTER CYLINDER

**NOTE** — On F10 models, separate reservoir tank assembly.

**Disassembly** — Remove master cylinder reservoir caps and filters and drain brake fluid. Using a screwdriver, pry off stopper ring. Remove stopper screw and pull out primary piston assembly, spring and secondary piston assembly. Remove plugs and pull out front and rear check valves.

**NOTE** — On all except F10 models, do not remove reservoir tanks. If tanks are removed for any reason, discard and install new ones.

**Fig. 4   Exploded View of Datsun Wheel Cylinder Used on F10, 200SX and B210 Models**

**Fig. 5   Exploded View of Datsun 200SX and B210 Master Cylinder — F10 Models Have Different Reservoir Arrangement**

# Brakes

## DATSUN F10, 200SX, B210 (Cont.)

**Inspecting** — Thoroughly clean all components in approved grade brake fluid. Inspect all components for excessive wear or damage and replace parts as necessary.

**Reassembly** — Reverse disassembly procedure and note the following: Coat all parts with brake fluid (rubber parts with brake grease) when assembling.

### POWER BRAKE UNIT

**Disassembly** — 1) Place power unit in a soft jaw vise with operating rod pointing up. Scribe an alignment mark on front and rear shell to assure reassembly in original position, then remove lock nut, clevis and dust boot from rear shell.

2) Place suitable wrench (ST08080000) over rear shell mounting studs. Press down on wrench while rotating counterclockwise and remove rear shell, then lift out diaphragm plate assembly, diaphragm spring and push rod assembly. Pry off retainer and remove bearing and valve body seal assembly.

3) Remove diaphragm from diaphragm plate assembly, then pry off air silencer retainer and remove silencer and filter. Rotate diaphragm plate assembly until valve plunger key slot is down, then press in on plunger and shake out stop key. Remove reaction disc from plate assembly. Detach flange from front shell and remove front seal assembly.

**Cleaning & Inspection** — Clean all parts in denatured alcohol and blow dry with compressed air. Inspect front and rear shells for wear or damage. If slight rust is found on inside surface of shells, polish clean with fine emery cloth. Inspect all parts for cracks, nicks, distortion or other damage and replace as necessary.

**Reassembly** — Reverse disassembly procedure and note the following: Apply a thin coat of silicone grease to parts before installation. When assembling front shell to rear shell ensure marks made during disassembly are aligned. After reassembly, measure distance from master cylinder mounting surface of power unit to end of power unit push rod; distance should be .38-.39" (9.8-10.0 mm). If distance is not to specifications, correct by adjusting end of push rod.

### TIGHTENING SPECIFICATIONS

| Application | Ft. Lbs. (mkg) |
| --- | --- |
| Master Cylinder Attaching Nuts | 6-9 (.8-1.2) |
| Hydraulic Lines | 11-13 (1.5-1.8) |
| Rotor-to-Hub | |
| 200SX & B210 | 28-38 (3.9-5.3) |
| F10 | 18-25 (2.5-3.4) |
| Caliper Mounting Bolts | |
| 200SX & B210 | 53-72 (7.3-9.9) |
| F10 | 40-47 (5.5-6.5) |

*Fig. 6   Sectional View of Datsun Master Vac*

# Brakes

## DATSUN F10, 200SX, B210 (Cont.)

### DISC BRAKE ROTOR SPECIFICATIONS

| Application | Disc Diameter In. (mm) | Lateral Runout In. (mm) | Parallelism In. (mm) | Original Thickness In. (mm) | Minimum Refinish Thickness In. (mm) | Discard Thickness In. (mm) |
|---|---|---|---|---|---|---|
| F10 | 9.45 (240) | .005① (.13) | ..... | ..... | .339 (8.6) | ② |
| B210 | 9.65 (245) | .0047① (.12) | ..... | .374 (9.5) | .331 (8.4) | ② |
| 200SX | 9.65 (245) | .0047① (.12) | ..... | .394 (10.0) | .331 (8.4) | ② |

① — Maximum.
② — Less than minimum refinish thickness.

### BRAKE LINING SPECIFICATION

| Application | Drum Dia. In. (mm) | Width | | Length | | Thickness | |
|---|---|---|---|---|---|---|---|
| | | Front In. (mm) | Rear In. (mm) | Primary In. (mm) | Secondary In. (mm) | Primary In. (mm) | Seondary In. (mm) |
| F10 & B210 | 8.00 (203) | ① | 1.378 (35) | 7.68 (195) | 7.68 (195) | .189 (4.8) | .189 (4.8) |
| 200SX | 9.00 (228.6) | ① | 1.575 (40) | 8.64 (219.5) | 8.64 (219.5) | .177 (4.5) | .177 (4.5) |

① — Front disc equipped.

### BRAKE DRUM SPECIFICATIONS

| Application | Drum Diameter In. (mm) | Original Diameter In. (mm) | Maximum Refinish Diameter In. (mm) | Discard Diameter In. (mm) |
|---|---|---|---|---|
| F10 & B210 | 8.00 (203) | 8.00 (203) | 8.051 (204) | ① |
| 200SX | 9.00 (228.6) | 9.00 (228.6) | 9.055 (230) | ① |

① — More than Maximum Refinish Diameter.

### BRAKE SYSTEM SPECIFICATIONS

| Application | Drum Diam. In. (mm) | Wheel Cylinder Diameter | | Master Cylinder Diameter In. (mm) |
|---|---|---|---|---|
| | | Front In. (mm) | Rear In. (mm) | |
| F10 | 8.00 (203) | 1.894 (48.1) | .687 (17.46) | .750 (19.05) |
| B210 | 8.00 (203) | 2.012① (51.1) | .813 (20.64) | .750 (19.05) |
| 200SX | 9.00 (228) | ①2.012 (51.1) | .813 (20.64) | .750 (19.05) |

① — Caliper cylinder diameter.

## DATSUN 280Z

### 280Z

## DESCRIPTION

Brake system is hydraulically operated, using a tandem master cylinder and a Master-Vac power brake unit. Front brakes are Girling-Sumitomo dual piston fixed caliper type. Rear brakes are leading-trailing, shoe/drum type. Brake system is equipped with a combination valve to prevent premature locking of rear wheels. A brake warning light works off the combination valve and indicates when a pressure drop occurs in either front or rear circuit. Parking brake is mechanically actuated through cables and levers. Parking brake locks rear drums.

## ADJUSTMENT

### BRAKE PEDAL

Loosen lock nut, turn push rod clevis, and adjust push rod length so that height of pedal, measured from pedal pad to floor, is 8.11" (206 mm). **NOTE** — *Make sure pedal stopper (stop light switch) does not contact pedal arm at this time.* With push rod adjusted, adjust stop light switch until pedal height is reduced to 7.99" (203 mm).

### FRONT DISC BRAKE PADS

Front disc brakes are self-adjusting, therefore, no adjustment in service is required.

### REAR DRUM BRAKE SHOES

Rear drum brakes are self-adjusting (actuated by parking brake), therefore, no adjustment in service is required.

### PARKING BRAKE

Adjust shoe-to-drum clearance on rear brakes. Loosen adjusting rod lock nut and rotate adjuster nut to reduce linkage play. Actuate parking brake lever several times to stabilize cable. Make sure cables are free to operate.

**Fig. 1  280Z Parking Brake Adjustment Point Adjuster Rod**

### COMBINATION VALVE

**Function Test** — Accelerate engine to 30 mph and quickly apply brakes. If rear wheels lock before front wheels, malfunction of combination valve is indicated.

**Warning Light Operation and Reset** — Instrument panel light will come on when a pressure difference of between 71-244 psi is evident between front and rear hydraulic systems. Combination valve shuttle moves to side of low pressure and grounds electrical circuit, causing waring light to come on. When hydraulic problem has been corrected and brakes have been bled, system should have normal psi. Shuttle will then return to position and light will go out.

## REMOVAL & INSTALLATION

### FRONT DISC BRAKE PADS

**Removal** — Remove tire and wheel. Remove clip, retaining pin, damper spring and remove pad with shim.

**Installation** — Depress piston into cylinder so new pad may be inserted. Install pad, shim, damper spring and retaining pin securing with clip. Depress pedal several times to position new pads.

### FRONT DISC BRAKE CALIPER

**Removal** - With disc pads removed, disconnect hydraulic line from caliper and plug openings. Remove caliper mounting bolts and separate caliper from steering knuckle and rotor.

**Installation** — Reverse removal procedure, tighten caliper mounting bolts securely, and bleed hydraulic system.

### FRONT DISC BRAKE ROTOR

**Removal** — With caliper assembly removed, remove wheel hub dust cap, cotter pin, and adjusting nut. Remove wheel hub and rotor assembly, wheel bearing, and washer from spindle as an assembly. Remove bolts attaching rotor to wheel hub, and detach rotor.

**Installation** — Reverse removal procedure and adjust front wheel bearings. *See Wheel Bearing Adjustment in WHEEL ALIGNMENT Section.*

### REAR BRAKE SHOES

**Removal** — Remove tire. Pull off brake drum. If drum is hard to remove, apply parking brake and drive out clevis pin. Release brake and pull on drum. Once drum is removed, disconnect all springs, clips and release brake shoes. Wheel cylinders are now accessible.

**Installation** — Apply brake grease to adjuster and all pivot points on backing plate. Refit brake shoes, springs, and clips. Refit drum. Connect parking brake and continually apply until click sound from adjuster is gone.

## DATSUN 280Z (Cont.)

Brake Shoes & Hardware — Backing Plate — Operating Lever
Anchor Block — Dust Cover
Wheel Cylinder Assembly
Adjuster

**Fig. 2   Exploded View of Rear Brake Assembly**

### REAR WHEEL CYLINDER

**Removal** — Remove rear brake shoes. Disconnect and plug hydraulic line. Separate parking brake linkage. Remove mounting bolt and slide off cylinder.

**Installation** — Reverse removal procedure and note the following: Apply brake grease (or equivalent) to wheel cylinder, backing plate, and adjusting plate sliding surfaces; also lubricate wheel cylinder lever fulcrum and ensure wheel cylinder assembly operates freely.

### MASTER CYLINDER

**Removal** — Disconnect hydraulic lines from master cylinder, remove nuts attaching cylinder to power unit, and separate master cylinder from power brake unit.

**Installation** — Reverse removal procedure, adjust brake pedal height, and bleed hydraulic system.

### POWER BRAKE UNIT

**Removal** — Disconnect power unit push rod from brake pedal by removing clevis pin. Disconnect hydraulic lines from master cylinder, vacuum line from power unit, remove master cylinder mounting nuts, and remove master cylinder. Remove nuts attaching power unit to firewall, and remove power unit from engine compartment.

**Installation** — Reverse removal procedure, adjust brake pedal height, and bleed hydraulic system.

**Check Valve Replacement** — Check valve is located in vacuum line between intake manifold and power unit on firewall. To remove, disconnect retaining clip from firewall, remove hose clamps, separate hoses from valve, and remove check valve. To install, reverse removal procedure.

### COMBINATION VALVE

**Removal** — Disconnect all hydraulic lines from combination valve. Plug openings. Remove mounting bolts and take off valve.

**NOTE** — 280Z combination valve looks similar to some used on other models. DO NOT mix-up or interchange valves.

**Installation** — To install, reverse removal procedure and note: "F" mark indicates where front brake circuit is attached. Arrows indicate where to attach rear brake circuit. Note that there are arrows to show where inlet and outlet lines attach.

## OVERHAUL

### FRONT DISC BRAKE CALIPER

**Disassembly** — Clean exterior of brake caliper. Remove retaining ring and dust seal. Using a small block of wood, (or equivalent), hold one piston and blow air into brake line inlet to force piston from bore. Remove piston seal from cylinder bore. Remove other piston in similar manner.

Caliper Assembly
Pad
Retaining Ring
Dust Cover
Piston
Mounting Bolt
Piston Seal
Retaining Pin

**Fig. 3   Exploded View of Front Disc Brake Caliper**

**Cleaning & Inspection** — Clean all parts in alcohol or brake fluid. **CAUTION** — DO NOT use mineral based solvents. Inspect caliper bores for wear, rust, corrosion, or other damage; minor deposits or scratches may be removed with fine emery cloth. Check piston for wear or damage. **NOTE** — DO NOT use abrasives on piston plated surfaces.

**Reassembly** — **NOTE** — Manufacturer recommends replacing rubber parts whenever caliper is being overhauled. Coat piston seal with rubber grease and install into caliper bore. Install dust seal on piston, insert piston into caliper, and install retaining ring. Install opposite piston assembly in same manner.

### REAR WHEEL CYLINDER

**Disassembly** — Remove dust boots. Pull out cylinder pistons and return spring.

**Cleaning & Inspection** — Clean all parts in alcohol or brake fluid. **CAUTION** — DO NOT use mineral based solvents. Check all parts for wear or damage; replace parts as necessary. Check clearance between cylinder bore and piston; if clearance exceeds .006", replace cylinder or piston as

## DATSUN 280Z (Cont.)

necessary. Check spring for damage or distortion. **NOTE** — *Manufacturer recommends replacing seal whenever wheel cylinder has been disassembled.*

**Reassembly** — Reverse disassembly procedure and note the following: Apply rubber grease to all parts when reassembling to prevent damage.

### MASTER CYLINDER

**Disassembly** — Remove reservoir filler caps, drain brake fluid, and remove secondary piston stop bolt. Remove snap ring and withdraw primary piston, secondary piston and return springs. Remove valve caps and withdraw check valve assemblies. **NOTE** — *Do not remove reservoirs unless necessary.*

**Fig. 4   Master Cylinder Reservoir, Body and Piston Assembly**

**Cleaning & Inspection** — Clean all parts in alcohol or brake fluid and inspect for wear or damage. Check clearance between cylinder bore and pistons; if clearance exceeds .006", replace cylinder or pistons as necessary. **NOTE** — *Manufacturer recommends replacing piston cups, gaskets, and valves whenever master cylinder has been disassembled.*

**Reassembly** — Reverse disassembly procedure and note the following: Apply rubber grease to all rubber parts and brake fluid to remaining parts when assembling to prevent damage.

### POWER BRAKE UNIT

**Disassembly** — 1) Place power unit in a soft jawed vise with operating rod pointing up. Scribe alignment marks on front and rear shells to assure reassembly in original position. Remove operating rod lock nut and clevis, then remove dust boot from rear shell.

2) Place a suitable wrench (ST08080000) over rear shell mounting studs. Press down on wrench while rotating counterclockwise and remove rear shell, then remove diaphragm plate assembly, diaphragm spring and push rod assembly. Pry off retainer and remove bearing and valve body seal from rear shell.

3) Remove diaphragm from diaphragm plate assembly, then pry off air silencer retainer and remove silencer and filter. Rotate diaphragm plate assembly until valve plunger key slot is down, then press in on plunger and shake out stop key. Remove reaction disc from plate assembly. Detach flange from front shell and remove plate and seal assembly.

**Cleaning & Inspection** — Clean all parts in denatured alcohol and blow dry with compressed air. Inspect inside of front and rear shells for wear or damage and replace as necessary. If slight rust is found on inside surface of shells, polish clean with fine emery cloth. Inspect all parts for cracks, nicks, distortion or other damage and replace as necessary.

**Reassembly** — Reverse disassembly procedure and note the following: Apply a thin coat of silicone grease to parts before installation. When assembling front shell to rear shell ensure marks made at disassembly are aligned. After reassembly, measure distance from master cylinder mounting surface to end of power unit push rod; distance should be .38-.39" (9.8-10.0 mm). If distance is not to specifications, correct by adjusting end of push rod.

### TIGHTENING SPECIFICATIONS

| Application | Ft. Lbs. (mkg) |
| --- | --- |
| Caliper-to-Knuckle Flange | 53-72 (7.3-9.9) |
| Rotor-to-Hub | 28-38 (3.9-5.3) |
| Hydraulic Lines | 11-13 (1.5-1.8) |
| Master Cylinder | |
|   Piston Stop Screw | 3-4 (.4-.5) |
|   Check Valve Caps | 58-65 (8-9) |
| Anchor Block-to-Backing Plate | 10-13 (1.4-1.8) |

### BRAKE SYSTEM SPECIFICATIONS

| Application | Drum Diam. In. (mm) | Wheel Cylinder Diameter | | Master Cylinder Diameter In. (mm) |
| --- | --- | --- | --- | --- |
| | | Front In. (mm) | Rear In. (mm) | |
| 280Z | 9.00① (229) | 2.125② (53.9) | .875 (22.2) | .875 (22.2) |

① — Rear drum.
② — Caliper bore diameter.

# Brakes

## DATSUN 280Z (Cont.)

### DISC BRAKE ROTOR SPECIFICATIONS

| Application | Disc Diameter In. (mm) | Lateral Runout In. (mm) | Parallelism In. (mm) | Original Thickness In. (mm) | Minimum Refinish Thickness In. (mm) | Discard Thickness In. (mm) |
|---|---|---|---|---|---|---|
| 280Z | 10.67 (271) | .0059 (.15) | .0028① (.07) | .492 (12.5) | .413 (10.5) | ② |

① — Maximum allowable.
② — Less than Minimum Refinish Thickness.

### BRAKE LINING SPECIFICATION

| Application | Drum Dia. In. (mm) | Width | | Length | | Thickness | |
|---|---|---|---|---|---|---|---|
| | | Front In. (mm) | Rear In. (mm) | Primary In. (mm) | Secondary In. (mm) | Primary In. (mm) | Secondary In. (mm) |
| 280Z (Rear) | 9.0 (229) | ① | 1.575 (40) | 8.64 (220) | 8.64 (220) | .177 (4.5) | .177 (4.5) |

① — Front disc brake equipped.

### BRAKE DRUM SPECIFICATIONS

| Application | Drum Diameter In. (mm) | Original Diameter In. (mm) | Maximum Refinish Diameter In. (mm) | Discard Diameter In. (mm) |
|---|---|---|---|---|
| 280Z (Rear) | 9.0 (229) | 9.0 (229) | 9.055 (230) | ① |

① — More than Maximum Refinish Diameter.

## DATSUN 510 (Cont.)

**510**

## DESCRIPTION

Brake system is hydraulically operated, utilizing a tandem master cylinder and Master-Vac power brake unit. Front disc brakes consist of rotors attached to wheel hubs, and single cylinder, dual-piston, floating-calipers attached to steering knuckles. Rear brakes are leading-trailing shoe/drum type, using a dual piston wheel cylinder. Parking brake is cable actuated, operating on rear wheels.

## ADJUSTMENT

### PEDAL HEIGHT

Adjust pedal height to specifications by maneuvering brake light switch and operating rod. Secure switch and rod after adjustment.

#### Pedal Height Specifications

| Application | Man. Trans. | Auto. Trans. |
|---|---|---|
| Datsun 510 | 6.06-6.30" | 6.14-6.38" |
| | (154-160 mm) | (156-162 mm) |

### FRONT DISC BRAKE PADS

Front disc brakes are self-adjusting, therefore, no adjustment in service is required.

### REAR BRAKE SHOES

Normally, no adjustment is required. Clearance between drum and shoes is automatically compensated when parking brake is operated.

### PARKING BRAKE

With rear brakes properly adjusted, adjust parking brake cable turnbuckle until rear brakes are locked when parking brake lever is pulled to sixth or seventh ratchet stop. Release parking brake lever and ensure rear wheels turn freely and that all parts are returned to their original position.

### BRAKE WARNING LIGHT

Light indicates parking brake is engaged. To adjust light operation, bend switch plate down until light comes on when brake lever is pulled up 1 notch and goes out when lever is released.

### COMBINATION VALVE

**Function Test** — Accelerate to about 30 mph on a dry concrete surface and harshly apply brakes. If rear wheels lock at same time as fronts do, or if front wheels lock before rears, combination valve is operating properly. If rear wheels lock first, combination valve is malfunctioning; replace valve.

### HYDRAULIC SYSTEM BLEEDING

Attach a bleed tube to bleeder screw and immerse opposite end of tube in a container partially filled with brake fluid. Pump brake pedal two or three times, keep pedal fully depressed, open bleeder screw and exhaust air, close bleeder screw, and return brake pedal. Repeat operation until air bubbles are no longer seen in discharged fluid. Repeat procedure on remaining brake lines. Bleed master cylinder first, rear wheels second, and front wheels last.

## REMOVAL & INSTALLATION

### FRONT DISC BRAKE PADS

**Removal** — Raise front of vehicle and support with safety stands. Remove wheels. Remove clip securing pad mounting pins. Retain anti-squeal springs with fingers and slide pads out of caliper. Remove anti-squeal springs.

**Inspection** — Clean pads. If any pad is worn to less than .08"(2 mm) all must be replaced. Always replace pads in sets (pad kit).

**Installation** — 1) Clean piston end and area around gripper. *See Fig. 1.* Loosen bleeder, push in outer piston until dust seal groove aligns with end of retaining ring on dust seal. Tighten bleeder. Insert inner pad.

2) Push inner piston in by pulling yoke. Fit outer pad. Grease following locations:

- Cylinder body-to-pad clearance.
- Pad pin-to-pad clearance.
- Pad pin-to-bracket clearance.

3) Refit anti-squeal spring and pad retaining pins. Insert keeper clips. Depress pedal several times to ensure proper operation.

**Fig. 1  Exploded View of Datsun 510 Front Disc Brake Assembly**

## DATSUN 510 (Cont.)

### FRONT DISC BRAKE CALIPER

**Removal** — Raise vehicle and suitably support on safety stands: remove tire and wheel. Remove brake friction pads as previously described. Disconnect brake line from caliper cylinder. Withdraw caliper mounting bolt and separate caliper from strut.

**Installation** — To install brake caliper assembly, reverse removal procedures, noting the following: Bleed hydraulic system.

### FRONT DISC BRAKE ROTOR

**Removal** — With caliper removed, remove hub dust cap, cotter pin and nut. Remove hub and rotor assembly with wheel bearing and washer in place. Remove bolts attaching rotor to wheel hub, and separate rotor from hub.

**Installation** — Reverse removal procedure, tighten rotor-to-hub bolts securely, and adjust wheel bearings.

### REAR BRAKE ASSEMBLY

**Removal** — Raise and support rear of vehicle. Remove brake drum as follows:
- Engage brake lever.
- Pull pin out. See Fig. 2. Remove stopper from lever.
- Disengage parking brake lever.

Disconnect brake line and plug open end. Disengage parking brake from back plate. Remove anti-rattle spring and pin. Take off return spring. Remove dust cover and lever with adjuster assembly. Remove wheel cylinder.

**Inspection** — Replace brake shoes that have worn to .059" (1.5 mm). Examine springs and replace those cracked or fatigued. Piston-to-wheel cylinder clearance must not exceed .059" (1.5 mm).

**Installation** — Reverse removal process to assemble and install rear brakes. Note that there are left and right hand threaded adjusters.

### MASTER CYLINDER

**Removal** — Disconnect front and rear brake lines from master cylinder. Remove master cylinder attaching nuts and remove master cylinder.

*Fig. 3   Exploded View of Tikico Made Master Cylinder. Nabco Made Master Cylinder is Similar But Has Different Piston Configuration*

*Fig. 2   Exploded View of Rear Brake Assembly*

## DATSUN 510 (Cont.)

**Installation** — To install master cylinder, reverse removal procedures, noting the following: Bleed hydraulic system and check pedal height.

### POWER BRAKE UNIT

**Removal** — Disconnect power unit push rod from brake pedal by removing clevis pin. Disconnect hydraulic lines from master cylinder and vacuum line from power unit, remove master cylinder attaching nuts, and remove master cylinder. Remove nuts attaching power unit to firewall, and remove power unit from engine compartment.

**Installation** — Reverse removal procedure, adjust brake pedal height, and bleed hydraulic system.

## OVERHAUL

### FRONT DISC BRAKE CALIPER

**Disassembly** — 1) Remove brake fluid from caliper cylinder body. Remove brake pads as previously outlined. Remove gripper pin mounting nuts. See *Fig. 1*.

2) Separate yoke from cylinder body. Take yoke holder out of piston. Remove retainer ring and dust seal from each piston.

3) Force pistons from cylinder using air pressure. Remove piston seals from grooves in cylinder. Only remove gripper if necessary.

**Inspection** — Check cylinder bore for damage (cracks, wear, etc.) and replace as necessary. Minor emery cloth work is acceptable. Check piston condition. Emery cloth polishing is not to be done on piston because sliding surface is plated.

**Reassembly** — 1) Fit new piston seals into place. Lightly coat pistons and cylinder with brake fluid. Insert pistons, one at a time, into cylinder body. Make sure outer piston yoke groove aligns with cylinder yoke groove.

2) Fit dust seals into position and secure with retainer rings. Install yoke holder to inner piston (*See Fig. 1*). Place gripper on yoke and drive in gripper pin. Install yoke to yoke holder while supporting outer piston, then press yoke into holder with a force not to exceed 60 lbs. (27 kg).

### WHEEL CYLINDER

**Disassembly** — Pull back dust covers. Push inward on one side until opposite side piston is forced out. Slide out cup and spring. Push through opposite direction and force out remaining cup and piston.

**NOTE** — *There are 2 types of wheel cylinders: Nabco and Tokico. Components are not interchangeable.*

**Reassembly** — Install spring. Fit cups and pistons with flat surfaces facing each other. Slide dust covers over wheel cylinder housing until they engage retainer groove.

### MASTER CYLINDER

**NOTE** — *Master cylinders are made by 2 different manufactures: Nabco and Tokico. Parts are not interchangeable.*

**Disassembly** — 1) Drain fluid out of reservoirs. Using a screwdriver force out stopper rings. Remove stop screw from cylinder body. Pull out primary piston assembly and spring. **2)** Slide secondary piston assembly and spring by stop screw hole and out of housing. Pistons can be further disassembled at this time. Also, inspect return springs for wear.

3) Remove plugs from bottom of cylinder housing to gain access to check valves. Replace check valves or springs found bad.

**Inspection** — Wash all components in clean brake fluid. Check piston-to-cylinder fit. There should be less than .006" (.15 mm) clearance between piston and cylinder bore.

**Reassembly** — Reverse disassembly procedure and note: Make sure proper kit is being used to replace worn parts. Bleed master cylinder and brake system.

### POWER BRAKE UNIT

**Disassembly** — 1) Place power unit in a soft jaw vise with operating rod pointing up. Scribe alignment marks on front and rear shells to assure reassembly in original position. Remove operating rod clevis, lock nut and dust boot.

2) Place Master-Vac wrench (ST08080000) over rear shell mounting studs. Press down on wrench while rotating counterclockwise and separate rear shell from front shell, then remove diaphragm plate assembly, diaphragm spring and push rod assembly. Pry off retainer and remove bearing and valve body seal from rear shell.

3) Remove rubber diaphragm from diaphragm plate assembly, then pry off air silencer retainer and remove silencer and filter. Rotate plate assembly until valve plunger key slot is down, then press in on plunger and shake out stop key. Remove reaction disc from plate assembly. Detach flange from front shell and remove plate and seal assembly.

**Cleaning & Inspection** — Clean all parts in denatured alcohol and blow dry with compressed air. Inspect front and rear shells for wear or damage. If slight rust is found on inside surface of shell, polish clean with fine emery cloth. Inspect all parts for cracks, nicks, distortion or other damage and replace as necessary.

**Reassembly** — Reverse disassembly procedure and note the following: Apply a thin coat of silicone grease to parts before reassembly. When assembling front shell to rear shell, ensure marks made during disassembly are aligned. After reassembly, measure distance from master cylinder mounting surface of power unit to end of power unit push rod; distance should be .38-.39" (9.8-10.0 mm). If distance is not to specifications, correct by adjusting tip of push rod.

# Brakes

## DATSUN 510 (Cont.)

### DISC BRAKE ROTOR SPECIFICATIONS

| Application | Disc Diameter In. (mm) | Lateral Runout In. (mm) | Parallelism In. (mm) | Original Thickness In. (mm) | Minimum Refinish Thickness In. (mm) | Discard Thickness In. (mm) |
|---|---|---|---|---|---|---|
| 510 | 9.625 (245) | .0047① (.12) | .0028 (.07) | .394 (10.0) | .331 (8.4) | ② |

① — Maximum.

② — Less than minimum refinish thickness.

### BRAKE DRUM SPECIFICATIONS

| Application | Drum Diameter In. (mm) | Original Diameter In. (mm) | Maximum Refinish Diameter In. (mm) | Discard Diameter In. (mm) |
|---|---|---|---|---|
| 510 | 9.00 (228.6) | 9.00 (228.6) | 9.055 (230) | ① |

① — More than maximum refinish diameter.

### BRAKE SYSTEM SPECIFICATIONS

| Application | Drum Diam. In. (mm) | Wheel Cylinder Diameter | | Master Cylinder |
|---|---|---|---|---|
| | | Front In. (mm) | Rear In. (mm) | Diameter In. (mm) |
| 510 | 9.00 (228.6) | ①2.012 (51.1) | .811 (20.6) | .811 (20.6) |

① — Caliper cylinder diameter.

## DATSUN PICKUP & 810

**Pickup**
**810**

### DESCRIPTION

Brake system is hydraulically operated, using a tandem master cylinder and a Master-Vac power brake unit. Front brakes are single cylinder, dual piston type. Rear brakes are leading-trailing drum type. A combination valve is used in brake system to prevent premature locking of rear brakes. Parking brake is cable operated by an actuating lever. Parking brake works on rear wheels only.

### ADJUSTMENT

#### BRAKE PEDAL HEIGHT & FREE PLAY ADJUSTMENT

Adjust brake light switch bolt until end face is flush with front face of bracket, then tighten lock nut. Adjust pedal stopper until pedal height, measured from pedal pad to floor, is 6.06" (154 mm) for Pickup or 7.09" (180 mm) for 810 models. Adjust master cylinder push rod length until free play, measured at pedal, is .030-.197" (1-5 mm).

#### FRONT DISC BRAKE PADS

Front disc brakes are self-adjusting; therefore, no adjustment in service is required.

#### REAR BRAKE SHOES

**Pickup** — With parking brake fully released, depress brake pedal several times so that shoes are settled to normal positions. Remove dust boot from backing plate. Lightly tap on adjuster housing to move it forward. Rotate adjuster using a screwdriver until brake drum locks. Back off adjuster about 12 notches to provide correct shoe-to-drum clearance.

**810** — No adjustment is required. Brakes are adjusted when parking brake is applied.

#### PARKING BRAKE

**Pickup** — Adjust rear service brakes. Raise vehicle until rear wheels clear floor. Apply parking brake lever 3.15-3.94". Adjust equalizer link with adjusting nut until rear wheels are locked. Release parking brake and ensure rear wheels turn freely.

**Station Wagon** — Make sure rear brakes are correctly adjusted. Adjust front cable adjusting nut so that when parking brake lever is pulled with specified force (see specifications), the lever stroke or the number of notches is as specified (see specifications). With parking brake off, make sure cables are slack and the rear levers are in their original positions.

**Sedan** — Make sure rear brakes are correctly adjusted. Adjust front cable adjusting nut so that when parking brake is off, dimension "A" (see *Fig. 1*) is .28" (7 mm). Tighten lock nut. Now adjust rear cable adjuster so that when parking brake lever is pulled with specified force (see specifications) the lever stroke or the number of notches is as specified (see specifications). With parking brake off, make sure cables are slack and the rear levers are in their original positions.

### Parking Brake Adjustment Specifications

| Adjustment | Station Wagon | Sedan |
|---|---|---|
| Pulling Force① | 53 lbs. (24 kg) | 44 lbs. (20 kg) |
| Lever Stroke | 4.49" | 4.02-4.49" |
| | (114 mm) | (102-114 mm) |
| No. of Notches | 6 | 5-6 |

① — Measured 1.97" (50 mm) from the end of the parking brake lever (less release button).

**Fig. 1  Adjusting Center Lever (Sedan Models)**

### BRAKE WARNING LIGHT

**810** — Light indicates parking brake is engaged. To adjust warning light, bend switch plate down until light operates when ratchet handle is pulled up one notch and so that light goes out when handle is returned to normal position.

### COMBINATION VALVE

**Function Test** — Accelerate to about 30 mph on a dry concrete surface and harshly apply brakes. If rear wheels lock at same time as fronts do, or if front wheels lock before rears, combination valve is operating properly. If rear wheels lock first, combination valve is malfunctioning; replace valve.

**Warning Light Operation & Reset** — Instrument panel light will come on when a pressure difference of between 71-224 psi is evident between front and rear hydraulic systems. Combination valve shuttle moves to side of low pressure and grounds electrical circuit causing warning light to come on. When hydraulic problem has been corrected and brakes have been bled, system should have 427 psi. Shuttle will then return to centered position and light will go out.

# Brakes

## DATSUN PICKUP & 810 (Cont.)

### HYDRAULIC SYSTEM BLEEDING

Attach a bleed tube to bleeder screw and immerse opposite end of tube in container partially filled with brake fluid. Depress pedal, open bleeder allowing air to escape, close bleeder screw, and allow pedal to return slowly. Continue operation until air bubbles are no longer seen in discharged fluid. Repeat procedure on remaining brake lines until all air is bled from system.

| Bleeding Sequence Chart | |
|---|---|
| **Application** | **Sequence** |
| 810 ................................. | Master Cylinder, Rear Brakes, Front Brakes |
| Pickup............ | Master Cylinder; Combination Valve, Front; Front Wheels; Left Rear; Right Rear; Combination Valve, Rear then Center |

## REMOVAL & INSTALLATION

### FRONT DISC BRAKE PADS

**Removal** — Raise and support front of vehicle. Remove retaining spring clip. Remove disc pad pins retaining anti-squeal springs. Pull pads from caliper cavity. If pad thickness is less than .079" (2 mm), replace pads.

**NOTE** — *Pads must always be replaced in sets.*

**Installation** — Clean cavity and area surrounding caliper. Loosen bleeder screw and seat outer piston in cylinder until dust seal groove of piston aligns with end surface of retaining ring on dust seal. **NOTE** — *Make sure piston groove does not go inside piston seal.* Tighten bleeder screw and fit new inner pad. Force inner piston into cylinder and install new outer pad. Install anti-squeal spring and insert pad pins, then put spring clip into position.

### FRONT DISC BRAKE CALIPER

**Removal** — Raise and support vehicle and remove tire and wheel assembly. Disconnect hydraulic line from caliper and plug openings. Remove bolts securing caliper to steering knuckle and remove caliper.

**Installation** — Reverse removal procedure, tighten mounting bolts securely, and bleed hydraulic system.

### FRONT DISC BRAKE ROTOR

**Removal** — With caliper assembly removed, remove hub dust cap, adjusting cap, adjustment nut and washer. Slide hub and rotor assembly from spindle taking care not to lose outer wheel bearing. Remove bolts attaching rotor to hub, then separate.

**Installation** — Reverse removal procedure, tighten rotor mounting bolts securly, and adjust wheel bearings. See *Wheel Bearing Adjustment* in *WHEEL ALIGNMENT* Section. Using a dial indicator, measure rotor runout. If runout exceeds .0059" (.15 mm), resurface or replace rotor.

### REAR BRAKE SHOES

**Removal (Pickup)** — 1) Raise rear of vehicle. Place vehicle on safety stands. Remove rear wheel. Remove rear brake drum.

**2)** Push in on mounting pin springs and cup washers. Remove pins. Remove strut. Disengage return springs. Remove primary shoe and adjuster assembly. Disconnect parking brake cable and remove secondary shoe with toggle lever.

**Installation** — To install, reverse removal procedure and note: Apply brake grease to moving parts of adjuster mechanism. If toggle lever has been separated from brake shoe, adjust clearance during reassembly to 0-.012" (0-.3 mm). Toggle pin washers (shims) are available in 5 sizes.

*Fig. 2 Rear Brake Assembly for Datsun Pickup. Note Detail of Adjuster Mechanism for Reassembly*

**Removal, 810 Sedan** — 1) Raise rear of vehicle, remove tire and brake drum. Apply parking brake. Lightly tap stopper head. Remove stopper and fastner as an assembly. Release parking brake.

**2)** If necessary, remove rear axle to gain access to rear brake components. Remove anti-rattle spring and pin. Remove return springs and brake shoes. Remove parking brake cable from lever. Pry off snap ring and remove lever from brake shoe.

**Installation** — To install, reverse removal procedure. Apply grease to adjuster nut and threads on rod. Also, apply grease to mating surfaces between adjuster and back plate.

**Removal, 810 Station Wagon** — 1) Raise rear of vehicle, remove tire and brake drum. Apply parking brake. Pull out pin and remove stopper from toggle lever. Release parking brake.

## DATSUN PICKUP & 810 (Cont.)

FRONT

WHEEL CYLINDER
Piston-to-Bore:
.006" (.15 mm) Max.

**Fig. 3   Exploded View of Rear Brake Assembly for Datsun 810 Sedan Models. 810 Station Wagon Models Are Similar But Have Different Brake Adjuster Mechanism Configuration**

**2)** If necessary, remove rear axle shaft to gain access to brake components. Remove anti-rattle spring and pin. Remove return springs and brake shoes. Remove parking brake return spring, then remove cross-rod cotter pin. Remove dust cover and toggle lever with adjuster assembly.

**Installation** — To install, reverse removal procedure. Apply grease to adjuster nut and rod threads. Also apply grease to mating surface between adjuster and toggle lever.

### WHEEL CYLINDER

**Removal (Pickup)** — With brake drum and shoe removed, disconnect brake fluid line and plug opening. Remove cylinder mounting nuts and slide wheel cylinder off backing plate.

**NOTE** — *For disassembly refer to Fig. 4.*

**Installation** — To install, reverse removal procedure and bleed brake system.

**Removal, 810** — With brake drum and shoes removed, disconnect hydraulic line at rear of wheel cylinder. Remove bolt securing wheel cylinder to backing plate and remove cylinder.

**Installation** — To install, reverse removal procedure. Bleed hydraulic system after installation.

### MASTER CYLINDER

**Removal** — Disconnect and plug front and rear hydraulic lines from master cylinder and drain brake fluid from cylinder. Remove master cylinder attaching nuts and lift off master cylinder.

WHEEL CYLINDER FOR PICKUP

WHEEL CYLINDER FOR 810

**Fig. 4   Exploded View of Wheel Cylinders**

**Installation** — Reverse removal procedure and bleed hydraulic system.

### POWER BRAKE UNIT

**Removal** — With master cylinder removed, disconnect vacuum line from power unit. From inside vehicle, disconnect pedal return spring, push rod from brake pedal, and power unit mounting nuts. Remove power unit from engine compartment.

**Installation** — Reverse removal procedure, adjust pedal height and free play, and bleed hydraulic system.

**Check Valve Replacement** — On 810 models, valve is located near identification plate on firewall. On Pickup models, valve is located in vacuum line between intake manifold and power booster unit. To remove, loosen hose clamps, separate hoses from valve, and remove valve. To in-

### OVERHAUL

### FRONT DISC BRAKE CALIPER

**Disassembly** — Drain any remaining fluid from cylinder. Remove holding mounting nut, See Fig. 5. Separate yoke and cylinder body. Remove yoke holder from piston. Take off retaining ring and dust seals from both inner and outer pistons. Force pistons from cylinder using compressed air. Carefully pry out piston seals.

# Brakes

## DATSUN PICKUP & 810 (Cont.)

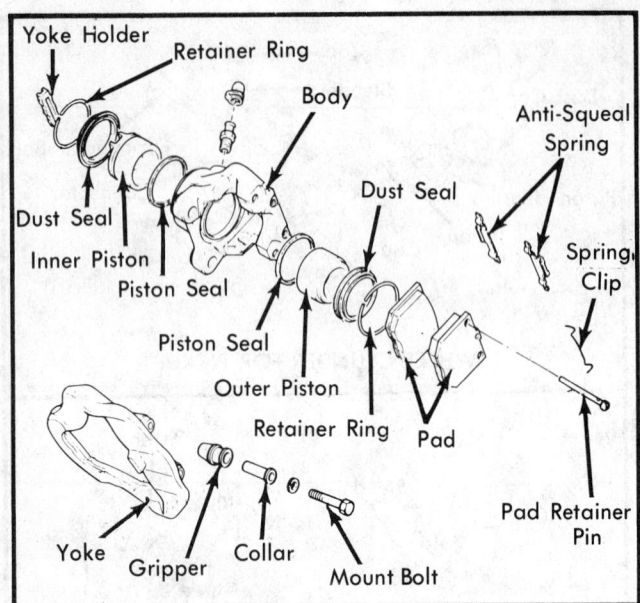

**Fig. 5   Exploded View of Front Disc Brake Caliper**

**Inspection** — Clean all components in brake fluid. Inspect for rust, score marks, damage, or wear. Minor damage can be polished out with a fine emery cloth, except on piston head.

**Reassembly** — Carefully refit piston seals. Apply a light coat of brake fluid to sliding surfaces. Insert inner piston so yoke groove aligns with groove in cylinder. Fit dust seal and insert retainer ring. Fit yoke holder to inner piston. Drive in holding pin. Support end of piston, then press yoke into holder.

### MASTER CYLINDER

**Disassembly** — Remove reservoir cap and drain fluid. Remove dust cover, retaining ring and piston stop screw. Remove washer, primary piston assembly, secondary piston assembly and return spring. Remove valve plugs and remove check valves. **NOTE** — *Do not remove master cylinder reservoir tanks; if removed new tanks must be reinstalled.*

**Cleaning & Inspection** — Clean all parts in alcohol or brake fluid, and inspect for wear or damage; replace parts as required. Check clearance between cylinder bore and piston; if greater than .006" (.15 mm) replace cylinder or piston a required. **NOTE** — *Manufacturer recommends replacing cylinder cups and valves whenever master cylinder has been disassembled.*

**Reassembly** — Coat all parts with clean brake fluid and reverse disassembly procedure.

### POWER BRAKE UNIT

**Disassembly** — 1) Place power unit in a soft jaw vise with operating rod pointing up. Scribe alignment marks on front and rear shells to assure reassembly in original position. Remove operating rod clevis, lock nut and dust boot.

2) Place Master-Vac wrench (ST08080000) over rear shell mounting studs. Press down on wrench while rotating counterclockwise and separate rear shell from front shell, then remove diaphragm plate assembly, diaphragm spring and push rod assembly. Pry off retainer and remove bearing and valve body seal from rear shell.

3) Remove rubber diaphragm from diaphragm plate assembly, then pry off air silencer retainer and remove silencer and filter. Rotate plate assembly until valve plunger key slot is down, then press in on plunger and shake out stop key. Remove reaction disc from plate assembly. Detach flange from front shell and remove plate and seal assembly.

**Fig. 6   Exploded View of 810 Master Cylinder**

**Fig. 7   Exploded View of Pickup Master Cylinder**

## DATSUN PICKUP & 810 (Cont.)

**Cleaning & Inspection** — Clean all parts in denatured alcohol and blow dry with compressed air. Inspect front and rear shells for wear or damage. If slight rust is found on inside surface of shell, polish clean with fine emery cloth. Inspect all parts for cracks, nicks, distortion or other damage and replace as necessary.

**Reassembly** — Reverse disassembly procedure and note the following: Apply a thin coat of silicone grease to parts before reassembly. When assembling front shell to rear shell, ensure marks made during disassembly are aligned. After reassembly, measure distance from master cylinder mounting surface of power unit to end of power unit push rod; distance should be .38-.39" (9.8-10.0 mm). If distance is not to specifications, correct by adjusting tip of push rod.

### TIGHTENING SPECIFICATIONS

| Application | Ft. Lbs. (mkg) |
|---|---|
| Master Cylinder-to-Master Vac | 6-8 (.8-1.1) |
| Caliper Mounting Bolts | 53-72 (7.3-9.9) |
| Backing Plate Bolts | |
| Pickup | 39-46 (5.4-6.4) |
| 810 St. Wgn. | 16-20 (2.2-2.7) |
| 810 Sedan | 20-27 (2.7-3.7) |
| Rotor-to-Hub | 28-38 (3.9-5.3) |

### BRAKE SYSTEM SPECIFICATIONS

| Application | Drum Diam. In. (mm) | Wheel Cylinder Diameter | | Master Cylinder Diameter In. (mm) |
|---|---|---|---|---|
| | | Front In. (mm) | Rear In. (mm) | |
| Pickup | 10 (254) | 2.125① (53.98) | .625 (15.88) | .813 (20.6) |
| 810 | 9 (229) | 2.125① (53.98) | .813 (20.6) | .813 (20.6) |

① — Disc Brakes.

### DISC BRAKE ROTOR SPCIFICATIONS

| Application | Disc Diameter In. (mm) | Lateral Runout In. (mm) | Parallelism In. (mm) | Original Thickness In. (mm) | Minimum Refinish Thickness In. (mm) | Discard Thickness In. (mm) |
|---|---|---|---|---|---|---|
| Pickup | 10.67 (271) | .0059 (.15) | ..... | .492 (12.5) | .413 (10.5) | ..... |
| 810 | 10.67 (271) | .0059 (.15) | .0012 (.03) | .492 (12.5) | .413 (10.5) | ..... |

### BRAKE DRUM SPECIFICATIONS

| Application | Drum Diameter In. (mm) | Original Diameter In. (mm) | Maximum Refinish Diameter In. (mm) | Discard Diameter In. (mm) |
|---|---|---|---|---|
| Pickup | 10 (254) | 10.000 (254) | 10.059 (255.5) | ① |
| 810 | 9 (229) | 9.000 (229) | 9.055 (230) | ① |

① — More than maximum refinish diameter.

# Brakes

## FIAT

124 Spider
128
131
 Brava
 Super Brava
X1/9

## DESCRIPTION

Brake system is hydraulically actuated, using a tandem master cylinder and a Master Vac power brake unit. All front brakes are single piston, sliding caliper type. 128 and 131 models use leading-trailing rear drum brakes, while 124 and X1/9 models use single piston rear disc brakes. All models except X1/9 use pressure differential valves. Parking brakes are cable operated and work either on rear drums or rear brake calipers.

## ADJUSTMENT

### DISC BRAKE PADS

Front disc brakes are self-adjusting, no in-service adjustment is required.

### REAR BRAKE SHOES

Rear drum brakes are self-adjusting, no in-service adjustment is required.

### PARKING BRAKE

Fully release parking brake lever, then pull up approximately two notches. On 124 and X1/9 models, tighten nut on equalizer until cable is tight. X1/9 models have an opening provided in floor pan under body for access to equalizer. On 128 models, loosen lock nut on tensioner located along under body and tighten adjuster nut until rear wheels are locked. On 131 models, loosen lock nut located near parking brake handle and tighten until rear wheels lock.

### BRAKE PRESSURE REGULATOR

**124 Spider** — 1) Bring end of torsion bar (E) to distance (X) from rubber buffer resting surface.

2) Lift dust boot (C) and check contact of regulator piston (D) with torsion bar end (E).

3) Pivot regulator body on screw (A) until piston (D) is just touching torsion bar end (E).

4) First, tighten screw (B) and then screw (A) in all the way. Connect link (G) to torsion bar eye end (E) with screw and nut while inserting rubber bushings and spacer.

**NOTE** — *Fluid inlet from master cylinder must be connected to lower union (R) and fluid line to rear brakes must be connected to upper union (S).*

**Fig. 1   Brake Pressure Regulator Measurement and Adjustment Points for 128**

**Fig. 2   Brake Pressure Regulator Measurement and Adjustment Points for 124**

## FIAT (Cont.)

**128** — With pressure regulator mounting bolts loosened and link (4) disconnected from control arm anchor pin (5), check that the axis of torsion bar end (3b) is 2.126″±.197″ from center of rubber buffer seat (2). Once obtained, position pressure regulator with piston (8) just touching torsion bar end (3a). Tighten regulator mounting bolts (7) on bracket (12), then connect link (4) to control arm anchor pin (5).

**131** — Install regulator and leave mounting bolts loose. Bring torsion bar (7) to dimension (X) from the base of buffer end (11). Remove rubber boot (3) from regulator, then rotate regulator until piston (6) is just touching torsion bar (1). Tighten mounting bolts.

*Fig. 3   Brake Pressure Regulator Measurement and Adjustment Points for 131 Models*

### HYDRAULIC SYSTEM BLEEDING

Attach a bleed tube to wheel cylinder bleeder screw and immerse opposite end of tube in a container partially filled with brake fluid. Loosen bleeder screw, depress brake pedal quickly and allow to return slowly. Continue operation until air bubbles are no longer seen in discharge fluid. Tighten bleeder screw on a down stroke of pedal application. Repeat procedure on remaining brake lines until all air is bled from system.

## REMOVAL & INSTALLATION

### DISC BRAKE CALIPERS & PADS

**Removal** — Raise and support vehicle; remove wheels. Plug master cylinder outlet ports. Disconnect brake line from caliper assembly. Remove cotter pins from locking blocks, drive out locking blocks and remove caliper. Take out disc pads and springs. On models with rear disc brakes, parking brake must be disconnected.

**NOTE** — *Pads MUST be replaced when worn to .079″ (2 mm) from original thickness.*

**Installation** — To install caliper and pad assemblies, reverse removal procedure and note the following: Inside and outside pads may be different. When fitting pads to calipers, ensure distance between inner surfaces is not less than .413″ (10.5 mm). In most instances two kinds of pads are available, be sure index paint stripes are not mixed.

### BRAKE ROTOR

**Removal** — Remove caliper as previously outlined. Before removing rotor check runout against specification. Runout should not exceed .006″ (.15 mm). Remove caliper support

bracket from support plate (front) or from axle housing (rear). Remove bolts mounting rotor to wheel hub, remove hub plate, then remove rotor using a suitable drift or puller.

**Installation** — Fit rotor onto wheel hub, install attaching bolts and tighten evenly.

### REAR BRAKE SHOES

**Removal** — Raise and support rear of vehicle and remove wheels. Remove bolts attaching drum. Install a suitable tool to retain wheel cylinder pistons, remove upper and lower shoe return springs, shoe guide pins, springs, and cups, then remove brake shoes.

*Fig. 4   Typical Rear Drum Brake Assembly for 128 Models*

**Installation** — Reverse removal procedure making sure shoe ends are correctly positioned in wheel cylinder pistons.

### REAR WHEEL CYLINDER

**Removal** — With rear brake shoes removed, disconnect hydraulic line from wheel cylinder, remove bolts attaching wheel cylinder to backing plate and remove wheel cylinder assembly.

**Installation** — To install, reverse removal procedure and bleed hydraulic system.

### MASTER CYLINDER

**Removal, Exc. X1/9** — On all models except 131, remove reservoir cover and plug fluid outlet line to prevent fluid loss. On 131 models only, drain fluid from reservoir and extract reservoir om master cylinder, using side-to-side rocking motion. On 128 models, remove spare tire. Disconnect fluid supply line at cylinder, hydraulic lines to front and rear brakes, and nuts retaining master cylinder to power unit.

**Installation** — To install, reverse removal procedure and bleed hydraulic system.

**Removal, X1/9** — Remove steering column. *See Steering Column Removal in STEERING Section.* Disconnect hydraulic lines from reservoir. Remove mounting nuts and slide unit off supports. Disconnect outlet lines from master cylinder.

## FIAT (Cont.)

**Installation** – To install, reverse removal procedure and bleed hydraulic system.

## OVERHAUL

**Disassembly, Front** – With caliper assembly on bench, remove dust boot. Apply light air pressure to brake fluid inlet union and gently force piston from caliper. Remove piston seal from groove in piston cylinder bore. **NOTE** – *Be sure bore is not scratched during removal process.*

**Inspection** – Clean all components in suitable solvent (Fiat LDC). Inspect each part for damage or excessive wear. Replace all piston seals and dust boots.

**Reassembly** – Fit piston seal in caliper. Insert piston to bottom end of cylinder bore. Position dust boot on caliper body. Fit caliper body into caliper bracket and reinstall on vehicle.

**Fig. 5   Front Brake Caliper Assembly for 124 and 131 Models**

**Disassembly, Rear** – With caliper assembly on bench, remove dust boot. With a screwdriver, separate piston from plunger. Remove piston seal from groove in piston cylinder bore. Remove cam lever, pivot pin, and lever. Lift out self-adjusting plunger, plunger seal, disc spring, and spring thrust washer.

**Inspection** – Clean all components in suitable solvent (Fiat LDC). Inspect each part for damage or excessive wear. Replace all piston seals and dust boots.

**Reassembly** – Fit self-adjusting plunger complete with seal, disc springs, and thrust washer. Fit parking brake cam lever complete with pivot pin. Fit pivot pin bushing and snap ring. Fit piston sealing ring into caliper cylinder. Screw piston into cylinder until fully seated. Align piston slot so it is opposite bleed connection. Refit dust boot.

**Fig. 6   Front Brake Caliper Assembly for 124 Models**

## REAR WHEEL CYLINDER

**Disassembly** – Remove boots, then remove pistons, seal rings, backing washers and reaction spring. Take out bleeder valve.

**Inspection** – Clean and dry all parts and inspect for excessive wear or damage. Light damage may be removed by honing; make sure bore size is not altered. Replace all rubber components at each overhaul.

**Fig. 7   Exploded View of Rear Brake Caliper for 124 Models**

## FIAT (Cont.)

*Fig. 8   Disassembled View of X1/9 Master Cylinder*

*Fig. 9   Fiat Rear Wheel Cylinder Assembly*

**Reassembly** — To reassemble, reverse disassembly procedure and note the following: Lightly coat all parts with brake fluid when assembling to prevent damage. Once assembled, move pistons to ensure they slide freely in cylinder bore.

### MASTER CYLINDER

**Disassembly** — Separate fluid inlet union from master cylinder. Disengage boot from cylinder body. Back out set screws and end plug (if equipped). Remove the following components: Piston assemblies, return springs, cups, seal rings, and spacers.

**Inspection** — Clean and thoroughly dry all parts, then inspect for wear or damage. Light scoring may be removed by honing, make sure honing does not alter size of cylinder diameter. Replace all rubber pieces each time overhaul is performed.

**Reassembly** — To reassemble, reverse disassembly procedure and lightly coat all components with brake fluid before reassembly.

*Fig. 10   Sectional View of Master Cylinder Assembly for 128 models*

# Brakes

## FIAT (Cont.)

### BRAKE DRUM SPECIFICATIONS

| Application | Drum Diameter | Original Diameter | Maximum Refinish Diameter | Discard Diameter |
|---|---|---|---|---|
| 128 Rear (Exc. X1/9) | 7.3 (185) | 7.293-7.304 (185.2-185.5) | 7.325 (186) | 7.355 (186.6) |
| 131 Rear | 9.0 (228.6) | 8.988-9.000 (228.3-228.6) | 9.03 (229.4) | 9.055 (230) |

### BRAKE SYSTEM SPECIFICATIONS

| Application | Drum Diam. In. (mm) | Wheel Cylinder Diameter | | Master Cylinder |
| | | Front In. (mm) | Rear In. (mm) | Diameter In. (mm) |
|---|---|---|---|---|
| 128 (Exc. X1/9 | 7.3① (185) | 1.89② (48) | .750 (19.05) | .750 (19.05) |
| 124 & X1/9 | ..... | 1.89② (48) | 1.34③ (34) | .750 (19.05) |
| 131 | 9.00① (228.6) | 1.89② (48) | .874 (22.2) | .750 (19.05) |

① — Rear.
② — Caliper Bore Diameter.
③ — Rear Caliper Bore Diameter.

### DISC BRAKE ROTOR SPECIFICATIONS

| Application | Disc Diameter In. (mm) | Lateral Runout In. (mm) | Parallelism In. (mm) | Original Thickness In. (mm) | Minimum Refinish Thickness In. (mm) | Discard Thickness In. (mm) |
|---|---|---|---|---|---|---|
| All Models | 8.937 (227) | .0059 (.15) | .0019① (.05) | .392-.400 (9.95-10.2) | .368② (9.35) | .354 (9.0) |

① — 128 3P Only.
② — 124 Rear is .372" (9.45 mm).

## FIESTA

Fiesta

### DESCRIPTION

The Fiesta braking system is hydraulically operated on all four wheels. All models incorporate disc brakes on the front and drum type brakes on the rear. The hydraulic pressure originates at the master cylinder as the brake pedal is depressed.

Fiesta braking system is different than other Ford models in that the system is split diagonally. In most dual-circuit brake systems, the front and rear wheels are separated by the two circuits. The Fiesta system ties the left front and right rear wheel into one circuit, and the right front and left rear wheel into the other circuit.

Front disc brake calipers are a single piston design and are not adjustable. The rear drum brakes consist of a primary and secondary shoe operated by a double-acting cylinder. Rear brakes are self-adjusting. The parking brake operates the rear brakes only.

The master cylinder is a tandem type, located on left side of engine compartment. Primary chamber provides fluid pressure for the right front/left rear circuit, while the secondary chamber provides fluid for the left front/right rear circuit.

Rear Drum Brakes

Master Cylinder

Wheel Cylinder

Brake Servo Unit
(Some Models)

Front Disc Brakes

BRAKE LINE CIRCUIT — Right Front/Left Rear

BRAKE LINE CIRCUIT — Left Front/Right Rear

*Fig. 1   Fiesta Brake System — Overall View*

### BRAKE WARNING SYSTEM

A low fluid level indicator, operating from either circuit, will warn the vehicle operator of a fluid loss. The warning light is located on the dash panel. Check fluid level if warning light is ON with engine running and parking brake released.

Warning light can be tested by depressing switch on top of master cylinder filler cap. Light should come ON, with engine running. If not, replace bulb or check cap assembly for defects.

### ADJUSTMENTS

**FRONT DISC BRAKE PADS**

Front disc brakes are self-adjusting; therefore, no adjustment in service is required.

**REAR BRAKE SHOES**

After brake shoe installation, brakes can be adjusted by depressing brake pedal several times. Check brakes on road test.

**PARKING BRAKE**

1) Jack up vehicle and place on safety stands.

2) Release parking brake.

3) Loosen adjuster nut "A" *See Fig. 2.*

4) Rotate cable adjuster "B" to allow slack in cable.

5) With parking brake in OFF position, tighten cable by turning adjuster until all slack is out of cable.

6) After parking brake levers have just begun to move, turn adjuster THREE MORE complete turns and secure lock nut "A".

**NOTE** — *When adjustment is completed, machined groove "C" must not protrude past lock nut "A".*

"C" — Machined Groove          "B" — Cable Adjuster

"A" — Adjuster Lock Nut

*Fig. 2   Fiesta Parking Brake Adjuster*

**BRAKE BLEEDING**

1) Cover fenders and raise vehicle.

2) Remove brake fluid reservoir cap and fill as necessary.

3) Both chambers should be full of suitable brake fluid.

**CAUTION** — *If brake fluid comes in contact with painted surfaces, wash with cold water immediately.*

4) Remove rubber dust cap from left front wheel brake bleeding nipple. Install suitable bleed tube.

5) Run other end of bleed tube into fluid resistant container partially filled with approved brake fluid (clean).
**NOTE** — *Keep end of bleed tube immersed in fluid during entire bleeding operation.*

6) Unscrew bleed valve about ½ turn. Depress brake pedal completely. Allow pedal to return to normal OFF position.

## FIESTA (Cont.)

7) Brake fluid or air bubbles should have been pumped into container. If not, open bleed valve further and repeat procedure.

8) With a three second pause between strokes, continue to depress and release brake pedal until fluid entering container is clear and free of air bubbles.

9) Press pedal to floor and hold while tightening bleed valve.

10) Check master cylinder fluid level and fill as needed.

11) Remove bleed tube and install rubber dust cap.

12) Bleed right rear wheel brake following same procedure. **NOTE** — *When bleeding rear brakes, parking brake should be ON.*

13) Release parking brake.

14) Bleed right front wheel brake following same procedure.

15) Apply parking brake and bleed left rear wheel brake.

16) Release hand brake. Fill master cylinder with approved brake fluid. **CAUTION** — *Do not fill master cylinder reservoir above 'MAX' mark.*

17) Check brake operation during road test.

| Brake Line Bleeding | |
|---|---|
| **Sequence** | **Wheel** |
| First | Left Front |
| Second | Right Rear |
| Third | Right Front |
| Fourth | Left Rear |

## REMOVAL & INSTALLATION

### FRONT DISC BRAKE PADS

**Removal** — 1) Raise and support front of vehicle.

2) Remove wheel and tire assembly.

**Fig. 3   Removing Disc Brake Caliper**

3) Remove caliper retaining pins and discard.

4) Apply light pressure to piston housing against caliper tension springs. Slide out keys and discard.

5) Remove piston housing (caliper) from rotor. Suspend caliper assembly from vehicle body using suitable wire.

**NOTE** — *Do not let piston housing (caliper) assembly hang by brake line.*

6) Remove old brake pads and anti-rattle clips from pad housing.

**Installation** — 1) Ensure new pads are correct type. All parts (pads, clips, key and disc) must be clean.

2) Carefully apply pressure to face of piston, pushing it back into its bore. Do not damage piston face.

3) Install new disc brake pads and anti-rattle clips into pad housing.

**NOTE** — *Anti-rattle clips must be fitted to top of brake pad.*

4) Install piston housing (caliper), ensuring that it is mounted above caliper tension springs.

5) Apply pressure to piston housing against caliper tension springs and slide in NEW keys.

**NOTE** — *Be sure that retaining pin holes in key and in piston housing are aligned.*

6) Insert new retaining pins from disc side and secure.

7) Depress and release brake pedal several times to bring pads into proper adjustment.

8) Replace wheel and tire assembly.

9) Lower vehicle and tighten lug nuts.

### FRONT DISC BRAKE CALIPER

**Removal** — 1) Raise vehicle and support with safety stands.

2) Remove wheel and tire assembly.

3) Disconnect brake fluid flexible hose from caliper. Plug open brake line.

4) Remove both caliper retaining bolts and remove caliper.

**Installation** — 1) Mount caliper assembly in position.

2) Install and tighten (2) retaining bolts.

3) Remove plug and connect flexible brake line hose.

4) Install wheel, lower vehicle and tighten lug nuts.

5) Bleed brake system. *See Brake Bleeding in this article.*

## FIESTA (Cont.)

**Fig. 4    Exploded View of Front Disc Brake Caliper**

### FRONT DISC BRAKE ROTOR

**Removal** — 1) With caliper assembly removed and suspended from body with suitable length of wire, remove disc retaining screw.

2) Carefully remove rotor assembly.

**Fig. 5    Fiesta Disc Brake Rotor & Caliper
Front Wheels Only**

**Installation** — 1) Ensure all parts are clean.

2) Mount disc assembly in position and secure retaining screw.

3) Install caliper assembly. *See Front Disc Brake Caliper Installation in this article.*

### REAR BRAKE SHOES

**Removal** — 1) Raise vehicle and support with safety stands.

2) Remove rear wheels.

3) Release parking brake fully.

4) Disconnect parking brake cable from brake assembly by removing spring clip and pulling out clevis pin.

5) Remove parking brake lever rubber dust cover from brake carrier plate.

6) Remove the following parts in order given:
    Spindle and bearing dust cap
    Cotter pin
    Adjusting nut retainer
    Adjusting nut
    Washer
    Outer bearing

7) Slide hub and drum assembly clear of spindle.

**Fig. 6    Exploded View of Fiesta Rear Brake Assembly**

## FIESTA (Cont.)

**8)** Remove hold-down spring from primary shoe by depressing and turning washer 90°. Remove spring and washer. Pull pin from carrier plate.

**9)** Twist primary shoe (shoe nearest rear of vehicle) out and up away from carrier plate. Use care not to damage cylinder dust cover.

**10)** Detach shoe and remove springs.

**11)** Remove hold-down spring from secondary shoe.

**12)** Slide lower end of spacer strut out from carrier plate slot.

**13)** Twist secondary shoe up and away from carrier plate. Remove parking brake lever and shoe assembly from carrier plate.

**14)** Disassemble primary shoe assembly.

**15)** Separate secondary shoe from strut by twisting, and remove spring.

**Installation** — Reverse removal procedure while noting the following:

**1)** Be sure parking brake lever rotates freely to spacer strut. Pin should rotate in strut hole and be riveted tightly to lever.

**2)** When assembling primary brake shoe, proceed as follows:
  **a.** Mount smaller ratchet and spring on shoe pivot. Slide two .008" (.2 mm) feeler gauges (one on each side of pivot) between brake shoe and ratchet. Install new spring retaining washer. Retaining tabs must be secure. Remove feelers. Ratchet should rotate freely on pivot and return freely with spring pressure.
  **b.** Mount larger ratchet to brake shoe. Secure with new spring clip. Push clip in fully. Ratchet should rotate freely.
  **c.** Position two ratchets relative to each other with an overlap. See Fig. 7

**Fig. 7   Assembling Large & Small Ratchets on Primary Brake Shoe**

**3)** Stronger of the two brake return springs mounts between shoes at pivot end, opposite from wheel cylinder.

**4)** Weaker of the two brake return springs mounts between shoes at wheel cylinder ends.

**5)** Install outer wheel bearing by tightening nut to 37 ft. lbs. (5.1 mkg) while turning drum. Back nut off 90° and install nut retainer. Install new cotter pin. Install dust cap.

**6)** Adjust rear brake by depressing brake pedal and releasing several times. Road test for brake operation.

### REAR BRAKE WHEEL CYLINDER

**Removal** — **1)** Remove rear brake shoe assembly. See Rea Brake Shoes — Removal in this article.

**2)** Disconnect brake fluid line and plug line.

**3)** Remove (2) retaining bolts from back of carrier plate anc remove wheel cylinder.

**Installation** — **1)** Ensure all parts are clean.

**2)** Replace wheel cylinder on carrier plate and install (2) retaining bolts.

**3)** Reconnect fluid line.

**4)** Install rear brake shoe assembly.

**5)** Bleed brake system. See Brake Bleeding in this article.

### MASTER CYLINDER

**Removal** — **1)** Disconnect battery and cover fenders.
**NOTE** — If brake fluid contacts any painted surfaces, wash immediately with cold water.

**2)** Remove filler cap from master cylinder.

**3)** Draw brake fluid from reservoir.

**4)** Tip reservoir assembly sideways and remove from cylinder.

**5)** Remove (2) rubber seals from cylinder assembly. Replace if necessary.

**6)** Detach fluid lines by carefully unscrewing union nuts. Install plugs.

**7)** Disconnect electrical wires from switch in differential valve (if equipped).

**8)** Remove spring clip. Withdraw clevis pin and bushing from pedal shaft and master cylinder push rod.

**9)** Remove (2) nuts and spring washers holding master cylinder to firewall. Remove master cylinder.

# Brakes

## FIESTA (Cont.)

**Fig. 9   Separating Reservoir from Master Cylinder**

**Installation** — Reverse removal procedure and note the following:

**1)** All parts must be absolutely clean before installation.

**2)** Torque fluid line union nuts.

**3)** After filling master cylinder with suitable brake fluid, bleed brake system. *See Brake Bleeding in this article.*

**4)** Check brake system operation on road test.

## POWER BRAKE SERVO UNIT

**Removal** — **1)** Remove spring clip and clevis pin holding actuating rod to brake pedal.

**2)** Cover fenders for paint protection.

**3)** Disconnect vacuum hose from non-return valve on front of servo unit.

**4)** Disconnect brake lines and install plugs.

**CAUTION** — *Block vent hole in reservoir cap with tape to prevent excessive fluid loss. If fluid contacts painted surface, wash immediately with cold water.*

**5)** Remove (2) nuts and washers attaching master cylinder unit to servo.

**6)** Remove master cylinder from servo.

**7)** Remove (4) attaching nuts and washers from servo unit and remove servo.

**Installation** — Reverse removal procedure and note the following:

**1)** Torque fluid line union nuts.

**2)** Remove tape from reservoir vent hole.

**3)** After filling master cylinder with suitable brake fluid, bleed brake system. *See Brake Bleeding in this article.*

## OVERHAUL

### FRONT DISC BRAKE CALIPER

**Disassembly** — Remove piston rubber bellows. To remove piston force air pressure or low hydraulic pressure to piston via brake fluid inlet port. Using pointed tool, dig out piston seal from groove in piston housing. See *Fig. 4.*

**Inspection** — Wash piston and piston housing bore in suitable cleaner (alcohol). Make sure piston and bore do not have scratches or score marks.

**Reassembly** — Fit piston seal in piston housing groove. Lightly coat piston with brake fluid. Push piston into bore until fully seated. Make sure piston seal is not damaged as piston is seated. Fit piston rubber bellows between piston housing and piston seal.

### MASTER CYLINDER

**Disassembly** — **1)** With master cylinder removed, pry reservoir off and remove rubber seals. Support cylinder in a soft jaw vise. Depress push rod to relieve piston stop pin pressure, then remove stop pin.

**2)** Using a pair of pliers, remove retaining clip located under dust boot of push rod. Take off push rod, boot, and washer.

**3)** Slide out primary piston assembly. Tap master cylinder softly in palm of hand to jar out secondary piston assembly. Disassemble primary and secondary pistons. *See Fig. 10 and Fig. 11.*

**Fig. 10   Parts Relationship of Primary Piston Assembly**

## FIESTA (Cont.)

**Inspection** — Check cylinder bores and pistons for obvious signs of score marks, ridges, or corrosion. Replace components if necessary. Clean pistons assemblies in commercial alcohol. Replace rubber parts.

**Reassembly** — **1)** Install new secondary piston seals and secure in place with retainer and spring to piston. Refer to *Fig. 11* for correct seal installation. Lightly coat secondary piston assembly in brake fluid and slide into cylinder bore.

**2)** Fit new primary piston seals ( *See Fig. 10* ) and secure in place with retainer, spring, sleeve and screw. Lightly coat primary piston assembly in brake fluid and slide into cylinder bore.

**3)** Refit push rod and boot to master cylinder. Depress push rod enough to insert piston stop pin into secondary inlet port. Install new rubber seals to inlet ports and fit reservoir.

*Fig. 11   Parts Relationship of Secondary Piston Assembly*

### WHEEL CYLINDER

**Disassembly** — Remove dust covers. Force out piston assemblies from cylinder bore. Separate piston seals from spring and flat side of piston. Remove bleed screw, if necessary.

**Inspection** — Clean cylinder bore and pistons. Check pistons and cylinder bore for score marks or grooves. Replace components as necessary.

**Reassembly** — Fit dust covers to pistons. Insert one piston and dust cover into position. Working from opposite end, slide in the following parts:
- Piston seal, flat side first.
- Spring.
- Piston seal, flat side first.
- Piston and dust cover.

### TIGHTENING SPECIFICATIONS

| Application | Ft. Lbs. (mkg) |
|---|---|
| Caliper-to-Front Suspension Unit | 38-45 (5.3-6.2) |
| Carrier Plate-to--Axle Housing | 15-18 (2.1-2.5) |
| Fluid Line-to-Master Cylinder Union Nuts | 8-11 (1.2-1.5) |
| Bleed Valves | 8 (1.0) Maximum[1] |

[1] — Tighten sufficiently to seal.

### BRAKE SYSTEM SPECIFICATIONS

| Application | Drum Diam. In. (mm) | Wheel Cylinder Diameter | | Master Cylinder |
|---|---|---|---|---|
| | | Front In. (mm) | Rear In. (mm) | Diameter In. (mm) |
| Fiesta | 7.00[1] (177.8) | 1.89 (48.0) | .59 (15.0) | ..... |

[1] — Drum brakes on rear only.

### DISC BRAKE ROTOR SPECIFICATIONS

| Application | Disc Diameter In. (mm) | Lateral Runout In. (mm) | Parallelism In. (mm) | Original Thickness In. (mm) | Minimum Refinish Thickness In. (mm) | Discard Thickness In. (mm) |
|---|---|---|---|---|---|---|
| Fiesta | 5.8[1] (148.0) | .006 (.15) | ..... | .39 (10.0) | .34[2] (8.7) | [3] |

[1] — Inner diameter shown. Outer diameter is 8.7" (221 mm).
[2] — Minimum allowable.
[3] — Less than minimum thickness.

# Brakes

## HONDA

Civic
Civic CVCC
Accord

## DESCRIPTION

Brake system is hydraulically actuated, using a tandem master cylinder and a power brake booster unit. On Civic models and Civic CVCC sedan models, front brakes are dual piston floating caliper type. CVCC station wagon models and Accord models utilize single piston front disc brakes. All models use leading-trailing shoe/drum type rear brakes actuated by a dual piston wheel cylinder. Parking brake is cable and lever operated, actuating shoes of rear brake assemblies. All models use proportioning valve arrangements to differentiate pressure to rear wheels. All vehicles are equipped with a brake warning light that indicates hydraulic pressure loss and when parking brake is engaged.

## ADJUSTMENT

### PEDAL FREE PLAY

Brake pedal free play is distance pedal travels from pedal stop (brake light switch) before push rod contacts vacuum booster. Adjust pedal free play to .039-.196" (1-5 mm), measured at pedal pad, by adjusting brake light switch.

### FRONT DISC BRAKE PADS

Front disc brakes are self-adjusting, therefore, no adjustment in service is required.

### REAR BRAKE SHOES

With parking brake released, depress brake pedal two or three times and release. Turn adjuster on backing plate clockwise until wheel no longer turns. Back off adjuster two clicks and ensure wheel rotates freely. If brakes are dragging, back off one additional click.

### PARKING BRAKE

With rear brakes adjusted, pull parking brake lever to check operation. Rear wheels should be locked when lever is pulled one to five notches on ratchet. Adjustment is made at equalizer located between rear lower control arms.

### HYDRAULIC SYSTEM BLEEDING

1) Attach a bleed tube to cylinder bleed screw and immerse opposite end of tube in a container partially filled with brake fluid.

2) Pump pedal several times. Hold steady pressure on pedal. Open bleed screw. Allow air to escape into container. Close bleed screw with pedal still depressed. Let pedal return unassisted.

3) Repeat procedure on remaining brake cylinders until all air is bled from system. Bleeding sequence is left front, right rear, right front, right rear.

## REMOVAL & INSTALLATION

### FRONT DISC BRAKE PADS

**Removal; Civic & CVCC Sedan** — Raise and support front of vehicle; remove front wheels. Remove pin retaining clip, retaining pins and springs. Note that springs are not interchangeable, reference mark for reassembly. Remove disc pads and shims from one side. DO NOT remove pads from both sides at one time.

**Installation** — Clean exposed portions of caliper pistons and cavity. Manually seat caliper pistons in cylinders. Check disc pad thickness. If less than .240" (6.1 mm), replace with new pads. If thickness variation between disc pads sets exceeds .079" (2 mm), replace pads. Install pads, shims (index arrow facing up), pad springs, and retaining pins. Secure retaining pin with clips.

**Removal; CVCC Station Wagon** — Raise and support front of vehicle; remove front wheels. Remove pad shield. Take off pad retainer clips. Drive out retaining pins and pull pads from caliper housing.

*Fig. 1  Honda Rear Drum Brake Assembly — Civic Shown — Others Similar*

# Brakes

## HONDA (Cont.)

**Installation** − To install, reverse removal procedure and note: Make sure all rust has been removed from brake pad retaining pins. Inspect brake pad thickness. If pads are worn so that thickness is less than .300″ (6.5 mm) or if thickness variation between disc pad sets exceeds .079″ (2 mm), replace pads.

**Removal; Accord** − Raise and support front of vehicle. Remove wheel. Using a pair of pliers, remove spring clips. Pull off top and bottom side plates. Lift off caliper and suspend out of way. Remove disc pad anti-rattle clip and slide off pads.

**Installation** − To install, reverse removal procedure and note: Clean exposed areas of caliper. Check disc pad thickness. If pad thickness is less than .236″ (6 mm) or if thickness variation between disc pad sets exceeds .079″ (2 mm), pads must be replaced.

### FRONT DISC BRAKE CALIPER

**Removal; Civic & CVCC Sedan** − Raise and support front of vehicle. Remove front wheels. Disconnect hydraulic line at caliper, remove bolts retaining caliper to steering knuckle. Lift off caliper assembly.

**Installation** − Reverse removal procedure and bleed hydraulic system.

**Removal; CVCC Station Wagon** − Raise vehicle and remove disc pads as previously outlined. Disconnect and plug brake fluid line. Remove caliper mounting bolt and lift off vehicle.

**Installation** − To install, reverse removal procedure and bleed brake system.

**Removal; Accord** − Raise and suitably support front of vehicle. Remove wheel. Disconnect and plug brake lines. Remove spring pins and caliper side plate covers. Pull off caliper cylinder. Mounting bracket can now be removed if necessary.

**Installation** − To install, reverse removal procedure and bleed brake system.

### DISC BRAKE ROTOR

**Removal** − 1) Raise and support front of vehicle; remove front wheel. Before continuing removal procedure, check rotor runout and compare to specifications. Remove spindle nut and caliper assembly.

**NOTE** − *Do not allow caliper to hang by brake line.*

2) Using a slide hammer with hub puller attachment, remove hub and rotor assembly. Index mark hub and rotor, then remove bolts and separate.

**NOTE** − *Since removing hub and rotor assembly involves use of a slide hammer and subjects wheel bearings to severe loads, it is suggested that both inner and outer wheel bearings be replaced each time hub and rotor assembly is removed.*

**Installation** − Reverse removal procedure, tighten rotor-to-hub bolts evenly, and bleed hydraulic system if necessary.

### REAR BRAKE DRUM

**Removal** − Raise and support rear of vehicle and remove rear wheels. Remove bearing retaining cap and rear axle nut, then remove brake drum. **NOTE** − *If drum is difficult to remove, use a slide hammer with a hub puller attachment.*

**Installation** − Reverse removal procedure and tighten axle nut.

### REAR BRAKE SHOES

**NOTE** − *All models have same basic brake system design; however, there may be some minor differences.*

**Removal** − With rear brake drum removed, remove tension pin clips and brake shoe return springs, and remove brake shoes.

**Installation** − 1) Reverse removal procedure and note the following: Upper and lower return springs are not interchangeable.

2) On Civic models, upper spring is identified by tight bends on each end and is designed so spring coils are located on outside of shoes when installed. Lower springs are designed so spring coils ride inside of shoes.

3) On all other models, 2 upper return springs are used to support shoes.

**Fig. 2   Disc Brake Assembly for Civic and CVCC Sedan**

### REAR BRAKE WHEEL CYLINDER

**Removal** − With rear brake drum and brake shoes removed, disconnect hydraulic line from wheel cylinder at rear of backing plate. Remove retaining nuts and wheel cylinder assembly.

**Installation** − Reverse removal procedure, tighten retaining nuts, and bleed hydraulic system.

## HONDA (Cont.)

### MASTER CYLINDER

**Removal** — Disconnect hydraulic lines at master cylinder, remove retaining nuts, and remove master cylinder from power brake unit.

**Installation** — Reverse removal procedure and bleed hydraulic system.

### POWER BRAKE UNIT

**Removal** — Disconnect vacuum hose at power brake unit, and hydraulic lines at master cylinder. Remove clevis pin retaining power brake unit push rod to brake pedal, and bolts attaching power unit to firewall, then remove power brake unit and master cylinder as an assembly.

**Installation** — Reverse removal procedure, tighten all nuts and bolts, and bleed hydraulic system.

## OVERHAUL

### DISC BRAKE CALIPER

**Disassembly; Civic & CVCC Sedan** — Holding caliper assembly in hands, press caliper down to compress piston. Keep pistons compressed and lift up on caliper removing yoke. Remove yoke return springs. Using light air pressure, force out pistons. Remove seals from cylinder bore grooves being careful not to scratch bore. **NOTE** — *Calipers are marked left "L" and right "R".*

**Inspection** — Clean and thoroughly dry all parts. Inspect all components for wear or damage. Check piston and cylinder bore scratching. Do not reuse inner seals, replace them.

**Reassembly** — 1) Install piston seals into grooves in cylinder. Lubricate pistons with brake fluid and install into cylinder. Install yoke guide into inboard piston. Hold yoke with retaining pin bracket facing up, and install yoke springs so long thin portion of spring is on upper side.

2) Hold yoke with retaining pin bracket facing up and to left. Place cylinder so that inlet port is facing up and to right. Slide yoke over cylinder. When yoke springs contact cylinder sliding surface, push down firmly and slide yoke to left until securely engaged with cylinder. Install disc pads, springs, pins and retainer.

**Disassembly; CVCC Station Wagon** — Remove caliper bridge bolt and carefully separate inner caliper with piston from torque plate and outer caliper. Remove rubber bushing insert from inner caliper housing. Take out retainer ring and wiper seal. Remove snap ring and dust seal, then force from cylinder. Using a pointed, but not sharp tool, remove "O" ring seal.

**Inspection** — Clean all components in brake fluid and inspect for excessive damage or wear. Replace all rubber parts. Look inside cylinder bore for signs of scoring or rough surfaces. Check outer caliper for cracks or metal fatigue.

**Reassembly** — Reverse disassembly procedure and note: Lightly grease shafts of torque plate. Lightly lubricate all internal components with brake fluid before reassembly. Make sure "O" ring seal is not twisted in cylinder groove.

*Fig. 4  Exploded View of CVCC Station Wagon Disc Brakes*

**Disassembly; Accord** — Remove snap ring retainer and piston boot. Apply light air pressure to caliper through brake fluid inlet port. Using a pointed tool, remove piston seal.

**Inspection** — Examine cylinder piston and bore for scoring, rough spots or excessive wear. Replace all rubber components.

*Fig. 3  Exploded View of Accord Disc Brake Assembly*

## HONDA (Cont.)

**Reassembly** — Reverse disassembly procedure and note: Make sure seal is properly fitted to cylinder groove.

### REAR WHEEL CYLINDER

**Disassembly** — Remove dust seals and pistons. Remove cylinder cups from pistons. If necessary, remove bleeder screw.

**Cleaning & Inspection** — Clean and dry all parts and inspect for wear or damage; replace parts as necessary. Check cylinder bore-to-piston clearance; if clearance exceeds .005", replace piston or cylinder as necessary.

**Reassembly** — Coat cylinder walls, pistons, and cups with brake fluid and install into cylinder bore. **NOTE** — *Install cups on pistons so that lips of cups face center of cylinder. Install dust covers making sure lips engage grooves on cylinder body.*

### MASTER CYLINDER

**NOTE** — *Accord and Civic models have some minor external modifications that make physical appearance different. Overhaul Procedures are same as for earlier models.*

**Disassembly** — Remove reservoir caps and floats and drain brake fluid. Loosen retaining clamps and remove reservoirs. Remove primary piston stop bolt, retaining clip, and washer, then remove primary piston. Hold a finger over stop bolt hole, apply compressed air to secondary outlet, and remove secondary piston. Remove two union caps, washers, check valves, and springs.

*Fig. 5   Exploded View of Master Cylinder*

**Cleaning & Inspection** — Clean and dry all parts and inspect for wear or damage. Check clearance between master cylinder bore and pistons; if greater than .005", replace pistons or cylinder assembly as required. Check for clogged orifices in pistons and cylinder. **NOTE** — *Manufacturer recommends replacing piston cups and check valves whenever cylinder has been disassembled.*

**Reassembly** — Reverse disassembly procedure and note the following: Coat all parts with brake fluid when assembling. When installing pistons, push in while rotating to prevent damaging cups.

### POWER BOOSTER UNIT

**Disassembly** — 1) Separate master cylinder from booster assembly, but leave retaining plate attached to booster shell. Remove spring clip and booster shell retaining tab, then separate push rod from master cylinder.

**2)** Place booster assembly in vise. Index-mark shell halves and separate halves with suitable tool. Turn tool clockwise, noting that shell is spring-loaded. Take booster from vise and remove master retaining plate, check valve, seal retainer and seal.

**3)** Remove booster push rod and boot. Separate housing from diaphragm and piston. Take off seal retainer, seal (note position), and bushing. Disengage snap ring, spring, and seat, then pull out diaphragm.

**4)** Remove retaining cover, push rod actuator, retaining plate, center seat, and spring washer (note position). Push piston from diaphragm plate. Extract "O" ring from inside piston. Remove filter retaining clip, then take off filter, push plate, spring, and poppet valve.

**Inspection** — Thoroughly wash all components in alcohol and blow dry with compressed air. Check all parts for wear and carefully look at booster plate and piston for scratches.

**Reassembly** — Reverse disassembly and note the following: Coat lip of seal with silicon before installing into booster housing. Be sure bushing fully seats into position. Make sure piston "O" ring has a perfect fit. Install reaction plates with curved side facing up. Lightly coat piston with silicon before installing in booster housing. After fitting master cylinder push rod, measure distance between booster shell and end of push rod. Clearance should be .024" (.6 mm).

### PROPORTIONING VALVES

**NOTE** — *Some models use two proportioning valves. Proportioning valves are NOT to be overhauled; if determined defective, replace.*

## TIGHTENING SPECIFICATIONS

| Application | Ft. Lbs. (mkg) |
|---|---|
| Caliper Mounting Bolts | |
|     Civic & CVCC Sedan | 29 (4.0) |
|     CVCC Wagon | 63 (8.5) |
|     Accord | 58-66 (8.0-9.0) |
| Rear Axle Nut | |
|     Except Accord | 83 (11.5) |
| Master Cylinder Nuts | 9 (1.2) |

## HONDA (Cont.)

**Fig. 6 Exploded View of Honda Accord Power Brake Unit**

**Fig. 7 Exploded View of Civic CVCC Power Booster Unit**

# Brakes

## HONDA (Cont.)

**Fig. 8 Exploded View of Honda Civic Power Booster Unit**

## DISC BRAKE ROTOR SPECIFICATIONS

| Application | Disc Diameter In. (mm) | Lateral Runout In. (mm) | Parallelism In. (mm) | Original Thickness In. (mm) | Minimum Refinish Thickness In. (mm) | Discard Thickness In. (mm) |
|---|---|---|---|---|---|---|
| Civic | ..... | .006 (1.5) | .003 (.07) | .378 (9.6) | .354 (9.0) | .343 (8.7) |
| CVCC Sedan | ..... | .006 (.15) | .003 (.07) | .378 (9.6) | .354 (9.0) | .343 (8.7) |
| Sta. Wgn. | ..... | .006 (.15) | .003 (.07) | .473 (12.0) | .449 (11.4) | .437 (11.1) |
| Accord | ..... | .006 (.15) | ① | .473 (12.0) | .449 (11.4) | .437 (11.1) |

① — Max. difference between measurements .006" (.15 mm).

## BRAKE DRUM SPECIFICATIONS

| Application | Drum Diameter In. (mm) | Original Diameter In. (mm) | Maximum Refinish Diameter In. (mm) | Discard Diameter In. (mm) |
|---|---|---|---|---|
| Civic | 7.08 (180) | 7.08 (180) | 7.13 (181) | 7.15 (181.5) |
| CVCC Sedan | 7.08 (180) | 7.08 (180) | 7.13 (181) | 7.15 (181.5) |
| CVCC St.Wgn | 7.87 (200) | 7.87 (200) | 7.91 (201) | 7.93 (201.5) |
| Accord | 7.08 (180) | 7.01 (180) | 7.13 (181) | 7.15 (181.5) |

## JAGUAR

**XJ6**
**XJ12**
**XJS**

## DESCRIPTION

Brake system utilizes four wheel disc brakes and a tandem master cylinder connected to a power unit (servo). Front calipers are four piston type. Master cylinder supplies hydraulic pressure to two individual brake circuits (front and rear). A combination valve is used to indicate a pressure difference between brake circuits. Front calipers are mounted on stub axle carriers and rear calipers are mounted inboard on differential housing. Rear rotors are connected to differential drive shaft flanges. Each front caliper consists of four pistons (two inboard and two outboard) and each rear caliper has two opposing pistons. Parking brake consists of independent, lever operated, disc pads mounted on rear calipers. Parking brake pads operate on rear brake rotor.

## ADJUSTMENT

### DISC BRAKE PADS

Due to self-adjusting feature of calipers, no adjustment in service is required.

### PARKING BRAKE

**Parking Brake Caliper** — Caliper is self-adjusting to compensate for pad wear, therefore, no adjustment is required.

**Parking Brake Cable (XJ6)** — Put parking brake in fully released position. Loosen lock nut on front yoke. Disconnect yoke from bell crank lever at clevis pin. Rotate yoke on adjusting rod so that when yoke is reconnected there is a slight amount of slack in cable. Reconnect yoke and tighten lock nut.

**Parking Brake Cable (XJ12)** — Working under vehicle, loosen lock nut. Remove clevis pin. Make sure parking brakes are fully released. Rotate adjusting nut until parking brake cable has just a slight amount of slack. Reconnect clevis pin. Tighten lock nut.

*Fig. 1  XJ12 Parking Brake Cable Adjustment Points*

**Parking Brake Cable (XJS)** — Pull back carpet near rear of drivers seat to gain access to adjustment components. Place parking brake in fully released position. Loosen cable lock nut. Rotate adjusting nut until cable has only a slight amount of slack. Tighten lock nut.

## HYDRAULIC SYSTEM BLEEDING

1) Keep hydraulic fluid reservoirs filled with clean brake fluid during bleeding operation. Attach a bleed tube to bleeder screw on left-rear brake caliper, and immerse opposite end of tube in a container partially filled with brake fluid.

2) Run engine at idle speed. Loosen bleeder screw, operate pedal through full stroke until discharged fluid is free of air bubbles, close bleeder screw. Repeat procedure on right-rear caliper and front calipers.

## COMBINATION VALVE

**Operation Testing** — 1) Put gear selector lever in Park. When ignition switch is on and parking brake is applied, brake warning light should be on. Run engine at idle. Release parking brake. Apply pedal hard.

2) Open any bleeder screw. Brake warning light should light. Close bleeder, then release and reapply brake pedal. Brake warning light should go out. Carefully repeat procedure if warning light will not go on. Replace component as necessary.

## REMOVAL & INSTALLATION

### DISC PADS (SERVICE BRAKES)

**Removal** — Raise vehicle and remove wheels. Remove pin clips, pad retaining pins, anti-chatter springs (if equipped) and lining pads.

*Fig. 2  Removing Front Disc Brake Pads*

**Installation** — Draw out about half the brake fluid from reservoir(s). This will enable caliper pistons to be pushed back into cylinders without overflowing fluid. Lever pistons back, insert new pads, springs and replace retaining pins and clips. Check pads for freedom of movement within caliper. Check reservoirs for correct fluid level.

### DISC PADS (PARKING BRAKE)

**Removal & Installation** — Parking brake calipers must be removed to replace disc pads. *See Parking Brake Caliper Removal & Installation.*

## JAGUAR (Cont.)

### PARKING BRAKE CALIPER

**Removal** — 1) Raise and support vehicle. On XJS models only, adjust some slack into parking brake cable. Remove nuts and bolts attaching rear suspension mounting plate to rear suspension unit and remove plate from vehicle. Disconnect parking brake cable and return spring from caliper.

2) Remove caliper mounting bolts and release lever, then slide caliper around rotor and remove through hole left by suspension plate. To remove disc pads, remove nut and spring washer securing pads to pad carriers.

**Fig. 3    Detail of Parking Brake Caliper**

**Installation** — 1) To install, reverse removal procedure and note the following: On XJ6 and XJ12 models only, adjust caliper if new pads have been installed or if caliper has been overhauled. Adjust by holding one pad carrier stationary and turning remaining carrier until there is a clearance of .75" (19.0 mm) between disc pad surfaces.

2) On all models, operate caliper actuating lever until adjuster ratchet stops clicking. Install remaining components and check operation of brakes.

### SERVICE BRAKE CALIPER

**NOTE** — *Do not separate caliper halves for repair. If a leak exists between halves, replace caliper*

**Removal (Front)** — Raise vehicle and remove wheels. Disconnect caliper fluid line and plug. Discard locking wire from mounting bolts. Remove caliper.

**NOTE** — *Check position and number of shims between steering arm and caliper; replace shims in order.*

**Installation** — 1) Place caliper in position. If original caliper is being reinstalled, refit shims. Install mounting bolts and safety wire. Bleed brakes.

2) If new caliper is being used, check gap between caliper abutment and rotor face. Gap should be no more than .010" (.25 mm). Gap on upper and lower abutment on SAME SIDE must be equal. If rotor is not centered, remove one caliper mounting bolt and add or subtract shims as necessary. Repeat procedure on other bolt.

**Fig. 4    Components to Remove to Allow Brake Caliper to be Removed.**

**Removal (Rear)** — Remove parking brake caliper as previously outlined. Disconnect and plug hydraulic line from caliper mounting bolts and lock wire. Slide caliper around brake rotor and out hole left by suspension plate.

**Installation** — Place caliper in position, install shims if equipped, and secure bolts. Torque bolts to 49-55 ft. lbs. Check rotor for center between caliper. If necessary, adjust shims between drive flange and rotor. If shim adjustment is performed, rear wheel camber must be checked. *See Jaguar Rear Wheel Camber Adjustment in WHEEL ALIGNMENT Section.* Complete installation by reversing removal procedures.

### BRAKE ROTOR

**Removal (Front)** — 1) Remove brake caliper as previously outlined. Remove hub-to-rotor attaching bolts and washers. Remove hub dust cap, then remove cotter pin, axle nut and washer from axle stub and remove hub.

2) Insert a punch through access hole in splash sheild and lightly tap on it to free water deflector. Remove rotor assembly by sliding it from caliper jaws and over axle stub.

**Installation (Front)** — To install, reverse removal procedure and note the following: Pack hub and wheel bearings with suitable grease and adjust wheel bearing end play. *See Wheel Bearing Adjustment in WHEEL ALIGNMENT Section.*

**Removal (Rear)** — Remove brake caliper as previously outlined. Disconnect shock absorber from lower mount and remove radius arm locking bolt and lower control arm outer grease fitting. Place stands under hub assembly and slide radius arm from anchor point. Loosen clamp and slide boot

## JAGUAR (Cont.)

away from inner universal joint, then remove universal joint-to-rotor attaching bolts and separate universal joint from rotor.

**NOTE** — *DO NOT move shims mounted between drive axle flange and brake rotor.*

**Installation** — To install, reverse removal procedure and note the following: Ensure caliper is centered on rotor; adjust by adding or removing shims between rotor and drive axle flange. Caliper is centered when gap is not more than .010" (.25 mm). Check rear wheel camber and adjust if necessary. *See Camber Adjustment in WHEEL ALIGNMENT Section.*

### MASTER CYLINDER

**Removal & Installation** — Disconnect electrical wires from master cylinder reservoir. Remove filter. Disconnect clips mounted to cylinder. Separate all hydraulic lines and plug openings. Remove nuts mounting cylinder to power unit studs. To install, reverse removal procedure.

### POWER BRAKE UNIT (SERVO)

**Removal** — 1) On XJ6 and XJ12, disconnect battery and remove air cleaner. On all models, disconnect and plug master cylinder lines. Pry vacuum hose from power unit. Remove fluid reservoir.

2) On XJS models, swing pedal box bracket into vertical position. Remove 4 pedal box mounting nuts. Slide off master cylinder. Lift off pedal box and power unit, then separate.

3) On XJ6 and XJ12 models, disconnect choke cable clips. Remove bolt securing upper pedal box. Remove reservoir mounting bracket. Remove stop light switch. Remove 6 bolts

attaching pedal box. Remove brake pedal pad. Withdraw pedal box, master cylinder, and power brake unit as an assembly, then separate.

**Installation** — To install, reverse removal procedure and bleed hydraulic system.

### COMBINATION VALVE

**Removal & Installation** — Disconnect battery. Remove air cleaner. Disconnect electrical lead. Separate fluid lines and plug openings. Remove mounting nut and bolt. To install, reverse removal procedure and bleed brakes.

## OVERHAUL

### BRAKE CALIPER

**NOTE** — *DO NOT separate caliper halves for service; pistons and seals may be changed without splitting caliper. If a leak is detected between caliper halves, replace caliper as a unit.*

**Disassembly** — With disc pads removed, install a suitable piston clamp to retain outboard piston(s), then apply compressed air to fluid inlet port and remove inboard piston(s). Pull dust seal from piston(s) and caliper grooves. Carefully remove piston seal from cylinder. **NOTE** — *Inboard piston(s) must be installed before outboard piston(s) can be removed.*

**Cleaning & Inspection** — Clean all parts in alcohol and inspect for wear or damage. Check cylinder bore and pistons for scratches, rust or corrosion; replace all damaged parts.

**Reassembly** — Coat cylinder, piston and seal with brake fluid before installing. Place piston seal in bore. Install dust seal over cylinder groove and carefully insert piston through dust

*Fig. 5   Exploded View of Rear Brake Caliper with Detail of Parking Brake Assembly*

## JAGUAR (Cont.)

seal. Pull dust seal into groove in piston. Use piston clamp to press piston completely into cylinder. Repeat procedure for outer piston seal replacement. Install caliper as previously outlined.

away from spring lock. Install master cylinder and bleed brake system.

**Fig. 6   Exploded View of 4 Piston Front Disc Brake Assembly**

**Fig. 7   Exploded View of Dual Piston Master Cylinder**

### MASTER CYLINDER

**Disassembly** — With master cylinder removed from vehicle, carefully pry hose adaptors from sealing grommets and grommets from master cylinder. Push in on primary piston and remove secondary piston stop pin from forward grommet housing. Remove spring lock, then tap flange end of cylinder to remove primary and secondary piston assemblies. Disassemble springs, spring seats, seals and washers from piston assemblies.

**Cleaning & Inspection** — Clean all parts in alcohol and dry with a lint-free cloth. Inspect pistons and bore for wear, scores, or corrosion; replace damaged parts as necessary.

**Reassembly** — To reassemble, reverse disassembly procedure and note the following: Lubricate all parts with clean brake fluid. Install secondary piston inner seal with lip facing away from primary piston and install outer seal with lip facing primary piston. Install primary piston seal with lip facing

### COMBINATION VALVE

**NOTE** — *Combination valve CANNOT be overhauled.*

### POWER BRAKE UNIT (SERVO)

**NOTE** — *Power brake unit CANNOT be overhauled; if determined defective, replace entire unit.*

### TIGHTENING SPECIFICATIONS

| Application | Ft. Lbs. (mkg) |
|---|---|
| Pedal Box-to-Body | 11-13 (1.5-1.8) |
| Caliper Mounting Bolts | |
| Front | 50-60 (7.0-8.3) |
| Rear | 49-55 (6.7-7.6) |
| Wheel Lug Nuts | 40-60 (5.5-8.3) |

### DISC BRAKE ROTOR SPECIFICATIONS

| Application | Disc Diameter In. (mm) | Lateral Runout In. (mm) | Parallelism In. (mm) | Original Thickness In. (mm) | Minimum Refinish Thickness In. (mm) | Discard Thickness In. (mm) |
|---|---|---|---|---|---|---|
| All Models | | | | | | |
| Front | 11.18 (284) | .004 (.1) | .... | .950 (24.1) | .... | .... |
| Rear | 10.38 (263.5) | .004 (.1) | .... | .500 (12.7) | .... | .... |

# LANCIA

**Lancia
Except Scorpion**

## DESCRIPTION

Brake system is hydraulically operated. System utilizes a tandem (dual piston) master cylinder and on some models, a power brake assist unit. Front and rear brakes are disc type. The brake system is fitted with an adjustable brake pressure limiter valve which regulates brake operating pressure on rear wheels. Parking brake is lever operated with cables acting on rear calipers. All models are equipped with brake wear limit indicator on front wheels. When brake lining reaches wear limit a warning light on instrument panel comes on.

## ADJUSTMENT

### PARKING BRAKE

Raise and support vehicle. Make sure brake system has no air trapped in lines. Apply parking brake three notches up from full released position. Loosen lock nut, turn adjuster rod until control cable is stretched and wheels are locked. Tighten lock nut. Check operation.

### PRESSURE LIMITER

**1)** Raise and support vehicle. Leave vehicle in unloaded state (fuel tank empty, spare tire and jack assembly removed, no driver). Remove limiter dust cover. Loosen limiter mounting bolts. Twist limiter housing counterclockwise until there is .001" (.03 mm) clearance between control rod and limiter plunger.

**2)** Rotate limiter housing clockwise until feeler gauge contact is broken. Do not load control rod. Tighten mounting bolts and recheck clearance. Refit dust cover.

## BRAKE BLEEDING

**1)** Begin work on either one of the front calipers. Attach bleeder tube to inner (closest to caliper support) bleeder screw. Immerse opposite end of tube in a container partially filled with brake fluid.

**2)** Pump pedal several times. Keep pressure on pedal. Open bleed screw and allow air to be forced out of system. Make sure that as pedal moves toward floor, it does not swing the full travel. Close bleed screw with pedal down. Allow pedal to return unassisted before next stroke.

**3)** Repeat procedure until all air is bled from system. Use the following sequence for bleeding: Front; either caliper first, rear; either one first.

## REMOVAL & INSTALLATION

### FRONT & REAR DISC BRAKE PADS

**Removal — 1)** Remove wheels. Remove spring clips. Drive out component keeping pad carrier to caliper. Remove pad carrier then slip out disc pads. Do not lose mounting springs.

**2)** Check disc pads for wear. Replace pads if they have less than .039" (1 mm) of lining left. Always replace pads in sets.

**NOTE** — *Front caliper assemblies are fitted with pad wear warning devices. Unit must be replaced when pads are renewed.*

**Installation —** Thoroughly clean brake rotor. Completely seat pistons in cylinders. On rear calipers, pistons must be turned clockwise in cylinder while pushing to fully seated position. Fit new pads and spring clips. If old pads are being reinstalled, make sure they are put back in original position. Reverse removal procedure for remaining components.

*Fig. 1  Installed View from Under Vehicle Showing Adjustment Direction of Rear Brake Pressure Limiter*

# Brake System

## LANCIA (Cont.)

### FRONT & REAR BRAKE CALIPER

**Removal** — Raise and support vehicle. Remove wheel. Disconnect hydraulic inlet lines at caliper cylinder. On rear calipers, disconnect parking brake from control lever. Pull out spring clips. Drive off retaining component and remove pad carrier. Disconnect electrical lead on front caliper. Remove caliper mounting bolts and slide assembly from mounting.

**Installation** — To install caliper assembly, reverse removal procedure and note: Bleed hydraulic system. Check parking brake operation.

### FRONT & REAR ROTOR

**Removal** — Raise and support vehicle. Remove wheel. Remove caliper assembly, but do not disconnect hydraulic line; lay caliper out of way. Remove rotor mounting bolts and pull rotor off. It may be necessary to use a puller to free rotor before sliding it off vehicle.

**Installation** — To install rotor, reverse removal procedure and check runout. On front wheels, attach dial gauge to front strut. On rear wheels, attach dial gauge to support tool 88095768 (or equivalent). Clean rotor surface and set gauge .08″ (2 mm) from outer diameter. Slowly turn rotor and record reading. Runout must not exceed .002″ (.05 mm).

### MASTER CYLINDER & POWER ASSIST UNIT (SERVO)

**Removal** — Disconnect battery. Disconnect electrical leads from master cylinder. Separate hydraulic lines and remove master cylinder from servo. Disconnect vacuum hose from power assist unit. Work under instrument panel and unhook brake pedal return spring. Remove operating rod from brake pedal. Remove servo from support by extracting mounting nuts and sliding servo off.

**Installation** — To install, reverse removal procedure and note: Adjust control rod length. Bleed hydraulic system.

### PRESSURE LIMITER

**Removal** — Raise vehicle and place on safety stands. Remove top bolt connecting control rod to mounting (shackle support), then loosen bottom bolt. Remove torsion control rod clamp from underbody. Loosen hydraulic fittings. Separate pressure limiter and take off with control rod. Remove rubber cover from pressure limiter, take out bolt mounting plate to limiter and separate control rod from plate.

**Installation** — To install, reverse removal procedure and note: Adjust pressure limiter. Bleed hydraulic system.

### PRESSURE LIMITER TORSION CONTROL ROD

**Removal** — Remove top bolt connecting control rod to shackle support. Remove torsion control rod clamp from underbody. Remove rubber cover from pressure limiter. Remove bolts keeping pressure limiter to bracket. Leave hydraulic lines connected. Lower control rod limiter, remove control rod and bracket from underbody.

**Installation** — To install, reverse removal procedure and adjust brake limiter.

## OVERHAUL

### FRONT DISC BRAKE CALIPER

**Disassembly** — 1) Completely clean outside of caliper. Fit caliper in vice. Remove pad carrier. Take off both bleeder screws. Slide off dust guard. Force compressed air into inner inlet port to remove piston from cylinder.

**Fig. 2   Sectional View of Lancia Front Disc Brake Assembly**

2) Take out front piston seal. Use a small diameter tool to lift edges and remove retainer. Access to retainer is gained through bleeder screw hole.

3) Refit piston to caliper. Again apply compressed air to inner inlet port this time removing front piston and separating piece. Force air pressure into outer bleeder screw and remove back piston. Remove seals from cylinder.

**Inspection** — Look at both pistons and replace if severely scored or pitted. Examine cylinder for signs of scoring, if excessively damaged, replace cylinder. Free any restriction in bleed screws.

**Reassembly** — Insert back piston and separating piece in cylinder. Fit retainer. Make sure retainer gap aligns with bleed hole. Refit cylinder to carrier. Reverse disassembly procedures for remaining components.

## LANCIA (Cont.)

### REAR DISC BRAKE CALIPER

**Disassembly — 1)** Thoroughly clean outer cylinder housing of grease before beginning disassembly. Fit caliper in vise. Remove pad carrier and retaining spring. Turn piston counterclockwise and separate dust shield. Apply air pressure to brake fluid inlet port and remove piston.

**2)** Remove snap ring from inside piston, then remove washer, bearing, self-adjuster and piston return spring. Take out parking brake snap ring and remove control lever, return spring, and drive block.

**3)** Take out brake adjusting rod and washers from cylinder. Remove seals from adjuster rod and from inside cylinder. When removing seals avoid scratching cylinder with tool.

**Inspection —** Check piston and cylinder for scoring or seizure marks, replace as necessary. Make sure seal seating grooves are not distorted, replace if necessary. Make sure bleed screws are not restricted.

**Reassembly —** Lightly coat all internal components with brake fluid. Refit parking brake control lever with spring and drive block to caliper cylinder using press and suitable tool 88053067. Turn piston clockwise and seat. Notch in piston must be facing top. Refit carrier block. Reverse disassembly procedure to assemble remaining components.

### MASTER CYLINDER

**Disassembly — 1)** Remove fluid reservoir. Clean outside of cylinder body. Fit master cylinder to vise. Remove snap ring.

Remove back piston assembly. Separate following components from piston:

- Washers
- Seals
- Guide bushing seal
- Piston guide bushing
- Floating spacer and piston seal
- Seal spring
- Spring caps and return spring

**2)** Back out piston stop screw. Remove front piston in assembled state. Separate following components from piston: (Also, refer to Fig. 3)

- Spring thrust washer
- Piston seals
- Seal spring
- Spring caps
- Piston return spring

**Inspection —** Check that all components slide freely in cylinder. Make sure both pistons and cylinders are free of score marks. Replace components if scoring is evident.

**Reassembly — 1)** Before reassembling pistons, lightly coat components with Castrol B.N.G. grease (or equivalent) Reassemble pistons in reverse of disassembly procedure. Make sure to replace all seals with new parts.

**2)** Fit front piston in master cylinder with groove aligning with threaded bore. Install stop screw and tighten. Check piston for free movement. Slide back piston into bore and fit snap ring. Fit grommets and install fluid reservoir.

**Fig. 3   Exploded View of Master Cylinder Internal Components. Primary and Secondary Pistons are Shown Removed, but Assembled**

## LUV

### LUV

## DESCRIPTION

Brake system is hydraulically actuated using a tandem master cylinder and a Master Vac power brake unit. Front brakes are single piston, floating disc type. Rear brakes are leading-trailing, shoe/drum type. Drum brakes are actuated by dual piston wheel cylinder. Parking brake is cable and lever operated, actuating shoes of rear drum.

## ADJUSTMENT

### PEDAL HEIGHT

Pedal height, measured from top of pedal pad to floor, should be 5.9-6.3". If adjustment is required, disconnect battery ground cable and stop lamp switch wiring harness. Remove stop lamp switch from bracket, then rotate master cylinder push rod until proper pedal height is obtained. Install stop lamp switch, then adjust clearance between switch housing (not actuating pin) and brake pedal tab to .02-.04". Tighten lock nuts and connect stop lamp switch wiring harness.

### FRONT DISC BRAKE PADS

Disc brakes are self-adjusting

### REAR BRAKE SHOES

Rear brakes have a self-adjusting mechanism. No in-service adjustment is required. Initial adjustment may be necessary after changing brake lining. Pull adjuster mechanism out of star. Rotate star until shoes just contact drum. Final adjustment will be accomplished with self-adjuster mechanism.

### PARKING BRAKE

Apply parking brake two notches from fully released position. Loosen equalizer check nut and adjust front jam nut until a light to moderate drag is felt when rear wheels are rotated forward. Tighten nuts securely, release parking brake lever, and ensure no drag is present.

### HYDRAULIC SYSTEM BLEEDING

NOTE — *Make sure engine is running while bleeding brakes. This will prevent damage to push rod.*

Attach a bleed tube to wheel cylinder bleeder screw and immerse opposite end of tube in a container partially filled with brake fluid. Open bleeder screw ¾ turn, depress pedal, close bleeder screw before bottom of pedal stroke, and allow pedal to return slowly. Continue operation until no air bubbles are seen in discharged fluid. Bleed wheel cylinder closest to master cylinder first, then repeat procedure at remaining cylinders, ending with cylinder furthest from master cylinder.

## REMOVAL & INSTALLATION

### FRONT DISC BRAKE PADS & BRAKE CALIPER ASSEMBLY

**Removal** — Raise and support vehicle. Remove tire and wheel. Take out caliper pin stops and remove stops. Remove caliper off support, take out stop plates, then suspend caliper from frame with wire. Remove pads and shims. Mark pad location for reassembly, if necessary. Separate anti-rattle springs from support.

**Inspection** — Replace disc pads when thickness is reduced to .039" (1 mm). Always replace pads in axle sets. Check caliper supports and adaptors for distortion or cracking. Inspect inside caliper cavity for leaks. Replace any parts found defective.

**Installation** — To install, reverse removal procedure and note the following: Original pads must be installed according to in-

*Fig. 1  Assembled View of Rear Drum Brake Assembly*

## LUV (Cont.)

dex marks. Install pads to supports with wear indicators facing LOWER SIDE. Make sure brake lubricant is applied to sliding portion of caliper.

### FRONT DISC BRAKE ROTOR

**Removal** — Raise and support vehicle. Remove tire and wheel. Remove caliper assembly. Remove grease cap, nut, and outer bearing. Pull hub and rotor assembly from vehicle. It is not necessary to separate hub and rotor, except to replace either component.

**Inspection** — Adjust all play out of wheel bearings and inspect rotor runout using a dial gauge. If runout exceeds .005" (.13 mm), replace or resurface. Check parallelism at four or more points. Value obtained must not exceed .0005" (.001 mm) in 360°. Make all measurements at same distance from edge of rotor.

**Installation** — To install, reverse removal procedure and note the following: Adjust wheel bearings. *See Wheel Bearing Adjustment in WHEEL ALIGNMENT Section.*

### REAR BRAKE SHOES

**Removal** — Remove tire and wheel. Remove tension from parking brake cable, remove retaining screws and remove brake drum. **NOTE** — *Mark drum for reassembly reference.* Remove return springs, hold-down springs, and self-adjuster assembly. Separate primary and secondary brake shoes, adjuster mechanism, return spring, and parking brake strut.

**Fig. 2   Exploded View of Front Disc Brake Assy.**

Separate parking brake lever and rear cable, and remove lever from secondary shoe.

**Installation** — Install parking brake lever to secondary shoe and rear cable to lever. Connect brake shoes together with return spring, and place adjuster screw into position, making sure star wheel is nearest secondary shoe. Install parking brake strut with spring on primary shoe end, then fit shoes to wheel cylinder push rods. Install hold-down springs, self-adjuster assembly, and return springs.

### WHEEL CYLINDER

**Removal** — With brake drum removed, disconnect brake shoe return springs. Disconnect hydraulic line and bolts retaining cylinder to backing plate. Disengage cylinder push rod(s) from brake shoe(s) and remove cylinder.

**Installation** — Reverse removal procedure and bleed hydraulic system.

### MASTER CYLINDER

**Removal** — Disconnect battery ground cable. Disconnect hydraulic lines at master cylinder and cover ends to prevent entry of dirt. Remove bracket bolt at front end of cylinder, and nuts retaining cylinder to power unit, then remove master cylinder and gasket from power unit.

**Installation** — Reverse removal procedure, bleed hydraulic system and adjust pedal height if necessary.

### POWER BRAKE UNIT

**Removal** — Disconnect battery ground cable. Disconnect hydraulic lines at master cylinder and cover ends to prevent entry of dirt. Remove bolts attaching bracket to master cylinder and fender and remove bracket. Disconnect vacuum line at power unit and place out of way. Disconnect brake pedal return spring and push rod. Remove nuts attaching power unit to firewall, and remove power unit and master cylinder as an assembly.

**Installation** — Reverse removal procedure, bleed hydraulic system, and adjust pedal height if necessary.

## OVERHAUL

### FRONT DISC BRAKE CALIPER

**Disassembly** — Remove flex hose from caliper. Using pointed, but blunt instrument, remove seal from caliper. Place a block of wood between piston and caliper cavity wall, then apply enough compressed air pressure to force piston from cylinder. Remove and discard piston ring seal.

**Inspection** — Replace dust seal and piston seal. Check cylinder bore for wear, scuffing or corrosion. Inspect cylinder piston for damage or wear. Never attempt to refinish piston. Replace any parts found defective.

**Assembly** — Lubricate piston seal and insert into caliper bore. Carefully insert piston into caliper assembly. Install dust seal to piston and caliper. Fit seal ring into dust seal.

# Brakes

## LUV (Cont.)

### WHEEL CYLINDER

**Disassembly** — Remove boots from cylinder ends. Remove pistons and cups. Remove expander springs, if equipped.

**NOTE** — *Front wheel cylinder pistons and cups are serviced as an assembly.*

**Cleaning & Inspection** — Clean all parts in clean brake fluid. **NOTE** — *Do not use mineral based solvents.* Inspect cylinder bore and pistons for rust, corrosion, or other damage; replace parts or cylinder as necessary. Measure clearance between piston and cylinder bore; if clearance exceeds .006", replace wheel cylinder assembly.

**Reassembly** — Lubricate cylinder bore with clean brake fluid. Install spring expander into bore, then install new cups with flat surfaces toward outside. Install new pistons into cylinder with flat surfaces toward inside. **NOTE** — *Do not lubricate pistons or cups before installation.* Press new boots onto cylinder.

### MASTER CYLINDER

**Disassembly** — Remove reservoir caps, plates and strainers and drain brake fluid. Place cylinder in a vise and remove reservoirs. Remove connector bolt, connector and gaskets from rear outlet, then withdraw end plug, gasket, check valve, return spring and spring seat. Remove check valve assembly from front outlet. Push in on primary piston, remove stop bolt and snap ring, and remove primary and secondary piston assemblies.

**Cleaning & Inspection** — Wash all parts in clean brake fluid and dry using compressed air. Blow out all passages, orifices and valve holes. If slight rust is found, polish clean with crocus cloth or emery paper. Inspect cylinder bore for scoring, pitting, or other damage. Check clearance between pistons and cylinder bore; if greater than .006", replace cylinder. **NOTE** — *Manufacturer recommends replacing rubber parts whenever master cylinder has been disassembled.*

**Reassembly** — Lubricate cylinder bore and all parts with clean brake fluid, reverse disassembly procedure, and note the following: Use all new gaskets and seals when reassembling. When reassembly is complete, bench bleed master cylinder as follows: Install plugs in all outlet ports of cylinder, fill reservoirs with clean brake fluid, and press in and out on primary piston until air bubbles are no longer seen in fluid.

### POWER BRAKE UNIT

**Disassembly** — 1) Remove master cylinder reservoir and drain remaining brake fluid from cylinder. Scribe alignment marks on front and rear shells to assure reassembly in original position. Clamp flange of master cylinder in a vise with power unit up. Loosen push rod clevis lock nut and remove clevis and lock nut, then remove push rod boot.

2) Place suitable wrench (J-9504) over rear shell mounting studs. Press down on wrench while rotating counterclockwise and remove rear shell, piston rod, power piston, return spring and spring retainer. Remove nuts and lock washers and separate master cylinder and power unit front shell, then remove and discard gasket.

3) Pry retainer off power piston and remove air silencer and filter, then remove rubber diaphragm from piston. Rotate power piston until push rod retainer slot is down, then press in on rod, allowing retainer to fall out of power piston. Remove push rod assembly and reaction disc. **NOTE** — *Do not disassemble push rod assembly; if defective, replace complete assembly.*

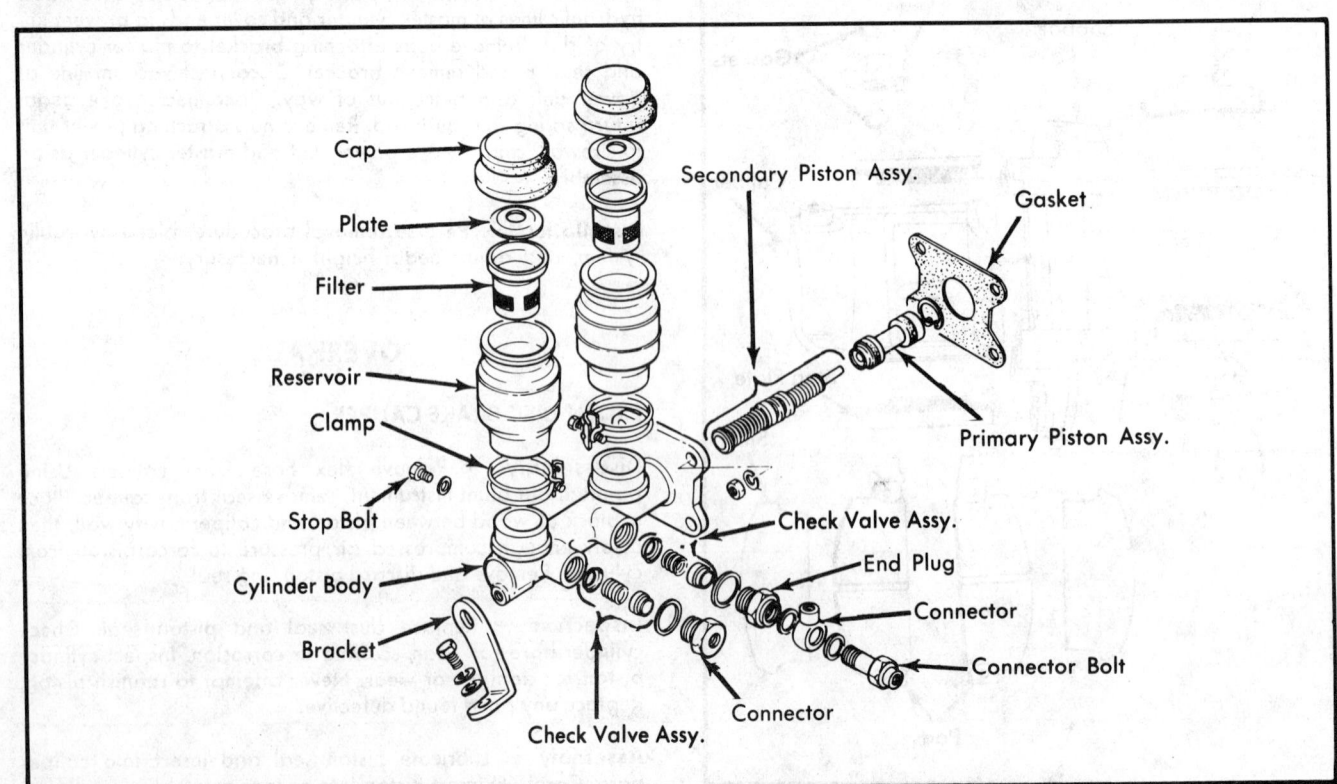

*Fig. 3   Master Cylinder Reservoir, Body and Piston Assembly*

## LUV (Cont.)

Fig. 4 Exploded View of Power Brake Assembly

**4)** If rear shell is defective, pry out seal retainer and remove spacer and seal assembly. If front seal is defective, pry out retainer and remove seal. If vacuum check valve is defective, remove using a twisting motion, then remove grommet.

**Cleaning & Inspection** — Clean all parts in denatured alcohol and blow dry with compressed air. **NOTE** — *Do not clean parts with a mineral based solvent.* Inspect inside surface of front and rear shell for wear or damage. If slight rust is found on inside surface, polish clean with crocus cloth or fine emery cloth. Inspect all parts for cracks, nicks, distortion or other damge and replace as necessary.

**Reassembly** — Reverse disassembly procedure and note the following: Apply a coat of silicone grease to parts before installation. When assembling front shell to rear shell, ensure marks made at disassembly are aligned. When reassembly is completed, remove master cylinder from power unit. Place suitable gauge (J-24568) over piston rod so that legs rest on master cylinder mounting surface. Piston rod should touch cutout portion of gauge. If rod must be adjusted, hold rod at serrated portion and turn threaded end. **NOTE** — *Push rod must be bottomed in power unit before making adjustment.*

| DISC BRAKE ROTOR SPECIFICATIONS | | | | | | |
|---|---|---|---|---|---|---|
| Application | Disc Diameter In. (mm) | Lateral Runout In. (mm) | Parallelism In. (mm) | Original Thickness In. (mm) | Minimum Refinish Thickness In. (mm) | Discard Thickness In. (mm) |
| LUV | ..... | .005 (.13) | .0005 (.013) | .709 (18.0) | .668 (16.97) | .653 (16.6) |

| BRAKE SYSTEM SPECIFICATIONS | | | | |
|---|---|---|---|---|
| Application | Drum Diam. In. (mm) | Wheel Cylinder Diameter | | Master Cylinder |
| | | Front In. (mm) | Rear In. (mm) | Diameter In. (mm) |
| LUV | 10 (254) | 1.06 (26.9) | .75 (19.0) | .875 (22.2) |

# Brakes

## LUV (Cont.)

| BRAKE DRUM SPECIFICATIONS | | | | |
|---|---|---|---|---|
| Application | Drum Diameter In. (mm) | Original Diameter In. (mm) | Maximum Refinish Diameter In. (mm) | Discard Diameter In. (mm) |
| LUV | 10 (254) | 10.000 (254) | 10.059 (255) | 10.079 (256) |

### TIGHTENING SPECIFICATIONS

| Application | Ft. Lbs. (mkg) |
|---|---|
| Backing Plate-to-Axle Housing | 55 (7.7) |
| Wheel Cylinder | 10 (1.4) |
| Master Cylinder | |
|   End Plug | 90 (12.4) |
|   Connector Bolt | 35 (4.8) |
|   Stopper Bolt | 14 (1.9) |
|   Mounting Nuts | 10 (1.4) |
| Power Brake Unit Mounting Nuts | 10 (1.4) |
| Rotor-to-Hub | 36 (5.0) |
| Caliper Connector | 22 (3.0) |
| Support-to-Adaptor | 64 (9.0) |
| Caliper Assembly-to-Knuckle | |
|   Large Bolt | 55 (7.6) |
|   Small Bolt | 35 (4.8) |

## MAZDA

GLC
RX-4
Cosmo
B1800

## DESCRIPTION

Brake system is hydraulically actuated using a dual piston master cylinder and power brake unit. All models use single piston front disc brakes. Cosmo models have single piston rear disc brakes with integral parking brake shoes covered by hub/rotor assembly. All other models are equipped with leading-trailing drum brakes. All models use lever and cable operated parking brake actuating shoes of rear brake assemblies or, on Cosmo models, operating the separate parking brake shoes. All models are equipped with a proportioning valve to regulate brake pressure to rear wheels and prevent rear wheel lockup.

## ADJUSTMENT

### BRAKE PEDAL FREE PLAY

Brake pedal free play must be set to specifications (see table) to ensure compensating port is not covered by master cylinder piston. To adjust free play, loosen lock nut, adjust brake pedal push rod until proper free play is obtained, and tighten lock nut.

#### Brake Pedal Free Play Adjustment

| Application | Inches (mm) |
| --- | --- |
| All Models ...................................................... | .28-.35 (7-9) |

### FRONT DISC BRAKE PADS

Front disc brakes are self-adjusting; therefore, no adjustment in service is required.

### REAR DISC BRAKE PADS

No adjustment is required.

**NOTE** – *On self-adjusting brakes, perform adjustment procedures only after overhaul or when servicing other components affects brake adjustment.*

### REAR DRUM BRAKES

1) Raise and support rear of vehicle. Release parking brake. Remove adjusting hole plugs from back plate. Use suitable tool and expand one shoe at a time by rotating star adjuster until wheel locks.

**NOTE** – *Direction for star rotation may be marked on back plate.*

2) Back off adjuster about 4-6 notches or until wheel rotates freely without drag. Repeat procedure on each adjuster mechanism.

### PARKING BRAKE

**RX-4, GLC** – With rear brakes properly adjusted, raise parking brake lever boot inside vehicle and turn lever adjusting screw so parking brake begins to apply when pulling lever 3-7 notches.

**Cosmo** – 1) Raise rear of vehicle and place on safety stands. Release parking brake. Remove dust plug and rotate star wheel in direction printed on backing plate. When drum locks, back off 7 to 9 notches. Clearance between shoe and drum should be .006-.008" (.15-.20 mm).

2) Work inside vehicle and free shift lever boot. Adjust brake lever screw so rear wheels will lock when lever is pulled 5 to 7 notches with normal application force.

**B1800 Pickup** – With rear brakes properly tightened, adjust length of front cable with adjusting nut (located under vehicle where cable guide attaches to threaded shaft) so rear wheels lock when parking brake is pulled 5-10 notches. Apply parking brake several times, release, and check that rear wheels rotate freely.

### BRAKE FAILURE SWITCH RESET

**All Models** – Turn ignition switch "On". Depress brake pedal and piston will center itself and light will go out. Turn ignition switch to "Off".

### HYDRAULIC SYSTEM BLEEDING

**NOTE** – *DO NOT use secondary stop bolt to bleed hydraulic system.*

Bleed hydraulic system in sequence starting with line furthest from master cylinder, and ending with line closest to master cylinder. Attach a bleed tube to wheel cylinder or caliper bleeder screw, and immerse opposite end of tube in a container partially filled with brake fluid. Pump brake pedal several times, and with pedal depressed, open bleeder screw ¾ turn allowing air to escape, tighten bleeder screw, and release brake pedal. Continue operation until air bubbles are no longer seen in discharged fluid. Repeat procedure at remaining brake lines until all air is bled from system.

## REMOVAL & INSTALLATION

### FRONT DISC BRAKE PADS

**Removal, Cosmo, RX-4, GLC, Pickup** – Raise and support front of vehicle. Remove retainers and take out stopper plate. Take off caliper and anti-rattle spring. DO NOT allow caliper to hang by brake hose. Pull out disc pads and shims. If pad lining has worn to less than .276" (7 mm), replace disc pads. Make sure to always replace pads in sets of same make.

**Installation** – To install, reverse removal procedure and note: It may be necessary to open bleed valve and seat piston into caliper bore so disc pads can be inserted.

## MAZDA (Cont.)

### FRONT DISC BRAKE CALIPER

**Removal, Cosmo, RX-4, GLC, Pickup** — 1) Raise and support vehicle. Remove front wheel(s). Disconnect brake hose from caliper and plug openings to prevent entry of dirt and loss of fluid.

2) Remove fastening clips and stopper plates, then remove caliper and anti-rattle spring. Remove disc pads. If necessary, lift off disc pad (caliper) bracket.

**Installation** — If removed, reinstall caliper bracket. Attach a bleed tube to caliper bleeder screw, open bleeder screw, press caliper piston to bottom of bore, and tighten bleeder screw. Install disc pads and replace anti-rattle spring, caliper, stopper plates, and fastening clips. Install hydraulic line and bleed hydraulic system.

### FRONT DISC BRAKE ROTOR

**Removal** — With caliper assembly removed, remove wheel hub grease cap, cotter pin, nut lock, and bearing adjusting nut. Remove thrust washer and outer bearing from hub, then slide hub and rotor assembly from spindle. Remove bolts attaching rotor to hub, and separate.

**Installation** — Reverse removal procedure, tighten rotor-to-hub bolts evenly, and adjust wheel bearings. *See Wheel Bearing Adjustment in WHEEL ALIGNMENT Section.*

### REAR DISC BRAKE PADS

**Removal, Cosmo** — Raise vehicle and place on safety stands. Remove wheel. Remove lock pins, then take out stopper plates. Slide off caliper and anti-rattle springs. DO NOT hang caliper from chassis by rubber brake hose. Pull out disc pads and shims. If pads have worn to .276" (7 mm) or less, disc pads must be replaced. Always replace all pads at one time and do not mix lining types.

**Installation** — To install, reverse removal procedure.

### REAR DISC BRAKE CALIPER

**Removal, Cosmo** — Raise rear of vehicle and place on safety stands. Disconnect brake line from caliper and plug openings. Remove lock pins, then take out stopper plates. Slide off caliper and anti-rattle spring.

**Installation** — To install, reverse removal procedure and bleed brakes.

### REAR DISC BRAKE ROTOR

**Removal, Cosmo** — Raise and support rear of vehicle. Remove caliper mounting bolts and remove caliper and mounting bracket assembly. Suspend caliper out of way with a wire hanger. Fully release parking brake. Unscrew hub/rotor mounting screws. Insert screws into tappered holes and tighten

evenly until hub/rotor is free. Before removal of hub/rotor index mark axle shaft flange and hub/rotor assembly.

**Installation** — To install, reverse removal procedure and note following: Make sure index marks on axle shaft flange and hub/rotor assembly are aligned.

### BRAKE DRUM

**Removal** — Raise and support vehicle and remove wheels to be serviced. Remove set screws securing drum to wheel hub or axle flange, fit screws into tapped holes in drum, and tighten evenly to force drum from hub or flange.

**Installation** — Mount brake drum to hub or axle flange, install and tighten set screws, and adjust brake shoes.

### REAR BRAKE SHOES

**Removal** — With brake drum removed, remove brake shoe return springs. Remove brake shoe retaining springs and guide pins by compressing retaining spring and turning guide pin 90°. Remove brake shoes. Remove parking brake strut and disengage parking brake cable from operating lever of secondary shoe.

*Fig. 1  Disassembled View of GLC Rear Brakes Other Models Similar*

**Installation** — 1) Lubricate adjusting screw threads and contact surfaces of shoes and backing plate with brake grease. Install parking brake operating lever to secondary shoe and secure with clip. Engage lever in parking brake cable.

2) Position operating strut between slots of shoes. Mount assembly to backing plate so slots in shoes are toward adjusting screws. Install return springs and retainer springs.

### WHEEL CYLINDERS

**Removal** — With brake drum and shoes removed, remove hydraulic lines from cylinders at rear of backing plate and cover openings to prevent entry of dirt and loss of fluid. Remove nuts and/or bolts securing wheel cylinder to backing plate, and remove cylinders.

**Installation** — Reverse removal procedure. With brake shoes and drum installed, bleed hydraulic system.

## MAZDA (Cont.)

### PARKING BRAKE SHOES

**Removal, Cosmo** — Remove rear hub/rotor assembly as previously outlined. Disengage parking brake shoe return springs. Take off secondary brake shoe mounting spring, pin, and retainer. Pull out brake shoe. Repeat procedure on primary shoe.

**Installation** — To install, reverse removal procedure.

### PROPORTIONING VALVE

**Removal & Installation** — Disconnect and plug all hydraulic lines. Remove mounting bolts and lift off valve. When installing valve make sure lines are connected as shown in *Fig. 2*.

**Fig. 2 Points Where Hydraulic Lines Attach to Proportioning Valve**

### MASTER CYLINDER

**Removal** — Disconnect hydraulic lines at master cylinder and plug openings to prevent entry of dirt and loss of fluid. Remove nuts attaching cylinder to firewall or power brake unit and remove master cylinder from vehicle.

**Installation** — Reverse removal procedure and bleed hydraulic system.

### POWER BRAKE UNIT

**Removal** - Disconnect hydraulic lines at master cylinder, and vacuum line at power brake unit. From inside vehicle, remove cotter pin and clevis pin retaining push rod to brake pedal, and separate. Remove nuts retaining power unit to firewall, and remove power brake unit and master cylinder as an assembly from engine compartment.

**Installation** — Reverse removal procedure and bleed hydraulic system.

## OVERHAUL

### DISC BRAKE CALIPER

**Disassembly** — Thoroughly clean exterior of caliper and remove retainer and dust boot. Place a piece of wood in front of piston, apply compressed air to fluid inlet, and remove piston. Remove piston seal from caliper bore. Remove bleed screw if necessary.

**NOTE** — *If piston is stuck, tap lightly with hammer while forcing compressed air into caliper.*

**Cleaning & Inspection** — Wash all parts in clean alcohol or brake fluid and air dry. Inspect cylinder bore and piston for scoring, scratches or rust; replace piston or caliper as necessary. Minor damage may be removed using crocus cloth. **NOTE** — *Manufacturer recommends replacing piston seal and dust boot whenever caliper has been disassembled.*

**Fig. 3 Exploded View of Front Disc Brake Caliper**

**Reassembly** — Apply clean brake fluid to cylinder bore, piston and piston seal, then seat piston seal in caliper bore. Install piston carefully into cylinder bore and install dust boot and retainer.

### WHEEL CYLINDERS

**Disassembly** — Remove rubber dust boots and withdraw pistons with adjuster assemblies. Press in on piston cup allowing cups, filling blocks and return spring to be removed.

**Cleaning & Inspection** — Clean all parts in alcohol or brake fluid. **CAUTION** — *DO NOT use gasoline or kerosene.* Check cylinder bore, pistons and/or adjusters for scores, roughness, or wear. Check clearance between cylinder bore and pistons; replace if clearance exceeds .006". Check cups for softening, swelling, wear, or other damage; replace as necessary.

**Reassembly** — Reverse disassembly procedure and note the following: Coat all parts with clean brake fluid before reassembly. When installing cylinder cups, make sure flat side of cup faces outward. On models so equipped, coat threads of adjuster with brake grease and install into piston.

### MASTER CYLINDER

**Disassembly** — Thoroughly clean exterior of cylinder and pour out any remaining brake fluid. If equipped, remove reservoir and dust boot. Depress primary piston assembly, remove retaining ring from rear of cylinder bore, and remove washer, primary piston assembly, and return spring. Depress secondary piston, loosen, DO NOT remove, secondary piston stop bolt, and carefully withdraw secondary piston assembly and return

## MAZDA (Cont.)

**Fig. 4    Exploded View of Master Cylinder Assembly. All Models are Similar.
Major Difference Occurs in Area of Piston Shape and
Reservoir Attachment.**

spring. Remove joint bolts from outlets, and withdraw check valves and return springs.

**Cleaning & Inspection** — Clean all parts in alcohol or brake fluid. **CAUTION** — *DO NOT use gasoline or kerosene.* Check all parts for scoring, roughness or wear. Check clearance between cylinder bore and piston; if clearance exceeds .006", replace parts as required. Check all recesses, openings and internal passages for foreign matter; remove with compressed air. Check cylinder cups for softening, swelling, or wear; replace as necessary.

**Reassembly** — Reverse disassembly procedure and note the following: Coat all parts with clean brake fluid before reassembly. Use new gaskets at all hydraulic unions. When assembled, make sure piston cups do not cover compensating ports. Make sure valve with hole in center faces front side outlet hole.

### POWER BRAKE UNIT

**Disassembly** — 1) Remove master cylinder and check valve from power unit, then place power unit in a vise with push rod up. Scribe alignment marks on front and rear shells to assure reassembly in original position. Remove clevis, lock nut and dust boot from rear shell.

**2)** Attach suitable removal tool to rear shell mounting studs, then press down on tool while rotating clockwise to unlock rear shell. **NOTE** — *Loosen shell carefully because it is under spring tension.* Lift rear shell assembly from power unit, then separate diaphragm and power piston assembly, valve rod and plunger assembly from rear shell. Remove return spring from power unit.

**3)** Remove diaphragm from power piston, then lift air silencer and filter from piston. Press in on valve rod and remove retainer key, then remove valve rod and plunger assembly. Press reaction disc from power piston. Remove push rod from front shell and if necessary, remove front seal.

**Cleaning & Inspection** — Clean all parts and blow dry with compressed air. Inspect all rubber parts for cuts, nicks, deterioration or other damage. Check power piston for

cracks, distortion, chipping and damaged seats. Inspect front and rear shells for scratches, scores, pits, dents or other damage. Replace any defective parts.

**Reassembly** — Reverse disassembly procedure and note the following: Apply clean brake fluid to parts before reassembly.

**Fig. 5    Exploded View of Power Brake
Unit. All Models are Similar. Some Models May
Have Slightly Different Internal Design.**

When assembling rear shell assembly to front shell, ensure marks made during disassembly are aligned. Before installing master cylinder to power unit, measure clearance between master cylinder primary piston and power unit push rod. Clearance should be .004-.020" (.1-.5 mm). If clearance is not within specifications, correct by adjusting push rod length.

## MAZDA (Cont.)

### TIGHTENING SPECIFICATIONS

| Application | Ft. Lbs. (mkg) | Application | Ft. Lbs. (mkg) |
|---|---|---|---|
| Rotor-to-Hub | | 10 mm Bolt/Nut | 23-34 (3.2-4.7) |
| Cosmo, B1800 | 40-47 (5.5-6.5) | 12 mm Bolt/Nut | 41-59 (5.6-8.2) |
| RX-4 | 36-43 | 14 mm Bolt/Nut | 56-76 (7.7-10.5) |
| GLC | 33-40 (4.5-5.5) | 8T Bolts/Nuts | |
| | | 6 mm Bolt/Nut | 6-9 (.8-1.2) |
| UNLESS OTHERWISE SPECIFIED: | | 8 mm Bolt/Nut | 13-20 (1.8-2.7) |
| 6T Bolts/Nuts | | 10 mm Bolt/Nut | 27-40 (3.7-5.5) |
| 6 mm Bolt/Nut | 5-7 (.7-1) | 12 mm Bolt/Nut | 46-69 (6.4-9.5) |
| 8 mm Bolt/Nut | 12-17 (1.6-2.3) | 14 mm Bolt/Nut | 75-101 (10.4-14) |

### DISC BRAKE ROTOR SPECIFICATIONS

| Application | Disc Diameter In. (mm) | Lateral Runout In. (mm) | Parallelism In. (mm) | Original Thickness In. (mm) | Minimum Refinish Thickness In. (mm) | Discard Thickness In. (mm) |
|---|---|---|---|---|---|---|
| RX-4 | 9.055 (230) | .004① (.10) | ..... | .472 (12) | .433 (11) | ② |
| Cosmo Front | 9.843 (250) | .004① (.10) | ..... | .709 (18) | .669 (17) | ② |
| Rear | 11.024 (280) | .004① (.10) | ..... | .394 (10) | .354 (9) | ② |
| Pickup | 10.079 (256) | .004① (.10) | ..... | .472 (12) | .433 (11) | ② |
| GLC | 8.150 (207) | .002① (.06) | ..... | .512 (13) | .472 (12) | ② |

① — Maximum allowable.　　　　② — Less than Minimum Refinish Thickness

### BRAKE DRUM SPECIFICATIONS

| Application | Drum Diameter In. (mm) | Original Diameter In. (mm) | Maximum Refinish Diameter In. (mm) | Discard Diameter In. (mm) |
|---|---|---|---|---|
| RX-3SP, 808, GLC | 7.874 (200) | 7.874 (200) | 7.914 (201) | ① |
| RX-4 | 9.000 (228.6) | 9.000 (228.6) | 9.040 (229.6) | ① |
| Rotary Pickup | 10.236 (260) | 10.236 (260) | 10.276 (261) | ① |
| Cosmo | ..... | ..... | ..... | ② |

① — More than Maximum Refinish Diameter.　　② — Max refinish diameter for PARKING BRAKE drum 6.535" (166 mm).

### BRAKE SYSTEM SPECIFICATIONS

| Application | Drum Diam. In. (mm) | Wheel Cylinder Diameter | | Master Cylinder |
|---|---|---|---|---|
| | | Front In. (mm) | Rear In. (mm) | Diameter In. (mm) |
| GLC | 7.874① (200) | 2.0② (50.8) | .750 (19.05) | .813 (20.6) |
| RX-4 | 9.00① (228.6) | 2.125② (54) | .687 (17.5) | .875 (22.2) |
| Cosmo | ..... | 2.0② (50.8) | 1.375② (34.9) | .875 (22.2) |
| Pickup | 10.236 (260) | 2.125② (54) | .750 (19.05) | .875 (22.2) |

① — Rear.　　　　② — Caliper bore diameter.

## MERCEDES-BENZ

230
240D
280 Series
300D
450 Series
6.9

### DESCRIPTION

Service brake system utilizes 4-wheel disc brakes, hydraulically operated by a step-type tandem, or tandem master cylinder, connected to a power unit. Step-type master cylinder can be identified by stop screw location, top center of master cylinder. Tandem master cylinder stop screw is located at bottom center of master cylinder. Brakes are manufactured by Teves or Bendix and incorporate a two or three chamber reservoir with a fluid level sensor contact built into each chamber. Warning light is activated when fluid level is low. Parking brakes are cable actuated, internal expanding shoe type, housed in rear brake rotors.

### ADJUSTMENT

#### PEDAL HEIGHT

Adjust pedal height by loosening 2 hex nuts and turning stop light switch. Proper pedal free position is approximately 5.91" (150 mm) from pedal stop.

#### PEDAL FREE PLAY

Adjust pedal free play to .197-.591" (5-15 mm) by loosening 2 hex nuts and turning stop light switch. Stop light switch contact button should extend .236-.315" (6-8 mm) when adjusted.

#### DISC PADS

Self-adjusting, no adjustment required.

#### PARKING BRAKE

Remove one wheel lug bolt at each rear wheel. Raise and support vehicle, and rotate wheels until lug bolt hole is positioned over parking brake adjuster (approximately 45° in upward and forward direction from wheel center). Using a screwdriver

inserted through lug bolt hole, turn adjuster until wheel cannot be turned by hand. Back off adjuster until wheel can be turned by hand without restriction.

### HYDRAULIC SYSTEM BLEEDING

Beginning with cylinder farthest from master cylinder, attach one end of bleeder tube to bleeder screw, and submerge opposite end in a jar half full of clean brake fluid. Pump brake pedal several times, and with pedal at bottom of stroke, open bleeder screw. Close bleeder screw when fluid stops flowing from tube, then release pressure on brake pedal. Repeat procedure until fluid flowing from tube shows no sign of air.

### REMOVAL & INSTALLATION

#### DISC PADS

**Removal** — Raise vehicle, support with safety stands and remove wheels. If equipped, remove shaft cover plate from caliper. Drive out retaining pins toward inside of vehicle and remove cross spring. Loosen bleed fitting and using suitable extractor tool, remove disc pads from caliper assembly.

**NOTE** — *All bolts are self-locking, hex-head and should be used once only.*

NOTE — Drive Pin In Toward Vehicle

*Fig. 2   Knocking Out Disc Pad Mounting Pins On Teves Model Brakes*

Apply Molykote Paste "U" Where Indicated By Arrows

*Fig. 3   Typical Mercedes-Benz Disc Brake Pad Illustration Shows Molykote Application Points*

*Fig. 1   Fitting Parking Brake Adjuster Tool Into Adjusting Mechanism*

## MERCEDES-BENZ (Cont.)

**Installation** — Using a cylinder brush, clean disc pad guide surface in caliper. Siphon sufficient fluid from master cylinder reservoir to prevent overflowing, then press pistons to bottom of bores. Install disc pads, cross spring, retaining pins and cover plate (if equipped). After installation, depress brake pedal several times to position pads against rotor.

### BRAKE CALIPER

**Removal** — Raise and support vehicle, and remove wheel. Disconnect brake lines at caliper assembly, and plug lines to prevent entry of foreign matter. Remove caliper attaching bolts, and remove caliper assembly from vehicle.

**Installation** — Reverse removal procedure ensuring that calipers are replaced in matched pairs from either manufacturer. Tighten all nuts and bolts and bleed hydraulic system.

### BRAKE ROTOR

**Removal & Installation (Front)** — With caliper assembly removed, remove hub grease cap. Remove contact spring for radio shielding, loosen socket screw on clamping nut on wheel spindle, remove clamping nut and washer, then remove wheel hub and rotor assembly. Remove Allen head bolts securing rotor to hub and remove rotor. To install, reverse removal procedure, tighten all bolts and fittings evenly, and bleed hydraulic system if necessary. Adjust front wheel bearing. See *Wheel Bearing Adjustment in WHEEL ALIGNMENT Section.*

**Removal & Installation (Rear)** — Remove rear wheel and caliper assembly, then pull rotor out from axle shaft flange. To install, reverse removal procedure, tighten all bolts and fittings evenly, and bleed hydraulic system if necessary.

*Fig. 4  Assembled View of Rear Hub and Caliper*

### MASTER CYLINDER

**Removal** — Drain master cylinder of brake fluid. Disconnect and plug brake lines, disconnect electrical wires. Remove bolts securing master cylinder to power booster and remove master cylinder.

**Installation** — Reverse removal procedure and note the following: Always replace rubber "O" ring seal between master cylinder and power unit. Bleed hydraulic system and check complete system for fluid leaks.

### POWER BRAKE UNIT

**Removal** — Drain master cylinder brake fluid, and remove master cylinder from vehicle. Disconnect vacuum line at power booster, and disconnect push rod at brake pedal. Remove power brake unit attaching hardware, and remove assembly from vehicle.

**Installation** — To install, reverse removal procedure, tighten all nuts and bolts, and bleed hydraulic system.

## OVERHAUL

### BRAKE CALIPER

**Disassembly** — With caliper removed from vehicle and disc pads removed from caliper, remove dust cap from piston housing. Hold one piston in place using a suitable clamp, then apply compressed air to fluid inlet and remove opposite piston. Remove piston seal from groove of cylinder bore. Remove remaining piston and seal in same manner. **CAUTION** — *Do not separate caliper halves.*

**Cleaning & Inspection** — Remove deposits on piston with a soft brass wire brush. **NOTE** — *Do not use polishing or emery cloth on pistons, as they could damage chrome plated surface.* Check cylinder bore of caliper for wear or damage. Small rust spots in bore can be removed with polishing cloth and heavier rust spots in front of piston seal groove with fine emery paper.

*Fig. 5  Disassembled View of Typical Mercedes-Benz Brake Caliper*

**Reassembly** — Coat piston and caliper bore with ATE brake cylinder paste (or equivalent), install piston seal into groove of bore, then install piston. **NOTE** — *Install piston so that elevation on piston is facing downward.* Install dust cap. Install heat shield into piston with recess in shield fitting into elevation of piston. **NOTE** — *Elevation should project at least .004" (.1 mm) above shield.*

# Brakes

## MERCEDES-BENZ (Cont.)

### MASTER CYLINDER

**CAUTION** — *Bendix master cylinder, spray painted blue, cannot be repaired.*

**Disassembly (Tandem and Step Tandem)** — Remove reservoir, push piston in with screwdriver, then remove stop screw and "O" ring. Remove lock ring from housing, then remove piston, stop washer, 2 vacuum seals and intermediate ring. Remove intermediate piston by rapping lightly with a wooden board.

**NOTE** — *Teves reservoir only, remove cap, end covers, strainer, splash guard, "O" rings and contact inserts. Bendix model, remove strainer from cover. DO NOT remove contact inserts. All models, master cylinder diameter should be .937" (23.81 mm).*

**Inspection** — Clean all parts with alcohol or brake fluid. Check bore in housing and piston for scoring and rust. Small rust spots in housing may be removed with polishing cloth. Scored or badly rusted parts cannot be repaired, replace complete master cylinder.

**Reassembly** — Reverse disassembly procedure and bleed hydraulic system.

### TIGHTENING SPECIFICATIONS

| Application | Ft. Lbs. (mkg) |
|---|---|
| Front Caliper Mounting Bolts | 83 (11.5) |
| Rear Caliper Mounting Bolts | 65 (9) |
| Master Cylinder Attaching Bolts | 9-10 (1.2-1.4) |
| Rotor-to-Wheel Hub Bolts | 83 (11.5) |
| Hydraulic Line Fittings | 11 (1.5) |

1 Container plug
3 Piston (push rod circuit)
4 Stop washer
5 Locking ring
6 Vacuum seal
7 Intermediate ring
8 Bearing ring
9 Filling washer
10 Primary sleeve
11 Supporting ring
12 Spring retainer
14 Connecting screw
15 Stop screw
17 Compression spring
18 Ring sleeve
19 Spring plate
20 Piston (intermediate piston)
21 Compression spring
22 Housing
23 Splash guard
24 Strainer
25 Closing cover
26 Compensating tank
27 Contact insert
28 O-ring
29 End cover
30 Float
31 Sealing ring

A Leak hole
B Filler hole
C Compensating hole

**Fig. 6 Sectional View of Late Model Mercedes-Benz Tandem Master Cylinder**

### DISC BRAKE ROTOR SPECIFICATIONS

| Application | Disc Diameter In. (mm) | Lateral Runout In. (mm) | Parallelism In. (mm) | Original Thickness In. (mm) | Minimum Refinish Thickness In. (mm) | Discard Thickness In. (mm) |
|---|---|---|---|---|---|---|
| **240D, 300D, 230 280E, 280CE, 300CD** | | | | | | |
| Front | 10.98 (279) | .0047 (.12) | .0008 (.02) | .496 (10) | .457 (9.4) | .435 (9.02) |
| Rear | 10.98 (279) | .0047 (.12) | .0008 (.02) | .394 (10) | .370 (9.4) | .355 (9.02) |
| **280SE, 450SEL, 6.9 450SC, 450SLC** | | | | | | |
| Front | 10.94 (278) | .0047 (.12) | .0004 (.01) | .866 (22) | .827 (21) | .737 (20) |
| Rear | 10.98 (279) | .0047 (12) | .0004 (.01) | .394 (10) | .370 (9.4) | .355 (9.02) |

## MGB

**MGB**

### DESCRIPTION

Lockheed type brake system consists of a tandem type master cylinder, self-adjusting disc brakes, manually adjusted leading-trailing type drum rear brakes, and a lever operated parking brake. Front brakes are of rotating disc and rigid mounted caliper type. Each caliper carries two disc pad assemblies, one on each side of the rotating disc. Rear brakes are internal expanding, shoe and drum type. Rear brakes are operated by a single wheel cylinder which is hydraulically actuated by a foot pedal. A brake pressure warning switch is mounted to master cylinder and connected to a warning light on instrument panel.

### ADJUSTMENT

#### DISC BRAKES

Disc brakes are self-adjusting, therefore no adjustment in service is required.

#### DRUM BRAKES

Raise and support rear of vehicle and fully release parking brake. Turn shoe adjuster clockwise until wheel is locked. Back off adjuster until wheel is free to rotate without binding.

**NOTE** — *Adjustment on drum brakes also tightens up parking brake.*

**Fig. 1  Rear Drum Brake Shoe Adjuster Location**

#### PARKING BRAKE

With service brakes properly adjusted, check for excessive parking brake cable stretch. Turn brass cable adjuster nut until total parking brake lever travel required to fully set parking brake is three to four serrations.

Adjust This Nut

Hold Here with Wrench

**Fig. 2  Parking Brake Cable Adjustment Location**

#### BRAKE SYSTEM BLEEDING

**1)** Release parking brake. Disconnect electrical wiring from brake failure switch. Unscrew switch about 3 ½ turns to ensure switch plunger is clear.

**2)** Fit bleed tube to caliper nearest master clyinder. Submerge opposite end of tube into a container partially filled with brake fluid. Open bleed screw about ½ turn.

**3)** Depress pedal rapidly through several full strokes allowing pedal to return unassisted. Repeat procedure (pedal pumping) with short pauses between each full stroke. Continue until all air bubbles stop. Tighten bleed screw with pedal on down stroke.

**4)** Repeat above procedure on other front caliper and each rear wheel cylinder. Tighten brake failure switch and connect wiring. It warning light remains on with parking brake released and pedal applied, repeat bleeding procedure.

### REMOVAL & INSTALLATION

#### FRONT DISC BRAKE PADS

**Removal** — Raise vehicle and remove tire and wheel. Depress pad retaining springs and remove cotter pins with retaining springs. Carefully lift out pads from caliper. Measure pad lining and replace if lining is worn to .063" (1.59 mm).

**Installation** — Before inserting disc pads, clean any foreign material from piston head and caliper cavity. Using suitable clamp, seat piston in cylinder bore. **NOTE** — *During this operation fluid level will rise.* Ensure machined portion of piston face is correctly positioned at inner end of caliper. Insert friction pads, reposition retaining springs and fit cotter pins. Check that pads have some degree of movement in caliper. It is acceptable to file high spots from friction pads if necessary. Pump brake pedal several times to readjust pistons.

#### REAR BRAKE SHOES

**Removal** — **1)** Raise and support rear of vehicle. Remove wheel. Release parking brake. Loosen brake shoe adjuster. Remove screws and pull off brake drum.

# Brakes

## MGB (Cont.)

**2)** Make note of how springs at wheel cylinder end attach. Separate parking brake lever spring. Remove each brake shoe mounting pin, retainer, and spring. Pry (by spreading return springs) brake shoes out of adjuster and wheel cylinder. Lift off shoes. If necessary, wheel cylinder and parking brake mechanism can now be removed.

**Fig. 3   Installed View of Rear Brake Drum Assembly**

**Installation** — To install, reverse removal procedure and note: Apply suitable brake grease to shoe contact points. Adjust brake shoes.

### BRAKE CALIPER

**Removal** — Raise vehicle and remove tire, wheel, and friction pads. Drain fluid through bleed screw. Disconnect fluid hoses on mounting half of caliper and plug end of hose. Bend locking ears and withdraw mounting bolts. Lift off caliper.

**Installation** — To install, reverse removal procedure noting the following: Torque mounting bolts to 43 ft. lbs. (6.0 mkg).

### MASTER CYLINDER

**Removal** — After removing pedal box cover drain fluid from master cylinder reservoir. Disconnect hydraulic lines from master cylinder and separate electrical connections from warning switch. move two nuts mounting master cylinder to power brake unit, then remove cylinder.

**Installation** — To install, reverse removal procedure. Start hydraulic lines before tightening master cylinder. Bleed hydraulic system and adjust brakes, if necessary.

### WHEEL CYLINDER

**Removal** — Remove rear brake shoes as previously outlined. Disconnect wheel cylinder fluid line. Pull line clear of cylinder and plug opening. Remove bleed screw. Pry out spring clip holding wheel clyinder to back plate. Slide out wheel cylinder.

**Fig. 4   Power Brake Unit Components**

## MGB (Cont.)

**Installation** — Coat face of wheel cylinder with heat resistant grease. Slide wheel cylinder through back plate and install new spring clip. Insert bleed screw. Reconnect brake line. To install remaining components, reverse removal procedure.

### POWER BRAKE UNIT

**Removal** — Disconnect throttle return spring from air cleaner, then remove air cleaner from vehicle. Remove pedal box cover. Disconnect hydraulic lines from mounting clips. Separate master cylinder from power brake unit and support cylinder out of way. Disconnect vacuum source and pedal return spring, then remove pin securing pedal to push rod. Remove nuts and spring washers mounting power brake unit to pedal box and lift out unit.

**Installation** — To install, reverse removal procedure and bleed hydraulic system.

## OVERHAUL

### BRAKE CALIPER

**Disassembly** — 1) Remove brake caliper, leaving inlet hose connected. Clamp piston in mounting half of caliper and gently apply service brakes. This procedure will force rim half piston out enough to be removed by hand.

**Fig. 5   Exploded View of Brake Caliper**

2) Using a blunt instrument, remove fluid seal, taking care not to damage bore or retaining groove. To remove dust seal, insert a screwdriver between retainer and seal, and gently pry retainer from mouth of caliper bore. Disassembly procedure is same for mounting half. **NOTE** — *Caliper rim half must be reassembled before disassembling mounting half.*

**Reassembly** — 1) Coat new seal with brake fluid and ease seal into groove. Loosen bleed screw in rim half one turn. Coat piston with brake fluid and locate piston squarely in cylinder bore with cut-away portion facing inner edge of caliper.

2) Press piston down until 5/16" protrudes from bore. Fit dust seal into retainer. Position seal assembly on extended portion of piston with seal innermost. Seat piston and seal assembly with clamp and retighten bleed screw. Rim half of caliper is reassembled in same manner.

### POWER BRAKE UNIT

**Disassembly** — Remove seal and retainer from servo (power brake unit). Fix servo into a vice and mark both cover and shell. Remove dust cover and pull out filter. Remove end cover by pressing down and turning counterclockwise. **NOTE** — *Cover is under spring tension.* Remove seal retainer, bearing, and seal from cover. Remove diaphragm from valve body. Push in on valve rod and plunger to release retaining key. Remove remaining components.

**Inspection** — Clean all components in brake fluid. Examine components for damage and wear. Replace all retainers and rubber parts. Valve rod and plunger must be replaced as an assembly.

**Reassembly** — To reassemble, reverse disassembly procedure and note the following: Coat all rubber components with brake fluid. Ensure push rod protrusion from servo is .400" (10.16 mm). One turn on adjuster alters rod length .035" (.088 mm)

### WHEEL CYLINDER

**Disassembly** — Pry off dust seals from each end of wheel cylinder. Slide pistons out. Remove seals taking care not to damage the seal groove.

**Inspection** — Clean all components in alcohol and allow to dry. If cylinder bore shows any signs of scoring or roughness, replace wheel cylinder.

**Fig. 6   Exploded View of Rear Wheel Cylinder**

## MGB (Cont.)

**Reassembly** — Lightly coat all internal components with brake fluid. Slide in each seal with flat surface toward slotted end of piston. Push piston into bore. Pull seal over end of assembly.

### MASTER CYLINDER

**Disassembly** — 1) Remove brake pressure failure switch. Place cylinder in vice and remove reservoir. Take out seal and adaptor assembly from primary feed port, then remove secondary port seal. Extract spring clip from cylinder bore and take out primary piston, return spring, and cup.

2) Insert a rod into bore and depress secondary piston, take out stop plug from secondary feed port and withdraw secondary piston assembly. Remove pressure differential piston assembly. Pull rubber seals from pistons.

**Inspection** — Clean all components in brake fluid. Examine cylinder bore for scoring or ridges, replace components as necessary.

**Reassembly** — 1) Lubricate all components with brake fluid. Fit "O" ring seals to pressure warning piston. Place a shim on primary and secondary pistons. Install seal to both pistons, lip facing away from shim. Fit the thinner of remaining seals to secondary piston with lips toward primary seat. Fit the secondary seal to primary piston with lip toward first seal. Fit return spring and cup to secondary piston and insert assembly.

2) Depress secondary piston and insert stop plug when piston head has passed feed port. Fit return spring and cup to primary piston and insert assembly. Refit spring clip.

3) Reinstall pressure differential valve into its bore and fit end plug. Fit "O" ring and seal to primary feed port adaptor and install into port recess. Install secondary feed port seal, round edge first. Reposition reservoir and brake pressure switch.

## TIGHTENING SPECIFICATIONS

| Application | Ft. Lbs. (mkg) |
| --- | --- |
| Caliper Mounting Bolts | 43 (6.0) |
| Master Cylinder End Plug | 33 (4.5) |
| Master Cylinder Reservoir Screws | 5 (.70) |
| Brake Hub-to-Rotor | 43 (6.0) |

**Fig. 7  Master Cylinder Reservoir, Body and Piston Assemblies**

## MG MIDGET

**Midget**

## DESCRIPTION

Midget brake system is made up of two independent curcuits: a hydraulic foot brake and a mechanical hand brake. Hand brake is lever operated and, when set, locks rear wheels. Foot brakes are either leading-trailing drum type or dual piston caliper disc type. Rear brakes in all instances are leading-trailing drum type with manual adjusters. Master cylinder is tandem type with each of its halves feeding a separate circuit. There is a brake warning light located on instrument panel to indicate fluid loss in either side of master cylinder.

## ADJUSTMENT

### DISC BRAKES

Disc brakes are self-adjusting, therefore no adjustment in service is required.

### DRUM BRAKES

Raise and support vehicle, and remove wheel to be serviced. Rotate drum until front hole and adjuster mechanism are aligned. Using a screwdriver, turn adjuster clockwise until brake shoe contacts drum. Back off adjuster until drum is just free to turn. Repeat adjustment on rear shoe adjuster.

### PARKING BRAKE

With service brakes correctly adjusted, apply parking brake three ratchet notches. Adjust sleeve nut on parking brake cable until drum can just be rotated.

### BLEEDING HYDRAULIC SYSTEM

Fit a bleeder tube to both right front and right rear wheel cylinders, then submerge free ends into a partially filled container of brake fluid. Pump brake pedal, but do not go entire pedal stroke. Repeat bleeding process until all air is expelled from system. With pedal down, and on next to last stroke, close bleeder screws. Perform same procedure on left front and left rear wheels.

### COMBINATION VALVE

**Reset** — Make sure brake fluid reservoir is full. Correct any hydraulic leaks. Bleed brakes to make sure all air is out of system. Bleed brakes of one wheel of system that was not at fault. Slowly depress pedal, as soon as light goes out, release pedal and close bleeder screw. **NOTE** — *If pedal isn't released immediately, piston will move too far and procedure will have to be repeated.*

### FRONT DISC BRAKE PADS

**Removal** — Remove tire and wheel. Depress friction pad retaining spring and remove cotter pins. Remove retaining springs. Carefully twist friction pads and remove damper shims. Lift out friction pads. Using a clean rag, wipe any foreign material from piston head and cylinder cavity.

**Installation** — Using suitable clamp, fully seat piston in cylinder bore. **NOTE** — *Fluid level will rise during this procedure.* Insert friction pads into caliper and ensure they have free movement. Install damper shims between pistons and friction pads. Fit pad retaining springs, press down spring and insert cotter pins. Install tire.

### BRAKE SHOES

**Removal** — Remove tire. Loosen brake shoes at adjuster and remove drum. Disconnect brake mounting springs. Pull trailing shoe against tension of return springs and away from its abutment at either end. With return spring tension released, detach mounting springs and remove both shoes. Remove brake adjuster.

**Installation** — To install, reverse removal procedure and ensure adjuster is in slot in shoe.

**Fig. 1   MG Midget Rear Drum Brake Assembly**

## REMOVAL & INSTALLATION

### BRAKE CALIPER

**Removal** — Remove tire and wheel. Remove friction pads. Disconnect brake caliper line. Remove nuts securing caliper hose mounting plate to caliper. Remove studs securing caliper to axle stud and lift off caliper.

**Installation** — To install, reverse removal procedure, tighten all nuts and bolts, and bleed hydraulic system.

### FRONT DISC BRAKE ROTOR

**Removal** — Remove tire and wheel. Extract friction pads and brake caliper. Remove dust cover cap, cotter pin, locking nut and washer. Withdraw hub assembly from axle, using suitable puller (18G-304 with adaptors 18G-304-F for standard wheels, or 18G-363 for wire wheels, early models, or 18G-1032 for wire wheels, late models). Remove bolts securing brake rotor to hub and remove rotor.

**Installation** — To install, reverse removal procedure.

## MG MIDGET (Cont.)

### MASTER CYLINDER

**Removal** — Disconnect high tension lead from ignition coil and blue-white lead from resistor. Remove four screws and pull cover plate with ignition coil from vehicle. Remove cotter pin and clevis from push rod. Disconnect and separate hydraulic lines from master cylinder, then plug open lines. **NOTE** — *Keep brake fluid off paint.* Remove bolts securing master cylinder pedal box and pull out cylinder.

**Installation** — To install master cylinder, reverse removal procedure and bleed brake system.

### REAR WHEEL CYLINDER

**Removal** — Remove rear wheel and brake drum. Disconnect the brake line at wheel cylinder and plug line opening. Remove cylinder bleed screw. Take out spring clip and washer retaining wheel cylinder to back plate and withdraw cylinder assembly.

**Installation** — To install, reverse removal procedure and bleed brakes.

### COMBINATION VALVE

**Removal** — Thoroughly clean all line connections. Disconnect electrical wiring. Disconnect and plug all hydraulic lines entering combination valve. Remove mounting bolts and take off assembly.

**Installation** — To install, reverse removal procedure and note: Make sure all hydraulic lines fully seat before final tightening. It is important that valve is fully seated in approximately horizontal position.

## OVERHAUL

### BRAKE CALIPER

**Disassembly** — 1) Remove brake caliper as previously described. Clean outside of caliper and note position of relieved portion of piston face. Using suitable clamp, retain piston in mounting half of caliper.

2) Holding caliper on bench, apply compressed air to hydraulic inlet port until dust seal retainer and seal can be removed. Remove fluid seal from groove in caliper bore. **NOTE** — *Exercise care not to score caliper bore.* Refit piston into caliper bore and install suitable clamp.

3) Remove mounting half dust seal, piston, and fluid seal. Remove clamp and piston. **NOTE** — *Do not separate caliper halves.*

**Inspection** — Clean all components with brake fluid. Check pistons and cylinder bores for wear or damage, replace parts as necessary.

**Reassembly** — Lubricate pistons and all new seals in brake fluid. Insert fluid seals into grooves fit pistons in bore with relieved portion toward bleed screw. Install dust seal and retainer.

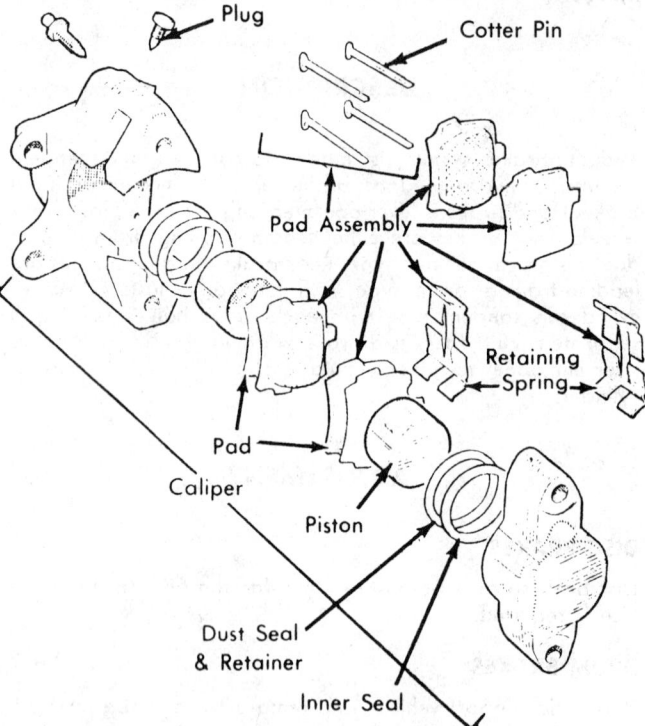

**Fig. 2** *Exploded View of Front Disc Brake Caliper Assembly*

### REAR WHEEL CYLINDER

**Disassembly** — Separate dust cover boot from both ends of wheel cylinder. Pull out both pistons with seals and inspect pistons for excessive wear or damage. Separate seals from pistons and replace seals.

**Reassembly** — After cleaning cylinder bore and related components in brake fluid, check wheel cylinder bore for scoring or pitting. While components are still damp, fit new seals to pistons with flat surfaces of seals facing slotted end of piston. Insert new pistons into wheel cylinder bore, plain end first. Install new dust cover boots.

**Fig. 3** *Disassembled View of Rear Wheel Cylinder*

## MG MIDGET (Cont.)

### COMBINATION VALVE

**Disassembly** — Remove the end plug and discard copper washer. Unscrew nylon switch. Remove shuttle valve piston from assembly bore. Use air pressure to force out piston. Remove two piston seals and discard.

**Inspection** — Thoroughly clean all components in clean brake fluid. Check bore of assembly for scoring or ridges. New seals can be used if bore isn't damaged.

**Reassembly** — Lightly coat all components in brake fluid. Install both new seals with lips facing outward from piston center. Fit piston into bore, taking care that lead seal is not cocked. Fit new copper seal and tighten end plug to 200 INCH lbs. (230 cmkg). Refit nylon switch and torque to 15 INCH lbs. (17.25 cmkg).

### MASTER CYLINDER

**Disassembly** — Thoroughly clean dirt from outside of cylinder. Detach rubber boot and remove snap ring. Compress return spring and remove circlip. Move piston around in bore to free nylon guide bearing and cap seal. Remove bearing seal and plain washer. Remove inner circlip. Withdraw primary and secondary piston assemblies complete with stop washers. When component parts have been removed, they can be further disassembled.

**Cleaning & Inspecting** — Clean all parts in approved grade brake fluid. Examine all components for signs of rust, grooves or distortion. Replace any parts found out of tolerance.

**Reassembly** — To reassemble, reverse disassembly procedure.

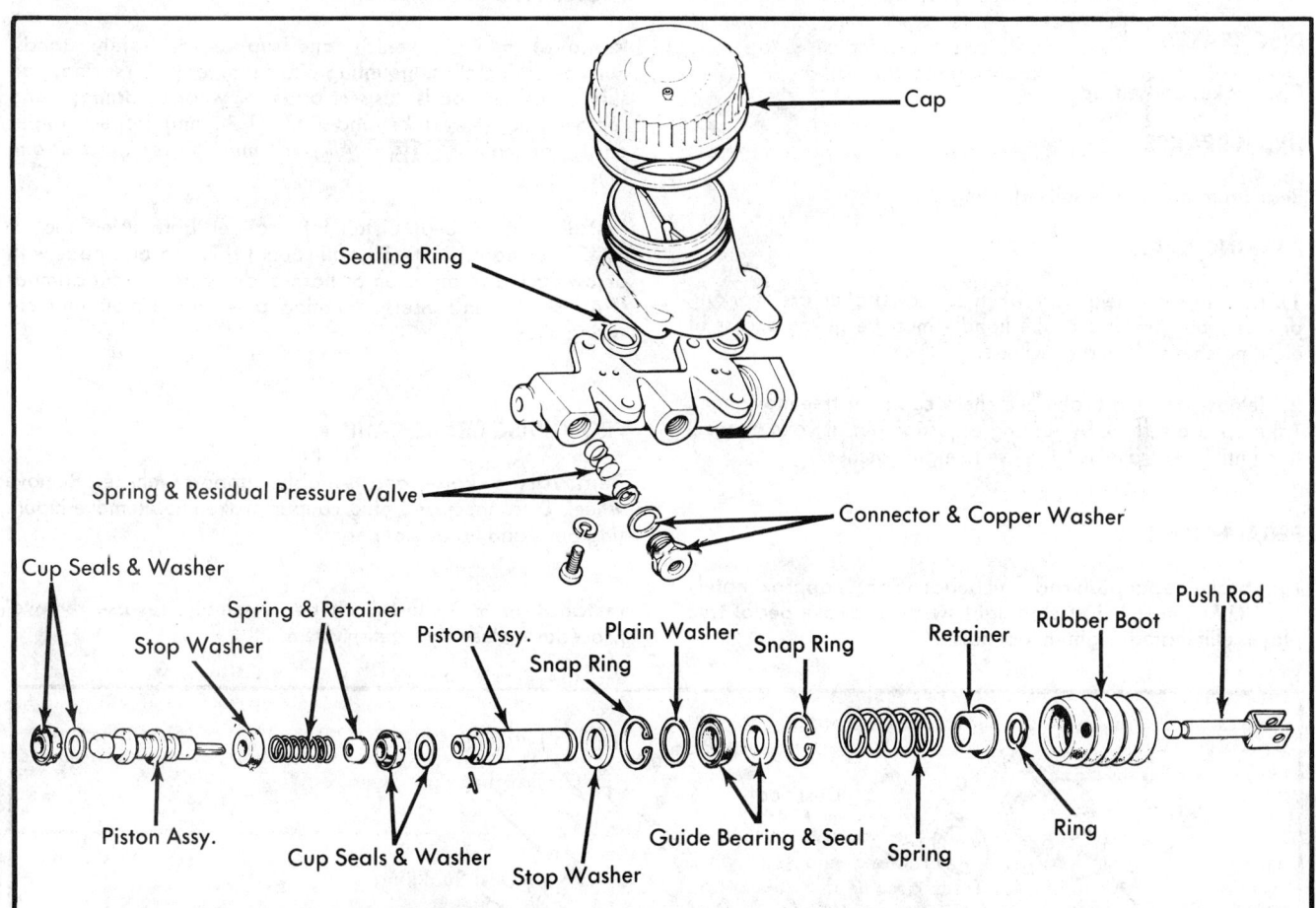

**Fig. 4    Exploded View of Master Cylinder Reservoir, Body and Piston Assemblies**

## BRAKE SYSTEM SPECIFICATIONS

| Application | Drum Diam. In. (mm) | Wheel Cylinder Diameter | | Master Cylinder |
| | | Front In. (mm) | Rear In. (mm) | Diameter In. (mm) |
| --- | --- | --- | --- | --- |
| Midget | 7 (177.8) | ① | .687 (17.46) | .750 (19.05) |

① — Front wheel disc brakes

## OPEL

**All Models**

### DESCRIPTION

Brake system has a two-part circuit. Front brakes are one circuit, consisting of a dual piston caliper and a rotor. Leading-trailing, rear drum brakes make up other circuit. Drum brakes are self-adjusting. A dual piston master cylinder supplies the hydraulic pressure for brake system. Some models may be equipped with a Master-Vac power brake unit. All models are fitted with a mechanical parking brake. Control handle for parking brake is mounted between front seats and, when actuated, locks rear wheels.

### ADJUSTMENT

**DISC BRAKES**

Disc brakes are self-adjusting.

**DRUM BRAKES**

Rear drum brakes are self-adjusting.

**PARKING BRAKE**

1) Adjustment is required when service brakes are working properly but parking brake handle must be pulled excess of eight notches to lock rear wheels.

2) Release parking brake and check cable for free movement. Take up cable slack by turning adjusting nut at yoke connection until lever travel is from five to eight notches.

**PEDAL HEIGHT**

Turn brake pedal push rod until pedal height is approximately 6¾" (171 mm). Adjust stop light switch so brake pedal free play is eliminated. Tighten lock nuts.

### HYDRAULIC SYSTEM BLEEDING

**NOTE** – *To avoid damage to push rod seal, engine must be running during bleeding operation.*

Attach a bleeder tube to bleeder screw and immerse opposite end of tube in a container partially filled with brake fluid. Open bleeder screw and allow pedal to be pushed through its full travel. Close bleeder screw and let pedal return to normal height. Continue procedure until all air is expelled from cylinder. Repeat bleeding procedure at remaining wheels.

### REMOVAL & INSTALLATION

**FRONT DISC BRAKE PADS**

**Removal** – Raise vehicle and support on safety stands. Remove spring clips, mounting pins, damper ("M") spring, pad shims, and disc pads. Inspect pads for wear or damage and replace pads if worn beyond .067" (1.70 mm). Inspect caliper cavity for leaks. **NOTE** – *All pads must be replaced at one time.*

**Installation** – Seat piston into caliper bore using tool J-22430 (or equivalent). Fit anti-squeal shims to disc pads with arrow facing in direction of normal disc rotation. Fit damper ("M") spring and insert mounting pins. Install mounting pin spring clips.

**FRONT DISC BRAKE CALIPER**

**Removal** – Raise and suitably support vehicle. Remove wheel. Disconnect and plug caliper brake line. Remove mounting bolts and lift off caliper.

**Installation** – To install caliper assembly, reverse removal procedure. Bleed hydraulic system.

*Fig. 1  Exploded View of Opel Front Disc Brake Assembly*

## OPEL (Cont.)

### FRONT DISC BRAKE ROTOR

**Removal** – Raise and suitably support vehicle. Remove wheel. Remove caliper without disconnecting brake fluid line. Suspend caliper from upper control arm using a wire hanger. Remove grease cap and take out the outer wheel bearing assembly. Pull hub and rotor assembly from spindle. Remove bolts mounting rotor to hub and index mark before separating.

**Installation** – To install, reverse removal procedure and note the following. Make sure wheel bearings are properly tightened. *See Wheel Bearing Adjustment in WHEEL ALIGNMENT Section.* Measure brake rotor runout. If runout exceeds .006" (.15 mm), resurface or replace rotor.

### REAR BRAKE SHOES

**Removal** – Raise and suitably support vehicle on safety stands. Remove wheel and drum. Remove return springs, shoe hold down pins, retainers and springs. Fully expand adjuster mechanism and disconnect strut. Remove primary shoe. Disconnect parking brake lever from cable; then remove secondary shoe. If necessary, wheel cylinder can now be removed.

*Fig. 2   Exploded View of Rear Brake Assembly*

**Installation** – To install brake shoes, reverse removal procedure and note the following: Make sure brake shoes do not scratch wheel cylinder boots during installation. Halves of adjuster mechanism are not reversible. Right and left side self-adjuster components are not interchangeable.

### MASTER CYLINDER

**Removal** – Disconnect front and rear brake lines from master cylinder. Take off nuts mounting cylinder to power brake unit support bracket. Separate brake fluid reservoir bracket and lift off master cylinder assembly complete with fluid reservoir and hoses.

**Installation** – To install master cylinder, reverse removal procedure.

### POWER BRAKE UNIT

**Removal** – Remove master cylinder as previously outlined. Disconnect vacuum hose from check valve. Remove clevis pin and brake pedal arm. Remove nuts mounting power brake unit to fire wall spacer and lift unit from vehicle.

**Installation** – To install, reverse removal procedure and note the following: Adjust push rod length to .733" (18.6 mm). Adjust brake pedal height as previously outlined.

*Fig. 3   Power Brake Unit Push Rod Measurement Points for Adjustment*

## OVERHAUL

### FRONT DISC BRAKE CALIPER

**Disassembly** – Remove each piston dust seal ring, then take out dust seal. Fit clamp J-2242 (or equivalent) to caliper mounting half piston, then force air pressure into fluid inlet to push rim half piston from caliper bore. Repeat procedure on opposite side to remove other piston. Remove seals from grooves in piston bores. **NOTE** – *Use a pointed, but not sharp instrument to dig out seal.*

**Inspection** – Inspect cylinder bores for signs of wear or scoring. Check calipers and adaptor plates for distortion, replace as necessary.

**Installation** – Lightly coat seals and cylinder bore walls with suitable grease. Fit new seals to grooves in caliper bore. Insert one piston and push to bottom of caliper bore. Install dust seal and seal ring. Repeat procedures on opposite side piston.

# Brakes

## OPEL (Cont.)

**Fig. 4  Exploded View of Opel Master-Vac Power Brake Assembly**

## REAR WHEEL CYLINDER

**Disassembly** — Pull off rubber dust boots. Push from one side until pistons, cups, and return spring are forced from cylinder.

**Inspection** — Check cylinder bore for damage, wear or score marks. Check clearance between cylinder and bore. Clearance should not exceed .006" (.15 mm).

**Reassembly** — Lightly coat pistons, cups, and return spring, then reverse disassembly procedure for remaining components.

## MASTER CYLINDER

**Disassembly** — Empty excess brake fluid from master cylinder reservoir. Separate reservoir from cylinder body. Remove brake line connectors and take out check valves, springs and retainers. Insert screwdriver and push in primary piston enough to remove secondary stop bolt and snap ring. Withdraw both piston assemblies and separate remaining components.

**Inspection** — Clean all parts in brake fluid and dry with compressed air. Inspect master cylinder bore for damage or wear. Measure bore diameter, value should be .875" (22.2 mm). If pistons are found defective or damaged, replace entire piston assembly. Always replace piston cup during overhaul. Master cylinder to piston clearance should be no more than .006" (.15 mm).

**Reassembly** — To reassemble, reverse disassembly procedure and not the following: Lightly coat all components with brake fluid before reassembling. Make sure check valve with hole is installed on front side. Insert primary piston and fit snap ring, then push in with screwdriver and install stop bolt.

## POWER BRAKE UNIT

**Disassembly** — 1) Index mark shell halves. Remove nuts and spacer from rear shell. Remove clevis. Use tool J-22805-01 (or

equivalent) and clamp front shell in vise. Use tool J-9504-01 (or equivalent) and turn rear shell counterclockwise to remove. Take off rear shell and diaphragm retaining spring.

2) Take out diaphragm plate assembly. Remove retainer from rear shell, then take out plate and seal. Slip off diaphragm and silencer retainer, then pull out stop key. Remove plunger assembly and reaction disc. Pull push rod, retainer and seal from front shell assembly.

**Inspection** — Clean all components and dry with compressed air. Check all diaphragms and seals for signs of weakening; replace as necessary. Check plunger for wear; replace if worn.

**Reassembly** — 1) Apply silicone grease to sliding surfaces of all components. Install plate, seal, and retainer. Install plunger assembly complete with filter and silencer. Be sure poppet valve is not projected beyond retainer. Install diaphragm plate. Fit retainer and diaphragm on diaphragm plate. Put diaphragm assembly on rear shell, then fit boot and clevis.

2) Install seal assembly to front shell. Install retainer and push rod. Use holding tool J-22805-01 (or equivalent) and mount front shell in vise. Install diaphragm spring between shell halves, then force in and rotate rear shell clockwise until fully seated and aligned with index marks.

### TIGHTENING SPECIFICATIONS

| Application | Ft. Lbs. (mkg) |
|---|---|
| Caliper Mounting Bolts | 36 (4.9) |
| Caliper Brake Line | 11 (1.5) |
| Master Cylinder-to-Power Brake Unit | 10 (1.4) |
| Master Cylinder Brake Line | 12 (1.6) |
| Master Cylinder Brake Line Connector | 87 (12.0) |
| Master Cylinder Stop Bolt | 14 (1.9) |
| Wheel Cylinder Mounting Bolt | 7 (.97) |

## OPEL (Cont.)

### BRAKE SYSTEM SPECIFICATIONS

| Application | Drum Diam. In. (mm) | Wheel Cylinder Diameter | | Master Cylinder |
| | | Front In. (mm) | Rear In. (mm) | Diameter In. (mm) |
| --- | --- | --- | --- | --- |
| All Models | 8.980 (228.1) | ① | .812 (20.6) | .875 (22.2) |

① — Front disc brakes.

### BRAKE DRUM SPECIFICATIONS

| Application | Drum Diameter In. (mm) | Original Diameter In. (mm) | Maximum Refinish Diameter In. (mm) | Discard Diameter In. (mm) |
| --- | --- | --- | --- | --- |
| All Models | 8.980 (228.1) | 8.980 (228.1) | 9.040 (229.6) | 9.060 (230.1) |

## PORSCHE

**911SC & Turbo**
**924**
**928**

## DESCRIPTION

Brake systems are hydraulically operated, utilizing a tandem master cylinder and a power brake unit. 911 and 928 models are equipped with front and rear disc brakes. 924 models are equipped with front disc brakes and rear shoe brakes. All models utilize mechanical parking brakes that operate off the rear brakes. All models have a brake warning light that is activated when there is a pressure drop in the hydraulic system. Warning light on instrument panel comes on and will not go off until the problem is corrected.

Master Cylinder Reservoir
To Rear Brakes
Master Cylinder
To Front Brakes

**Fig. 1  Hydraulic Fluid Distribution for Dual Circuit Brake System**

## ADJUSTMENT

### DISC BRAKES

Disc brakes are self adjusting, therefore no adjustment in service is required.

### REAR BRAKE SHOES

**924 (Rear Brakes)** — Turn adjuster until a slight drag is felt when rotating brake drum. Back off adjuster until drum is just free to rotate.

### PARKING BRAKE

**911 Models** — Raise and support vehicle, and remove rear wheels. Release parking brake lever and push pistons and pads into caliper to allow rotor to turn freely. Loosen parking brake cable lock nuts until cable is slack. Working through access hole in parking brake drum, turn star wheel adjuster until rotor can no longer be turned by hand. Adjust parking brake cable at rear cable end until it just begins to pull and tighten lock nuts. Back off on star wheel adjuster until rotor turns freely without drag. Repeat procedure on opposite wheel and check parking brake operation.

**924 Models** — Raise and support vehicle and ensure rear brakes are properly adjusted. From inside of vehicle, pull parking lever up by two notches. At base of lever adjust nut until both wheels can just be turned by hand.

**928 Models** — Parking brake adjustment is the same as on the 911.

## BLEEDING SYSTEM

**Bleeding Sequence** — If equipped with outer and inner caliper half bleed screws, always bleed outer caliper half fist and inner half second. Bleed brakes as follows: Left rear first, right rear second, right front third, and left front last.

**CAUTION** — *When any fluid fitting is disconnected, fluid will drain from reservoir through master cylinder and out open fitting. To avoid this, depress brake pedal far enough so piston cup will pass the compensating (resupply) port.*

**Pressure Bleeding** — Fill pressure bleeder with brake fluid and pressurize tank to 32.3 psi (2.2 atm). Connect bleeder to reservoir and connect a small bleed hose to first bleed screw. See *Bleeding Sequence.* Place other end in container partially filled with brake fluid. Open bleed screw 1/2 — 3/4 turn and allow fluid to drain until no air bubbles are apparent in fluid. Close bleed screw and repeat operation for each bleed screw in turn.

**NOTE** — *If brake system was completely drained, it may be necessary to perform bleeding, in sequence, more than once.*

**Manual Bleeding** — Fill reservoir with brake fluid and connect a small hose to first bleed screw. See *Bleeding Sequence.* Place other end in container partially filled with brake fluid. Have an assistant rapidly pump brake pedal until slight pressure is felt, then hold pedal depressed. Open bleed screw and allow fluid to drain. Close bleed screw before slowly releasing pedal. Repeat pedal action until fluid flows into container with no bubbles. Repeat at each bleed screw in turn.

## REMOVAL & INSTALLATION

**NOTE** — *Rear brake calipers are now mounted on the trailing arms at the rear rather than at the front. Trailing arms have been modified with mounting holes at the rear to accommodate this change. Rear brake lines are now secured to the trailing arms with a retaining clip to prevent vibration.*

### DISC PADS

**NOTE** — *Mark pads and calipers before removal. If pads are to be reused, they must be installed in original location. If only one pad on front or rear needs replacing, all four pads must be replaced.*

**Removal** — Raise and support vehicle and remove wheels. On 911 models, squeeze spreader spring together until it is disengaged. Pull pads out with suitable wire hook. On 924 models, remove inside brake pad first. Outside brake pad is guided by a tab on caliper frame. Press out this frame to pull out brake pad. On 928 models, remove brake pad sensor from backing plate. Remove spring lock and retaining pins. Remove inner brake pad with hook. Remove outer brake pad.

**NOTE** — *Depress spreader spring if required. Using a suitable extractor (P86) pull pads from caliper.*

**CAUTION** — *If fluid level is too high in reservoir, overflow will result when pistons (during installation) are pushed back into calipers.*

**Installation** — Push piston back into caliper using suitable tool (P83), or wooden block. Remove anti-rotation locks (if equipped) and clean all parts with alcohol. Inspect all parts for damage or wear. Ensure piston 20° position is correct using suitable gauge (P84). Install remaining parts in reverse order of removal, replace parts as necessary.

## PORSCHE (Cont.)

**Fig. 2   Using a 20° Gauge to Properly Position Caliper Piston**

### BRAKE CALIPER

**CAUTION** — *When any fluid fitting is disconnected, fluid will drain from reservoir through master cylinder and out open fitting. To avoid this, depress brake pedal far enough so piston cup will pass the compensating (resupply) port.*

**Removal (Front & Rear)** — Raise and support vehicle, and remove wheels. Remove brake pads as previously outlined. Remove splash shield (if necessary), disconnect hydraulic line. Remove mounting bolts and remove caliper assembly.

**Installation (Front & Rear)** — To install, reverse removal procedure and note the following: Clean and inspect all parts for wear or damage and replace as necessary. Tighten all bolts and fittings to specifications and bleed complete brake system.

### BRAKE ROTOR

**Removal (Front)** — Remove caliper assembly as previously outlined. Remove dust cap from wheel hub, loosen clamp lock screw, then remove clamp nut and thrust washer. Remove rotor and wheel bearings as a unit. On 911 models, mark rotor and hub for reassembly reference, remove attaching bolts and separate rotor from hub.

**Removal (Rear)** — Remove caliper assembly as previously outlined. Remove the two rotor attaching bolts and pull rotor from hub.

**NOTE** — *If rotor cannot be removed by hand, insert two 8mm bolts into attaching screw holes and alternately tighten bolts to press rotor from hub.*

**Installation (Front & Rear)** — To install, reverse removal procedure, bleed brakes and adjust front wheel bearing free play. *See Wheel Bearing Adjustment in WHEEL ALIGNMENT Section.*

**NOTE** — *Rotors must be installed in original position due to cooling holes and internal ventilation channels. These holes and channels are different for right and left sides.*

### REAR BRAKE SHOES

**Removal** — Raise and support vehicle and remove wheels. Using suitable puller (40-107) remove brake drum. Remove shoe hold down springs. Remove upper and lower return springs and pressure rod. Remove emergency brake rod from brake shoe.

**Installation** — Reverse removal procedures and note the following: Lubricate adjusting screws and sliding surfaces of brake shoes slightly. Use new bearing pin and clip when installing emergency brake rod.

**Fig. 3   Exploded View of 924 Rear Wheel Brakes**

## PORSCHE (Cont.)

### REAR WHEEL CYLINDER

**Removal** — With rear drum and brake shoes removed, disconnect brake line from wheel cylinder at rear of backing plate, remove bolts attaching cylinder and remove cylinder.

**Installation** — Reverse removal procedure, tighten mounting bolts and bleed hydraulic system.

### PARKING BRAKE ASSEMBLY

**Removal & Installation** — On 911 models, remove cotter pin, castle nut and washer from cable, then remove cable from brake assembly. Remove expander and springs and shoe retaining pins, then springs from upper shoes. Raise upper shoe, withdraw adjuster and spring. Remove shoe retainer from lower shoe and remove both shoes from vehicle. On 924 models, loosen mounting screws and remove entire parking brake lever. It may be necessary to remove tension spring and adjusting rod to remove assembly. On 928 models, remove caliper, loosen adjuster and remove screws and brake disc. Remove spreader, shoes, springs and adjuster. To install, reverse removal procedures.

### BRAKE PRESSURE REGULATOR

**Removal** — Disconnect brake lines at pressure regulator. Remove bolts from regulator flange and take out unit.

**Checking** — Step down hard on the brake pedal while feeling the regulator body; note if piston in regulator is moving. When the brake pedal is released, a slight "knock" should be felt on regulator body.

**Installation** — To install, reverse removal procedure and bleed brake system.

**NOTE** — *Brake pressure units can not be overhauled.*

### MASTER CYLINDER

**Removal** — On 911 models, raise and support vehicle and drain fluid from reservoir. Pull back on accelerator pedal to detach pedal from rod. Remove floor mat and floor board and withdraw boot from master cylinder. Remove underpanel covering front axle, remove brake lines, electrical leads and reservoir tubes from cylinder and remove master cylinder from vehicle. On 924 models, remove hydraulic lines from master cylinder and remove electrical connections. Remove mounting nuts and remove master cylinder.

**Installation** — Reverse removal procedures and note the following: On 911 models, be sure push rod is correctly installed and that clearance between push rod and piston is about .04" (1mm). Use a sealing material on cylinder flange to prevent water leakage into drivers compartment. Bleed both systems as previously outlined.

**Fig. 4  Illustrating Push Rod-to-Master Cylinder Piston Clearance on 911 Models**

### POWER BRAKE UNIT

**NOTE** — *Before removal or overhaul test check valve and power brake unit for operation. To check valve, pull off vacuum hose, place finger over check valve and crank engine, vacuum should be created. To check power brake unit, push on brake pedal several times with engine stopped, hold pedal down and start engine. If power brake unit is operating properly brake pedal will drop slightly.*

**Removal** — With master cylinder removed, disconnect vacuum hose from power brake unit. Remove pin connecting power brake unit operating rod to brake pedal assembly, remove nuts and remove power brake unit from vehicle.

**Installation** — Reverse removal procedures and note the following: Apply a suitable sealer to power brake unit mounting surface and vacuum line connections. Adjust pedal height and bleed hydraulic system.

## OVERHAUL

### BRAKE CALIPER

**NOTE** — *Cylinders can only be overhauled one at a time, because with one piston removed air pressure is unattainable in second cylinder.*

**Disassembly** — With pads and piston retaining plates removed, clamp caliper (by mounting flange) in vise. Remove dust cover retaining ring and dust cover. Install suitable piston

Apply Light Air Pressure Here

Small, Hard Wood Block Inserted Between Tool & Piston

Piston Retaining Tool Shown Holding Piston In Seated Position

**Fig. 5  Using Air Pressure to Remove Piston from Caliper Assembly**

## PORSCHE (Cont.)

retaining tool (P83) to one piston and place a thin wood block between tool and piston to be removed. Apply air pressure to fluid inlet hole to remove piston. Remove cylinder to piston seal using a plastic or hard rubber tool.

**928** — Remove spring lock, retaining pin, spreader spring and inner brake pad. Remove sensor and outer brake pad. Press caliper frame off mounting frame. Drive brake cylinder off frame by tapping it lightly with a plastic hammer. Press piston out with compressed air. Remove seal.

**930** — Clamp caliper in vise and detach connecting line. Unscrew holding bolts, drive off caliper halves from bridges by tapping with plastic hammer. Heat screws holding spring plate to 300 °F (150 °C), to prevent stripping of threads. Remove screws.

**Cleaning & Inspection** — Clean all parts in alcohol or clean brake fluid. Check all parts for wear or damage and replace as necessary. If caliper piston or bore show any signs of wear or damage, complete caliper assembly must be replaced.

**Separating Caliper Halves** — Caliper halves should only be separated if "O" ring seals between caliper halves show signs of leaking. To separate, remove bolts attaching caliper halves, separate caliper and discard "O" ring seals. To reassemble, install new "O" ring seals and reassemble caliper using new bolts, spring washers and nuts.

**NOTE** — *Install shorter bolts in outside holes. Tighten two inside bolts first and then tighten outside bolts. Bolts must be tightened in two stages; first to 50% of torque value, then to 100% of torque value.*

**Reassembly** — Reverse disassembly procedure and note the following: Use new rubber components, dust cover retaining ring and pad retaining plates. Apply brake cylinder paste to piston, and cylinder seal. Assure piston is straight with cylinder by using a suitable piston installing clamp. Check 20° position of piston with suitable gauge and correct using piston rotating pliers (if required). On 930 and 911 models, apply Loctite before replacing spring plate screws. Replace seals on hollow bolt and adapter.

**Fig. 6   Cross Sectional View of Porsche Brake Caliper Assembly**

## MASTER CYLINDER

**Disassembly** — Push in on primary piston to remove lock ring, then remove stop plate and primary piston assembly. Remove piston stop screw, and using compressed air, remove

## DISC BRAKE ROTOR SPECIFICATIONS

| Application | Disc Diameter In. (mm) | Lateral Runout In. (mm) | Parallelism In. (mm) | Original Thickness In. (mm) | Minimum Refinish Thickness In. (mm) | Discard Thickness In. (mm) |
|---|---|---|---|---|---|---|
| **911 Models** | | | | | | |
| Front | 11.96 (304) | .008 (.2) | .0012 (.03) | 1.25 (32) | 1.20 (30.6) | 1.18 (30) |
| Rear | 12.16 (309) | .008 (.2) | .0012 (.03) | 1.10 (28) | 1.04 (26.6) | 1.02 (26) |
| **924 Models** | | | | | | |
| Front | 10.1 (257) | .... | .... | .5 (13) | .47 (12) | .45 (11.5) |
| **928 Models** | | | | | | |
| Front | 11.10 (282) | .... | .... | .78 (20) | .732 (18.6) | .70 (18) |
| Rear | 11.37 (289) | .... | .... | .78 (20) | .732 (18.6) | .70 (18) |

# Brakes

## PORSCHE (Cont.)

### BRAKE SYSTEM SPECIFICATIONS

| Application | Drum Diam. In. (mm) | Wheel Cylinder Diameter | | Master Cylinder Diameter In. (mm) |
| | | Front In. (mm) | Rear In. (mm) | |
| --- | --- | --- | --- | --- |
| 924 Models | 9.05 (230) | ..... | .75 (19.05 | .81 (20.64) |

secondary piston. Remove secondary piston support washer, spring seat and return spring. To remove hydraulic warning system assembly, remove sending unit and retaining bolt from master cylinder, and using compressed air, remove pistons and springs.

**Cleaning & Inspection** — Clean all parts with alcohol. Check all pistons and cylinders for out-of-round, corrosion or damage. Inspect all other parts for scoring, excessive wear, corrosion or other damage.

**Reassembly** — To install reverse disassembly procedure using illustration as a reference and note the following: Lightly coat all parts with a suitable brake cylinder paste before installation. Use new "O" ring seals on warning system sending unit and retaining bolt. Tighten all brake lines and fittings and bleed complete brake system.

### TIGHTENING SPECIFICATIONS

| Application | Ft. Lbs. |
| --- | --- |
| **911 Models** | |
| Master Cylinder Mounting Bolts | 18 (2.5) |
| Brake Line Connections | 10 (1.4) |
| Caliper Mounting Bolts (Front & Rear) | 50 (7.0) |
| Caliper Housing Bolts, Front | 43 (6.0) |
| Rotor to Hub | 17 (2.3) |
| Splash Shield Bolts | 18 (2.5) |
| **924 Models** | |
| Master Cylinder Mounting Bolts | 9 (1.3) |
| Brake Line Connections | 9 (1.2) |
| Caliper Mounting Bolts | 60 (8.5) |
| Rear Brake Cylinder to Backing Plate Bolts | 15 (2.1) |
| Rear Wheel Brake Drum Shaft Nut | 220-290 (30-40) |
| **928 Models** | |
| Brake Line Connections | 10 (1.4) |
| Master Cylinder | 17 (2.3) |
| Caliper Bleeder Screw | 2.5 (.35) |
| Caliper to Spindle | 61 (8.5) |
| Caliper to Hub Carrier | 61 (8.5) |
| Splash Shield to Spindle | 11 (1.5) |
| Ratchet to Parking Brake Lever | 18 (2.5) |

## RENAULT

### R-5 Le Car

## DESCRIPTION

Brake system is hydraulically operated by a tandem master cylinder. Some vehicles may be equipped with a power brake unit. All models are fitted with front disc brakes and rear drum brakes. A pressure limiter valve is used to regulate pressure to rear wheels and prevent rear wheel lock-up. Parking brake cable is lever operated from between the front seats.

## ADJUSTMENT

### DISC BRAKES

Disc brakes are self adjusting; therefore, no adjustment in service is required.

### DRUM BRAKES

**NOTE** — *Some late R-5 models have self-adjusting rear drum brakes.*

Remove plastic dust plug and insert screwdriver into opening. Turn star wheel until linings just contact drum. Back off adjuster until wheels rotate freely.

### PARKING BRAKE

**R-5** — Adjust brake shoes. Fully release parking brake lever. Loosen lock nut on adjustment rod. Tighten adjustment nut until lining just meets drum. At this point parking brake lever travel should be about 6 notches. Tighten lock nut. Check operation.

**Fig. 1  R-5 Parking Brake Adjustment Points**

### REAR BRAKE PRESSURE LIMITER

**NOTE** — *Limiter must always be checked and adjusted with vehicle on level ground, trunk empty and drivers seat occupied.*

**R-5** — 1) To check limiter, remove one rear wheel cylinder bleeder screw and connect a pressure gauge into vacant hole. Bleed brake system. Depress brake pedal and check pressure obtained at wheel cylinder. Pressure should be as shown in table.

**Fig. 2  Pressure Limiter Adjustment Points**

2) To adjust limiter, release lock nut and tighten adjustment nut to **increase** pressure or loosen it to **reduce** pressure.

3) Apply brake pedal several times and recheck adjustment. Remove pressure gauge and bleed brake system.

**Pressure Limiter Adjustment**

| Application | ①psi |
|---|---|
| R-5 | 405-45 |

① — With fuel tank full.

### HYDRAULIC SYSTEM BLEEDING

**NOTE** — *On vehicles equipped with power assisted brakes, release vacuum from servo unit prior to bleeding brakes.*

Fill brake reservoir, and connect pressure bleeder. **NOTE** — *Do not exceed 30 psi with pressure bleeder.* Check each bleeder screw for fluid flow. Close bleeder screw when fluid flowing from screw is free of air. Remove pressure bleeder, and check fluid level in reservoir.

## REMOVAL & INSTALLATION

### DISC BRAKE PADS

**Removal & Installation** — Caliper must be removed to replace disc pads. See *Disc Brake Caliper Removal & Installation.*

### DISC BRAKE CALIPER

**Removal** — Raise and support vehicle and remove front wheels. Remove spring clips and slide keys out of caliper and mounting bracket. Disconnect brake line fitting from flexible hose and remove hose retaining clip from body. **NOTE** — *Brake lines and hoses should not be disconnected for removal of brake pads.* Remove caliper from mounting bracket and disconnect flexible hose from caliper. Remove brake pads and pad spring from caliper.

## RENAULT (Cont.)

**Installation** — To install, reverse removal procedure and note the following: Install longest pad spring on outside of caliper. Tighten all fittings and bleed hydraulic system.

### DISC BRAKE ROTOR

**Removal & Installation** — Remove caliper assembly and pad mounting bracket from vehicle. Take out the three screws securing brake disc. Remove stub axle nut. Fit slide hammer and remove disc/hub assembly. To install, reverse removal procedure.

**NOTE** — *Brake rotor on R-5 cannot be machined. When rotor has worn to .355" (9 mm), replace rotor.*

### BRAKE DRUM

**Removal** — Remove plug in backing plate and insert a screwdriver through hole. Push parking brake operating lever in until peg on lever is clear of brake shoe, then push lever to rear to back off brake shoes. Remove hub grease cap and attaching hardware. Remove drum assembly using a suitable puller.

**Installation** — To install reverse removal procedure and note the following: Apply a suitable grease to wheel bearings. After installing drum assembly, adjust wheel bearings. See *Wheel Bearing Adjustment in WHEEL ALIGNMENT Section.* Apply brake pedal several times to adjust brake shoes.

### DRUM BRAKE SHOES

**Removal & Installation** — Remove wheel and brake drum from vehicle. Install wheel cylinder clamp, then remove upper brake shoe return spring. On rear brake assembly, disconnect parking brake cable. Unhook shoe hold down springs, and tilt long self-adjuster lever inward. Ease leading shoe away from backing plate, and pull cross lever from shoe. Turn leading shoe at right angle to backing plate and remove lower return spring. Remove both brake shoes. To install, reverse removal procedure.

### WHEEL CYLINDER

**Removal & Installation** — Remove brake drum and brake shoes from vehicle. Disconnect brake line from wheel cylinder, and remove cylinder attaching bolts. Remove cylinder from vehicle. To install, reverse removal procedure and bleed hydraulic system.

### MASTER CYLINDER

**Removal & Installation** — Syphon fluid from master cylinder reservoir. Disconnect hydraulic lines at master cylinder and plug open ends. Rremove pressure loss indicator bolt (if equipped.) Disconnect push rod from brake pedal if vehicle is not equipped with power unit. Remove cylinder mounting hardware and remove cylinder from vehicle. To install reverse procedure and adjust push rod clearance. On R-5 models push rod clearance is measured between piston and push rod. Clearance should be .203" (5 mm).

### POWER BRAKE UNIT

**NOTE** — *Power brake unit is not serviceable, only the air filter and check valve can be serviced.*

**Removal** — Disconnect battery, and remove fluid from master cylinder. Remove engine air filter (if necessary). Disconnect hydraulic lines at master cylinder, and remove pressure loss indicator valve bolt (if equipped). Disconnect vacuum hose, and remove clevis from brake pedal. Remove power brake unit attaching nuts from pedal side of firewall, and remove master cylinder and power brake unit as an assembly. Separate master cylinder from power brake unit.

**Installation** — Measure push rod-to-master cylinder clearance at master cylinder mounting flange, and adjust by turning push rod nut. To install power brake unit, reverse removal procedure, and bleed hydraulic system.

## OVERHAUL

**NOTE** — *Master Cylinder, Power Brake Unit, and Brake Pressure Limiter cannot be Overhauled.*

### DISC BRAKE CALIPER

**Disassembly** — Remove caliper assembly from vehicle, and remove piston dust cover. Using compressed air, introduced at

*Fig. 3   Assembled View of R-5 Rear Brake Assembly*

Wheel Cylinder
Return Spring
"C" Shaped End of Adjuster
Adjustment Star
Mounting Spring, Cup, Pin
"U" Shaped End of Adjuster
Brake Shoe
Brake Shoe
Lower Anchor Point

*Fig. 4   Prying Out Seal from Caliper Cylinder Bore*

## RENAULT (Cont.)

caliper fluid port, carefully remove piston from caliper assembly. Remove piston seal from cylinder. Using a wedge, spread legs of caliper piston bracket a small amount. Remove caliper stop peg from piston bracket. Slide cylinder assembly from bracket.

**Inspection** — Clean all parts in denatured alcohol, and inspect for piston and cylinder wear. Replace worn parts as necessary. Replace all rubber seals.

**Reassembly** — Lubricate cylinder bore, piston, and seals with brake fluid prior to reassembly. To reassemble, reverse disassembly procedure.

### WHEEL CYLINDER

**Disassembly & Reassembly** — Using the following illustration, disassemble wheel cylinder and examine com-

ponents for damage or excessive wear. Before reassembly, dip pistons and cups in brake fluid.

### TIGHTENING SPECIFICATIONS

| Application | Ft. Lbs. (mkg) |
|---|---|
| Caliper Bracket-to-Stub | |
| Axle Carrier (R-5) | 50 (6.5) |
| Rotor-to-Hub (R-5) | 20 (.25) |
| Stub Axle Nut (R-5) | 90 (12.0) |

### DISC BRAKE ROTOR SPECIFICATIONS

| Application | Disc Diameter In. (mm) | Lateral Runout In. (mm) | Parallelism In. (mm) | Original Thickness In. (mm) | Minimum Refinish Thickness In. (mm) | Discard Thickness In. (mm) |
|---|---|---|---|---|---|---|
| R-5 | 9.000 (228.5) | .004 (.1) | ..... | .395 (10) | ..... | .355① (9) |

① — Rotor cannot be machined; it must be replaced.

### BRAKE DRUM SPECIFICATIONS

| Application | Drum Diameter In. (mm) | Original Diameter In. (mm) | Maximum Refinish Diameter In. (mm) | Discard Diameter In. (mm) |
|---|---|---|---|---|
| R-5 | 7.087 (180) | 7.087 (180) | 7.136 (181) | ..... |

### BRAKE SYSTEM SPECIFICATIONS

| Application | Drum Diam. In. (mm) | Wheel Cylinder Diameter | | Master Cylinder |
| | | Front In. (mm) | Rear In. (mm) | Diameter In. (mm) |
|---|---|---|---|---|
| R-5 | 9.000 (228.5) | 1.772① (45) | .866 (22) | .811 (20.6) |

① — Caliper Cylinder.

# Brakes

## SAAB

### 99

## DESCRIPTION

Brake system is hydraulically operated by a tandem master cylinder and power brake unit. As a new feature, master cylinder contains a float that senses the brake fluid level in the reservoir. If leakage occurs, float actuates switch in reservoir cover and warning light comes on. This new feature changes the reservoir configuration from last years model. Front disc brakes are Girling type consisting of a brake rotor and dual piston, sliding yoke type caliper. Rear brakes are either Girling type with sliding yoke or ATE dual piston type. Note that parking brake is mechanically actuated and works on **front** brake assemblies.

## ADJUSTMENT

### DISC BRAKES

Disc brakes are self adjusting; therefore, no adjustment in service is required.

### PARKING BRAKE CABLE

Before adjusting cable, apply brake lever several times to stretch cables. Rotate cable adjusting nuts located at rear of parking brake lever under plastic cover until distance between lever on front caliper and yoke is .016-.022" (.41-.56 mm). Check distance with parking brake fully released.

**NOTE** — *Parking brake cables are crossed, so to adjust left parking brake mechanism (cable), right adjusting nut must be rotated and vice versa.*

### HYDRAULIC SYSTEM BLEEDING

Connect bleeder tube to bleeder screw, and submerge open end of tube in a jar half full of clean brake fluid. Open bleeder screw, and push brake pedal down quickly, allowing it to return slowly. Repeat procedure until fluid flows from bleeder tube with no sign of air. On last downward stroke, close bleeder screw. Bleeding sequence is left-rear, right-front, right-rear, left-front.

## REMOVAL & INSTALLATION

### DISC BRAKE PADS

**Removal, Girling Type** — Rotate brake rotor until one of the recesses in edge of rotor is aligned with brake pads. Remove damper spring, pin retaining clips and retaining pins, then lift out brake pads.

**Installation** — Open bleeder screw and press pistons back into caliper bore, then close bleeder screw. **NOTE** — *On the front brakes, it will be necessary to rotate direct piston while pressing it into caliper bore.* Insert brake pads into caliper, then install retaining pins, clips and damper spring. After installation, apply brake pedal several times to position pads against rotor.

**Removal, ATE Type** — Clean outside of caliper housing. Turn rotor until recess in edge of rotor is inline with pad. Remove cover plate, mounting pins and spring that retains brake pads. Pull pads out of caliper.

**NOTE** — *If pads are siezed, use suitable extractor tool (8995771) to remove pads.*

**Installation** — Seat pistons in bores. Insert new pads. Install spring, lock pins, and cover plate. Pump pedal several times to ensure proper brake operation is taking place.

### DISC BRAKE CALIPER

**Removal** — Raise and support vehicle and remove wheels. On front wheel calipers, disconnect parking brake cable from lever on caliper. On all wheels, disconnect hydraulic line from hose, then plug lines to prevent entry of dirt and loss of fluid. Remove caliper attaching bolts and lift off caliper.

**Installation** — To install, reverse removal procedure and note the following: Tighten all attaching bolts, bleed hydraulic system and adjust parking brake cables.

### DISC BRAKE ROTOR

**Removal (Front)** — Apply parking brake and remove rotor and hub attaching nut from spindle, then release parking brake. Remove caliper assembly (without disconnecting hydraulic line) and support out of way. Using a puller, remove rotor and hub assembly from spindle. Remove the four attaching bolts and separate rotor from hub.

**Removal (Rear)** — Remove caliper assembly (without disconnecting hydraulic line) and support out of way. Remove the two rotor attaching bolts and lift off rotor.

**Installation (Front & Rear)** — To install, reverse removal procedure and note the following: Tighten all nuts and bolts and adjust parking brake if necessary.

### MASTER CYLINDER

**Removal** — Disconnect electrical lead to warning switch on master cylinder. Disconnect clutch master cylinder hose from fluid reservoir, then plug reservoir nipple to prevent loss of fluid. Disconnect hydraulic lines from master cylinder. Remove master cylinder-to-power brake unit attaching nuts and lift off master cylinder.

**Installation** — To install, reverse removal procedure and bleed hydraulic system.

### POWER BRAKE BOOSTER

**Removal** — From inside engine compartment, remove upper circlip from brake pedal push rod. Disconnect all electrical leads, hydraulic lines and vacuum lines from master cylinder and power brake unit. Remove the four attaching nuts and lift off master cylinder and power unit as an assembly. **NOTE** — *Three attaching nuts are removed from inside vehicle while the fourth nut is removed from engine compartment.* Separate master cylinder from power unit.

**Installation** — To install, reverse removal procedure and bleed hydraulic system.

## OVERHAUL

### FRONT CALIPER ASSEMBLY

**Disassembly, Girling Type** — 1) With caliper removed from vehicle, mount assembly in a soft jawed vise. Remove parking brake return spring. Then remove yoke from caliper assembly and spring and parking brake lever from yoke.

## SAAB (Cont.)

**2)** Remove retaining ring and dust boot, then using compressed air, force out indirect piston assembly from caliper. Press direct piston push rod and remove piston from caliper. Remove "O" rings and seal rings from caliper bore and pistons.

**Cleaning & Inspection** — Clean all parts, except indirect piston assembly, in clean brake fluid and dry with a clean, lint-free cloth. **NOTE** — *Indirect piston assembly should only be wiped clean to prevent washing off parking brake mechanism lubricant. Inspect all parts for wear, damage or corrosion and replace as necessary.* **NOTE** — *Manufacturer recommends replacing all rubber parts whenever caliper assembly has been disassembled.*

**Fig. 1    Exploded View of Girling Front Brake Caliper**

**Reassembly** — **1)** Lubricate pistons and caliper bore with clean brake fluid, then install new "O" rings and seal rings to pistons and caliper bore. Install indirect piston into caliper with recess for yoke aligned with groove in caliper housing, then install direct piston in the same manner. Press in indirect piston and screw in direct piston until edges of dust boot grooves are flush with caliper housing.

**2)** Install dust boots and retaining rings. Fit yoke spring and parking brake lever to yoke, then align yoke guide edges with groove on caliper housing and install yoke. Lift parking brake lever and install axle pin into hole in indirect piston. **NOTE** — *Ensure yoke fits into recess of indirect piston.* Install parking brake return spring. Check clearance between sliding surfaces

of yoke and caliper housing; clearance on one side should be .006-.012" (.15-.30 mm), while there should be no clearance on the other side (see illustration).

**Fig. 2    Girling Front Brake Caliper Clearance Measuring Points**

### REAR CALIPER ASSEMBLY

**Disassembly, Girling Type** — **1)** With caliper assembly removed from vehicle, mount assembly in soft jawed vise. Remove yoke from caliper assembly by lifting it toward bleeder screw. Then remove yoke spring.

**2)** Remove retaining ring and dust boot. Using compressed air, force indirect piston from caliper assembly. Push direct piston from caliper assembly. Remove piston seals from caliper bore.

**Fig. 3    Disassembled Girling Rear Brake Caliper Showing Internal Component Relationships**

## SAAB (Cont.)

**Cleaning & Inspection** — Clean all parts in clean brake fluid and dry with a clean, lint-free cloth. Inspect all parts for wear, damage or corrosion and replace as necessary.

**Reassembly** — Lubricate caliper bore with clean brake fluid and install new piston seals. Press pistons into caliper bore, then rotate indirect piston until recess for yoke is aligned with groove in caliper housing. Install new dust boot and retaining ring. Install yoke spring on yoke, then install yoke into groove of caliper housing and indirect piston. Check clearance between sliding surfaces of yoke and caliper housing; clearance should be .006-.012" (.15-.30 mm) on bleeder screw side of caliper housing (see illustration).

**Fig. 4  Girling Rear Brake Caliper Clearance Measuring Points**

**Disassembly, ATE Type** — 1) Clean outside of caliper assembly. Remove pads and caliper as previously outlined. Using suitable clamp (7841323), secure one piston in bore. Apply air pressure to fluid inlet port and force out piston.

**Fig. 5  Exploded View of ATE Type Rear Caliper**

2) Carefully remove seals from cylinder bore using a pointed but not sharp instrument. Make sure seal groove is not damaged when removing seal.

**NOTE** — *Before second piston can be removed and seal replaced, reassembly operation must be completed on first piston.*

**Reassembly** — Lubricate caliper bore with clean brake fluid and slide new seal into machined groove. Lubricate piston with brake fluid and fit it into cylinder. Install new dust seal and retainer ring. Seat piston into bore and begin disassembly of other piston.

### MASTER CYLINDER

**Disassembly** — 1) With master cylinder removed from vehicle, drain brake fluid from reservoir. Mount cylinder in a soft jaw vise. Remove retaining pins and separate reservoir from master cylinder (pins may have to be driven out). Remove rubber seals from reservoir mounting holes in cylinder.

**Fig. 6  Master Cylinder Reservoir, Housing and Pistons**

2) Push in on primary piston and pull secondary piston stop pin from forward reservoir mounting hole. Remove circlip and take out primary piston assembly and spring. Remove cylinder from vise and carefully knock it against a block of wood to remove secondary piston assembly and spring. Remove brake warning switch from master cylinder, then remove end plug and lift out warning valve assembly.

**Cleaning & Inspection** — Wash all parts in clean brake fluid and dry with a clean, lint-free cloth. Inspect all parts for wear, damage or corrosion and replace as necessary. **NOTE** — *Manufacturer recommends replacing all rubber parts whenever master cylinder is disassembled.*

# Brakes

## SAAB (Cont.)

**Reassembly** — Reverse disassembly procedure and note the following: Coat all parts with clean brake fluid prior to reassembly. Use care not to damage piston seals when fitting to pistons or when installing pistons into cylinder bore. Refer to *Figs. 7* and *8* for correct seal installation.

### POWER BRAKE UNIT

**NOTE** — *Power brake unit is serviced as a complete assembly only. Do not attempt to overhaul.*

**Fig. 7  Primary Piston with Installation Direction of Seals Illustrated**

**Fig. 8  Secondary Piston with Installation Direction of Seals Illustrated**

## DISC BRAKE ROTOR SPECIFICATIONS

| Application | Disc Diameter In. (mm) | Lateral Runout In. (mm) | Parallelism In. (mm) | Original Thickness In. (mm) | Minimum Refinish Thickness In. (mm) | Discard Thickness In. (mm) |
|---|---|---|---|---|---|---|
| Model 99 Front | 11.024 (280) | .004 (.10) | ..... | .500 (12.7) | .461 (11.7) | .460 (11.6) |
| Rear | 10.614 (269.5) | .004 (.10) | ..... | .413 (10.5) | .374 (9.5) | .373 (9.4) |

## BRAKE SYSTEM SPECIFICATIONS

| Application | Drum Diam. In. (mm) | Wheel Cylinder Diameter | | Master Cylinder |
| | | Front In. (mm) | Rear In. (mm) | Diameter In. (mm) |
|---|---|---|---|---|
| Model 99 Girling | ..... | 2.126① (54) | 1.063① (27) | .875 (22.3) |
| ATE | ..... | ..... | 1.181① (30) | ..... |

① — Disc brakes

# Brakes

## SUBARU

**Subaru**

## DESCRIPTION

Service brake system is a diagonally split dual hydraulic circuit with a tandem master cylinder and vacuum suspended type power brake unit. Front disc brakes on all models are Bendix type, automatic adjusting, and rear brakes are leading trailing drum type. Parking brake operates on front brakes and is mechanically actuated.

## ADJUSTMENT

### PEDAL HEIGHT

Adjust pedal height to 2.76" (70 mm) depressed and no less than 1.97" (50 mm), by disconnecting wiring from stop light switch and turning switch. Proper pedal free postion is 7.09-7.48" (180-190 mm).

### PEDAL FREE PLAY

Adjust pedal free play to .20-.43" (5-11 mm) by disconnecting wiring from stop light switch and turning switch.

### FRONT DISC BRAKE PADS

Self-adjusting, no adjustment required.

### REAR DRUM BRAKE SHOES

Raise vehicle and loosen lock nut. Turn adjusting wedge until wheel locks, then back-off to clearance of .0004-.0006" (.1-.15 mm).

### PARKING BRAKE

With service brake system fully adjusted, engage parking brake lever several times, then loosen cable lock nut and adjust cable length for lever ratchet travel of 6-9 notches under normal application.

### HYDRAULIC SYSTEM BLEEDING

Begin bleeding with wheel furthest from master cylinder and end with wheel nearest master cylinder. With pressure on pedal, open bleed fitting and push pedal its full travel. When pedal is fully depressed, close fitting and let pedal return to fully released position. Repeat procedure until all air is bled from system.

## REMOVAL & INSTALLATION

### FRONT DISC BRAKE PADS

**Removal** — Disconnect handbrake cable. Remove pin and stop plug. Force caliper body from brake pad and lift-off pad.

**NOTE** — *It is not necessary to disconnect brake line to change pads.*

**Installation** — Return piston to bottom of caliper bore by turning it clockwise with a screwdriver or suitable tool (925370000). Place new disc pad in position then reinstall stop plug (coated on both sides with high temperature grease), pin and connect handbrake cable.

**Fig. 1  Exploded View of Front Disc Brake Assembly**

### FRONT DISC BRAKE CALIPER

**Removal** — Raise and support vehicle and remove wheel assembly, brake line and pads from caliper assembly. Remove parking brake cable and mounting bracket bolts and remove caliper assembly.

**Installation** — Reverse removal procedure ensuring caliper-to-rotor clearance of 1.5" (39 mm). Bleed hydraulic system.

### FRONT DISC BRAKE ROTOR

**Removal** — Remove wheel, handbrake cable, stoppers and caliper assembly. Remove 2 bolts and lift off caliper bracket. Pull rotor from axle using suitable tool (925200000). Remove 4 bolts to separate rotor from hub.

**NOTE** — *Mounting bracket should be replaced if rotor is replaced.*

**Installation** — To install, reverse removal procedure.

### REAR BRAKE DRUM

**Removal** — Remove wheel cap and loosen wheel nuts. Raise vehicle and remove wheel. Remove 3 cap bolts, washers, cap

## SUBARU (Cont.)

and stopper plate. Remove cotter pin and castle nut. Remove brake drum using suitable puller (925240000).

**Installation** — To install, reverse removal procedure.

### REAR BRAKE SHOES

**Removal** — Remove brake drum. Remove 3 bolts securing back plate and remove brake assembly. Remove shoe setting spring and anchor side of shoe first.

**Installation** — To install, reverse removal procedure.

### REAR BRAKE WHEEL CYLINDER

**Removal** — With rear drum and brake shoes removed, disconnect hydraulic line from wheel cylinder at rear of backing plate, remove cylinder attaching bolts, and remove wheel cylinder.

**Installation** — Reverse removal procedure and bleed hydraulic system.

### MASTER CYLINDER

**NOTE** — *BRAT models are equipped with a brake fluid level sensor built into rear reservoir cap. Warning light actuates when fluid is low. To test, remove cap and allow float to drop. Indicator bulb should light.*

**Removal** — Remove nuts securing brake lines to cylinder. Remove nuts securing cylinder-to-firewall and remove master cylinder.

**Installation** — To install, reverse removal procedure.

**Fig. 2  Exploded View of Rear Drum Brake Assembly**

***Fig. 3   Exploded View of Components in Tandem Master Cylinder***

## SUBARU (Cont.)

### POWER BRAKE UNIT

**Removal** — Extract cotter key, pull out lock pin and separate brake pedal from push rod. Disconnect power brake unit vacuum hose and remove master cylinder mounting nuts. If equipped, disconnect wiring harness at master cylinder. Remove power brake unit attaching hardware and lift unit from engine compartment, leaving supported master cylinder in vehicle.

**Installation** — To install, reverse removal procedure. Arrow on power brake unit should face toward engine.

### OVERHAUL

### FRONT DISC BRAKE CALIPER

**Disassembly** — 1) Thoroughly clean exterior of caliper with clean brake fluid or alcohol, and remove bleed valve, retainer and dust boot. Apply compressed air or liquid to fluid inlet and gradually remove piston.

2) Carefully remove piston seal, lever cap retainer and lever cap, then remove circlip from spindle. Using suitable puller tool (925470000) release spring washer load, remove connecting link, spindle and parking brake lever assembly.

**Cleaning & Inspection** — Clean all components with brake fluid and ensure that inner cylinder wall is not scratched or corroded. Replace any damaged parts.

**Reassembly** — 1) To reassemble, hand insert piston seal (lightly coated with silicon grease) into cylinder, then hand insert piston (coated with brake fluid). Lubricate cylinder wall and piston grooves then insert piston boot and retainer.

2) Lightly coat spindle and "O" ring with silicon grease, insert spindle and using suitable puller tool (925470000) install 6 spring washers. Lubricate and install connecting link (thick side in slot). Install parking brake lever assembly, circlip, lever cap and retainer. Bleed hydraulic system after installation.

### REAR WHEEL CYLINDER

**Disassembly** — Remove boot and take out wheel cylinder piston with cup. DO NOT separate cup unless replacement is to be made.

**Cleaning & Inspection** — Clean all components in brake fluid. Inspect piston-to-cylinder bore for .001-.004" (.025-.102 mm) clearance. If cylinder is out of round or burred, replace, DO NOT hone.

**Reassembly** — To reassemble, reverse disassembly procedure, making certain cup is not installed in reverse.

### MASTER CYLINDER

**Disassembly** — Remove boot from cylinder, then remove stop ring and plate. Remove stopper pin and gasket, pull out primary and secondary piston assembly. Remove return spring, screw, retainer and secondary cup.

**Cleaning & Inspection** — Clean all components in brake fluid. Inspect cylinder bore for smoothness and roundness. Replace cylinder if scored or out of round. DO NOT hone cylinder. Inspect piston-to-cylinder clearance and replace if worn.

**Reassembly** — To reassemble master cylinder, reverse disassembly procedure.

### POWER BRAKE UNIT

**Disassembly** — Disassembly procedures not available.

### TIGHTENING SPECIFICATIONS

| Application | Ft. Lbs. (mkg) |
|---|---|
| Front Brake Mounting Bolt | 36-51 (5.0-7.0) |
| Backing Plate Mounting Bolts | 22-35 (3.0-4.8) |
| Brake Lines | 11-14 (1.5-2.0) |
| Wheel Bearing Nut | 174 (24.0) |
| Power Cylinder-to-Firewall | 5-9 (0.7-1.2) |
| Master Cylinder-to-Power Cylinder | 5-9 (0.7-1.2) |

### DISC BRAKE ROTOR SPECIFICATIONS

| Application | Disc Diameter | Lateral Runout | Parallelism | Original Thickness | Minimum Refinish Thickness | Discard Thickness |
|---|---|---|---|---|---|---|
| All Models | 7.2 (184) | .006 (.15) | ..... | .39 (10) | .33 (8.5) | ..... |

### BRAKE DRUM SPECIFICATIONS

| Application | Drum Diameter In. (mm) | Original Diameter In. (mm) | Maximum Refinish Diameter In. (mm) | Discard Diameter In. (mm) |
|---|---|---|---|---|
| All Models Rear | 7.09① (180) | 7.09 (180) | 7.17 (182) | ..... |

① — All models use front disc brakes.

## SUBARU (Cont.)

### BRAKE LINING SPECIFICATION

| Application | Drum Dia. In. (mm) | Width | | Length | | Thickness | |
|---|---|---|---|---|---|---|---|
| | | Front In. (mm) | Rear In. (mm) | Primary In. (mm) | Secondary In. (mm) | Primary In. (mm) | Secondary In. (mm) |
| All Models | 7.09 (180) | ① | 1.18 (30) | 5.55 (141) | 5.55 (141) | .20 (5) | .20 (5) |

① — All models use front disc brakes.

### BRAKE SYSTEM SPECIFICATIONS

| Application | Drum Diam. In. (mm) | Wheel Cylinder Diameter | | Master Cylinder Diameter In. (mm) |
|---|---|---|---|---|
| | | Front In. (mm) | Rear In. (mm) | |
| All Models | 7.09 (180) | 2.125 (53.9) | .625① (15.9) | .750 (19.0) |

① — Station Wagon and 4-Wheel Drive Wagon .687" (17.46 mm), BRAT models use .750" (19.05 mm).

# Brakes

## TOYOTA

Celica
Corolla
Corona
Cressida
Pickup
Land Cruiser

## DESCRIPTION

All models use front disc brakes and drum rear brakes. Dual piston master cylinders are used on all models. All vehicles are equipped with some kind of pressure differential valve (combination valve). Any model can be fitted with a power assist unit. Not all power units are the same. All parking brakes are cable actuated, internal expanding shoe type. Land Cruiser parking brake is mounted on rear of transfer case, all other models use a parking brake incorporated in rear wheel brakes. Land Cruiser models use a separate vacuum pump to supply vacuum to power assist unit.

## BRAKE APPLICATION TABLE

| Application | Brake System① |
| --- | --- |
| Corona, Corolla (2T-C Eng.), Celica | "F" Type |
| Corona, Cressida, Pickup | Girling Type |
| Corolla (3K-C Eng.) | "PS" Type |

① — Land Cruiser information unavailable.

## ADJUSTMENTS

### BRAKE PEDAL HEIGHT

**All Models (Exc. Land Cruiser)** — Loosen stop light switch lock nut and turn switch to obtain correct brake pedal height. If correct height cannot be obtained by adjusting switch, loosen push rod lock nut and lengthen or shorten push rod as necessary to obtain correct height.

### Brake Pedal Height

| Application | Height In. (mm) |
| --- | --- |
| Celica | 6.48 (164.5) |
| Corolla | 6.65 (169) |
| Corona | 6.2-6.6 (157-168) |
| Cressida | 6.1-6.5 (156-166) |
| Pickup | |
| Man. Trans. | 6.3 (160) |
| Auto. Trans. | 6.5 (166) |

**Land Cruiser** — On models with power brake unit, loosen stop light switch and adjust pedal height with push rod. Readjust stop light switch to make proper contact. On models without power brake unit, loosen push rod and adjust pedal height by turning stop light switch.

*Fig. 1  Exploded View of Girling Type Disc Brake Components*

## TOYOTA (Cont.)

### Brake Pedal Height

| Application | Height In. (mm) |
| --- | --- |
| FJ40 Series | 8.46 (215) |
| FJ55 Series | 7.28 (185) |

### DISC BRAKES

Disc brakes are self-adjusting; therefore, no adjustment in service is required.

### DRUM BRAKES

**Manual Adjusting** — One or two adjusting screws may be used on some vehicles. **CAUTION** — *On double adjusting screw type, do not adjust both screws at the same time.* Pump brake pedal several times, and ensure brake cylinder reservoir is full. Raise vehicle and remove adjusting hole plug from backing plate. Using a suitable adjusting tool, turn adjusting screw until shoes make full contact with brake drum, and wheel will not turn. Pump brake pedal, then turn adjuster back until wheel turns with light shoe drag.

### PARKING BRAKE

**Land Cruiser** — With brake handle fully released, turn shaft of adjusting cam (on brake backing plate) counterclockwise until shoe seats against drum. Back off adjuster one notch at a time until drum locks when foot brake is applied, and spins freely when released. After adjusting shoes, adjust brake handle for travel of 6-9 notches from released to applied position. Adjust by turning cable adjusting nut or turnbuckle.

**Corolla** — Correct adjustment is obtained when rear wheels are locked and brake lever travel is 5-8 notches. To adjust, remove cable adjusting cap at rear of lever and turn cable adjusting nut until correct lever travel is obtained. Replace and lightly tighten adjusting cap. Check and adjust brake warning light switch so that light is off when brake lever is released.

**Celica, Corona, Cressida** — Fully release parking brake lever. Working under vehicle, loosen brake cable lock nut and tighten turn buckle about 1" (.039 mm). Tighten lock nut. If equipped with "U" shaped cable equalizer, adjust so slack is taken up from cable. Parking brake is properly adjusted when lever travels of 3-8 notches locks rear brakes.

**Pickup** — With brake handle fully released, turn cable adjusting nut at equalizer on frame until cables to rear wheels are slightly slack and there is no drag on rear wheels. After adjustment, brake handle travel should be about 8 notches and brake warning light should go out. If light remains on, adjust switch position so light goes on when brake is applied and off when handle is released.

### BRAKE BLEEDING

**NOTE** — *Master cylinder reservoir(s) must be kept full at all times during bleeding.* Starting at wheel cylinder farthest from master cylinder, connect a tube to bleeder screw and put other end of tube in a glass container half full of clean brake fluid. Slowly pump brake pedal several times, then hold pedal in depressed position. Open bleeder screw slightly, and close screw when fluid starts to flow from tube. Repeat procedure until fluid coming from tube shows no signs of air.

## REMOVAL & INSTALLATION

### DISC BRAKE PADS

**Removal, F Type** — Raise and support front of vehicle; remove wheel. Pull four spring clips out and remove cylinder guides. Hang disc cylinder assembly out of way. Remove disc pads and inspect for wear.

*Fig. 2 Expanded View of F Type Disc Brake Components*

**Installation** — Clean piston and cylinder assembly, then seat piston into cylinder bore. If piston won't easily reseed into cylinder bore, crack bleed valve to relieve pressure. Insert cylinder assembly into position. Refit new disc pads, cylinder guides, and spring clips. If hydraulic line has been disconnected, bleed brake system.

**Removal, Girling Type** — Raise and support front of vehicle; remove wheel. Remove clips, pins, and springs; then take out pads and anti-squeal shims. If vehicle is equipped with Electrical Sensor Panel, separate wire harness from steering knuckle wire harness clamp. Pull out pads and separate connection between pad and wear sensor.

**Installation** — Install by fitting anti-squeal shim so folded portion will be facing pad and arrow will face in direction of rotation. If ESP equipped, mount wear sensor in inner side pad before installing pad. Install springs, pins, and clips. Refit ESP wiring, ensuring wiring harness is not kinked.

## TOYOTA (Cont.)

**Fig. 3   Exploded View of Toyota Pickup Rear Brake Assembly**

**Removal & Installation, PS Type** — Raise and support front of vehicle; remove wheel. Take out pad protector, anti-rattle springs, spring pins, and pads. Clean dirt from pin portion of torque plate. After cleaning piston assembly, seat into cylinder bore. Insert pads and install retaining pins, anti-rattle springs, and protector.

**Installation** — To install, reverse removal procedure and note: Tighten mounting bolts. Make sure brake tube is properly seated and that anti-rattle spring is tight.

**Fig. 4   Exploded View of PS Type Disc Brake Assembly**

**Fig. 5   Exploded View of Land Cruiser Front Disc Brakes**

### FRONT DISC CALIPER & PADS

**Removal, Land Cruiser** — Raise and suitably support front of vehicle. Disconnect and plug brake fluid line and inlet port. Remove caliper mountings and lift off rotor. Remove clip, mounting pin, and anti-rattle spring. Pull disc pads from caliper cavity.

**Inspection** — Wipe all dirt from caliper cavity and look for possible leaks. Replace disc pads if worn beyond .039" (1 mm).

### DISC BRAKE CALIPER

**Removal, F Type** — Raise and support front of vehicle; remove wheel. Pull four clips out and remove cylinder guides.

## TOYOTA (Cont.)

Hang disc cylinder assembly out of way. Remove disc pads. Remove two bolts from rear of disc brake cylinder mounting and remove mounting along with cylinder support springs and pad support plates.

**Installation** — To install F type brake caliper, reverse removal procedure and note the following: It may be necessary to manually seat piston in cylinder bore to ease installation. Ensure cylinder guides and clips are in good condition.

**Removal, All Others** — Raise and support front of vehicle; remove wheel. Remove disc brake pads as previously outlined. Disconnect hydraulic fluid line from caliper inlet port. Remove caliper mounting bolts and carefully lift off caliper assembly.

**Installation** — To install, reverse removal procedure and note the following: Ensure caliper mounting bolts are properly torqued. Make sure disc pads are installed according to prevoiusly outlined procedure.

### DISC BRAKE ROTOR

**Removal, Except Land Cruiser** — Raise and support vehicle; remove tire. Before removing rotor, measure runout and check against specifications. Proceed by removing hub grease cap, cotter pin, washer, and castle nut; carefully ease outer wheel bearing from hub. Remove caliper assembly as previously outlined. Pull hub and rotor from vehicle as an assembly. If necessary, hub and rotor can be further disassembled after index marking relationship.

**Installation** — To install hub and rotor assembly, reverse removal procedure and note the following: Ensure wheel bearings are packed with grease and that wheel bearing grease seal is satisfactory. Make sure wheel bearings are properly adjusted. *See Wheel Bearing Adjustment in WHEEL ALIGNMENT Section.*

**Removal, Land Cruiser** — Remove caliper assembly as previously outlined. Remove hub grease cap and take off snap ring. Remove cover nuts, washers and cone washers. Using suitable socket or wrench SST 09607-60020, remove lock nut, lock washer and wheel bearing adjusting nut. Slide off rotor and hub assembly. If necessary, index mark rotor and hub, then separate.

**Inspection** — Before rotor removal check runout. Set up dial indicator, remove play from wheel bearings, and take measurement. Runout must not exceed .005" (.13 mm). With rotor removed, measure thickness. Rotor thickness must not be less than .790" (20 mm).

**Installation** — To install, reverse removal procedure and note: Adjust wheel bearings. *See Wheel Bearing Adjustment in WHEEL ALIGNMENT Section.*

### BRAKE DRUM

**Removal, All Models Rear** — Raise and support rear of vehicle; remove wheel. Remove set screws from brake drum, if equipped. Using hands only, pull drum from vehicle. It may be necessary to first loosen brake shoes if an adjustment hole is provided.

**Installation** — To install, reverse removal procedure and readjust brake shoes, if necessary.

### BRAKE SHOES

**Removal, All Models Rear** — Raise and support vehicle. Remove wheel and brake brum. Remove parking brake cable from lever, and remove tension springs from shoes. Remove self–adjuster mechanism (if equipped). Remove shoe guide plate, shoe hold down pins and springs. Take out parking brake strut. Remove brake shoes from backing plate. Remove parking brake actuating lever, self-adjusting lever, and latch from brake shoe.

**Installation** — To install, reverse removal procedure and bleed hydraulic system.

**Fig. 6 Exploded View of Cressida Rear Brake Assembly with Automatic Adjuster Lever Shown**

### PARKING BRAKE

**Removal, Land Cruiser** — Drain oil from transfer case. Disconnect front of drive shaft and wire out-of-way. Remove drum mounting nut and slide drum off splines. Remove return springs and tension springs, then take off hold down springs and pins. Disconnect parking brake cable from shoes.

**Inspection** — Inspect shoes for excessive damage or wear. Replace shoes when lining thickness is less than .06" (1.5 mm).

## TOYOTA (Cont.)

**Installation** — To install, reverse removal procedure and note: Make sure lower tension spring is installed so it lies between back plate and shoes. Refill transfer case with 1.8 quarts of SAE 90. Tighten drum mounting nut.

### VACUUM PUMP

**Removal, Land Cruiser** — Disconnect vacuum line from pump assembly. Disconnect and plug oil lines. Remove mounting nuts and gently pry pump off studs.

Drive End Frame  Case  Blade  End Cover  Rotor  "O" Ring  Dowel Pins  "O" Ring

**Fig. 7  Exploded View of Vacuum Pump for Land Cruiser**

**Installation** — To install, reverse removal procedure and note: Run engine at idle speed. Loosen screw at vacuum pump outlet and check that oil is circulating.

### MASTER CYLINDER

**Removal, All Models** — Disconnect any electrical lead from master cylinder switches. Separate hydraulic outlet lines and plug open ends of line. Remove nuts mounting master cylinder to power unit, if equipped. If vehicle is not power brake equipped, disconnect master cylinder push rod and lift from vehicle.

**Installation** — To install, reverse removal procedure and bleed hydraulic system.

### POWER BRAKE UNIT

**Removal & Installation** — Remove master cylinder assembly from vehicle. Disconnect push rod clevis at brake pedal. Remove power booster attaching hardware, and remove booster assembly from vehicle. To install, reverse removal procedure.

## OVERHAUL

**NOTE** — *When overhauling caliper, wheel cylinder, or master cylinder assemblies, all rubber components should be replaced. If cylinder bores in any part are pitted, or scored more than light honing will repair, entire assembly should be replaced.*

Primary Booster Body Seal  Reaction Retainer  Diaphragm
Vacuum Valve  Reaction Plate  Piston
Grommet  Snap Ring  Air Cleaner Separator
Damper  Air Cleaner Element
Outside Star Washer  Diaphragm Retainer
Adjusting Rod  Ring Retainer
Reaction Retainer  Washer  Air Booster Valve Assembly
Reaction Lever
Seal Reatiner  Piston Return Spring
Primary Valve Booster Body
Ring
Booster Piston Bearing  Body  Silencer  Band
Secondary Booster Body Seal

**Fig. 8  Exploded View of ASCO Type Brake Booster Unit**

## TOYOTA (Cont.)

Housing

Brake Light Switch

Spring
Check Valve
Outlet Plug

MASTER CYLINDER

Sleeve
Spring Retainer
Secondary Piston
Retainer
Primary Piston
Snap Ring
Push Rod
Spring
Spring
Primary Spring Retainer
Boot

PICKUP

Secondary Piston Assy.
Primary Piston Assy.
Snap Ring
Boot

CELICA

Secondary Piston Assy.
Primary Piston Assy.
Boot
Spring
Snap Ring
Spring

CRESSIDA

Stopper
Secondary Piston Assy.
Primary Piston Assy.
Boot
Spring
Spring
Snap Ring

CORONA

Spring
Retainer
Spacer
Spring
Clip
Piston Stopper
Clip
Cup
Cups
Secondary Piston
Retainer
Cup
Spring
Spacer
Cup
Primary Piston
Cup
Boot
Snap Ring

COROLLA

Stopper
Secondary Piston Assy.
Primary Piston Assy.
Spring
Spring

LAND CRUISER

**Fig. 9   Exploded View of Typical Master Cylinder Body and Detail of Each Model Primary and Secondary Piston Assemblies**

## TOYOTA (Cont.)

### DISC BRAKE CALIPER

**Disassembly, F Type** — Remove retainer ring and take off cylinder boot. Apply light air pressure to fluid inlet port and force piston from cylinder. Remove seal from cylinder, being careful not to damage cylinder bore.

**Inspection** — Clean and inspect all components. Replace any parts found defective.

**Reassembly** — To reassemble, reverse disassembly procedure and note the following: Apply light coat of suitable grease/brake fluid to all components before reassembly. Bleed hydraulic system after installation.

**Disassembly, Girling Type** — Remove retainer ring from dust boot and pull off dust boot. Insert a small block of wood between pistons and apply light air pressure to inlet port to force pistons from cylinder bores. Remove seals from grooves in cylinder bores. **NOTE** — *Do not separate caliper halves.*

**Inspection** — Clean and inspect all components. Replace any parts found defective.

**Reassembly** — Lightly coat all components with brake fluid, then insert seal into cylinder bore groove. Carefully push pistons into cylinder, install rubber dust boots and retainer rings.

**Disassembly, PS Type** — Loosen both bridge bolts (caliper half mounting bolts) and separate cylinder casting from outer body. Pull out torque plate. Remove retainer ring and dust boot. Force light air pressure through fluid inlet port and expel piston. From caliper, remove following: Piston seal, bushings, hole plug, retainers and dust seals.

**Inspection** — Inspect all parts for wear or damage and replace as necessary. If torque plate pins are excessively worn or if pin weld parts are abnormally corroded, caliper must be replaced.

**Reassembly** — 1) Lightly coat all parts prior to reassembly with clean brake fluid. Fit dust seal, retainers, and bushings to cylinder. Ensure pin sliding surfaces and bushing bores are clean and smear with suitable grease from repair kit.

2) Fit piston seal on cylinder and push piston in by hand. Install dust boot and ring. Reassemble torque plate pins in cylinder body. Make sure torque plate is free to slide smoothly. Install bridge bolts and torque.

**Disassembly, Land Cruiser** — Remove caliper assembly and take out disc pads. Remove dust seal retainer ring and dust seal. Place a small block of wood into caliper cavity. Blow compressed air into brake fluid inlet port until piston is forced out; repeat procedure on opposite side. Using a pointed, but blunt tool, dig piston seal from caliper groove. **NOTE** — *Do not separate caliper halves.*

**Inspection** — Check cylinder bore and piston for excessive wear, damage or corrosion; replace parts as necessary. Inspect pad thickness, pad must not be worn beyond .039" (1 mm).

**Reassembly** — Lightly coat all components with brake fluid. Insert new piston seal, being careful that seals properly enter grooves. Fit piston and slide dust seal into position. With dust seal seated, fit retainer ring.

### MASTER CYLINDER

**Disassembly, All Models** — Remove pressure switches and clamp cylinder flange in a soft jawed vise. Remove unions and bolts, outlet plugs, valves, and springs. Remove push rod boot. Take off snap ring, then remove push rod and rear piston assembly. Remove stop bolt from side of cylinder and remove front piston. Remove inlet valve seat and inlet valve. Disassemble pistons by removing springs, retainers, and cups.

**Reassembly** — To reassemble, reverse disassembly procedure using all new rubber parts and lubricating all components with clean brake fluid.

### WHEEL CYLINDER

**NOTE** — *Removal of wheel cylinder from backing plate is not necessary, except when replacement of cylinder assembly is required.*

**Disassembly** — Remove adjuster lock spring and adjuster (if equipped). Remove bleeder screw. Remove cylinder boot(s), piston(s), cup(s), spring seat (if equipped), and spring.

**Inspection** — Clean all parts with solvent, and blow dry with compressed air. Check cylinder bore for out-of-round, corrosion, or scoring.

**Reassembly** — To reassemble, reverse disassembly procedure, using new rubber parts.

### VACUUM PUMP

**Disassembly, Land Cruiser** — Drive dowel pins from end cover toward case. Separate end cover. Continue to drive dowels through case and stop with them flush with end frame. Remove end frame with pins still fitted. Remove both "O" rings and discard. Slide rotor and blades from case.

**Inspection** — Inspect end cover and casing for damage or wear. Casing bore must not be worn beyond 2.29" (5.82 mm). Check rotor-to-alternator shaft spline play. Rotor wear must not exceed .095" (2.4 mm). Inspect rotor blades for following wear limits: Height .47" (12 mm); length 1.377" (34.98 mm); width .036" (.92 mm). Check end frame bushing and oil seal. Bushing bore must not exceed .635" (16.14 mm). Replace oil seal by prying out and pressing in new one.

**Reassembly** — Lightly coat new "O" rings and insert into grooves. Refit rotor and blades. Drive in dowel pins.

### POWER BRAKE UNIT

**Disassembly, ASCO Type** — Remove booster push rod. Remove clamping band and separate primary and secondary booster body halves. Remove boot and booster piston assembly from secondary body half. Remove outside star washer from secondary body and remove bearing and body seal. From primary body, remove seal and retainer. Disassemble booster piston by removing reaction retainers, lever, air valve, air cleaner element and separator. Using suitable remove tool (SST 09736-30020), take out diaphragm rotating it 45°, then remove diaphragm from piston. Remove vacuum check valve and grommet from booster body.

## TOYOTA (Cont.)

Secondary Shell & Stud
Silencer
Bearing Seal
Filter
Boot
Diaphragm
Retainer
Plunger Stop Key
Valve Rod & Plunger
Push Rod
Valve Body & Diaphragm Plate
Retainer
Reaction Disc
Plate & Seal
Primary Shell & Stud
Spring

**Fig. 10  Exploded View of JKK Brake Booster Unit**

**Inspection** — Wash all parts in suitable cleaner. Inspect all components for excessive wear or damage and replace those that are found damaged.

**Reassembly** — To reassemble, reverse disassembly procedure and note the following: When assembling booster body seal to seal retainer, ensure seal retainer side is in the body inner side. When assembling body halves, align index marks.

**Disassembly, JKK Type** — Remove push rod clevis, nut, and boot. Index mark primary and secondary shell halves. Separate halves using suitable tool (SST 09738-22012). Remove diaphragm spring and push rod. Take out diaphragm plate and diaphragm spring from secondary shell half.

Disengage the diaphragm from plate, then remove silencer. Remove plunger stop key by lining up valve rod and plunger toward key hole with pieces facing downward; then remove valve and plunger rod from diaphragm plate. **NOTE** — *Valve rod and plunger assembly can not be further disassembled.* Remove reaction disc from diaphragm plate. If necessary, remove retainer and seal from primary shell. With a press, force bearing seal from secondary shell.

**Inspection** — Wash all parts in suitable cleaner. Inspect all components for any damage and replace those found defective. Ensure all rubber pieces are replaced during each overhaul.

Check Valve
Grommet
Compression Ring
Reaction Retainer
Reaction Plate
Reaction Lever
Snap Ring
Booster Diaphragm
Diaphragm Retainer
Secondary Shell Half
Connector Lock
Booster Body Connector
Primary Shell Half
Booster Piston
Plate Washer
Air Cleaner Element
Booster Piston Rod
Booster Body Seal Retainer
Outside Star Internal Ring
Booster Body Seal
Booster Piston Bearing
Air Valve
Air Cleaner Separator
Boot
Silencer
Outside Star Washer Retainer

**Fig. 11  Exploded View of Aisan Type Brake Booster Assembly**

# Brakes

## TOYOTA (Cont.)

Check Valve

Grommet

Retainer, Filter & Silencer

Dust Boot

Clevis

Mounting Nut

Nut

Spring

Front Shell

Front Diaphragm Assy.

Center Plate

Rear Diaphragm Assy.

Rear Diaphragm Retainer

Rod

Reaction Disc

Reaction Disc Hub

Spring

"O" Ring

Valve Body

Rear Shell

**Fig. 12  Exploded View of Land Cruiser Power Brake Booster Assembly**

# Brakes

## TOYOTA (Cont.)

**Reassembly** — To reassemble, reverse disassembly procedure and note the following: Ensure retainer is fully seated in secondary shell half. Properly locate plunger key stop. Coat reaction disc with silicon grease. Make sure diaphragm edge has oil coating before final tightening.

**Disassembly, Aisan Type** — 1) Remove booster push rod, clips mounting booster body connector, and push rod clevis. Using suitable tool (SST 09738-20010) and a press, apply pressure to body; then turn booster body connector until slots (and body halves) are disengaged.

2) Remove the following from secondary shell half: Boot, booster piston assembly, and bearing. From primary shell side, remove outside star washer retainer ring and body seal.

3) Disassemble following parts from front of booster piston: Reaction retainer, plate, lever, and snap ring. From rear of booster piston take off: Mounting ring, air cleaner elements, separators and booster air valves. Remove diaphragm retainer using suitable tool (SST 09736-30020) and rotating retainer 45°. Take off diaphragm from piston.

**Inspection** — Wash all parts in suitable cleaner. Inspect all components for any damage and replace those found defective.

**Reassembly** — To reassemble, reverse disassembly procedure and note the following: Ensure that seal retainer is assembled to inner primary shell. Make sure when assembly is installed on dash panel, sunken part of primary body will be positioned downward.

**Disassembly, Land Cruiser** — Remove check valve and rubber grommet. Take off clevis mounting nut and withdraw clevis, rubber dust boot, retainer, and filter/silencer assembly. Using a suitable tool (SST 09738-22012 & 09753-22010), separate front shell housing and diaphragm spring. Remove diaphragm nut and diaphragm retainer, then slide assembly apart. Remove hub bolts and take off rear diaphragm plate. Reaction disc assembly can now be removed along with valve body and "O" ring.

**NOTE** — Index mark front and rear diaphragms. Also, index mark front and rear shells for reassembly.

**Inspection** — Inspect shell cylinder, diaphragms, and center plate for cracks, damage or wear. Apply silicone grease to front and rear shell seals.

**Reassembly** — Reverse disassembly procedure and note: Fit reaction disc with protrusion directed toward valve body. Position center plate on hub with large groove facing front side. Make sure that front and rear shells are aligned with index marks. Adjust push rod length to .004-.020" (.1-.5 mm)

## TIGHTENING SPECIFICATIONS

| Application | Ft. Lbs. (mkg) |
|---|---|
| Caliper Mounting Hardware Land Cruiser, Cressida, Corona (Girling) | 67-86 (9.3-11/9) |
| Celica, Corolla (2T-C) | 40-54 (5.5-7.5) |
| Corolla (3K-C) | 29-40 (4.0 5.5) |
| Rotor-to-Hub | 20-40 (4.0-5.5) |
| Brake Durm Backing Plate | 43-53 (6.0-7.3) |
| Bridge Bolt (Corolla (2T-C) | 58-69 (8.0-9.5) |

## DISC BRAKE ROTOR SPECIFICATIONS ①

| Application | Disc Diameter | Lateral Runout | Parallelism | Original Thickness | Minimum Refinish Thickness | Discard Thickness |
|---|---|---|---|---|---|---|
| Celica F Type | ..... | .006 (.15) | ..... | .492 (12.5) | .453 (11.5) | ..... |
| Corolla F Type & PS Type | ..... | .006 (.15) | ..... | .394 (10) | .354 (9.0) | ..... |
| Corona F Type | ..... | .006 (.15) | ..... | .492 (12.5) | .453 (11.5) | ..... |
| Girling Type | ..... | .006 (.15) | ..... | .492 (12.5) | .453 (11.5) | ..... |

① — All measurements given in Inches with millimeters in parens.

# Brakes

## TOYOTA (Cont.)

### DISC BRAKE ROTOR SPECIFICATIONS

| Application | Disc Diameter In. (mm) | Lateral Runout In. (mm) | Parallelism In. (mm) | Original Thickness In. (mm) | Minimum Refinish Thickness In. (mm) | Discard Thickness In. (mm) |
|---|---|---|---|---|---|---|
| Cressida, Pickup Girling | ..... | .006 (.15) | ..... | .492 (12.5) | .453 (11.5) | ..... |
| Land Cruiser | ..... | .0047 (.12) | ..... | .790 (20.1) | .740 (19) | ..... |

### BRAKE DRUM SPECIFICATIONS

| Application | Drum Diameter In. (mm) | Original Diameter In. (mm) | Maximum Refinish Diameter In. (mm) | Discard Diameter In. (mm) |
|---|---|---|---|---|
| Corolla (3K-C) | 7.87 (200) | 7.87 (200) | ..... | 7.953 (202) |
| Corolla (2T-C), Celica, Corona, Cressida | 9.0 (228.6) | 9.0 (228.6) | ..... | 9.079 (230.6) |
| Pickup | 10.0 (254) | 10.0 (254) | ..... | 10.078 (256) |
| Land Cruiser | ..... | ..... | ..... | 11.50 (292) |

## TRIUMPH

**Spitfire**
**TR7**

### DESCRIPTION

All models use front disc and rear drum brakes. A tandem piston master cylinder which consists of two independent and complete hydraulic circuits is used. A pressure differential valve is used on all models to detect low pressure in either front or rear brake systems. When a pressure differential exists between the two circuits, indicating a failure, the pressure differential valve completes the circuit to the brake failure warning light on the instrument panel. A vacuum servo unit for power braking is also used on some models.

### ADJUSTMENT

**DISC BRAKES**

No adjustment required.

**DRUM BRAKES**

**Spitfire** — Release parking brake and raise rear wheels off ground. Rotate rear wheel clockwise while tightening adjuster. After wheel locks back off adjuster until wheel is just free to turn.

**PARKING BRAKE**

**NOTE** — *Adjustment of rear brakes will normally provide satisfactory parking brake adjustment. If cables are stretched, further adjustment is performed as follows:*

1) Hoist vehicle in rear, release parking brake and lock both rear brake drums with adjusters. Remove clevis pins from levers on brake back plates.

2) Adjust each clevis equal amounts until clevis pin can be easily inserted to relay levers. Secure clevis pins and check operation. **NOTE** — *If system is equipped with return spring, adjust bracket to provide proper tension.*

**HYDRAULIC SYSTEM BLEEDING**

**NOTE** — *TR7 system incorporates a self-centering Pressure Differential Shuttle. On all others, hard pedal application will cause shuttle to go over-center and warning light be activated.*

1) Refer to Bleeding Sequence Chart, then attach a bleed tube to correct wheel cylinder. Submerge free end of tube into a half full container of brake fluid.

2) On TR7 models, remove pressure differential switch. Open bleed valve and FULLY depress brake pedal, then follow with three rapid, successive strokes.

3) On Spitfire models, open bleed valve and lightly depress brake pedal, but DO NOT allow pedal to make complete stroke.

4) Continue either step **2** or **3** until all air is bled from brake system. On last stroke (at each cylinder) close bleed valve. On TR7 models, reinstall pressure differential switch.

### Bleeding Sequence

| Application | Sequence |
| --- | --- |
| Spitfire ................................................. | RR,LR,RF,LF |
| TR7 ...................................................... | RF,LF,RR,LR |

### REMOVAL & INSTALLATION

**DISC BRAKE PADS**

**Removal** — Raise vehicle and remove front wheels. Withdraw the two retaining pins and springs. Lift out brake pads complete with damper shims.

**Installation** — Clean surfaces of pistons and caliper cavity. Ease caliper pistons into bores to provide clearance. **NOTE** — *Brake fluid will raise during this operation.* Insert new pads and shims. On TR7 models only, larger cut outs face upper most in cylinder recess. On Spitfire models only, arrow on disc pad faces UP. Insert retaining pins and secure in place.

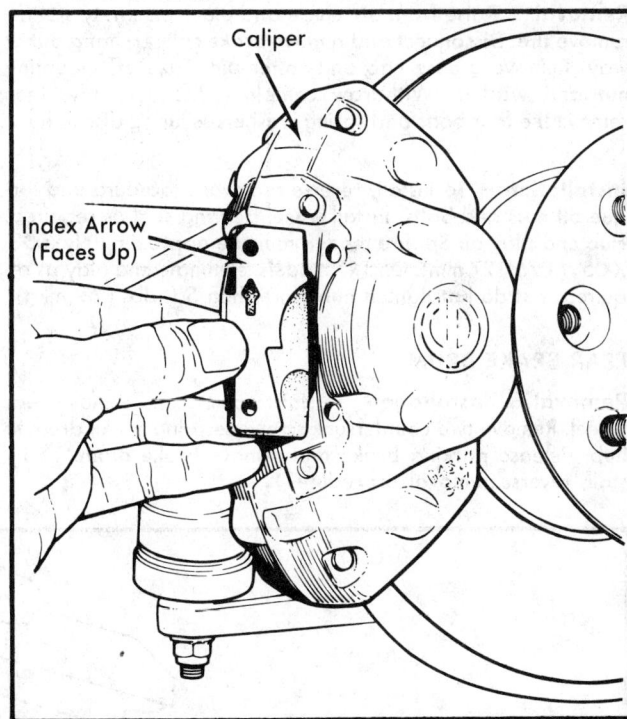

Caliper

Index Arrow
(Faces Up)

**Fig. 1   Installing Disc Brake Pad on Spitfire Models**

**MASTER CYLINDER**

**Removal** — Disconnect all hydraulic lines from master cylinder. On models equipped with power brake unit, remove mounting nuts and spring washers, then pull cylinder off studs. On models without power unit, disconnect master cylinder push rod from brake pedal. Remove four mounting bolts securing cylinder to mounting bracket. Take off bolt mounting master cylinder flange to bracket and withdraw entire assembly.

**Installation** — To install master cylinder assemblies, **reverse** removal procedure and bleed brake system.

## TRIUMPH (Cont.)

### VACUUM SERVO UNIT

**Removal & Installation** — Remove master cylinder as previously outlined. Disconnect vacuum hose from check valve. Remove clevis pin from servo operating rod and brake pedal lever. Remove servo with spacer. To install, reverse removal procedure.

### DISC BRAKE CALIPER

**Removal** — Disconnect brake union at caliper and plug opening in line. On Spitfire models, remove two bolts mounting caliper assembly to stub axle. On TR7 models, remove two bolts mounting steering arm and caliper lower mounting to stub axle assembly. Push steering clear, then remove upper mounting.

**Installation** — To install caliper assembly, reverse removal procedure and torque mounting bolts. Bleed hydraulic system.

### BRAKE DISC (ROTOR)

**Removal** — Raise front of vehicle and place on safety stands; remove tire. Disconnect and remove brake caliper; hang out of way. Remove grease cap and cotter pin. Take off mounting nut and washer. Withdraw complete disc assembly, then remove the four bolts and spring washers securing disc to hub.

**Installation** — To install, reverse removal procedure and torque all nuts and bolts. Install wheel bearing seal as required. Hub end play on Spitfire models must be approximately .003-.005" (.076.127 mm). On TR7 models, eliminate end play as required, but do not tighten hub more than 5 ft. lbs (.69 mkg).

### REAR BRAKE DRUM

**Removal & Installation** — Hoist vehicle and remove rear wheel. Remove two countersunk screws securing brake drum to hub. Release parking brake and remove brake drum. To install, reverse removal procedure.

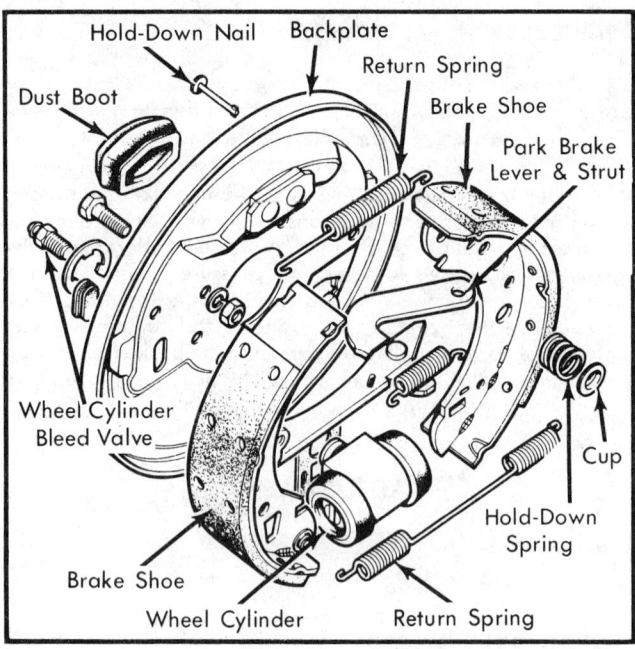

**Fig. 2   Exploded View of Triumph TR7 Rear Brake Assembly**

### REAR BRAKE SHOES

**Removal** — Remove brake drum as previously outlined. Remove parking brake cotter pin, shoe anchor pins, cups and springs. Disconnect return springs and lift shoes from abutments. Disconnect return springs and lift soes from abutments. Disconnect front soe from parking brake lever and remove shoes.

**Installation** — Reverse removal procedure and lightly apply white grease (zinc base) to ends of shoes and cam faces. **CAUTION** — *Do not allow grease to contact lining material.* Readjust brakes when lining replacement is complete.

**Fig. 3   Exploded View of Master Cylinder — Spitfire Shown**

# Brakes

## TRIUMPH (Cont.)

### REAR BRAKE WHEEL CYLINDER

**Removal & Installation** — Remove brake shoes as previously outlined. Drain fluid, disconnect flex hose from steel line and unscrew hose from cylinder. Disconnect parking brake cable clevis, remove dust cover, retaining plate and spring clips. Remove wheel cylinder. To install, reverse removal procedure and bleed brakes.

### PRESSURE DIFFERENTIAL VALVE

**Removal & Installation** — Disconnect electrical leads. Disconnect inlet and outlet lines and plug all ports to prevent loss of fluid and entry of dirt. Remove bolt securing valve and remove unit. To install, reverse removal procedure, bleed brakes and if necessary, center valve shuttle.

## OVERHAUL

### DISC BRAKE CALIPER

**Disassembly** — Using low air pressure, force pistons from caliper bores. If pistons are seized, the whole caliper assembly must be renewed. Carefully pry wiper seal retainer from groove, using a blunt instrument. **NOTE** — *Spitfire uses circlips for retainers.* Take out wiper seal and then fluid seal.

**Inspection** — Clean caliper bores and inspect for deep scratches or pitting. Look at pistons and ensure they are not corroded or damaged. Replace components as necessary.

**Reassembly** — Fit new fluid seals into caliper bores, making sure they are properly located. Lightly coat bores with clean brake fluid. Insert pistons into calipers, with approximately $\frac{5}{16}$" (7.94 mm) of each piston protruding from mouth of each bore. Fit new wiper seal into each retainer, then slide assembly, seal first, into mouth of bore. **NOTE** — *Use piston as a guide for seal.* On Spitfire models, insert dust seals and install circlip. Fully seat pistons, ensuring retainers are not distorted.

NOTE — Spitfire Models Have Circlips

Caliper — Fluid Seal — Piston — Wiper Seal — Retainer

**Fig. 4  Disassembled Front Disc Brake Caliper Spitfire Shown**

### REAR WHEEL CYLINDER

**Disassembly** — Remove wheel cylinder as previously outlined. Remove dust cover and withdraw piston. Remove seal from piston using fingers only.

**Cleaning & Inspection** — Clean all parts in alcohol or brake fluid and examine cylinder bore and piston for score marks, ridges or corrosion. If either bore or piston is damaged, replace entire cylinder assembly.

**Reassembly** — Install new seal with lip towards bottom of cylinder. Lubricate seal with clean brake fluid, insert piston into cylinder and install dust cover. Reinstall cylinder and bleed brakes.

### VACUUM SERVO UNIT

**NOTE** — *Overhauling unit consists of changing check valve, filter, dust cover, seal and plate assembly. Any other component failure requires complete unit replacement. Replacing filter is the only normal service required. A service repair kit is available for limited service.*

**Disassembly** — 1) Remove servo unit as previously outlined. To remove check valve, note angle of valve in relation to servo housing. Use a suitable wrench to press down on valve and rotate counterclockwise $\frac{1}{3}$ turn.

2) Remove filter by pulling back dust cover and pulling out filter. For ease of filter installation, cut new filter diagonally.

Seal & Plate — Front Shell — Rear Shell — Diaphragm — Diaphragm Plate — Retainer — Sprag Washer — Dust Cover — Filter — End Cap — Hydraulic Push Rod — Valve Operating Rod — Seal — Bearing — Retainer — Valve Retaining Plate — Reaction Disc — "O" Ring — Diaphragm Return Spring — Check Valve

**Fig. 5  Sectional View of Vacuum Servo Unit**

## TRIUMPH (Cont.)

**3)** Remove seal and plate assembly from front shell recess by gripping center rib with needle nose pliers. Use grease supplied in service kit to lubricate new seal and plate assembly when installing.

**4)** To check push rod for wear, place a straight edge across front shell recess. Measure clearance between end of push rod and straight edge. Clearance should be .011-.016" (.28-.41mm). Replace servo unit if clearance is incorrect.

**NOTE** — *Servo push rod to master cylinder clearance is set by factory and secured with Locktite. No attempt should be made to alter setting.*

**Reassembly** — To reassemble components to servo unit, reverse disassembly procedures.

### MASTER CYLINDER

**Disassembly, Spitfire** — **1)** Remove master cylinder as previously outlined. Drain and discard fluid. Remove screws securing reservoir to cylinder. Depress push rod, remove snap ring and withdraw push rod with abutment plate. Use an Allen wrench to unscrew tipping valve securing nut and remove seal. Depress primary plunger and remove tipping valve.

**2)** Remove internal parts either with compressed air at inlet or by shaking cylinder body. Separate plunger and intermediate spring. Lift leaf of spring retainer, remove spring and center

valve sub-assembly from secondary plunger. From valve stem, remove spring, valve spacer, spring washer and valve seal. Remove seals from primary and secondary plungers.

**Cleaning & Inspection** — Clean all serviceable parts in brake fluid or alcohol. Examine cylinder bore for score marks, ridges or corrosion. Discard cylinder body even if only slight imperfections are found.

**NOTE** — *Replace all seals with those contained in service repair kit. Prior to assembly, lubricate all parts in clean brake fluid.*

**Reassembly** — **1)** Install seal on primary and secondary plungers. Install seal, smaller diameter leading, to valve head. Place spring washer on valve stem ensuring that convex side of washer is to valve. Place spring retainer to valve stem with keyhole leading. Slide secondary spring over spring retainer and up to secondary plunger.

**2)** Place secondary plunger and valve assembly between protected jaws of a vise and compress spring. Use a small screwdriver to press leaf spring retainer against secondary plunger and then compress leaf spring retainer with needle nose pliers against plunger. Remove plunger and valve assembly from vise and check retainer spring.

**3)** Install intermediate spring between primary and secondary plungers and insert into cylinder. Replace push rod, snap

**Fig. 6  Exploded View of Master Cylinder Assembly**

## TRIUMPH (Cont.)

ring and rubber boot. Depress push rod and insert tipping valve. Install seal, secure nut and torque to specifications. Install reservoir and seal. Install master cylinder and bleed brakes.

**Disassembly, TR7 — 1)** Separate fluid reservoir from master cylinder. Pull out rubber seals from cylinder body. Take off metal cap and rubber boot, then disengage circlip and pull out primary piston assembly.

**2)** Insert a rod into bore and depress secondary piston. This releases stop pin for removal. Withdraw secondary piston, spring retainer and return spring.

**3)** Unscrew failure switch from cylinder body. Remove end plug and extract washer, spacer and piston with spring. Carefully separate rubber seals.

**Inspection —** Clean all components in brake fluid, then thoroughly dry. Carefully inspect all components for wear. If cylinder bore is even slightly corroded, cylinder must be replaced. Ensure all fluid passages are unobstructed.

**Reassembly — 1)** Fit new seals and washers to primary and secondary pistons. Insert secondary return spring, spring retainer, and piston into cylinder bore.

**2)** Using a rod, depress secondary piston until head of piston passes secondary fluid port, then fit stop bolt. Fit primary return spring, spring retainer and piston into bore. Be sure lip of seal is not bent back.

**3)** Fit circlip at mouth of cylinder and check for correct seating in groove. Reinstall both rubber seals into cylinder body recesses. Ensure reservoir is clean and fit to master cylinder.

**4)** Fit new "O" rings into grooves on pressure warning switch piston and spring assembly. Insert assembly into bore and take care not to damage "O" rings. Install spacer, fuel line, copper washer, and end plug.

### TIGHTENING SPECIFICATIONS

| Application | Ft. Lbs. (mkg) |
|---|---|
| Disc Brake Rotor-to-Hub | |
|    Spitfire | 26-34 (3.6-4.7) |
| Caliper Mounting Bolts | |
|    Spitfire | 50-65 (7.0-9.0) |
|    TR7 | 74 (10.2) |

### DISC BRAKE ROTOR SPECIFICATIONS

| Application | Disc Diameter In. (mm) | Lateral Runout In. (mm) | Parallelism In. (mm) | Original Thickness In. (mm) | Minimum Refinish Thickness In. (mm) | Discard Thickness In. (mm) |
|---|---|---|---|---|---|---|
| Spitfire | 9.000 (229) | ... | ... | ... | ... | ... |
| TR7 | 9.76 (247.6) | ... | ... | .375 (9.5) | ... | ... |

### BRAKE DRUM SPECIFICATIONS

| Application | Drum Diameter In. (mm) | Original Diameter In. (mm) | Maximum Refinish Diameter In. (mm) | Discard Diameter In. (mm) |
|---|---|---|---|---|
| Spitfire | 7.000 (178) | 7.000 (178) | ... | ... |
| TR7 | 7.995-8.000 (203.2-203.3) | 7.995-8.000 (203.2-203.3) | ... | 8.050 (204.5) |

## VOLKSWAGEN

Type 1
Type 2
Dasher
Rabbit
Scirocco

## DESCRIPTION

Brake system is hydraulically actuated, using a tandem master cylinder and on some models, a power brake unit. Type 1 models are equipped with drum brakes on all four wheels. All other models are equipped with disc brakes on the front wheels and drum brakes on rear wheels. Dasher models incorporate new Girling calipers this year. All models with disc brakes are equipped with a pressure regulator in the rear brake circuit. The pressure regulator limits pressure to the rear brakes when foot brake is applied, preventing rear wheel lock-up. All models are equipped with a mechanical parking brake, operating on the rear brakes.

## ADJUSTMENT

### DISC BRAKES

Disc brakes are self-adjusting; therefore, no adjustment in service is required.

### DRUM BRAKES

**Type 2 (Rear Brakes)** — Turn adjusting nut for both shoes three notches at a time, alternating from one nut to the other, until both shoes are rubbing on brake drum. Turn both nuts back alternately, until brake drum just rotates freely.

**NOTE** — *On Rabbit, Scirocco and Dasher models, make sure residual pressure is released from right brake before making adjustment.*

**All Others** — Turn adjuster until a slight drag is felt when rotating brake drum. Back off adjuster 3-4 notches, or until drum is just free to rotate.

### PARKING BRAKE

**Type 2 & Dasher** — Raise and support vehicle and ensure rear brakes are properly adjusted. From under vehicle, loosen parking brake cable lock nut(s). Pull parking brake handle up six notches (Type 2), or two notches (Dasher) and tighten cable adjusting nut(s) until rear wheels can just be turned by hand. Tighten lock nut(s) and ensure rear wheels rotate freely with parking brake fully released.

**All Others** — Raise and support vehicle and ensure rear brakes are properly adjusted. Pull back rubber (plastic) boot at base of parking brake handle and loosen parking brake cable lock nuts. Pull handle up three notches and tighten each adjusting nut until rear wheels just lock. Tighten lock nuts and refit rubber (plastic) boot. Ensure rear wheels rotate freely with parking brake fully released.

### HYDRAULIC SYSTEM BLEEDING

**Pressure Bleeding** — Attach bleeder connector cap to cylinder reservoir, and pressurize system to 43 psi. Attach one end of bleeder tube to cylinder bleeder screw, and submerge opposite end of tube in a jar half full of clean brake fluid. Open each bleeder screw in turn, and allow fluid to flow into container until fluid flows with no sign of air in fluid.

**Manual Bleeding** — Attach one end of bleeder tube to bleeder screw, and submerge opposite end in a jar half full of clean brake fluid. Pump brake pedal several times, and with pedal at bottom of stroke, open bleeder screw. Close bleeder screw, then release pressure on brake pedal. Repeat procedure until fluid flows from bleeder tube with no sign of air in fluid.

## BRAKE PRESSURE REGULATOR

**Type 2 — 1)** Install a hydraulic pressure gauge that will record 0-2300 psi in front and rear circuit. Bleed both hoses through gauge bleeder valves.

**2)** Pump pedal several times. Depress pedal until there is 1420 psi in each circuit. Release pedal. Loosen pressure regulator mounting bolts.

**3)** Apply pressure to pedal until both gauges read 710 psi. Tilt front of pressure regulator about 30° down from installed position. Leave regulator on angle and depress pedal until front brake circuit pressure reaches 1420 psi. Rear circuit MUST have 786-929 psi. If correct pressure is not obtained in rear circuit, replace regulator.

**Dasher & Rabbit — 1)** Remove everything from luggage compartment. Fill fuel tank. Load drivers seat with about 165 lbs. Bounce vehicle several times and allow to settle normally.

**2)** Measure distance from top of tire rim to lower edge of fender lip. Make sure measurement is made on both sides. Install spring tensioners under shock absorbers and attach at top to frame. See Fig. 1. Tensioners will hold vehicle in settled position. Check measurement several times druing adjustment operation.

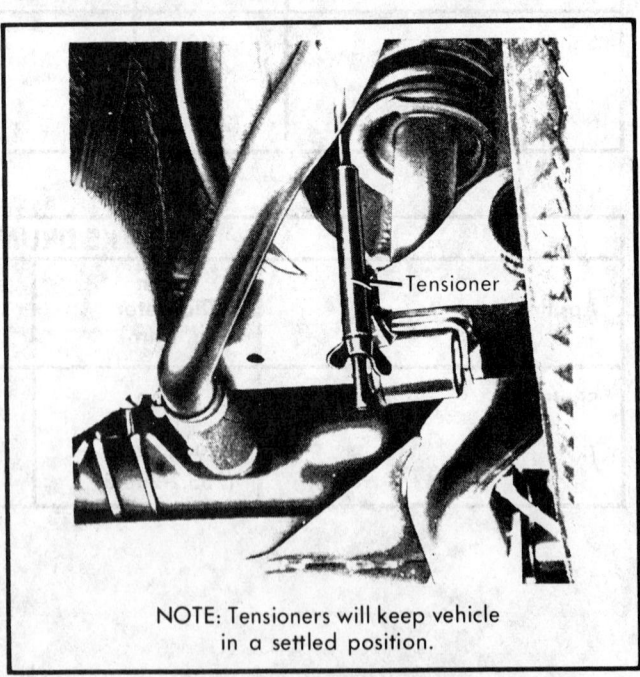

NOTE: Tensioners will keep vehicle in a settled position.

*Fig. 1  Tensioner with Wing Nut Fitted on Left Side Shock Absorber of Rabbit*

**3)** Connect one 1500 psi minimum pressure gauge to right rear wheel cylinder and connect another to left front brake caliper. Bleed gauges.

## VOLKSWAGEN (Cont.)

**4)** Pump pedal several times. Depress pedal until front wheel gauge reads 710 psi. Check rear wheel gauge for pressure of 440-497 psi.

**5)** Continue to depress pedal until front gauge reads 1400 psi. Rear gauge must read 753-810 psi.

**NOTE** — *Do NOT adjust spring tension with brake pedal depressed.*

**6)** If both pressures in test were too high on rear wheel, loosen regulator clamp bolt and REDUCE spring tension. If both pressures were consistently low, INCREASE spring tension. If correct specifications cannot be obtained by adjusting spring tension, replace pressure regulator.

## REMOVAL & INSTALLATION

### FRONT DISC BRAKE PADS

**Removal: Girling, Exc. Dasher — 1)** Raise and support vehicle. Remove wheel. Pry off spreader spring. On Rabbit and Scirocco models, remove spring retainer bolt. Using a pair of pliers, pull out pad retainer pins.

**NOTE** — *Some models have "U" shaped retainer.*

**2)** With a disc pad extractor tool, pull out pads. Inspect pads for wear or damage. Replace pads if lining thickness is less than .080" (2.0 mm).

**Installation** — To install Girling disc brake pads, reverse removal procedure and note: Tighten spring retainer bolt. Make sure spreader spring arrow faces upward.

**Fig. 2   Using a 20° Gauge to Properly Position Piston in Caliper Bore**

**Removal: Girling, Dasher — 1)** Raise vehicle and place on safety stands. Remove front wheel. Using hand pressure force caliper to slide outward (toward outer wheel bearing). This forces piston into cylinder housing. Some brake fluid may need to be siphoned out of reservoir during this procedure.

**2)** Take an open end wrench and hold guide pin head while removing lower mounting bolt. *See Fig. 9.* Rotate caliper cylinder upward. Take out disc pads.

**Installation — 1)** Clean area where pads rest. Make sure grommets on guide pins are not damaged. Guide pins must slide smoothly in housing. Install brake pads. Swing caliper housing down.

**2)** Make sure pads do not hit piston, force piston deeper into housing if necessary. Tighten lower mounting bolt. Depress brake pedal several times to seat pads against rotor.

**Removal: ATE; Dasher, Rabbit and Scirocco — 1)** Raise and support vehicle. Remove wheel. Remove spring clips from retaining pins. Using a punch, drive out retaining pins. Remove damper spring. With a disc pad extractor tool, remove inner pad. Outer pad is positioned in a notch and must be moved out of notch before removal.

**2)** Inspect disc pads for wear or damage. Replace pads if lining thickness is less than .008" (2.0 mm). Remove piston retaining plate and clean in denatured alcohol. Inspect plate for damage and replace as necessary.

**Installation** — Using a suitable piston retaining device, push piston to bottom of cylinder bore. Check position of piston using a 20° gauge. Install piston retaining plate, insert disc pads and a NEW damper spring. Using a hammer, install retaining pins into caliper. Depress brake pedal several times to seat pistons and disc pads.

**Removal: ATE; Type 2 —** Raise and support vehicle. Remove wheel. Pry off spreader spring. Using a pair of pliers, pull out pad retainer pins. Using a disc pad extractor tool, pull out pads. Inspect pads for wear or damage. Replace pads if lining thickness is less than .080" (2.0 mm).

**Installation** — To install disc pads, reverse removal procedure and note: Make sure spreader spring faces up.

### DISC BRAKE CALIPER

**Removal** — Raise and support vehicle and remove wheel. Disconnect brake line from caliper and plug opening to prevent entry of dirt and foreign matter. Bend back locking tabs (if equipped) on mounting bolts. Remove caliper mounting bolts and take off caliper assembly.

**Installation** — To install, reverse removal procedure, using new lock plates and mounting bolts.

### DISC BRAKE ROTOR

**Removal** — Raise and support vehicle, remove wheel. Remove caliper mounting bolts and hang caliper from tie rod with wire. Remove wheel bearing mounting hardware and carefully pull hub and rotor assembly (with outer bearing) from spindle. **NOTE** — *On Type 2 models, if hub is stuck, DO NOT pound with hammer, screw bolts into three holes provided until assembly breaks loose. Rotor can be separated from hub by removing the Allen head bolts.*

## VOLKSWAGEN (Cont.)

**Installation** — To install hub and rotor assembly, reverse removal procedure and adjust wheel bearings. *See Wheel Bearing Adjustment in WHEEL ALIGNMENT Section.*

### FRONT BRAKE DRUM

**Removal** — Raise and support vehicle, and remove wheel. Remove retainer from speedometer cable. Remove dust cap from hub, then remove wheel bearing adjusting nut, and outer wheel bearing. Back off brake shoe adjusters, and remove hub and drum assembly from vehicle.

**Installation** — To install, reverse removal procedure. Adjust and lubricate wheel bearings, and adjust brake shoes.

### REAR BRAKE DRUM

**Removal (Type 1)** — Remove cotter pin and castellated nut. Loosen castellated nut while vehicle is on ground. Raise and support vehicle, then take off wheel. Release parking brake and back off adjusters. Fit puller to drum and take off drum.

**Installation** — To install, reverse removal procedure and note: Make sure castellated nut is tightened with vehicle on floor.

**Removal (Type 2)** — Raise and support vehicle, remove wheel. With parking brake released, back off on brake shoe adjuster. Remove two Allen head screws and pull brake drum from wheel hub.

**Installation** — To install, reverse removal procedure and make sure Allen head screws are tight.

**Removal (Rabbit, Scirocco, Dasher)** — Raise and support vehicle. Back off brake shoe adjusters. Remove grease cap and cotter pin. Loosen, then remove adjustment nut and washer. Slide drum off spindle being careful not to drop outer bearing.

**Installation** — To install, reverse removal procedure and note: Clean spindle and threads. Make sure wheel bearing is lubricated. Adjust wheel bearings. *See Wheel Bearing Adjustment in WHEEL ALIGNMENT Section.* Adjust brake shoes.

*Fig. 4    Type 1 Front Brake Assembly with Brake Drum Removed*

### BRAKE SHOES

**Removal (Front)** — Raise and support vehicle. Remove wheel, and brake drum. Remove brake shoe hold down pins and springs. Remove brake shoe return springs, and pry shoes from adjusting screws. Remove brake shoes from vehicle.

*Fig. 3    Volkswagen Type 2 ATE Front Disc Brake Assembly. Girling Caliper Internal Design is Only Slightly Different. Girling Has a Retainer Ring for Dust Seal that is not Integral with Seal.*

# Brakes

## VOLKSWAGEN (Cont.)

Wheel Cylinder — Backing Plate

Shoe & Lining

Parking Brake Link

Return Spring

Lever

Cable

Hold Down Spring

Return Spring

Adjuster

Star Wheel — Anchor Block

**Fig. 5 Volkswagen Type 1 & 2 Rear Brake Assembly with Brake Drum Removed**

**Removal (Rear)** — Raise and support vehicle. Remove wheel, and brake drum. Remove brake shoe hold down pins and springs. Remove lower shoe return spring, and disconnect parking brake cable from lever. Remove brake shoes, connecting link, upper return spring, and clip from vehicle as an assembly. Separate shoes from attaching hardware.

**Installation (All Models)** — To install reverse removal procedure. Adjust brakes and bleed hydraulic system if necessary.

### MASTER CYLINDER

**NOTE** — Removal and installation of all master cylinders is basically the same. The following variations may apply: Loca-

tion of cylinder, removal of wheel for accessibility, number of fluid connections, and number of electrical connections.

**Removal** — Drain or siphon fluid from reservoir(s). Raise and support vehicle, and remove cover plate (if equipped). Disconnect fluid lines at master cylinder. Disconnect electrical connections at cylinder, and remove push rod at brake pedal connection. Remove master cylinder attaching bolts, and remove master cylinder from vehicle. **NOTE** — If spacers are used on attaching bolts, do not allow spacers to drop into pedal assembly recess.

**Installation** — To install, reverse removal procedure and note the following: On vehicles equipped with a power brake unit, install a new "O" ring seal between master cylinder and power unit. After installation, bleed hydraulic system.

### POWER BRAKE BOOSTER

**Removal & Installation** — Remove master cylinder from power brake unit. Remove vacuum hoses and cover plate, then back off push rod lock nut at power booster end. Disconnect push rod at brake pedal, pull rod to one side, and unscrew push rod from booster. Remove booster attaching hardware, and pull booster out and back. To install booster, reverse removal procedure.

## OVERHAUL

### DISC BRAKE CALIPER

**Disassembly: ATE & Girling; Type 2 — 1)** Remove disc pads and retaining plates from caliper assembly. Clamp mounting flange in a vise. Remove retainer and dust seal from caliper assembly.

Piston Seal

Lock Ring

Piston

Rotor

Guide Spring

Dust Boot

Brake Cylinder

Locking Spring

Pad Mounting Pin

Mounting Frame

Floating Frame

Piston Retainers

Brake Pads

**Fig. 6 Exploded View of ATE Disc Brake Assembly Used on Dasher, Rabbit and Scirocco**

## VOLKSWAGEN (Cont.)

**2)** Install a piston retaining tool on one piston and fit a thin block of wood between tool and piston to be removed. Carefully apply air pressure to fluid inlet port and remove piston. Remove piston seal from groove with a pointed tool.

**Inspection** — Clean all parts in brake fluid. Check piston and caliper bore for wear or damage; replace as necessary. NOTE — *Manufacturer recommends replacing rubber parts during caliper overhaul.*

**Reassembly** — Apply light coat of brake paste to piston and seal. Fit seal in groove. Install piston and clamp at bottom of bore. Lightly coat inside of dust seal with paste and fit to piston. Using suitable tool (VW 442), press seal and piston into caliper. Fit retaining plate and position piston in bore. Repeat procedure on other half of caliper.

**Disassembly: ATE; Dasher, Rabbit, Scirocco** — Remove disc pads. Pry mounting frame and piston assembly off floating frame. Separate guide spring and brake cylinder. Remove clamp and dust cap from brake cylinder, then withdraw piston. Compressed air may be used to force out piston.

**Inspection** — Clean all parts in brake fluid. Check piston and caliper bore for damage or wear; replace as necessary. NOTE — *Manufacturer recommends replacing all rubber parts during overhaul.*

**Reassembly** — To reassemble, reverse disassembly procedure and note following: Coat piston with brake paste. Use a vise to seat piston. Use a brass drift to fit brake cylinder to floating frame. Make sure two grooves in mounting frame are pushed over ribs on floating frame. Ensure piston is in proper position.

**Fig. 7  *Exploded View of Girling Disc Brake Assembly Used on Rabbit and Scirocco***

# Brmes

## VOLKSWAGEN (Cont.)

**Disassembly: Girling; Rabbit & Scirocco** — Press brake cylinder out of yoke. Hold brake cylinder between two jaws of a vise with a slight gap. This will prevent piston from flying out of cylinder when compressed air is introduced into fluid port to remove pistons. With a pointed tool, remove sealing rings.

**Inspection** — Clean all parts in brake fluid. Check piston and caliper bore for damage or wear; replace as necessary. **NOTE** — *Manufacturer recommends replacing all rubber parts at time of overhaul.*

**Reassembly** — To reassemble, reverse disassembly procedure and note: Coat pistons and seals with brake paste before refitting.

**Disassembly: Girling; Dasher** — 1) Remove caliper and clean outside surfaces. Remove both cylinder housing mounting bolts. Place a block of wood between piston and housing. Blow compressed air into cylinder housing to dislodge piston.

2) Remove dust seal. Using a plastic instrument, carefully dig piston seal from groove in cylinder housing.

**Inspection** — Check housing and piston. Housing cannot be honed. Replace housing and cylinder in sets. Boots, guide pins and miscellaneous pieces are only available with new pad carrier.

**Reassembly** — Coat piston, cylinder bore, and new seal with suitable brake paste. Fit seal into cylinder. Slide dust seal onto piston. Slowly insert piston into cylinder fitting inner lip of dust seal into cylinder housing groove. Fully seat piston into cylinder. Engage outer lip of dust seal into groove of piston.

**Fig. 8    Exploded View of Girling Disc Brake Assembly Used on Dasher**

## WHEEL CYLINDER

**Disassembly** — With wheel cylinder removed from vehicle, remove dust boot(s), piston(s), expander spring, and cups.

**Fig. 9    Volkswagen Type 1 Wheel Cylinder Assembly**

**Inspection** — Clean all parts with clean brake fluid or denatured alcohol. Check piston and cylinder bore for out-of-round, corrosion, or damage.

**Reassembly** — To reassemble, reverse disassembly procedure, using new rubber components. Replace piston(s) and spring as necessary. Use brake cylinder paste on pistons and cups.

## MASTER CYLINDER

**Disassembly** — Remove front brake circuit piston stop screw. On Type 2 vehicles with power booster, remove snap ring and stop washer. On all other models, remove dust boot, stop ring, and stop washer. Remove both pistons and springs from cylinder by tapping open end of cylinder on a wood surface, or by carefully applying air pressure to front brake circuit fluid port will all other openings plugged. Remove all externally mounted fittings and switches from cylinder housing.

**Inspection** — Clean all parts with clean brake fluid or denatured alcohol. Check all pistons and cylinder for out-of-round, corrosion, or damage. If light honing will not remove blemishes from cylinder, replace cylinder. Inspect all other parts for scoring, wear, corrosion, or other damage.

**Reassembly** — 1) Install cups on pistons. Place cup washer, primary cup, support washer, spring retainer, and spring onto front piston, and insert piston assembly into cylinder bore. Assemble cup washer, primary cup, support washer, spring retainer, spring, and stop sleeve onto rear piston. Secure assembly with stroke limiting screw.

2) Except on Type 2 vehicles with power booster, install rear piston assembly into cylinder. Install stop washer, and lock ring. On Type 2 vehicles with power booster, install rear piston

## VOLKSWAGEN (Cont.)

with washer, cup, plastic washer, second cup, and second washer into cylinder, followed by snap ring.

3) Install piston stop screw, pushing front piston assembly forward as required to clear stop screw hole. Install all externally mounted switches and fittings. Tighten all nuts and bolts.

### POWER BRAKE UNIT & PRESSURE REGULATING VALVE

Replace these units as an assembly, do not try to overhaul units. When installing booster, use new boot, filter, damping washer, and sealing ring.

### TIGHTENING SPECIFICATIONS

| Application | Ft. Lbs. (mkg) |
|---|---|
| Master Cylinder-to-Booster | 9 (1.3) |
| Master Cylinder-to-Frame | |
| Type 1 & 2 | 18 (2.5) |
| Master Cylinder Piston Stop Screw | |
| Type 1 & 2 | 3.5-7.0 (.5-1.0) |
| Dasher, Rabbit, Scirocco | 11-14 (1.5-2.0) |
| Caliper Mounting | |
| Type 2 | 116 (16.0) |
| Dasher, Rabbit, Scirocco | 43 (6.0) |
| Slotted Axle Shaft Nut (Type 2) | 253 (35.0) |

NOTE: Master Cylinder Shown is for Models with Brake Booster. Other Cylinders Have Different Primary Piston Configuration.

Plug Coat With Brake Fluid

Stop Screw Remove Before Detaching Circlip

Brake Master Cylinder Housing

Seal

Seal

Brake Light Switches

Return Spring Do Not Interchange With Primary Return Spring

Spring Seat

Primary Cup

Washer

Secondary Piston

Secondary Cups Insert With Sealing Lips Facing Opposite Directions

Stop Sleeve

Stroke Limiting Screw

Primary Return Spring

Spring Seat

Primary Cup

Washer

Primary Piston

Washer

Secondary Cups Always Replace With Sealing Lip Pointing Toward Cylinder

Washer

Plastic Washer

Washer

Circlip

*Fig. 10　Master Cylinder Component Relationship — Rabbit, Scirocco, Dasher Shown*

# Brakes

## VOLKSWAGEN (Cont.)

### BRAKE SYSTEM SPECIFICATIONS

| Application | Drum Diam. In. (mm) | Wheel Cylinder Diameter | | Master Cylinder Diameter In. (mm) |
| | | Front In. (mm) | Rear In. (mm) | |
|---|---|---|---|---|
| Type 1 | ② 9.055 (230) | .874 (22.2) | .678 (17.5) | .750 (19.05) |
| Type 2 | 9.921 (252) | 2.126① (54) | .937 (23.8) | .874 (22.2) |
| Dasher | 7.87 (200) | ① | ..... | .813 (20.6) |
| Rabbit & Scirocco | 7.1 (180) | ① | ..... | ..... |

① — Front disc brakes.

② — Front and rear.

### DISC BRAKE ROTOR SPECIFICATIONS ①

| Application | Disc Diameter | Lateral Runout | Parallelism | Original Thickness | Minimum Refinish Thickness | Discard Thickness |
|---|---|---|---|---|---|---|
| Type 2 | 10.95 (278) | .004 (.10) | .0008 (.02) | .512 (13) | .472 (12) | .452 (11.5) |
| Dasher | 9.41 (239) | .002" (.06) | .0008 (.02) | .472 (12) | .433 (11) | .410 (10.5) |
| Rabbit & Scirocco | ... | ... | ... | .472 (12) | .433 (11) | .410 (10.5) |

① — In. (mm)

### BRAKE DRUM SPECIFICATIONS

| Application | Drum Diameter In. (mm) | Original Diameter In. (mm) | Maximum Refinish Diameter In. (mm) | Discard Diameter In. (mm) |
|---|---|---|---|---|
| Front | | | | |
| Type 1 | 9.055 (230) | 9.055 (230) | 9.114 (231.5) | ..... |
| Rear | | | | |
| Type 1 | 9.055 (230) | 9.055 (230) | 9.114 (231.5) | ..... |
| Type 2 | 9.921 (252) | 9.921 (252) | 9.980 (253) | ..... |
| Dasher | 7.87 (200) | 7.87 (200) | 7.89 (200.5) | 7.91 (201) |
| Rabbit & Scirocco | 7.08 (180) | 7.08 (180) | 7.10 (180.5) | 7.125 (181) |

# Brakes

## VOLVO

**240 Series**
**260 Series**

### DESCRIPTION

Volvo models may be equipped with either Girling disc brake calipers on all 4 wheels or with Girling calipers on front wheels and ATE calipers on rear wheels. Brake system incorporates 2 separate circuits: Hydraulic disc brake and mechanical parking brake. Service brakes are operated by a tandem master cylinder attached to a vacuum operated power assist unit. Master cylinder feeds hydraulic pressure to each circuit. One circuit feeds lower front caliper pistons and right rear caliper. Other circuit feeds upper front caliper pistons and left rear caliper. Additionally, valves are installed in both circuits to equally distribute braking power. A warning light, mounted on instrument panel, indicates pressure differences between circuits.

### ADJUSTMENT

#### DISC BRAKES

Disc brakes are self-adjusting; therefore, no adjustment in service is required.

#### PARKING BRAKE

**1)** Remove center console rear ash tray, then working through ash tray hole, loosen parking brake cables adjusting screw until cables are slack. Raise and support rear of vehicle, then remove wheels. Align hole in parking brake drum with starwheel adjuster.

**2)** Tighten starwheel until drum can just be rotated by hand, then back off adjuster until drum just rotates freely. Install rear wheels. Tighten parking brake cable adjusting screw until parking brake is fully applied when lever is pulled three or four notches. Install ash tray and lower vehicle.

### HYDRAULIC SYSTEM BLEEDING

**NOTE** — *To ensure the best possible results, bleed brakes in proper sequence.*

**1)** Start at left front brake. Connect bleed tubes to all three bleeder screws and immerse opposite end of tubes in a container partially filled with brake fluid. Pump brake pedal ten times, then keep pedal depressed and using assistants, open all three bleeder screws simultaneously. When pedal reaches end of travel, close all bleeder screws. Continue operation until all air is bled from caliper assembly. Repeat procedure on right front brake.

**2)** Depress brake pedal several times to level out master cylinder. Connect a bleed tube to right rear brake bleeder screw and immerse opposite end of tube in a container partially filled with brake fluid. Open bleeder screw and gravity bleed (no pumping of pedal) caliper assembly. Close bleeder screw when brake fluid is free of air bubbles. Repeat procedure on left rear brake.

### REMOVAL & INSTALLATION

#### DISC PADS

**Removal (All Types)** — Raise and support vehicle. Remove wheel. Remove spring locks. Pull out one lock pin and hold damper springs in place. Remove springs and other lock pin. Use tool 2917 (or equivalent) and pull disc pads from caliper. If pads are to be reinstalled, index mark.

**Installation, All; Front** — Using tool 280 (or equivalent), seat pistons in caliper bore. **NOTE** — *Use of screwdriver is discouraged because pads, seals or piston can be easily damaged.* Insert pads and fit guide or lock pins, spring locks and tension springs.

**Installation, Rear; ATE** — Press pistons into caliper until bottomed in bore. Before installing disc pads, ensure pistons are in proper position to prevent brake squeal; piston recess should incline 20° in relation to lower guide area on caliper (See Fig. 2). Check piston angle using template SVO 2919 (or equivalent) and correct if necessary. Install disc pads and one guide pin. Install damper spring and remaining guide pin and secure with locking clips. After installation, depress brake pedal several times to position pads against rotor.

**Fig. 1  Schematic of Bleeding Sequence**

**Fig. 2  Checking Piston Angle on Rear Brakes**

## VOLVO (Cont.)

**Installation, Rear; Girling,** — Select new disc pads and fit to caliper. If caliper is equipped with intermediate plates between pad and caliper, reinstall plates. If round damper washers are used, reinstall with smaller contact face toward pad. **NOTE** — *DO NOT install intermediate plates in caliper with round damper washers.* Fit one lock pin and install damper spring, then insert last lock pin. Check free movement of pads.

### CALIPER ASSEMBLY

**Removal** — Raise and support vehicle, and remove wheel. Disconnect brake line connections at caliper, and cap lines to prevent entry of foreign matter. Remove caliper mounting bolts and lift caliper from vehicle.

**Installation** — Position caliper assembly on mounting bracket, and install attaching bolts. After installing bolts, check clearance between disc pads and rotor on both sides of rotor; maximum deviation between sides should not exceed .022" (.01 mm). If clearance is not within specifications, correct by adding shims to caliper. Connect hydraulic lines to caliper and bleed brakes.

### DISC BRAKE ROTOR

**Removal** — Raise and support vehicle, remove wheel. Remove caliper assembly as previously outlined. Unscrew rotor lock bolts. Pull rotor from wheel hub.

**Inspection** — Before removing rotor, mount a dial indicator and check rotor runout. Runout must not exceed .004" (.1 mm). Measure rotor thickness through one revolution, thickness must not vary more than .001" (.03 mm).

**Installation** — To install, reverse removal procedure.

### PARKING BRAKE SHOES

**Removal** — Remove center console rear ash tray and loosen parking brake cable adjusting nut until cables are slack. Raise and support rear of vehicle and remove wheels. Remove caliper (without disconnecting hydraulic line) and support out of way, then remove rotor. Remove brake shoe return springs and lift off shoes and adjuster.

**Installation** — Reverse removal procedure and note the following: Replace brake drum (rotor) if out-of-round more than .008" (.2 mm). Apply a thin coat of heat resistant graphite grease to brake shoe sliding surfaces and to adjusting starwheel. After installation, adjust parking brake. See *Parking Brake.*

**Fig. 3   Exploded View of Parking Brake Assembly**

### MASTER CYLINDER

**Removal & Installation** — Disconnect hydraulic lines at master cylinder and cap openings to prevent entry of foreign matter. Remove cylinder attaching hardware, and remove cylinder assembly from vehicle. To install, reverse removal procedure, and bleed hydraulic system.

### POWER BRAKE UNIT

**Removal** — Remove master cylinder from vehicle. Disconnect vacuum hose and support unit at power brake unit. Remove power booster attaching hardware, then remove yoke lock nut and yoke. Tilt power booster forward slightly, and remove unit from vehicle.

**Fig. 4   ATE Rear Caliper Assembly Components**

## VOLVO (Cont.)

**Installation** — Position power brake unit on vehicle, and attach yoke to push rod. Install and tighten push rod lock nut.

Install and tighten power booster mounting hardware, and install master cylinder to booster. Install vacuum hose, and bleed hydraulic system.

**Check Valve Replacement** — Remove vacuum hose clamps at check valve, and remove check valve from vehicle. When installing check valve into vacuum hose, install valve with arrow on valve housing pointing toward intake manifold.

**Fig. 5   Girling Front Caliper Assembly**

**Filter Replacement** — Remove power brake unit from vehicle. Remove rubber dust boot, and filter retainer washer. Withdraw silencer and filter from end of booster. To install, reverse removal procedure, making sure slots in filter and silencer are 180° apart.

## OVERHAUL

### BRAKE CALIPER

**Disassembly** — Remove caliper from vehicle. Remove disc pads from caliper. Remove piston dust covers and retaining clips. Position a piece of wood between pistons, and carefully apply compressed air at fluid inlet port to force pistons out of cylinder bores. Remove piston seal from cylinder bore, then remove bleeder screw. **NOTE** — *DO NOT separate caliper halves.*

**Inspection** — Clean all parts in brake fluid or denatured alcohol. Inspect cylinder bores for scoring, grooving, or corrosion. If any cylinder bore is found to be damaged, replace caliper housing.

**Reassembly** — Lubricate all parts with clean brake fluid just prior to reassembly. Fit new piston seals in cylinder bore, then

**Fig. 6   Girling Rear Caliper**

install pistons. On ATE rear brakes, ensure piston is at 20° incline as shown in *Fig. 2*. Install rubber dust boots and retaining clips. Install bleeder screw, then fit disc pads.

### MASTER CYLINDER

**Disassembly** — Remove master cylinder from vehicle, and clamp mounting flange in a vise. Remove reservoir from cylinder, and remove rubber sealing rings. Remove piston stop screw, and remove retainer ring from end of cylinder bore. Remove pistons from cylinder bore.

**Inspection** — Clean all parts in clean brake fluid or denatured alcohol and blow dry with compressed air. Inspect cylinder bore for scratches, scoring or corrosion. If cylinder is scored or scratched, it should be replaced.

**Fig. 7   Master Cylinder Assembly**

**Reassembly** — Lubricate all parts with clean brake fluid prior to reassembly. Position washer, seal, and back-up ring on

# Brakes

B R A K E S

## VOLVO (Cont.)

secondary piston. Install spring thrust washer on piston, and install piston assembly into cylinder bore. Install washer, seal, and back-up ring on primary piston. Install spring, with plate and sleeve on piston, then install piston assembly into cylinder bore. Push piston into cylinder bore, and install piston stop screw. Install reservoir sealing rings, and install reservoir.

### VACUUM PUMP

NOTE — *Repair kits are available for valve and diaphragm.*

**Disassembly** — 1) Place pump in soft jawed vise. Index mark valve housing with cover. Remove valve housing. Remove diaphragm, washers, and spring from pump.

2) Turn pump over. Remove bottom cover. Remove actuating lever pin. Slide out pump lever, pump rod and nylon bushing.

**Reassembly** — 1) Place bushing on pump rod. Put rod in pump housing. Fit lever and pin. Install bottom cover and gasket.

2) Place washer and "O" ring on diaphragm screw. Remember to lightly coat end of screw with suitable thread locking compound. Install diaphragm assembly. Insert valve housing aligned with index marks. Fit valves and seals. Make sure domed side disc faces diaphragm. Install valve housing cover with spring and gasket.

### TIGHTENING SPECIFICATIONS

| Application | Ft. Lbs. (mkg) |
|---|---|
| Front Caliper Mounting Bolts | 65-70 (9.0-9.7) |
| Rear Caliper Mounting Bolts | 45-50 (6.2-6.9) |
| Wheel Nuts | 70-95 (9.7-13.1) |
| Master Cylinder Bolts | 20-35 (2.8-4.8) |
| Brake Fluid Lines | 6-9 (.83-1.2) |

### DISC BRAKE ROTOR SPECIFICATIONS

| Application | Disc Diameter In. (mm) | Lateral Runout In. (mm) | Parallelism In. (mm) | Original Thickness In. (mm) | Minimum Refinish Thickness In. (mm) | Discard Thickness In. (mm) |
|---|---|---|---|---|---|---|
| 240 Front | 10.35 (263) | .004 (.10) | .0012 (.03) | .563 (14.3) | .557 (13.14) | ... |
| Rear | 11.06 (281) | .004 (.10) | .0012 (.03) | .378 (9.6) | .331 (8.4) | ... |
| 260 Front | 10.35 (263) | .004 (.10) | .0012 (.03) | .95 (24) | .90 (22.8) | ... |
| Rear | 11.06 (281) | .004 (.10) | .0012 (.03) | .378 (9.6) | .331 (8.4) | ... |

# Section 8
# WHEEL ALIGNMENT

## Contents

*NOTE — ALSO SEE GENERAL INDEX.*

## WHEEL ALIGNMENT TROUBLE SHOOTING

**NOTE** — *This is a general trouble shooting guide. When using this guide, locate the condition in column one that corresponds to your problem and determine the possible causes in column two. Match the number of the possible cause with the same number in column three, and you will have the suggested correction.*

| CONDITION | POSSIBLE CAUSE | CORRECTION |
|---|---|---|
| ▶ Tire wear | 1) Tire pressure too low<br>2) Wheel alignment out of tolerance<br>3) Excessively worn wheel bearings<br>4) Improper or no tire rotation | 1) Check manufacturer's recommended pressure and set to specifications.<br>2) Check alignment and set to specs or replace components<br>3) Check, adjust or replace bearings<br>4) Follow manufacturer's recommended procedures. Perform a 4 or 5-tire rotation |
| ▶ Grating tire noise | 1) Improper tire pressure<br>2) Wheel alignment out of tolerance<br>3) Damaged or defective spindle or suspension components | 1) Check manufacturer's recommended pressure and set to specifications<br>2) Reset alignment or replace necessary suspension components<br>3) Inspect and replace components |
| ▶ Uneven tire wear | 1) Uneven tire pressure<br>2) Tire pressure too low (shoulders on tire worn)<br>3) Tire pressure too high (center of tred worn)<br>4) Bent rotor or wheel<br>5) One side of front tred worn<br>6) Inside of tred worn<br>7) Outside of tred worn<br>8) Excessive wheel bearing play<br>9) Brake operation on only one side | 1) Check manufacturer's recommended pressure and set to specifications<br>2) See correction 1<br>3) See correction 1<br><br>4) Check and replace part<br>5) Inadequate camber<br>6) Inadequate toe-in<br>7) Excessive toe-in<br>8) Inspect and adjust bearings<br>9) Check and adjust brakes |
| ▶ Road noise | 1) Abnormal tire wear<br>2) Tire out of balance<br>3) Tire pressure too low | 1) Replace tire<br>2) Rebalance tire<br>3) Check manufacturer's recommended pressure and set to specifications |

| WHEEL ALIGNMENT SPECIFICATIONS | | | | |
|---|---|---|---|---|
| Application | Caster (Degrees) | Camber (Degrees) | Toe-In (Inches) | Remarks |
| **ARROW** All Models | $2^1/_{12}\pm\frac{1}{2}$ | $1\pm\frac{1}{2}$ | $\frac{5}{64}$ to $\frac{15}{64}$ | |
| **AUDI** Fox | | | | ① Toe-in given in degrees. |
|   Front | $\frac{1}{2}\pm\frac{1}{2}$ | $\frac{1}{2}\pm\frac{1}{2}$ | $-\frac{1}{12}$ to $+\frac{5}{12}$① | |
|   Rear | ..... | $-\frac{1}{2}\pm\frac{1}{2}$ | $-\frac{5}{6}$ to $+\frac{5}{6}$① | |
| 5000 | | | | |
|   Front | $-\frac{1}{6}\pm\frac{1}{2}$ | $-\frac{1}{2}\pm\frac{1}{2}$ | $-\frac{1}{6}$ to $\frac{1}{12}$① | |
|   Rear | ..... | $-\frac{1}{2}\pm\frac{1}{2}$ | $+\frac{1}{6}$ to $+\frac{5}{12}$① | |
| **BMW** 320i | | | | |
|   Front | $8^1/_3\pm\frac{1}{2}$ | $0\pm\frac{1}{2}$ | $\frac{3}{64}$ to $\frac{3}{32}$ | |
|   Rear | ..... | $-2\pm\frac{1}{2}$ | $0$ to $\frac{5}{64}$ | |
| 530i | | | | |
|   Front | $7^2/_3\pm\frac{1}{2}$ | $\frac{1}{2}\pm\frac{1}{2}$ | $\frac{3}{64}$ to $\frac{3}{32}$ | |
|   Rear | ..... | $-2\pm\frac{1}{2}$ | $0$ to $\frac{5}{6}$ | |
| 633CSi & 733i | | | | |
|   Front | $9\pm\frac{1}{2}$ | $0\pm\frac{1}{2}$ | $0$ to $\frac{1}{16}$ | |
|   Rear | ..... | $-1\pm\frac{1}{2}$ | $\frac{5}{64}$ to $\frac{9}{64}$ | |
| **CAPRI** All Models | $1\frac{5}{8}\pm\frac{5}{8}$ | $1\frac{1}{2}\pm\frac{3}{4}$ | $\frac{1}{4}$ to $\frac{3}{8}$ | |
| **CHALLENGER** All Models | $2\frac{2}{3}\pm\frac{1}{2}$ | $1\frac{1}{2}\pm\frac{1}{2}$ | $\frac{5}{64}$ to $\frac{23}{64}$ | |
| **COLT** All Models | $2^1/_{12}\pm\frac{1}{2}$ | $1\pm\frac{1}{2}$ | $\frac{5}{64}$ to $\frac{15}{64}$① | ① Wagon is $\frac{5}{64}$ to $\frac{11}{32}$ |
| **COURIER** All Models | $1\pm\frac{1}{4}$ | $\frac{7}{8}\pm\frac{3}{8}$ | $0$ to $\frac{1}{4}$ | |
| **DATSUN** F10 | $1\frac{1}{2}\pm\frac{3}{4}$ | $1^7/_{12}\pm\frac{3}{4}$ | $0$ to $\frac{5}{64}$① | ① Radial tires; $\frac{13}{64}$ to $\frac{9}{32}$ for bias tires |
| B210 | $\frac{3}{4}\pm\frac{3}{4}$ | $1\frac{1}{6}\pm\frac{3}{4}$ | $\frac{5}{64}$ to $\frac{5}{32}$ | |
| 200SX | $1\frac{5}{6}\pm\frac{3}{4}$ | $1\pm\frac{5}{6}$ | $\frac{5}{64}$ to $\frac{5}{32}$ | ② A toe-in to a toe-out range. |
| 510 | $\frac{3}{4}\pm\frac{1}{2}$ | $1^7/_{12}\pm\frac{3}{4}$ | $\frac{3}{64}$ to $\frac{1}{8}$ | |
| 810 | $1^{11}/_{12}\pm\frac{3}{4}$ | $\frac{3}{4}\pm\frac{3}{4}$ | $0$ to $\frac{5}{64}$ | |
| 280Z | | | | |
|   Front | $2\frac{3}{4}\pm\frac{3}{4}$ | $1\frac{1}{6}\pm\frac{3}{4}$ | $0$ to $\frac{1}{8}$ | |
|   Rear | ----- | $\frac{3}{4}\pm\frac{3}{4}$ | $-\frac{13}{64}$ to $\frac{13}{64}$② | |
| 280Z 2+2 | | | | |
|   Front | $2\frac{3}{4}\pm\frac{3}{4}$ | $1\frac{1}{6}\pm\frac{3}{4}$ | $0$ to $\frac{1}{8}$ | |
|   Rear | ----- | $-\frac{3}{4}\pm\frac{7}{12}$ | $-\frac{13}{64}$ to $\frac{13}{64}$② | |
| Pick-up | $1\frac{5}{6}\pm\frac{2}{3}$ | $1\frac{1}{4}\pm1$ | $\frac{5}{64}$ to $\frac{1}{8}$ | |
| **FIAT** 124 Sport Spider | $3\frac{1}{2}\pm\frac{1}{2}$ | $\frac{1}{2}\pm\frac{1}{2}$ | $\frac{5}{64}$ to $\frac{1}{8}$ | |
| 128 | | | | |
|   Front | $2\frac{1}{4}\pm\frac{1}{2}$ | $1\frac{1}{2}\pm\frac{1}{2}$ | $-\frac{5}{64}$ to $\frac{5}{64}$ | |
|   Rear | ..... | $-3\frac{1}{4}\pm\frac{1}{2}$ | $\frac{1}{64}$ to $\frac{5}{64}$ | |
| 128 3P | | | | |
|   Front | $2\frac{1}{4}\pm\frac{1}{2}$ | $\frac{3}{4}\pm\frac{1}{2}$ | $-\frac{5}{64}$ to $\frac{5}{64}$ | |
|   Rear | ..... | $-3\frac{1}{2}\pm\frac{1}{2}$ | $\frac{5}{64}$ to $\frac{15}{64}$ | |
| 131 Brava | $3\frac{1}{2}\pm\frac{1}{2}$ | $\frac{1}{2}\pm\frac{1}{2}$ | $\frac{5}{64}$ to $\frac{13}{64}$ | |
| X1/9 | | | | |
|   Front | $7\pm\frac{1}{2}$ | $-1\pm\frac{1}{3}$ | $\frac{3}{64}$ to $\frac{13}{64}$ | |
|   Rear | ..... | $-2\pm\frac{1}{3}$ | $\frac{5}{32}$ to $\frac{15}{64}$ | |

| WHEEL ALIGNMENT SPECIFICATIONS (Cont.) | | | | |
|---|---|---|---|---|
| Application | Caster (Degrees) | Camber (Degrees) | Toe-In (Inches) | Remarks |
| **FIESTA** All Models | $-\frac{3}{4}$ to $+1$ | $+1$ | $\frac{3}{64}$ to $\frac{9}{64}$ | |
| **HONDA** Accord | | | | ① A toe-in to a toe-out range. |
| Front | $2\pm1$ | $\frac{1}{2}\pm1$ | $-\frac{5}{64}$ to $+\frac{5}{32}$ ① | |
| Rear | ----- | ----- | $-\frac{3}{64}$ to $+\frac{1}{8}$ ① | |
| Civic | | | | ② Toe-out. |
| Front | $1\frac{3}{4}$ | $\frac{1}{2}$ | $\frac{3}{64}$ ② | |
| Rear | ----- | $\frac{1}{2}$ | $0$ | |
| CVCC Sedan | | | | |
| Front | $1\frac{1}{2}\pm\frac{1}{2}$ | $\frac{1}{2}\pm\frac{1}{2}$ | $0$ to $\frac{5}{64}$ ② | |
| Rear | ----- | $\frac{1}{2}\pm\frac{1}{2}$ | $0$ to $\frac{5}{64}$ ② | |
| CVCC Wagon | $1\pm\frac{1}{2}$ | $\frac{1}{2}\pm\frac{1}{2}$ | $0$ to $\frac{5}{64}$ ② | |
| **JAGUAR** XJ6 | | | | ① Toe-out. |
| Front | $2\frac{1}{4}\pm\frac{1}{4}$ | $\frac{1}{2}\pm\frac{1}{4}$ | $\frac{1}{16}$ to $\frac{1}{8}$ | |
| Rear | ..... | $-\frac{3}{4}\pm\frac{1}{4}$ | $0\pm\frac{1}{32}$ | |
| XJ12 & XJS | | | | |
| Front | $3\frac{1}{2}\pm\frac{1}{4}$ | $\frac{1}{2}\pm\frac{1}{4}$ | $0$ to $\frac{1}{16}$ ① | |
| Rear | ..... | $-\frac{3}{4}\pm\frac{1}{4}$ | $0\pm\frac{1}{32}$ | |
| **LANCIA** All Models | | | | ① Sedan is $-\frac{3}{4}\pm\frac{1}{3}$ |
| Front | $1\frac{1}{2}\pm\frac{1}{3}$ | $\frac{1}{2}\pm\frac{1}{3}$ | $\frac{3}{64}$ to $\frac{3}{32}$ | |
| Rear | ..... | $-\frac{7}{8}\pm\frac{3}{8}$ ① | $\frac{1}{64}$ to $\frac{5}{32}$ | |
| **LUV** All Models | $\frac{1}{2}\pm\frac{1}{2}$ | $\frac{1}{2}\pm\frac{1}{2}$ | $0$ to $\frac{1}{8}$ | |
| **MAZDA** | | | | ① With power steering $2\frac{1}{4}\pm\frac{3}{4}$. |
| RX4 | | | | |
| Sedan | $1\frac{5}{6}\pm\frac{3}{4}$ | $1\pm1$ | $0$ to $\frac{1}{4}$ | |
| Hardtop | $1\frac{5}{6}\pm\frac{3}{4}$ | $1\pm1$ | $0$ to $\frac{1}{4}$ | |
| Wagon | $1\frac{5}{6}\pm\frac{3}{4}$ | $1\frac{1}{4}\pm1$ | $0$ to $\frac{1}{4}$ | |
| Cosmo | $1\frac{5}{6}\pm\frac{3}{4}$ ① | $1\pm1$ | $0$ to $\frac{1}{4}$ | |
| GLC | $1\frac{7}{12}\pm\frac{3}{4}$ | $\frac{2}{3}\pm1$ | $0$ to $\frac{1}{4}$ | |
| B1800 | $1\pm\frac{1}{3}$ | $\frac{5}{6}\pm\frac{5}{12}$ | $0$ to $\frac{1}{4}$ | |
| **MERCEDES BENZ** | | | | |
| 230,240D,280E,300D | $8\frac{3}{4}\pm\frac{1}{2}$ | $0\pm\frac{1}{6}$ | $\frac{3}{32}$ to $\frac{5}{32}$ | |
| 280SE,450SEL | $10\pm\frac{1}{2}$ | $-\frac{1}{6}\pm\frac{1}{6}$ | $\frac{3}{32}$ to $\frac{5}{32}$ | |
| 450SL,450SLC | $3\frac{2}{3}\pm\frac{1}{3}$ | $-\frac{1}{2}\pm\frac{1}{4}$ | $\frac{5}{64}$ to $\frac{7}{64}$ | |
| 6.9 Sedan | $10\frac{1}{4}\pm\frac{1}{2}$ | $-\frac{1}{3}\pm\frac{1}{6}$ | $\frac{3}{32}$ to $\frac{5}{32}$ | |
| **MG** | | | | |
| Midget | $3$ | $\frac{3}{4}$ | $0$ to $\frac{1}{8}$ | |
| MGB | $6\frac{1}{8}\pm1\frac{1}{8}$ | $\frac{1}{2}\pm\frac{3}{4}$ | $\frac{1}{16}$ to $\frac{3}{32}$ | |

| WHEEL ALIGNMENT SPECIFICATIONS (Cont.) | | | | |
|---|---|---|---|---|
| Application | Caster (Degrees) | Camber (Degrees) | Toe-In (Inches) | Remarks |
| **OPEL** <br> All Models | $5 \pm 1$ | $0 \pm \frac{1}{2}$ | $\frac{5}{64}$ to $\frac{11}{64}$ | |
| **PEUGEOT** <br> 504 <br> Front <br> Rear <br><br> 604 <br> Front <br> Rear | <br><br> $2\frac{2}{3} \pm \frac{1}{2}$ <br> ..... <br><br><br> $3\frac{1}{2} \pm \frac{1}{2}$ <br> ..... | <br><br> $\frac{2}{3} \pm \frac{1}{2}$ <br> $-1 + \frac{2}{3}$ <br> $-\frac{1}{3}$ <br><br> $-\frac{1}{2} \pm \frac{3}{4}$ <br> $-\frac{1}{2} \pm \frac{1}{2}$ | <br><br> $\frac{1}{8} \pm \frac{1}{32}$ <br> $\frac{9}{64}$ <br><br><br> $\frac{1}{8} \pm \frac{1}{32}$ <br> $\frac{5}{64} + \frac{5}{64}$ <br> $-\frac{1}{32}$ | |
| **PORSCHE** <br> 911S <br> Front <br> Rear <br> Turbo-Carrera <br> Front <br> Rear <br> 924 <br> Front <br> Rear <br> 928 <br> Front <br> Rear | <br><br> $6\frac{1}{12} \pm \frac{1}{2}$ <br> ..... <br><br> $5\frac{1}{2} \pm \frac{1}{2}$ <br> ..... <br><br> $2\frac{3}{4} \pm \frac{1}{2}$ <br> ..... <br><br> $3\frac{1}{2} \pm \frac{1}{2}$ <br> ..... | <br><br> $\frac{1}{2} \pm \frac{1}{6}$ <br> $0 \pm \frac{1}{6}$ <br><br> $\frac{1}{2} \pm \frac{1}{6}$ <br> $0 \pm \frac{1}{6}$ <br><br> $-\frac{1}{3} \pm \frac{1}{4}$ <br> $-1 \pm \frac{1}{2}$ <br><br> $-\frac{1}{2} \pm \frac{1}{6}$ <br> $-\frac{2}{3} \pm \frac{1}{6}$ | <br><br> 0 <br> 0 to $\frac{1}{3}$① <br><br> 0 <br> $\frac{1}{3} \pm \frac{1}{3}$① <br><br> $-\frac{1}{4}$ to $+\frac{1}{12}$① <br> $-\frac{1}{6}$ to $\frac{1}{6}$① <br><br> $0 \pm \frac{1}{12}$① <br> $\frac{1}{6} \pm \frac{1}{12}$① | ① Toe-in given in degrees. |
| **RENAULT** <br> R-5 <br> Front <br> Rear | <br><br> $13\frac{1}{2} \pm \frac{1}{2}$ <br> ..... | <br><br> $\frac{1}{2} \pm \frac{1}{2}$ <br> $\frac{3}{4} \pm \frac{3}{4}$ | <br><br> $\frac{3}{64}$ to $\frac{3}{16}$① <br> $\frac{3}{64}$ to $\frac{1}{8}$ | ① Toe-out. |
| **SAAB** <br> All Models | $1 \pm \frac{1}{2}$ | $\frac{1}{2} \pm \frac{1}{2}$ | 0 to $\frac{3}{32}$① | ① With power steering $-\frac{3}{4}$ to $+\frac{3}{4}$; a toe-in to a toe-out range. |
| **SAPPORO** <br> All Models | $2\frac{2}{3} \pm \frac{1}{2}$ | $1\frac{1}{2} \pm \frac{1}{2}$ | $\frac{5}{64}$ to $\frac{23}{64}$ | |
| **SUBARU** <br> 1600 <br> Front <br> Rear <br> 4WD Station Wagon <br> Front <br> Rear <br> Brat <br> Front <br> Rear | <br><br> $-\frac{5}{6} \pm \frac{3}{4}$① <br> ..... <br><br> $-\frac{5}{6} \pm \frac{3}{4}$ <br> ..... <br><br> $-3\frac{1}{4} \pm 1\frac{2}{3}$ <br> ..... | <br><br> $1\frac{1}{2} \pm \frac{3}{4}$② <br> $\frac{1}{3} \pm \frac{3}{4}$③ <br><br> $2\frac{1}{6} \pm \frac{3}{4}$ <br> $1\frac{1}{3} \pm \frac{3}{4}$ <br><br> $1\frac{2}{3} \pm \frac{1}{4}$ <br> $1\frac{1}{3} \pm \frac{3}{4}$ | <br><br> $\frac{5}{64}$ to $\frac{5}{16}$ <br> $\frac{3}{64}$ to $\frac{13}{64}$④ <br><br> $\frac{15}{64}$ to $\frac{15}{32}$ <br> $\frac{5}{64}$ to $\frac{15}{64}$ <br><br> $\frac{15}{64}$ to $\frac{15}{32}$ <br> $\frac{5}{64}$ to $\frac{15}{64}$ | ① Wagon is $-\frac{1}{6} \pm \frac{3}{4}$ <br> ② Wagon is $1\frac{3}{4} \pm \frac{3}{4}$ <br> ③ Wagon is $1\frac{1}{6} \pm \frac{3}{4}$ <br> ④ Wagon is $\frac{5}{64}$ to $\frac{15}{64}$ |

| WHEEL ALIGNMENT SPECIFICATIONS (Cont.) | | | | |
|---|---|---|---|---|
| Application | Caster (Degrees) | Camber (Degrees) | Toe-In (Inches) | Remarks |
| **TOYOTA** | | | | ① Radial tires; $5/64$ to $3/32$" with bias tires. |
| Corolla 1100 cc | $1 5/6 \pm 1/2$ | $1 \pm 1/2$ | 0 to $5/64$ ① | |
| Corolla 1600 cc | $1 5/6 \pm 1/2$ | $1 \pm 1/2$ | 0 to $5/64$ | ② Radial tires; $1/8$ to $13/64$" with bias tires. |
| Corona | $1 5/6 \pm 1/2$ | $1 \pm 1/12$ | $3/64$ to $1/8$ ② | |
| Celica | $1 3/4 \pm 1/2$ | $1 \pm 1/2$ | 0 to $5/64$ | |
| Cressida | $1 1/4 \pm 1/2$ | $5/6 \pm 1/2$ | $5/64$ to $5/32$ | |
| Hi-Lux | $1/2 \pm 1/2$ | $1 \pm 1/2$ | $13/64$ to $11/64$ | |
| Land Cruiser | 1 | 1 | $1/8$ to $13/64$ | |
| **TRIUMPH** | | | | |
| Spitfire | | | | |
| Front | $4 1/2 \pm 1/2$ | $2 \pm 1/2$ | 0 to $1/16$ | |
| Rear | ..... | $-3 3/4 \pm 1/2$ | 0 to $1/16$ | |
| TR7 | $3 1/2 \pm 1$ | $-1/4 \pm 1$ | 0 to $1/16$ | |
| **VOLKSWAGEN** | | | | ① Toe-in given in degrees. Some models give a toe-in to a toe-out range. |
| Type 1 | | | | |
| Front | $2 \pm 1/12$ | $5/6 \pm 1/2$ | $1/4$ to $3/4$ ° ① | |
| Rear | ----- | $-1 \pm 2/3$ | $-1/4$ to $+1/4$ ° ① | |
| Type 2 | | | | |
| Front | $3 \pm 2/3$ | $2/3 \pm 1/3$ | 0 to $1/2$ ° ① | |
| Rear | ----- | $-5/6 \pm 1/2$ | $-1/6$ to $+1/2$ ° ① | |
| Dasher | | | | |
| Front | $1 5/6 \pm 1/2$ | $1/3 \pm 1/2$ | $-1/12$ to $+5/12$ ° ① | |
| Rear | ----- | $-1/2 \pm 1/2$ | $-5/6$ to $+5/6$ ° ① | |
| Rabbit/Scirocco | | | | |
| Front | $1 5/6 \pm 1/2$ | $+1/3 \pm 1/2$ | $-1/2$ to $+1/12$ ° ① | |
| Rear | ----- | $-1 1/4 \pm 5/6$ | $-1/6$ to $+5/6$ ° ① | |
| **VOLVO** | | | | ① 240 without power steering; $1/4 \pm 1/6$ for 240 with power steering and 260 series. |
| All Models | $2 1/2 \pm 1/2$ | $1 1/4 \pm 1/4$ | $1/3 \pm 1/6$ ① | |

## ARROW, CHALLENGER, COLT & SAPPORO

## ADJUSTMENT

### TIRE INFLATION (COLD)

Before attempting to check or adjust wheel alignment, ensure that tires are properly inflated. Refer to specifications in owners handbook for proper inflation procedures.

### CASTER

Generally caster is stated as nonadjustable, and that if not within specifications parts are to be replaced. However, in some instances when slight adjustment will alleviate the problem, adjustment of strut bar nut is permitted. If caster is altered, wheel base must stay within approximately 92.1" (Arrow and Colt; Exc. Colt Wagon) or approximately 99" (all others).

### CAMBER

Camber is nonadjustable. If not within specifications, check front suspension for damage. Repair or replace parts as necessary.

### TOE-IN

Position wheels in straight-ahead position. If toe-in is not within specifications, loosen locking nuts on tie rod turn buckles. Rotate buckles until toe-in is within specifications. Tighten lock nuts.

**NOTE** — Adjustment must be made equally to both sides of vehicle. Equal adjustment maintains correct wheel lock angles. Difference between adjusted tie rod lengths should not exceed .20" (5.1 mm).

## AUDI

## ADJUSTMENT

### TIRE INFLATION (COLD)

Before attempting to check and adjust wheel alignment, ensure tires are properly inflated. 5000 models require 27 psi for front and rear tires under normal conditions and 27 psi for front and 31 psi for rear under maximum load conditions. Fox models require 27 psi for front and rear tires under normal conditions and 30 psi for front and rear tires under maximum load conditions.

### CASTER

Caster angle is not adjustable. If caster is not within specifications, check suspension components for excessive wear or damage. Replace components as necessary to bring caster into specifications.

### CAMBER

**Fox** — With vehicle loaded down or placed on blocks, measure camber angle. If not to specifications, loosen ball joint nuts and attach tool US 4471 (or equivalent). Tighten tool nut to break loose joint from control arm.

**NOTE** — When tool nut is loosened weight of vehicle will move wheel to negative camber. After adjustment retorque ball joint nuts to 47 ft. lbs. (6.5 mkg).

**5000** — Work under hood and loosen the 3 upper strut mounting nuts. Place a socket over suspension strut nut. Move strut around in slots until camber is correct. Tighten nuts. Recheck camber after nuts are tight.

Tool US 4471

**Fig. 1  Camber Adjusting Tool for Audi Fox**

### TOE-IN

Loosen adjustable tie rod lock nuts (5000) or clamp and lock nut (Fox). Rotate threaded collar (5000) or rod (Fox) until toe-in is within specifications. Tighten locking components. If necessary, remove steering wheel and reposition so wheel spokes are horizontal when front wheels point straight ahead.

## BMW

### ADJUSTMENT

#### TIRE INFLATION (COLD)

Before attempting to check or adjust wheel alignment, ensure tires are properly inflated. The 320i series requires 27 psi front and rear. The 530i series requires 28 psi front and 26 psi rear.

The 633CSi series require 33 psi in front tires and 31 psi in rear tires. The 733i models require 32 psi in front and rear tires.

#### CASTER & CAMBER

**All Models** — Before checking caster and camber, vehicle must be in loaded condition. Refer to table for correct loading of vehicle. If caster or camber are not within specifications, check suspension components for damage.

### Vehicle Loading Table

| Application | ①Lbs. (kg) |
| --- | --- |
| Each Front Seat | 150 (68) |
| Rear Seat | 150 (68) |
| Luggage Compartment | 46 (21) |

① — Fuel tank full.

#### TOE-IN

**All Models** — Before checking toe-in, vehicle must be in loaded condition (see Caster & Camber). Check toe-in with front wheels in straight ahead position. If not within specifications, loosen tie rod clamping bolts. Rotate both tie rod tubes until toe-in is within specifications. Tighten clamping bolts.

## CAPRI

### ADJUSTMENT

#### TIRE INFLATION (COLD)

Before attempting to check or adjust wheel alignment, make sure that tires are properly inflated. Refer to manufacturers specifications, located inside glove box door.

#### CASTER

**All Models** — Caster is nonadjustable. If not within specifications, check front suspension for damage. Repair or replace parts as necessary.

#### CAMBER

**All Models** — Camber is nonadjustable. If not within specifications, check front suspension for damage. Repair or replace parts as necessary.

#### TOE-IN

**All Models** — Position wheels in straight-ahead position and loosen tie rod end lock nut and clips securing bellows. To adjust toe-in, rotate tie rods until specifications are within limits. Tighten lock nuts and secure clips. Tie rods lengths should be equal within 1/4".

## COURIER

### ADJUSTMENT

#### TIRE INFLATION

Before attempting caster or camber adjustments, ensure tires are correctly inflated. Specifications are located on glove box door; especially consider radial tires, they require a different pressure than conventional tires.

**NOTE** — *Vehicle must be unloaded, except fuel, water, and oil should be at their proper levels.*

#### CASTER

To correct caster, adjust shims between upper control arm and frame or turn control arm shaft until correct angle is obtained (see specifications).

#### CAMBER

The camber is adjusted by adding or subtracting shims between the upper control arm and frame. Shims are available in the following sizes: .039", .063", .079", and .126". Set camber to specifications as shown in chart.

#### TOE-IN

1) Raise vehicle until front wheels clear ground. Turn wheel by hand and scribe a line in center of each tire tread. Measure distance between marked lines in front of front wheel and at rear of front wheel. Both measurements must be taken at equal distances from ground.

2) If distance between wheels at rear is greater than that at front, but within specifications, adjustment is correct. If adjustment is wrong, loosen clamp bolts and adjust tie rod to specifications.

**NOTE** — *Tighten clamping bolts with bolts horizontal and below steering link to prevent interference with center steering link.*

## DATSUN

## ADJUSTMENT

### TIRE INFLATION (COLD)

Before attempting to check or adjust wheel alignment, make sure that tires are properly inflated. Refer to manufacturer's specifications given in owner's manual.

### RIDING HEIGHT

**Pickup** — Make measurement illustrated in *Fig. 1* with vehicle in unladen state. If measured specification does not agree with one shown in illustration, adjustment will be necessary.
* Raise vehicle and place on safety stands.
* Loosen lock nut and turn anchor bolt adjusting nut to obtain specified dimension.

*Fig. 1  Riding Height Measurement and Adjustment Locations*

### CASTER

**All Models Exc. Pickup** — Preset at factory and cannot be adjusted. If not to specifications, check suspension for wear or damage and repair or replace components as necessary.

**Pickup** — Caster is adjusted by increasing or decreasing thickness of shims inserted between upper link spindle and upper link mounting bracket. When front shim thickness increases, caster decreases.

**NOTE** — *Total thickness of shims must be within .236" (6.0 mm) and must not collectively total more than 3 individual shims. Difference of total thickness between front and rear must be within .079" (2.0 mm).*

### CAMBER

**All Models (Exc. Pickup)** — Preset at factory and cannot be adjusted. If not to specifications, check suspension for wear or damage and repair or replace components as necessary.

**Pickup** — Camber is adjusted by increasing or decreasing the thickness of shims inserted between upper link spindle and upper link mounting bracket. Adding thicker shims to front and rear decreases camber 3'. When rear shim is .039" (1.0 mm) thicker than front one, camber decreases 7'.

### TOE-IN

**280Z** — Working under vehicle, loosen side rod lock nut. Adjust side rod so distance between extreme edges of lock nuts is 1.49" (37.9 mm). Both sides should be equally adjusted.

**810** — Place front wheel facing straight ahead. Ensure steering gear faces same direction. Adjust side rod (tie rod) so that steering gear side has a distance of 14.35" (364.5 mm) between ball joints. Adjust idler arm side so distance between ball joints is 14.19" (360.5 mm). Tighten clamp bolts after adjustment.

**Pickup** — Adjust by loosening steering cross link lock nuts, and adjusting steering cross link to change toe-in. Tighten lock nuts.

**All Others** — Place wheels in straight-ahead position, then make sure steering spokes are horizontal. Adjust toe-in by varying the length of steering side rods (tie rods). Loosen lock nuts and rotate rods evenly until toe-in is within specifications.

| Application | Normal Distance Between Lock Nuts | Normal Distance Between Ball Joints |
| --- | --- | --- |
| 510 | 5.0" (127 mm) | ..... |
| B210 | 4.0" (102 mm) | ..... |
| 200SX | 4.0" (102 mm) | 12.05" (306 mm) |

Specifications for F10 not available.

## FIAT

### ADJUSTMENT

#### TIRE INFLATION (COLD)

Before attempting to check or adjust wheel alignment, make sure tires are properly inflated. Refer to manufacturers specifications given in owner's manual.

#### CASTER

**Model 128 & 131 (Except 128 3P)** — If caster is not to specifications, raise front of vehicle. Remove stabilizer bar-to-control arm nut and disconnect control arm from body. Remove end of stabilizer bar from control arm. To adjust caster, addition of shims between end of stabilizer bar and rubber pad of control arm will decrease caster angle and removal of shims will increase caster angle. Reverse removal procedure and recheck caster.

**Model 124** — If caster is not within specifications, raise front of vehicle and remove wheel and shock absorber. Using suitable tool (A.74174), compress spring to relieve lower control arm and loosen nuts holding control arm pivot bar to crossmember. To adjust caster, remove shims from front stud and move to rear stud to increase caster. To decrease caster, remove shims from rear stud and move shims to front stud. Reverse removal procedure and check caster.

**Model X1/9** — If caster is not to specifications, adjust by adding or removing shims located between stabilizer bar and stabilizer bar support.

#### CAMBER

**Model 124** — If camber is not within specifications, adjust by changing shims. Raise front of vehicle, remove wheel and shock absorber. Using suitable tool (A.74174), compress spring to relieve lower control arm and loosen nuts holding control arm pivot bar to crossmember. To increase camber, remove equal amount of shims from both studs and add equal amount of shims to decrease camber. **NOTE** — *Adding or removing equal amounts of shims will not affect caster.* Reverse removal procedure and check camber.

**Model 128 & 131 Front** — Camber is nonadjustable. If not within specifications, inspect suspension for damage and repair or replace parts as necessary.

**Model 128 Rear** — If rear camber is not within specifications raise rear of vehicle and compress one end of leaf spring, shifting it from flexible guide anchoring spring to control arm. Remove guide and slowly release spring. Remove nuts attaching pivot to body and loosen screw to free adjustment shims. To increase camber, add an equal number of shims on both screws attaching control arm to body. To decrease, remove equal number of shims from both screws. Reverse removal procedure and check camber.

**Model X1/9 Front & Rear** — Camber is nonadjustable. If not within specifications, inspect suspension for damage and repair or replace parts as necessary.

#### TOE-IN

**Model 124 Front** — Place front wheels in straight-ahead position. If toe-in is not within specifications, loosen four clamps securing sleeves on tie rods. Rotate tie rods in opposite direction (by equal amounts) to set toe-in to specifications. Tighten clamp nuts. **NOTE** — *Expansion slot in sleeve must coincide with clamp joint when clamp is fully tightened.*

**Model 128, 131 & X1/9 Front** — Place front wheels in straight-ahead position. If toe-in is not within specifications, loosen sleeve locking nut on tie rods. To adjust, rotate hexagon on ball pin to set toe-in to specifications. Hold hexagon in position and lock nut against tie rod sleeve.

**Model 128 Rear** — If rear toe-in is not within specifications raise rear of vehicle and compress one end of leaf spring, shifting it from flexible guide anchoring spring to control arm. Remove guide and slowly release spring. Remove nuts attaching pivot to body and loosen screws to free adjustment shims. To increase toe-in, add shims to rear screw or remove shims from front screw. To decrease, add shims to front screw or remove shims from rear screw.

**Model X1/9 Rear** — If rear wheel toe-in is not within specifications, loosen clamps securing sleeves to reaction rods. Adjust toe-in by lengthening or shortening reaction rods. Tighten clamps and recheck toe-in.

## FIESTA

### ADJUSTMENT

#### TIRE INFLATION (COLD)

Before attempting to check and adjust wheel alignment, make sure tires are properly inflated. Refer to manufacturer's specifications given in owner's manual.

#### CASTER

Caster is not adjustable. If caster is not to specifications, inspect suspension system for wear or damage and repair or replace components as necessary.

#### CAMBER

Camber is not adjustable. If camber is not to specifications, inspect suspension system for wear or damage and repair or replace components as necessary.

#### TOE-IN

Loosen lock nuts on outer ends of tie rods. Lock nuts are located next to ball joints. Loosen clamps on outer ends of steering gear bellows. Adjust both tie rods equal amounts until toe-in is within specifications. Tighten lock nuts. Install new clips to outer ends of bellows.

# Wheel Alignment

## HONDA

### ADJUSTMENT

#### TIRE INFLATION (COLD)

Before checking or adjusting wheel alignment, make sure tires are correctly inflated. Refer to manufacturers specifications located in glove box.

#### RIDING HEIGHT

Make sure tires are properly inflated.Measure from bottom of side marker lamps to ground. If height measurement is not within specifications, check rear height before attempting to repair front suspension.

**Riding Height Specifications**

| Application | Front | Rear |
|---|---|---|
| Civic | 25.98" | 23.03" |
| | (660 mm) | (585 mm) |
| CVCC | | |
| Sedan | 24.2" | 20.7" |
| | (615 mm) | (525 mm) |
| Station Wgn. | 24.2" | 22.9" |
| | (615 mm) | (583 mm) |
| Accord | 24.0" | 25.4" |
| | (610 mm) | (645 mm) |

**NOTE** — *CVCC and Accord specifications are service limit specifications.*

### CASTER

Caster is nonadjustable. If alignment is not within specifications, inspect for damaged parts and replace as necessary.

### CAMBER

Camber is nonadjustable. If alignment is not within specifications, inspect for damaged parts and replace as necessary.

### TOE-OUT

**Front, CVCC and Accord** — Loosen lock nuts at each end of tie rods. Turn tie rod until toe-out is within specifications. Use same procedure for both sides. To center steering wheel after toe has been adjusted, turn both tie rods in same direction until steering wheel (spokes) are centered. Tighten lock nuts.

### TOE-IN

**Rear, CVCC and Accord** — To adjust toe-in, loosen nuts on radius rods. Rotate radius rods until toe-in is within specifications, then tighten lock nuts. **NOTE** — *Each notch on cam plate is equal to 5/64" movement.*

## JAGUAR

### ADJUSTMENT

#### TIRE INFLATION (COLD)

Before attempting to check or adjust wheel alignment, make sure tires are properly inflated. Refer to owner's manual for manufacturer's specifications.

#### RIDING HEIGHT

**All Models (Front)** — **1)** Check that vehicle is full of fuel, oil, and water, and that tires are properly inflated. Press down on front bumper and slowly release, then lift up on bumper and slowly release, this will settle front suspension.

**2)** On XJ6 and XJ12 models, measure distance between center of outer headlight and ground on both sides of vehicle. Height should be 24.6" (611 mm) minimum.

**3)** On XJS models, measure distance between lower face of crossmember and ground on both sides. Height should be 6.0" (152 mm) minimum, plus thickness of slip plates.

**4)** On all models, adjust by installing or removing spring spacers from front coil springs. **NOTE** — *Spring spacers are 1/8" (3.2 mm) thick and will change riding height approximately 5/16" (7.9 mm).*

**All Models (Rear)** — Check that vehicle is full of gasoline, water and oil, and that tires are properly inflated. Roll vehicle forward three car lenghts to settle suspension system. Measure distance between lower surface of rear crossmember and ground on both sides of vehicle. Correct height should be 7.45±.25 (189±6 mm). If height is correct, it will be unnecessary to proceed further, however if height is incorrect, all four rear springs will need to be replaced.

### PREPARATION FOR CASTER & CAMBER ADJUSTMENT

**1)** Ensure vehicle is on level ground and that tires are properly inflated. Before checking or adjusting caster or camber it will be necessary to fabricate two setting tools *(See Fig. 1).*

**2)** Compress front suspension and insert tools under upper control arms, adjacent to control arm rubber stops and over brackets welded to bottom of control arms.

# Wheel Alignment

## JAGUAR (Cont.)

**Fig. 1  Dimensions for Fabricating the Two Necessary Setting Tools**

3) Compress rear suspension and install suitable suspension setting links (J. 25), to lock rear suspension in place *(See Fig. 2)*. Vehicle is now locked in half-loaded condition and caster and camber can be checked and adjusted.

**Fig. 2  Rear Suspension in Locked Position with Special Tool**

## CASTER

**NOTE** — *Before adjusting caster angle, make sure car is standing at normal riding height.*

**All Models** — If caster angle is not within specifications, adjust by moving shims on front and rear of upper control arm ball joint. To increase caster, loosen bolts securing upper ball joint and move shims from rear of ball joint to front of ball joint. To decrease caster, reverse procedure. Tighten ball joint attaching bolts and recheck caster angle.

## CAMBER

**NOTE** — *Before attempting to check or adjust camber angle it will be necessary to make sure that vehicle is in half-loaded condition.*

**All Models (Front)** — Place wheels in straight-ahead position. Measure camber angle. Make sure front wheels are within $\frac{1}{4}°$ of each other. Adjustment is accomplished by adding or subtracting shims. *See Fig. 3.* Adding shims increases camber angle. Make sure same number of shims are used on each bolt.

**Fig. 3  Shim Placement for Front Camber Angle Adjustment**

**All Models (Rear)** — Before checking rear wheel camber, rear suspension must be in the half-loaded position. **See**

**Fig. 4  Placement of Shims for Rear Camber Angle Adjustment**

## JAGUAR (Cont.)

*Preparation for Caster & Camber Adjustment.* To adjust, remove suspension setting links (JD.25), raise and support rear of vehicle and remove wheels. Loosen nuts securing half-shaft to brake disc, then add or remove shims as reqired to bring camber angle within specifications.

**NOTE** — *Addition of one .020" (.5 mm) shim will alter camber ¼ °.*

## ADJUSTMENT

### TIRE INFLATION

Before checking or adjusting wheel alignment, ensure tires are correctly inflated. Refer to manufacturers specifications located in glove box or on right hand door jam.

### RIDING HEIGHT

1) Place vehicle on smooth level surface. Bounce vehicle several times. Raise vehicle and allow to settle at normal height. Measure distance as shown in *Fig. 1 and 2.*

**Fig. 1    Rear Suspension Riding Height Measuring Point**

**Fig. 2    Front Suspension Riding Height Measuring Point**

**NOTE** — *Height check should be made with a full tank of gas, spare tire installed, and jack included. No passengers should be in vehicle.*

### TOE-IN

**All Models** — Place vehicle in straight-ahead position. Remove grease nipple from rack adjuster nut. Put centralizing tool 12279 (or equivalent) into locating hole. Push tool on to back of rack bar. Slowly turn steering wheel until tool drops into back of rack bar. Measure toe-in. If toe-in is not within specifications, adjust by loosening steering link lock nuts and rotating adjuster sleeves equal amounts, as necessary. Tighten lock nuts and recheck toe-in.

## LUV

2) Difference between measurements of each side must not be more than 1/2". If an adjustment is necessary, it can be made at bolt on height control arm.

### Riding Height Specifications

| Application | Front | Rear |
|---|---|---|
| LUV | 4.6" | 6.0" |
| | (116.8 mm) | (152.4 mm) |

### TORSION BAR SPRING

1) Park vehicle on level surface. Jounce vehicle several times and allow to return to settled position.

2) Measure buffer clearance between rubber bumper and lower control arm. Using bolt located on height control arm, adjust buffer clearance to about .866" (22 mm).

**NOTE** — *Rotating bolt inward increases vehicle height.*

### CASTER

Adjustment is made with shims inserted between upper control arm pivot shaft and frame. Adding or subtracting shims from either front or rear bolts will effect a change in caster. Shims may be transfered from front to rear or from rear to front. Transfer of one shim from front bolt to rear bolt will decrease positive caster. For correct specifications, refer to table.

### CAMBER

Camber is adjusted by adding or subtracting shims. Adding an equal number of shims at both front and rear of pivot shaft will decrease positive camber. For correct specifications, refer to table.

### TOE-IN

**NOTE** — *Toe-in must be adjusted after caster and camber adjustment.*

Toe-in can be adjusted by rotating the intermediate rod after loosening lock nuts. Rotating intermediate rod towards front of vehicle reduces toe-in and towards rear of vehicle increases toe-in. For correct specifications, refer to specifications table.

# Wheel Alignment

## MAZDA

### ADJUSTMENT

#### TIRE INFLATION (COLD)

Before attempting to check or adjust wheel alignment, make sure tires are properly inflated. Refer to manufacturer's specifications given in owner's manual.

#### CASTER

**GLC** — Caster is not adjustable. If caster is not to specifications, inspect suspension for excessive wear or damage. Replace components as necessary.

**RX4 and Cosmo** — Caster and camber angles are adjusted by changing position of shock absorber support. To adjust, remove four nuts attaching shock absorber support to fender apron. Raise front of vehicle and support with jack stands, then remove wheel on side to be adjusted.

2) Press shock absorber downward and change position of support according to table and *Fig. 1*. Tighten shock absorber support mounting nuts. Install wheel, lower vehicle and recheck caster and camber.

| Caster and Camber Adjustment | | | |
|---|---|---|---|
| Adjustment | | Variation | |
| | Shock Absorber Support | Caster | Camber |
| A | 0 | 0 | 0 |
| B | 90° | ½° | 0 |
| C | 180° | ½° | ½° |
| D | -90° | 0 | ½° |

**Pickup** — To adjust, change shims between upper arm shaft and support bracket or turn upper arm shaft until specifications are obtained.

#### CAMBER

**GLC** — Camber is not adjustable. If caster is not to specifications, inspect suspension for excessive wear or damage. Replace components as necessary.

**RX4 and Cosmo** — *See procedure given under Caster adjustment.*

**Pickup** — To adjust, change shims between upper arm shaft and support bracket until specifications for camber are within limits.

*Fig. 1  RX4 & Cosmo Caster and Camber Adjusting Pad (Position "B" Shown)*

#### TOE-IN

**All Models** — 1) Raise front of vehicle. Turn wheels by hand and mark a line in center of each tire tred. Place vehicle in straight-ahead position and lower vehicle to ground.

2) Measure distance between marked lines at both front and rear of wheel. Make sure measurements are made equal distances from ground. Distance at rear of wheel should be .24" (6 mm) more than that at front wheels. Loosen lock nuts and turn tie rods until adjustment is correct.

## MERCEDES-BENZ

### ADJUSTMENT

#### TIRE INFLATION (COLD)

Before attempting to check or adjust wheel alignment, make sure tires are properly inflated. Refer to manufacturers specifications given in owner's manual.

#### CASTER

**All Models (Front)** — Test under loaded condition. Load vehicle with two 143 lb. weights on rear seat and full tank of gasoline. If caster is not to specifications, loosen lock nut on eccentric bolt on front side of lower control arm. To adjust, rotate eccentric bolt until caster angle is to specifications. Hold eccentric bolt in place and tighten lock nut.

#### CAMBER

**All Models (Front)** — Test under loaded condition. Load vehicle with two 143 lb. weights on front seat, one 143 lb. weight on rear seat and full tank of gasoline. If camber is not to specifications, loosen lock nut of eccentric bolt on rear side of lower control arm. To adjust, rotate eccentric bolt until camber is within specifications. Hold eccentric bolt in place and tighten lock nut.

#### TOE-IN

**All Models (Front)** — Place wheels in straight-ahead position. If toe-in is not within specifications, adjust by loosening lock nuts on outer steering links and rotating links to obtain specified toe-in. Make sure steering links are adjusted equally.

## MG

### ADJUSTMENT

#### TIRE INFLATION (COLD)

Before attempting to check or adjust wheel alignment, make sure tires are properly inflated. Refer to manufacturers specifications given in owner's manual.

**NOTE** — *All checks must be made with vehicle unloaded, tires properly inflated and steering wheel in straight-ahead position. Before making checks, ensure suspension components are in good condition. If necessary, repair damaged components before making wheel alignment checks.*

#### CASTER

**All Models** — Caster is nonadjustable. If alignment not within specifications, inspect for damaged suspension parts and repair or replace as necessary.

#### CAMBER

**All Models** — Camber is not adjustable. If alignment is not within specifications, inspect suspension parts for wear or damage and repair or replace components as necessary.

#### TOE-IN

**All Models** — Turn front wheels to straight-ahead position and check toe-in measurement. Move vehicle ahead so front wheels rotate 180° and take second reading. Take average of two readings to check toe-in. If not within specifications, loosen lock nut for each tie rod and loosen clips securing rubber gaiters to tie rods. To adjust, rotate both tie rods equally to set toe-in to specifications. **NOTE** — *Tie rods must be equal lengths.* Tighten lock nuts and clips on tie rods.

## OPEL

### ADJUSTMENT

#### TIRE INFLATION (COLD)

Before attempting to check or adjust wheel alignment, make sure tires are properly inflated. Refer to manufacturer's specifications given in owner's manual.

#### CASTER

1) If caster is not within specifications, adjust by changing washers on upper control arm shaft. Raise vehicle and place jack stands under lower control arms. Remove wheel on side which requires caster adjustment.

**NOTE** — *The replacement of washers requires the same diameter as those being changed and a combination such that the total thickness of front and rear equals 12 mm. If specifications are not achieved, frame alignment is required.*

2) Loosen hex. nut from upper control arm shaft and remove shaft. Adjust caster by replacing washers on control arm shaft. Put smaller washer on leg nearest front of vehicle.

#### CAMBER

Raise front of vehicle and place jack stands below lower control arms. Remove wheel on side to be adjusted. Remove ball joint from upper control arm and front steering knuckle. To adjust camber, lift upper control arm and rotate ball joint flange 180°. **NOTE** — *Only two adjustments are possible. Rotating ball joint flange will make camber more negative.*

#### TOE-IN

1) Position front wheel in straight-ahead position. Remove clamp on tie rod bellows and push bellows back. Loosen tie rod clamping bolts. To adjust, rotate tie rod sleeves equally to obtain specified toe-in. **NOTE** — *Never grip tie rod on inner ball joint stud.*

2) Pull bellows over tie rods and secure wire clamps. Bellows must not be twisted and wire ends showing towards steering gear adjusting screw opening. Tighten clamp bolts. Rotate wheel back and forth several times to check bellows for correct attachment to tie rods.

## PORSCHE

### ADJUSTMENT

#### TIRE INFLATION (COLD)

Before attempting to check or adjust wheel alignment, make sure tires are properly inflated. Refer to manufacturer's specifications given in owner's manual.

#### RIDING HEIGHT

**NOTE** — *Riding height should be set with fuel tank full and spare tire included.*

**911 (Front)** — 1) Checking or adjusting riding height can only be performed with vehicle on level surface. Mark center of front wheel hub cap (grease retainer cup). Jounce vehicle several times to settle suspension. Measure distance "A" shown in *Fig. 1.* Measure distance "B" in same figure. Difference between measurements should be as shown in table.

2) If necessary, loosen or tighten torsion bar adjusting bolt until correct height is obtained. Jounce vehicle several times and recheck height. Make sure difference between right and left side measurements does not exceed .20" (5 mm).

# Wheel Alignment

### Riding Height Specifications①

| Application | Front | Rear |
|---|---|---|
| 911/SC | 4.25±.20" | .468±.20" |
| | (108±5 mm) | (12±5 mm) |
| Turbo | 3.3±.20" | 1.5±.20" |
| | (84.5±5 mm) | (37±5 mm) |

① — Measurement is difference between "A" and "B".

**Fig. 1  Front Suspension Riding Height Measuring Points**

**Fig. 2  Porsche 911/SC Rear Suspension Riding Height Measuring Points and Dimensions**

**911 Series (Rear)** — Checking or adjusting riding height can only be performed with vehicle on level surface. Mark center of rear wheel. Bounce vehicle several times to settle suspension. Measure distance "a" as shown in illustration. Distance "a" plus .468" (12 mm) equals "b"; however, distance "b" is difficult to measure because the torsion bar is mounted off center in its rubber bushing. Therefore it is necessary to measure distance "b1" and add .585" (14.8 mm), radius of bushing. This total should be equal to "b". After calculating "b", difference between "a" and "b" should be .468"±.20" (12±5mm). Difference in height from left to right should not exceed .197" (5 mm). If values are not within specifications, check front height and rear torsion bar adjustment. Correct as required.

**NOTE** — If spring plate angle is 19° (with stabilizer bar) or 23° 40' (without stabilizer bar), vehicle height will be correct.

**924 (Rear)** — Rear height is adjusted at 2-piece spring plate; spring plate removal is not required. Loosen mounting bolt (Fig. 3) and adjust vehicle height with eccentric bolt. Height should be .315" ±.004" (8 mm ±.10 mm) when measured from torsion bar center to center of wheel.

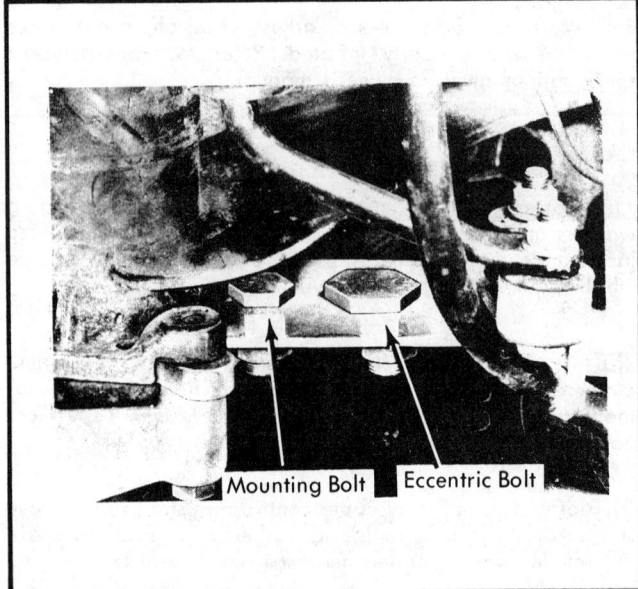

Mounting Bolt    Eccentric Bolt

**Fig. 3  Location of 924 Rear Riding Height Adjusting bolt**

**928 (Front)** — Park vehicle on level ground. Place wheels in straight-ahead position. Measure distance from boss (on forward underside of lower control arm) to ground. Distance should be about 7.48" (190 mm). Height is determined by coil spring and is not adjustable at front axle.

**928 (Rear)** — Park vehicle on level ground. Place front wheels to face straight ahead. Measure distance from boss located on

## PORSCHE (Cont.)

underside of lower control arm (inner arm) mounting bracket to ground. Distance should be about 7.20″ (183 mm).

- To adjust vehicle upward turn coil spring adjusting nut (located at under side of lower spring retainer) clockwise.
- Rear height must be adjusted to match front height. EXAMPLE: If front height is .394″ (10 mm) too high, rear height must be raised .394″ (10 mm).

### CASTER

**911 Series & Turbo Carrera** — If caster angle is not to specifications, it will be necessary to remove adjuster plate which attaches to front shock absorber. Remove enough front compartment carpet to allow access to top of each shock absorber. Mark position of each movable plate, located below each Allen screw. Loosen each screw and upper shock absorber nut. Move assembly lengthwise to obtain correct caster angle. Tighten all three screws and shock absorber nut.

**924** — Adjust caster by moving the rear of suspension control arm form side-to-side. See Fig. 4.

**Fig. 4   924 Caster Adjustment Location**

**928** — Caster is adjusted at eccentric located on lower control arm. To adjust caster, use eccentric closest to brake disc.

### CAMBER

**911 Series & Turbo Carrera (Front)** — If camber angle is not to specifications, it will be necessary to move adjuster plate which attaches to front shock absorber. Remove enough carpet to allow access to top of each shock absorber. Mark position of each movable plate located below each Allen screw. Loosen each screw and upper shock absorber nut. Move assembly from side to side-to-obtain correct camber angle. Tighten all three screws and shock absorber nut.

**911 Series (Rear)** — In order to obtain correct camber value at rear wheels, it is necessary that rear torsion bars be adjusted first. See Torsion Bar Adjustment. Now, loosen nuts on retaining bolts and on eccentric bolt at rear axle flange. Turn camber eccentric until camber angle is within specifications. Tighten retaining nuts and eccentric bolt nuts.

**924 (Front)** — Adjust camber by turning eccentric bolt shown in Fig. 5.

**924 (Rear)** — Loosen bolts between spring plate and diagonal arm flange. Bring camber to specification by turning eccentric.

**Fig. 5   924 Camber Eccentric Bolt Location**

**928 (Front)** — Camber is adjusted at eccentric located on lower control arm. To adjust camber, use eccentric furtherest away from brake disc.

**928 (Rear)** — Make camber adjustments at eccentric bolt located on inner control arm bushing.

**Fig. 6   911 Rear Camber Adjustment Points**

### TOE-IN

**All Models (Front)** — Place front wheels in straight-ahead position. Adjust left and right steering links (tie rods) equally to obtain specified setting. Coat each steering link with anti-corrosive compound after adjustment.

## PORSCHE (Cont.)

**911 Series (Rear)** — To adjust rear wheel toe-in, loosen nuts on retaining bolts and adjusting eccentrics at rear axle flange. Turn toe-in eccentric until toe-in is set to specifications. Hold eccentric stationary and tighten all lock nuts.

**924 (Rear)** — Adjust toe-in by repositioning control arm flange in slots of spring plate. Use of special tool 1979 is suggested.

**928 (Rear)** — Rear to adjustments are made at eccentric bolt located on front control arm bushing.

### TORSION BAR ADJUSTMENT

**911 Series (Rear)** — Place torsion bar into transverse tube with inner end splines first. Slip radius arm onto outer end splines of torsion bar. Place suitable leveling tool (VW 261) on lower edge of door opening and adjust level so bubble is in center of glass. Check adjustment (degrees) of free hanging radius arm with same leveling tool. If not to specifications, adjust by turning torsion bar and radius arm in opposite directions. Adjustment of both radius arms must each equal 36°45′±15′.

## RENAULT

### ADJUSTMENT

#### TIRE INFLATION (COLD)

Before attempting to check or adjust wheel alignment, make sure tires are properly inflated. Refer to manufacturers specifications given in owner's manual.

*Fig. 1   Riding Height Measurement Points*

#### CASTER

**R-5 — 1)** Vehicle riding height must be calculated before adjusting caster. Measure distance between ground and rear side member (H5, *Fig. 1*). Measure distance between ground and front side member in line with wheel centers (H2, *Fig. 1*). Subtract measurements and refer to table for correct caster angle.

**2)** With caster angle determined, loosen both lower control arm mounting bolts. Add or remove caster shims to bring adjustment within specifications. One shim is equal to about 1°.

**NOTE** — *Never use more than two shims between bushing and side member. Always check steering box height after adjustment.*

#### Caster Angle Table

| Subtracted Value | Caster Angle |
|---|---|
| 1⁹⁄₁₆″ (40 mm) | 12½° |
| 2³⁄₈″ (60 mm) | 12° |
| 3⅛″ (80 mm) | 11½° |
| 3¹⁵⁄₁₆″ (100 mm) | 11° |
| 4¾″ (120 mm) | 10½° |
| 5½″ (140 mm) | 10° |

#### CAMBER

Camber angle is not adjustable. If not within specifications, inspect front suspension for wear or damage and repair or replace components as necessary.

#### TOE-IN

If toe-in is not to specifications, disconnect steering arm at rack end. Loosen lock nut on steering end fitting. To increase toe-in, unscrew end fitting. To decrease, screw in fitting. Tighten lock nut and connect steering arm. Recheck toe-in.

## SAAB

### ADJUSTMENT

#### TIRE INFLATION (COLD)

Before attempting to check or adjust wheel alignment, make sure tires are properly inflated. Refer to manufacturers specifications given in owner's manual.

#### CASTER

**All Models** — To adjust caster, add or remove shims under upper control arm bushing brackets. Changing shims from front to rear bracket increases caster angle. Moving shims from rear to front decreases caster angle. **NOTE** — *Same thickness of shims removed from front must be placed under rear and vice versa. Change in caster also effects camber.*

## SAAB (Cont.)

### CAMBER

**All Models** — To adjust camber, add or remove shims under upper control arm bushing brackets. Increasing shims under both brackets reduces camber angle and removing shims under both increases camber. **NOTE** — *Always add or remove same thickness of shims at front and rear or caster angle will be affected.*

### TOE-IN

**All Models** — With wheels in straight-ahead position, loosen steering link (tie rod) lock nut and turn adjustable sleeve until correct toe-in is obtained. Tighten lock nuts and recheck toe-in.

**NOTE** — *After adjustment of toe-in, measurement "A" (Fig. 1) of tie rod must not exceed 1.0" (25 mm) or 1.02" (26 mm) for power steering models. For tie rods opposite each other, the difference between measurements "A" must not exceed .08" (2 mm).*

**Fig. 1    View Showing Tie Rod Length Measurement**

## SUBARU

### ADJUSTMENT

#### TIRE INFLATION (COLD)

Before attempting to check or adjust wheel alignment, make sure tires are properly inflated. Refer to manufacturers specifiction given in owner's manual.

#### RIDING HEIGHT (REAR)

Riding height is adjusted by changing the size of the angle between trailing arm center line and the markings on outer bracket. See *Fig. 1*. The trailing arm and outer bracket have full serrations around the torsion bar mounting hole, while torsion bar has one missing serration, thus allowing torsion bar to be inserted at any angle.

Raising vehicle height is accomplished by turning outer end and inner end of torsion bar in direction opposite to cast-in arrow on outer end of bar. Height changes .20" (5mm) per each serration shifted.

1) Initially set vehicle rear riding height by inserting torsion bar with its missing serration aligned with markings on outer bracket surface and trailing arm inner surface. This will give approximately the specified riding height as indicated in table.

2) Measure road clearance from center of trailing arm bushing to ground. **NOTE** — *Vehicle must be in unloaded condition.* Raise rear of vehicle and remove rear wheel.

3) Unscrew shock absorber lower mounting nut and remove it from trailing arm. Unscrew lock bolt on outer bushing.

4) Scribe mark position of torsion bar by making a mark on upper half of inner end surface and lower half of outer end surface. Outer end surface mark should be continued onto trailing arm shaft and outer bracket boss.

5) Holding trailing arm so torsion bar does not twist, disengage serrations by tapping inner end surface of torsion bar *See Fig. 2.*

**Fig. 1    Installed View of Torsion Bar Outer End Attachment**

**Fig. 2    View Showing Removal Procedure for Torsion Bar**

## SUBARU (Cont.)

**6)** Pull torsion bar out of trailing arm. Determine amount of turn necessary to make proper height adjustment and turn inner end of torsion bar to this value. Then, insert outer end of torsion bar to its proper adjusted position.

**7)** Install rear wheel and lower vehicle. Reattach lower end of shock absorber. Recheck vehicle rear ground clearance as originally measured. If correct, tighten lock bolt on outer trailing arm bushing. If incorrect, repeat adjustment.

### Riding Height Specifications

| Application | Specification In. (mm) |
|---|---|
| 1600 | |
| Sedan, Coupe | |
| Hardtop | 11.22-12.01 (285-305) |
| Station Wagon | 12.20-12.99 (310-330) |
| 4WD | 13.58-14.37 (345-365) |

## CASTER

Caster angle is not adjustable. If angle is not to specifications, inspect suspension for wear or damage and repair or replace components as necessary.

## CAMBER

**All Models (Front)** — Camber angle is not adjustable. If angle is not to specifications, inspect suspension for wear or damage. Repair or replace components as necessary.

**All Models (Rear)** — Camber angle is adjusted by altering number of shims inserted between torsion bar bracket and chassis mounting. Fitting shims changes camber to negative and removing shims changes camber to positive. One shim corresponds to $\frac{1}{4}°$ adjustment.

## TOE-IN

**All Models (Front)** — If toe-in is not within specifications, loosen steering link (tie rod) lock nut and turn sleeve until correct toe-in is obtained.

**All Models (Rear)** — If toe-in is not within specifications, loosen bolts holding torsion bar bushing to body. Bushing is fixed to body at elongated holes. Moving bushing forward decreases toe-in and moving it rearward increases toe-in. Tighten bolts and recheck toe-in.

# TOYOTA

## ADJUSTMENT

### TIRE INFLATION (COLD)

Before attempting to check or adjust wheel alignment, make sure tires are properly inflated. Refer to manufacturers specifications given in owner's manual.

### CASTER

**Corona** — NOTE — *Camber and caster adjustments should always be made in one operation.* If caster angle is not within specifications, adjust eccentric on front of lower control arm.

**Pickup** — NOTE — *Camber and caster adjustments should always be made in one operation.* If caster angle is not within specifications, adjust by adding or removing shims between the upper control arm shaft and the front suspension crossmember. To increase caster, add shims to rear side of the upper control arm shaft mounting bolt or remove shims from the front side. To decrease caster, reverse procedure.

**All Other Models** — Caster angle is not adjustable. If caster angle is not within specifications, inspect front suspension for wear or damage and repair or replace components as necessary.

## RIDING HEIGHT

**Celica, Corona, & Cressida** — Place vehicle on level surface. Jounce body several times and allow suspension to settle. Check riding height according to *Fig. 1 or 2* and table.

| Riding Height Specifications | |
|---|---|
| **Application** | **Specification In. (mm)** |
| Celica | |
| Front | |
| GT | 9.33 (237) |
| ST | 9.72 (247) |
| Rear | |
| GT | 9.37 (238) |
| ST | 9.76 (248) |
| Rear | |
| St. Wgn. | 8.74 (222) |
| Cressida | |
| Front | 8.31 (211) |
| Rear | 8.11 (206) |
| Rear (St. Wgn) | 7.64 (194) |
| Corona | |
| Front | |
| W/175 SR Tires | 9.06 (230) |
| W/B78 Tires | 9.29 (236) |
| Rear | |
| W/175 SR Tires | 9.61 (230) |
| W/B78 Tires | 9.84 (250) |

# Wheel Alignment

## TOYOTA (Cont.)

**Fig. 1   Riding Height Measurement Points for Celica and Cressida**

### CAMBER

**Corona — NOTE —** *Caster and camber adjustments should always be made in one operation.* If camber angle is not within specifications, adjust eccentric on rear of lower control arm.

**Pickup — NOTE —** *Caster and camber adjustments should always be made in one operation.* If camber angle is not within specifications, adjust by adding or removing shims between upper control arm shaft and the front suspension crossmember. To increase camber angle, remove shims from, upper control arm shaft bolts in equal amounts. To decrease camber, reverse procedure.

**All Other Models —** Camber angle is not adjustable. If camber angle is not with specifications, inspect front suspension for wear or damage and repair or replace components as necessary.

### TOE-IN

**All Models —** If toe-in is not within specifications, loosen steering link (tie-rod) clamping bolts and rotate adjusting sleeves an equal amount until correct toe-in is obtained. Position clamp bolts at right angles to slot in tie rod and tighten bolts.

**Fig. 2   Corona Riding Height Measurement**

## TRIUMPH

### ADJUSTMENT

#### TIRE INFLATION (COLD)

Before attempting to check or adjust wheel alignment, make sure tires are properly inflated. Refer to manufacturers specifications given in owner's manual.

#### CASTER

**All Models —** Caster angle is not adjustable. If caster angle is not to specifications, inspect suspension system for wear or damage and repair or replace components as necessary.

### CAMBER

**All Models (Exc. TR7) —** Before adjusting camber angle, inspect suspension for wear or damage and repair or replace components as necessary. To adjust, raise vehicle and support chassis on jack stands. Loosen nuts securing lower control arm bracket to chassis. Add shims equally to front and rear of bracket to decrease camber, or remove shims equally to increase camber angle. After each adjustment is made, tighten bracket-to-chassis bolts, remove jack stands and measure camber angle.

## TRIUMPH (Cont.)

**TR7** — Camber angle is not adjustable. If camber angle is not within specifications, inspect suspension system for wear or damage and repair or replace components as necessary.

### TOE-IN

**All Models (Front)** — Set front wheels in straight ahead position. If adjustment is necessary, loosen steering link (tie rod) lock nuts and gaiter clips. Rotate adjusting sleeves equal amounts until correct toe-in is obtained. Tighten lock nuts and recheck toe-in.

**Spitfire (Rear)** — If toe-in is not to specifications, loosen bolts holdings strut front support. Adjust as necessary by adding to or removing from the shims fitted between support and body. Tighten bolts and recheck toe-in.

## VOLKSWAGEN

### ADJUSTMENT

#### TIRE INFLATION (COLD)

Before attempting to check or adjust wheel alignment, make sure tires are properly inflated. Refer to manufacturers specifications given in owner's manual.

#### CASTER

Caster angle is part of front axle design and is not adjustable. If not within specifications, inspect front suspension for wear or damage and repair or replace components as necessary.

#### CAMBER

**Type 1 (Front)** — Bolt mounting inner end of control arm is also eccentric bolt for camber adjustment. Loosen lock nut and turn eccentric until camber is within specifications. Tighten lock nut.

**Type 2 (Front)** — Loosen self-locking nut in bottom of ball joint stud. Adjust camber by turning bushing with appropriate wrench. Bushing can be turned a maximum of 90° to either side.

**NOTE** — *Basic setting is achieved when eccentric notch faces in forward position.*

**Dasher (Front)** — If adjustment is necessary, loosen nuts attaching ball joint to track control arm. To adjust, insert suitable adjusting tool (40-200) in adjusting holes in control arm and pry ball joint sideways until camber is set to specifications. **NOTE** — *Difference in camber between wheels should not vary more than 1°. Tighten attaching nuts and recheck camber.*

**NOTE** — *On Dasher models, insert tool from front on right side and from rear on left side.*

**Rabbit & Scirocco (Front)** — If adjustment is necessary, loosen nuts of suspension strut-to-wheel bearing housing mounting bolts. Turn eccentric bolt (upper mounting bolt) until specified camber angle is obtained. Tighten mounting bolt nuts and recheck camber angle.

**Type 1 (Rear)** — Camber angle is dependent on torsion bar adjustment. If camber angle is not within specifications, *see Torsion Bar Adjustment.*

**Type 2 (Rear)** — If minor adjustment is necessary, loosen bolts attaching bearing housing to spring plate and diagonal arm. Adjust by changing position of bearing housing in elongated holes in spring plate. Tighten bolts and recheck camber.

**NOTE** — *Range that this procedure covers is small. Also, see Torsion Bar Adjustment.*

**Dasher, Rabbit & Scirocco (Rear)** — Rear camber is not adjustable. If camber angle is not to specifications, inspect rear suspension for wear or damage and repair or replace components as necessary.

### TOE-IN

**Type 1 (Front)** — Loosen lock nuts and hex tapered rings at each end of right side tie rod. Turn right side tie rod until each wheel is set to half the specified toe. Rotating tie rod toward front of vehicle increases toe. Opposite direction rotation decreases toe.

***Fig. 1    Direction of Tie Rod Rotation to Align
Steering Wheel (Type 1 Only)***

## VOLKSWAGEN (Cont.)

**Type 2 (Front)** — Loosen both clamp bolts on right side tie rod. Rotate right side tie rod until toe is within specifications. Rotating tie rod toward front of vehicle increases toe. Opposite direction rotation decreases toe.

**Dasher, Rabbit, Scirocco (Front)** — Place front wheels in straight-ahead position. Loosen lock nut on adjustable tie rod end (left side, Dasher; right side, Rabbit and Scirocco). Hold axle boot to avoid twisting. Adjust tie rod until specified toe-in is obtained. Tighten lock nut and recheck toe-in.

**Type 1 (Rear)** — If adjustment is necessary, remove nuts securing spring plate but do not remove bolts. To adjust, move diagonal arm forward or backward in slotted spring plate mounting holes until toe-in is set to specifications. Install spring plate attaching nuts and recheck toe-in.

**Type 2 (Rear)** — If adjustment is necessary, loosen bolts attaching bearing housing to spring plate and diagonal arm. Change position of bearing housing in elongated holes on spring plate. Tighten bolts and recheck toe-in.

**All Other Models (Rear)** — Toe-in is not adjustable. If toe-in is not within specifications, inspect rear suspension for wear or damage and repair or replace components as necessary.

### TORSION BAR ADJUSTMENT (REAR)

**Type 1** — Using a suitable protractor, find deviation of vehicle from horizontal plane and note reading which will be used in setting angle of spring plate. Install spring plate on torsion bar and measure position with protractor. If not within specifications, adjust by moving torsion bar, one spline at a time, forward or backward until correct position is obtained.

**Type 2** — Using a suitable protractor, check horizontal position of vehicle on one frame side member. Reading should be noted; it will be used in setting spring plate angle. Insert inner end of torsion bar in center anchor and press spring plate on outer end of torsion bar. Adjust protractor on unloaded spring plate until bubble is in center position. Adjust torsion bar one spline forward or rearward until correct specifications are obtained.

### Torsion Bar Specifications

| Application | Setting (Degrees) |
|---|---|
| Type 1 | $21\frac{1}{3} \pm \frac{5}{6}$ |
| Type 2 | |
| Kombi & Campmobile | |
| From Chassis 218 000 002 | ①$21 \pm \frac{5}{6}$ |
| From Chassis 212 2000 001 | ①$20 \pm \frac{5}{6}$ |
| Station Wagon | |
| From Chassis 218 000 002 | ②$23 \pm \frac{5}{6}$ |
| From Chassis 212 2000 001 | ②$23 \pm \frac{5}{6}$ |

① — Man. Trans.
② — Man. Trans. and Auto. Trans.

# VOLVO

## ADJUSTMENT

### TIRE INFLATION (COLD)

Before attempting to check or adjust wheel alignment, make sure tires are properly inflated. Refer to manufacturers specifications given in owner's manual.

### CASTER

Caster cannot be adjusted. If not within specifications, check front end components for damage.

### CAMBER

If camber is not within specifications, loosen nuts at strut assembly upper attachment. Use special tool 5038 (or equivalent) at strut upper attachment to adjust camber. Tighten lock nuts. Recheck camber.

### TOE-IN

Place wheels in straight-ahead position and loosen lock nut and rubber dust boot outer clamp. Turn tie rods until toe is within specifications. Make sure length of tie rods does not differ more than .08" (2 mm). Measure difference between groove in tie rod and lock nut.

# Wheel Bearing Adjustment

## ARROW, CHALLENGER, COLT SAPPORO

**All Models** — Tighten adjusting nut to 14.5 ft. lbs. After seating bearing components, loosen nut to 0 ft. lbs. Now make final adjustment to 3.6 ft. lbs. After installing lock cap, insert cotter pin.

**NOTE** — *Do not loosen adjusting nut more than 15° to align spindle holes.*

## AUDI

**5000 (Front)** — Adjustment not required. Torque spindle nut to 203 ft. lbs. (28 mkg).

**5000 (Rear)** — Tighten adjustment nut firmly while rotating wheel. Make sure bearing is fully seated. Back off nut until thrust washer can be moved with screwdriver. Insert cotter key.

**Fox (Front)** — Adjustment not required. Torque spindle nut to 145 ft. lbs. (20 mkg) for M 18x1.5 nuts or 175 ft. lbs. (24 mkg) for M 20x1.75 nuts

**Fox (Rear)** — Remove grease cup, cotter pin and castle nut. Tighten spindle nut and loosen for adjustment. Adjust by lightly tightening spindle nut until plain washer (beneath spindle nut) can just be moved from side to side, using screwdriver. This adjustment will correspond to .0012-.0027" (.03-.06 mm) wheel bearing play.

## BMW

**Except 733i** — While rotating wheel hub, tighten castle nut to 22-24 ft. lbs. (3.0-3.3 mkg), then rotate hub at least 2 more times. Loosen castle nut until bearing end play is noticed. Tighten castle nut to a maximum of about 2 ft. lbs. (.28 mkg), then loosen to nearest hole and install cotter key.

**NOTE** — *After adjustment, slotted washer should move easily, without noticeable resistance.*

**733i** — Tighten castle nut to 22-24 ft. lbs. (3.0-3.3 mkg) while continuously rotating wheel. Loosen castle nut until there is visible axial bearing play. Again rotate wheel and tighten bearing, this time to 2 ft. lbs. (.3 mkg). Insert cotter key. Thrust washer should have movement with only slight resistance after adjustment.

## CAPRI

**All Models** — Rotate wheel, hub and drum assembly while turning adjusting nut to 17-25 ft. lbs. Back adjusting nut off 120°. Install cotter pin and check front wheel rotation.

## COURIER

**All Models** — While rotating wheel, hub and drum assembly, tighten adjusting nut to 17-25 ft. lbs. Back adjusting nut off ¼ turn and retighten nut where castellations on the lock nut are aligned with cotter pin hole in spindle. Install new cotter pin and check wheel rotation.

## DATSUN

**All, Except F10** — Tighten spindle nut to torque specifications in table. Spin wheel and retorque spindle nut. Loosen nut according to specifications in table and then tighten to align cotter key hole. Insert cotter key.

### Wheel Bearing Adjustment

| Application | Torque (Ft. Lbs.) | Loosen |
|---|---|---|
| B210 | 18-22 | 90° |
| Pickup | 25-29 | 45° |
| 510 | 22-25 | 90° |
| 200SX, 810, 280Z | 18-22 | 60° |

**F10** — Raise vehicle and place on safety stands. Remove tire and wheel. Make sure mounting nut is torqued to 87-145 ft. lbs. (12-20 mkg). Spin wheel hub several times in both directions to ensure free rotation.

## FIAT

**Model 124 & 131** — While rotating hub, torque spindle nut to 14.5 ft. lbs. Completely loosen nut and retighten to 5 ft. lbs. Loosen nut 30° and stake collar of spindle nut into machined slot on spindle. Attach dial indicator with magnetic base on brake drum and actuating foot on spindle. Hub end play should not exceed .004". **NOTE** — *When ever spindle nut has been removed it must be replaced with a new nut.*

**Models 128 & X1/9** — Tighten front and rear spindle nuts to 112 ft. lbs. When spindle nuts are properly tightened, stake collar of spindle nut into machined slot on spindle.

## FIESTA

**Front** — No adjustment required. Tighten front spindle nut to 173.5-195 ft. lbs. (24-27 mkg).

**Rear** — Adjust rear bearing by tightening nut to torque of 27 ft. lbs. (3.7 mkg) while rotating drum. Loosen nut 90° and fit retainer nut with cotter key.

## HONDA

**All Models (Front)** — Front wheel bearings are not adjustable. Torque front spindle nut to 87-130 ft. lbs. (Civic and Accord) or 109 ft. lbs. (Civic CVCC).

**All, Except Accord (Rear)** — Rear wheel bearings are not adjustable. Torque rear spindle nut to 72-94 ft. lbs. (Civic) or 83 ft. lbs. (Civic CVCC).

**HONDA (Cont.)**

**Accord (Rear)** — Tighten spindle nut to 18 ft. lbs. (2.5 mkg) and rotate drum several times. Loosen lock nut. Tighten spindle nut to 1.1-3.6 ft. lbs. (.15-.5 mkg). Insert cotter pin.

## JAGUAR

**All Models** — While rotating hub, tighten nut until no end play is evident. Loosen nut 1 or 2 flats to line up cotter key and install cotter key. End play should be measured with a dial indicator and should be .002-.006". If not within specifications, adjust axle nut to correct end play.

## LANCIA

**All Models** — Front wheel bearing and rear wheel bearings are pressed into stub axle housings. Stub axle must be removed to replace bearings. Spindle nut torque not available.

## LUV

**All Models** — While rotating wheel, tighten spindle nut to 22 ft. lbs. Turn hub through two or three turns and loosen nut until just finger tight. Check free play. Using a pull scale attached to wheel stud, measure turning torque; adjust nut until pull recorded on scale is 1.1-2.6 lbs. when wheel begins to rotate.

## MAZDA

**GLC** — Tighten adjustment nut to 14-18 ft. lbs. (2.0-2.5 mkg). Rotate brake discs several times in both directions. Loosen adjustment nut. Using a spring pull scale, set bearing preload (using adjustment nut) to .33-1.32 lbs. (.15-.60 kg).

**All Models (Exc. GLC)** — With vehicle raised and supported under lower control arms, tighten adjusting nut until hub locks. Back off nut until hub is just free to turn. Rotate hub several times in each direction. Attach pull scale to hub. Preload should be 1.3-2.4 lbs (Pickup) or .88-2.0 lbs. (other models). If preload is not to specifications adjust spindle nut. Align slot in spindle nut with hole in spindle and install cotter key.

## MERCEDES-BENZ

**All Models** — While rotating hub, tighten clamping nut until hub can just be turned. Loosen clamping nut and release bearing tension by striking steering knuckle spindle with plastic hammer. Using a suitable dial indicator, check wheel bearing end play. End play should be .0004-.0008". Adjust clamping nut until end play is within limits. Tighten socket bolt of clamping nut. Washer between outer bearing and clamping nut should rotate with light pressure applied to it.

## MG

**Midget** — Raise front of vehicle and remove each wheel. Remove caliper assembly, but do not disconnect hydraulic brake hose. Support caliper to prevent damage to hose. Attach suitable dial indicator and measure runout of hub at outer edge of brake rotor. If runout exceeds .006" remove rotor and reposition on hub. Torque spindle nut to 46 ft. lbs. and recheck runout.

**MGB** — Raise front of vehicle and remove front wheels. Using suitable dial indicator, measure hub end play. Correct end

**MG (Cont.)**

play is .002-.004" (.05-.10 mm). If not within specifications, remove spindle nut, washer, and outer bearing. Add or remove shims behind outer bearing until correct end play is obtain with spindle nut torqued to 40 ft. lbs. (5.5 mkg)

## OPEL

**All Models** — Raise and support front of vehicle. While rotating wheel, torque spindle nut to 21 ft. lbs. Back off spindle nut completely. Now turn the nut all the way in using fingers only. If slot and hole are not aligned, tighten enough to align and install cotter key.

## PORSCHE

**All Models (Front)** — Tighten adjusting nut while turning hub. Loosen adjusting nut until thrust washer can just be moved by exerting hand pressure with a screwdriver. Tighten socket head bolt (pinch bolt).

**930 (Rear)** — Torque axle nut to 217 ft. lbs. (30 mkg) and check axial play. Adjust axle nut in small steps until axial play is about .001" (.04 mm) (torque may be increased to 325 ft. lbs.; 45 mkg, during this procedure). Loosen axle nut. Retorque nut to 217 ft. lbs. (30 mkg) and insert cotter pin.

## RENAULT

**R5 (Front)** — Nonadjustable. Torque stub axle nut to 90 ft. lbs. (12.4 mkg).

**R5 (Rear)** — Tighten stub axle nut to 25 ft. lbs. (3.5 mkg). Loosen nut about ¼ turn. Check bearing end play, it should be between .0004-.002" (.01-.05 mm). Adjust stub axle as necessary. Fit lock plate and cotter pin. Refill hub dust cover cap with ⅓ oz. of grease.

## SAAB

**All Models (Front)** — Front wheel bearings are not adjustable. Torque front spindle nut to 246-261 ft. lbs. (34-36 mkg).

**All Models (Rear)** — Install washer and lock nut. Tighten lock nut to 36 ft. lbs. (5 mkg) to seat bearings. Loosen lock nut completely, then tighten nut to 1.4-2.9 ft. lbs. (.2-.4 mkg) and lock nut in place by bending flange into slot of lock nut.

## SUBARU

**All Models (Front)** — Front wheel bearing is not adjustable. Tighten spindle nut to 174 ft. lbs.

**4WD (Rear)** — No adjustment required. Tighten axle nut to 174 ft. lbs. (24 mkg). After tightening nut, punch flange portion of axle nut toward groove in rear axle shaft.

**All Other Models (Rear)** — While rotating brake drum, snug down spindle nut to seat bearings. Back spindle nut off ⅛ turn and bend down tab of locking washer to secure spindle nut. If adjustment is correct, a force of 2.2-3.1 lbs. (1.0-1.4 kg) will be required to rotate wheel.

**NOTE** — *A force of 1.9-3.2 lbs. (.85-1.45 kg) is required to rotate wheel when measured at axle nut.*

## TOYOTA

**Land Cruiser** — Rotate drum and tighten adjustment nut to 43 ft. lbs (6 mkg). This will seat bearings. Loosen adjustment nut about ⅛ turn. If brake drum rotates properly, install lock washer and tighten lock nut.

**Pickup** — Tighten front axle castle nut to 36 ft. lbs. to seat bearings, then back off until nut is finger tight. Retighten nut to 36 ft. lbs. and back off ⅙-⅓ turn and install cotter key. When properly adjusted, bearing preload should be as shown in table, when checked with pull scale attached to hub bolt.

**All Other Models** — Tighten castle nut bearing retainer nut 18.8-23.2 ft. lbs. and turn brake drum back and forth to seat bearing. Loosen nut until can be turned with fingers. Tighten nut to finger tight using a socket without the handle. If not aligned for cotter key installation, tighten until installation possible. Preload at hub (hub rotating) should be within specifications.

### Bearing Preload Specifications

| Application | Preload Lbs. (kg) |
| --- | --- |
| Corona | .77-1.9 (.35-.86) |
| Pickup | .66-1.98 (.30-.90) |
| Corolla, Celica | .66-1.5 (.30-.68) |
| Cressida | 2.3-3.5 (1.0-1.6) |

## TRIUMPH

**TR7** — Raise and support front of vehicle, then remove wheel and tire. Check hub for excessive end play. If adjustment is necessary, remove grease cap and cotter key. Tighten spindle nut to 5 ft. lbs. (.7 mkg), then back nut off one flat and install cotter key.

**All Others** — Raise and support front of vehicle, then remove wheel and brake caliper. Attach a dial indicator and measure wheel bearing end play. If end play exceeds .003-.005" (.08-.13 mm), remove cotter key and loosen or tighten spindle nut until end play is within specifications. Install new cotter key.

**NOTE** — *Do not exceed 5 ft. lbs. (.7 mkg) when torquing spindle nut.*

## VOLKSWAGEN

**Type 1 (Front)** — Torque adjusting nut to 7 ft. lbs. (1.0 mkg) while hand turning drum. Measure bearing play using a dial indicator. Hand tighten adjustment nut until bearing play is about .001-.005" (.03-.12 mm). Tighten retainer clamp.

**Type 2 (Front)** — Adjust clamp nut while rotating wheel. Adjustment is completed when thrust washer can be moved with a screwdriver and finger pressure.

**All Others (Front)** — Front wheel bearings are pressed into bearing housing and no adjustment is required. Tighten front axle nut on Dasher to 145 ft. lbs. (20 mkg) for M 18x1.5 nuts or 175 ft. lbs. (24 mkg) for M 20x1.5 nuts. For Rabbit and Scirocco models tighten nuts to 175 ft. lbs. (24 mkg).

**Dasher, Rabbit & Scirocco (Rear)** — Wheel bearings are correctly adjusted if thrust washer can be moved slightly with a screwdriver. **NOTE** — *This will provide axial play of approximately .001-.003".*

## VOLVO

**All Models** — While rotating hub, torque nut to 50 ft. lbs. Loosen nut 1/3 turn and check for hub rotating freely with no end play. If necessary to align cotter key holes loosen nut and install cotter key.

**Fig. 1** *Using a Pull Scale to Measure Wheel Bearing Starting Torque*

**Fig. 2** *Exploded View of Wheel Bearing Components with Disc Brakes*

## ARROW, CHALLENGER, COLT SAPPORO

**All Models** — With components removed from control arm and ball joint still installed, check following: Horizontal and vertical free play (0″), and ball joint rotation starting torque 4-6 ft. lbs. (.83 mkg). Replace ball joints if correct specifications are not obtained.

## AUDI

**Fox** — Movement of ball joint with pressure applied by leverage should be about .098″ (2.5 mm). If not within specifications, replace ball joint.

## COURIER

**All Models** — Check working surfaces of ball joints and studs for wear or damage. End play should not exceed .031″ (.8 mm). If end play is excessive, replace ball joint. *See Courier in SUSPENSION Section.*

## DATSUN

Remove lower control arm. *See Datsun in SUSPENSION Section.* Use appropriate spring tension gauge and attach it to top of ball joint stud nut. Measure force (INCH lbs.) required to move ball joint stud laterally. If measurement is not within specifications, replace ball joint.

**Ball Joint Lateral Movement①**

| Application | New In. Lbs. (cmkg) | Used In. Lbs. (cmkg) |
|---|---|---|
| 510 | 35-87 (40-100) | 17 (20) |
| 810 | 52-104 (6-120) | 35 (40) |
| 200SX, B210, 280Z | 65-109 (75-125) | 50 (43) |
| Pickup Upper | 8.7-43.3 (10-50) | More Than 8.7 (10) |
| Lower | 8.7-34.7 (10-40) | More Than 8.7 (10) |

① — For F10 models 30.4 INCH lbs. (35 cmkg) is standard 8.7 INCH lbs. (10 cmkg) is minimum.

## FIAT

**All Models** — With vehicle raised and supported under lower control arms, grasp wheel at top and bottom and try to shake wheel. If any movement is noted, control arm must be removed for further inspection. *See Fiat in SUSPENSION Section.*

## HONDA

**All Models** — Raise and support front of vehicle. Attach dial indicator onto lower control arm with indicator tip on steering knuckle near ball joint. Place pry bar between lower control arm and steering knuckle. **NOTE** — *Take care not to damage ball joint rubber boot.* Push on pry bar and observe movement on dial indicator. If movement is in excess of .020″ (.5 mm), ball joint must be replaced. *See Honda in SUSPENSION Section.*

## JAGUAR

**All Models** — Ball joints must be replaced if signs of wear are evident. Lower ball joint does use shims. These shims are not to be used to compensate wear. The shims are designed to provide adjustment for ball joints during overhaul reassembly.

## LANCIA

**All Models** — If ball joint shows excessive amounts of wear (play), replace ball joints. *See Lancia in SUSPENSION Section.*

## LUV

With vehicle raised and supported under lower control arms, grasp wheel at top and bottom, then try to move wheel. Replace lower ball joint or upper control arm with ball joint if movement exceeds .06″ (1.52 mm).

## MERCEDES-BENZ

There should be no lateral movement of ball joint. Vertical movement is adjusted by adding or removing washers.

## MAZDA

**All Models** — Check ball joint dust seal for wear or damage and, if necessary, replace seal. Ball joint end play must not exceed .039″ (1 mm). If end play exceeds specifications, replace ball joint. *See Mazda in SUSPENSION Section.*

## OPEL

Raise and support front of vehicle. Inspect ball joint boots for damage and replace if necessary. If lower ball joints exceed maximum permissible axial play of .040″ (1.0 mm) components must be replaced. Specification refers generally to older ball joints.

## PORSCHE

**924** — Measure distance between uppper edge of control arm and lower edge of steering knuckle using a vernier caliper. Place a lever under ball joint and pry upward. Record any movement. New ball joints should have no play. Wear limit for other ball joints is about .098″ (2 mm).

## RENAULT

**All Models** — Inspect ball joints for wear or excessive play. Replace ball joints as necessary.

# Ball Joint Checking

## TOYOTA

**Corona & Pickup (Lower)** — Raise vehicle under lower control arm. Check ball joint looseness by moving wheel vertically and horizontally. Movement limit in vertical direction must be less than .04" (1 mm) for Corona and .20" (5 mm) for Pickup. Horizontal limit is .08" (2 mm) for Corona and .09" (2.3 mm) for Pickup.

**Corona & Pickup (Upper)** — Make sure all suspension components are tight. Disconnect upper control arm from steering knuckle. Turn ball stud and check for excessive looseness or tightness. Replace ball joint and control arm if ball joint is excessively loose or tight.

**All Other Models** — Check for excessive looseness, proper operation and damaged ball stud. Replace as necessary.

## TRIUMPH

**All Models** — Inspect ball joints for excessive wear or play. Replace ball joint as necessary. *See Triumph in SUSPENSION Section.*

## VOLKSWAGEN

**Type 1 & 2** — Measure distance between top of lower ball joint and steering knuckle using a vernier caliper. Record measurement. Lever wheel or suspension so as to move ball joint. Record ball joint movement. Difference between measurements is ball joint play. Refer to table for wear limits.

**All Other Models** — Raise and support, then turn steering to one side. Install suitable levering tool so that ball joint spring may be compressed. With spring compressed, postion a vernier caliper with lower jaw on ball joint stud and upper jaw on top of clamping bolt for ball joint stud. Note reading. Slowly release tension from spring and note travel of caliper. This reading indicates ball joint play. If specified play is exceeded, replace ball joint. *See Volkswagen in SUSPENSION Section.*

| Ball Joint Specifications | | |
|---|---|---|
| **Application** | **New** | **Used** |
| Type 1 | | |
|   Upper Ball Joint | .020" (.50 mm) | .040" (1.0 mm) |
|   Lower Ball Joint | .020" (.50 mm) | .080" (2.0 mm) |
| Type 2 (All) | .020" (.50 mm) | .080" (2.0 mm) |
| Dasher, Rabbit | | |
|   Scirocco | .040" (1.0 mm) | .100" (2.5 mm) |

## VOLVO

**All Models** — Maximum permitted axial play for lower ball joint is .12" (3 mm). Check ball joint by prying back and forth with a bar. If specifications are exceeded, replace ball joints. *See Volvo in SUSPENSION Section.*

## ALL MANUFACTURERS

**NOTE** — *These illustrations are not intended to represent exact structure of the manufacturer's frame, underbody, or body outline. These are presented only to give the mechanic some point of reference.*

### FRAME & UNDERBODY

The following illustrations indicate areas (parts) of the underbody and frame which may be used to raise and support the vehicle, using either floor jack or hoist. These points are indicated by shaded areas on the frame (see sample illustration).

### OUTERBODY

Those points designated on the outline of the body were specifically designed to facilitate the use of the vehicle's own jack, but may also be used to raise and support the vehicle by means of a floor jack or hoist. These jacking points are indicated by circular dots on the outline of the body (see sample illustration). If floor jack or hoist is employed, extreme care should be exercised to prevent damaging the outer body shell.

Floor Jack & Hoist

For Vehicle Jack

**Fig. 1  Sample Jacking & Hoisting Points**
**(Typical Illustration)**

**Arrow/Colt**
**Challenger/Sapporo**

**Audi**

**BMW**

**Capri**

**Courier**

**Datsun (Except Pickup & F10)**

**Datsun Pickup**

# Jacking & Hoisting

Datsun F10

Honda

Fiat 124

Jaguar

Fiat 128 & 131

Lancia

Fiat X1/9

LUV

Fiesta

Mazda

Mercedes-Benz

Renault

MG

Saab

Opel

Subaru

Porsche (Except 928)

Toyota (Except Land Cruiser & Pickup)

Porsche 928

Toyota Land Cruiser & Pickup

# Jacking & Hoisting

Triumph

Volkswagen Dasher, Rabbit & Scirocco

Volkswagen Type 1 & 2

Volvo

# Section 9
# SUSPENSION

# Contents

*NOTE — ALSO SEE GENERAL INDEX IN BACK OF MANUAL*

# Suspension

## SUSPENSION TROUBLE SHOOTING

**NOTE** — *This is a general trouble shooting guide. When using this guide, locate the condition in column one that corresponds to your problem and determine the possible causes in column two. Match the number of possible cause with the same number in column three, and you will have the suggested correction.*

| CONDITION | POSSIBLE CAUSE | CORRECTION |
|---|---|---|
| ▶ Hard Steering | 1) Tire pressure too low<br>2) Front wheels out of alignment<br>3) Lower control arm ball joint siezed | 1) Check manufacturers recommended pressure and set to specifications<br>2) Check alignment and set to specifications or replace parts<br>3) Check specifications set or replace parts |
| ▶ Pulls to one side | 1) Crossmember broken, cracked or loose<br>2) Left and right side wheel base uneven<br>3) Loose or excessively worn wheel bearings<br>4) Loose wheel lug nuts | 1) Replace crossmember<br>2) Check frame and repair<br>3) Adjust wheel bearings or replace<br>4) Tighten lug nuts |
| ▶ Steering wheel wander | 1) Excessive ball joint wear<br>2) Lower control arm and strut<br>3) Lower control arm pivot bolt (shaft) loose or sloppy<br>4) Lower control arm and strut damaged or worn | 1) Replace ball joint or adjust if possible<br>2) Replace defective component bar(s) damaged<br>3) Tighten or replace parts<br>4) Inspect bushings and replace as required |
| ▶ Body roll | 1) Stabilizer broken or damaged<br>2) Shock absorbers worn out | 1) Replace parts<br>2) Check and replace |
| ▶ Noise | 1) Coil spring broken<br>2) Bad shock absorber<br>3) Insufficient lubrication<br>4) Components loose or excessively worn<br>5) Damaged wheel bearing<br>6) Improper tire pressure | 1) Replace, may be matched set<br>2) Check operation and replace<br>3) Grease fittings<br>4) Tighten or replace<br>5) Adjust or replace wheel bearings<br>6) Check inflation |
| ▶ Steering hard to control | 1) Broken front coil spring<br>2) Defective shock absorber<br>3) Loose control arm bushings<br>4) Strut assembly loose<br>5) Tire pressure<br>6) Wheel alignment out of tolerance<br>7) Damaged suspension links | 1) Replace coil spring<br>2) Replace shock absorber<br>3) Replace bushings<br>4) Tighten or replace assembly<br>5) Check and set to specifications<br>6) Check and adjust or replace components<br>7) Replace parts |

# Front Suspension

## ARROW, COLT, CHALLENGER & SAPPORO

Arrow
Colt
Challenger
Sapporo

### DESCRIPTION

Strut type suspension consists of a vertically mounted strut assembly, lower control arm, and stabilizer bar. Strut assembly is mounted to top of fender panel by a thrust bearing. Strut assembly mounts at bottom to steering arm and pivots in ball joint. Strut components are: shock absorber built into strut outer tube, coil spring around outside of strut tube, and wheel spindle integral with bottom of strut tube. A stabilizer bar is attached to front chassis members and at ends to lower control arms. Some models are also equipped with strut bars.

### ADJUSTMENT

#### WHEEL ALIGNMENT SPECIFICATIONS & PROCEDURES

*See Wheel Alignment Specifications & Procedures in WHEEL ALIGNMENT Section.*

#### WHEEL BEARING ADJUSTMENT

*See Wheel Bearing Adjustment in WHEEL ALIGNMENT Section.*

#### BALL JOINT CHECKING

*See Ball Joint Checking in WHEEL ALIGNMENT Section.*

### REMOVAL & INSTALLATION

#### STABILIZER & STRUT BAR

**Removal** — Raise vehicle and support on safety stands. Disconnect stabilizer and strut bars from mountings on lower control arm. Remove strut bracket from body mounting position. Remove stabilizer bracket on each side and take off stabilizer. Next, lift off strut bar after noting position of all washers and bushings.

**Installation** — To install, reverse removal procedure and note the following: Make sure distance between strut bar end and lock nut is 3.1" (78.7 mm). Install strut bar bushing with convex surface to front side.

**Fig. 1** *Showing Mounting Positions and Components for Stabilizer Bar and Strut Bar*

### LOWER CONTROL ARM

**Removal** — 1) Raise and support front of vehicle. Remove front wheel(s).

2) Disconnect stabilizer bar and strut bar from lower control arm. Remove strut assembly.

3) Using suitable puller, detach tie rod ball joint from steering knuckle arm.

4) Remove bolt retaining strut assembly and steering knuckle arm. Separate them using a soft-faced hammer.

5) Turn steering wheel to gain clearance for removing lower control arm from crossmember. Using puller, disconnect knuckle arm from lower control arm ball joint.

**Fig. 2** *Exploded View of Front Suspension Showing Relationship of Strut Assembly and Lower Control Arm*

**Ball Joint Replacement** — 1) Pry out ball joint dust seal.

2) Remove snap ring from groove in ball joint seat.

3) Press ball joint from control arm.

4) Select new ball joint. Position ball joint in control arm. Seat ball joint into position so ball joint and lower control arm reference marks are aligned.

**NOTE** — *It should take approximately 11,000 lbs. (5000 kg) to fully seat ball joint.*

## ARROW, COLT, CHALLENGER & SAPPORO (Cont.)

**5)** Fit new snap ring into ball joint groove. It may be necessary to tap snap ring into place.

**NOTE** — *Make sure not to open snap ring wider than necessary.*

**6)** Apply packing sealer inside of dust cover metal ring. Seat metal ring into snap ring surface by tapping with hammer.

**Installation** — To install, reverse removal procedure and note the following:

- When connecting strut assembly to steering knuckle arm, apply suitable sealer to flanged mating surface.
- When installing lower control arm shaft, tighten shaft nut temporarily and shaft flange nut to full torque setting. After vehicle is on ground at full weight, then tighten shaft nut to specified torque.

### STRUT ASSEMBLY

**Removal — 1)** Raise and support front of vehicle allowing suspension to hang free. Remove front wheel.

**2)** Remove caliper assembly and front hub assembly.

**3)** Disconnect stabilizer link and lower control arm. Remove strut assembly, knuckle arm and strut insulator retaining bolts. Remove strut assembly from vehicle.

**Fig. 3   Breakdown of Strut Assembly Components**

**Disassembly — 1)** Clamp strut assembly in vise and use proper tool to compress coil spring. Remove dust cover. Remove nuts holding insulator to strut sub-assembly. Remove insulator and then coil spring.

**NOTE** — *Steering knuckle is welded to strut sub-assembly and cannot be separated.*

**2)** If oil loss is found, disassemble sub-assembly after thoroughly cleaning it. Place sub-assembly vertically in vise. Use special wrench (CT-1112) to remove seal assembly. Compress piston rod to lowest position during this procedure.

**3)** Drain fluid. Using small screwdriver, remove square-cut "O" ring from rod and draw out rod assembly and guide. Remove guide from piston rod.

**Reassembly — 1)** Clean and replace all components as required. Apply hydraulic fluid to sliding surfaces. Insert piston rod in cylinder. Compress piston ring with fingers as it slides into cylinder.

**2)** Assemble cylinder and piston assembly with strut outer casing. Fill unit with new fluid (approximately .72 pint or 300 cc).

**3)** With guide flange at top, insert piston rod until guide flange contacts shock absorber cylinder end. Install "O" ring between guide and strut outer cylinder (always use new "O" ring).

**4)** Cover piston rod end with seal guide (CT-1111B), slide in seal after applying oil to seal lip and tighten seal assembly until seal nut edge contacts strut outer cylinder.

**NOTE** — *Be sure to replace seal assembly when shock absorber has been disassembled.*

**5)** Attach compressor to coil spring and place spring onto strut assembly. Pull shock absorber fully out and position bumper rubber and spacer.

**6)** Align "D" shaped hole in spring seat upper assembly with indentation on piston rod. Install insulator assembly. Install self-locking nut and tighten temporarily.

**NOTE** — *If replacing coil springs, be sure to use same color-code class as original.*

**7)** After seating upper and lower end of coil spring on grooves of spring seats, remove spring compressor. Using special tool (CT-1112) tighten spring seat and self-locking nut to specified torque.

**Installation** — To install, reverse removal procedure, noting the following:

- Secure top of strut assembly to mounting bracket first. Apply sealant to lower end of assembly and connect it to knuckle arm, using dowel pins as locating guides.
- Pack strut upper bearing with grease and install dust cap. Install stabilizer, hub assembly and wheel.

### TIGHTENING SPECIFICATIONS

| Application | Ft. Lbs. (mkg) |
|---|---|
| Knuckle Arm-to-Ball Joint | 29-43 (4.0-5.7) |
| Knuckle Arm-to-Tie Rod Ball Joint | 29-36 (4.0-5.0) |
| Control Arm Flange Bolt | 6-9 (0.8-1.2) |
| Control Arm Shaft Nut | 43 (5.7) |
| Stabilizer-to-Control Arm | 18-25 (2.5-3.5) |
| Strut Bar-to-Control Arm | 36-43 (5.0-5.7) |

# Front Suspension

## AUDI

Fox
5000

## DESCRIPTION

Suspension is independent type, having strut assembly, control arm and stabilizer bar. Strut assembly consists of shock absorber surrounded by a coil spring. It is attached to inner fender panel at top and is integral with steering knuckle at bottom. Lower control arm is connected by ball joint to steering knuckle and by bushing connection to frame (note configuration differences in *Fig. 1*). Stabilizer bar is connected by brackets to subframe and by bracket to control arm on Fox and by bushing and bolt on 5000.

**Fig. 1 Exploded View of Audi Front Suspension. Note Inset of 5000 Control Arm. Other Components Similar on Both Models.**

## ADJUSTMENTS

### WHEEL ALIGNMENT SPECIFICATIONS & PROCEDURES

*See Wheel Alignment Specifications and Procedures in WHEEL ALIGNMENT section.*

### WHEEL BEARING ADJUSTMENT

*See Wheel Bearing Adjustment in WHEEL ALIGNMENT section.*

### BALL JOINT CHECKING

*See Ball Joint Checking in WHEEL ALIGNMENT section.*

## REMOVAL & INSTALLATION

**NOTE** — *During any removal and installation procedure, if axle nut is removed or installed, do so with vehicle resting on ground at full curb weight.*

### STRUT ASSEMBLY

**Removal — 1)** Remove axle nut. Raise and support vehicle and remove wheel. Without detaching brake hose or line, unbolt brake caliper and suspend out of way. Remove rotor.

**2)** On Fox, index mark ball joint bracket on control arm and remove. On 5000, remove ball joint retaining bolt holding joint to hub assembly and remove. Using suitable tool, separate tie rod ball joint from strut arm. Remove stabilizer-to-frame brackets.

**3)** Using suitable puller attached to hub studs, apply pressure to drive axle shaft to separate strut assembly from drive axle.

**NOTE** — *If work is being done on right side, it may be necessary to remove exhaust pipe from manifold and bracket on transmission.*

**4)** While holding strut assembly from below, remove upper retaining nuts at fender panel (not strut plate nuts). Remove strut assembly.

**Disassembly — 1)** With strut assembly on bench, attach suitable spring compressor to coil spring and compress enough to remove upper piston rod retaining nut. Remove strut top plate.

**2)** Slowly release tension from coil spring and remove spring.

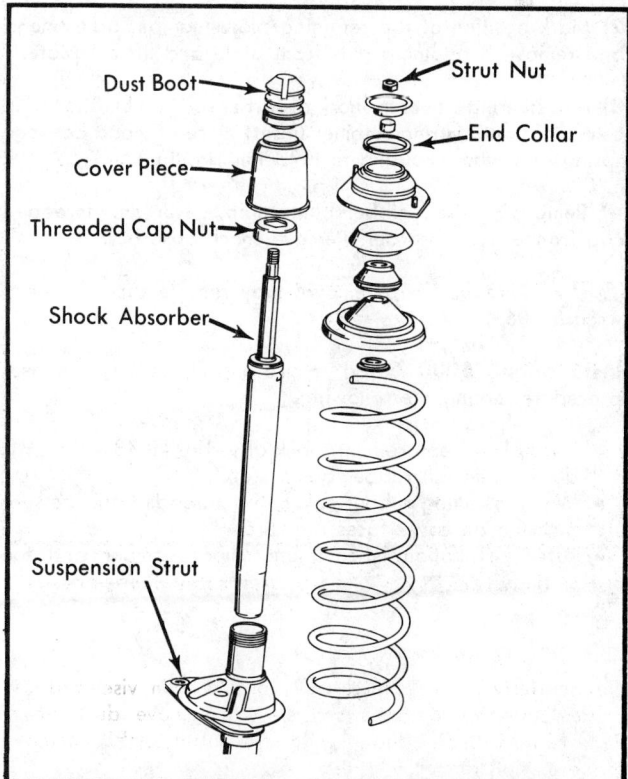

**Fig. 2 Disassembled View of Strut Assembly (Fox Shown; 5000 Similar)**

# Front Suspension

## AUDI (Cont.)

**3)** Use suitable tool (40-201, Fox; 2069, 5000) to remove threaded cap from top of shock absorber. Remove shock absorber.

**NOTE** — *Manufacturer suggests that a 3/8" diameter hole be drilled in bottom center of strut housing and into shock absorber to drain oil before shock absorber removal. Have container ready to catch oil. Do this only if shocks are being replaced. For 5000, replacement shock absorber kit (431 498 091) has been modified to include a cover over threaded cap and rubber boot above that. If replacing with this type, manufacturer notes that rubber bump stop should not be reinstalled.*

**Reassembly & Installation** — To reassemble and install, do so in reverse of disassembly and removal procedure, noting the following:

- On 5000 models, be sure damping ring locating tabs are mated with indentations on upper spring retainers.
- If nuts or bolts are covered with undercoat or grease, clean threads thoroughly before installation.
- Drive axle splines must be grease-free. Also, apply a narrow ring of suitable locking compound (D6) around outer end of drive shaft splines and allow 1 minute to dry before installing.
- Tighten drive axle nut with vehicle resting on ground.

## SHOCK ABSORBER (ON-CAR)

**Removal (5000 Only)** — **1)** Leave vehicle sitting on ground at full curb weight. Remove top shock absorber nut.

**2)** Mark position of top retaining plate (camber adjustment) and remove 3 retaining nuts from plate and lift off plate.

**3)** Turn steering wheel so shock absorber rod can be aligned in center of upper spring retainer (insert piece of wood between spring and wheel housing to hold this position).

**4)** Remove washer, rubber bump stop, cover and threaded cap from shock absorber. Remove shock absorber.

**NOTE** — *Threaded cap removal may require use of special wrench 2069.*

**Installation (5000 Only)** — To install, reverse removal procedure, noting the following:

- If installing replacement shock absorbor kit 431 498 091, do not reinstall rubber bump stop.
- When installing rubber cover over threaded nut, be sure marking on cover faces outward.
- After installation is complete, check camber and toe settings.

## LOWER CONTROL ARM

**Removal — 1)** Raise and support front of vehicle. Place additional support under strut assembly.

**2)** Detach stabilizer bar from control arm. It may be necessary to remove stabilizer bar clamps from frame to gain movement.

**3)** Loosen control arm mounting bolts. Remove axle drive shaft if necessary.

**4)** On Fox, index mark ball joint nuts and bracket. Remove ball joint mounting nuts, bolts and bracket (Fox) and separate ball joint from strut. Remove control arm.

**Bushing Replacement** — Using suitable support (40-21, Fox; VW415a, 5000), driver (VW409, Fox; 2040, 5000) and press, remove old bushings from control arm. Using same tools, lubricate and press in new bushings.

**Installation** — To install lower control arm, reverse removal procedure, noting the following:

- On Fox, if ball joint is not replaced at this time, be sure index marks made during removal are aligned.
- Tighten all nuts and bolts to specifications.
- Check alignment.

## TIGHTENING SPECIFICATIONS

| Application | Ft. Lbs. (mkg) |
|---|---|
| Stabilizer ar Bracket | |
| Fox | |
|   6 mm Bolt | 7 (1) |
|   8 mm Bolt | 14 (2) |
| 5000 | 76 (10.5) |
| Stabilizer Bar-to-Control Arm (5000) | 80 (11) |
| Control Arm-to-Subframe | |
| Fox | 50 (7) |
| 5000 | 80 (11) |
| Ball Joint-to-Strut Nut | |
| Fox | 25 (3.5) |
| 5000 | 47 (6.5) |
| Ball Joint Bracket Nuts (Fox) | 47 (6.5) |
| Axle Nut | |
| Fox | |
|   M18x1.5 | 145 (20) |
|   M20x1.5 | 175 (24) |
| 5000 | 203 (28) |
| Strut Upper Retaining Nuts | 18 (2.5) |
| Shock Absorber Threaded Cap | |
| Fox | 108 (15) |
| 5000 | 130 (18) |
| Shock Piston Rod Nut | 43 (6) |
| Strut Upper Plate (5000) | 18 (2.5) |

# Front Suspension

## BMW

320i
530i
633CSi
733i

### DESCRIPTION

Strut type suspension consisting of a vertically mounted strut assembly. Strut assembly is mounted to chassis frame at top by means of thrust bearing. Lower end of strut assembly is mounted to ball joint which is bolted to lower control arm. Strut assembly connects to ball joint by means of a steering knuckle which is bolted to strut assembly and ball joint. Strut assembly consists of a shock absorber built into strut tube. A coil spring is mounted on outside of strut assembly. A stabilizer bar is mounted to front of crossmember and is connected at ends to lower control arms. A strut rod connects lower control arm to crossmember.

**Fig. 1  BMW 320i Front Suspension Assembly**

### ADJUSTMENT

#### WHEEL ALIGNMENT SPECIFICATIONS & PROCEDURES

*See Wheel Alignment Specifications and Procedures in WHEEL ALIGNMENT Section.*

#### WHEEL BEARINGS

*See Wheel Bearings in WHEEL ALIGNMENT Section.*

#### BALL JOINT CHECKING

*See Ball Joint Checking in WHEEL ALIGNMENT Section.*

### REMOVAL & INSTALLATION

#### FRONT SUSPENSION ASSEMBLY

**Removal — 1)** Raise and support vehicle. Remove front wheels. Detach brake line mounting brackets from strut tube. On 733i, detach brake indicator light wiring from caliper clip. On all models, remove caliper and suspend out of way. On 320i, disconnect stabilizer bar at frame.

**2)** Disconnect steering shaft pinch bolt at universal joint. Index mark shaft and separate from "U" joint. Drain power steering unit, detach power steering hoses and plug openings. Remove nuts from engine dampers, heat shields and engine mounts (as equipped). Remove clamps from automatic transmission cooling lines (if equipped).

**3)** Check along front axle for engine ground wire. If attached at this location, remove wire. Detach top strut-to-fender mountings. Using overhead hoist to support engine and a floor jack to support suspension, detach right end of front axle from frame member and lower suspension from vehicle.

**Fig. 2  BMW 530i, 633CSi and 733i Front Suspension**

**Installation —** To install reverse removal procedure and note the following: Make sure shoulder of engine mount engages

# Front Suspension

## BMW (Cont.)

properly in opening. Reconnect steering shaft while front wheels are pointing straight ahead. Ensure steering shaft index marks are aligned and that mounting screw engages safety groove. Check wheel alignment and bleed power steering unit, if equipped.

### LOWER CONTROL ARM

**Removal — 1)** Raise vehicle and remove front wheel. Disconnect stabilizer link or bar from control arm. If strut rod connects to control arm, remove from arm.

**2)** Detach inner end of control arm from axle carrier. On models held with castle nut only, remove castle nut and press control arm from steering knuckle. If held with safety wire, remove wire, then separate control arm and steering knuckle from shock absorber assembly.

**3)** Detach tie rod ball joint. Remove castle nut from steering knuckle arm (if not done so in previous step) and press control arm free.

**Inspection —** Check axial play of ball joint. If play exceeds specified measurements, replace control arm assembly.

#### Ball Joint Axial Play

| Application | In. (mm) |
| --- | --- |
| 320i, 633CSi, 733i | .055 (1.4) |
| 530i | .094 (2.4) |

**Installation —** To install, reverse removal procedure, replacing all self-locking nuts.

### STRUT TUBE ASSEMBLY

**Removal — 1)** Raise front of vehicle and remove front wheel. Detach stabilizer bar from control arm. Detach brake line brackets from strut tube. Remove caliper from rotor and suspend out of way. If equipped, detach brake warning indicator wire from caliper.

**2)** Detach tie rod ball joint from steering knuckle arm. Remove lower strut mounting bolts. Remove 3 upper strut mounting bolts and remove strut tube assembly.

**Disassembly — 1)** Place strut tube assembly in spring compressor. Slightly collapse spring. Remove end cap. Unscrew piston rod lock nut. Slowly release spring pressure and remove upper spring seat bearing and mounting hardware.

**2)** Remove auxiliary spring off piston rod. Remove shock absorber cap nut. Slide out shock absorber. Pour out used fluid.

**Reassembly — 1)** Fill strut housing with 1-1.5 ounces of SAE 30 oil.

**2)** Fit shock absorber. Tighten cap nut. Slide auxiliary spring into place. Guide coil spring into lower spring seat. Set upper bearing mount (upper spring seat) on top of coil spring. Slide piston rod through opening, after extending rod as far as possible. Attach compressor and collapse spring enough to install upper mounting nut.

**Installation —** To install, reverse removal procedure and tighten all nuts and bolts.

### STABILIZER BAR

**Removal, 320i and 733i —** Raise and support vehicle. Remove front wheels for easier access. Detach stabilizer link or bar from control arms. Remove stabilizer bar brackets and take stabilizer bar from vehicle.

**NOTE** — *Before installation, inspect bushings for excessive wear and replace as necessary.*

**Installation —** To install, reverse removal procedure.

### STRUT ROD (TRAILING ARM)

**Removal, 530i and 633CSi — 1)** Raise vehicle and place on safety stands. Remove front wheels.

**2)** Separate stabilizer bar from control arm. Remove nut and thrust washer mounting strut rod to control arm.

**3)** Remove opposite end strut rod nut. Separate control arm from crossmember (axle carrier) and remove strut rod.

**Installation —** To install, reverse removal procedure and note: Convex side of thrust washer faces nut.

---

### TIGHTENING SPECIFICATIONS

| Application | Ft. Lbs. (mkg) |
| --- | --- |
| Stabilizer Bar or Link-to-Control Arm | |
|   320i | 50-65 (6.9-9.0) |
|   733i | 18-20 (2.5-2.8) |
| Stabilizer Link-to-Stabilizer Bar | |
|   733i | 36-40 (5.0-5.5) |
| Control Arm-to-Axle Carrier | |
|   733i | 59-66 (8.2-9.2) |
| Stabilizer Bar Brackets | 34-37 (4.3-4.8) |
| Front Axle-to-Engine Carrier | |
|   320i | 31-35 (4.3-4.8) |
|   530i & 633CSi | 58-65 (8.1-9.0) |
| Shock Absorber Cap Nut | 87-101 (12-14) |
| Tie Rod Castle Nut | 25-29 (3.5-4.0) |

## CAPRI

**Capri**

### DESCRIPTION

Strut type suspension with strut assemblies mounted vertically between lower control arms and upper body members. Strut assemblies are mounted to lower control arms by means of ball joints. Strut assembly consists of a coil spring mounted over strut tube with a hydraulic shock absorber built into strut tube. A wheel spindle is integral with bottom of strut tube. A stabilizer bar is mounted to front chassis members and at ends to lower control arms.

### ADJUSTMENT

#### WHEEL ALIGNMENT SPECIFICATIONS & PROCEDURES

See Wheel Alignment Specifications & Procedures in WHEEL ALIGNMENT Section.

#### WHEEL BEARING ADJUSTMENT

See Wheel Bearing Adjustment in WHEEL ALIGNMENT Section.

#### BALL JOINT CHECKING

See Ball Joint Checking in WHEEL ALIGNMENT Section.

### REMOVAL & INSTALLATION

#### STABILIZER BAR

**Removal** — Raise vehicle and place safety stands under chassis members. Disconnect clamps holding stabilizer bar to chassis and remove cotter pins and nuts retaining stabilizer bar to control arms. Slide stabilizer bar forward and remove from vehicle.

*Fig. 1  Front Suspension Assembly with Detail of Lower Ball Joint*

**Installation** — To install, reverse removal procedure noting the following: Tighten all nuts and bolts when vehicle weight is on ground.

#### LOWER CONTROL ARM

**Removal** — Raise vehicle and place safety stands under chassis members. Disconnect stabilizer bar from control arm as previously outlined. Remove self-locking nut and flat washer and slide out control arm pivot bolt. Remove cotter pin and nut from ball joint stud and separate ball joint from steering knuckle. Remove control arm from vehicle.

**Installation** — To install, reverse removal procedure noting the following: Tighten all nuts and bolts. Bleed brakes when all operations are completed.

#### STRUT ASSEMBLY

**Removal** — Raise vehicle and place safety stands under chassis members. Remove tire and wheel. Disconnect brake flex line from bracket on strut tube. Place a jack under control arm and raise enough to release connecting rod from steering arm when cotter pin and nut are removed. Lower jack and remove. Remove cotter pin and nut from ball joint stud and separate ball joint from strut assembly. Remove three bolts securing strut assembly top mount to fender panel and remove strut assembly from vehicle.

**Disassembly** — Using a suitable spring compressor (T70P-5045), compress spring enough to remove piston rod nut. **NOTE** — *Force nut collar out of keyway by using a small punch.* Remove cranked retainer. Remove top mount, then lift off spring upper seat, suspension spring, and rubber bumper. Use a suitable wrench to remove the shock cartridge.

**Reassembly** — Install shock cartridge into top of outer casing, then tighten to specifications using a suitable wrench. Install coil spring, rubber bumper, plug, and spring upper seat. Assemble top mount and cranked retainer, then install collared piston rod nut. Tighten nut to 5-10 ft. lbs. (.7-1.4 mkg) but do not bend collar. Remove coil spring retainers from front spring.

**Installation** — Reverse removal procedure for installation while noting the following: Tighten piston rod nut when unit is installed in vehicle and weight of vehicle is on front wheels, then force collar into keyway with a small punch. Bleed brakes when all operations are completed.

### TIGHTENING SPECIFICATIONS

| Application | Ft. Lbs. (mkg) |
|---|---|
| Piston Rod Nut | ①28-32 (3.9-4.4) |
| Strut Assembly Upper Mount | 15-18 (2.1-2.5) |
| Ball Joint Stud Nut | 30-35 (4.2-4.9) |
| Connecting Rod-to-Steering Arm | 18-22 (2.5-3.0) |
| Lower Control Arm Pivot Bolt | 22-27 (3.0-3.7) |
| Stabilizer Bar Clamps | 15-18 (2.1-2.5) |
| Stabilizer Bar-to-Control Arm Nut | ①15-45 (2.1-6.2) |
| Brake Caliper Bolts | 45-50 (6.2-6.9) |

① — Tighten with front wheels straight ahead.

## COURIER

### Courier

## DESCRIPTION

Independent type suspension, consisting of upper and lower control arms and wheel spindle mounted between upper and lower arms by means of ball joints. Upper control arm pivots on a shaft attached to frame, lower control arm pivots on a shaft mounted to crossmember. A coil spring is mounted between lower control arm and frame. Shock absorber is hydraulic double action type, mounted between lower control arm and frame inside coil spring.

**Fig. 1 Exploded View of Front Suspension Assembly**

## ADJUSTMENT

### WHEEL ALIGNMENT SPECIFICATIONS & PROCEDURES

*See Wheel Alignment Specifications & Procedures in WHEEL ALIGNMENT Section.*

### WHEEL BEARING ADJUSTMENT

*See Wheel Bearing Adjustment in WHEEL ALIGNMENT Section.*

### BALL JOINT CHECKING

*See Ball Joint Checking in WHEEL ALIGNMENT Section.*

## REMOVAL & INSTALLATION

### SHOCK ABSORBERS

**Removal** – Remove nut, rubber bushing and washer attaching upper end of shock absorber to crossmember. Remove lower retaining bolts holding shock absorber to lower control arm, and remove shock absorber from vehicle.

**Installation** – Reverse removal procedure and tighten mounting bolts to specifications.

### UPPER BALL JOINT & CONTROL ARM

**Removal** – 1) Raise and suitably support vehicle under lower control arm. Lower vehicle until arm is off rubber bumper stop. Remove tire and wheel. Remove cotter pin and nut attaching upper ball joint to spindle.

2) Strike tapered fit with a hammer to break loose and separate ball joint from spindle. Remove three retaining nuts and bolts and remove ball joint from control arm. To remove, open hood and remove two upper arm retaining bolts, then remove control arm from vehicle.

**Installation** – Position ball joint in upper arm and tighten bolts to specifications. Install control arm in vehicle and tighten bolts to specifications. Install spindle on ball joint, tighten nut to specification and install cotter pin. Install tire and wheel, remove safety stands and lower vehicle. Check caster, camber and toe-in.

### LOWER CONTROL ARM, BALL JOINT & COIL SPRING

**Removal** – 1) Raise vehicle and place safety stands under frame behind both lower control arms. Remove wheel and tire. Remove lower shock absorber bolts and collapse shock absorber up into spring. Remove retaining bolt attaching stabilizer bar to lower control arm.

2) Install a floor jack under spring area of lower arm and raise arm to relieve spring pressure. Remove cotter pin and nut attaching lower control arm to spindle, strike tapered fit with hammer and separate ball joint from spindle.

3) Remove three bolts and nuts retaining ball joint to lower control arm and remove ball joint. Release jack and lower arm enough to remove coil spring. Remove three bolts and nuts retaining lower control arm to crossmember and remove arm from vehicle.

**Installation** – 1) Place lower control arm in position, install three retaining bolts and nuts, DO NOT tighten. Place coil spring in position in lower arm and hold in place with a "C" clamp. Place upper end of spring in pocket in frame and raise lower control arm with a jack.

2) Position ball joint in lower arm and tighten bolts. Raise lower control arm with jack enough to install ball joint in spindle, refit nut.

3) Tighten three lower arm retaining bolts left loose. Pull shock absorber down and tighten retaining bolts. Install stabilizer bar as previously outlined. Install tire and wheel, remove safety stands and lower vehicle. Check caster, camber and toe-in.

### TIGHTENING SPECIFICATIONS

| Application | Ft. Lbs. (mkg) |
|---|---|
| Upper Ball Joint Stud | 47(6.5) |
| Lower Ball Joint Stud | 65(9.0) |
| Ball Joint-to-Upper Arm | 17(2.4) |
| Ball Joint-to-Lower Arm | 65(9.0) |
| Shock Absorber | |
| Lower Mount | 14.5(2.0) |
| Upper Mount | ① |
| Control Arm-to-Frame | |
| Lower | 62(8.6) |
| Upper | 69(9.5) |
| Lower Arm Shaft-to-Lower Arm | 61.5(8.5) |
| Bumper-to-Lower Arm | 65(9.0) |
| Bumper-to-Upper Arm | 17(2.4) |

① – Distance from top of lock nut to top of shock absorber stud should be .256" (6.5 mm).

## DATSUN F10

**F10**

### DESCRIPTION

All models use a strut type front suspension system. Shock absorbers are built into each strut. Upper end of strut is mounted to inner fender panel. Lower end is connected by a ball joint to lower control arm. Control arm mounts at two points on subframe. Steering knuckle is removable from strut. Knuckle bolts to strut with four bolts and has a hole for axle drive shafts to pass through.

### ADJUSTMENTS

#### WHEEL ALIGNMENT SPECIFICATIONS & PROCEDURES

See Wheel Alignment Specifications and Procedures in WHEEL ALIGNMENT Section.

#### WHEEL BEARING ADJUSTMENT

See Wheel Bearing Adjustment in WHEEL ALIGNMENT Section.

#### BALL JOINT CHECKING

See Ball Joint Checking in WHEEL ALIGNMENT Section.

### REMOVAL & INSTALLATION

#### CONTROL ARM

**Removal** — Raise and support vehicle with safety stands. Remove tire and wheel. Remove bolts securing lower control arm to ball joint. Take off nut mounting stabilizer bar to control arm. Disconnect control arm from subframe by removing two mounting bolts.

**Fig. 1    Exploded View of Control Arm and Stabilizer Bar**

**Inspection** — Inspect arm for distortion. Replace control arm bushings using a press. Make sure new bushings extend evenly on both sides of hole.

**Installation** — To install, reverse removal procedure and note: Control arm bolts must be tightened with weight of vehicle on ground.

#### STEERING KNUCKLE (INNER BEARING HOUSING)

**Removal** — Raise vehicle and place on safety stands. Remove tire and wheel. Remove caliper and suspend out of way. Remove stub axle. Remove rotor. Disconnect ball joint and support control arm. Remove four bolts securing steering knuckle (inner bearing housing) to strut.

**Fig. 2    Exploded View of Steering Knuckle and Strut**

**Installation** — To install, reverse removal procedure an note: Adjust wheel bearings.

#### BALL JOINT

**Removal** — Raise vehicle and support on safety stands. Remove tire and wheel. Remove ball joint stud nut. Use ball joint driver and hammer to remove ball joint. **NOTE** — Avoid damage to ball joint dust cover. Remove bolts securing ball joint to lower control arm.

**Installation** — To install ball joint, reverse removal procedure and make sure new cotter pin is installed. Replace ball joint dust cover if cracked.

#### STABILIZER BAR

**Removal** — Raise and support vehicle with safety stands. Remove nuts mounting stabilizer bar to control arm. Disconnect and remove brackets mounting stabilizer bar to subframe.

**Installation** — To install, reverse removal procedure and replace any bushing that is worn or cracked.

# Front Suspension

## DATSUN F10 (Cont.)

### STRUT ASSEMBLY

**Removal – 1)** Raise vehicle and suitably support with safety stands. Remove tire and wheel. Working from inside engine compartment, remove cap. Partially loosen lock nut mounting piston rod. Disconnect brake line and plug opening. Detach tie rod from steering knuckle.

Packing Gland

"O" ring

Piston Rod

Cylinder

Strut →

Cap

Mounting

Plate

Seat

Dust Seal

Spring Seat

Dust Cover

Coil Spring

Bumper

*Fig. 3   Exploded View of F10 Strut Assembly*

**2)** Place safety stand under control arm for support. Remove four bolts mounting strut to steering knuckle. Remove three nuts keeping upper portion of strut to inner fender panel. Maneuver strut and coil spring assembly from vehicle.

**Disassembly – 1)** Place strut in a vise and slightly compress coil spring. Remove piston rod nut and take off all upper mounting hardware. *See Fig. 2.*

**2)** Remove packing gland. Remove "O" ring, then remove piston rod assembly and guide bushing. Drain oil from inner shock absorber cylinder, then pull out cylinder.

**Inspection –** Inspect all components for damage or excessive wear. Always replace packing gland and "O" ring.

**Reassembly –** Install cylinder and piston rod in strut. Add 7 ounces (210 cc) of shock absorber oil for AMPCO struts or 7 1/3 ounces (220 cc) of oil for K.Y.B. struts. Fit guide bushing in cylinder. Slide "O" ring over guide bushing. Install new packing gland. **NOTE** – *Lubricate sealing lip with multi-purpose grease.* Torque packing gland. Pump piston rod several times and bleed air from cylinder. Refit coil spring. **NOTE** – *Only torque piston rod nut after strut has been reinstalled.*

**Installation –** To install strut assembly, reverse removal procedure and note following: Make sure all contact surfaces are clean and dirt free.

### TIGHTENING SPECIFICATIONS

| Application | Ft. Lbs. (mkg) |
| --- | --- |
| Packing Gland | 58-80 (8.0-11.0) |
| Piston Rod Nut | 46-53 (6.3-7.3) |
| Strut-to-Steering Knuckle | 24-33 (3.3-4.5) |
| Ball Joint Stud Nut | 22-29 (3.0-4.0) |
| Ball Joint-to-Control Arm | 40-47 (5.5-6.5) |
| Caliper Mounting Bolt | 40-47 (5.5-6.5) |
| Control Arm Mounting Nut | 42-51 (5.8-7.0) |
| Stabilizer Bar | 6-9 (.8-1.2) |

# Front Suspension

## DATSUN B210, 200SX, 280Z, 510, & 810

B210
200SX
280Z
510
810

### DESCRIPTION

Strut type suspension consisting of a vertically mounted strut assembly, lower control arm, stabilizer bar and compression rod. Strut assembly is mounted at top to chassis frame by a thrust bearing and at bottom to lower control arm by a ball joint. Strut assembly consists of a shock absorber built into outer strut tube, a coil spring mounted on outside of strut tube, and a wheel spindle integral with bottom of strut tube. Compression rod is mounted between lower control arm and chassis. Stabilizer bar is mounted to front chassis member and is connected at end of lower control arm.

### ADJUSTMENT

#### WHEEL ALIGNMENT SPECIFICATIONS & PROCEDURES

*See Wheel Alignment Specifications & Procedures in WHEEL ALIGNMENT Section.*

#### WHEEL BEARING ADJUSTMENT

*See Wheel Bearing Adjustment in WHEEL ALIGNMENT Section.*

#### BALL JOINT CHECKING

*See Ball Joint Checking in WHEEL ALIGNMENT Section.*

### REMOVAL & INSTALLATION

#### SPRING & STRUT ASSEMBLY

**Removal — 1)** Raise and support front of vehicle. Remove front wheels. Detach brake hose from bracket on front strut (if required). Remove caliper assembly retaining bolts and remove caliper from axle.

**2)** Remove bolts holding strut to knuckle arm. Detach knuckle arm from bottom of strut by forcing off with suitable pry bar.

**3)** Place jack under strut to support it when nuts are removed. Remove 3 nuts holding strut to hood ledge and remove strut and spring as an assembly.

**Disassembly — 1)** Thoroughly clean strut assembly. Fix assembly in suitable holding tool (KV48100300) and clamp tool in vise.

**2)** With spring compressor, press spring down just far enough to permit turning of strut mounting insulator and remove self-locking nut.

*Fig. 1  Assembled View of B210 Front Suspension, with Some Items Shown in Detail*
*(All Other Models Are Similar)*

## DATSUN B210, 200SX, 280Z, 510 & 810 (Cont.)

**NOTE** – *Be sure spring tool evenly engages on at least 3 coils. Do not hit piston rod of strut with spring tool.*

3) Take out strut insulator, bearing, dust seal, upper spring seat, spring and rubber bumper.

4) Push piston rod down until it bottoms. Remove gland packing using suitable wrench (ST35500001). Remove "O" ring from top of piston rod guide and lift out piston rod and cylinder.

**NOTE** – *The piston rod, piston rod guide and cylinder are furnished as a matched set with precision mating surfaces.*

5) Drain fluid from inner and outer cylinder and discard. Wash all parts in solvent.

**Reassembly – 1)** Install strut outer casing onto suitable holding tool (KV48100300). Install cylinder and piston rod assembly (shock absorber kit) in outer casing.

2) Remove piston rod guide from cylinder and pour in specified amount of new fluid (outer casing).

### Oil Replacement Amounts

| Application | Ounces |
| --- | --- |
| B210 & 510 | 11.0 |
| 280Z | 11.5 |
| 200SX & 810 | 10.0 |

3) Install piston rod guide, taking care not to damage guide with threaded portion of rod. Install new "O" ring over rod guide. Lube inner edge of sealing lips of gland packing and install packing, using suitable wrench (ST35530000). Tighten gland packing to specification.

4) To correctly bleed strut assembly, stand strut vertically with spindle end down and pull piston rod up to end of stroke. Turn strut assembly until spindle end is up and depress piston rod to end of stroke. Repeat several times until there is no variation of pressure between pushing and pulling piston rod.

5) Pull piston rod fully out and install rubber bumper. Place spring on lower spring seat and compress with proper tool (ST35651001). Lubricate dust seal and then install dust cover, spring seat, dust seal, mounting bearing and insulator.

6) Tighten new self-locking nut to specification. To prevent entry of dirt, apply thick coat of multi-purpose grease around upper seal. After positioning spring between upper and lower seats, release spring compressor slowly. Raise rubber bumper to upper spring seat.

**Installation** – To install, reverse removal procedure, tightening nuts and bolts to specification.

### LOWER CONTROL ARM & BALL JOINT

**Removal – 1)** Raise vehicle. Support with stands. Remove tire, wheel and splash guard (if equipped).

2) Detach tie rod at ball socket. Remove steering knuckle arm bolts and separate arm from bottom of strut. Separate compression rod and stabilizer bar from lower control arm. Remove bolt connecting lower control arm to crossmember. Remove lower control arm with ball joint and knuckle arm.

3) Place arm in vise, loosen control arm ball joint bolts and remove ball joint. Place steering knuckle arm in vise and remove cotter pin and nut. Remove knuckle from control arm.

4) With suitable tool (ST36720000), extract bushing, from lower control arm.

**NOTE** – *On 810 models, steering gear arm must be separated from sector shaft and steering linkage lowered to remove lower control arm from driver's side. On passenger side, idler arm assembly must be separated from frame and linkage lowered.*

**Installation** – Using suitable bushing replacement tool set (ST36700000) press bushing into control arm. To install lower control arm, reverse removal procedure. Do not tighten nuts and bolts to final torque until weight of vehicle is on front wheels.

### COMPRESSION RODS

**Removal** – Raise vehicle and support with safety stands; remove tire and wheel. Remove splash board, back off nuts securing compression rod to mounting bracket. Remove bolts attaching compression rod to lower control arm. Rod can now be maneuvered from vehicle.

**Installation** – To install, reverse removal procedure and tighten nuts and bolts.

### TIGHTENING SPECIFICATIONS

| Application | Ft. Lbs. (mkg) |
| --- | --- |
| Gland Packing | 51-94 (7-13) |
| Piston Rod Self-Locking Nut | 43-54 (6.0-7.5) |
| Strut-to-Body Nuts | 18-25 (2.5-3.5) |
| Steering Knuckle Arm-to-Strut | 53-72 (7.3-9.9) |
| Stabilizer Bar Bracket Bolts | |
| B210 & 200SX | 12-15 (1.6-2.1) |
| 280Z | 9-20 (1.2-2.7) |
| 810 | 20-27 (2.7-3.7) |
| 510 | 52-31 (3.2.4.3) |
| Compression Rod-to-Lower Control Arm | |
| B210 & 200SX | 35-46 (4.9-6.3) |
| 280Z | 44-51 (6.1-7.1) |
| 810 | 33-40 (4.5-5.5) |
| 510 | 37-44 (5.2-6.1) |
| Compression Rod Nut | 33-40 (4.5-5.5) |
| Lower Control Arm-to-Crossmember | |
| B210 & 200SX | 65-72 (9.0-10.0) |
| 280Z | 80-101 (11.1-14.0) |
| 810 & 510 | 58-80 (8.0-11.0) |
| Ball Joint-to-Lower Control Arm | |
| B210 & 200SX | 35-46 (4.9-6.3) |
| 280Z | 40-55 (6.5-7.6) |
| 810 | 33-40 (4.5-5.5) |
| 510 | 37-44 (5.1-6.1) |
| Tie Rod Ball Joint | 40-55 (5.5-7.6) |

## DATSUN PICKUP

**Pickup**

## DESCRIPTION

Front suspension is an independent type with upper and lower control arms which are connected by ball joints. This suspension also incorporates a torsion bar which connects to lower control arm inner end and to frame bracket, a strut rod which connects to lower control arm outer end and an optional stabilizer bar. A double-acting shock absorber is also used. See Fig. 1.

## ADJUSTMENT

### WHEEL ALIGNMENT SPECIFICATIONS & PROCEDURES

See Wheel Alignment Specifications & Procedures in WHEEL ALIGNMENT Section.

### WHEEL BEARING ADJUSTMENT

See Wheel Bearing Adjustment in WHEEL ALIGNMENT Section.

### BALL JOINT CHECKING

See Ball Joint Checking in WHEEL ALIGNMENT Section.

## REMOVAL & INSTALLATION

### SHOCK ABSORBER

**Removal** — 1) Raise and support front of vehicle. Remove wheel assembly.

2) While holding upper stem of shock absorber, remove lock nut, adjusting nut, washer and bushing from upper end of shock. Remove nut and bolt at lower end and remove shock absorber.

**Installation** — To install, reverse removal procedure and tighten nuts and bolts to specifications.

### TORSION BAR

**Removal** — 1) Raise and support front of vehicle. If removing left torsion bar, remove catalytic converter first.

**Fig. 1  Exploded View of Datsun Pickup Front Suspension**

## DATSUN PICKUP (Cont.)

**2)** Loosen nuts at anchor arm bolt. Remove dust cover at back end of torsion bar and detach snap ring. Pull anchor arm rearward and withdraw torsion bar.

**Installation — 1)** Coat serrated portions of torsion bar with grease and position bar into torque arm.

**NOTE** — *Torsion bars are identified for left and right installations with an "R" and "L" on end of bar.*

**2)** Install anchor arm and tighten adjusting nut to obtain specified dimension for "A" when bar is in contact with rebound bumper. See Fig. 2.

**3)** Install snap ring and dust cover. Temporarily tighten adjusting nut until dimension "B" is obtained.

**4)** Install wheel assembly and lower vehicle. Be sure vehicle is at curb weight (full fuel tank and no passengers). Tighten anchor arm bolt lock nut to specification.

### Dimensions for Setting Torsion Bar

| Application | In. (mm) |
| --- | --- |
| Dimension "A" | .28-.67 (7-17) |
| Dimension "B" | 2.36-2.76 (60-70) |

**Fig. 2   View Showing Measuring Points for Installation of Anchor Pin**

### UPPER CONTROL ARM & BALL JOINT

**Removal — 1)** Raise and support front of vehicle. Remove wheel assembly. Loosen torsion bar anchor arm lock nut and adjusting nut.

**2)** Remove cotter pin and nut from upper ball joint and separate ball joint from steering knuckle with suitable tool.

**3)** Loosen bolts holding upper ball joint to upper control arm and remove ball joint.

**4)** Remove bolts retaining upper link spindle and remove spindle and upper control arm from mounting, collecting all camber adjusting shims present.

**5)** Remove nuts and washers at both ends of upper link spindle. Place assembly on a vise and press upper link spindle from one end and remove rubber bushing. Press from other end and remove other bushing. Remove spindle from upper control arm.

**Installation — 1)** Apply soapy solution or other lubricant to rubber bushing and press into place from outer side of control arm until bushing protrudes as specified for dimension "C".See Fig. 3.

**2)** Position upper link spindle into control arm, with spindle washer having its beveled edge inward as shown.

**3)** Press-fit bushing on other end of spindle and control arm as described in step **1)** above.

**4)** After bushings are installed, check dimensions "C" "D" and "E" to be sure they match given specifications.

### Dimensions for Installing Upper Control Arm Bushings

| Application | In. (mm) |
| --- | --- |
| Dimension "C" | .18 (4.5) |
| Dimension "D" | 5.7-5.8 (144.6-146.6) |
| Dimension "E" | 1.1 (28.3) |

**Fig. 3   Showing Installed Positions of Bushings for Upper Control Arm**

**5)** Install upper control arm assembly to its mounting by setting upper link spindle-to-control arm position as shown. See Fig. 4. Tighten mounting bolts to specifications, installing camber shims to original positions.

**6)** Install upper ball joint to upper control arm, tightening mounting nuts to specifications.

**7)** Position upper ball joint stud into steering knuckle hole and install retaining nut and cotter pin. Be sure grease does not contact tapered area of ball joint stud and knuckle or ball joint stud threads.

**8)** Install tire and wheel. Adjust vehicle riding height. See *"Riding Height" under appropriate article in WHEEL ALIGNMENT section.* Check and adjust wheel alignment.

**Fig. 4   Side View of Upper Control Arm Showing Alignment of Spindle in Relation to Control Arm Centerline**

## DATSUN PICKUP (Cont.)

### LOWER CONTROL ARM & BALL JOINT

**Removal** – 1) Raise and support front of vehicle. Remove wheel assembly. Remove shock absorber as described in this article.

2) Loosen torsion bar anchor arm lock nut and adjusting nut and remove anchor arm bolt. Remove dust cover and snap ring and move anchor arm and torsion bar rearward as far as possible.

3) Detach stabilizer connecting rod from lower control arm. Remove strut rod from lower control arm. Remove cotter pin and nut and remove lower ball joint from knuckle.

4) Remove lower control arm spindle by tapping on front end of spindle and driving toward rear. Move torsion bar down as required. Remove spindle.

5) Remove lower ball joint by removing retaining nuts and bolts. Using suitable drift (ST36070000), drive out lower control arm bushings. *Fig. 5*. Remove bolt attaching torque arm to lower control arm and remove torque arm.

*Fig. 5  Removing Bushings from Lower Control Arm*

**Installation** – To install, reverse removal procedure, tightening nuts and bolts to specifications. Be sure grease does not contact tapered area of ball joint stud or knuckle hole and does not contact ball joint threads. Adjust vehicle riding height. *See appropriate article in WHEEL ALIGNMENT section.*

### STRUT ROD

**Removal** – Remove bolt holding strut rod to lower control arm and separate these parts. Remove nut attaching strut rod to bracket and remove rod with bushings, collar and washers.

**Installation** – To install, reverse removal procedure, noting the following: Swing strut rod a few times to settle bushings and washers; do not allow grease or oil to contact rubber bushings; tighten retaining nuts and bolts to specifications.

### STABILIZER BAR

**Removal** – Remove nut holding stabilizer connecting rod to lower control arm. Remove bolt holding stabilizer mounting bracket to frame. Remove nut attaching stabilizer and connecting rod and remove these parts.

**Installation** – To install, reverse removal procedure, noting the following: Install stabilizer so white paint mark is on left side and be sure locating mark is positioned inside frame mount bushing.

## TIGHTENING SPECIFICATIONS

| Application | Ft. Lbs. (mkg) |
|---|---|
| Shock Absorber Upper Nut | 12-16 (1.7-2.2) |
| Shock Absorber Lower Nut | 22-30 (3.1-4.1) |
| Anchor Bolt Lock Nut | 22-30 (3.1-4.1) |
| Upper Control Arm Spindle Nut | 56-76 (7.7-10.5) |
| Upper Link Spindle-to-Frame | 80-108 (11.1-15.0) |
| Upper Ball Joint-to-Control Arm | 12-16 (1.7-2.2) |
| Upper Ball Joint-to-Knuckle | 58-72 (8-10) |
| Lower Ball Joint-to-Control Arm | 28-38 (3.9-5.3) |
| Torque Arm-to-Lower Control Arm | |
|   Outer Nut | 20-27 (2.7-3.7) |
|   Inner Nut | 26-33 (3.6-4.6) |
| Lower Control Arm Spindle Nut | 80-108 (11.1-15.0) |
| Lower Ball Joint-to-Knuckle | 127-141 (17.5-19.5) |
| Strut Rod-to-Lower Control Arm | 28-38 (3.9-5.3) |
| Strut Rod-to-Bracket | 22-30 (3.0-4.2) |

## FIAT X1/9

**X1/9**

### DESCRIPTION

Independent type front suspension consisting of lower control arms and hydraulic shock absorbers, surrounded by coil springs. Steering knuckle is attached to lower control arm at sealed ball joint. Shock absorber is attached to steering knuckle at bottom and to fender panel at top. Lower control arm pivots in rubber bushings attached to crossmember. Stabilizer bar is mounted to lower control arm and at front, to frame.

**Fig. 1  Sectional View of Front Suspension Assembly**

### ADJUSTMENT

#### WHEEL ALIGNMENT SPECIFICATIONS & PROCEDURES

*See Wheel Alignment Specifications and Procedures in WHEEL ALIGNMENT Section.*

#### WHEEL BEARING ADJUSTMENT

*See Wheel Bearing Adjustment in WHEEL ALIGNMENT Section.*

#### BALL JOINT CHECKING

*See Ball Joint Checking in WHEEL ALIGNMENT Section.*

### REMOVAL & INSTALLATION

#### FRONT SUSPENSION ASSEMBLY

**Removal** — Raise and support vehicle; remove tire and wheel. Remove front disc brake caliper assembly. **NOTE** — *See appropriate article in BRAKE Section.* Remove bolts and plate holding shock absorber tube to steering knuckle.

Separate shock absorber at top by removing upper mounting nuts. Disconnect lower control arm from stabilizer bar bracket and ball joint. Remove tie rod nut and force tie rod from steering knuckle. Maneuver assembly from vehicle.

**Inspection** — Check rubber bushings in control arm and replace any that appear worn. Inspect ball joints for excessive play or damage; replace as necessary.

**Installation** — To install suspension assembly, reverse removal procedure ensuring all nuts and bolts are properly torqued.

### STRUT ASSEMBLY

**Removal** — Raise and support vehicle under chassis. Disconnect upper strut assembly mount from inner fender panel. Remove bolts securing strut assembly to steering knuckle and carefully maneuver strut from vehicle.

**Disassembly** — 1) Install strut assembly in suitable spring compressor and collapse coil. Remove nut from center of upper mount. Release spring compressor and remove upper mount and coil spring.

2) Inspect springs for cracks or distortion. Springs are manufactured in two classes and identified by paint markings. Class A springs are marked with a yellow stripe on outside of center coils and class B springs are marked with a green stripe. If springs are replaced for any reason, use a spring of same class.

**Reassembly** — Using same spring compressor as previously outlined, reverse disassembly procedure to assemble strut assembly.

**Installation** — To install strut assembly, reverse removal procedure. Do not tighten strut assembly lower mount until weight of vehicle is on ground.

### CONTROL ARM, BUSHINGS & BALL JOINTS

**Removal** — Remove complete front suspension assembly as previously outlined. Remove ball joint stud nut and separate ball joint from steering knuckle with a suitable puller.

**Disassembly** — Inspect ball joint for wear or distortion. If ball joint is defective, complete control arm must be replaced. Inspect bearings for wear or damage. If defective, drill out metal sleeve from inside rubber bushing and extract bushing.

**Reassembly** — Position outer washer, bushing and sleeve on centering pin of a suitable bushing installation tool. Place control arm over bushing and washer for opposite side. Place control arm, components and tool into a press. Position remaining tool components in sleeve and press into position with a pressure of approximately 2200-2645 pounds.

**Installation** — To install control arm, attach to steering knuckle, tighten ball joint stud nut and install suspension assembly as previously outlined.

## FIAT X1/9 (Cont.)

Fig. 2 Exploded View of Lower Control Arm Assembly

Fig. 3 Exploded View of Stabilizer Bar Assembly

**Installation** — To install stabilizer bar, reverse removal procedure noting the following: Replace any rubber grommet that appears distorted or severely worn.

**STABILIZER BAR**

**Removal** — Raise and support vehicle. Disconnect stabilizer mounting bolt from lower control arm. Remove stabilizer attaching hardware from front end of stabilizer and carefully maneuver bar from vehicle.

## TIGHTENING SPECIFICATIONS

| Application | Ft. Lbs. (mkg) |
|---|---|
| Tie Rod Nut | 58 (8.0) |
| Stabilizer Bar-to-Lower Control Arm | 51 (7.0) |
| Lower Control Arm-to-Crossmember | 29 (4.0) |

## FIAT 124

**124 Spider**

### DESCRIPTION

Independent wishbone type suspension with coil springs and telescopic, hydraulic, double acting shock absorbers. Shock absorbers are mounted inside coil springs between upper and lower control arms. Control arms are connected to steering knuckle with ball joints.

Ball Joints — Shock Absorber — Upper Control Arm

Ball Joints — Coil Spring — Lower Control Arm

**Fig. 1  Sectional View of Front Suspension Assembly**

### ADJUSTMENT

#### WHEEL ALIGNMENT SPECIFICATIONS & PROCEDURES

*See Wheel Alignment Specifications and Procedures in WHEEL ALIGNMENT Section.*

#### WHEEL BEARING ADJUSTMENT

*See Wheel Bearing Adjustment in WHEEL ALIGNMENT Section.*

#### BALL JOINT CHECKING

*See Ball Joint Checking in WHEEL ALIGNMENT Section.*

### REMOVAL & INSTALLATION

#### FRONT SUSPENSION ASSEMBLY

**Removal** — Raise and support vehicle. Place cross-support over engine compartment and attach to engine. Remove wheels and shock absorbers. Using suitable tool (A. 74174) compress spring to relieve lower control arm. Disconnect stabilizer bar from lower control arm. Block brake lines and disconnect from brake cylinder. Disconnect tie rod from steering knuckle arm using suitable puller (A. 47044). Remove pivot

bolt and detach upper control arm from body. Remove nuts and bolts securing lower control arm to crossmember and remove suspension.

**Installation** — To install, reverse removal procedure. Tighten all nuts and bolts, bleed brakes and check wheel alignment.

#### STEERING KNUCKLE

**Removal** — 1) Raise and support vehicle. Remove wheel, brake caliper, brake disc and plate. Using suitable puller, remove front grease cap. Remove hub using puller A.47015 (or equivalent). Remove inner race from inside hub bearing with a puller. Remove arm from steering knuckle.

2) Remove nut attaching lower control arm to steering knuckle and place suitable tool (A.47042) between control ball joints, then remove lower ball joint. Remove nut attaching upper ball joint to steering knuckle. Separate upper ball joint from steering knuckle.

**Installation** — Inspect all parts for signs of wear or damage. To install, reverse removal procedure and tighten all nuts and bolts.

#### COIL SPRINGS

**Removal** — Raise and support vehicle so that suspension hangs freely. Remove wheels and shock absorbers. Disconnect stabilizer bar from lower control arm. Support lower control arm with a jack and disconnect lower ball joint stud from steering knuckle. Install suitable spring compressor tool and rotate lower control arm down carefully. Coil spring may now be removed.

**Installation** — To install reverse removal procedure.

#### STABILIZER BAR

**Removal** — Remove front stabilizer bar by removing nuts and bolts securing bar to crossmember. Remove nuts and bolts attaching ends of stabilizer bar to lower control arms and remove stabilizer bar.

**Installation** — To install, reverse removal procedure.

---

### TIGHTENING SPECIFICATIONS

| Application | Ft. Lbs. (mkg) |
|---|---|
| Lower Control Arm Pin-to-Crossmember | 43 (6.0) |
| Lower Control Arm-to-Crossmember | 72 (10.0) |
| Upper Control Arm | 65 (9.0) |
| Lower Shock Absorber | 43 (6.0) |
| Steering Arm-to-Steering Knuckle | 43 (6.0) |
| Brake Caliper | 36 (5.0) |
| Crossmember-to-Side Member | 69 (10.0) |

## FIAT 128

128
Sedan
Station Wagon
3P

### DESCRIPTION

Suspension is independent, strut type. Consists of double-action shock absorbers with surrounding coil springs. Strut assemblies are mounted to inner fender panel at top and to steering knuckle at bottom. Steering knuckle is also bearing carrier for drive axles. Lower control arm is connected to knuckle by ball joint. Stabilizer bar is also incorporated.

**Fig. 1  Assembled View of Fiat 128 Front Suspension**

### ADJUSTMENTS

#### WHEEL ALIGNMENT SPECIFICATIONS & PROCEDURES

See Wheel Alignment Specifications and Procedures in WHEEL ALIGNMENT section.

#### WHEEL BEARING ADJUSTMENT

See Wheel Bearing Adjustment in WHEEL ALIGNMENT section.

#### BALL JOINT CHECKING

See Ball Joint Checking in WHEEL ALIGNMENT section.

### REMOVAL & INSTALLATION

#### COMPLETE SUSPENSION ASSEMBLY

**NOTE** — This procedure is for complete suspension assembly on one side only.

**Removal — 1)** Raise and support front of vehicle. Remove brake caliper, without detaching brake hose, and suspend out of way (be sure there is no strain on hose or line).

**2)** Remove nut from tie rod end stud and separate tie rod end from steering knuckle. Remove nut from stabilizer bar at control arm. Note any shims at this connection.

**3)** Remove control arm pivot bolt from chassis mount. Detach upper strut assembly mount from fender panel. Remove axle nut from hub. Pull out on suspension assembly to separate axle from hub. Remove suspension assembly and secure axle to prevent pulling out of differential.

**Installation** — To install, reverse removal procedure, tightening axle nut before lowering vehicle and tightening all other nuts and bolts with vehicle resting on ground. Be sure stabilizer shims are in proper position.

#### STRUT ASSEMBLY

**Removal** — Raise and support front of vehicle. Detach upper strut mount from fender panel. Remove bolts holding strut to steering knuckle. Pull knuckle down to separate and remove strut assembly.

**Disassembly and Reassembly** — Install suitable spring compressor and compress spring enough to remove upper strut nut. Slowly release spring and remove upper mount and spring. To reassemble, reverse disassembly procedure.

**NOTE** — If replacing coil springs, be sure same color-coded class of spring is installed (different colors show different weights).

**Installation** — To install, reverse removal procedure, tightening nuts to specifications. Be sure lower mount nuts are tightened after vehicle is at curb weight.

#### CONTROL ARM, BUSHINGS & BALL JOINTS

**Removal** — Remove complete suspension assembly as outlined. Remove ball joint stud nut and separate from steering knuckle.

**Disassembly** — To replace control arm bushings, drill out metal sleeve from inside rubber bushings and remove bushings. If ball joint is defective, replace entire control arm assembly.

**Reassembly** — Place outer washer, bushing and sleeve on centering pin of suitable bushing installation tool (A.74221). Place control arm over bushing. Position inner bushing and washer on control arm. Place this assembly in a vise and press into place. Sleeve will bellow out over washers, securing bushings in control arm.

**Installation** — To install, reverse removal procedure.

### TIGHTENING SPECIFICATIONS

| Application | Ft. Lbs. (mkg) |
|---|---|
| Front Axle-to-Hub Nut | |
| Exc. 3P | 101 (14.0) |
| 3P | 112 (15.5) |
| Control Arm Pivot Bolt | |
| Exc. 3P | 18 (2.5) |
| 3P | 32 (4.5) |
| Stabilizer Bar-to-Control Arm | 43 (6.0) |
| Stabilizer Bar-to-Chassis | 22 (3.0) |
| Strut-to-Control Arm (3P) | 51 (7.0) |
| Ball Joint Nut | 58 (8.0) |
| Strut Assembly Mount | |
| Upper | 18 (2.5) |
| Lower | 43 (6.0) |

# Front Suspension

## FIAT 131

**131**

### DESCRIPTION

Strut type front suspension consisting of a vertically mounted strut assembly. Strut assembly is mounted to body at the top by means of a thrust bearing and lower end of strut is connected to steering knuckle. Strut assembly consists of hydraulic shock absorber with a coil spring mounted over outside. Lower control arm is connected to steering knuckle through ball joint and to front crossmember. A stabilizer bar is mounted to lower control arm and to frame.

**Fig. 1  Fiat 131 Front Suspension Assembly**

### ADJUSTMENTS

#### WHEEL ALIGNMENT SPECIFICATIONS & PROCEDURES

*See Wheel Alignment Specifications and Procedures in WHEEL ALIGNMENT Section.*

#### WHEEL BEARING ADJUSTMENT

*See Wheel Bearing Adjustment in WHEEL ALIGNMENT Section.*

#### BALL JOINT CHECKING

*See Ball Joint Checking in WHEEL ALIGNMENT Section.*

### REMOVAL & INSTALLATION

#### FRONT SUSPENSION ASSEMBLY

**Removal** — Raise vehicle, support with safety stands, and remove wheel and tire. Disconnect brake hose from tube at clip mounted in fender well. Disconnect tie rod from steering knuckle. Disconnect stabilizer bar from lower control arm. Remove control arm-to-crossmember attaching bolt and separate control arm from crossmember. Position a jack under suspension assembly, then remove nuts and washers attaching top of strut assembly to body. Carefully lower suspension assembly from vehicle. Individual components may be removed from suspension assembly as follows: Disconnect control arm by removing ball joint stud nut and separating ball joint and lower control arm from steering knuckle. Remove shock absorber assembly by removing nuts and bolts attaching assembly to steering knuckle. Remove coil spring by using a coil spring compressor to compress the spring and removing spring retainer attaching nut.

**Installation** — Install suspension assembly in vehicle and secure strut assembly to body. Install control arm to stabilizer bar, and then to crossmember. Install attaching nuts and bolts loosely. Install tie rod to steering knuckle, and connect brake hose to tube. Install wheel and tire. Lower vehicle and tighten nuts and bolts to specifications with weight of vehicle on ground. Check wheel alignment.

#### CROSSMEMBER

**Removal** — Remove (4) bolts mounting steering box to crossmember. Remove engine mount bolts and suitably support engine. Disconnect lower control arms from crossmember. Remove (4) crossmember to frame bolts and remove crossmember.

**Installation** — To install, reverse removal procedure.

#### STRUT ASSEMBLY

**Removal** — 1) Remove (3) nuts mounting strut assembly to inner fender panel. Raise vehicle and place on safety stands. Remove wheel. Remove nuts and bolts mounting strut to steering knuckle. Remove strut complete with coil spring.

2) To remove coil spring from strut, proceed as follows: Use a spring compressor (A74277) and collapse coil until tension is relieved. Remove retainer mounting nut from top end of strut. Release spring compressor and remove coil.

**Installation** — To install, reverse removal procedure.

#### TIGHTENING SPECIFICATIONS

| Application | Ft. Lbs.(mkg) |
|---|---|
| Ball Joint-to-Steering Knuckle | 58(8) |
| Control Arm-to-Crossmember | 65(9) |
| Strut Assembly-to-Knuckle | 36(5) |
| Strut Assembly-to-Upper Mount | 43(6) |
| Strut Upper Mount-to-Body | 18(2.5) |
| Stabilizer Bar-to-Crossmember | 65(9) |
| Stabilizer Bar-to-Control Arm | 43(6) |

*Labels in figure: Steering Knuckle, Coil Spring, Strut Assembly, Strut Mounting, Lower Control Arm, Lower Ball Joint*

## FIESTA

**Fiesta**

## DESCRIPTION

Front suspension is MacPherson strut type. A shock absorber is mounted to steering knuckle at bottom and to inner fender panel at top. It is surrounded by a coil spring. A tie rod ball joint connects steering knuckle arm to rack-and-pinion steering assembly. Lower ball joint connects underside of knuckle to lower control arm which attaches to frame member. A stabilizer bar attaches to same mounting as lower ball joint and connects to bushing mount at front of vehicle.

*Fig. 1  Fiesta Front Suspension Assembly Components*

## ADJUSTMENTS

### WHEEL ALIGNMENT SPECIFICATIONS & PROCEDURES

*See Wheel Alignment Specifications and Procedures in WHEEL ALIGNMENT section.*

### WHEEL BEARING ADJUSTMENT

*See Wheel Bearing Adjustment in WHEEL ALIGNMENT section.*

### BALL JOINT CHECKING

*See Ball Joint Checking in WHEEL ALIGNMENT section.*

## REMOVAL & INSTALLATION

### STEERING KNUCKLE & STRUT ASSEMBLY

**Removal — 1)** Loosen wheel bolts. Raise and support front of vehicle and remove front wheel. Apply foot brake and remove drive axle retaining nut.

**2)** Detach flexible brake hose at coupling on holding clip and plug hose to prevent fluid loss.

**3)** Remove 3 bolts retaining stabilizer bar bracket to frame.

**4)** Detach tie rod end ball joint from steering knuckle arm.

**5)** Remove lower control arm pivot bolt. Remove 2 upper strut-to-fender retaining bolts and withdraw suspension and knuckle assembly.

**Installation —** To install, reverse removal procedure.

### STRUT ASSEMBLY

**Removal — 1)** Loosen wheel bolts, raise and support front of vehicle. Remove front wheel.

**2)** Remove 2 bolts holding lower strut mounting to steering knuckle. Remove 2 upper strut-to-fender panel bolts and withdraw strut assembly from vehicle.

**Disassembly — 1)** Attach a suitable spring compressor to coil spring and compress enough to remove tension from top mount assembly.

*Fig. 2  Exploded View of Top Mount Components for Fiesta Strut Assembly*

# Front Suspension

## FIESTA (Cont.)

**Reassembly & Installation** — To reassemble and install strut assembly, reverse appropriate procedures and note the following:

- Strut assembly is retained to steering knuckle with special bolts which have double-knurled design. If not installed, manufacturer recommends that these bolts be used to assure proper alignment of strut-to-knuckle (part no. E800622-S72).
- Be sure to hold piston rod with Allen wrench while installing top retaining nut.
- Reset toe alignment if necessary.

**2)** Remove top mount retaining nut by holding inner spindle with Allen wrench and turning nut off with box-end wrench.

**NOTE** — *Newer designs of strut assembly incorporate a fully sealed shock absorber (not serviced by replacement cartridges). It is a "lifetime" type of unit. It is important to use Allen wrench to keep shock absorber rod from turning while removing and installing top nut; otherwise, gland seal will be damaged and leak.*

**3)** Remove top mount assembly components. Remove tension from coil spring compressor and lift off coil spring.

## LOWER CONTROL ARM

**Removal** — **1)** Raise and support front of vehicle. Remove lower control arm pivot bolt.

**2)** Remove clinch bolt from ball joint stud at lower steering knuckle connection. Separate ball joint from knuckle.

**3)** Remove 2 bolts holding stabilizer bar to lower control arm. Remove control arm from vehicle.

**Bushing Replacement** — Using suitable driver, with control arm in vise, push out old bushings. Lubricate new bushings and press into place.

**NOTE** — *It is important that bushings be pressed in quickly to keep bushing from deforming while being installed.*

**Installation** — To install, reverse removal procedure, noting the following:

- Install stabilizer-to-control arm bolts loosely until rest of assembly is fully installed, then tighten bolts fully.

**Fig. 3   Lower Control Arm Illustration Showing Mounting Bolts and Related Components**

## STABILIZER BAR

**Removal** — **1)** Raise and support front of vehicle. Remove stabilizer bar-to-bracket nut and washer from front end of stabilizer bar.

**2)** Remove stabilizer bar-to-lower control arm retaining nuts. Pull downward on lower arm to free stabilizer bar and remove bar from vehicle. Remove remaining washer on front of stabilizer bar.

**Installation** — **1)** Position inner washer on front of stabilizer bar on lower control arm (with "Ford" marking upward) and install retaining bolts loosely.

**2)** Install outer washer and retaining nut on front end of stabilizer bar and tighten to specification.

**3)** Tighten stabilizer-to-lower control arm bolts and nuts.

## TIGHTENING SPECIFICATIONS

| Application | Ft. Lbs. (mkg) |
| --- | --- |
| Hub Retaining Nut | 180-200 (24-27) |
| Control Arm Pivot Bolt | 30-33 (4.2-4.6) |
| Ball Joint Clinch Bolt | 5-18 (2.0-2.6) |
| Ball Joint-to-Control Arm | 40-48 (5.6-6.6) |
| Strut-to-Steering Knuckle | 74-88 (10.2-12.2) |
| Stabilizer Bar-to-Ft. Bracket | 32-40 (4.5-5.6) |
| Stabilizer Bracket-to-Frame | 30-38 (4.2-5.2) |
| Shock Absorber Top Nut | 30-38 (4.2-5.2) |
| Top Mount-to-Fender | 15-18 (2.0-2.4) |
| Allen Bolts-to-CV Joint | 28-32 (3.8-4.5) |

## HONDA

### DESCRIPTION

Strut type front suspension consisting of a vertically mounted strut assembly. Strut assembly is mounted to body at the top by means of a thrust bearing. Lower end of strut is connected to steering knuckle which is mounted to lower control arm by means of a ball joint. Strut assembly consists of a shock absorber built into strut outer tube and a coil spring mounted to outside upper portion of strut tube. A two-piece stabilizer bar (with control spring) is attached to crossmember and to lower control arms. Control spring mounts with brackets to stabilizer bar and crossmember.

### ADJUSTMENT

#### WHEEL ALIGNMENT SPECIFICATIONS & PROCEDURES

See Wheel Alignment Specifications & Procedures in WHEEL ALIGNMENT Section.

#### WHEEL BEARING ADJUSTMENT

See Wheel Bearing Adjustment in WHEEL ALIGNMENT Section.

#### BALL JOINT CHECKING

See Ball Joint Checking in WHEEL ALIGNMENT Section.

### REMOVAL & INSTALLATION

#### STEERING KNUCKLE

**Removal** — **1)** Raise and support vehicle and remove wheel. Remove spindle nut and brake caliper. Install hub puller with slide hammer and remove hub with brake disc attached, from steering knuckle.

**2)** Disconnect tie rod from steering knuckle, using suitable removal tool. Taking care not to damage ball joint seals, detach lower control arm from steering knuckle at ball joint.

**3)** Loosen lock bolt holding steering knuckle to strut assembly and slide steering knuckle off axle.

**NOTE** — *Since removing hub assembly involves use of slide hammer and subjects wheel bearings to severe loads, both inner and outer wheel bearings must be replaced each time hub assembly is removed.*

**Installation** — To install, reverse removal procedure and note. Wheel bearing and seal must be replaced. Press out old bearing, then insert new one using a press to fully seat bearing and seal.

**Fig. 1  Assembled View of Honda Front Suspension Showing Component Relationships**
**Honda Civic Shown**

## HONDA (Cont.)

### STRUT ASSEMBLY

**Removal** — Raise and support vehicle then remove wheel. Disconnect brake line at strut assembly and remove retaining clip. Loosen lock bolt securing strut assembly to steering knuckle and separate knuckle from strut. Remove nuts retaining upper end of strut to body and remove strut.

**Disassembly** — Using suitable tool, compress coil spring to relieve tension from upper shock absorber retaining nut. Remove nut, seals, spacers, etc. (noting arrangement), beneath upper mounting plate. Slowly remove pressure from spring and lift spring off. Shock absorber may now be replaced, if necessary.

**Fig. 2  Exploded View of Honda Strut Assembly (Accord Shown; Civic Models Similar)**

**Reassembly** — Reverse disassembly procedure using Fig. 2 as a guide. Also, make sure shock absorber components do not show any signs of leaking.

**Installation** — Reverse removal procedure and note: Make sure slot in steering knuckle is engaged in tab on shock (strut) housing before seating it into steering knuckle.

### LOWER CONTROL ARM

**Removal** — Raise and support vehicle. Remove front wheel. Disconnect lower ball joint from steering knuckle, using ball joint remover tool. Disconnect stabilizer retaining bolts and nuts from control arm (it may be necessary to loosen front stabilizer retaining brackets). Remove lower control arm pivot bolt and remove control arm.

**Installation** — To install, reverse removal procedure and note: On Accord models only, make sure bolt mounting lower control

arm to crossmember is tightened with weight of vehicle on jack. This simulates normal riding height.

**Fig. 3  Exploded View Showing Stabilizer Bar and Control Spring (Sway Bar). Note Mounting Locations. Accord Model Shown**

### STABILIZER BAR & CONTROL SPRING

**Removal** — Disconnect stabilizer bar mounting at lower control arm on both sides. Separate bracket and bushing mounting stabilizer bar control spring to stabilizer bar. Remove bracket securing control spring to crossmember. Loosen and remove stabilizer bar mounting at crossmember and slide both pieces from vehicle.

**Inspection** — Inspect all rubber bushings and metal sleeves for excessive wear or damage.

**Installation** — To install stabilizer and control spring, reverse removal procedure.

### TIGHTENING SPECIFICATIONS

| Application | Ft. Lbs. (mkg) |
|---|---|
| **Spindle Nut** | |
| Civic & Accord | 87-130 (12-18) |
| CVCC | 109 (15) |
| **Ball Joint** | |
| Civic | 22-29 (3-4) |
| CVCC | 25 (3.5) |
| Accord | 29-36 (4-5) |
| **Strut-to-Knuckle** | |
| Civic | 36-43 (5-6) |
| CVCC | 40 (5.5) |
| Accord | 43-51 (6-7) |

## JAGUAR

XJ6
XJ12
XJS

## DESCRIPTION

Suspension consists of upper and lower control arms, double acting hydraulic shock absorbers, coil springs, stabilizer bar and steering knuckles. The upper control arms are mounted inboard to fulcrum shafts and are mounted outboard to steering knuckles by upper ball joints. Lower control arms are mounted inboard to crossmember and outboard to steering knuckles by lower ball joints. Coil springs are mounted between lower control arms and crossmember. Shock absorbers are attached at the bottom to lower control arms and at the top to body. Stabilizer bar is attached to lower control arms and crossmember.

**Fig. 1 Sectional View of Front Suspension Assembly**

## ADJUSTMENT

### WHEEL ALIGNMENT SPECIFICATIONS & PROCEDURES

See Wheel Alignment Specifications and Procedures in WHEEL ALIGNMENT Section.

### WHEEL BEARING ADJUSTMENT

See Wheel Bearing Adjustment in WHEEL ALIGNMENT Section.

### BALL JOINT CHECKING

See Ball Joint Checking in WHEEL ALIGNMENT Section.

### FRONT SUSPENSION ASSEMBLY

**Removal** — 1) Disconnect battery and remove air cleaners. Disconnect the upper end of shock absorber. Drain and discard power steering fluid. Disconnect and plug power steering inlet and outlet hoses.

2) Remove nuts securing engine mounts to brackets on frame crossmember. Disconnect rear crossmember mountings, then separate stabilizer bar from link. On XJS models, attach

engine lifting device and remove weight from front engine mounts.

3) On XJS models, loosen pinch bolts holding "U" joint to upper and lower steering columns, and remove upper bolt. Remove clip holding boot to lower column. On all models, turn steering until pinch bolt holding lower "U" joint to pinion shaft is accessible. Remove bolt.

4) Return steering to straight-ahead position. Set ignition to "LOCK" and remove key. Separate lower steering column from upper "U" joint, then from pinion shaft.

5) Raise and support vehicle. Remove front wheels. Disconnect brake hoses and lines. Detach ground strap from engine. On XJS, remove 2 screws and 13 plastic fasteners holding spoiler undertray to body and spoiler.

6) Remove suspension mounting bolts. Collect and note location of all washers, spacers and bushings. Slowly lower jack and remove suspension assembly from vehicle.

**Installation** — To install, reverse removal procedure and note the following:

- Be sure brake lines and hoses are properly routed without bends or kinks.
- It may be helpful to remove protective heat shield covering boot on rack and pinion steering prior to positioning suspension into place.
- Be sure power steering reservoir is full before starting engine after installation.
- If additional information is required on steering column installation, see appropriate article in STEERING section of this manual.
- Bleed brake system.

### SHOCK ABSORBERS

**Removal** — Detach upper shock absorber mounting. Raise and support vehicle. Remove front wheel if necessary for access to lower mounting. Remove lower shock absorber mounting and remove from vehicle.

**Installation** — To install, reverse removal procedure.

### COIL SPRINGS

**Removal** — Raise and support vehicle, then remove tire and wheel. Fit a spring compressor (JD-6D & adaptor JD-6D-1) and collapse spring coil enough to allow load on pan seat to be relieved. Remove hardware mounting spring pan to lower control arm. Slightly loosen spring compressor and remove assembly complete.

**NOTE** — Be sure to note number and location of any packing shims.

**Installation** — To install coil spring, reverse removal procedure noting the following: Floor jack can be placed under lower ball joint to aid in aligning spring pan bolt. A maximum of three packers may be placed in spring pan and no more than two can be fitted on crossmember.

### LOWER CONTROL ARM

**Removal** — 1) Remove complete suspension assembly as described in this article.

**2)** On XJS, with assembly on bench, attach suitable coil spring compressor to spring. Compress, remove spring mounting plates and lift out coil spring. Note number and position of spring packing pieces. Detach tie rod end ball joints from knuckle.

**3)** On XJ6 and XJ12, with assembly on bench, detach tie rod ball joints from steering knuckle, then detach and remove steering rack from crossmember. Use suitable tool and remove coil spring, as described in this article.

**4)** On all models, separate upper ball joint, noting location of all caster shims. Detach lower ball joint.

**5)** On XJ6 and XJ12, remove stabilizer bar support bracket and shock absorber lower mounting.

**6)** On XJS, detach hub and rotor assembly, then lift shock absorber and lower mounting clear of lower control arm. Remove steering rack upper mounting bolt and loosen lower bolts. Pivot rack assembly around lower bolts to clear lower control arm pivot shaft.

**7)** On all models, remove split pin at pivot shaft nut. Remove nut and washer. Drive pivot shaft from crossmember and collect spacers.

**Installation** — To install, reverse removal procedure. Do not tighten pivot shaft nut until vehicle is resting on ground at full curb weight.

### UPPER CONTROL ARM

**Removal** — **1)** Raise and support vehicle. Remove front wheel. Detach upper ball joint from control arm. Note number of all caster adjusting shims present.

**2)** Wire steering knuckle to coil spring and remove bolts holding upper control arm pivot shaft to vehicle. Note number and location of all camber adjusting shims. Remove control arm from vehicle.

*Fig. 2  Showing Upper Control Arm Mounting Points on XJ6 and XJ12*

**Installation** — To install upper control arm, reverse removal procedure and tighten all nuts and bolts. Recheck wheel alignment.

### STABILIZER BAR

**Removal (XJ6 and XJ12)** — Raise and support vehicle. Remove both front wheels. Detach both ends of stabilizer bar from mounting links. Remove both mounting brackets from frame. Separate bar from all mounting bushings. Detach one tie rod end from steering knuckle and maneuver stabilizer bar from vehicle.

**Removal (XJS)** — **1)** Raise and support vehicle. Remove both front wheels. Pry out plastic retainers holding vertical diaphragms in wheel wells. Remove 13 fasteners and 2 screws holding spoiler undertray in place.

**2)** Detach nut holding left tie rod to steering knuckle and separate ball joint at this point. Remove self-locking nuts, washers and rubber pads retaining stabilizer bar to its links on both sides.

**3)** Remove front suspension mounting bolts. Lower jack and collect washers, spacers and bushings. Remove nuts and bolts holding stabilizer bar to frame. Detach retaining brackets. Remove rubber bushings from stabilizer links and remove stabilizer out past left hub assembly.

**Installation (All Models)** — To install, reverse removal procedure, fully tightening stabilizer bar-to-link nuts after vehicle is resting on ground.

### LOWER BALL JOINT

**Removal** — **1)** Raise front of vehicle and place on safety stands. Remove wheel. Disconnect brake line from caliper and plug openings. Disconnect tie rod from steering arm. Twist stub axle carrier to gain access to bolts securing upper ball joint to control arm, then remove bolts. Note position and number of shims.

**2)** Remove nut mounting lower ball joint to control arm. Use tool JD 24 (or equivalent) to separate ball joint from control arm, then maneuver assembly from vehicle.

**Disassembly & Reassembly** — **1)** Pry back tab washers and remove four screws keeping ball pin cap. Lift out ball pin. Release clip and remove upper socket from stub axle.

**2)** Clean all components and inspect for excessive wear or damage.

**3)** Install new upper socket to stub axle. Fit lip of boot clip in recess in socket. Lip MUST be near lower face of clip. Install new boot to clip and attach with plastic retaining ring. Grease new ball pin and put into position.

**4)** Put ball pin cap into vise and cut out lower socket. Clean shavings and fit new socket. Refit shims and replace ball cap. Fit four setscrews with lock tabs and tighten, continually checking ball joint movement.

**5)** If ball pin is loose in socket, remove shims. If pin is excessively tight, add shims until movement is correct. Movement should be slightly stiff.

**Installation** — Insert ball joint in lower control arm and tighten lock nut. Align stub axle with upper control arm and insert bolts (bolt heads MUST face front). Make sure packing pieces and shims are properly installed. Reconnect tie rod. Attach brake lines and bleed brakes. Check camber and caster angles.

## JAGUAR (Cont.)

*Fig. 3   Exploded View of Ball Joint*

Labels: Upper Ball Joint Mounting, Upper Socket, Boot & Clips, Ball Pin, Ball Pin Cap, Shims, Lower Socket, Mounting Hardware

### UPPER BALL JOINT

**NOTE** — *Upper control arm ball joint cannot be overhauled. If ball joint is excessively worn, assembly must be replaced.*

**Removal** — 1) Raise vehicle and place on safety stands. Remove wheel. Twist steering to full lock position. Wire stub axle to crossmember to prevent tension on brake hose when ball joint is separated.

2) Remove bolt mounting upper ball joint to control arm. Note number of shims and position of packing pieces. Remove ball joint lock nut and separate ball joint from control arm. Maneuver assembly from vehicle. Withdraw ball joint from stub axle.

**Installation** — Apply grease to replacement ball joint and place in position in stub axle. Hold ball joint against taper fit washer and tighten retaining nut. Refit upper control arm mounting bolts (bolt heads must face forward) and caster shims. Check camber and caster angles.

### TIGHTENING SPECIFICATIONS

| Application | Ft. Lbs. (mkg) |
| --- | --- |
| Upper Pivot Shaft-to-Crossmember | 49-55 (6.8-7.6) |
| Upper Ball Joint-to-Control Arm | 26-32 (3.6-4.4) |
| Pivot Shaft-to-Upper Control Arm | 45-55 (6.3-7.6) |
| Pivot Shaft-to-Lower Control Arm | 32-50 (4.4-6.9) |
| Upper Shock Absorber | 27-32 (3.8-4.4) |
| Lower Shock Absorber | 32-36 (4.4-5.0) |
| Spring Pan | 27-32 (3.8-4.4) |
| Stabilizer-to-Link | 14-18 (2.0-2.5) |
| Tie Rod Nut | 35-50 (4.8-6.9) |

## LANCIA

**Lancia**

### DESCRIPTION

Vehicles are equipped with front wheel drive and independent hydraulic strut type shock absorbers. Axles are supported by lower control arms and vertically mounted strut assemblies. Strut assemblies have shock absorbers with coil springs mounted over outside. Top of strut is attached at fender with four studs. Bottom is attached to steering knuckle (bearing retainer housing). Tie rods are connected to steering knuckle. Stabilizer bar mounts at lower control arm and frame.

**Fig. 1  Sectional View of Lancia Front Suspension Showing Component Relationship**

### ADJUSTMENT

#### WHEEL ALIGNMENT SPECIFICATIONS & PROCEDURES

See Wheel Alignment Specifications and Procedures in WHEEL ALIGNMENT Section.

#### WHEEL BEARING ADJUSTMENT

See Wheel Bearing Adjustment in WHEEL ALIGNMENT Section.

### BALL JOINT CHECKING

See Ball Joint Checking in WHEEL ALIGNMENT Section.

### REMOVAL & INSTALLATION

#### STRUT ASSEMBLY

**Removal** — Raise and support vehicle. Remove front wheel. Remove brake line bracket to strut base. Remove strut from mounting at steering knuckle. Remove nuts holding strut top mounting plate. Pull strut free and out fender opening.

**Disassembly** — 1) Using a coil spring compressor, collapse coil off top seat. Remove mounting nut and washer. Withdraw bumper and thrust plate. Release tension on coil. Separate base from strut and remove. Slide off coil spring, gasket, upper seat, and bumper.

2) Grip base of strut in vice. Remove retaining ring nut. Extract seals, cap and hose. Drain fluid from strut. Pull shaft assembly from strut tube. Remove buffer valve.

**Reassembly** — Reassemble buffer valve. See Fig. 2. Refill strut tube with fluid (10 oz. for Coupe and 7 oz. for other models). Slowly insert strut assembly into tube, exhausting air. Fit top cap assembly over strut shaft, sealing tube. Make sure seals and hose fit properly. Tighten lock ring nut and stake in 3 places.

**Fig. 2  Reassembly Sequence for Buffer Valve. Assemble Components Over Strut Shaft Stem. Refer to Table for Correct Shim Thickness.**

**Installation** — To install strut assembly, reverse removal procedure and tighten all nuts and bolts.

## LANCIA (Cont.)

### Buffer Valve Shim Table

| Application | Thickness In. (mm) |
|---|---|
| **Early Coupe Models** | |
| Shim A,C,D | .008 (.20) |
| Shim B | .006 (.15) |
| **Late Coupe Models** | |
| Shim A,D | .008 (.20) |
| Shim B | .004 (.10) |
| Shim C | .006 (.15) |
| **Saloon** | |
| Shim A | .020 (.50) |
| Shim B | .004 (.10) |
| Shim C,D | .008 (.20) |

### LOWER CONTROL ARM

**Removal** − Raise and support vehicle. Remove wheel. Disconnect axle drive shaft. Separate stabilizer bar from control arm. Disconnect headlight aiming link from left side control arm (if equipped). Using remover tool 88042104 (or equivalent), drive ball joint from steering knuckle. Remove bolts mounting control arm to subframe and pull control arm from vehicle.

**Installation** − To install, reverse removal procedure.

### STABILIZER BAR

**Removal** − Raise and support vehicle. Remove front wheels. Remove clamps mounting stabilizer bar to lower control arms and subframe.

**Installation** − To install, reverse removal procedure.

### TIGHTENING SPECIFICATIONS

| Application | Ft. Lbs. (mkg) |
|---|---|
| Lower Control Arm-to-Frame | 43 (6.0) |
| Stabilizer-to-Control Arm | 17 (2.3) |
| Ball Joint-to-Control Arm | 18 (2.5) |
| Ball Joint Stud Nut | 69 (9.5) |
| Strut-to-Steering Knuckle | 72 (10.0) |
| Upper Plate-to-Strut | 65 (9.0) |
| Strut-to-Fender Panel | 13 (1.8) |
| Shock Absorber Ring Nut | 94 (13.0) |

## LUV

### LUV

## DESCRIPTION

Independent type suspension, using torsion bars. Upper control arms are mounted to bracket which is part of shock tower. Lower control arm is mounted to crossmember. Ball joints attach both upper and lower control arms to steering knuckles, which are part of the front wheel spindle. Torsion bars are connected in front to lower control arm and at rear to frame crossmember. Back and forth movement of front suspension is regulated by a strut bar connecting lower control arm to frame, by means of a rubber bumper at frame end of strut.

## ADJUSTMENT

### WHEEL ALIGNMENT SPECIFICATIONS & PROCEDURES

*See Wheel Alignment Specifications & Procedures in WHEEL ALIGNMENT Section.*

### WHEEL BEARING ADJUSTMENT

*See Wheel Bearing Adjustment in WHEEL ALIGNMENT Section.*

### BALL JOINT CHECKING

*See Ball Joint Checking in WHEEL ALIGNMENT Section.*

## REMOVAL & INSTALLATION

### UPPER CONTROL ARM & BALL JOINT

**Removal** — 1) Raise and support front of vehicle. Remove tire and wheel.

2) Remove upper ball joint cotter pin and nut. Separate ball joint from steering knuckle arm. Safety wire steering knuckle and brake assembly so it does not hang loose.

3) Note number and placement of shims at upper control arm bracket. Remove 2 bolts holding control arm bracket to frame and remove control arm from vehicle.

**Inspection** — Check control arm and pivot shaft for cracks or distortion. Replace both pivot shaft and bushings if either is found defective. Replace ball joint and control arm as an assembly if either is defective.

**Installation** — 1) Install boots on upper control arm pivot shaft. Pack inside of bushings with molybdenum disulfide grease and alternately tighten right and left bushings into place (a spacer tool such as J-24258 should be placed over pivot shaft when tightening bushings).

2) Install grease fittings and lubricate all parts. Place ball joint stud through steering knuckle arm. Install retaining nut and cotter pin (if cotter pin hole does not align after tightening to specification, tighten nut further to align hole; do not loosen).

3) Install upper control arm to frame, making sure any shims removed are installed in original position. Tighten mounting bolts to specifications, torquing bolt at thin shim pack first to achieve best control arm-to-frame retention.

4) Install dust cover, wheel assembly, and lower vehicle. Check alignment if required.

**Fig. 1   Exploded View of LUV Front Suspension**

### LOWER CONTROL ARM & BALL JOINT

**Removal** — 1) Raise front of vehicle and place safety stands under frame. Remove front wheel.

2) Remove strut bar, torsion bar and stabilizer bar as described in this article.

3) Detach lower end of shock absorber. Remove cotter pin and nut from lower ball joint stud. Remove lower control arm retaining nuts and bolts and remove lower control arm om vehicle.

**Inspection** — Check all parts for distortion, cracking or excessive wear. Replace all worn parts.

**Installation** — 1) If ball joint was removed from lower control arm (it can be replaced separately), install new ball joint to control arm.

2) Place ball joint stud in steering knuckle spindle, tighten nut and install new cotter pin.

**NOTE** — *If cotter pin hole does not align after tightening ball joint nut to specification, tighten further to align hole; do not loosen nut.*

3) Install torsion bar, strut bar and stabilizer bar as described in this article. Install front wheel, remove stands and lower vehicle.

## LUV (Cont.)

### SHOCK ABSORBER

**Removal** − Raise vehicle. Hold shock absorber upper stem with a wrench and remove retaining nut, retainer and rubber grommet. Remove lower shock absorber pivot bolt from lower control arm and remove shock absorber.

**Installation** − Check shock absorber and replace if necessary. Fully extend shock absorber, place lower retainer and grommet on stem and slide shock absorber into position. Install upper grommet and retainer on stem and tighten nut to specification. Slide bolt thru lower shock absorber mount and shock absorber. Tighten bolt to specification and lower vehicle.

### STABILIZER BAR

**Removal** − Raise vehicle and disconnect stabilizer bar from lower control arm. Remove brackets holding bar to frame and remove bar. Remove link bolt, spacers and rubber grommets from lower control arm or stabilizer bar. Inspect all parts for wear or damage and replace if necessary.

**Installation** − Bolt brackets to frame over rubber bushings installed over stabilizer bar but do not tighten. Connect link bolts to lower control arm, making sure washers are installed in correct position. Connect link bolts to stabilizer, and tighten to specifications. Tighten bracket bolts to specifications.

### TORSION BAR

**Removal** − Raise vehicle and place safety stands under front of vehicle. Mark position of height control arm adjusting bolt, then remove bolt. Remove height control arm from torsion bar and crossmember. Mark position, then remove torsion bar from lower control arm.

**Installation** − 1) Thoroughly grease serrated portions at both ends of torsion bar. Raise lower control arm with jack to position rubber bumpers in contact with lower control arm. Install front end of torsion bar into control arm.

*Fig. 2   Exploded View of Torsion Bar, Stabilizer Bar, Strut Bar and Shock Absorber*
*Illustration Shows Component Relationships and Part Identification*

## LUV (Cont.)

2) Install height control arm into position so its end reaches height control bolt (grease portion of height control arm which fits into frame).

3) Turn height control adjusting bolt to position marked during removal. Check riding height. See *appropriate article in WHEEL ALIGNMENT section.*

### LOWER CONTROL ARM STRUT BAR

**Removal** — Raise vehicle and remove double nuts, washers and rubber bushings from front side of strut bar. Remove two bolts holding strut bar to lower control arm and remove strut bar.

**Installation** — Place washer and bushing on strut bar and slide rod through frame bracket. Place second set of washers and bushings on end through bracket, then start on washer and one nut, but do not tighten. Bolt other end of strut to lower control arm and tighten to specifications. Lower vehicle and tighten bracket nut, install second nut and tighten to specifications.

### STEERING KNUCKLE

**Removal** — Raise vehicle and place safety stands under front of vehicle. Remove tire and wheel. Disconnect brake hose from wheel cylinder. Remove dust cap, cotter pin, nut retainer, and spindle nut. Remove brake drum. Remove two bolts attaching tie rod end link, and position link to one side. Remove remaining two bolts, then remove brake backing plate assembly. Remove cotter pins and attaching nuts for upper and lower ball joints. Disconnect knuckle from ball joints, then remove steering knuckle from vehicle.

**Installation** — To install, reverse removal procedures while noting the following: Adjust wheel bearings. Bleed brakes after connecting brake hose to wheel cylinder. Tighten all bolts to specifications.

### TIGHTENING SPECIFICATIONS

| Application | Ft. Lbs. (mkg) |
|---|---|
| Backing Plate-to-Knuckle | |
| Small Bolts | 35(4.8) |
| Large Bolts | 55(7.5) |
| Ball Joint-to-Lower Control Arm | 45(6.2) |
| Ball Joint Stud Nut | 75(10.4) |
| Control Arm Pivot-to-Frame | |
| Lower | 130(18.0) |
| Upper | 50(6.9) |
| Lower Control Arm-to-Crossmember | 130(18.0) |
| Shock Absorber | |
| Lower End | 45(6.2) |
| Upper End | 18(2.5) |
| Stabilizer Bar | |
| Nuts | 7(1.0) |
| Lock Nuts | 18(2.5) |
| Strut Bar-to-Frame | |
| Nut | 15(2.1) |
| Lock Nut | 50(6.9) |
| Strut Bar-to-Lower Control Arm | 45(6.2) |
| Upper Control Arm Shaft Bushings | 220(30.4) |

## MAZDA RX-4, COSMO & GLC

RX-4
Cosmo
GLC

### DESCRIPTION

Independent hydraulic strut type suspension with coil springs. Strut assemblies mount between lower control arms and upper fender panels. Strut assemblies consist of: hydraulic shock absorbers (built into strut tube), coil springs around outside of strut tube housing, and a steering knuckle that is connected to both lower control arm and strut. Lower control arms pivot at crossmember and are connected by ball joints to steering knuckle. A stabilizer bar is attached to chassis and at each end to lower control arm.

### ADJUSTMENT

#### WHEEL ALIGNMENT SPECIFICATIONS & PROCEDURES

See Wheel Alignment Specifications & Procedures in WHEEL ALIGNMENT Section.

#### WHEEL BEARING ADJUSTMENT

See Wheel Bearing Adjustment in WHEEL ALIGNMENT Section.

#### BALL JOINT CHECKING

See Ball Joint Checking in WHEEL ALIGNMENT Section.

### REMOVAL & INSTALLATION

#### LOWER CONTROL ARM

**Removal — 1)** Raise vehicle. Support weight with safety stands. Remove tire and wheel.

**2)** Remove cotter pin from tie rod nut. Remove nut. Separate tie rod ball joint using a puller.

**3)** Remove bolts mounting steering knuckle to strut tube. Remove nut from front of stabilizer bar. Begin to separate stabilizer bar from control arm.

**4)** Remove lower control arm pivot bolt mounting arm to crossmember. Pull strut outward and force control arm out of vehicle.

**Ball Joint Replacement — 1)** Remove cotter pin and nut from ball joint stud. Separate ball joint from steering arm using a puller.

**2)** Remove retainer ring and dust seal from ball joint. Press joint from control arm.

**3)** Select new ball joint. Clean mounting bore in control arm. Press new ball joint into control arm. Position steering knuckle on ball joint and tighten nut.

**Fig. 1  Exploded View of RX-4 and Cosmo Front Suspension Assembly**

**Installation —** To install, reverse removal procedure and tighten all nuts and bolts. Do not use more than two adjusting plates at one side when installing coil spring.

#### STRUT ASSEMBLY

**Removal — 1)** Raise and suitably support vehicle. Remove tire and wheel.

**2)** Remove nuts (3 or 4) retaining strut to upper fender panel. Nuts are accessible from inside engine compartment.

**3)** Remove clip mounting brake hydraulic line to strut housing (if equipped). Remove bolts attaching caliper (bracket) and pull caliper assembly off disc. Hang caliper out of way using a short wire.

**4)** Remove hub grease cap, cotter pin, nut lock and bearing adjustment nut from spindle. Remove thrust washer and outer bearing. Pull off hub and brake assembly. Remove any remaining brake system components from steering knuckle.

**5)** Remove bolts mounting strut to steering knuckle. Drop lower control arm down. Slide strut assembly with coil spring out of vehicle.

**Disassembly — 1)** Clamp strut in vise. Use spring compressor and collapse coil. Remove lock nut and washer from top of piston rod.

**2)** Remove shock absorber support, spring seat, coil spring, dust boot and damper stopper.

## MAZDA RX-4, COSMO & GLC (Cont.)

*Fig. 2  Exploded View of GLC Front Suspension Assembly*

**NOTE** — *Check hydraulic strut (shock absorber) by forcing piston rod in and out several times. If resistance is weak or there is a free travel spot somewhere in the stroke, strut must be replaced or repaired.*

3) Place strut in a soft jawed vise. Remove cap nut and seal. Pry "O" ring from guide rod. Pull piston rod and pressure tube assembly out of strut (reservoir tube).

4) Remove piston rod, guide, base valve and pressure tube assembly from reservoir tube. Take strut from vise and drain hydraulic fluid.

**NOTE** — *Piston rod, guide and base valve are serviced as an assembly only. Do not remove items listed in step 4) from pressure tube.*

**Inspection** — 1) Check reservoir tube for cracks or damage. Replace tube if necessary.

2) Check mounting rubbers, replace if deteriorated.

3) Inspect coil spring for signs of fatigue, cracks or damage.

**Reassembly** — 1) Hold reservoir tube in a vise. Insert pressure tube, piston rod and base valve assembly into tube as a set. Pour approximately 4 ounces (270 cc) hydraulic fluid into reservoir.

2) Install piston rod guide into pressure tube. Fit new "O" ring between rod guide and reservoir tube.

3) Fit a pilot (49 0370 590) over threads of piston rod. Apply grease to lip of oil seal, insert cap nut through pilot onto piston rod.

*Fig. 3  Exploded View of Strut Assembly*

4) Tighten cap nut and pull out piston rod. Seat piston and torque cap nut. Install coil spring and remaining components in reverse of removal procedure.

**Installation** — To install, reverse removal procedure.

### TIGHTENING SPECIFICATIONS

| Application | Ft. Lbs. mkg) |
| --- | --- |
| Control Arm-to-Frame | |
| RX-4 and Cosmo | 54-69 (7.5-9.5) |
| GLC | 29-40 (4.0-5.5) |
| Steering Knuckle-to-Strut | |
| RX-4 and Cosmo | 75-101 (10.4-14.0) |
| GLC | 46-69 (6.4-9.5) |
| Ball Joint-to-Knuckle | |
| All Models | 43-58 (6.0-8.0) |

## MAZDA PICKUP

### B1800

## DESCRIPTION

Independent type suspension, consisting of upper and lower control arms and wheel spindle mounted between upper and lower arms by means of ball joints. Upper control arm pivots on a shaft attached to frame, lower control arm pivots on a shaft mounted to crossmember. A coil spring is mounted between lower control arm and frame. Shock absorber is hydraulic double action type, mounted between lower control arm and frame inside coil spring. A stabilizer bar is also incorporated which connects to the lower control arm on each side by bushings and links.

**Fig. 1  Exploded View of Front Suspension Assembly for Component Identification**

## ADJUSTMENTS

### WHEEL ALIGNMENT SPECIFICATIONS & PROCEDURES

See Wheel Alignment Specifications & Procedures in WHEEL ALIGNMENT section.

### WHEEL BEARING ADJUSTMENT

See Wheel Bearing Adjustment in WHEEL ALIGNMENT section.

### BALL JOINT CHECKING

See Ball Joint Checking in WHEEL ALIGNMENT section.

## REMOVAL & INSTALLATION

### SHOCK ABSORBERS

**Removal** — Remove nut, rubber bushing and washer attaching upper end of shock absorber to crossmember. Remove lower retaining bolts holding shock absorber to lower control arm, and remove shock absorber from vehicle.

**Installation** — Reverse removal procedure and tighten mounting bolts.

### COMPLETE SUSPENSION ASSEMBLY

**Removal** — 1) Raise and support front of vehicle with safety stands placed just behind lower control arms. Remove front wheel. Remove shock absorber.

2) Detach upper ball joint from steering knuckle. From under hood, remove upper control arm retaining bolts and nuts, noting number and position of alignment shims. Remove upper control arm from vehicle.

3) Remove 3 nuts and bolts holding ball joint to upper control arm and remove ball joint.

4) Remove stabilizer bar retaining nut, washers and bushings. Detach stabilizer bar from lower control arm.

5) Position floor jack under lower control arm and raise arm to relieve pressure. Using suitable tool, compress coil spring, then detach lower ball joint from steering knuckle.

6) Lower floor jack under lower control arm and remove coil ring from vehicle. Remove 2 lower control arm retaining bolts and remove arm from vehicle. Remove ball joint from lower control arm.

**Installation** — To install, reverse removal procedure.

| TIGHTENING SPECIFICATIONS | |
|---|---|
| **Application** | **Ft. Lbs. (mkg)** |
| Ball Joint-to-Knuckle | 51-65 (7.0-9.0) |
| Ball Joint-to-Lower Cont. Arm | 60-70 (8.8-9.7) |
| Control Arm-to-Frame (Both) | 54-69 (7.5-9.5) |

## MERCEDES-BENZ, EXCEPT 450SL & 450SLC

**230**
**240D**
**280CE, E & SE**
**300CD & D**
**450SEL**
**6.9**

**NOTE** — *Some 6.9 models use a "Hydropneumatic" suspension system. See article at end of this section.*

### DESCRIPTION

Front suspension consists of upper and lower control arms, coil springs, shock absorbers, steering knuckles and a stabilizer bar.

### ADJUSTMENTS

#### WHEEL ALIGNMENT SPECIFICATIONS & PROCEDURES

*See Wheel Alignment Specifications and Procedures in WHEEL ALIGNMENT section.*

#### WHEEL BEARING ADJUSTMENT

*See Wheel Bearing Adjustment in WHEEL ALIGNMENT section.*

#### BALL JOINT CHECKING

*See Ball Joint Checking in WHEEL ALIGNMENT section.*

### REMOVAL & INSTALLATION

**NOTE** — *Manufacturer requires that shock absorber mountings and stabilizer attachments not be loosened or tightened unless vehicle is resting on ground or axle is supported to simulate vehicle load.*

#### SUSPENSION ASSEMBLY (ONE SIDE)

**Removal — 1)** Remove front shock absorber by detaching upper mounting first, then lower mounting. Raise front of vehicle, with jacks placed under outer edge of lower control arms. Remove front wheel.

**2)** Remove coil spring, as described in this article. Use suitable tool to separate tie rod ball joint from steering knuckle arm.

**3)** Detach flexible brake hose from brake line at connection on fender well. Loosen plug connection of brake lining wear indicator on caliper. Remove bolts holding brake support to frame.

**4)** Support front axle half. Mark position of lower control arm eccentric to crossmember for reinstallation purposes. Remove eccentric bolt.

**5)** Remove stabilizer bar support from upper control arm. Remove hex bolt holding upper control arm bushing to body. Remove front suspension assembly.

**Installation — 1)** Position front suspension in vehicle and mount upper control arm to body and stabilizer bar, but do not fully tighten bolts. Raise opposite side of vehicle as required to obtain proper stabilizer bar position.

**2)** Attach upper control arm to frame crossmember. Attach brake support to frame. Reconnect brake line to hose and plug connection of caliper wear indicator.

**3)** Install coil spring. Install shock absorber loosely. Attach tie rod ball joint to steering knuckle arm.

**4)** Bleed brake system. Install front wheel and lower vehicle to ground.

**5)** Place eccentric bolt of camber adjustment to original position and tighten.

**6)** Tighten upper control arm-to-body bolt and stabilizer bar-to-control arm support bolt. Tighten shock absorber mounting bolts. Check axle height and front wheel alignment. See *WHEEL ALIGNMENT* section.

#### UPPER CONTROL ARM

**NOTE** — *Loosen hex nuts on ball joints with coil spring installed ONLY when supporting jacks are under lower control arm and not body. If jack cannot be so positioned, remove coil spring.*

**Fig. 1  Assembled View of Mercedes-Benz Front Suspension**
**(280 Series Shown; Others Similar with Major Difference in Stabilizer Bar Configuration and Mounting)**

## MERCEDES-BENZ, EXCEPT 450SL & 450SLC (Cont.)

**Removal — 1)** Raise front of vehicle, placing jacks under outer edges of control arms.

**2)** Remove upper ball joint nut. Using suitable tool, detach ball joint from steering knuckle arm. Wire steering knuckle to frame so it will not drop.

**3)** Remove upper control arm support from stabilizer bar and from body. Remove upper control arm.

**Installation — 1)** Position upper control arm in vehicle and attach control arm-to-body bolt. Connect upper ball joint to steering knuckle.

**2)** Mount stabilizer bar support to upper control arm, attaching bolt loosely. Lower vehicle to ground and tighten all bolts to specifications. Check front end alignment.

### LOWER CONTROL ARM

**Removal — 1)** Loosen top shock absorber mounting, then lower mounting. Remove shock absorber. Raise front of vehicle, with jacks placed under outer edge of control arm.

**2)** Remove front wheel. Remove coil spring as described in this article. Detach tie rod ball joint from steering knuckle arm.

**3)** Mark position of lower control arm eccentric bolt and bushing to crossmember for reassembly reference.

**4)** Remove bolts holding brake support to frame. Remove lower control arm eccentric bolt. Detach lower ball joint from control arm. Remove lower control arm with brake support.

**Installation — 1)** Mount lower control arm to ball joint. Position control arm bushing to frame.

**2)** Attach brake support to frame. Install coil spring. Install shock absorber, loosely. Mount front wheel and lower vehicle to ground.

**3)** Tighten shock absorber mountings. Position eccentric bolt to original position and tighten to specifications.

**4)** Attach tie rod ball joint to steering knuckle arm. Check wheel alignment.

### COIL SPRING

**Removal — 1)** Release upper shock absorber mount. Raise front of vehicle with jack placed under lower control arm. Remove front wheel.

**2)** Attach suitable coil spring compressor. Tighten spring compressor while raising jack under lower control arm to assist compressing operation. Slowly lower jack and remove the coil spring and rubber mounting.

**Installation — 1)** Position rubber mount on coil spring. With spring compressed, position in vehicle. Slowly release spring, being sure it rests in mounting groove.

**2)** Mount front wheel and lower vehicle to ground. Attach upper shock absorber mount.

### STABILIZER BAR

**Removal — 1)** Raise front of vehicle, with jacks placed under lower control arms. Remove front wheels.

**2)** Detach upper control arm support from stabilizer bar.

**3)** Remove master cylinder and booster. Remove heater hoses, air cleaner, regulator linkage, vacuum lines and electrical wiring as required to allow clearance for stabilizer bar removal.

**4)** Remove stabilizer bar mounting brackets and bushings. Remove end covers and remove stabilizer bar.

**Installation — 1)** Position stabilizer bar in vehicle and loosely attach bar support to upper control arm.

**2)** Position rubber bushings on stabilizer bar, with splits facing against frame. Install brackets loosely.

**3)** Attach left and right end covers and replace all hoses, linkage, wiring and brake components removed. Mount front wheels and lower vehicle to ground.

**4)** Tighten stabilizer bar-to-control arm support bolt. Tighten mounting brackets. Check Front wheel alignment.

**Fig. 2   Showing Attachment of Upper Control Arm and Stabilizer Bar**

### STEERING KNUCKLE

**Removal — 1)** Raise front of vehicle, with jacks placed under outer edge of lower control arm. Remove front wheels.

**2)** Detach steering knuckle arm from steering knuckle. Remove caliper from steering knuckle and suspend out of way with wire. Remove front wheel hub.

**3)** Loosen brake hose holder on backing plate. Remove nut from upper ball joint and separate from steering knuckle.

**4)** Remove nut from lower ball joint. Swivel upper end of steering knuckle slightly outward and use suitable tool to detach steering knuckle from lower ball joint. Remove knuckle from vehicle.

**Installation —** To install, reverse removal procedure.

## TIGHTENING SPECIFICATIONS

| Application | Ft. Lbs. (mkg) |
|---|---|
| Lower Shock Absorber Mount | 18 (2.5) |
| Stabilizer Bar Bracket Bolts | 18 (2.5) |
| Steering Linkage Bolts | 25 (3.5) |
| Steering Knuckle Arm Bolts | 58 (8.0) |
| Upper Control Arm Eccentric Bolts | 43 (6.0) |
| Lower Control Arm Eccentric Bolts | 87 (12.0) |
| Upper Ball Joint Nut | 43 (6.0) |
| Lower Ball Joint Nut | 58 (8.0) |

## MERCEDES-BENZ 450SL & 450SLC

450SL
450SLC

### DESCRIPTION

Front suspension assembly is a coil spring type, having separately-mounted coil springs and shock absorbers between upper and lower control arms. Other front suspension components include steering knuckle, tie rods and a stabilizer bar.

### ADJUSTMENTS

#### WHEEL ALIGNMENT SPECIFICATIONS & PROCEDURES

See Wheel Alignment Specifications and Procedures in WHEEL ALIGNMENT section.

#### WHEEL BEARING ADJUSTMENT

See Wheel Bearing Adjustment in WHEEL ALIGNMENT section.

#### BALL JOINT CHECKING

See Ball Joint Checking in WHEEL ALIGNMENT section.

### REMOVAL & INSTALLATION

NOTE — Manufacturer requires that shock absorber mountings and stabilizer bar attachments not be loosened or tightened unless vehicle is resting on ground or axle is supported enough to simulate full vehicle load.

#### SHOCK ABSORBERS

Removal — With vehicle on ground, detach upper and lower shock absorber mountings. Compress shock absorber to gain clearance and remove from vehicle.

Installation — To install, reverse removal procedure.

#### COIL SPRING

Removal — 1) Loosen lower shock absorber mounting and stabilizer bar connecting linkage. Raise front of vehicle. Remove front wheel.

2) Mark position of lower control arm eccentric bolts on inner end of arm for reinstallation reference. Attach and engage a suitable coil spring compressor. Remove eccentric bolts.

3) Place suitable cradle-type support beneath lower control arm directly below coil spring position. Slowly lower cradle, allowing inner end of control arm to drop down, and remove coil spring.

Installation — To install, reverse removal procedure, fully tightening stabilizer bar mountings and lower shock absorber mounting after vehicle is resting on ground.

#### STABILIZER BAR

Removal — Loosen stabilizer bar connecting linkage from both lower control arms. Remove stabilizer bar-to-frame mounting brackets and remove torsion bar.

Installation — To install, reverse removal procedure.

#### STEERING KNUCKLE

Removal — 1) Install coil spring compressor on spring. Raise and support front of vehicle. Remove front wheel.

2) Remove bolt holding steering knuckle arm to steering knuckle. Detach flexible brake hose from brake line and plug openings. Remove caliper.

NOTE — On some models, it may be possible to remove caliper from rotor and suspend out of way without detaching brake hose. This will eliminate necessity of bleeding brake system after installation.

3) Remove nuts from upper and lower ball joint studs. Detach both ball joints from steering knuckle. Remove steering knuckle.

Installation — To install, reverse removal procedure, bleed brakes and check front wheel alignment.

#### UPPER CONTROL ARM

Removal — 1) Attach suitable spring compressor to coil spring. Raise and support front of vehicle. Remove front wheel.

NOTE — Shock absorber remains installed.

2) Remove bolt holding steering knuckle to steering knuckle arm. Detach brake hose from brake line and plug openings.

3) Remove nuts from upper and lower ball joint studs. Using suitable tool, detach upper ball joint from steering knuckle.

4) Remove both upper control arm mounting nuts and remove arm.

Installation — To install, reverse removal procedure. Bleed brakes and check front wheel alignment.

#### LOWER CONTROL ARM

Removal — 1) Loosen and detach lower shock absorber mounting. Raise front of vehicle and remove front wheel.

2) Detach steering knuckle arm from steering knuckle. Separate brake hose from brake line and plug openings. Remove brake hose retaining clip.

3) Remove coil spring as described in this article.

4) Remove nuts from upper and lower ball joint studs. Detach lower control arm from lower ball joint. Remove control arm.

Installation — To install, reverse removal procedure, bleed brake system and tighten shock absorber mounting (after vehicle is resting on ground). Check front wheel alignment.

### TIGHTENING SPECIFICATIONS

| Application | Ft. Lbs. (mkg) |
|---|---|
| Lower Shock Absorber Mount | 14 (2.0) |
| Upper Ball Joint Nut | 29 (4.0) |
| Lower Ball Joint Nut | 29 (4.0) |
| Tie Rod Ball Joint Nut | 14 (2.0) |
| Lower Control Arm-to-Frame | 130 (18.0) |
| Steering Arm-to-Steering Knuckle | 57 (8.0) |
| Upper Control Arm Clamping Bolt | 21 (3.0) |
| Upper Control Arm-to-Body | 60 (8.0) |

## MGB

**MGB**

### DESCRIPTION

Suspension consists of a lower control arm assembly, on which a coil spring is mounted. A kingpin connects lower control arm to steering knuckle. A shock absorber assembly is mounted on top of steering knuckle. A stabilizer bar is connected to lower control arm.

### ADJUSTMENT

#### WHEEL ALIGNMENT SPECIFICATIONS & PROCEDURES

*See Wheel Alignment Specifications and Procedures in WHEEL ALIGNMENT Section.*

#### WHEEL BEARING ADJUSTMENT

*See Wheel Bearing Adjustment in WHEEL ALIGNMENT Section.*

### REMOVAL & INSTALLATION

#### COIL SPRING

**Removal** — Raise and support vehicle on safety stands, remove wheels. Remove stabilizer bar link from spring pans. Using suitable spring compressor (18G 693), compress spring and remove spring pan bolts from lower control arm. Release spring compressor, remove spring pan and spring.

**Fig. 1   MGB Front Suspension Assembly Shown as an Exploded View**

**Inspection** — Before reinstalling coil spring make sure free length of coil spring is 10.6" (269 mm). Also, check that under a load of approximately 1010-1050 lbs. (581-599 kg) spring height is 7.4" (190 mm).

**Installation** — To install, reverse removal procedure and note: Shortest spring pan screw must be fitted to rear hole closest to wheel.

#### SHOCK ABSORBERS

**Removal** — 1) Raise and support front of vehicle. Place floor jack under spring pan and raise until shock absorber is clear of rebound bumper.

2) Remove cotter pin and remove castle nut from fulcrum bolt. Loosen clamp bolt and center bolt on shock absorber arm.

3) Drive out fulcrum pin. Pry shock absorber halves apart and swing trunnion out of way. Wire steering knuckle to crossmember in an upright position. Remove 4 bolts mounting shock absorber to crossmember and slide out shock.

**Fig. 2   Shock Absorber Removal**

**Inspection** — 1) Place shock absorber vertically in vise. Remove filler plug. Move shock absorber levers back and forth to ensure they are firm and also to bleed air from housing. Recheck fluid level, fill to plug opening.

2) Check trunnion bushings to make sure they are not deteriorated or severely worn. Replace bushings if necessary.

**Installation** — To install, reverse removal procedure and note: Grease kingpin.

#### LOWER CONTROL ARMS

**Removal** — 1) Raise and support front of vehicle. Remove tire and wheel. Remove coil spring as previously outlined.

2) Remove cotter pin and castle nut mounting lower control arm link at kingpin. Remove cotter pin and castle nut mounting control arm link to pivot shaft.

## MGB (Cont.)

**3)** Support hub assembly. Pull off front control arm link. Pull out control arm link mounting bolt at kingpin and force off back control arm link.

**Inspection —** Replace any bushings that show signs of excessive wear.

**Installation —** To install, reverse removal procedure and note: Make sure thrust washers face bushing correctly. Tighten castle nuts with vehicle weight on ground. If cotter pin cannot be fitted, tighten nut to next opening. Grease kingpin.

**Fig. 3   Lower Control Arm Removal**

### STEERING KNUCKLE

**Removal — 1)** Raise and support vehicle on safety stands. Remove tire and wheel. Detach caliper and support to avoid damage to brake hose. Remove hub and rotor. Remove steering lever and rotor dust cover. Remove coil spring as previously outlined. Remove cotter pins and nuts from upper and lower fulcrum shafts. Remove shock absorber lever arm center bolt and clamp bolt. Ease arm off.

**2)** Raise jack under spring pan. Loosen 2 bolts mounting lower arm link to the spring pan. Remove kingpin fulcrum bolt. Separate lower control links. Remove kingpin and spindle assembly. If necessary, kingpin can be separated from spindle assembly.

**Installation —** Check all parts for wear or damage. Check fulcrum shafts for out of round. Replace parts and shafts as necessary. To install, reverse removal procedure. Tighten nuts and bolts.

### STABILIZER BAR

**Removal — 1)** Raise and support front of vehicle. Disconnect stabilizer bars at lower control arm links.

**2)** Remove bolts mounting bushing clamps to body. Slide stabilizer bar from vehicle.

**3)** Pry mounting clamps away from bushings and slide bushings off stabilizer bar. Force link mounting bushings from each end of stabilizer bar. If bushings show signs of wear or severe deterioration, replace with new parts.

**Installation —** To install, reverse removal procedure. If bar is replaced, put old locaters $9\frac{5}{16}''$ from center of stabilizer bar.

### FRONT SUSPENSION ASSEMBLY

**Removal — 1)** Raise and support vehicle. Remove tire and wheel. Disconnect tie rods from steering knuckle. Disconnect stabilizer bar at lower control arm connecting links.

**2)** Remove 4 bolts mounting steering rack to crossmember. Tie rack to stabilizer bar.

**3)** Disconnect brake hose at bracket. Plug openings. Place floor jack under crossmember.

**4)** Put rods through holes in crossmember to retain body to crossmember studs. Loosen both REAR stud lock nuts keeping crossmember to body.

**5)** Work inside of engine compartment and remove lock nuts and washers from both FRONT mounting studs. Remove mounting pad from each rear stud. Lower suspension from vehicle.

**Installation —** To install suspension assembly, reverse removal procedure and note: Make sure all mounting pads are aligned. Make sure that REAR stud clamp plates have depressions facing toward mounting pad. Bleed brake system.

### TIGHTENING SPECIFICATIONS

| Application | Ft. Lbs. (mkg) |
| --- | --- |
| Shock Absorber Bolts | 44 (6.1) |
| Brake Caliper Mounting Bolts | 43 (6.0) |
| Crossmember-to-Body | 55 (7.6) |
| Shock Absorber Pinch Bolt | 28 (3.9) |
| Lower Control Arm Nuts | 28 (3.9) |
| Stabilizer Bar Link Nut | 60 (8.3) |
| Kingpin Nut | 68 (8.3) |

# Front Suspension

## MG MIDGET

**Midget**

### DESCRIPTION

Suspension is a control arm coil spring type. Shock absorber is a lever arm type and acts as upper control arm. Shock absorber is bolted to crossmember and attached to steering knuckle. Lower control arm is attached to frame and steering knuckle with fulcrum shafts. A coil spring is mounted between lower control arm and crossmember. A stabilizer bar is attached at each side to the lower control arm by a link.

### ADJUSTMENT

#### WHEEL ALIGNMENT SPECIFICATIONS & PROCEDURES

See *Wheel Alignment Specifications & Procedures* in WHEEL ALIGNMENT Section.

#### WHEEL BEARING ADJUSTMENT

See *Wheel Bearing Adjustment* in WHEEL ALIGNMENT Section.

### REMOVAL & INSTALLATION

#### COIL SPRINGS

**Removal** — 1) Place a wood block under shock absorber lever arm rubber stop. Raise and support vehicle on jack stands. Remove wheels.

2) Using a suitable compressor (18G 153) collapse spring. Remove nuts and bolts securing spring seat to lower control arm. Release spring pressure and remove spring.

**Inspection** — Before reinstalling coil spring make sure free length of coil spring is 9.85" (250 mm). Also, check that under a load of approximately 735-765 lbs. (331-343 kg) spring height is 7.08" (180 mm).

**Fig. 1  Where to Place Tool When Compressing Front Spring for Removal**

**Installation** — To install, reverse removal procedure. Remember to remove wood block.

#### STABILIZER BAR

**Removal** — Raise front of vehicle and place jack stands under front suspension. Remove screws and nuts to release end stops from stabilizer bar. Remove bolts mounting stabilizer bar rubber bushing bracket. Remove nuts mounting stabilizer bar links and remove from vehicle.

**Installation** — To install, reverse removal procedure and tighten all mounting hardware.

#### STUB AXLE ASSEMBLY

**Removal** — 1) Remove front spring as previously outlined. Separate tie rod ball joint. Remove brake assembly. See *Midget in BRAKE Section.*

2) Remove dust shield. Separate stabilizer bar from lower arm. Remove clamp bolt at shock absorber. Remove trunnion link bolt. Remove bushings from trunnion link.

**Fig. 2  Exploded View of Front Suspension Components**

# Front Suspension

## MG MIDGET (Cont.)

3) Remove nuts, washers, and fulcrum shaft from inside end of lower control arm. Force lower control arm down and remove from vehicle. Remove lower control arm bushings.

4) Remove upper kingpin mounting nut. Remove trunnion link with thrust washers and shims. Pivot out kingpin and separate spindle from kingpin.

5) Remove nut and take out fulcrum shaft. Tap out kingpin. Separate dust seal. Remove "O" ring. Take out steering arm mounting bolts and separate steering arm from spindle (steering knuckle).

**Installation — 1)** Install new bushings with lubricating hole in bushing aligned with hole in kingpin. One end of bushing will easily enter housing. Bottom bushing must be flush with recess in housing. Ream bushings as necessary.

**2)** Fit dust seal. Install steering arm. Assemble kingpin to lower link arm by screwing fulcrum shaft into lower link. Use new dust seals. Install cotter pin.

**3)** Coat new "O" ring with oil and fit in bottom of kingpin. Fit thrust washers over kingpin. Refit shims.

4) Install trunnion with bore toward kingpin. Fit mounting nut. Check movement of kingpin from stop to stop, slight resistance should be felt. Make sure there is no vertical movement. Add or subtract shims to increase or decrease resistance.

5) To install the remaining components, reverse removal procedure.

### SHOCK ABSORBERS

**Removal — 1)** Raise and support front of vehicle. Remove front wheels. Place jack under outer end of control arm and raise until shock lever arm is off its rubber stop.

**2)** Remove nut and bolt from fulcrum shaft and remove shaft. Remove bolts holding shock absorber to frame. Remove shock absorber.

**NOTE** — *Jack must remain under lower control arm while shock absorber is removed from vehicle.*

**Installation** — To install, reverse removal procedure and tighten bolts securing shock absorber to frame to 25-30 ft. lbs. (3.5-4.2 mkg).

## OPEL

**All Models**

### DESCRIPTION

Independent type suspension consisting of upper and lower control arms. Upper control arm pivots on a shaft bolt attached to crossmember and is connected to steering knuckle by a ball joint. Lower control arms are connected in same manor. A coil spring is mounted between lower control arm and crossmenber. Shock absorbers mount between top of upper control arm and inner fender panel. All vehicles are equipped with stabilizer bars.

Shock Absorber

Upper Ball Joint

Stabilizer Bar

Upper Control Arm

Crossmember

Lower Control Arm

Lower Ball Joint

**Fig. 1    Front View of Suspension Components Showing Relationship of Parts**

### ADJUSTMENTS

#### WHEEL ALIGNMENT SPECIFICATIONS & PROCEDURES

*See Wheel Alignment Specifications and Procedures in WHEEL ALIGNMENT Section.*

#### WHEEL BEARING ADJUSTMENT

*See Wheel Bearing Adjustment in WHEEL ALIGNMENT Section.*

#### BALL JOINT CHECKING

*See Ball Joint Checking in WHEEL ALIGNMENT Section.*

### REMOVAL & INSTALLATION

#### SHOCK ABSORBER

**Removal** — Raise vehicle and suitably support with safety stands. Remove tire and wheel. Disconnect shock absorber from upper control arm. Working from inside engine compartment, remove shock absorber mounting nuts. Maneuver shock absorber from vehicle.

**Installation** — To install shock absorber, reverse removal procedure.

#### STABILIZER BAR

**Removal** — Raise vehicle and suitably support with safety stands. Remove protective under cover. Remove stabilizer bar mounting on lower control arm. Disconnect and remove clamps securing stabilizer bar to body.

**Installation** — Install new bushing on stabilizer bar. Install stabilizer bar and hold in place with mounting clamps. Fit stabilizer bar to lower control arms and tighten nut to end of bolt threads.

#### UPPER CONTROL ARM & BALL JOINT

**Removal** — 1) Raise vehicle and suitably support on safety stands. Remove tire and wheel. Remove upper brake caliper bolt and move hose clip back about ½". Disconnect lower end of shock absorber and compress upward. Using a jack, raise lower control arm until level, then support with jack stand.

**2)** Loosen upper ball joint and disconnect from steering knuckle using tool J-26407-1 (or equivalent). If only ball joint is being removed, take off two bolts connecting ball joint and control arm. If entire control arm is being taken off, remove pivot shaft bolt. Maneuver control arm from vehicle.

**Installation** — To install upper control arm and ball joint, reverse removal procedure and note the following. Fit ball joint so straight cut edge is outward.

#### LOWER CONTROL ARM, BALL JOINT AND COIL SPRING

**Removal** — 1) Raise vehicle and suitable support with jack stands. Remove tire and wheel. Disconnect tie-rod from steering knuckle. Disconnect and remove stabilizer bar from lower control arm. Remove upper caliper mounting bolt and slide hose clip back about ½".

**2)** Disconnect shock absorber lower mount and compress shock upward. Place a jack at outer edge of control arm and disconnect ball joint from steering knuckle. Suspend steering and hub assembly out of way.

**3)** With coil spring compressed until spring clears seat, lower jack under control arm. Using tools J-9519 and J-9519-14 (or equivalent) ball joint can be removed from control arm. If control arm is being removed, remove bolts connecting lower control arm to crossmember and body. Coil spring can now be removed.

**Installation** — To install, reverse removal procedure and note: Use installer J-9519 and receiver J-9519-4 (or equivalent) to install ball joint. **NOTE** — *DO NOT hammer on ball joint bottom.*

**Fig. 2   Exploded View of Opel Front Suspension Components**

## STEERING KNUCKLE

**Removal — 1)** Raise vehicle and support on safety stands. Disconnect and compress shock absorber upward. Disconnect and remove caliper assembly, then hang with wire out of way. Disconnect tie rod from steering knuckle. Remove hub and rotor assembly from steering knuckle.

**2)** Raise lower control arm until level, then support at outside edge. Disconnect upper and lower ball joints from steering knuckle. Removal backing plate.

**Installation —**. To install, reverse removal procedure and adjust wheel bearings.

## TIGHTENING SPECIFICATIONS

| Application | Ft. Lbs. (mkg) |
|---|---|
| Lower Control Arm Ball Joint-to-Steering Knuckle | 58 (8.0) |
| Lower Control Arm-to-Crossmember | 47 (6.5) |
| Lower Control Arm-to-Body | 47 (6.5) |
| Upper Control Arm Ball Joint-to-Steering Knuckle | 40 (5.5) |
| Upper Control Arm Ball Joint-to-Upper Control Arm | 29 (4.0) |
| Shock Absorber-to-Upper Control Arm | 29 (4.0) |
| Brake Caliper-to-Steering Knuckle | 36 (5.0) |

## PORSCHE 911SC & TURBO

**911SC**
**Turbo**

### DESCRIPTION

Independent strut type suspension with torsion bars. Strut assemblies are mounted to inner fender panels at top by thrust bearings. Bottom of strut assemblies are mounted to control arms by ball joints. Steering knuckle and shock absorbers are integral with individual strut assembly. Control arms pivot in mounts connected to body at front and in mounts integral with suspension crossmember at rear. Torsion bars anchor to control arm at front and to suspension crossmember at rear. Suspension crossmember also serves as mount for steering gear and is removable.

### ADJUSTMENT

#### WHEEL ALIGNMENT SPECIFICATIONS & PROCEDURES

See Wheel Alignment Specifications & Procedures in WHEEL ALIGNMENT Section.

#### WHEEL BEARING ADJUSTMENT

See Wheel Alignment Specifications & Procedures in WHEEL ALIGNMENT Section.

#### BALL JOINT CHECKING

See Ball Joint Checking in WHEEL ALIGNMENT Section.

### REMOVAL & INSTALLATION

#### STRUT ASSEMBLY AND THRUST BEARING

**Removal — 1)** Raise vehicle and place safety stands under body. Remove wheel and tire. Remove brake rotor and brake caliper.

**NOTE** — If necessary, refer to appropriate article in BRAKE SYSTEMS section.

**2)** Remove tie rod end strut nut and separate tie rod end from steering arm. Unscrew adjusting screw from torsion bar adjusting lever and remove lever. Remove ball joint retaining bolt at bottom of strut assembly and push control arm down to separate strut assembly from ball joint.

**3)** Remove center nut from upper strut assembly mount from inside luggage compartment. Remove lock washer, tab washer and strut assembly. Mark position of pressure plates on fender panel and remove Allen head bolts and pressure plates. Remove thrust , bearing and support.

**NOTE** — Thrust bearing can be removed without completely removing strut assembly by disconnecting upper mount and pulling down on control arm to separate from thrust bearing.

**Fig. 1   Exploded View of Front Suspension Assembly**

# Front Suspension

## PORSCHE 911SC & TURBO (Cont.)

**Installation** — 1) Install thrust bearing and support. Place pressure plates in proper position and tighten Allen head bolts. Inspect strut assembly for leaks, if leak is discovered, strut assembly must be replaced.

2) Push rod to bottom of stroke, if flange does not bottom out against strut tube, replace strut assembly. There should be no variation of pressure when pushing in or pulling out on rod.

3) Install strut assembly in proper position in vehicle. Install hollow rubber spring, new lock washer, and tighten nut. Fit strut assembly to ball joint and tighten nut.

**NOTE** — *Make sure steel washer is between ball joint and stud.*

4) Push control arm lever down to stop and install adjusting lever on torsion bar. Grease threads of adjusting screw with suitable grease and install screw. Make sure closing cover is correctly seated against adjusting lever.

5) Install tie rod and retighten nut. Install remaining components. *See appropriate article in BRAKE SYSTEM Section.* Tighten all nuts and bolts, bleed brake system, check wheel alignment and riding height.

### CONTROL ARM & BALL JOINT

**Removal** — 1) Raise vehicle and place safety stands under body. Remove wheel and tire. Remove adjusting screw from torsion bar lever and remove lever. Disconnect strut assembly from control arm as previously outlined. Remove rear control arm mounting bolt at suspension crossmember. Remove two bolts securing front control arm mount to body. Slide control arm with torsion bar out of suspension crossmember.

**CAUTION** — *If both control arms are being removed, reinstall rear control arm mounting bolt in suspension crossmember before removing opposite side.*

2) Secure control arm in a vise and remove ball joint retaining nut using a suitable wrench. Remove ball joint from control arm. Control arm should pivot smoothly in mounts. If control arm binds or is distorted, it must be replaced.

3) Inspect torsion bars for damaged serrations. Check sealing bellows on ball joint, replace if damaged or cracked. Remove sealing bellows with a flat chisel and install using suitable mandrel to press bellows on with.

**Installation** — 1) Install ball joint in control arm and tighten grooved nut. Secure nut by bending over tab on lock washer. Grease entire torsion bar and install in control arm. Place control arm in proper position in vehicle and tighten mounting bolts (front to rear).

2) Install strut assembly on ball joint and tighten retaining bolt. Push down on control arm until it contacts stops and install torsion bar seal and adjusting lever. Slide adjusting lever against torsion bar until it reaches stop. Grease adjusting bolt threads and install in lever. Make sure closing cover is correctly seated against adjusting lever. Install control arm protective cover. Install wheel and tire, lower vehicle and check riding height and wheel alignment.

### SUSPENSION CROSSMEMBER

**Removal** — Raise vehicle and place safety stands under vehicle. Remove front axle protective cover. Remove steering gear bolts from crossmember. Remove rear control arm mounting bolts as previously outlined and remove suspension crossmember. Place crossmember on level surface and check for distortion. Inspect for cracks or damage.

**Installation** — Place crossmember in proper position in vehicle and install control arm mounting bolts as previously outlined. Install steering gear bolts and tighten. Install front suspension protective cover. Lower vehicle and check riding height and wheel alignment.

### FRONT AXLE STABILIZER

**Removal** — Remove stabilizer shackles. Unbolt stabilizer lever retaining nuts and extract lever. Remove stabilizer mounting cover hardware and gently pry cover from vehicle.

**Installation** — Check all rubber grommets for signs of wear and replace components as necessary. Coat rubber parts with suitable lubricant. Reinstall stabilizer mounting cover, center stabilizer, then tighten attaching bolts. Seat stabilizer lever in position so stabilizer protrudes approximately .118" (3 mm) beyond lever. Tighten retaining nuts and install shackles.

### FRONT AXLE ASSEMBLY

**Removal** — Disconnect brake hose and plug opening. Disconnect stabilizer bar at crossmember. Remove tie rod shield. Remove bolts at carrier and control arm brackets. Place jack under crossmember. Disconnect steering shaft. Remove upper strut mounting hardware. Carefully pull front axle assembly from vehicle.

**Installation** — To install, reverse removal procedure.

### TIGHTENING SPECIFICATIONS

| Application | Ft. Lbs. (mkg) |
| --- | --- |
| Strut Assembly-to-Ball Joint Securing Bolt | 47 (6.5) |
| Strut Assembly Thrust Bearing | 58 (8.0) |
| Pressure Plate Allen Head Bolts | 34 (4.7) |
| Front Control Arm Mount | 34 (4.7) |
| Control Arm & Suspension Crossmember Mounting Bolt | 65 (9.0) |
| Steering Gear Bolts | 34 (4.7) |
| Ball Joint-to-Control Arm Grooved Nut | 108 (14.9) |
| Front Protective Clamp Allen Head Bolt | 32 (4.4) |
| Suspension Protective Cover-to-Body Bolts | 34 (4.7) |
| Suspension Protective Cover-to-Crossmember Bolts | 11 (1.5) |
| Tie Rod End Strut Nut | 32 (4.4) |

## PORSCHE 924

924

## DESCRIPTION

Vehicle uses independent strut type front suspension. Lower control arms mount with a ball joint to steering knuckle. Back branch of control arm mounts to frame with "U" clamp around control arm pivot shaft. Front branch attaches to frame with bushings and pivot bolt. Strut assembly mounts at top to body with 3 nuts and at bottom to steering knuckle with 2 bolts. Tie rod mounts to steering knuckle with ball joint.

## ADJUSTMENTS

### WHEEL ALIGNMENT SPECIFICATIONS & PROCEDURES

See Wheel Alignment Specifications and Procedures in WHEEL ALIGNMENT Section.

### WHEEL BEARING ADJUSTMENT

See Wheel Bearing Adjustment in WHEEL ALIGNMENT Section.

### BALL JOINT CHECKING

See Ball Joint Checking in WHEEL ALIGNMENT Section.

## REMOVAL & INSTALLATION

### STRUT ASSEMBLY

**Removal** — 1) Raise vehicle so front suspension and front wheels are not supported.

2) Remove bolts mounting suspension strut to steering knuckle. Note that top bolt is one used to adjust front wheel camber.

3) Remove brake caliper assembly and suspend out of way. Pry or force suspension strut out of steering knuckle.

4) Support front suspension by hand. Also, support lower control arm and related components. Work inside engine compartment and remove upper strut mounting nuts. Guide out assembly.

**Disassembly** — 1) Fit strut to spring compressor. Slightly collapse coil spring. Remove shock absorber piston rod nut. Take off the following:
- Stop
- Seal
- Bearing flange
- Bearing
- Spring seat

2) Slowly release spring pressure, remove coil spring. Lift off rubber buffer and protective sleeve. Hold shock absorber upright and work piston rod through entire stroke several different times. Equal pressure must be felt in both directions. Remove cap nut and take out shock absorber.

**Reassembly** — 1) Place shock absorber in strut tube and fit cap nut. Slide on protective sleeve and buffer. Position coil spring into lower seat.

**NOTE** — If new coil is being installed, make sure it is same class of one on opposite side. Springs are available in 3 classes and each class is identified by RED paint stripe(s).

**Fig. 1  Exploded View of Strut Assembly**

2) Fit coil spring to compressor and collapse coil enough to allow piston rod threads to be exposed after upper mounting hardware is fitted. Tighten piston rod lock nut. Release spring pressure.

**Installation** — To install, reverse removal procedure and check front wheel alignment.

# Front Suspension

## PORSCHE 924 (Cont.)

Steering Knuckle — Mountings for Brake Caliper

Upper Mounting (Bearing Flange)

Coil Spring

Tie Rod

Ball Joint

Control Arm Pivot Shaft

Pivot Bolt

Bushings

"U" Clamp

Strut Tube

Control Arm

Brake Line Bracket
for Mounting

**Fig. 2   Exploded View of 924 Front Suspension**

### CONTROL ARM & BALL JOINT

**NOTE** — *If there is enough access room to work, lower control arm does not have to be removed to replace ball joint.*

**Removal** — 1) Raise vehicle and support so suspension is free. Remove pinch bolt mounting ball joint in bottom of steering knuckle. Pull ball joint out of steering knuckle.

Mounting Bolt

Slot for Ball Joint

Replacement Ball Joint

Original Equipment Rivets

Lock Washer

Lock Nut

**Fig. 3   Ball Joint Location in Control Arm**

2) If control arm is not being removed, drill through ball joint rivets with about $^{15}/_{64}$" (6 mm ) bit. Chisel off rivet heads. Fit new ball joint into slot on control arm and install bolts so heads are on top.

3) If control arm is being removed, take out mounting pivot bolt and "U" clamp housing inner pivot pin. Slide out control arm. For ball joint replacement, refer to step 2).

**Inspection** — Check control arm bushings. If bushings are bad they can be replaced. Press out worn bushings. Select new bushing and press into position. Make sure new bushings do not twist when seating into position.

**Installation** — To install, reverse removal procedure.

### TIGHTENING SPECIFICATIONS

| Application | Ft. Lbs. (mkg) |
|---|---|
| Control Arm-to-Crossmember | 40-54 (5.5-7.5) |
| "U" Clamp Bolts | 30 (4.2) |
| Toe Rod Castle Nut | 21 (2.9) |
| Piston Rod Nut | 56-58 (7.7-8.8) |
| Strut-to-Steering Knuckle | 51-72 (7.0-10.0) |
| Upper Strut Mount | 15-21 (2.1-2.9) |
| Ball Joint-to-Control Arm (Replacement) | 18 (2.5) |
| Ball Joint Pinch Bolt | 36-43 (5.0-6.0) |

# Front Suspension

## PORSCHE 928

**928**

### DESCRIPTION

Front suspension is an independent type strut suspension. It consists of a strut assembly, surrounded by a coil spring. This assembly is connected at top to inner fender panel and at bottom to lower control arm. Lower control arm connects at outer end to steering knuckle through a ball joint. At inner end of the "T" shaped control arm, 2 bushings connect arm to frame member. An upper control arm is attached by ball joint to steering knuckle and by pivot shaft to frame member. A stabilizer bar is connected via a link to lower mounting of strut assembly.

**Fig. 1  Exploded View of Porsche 928 Front Suspension Assembly**

### ADJUSTMENTS

#### WHEEL BEARING ADJUSTMENT

*See Wheel Bearing Adjustment in WHEEL ALIGNMENT section.*

#### WHEEL ALIGNMENT SPECIFICATIONS & PROCEDURES

*See Wheel Alignment Specifications and Procedures in WHEEL ALIGNMENT section.*

#### BALL JOINT CHECKING

*See Ball Joint Checking in WHEEL ALIGNMENT section.*

### REMOVAL & INSTALLATION

#### STRUT ASSEMBLY & UPPER CONTROL ARM

**Removal — 1)** Remove 3 self-locking nuts securing top of strut assembly to inner fender panel in engine compartment. Raise and support vehicle. Remove front wheel.

**2)** Unscrew flange locknut and use suitable tool to separate upper control arm ball joint from steering knuckle. Remove self-locking nuts holding upper control arm pivot shaft to body (access in engine compartment).

**3)** Remove strut lower mounting bolt and maneuver strut assembly and upper control arm out of vehicle.

**Disassembly — 1)** Place strut assembly in vise and attach coil spring compressor. Apply enough tension to coil spring to allow removal of top self-locking nut, washer and mounting plate.

**2)** Release spring compressor. Remove upper spring retainer, coil spring and components from piston rod.

**3)** Mark position of lower spring retainer to shock absorber for proper reassembly reference.

**Reassembly — 1)** Reassemble strut assembly components in reverse order of disassembly. If replacing coil spring, be sure proper weight class springs are used.

**2)** If replacing lower spring retainer, coil spring or shock absorber, position of spring retainer to shock absorber must be determined. Install assembly in vehicle by attaching upper retainers. Position upper end of spring against upper retainer stop. Position lower retainer and turn until against stop. Mark position.

**3)** Remove strut assembly back to vise and complete reassembly.

**Installation —** To install, reverse removal procedure.

## TIGHTENING SPECIFICATIONS

| Application | Ft. Lbs. (mkg) |
| --- | --- |
| Upper Control Arm-to-Body | 101 (14) |
| Lower Control Arm-to-Body | |
|   Front | 61 (8.5) |
|   Rear | 87 (12) |
| Stabilizer Bar-to-Body | 33 (4.6) |
| Stabilizer Link Nut | 61 (8.5) |
| Ball Joints-to-Knuckle | 61 (8.5) |

## RENAULT R-5

### R-5

### DESCRIPTION

Independent type suspension, consisting of upper and lower control arms with stub axles mounted between upper and lower control arms by ball joints. Upper control arm pivots on shaft attached to frame. Lower arm pivots on shaft secured to crossmember. Shock absorbers mount off body brackets at top and off purchases built into control arm on bottom.

Upper Shock Absorber Mounting

Upper Ball Joint

Upper Control Arm Mount

Upper Control Arm

Axle Drive Shaft

Stub Axle

Lower Shock Absorber Mounting

Lower Control Arm

Axle Nut

**Fig. 1  Cut-Away View of Renault R-5 Front Suspension**

### ADJUSTMENT

#### WHEEL ALIGNMENT SPECIFICATIONS & PROCEDURES

*See Wheel Alignment Specifications & Procedures in WHEEL ALIGNMENT Section.*

#### WHEEL BEARING ADJUSTMENT

*See Wheel Bearing Adjustment in WHEEL ALIGNMENT Section.*

#### BALL JOINT CHECKING

*See Ball Joint Checking in WHEEL ALIGNMENT Section.*

#### RIDING HEIGHT ADJUSTMENT

*See Riding Height Adjustment in WHEEL ALIGNMENT Section.*

### REMOVAL & INSTALLATION

#### SHOCK ABSORBERS

**Removal** — Raise vehicle and suitably support vehicle with safety stands. Remove lock nut, mounting nut, and bushing attaching shock absorber to upper bracket. Remove lower retaining bolt holding shock absorber to lower control arm. Maneuver shock absorber from vehicle.

**Installation** — To install, reverse removal procedure.

#### UPPER CONTROL ARM & BALL JOINT

**Removal** — Take out overflow tank and remove ignition coil. Using tool T. Av. 476 (or equivalent) disconnect upper ball joint. Remove nut from inboard edge of pivot shaft. Place a lock nut on outer end of pivot shaft and turn mounting nut to remove shaft. Pivot shaft will clear brake lines. Maneuver control arm from vehicle.

**Inspection & Replacement** — Inspect rubber bushings for cracks or distortion. Use a press and mandrel to remove and replace worn bushings. To replace ball joint, place control arm in a vise and drill out rivet heads. Fit new ball joint with shim placed on top of control arm. Tighten nuts and bolts (those that replaced rivets). Make sure bolt head is installed on dust cover side of joint.

**Installation** — To install, reverse removal procedure and note following: Apply a light coat of grease to pivot shaft before inserting in control arm. If ball joint has been replaced, check wheel alignment and steering box height.

#### LOWER CONTROL ARM & BALL JOINT

**Removal** — 1) Raise front of vehicle and place on safety stands. Remove stub axle nut. Disconnect and remove torsion bars. Disconnect sway bar from brackets and mounting on control arm. Separate bottom of shock absorber from mounting.

**2)** Remove lower control arm from crossmember. Put tool T. Av. 235 (or equivalent) in brake drum or hub. With a spacer located between thrust screw and axle drive shaft, force shaft inward and free ball joint from stub axle carrier.

NOTE — *Make sure axle drive shaft is not removed.*

**Inspection & Replacement** — 1) Inspect rubber bushings and sleeve inserts for cracks, excessive damage or wear. Use a mandrel and press to replace bushings. Make sure each bushing is centered and has adequate protrusion out each side of control arm.

**2)** Place control arm in suitable holding fixture (vise). Chisel or drill out rivet heads. Remove nuts, if necessary. Separate joint from control arm. Fit new ball joint into control arm. Make sure bolt heads face dust cover side.

**Installation** — To install, reverse removal procedure and note following: Make sure castor adjusting shims are under bushing. Check wheel alignment after reinstallation.

#### STUB AXLE

**Removal** — Raise vehicle and place on safety stands. Remove hub and disc assembly. Using tool T. Av. 476 (or equivalent) disconnect upper and lower ball joints, then separate steering arm ball joint. Use a slide hammer and withdraw drum/hub assembly. Make sure axle drive shaft does not drop.

**Installation** — Install stub axle into position while guiding ball joints into position. Pull drive shaft into carrier housing. Refit brake components. Tighten stub axle nut.

# Front Suspension

## RENAULT R-5 (Cont.)

### TORSION BAR

**Removal — 1)** Slide seat forward and tilt seat. Loosen lock nut and turn cam screw counterclockwise to zero. Raise vehicle and place on safety stands. Remove dust cover from adjusting lever. Fit special tool 545 (or equivalent) in adjusting lever. From inside vehicle, remove lever housing attachment bolts. Remove housing cover cam assembly from adjusting lever, then slowly release pressure on wrench.

**Fig. 2   Exploded View of Torsion Bar Assembly**

**2)** Index mark position of adjusting lever with floor crossmember. Mark position of torsion bar on lower arm anchor sleeve. Disconnect stabilizer bar brackets. Remove bar from arm and check that mark made on lower arm anchor sleeve is aligned with punch mark on torsion bar. If punch marks do not align, count number of revolutions and spines displaced to align marks.

**Fig. 3   Scribe Marks on Floor Crossmember**

**Installation — 1)** Lightly grease torsion bar ends with grease. Reassemble cover seal, cam housing, and adjusting lever over torsion bar. Insert bar into lower control arm, aligning index mark made during installation. Fit adjusting lever on splines, aligning with mark on floor crossmember.

**Fig. 4   Lower Arm Anchor Sleeve Scribe Mark**

**2)** Place adjusting lever ⅜-¾" (10-20 mm) as shown in *Fig. 5*. Insert wrench 545 (or equivalent) and take up tension on bar. Center the cover by resetting cam. Hold assembly with vise grips and insert mounting bolts. Adjust under body height by turning adjusting cams.

**Fig. 5   Position of Adjusting Lever**

## TIGHTENING SPECIFICATIONS

| Application | Ft. Lbs. (mkg) |
| --- | --- |
| Lower Shock Absorber Bolt | 30 (4.2) |
| Lower Ball Joint | 40 (5.5) |
| Upper Ball Joint | 25 (3.5) |
| Lower Control Arm Nuts | 75 (10.4) |
| Axle Nut | 90 (12.4) |

## SAAB

99

### DESCRIPTION

Independent front suspension with coil springs. Wheel is supported by steering knuckle mounted between upper and lower control arms by means of ball joints. Both upper and lower control arms pivot on shafts connected to body. Coil springs fit in pockets built into body at top and in supports attached to upper control arms at bottom. Hydraulic shock absorbers mount between lower control arm and body. If stabilizer bar is used, it is attached to frame and connected at ends to lower control arms.

**Fig. 1    Saab Front Suspension Assembly with Relationship of Components**

### ADJUSTMENT

#### WHEEL ALIGNMENT SPECIFICATIONS & PROCEDURES

*See Wheel Alignment Specifications and Procedures in WHEEL ALIGNMENT Section.*

#### WHEEL BEARING ADJUSTMENT

*See Wheel Bearing Adjustment in WHEEL ALIGNMENT Section.*

#### BALL JOINT CHECKING

*See Ball Joint Checking in WHEEL ALIGNMENT Section.*

### REMOVAL & INSTALLATION

#### SHOCK ABSORBERS

**Removal** — Raise vehicle and place safety stands under frame. Remove wheel and tire. Remove nuts securing shock absorber and remove shock.

**Installation** — To install, reverse removal procedure.

#### UPPER CONTROL ARM

**Removal** — Raise and support front of vehicle. Remove tire and wheel. Remove shock absorber. Compress coil spring using a suitable compressor (8995839). Remove two bolts attaching upper ball joint to upper control arm. Remove bolts

attaching upper control arm bearing brackets, remove compressed coil spring, upper control arm and bearings. **NOTE** — *Save spacers under bearings, and note number of spacers under each reassembly reference.*

**Installation** — Replace worn or damaged components. If bearings have been removed from control arm, position onto control arm so when both nuts are tightened and locked, angle between arm and bearing will be 52°±2°. Install upper control arm but do not install bearing locating bolts. Make sure spacer and support ring of upper spring seat are in position, then locate compressed coil spring with rubber buffer, and mount ball joint and lower spring seat onto control arm. Install bearing attaching bolts while ensuring that spacers are in position. Slowly release compressor tool to release coil spring. Install shock absorber, wheel and tire. Recheck wheel alignment.

**Fig. 2    Assembled Angle of Upper Control Arm-to-Bearing**

### LOWER CONTROL ARM

**Removal** — Raise vehicle, then remove wheel and tire. Disconnect shock absorber lower mounting. Remove two bolts attaching lower ball joint to lower control arm. Remove lower control arm-to-engine compartment attaching bolts, then remove lower control arm and brackets.

**Installation** — Replace worn or damaged components. If bearings have been removed from control arm, position onto control arm so when both nuts are tightened and locked, angle between arm and bearing will be 18°±2°. Install control arm and brackets, attach ball joint to control arm and tighten all attaching bolts. Install wheel and tire. Recheck wheel alignment.

**Fig. 3    Lower Control Arm-to-Bearing Angle**

### BALL JOINTS

**Removal** — Raise vehicle. Remove tire and wheel. Remove caliper and hang out of way. Remove ball joint nut. Using suitable tool (8995409) separate ball joint from steering knuckle.

**Installation** — Fit new ball joint to steering knuckle. Tighten nut. Insert ball joint mounting bock into control arm and tighten using new lock nuts. Reinstall brake caliper.

## SUBARU

**1600**
**Brat**

### DESCRIPTION

Suspension is strut type, utilizing a hydraulic shock absorber/coil spring assembly forming a strut. Strut is secured at top to body and at bottom to steering knuckle. Steering knuckle pivots on ball joint attached to lower control arm. Lower control arms are attached to front crossmember. Radius rods are welded to lower control arms and attached to rear crossmember with rubber bushings, washers, and nuts. A stabilizer bar is also used and attached to rear crossmember and to radius rods with clamps and rubber bushings.

**Fig. 1  Exploded View of Front Suspension**

### ADJUSTMENT

#### WHEEL ALIGNMENT SPECIFICATIONS & PROCEDURES

*See Wheel Alignment Specifications and Procedures in WHEEL ALIGNMENT Section.*

#### WHEEL BEARING ADJUSTMENT

*See Wheel Bearing Adjustment in WHEEL ALIGNMENT Section.*

#### BALL JOINT CHECKING

*See Ball Joint Checking in WHEEL ALIGNMENT Section.*

### REMOVAL & INSTALLATION

#### FRONT SUSPENSION

**Removal — 1)** Detach battery ground cable. Raise and support vehicle and remove front wheel(s).

**2)** Remove parking brake cable hanger from tie rod end, remove cable end from caliper lever, remove outer cable clip from caliper, remove cable bracket from housing and remove cable mounting bracket from lower control arm.

**3)** Drive out spring pins from inner end of drive axle nearest transaxle housing.

**4)** Remove self-locking nut and bolt holding control arm to crossmember. Pull control arm downward from crossmember.

**5)** Use suitable tool to separate tie rod end from steering knuckle arm.

**6)** Detach radius rod from rear crossmember. Remove stabilizer bar brackets.

**7)** Remove upper strut assembly mounting nuts. Pull drive shaft from transaxle and remove suspension assembly from vehicle.

**Installation —** To install, reverse removal procedure, noting the following points:

- Be sure to align spring pin holes in drive axle before installing.
- When installing strut top mounting, be sure the stud marked "S" is forward on Sedan, Coupe and Hardtop models, while stud marked "V4" is forward on Station Wagon and 4-Wheel Drive models.
- When installing stabilizer, be sure slit in bushing is facing downward in clamp.
- Replace all self-locking nuts.
- Before installing radius rod bushing, soak it in soapy solution or rubber lubricant to assist installation.
- When installing castellated nuts on ball joints, tighten nut, as required, beyond specified torque setting to align cotter pin hole.
- Always use new spring pins for attaching inner end of drive shaft.

#### STRUT ASSEMBLY

**Removal — 1)** Raise and support vehicle. Remove front wheels. Remove bolts attaching strut tube to steering knuckle.

**2)** Detach tie rod end from steering knuckle arm. Pull strut out of mounting on steering knuckle. Remove upper strut mounting nuts. Remove strut assembly from vehicle.

**Disassembly — 1)** Attach special puller and wrench tool (925160000) to strut assembly and hold in horizontal position. Use tool to compress coil spring until upper seat is separated from coil spring.

**2)** Use wrench portion of tool to hold upper mounting plate while removing self-locking nut from top end of strut. Remove thrust washer, oil seal and thrust bearing. Remove the upper spring seat from rod.

## SUBARU (Cont.)

**3)** Carefully remove tension from coil spring and remove tool and spring from strut.

**Reassembly** — To reassemble, reverse diassembly procedures, replacing self-locking nut with a new one. Place small amount of grease on thrust washer.

**Installation** — To install, reverse removal procedure, noting the following:

- Be sure upper strut mounting plate is facing in proper direction as described under "Front Suspension" installation procedure in this article.
- When reattaching brake line and hose, be sure to allow enough clearance from wheel apron.

### STABILIZER BAR

**Removal** — Raise front of vehicle, and support with safety stands. Remove clamps securing stabilizer bar to radius rod. Remove clamps attaching stabilizer bar to rear crossmember.

**Installation** — Check all bushings for wear or damage and replace as necessary. Check stabilizer bar for possible cracking. To install, reverse removal procedure.

### LOWER CONTROL ARM

**Removal** — Raise front of vehicle, support with safety stands, and remove wheel and tire. Disconnect brake cable bracket from control arm. Disconnect stabilizer bar from radius rod. Disconnect radius rod from rear crossmember. Remove control arm-to-front crossmember attaching bolt. Remove ball joint-to-steering knuckle attaching nut and separate from knuckle. Remove control arm from vehicle.

**Installation** — Check ball joint for wear or damage. Check pivot bushing for wear or damage. To install lower control arm, reverse removal procedure and note: Torque ball joint castle nut, insert cotter pin, and tighten nut an additional turn.

### TIGHTENING SPECIFICATIONS

| Application | Ft. Lbs. (mkg) |
| --- | --- |
| Stabilizer Bracket Nuts | 13-16 (1.8-2.2) |
| Radius Rod-to-Rear Crossmember | 51-62 (7.0-8.5) |
| Tie Rod End Ball Joint Nut | 18-36 (2.5-5.0) |
| Wheel Nuts | 58-72 (8.0-10.0) |
| Upper Strut Mounting Nuts | 22-29 (3.0-4.0) |
| Strut-to-Piston Rod Nut | 43-54 (6.0-7.5) |
| Lower Strut End-to-Housing | 22-29 (3.0-4.0) |
| Control Arm-to-Crossmember | 47-54 (6.5-7.5) |
| Control Arm Ball Joint Nut | 80-94 (11.0-13.0) |
| Ball Joint-to-Control Arm | 35-40 (4.8-5.5) |

# Front Suspension

## TOYOTA CELICA, COROLLA & CRESSIDA

Celica
Corolla
Cressida

### DESCRIPTION

Independent strut type suspension consisting of vertically mounted strut assemblies, lower control arms, strut rods and a stabilizer bar. Individual strut assembly is mounted at top to inner fender by a thrust bearing and at bottom to lower control arm by means of a ball joint. Strut assembly consists of a shock absorber built into strut outer tube, a coil spring mounted on outside of strut tube and a steering knuckle integral with bottom of strut tube. A strut rod is mounted between lower control arm and frame. A stabilizer bar is mounted to front frame members and connected at ends to lower control arms. The suspension crossmember that serves as support for all suspension components is removable.

**Fig. 1  Assembled View of Front Suspension Assembly (Corolla Shown; Celica & Cressida Similar)**

### ADJUSTMENT

#### WHEEL ALIGNMENT SPECIFICATIONS & PROCEDURES

*See Wheel Alignment Specifications & Procedures in WHEEL ALIGNMENT Section.*

#### WHEEL BEARING ADJUSTMENT

*See Wheel Bearing Adjustment in WHEEL ALIGNMENT Section.*

#### BALL JOINT CHECKING

*See Ball Joint Checking in WHEEL ALIGNMENT Section.*

## REMOVAL & INSTALLATION

### STRUT ASSEMBLY

**Removal — 1)** Raise and support vehicle. Remove front wheel. Disconnect brake tube and flexible hose.

**2)** Remove 3 nuts retaining top of strut assembly to vehicle. Remove bolts holding lower end of strut tube to steering knuckle.

**3)** Pull down on control arm to gain clearance and remove strut assembly (with brake and hub assembly attached) from vehicle.

**Disassembly — 1)** Install assembly in vise, clamping portion of strut tube below flange.

**2)** Use suitable spring compressor to collapse spring enough to remove strut rod top nut. Relieve pressure on spring, remove spring and disassemble shock absorber top end retaining components.

**3)** Lift shock absorber piston rod from cylinder. On Corolla, lower end components may be disassembled. *Fig. 2.* On other models, piston valve assembly on lower end is integral with piston rod.

**Fig. 2  Lower End Components of Piston Rod for Corolla Models**

**Reassembly —** Thoroughly clean and inspect all components. Replace any damaged parts. Install shock absorber components into cylinder in reverse of disassembly procedure, noting the following:

- Follow appropriate illustration for reassembling Corolla piston rod components. *Fig. 2.*
- After installing piston nut, stake it in place.
- When installing base valve onto cylinder, use a soft-face hammer to drive into place.
- Add specified amount of new shock absorber oil to cylinder.
- Before fully tightening ring nut, pull piston rod out of cylinder about 3-4".

## TOYOTA CELICA, COROLLA & CRESSIDA (Cont.)

### Shock Absorber Oil Amount

| Application | Ounces (cc) |
| --- | --- |
| Celica | 12.0 (325) |
| Corolla | |
| With 1100 cc Engine | 9.5-9.8 (280-290) |
| With 1600 cc Engine | 10.6 (315) |
| Cressida | 10.8 (320) |

**Installation** — To install strut assembly in vehicle, reverse removal procedure, noting the following:

- After top end of strut is attached to mounting, fill bearing recess, which protrudes into engine compartment, with multi-purpose grease.
- Always use new self-locking nut on top of piston rod.

### CONTROL ARM

**Removal** — 1) Raise and support front of vehicle. Remove front wheel. Remove strut assembly-to-knuckle mounting bolts.

2) On Corolla and Cressida, detach tie rod end ball joint from steering arm. On Celica, detach ball joint from steering arm.

3) On all models, separate stabilizer bar and strut bar from control arm (stabilizer bar shield may have to be removed first on some models).

4) Remove control arm pivot bolt and remove control arm and ball joint assembly from vehicle.

**Disassembly** — 1) On Corolla and Cressida, place control arm assembly in vise and use suitable puller to remove steering arm from ball joint.

2) Pry dust cover from ball joint and discard (also discard dust cover snap ring or retaining wire).

3) Press bushing out of control arm toward front side of arm, using suitable press and arbor.

**Reassembly** — Use suitable support and press in new bushing. Position new ball joint dust cap and install new retaining wire or snap ring.

**Installation** — To install, reverse removal procedure.

### STABILIZER BAR

**Removal** — Disconnect stabilizer bar from both control arms. Remove engine protective cover, if equipped. Remove bolts securing mounting brackets to chassis and remove stabilizer bar.

**Installation** — To install, reverse removal procedure. Make sure components connecting stabilizer bar to control arms are installed properly.

### STRUT ROD

**Removal** — Raise vehicle and place safety stands under vehicle. Remove nut from front of strut rod and remove washer, retainer, and rubber grommet. Remove bolts connecting strut rod to control arm and remove rod from vehicle.

**Installation** — On Corolla, install inside retaining nut so its inner edge is 3.43" (87.2 mm) from outer end of threaded portion of strut rod. On Celica, set distance between outer side of staked nut and inner mounting hole on other end of rod at 14.9" (379 mm); on Cressida, set this distance at 15.9" (405 mm). Place rod in vehicle and tighten mounting hardware.

### SUSPENSION CROSSMEMBER

**Removal** — Disconnect control arms as previously outlined. Place a jack under engine for support and remove nuts securing motor mounts to crossmember. Remove protective cover from under engine. Remove bolts securing crossmember to body and remove crossmember.

**Installation** — To install, reverse removal procedure. Make sure components connecting stabilizer bar to control arms are installed in correct order.

### TIGHTENING SPECIFICATIONS

| Application | Ft. Lbs. ( mkg) |
| --- | --- |
| Control Arm-to-Crossmember | |
| Celica, Corolla | 51-65 (7.0-9.0) |
| Cressida | ①65-94 (9.0-13.0) |
| Control Arm-to-Strut | |
| Celica, Corolla | 29-40 (4.0-5.5) |
| Cressida | 43-53 (6.0-7.4) |
| Control Arm-to-Stabilizer | 11-15 (1.4-2.2) |
| Ball Joint-to-Knuckle Arm | 51-65 (7.0-9.0) |
| Knuckle Arm-to-Strut Tube | |
| Corolla | 51-65 (7.0-9.0) |
| Celica, Cressida | 58-86 (8.0-12.0) |
| Piston Rod-to-Mounting Plate | 29-40 (4.0-5.5) |
| Piston Rod Ring Nut | 73-108 (10.0-15.0) |
| Lower Piston Nut (Corolla Only) | |
| KE Series | 43-54 (6.0-7.5) |
| TE Series | 14-22 (1.9-3.1) |

① — With vehicle at full curb weight.

# Front Suspension

## TOYOTA CORONA

Corona

## DESCRIPTION

Front suspension is independent type. Wheel is supported by steering knuckle mounted by ball joints to upper and lower control arms. Upper control arm pivots on shaft bolted to upper frame member. Lower control arm pivots on shaft bolted to lower frame member. Shock absorbers attach at bottom to lower control arm, are surrounded by a coil spring and are bolted at top to body. A stabilizer bar is also used and attaches at each end to lower control arms and also to body brackets.

**Fig. 1  Exploded View of Front Suspension Assy.**

## ADJUSTMENT

### WHEEL ALIGNMENT SPECIFICATIONS & PROCEDURES
See Wheel Alignment Specifications & Procedures in WHEEL ALIGNMENT Section.

### WHEEL BEARING ADJUSTMENT
See Wheel Bearing Adjustment in WHEEL ALIGNMENT Section.

### BALL JOINT CHECKING
See Ball Joint Checking in WHEEL ALIGNMENT Section.

## REMOVAL & INSTALLATION

### STEERING KNUCKLE

**Removal — 1)** Raise and support vehicle. Remove front wheel. Remove and suspend brake caliper out of way. Remove hub assembly. Remove backing plate.

**2)** Remove cotter pin and nut and separate tie rod end ball joint from steering knuckle.

**3)** Place jack under lower arm spring seat. Raise jack to compress coil spring. Remove cotter pins and nuts from upper and lower ball joints and detach ball joints from steering knuckle. Remove knuckle from vehicle.

**Installation —** To install, reverse removal procedure.

### LOWER CONTROL ARM, COIL SPRING & BALL JOINT

**Removal — 1)** Raise vehicle and place safety stands under body. Remove tire and wheel. Disconnect stabilizer bar from lower control arm. Remove shock absorber. Using a spring compressor, collapse coil spring until there is no pressure on lower control arm. On models with ESP, disconnect wiring harness for brakes and separate clamp from arm.

**2)** Remove nut securing ball joint stud to steering knuckle. Using a puller, separate ball joint from steering knuckle. Push down on control arm, release spring pressure, and remove coil spring. Remove bolts securing control arm pivot shaft to suspension crossmember and remove control arm from vehicle.

**Installation —** To install, reverse removal procedure, noting the following:

- Attach control arm to frame, installing cams in original positions, with nuts tightened only partially.
- Position coil spring in lower plate against stop.
- Attach coil spring compressor and collapse spring, jack up lower control arm and connect ball joint to steering knuckle.
- After vehicle is resting on ground, tighten control arm mounting nuts.
- Check front end alignment.

### UPPER CONTROL ARM & BALL JOINT

**Removal — 1)** From inside engine compartment, remove upper control arm attaching nuts, but do not pull out bolts.

**2)** Raise and support vehicle, with jack placed under lower control arm. Remove front wheel.

**NOTE** — On vehicles with ESP, detach wire harness clamp from upper control arm.

**3)** Raise jack under control arm to compress coil spring. Remove ball joint nut, then use puller to separate ball joint from upper control arm.

**NOTE** — Safety wire steering knuckle to suspension so it does not drop and strain brake hose.

**4)** Remove bolts from upper control arm and pull arm from vehicle.

**Installation —** To install, reverse removal procedure and note the following:

- Do not fully tighten upper control arm-to-body mounting nuts until vehicle is resting on ground.

## TIGHTENING SPECIFICATIONS

| Application | Ft. Lbs. (mkg) |
|---|---|
| Upper Ball Joint | 40-50 (5.5-7.0) |
| Lower Ball Joint | 40-52 (5.5-7.2) |
| Upper Arm-to-Body | 65-87 (9.0-12.0) |
| Lower Arm-to-Body | 94-130 (13.0-18.0) |
| Wheel Nuts | 65-87 (9.0-12.0) |

# Front Suspension

**Pickup**

## DESCRIPTION

Independent front suspension with coil springs. Wheel is supported by steering knuckle mounted between upper and lower control arms by ball joints. Upper control arms pivot on shafts connected to frame. Lower control arms pivot on shafts connected to crossmember. Coil springs fit in pockets built into frame at top and in pockets built into lower control arms at bottom. Hydraulic shock absorbers mount between lower control arm and frame and are inside coil spring. A stabilizer bar is mounted to frame and connected at ends to lower control arms.

**Fig. 1  Sectional View of Front Suspension Assembly**

## ADJUSTMENT

### WHEEL ALIGNMENT SPECIFICATIONS & PROCEDURES

*See Wheel Alignment Specifications & Procedures in WHEEL ALIGNMENT Section.*

### WHEEL BEARING ADJUSTMENT

*See Wheel Bearing Adjustment in WHEEL ALIGNMENT Section.*

### BALL JOINT CHECKING

*See Ball Joint Checking in WHEEL ALIGNMENT Section.*

## REMOVAL & INSTALLATION

### SHOCK ABSORBERS

**Removal** — Raise vehicle and place on jack stands under frame. Remove wheel and tire. Remove nuts from upper shock absorber stem. Remove bolts securing shock absorber lower mount to lower control arm.

**Installation** — To install, reverse removal procedure. Tighten all nuts and bolts.

## UPPER CONTROL ARM & BALL JOINT

**Removal** — Raise vehicle by placing jack under lower control arm. Place safety stands under frame and leave jack in place. Remove wheel and tire. Remove cotter pin and nut from upper ball joint stud. Using a suitable puller (09628-62010) separate ball joint from steering knuckle. Remove bolts securing upper control arm mount, noting size and number of shims between pivot shaft and mount. Remove control arm from vehicle. Remove bolts securing ball joint to control arm, and remove ball joint. Unscrew pivot shaft bushings and remove bushings and shaft.

**Fig. 2  Exploded View of Upper Control Arm Assembly**

**Installation** — Inspect all components for wear or distortion. Install pivot shaft with offset mounting hole to front. Reverse removal procedure for installation making sure wheel alignment shims are installed in correct position. Tighten all bolts and nuts to specifications. Check wheel alignment.

### LOWER CONTROL ARM, COIL SPRING & BALL JOINT

**Removal** — **1)** Raise vehicle by jacking up under lower control arm. Place jack stands under frame and leave jack in place. Remove wheel and tire. Disconnect stabilizer bar from control arm. Remove cotter pin and nut from tie rod end stud and using a puller separate tie rod from steering arm. Remove shock absorber as previously outlined.

**2)** Remove cotter pin and nut from lower ball joint stud and using a puller, separate ball joint from steering knuckle. Lower jack slowly and remove coil spring and insulator. Remove bolts securing control arm to crossmember and remove control arm from vehicle. Secure control arm in a vise and remove ball joint from control arm. Remove bushings from both ends of pivot shaft and remove shaft.

**Installation** — **1)** Install pivot shaft in control arm. Install bushings and tighten alternately and evenly. Install ball joint in control arm. Install control arm and tighten pivot shaft bolts. Install coil spring insulator in pocket.

**2)** Install a coil spring compressor on coil. Collapse coil spring until control arm can be connected to steering knuckle with coil spring in vehicle. With ball joint stud installed in steering knuckle, tighten nut.

## TOYOTA PICKUP (Cont.)

Pivot Bushing  Pivot Shaft
Dust Seal

Bumper

Lower
Control Arm

Ball Joint

Dust Cover

Snap Ring

**Fig. 3    Exploded View of Lower Control Arm
and Related Components**

**3)** Connect stabilizer bar to control arm. Connect tie rod end to steering arm and tighten nut. Install wheel and tire, lower vehicle and grease lower control arm bushings. Check front wheel alignment.

### STEERING KNUCKLE

**Removal — 1)** Raise vehicle and place jack stands under frame. Remove wheel and tire. Remove brake system components from steering knuckle. **NOTE** — See *appropriate information in BRAKE SYSTEMS Section for removal.* Jack up under control arm to release spring tension from lower arm.

**2)** Remove cotter pin and nut from lower ball joint stud and using a suitable puller separate ball joint from steering knuckle. Separate upper ball joint from steering knuckle in same manner. Lower jack and remove steering knuckle.

**Installation —** To install, reverse removal procedure. Check wheel alignment.

### FRONT SUSPENSION CROSSMEMBER

**Removal — 1)** Raise front of vehicle and support with jack stands. Remove front wheels. Disconnect tie rod ends from both steering knuckles. Disconnect each end of stabilizer bar from suspension lower arms. Remove engine compartment hood.

**2)** Disconnect brake system components from steering knuckle. **NOTE** — See *BRAKE SYSTEMS Section for removal procedure.* Remove bolts retaining front engine mounts. Separate brake line from crossmember. Support engine from overhead. Support front crossmember with jack. Remove four bolts from front suspension crossmember and slide from vehicle.

**Installation —** To install, reverse removal procedure and tighten all nuts and bolts.

### TIGHTENING SPECIFICATIONS

| Application | Ft. Lbs. (mkg) |
|---|---|
| Lower Ball Joint-to Steering Knuckle | 87-123 (12.0-17.0) |
| Upper Ball Joint-to Steering Knuckle | 65-94 (9.0-13.0) |
| Pivot Shaft-to-Upper Control Arm | 94-152 (13.0-21.0) |
| Pivot Shaft-to-Lower Control Arm | 22-32 (3.0-4.5) |
| Ball Joint-to-Upper Control Arm | 14-22 (1.9-4.5) |

# Front Suspension

## TRIUMPH TR7

**TR7**

### DESCRIPTION

Suspension is strut type with a coil spring around strut tube. Strut is secured at top to inner fender and at bottom to control arm link. A stabilizer bar is connected to chassis and lower control link. Control arm links are mounted by a ball joint at stub axles and through bolts at chassis.

### ADJUSTMENT

#### WHEEL ALIGNMENT SPECIFICATIONS & PROCEDURES

See Wheel Alignment Specifications and Procedures in WHEEL ALIGNMENT Section.

#### WHEEL BEARING ADJUSTMENT

See Wheel Bearing Adjustment in WHEEL ALIGNMENT Section.

#### BALL JOINT CHECKING

See Ball Joint Checking in WHEEL ALIGNMENT Section.

### REMOVAL & INSTALLATION

#### LOWER CONTROL LINK

**Removal — 1)** Raise and support vehicle with safety stands. Remove tire and wheel. Remove mounting hardware from end of stabilizer bar. Remove bolts holding steering arm to stub axle and move out of way. Remove nut and separate ball joint. Remove bolt and nut securing lower control link to chassis, then take out link.

**Fig. 1** *Detail of Components to Remove in Order to Take Off Lower Control Link and Strut Assembly*

**2)** Remove plastic and rubber ring from ball joint. Remove snap ring retaining ball joint housing to bottom link. Press or drive out ball joint and housing. Install new ball joint, fit snap ring, plastic, and rubber ring.

**Installation** — To install reverse removal procedure and tighten lower control link when vehicle weight is on ground.

**Fig. 2** *Exploded View of Ball Joint Assembly*

#### STRUT ASSEMBLY

**Removal — 1)** Raise vehicle and support with jack stands. Remove tire and wheel. Separate steering arm from stub axle assembly by removing two bolts. Disconnect brake hose from bracket on strut tube. Disconnect brake caliper and hang out of way.

**2)** Remove ball joint nut and separate from stub axle. Remove three nuts mounting strut assembly to inner fender panel. Pull strut downward and maneuver from vehicle.

**3)** Using a spring compressor, collapse coil and remove slotted nut from top of strut assembly. Take out spring pan complete with top mounting and swivel assembly. Remove spring from strut.

**Disassembly** — Remove retainer securing strut tube to plug nut using a 1/8" diameter drill. Using a suitable tool, remove plug nut. Slide shock absorber (damper) from strut tube.

**Reassembly** — Drill 1/4" diameter hole 1/16" deep at a 90° angle to the existing recess in plug nut. Fit shock absorber (damper) assembly to strut tube, then fit plug nut and tighten. Using center punch, stake strut tube into recess in plug nut.

## TRIUMPH TR7 (Cont.)

- Coil Spring
- Lower Insulating Ring
- Plug Nut
- Stake Here
- Strut Tube
- Stub Axle
- Mounting Hardware
- Upper Insulating Ring
- Dust Boot
- Shock Absorber (Damper)

**Fig. 3    Disassembled View of Strut**

**Installation** – 1) Compress coil spring and ensure bumper stop is correctly positioned. Fully extend strut rod and fit the following: lower insulating ring, rubber seal, spring, upper insulating ring, and spring pan. Fit seal to thrust collar and place on upper spring pan.

**2)** Install plain washer, ground surface facing spring pan. Insert rubber mounting to strut and secure with dished washer and slotted nut. To complete installation, reverse removal procedure. Bleed brake system.

### STABILIZER BAR

**Removal** – Raise vehicle and place on safety stands. Remove bolts and brackets mounting stabilizer bar to chassis. Remove mounting nut and rubber bushing securing stabilizer bar to lower control link. Pull out stabilizer, adjusting vehicle height as necessary. If necessary, inner bushing and mounting bushings can now be removed and replaced.

**Installation** – Refit inner dished washer with dish facing bushing, then install inner bushing on each end of stabilizer bar. Insert stabilizer bar and fit outer rubber bushings with dished washers. Reinstall mounting brackets and tighten all nuts and bolts.

## TIGHTENING SPECIFICATIONS

| Application | Ft. Lbs. (mkg) |
|---|---|
| Stabilizer Bar-to-Chassis | 30-37 (4.2-5.1) |
| Stabilizer Bar-to-Lower Control Link | 48-59 (6.7-8.1) |
| Strut Mounting-to-Body | 16-21 (2.3-2.9) |
| Strut-to-Mounting | 30-44 (4.2-6.0) |
| Tie Rod-to-Stub Axle | 59-74 (8.2-10.2) |
| Strut Tube Plug Nut | 50 60 (7.0-8.2) |

## TRIUMPH SPITFIRE

**Spitfire**

### DESCRIPTION

Independent type front suspension consisting of upper and lower control arms, coil spring and shock assemblies and steering knuckles. Control arms pivot in mounts connected to chassis. Coil spring and shock assemblies are mounted between lower control arms and mounts integral with chassis. Steering knuckles are connected to upper control arms by means of ball joints and to lower control arms by means of trunion joints. Later models are equipped with a stabilizer bar.

**Fig. 1    Assembled View of Spitfire Front Suspension**

### ADJUSTMENT

#### WHEEL ALIGNMENT SPECIFICATIONS & PROCEDURES

*See Wheel Alignment Specifications & Procedures in WHEEL ALIGNMENT Section.*

#### WHEEL BEARING ADJUSTMENT

*See Wheel Bearing Adjustment in WHEEL ALIGNMENT Section.*

#### BALL JOINT CHECKING

*See Ball Joint Checking in WHEEL ALIGNMENT Section.*

### REMOVAL & INSTALLATION

#### COIL SPRING & SHOCK ABSORBER

**Removal** — Raise and support vehicle. Place safety stands behind front wheels and remove wheel and tire. Loosen bolts securing lower control arm to trunion joints. Remove bolts securing bottom spring assembly mount to control arm. Remove three nuts securing upper spring assembly mount to chassis and remove spring and shock absorber as an assembly.

**Disassembly** — Using a suitable spring compressor, compress coil spring until spring is not contacting upper spring seat. Remove nut securing shaft from shock absorber to mount and remove rubber mounts, mount seats and mounting flange. Release spring compressor and remove coil spring.

**Fig. 2    Coil Spring and Shock Absorber Assembly**

**Assembly** — Push shock absorber shaft in and out a few times, pressure should be constant and equal on either stroke. If little or no resistance is felt, or if shaft cannot be moved, replace shock absorber. To assemble coil spring and shock assembly, reverse disassembly procedure.

**Installation** — To install coil spring and shock absorber assembly, reverse removal procedure.

#### UPPER CONTROL ARMS

**Removal** — Raise vehicle, position safety stands behind front wheels and remove wheel and tire. Remove coil spring and shock assembly as previously outlined. Remove bolts securing upper control arms to ball joint. Remove both upper control arm pivot bolts and separate control arms from pivot mounts and ball joint.

**Installation** — To install upper control arms, reverse disassembly procedure. Do not tighten pivot bolts until weight of vehicle is on front wheels.

## LOWER CONTROL ARMS

**Removal** – Raise vehicle, position safety stands behind front wheels and remove wheel and tire. Disconnect stabilizer bar link from lower control arm. Disconnect bottom spring assembly mount from control arm. Remove bolt securing control arms to trunion joint. Remove inner pivot bolts and remove control arms.

*Fig. 3   Nuts and Bolts to Remove Before Taking Out Lower Control Arm*

**Installation** – To install lower control arms, reverse removal procedure. Do not tighten inner pivot bolts until weight of vehicle is on front wheels.

## UPPER BALL JOINT

**Removal** – Raise vehicle and place on safety stands; remove tire and wheel. Remove ball joint stud nut and separate ball joint from steeing knuckle. Remove bolts securing ball joint to control arm and remove ball joint.

**Installation** – To install ball joint, reverse removal procedure.

## LOWER TRUNION JOINT

**Removal** – Raise vehicle, position safety stands behind front wheels and remove wheel and tire. Remove wheel hub and dust shield. Remove bolt securing trunion joint to lower control arm. Disconnect shock absorber mount from lower control arm. Pull trunion and steering knuckle from lower control arm and unscrew trunion from steering knuckle.

**Disassembly** – Pry loose 2 end washers. Slide out both dust seals. Lightly press out single spacer piece. Force out each of the nylon bearings and remove inner washers. Check all pieces for excessive wear and replace as necessary.

*Fig. 4   Exploded View of Lower Trunion Assembly*

**Reassembly** – Reverse disassembly procedure after lightly greasing nylon bearings with suitable grease.

**Installation** – To install trunion joint, screw trunion on steering knuckle as far as possible and back off to first working position. This will allow full turning radius. Reverse removal procedure to finish installation.

## STEERING KNUCKLE

**Removal** – Raise vehicle, position safety stands behind front wheels and remove wheel and tire. Remove brake caliper, disc hub and dust shield from steering knuckle. Remove steering arm from knuckle. Remove ball joint stud nut and separate ball joint from steering knuckle. Disconnect shock absorber from lower control arm. Remove bolt securing trunion joint to control arm and remove steering knuckle. Remove trunion from steering knuckle. If necessary, remove nut securing spindle to steering knuckle and press spindle from knuckle.

**Installation** – To install steering knuckle, reverse removal procedure.

## STABILIZER BAR

**Removal** – Remove nuts securing stabilizer bar to lower control arm. Remove nuts and plain washers holding bushing brackets to chassis. Remove bushing and withdraw stabilizer bar from vehicle.

**Installation** – To install stabilizer bar, reverse removal procedure.

## TIGHTENING SPECIFICATIONS

| Application | Ft. Lbs. (mkg) |
|---|---|
| Stabilizer Bar Stud | 14 (1.9) |
| Ball Joint-to-Upper Control Arm | 20 (2.8) |
| Ball Joint Stud Nut | 38 (5.2) |
| Tie Rod End Ball Joint | 32 (4.4) |
| Trunnion-to-Lower Control Arm | 45 (6.2) |
| Lower Control Arm-to-Frame | 25 (3.5) |

## VOLKSWAGEN TYPE 1

### Type 1

## DESCRIPTION

Independent strut type suspension consisting of vertically mounted strut assemblies, lower control arms and a stabilizer bar is used on Type 1 vehicles. Struts mount at top to fender panel and at bottom to side of steering knuckle. Steering knuckle mounts to a ball joint that is pressed into lower control arm. Control arm pivots in bushing mounted at chassis tube. Strut assembly consists of a shock absorber inside strut housing, coil spring mounted over strut housing, and a thrust bearing mounted on top attaching assembly. A stabilizer bar mounts to chassis and through lower control arms.

Coil Spring

Shock Absorber Piston Rod

Lower Spring Seat

Strut Assembly

Mounting Bolts:
Strut-to-Steering Knuckle

Control Arm

Pinch Bolt

Pivot at Chassis

Stabilizer Bar Mounts Here

Ball Joint
Pressed into Control Arm

*Fig. 1  Sectional View of Front Suspension*

## ADJUSTMENT

### WHEEL ALIGNMENT SPECIFICATIONS & PROCEDURES

*See Wheel Alignment Specifications & Procedures in WHEEL ALIGNMENT Section.*

### BALL JOINT CHECKING

*See Ball Joint Checking in WHEEL ALIGNMENT Section.*

### WHEEL BEARING ADJUSTMENT

*See Wheel Bearing Adjustment in WHEEL ALIGNMENT Section.*

## REMOVAL & INSTALLATION

### STRUT ASSEMBLY

**Removal** — Raise vehicle and place safety stands under body. Remove wheel and tire. If left side strut assembly is to be removed pull speedometer cable out of steering knuckle. Pry loose brake hose retaining clip from strut. Remove two nuts and bolts that mount steering knuckle to strut and separate knuckle from strut. From inside luggage compartment, remove nuts securing assembly to fender panel and guide strut assembly from vehicle.

**Disassembly** — 1) Fit strut to suitable spring compressor. Pry off thrust bearing dust cap. Slightly compress coil.

2) Remove piston rod lock nut. Relieve spring pressure. Remove thrust bearing assembly. Separate coil spring from strut. Remove thrust bearing assembly. Take out rubber bumper and protective sleeve.

**Inspection** — 1) Hold shock absorber in assembled position. Work shock absorber back and forth; resistance must be uniform. Replace as necessary.

2) If new coil spring must be used make sure that both springs have the same identification markings.

#### Coil Spring Chart

| Application | Spring Pressure Lbs. (kg) |
|---|---|
| 1 Red Mark | 500-514 (227-233) |
| 2 Red Marks | 516-529 (234-240) |
| 3 Red Marks | 531-545 (241-247) |

**Reassembly** — Fit buffer and protective sleeve. Fit shock absorber and coil spring to compressor. Tighten compressor until piston rod threads project about $5/16$-$3/8$ (8-10 mm) over spring seat. Install thrust bearing assembly. Fit new piston rod lock nut.

**Installation** — Reverse removal procedure to refit strut assembly to vehicle.

### CONTROL ARM

**NOTE** — *It is not necessary to remove suspension strut assembly or stabilizer bar when replacing control arm.*

**Removal** — 1) Loosen ball joint pinch bolt. Pull control arm down and free from steering knuckle. Remove cotter pin and castle nut from stabilizer bar. Remove nut from control arm pivot bolt.

2) Force stabilizer bar off mounting at control arm. Tap out control arm pivot bolt. Remove control arm from vehicle.

**Installation** — Check control arm for obvious cracks or distortion. Inspect rubber bushings and replace as necessary using suitable press. To install, reverse removal procedure and tighten all nuts and bolts. Check wheel alignment.

## VOLKSWAGEN TYPE 1 (Cont.)

### STEERING KNUCKLE

**Removal** — 1) Raise and support vehicle. Remove wheel and tire. Remove speedometer through back of steering knuckle.

2) Remove wheel bearing pinch bolt nut. Remove brake caliper and hang with wire hook out of way. Remove hub and rotor assembly. *See Volkswagen in BRAKE Section.*

3) Remove tie rod nut from end stud. Press tie rod out of steering arm.

4) Loosen pinch bolt on suspension ball joint stud. Pull lower control arm complete with ball joint down from steering knuckle.

5) Take out both bolts securing steering knuckle to strut assembly. Remove knuckle from vehicle.

**Installation** — Reverse removal procedure and note: Adjust wheel bearings and check front wheel alignment.

### BALL JOINT

**Removal** — Raise vehicle and place safety stands under body. Remove control arm as previously described. Using a suitable press type tool, press ball joint downward and free from control arm.

**Installation** — Select new ball joint and press into control arm from deep side of arm. Reverse removal procedure for remaining components.

### STABILIZER BAR

**Removal** — Remove cotter pin and nut from stabilizer bar end at control arm. Remove bolts from brackets securing stabilizer bar to chassis member. Pull stabilizer bar out of control arm and remove from vehicle.

**Installation** — Inspect rubber mounting components for wear or cracking. Reverse removal procedure for installation. Tighten all bolts and nuts to specifications.

### TIGHTENING SPECIFICATIONS

| Application | Ft. Lbs. (mkg) |
|---|---|
| Ball Joint Pinch Bolt | 25 (3.5) |
| Stabilizer Bar Mounting Bracket Bolts | 29 (4.) |
| Stabilizer Bar-to-Control Arm | ①22 (3.0) |
| Strut Assembly-to-Body | 14 (2.0) |
| Steering Knuckle-to-Strut | 61 (8.5) |
| Control Arm-to-Chassis | 29 (4.0) |
| Piston Rod Lock Nut | 43 (6.0) |

① — Turn until cotter pin hole is accessible.

## VOLKSWAGEN TYPE 2

**Type 2**

### DESCRIPTION

Independent ball joint type suspension with torsion bars. Front axle beam consists of two horizontal tubes held together at ends by endplates welded to tubes. Torsion bars are mounted inside tubes and anchor in center. Torsion arms are connected to end of torsion bars and mount to steering knuckles by means of ball joints. Hydraulic shock absorbers are mounted between lower torsion arms at bottom and to axle beam endplates at top. A stabilizer bar is mounted to lower torsion arms. Complete front axle assembly is removable.

### ADJUSTMENT

#### WHEEL ALIGNMENT SPECIFICATIONS & PROCEDURES

See Wheel Alignment Specifications & Procedures in WHEEL ALIGNMENT Section.

#### WHEEL BEARING ADJUSTMENT

See Wheel Bearing Adjustment in WHEEL ALIGNMENT Section.

#### BALL JOINT CHECKING

See Ball Joint Checking in WHEEL ALIGNMENT Section.

### REMOVAL & INSTALLATION

#### FRONT SUSPENSION ASSEMBLY

**NOTE** – Most front suspension repairs can be accomplished without removing entire suspension.

**Removal** – 1) Raise vehicle and place safety stands under body. Remove tires and wheels. Disconnect brake fluid flex lines at brackets. Plug openings. On vehicles equipped with brake servo, remove push rod and take out servo.

2) Disconnect speedometer at left steering knuckle. Remove cover plate under pedal assembly. Engage 1st or 3rd gear. Remove gearshift rod lever at coupling.

3) On manual transmission models, remove gearshift lever and front rod. On automatic transmission models, remove gearshift rod from lower selector lever. Disconnect clutch cable pedal. Separate parking brake cables at parking brake lever.

4) Separate drag link from pitman arm. Remove steering damper from axle tube bracket and swing damper out of way.

5) Place floor jack (and adaptor VW 610) under axle. Raise jack until contact is made. Remove 4 axle beam mounting bolts. Lower jack and guide assembly from vehicle.

**Installation** – Reverse removal procedure. Tighten nuts and bolts. Bleed brake system. Check front wheel alignment.

**Fig. 1  Exploded View of Front Suspension Assembly**

## VOLKSWAGEN TYPE 2 (Cont.)

### STEERING KNUCKLE

**Removal** — 1) Raise vehicle and place safety stands under body. Remove wheel and tire. If left side knuckle is being removed, pull out speedometer cable. Disconnect brake caliper and support out of way. Remove cotter pin and castellated nut from tie rod end. Use a press type tool and separate tie rod from steering knuckle.

2) Remove splash shield from steering knuckle. Take off lower ball joint nut and press joint from knuckle. Remove upper ball joint nut, then with suitable wrench, turn camber eccentric adjusting bushing until joint is free from knuckle. See Fig 2.

**Fig. 2   Removing Upper Ball Joint from Steering Knuckle**

**Installation** — 1) Inspect all components for wear or distortion. Loosely attach steering knuckle to lower torsion ball joint. Raise lower torsion arm until steering knuckle engages upper ball joint.

**CAUTION** — *Position notch on camber adjusting bushing so it faces forward.*

2) Install all new self locking nuts to ball joints. Insert cotter pin in tie rod stud. Install brake components. Adjust wheel bearings and check wheel alignment.

**Fig. 3   Align Notch in Ball Joint with Boss on Torsion Arm**

### STABILIZER BAR

**Removal** — Knock retaining clip from clamp. Bend up clamp and remove plates. Remove nut from retaining bolt and remove bolt. Remove stabilizer bar from vehicle.

**Installation** — Inspect rubber components for wear or cracking. Inspect stabilizer bar for wear or distortion. Install stabilizer bar and retaining bolt and tighten nut to specification. Install clamp with cutout facing wheel. Press edges of clamp together with a pair of pliers and install clip. Make sure tongue edge of clip is facing axle beam. Lock clip by bending over tongue.

### TORSION ARMS & BALL JOINTS

**Removal** — Raise vehicle and place safety stands under body. Remove wheel and tire. Remove steering knuckle and stabilizer bar as previously outlined. Back lock nuts from set screws and remove set screws. Pull torsion arms out of axle tubes. Press ball joints out of torsion arms.

**Installation** — Press ball joints into torsion arms. When pressing ball joints into control arms make sure that notches in shoulder of ball joint align with forged projections on torsion arm. Install a suitable peening tool (VW471) on press and peen ball joint 3 times with a pressure of 6 tons to insure ball joint is properly seated in torsion arm. Thoroughly grease pivot portion of torsion arm and install in axle tube. Reverse removal procedure for installation of remaining components. Tighten all bolts and nuts to specifications. Bleed brake system and check wheel alignment.

### SHOCK ABSORBER MOUNTING STUD

**Removal** — Remove lower torsion arm as previously outlined. Drive dowel pin out and pull stud from torsion arm. If stud is broken, center punch in center of remaining piece and drill a .12" pilot hole in stud. Then drill remaining piece out with a .423" drill.

**Installation** — Replacement studs are oversized. Drill out hole with a .483" drill and ream to .4904-.4914" (12.45-12.8 mm). A press fit of .0004-.002" (.01-.05 mm) is required for proper fit. Press stud in arm until distance between shoulder of arm and end of stud is 1.77-1.79" (45.0-45.5 mm). Drill through dowel pin hole with .157-.161"(4.0-4.1 mm) drill and drive in dowel pin. Install torsion arm in vehicle as previously outlined.

### SHOCK ABSORBER

**Removal** — Raise and suitably support vehicle. Remove tire and wheel. Remove upper mounting nut and bolt. Pull shock absorber top rearward and remove nut holding lower end of shock absorber on stud.

**Installation** — To install shock absorber, reverse removal procedure and note: With vehicle still raised, incline shock absorber 30° to rear while torquing nuts. This will prevent lower rubber bushing from twisting as suspension moves upward.

**CAUTION** — *DO NOT incline shock absorber if vehicle weight is on ground.*

## VOLKSWAGEN TYPE 2 (Cont.)

### TORSION BARS, AXLE BUSHINGS & BEARINGS

**Removal — 1)** Raise vehicle and place on safety stands. Remove both tires and wheels. Remove steering knuckle from both sides. Remove torsion arm from one end of torsion bars. If lower bar is being removed, remove shock absorber. If upper bar is being removed, remove gearshift rod at coupling and set to one side.

**2)** Loosen lock nut and remove screw from center of axle tube. Pull out torsion bar. Remove torsion arm from bar.

**Bearing Assembly Replacement — 1)** Use a slide hammer and remove bearing. Measure metal bushing. If diameter of bushing exceeds 1.71" (43.4 mm), use slide hammer with fingers or washer inserted behind bushing and pull out bushing.

**CAUTION** — *DO NOT damage or pull out plastic sleeve in axle tube. Replacement sleeves are not available, axle tube must be replaced.*

**2)** Clean off needle bearing seat. Measure inside diameter of bearing seat. If measurement is between 2.243-2.244" (56.97-56.99 mm), use standard bearings. If measurement is between 2.251-2.252" (57.17-57.19 mm), install oversize bearings. Oversize bearings are stamped with letter "U". Axle tubes that will not accept oversize bearing must be replaced.

**3)** Clean bearing and bushing seats. Insert bearing with hardened surface facing out. Drive bearing in using special drift VW 772 (or equivalent) until drift shoulder just meets outside edge of axle tube.

**4)** Use bearing as drift pilot and drive metal bushing into place. Fit new seal retainer to axle tube with lug in vertical position. Oversize seal retainers are available and can be identified by notch in lip. Fit new seals.

**Installation** — Reverse removal procedure and note: White stripe paint mark on end of torsion bar identifies left side bar.

Axle Tube — Slide Hammer Shaft — Washer — Metal Bushing — Plastic Sleeve

*Fig. 4   Section View Showing Front Axle Tube*

### TIGHTENING SPECIFICATIONS

| Application | Ft. Lbs. (mkg) |
| --- | --- |
| Ball Joint Stud Nuts | 72 (10.0) |
| Torsion Arm Set Screw | 29 (4.0) |
| Torsion Arm Set Screw Lock Nut | 29 (4.0) |
| Stabilizer Bar Retaining Nut | 31 (4.3) |
| Shock Absorber | |
|   Lower Mount Nut | 18-25 (2.5-3.5) |
|   Upper Mount Nut | 36 (5.0) |
| Torsion Bar Set Screw | 29 (4.0) |
| Torsion Bar Set Screw Lock Nut | 29 (4.0) |
| Axle Assembly-to-Body | 65-90 (9.0-12.5) |
| Tie Rod End Stud Nut | 22 (3.0) |

## VOLKSWAGEN DASHER

**Dasher**

### DESCRIPTION

Volkswagen Dasher is front wheel drive with independent strut type front suspension. Axles are supported by lower control arms, vertically mounted strut assemblies, and a stabilizer bar. Strut assemblies consist of double action shock absorbers with coil springs mounted over the outside. The top part of strut is attached to the inner fender panel and the lower portion is attached directly to steering knuckle. Tie rods are connected to supports under coil springs. Stabilizer bar is connected to lower control arms at each end and to crossmember below engine.

### ADJUSTMENT

#### WHEEL ALIGNMENT SPECIFICATIONS & PROCEDURES

See Wheel Alignment Specifications & Procedures in WHEEL ALIGNMENT Section.

#### WHEEL BEARING ADJUSTMENT

See Wheel Bearing Adjustment in WHEEL ALIGNMENT Section.

#### BALL JOINT CHECKING

See Ball Joint Checking in WHEEL ALIGNMENT Section.

### REMOVAL & INSTALLATION

#### STRUT & COIL SPRING ASSEMBLY

**Removal — 1)** Loosen axle nut and wheel lugs. Raise and support vehicle; remove wheel and tire. Remove brake hose clips, disconnect brake caliper and move out of way.

**2)** Loosen bolt holding suspension ball joint stud in bottom of strut assembly. Using suitable tool, remove tie rod end from mounting under coil spring seat. Disconnect stabilizer bar from lower control arm.

**3)** Force lower control arm down until ball joint stud is removed from suspension strut. Remove axle nut. Support axle drive shaft so it won't fall. Pull strut outward until off axle drive shaft. Remove both upper mounting nuts. Guide strut from vehicle.

**Disassembly — 1)** Place strut in a vise and install coil spring compressor. Tighten compressor until pressure is taken off upper retainer. Remove upper collar mounting nut. Take off upper mounting hardware. Release spring compressor and remove coil spring.

**2)** Hold shock absorber cartridge center shaft with suitable tool. Loosen and remove threaded cap nut. If shock absorber cartridge will not easily pull front strut tube, thread a nut on center shaft and tap until corrosion breaks free.

**Fig. 1 Exploded View of Front Suspension Strut**

Labels: Boot, Boot, Threaded Cap, Shock Absorber Cartridge Piston Rod, Cap Nut Threads to Strut Here, Tie Rod Mounts Here, Piston Rod Nut, End Collar, Upper Strut Mounting, Rubber Damper, Upper Spring Seat, Coil Spring

**Reassembly —** To reassemble, reverse disassembly procedure, noting the following:

- Coil springs may be replaced one at a time, but paint color codes must be matched. Original springs will have 1 or 2 stripes of orange or 1, 2 or 3 stripes of gray paint. Replacement springs all have 2 stripes of paint. Match to original gray or orange color.

**Installation —** To install, reverse removal procedure and note the following. When assembling ball joint to lower control arm always use a new bolt and nut. Face bolt head toward front of vehicle.

#### LOWER CONTROL ARM

**Removal — 1)** Raise vehicle so that front wheel and suspension are not supported.

**2)** Disconnect stabilizer bar at control arm and subframe. Slide stabilizer bar out of vehicle.

**3)** Loosen ball joint clamp bolt. Force lower control arm down until ball joint stud is removed from suspension strut. Remove bolt mounting control arm to subframe. Guide arm from vehicle.

**Bushing Replacement — 1)** Check bushing in control arm for signs of excessive wear or damage. If bushings are bad they can be replaced.

**2)** Support wide points on control arm. Press bushings from each side of control arm.

## VOLKSWAGEN DASHER (Cont.)

Subframe Bushing

Lower Control Arm

Bolts

Control Arm Bushing

Bolt

Spring Washer

Nuts    Ball Joint

*Fig. 2    Exploded View of Lower Control Arm*

**3)** Select new bushings. Lightly coat each bushing with brake paste. Press bushing into position in control arm. Make sure bushing does not twist when pressing into place. Use bushing guide if necessary.

**Installation** — Reverse removal procedure and note: Use water pump pliers to compress clamps around bushing when trying to start bolts. Check front wheel alignment.

### STABILIZER BAR

**Removal** — **1)** Raise vehicle and suitably support with safety stands. Remove brackets mounting stabilizer bar to lower control arm .

**2)** Loosen and remove "U" brackets mounting stabilizer bar to subframe. Guide stabilizer bar from vehicle. Inspect rubber bushings for damage or excessive wear and replace as necessay.

**Installation** — To install, reverse removal procedure.

## TIGHTENING SPECIFICATIONS

| Application | Ft. Lbs. (mkg) |
| --- | --- |
| Axle Nut | |
|   18 mm Nut | 145 (20.0) |
|   20 mm Nut | 175 (24) |
| Lower Control Arm-to-Subframe | 50 (7.0) |
| Upper Strut Assembly-to-Body | 18 (2.5) |
| Stabilizer Bar-to-Subframe | 7 (.9) |
| Piston Rod Nut | 43 (6) |
| Shock Absorber Cap Nut | 108 (15.0) |
| Stabilizer Bar-to-Lower Control Arm | 7 (.9) |
| Ball Joint-to-Suspension Strut | 36 (5.0) |
| Tie Rod Castle Nut | 29 (4.0) |
| Ball Joint-to-Lower Control Arm | 47 (6.5) |

# Front Suspension

## VOLKSWAGEN RABBIT & SCIROCCO

**Rabbit**
**Scirocco**

### DESCRIPTION

Vehicles are equipped with front wheel drive and independent strut type front suspension. Axles are supported by lower control arms, and vertically mounted strut assemblies. Strut assemblies consist of double action shock absorbers with coil springs mounted over the outside. The top portion of strut is attached to inner fender panel and lower portion is attached directly to steering knuckle. Tie rods are connected to steering knuckle.

### ADJUSTMENT

#### WHEEL ALIGNMENT SPECIFICATIONS & PROCEDURES

See Wheel Alignment Specifications & Procedures in WHEEL ALIGNMENT Section.

#### WHEEL BEARING ADJUSTMENT

See Wheel Bearing Adjustment in WHEEL ALIGNMENT Section.

#### BALL JOINT CHECKING

See Ball Joint Checking in WHEEL ALIGNMENT Section.

### REMOVAL & INSTALLATION

#### STRUT ASSEMBLY

**NOTE** — Suspension strut does not need to be removed to replace end collar. Only requirement is to leave vehicle on ground.

**Removal — 1)** Raise vehicle so front suspension and front wheels are not supported.

**2)** Remove bolts mounting suspension strut to steering knuckle. Note that top bolt is one used to adjust front wheel camber.

**3)** Remove brake caliper assembly and suspend out of way. Pry or force suspension strut out of steering knuckle.

**4)** Support front suspension by hand. Also, support lower control arm and related components. Work inside engine compartment and remove upper strut mounting nuts. Guide out assembly.

**Disassembly — 1)** Fit strut to spring compressor. Slightly collapse coil spring. Remove shock absorber piston rod nut. Slowly release spring pressure. Take off upper mounting hardware and coil spring.

**2)** Hold shock absorber cartridge center shaft with suitable tool. Loosen and remove threaded cap nut. If shock absorber cartridge will not easily pull from strut housing, thread a piston rod nut onto shaft and tap until corrosion breaks free.

**Reassembly — 1)** Fit protective sleeve and buffer over piston rod. Insert shock absorber cartridge to strut housing and tighten cap nut.

**NOTE** — Both coil springs must be of same class. If set cannot be matched, both springs will have to be replaced. Springs are color coded.

**2)** Position coil spring into lower spring seat. Install the upper spring retainer. Fit entire assembly into spring compressor and collapse coil gradually until whole threaded portion of piston rod is exposed.

**3)** Put on bearing, rubber bumper and remaining upper mounting components. Hold piston rod and tighten piston rod lock nut.

**Installation** — Reverse removal procedure and check front wheel alignment.

**Fig. 1 Exploded View of Rabbit/Scirocco Front Suspension**

#### FRONT SUSPENSION ASSEMBLY

**Removal — 1)** Raise vehicle so front suspension and wheels are not supported. Disconnect brake line, leave flex line in place, and plug openings.

**2)** Remove tie rod castle nut. Press tie rod from steering knuckle. Remove bolts mounting inner portion of constant velocity joint to transaxle drive flange.

**3)** Remove lower control arm front pivot bolt. Remove 2 bolts mounting "U" shaped bracket holding control arm rear pivot.

**NOTE** — On vehicles equipped with automatic transmissions, engine may have to be slightly raised to gain access to pivot bolts.

## VOLKSWAGEN RABBIT & SCIROCCO (Cont.)

**4)** Support suspension assembly. Remove upper strut mounting nuts located in engine compartment. Guide assembly from vehicle.

**Installation** — Reverse removal procedure and note: Make sure convex side of thrust washer faces pivot bolt head.

### LOWER CONTROL ARM & BALL JOINT

**NOTE** — *Ball Joint can be replaced while control arm is in vehicle.*

**Removal** — **1)** Raise vehicle and suitably support with front suspension free. Remove nut and clamp bolt mounting ball joint in bottom of steering knuckle. Force ball joint out of steering knuckle. Leave control arm hanging in mounts at subframe.

**2)** If control arm is not being removed, drill out 3 ball joint rivets with a $^9/_{32}$" (7 mm) drill. After drilling it still may be necessary to chisel off rivet heads. Remove ball joint.

**3)** If control arm is being removed, take out pivot bolt and "U" bracket housing inner pivot pin. Slide out control arm.

**NOTE** — *On vehicles equipped with automatic transmissions, engine may have to be slightly raised to gain access to pivot bolts.*

**Inspection** — Check lower control arm bushings. If bushings are bad they can be replaced. Press out worn bushing. Select new bushing and press into position. Make sure bushing does not twist when seating into place.

**Installation** — Slide new ball joint into slot in control arm. Tighten ball joint mounting bolts. Refit lower control arm to subframe (chassis). Install ball joint into lower section of suspension strut.

**Fig. 2  New Ball Joint Installation Location in Lower Control Arm**

## TIGHTENING SPECIFICATIONS

| Application | Ft. Lbs. (mkg) |
|---|---|
| Ball Joint Clamp Bolt-to Suspension Strut | 22 (3.0) |
| Tie Rod Castle Nut | 22 (3.0) |
| New Ball Joint-to-Control Arm | 18 (2.5) |
| Suspension Strut-to-Inner Fender | 14 (2.0) |
| Control Arm-to-Subframe (Chassis) | 43 (6.0) |
| Pivot Pin "U" Bracket | 22 (3.0) |
| Axle Drive Shaft-to-Transaxle | 32 (4.5) |
| Suspension Strut-to-Steering Knuckle | 58 (8.0) |
| Piston Rod Nut | 58 (8.0) |
| Axle Shaft Nut | 173 (24.0) |

# Front Suspension

## VOLVO

240 Series
260 Series

## DESCRIPTION

Strut type suspension consisting of a vertically mounted strut assembly. Strut assembly is mounted to chassis frame at top by means of a thrust bearing. Lower end of strut assembly is mounted to a ball joint which is bolted to lower control arm. Steering knuckle is an integral part of strut assembly. Strut assembly consists of a shock absorber built into strut outer tube; a coil spring mounted on outside of strut assembly; and a spindle integral with bottom of strut. A stabilizer bar connects the control arms through rubber mounted links.

## ADJUSTMENT

### WHEEL ALIGNMENT SPECIFICATIONS & PROCEDURES

*See Wheel Alignment Specifications & Procedures in WHEEL ALIGNMENT Section.*

### WHEEL BEARING ADJUSTMENT

*See Wheel Bearing Adjustment in WHEEL ALIGNMENT Section.*

### BALL JOINT CHECKING

*See Ball Joint Checking in WHEEL ALIGNMENT Section.*

Fig. 1   *Exploded View of Front Suspension Assembly*

## REMOVAL & INSTALLATION

### CONTROL ARM

**Removal** — Raise vehicle and support on safety stands, then remove wheel and tire. Disconnect stabilizer bar-to-link assembly. Disconnect ball joint from control arm at three attaching bolts. Remove front attaching bolt for control arm. Remove bracket attaching rear of control arm to chassis, then remove control arm from vehicle. If control arm bushing is being replaced, press out using proper adapter (9995085) and driver (9995091).

**Installation** — Inspect all components for wear or damage. Use proper adapter (9995085) and driver (5555084) to install new bushings if necessary. If bushing in bracket is replaced, ensure that small slots on new bushing will point in a horizontal position when bracket is installed on vehicle. Install bracket, with control arm, to chassis but do not tighten bolts. Install front attaching bolt for control arm but do not tighten. Install ball joint to control arm and tighten bolts. Position a jack under control arm and raise so coil spring is compressed. Connect stabilizer bar to link. Tighten control arm attaching nuts and bolts. Install wheel and tire.

### SHOCK ABSORBER

**Removal** — 1) Raise vehicle and support on safety stands, then remove wheel and tire. Position jack under control arm and raise slightly to provide support. Using a spring compressor, compress coil spring being sure to engage five coils with tool. Disconnect steering rod from steering arm and stabilizer bar from link at control arm. Remove bolt attaching brake line bracket. Remove cover on upper end of strut and spring assembly. Remove center nut using tool as indicated in Fig. 2.

Fig. 2   *View Showing Removal of Strut Assembly Center Nut*

**2)** Lower jack supporting control arm while supporting strut assembly so brake lines and hoses are not damaged. Hook special tool (9995045) to strut assembly and stabilizer to support unit during remaining removal procedures. Remove the spring seat and rubber bumper. Remove coil spring with compressor tool attached. Remove shock absorber retaining nut while holding strut outer casing at the weld. Pull shock absorber from casing.

## VOLVO (Cont.)

**Installation** — 1) Install new shock absorber and retaining nut while holding strut outer casing at the weld. Pull shock absorber spindle to fully extended position. Install coil spring onto strut assembly making sure spring end is properly aligned on strut bracket. Install rubber bumper and install spring seat on coil spring. Guide strut assembly into upper mount and shock absorber spindle through upper mount. Connect stabilizer bar to stabilizer link.

Strut Support Tool
Removal Tool
Retaining Tool

**Fig. 3   View Showing Removal of Shock Absorber Nut**

2) Position jack under control arm and raise slightly. Install and tighten washer and nut to shock absorber spindle while using proper retaining tool. Install cover, then connect brake line bracket to chassis. Connect steering arm to steering rod and remove coil spring compressor tool slowly. Install wheel and tire.

## BALL JOINTS

**Removal** — Raise vehicle and support with safety stands. Loosen shock absorber nut. Remove 4 bolts attaching ball joint to strut assembly. Remove ball joint from control arm, then remove ball joint nut and separate from attachment.

**Installation** — Position new ball joint to attachment and tighten nut. Install ball joint assembly to strut assembly and to control arm. Tighten shock absorber retaining nut.

**Fig. 4   View Showing Ball Joint Retaining Bolts**

## TIGHTENING SPECIFICATIONS

| Application | Ft. Lbs.(mkg) |
|---|---|
| Ball Joint-to-Control Arm | 70-95(9.7-13.1) |
| Ball Joint Assembly-to-Strut | 11-18(1.5-2.5) |
| Ball Joint-to-Bracket | 35-50(4.8-6.9) |
| Control Arm-to-Bracket (Rear) | 36-43(5.0-5.9) |
| Control Arm-to-Chassis | 40-70(5.5-9.7) |
| Control Arm Bracket-to-Frame | 22-36(3.0-5.0) |

## AUDI

**Fox
5000**

## DESCRIPTION

Suspension on all Audi models consists of coil springs, shock absorbers, transverse rod and trailing arms. Some design differences occur between models.

On Fox Wagon and 5000 models, rear suspension arrangement is illustrated in *Fig. 1*. On these models, coil spring is mounted directly on rear axle and shock absorber is mounted separately. On Fox Wagon, transverse rod mounts diagonally in front of axle beam. On 5000, it mounts behind axle beam. Also on 5000, top end of shock absorber is a stud-type mount and incorporates a rubber damper assembly.

On Fox Sedan models, coil spring and shock absorber are combined into a single, strut-type assembly. A transverse rod is also used and mounts diagnoally in front of axle beam. *Fig. 2.*

**Fig. 1   Exploded View of Audi Fox Wagon
Rear Suspension. 5000 Models Similar.
See Text for Differences**

## ADJUSTMENTS

### WHEEL ALIGNMENT SPECIFICATIONS & PROCEDURES

*See Wheel Alignment Specifications and Procedures in WHEEL ALIGNMENT Section.*

### WHEEL BEARING ADJUSTMENT

*See Wheel Bearing Adjustment in WHEEL ALIGNMENT Section*

## REMOVAL & INSTALLATION

### REAR AXLE ASSEMBLY

**Removal, Fox — 1)** Raise vehicle and place supports under frame. Remove nuts from parking brake linkage equalizer line. Force parking brake plastic cable guide bushing from clip. Pry down and unhook muffler from front bracket. Separate all brake cables from body holders.

**Fig. 2   Exploded View of Audi Fox Sedan
Rear Suspension**

**2)** Detach brake hoses and plug openings. Using a jack, raise axle slightly. Unhook muffler at rear. Disconnect transverse rod. Disconnect lower end of shock absorber.

**3)** Slowly lower rear axle assembly from vehicle, watching coil springs while lowering.

**Bushing Replacement, Fox —** Place trailing arm in press and force bushings from arm. Reverse process to install new bushings. Make sure new bushings are installed with slots positioned horizontally in trailing arm.

**Installation, Fox — 1)** To install rear axle, reverse removal procedure and note the following: Make sure trailing arm bushings are free of tension when installed. Before tightening trailing arm bolts insure arms are in middle of moving range.

## AUDI (Cont.)

**Fig. 3   Measurement Points for Installing Fox Rear Axle Beam**

**2)** Lift axle beam until center of axle *(See Fig. 2)* is 2.75" (70 mm) higher than center of bushing in trailing arm. Check distance between axle center to lower edge of fender lip. Distance should be 10.6" (270 mm). Tighten mounting bolts only after axle is located with measurements set as described.

**Removal, 5000 - 1)** Loosen, but do not remove wheel bolts. Raise and support vehicle. Remove bolt from transverse rod at axle mounting. Detach right brake hose at coupling with steel tubing. Plug openings.

**2)** Detach brake pressure regulator spring (hooked to lower mounting bolt of shock absorber). Detach left brake hose at connection with tubing and plug openings.

**3)** Remove right fuel tank retaining strap. Remove parking brake cable from guide on fuel tank. Loosen left side parking brake cable bolt. Loosen parking brake adjusting nut and disconnect parking brake cable.

**4)** Remove rear mounting for exhaust system. Lower vehicle to ground. Remove both shock absorber top nuts. Using frame jack, raise vehicle slowly until coil spring can be removed from axle mountings. Remove rear wheels.

**5)** Remove trailing arm mounting bolts, with rear axle suitably supported on a jack. While slowly lowering axle assembly from vehicle, guide parking brake cable over exhaust pipe.

**Installation, 5000 — 1)** Raise vehicle and position rear axle in vehicle. Install and lightly tighten trailing arm mounting bolts. Install both rear wheels and lower vehicle to ground.

**2)** Position rubber damper rings on coil springs, jack up vehicle body, position springs and slowly lower body to hold springs (3 persons may be required to perform this step).

**3)** Tighten shock absorber top mounting nuts. Raise vehicle and check position of coil springs. If necessary, turn springs in mounting to correct their positions.

**4)** With vehicle resting on ground, tighten trailing arm bolts. Install transverse rod, brake hoses, spring for brake pressure regulator and fuel tank retaining strap.

**5)** Bleed brake system, attach and adjust parking brake cable.

### TRANSVERSE ROD

**Removal, All Models —** Raise and support vehicle. Remove nuts from transverse rod bolts and tap bolts out of holes. Inspect bushings and sleeves for wear and replace if necessary.

**Installation, All Models —** To install, reverse removal procedure.

### SHOCK ABSORBERS

**Removal, All Models — 1)** On Fox Sedan models, remove rear seat cushion, locate and bend up tabs holding rear seat back in place. Remove rear seat back to gain access to top shock absorber mounting nut. Remove nut.

**2)** On Fox Wagon models, raise vehicle and remove lower shock absorber mounting first (it may not be necessary to raise vehicle to gain access).

**3)** On 5000 models, keep vehicle resting on ground at all times and remove top shock absorber mounting.

**4)** On all models, remove upper or lower shock absorber mounting not previously removed. On Fox Sedan models, raise vehicle to relieve spring pressure. On all models, remove shock absorber from vehicle.

**Installation, All Models —** To install, reverse removal procedure. Be sure, on Fox Wagon models, to install upper bolt before attaching lower mounting.

**NOTE** — *When installing shock absorber on Fox Sedan models, be sure top protection cap is properly installed. A missing or misaligned cap will allow dirt and water to enter shock absorber and cause damage.*

### TIGHTENING SPECIFICATIONS

| Application | Ft. Lbs. (mkg) |
| --- | --- |
| **Shock Absorbers** | |
| Fox Wagon | |
|   Upper & Lower | 43 (6.0) |
| Fox Sedan | |
|   Upper 21 (3.0)   Lower 43 (6.0)   5000 | |
|   Upper | 14 (2.0) |
|   Lower | 40 (5.5) |
| **Transverse Rod** | |
| Fox (All) | 50 (7.0) |
| 5000 | 65 (9.0) |
| **Trailing Arm** | |
| Fox (All) | 43 (6.0) |
| 5000 | 51 (7.0) |

# Rear Suspension

## BMW

320i
530i
633CSi
733i

## DESCRIPTION

Independent type rear suspension with rear struts. Semi-trailing control arms pivot on crossmember and are integral with axle shaft bearing housing. Shock absorber (strut assembly) mounts to purchase on top of control arm and to body. A stabilizer bar is attached to each trailing arm and at two points on crossmember.

## ADJUSTMENTS

### WHEEL ALIGNMENT SPECIFICATIONS & PROCEDURES

*See Wheel Alignment Specifications and Procedures in WHEEL ALIGNMENT Section.*

## REMOVAL & INSTALLATION

### STRUT ASSEMBLIES (SHOCK ABSORBERS)

**Removal, Exc. 733i** — Raise vehicle and remove rear wheel. Place jack under control arm. Disconnect shock at lower mounting. Remove centering shell and mounting nuts from top of shock absorber. Remove assembly from vehicle.

**Removal, 733i** — Remove rear seat backrest. Raise and support vehicle under control arms. Detach lower mounting. Remove package shelf and detach centering shell at wheel housing. Remove shock absorber from vehicle.

**Disassembly, All** — Using a spring compressor, collapse spring and remove centering shell. Remove coil spring and boot. Pull retainer and auxiliary spring off shock absorber. Inspect and replace any defective parts.

**Reassembly, All** — Reverse disassembly procedure, making sure coil spring is properly aligned before releasing spring compressor. Vent opening on spring faces inside retainer.

**Fig. 2   Exploded View of BMW Rear Suspension Strut Assembly — 320i Shown**

**Installation, All** — To install, reverse removal procedure. Tighten nuts and bolts after vehicle is resting on ground.

### SEMI-TRAILING CONTROL ARM

**Removal, Exc. 733i — 1)** Raise vehicle and remove rear wheels. Remove parking brake lever. Disconnect and plug brake line at union bracket. Detach brake pad wear sensor from right control arm (if equipped).

**2)** Remove stabilizer bar from control arm. Remove strut assembly (shock absorber) from vehicle. Disconnect axle drive shaft from bearing carrier. Place jack under control arm. Remove trailing arm pivot bolts at crossmember and lower arm to ground.

**Fig. 1   Overhead View of BMW Rear Suspension**

## BMW (Cont.)

**Removal, 733i — 1)** Raise and support vehicle. Remove rear wheel. Pull up parking brake lever and detach output shaft at drive flange. Remove parking brake lever.

**2)** Using a syringe, draw off fluid from reservoir and detach and plug brake lines. Detach control arm from rear axle carrier. Detach shock absorber and remove control arm.

Inspection Mandrel

Semi-Trailing Control Arm

Support Plate

**Fig. 3    Trailing Arm Fitted to Support Plate to Check Alignment**

**Inspection, All — 1)** Visually inspect bushings and replace as necessary. Before pressing out worn bushings, cut off collar. When pressing in new bushings, lubricate them with oil. Note that collared edge faces out.

**2)** Check trailing arm alignment. Place arm in support plate. See *Fig. 3.* Slide inspection mandrel through control arm to crossmember mounting bushings bores (bushings removed). If control arm is out of alignment it can be straightened if there is no other damage to arm.

**Installation, All —** To install, reverse removal procedure and tighten nuts fully after vehicle is resting on ground. Bleed and adjust brakes.

### TIGHTENING SPECIFICATIONS

| Application | Ft. Lbs. (mkg) |
|---|---|
| Lower Shock Absorber Mount | |
| 320i ............................................. | 36-39 (4.-5.4) |
| 530i, 633CSi and 733i .......................... | 87-94 (12-13) |
| Upper Shock Absorber Mount | |
| All Models ....................................... | 18-20 (2.5-2.8) |
| Trailing Arm-to-Crossmember | |
| 320i ............................................. | 58-65 (8.1-9.0) |
| 530i, 633CSi and 733i .......................... | 49-54 (6.7-7.5) |

# Rear Suspension

## DATSUN 280Z

### 280Z

## DESCRIPTION

Rear suspension is a strut type independent suspension. Rear wheels are supported with strut and transverse link. The gear carrier is aligned independently and separately from the suspension, and gear carrier is mounted directly to body with rubber insulators. Rear axle housing is welded on lower end of strut which contains a shock absorber, and its lower side is connected to the transverse link through rubber bushings. At strut midpoint, the body is suspended with coil springs. The transverse link is attached to the body with rubber cushions.

**Fig. 1  Datsun 280Z Rear Suspension Assembly**

## REMOVAL & INSTALLATION

### STRUT & COIL SPRING

**Removal** — 1) Block front wheels, raise rear end of vehicle, and support at body with stands. Remove rear wheels. Disconnect brake line coupler (body side) and parking brake linkage. Disconnect stabilizer bar from transverse link.

2) Remove transverse link outer self-locking nuts and bolt from lower end of bearing housing. Withdraw spindle and separate transverse link from strut assembly.

3) Disconnect drive half-shaft at wheel side. Remove strut mounting nuts from passenger side and remove strut assembly downward. **NOTE** — When removing strut assembly, apply a jack to lower end of strut and remove it gradually.

4) For removal of coil spring, clamp strut assembly in vise with suitable strut attachment (ST35650000). Compress coil spring until strut mounting insulator can be turned by hand, then remove self-locking nut. Remove strut insulator, mounting bearing, and upper spring seat. Remove coil spring with tool still attached to spring.

**Installation** — To install, reverse removal procedure, noting the following: Tighten transverse link outer self-locking nut after rear wheels are installed and vehicle is lowered to ground.

### TRANSVERSE LINK

**Removal** — 1) Block front wheels, raise rear end of vehicle, and remove rear wheels. Remove stabilizer bar from transverse link. Separate transverse link from strut assembly. Refer to Strut & Coil Spring above. Support gear carrier with a jack.

2) Loosen transverse link inner bolts for both front and rear. Remove differential mount front insulator installation nut. Remove mount front member installation nuts, and remove differential mount front member.

3) Remove link mount rear bracket and withdraw the transverse link. Detach inner bushing and outer bushing from link.

**Installation** — To install, reverse removal procedure, noting the following: Tighten transverse link inner bolts and outer self-locking nut only after rear wheels are replaced and vehicle is under standard load (on the ground).

### REAR SUSPENSION ASSEMBLY

**Removal** — 1) Remove strut assemblies from both sides as previously outlined. Detach main muffler. Disconnect stabilizer bar from body. Separate propeller shaft from final drive. Loosen transverse link inner bolts for front and rear. Support gear carrier with jack.

2) Remove differential mount front member installation bolts. Unscrew link brace mounting bolt and differential mount rear insulator attaching bolt (for both sides). Lower jack slowly and remove rear suspension assembly.

**Disassembly** — 1) Remove link mount rear bracket and remove transverse link (for both sides). Unscrew drive shaft installation bolt (in gear carrier side), and separate drive shaft from gear carrier (both sides).

2) Extract inner and outer bushings from transverse link. Remove differential mount rear member and differential mount front insulator from gear carrier. Drift out differential mount rear insulator from rear member.

**Reassembly & Installation** — Assemble and install rear suspension assembly in reverse of disassembly and removal procedures, while noting the following: When replacing transverse link inner bushing, position bushing to link shaft and align projection on bushing horizontally. Align center of bushing to center of bracket and temporarily tighten transverse link inner bolts. Do not fully tighten inner bolts until installation is complete and vehicle has been lowered to ground. When differential carrier front insulator is installed, ensure arrow points toward front.

| TIGHTENING SPECIFICATIONS | |
|---|---|
| **Application** | **Ft. Lbs.(mkg)** |
| Transverse Link Outer | |
|   Self-Locking Nut | 54-68(7.5-9.4) |
| Transverse Link Inner Bolt | 101-106(14-16) |
| Strut Upper Mounting Nuts | 18-25(2.5-3.5) |
| Strut Rod Self-Locking Nut | 54-69(7.5-9.5) |
| Gland Packing | 51-94(7-13) |
| Drive Shaft Installation Bolts | 36-43(5-6) |

## FIAT X1/9

### X1/9

#### DESCRIPTION

Fiat X1/9 is a rear engine mounted and rear wheel driven vehicle utilizing independent rear suspension. All rear suspensions consists of the following: Lower control arms, bearing housings, and hydraulic, strut type, shock absorbers. Control arms are attached to chassis in rubber bushings and to bearing housing with a ball joint. Hydraulic strut assembly attaches to bearing housing just above axle shaft and mounts at top to inside of engine compartment. A reaction rod is also attached to bearing housing and is used to adjust rear wheel alignment.

**Fig. 1  Sectional View of Fiat X1/9 Rear Suspension Assembly**

#### ADJUSTMENT

##### WHEEL ALIGNMENT SPECIFICATIONS & PROCEDURES

*See Wheel Alignment Specifications and Procedures in WHEEL ALIGNMENT Section.*

##### WHEEL BEARING ADJUSTMENT

*See Wheel Bearing Adjustment in WHEEL ALIGNMENT Section.*

#### REMOVAL & INSTALLATION

##### SUSPENSION ASSEMBLY

**Removal** — Raise and support vehicle; remove tire and wheel. Remove rear brake caliper and disconnect parking brake. **NOTE** — *See appropriate article in BRAKE Section.* Remove exhaust pipe. Note number and position of shims on control arm. Separate front and rear ends of lower control arm from chassis; do not lose shims. Remove hub nut and washer. Remove nuts mounting strut assembly at top. Slide suspension off axle shaft and secure axle to prevent pulling out of differential.

**Installation** — To install suspension assembly, reverse removal procedure. Make sure axle nut is properly torqued before lowering vehicle. Tighten all remaining bolts with weight of vehicle on all four wheels. Ensure correct amount of shims are installed.

##### STRUT ASSEMBLY

**Removal** — Raise and support vehicle; remove tire and wheel. Disconnect upper strut assembly mounts from inside engine compartment. Remove bolts mounting strut to bearing housing and carefully maneuver strut assembly from vehicle.

**Disassembly** — 1) Using a suitable spring compressor, collapse spring coil. With spring compressed, remove nut from center of upper mount. Release spring compressor and remove upper mount and coil spring.

2) Inspect springs for cracks or distortion. Springs are manufactured in two classes and identified by paint marks. Class A springs are marked with a yellow stripe on outside of center coils and class B springs are marked with a green stripe. If springs are replaced, use one of same class.

**Reassembly** — Using same spring compressor as previously implemented, reverse disassembly procedure.

**Installation** — To install strut assembly, reverse removal procedure. Do not tighten strut assembly lower mount until weight of vehicle is on ground.

#### CONTROL ARM, BUSHINGS & BALL JOINTS

**Removal** — Remove complete front suspension assembly as previously outlined. Remove ball joint stud nut and separate ball joint from bearing housing using suitable puller.

**Disassembly** — Inspect ball joint for wear or excessive play. If ball joint is defective, replace complete control arm. Inspect bushings for wear or damage. If defective bushings are found, drill out bushing metal sleeve and force rubber from control arm.

**Fig. 2  Exploded View of Control Arm Assembly**

**Reassembly** — Position outer washer, bushing and sleeve on centering pin of a suitable installer (mandrel). Place control arm over bushing and install bushing and washer for opposite side. Using suitable mandrel and necessary adaptors press in new bushing until properly seated. Repeat procedure for other side.

**Installation** — To install control arm, attach to bearing housing, tighten ball joint stud nut, and position suspension assembly as previously outlined.

#### TIGHTENING SPECIFICATIONS

| Application | Ft. Lbs. (mkg) |
| --- | --- |
| Wheel Hub Nut | 112 (15.5) |
| Reaction Rod-to-Control Arm | 50.6 (7.0) |
| Ball Joint Nut | 72.3 (10.0) |
| Control Arm Pivot Pin Nut | 72.3 (10.0) |
| Strut-to-Bearing Housing Bolts | 43.4 (6.0) |
| Brake Caliper-to-Bearing Housing | 36.2 (5.0) |
| Wheel Bearing Nut | 43.4 (6.0) |

# Rear Suspension

## FIAT 124

**124 Spider**

### DESCRIPTION

Link type rear suspension with coil springs. System uses upper and lower strut rods to attach rear axle to body. Brackets on rear axle and body support coil springs with hydraulic, double acting shock absorbers mounted inside coil spring. A stabilizer bar pivots on rear axle and body.

### REMOVAL & INSTALLATION

#### UPPER & LOWER STRUT RODS

**Removal** — Raise and support vehicle. Place support under rear axle. Remove nuts and bolts attaching strut rods to axle and to body. Remove strut rods.

**Installation** — Before installing, inspect all parts for signs of damage or wear and replace as necessary. To install, reverse removal procedure.

#### SHOCK ABSORBERS

**Removal** — Remove shock absorber upper retaining nuts from inside luggage compartment. Remove nuts attaching shock absorber to spring seat plate and remove shock absorber.

**Installation** — To install, reverse removal procedure and tighten all nuts and bolts.

### COIL SPRINGS

**Removal** — Raise rear of vehicle and support. Remove wheels and disconnect brake lines. Disconnect parking brake. Remove nuts attaching shock absorbers to body. Disconnect pressure regulator link from axle housing. Support axle with jack, disconnect upper and lower control arms and stabilizer bar. Lower suspension assembly and remove springs.

**Installation** — Before installing, inspect all parts for signs of excessive wear or damage and replace as necessary. To install, reverse removal procedure and tighten all nuts and bolts. Bleed and adjust brakes if necessary.

### STABILIZER BAR

**Removal** — Remove nuts and bolts attaching stabilizer bar to rear axle and body and remove bar.

**Installation** — Inspect all parts for signs of distortion, wear or damage. To install, reverse removal procedure and tighten all nuts and bolts.

### TIGHTENING SPECIFICATIONS

| Application | Ft. Lbs. (mkg) |
| --- | --- |
| Stabilizer Bar | 58 (8.0) |
| Upper Strut Rod-to-Body | 25 (3.5) |
| Lower Strut Rod-to-Body | 58 (8.0) |
| Upper and Lower Strut Rods-to-Axle | 72 (10.0) |
| Shock Absorber Mountings | 36 (5.0) |

**Fig. 1  Installed View of Fiat 124 Rear Suspension Assembly**

## FIAT 128

128
Sedan
Station Wagon
3P

### DESCRIPTION

Independent type rear suspension utilizing a transverse leaf spring. Wheel bearing carriers are supported by control arms connected to chassis and by hydraulic double action shock absorbers connected at top to inner fender panel. Transverse leaf spring is connected to chassis at center and to control arms at outside.

### ADJUSTMENT

#### WHEEL ALIGMENT SPECIFICATIONS & PROCEDURES

*See Wheel Alignment Specifications & Procedures in WHEEL ALIGNMENT Section.*

#### WHEEL BEARING ADJUSTMENT

*See Wheel Bearing Adjustment in WHEEL ALIGNMENT Section.*

### REMOVAL & INSTALLATION

#### SHOCK ABSORBER & CONTROL ARM

**Removal — 1)** Raise rear of vehicle, position safety stands under chassis and remove rear wheels. Disconnect and plug brake flex line. Disconnect parking brake cable from lever on back of backing plate. Position a jack under control arm, raise slightly and disconnect upper shock absorber mount, accessible from inside luggage compartment.

**2)** Remove outer mount pad securing spring to control arm. Remove nuts securing control arm pivot shaft to chassis. Lower jack and remove shock absorber and control arm. Note number and position of wheel alignment shims between control arm pivot shaft and body mount for installation.

**Installation —** To install control arm and shock absorber, reverse removal procedure. Bleed brake hydraulic system. Tighten control arm pivot shaft nuts with weight of vehicle on rear wheels.

#### CONTROL ARM BUSHINGS

**Removal —** Remove shock absorber and control arm as previously outlined. Remove pivot bolt securing control arm to bearing carrier and shock absorber mount. Remove inner pivot shaft nuts at control arm. Using a press and a suitable mandrel (A. 47057), press out on pivot shaft until bushing is partially removed. This allows for removing tool to properly center on opposite bushing. Using same procedure, remove other bushing. Remove control arm from press and extract remaining bushing. Remove bearing carrier bushings in control arm with a suitable puller (A. 47057).

**Installation — 1)** Using same tools as used for removal in addition to a suitable spacer (A. 74220) installed between inner legs of control arm, press bushings into control arm onto pivot shaft. Use same tool as used for removal to reinstall bearing carrier bushings into control arm.

**2)** When reconnecting control arm to bearing carrier, the correct shim thickness between control arm and shock absorber mount must be determined. *See Control Arm Shim Determination.* Reinstall control arm, bearing carrier and shock absorber as previously outlined. Tighten control arm to bearing carrier pivot bolt with weight of vehicle on rear wheels.

Shock Absorber

Transverse Leaf Spring

Control Arm

*Fig. 1  Installed View of Fiat 128 Rear Suspension Assembly*

## FIAT 128 (Cont.)

### CONTROL ARM SHIM DETERMINATION

Measure distance ("A" see illustration) between outer bushings on control arm. Measure width ("B" see illustration) of shock absorber mount. Add .118" (3 mm) to the difference of measurements "A" and "B". This will give the thickness required for both shims. Shim thickness must not vary more than .020" (.5 mm) between left and right side.

**Fig. 3   Shim Thickness Measuring Dimension "B" on Control Arm**

**Fig. 2   Shim Thickness Measuring Dimension "A" on Control Arm**

### TRANSVERSE LEAF SPRING

**Removal** — Raise rear of vehicle, position on safety stands and remove wheels. Place a jack under left end of spring and raise enough to release spring from rubber mounting pad on control arm. Remove cotter pin and disconnect rod linking spring to brake regulator (if equipped). Remove mount for rubber pad on bottom of control arm and lower jack to release spring. Repeat same procedure for opposite side. Remove two guides securing spring to chassis and remove spring.

**Installation** — Inspect spring making sure there are not any cracked or broken leaves. Inspect all rubber mounts and inter leaf shims for wear or damage. To install transverse leaf spring, reverse removal procedure.

### TIGHTENING SPECIFICATIONS

| Application | Ft. Lbs. (mkg) |
|---|---|
| Rear Wheel Hub Nut | 112 (15.5) |
| Leaf Spring Mounting Pad-to-Control Arm | 22 (3.0) |
| Control Arm-to-Bearing Carrier Pivot Bolt | 58 (8.0) |
| Control Arm-to-Chassis Pivot Bolt | 36 (5.0) |
| Control Arm Pivot Shaft End Nuts | 32 (4.4) |
| Upper Shock Absorber Mount | 18 (2.5) |
| Lower Shock Absorber Mount | 43 (6.0) |
| Brake Backing Plate Assembly-to-Bearing Carrier | 18 (2.5) |

## FIAT 131

**131**

### DESCRIPTION

Rear suspension consists of upper and lower reaction struts, shock absorbers encased by coil springs and a track bar. Lower reaction struts mount near wheels under axle housing and at forward end to car body. Upper reaction struts mount off bracket on axle housing and at front end to bracket on body. A track bar is connected at one end to bracket mounted off frame and at opposite end to bracket below axle housing. Coil springs mount between axle assembly and frame. Hydraulic shock absorbers are used and are mounted between axle and body, inside of coil spring.

### REMOVAL & INSTALLATION

#### REAR SUSPENSION ASSEMBLY

**Removal** — Raise vehicle, support with safety stands, and remove rear wheels. Disconnect propeller shaft from rear axle.

Coil Spring

Shock Absorber

Lower Reaction Strut

Track Bar

Upper Reaction Struts

Lower Reaction Strut

*Fig. 1  Fiat 131 Rear Suspension Assembly*

Disconnect parking brake cable from cable housing assembly. Disconnect track bar from frame. Position a jack under axle assembly and raise jack enough to support axle. Disconnect lower strut rods from frame bracket, then remove brake cable and brake regulator rod from bracket. Disconnect brake hose from "T" fitting on rear axle. Disconnect upper reaction struts from frame bracket. Disconnect shock absorber from upper mount and upper mount from body. Lower rear axle with suspension from vehicle.

**Installation** — To install rear axle, reverse removal procedure while noting the following: Tighten nuts and bolts to specifications with weight of vehicle on ground. Bleed brake system after installation.

### SHOCK ABSORBERS

**NOTE** — *To remove shock absorber from sedan models, rear suspension must be removed.*

**Removal & Installation, St. Wgn.** — Remove mounting bolts and nuts from top and bottom of shock absorbers, then remove. To install, reverse removal procedure.

### STRUT RODS

**Removal (Lower)** — Remove nut and bolt mounting strut in rear axle bracket. Disconnect parking brake cable from bracket on strut. Remove strut from front bracket and lift out.

**Removal (Upper)** — Remove hardware mounting strut in rear bracket, then separate strut from front bracket and remove.

**Installation (Upper and Lower)** — To install, reverse removal procedure.

### TIGHTENING SPECIFICATIONS

| Application | Ft. Lbs.(mkg) |
| --- | --- |
| Shock Absorber-to-Upper Mount | 11(1.5) |
| Upper Mount-to-Body | 18(2.5) |
| Shock Absorber Lower Mount | 36(5) |
| Track Bar-to-Rear Axle | 72(10) |
| Track Bar-to-Body | 58(8) |
| Reaction Strut Rods | 58(8) |

## FIESTA

**Fiesta**

### DESCRIPTION

Rear suspension assembly components mount on a tubular steel axle and consist of separately mounted coil springs, shock absorbers, transverse rod, trailing arms and a stabilizer bar (some applications).

### ADJUSTMENTS

#### WHEEL ALIGNMENT SPECIFICATIONS & PROCEDURES

See *Wheel Alignment Specifications and Procedures* in WHEEL ALIGNMENT section.

#### WHEEL BEARING ADJUSTMENT

See *Wheel Bearing Adjustment* in WHEEL ALIGNMENT section.

Stabilizer Bar (Optional)
Shock Absorber
Coil Spring
Transverse Rod
Parking Brake Adjuster
Trailing Arm

**Fig. 1  Assembled View of Fiesta Rear Suspension**

### REMOVAL & INSTALLATION

#### REAR AXLE & SUSPENSION ASSEMBLY

**Removal — 1)** Raise and support vehicle. Detach parking brake cable from adjuster. Remove bolts holding transverse rod to body and axle and remove transverse rod.

**2)** Detach flexible brake lines from axle connections and plug openings. Working from engine compartment, disconnect exhaust pipe from manifold, then from both rear supports. Remove pipe.

**3)** Place jack under center of rear axle. Remove bolts holding trailing arms to body. Remove stabilizer bar-to-body bolts.

**4)** Raise tailgate and package tray, remove plastic caps and remove shock absorber upper retaining nuts. Slowly lower jack (watching coil springs) and remove complete axle and suspension assembly.

**Installation — 1)** Position axle assembly and, with coil springs in position, support with jack and attach trailing arm-to-body bolts.

**2)** Install and tighten shock absorber top mounts. Reposition stabilizer bar and tighten locknuts. Loosely install trailing arm-to-axle bolts. Remove jack.

**3)** Install transverse rod and secure both ends. Connect handbrake cable to adjuster and set to proper operating tension. Reconnect brake lines and bleed brake system. Install exhaust pipe.

**4)** Lower vehicle to ground and fully tighten trailing arm bolts and nuts.

#### COIL SPRINGS

**Removal — 1)** Raise and support vehicle. Remove rear wheels. Positon a jack below center of rear axle.

**2)** From beneath package tray, remove shock absorber top mountings. Remove trailing arm-to-axle bolts. Detach 2 stabilizer bar-to-body nuts.

**3)** Slowly lower jack and remove coil springs and insulators.

**Installation —** To install, reverse removal procedure, but do not fully tighten trailing arm-to-axle bolts until vehicle is resting on ground.

#### TRAILING ARM

**Removal —** Raise and support vehicle. Remove trailing arm-to-body bolts. Remove trailing arm-to-axle bolts and remove arm.

**Installation —** To install, reverse removal procedure, noting the following:
- Be sure trailing arm flanges point toward centerline of vehicle.
- Do not fully tighten trailing arm-to-axle bolts until vehicle is resting on ground.

#### STABILIZER BAR

**Removal —** Remove nuts from body mounting brackets. Remove bolts at each end of stabilizer bar (same as lower shock absorber mounting). Remove stabilizer bar.

**Installation —** To install, reverse removal procedure.

**NOTE** — *Right end of stabilizer bar is stamped with an arrow and the word "TOP".*

#### SHOCK ABSORBERS

**Removal — 1)** Raise and support vehicle. Position a jack below rear axle and raise slightly. From beneath package tray, remove mounting pieces, noting position of upper insulators for reinstallation reference.

**2)** Remove nut and bolt from lower mounting. Use a lever and pry lower end of shock absorber from locating peg. Remove from vehicle.

**Installation —** To install, reverse removal procedure.

| TIGHTENING SPECIFICATIONS | |
| --- | --- |
| **Application** | **Ft. Lbs. (mkg)** |
| Transverse Rod Bolts | 40-48 (5.4-6.4) |
| Trailing Arm Bolts | 40-48 (5.4-6.4) |
| Shock Absorber | |
|     Upper | 18-22 (2.5-3.5) |
|     Lower | 40-48 (5.4-6.4) |
| Stabilizer Bar-to-Body | 15-18 (2.1-2.5) |

## HONDA

**Civic**
**Civic CVCC**
  **Except St. Wgn.**
**Accord**

### DESCRIPTION

Rear suspension system on all models is an independent type. Major components are: Control arm (lower), shock absorber with coil spring assembly, radius rod, and rear hub carrier. Radius rod controls rear wheel alignment.

### REMOVAL & INSTALLATION

#### SHOCK ABSORBER

**Removal** — 1) Raise vehicle and suitably support on safety stands. Remove rear wheels. Disconnect brake line from bracket on shock absorber housing. Plug open ends and place lines out of way. Disconnect parking brake cable from lever on backing plate.

2) Remove bolt mounting shock absorber to knuckle. Remove cotter pin and loosen outer control arm pivot bolt. Remove two upper shock absorber retaining nuts. Lower shock absorber and coil spring from vehicle.

**Disassembly** — Fit spring compressor and slightly compress coils. Remove lock nut and piston rod center nut. Take off upper mounting hardware and coil spring.

**Inspection** — Check piston rod for smooth, even operation. Inspect for signs of oil leaks. Listen for noise or unusual binding during inspection.

**Reassembly** — Select new shock absorber. Fit coil spring to lower spring seat. Refit spring compressor. Collapse coil enough to insert upper mountings and tighten piston rod. Release coil spring.

**Installation** — To install, reverse removal procedure and note: Fit top of shock absorber first. Make sure tab on shock absorber engages slot in bearing carrier. Bleed brake system.

#### REAR WHEEL HUB CARRIER

**Removal** — Raise vehicle and place on safety stands. Remove wheel and brake drum. Disconnect and plug brake lines. Remove bolt mounting shock absorber to hub carrier. Disconnect control arm and radius rod from hub carrier. Maneuver hub carrier from vehicle.

**Fig. 1  Exploded View of Accord Shock Absorber Assembly — Other Models Are Similar**

**Fig. 2  Exploded View of Accord Rear Suspension Other Models Are Similar**

**Installation** — To install hub carrier, reverse removal procedure and note following: Bleed brake system and check rear wheel alignment.

## HONDA (Cont.)

### RADIUS ROD

**Removal** — Raise and suitably support vehicle. Remove bolt mounting radius rod to hub carrier. Remove bolt mounting opposite end of radius rod to body bracket.

**Inspection** — Inspect all radius rod bushings and grommets for damage or excessive wear. Replace parts found defective. Make sure radius rod adjusting bolt is not damaged

**Fig. 3   Radius Control Rod with Bushings and Adjustment Bolt — Accord Shown Others Similar**

**Installation** — To install, reverse removal procedure and note: Either lower vehicle to ground or raise rear of vehicle to simulate normal weight before tightening radius control rod. Check and adjust wheel alignment as required.

**Fig. 4   Lower Control Arm with Detail of Mounting Bushings**

### CONTROL ARM

**Removal** — Raise vehicle and place on safety stands. Remove wheel and brake drum. Remove brake hoses from shock absorber mounting, then plug openings. Remove brake backing plate. Remove bolt mounting shock absorber to hub carrier. Remove both inside and outside control arm pivot bolts. Pull out control arm.

**Inspection** — Inspect all control arm bushings for damage or excessive wear. Replace any parts found defective. Always replace bolt lock tabs.

**Installation** — To install, reverse removal procedure and note following: Bleed brake system and check rear wheel alignment.

### TIGHTENING SPECIFICATIONS

| Application | Ft. Lbs. (mkg) |
| --- | --- |
| **Outer Pivot Bolt** | |
| Accord | 54-65 (7.5-9.0) |
| CVCC | 58 (8.0) |
| **Inner Pivot Bolt** | |
| Accord and Civic | 25-36 (3.5-5.0) |
| CVCC | 33 (4.7) |
| **Shock Absorber Lower Mount Bolt** | |
| Accord | 36-43 (5.0-6.0) |
| Civic | 26-35 (3.6-4.8) |
| CVCC | 33 (4.6) |
| **Shock Absorber Piston Nut** | |
| Accord | 22-25 (3.0-3.5) |
| Civic | 40-50 (5.5-7.0) |
| CVCC | 44 (6.1) |
| **Radius Rod-to-Bearing Carrier** | |
| Accord | 54-65 (7.5-9.0) |
| Civic | 40-54 (5.5-7.5) |
| CVCC | 33 (4.7) |
| **Radius Rod-to-Body** | |
| Accord | 43-54 (6.0-7.5) |
| Civic | 25-36 (3.5-5.0) |
| CVCC | 33 (4.7) |

## JAGUAR

XJ6
XJ12
XJS

### DESCRIPTION

Independent, coil spring type suspension. Outer bearing carrier and hub assembly is supported by control arms at bottom and utilizes drive axles as upper support. Suspension is controlled by two coil spring/shock absorber assemblies mounted at each rear wheel. Movement of lower control arms are controlled by radius arms connected to control arms at rear and to chassis members at front.

Fig. 1  Jaguar Rear Suspension Assembly

### ADJUSTMENTS

#### WHEEL ALIGNMENT SPECIFICATIONS & PROCEDURES

*See Wheel Alignment Specifications and Procedures in WHEEL ALIGNMENT Section.*

### REMOVAL & INSTALLATION

#### COIL SPRING & SHOCK ABSORBER

**NOTE** — *Rear springs can be removed with rear suspension installed in vehicle.*

**Removal** — Raise vehicle and support at lift points with jack stands. Position floor jack under control arm. Remove nut and bolt mounting top of shock absorbers to the suspension assembly crossmember. Remove washers and nuts securing shock absorbers to lower mounting. Using a drift, remove mounting piece. Withdraw shock absorber and coil spring assembly. Using a spring compressor, collapse spring until collets and spring seat can be removed. Release pressure and separate shock absorber from spring.

**Installation** — To install spring and shock absorber assembly, reverse removal procedure and tighten all nuts and bolts.

### RADIUS ROD

**Removal — 1)** Raise and support vehicle on safety stands forward of radius rods. Remove tire and wheel. Remove bolt and spring washer securing safety strap to body. Remove lock wire and bolt securing radius rod to body, then remove safety strap.

Fig. 2  *Installed Position of Radius Rod*

**2)** Remove forward lower shock absorber mounting pin. Using a punch, remove pin rearward. Bend tab washer and remove bolt mounting radius rod to control arm.

**Installation** — Replace any damaged radius rod bushings. When pressing bushings into radius rod, bushing should protrude from each side equal amounts. To install, reverse removal procedure.

### REAR SUSPENSION ASSEMBLY

**Removal — 1)** Raise and support vehicle forward of radius rods. Remove tires and wheels. Place floor jack (with adaptor to hold suspension assembly) under rear suspension.

**2)** Disconnect intermediate exhaust pipes at both ends. On XJS models, remove rear mufflers.

**3)** On XJ12 and XJ6 models, remove intermediate exhaust pipe from vehicle. Block rear mufflers out of way.

**4)** Disconnect radius rod-to-body mounting hardware.

**5)** On XJS models, separate stabilizer bar from radius rods.

**6)** Separate brake line union from body bracket. Disconnect brake lines at flexible hoses and plug openings. Disconnect propeller shaft at differential. Lower shaft out of way.

**7)** Release parking brake. Separate actuating lever cable. Disconnect opposite side cable at trunnion and retain cable out of way.

**8)** On models equipped with overdrive units, disconnect speedometer and electrical wire.

**9)** On XJS models, remove bolts attaching suspension mounting rubbers to body.

## JAGUAR (Cont.)

10) On XJ12 and XJ6 models, remove 8 self-locking nuts and bolts and 4 nuts keeping mounting brackets to body.

11) Lower suspension to ground and slide from vehicle. Guide intermediate exhaust pipe from suspension assembly.

**Installation** — Reverse removal steps and bleed brake system.

### LOWER CONTROL ARM

**Removal, XJ12 and XJ6 — 1)** Drain differential. Remove suspension assembly as previously described. Place suspension on bench in an inverted state.

2) Remove 6 nuts mounting support plate to crossmember. Remove 8 bolts mounting support plate to lower control arm inner fulcrum brackets.

3) Remove fulcrum shaft and refit dummy shaft. Collect shims and oil seal retaining washers from each side of shaft. Remove lock nut from shock absorber fulcrum pivot and drift shaft rearward through control arm. Move shock absorber toward suspension middle.

4) Disconnect radius rod from control arm and remove shock absorber pivot assembly. Remove nut from lower control arm inner fulcrum shaft and tap shaft out. Guide control arm from vehicle.

5) Collect all thrust washers, seal retainers, seals, bearing tubes, needle bearings and spacer from each inner control arm boss.

**Installation — 1)** Lightly coat bearing cage with grease and press into inner fulcrum shaft boss. Stamped markings face outward. Insert bearing tube and press in other bearing. Repeat procedure for each boss.

2) Fit thrust washers to control arm. Insert control arm to inner fulcrum mounting bracket. Make sure radius rod bracket faces front of suspension.

3) Fit dummy shaft from each end to keep bearings and insert control arm with mounting bracket. Tap in fulcrum shaft.

NOTE — Be careful not to drop thrust washers off control arm.

4) Reverse removal procedure for installation of remaining components.

**Fig. 3    Fitting Dummy Pivot Shaft**

**Removal, XJS — 1)** Raise and support vehicle with stand placed ahead of radius rods. Remove tire and wheel.

2) Remove lock nut and drift out bearing carrier fulcrum shaft. Fit dummy shaft for support. Collect shims and oil seal retainers.

3) Lift bearing carrier up, clear of control arm. Keep in position with heavy wire attached to crossmember. Remove bolt mounting stabilizer bar link to radius rod. Move link out of way. Separate radius rod from body.

**Fig. 4    Bolts and Setscrews Mounting Support Plate to Crossmember and Inner Fulcrum Brackets**

4) Remove 14 bolts mounting support plate to crossmember and inner fulcrum brackets. Separate shock absorber at upper mount. Drift out pivot pin.

5) Separate inner fulcrum from control arm. Guide out control arm and radius rod.

**Installation — 1)** Smear bearing cage with grease and force bearing into lower control arm. Marking cast on bearing faces out. Insert bearing tube for other end and force in opposite end bearing. Repeat procedure for other boss.

**Fig. 5    Fulcrum Boss Assembly**

2) Assemble radius rod to control arm. Lightly coat thrust washers, new oil seals and oil seal retainers with grease. Fit assemblies into place on control arm.

## JAGUAR (Cont.)

3) Insert control arm to inner fulcrum mounting bracket. Make sure radius rod bracket faces toward front of suspension.

4) Insert dummy shaft from each end to keep bearings positioned then locate control arm in bracket. Slip in fulcrum shaft while pushing out dummy shaft. Install lock nut.

**Fig. 6 Locating Control Arm in Mounting Bracket with Dummy Shafts**

5) To install remaining components, reverse removal procedure.

### STABILIZER BAR & LINKS

**Removal, XJS** — Raise vehicle and place on safety stands. Remove left rear wheel. Loosen exhaust pipe clamp nuts on right side forward of crossmember. Remove bolts mounting stabilizer bar to top of connecting links. Remove brackets mounting stabilizer bar to floorpan. Pull exhaust pipe apart. Maneuver stabilizer through left fender opening. Remove nuts and bolts mounting connecting link, then separate from radius rod.

**Fig. 7 Installed View of Stabilizer Bar and Connecting Link**

**Installation** — To install stabilizer bar and connecting links, reverse removal procedure. Make sure exhaust system does not leak.

### TIGHTENING SPECIFICATIONS

| Application | Ft. Lbs. (mkg) |
|---|---|
| Radius Rod-to-Control Arm | 60-70 (8.3-9.7) |
| Radius Rod-to-Body | 40-45 (5.5-6.2) |
| Shock Absorbers | 32-36 (4.4-5.0) |
| Support Plate-to-Crossmember and Inner Fulcrum Mounting | 14-18 (1.9-2.5) |
| Inner Fulcrum Shaft | 45-50 (6.2-6.9) |
| Stabilizer Bar Bracket-to-Body | 14-18 (1.9-2.5) |

## LANCIA

**Lancia Beta**
**Except Scorpion**

### DESCRIPTION

Rear suspension is strut type. Strut is hydraulic and is fitted with coil spring. Strut mounts off bearing housing and at top to inner fender. Control arms (links) mount at bearing housing and crossmember. A stabilizer bar mounts off bearing housing and in at least two places on body brackets.

### ADJUSTMENT

#### WHEEL ALIGNMENT SPECIFICATIONS & PROCEDURES

**NOTE** – *Procedures not available. See WHEEL ALIGNMENT Section for Specifications.*

### REMOVAL & INSTALLATION

#### CROSSMEMBER

**Removal** – Raise and support vehicle. Place a hydraulic jack under center of crossmember. Remove nuts from crossmember mounting bolts. Remove mounting crossmember from body. On models with automatic headlight aiming device, remove rear sensor and support bracket. Separate crossmember from floor pan and lower jack. Take out bolts from crossmember mounting while lowering jack. Remove spacers and washers from mounting point. Control arm links may be wedged and have to be pried against.

**Installation** – To install, reverse removal procedure.

#### STABILIZER BAR

**Removal** – Raise and support vehicle. Remove brake rear limiter valve control lever from stabilizer bar. Disconnect stabilizer bar ends from mountings. Attach tool 8803342 (or equivalent) and compress bar enough to remove from vehicle. Make sure bar clears muffler and hardware. If mounting grommets need replacing, use a press to force from mounting brackets.

**Installation** – To install, reverse removal procedure. Make sure all grommets are properly aligned with brackets.

#### CONTROL ARM (LINK)

**Removal** – Raise and support vehicle. Remove plate covering crossmember bolts. On vehicles with automatic aiming sensor, remove headlight ball pin for left side control link. Remove nuts and bolts mounting control link to crossmember and bearing carrier. Separate links from crossmember mounting. Remove wheel. Guide links from vehicle.

**Installation** – To install, reverse removal procedure and note: Make sure crossmember mounting bolt heads face front of vehicle. Check and reset toe-in.

**Fig. 1   Cross Section View of Rear Suspension**

Labels in figure: Coil Spring; Bumper; NOTE – Static Load Distance: Saloon; 2.77" (70.5 mm) Coupe; 2.54" (64.5 mm); Strut Assembly; Crossmember; Stabilizer Bar; Brake Rotor; Control Arm (Link)

#### STRUT ASSEMBLY

**Removal** – Raise and support vehicle. Remove wheel. Fit tool 88033412 (or equivalent) to stabilizer bar and lightly tighten. Remove bolts mounting strut to bearing carrier and control links. Separate strut from mounting. Hang wheel hub and brake caliper to body. Make sure brake hose is not stretched. Work inside vehicle and remove mounting nuts from top strut plate. Draw strut out bottom of vehicle.

**Installation** – To install, reverse removal procedure and check static load. *See Fig. 1.*

#### TIGHTENING SPECIFICATIONS

| Application | Ft. Lbs. (mkg) |
| --- | --- |
| Crossmember | 18 (2.5) |
| Strut-to-Control Link | 31 (2.3) |
| Stabilizer Bar Bolts | 17 (2.3) |

## MERCEDES-BENZ

230
240D
280 Series
300D
450 Series
6.9

### DESCRIPTION

Rear suspension is independent with coil springs and semi-trailing arms. Rear axle carrier is mounted to body at three points and supports rear axle assembly. Axle shafts serve as upper control arms to rear wheels. Wheel hubs are supported by semi-trailing arms which run forward to pivot points on rear axle carrier and body. Shock absorbers are mounted inside of coil springs, attached to body on top and to semi-trailing arms on bottom. Stabilizer bar is mounted to body and to wheel hubs at ends.

### ADJUSTMENT

#### WHEEL ALIGNMENT SPECIFICATIONS & ADJUSTMENTS

*See Wheel Alignment Specifications & Adjustments in WHEEL ALIGNMENT Section.*

### REMOVAL & INSTALLATION

#### SHOCK ABSORBERS

**NOTE** — *Shock absorbers should be removed only when vehicle is on wheels or when semi-trailing arm is supported.*

*Fig. 1  Rear Spring and Shock Configuration*

*Fig. 2  Rear to Front View of Typical Mercedes Benz Rear Suspension*

## MERCEDES-BENZ (Cont.)

**Removal** — On vehicles with coupe top, remove top and open flap. On all models, remove rear seat and backrest. Remove locking lever from top flap and unscrew lining. Remove nut and rubber ring of upper shock mount. Remove lower shock mount on semi-trailing arm. Remove shock absorber in a downward direction.

**Installation** — To install, reverse removal procedure.

### COIL SPRINGS

**Removal** — Remove shock absorbers as previously outlined. Raise and support rear of vehicle on safety stands. Raise semi-trailing arm until approximately level. Using suitable spring compressor, compress spring. Carefully lower semi-trailing arm and remove spring with rubber mounting.

**Installation** — To install, reverse removal procedure.

### REAR STABILIZER BAR

**Removal** — Raise and support rear of vehicle with safety stands. Remove wheels. Detach connecting rod from stabilizer

Connecting Rod

Stabilizer Bar

Holding Bracket

**Fig. 3   Stabilizer Bar and Mounting Locations**

on both sides of vehicle. Remove stabilizer bar holding brackets. Loosen exhaust pipe mounts (rubber rings) and lower slightly. Remove stabilizer bar in a downward direction.

**Installation** — To install, reverse removal procedure.

**NOTE** — *When installing rear stabilizer bar, ensure that bend of bar is pointing upward.*

### REAR SUSPENSION & AXLE

**Removal — 1)** Raise and support vehicle with safety stands. Remove wheels. Disconnect exhaust system. Detach parking brake control cables at frame and compensating lever.

**2)** Loosen clamp nut and disconnect drive shaft intermediate bearing from frame. Disconnect rear of drive shaft and slide forward, out of centering position.

**NOTE** — *On 3-piece drive shaft, loosen front clamp nut only.*

**3)** Remove shock absorber and coil spring. Detach and plug brake lines. Disconnect stabilizer bar holding clamps.

**4)** Place suitable support jack under rear suspension. Disconnect supporting plates and front and rear rubber mounts from frame. Carefully lower jack and remove rear suspension from vehicle. Remove rear rubber mount from axle.

**CAUTION** — *When lowering and removing rear suspension, be sure cover plates of disc brakes are not damaged.*

**Installation** — To install, reverse removal procedure.

### DIFFERENTIAL WITH AXLE SHAFTS

**Removal — 1)** Drain fluid from differential. Detach brake caliper from right rotor and wire out of way. Remove axle shaft-to-flange attaching bolts (both sides) and force rear shafts out of shaft flanges.

Differential

Axle Shaft

Semi-Trailing Arm

Rear Axle Carrier

**Fig. 4   Typical Mercedes Benz Rear Suspension with Components Removed**

# Rear Suspension

## MERCEDES-BENZ (Cont.)

**NOTE** — *If required, loosen right shock absorber upper mount and lower semi-trailing arm to deflection stop.*

**2)** If required, remove exhaust system. Loosen clamp nut and detach drive shaft intermediate bearing from frame. Remove drive shaft from differential and push from centering alignment.

**NOTE** — *On 3-piece drive shaft, loosen front clamp nut only.*

**3)** Support differential with jack and suitable support (115 589 35 63 00). Disconnect rear rubber mount from body. Disconnect differential from rear axle carrier. Lower jack and remove differential with axle shafts.

**CAUTION** — *When moving differential with axle shafts, make sure that axle shafts are supported and DO NOT drop down, as this might damage inner joints.*

**Installation** — Check all rubber parts and replace as necessary. To install differential with rear axle shafts, reverse removal procedure. Tighten down all nuts and bolts, except when connecting drive shaft to differential. These bolts must be torqued after vehicle has been rolled forward and backward to seat parts. Install exhaust system, if removed.

### REAR AXLE CARRIER

**Removal** — Remove rear suspension, differential with rear axle shafts and semi-trailing arms as previously outlined.

**Fig. 5   Proper Washer Placement for Rear Axle Carriers without Spot Welds**

**Inspection** — Using inspection tool (*Fig. 6*), check rear axle carrier. When checking rear axle carriers without spot welded washers, place a .098" (2.5 mm) thick washer under receiving bolt (*Fig 5*).

**Installation** — To install rear axle, reverse removal procedure.

Inspection Device

**Fig. 6   Inspection Tool 115 589 04 23 00**

## TIGHTENING SPECIFICATIONS

| Application | Ft. Lbs. (mkg) |
|---|---|
| Shock Absorber Lower Mount | 33 (4.6) |
| Torsion Bar Bearing Bolts | 47 (6.5) |
| Torsion Bar Connecting Rod Ball Joints | 33 (4.6) |
| Rear Rubber Mount-to-End Cover | 101 (14.0) |
| Rear Rubber Mount-to-Frame | 18 (2.5) |
| Front Rubber Mounts-to-Frame | 29 (4.0) |
| Supporting Plate-to-Frame | 23-29 (3.2-4.0) |
| Drive Shaft Clamp Nut (Two Piece) | 145 (20.0) |
| Drive Shaft Clamp Nut (Three Piece) Front | 23-29 (3.2-4.0) |
| Rear | 145 (20.0) |
| Semi-Trailing Arm-to-Rear Axle Carrier | 87 (12.0) |
| Axle Shaft-to-Axle Shaft Flange | 69 (9.5) |
| Differential-to-Rear Axle Carrier | 72 (10.0) |
| Brake Caliper Bolts | 23-29 (3.2-4.0) |

# Rear Suspension

## OPEL

**All Models**

### DESCRIPTION

Rear suspension system consists of: Control arm link, coil spring, track rod, and shock absorber. Track rod is connected to rear axle housing and body. Track rod helps control lateral movement of rear axle. Control arms limit the back and forth movement of rear axle.

### REMOVAL & INSTALLATION

#### SHOCK ABSORBER

**Removal & Installation** — Raise vehicle and place on safety stands. Remove rear wheel. Disconnect shock absorber lower end from mounting position on rear axle housing. Working form inside trunk, remove fuel tank cover and disconnect upper end of shock absorber. To insall, reverse removal procedure.

#### CONTROL ARM LINK

**Removal & Installation** — Raise vehicle and place on safety stands. Remove rear wheel. Remove bolts mounting control arm to axle housing. Remove bolt connecting control arm link

to body. Maneuver control arm link from vehicle. To install, reverse removal procedure.

#### COIL SPRINGS

**Removal & Installation** — Raise vehicle and place on safety stands. Place jack under rear axle. Disconnect lower end of shock absorber. Lower jack until coil spring can be removed. To install, reverse removal procedure and note: Spring can be compressed enough by hand to be installed.

### TIGHTENING SPECIFICATIONS

| Application | Ft. Lbs. (mkg) |
|---|---|
| Shock Absorber-to-Rear Axle Housing | 29 (4.0) |
| Track Rod-to-Body Bracket | 47 (6.5) |
| Track Rod-to-Rear Axle Housing | 54 (7.5) |
| Control Arm Link Bolts | 29 (4.0) |

*Fig. 1  Exploded View of Rear Suspension Components*

# Rear Suspension

## PORSCHE 911SC & TURBO

**911SC & Turbo**

### DESCRIPTION

Independent torsion bar type rear suspension. Torsion bars are mounted inside rear crossmember tube and anchored in center by a splined hub. Outer end of torsion bars mount into splined hubs integral with spring plates which connect at ends to control arms. Control arms pivot in mounts integral with body and also serve as rear wheel bearing carriers. Hydraulic shock absorbers mount between control arms and inner fender panel. A stabilizer bar is installed on some models.

### ADJUSTMENT

#### WHEEL ALIGNMENT SPECIFICATIONS & PROCEDURES

*See Wheel Alignment Specifications & Procedures in WHEEL ALIGNMENT Section.*

### REMOVAL & INSTALLATION

#### SHOCK ABSORBERS

**Removal — 1)** Raise vehicle and place safety stands in a position so weight of vehicle is still on rear wheels. Remove rubber cap from upper mount (accessible from inside engine compartment) and remove nut from shock absorber stem.

**2)** Remove bolt securing shock absorber to control arm and remove shock absorber. Remove rod cover and rubber buffer from shock absorber.

**Installation —** Inspect rubber buffer for wear or cracking and replace if necessary. Make sure that stop disc grooves face bottom of shock absorber when assembling. Install rubber buffer and cover and reverse removal procedure to install remaining components. Tighten upper and lower mounts.

*Fig. 1  Exploded View of Porsche Rear Suspension*

Labels: Spring Plate, Toe-In Adjuster, Hub, Camber Adjuster Bolt, Brake Line, Eccentric Bolt, Spacer, Bearing, Control Arm, Shock Absorber, Spring Plate Hub Cover, Axle Drive Shaft

#### CONTROL ARM

**Removal — 1)** Raise vehicle and place safety stands under body. Remove rear wheels. Detach brake system components from rear wheel hub. *See Porsche in BRAKE Section.* Remove axle hub cotter pin and nut. Remove Allen head bolts from axle shaft flanges and remove axle shaft.

**2)** Using a suitable driver, remove rear wheel hub from control arm. Remove cotter pin and nut from parking brake cable and pull cable out toward center of vehicle. Remove

bolts securing parking brake assembly to control arm and remove assembly.

**3)** Raise torsion bar spring plate to take tension from shock absorber with a suitable tool. Remove lower shock absorber mount. Remove bolts securing spring plate to control arm. Disconnect brake hose from bracket on control arm. Remove nut from control arm pivot bolt and drive bolt out with a punch. Remove control arm from vehicle.

**Installation —** Reverse removal procedure and note the following: Use new self-locking nuts and tighten all bolts and nuts. Check wheel alignment and bleed brake system.

#### TORSION BAR & SPRING PLATE

**Removal — 1)** Raise vehicle and place safety stands under body. Remove wheel and tire. Raise torsion bar spring plate using suitable equipment. Remove lower shock absorber mounting bolt. Remove bolts securing spring plate to control arm. Pull back on control arm to separate from spring plate.

**2)** Remove torsion bar hub cover bolts and remove cover by prying off with a screwdriver. Remove torsion bar tensioner tool. Remove plug from body, remove spring plate and withdraw torsion bar. If torsion bar is broken, opposite side torsion bar will have to be removed in order to drive out broken piece.

**Installation — 1)** Inspect all components for wear or damage. Coat torsion bar with lithium grease before installing. Torsion bars are marked left and right; install accordingly. Coat rubber components with glycerin paste. Install torsion bar and spring plate in correct position.

**2)** Adjust torsion bars as follows: using suitable protractor (VW261), place onto lower edge of door sill. Adjust protractor so that bubble in glass tube marked "Axle Housing/Angle" is in the center.

**3)** Reset glass tube carrier by value specified. Place protractor onto spring plate and adjust to, on 911S models, .468±.20" (12±.5 mm), on Turbo Carrera 1.5±.20" (37±.5 mm), by turning eccentric screw on spring plate.

**NOTE —** *Difference between right and left measurement must not exceed .20" (.5 mm).*

**4)** Install hub cover and start three bolts that are accessible. Raise spring plate until remaining bolt can be installed. Reverse removal procedures for remaining components. Check rear wheel alignment.

### TIGHTENING SPECIFICATIONS

| Application | Ft. Lbs. (mkg) |
| --- | --- |
| Control Arm Pivot Bolt | 87 (12.0) |
| Spring Plate-to-Control Arm Bolts | 65 (9.0) |
| Camber Adjusting Bolt | 43 (6.0) |
| Tracking Adjusting Bolt | 36 (5.0) |
| Lower Shock Absorber Mount | 54 (7.5) |
| Hub Nut | 235 (32.5) |
| Axle Shaft Allen Head Bolts | |
| M10-8G | 34 (4.7) |
| M8-12K | 31 (4.3) |
| M10x55-12K | 60 (8.3) |
| Torsion Bar Hub Cover Bolts | 34 (4.7) |

# Rear Suspension

## PORSCHE 924

924

### DESCRIPTION

Independent torsion bar type rear suspension. Torsion bars mount in rear crossmember tube and anchor in center of tube by a splined hub. Outer ends of torsion bar mount into splined hubs integral with spring plates. Spring plates are bolted to control arm at a flange. Control arms pivot in mounts on crossmember tube and are integral with stub axle housing. Hydraulic shock absorbers mount on control arm and to upper body.

### ADJUSTMENTS

#### WHEEL ALIGNMENT SPECIFICATIONS & PROCEDURES

*See Wheel Alignment Specifications and Procedures in WHEEL ALIGNMENT Section.*

### REMOVAL & INSTALLATION

#### SHOCK ABSORBERS

**Removal** — Raise vehicle and place on safety stands. Remove wheel. Remove both bottom and top mounting nuts and bolts, then slide shock absorber from vehicle.

**Installation** — Inspect for hydraulic leaks and replace shock absorber if excessive leaking is apparent. Check shock absorber for smooth, even operation. To install, reverse removal procedure.

#### CONTROL ARM

**Removal** — 1) Remove cotter pin and loosen rear hub nut. Raise vehicle and place on safety stands. Remove wheel. Remove shock absorber.

2) Remove bolts mounting axle drive shaft to stub axle. Separate axle drive shaft from stub axle and wire out of way. Use protective cap to cover exposed end of axle drive shaft.

*Fig. 1   Exploded View of 924 Rear Suspension*

## PORSCHE 924 (Cont.)

3) Remove drum and disconnect parking brake and hydraulic lines. Index mark spring plate in relation to a point on control arm. Remove control arm pivot bolt and remove arm from vehicle.

**Installation** — To install, reverse removal procedure. Tighten pivot bolt and lock in place by staking to edge to metal shoulder on bracket. Align spring plate marks with those on control arm. Bleed brake system.

### TORSION BARS & SPRING PLATES

**Removal** — 1) Raise and support vehicle. Take off wheel. Scribe mark alignment position of spring plate in control arm for reassembly. Disconnect spring plate from control arm.

2) Remove bolts mounting spring plate cover. Pry off lower stop cast into torsion bar housing. Remove spring plate and withdraw torsion bar. If torsion bar is broken, opposite side torsion bar must be removed to drive out broken piece.

**Installation** — 1) Inspect torsion bar and spring plate for wear or distortion. Inspect rubber mounts for cracking or wear. Torsion bars are marked left and right and should be installed accordingly.

2) Coat torsion bar splines with grease and install into vehicle. Coat rubber supports with talcum powder. Make sure part of rubber support marked "Oben" is installed facing up. Not all supports are marked.

3) Install spring plate in position. *See Torsion Bar Adjustment in this article.* Install hub cover and secure with 2 bolts.

4) Use a suitable jack or spring compressor (VW655/3) to raise spring plate and install remaining hub cover bolts. To install remaining components, reverse removal procedure. Recheck rear wheel alignment.

### TORSION BAR ADJUSTMENT

**NOTE** — *Adjust both torsion bars on vehicles with high milage.*

1) Using suitable protractor (VW261), place protractor on lower edge of door sill. Adjust protractor so bubble in glass tube marked "Axle Housing/Angle" is in center. Note reading that will indicate vehicle deviation from horizontal.

2) Rotate level carrier on protractor by specified value for spring plate angle (23°). With spring plate cover removed, place protractor on spring plate. Lift spring plate enough to remove play from splines.

3) If front of vehicle is lower, add door sill measurement to spring plate value. If rear of vehicle is lower than front, subtract door sill measurement from spring plate value. Correct spring plate angle if measured value differs from specified value by more than ⅝".

---

### TIGHTENING SPECIFICATIONS

| Application | Ft. Lbs. (mkg) |
|---|---|
| Torsion Bar Crossmember Tube-to-Body | 54 (7.5) |
| Spring Plate Cover | 25 (3.5) |
| Control Arm-to-Torsion Bar Crossmember Tube | 44 (6.1) |
| Spring Plate-to-Control Arm | 76-90 (10.5-12.5) |
| Lower Shock Absorber Mounting | 44 (6.1) |
| Upper Shock Absorber Mounting | 44 (6.1) |

# Rear Suspension

## PORSCHE 928

**928**

## DESCRIPTION

Porsche 928 rear suspension is a strut type, consisting of a strut assembly (shock absorber and coil spring) which is mounted at bottom to the rear wheel hub and lower control arm and at top to vehicle body. An upper control arm is also incorporated. A stabilizer bar is connected by a link to the lower control arm.

## ADJUSTMENTS

### WHEEL ALIGNMENT SPECIFICATIONS & PROCEDURES

*See Wheel Alignment Specifications and Procedures in WHEEL ALIGNMENT section.*

## REMOVAL & INSTALLATION

### REAR SUSPENSION ASSEMBLY

**Removal – 1)** Raise and support vehicle. Detach axle shaft from differential by removing Allen-head bolts.

**2)** Detach caliper from rotor. Remove 2 countersunk screws and take off rotor. Remove parking brake shoes and spreader lever. Pull parking brake cable out of guide in hub assembly.

**3)** Remove hub assembly with upper control arm attached after removing control arm retaining bolt.

**4)** Remove lower control arm retaining nuts and bolts and remove control arm from vehicle. Remove stabilizer bar and link, if necessary.

**Installation –** To install, reverse removal procedure.

**Fig. 1   Exploded View of 928 Rear Suspension**

### STRUT ASSEMBLY

**Removal – 1)** Working from luggage compartment, remove 3 self-locking nuts from upper strut mounting plate. Raise and support vehicle and remove rear wheel(s).

**2)** While counterholding rear nut, remove front nut from pivot pin of lower control arm (it may be necessary to counterlock the rear nut with another M14x1.5 nut). Remove pivot pin.

**3)** Remove stabilizer bar link from its attachment at lower control arm to gain additional clearance, then remove strut assembly from vehicle.

**Disassembly – 1)** Attach a suitable coil spring compressor to coil spring and compress enough to allow removal of top piston rod nut. Loosen spring compressor slowly, and remove coil spring.

**2)** Lift off cover pieces, unscrew adjusting nut and remove threaded sleeve.

**Reassembly –** Reassemble in reverse of disassembly procedure, using appropriate illustration as a guide. *Fig. 2.*

**Installation –** To install, reverse removal procedure.

**Fig. 2   Disassembled View of 928 Strut Assembly**

## TIGHTENING SPECIFICATIONS

| Application | Ft. Lbs. (mkg) |
| --- | --- |
| Caliper-to-Hub Bolt | 61 (8.5) |
| Lower Control Arm-to-Hub | 101 (14.0) |
| Upper Control Arm-to-Crossmember | 33 (4.6) |
| Upper Control Arm-to-Hub | 33 (4.6) |
| Hub-to-Stub Axle | 333 (46.0) |
| Wheel Nuts | 93 (13.0) |
| Upper Strut Mount-to-Body Locknuts | 33 (4.6) |
| Stabilizer Bar-to-Body | 33 (4.6) |
| Stabilizer Bar-to-Link | 33 (4.6) |
| Stabilizer Link-to-Control Arm | 33 (4.6) |
| Lower Control Arm-to-Link Pin | 61 (8.5) |
| Shock Absorber-to-Upper Strut Mount | 42 (5.8) |

## RENAULT R-5

**R-5**

### DESCRIPTION

System is torsion bar type with a trailing arm. Trailing arms are mounted off chassis and have torsion bars connected to inboard edge.

### ADJUSTMENT

#### WHEEL ALIGNMENT SPECIFICATIONS & PROCEDURES

*See Wheel Alignment Specifications and Procedures in WHEEL ALIGNMENT Section.*

#### RIDING HEIGHT ADJUSTMENT

*See Riding Height Adjustment in WHEEL ALIGNMENT Section.*

### REMOVAL & INSTALLATION

#### TRAILING ARM

**Removal** — Raise rear of vehicle and place on safety stands. Disconnect, then carefully remove sway bar. Remove shock absorber. Disconnect brake lines and plug openings. Put torsion bar adjusting cams in zero position. Remove torsion bars from both sides. Remove mounting bolts and slide complete arm assembly from vehicle.

**Fig. 1   Trailing Arm and Torsion Bar Assembly**

**Inspection** — Check all bushings and spacers for obvious signs of wear or damage. Use suitable puller and/or mandrel (with press) to replace bushings.

**Installation** — To install, reverse removal procedure and note: Bleed brake system. Recheck brake pressure equalizer. Check rear wheel alignment.

### TORSION BAR

**Removal** — Raise vehicle and place on safety stands. Loosen lock nut on cam and adjust until cam is zeroed. Remove shock absorber. Fit fabricated tool where shock absorber has been removed. Tighten nut until adjuster lever is raised from cam. Remove torsion bar.

**Fig. 2   Specifications for Tool Fabrication**

**NOTE** — *Before installing torsion bar, adjust nut on tool to 23¼" (590 mm), right side and/or 23⅝" (600 mm), left side. This will allow torsion bar to be inserted.*

**Installation** — Put adjuster lever so it touches cam. Lightly coat torsion bar splines with grease, then insert into lever and arm. Tighten cam lock nut. Take off tool. Install shock absorber. Lower vehicle. Measure under body (riding height).

### SHOCK ABSORBER

**Removal** — Work from inside trunk and remove upper nuts. Raise vehicle and place on safety stands. Remove lower mounting nut and take off shock absorber.

**Installation** — To install, reverse removal procedure. Make sure upper mounting is attached first.

## SAAB

### DESCRIPTION

Tube type rear axle with coil springs. Rear axle is straight tube with stub axles press fitted into the ends. Axle is mounted to body by two lower control arms, which are connected at rear to the axle tube and to the body at front. Rear links are also used which mount rearward from stub axle assembly to body. A cross bar is mounted from right side of axle and attaches to body support in center. Coil springs are mounted between lower control arms and body. Telescopic shock absorbers are used which are attached between lower control arms and body.

**Fig. 1  Saab Rear Suspension Assembly**

### ADJUSTMENT

#### REAR WHEEL BEARINGS

*See Wheel Bearing Adjustment in WHEEL ALIGNMENT Section.*

### REMOVAL & INSTALLATION

#### SHOCK ABSORBERS

**Removal, Standard Type —** Raise vehicle and place on safety stands. Remove tire and wheel. Disconnect shock absorbers from upper and lower mounting brackets. Remove shock absorber.

**Installation —** Reverse removal procedure and note: Bleed new shock absorber before installing. Place shock absorber straight up and down. Work it through full cycle several times. Make sure nuts are not overtightened. There should just be enough tension against rubber bushing to provide a solid fit.

**Removal, Pneumatic Type — 1)** Raise vehicle and place on safety stand at rear jacking point. Fit another safety stand under rear axle. This will stop axle from suddenly dropping.

**2)** Place a hydraulic jack under control arm near rear axle. Remove shock absorber mounting nuts. Remove bolts mounting control arm to rear axle. Lower control arm with jack until shock absorber can be removed.

**Installation —** To install, reverse removal procedure.

### REAR AXLE ASSEMBLY

**Removal —** Raise rear of vehicle and support on safety stands. Remove wheels and tires. Disconnect rear brake hoses, lower shock absorber attachments, and cross bar. Position a jack under rear axle, lower axle and remove rear springs. Remove screws of spring link rear bushings and remove axle assembly from vehicle.

**Installation — 1)** To install, reverse removal procedure and note: When repositioning axle tube, DO NOT place jack in center of axle tube. Either use two jacks (one at each end) or one jack and one safety stand.

**2)** DO NOT tighten bearings until car weight is on suspension to ensure bushings are aligned correctly. Cross bar-to-body mounting bolt must be installed with nut facing forward. Bleed brake system.

### COIL SPRING

**NOTE** — *DO NOT place floor jack under rear axle.*

**Removal — 1)** Set parking brake. Raise vehicle and place safety stands under rear axle. Remove wheel.

**2)** Place jack centered under control arm near coil spring. Slightly raise jack and disconnect lower end of shock absorber. Disconnect control arm from body. Let control arm down on jack until spring can be removed.

**Inspection —** Check spring for obvious signs of weakening or damage. Check free length of spring using table.

**Coil Spring Table**

| Application | Free Length |
| --- | --- |
| Coil with GREEN Stripe | 12.7" (323 mm) |
| Coil with YELLOW Stripe | 12.9" (329 mm) |
| Coil with WHITE Stripe | 12.4" (315 mm) |
| Coil with BLUE Stripe | 12.8" (324 mm) |

**Installation —** Reverse removal procedure. Make sure to use new lock nuts where control arm attaches to body.

## SUBARU

**1600**
**Brat**

### DESCRIPTION

Rear suspension consists of a control arm, shock absorber and torsion bar as 3 main components of each side. *Fig. 1.*

**Fig. 1   Subaru Rear Suspension Components**

### ADJUSTMENT

#### WHEEL ALIGNMENT SPECIFICATIONS & PROCEDURES

*See Wheel Alignment Specifications and Procedures in WHEEL ALIGNMENT Section.*

### REMOVAL & INSTALLATION

#### REAR SUSPENSION ASSEMBLY

*NOTE — To repair or replace any rear suspension components, with the exception of shock absorbers, suspension assembly, for side being repaired, must be removed.*

**Removal** — Raise rear of vehicle and support with safety stands. Remove rear wheels and disconnect brake line from flex line. Disconnect lower shock absorber mount. Remove bolts securing inner control arm pivot shaft mount to body. Loosen

lock bolt at outer bushing. Remove outer control arm pivot shaft mount bolts and remove suspension assembly for one side.

**Disassembly** — With lock bolt removed, pull outer bracket from bushing and pull torsion bar from control arm. Remove outer bushing with a suitable puller (925210000). Inner bushing can be removed in same manner.

**Reassembly** — Press bushing onto control arm, making sure bushings are flush with ends of control arm. Apply grease to serrations on end of torsion bar. Torsion bars are marked "R" and "L", they should be installed accordingly. The angle between center line of bushing and control arm should be as specified. *See Chart and Fig. 2.*

#### Bushing Installed Angle

| Application | Degrees |
| --- | --- |
| Sedan, Coupe, Hdtop. | 6 |
| Station Wagon | 7 |
| 4-Wheel Drive | 16.5 |

**Fig. 2   Measuring Angle Between Centerline of Bushing and Control Arm**

**Installation** — To install suspension assembly, reverse removal procedure. Tighten all bolts and nuts to specifications. Bleed hydraulic brake system and check wheel alignment.

### TIGHTENING SPECIFICATIONS

| Application | Ft. Lbs. ( mkg) |
| --- | --- |
| Lower Control Arm | |
|     Inner Bushing Bolt | 33-38 (4.5-5.3) |
|     Outer Bracket Bolts | 87-108 (12.0-15.0) |
|     Outer Bushing Bolt | 13-18 (1.8-2.5) |
|     Shock Absorber Lower Nut | 22-32 (3.0-4.5) |

## TOYOTA CELICA & CRESSIDA

Celica
Cressida (Exc. Station Wagon)

### DESCRIPTION

Coil spring type suspension utilizing upper and lower control arms as pivot supports. Coil springs are mounted between axle housing and chassis member. Shock absorbers are connected to axle housing at bottom and to chassis members at top. A stabilizer bar is mounted to rear side of axle and runs parallel with axle to mount at side of body.

**Fig. 1   Rear Suspension Arrangement for Toyota Celica and Cressida**

### REMOVAL & INSTALLATION

#### SHOCK ABSORBERS

**Removal** — Raise vehicle and place safety stands under axle housing. Remove nut from upper shock absorber mounting stud. Remove bolt from lower mount and remove shock absorber from vehicle.

**Installation** — Reverse removal procedure for installation. Tighten all bolts and nuts to specifications.

#### COIL SPRINGS

**Removal** — Raise and support vehicle. Place a support jack under rear axle. Detach shock absorber lower mount. Remove stabilizer bar mounting from axle. Slowly lower axle jack and remove coil springs and insulators.

**Installation** — To install, reverse removal procedure.

### CONTROL ARMS

**Removal — 1)** Raise and support vehicle at frame. Place an additional support jack under rear axle.

**2)** To remove upper control arm, remove bolt holding upper control arm to body and bolt holding control arm to axle housing. Remove upper control arm.

**3)** To remove lower control arm, remove arm-to-body bolt and arm-to-axle housing bolt. Remove control arm.

**Installation** — To install, temporarily attach both upper and lower control arms, then raise axle jack until vehicle is lifted from body stands. Tighten control arm bolts to specifications. Lower vehicle to ground.

### STABILIZER BAR

**Removal** — Raise vehicle at rear axle and place support stands beneath axle. Remove bolts from body and axle and remove stabilizer bar.

**Bushing Replacement** — Bushings are replaceable in both ends of stabilizer bar. Use suitable drift and press to remove and install bushings.

**Installation** — Attach stabilizer bar to body and axle mounts, leaving slightly loose. Lower vehicle to ground and jounce several times to settle stabilizer bar bushings. Torque stabilizer bar bolts to specifications.

### TIGHTENING SPECIFICATIONS

| Application | Ft. Lbs. (mkg) |
|---|---|
| Upper Control Arm-to-Axle | |
| Celica | 72-108 (10.0-15.0) |
| Cressida | 87-123 (12.0-17.0) |
| Upper Control Arm-to-Body | |
| Celica | 87-123 (12.0-17.0) |
| Cressida | 109-137 (15.0-19.0) |
| Lower Control Arm-to-Axle | |
| Celica | 72-108 (10.0-15.0) |
| Cressida | 87-123 (12.0-17.0) |
| Lower Control Arm-to-Body | |
| Celica & Cressida | 87-123 (12.0-17.0) |
| Stabilizer Bar-to-Axle | |
| Celica | 30-56 (4.1-7.7) |
| Cressida | 54-80 (7.5-11.0) |
| Stabilizer Bar-to-Body | |
| Celica | 51-65 (7.0-9.0) |
| Cressida | 65-98 (9.0-13.5) |

## TRIUMPH TR7

### TR7

### DESCRIPTION

Rear suspension system consists of a control arm (trailing arm), radius rod, and a stabilizer bar. A coil spring is mounted between body and control arm. Shock absorbers mount off axle housing at bottom and at top to body.

### ADJUSTMENT

#### WHEEL ALIGNMENT SPECIFICATIONS & PROCEDURES

*See Wheel Alignment Specifications in WHEEL ALIGNMENT Section.*

### REMOVAL & INSTALLATION

#### COIL SPRING & CONTROL ARM

**Removal** — Raise vehicle and place on safety stands. Remove wheel. Place jack under suspension control arm and compress spring ensuring vehicle does not come off stands. Remove two nuts and bolts mounting stabilizer bar to control arm. Remove nut and bolt securing rear end of suspension arm to axle bracket. Lower jack and remove spring and insulating rubbers. Detach suspension control arm front mounting and remove arm.

Lower Shock Absorber Mount

Stabilizer Bar

Body Bracket

Axle Bracket

Control Arm (Trailing Arm)

***Fig. 1 Detailed View of Control Arm Removal***

**Installation** — Insure spring insulators are in correctly, then fit spring. With jack positioned under control arm and front (body bracket end) of control arm installed, fit rear end of suspension control arm in axle bracket. Reconnect stabilizer bar to suspension arm and install wheel. Tighten suspension components with vehicle weight on ground.

### SHOCK ABSORBERS

**Removal** — Jack up vehicle and place on safety stands; remove wheel. On right side, remove fuel filler assembly. On left side, remove upper access plate. On both sides, disconnect upper end of shock absorber and remove hardware. Disconnect and remove lower shock absorber mounting, then pull shock absorber from vehicle.

**Installation** — To install, reverse removal procedure and tighten nuts.

### STABILIZER BAR

**Removal & Installation** — Raise vehicle and place on safety stands. Remove the four bolts mounting stabilizer bar to rear suspension arms. Remove stabilizer bar with shims, if equipped. To install, reverse removal procedure and ensure shims are refitted.

### RADIUS ROD

**Removal & Installation** — Raise vehicle and place on safety stands. Disconnect radius rod from rear axle bracket and from bracket attached to body; then remove radius rod. If bushings are damaged, press out of rod and install new ones. To install, reverse removal procedure.

Axle Bracket

Radius Rod

Body Bracket

***Fig. 2 Detailed View of Radius Rod Removal***

### TIGHTENING SPECIFICATIONS

| Application | Ft. Lbs. ( mg) |
| --- | --- |
| Stabilizer Bar-to-Control Arm | 30-37 (4.2-5.1) |
| Shock Absorber-to-Control Arm | 10-14 (1.4-1.9) |
| Shock Absorber-to-Body | 10-14 (1.4-1.9) |
| Suspension Arm-to-Axle Bracket | 38-48 (5.3-6.6) |
| Suspension Control Arm-to-Body Bracket | 38-48 (5.3-6.6) |

# Rear Suspension

## TRIUMPH SPITFIRE

**Spitfire**

### DESCRIPTION

Semi-trailing arm, independent type with a transverse leaf spring. Strut rods are connected at front to chassis and at rear to axle bearing carrier. Transverse leaf spring is mounted in center to differential and at ends to mounts connected to bearing carrier. Hydraulic shock absorbers are mounted between bearing carrier at bottom and chassis at top.

**Fig. 1  Exploded View of Rear Suspension Assembly**

### ADJUSTMENT

#### WHEEL ALIGNMENT SPECIFICATIONS & PROCEDURES

See Wheel Alignment Specifications and Procedures in WHEEL ALIGNMENT Section.

### REMOVAL & INSTALLATION

#### TRANSVERSE LEAF SPRING

**Removal** — Raise vehicle, position safety stands under chassis and remove both rear wheels. Remove bolts connecting transverse leaf spring to bearing carrier mount. Place a jack under lower shock absorber mount and disconnect lower shock absorber from mount on bearing carrier. From inside luggage compartment, remove plate covering spring mount on differential. Remove nuts and clamp plate from spring mount. Remove mounting studs from differential and pull spring out through side of fender well.

**Installation** — To install transverse leaf spring, reverse removal procedure. Spring is marked "FRONT" and must be installed correctly. Do not tighten spring to bearing carrier bolts until weight of vehicle is on rear wheels.

#### STRUT RODS

**Removal** — Raise vehicle, position safety stands under chassis and remove wheels. Place a jack under lower shock absorber mount and raise jack until strut rod bolts can be removed easily. If shims are removed from strut rod mount on chassis, make sure the same amount of shims are reinstalled.

**Installation** — To install strut rod, reverse removal procedure. Install same amount of shims at front mount as were removed and check rear wheel alignment.

#### BEARING CARRIER MOUNTS

**Removal** — Raise vehicle, position safety stands under chassis and remove wheel and tire. Disconnect strut rod from bearing carrier mount. Disconnect lower shock absorber mount. Remove bolt securing transverse leaf spring to bearing carrier mount. Remove pivot bolt securing mount to bearing carrier and remove mount.

**Installation** — To install bearing carrier mounts, reverse removal procedure.

**Fig. 2  Components to Remove to Take Out Bearing Carrier Mount**

### TIGHTENING SPECIFICATIONS

| Application | Ft. Lbs. (mkg) |
| --- | --- |
| Lower Shock Absorber Mount | 28-38 (3.9-5.3) |
| Upper Shock Absorber Mount | 38-48 (5.3-6.6) |
| Strut Rod Pivot Bolts | 24-32 (3.3-4.4) |
| Strut Rod Bracket-to-Chassis | 24-32 (3.3-4.4) |
| Mounts-to-Bearing Carrier | 38-48 (5.3-6.6) |
| Transverse Spring Pivot Bolts | 38-48 (5.3-6.6) |

## VOLKSWAGEN TYPE 1

### Type 1

## DESCRIPTION

Independent torsion bar type rear suspension. Torsion bars are mounted inside rear crossmember tube and anchor in center by means of a splined hub. Outer ends of torsion bars mount into splined hubs integral with spring plates. Control arm and spring plate mount together. Control arms pivot in mounts connected to crossmember tube and also serve as rear wheel bearing carriers. Hydraulic shock absorbers mount off control arms.

**Fig. 1  Volkswagen Type 1 Rear Suspension Components**

## ADJUSTMENT

### WHEEL ALIGNMENT SPECIFICATIONS & PROCEDURES

*See Wheel Alignment Specifications and Procedures in WHEEL ALIGNMENT Section.*

## REMOVAL & INSTALLATION

### SHOCK ABSORBERS

**Removal** — Raise vehicle and place on safety stands. Remove wheel. Remove both bottom and top mounting nuts and bolts, then slide shock absorber from vehicle.

**Installation** — Inspect for hydraulic leaks and replace shock absorber if excessive leaking is apparent. Check shock absorber for smooth, even operation. To install, reverse removal procedure.

### CONTROL ARMS

**Removal** — 1) Remove cotter pin and loosen rear hub nut. Raise vehicle and place safety stands under body. Remove wheel. Remove shock absorber. Remove bolts mounting axle drive shaft to stub axle. Separate axle drive shaft from stub axle and wire out of way. Use protective cap to cover exposed end of axle drive shaft.

2) Remove drum and disconnect parking brake and hydraulic lines. Index mark spring plate in relation to a point on control arm. Remove control arm pivot bolt and remove control arm from vehicle.

**Installation** — To install, reverse removal procedure. Tighten pivot bolt and lock in place by staking edge to metal shoulder on bracket. Align spring plate marks with those on control arm. Bleed brake system.

### TORSION BARS & SPRING PLATES

**Removal** — 1) Disconnect control arm from spring plate as previously described. Remove bolts securing hub cover and remove cover.

2) Pry spring plate off lower stop cast into torsion bar housing. Remove spring plate and withdraw torsion bar. If torsion bar is broken, opposite side torsion bar must be removed to drive out broken piece.

**Installation** — 1) Inspect torsion bar and spring plate for wear or distortion. Inspect rubber mounts for cracking or wear. Torsion bars are marked left and right and should be installed accordingly. Coat torsion bar splines with grease and install in vehicle. Coat rubber supports with talcum powder. Make sure part of rubber support marked "Oben" is installed facing up.

**NOTE** — *See appropriate article in WHEEL ALIGNMENT section for setting torsion bar.*

2) Install spring plate in position. Install hub cover and secure with 2 bolts. Raise spring plate using a spring compressor and install remaining hub cover bolts. Install remaining components in reverse of removal procedure. Recheck wheel alignment.

## TIGHTENING SPECIFICATIONS

| Application | Ft. Lbs. (mkg) |
|---|---|
| Shock Absorber Upper and Lower Mounts | 43 (6.0) |
| Control Arm Pivot Bolt | 87 (12.0) |
| Spring Plate-to-Control Arm | 80 (11.0) |
| Spring Plate Hub Cover Bolts | 25 (3.5) |
| Axle Drive Shaft-to-Stub Axle | 25 (3.5) |
| Rear Axle Hub Nut | 217 (30.0) |

## VOLKSWAGEN TYPE 2

Type 2

### DESCRIPTION

Independent torsion bar type rear suspension. Torsion bars mount in rear crossmember tube and anchor in center of tube by means of a splined hub. Outer ends of torsion bars mount into splined hubs integral with spring plates. Control arms are connected to spring plates. Control arms pivot in mounts connected to crossmember tube and connect at ends to rear wheel bearing housing. Hydraulic shock absorbers mount between control arms and bracket integral with chassis.

**Fig. 1    Exploded View of Rear Suspension Assembly**

### ADJUSTMENT

#### WHEEL ALIGNMENT SPECIFICATIONS & PROCEDURES

*See Wheel Alignment Specifications and Procedures in WHEEL ALIGNMENT Section.*

### REMOVAL & INSTALLATION

#### CONTROL ARMS

**Removal** — 1) Remove cotter pin and loosen rear axle hub nut. Raise vehicle and place safety stands under body. Remove

wheel and tire. Remove bolts from axle drive shaft at stub axle and separate axle drive shaft from stub axle. Disconnect shock absorbers from control arm.

2) Disconnect brake line and parking brake cable from backing plate. Mark position of spring plate in relation to control arm. Remove bolts securing spring plate to control arm. Remove control arm pivot bolt and remove control arm from vehicle.

**Installation** — 1) Install control arm in vehicle in an extended position, then tighten pivot bolt. Attach control arm to spring plate with index marks make during removal properly aligned; tighten bolts.

2) To install remaining components, reverse removal procedure and tighten all nuts and bolts. Check wheel alignment if new control arm has been installed.

#### SPRING PLATES & TORSION BARS

**Removal** — Disconnect spring plate from control arm as previously outlined. Remove bolts securing hub cover to crossmember and remove hub cover. Pry spring plate off lower stop (cast in housing) and pull spring plate out. Withdraw torsion bar. If broken torsion bar is being removed, opposite side torsion bar must be removed to drive out broken piece.

**Installation** — 1) Inspect torsion bar and spring plate for wear or distortion. Inspect rubber support bushings for wear or cracking. Grease torsion bar splines and install in vehicle. Torsion bars are marked left and right, install accordingly. Coat rubber bushings with talcum powder before installation.

**NOTE** — *See appropriate article in WHEEL ALIGNMENT section for setting torsion bar.*

2) Install spring plate on torsion bar. Install rubber bushing and hub cover and secure hub cover with 2 bolts. Raise spring plate using spring compressor type tool. Install remaining bolts and tighten. Install remaining components and check wheel alignment.

### TIGHTENING SPECIFICATIONS

| Application | Ft. Lbs. (mkg) |
| --- | --- |
| Control Arm-to-Bearing Housing | 94 (13.0) |
| Control Arm Pivot Bolt | 43 (6.0) |
| Rear Axle Hub Nut | 253 (35.0) |
| Shock Absorber Mounting Bolts | 43 (6.0) |
| Torsion Bar Hub Cover | 35 (4.5) |
| Axle Drive Shaft-to-Stub Axle | 25 (3.5) |

# Rear Suspension

## VOLKSWAGEN DASHER

**Dasher**

### DESCRIPTION

Rear suspension is coil spring type utilizing a transverse mounted suspension rod and a trailing arm. Suspension rod is used to improve stability. Shock absorbers mount off bracket on axle beam and to upper body. Coil spring rides in spring seat welded to axle beam and wedges against damper ring at chassis/body.

### ADJUSTMENTS

#### WHEEL ALIGNMENT SPECIFICATIONS & PROCEDURES

See *Wheel Alignment Specifications and Procedures* in *WHEEL ALIGNMENT* Section.

#### WHEEL BEARING ADJUSTMENT

See *Wheel Bearing Adjustment* in *WHEEL ALIGNMENT* Section

### REMOVAL & INSTALLATION

#### REAR AXLE BEAM ASSEMBLY

**Removal** — **1)** Raise vehicle and place safety stands under body. Take nuts off parking brake linkage equalizer bar. Force parking brake plastic cable guide bushing from clip holder. Pry down and unhook muffler from front bracket. Separate all brake cables from body mountings.

**Fig. 1    Exploded View of Dasher Rear Suspension**

Labels: Damping Ring, Shock Absorber, Coil Spring, Transverse Suspension Rod, Axle Beam, Trailing Arm, Rubber Bushing & Sleeve, Rubber Bushing & Sleeve

**2)** Disconnect brake lines and plug open ends. Remove trailing arm mounting bolts from body. Detach muffler from rear mounting. Remove suspension rod-to-axle mounting bolt. Detach lower end of shock absorber and guide rear axle assembly (on a jack) from vehicle.

**Bushing Replacement** — Place trailing arm in press and force bushing from arm. Make sure when installing new bushings that bushing slots are aligned horizontally in arm.

**Installation** — **1)** To install rear axle assembly, reverse removal procedure and note the following: Make sure trailing arm bushings are free of tension. Before tightening trailing arm bolts ensure arms are in middle of moving range.

**Fig. 2    Measurement Points for Installing Rear Axle Beam**

Labels: Lower Edge of Fender Lip, 10.6" (270 mm), Center of Axle, 2.75" (70 mm), Bushing Center

**2)** Lift axle beam until center of axle (See *Fig. 2*) is 2.75" (70 mm) higher than center of bushing in trailing arm. Check distance between axle center to lower edge of fender lip. Distance should be 10.6" (270 mm). Tighten bolts.

**NOTE** — *Only tighten bolts with axle in this position.*

#### TRANSVERSE SUSPENSION ROD

**Removal & Installation** — Raise vehicle and place on safety stands. Remove suspension rod mounting bolts and tap bolts free from mounting bushings. Inspect mounting bushings and sleeves for excessive wear or damage; replace as necessary. To install, reverse removal procedure.

#### SHOCK ABSORBER

**Removal & Installation** — Raise vehicle and place on safety stands. Remove shock absorber lower mounting bolt. Remove upper mount bolt and slide shock absorber from vehicle.
**NOTE** — *Lower mounting bolt must be removed first. Upper mounting bolt must be installed first.*

### TIGHTENING SPECIFICATIONS

| Application | Ft. Lbs. (mkg) |
| --- | --- |
| Shock Absorber Mounting Bolts | 43 (6.0) |
| Suspension Rod Mounting Bolts | 50 (7.0) |
| Trailing Arm Bolt | 43 (6.0) |

## VOLKSWAGEN RABBIT & SCIROCCO

**Rabbit**
**Scirocco**

### DESCRIPTION

Rear suspension is a link type with coil springs and using control arms and torsion beam for stabilization. Control arm and torsion beam are combined as one unit. Hydraulic shock absorbers are mounted inside coil springs and attached to control arm at the bottom and to vehicle body at the top.

### REMOVAL & INSTALLATION

#### SUSPENSION STRUT & COIL SPRING

**Removal** – 1) Leave vehicle on ground. Take off plastic cap covering rear strut upper mounting nuts. Remove nuts.

2) Slowly raise vehicle until weight is off spring. Remove bolt holding lower end of strut shock absorber to axle beam mount. Raise vehicle until strut can be removed.

**NOTE** – *It is not necessary to use spring compressor to disassemble strut.*

**Disassembly** – Set strut assembly in vise. Hold piston rod and remove strut mounting nut. Take off components down to slotted nut. Remove slotted nut. Take off spacer and coil spring.

**Inspection** – 1) Hand check shock absorber for even resistance through entire piston stroke. Worn shock absorbers cannot be overhauled.

2) There are three spring classes used in production. Springs are identified with 1, 2, or 3 paint stripes. Replacement springs come only with 2 paint stripes and can be used in conjunction

*Fig. 1  Exploded View of Rabbit/Scirocco Rear
Suspension Components*

## VOLKSWAGEN RABBIT & SCIROCCO (Cont.)

with any spring (Scirocco only). On Rabbit models only, springs must be matched sets with corresponding matched rubber bumpers.

**NOTE** — *Be sure protective cap is properly installed or dirt and water can enter shock absorber and cause damage.*

**Reassembly** — 1) Fit protective cap on shock absorber. Install rubber buffer, with small diameter end downward. Insert snap ring and washer.

2) Place spring into lower seat. Fit upper retainer with spacer sleeve. Tighten slotted nut holding piston rod. Put on remaining upper mounting hardware and tighten piston rod.

**Installation** — Reverse removal procedure.

### SUSPENSION ASSEMBLY

**Removal** — 1) Leave vehicle on ground. Disconnect upper strut mounting at body. Raise vehicle and support at rear with jack stands.

2) Disconnect parking brake at holder near rear axle mount. Disconnect and plug brake lines. Leave flex hose attached to suspension.

3) Separate brake pressure regulator spring from axle beam on models so equipped. Remove both nuts mounting axle beam on each side to body.

**Installation** — 1) If axle beam mounting has been removed, use *Fig. 2* to correctly adjust mounting pad. If pad is not correctly aligned, torsional preload of mounting bushings will be incorrect.

2) Position rear suspension on body. Refit nuts keeping axle beam to body. Raise wheel and guide upper end of strut into body mounting.

3) Connect parking brake cables. Connect brake lines. Lower vehicle and tighten upper strut mounting nuts. Bleed brake system.

### AXLE BEAM PIVOT BUSHING

**NOTE** — *Procedure given is for replacing bushing with axle beam installed in vehicle.*

**Removal** — 1) Raise and support vehicle so axle beam pivot bolt is not under load.

2) Remove 2 nuts holding axle beam to body and tap out pivot bolt.

3) Press out bushing. Select new bushing and press bushing into place. Loosely install mounting on axle beam. Concave washer and bolt head must face toward outside of vehicle. Bolt head must recess into washer.

4) Align mount as shown in *Fig. 2*. Tighten pivot bolt nut. Lower vehicle.

Align Mounting Surface "A"
with Imaginary Line "B"
Torque Pivot Bolt "C"
43 ft. lbs. (6.0 mkg)

**Fig. 2   Drawing Showing Correct Mounting Pad Alignment**

## TIGHTENING SPECIFICATIONS

| Application | Ft. Lbs. (mkg) |
| --- | --- |
| Shock Absorber-to-Axle Beam | 32 (4.5) |
| Piston Shock Absorber Top Mounting | 25 (3.5) |
| Coil Spring Retainer-to-Piston Rod | 14 (2.0) |
| Rear Axle Beam-to-Mounting Pad | 43 (6.0) |
| Rear Axle Mounting-to-Body | 32 (4.5) |

## VOLVO

**240 Series**
**260 Series**

### DESCRIPTION

Rear suspension consists of coil springs mounted between control arms and body rubber mounts, double-acting shock absorbers mounted on control arms and to body, a stabilizer bar attached at both ends to control arms, two torque rods running forward from axle brackets and a track bar attached nearly parallel to axle housing.

*Fig. 1  Exploded View of Volvo Rear Suspension*

### REMOVAL & INSTALLATION

#### COIL SPRINGS

**Removal** — Raise vehicle and place on safety stands. Remove tires and wheels. Place jack under rear axle housing and jack up axle until spring compresses. Disconnect lower shock absorber mounting, then remove spring lower retaining nut. Lower jack and remove coil spring.

**Installation** — To install, reverse removal procedure and tighten all nuts and bolts. Make sure rubber spring support is in correct position.

### SHOCK ABSORBER

**Removal** — Raise rear of vehicle and support on safety stands. Remove wheel and tire. Use jack to raise rear axle. Remove upper and lower attaching nuts, then remove shock absorber.

**Installation** — To install, reverse removal procedure and make sure spacer sleeve is in correct position.

### CONTROL ARMS

**Removal** — Raise rear of vehicle and position on safety stands. Position jack under rear axle housing and jack up axle until spring compresses. Disconnect shock absorber from control arm. Remove coil spring lower retaining nut, then remove spring. Remove control arm attaching bolts, and control arm.

**Installation** — Install attaching bolts for forward end of control arm, then install rear control arm bolts (only finger tight). Install coil spring and lower plate attaching nut. Raise rear axle while guiding coil spring into position. Attach shock absorber lower mount. Lower vehicle to ground and tighten control arm bolts to specifications.

### STABILIZER BAR

**Removal** — Raise vehicle and place safety stand just in front of rear jack supports. With a jack, raise rear axle to take load off shock absorbers. Disconnect stabilizer bar mountings and guide stabilizer bar from vehicle.

**Installation** — Fit stabilizer bar in position on brackets. Put nuts on finger tight. Remount lower end of shock absorber. Maneuver stabilizer bar so it settles in bracket. Tighten all nuts.

### TORQUE RODS & TRACK BAR

**Removal** — Raise rear of vehicle and place on safety stands. Disconnect track rod from mounting on body and rear axle. Inspect both bushings and sleeves for damage or excessive wear.

**Installation** — To install, reverse removal procedure.

## TIGHTENING SPECIFICATIONS

| Application | Ft. Lbs. (mkg) |
|---|---|
| Track Bar-to-Axle | 43 (6.0) |
| Track Bar-to-Body | 61 (8.5) |
| Shock Absorber Bolts | 61 (8.5) |
| Stabilizer Bar | |
| M10 Thread Bolt | 33 (4.5) |
| M12 Thread Bolt | 61 (8.5) |
| Control Arm Bolts | 94 (13.0) |
| Torque Rod Bolts | 61 (8.5) |

# Pneumatic Suspension

## MERCEDES-BENZ 6.9

### DESCRIPTION

The hydropneumatic suspension is a gas pressure suspension system with hydraulic level control. The vehicle load is supported by four struts, which also serve as shock absorbers. Suspension is accomplished by the compression and decompression of the gas cushion in the pressure reservoirs. To regulate the vehicle level, the oil volume in the suspension struts is increased or reduced by means of a hydraulic system. The hydraulic system is comprised of; oil pump, pressure regulator, main pressure reservoir and oil reservoir. The pressure regulator and level selector valve are combined into one valve unit.

### OPERATION

The hydraulic oil pump delivers oil from the oil reservoir to the main pressure reservoir via pressure regulator of valve unit. When the maximum oil pressure is reached, the pressure regulator revereses the oil flow. If the main oil pressure drops to the minimum, pressure regulator will reverse the flow and oil will be pumped into the main pressure reservoir until maximum pressure is again reached. If vehicle level drops due to increased load, levelling valve will open. Oil flowing into suspension struts will lift vehicle until normal level is reached. If load is reduced, levelling valve will permit oil to flow from suspension

1 — Hydraulic Oil Pump
2 — Hydraulic Oil Reservoir
3 — Valve Unit
3a — Pressure Regulator of Valve Unit
3b — Level Selector Valve of Valve Unit
3e — Control Knob
4 — Main Pressure Reservoir
5 — Electir Pressure Switch
6 — Levelling Valve, Front Axle
11 — Pressure Reservoir, Left Front
12 — Pressure Reservoir, Right Front
13 — Suspension Strut, Left Front
20 — Suspension Strut, Right Front
23 — Warning Light
24 — Levelling Valve, Rear

28 — Pressure Reservoir, Left Rear
29 — Pressure Reservoir, Right Rear
30 — Suspension Strut, Left Rear
31 — Suspension Strut, Right Rear
A — Suction Line
B1 — Pressure Line
B2 — Pressure Line, Regulator Valve to Main Pressure Reservoir
B3 — Pressure Line, Main Pressure to Selector Valve
B4 — Pressure Line, Selector Valve to Levelling Valve
B5 — Pressure Line, Levelling Valve to Pressure Reservoir
B6 — Pressure Line, Pressure Reservoir to Suspension Struts
C — Control Pressure Line
D1 — Return Line, Levelling Valve to Pressure Regulator
D2 — Return Line

*Fig. 1  Mercedes-Benz Hydropneumatic Suspension System*

## MERCEDES-BENZ 6.9 (Cont.)

struts until vehicle is back to normal level. The oil flowing from struts, is returned to oil reservoir after going through a filter.

**NOTE** — *When towing vehicle equipped with Hydropneumatic Suspension, instrument panel switch must be placed in "S" (Detent) position.*

## REMOVAL & INSTALLATION

### FRONT SHOCK ABSORBERS

**Removal** — Move switch on instrument panel to the normal position. Jack up front of vehicle and remove front wheel. Separate high-pressure hose and leak hose from lines in wheel housing. Loosen upper shock attaching bolt. Remove lower attaching bolt and remove shock.

**Inspection** — Check high-pressure hose, leak oil hose rubber mount and ball joint. Replace if required.

**Installation** — Install in reverse of removal procedure.

*Fig. 2 Adjusting Switch for Valve Unit*

### REAR SHOCK ABSORBERS

**Removal** — Remove rear seat and back rest, remove rear trunk cover. Loosen nut on upper shock mount, remove washer and rubber ring. Jack up rear of vehicle. Remove high-pressure hose on reservoir and disconnect leak oil hose from line. Loosen lower attaching bolt and remove rear shock.

**Inspection** — Check high-pressure hose, leak oil hose rubber mount and ball joint. Replace if required.

**Installation** — 1) Insert shock into dome on frame floor. Mount lower attaching bolt, install upper attaching bolt, do not tighten. Align high-pressure hose and leak hose, by turning shock.

2) Lower vehicle, tighten upper attaching bolt and replace cover. Install rear seat and back rest. Check oil level in system and correct.

### FRONT PRESSURE RESERVOIR

**Removal** — 1) Move switch on instrument panel to normal postion. Jack up front of vehicle. Remove left wheel, disconnect

pressure lines on pressure reservoir. Loosen pressure reservoir and remove.

2) Remove battery and battery frame, from right side of vehicle. Disconnect pressure line from pressure reservoir. Remove reservoir.

**Installation** — Install in reverse of removal procedure.

**NOTE** — *When vehicle is lowered, the lever of the level controller will move into "filling postion". Since the capacity of the central reservoir is not enough for filling the suspension components, keep the engine operating.*

### REAR PRESSURE RESERVOIR

**Removal** — With switch in normal position, jack up rear of vehicle. Disconnect pressure lines from reservoir. Remove reservoir.

**Installation** — Install in reverse of removal procedure.

### CENTRAL RESERVOIR

**Removal** — 1) Disconnect puller for adjusting switch upon removal of locking ring and move disc of adjusting switch into assembly position. Jack up vehicle at front and remove left front wheel.

2) Disconnect pressure lines from central reservoir. Disconnect cable plug connection on front end. Pull cable with plug and rubber sleeve into wheel house. Loosen reservoir at front end and remove. Unscrew electrical pressure switch from central reservoir, while marking position of ring fitting.

**Installation** — Install in reverse of removal procedure.

### OIL PUMP

**Removal** — Disconnect suction and pressure lines from pump. Loosen attaching bolts and remove pump.

**Inspection** — Check driver and clutch components replace as required.

**Installation** — Install in reverse of removal procedure.

### VALVE UNIT

**Removal** — Disconnect puller for adjusting switch. Move control disc into position M (assembly). Loosen clip for puller, while applying counterhold at holder by using a hex socket wrench. Disconnect pressure lines from valve unit. Loosen attaching bolts of pressure regulator to oil reservoir and remove valve unit.

**Installation** — Install in reverse of removal procedure. noting the following: Install new sealing rings for sealing pressure regulator to oil reservoir.

### FRONT STABILIZER BAR

**Removal** — 1) Move adjusting switch on instrument panel (suspension valve switch) to "S" (Detent) position. This will lock in suspension pressure and hold it when vehicle is raised off ground.

2) Raise vehicle, with jacks placed under outer edges of lower control arms. Remove front wheels.

## MERCEDES-BENZ 6.9 (Cont.)

**3)** Loosen Allen screw on clamping piece of stabilizer bar-to-control arm. Remove large hex bolt from end of stabilizer bar. Remove 2 remaining hex bolts on clamping piece and remove clamping piece.

**4)** Remove master cylinder, booster, air cleaner, Climate Control (A/C) regulating valve, heater hoses and pipes, as required to gain clearance for stabilizer bar removal. Discharge A/C system and disconnect A/C lines and oil pressure line. Pull vacuum line of master vacuum system from pipe. Remove regulating linkage.

**5)** Detach connecting rod on lever of level controller (loosen hex nut while counterholding ball pin with 10 mm open-end wrench).

**NOTE** — *Do not pull ball pin out of socket.*

**6)** Remove stabilizer bar brackets. Mark rubber insulating mounts for reinstallation in proper position and on proper side. Remove stabilizer bar end covers from wheel wells. Remove stabilizer bar.

**7)** If necessary, remove actuating linkage for level controller at this time: detach clamping nuts and bracket from stabilizer bar. When reattaching, be sure lever of connecting shaft is against stabilizer bar.

**Fig. 3   Showing Positions of Level Controller Switch on Instrument Panel**

**Installation — 1)** Position stabilizer bar in vehicle. Attach stabilizer clamping pieces on ends with sleeves flush to bar. Attach support of upper control arm to stabilizer bar, tightening large end bolt as far as possible.

**2)** Install end covers to wheel wells. Position rubber bushings with splits rearward and install mounting brackets.

**3)** Attach connecting rod toward level controller. Install regulating linkage, water hoses and pipes. Connect vacuum hoses, A/C hoses and oil pressure line.

**4)** Install regulating valve for Climate Control (A/C) system. Install air cleaner, master cylinder and booster. Mount front wheels and lower vehicle to ground.

**5)** Completely tighten stabilizer-to-control arm support bolts and bracket mounting bolts.

**6)** Move suspension control switch to "NORMAL LEVEL" position. Recharge A/C system. Check and adjust vehicle level.

### REAR STABILIZER BAR

**Removal — 1)** Move adjusting switch to "S" (Detent) position. This will hold vehicle at normal riding level after it has been raised off ground.

**2)** Remove expanding bolts of wheel carrier support, on both sides. Detach connecting rod from lever of level controller by unscrewing hex nut while counterholding ballpin with 10 mm open-end wrench.

**NOTE** — *Do not pull ball pin from socket.*

**3)** Raise vehicle and remove right rear wheel. Remove rubber rings of rear axle suspension. Slightly lower and support exhaust pipe to allow additional clearance.

**4)** Unscrew hex bolts of stabilizer bar brackets. Pull stabilizer bar out toward right side. Remove actuation lever of level controller from stabilizer bar, if necessary.

**Installation — 1)** Attach level controller lever to stabilizer bar, making sure lever rests against bar.

**2)** Install rubber insulators on stabilizer bar with splits facing upward. Attach stabilizer bar mounting brackets. Reconnect exhaust pipe to original position.

**3)** Lower vehicle to ground. Connect stabilizer bar to wheel carriers, but do not fully tighten expanding bolts.

**NOTE** — *Be sure bolt contact surfaces are clean and grease-free.*

**4)** Attach connecting rod of level controller. Move level control switch, on instrument panel, to "N" (normal level) position. Check and adjust vehicle level. Fully tighten expanding bolts after all adjustments are complete.

**Fig. 4   Location of Hydropneumatic Level Controller Components on Rear Stabilizer Bar**

| System Capacity | |
| --- | --- |
| **Application** | **Pints (liters)** |
| Total System Oil Capacity ............................... | 12.3 (5.8) |
| Filling Capacity (On Dipstick) | |
| Maximum ................................ | 7.6 (3.6) |
| Minimum ................................ | 5.5 (2.6) |

# Section 10
# STEERING

# Contents

*NOTE – ALSO SEE GENERAL INDEX.*

# Steering

## MANUAL STEERING TROUBLE SHOOTING

| CONDITION | POSSIBLE CAUSE | CORRECTION |
|---|---|---|
| ▶ Hard steering | 1) Incorrect tire pressure<br>2) Gear housing lubricant low<br>3) Insufficient lubrication or abnormal wear on steering linkage<br>4) Siezed or damaged ball joints<br>5) Steering shaft too tight<br>6) Steering column incorrectly aligned | 1) Inflate tires to recommended psi<br>2) Refill and check for leaks<br>3) Lubricate or replace components<br>4) Replace ball joints<br>5) Readjust<br>6) Realign column |
| ▶ Drifting | 1) Incorrect tire pressure<br>2) Loose lug nuts<br>3) Mismatched tires<br>4) Worn or loose wheel bearings<br>5) Brake drag<br>6) Faulty shock absorbers or coil springs<br>7) Pitman arm binding<br>8) Loose steering gear<br><br>9) Vehicle uneven riding height | 1) Inflate tires to correct psi<br>2) Tighten<br>3) Replace and match<br>4) Replace or tighten<br>5) Check and readjust brakes<br>6) Replace broken or faulty parts<br>7) Adjust or replace arm<br>8) Check for worn parts replace and adjust<br>9) Adjust level |
| ▶ Excessive steering wheel play | 1) Steering wheel shaft loose or worn<br>2) Steering linkage loose or worn<br>3) Worn wheel bearings<br>4) Worn ball joints<br>5) Worm shaft bearing out of adjustment<br>6) Loose steering gear housing | 1) Adjust shaft or replace<br><br>2) Adjust or repalce<br>3) Replace bearings<br>4) Replace or adjust ball joints<br>5) Readjust<br><br>6) Tighten housing |
| ▶ Steering wheel slides | 1) Worm shaft or ball damaged<br>2) Sector shaft damaged | 1) Replace components<br>2) Replace components |
| ▶ Vibration or shimmy | 1) Incorrect tire pressure<br>2) Tire out of balance<br>3) Worn shock absorbers or springs<br>4) Loose steering gear housing<br>5) Loose steering linkage | 1) Inflate to correct psi<br>2) Balance tire<br>3) Replace defective parts<br>4) Tighten<br>5) Adjust or replace linkage |
| ▶ Noise | 1) Incorrect tire pressure<br>2) Wheel bearings loose or worn<br>3) Hub caps or rims loose | 1) Inflate tires to correct psi<br>2) Repair or replace<br>3) Tighten or replace |

## POWER STEERING TROUBLE SHOOTING

| CONDITION | POSSIBLE CAUSE | CORRECTION |
|---|---|---|
| ▶ Hard Steering | 1) Shipping spacers between column tube and shaft or in flexible couplings<br>2) Fluid level low<br>3) Control valve binding<br>4) Kinked or broken hoses<br>5) Fluid lines blocked<br>6) Air in system<br>7) Low pump pressure<br><br>8) Loose drive belt | 1) Remove spacers<br><br><br>2) Add fluid, check for leaks<br>3) Replace or repair control valve<br>4) Straighten or replace<br>5) Check, clean, or replace lines<br>6) Bleed, refill and check for leaks<br>7) Check pump for worn or damaged parts<br>8) Adjust or replace belt |
| ▶ Noise | 1) Loose drive belt<br>2) Low fluid<br>3) Faulty valves or pump wear | 1) Check, tighten, or replace belt<br>2) Check and add fluid<br>3) Repair or replace |
| ▶ Excessive steering wheel play | 1) Control valve binding | 1) Repair or replace valve |
| ▶ Sticking steering wheel | 1) Binding control valve | 1) Repair or replace valve |

## ARROW, CHALLENGER, COLT & SAPPORO

Arrow
Challenger
Colt
Sapporo

### REMOVAL & INSTALLATION

#### HORN BUTTON & STEERING WHEEL

Pry off horn pad. Mark relative position of steering wheel on the shaft for reassembly reference. Remove steering wheel nut, then use a puller (CT-1126) to remove steering wheel.

**CAUTION** — *Do not use excessive force to remove the steering wheel from the shaft.*

#### COMBINATION SWITCH (TURN SIGNAL, WIPER/WASHER, HAZARD, DIMMER)

To remove the combination switch assembly, tilt steering wheel to its lowest position, remove cover from switch assembly, disconnect switch wiring and withdraw switch assembly from column.

## AUDI

Fox
5000

### REMOVAL & INSTALLATION

#### STEERING WHEEL & HORN

**5000** — Disconnect battery ground. Using hand pressure, force off steering wheel center pad. When withdrawing pad make sure horn leads slide out of recess in steering wheel. Unscrew steering wheel nut and use wheel puller to remove steering wheel.

**Fox** — Pull off steering wheel horn control pad by hand. Disconnect ground wire at horn button. Unscrew mounting nut and remove steering wheel.

#### TURN SIGNAL, WIPER/WASHER HAZARD, DIMMER

**5000** — Remove steering wheel. Working through hole in bottom of column shrouding, release mounting and take off shroud. Disconnect electrical wire connectors and undo switch mounting screws. Lift out switches.

#### TURN SIGNAL, WIPER/WASHER, DIMMER

**Fox** — Remove steering wheel. Unscrew 3 steering column switch housing mounting screws and pull housing off column tube. Make sure electrical wires are disconnected before completely pulling off switch housing. Remove switch mounting screws and take out switches.

Fig. 1   Audi 5000 Steering Wheel Assembly

Labels: 36 Lbs. (5 mkg) All Models; Center Pad (Horn Bar); Steering Column Switch Housing; Carbon Brushes Lube Before Installation

#### STEERING COLUMN LOCK

**All Models** — Remove lower cover. Disconnect electrical wires from back of ignition switch. Drill out shear bolts. Separate lock from column. Refit lock assembly in reverse of removal procedure. Make sure lugs on steering lock engage column tube. Tighten mounting bolts until heads shear off.

## BMW

320i
530i
633CSi
733i

### REMOVAL & INSTALLATION

#### STEERING WHEEL

**Removal** — Place wheels in straight-ahead position. Pry steering wheel cover off to expose wheel mounting nut. Index mark wheel and main shaft. Remove mounting nut and pull steering wheel off main shaft.

**Installation** — To install, reverse removal procedure and refer to reference marks made during removal.

#### HORN CONTROLS

**Horn Button** — Remove screw on back side of steering wheel spoke to free horn button.

**Contact Spring** — Pry off cover concealing contact spring. Replace spring if broken or if spring is unable to provide adequate contact. Make sure contact pins face inward when reinstalling existing spring or fitting new one.

**Slip Ring** — Disconnect electrical lead at each spoke. Remove 2 slip ring mounting screws and slide slip ring off steering wheel.

## BMW (Cont.)

**Fig. 1 Screws to Take Out for Slip Ring Removal**

### TURN SIGNAL & DIMMER SWITCH

**Removal** — Disconnect battery ground cable. Remove 3 mounting screws and pull down lower shroud. Remove steering wheel as previously outlined. Separate wiring from mounting straps on steering column. On 320i models, disconnect electrical plug under instrument panel. On other models, disconnect central fuse/relay plug. Remove 4 switch mounting screws and slide off switch with harness.

**Installation** — To install, reverse removal procedure and note: Make sure steering wheel is lined up with reference marks. Ensure turn signal assembly is centered. Finger on cancelling cam must face toward center. Distance between switch and finger should be about .118" (3 mm).

**Fig. 2 Cancelling Cam and Finger with Clearance Shown**

### IGNITION SWITCH

**Removal (Exc. 733i)** — 1) Disconnect battery ground cable. Remove 3 mounting screws and pull off lower plastic shroud. Remove hollow set screw and slide out ignition switch. Disconnect horn wires on 320i models only.

**2)** Disconnect steering column wire holders. On 530i and 633CSi models only, disconnect central fuse/relay plate plug and plug connector. On 320i models only, disconnect central plug. Ignition switch is free for removal.

**Installation** — To install, reverse removal procedure and note following: Make sure to turn ignition key all the way back before inserting. Set ignition switch at "O" position before installing. On 320i models only, marks on ignition switch must oppose each other.

**Fig. 3 Location of Shear Bolts. View Looking Up From Under Steering Column. All Models Except 320i**

### STEERING LOCK

**Removal (Exc. 320i)** — 1) Disconnect battery ground. Remove steering wheel. Remove 3 screws holding lower steering column shroud. Disconnect and remove turn signal and wiper/washer switch plate.

**2)** Remove shear bolts from switch plate with chisel. Remove set screw on outside of steering column tube. Pull out ignition switch. Remove steering lock plate shear bolt and pull out steering lock.

**Installation** — To install, reverse removal procedure.

**Removal; 320i** — Disconnect electrical wires from under instrument panel. Remove shroud. Remove shear bolt from lock plate and pull out steering lock.

**Installation** — To install, reverse removal procedure.

## CAPRI

### Capri

## REMOVAL & INSTALLATION

### STEERING WHEEL

**Removal** — Align wheels in straight-ahead position. Remove two screws securing steering column shroud and detach both halves. Pry out steering wheel center emblem. Unscrew steering wheel nut. Note alignment marks on wheel and shaft. Pull off steering wheel, using hand pressure only.

**Installation** — To install, reverse removal procedure, noting the following: Realign positioning marks of steering wheel and shaft. Ensure turn signal cancelling cam is engaged in groove on underside of steering wheel.

### TURN SIGNAL & IGNITION SWITCHES

**Removal** — Disconnect battery. Remove steering column shroud upper and lower halves. Remove turn signal switch retaining screws, disconnect electrical plug and remove turn signal switch. Place ignition key in the "O" position, then remove screws from the lower left trim panel. Disconnect electrical plug from emergency flasher then remove trim panel. Disconnect ignition wires at connector then remove screws securing ignition switch to lock and remove ignition switch.

**Installation** — To install, reverse removal procedure, making sure that ignition key is in the "O" position and all wires are reconnected.

**Fig. 1   Capri Steering Wheel Components**

## COURIER

### Courier

## REMOVAL & INSTALLATION

### STEERING WHEEL & COMBINATION SWITCH

**Removal** — 1) Disconnect battery ground cable. Remove steering wheel nut cover. Index mark main shaft and steering wheel. Disconnect electrical leads. Pull steering wheel from shaft.

2) Remove plastic hazard light indicator and steering column shroud. Disconnect electrical wires at base of steering column. Remove headlight switch knob from shaft.

3) Remove snap ring retaining switch and force turn indicator cancelling cam off shaft. Take out single bolt, near bottom of switch, and pull out complete switch assembly.

**Installation** — 1) Fit switch assembly on steering column then, refit one retaining bolt. Place turn indicator cancelling cam into position and install snap ring. Reconnect electrical plug at column base.

2) Insert and tighten headlight knob switch. Install column shroud and plastic hazard light indicator. Refit steering wheel with index marks aligned. Connect battery ground cable.

**Fig. 1   Top View of Steering Column with Steering Wheel Removed to Expose Combination Switch**

## DATSUN

B210
F10
200SX
280Z
510
810
Pickup

## REMOVAL & INSTALLATION

### STEERING WHEEL & HORN PAD

**Removal** — 1) Use following list for removal of steering wheel for particular model:

- On B210 models, disconnect battery ground cable. On resin model steering wheels, remove bolts on rear side of steering wheel bar. Pull out pad. Disconnect electrical wires. On 3 spoke steering wheels pad just pulls (pops) off.
- On F10 models, disconnect battery ground. On Hatchback models, remove horn pad, contact plates and spring, and contact base plate. On other models, horn pad is removed by unscrewing bolts from rear side of steering wheel.
- On 200SX and 280Z models, disconnect battery ground. Push in on horn pad and rotate counterclockwise.
- On 510, 810 and Pickup models, disconnect battery ground. Remove 2 bolts on rear side of steering wheel bar and slide off horn pad.

2) Index mark top of steering column with steering wheel. Remove wheel mounting nut. Use suitable puller and extract steering wheel.

**NOTE** — *Do not hammer on steering wheel. Pounding may cause damage to collapsible steering column.*

**Installation** — On all models, reverse removal procedure. Grease any sliding components. Match index marks made during removal. Check operation.

### TURN SIGNAL SWITCH & DIMMER SWITCH

**Removal (Except F10, 280Z, 810)** — Disconnect battery ground cable. Remove steering wheel as previously outlined. Remove screws holding upper and lower shrouding together. Disconnect switch connector. Remove screws holding switch to column and lift switch off shaft.. Switch may come apart in 2 pieces.

**NOTE** — *On Pickup models switch connector is near lower edge of instrument panel.*

**Installation** — To install, reverse removal procedure. Make sure switch tab locates in hole in column.

**Removal & Installation; F10** — Removal of turn signal switch is same as outlined for other models. To remove dimmer switch, disconnect battery ground. Remove column cover. Disconnect wiring connector. Remove both retaining screws. Slide out switch. Refit by reversing removal procedure.

### COMBINATION SWITCH

**NOTE** — *On 280Z and 810 models combination switch controls Turn Signal, Dimmer, Wiper/Washer.*

**Removal (280Z and 810)** — Disconnect battery ground cable. Remove shroud cover mounting screws and take shrouding away from steering column. Disconnect lead wires from combination switch (5 connectors). Remove mounting screws and separate switches from steering column mounting. Switches will come apart in 2 pieces.

### HAZARD WARNING SWITCH

**Removal (F10, B210, 510)** — Disconnect battery ground cable. Remove mounting screws and take off top shrouding from steering column. Disconnect lead wires at connector. Remove retaining screws and take switch out of shroud.

**Installation** — To install, reverse removal procedure.

**Installation** — To install, reverse removal procedure.

**Removal (Pickup)** — Disconnect battery ground. Disconnect multi-plug connector lead wire from instrument harness wiring. Remove upper shrouding. Remove screws mounting switch to lower shrouding cover. Remove switch.

**Installation** — To install, reverse removal procedure.

*Fig. 1  Steps for Removing and Installing Steering Wheel and Combination Switch*

## DATSUN (Cont.)

### STEERING LOCK & IGNITION SWITCH

**Removal** — Disconnect battery ground. Remove steering column shrouding. Drill out shear bolts. Steering lock should be free to separate from steering column. If ignition switch is to be removed from lock, separate electrical connector then remove small set screw holding switch body. Switch should now slide free.

**Installation** — To install, reverse removal procedure. Fit ignition switch to lock mechanism before installing lock.

**NOTE** — *It should be possible to remove ignition switch without removing steering lock. Remove small set screw.*

124
128
131
X1/9

*Fig. 2   Steering Lock and Ignition Switch*

## FIAT

### REMOVAL & INSTALLATION

#### HORN BUTTON & STEERING WHEEL

Remove battery cables. Pry off or unscrew horn button (center emblem) as necessary. Remove horn cable. On 128 and 131 models it will be necessary to remove steering column cover. On all models, unscrew steering wheel retaining nut and pull off steering wheel.

#### TURN SIGNAL SWITCH

After removing steering wheel as described, disconnect turn signal switch electrical wiring, loosen switch retaining nut (or screws), and remove switch from steering column.

*Fig. 1   Using a Torque Wrench to Tighten Steering Wheel Nut*

## FIESTA

**Fiesta**

#### STEERING WHEEL

Disconnect battery ground. Pry out insert in center of steering wheel. Remove retaining nut. Pull off steering wheel along with turn signal indicator cam.

#### IGNITION SWITCH CYLINDER

Disconnect battery cables. Remove upper and lower column shrouds. Be careful when sliding lower shroud past choke control. Place key in accessories (I) position. Use a small screwdriver inserted through hole on under side of ignition housing to push up retaining spring clip. While clip is free pull out cylinder with key.

#### IGNITION SWITCH

Disconnect battery cables. Remove upper and lower steering column shrouds. Remove ignition switch retaining screws located on back side of switch near electrical plug. Disconnect wires. Remove switch from lock assembly.

#### IGNITION/STEERING COLUMN LOCK

Disconnect battery cables. Remove upper and lower steering column shrouds. Disconnect electrical wires. Drill out steering column/ignition lock shear bolts and remove lock mechanism.

*Fig. 1   Steering Column Lock Assembly and Ignition Switch*

# HONDA

Civic
Civic CVCC
Accord

## REMOVAL & INSTALLATION

### HORN PAD & STEERING WHEEL

**1)** Pry off steering wheel horn pad. With front wheels in straight-ahead position, mark position of steering wheel to shaft then remove steering wheel retaining nut.

**2)** Steering wheel may then be pulled from shaft, using a puller tool or by hitting with hand on backside of wheel.

**CAUTION** Do not apply a heavy hitting force or the shear pins within the column may be damaged.

**3)** Steering wheel components may then be disassembled and replaced if necessary (see *appropriate exploded view illustration*).

### TURN SIGNAL, WIPER/WASHER, DIMMER

**Removal** — Remove steering pad. Remove column shrouding. Disconnect electrical connectors. Remove steering wheel. On Civic models, loosen lock screw and tap on screw head to free locking component. On all models, remove remaining mounting screw and lift out switches. Washer/Wiper switch can now be separated from turn signal switch. Do not drop out or lose turn signal cancel cam key when lifting out switches.

**Installation** — To install switches, reverse removal procedure and note: Insert the lug on the turn signal switch assembly into recess in steering column . On Civic models only, make sure lock component fits squarely into its recess along column. Make sure turn signal cancel key 2 lugs fit into recess in steering wheel. Make sure horn switch spring terminal contacts steering wheel contact ring.

### HAZARD SWITCH

Switch is located in the top column shrouding. Remove top shrouding, disconnect electrical wires and remove switch from mounted position.

**NOTE** — *Accord models also have an indicator light switch located in the upper column shrouding. The switch, when depressed, will allow all indicator lights to function. Procedures for Hazard switch apply.*

## STEERING LOCK & IGNITION SWITCH

**Removal** — Remove steering column upper and lower shrouding. Disconnect ignition switch electrical wiring at lower end of steering column. Center punch shear bolts. Drill out shear head bolts and extract from lock bracket. Remove ignition switch.

**Fig. 2   Exploded View of Accord Steering Wheel and Related Components**

**Installation** — Insert new ignition switch. Hand tighten new shear bolts. Check switch operation at this time. Tighten shear bolts. Reconnect switch electrical leads.

**Fig. 1   Exploded View of Civic Steering Wheel and Related Components**

**Fig. 3   Disassembled View of Upper Column Components — Accord Shown; Others Similar**

## JAGUAR

XJ6
XJ12
XJS

## REMOVAL & INSTALLATION

### HORN PAD & STEERING WHEEL

**Removal (XJ6 & XJ12) — 1)** Set front wheels in straight-ahead position. Mark this position on steering wheel and do not turn wheel again.

**2)** Remove three screws securing lower switch cover and detach cover.

**3)** Working from below, remove clamp bolt securing split collet adaptor *(Fig. 1)* to steering column. Loosen lock nut set screw lock nut 2 turns.

**4)** Withdraw steering wheel, complete with hand lock nut, impact rubber bumper, collet adaptor, and shaft.

**Fig. 1   Components Located Behind Steering Wheel. XJ6 and XJ12 Shown**

**Dismantling — 1)** Unscrew two self-tapping screws from lower face of steering wheel boss and lift off padded horn contact.

**2)** Unscrew nylon nut from top of steering wheel shaft and remove it carefully, taking out the horn contact tube also.

**3)** Remove self-locking nut and plain washer which retain steering wheel. Carefully pull steering wheel from the shaft, collecting both halves of the split cone.

**Installation —** To install, reverse removal procedure and note the following: Be sure that front wheels are always kept in a straight-ahead position. When tightening collet clamp, tighten grub screw finger-tight, snug down its lock nut and torque clamp bolt to 10-12 ft. lbs. (1.4-1.6 mkg).

**Removal (XJS) — 1)** Loosen steering wheel adjustment lock nut. Grasp wheel and pull outward to the maximum extended position. Remove 2 horn pad-to-steering wheel mounting screws, then lift pad from wheel.

**2)** Place front wheels in straight ahead position. Engage steering column lock. Make sure key is removed. Remove the horn contact (rod) from upper column. Take off steering wheel mounting nut. Tap steering wheel off column. Do not lose split pins.

**Installation —** To install, reverse removal procedure.

### STEERING LOCK

**Removal —** Take off upper column shrouding. Using a center punch, make several dimples in shear bolt and rotate bolt out.

**Installation —** Reverse removal procedure.

### IGNITION SWITCH

**Removal —** Disconnect battery ground. Separate column shrouding from switch side. On XJ6 and XJ12 models only, disengage retaining ring holding ignition switch in housing. On XJS models only, maneuver shrouding until access to ignition switch set screw is gained; loosen screw. Force switch and wiring clear of housing. On all models, disconnect ignition switch wiring at multi-pin connector. Remove switch and harness.

**Installation —** To install, reverse removal procedure. On XJS models only, make sure lock tab on retaining ring engages slot.

### TURN SIGNAL, WIPER/WASHER, HAZARD, DIMMER

**Removal; XJ12 & XJ6 —** Disconnect battery ground. Take off steering column lower shroud. Remove steering wheel as previously outlined. Take off steering column upper shroud. Take cover out from below instrument panel. Loosen pinch bolt and pull combination switch assembly from steering column. Disconnect electrical wiring. Hazard flasher can now be separated by disconnecting wires, depressing tangs and pushing switch through mounting plate.

**Installation —** To install, reverse removal procedure.

**Fig. 2   Combination Switch Assembly XJS Shown**

## JAGUAR (Cont.)

**TURN SIGNAL, WIPER/WASHER, DIMMER**

**Removal (XJS)** — **1)** Disconnect battery ground. Loosen steering wheel hand adjustment ring, then extend wheel as far into passenger compartment as possible. Remove steering column lower shrouding. Remove steering wheel.

**2)** Remove upper shroud screw from bracket on column. Loosen pinch screw holding switch assembly to column. See Fig. 2. Separate shroud from switch assembly. Remove switch mounting screw. Separate ground at electrical quick-disconnect. Separate turn signal and wiper/washer switches.

**Installation** — To install, reverse removal procedure.

## LANCIA

### Lancia

## REMOVAL & INSTALLATION

### STEERING WHEEL

**Removal** — Place front wheels in straight ahead position. Disconnect battery. Remove horn cover mounting screws from below steering wheel spokes. On Coupe models only, horn cover will pry off. Remove spring. Mark steering wheel and shaft. Remove mounting nut. Fit puller 88062038 (or equivalent) and remove steering wheel.

**NOTE** — *On some early models it will be necessary to drill and tap two holes for puller.*

**Installation** — To install, reverse removal procedure. Make sure index marks on steering wheel and shaft align.

### STEERING COLUMN LOCK AND IGNITION SWITCH

**Removal** — **1)** Disconnect battery. Place front wheels in straight ahead position. Remove steering shaft mounting bolt and take off lower column casing. Disconnect multi-plug from socket. Remove steering column cover nuts and lift off complete with controls and steering wheel.

**2)** Use a .236" (6 mm) drill and remove shear bolts mounting column lock. Punch out bolts (if necessary) and lift out lock. Remove bolt keeping ignition switch to column lock support. Fit key and turn switch to "GAR", remove key. Use a metal pointed tool, depress lock spring, and slip out lock at same time.

**Installation** — Reassemble ignition switch. Fit column lock into position on steering column. Tighten mounting bolts until heads shear. Refit steering shaft lower end and tighten nut. Install upper cover to steering column and tighten mounting nuts. Reconnect multi-plug. Install steering column lower cover. Connect battery.

### STEERING COLUMN ADJUSTER

**Removal** — **1)** Disconnect battery. Disconnect speedometer at transaxle. Remove instrument cluster bolts and knobs. Disconnect speedometer cable from under dash. Separate electrical connections and lift off cluster.

**2)** Remove lower column cover. Remove nuts mounting steering shaft to adjustable bracket. Place steering shaft out of way. Remove mounting nuts and take off adjuster handle. Remove nuts mounting bracket to pedal support and lift off unit.

**Installation** — To install, reverse removal procedure.

## LUV

### LUV

**CAUTION** — *Steering shaft is an energy-absorbing unit. During any service operation, avoid jarring or leaning on any portion of column.*

## REMOVAL & INSTALLATION

### HORN BUTTON & STEERING WHEEL

**1)** Disconnect battery. Remove horn pad and spring by pushing in on pad and turning counterclockwise.

**2)** Remove horn contact ring and wire. Unscrew steering wheel retaining nut. Mark position of steering wheel on column shaft. Remove steering column cowling (4 screws).

**3)** Using appropriate puller (J-24292 for standard wheel or J-2927/J-2927-10 for sport type wheel), remove steering wheel.

### TURN SIGNAL/DIMMER SWITCH

Switch is a combination turn signal and headlight dimmer assembly. Disconnect battery ground and remove steering column cowling. Disconnect wires to switch harness. Remove switch by separating from clamp on mast jacket (two screws). To install, reverse removal procedures.

*Fig. 1  LUV Steering Wheel Assembly*

Spring

Horn Shroud

Horn Shroud Seat

Column Cowling

## LUV (Cont.)

### HAZARD WARNING SWITCH

Disconnect battery ground cable. Remove steering column cowling screws. Hazard warning switch is retained on upper half of cowling by two screws. Disconnect switch wiring harness at connector, remove mounting screws, and withdraw switch. To install, reverse removal procedure.

## ADJUSTMENT

### STEERING WHEEL ALIGNMENT

1) Set front wheels in straight-ahead position. Check location of spot on wormshaft which indicates gear "high point" (this should be at top center).

GLC
Cosmo
RX4
B1800

## REMOVAL & INSTALLATION

### STEERING WHEEL & COMBINATION SWITCH

**Removal** — 1) Disconnect battery ground cable. Pull off horn cap. Place front wheels in straight-ahead position. Index mark column shaft and steering wheel.

2) Remove steering column shrouding. Disconnect electrical connectors. On models so equipped, remove stop ring from steering shaft. Take out screw(s) mounting combination switch and lift assembly from vehicle.

NOTE — *Wiper switch can be removed with combination switch or separated from it.*

**Installation** — To install, reverse removal procedure.

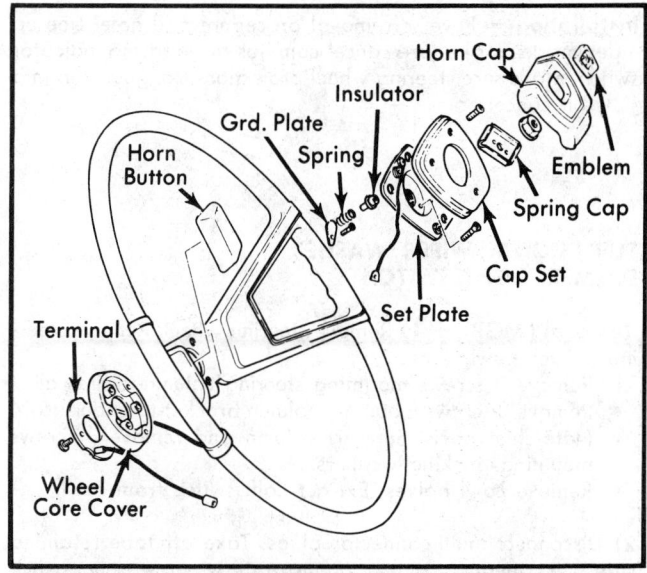

**Fig. 1     Typical Mazda Steering Wheel Assembly**

2) If gear is not in this position, loosen adjusting locknuts on both left and right sides of intermediate connecting rod.

3) Remove intermediate rod with inner tie rod ends attached. Turn ends an equal amount in the same direction to bring steering gear back to high point.

NOTE — *Turning ends unevenly will disturb toe-in setting; however, toe-in should be rechecked after adjustment is made and set as required.*

4) Note position of steering wheel spokes. They should be equally balanced. If they are off-center, remove steering wheel and reposition to proper alignment.

## MAZDA

### IGNITION SWITCH

**Removal; RX4 & Cosmo** — Remove steering wheel as previously outlined. Remove column shrouding. Remove combination switch. Disconnect electrical connector. Remove screw attaching switch contact (See Fig. 2) housing to steering lock body and slide out contact housing.

**Installation** — Reverse removal procedure.

**Fig. 2     RX4 and Cosmo Ignition Switch Contact Housing**

### KEY CYLINDER

**Removal & Installation; RX4 & Cosmo** — Remove steering wheel. Remove steering column shrouding. Remove set screw holding key cylinder. Insert key into cylinder and place in "ON" position. Push in on lock button and pull out key with cylinder. Reverse removal procedure to install key cylinder.

### STEERING LOCK

**Removal (RX4 & Cosmo)** — Remove steering wheel, column shrouding and combination switch. Remove 2 bolts mounting steering column bracket to instrument panel. Move shaft out from instrument panel about 1" (.039 mm). Put a groove in bolt attaching steering lock body to column shaft and remove bolt. Steering lock should be free to remove.

**Installation** — To install, reverse removal procedure and tighten new shear bolts until heads break.

## MERCEDES-BENZ

230
240D
280, C, S
300D
450 Series
6.9

### REMOVAL & INSTALLATION

#### HORN PAD & STEERING WHEEL

**Removal, with Polyurethane Wheel (Soft Rubber) — 1)** Grip horn pad near one corner and pull straight up until free. Pull up other corner. Remove pad from steering wheel.

**2)** Unscrew steering retaining nut, remove spring washer and pull steering wheel from shaft.

**Installation** — Prior to steering wheel installation, be sure scribe mark on shaft is straight up. Position wheel on shaft with spokes horizontal. Install retaining nut.

**Removal, with Rigid Plastic (Bealit) Wheel — 1)** Remove vehicle emblem from horn pad. Unscrew steering wheel retaining nut and pull wheel from shaft with pad still attached.

**2)** Unscrew hex nuts on backside of wheel and separate steering wheel from pad.

**NOTE** — *Horn wire is still attached to steering wheel, so care must be taken to avoid breaking it.*

**3)** Detach horn wire from contact ring and remove steering wheel.

**4)** Unscrew countersunk screws from steering wheel hub and remove centering pad of contact ring.

**5)** Remove horn ring from steering wheel. Remove locking ring from hub of pad, then remove slip ring.

**Installation** — To install, reverse removal procedure, noting that front wheels are always kept in a straight-ahead position and that steering wheel spokes are horizontal.

**Fig. 1** *Mercedes-Benz Steering Wheel with Cover Removed*

## MG

MGB
Midget

### REMOVAL & INSTALLATION

#### STEERING WHEEL

**Removal & Installation; Midget** — Disconnect battery ground. Pry off steering pad and remove horn contact plunger from seat. Remove six bolts holding steering wheel and lock

**Fig. 1** *Midget Steering Wheel and Related Components*

ring to hub. Lift wheel from hub and set aside. Loosen hub nut. Scribe index mark on hub and column. Fit puller (*Fig. 1*) and work hub until loose. Remove nut and hub.

**Removal (MGB)** — Remove steering wheel pad. Remove mounting nut. Index mark wheel hub and steering column. Use puller (18 G 1317) to remove steering wheel off column shaft.

**Installation** — Reverse removal procedure and note: Line up index marks. Make sure cancel cam has ridge facing indicator switch. Make sure steering wheel projections (tongues) slip into slots on cancel cam.

#### TURN SIGNAL, WIPER/WASHER DIMMER, LIGHT SWITCH

**Removal (MGB) — 1)** Remove steering wheel. Remove steering column cowl:
- Remove 3 screws mounting steering column-to-firewall.
- Remove 3 screws mounting column bracket-to-under dash.
- Note shim pack. Support column and remove 3 screws mounting packing washers.
- Remove cowl halves. Extract light switch from cowl.

**2)** Disconnect multi-connector plugs. Take off tape retaining wires to steering column. Remove 3 wiper/washer switch mounting screws.

## MG (Cont.)

3) Remove switch clamp screw located behind wiper switch. Lift off turn signal and wiper switch assemblies.

**Installation** – To install, reverse removal procedure making sure lugs on switch engage slot in steering column.

### TURN SIGNAL, WIPER/WASHER, DIMMER

**Removal (Midget)** – 1) Disconnect battery. Take off heater intake hose. Remove steering column pinch bolt at lower end on column.

2) Remove 3 bolts mounting column-to-firewall. Note shim pack located between column mounting and mounting bracket. Remove mounting bolts from bracket. Pull steering column back so cowl clears facia.

3) Remove cowl halves. Remove 2 wiper/washer switch mounting screws and lift up switch. Disconnect electrical wiring at plug. and remove wiper/washer switch.

4) Remove 2 turn signal mounting screws. Disconnect electrical wiring. Disconnect electrical lead from horn slip ring terminal. Remove switch.

**Installation** – To install switches, reverse removal procedure.

### STEERING COLUMN LOCK & IGNITION SWITCH

**NOTE** – *Steering column must be removed before lock or switch can be removed.*

**Removal** – Remove necessary shrouding to gain access to lock. Make sure steering lock is disengaged. Disconnect ignition switch multi-pin connector. Drill out and remove shear bolts from lock bracket. Remove steering screw holding switch in lock and remove switch.

**Installation** – Center locking mechanism on column. Hand tighten new shear bolts. Reconnect multi-pin connector. Check switch and lock operation. Tighten shear bolts until heads break.

**Fig. 2   Bottom View of Steering Column Showing Ignition Switch and Column Lock – MGB Shown**

## OPEL

**All Models**

## REMOVAL & INSTALLATION

### HORN PAD & STEERING WHEEL

**Removal** – 1) Disconnect battery cable. Remove two screws from backside of steering wheel which hold the horn pad in place.

2) Remove horn pad from its position and disconnect the horn contact wire from the hub connection.

3) Remove steering wheel retaining nut and washer. Position suitable puller and remove the steering wheel.

**NOTE** – *On sport steering wheels: Remove center pad. Remove mounting nut. Index shaft and wheel. Pull off wheel with tool J-23072 (or equivalent).*

**Installation** – To install, reverse removal procedure after making sure that front wheels are in straight-ahead position and that steering wheel spokes are horizontal when steering wheel is installed. Make sure cancelling cam of turn signal switch engages properly.

### COMBINATION SWITCH & IGNITION LOCK

**Removal** – 1) Remove screws holding upper and lower steering column covers in place. Remove the hazard warning button.

2) Detach the combination turn signal/lighting switch by removing the four retaining screws. Remove two retaining screws to take off the washer/wiper switch.

3) Remove the lock cylinder by removing the snap ring and three attaching bolts on the column flange. Lift off the cylinder housing, lower washer and shaft. Use a screwdriver to pry out the lower column rubber bushing.

**Installation** – To install, reverse removal procedure, noting that lock cylinder engages shaft properly and that cancelling cam of turn signal switch engages steering wheel properly.

## PORSCHE

911 Series
924
928

## REMOVAL & INSTALLATION

### HORN PAD & STEERING WHEEL

**NOTE** — *On models equipped with a collapsable "can" behind the steering wheel, care must be taken in all service procedures. Do not apply excessive or striking forces to the steering wheel or steering column.*

**Removal; 911 Series — 1)** Align front wheels in straight-ahead position. Disconnect battery ground cable.

**2)** Grasp horn pad and rotate counterclockwise while pushing in. When horn pad is free, lift from steering wheel and disconnect horn contact finger.

**3)** Loosen steering wheel retaining nut. Mark position of steering wheel to steering shaft. Attach a suitable puller and remove the steering wheel.

**Installation** — To install steering wheel, reverse removal procedure and note the following: Lightly lubricate horn contact finger with electrical contact grease before reinstalling.

**Removal & Installation; 924** — Disconnect battery. Carefully pry off horn pad. Unscrew wheel retaining nut. Pull wheel upward and off the shaft. To refit wheel, reverse removal procedure.

**Removal (928)** — Disconnect battery ground. Place wheels in straight-ahead position. Take off horn pad. Disconnect horn wires. Index mark steering wheel and column shaft. Unscrew mounting nut. Remove steering wheel.

**Installation** — Align index marks and replace steering wheel so spokes are horizontal. Install mounting nut. Fit horn wires into place in pad. Press horn pad onto retaining pins.

### STEERING WHEEL COMBINATION SWITCH

**Removal; 924 — 1)** Disconnect battery ground. Using hand pressure, lift up steering pad. Remove steering wheel mounting nut. Pull steering wheel off shaft.

**2)** Remove shroud from around switch housing. Pull up on switch plate and disconnect electrical wires. Remove entire switch assembly then, separate wiper/washer switch from turn signal switch by taking out screw that mounts them together.

**Installation** — Refit switches together with screw. Slide switch assemblies back into place refitting spacer at same time. Make sure spacer is driven in until there is a distance of 1.6" (41 mm)

from face (top edge) of spacer to top edge of shaft. This distance will ensure there is .08-.15" (2-4 mm) between steering wheel and steering column switches. Reverse removal procedure to install remaining components.

**Removal (928)** — Disconnect battery ground. Remove steering wheel. Remove cover from under steering column switch. Remove steering column switch mounting screw. Remove instrument cover mounting screws. Maneuver instrument cover until electrical wires can be disconnected. Remove column switch.

**Installation** — To install, reverse removal procedure.

### STEERING COLUMN LOCK, KEY CYLINDER & IGNITION SWITCH

**Removal — 1)** Remove combination switch as previously outlined.

**2)** Drill out shear bolts.

**3)** Disconnect ignition switch wiring.

**4)** Disengage snap ring and slide out switch housing with bearing.

**5)** Use a pointed tool (scribe) and push cylinder lock retainer in to release cylinder. With key inserted and retainer depressed, pull cylinder from housing.

**6)** Take out ignition switch set screw and pull ignition switch back out of housing.

**Installation** — To install, reverse removal procedure.

*Fig. 1  Porsche 911 Steering Wheel and Related Components*

## RENAULT

**R-5**

### REMOVAL & INSTALLATION

#### HORN PAD & STEERING WHEEL

**Removal, All Models** — Disconnect battery. Remove horn pad. Unscrew steering wheel retaining nut. Use a suitable puller (Dir. 21.A or equivalent) to free steering wheel from shaft.

**Installation, All Models** — When installing steering wheel, set front wheels in straight-ahead position and place steering wheel on shaft with spokes horizontal. Torque steering wheel nut. Replace horn pad.

#### TURN SIGNAL & LIGHTING SWITCH

**NOTE** — *For the following procedure, steering wheel does not have to be removed.*

**Removal, R-5** — 1) Disconnect battery. Remove instrument panel housing screws. Remove screws from bottom shell of switch cover.

2) Remove screws securing turn signal/lighting switch to column. Disconnect electrical couplings and remove switch.

**Installation, R-5** — To install, reverse removal procedure. Make sure electrical connections are made in their original locations.

**Fig. 1  Top View of Steering Wheel with Detail of Horn Pad Mounting Pins**

#### IGNITION SWITCH/COLUMN LOCK

**Removal, All Models** — 1) Disconnect the battery. Remove shell cover from around switch assemblies. Disconnect electrical couplings. Turn ignition key to "G" (Garage) and remove it.

2) Unscrew the set screw and press retaining catch in with a small punch. Push switch body from backside to release it.

**Installation, All Models** — To install, reverse removal procedure.

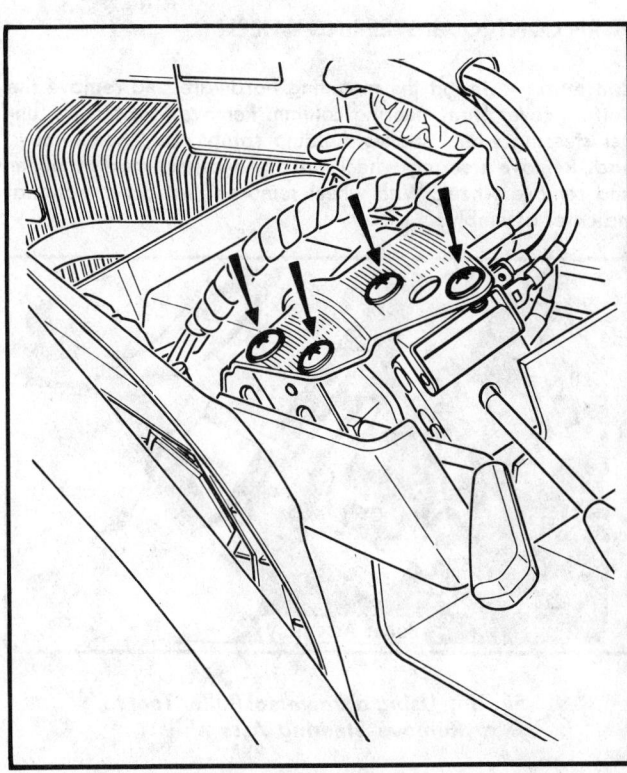

**Fig. 2  Location of Switch Assembly Retaining Screws — R-5 Shown**

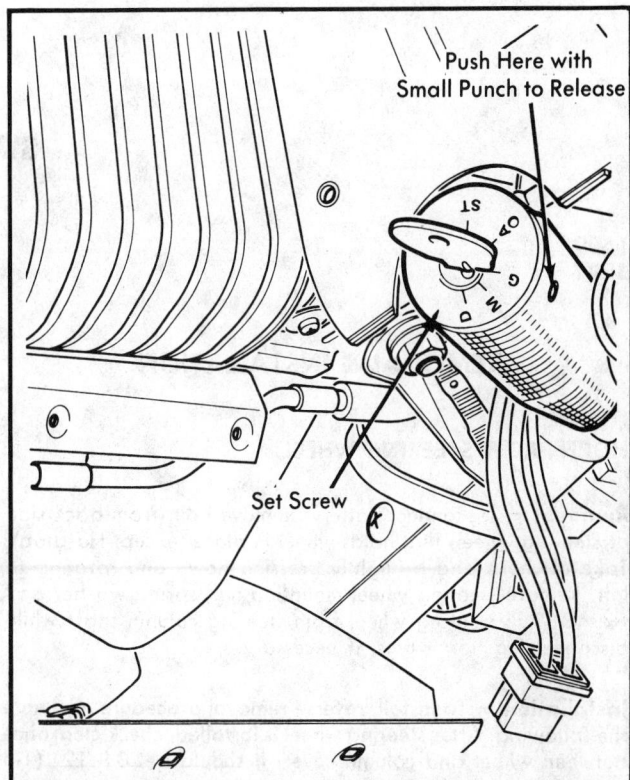

Push Here with Small Punch to Release

Set Screw

**Fig. 3  Ignition Switch Removal — R-5 Shown**

## SAAB

### 99

### REMOVAL & INSTALLATION

#### HORN CONTROL & STEERING WHEEL

**Removal** — Unbolt the mounting hardware and remove the bottom cover from steering column. Remove four screws, under steering wheel spokes, holding safety pad, then remove pad. Remove steering wheel nut and washer, then fit puller and remove wheel. With wheel removed, extract directional indicator assembly.

*Fig. 1   Using a Universal Puller Tool to Remove Steering Assembly*

**Installation** — Refit directional signal assembly ensuring index line coinsides with centerline of assembly housing. Install plastic sleeve over driver. Put steering wheel on with front wheels straight ahead and spokes horizontal. To complete reassembly, reverse removal procedure.

**Removal (99 EMS Models Only)** — Disconnect battery ground. Remove center pad, then reach under and disconnect horn leads from center pad while hand supporting pad. Remove steering wheel nut. Use a universal steering wheel puller to remove steering wheel.

**Installation** — To install, reverse removal procedure.

*Fig.2   Exploded View of Saab Steering Wheel Except EMS Models*

## SUBARU

### 1600 BRAT

### REMOVAL & INSTALLATION

#### HORN PAD & STEERING WHEEL

**Removal** — Disconnect battery. Remove bolt (from back side of steering wheel) that holds wheel in place (except Hardtop). Take off horn pad by lightly pressing down and rotating to left. Remove steering wheel mounting nut, spring washer and washer. Pull steering wheel from steering column shaft while disconnecting horn wires, if necessary.

**Installation** — To install, reverse removal procedure and note the following: After steering wheel is installed, check clearance between wheel and column cover; it should be .04-.12" (1-3 mm). If beyond this range, loosen column cover screws and adjust.

#### COMBINATION SWITCH

**Removal** — Remove steering wheel as previously described. Unscrew hazard warning knob from steering column. Remove two switch retaining screws and lift assembly from steering column.

**Installation** — To install, reverse removal procedure.

*Fig. 1   Removing Horn Pad from Steering Wheel*

## TOYOTA

Celica
Corolla
Corona
Cressida
Pickup
Land Cruiser

### REMOVAL & INSTALLATION

#### STEERING WHEEL

**NOTE** — *Steering wheel removal procedure is a general one. It should be noted that all steps may not apply to every model.*

**CAUTION** — *Some models are equipped with collapsible type steering, DO NOT apply excessive pressure or impact to mainshaft.*

**Removal** — 1) Disconnect battery ground. From lower portion of steering column, disconnect any electrical wiring for indicator lights, horn or dimmer switch.

2) Remove screws holding steering wheel protective pad or plastic cover. On some models, pad will pry off.

3) Remove steering wheel mounting nut and washer (if equipped), then using suitable puller, extract steering wheel from shaft *(Fig. 1)*.

**Installation** — To install, reverse removal procedure.

**Fig. 1   Using Puller to Remove Steering Wheel**

#### COMBINATION SWITCH

**Removal** — After removing steering wheel as previously outlined, combination switch may be removed by detaching steering column covers, removing retaining screws from face of switch assembly and unplugging necessary electrical connectors.

**Installation** — To install, reverse removal procedure and make sure all electrical connections are properly made. Check cancelling operation of turn signal switch.

#### COLUMN LOCK & IGNITION SWITCH

**Removal** — 1) Disconnect battery ground. Remove steering wheel as previously outlined.

**NOTE** — *Steering wheel removal is optional if only the ignition switch portion is being removed. Removal of wheel makes access to this operation easier.*

**Fig. 2   Disengaging Key Cylinder from Position on Mainshaft**

2) Remove screws mounting upper and lower column covers and disconnect any electrical couplings not detached during steering wheel removal.

**NOTE** — *On some models, access to ignition switch for its removal is gained by removing lower cover only. It is easier to perform this operation, however, by removing both cover halves.*

**Fig. 3   Drilling Out Shear Head Bolt to Remove Steering Lock from Shaft**

3) Remove turn signal switch assembly as previously described. (required only if column lock assembly is being removed).

4) Remove mainshaft bearing retainer and snap ring (if required).

## TOYOTA (Cont.)

5) Put ignition key in "ACC" position. Use a small pointed tool to press down stop pin on side of cylinder to free the mechanism. Pull cylinder from housing. (*Fig. 2*)

6) After removing switch cylinder, column lock may be removed as follows:
- **Except Corona & Cressida** — Drill out shear bolts holding lock mechanism around steering column.
- **Corona & Cressida** — Lock mechanism is part of upper column bearing assembly. Remove 3 bolts mounting upper bearing carrier (housing lock) and slide off assembly.

**Installation** — 1) To install column lock and switch assembly, reverse removal procedure. Tighten lock housing shear-head bolts (new) until the heads shear off.

2) Fit key cylinder so ignition switch and cylinder will be aligned in "ACC" position. Insert into housing and check for proper locking operation and key movement.

3) Replace all other components (combination switch assembly, bearing retainer, steering wheel) as removed. Check for proper turn signal switch cancelling operation and smoothness of steering wheel movement.

# TRIUMPH

TR7
Spitfire

## REMOVAL & INSTALLATION

### STEERING WHEEL

Place wheels in straight-ahead position. Pry off steering wheel pad. Remove mounting nut. Index mark wheel and column shaft. Use puller and remove steering wheel.

Column Cover

Combination Switch

Ignition Lock & Switch

Column Cover

Electrical Connectors

*Fig. 1  TR7 Steering Wheel and Column Switches*

### TURN SIGNAL & WIPER SWITCHES

**Removal** — 1) Disconnect battery. Unscrew retaining screws for column cover halves and remove covers. Remove steering wheel as previously described.

2) Note the location of all wiring harnesses. Remove the wire harness clip securing the switch harnesses. Disconnect the two harness plugs. Loosen the switch clamp screw and remove switch assembly.

3) Individual switches may be replaced at this time, but note that the two center cross-head screws are not to be removed. Switches are separated by drilling out the two retaining rivets and removing the one cross-head screw (on right side of switch face).

**Installation** — To install, reverse removal procedure and note: Switch assembly must engage outer column assembly. Turn signal cancel collar must align in steering wheel.

### IGNITION SWITCH AND STEERING COLUMN LOCK

**Removal** — On Spitfire only, remove nuts and washers securing steering lock shroud and withdraw shroud and column support. On all models, center punch both shear bolts mounting steering lock to column. Using a small chisel or suitable tool arrangement, remove bolts. Disconnect electrical plug and remove steering lock.

**NOTE** — *It is possible to remove ignition switch without taking out column lock. There are 2 set screws mounting switch assembly in column lock housing.*

**Installation** — To install ignition switch and steering column lock, reverse removal procedure and note the following: Ensure dowel pin aligns in column drilling. Fit new shear head bolts and tighten evenly.

## VOLKSWAGEN

Type 1
Type 2
Dasher
Rabbit
Scirocco

## REMOVAL & INSTALLATION

### HORN PAD & STEERING WHEEL

**All Models** – Disconnect battery. Carefully pry off horn pad. Unscrew steering wheel retaining nut. Pull wheel upward and off the shaft.

**CAUTION** – *Steering wheel or column has a collapsible section. Care must be taken when working with these components.*

**Fig. 1** *Typical Volkswagen Steering Wheel Rabbit and Scirocco Shown*

### TURN SIGNAL & WIPER SWITCH

**Removal; Type 1** – Disconnect battery ground. Place ignition key in on position. Remove steering as previously outlined. Remove circlip from groove below steering wheel splines. Disconnect electrical wiring from combination switch. Remove mounting bolt and pull switch assembly up and out.

**NOTE** – *Wiper switch must be removed together then, separated. Make sure to bleed air pressure from washer reservoir before disconnecting hose of valve on switch.*

**Installation** – To install, reverse removal procedure and note: Make sure turn signal wires are not crushed by windshield wiper switch. Adjust distance between steering wheel hub and steering column switch to 1/16-1/8" (2-3 mm) by loosening both switch mounting screws.

**Removal (Type 2)** – 1) Disconnect battery ground. Using hand pressure, lift up steering pad. Remove steering wheel mounting nut. Pull steering wheel off shaft.

2) Remove spring and spacer from top end of steering column. Remove 4 screws holding turn signal switch and wiper switch on steering lock housing. Collect 4 spacers located between switches.

3) Disconnect water hoses from valve on wiper switch. Remove turn signal switch, wiper switch and switch housing upper trim from steering column.

**Installation** – To install, reverse removal procedure.

**Fig. 2** *Dimensions for Installing Spacer Sleeve*

**Removal (Rabbit & Scirocco)** – Disconnect battery ground. Remove steering wheel. Remove 2 screws and 1 bolt from recess in switch housing bottom. Take off housing bottom half. Force switch assembly toward instrument panel as far as possible. Pry off spacer sleeve. Pull up on switch and disconnect wires. Remove switch, then separate turn signals and wipers.

**Installation** – Refit switches together with screw and spacer sleeve. Slide switch assembly onto column and hook up wires. Refer to *Fig. 2* for how far to drive on spacer sleeve.

**Removal (Dasher)** – Disconnect battery ground. Remove steering wheel. Remove 2 screws mounting lower switch housing. Disconnect electrical wires. Remove 3 screws attaching turn signal and wiper switches to ignition switch mounting. Remove switches.

**Installation** – To install, reverse removal procedures and note: Drive spacer sleeve on until upper end of spacer is flush with bevel on steering column. Make sure steering wheel is installed with lug for turn signal cancel mechanism facing left side of vehicle.

### STEERING/IGNITION LOCK

**Removal (Type 1)** – 1) Remove steering wheel. Remove clip and plastic bushing from steering column. Remove turn signal switch and wiper switch. Remove steering/ignition lock retainer plate.

## VOLKSWAGEN (Cont.)

**2)** Disconnect wiring harness from switch. If no hole is present in lock mechanism housing, one must be drilled. Refer to *Fig. 3.*

Fig. 3 *Measurements for Drilling into Steering Lock Cylinder — Type 1 Only*

**3)** Using a small, pointed tool, work through drilled hole and push down on cylinder lock retaining pin. Insert ignition switch key. Turn key and pull cylinder out of housing.

**Installation** — To install, reverse removal procedure and note: Insert lock cylinder by pushing into place without key installed. Then, use key to turn cylinder to **left.** Check operation.

## STEERING LOCK & CYLINDER

**Removal (Except Type 1)** — **1)** It is necessary to drill into cylinder lock to gain access to cylinder release pin. Refer to *Fig. 3* to determine where $\frac{1}{8}$" hole must be drilled.

**NOTE** — *On Type 2 models, hole for cylinder removal is accessible when cover plate has been removed. Note that not all models have pre-drilled hole.*

Fig. 4 *Measurements for Drilling into Steering Lock Cylinder*

**2)** Insert a pin through hole and press down spring holding lock cylinder in housing. It may be necessary to insert key to pull out cylinder.

**Installation** — To install, press cylinder in until it snaps into position. Reverse removal procedure for remaining components.

## IGNITION SWITCH

**Removal (All Except Type 1)** — Remove shear bolt and remove switch housing. There is 1 set screw on back side of switch (near wire connector) holding ignition switch in housing.

# VOLVO

240
260

## REMOVAL & INSTALLATION

### HORN PAD & STEERING WHEEL

**Removal** — **1)** Using a screwdriver, pry up both lower corners. Do not lever screwdriver against steering wheel.

**2)** Grip contact plate and padding then, snap out upper corners. Disconnect electrical wire. Remove steering wheel nut. Attach suitable steering wheel puller and remove steering wheel.

**Installation** — To install, reverse removal procedure.

### TURN SIGNAL & WIPER SWITCHES

**Removal** — Remove steering wheel as previously described. Remove column covers from around switches. Disconnect wiring from switch(es) to be replaced.

**Installation** — Attach wiring to replacement switch(es). Replace covers and replace steering wheel. Check switch operation.

Fig. 1 *Using Puller to Remove Steering Wheel*

## ARROW, CHALLENGER, COLT, SAPPORO

Arrow
Challenger
Colt
Sapporo

### DESCRIPTION

Collapsible steering system is comprised of a two-piece (upper and lower) column shaft, joined by a collapsible section. This section contracts axially under impact without affecting turning motion. Upper column cover incorporates slits, allowing it to collapse under impact.

### REMOVAL & INSTALLATION

#### STEERING COLUMN

NOTE – *During any service operations of collapsible columns or components avoid jarring or leaning on any portion of column.*

**Removal – 1)** Remove air cleaner and unbolt clamp connecting shaft to gear box. If vehicle is equipped with air conditioning, perform this step from underneath vehicle. Remove horn pad, steering wheel nut, and pull steering wheel off. Loosen tilt lock lever or knob and lower wheel. Remove column cover and floor dust cover.

**Fig. 1  Exploded View of Steering Column
Arrow & Colt (Except Station Wagon)**

**2)** Unplug column switch connectors and pull out switch. Remove tilt bracket bolts and remove column as an assembly. On Colt Station Wagon, Challenger and Sapporo models, remove rubber stopper from tilt bracket and unscrew lock lever and bushing from bolt. Pull out bolt to remove tilt bracket.

**Fig. 2  Exploded View of Steering Column
Challenger, Sapporo & Colt Station Wagon**

**Disassembly – 1)** Pull the lower shaft bushing out of column and remove shaft. Remove cover from the steering shaft joint socket; remove stopper and joint pin retainer. With steering shaft held upright, press down on shaft and remove joint retaining pin with a magnet. Do not drive pin out. Remove joint socket.

**2)** Loosen column tube clamp, draw out column tube, and remove the column bushing. When removing the tilt bracket, cut a slot in head of retaining studs, then unscrew studs, and remove steering lock. Lightly tap the tilt bracket with a wooden hammer to drive the bracket assembly from the upper end of column tube.

**Inspection and Replacement –** Make following checks before beginning reassembly of components:

**1)** Check clearance between upper coupling joint pin and bearing. Also, check clearance between upper coupling joint pin and socket. Clearance should be .0006-.002" (.016-.056 mm) for both measurements.

**2)** Check interference fit between lower coupling joint pin and shaft. Fit should be .0001-.0013" (.003-.034 mm). Check free play of lower joint pin and bearing. Free play should be .0006-.002" (.016-.056 mm).

**3)** Check steering shaft bend. Distortion must not exceed .020" (.5 mm).

## ARROW, CHALLENGER, COLT, SAPPORO (Cont.)

**4)** Hold lower end of steering shaft and move upper shaft. Note any excessive movement. Replace components as necessary.

**5)** Check column tube bushing stop. Replace bushing if wear is excessive.

**6)** Inspect upper and lower steering column bearings. Replace if excessively worn. Clearance between shaft and bearings is .0001-.0045" (.003-.115 mm).

**7)** Check tilt bracket. Slots give and break through when driver impact hits steering wheel. Make sure slots are not damaged.

**Reassembly – 1)** Install bearing on steering shaft lower end with flange facing upward, then insert pin. Make sure pin does not interfere with bearing operation.

**2)** Grease socket, dust cover and seat. Insert spring seat and spring into socket. Place steering shaft vertically and hold other portion of steering shaft down, fit lock pin. Make sure shaft and socket rotate freely.

**Fig. 3   Tilt Lever Installation**
**Challenger, Sapporo & Colt Station Wagon**

**3)** Fit spacer on shaft and install in steering column. Wipe grease off lower bearing retainer and inside of column. Apply a thin coat of adhesive to end of column.

**4)** On Arrow and Colt models (except station wagon), place tilt bracket on column, insert spacers, bolt, washers and tilt knob.

**5)** On Challenger, Sapporo, and Colt wagon, align tilt bracket with column tube and insert bolt. Tighten bushing on tilt lever until it stops, then back off ½ turn. Install tilt lever on bolt and adjust bushing until tilt lever locks column without hitting bracket. See Fig. 3.

**6)** Install shaft assembly in car. Fit column tube bushings onto upper and lower column tubes until stop touches column tube end. Tighten clamp bolt. Align column tube hole with steering wheel lock guide dowel. Insert ignition key and check operation. Tighten bolts after installing tilt bracket.

**Installation – 1)** Be sure shaft can easily be turned within the column, insert column assembly, and position against instrument panel. Connect shaft to steering gear housing mainshaft with clamp bolt head upward. Position tilt bracket so upper end of steering shaft to upper column end measurement is 3.60-3.64" (91.5-92.5 mm). Tighten tilt bracket bolts and install dust cover, applying sealant to the bolt.

**2)** Install column switch, routing harness along center of column tube, then replace cover. With front wheels in straight ahead position, install steering wheel. On Challenger, Sapporo, and Colt wagon, fit the three cancel pins on the column switch into the bottom of the steering wheel with a screwdriver. Tighten retaining nut to specification and make sure free play at wheel rim does not exceed .04" (1.0 mm).

### TIGHTENING SPECIFICATIONS

| Application | Ft. Lbs. (mkg) |
| --- | --- |
| Column Tube Clamp | 4-6 (.55-.83) |
| Steering Shaft Clamp | 15-18 (2.0-2.5) |
| Steering Wheel Nut | 25-33 (3.5-4.6) |
| Steering Wheel Lock | ①5 (.70) |

①Minimum.

## AUDI FOX

**Fox**

### DESCRIPTION

The Audi Fox uses a two piece safety steering column with a slip joint flange connection. A metal lattice column support is also used to help absorb shock in the event of a collision.

### REMOVAL & INSTALLATION

**STEERING COLUMN**

**Removal — 1)** Disconnect battery ground strap. Remove steering wheel. See Audi Fox under STEERING WHEELS & COLUMN SWITCHES in this Section.

**2)** Remove all steering column switches.

**3)** From under hood, remove pinch bolt holding steering column flange to pinion shaft.

**4)** Work under brake pedal and unbolt mounting flange from bracket. Disconnect electrical wires from ignition switch. Put ignition switch in "ON" position.

**5)** Centerpunch shear bolts holding steering lock on steering column. Drill out shear bolts. Remove steering lock. Remove steering column and shaft as a unit. It may be necessary to drive flange tube off pinion shaft with a drift.

**Fig. 1  Expanded View of Fox Steering Column**

**Disassembly —** Pull off steering wheel spacer ring and snap ring. Remove flat washer and spring. Pull steering shaft out through bottom of column. Press race out of column.

**Reassembly —** Examine race and replace if excessively worn. Slide steering shaft back into column then refit spring and snap ring.

**Fig. 2  Using a Drill to Remove Steering Column Shear Bolts**

**Installation — 1)** Position column assembly back in vehicle. Install steering column lock. Make sure lock lug will snap into recess in steering column. Fit new shear bolts finger tight.

**2)** Bolt steering column mounting flange onto bracket so long side of flange faces right side of vehicle. Snug up flange bolts and shear bolts.

**3)** Connect electrical wires to ignition switch. Fit column trim. Place front wheels straight-ahead.

**4)** Make sure column bushings are in position on pins at lower end of steering column. Line holes in flange so flange will slide down over pins on steering column. It will be necessary to use drift to drive flange tube onto steering gear pinion shaft. Make sure flange seats to stop on pinion. Tighten pinch bolt.

**5)** Maneuver steering column until steering lock operates effectively. Tighten shear bolts until head snap off. Refit steering wheel.

### TIGHTENING SPECIFICATIONS

| Application | Ft. Lbs. (mkg) |
| --- | --- |
| Steering Gear Box-to-Frame | 14 (2.0) |
| Column Mounting Flange Bolts | 7 (1.0) |
| Steering Wheel Nut | 36 (5.0) |
| Gear Box Pinch Bolt | 22 (3.0) |

## AUDI 5000

**5000**

### DESCRIPTION

The Audi 5000 uses a two-piece steering column/shaft assembly. The steering shaft is designed with an offset slip joint that engages the flange tube. In a collision, the gear box and flange tube may be moved rearward, but the force will not be transmitted through the upper column shaft. An anti-theft locking device prevents the steering wheel from turning when the ignition key is removed.

### REMOVAL & INSTALLATION

**Removal — 1)** Disconnect battery ground wire and loosen flange tube-to-pinion shaft clamp bolt. Pull off horn pad by hand and remove steering wheel with suitable puller.

**2)** Insert screwdriver through access hole at bottom of switch cover and loosen clamp. Remove switch assembly and disconnect ignition switch wiring. Place ignition switch in "ON" position.

**3)** Centerpunch shear bolts holding steering lock. Drill out shear bolts. Remove switch and unbolt mounting flange from under dash. Remove steering column and shaft as a unit.

**Disassembly —** Remove retaining ring, spring and support ring. Pull steering shaft out of column from the bottom. If necessary, press bearing race out of column.

**Reassembly —** Examine race and replace if excessively worn. Slide steering shaft back into column tube, then replace support ring, spring, and use a new retaining ring to lock in place.

**Installation — 1)** Place column assembly in vehicle. Install steering lock shear bolts finger tight and check operation of lock. Bolt mounting flange onto bracket.

**2)** Connect ignition wiring. Install flange tube over steering column pins and press on pinion shaft. Hold flange tube and shaft together with pliers and check length of shaft protruding from upper end of column. Adjust by moving flange tube on pinion shaft until distance is 2.56" (65 mm). See Fig. 2.

**Fig. 2  Steering Shaft Installation Measurement**

**3)** Tighten shear bolts until heads break. Install switch assembly flush with dashboard. With wheels in straight position, turn signal lever in middle position and cancelling lug to right, install steering wheel. Gap between wheel and switch assembly should be .125" (3.0 mm). Adjust if necessary and tighten flange clamp bolt on pinion shaft.

**Fig. 1  Exploded View of Audi 5000 Steering Column**

## BMW

320i
530i
633CSi
733i

### DESCRIPTION

Steering column consists of a padded steering wheel with horn contact, turn signal/headlight dimmer switch, windshield wiper switch and an anti-theft steering column lock/ignition switch. Columns on 530i, 633CSi, and 733i are telescoping, while the 320i column is fixed in position. Column is connected to steering gear by universal joints and flexible coupling.

### REMOVAL & INSTALLATION

**STEERING COLUMN**

**Removal, 320i — 1)** Disconnect battery ground cable. Remove lower half of steering column casing. Lift off pad from center of steering wheel and remove steering wheel.

**2)** Remove windshield wiper and turn signal switches at switch plate. Loosen set screw and pull out ignition switch.

**3)** Detach steering spindle at universal joint next to firewall in engine compartment. Loosen casing tube clamp at base of tube in driver's compartment. Drill or chisel off shear head bolts holding steering column to instrument panel. Remove steering column.

**NOTE** — On 320i only, lower bearing may be replaced by driving shaft and bearing out from top. Remove snap ring, split ring and bearing. When reinstalling, stem of split ring must face bearing and snap ring must fit in locking groove.

**Installation** — To install, reverse removal procedure and note the following: Upper column casing and tube must be aligned prior to tightening. When installing turn signal switch, wheels must point straight ahead with switch in center position. With dog pointing to center of cancelling cam, adjust switch so that dog is about .12" (3 mm) from cancelling cam.

**Removal, 530i & 633CSi — 1)** Disconnect battery ground cable and remove steering wheel. Detach lower half of housing below column, then remove turn and wiper switches.

**2)** Remove spindle shaft holder at top of column. Loosen adjusting nut and mark position of upper and lower shafts. Carefully pry spindle shaft bearing from top of column and pull shaft out from above.

**3)** To remove upper outer tube, disconnect horn wire at carbon brush. Drill or chisel off switch plate shear screws and disconnect wiring harnesses. Loosen clamp bolt and support screws, then slide down lower outer tube. Lift up outer casing and pull out outer tube.

**Installation** — To install, reverse removal procedures noting the following: Prior to tightening clamp bolt, assure that distance from centerline of clamp bolt to end of upper outer tube is between 1.65" and 1.77" (42-45 mm). Align upper and lower spindle marks and tighten adjusting nut.

**Fig. 1  Outer Tube and Clamp Bolt (530i & 633CSi)**

**Fig. 2  Upper Column Spindle and Bearing (All Models Except 733i)**

## BMW (Cont.)

**Fig. 3   Exploded View of Steering Column (733i)**

**Removal, 733i — 1)** Disconnect ground lead at battery and remove steering wheel. Remove lower instrument panel cover and steering column housing. Disconnect switches and remove all wiring and ignition switch.

**2)** Remove clamp bolt and detach lower shaft. Remove 5 bolts holding column assembly to dash and pedal bracket. Remove upper shroud and shaft. Disconnect lower shaft from clamp in engine compartment and pull into passenger compartment.

**3)** Remove inner steering shaft by taking off collar, snap ring, washer, spring, and lock ring. Pry out upper bearing with screwdrivers. Pry out lower bearing and remove shaft. Remove snap ring, collar, ring and bearing.

**Installation** — To install, reverse removal procedure. Wheels must be in straight ahead position when shafts are connected. Ensure all washers and spacers are replaced. Ignition switch must be in "O" position when installed.

### TIGHTENING SPECIFICATIONS

| Application | Ft. Lbs. (mkg) |
| --- | --- |
| Steering Wheel Nut | 62-69 (8.5-9.5) |
| Universal Joint-to-Spindle | 18-20 (2.5-2.8) |
| Casing Tube Clamp Bolt | |
|   320i | 12-14 (1.7-1.9) |
|   530i & 633CSi | 16-17 (2.2-2.4) |
| Column-to-Housing | 10 (1.5) |
| Column Bracket-to-Dashboard | 16 (2.2) |
| Lower-to-Upper Shaft Bolt (733i only) | 18 (2.5) |

**S T E E R I N G**

## CAPRI

**Capri**

### DESCRIPTION

Steering column is a collapsible safety type. Steering wheel is mounted to a convoluted can which will collapse under impact. Can assembly is integral with steering wheel and is removed with the wheel.

### REMOVAL & INSTALLATION

#### STEERING COLUMN

**NOTE** — *Steering column and steering column shaft are removed as a single unit.*

**Removal** — Disconnect battery. Remove upper and lower coupling clamp bolts (mark shafts for installation alignment). Tap coupling shaft down to remove from steering column. Remove steering column shroud, steering wheel and turn signal cancelling cam. Lower trim panel and remove turn signal switch. Disconnect ignition switch wires at connector. Remove steering column retaining bolts, then remove steering column with steering column shaft and grommet.

**Installation** — To install, reverse removal procedure and note the following: wheels should be in straight ahead position, marks on splines are aligned and couplings are not distorted.

#### STEERING COLUMN SHAFT

**NOTE** — *Steering column shaft is removed from steering column after steering column is removed from vehicle.*

**Removal** — Remove steering wheel and steering column as previously outlined. Remove steering lock by drilling out headless bolts. Remove clip, washer and spring from lower end of steering column shaft. Tap lower end of shaft with soft mallet to remove upper bearing, then use shaft to tap lower bearing out of steering column.

**Installation** — Place shaft in column and install lower bearing, spring, washers and clip. Push lower bearing in place and install upper bearing. Install steering lock with shear head bolts, then use steering lock to align shaft in column. Install steering column and steering wheel as previously outlined.

**Fig. 1  Exploded View of Steering Column Assembly**

### TIGHTENING SPECIFICATIONS

| Application | Ft. Lbs (mkg) |
| --- | --- |
| Steering Wheel Nut | 25-30 (3.5-4.2) |
| Universal Joint-to-<br>  Shaft Spline | 12-15 (1.7-2.1) |

## DATSUN F10, 200SX, B210, 510 & 810

F10
200SX
B210
510
810

### DESCRIPTION

Steering column used on Datsun vehicles are safety, collapsible type. These columns compress on impact. F10 models use two universal joints between column and steering gear. These joints provide steering wheel most desirable position and angle. On all other models, a flexible rubber coupling attaches column to steering gear assembly.

### REMOVAL & INSTALLATION

**NOTE** — *During any service procedure involving the steering assembly, do not hammer or exert extreme pressure on the steering column or damage to the collapsible section may result.*

**Removal, F10 — 1)** Disconnect lower column "U" joint from steering gear assembly. Remove steering wheel. *See Datsun under STEERING WHEEL & COLUMN SWITCHES in this Section.*

**2)** Remove steering column cover. Separate turn signal switch assembly and combination light switch from column.

**3)** Hold steering column upper portion by hand. Remove upper and lower steering column clamp mounting bolts. Remove screws keeping column hole cover assembly to instrument panel. Slide out steering column through passenger compartment.

**NOTE** — *Do not further disassemble collapsible steering column. If components are damaged and require replacement, entire assembly must be replaced.*

**Inspection — 1)** Check column bearings for smooth even operation. If necessary, grease bearings with suitable lubricant.

**2)** Check column tube for deformation or breaks. Replace components as required.

**3)** Check column shaft spring. Spring length should be about .512" (13 mm) under a load of about 66 lbs. (30 kg).

**4)** Measure distance between top end of upper column tube and top end of lower column tube. Distance should be 11.63" (295.5 mm). *See Fig. 1.*

**Installation — 1)** Set steering gear in straight-ahead position. Connect lower joint to steering column. Slide steering assembly through hole in floor board.

**2)** Tighten column tube mounting bolts. Loosen splined shaft set screw and connect shaft to joint. Connect opposite end to steering gear. Tighten pinch bolt and set screw.

**3)** Make sure column tube hole seal is not twisted and that lower lip makes contact with joint shaft.

**Fig. 1  Datsun F10 Steering Column Assembly**

**Removal, Except F10 — 1)** Remove steering shaft pinch bolt. Remove steering wheel. *See Datsun under STEERING WHEEL & COLUMN SWITCHES in this Section.*

**2)** Remove upper and lower steering column shroud covers. Loosen screws and take off turn signal switch assembly.

**3)** Remove 4 bolts mounting steering column tube cover to floor board. From under instrument panel, remove bolts mounting column clamp and remove clamp. Pull steering assembly from vehicle by removing it through passenger compartment.

**Fig. 2  Column Tube Measurement Specification**

**Inspection — 1)** Check column bearings for smooth even operation. If necessary, grease bearings with suitable lubricant.

**2)** Check column tube for deformation or breaks. Replace components if necessary.

## DATSUN F10, 200SX, B210, 510 & 810 (Cont.)

**Fig. 3   Sectional View of Collapsible
Steering Column — All Except F10**

**3)** Check column shaft spring and replace spring if it seems weak.

**4)** On all models except 810, measure distance between column clamp and top end of lower column tube. Distance should be 7.04" (179 mm) for 200SX and B210, or 7.25" (184 mm) for 510 models. See *Fig. 2, measurement A.*

**5)** On 810 models, measure distance between top end of upper column tube and top end of lower column tube. Distance should be about 16.27" (413.5 mm).

**Installation — 1)** Place steering gear so wheels point straight-ahead.

**2)** Slide steering column in postion through passenger compartment. Guide column over worm shaft. Make sure punch mark faces up, then tighten pinch bolt.

**3)** Fix column under instrument panel. Refit column tube cover at floor board. Reverse removal procedure for remaining components. Make sure steering wheel rotates freely.

## OVERHAUL

**NOTE** — *This article does not outline an overhaul procedure; it is recommended that, should damage to the column occur, it be replaced as an assembly.*

### TIGHTENING SPECIFICATIONS

| Application | Ft. Lbs. (mkg) |
|---|---|
| **Steering Wheel Nut** | |
| F10 | 14-18 (2.0-2.5) |
| 200SX, B210 | 22-25 (3.0-3.5) |
| 510, 810 | 27-38 (3.7-5.3) |
| **Steering Column Clamp Bolt** | |
| F10 | 7-10 (1.0-1.4) |
| 200SX, B210 | 11-13 (1.5-1.8) |
| 510, 810 | 9-13 (1.2-1.5) |
| **Column Tube-to-Instrument Panel** | |
| B210, 810 | 3-3.3 (.35-.45) |
| **Rubber Coupling-to-Worm Shaft** | 29-36 (4.0-5.0) |
| **Upper Joint Shaft-to-Column Bolt** | |
| F10 | 14-17 (1.9-2.4) |
| **Lower Joint-to-Steering Gear** | |
| F10 | 14-17 (1.9-2.4) |

## DATSUN 280Z

### 280Z

#### DESCRIPTION

The steering column assembly used on the 280Z is a safety, collapsible type. A rubber coupling is used to prevent road vibrations from reaching the steering wheel. Two universal joints are incorporated between the steering gear and steering wheel to give the most suitable steering wheel position and angle. The column is a steel ball type which is designed to compress on impact, absorbing the collision shock.

#### REMOVAL & INSTALLATION

##### STEERING COLUMN

**NOTE** — *During any service procedure involving the steering assembly, do not hammer or exert extreme pressure on the steering column or damage to the collapsible section may result.*

**Fig. 1  Separating Upper and Lower Shafts**

**Removal** — Disconnect column assembly from lower joint shaft at rubber coupling (remove clamp bolt). Remove steering wheel. See *Datsun under STEERING WHEEL & COLUMN SWITCHES in this section.* Detach column shroud halves and remove lighting switch assembly. Unscrew bolts retaining column tube flange plate to toeboard. Support steering column at upper end and remove column clamp bolts. Draw out steering column assembly from passenger compartment side. Loosen clamp bolt at pinion shaft and remove lower steering joint section.

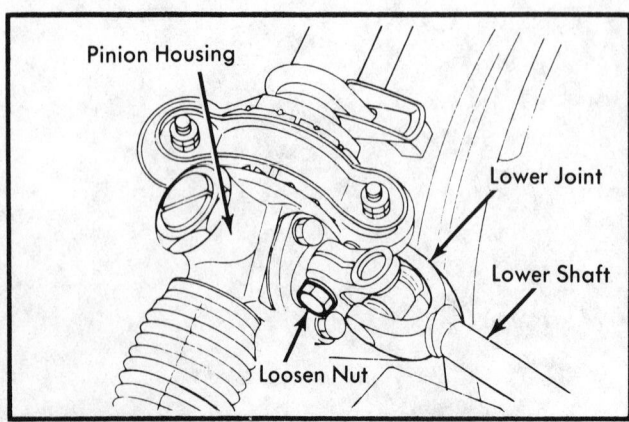

**Fig. 2  Separating Lower Shaft from Pinion Gear**

**Inspection** — Check for smoothness of rotation at all steering components. Inspect jacket tube for deformation or breakage (replace if necessary). Check column shaft spring for proper tension: free length, 1.075" (27.3 mm); loaded length, .059" @ 66 lbs. (15 mm @ 30 kg). Measure distance from upper end of tube collapsible section to lower side of column support clamp. If this measurement is less than 6.933" (176.1 mm), collapsing of column has occurred and column should be replaced. Also inspect inserts in column support clamp. If they protrude beyond the clamp, damage to column may be suspected.

**Installation** — Install lower joint section after installation of steering column. Set front wheels in straight-ahead position, line up slits of universal joints with punch mark on upper end of steering shaft (punch mark should be on top), then connect column and tighten bolts as required. After installation, ensure steering wheel rotates smoothly.

**Fig. 3  Lining Up "U" Joint Slits with Steering Shaft Punch Mark**

#### OVERHAUL

**NOTE** — *Refer to Inspection in this article for description of components which may be replaced; however, if damage to the collapsible section is suspected, steering column replacement is recommended.*

#### TIGHTENING SPECIFICATIONS

| Application | Ft. Lbs. (mkg) |
| --- | --- |
| Steering Wheel Nut | 29-36 (4.0-5.0) |
| Column Clamp Bolt | 6-8 (0.8-1.1) |
| Rubber Coupling Securing Bolt | 12-14 (1.7-2.0) |
| Lower Joint-to-Rubber Coupling | 17-20 (2.3-2.7) |
| Lower Joint-to-Pinion Shaft | 29-36 (4.0-5.0) |

# Steering Columns

## DATSUN PICKUP

**Pickup**

### DESCRIPTION

The steering column is a conventional, non-collapsible type. It is supported under the instrument panel by a post clamp. The lower end of the steering column tube is bolted directly to the gear box. The worm assembly, within the gear housing, is an integral extension of the steering shaft.

### REMOVAL & INSTALLATION

Since the worm gear is an integral, non-separable part of the steering shaft, the shaft must be removed as an assembly with the gear. See *appropriate article under STEERING GEARS & LINKAGE in this section.*

### OVERHAUL

Replacement of bearings or bushings may be accomplished during steering gear overhaul. See *appropriate article under STEERING GEARS & LINKAGE in this section.*

**Fig. 1   Steering Column and Gear Assembly for Datsun Pickup**

## FIAT 124

### 124 Spider

#### REMOVAL & INSTALLATION

**Removal** — After removing steering wheel, horn button, and turn signal switch, remove steering column bracket by disconnecting column front ignition switch and removing four column-to-instrument panel retaining screws. Unbolt clamp securing steering column to worm shaft and pull column up into passenger compartment.

**Installation** — Insert column through opening in instrument panel. Fit worm shaft to steering column and lock with clamp. Replace column support bracket to steering column and connect with attaching screws (loosely). Replace steering wheel temporarily and turn two or three times side to side. Attach directional signal switch, then torque column bracket bolts to 11 ft. lbs. (1.5 mkg). Tighten steering wheel nut and connect switch wiring. Replace remaining components in reverse of removal procedure.

*Fig. 1    Detail of Flexible Coupling Connecting Upper and Lower Portions of Steering Shaft*

---

## FIAT X1/9, 128 AND 131

### X1/9
### 128
### 131

#### DESCRIPTION

The steering column is composed of two sections. The top section is mounted on two ball bearings, while the lower section is equipped with two universal joints.

#### REMOVAL & INSTALLATION

##### STEERING COLUMN (ALL MODELS)

**Removal** — Disconnect battery. Remove screws holding column cover halves. On 131 models, remove steering column adjustment knob. Detach electrical connectors at steering column. Remove nuts and washers retaining column at support bracket below instrument panel. Unscrew pinch bolt holding lower end of steering shaft to gear box. Remove column assembly from vehicle. Dismantle steering wheel and turn signal unit, if necessary.

**Installation** — To install, reverse removal procedure.

##### UPPER COLUMN BEARING REPLACEMENT (128 MODELS)

**Removal** — 1) Remove screws attaching horn button cover and screws attaching steering column cover. Unscrew steering wheel nut and take off wheel. Loosen turn signal switch retaining nut and disconnect electrical wiring, then remove nut and switch.

2) Withdraw retaining ring and allow spring to extend. Remove nuts attaching steering column support to instrument panel. Disconnect universal joint between upper and lower column sections. On bench, push out top end of column and remove bearing, then repeat on lower end bearing.

**Installation** — Replace bearings in reverse of removal procedure.

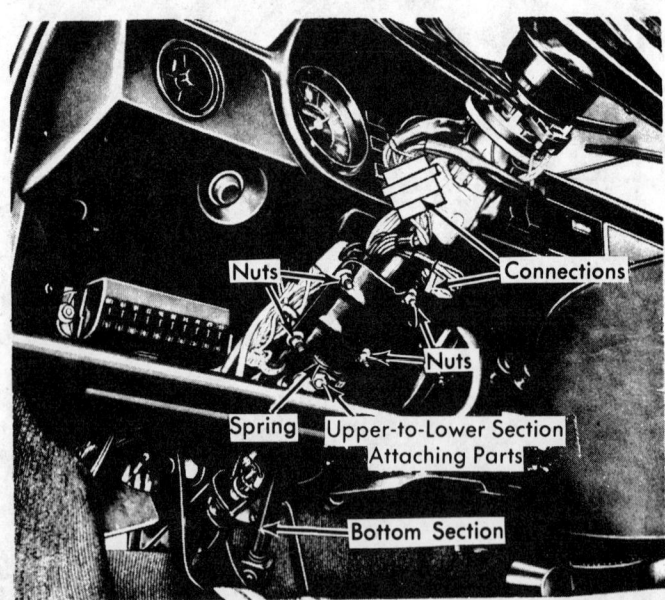

*Fig. 1    Installed View of Steering Column as Viewed from Under Instrument Panel*

## FIESTA

### DESCRIPTION

Steering column is two-piece, with a slip joint that allows either part to move without transmitting force to the other end. A steering column jacket over the upper part of the steering shaft will also collapse under impact. No universal joints or flexible couplings are used between the shaft and steering gear.

### REMOVAL & INSTALLATION

#### STEERING COLUMN

**Removal — 1)** Disconnect battery ground strap. Remove pinion-to-steering shaft clamp bolt. Inside vehicle, remove upper and lower steering column shrouds and lower dash insulation panel.

**2)** Loosen two screws retaining switch assembly to column and unplug wiring connectors. Remove column mounting bolts and nuts. Carefully remove column and shaft assembly from vehicle.

**3)** Remove steering wheel from assembly. Remove directional signals cam and bearing tolerance ring from shaft. Lift off column tube, remove washers and spring, then disconnect halves of shaft.

**Installation — 1)** Assemble upper and lower shafts, replace washers and spring, then insert shaft into column. Position bearing tolerance ring and install steering wheel.

**2)** Place column assembly in vehicle, with lower shaft loosely over pinion shaft. Secure column in place with supporting nuts and bolts. Reconnect ignition and replace column switches and wiring.

**3)** Ensure pins on lower shaft are fully engaged in upper shaft bushings. Tighten clamp bolt after checking steering wheel position. Replace column shrouds and dash insulation cover. Reconnect battery. Column upper shroud should have .28" (7.0 mm) clearance from steering wheel. Adjust as necessary.

### TIGHTENING SPECIFICATIONS

| Application | Ft. Lbs. (mkg) |
|---|---|
| Steering Wheel Nut | 30-37 (4.1-5.1) |
| Column-to-Pinion Shaft Clamp Bolt | 33-41 (4.6-5.7) |

***Fig. 1  Exploded View of Fiesta Steering Column Assembly***

# Steering Columns

## HONDA

**Accord**
**Civic**
**Civic CVCC**

### DESCRIPTION

Steering columns are mounted with an impact absorbing plate on the upper bracket that deforms under pressure. A plastic bracket collar at the lower end of the column allows the assembly to slide, and double universal joints absorb impact without the need for a collapsing column.

### REMOVAL & INSTALLATION

#### STEERING COLUMN

**Removal, Civic and Civic CVCC** — Disconnect steering joint at splines by removing clamp bolt. Remove wire connectors below column. Remove 4 attaching bolts (upper 2 first) and take entire assembly out of vehicle.

**Installation, Civic and Civic CVCC** — To install, reverse removal procedure and ensure that front wheels are straight when steering wheel is replaced.

**Removal, Accord** — Disconnect wire harness. Remove middle clamp bolt in universal joint shaft. Detach lower dash panel. Remove nuts securing column to mounting brackets (remove upper nuts first). Remove column from vehicle.

**NOTE** — *If steering wheel has been removed, ignition switch must be in "LOCK" position to retain steering shaft during column removal.*

**Installation, Accord** — Insert column in vehicle and loosely connect universal joint shaft. Pull down on column to ensure bending plate is against hook, then tighten bracket nuts. Check plastic collar to ensure it is all the way on column, then install lower column bracket. On models with manual steering, tighten universal joint clamp bolt. On power steering models, install special tool (07973-6710000) on top of steering shaft. Pull down on universal joint shaft while tightening.

*Fig. 1  Exploded View of Civic Steering Column (CVCC Similar)*

## HONDA (Cont.)

**Fig. 2   Exploded View of Accord Steering Column**

## OVERHAUL

**Disassembly — 1)** Remove steering wheel and column switches. *See Honda under STEERING WHEEL & COLUMN SWITCHES in this Section.*

**2)** Pull steering shaft out from bottom of column. Remove bushings and horn ground ring. Ignition switch bolts must be drilled and removed with screw extractor.

**Reassembly — 1)** Install horn ground ring, serrated bushing and upper column bushing in steering column. On all models, flat side of bushing should be centered with notch in column.

**2)** Grease top end of shaft and insert in column. Fill bottom of tube with grease and install column hanger bushing. On Civic and Civic CVCC, install washer and bracket collar. On Accord models with power steering, install circlip, washer, spring, washer, and bushing. Slip bracket collar over column tube.

**3)** On Civic models, install universal joint shaft flush against lower thrust washer. On CVCC and Accord, insert splined end of steering shaft into universal joint shaft clamp, install bolt, and pull joint shaft down so bolt bottoms against lower edge of flat on steering shaft. Tighten clamp bolt.

**4)** Replace turn signal switch and ignition switch (if removed). Use rubber bands to retain upper bracket and bending plate to column, and install upper and lower covers. Install in vehicle.

### TIGHTENING SPECIFICATIONS

| Application | Ft. Lbs. (mkg) |
|---|---|
| **Clamp Bolt** | |
| Civic, Accord | 20-23 (2.8-3.2) |
| Civic CVCC | 16 (2.2) |
| **Upper Column Bracket Nuts** | |
| Civic | 7-12 (1.0-1.6) |
| Civic CVCC | 16 (2.2) |
| Accord | 10 (1.3) |
| **Lower Column Bracket Bolts** | |
| Civic | 14-18 (2.0-2.5) |
| Civic CVCC, Accord | 16 (2.2) |

## JAGUAR

XJ6
XJ12
XJS

### DESCRIPTION

The upper and lower steering columns are the collapsible type, designed to comply with safety regulations. The collapse points are retained by nylon plugs which will shear on impact, allowing steering wheel and columns to move forward. The upper column is composed of two separate sliding shafts, with the column tube on later models being formed with an expanded metal section. The column shaft is supported on two prelubricated roller bearings. The lower column section is also comprised of two sliding portions, which are retained in a fixed length by nylon plugs.

### REMOVAL & INSTALLATION

#### UPPER STEERING COLUMN

**Removal, Except XJS — 1)** Disconnect battery. Remove steering wheel, see *Jaguar under STEERING WHEEL & COLUMN SWITCHES in this Section.* Remove speedometer as follows: Remove instrument panel casing. Behind speedometer, unscrew knurled nut from right-angle bracket to gear box and disconnect speedometer drive cable. Disconnect trip record reset control cable by unscrewing knurled nut. Apply pressure to instrument panel bezel, rotate speedometer clockwise until it releases, and withdraw from panel. Withdraw headlight warning light and illuminator lights. Disconnect ground lead.

**2)** Remove tachometer as follows: Apply pressure to instrument bezel and rotate counterclockwise until tachometer releases. Disconnect electrical plug and socket. Remove ground lead. Withdraw illumination light holder.

**3)** Remove trim panel below the upper steering column. Disconnect electrical switch connections (three socket and plug connections). Detach horn contact at upper column. Unscrew self-locking nut and remove pinch bolt securing upper universal joint to lower steering column.

**4)** Loosen 2 set screws holding lower end of upper column. Reach through instrument openings and remove two nuts holding top of column. Collect washers, shims, and nuts, and support column. Remove 2 set screws previously loosened and carefully remove complete steering column assembly from vehicle.

**CAUTION** — *Do not use excessive force when separating upper column from lower column.*

**Inspection** — Examine column for straightness. Any wear, damage, or variation in length means the column should be replaced. Length from end to end (without "U" joint) should be between 21.56-21.70" (547.7-551.0 mm).

**Installation** — If universal joint and/or adjusting clamp have been removed, refit, then reverse removal procedure and note the following: Check that ⅜" (9.5 mm) clearance exists axially in lower universal joint; if necessary, move upper universal joint further along lower column to increase clearance. Ensure self-cancelling operation of turn signals functions properly and that steering wheel spokes are horizontal when straight-ahead position is set; if not adjust as necessary.

**Removal, XJS — 1)** Disconnect battery. Remove cover panel from under instrument panel. Remove trim from around instrument cluster. Remove screws mounting instrument panel to facia. Disconnect speedometer cable. Lay cluster forward and disconnect wires from behind cluster. Lift off entire cluster.

**2)** Remove steering column lower shroud. Lock steering wheel in straight-ahead position. Remove column adjusting mount bolt, then loosen set screw and take out adjusting assembly.

**3)** Disconnect ignition switch from main harness. Disconnect main harness from auxiliary controls. Remove upper "U" joint bolt. Remove bolts mounting column at lower mounting.

**4)** Disconnect horn. Remove upper column mounting bolts. Maneuver column free of "U" joint and vehicle. Remove other shroud half. Unscrew auxiliary switches from column, slide assemblies out of column.

**5)** Remove bolts securing ignition switch and lock assembly to column. Remove bolt securing horn feed and take off from column.

**NOTE** — *Remaining components can not be individually replaced.*

**Installation** — Reverse removal procedure and note: Loosely fit upper and lower mounting bolts and spacers. Adjust column so groove on inner splined shaft aligns with bolt hole in "U" joint. Make sure upper section of column fits in center of housing facia. Tighten mounting bolts. Reverse removal procedure for remaining components.

#### LOWER STEERING COLUMN

**Removal, Except XJS — 1)** Raise vehicle on hoist and remove pinch bolt securing lower "U" joint to pinion shaft. Lower vehicle. Detach lower parcel shelf. Remove both pinch bolts from upper-to-lower "U" joint.

**2)** Unscrew lower mounting screws of upper column. Pull lower steering column from upper "U" joint. Raise vehicle. Remove "U" joint from pinion shaft and withdraw lower steering column.

*Fig. 1  Disconnecting Lower Steering Column from Pinion Shaft*

## JAGUAR (Cont.)

**Installation** — To install, reverse removal procedure and ensure gap of ⅜" (9.5 mm) exists in universal joint. **NOTE** — *Front wheels should be kept in straight-ahead position during this operation.*

**Removal, XJS** — 1) Place front wheels in straight-ahead position. Remove exhaust heat shields near head pipe. Remove right side heat shield near steering rack.

2) Remove nut and bolt mounting lower "U" joint to pinion shaft. Work inside passenger compartment and separate "U" joint from upper and lower column. Pull "U" joint free from upper column.

3) Remove "U" joint from lower shaft. From under vehicle, push lower column through firewall until "U" joint separates from pinion shaft. Pull "U" joint clear of pinion shaft and withdraw lower column assembly.

**Installation** — Reverse removal procedure and note: Make sure steering wheel is in center position before installing lower column. Also, Do not use excessive force to fit lower column to upper column; nylon shear plug may be damaged.

### STEERING COLUMN ADJUSTING CLAMP

**Removal** — Remove steering wheel. Pull impact rubber from steering wheel shaft. Unscrew three small cheese-head screws from beneath adjusting clamp (lock nut) and withdraw retaining plate. Unscrew collet adaptor completely and remove from shaft. Remove circlip from within upper side of adjuster. Withdraw adjuster (lock nut) collecting stop button. Slide split collet off shaft.

Collet Adaptor
Split Collet
Circlip
Retaining Plate
Stop Button
Impact Rubber
Adjusting Clamp (Lock Nut)

**Fig. 2  Exploded View of Steering Column Adjusting Clamp**

**Installation** — Clean parts thoroughly and remove any burrs with a file. Lightly lubricate all enclosed metal components. Install by reversing removal procedure.

### STEERING COLUMN LOWER SEAL

**Removal, Except XJS** — Remove upper steering column, as previously outlined. Loosen hose clip attaching upper sealing sleeve to lower column; remove clip and sleeve. Remove 3 screws securing seal retainer to instrument panel. Slide seal, retainer, and sealing sleeve up and off lower column.

**Installation** — Fit assembly of sealing sleeve, seal, and retainer over end of lower column carefully. Insert and tighten three retaining set screws. Carefully slide second sealing sleeve, flanged end first, over lower column as far as first sealing sleeve; position hose clip, but do not tighten. Move second sealing sleeve approximately ¼" (6 mm) toward dash, to preload it against first sealing sleeve. Secure this position with hose clip. Replace upper column assembly.

## OVERHAUL

### UPPER & LOWER STEERING COLUMNS

**NOTE** — *No repairs, adjustments, or overhaul procedures are given by the manufacturer. If damage is evident or suspected, replacement of assemblies is necessary.*

### TIGHTENING SPECIFICATIONS

| Application | Ft. Lbs. (mkg) |
|---|---|
| Universal Joint Bolts | 14-18 (1.9-2.5) |
| Steering Wheel-to-Shaft | 25-30 (3.5-4.1) |
| Column-to-Bracket Bolts | 14-18 (1.9-2.5) |
| Column-to-Bracket Nuts | 14-18 (1.9-2.5) |
| Lower Column-to-Body | 6-7 (0.8-1.0) |

## LANCIA

**Lancia Beta**
**Except Scorpion**

### DESCRIPTION

All models use energy absorbing safety type steering column assemblies. Steering column is two piece. "U" joints connect upper steering column to lower shaft and lower shaft to steering gear. Upper steering column has a two inch variable adjustment. This allows column and steering wheel to be placed in most desirable position.

### REMOVAL & INSTALLATION

#### STEERING COLUMN

**Removal — 1)** Disconnect battery. Place front wheels in straight ahead position. Disconnect lower steering shaft from steering gear by removing nut and bolt, then separating. Disconnect multi-plug connector from socket.

**2)** Remove nuts mounting steering column cover and lift off cover with steering wheel. *See Steering Wheel in this section.* Remove entire steering column assembly and place on bench.

**Installation —** To install steering column, reverse removal procedure and note. Make sure turn signal cancellation groove in shaft is facing right side.

### OVERHAUL

**Disassembly — 1)** Index mark steering shaft and lower shaft. Remove bolt mounting steering column shaft with lower shaft and separate. Do not lose spring.

**2)** Remove mounting screw and take off turn signal light assembly and windshield wiper control. Remove snap ring, tap on steering shaft and drive out lower bearing.

**3)** Remove steering shaft, turn it upside down and refit in steering column. Drive upper bearing from steering column. Inspect both bearings and replace if found defective.

**Reassembly —** To reassemble steering column components, reverse disassembly procedure. Make sure bolt mounting steering column shaft and lower shaft faces vertically.

*Fig. 1  Sectional View of Lancia Beta Steering Column for Component Identification*

## LUV

### LUV

### DESCRIPTION

Column is fastened to steering gear through a flexible coupling. The energy-absorbing shaft will collapse during frontal impact under predetermined loads, by shearing plastic pins.

**Fig. 1  Exploded View of Steering Column Assembly**

### REMOVAL & INSTALLATION

**NOTE** — Before beginning removal and installation, inspect steering shaft shear pins. If steering shaft plastic pins have been sheared, shaft will rattle when struck lightly from side.

### STEERING COLUMN

**Removal** — 1) Disconnect battery ground. Remove horn cover and spring. Remove steering column shrouding and hazard warning light switch. Remove combination switch. Remove steering wheel. See LUV under STEERING WHEEL & COLUMN SWITCHES in this Section.

**NOTE** — Avoid impact to steering wheel at all times.

2) Raise front of vehicle and support. Remove pinch bolt holding shaft to lower coupling flange. Remove 3 mast jacket to firewall bolts. Remove 2 steering column to instrument panel bolts.

3) Separate rubber coupling from steering shaft. Carefully slide steering shaft toward inside of passenger compartment and remove from vehicle.

**Installation** — To install, reverse removal procedure, noting the following: Leave column-to-panel bolts slightly loose until vehicle is lowered to ground.

### FLEXIBLE COUPLING

**Removal** — 1) Raise front of vehicle. Remove coupling through bolts (only two can be removed). Remove coupling assembly by loosening clamp bolts.

2) If necessary to remove clamps, steering column must be loosened. Remove column mounting screws at cowl. Remove instrument panel mount bolts and slide column rearward about 1" (25 mm), then remove steering column flexible coupling.

**Installation** — Replace clamps without pinch bolts. Position rubber coupling and tighten through-bolts as required. Install and tighten clamp pinch bolts. If column was loosened, lower vehicle to floor and slightly tighten column-to-instrument panel screws. Install column cowling, then completely tighten column support screws.

### TIGHTENING SPECIFICATIONS

| Application | Ft. Lbs. (mkg) |
| --- | --- |
| Steering Wheel Nut | 25 (3.5) |
| Coupling Through-Bolts | 18 (2.5) |
| Shaft Coupling Clamp | 20 (2.8) |
| Coupling-to-Wormshaft Clamp | 20 (2.8) |
| Column-to-Cowl | 10 (1.4) |

## MERCEDES-BENZ

230
240D
280E
280SE/280CE
300D/300CD
450SEL
450SL/450SLC
6.9

### DESCRIPTION

Steering column assembly includes an impact absorbing steering wheel, upper and lower column shafts and flexible coupling. Lower shaft on 123 Series models is corrugated for additional impact protection.

### CHASSIS IDENTIFICATION

| Application | Chassis Type |
|---|---|
| 230, 240D, 280E, 280CE, 300D, 300CD | 123 |
| 450SL, 450SLC | 107 |
| 280SE, 450SEL, 6.9 | 116 |

### STEERING COLUMN

**Removal** — 1) On 123 Series, remove screws holding upper and lower cover on instrument panel and remove covers. On all models, disconnect battery and remove steering wheel. Remove instrument cluster by pulling outward as far as possible and loosening tachometer, temperature, and oil pressure connections.

2) On all models, remove steering lock. Disconnect wiring connectors. Remove Allen head screw of flexible coupling and all nuts and screws holding casing and column to dashboard. Remove steering column housing.

**Installation** — To install, reverse removal procedure. On 450 and 6.9 models, hold steering shaft in place with pin through hole in jacket tube. Check that lower tube on 123 Series is not bent or distorted. Use caution when installing jacket tube to prevent damage to this shaft.

### STEERING COLUMN SHAFT

**Removal, 123 Series (Lower)** — 1) From engine compartment, remove both Allen head screws holding flexible coupling to worm shaft and steering shaft. Slide coupling down on worm shaft and off steering shaft.

2) From inside car, remove upper and lower cover from instrument panel/steering column. Remove Allen screws at upper coupling and slide coupling and lower shaft off of upper shaft.

**Fig. 1  Lower Steering Shaft (123 Models)**

**Installation** — To install, lubricate inner lips of bellows seal at firewall and reverse removal procedures.

**NOTE** — *Wheels must be in straight ahead position and notch on upper shaft must point directly upward during installation.*

**Removal, 123 Series (Upper)** — 1) With column out of car, remove combination switch. Remove jacket tube casing, then remove spacing ring from steering shaft.

2) Remove gripper ring, compression spring, supporting ring and ball bearing from steering shaft. Knock steering shaft upward out of jacket tube with plastic hammer.

**Installation** — Inspect and replace bearings and races if required. Reverse removal procedure and reinstall upper steering shaft.

**Fig. 2  Typical Steering Wheel and Shaft**

**Removal, 107 and 116 Series** — 1) Remove steering wheel and combination switch rubber cover. Loosen switch mounting screws on bearing body and pull switch out slightly. Loosen screws holding cable of contact carbon on combination switch.

2) Remove Allen screw from upper end of steering coupling. Remove screws from jacket tube and pull steering shaft with bearing body out of jacket tube.

**Installation** — Replace bearings and races as required and reverse removal procedure. Check shaft adjustment; pin inserted through hole in jacket casing should locate check bore of steering shaft. Mark on end of shaft should be up when installing.

**NOTE** — *Steering shaft length should be 31.7" (805 mm); tap gently with plastic mallet to adjust length before installation.*

### TIGHTENING SPECIFICATIONS

| Application | Ft.Lbs. (mkg) |
|---|---|
| Steering Wheel | 37 (5) |
| Jacket Tube-to-Cross Member | 7 (1.0) |
| Jacket Tube-to-Lower Bracket | 18 (2.5) |
| Flexible Coupling (Allen) | 18 (2.5) |

# Steering Columns

## MGB

**MGB**

### REMOVAL & INSTALLATION

**STEERING COLUMN**

**Removal** – Remove steering wheel. See MGB under STEERING WHEEL & COLUMN SWITCHES in this section. Remove pinch bolt clamping steering column to "U" joint. Disconnect column wiring at multi-wire connector. Remove column bracket mounting bolts and note position of packing washers. Remove column from vehicle.

**Disassembly** – Remove column covers, take off wiring and combination switch. Drill and use screw extractor to remove ignition switch bolts. Remove switch.

**Reassembly** – Reverse disassembly procedure.

**Installation** – **1)** Fit column into vehicle. Replace packing washers and loosely attach column clamp bolts under instrument panel. If packing washers have been lost or if new column is being installed, column must be realigned. See Column Alignment in this Section.

**2)** Connect wiring plug and set wheels straight ahead. Slide steering shaft into "U" joint, making sure grooves align with pinch bolt holes. Fit pinch bolt and tighten.

### ADJUSTMENTS

**STEERING COLUMN ALIGNMENT**

**1)** Remove "U" joint. Fit alignment gauge shown in Fig. 2. Make sure setscrew seats in splined groove.

**2)** Fit 1 packing washer between each upper column mounting bracket. Tighten bolts until washers are just pinched. Tighten column plate bolts just enough to retain column in center of hole. Make sure rack has original amount of shims. Tighten bolts.

**3)** To correct horizontal misalignment, move end of column, then tighten column plate bolts.

**4)** To correct vertical misalignment, use shims placed between rack mounting brackets and bring left and right alignment into tolerance. Do not use more than 3 shims on either bracket. Refit rack and tighten mounting bolts.

**Fig.1  Exploded View of Steering Column and Related Components**

## MGB (Cont.)

5) Check gauge alignment. Make sure pinion has clearance. If there is interference, adjust shims. If alignment is still not adequate, readjust upper shims (packing washers). Make sure not to exceed .235" (6 mm) thickness with shims. Tighten top bolts. Take off gauge set.

6) Measure gap between column upper mounting flange and body bracket at third bolt position. Fit packing shims equal to gap. Tighten bolt. Make sure to rivet shims to rack mounting bracket before completing job.

### TIGHTENING SPECIFICATIONS

| Application | Ft. Lbs. (mkg) |
| --- | --- |
| Upper Column Mounting Bolts | 12-17 (1.7-2.4) |
| Universal Clamp Bolts | 20-22 (2.8-3.0) |
| Steering Wheel Nut | 27-29 (3.7-4.0) |

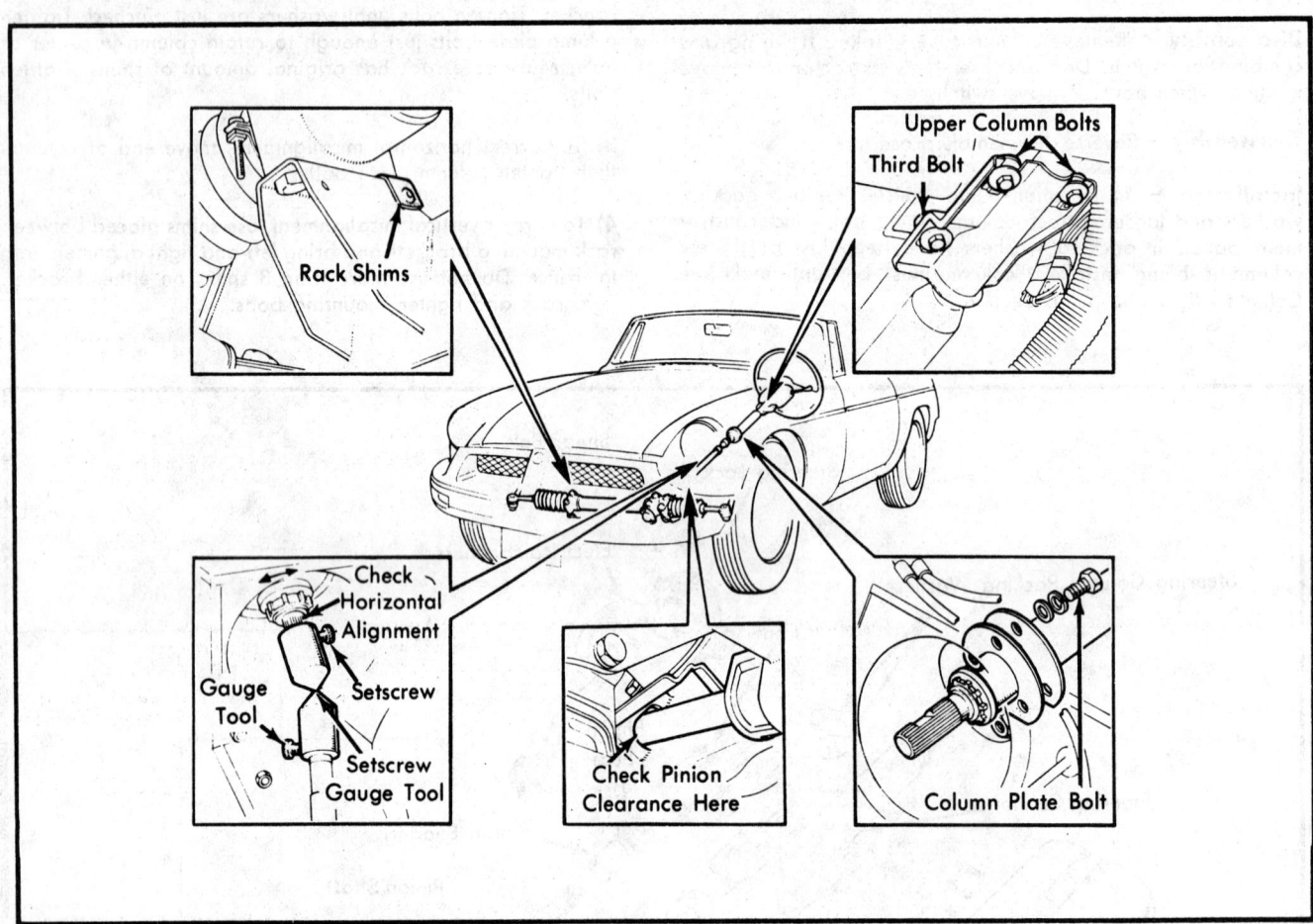

**Fig. 2  Steering Column Alignment Steps**

# Steering Columns

## MG MIDGET

**Midget**

### REMOVAL & INSTALLATION

**STEERING COLUMN**

**Removal** — 1) Disconnect battery cable. Remove heater air intake hose. Remove pinch bolt securing steering column clamp to steering gear pinion shaft, then remove screws securing floor board cover plate.

2) Note location, quantity, and thickness of spacing washers between upper column mount and body mount. Remove 3 nuts, bolts, and washers keeping column to upper flange and body bracket. Gather packing washers.

3) Disconnect steering column wiring harness at connector below facia. Remove steering column with steering wheel and switches.

**Disassembly** — 1) Remove steering wheel. See *Midget* under *STEERING WHEELS & COLUMN SWITCHES* in this Section.

2) Remove 4 small screws attaching shroud halves to steering column. Remove shrouds. Remove 2 small screws mounting wiper switch and slide switch out.

3) Remove 2 screws holding turn signal combination switch, disconnect horn slip ring and remove switch. Disconnect key warning buzzer lead at steering column, then remove ignition switch. Note position of turn signal canceller and remove from column.

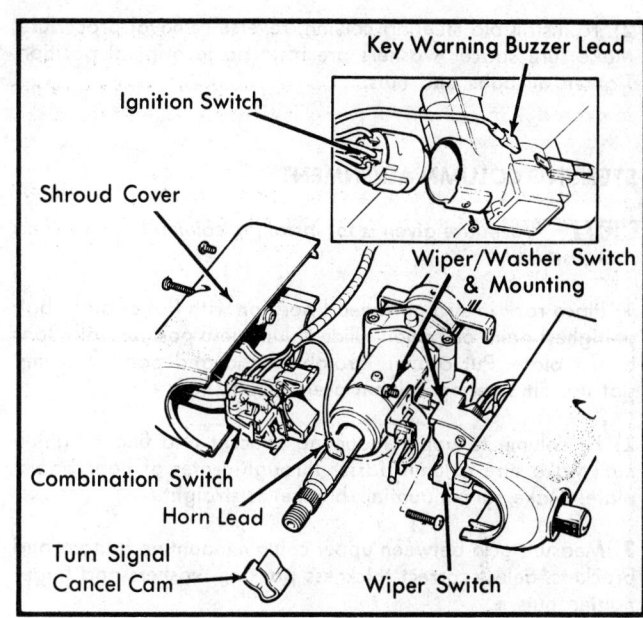

**Fig. 1  Items to Remove for Disassembly of Steering Column**

**Reassembly** — Reverse disassembly procedure.

**Installation** — 1) If a new steering column is being installed or if spacer washers were lost, steering column must be aligned. See *Steering Column Alignment*.

**Fig. 2  Preparation and Steps for Completing Steering Rack and Column Alignment**

## MG MIDGET (Cont.)

2) To install old steering column, reverse removal procedure. Make sure spacer washers are installed in original position. Tighten all bolts and nuts.

### STEERING COLUMN ALIGNMENT

**NOTE** — *Procedure given is for installing column to an existing rack assembly.*

1) Place rack in straight-ahead position with flat of pinch bolt at highest point on pinion. Slide column into position with floor board plate. Put column straight-ahead and position clamp slot up. Fit steering column over pinion shaft.

2) Fit column to upper mounting bracket and finger tighten nut. Make sure column passes through center of floor board plate. Make sure mounting bracket is straight.

3) Measure gap between upper column mounting flanges and brackets. Select correct thickness packing washers and finger tighten nuts.

4) Tighten cover plate at floor board. Tighten pinion shaft pinch bolt.

5) Rotate steering wheel from stop to stop. Note movement of rack assembly in relation to crossmember. Slowly move steering wheel in each direction until neutral position of rack is located.

6) Measure distance between rack mounting bracket at pinion end and front face of body crossmember. Install packing washers thickness of gap.

7) Remove pinion pinch bolts and floor board plate bolts. Push and pull on steering column and make sure column is free to slide. If column is too tight on pinion rack, recheck alignment. When alignment is correct tighten nuts and bolts.

### TIGHTENING SPECIFICATIONS

| Application | Ft. Lbs. (mkg) |
|---|---|
| Upper Column Mounting Bolts | 12-17 (1.7-2.4) |
| Pinion Shaft Pinch Bolt | 9-12 (1.2-1.7) |
| Steering Wheel Nut | 37 (5.1) |

## OPEL

### All Models

## DESCRIPTION

Steering column is a ball type energy absorbing unit with a plastic pin type shaft. Column and shaft will collapse during a front end collision by the shearing of the injected plastic pins. The column is attached at the instrument panel and by a flexible joint at the steering gear.

**Fig. 1  Assembled View of Steering Column Assembly**

## REMOVAL & INSTALLATION

**Removal** — Disconnect battery negative cable. Remove flexible joint bolt and two lower column guide bolts. Remove two column-to-instrument panel nuts and disconnect electrical connections. Withdraw column and shaft assembly.

**Fig. 2  Flexible Joint Connecting Steering Shaft with Steering Gear**

**Installation** — Install steering column assembly and loosely install two upper column-to-instrument panel nuts. Insert steering shaft into flexible coupling and torque key bolt nut to specification. Slide lower column guide down and bolt to floor pan. Position front wheels straight ahead and install steering wheel, making sure the turn signal cancelling pin is in the hole in the back of steering wheel. Install steering wheel washer and nut, then torque nut to specification.

## OVERHAUL

**Disassembly** — 1) Remove two horn button retaining screws, disconnect horn contact, then remove steering wheel nut and washer. Use suitable steering wheel puller and remove steering wheel. Remove screws from upper and lower column covers and hazard warning switch and remove switch unit.

**Fig. 3  Steering Column Shaft Measurement Locations**

2) Remove two retaining screws and take out windshield washer and wiper switch. Remove snap ring, washer and three attaching bolts on column flange, then remove lock cylinder housing, lower washer and shaft. Pry out lower column rubber bushing with a screwdriver.

**Inspection** — Check measurement of lower column and steering column shaft for correct measurement (See Fig. 3). If not to specifications replace component.

**Assembly** — 1) Assemble flat washer, lock cylinder housing, washer and snap ring on the shaft. Then install shaft assembly in the steering column and install lock cylinder retaining screws.

2) Install windshield wiper/washer switch and combination turn signal, headlight dimmer, and hazard warning flasher switch. Install upper and lower column covers and hazard warning button.

## TIGHTENING SPECIFICATIONS

| Application | Ft. Lbs. (mkg) |
| --- | --- |
| Key Bolt | 19 (2.6) |
| Steering Wheel Nut | 22 (3.0) |

# Steering Columns

## PORSCHE

911SC
924
930 Turbo

### DESCRIPTION

The steering column assemblies on all Porsche models are essentially the same, consisting of a three-piece, energy-absorbing unit, with the three pieces connected by two universal joints. The offset design of the steering shaft and the collapsible element in the steering column provide the energy-absorbing protection for the driver. An energy absorbing steering wheel with rebound chambers and padded hub cover provides additional protection.

**NOTE** — At the time of publication, no information was available for Porsch 928 steering column removal and installation procedures.

### REMOVAL & INSTALLATION

**Removal, 911SC & 930 — 1)** Disconnect battery. From front compartment, remove blower, ducting and steering shaft cover. Remove universal joint retaining bolt.

**2)** From driver's compartment, remove knee strip, light switch and tachometer. Drill or grind off shear bolts holding ignition switch/steering lock in panel mounting.

**3)** Lift off hub cover and remove steering wheel. Detach wire connection and remove steering column switch assembly along with steering shaft and tube.

**Installation** — To install, reverse removal procedure and tighten attaching shear bolts until heads break off.

**Removal, 924 — 1)** Disconnect battery and lift off steering wheel pad. Remove steering wheel. Remove upper universal joint retaining bolt.

**2)** Disconnect wiring plugs from rear of switches. Drill out casing tube shear bolts holding column to instrument panel. Remove upper steering column and switches as an assembly.

**Installation** — To install, reverse removal procedure noting the following: Tighten shear bolts holding column to panel until heads break off. Steering must be centered and hub lubricated when installing steering wheel. Tighten to specified torque with spokes in horizontal position.

### STEERING COLUMN ASSEMBLY

**Disassembly, 911S & 930 — 1)** With column out of vehicle and switches removed from column, drive steering shaft out of tube. Remove lower end circlip and lower ball bearing.

**2)** Press Seeger ring out of top end of steering shaft tube. Remove ball bearing and contact ring.

**Reassembly — 1)** Install ball bearing against circlip at lower end of steering column and seat bottom circlip against bearing. Circlips must seat in recessed grooves. Place contact ring and upper bearing together on steering shaft.

**2)** With section of pipe, drive bearing into place on shaft. Pipe should contact inner race only. Complete assembly in reverse order of disassembly.

**Disassembly, 924 —** Remove turn signal and windshield wiper switches. Remove circlip and upper ball bearing from housing.

**Reassembly — 1)** Reverse disassembly procedures and note the following: Drive ball bearing in up to stop in housing. Switches must be in OFF position when installed.

**2)** Lubricate needle bearing at lower end with multi-purpose grease. Use light coat of silicone grease or talcum powder on rubber bearing.

**3)** Drive steering shaft spacer sleeve onto shaft so that top of sleeve is 1.614" (41 mm) below top of shaft. Cancelling tab of turn signal release ring must face to right.

### TIGHTENING SPECIFICATIONS

| Application | Ft. Lbs. (mkg) |
| --- | --- |
| Universal Joint Bolts | 18-25 (2.5-3.5) |
| Steering Wheel Nut | |
| 911 & 930 | 54 (7.5) |
| 924 | 25-40 (3.5-5.5) |
| Steering Column Switch to Casing (Allen) | 8-14 (1-2) |

*Fig. 1   Porsche 924 Steering Column*

## RENAULT

**R-5**

### DESCRIPTION

Vehicles are equipped with an energy-absorbing collapsible column. The steering column is designed in two separate sections, which are joined by a universal joint. The upper portion of the column is designed with a sliding section which compresses on vehicle impact. At the lower end of the bottom section, the steering column is connected to the pinion flange of the steering gear through a flexible rubber coupling.

### REMOVAL & INSTALLATION

#### STEERING COLUMN

**Removal — 1)** Disconnect battery and unclip speedometer cable in engine compartment. Remove instrument cluster cowl. Pry clips on sides of cluster inward and pull cluster forward. Disconnect wiring and speedometer cable, then remove cluster.

**2)** Remove steering wheel pad and steering wheel. Detach lower column cover, remove screws and lift off combination switch from column. Disconnect wiring from switch. Remove fuse box screws and place box to one side. Disconnect universal joint.

**Fig. 1  Renault Steering Column with Related Components**

**3)** Mark column clamp position, remove shaft flexible coupling at steering box, and remove clamps from column tube. Pull column assembly free from dashboard.

**Installation — 1)** To install, reverse removal procedures, noting the following: Tighten upper column clamp at the end of installation. Set gear at center position before connecting universal joint in the following manner:

**2)** Raise front end of vehicle. Set steering box at center point. Tighten bottom joint pin. Turn steering ¼ turn to left or right, then tighten upper universal joint pin.

**3)** Reconnect all wiring, tighten bolts securely and check shaft for binding or rubbing.

**Fig. 2  Removing Upper Column Bushing**

### OVERHAUL

#### REPLACING COLUMN BUSHINGS

**Disassembly —** Tap upper end of steering shaft until lower bushing comes out of column tube. Remove snap ring from top of column tube and carefully pry out bushing with screwdriver.

**Assembly — 1)** Coat new bushings with suitable grease. Position lower split bushing on steering shaft and fit an old bushing below it (which has been turned down .079", 2 mm in diameter).

**2)** Insert lower bushing by pulling steering shaft upward, then push it back slightly to recover used bushing. Using a suitable sleeve, replace upper bushing. Insert snap ring and install column in vehicle.

## SAAB

**99**

### DESCRIPTION

Steering columns used on this model is a safety, telescopic type. The lower portion of the steering shaft is designed to retract into the upper portion when frontal impact is experienced. Steering column tube is mounted at one end to pedal bracket and at other end to body. An intermediate shaft, with "U" joints at each end, transmit steering column movement to steering gear. Models with power steering units are provided with a double "U" joint.

### REMOVAL & INSTALLATION

#### STEERING COLUMN

**Removal** — Unscrew locking bolt at universal joint. Remove two lower retaining screws at pedal bracket and two upper column-to-instrument panel retaining screws. Detach quick-release wiring connection and lift out steering column assembly.

**CAUTION** — *Steering wheel must be mounted on shaft before column is installed. Otherwise, tension on wheel and column may result.*

**Installation** — Position steering column tube in place with steering shaft and wheel attached. Bolt steering shaft to "U" joint. Make sure mounting bolt is opposite groove in steering shaft. Tighten bolt. Mount steering column tube to pedal bracket and body. Connect electrical harness. Adjust steering wheel.

### INTERMEDIATE SHAFT SEALING BELLOWS

**Removal** — Remove cover under instrument panel. Unscrew steering column-to-intermediate shaft retaining screw. Unbolt column tube from instrument panel. Pull steering column from intermediate shaft. Cut off old sealing bellows.

**Installation** — Lubricate suitable installation tool (899581) with vaseline or soapy water. Place tool against intermediate shaft. Ease new bellows over tool and joint. Ensure bellows are not damaged in this process. Replace steering column into intermediate shaft. Make sure that shaft is pushed in so that screw is located directly opposite the groove. Tighten retaining screw. Attach steering column to instrument panel. Check position of steering wheel and adjust if necessary. Fit bellows in dash panel. Replace cover under instrument panel.

### OVERHAUL

#### STEERING COLUMN

**Disassembly** — Remove three retaining screws and remove plastic cover under steering wheel. Pull steering wheel shaft out of tube. Withdraw two rubber bushings with steering wheel shaft bushings and washers.

**Assembly** — To assemble, reverse disassembly procedure, after replacing required bushings.

*Fig. 1 Exploded View of Steering Column Assembly*

## SUBARU

### DESCRIPTION

Steering column assembly consists of a steering wheel incorporating a horn control, a combination turn signal, hazard warning, and headlight dimmer switch assembly, and an energy absorbing steering shaft. The steering column is connected to the steering gear through a universal joint coupling. The energy absorbing steering shaft is designed to collapse during a front end collision. An anti-theft locking mechanism is used to prevent steering shaft from turning when key is removed.

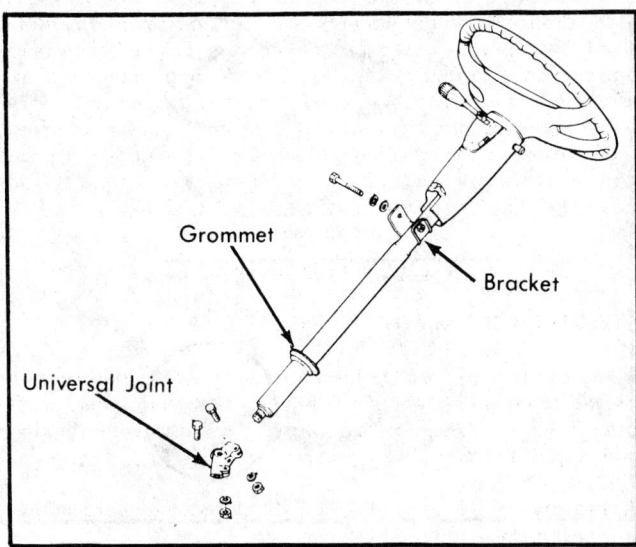

**Fig. 1  Subaru Steering Column Assembly**

### REMOVAL & INSTALLATION

**Removal — 1)** Disconnect battery ground strap. Loosen the universal joint clamp bolt and separate shaft from joint.

**2)** Unplug all wiring connectors to the steering column switches. Remove steering shaft bolt from instrument panel and pull steering column from floorboard.

**Installation —** Insert column through floorboard into universal joint. Install column bolt into dashboard finger tight, then tighten universal joint clamp bolt in engine compartment. Connect all wiring and tighten dashboard bolt.

### OVERHAUL

**Disassembly — 1)** Clamp steering column carefully in vise. Check back side of steering wheel for horn pad retaining bolt and remove if present. Remove pad by turning to left. Pull off steering wheel and remove column cover and hazard light knob.

**2)** Remove screws retaining bearing to steering column. Pull out shaft from the bottom of cover and remove snap ring, washer, "O" ring and bearing.

**Inspection — 1)** Universal joint should have no play in any direction. Replace if any play exists. Flex universal joint and check for binding. Replace if torque required to flex joint exceeds 0.43 ft. lbs. (0.06 mkg). Check plastic washer for damage, and serration for wear.

**Fig. 2  View of Steering Shaft Components**

**2)** Check steering shaft run-out and length. Run-out should be less than .02" (0.6 mm). Shaft for Subaru BRAT should be 32.84-32.92" (834.1-836.1 mm) in length. All others should measure 33.03-33.11 (839.1-841.1 mm). Replace shaft if damage is found. Check bearings for wear and replace if necessary.

**Reassembly —** To reassemble, reverse disassembly procedure and note the following: With steering wheel in place, check clearance between wheel and cover. If clearance exceeds .04-.12" (1.0-3.0 mm), loosen column cover screws and adjust cover.

### TIGHTENING SPECIFICATIONS

| Application | Ft. Lbs. (mkg) |
| --- | --- |
| Steering Wheel Nut | 20-29 (2.8-4.0) |
| Column Bracket Bolt | 12-15 (1.6-2.0) |
| Universal Joint Bolt | 16-19 (2.2-2.6) |

# Steering Columns

## TOYOTA COROLLA & CORONA

Corolla
Corona

### DESCRIPTION

Columns used on Corolla and Corona models are collapsible two-piece design. Some models use plastic shear pins to absorb collision impact; other models have a collapsible bellows-type column. A flexible coupling connects the shaft to steering gear.

### REMOVAL & INSTALLATION

#### STEERING COLUMN

**Removal — 1)** Working from inside engine compartment, remove bolt mounting steering mainshaft to steering gear box (*Fig. 1*). Before separating units, index mark for reinstallation and place front wheels in straight-ahead position.

**Fig. 1 Pinch Bolt Mounting Mainshaft to Steering Gear**

**2)** Remove steering wheel and turn signal switch. *See Steering Wheel and Column Switch in STEERING Section.* From inside passenger compartment, remove bolts mounting hole cover to firewall. Remove nuts and bolts mounting the break-away bracket (*Fig. 2*) then withdraw steering column assembly into passenger compartment and free from vehicle.

Break-Away Bracket

Steering Column

**Fig. 2 Column Mounting Bracket
(Corolla Shown, Corona Similar)**

**Installation —** Working from inside passanger compartment, insert steering column assembly through column hole in firewall. Align index marks made during removal and tighten pinch bolt. Fit break-away bracket, but leave bolts finger tight. Position column hole cover in place with a new "O" ring seal. Push in column tube until fully seated, then tighten nuts mounting break-away bracket. Make sure hole cover locating pin contacts cover as shown in *Fig. 3*.

Corona Models

Corolla Models

**Fig. 3 Proper Installation of Steering Column Locating Pin**

### OVERHAUL

#### STEERING COLUMN

**Disassembly —** Remove upper steering column bracket. From column tube, pull out mainshaft, then remove dust seal. From lower end of mainshaft, remove flexible coupling unit. Remove bolts attaching column plate, rotate column tube counterclockwise and remove it from column hole cover.

**Inspection —** Check mainshaft for out-of-alignment and looseness in plastic pin. Inspect column tube for deformation. Look closely at flexible coupling for deterioration, also check dust seal "O" ring for damage.

**Reassembly —** To reassemble components, reverse disassembly procedure and note the following: Apply a light coat of grease to both sides of "O" ring.

| TIGHTENING SPECIFICATIONS | |
|---|---|
| Application | Ft. Lbs. (mkg) |
| Steering Gear-to-Frame............................ | 25-36 (3.5-5.0) |
| Pitman Arm-to-Sector Shaft ..................... | 72-101 (10-14) |
| Column Tube Clamp ................................. | 22-33 (3.0-4.5) |
| Steering Wheel Nut .................................. | 22-29 (3.0-4.0) |
| Pinch Bolt.............................................. | 14.5-22 (2.0-3.0) |

# Steering Columns

## TOYOTA CELICA, CRESSIDA & PICKUP

Celica
Cressida
Pickup

### DESCRIPTION

Passenger cars incorporate energy absorbing steering columns which collapse on impact. Steering shaft and column tube both telescope. Pickup steering shaft is solid and does not collapse. All columns attach to lower edge of instrument panel with a bolt-on bracket.

Fig. 1  Pinch Bolt Separation Point and Index Marking

### REMOVAL & INSTALLATION

**NOTE** — *Removal and installation procedures are of a general nature and can be used for all models.*

**Removal** — 1) Loosen pinch bolt *(Fig. 1)* attaching coupling yoke to worm shaft. Index mark coupling yoke and worm shaft. Loosen steering wheel nut and using a puller, remove steering wheel. *For additional information, See Steering Wheel and Column Switches in STEERING Section.*

2) Disconnect wiring harnesses for ignition switch, turn signals, horn, and dimmer switch. Remove switches. Unscrew column floor cover bolts. Remove lower instrument panel cover and air conditioning duct (if equipped). Remove bracket bolts and pull column out of vehicle.

**Installation** — 1) Insert steering column through column hole from inside of vehicle, align coupling yoke on steering worm, and tighten pinch bolt. **NOTE** — *Yoke and worm are in proper alignment when yoke bolt hole is aligned with cut-away portion of worm spline.*

2) Coat break-away bracket center portion with suitable weatherstrip adhesive. Finger tighten break-away bracket bolts. Tighten column hole cover bolts and break-away bracket nuts, then insert and tighten center bracket retaining bolt.

Fig. 2  Toyota Energy Absorbing Steering Column

# Steering Columns

## TOYOTA LAND CRUISER

**Land Cruiser FJ40**
**Land Cruiser FJ55**

### DESCRIPTION

The steering shaft assembly on Land Cruiser models consists of a main shaft rotating inside a column tube. FJ40 models use a one-piece main shaft with a flexible coupling at the steering box. FJ55 uses a collapsible shaft and column tube. A second, intermediate shaft connects the steering box to the main shaft. Both models bolt to the instrument panel and floorboard.

### REMOVAL & INSTALLATION

#### MAIN SHAFT

**Removal — 1)** Place index marks on steering shaft and flexible coupling or universal joint. Loosen screws and remove steering wheel pad. Place marks on wheel and shaft, then pull off steering wheel. Disconnect wiring plugs under column.

**2)** Remove lock bolt at bottom of main shaft. Remove bolts attaching floor cover to firewall. Loosen upper bracket bolts and pull steering column from vehicle.

**Installation —** To install, reverse removal procedure.

#### INTERMEDIATE SHAFT

**Removal —** Raise front of vehicle and support with stands. Pry off wheel cap and remove left front wheel. Remove bolts securing steering worm yokes to worm and main shaft. Remove intermediate shaft.

**Installation —** To install, reverse removal procedure.

**Fig. 2   Assembled View of Intermediate Shaft Coupling**

### OVERHAUL

**Disassembly — 1)** Remove turn signal switch from top of column tube. Remove bearing retainer bolts and retainer. Remove snap ring from main shaft.

**2)** On FJ40 models, remove flexible coupling from bottom of shaft and pull shaft from column housing. On FJ55 models, remove floor plate from bottom of housing, remove snap ring, and pull shaft from column housing.

**Inspection —** Check shaft, coupling, and bearings for damage, wear, and cracks. Replace bearings if rough.

**Reassembly —** Grease upper bearing and assemble shaft components in reverse order of disassembly.

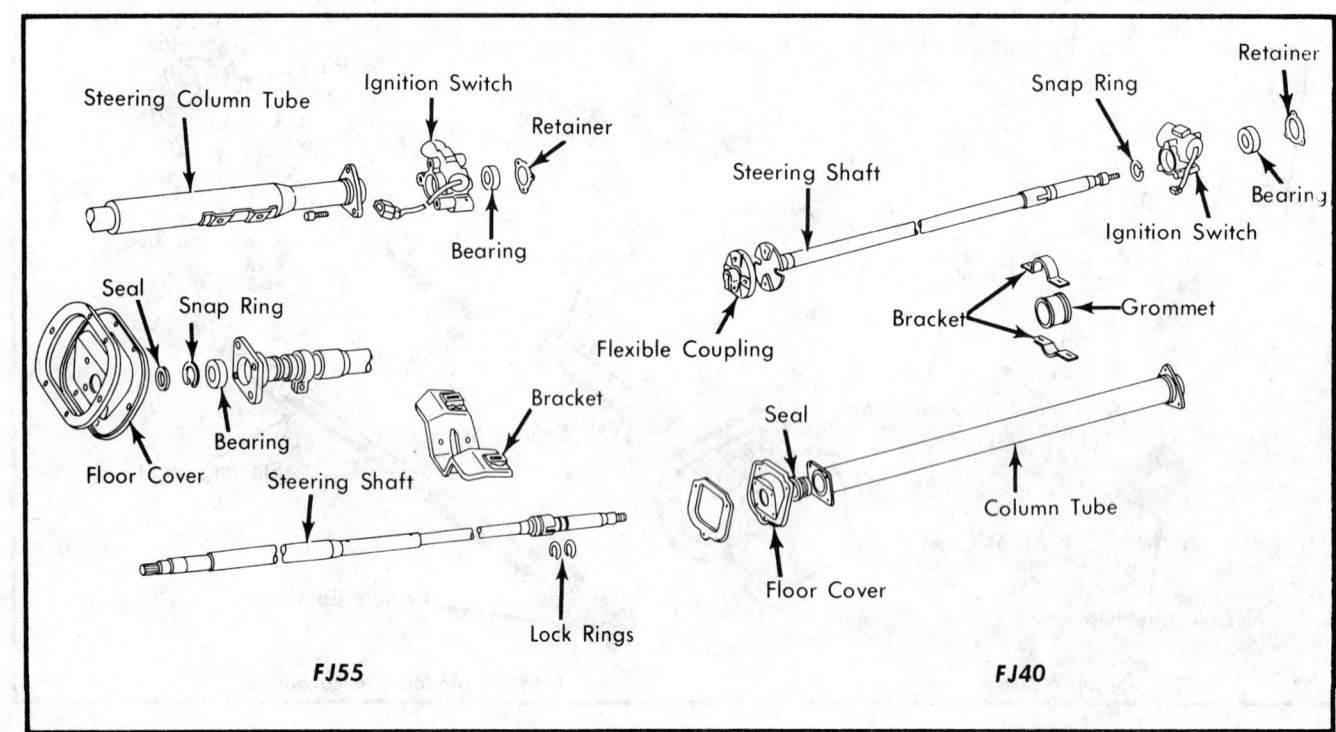

**Fig. 1   Land Cruiser Steering Column Assembly**

## TOYOTA LAND CRUISER (Cont.)

### INTERMEDIATE SHAFT

**Disassembly** — Remove cup stopper plates *(Fig. 2)*, then remove "U" bolts securing universal joint spider bearing to steering worm yoke. Separate worm yoke from sliding yoke and shaft. Remove hole snap rings from bearing holes, then remove spider bearing.

**Reassembly** — 1) Pack spider bearing cups with suitable grease and assemble bearing rollers. Press bearing into one side of sliding shaft. Install bearing seal and complete the in-

stallation of spider bearing. Install suitable snap rings in one of the following sizes: .047" (1.20mm), .049" (1.25mm), .051" (1.30mm). Check joint for smooth operation.

2) Connect sliding shaft to steering worm yoke. Install cup stopper plates and "U" bolts. Assemble joint spider bearing onto sliding yoke in same manner. Pack inside hole of sliding yoke with suitable grease. Align cup stopper plates on sliding yoke side and sliding shaft side. Install dust cover and connect sliding shaft with yoke.

*Fig. 3 Exploded View of Land Cruiser FJ55 Intermediate Steering Shaft Components*

# Steering Column

## TRIUMPH TR7

**TR7**

### DESCRIPTION

Steering column houses ignition switch, column lock, and light and wiper controls. The steering column is divided into upper and intermediate shafts which are coupled by universal joints.

### REMOVAL AND INSTALLATION

**STEERING COLUMN ASSEMBLY**

**Removal** — 1) Disconnect battery ground. Take out pinch bolt securing upper universal to steering mast. Disconnect electrical harness from steering column and separate plug connectors (*Fig. 1*). Remove plastic cover from around steering column.

2) Center punch shear head bolts and use a small chisel to remove. With wheels facing in a straight ahead position, withdraw steering column, noting number and position of flat and concave washers.

**Installation** — 1) To install steering column assembly, reverse removal procedures, noting the following: Make sure front wheels are in straight ahead position and steering wheel is centered. Check for proper positioning of flat and concave washers.

2) Align steering column mounting holes, then install new bolts and tighten evenly until heads shear. Tighten upper universal pinch bolt to specification.

**INTERMEDIATE SHAFT**

**Removal** — Remove pinch bolt mounting intermediate shaft to upper universal coupling and pinch bolt securing universal joint to rack pinion. With front wheels in straight ahead position, slide intermediate shaft upward to remove it from pinion shaft universal joint, then pull shaft downward to disengage from upper universal joint.

**Installation** — To install intermediate shaft, reverse removal procedure, noting the following: Make sure steering wheel is in straight ahead position and splines on intermediate shaft and rack pinion are fully engaged. Tighten pinch bolts to specification.

### OVERHAUL

**STEERING COLUMN ASSEMBLY**

**Disassembly** — With steering column assembly removed from vehicle, remove the steering wheel spoke pad. Remove steering wheel from column. Remove shear head bolts. Withdraw column housing from steering mast. Remove nut and bolt securing clamp to steering mast and remove clamp. With a drift, remove top and bottom bushings from steering column housing.

**Reassembly** — Align slots in bushings with lugs in column housing, then press in bushings. Install steering lock in column housing and secure with shear bolts. Refit all electrical connectors and indicator control cams and arms. Tighten steering hub and wheel into position, then refit spoke cover.

### TIGHTENING SPECIFICATIONS

| Application | Ft. Lbs. (mkg) |
|---|---|
| Steering Wheel Nut | 30-37 (4-5) |
| Column Clamp-to-Column | 6-9 (.8-1.2) |
| Universal Joint Pinch Bolts | 16-21 (2.2-2.9) |

*Fig. 1  Partially Disassembled View of TR7 Upper Steering Column*

## TRIUMPH SPITFIRE

**Spitfire**

### DESCRIPTION

Steering column is a telescoping, safety unit which is designed to compress on impact. The lower section of column will move into the steering column, absorbing impact shock. Column is connected to pinion gear through a flexible coupling and is mounted to the instrument panel on two column supports. A grub screw is inserted through the lower support clamp and retains the lower telescoping portion in place.

### REMOVAL & INSTALLATION

**Removal — 1)** Disconnect battery. Remove driver's parcel shelf. Unscrew pinch bolts securing steering mast to flexible coupling at gear housing. Remove nuts and washers from two bolts securing steering column forward bracket. Withdraw forward support housing and felt liner.

**2)** Disconnect electrical couplings for horn, turn signal switch, lights, and column lock. Remove two cap screws securing steering column rear bracket, then withdraw both clamp halves and upper plate. Remove steering column assembly with tie bar.

**Installation — 1)** Set front wheels in straight-ahead position. Hold steering wheel with center spoke straight down, then engage lower end of steering mast in splines of flexible coupling. Slide cardboard tube rearward and fit felt over steering mast housing, ensuring ends of felt are below mast housing.

**2)** Engage forward ends of tie bar in mounting bolt. Fit felt housing and engage forward mounting bolts, using spring and plain washers under nuts. Ensure spring clip is fitted on mast housing to align with rear clamp bracket. Attach upper and lower clamp halves to mast housing.

**3)** Place plate in bracket above clamp halves. Enter clamp bolts through tie bar, clamp halves, and mounting bracket. Tighten nuts securing forward bracket. Reconnect electrical leads for horn, turn signal switch, lights, and steering lock. Replace parcel shelf. Connect battery.

### OVERHAUL

**Disassembly — 1)** Remove steering wheel. Detach column switches. Unlock steering column lock. Remove two set bolts and spring washers securing safety clamp, and remove safety clamp and thrust washer.

**2)** Withdraw lower steering mast. Pull cap from lower end of steering column tube and remove tubular cardboard spacer. Push column housing upward and withdraw turn signal cam. Pull housing toward lower end of column until it presses against column bushing. Depress rubber locating tabs on column lower bushing and withdraw steering mast and lower bushing. Pull bushing from mast. Remove upper bushing.

**Assembly —** To assemble, reverse disassembly procedure, noting that rubber dots on bushings are facing bottom of tube.

**Fig. 1  Spitfire Telescoping Steering Column and Related Components**

## VOLKSWAGEN TYPE 1

### Type 1

## DESCRIPTION

Two universal joints are used in the steering column to keep the column from being in line with the steering box. The offset prevents collision impact forces from being transmitted up through column to the driver. No collapsible sections are necessary with this design.

## REMOVAL & INSTALLATION

**Removal** — Disconnect battery ground strap and remove fuel tank. Remove the clamp bolt securing upper universal joint to steering column.

**2)** Disconnect all wiring from column switches and pull wiring toward passenger compartment. Remove horn pad and steering wheel, then circlip and spacer from column.

**3)** Remove 2 upper column support bolts from dashboard. Pull column tube into passenger compartment. Remove bolt holding column switch assembly to tube and remove switches. Pull shaft out of housing.

**Installation** — **1)** Place shaft in column tube and ensure bearing seat contacts needle bearing in tube. Install contact ring on top of shaft. Push column switch assembly on and tighten socket head screw. Reinstall circlip and spacer.

**2)** Slide sealing collar onto tube, then dust sealing ring with talcum powder and install over lower end of shaft. Place column in vehicle and insert support washer (plastic coated side down) between bottom of column tube and universal joint.

**3)** Align steering column groove with universal joint bolt and tighten new locking nut to 18 ft. lbs. (2.5 mkg). Install upper column bolts to dashboard finger tight. Center wheels and install steering wheel. Slide column up or down to adjust gap between wheel and column switch assembly to .063-.156" (2-4 mm). Tighten column bolts to 11-14 ft. lbs. (1.5-2.0 mkg)

## TIGHTENING SPECIFICATIONS

| Application | Ft. Lbs. (mkg) |
| --- | --- |
| Steering Wheel Nut | 36 (5.0) |
| Universal Joint Clamp Bolt | 18 (2.5) |
| Column Switch Socket Head Screw | 4-7 (.5-1.0) |
| Column-to-Dashboard | 11-14 (1.5-2.0) |

**Fig. 1   Exploded View of Type 1 Steering Column**

## VOLKSWAGEN TYPE 2

**Type 2**

### DESCRIPTION

Type 2 Volkswagen models use an energy-absorbing steering column assembly. Mounting support and energy-absorbing bracket are welded to steering column. When frontal impact is encountered, column support detaches from under instrument panel. Bracket then collapses to a predetermined location and support is deflected to side. Steering shaft can be removed separately or entire steering column (with shaft) can be removed as a unit.

### STEERING COLUMN ASSEMBLY

**Removal — 1)** Disconnect battery ground. Disconnect all electrical wires from steering column.

**2)** Work under vehicle and disconnect horn ground wire. Unbolt steering shaft from coupling at steering gear box pinch bolt.

**3)** Work between pedals and remove column cover plate. From under instrument panel, unbolt column tube support. Pull steering column assembly out of vehicle as an assembly.

**NOTE** — *If vehicle has been damaged, entire steering column must be replaced. Do not attempt any repairs.*

**Installation —** To install, reverse removal procedure and note: Make sure plastic-coated washers are replaced.

### STEERING SHAFT

**Removal — 1)** Disconnect battery. Remove steering wheel. *See Volkswagen under STEERING WHEEL & COLUMN SWITCHES in this Section.* Put ignition/steering lock switch in "ON" position.

**2)** Work between pedals and remove steering column cover plate. Bend up lock plate then remove bolt keeping steering shaft coupler to steering gear.

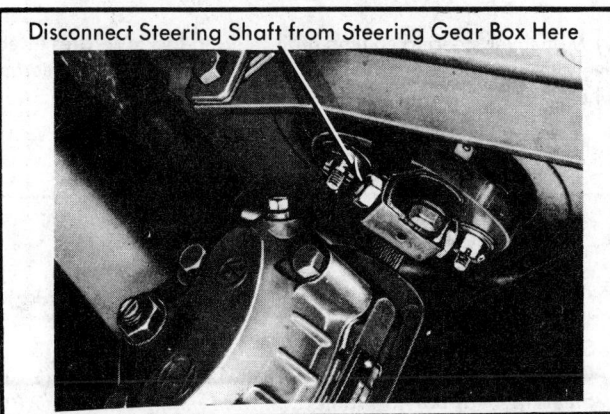

**Fig. 1    Steering Shaft to Gear Box Coupling Viewed from Under Vehicle**

**3)** Remove drag link and pitman arm. Remove 4 bolts mounting steering gear box to frame. Force steering shaft up enough so gear box can be removed.

**4)** Slide shaft downward and out of vehicle complete with steering coupling.

**Installation —** To install, reverse removal procedure and note: From chassis number 212-2038-133 there are 2 pitman arm alignment marks. Make sure the "L" (left-hand drive) mark in pitman arm aligns with index mark cast in steering gear shaft.

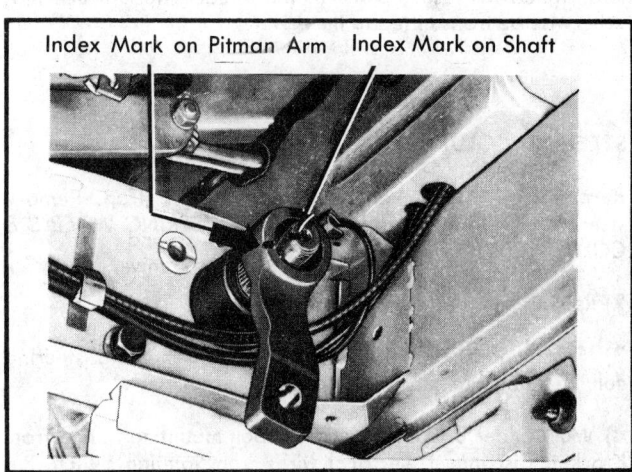

**Fig. 2    Pitman Arm and Steering Gear Shaft Alignment Marks**

**Fig. 3    Type 2 Steering Column and Bracket Assembly**

## TIGHTENING SPECIFICATIONS

| Application | Ft. Lbs. (mkg) |
| --- | --- |
| Steering Wheel Nut | 36 (5.0) |
| Flexible Coupling-to-Flange | 11 (1.52) |
| Column Cover Plate | 3.5 (.48) |
| Bracket Attaching Bolts | 10-11 (1.38-1.52) |
| Coupling, Flange-to-Worm Shaft | 14 (1.94) |

# VOLKSWAGEN DASHER

**Dasher**

## DESCRIPTION

The Volkswagen Dasher uses a two-piece safety steering column which incorporate a flange connection. A lattice metal column support is used under the instrument panel. This device is designed to absorb some of the impact shock which may otherwise be transmitted to the driver.

## REMOVAL & INSTALLATION

### STEERING COLUMN

**Removal − 1)** Disconnect battery ground strap. Remove steering wheel. See *Volkswagen under STEERING WHEELS & COLUMN SWITCHES in this Section.*

**2)** Remove all steering column switches.

**3)** From under hood, remove pinch bolt holding steering column flange to pinion shaft.

**4)** Work under brake pedal and unbolt mounting flange from bracket. Disconnect electrical wires from ignition switch. Put ignition switch in "ON" position.

**5)** Centerpunch shear bolts holding steering lock on steering column. Drill out shear bolts. Remove steering lock. Remove steering column and shaft as a unit.

*Fig. 1   Expanded View of Dasher Steering Column*

**Disassembly −** Pull off steering wheel spacer ring and snap ring. Remove flat washer and spring. Pull steering shaft out through bottom of column. Press race out of column.

**Reassembly −** Examine race and replace if excessively worn. Slide steering shaft back into column then refit spring and snap ring.

*Fig. 2   Using a Drill to Remove Steering Column Shear Bolts*

**Installation − 1)** Position column assembly back in vehicle. Install steering column lock. Make sure lock lug will snap into recess in steering column. Fit new shear bolts finger tight.

**2)** Bolt steering column mounting flange onto bracket so long side of flange faces right side of vehicle. Snug up flange bolts and shear bolts.

**3)** Connect electrical wires to ignition switch. Fit column trim. Place front wheels straight-ahead.

**4)** Make sure column bushings are in position on pins at lower end of steering column. Line holes in flange so flange will slide down over pins on steering column. It will be necessary to use drift to drive flange tube onto steering gear pinion shaft. Make sure flange seats to stop on pinion. Tighten pinch bolt.

**5)** Maneuver steering column until steering lock operates effectively. Tighten shear bolts until head snap off. Refit steering wheel.

## TIGHTENING SPECIFICATIONS

| Application | Ft. Lbs. (mkg) |
|---|---|
| Steering Wheel Nut | 36 (5.0) |
| Column Mounting Flange-to-Body | 14 (2.0) |
| Steering Gear Box-to-Frame | 14 (2.0) |
| Gear Box Pinch Bolt | 22 (3.0) |

## VOLKSWAGEN RABBIT & SCIROCCO

**Rabbit**
**Scirocco**

### DESCRIPTION

Volkswagen Rabbit and Scirocco use a swing-away type of steering column. The column is held in place by a clamp and leaf spring. On impact, the lower, angled portion of the column pushes upper column against leaf spring. The spring allows the column to disengage and swing to the side.

### REMOVAL & INSTALLATION

#### STEERING COLUMN ASSEMBLY

**NOTE** — *Do not attempt to remove steering shaft from column without first removing entire assembly from the vehicle.*

**Removal – 1)** Disconnect battery ground. Remove steering wheel. See *Volkswagen* under *STEERING WHEEL & COLUMN SWITCHES* in this Section.

**2)** Remove socket head bolt and Phillips head screw from switch housing recess. Tilt switch unit toward instrument panel. Pry off spacer sleeve on steering column. Pull switch unit up enough to disconnect wires. Remove switch unit from column.

NOTE: Later Models Have Internal Mounting Rings. Mounting Ring Lugs Must Fit Into Column Tube Slots.

Spacer Sleeve

Steering Column Switch Unit

Damping Grommet

"U" Joint Shaft

Pinch Bolt

Boot

Spring

Steering Column Bearing

Mounting Ring

Support Ring

Shear Bolt

Pinch Bolt

Steering Shaft

Bearing Support Ring

*Fig. 1  Exploded View of Rabbit and Scirocco Steering Column*

## VOLKSWAGEN RABBIT & SCIROCCO (Cont.)

Distance Should be
1.63" (41.5 mm)

Spacer Sleeve

Gap Should be
.08-.16" (2-4 mm)

**Fig. 2   Spacer Sleeve Adjustment Dimensions**

**3)** Disconnect steering shaft from "U" joint shaft. Disconnect brake pedal push rod. Separate clutch pedal from actuating cable under instrument panel.

**4)** Push leaf spring retainer clip down with a screwdriver and disengage it from mounting slot. Remove bolts mounting column under instrument panel. Shear bolts will have to be centerpunched and drilled out. Pull entire column (with shaft) out of vehicle.

**Bearing Replacement** — Drive steering shaft from column. Remove bearings. Press in steering shaft and bearings. It should not take more than a force of 100-200 lbs. (45-90 kgs) to properly seat bearings into position.

**Installation** — To install, reverse removal procedure and note: Make sure front wheels point straight-ahead before tightening pinch bolt. Before fitting column switch unit, install spacer to dimensions shown in *Fig. 2*. Adjust both brake pedal and clutch pedal height.

## "U" JOINT SHAFT

**Removal** — **1)** Separate manual gearshift linkage from steering box.

**2)** Remove pinch bolt connecting lower end of "U" joint shaft with steering gear pinion shaft.

**3)** Remove nuts mounting steering gear box to frame. Pull box down to separate from lower "U" joint. Remove rubber boot from lower "U" joint.

**4)** Remove pinch bolt connecting upper "U" joint to steering shaft. Pull down on joint and remove shaft with "U" joints from vehicle.

**NOTE** — *Identification is stamped on the lower end of shaft where it connects to "U" joint. Rabbit models are identified by 17L cast into shaft. Scirocco models are identified by circular knurl and 53L cast into shaft.*

**Installation** — **1)** Fit "U" joint to steering shaft. Make sure notch in steering shaft aligns with slot in lower "U" joint.

**2)** Install boot and damping grommet. Fit steering gear box to frame while guiding pinion shaft into lower "U" joint. Finger tighten gear box nuts.

**3)** Place front wheels straight-ahead. Align pinion shaft and "U" joint. Tighten pinch bolt. Tighten gear box nuts. Connect manual gearshift linkage to gear box. Check linkage operation.

### TIGHTENING SPECIFICATIONS

| Application | Ft. Lbs. (mkg) |
|---|---|
| Steering Wheel Nut | 36 (5.0) |
| Steering Column-to-Instrument Panel | |
|   Mounting Bolt | 14 (2.0) |
|   Shear Bolts | ① |
| Pinch Bolts | 22 (3.0) |

① — Until bolt head snaps.

## VOLVO

**240 Series**
**260 Series**

### DESCRIPTION

Steering column is divided in two sections. Upper and lower sections are joined by means of a flange. A heavy frontal impact would cause flange to break from upper column. The upper portion of steering column would retain its position, eliminating possibility of its being forced toward driver. Upper part of column is carried in two ball bearings located in jacket tube. Lower end of steering column is connected to steering shaft by a flange.

### REMOVAL & INSTALLATION

**STEERING COLUMN**

**Removal — 1)** Disconnect battery ground. Remove steering wheel. *See Volvo under STEERING WHEEL & COLUMN SWITCHES in this Section.*

**2)** Work inside engine compartment and disconnect clamp holding column shaft to lower shaft universal joint. Pry clamp apart with screwdriver, do not tap with hammer.

**3)** Remove column covers. Disconnect wiring and remove turn signal and wiper switches. Remove switch retainer, spring, and bearing race.

**4)** Drill steering column lock bolts and remove with a screw extractor.

**5)** Slide out steering column rubber grommet at firewall. Remove steering column lower mounting bolts. Force steering column through firewall until clear of lower portion of instrument panel. Pull column toward passenger compartment and remove from vehicle.

**6)** Place steering column assembly in a soft jawed vise and remove steering lock mechanism.

3.8" (97 mm)

Steering Wheel Lock

Steering Column

**Fig. 1   Steering Wheel Lock Position**

**Installation — 1)** Measure steering column to ensure length is 27.08-27.17" (688-690 mm). Position steering wheel lock on column so lock upper edge is 3.8" (97 mm) from upper edge of steering column. *See Fig. 1.*

**2)** Place rubber seal on column and insert column through firewall. Make sure both plastic guides are in position on the dashboard and install bolts loosely in upper and lower attachments.

**3)** Adjust column position. Steering wheel lock should protrude from dashboard .53-.65" (13.5-16.5 mm) when measured at key position "III" at the lock. Check for binding and rubbing, and adjust dashboard beam if necessary. Tighten lower bolts to 15-22 ft. lbs. (2-3 mkg).

Switch Bracket Ground

**Fig. 2   Switch Bracket Ground on Steering Column**

**4)** Install switch bracket. Make sure to use one of mounting screws as a ground. Install race and spring for upper race. Install turn signal, wiper switch and ignition switch. Connect horn wire lead.

Race

Upper Spring

**Fig. 3   Install Upper Bearing Race and Spring to Steering Column**

**5)** Replace column covers after tightening upper bolts until the heads shear off. Install steering wheel and tighten nut to 33-55 ft. lbs. (4.6-7.6 mkg). Tighten lower column clamp bolt in engine compartment to 15-22 ft. lbs. (2-3 mkg).

**NOTE** — *Rattling in steering column can be corrected by placing 1 or 2 flat washers between steering wheel and upper bearing spring.*

## ARROW, CHALLENGER, COLT, SAPPORO RECIRCULATING BALL

**Arrow**
**Challenger**
**Colt**
**Sapporo**

### DESCRIPTION

Steering system uses a recirculating ball gear of variable ratio. This type of gear minimizes gear ratio at the straight-ahead position, resulting in high stability at center; however, as the wheel is turned from center, gear ratio increases, allowing easy maneuvering.

Two sizes of steering box are used: a small box on models equipped with the 1600 cc engine, and a larger box for models equipped with the 2000 and 2600 cc engines. Both are serviced by the same procedures.

### REMOVAL & INSTALLATION

#### STEERING GEAR

Disconnect steering shaft from gear box main shaft. Using suitable puller, separate relay rod from pitman arm. Remove gear box from frame. Pull pitman arm from cross shaft. To install, reverse removal procedure.

#### TIE ROD ASSEMBLY

**Removal** — Disconnect tie rod ends from steering knuckle, using suitable puller (MB990635). Unscrew tie rod ends from tie rod.

**Installation** — Grease tie rod end dust cover and coat lower edge of cup with packing sealer before installation. Temporarily install tie rod ends to rod, so distance from center to center of tie rod ends is 11.89" (302 mm) for Arrow and Colt, except station wagon. Distance should be 12.36" (314 mm) for Challenger, Sapporo and Colt wagon. Amount of threads showing on each side of tie rod sleeve should be equal. Install on vehicle and check toe-in. See WHEEL ALIGNMENT Section.

**Fig. 1  Exploded View of Steering Linkage
Colt & Arrow (Exc. Station Wagon)**

#### RELAY ROD

**Removal** — Disconnect tie rod ends from steering knuckle arms using suitable puller (MB990635). Detach pitman arm and idler arm, using same puller. Remove relay rod.

**Installation** — To install, reverse removal procedure, noting the following: Ensure dust covers are well greased and that lower edge of covers are coated with packing sealer.

**Fig. 2  Exploded View of Steering Linkage
Challenger, Sapporo, Colt Station Wagon**

#### IDLER ARM

**Removal** — Disconnect idler arm from relay rod, using suitable puller (MB990635). Remove idler arm assembly from frame.

**NOTE** — *Do not disassemble idler arm and support unless absolutely necessary.*

**Installation** — Apply soapy water to bushings and idler arm. Push bushings into arm, using a vise if necessary. Grease bracket shaft and inner surface of bushing, then insert shaft into idler arm. Install washer with knurled side toward bushing and using a new self-locking nut, tighten to specification.

#### PITMAN ARM

**Removal** — After removing steering gear, disconnect pitman arm from cross shaft, using a suitable puller (CT-1106).

**Installation** — During installation, ensure slit on cross shaft aligns with pitman arm mark.

### OVERHAUL

#### STEERING GEAR

**Disassembly** — 1) Prior to disassembly, record starting torque of main shaft (as guide during assembly). Remove adjusting screw lock nut, turn screw counterclockwise (partial turn), then remove cover. When cover is free of sector shaft, remove adjusting screw. Set gear in straight ahead (center) position and withdraw sector shaft from gear box.

2) Measure and record main shaft starting torque with sector shaft removed. Remove end cover and record thickness of shim. Carefully remove main shaft, ball nut assembly, and bearings.

**CAUTION** — *Do not disassemble the mainshaft and ball nut assembly.*

## ARROW, CHALLENGER, COLT, SAPPORO RECIRCULATING BALL (Cont.)

**Inspection** — Check components for excess wear or free play. If rough rotation or excess play is found in main shaft or ball nut, replace both as an assembly. Do not force ball nut to either end of main shaft.

**Assembly & Adjustment — 1)** Place gear box in vise with main shaft in horizontal position. Replace end cover with shim (same as removed) and torque to specifications. Measure main shaft preload. If less or greater than 3.0-4.8 INCH lbs. (.42-.66 cmkg), reduce or increase shim size to obtain proper preload.

**2)** Install adjusting screw and proper shim in groove on sector shaft. Be sure axial play of shaft is no greater than .002" (.051 mm). If greater, change shim size. Lubricate and install sector shaft in housing. Replace cover and cover bolts. Turn sector shaft several times from side to side, then turn adjusting screw in and out several times, to set proper gear mesh.

**Fig. 3 Exploded View of Recirculating Ball & Nut Steering Gear — Small Gear Box**

**3)** Loosen adjusting screw until no play is noticed at main shaft when gear is in central position. Tighten lock nut. Recheck main shaft preload; it should now be 5.7-7.4 INCH lbs. (.79-1.02 cmkg). Fill gear box with SAE 90 gear oil. Check oil level through lower right bolt hole. Proper level from hole is

0.7" (18 mm) for small steering gear box and .87" (22 mm) for large box.

**Fig. 4 Exploded View of Recirculating Ball & Nut Steering Gear — Large Gear Box**

### TIGHTENING SPECIFICATIONS

| Application | Ft. Lbs. (mkg) |
|---|---|
| Gear Box-to-Frame | |
| Small Box | 25-29 (3.5-4.0) |
| Large Box | 32-36 (4.4-5.0) |
| Gear Box End Cover | 11-14 (1.5-2.0) |
| Pitman Arm-to-Gear Box | 94-108 (13-15) |
| Idler Arm Bracket-to-Frame | 29-43 (4.0-6.0) |
| Tie Rod Stud Nuts | 36-40 (5.0-5.5) |
| Tie Rod End Lock Nuts | |
| Arrow, Colt | 25-33 (3.5-4.5) |
| Challenger, Sapporo | 29-36 (4.0-5.0) |
| Relay Rod-to-Pitman Arm | |
| Arrow, Colt | 25-33 (3.5-4.5) |
| Challenger, Sapporo | 29-36 (4.0-5.0) |

## AUDI FOX RACK & PINION

Fox

### ADJUSTMENT

#### RACK ADJUSTMENT

Loosen lock nut on steering gear cover. Hand tighten adjusting screw until it touches thrust washer. Hold screw in position and tighten lock nut. If steering is too tight or does not self center, readjust. If gear rattles when driven, adjustment is too loose.

**CAUTION** — *Do not turn gear hard against either lock when vehicle is raised off ground or damage may result.*

### REMOVAL & INSTALLATION

#### STEERING GEAR

**Removal** — After removing both tie rod mounting bolts from rack, pry tie rods off steering gear. Remove lower instrument panel trim. Loosen bottom steering column mounting bolt and pry off clip. Drive bottom of column off gear, using a brass mandrel. Remove gear mounting bolts from body. Turn front wheels to right lock and remove steering gear through opening in right wheel well.

**Installation** — Before installing steering gear in vehicle, install the slider (in which both sealing sleeves are welded into the cup — see illustration). Install steering gear. To facillitate installation of tie rods, remove one bolt from the slider, install tie rod, and reinstall bolt. Repeat procedure for other tie rod. After tightening bolts, secure with lock plate.

**Fig. 2   Cross Sectional View of Pinion Shaft with Rack Adjustment**

#### STEERING DAMPER

**NOTE** — *Replacement of steering damper is the only service procedure recommended. Do not attempt repairs on this unit.*

### OVERHAUL

**NOTE** — *Manufacturer does not recommend overhaul of this rack and pinion steering unit. If unit is determined defective, replace as assembly.*

**Fig. 1   Audi Fox Rack and Pinion Assembly**

## BMW RACK & PINION

**320i**

### DESCRIPTION

Direct-acting manual rack and pinion gear on resilient rubber mounts is of ZF design. Steering is dampened by a single tube-type hydraulic damper. Tie rods attached at outer end of central steering rack connect to steering knuckles.

### ADJUSTMENT

Steering gear assembly should be removed for proper adjustment. See *OVERHAUL* procedures in this article.

### REMOVAL & INSTALLATION

#### STEERING GEAR

**Removal and Installation** — Disconnect tie rods from steering knuckles with special tool (32 2 050). Detach steering gear mounting bolts at front axle support. Remove pinch bolt from steering spindle and pull steering gear loose from universal coupling. To install, reverse removal procedure noting that wheels must point straight ahead and raised mark on dust seal must align between raised marks on steering gear box.

### OVERHAUL

**Disassembly — 1)** Mount gear in suitable holding fixture held in a vise. Bend open right lockplate and slide rack in up to stop. Detach damper at holder.

**2)** Using special tool (32 2 110), detach right tie rod at rack. Loosen bellows clamp and slide bellows off housing. Move rack in far enough to apply special tool (32 2 100) to left side of rack. Loosen clamp and slide back bellows onto rack. Bend open lockplate and detach left tie rod at rack.

**3)** Remove cap from pinion housing, then pull out cotter pin holding set screw. Unscrew set screw with special tool (32 1 040) and remove spring retainer and spring. Lift rack to remove pressure pad and "O" ring from housing.

**4)** Remove pinion shaft dust cover, "V" lock ring and notched ring. Remove pinion shaft set screw with special tool (32 1 040), then pull out "O" ring and washer.

**Fig. 1  Exploded View of BMW Rack & Pinion Steering Gear Assembly**

## BMW RACK & PINION (Cont.)

**5)** Clamp drive pinion spline in soft jawed vise and remove drive pinion from housing by tapping housing with plastic hammer. Remove circlip from pinion shaft and press ball bearing off of drive pinion shaft.

**6)** Needle bearing may be removed from housing with suitable screw type puller (Kukko 00 8 510). Remove rack bushings from housing by prying out with two screwdrivers.

**Assembly — 1)** Place new "O" rings on rack bushings and install bushings in steering box. Locking tabs must enage in housing lock holes. Drive needle bearing, flat side down, into box using suitable mandrel.

**2)** Press ball bearing onto drive pinion with closed end facing spline and install circlip. Apply thick coat of grease to spline surface of rack and thin coating to remainder of surface. Insert rack into box. Dip assembled pinion shaft in grease and install in box.

**3)** Tighten set screw to specifications. Insert "V" ring up to groove and press notched ring up to stop. Center rack in housing. Right end of rack should extend 3.031" (77 mm) beyond housing. Place dust seal on shaft so mark on seal is between marks on housing. Place "O" ring into pressure pad and slide pad into steering box.

**4)** Place spring and retainer on pressure pad. Tighten notched set screw against stop, then back off socket head set screw until it extends approximately ½" (12 mm) above edge of housing.

**Adjustment — 1)** Tighten notched set screw to 4 ft.lbs. (.6 mkg), then back off by one full castle slot to cotter pin hole. Install adapter (32 1 000) and torque wrench (00 2 000) on pinion shaft. Turn rack over entire length to check for sticking or binding. Set screw may be backed off no more than one notch in event of sticking or binding.

**2)** Move rack to center position and determine turning torque. If not within specifications, self locking set screw may be turned right to increase or to left to decrease friction.

**3)** Use new seals and lock plates and complete assembly procedure in reverse order of disassembly.

**NOTE** — *Shoulder of lock plates must engage opening of rack when installing tie rods. If replacing rubber bushing supporting steering damper, short spacers must be in place prior to tightening cover plate.*

### TIGHTENING SPECIFICATIONS

| Application | Ft. Lbs. (mkg) |
| --- | --- |
| Tie Rod to Rack | 51-56 (7-8) |
| Tie Rod to Steering Knuckle | 25-29 (3.5-4.0) |
| Steering Gear to Axle | 35-39 (4.9-5.4) |
| Pinion Shaft Pinch Bolt | 18-20 (2.5-2.8) |
| Pinion Shaft Set Screw | 16-19 (2.2-2.6) |
| Steering Damper Mounting | 11-13 (1.5-1.8) |
| Steering Gear Turning Torque | |
| At Center | 7.8-11.2 INCH lbs. (9-13 cmkg) |
| Beyond Center (Max.) | 17.4 INCH lbs. (20 cmkg) |

## CAPRI RACK & PINION

Capri

## DESCRIPTION

Rack and pinion steering gear is mounted in rubber insulators on brackets attached to front crossmember. Movement of steering wheel is transmitted by steering shaft through universal joint and flexible coupling to helical pinion. Rotation of pinion causes rack to move laterally where connecting rods, attached to rack, transmit this movement to spindle arms, causing front wheels to change direction. Connecting rod inner ball joints are protected by convoluted rubber bellows. Design of steering gear provides for two adjustments: rack damper adjustment and pinion bearing preload adjustment. Both adjustments are obtained by varying the thickness of shim packs under cover plates.

## ADJUSTMENT

**NOTE** — *Adjustments can be made only after steering gear assembly is removed from vehicle.* Place gear in padded vise with rack preload cover plate on top and rack in horizontal position. Remove rack preload cover plate, shim pack and gaskets. Withdraw spring and slipper. Remove pinion bearing preload cover plate, shim pack and gaskets, then make adjustments as follows:

### PINION BEARING PRELOAD

Position shim pack and pinion cover plate on bearing. **NOTE** — *Shim pack must have at least three shims with one shim .093" (2.36 mm) thick against cover plate.* Tighten cover bolts then loosen until cover plate just touches shim pack. Measure distance between cover plate and steering gear housing.

Distance should be .011-.013" (.28-.33 mm), if not to specifications, add or remove shims to obtain this clearance. **NOTE** — *The .093" (2.36 mm) shim must be used next to the cover plate.* When correct specification is obtained, tighten cover plate bolts.

### RACK DAMPER ADJUSTMENT

Assemble slipper to rear of rack and push fully into bore. Using straightedge and feeler gauge, measure distance between top of slipper and cover plate mounting surface. Assemble a shim pack, including two gaskets, .0005-.0035" (.013-.089 mm) GREATER than measurement. Replace slipper spring, position shim pack, replace cover plate, and tighten bolts.

### STARTING TORQUE CHECK

Install a suitable torque wrench to splined end of pinion shaft. Measure torque required to start pinion rotating. If this torque is not 10-18 INCH lbs. (11.5-20.7 cmkg), check for improper adjustment or gear assembly malfunction (causing friction increase).

## REMOVAL & INSTALLATION

### STEERING GEAR

**Removal** — 1) Set steering wheel in center position. Raise and support front of vehicle (use wheel stands or hoist, not chassis stands). Unbolt flexible coupling from pinion spline. Bend back lock tabs and unscrew steering gear mounting brackets from crossmember.

2) Loosen castellated nuts securing connecting rod ends to spindle arms. Remove castellated nuts, turn wheel to either lock (to permit sideways movement), and remove gear assembly.

*Fig. 1  Exploded View of Capri Rack & Pinion Steering Gear Assembly*

## CAPRI RACK & PINION (Cont.)

**3)** Remove connecting rod ends and lock nuts, noting number of turns required for removal.

**Installation** — **1)** Replace connecting rod ends and lock nuts (use same number of turns as during removal). Check steering wheel and gear in straight-ahead position. Place gear and splines on flexible coupling.

**2)** Secure gear assembly to crossmember (use new locking plates under screw heads). Torque screws to specification. Tighten flexible coupling-to-pinion shaft securing bolt to specification. Lower vehicle and check toe-in.

### CONNECTING ROD END

**Removal** — Raise vehicle on hoist. Loosen lock nut on outer end of connecting rod, adjacent to ball joint. Remove nut securing connecting rod end to spindle arm, then use suitable puller (3290-C) to separate connecting rod end from spindle arm. Unscrew connecting rod end, noting number of turns required for removal.

**Installation** — To install, reverse removal procedure, noting the following: Note that rod end is screwed on exact same number of turns as required for removal. Torque nut on spindle arm. Recheck toe-in and wheel lock angles. Tighten lock nut on connecting rod end.

## OVERHAUL

### STEERING GEAR

**Disassembly** — **NOTE** — *Pinion bearings utilize bearing races and loose balls (28); take care not to lose bearings into gear assembly.* Remove pinion dust seal. Withdraw pinion and lower bearing assembly. Remove remainder of bearing from inside pinion housing. **NOTE** — *Preferably withdraw rack from pinion end of housing.*

**Reassembly** — Remove pinion oil seal from housing and install new seal. Install new upper pinion bearing. Slide rack into

housing and locate it so that teeth are adjacent to pinion location. Position rack shaft in center of travel. Assemble lower bearing to pinion and install assembly into housing with alignment mark on pinion in vertical position (as installed in car).

### STEERING GEAR BELLOWS

**NOTE** — *Removal and replacement of bellows should be done on one end at a time.*

**Disassembly** — Remove connecting rod end and lock nut from appropriate connecting rod, noting number of turns required for removal. Loosen bellows clamps. **NOTE** — *In production, some bellows may have been secured with wire. Replace with screw clamp.* Pull bellows off rod and housing, keeping bellows higher than gear housing to avoid spilling lubricant. Drain lubricant from assembly by traversing rack from lock to lock several times.

**Reassembly** — Mount steering gear in padded vise with end (from which bellows has been removed) higher than gear housing. Traverse rack to fully extend upper connecting rod. Pour 0.3 pint SAE 90 EP oil into gear housing under inner ball joint. Move rack laterally to assist oil flow. Install new bellows and securing clamps. Reinstall lock nut and connecting rod end (using same number of turns as during removal).

### TIGHTENING SPECIFICATIONS

| Application | Ft. Lbs. (mkg) |
|---|---|
| Pinion Cover Plate | 6-8 (.83-1.11) |
| Rack Damper Cover Plate | 6-8 (.83-1.11) |
| Gear-to-Crossmember | 15-18 (2.07-2.49) |
| Connecting Rod-to-Spindle Arm | 18-22 (2.49-3.04) |
| Coupling-to-Pinion Shaft | 12-15 (1.66-2.07) |
| "U" Joint Pinch Bolt | 12-15 (1.66-2.07) |
| Connecting Rod End-to-Connecting Rod | 30-35 (4.15-4.84) |

## COURIER RECIRCULATING BALL

**Courier**

## DESCRIPTION

Steering gear is a recirculating ball and nut type. Two tubes carry the balls through worm channels, thus transmitting the turn action of the steering shaft. Worm bearing preload and ball-nut meshload have adjustments provided, to maintain smooth steering operation.

*Fig. 1   Exploded View of Recirculating Ball & Nut Steering Gear*

## ADJUSTMENT

### WORM BEARING PRELOAD

Drain gear box. Disconnect pitman arm from gear. Loosen sector adjusting screw lock nut and turn screw counterclockwise. Using torque wrench, rotate worm shaft. Preload should be 5.2-7.8 INCH lbs. (6.0-9.0 cmkg). If not within specification, remove end cover and shims. If preload is below minimum, reduce shim size. If above maximum, increase shim size.

### SECTOR SHAFT & BALL-NUT MESHLOAD

Adjusting screw in side cover sets sector shaft to provide proper mesh between sector gear teeth and ball-nut rack. Adjustment is made only after setting worm bearing preload. Disconnect pitman arm from center link. Loosen sector adjusting screw lock nut. Turn steering wheel slowly to either stop, then turn to opposite stop. Count steering wheel rotations and turn wheel to center position. Turn adjusting screw in or out until adjustment is obtained. There should be no backlash. Hold adjusting screw in position and tighten lock nut. Recheck mesh load. Connect pitman arm to center link.

## REMOVAL & INSTALLATION

### STEERING GEAR

**Removal — 1)** Remove steering wheel and switches. See *Courier* in *STEERING WHEELS & COLUMN SWITCHES* in this Section. Remove support bracket, move floor mat away from column, and separate toe plate/boot from dash. Remove column jacket from shaft.

**2)** Take off air cleaner assembly. Disconnect heater hoses. Remove hydraulic lines from brake and clutch master cylinders, plug ports on both cylinders and remove from vehicle.

**3)** Raise vehicle on hoist. Disconnect pitman arm from sector shaft. Remove steering gear retaining bolts. Lower vehicle and remove gear and shaft assembly.

**Installation — 1)** Position gear to frame and install mounting bolts finger tight. Replace column jacket and dash panel boot and toe plate. Reposition floor covering. Install cancelling cam and snap ring on steering shaft, then connect directional signal/dimmer switch wires.

**2)** Install steering wheel (align marks made during removal). Replace spring and horn button. Install brake and clutch master cylinders and hydraulic lines. Reattach heater hoses and install air cleaner assembly.

**3)** Raise vehicle and tighten steering gear mounting bolts. Bleed clutch system. Attach pitman arm to sector shaft. Lower vehicle and bleed brake system.

### STEERING LINKAGE

Center link can be removed from both tie rods, pitman arm, and idler arm by removing ball joint nuts and using suitable puller. After center link removal, pitman arm can be removed from sector shaft. Tie rods can also be removed with puller. Toe-in must be reset when tie rods or ball joints are replaced.

*Fig. 2   Exploded View of Courier Steering Linkage*

## COURIER RECIRCULATING BALL (Cont.)

### OVERHAUL

**STEERING GEAR**

**Disassembly** — With gear removed and drained, position gear in vise. Remove pitman arm from gear. Remove sector shaft adjusting screw lock nut. Take off side cover by removing bolts and turning adjusting screw clockwise. Remove adjusting screw and shim from sector shaft. Extract shaft from housing. Remove worm shaft and ball-nut assembly through bottom of housing after end cover and shims are removed.

**Inspection** — Check operation of ball-nut assembly on worm shaft. If travel is not smooth or any part is worn, replace entire assembly. Check and replace all other components as necessary.

**Assembly & Adjustment** — 1) Insert worm shaft and ball-nut assembly into gear housing. Install end cover and shims. Adjust bearing preload, as previously described. Place adjusting screw in slot of sector shaft and check end clearance with feeler gauge; adjust to 0-.004" (0-.1 mm) by adding or subtracting shims.

**2)** Turn worm shaft and place rack in center position of worm. Insert sector shaft and adjusting screw into gear housing, being careful not to damage bushings or seal. Align center of sector gear with center of rack. Place side cover on adjusting screw, turn screw to position cover, then install cover retaining bolts.

**3)** Adjust sector gear and rack backlash, as previously described. Tighten adjusting screw lock nut. Install pitman arm to sector shaft and torque to specification.

### TIGHTENING SPECIFICATIONS

| Application | Ft. Lbs. (mkg) |
| --- | --- |
| Gear-to-Frame | 33-42 (4.56-5.81) |
| Side Cover Bolts | 12-17 (1.66-2.35) |
| Steering Wheel Nut | 22-29 (3.04-4.01) |
| Column Support Bracket | 12-17 (1.66-2.35) |
| Pitman Arm-to-Gear | 109-130 (15.1-18.0) |
| Column Jacket Clamp-to-Gear | 7-9 (0.97-1.24) |

## DATSUN F10 RACK & PINION

**F10**

### DESCRIPTION

Steering assembly is a direct-acting rack and pinion system with a gear ratio of 18.0:1. This unit consists of a rack bar and toothed pinion. Backlash is held to zero by the retainer and the retainer spring.

### REMOVAL & INSTALLATION

**Removal** — 1) Raise and support front of vehicle; remove front wheels. Remove cotter pins and nuts from tie rods, then pull tie rods from steering knuckle. Loosen bolt securing lower joint assembly to pinion, then remove bolt from lower joint assembly.

2) Remove bolts securing steering gear housing to front member, then remove steering gear and linkage by pulling them out to the side.

**Installation** — Install in reverse order of removal procedure noting the following: Be sure to align bracket with gear housing mount correctly and check that black clip is installed on gear housing and white clip is on rubber mount.

### ADJUSTMENT

**NOTE** — *Adjustments are performed during gear assembly. See Overhaul as outlined.*

### OVERHAUL

**Disassembly** — 1) Clamp rack and pinion assembly in a vise, using pads on steering gear housing to prevent damage. Remove boot clamps, then loosen tie rod lock nut and inner

socket assembly. **NOTE** — *Do not disassemble inner socket assembly or tie rod assembly. Remove tie rod assembly from rack.*

2) Loosen rack adjuster lock nut (on housing), then remove adjuster, spring, and rack damper. Remove oil seal from pinion shaft, then pry snap ring from pinion housing and withdraw pinion assembly. Pull rack from gear housing.

3) Remove snap ring securing pinion bearing, then press out bearing from pinion shaft. Remove rubber mounts by striking with wood hammer. Pry snap ring from steering gear housing and remove rack bushing.

**Fig. 2   Cutaway View of Steering Gear**

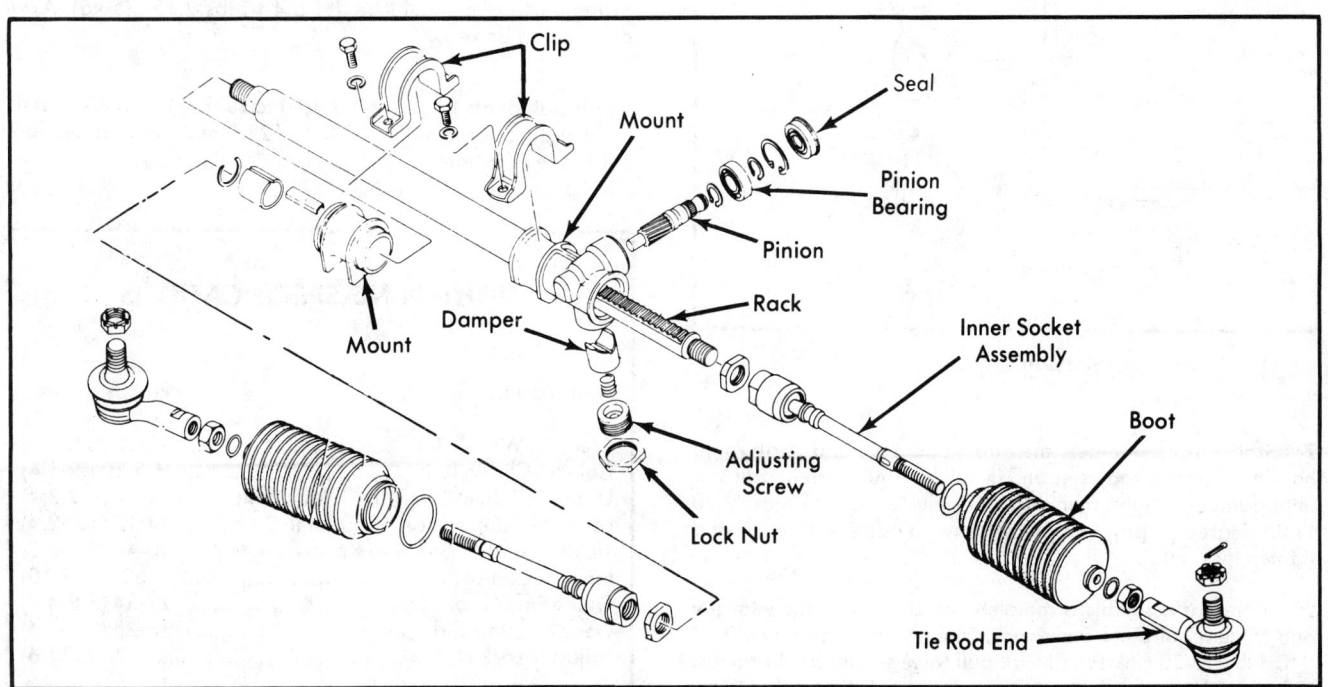

**Fig. 1   Exploded View of Rack & Pinion Steering Gear Assembly**

## DATSUN F10 RACK & PINION (Cont.)

**Assembly & Adjustment** — 1) Press bearing onto pinion gear, then install .047-.049" (1.119-1.24 mm) snap ring in shaft ring groove (inner side of bearing). Install snap ring of proper thickness in shaft ring groove (outer side of bearing), to limit bearing end play to .0039" (0.1 mm). Snap rings are available in the following thicknesses: .041-.043" (1.04-1.09 mm), .043-.045" (1.09-1.14 mm), .045-.047" (1.14-1.19 mm), .047-.049" (1.19-1.24 mm), and .049-.051" (1.24-1.29 mm).

2) Drive rack bushing into tube and secure with snap ring. Install rubber mount with plate onto tube, making sure that cut-out section in mount is aligned with hole in tube and ventilation hole is not clogged.

3) With gear clamped in vise, thinly coat rack teeth and sliding surfaces with multi-purpose grease and install rack into tube from gear housing side. Coat pinion teeth and bearing with multi-purpose grease, then mesh pinion with rack and insert pinion assembly into housing.

4) Secure bearing in housing with a snap ring of proper thickness to take up clearance. Snap rings are available in the following thicknesses: .067-.069" (1.70-1.75 mm), .065-.067" (1.65-1.70 mm), .063-.065" (1.60-1.65 mm), and .061-.063" (1.55-1.60 mm).

5) Press oil seal into housing, then pack sealing lips with grease. Check that pinion assembly rotates smoothly.

6) Check pinion for minimal end play using a dial gauge. Play must not exceed .012" (.3 mm). If it does, recheck gear, rack teeth, and adjusting snap rings.

**Fig. 3   Measuring Pinion Axial Play**

7) Grease rack damper, then insert damper and spring into housing. Screw in adjuster and install lock nut. Turn in adjuster until damper is tight, then back off adjuster approximately 20 to 25 degrees. Apply suitable sealant on adjuster threads and tighten lock nut.

8) After gear assembly is complete, check pinion rotary torque and force required to move rack. Pinion torque should be 0-17 INCH lbs. (0-20 cmkg) and rack pull force should be 33-66 lbs. (15-30 kg). If steering gear does not meet specifications, readjust rack damper adjuster.

**Fig. 4   Measuring Rack Pulling Force**

9) Install boot to inner socket assembly, then connect socket assembly to tie rod socket and tighten lock nut temporarily. Screw in inner socket as far as it will go. Apply locking agent to threaded part of lock nut and tighten to specification.

**Fig. 5   Tie Rod Length Adjustment**

10) Install boot and clamp on tie rod assembly, then measure swinging torque and axial play of inner socket assembly. Swinging torque should be 1.1-5.4 ft. lbs. (.15-.75 kg). Axial play should be zero.

11) Install boots to gear housing and rubber mount. Adjust tie rod length at each side to 5.02" (127.5 mm) and tighten lock nut to specifications.

## TIGHTENING SPECIFICATIONS

| Application | Ft. Lbs. (mkg) |
|---|---|
| Steering Wheel Nut | 20-25 (3.0-3.5) |
| Column Clamp Bolt | 6.5-10 (.9-1.4) |
| Upper "U" Joint Shaft-to-Column Bolt | 14-17 (1.9-2.4) |
| Lower "U" Joint Shaft-to-Column Bolt | 14-17 (1.9-2.4) |
| Tie Rod Stud-to-Steering Knuckle Nuts | 40-47 (5.5-6.5) |
| Inner Socket Lock Nut | 58-72 (8-10) |
| Outer Socket Lock Nut | 27-34 (3.8-4.7) |
| Gear Housing Clamp Bolt | 16-25 (2.2-3.4) |
| Adjuster Lock Nut | 29-43 (4-6) |

## DATSUN 200SX, B210, 510 & 810 RECIRCULATING BALL

200SX
B210
510
810

### DESCRIPTION

The steering gear used on these vehicles is a recirculating ball type. The worm shaft is joined to the steering shaft by a rubber shock-absorbing coupling. The steering linkage is a relay design, with the steering gear attached by a pitman arm to one end of the center link (cross shaft), while the other end of the center link moves on the idler arm.

### REMOVAL & INSTALLATION

#### STEERING GEAR

**Removal** — Unbolt and remove heat shield from around steering gear (if equipped). On 200SX and 510, disconnect exhaust tube from manifold. On 200SX, remove bolt to transmission insulator. Remove flexible coupling bolt. Pull pitman arm off steering gear sector shaft, then unbolt and remove steering gear.

**Installation** — To install, reverse removal procedure, aligning markings on pitman arm with markings on sector shaft.

**Fig. 1  Datsun Steering Gear Linkage
(B210 Shown, Others Similar)**

#### STEERING LINKAGE

**Removal** — Jack up front of vehicle and support with stands. Detach both outer tie rod ends from steering knuckles. Separate cross shaft from idler arm and pitman arm, then remove cross shaft and tie rods as an assembly. Idler assembly may be removed from side member, if necessary to replace bushing.

**Installation** — To install, reverse removal procedure, noting the following: Set tie rod end length to the prescribed setting, then check wheel alignment. See Datsun in WHEEL ALIGNMENT section.

#### Tie Rod Settings

| Application | ① In. (mm) |
|---|---|
| 200SX, B210 | 12.05 (306.0) |
| 510 | 12.40 (315) |
| 810 | |
| Steering Gear Arm Side | 14.35 (364.5) |
| Idler Arm Side | 14.19 (360.5) |

① — As measured from center-to-center of tie rod ball studs.

### ADJUSTMENT

**NOTE** — Steering gear adjustments are performed during reassembly. See Overhaul as outlined below.

### OVERHAUL

#### STEERING GEAR

**Disassembly —1)** Drain gear box of oil, then place unit in padded vise or on suitable holding fixture mounted in a vise.

**2)** Loosen adjusting screw lock nut and remove sector shaft cover screws. Turn adjusting screw a few turns clockwise and withdraw sector shaft. Remove rear cover. Withdraw bearing shims and worm assembly. Remove oil seal. **NOTE** — Do not remove sector shaft needle bearings from housing. If defective, replace housing assembly. Do not disassemble ball nut; replace, if necessary, with worm shaft assembly.

**Fig. 2  Sectional View of Datsun Recirculating
Ball Steering Gear**

**Inspection** — Inspect gear teeth on sector shaft and ball nut for wear or damage; replace as necessary. Check bearings for wear or roughness during rotation. Ensure ball nut moves smoothly over its entire length of travel.

## DATSUN 200SX, B210, 510 & 810 RECIRCULATING BALL (Cont.)

**Assembly & Adjustment** — **1)** Lubricate bearings, gear, and other moving parts with gear oil. Apply suitable grease to oil seal lip and press seal into rear cover. Install "O" ring, worm shaft assembly, and worm bearing shims to gear housing. **NOTE** — *Be sure to install thicker shims to gear housing side.*

**2)** By selecting suitable shims, adjust worm bearing preload so that initial turning torque of worm shaft is as specified (see illustration). Rotate worm shaft a few turns to properly settle worm bearing before taking preload measurement.

### Worm Bearing Preload

| Application | Inch Lbs. (cmkg) |
|---|---|
| B210 | 3.5-5.2 (4-6) |
| 200SX, 510 & 810 | 3.5-6.9 (4-8) |

**Fig. 3   Measuring Steering Gear Initial Turning Torque**

**3)** Insert adjusting screw into "T" groove of sector shaft and adjust end play between shaft and screw head to .0004-.0012" (.01-.03 mm) by selecting appropriate shim size.

**4)** Rotate worm shaft until ball nut is in center of travel, then install sector shaft and adjusting screw in gear housing. Ensure center tooth of sector shaft is engaged with center of ball nut. Apply sealant and gasket material to sector shaft attaching face.

**5)** Turn adjusting screw counterclockwise to set cover on gear housing. Temporarily install retaining bolts. Turn adjusting screw further counterclockwise until sector shaft is drawn upward about .08-.12" (2-3 mm). Fully tighten cover bolts.

**6)** Push sector shaft against ball nut by gradually turning adjusting screw until sector shaft gear lightly meshes with ball nut gear, and temporarily secure adjusting screw with lock nut.

**7)** Install pitman arm to sector shaft and move it side-to-side several times to ensure smooth operation. Set pitman arm at center point and adjust backlash (by turning adjusting screw) such that free movement at top end of pitman arm is .004" (0.1 mm).

**8)** Turn adjusting screw clockwise approximately ⅛-⅙ turn and tighten lock nut securely, after moving sector shaft several times. Fill gear housing with approximately ⅝ pint (.27 litre) of suitable gear oil. Install filler plug.

**Fig. 4   Measuring Sector Shaft-to-Adjusting Screw End Play**

## TIGHTENING SPECIFICATIONS

| Application | Ft. Lbs. (mkg) |
|---|---|
| Pitman Arm-to-Gear | |
| All Models | 94-108 (13.0-14.9) |
| Front & Rear Cover Bolts | |
| B210 | 12-20 (1.7-2.8) |
| All Others | 11-18 (1.5-2.5) |
| Adjusting Screw Lock Nut | |
| B210 | 18-25 (2.5-3.5) |
| All Others | 12-18 (1.7-2.5) |
| Gear-to-Frame | |
| B210 | 43-58 (6.0-8.0) |
| 200SX & 510 | 51-58 (7.0-8.0) |
| 810 | 38-46 (5.3-6.3) |
| Idler Arm-to-Frame | |
| 200SX & 510 | 51-58 (7.0-8.0) |
| B210 | 43-58 (6.0-8.0) |
| 810 | 32-44 (4.4-6.1) |
| Ball Stud Nuts | |
| B210 | 40-55 (5.5-7.6) |
| 200SX, 510 & 810 | 40-72 (5.5-10.0) |
| Tie Rod Lock Nuts | |
| All Models | 58-72 (8.0-10.0) |
| Worm Shaft Coupling Bolt | |
| All Models | 29-36 (4.0-5.0) |

## DATSUN 280Z RACK & PINION

**280Z**

### DESCRIPTION

Steering assembly is a direct-acting rack and pinion system, with a gear ratio of 18.0:1. This unit consists of a rack bar and toothed pinion, both working in the plain bearing of the housing. Backlash is held to zero by the retainer and the retainer spring.

### REMOVAL & INSTALLATION

**Removal** — Raise and support front of vehicle; remove front wheels. Disconnect column joint from rubber coupling (two bolts). Unbolt lower joint from gear pinion and remove lower shaft assembly. Remove splash shield, then pull tie rods from steering knuckle arms. Unbolt gear housing from front member and remove rack and pinion assembly.

**Installation** — Install in reverse order of removal procedure. Check wheel alignment. For wheel alignment procedures, see *Datsun in WHEEL ALIGNMENT section.*

### ADJUSTMENT

**NOTE** — *Adjustments are performed during gear assembly process. See Overhaul as outlined.*

### OVERHAUL

**Disassembly** — **1)** Clamp gear housing horizontally in a padded vise. Unclamp dust boot and pull boot outward to expose inner end of tie rod. Loosen tie rod retaining nut, detach tie rod socket, and remove tie rod from rack. Withdraw spring seat and tie rod spring.

**2)** Loosen rack adjuster lock nut (on housing), then remove adjuster, spring, and rack damper. Pry oil seal from pinion shaft, then remove pinion cover bolts, cover, and adjusting shims. Draw out pinion assembly, then rack, from housing. Pry pinion lower bearing from housing, then press pinion upper bearing from pinion gear.

**Assembly & Adjustment** — **1)** Press bearing onto pinion gear. With gear horizontal in padded vise, thinly coat rack teeth and sliding surfaces with suitable multi-purpose grease. Install pinion lower bearing into housing, with seal side upward, then insert pinion.

**2)** Set initial pinion turning torque, by selecting an adjusting shim which will give 2.6-5.2 INCH lbs. (3-6 cmkg) when pinion cover is installed and bolts are tightened (rack is not installed). Shims are available in the following sizes: .002" (.05 mm), .005" (.127 mm), .01" (.25 mm), .02" (.5 mm), and .04" (1 mm).

**3)** Remove pinion cover and pinion gear. Insert rack into housing, making sure rack protrudes same amount from each end. Coat pinion gear and bearing with suitable multi-purpose grease. Install pinion and properly mesh pinion gear with rack teeth. Recheck rack for equal protrusion at ends of housing. Reinstall and tighten pinion cover (with shim). Install pinion oil seal.

**4)** Check pinion for smooth rotation and minimal axial play. Measure axial play with a dial gauge. Play must not exceed .012" (.3 mm). If it does, recheck condition of gear and rack teeth, bearings, and adjustment shim.

*Fig. 1  Exploded View of Rack & Pinion Steering Gear Assembly*

# Steering Gears & Linkage

## DATSUN 280Z RACK & PINION (Cont.)

5) Grease rack damper, then insert damper and spring into housing. Screw in adjuster and install lock nut. Turn in adjuster until damper is tight. Check pinion rotary torque. If beyond 0-17 INCH lbs. (0-20 cmkg), select a suitable adjuster shim for placement on top of rack damper, which will bring rotary torque within limits. Shims are available in the following sizes: .01" (.25 mm), and .04" (1 mm). Apply sealer around lock nut.

**Fig. 2   Measuring Pinion Shaft Rotary Torque**

6) After gear assembly is complete, recheck pinion rotary torque and force required to move rack. Pinion rotary torque should remain same as previously described, and rack pull force should be 31-37 lbs. (14-17 kg). If these torques are not within limits, readjust rack damper adjuster.

**Fig. 3   Measuring Steering Gear Rack Pulling Force**

7) Position dust boots on tie rod. Thread lock nut spacer and lock nut over threaded portion of rack. Coat sliding surfaces of tie rod inner socket and spring seat. Fit tie rod assembly to rack end with inner spring and spring seat. **NOTE** — Ensure proper tie rod is installed on correct side. Left tie rod is marked with an "L", right tie rod has no marking.

8) Screw inner socket portion until ball seat reaches rack end, then tighten lock nut securely. Upon completion of tie rod assembly, measure swinging torque and axial play of inner ball joint. Swinging torque (measured at outer end of tie rod) should be 0-43 INCH lbs. (0-50 cmkg). Axial play of inner ball joint should not exceed .002" (.05 mm).

**Fig. 4   Measuring Steering Gear Rack Protrusion**

9) Measure rack protrusion. It should be 2.39" (60.7 mm). Attach boot and clamps, insert grease nipples at both ends of housing, and lubricate gear assembly (until a small amount of grease appears at boot outlet hole). Adjust tie rod length so that distance from outer side of lock nut to end of boot mounting groove is 1.492" (37.9 mm).

**Fig. 5   Adjusting Steering Gear Tie Rod Length**

## TIGHTENING SPECIFICATIONS

| Application | Ft. Lbs. (mkg) |
| --- | --- |
| Pinion Cover Bolts | 14-22 (1.94-3.04) |
| Adjuster Lock Nut | 29-36 (4.01-4.98) |
| Inner Socket Lock Nut | 58-72 (8.02-9.95) |
| Tie Rod Lock Nut | 58-72 (8.02-9.95) |
| Column-to-Gear Clamp Bolt | 6-8 (0.83-1.11) |
| Rubber Coupling Bolt | 12-14 (1.66-1.94) |
| Lower Joint-to-Rubber Coupling Bolt | 17-20 (2.35-2.77) |
| Lower Joint-to-Pinion Clamp Bolt | 29-36 (4.01-4.98) |

## DATSUN PICKUP RECIRCULATING BALL

**Pickup**

### DESCRIPTION

The steering system is comprised of a recirculating ball type steering gear and a relay design steering linkage. The linkage connects the pitman arm to one end of an adjustable center link. The other end of the center link is connected to the idler arm assembly. Two nonadjustable tie rods connect both ends of the steering linkage to the steering knuckles.

### REMOVAL & INSTALLATION

#### STEERING GEAR

**Removal** — **1)** Disconnect battery ground cable. Remove steering wheel, upper and lower column shell covers, and turn signal switch assembly. Unscrew two retaining bolts at column support clamp under instrument panel. Remove screws holding column grommet to dash panel.

**2)** Unscrew pitman arm retaining nut, scribe a mark for arm-to-sector shaft position and detach pitman arm. Remove three bolts securing gear housing to frame. Withdraw steering gear.

**Installation** — To install, reverse removal procedure, noting the following: Align pitman arm-to-sector shaft scribe marks after first setting front wheels and steering wheels in straight-ahead position.

#### STEERING LINKAGE

**Removal** — **1)** Jack up front of vehicle and support on stands. Remove cotter pins and nuts retaining outer tie rod end to steering knuckles. Separate knuckles from rod ends. Detach idler arm and pitman arm from cross shaft. Remove cross shaft and tie rod assembly from vehicle.

**Fig. 1  Exploded View of Recirculating Ball Steering Gear Assembly**

**2)** Unbolt idler assembly from vehicle. Disconnect both tie rods from cross shaft. Remove idler arm nut and disassemble idler unit.

**Installation** — Reassemble and install steering linkage in reverse of removal procedure, noting the following: Installed length of center link (as measured from center-to-center of ball studs) should be 20.7" (516 mm). Adjust toe-in and steering angle. *See Datsun in WHEEL ALIGNMENT section.*

### ADJUSTMENT

**NOTE** — *Adjustments are performed as part of reassembly procedure. See Overhaul as outlined below.*

### OVERHAUL

#### STEERING GEAR

**Disassembly** — **1)** Drain steering gear of oil, then place assembly in padded vise. Loosen lock nut and turn sector shaft adjusting screw a few turns counterclockwise. Remove sector shaft cover bolts. Now turn adjusting screw clockwise until cover is free, then pull sector shaft and cover from gear housing. Separate sector shaft, adjusting screw, and shim from cover.

**2)** Unscrew column tube retaining screws and remove tube. Withdraw worm assembly from housing. Detach worm bearings and adjusting shims from assembly and column tube. **CAUTION** — *Do not allow ball nut to run freely to either end of travel on worm or ball guides may be damaged.*

**3)** Pry out sector shaft oil seal from housing (discard seal). Remove "O" ring from rear cover and column tube (discard "O" ring). Remove column tube bushing.

**NOTE** — *Do not remove sector shaft bushing from housing. If bushing is defective, replace entire worm gear assembly.*

**NOTE** — *Do not disassemble ball nut. If found to be defective, replace entire worm gear assembly.*

**Assembly & Adjustment** — **1)** Fit column tube bushing into position (coated with suitable adhesive on exterior of bushing and grease on interior). Fill space of new sector shaft oil seal lips with grease, then install seal. Place worm assembly, with bearings, into housing. Install column tube with new "O" ring and original amount of column tube shims. **NOTE** — *Be sure thicker shim is to gear housing side.*

**2)** Adjust worm bearing preload by selecting suitable bearing shims so that initial turning torque of steering column shaft is 2-4 INCH lbs. (2.4-4.4 cmkg) when measured at steering shaft, and 5-8 oz. (.12-.22 kg) when measured with pull scale at steering wheel circumference. **NOTE** — *Measurements given are with original bearings installed. If new bearings are used on the worm, the values should be 3.5-5 INCH lbs. (4-6 cmkg) and 6.6-11 oz. (.4-.7 kg) respectively.*

## DATSUN PICKUP RECIRCULATING BALL (Cont.)

3) Install adjusting screw into "T" groove at sector shaft head. Choose suitable shim for placement beneath adjusting screw which will give an end play of .0004-.0012" (.01-.03 mm) at adjusting screw.

4) Rotate ball nut by hand until it is in center of its travel, then install sector shaft, engaging center sector tooth with center of ball nut. Coat sector cover packing faces with sealant, then install cover. Turn adjusting screw counterclockwise to bring cover into mounting position. Temporarily install cover bolts.

5) Turn adjusting screw an additional amount to bring sector shaft toward cover approximately .08-.12" (2-3 mm). Fully tighten sector cover bolts. Now gradually turn adjusting screw clockwise to push sector shaft against ball nut. When a light mesh is felt, secure lock nut.

6) Install pitman arm to sector shaft and move arm several times side to side to ensure smooth movement. Adjust backlash at neutral position of pitman arm by turning adjusting screw in or out until less than .004" (.1 mm) free play is measured at outer end of arm.

7) Turn adjusting screw approximately ⅛-⅙ turn clockwise and retighten lock nut. Fill gear housing with suitable oil (¾ pt.).

### TIGHTENING SPECIFICATIONS

| Application | Ft. Lbs. (mkg) |
|---|---|
| Column Tube-to-Gear | 11-18 (1.52-2.49) |
| Sector Shaft Cover | 11-18 (1.52-2.49) |
| Adjusting Screw Lock Nut | 22-29 (3.04-4.01) |
| Gear-to-Frame | 33-38 (4.56-5.25) |
| Steering Wheel Nut | 51-54 (7.05-7.47) |
| Pitman Arm-to-Gear | 94-108 (13.0-14.9) |
| Steering Linkage Connections | 40-72 (5.53-9.95) |

Fig. 2   Removing Sector Shaft Cover

Fig. 3   Removing Sector Shaft

Fig. 4   Removing Steering Gear Worm

## FIAT 124 WORM & ROLLER

**124 Spider**

### DESCRIPTION

**STEERING GEAR**

The steering gear is a worm and roller type, having a gear ratio of 16.4:1. The steering gear box is mounted on the crossmember inside the firewall.

*Fig. 1  Exploded View of Fiat Worm & Roller Steering Gear*

### ADJUSTMENT

**NOTE** — *Adjustments are performed as part of gear reassembly. See Overhaul as outlined below.*

### REMOVAL & INSTALLATION

**STEERING GEAR**

**Removal** — Using suitable puller, remove tie rod and center link from Pitman arm. Loosen steering column clamp on worm shaft. Remove three bolts holding steering gear to body, noting number and position of shims. Remove steering box.

**Installation** — Bolt steering box to body, but do not tighten bolts. Clamp steering column on worm shaft and reconnect tie rod and center link. Turn steering wheel from side to side several times to align shaft and box, then tighten bolts to specification.

### OVERHAUL

**STEERING GEAR**

**Disassembly** — 1) Unscrew oil plug and drain gear oil, then mount assembly on suitable overhaul stand (A. 74076/1 with adaptor A. 74076/2). Detach pitman arm from roller shaft, using suitable puller (A. 47043).

2) Remove nuts and washers attaching roller shaft cover to gear box, then take off cover with roller shaft adjusting screw, adjusting disc, lock washer, and lock nut. Extract roller shaft assembly from gear housing.

3) Remove worm shaft thrust cover and shims. Turn shaft and remove bearing. Using a suitable puller (A. 47004), remove worm shaft rear bearing. This will release shims located behind bearing. Remove roller shaft oil seal, and bearings if necessary with puller (A. 74105).

**Assembly & Adjustment** — 1) If installing new roller shaft bearings, drive into place with drift. Ream to correct bore diameter, 1.1298-1.1306" (28.698-28.720 mm). Replace shims and rear worm shaft bearing.

**NOTE** — *If proper center mesh position was found during inspection, install same shims. If not, adjust shim pack.*

2) Fit worm bearing races and install worm into gear box. Drive front ball bearing race into gear box and replace thrust cover with shims. Check starting torque of worm shaft. It must not exceed 4.3 INCH lbs. (5.0 cmkg). If torque is higher, shimming must be increased; if lower than specified, reduce shimming.

3) Insert roller shaft oil seal, roller shaft, and cover plate with gasket and shims. Replace pitman arm temporarily to roller shaft. The roller shaft should be free to rotate through 30° on either side of center. Eliminate any clearance using adjusting screw. Turning torque after adjustment should be 7.8-10.4 INCH lbs. (9-12 cmkg).

4) When adjustment is complete, tighten pitman arm retaining nut to specification. Fill steering box with 7.25 oz. of SAE 90 EP lubricant.

### TIGHTENING SPECIFICATIONS

| Application | Ft. Lbs. (mkg) |
|---|---|
| Steering Column Bracket Bolts | 11 (1.52) |
| Linkage-to-Pitman Arm | 22 (3.04) |
| Steering Gear-to-Body | 29 (4.01) |
| Steering Wheel Nut | 36 (4.98) |
| Pitman Arm-to-Gear | 174 (24.1) |

## FIAT X1/9 & 128 RACK & PINION

X1/9
128

### DESCRIPTION

Rack and pinion type steering gear is mounted in rubber insulators and attached to body. Gear is attached to steering shaft through universal joints. Adjustments are provided for pinion bearing play and rack yoke free play. At each end of steering rack, tie rods connect steering mechanism to front wheels.

### ADJUSTMENT

**NOTE** — *Adjustments of the pinion bearing and rack yoke are performed during rebuilding. See Overhaul procedure.*

### REMOVAL & INSTALLATION

**STEERING GEAR**
**Removal** — **1)** Disconnect battery leads. Raise and support front end of vehicle, then remove front wheels. On 128 models it may be necessary to remove the spare tire. Remove three screws holding gasket cover to steering box (at toe board).

**2)** Disconnect drive pinion from lower steering column section by detaching universal joint inside vehicle. Using a suitable puller (A. 47035), remove tie rods from steering knuckles.

**3)** Remove stone shield, then unbolt and remove steering gear assembly by sliding out from right hand side of vehicle.

**Installation** — Fill gear with suitable oil before inserting into vehicle. Set front wheels in straight-ahead position, then connect drive pinion to steering column. Remount gear to body. Connect tie rods to steering knuckles and torque attaching nuts to 58 ft. lbs. Replace stone shield and front wheels.

### OVERHAUL

**Disassembly** — **1)** Disconnect tie rods from ball joints (inner end of tie rods). Loosen rubber dust boot retaining clamps, then drain oil from gear. Remove dust boots, then brackets and rubber cushions attaching gear to body.

**Fig. 1   View Showing Measurement "A" for Pinion Bearing Shim Thickness**

**2)** Detach rack yoke cover plate and withdraw gasket, spring, shims, and yoke. Remove pinion cover plate and withdraw gasket, shims, and drive pinion (with upper ball bearing).

**3)** Mount steering gear in vise, unscrew ball joint ring nuts, then slide off joints with sockets and springs. Slide rack out of steering box, then remove lower drive pinion bearing.

**Assembly & Adjustment** — **1)** Set steering box in horizontal position in padded vise, with pinion flange on top. Insert lower pinion bearing, using a suitable driver (A. 74219). Replace bushing in steering box. Slide rack into position with smooth side facing pinion seating. When rack is fully in place, turn teeth to face axis of pinion seating.

**2)** Insert pinion, ensuring it mates properly with rack teeth, then install upper pinion bearing. Apply force to pinion to eliminate axial play, then with a suitable measuring device, measure distance "A" as shown in illustration. To this measurement, add .001-.005" (.025-.13 mm). This will give the total shim thickness to be used. Remove tool, install shim, cover plate, and oil seal. Check turning torque of pinion. It should be .3 ft. lb. (.04 mkg) or less.

**3)** Set rack to center position, insert rack damper yoke in its seat, install cover plate (without shims) and turn pinion 180° in both directions to settle rack and yoke. Measure gap between rack yoke cover plate and mounting surface ("B" as shown in illustration). To this measurement, add .002-.005" (.05-.13 mm). This will give total shim thickness to be used. Remove cover, insert spring, "O" ring, shim (coated with liquid adhesive), and cover. Tighten bolts as required. Ensure ground wire is in place.

**Fig. 2   View Showing Measurement "B" for Rack Yoke Shim Thickness**

**4)** Screw ball joint ring nuts onto rack to end of threaded portion. Assemble springs and socket. Lubricate ball pins with suitable oil, and assemble to rack. Install adjustable ball joint heads and tighten until a force of 1.5-3.75 ft. lbs. (.2-.5 mkg) is required to turn the pins. Lock heads in position with nuts, then stake-lock the nut collars and ball heads. Replace rubber dust boots and clamp in place. Ensure clamp screws are positioned such that they will be accessible when gear assembly is installed in vehicle. Fill gear with 4.75 oz. (140 cc) of suitable gear oil.

**NOTE** — *Lubricate dust boots with a silicone spray and be sure they are not twisted after installation.*

## FIAT 131 RACK & PINION

131

### DESCRIPTION

Rack and pinion type steering gear is mounted in rubber insulators and attached to frame. Gear is attached to steering shaft through universal joints. Adjustment is provided for pinion bearing preload. At each end of steering rack, tie rods connect steering mechanism to front wheels.

### ADJUSTMENT

**NOTE** — *Adjustments of the pinion bearing preload are performed during overhaul. See Overhaul procedure.*

### REMOVAL & INSTALLATION

#### STEERING GEAR

**Removal** — With wheels in straight ahead position, disconnect tie rod ball joints from steering knuckles. Disconnect steering column universal joint from pinion shaft. Remove bolts securing steering gear assembly to frame and remove steering gear from vehicle.

**Installation** — Make sure steering wheel is in center position, wheels are straight ahead and pinion gear is centered. Install steering gear assembly to frame. Connect steering column universal joint to pinion shaft and tie rod ball joints to steering knuckles. Check wheel alignment. *See Fiat in WHEEL ALIGNMENT section.*

### OVERHAUL

**Disassembly** — **1)** Loosen clamps securing dust boots to tie rod and gear housing. Slide boots onto the tie rod and position gear assembly into vise so that rack is securely clamped. Remove one tie rod inner ball joint from rack.

**NOTE** — *Ball joints are staked to rack, do not remove other ball joint unless replacement is necessary.*

**2)** Remove rack piston retainer plate, plug, spring, and rack piston. Slide rack out of gear housing. Remove pinion shaft and bearing.

**Assembly & Adjustment** — **1)** Inspect bearing on pinion shaft and in housing. Replace if necessary.

**2)** Slide rack into gear housing. Install pinion and bearing. Tighten pinion nut to specification. Check pinion shaft torque with rack installed. Effort required to turn pinion should not exceed 4 ft. lbs. (.5 mkg). With torque correct, stake pinion nut in place.

*Fig. 1  Sectional View of Rack Piston Assembly*

**3)** Center rack in gear assembly. Install rack piston, spring, plug and retainer. With dust boots on tie rods, lubricate tie rod inner ball joint with oil and install on rack. Tighten ball joint collar to specification, then stake to rack.

**4)** Slide one dust boot onto gear housing and secure to gear housing and tie rod with clamps. Stand steering gear assembly on end and pour 5-5.2 oz. (145-155 cc) of oil (SAE 90 EP) into gear housing. Install other dust boot.

**NOTE** — *Lubricate dust boots with a silicone spray and be sure they are not twisted after installation.*

### TIGHTENING SPECIFICATIONS

| Application | Ft. Lbs. (mkg) |
| --- | --- |
| Pinion Shaft Nut | 22-23 (3-3.2) |
| Tie Rod Inner Ball Joint | 11 (1.5) |

*Fig. 2  Sectional View of Rack & Pinion Steering Gear Assembly*

## FIESTA RACK & PINION

**Fiesta**

### DESCRIPTION

Rack and pinion steering gear is mounted to firewall by rubber-insulated clamps. Pinion shaft is supported by a bushing and a ball bearing, eliminating the need for preload adjustment. Excessive rack play is prevented by a spring loaded slipper that bears against rack. Rubber boots seal ends of gear, and tie rods transfer turning motion to front wheels.

### ADJUSTMENT

#### RACK

**1)** Mount rack in vise with padded jaws, with rack slipper bearing cover up. Remove bolts and cover, shims and gasket. Using dial indicator, measure amount rack slipper protrudes from face of housing.

**2)** Assemble shim pack (including gasket) which is .002-.005" (.05-.125 mm) thicker than measurement obtained. Fit shims and gasket to housing and tighten cover bolts to 55-80 INCH lbs. (63.25-92.0 cmkg). Measure pinion turning torque to check adjustment. Torque should measure 5-18 INCH lbs. (5.8-20.8 cmkg).

### REMOVAL & INSTALLATION

**Removal — 1)** Place front wheels in center position. Raise and support vehicle, then remove clamp bolt securing steering shaft to pinion shaft. Remove tie rod outer ball joints from steering arms.

**2)** Bend lock tabs and remove steering gear bolts and clamps. Remove steering gear from vehicle, then loosen lock nuts and detach tie rod ends from gear.

*Fig. 1  Exploded View of Fiesta Steering Gear*

## FIESTA RACK & PINION (Cont.)

**Installation** — To install, reverse removal procedure and install new lock plates and cotter pins. Check wheel alignment and steering wheel position.

### OVERHAUL

**Disassembly** — 1) Remove bellows and drain fluid lubricant from steering gear, then mount in padded vise. Drill out pins securing tie rod ball joint housings to rack, using 5/32" drill bit.

**CAUTION** — *Do not drill deeper than .4" (9.5 mm).*

2) Separate ball joint housing and lock ring, then remove housings, tie rods and ball seats. Remove rack slipper cover plate, shims, gasket, spring and slipper.

3) Remove pinion bearing cover plate, gasket, and seal. Remove pinion and bearing assembly. If necessary, use suitable tool (T77F-3504-F) and slide hammer to remove pinion bushing. Remove rack from housing.

*Fig. 2  Checking Tie Rod Effort*

**Inspection** — Clean all parts and inspect for wear. Pinion shaft and bearing are serviced as an assembly and must be replaced if damaged. Rack support bushing at end of housing can be replaced separately if necessary.

**Reassembly** — 1) Position rack in housing. With rack centered, insert pinion and bearing assembly. Flat on pinion must face right hand side of vehicle and be at 90° to centerline of rack. Install pinion shaft gasket, cover and seal, applying sealer to bolts. Tighten to specification.

2) Install rack slipper, spring, shims, gasket and cover plate. Select shims as described in *Adjustment* in this article.

3) Grease tie rod ball and seat and assemble on end of rack. Tighten ball seat until effort required to move tie rod is 5.1 lbs. (2.3 kg) when measured 1/4" from end of rod. See *Fig. 2*.

4) Centerpunch and drill 5/32" hole .4" (9.5 mm) deep at housing and lock nut joint. Install retaining pins and peen metal to lock in place. Grease bellows inner ends and install. Use screw clamps in place of some production wire clamps. Add .2 pt. of fluid grease and tighten clamps.

5) Turn pinion to move rack side to side 5 times. Using torque gauge, measure rotating torque. Effort should be between 5-18 INCH lbs. (5.8-20.8 cmkg). Check adjustment and correct if necessary.

## TIGHTENING SPECIFICATIONS

| Application | Ft. Lbs. (mkg) |
|---|---|
| Steering Gear-to-Firewall | 33-37 (4.6-5.1) |
| Tie Rod End-to-Steering Arm | 18-22 (2.5-3.0) |
| Coupling-to-Pinion Clamp | 33-41 (4.6-5.7) |
| Tie Rod End Lock Nut | 42-50 (5.8-6.9) |
| Pinion Bearing Cover Bolts | 13-18 (1.7-2.4) |
| Rack Slipper Cover Bolts | 4.5-6.7 (0.6-0.9) |
| Ball Joint Housing Lock Nut | 33-38 (4.6-5.1) |

# Steering Gears & Linkage

## HONDA RACK & PINION

Civic
Civic CVCC
Accord

### ADJUSTMENT

**NOTE** — *Rack piston must be adjusted whenever steering gear assembly is removed and installed.*

Make sure gear is well lubricated. Loosen rack piston adjusting screw lock nut. Tighten adjusting screw until lightly bottomed. Back off screw 45° and hold in that position while tightening lock nut. Recheck play. Move front wheels from lock-to-lock to make sure rack moves freely. Recheck steering force.

### REMOVAL & INSTALLATION

#### STEERING GEAR

**Removal — 1)** Raise front of vehicle and support with safety stands. Remove front wheels. Attach suitable engine hoist (07966-634011) to torque rod bolt and to bolt just left of distributor, and lift engine far enough to take load off engine mounts.

**2)** Remove tie rod ends from steering knuckles. Disconnect linkage at engine on standard transmissions or the control cable at transmission on automatic transmissions. Disconnect exhaust pipe at manifold. Make sure engine is properly supported and remove center support member.

**3)** Turn steering wheel to a full lock position and remove steering shaft universal joint from pinion shaft. Unscrew steering gear retaining bolts. Bend left tie rod upward and lower rack until pinion shaft clears vehicle body. Rotate steering gear assembly until pinion shaft is facing down. Move rack toward one side until tie rod can be lowered out bottom. Remove gear assembly through bottom of subframe.

**4)** On Accord models, turn steering wheel to full left lock position. Remove steering shaft connector bolt and washer, then remove steering gear box mounting bracket. Move gearbox as far right as possible, disconnect left end and remove assembly from vehicle.

**Installation** — To install, reverse removal procedure.

### OVERHAUL

#### STEERING GEAR

**Disassembly — 1)** Disconnect air tube at tie rod dust seal clamps and move rubber boots to expose tie rod and rack joints. Straighten tie rod lock washer tabs. Remove both tie rods.

**2)** Remove rack screw lock nut, rack piston screw, pressure spring, and piston. Rack piston can be removed with snap ring pliers, if necessary. Remove pinion dust seal by carefully prying around pinion shaft. **CAUTION** — *Do not pry at outer edge, as housing will be damaged.*

**Inspection** — Check all components for wear and replace as necessary. Measure rack piston length. New spring should be 1.028" (26.1 mm) and used spring should be .945" (24 mm) for Accord and 1.087" (27.6 mm) new, .984" (25 mm) used for all others. Replace if necessary.

**Assembly** — Before assembling, coat each sliding component with grease, then reverse disassembly procedure, noting the following: First install steering rack to gear box. Install pinion in place and mesh it with rack. Position internal snap ring and then a new pinion dust seal. Install rack guide in proper position (note contour of guide over rack). Position pressure spring, new "O" ring on guide screw, and install screw. Adjust rack guide screw as described under Adjustment.

**Fig. 1  Exploded View of Honda Rack & Pinion Steering Gear Assembly**

Labels in figure:
Outer Dust Seal
Inner Dust Seal
Pinion Dust Seal
35 mm Snap Ring
External Snap Ring
Bearing
Pinion Washer
Pinion
Rack
Rack Piston
Air Tube Clips
Pressure Spring
"O" Ring
Lock Nut
Piston Screw
Gear Housing
Mounting Cushion
Bracket
Tie Rod Stop Washer
Tie Rod Lock Washer
Air Tube
Tie Rod
Bellow Clamp
Ball Joint Seal
Circlip
Grease Fitting
Dust Boot
Tie Rod End

### TIGHTENING SPECIFICATIONS

| Application | Ft. Lbs. (mkg) |
|---|---|
| Mounting Bracket (CVCC Only) | |
|   Pinion Shaft Side | 16 (2.2) |
|   Tube Side | 22 (3.0) |
| Mounting Bracket (Accord and Civic) | |
|   Both Sides | 14-18 (1.9-2.5) |
| Rack Piston Lock Nut | 33 (4.5) |
| Tie Rod Lock Nut | 33 (4.5) |
| Tie Rod-to-Steering Knuckle | 25 (3.5) |
| Universal Joint Clamp Bolt | 17-22 (2.5-3.0) |

## LANCIA RACK & PINION

Lancia Beta
  Coupe
  Sedan
  HPE

### DESCRIPTION

All models use a rack and pinion steering gear. The steering wheel turning motion is transmitted by the pinion gear to the rack, causing it to move side-to-side to turn the road wheels. A steering gear damper is also attached to this rack housing. This dampens road shocks.

**NOTE** — *Power-assisted rack and pinion is also available on all models. See appropriate article under POWER STEERING in this section.*

### ADJUSTMENT

**NOTE** — *Adjustments are included within the Overhaul procedure contained in this article.*

### REMOVAL & INSTALLATION

**Removal** — **1)** Remove hub caps and loosen wheel nuts. Remove bolt from steering column coupling, located inside passenger compartment just above floor board.

**2)** Install suitable holding device on steering wheel to retain wheel in straight-ahead position (spokes horizontal). Raise front of vehicle and support with frame stands. Remove front wheels.

**3)** Separate tie rod end (steering rod) ball joints from steering knuckles. Remove steering rack housing mounting bolts and clamps, and remove rack and pinion steering assembly from vehicle.

**Installation** — **1)** Move rack from lock-to-lock and count number of turns on pinion as rack travels the distance. Determine the halfway point and move rack back to this position (this will set the center point).

**2)** Position rack and pinion assembly to its mounting and install retaining clamps and bolts. Connect tie rod end ball joints and torque retaining nuts.

**3)** Attach pinion shaft to steering shaft coupling. Remove the holding device from steering wheel. Replace front wheels and lower vehicle.

### OVERHAUL

**Disassembly** — **1)** After removing rack and pinion steering gear, loosen clamp from one end of bellows and drain oil.

**2)** Clamp housing in soft-jawed vise. Straighten locking tabs and remove bolts holding tie rod ends to housing. Remove tie rod ends.

**3)** Remove rubber mounting insulators. Loosen clips and remove rubber caps and guard from housing.

**4)** Remove damper cover, gasket, shims, spring and damper. Remove pinion cover, gasket, shims and pinion (with upper bearing).

**5)** Withdraw rack and plastic bushing from housing. Remove lower pinion bearing.

**6)** Inspect all components for any wear. Replace as necessary.

**NOTE** — *It is recommended that pinion housing seal be replaced.*

**Assembly & Adjustments** — **1)** Insert plastic bushing into rack housing and position it in locating grooves.

**2)** Install lower pinion bearing, pinion and upper bearing thrust piece, upper bearing and a .09" (2.3 mm) spacing washer.

**3)** Set pinion bearing preload as follows:

  1. Position dial gauge (set to zero) on pinion housing and measure distance between pinion cover mounting surface and top of washer.
  2. To obtain a preload (turning torque) of .15-.29 ft. lbs. (.02-.04 mkg), the measured distance must be .001-.005" (.025-.130 mm). Insert shims or use thinner washer as required to set proper distance.

**4)** When preload is set, remove pinion, shims and upper bearing. Insert rack into housing from pinion housing end, placing rack in center position.

**5)** Insert pinion, meshing it with rack teeth. Install shims between upper bearing and washer. Install pinion cover and retaining bolts with lock-tab washers. Torque bolts to .15 ft. lbs. (.02 mkg).

**6)** Now, set rack backlash as follows:

  1. Insert rack damper and position damper cover without gasket or shims. Use a feeler gauge and measure gap between cover and mounting face.
  2. To the amount of gap, add the amount of specified backlash of .002-.004" (.05-.10 mm). Now subtract the amount of thickness of the cover gasket.
  3. This amount will equal the thickness of shims to be installed in order to give a rack backlash of .002-.004" (.05-.10 mm).

**7)** Remove damper cover. Insert spring, shims, cover gasket and cover. Coat retaining bolts and edges of shims with sealing compound. Torque bolts to .15 ft. lbs. (.02 mkg).

**8)** Position bellows and rubber dust caps to rack housing (leave end of one bellow loose until housing is filled with oil). Install spacers before tightening rubber guard securing clips. Lock the clips.

**9)** Fit steering rods to rack housing with washers, positioning them horizontally. Tighten mounting bolts.

**10)** Fill rack housing with suitable steering gear oil. Position and tighten end of bellows left loose. Use torquemeter or other suitable device to measure and ensure a pinion turning torque of .15-.29 ft. lbs. (.02-.04 mkg).

## LUV RECIRCULATING BALL

### LUV

## DESCRIPTION

### STEERING GEARS

Steering gear is a recirculating ball and nut type. A worm gear is incorporated on lower end of steering shaft and is engaged with ball-nut through a number of recirculating balls. These balls carry the turning motion of steering shaft onto the sector shaft with minimal loss of friction. The balls circulate through the ball-nut outlet to a ball tube and back to ball-nut inlet. Adjustment is provided for backlash between sector gear and rack by a tapered sector gear in steering unit (adjustment screw is on sector shaft).

**Fig. 1** *Exploded View of Recirculating Ball Steering Gear Assembly*

### STEERING LINKAGE

Linkage consists of splined pitman arm connected to adjustable center link and a tie rod. Center link is connected to idler arm at right end, which in turn is connected to other tie rod and idler arm pivot shaft. Shaft is fastened to frame by a bracket. Tie rods are non-adjustable and connected to brake backing plates by tie rod links. All ball stud connections and idler arm have lubrication fittings. Toe-in is set by adjustable intermediate rod.

## ADJUSTMENT

### PRELOAD & LASH

1) Disconnect battery ground cable. Remove pitman arm nut and mark relative position of arm to shaft. Remove arm using suitable tool. Remove horn shroud and spring.

2) Turn steering wheel in one direction until stopped by gear, then turn back half way. **CAUTION** — *Do not turn wheel hard against stops, as damage to ball guides may result.* Measure and record "bearing drag" by applying torque wrench to steering wheel nut and rotate through 90° arc.

**NOTE** — *Do not use a torque wrench having a maximum reading of more than 50 INCH lbs.*

3) Adjust sector lash by turning steering wheel from one stop to the other, turn wheel back exactly halfway (to obtain center position), then turn sector adjusting screw clockwise to eliminate backlash between ball-nut and sector gear. Tighten lock nut.

4) Check torque at steering wheel nut, taking highest reading as steering wheel turns through center. Torque should be 3.5-8.5 INCH lbs. (4.0-9.8 cmkg). If not, loosen lock nut and readjust sector screw. Tighten lock nut and recheck torque at steering wheel.

5) If maximum specification is exceeded, turn adjusting screw counterclockwise, then turn adjuster lock nut clockwise. Reassemble pitman arm to shaft, lining up marks made during removal. Tighten pitman shaft nut to specifications. Install horn spring and shroud. Connect battery cable.

## REMOVAL & INSTALLATION

### STEERING GEAR

**Removal** — Raise vehicle on hoist. Remove Pitman arm nut and mark relative position of pitman arm to shaft. Using suitable tool, remove arm from shaft. Remove engine protection shield. Remove lower clamp-to-flexible coupling bolts. Remove gear.

**Installation** — Place gear in position and start (do not torque) gear mounting bolts. Install clamp-to-coupling bolts and torque. Tighten gear mounting bolts. Install pitman arm, aligning index marks and tighten nut. Install engine protection shield.

**Fig. 2** *Adjusting Sector Gear Lash*

# Steering Gears & Linkage

## LUV RECIRCULATING BALL (Cont.)

### OVERHAUL

#### STEERING GEAR

**NOTE** — *Recirculating ball and nut assembly parts are selectively combined. Ball tube clamp plate is sealed with paint to avoid disturbing. Any worn part, therefore, necessitates entire assembly replacement.*

**Disassembly** — 1) Remove steering gear as previously described. Disconnect flexible coupling from worm shaft. Drain gear box through filler plug hole (no drain hole is provided). Bring steering shaft into straight-ahead position.

2) Remove top cover bolts and adjusting screw lock nut. Separate top cover from gear box by turning adjusting screw clockwise. Hold sector shaft in straight-ahead position during removal and DO NOT drive shaft off gear box by impact.

3) Remove adjusting screw and sector shaft from gear case. Remove end cover bolts and shims. Pull worm and ball-nut assembly from gear box and take out lower bearing.

**CAUTION** — *Keep assembly in horizontal position or ball-nut will fall onto end of worm gear, damaging ball tubes.*

**Inspection** — Check all parts for wear or other abnormalities; replace if conditions are noticeable. Ball-nut noise or roughness necessitates replacement of entire steering shaft assembly.

**Reassembly & Adjustment** — 1) Insert lower bearing into position in gear box. Install worm shaft assembly in box. Check lower end of worm shaft for proper fit in lower bearing.

2) Assemble upper bearing onto worm shaft and install adjusting shims between gear box and end cover. Install and torque bolts.

**NOTE** — *Apply liquid gasket to end cover during installation.*

3) At this point, measure starting torque of pinion shaft (see illustration). Reading should be 2.9-6.0 lbs. (1.3-2.7 kg) when coupling begins to rotate. If not within limits, add or remove shims as necessary.

4) Bring ball-nut to center of worm and insert sector shaft into gear box. Engage center tooth of shaft with center tooth of worm. Insert adjusting screw in sector shaft slot. Screw should slide freely within the slot and have no more than .001" (.025 mm) clearance. If clearance is excessive, insert adjusting shim. Install sector cover while turning adjusting screw out. Tighten lock nut.

5) Check total gear preload (starting torque) using pull scale shown in illustration. If reading is between 4.9-11.7 lbs. (2.2-5.3 kg), no further adjustments are required. If correct specification is not obtained, turn adjusting screw until preload is within specifications. Tighten lock nut.

6) Connect sector shaft to pitman arm (align marks made during removal) and torque pitman arm. Install and torque pinch bolt. Fill gear box with 10 oz. lubricant. Do not overfill.

*Fig. 3   Measuring Steering Gear Starting Torque*

#### PITMAN SHAFT SEAL REPLACEMENT

If replacement has been determined as necessary, it may be done without removing the steering gear as follows:

Raise vehicle on hoist. Remove pitman arm, as previously described. Clean area around seal. Pry out old seal, being careful not to damage housing bore. **CAUTION** — *Check gear lubricant for contamination. If contamination of any kind is detected, gear overhaul is necessary.* Coat new seal with gear lubricant and tap into position. Install pitman arm. Lower vehicle and check lubricant level in gear box (10 oz.).

### TIGHTENING SPECIFICATIONS

| Application | Ft. Lbs. (mkg) |
|---|---|
| Pitman Arm-to-Gear | 160 (22.1) |
| Gear & Idler Arm-to-Frame | |
| Large Bolts | 50 (6.9) |
| Small Bolts | 20 (2.8) |
| Adjusting Screw Lock Nut | 20 (2.8) |
| Linkage Ball Joints | 44 (6.1) |
| Center Link Lock Nuts | 90 (12.4) |
| Coupling Pinch Bolt | 20 (2.8) |

## MAZDA RECIRCULATING BALL

GLC
RX4
Cosmo
B1800 Pickup

### DESCRIPTION

Steering gear is a recirculating ball type with a variable ratio, depending on turning angle of sector shaft. The pinion shaft and steering shaft are an integral (nonseparable) unit on some models, while the shaft is separable from the pinion on others. Steering linkage is basically the same for all models, having a nonadjustable center link, two adjustable tie rods, an idler arm assembly, and pitman arm.

### ADJUSTMENT

**NOTE** — *Adjustments are performed during assembly portion of overhaul. See Overhaul procedure in this article.*

### REMOVAL & INSTALLATION

#### STEERING GEAR

**Removal (GLC, B1800 Pickup)** — 1) Disconnect negative battery cable. Remove steering wheel and switches. *See Mazda under STEERING WHEEL & COLUMN SWITCHES in this Section.* Remove bolts holding column to dash. Loosen dust cover screws, any other column bolts, and pull column jacket off shaft.

2) On GLC, disconnect center link from pitman arm with puller. Remove steering gear mounting bolts and pull gear forward after raising vehicle.

3) On B1800 Pickup models, remove air cleaner, brake master cylinder and power booster, clutch master cylinder, and EGR pipes and hoses. Drain coolant, then remove hoses and lines from intake manifold. Remove manifold and carburetor assembly.

4) Raise and support vehicle. Remove left front wheel, then disconnect and remove pitman arm. Place jack under lower left control arm and support. Remove upper left control arm, noting position of shims. Unbolt steering gear and pull up out of vehicle.

**Removal (RX4, Cosmo)** — Raise and support front of vehicle on stands. Remove front wheel and detach pitman arm from center link. Remove bolt securing flexible coupling to worm shaft. Detach pitman arm from gear. Remove speedometer cable from clips attached to gear housing and power brake unit. Unbolt and remove gear housing.

**Installation (All Models)** — To install, reverse removal procedure, ensuring any shims which were removed are installed in original positions.

**NOTE** — *To avoid damage to steering column components, do not apply bending or striking forces to steering shaft or column.*

#### STEERING LINKAGE

Steering linkage may be removed as an assembly or as individual components. Whenever tie rod setting is disturbed, toe-in must be reset. *See Mazda in WHEEL ALIGNMENT section.*

### OVERHAUL

#### STEERING GEAR

**Disassembly** — Drain gear oil from housing. Remove pitman arm from sector shaft if not removed previously. Unscrew side cover attaching bolts and loosen adjusting screw lock nut. Turn adjusting screw in to remove side cover from housing. Take adjusting screw and shim from slot in sector shaft. Withdraw sector shaft. Unbolt end cover, then remove worm and ball nut assembly. On GLC, worm and ball nut assembly is held in place by adjuster plug and lock nut.

**Inspection** — Check ball nut rotation on worm. If movement is not smooth for full length of travel, replace worm and ball nut assembly. Ball nut is not to be serviced separately. Check worm bearings and cups, sector shaft gear surface, and oil seal. If any component is defective, replace it.

**Fig. 1 Exploded View of GLC Steering Gear**

**Fig. 2 Checking Adjusting Screw End Clearance**

## MAZDA RECIRCULATING BALL (Cont.)

**Assembly & Adjustment — 1)** Replace oil seal in housing. Insert worm shaft and ball nut assembly into gear housing. Position end cover (or column jacket) with bearing preload adjusting shims and tighten cover (jacket) bolts. Attach an INCH lbs. torque wrench to shaft and check preload. If below specification, reduce the shims; if above, increase the shim. On GLC, tighten adjuster plug to set preload.

### Initial Worm Bearing Preload Torque

| Application | INCH lbs. (cmkg) |
| --- | --- |
| RX4 | 0.9-3.5 (1-4) |
| Cosmo, GLC, B1800 | 1.7-4.3 (2.0-5.0) |

**Fig. 3   Aligning Sector Gear & Rack**

**2)** Insert sector shaft into gear housing, using care not to damage oil seal. Ensure center of sector gear is aligned with center of worm gear. **See Fig. 3.** Insert adjusting screw into slot in end of sector shaft. Check end clearance as illustrated and add appropriate shim to bring clearance within 0-.004" (0-.1 mm). Place side cover and gasket over adjusting screw and turn adjusting screw until cover is in place, install attaching bolts.

**3)** Install pitman arm onto sector shaft, aligning marks. Install and tighten retaining nut. Measure pitman arm backlash. If necessary, turn sector adjusting screw until zero backlash is obtained. Tighten adjusting screw lock nut, taking care not to disturb backlash adjustment.

**4)** Check worm shaft rotating torque. Attach an INCH lbs. torque wrench to worm shaft. If not to specifications, adjust as necessary. Fill gear housing with lubricant (SAE 90 EP).

### Final Worm Bearing Preload Torque

| Application | INCH lbs. (cmkg) |
| --- | --- |
| GLC, Cosmo | 5.2-10.4 (6-12) |
| RX4 | 7.9-10.4 (9-12) |
| B1800 | 5.2-7.8 (6-9) |

**Fig. 4   Exploded View of RX4 Recirculating Ball Steering Gear (Others Similar)**

### TIGHTENING SPECIFICATIONS

| Application | Ft. Lbs. (mkg) |
| --- | --- |
| Gear Box-to-Frame | 32-40 (4.4-5.5) |
| Steering Wheel Nut | 22-29 (3-4) |
| Pitman Arm-to-Sector Shaft | |
| RX4, Cosmo, B1800 | 108-130 (15-18) |
| GLC | 58-87 (8-12) |
| Pitman Arm-to-Center Link | |
| GLC, RX4, Cosmo | 22-33 (3-4.5) |
| B1800 | 22-29 (3-4) |

# Steering Gears & Linkage

## MGB RACK & PINION

**MGB**

### DESCRIPTION

Steering gear is a direct-acting rack and pinion type. Gear consists of rack bar and toothed pinion mounted on front suspension crossmember. No adjustment for bearing wear in gear box is provided. Steering column is attached to pinion by "U" joint coupling.

### REMOVAL & INSTALLATION

**Removal** — Raise and support front of vehicle and remove both front wheels. Detach tie rod ends from steering arms. Turn steering to right lock and remove "U" joint lower pinch bolt. Remove nuts and bolts securing rack assembly to crossmember, noting that front bolts are attached with self-locking nuts and that shims may be found between rack assembly and frame brackets. Withdraw rack assembly downward and remove from vehicle.

**Installation** — To install, reverse removal procedure after first setting steering gear and steering column in straight-ahead position. **NOTE** — *If new rack is being installed, it must be aligned. See Alignment in MGB article under Steering Columns in this section.*

### OVERHAUL

**Disassembly** — 1) Clamp rack in padded vise. Remove pinion end cover and joint washer, placing container beneath assembly to catch oil. Remove damper cover and shims. Extract yoke, damper pad, and spring, then withdraw pinion.

2) Unlock tie rod outer lock nuts and remove tie rod ends. Unclamp and remove both rubber bellows. Release bellows seal clips and withdraw seals. Pry up tab on locking rings, slacken rings, and unscrew housing to release tie rod, ball seat, and spring.

3) Pull rack out pinion end of housing. To remove rack housing bushing, unscrew self-tapping screw and carefully drive out bushing.

**Inspection** — Thoroughly clean all parts and examine for wear. Particularly, note condition of rubber bellows; if they show any sign of wear, replace them. Outer ball socket assembly cannot be disassembled; if worn, it must be replaced as assembly.

**Assembly** — 1) Insert rack bushing and carefully drive it in until flush with housing end. Drill outer housing of bushing through screw hole with a $\frac{7}{64}$" (2.78 mm) drill to a depth of .24" (6.3 mm) so that a new retaining screw may be inserted. Coat screw head with sealing compound before tightening.

2) Replace rack from pinion end. Position seat spring, ball seat, tie rod, and ball housings. Coat ball seats liberally with SAE 90 oil. Tighten ball housings until tie rods are held firmly, without free play. This tightening is correct when a force of 32-52 Inch lbs. is required to move the tie rods. Tighten new locking rings and bend tabs.

3) Insert pinion complete with ball races and locking nut into housing. Replace pinion end cover and seal, using sealing compound on mounting edges. Peen outer edge of ball race lock nut into slot in pinion shaft, if lock nut has been removed.

4) To adjust rack damper, replace plunger in housing and tighten cover, without spring or shims, until it is just possible to rotate pinion shaft by drawing rack through housing. With a feeler gauge, measure clearance between cover and housing. To this measurement add .0005-.003" (.013-.076 mm). This figure will be the correct thickness of shims to place beneath damper cover. Remove cover and plunger, insert spring and shims with plunger and cover. Coat cover with sealing compound and tighten.

5) Replace rubber bellows; before securing bellow clip on tie rod at pinion end, stand assembly on end and pour in 1/3 pint (.2 litre) of suitable SAE 90 oil. Replace bellow clip.

*Fig. 1  Exploded View of MGB Rack and Pinion Assembly*

## MG MIDGET RACK & PINION

**Midget**

### DESCRIPTION

Steering gear is a rack and pinion type and is secured above front frame crossmember, immediately behind the radiator. Tie rods, operating swivel arms, arm attached to each end of rack by ball joint enclosed in rubber bellows. Steering column engages splined end of pinion. Pinion end play is eliminated by adjustment of shims beneath pinion lower bearing. A damper pad, inserted in rack, controls backlash between pinion and rack.

**Fig. 1  MG Midget Rack & Pinion Assembly**

### REMOVAL & INSTALLATION

**Removal** — **1)** Remove radiator. Detach tie rod ball joints from swivel arms. Remove column-to-pinion pinch bolt. Unscrew six bolts securing rack assembly to body crossmember.

**2)** Move rack assembly forward as far as possible, collecting any shims between mounting bracket and body. Note location and number of these shims for reassembly reference. **NOTE** — *If these shims are lost or unmarked for reinstallation, steering rack and column must be realigned. See Alignment in MG Midget article under STEERING COLUMNS in this section.*

**3)** Unscrew three toe plate bolts. Slacken three upper column attaching bolts and pull column back sufficiently to disengage column sleeve from pinion. Remove front wheels and pull rack assembly from vehicle.

**Installation** — To install, reverse removal procedure, noting the following: Ensure shims are returned to original positions. When joining column to pinion, check that rack and column are both in straight-ahead position. If new rack is being installed, column and rack alignment is necessary. See *Alignment in MG Midget article under STEERING COLUMNS in this section.*

### OVERHAUL

**Disassembly** — **1)** Loosen lock nuts and remove tie rod end assemblies. Release retaining clips and wires, then remove bellows and protective shields.

**2)** Loosen lock nuts and unscrew tie rod inner ball joint assemblies. Remove coil spring and remove lock nuts from each end of rack.

**3)** Disassemble inner ball joint assembly by unlocking tab washer and unscrewing sleeved nut. Remove grease plug, cap, and shims, then withdraw spring and plunger from housing. Remove circlips and withdraw pinion assembly with dowel, then press lower bushing and end plug from housing bore.

**Inspection** — Thoroughly clean all components and check rack and pinion for wear, cracks or damage. Examine seals and replace any faulty parts.

**Reassembly** — **1)** Reassemble by reversing disassembly procedure, noting the following: Heat the pinion bushing and plunger in 212°F (100°C) SAE 20 engine oil for 2 hours and allow to cool to ensure pores of bushing and plunger are properly lubricated.

**2)** Install large bushing on pinion shaft. Place end plug into recess in lower bushing and install on pinion shaft. Position pinion housing over bushing and press housing onto bushing.

**3)** Insert thrust washer, chamfered bore up, into housing. Coat rack with grease and fit into housing, making sure 3½" (88.9 mm) of teeth end protrude from inner face of housing.

**4)** Tape locating plug against flat of rack (plug will be held in place by mounting bracket after rack is installed). With the rack in the straight-ahead position make sure the flat on pinion is within 30° of either side of pinion housing centerline on plunger cap side.

**5)** Insert reassembled pinion assembly into housing and adjust end play by measuring with dial guage and fitting proper shims to bring end play to .010" (0.25 mm).

**6)** To adjust preload, fit plunger and cap to rack housing and tighten threaded cap until end play is eliminated. Measure the clearance between cap and rack housing with a feeler gauge.

**7)** Make up a shim pack equal to previous clearance measurement, plus .004" (.1 mm). It is important to have at least one .004" (.1 mm) shim in assembly.

## MG MIDGET RACK & PINION (Cont.)

**Fig. 2  Checking Rack Damper Clearance Preload Adjustment**

8) Remove cap and plunger, grease plunger, then install cap, plunger and shims on the housing and tighten cap.

9) Replace grease plug with fitting and inject ½ to ¾ ounce of grease into unit. Replace grease plug, then check pinion shaft torque for 2 ft. lbs. (.91 mkg). Adjust by adding or subtracting shims.

10) Lubricate tie rod inner ball joint with graphite grease and reassemble by reversing disassembly procedures noting the following: Use a new tab washer and adjust ball end movement by measuring clearance between cap nut and tab washer.

11) Add or subtract shims to arrive at the following torque values: For steel cups 40 INCH lbs. (.46 cmkg) or for nylon cups 15-50 INCH lbs. (.17-.57 cmkg).

12) Install bellows, clips and wires and screw lock nuts on rack, making sure the distance between faces of lock nuts is 23.2" (589.3 mm).

13) Insert thrust springs into ends of rack (steel cup type only) and screw tie rod end assembly as far as possible up to the lock nut. Tighten lock nuts to 80 ft. lbs. (11.1 mkg), push bellows onto tie rods, grease ball joints, and secure bellows with clips and wires.

14) Screw tie rod end assemblies onto tie rods and check that there is 42.7" (1084.1 mm) between ball stud centers. Tighten locknuts to 30-35 ft. lbs. (4.2-4.8 mkg).

**Fig. 3  MG Midget Rack Assembly Adjustments**

## OPEL RACK & PINION

**All Models**

### DESCRIPTION

Steering gear is a rack and pinion type. Gear housing is held to crossmember by rubber bushing and clamps. Pinion shaft is seated in upper portion of gear housing and is supported by a needle bearing in upper housing and a bushing in lower housing. Pinion is not adjustable. Rack and pinion are held in mesh by a thrust spring and shell.

### ADJUSTMENT

#### STEERING GEAR BACKLASH

Set gear to high point by positioning front wheels straight-ahead. Flexible coupling bolt holes will be positioned parallel to the rack. Thread adjusting screw into gear housing until a resistance is felt. Back off screw ⅛-¼ turn. Tighten lock nut. Fill area under pinion shaft rubber boot with gear lubricant and slide boot into position.

### REMOVAL & INSTALLATION

#### STEERING GEAR

**Removal** — Remove splash shield from lower deflector panel and both side members. Remove clamp bolt securing flexible coupling to steering shaft. Detach tie rods from steering arms. Unbolt, then remove gear assembly and tie rods from vehicle.

**NOTE** — *If fasteners or attaching parts are replaced, it is imperative that ones of equivalent grade are used.*

**Installation** — To install, reverse removal procedure, noting the following: First set gear and steering wheel in center positions, and ensure slot of lower steering mast matches bolt hole of flexible coupling pinion flange.

### OVERHAUL

#### STEERING GEAR

**Disassembly** — 1) Clamp gear assembly in padded vise. Disconnect tie rod ends from axial joints (at lock nuts). Unclamp and remove bellows. Ball joint is maintenance-free and must be replaced if damaged.

2) Disconnect ball stud of axial joint from rack. Hold rack securely while removing, or rack teeth may be damaged. If axial joint is damaged, it must be replaced.

3) Loosen adjusting screw lock nut, remove adjusting screw; withdraw thrust spring and bearing. Remove sheet metal cap from gear housing and remove hex nut from pinion. Do not turn pinion in end position. Pull pinion and rack from housing.

**Assembly** — 1) With gear housing in padded vise, coat all parts with multi-purpose grease. Fill long part of housing with about 1¼ oz. lubricant.

2) Insert long, smooth end of rack into short end of housing until rack ends protrude evenly from housing. Ensure that three air channels of sintered bushing are not blocked by lubricant.

3) Reassemble pinion shaft into gear housing so spline in pinion shaft meshes with twelfth tooth of rack. Ensure pinion is positioned so bolt hole in flexible coupling is on top and parallel with rack.

4) Assemble flat washer and pinion nut to shaft. Torque nut to 20 ft. lbs. (2.8 mkg). DO NOT exceed this specification or gear may jam. Assemble screw cap and lock nut on gear assembly. Torque cap to 43 ft. lbs. (6.0 mkg) and lock.

5) Place bearing shell in gear housing and fill hole with lubricant. Replace thrust ring, adjuster screw, and locknut in gear housing. Adjust and tighten locknut to specification.

6) Screw ball stud of axial joint together with stop plate onto both ends of rack (hold rack from turning). Slide rubber bellows into position and clamp such that clamp screws are facing same direction as adjuster screw.

*Fig. 1  Exploded View of Opel Steering Gear Assembly*

### TIGHTENING SPECIFICATIONS

| Application | Ft. Lbs. (mkg) |
|---|---|
| Flexible Coupling Clamp | 19 (2.6) |
| Axial Joint Ball Stud-to-Rack | 65 (9.0) |
| Gear Housing-to-Crossmember | 14 (1.9) |
| Adjusting Screw Lock Nut | 49 (6.8 mkg) |
| Pinion Lock Nut | 20 (2.8) |
| Tie Rod-to-Steering Arm | 29 (4.0) |

## PORSCHE

911SC
924
930 Turbo

### DESCRIPTION

Porsche models use rack and pinion steering. 911SC tie rods attach to rack with yoke and eyebolts, while 924 and 930 use ball swivel joints. Pinion on 924 is offset to the left of center; 911SC and 930 have pinion shaft centered in rack housing. Pinion shafts on all models are supported by ball bearings.

### ADJUSTMENT

#### STEERING GEAR

Steering gear adjusting methods vary according to type of steering rack pressure block: (1) Steel pressure block with plastic contact surface and external housing dust boot seat; (2) Plastic pressure block with no external housing dust boot seat; (3) Adjusting screw on 924 extends through cover to take play out of steering rack.

**Fig. 1  Adjusting Nut with Cover**

**Steel Pressure Block Type** — 1) With housing assembly in padded vise, detach base plate. Tighten adjusting nut seating contact. **NOTE** — *Base plate has integral pins which may be used as a wrench for this adjustment. Back nut off contact by three teeth.*

2) Check steering gear drag at pinion flange, using an INCH-lb. torque wrench. A measurement of 6.94 INCH lbs. (8 cmkg) should be obtained. If beyond this measurement, loosen adjusting nut; however, if this measurement is not less than 3.47 INCH lbs. (4 cmkg), do not retighten adjusting nut. Install base plate with gasket.

**NOTE** — *When installing base plate, pin in plate must fit easily between teeth of adjusting nut. If necessary, move nut slightly.*

**Plastic Pressure Block Type** — Remove base plate and tighten adjusting nut until 6.94 INCH lbs. (8 cmkg) torque is obtained, using method as described above. Install base plate with gasket.

**External Adjustment (924 Only)** — With rack centered, loosen lock nut and tighten adjusting screw until it just touches thrust washer. Hold screw and tighten lock nut.

**Fig. 2  Plastic Pressure Block Housing Assembly**

### REMOVAL & INSTALLATION

#### STEERING GEAR

**Removal** — 1) Remove bottom bolt attaching universal joint to pinion shaft. Remove nuts and detach tie rod ball joints from steering knuckles.

2) Remove steering housing retaining bolts and extract entire steering housing from right side of vehicle. Detach track rods from rack.

**Installation** — To install, reverse removal procedures noting that indentation in pinion shaft must line up with bolt hole in lower universal joint. On 924 only, insert special centering bolt (9116) to center gear during installation.

### OVERHAUL

#### STEERING GEAR

**Disassembly** — 1) Mount steering housing in padded vise and remove base plate retaining bolts. Unscrew adjusting nut (base plate may be used as wrench). Remove pressure block and spring.

2) Move steering rack to either lock position and remove castellated nut. Using suitable puller (P 293), remove flange from pinion. Remove oil seal, lock ring and spacer. Using suitable puller (P 282), remove pinion from pinion carrier (ensure bearing does not bind against housing). Remove Woodruff key from pinion and press bearing off pinion.

3) Mark position of rack (for assembly), remove from housing, and withdraw pinion carrier. Press bearing out of pinion carrier. Remove rack bushing spring retainer from end of housing. Extract support ring and drive rack bushing out.

## PORSCHE RACK & PINION (Cont.)

**Reassembly** — Reverse disassembly procedure, noting the following: During assembly, coat all components with suitable gear lubricant. Use shims, if necessary, to adjust axial play of pinion to zero. Fill housing with suitable gear lubricant, either before installing pinion or after, by means of bolt hole opposite base plate.

### EYEBOLT (911SC ONLY)

**CAUTION** — *Eyebolt must be installed in precise position to ensure free movement of steering components and exact guiding of track rod.*

**Disassembly** — Clamp gear into special tool (P 285b) without washers. Remove clamps on outer end of bellows and pull bellows off holder. Loosen bellows holder with hook spanner and unscrew eyebolt and bellows holder.

**Inspection** — Check eyebolt, bellows and clamps for visible wear. Replace as required.

**Assembly** — Mount bellows on housing. Screw bellows holder on eyebolt. Coat eyebolt threads and rack face end with sealer. Install eyebolts. Attach steering gear, without washers, to original holding tool (P 285b). Locating pins should slide easily into eyebolts, with flattened end resting against outer pin. Tighten bellows holder. Clamp bellows to gear assembly.

**Fig. 4    Exploded View of Porsche 924 Steering Gear Assembly**

*(Labels: Lock Nut, Pinion Shaft, Housing, Rack, Pressure Block, Spring, Adjusting Screw, Lock Nut)*

**Fig. 3    Exploded View of 911SC and 930 Turbo Steering Gear Assembly**

*(Labels: Boot, Holder, Tie Rod, Dust Boot Seat, Spacer, Rack, Rack Housing)*

## TIGHTENING SPECIFICATIONS

| Application | Ft.Lbs. (mkg) |
|---|---|
| **Housing to Crossmember** | |
| 911SC & 930 | 34 (4.7) |
| 924 | 14-17 (2.0-2.4) |
| **Tie Rod to Steering Knuckle** | |
| 911SC & 930 | 33 (4.5) |
| 924 | 21 (2.9) |
| **Tie Rod to Rack (Locknut)** | |
| 911SC & 930 | 34 (4.7) |
| 924 | 29 (4.0) |
| **"U" Joint Coupling Bolt** | |
| All Models | 25 (3.5) |
| **Bearing Cover** | |
| 911SC & 930 | 11 (1.5) |
| 924 | 4-6 (.6-.8) |

# Steering Gears & Linkage

## RENAULT RACK & PINION

**R-5**

### DESCRIPTION

Vehicles are fitted with a rack and pinion steering gear, which has direct steering linkage (tie rods) to each front wheel. Steering housing is mounted to front crossmember and connected to steering column through a flexible coupling.

### ADJUSTMENT

#### STEERING GEAR HEIGHT (TOE-OUT)

Steering gear on R5 is mounted with slotted shims. Whenever steering gear is removed or replaced, it must be adjusted.

**1)** Place vehicle on lift, or alignment rack, with front wheels on radius gauges. Attach a brake press to pedal (to prevent rolling movement of wheels). Set steering at center point and lock in position with suitable holding tool (MS. 504) attached to steering wheel.

**2)** Load front of vehicle until measurement from centerline of front wheel to bottom of lower frame member (at front wheel) is $4\frac{5}{16}$" (110 mm). Mount scale boards (T. Av. 552) on side of body so distance from wheel center to board is $51\frac{3}{16}$" (1.30 m). See *Fig. 1*.

**3)** Mount measuring tools on both front wheels of vehicle so pointers are in line with crosses on scale boards. Remove load from vehicle (and raise with jack if necessary) so position is $3\frac{1}{8}$" (80 mm) higher than loaded position. Pointer should move to 6-7.75 on scale board. If not, steering gear must be adjusted.

**Fig. 1  Measurements for Steering Gear**

**4)** Slotted shims are used to adjust steering gear. Position of slot in shim varies to move gear up and down. To replace or adjust shims, remove transaxle cover. Loosen steering gear bolts and remove adjusting shims. See *Fig. 2*.

**Fig. 2  Shim Position on R5**

### SETTING STEERING CENTER POINT

To find center steering point, set center of rivet head on flexible coupling in line with index mark on pinion housing. This should result in a measurement of $2\frac{13}{16}$" (71.5 mm).

**Fig. 3  Steering Center Measurement**

### REMOVAL & INSTALLATION

**Removal** — Remove spare tire and disconnect battery. Remove air cleaner and cooling fan relay, without disconnecting wiring. Remove governor, connector, valve, and air pump pipe. Remove air filter bracket bolts and place assembly on engine. Remove air pump filter. Remove steering shaft flexible coupling bolts and gear mounting bolts. Disconnect tie rod ends and remove steering gear. Mark shim location to reinstall in correct position.

## RENAULT RACK & PINION (Cont.)

**Installation** — To install, reverse removal procedure, noting the following: Coat tie rod end connections with grease. Check condition of bellows and clamps. Align tie rod connecting bolts horizontally. After steering gear is installed, check height setting and alignment.

## OVERHAUL

**Disassembly** — **1)** Loosen rack and locknut. Remove rack end fitting, opposite pinion, noting the number of turns required. Take off bellows, circlip, and thrust washer. Pry out rubber washer.

**Fig. 4  Exploded View of R5 Rack and Pinion Steering**

**2)** Make a bearing removal tool by drilling two $5/32''$ holes $1\frac{1}{16}''$ apart in a piece of steel strap. Turn two $1/8''$ screws into old bearing and turn pinion shaft to remove bearing.

**Fig. 5  Removal of Rack Bearing**

**3)** Remove plunger cover, washers, spring and plunger. Pry out pinion seal plug, then remove pinion nut and washer. Pull out pinion and rack. Remove circlip and tap out bearings.

**Inspection** — Clean all parts with soft cloth and check for excessive wear or damage. Replace parts if necessary.

**Reassembly & Adjustment** — **1)** Tap pinion bearings into place. Replace thrust washers, rubber rings and bushing in end of rack housing. Be sure slot is clear, and refit circlip. Spread Molykote grease over rack and pinion, then center rack in housing and install pinion. Replace washer, nut, and seal.

**2)** Grease plunger, spring and washers, and replace in housing. Fabricate a dial indicator bracket using a spare plunger cover. Drill a hole in the center and weld on a flange to hold indicator outer shaft. *See Fig. 6.*

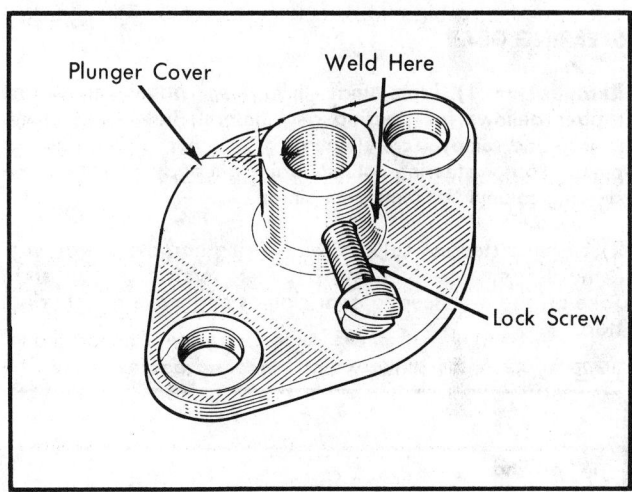

**Fig. 6  Tool for Rack Play Measurement**

**3)** Measure plunger movement while turning pinion. Set rack at position of greatest measurement, then reset dial indicator to zero. Pry rack back and forth without moving from position, and measure play on indicator.

**4)** Select a shim .0016" (.04 mm) smaller than measured play, then remove spare cover, insert shim, and replace plunger cover. Tighten cover bolts to specification.

## TIGHTENING SPECIFICATIONS

| Application | Ft. Lbs. (mkg) |
| --- | --- |
| Plunger Cover Bolts | 7.5 (1.0) |
| Pinion Nut | 7.5 (1.0) |
| Flexible Coupling Bolts | 11 (1.5) |
| Tie Rod-to-Rack Bolts | 25 (3.5) |
| Gear-to-Frame Bolts | 25 (3.5) |

## SAAB RACK & PINION

99

**NOTE** — *Power steering may be used on some models as optional equipment. See Saab Power-Assisted Rack & Pinion under POWER STEERING in this section.*

### DESCRIPTION

Steering gear is the rack and pinion type. Rack is protected from dirt by rubber bellows. The pinion bearing uses an adjustable spring-loaded plunger. The gear is oil-lubricated. The steering linkage is a direct link from the steering rack to the steering knuckles, consisting of tie rods and ball joints.

### ADJUSTMENT

**NOTE** — *See Overhaul procedure in this article.*

### REMOVAL & INSTALLATION

#### STEERING GEAR

**Removal — 1)** From under instrument panel, loosen the rubber bellows for steering gear intermediate shaft. Raise vehicle and remove screw mounting "U" joint to steering gear pinion. Loosen steering column tube from body, then separate steering column "U" joint from pinion.

**2)** Suspend steering column, with wiring harness, out of way. Remove front wheels. Using a puller, remove tie rod ends. Take off the two steering gear clamps and move rack to right stop.

**NOTE** — *Be sure bellows is not damaged against body.*

**3)** Place steering gear far enough to the right to allow tie rod to be bent down into body opening. Pull rack maximum stroke to left and lift steering gear through body opening.

**Installation** — To install, reverse removal procedure and check toe-in and steering wheel alignment.

### OVERHAUL

#### STEERING GEAR

**Disassembly** — Remove tie rod ends and rubber bellows. Drill out lock pins from inner ball joints, using a 4 mm bit and drilling only ⅜" deep. Remove outer bearing cups and lock nuts. Remove rack adjustment screw, cap with gasket, shims, spring, and plunger. Remove pinion and cap with gasket shims, and upper bearing. Pull rack out from housing. Tap out lower pinion bearing.

**Fig. 1    Procedure for Removing Outer Bearing Cap Lock Nut**

**Fig. 2    Exploded View of Saab Rack & Pinion Steering Gear Assembly**

## SAAB RACK & PINION (Cont.)

**Assembly – 1)** Ensure all parts are thoroughly cleaned before proceeding with assembly. Lubricate all parts during assembly. Seat the lower pinion bearing.

**NOTE** – *Be sure extended parts of the inner bearing tracks are facing each other.*

**2)** Assemble inner ball joint on pinion end of rack as follows: Thread lock nut onto rack. Fit outer bearing cup on rack and fill with suitable gear oil. Insert spring and inner bearing cup. Tighten bearing cup so that there is no looseness in ball joint, but without tightness. If rack, with tie rod mounted, is held horizontally, the tie rod should be able to be placed in any position without falling under its own weight. Tighten lock nut against bearing cup and recheck ball joint tightness. Drill a new 4 mm hole ⅜ " deep and insert and stake lock a new lock pin.

**Fig.3    Exploded View of Ball Joint Assembly**

**3)** Insert rack into housing, then fit pinion and upper bearing. Adjust pinion with shims so that there is no axial play when pinion gasket and cap are attached. Various shim sizes are available.

**4)** Adjust radial play of rack as follows: Insert plunger without spring and gasket, then attach cap with bolts (fingertight only). Measure clearance which exists between the cap and the housing face. To this measurement add .002-.006" (.05-.15 mm), to allow for play after completion of adjuster assembly. This total thickness will be the thickness of gasket and shims required. Measure shims and gasket together, then remove cap and install shims, gasket, and cap. Check rack for free movement by rotating pinion.

**Fig. 4    Measuring Clearance Between Cap and Gear Housing**

**5)** Assemble and adjust other ball joint in same manner as previously described. Attach bellows after lubricating contact area between bellows and tie rod (use silicone grease). Attach both inner clamps. Stand gear on end and pour 7.8 oz. of suitable EP 90 gear oil into bellows. Attach outboard bellows with clamps. Screw on lock nuts and mount tie rod assemblies.

**NOTE** – *Outer bellows clamps should be protected with rubber caps.*

## SUBARU RACK & PINION

**1600**

### DESCRIPTION

Steering gear, mounted on crossmember, is a rack and pinion type, with backlash automatically adjusted. Pinion is connected to steering shaft by a flexible rubber coupling. Steering knuckle arms are connected to rack by tie rods which are threaded onto ball joint studs at each end of rack.

### ADJUSTMENT

**Backlash** — Backlash is automatically held to a minimum by a spring loaded sleeve which bears against rack. Adjustment is not normally required. End play of sleeve may be corrected if necessary by turning adjusting screw in until it contacts plate,

and then backing screw out 1/8 turn to obtain .006" (0.16 mm) end play. Tighten lock nut.

### REMOVAL & INSTALLATION

**Removal** — Raise vehicle and remove front wheels. Remove tie rod ends from steering knuckles. Disconnect parking brake cable hanger from tie rod. Unbolt rubber coupling from steering pinion. Remove exhaust cover under front crossmember, and remove bolts holding gear box to crossmember. Pull out gear box toward the left side of vehicle.

**Installation** — To install, reverse removal procedure and note the following: tighten right bracket first when installing gear box. Torque tie rod end lock nuts to specification, then turn until cotter pin can be inserted.

*Fig. 1   Exploded View of Subaru Rack & Pinion Steering Gear Assembly*

## SUBARU RACK & PINION (Cont.)

### OVERHAUL

**Disassembly** — Loosen lock nuts and remove tie rod ends. Remove air vent tube from boots. Remove snap rings from boots and pull boots from gear housing. Straighten lock washers and remove ball joints from rack ends. Loosen lock nut, completely back out adjusting screw, then remove cover, gasket, sleeve spring, sleeve plate, and sleeve. Remove pinion from rack, then remove rack from gear housing.

**Inspection** — Steering rack should be straight within .010" (0.3 mm). Ball joint play should not exceed .010" (0.3 mm) at 154 lbs. (70 kg). Inspect all parts and replace if worn, damaged, or not within specifications.

**Fig. 2  View Showing Method of Centering Rack in Gear Housing**

**Reassembly** — 1) Grease the toothed and sliding portions of rack and install rack into gear housing. Locate end of rack so that it measures 2.83" (72 mm) from end of gear housing, then grease and install pinion. Tighten pinion assembly to gear housing. In this position, rack and pinion will be centered for vehicle straight-ahead position. When center position has been established, mark the gear housing and pinion with white paint so that marks will align for center position reference.

2) Install sleeve, plate, spring, gasket, and cover to gear housing and tighten bolts. Turn adjusting screw in until it contacts plate and back off 1/8 turn to obtain .006" (0.16 mm) end play. Tighten lock nut. **NOTE** — *Use a suitable locking compound on bolt and adjusting screw threads.*

**Fig. 3  View Showing Lubrication Points and Backlash Adjustment**

3) Install lock washers and ball joints on rack ends. Tighten ball joints and bend lock washers over to secure joints. Install boots on gear housing and retain with snap rings. Install air vent tube into boots while aligning it with embossed mark on gear housing. Install tie rod ends with lock nuts, and temporarily tighten lock nuts. Rotate pinion and check operation of gear assembly. Pinion operating torque in straight ahead position should be less than 1.1 ft. lbs. (0.15 mkg) at ±1.18" (±30 mm) of rack displacement. Maximum torque should not exceed 1.59 ft. lbs. (0.22 mkg).

### TIGHTENING SPECIFICATIONS

| Application | Ft. Lbs. (mkg) |
|---|---|
| Pinion Flange-to-Gear Housing | 11 (1.5) |
| Rack Adjuster Cover | 11 (1.5) |
| Rack Adjuster Lock Nut | 15-18 (2.1-2.5) |
| Ball Joint Assembly-to-Rack | 58 (8.0) |
| Gear-to-Crossmember | 33-40 (4.5-5.5) |
| Rubber Coupling Self-Locking Nut | 15-18 (2.1-2.5) |
| Tie Rod End Castellated Nut | 18-22 (2.5-3.0) |
| Tie Rod End-to-Ball Joint Lock Nut | 58-65 (8.0-9.0) |

## TOYOTA (EXC. LAND CRUISER) RECIRCULATING BALL

Celica
Corona
Corolla
Pickup

## DESCRIPTION

### STEERING GEAR

Steering gear is a variable ratio, recirculating ball type. Ball bearings circulate within grooves in worm and nut. As worm shaft turns, ball nut moves up or down, turning the sector shaft and pitman arm.

### STEERING LINKAGE

Linkage consists of idler arm, center relay rod, two adjustable tie rods, and two steering knuckles. The connection between each component is through ball joints. The linkage assembly is joined to the steering gear at the pitman arm.

**Fig. 1  Toyota Steering Linkage with Bushings and Retainers (Typical Illustration)**

## ADJUSTMENT

*See Overhaul procedures in this article.*

## REMOVAL & INSTALLATION

### STEERING GEAR

**Removal** — Remove clamp bolt attaching steering shaft to worm shaft. On Corona models, remove two bolts in flexible coupling after removing air cleaner for access. Using a suitable puller, detach relay rod from pitman arm. Unbolt gear housing from frame and remove from vehicle.

**Installation (All Models)** — Reverse removal procedure, aligning worm shaft cut portion with flexible coupling yoke.

### STEERING LINKAGE

**Removal** — Using a suitable puller, disconnect pitman arm from sector shaft. Remove idler arm support from frame. Detach tie rod ends from steering knuckles, using a suitable puller. Remove steering linkage assembly from vehicle.

**Installation** — Connect tie ends to steering knuckles and torque retaining nuts to specification. Install pitman to sector shaft (ensure correct positioning of aligning marks as illustrated). Tighten nut to specified torque. Place idler arm support on frame and tighten retaining bolts to specification. Adjust toe-in.

## OVERHAUL

### STEERING GEAR

**Disassembly** — Using a suitable puller, remove pitman arm. Loosen sector shaft adjusting screw lock nut. Remove bolts attaching end cover, then remove cover and sector shaft. Loosen worm bearing adjusting screw lock nut and remove worm assembly with bearing.

**NOTE** — *Do not disassemble ball nut from worm. If recirculating ball assembly has damaged or worn components, replace entire assembly.*

**Fig. 2  Exploded View of Recirculating Ball Type Steering (Corona Shown, Others Similar)**

**Inspection** — Check all components for wear or damage and replace as necessary. Check sector shaft-to-bushing clearance: it must not exceed .0020" (.05 mm). If clearance is exceeded, replace bushing or shaft.

**Assembly & Adjustment — 1)** Lubricate all bearings and sliding portions of gear assembly. Install worm into gear housing, then install adjusting screw and lock nut. Check worm bearing preload with an INCH-lb. torque wrench. Turn adjusting screw as required to bring preload within limits. Tighten lock nut and recheck preload.

## TOYOTA (EXC. LAND CRUISER) RECIRCULATING BALL (Cont.)

### Initial Worm Bearing Preload

| Application | INCH-lbs. (cmkg) |
|---|---|
| Celica | 2.6-3.5 (3-4) |
| Corolla & Corona | 3.5-5.2 (4-6) |
| Pickup | 2.6-5.2 (3-6) |

**Fig. 3   Measuring Worm Bearing Preload**

**2)** Install adjusting screw and thrust washer into sector shaft and measure thrust clearance (between head of adjusting screw and bottom of "T" slot). Maximum clearance is .002" (.05 mm). If clearance is exceeded, replace thrust washer with one of correct size to bring clearance within limits.

**NOTE** — *Ensure ball nut is at center of travel before inserting sector shaft. Loosen adjusting screw completely before shaft insertion.*

**3)** Install sector shaft to end cover. Coat gasket with sealer, then install assembly into gear housing. After sector shaft cover is bolted into place, repeat worm bearing preload test. Use sector shaft adjusting screw to obtain correct preload.

### Final Worm Bearing Preload

| Application | INCH-lbs. (cmkg) |
|---|---|
| Celica | 2.6-3.5 (3-4) |
| Corolla & Corona | 6.9-9.5 (8-11) |
| Pickup | 6.1-9.5 (7-11) |

**Fig. 4   Aligning Pitman Arm to Sector Shaft**

**4)** Install pitman arm (aligning mating marks); attach a dial gauge to measure pitman arm backlash. Backlash, as measured at pitman arm outer end, should not exceed 5° from either side of center. After checking, tighten adjusting screw lock nut securely.

### TIGHTENING SPECIFICATIONS

| Application | Ft. Lbs. (mkg) |
|---|---|
| Steering Gear-to-Frame | |
| Celica & Corona | 36-51 (5-7) |
| Corolla & Pickup | 25-36 (3.5-5) |
| Pitman Arm-to-Sector Shaft | |
| Celica & Corona | 80-101 (11-14) |
| Corolla | 72-101 (10-14) |
| Pickup | 80-90 (11-12.5) |
| Worm Adjusting Screw Lock Nut | |
| Celica & Corolla | 95-122 (13-17) |
| Corona & Pickup | 58-72 (8-10) |
| Sector Shaft Adjuster Lock Nut | |
| All Models | 14-22 (2-3) |
| Sector Shaft Cover Bolts | |
| All Models | 11-16 (1.5-2.2) |
| Pitman Arm-to-Relay Rod | |
| Pickup | 54-80 (7.5-11) |
| All Other Models | 36-51 (5-7) |
| Relay Rod-to-Idler Arm | |
| Pickup | 54-80 (7.5-11) |
| All Other Models | 36-51 (5-7) |
| Tie Rod-to-Steering Knuckle | |
| Pickup | 54-80 (7.5-11) |
| All Other Models | 36-51 (5-7) |

## TOYOTA LAND CRUISER RECIRCULATING BALL

**FJ40**
**FJ55**

### DESCRIPTION

#### STEERING GEAR

Steering gear mechanism is of the recirculating ball type. Gear mounts off a bracket that is attached to frame. Adjustment screws are provided for backlash and preload. Initial preload is achieved with shims.

#### STEERING LINKAGE

Steering linkage consists of the following: pitman arm, relay rod, tie rod, damper, center arm and drag link. Tie rod and relay rod are adjustable to correct wheel alignment.

### ADJUSTMENT

**NOTE** — *Adjustments are done during reassembly after overhaul. For adjustments, refer to Overhaul in this article.*

### REMOVAL & INSTALLATION

#### STEERING GEAR

**Removal** — Scribe mating marks on all steering shaft couplings to aid in reassembly. Remove coupling clamp bolt. Remove steering wheel and snap ring at top of column, then pull main shaft back from steering gear. Remove steering gear mounting bolts and pitman arm using suitable puller. Remove gear from frame.

**Installation** — To install, reverse removal procedure and tighten all mounting bolts.

*Fig. 1   Toyota Land Cruiser Steering Gear*

#### STEERING LINKAGE

**Removal** — 1) — Raise and support front of vehicle, then remove front wheels. Index mark relative position of pitman arm to sector shaft and remove arm, using suitable puller. Disconnect steering drag link from steering center arm.

*Fig. 2   Toyota Land Cruiser Front Steering Linkage with Detail of Both FJ40 and FJ55*

## TOYOTA LAND CRUISER RECIRCULATING BALL (Cont.)

**2)** Disconnect tie rod ends from both sides. Disconnect relay rod from steering center arm, then remove tie rod assembly with relay arm assembly. Disconnect end of steering damper from bracket on crossmember. Loosen and remove center arm from bracket (with steering damper). Remove steering center arm bracket from frame.

**Installation** – To install, reverse removal procedure and note the following: Adjust tie rod and relay rod as shown in *Fig. 3.*

32.56" (827 mm)

Relay Rod

47.44" (1205 mm)

Tie Rod

**Fig. 3   Relay Rod and Tie Rod Length Adjustments for Installation**

## OVERHAUL

**Disassembly** – Drain gear lubricant, then secure housing in a vise. Remove sector shaft end cover and gasket. With sector shaft positioned at rotational center, pull assembly out of gear housing. Note number and placement of shims as they are removed. Remove gear housing end cover and gasket. Take out worm assembly, keeping bearings in sequence and don't attempt to disassemble worm assembly.

**Inspection** – Wash all disassembled parts and inspect for wear or damage; replace as necessary. If inner or outer races are scored or pitted, replace as required. Inspect sector shaft and bushings for wear. If replacement is necessary, use a press to remove and replace bushings. Hone bushings until clearance between bushing and sector shaft is .0004-.0024" (.009-.060 mm). Install new oil seal. Measure sector shaft thrust clearance, then select thrust washer that provides minimum clearance between sector shaft and adjustment screw: .004" (.1 mm).

**Reassembly** – **1)** Install cover with same number of shims that were removed, then tighten bolts. **NOTE** – *When tightening cover bolts keep checking worm to see that it will turn properly.*

**2)** Using a pull scale, measure initial (starting) worm bearing preload for 8.8-13.2 lbs (4-6 kg). If preload is not within specifications, correct by selecting proper thickness shim(s).

**3)** Position worm ball nut at center, then insert sector shaft ensuring ball nut and sector mesh together at center. Loosen ball adjusting bolt all the way and install cover.

**4)** Set worm shaft preload to 17.6-24.2 lbs. (8-11 kg) with adjusting bolt. Make sure measurement is made with meshing positioned at center.

**5)** Install pitman arm and check backlash. There should be zero backlash when worm is rotated within 45° to either side. Tighten adjustment screw lock nut and recheck preload.

## TIGHTENING SPECIFICATIONS

| Application | Ft. Lbs. (mkg) |
|---|---|
| Sector End Cover Bolts | 21.7-32.5 (3.0-4.5) |
| Worm Bearing Cap | 21.7-32.5 (3.0-4.5) |
| Gear Box Bracket | 28.9-39.8 (4.0-5.5) |
| Pitman Arm Nut | 119-141 (16.5-19.5) |

# Steering Gears & Linkage

## TRIUMPH RACK & PINION

**TR7**
**Spitfire**

### DESCRIPTION

Steering gear is a rack and pinion type with direct linkage (tie rods) to steering arms. Gear housings are mounted by bolts through frame on TR7; by "U" bolts on Spitfire models. A flexible coupling links the steering gears to steering shaft.

### ADJUSTMENTS

Rack and pinion free play are adjusted through the use of shims on the rack damper and pinion shaft. These adjustments are performed as part of overhaul procedure. See Overhaul below.

### REMOVAL & INSTALLATION

#### RACK AND PINION

**Removal — 1)** Raise vehicle and place on safety stands. Scribe an index mark on pinion shaft and lower steering coupling for installation purposes. Disconnect tie rod ends from steering knuckle.

**2)** Remove pinch bolt attaching lower steering coupling to rack pinion. On TR7 models only, withdraw bolts mounting pinion end of rack to chassis. On all other models, "U" bolts mount steering rack to chassis.

**3)** On TR7 only, remove remaining rack mounting hardware, disconnect lower pinion shaft coupling and take rack out driver's side. On all others, slide rack forward disengaging rack pinion splines from flexible coupling. Disconnect ground strap from rack plug and withdraw steering rack.

**Installation — 1)** If rack has been disassembled, it must be centralized before reinstallation: Remove center plug from thrust pad and, using a piece of welding rod, locate dimple in rack shaft. When dimple in rack shaft is aligned with plug hole rack is centralized.

**Fig. 1   Installed View of TR7 Rack Assembly**

**2)** Carefully slide rack assembly into position but DO NOT disturb rack shaft. On TR7 models only, secure rack to chassis with mounting hardware, refit tie rod ends and tighten pinion coupling pinchbolt.

**3)** On all other models, hold steering wheel in straight-ahead position and engage rack pinion shaft splines in flexible coupling. Install and tighten pinch bolt. Keep rubber grommets correctly positioned on inboard side of rack flanges with lip under straight face of flange, then fit "U" bolts (Fig. 2). Refit tie rod outer ends to steering arms.

**Fig. 2   Spitfire Rack with Rubber Grommets**

**4)** Make sure all nuts and bolts are tightened and check front wheel alignment. See Triumph in WHEEL ALIGNMENT Section.

### OVERHAUL

#### RACK AND PINION

**Disassembly — 1)** Release clip and slide bellows toward outer ball joint. Slacken inner lock nut and unscrew tie rod assembly from rack. Withdraw spring from rack end. Straighten tab washer, unscrew sleeve nut, and remove tab washer, shims, and cup.

**2)** Slacken outer lock nut and unscrew tie rod end from tie rod. Remove outer lock nut, bellows, and cup nut. Remove inner lock nut from rack. Repeat on other end.

**3)** Remove damper plug, spring, shims and damper. On Spitfire models, remove circlip from top of pinion and carefully pull out pinion, retainer, shims, bushing and thrust washer. Remove "O" ring from retainer. Be careful not to lose dowel pin. On TR7 models, remove rubber seal and pinion retaining plug then pull out pinion shaft and bearing. Remove circlip to slide bearing off pinion shaft.

**4)** Pull out rack and remove bushings from housing if necessary.

## TRIUMPH RACK & PINION (Cont.)

**Reassembly — 1)** Install end cover and lower bushing in rack housing (if removed). Place rack shaft in housing with teeth toward pinion end. Install lock nuts, tie rods, springs and shims, then tighten. Pack inner joints with grease, then install bellows and clips.

**2)** Rotate rack shaft until teeth mesh with pinion. On Spitfire models, install pinion. Replace thrust washer, bushing, shims, and retaining ring with new "O" ring. Fit circlip and check to see that end play does not exceed .010" (.254 mm). Adjust shim pack if necessary. See Fig. 3.

**Fig. 3   Exploded View of Spitfire Pinion Assembly**

**3)** On TR7 models, slide ball bearing on pinion and secure with circlip. Lubricate pinion shaft and insert into housing. Tighten end plug and replace rubber seal.

**4)** On all models, install rack damper, shims, spring and cap. Adjust rack side play by adding shims so movement does not exceed .004-.008" (.1-.2 mm) for Spitfire, or .001-.007 (.03-.18 mm) for TR7. Install rack in vehicle and reconnect ground strap (if removed).

**Fig. 4   Exploded View of TR7 Pinion and Damper**

## TIGHTENING SPECIFICATIONS

| Application | Ft. Lbs. (mkg) |
|---|---|
| Steering Gear-to-Frame | |
| TR7 | 22-29 (3.0-4.0) |
| Spitfire | 16 (2.2) |
| Tie Rod Lock Nuts | |
| TR7 | 30-37 (4.1-5.1) |
| Spitfire | 38 (5.2) |
| Universal Joint Pinch Bolts | |
| TR7 | 16-21 (2.2-2.9) |
| Spitfire | 14 (1.9) |

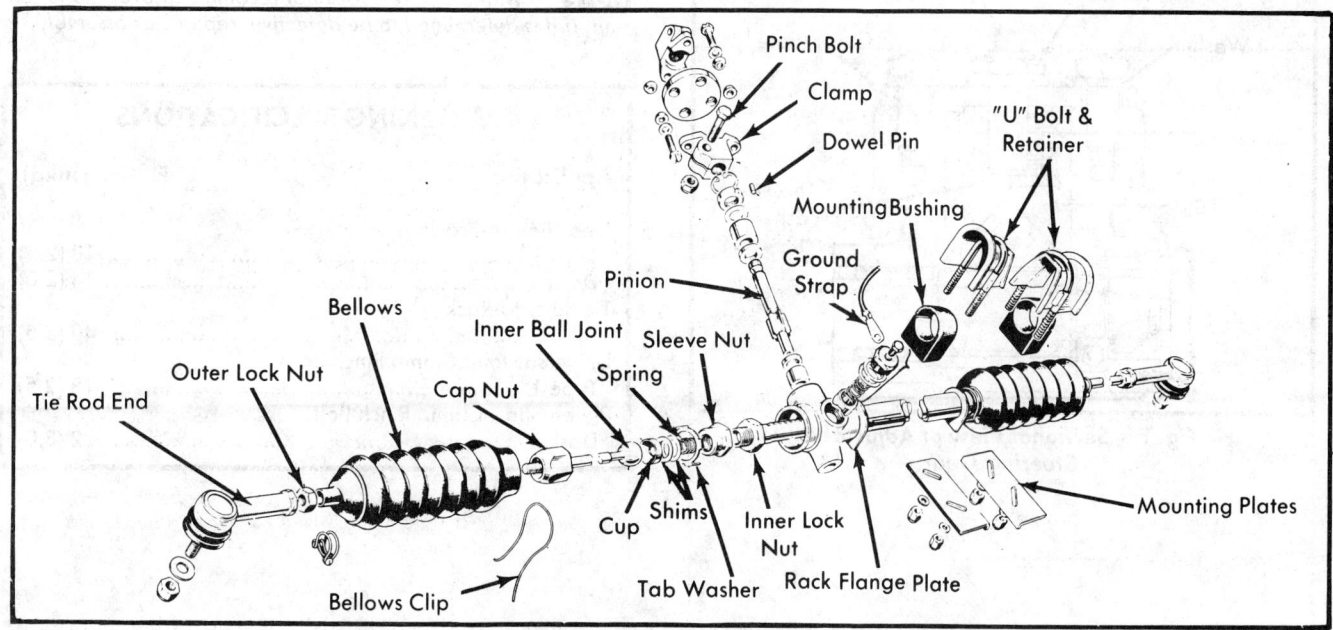

**Fig. 5   Triumph Spitfire Rack and Pinion Steering**

## VOLKSWAGEN TYPE 1 & DASHER RACK & PINION

Type 1
Dasher

### DESCRIPTION

These vehicles are equipped with an adjustable rack and pinion steering gear. Attached to center of the rack housing are two tie rods (one adjustable and one non-adjustable). The Dasher uses a steering damper.

### REMOVAL & INSTALLATION

**Removal, Dasher — 1)** Bend back tabs on locking plate at center of rack housing and remove both tie rod bolts. Move tie rods so that gear will have clearance for removal.

**2)** Unbolt pinch clamp at pinion-to-column connection. Remove lower instrument panel. Loosen steering column flange at toe board. Drive steering flange tube off of steering gear.

**3)** Remove gear mounting screw at right end of rack housing, then unbolt rack mounting at left end. Turn front wheels to right lock, and remove steering gear through right wheel housing.

**Removal, Type 1 — 1)** Raise vehicle and remove front wheels. Uncover lower universal joint by moving boot, then remove universal joint clamp bolt.

**2)** Pry universal joint shaft off pinion. Bend up lock plate and remove bolts holding tie rod inner end to steering rack.

**3)** Disconnect tie rods. Remove nuts and bolts holding ends of steering rack housing to brackets, then remove rack and pinion assembly from vehicle.

**NOTE** — *For earlier non-adjustable models, there is a change-over kit available. When installing kit follow manufacturers instructions and DO NOT reinstall shims between housing and cover plate.*

**Fig. 1    Sectional View of Adjustable Steering Gear**

**Installation** — Reverse removal procedure and torque nuts and bolts to specifications.

**NOTE** — *Gain access to adjusting screw on Dasher by removing cover on access hole located in spare wheel well.*

### ADJUSTMENT

With components installed on vehicle, tighten adjusting screw by hand until screw just contacts thrust washer. Hold adjusting screw in position and tighten lock nut *(Fig. 1)*.

**Fig. 2    Volkswagen Dasher Rack and Pinion Assembly (Type 1 Similar)**

### OVERHAUL

**NOTE** — *Manufacturer does not recommend overhaul of this unit. If it is determined to be defective, replace as assembly.*

### TIGHTENING SPECIFICATIONS

| Application | Ft. Lbs. (mkg) |
| --- | --- |
| Gear Box-to-Brackets | |
| Type 1 | 18 (2.5) |
| Dasher | 14 (2.0) |
| Tie Rods-to-Rack | |
| All | 40 (5.5) |
| Universal Joint Clamp Pinch Bolts | |
| Type 1 | 18 (2.5) |
| Pinion Shaft Clamp Pinch Bolt | |
| Dasher | 22 (3.0) |

## VOLKSWAGEN TYPE 2 WORM & ROLLER

**Type 2**

### DESCRIPTION

Beginning with 1973 models, Type 2 vehicles incorporated a worm and roller steering unit. This replaced the previously used worm and peg assembly. Steering linkage remains the same as on earlier models, consisting of an adjustable drag link, two maintenance-free tie rods (one adjustable), and a hydraulic steering damper.

### ADJUSTMENT

#### STEERING GEAR

1) Check for excessive free play in steering by raising front of vehicle, placing wheels in straight-ahead position, and lightly turning steering wheel back and forth while holding one of the steering wheel spokes at outer end. Free play should not exceed ⅝" (15 mm) before resistance is felt in the steering wheel.

2) If free play is excessive, check for loose or worn steering linkage components, check for tight mounting of gear box, and check for proper tightness of gear box cover. If these are found to be in good condition and properly tightened, continue to next step.

**Fig. 1   Steering Gear Aligned in Central Position**

3) Disconnect drag link from pitman arm. Turn steering wheel 180-200° from center, in either direction. **NOTE** — *Center position is determined when pointer on worm spindle dust cap is in line with square boss on worm cover plate.* Loosen adjusting screw lock nut and turn adjusting screw out one full turn.

4) Working under vehicle, move pitman arm back and forth while gradually tightening adjusting screw. Repeat until no play is felt at pitman arm (without stiffness). Hold adjusting screw in this position and tighten lock nut.

5) Take off horn button and disconnect horn wire. Attach a torque gauge to steering wheel nut. Turn steering wheel through centerpoint. Steering is correctly adjusted if torque gauge reads 7-11 INCH lbs. (8-12 cmkg). If necessary, repeat and recheck adjustment.

### REMOVAL & INSTALLATION

#### STEERING GEAR

**Removal** — From under vehicle, remove cover plate that is below pedal cluster. Detach drag link and remove pitman arm using suitable puller. Bend back lock plate and remove clamp bolt holding coupling flange on worm spindle. Remove gear box mounting bolts and push steering column slightly upward while extracting gearbox from frame.

**Installation** — To install, reverse removal procedure noting that mark on drop arm is aligned with mark on shaft.

### OVERHAUL

**NOTE** — *Manufacturer does not recommend overhaul of the worm and roller steering gear, however a defective roller shaft oil seal may be replaced without removing steering gear box from vehicle.*

#### OIL SEAL REPLACEMENT

To replace seal, remove pitman arm, See *Removal,* and pry out defective seal. Clean shaft and seal recess, then lubricate new seal. Center seal on shaft and drive into recess with suitable tube. Reinstall pitman arm, and using new lock plate, tighten lock nut to 101 ft. lbs. (14 mkg). Place steering gear in full right lock position and check that steering roller shaft is covered with oil.

**Fig. 2   Cutaway View of Worm & Roller Gearbox**

### TIGHTENING SPECIFICATIONS

| Application | Ft. Lbs. (mkg) |
|---|---|
| Steering Gear-to-Frame | 25-36 (3.5-5.0) |
| Pinion Shaft Nut | 101 (14) |
| Pitman Arm-to-Drag Link | 22 (3) |
| Adjuster Locknut | 36-43 (5-6) |
| Flange-to-Wormshaft | 14 (2) |

# Steering Gears & Linkage

## VOLKSWAGEN RABBIT, SCIROCCO RACK & PINION

Rabbit
Scirocco

### DESCRIPTION

Steering gear is a rack and pinion type. Tie rods attach to ends of rack. Late production racks are mounted with "U" bolts and rubber bushings rather than welded mounting plates.

### REMOVAL & INSTALLATION

**Removal** — Disconnect shift linkage bearing plate from rack housing. Loosen pinch bolts on steering shaft and remove shaft from pinion. Disconnect tie rod ends from steering linkage, using suitable puller. Remove mounting bolts and remove rack with tie rods attached.

**Installation** — When installing steering gear assembly, correctly align and insert pinion shaft with steering shaft lower universal joint before securing steering gear housing clamp bolts. Connect tie rod outer ends to steering linkage. Tighten upper and lower universal joint pinch bolts. Connect and adjust shift linkage bearing plate to gear housing.

### ADJUSTMENT

#### RACK & TIE RODS

1) Center rack in housing so rack protrudes an equal amount from each end of housing.

**Fig. 1  Centering Rack in Steering Gear Housing**

2) If replacing the non-adjustable left tie rod with adjustable type, adjust tie rod length "D" to 14.92" (379 mm).

3) Screw tie rods onto rack and adjust to specified dimensions without moving rack from center position. When adjustment is correct, secure tie rods with lock nuts and install rubber boots. See *Fig. 2*.

**Tie Rod Specifications**

| Application | Dimension "B" | Dimension "C" |
|---|---|---|
| Man. Trans. | 2.72" (69 mm) | 2.72" (69 mm) |
| Auto. Trans. | 2.64" (67 mm) | 2.72" (69 mm) |

**Fig. 2  Installation Adjustment of Tie Rods on Rack**

4) Loosen pinion shaft adjusting screw lock nut, then turn adjusting bolt until it just contacts thrust washer. Tighten lock nut.

### TIGHTENING SPECIFICATIONS

| Application | Ft. Lbs. (mkg) |
|---|---|
| Tie Rod End to Steering Arm | 22 (3.0) |
| Tie Rod End Locknut | 29 (4.0) |
| Gear Box Mounting Bolts | |
|   Welded Mounts | 14 (2.0) |
|   Rubber Bushing Mounts | 22 (3.0) |
| Universal Joint Pinch Bolt | 22 (3.0) |

**Fig. 3  Disassembled View of Rack & Pinion Steering Gear Assembly**

## VOLVO RACK & PINION

**240 Series**
**260 Series**

**NOTE** — *For models equipped with power steering, refer to appropriate article under Power Steering in this section.*

## DESCRIPTION

Rack and pinion steering gear is mounted in rubber insulators to front crossmember. Movement of steering wheel is transmitted by steering shaft assembly to helical pinion. Rotation of pinion causes rack to move laterally where tie rods, attached to rack, transmit this movement to spindle arms, causing front wheels to change direction. Two types of steering gears are used by Volvo. The first is a Cam Gear unit which may be recognized by the two bolt rack damper cover. The second type is a ZF unit which has a plug type rack damper cover.

## REMOVAL & INSTALLATION

### STEERING GEAR

**Removal** — Remove lock bolt and nut from pinion flange. Bend flange apart slightly. Raise and support front of vehicle and remove wheels. Remove tie rod nuts and disconnect ball studs from spindle using ball joint removal tool (9995043). Remove splash guard and bolts securing steering gear to crossmember. Disconnect gear from flange and remove gear.

**Installation** — To install, reverse removal procedure making sure that recess on pinion shaft is aligned towards lock bolt opening in flange.

### TIE RODS

**Removal** — Raise vehicle and remove wheel(s). Remove tie rod nuts and disconnect ball studs from spindle using ball joint removal tool (5043). Remove splash guard. On cam gear units, loosen inner clamps for both rubber bellows and drain oil, then re-attach clamp on side not being removed (if applicable). Bend up tie rod lock and disconnect rod from steering gear. Clamp ball stud in vise, loosen lock nut and unscrew rod, counting number of thread turns. Remove outer clamp for rubber bellows and remove bellows.

**Installation** — Install rubber bellows and outer clamp. Screw on lock nut same number of turns as when removed. Install ball stud and tighten lock nut. Attach tie rod to steering gear and punch ball stud edge or lock washer tab into rack groove. On cam gear units, fill a suction gun with 6.75 oz. (200 cc) of 20W-50 engine oil and inject oil into steering gear through rubber bellows inner end. Install inner bellows clamp and tighten clamp after turning tie rod so that ball stud is up. Connect tie rod to spindle making sure that both rods are the same length within .08" (2 mm).

## ADJUSTMENT

**NOTE** — *Adjustments are performed during gear assembly process. See Overhaul as outlined.*

## OVERHAUL

### CAM GEAR

**Disassembly** — 1) Clean steering gear exterior and check inner ball joints for wear. Loosen pinion side rubber bellows and drain oil. Remove pinion side ball stud, lock nut and rubber bellows. Bend up locked portion of ball joint and unscrew pinion side tie rod. Repeat procedure on opposite side of gear.

2) Remove rack damper cover, spring, "O" ring and piston. Remove pinion cover and lift out pinion assembly. Pull out rack from pinion side of gear housing and remove rack bushing using a puller (4078). Use a puller (5047) to remove pinion lower bearing. Clean all parts and check for wear. Replace all seals, rack bushing and worn parts.

**Assembly & Adjustment** — 1) Oil all parts prior to assembly with 20W-50 engine oil. Install new rack bushing so that locks align with gear housing slots, using driver tool (2993). Install pinion lower bearing using driver tool (5048). Install pinion with upper bearing, but no shims, in housing. Install pinion spacer sleeve and cover with gasket but no seal. Use a dial indicator to measure pinion end play and record for later use. Remove pinion assembly.

2) Insert rack in gear housing from pinion side using care that rack teeth do not damage rack bushing. Apply a nonhardening gasket compound to pinion cover seal and install seal in cover using suitable driver (2734). Calculate required pinion shim thickness by adding .004-.010" (.10-.25 mm) to pinion end play previously measured. This will give correct amount of pinion preload. Install pinion, shims and spacer sleeve with shims between upper bearing and spacer sleeve. Install pinion cover with gasket and seal.

3) Place rack damper piston in housing without "O" ring or spring. Using straight edge and feeler gauge, measure end play between end of piston and housing (see Fig. 1). Measure thickness of gasket and calculate shim thickness required to obtain a total thickness, between gasket and shim, of .001-.006" (.02-.15 mm) greater than the measured piston end play to obtain correct preload. Install spring and "O" ring in piston, install shims, gasket and cover.

Straight Edge

Feeler Gauge

**Fig. 1  Measuring Rack Damper Piston End Play (Cam Gear)**

## VOLVO RACK & PINION (Cont.)

**4)** Using suitable torque gauge (5053), crank rack back and forth from one end to the other. Torque reading should be 8-14 INCH lbs. (9-16 cmkg). Install pinion side tie rod and punch ball joint edge into rack groove.

**NOTE** – *When installing old tie rod, place a thin shim between ball joint and rack shoulder so unused portion of ball can be used for punch locking.*

**5)** Install pinion side rubber bellows with inner clamp only. Install lock nut and ball stud. Repeat procedure for other side of gear and adjust both rods to the same length within .08" (2 mm). Use a suction gun to inject 6.75 ozs. (200 cc) of 20W-50 engine oil through outer end of pinion side rubber bellows. Install outer clamps on bellows.

*Fig. 2 Exploded View of Cam Gear Steering Gear Assembly*

### ZF STEERING GEAR

**Disassembly** – **1)** Clean exterior of steering gear and check inner ball joints for wear. Remove pinion side rubber bellows. Bend up locked portion of ball joint and unscrew tie rod from rack. Remove opposite side tie rod in like manner. Remove dust seal and cotter pin for rack damper, then remove cover and spring using suitable tool (5119). Remove rack damper piston, knocking on rack with palm of hand to aid removal.

**2)** Remove pinion shaft dust seal. Unscrew the pinion shaft nut using suitable tool (5119). Clamp pinion shaft in a soft

jawed vise and tap lightly on housing with soft mallet to remove pinion. Remove rack from pinion side of housing and remove rack bushing by pressing in locking tabs and prying bearing out. Press pinion thrust washer and bearing from shaft. Clean all parts and check for wear. Replace all "O" rings and worn parts.

**Assembly & Adjustment** – **1)** Press bearing onto pinion and install snap ring and thrust washer. Install new "O" rings on rack bushing and press bushing into housing making sure that tabs on bushing fit correctly into slots in housing. Grease rack with Calypsol D 4024-OK grease or equivalent. Insert rack into pinion side of housing using care not to damage rack bushing with rack teeth. Grease pinion using same grease as for rack and install pinion with bearing.

**2)** Install new "O" ring in pinion nut and install nut using suitable tool (5119). Torque to 18±1.5 ft.lbs. (2.5±.2 mkg). Fill cavity on top of nut with grease and install dust seal. Install new "O" ring on rack damper piston, grease piston and install piston and spring. Install, but do not tighten rack damper cover (tool 5119). Using torque gauge, crank rack back and forth between end positions. Torque should be 8-14 INCH lbs. (9-16 cmkg). To increase torque, screw in rack damper cover. Lock cover in correct position with cotter pin and install dust cover.

**3)** Crank out rack fully and fill rack tooth spaces with Calypsol D 4024-OK grease or equivalent. Crank rack in and then out again and repeat grease application. Approximately 1 oz. (25 g) of grease should be used. Install tie rods using new lock washers and bend washer to lock rod in place. Install rubber bellows.

*Fig. 3 Exploded View of ZF Steering Gear Assembly*

## AUDI 5000 POWER-ASSISTED RACK & PINION

**5000**

### DESCRIPTION

A power-assisted rack and pinion steering gear is used on Audi 5000 models. The system consists of a vane pump, rotary piston pinion gear assembly and an oil reservoir. The vane pump draws fluid from the reservoir and supplies it to the flow control valve. The control valve supplies fluid to the proper side of the rack-piston as the steering wheel is turned. The pump is belt driven and mounted on the front of the engine. The reservoir is located near the firewall.

### GENERAL SERVICE

**Capacity** — 1 qt.

**Lubricant** — ATF Dexron or Dexron II

**Oil Level Check** — Remove reservoir cover, start engine and check fluid level. Fluid level should be at mark on upper inside of reservoir.

**Hydraulic System Bleeding** — Start engine and allow to idle. Check that fluid is at proper level. Turn steering wheel lock to lock several times quickly. Continue until fluid level remains at reservoir mark. Make sure that no bubbles appear in reservoir when steering wheel is turned. Shut off engine and check that oil level does not rise more than 3/8" above mark.

**Fig. 1   Audi Power Steering Gear Exploded View**

### Oil Filter Replacement

**NOTE** — *Oil filter insert must be replaced whenever repairs are made to power steering system.*

Remove outer cover, gasket and spring from reservoir. Remove inner filter cover and filter insert. Replace filter. Install new filter, replace filter cover, spring, gasket and cover. Check fluid level.

### ADJUSTMENT

#### PUMP BELT

Remove "V" belt from alternator and air conditioning compressor. Loosen two nuts on pump mounting bracket as shown in *Fig. 3*. Turn adjusting nut on bracket until belt deflection is 3/8" at center. Tighten nuts. Reinstall alternator "V" belt.

#### STEERING GEAR

Loosen lock nut on steering gear. Hand tighten adjusting screw until it touches the thrust plate. Hold adjusting screw and tighten lock nut. Check adjustment with engine idling. No play should be felt. Readjust if necessary.

**Fig. 2   Steering Gear Adjustment**

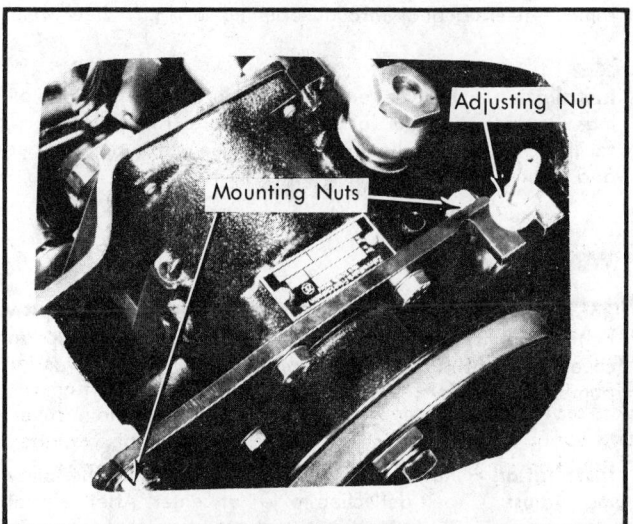

**Fig. 3   Power Steering Belt Adjustment**

## AUDI 5000 POWER-ASSISTED RACK & PINION (Cont.)

### TESTING

#### SYSTEM PRESSURE TEST

Install pressure gauge (US1074), between expansion hose and connecting pipe of valve housing, with the valve open. Run engine at idle. Turn steering wheel lock to lock several times. Check pressure. Correct pressure is 967-1166 psi. If pressure is not within limits, replace steering gear.

#### PUMP PRESSURE TEST

**1)** With pressure gauge installed, start engine and idle. Close valve (no longer than 5 seconds) and check pressure. Correct pressure is 967-1166 psi. If pressure differs, check pressure/flow limiting valve. If valve is all right, replace power steering pump.

**2)** To check limiting valve, inspect bores in valve and piston for obstructions, and that piston moves freely in housing. Install new valve if necessary.

#### LEAKAGE TEST

With engine idling, turn steering wheel to full lock and hold in position. Inspect all connections and tighten if necessary. If leak shows at steering pinion, replace pinion housing seal and both intermediate cover seals. If piston rod is leaking fluid will have entered steering housing. Check for fluid by loosening outer clamp on right steering boot and pushing boot in. If seal is leaking, disassemble steering gear and replace all seals.

### REMOVAL & INSTALLATION

#### STEERING GEAR

**Removal —** Drain fluid from system. Disconnect pressure hose and return line. Cap openings. Remove tie rod lock plate and both tie rod mounting bolts. Pry tie rods off steering gear. Disconnect steering damper. Disconnect flange tube clamp from steering gear and remove flange tube. Remove steering gear mounting bolts from body. Turn front wheels to right lock and remove steering gear through opening in right wheel well.

**Installation —** Reverse removal procedures, noting the following: Replace tie rod lock plate before reinstallation. To facilitate tie rod installation, install one tie rod to steering gear and tighten before installing other tie rod.

#### VANE PUMP

**Removal —** Remove alternator "V" belt and vane pump "V" belt. Disconnect pressure and suction lines from pump and cover openings. Remove mounting bolts from bracket and lift pump from engine.

**Installation —** Reverse removal procedures noting the following: Adjust "V" belt deflection to ³/₈" at center. After reinstalling pressure and suction lines, start engine and turn steering wheel to full lock and check for leaks in connections.

### OVERHAUL

**NOTE** — *Manufacturer does not recommend overhaul of steering gear. Leaking seals may be replaced, however. Check output and system pressure before removing steering gear. Steering gear must be removed to replace seals.*

#### PINION HOUSING SEALS

**Disassembly — 1)** Remove attaching bolts from valve housing and remove housing. Remove pinion gear and intermediate cover.

**2)** Remove "O" ring from intermediate cover, and using suitable tool, drive out intermediate cover oil seal. Anchor housing in padded vise and drive out oil seal from the back.

**Fig. 4　Power Steering Pinion Shaft Assembly Exploded View**

**3)** Install new seals from the inside on cover and housing. Make sure that seal lip on housing seal faces intermediate cover, and seal lip of cover seal faces valve housing. Replace intermediate cover "O" ring.

**Reassembly —** Reverse removal procedure noting the following: Protect pinion teeth on shaft when replacing intermediate cover. Do not damage "O" rings during reinstallation.

#### STEERING HOUSING SEALS

**Disassembly —** With steering gear removed from vehicle, drive out right end of steering housing with drift and remove seals. Clamp rack in vise and remove self locking nut and piston. Insert special tool (VW771), into right steering housing and remove oil seal and shims.

## AUDI 5000 POWER-ASSISTED RACK & PINION (Cont.)

**Reassembly** — Using special tool (2082), install shims and seal with thin shim behind seal, and seal lip facing piston. Replace piston and self locking nut. Tighten to specification. Replace seals and end housing.

inner circlip. Carefully drive pump shaft onto seat with plastic hammer, watching alignment of pump shaft and impeller splines. Install outer circlip, woodruff key and pulley.

Tool VW771

**Fig. 5   Steering Housing Oil Seal Removing**

Tool 2082

Shims

Seal

**Fig. 6   Steering Housing Oil Seal Installation**

### VANE PUMP OIL SEAL

**Disassembly — 1)** With pump removed from vehicle, remove pulley and woodruff key from pinion shaft. Disengage outer circlip with pliers and screw pulley nut onto pinion shaft.

**2)** Anchor pulley nut and shaft in padded vise, and strike pump housing with plastic mallet to drive out shaft. Remove from vise and disengage inner circlip with pliers. Insert extractor into housing. Tighten nut on extractor until two jaws on extractor engage on metal case of seal.

**3)** Anchor nut of extractor in vise and strike pump housing with plastic hammer to drive out seal.

**Reassembly** — Lubricate space between lips of new seal. Drive seal onto seat with lips facing interior of housing. Install

### TIGHTENING SPECIFICATIONS

| Application | Ft. Lbs. (mkg) |
|---|---|
| Pulley to Pump Shaft | 36 (6) |
| Pump Mounting Bolts | 14 (2) |
| Pinion Shaft Nut | 14 (2) |
| Steering Damper | 29 (4) |
| Tie Rod to Steering Gear | 43 (6) |
| Valve Housing Bolts | 7 (1) |
| Tie Rod Locking Nut | 43 (6) |
| Steering Housing Locking Nut | 29 (4) |
| Expansion Hose | 29 (4) |
| Suction Hose | 29 (4) |
| Flange Tube to Steering Gear | 22 (3) |

Inner Circlip

Pinion Shaft

Pulley Nut

**Fig. 7   Vane Pump Oil Seal Removal**

# Power Steering

## BMW POWER-ASSISTED WORM & SECTOR

530i
633CSi
733i

## DESCRIPTION

### STEERING GEAR

Power steering gear consists of a gear housing containing a sector shaft with sector gear, a power piston with gear teeth in side of piston which is in constant mesh with sector shaft teeth, and a worm shaft connecting steering shaft to power piston through a universal joint coupling. Worm shaft is geared to piston through recirculating ball contact; and a steering valve is incorporated into upper end of worm gear assembly.

### STEERING PUMP

Power steering pump is a high pressure, belt driven, vane type pump. A fluid reservoir incorporating a filter element supplies hydraulic fluid to pump. Pump maintains hydraulic pressure to power steering gear assembly.

## LUBRICATION

### CAPACITY

**System Capacity** — 3.8 pints.

### LUBRICANT TYPE

**Initial or Subsequent Filling** — BMW recommends Shell ATF Dexron B (or equivalent).

**Subsequent Filling (Max. ½ pint)** — Veedol Automatic Transmission Fluid Type A Suffix A AQ 1407 A, or suitable equivalent.

### FILTER REPLACEMENT

Remove brake booster return hose and cap opening in reservoir. Fill reservoir with fluid. Run engine 10 minutes and turn wheel lock to lock several times. Depress brakes quickly 10 times and collect fluid from return hose. Stop engine, drain fluid from reservoir. Remove washer, spring, screen, filter, washer and bottom filter from reservoir. Replace filter cartridge. Install filters and washers in reservoir and connect brake booster hose. Fill tank.

## ADJUSTMENT

### PUMP BELT

Loosen adjustment bolts and shift pump to tighten belt. Adjustment is correct when it is possible to press in belt 0.2-0.4" (5-10 mm) with the thumb.

*Fig. 1  Power Steering Belt Adjustment Locations*

## HYDRAULIC SYSTEM BLEEDING

1) Power steering must be bled whenever system is opened, or oil level falls so low that the vane type pump picks up air. Fill reservoir to upper mark with fluid. Turn engine over with starter and continue to add fluid. When oil level no longer falls, start and run engine at idle speed.

2) Turn steering wheel rapidly from lock to lock and back until no further air bubbles rise in reservoir. During this operation, and when completed, fluid level must remain at upper mark.

### SECTOR SHAFT

**Adjustment (In Vehicle)** — **1)** Position front wheels straight ahead. Remove cotter pin and castle nut from tie-rod. Press off center tie-rod from steering arm. Remove BMW emblem from steering wheel. Turn wheel counterclockwise 1 turn from center. Install torque wrench on nut, turn wheel clockwise and read frictional torque.

**2)** Torque should be 2.7-3.5 INCH lbs. (3.1-4 cmkg). To adjust, turn steering wheel counterclockwise from center 1 turn. Loosen locknut on steering gear and turn adjusting screw clockwise until correct torque is reached when passing through center position. Tighten locknut and recheck adjustment. Replace cotter pin and castle nut.

*Fig. 2  Sector Shaft Adjusting Screws*

## TESTING

### STEERING PUMP PRESSURE

1) Disconnect pressure line from pump. Install pressure line from pressure gauge 32-4-000 (or equivalent) in its place. Connect pump pressure line to gauge. Disconnect pressure line from control regulator and connect it to pressure gauge.

2) Shut cut-off valve on gauge. Open shut-off valve on pressure line (See Fig. 6), and bleed system with engine running at idle. After bleeding, close valve in pressure line for 10 seconds maximum and read pressure. Pressure should be $1560 \pm 156$ psi ($109.7 \pm 11$ kg/cm$^2$). If pressure is not within limits, check belt tightness. Replace pump if belt adjustment does not help.

## BMW POWER-ASSISTED WORM & SECTOR (Cont.)

Curved Ring
Impeller
Valve Piston
Pressure Relief Valve
Pressure Check Valve
Throttle Element

Gear Housing
Piston
Balls
Circulation Tube
Worm

Wheel Locking Valve
Sector Shaft
Torsion Bar
Shaft

**Fig. 3   Cross-Sectional View of Power Steering Gear Assembly**

Drive Shaft
Seal
Circlip
Snap Rings
Ball Bearing
Spring
Bearing Sleeve
Dowel Pin
Face Plate
Rotor Set
Cover End Face Plate
"O" Ring
Valve Piston
Spring
Cover
"O" Ring
Hook Snap Ring

**Fig. 4   Cross-Sectional View of Power Steering Pump**

## BMW POWER-ASSISTED WORM & SECTOR (Cont.)

### STEERING GEAR PRESSURE

Raise front of car and support with safety stands. Install pressure tester 32-4-000 (or equivalent), in same position as pump pressure test. Limit steering from reaching full lock position by ½-¾ turn. With engine running, pull steering wheel against final lock with 22 lbs. (9.9 kg) pressure for 5 seconds. Read pressure. Correct reading should be 1560 psi. Check opposite side pressure. Replace steering gear if pressure not up to specifications.

**Fig. 5   Power Steering Pump Pressure Gauge Installation**

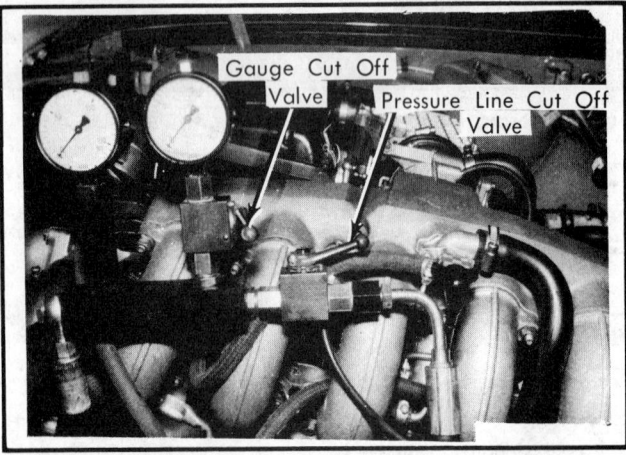

**Fig. 6   Power Steering Pump Pressure Check**

### REMOVAL & INSTALLATION

#### STEERING GEAR

**Removal — 1)** Turn steering to full left lock. This moves piston to top of travel. Discharge hydraulic fluid by depressing brake pedal approximately 20 times. Detach pressure and return hoses from steering gear and cap openings.

**CAUTION** — *Do not reuse fluid drained from system.*

**2)** Remove cotter pin and nut from tie rod end. Press off tie rod from steering arm. Remove bolt from locking groove of steering shaft (See Fig. 7). Push up pivot flange with steering column. Detach steering gear from front axle carrier.

**Installation** — To install, reverse removal procedures, noting the following: Replace hose seals. Position steering wheel straight ahead. Align marks on pivot flange with steering shaft. Make sure bolt is in locking groove of steering shaft. Tighten all connections to proper torque. Bleed system.

### STEERING PUMP

**Removal** — Discharge hydraulic fluid by depressing brake pedal approximately 20 times. Detach hoses from pump. Loosen pump mounting bolts and remove "V" belt. Remove mounting bolts and remove pump.

**Installation** — To install, reverse removal procedures, noting the following: Install hoses so that they do not rub on engine carrier. Torque to specifications. Bleed system.

## OVERHAUL

### STEERING GEAR

**NOTE** — *Power steering gear assembly cannot be repaired except in exceptional cases. BMW recommends replacing the entire unit if malfunctions occur in the steering gear.*

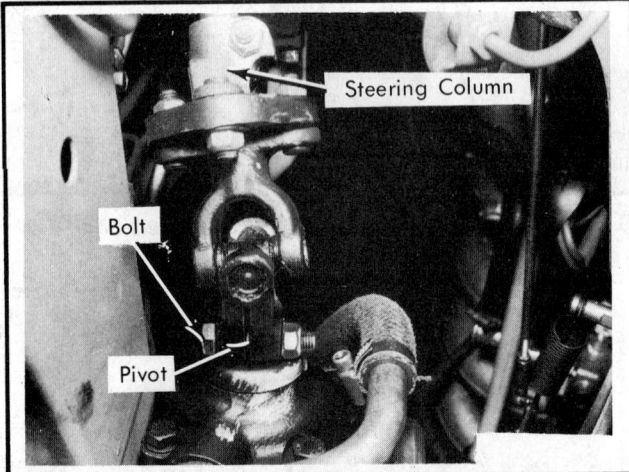

**Fig. 7   Removing Steering Shaft Flange**

**Fig. 8   Steering Gear to Front Axle Removal**

## BMW POWER-ASSISTED WORM & SECTOR (Cont.)

### POWER STEERING PUMP

**NOTE** — *Disassembly procedures are for model 530i only. For model 733i, BMW recommends replacing power steering pump if malfunctions occur. Overhaul procedures for model 633CSi were not available at time of printing. Two versions of the power steering pump are available on 530i models. One has a speed controlled pump and one does not. Differences in disassembly are noted in italics for the version with a speed controlled pump.*

**1)** Press cover in slightly and remove retaining ring. Remove cover, coil spring and "O" ring. Remove end plate and "O" ring, noting location of pin in one of the small holes in end plate.

**Fig. 9    Pin Location Inside of Pump Housing**

**2)** Tilt housing and remove cam ring and rotor. Note that side of rotor with recessed hole faces drive shaft, the rounded off side of rotor faces cam ring, and the cast-in half arrow indicates direction of rotor rotation.

**Fig. 10    Mark Showing Direction of Rotation**

**3)** Remove drive end face plate and "O" ring. If it should be necessary to remove input shaft, proceed as follows: Remove pulley, *(shaft seal in models with speed controlled pump)*, and circlip from housing. Force out input shaft from housing. Inspect seal and needle roller bearing and replace if necessary. Replace ball bearing on drive shaft if necessary. *(In speed controlled version press out bearing sleeve with mandrel, and when replacing, press in flush.)*

**NOTE** — *Installed depth of needle roller bearing is 1.457" + .008" (37 + 0.2 mm)*

**Fig. 11    Location of Needle Roller Bearing in Housing**

**4)** Remove plug from pressure valve bore, then remove coil spring and valve piston. Note that threaded section on valve piston faces coil spring. **CAUTION** — *Do not alter length of coil spring or thickness of plug sealing ring.*

**5)** The valve tolerance group (1 or 2) is stamped into housing adjacent to pressure valve bore and valve barrel should be scribed with one or two marks (lines) agreeing with group number stamped into housing. **CAUTION** — *If valve must be replaced, install valve of same tolerance group.*

**6)** Clean and inspect all parts. Clean restrictor insert in pump outlet passage. Valve piston may be disassembled for cleaning. **CAUTION** — *When disassembling piston, do not clamp across the sliding surfaces.* A pressure valve is located inside valve piston (flow limit valve), and thickness of washers determines cut-in range of pressure valve. Maximum pump pressure should not be more than 10% below the value stated on manufacturer's plate attached to pump.

**7)** Clean power steering reservoir, wipe dry with lint free cloth, and install new filter element.

### REASSEMBLY

To reassemble, reverse disassembly procedure.

### ADJUSTMENT TORQUE

| Application | INCH Lbs. (cmkg) |
|---|---|
| Worm in Piston | 1.7-3.5 (2-4) |
| Worm Bearing in Valve Housing | 1.3-2.2 (1.5-2.5) |
| Total for Worm Gear | 3.5-5.2 (4-6) |
| Worm in Intermediate Housing | 0.9-1.7 (1-2) |

### TIGHTENING SPECIFICATIONS

| Application | Ft. Lbs. (mkg) |
|---|---|
| Steering Gear to Front Axle | 32-35 (4.4-4.8) |
| Worm End Cover | 25 (3.5) |
| Sector Shaft End Cover | 23 (3.1) |
| Adjusting Screw Counternut | 22 (3.0) |
| Adjusting Screw Lock Nut for Piston Movement | 4 (.5) |
| Steering Pump Mounting | 17 (2.4) |
| Hose Connections | 33-37 (4.5-5.1) |

## CAPRI POWER-ASSISTED RACK & PINION

Capri

### DESCRIPTION

Power steering gear is a hydraulic-mechanical unit using an integral piston and rack design to provide power assisted steering control. Internal valving directs pump flow and controls pressure to reduce steering effort. Unit contains rotary hydraulic fluid control valve integrated to input shaft and a boost cylinder integrated with rack.

### TESTING

#### STEERING SYSTEM TEST

1) Check belt tension, tire pressure and fluid level and adjust as necessary. Run engine at 1500 RPM and slowly turn steering wheel from lock to lock to bring power steering fluid to 158°F (70°C).

**NOTE** — *Do not turn wheels from lock-to-lock more than five times.*

2) Place steering wheel in straight ahead position and make sure wheels are on a clean dry surface. With a torque wrench on the steering wheel nut, measure torque required to keep steering wheel turning. Torque should be 6 ft. lbs. (.8 mkg).

#### PUMP PRESSURE TEST

1) Disconnect pressure line from pump and connect gauge side of a suitable power steering pressure tester to pump and pressure line to valve side of tester. Make sure valve on tester is open and fluid is at proper level. Start engine and turn steering wheel lock to lock a few times to remove any air in system. Add fluid if necessary.

2) With power steering fluid at 158°F (70°C) and engine running at 1500 RPM, turn steering wheel to lock and hold momentarily. Pressure should be 740 psi (52 kg/cm²). If pressure is below specification, hydraulic system is faulty. With engine at 1500 RPM and wheels in straight ahead position, slowly close valve on tester. If pressure drops below specification, pump is faulty. If pressure rises above specification, steering gear control valve, rack piston or piston seals are faulty.

*Fig. 1  Capri Power Steering Pump*

### REMOVAL & INSTALLATION

#### STEERING GEAR

**Removal** — Disconnect fluid lines from steering gear and allow fluid to drain. Remove steering coupler lower clamp bolt (mark splines for alignment on installation) and disconnect tie rod ends from steering arms. Remove steering gear assembly-to-frame mounting bolts and remove steering gear from vehicle. Remove the tie rod ends from tie rods (note number of turns for installation alignment).

**Installation** — Install tie rod ends with the same number of turns noted when removed. Position steering gear assembly in vehicle, aligning pinion shaft splines with lower coupler, and secure with bolts.

#### POWER STEERING PUMP

**Removal** — Disconnect fluid lines and allow fluid to drain. On 2300 cc engines, disconnect fuel pump and position out of way (it is not necessary to disconnect fuel lines from pump). Remove power steering pump (on 2800 cc engines, remove pump with bracket assembly) from vehicle.

**Installation** — To install, reverse removal procedure and fill pump or reservoir with suitable power steering fluid (D2AZ-19582-A).

*Fig. 2  Disassembled View of Capri Power Steering Pump*

### OVERHAUL

#### STEERING PUMP

**Disassembly** — With pump removed from vehicle, remove hub and key from pump shaft. On 2300 cc engines, remove pressure line from reservoir. Mark pump to pump housing for alignment during assembly. Remove snap ring and tap on pump shaft to remove pump unit from housing. Remove the two screws holding end plate to pump unit and remove end plate. **NOTE** — *Do not remove the Allen screw at rear of pump.* Remove "O" ring from end plate. Remove rotor shaft, annulus, locating pin, and port plate from valve body. Remove snap ring retaining bearing in valve body, then remove bearing and seal.

## CAPRI POWER-ASSISTED RACK & PINION (Cont.)

**Assembly** — Install seal (with seal lip facing into body) in valve body. Lubricate port plate, locating pin, and annulus with power steering fluid and install to valve body. Install rotor shaft with rollers in annulus. Lightly grease "O" rings and position on end plate, then install end plate with screws. Install pump unit to pump housing, aligning scribe marks, and secure with snap ring.

**Fig. 3   Tie Rod Housing Removal**

### STEERING GEAR

**Disassembly** — 1) With steering gear removed from vehicle, remove rubber boots from tie rods and drain fluid. Mount assembly in a vise and loosen lock nut holding tie rod ball housing. To loosen lock nut use special tool T75P-3504-B with a $\frac{5}{32}$" drill and drill collar. Install special tool (see *Fig. 4*) and drill out lock pins. **NOTE** — *Special tool has a depth hole to set drill collar on drill bit.* Then remove housing with tie rod, nylon seat, washer and spring. Remove fluid lines from control valve to rack assembly.

**Fig. 4   Exploded View of Tie Rod Assembly**

2) Remove control valve cover plate, bearing, seal, carrier assembly and spool preload spring from control valve body, then remove control valve body from pinion shaft. Remove rack adjusting bearing cover plate, shim pack, sealing ring, spring, and adjusting bearing.

**Fig. 5   Rack Adjusting Bearing Assembly**

3) Position gear assembly in a vise and using a suitable tool that will lock onto splines of pinion shaft (tool T75P-3504-E), remove pinion bearing nut. Remove bearing outer race, then turn gear housing so pinion bearing is up. Remove bearing from pinion shaft and shaft from housing. Remove bearing inner race from housing.

**Fig. 6   Pinion Shaft Disassembled**

4) Remove clip and spool valve from pinion shaft. Remove locating pegs from gear housing. Tap end housing and separate joint at rack tube. Pull rack towards end housing and remove rack and support bearing. Remove inner tube from rack tube. *Note seal, washer and snap ring order.*

# Power Steering

## CAPRI POWER-ASSISTED RACK & PINION (Cont.)

Fig. 7    Steering Rack Disassembled

**5)** Clean and inspect all components. Check rack and pinion teeth for damage or wear. Check bearings for wear, pitting or scoring. Replace components as necessary.

**NOTE** — *Use new seals when assembling power steering gear assembly.*

**Assembly** — **1)** Install washers, seal and snap ring onto gear end of rack. Then slide inner tube onto rack. Install seal on a suitable seal protector (T75P-3504-H) and slide protector past rack teeth to smooth part of rack, slide seal off and remove seal protector. Lubricate two seals with power steering fluid and install in gear housing. Install snap ring and washer on inner tube then push tube into gear housing.

**2)** Slide rack through inner tube and gear housing. Install seals on inner tube and slide washers on rack to inner tube, then install snap ring. Soak "O" ring and nylon piston ring in power steering fluid. Install "O" ring and piston ring in groove of piston on rack. Compress piston ring and slide rack outer tube over piston and into gear housing. Rack tube end with one round and one oval hole should be towards gear housing. Align locating peg holes and install pegs.

**3)** Install outer seals to rack support bearing and slide bearing onto rack aligning peg holes. Using seal protector, install inner seals to rack support bearing. Lubricate large washer and "O" rings with power steering fluid and install in end housing. Position seals on transfer pipe and install pipe in gear housing. Slide end housing over rack, rack tube and transfer pipe. Align locating peg holes and install peg and washer.

**4)** Install inner bearing race to gear housing. Install spool valve to pinion shaft and secure with clip. Install oil seal next to middle pinion shaft bearing. Position lower bearing half cup to gear housing and position rack in steering gear assembly so that equal amounts extend from each end of steering gear assembly. Slide pinion shaft into gear housing, make sure that flat on pinion shaft faces center of rack assembly.

**5)** Screw lower bearing seat onto pinion shaft. Adjust bearing so that when pinion shaft float is removed, there is 1.62" (41.15 mm) between gear housing flange and top of spool valve (see *Fig. 9*). Install shim and pinion shaft end cover to gear housing, torque bolts to 9-12 ft. lbs. (1.2-1.7 mkg). Recheck gear housing flange to top of spool valve. If measure-

ment changed, measure gap between cover plate and gear housing (take measurement adjacent to bolts). Install shims .001-.002" (.025-.051 mm) thicker than measurement. If shims were needed, readjustment of gear housing flange to spool valve measurement is necessary.

Fig. 8    Pinion Shaft Adjustment Procedure

**6)** Install control valve body, pinion bearing preload spring and bearing, and valve body cover plate. Tighten bolts. Attach fluid lines from control valve body to steering gear assembly.

**7)** Place rack adjusting bearing in gear housing, then using dial gauge and mounting block (T75P-3504-J) measure bearing deflection. Zero dial gauge and mount block on rack adjusting bearing, then turn pinion shaft so rack goes from lock to lock and record maximum gauge deflection from zero. Assemble a shim pack that is .001-.005" (.025-.27 mm) thicker than maximum deflection. With shim pack assembled, install spring, seal, shim pack and cover plate. Tighten cover plate bolts.

Fig. 9    Measuring Rack Adjusting Bearing Deflection

## CAPRI POWER-ASSISTED RACK & PINION (Cont.)

Control Valve Body

Valve Body Cover Plate

Preload Spring

Seal

Bearing

Seal

Spool Valve

Pinion Shaft

Cover Plate

Shims

Seal

Spring

Rack Adjusting Bearing

Pinion Shaft

Snap Ring

Washers

Inner Tube

Washers

Seals

Seal

Seal

Lock Nut

Spring

Nylon Seat

Tie Rod

Ball Housing

Seals

Rack Support Bearing

Washer

Rack Piston

Gear Housing

Rack

Outer Race

Inner Race

Control Valve Adjustment Bearing

Thrust Bearing

Ball Housing

Rubber Boot

Ball Housing

Tie Rod

Nylon Seat

Spring

Lock Nut

End Housing

Seals

Cover Plate

Shim

Tie Rod End

Rack Tube

Transfer Pipe

Crossmember

Steering Gear Housing

*Fig. 10  Capri Power Assisted Rack & Pinion Steering (Exploded View)*

# Power Steering

## CAPRI POWER-ASSISTED RACK & PINION (Cont.)

8) Lubricate and assemble tie rods then install tie rods to rack. Check turning effort of tie rods by locking two nuts to tie rod ends and turning with a torque wrench. Turning torque should be 5 ft. lbs. (.7 mkg). If torque is greater loosen ball housing and if less tighten ball housing. Recheck turning torque.

9) Hold ball housing from rotating on tie rod and tighten lock nut against ball housing to 25-35 ft. lbs. (3.5-4.8 mkg). Using special tool T75P-3504-B installed on ball housing and lock nut, drill a 5/32" hole in line of contact between lock nut and ball housing. Use the depth measurement hole on special tool for depth to drill hole. Drill hole opposite existing hole. Insert pin and stake hole to secure pin.

10) Install one rubber boot, add 1/3 pint of lubricant (SAE 40 engine oil) and install other rubber boot. Do not tighten boot clamps until gear assembly is installed in vehicle. Install gear assembly in vehicle.

11) To check control valve adjustment, connect pump pressure test gauge as described in PUMP PRESSURE TEST. Start engine and allow power steering fluid to reach normal operating temperature. With engine running, turn wheels from lock to lock. When wheels are in each lock position apply 34 INCH lbs. (39 cmkg) of torque to steering wheel nut and record pressure from gauge. Pressure should be 160 psi (11.25 kg/cm$^2$) in the lock position with a maximum difference of 12 psi (.8 kg/cm$^2$) from side to side.

12) If pressure is not within specifications, turn lower bearing to equalize pressure. Turning bearing 20° will change pressure by 25 psi (1.8 kg/cm$^2$). With pressure equalized at 160 psi (11.25 kg/cm$^2$) at each lock position, install cover plate and check fluid level.

### TIGHTENING SPECIFICATIONS

| Application | Ft. Lbs. (mkg) |
|---|---|
| Fluid Lines | |
| Pressure | 19-23 (2.6-3.2) |
| Return | 12-15 (1.7-2.1) |
| Pinion Bearing Cover Plate | 7.5-9 (1-1.2) |
| Rack Slipper Cover Plate | 7.5-9 (1-1.2) |

# Power Steering

## CHRYSLER CORP. IMPORTS POWER-ASSISTED RECIRCULATING BALL

Challenger
Colt Wagon
Sapporo

### LUBRICATION

**Capacity** — 1.10 qts.

**Type** — ATF Type Dexron

### DESCRIPTION

#### POWER STEERING GEAR BOX

The power steering gear box displaces fluid to provide hydraulic pressure assist when turning. A torsion bar transmits road feel to the driver. A one piece rack-piston nut is geared to the sector shaft. An adjusting screw on the shaft maintains backlash between the shaft and the rack-piston.

#### POWER STEERING PUMP

The power steering pump is a constant displacement vane type. The pump has a rotor with 12 radial vanes and is belt driven by the crankshaft.

### ADJUSTMENTS

#### BELT TENSION ADJUSTMENT

With 22 lbs. (10 kg) pressure applied, belt deflection at center of belt should be .28-.39" (7-10 mm).

#### STEERING WHEEL PLAY

Raise front of vehicle. Start engine and idle at 1000 RPM. With steering wheel in center position check that free play is within 1" (25 mm). If necessary, adjustment can be made at the steering gear housing adjusting bolt.

*Fig. 1  Power Steering Gear Box Exploded View*

## CHRYSLER CORP. IMPORTS POWER-ASSISTED RECIRCULATING BALL (Cont.)

### FLUID REPLACEMENT

1) Disconnect suction hose at reservoir and drain fluid. Crank engine several times, but do not start. Disconnect pressure hose at pump and drain fluid.

2) Raise front of vehicle and turn steering wheel from lock to lock to drain gear box. Connect hoses to pump and reservoir and fill with fluid. Bleed system.

### AIR BLEEDING

**NOTE** — *Make sure reservoir is filled before bleeding. Add fluid as needed during bleeding.*

1) Raise front of vehicle. Turn steering wheel lock to lock until no air bubbles appear in reservoir fluid.

2) Lower vehicle and turn the wheel lock to lock several times while engine is idling. Attach 1'6" long tube to bleeder screw of gear box. Place other end of tube in container to drain.

3) Start engine, set to idle. Turn steering wheel fully to right and loosen bleeder screw. Continue loosening until no air bubbles come out of drain tube. Tighten bleeder screw to specifications. Check fluid level and replace as necessary.

**CAUTION** — *Abrupt rising of fluid level after engine is shut off signals incomplete bleeding. Repeat procedure as needed.*

### FLUID PRESSURE TESTING

1) Remove pressure hose from oil pump and attach adapter for special pressure gauge (MB990662). Start engine and place thermometer in reservoir until fluid temperature reaches 122°F. Bleed system if necessary.

2) Start engine and let idle. Close and then fully open the shut-off valve of the pressure gauge and read fluid pressure. Pressure with valve closed should be 925 to 1067 psi. With valve open pressure should be 142 psi.

3) Reinstall pressure hose, taking care not to twist it or make it interfere with adjacent parts.

**CAUTION** — *Do not keep shut-off valve closed more than three seconds at a time. Do not keep steering wheel fully turned more than 10 seconds at a time.*

## REMOVAL & INSTALLATION

### POWER STEERING GEAR BOX

**Removal — 1)** Disconnect steering shaft from gear box. Disconnect tie rod from relay rod and the pitman arm from relay rod. Remove air cleaner. Disconnect the pressure and return hoses from gear box. Remove under-cover.

2) Loosen steering shaft joint bolt, kickdown linkage shield and bolts, and remove gear box downward. Remove pitman arm from gear box.

**Fig. 2  Oil Pump Exploded View**

# Power Steering

## CHRYSLER CORP. IMPORTS POWER-ASSISTED RECIRCULATING BALL (Cont.)

**Installation** — 1) Install in reverse of removal procedures, noting the following: When connecting cross shaft to pitman arm, align slit of cross shaft tip to marking of pitman arm. Insure that clearance between bolt hole at bottom of gear box and pitman arm is within tolerance. Standard value is .77" +.16" or −.04"

### POWER STEERING OIL PUMP

**Removal** — Loosen pulley nut before removing belt. Remove pulley and belt. Disconnect pressure and suction hoses and cap openings. Remove oil pump attaching bolts and remove pump.

**Installation** — Install in reverse of removal procedures, noting the following: Check oil pump bracket for slack and tighten if necessary. Start engine after reinstallation and run at 2000 RPM for 5 minutes to check for fluid leaks.

### OVERHAUL

#### POWER STEERING GEAR BOX

**Disassembly** — 1) Loosen adjusting lock nut and remove. Remove side cover bolts and screw in the adjusting bolt 2 or 3 turns. With gear in neutral position, tap bottom of cross shaft with plastic hammer and remove.

2) Remove valve housing nut and bolts. Remove valve housing and rack piston, holding rack-piston up to avoid rotation and to prevent piston from falling.

3) Place valve housing in vise and move rack-piston up and down to check backlash between circulator balls and rack-piston gutter. Turn the rack-piston fully into the valve housing and then loosen two turns to measure backlash. Backlash service limit is .0039" (.10 mm). If backlash exceeds limit replace ball screw unit and rack-piston as an assembly.

**Fig. 3   Measuring Backlash of Gutter and Ball**

4) Remove rack-piston by turning counterclockwise. Do not lose circulator balls. Remove top cover and "O" ring from valve housing. Remove input worm unit from housing. Remove circulator, circulator holder, seal ring and "O" ring from the rack-piston. Remove bearings, plates and rings from input worm unit and valve housing.

**NOTE** — *Replace all "O" rings, seal rings and oil seals once they have been removed. When replacing, lubricate with power steering fluid before insertion.*

**Inspection** — 1) Inspect cross shaft bearing surface for peeling or pitting. Check stepped wear of adjusting bolt shank. Inspect for damage to gear teeth on cross shaft and rack-piston.

2) Inspect for uneven wear of circulator rolling surface on rack-piston. Check for damage to balls. Inspect for peeling or pitting on thrust needle roller bearing, and bearing surface of thrust plate on worm unit. Check ball rolling surface of worm shaft for peeling and sealing surface of input shaft for damage. If thrust bearing or thrust plate is defective, replace both as a set.

3) Inspect valve housing for damage to seal ring-to-housing contact surface. Inspect "O" ring sealing surface of seal housing, valve housing and side cover.

**Reassembly** — 1) Lubricate bearing surface of side cover and install needle roller bearings. Insert adjusting bolt and plate into the" T" slot on top of cross shaft, and set play with adjusting shims. Cross shaft play is 0-.002" (0-0.5 mm). When installing adjusting shims place chamfered edge of adjusting plate to contact surface of cross shaft. Install side cover "O" ring.

**Fig. 4   Adjusting the Cross Shaft "T" Slot**

2) Align cross shaft with side cover and tighten with adjusting bolt. Tighten lock nut temporarily. Install ball bearing and oil seal in top cover. Gently insert "O" ring and seal ring into seal housing and install housing in gear box with "O" ring side toward the main shaft. Install oil seal back-up ring and snap ring in gear box.

3) Install "O" ring and seal ring to input worm shaft. Install thrust plates and needle bearings in input worm unit.

**NOTE** — *Install top cover side thrust plate with smaller outside diameter first.*

## CHRYSLER CORP. IMPORTS POWER-ASSISTED RECIRCULATING BALL (Cont.)

**4)** Install "O" ring and seal ring into valve housing. Fit two "O" rings in groove at end of valve housing. Install input worm unit in valve housing. Fit top cover "O" ring, and install top cover to valve housing. Measure input worm unit preload. Torque is 3.5-6.9 INCH lbs. Adjust if necessary, by loosening valve housing nut.

**5)** Fit "O" ring and seal ring to rack-piston. Insert rack-piston into worm shaft and turn worm unit to align ball sliding surfaces. Install 20 circulator balls into rack-piston through the two openings.

**Fig. 5    Installing the Circulator Balls**

**NOTE** — *Do not move rack-piston when installing balls, as balls may fall into wrong groove.*

**6)** After installing 20 balls measure distance from rack-piston to the ball. If distance is more than .08" (2 mm), remove rack-piston and reinstall balls. Insert remaining 8 balls and install circulator holder. Install rack-piston of the ball screw unit assembly to gear box and tighten. Install seal ring of rack-piston and place rack-piston in neutral (center) position. Install cross shaft and side cover and tighten.

**7)** Measure starting torque of input shaft and adjust to 5.2-8.7 INCH lbs. Tighten valve housing nut. Measure preload after tightening. Connect cross shaft with pitman arm.

### POWER STEERING OIL PUMP

**Disassembly — 1)** Remove woodruff key from shaft. With pump anchored in vise, remove cover and snap ring. Take out the following parts from the pump body: collar, cam ring, rotor, vane, "O" rings, dowel, side plate and side plate spring.

**2)** Measure clearance between shaft and pump body. If clearance is more than .0035" (.09 mm), replace pump body as an assembly. Remove shaft by tapping it with a plastic hammer. Remove "O" ring, oil seal and suction connector. Remove flow control spring, control valve assembly and "O" ring.

**Inspection — 1)** Inspect pump shaft oil seal lip and bushing end for damage. Inspect groove of rotor vane and cam surface for stepped wear. Check vane for damage and cam ring and rotor sides for grooving. Replace entire assembly if any damage is seen.

**2)** Inspect side plate and pump cover for grooving. Check side plate spring and flow control spring for sagging. Check sliding surfaces and ports of flow control valve for obstruction.

**Reassembly — 1)** Install flow control spring and control valve assembly to pump body and tighten connector. Install oil seal

**Fig. 6    Measuring Clearance Between Shaft and Pump Body**

into pump body. Insert shaft into pump body and install the following parts into pump body: "O" rings (2), side plate spring, side plate, dowel, cam ring, rotor and 12 vanes.

**NOTE** — *When installing cam ring, direct arrowhead on outer surface toward side plate. Place chamfered face of rotor toward side plate. Vanes must be positioned so that round tip is toward sliding surface of cam ring.*

**2)** Install collar and snap ring with chamfered edge to rotor. Check that clearance between pump shaft and body does not exceed .0035" (.09 mm). Install "O" ring to pump body and tighten cover. Install "O" ring and suction connector. Install woodruff key in shaft.

**Fig. 7    Distinction of Cam Ring and Rotor**

### TIGHTENING SPECIFICATIONS

| Application | Ft. Lbs. (mkg) |
| --- | --- |
| Gear Box to Frame | 40-47 (5.5-6.5) |
| Pitman Arm to Cross Shaft | 94-109 (13-15) |
| Bleeder Screw | 4.3-6.5 (.59-.89) |
| Oil Pump Bracket to Housing Bolt | 20-30 (2.7-4.1) |
| Oil Pump Bracket to Cylinder Block Bolts | 10-15 (1.3-2) |
| Oil Pump Brace to Oil Pump Housing | 20-30 (2.7-4.1) |
| Oil Pump Brace to Cylinder Block Bolts | 10-15 (1.3-2) |
| Oil Pump Pulley to Shaft | 12-15 (1.6-2) |
| Return Pressure Hose | 29-36 (3.9-4.9) |
| Input Pressure Hose | 36-43 (4.9-5.9) |
| Oil Pump Cover | 22-29 (3-4) |
| Tie Rod to Relay Rod | 29-36 (3.9-4.9) |
| Valve Housing | 33-40 (4.5-5.5) |
| Side Cover | 33-40 (4.5-5.5) |
| Valve Housing Nut | 130-166 (17.9-22.9) |
| Flow Control Connector | 51-72 (7-9.9) |
| Suction Connector | 4-7 (.55-.96) |
| Input Worm Unit Preload | 3.5-6.9 (.48-.96) |

# Power Steering

## DATSUN POWER-ASSISTED RECIRCULATING BALL

810

## DESCRIPTION

Power steering is composed of power steering pump and steering gear. The pump has an integral oil reservoir and is engine driven. The steering gear incorporates a control valve and power cylinder which is pressure operated from the power steering pump by flexible lines.

## GENERAL SERVICE

### HYDRAULIC SYSTEM LUBRICANT

**Capacity** – 1½ qts.

**Type** – ATF Type DEXRON

### BELT TENSION ADJUSTMENT

Apply thumb pressure of 22 lbs. midway between idler pulley and power steering pump pulley. Deflection should be, 0.31-0.47" (8-12 mm).

### HYDRAULIC SYSTEM PRESSURE CHECK

**1)** Disconnect pressure line at pump and connect pressure gauge and shut off valve. Check fluid level, open shut off valve and run engine for about five seconds. Check fluid level and restart engine.

**2)** Turn steering wheel from lock-to-lock several times to expel air from system. Slowly close shut off valve. Pressure should be 953-1123 psi at idle.

**NOTE** – *Do not close shut-off valve for more than 15 seconds as this may result in undue pump wear and abnormally increased lubricant temperature.*

**3)** If pressure is below specifications the pump is faulty. If pressure is above specifications the pressure relief valve in pump is faulty.

### HYDRAULIC SYSTEM BLEEDING

Check fluid level in reservoir, raise and support front of vehicle. With engine not running, turn steering wheel from lock-to-lock several times. Check fluid level, start engine and turn steering wheel from lock-to-lock several times. If system is not bled turn steering wheel to left lock and open bleeder screw to expel remaining air.

## ADJUSTMENT

### BACKLASH

**NOTE** – *Always check and adjust backlash before removing steering gear for replacement.*

**On Car – 1)** Disconnect gear arm from steering gear, remove steering wheel horn pad. Locate steering wheel at its center of travel. Punch mark on column shaft should be upward. Turn wheel one complete turn from center and attach socket to steering wheel nut.

**2)** With gauge ST3127S0000, turn nut less than 20° and determine torque required for column shaft rotation. Read turning torque with wheel in center position. Turn wheel 360° in both directions and read torque at both points. With steering wheel in center position, required turning torque should be 0.9 to 1.7 INCH lbs. (1 to 2 kg/cmkg) higher than at 360°. When steering wheel is turned 360° in either direction from center, turning torque should be less than 10 INCH lb (12 kg/cmkg).

**3)** If torque is within specifications, backlash adjustment is not neccessary. If torque is outside specifications, remove column assembly and adjust backlash on steering gear unit alone.

**Off Car – 1)** Loosen lock nut on steering gear, and turn adjusting screw until worm shaft turning torque is within specifications. Tighten lock nut.

## REMOVAL & INSTALLATION

### STEERING GEAR

**Removal – 1)** Remove air cleaner, remove bolt from universal joint to worm shaft. Disconnect fluid lines and block off. Remove nut and washer from steering gear arm.

**2)** Using steering gear arm puller ST29020001, remove arm from sector shaft. Remove mounting bolts from gear housing and remove housing from vehicle.

**Installation** – To install reverse removal procedure and note the following: Align groove in worm shaft with bolt hole in universal joint and pass bolt through undercut section of worm shaft.

### STEERING PUMP

**Removal** – Disconnect fluid lines at pump and block off fittings. Remove pump mounting bolts and remove drive belt from pulley. Remove pump from vehicle.

**Installation** – To install reverse removal procedure.

## OVERHAUL

**NOTE** – *Overhaul of steering gear is limited to oil seal replacement. If any further repair is neccessary, replace entire steering gear assembly. According to location of oil leak, disassembly is divided into three catagories as shown Fig. 1.*

### ADJUSTING SCREW SEAL REPLACEMENT

Measure turning torque of stub shaft. Remove lock nut. Lubricate and replace "O" ring. Reinstall lock nut, replacing copper washer. Adjust backlash.

## DATSUN POWER-ASSISTED RECIRCULATING BALL (Cont.)

### SECTOR SHAFT SEAL REPLACEMENT

**Disassembly — 1)** Install gear assembly on attachment KV48100300 and anchor in vise. Check preload, remove sector cover bolt. Install gear arm lock nut. With plastic mallet, knock out end of sector shaft approximately ¾". Cover shaft with plastic film to prevent needle bearing loss.

**2)** Pull out sector shaft, remove snap ring and oil seal on low pressure side. Remove high pressure oil seal and stopper.

**NOTE** — *Do not reuse snap ring, oil seals or stopper once removed.*

**Assembly —** Lubricate and install oil seals, snap ring and sector cover "O" ring. Guide sector shaft into gear housing. Push sector cover in by hand. Tighten cover bolts. Check stub shaft turning torque. Check and adjust backlash.

### REAR HOUSING SEAL REPLACEMENT

**Disassembly — 1)** Install gear assembly on attachment and anchor in vise. Measure stub shaft turning torque. Loosen rear cover bolts, but do not remove cover.

**2)** Turn stub shaft clockwise to bring piston to rear side. Install gear arm lock nut on sector shaft, and turn slightly clockwise to raise intermediate cover through piston. Remove lock nut and turn shaft counterclockwise to place piston in neutral position. Remove sector shaft. Move piston to rear side, pull out worm assembly.

**NOTE** — *When worm assembly is removed, piston may turn and come off under its own weight. Hold piston to prevent this. Do not damage Teflon ring at piston end when removing.*

**3)** Lightly tap stub shaft end to remove rear housing. Remove rear housing oil seal. Remove sector shaft oil seal. Remove all "O" rings.

**Assembly — 1)** Lubricate and install rear housing oil seal, sector shaft oil seal and intermediate cover "O" rings. Replace worm assembly into rear housing, then into gear housing. Tighten rear housing bolts in a crisscross fashion.

**CAUTION** — *Tighten housing bolts with assembly in a level position, to avoid damaging inner seals.*

**2)** Inspect sector shaft. Check stub shaft turning torque. Check and adjust backlash.

**Fig. 2   Datsun Powet Steering Components**

NOTE: No. 1 to 11, once removed, must not be used again.

**Fig. 1   Power Steering Gear Exploded View**

### TIGHTENING SPECIFICATIONS

| Application | Ft. Lbs. (mkg) |
| --- | --- |
| Universal Joint to Worm Shaft Bolt | 24-28 (3.3-3.9) |
| Steering Gear Arm Lock Nut | 94-108 (13-15) |
| Pump Bleeder Screw | 5-7 (.7-.9) |
| Pump Mounting Bolts | 14-19 (1.9-2.6) |
| Sector Cover Bolts | 20-24 (2.7-3.3) |

# Power Steering

## HONDA ACCORD POWER-ASSISTED RACK & PINION

**Accord CVCC (LX)**

### DESCRIPTION & OPERATION

Power steering is rack and pinion with the power assist proportional to both vehicle speed and steering load. Power assist is high when vehicle speed is low and reduces as vehicle speed increases. Pump uses a metered orifice and a combination flow control/relief valve to keep pressure below 980 psi (70 kg/cm²). Power steering fluid is used to lubricate pump bushings.

Valve body is mounted to lower part of rack and pinion housing. A spool valve is attached to steering shaft and supported by needle bearings and thrust washers. These keep spool valve entered. Spool valve movement comes from the thrust produced by one helical gear (pinion) driving another (rack). When steering wheel is turned, spool valve is forced to move up or down. This movement allows fluid (under high pressure) to enter either right or left rack housing, assisting in turning wheels. When steering wheel is no longer turned, spool valve centers itself and stops fluid flow to rack housing. This stops power assist.

The speed sensor is a trochoid rotor hydraulic pump. The sensor is combined with the speedometer drive and mounted in transmission housing. Two internal relief valves connect sensor inlet and outlet. One valve allows fluid to recirculate when vehicle is in reverse and the other relieves low pressure at the inlet while driving at high speed. With engine running and in neutral or PARK, pressure closes the cut-off valve which keeps pressure in reaction chambers at a minimum. When vehicle starts moving, pressure drops and opens the cut-off valve. As

pressure rises, plunger resistance to spool valve movement increases. This decreases power assist. When vehicle speed decreases, the reverse happens and increases power assist. This opening and closing of the cut-off valve is very rapid (actually vibrating) making the changing pressures a gradual smooth transition.

*Fig. 2  Sectional View of Power Steering Pump and Power Steering Gear*

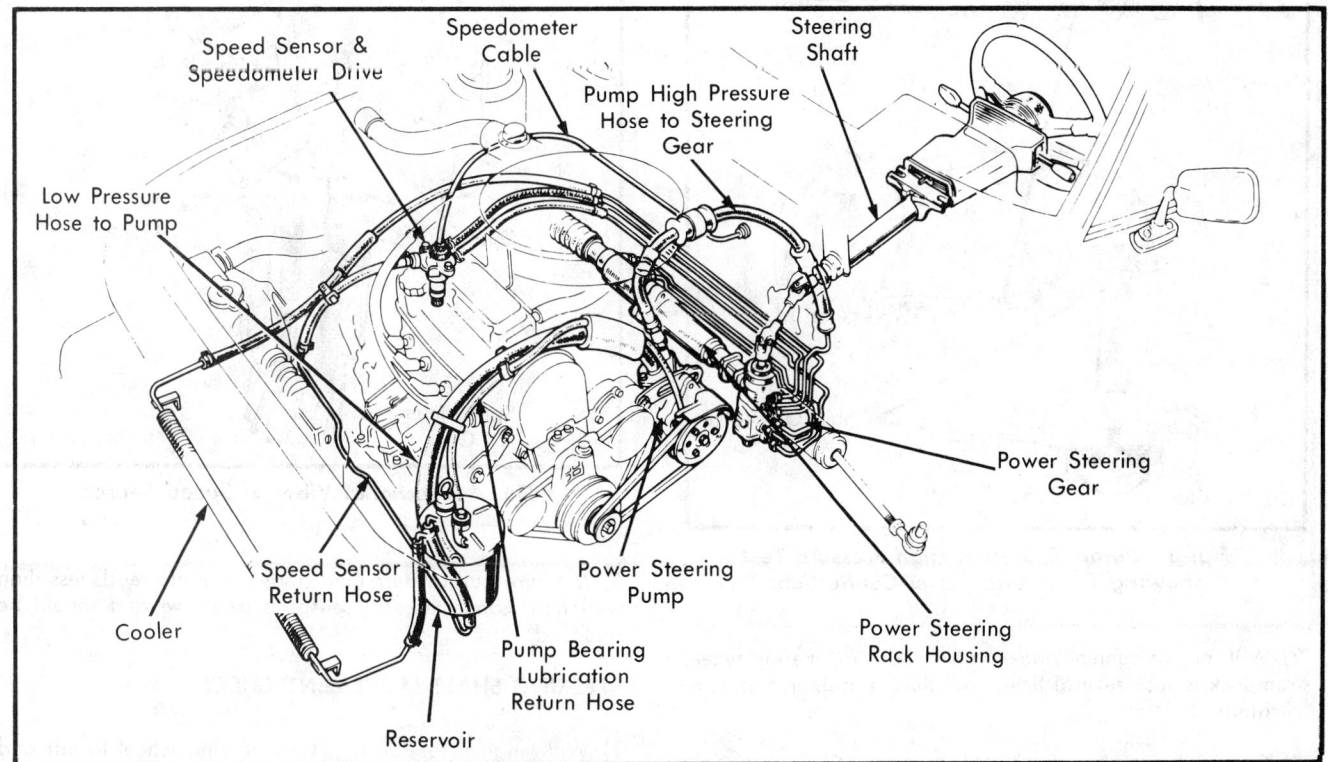

*Fig. 1  Power Steering System for Honda Accord Models*

## HONDA ACCORD POWER-ASSISTED RACK & PINION (Cont.)

### GENERAL SERVICE

#### HYDRAULIC SYSTEM LUBRICANT

**Capacity**

Reservoir ...................................... .85 qts. (.8 liter)
Complete System .................................. 2.1 qts. (2 liters)

**Fluid Type**

**CAUTION** — *Use only genuine Honda power steering fluid. The use of any other fluids, such as ATF or other manufacturer's power steering fluid, will cause damage to the system.*

#### BELT TENSION ADJUSTMENT

1) Measure pump belt deflection midway between pulleys. Deflection should be $^9/_{16}$" at 22 lbs. pressure (13 mm at 10 kg) on used belt or $^7/_{16}$" at 22 lbs. pressure (11 mm at 10 kg) on a new belt.

2) Replace belt when pump adjusting bolt reaches "bump" on adjusting bracket.

#### HYDRAULIC SYSTEM PRESSURE CHECK

1) Disconnect outlet hose from pump. Install ressure gauge and valve (07406-0010000). *See Fig. 3.*

**Fig. 3   Pump & System High Pressure Test Showing Tester and Tester Connections**

2) With engine running, open valve and turn steering wheel from lock to lock several times until fluid is at operating temperature.

3) Check idle speed and adjust if necessary. Close valve and read pressure gauge.

**CAUTION** — *Do not keep valve closed for more than 5 seconds or pump could be damaged by overheating.*

4) Pump pressure should be at least 840 psi (60 kg/cm$^2$). If pump pressure is too low, replace pump.

5) Open valve fully and turn steering wheel to full left lock. Read gauge, then turn wheel to full right lock and read gauge. Both readings should be at least 840 psi (60 kg/cm$^2$). A low reading indicates rack and pinion housing or speed sensor is defective. Check speed sensor (as described later), if sensor is OK, replace rack and pinion gears and housing.

#### SPEED SENSOR CHECK

1) Start engine and let idle. Attach spring tension scale to steering wheel (outer end of spoke). Vehicle should be on a clean dry surface. Turn steering wheel with the tension gauge and record reading.

2) Reading should be no more than 6 lbs. (2.7 kg).

4) If reading is higher than specified, disconnect and plug large diameter hose running from steering gear to speed sensor.

**Fig. 4   Sectional View of Speed Sensor**

5) Measure pull as described above. If scale reads less than with hose connected, the sensor is defective and should be replaced.

#### STEERING SHAFT MOVEMENT CHECK

1) With engine not running, turn steering wheel to left and then to right. Steering wheel cover should move closer to or further away from turn signal cover. *See Fig. 5.*

## HONDA ACCORD POWER-ASSISTED RACK & PINION (Cont.)

**Fig. 5   Checking Steering Shaft Movement**

2) Movement of steering wheel should be at least .079" (2 mm) for proper spool valve operation.

3) If the steering wheel moves only in or only out, but not both, loosen the 3 bolts in the steering shaft connector. Adjust shaft and make sure that shaft slides freely in column. Retighten bolts.

4) If adjustment does not allow correct movement of steering wheel, replace rack and pinion gears.

## REMOVAL & INSTALLATION

### STEERING GEAR

**Removal — 1)** Disconnect tie rods from steering knuckles. Disconnect exhaust pipe at manifold.

2) On manual transmission models only, disconnect shift linkage by driving out pin. Remove cross (center) member. Disconnect shift lever torque arm from transmission.

3) On automatic transmission models only, remove center engine mount and transmission splash guard. Disconnect control cable from transmission.

4) Disconnect the following lines from power steering gear:

- Hose to right side of power cylinder.
- Hose to left side of power cylinder.
- Hose from power steering pump.
- Hose to power steering cooler.
- Hose to speed sensor.
- Hose from speed sensor.

5) Turn steering wheel to full left and remove bottom bolt in steering shaft connector. Remove steering gear brackets.

6) Lower steering gear to pull pinion out of connector, then move to right until left tie rod drops out of subframe. Remove steering gear to left.

**Installation** — To install steering gear, reverse removal procedure.

### STEERING PUMP

**Removal — 1)** Drain fluid from system. Disconnect inlet and outlet hoses at pump. Remove power steering belt by loosening the pump pivot and adjusting bolts.

2) Remove pump mounting bolts, bracket and power steering pump.

**Installation — 1)** Install pump, bracket and bolts. Fill reservoir with new fluid, to the full mark on dipstick.

**CAUTION** — *Use only genuine Honda power steering fluid. The use of other fluids, such as ATF or other manufacturer's power steering fluid, will cause damage to the system.*

2) Start engine and let run at fast idle while turning the steering wheel lock to lock several times to bleed air from system.

### SPEED SENSOR

**Removal — 1)** Lift speedometer cable boot up to gain access to retaining clip. Remove retaining clip and pull out cable.

2) Disconnect and plug speed sensor hoses, back off speedometer gear set bolt. Lift speed sensor out.

**Installation** — After installing new sensor, turn steering wheel from lock to lock several times (engine idling), to bleed air from system.

## OVERHAUL

**NOTE** — *Power steering pump, steering gear and speed sensor cannot be overhauled. These items must be replaced as an assembly. Steering pump shaft seal can be replaced.*

### POWER STEERING PUMP SHAFT SEAL

1) Remove power steering pump belt. Remove pump pulley. Remove old seal. Coat new seal and pump shaft with clean fluid and install seal on pump shaft. Be careful not to scratch or damage inner part of seal.

# Power Steering

## JAGUAR POWER-ASSISTED RACK & PINION

XJ6
XJ12
XJS

### DESCRIPTION

Vehicles are equipped with a power assisted rack and pinion type steering system. The system consists of two main components: the rack and pinion steering gear and the power assist pump. The two components are connected by flexible fluid lines. The power assist pump and fluid reservoir are combined.

### LUBRICANT

**Type** — ATF Dexron II

**Intervals** — Check power steering fluid every 3,000 miles.

### TESTING

**Control Valve & Pinion** — 1) Connect a 100 psi (7 kg/cm²) pressure gage into the pump return line, start engine and allow to idle. Pressure reading should be approximately 40 psi (2.8 kg/cm²). Turn steering gear left and right a small amount. **CAUTION** — *Gauge will be damaged if steering gear is turned excessively. Pressure increase, as wheel is turned, should register an equal amount on either side of center.*

**Fig. 1  Pressure Gauge Connection**

2) Stop and restart engine and check that steering does not kick to one side.

**Hydraulic System** — 1) Connect a 1500 psi (100 kg/cm²) pressure gauge into the pump pressure line, start engine and allow to idle.

2) Turn steering to full lock and exert pressure on steering gear until gauge pressure ceases to rise. Pressure should be between 1100 psi (77.5 kg/cm²) and 1200 psi (84.4 kg/cm²).

**NOTE** — *If pressure is below 1100 psi (77.5 kg/cm²) at idle, but rises with engine speed increase, the problem is either a defective pump control valve or internal leakage in rack and pinion. The following test will determine the location.*

3) Connect a suitable tap (JD. 10-2) between pump and pressure gauge, isolating rack from pump.

**Fig. 2  Jaguar Power Assisted Rack and Pinion**

## JAGUAR POWER-ASSISTED RACK & PINION (Cont.)

**4)** Open tap, start engine and allow to idle. Turn steering gear to full lock and check that gauge exceeds 1100 psi (77.5 kg/cm²). If pressure is below this figure, CLOSE TAP AT ONCE, and note reading when tap reaches OFF position.

**CAUTION** — *Tap must not be held closed for more than 5 seconds when engine is running.*

**5)** If gauge reading increases to at least 1100 psi (77.5 kg/cm²) with tap off, leaks are located in steering unit, requiring overhaul. See OVERHAUL in this article.

**6)** If gauge reading is above 1200 psi (84.4 kg/cm²), problem is a blocked filter located in pump discharge port.

**Fig. 3   Pressure Gauge and Tap Connection**

### SYSTEM BLEEDING

Turn wheels to full left lock, add fluid to "COLD" level mark on dipstick. Start engine and idle. Turn steering wheel lock to lock to expell air. Check fluid level. Straighten wheels and run engine for several minutes. Turn off engine, check fluid level. Fluid should be up to "HOT" mark on dipstick.

## REMOVAL & INSTALLATION

### STEERING GEAR

**NOTE** — *Amount and location of all washers and spacers must be noted for correct installation.*

**Removal** — **1)** Remove lower steering column. Drain fluid from pump. Disconnect pressure and return lines, cap openings. Remove tie-rod to steering arm nut on right and left sides. Separate tie-rods from steering arms.

**2)** Remove bolt securing rack to suspension. Save heatshield mounting bracket and spacers. Remove remaining bolts from rack mounting. Save washers. Withdraw rack from suspension.

**Installation** — **1)** Position rack against mounting brackets. Center lugs on bracket and insert shims between lug and bracket to insure a gap of .05" (1.3 mm) on either side of rack lug and mounting bracket. Insert mounting bolts but do not tighten.

**2)** Repeat step **1)** on upper and lower mountings on pinion side of rack, ensuring that heatshield mounting bracket is located on upper mounting bolt. Remove clip securing rubber bellows to rack housing. Fold back bellows to expose inner ball joints.

**Fig. 4   Installing Rack and Pinion Gear**

**3)** Locate attachment brackets of alignment tool JD36A over large hex head bolts on lower control arms. It may be necessary to bend shields slightly to locate tool correctly

**4)** Release locking screw and slide collar along tool to front of suspension unit until slot engages front weld flange of crossbeam. Lock slide in this position. Rotate alignment tool until legs rest on tie-rods. To adjust slack, loosen lock nut of single bolt mounting and raise or lower same side of rack assembly.

**5)** Remove tool, fully tighten rack mounting lock nuts. Reposition bellows and secure clips. Reinstall tie-rods and hoses. Refill and bleed system. Check wheel alignment.

### POWER STEERING PUMP

**Removal** — **1)** Remove right air cleaner. Partially drain radiator. Remove upper radiator hose. Drain fluid from pump. Disconnect pressure and return hose from rear of pump. Loosen nut securing adjuster rod to timing cover.

**2)** Remove bolt securing adjuster rod to pump, swing adjuster clear of pump. Remove lower pump pivot nut. Move pump toward engine and remove belt. Remove lower pivot bolt. Lift pump from car.

**Installation** — Replace pump in reverse of removal procedures, noting the following: Make sure hose connections are clean. Adjust drive belt deflection to .16" (4.1 mm) at mid point. Bleed system.

### CONTROL VALVE AND PINION

**NOTE** — *No adjustment or repair is possible except the replacement of the pinion seal.*

**Removal** — Remove rack assembly. Clean rack and pinion housing. Loosen nuts securing pressure and return lines. Remove nuts holding pinion housing to rack tube. Remove pinion assembly from rack. Discard gasket.

**Installation** — Reverse removal procedures, noting the following: Replace gasket in joint of pinion assembly to rack. Ensure that recess on pinion shaft is in position with pinion housing.

## JAGUAR POWER-ASSISTED RACK & PINION (Cont.)

### OVERHAUL

#### RACK ASSEMBLY

**Disassembly – 1)** Clean rack and pinion housing. Remove clips holding bellows and fold bellows back to expose inner ball joints. Do not disturb outer ball joints. Straighten lock tab of washer securing tie-rod inner lock nuts. Loosen lock nuts and unscrew tie-rod assemblies from rack. Retain thrust springs and packing washers.

**2)** Remove fluid feed lines from rack housing. Remove pinion housing from rack tube. Remove and discard pinion seals in housing recess. Remove Allen screw from end cap. Remove locking ring from end cap and remove end cap. Remove air transfer pipe from rack.

**3)** Remove end cap "O" ring seal, washer, nylon spacer, seal and seal seat. Remove rack damper plate, seal and spring. Remove damper from rack tube, carefully remove rack from tube.

**4)** Remove rack inner sleeve from tube. Remove circlip from inner sleeve along with nylon washer, seal and seal seat. Remove "O" ring from inner sleeve and seal from seal carrier from rack bar.

**Reassembly – 1)** Lubricate all seals and "O" rings before installation. Fit seal seat, seal and nylon washer to inner sleeve and replace circlip. Fit "O" ring to inner sleeve. Insert grooved end of inner sleeve into rack tube and align inner sleeve hole with rack tube hole.

**2)** Fit locating bolt to end casing. Install new nylon seal to seal carrier on rack bar. Tape rack teeth, carefully insert rack into rack tube and inner sleeve. Install seal seat, seals, nylon washer, metal washer and "O" ring to end cap. Fit "O" rings to air transfer pipe.

**3)** Install end cap making sure that holes in rack tube and end cap line up. Fit locating bolt to end cap. Install air transfer pipe. Rotate threaded sleeve and secure end cap to rack tube. Fit Allen screw to sleeve. Remove tape from rack teeth.

**4)** Install washer, "O" ring and seal to pinion housing. Insert pinion assembly into housing, aligning teeth with pinion shaft. Secure pinion to housing. Replace damper to housing. Fit "O" ring, seal and spring to damper. Replace damper cover plate. Install pressure and return hoses. Replace tie-rods. Coat inner ball joints with grease. Adjust rack damper and lubricate.

#### POWER STEERING PUMP

**Disassembly – 1)** Remove rear mounting plate and pulley from pump. Remove front mounting plate from pump and clean pump body. Remove pressure outlet union and mounting plate studs from rear of pump. Tip pump and remove flow control valve and spring.

**2)** Place pump in padded vise and tap pump casing from body. Remove "O" rings from pump body and magnet from flange. With suitable pin punch, push retaining ring free from groove and lever from body. Remove spring retaining plate and spring. Remove "O" ring from recess in pump body.

**Fig. 5   Rack End Play Adjustment**

Lock Nut

Grease Plug          Adjusting Plug

**3)** Remove woodruff key from shaft. Tap roller spindle toward body and remove pump assembly from body. Remove "O" ring from recess in pump body. Remove dowel pins.

**4)** Remove rotor housing top plate and rotor housing. Remove rotor vanes and circlip securing rotor to drive shaft. Remove drive shaft oil seal from pump body.

**Inspection –** Clean all parts. Replace all "O" rings, seals, rotor housing and vanes. Check flow control valve for free movement in bore.

**Reassembly – 1)** Lubricate drive shaft seal and fit into pump shaft housing. Fit "O" ring to lower recess in pump body. Place dowel pins in locating holes. With cutaway face uppermost, fit bottom plate to drive shaft.

**2)** Fit rotor over splines of drive shaft and secure with circlip. Insert vanes in rotor with curved edge out. Fit drive shaft and rotor to pump body, ensuring that dowel pins locate through smallest holes of bottom plate. With arrow up place pump ring chamber over rotor and dowel pins.

**Fig. 6   Prying Out End Plate Ring**

# Power Steering

## JAGUAR POWER-ASSISTED RACK & PINION (Cont.)

**3)** With spring recess up, fit chamber top plate over dowel pins. Push complete pump assembly home. Fit "O" ring into upper recess of pump body. Fit spring to recess in top plate. Place retaining plate over spring and push into body. Fit "O" rings to port recess, and large "O" ring to outside pump body and magnet to flange.

**4)** Place pump casing over body. Locate mounting studs into outer casing and into pump body. Place outer casing over pump body. Tighten mounting studs. Install spring and flow control valve. Fit pressure outlet union. Place Woodruff key in drive shaft spindle. Replace pulley and mounting plates.

**5)** Refill system with fluid and bleed.

*Fig. 7   Placing Vanes in Rotor Plate*

*Fig. 8   Exploded View of Jaguar Power Steering Pump*

## LANCIA POWER-ASSISTED RACK & PINION

Lancia Beta
  Coupe
  Sedan
  HPE

### DESCRIPTION

Lancia models have an optional power-assisted rack and pinion steering system. The power assist pump is located just to the right of the engine crankshaft and is belt-driven. The non-integral fluid reservoir is situated directly above the pump.

### MAINTENANCE

#### PUMP BELT

Vehicles built after the following serial numbers have modified cog belts to eliminate excessive whining noise: Sedan-504571, Coupe-607379, HPE-701572. Cars built before these serial numbers may have a slight whining noise from the belt. This is normal. Do not replace belt on these cars unless belt is worn or damaged.

#### CHANGING & BLEEDING FLUID

1) Remove banjo bolts from power steering pump inlet and outlet ports. Take cover from reservoir. Disconnect ignition coil high tension lead.

**NOTE** — *On air conditioned vehicles it will be necessary to remove right front wheel and splash guard to gain access to banjo bolts.*

2) Turn steering wheel from lock-to-lock and crank engine intermittently to ensure all fluid is drained. Replace banjo bolts, using new washers.

**CAUTION** — *When fluid is drained, DO NOT continue to crank engine as power steering pump will be damaged.*

3) Check pump fluid reservoir filter and replace if necessary.

4) Fill reservoir with fresh fluid while intermittently cranking engine to draw fluid into pump.

5) When fluid level indicates full and remains constant, stop cranking engine and connect ignition coil lead.

6) Start engine and run at idle. Watch level of fluid in reservoir. Refill as required to maintain full level.

7) While idling engine, turn steering wheel from lock-to-lock several times until no air bubbles are seen in fluid reservoir.

8) Check all hose connections for any leakage. Stop engine and note that fluid level will rise slightly. Install reservoir cover.

### REMOVAL & INSTALLATION

#### FLUID RESERVOIR

**Removal** — 1) Remove power steering pump fluid inlet banjo bolt and allow reservoir to drain. If equipped with A/C, remove right front wheel and splash guard to gain access to bolt.

2) Remove cover from reservoir, remove clips and detach hoses from reservoir. Remove support bracket and reservoir from vehicle.

**Installation** — To install, reverse removal procedure, using new washers for banjo bolts. Fill and bleed system.

#### POWER STEERING PUMP

**Removal** — 1) Raise front of vehicle and support on frame stands. Remove right front wheel and splash guard. Remove wheelhousing guard.

2) Place container under pump, remove inlet banjo bolt from pump and drain fluid.

3) In non-A/C, hold pump drive belt and remove pulley nut. Unscrew top bracket adjusting bolt and remove belt. Remove outlet banjo bolt. Slacken alternator and remove pump mounting through-bolt. Lift pump assembly and bracket from vehicle.

4) If equipped with A/C, remove air cleaner and loosen compressor mounting. Remove pump pulley nut and remove cogged drive belt. Take off pump pulley. Remove outlet banjo bolt and rear bracket. Remove pump mounting screws and remove pump.

**Installation** — To install, reverse removal procedure, using new banjo bolt washers. Also, set pump belt to proper tension. Fill and bleed fluid system.

#### POWER-ASSISTED RACK & PINION ASSEMBLY

**Removal** — 1) Disconnect battery. Remove steering shaft joint bolt, located inside passenger compartment. Remove steering column lower casing, disconnect column from dash and rest on front seat.

2) Raise front of vehicle and support on frame stands. Remove front wheels.

3) Remove cooling system overflow tank. Place container under steering rack, remove fluid outlet tubing from housing and drain fluid.

4) Detach tie rod end ball joints from steering knuckles. Remove guards from tie rod housing. Remove EGR system lower piping and exhaust pipe front heat shield.

5) Remove rack and pinion steering assembly mounting bolts and lift assembly out left side of vehicle.

**Installation** — To install, reverse removal procedure, after setting rack in central position. Use new banjo bolt washers. Refill and bleed fluid system.

### OVERHAUL

#### RACK ASSEMBLY

**Disassembly, TRW Models** — 1) Loosen clip on rubber cap at end of housing and drain oil. Install housing in vise, knock down lock plate, remove bolts and lift off steering rods from rack housing.

## LANCIA POWER-ASSISTED RACK & PINION (Cont.)

**2)** Remove mounting clamp insulators, loosen clips and remove rubber cap and guard from housing. Remove bolts from locating support cover and withdraw shims with seal, spring, and rack locating support.

**3)** Straighten lock and remove pinion cover, seal, shims, and drive pinion together with upper bearing. Slide out rack and plastic bushing from housing. Remove lower bearing.

**Fig. 1   Sectional View of TRW Steering Rack Housing**

**Fig. 2   Setting Bearing Pre-Load**

**Fig. 3   Setting Backlash**

**Reassembly — 1)** Using seal replacement tool (88062031), replace seal in pinion cover. Insert plastic bushing in rack housing and position so three locating gears engage seats in housing. Install drive pinion together with bearing and .09" (2.3 mm) washer to steering box.

**2)** Check bearing pre-load by installing support tool (88065001) on rack housing, then install depth gauge (88095851) with 4.7" (120 mm) long stem. Using dial indicator, set indicator on rack housing surface and measure between housing surface and washer.

**3)** Add value indicated to thickness of cover gasket, .010" (0.25 mm), and to value required to obtain pre-load, .001-.005" (.025-.13 mm). Install required shims, washer, cover, and mounting bolts. Torque bolts to 14.5 ft. lbs. (2 Mkg).

**NOTE** — *Shims are available in .005" (.13 mm), .007" (.19 mm), .010" (0.25 mm) and .09" (2.30 mm) thicknesses.*

**4)** Using extension and torque wrench, check turning torque for .6 ft. lbs. (.085 Mkg). To check backlash, remove cover, pinion with shims and upper bearing and insert rack. Install pinion, meshing it with rack teeth. Install shims between bearing and washer and install cover and bend lock plate.

**5)** Install support tool (88065001) and using dial indicator measure between housing face and top of support sticking out of housing. Add this value to backlash specifications, .002-.004" (.05-.10 mm). Then subtract thickness of cover seal, .009" (0.25 mm). This will give shim thickness required.

**NOTE** — *Shims are available in .002" (0.06 mm), .005" (.13 mm) and .01" (.25 mm).*

## LANCIA POWER-ASSISTED RACK & PINION (Cont.)

6) Install spring to rack locating support. Install shims, cover and pinion cover mounting bolt. Torque bolt to 14.5 ft. lbs. (2 Mkg). Install rubber cover and cap to housing end. Install spacers and lock clips.

**NOTE** — *To ensure tightness to rack housing, coat bolts and edges of shims with sealing compound.*

**Disassembly, Z.F. Models** — 1) Remove damper from steering rack housing. Remove caps and install housing in vise. Knock down tabs and remove screws, disconnect steering rods. Remove buffers from housing. Remove clips, dust covers, sleeve and link from recess in housing.

2) Remove cap and cotter pin. Using spanner tool (88061024) remove adjuster and take out spring and support. Remove rack from housing, position housing with worm shaft facing upwards, remove cap and lift up retainer ring. Using spanner tool, remove adjuster.

3) Install worm shaft in vise, using rawhide or rubber mallet, hit housing lightly and remove worm shaft with bearing. Remove plastic bushing and rack "O" ring.

**Reassembly** — 1) Install new "O" ring and plastic bushing in rack housing, so that two locating gears engage with seats in housing. Using bearing installer (88022093), install worm shaft and bearing. Install screw in adjuster.

2) Lightly grease rack and insert into housing and grease teeth of rack. Mesh rack with worm shaft and set steering rod mounting bores at center of slot. Grease and install support and spring. Tighten adjuster.

3) Install connector (88063006) to worm shaft. Using torque wrench, check turning torque, .6 ft.lbs. (.085 Mkg). Loosen adjuster as needed to install cotter pin and disconnect connector from worm shaft. Install retainer ring, fill recess in ring with grease and install caps. Install link to rack, dust covers and sleeve. Tighten mounting clips and install rubber caps.

4) Fit the steering rods and damper support bracket by inserting the washers. Locate steering rods horizontally, tighten screws and bend lock plate. Fit the damper.

*Fig. 4    Z.F. Model Steering Rack Housing*

*Fig. 5    Sectional View of Z.F. Model Steering Rack Housing*

## MAZDA POWER-ASSISTED RECIRCULATING BALL

**RX4**
**Cosmo**

### DESCRIPTION

This torsion-bar type hydraulic assisted system furnishes power to reduce the amount of effort needed to turn the steering wheel. The system also reduces road shock and vibration. The power steering system includes a worm and one-piece rack piston which is meshed to the gear teeth on the steering sector shaft. The unit also incorporates a hydraulic valve, valve actuator, stub shaft and torsion bar which is mounted on the end of the worm shaft and operated by the twisting action of the torsion bar.

### GENERAL SERVICE

#### LUBRICANT TYPE

ATF Type F (M2C33-F)

#### SERVICE INTERVALS

Check and add (if necessary) at first 2000 miles and every 6250 miles or 6 months. Change every 25,000 miles or 24 months whichever occurs first.

**Fig. 1    Mazda Power Steering Components**

#### HYDRAULIC SYSTEM BLEEDING

**1)** Fill the reservoir to the "FULL" mark and raise the front end of vehicle. To avoid foaming of the fluid during filling and testing, fabricate a stick, using the dimensions shown in *Fig. 2*.

**2)** Install the fabricated stick in reservoir with short end down into fluid return port on bottom of reservoir. Raise and support front of vehicle. With stick in position, turn steering wheel lock-to-lock at least ten times. Check fluid level and add if necessary.

**NOTE** – *Do not let the reservoir run dry.*

**Fig. 2    Fabricated Tool**

**3)** Attach a tube to the bleeder screw on the power steering gear. Insert open end of tube into a container partially filled with fluid.

**4)** Start engine and turn steering wheel to left lock position and open bleeder screw. Run engine until air bubbles cease to appear. Repeat operation with the steering wheel in the right lock position.

**NOTE** – *Do not let the reservoir run dry.*

**5)** Close the bleeder screw and fill reservoir to between the "FULL" and "LOW" level marks. *NOTE - Do not overfill* .

#### PUMP BELT ADJUSTMENT

Belt deflection should be .35±.04" (9±1 mm) when pressure of approximately 22 lbs. (10 kg) is applied to belt halfway between pulleys. Adjust tension by turning adjusting bolt on idler pulley.

#### PUMP PRESSURE TEST

**1)** Install a pressure gauge with shut off valve in series with the pressure hose. Start the engine and set idle between 600-700 RPM. Check that fluid temperature in the reservoir is maintained between 122°-140°F (50-60°C).

**2)** Close pressure gauge shut off valve and check a that pressure is between 782-896 psi (55-63 kg/cm²). If pressure is less than specifications, check for faulty pump or a sticking flow control valve.

**3)** Open shut off valve. Pressure should drop at least 71 psi (5 kg/cm²). If pressure drops more than this, check for bent or kinked lines or contaminated fluid.

**4)** With shut off valve open, turn steering wheel to full lock position, then release. If pressure drops more than 71 psi (5 kg/cm²), check for faulty valve in steering gear.

**5)** Turn steering wheel to full right and full left lock position. If pressure drops more than 71 psi (5 kg/cm²) with shut off valve open, look for excessive internal leakage in the power steering gear, caused by excessive valve clearances or broken seals.

### REMOVAL & INSTALLATION

#### POWER STEERING GEAR

**Removal – 1)** Disconnect negative battery cable then remove engine oil filter cartridge to gain clearance for removal of the fluid lines. Disconnect and tag pressure and

# Power Steering

## MAZDA POWER-ASSISTED RECIRCULATING BALL (Cont.)

return lines for correct reassembly, then plug both lines and steering gear ports to prevent entry of dirt.

2) Raise vehicle and disconnect center link at pitman arm, then remove bolts and nuts securing steering gear housing to frame. Remove clamp bolt holding flexible coupling to steering gear, slide gear off coupling and remove steering gear from vehicle.

**Installation** — To install steering gear, reverse removal procedure, noting the following: Fill and bleed system, then start engine and check for leaks by turning steering wheel to left and right.

**Fig. 4    Location of Identification Mark**

3) Remove side cover attaching bolts. Tap lower end of sector shaft with soft hammer to loosen, then remove cover and shaft as an assembly. Turn side cover counterclockwise to remove cover from adjusting screw.

4) Remove adjuster plug lock nut, then loosen, but do not remove the adjuster plug. Unscrew valve housing attaching bolts and remove valve housing and worm shaft as an assembly from steering gear housing.

**Fig. 3    Exploded View of Mazda Power Steering Gear**

**Fig. 5    Loosening Adjuster Plug**

5) Stand valve body and piston on end with piston end down. Rotate worm shaft counterclockwise out of the piston letting the ball bearings drop into the piston. Turn the piston upside down and catch the 26 balls in a container. Unscrew ball guide cover screws, then remove cover and ball guides.

## OVERHAUL

### POWER STEERING GEAR

**Disassembly** — 1) Thoroughly clean the exterior of gear with solvent. Hold gear upside down over a drain pan and turn worm shaft back and forth several times to drain fluid, then secure gear on a work stand.

2) Remove pitman arm nut and using puller (49 0223 695D), remove pitman arm. Remove sector shaft adjusting screw lock nut. To center the gear, turn worm shaft until identification mark is in the position shown in *Fig. 4*.

### STEERING GEAR HOUSING

**Disassembly** — Clean and inspect housing. Replace seals, if necessary, as follows: Pry lower seal from lower end of housing and remove upper seal snap ring, spacer washer, and upper seal.

**Reassembly** — Dip new seals in gear lubricant and coat seal bore of housing with lubricant. Place upper seal in bore with lip facing inward. Install spacer washer, then seat snap ring in groove. Insert lower seal in bore with rubber side facing out and press into place.

## MAZDA POWER-ASSISTED RECIRCULATING BALL (Cont.)

### VALVE HOUSING, WORM SHAFT & VALVE

**Disassembly** — Unscrew adjuster plug from valve housing, then remove outer bearing race, thrust bearing and inner bearing race. Remove valve and worm shaft assembly, bearing races and thrust bearing from housing. Remove worm shaft bearing and pry oil seal and dust seal from adjuster plug. Remove Teflon ring and "O" ring from piston and ball nut.

**Reassembly** — **1)** Install new Teflon ring and "O" ring in valve housing. Coat new Teflon rings and "O" rings in gear lubricant and install on valve body and worm shaft. Dip bearing races and needle bearing in power steering fluid and position on worm.

**2)** Lubricate Teflon ring and "O" ring with power steering fluid, then carefully install worm and valve in housing. Coat new dust seal and oil seal with power steering fluid, then install dust seal with rubber side facing out and oil seal with lip facing inward on adjusting plug.

**3)** Drive worm shaft bearing into adjuster plug until it seats on bottom surface of bearing bore. Coat bearing races and thrust bearing with power steering fluid, then align grooves on race with pins, thrust bearing, and outer race, install on valve body.

**4)** Lubricate and install "O" ring in adjuster plug groove and place adjuster plug over end of stub shaft. Tighten adjuster plug enough to properly seat all parts, then tighten until initial preload is to specifications. Install, but do not tighten adjuster plug lock nut.

**5)** Coat new "O" ring in gear lubricant, then install "O" ring and new Teflon ring on piston and ball nut.

**NOTE** — *Do not stretch Teflon ring more than necessary.*

### STEERING GEAR ASSEMBLY

**1)** Lubricate and install "O" ring in valve housing. Insert worm shaft into piston so that three grooves are visible between valve housing and ball nut, then place 19 balls into hole near Teflon ring as worm is turned clockwise. Insert remaining seven balls into one side of ball guide, hold in place with Vaseline, then position other half of ball guide over balls and install in piston.

**2)** Apply Vaseline to new "O" ring and install on cover. Make sure neoprene pad is in cover, then position cover on ball nut and tighten attaching screws to specification. Use a straightedge to make sure guide cover head is not higher than Teflon ring. File off high spots.

**NOTE** — *Do not rotate piston or stub shaft after balls are inserted, as balls may fall out of circuit.*

**3)** Coat new "O" ring with Vaseline and install in pressure port of gear housing. Coat Teflon seal with Vaseline and install on piston, then insert piston and valve into gear housing. Align lube passages in valve housing with passages in gear housing and install, but do not tighten, attaching bolts.

**4)** Rotate ball nut until teeth mesh with sector teeth then tighten valve housing bolts to specification. Insert side cover "O" ring in steering gear housing, then turn stub shaft to

center the piston. Screw side cover onto adjusting screw until it bottoms, then back out one and one half turns.

**5)** Lubricate sector shaft bearing and journal, then install sector shaft with center gear tooth meshing with center groove of rack piston. Install side cover attaching bolts and lock washers and tighten to specification.

**NOTE** — *Make sure cover "O" ring is in place before tightening bolts.*

**6)** Turn stub shaft completely to left or right, then back 90°, then using pull scale, recheck that initial preload is to specifications. Turn sector shaft adjusting screw to adjust final preload to specifications. Install new rubber seal and adjusting screw lock nut, then tighten lock nut to specifications. Align identification marks and install pitman arm on sector shaft and tighten nut to specifications.

### POWER STEERING PUMP

**Disassembly** — **1)** Clean pump exterior and drain fluid. Clamp pump in padded vise. Remove pulley and Woodruff key. Unscrew suction line connector attaching bolts and remove connector. Remove flow control plug, valve and spring from housing.

**Fig. 6  *Exploded View of Mazda Power Steering Pump***

**2)** Remove end cover attaching bolts and end cover. Take off snap ring then remove collar, vanes and rotor from shaft. Remove cam ring, and tapping drive end of shaft with plastic hammer, drive out pressure plate and shaft.

**3)** Remove dowel pins from housing. Pry shaft seal from housing (if defective)

**NOTE** — *The seal will be destroyed if removed.*

**Inspection** - Clean parts thoroughly and check for cracks, wear or burned areas. Rotor, vanes and ring must be replaced as an assembly if defective. Check flow control valve and plug orifices.

# Power Steering

## MAZDA POWER-ASSISTED RECIRCULATING BALL (Cont.)

**Reassembly — 1)** If shaft seal was removed, install new seal with metal backing facing pump end of shaft. Seat seal properly in shaft hub.

*Fig. 7   Installing Dowel Pin and Spring*

2) Lubricate new "O" ring with power steering fluid and install in groove on pump body. Install both dowel pins and spring, then insert shaft in housing. Install new "O" ring on pressure plate, then coat plate and "O" ring with power steering fluid. Install pressure plate on dowel pins with recess facing out and press into place. Place cam ring on dowel pins with rotation arrow toward pressure plate.

*Fig. 8   Installing Pressure Plate*

*Fig. 9   Cam Ring Locating Mark*

3) Coat rotor with gear lubricant and install on shaft with recessed chamfer side of bore toward pressure plate. Install vanes in rotor slots with rounded edge of vanes facing out. Make sure vanes move freely. Install collar and snap ring on splined end of shaft, sliding snap ring down until seated into ring groove.

4) Lubricate new "O" rings with power steering fluid and install on housing, then install end cover and tighten attaching bolts to specification. Place flow control valve spring and valve in hole, making sure pin end of valve is toward plug. Lubricate new "O" rings and install on plug, then install plug in housing tighten to specification.

5) Lubricate new "O" rings and install on pressure connector and suction line connector. Tighten pressure connector and suction line connector bolts to specification. Tap Woodruff key into shaft and install pulley on pump.

### TIGHTENING SPECIFICATIONS

| Application | Ft. Lbs. (mkg) |
| --- | --- |
| Valve Housing Bolts | 29-36 (3.8-5.0) |
| Side Cover Bolts | 29-36 (3.8-5.0) |
| Pitman Arm Nut | 108-130 (15-18) |
| Pump End Cover Bolts | 22-29 (3-4) |
| Pump Control Valve Plug | 50-72 (7-10) |
| Pump Pressure Connector | 50-72 (7-10) |
| Pump Suction Connector Bolts | 5-7 (.7-1.0) |

| Application | INCH Lbs. (cmkg) |
| --- | --- |
| Worm Shaft Initial Preload | 5-9.5 (6-11) |
| Worm Shaft Final Preload | 9-14 (10-16) |

# Power Steering

## MERCEDES-BENZ POWER-ASSISTED RECIRCULATING BALL

**All Models**

### DESCRIPTION

Power steering is composed of power steering pump and steering gear. Some models use a VT27 pump which has a separate oil reservoir, and some models use a ZF and VT49 pump, which has an integral oil reservoir.

All power steering pumps are engine driven vane type with a control valve. The purpose of the power steering gear pump is to supply fluid (under pressure) to the steering gear.

Steering gear has integral piston/steering nut. Fluid pressure to each side of piston/steering nut is controlled by a control valve which is moved by a lever from steering column shaft.

### LUBRICATION

**Capacity** — 2.6 pts. (1.5 lts.) automatic transmission fluid.

### REMOVAL & INSTALLATION

#### POWER STEERING PUMP

**NOTE** — *A modified power steering pump is used on 6.9 models. An asterisk is stamped on the blue identification plate to signify this.*

**Removal** — 1) Remove power steering tank cover, spring and damping plate. Drain tank with a syringe. Disconnect and plug high pressure and return hoses.

2) Loosen fastening bolts and push pump towards engine, remove "V" belts from pulley. Remove remaining bolts and remove pressure pump with carrier.

**Installation** — To install power steering pump, reverse removal procedures. Fill system with recommended fluid.

#### POWER STEERING GEAR

**NOTE** — *All models are equipped with a modified power steering gear. The stop for the full lock position is incorporated into the housing itself, not on the steering arms as before. When replacing steering gears, install only the newer type gear. This gear can be recognized by an "A" \* stamped on the housing.*

**Removal** — 1) Drain fluid from power steering pump. Disconnect and plug pressure line and return line from steering gear. Remove bolts from steering coupling. Remove rear exhaust system and left hand exhaust pipe at manifold (all 450 models). Disconnect center link and tie rod from pitman arm. Remove bolts securing steering gear to frame, force steering gear from steering column shaft, in a downward direction.

2) Drain fluid from steering gear, remove steering coupling and pitman arm from gear (be sure to mark pitman shaft-to-pitman arm position for proper assembly).

**Installation** — To install steering gear, reverse removal procedure. Replace locking nuts and bolts, tighten to specifications. Fill system with recommended fluid.

### OVERHAUL

#### POWER STEERING PUMP

**Disassembly, VT27 Pump** — 1) Remove knurled nut and tank cover with seal. Remove spring, damping plate and filter ring. Remove bolt and hollow screw, then remove tank with "O" rings from pump housing.

**Fig. 1  Exploded View of VT27 Power Steering Pump**

2) Remove bolts connecting pump cover to pump body. Remove compression spring from pressure plate. Mark pressure plate and vane body and then lift off pressure plate from pins on vane body.

3) Remove vane rotor with vanes and vane body. Remove all "O" rings then remove control valve from pump body. Dismantle control valve and check for worn, damaged or missing parts.

**Fig. 2  Removing VT27 Pump Control Valve Assembly**

## MERCEDES-BENZ POWER-ASSISTED RECIRCULATING BALL (Cont.)

**Inspection, VT27 Pump** — 1) Check vanes and rotor for damage or wear: vanes should slide easily in rotor. If necessary, replace vanes and rotor. Check vane body for excessive wear. If necessary to replace vane body, vanes and rotor must also be replaced.

2) Check running surfaces of housing cover. If worn, replace entire pump. Check surface of pressure plate and replace if worn. Check control valve. If worn, replace entire pump. Install shell halves on shaft and check end play. If end play exceeds specifications, replace entire pump.

**Assembly, VT27 Pump** — To assemble steering pump, reverse disassembly procedure.

**Fig. 3   Exploded View of VT27 Pump Control Valve Components**

**Disassembly, VT49 Pump** — 1) Remove wing nut and cover from reservoir. Remove compression spring, two damping plates and filter ring. Remove woodruff key from input shaft.

2) Install puller 1104-7251 on input shaft. Screw bolt back on puller enough to install clamping shoes 11004-6304 between puller and seal. Turn clamping cone of puller to the right up to stop and remove seal ring out of housing.

3) On rear of housing, push in cover and insert a punch through hole in housing (See Fig. 4), push in on punch and remove circlip and cover. Remove spring and "O" ring from housing. Push input shaft with pressure plate at cover end, rotor, cam ring and pressure plate at input end out of housing in rearward direction.

**Fig. 4   Circlip Punch Hole Location & Removing Locking Pin on VT49 Pump**

4) Remove pressure plate, cam ring and blades. Remove locking clip from input shaft, then remove rotor and pressure plate. Remove cylinder pins from housing. Using a punch, knock out locking pins in housing. (See Fig. 4).

5) Remove closing plug, volume control valve and compression spring from housing. Clamp volume control valve in vise and disassemble valve. Check spacer washer, valve cone and compression spring.

**Inspection** — Check pressure plates, input shaft, and bearing bushing for wear. Check blades for easy sliding in rotor. Check surfaces of volume control valve and bore in pump housing for wear or damage.

**NOTE** — *Never replace volume control valve only, replace power steering pump.*

**Reassembly, VT49 Pump** — To install power steering pump, reverse removal procedure. Fill system with recommended fluid.

**Disassembly, ZF Pump** — 1) Remove woodruff key from input shaft. Install puller 1104-7251 on shaft. Screw bolt back on puller enough to install clamping shoes 11004-6304 between puller and seal.

2) Turn clamping core of puller to the right up to stop, remove tool, seal and washer from housing. Remove knurled nut and cover from housing. Remove retaining and compression springs. Remove upper damping plate, filter ring, and lower damping plate.

3) On rear of housing, push in cover plate and using a screwdriver remove circlip and cover. Remove "O" ring, compression spring, and pressure plate. Remove rotor with blades from input shaft and "O" ring and cam ring.

4) Remove lock ring from forward end of shaft. Press out input shaft from rear of housing. Remove circlip from shaft and remove bearing by pressing off toward rear of shaft. Remove needle bearing from housing.

5) Remove closing plug from housing. Remove compression spring and volume control valve. Clamp volume control valve in vise, disassemble and check spacer washers, ball, and compression spring.

**Inspection** — Check pressure plates, input shaft, bearing housing, and bushing for wear. Check blades for easy sliding in rotor. Check surfaces of volume control valve and bore in pump housing for wear or damage.

**NOTE** — *Never replace volume control valve only, replace power steering pump.*

**Reassembly, ZF Pump** — To install power steering pump, reverse removal procedure. Fill system with recommended fluid.

### POWER STEERING GEAR

**Disassembly** — 1) Attach steering gear to a suitable assembly plate (116 589 01 59 00). Remove lock nut from adjusting screw and remove copper seal ring. Remove bolts attaching pitman shaft cover to steering case.

## MERCEDES-BENZ POWER-ASSISTED RECIRCULATING BALL (Cont.)

**Fig. 5  Sectional View of Adjusting Screw**

**2)** With steering in center position, turn adjusting screw clockwise. This forces pitman shaft, with housing, from steering gear case. Remove pitman shaft with cover. Remove "O" rings from cover. Remove lock ring and seal ring. Remove lock ring from pitman shaft and remove adjusting screw with thrust washers. (See Fig. 5).

**3)** Remove bolts securing bearing cap to steering gear case. Turn worm gear counterclockwise until bearing cap is forced out of steering gear case.

**NOTE** – Balls will fall out of ball guide if worm gear is turned too far.

**4)** Remove bearing cap and worm gear with piston/steering nut from steering gear case.

**5)** Unscrew worm gear with bearing cap from piston/steering nut.

**CAUTION** – Do not lose circulator balls.

**6)** Remove "O" ring from bearing cap and attach bearing cap to a suitable assembly fixture.

**Fig. 6  Removing Bearing Insert from Bearing Cap**

**7)** Unscrew slotted nut, using hook wrench, from bearing insert.

**8)** Remove bearing insert from bearing cap using spanner wrench (See Fig. 6). Remove steering worm and washer from bearing cap. Remove roller cage from steering worm, along with seal and "O" rings.

**9)** Remove bearing and disc from bearing cap. Remove bolts, clamp, and both ball guide halves from piston/steering nut.

**Fig. 7  Removing Worm Gear Nut from Piston Steering Nut**

**10)** Using suitable clamp and tools (Fig. 7), remove worm gear nut from piston/steering nut. Remove seal ring and "O" ring from worm gear nut. On early models, remove axial disc from worm gear nut

**11)** Remove bearings from piston/steering nut. (See Fig. 8)

**12)** Remove lock ring, cover and control valve from steering gear case. (See Fig. 8).

**Fig. 8  Cross Sectional View of Steering Gear**

## MERCEDES-BENZ POWER-ASSISTED RECIRCULATING BALL (Cont.)

**Inspection** — 1) On worm gear, check ball paths and bearings surfaces for wear and damage, replace if necessary.

Control Valve

Steering Gear Case

*Fig. 9   Steering Gear Case with Detail of Control Valve*

**2)** On piston/steering nut, remove seal rings, "O" rings, bearings and races, and worm gear nut. Inspect for wear or damage and replace as necessary.

**3)** Check pitman shaft for wear or damage on bearing surfaces, check for bent or warped shaft and replace as necessary. Check steering case, cover, and bearing insert for wear or damage and replace as necessary.

**4)** On control valve, check reaction piston in control valve for free movement. If necessary remove pistons from control valve by removing lock rings.

**Assembly** — To assemble steering gear, reverse disassembly procedure. Replace all "O" rings and sealing rings. Adjust gear to specifications.

### SPECIFICATIONS

| Application | Dimensions |
|---|---|
| Steering Wheel Free Play | 1" Maximum |
| Pump Circulation Pressure | 28.4-71 psi |
| Number of Balls in Ball Circuit | 24 |
| End Play of Pump Shaft | |
| New | .028" Maximum |
| Used | .039" Maximum |

### TIGHTENING SPECIFICATIONS

| Application | Ft. Lbs. (mkg) |
|---|---|
| Steering Gear to Frame | 50-57 (7-8) |
| Pitman Arm to Pitman Shaft | 116-145 (16-19) |
| Slotted Nut to Bearing Cap | 101-115 (14-16) |
| Adjusting Screw Nut | 22-25 (3-3.5) |
| Pump Housing Bolts | 25-29 (3.5-4) |

# Power Steering

## PORSCHE POWER-ASSISTED RACK & PINION

928

### DESCRIPTION

A power-assisted rack and pinion steering gear is used as standard equipment on Porsche 928 models. The power assistance decreases with engine speed to provide a better road feel at high speeds. The system consists of a belt driven vane pump mounted on the engine, a fluid reservoir located in the left front engine compartment, and a rotary piston pinion steering gear.

### GENERAL SERVICE

**Lubricant** — ATF Dexron Type

**Oil Level Check** — Remove reservoir cap and start engine. Check that fluid level is up to embossed mark on inside of reservoir.

**Hydraulic System Bleeding** — Start engine, set to idle. Check fluid level. Turn steering wheel lock to lock several times quickly. Do not turn wheel harder than necessary. Check fluid and add if needed. No air bubbles should rise in reservoir. Shut off engine. Check that fluid level does not rise more than 3/8" (10 mm). If level rises, repeat procedure.

### ADJUSTMENTS

#### PUMP BELT

Check belt deflection at center of belt between pump pulley and crankshaft pulley. Correct deflection is 3/8" (10 mm). Adjust by loosening pump mounting bolts and moving pump.

#### SYSTEM LEAKS

With engine running, turn steering to full lock position and hold. This produces maximum pressure in lines. Check all hose connections and tighten if necessary.

### REMOVAL & INSTALLATION

#### STEERING GEAR

**Removal — 1)** Drain fluid from system. Raise front of vehicle and support on safety stands. Press out tie rods with standard extractor. Remove bolt holding hose strap, and pull back hose and harness.

Steering Gear

Round Cord Seal

Hollow Bolt

Bolt

Seal

Tie Rod Assembly

Reinforcement Plate

Dust Boot

Tie Rod

Tie Rod End

*Fig. 1  Power Steering Gear Porsche 928*

# Power Steering

## PORSCHE POWER-ASSISTED RACK & PINION (Cont.)

**Fig. 2   Tie Rod Removal**

**2)** Remove bolts from stabilizer bar mounts. Allow stabilizer to hang down. Disconnect pressure and return lines from steering gear.

**Fig. 3   Stabilizer Bar Mounting**

**3)** Remove 5 bolts holding reinforcement plate on engine crossmember. Loosen 4 self-locking nuts on steering gear, but do not remove.

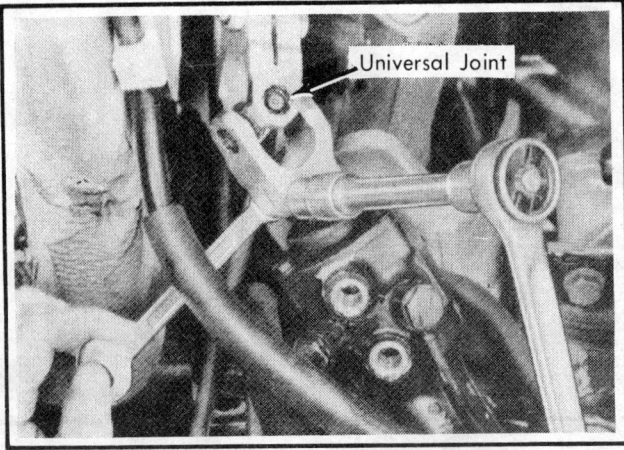

**Fig. 4   Steering Intermediate Shaft Removal**

**4)** Remove bolt on universal joint which connects to steering intermediate shaft and pull off shaft. Remove 4 nuts on steering gear and lower steering gear out of studs on engine crossmember.

**Installation — 1)** Reverse removal procedures, noting the following: Position steering intermediate shaft correctly and install bolt to universal shaft. Add fluid to reservoir. Check for leaks after reinstalling. Adjust toe if necessary.

### STEERING PUMP

**Removal — 1)** Detach intake hose from air cleaner on left side. Drain fluid from reservoir. Remove splash shield. Loosen front bolts on pump, but do not remove.

**2)** Remove rear bolt from pump. Remove "V" belt. Take off upper left section of drive belt cover. Disconnect pressure hose from pump.

**Fig. 5   Drive Belt Cover Removal**

**3)** Loosen clip holding suction hose and remove hose. Remove front bolts holding pump. Remove pump.

**Installation —** Reverse removal procedures, noting the following: Install pressure hose so that not more than 1" (25 mm) is provided between inner wheel well and hose when pump is installed. If hose is too close to exhaust manifold it could slip from its holder. Adjust belt tension, add fluid and bleed system. Check for leaks.

## OVERHAUL

**NOTE** — *Information regarding overhaul of steering gear and vane pump not available at time of publication.*

### TIGHTENING SPECIFICATIONS

| Application | Ft. Lbs. (mkg) |
|---|---|
| Tie Rod to Steering Arm | 61 (8.5) |
| Tie Rod to Steering Rack | 108 (15) |
| Tie Rod End to Tie Rod | 33 (4.5) |
| Universal Joint to Steering Column | 17 (2.3) |
| Steering Rack to Cross Member | 33 (4.6) |
| Pressure/Return Lines to Steering Rack | 22 (3) |

## SAAB POWER-ASSISTED RACK & PINION

99

### DESCRIPTION

Power steering is added to some vehicles as optional equipment. The assembly consists of a rack and pinion steering gear with a servo valve which regulates the oil flow to a servo plunger on the rack. The hydraulic pressure is generated by an oil pump which is driven by a belt attached to the crankshaft pulley. A separate oil reservoir located by the left wheel housing supplies the system with hydraulic oil. A tube running between the two ends of the steering gear housing leads the oil past the hydraulic portion of the rack.

### REMOVAL & INSTALLATION

**Removal** — 1) Loosen servo pump and lift away from mounting. Turn steering wheel a full turn left and remove clamping screw holding universal joint to steering gear. Block up the engine and remove left side engine mounting. Remove left cover under instrument panel and remove bearing bracket mounting from body.

2) Lift steering column with universal joint and support out of way. Raise and support front of vehicle. Remove front wheels. Using tie rod remover tool (8995409), detach tie rod end assemblies from control arms. Unscrew left tie rod end assembly from tie rod.

3) Disconnect speedometer cable from transmission. Disconnect left side handbrake cable at brake yoke and vehicle housing. Remove right side handbrake cable clamp on steering gear. Remove steering gear mounting from body.

4) From left side, remove two retaining screws from steering gear, and remove intermediate piece. On right side, remove yoke and intermediate piece. Disconnect delivery and return lines from servo valve.

5) Move steering gear over to right far enough so left tie rod can be pulled down through the body opening while twisting the valve housing backward. Take steering assembly out by moving it down and to the left.

**Installation** — Installation, is a reversal of removal procedure; however, tie rod ends are to be connected after gear assembly has been fully installed. Adjust toe-in.

### OVERHAUL

#### POWER STEERING GEAR

**Disassembly** — 1) Clean exterior of gear assembly thoroughly before beginning work. Back off lock nut and remove tie rod end assemblies. Loosen clamps and take off rubber bellows. Bend up lock plate between end piece and rack.

2) Clamp toothed end of rack in a vise. Unscrew lock nut and adjusting screw. Withdraw adjusting screw retaining plate, spring "O" ring, and plunger. Remove tubes between servo valve and servo cylinder.

3) Unscrew three lock nuts, then detach valve housing and servo valve with pinion. Keep servo valve in a clean plastic bag. Remove ring nut locking screws. Clamp gear end of housing vertically in padded vise and remove ring nut using a suitable spanner (8995961).

*Fig. 1   Exploded View of Saab Power Steering Components*

## SAAB POWER-ASSISTED RACK & PINION (Cont.)

*Fig. 2   Removing Ring Nut Locking Screw from Steering Gear End*

**4)** Remove steering gear end from the cylinder and the rack while removing the bleeder tube. Set aside loose cone in hole for oil tube. Remove sealing ring, washer, and servo seal from steering gear end. Pull rack out of steering gear housing. Remove knurled sleeve, servo seal, and washer from cylinder. Remove plunger seal and snap ring.

**NOTE** — *Plunger cannot be detached from rack.*

**Reassembly — 1)** Apply Loctite to needle bearing seat and push in the needle bearing, if it has been removed. Fit snap ring and new teflon ring onto rack plunger. Slide knurled sleeve onto rack. Fit servo seal on fitting sleeve using the special cone tools (8995938 and 8995946). Slide sleeve with seal past teeth on rack. Remove tools. Turn notch in seal toward servo plunger.

**2)** Push rack into servo cylinder until knurled sleeve can be seen in hole for tube connection. Use a screwdriver to turn sleeve to expose its threaded hole. Screw in connecting screw temporarily to hold the washer in place.

**NOTE** — *Do not tighten screw completely, or rack will be damaged.*

**3)** Insert servo seal into its seat. Turn notch in seal toward servo plunger. Slip on the washer. Turn smaller diameter of washer toward the servo seal. Fit flat sided seal. Put cone into tube connection hole and lock cone using special screw (8995953). Cylindrical part of cone (inside steering gear end) serves to fix position of gear end in relation to servo cylinder. Screw fitting cone (8995987) onto rack end and position steering gear end onto rack and servo cylinder while inserting the vent tube. Cylindrical portion of cone fits into "U" shaped recess in end of servo cylinder. Tighten ring nut with suitable wrench. Lock the nut with socket head screw.

**4)** Install washer and seal between pinion and servo valve in gear housing. Position servo valve in housing. Position gasket (earlier design), or "O" ring (later design), between valve housing and gear housing. Insert sealing ring, plastic washer and lock ring in valve housing. Place installation tool (8995979), over shaft end of valve. Attach valve housing.

**5)** Remove special locking screw (8995953) from connection hole in steering gear end. Install tubes between servo valve and two sides of cylinder. Position new gaskets on banjo connection of the shorter tube to the cylinder. Install rack plunger, "O" ring, spring, cover, adjusting screw, and lock nut for radial adjustment of rack.

*Fig. 3   Fitting Steering Gear End to Rack Housing*

**6)** Clamp toothed end of rack in a padded vise, and install complete end pieces with thrust washer, spring, and lock washer. Lock the washer.

**7)** Adjust the radial play of the rack as follows: Screw in adjusting screw until resistance of the gear is felt. Back off screw 1/6 turn. Check that steering gear can be turned from lock to lock without jamming. Tighten adjusting screw lock nut.

*Fig. 4   Adjusting Rack Radial Play*

**8)** Position rubber bellows and install (tighten) all clamps except one outer one. Hold steering gear vertically, with unclamped end up, and inject 6.5 fl. oz. of suitable EP 90 gear oil into the bellows. Attach remaining clamp. Install lock nuts and tie rod end assemblies.

## TIGHTENING SPECIFICATIONS

| Application | Ft. Lbs. (mkg) |
| --- | --- |
| Gear End Ring Nut | 130-135 (18-19) |
| Valve Housing Lock Nuts | 16.6 (2.3) |
| End Pieces (Inner Ball Joints) | 47-54 (6.5-7.5) |
| Adjusting Screw Lock Nut | 50-60 (7-8) |

# Power Steering

## TOYOTA POWER-ASSISTED WORM AND SECTOR

Corona
Celica
Cressida

### DESCRIPTION

#### POWER STEERING PUMP

The power steering pump is a vane type composed of an engine driven eccentric rotor, a fixed ring (having six slotted grooves), and a flow control valve (to regulate maximum oil pressure and amount of oil flow). Slippers are fitted in each slotted groove and are pressed against rotor outside surface by pressure produced in adjoining slots and by spring tension. As rotor rotation increases or decreases, then space between the rotor and fixed ring changes accordingly, in order to control oil flow.

#### POWER STEERING GEAR

Power steering gear consists of a mechanism which converts steering wheel torque to cross shaft torque by means of worm and power piston nut, and of a mechanism which detects hydraulic pressure developed by vane pump and controls this pressure in proportion to the steering effort. The worm shaft is separated at the center and power is transmitted from the steering wheel to worm gear through a small diameter torsion bar.

### LUBRICATION

**Capacity** – 1.7 pts. (800 cc)

**Type** - ATF type Dexron

With 22 lbs. (10 kg) pressure applied, belt deflection for Cressida between crank and vane pulley is: .71-.84" (18-21.5 mm). Celica between crank and vane pulley, .3-.5" (8-12. mm). Corona between water pump and vane pulley, .35-.43" (9-11 mm): Corona (with A/C) between air pulley and vane pulley, .31-.39" (8-10 mm).

#### STEERING GEAR AIR REMOVAL

1) Jack up front of vehicle and support with safety stands. Fill fluid to proper level in vane pump reservoir (turn wheels fully in both directions and recheck fluid level).

2) Start engine and let idle. Turn steering from lock to lock 2 or 3 times. Lower vehicle. Run engine at 1000 RPM or less. Turn wheel from lock to lock 2 or 3 times. Center steering wheel. If fluid level does not rise and no foaming of fluid is evident, bleeding is complete. If level rises, or foaming is evident, repeat procedure until air is released.

#### FLUID REPLACEMENT

Raise and support front of vehicle. Disconnect return hose and drain fluid into container. Turn steering wheel from lock to lock while draining. Connect return hose, add fresh fluid and bleed system.

### HYDRAULIC PRESSURE TESTING

1) Disconnect pressure lines from steering gear case and vane pump. Attach pressure gauge with gauge side connected to vane pump. Attach valve side of gauge to pressure line. Bleed air from system and check fluid level.

2) Set engine to idle speed. Check fluid pressure reading with pressure gauge valve closed. Correct pressure should be 1022 psi. If pressure does not reach specifications within 10 seconds, there is a problem with the vane pump.

**NOTE** – *Do not keep pressure gauge valve closed for more than 10 seconds. Fluid testing temperature should be 176°F (80° C)*

3) Open pressure valve. With steering wheel at full lock position, check oil pressure. Correct pressure is 1022 psi. Measure oil pressure with engine at 1000 RPM, and again at 3000 RPM. Pressure difference should be less than 71 psi. If pressure is more than this, check flow control valve.

4) With vehicle on flat surface, turn steering wheel to midpoint. With engine idling, measure steering power at the steering wheel circumference over one turn to full lock both sides of midpoint. Left and right steering effort should be 8.8 lbs (4 kg), maximum.

### REMOVAL & INSTALLATION

#### POWER STEERING PUMP

**Removal** – Loosen pulley mounting nut before loosening drive belt. Disconnect pressure feed line from pump housing. **NOTE** – *Keep disconnected hose at high level to prevent fluid from draining out. Also plug pump housing hose fitting.* Disconnect inlet fluid line. Remove pump assembly from mounting bracket and adjusting strap.

**Installation** – Install in reverse of removal procedures, noting the following: Adjust drive belt tension as previously described, then perform Air Removal procedure.

#### POWER STEERING GEAR

**Removal** – Disconnect pressure feed hose and inlet return line from steering gear housing. Remove bolt securing the intermediate shaft to flexible coupling. Unscrew nut from cross shaft. Disconnect pitman arm from steering relay rod using tool 09611-20014, (Celica). Remove pitman arm with tool 09610-20011, (Cressida). Remove gear housing from vehicle.

**Installation** – Reverse removal procedure. Perform air removal procedure as previously described.

### OVERHAUL

#### POWER STEERING PUMP

**Disassembly** – 1) Pump disassembly will be made easier if a suitable holding tool is used (09630-30041). Clamp tool in vise and attach pump to it. After marking front housing alignment, remove front housing with soft hammer. Do not allow slippers or springs to fall out.

# Power Steering

## TOYOTA POWER-ASSISTED WORM AND SECTOR (Cont.)

**2)** Remove rotor shaft, slippers and springs. Remove rear housing from fixed ring with a soft hammer, being careful not to tap flow control valve. Remove screw, washer and snap ring from in front of flow control valve. Reinstall screw and grip with pliers to remove flow control valve. Remove side plate from front and rear housings, along with "O" rings.

**Inspection – 1)** Clean all disassembled parts in solvent and blow dry. Inspect oil seal lip and bushing sliding surface for wear or damage. Check rotor outer surface for wear or scoring. Inspect rotor-to-side plate contact surface.

**2)** Measure overall length of rotor (between end faces) and overall length of fixed ring. If overall length of rotor is more than .0024" (.06 mm) shorter than fixed ring overall length, replace with new rotor shaft sub-assembly.

**3)** Inspect slipper for wear: Measure length and thickness. If thickness is less than .0551" (1.4 mm) or if length is less than 1.571" (39.920 mm), replace entire set.

**4)** Inspect front and rear housing bushings. Bushing-to-rotor shaft clearance must not exceed .0012" (.03 mm). Inspect internal surface of fixed ring. If worn, scratched, or scored, replace ring. Check front and rear side plates at sliding surfaces. Bushings cannot be replaced separately. Replace entire housing.

**Fig. 2   Rotor Shaft Sub-Assembly Inspection Points**

**5)** Measure free length of slipper compression springs. If less than .51" (13 mm) replace individually. If free length varies more than .02" (0.5 mm) between springs, replace entire set.

**6)** If flow control valve is scratched or otherwise damaged, replace it with one having the same production number. Measure compression spring for flow control valve. If free length measures less than 1.85" (47 mm), replace spring. Inspect ball and relief spring.

**7)** Inspect reservoir for leakage. Inspect "S" type oil seal and replace if damaged: Remove with screwdriver. Apply a suitable lubricant to lip of new seal and install using special tool 09630-30041.

**Fig. 1   Exploded View of Toyota Power Steering Pump Assembly**

# Power Steering

## TOYOTA POWER-ASSISTED WORM AND SECTOR (Cont.)

**Fig. 3   Flow Control Valve and Rear Housing Index Marks**

**Fig. 4   Using Gauge to Check Ball Clearance**

**Reassembly – 1)** Replace all "O" rings. Unless otherwise noted, coat all sliding surfaces and "O" rings with power steering fluid. Ensure that number on flow control valve matches number scribed on rear housing. Install flow control valve assembly. Check operation of valve by pushing into bore with finger.

**2)** Install side plate with large beveled width facing rear housing. Drive in fixed ring evenly with soft hammer. Lubricate and install rotor into rear housing. Assemble spring seat, springs and slipper. Install slipper assembly with open side facing counter clockwise.

**3)** Install second side plate with large beveled side facing front housing. Fit front housing over shaft assembly and align marks. Tighten front housing bolts evenly 3 or 4 times to specifications. Mount pulley on rotor shaft and check preload. Preload, while turning, should be less than 6.2 lbs (2.8 kg).

## POWER STEERING GEAR

**NOTE** – *It is recommended that Toyota tool kit part number 09630-22010 be used in disassembling and assembling power steering gear.*

**Disassembly – 1)** Attach gear housing to holding tool, and anchor in vise. Remove pitman arm (Celica). Tighten adjusting screw until end cover "O" ring is removed. Remove cross-shaft by tapping bottom end with hammer. Remove bolts attaching gear housing to valve housing.

**2)** Hold power piston nut with hand and turn worm shaft clockwise, then remove valve assembly and power piston.

**CAUTION** – *Ensure that power piston nut does not come off worm shaft. Do not disassemble valve body or remove power piston from worm shaft.*

**3)** Install valve assembly in vise. Using a dial indicator measure ball clearance. If clearance exceeds .006" (.15 mm) replace valve assembly.

**4)** Install cross shaft in vise. Using dial indicator check cross shaft adjusting screw for thrust clearance .001.002" (.03-.05 mm). To adjust thrust clearance, remove seal from shaft. Using lock nut tool, loosen lock nut and turn adjusting bolt to set clearance. Install seal on cross shaft.

**Fig. 5   Checking Thrust Clearance**

**5)** Temporarily install valve assembly in gear housing and install mounting bolts. Using lock nut tool, remove lock nut and adjusting bolt from gear assembly. Remove and replace as needed, oil seal, "O" ring, and bearing assembly. Install lock nut and tighten. Remove valve assembly from gear housing

**Inspection – 1)** Clean and dry all disassembled components. Unless otherwise mentioned, coat all sliding parts, "O" rings, and teflon rings with power steering fluid upon reassembly.

**2)** Inspect cross shaft for peeling or pitting at ball rolling surface. Check power piston nut mesh with cross shaft. Look for damaged tooth surfaces or ball rolling surfaces.

**3)** Gear housing bearings must be replaced if bearing rollers are pitted or peeled. Also replace housing bearings if it was noticed that cross shaft bearing surfaces had been scored or pitted.

# Power Steering

## TOYOTA POWER-ASSISTED WORM AND SECTOR (Cont.)

Pump Inlet Hose

Cooler
Inlet Hose

Oil Cooler

Cooler Inlet Pipe

Pump Outlet
Line & Hose

Gear Inlet Hose

Gear Outlet Pipe

**Fig. 6    Componet View of Power Steering Line and Hose Placement**

Cross Shaft Cover

Valve Housing

Cross Shaft Ajusting

Worm Shaft

Cross Shaft

Gear Housing

Power Piston

Needle Bearings

**Fig. 7    Exploded View of Power Steering Gear**

## TOYOTA POWER-ASSISTED WORM AND SECTOR (Cont.)

**4)** Remove teflon ring and "O" ring from gear housing. Using needle bearing removing tool, remove needle bearings.

**Reassembly — 1)** Install needle bearings with longer edge of outer race facing outwards and ensure bearing top end aligns with housing end surface. Install lower bearing so that it is positioned 0.764" (19.4 mm) away from housing inner end surface.

**2)** Install "O" ring, teflon ring and spacer in gear housing. Install "O" ring, valve housing, and mounting bolts. Tighten bolts to specifications. To adjust preload on worm shaft, loosen lock nut and install shaft tool and torque wrench on shaft. Preload should be 3.5-5.6 INCH lbs. (4-6.5 cmkg). Hold power piston nut to prevent it from turning.

**3)** Insert shaft holding tool inside of lock nut tool and tighten lock nut on worm shaft. Wrap a piece of vinyl tape around spline area of cross shaft. Align shaft gear with power piston nut gear and insert cross shaft in gear housing.

**CAUTION** — *Do not turn cross shaft, because of possible damage to "O" ring.*

**4)** Insert cross shaft (with cover attached) into housing and install mounting bolts. Tighten bolts to specifications. To adjust preload of cross shaft, set worm shaft to midpoint position. Determine total number of shaft turns and return from full lock by half that number.

**5)** Install shaft tool over shaft and attach a torque wrench. Using a screwdriver turn cross shaft adjusting bolt to specified preload, 2.6-3.5 INCH lbs. (3-4 cmkg). Install seal and nut on adjusting bolt, tighten nut to specifications.

**6)** Recheck worm gear preload to see that both right and left rotations are identical. Align marks and install pitman arm (Celica). Stake worm gear lock nut at three points. Insure that the pitman arm end has no play at the neutral position (Celica).

### TIGHTENING SPECIFICATIONS

| Application | Ft. Lbs. (mkg) |
|---|---|
| Pump Housing & Bracket Bolts | 18-25 (2.5-3.5) |
| Hose Union to Pump Housing | |
|    Return Hose | 24-30 (3.2-4.2) |
|    Pressure Hose | 29-36 (4-5) |
| Rear Reservoir Bolts | 3-5 (0.4-0.7) |
| Worm Bearing Adj. Screw | |
|    Lock Nut | 29-40 (4-5.5) |
| Cross Shaft End Cover | 29-40 (4.0-5.5) |
| Valve Housing-to-Gear Housing | 29-40 (4.0-5.5) |
| Gear Housing-to-Frame | 36-51 (5.0-7.1) |
| Cross Shaft-to-Pitman Arm | 80-101 (11.1-14.0) |
| Pulley-to-Pump | 25-39 (3.5-5.4) |
| Pitman Arm (Celica) | 37-50 (5-7) |

# Power Steering

## VOLVO POWER-ASSISTED RACK & PINION

### DESCRIPTION

Rack and pinion type cam gear power steering is standard on 260 models and on 240 station wagons. This power steering unit consists of a rack and pinion steering gear and a power assist pump interconnected by flexible lines. The 240 and 260 series use a Saginaw type pump with a separate fluid reservoir. The 240 series also uses a ZF type pump with a separate fluid reservoir.

### GENERAL SERVICE

#### STEERING GEAR LUBRICANT

**Type** — Engine oil SAE 20W-40 or SAE 20W-50.

**Capacity** — 6¾ oz.

#### HYDRAULIC SYSTEM LUBRICANT

**Type** — ATF Type A or Dexron.

**Capacity** — 2.3 pts.

#### STEERING GEAR FILLING

Remove inner clamp on right side rubber bellows, and using a suction gun, fill gear with recommended lubricant through side of bellows. Reinstall clamp, then carefully compress bellows so some oil will flow to other side.

#### HYDRAULIC OIL FILLING AND BLEEDING

Fill the reservoir with approved oil, then start engine and allow to idle, adding oil as level drops. Turn steering wheel left and right lock to lock in a slow even motion to allow the pump to operate at low pressure. Continue turning steering wheel until oil in reservoir is almost free of air bubbles. Check that oil is at the level mark, then install reservoir cap.

#### SERVO BALANCE TESTING AND ADJUSTING

**Testing** — 1) Connect a pressure gauge as shown in *Fig. 1*). Make sure oil in reservoir is at level mark.

*Fig. 1    Pressure Gauge Test Set Up*

2) Remove steering wheel impact guard by compressing sides slightly. Install a torque wrench on steering wheel nut.

3) With engine at idle, turn steering wheel (using torque wrench) slowly to right and read torque the moment pressure reaches 170 psi (12 kg/cm²). Repeat operation turning steering wheel to left. Torque should be 30-40 INCH lbs. (35-46 cmkg) as pressure approaches 170 psi (12 kg/cm²). The difference between right and left sides may not exceed 8 INCH lbs. (9 cmkg).

4) If the difference between the sides exceeds this amount, use the following procedures for correction.

**Adjusting** — 1) Turn off engine and remove lock nut and lock washer from pinion lower bearing *(See Fig. 2)* Lock washer will have one tab bent down to lock adjustment nut (bearing race).

*Fig. 2    Lock Washer Adjustment*

2) To increase torque for left side, straighten existing bent tab and bend first tab to left. To increase torque for right side, bend first tab to right.

**NOTE** — *Changing tabs increases torque for one side and decreases torque an equal amount the other side. The value of torque increase or decrease is 4 INCH lbs. (4.6 cmkg).*

3) After bending tab, use suitable tool (9995049) to turn adjustment nut until groove fits lock washer tab. Reinstall lock washer and lock nut. Install pinion cover and gasket.

#### PUMP PRESSURE TEST

1) — With pressure gauge connected as shown in *Fig. 1*, and engine at idle, turn steering wheel fully to left, then fully to right, pressing at end position for a maximum of 10 seconds. Correct pressure should be 895-995 psi (63-69 kg/cm²) for the Saginaw pump and 825 psi (58 kg/cm²) for the ZF pump.

2) To test system maximum pressure, close pressure gauge valve and block oil flow for maximum of 10 seconds. If pressure does not reach the values in the preceeding paragraph, the pump is defective and must be repaired or replaced, *see Overhaul in this article.*

**NOTE** — *The manufacturer does not recommend repair of the Saginaw pump, replace if defective.*

## VOLVO POWER-ASSISTED RACK & PINION (Cont.)

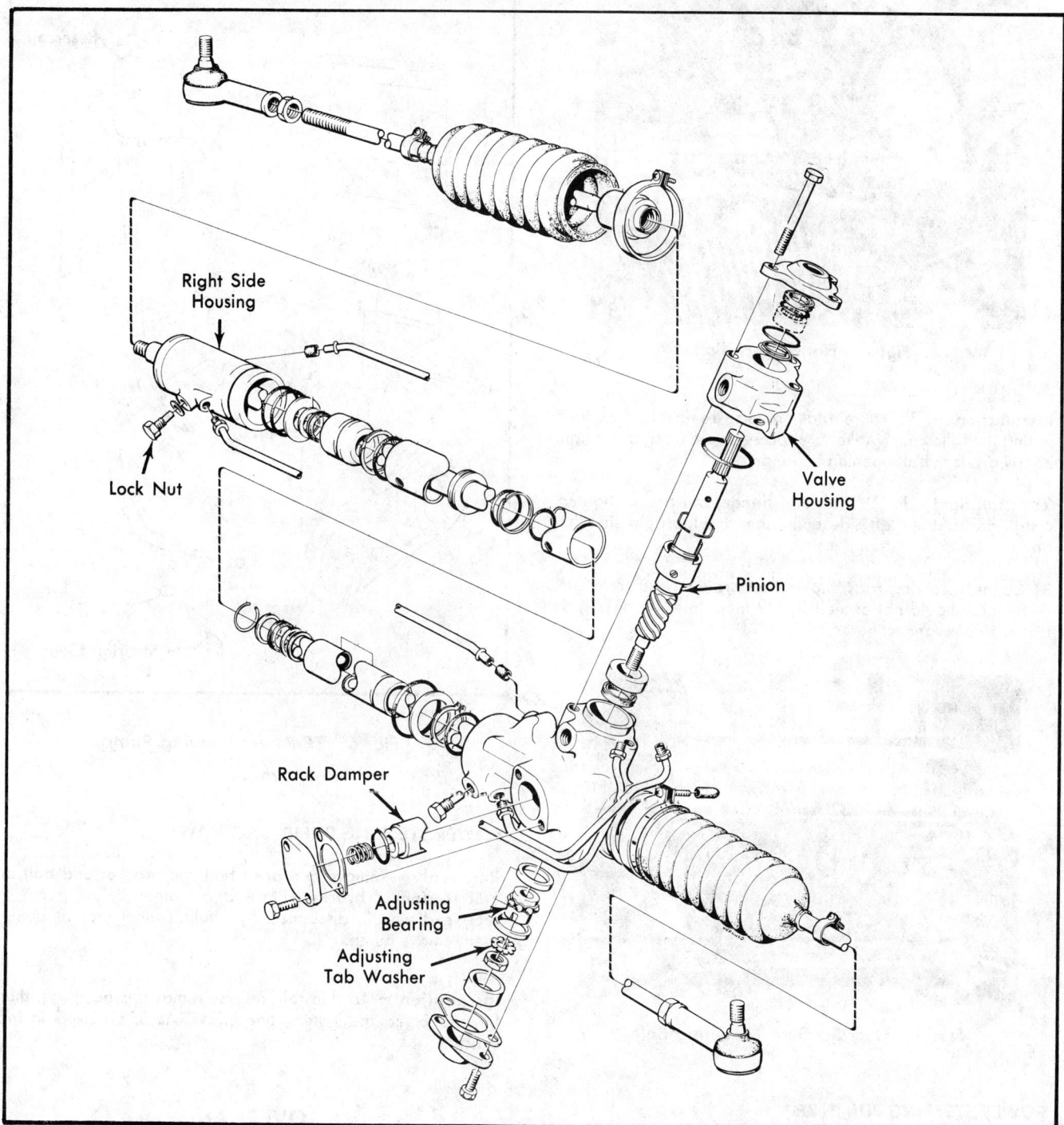

Right Side
Housing

Lock Nut

Valve
Housing

Pinion

Rack Damper

Adjusting
Bearing

Adjusting
Tab Washer

*Fig. 3   Exploded View of Volvo Power Steering Components*

## REMOVAL & INSTALLATION

### STEERING GEAR

**Removal** — **1)** Remove lock bolt and nut from pinion flange. Bend flange apart slightly. Raise and support front of vehicle and remove wheels. Remove tie rod nuts and disconnect ball

studs from spindle using suitable ball joint removal tool (5043). Remove splash guard.

**2)** Disconnect hoses at steering gear and install plugs in hose connections to protect against contamination. Remove bolts securing steering gear to front axle member. Pull steering gear down until free of steering shaft flange, then remove steering gear on left side of vehicle.

# Power Steering

## VOLVO POWER-ASSISTED RACK & PINION (Cont.)

Fig. 4    Flange Lock Bolt

**Installation** — 1) To reinstall, reverse removal procedure, noting the following: Make sure recess on pinion shaft is aligned toward lock bolt opening in flange.

2) Install right side "U" bolt and flange, but do not tighten. Install and tighten left side bolts, then tighten right side "U" bolt.

3) Connect steering rods, making sure rods are same length. Difference should not exceed $\frac{1}{16}$" (2 mm). Install lock bolt on flange and reconnect hoses.

Fig. 5    Steering Gear Mounting Bolts

### POWER STEERING PUMP (ZF)

**Removal** — Place a container below the pump to receive drain oil, then disconnect hydraulic connections. Remove nuts on two long bracket bolts and tensioner locking screws on both sides of pump. Remove drive belt.

2) Turn pump up and remove three screws retaining bracket to engine block, then remove pump and bracket.

**Installation** — 1) To reinstall, reverse removal procedures, noting the following: Use new copper washers when reconnecting pump hoses. Fill the system with new oil that meets specifications. See GENERAL SERVICING in this article.

Fig. 6    ZF Power Steering Pump

### POWER STEERING PUMP (SAGINAW)

**Removal** — Remove two pivot bolts on bracket and bolt on belt tensioning bracket. Place a container below pump to receive drain oil, disconnect hydraulic connections at pump, then remove pump.

**Installation** — To reinstall, reverse removal procedures, then fill and bleed the system, See GENERAL SERVICING in this article.

## OVERHAUL

### STEERING GEAR

**Disassembly** — 1) Clean steering gear exterior and check inner ball joints for wear. Loosen pinion side rubber bellows and drain oil. Remove steering rod using a 32 mm open end wrench, take load off of pinion with an adjustable wrench. When unscrewing steering rod, lock tab will bend up.

2) Remove oil lines, rack damper cover, piston, "O" ring, and spring. Remove pinion cover and spacer sleeve. Bend up locking tab and remove nut. Using tool (5049), unscrew inner bearing race with ball retainer and outer race from pinion.

## VOLVO POWER-ASSISTED RACK & PINION (Cont.)

**Fig. 7    Inner Bearing Race**

**3)** Unscrew three screws from valve housing cover and remove cover and spring, then lift off valve housing and lift out pinion.

**4)** Unscrew right side housing lock bolt and remove housing and connecting tube from outer tube, then pull out rack and bearing sleeve. Remove bearing sleeve rack.

**5)** Unscrew left side housing lock bolt, then remove outer and inner tube from housing. Using suitable tool (1819) remove upper bushing from housing. Use two narrow screwdrivers and remove lower pinion bearing outer race. Remove left side housing from fixture.

**CAUTION** — *Do not use tool (5051) to remove upper bushing.*

**Fig. 8    Removing Upper Bushing**

**6)** Remove "O" rings and spacer from right side housing. Use suitable tool (5051) to remove bearing and seal from valve housing cover. Remove "O" ring from cover and "O" ring, seal, and plastic rings from rack bearing sleeve.

**7)** Remove plastic ring and "O" ring from rack only if, damaged, worn or rack has more than 24,000 miles on vehicle. Remove oil seal from inner tube. Remove washer and snap ring from tube.

**Reassembly** — **1)** Coat all parts with oil before reassembling. Replace all seals, "O" rings, and defective parts. Using tool (5050) install oil seal, bearing and "O" ring in valve cover. Seal should be glued into cover or cover and seal should be changed.

**NOTE** — *If the rack bearing is replaced, the bearing sleeve should also be replaced.*

**2)** Install plastic ring and "O" ring on rack bearing sleeve with "O" ring on tapered side of sleeve. Install snap ring on inner

tube, then install "O" ring and plastic ring on rack piston with the "O" ring under the plastic ring.

**3)** Assemble spacer sleeve, oil seal, and plastic ring on rack (from tooth side). Use tape over teeth to avoid damaging oil seal, then remove tape and install spacer sleeve on rack.

**4)** Insert seal in left side housing with lip facing out, then press in bushing using suitable tool. Install two "O" rings in left side housing, then install the two "O" rings and spacer washer in right side housing.

**5)** Lubricate end of inner tube and install with spacer into left housing, then push rack (with seal and spacer rings) into inner tube. Place tool (5056) on rack and using rack and tool, press seal and spacer rings into housing. Withdraw rack approximately ¾" (20 mm) and remove tool, install lock ring.

**Fig. 9    Installing Seals & Spacer Rings**

**6)** Insert outer tube in left housing, align lock bolt holes in housing and tube, lubricate tube and plastic seal on rack piston, then insert lock bolt with seal. Torque bolt to 9-12 ft. lbs. (1.24-1.66 mkg). Lubricate and insert bearing sleeve in outer tube.

**Fig. 10    Lock Bolt Hole Alignment**

**7)** Align sleeve hole with outer tube hole, tape threaded edges and install seal. Remove tape and install plastic ring in bearing sleeve. Lubricate end of connecting tube and insert tube with rubber seal in right side of housing.

**8)** Install right housing with connecting tube and rubber seal. Align hole in right side of housing with hole in outer tube and install lock bolt. Torque bolt to 9-12 ft. lbs. (1.24-1.66 mkg).

**9)** Install upper race for pinion lower bearing and insert pinion. To avoid readjusting the steering wheel, center the rack. Insert the pinion with the flat outwards (to the left). Screw on sleeve tool (5049) until .31" (8 mm) of the axle end comes through the retainer. Remove tool.

# Power Steering

## VOLVO POWER-ASSISTED RACK & PINION (Cont.)

**10)** Install outer race and spacer sleeve in housing. Press down spacer sleeve so it bottoms on bearing race, then use feeler gauge and straight edge to measure distance between spacer ring and housing. Select gasket(s) of proper thickness, then temporarily install gaskets and cover plate. Gaskets range in thickness from .008-.028" (.2-.7 mm).

*Fig. 11    Measuring for Gasket(s)*

**NOTE** — *Cover plate will have to be removed to make servo balance adjustment after steering gear is installed on vehicle. See GENERAL SERVICING in this article.*

**11)** Insert "O" ring in valve housing, then install valve housing on gear. Install tool (5171) over splines. Place coil spring in valve housing, large end first. To eliminate the possibility of spring being caught in top groove of valve housing, adjust pinion upwards until spool covers the groove completely.

**12)** Install valve housing cover, check that coil spring is not squeezed between cover and housing. Pinion shaft shoulder should be .06" (1.5 mm) above cover face. Adjust by using tool (5049) and moving lower bearing inner race. Install lock ring and lock nut.

**13)** Install damper piston (without "O" ring) in housing. Press piston against rack, then use feeler gauge and straight edge to measure clearance between piston face and housing. Adjust by using shims equal to measured clearance plus .002-.006" (.05-

.15 mm). Shims are available in the following thicknesses: .002" (.051 mm), .0035" (.089 mm), .005" (.127 mm), and .010" (.254 mm).

*Fig. 12    Pinion Shaft Shoulder Measurement*

**14)** Install "O" ring damper, spring, shims, and cover on housing. Use brass shims as the outer ones in stack. Connect an INCH lbs. torque wrench to pinion shaft and rotate shaft in both directions to stop. Torque should be 8-14 INCH lbs. (9-16 cmkg). If torque is excessive at any point, stop rack in that position and readjust by adding shims.

**NOTE** — *If rack jams with damper removed, rack is warped, and must be replaced.*

**15)** Install oil lines, reinstall left and right steering rods. If installing previously used rods, a thin shim may be placed between ball joint and rack shoulder or the two rods may be swapped in order to obtain an unused portion of the rod for locking.

**16)** Lock ball joint in rack recess and install bellows, clamps, and tie rod ends, then install steering gear on vehicle. Refill steering gear and power steering unit and check servo balance. See *General Servicing* in this article.

*Fig. 13    Exploded View of ZF Power Steering Pump*

## VOLVO POWER-ASSISTED RACK & PINION (Cont.)

### POWER STEERING PUMP

**NOTE** — *Procedures are for the ZF type pump only, manufacturer recommends replacement of the Saginaw type pump if found defective.*

**Disassembly — 1)** With pump removed from vehicle, pry front seal from housing. Remove rear cover snap ring and cover. Take out pressure plate and spring.

**2)** Turn pump over and tap on end until parts fall free. Remove ball bearing retaining ring, then push shaft out of housing. Push out thrust plate and cam ring, if still in housing.

**3)** Remove plug, control valve, spring and all "O" rings from housing. Check all parts for wear and scratches. Replace all worn or damaged parts and all "O" rings.

**NOTE** — *If pump housing bushing is defective, replace housing assembly. Rotor, vanes and cam ring are also replaced as an assembly.*

**Reassembly — 1)** Install bearing on shaft (if replaced). Bearing is held by rings on each side. Press bearing and shaft into housing.

**2)** Snap bearing retaining ring into housing. Install thrust plate in housing making sure dowel is through one of the holes in thrust plate, then place cam ring on dowel, arrow facing up.

**Fig. 14   Cam Ring Installation**

**3)** Install "O" rings in housing, small "O" ring nearest cam ring. Place rotor in housing, then insert vanes in rotor (rounded ends toward cam ring). Install pressure plate with dowel aligned in one of the holes.

**4)** Insert "O" ring, spring and cover, then press in cover and install retaining ring. Install control valve, spring and plug, then place shaft seal into housing and tap seal lightly until properly seated.

**5)** Install pump assembly on vehicle, then refill and bleed system. See *GENERAL SERVICING* in this article procedure.

# English-Metric Conversion Chart

## FRACTIONS TO INCHES & METRIC EQUIVALENTS

| Fractions | Inches | MM |
|---|---|---|
| 1/64 | .016 | .397 |
| 1/32 | .031 | .794 |
| 3/64 | .047 | 1.191 |
| 1/16 | .063 | 1.588 |
| 5/64 | .078 | 1.984 |
| 3/32 | .094 | 2.381 |
| 7/64 | .109 | 2.778 |
| 1/8 | .125 | 3.175 |
| 9/64 | .141 | 3.572 |
| 5/32 | .156 | 3.969 |
| 11/64 | .172 | 4.366 |
| 3/16 | .188 | 4.763 |
| 13/64 | .203 | 5.159 |
| 7/32 | .219 | 5.556 |
| 15/64 | .234 | 5.953 |
| 1/4 | .250 | 6.350 |
| 17/64 | .266 | 6.747 |
| 9/32 | .281 | 7.144 |
| 19/64 | .297 | 7.541 |
| 5/16 | .313 | 7.938 |
| 21/64 | .328 | 8.334 |
| 11/32 | .344 | 8.731 |
| 23/64 | .359 | 9.128 |
| 3/8 | .375 | 9.525 |
| 25/64 | .391 | 9.922 |
| 13/32 | .406 | 10.319 |
| 27/64 | .422 | 10.716 |
| 7/16 | .438 | 11.113 |
| 29/64 | .453 | 11.509 |
| 15/32 | .469 | 11.906 |
| 31/64 | .484 | 12.303 |
| 1/2 | .500 | 12.700 |

| Fractions | Inches | MM |
|---|---|---|
| 33/64 | .516 | 13.097 |
| 17/32 | .531 | 13.494 |
| 35/64 | .547 | 13.891 |
| 9/16 | .563 | 14.288 |
| 37/64 | .578 | 14.684 |
| 19/32 | .594 | 15.081 |
| 39/64 | .609 | 15.478 |
| 5/8 | .625 | 15.875 |
| 41/64 | .641 | 16.272 |
| 21/32 | .656 | 16.669 |
| 43/64 | .672 | 17.066 |
| 11/16 | .687 | 17.463 |
| 45/64 | .703 | 17.859 |
| 23/32 | .719 | 18.256 |
| 47/64 | .734 | 18.653 |
| 3/4 | .750 | 19.050 |
| 49/64 | .766 | 19.447 |
| 25/32 | .781 | 19.844 |
| 51/64 | .797 | 20.241 |
| 13/16 | .813 | 20.638 |
| 53/64 | .828 | 21.034 |
| 27/32 | .844 | 21.431 |
| 55/64 | .859 | 21.828 |
| 7/8 | .875 | 22.225 |
| 57/64 | .891 | 22.622 |
| 29/32 | .906 | 23.019 |
| 59/64 | .922 | 23.416 |
| 15/16 | .938 | 23.813 |
| 61/64 | .953 | 24.209 |
| 31/32 | .969 | 24.606 |
| 63/64 | .984 | 25.003 |

## CONVERSION FACTORS

| Unit | To | Unit | Multiply By |
|---|---|---|---|
| **LENGTH** | | | |
| Millimeters | | Inches | .03937 |
| Inches | | Millimeters | 25.4 |
| Meters | | Feet | 3.28084 |
| Feet | | Meters | .3048 |
| Kilometers | | Miles | .62137 |
| Miles | | Kilometers | 1.60935 |
| **AREA** | | | |
| Square Centimeters | | Square Inches | .155 |
| Square Inches | | Square Centimeters | 6.45159 |
| **VOLUME** | | | |
| Cubic Centimeters | | Cubic Inches | .06103 |
| Cubic Inches | | Cubic Centimeters | 16.38703 |
| Liters | | Cubic Inches | 61.025 |
| Cubic Inches | | Liters | .01639 |
| Liters | | Quarts | 1.05672 |
| Quarts | | Liters | .94633 |
| Liters | | Pints | 2.11344 |
| Pints | | Liters | .47317 |
| Liters | | Ounces | 33.81497 |
| Ounces | | Liters | .02957 |

| Unit | To | Unit | Multiply By |
|---|---|---|---|
| **WEIGHT** | | | |
| Grams | | Ounces | .03527 |
| Ounces | | Grams | 28.34953 |
| Kilograms | | Pounds | 2.20462 |
| Pounds | | Kilograms | .45359 |
| **WORK** | | | |
| Centimeter Kilograms | | Inch Pounds | .8676 |
| Inch Pounds | | Centimeter Kilograms | 1.15262 |
| Meter Kilograms | | Foot Pounds | 7.23301 |
| Foot Pounds | | Meter Kilograms | .13826 |
| **PRESSURE** | | | |
| Kilograms/ Sq. Centimeter | | Pounds/Sq.Inch | 14.22334 |
| Pounds/Sq.Inch | | Kilograms/Sq.Centimeter | .07031 |
| Bar | | Pounds/Sq.Inch | 14.504 |
| Pounds/Sq.Inch | | Bar | .06895 |
| Atmosphere | | Pounds/Sq.Inch | 14.696 |
| Pounds/Sq.Inch | | Atmosphere | .06805 |
| **TEMPERATURE** | | | |
| Centigrade Degrees | | Fahrenheit Degrees | $(C° \times 9/5)+32$ |
| Fahrenheit Degrees | | Centigrade Degrees | $(F°-32) \times 5/9$ |

# Torque & Drill Conversion Chart

## TORQUE CONVERSIONS
### FOOT POUNDS TO METER KILOGRAMS

| Ft. Lbs. | Mkg | Ft. Lbs. | Mkg | Ft. Lbs. | Mkg | Ft. Lbs. | Mkg |
|---|---|---|---|---|---|---|---|
| 1 | .14 | 26 | 3.60 | 51 | 7.05 | 76 | 10.51 |
| 2 | .28 | 27 | 3.73 | 52 | 7.19 | 77 | 10.65 |
| 3 | .41 | 28 | 3.87 | 53 | 7.33 | 78 | 10.78 |
| 4 | .55 | 29 | 4.01 | 54 | 7.47 | 79 | 10.92 |
| 5 | .69 | 30 | 4.15 | 55 | 7.60 | 80 | 11.06 |
| 6 | .83 | 31 | 4.29 | 56 | 7.74 | 81 | 11.20 |
| 7 | .97 | 32 | 4.42 | 57 | 7.88 | 82 | 11.34 |
| 8 | 1.11 | 33 | 4.56 | 58 | 8.02 | 83 | 11.48 |
| 9 | 1.24 | 34 | 4.70 | 59 | 8.16 | 84 | 11.61 |
| 10 | 1.38 | 35 | 4.84 | 60 | 8.30 | 85 | 11.75 |
| 11 | 1.52 | 36 | 4.98 | 61 | 8.43 | 86 | 11.89 |
| 12 | 1.66 | 37 | 5.12 | 62 | 8.57 | 87 | 12.03 |
| 13 | 1.80 | 38 | 5.25 | 63 | 8.71 | 88 | 12.17 |
| 14 | 1.94 | 39 | 5.39 | 64 | 8.85 | 89 | 12.31 |
| 15 | 2.07 | 40 | 5.53 | 65 | 8.99 | 90 | 12.44 |
| 16 | 2.21 | 41 | 5.67 | 66 | 9.13 | 91 | 12.58 |
| 17 | 2.35 | 42 | 5.81 | 67 | 9.26 | 92 | 12.72 |
| 18 | 2.49 | 43 | 5.95 | 68 | 9.40 | 93 | 12.86 |
| 19 | 2.63 | 44 | 6.08 | 69 | 9.54 | 94 | 13.00 |
| 20 | 2.77 | 45 | 6.22 | 70 | 9.68 | 95 | 13.13 |
| 21 | 2.90 | 46 | 6.36 | 71 | 9.82 | 96 | 13.27 |
| 22 | 3.04 | 47 | 6.50 | 72 | 9.95 | 97 | 13.41 |
| 23 | 3.18 | 48 | 6.64 | 73 | 10.09 | 98 | 13.55 |
| 24 | 3.32 | 49 | 6.77 | 74 | 10.23 | 99 | 13.69 |
| 25 | 3.46 | 50 | 6.91 | 75 | 10.37 | 100 | 13.83 |

## DRILL SIZE & IDENTIFICATION

| Drill Diam. | Drill Size | Drill Diam. | Drill Size | Drill Diam. | Drill Size | Drill Diam. | Drill Size |
|---|---|---|---|---|---|---|---|
| .413" | Z | .2280" | 1 | .1440" | 27 | .0550" | 54 |
| .404" | Y | .2210" | 2 | .1405" | 28 | .0520" | 55 |
| .397" | X | .2130" | 3 | .1360" | 29 | .0465" | 56 |
| .386" | W | .2090" | 4 | .1285" | 30 | .0430" | 57 |
| .377" | V | .2055" | 5 | .1200" | 31 | .0420" | 58 |
| .368" | U | .2040" | 6 | .1160" | 32 | .0410" | 59 |
| .358" | T | .2010" | 7 | .1130" | 33 | .0400" | 60 |
| .348" | S | .1990" | 8 | .1110" | 34 | .0390" | 61 |
| .339" | R | .1960" | 9 | .1100" | 35 | .0380" | 62 |
| .332" | Q | .1935" | 10 | .1065" | 36 | .0370" | 63 |
| .323" | P | .1910" | 11 | .1040" | 37 | .0360" | 64 |
| .316" | O | .1890" | 12 | .1015" | 38 | .0350" | 65 |
| .302" | N | .1850" | 13 | .0995" | 39 | .0330" | 66 |
| .295" | M | .1820" | 14 | .0980" | 40 | .0320" | 67 |
| .290" | L | .1800" | 15 | .0960" | 41 | .0310" | 68 |
| .281" | K | .1770" | 16 | .0935" | 42 | .0292" | 69 |
| .277" | J | .1730" | 17 | .0890" | 43 | .0280" | 70 |
| .272" | I | .1695" | 18 | .0860" | 44 | .0260" | 71 |
| .266" | H | .1660" | 19 | .0820" | 45 | .0250" | 72 |
| .261" | G | .1610" | 20 | .0810" | 46 | .0240" | 73 |
| .257" | F | .1590" | 21 | .0785" | 47 | .0225" | 74 |
| .250" | E | .1570" | 22 | .0760" | 48 | .0210" | 75 |
| .246" | D | .1540" | 23 | .0730" | 49 | .0200" | 76 |
| .242" | C | .1520" | 24 | .0700" | 50 | .0180" | 77 |
| .238" | B | .1495" | 25 | .0670" | 51 | .0160" | 78 |
| .234" | A | .1470" | 26 | .0635" | 52 | .0145" | 79 |
|  |  |  |  | .0595" | 53 | .0135" | 80 |

# English-Metric Conversion Chart

## MILLIMETERS TO INCHES

Conversion Factor — Multiply known millimeter figure by .03937

| MM | Inches | MM | Inches | MM | Inches | MM | Inches | MM | Inches |
|---|---|---|---|---|---|---|---|---|---|
| 1 | .039 | 21 | .827 | 41 | 1.614 | 61 | 2.402 | 81 | 3.189 |
| 2 | .079 | 22 | .866 | 42 | 1.654 | 62 | 2.441 | 82 | 3.228 |
| 3 | .118 | 23 | .906 | 43 | 1.693 | 63 | 2.480 | 83 | 3.268 |
| 4 | .157 | 24 | .945 | 44 | 1.732 | 64 | 2.520 | 84 | 3.307 |
| 5 | .197 | 25 | .984 | 45 | 1.772 | 65 | 2.559 | 85 | 3.346 |
| 6 | .236 | 26 | 1.024 | 46 | 1.811 | 66 | 2.598 | 86 | 3.386 |
| 7 | .276 | 27 | 1.063 | 47 | 1.850 | 67 | 2.638 | 87 | 3.425 |
| 8 | .315 | 28 | 1.102 | 48 | 1.890 | 68 | 2.677 | 88 | 3.465 |
| 9 | .354 | 29 | 1.142 | 49 | 1.929 | 69 | 2.717 | 89 | 3.504 |
| 10 | .394 | 30 | 1.181 | 50 | 1.969 | 70 | 2.756 | 90 | 3.543 |
| 11 | .433 | 31 | 1.220 | 51 | 2.008 | 71 | 2.795 | 91 | 3.583 |
| 12 | .472 | 32 | 1.260 | 52 | 2.047 | 72 | 2.835 | 92 | 3.622 |
| 13 | .512 | 33 | 1.299 | 53 | 2.087 | 73 | 2.874 | 93 | 3.661 |
| 14 | .551 | 34 | 1.339 | 54 | 2.126 | 74 | 2.913 | 94 | 3.701 |
| 15 | .591 | 35 | 1.378 | 55 | 2.165 | 75 | 2.953 | 95 | 3.740 |
| 16 | .630 | 36 | 1.417 | 56 | 2.205 | 76 | 2.992 | 96 | 3.780 |
| 17 | .669 | 37 | 1.457 | 57 | 2.244 | 77 | 3.031 | 97 | 3.819 |
| 18 | .709 | 38 | 1.496 | 58 | 2.283 | 78 | 3.071 | 98 | 3.858 |
| 19 | .748 | 39 | 1.535 | 59 | 2.323 | 79 | 3.110 | 99 | 3.898 |
| 20 | .787 | 40 | 1.575 | 60 | 2.362 | 80 | 3.150 | 100 | 3.937 |

## INCHES TO MILLIMETERS

Conversion Factor — Multiply known inch figure by 25.40

| Inches | MM | Inches | MM | Inches | MM | Inches | MM | Inches | MM |
|---|---|---|---|---|---|---|---|---|---|
| .001 | .025 | .040 | 1.016 | .340 | 8.636 | .640 | 16.256 | .940 | 23.876 |
| .002 | .051 | .050 | 1.270 | .350 | 8.890 | .650 | 16.510 | .950 | 24.130 |
| .003 | .076 | .060 | 1.524 | .360 | 9.144 | .660 | 16.764 | .960 | 24.384 |
| .004 | .102 | .070 | 1.778 | .370 | 9.398 | .670 | 17.018 | .970 | 24.638 |
| .005 | .127 | .080 | 2.032 | .380 | 9.652 | .680 | 17.272 | .980 | 24.892 |
| .006 | .152 | .090 | 2.286 | .390 | 9.906 | .690 | 17.526 | .990 | 25.146 |
| .007 | .178 | .100 | 2.540 | .400 | 10.160 | .700 | 17.780 | 1.000 | 25.400 |
| .008 | .203 | .110 | 2.794 | .410 | 10.414 | .710 | 18.034 | 2.000 | 50.800 |
| .009 | .229 | .120 | 3.048 | .420 | 10.668 | .720 | 18.288 | 3.000 | 76.200 |
| .010 | .254 | .130 | 3.302 | .430 | 10.922 | .730 | 18.542 | 4.000 | 101.600 |
| .011 | .279 | .140 | 3.556 | .440 | 11.176 | .740 | 18.796 | 5.000 | 127.000 |
| .012 | .305 | .150 | 3.810 | .450 | 11.430 | .750 | 19.050 | | |
| .013 | .330 | .160 | 4.064 | .460 | 11.684 | .760 | 19.304 | | |
| .014 | .356 | .170 | 4.318 | .470 | 11.938 | .770 | 19.558 | | |
| .015 | .381 | .180 | 4.572 | .480 | 12.192 | .780 | 19.812 | | |
| .016 | .406 | .190 | 4.826 | .490 | 12.446 | .790 | 20.066 | | |
| .017 | .432 | .200 | 5.080 | .500 | 12.700 | .800 | 20.320 | | |
| .018 | .457 | .210 | 5.334 | .510 | 12.954 | .810 | 20.574 | | |
| .019 | .483 | .220 | 5.558 | .520 | 13.208 | .820 | 20.828 | | |
| .020 | .508 | .230 | 5.842 | .530 | 13.462 | .830 | 21.082 | | |
| .021 | .533 | .240 | 6.096 | .540 | 13.716 | .840 | 21.336 | | |
| .022 | .559 | .250 | 6.350 | .550 | 13.970 | .850 | 21.590 | | |
| .023 | .584 | .260 | 6.604 | .560 | 14.224 | .860 | 21.844 | | |
| .024 | .610 | .270 | 6.858 | .570 | 14.478 | .870 | 22.098 | | |
| .025 | .635 | .280 | 7.112 | .580 | 14.732 | .880 | 22.352 | | |
| .026 | .652 | .290 | 7.366 | .590 | 14.986 | .890 | 22.606 | | |
| .027 | .686 | .300 | 7.620 | .600 | 15.240 | .900 | 22.860 | | |
| .028 | .711 | .310 | 7.874 | .610 | 15.494 | .910 | 23.114 | | |
| .029 | .737 | .320 | 8.128 | .620 | 15.748 | .920 | 23.368 | | |
| .030 | .762 | .330 | 8.382 | .630 | 16.002 | .930 | 23.622 | | |

**NOTE** — *The latest changes and corrections represent a collection of last minute 1978 information which arrived too late to be incorporated into the body of the manual. In addition, we have included information on prior year models which we've received since the publication of the 1977 edition.*

## TUNE-UP & FUEL SYSTEMS

▶ *AUDI FOX, ALL MODELS WITH CIS* — When checking control pressure regulator on injection system, connect ohmmeter between terminals in socket. Resistance on all models must be between 16-22 ohms. All previous specifications are incorrect.

▶ *1977-78 CAPRI II, COURIER & FIESTA: PCV VALVE REPLACEMENT* — When vehicle has over 20,000 miles, manufacturer recommends a high volume flow rate PCV valve should be installed as a service replacement.

▶ *1977 & EARLIER COURIER, VEHICLES CALIBRATED FOR NON-HIGH ALTITUDE OPERATION: RESETTING IDLE SPEED* — On vehicles calibrated for non-high altitude operation (sea level), if driving into a high altitude region, loss of engine idle speed will result and may cause rough operation or stalling.

This condition may be temporarily corrected by resetting idle speed to RPM specified on Emission Control Decal if high altitude driving is to be done for any length of time. Reset idle speed upon reaching low altitude region.

▶ *1978 & EARLIER FIAT (EXCEPT X1/9)* — Some hesitation problems, especially in cold or damp weather conditions, may be caused by an improperly set air cleaner. The air cleaner top has two separate air intake positions: "COLD" and "WARM". When driving in cold climates, line up mark "I" with arrow on air cleaner duct. In hot climates, line up reference mark "E" with air cleaner duct arrow.

▶ *1978 FIAT (ALL MODELS)* — To check for proper diverter valve operation, use the following procedure:

**1)** Warm engine to normal operating temperature and check vacuum signal line from manifold to diverter valve. Be sure line is not leaking or blocked.

**2)** Clamp vacuum signal line closed and raise engine speed to 1500-2000 RPM for 131 and 124 models; 2000-2500 RPM for 128 and X1/9 models.

**3)** Unclamp vacuum signal line and see if air is exhausted from diverter valve discharge port. If no air is released, make sure signal line is completely unclamped. If it is, replace diverter valve.

▶ *1977-78 HONDA CIVIC CVCC AND ACCORD: ENGINE STALLING AND MISSING AFTER AIR FILTER REPLACEMENT* — Be sure to use only the specified replacement filter for this model. Substitution of earlier year model filters will result in an improper fit, allowing air and dirt to flow around filter and into the carburetor.

▶ *1977-78 MERCEDES-BENZ 280 SERIES (110 ENGINE): VACUUM LINE DISLODGING DURING OIL FILTER CHANGE* — On these models with CIS fuel injection, the manufacturer notes that it is possible to knock loose the vacuum line to the warm-up regulator when changing the oil filter. A rough-running engine will result and the cause may be difficult to detect. Be sure this vacuum line is in place after changing oil filter.

▶ *1977 PORSCHE 911S: MODIFICATIONS TO FUEL INJECTION SYSTEM* — In 1977, 911S models had some modifications made to the fuel injection system over previous years. The sensor plate lever has a riveted leaf spring, which holds the CO adjustment screw against the sensor plate lever. The sensor plate lever stop has been modified so that the rubber block is higher, limiting downward movement of the lever. The wire clip for sensor plate height adjustment has been replaced by a screw and lock nut.

▶ *1977 AND LATER VOLKSWAGEN RABBIT DIESEL: FUEL SYSTEM MAINTENANCE CHANGES* — Note that the following fuel maintenance procedures have recently been released by Volkswagen and supersede earlier literature:

### FUEL SYSTEM BLEEDING

**1)** No bleeding is required.

**2)** Crank engine until it starts.

**3)** Accelerate engine several times (until engine runs smoothly).

### FUEL FILTER REPLACEMENT

**Removal** — **1)** Remove both filter support mounting nuts.

**2)** Rotate filter until upside down on studs.

**3)** Carefully loosen filter; avoid any fuel leakage.

**4)** Rotate filter from upside down position, unscrew filter by hand, remove and discard filter.

**Installation** — **1)** Lightly coat new filter gasket with diesel fuel.

**2)** Fit filter on to support and tighten by hand.

**3)** Tighten filter onto mounting studs.

**4)** Crank engine until it starts; accelerate several times to smooth out operation.

**5)** Check for leaks.

### FUEL FILTER WATER DRAIN

Fuel filters with primer pump and vent screw, and fuel filters with only vent screw:

- Loosen vent screw.

FOR 1978 & PREVIOUS MODELS

## TUNE-UP & FUEL SYSTEMS (Cont.)

- Loosen drain plug and allow approximately 100 cc fuel to flow from filter.

Fuel filters without vent screw or primer pump:

- Remove fuel return line at injection pump (side with out clamp).
- Loosen drain plug on bottom of fuel filter and allow approximately 100 cc fuel to drain out.

## ELECTRICAL

▶ *1978 FIAT X1/9: WIRING HARNESS CHANGE* — The wiring harness connecting the alternator to voltage regulator has three wires: Red to positive brush, green to negative brush, and black to ground. Some 1978 models have a white wire in place of the green wire specified on the wiring diagrams. All other connections and colors remain the same.

☐1

▶ *1978 FIESTA: DISTRIBUTOR ARMATURE PIN* — The distributor armature assembly is secured with an expanding type drive pin. If this pin is loose or missing, the armature will move out of position, causing a no-start condition. Secure a loose pin with Loctite-type material.

☐2

▶ *1977 VOLVO WITH V6 ENGINE: DISTRIBUTOR CAP REMOVAL NOTE* — When distributor cap has to be removed for service or repair it can be inadvertently cracked when being forced by fuel distributor. To avoid cracking cap, loosen the fuel distributor mounting bolts (two Allen head, one hex head) and lift upward on fuel distributor while removing ignition distributor cap.

☐3

## ENGINES

▶ *1978 ARROW, COLT, CHALLENGER & SAPPORO: SILENT SHAFT CHAIN ADJUSTMENT* — A mid-year production change was made to Silent Shaft engines available on these models. An adjustment window has been provided that eliminates the need to remove the chain case cover when adjusting the Silent Shaft drive chain. A revised service procedure is now used for this adjustment:

☐1

1) Remove cover from adjusting window of chain case cover. Loosen bolt shown in illustration.

2) Push projection on chain guide down as far as possible. Use ONLY finger pressure. Chain will be noisy if set too tight.

3) Tighten bolt to 11-16 ft. lbs. and install cover with new gasket.

▶ *1977 AUDI FOX, VOLKSWAGEN RABBIT, SCIROCCO, DASHER: CYLINDER HEAD BOLT CHANGE* — New 11 mm cylinder head bolts with 12 mm polygon socket heads have replaced the earlier 10 mm head bolts that had hexagon socket heads. New bolts MUST be used in complete sets if utilized as repair parts for early models. Make sure NOT to retorque polygon head bolts at the 1000 mile maintenance service or the first 1000 miles following repair. Note that new polygon bolts do not have to be replaced during repair work.

☐2

▶ *1978 FIESTA: ENGINE MOUNT CONSTRUCTION* — The Fiesta engine mount is constructed of two rubber blocks encased by a metal bracket. There is no bond between the two blocks in the mount, and this construction has led to the incorrect diagnosis that the mount needs replacement. The condition is normal and does not indicate a need for replacement.

☐3

Chain Guide

Projection

Bolt

Push Here

Adjusting Window
(Cover Removed)

**Silent Shaft Chain Adjustment**

Metal Casing

No Bond

Rubber/Metal Bond

**Fiesta Engine Mount**

## ENGINES (Cont.)

**4** ▶ *1978 HONDA CIVIC CVCC AND ACCORD: ENGINE COMPARTMENT BUZZING NOISE* — Engine compartment buzzing vibration noise may be caused by manifold insulator plate interfering with intake manifold gasket at head. To correct this condition, bend edge of manifold insulator plate up to clear the head and gasket.

**5** ▶ *1977 AND LATER MERCEDES-BENZ: OIL SUMP PROTECTION COVER* — In instances when vehicle is being operated for sustained periods of time on rough roads, it may be necessary or desirable to install an underpan (oil sump protection cover) to reduce the possibility of damage to oil sump. Each Mercedes-Benz series of vehicles has an underpan available.

**6** ▶ *1976-1978 OPEL: OIL CAPACITY* — Specifications in the Owner's Manuals for Opel give the oil capacity for a new or rebuilt engine. When oil is changed in service, the amount required for refill is less. The correct crankcase capacities are shown below:

New or Rebuilt Engine .......................... 5.7 qts.
Change with Filter ................................ 4.4 qts.
Change without Filter ........................... 4.0 qts.

**7** ▶ *ALL PORSCHE 911 AND TURBO MODELS* — Two piece oil return pipes are available. These service parts (Number 930.107.040.00) eliminate the need to dismantle the engine to replace a leaking pipe. The replacement procedure is as follows:

**1)** Clean underside of engine and remove EGR filter. Cut existing oil return pipe with sheet metal shears and remove pieces from engine.

**2)** Clean sealing surfaces on engine and cylinder head. Lightly oil "O" rings and seals. Slide the retaining ring down pipe so the sections can telescope together.

**3)** Install pipe with short piece toward crankcase. Extend pipe sections and refit retaining ring in its groove. Turn pipe slightly to ensure a proper fit.

**Porsche Oil Pipe Replacement**

*(Labels: Short Oil Pipe (Toward Crankcase); Long Oil Pipe (Toward Cylinder Head); Round Seal; "O" Rings; Retaining Ring)*

**4)** Install EGR filter. Start engine and check installation for leaks.

**8** ▶ *1977 VOLKSWAGEN DIESEL ENGINE: CYLINDER HEAD GASKET* — Beginning with engine number CK 024 944 a thicker cylinder head gasket has been introduced. New gasket is .008" (2 mm) thicker to compensate for piston projection above top of cylinder block. Measure piston projection and select gasket thickness according to table.

### Cylinder Head Gasket Table

| Piston Projection In (mm) | Gasket Thickness In. (mm) | Identification Number |
|---|---|---|
| .017-.025 (.43-63) | .051 (.13) | 2 |
| .025-.032 (.63-.82) | .055 (1.4) | 3 |
| .032-.036 (.82-.92) | .059 (1.5) | 4 |
| .036-.040 (.92-1.02) | .063 (1.6) | 5 |

**9** ▶ *1977 AND LATER VOLKSWAGEN RABBIT WITH DIESEL ENGINE: PISTON CHANGE* — Beginning with engine number CK 024 944 a new piston with increased height was introduced. Refer to illustration for new height measurement.

NOW: 1.768" (44.9 mm)

WAS: 1.759" (44.7 mm)

**Piston Height Measurement**

Also, new pistons are identified by the number "9" stamped next to installation direction arrow. If new pistons are installed in early models engines, sets of four must be used.

FOR 1978 & PREVIOUS MODELS

## ENGINES (Cont.)

**Top of New Piston with Identification Mark**

▶ 1977 AND LATER VOLVO MODELS WITH B21 ENGINE: VALVE SPRING WASHER CHANGE — A new valve spring washer has been released in production. The new washer can be identified by its slightly different shape. New washer will withstand greater loads. Only new washer is available as a replacement part.

▶ 1977 VOLKSWAGEN RABBIT WITH DIESEL: INJECTION PUMP SPROCKET REMOVAL ADDITION — Loosen sprocket mounting nut a few turns. Attach puller or equipment tool shown in illustration. Make sure puller jaws are at right angles to cross piece and that they point in direction of rotation. Tighten puller bolt head (shown by arrow) with several light taps until sprocket comes loose from shaft. Remove puller and nut.

**Puller Installed on Injection Pump Sprocket**

## CLUTCHES

▶ 1976 CAPRI II CLUTCH "SHUDDER" NOTE — If normal checks are negative and a rubbing or "scrubby" feel at clutch pedal is evident, engine heat may be creating an interference between inner cable plastic covering and outer casing plastic lining. This problem may not be evident when engine is cold. Correct problem by repositioning clutch cable as far away from exhaust pipe as possible. If problem presists, clutch disc must be inspected.

▶ 1976 CAPRI II: CLUTCH CABLE CHANGE — A revised clutch cable, part number D7RY-7KB53-A, has become available. The new cable is designed to reduce pedal application effort and to be able to be fitted without any modifications.

▶ 1978 MERCEDES-BENZ: CLUTCH MODIFICATIONS — Beginning with June 1978 production, all 240D models are fitted with a modified throw-out bearing and a pressure plate without thrust ring. When replacing clutch parts, only the modified bearing may be used on pressure plates without the thrust ring. However, earlier model pressure plates may be used with the new design bearing if the thrust ring is removed from the pressure plate fingers.

## BRAKES

▶ 1978 CHALLENGER, SAPPORO & COLT WAGON — Squeal in the front disc brakes, normally caused by vibration of the pad assemblies, can be reduced by fitting shims. To correct this condition, perform the following procedure:

1) Remove disc calipers and pad. Measure total thickness of both inner and outer pads. If total measurement is more than 1.2" (30.5 mm) file pads until dimension is obtained.

2) Fit shim MB150749 behind outer pad, and shim MB150748 behind the inner pad in piston pocket. Reinstall caliper assembly.

3) Check brake dragging torque by bottoming a nut on one of wheel studs. Start engine and apply brakes, then release. Torque required to turn rotor should be less than 9 INCH-lbs. If not, file pads more until proper torque is obtained.

▶ 1978 FIESTA: BRAKE ROTOR REPLACEMENT — When replacing a disc brake rotor on Fiesta, identify the engineering number stamped on outer edge of rotor and install a replacement part having the same engineering number. If replacing both rotors, any pair of replacement rotors may be used as long as they both have the same engineering number. Under

### BRAKES (Cont.)

NO circumstances should rotors with different engineering numbers be used on the same vehicle.

| Replacement Part Number | Engineering Number |
| --- | --- |
| D8RZ-1125-A | 77FB-1125-ABA |
| D8RZ-1125-B | 77FB-1125-ACA |
| D8RZ-1125-C | 77FB-1125-ADA |
| D8RZ-1125-D | 77FB-1125 AEA |

▶ **3** *1977 AND EARLIER HONDA MODELS: BRAKE SYSTEM MALFUNCTION CORRECTION* — Models suffering premature brake pad wear, dragging brakes or low brake pedal may be faced with improper clearance between master cylinder push rod and secondary piston. Before confirming diagnosis make following general checks:

- Rear brake adjustment
- Pad/shoe thickness
- Caliper action
- Air in hydraulic system

If everything checks out satisfactory proceed with master cylinder push rod adjustment:
1) Separate master cylinder from booster.

2) Face knurled end up. Place rod bolt adjustment gauge 6340000, Civic or 65700, CVCC (or equivalent) on master cylinder. Rotate screw until contact is just made with secondary piston.

**NOTE** — *CVCC adjustment gauge can be used on Civic models if retainer plate is left attached to booster when measurement is taken.*

3) Do not disturb gauge setting. Turn adjustment gauge upside down, then place it in the booster shell with master cylinder push rod fully seated. Using a feeler guage, measure distance between push rod and gauge. Gap should be .004-.024" (.1-.6 mm).

4) If required specification is not obtained, remove master cylinder push rod, loosen lock nut and reset adjustment rod. Install and recheck clearance.

▶ **4** *1977 AND LATER MERCEDES-BENZ: BRAKE DISC WEAR LIMIT* — On vehicles equipped with calipers of 2.36" (60 mm), 1.50" (38 mm) or 1.65" (42 mm), the wear limit of brake discs has been changed. A maximum wear limit of .08" (2.0 mm) is permissible for front wheel brake discs and a maximum of .07" (1.7 mm) is permissible for rear wheel brake discs.

▶ **5** *1977 AND LATER VOLVOS: REVISED BRAKE LINE ROUTING* — A new brake line with a different routing to right side rear brake caliper has been in production since about 4/77. The new brake line is mounted to rear axle with a protective sleeve and clamp. If brake line must be replaced on earlier model, new line must be adapted.

▶ **6** *1978 VOLKSWAGEN RABBIT & SCIROCCO: EXCESSIVE BRAKE EFFORT* — If brake pedal pressure is too great, the vacuum booster may need adjustment. Check vacuum at dis-

tributor hose to ensure there is at least 7.4 in. Hg. If not, check vacuum system for leaks. If adequate vacuum is present at distributor, remove and plug hose from vacuum booster. Loosen lock nut on booster and attach vacuum gauge. Turn booster adjustment screw to obtain vacuum of at least 11.8 in. Hg. Tighten lock nut and replace vacuum hose.

**Vacuum Booster Adjustment**

▶ **7** *1978 VOLVO: BRAKE LINE ATTACHMENT CHANGE* — Beginning January 1978 a redesigned attachment for front brake lines and hoses was introduced into production. Refer to illustration for details of modification.

**Components of Newly Designed Brake Line Attachment**

## FOR 1978 & PREVIOUS MODELS

## WHEEL ALIGNMENT & SUSPENSION

▶ 1 *1977 AND EARLIER CAPRI II MODELS: WHEEL BEARING ADJUSTMENT CHANGE* — Procedure for adjusting front wheel bearings now requires that adjustment nut be backed off 120° after torquing. Previously it was only necessary to back off nut 90°.

▶ 2 *1972-75 VOLVO MODELS: REVISED WHEEL ALIGNMENT SPECIFICATIONS* — Listed below are the revised wheel alignment specifications for Volvo models. New specifications should be put into effect immediately.

### Revised Wheel Alignment Specifications

| Application | Camber | Caster |
|---|---|---|
| **Through 1972** | | |
| 140 & 164 Series | | 0 to +1° |
| **1973** | | |
| 140 & 164 Series | | +1 to +2° |
| **1974** | | |
| 140 W/Man. Str. | | +1.5 to +2.5° |
| 140 W/Pwr. Str. | | ① +2 to 3° |
| 164 | | +1.5 to +2.5° |
| **1975** | | |
| 164 | $-1 \pm \frac{1}{4}°$ | $+1 \pm \frac{1}{2}°$ |

① — Only use one spacer per adjustment location.

▶ 3 *1978 ARROW & COLT: FRONT STRUT REPLACEMENT* — When replacing front strut assembly with a new unit, be sure all factory applied coating material (rust preventative) is removed from strut and steering knuckle mating surfaces. A clean surface must be maintained to ensure a tight fit.

▶ 4 *1977 AND LATER MERCEDES-BENZ: SUSPENSION RATTLE CORRECTION* — On all models except 450 SL and 450 SLC a rattle may develop in the rear suspension area. Generally, the cause for the rattle is insufficient tightening of connecting linkage between sway bar and semi-trailing arm. To correct, take off connecting linkage and clean mounting surface of semi-trailing arm. Refit connecting linkage and use a lock washer between sway bar and hex nut. Tighten linkage at semi-trailing arm to 25-37 ft. lbs. (3.5-5.1 mkg) and to 24-32 ft. lbs. (3.3-4.4 mkg) at sway bar.

▶ 5 *1977 AND LATER MERCEDES-BENZ: UPPER CONTROL ARM BUSHING CHANGE* — As of 1/77 all models except 450 SL and 450 SLC have been fitted with a two piece upper control arm bushing. Make sure when repair is required that only one type of bushing is used (either one-piece or two-piece version). Make sure two-piece bushing is installed if vehicle has steel (not aluminum) upper control arms.

▶ 6 *1978 VOLKSWAGEN RABBIT & SCIROCCO: FRONT SUSPENSION CHANGES* — Mid-way through the 1978 model year, the front ball joint pin diameter was increased from 15 to 17mm. The clamping hole in the front wheel bearing housing was also enlarged to match the ball joint change. 15 mm ball joints will still be available, but only 17 mm wheel bearing housings will be supplied as replacement parts. In the event one wheel bearing housing must be changed, manufacturer allows the use of old, 15 mm housing on the other side of vehicle. New tightening torque for clamping bolt is 37 ft. lbs. (5 mkg).

▶ 7 *1978 VOLVO: FRONT SUSPENSION STRUT REPLACEMENT* — If the original front suspension struts (hydraulic) are replaced with gas pressurized units, a spacer must be removed to allow for the replacement strut's extra length. Removal of this spacer will allow the strut to seat against the retaining ring directly below it.

*Volvo Strut Detail*

▶ 8 *ALL PEUGEOT MODELS 504 & 604: REVISED WHEEL ALIGNMENT SPECIFICATIONS* — The following specifications apply to all Peugeot 504 models sold in the United States to 1978, and all 604 models sold in the United States from 1977 on.

### Revised Wheel Alignment Specifications

#### 504 Models

**Front End Specifications**

| | |
|---|---|
| Toe-In | $\frac{1}{8}" \pm \frac{1}{32}"$ |
| Camber Neg. | $\frac{2}{3}° \pm \frac{1}{2}°$ |
| Castor | $2\frac{2}{3}° \pm \frac{1}{2}°$ |
| Swivel Pin Angle | $8\frac{5}{6}° \pm \frac{1}{2}°$ |
| Steering Lock Angle | |
|   Inner Wheel | 20° to 22° |
|   Outer Wheel | $18\frac{1}{3}°$ to 20° |

**Rear End Specifications**

| | |
|---|---|
| Camber Neg | $-1° + \frac{2}{3}° - \frac{1}{3}°$ |
| Toe-In | ① $\frac{11}{64}" \pm \frac{1}{64}"$ |
| Toe-In | ② $\frac{9}{64}" \pm \frac{1}{64}"$ |

#### 604 Models

**Front End Specifications**

| | |
|---|---|
| Toe-In | $\frac{1}{8}" \pm \frac{1}{32}"$ |
| Camber Neg. | $-\frac{1}{2}° \pm \frac{3}{4}°$ |
| Castor | $3\frac{1}{2}° \pm \frac{1}{2}°$ |
| Swivel Pin Angle | $10° \pm \frac{1}{2}°$ |
| Steering Lock Angle | |
|   Inner Wheel | $20°$ to $21\frac{1}{6}°$ |
|   Outer Wheel | 19° to 20° |

**Rear End Specifications**

| | |
|---|---|
| Camber | $1\frac{1}{2}° \pm 1\frac{1}{2}°$ |
| Toe-In | $\frac{5}{64}" + \frac{5}{64}" - \frac{1}{32}"$ |

① — Up to Sept. 1970.
② — From Sept. 1970 on.

## FOR 1978 & PREVIOUS MODELS

### STEERING

**1** ▶ *1977 AND LATER MERCEDES-BENZ: STEERING STOP CHANGE* — A new power steering unit has been installed on 230, 280E, 240D & 300D models. New unit has internal steering stops located in steering gear housing. Previously stops were on crossmember and pitman arm. New unit part number is preceeded with "A*". Note that 300CD and 280CE models are equipped with new unit from start of production. When new unit was introduced slight modifications to steering linkage were made. Make certain an early version system is never installed into a vehicle that does not have stops on crossmember, pitman arm, and idler arm.

**Linkage Used with Early Power Steering Unit**

**Steering Linkage Used with Late Power Steering Unit**

**2** ▶ *1977 AND LATER VOLKSWAGEN TYPE 2: ROLLER SHAFT OIL SEAL REPLACEMENT* — It is now possible to replace a leaking roller shaft oil seal instead of replacing steering gear. Perform seal replacement as follows:

**1)** Remove steering drop arm. Use a sharp tool to pry out oil seal. DO NOT scratch or damage roller shaft.

**2)** Clean oil seal seats in housing and shaft. Clean splines on shaft. Cover splines with cardboard or tape to prevent new seal from being damaged during installation.

**3)** Coat oil seal lip with multi-purpose grease. Slide seal on roller shaft and carefully drive into place.

**4)** Reinstall drop arm, install new lock plate and tighten nut to 100 ft. lbs. (14 mkg). Check oil level and add if needed.

**Steering Gear Assembly Showing Oil Seal Location**

**3** ▶ *1977 AUDI FOX: TIE ROD MODIFICATIONS* — Three changes have been made to the tie rods:
- Threaded shaft has been increased from $9/16$" (14 mm) to $11/16$" (17.5 mm).
- Cotter pin hole in shaft has been deleted.
- Self-locking nut has replaced castle nut and cotter pin. Nut torque is 22 ft. lbs. (3.0 mkg).

**4** ▶ *1977 VOLVO 240: POWER STEERING SERVO NOISE* — Some subject vehicles may encounter a vibration or audiable noise coming from the power steering servo area. Noise

# Latest Changes & Corrections

## STEERING (Cont.)

usually occurs between 3,100 and 4,100 RPM. The noise may even be heard when vehicle is stationary. Volvo has released a new pump mounting bracket with rubber grommets to eliminate this noise. Part number for new bracket is 1219522-8. Bracket was introduced in production at approximately the following chassis numbers: 242, 76000; 244, 120000; 245, 76000.

▶ *1977 AND LATER VOLVO 260 MODELS: POWER STEER-ING HOSE CHAFING CAUTION* — The location of the power steering reservoir has been changed. This relocating changes the fluid hose routing so it runs close to the battery purchase.

To prevent premature hose failure, ensure the strip clamp mounting hose is adequately positioned.

▶ *1976 AND LATER VOLVO MODELS: STEERING WHEEL NOISE* — Models equipped with the new design "off center cover pad" are suject to a "creaking" noise during maneuvers where excessive steering effort is required. Proceed as follows to eliminate noise:

* Remove steering wheel padding.
* Lubricate the four sleeves where pad attaches to steering wheel.
* Refit padding.

# General Index

*NOTE — ALSO SEE INDIVIDUAL SECTION CONTENTS PAGE*

*NOTE — ALSO SEE INDIVIDUAL SECTION CONTENTS PAGE*

## – C –

## – C –

*NOTE – ALSO SEE INDIVIDUAL SECTION CONTENTS PAGE*

*NOTE — ALSO SEE INDIVIDUAL SECTION CONTENTS PAGE*

*NOTE – ALSO SEE INDIVIDUAL SECTION CONTENTS PAGE*

*NOTE – ALSO SEE INDIVIDUAL SECTION CONTENTS PAGE*

*NOTE − ALSO SEE INDIVIDUAL SECTION CONTENTS PAGE*

*NOTE – ALSO SEE INDIVIDUAL SECTION CONTENTS PAGE*

*NOTE – ALSO SEE INDIVIDUAL SECTION CONTENTS PAGE.*

*NOTE — ALSO SEE INDIVIDUAL SECTION CONTENTS PAGE*

*NOTE – ALSO SEE INDIVIDUAL SECTION CONTENTS PAGE.*

*NOTE — ALSO SEE INDIVIDUAL SECTION CONTENTS PAGE*

*NOTE – ALSO SEE INDIVIDUAL SECTION CONTENTS PAGE*

*NOTE — ALSO SEE INDIVIDUAL SECTION CONTENTS PAGE.*

*NOTE – ALSO SEE INDIVIDUAL SECTION CONTENTS PAGE*

## "WE LISTEN!"

We will greatly appreciate receiving your comments or corrections so that we may continue to publish the world's best automotive manuals. **Mail this card today. We'd like to hear from you!**

☐ Domestic  ☐ Imported  ☐ Trucks  ☐ AC Service
☐ Tune-Up  ☐ Mechanical  ☐ Transmissions  ☐ Emission Control

Section No._____  Page No._____  Vehicle model, year_____

Comments:_____
_____
_____
_____

(Please print Co. name and address on the reverse side.)

---

## "WE LISTEN!"

We will greatly appreciate receiving your comments or corrections so that we may continue to publish the world's best automotive manuals. **Mail this card today. We'd like to hear from you!**

☐ Domestic  ☐ Imported  ☐ Trucks  ☐ AC Service
☐ Tune-Up  ☐ Mechanical  ☐ Transmissions  ☐ Emission Control

Section No._____  Page No._____  Vehicle model, year_____

Comments:_____
_____
_____
_____

(Please print Co. name and address on the reverse side.)

---

## "WE LISTEN!"

We will greatly appreciate receiving your comments or corrections so that we may continue to publish the world's best automotive manuals. **Mail this card today. We'd like to hear from you!**

☐ Domestic  ☐ Imported  ☐ Trucks  ☐ AC Service
☐ Tune-Up  ☐ Mechanical  ☐ Transmissions  ☐ Emission Control

Section No._____  Page No._____  Vehicle model, year_____

Comments:_____
_____
_____
_____

(Please print Co. name and address on the reverse side.)

# BUSINESS REPLY CARD

FIRST CLASS          PERMIT NO. 3701          SAN DIEGO, CA

POSTAGE WILL BE PAID BY ADDRESSEE

## MITCHELL MANUALS, INC.

P.O. BOX 80427
San Diego, California 92138

---

# BUSINESS REPLY CARD

FIRST CLASS          PERMIT NO. 3701          SAN DIEGO, CA

POSTAGE WILL BE PAID BY ADDRESSEE

## MITCHELL MANUALS, INC.

P.O. BOX 80427
San Diego, California 92138

---

# BUSINESS REPLY CARD

FIRST CLASS          PERMIT NO. 3701          SAN DIEGO, CA

POSTAGE WILL BE PAID BY ADDRESSEE

## MITCHELL MANUALS, INC.

P.O. BOX 80427
San Diego, California 92138

# Now . . . Save Time, Expand Your Business, Increase Profits

## with Mitchell's time-saving profit builders!

Turn Page ➜

# YES!
I want to save time and increase my shop profits—at no risk to me at all for 30 days. Please send me the manuals I have checked off below. I understand that if I am not completely satisfied, I can return the books within 30 days of delivery for a full refund.

## AIR CONDITIONING & HEATING SERVICE MANUAL

The manual that's used and respected by the people who KNOW the air conditioning industry. Now you can service any air conditioning or heating system—profitably! You get everything you need to make system servicing quick and easy: in-depth trouble shooting and diagnosis . . . servicing, repair and overhaul data . . . thousands of illustrations . . . hundreds of spec tables and charts . . . factory bulletins . . . labor estimating section . . . and more! Total coverage for all factory-installed systems produced in this country since 1966! Big two-volume set! **Price: only $50.00**

## AIR CONDITIONING BASIC TRAINING MANUAL

Now you can have the most complete basic training manual available for air conditioning systems! This book covers all the important aspects of air conditioning service: Theory, components, operation, diagnosis, servicing, and compressor repair. A handy trouble-shooting wall chart is also included! **Price: only $4.95**

## DOMESTIC EMISSION CONTROL SERVICE MANUAL

Tough new pollution laws mean big profits for you in emission control servicing! Cash in on it with Mitchell! You get the most complete and current data available . . . anywhere! Description, operation, trouble-shooting, maintenance, repair and overhaul info for all domestic car emission systems produced since 1966! PLUS—you get a complete fuel system section, engine I.D., all system wiring and vacuum diagrams. Also included: handy system application charts that give you instant access to the data you need! **Price: only $42.00**

## IMPORTED EMISSION CONTROL SERVICE MANUAL

Imported cars need pollution control servicing too . . . and that means more profit opportunities for your shop! Cash in on it with this fantastic coverage—over 30 foreign manufacturers are covered in complete detail. Description, operation, trouble-shooting, maintenance, repair, and overhaul—you get it all with Mitchell PLUS . . . you get a complete carburetion and fuel injection section, emission system wiring and vacuum diagrams, and more! Over 2,000 pages—it's the most in-depth, money-making repair tool you'll find. Start enjoying big emission control servicing profits today! **Price: only $44.00**